BRITANNICA
BOOK OF THE YEAR
1960

BRITANNICA
BOOK OF THE YEAR
1960

1768

ENCYCLOPÆDIA BRITANNICA, LTD.

CHICAGO · LONDON · TORONTO

©

ENCYCLOPÆDIA BRITANNICA, LTD.
LONDON, 1960

★

PRINTED AND BOUND BY
KNIGHT & FORSTER LTD.
LEEDS

PREFACE

APART from flurries of excitement over the GENERAL ELECTION (*see* frontispiece), the Devlin report and the opening to traffic of M.1 Great Britain's chief memory at home of 1959 was a glorious summer unparalleled for a number of years. For publishers, however, summer glories were dimmed by the cloud of the printing dispute which put all of them well behind with autumn schedules and made binderies towards Christmastide scenes of internecine strife.

Especially in our thoughts during the year, and not forgetting nuclear disarmament marchers and protesters, was the slow approach to the SUMMIT CONFERENCE, fully reported and illustrated in this year's *Britannica Book of the Year*. Other special articles on current problems in this year's book are ACCIDENTS, particularly road accidents, CRIME, NEW TOWNS, REFUGEES and an important background piece on the SINO-INDIAN FRONTIER DISPUTE. There are also postwar surveys of the CINEMA, MUSIC and the THEATRE. Two regular titles, CAPITAL INVESTMENT and INDUSTRIAL DESIGN, are included for the first time.

Once again a change has been made to the index. The extra ten-year indexes of biographies and obituaries have clearly proved valuable. Now, in the main index, article headings in bold type refer to articles appearing during the past ten years and not solely in the current volume. Thus the bold heading ADVERTISING, without dates, means that an article on Advertising appears in all the last ten volumes; whereas AFRO-ASIAN CONFERENCE 56, means that an article of that name appeared only in the 1956 *Book of the Year*.

JOHN ARMITAGE

London Editor.

EDITORS AND CONTRIBUTORS

JOHN ARMITAGE, London Editor of Encyclopædia Britannica

R. M. GOODWIN, SHELAGH M. FREEMAN, Assistant Editors

The initials and names of contributors to the Britannica Book of the Year with the principal articles written by them are given below. The arrangement is alphabetical by initials.

A.B.   **Japan**
ARDATH WALTER BURKS. Associate Professor of Political Science, Rutgers University, New Brunswick, New Jersey. Author of " Japan ", in P. M. A. Linebarger, Djang Chu and A. W. Burks, *Far Eastern Governments and Politics*, Part II; etc.

A.B.MacC.   **Advertising** (*in part*)
ALISTAIR BRUCE MacCOLL. Director, Arlington Television and Radio, Ltd., London; Director, Royds Overseas Advertising and Marketing, Ltd.; Director, Young Advertising and Marketing Ltd., Singapore.

A.C.   **Salvation Army**
ARTHUR E. CARR. Salvation Army Officer, International Headquarters, London.

A.C.F.H.   **Chambers of Commerce** (*in part*)
ALBERT CHARLES FIELDING HEY. Secretary, Association of British Chambers of Commerce. Associate Editor, *The Chambers of Commerce Manual*.

A.D.E.   **Aircraft Manufacture**
ALUN DAVIES EDWARDS, B.Sc. Principal Scientific Officer, Ministry of Supply.

A.D.Ls.   **Entomology**
ANTHONY DAVID LEES, M.A., Ph.D. Principal Scientific Officer, Agricultural Research Council Unit of Insect Physiology, Cambridge.

A.Dr.   **Textile Industry**
ALFRED DAWBER, Mem. Text. Inst. Director, Emmott and Company Ltd., technical publishers, Manchester. Editor, *Textile Manufacturer*, Manchester; compiler of *Textile Manufacturer Year Book*; etc.

A.E.Dd.   **Business Review** (*Pottery and Porcelain*)
ARTHUR EDWARD DODD, M.B.E., M.Sc., Ph.D., F.R.I.C., F.I.Ceram. Information Officer, British Ceramic Research Association.

A.E.Ps.   **Colombo Plan**
ALBERT EDWARD PARSONS, O.B.E. Principal, Commonwealth Relations Office, London.

A.E.Tr.   **Ecuador; etc.**
AMOS E. TAYLOR. Director, Department of Economic and Social Affairs, Pan American Union, Washington.

A.E.Y.   **Turkey**
AHMET EMIN YALMAN, M.A., Ph.D. Editor, *Vatan*, Istanbul. Author of *Turkey in the World War*; *The Development of Modern Turkey as Measured by its Press*; *Turkey in My Time*.

A.F.T.-D.   **Chemistry** (*in part*)
AUBREY FIENNES TROTMAN-DICKENSON, M.A., Ph.D. D.Sc. Lecturer, University of Edinburgh. Author of *Gas Kinetics*; *Free Radicals*.

A.G.   **Malta**
ALBERT GANADO, B.A., LL.D. Lawyer, Malta.

A.G.F.C.B.   **Music** (*in part*)
ALAN GEOFFREY FREDERIC CECIL BLYTH, B.A. Music Critic, London.

A.Gg.   **Air Forces of the World** (*in part*)
ALFRED GOLDBERG. Chief, Current History Branch, United States Air Force, Historical Division. Editor, *A History of the U.S. Air Force, 1907-1957*.

A.G.Hr.   **Nuclear Energy**
ALEC GEOFFREY HESTER, B.Sc., A.R.C.S., A.Inst.P. Publicity Department, The General Electric Co., Ltd., Erith, Kent.

A.H.D.   **Theatre** (*in part*)
ALAN HOLMES DENT. Dramatic Critic, the *News Chronicle*. Author of *Preludes and Studies*; *Nocturnes and Rhapsodies*; *My Dear America . . .*; *Mrs. Patrick Campbell: a Biography*.

A.H.H.   **Diseases** (*Venereal Diseases* [*in part*])
ARTHUR HERBERT HARKNESS, F.R.C.S. Director (Venereology), Institute of Urology, London; Consulting Venereologist, St. Charles' Hospital, London; Civil Consultant in Venereal Diseases to the Royal Navy. Author of *Non-gonococcal Urethritis*.

A.H.Ld.   **Forestry** (*in part*)
ARTHUR HENRY LLOYD, O.B.E., M.A. Lecturer in Forestry, University of Oxford. Author of *Engineering for Forest Rangers*; *The Use of Cableways for the Extraction of Timber*.

A.Hw.   **Diseases** (*Cancer*)
ALEXANDER HADDOW, M.D., D.Sc., Ph.D., F.R.S. Professor of Experimental Pathology, University of London, and Chairman, Academic Board, Institute of Cancer Research; Director, Chester Beatty Research Institute, London.

A.J.Kd.   **Fairs, Shows and Exhibitions**
ALAN JOHN KENNARD. Managing Editor, Newman Neame, Publishers, London.

A.J.S.   **British Guiana**
ARTHUR JAMES SEYMOUR. Chief Information Officer, Government Information Services, Georgetown, British Guiana. Author of *The Guiana Book*; *Caribbean Literature*. Editor of *Kyko-veral*.

A.Kg.   **Presbyterian Churches**
ALEXANDER KING, D.D. Secretary, the Colonial and Continental Committee of the Church of Scotland.

A.Kn.   **Spanish Literature**
(THOMAS) ANTHONY KERRIGAN. American editor, *Goya* (Madrid). Editor and translator of Pio Baroja's *The Restlessness of Shanti Andia and Other Writings*; Miguel de Unamuno's *Abel Sanchez and Other Stories*.

A.L.A.   **British Honduras**
ANGEL LIBORIO AYUSO. Programme Organizer, Broadcasting Service, Belize, British Honduras.

A.L.Hl.   **Dance** (*in part*)
ARNOLD LIONEL HASKELL, C.B.E., M.A. Chevalier of the Legion of Honour. Director, The Royal Ballet School, London. Author of *Balletomania*; *Diaghileff*; *Ballet Panorama*; etc.

A.M.Dt.   **Scotland**
ALASTAIR MACTAVISH DUNNETT. Editor, *Scotsman*. Author of *Quest by Canoe*; *Heard Tell*.

A.M.F.   **Exploration and Discovery**
ANTHONY MARGARET FERRAR, B.Sc. Map Curator in the Department of Geography, University of Leeds.

A.Mn.   **Industrial Health**
ANDREW MEIKLEJOHN, M.D., M.R.C.P., D.P.H., F.R.S.E. Senior Lecturer in Industrial Health, University of Glasgow.

A.Mo.   **Business Review** (*Tourist Trade*)
SIR ARTHUR MORSE, C.B.E. Chairman, British Travel and Holidays Association.

A.P.H.   **Cinema** (*Postwar Survey*)
ANN PENELOPE HOUSTON. General Editor of Publications, British Film Institute. Editor of *Sight and Sound*.

A.Pr.   **France; etc.**
ANDRE PIERRE, A.de l'U. Member of editorial staff, *Le Monde*, Paris. Author of *Vie de Tolstoi*; *U.R.S.S.*; *Staline contre Hitler*; *Qui succédera à Staline?*

A.P.S. **British Council**
SIR (ALGERNON) PAUL SINKER, K.C.M.G., C.B. Director-General, British Council.

A.R.A. **Cricket**
ARTHUR REX ALSTON, M.A. B.B.C. Staff Sports Commentator and Reporter. Author of *Taking the Air*; *Over to Rex Alston*; *Test Commentary*.

Ar.Mo. **Electrical Industries** (*in part*)
ARY MOSSIMAN. Manager, Market Research and Statistics, Anaconda Wire and Cable Co., New York.

A.R.W. **Panama**
ALMON R. WRIGHT. Senior Historian, Department of State, Washington, D.C.

A.Ste. **Exchange Control and Exchange Rates**
ALEXANDER STEVENSON. Department of Operations (Europe, Africa and Australasia), International Bank for Reconstruction and Development, Washington, D.C.

A.Stn. **Budgets** (*in part*); **etc.**
AUBREY SILBERTSON, M.A. Lecturer in Economics and Fellow of St. John's College, Cambridge University. Contributor to the *Economic Journal*, London. Author of *Education and Training for Industrial Management*. Part-author of *The Motor Industry*.

A.T.Cl. **New Zealand**
ARTHUR TREVOR CAMPBELL, M.A. Public Relations Officer, New Zealand High Commission, London.

A.T.E. **Business Review** (*Clothing Industry* [*in part*])
ALEC THOMAS ELVY. Technical Services and Information Officer, Apparel and Fashion Industry's Association.

A.Tl. **Cotton**
ARTHUR TATTERSALL. Cotton Trade Expert and Statistician, Manchester.

A.T.M. **Historical Studies**
ALEXANDER TAYLOR MILNE, M.A., F.R.Hist.S. Secretary and Librarian, Institute of Historical Research, University of London. Compiler of *Writings on British History* (annual).

A.W.Bx. **Labour Party**
ARTHUR WILLIS BAX. Secretary, Press and Publicity Department, Labour Party.

A.W.Pl. **Television** (*in part*)
ANTHONY WILLIAM PRAGNELL, LL.B. Secretary, Independent Television Authority, London.

Ay.Sy. **British South African Territories**
ANTHONY SILLERY, M.A. Secretary to the Curators of the Taylor Institution, University of Oxford. Author of *The Bechuanaland Protectorate*; *Sechele*.

B.A.Gh. **Motor Transport** (*in part*)
BERNARD A. GOODRICH. Manager of Press Relations, American Trucking Associations.

B.Ca. **Friends, The Religious Society of**
BERNARD HALL CANTER, B.A. Editor, *The Friend*, London.

B.C.R. **Trade Unions** (*in part*); **etc.**
BENJAMIN CHARLES ROBERTS, M.A. Reader in Industrial Relations, London School of Economics, University of London.

Be.B. **X-Ray and Radiology**
BERNARD BAKER, M.D. Assistant Clinical Professor, Department of Radiology, University of Illinois College of Medicine, Chicago.

B.E.J.P. **Astronomy; Space Exploration**
BERNARD EPHRAIM JULIUS PAGEL, M.A., Ph.D. Principal Scientific Officer, Royal Greenwich Observatory, Herstmonceux, Sussex.

B.E.W. **Business Review** (*Shoe Industry*)
BRYAN ERNEST WALLIS. Export Manager, British Footwear Manufacturers Federation.

B.Fy. **Machinery and Machine Tools** (*in part*)
BURNHAM FINNEY. Editor, *American Machinist*, New York.

B.L. **Timber** (*in part*)
(EDWARD) BRYAN LATHAM. Member of the Forestry Commission. Past President and Member of Executive Council, Timber Trade Federation of the United Kingdom. Founder President and Member of Council, Institute of Wood Science. Member of Education Committee, Federation of British Industries. Fellow of the Forest History Foundation, Inc., Minnesota, U.S. Author of *Timber: Its Development and Distribution: A Historical Survey*.

B.P.W. **Profits and Dividends**
BRIAN PAUL WHITEHOUSE, M.A. (Oxon.). Editor, *Investors' Chronicle, Market News-Letter*.

B.R.W. **Automation**
BRUCE RODDA WILLIAMS. Professor of Economics, University College of North Staffordshire. Editor, *Sociological Review*.

B.S. **Antarctica**
BERNARD STONEHOUSE, B.Sc., D.Phil. Edward Grey Institute of Field Ornithology, Oxford, and Falkland Islands Dependencies Scientific Bureau, London.

B.S.-E. **Central Treaty Organization; etc.**
BICKHAM SWEET-ESCOTT. Writer and Broadcaster on Middle Eastern and Balkan affairs. Manager, Ionian Bank Ltd., 1950-57. Author of *The Balkan States, an economic and financial survey*; *Greece, a political and economic survey*.

C.A.G.S. **Chambers of Commerce** (*in part*)
C. A. G. SAVIDGE, M.B.E., M.A. Director, British National Committee, International Chamber of Commerce.

C.A.Hh. **Business Review** (*Catering Industry* [*in part*])
CHARLES A. HORRWORTH. Executive Vice-President, American Hotel Association, New York.

C.B.Ss. **Business Review** (*Dyestuffs*)
CYRIL BEYNON STEVENS, B.Sc., Ph.D. Lecturer in Dyeing, University of Leeds.

C.C.N.V. **Physiology**
CHARLES CYRIL NORROY VASS, M.B., M.Sc., Ph.D., Ch.B. Reader in Physiology, University of London (at St. Thomas's Hospital Medical School). Part-author of *Synopsis of Physiology* (4th ed.).

C.D.He. **Mexico**
C. DAVID HELLYER. Latin-American Editor, *The San Diego Union*, California.

C.D.M. **Book Sales**
CHARLES DUDLEY MASSEY. Managing Director, Pickering and Chatto, antiquarian booksellers, London.

C.E.R. **Timber** (*in part*)
CHARLES EDGAR RANDALL, A.B., M.A. Information Specialist, Division of Information and Education, Forest Service, U.S. Department of Agriculture, Washington. Author of *Our Forests*; etc.

C.E.R.S. **Railways** (*in part*)
CHARLES ELY ROSE SHERRINGTON, O.B.E., M.A. Secretary, Railway Research Service, and Director, Research Information Division, British Transport Commission, London. Author of *Economics of Rail Transport in Great Britain*; *100 Years of Inland Transport*.

C.E.T. **Mineralogy**
CECIL EDGAR TILLEY, D.Sc., Ph.D., F.R.S. Professor of Mineralogy and Petrology, University of Cambridge; Fellow of Emmanuel College, Cambridge.

C.F.Sz. **Budgets** (*in part*); **etc.**
CHARLES F. SCHWARTZ. Assistant Director, Office of Business Economics, U.S. Dept. of Commerce, Washington, D.C.

C.G.C. **Jet Propulsion and Gas Turbines** (*in part*)
CYRIL GORDON CONWAY, B.Sc. Engineer, Great Lakes Carbon International Ltd., London. Author of *Data Book on Heat-Resisting Steels*.

A. H. Lloyd   *Bernard Pagel*   *B. R. Williams*   *C. G. Conway*

C. H. G. Tether

Brig. C. N. Barclay

E. M. Barker

F. S. Russell

C.G.My.   **Poultry**
CLARENCE GEORGE MAY. Editor, *Poultry World*, London. Author of *Natural Hatching and Rearing*; *Bantams for Eggs*.

C.H.Bu.   **Machinery and Machine Tools** (*in part*)
CHARLES HENRY BURDER, M.B.E., B.A. Director and Editor, *Machinery*, London.

C.H.G.T.   **Banking** (*in part*); **Bank of England; etc.**
C. H. GORDON TETHER. Money Market Editor, *Financial Times*, London.

C.L.B.   **Psychology**
SIR CYRIL LODOWIC BURT, M.A., D.Sc., Hon.LL.D., Hon. D.Litt., F.B.A. Hon. Fellow, Jesus College, Oxford. Professor Emeritus of Psychology, University of London. Author of *The Young Delinquent*; *The Backward Child*; *Factors of the Mind*; etc.

C.L.Be.   **Wild Life Conservation** (*in part*)
CHARLES LEOFRIC BOYLE, Lieut.-Col., R.A. (retd.). Secretary, Fauna Preservation Society, London.

C.L.W.C.   **Law and Legislation** (*in part*)
CHARLES LEONARD WINTERFORDE CODRINGTON, M.A., LL.B. Solicitor.

C.L.Wi.   **National Parks** (*in part*)
CONRAD L. WIRTH. Director, National Park Service, Washington, D.C.

C.M.B.   **United Nations Educational Scientific and Cultural Organization**
CLAUD MOWBRAY BERKELEY, B.A. Executive Secretary, U.N.E.S.C.O.

C.McG.   **Cuba; Dominican Republic; etc.**
CONSTANTINE EDWARD McGUIRE. Economic Adviser (U.S.). Author of *Italy's International Economic Position*; etc.

C.N.B.   **Commonwealth Armies**
CYRIL NELSON BARCLAY, C.B.E., D.S.O., Brig. (retd.). Editor, *Army Quarterly and Defence Journal* and Army Section, *Brassey's Annual—The Armed Forces Year Book*. Author of *The New Warfare*; *History of the Commonwealth Division in Korea, 1950-53.*

Cn.Mn.   **Music** (*Postwar Survey*)
COLIN MASON. Music Critic of *The Guardian*.

C.Os.   **Puerto Rico.**
CANDIDO OLIVERAS. Chairman, Puerto Rico Planning Board, Santurce, Puerto Rico.

C.S.Ba.   **Bermuda**
COLONIAL SECRETARIAT, BERMUDA.

C.T.   **Channel Islands**
CAREL TOMS. Editor, *Weekly Press and Advertiser*, Guernsey; Assistant Editor, *Evening Press*, Guernsey.

C.W.A.   **Bolivia**
CHARLES W. ARNADE. Assistant Professor of History, University of Florida, Gainesville, Florida.

C.W.B.H.   **Philately**
CHARLES WILFRID BUCKENHAM HAWORTH, M.A. Editor, *Philatelic Journal of Great Britain*. Author of *Postal History and Postage Stamps of Chile*; *Postage Stamps of the Hejaz*; etc.

D.A.G.R.   **Building and Construction Industry**
DONALD A. G. REID, B.Sc.(Eng.), M.I.C.E., M.I.Struct.E. Principal, L.C.C. Brixton School of Building, London. Author of *Building Science*.

D.A.Ws.   **West Indies, The** (*Barbados*)
DONALD ALONZO WILES, B.A., B.L.S. Permanent Secretary to the Minister of Communications, Barbados.

D.B.F.   **Fisheries**
DONOVAN BARTLEY FINN, C.M.G., M.Sc., Ph.D., F.R.S.C., F.C.I.C. Director, Fisheries Division, Food and Agriculture Organization of the United Nations, Rome.

D.B.S.   **Bridges** (*in part*)
DAVID BARNARD STEINMAN, A.M., C.E., Sc.D., Ph.D., F.R.S.A. U.S. authority on the design and construction of long-span bridges.

D.Cr.   **Commonwealth Air Forces**
DOUGLAS COLYER, C.B., C.M.G., D.F.C., M.A., Air Marshal, R.A.F. (retd.). Civil Aviation Representative, Western Europe, Ministry of Transport and Civil Aviation.

D.Cw.   **Cinema** (*in part*)
H. DUNCAN CROW. Member of National Film Archive, History Selection Committee. Author of *The British Film Industry*.

D.D.   **Business Review** (*Canning Industry* [*in part*])
DENIS DICKINSON, M.Sc., Ph.D., F.R.I.C., F.R.S.H. Chief Chemist, Fruit and Vegetable Canning Research Association. Author of *Chemical Analysis of Waters*, etc. Part-author of *Laboratory Inspection of Canned and Bottled Foods*.

Dd.A.M.   **International Labour Organization**
DAVID A. MORSE. Director-General, International Labour Office, Geneva. Former Acting Secretary of Labor of the United States.

Dd.A.W.   **Soil Conservation**
DONALD A. WILLIAMS. Administrator, Soil Conservation Service, U.S. Department of Agriculture, Washington, D.C.

D.D.M.   **Business Review** (*Furniture Industry*)
DAVID DALRYMPLE MITCHELL. Secretary, British Furniture Manufacturers' Federated Associations and B.F.M. Exhibitions Ltd. Joint Secretary, British Furniture Trade Confederation and British Furniture Trade Joint Industrial Council.

D.F.   **Union of Soviet Socialist Republics; etc.**
DAVID FLOYD, B.A. Special Correspondent on Communist affairs, *Daily Telegraph*, London.

D.F.C.   **Metallurgy**
DONALD FREDERIC CLIFTON. Assistant Professor of Metallurgy, University of Idaho, Moscow, United States.

D.F.Ky.   **Angling**
DONOVAN FRANK KELLEY. Writer on angling, Plymouth.

D.F.R.   **Anthropology** (*in part*)
DEREK FRANK ROBERTS, M.A., D.Phil. University Demonstrator in Physical Anthropology, Oxford.

D.Hl.   **Architecture** (*in part*)
DOUGLAS HASKELL. Editor, *Architectural Forum*, New York.

D.H.McC.   **National Trust**
DONALD HAMILTON McCULLOUGH, M.A. Public Relations Consultant and Company Director. Author of *You Have Been Warned* (with Fougasse); *Question Mark*.

D.Hn.   **Newspapers and Magazines** (*in part*)
DEREK HUDSON, M.A. Publisher's editor. Formerly member of staff, *The Times* and *Spectator*, London. Author of *Thomas Barnes of " The Times "*; *British Journalists and Newspapers*; etc.

D.J.R.   **Ireland, Republic of**
DAVID JOSEPH RYAN, F.Inst.J. Chief Editorial Writer, *Cork Examiner*.

D.L.B.   **Missiles** (*in part*); **etc.**
DONALD LEONARD BEATON, B.A. (McGill), B.A. (Cantab.). Defence and Air Correspondent of *The Guardian*.

D.L.Fr.   **Obituaries** (*Berenson*)
DENNIS LARRY ASHWELL FARR. Assistant Keeper, Tate Gallery, London.

D.Mn.   **Political Parties, European** (*in part*)
DERICK MIRFIN, M.A. Secretary-General, Liberal International. Editor, *Pall Mall Quarterly*.

D.R.Pn.   **Liberia**
DONALD RAHL PETTERSON. Professor of Geography, East Carolina College, Greenville, North Carolina, United States.

D.Rr.   **Business Review** (*Glass Industry*)
DENNIS LIONEL RIDER. Director, Glass Manufacturers' Federation, etc., London.

D.R.Wn.   **Ornithology**
DAVID RONALD WILSON, B.A. Secretary, British Trust for Ornithology, Oxford.

E.A.J.D.   Canals and Inland Waterways; Docks and Harbours; etc.
ERNEST ALBERT JOHN DAVIES, Assoc.Inst.T. Author of *National Capitalism*; *National Enterprise*; etc.

E.C.Sd.   Aviation, Civil (*in part*)
EDWIN COLSTON SHEPHERD, B.A., B.Litt. Air Correspondent, *Sunday Times*, London; formerly Aeronautical Correspondent, *The Times*, and Editor, *Aeroplane*, London. Author of *The R.A.F. Today*; *Great Flights*.

E.C.T.   Parliament, Houses of
ERIC CLIFFORD THOMPSON, M.A. Senior Library Clerk (Statistician) in the Library of the House of Commons, London.

E.Ey.   Newspapers and Magazines (*in part*)
EDWIN EMERY. Professor of Journalism, University of Minnesota, Minneapolis. Author of *The Press and America*; etc. Associate editor, *Journalism Quarterly*.

E.F.Rg.   Diseases (*Rheumatic Diseases*)
EDWARD F. ROSENBERG, M.D. Assistant Professor of Medicine, Chicago Medical School; Chief, Arthritis Clinic, Michael Reese Hospital, Chicago.

E.Gd.   Business Review (*Fur Trade* [*in part*])
ED GOLD. Fur News Editor, *Women's Wear Daily*, New York.

E.G.E.   Petroleum
ERIC GEORGE ELLIS, B.Sc., F.Inst.Pet. Petroleum Technologist and Consultant. Author of *Lubricant Testing*.

E.G.S.E.   Town and Country Planning
ERNEST GERALD SUTHERLAND ELLIOT, O.B.E., M.A., M.T.P.I. Formerly Chief Technical Planner, Ministry of Housing and Local Government.

E.H.Gn.   Narcotics (*in part*)
EDWARD HAROLD GWYNN. Assistant Under Secretary of State, Home Office.

E.Hin.   Zoological Gardens; Zoology
EDWARD HINDLE, M.A., Sc.D., Ph.D., F.R.S., Hon. Fellow of the Imperial College of Science and Technology. Formerly Scientific Director, Zoological Society of London, and Regius Professor of Zoology, University of Glasgow. Author of *Flies and Disease-Biting Flies*; *A Laboratory Notebook of Zoology*.

Eh.M.B.   Summit Conference, Approaches to
ELISABETH MARY BARKER. Diplomatic Correspondent, External Services, B.B.C. Author of *Truce in the Balkans*; *Macedonia*.

E.H.O.   Printing (*in part*)
EDWARD H. OWEN. Associate Editor, *Printing Production Magazine*, Cleveland, Ohio.

E.H.R.   Wales
EMRYS HADDON ROBERTS, O.B.E., M.A., M.Sc., J.P. Headmaster, Grove Park school, Wrexham. Editor, *Welsh Secondary Schools Review*.

E.H.S.   Man, Isle of
ERNEST HENRY STENNING, M.B.E., T.D., M.A. Archdeacon of Man, Chaplain to the Queen. Formerly Vice-Principal, King William's college, Castletown, Isle of Man. Author of *The Isle of Man*; *Portrait of the Isle of Man*.

E.H.S.S.   Thailand
EDWARD HAROLD STUART SIMMONDS, M.A. (Oxon.). Lecturer in Thai, School of Oriental and African Studies, University of London.

E.I.U.   Vital Statistics
ECONOMIST INTELLIGENCE UNIT, Economist Newspaper, Ltd., London.

E.Ke.   Youth Employment (*in part*)
ELLA CATHCART KETCHIN. Acting Chief, Division of Child Labor and Youth Employment, Bureau of Labor Standards, U.S. Department of Labor, Washington, D.C.

E.L.   Festivals; Music (*in part*); etc.
EDWARD LOCKSPEISER, Officier d'Académie, Paris. Author of *Debussy*; *The Literary Clef*.

E.L.C.   Caribbean Commission
EDWARD LLOYD COZIER. Information Officer, Caribbean Commission.

E.L.Cy.   Hospitals (*in part*)
EDWIN L. CROSBY, M.D. Director, American Hospital Association.

En.M.T.   Broadcasting, Sound (*in part*); Television (*in part*)
EVELYN MARY THOMAS. Assistant to Head of Publicity, B.B.C., London.

E.O.G.   Foodstuffs (*Cocoa; Coffee*); Tobacco
EDGAR OTTO GOTHSCH, B.Sc.(Econ.). Economic Assistant, Commonwealth Economic Committee, London.

E.P.T.   Organization for European Economic Co-operation
EDWARD PETER TEWSON. Information Officer, Organization for European Economic Co-operation.

E.R.Bk.   International Bank for Reconstruction and Development
EUGENE R. BLACK. President, International Bank for Reconstruction and Development, Washington, D.C.

E.R.La.   Seismology
ERNEST RALPH LAPWOOD, M.A., Ph.D. Fellow, Emmanuel College, Cambridge.

E.S.A.   Arab League; United Arab Republic; etc.
EDWARD SELIM ATIYAH, B.A. Writer and Broadcaster. Author of *An Arab Tells his Story*; *The Arabs*; *Black Vanguard*; *Lebanon Paradise*; etc.

E.Sl.   Psychiatry
ERWIN STENGEL, M.D., F.R.C.P. Professor of Psychiatry in the University of Sheffield; Consultant Psychiatrist to the United Sheffield Hospitals.

E.T.Ss.   Great Britain
EDWARD TRERISE SYMONS. Editor, *Evening News*, Portsmouth. Member of the General Council of the Press. Ex-President of the Guild of British Newspaper Editors.

E.W.G.   Electrical Industries (*in part*); etc.
EDWARD WILLIAM GOLDING, O.B.E., M.Sc.Tech., M.I.E.E., M.A.I.E.E., F.R.G.S. Head of Rural Electrification and Windpower Department, Electrical Research Association, London. Author of *Electrical Measurements and Measuring Instruments*; *Electrification of Agriculture and Rural Districts*; etc.

E.Wi.   Italy; Switzerland; etc.
ELIZABETH WISKEMANN, M.A., M.Litt., Associate of Newnham College, Cambridge. Montague Burton Professor of International Relations in the University of Edinburgh. Contemporary historian and writer on foreign affairs, London. Author of *Czechs and Germans*; *Undeclared War*; *Italy*; *The Rome-Berlin Axis*; *Germany's Eastern Neighbours*; *A Great Swiss Newspaper: The Story of the "Neue Zürcher Zeitung"*.

F.A.O.   Food and Agriculture Organization
Article compiled by a member of the staff of the Food and Agriculture Organization of the United Nations, Rome.

F.A.Sw.   Art Exhibitions (*in part*)
FREDERICK A. SWEET. Curator of American Painting and Sculpture, Art Institute of Chicago.

F.B.H.   Portugal; etc.
FRED BRABY HILLS. Programme Organizer, Uganda Broadcasting Service, Kampala.

F.B.Lt.   Cinema (*in part*); Television (*in part*)
FREDA BRUCE LOCKHART. Television Critic, *Time and Tide*, London; Film and Television Correspondent, *Woman*.

F.Br.   Biographies (*Johansson*); Boxing (*in part*)
FRANK BUTLER. Sports Columnist, *News of the World*. Author of *The Fight Game*; *Success at Boxing*; *Success at Soccer*.

F.B.R.   Engineering Techniques, Developments in
FREDERICK BROWNE ROBERTS, M.B.E., M.I.Mech.E., A.M.I.Loco.E. Editor, *Engineering*, London.

F.E.S.   Ethiopia; etc.
FRANK EDMUND STAFFORD, C.M.G., C.B.E. Advisor to the Ethiopian Government.

F.H.L.T.   Business Review (*Paper and Pulp Industry*)
F. H. LLEWELLYN THOMAS, M.A., LL.B. Secretary, British Paper and Board Makers' Association and Associated Bodies and Companies. Part-author of *Papermaking*.

F.Ho.   Congregational Churches (*in part*)
FRED HOSKINS, D.D. Minister and Secretary of the General Council of Congregational Christian Churches. Co-president, United Church of Christ.

F.H.Sd.   Universities and Colleges (*in part*)
SIR FOLLIOTT HERBERT SANDFORD, K.B.E., C.M.G., M.A. Registrar of Oxford University. Fellow of New College, Oxford.

F.J.Se.   Nutrition (*in part*)
FREDERICK J. STARE, M.D. Professor of Nutrition, Schools of Medicine and Public Health, Harvard University.

F.K.En.   Water Supply (*in part*)
FREDERICK K. ERICKSON. Sanitary Engineer Director, Office of Engineering Resources, U.S. Public Health Service, Department of Health, Education and Welfare, Washington, D.C.

F.L.Lr.   Diseases (*Ear, Nose and Throat Diseases*)
FRANCIS LOEFFLER LEDERER, M.D. Professor and Head of Department of Otolaryngology, University of Illinois College of Medicine, Chicago. Author of *Basic Otolaryngology*; *Diseases of the Ear, Nose and Throat*; etc.

F.M.H.   Malaya, Federation of
FREDERIC MARTIN HUTTON. Editor, *Malay Mail*, Kuala Lumpur, Malaya.

F.Mi.   Italian Literature
FRANCESCO PAOLO MEI, M.A., Ph.D. Instructor at the Italian Institute, London.

F.N.Hr.   Botanical Gardens
FRANK NIGEL HEPPER, B.Sc., F.L.S. Senior Scientific Officer, Herbarium, Royal Botanic Gardens, Kew.

F.P.M.   Austria
FRITZ P. MOLDEN. Editor of *Die Presse*, Vienna.

F.P.W.   Iron and Steel
FREDERICK PETER WEBSTER, M.A. Head of International Relations Department, British Iron and Steel Federation.

F.S.R.   Marine Biology
FREDERICK STRATTEN RUSSELL, C.B.E., LL.D., F.R.S. Director, Plymouth Laboratory, Marine Biological Association of the United Kingdom. Author of *The Seas* (with C. M. Yonge); *The Medusae of the British Isles*.

F.S.V.D.   Burma
FRANK SIEGFRIED VERNON DONNISON, M.A. (Oxon.). Official Historian, Cabinet Office, London. Author of *Public Administration in Burma*; *British Military Administration in the Far East*.

F.T.L.   Baptist Church
FRED TOWNLEY LORD, D.D., D.Litt. Formerly Editor of *Baptist Times* and President of the Baptist World Alliance. Now visiting professor at Furman University, South Carolina.

F.V.W.   **Business Review** (*Soaps, Perfumery and Cosmetics*)
FREDERICK VICTOR WELLS, F.C.S., M.R.I. Consulting Chemist and Perfumer. Editor, *Soap, Perfumery and Cosmetics*, London; Founder-President, Society of Cosmetic Chemists of Great Britain; Member, Society of Cosmetic Chemists, U.S., and Société Française de Cosmétologie.

F.W.W.-S.   **Art Exhibitions** (*in part*); **Drawing, Engraving and Illustration**
FRANCIS WILLIAM WENTWORTH-SHEILDS, N.R.D. Designer; Senior lecturer, School of Printing and Graphic Design, Twickenham Technical College, Middlesex.

G.A.L.   **St. Helena**
GEORGE ALBERT LEWIS, M.B.E. Government Secretary, St. Helena.

G.D.H.L.   **Air Races and Records**
GEORGE DAVID HOUGH LINTON. Former Joint Editor, *The Airport Visitor*, London.

G.D.M.   **Chemistry** (*in part*)
GEORGE DENIS MEAKINS, M.A., B.Sc., D.Phil. Graduate Research Assistant in Dyson Perrins Laboratory, Oxford.

G.E.C.   **Rubber**
GODFREY E. COOMBS, B.Sc. Secretary, British Rubber Producers' Research Association, London.

G.E.R.D.   **Oceanography**
GEORGE EDWARD RAVEN DEACON, C.B.E., D.Sc., F.R.S. Director, National Institute of Oceanography, Great Britain.

G.F.   **London**
GERARD FAY. London Editor, *The Guardian*. Author of *The Abbey Theatre: Cradle of Genius*.

G.F.A.   **Business Review** (*Gems*)
GORDON FREDERICK ANDREWS, F.G.A. Secretary, Gemmological Association of Great Britain. Editor, *Journal of Gemmology*.

G.G.R.   **Business Review** (*Leather*)
GUY GARLAND REAKS, B.A. Director, British Leather Federation.

G.H.Bl.   **Local Government**
SIR (GEORGE) HAROLD BANWELL. Secretary, Association of Municipal Corporations, London.

G.H.I.   **Telecommunications** (*in part*)
SIR GODFREY HERBERT INCE, G.C.B., K.B.E., B.Sc., LL.D. Fellow of University College, London; Chairman, Cable and Wireless Limited; former Permanent Secretary, Ministry of Labour and National Service. President, British Association for Commercial and Industrial Education.

G.H.N.B.   **Islam**
GEOFFREY H. NEVILLE BAGOT. Contributor to the *Islamic Review*.

G.Hs.   **Business Review** (*Hemp and Jute*)
GORDON HUGHES. Managing Director, British-Continental Trade Press, Ltd., London. Editor, *Jute and Canvas Review, Jute Market Prices, Waste and Reclamation Trades Review*, etc., London.

G.P.   **Argentina; Brazil**
GEORGE PENDLE, M.A. Writer and broadcaster on Latin American affairs, London. Author of *Much Sky: Impressions of South America*; *Uruguay: South America's First Welfare State*; *Paraguay: a Riverside Nation*; *Argentina*; *South America: A Visual Geography*.

G.P.O.   **Post Office; Telecommunications** (*in part*)
Articles compiled through the courtesy of the Postmaster-General, London.

G.R.McR.   **Diseases** (*Tropical Diseases*)
SIR GEORGE REID McROBERT, C.I.E., M.D., F.R.C.P. Senior Physician, Tropical Diseases Hospital, University College Hospital, London. Consulting Physician to the Colonial Office. Part-author of *Tropical Medicine*.

G.R.N.   **Physics**
GEORGE ROBERT NOAKES, M.A., F.Inst.P. Senior Physics Master, Uppingham School, Rutland. Editor of *Contemporary Physics*. Author of *A Textbook of Electricity and Magnetism*; *A Textbook of Heat*; *General Physics*; *New Intermediate Physics*.

G.S.Ss.   **Art Sales**
GEORGE SOMMERVILLE SANDILANDS, Hon. A.R.C.A., Officier d'Académie (France). Art Critic of *The Artist*. Author of *Masters of English Water-Colours: Bonington, Turner, Brangwyn, Russell Flint*; *The Lakes, An Anthology of Lakeland Life and Landscape*.

G.T.Wk.   **Speleology**
GORDON THOMAS WARWICK, M.B.E., B.Sc., Ph.D., F.R.G.S., F.G.S. Lecturer in Geography, University of Birmingham; Hon. Secretary, Cave Research Group of Great Britain. Part-author of *British Caving*.

G.W.Ey.   **Banking** (*in part*)
GROVER WILLIAM ENSLEY. Executive Vice-President, National Association of Mutual Savings Banks, New York. Author of *Potential Economic Growth of the United States, 1954*.

G.Wr.   **Broadcasting, Sound** (*in part*); etc.
GORDON (GUSTAV-ADOLF) WINTER. Formerly official of the British Broadcasting Corporation, London.

G.W.St.   **Diseases** (*Tuberculosis*)
GEORGE WALTER SCOTT, M.D., M.R.C.P. Clinical Tutor, Guy's Hospital, London. Clinical Assistant, Brompton Hospital, London.

H.A.Cn.   **Business Review** (*Clothing Industry* [*in part*])
HARRY A. COBRIN. Executive Secretary, Clothing Manufacturers Association of the United States of America, New York.

H.A.P.F.   **International Court of Justice**
H. A. P. FISHER, M.A. Barrister-at-Law. Fellow of All Souls College, Oxford.

H.Bfe.   **Motor Cycle and Cycle Industry**
HAROLD BRIERCLIFFE. Editor, *Motor Cycle and Cycle Trader*, London.

H.C.D.   **Education** (*in part*); **Universities and Colleges** (*in part*); etc.
HAROLD COLLETT DENT, B.A., Hon.F.E.I.S., F.R.S.A. Professor of Education, University of Sheffield. Author of *A New Order in English Education*; *Education in Transition*; *Secondary Education for All*; etc. Editor of *Year Book of Technical Education and Careers in Industry*.

H.D.Hs.   **West Indies, The** (*Jamaica; etc.*)
HASTINGS DUDLEY HUGGINS, M.A., M.Sc., Ph.D. Director, Institute of Social and Economic Research, University College of the West Indies, Kingston, Jamaica.

H.D.M.   **Tunnels**
HORACE DENTON MORGAN, M.Sc.(Eng.), M.I.C.E. Senior partner, Sir William Halcrow and Partners, London.

Hd.S.   **English Literature** (*in part*)
HOWARD SERGEANT. Company Secretary and Editor of *Outposts*. Author of *The Cumberland Wordsworth*; *Tradition in the Making of Contemporary Modern Poetry*; *A Critical Survey of South African Poetry*.

Hd.Sw.   **Refugees: A Postwar Survey**
HAROLD SHAW, M.B.E. Organizing Secretary, United Kingdom Committee, World Refugee Year.

H.E.Cn.   **West Indies, The** (*Trinidad and Tobago*)
HUGH ELLIOT CAMERON, D.P.A. Formerly Information Officer, Trinidad and Tobago.

H.G.H.   **Netherlands Overseas Territories** (*in part*)
HANS G. HERMANS. Senior Official of the Netherlands Government Charged with Information and Cultural Relations in the Netherlands Antilles.

H.G.N.   **Congress, U.S.**
HERBERT GEORGE NICHOLAS, M.A. Fellow of New College, Oxford; Reader in the Comparative Study of Institutions, University of Oxford. Author of *The American Union*; *The British General Election of 1950*; *To the Hustings*; *The United Nations as a Political Institution*.

H.H.Lb.   **Meteorology** (*in part*)
HUBERT HORACE LAMB, M.A., F.R.Met.S., F.R.G.S. World Climatology Research Unit, Meteorological Office, London.

H.J.A.   **Narcotics** (*in part*)
H. J. ANSLINGER, Commissioner of Narcotics, U.S. Treasury Department, Washington, D.C.; U.S. Representative, U.N. Commission on Narcotic Drugs. Author of *The Physician and the Federal Narcotic Law*; co-author of *The Traffic in Narcotics*.

H.J.J.   **Insurance** (*in part*)
HOLGAR J. JOHNSON. President, Institute of Life Insurance, New York.

H.Ln.   **Denmark; Greenland; etc.**
HELGE LARSEN, M.A. Teacher at Nykøbing Kathedralskole, Denmark. Author of *Politiske Grundtanker* (" Political Ideas "); Contributor to *De fem lange år* (" The Five Long Years ").

H.L.Sr.   **Business Review** (*Canning Industry* [*in part*])
H. L. STIER. Director, Division of Statistics, National Canners Association, U.S.

H.M.As.   **National Parks** (*in part*)
HAROLD MAURICE ABRAHAMS, M.A., LL.B. Secretary, National Parks Commission, London.

H.M.F.M.   **Wool**
HUGH MICHAEL FINER MALLETT, M.A. Editor, *Weekly Wool Chart*, Bradford, Yorkshire.

H.M.H.   **American Literature**
HARRISON M. HAYFORD, Ph.D. Assistant Professor of English, Northwestern University, Evanston, Illinois.

H.Mm.   **Crime** (*Postwar Survey*)
HERMANN MANNHEIM. Dr.jur., Hon. LL.D. (Utrecht), O.B.E. Hon. Director, Criminological Research Unit, London School of Economics and Political Science, London University. Author of *Social Aspects of Crime in England between the Wars*; *Criminal Justice and Social Reconstruction*; *Group Problems in Crime and Punishment*; etc.

H.My.   **Motor Industry** (*in part*)
HARRY MUNDY, A.M.I.Mech.E., M.S.A.E. Technical Editor, " Racing Engine Design " (Lonsdale Library *Motor Racing*).

H.Pn.   **Beekeeping**
HENRY PAGAN, B.A. Commercial Beekeeper.

H.Ra.   **Diseases** (*Skin Diseases*)
HERBERT RATTNER, M.D. Professor and Chairman, Department of Dermatology, Northwestern University Medical School, Chicago. Editor, *A.M.A. Archives of Dermatology*.

H.S.B.   **Cost of Living; Prices; etc.**
HAROLD SCOTT BOOKER. Senior Lecturer in Economic Statistics, University of London. Author of *The Problem of Britain's Overseas Trade*.

Hermann Mannheim   *J. du Plat Taylor*   *J. E. Nichols*   *Lord Silkin*

H.S.Js. **International Geophysical Co-operation**
SIR HAROLD SPENCER-JONES, M.A., Sc.D., LL.D., D.Phil., F.R.S. Editor, *I.C.S.U. Review*, International Council of Scientific Unions. (Astronomer Royal, 1933-55.) Author of *General Astronomy*; *Worlds without End*; *Life on Other Worlds*.

H.Sn. **Northern Ireland**
HUGH SHEARMAN, B.A., Ph.D. Author of *Anglo-Irish Relations*; *Ulster*; *Finland*; *Modern Ireland*; etc.

H.S.R. **German Literature**
HANS SIEGBERT REISS, B.A., Ph.D. Professor of German Language and Literature, McGill University, Montreal, Quebec, Canada. Author of *Franz Kafka, eine Betrachtung seines Werkes*. Editor of *The Political Thought of the German Romantics*.

H.S.S. **Bridges** (*in part*)
HUBERT SHIRLEY SMITH, O.B.E., M.I.C.E., M.Am.Soc.C.E., B.Sc.(Eng.), A.C.G.I., D.I.C. Director and London Manager of the Cleveland Bridge and Engineering Co. Ltd.; Council Member of the Institution of Civil Engineers. Author of *The World's Great Bridges*.

Hu.De. **Algeria; French Community; Tunisia; etc.**
HUBERT DESCHAMPS. Former French Colonial Governor. Professor at l'Ecole de la France d'Outremer and l'Institut d'Etudes Politiques (University of Paris). Author of *Madagascar*; *Champlain*; *l'Union Française*; *Méthodes et Doctrines coloniales de la France*; etc.

H.W.D. **Music** (*in part*)
HUBERT W. DAVID. Weekly columnist and feature writer, *The Melody Maker*; *Dance News*. Council Director, the Songwriters' Guild of Great Britain.

H.W.Dg. **Red Cross**
HENRY W. DUNNING. Secretary-General, League of Red Cross Societies, Geneva.

H.W.Sy. **Betting and Gambling** (*in part*)
HERBERT WENTWORTH STOTESBURY, B.A. Assistant Secretary, Home Office.

H.W.Wr. **Libraries** (*in part*)
HOWARD WOODROW WINGER. Associate Professor, Graduate Library School, University of Chicago.

H.Z. **Wild Life Conservation** (*in part*)
HOWARD ZAHNISER. Executive Secretary, Wilderness Society (U.S.); Editor, *The Living Wilderness*; Book Editor, *Nature Magazine*.

I.C. **Jewry**
ISRAEL COHEN, B.A. Vice-Chairman, Foreign Affairs Committee, Board of Deputies of British Jews; formerly General Secretary, World Zionist Organization. Author of *Contemporary Jewry*; *A Short History of Zionism*; *A Jewish Pilgrimage*.

I.H.D.B. **Social Services** (*in part*)
IAN HUGH DONALD BROWN. Children's Officer for the City of Manchester.

I.T.U. **Telecommunications** (*in part*)
Article contributed by the International Telecommunications Union, Geneva.

I.W.B.G. **Diseases** (*Respiratory Diseases*)
IAN WILLIAM BALLANTYNE GRANT, M.B., F.R.C.P.E. Physician, Respiratory Diseases Unit, Northern General Hospital, Edinburgh.

I.W.R. **Words and Meanings, New** (*in part*)
I. WILLIS RUSSELL. Chairman of the Research Committee on New Words of the American Dialect Society which contributed to the United States section of the article.

J.An. **Police** (*in part*)
SIR JOHN ANDERSON, K.B.E., C.B. Secretary, Scottish Home Department, Edinburgh.

J.B.Kr. **Diseases** (*Gastric and Intestinal Diseases*)
JOSEPH B. KIRSNER, M.D. Professor of Medicine, University of Chicago.

J.Bx. **Shops and Department Stores**
JOHN BAXTER, B.Com., Ph.D.(Econ.). Economic consultant.

J.C.Mn. **Printing** (*in part*)
JAMES CHARLES MORAN. Editor, *Printing, Press and Publishing News* and *Book Design and Production*, London.

J.D.Bs. **Gibraltar**
JULIAN DARRELL BATES, C.M.G., C.V.O. Colonial Secretary, Gibraltar.

J.D.Mn. **Virgin Islands, U.S.**
JOHN D. MERWIN. Governor, Virgin Islands of the United States.

J.D.P.T. **Archaeology** (*in part*)
JOAN du PLAT TAYLOR. Librarian, University of London Institute of Archaeology. Author of *Myrtru-Pigadhes: A Late Bronze Age Sanctuary in Cyprus*.

J.E.D. **Accidents**
JAMES EDWIN DAVIS. Journalist.

J.E.N. **Livestock**
JAMES EDWARD NICHOLS, M.Sc., Ph.D., F.R.S.Ed. Professor of Agriculture (Animal Husbandry), University of Wales (at University College of Wales, Aberystwyth). Author of *Livestock Improvement*.

J.E.S. **Philippines**
JOSEPH E. SPENCER. Professor of Geography, University of California, Los Angeles.

J.F.Bd. **General Election; Obituaries** (*Halifax*)
JOHN FRANCIS BOYD. Political Correspondent of *The Guardian*. Author of *Richard Austen Butler*.

J.F.Ck. **Political Parties, European** (*in part*)
JOHN FRANKLIN CLARK, B.A. Administrative Officer, International Department, Labour Party, London.

J.G. **Plastics Industry** (*jointly*)
JOHN GADSBY, B.Sc., M.A., D.Phil. Manager, Technical Service and Development Department, Plastics Division, Imperial Chemical Industries.

J.Ge. **Meteorology** (*in part*)
JOHN GLASSPOOLE, I.S.O., M.Sc., Ph.D. Formerly head of British Climatology Branch, Meteorological Office, London. Author of *British Floods and Droughts* (with C. E. P. Brooks).

J.G.L. **Business Review** (*Fur Trade* [*in part*])
JOSEPH GLUCKSTEIN LINKS, O.B.E. Director, Calman Links Ltd. and Hudson's Bay Company. Author of *The Book of Fur*.

J.G.T. **Medicine**
JOHN GILBERT THWAITES, M.B., B.S. Assistant Editor, *British Medical Journal*. Author of *Into General Practice*; *Modern Medical Discoveries*.

J.Gy. **English Research Studies**
JOAN GRUNDY, M.A. Lecturer in English Literature, University of Liverpool. Author of " Keats and the Elizabethans " in *John Keats: A Reassessment*, edited by K. Muir.

J.H.Ht. **Commonwealth Navies**
JOHN HUGHES-HALLETT, M.P. Vice-Admiral, R.N. (retd.).

J.Hkn. **Ceylon**
JOHN HOCKIN. London Editor, *Times of Ceylon*.

J.H.P. **Ghana**
JOSEPH HENRY PRICE. Lecturer in Government, University College of Ghana. Author of *The Role of Islam in Gold Coast Politics*; *The Gold Coast Election of 1951*; *The Eastern Nigerian General Election of 1957*.

J.H.Ps. **Universities and Colleges** (*in part*)
J. HOOD PHILLIPS, M.A. Secretary to the Senate, University of London.

J.J.McN. **Vegetable Oils and Animal Fats** (*in part*)
J. J. McNERNEY, B.Sc.(Econ.). Economic Assistant, Commonwealth Economic Committee, London.

J.Kd.   Water Supply (*in part*)
JULIUS KENNARD, B.Sc.(Eng.), M.I.C.E., M.I.W.E., M.Cons.E. Chartered civil engineer: Senior Partner, Edward Sandeman, Kennard and Partners, London.

J.Ke.   Israel
JON KIMCHE. Editor, *Jewish Observer and Middle East Review*. Author of *Seven Fallen Pillars: the Middle East 1945-1953*; (with David Kimche) *The Secret Roads: the Migration of a People*.

J.Kg.   Business Review (*Book Publishing* [*in part*])
JESSIE KITCHING. Head of the Booklisting Department, *Publishers' Weekly*, New York.

J.K.K.   Electric Power (*in part*)
JEROME K. KUYKENDALL. Chairman, Federal Power Commission, Washington, D.C.

J.K.L.   Banking (*in part*)
JOHN K. LANGUM. President, Business Economics, Inc., Chicago. Former Vice-president, Federal Reserve Bank of Chicago.

J.K.R.   Agriculture (*in part*); etc.
JOHN KERR ROSE, A.M., Ph.D., J.D. Senior Specialist in Natural Resources and Conservation, Legislative Reference Service, Library of Congress, Washington, D.C.

J.Ky.   Unitarian Church
JOHN KIELTY. Secretary, General Assembly, Unitarian and Free Christian Churches, London.

J.Ln.   South Africa, Union of
JULIUS LEWIN, B.A., LL.B. Barrister-at-Law. Advocate of the Supreme Court of South Africa; Senior Lecturer in African Administration, University of the Witwatersrand, Johannesburg; Joint Editor, *African Studies*. Author of *Studies in African Native Law*; etc.

J.L.T.   Libraries (*in part*)
JOHN LEONARD THORNTON, A.L.A. Librarian, Medical College Library, St. Bartholomew's Hospital, London. Author of *Classics of Librarianship*; (jointly) *Scientific Books, Libraries and Collectors*; *Medical Books, Libraries and Collectors*; etc.

J.L.V.C.   Forestry (*in part*)
JOHN LLOYD VAN CAMP. General Manager, Canadian Forestry Association, Montreal, Quebec. Author of *Fifty Trees of Canada*.

J.Mu.C.   Country Life
SIR JOHN (MONTAGU) CRASTER. Chairman of the Association of Sea Fisheries Committees for England and Wales and Vice-chairman of the Farne Island Committee of the National Trust. Author of " The Birds of Northumberland " in *The Three Northern Counties of England*.

Jn.Rd.   English Literature (*in part*)
JOHN RAYMOND. Critic and journalist for the *Sunday Times* and *New Statesman*. Author of *England's on the Anvil* and *Dodge of Dover*.

Jo.Ms.   Social Services (*in part*)
JOHN MOSS, C.B.E. Barrister-at-Law. Author of *Hadden's Health and Welfare Services Handbook*. Editor, *Local Government Law and Administration*.

J.P.Hn.   Horticulture
JOHN PILKINGTON HUDSON, M.B.E., G.M., M.Sc., Ph.D., N.D.H., Professor of Horticulture, University of Nottingham School of Agriculture, Sutton Bonington, Loughborough. Editor of *Control of the Plant Environment*.

J.R.D.   Foodstuffs (*Spices; Sugar; Tea*)
JEFFREY ROY DELLOW, B.Sc.(Econ.). Economic Assistant, Commonwealth Economic Committee, London.

J.R.Se.   Lesser Eastern Churches; Lutherans; etc.
JOHN RICHARD SATTERTHWAITE, B.A. General Secretary of the Church of England Council on Interchurch Relations and Vicar of St. Dunstan in the West, Fleet Street, London.

J.S.Br.   Orthopaedics
JOHN STANLEY BATCHELOR, F.R.C.S. Orthopaedic Surgeon, Guy's Hospital, London, and St. Vincent's Orthopaedic Hospital, Pinner, Middlesex.

Js.D.   United States
JULIUS CARL DUSCHA. Reporter, *The Washington Post*, Washington, D.C.

J.Sto.   Electronics (*in part*)
JAMES STOKLEY, B.S.(Ed.), M.S. College of Communication Arts, Michigan State University. Editor, *Science Marches On*.

J.T.W.   Coal
JOHN THOMAS WHETTON, M.Sc. Professor of Mining, University of Leeds. Author of Sections on Prospecting, Boring and Sinking of Caxton's textbook *Coal Mining*.

J.W.G.   Theatre (*in part*)
JOHN W. GASSNER. Sterling Professor of Playwriting and Dramatic Literature, Yale University. Drama Critic, *Educational Theatre Journal*. Author of *Masters of the Drama*; *The Theatre in Our Times*; etc.

K.A.L.P.   Fire Service
KENNETH ALFRED LAMPORT PARKER, C.B. Assistant Under Secretary of State, Civil Defence and Fire Service Departments, Home Office, London.

K.B.P.   Aliens
KARLO BRUCE PAICE, M.A. Assistant Under Secretary of State, Aliens Department, Home Office, London.

K.C.S.   Veterinary Medicine (*jointly*)
KENNETH CHARLES SELLERS, Ph.D., B.Sc., M.R.C.V.S., D.V.S.M. Director, the Animal Health Trust, Farm Livestock Research Centre, Stock, Essex.

K.I.   East Africa High Commission; Kenya; etc.
KENNETH INGHAM, M.C., M.A., D.Phil. Professor of History, Makerere College, University College of East Africa, Kampala, Uganda. Author of *Reformers in India*; *The Making of Modern Uganda*.

K.M.S.   Eastern European Economic Planning; Poland; etc.
KAZIMIERZ MACIEJ SMOGORZEWSKI. Writer on contemporary history. Founder and Editor, *Free Europe*, London. Author of *The United States and Great Britain*; *Poland's Access to the Sea*; etc.

K.M.Wy.   Bahama Islands
KENNETH MAURICE WALMSLEY, C.M.G., O.B.E. Colonial Secretary of the Bahamas.

L.B.K.   Armies of the World
LYMAN BICKFORD KIRKPATRICK, Jr. Former member of editorial staff, *U.S. News and World Report*, Washington, D.C.; general staff officer on staff of General Omar Bradley, Europe, 1944-45.

L.C.-Le.   West Indies, The (*Windward Islands*)
LOUIS COOLS-LARTIGUE, O.B.E. Chief Secretary, Windward Islands, Grenada.

L.F.C.   Methodist Church
LESLIE FREDERIC CHURCH, B.A., Ph.D., F.R.Hist.S. Hon. Connexional Editor, Methodist Church in Great Britain. Author of *The Knight of the Burning Heart*; *The Early Methodist People*; etc.

L.F.R.W.   Pakistan
LAURENCE FREDERIC RUSHBROOK WILLIAMS, C.B.E., J.P., M.A., B.Litt. Sometime Fellow of All Souls college, Oxford. Author of *India Under the Company and the Crown*; *What about India?*; *The State of Israel*; *Kutch in History and Legend*; etc.

L.H.C.   Diseases (*Allergic Diseases*)
LEO HERMANN CRIEP, M.D. Chief Clinician, Allergy Clinic, and Associate Professor of Medicine, School of Medicine, University of Pittsburgh, Pennsylvania. Author of *Essentials of Allergy*.

L.H.M.   Epidemics
LAURENCE HENRY MURRAY, O.B.E., M.D., B.S., B.Hy., D.P.H. Principal Medical Officer, Ministry of Health.

L.J.A.   Insurance (*in part*)
LAURENCE J. ACKERMAN. Dean, School of Business Administration, University of Connecticut, Storrs. Dean, College of Insurance, University of Connecticut, Hartford. Author of *Risks We Face*; etc.

L.J.D.R.   Classical Studies
LEOPOLD JOHN DIXON RICHARDSON, M.A. Emeritus Professor of Greek, University of Wales (at University College of South Wales and Monmouthshire, Cardiff); Hon. Secretary, Classical Association.

L.J.G.   Dentistry
LESLIE JAMES GODDEN, F.D.S., R.C.S. (Edin), L.D.S. (Eng.). Editor, *British Dental Journal*. Author of *Handbook on Dental Radiography*.

L.J.Le B.   Bacteriology
LEON JOSEPH LE BEAU. Assistant Professor of Microbiology, University of Illinois College of Medicine, Chicago.

L.M.   Association Football; Rugby Football
LAURENCE MONTAGUE, B.A. Assistant Editor, *The Guardian*.

L.M.K.   Biochemistry
LLOYD M. KOZLOFF. Associate Professor, Department of Biochemistry, University of Chicago.

L.O.T.   Lawn Tennis; Obituaries (*Riseley*)
LANCELOT OLIVER TINGAY. Lawn Tennis Correspondent, *Daily Telegraph*, London.

L.R.A.   Biographies (*Noel-Baker*); Trust Territories
LESLIE RONALD ALDOUS. Head of Information Department, United Nations Association of Great Britain and Northern Ireland. Editor, *United Nations Association Yearbook*. Author of *World Health: The New Outlook*; *Let There Be Bread*; *Education for Peace*.

Ls.Sn.   New Towns
LORD (LEWIS) SILKIN, P.C. Solicitor. Deputy Leader of Official Opposition in the House of Lords. Partner in the firm of Lewis Silkin and Partners, Solicitors. Minister of Town and Country Planning, 1945-50.

L.S.Y.   Singapore
LEE SIEW YEE. Editor, *Straits Times*, Kuala Lumpur, Federation of Malaya.

L.W.F.   Prisons
SIR LIONEL WRAY FOX, C.B., M.C. Chairman, Prison Commission for England and Wales. Author of *The Modern English Prison*; *The English Prison and Borstal Systems*.

M.B.McC.   Nutrition (*in part*)
MARY B. McCANN. Instructor in Nutrition, School of Public Health, Harvard University.

M.C.Br.   Housing
MARGARET CHRISTINE BAKER, M.B.E., B.A. Secretary, The Housing Centre Trust, London.

M.Dk.   Roman Catholic Church; etc.
(JOHN) MICHAEL DERRICK. Assistant Editor, *Tablet*, London. Editor, *Dublin Review*.

Marcel Stijns   *Norman Macdonald*   *Paul Grainger*   *Gen. Sir Sidney Kirkman*

M.DuV.   **Panama Canal Zone**
MILES DuVAL, Jr. Captain U.S. Navy, retired. Author of Panama Canal Series and other writings on inter-oceanic canal problems.

M.Gt.   **National Income**
MILTON GILBERT, M.A., Ph.D. Director of Economics and Statistics, Organization for European Economic Co-operation. Author of *Comparative Natural Products and Price Levels*; *Currency Depreciation and Monetary Policy*.

M.Mr.   **Commonwealth of Nations** (*in part*)
MOLLY MORTIMER, B.Sc.(Econ.). Journalist on Commonwealth and International Affairs. Contributor to *The Times Colonial Quarterly*; *Times of India*. Author of *Trusteeship in Practice*.

M.Rj.   **Netherlands**
MAARTEN ROOIJ, LL.D., Econ.D. Professor of Mass Media, University of Amsterdam. Director, Institute for Press Science.

M.Sk.   **Switzerland**
MELANIE F. STAERK, M.A., Ph.D. Associate Editor, *Swiss Review of World Affairs* (*Neue Zürcher Zeitung*), Zürich.

M.Ss.   **Belgium; etc.**
MARCEL HENRI STIJNS, O.B.E. President, International Federation of Journalists; Honorary President, Belgian Press Association. Editor-in-Chief, *Het Laatste Nieuws*, Brussels.

M.S.Sh.   **Fertilizers**
MARGARET SARAH SMITH, B.Sc., Ph.D., A.R.I.C. Senior Lecturer in Chemistry, Wye College (University of London), Wye, Kent.

Ms.Sr.   **World Health Organization**
MORRIS SINCLAIR. Press Officer, World Health Organization, United Nations, Geneva.

M.V.P.   **Balance of Payments; Investments Abroad** (*in part*); **etc.**
MICHAEL VIVIAN POSNER, M.A. (Oxon.), M.A. (Cantab.). University Lecturer in Economics, Cambridge.

N.C.B.   **Civil Service**
RT. HON. SIR NORMAN (CRAVEN) BROOK, G.C.B., LL.D. Secretary of the Cabinet; Joint Permanent Secretary to the Treasury; and Official Head of the Home Civil Service.

N.Fl.   **Boxing** (*in part*)
NAT S. FLEISCHER. Publisher and editor, *The Ring*, New York. Treasurer and former president, National Boxing Writers' Association, New York. Author of *Nat Fleischer's All Time Ring Record Book*; etc.

N.J.P.   **Metallurgy** (*in part*)
NORMAN JAMES PETCH, B.Sc., B.Met., Ph.D. Professor of Metallurgy, Leeds University.

N.McW.   **Athletics**
NORRIS DEWAR McWHIRTER, M.A. Athletics Correspondent, *Observer*, *Star*, etc., London. Secretary-General of the Association of Track and Field Statisticians. Author of *Get to Your Marks* (with R. McWhirter).

N.P.Macd.   **Chile; Peru**
NORMAN PEMBERTON MACDONALD. Writer on Latin American affairs, London. Author of *Hitler over Latin America*; *The Land and People of Brazil*; *The Markets of Central America*.

N.S.   **News Stories; Royal Family**
NORMAN SHRAPNEL. Member of editorial staff, *The Guardian*.

N.S.D.   **Trade Unions** (*in part*)
NORMAN STEWART DOWD. Executive Secretary, Canadian Labour Congress. Editor and Manager, *Canadian Labour*.

Oa.S.   **Literary Prizes** (*in part*)
OLGA SVATIK. Editor of *Literary Prizes and Their Winners* (U.S.).

O.F.K.   **Norway**
OLE FERDINAND KNUDSEN, M.Sc.(Econ.). Editor, *Norway Exports*, Oslo.

O.J.W.   **Historic Buildings**
OWAIN JOHN WEAVER, M.A. Assistant Inspector of Ancient Monuments, Ministry of Works, London.

O.M.R.   **Australia; Broadcasting, Sound** (*in part*); **etc.**
OWEN MICHAEL ROE, M.A. (Melb.), B.A. (Cantab.). Research Student in Australian History, Australian National University.

O.Pl.   **Diseases** (*Heart Diseases*)
OGLESBY PAUL, M.D. Clinical Associate Professor of Medicine, University of Illinois College of Medicine.

O.R.K.   **West Indies, The** (*Leeward Islands*)
OSMUND RANDOLPH KELSICK, D.F.C. Chief Secretary, Leeward Islands.

O.T.W.P.   **Dairy Farming and Dairy Produce**
OWEN THOMAS WILLIAMS PRICE, B.Sc., M.A., D.Phil. Technical Officer in Charge, Intelligence Unit, Development Department, Central Agricultural Control, Imperial Chemical Industries Limited, London.

O.W.W.   **Crime** (*in part*); **Police** (*in part*)
ORLANDO WINFIELD WILSON. Dean and Professor of Criminology, School of Criminology, University of California, Berkeley. Author of *Police Administration*; *Police Planning*; *Police Records*.

P.A.B.G.   **Sweden**
PERCY AMOREY BEAUFORT GETHIN, B.A. Assistant in Scandinavian Studies, Scott Polar Research Institute, Cambridge.

P.A.Sd.   **Meteorology** (*in part*)
PERCIVAL ALBERT SHEPPARD, B.Sc., F.Inst.P. Professor of Meteorology, University of London (at Imperial College). Author of " The Earth's Atmosphere " in *A Century of Science*.

P.A.W.-T.   **Golf**
PAT AINSWORTH WARD-THOMAS. Golf Correspondent, *The Guardian*.

P.D.   **Shipping, Merchant Marine** (*in part*)
PETER JOHN DUFF. Editor, *Shipping World and World Shipbuilding*, London. Author of *British Ships and Shipping*.

P.E.G.   **Mineral and Metal Production**
PAUL EVELEIGH GRAINGER, B.Sc.(Econ.), F.S.S. Statistician, British Bureau of Non-Ferrous Metal Statistics, Birmingham.

P.H.   **Fashion and Dress** (*in part*); **Housewifery**
PHYLLIS WEST HEATHCOTE. Paris correspondent on women's topics, *The Guardian*, *Glasgow Herald* and *Punch*.

P.Hh.   **Shipping, Merchant Marine** (*in part*)
PATRICK JOHN FIELDING HOWARTH, B.A. Publicity Secretary, Royal National Life-Boat Institution, London. Author of *The Year is 1851*; *The Dying Ukrainian*; *A Matter of Minutes*; etc.

P.M.Re.   **Business Review** (*Man-Made Fibres*)
PHILIP MORTON ROWE. Press Officer, British Man-Made Fibres Federation.

P.R.Ba.   **Architecture** (*in part*); **Obituaries** (*Wright*)
(PETER) REYNER BANHAM, B.A. Assistant Editor (Literary), *Architectural Review*; Lecturer on History of Art at the Central School of Arts and Crafts, London.

P.Ss.   **Insurance** (*in part*)
PERCY STEBBINGS. Insurance Editor and Correspondent of the *Financial Times*; *Bankers' Magazine*; *Investors' Chronicle*; *Lloyd's List*, London; etc.

P.W.H.   **Photography**
PERCY WOOTTON HARRIS, F.I.B.P., Hon.F.R.P.S., F.P.S.A., M.R.I. Formerly President, Royal Photographic Society, London; Editor, *Modern Camera Magazine*, London.

Q.W.   **International Law**
QUINCY WRIGHT, A.M., Ph.D., LL.D. Emeritus Professor of International Law, University of Chicago. Author of *A Study of War*; *The Study of International Relations*; etc.

R.A.Bz.   **Juvenile Delinquency**
RALPH A. BRAUNHOLTZ. Department of Social Administration, University of Manchester.

R.A.Sh.   Liberal Party
REGINALD ARTHUR SMITH. Editor, *Liberal News* and Liberal Publication Department. Author of *A Liberal Window on the World*; *Towards a Living Encyclopaedia*; *King of Little Everywhere*.

R.B.Gt.   Endocrinology
ROBERT BENJAMIN GREENBLATT, M.D. Professor of Endocrinology, Medical College of Georgia, Augusta. Author of *Office Endocrinology*.

R.B.Pe.   Air Forces of the World (*in part*)
ROBERT B. PIRIE. Vice-Admiral, U.S.N. Deputy Chief of Naval Operations (Air), U.S. Department of the Navy, Washington, D.C.

R.Cn.   Industrial Design
ROGER COLEMAN, A.R.C.A. Free-lance journalist on industrial design and art subjects. Contributor to *Design* and *Architecture and Building*.

R.C.T.   Missiles (*in part*)
ROBERT C. TRUAX, Captain, U.S. Navy Advanced Research Projects Agency, Department of Defense, Washington, D.C.

R.D.B.   Rowing
RICHARD DESBOROUGH BURNELL, M.A. Rowing Correspondent, *The Times*. Author of *The Oxford and Cambridge Boat Race*; *Sculling*; *Henley Regatta: a History*; *Swing Together*.

Rd.F.   Theatre (*in part*)
RICHARD FINDLATER. Dramatic Critic. Author of *The Unholy Trade*; *Michael Redgrave: Actor*; *Six Great Actors*.

R.E.Br.   Business Review (*Book Publishing* [*in part*])
RONALD ERNEST BARKER. Secretary, Publishers' Association, London. Author of *Books for All: A Study of International Book Trade*; *Tendency to Corrupt*; etc.

R.F.G.C.   Congregational Churches (*in part*)
RALPH FORMAN GODLEY CALDER, M.A., B.D. Secretary, International Congregational Council, London. Former Editor, *Scottish Congregationalist*, Glasgow; *British Missionary*, London.

R.F.W.   New York
ROBERT F. WAGNER. Mayor of New York City.

R.H.Pd.   Genetics
ROBERT HUGH PRITCHARD, Ph.D., B.Sc. Medical Research Council, Microbial Genetics Research Unit, Hammersmith Hospital, London.

R.H.Sl.   Jet Propulsion and Gas Turbines (*in part*)
REGINALD HERBERT SCHLOTEL, C.B.E., F.R.Ae.S. Director of Engine Research and Development, Ministry of Supply, London.

R.J.L.   Aviation, Civil (*in part*)
ROBERT JOSEPH LANDRY. Secretary, Industrial Council, Air Industries and Transport Association of Canada.

R.J.Lh.   Foodstuffs (*Meat*)
RONALD JOSEPH LICKORISH. Member of the editorial staff, *The Meat Trades Journal*, London.

R.J.My.   Fashion and Dress (*in part*)
RONALD JOSEPH MURRAY. Assistant Editor, *Men's Wear*, London.

R.J.S.   Yachting
ROBIN JACK SALES, M.A. Journalist.

R.L.G.   Colombia
ROBERT L. GILMORE. Intelligence Research Specialist, Department of State, Washington, D.C.

R.L.Hs.   Hockey
RICHARD LYNTON HOLLANDS. Hockey Correspondent. Editor, *Hockey News* (official journal of the Hockey Association), London. Author (with R. Y. Fison) of *Hockey*.

R.L.S-R.   Radio, Scientific Developments in; etc.
REGINALD LESLIE SMITH-ROSE, C.B.E., D.Sc., Ph.D., F.C.G.I., D.I.C., A.R.C.S., M.I.E.E., F.I.R.E. Director of Radio Research, Department of Scientific and Industrial Research, London.

R.M.G.   Horse Racing
ROBERT MARSHALL GOODWIN. Assistant Editor (London), *Encyclopædia Britannica*.

R.M.Ry.   Universities and Colleges (*in part*)
ROBERT MANTLE RATTENBURY, M.A. Registrary of the University of Cambridge.

R.O.B.   Business Review (*Catering Industry* [*in part*])
REGINALD O. BAKER. Editor, *Caterer and Hotel Keeper*, London.

R.P.Gn.   British Borneo; etc.
RICHARD PHILLIP GILSON, A.B., M.A., M.Sc.(Econ.). Research Fellow, Department of Pacific History, Australian National University, Canberra.

R.Pn.   Wines
RENE PROTIN, Ingénieur Agronome. Director, International Vine and Wine Office, Paris.

R.R.Cy.   Business Review (*Silk*)
REGINALD RAYNER CATTY, B.Com. Director, Silk and Rayon Users Association, Richmond, Surrey.

R.R.W.E.   Foodstuffs (*Fruit*); Market Gardening; etc.
ROGER ROLAND WESTWELL FOLLEY, B.Sc., B.Com. Lecturer in Agricultural Economics, Wye College (University of London), Wye, Kent. Author of *The Economics of a Fruit Farm*; etc.

R.Sd.   Business Review (*Baking Industry* [*in part*])
RONALD WALTER SHEPPARD. Editor, *Bakers' Review*, London. Part-author of *The Story of Bread*.

R.S.E.   Anglican Communion
ROSAMUND SIBYL ESSEX, M.A. Editor, *Church Times*, London.

R.S.H.   Railways (*in part*)
ROBERT SELPH HENRY. Retired Vice-President, Association of American Railroads. Author of *This Fascinating Railroad Business*; *Trains*.

R.Ss.   Conservative Party
RONALD SIMMS. Chief Publicity Officer, Conservative Party.

R.V.B.B.   Navies of the World
RAYMOND VICTOR BERNARD BLACKMAN, A.M.R.I.N.A., A.I.Mar.E. Editor, *Jane's Fighting Ships*, London. Author of *Modern World Book of Ships*; *The World's Warships*.

R.W.Cr.   Television (*in part*)
RUFUS WILLIAM CRATER. Senior Editor, *Broadcasting Magazine*, New York.

R.W.Sl.   Geography
ROBERT WALTER STEEL, B.Sc., M.A. John Rankin Professor of Geography, University of Liverpool; formerly Fellow of Jesus College, Oxford, and Senior Lecturer in Colonial Geography, University of Oxford.

Ry.P.   European Coal and Steel Community; etc.
ROY PRYCE, M.A., Ph.D. Press Attaché, Delegation in the United Kingdom of the European Coal and Steel Community, London.

S.A.Ln.   Strikes (*in part*); Trade Unions
SAR A. LEVITAN. Specialist in Labour Economics and Industrial Development, Legislative Reference Service, Library of Congress. Author of *Federal Assistance to Labor Surplus Areas*; *Ingrade Wage Rate Progressions*.

S.C.Kn.   Civil Defence
SIR SIDNEY (CHEVALIER) KIRKMAN, G.C.B., K.B.E., M.C., General, Director-General of Civil Defence, Home Office, London.

S.E.J.   Dance (*in part*)
SARA E. JACKSON. Librarian of the English Folk Dance and Song Society, London.

S.Gl.   India
SARVEPALLI GOPAL, M.A., D.Phil. Director, Historical Division, Ministry of External Affairs, New Delhi. Author of *The Permanent Settlement in Bengal and its Results*; *The Viceroyalty of Lord Ripon, 1880-1884*; *The Viceroyalty of Lord Irwin, 1926-1931*.

S.G.Tn.   Aviation, Civil (*in part*)
STUART GUY TIPTON. President, Air Transport Association of America.

S.J.G.   Sociology
SAMUEL JULIUS GOULD, M. A. (Oxon.). Lecturer in Sociology, London School of Economics.

S.L.H.   Greece
STELIO LUCIAN HOURMOUZIOS. Journalist; Director, Greek Information Office, London, 1952-55. Author of *Salute to Greece*; *Starvation in Greece*.

S.M.F.   Comment of the Year
SHELAGH MARY FREEMAN, B.A. Journalist.

S.Nn.   English Literature (*in part*)
SYLVA NORMAN. Writer and critic, London. Author of *Cat Without Substance*; *Flight of the Skylark: the Development of Shelley's Reputation*; *Tongues of Angels*.

S.Nr.   Pacific Islands, U.S.; etc.
STANLEY NEHMER. International Bank for Reconstruction and Development, Washington, D.C. Professorial Lecturer, American University, Washington, D.C.

S.Pr.   Investments Abroad (*in part*)
SAMUEL PIZER. Chief, International Investment Section, Balance of Payments Division, Office of Business Economics, U.S. Department of Commerce, Washington, D.C.

S.R.Bn.   Advertising (*in part*)
SIDNEY R. BERNSTEIN. Editorial Director, *Advertising Age*, *Industrial Marketing* and *Advertising Requirements*. Vice-president, Advertising Publications Inc., Chicago.

S.Tf.   Television (*in part*)
SOL TAISHOFF. President, Editor and Publisher of *Broadcasting Magazine*, Washington, D.C.

S.Wn.   Show Jumping and Horse Trials
SHEILA WADDINGTON. Author of *Three Days Running*.

T.Bar.   Capital Investment; etc.
TIBOR BARNA, B.Sc.(Econ.), Ph.D. Assistant Director, National Institute of Economic and Social Research, London. Author of *Redistribution of Income through Public Finance in 1937*.

T.C.Pe.   Berlin; Germany
HON. TERENCE CORNELIUS PRITTIE, B.A. German correspondent, *The Guardian*. Author of *Escape to Freedom*; *Mainly Middlesex*; *Lancashire Hot-Pot*.

T.L.K.   Costa Rica
THOMAS L. KARNES, Ph.D. Assistant Professor of History, Tulane University, New Orleans.

T.L.T.L.   Gynaecology and Obstetrics
THOMAS LOFTUS TOWNSHEND LEWIS, M.B., B.Ch., F.R.C.S., M.R.C.O.G. Obstetric Surgeon, Guy's Hospital; Surgeon, Queen Charlotte's Maternity Hospital; Surgeon, Chelsea Hospital for Women. Author of *Progress in Clinical Obstetrics and Gynaecology*; (jointly) *The Queen Charlotte's Textbook of Obstetrics*, 9th ed.; *Midwifery by Ten Teachers*, 9th ed.; etc.

T.Q.C.   Theatre (*in part*)
THOMAS QUINN CURTISS. Drama critic, *New York Herald-Tribune*, Paris.

V.A.J.W.   **Foodstuffs** (*Vegetables*); **Market Gardening**
VERNON ALFRED JOHN WAKELY. Editor of *Commercial Grower*.

V.J.P.   **Cyprus**
VERNON JOHN PARRY, M.A. (Oxon.). Lecturer in the History of the Near and Middle East, School of Oriental and African Studies, University of London. Contributor to the *New Cambridge Modern History*; *Encyclopaedia of Islam*; etc.

V.Sr.   **Dance** (*in part*)
VICTOR SILVESTER. Chairman, Imperial Society of Teachers of Dancing; Director, B.B.C. and Television Dancing Clubs. Author of *Modern Ballroom Dancing*; *Old Time Dancing*.

V.W.P.   **Betting and Gambling** (*in part*)
VIRGIL WALLACE PETERSON. Operating Director, Chicago Crime Commission, Chicago, Illinois. Author of *Barbarians In Our Midst*; *Gambling: Should It Be Legalized?*

W.A.Re.   **Archaeology** (*in part*)
WILLIAM A. RITCHIE. State archaeologist, New York State Museum and Science Service, Albany, N.Y. Author of *The Pre-Iroquoian Occupations of New York State*.

W.B.Hd.   **Geology**
WALTER BRIAN HARLAND, M.A. Fellow of Gonville and Caius College, Cambridge; Lecturer in Geology, University of Cambridge.

W.C.B.   **Motor Racing**
WILLIAM CHARLES BODDY. Editor, *Motor Sport*. Full member, Guild of Motoring Writers. Author of *The Story of Brooklands*, vol. 1-3; *The 200 Mile Race*; *The World's Land Speed Record*; *Continental Sports Cars*; Motoring section, *Fifty Years of Brooklands*.

W.Cn.   **United Nations**
WALDO CHAMBERLIN. Professor of Government, New York University.

W.Dd.   **United States Foreign Aid**
WILLIAM DIEBOLD, Jr. Director of Economic Studies, Council on Foreign Relations, New York. Author of *New Directions in Our Trade Policy*; *The Schuman Plan*; etc.

Wd.E.   **Canada** (*in part*)
WILFRID EGGLESTON. Director, Department of Journalism, Carleton University, Ottawa, Canada. Author of *Scientists at War*; etc.

W.D.Hd.   **Law and Legislation** (*in part*)
WILLIAM DENNIS HAWKLAND. Professor of Law, Rutgers University School of Law, Newark, New Jersey. Author of *Cases on Bills and Notes*; *Sales under Uniform Commercial Code*.

W.Dk.   **Diseases** (*Diseases of the Blood*)
WILLIAM DAMESHEK, M.D. Professor of Medicine, Tufts University School of Medicine, Boston, Massachusetts. Editor-in-Chief, *Blood—the Journal of Hematology*, New York.

W.E.Hl.   **Hospitals** (*in part*)
WILLIAM EDWARD HALL, F.C.I.S., F.H.A. Director, Division of Hospital Facilities, King Edward's Hospital Fund for London.

W.E.Sn.   **Palaeontology**
WILLIAM ELGIN SWINTON, B.Sc., Ph.D., F.R.S.E. Principal Scientific Officer, British Museum (Natural History), London. Author of *The Dinosaurs*; *The Corridor of Life*; *Geology in the Museum*.

W.F.Q.   **Hawaii**
WILLIAM FRANCIS QUINN. Governor, Territory of Hawaii.

W.Gt.   **Anthropology** (*in part*)
WALTER GOLDSCHMIDT. Professor of Anthropology and Sociology, University of California, Los Angeles; Editor, *American Anthropologist*. Author of *Man's Way*; *A Preface to the Understanding of Human Society*; *Exploring the Ways of Mankind*.

W.Han.   **Motor Industry** (*in part*); **Motor Transport** (*in part*)
WOODTHORPE JUDE HARRISON, B.A. Economist, London.

W.H.C.   **Police** (*in part*)
WILLIAM HERBERT CORNISH, C.B. Assistant Under Secretary of State, Home Office, London.

W.H.Ctr.   **Council of Europe**; **Western European Union**
WILLIAM HORSFALL CARTER, M.A. Head of Publications Division, Council of Europe, Strasbourg; Editor, *The Fortnightly*, London, 1937-39. Co-author of *The Life of Leonid Krassin*; Translator of books from French, German and Spanish.

W.H.G.   **Roads** (*in part*)
WILLIAM HENRY GLANVILLE, C.B., C.B.E., D.Sc., M.I.C.E., F.R.S. Director of Road Research, Department of Scientific and Industrial Research Road Research Laboratory, Harmondsworth, Middlesex.

W.H.Is.   **Commonwealth of Nations** (*in part*); **etc.**
(WILLIAM) HAROLD INGRAMS, C.M.G., O.B.E. Formerly Adviser on Overseas Information, Colonial Office, London. Author of *Arabia and the Isles*; *Seven across the Sahara*; *Hong Kong*; etc.

W.Hl.   **Finland**
WENDY HALL, B.A. Author and journalist, London. Author of *Green Gold and Granite: A Background to Finland*; etc.

W.H.W.   **Philosophy**
WILLIAM HENRY WALSH. Senior Tutor, Merton College, Oxford; Lecturer in Philosophy, University of Oxford. Author of *Introduction to Philosophy of History*; *Reason and Experience*.

W.J.Bn.   **Diseases** (*Venereal Diseases* [*in part*])
WILLIAM JORDAN BROWN, M.D. Chief, Venereal Disease Branch, Communicable Disease Center, Atlanta, Georgia.

W.J.Bp.   **Biographies** (*Heyrovský*)
WILLIAM JOHN BISHOP, F.L.A. Editor, *Medical History*, London; formerly Librarian, Wellcome Historical Library, London. Part-author of *Notable Names in Medicine and Surgery*; etc.

W.J.Fy.   **Accountancy**
WILLIAM JOHN FINDLAY. Chartered Accountant, London.

W.J.S.   **Plastics Industry** (*jointly*)
WILFRED JOHN SUTTON, B.Sc. Chemist, Imperial Chemical Industries Ltd., Plastics Division.

W.K.F.   **Pharmacy**
WILLIAM KENNETH FITCH, M.P.S. Editor (1933-57), *Pharmaceutical Journal*, London; Publications Manager, Pharmaceutical Society of Great Britain. Author of *Gas Warfare*.

W.L.Be.   **Diseases** (*Eye Diseases*)
WILLIAM L. BENEDICT, M.D., LL.D. Emeritus Professor of Ophthalmology, University of Minnesota Graduate School, Mayo Foundation, Rochester, Minnesota.

Wm.C.   **Business Review** (*Linen and Flax*)
WILLIAM CARTER. Information Officer, Flax Development Committee, Belfast.

Wm.M.   **Agriculture** (*in part*)
WILLIAM MORGAN. On the staff of the Commonwealth Economic Committee, London.

W.N.   **Words and Meanings, New** (*in part*)
WALTER NASH, M.A. Lektor in English, University of Lund, Sweden.

Wn.A.S.   **Air Forces of the World** (*in part*)
WELMAN A. SHRADER. Director of Publications, Institute of the Aeronautical Sciences, New York. Author of *Fifty Years of Flight*; *Florida from the Air*; etc.

W.O.L.S.   **Youth Employment** (*in part*)
WILLIAM OWEN LESTER SMITH, LL.D., M.A. Formerly Professor of the Sociology of Education, University of London. Author of *To Whom do Schools belong?*; *Education in Great Britain*; etc.

W.P.Ma.   **Telecommunications** (*in part*)
WALTER P. MARSHALL. President, Western Union Telegraph Company, New York.

Wr.B.H.   **Theatre** (*in part*)
WALTER BERTRAM HERBERT. Executive Director, Canada Foundation, Ottawa, Ontario.

W.R.W.   **Veterinary Medicine** (*jointly*)
WALTER REGINALD WOOLDRIDGE, M.Sc., Ph.D., F.R.C.V.S., F.R.I.C. Scientific Director, Animal Health Trust, London. Author of *War Gases and Foodstuffs*; *Farm Animals in Health and Disease*.

W.Ss.   **Field Sports**
WILSON STEPHENS. Editor, *The Field*, London.

W.T.Ws.   **Defence Policy**; **Law and Legislation** (*in part*); **etc.**
WILLIAM THOMAS WELLS, B.A., Q.C., M.P. Member, Magistrates' Courts Rules Committee, and formerly of Lord Chancellor's Committee on the Practice and Procedure of the Supreme Court. Author of *How English Law Works*.

W.V.P.   **China**; **Hong Kong**; **Tibet**
WILFRED VICTOR PENNELL. Associate Editor, *South China Morning Post*, Hong Kong.

W.W.Bn.   **Education** (*in part*)
WILLIAM W. BRICKMAN. Professor of Education, New York University. President's Research Fellow, Brown University, Providence, Rhode Island, 1950-51. Editor, *School and Society*.

X.
Contributor wishing to remain anonymous.

Z.L.Sz.   **Hungary**
ZOLTÁN LADISLAS SZABÓ. Author, editor, radio correspondent. Honorary Secretary of the Hungarian Writers' Association Abroad. Author of *A Tardi Helyzet*; *Szerelmes Földrajz*; etc.

BOOK OF THE YEAR

ACCIDENTS. **On the Roads.** At the annual meeting of the Magistrates' association in Oct. 1959 Lord Kilmuir, the lord chancellor and president of the association, spoke of the number of deaths on the roads as one of the " tragic problems overshadowing the scientific and material advance of mankind ". In Great Britain 5,970 people were killed and 293,797 injured in road accidents in 1958 (Table I), an over-all increase in all road casualties of 9·5% on the previous year. Figures for the first nine months of 1959 indicated that the year's total would exceed by about 11% that for 1958. The cost to the community of road accidents in 1958, comprising compensation for personal injury, damage to and repair of property, and administrative costs, was estimated by the Royal Society for the Prevention of Accidents (Rospa) at £190 million (total expenditure on the roads in 1958 amounted to £133·2 million).

While the publicity given to road and travel accidents in general tends to obscure the fact that they claim only about one-third of all accidental deaths—more than 40% occur in the home—it is on the roads that the element of human fallibility which is the biggest factor in nearly all accidents is most apparent. From the detailed analyses of road accidents and their causes the salient fact emerges that it is the driver of a motor vehicle who is most frequently at fault. More than 2·5 million new driving licences were issued in 1959 and traffic conditions, to quote a former chief inspector of police in London, had brought about " a state of affairs in which you have something like 8 million motorists all hating each other." The motor car, besides being a symbol of success, is indeed all too often an instrument for the release of aggressive instincts, whereas the frustrating chaos of modern traffic

He thought he could drink and drive

The Royal Society for the Prevention of Accidents published this poster in 1959 to focus attention on a factor to which some experts attributed more road accidents than did official statistics.

TABLE I. ROAD CASUALTIES TO CHILDREN AND ADULTS

	1934	1945	1957	1958	1958 9 months	1959 9 months
CHILDREN*						
Deaths .	1,438	1,282	629	717	569	520
Injuries .	...	...	44,701	49,146	38,368	39,621
ADULTS						
Deaths .	5,905†	3,974	4,921	5,253	3,580	3,839
Injuries .	231,603†‡	133,042‡	223,607	244,651	176,543	197,712
TOTAL .	238,946†	138,298	273,858	299,767	219,060	241,692

* Under 15 yr. † Highest prewar figure. ‡ Including children.

TABLE II. MOTOR VEHICLES REGISTERED AND ROAD ACCIDENT DEATH RATES IN SELECTED COUNTRIES, 1957

Country	Vehicles Registered* ('000)	Deaths per 10,000 Vehicles	Deaths per 100,000 Population
Austria . . .	303	65·5	28·4
German Fed. Rep. .	3,306	37·7	24·5
Australia . . .	2,272	9·2	21·6
United States . .	67,135	5·5	21·4
France . . .	5,343	15·9	19·3
Italy . . .	1,643	42·2	14·4
Sweden . . .	974	9·7	12·8
Great Britain . .	5,450	10·2	11·1
Yugoslavia . .	60	123·0	4·1

* Excl. 2- or 3-wheeled motorcycles, trams, trolley-buses, ambulances, hearses, government and special purpose vehicles.

demands of all classes of road user an unrelaxing self-discipline. In conditions of ever-increasing vehicle density the greatest need is for higher standards of driving. Much of the work of Rospa, within the framework of the national road safety campaign begun by the government in 1945, has been designed to achieve this. The society has conducted special annual campaigns bearing on a particular aspect of road safety—" Road Courtesy ", " Mind That Child ", " Be a Better Driver ", etc.—and it has organized a national safe driving competition in which more than a quarter of a million professional drivers take part annually. Perhaps the greatest encouragement to the society and to others concerned with road safety has been that the number of children killed has been almost halved during the postwar years.

Criticism by magistrates, police officers and others of the lack of an effective deterrent to dangerous driving and driving while under the influence of drink gave interest to an amendment to the Norwegian traffic laws, passed in 1959, which made it illegal to have consumed alcohol within six hours of being involved in an accident, the object being to invalidate attempts to prove in court that drinking had taken place subsequent to and not before the accident. In Norway there is no alternative to a minimum sentence of three weeks' imprisonment and disqualification for a year if a driver has a concentration of alcohol in his blood exceeding $0 \cdot 05\%$ (representing a quite modest intake). Tests may be made during routine traffic checks and, if positive, the driver will incur the minimum penalty, though no accident has taken place. This clear-cut legislation is held in healthy respect.

In the Home. The chief victims of accidents in the home are the very young and the elderly, with women forming the majority of casualties in the three main categories—falls, poisoning and burns and scalds. Table III analyses the total number of deaths in 1957 by age, sex and cause of death. The number of injuries is not known, but has been estimated at between 75,000 and 100,000 serious and about 1 million slight. Falls cause many more deaths in the home than all other forms of accident combined and, in October, at the opening of its annual national safety congress, Rospa launched a six months' campaign with the slogan " Check That Fall ". Among the commonplace hazards to which attention was drawn was trailing flex from makeshift connections for numerous electrical apparatuses, including the varied armoury of the " do-it-yourself " enthusiast. The majority of fatal poisonings at home are by household gas, most of the victims

protect young and old from

HOME ACCIDENTS

A poster published by the Royal Society for the Prevention of Accidents in support of its 1959 campaign to reduce home accidents.

being elderly people. Burns and scalds can be divided into two main groups. The first consists of burns from clothing ignited by open and unguarded fires and direct burns from fires, chiefly suffered by women and elderly people. The second group consists of burns and scalds from hot substances, corrosive liquids and steam, of which young children are the most frequent victims.

Legislation for the prevention of domestic accidents, apart from that concerned with the design of houses and their equipment, is largely impracticable and by the end of 1959 was limited in the United Kingdom to the Children and Young Persons (Amendment) act of 1952 and the Heating Appliances (Fireguards) act of 1953, both acts being concerned solely with the danger from unguarded open fires and other heating appliances (the 1953 act prohibited the sale of electric and gas fires or oil heaters without guards). The Fabrics (Misdescription) act of 1913 has a bearing on home safety as it prohibits the sale of textile fabrics or garments described as non-flammable which do not conform to a prescribed standard. Its effect is negative, however, in that it does not prohibit the offer for sale of highly inflammable fabrics bearing no description.

The enforcement of any code of safety in the home being impossible, reduction of the accident rate can only be achieved through publicizing the risks involved and the means of minimizing them. Rospa has been instrumental, since 1932, in forming local home safety committees throughout Britain, which under the National Health act, 1946, and the Local Government act, 1948, became eligible for financial support from local authorities. Training in home safety is also carried out by health visitors and welfare workers and by voluntary organizations such as the British Red Cross society and the St. John Ambulance brigade. In 1947 the home secretary set up a standing interdepartmental committee to co-ordinate departmental action in connection with the prevention of accidents in the home and to maintain contact with unofficial organizations interested in the subject. Home accidents cause a heavy strain on hospital services, the annual cost of treatment being between £4 million-£5 million. A badly burned child may spend up to 400 days in hospital and in the early stages needs the constant attention of three to four doctors and five to six nurses to save its life.

TABLE III. ACCIDENTAL DEATHS IN THE HOME, 1957

Cause of Death	Age Group					Sex		Total Deaths
	0-4	5-14	15-44	45-64	65+	Male	Female	
Falls .	51	12	83	305	4,217	1,437	3,231	4,668
Poisoning .	23	9	178	354	699	558	705	1,263
Burns and Scalds	103	53	63	123	398	243	497	740
Suffocation .	522	11	41	60	62	404	292	696
Miscellaneous .	116	31	76	62	75	217	143	360
TOTAL .	815	116	441	904	5,451	2,859	4,868	7,727

SOURCE. Rospa.

At Work. Industrial accident prevention has its roots in legislation dating from an act of 1833 empowering the government to appoint inspectors of factories. The Factories acts of 1937 and 1948, with many associated regulations, constitute a comprehensive statutory code of industrial safety which has been supplemented by the work of Rospa and other voluntary bodies and of employers' and workers' organizations.

Fatal accidents at workplaces comprise about 6%-7% of all accidental deaths. Since 1955 there has been a general downward trend in the total accident figure for factories and premises subject to the factories acts (*see* Table IV). The 1958 total was the lowest since 1935, but the general trend does not apply to building operations and works of engineering construction, at which the total number of accidents has increased almost without break since 1952. About 80% of fatal accidents in building and civil engineering operations are caused by falls of persons and materials during demolition work, an indication that much of this work is carried out by insufficiently experienced labour. The introduction of new techniques in building construction has brought new hazards. An example is the use of the continental type of tower crane which has to be anchored to the structure at successive heights as work proceeds. Another danger connected with cranes stems from the use of remote radio control, which in many cases has proved unreliable for the purpose.

Safety precautions for the erection and operation of nuclear reactors and associated plant must of course be particularly stringent, and the risk from radioactive materials extends to an increasing number of factories (560 in 1958) which use radio-isotopes in sealed and unsealed forms for gamma radiography of castings and welds and various other purposes. Preliminary draft regulations under the factories acts for the protection of workers exposed to this risk were published in 1957 and were being revised during 1959. The International Atomic Energy agency also published a handbook on *Safe Handling of Radio-isotopes* in 1958.

The Industrial Health and Safety centre, a permanent public exhibition of methods, arrangements and appliances for promoting safety, health and welfare in industry, maintained in London by the factories department of the Ministry of Labour and National Service, had 16,000 visitors in 1958 and provided a meeting place for numerous accident prevention groups.

TABLE IV. REPORTED ACCIDENTS IN PREMISES SUBJECT TO THE FACTORIES ACTS

	1938	1952	1955	1956	1957	1958
Fatal accidents	944	792	703	687	651	665
Total accidents	180,103	177,510	188,403	184,785	174,713	167,697

TABLE V. CASUALTIES IN COAL MINES

	1933-42*	1950*	1955*	1956	1957	1958
Deaths .	877	493	425	328	396	327
Serious injuries	3,123	2,020	1,538	1,452	1,604	1,752
Total injuries .	140,297	237,833	217,305	219,783	198,129	206,855

* Incl. oil shale, stratified ironstone and fireclay mines.

During 1958 there were 327 fatal accidents in the 1,434 coal mines being worked (Table V), the lowest figure ever recorded, and a continuation of the trend of recent years. To some extent this reflected the reduction in the number of manshifts worked due to the fall in the demand for coal. On the other hand the number of serious injuries, at 1,752, continued an upward trend begun in 1956.

There is no reliable record of all non-fatal casualties requiring medical treatment, but the annual total in all forms of activity may be about 2·25 million. It was stated at the annual conference of the British Orthopaedic association in Oct. 1959 that existing accident services were " seriously inadequate " to deal with such numbers and that their organization should be undertaken by the state as a " quasi-military operation ". (J. E. D.)

ACCOUNTANCY. Electronic data processing was the theme of many addresses given at accounting conferences and meetings in 1959. Indeed, two professional bodies held special courses for their members exclusively on that subject. That by the Institute of Chartered Accountants of Scotland at Troon in April proved so popular that it had to be repeated later in the year. The Association of Certified and Corporate Accountants held a weekend school at Oxford, also in April, at which the theme was " the accountant as adviser and co-ordinator in electronic data processing ". The same body published in October the first two pamphlets of a series in which both general and specific aspects of the effect electronic computers were likely to have on business activities would be surveyed. Another opportunity for accountants to make themselves familiar with this striking development in commercial recording and analysis was afforded by the annual National Business Efficiency exhibition in London in May, when " every conceivable office gadget from a computer to a paper clip " was on show. In the United States, where so many accountants take a degree before beginning their office careers, the question of offering courses in computer instruction was being considered by a number of universities.

In answering a questionnaire prepared by the Metric committee of the British Association for the Advancement of Science, engaged on an inquiry into the desirability of introducing the metric system and decimal coinage into the United Kingdom, both the Institute of Chartered Accountants in England and Wales and the Scottish institute expressed full approval of any move towards reform in the direction of decimal coinage. Neither body thought that, as far as the profession was concerned, transitional difficulties would be great and each was in favour of a method of decimalization which would keep the £ as the basic currency unit with probable sub-divisions equal to one-tenth, one-hundredth and one-thousandth of a £.

From a record entry, the British Oxygen company and General Refractories Ltd. won the 1959 awards by *The Accountant* for merit in the presentation of company financial accounts. The presentation of the awards was made in the Mansion house by the lord mayor of London, Sir Harold Gillett, himself a chartered accountant.

A case of much interest to accounting and other professional bodies was decided during the year when the U.S. Court of Appeal upheld the right of the American Institute of Certified Public Accountants to issue statements on accounting principles. The plaintiffs, three public utility companies, had obtained an injunction restraining the institute from issuing a letter explaining the phrase " a deferred tax account " used in one of its accounting research bulletins. The allegedly offending paragraph ran:

" The committee used the phrase in its ordinary connotation of an account to be shown in the balance sheet as a liability or a deferred credit. A provision in recognition of the deferral of income taxes, being required for the proper determination of net income, should not at the same time result in a credit to earned surplus or to any other account included in the stockholders' equity section of the balance sheet."

The companies maintained that such treatment would interfere with their short-term borrowing powers and other financial activities and that the prestige of the institute was such that, in effect, the recommendation would become a rule. After a number of contradictory court rulings the injunction was finally set aside.

The Netherlands government, in 1959, had on hand a bill to regulate the accountancy profession in that country. This provided that a register should be established to contain the names of those who had passed a university accountancy examination or an examination conducted by a new professional organization to be established entitled the Netherlands Institute of Register-Accountants. Under the proposed new regime the mere title of " accountant " was not to be protected. The government of Ceylon also considered a bill designed to regulate the profession. The measure called for the establishment of a professional body to be named the Institute of Chartered Accountants of Ceylon. Existing recognized accountants were to be eligible for membership and, thereafter, the approach to qualification was normally to be by practical training and examination. Until such time as the new institute was in receipt of regular income the government was prepared to finance it.

In 1955 the Scottish institute issued a report on the training of apprentices and recommended that the middle one of the five years' training period should be regarded as an " academic year " in which apprentices would attend a university to take prescribed classes in accounting, law and economics. The scheme was accepted by the members after much discussion and, following upon protracted negotiations with university and other authorities, the institute announced in 1959 that the scheme would begin to operate in the autumn of 1960. The committee set up in 1958 by the English institute to consider and make recommendations on the most appropriate forms of education and training for entrants to the profession received evidence during the year from professional, educational, commercial and industrial sources.

The same institute, in 1959, issued its new members' handbook. Designed on the same loose-leaf principle as the American institute's C.P.A. handbook, this notable project—which cost £37,500 to inaugurate—would eventually contain all the institute's current publications in two volumes.

The particulars of the succession of mergers and amalgamations which were again a feature of British business in 1959, were closely studied by accountants as the profession was almost invariably represented, either by firms or by individuals, when the terms and mechanics of such deals were being negotiated. A general welcome was given, by experts and layment alike, to the pamphlet issued in November by the Issuing Houses association entitled *Notes on Amalgamations of British Business*, containing the views of a committee, appointed in July at the suggestion of the governor of the Bank of England, on the "principles and practices to be followed in such operations". (*See* also BANKING.)

(W. J. FY.)

ADEN. British colony and protectorate on south coast of Arabia. Total area: *c.* 112,110 sq.mi. Total pop.: (1957 est.) *c.* 800,000. Main imports: petroleum products, raw cotton, cotton piecegoods and foodstuffs. Main exports: refined petroleum products, ships' stores and bunkering, raw cotton, cotton piecegoods, coffee, sugar, skins and hides. Aden free port's trade is mainly entrepôt, trans-shipment and bunkering. Monetary unit: E. African shilling (20s. = £1 sterling) and, in protectorate, *riyal* or Maria Theresa dollar (= *c.* 5s. sterling).
    Colony. Area: 75 sq.mi. Pop.: (1955 census) 138,441, incl. Arabs 75·2%; Indians and Pakistanis 11·4%; Somalis 7·7%; (1957 est.) 140,000. Language: Arabic; also Indian languages, Somali. Religion: mainly Moslem. Chief towns (pop., 1955): Aden (Crater, etc.) 99,285; Sheikh Othman 29,879. Administration: governor; executive council; legislative council with elected majority. Governor, Sir William Luce. Also forming part of the colony are Perim island (5 sq.mi.) and the Kuria Muria islands (*c.* 28 sq.mi.). The Kuria Murias are administered for Aden by British Persian Gulf residency.
    Protectorate. Area: *c.* 112,000 sq.mi., incl. Socotra island (1,400 sq.mi.). Language: Arabic. Religion: Moslem. Administration: by rulers, with British political officers' advice.
    Western Area. Eight sultanates, two amirates and eight sheikhdoms. Total pop.: (1957 est.) 355,000. Headquarters of adviser and British agent: Lahej (pop.: *c.* 12,000). British agent, G. K. N. Trevaskis.
    Eastern Area. Five sultanates and two sheikhdoms (incl. the Hadhramaut). Total pop.: (1957 est.) 305,000 (Socotra island, *c.* 12,000). Chief towns: Mukalla (port, headquarters of resident adviser and British agent, pop.: *c.* 20,000); Saiun; Tamridah (Socotra). British agent, A. J. McIntosh.
    Kamaran (area 22 sq.mi.; pop. *c.* 2,200) is in Red sea off Yemen coast. Governor, governor of Aden *ex officio*; commissioner, Lieut.-Col. R. G. W. E. Alban.
    History. On Jan. 4, 1959, elections were held for 12 of the 23 seats in the colony's legislative council. There were 31 candidates, and 27% of the electorate voted. Nine of the successful candidates were Arabs, two were Somalis and one was an Indian. None claimed allegiance to any political party. The elections were boycotted by the Aden Trade Union congress.
    On Feb. 11 the chiefs of 6 of the 18 states comprising the Western Aden protectorate formally inaugurated the new Federation of Arab Amirates of the South. The secretary of state for the colonies, A. T. Lennox-Boyd, attended the ceremony which marked the culmination of discussions which had lasted intermittently for a number of years. By the terms of a treaty between the United Kingdom and the new federation Britain undertook to provide financial and military aid

to assist the federation towards ultimate independence. Yemen did not welcome this development since it appeared to place a further obstacle in the way of the realization of the imam of

A scout car of the Life Guards halts in a village of the western Aden protectorate during patrol duty along the Yemeni frontier.

Yemen's claim to the protectorate and colony. Nevertheless, in May a Yemeni delegation took part in discussions with the Aden government concerning the Aden-Yemeni frontier, but no positive conclusions were reached. The Aden Trade Union congress refused to recognize the federation, which was further strengthened in October by the admission of the sultanate of Lahej.
    Discussions took place in September to prepare the way for a search for oil in the Eastern Aden protectorate by Petroleum Concessions Ltd. In October the members of the General Port Workers union went on strike in the colony in an attempt to obtain redress for the workers' alleged grievances. (*See* also YEMEN.)   (K. I.)

ADVERTISING. In Aug. 1959 the Advertising association published a projection for 1958 of the figures from its survey *Advertising Expenditure 1956*. This estimated total advertising in 1958 at £364 million, an increase of £30 million on 1957. Press advertising at £172 million showed a rise of £10 million and television advertising at £48 million an increase of £21 million. In presenting these figures the association pointed out that the total expenditure was equal to 2% of the national income—the same proportion as in 1938—and that even those economists and others who were opposed to "competitive" advertising agreed that financial and classified advertising, and advertising by manufacturers to other manufacturers were "informative" and useful. If this distinction were made, then in 1958 the amount spent on advertising by manufacturers to consumers was estimated at three-fifths of the total, or £220 million.
    The *Statistical Review of Press Advertising* calculated that display advertising in the first six months of 1959 was 10·9% greater than in the same period of 1958, which in turn had shown a 9·7% rise over the first half of 1957 and a 15·4% increase over the first half of 1956. That the effect on the press of increased expenditure on television advertising was less marked was borne out by the rise in advertising revenues recorded for each category from the London-based national morning newspapers through provincial newspapers to trade journals. However, the tendency for the larger national newspapers, both daily and Sunday, to receive proportionately more of the total business was still evident. There was a setback through the printing strike, which began in the latter part of June and continued into August. Provincial newspapers, magazines and trade papers were compelled to suspend normal publication, while shortages of printing ink reduced

the sizes of the national newspapers and therefore the amount of advertising they could carry. While it was not easy to assess the effect of the strike on the various groups of media, it seemed likely that in July they lost in total about £3 million in advertising revenue.

Studies of the readership, as distinct from the circulations, of national newspapers and magazines had been available annually since 1947, when the Hulton magazine group sponsored its first survey of this kind. The Hulton surveys were discontinued in 1957, when the National Readership survey of the Institute of Practitioners in Advertising became a continuous investigation, with quarterly and later half-yearly reports. Advertisers and agencies had long criticized the failure of all but one or two publishing groups to provide similar information for provincial newspapers. In an attempt to fill the gap, the Newspaper society, the representative body for the provincial newspapers, published between the latter part of 1958 and the spring of 1959 ten sections of a survey of housewives' readership, each dealing with one of the regions of England and Wales. Since it was found necessary to give no more than the totals for all morning, evening and weekly provincial newspapers (aggregating several hundreds in some regions) the practical usefulness of the survey was restricted.

Commercial television continued to be in the news. In the House of Commons an abortive attempt was made to introduce legislation to reduce the amount of advertising time and control its placing in relation to programmes. In July the third report of the Committee on Public Accounts dealt with the Independent Television authority's report and accounts for 1957-58. The committee noted that in 1955 and 1956 the programme contractors had lost £10 million, that by the summer of 1957 the initial losses had been paid off, that in

1958 the annual trading profits (before tax) exceeded £20 million and that the indications were that trading profits of the same order would continue in 1959. In the light of this, and the announcement that Associated-Television's trading profit for the year ending April 30, 1959, had been £7·1 million, advertisers considered the notification of increased advertising rates that followed to be ill-timed.

Three new commercial television stations opened during the year—Tyne-Tees, Anglia and Ulster. At the end of Sept. 1959 the coverage of these was estimated by Television Audience Measurement (with which the television index activities of the A. C. Nielsen company had merged during the year) as in the following table. About 92% of the U.K. population was located within the service areas of the ten stations.

AUDIENCE FOR TV ADVERTISING, U.K., Sept. 1959

Station and date opened	Population served ('000)	All TV homes ('000)	ITV homes ('000)	Viewers in ITV homes ('000)
London (Sept. 22, 1955) .	12,638	2,870	2,190	7,340
Birmingham (Feb. 17, 1956) .	7,027	1,660	1,230	4,185
Manchester (May 3, 1956) ⎰ Yorkshire (Nov. 3, 1956) ⎱	13,000	2,910	2,340	8,110
Scotland (Aug. 31, 1957) .	3,871	740	600	2,150
Wales and West (Jan. 14, 1958)	3,140	750	490	1,670
Southern (Aug. 30, 1958) .	2,760	540	410	1,355
Tyne-Tees (Jan. 15, 1959) .	2,600	550	440	1,575
Anglia (Oct. 27, 1959) .	2,000	698	332	998
Ulster (Oct. 31, 1959) .	1,112	127	103	419

The Western Nigerian government in August gave Marconi's Wireless Telegraph company a contract for the supply and installation of transmitting and studio equipment for two television stations, one of 500 watts at Ibadan and one of 15 kilowatts at Abafon. A 15-year contract was also signed with Overseas Rediffusion for the provision of educational, public service and entertainment programmes and the sale of advertising time. The contract also provided for the later establishment of commercial sound radio and the sale of time spots. In the same month the Federal House of Representatives amended the ordinances of the Nigerian Broadcasting corporation to allow it to undertake commercial broadcasting.

In the United States, advertising expenditure for 1959 was estimated to exceed $11,000 million—an increase of about 7% from the previous high point of $10,300 million reached in 1957. Thus the substantial year-to-year increases in dollar volume which the business had marked up since the end of World War II continued, with the single exception of 1958, when there was a decline of less than 1% from the 1957 totals.

The *Advertising Age* report showed 33 U.S. and Canadian agencies each billing $25 million or more in 1958, compared with 32 in the previous year. Their combined billing in 1958 was $2,700 million. Although total 1958 advertising was down on 1957, 67 of the 100 leading advertisers increased their expenditures in 1958, 5 held even and 28, including the " big three " automobile manufacturers, cut back. In all, the 100 leaders invested a total of $2,300 million in advertising and promotion in 1958—4·6% more than during the preceding year. The largest advertiser, despite a drop for the third successive year, was General Motors, with a 1958 investment estimated at $137·5 million.

One aspect of the congressional investigation of quiz shows was the feeling that this would hasten the move towards what is known as the " magazine concept " in broadcasting advertising, meaning that radio and television stations and networks would assume full and complete control over programme content in the same manner that magazines control their editorial content, without advertisers having any direct connection with any particular programme.

An important legal decision affecting advertising was that

In the exceptionally hot, dry summer of 1959, the enticingly proffered dish of ice-cream in this press advertisement had a mirage-like quality.

In Britain competition among breakfast foods is keen. Cereals are a big item in advertising expenditure.

of the U.S. Supreme Court upholding the reasonableness of a Treasury Department ruling disallowing advertising designed to influence legislative action as a " necessary business expense ", even though the very existence of the advertiser's business was at stake.

As 1959 drew to a close, it became apparent that all media would share in the increased advertising for the year. In newspapers total advertising linage for the first eight months of 1959 was up 6·9% over the previous year, a sharp reversal from 1958, when in the same period linage was down 6·6% from 1957. General and farm magazines measured by the Publishers Information bureau carried $549,524,000 in advertising for the first nine months of 1959, an increase of 11·5% on the same period of 1958. The figure for the year was expected to approach a 12% increase. The Television Bureau of Advertising reported network television time sales for the first eight months of 1959 at $408,046,000, an increase of 10·2% on 1958. The same source reported spot (non-network) television sales at $315,323,000 for the first six months of 1959, a sharp rise of $249,415,000 on the previous year. For the year 1959, the Television bureau estimated a total 12% gain over 1958. Radio was also expected to continue its comeback during the year, but over-all gains would probably be relatively small. (A. B. MacC.; S. R. Bn.)

AFGHANISTAN.
Independent kingdom in central Asia, bounded N. by the U.S.S.R., W. by Persia, S. and S.E. by Pakistan and E. by China. Area: *c.* 250,000 sq.mi. Pop. (1957 est., no census ever taken): 12 million. Races: Pakhtu or Pathan 60%, Tajik 30·7%, Uzbek 5%, Hazara (Mongoloid) 3%. Languages: Pakhtu and Persian. Religion: Sunni (Hanafi) Moslem. Chief towns (pop., 1953 est.): Kabul (cap.) 310,000; Kandahar 195,000; Herat 150,000; Mazar-i-Sharif 100,000. King, Mohammed Zahir Shah; prime minister, Mohammed Daud Khan. Main imports: manufactured goods, petroleum products, sugar. Main exports: karakul skins, carpets, wool, raw hides, dried fruit. Monetary unit: *afghani* with a free exchange rate of Af.145·60 =£1 sterling.

History. There was no change during 1959 in the traditional Afghan policy of neutrality. On Aug. 24, speaking at Kabul, on the Afghan national day, King Mohammed Zahir Shah commented, also traditionally, on the problem of Pakhtunistan, " still awaiting a peaceful and just solution ". Mohammed Daud Khan, the prime minister, explained to the correspondent of a Japanese press agency that the Pakhtun problem had existed for a century and arose when part of Afghanistan had been annexed to British India—the Pakistan of today.

In February the Afghan prime minister visited New Delhi and in September Jawaharlal Nehru, the Indian prime minister, paid a return visit to Kabul. In May the Afghan prime minister was on an official visit in Moscow, where he conferred with N. S. Khrushchev. An agreement on the expansion of Soviet-Afghan economic and technical co-operation was signed on May 28. Among other things, it provided for Soviet assistance in the construction of the Kushka-Herat-Kandahar motor road, over 460 mi. long. In September Mohammed Naim, Afghan foreign minister, paid an official visit to Peking.

On Dec. 9, President Dwight D. Eisenhower paid a visit to Kabul.

The budget estimates for Sept. 23, 1958-Sept. 22, 1959 (1337-38 of the Afghan year), amounted to a revenue of Af.1,455,122,000 (including Af.521,192,000 from foreign loans) and to an expenditure of Af.1,455,107,962.

Between the fiscal years 1955-56 and 1957-58 the amounts of Afghan exports rose from Af.1,527 million to 1,984 million.

The Ariana Afghan Airlines extended in September their services from Kabul to Frankfurt (German Federal Republic), through Ankara and Prague. The reconstruction of the Kabul airport, with Soviet help, started in May.

See Edward Hunter, *The Past Present: A Year in Afghanistan* (London, 1959).

AGRICULTURE.
Production, Trade, Price and Policy Changes. World agricultural production, which had not increased for two years, resumed its upward trend in 1958-59. Excluding China, it was about 4% higher than in the previous year and the same rate of expansion was expected in 1959-60. Most of the increase was in North America, Australia, New Zealand and the U.S.S.R. A big increase was also reported from China. In several countries of southeast Asia and in parts of South America and Africa the growth in agricultural production barely kept pace with the growth in population. For the underdeveloped regions of the world taken as a whole, however, production increased nearly 1% faster than the population.

The economic recession experienced in industrial countries during the autumn and winter of 1958-59 had an adverse effect on world trade and on the prices of agricultural products. Trade for all agricultural products fell by 3% and world prices fell some 7%. For the raw materials group, trade declined by 8% and prices by 16%. The prices of foodstuffs as a group were less severely affected, although coffee prices fell by more than one-third and sugar prices reached their lowest point for 17 years. During the summer the improved industrial conditions in the major importing countries brought a revival in demand and in the price level of most commodities. By August the wholesale price of basic raw materials was nearly 1% higher than a year earlier. Rubber prices had risen to their highest point for two years; the wool season opened confidently and jute prices recovered to their level of a year earlier. Cotton, coffee and tea prices however remained depressed. The drought in Europe, which reduced the supplies of milk, drove up butter prices by October to 50% above their 1958 level.

A new three-year International Wheat agreement came into force in August. Italy, Mexico and Spain joined the major exporting countries in the scheme and Britain rejoined as the largest importing member. The new agreement eased the obligations of importers in two respects: they undertook to buy a " consented percentage " of their total imports instead of the former guaranteed quantities, and they might purchase their commercial supplies elsewhere when the price was held to the maximum. Exporters, however, undertook to supply the average import needs of members at the maximum price even when this was below the world commercial price. The agreement retained the former minimum price of 150 cents a bushel for standard Grade No. 1 Northern Manitoba wheat, but the maximum price was cut by 10 cents to 190 cents per bushel.

The International Sugar council, faced with big surpluses and low prices, announced in July that exporters could carry forward into 1960 up to 10% of their basic export tonnage. This action, coupled with heavy purchases of sugar by the U.S.S.R., steadied the sugar market in the third quarter of the year. The major coffee exporters reached an agreement on the limitation of exports but the scheme was not backed by production control.

United Kingdom. There were no major changes in the 1959 price review held in February-March to determine the level of guaranteed prices, and the government's policy of improving the competitive position of the industry rather than encouraging any further expansion of gross output remained unchanged. The guaranteed price of wheat was reduced by 6% and, in view of a further prospective rise in egg production in 1959-60, egg prices were again lowered by 1d. per dozen. Calf and hill cattle subsidies were increased in order to encourage the rearing of beef cattle. Following the reductions in guaranteed prices made in 1958 the cost of support for 1958-59 fell by £36 million to £248 million, and net farm incomes fell by £27·5 million to £327 million. Under these circumstances the government decided that there should be a small increase of £3 million in the total value of the guarantees. These were now to include the cost (about £9 million in a full year) of a new assistance scheme for small farmers who carried out approved farm improvement plans.

During the year the Fatstock Marketing corporation changed its buying and selling policy in the light of a fall in turnover from £97 million in 1957-58 to £88 million in 1958-59. More animals were bought live and advance prices for pigs were replaced by more competitive methods. A new contract between the corporation, which handled 65% of all pigs marketed, and bacon factories gave curers the right to buy from any source and the corporation permission to switch at any time to the factory offering the best prices. The report

On the smaller farms an increasing number of tasks—such as turning hay as seen here—are undertaken by agricultural contractors.

of the Committee on Grassland Utilization issued late in 1958 confirmed that grass and forage crops were the cheapest sources of animal foods, but stressed that the total output from grass and other home feeding-stuffs was scarcely keeping pace with the increasing livestock population.

Canada. In addition to nine mandatory commodities permanently price-supported under the Agricultural Stabilization act of 1958, 11 other commodities were price-supported in 1958-59. The total grain acreage was about 1·3 million ac. larger than in 1958, and by June Canadian hog numbers reached a record figure of 6·9 million. Farm cash receipts from the sale of farm products and participation payments on the previous year's crops were higher during the first half of 1959. Over the year cash incomes were expected to maintain their 1958 level, but with higher costs reducing net farm incomes slightly.

Australia and New Zealand. The drought of 1957-58 in Australia was followed by a favourable season and a record total production some 14% larger in 1958-59. Expectations of an even bigger harvest in 1959-60 were frustrated by bad weather and the wheat crop estimates were revised downwards to 140 million bu. as compared with 190 million bu. in 1958-59. Export prices, depressed throughout 1958, made a substantial recovery during the first half of 1959. In spite of a near-record wool clip for 1958-59, prices moved upwards towards the season's end in May. The new season in September opened favourably and consumption trends in the leading importing countries indicated that more wool would be absorbed during 1959-60. A move by some growers to introduce a stabilization scheme for wool was unsuccessful, but the stabilization schemes for wheat and dairy products were renewed for a further five years. Farm incomes in 1958-59 were estimated to be about 12% higher than in 1957-58 though they were well below the record incomes of 1956-57.

New Zealand agricultural production during 1958-59 was slightly above that of 1957-58 but farm incomes were about 15% lower, largely due to a further reduction of 10% in the guaranteed prices for dairy products following on the exhaustion of the Dairy Industry Reserve account at the end of 1957-58. Receipts from exported butter recovered strongly during the year with wholesale prices in the United Kingdom rising from 280s. to 430s. a cwt. between Nov. 1958 and Nov. 1959. Both Australia and New Zealand expressed concern at the reported discrimination against Commonwealth food and raw material exports in the European Economic community.

Africa. Agricultural production in Africa recovered in 1958-59 to about its 1956-57 level. Wheat production in

TABLE I. FORAGE CROPS, UNITED KINGDOM. ACREAGE AND PRODUCTION, 1939, 1957 AND 1958

	Acreage ('000 ac.)			Production ('000 tons)		
	1939	*1957*	*1958*	*1939*	*1957*	*1958*
Beans (for fodder) .	135	87	90	111	77	72
Peas (for fodder) .	37	14	15	23	10	7
Turnips and swedes .	712	512	497	10,084	8,610	8,689
Mangolds . . .	216	154	148	4,069	3,559	3,578
Other fodder crops (kale, fodder, beet, etc.) .	226	560	552	...	...	...
Temporary grassland						
For mowing* .	1,934†	3,142	3,224	2,588	4,092‡	4,318‡
For grazing .	2,191	3,206	3,127	—	—	—
Permanent grassland						
For mowing .	5,009	3,211	3,415	5,202	3,250‡	3,745‡
For grazing .	13,764	10,292	10,070	—	—	—
Rough grazing .	16,539	16,827	16,873	—	—	—

* Lucerne, clover and rotation grasses. † Includes lucerne grown in England and Wales only. ‡ Excl. grass and lucerne mown for silage, drying or seed in Great Britain.
SOURCE. *Monthly Digest of Statistics* (H.M.S.O., London, April 1959).

South Africa was lower by 17% but maize production was 10% greater than in the previous season. In Morocco, Tunisia and Algeria there was a small rise in grain production. The Nigerian groundnut crop was some 20% below the previous year's record. But cocoa and coffee production showed significant increases.

The United Kingdom continued to participate in various agricultural development programmes in the dependent territories. These included sisal, tea and wattle projects in Tanganyika, tobacco and tung in Nyasaland, sugar in Swaziland and rubber in Nigeria. In Kenya a further £600,000 was allocated under the Swynnerton plan for the intensification of African agriculture, bringing the total spent since 1955 to nearly £4·5 million. In the Portuguese African territories, agricultural and irrigation plans, including settlement projects in Angola and Mozambique, absorbed 35% of the total planned development expenditure of $290 million. Under the second five-year development plan (1959-64) in Ghana, £26 million of the total planned expenditure of £350 million was to be invested in agriculture and in the development of natural resources, in addition to over £100 million allocated to the Volta dam project. The agricultural programme included research to improve cocoa yields, plans to establish rubber and banana estates in the southwest, to develop the cattle industry and to irrigate the Volta flood plain. The United Ghana Farmers' council offered to accept a reduced price for dry cocoa beans for the next five years to enable the government to divert an extra £5 million a year to the development plan. At the sime time the government abandoned its £34 million five-year mass spraying programme against capsid infestation of cocoa. Instead, farmers were encouraged to do their own spraying with subsidized equipment.

India, Pakistan and Ceylon. Agricultural production in 1958-59 was only about 2% above the comparatively low level of 1957-58. Indian food grain production rose by 17% but the Pakistan rice crop fell by 12%. Crop prospects for the 1959-60 season were distinctly better in both countries.

A U.S. team of agricultural specialists visiting India drew attention to the widening gap between the food required and food production. To meet the food requirements of the 1965 population the rate of increase in production would need to be raised to 8·2% per annum, whereas the average from 1952-53 to 1958-59 was only 3·2% per annum. The Indian minister of food and agriculture stressed that the fulfilment of the second and successive plans would depend mainly upon the surpluses obtained from the land. A far-reaching policy change was announced in the National Development council's decision that all rural life should be organized in village councils (panchayats) and village co-operatives by the end of the third five-year plan. All states were urged to fix ceilings on land holdings by the end of 1959. Expropriated land was to be turned over to farm co-operatives which were to be strengthened and given crop loan facilities. During the year the agricultural credit department of the Reserve bank initiated an interesting experiment by issuing through land mortgage banks " rural debentures " to mobilize rural savings for specific development projects in the villages.

A new short-term plan designed to make Pakistan self-sufficient in food by 1960 was introduced at the beginning of 1959, but extensive floods in East Pakistan damaged 1959 harvest prospects and the finance minister announced that Pakistan could not be self-sufficient in food grains in the near future. Work on land reform, including ceilings on individual land holdings, proceeded during the year, and 2·5 million ac. were surrendered to the state by the end of the first phase. New loan and credit arrangements made by the West Pakistan government for equipping the new tenant farmers were expected to cost Rs.30 million (over £2 million).

Government policy in Ceylon emphasized that the country's economic development rested on its agricultural programmes though the first results of schemes for increased yields of rice in 1958-59 were disappointing. Land reforms were started in some areas and the government announced a plan to establish a co-operative development bank, began a pilot-crop insurance scheme and sought to broaden the agricultural economy by encouraging vegetable cultivation and the growth of a bigger livestock industry.

TABLE II. ROOT CROPS. OUTPUT OF MAJOR PRODUCING COUNTRIES
1958 AND 1948-52 AVERAGE

POTATOES ('000 metric tons)			SUGAR BEET ('000 metric tons)		
	1948-52	1958		1948-52	1958
Poland . .	29,727	35,836	U.S.S.R. .	17,500*	54,100
German Fed. Rep.	24,075	22,678	United States .	9,762	13,879
France . .	13,734	13,716	German Fed. Rep.†	5,824	12,000*
GermanDem.Rep.	13,164	12,489	France . .	8,344*‡	11,448§
United States .	10,676	11,965	Poland . .	5,746	7,621‖
Czechoslovakia	7,255	7,149	Czechoslovakia	5,420¶	6,775‖
United Kingdom	9,444	5,645	GermanDem.Rep.†	5,318	6,450

ONIONS ('000 long tons)			CARROTS ('000 long tons)		
United States .	907	1,049	United States .	668	658
Japan . .	601	756‖	France . .	326	389
Spain . .	440	576‖	United Kingdom	335	381
Egypt . .	277	473‖	German Fed. Rep.	147	94
Turkey . .	186	457‖	Netherlands .	85	93**

* Estimate. † Delivered to sugar factories. ‡ Beets processed in sugar factories. § Total production. ‖ 1957. ¶ Average of 3 yr. ** 1957-58.
SOURCE. F.A.O. *Monthly Bulletin of Agricultural Economics and Statistics*; Commonwealth Economic Committee.

Western Europe. There was a small increase in total agricultural production in 1958-59, though the grain output was 3% below the high level of 1957-58. Favourable harvesting conditions in most areas indicated that grain yields would be high for 1959-60. The dry summer of 1959 affected milk yields and the output of dairy products. There was a further rise in meat output but pig numbers levelled off in a number of countries during the first half of 1959. Egg production continued to rise and the traditional exporting countries, Denmark and the Netherlands, found themselves with an embarrassing surplus.

The six participating countries of the European Economic community (*q.v.*) agreed that the first major problem was to fix a common price for grain. Tariffs were reduced by 10% from January but later the Netherlands government criticized the inadequate import quotas granted by Belgium and the German Federal Republic for Dutch dairy produce. A treaty was drafted for a second free trade area between the " Outer Seven " countries—Austria, Denmark, Norway, Sweden, Switzerland, Portugal and the United Kingdom. Denmark, wishing to preserve both its major markets, agreed only reluctantly to join the " Seven " and was able to obtain some agricultural concessions from both groups. The United Kingdom agreed to abolish the 10% tariff on Danish bacon and to give Denmark a reduction in duties totalling Kr.150 million (£7·5 million) a year. From western Germany, Denmark obtained an agreement that the current level of Danish imports would be admitted for the following three years.

U.S.S.R. and Eastern Europe. The Food and Agriculture organization index of the volume of agricultural output in the U.S.S.R. and eastern Europe showed an increase of 9% in 1958-59, chiefly because of the exceptionally good grain crop in the U.S.S.R. which totalled nearly 140 million tons. The 1959 crop was affected by drought in the Ukraine and Byelorussia and, though heavy yields were reported from Kazakhstan and Siberia, harvesting was delayed by heavy rains and the total output in 1959-60 was not expected to exceed that of the previous year. But substantial increases were again claimed in the output of meat and dairy produce.

TABLE III. GRAIN CROPS (Thousand metric tons)

Country	Wheat Production 1948-52 average	1958	Import— Export+ 1955-58 average	Barley Production 1948-52 average	1958	Import— Export+ 1955-58 average	Oats Production 1948-52 average	1958	Import— Export+ 1955-58 average	Rye Production 1948-52 average	1958	Import— Export+ 1955-58 average	Maize Production 1948-52 average	1958	Import— Export+ 1955-58 average	Rice Production 1948-52 average	1958	Import— Export+ 1955-58 average
World total (excl. U.S.S.R.)	140,300	190,800	{+26,622[1] −26,487[1]/[2]	52,500	76,500	{+7,128[1] −6,941[1]/[2]	49,100	53,700	{+1,418[1] −1,404[1]	19,900	21,050	{+1,441[1]/[2] −1,568[1]/[2]	139,100	...	{+7,080[1] −7,179[1]	163,700	235,500	{+5,869[1] −6,067[1]
Europe																		
Austria	348	549	−222	210	335	−93	275	333	−4	343	397	−54	120	155	−375	—	—	−33
Belgium	525	794	−463[3]	244	318	−552[3]	483	443	−102[3]	222	200	−77[3]	782	910	+73[5]	—	—	−62[3]
Bulgaria	1,760	2,352	{−66[2] +19[2]	332	416	...	148	199[4]	...	240	117	...	782	910	...	...	...	...
Czechoslovakia	1,493	1,350	{−855[2] +13[2]	1,046	1,215	−242[2]	961	905	−15[2]	1,110	921	−72[2]	243	476	−135[2]	—	—	−55[2]
Denmark	285	275	−259	1,709	2,486	{−221 +229	922	650	{−60 +43	365	305	{−103 +1	—	—	−31	—	—	...
Finland	264	215	−286	201	406	...	718	798	−34[2]	201	111	−106	—	—	...	—	—	...
France	7,791	9,601	{−687 +1,348	1,534	3,892	{−102 +556	3,393	2,637	{−12 +27	573	430	{−5 +14	447	1,625	−311	46	145	−74
German Dem. Republic	1,243	1,362	{−746[2] +3[2]	593	929	−397[2]	1,188	1,144	−92[2]	2,516	2,353	−337[2]	...	...	...	—	—	−65[2]
German Fed. Republic	2,656	3,693	−2,644	1,397	2,414	−1,058	2,500	2,149	−214	3,042	3,728	{−100 +136	—	—	−655	—	—	−109
Greece	894	1,750	−280	211	282	...	119	191	...	47	47	...	225	226	{−18[2] +73	39	67	...
Hungary	1,909	1,487	{−237 +122	654	735	−132[2]	213	192	...	731	371	{−20[2] +22[2]	2,068	2,739	{−18[2] +73	40	...	...
Ireland	327	343	−148	163	312	...	617	433	...	4	2	...	—	—	−95	—	—	...
Italy	7,170	9,815	{−524 +278	258	296	−184	495	569	−62	123	105	−69	2,306	3,674	{−413 +13	725	705	+212
Netherlands	325	402	−787	202	315	{−634 +68	419	446	{−281 +47	455	427	{−127 +19	26	...	−742	—	—	−81
Norway	58	17	−310	109	340	−40	170	127	...	2	1	−52	—	—	−60	—	—	...
Poland	1,833	2,344	{−1,066[2] +3[2]	1,061	1,196	{−52[2] +17[2]	2,240	2,657	−2[2]	6,374	7,346	−241[2]	...	...	−15[2]	—	—	−30[2]
Portugal	499	749	−89	96	110	...	124	140	...	162	211	...	393	405	{−25 +35[2]	114	157	...
Rumania	2,778[6]	3,704[4]	{−191[2] +37[2]	412[6]	417[4]	...	369[6]	392[4]	...	177[6]	152[4]	...	2,495[6]	6,338[4]	...	35	36[4]	...
Spain	3,622	4,430	−251	1,909	1,770	...	519	520	...	482	530	...	520	950	...	272	381	+75
Sweden	677	614	{−87 +163	231	669	−48	804	927	{−42 +23	258	178	{−51 +21	—	—	−36	—	—	−23
Switzerland	260	352	−405	55	64	−200	68	56	−126	34	40	...	6	...	−72	—	—	−23
United Kingdom	2,397	2,755	−4,655	2,060	3,221	{−1,035 +93	2,852	2,172	−74	52	21	...	—	—	−1,771	—	—	−91
U.S.S.R.	...	75,300	{−198[2] +2,980[2]	...	...	+855[2]	...	...	+155[2]	...	...	−553[2]	...	...	+228[2]	...	...	+16[2]
Yugoslavia	2,171	2,453	−1,134[2]	323	470	...	286	259	−14[2]	248	241	...	3,078	3,950	{−9[2] +34[2]	6[6]	22	...
N. and Central America																		
Canada	13,472	10,035	+6,783	4,282	5,329	+1,530	6,328	6,183	+268	463	203	+196	384	759	−226	173	254	−35
Mexico	534	1,151	−24	160	...	...	47	...	...	—	—	...	3,090	4,953	−438	173	254	...
United States	31,066	39,796	{−248 +9,360[7]	5,843	10,243	{−461 +1,794[8]	18,970	20,643	{−199 +362[8]	524	825	{−85 +187[8]	81,971	96,520	+3,700[7] [8]	1,924	2,133	+660[7] [8]
South America																		
Argentina	5,175	6,720	+2,729	656	1,125	+501	743	930	+329	526	800	+247	2,509	4,806[4]	+974	152	220	+38[5]
Bolivia	26[9]	...	...	40[9]	45[4]	...	4[9]	...	...	—	—	...	138[10]	...	...	18[11]	...	−8[5]
Brazil	498	1,155	−1,516[2]	15	29	...	9	18	...	17	19	...	5,916	7,386[4]	+27[2]	3,025	3,988[4]	+35[5]
Chile	942	1,007	−148[2]	84	98	...	83	115	+2[5]	5	6[4]	...	68	110	...	76	91[4]	...
Colombia	124	...	−83	50	...	...	—	—	−5[5]	—	—	...	735	825	{−7[5] +1[5]	264	420	−1
Peru	146	150	−291[2]	208	200	...	...	...	...	2[6]	...	...	418	270	{−7[5] +1[5]	205	249[4]	...
Uruguay	462	525	+322[2]	23	53	...	44	53	...	—	—	...	157	170[4]	...	44	...	...
Asia																		
Burma	4[12]	...	...	—	—	...	—	—	...	—	—	...	28[13]	...	+21[5]	5,309[14]	6,397	+1,667
Cambodia	—	—	...	—	—	...	—	—	...	—	—	...	80[12]	100[4]	+93	1,372[5]	1,050	+226
China	15,915[6]	39,500	+34[2]	6,950[6]	20,000	...	—	—	...	—	—	...	13,450	14,200	+5[5]	58,181[6]	86,600[4]	{−121 +367
India	6,087	7,865	−1,763	2,384	2,274	...	—	—	...	—	—	...	2,165	3,113[4]	+1[5]	33,383	45,295	{−483 +37
Indonesia	—	—	...	—	—	...	—	—	...	—	—	...	1,536[12]	2,032	...	9,441[12]	12,300	−485[2]
Iraq	448	754	...	722	953	+282	—	—	...	—	—	...	14	...	+2[5]	203	137	{−11[5] +1[5]
Japan	1,375	1,281	−2,271	2,020	2,067	−767	120	196	...	6	2	...	57	100[15]	−467	11,991	14,991	−485[2]
Korea, South	92	122	−270	594	720[4]	...	4	...	...	21	19[4]	...	12	...	{−1[5] +1[5]	2,924	3,254	−40[5]
Lebanon	51	48	−73[2]	25	...	−20[2]	2	...	...	—	—	...	12	...	{−1[5] +1[5]	1	...	−15[2]
Malaya, Fed. of	—	—	...	—	—	...	—	—	...	—	—	...	6[9]	...	{−47[5] +10[5]	635	726	{−577[16] +104[16]
Pakistan	3,682	3,718	−487	150	176	...	—	—	...	—	—	...	384	473	...	12,400	11,407	{−301 +74
Persia	1,860	2,700	...	767	950	...	—	—	...	—	—	...	6	...	...	424	454	+16[5]
Philippines	762	562	+186	321	228	+188	6	7[4]	...	—	—	...	696	949	...	2,767	3,497	−53[5]
Syria	—	—	...	—	—	...	—	—	...	—	—	...	31	...	+1	13	...	−15
Thailand	—	—	...	2,270	3,600	+103	326	475	+9	500	700	...	31	...	+94	6,845	7,123	+1,348
Turkey	4,771	8,671	{−228 +89	2,270	3,600	+103	326	475	+9	500	700	...	747	900	...	109	...	...
Vietnam	—	—	...	—	—	...	—	—	...	—	—	...	195[17]	...	...	5,434[17]	3,500	+91
Africa																		
Algeria	996	1,250	−58	808	750	+66	136	80	...	1[12]	...	...	6	...	+2	971	1,027	{−3 +2
Egypt	1,113	1,412	−524	123	135	...	—	—	...	—	—	...	1,378	1,678	+43	6[11]	...	+261
Kenya	112[18]	106[18]	...	10[18]	...	...	6[18]	...	...	—	—	...	93[18]	102	+51	6[8] [19]	...	−3
Morocco	738[19]	980[19]	+137[19]	1,362[19]	1,282[19]	+226[19]	51[19]	19[19]	+7[19]	4[20]	4[20] [4]	—	296[19]	226[19]	+90[19]	—	—	+15[19]
Tunisia	452	610	{−73 +76	218	300	+21	15	6[4]	...	—	—	...	4[21]	...	...	—	—	−2
South Africa, Union of	558[18]	657[18]	−93	39[18]	22[18]	+3[5]	80[18]	...	...	11[18]	...	...	2,453[18]	3,687	+911	...	...	−37
Oceania																		
Australia	5,161	5,824	+1,487	531	1,135	+484	560	1,361	+115	12	9[4]	...	126	119	{+4 −1[5]	90	120	{+41 −3
New Zealand	139	184	−262	49	61	{−7[5] +1[5]	47	23	−10	2[6]	...	...	10	...	{+4 −1[5]	90	120	−3

NOTE. — indicates quantity nil or negligible; ... indicates quantity not known.
[1] Estimate of total world trade. [2] 1955-57 average. [3] Belgium-Luxembourg union. [4] 1957. [5] 1955-56 average. [6] Average of 4 years. [7] Commercial and government exports. [8] Incl. shipments under foreign aid programmes, but not to territories and possessions. [9] Average of 2 years. [10] 1949. [11] 1948. [12] Average of 3 years. [13] 1950. [14] Excl. Putas, Chin Hills, Shan states and Karenni. [15] Excl. maize harvested green. [16] Incl. Singapore. [17] 1934-38 average; area relating to Tonkin, Annam and Cochin China. [18] Farms and estates. [19] Former French zone. [20] Former French and Spanish zones. [21] Incl. sorghum.
SOURCE. F.A.O. *Monthly Bulletin of Agricultural Economy and Statistics.*

Combine harvesters eating their way through a 19-acre field of winter-sown barley on a farm at Stowell Park in the Cotswold hills, Gloucester-shire, towards the end of July. This was believed to be the earliest harvest since the end of World War II.

Under the new seven-year plan (1959-65) the planned increase in Soviet agricultural production by 1965 was 70% of the 1959 output, which F.A.O. regarded as more realistic than the superseded five-year plan. The planned outputs for the major products were: grain, 164 million tons (12% increase on 1958); cotton, 5·7 million tons to 6·1 million tons (35% to 45% increase on 1957); oil-bearing seeds, 5·5 million tons (70% increase on 1957); meat, 16 million tons (100% increase on 1958). More emphasis was to be placed on farm investment and increased yields than on the expansion of the cultivated area. Further changes in the organization of collective farms were designed to bring them nearer in structure to the state farms.

A new agricultural programme with a production target of 30% increase by 1965 was announced in Poland. While declaring that the socialization of agriculture was the eventual goal, Władysław Gomułka assured peasants that they would not be coerced into co-operatives as they were before 1956. Voluntary co-operation was to be encouraged through the revival of village " agricultural circles ". Agricultural development would be promoted and financed for the next seven years by these circles from a special development fund representing the difference between the farmers' compulsory delivery prices and the free market prices. The total investment in agriculture (including the farmers' own investments) during 1959-65 was expected to amount to Zł.28,000 million (about £25 million). It was planned that the circles would be self-supporting by 1965 when compulsory deliveries would cease.

China. Chou En-lai stated in August that the " big leap forward " in the national economy in the autumn and winter of 1958-59 was inseparably connected with the peoples' communes. By the beginning of 1959, 740,000 agricultural co-operatives had been transformed into 26,000 communes containing 20 million peasant families. Grain and cotton outputs in 1958-59 were reported to be 35% and 28% above their 1957-58 levels respectively. In the spring of 1959, 34

million ha. of farmland—nearly one-third of the total cultivated area—were affected by either flood or drought. These natural setbacks forced a reduction in the 1959 target for grain from 525 million tons to 275 million tons and a reduction in the cotton target from 5 million tons to 2·3 million tons. The market supply of meat, sugar and dairy products fell during the first half of 1959, largely owing to increased consumption and use in the rural communes, and the 1959 targets for these products were adjusted accordingly.

United States. It became clearer in 1959 that the existing U.S. agricultural resources, if they were to be operated without official production controls, and short of major natural catastrophe, might be expected to produce, year in and year out, for the next decade or longer, 5% to 10% more agricultural products than could be sold at fair prices. Total crop production fell only slightly short of the record level of 1958. The 340 million ac. planted were 2% above the low levels of 1957 and 1958, but well below other recent years. Harvested acreage, at 325 million ac., though slightly above the low levels of the previous three years, was nevertheless smaller than in other years since 1939. Most significant was the 15% increase in acreage planted to maize, a result largely of removal of official acreage allocations, with price support continued at what many considered to be a favourable level compared with competitive crops. The composite index of yield per acre was 134, second only to the 1958 record of 143 (1947-49= 100). Maize, cotton, sugar beet, sugar cane, dry peas and dry beans set new record yields.

The wheat carry-over was 1,277 million bu., compared with 881 million bu. a year earlier; the maize carry-over from previous crops had risen to 1,550 million bu., to which was added a huge 1959 crop of more than 4,400 million bu. Soya bean stocks were indicated at 55 million bu., compared with 21 million bu. a year earlier.

Lower average prices more than counterbalanced slightly larger farm marketings in 1959; in the first eight months farmers' cash receipts from marketings totalled $19,100 million, or 2% less than in the corresponding period of 1958. Realized gross farm income was approximately $1,000 million below the $38,300 million of 1958. As U.S. farming was increasingly mechanized, only 8,773,000 persons were employed on farms late in the summer of 1959, as compared with 9,183,000 persons a year earlier. Wage rates of persons hired by the month and furnished with house and other requisites averaged $196, compared with $181 per month in 1958.

Farm Machinery and Equipment. British and U.S. manufacturers devoted more attention to developing tractors and other farm equipment suitable for tropical areas and crops. Special high-clearance tractors for row-crop work in sugar-cane and young pineapple were successfully introduced. Soviet tractors displayed in European exhibitions showed that the U.S.S.R. was catching up in tractor design. From Hungary came news of a new roller plough design to replace sliding friction by rolling friction. New machines developed in the United Kingdom included a combined cleaner and elevator for beet; in the United States a bean harvester, a peach grader and a new silo unloader; in the U.S.S.R. a combine drill for flax; and in Israel a track-laying, tractor-drawn, banana-planting machine.

Experiments were carried out in Madagascar on weed control in rice fields by spraying from the air. A series of field experiments was started by the West African Cocoa Research institute to study the effects of virus infection on growth and yield of mature cocoa trees. A British company developed a new process of extracting a cheap and tasteless protein from vegetable materials. The process, called " impulse rendering ", had been tried out with nuts, oilseeds, grasses and wheat. It was expected that it would be applied in underdeveloped countries, short of protein but with adequate supplies of vegetable matter. (*See* also BEEKEEPING; DAIRY FARMING AND DAIRY PRODUCE; FERTILIZERS; FOOD AND AGRICULTURE ORGANIZATION; FOODSTUFFS; FORESTRY; LIVESTOCK; POULTRY.) (WM. M.; J. K. R.)

BIBLIOGRAPHY. A. Martin, *Economics and Agriculture* (London, 1958); W. W. Cochrane, *Farm Prices: Myth and Reality* (Minnesota, 1958); *Report of the 1950 World Census of Agriculture*, vol. ii, *Census Methodology* (F.A.O., Rome, 1958); *Third report on the Agricultural Policies in Europe and North America* (O.E.E.C., Paris, 1958); B. F. Johnston, *The Staple Food Economies of Western Tropical Africa* (Stanford, 1958); *Report of the Committee on Grassland Utilization* (H.M.S.O., London, 1958); *Report on India's Food Crisis and Steps to Meet it* (Ford Foundation Agricultural Production Team, New Delhi, 1959).

AIRCRAFT MANUFACTURE.

Great Britain. A further step in the development of the Bristol Britannia was achieved on Dec. 29, 1958, when the Mark 253, a 117-seater trooper, flew for the first time. First delivery to R.A.F. Transport command was in June. A new twin-boom freighter aircraft with four Rolls-Royce (R.-R.) Dart 7 engines, the Armstrong Whitworth (AW) Argosy, first flew on Jan. 8. It was being offered in four versions, the AW650 freighter-coach, the AW660 military transport, the AW670 car ferry and the AW671 air bus. The AW660 would be able to carry about 23,000 lb. freight over 1,100-mi. stages at 275 m.p.h. at 25,000 ft. The 139-seater Vickers Vanguard with four R.-R. Tyne turbo-prop engines of 5,300 h.p. first flew on Jan. 20. It was estimated to carry its capacity payload of 29,000 lb. over a stage of about 1,800 mi. at 410 m.p.h. A good airfield performance and a low operating cost were to be its special features. The 92-seater Comet Mark 4B first flew on June 27 and was estimated to carry its capacity payload of 23,000 lb. over stages of nearly 2,000 mi. at 530 m.p.h. at 23,500 ft. According to preliminary estimates, the Vickers VC.10 long-range jet aircraft would carry a payload of 38,000 lb. (including 150 passengers) over a stage of 4,450 mi., taking off from a runway of about 7,500 ft. at sea level. A new DC 3 replacement-type aircraft was the 36-44-seater Avro 748 which was

to have two 1,700-h.p. R.-R. Dart 6 engines and was intended to be ready for use in 1961. It was estimated to carry 8,000 lb. payload over a 600-mi. stage distance at 265 m.p.h. at 20,000 ft. Negotiations were being made for the Hindustan Aircraft company of Bangalore to build about 100 aircraft under licence for the Indian air force. The first project of the newly formed light aircraft division of Short Brothers and Harland

The Short SCI, an experimental vertical take-off and landing (V.T.O.L.) jet aircraft, on view at the Farnborough air show.

was the SC 7, a twin-piston-engined passenger/freighter braced-wing aircraft having short take-off and landing (S.T.O.L.) capabilities. It was estimated to carry a payload of 2,500 lb. over a range of 500 mi. at 160 m.p.h.

Demonstrated publicly for the first time on June 11 was the Hovercraft SRN 1, an experimental vehicle being developed by Saunders Roe. Weighing about 8,500 lb., it was a platform measuring 30 ft. by 24 ft. which rode about 1 ft. clear of ground or water on a cushion of air, contained by a peripheral jet curtain generated by a central fan driven by one Alvis Leonides 523 engine of 450 maximum continuous h.p. One of the several proposed developments of the Hovercraft was a 40,000-h.p. ferry vehicle about 220 ft. in length and weighing 400 tons which could carry 800 passengers and 80 cars for 350 mi. at about 100 m.p.h. at a clearance of about 5 ft. Its direct operating cost was calculated at approximately 1½d. per passenger mile.

A new supersonic tactical strike reconnaissance aircraft (TSR-2) was announced as a replacement for the Canberra. It was to be developed jointly by Vickers Armstrongs and English Electric and was to be powered by an advanced version of the Bristol Siddeley Olympus engine. The first production Hunting Jet Provost Mark 3 basic trainer aircraft (one Bristol Siddeley Viper 8 jet engine of 1,750 lb. static thrust) was handed over to R.A.F. Training command on June 26. A two-seater trainer version of the Folland Gnat first flew on Aug. 31.

The Bristol T.188 research aircraft of steel construction (two DH Gyron Junior jet engines of 10,000 lb. static thrust plus reheat) was being developed to explore flight behaviour and control and the endurance of materials at supersonic speeds. Developed versions of the Fairey Rotodyne weighing up to 60,000 lb. with more powerful R.-R. Tyne engines of 5,250 h.p. were being planned for inter-city or similar operations in 1964.

United States. Civil aircraft that began regular services were the Lockheed Electra, the Boeing 707-320 and the Douglas DC-8. Other new or developed civil jet aircraft being flight tested were the 109-seater Convair 880 having four General Electric CJ-805-3 turbo-fan engines of about 11,000 lb. static thrust; the Douglas DC-8 with R.-R. Conway engines; and the Boeing 707-420, also with R.-R. Conway engines. Military versions of the Boeing 707 were the VC-137A, to be used for personnel and high priority cargo, which was taken over by the U.S. air force in April; and the projected Boeing 735 which was to have new turbo-fan engines for better performance, and a swing tail for ease of loading bulky goods. The 735 was estimated to carry a capacity payload of 100,000 lb. over a stage of 2,700 mi. at about 550 m.p.h. at 40,000 ft.

Douglas announced a new short-medium-range 92-seater civil jet aircraft intended for continental service in 1963, the DC-9, which was estimated to carry about 20,000 lb. payload over 2,000-mi. stages at 530 m.p.h. at 35,000 ft. It was to be derived from the larger DC-8 aircraft, but was aimed to have an airfield performance no worse than that of the current DC-6B. The McDonnell 119 ten-seater executive jet transport first flew in February with four Westinghouse J-34 engines, but these were to be replaced by Pratt and Whitney JT-12 engines of 2,900 lb. static thrust on later models, which were estimated to carry eight passengers for a 2,300-mi. stage at 520 m.p.h. Another executive aircraft was the 12-seater twin-Dart-engined Grumman Gulfstream which was certificated in May and delivered to the first customer in June.

A development of the Lockheed Hercules (C-130) military freighter aircraft embodied boundary layer control in order to achieve S.T.O.L. performance. Wind tunnel model tests were completed and the first aircraft was due to fly by the end of the year. Another development was the Super Hercules (GL-207), a civil version with longer fuselage and greater wing span and having four Allison T-61 turbo-prop engines. The capacity payload of 78,000 lb. was estimated for stages of 1,350 mi. at about 375 m.p.h. for a direct operating cost of four cents per ton-mi. Alternatively, the use of external auxiliary fuel tanks of 1,500 gal. was to give a distance of 5,500 mi. with 32,000 lb. payload.

The Northrop Talon (T.38) supersonic trainer aircraft, having two General Electric J.85 jet engines of 2,500 lb. static thrust each, first flew in April and a lightweight fighter version, the N-156F Freedom fighter, first flew in July when it reached supersonic speed within 40 min. of take-off. The Deak Model 16 vertical take-off and landing experimental aircraft of about 2,600 lb. gross weight having a ducted propeller at each wing tip was reported in June to have made its first transition from vertical to horizontal flight. The propellers, driven by an 840-h.p. Lycoming T-53 turbine engine, could be rotated through 90° in flight to give either forward or vertical motion.

France. The Caravelle (SE210) started regular passenger services with Air France on the Paris-Istanbul route on May 12. A new executive and liaison 8-12-passenger aircraft which first flew on May 10 was the Dassault Communauté (MD-415) having two Turboméca Bastan turbo-prop engines of 800 h.p. Its range with 12 passengers was estimated to be about 900 mi. at 285 m.p.h. The latest of the Hurel Dubois projects employing the braced, long-span wing concept was the HD-37, a double-decker passenger/cargo aircraft having two Dart 527 engines of 2,100 h.p. and a wing of aspect ratio of 21. The estimated payload for a 350-mi. stage distance was about 18,000 lb. at 205 m.p.h. at 10,000 ft. for a take-off field length of 4,200 ft.

On order for the French army were 150 Nord 3400 two-seater liaison and spotting aircraft having one 260-h.p. Potez piston engine. Offering S.T.O.L. capabilities and a range of about 600 mi. at 125 m.p.h., it was to be suitable for carrying either one stretcher or 220 lb. of armament. The Dassault Mirage IV delta-wing Mach-2 strategic bomber having two Atar 9 jet engines of 13,200 lb. static thrust each with reheat first flew on June 17. The Sud Aviation Frelon (SA-3200), a 24-seater, single-rotor helicopter having three Turmo III engines of 750 h.p., first flew on June 9. Its proposed uses were for the carriage of 24 soldiers or 11 stretchers, or the towing of boats.

German Federal Republic. A trooper and supply aircraft

The experimental Saunders-Roe Hovercraft SR-N1 landing on the beach near Portsmouth on June 22, when it took part in amphibious warfare demonstrations before senior staff officers of the three services, Ministry of Defence officials and foreign military attachés.

(the C.160) for the German air force was projected by a consortium of three German firms, Blume Leichtbau und Flugtechnik, Hamburger Flugzeugbau, Weser Flugzeugbau, and the French firm Nord Aviation. It was to have two R.-R. Tyne turbo-prop engines and a cargo hold 43 ft. long by about 10 ft. square. Another new project was the RF-1 by Rhein Flugzeugbau, a light touring S.T.O.L. aircraft having two 245-h.p. Lycoming engines in the wing root, driving one ducted pusher propeller of about 8 ft. diameter. It was understood that plastics were to be extensively used and that its price would be about DM.200,000. The 4-6-seater Dornier DO.28, having a high main wing and two 180-h.p. Lycoming O-360 piston engines on stub wings, first flew on April 29 and was estimated to be able to cruise for 800 mi. at 155 m.p.h. (*See* also JET PROPULSION AND GAS TURBINES.)   (A. D. E.)

BIBLIOGRAPHY. N. J. Hoff (ed.), *High Temperature Effects in Aircraft Structures* (London, 1958); P. B. Walker, " Structural Design in British Aviation " (*Aircraft Engineering*, Aug. 1959, London); M. J. Zucrow, *Aircraft and Missile Propulsion*, vol. i and ii (London, 1958); P. B. Morice, *Linear Structural Analysis* (London, 1959).

AIR FORCES OF THE WORLD.

The integration of missiles with manned aircraft to form the most efficient defensive and offensive weapons systems possible was the objective and principal activity of all air forces throughout 1959. No appreciable changes were made in the numbers of aircraft or personnel in any of the world's air forces during the year as compared with 1958.

France. The unrealistic government air-power policies, which caused the cancellation of many projects in 1958, continued to plague the French air force and navy during most of 1959. The necessity for maintaining a fighting force in Algeria, the failure of the French aircraft industry to sell other Nato countries the Dassault Mirage III intercepter and Bréguet's Taon strike fighter, and the government's conservative attitude toward appropriations for research and development seriously handicapped both the industry and the armed services of France.

Towards the end of the year, however, the de Gaulle government came forth with some long-range plans and modest appropriations for building up the defensive and offensive potentialities of the nation. In July the French cabinet allocated £15·4 million for space research. A group of the nationalized aircraft companies, together with the French government, set up a new organization, the Société pour l'Etude et la Réalisation d'Engines Balistiques (S.E.R.E.B.), to further the development and production of ballistic missiles. With help from the United States, the French hoped to develop a strategic intermediate range ballistic missile that could be ready for production in two years.

In September the French air force received its first production model of the Mirage III fighter, equipped with SNECMA Atar jet engines; 100 of these were currently on order. France's front-line fighting forces in 1959 consisted mostly of F-1000s, Dassault Super-Mystère B2s, Douglas B-26 bombers and Sud Aviation's Vautour ground attack, night fighter and bomber versions.

German Federal Republic. Towards the close of 1958 the defence committee of the German federal parliament decided to adopt the Lockheed F-104 Starfighter and the Fiat G.91 lightweight strike fighter as standard equipment for the German air force. Negotiations with Lockheed, General Electric and Fiat were concluded during 1959 for the manufacture of the aircraft and engines under licence in Germany. The first 96 Starfighters, together with their J79 turbo-jet engines, were to be built and supplied by Lockheed and General Electric as quickly as possible. German plants were being tooled-up meanwhile for the production of the remaining 300 F-104s initially ordered by the Ministry of Defence. In

the case of the G.91, Fiat was to produce and deliver the first 50 aircraft. Another 150 were to be manufactured under licence in Germany.

Early in the year Honest John missiles with concrete warheads for training purposes were shipped into Germany from the United States. Heinkel, Messerschmitt and Bolkow, three German manufacturing companies, were also working together on the design of various missile projects of their own. Six thousand U.S. Sidewinder air-to-air missiles were scheduled for production in Europe, and Bodenseewerk Perkin-Elmer of Überlinger was to be the main contractor in August for supplying 5,000 of these.

On Oct. 22 the European allies granted the German Federal Republic permission to build its own surface-to-air and air-to-air missiles. Previously, these were on the list of weapons Germany was not allowed to build when it joined Nato.

Italy. In 1959 fighters of Italian design were integrated into the air force. These consisted of several squadrons of Fiat G.91 lightweight strike fighters which were put into active service in the spring and summer. Fiat-built North American F-86 K all-weather fighters were also rolling off the production lines and were scheduled to replace the F-86 Es currently in use. The G.91s eventually would replace the Italian air force's Republic F-84F Thunderstreaks.

The English Electric Lightning fighter over Farnborough on Sept. 7, when the annual flying display and exhibition began.

Pilots from Turkey, Greece, France, Germany and Italy were being trained at Pratica di Mare base to form Nato's international G.91 squadrons. The first of these was put into active service in the spring and was stationed in western Germany. Eventually, Nato expected to have 27 squadrons of G.91s established throughout Europe.

Sweden. At the beginning of the year, the Royal Swedish air force numbered about 20 wings. This included 27 squadrons of day-fighter units, equipped mostly with Saab J-29s and J-34 Hawker Hunters, 6 all-weather fighter squadrons flying J-32B Lansens and J-35 Drakens and 12 ground-attack units equipped with other versions of Lansens. Five reconnaissance squadrons, an air base wing, and a search and air-rescue unit made up the balance. The Royal Swedish air force totalled approximately 20,000 men and 1,200 aircraft.

A decision by the Swedish government early in the year to purchase U.S. Sidewinder missiles as primary armament for the J-35 Draken, J-32B Lansen and J-34 Hawker Hunter greatly increased the striking power of these three fighters. A new version of the Saab all-weather fighter, the J-35B, with a new Rolls-Royce engine and a Mach 2-plus capability, was being built and was expected to go into service in 1960.

United States. *Air Force.* The U.S. air force moved closer during 1959 towards its goal of a balanced and complementary force of manned aircraft and missile units. The first long-range units assigned to the Strategic Air command (SAC) were in place and operational at the end of the year. A wing of SM-62 Snark cruise missiles at Presque Isle air force base, Maine, and a squadron of SM-65 Atlas intercontinental ballistic missiles (ICBMs) at Vandenberg air force base, California, stood ready for action.

Manned aircraft strength decreased from 117 wings in July 1958 to 104 in July 1959, with the Tactical Air command (TAC) bearing the greater part of the reduction. As more missile units—Titan ICBMs and Bomarcs in addition to Snarks and Atlases—came into operation, the number of manned aircraft units was expected to decline still further. But improved aircraft performance and better weapons had greatly increased the combat strength of the individual manned aircraft unit, thereby making up in large part for the decline in number of units.

The most important operational problem was to ensure the ability of the strategic strike force to survive a surprise attack and retaliate on the shortest possible notice. The programme of dispersing bomber units—especially B-52s—over a larger number of bases progressed well, and SAC also maintained a portion of its force of bombers and tankers on a constant ground alert.

While timely warning of attack was vital to performance of SAC's mission, it was equally vital for the Air Defense command (ADC) and for the nation as a whole. The speed of the ICBM meant that warning time was reduced to the barest minimum—15 to 30 min. To provide warning of ICBM attack, the air force accelerated construction of its ballistic missile early warning system. The first two major installations, in Alaska and Greenland, were under way in 1959, and a third was to be built in the United Kingdom.

The total strength of the air force declined from 871,150 on June 30, 1958, to 840,435 on June 30, 1959. About 225,000 officers and airmen were stationed overseas on the latter date. The air force received from congress for fiscal year 1958-59 $18,767 million in new obligational authority. For fiscal year 1959-60 the air force received $18,270 million.

The role of the air force in the national astronautical effort was clarified in Sept. 1959 when the secretary of defense assigned to it responsibility for developing, producing and launching space boosters for all U.S. space satellites and

A U.S. B-58 bomber is lowered to the ground by hydraulic jacks as it leaves the elevated production line at Fort Worth, Texas.

vehicles. The air force was also given responsibility for the development of two major satellites—Midas, for early warning against ballistic missiles, and Samos, for reconnaissance.

Progress in missiles was steady. The air force declared the SM-65 Atlas ICBM operationally ready in Sept. 1959, and the first SM-68 Titan ICBM made its first successful flight in Feb. 1959. By Oct. 1959 the air force had named 12 bases to be constructed for operation of the Atlas and the Titan. The

air force speeded development of a third ICBM, the solid-propellent Minute-man, which would be relatively inexpensive and easily maintained and operated.

SM-75 Thor intermediate-range missiles were to be operated from British bases by R.A.F. squadrons. The first SM-75 Thor was in place in June 1959. The United States signed an agreement with Italy to use Italian bases for the SM-78 Jupiter intermediate-range missiles.

All intercontinental missiles were under the operational control of SAC, which also had the air-breathing SM-62 Snark units in its armoury of weapons. The first Snark

A new type of aircraft escape capsule being tested by personnel of the U.S. Wright air development centre off Key West, Florida.

missile wing attained operational readiness in the autumn of 1959. The IM-99 Bomarc interceptor missile, to be used by the ADC, also neared operational status.

SAC received its first B-52G in April 1959. This heavy bomber had more range and speed than its predecessors and would carry the long-range GAM-77 Hound Dog air-to-surface missile. The first supersonic jet bomber, the B-58, already in production, was eventually to replace a portion of SAC's B-47 medium bomber force.

Navy Air Element. On Jan. 1, 1959, there were 8,145 operating aircraft on hand, and 28,900 officers and 170,000 enlisted men in navy and marine corps aviation.

Two modern attack carriers, added to the fleet by the commissioning of the new U.S.S. " Independence " and the completion of the U.S.S. " Oriskany " conversion, permitted the reassignment of two older carriers to anti-submarine forces. Three of nine nuclear-powered ballistic missile submarines authorized by congress were launched, the first being the U.S.S. " George Washington ", launched June 9, 1959. Two destroyers, specially designed and built as missile ships, were launched in April. Three more guided missiles became operational as the air-to-air Sparrow III, the air-to-surface Bullpup and the Talos (effective against surface targets, aircraft and air-breathing missiles) were assigned to fleet units.

Tests of the ballistic missile Polaris demonstrated steady progress toward operational status. In August, a significant milestone was passed when the missile was fired on a limited 700-mi. flight from the U.S.S. " Observation Island ", at sea seven miles off the Atlantic missile range at Cape Canaveral, Florida.

New operational aircraft included the F8U-2 Crusader and the T2J jet trainer. The ZPG-3W airship, largest non-rigid airship ever built, was delivered on June 19. It was designed and heavily instrumented for early warning patrol. Carrier aircraft under development included the high performance F4H Phantom II interceptor; the A3J, a high-speed, long-range, high-altitude attack plane; the A2F low-altitude attack specialist, capable of delivering a variety of weapons; and the W2F early warning plane.

Emphasis on defence against submarines continued. In Oct. 1958, two additional anti-submarine groups were formed in the Atlantic for developing tactics and training assigned units in co-ordinated attack. Improved models of the HSS helicopter and S2F twin-engine aircraft made first flights. Contracts were let for installing new electronic detection and destruction systems in P5M and P2V patrol planes. The P3V version of the commercial transport Electra, featuring speed, long range and the latest in electronics, made its first flight.

U.S.S.R. There was no evidence during 1959 that the U.S.S.R. was changing the production of aircraft in favour of an unmanned, all-missile air force. On the contrary, every indication pointed to the fact that it was working hard to equip its existing forces with the latest model aircraft and missiles. Particular attention was being given to the development of an air-to-air rocket that would be as deadly and accurate as the U.S. Sidewinder.

Top priority was also assigned to the development of an intercontinental bomber to replace the Bear and Bison. Several prototype versions, given the code name Bounder by Nato, were known to have made experimental flights.

While several supersonic all-weather fighters and Mach 2 interceptors were being introduced into the Soviet air force, the Mig-19 Farmer was still the mainstay of the fighter squadrons. The successor to the Farmer was the Mig-21 Faceplate, a few of which were integrated into the air defence divisions during the year. A limited number of Sukhoi-15 Fishpot delta-wing fighters were also put into operation. The Yak-25 Flashlight remained as the principal all-weather interceptor, with its successor, the swept-wing Flashlight C, beginning to appear in limited quantities. The twin-jet Badger still served as the Soviet first-line medium bomber.

It was evident that the U.S.S.R. had established a number of intermediate-range missile bases at strategic points throughout its territory, as well as in some eastern European countries. Coupled with its ever-increasing network of radar warning stations and interceptor bases, the Soviet air force now had a combined missile-aircraft defence system of considerable depth.

People's Republic of China. A new agreement with the Soviet Union, made early in 1959, promised greater economic and technical co-operation with China's infant aircraft industry. During 1959, the Chinese flight-tested at least seven different types of planes of their own design. These were mostly light planes and inexpensive small transports. China's arsenal of aerial weapons had so far come from the U.S.S.R. and eastern Europe. (*See* also COMMONWEALTH AIR FORCES; JET PROPULSION AND GAS TURBINES; WEAPONS AND MILITARY EQUIPMENT.)   (WN. A. S.; A. GG.; R. B. PE.)

AIR RACES AND RECORDS.
The first crossing of the English channel by Louis Blériot in 1909 was commemorated during July 13-23, 1959, by a London-Paris race organized by the *Daily Mail* in conjunction with the Royal Aero club. Competitors were timed in either direction between the Marble Arch, London, and the Arc de Triomphe, Paris. The aircraft used for the major part of the journey ranged from jet-propelled fighters to ultra-light aeroplanes and a glider, and great ingenuity was shown in the means of covering the first and last stages of the route. The winner was Sqn. Ldr. C. G. Maughan who, aided by an R.A.F. team, achieved a time of 40 min. 44 sec. His method was: motorcycle from the Arc de Triomphe to Issy-les-Moulineaux; helicopter to Villacoublay; Hunter jet fighter to Biggin Hill, Kent; helicopter to Thames foreshore at Ranelagh, London; motorcycle to Marble Arch. Second was a civilian, J. E. Rylands, who used the new Westland heliport in London; third, Gp. Capt. E. N. Ryder, R.A.F. The prize for the " most praiseworthy " attempt went to the BEAline syndicate—largely

executives from British European airways—whose mean time of 62¼ min. showed the possibilities in public transport, notably in crossing from Northolt to Le Bourget in a DH Comet 4B airliner in 28 min.

At the British National Air races at Baginton, Coventry, in July, the King's cup was won by A. J. Spiller in a Percival Proctor; the over-all air racing champion for the year was Capt. N. Baldwick. M. F. Liardon (Switzerland) won the international aerobatic championships.

One absolute world record fell to France when, on June 18, G. Muselli, flying a Dassault Mirage, covered the 100-km. closed circuit at 1,100·4 m.p.h.—80 m.p.h. more than A. Turcat, also of France, on Feb. 25. New class records for jet-powered aircraft over 500-km. and 1,000-km. closed circuits went to U.S.A.F. pilots with the RF-101C Voodoo: 816·2 m.p.h. and 700 m.p.h. by Capt. G. A. Edwards and Colonel E. H. Taylor respectively. A significant Soviet achievement was a new aeroplane altitude record, officially admitted as 94,692 ft. The pilot was V. Ilyuishin, the machine a T-431 and the date July 14. Later in the year, the U.S.S.R. claimed the world air speed record for the first time; on Oct. 31 Colonel G. Mosolov flew an E66 fighter over an officially observed course at a speed put forward as 1,493 m.p.h. The British Fairey Rotodyne, with Sqn. Ldr. W. R. Gellatly (N.Z.) as chief pilot, set up the first record in the new convertiplane category—for aircraft capable of both vertical and normal forward propulsion. On Jan. 5, from White Waltham, the Rotodyne flew round a 100-km. circuit at 190·9 m.p.h.—much faster than the existing world speed record for helicopters. (For gliding results and records, *see* SPORTING RECORD.)   (G. D. H. L.)

ALBANIA. People's republic in the western part of the Balkan peninsula bounded N. and E. by Yugoslavia, S. by Greece and W. by the Adriatic sea. Area: 11,100 sq.mi. Pop.: (1950 census) 1,215,200; (1957 est.) 1,452,100. Language: literary Albanian and two spoken dialects, the Gheg north of the river Shkumbi and the Tosk in the south. Religion: Moslem 65%, Orthodox 23%, Roman Catholic 11%. Chief towns (Oct. 1955): Tirana (cap.) 108,182; Scutari (Shkodër) 38,564; Koritsa (Korçë) 31,833; Valona (Vlorë) 28,212. First secretary of the Albanian Workers' (Communist) party, Enver Hoxha; chairman of the presidium of the People's assembly, Haxhi Leshi; chairman of the council of ministers, Mehmet Shehu. Main imports: machinery, wheat, paper, window glass. Main exports: crude oil, chrome ore, copper ore. Monetary unit: *Lek* (L.140 = £1 sterling).

History. The principal event of the year 1959 was a ten-day visit (May 25-June 4) by Nikita Khrushchev, chairman of the Soviet council of ministers, in May. Talks between him and the leaders of the Albanian Communist party and government resulted in a reaffirmation of Albania's allegiance to the Soviet bloc, Soviet support for Enver Hoxha as the leader of Albanian Communism and an increase in Soviet economic aid. Khrushchev used the occasion to advocate the creation of a zone in the Balkans free of nuclear weapons, a proposal that the Albanian government supported. Albania's relations with both its neighbours remained strained. A frontier incident early in the year led to sharp exchanges with Greece, while relations with Yugoslavia remained unfriendly, with strongly worded propaganda directed against Marshal Tito. The Yugoslav minister in Tirana was formally recalled to Belgrade in March.

Figures published early in the year showed that industrial production in 1958 had risen by 20% compared with 1957. Figures for four major products were: crude oil 403,197 metric tons (a decrease of 18%); coal 255,677 tons; chrome ore 201,252 tons; electric power 150,000,000 kwh. In April retail prices on a wide range of foodstuffs and manufactured goods were reduced by amounts ranging from 5% to 20%. At the same time prices paid by the state to farmers for compulsory deliveries of crops were doubled and in some cases trebled. The compulsory delivery system was modified, deliveries from privately owned plots being abolished and a large proportion of arrears being wiped out. It was stated that, at the end of 1958, 63% of the peasants had been brought into collective farms, which accounted for 72% of the total arable land.

On July 3 agreements were signed at Tirana by which the Soviet government granted Albania a long-term credit of Rb.300 million and undertook to provide technical aid for the expansion of Albanian industry. (*See* also EASTERN EUROPEAN ECONOMIC PLANNING.)   (D. F.)

ALGERIA.

French territory of North Africa, situated between Morocco (W.) and Tunisia (E.), with the status of government-general of the French Republic. Total area: *c.* 921,620 sq.mi., administered in two parts: Algeria proper (117,760 sq.mi.), comprising 12 *départements*, and Algerian Sahara (803,860 sq.mi.), two *départements**. Pop. (1959 est.): 9,875,000, incl. 8,850,000 Arabs and Berbers (Moslem) and 1,025,000 Europeans (predominantly Roman Catholics). Chief towns (1954 census, urban agglomerations, Europeans in brackets): Algiers 355,040 (192,890)†; Oran 291,812 (173,157); Constantine 143,334 (40,675); Bône 112,010 (46,114). Delegate-general of the government, Paul Delouvrier. Main exports: wine, iron ore, citrus fruits, cereals, spring vegetables, phosphates. Monetary unit: Algerian *franc*=metropolitan *franc*.

* These two *départements*—Oasis (chief town, Ouargla) and Saoura (chief town, Colomb-Béchar)—are administered from Paris by the minister-delegate for the Organisation Commune des Régions Sahariennes; pop. (1959 est.) 501,000. (*See* SAHARA, FRENCH.)
† " Great Algiers " (1959 est.) had a population of 750,000, including *c.* 300,000 Europeans.

History. With a view to finding a political solution General Charles de Gaulle gradually freed himself from the hold of the French " activists " in Algeria—the supporters of " integration ". On Dec. 12, 1958, General Raoul Salan was replaced as delegate-general by Paul Delouvrier and, as commander-in-chief, by General Maurice Challe. On Jan. 8, 1959, on assuming the presidency of the republic, de Gaulle declared: " A place of honour is reserved for the Algeria of tomorrow, pacified and transformed, developing its own personality and closely associated with France." On Jan. 13, Messali Hadj,

President de Gaulle greets Moslem women at the small town of Saida during his four-day tour of the Algerian hinterland in August.

the leader of the Algerian autonomists, who had been interned at Belle-Ile, was set free; Mohammed ben Bella, the military commander of the Algerian insurgents (arrested by ruse on Oct. 22, 1956), was transferred from the " Santé " prison in Paris to the island of Aix; men condemned to death were pardoned.

On May 7, speaking at Bourges, de Gaulle declared that the " peace of brave men " (proclaimed by him on Oct. 23, 1958) remained a valid concept. At the commemoration ceremony on May 13 some activists shouted " down with de Gaulle ". Two days before, Pierre Lagaillarde, a deputy from Algiers, declared that the " peace of brave men " was a " fraud ". But the army supported the government. On

Aug. 27-30 de Gaulle made an inspection of the army in Algeria and concluded: " The army must continue pacification to the very end . . . The Algerians will work out their own destiny."

On Sept. 16, in a televised broadcast, he set forth his plans: after pacification and a transition period of four years a referendum would be held; the Algerians would then have the choice of three solutions: secession, integration or federation. He thus proclaimed the right of Algerians to " self-determination ".

The reactions of the French " activists " showed a certain confusion. The " provisional government of the Algerian republic ", replying from Tunis on Sept. 28, said: " We do not intend to neglect any opportunity which may bring peace; voting cannot take place under the pressure of the army and the administration; a discussion is necessary; the return to peace may be immediate ". On Nov. 11 de Gaulle declared that the leaders of the insurgents could go to France to discuss terms.

" Greater Algiers " was created by the inclusion of neighbouring communes, and on April 30 the new municipal council (41 Moslems, 34 Europeans) was elected. Mohammed Bouharaoua was elected mayor.

The elections to the Senate held in Algeria on May 31 resulted in a defeat for the " activists "; 20 Moslems and 12 Europeans were elected.

A large-scale military operation " Jumelles " (Binoculars) started in Ouarsenis and Kabylia on July 22. On Sept. 21 General Challe claimed that 4,400 rebels had been killed in the first two months of the operation. Acts of terrorism in France caused several deaths, including that of Chérif Benhabyles, a senator from Constantine. An attempt on the life of Messali Hadj (Sept. 17) failed.

In his press conference of Nov. 10, de Gaulle said that in the five-year civil war the rebels had killed 1,800 European and 12,000 Moslem civilians. Of the 1·4 million French soldiers who had served there 13,000 (less than 1%) had been killed on active service; 145,000 Algerians had been killed on the rebel side.   (HU. DE.)

ALIENS.

The number of aliens registered in the United Kingdom on June 30, 1959, was 394,573 (males 216,605, females 177,968). This compared with 388,231 (males 217,451, females 170,780) on June 30, 1958.

Among aliens not required to register and therefore not included in these figures were children under 16; members of diplomatic and consular services of foreign governments; certain officials of international organizations; foreign members of the armed forces of countries of the Commonwealth; members of Nato forces on duty in the United Kingdom; and tourists and other visitors who spent less than three months in the United Kingdom. The number of incoming foreign travellers to the United Kingdom in the 12 months ended Sept. 30, 1959, was 1,449,483, compared with 1,306,878, for the previous 12 months.

During the first nine months of 1959 more than 34,200 permits were issued to aliens to work in the United Kingdom for periods of varying lengths. More than 16,100 were for domestic employment in private households or institutions.

Between Oct. 1, 1958, and Sept. 30, 1959, 5,503 new applications for naturalization were lodged. Certificates granted numbered 4,150. During the same period 3,631 foreign women who had married British subjects and 1,153 minors acquired British nationality by registration as citizens of the United Kingdom and colonies. (*See* also IMMIGRATION AND EMIGRATION.)   (K. B. P.)

See *Statistics of Foreigners entering and leaving the United Kingdom, 1958* (H.M.S.O., 1959).

AMBASSADORS AND ENVOYS. The following is a list of the chief diplomatic representatives to and from the United Kingdom on Dec. 1, 1959.

The following is a list of high commissioners within the Commonwealth of Nations on Dec. 1, 1959.

To United Kingdom	Country	From United Kingdom
Mohammed Kabir Ludin	Afghanistan	M. C. Gillett
Rear Admiral Teodoro Hartung	Argentina	Sir John Ward
Dr. Johannes Schwarzenberg	Austria	Sir James Bowker
René van Meerbeke	Belgium	Sir George Labouchere
*Jorge H. Sanchez Peña	Bolivia	Sir James Henderson
Francisco de Assis Chateaubriand Bandeira de Mello	Brazil	Sir Geoffrey Wallinger
†Georgi Pétrov Zenguilékov	Bulgaria	†A. E. Lambert
U Aung Soe	Burma	R. H. S. Allen
Au Chheun	Cambodia	F. F. Garner
Victor Santa-Cruz	Chile	I. T. M. Pink
*Huan Hsiang	China	*M. N. F. Stewart
*Dr. Pablo Samper	Colombia	Sir James Joint
Alfredo Alfaro Sotela	Costa Rica	D. J. Mill Irving
Sergio Rojas Santamarina	Cuba	A. S. Fordham
Miroslav Galuška	Czechoslovakia	P. F. Grey
Vicens de Steensen-Leth	Denmark	Sir Roderick Barclay
Dr. Héctor García Godoy	Dominican Rep.	W. W. McVittie
Leonidas Plaza	Ecuador	C. A. G. Meade
*Ato Kebbede Abbebe	Ethiopia	D. A. H. Wright
Leo Olavi Tuominen	Finland	Sir Douglas Busk
Jean Chauvel	France	Sir Gladwyn Jebb
Hans von Herwarth	German F. R.	Sir Christopher Steel
George St. Seferiades	Greece	Sir Roger Allen
*Juan David Lambour	Guatemala	†T. Wikeley
Nabi Youla	Guinea	W. N. Hugh-Jones
Colbert Bonhomme	Haiti	Sidney Simmonds
‡Archbishop G. P. O'Hara	Holy See	†Sir Marcus Cheke
Antonio Bermúdez Milla	Honduras	G. H. S. Jackson
†Béla Szilágyi	Hungary	†N. J. A. Cheetham
Dr. Kristinn Gudmundsson	Iceland	A. G. Gilchrist
Dr. Sunario	Indonesia	Sir Leslie Fry
Abd-ul-Malik el-Zaibak	Iraq	Sir Humphrey Trevelyan
Hugh J. McCann	Ireland, Rep. of	Sir Ian Maclennan
*Arthur Liveran	Israel	P. F. Hancock
Vittorio Zoppi	Italy	Sir Ashley Clarke
Katsumi Ohno	Japan	Sir Oscar Morland
Anastas Hanania	Jordan	Sir Charles Johnston
Yu Taik Kim	Korea	H. J. Evans
Prince Khammao	Laos	A. H. Lincoln
Ibrahim el-Ahdab	Lebanon	P. M. Crosthwaite
George Tilman Brewer, Jr.	Liberia	G. H. Clarke
Abdussalam Busairi	Libya	D. M. H. Riches
André Clasen	Luxembourg	H. W. A. Freese-Pennefather
Pablo Campos Ortiz	Mexico	Sir Andrew Noble
Prince El Hassan Ben El Mehdi	Morocco	Sir Charles Duke
Rama Prasad Manandhar	Nepal	L. A. Scopes
Baron Adolph Bentinck	Netherlands	Sir Paul Mason
Erik Braadland	Norway	Sir Peter Scarlett
Carlos Fernando Alfaro	Panama	Sir Ian Henderson
R. Adm. J. Wenceslao Benítes E.	Paraguay	H. F. A. Gates
Hossein Ghods-Nakhai	Persia	Sir Geoffrey Harrison
Ricardo Rivera Schreiber	Peru	Sir Berkeley Gage
León María Guerrero	Philippines	J. A. Pilcher
Eugeniusz Milnikiel	Poland	Sir Eric Berthoud
Gen. Adolfo do Amaral Abranches Pinto	Portugal	Sir Charles Stirling
†Petre Bălăceanu	Rumania	†R. D. J. Scott Fox
José Antonio Meléndez Prado	Salvador, El	F. C. Everson
El Marqués de Santa Cruz	Spain	Sir Ivo Mallet
Mohammed Hamad El-Niel	Sudan	Sir Edwin Chapman-Andrews
Gunnar R. Hägglöf	Sweden	Sir Robert Hankey
Armin Daeniker	Switzerland	Sir William Montagu-Pollock
Mom Luang Peekdhip Malakul	Thailand	Sir Richard Whittington
Taieb Slim	Tunisia	A. C. E. Malcolm
Muharrem Nuri Birgi	Turkey	Sir Bernard Burrows
Yakov A. Malik	U.S.S.R.	Sir Patrick Reilly
*Kamel Khalil	Un. Arab Rep.	*C. T. Crowe
John Hay Whitney	United States	Sir Harold Caccia
*Marcos Brondi	Uruguay	M. S. Henderson
Dr. Ignacio Iribarren Borges	Venezuela	Sir John Walker
Ngo Dinh Luyen	Vietnam	R. W. Parkes
*Mohammed Bin Ibrahim	Yemen	*C. M. Pirie-Gordon
Ivo Vejvoda	Yugoslavia	Sir John Nicholls
—	United Nations	Sir Pierson Dixon

Unstarred, ambassador. * Chargé d'affaires. † Minister. ‡ Apostolic delegate.

From Australia to		
Canada		Sir Walter Cawthorn
Ceylon		J. C. G. Kevin
Federation of Malaya		T. K. Critchley
Ghana		S. Jamieson
India		W. R. Crocker
New Zealand		Sir John Collins
Pakistan		A. R. Cutler
South Africa		*O. L. Davis
United Kingdom		Sir Eric Harrison
From Canada to		
Australia		T. W. L. MacDermot
Ceylon		N. Cavell
Federation of Malaya		A. R. Menzies
Ghana		B. M. Williams
India		Chester A. Ronning
New Zealand		G. R. Heasman
Pakistan		H. O. Moran
South Africa		J. J. Hurley
United Kingdom		G. A. Drew
From Ceylon to		
Australia		
New Zealand		B. F. Perera
Canada		Sir Velupillai Coomaraswamy
Federation of Malaya		D. C. R. Gunawardena
India		Sir Richard Aluwihare
Pakistan		M. M. Maharoff
United Kingdom		P. R. Gunasekara
From the Federation of Malaya to		
Australia		Gunn Lay Teik
India		S. Chelvasingam MacIntyre
Pakistan		Haji Kamarudin bin Haji Idris
United Kingdom		Tunku Ya'acob ibni Al-Marhum Sultan Abd-ul-Hamid Halim Shah
From the Federation of Rhodesia and Nyasaland to		
South Africa		J. W. M. Fitt
United Kingdom		Sir Gilbert Rennie
From Ghana to		
India		Nana Kwabena Kena II
United Kingdom		E. O. Asafu-Adjaye
From India to		
Australia		Samarendranath Sen
New Zealand		
Canada		C. S. Venkatachar
Ceylon		Y. D. Gundevia
Federation of Malaya		S. K. Banerji
Ghana		B. K. Kapoor
Pakistan		Rajeshwar Dayal
United Kingdom		Mrs. Vijaya Lakshmi Pandit
From New Zealand to		
Australia		F. Jones
Canada		Foss Shanahan
Federation of Malaya		C. M. Bennett
United Kingdom		†G. R. Laking
From Pakistan to		
Australia		Ihsanulla Khan
New Zealand		
Canada		S. M. Burke
Ceylon		Brig. Hamid Hussein
Federation of Malaya		Maj.-Gen. Sher Ali Khan
Ghana		Mahmud Ahmad
India		Dr. O. H. Malik
United Kingdom		Lieut.-Gen. Mohammed Yousuf
From South Africa to		
Australia		A. A. M. Hamilton
Canada		R. Kirsten
Federation of Rhodesia and Nyasaland		H. L. T. Taswell
United Kingdom		Dr. A. J. R. van Rhijn
From United Kingdom to		
Australia		Sir William P. Oliver
Canada		Sir Saville Garner
Ceylon		Sir Alexander Morley
Federation of Malaya		Sir Geoffrey Tory
Federation of Rhodesia and Nyasaland		M. R. Metcalf
Ghana		A. W. Snelling
India		Malcolm Macdonald
New Zealand		F. E. Cumming-Bruce
Pakistan		Sir Alexander Symon
South Africa		Sir John Maud

* Designate. † Acting.

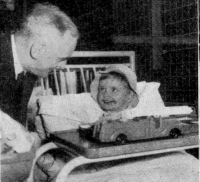

(*Left*) The Swiss ambassador, A. Daeniker, at the Gt. Ormond st. children's hospital, London, in October. (*Centre*) U Aung Soe, the Burmese ambassador, on his country's 11th independence day. (*Right*) S. R. Santamarina, the new Cuban ambassador, with his wife and daughter.

AMERICAN LITERATURE. The American literary mood of 1959 was retrospective and self-critical. Analysts of the role of the United States in international affairs were almost unanimous in condemning the current foreign policy of the government. They included Walter Lippmann, who, in *The Communist World and Ours*, dissected Nikita Khruschev's political thinking and urged that the United States should reappraise its political aims and needs. On the American scene, Vance Packard's *The Status Seekers* pointed out the hidden barriers and the visible signs of class consciousness in a theoretically classless society, while Jacques

Jacques Barzun   *Vance Oakley Packard*

Barzun, distinguishing intelligence from intellect in *The House of Intellect*, found that art, science and philanthropy were the enemies of contemporary intellect. A perennial subject, the American Civil War attracted even more writers than usual as its centennial approached, although many of the books appealed only to the specialist or monomaniac.

In fiction, many writers, including those whose chief purpose was not to attack the world they lived in, observed and recorded its follies. The flood of poetry continued, but many considered that one major source, the " beatniks ", occupied with reading their deliberately undisciplined, protesting verse in night clubs and hotel ballrooms, created more publicity than poetry.

The year's books also included the following:

The Foreign Scene. C. L. Sulzberger, *What's Wrong with U.S. Foreign Policy*; William Appleman Williams, *The Tragedy of American Diplomacy*; Charles Wright Mills, *The Causes of World War Three*; Adlai Stevenson, *Friends and Enemies*; Crane Brinton, *A History of Western Morals*; Hannah Arendt, *The Human Condition, a Study of the Central Dilemmas facing Modern Man*.

The American Scene. James Bryant Conant, *The American High School Today*; Hyman George Rickover, *Education and Freedom*; Howard Mumford Jones, *One Great Society* (a report on humane learning in the United States); Benjamin Ginzburg, *Rededication to Freedom* (an account of the damage suffered in recent years by personal liberty due to attacks on constitutional rights); William Peters, *The Southern Temper*; Elena Padilla, *Up from Puerto Rico*; Dan Wakefield, *Island in the City: the World of Spanish Harlem*; Richard Carter, *The Doctor Business* (an analysis of the business practices of the medical profession); W. Lloyd Warner, *The Living and the Dead* (a study of the symbolic life of a New England town); Thomas Griffith, *Waist-High Culture*; Eric Larrabee and Rolf Meyerson (eds.), *Mass Leisure*; Carl Bode, *The Anatomy of American Popular Culture, 1840-1861*; Allen Churchill, *The Improper Bohemians* (a portrait of Greenwich Village in its heyday); Harold Loeb, *The Way It Was*; Lawrence Lipton, *The Holy Barbarians* (" beatniks " in Venice, California); Aline Saarinen, *The Proud Possessors* (a history of America's great art collectors); Langston Hughes and Arna Bontemps (eds.), *The Book of Negro Folklore*; James Thurber, *The Years with Ross*; Kathleen O'Donnell Hoover and John Cage, *Virgil Thomson*; Margaret Mead (ed.), *An Anthropologist at Work* (the writings and correspondence of Ruth Benedict); Moss Hart, *Act One* (autobiography); Harry Golden, *For 2¢ Plain* (essays); James Agee, *Agee on Film* (a posthumous collection of criticism and essays).

Historical Works. Carl N. Degler, *Out of Our Past: the Forces that Shaped Modern America*; Daniel Boorstin, *The Americans: the Colonial Experience*; Henry Savage, *Seeds of Time* (a study of the roots of

Southern solidarity); Hodding Carter, *The Angry Scar* (an account of the Reconstruction); Arthur Schlesinger, Jr., *The Coming of the New Deal* (vol. ii of *The Age of Roosevelt*); Julian P. Boyd (ed.), *The Papers of Thomas Jefferson* (vol. xv); Alfred Owen Aldridge, *Man of Reason* (a life of Thomas Paine); Samuel Eliot Morison, *John Paul Jones* and *History of United States Naval Operations in World War II* (vol. xii); Shelby Foote, *The Civil War: a Narrative*; Burke Davis, *To Appomattox: Nine April Days, 1865*; Glen Tucker, *High Tide at Gettysburg*; Richard Nelson Current, *The Lincoln Nobody Knows*; Richard B. Harwell (ed.), *Union Reader* (a collection of contemporary writings and sources); Raymond Ginger, *Altgeld's America: the Lincoln Ideal Versus Changing Realities*; Edward Charles Wagenknecht, *The Seven Worlds of Theodore Roosevelt*; Michael Amrine, *The Great Decision* (an account of President Truman's decision to drop the atom bomb); John Brooks, *The Seven Fat Years* (an account of the stock market in the 1950s).

Fiction. Robert Penn Warren, *The Cave*; Saul Bellow, *Henderson the Rain King*; John O'Hara, *From the Terrace*; Peter DeVries, *The Tents of Wickedness*; Mark Harris, *Wake Up, Stupid*; Truman Capote, *Breakfast at Tiffany's*; Hamilton Basso, *The Light Infantry Ball*; Lilian Smith, *One Hour*; John Hersey, *The War Lover*; Frank Brown, *Trumbull Park*; Lorraine Hansberry, *Raisin in the Sun*; Richard Wright, *The Long Dream*; Allen Drury, *Advise and Consent*; George P. Elliott, *Parktilden Village*; John Updike, *The Poorhouse Fair* and *The Same Door*; Warren Miller, *The Cool World*; Bianca Van Orden, *Water Music*; Peter S. Feibleman, *The Daughters of Necessity*.

Scholarship. Ernest Samuel, *Henry Adams: the Middle Years*; Frances Winwar, *The Haunted Palace* (a life of Edgar Allan Poe); Oscar Sherwin, *Prophet of Liberty: the Life and Times of Wendell Phillips*; Sherman Paul, *The Shores of America: Thoreau's Inward Exploration*; Philip Butcher, *George W. Cable: the Northampton Years*; William Dean Howells, *The Realist at War: the Mature Years, 1885-1920* (vol. ii of the biography of Erwin Harrison Cady); Frederick George Bracher, *The Novels of James Gould Cozzens*; Walter Harding and Carl Bode (eds.), *The Correspondence of Henry David Thoreau*; Charles Neider, *The Autobiography of Mark Twain*; Philip S. Foner, *Mark Twain: Social Critic*; Minnie M. Brashear and Robert M. Rodney (eds.), *The Art, Humor and Humanity of Mark Twain*; Robert H. Elias (ed.), *Letters of Theodore Dreiser: a Selection*.

Poetry. Theodore Roethke, *Words for the Wind*; Robert Lowell, *Life Studies*; Langston Hughes, *Selected Poems*; David Wagoner, *A Place to Stand*; Michael Hamburger, *The Dual Site*; James Merrill, *The Country of a Thousand Years of Peace, and Other Poems*; James Wright, *Saint Judas*; Barbara Howes, *Light and Dark*; Donald Hall, *Dark Houses*; Louis O. Coxe, *The Wilderness*; May Swenson, *A Cage of Spines*; Barbara Gibbs, *The Green Chapel*; Ned O'Gorman, *The Night of the Hammer*; John Fandel, *Testament, and Other Poems*; Hyam Plutzik, *Apples from Shinar*; Irving Layton, *Laughter in the Mind*; Marianne Moore, *O to Be a Dragon*. (*See also* LITERARY PRIZES.)   (H. M. H.; X.)

ANDORRA. Autonomous principality between France and Spain, bounded N. by the *départements* of Ariège and Pyrénées Orientales and S. by the Spanish province of Lerida. Area: 191 sq.mi. Pop. (1959 est.): *c*. 6,000, excluding *c*. 1,400 foreigners, mainly Spaniards and Frenchmen. Language: Catalan. Religion: Roman Catholic. Capital: Andorra-la-Vella (Catalan) or la-Vieja (Spanish), pop. (1959 est.) 2,000. Co-princes: the president of the French republic and the bishop of Urgel, Spain, respectively represented by their *viguiers* (deputies). An elected general council of 24 members appoints one of its members as the *syndic général des vallées* (from 1946, Francisco Cairat). Currencies: French and Spanish.

History. The main event of 1959 was the closing, on Jan. 23, of the Spanish-Andorran frontier by the Spanish government. No official explanation was given, but it was generally believed that there were two reasons for this measure: illegal exports of Spanish currency and smuggling of consumer goods (mainly cars) into Spain. There was little doubt than many of the currency traffickers who formerly operated from Tangiers had moved to Andorra since Tangier had lost its international status. In spite of the closing of the Spanish frontier, the number of tourists who visited Andorra during the year was estimated at 660,000. A new general council was elected on Dec. 17.

ANGLICAN COMMUNION. The Anglican Communion is composed of dioceses all over the world, the bishops of which are summoned to the Lambeth conference, under the presidency of the archbishop of Canterbury. There are estimated to be 50 million members of the Anglican Communion in some 350 dioceses. Some of the dioceses are missionary, some belong to self-governing provinces having their own archbishop or metropolitan.

The church of St. Paul, Harlow New Town, which was consecrated by the bishop of Chelmsford on April 19. Features of interest are the belfry tower, which stands apart, and the 97-ft.-high precast concrete spire. Behind the altar is a large mosaic by John Piper.

In the Church of England the main news during 1959 was the discussions on Church relations with the Methodists, the need for raising money by " Christian stewardship " methods, Church relations with other Christian bodies which admitted women priests, the " seal " of confession, the stir raised by an " Anglican-Methodist " local church and the resignation in the Southwark diocese of a curate who was asked to discontinue the use of the Roman Catholic missal.

Church of England relations with the Church of Sweden were discussed in the convocations in January after the Church of Sweden had agreed to the ordination of women to the priesthood. No Swedish women, however, offered themselves for ordination during 1959. The English convocations were gravely disturbed since the ordination of women might impair the limited intercommunion with the Church of Sweden. No action was taken because the archbishop of Canterbury reported that he had sent a private letter to the Church of Sweden. In the Church of England itself the admittance of women as lay readers was recommended by the Church assembly. The proposal was to go later to the convocations. Relations with the Methodists were again discussed. Progress was so slow that it was said in the upper house of Canterbury that the Methodists might well think that the Church of England had " missed the 'bus altogether ". A statement was recorded showing the precise nature of the difficulties Anglicans had in allowing intercommunion. No recommendations or actual proposals for reunion were yet possible.

The bishops of the York convocation found themselves " uncomfortable " about the representation of our Lord in plays given in church. It was doubted if any man could fill such a role adequately, and if he did, whether it was a real help to faith.

The old Church Information board was superseded in February by a new Church Information office. It was to produce a 24-hr. Church news service, and this began in May. It was also decided to enlarge and reconstitute the C.A.C.T.M. (Central Advisory Council of Training for the Ministry). In the past it had dealt only with ordinands; in the future it was to take charge of training for lay ministries, including women's work in the Church. A new moderator for C.A.C.T.M. was appointed, the Right Rev. Frederick Craske, bishop of Gibraltar.

A mild furore was raised in the Church at the publication in March of a booklet *Getting Married*, issued by the British Medical association. One article suggested that there was nothing wrong with premarital intercourse between young people. Strong protest was made by Christian doctors and Church writers, and eventually the booklet was withdrawn.

In the May convocations the inviolability of the " seal " of confession was raised in the discussion of the new draft canons. The steering committee had recommended the withdrawal of the relevant canon, not because of any reluctance to affirm the principle of the seal, but because of difficulties in the way of seeking statutory authority for the principle by way of a canon. It was, however, hotly asserted that the withdrawal of the draft canon might appear to be a surrender of the principle and a sign of fear of what parliament might say or do. Others maintained that the inviolability of the seal was not in any case matter for a canon and that the seal was best left as it was in a country where its inviolability was taken for granted. The discussion ended inconclusively.

There was some controversy when news was received in July that a " joint Anglican and Methodist church " was to be built in Greenhill, in the diocese of Canterbury. The idea was mooted to save reduplicating funds by building both a new Methodist and a new Anglican church in a new locality. The church was to be the legal property of the Methodists, and all services except holy communion were to be shared. A joint Sunday school was also to be encouraged. Strong doubts were held by Church people concerning preaching (where two different formularies were involved), about sacramental teaching, confirmation and the training of children. An even wider-reaching storm raged over the resignation of an assistant priest at St. Andrew's, Carshalton, after the request first of the rector of Carshalton and then of the bishop of Southwark that he should cease to use the Roman Catholic missal, the Roman calendar and the practice, unacceptable in the Church of England, of communicating the people in one kind only. The assistant priest's licence was withdrawn for the diocese. The general dispute throughout the Church soon left the particular circumstances at Carshalton and concentrated on whether deviations from the 1662 prayer book were legal or allowable or desirable, how far bishops could or should make regulations about the liturgy and to what extent priests could refuse obedience. The whole subject of authority and canonical obedience was immediately called into question. On the one side priests asserted that after the Tractarian movement English Catholics could never have transformed the Church of England as they had done without exercising their own discretion over what book they would use for holy communion or what deviations they followed. On the other side it was strongly argued that a Church with episcopal authority must commend obedience to the bishops in matters such as these. The " Carshalton affair ", as it came to be called, strengthened the growing demand for an alternative holy communion to the 1662 rite, duly authorized and accepted.

The Peterborough Cathedral appeal closed at £71,500 and the second stage of the Leicester Cathedral appeal was launched to raise £100,000. A controversial statue, " Ecce Homo ", by Sir Jacob Epstein (*see* OBITUARIES), was offered to Selby abbey and accepted. Later, after a protest had been made, that the statue was "hideous, too modernistic and cruel", the chancellor of the diocese refused to grant a faculty.

A new post for an executive officer for the whole of the Anglican communion was created in 1959, and the first holder of it was the bishop of Olympia, United States, the

The nave of the new church of St. Cuthbert, North Wembley, London.

Right Rev. Stephen Bayne, who left his diocese to take on the new work. His task was to help in worldwide missionary strategy and to carry plans forward in the intervals between the Lambeth conferences. In India the Church Missionary

society transferred assets valued at £3 million either to the Church of India, Pakistan, Burma and Ceylon, or to the Church of South India. In April the Nippon Sei Ko Kai (Anglican Church in Japan) celebrated its centenary. The archbishop of Canterbury visited Japan and consecrated the new cathedral at Kobe. Protests were made throughout the Anglican communion when in March Guy Clutton Brock, adviser of St. Faith's mission, Southern Rhodesia, was detained by the Southern Rhodesian government following the proclamation of a state of emergency in Nyasaland. The bishop of Masasi, the Right Rev. Mark Way, resigned his see because the diocese as a whole voted not to enter the proposed new province of East Africa. The reason for the refusal was partly because of the diocese's fear of dominance by white people in Kenya, and partly because of the difference in churchmanship between dioceses supported by the Universities' Mission to Central Africa (Masasi is one) and the dioceses supported by the Church Missionary society, which would also join the new province.

Among the English appointments of the year were Prebendary J. Moorman to be bishop of Ripon, the Right Rev. G. F. Allen to be bishop of Derby, the Rev. Mervyn Stockwood to be bishop of Southwark and Canon Eric Abbott to be dean of Westminster. Appointments overseas included those of the Right Rev. James MacCann to be archbishop of Armagh and Canon A. Rogers to be bishop of Mauritius. The bishop of Norwich, the Right Rev. P. M. Herbert, resigned. Among deaths were those of Bishop H. Pakenham Walsh, formerly of Assam, Bishop C. S. Woodward, formerly of Bristol and Gloucester (*see* OBITUARIES), the Very Rev. E. G. Selwyn, former dean of Winchester and Dr. S. C. Carpenter, former dean of Exeter.   (R. S. E.)

ANGLING. River-fishing in 1959 was adversely affected by the exceptionally dry summer, but a good season was enjoyed by sea-anglers and by anglers fishing those lakes and ponds which were not seriously lowered by the drought. One lake which maintained its high reputation was the Bristol Waterworks reservoir at Chew valley, Somerset, where 6,784 trout averaging 2 lb. 6 oz. were caught. In four days' fishing there, in August, two anglers took 109 trout averaging nearly 3 lb. apiece.

The following record specimens were reported during the year; tench, 9 lb. 9 oz., from Staines, Middlesex, in July (this specimen was transferred alive to the London zoo aquarium); mako shark, 372 lb., from Looe, Cornwall, in July (A. Melhuish); blue shark, 218 lb., also from Looe in July (N. Sutcliffe); and three-bearded rockling, 2 lb., from Dartmouth, Devon, in February (E. Curl). A black bream of 8 lb. 5½ oz. —2 lb. over the existing record—was also reported, but adequate proof of identity was still awaited. Other large fish, all very close to the existing records and now the " runners-up ", were a carp of 40½ lb. (Redmire pool, Shropshire, July); bass, 17 lb. 9 oz. (Minehead, Somerset, September); mackerel, 3 lb. 15½ oz. (Newlyn, Cornwall, September); thresher shark, 268 lb. (Looe, August); and blue shark 198 lb. (Looe, June).

Bedford won the annual " All-England " contest fished on the River Nene at Peterborough in September, with an aggregate weight of 86 lb. The individual winner was J. Sharpe, of the Bedford team, with 57½ lb. The annual tournament of the British Casting association was merged into the Third World Casting championship at Scarborough, Yorkshire, which attracted expert casters from many countries on both sides of the Atlantic. Among many outstanding performances was a world-record trout fly-cast of 56 yd. by R. Fredriksson (Sweden). E. Horsfall Turner of Britain cast 53½ yd. in the same event to set up a new amateur record.

A sale of early angling books at Sotheby's, London, in October yielded over £15,000, including £3,300 for the *Treatyse*

A tranquil scene of anglers on the River Wiltham at Woodhall, Lancashire, which exemplifies the charm of this leisurely sport.

of Fysshinge with an Angle by Dame Juliana Berners (1494). A new monthly magazine, *Angling*, was launched by Caxton Press, under the editorship of K. Mansfield.   (D. F. KY.)

ANGOLA: *see* PORTUGUESE OVERSEAS TERRITORIES.

ANTARCTICA. A continent lying almost entirely within the Antarctic circle, nine-tenths covered by an ice-sheet. Area: nearly 6 million sq.mi. Uninhabited, but divided broadly into Ross dependency (New Zealand), Adelie Land (France), Australian Antarctic territory, Queen Maud Land (Norway), Falkland Islands dependencies (U.K.), Marie Byrd Land and James W. Ellsworth Land (U.S., but not officially claimed). There are overlapping Argentine and Chilean claims to most of the Falkland Islands dependencies.

History. On Dec. 1, 1959, representatives of Argentina, Australia, Belgium, Chile, France, Japan, New Zealand, Norway, South Africa, the United Kingdom, the United States and the U.S.S.R. signed a 30-yr. treaty establishing peaceful scientific co-operation in Antarctica. The main effects would be to suspend all territorial claims and disputes in the area south of latitude 60, to establish free use of the entire continent for scientific work and to set up a mutual inspection system to prevent any military activities. The treaty included the South Shetland islands and the South Orkney islands which were administered by Britain but claimed by Argentina and, in the case of the South Shetlands, by Chile also, but did not include the disputed Falkland islands.

With the conclusion of the International Geophysical Year (I.G.Y.) in Dec. 1958, several temporary stations were abandoned. The continued scientific work of 12 nations was co-ordinated under the guidance of the Special Committee on Antarctic Research (S.C.A.R.).

Argentina. Nine bases were maintained in the Falkland Islands Dependencies sector; in addition Ellsworth station on the Weddell Sea coast was transferred from United States to Argentine control. Men marooned on Robertson island in Jan. 1959 were rescued by the icebreaker " General San Martin ".

Australia. In a journey lasting three and a half months a five-man tractor party from Mawson base continued seismic sounding around the Prince Charles mountains. A geological survey party was flown to Amundsen bay late in Nov. 1958 with dogs and sledges and explored among the Leckie

mountains, returning to Mawson on Jan. 18, 1959. At Davis, biological observations continued among nearby islands. The " Thala Dan " left Melbourne for the bases on Dec. 6, 1958, relieving Davis on Jan. 16. The base was enlarged to accommodate eight men. Mawson was relieved early in Feb. 1959, extensive sea ice hampering operations. The relief ship sustained slight damage to the bows but temporary repairs were effected. The U.S. base on the Wilkes coast was relieved by " Magga Dan " on Jan. 24. The automatic weather reporting station on Lewis islet was serviced and made operational. In in spite of heavy pressure ice the " Magga Dan " succeeded surveying parts of the Oates Land coast, assisted by aerial reconnaissance. Landings were made near the Wilson hills, the first landings ever to succeed on this part of the Antarctic coastline. In April the new powerhouse at Mawson was destroyed by fire. Biological, ionospheric, geomagnetic and seismographic observations were continued on the sub-Antarctic station of Macquarie island.

Belgium. Field parties working from King Baudouin base explored the Sør Rondane range in Nov. and Dec. 1958. On Dec. 5, a reconnaissance aircraft crashed near one of the parties; the pilot and observer were picked up unhurt by a Soviet aircraft which flew in to assist from the Soviet base at Mirny, 1,800 mi. to the east. Late in December the relief ship " Polarhav " was trapped by pack ice 30 mi. off the coast. In spite of a damaged propeller the U.S. icebreaker " Glacier " gave assistance, breaking through to the base after a difficult struggle with very heavy pack. A wintering party of 22 was left at the base.

Chile. Routine observations were maintained at bases in the South Shetlands and on the Graham Land coast at Cape Legoupil. Three relief ships (including the new " Pilote Pardo ") visited the bases during the summer.

France. Observations were continued at Dumont d'Urville base. The inland subsidiary station Charcot was closed after two years' operation. The " Norsel " relieved Dumont d'Urville in Jan. 1959 and made a visit to Sir Douglas Mawson's old base at Cape Dennison for magnetic observations. A wintering party of 12 was left at the base.

Japan. Syowa base was reoccupied on Jan. 14, after lying empty for almost a year. The first party was greeted by two dogs which had survived after being abandoned when the base was closed in Feb. 1958. The 11-man wintering party and stores were flown in by helicopter across the pack ice in April. Sledging parties established a self-recording weather station 58 mi. inland from the base.

New Zealand. At Scott base routine observations on geomagnetism, aurora, seismology, meteorology, glaciology and sea level recording were continued. The base was relieved on Jan. 2 by H.M.N.Z.S. "Endeavour", which also made oceanographic observations between New Zealand and McMurdo sound. During the summer the New Zealand Geological and Survey expedition, with the help of U.S. aircraft, made geological and survey observations in the McMurdo sound region, establishing survey stations on mountain peaks. An expedition from Victoria university spent seven weeks in the Wright glacier area of South Victoria Land. Scientific observations were also maintained at the Joint United States-New Zealand Hallett base, which was relieved by U.S. ships early in January.

Norway. Topographical survey and glaciological work was continued among the mountains southeast of Norwaystation. The "Polarbjørn" relieved the base on Dec. 21, 1958, bringing two aircraft of the Royal Norwegian air force. An extensive photographic reconnaissance was made 600 mi. eastward to the Sør Rondane mountains and a wintering party of 14 was left at the base.

South Africa. Weather and aurora observation stations were maintained on the South Atlantic islands of Gough, Tristan da Cunha and Marion.

United Kingdom. During the southern spring of 1958-59 sledging parties from base E (Stonington island) established depots on Mushroom island and visited the entrance to King George VI sound. From base Y (Horseshoe island) surveying operations were continued in the Square bay area. From base W (Loubet coast) Lallemand fjord was surveyed and reconnaissance journeys were made to the Graham Land plateau. At base G (Admiralty bay) surveys of Livingston and Nelson islands were continued. Ornithological work was continued at base H (Signy island) where more than 1,000 giant petrel chicks were ringed. Local and field survey operations, geomagnetic, seismographic, meteorological, glaciological and biological work continued at 12 bases.

The annual relief ships were hampered by very severe ice conditions. Bases H (Signy island), D (Hope bay), B (Deception island), O (Danco coast), A (Port Lockroy) and G were relieved in Nov. and Dec. 1958 by R.R.S. "Shackleton", which sustained slight damage in Admiralty bay and was compelled to return to Port Stanley and Montevideo for repairs. After completing a programme of hydrographic survey in South Georgia, R.R.S. "John Biscoe" sailed southward in December to visit bases B and F (Argentine islands). A delay of 15 days due to ice conditions caused her return to Port Stanley for refuelling. In February she revisited base O and relieved base J (Ferin head); both bases were closed as planned for the winter. Assisted by U.S. icebreakers, the "John Biscoe" attempted to reach base Y.

Members of the Royal society's International Geophysical Year antarctic expedition at Halley bay on the Weddell sea were relieved in January by the Norwegian motor vessel "Tottan". On the way home thick pack ice in the Weddell sea held the "Tottan" fast for four days. These pictures show members of the crew and of the expedition trying to free the ship.

Fast ice remained in Marguerite bay; the party from base E sledged over sea ice to base Y, which was eventually relieved by helicopter. Base E was closed. The remaining Graham Land base, W, was temporarily evacuated in March after further difficulties with pack ice. The I.G.Y. station at Halley bay was transferred to Falkland Island Dependencies Survey (F.I.D.S.) control and became base Z. The base was relieved by the "Tottan" on Jan. 10 and a wintering party of 12 was left.

During the summer cruises, survey parties were established on Livingston, Deception and Snow islands for survey and physiographic work. H.M.S. "Protector", the Royal Naval guardship, assisted in these operations. Sea ice observations were maintained at all bases throughout the year. Sledging parties from base D surveyed Joinville island and carried out a magnetometer survey northeast of Mount Bransfield. Eight bases (A, B, D, F, G, H, Y, Z) remained in operation during the winter of 1959, with a total personnel of 59.

United States. Parties left Byrd station in Nov. 1958 to investigate the Horlick mountains and found sedimentary rocks with shells and coal beds overlying granite. Aerial survey flights were carried out between the Harold Byrd mountains and Executive Committee range, and seismographic soundings in this area showed steadily rising rock under the ice from 2,500 ft. to 1,000 ft. below sea level, confirming the existence of a channel. From McMurdo sound 67 air-dropping sorties were made to Byrd and Amundsen-Scott (south pole) bases during October and November. On Oct. 15, 1958, Sno-cat parties set out from Little America to cross the Ross ice shelf, investigating the Skelton glacier and arriving at McMurdo sound at the end of Jan. 1959, after a 1,600-mi. journey. Relief operations began in Dec. 1958. Little America V was evacuated by helicopter flights from icebreakers in the Ross sea on Jan. 19. An auxiliary station, Rockford (79° 35′ S., 152° 56′ W.) was opened for meteorological observations and aircraft support during the summer in Marie Byrd Land. The auxiliary meteorological station, Beardmore (83° 17′ S., 175° 45′ E.) was re-opened, also for the summer. The south pole station was replenished for a further winter's observations, with a wintering team of 15, glaciological observations in a deep ice cavern and programmes of ionospheric, auroral, geomagnetic and meteorological research being continued. A 23-man party was left to winter at Byrd and U.S. Naval Air facility at McMurdo sound was retained. A tractor-sledging party left Byrd base on Feb. 14, 1959, to survey Executive Committee range, which was originally described from aerial surveys during the U.S. Antarctic Service expedition 1939-41. The mountains were found to be of volcanic origin; the ice near some of the peaks was littered with rock debris as though from recent eruptions. As a result of ground surveys, considerable changes were made in the charted position of the range, the highest mountains recorded being 12,000 ft.

U.S.S.R. The inland station Vostok (south geomagnetic pole) was relieved late in Dec. 1958. From Mirny tractor parties established a temporary observation site at the pole of relative inaccessibility (approx. 82° S., 55° E.) occupying the station for 12 days and returning to Mirny in mid-January. Seismic soundings along the route suggested that a continental mass of considerable topographic irregularity extended under the ice in this region, with mountain ridges rising to 10,000 ft. completely hidden by the ice-sheet. Mirny was relieved on Dec. 22, 1958, by the icebreaker "Ob", assisted by "Mikhail Kalinin". Oazis was also visited and occupied temporarily by a Polish team. The inland stations of Pionerskaya and Sovietskaya were closed in January. On completing her work in the Australian sector, "Ob" sailed westward to establish a new Soviet station on the Queen Maud Land coast. The station, Lazarev (69° 58′ S., 12° 55′ E.) was completed

on March 10 and a wintering party of seven was left.

Whaling. The following nations were represented in Antarctic whaling activities during the season:

Nation	Factory Ships	Land Stations	Catchers
Argentina	—	1	7
Japan	6	—	69
Netherlands	1	—	12
Norway	9	1	100
United Kingdom	3	1	44
U.S.S.R.	1	—	24
	20	3	256

The maximum catch of 15,000 blue-whale units was permitted. More than 37,900 whales were caught, yielding a total of over 2·2 million barrels of oil. (*See* also EXPLORATION AND DISCOVERY; INTERNATIONAL GEOPHYSICAL CO-OPERATION.)
(B. S.)

See G. J. Dufek, *Through the Frozen Frontier* (*The Exploration of Antarctica*) (New York, 1959); F. Debenham, *Antarctica* (London, 1959).

ANTHROPOLOGY. During 1959 advance in knowledge of past human evolution especially concerned man's remote ancestors, and several studies appeared of early primate forms from various parts of the world. A most revealing discovery was of a small frontal bone of early Oligocene date, the oldest known fragment of an anthropoid skull. Although discovered in the Fayum deposits of Egypt in 1908 and sent to the American Museum of Natural History, it was not recognized as anthropoid until 1958. Only teeth and part of the lower jaw of a single specimen, *Propliopithecus*, were hitherto available to show that an anthropoid stock existed in Oligocene times; the new find shows that by this early date the anthropoids already possessed a vertically deepened forebrain, a fore-shortened muzzle and posteriorly closed orbital cavities, all advanced characters. A new Australopithecine fossil was reported from Olduvai, Tanganyika, the most northerly find to date; whereas it was formerly assumed that the Australopithecinae were only capable of tool-using, the clear association of the new fossil with artefacts of the primitive Oldowan culture confirmed what had been suggested by the discovery of pebble tools at the Australopithecine site at Sterkfontein, South Africa, that tool-making antedated brain enlargement. The publication of an extensive report clarified the evolutionary position of *Oreopithecus*.

Progress continued in the development of techniques for dating early human remains. Uranium estimation confirmed the findings of earlier fluorine analysis that several specimens of dubious antiquity (*e.g.*, the Ipswich and Dartford skulls) were in fact intrusive, and also threw doubt on the age claimed for the Kanam mandible. The potassium/argon method proved applicable to finds from volcanic soils, and the protein or amino-acid content a valuable guide to the relative dating of post-Pleistocene specimens.

In ethnology also the new methods of dating were revealing. Radiocarbon estimation indicated that the fringe groups of Polynesia were peopled much earlier than was formerly thought; for instance, there was settlement in the Marquesas by the 2nd century B.C., instead of the 2nd millenium A.D. as was previously held. Reports of rock paintings continued from many areas; *e.g.*, eastern Uganda, northeastern Somaliland, Geji in Nigeria and the Villars cave in the Dordogne, France; of particular interest were those from the Fezzan, Libya, depicting the way of life of an unknown white race and from the Niah caves in Borneo apparently depicting boats of the dead. Reports of rock gongs from as far east as Darfur, Sudan and Uganda showed that the area of their occurrence is more extensive than was formerly thought; an important series of ancient works of art in bronze or brass was discovered at Ita Yemoo, near Ife, Western Nigeria.

In social anthropology the studies made of European communities were highly stimulating; for instance, in ordinary urban London families it was found that the segregation of activities of husband and wife within the family varied directly with the connectedness of the social network in which it functioned, and among possible factors promoting a close-knit network were stability of residence, proximity of kin and homogeneity of class of neighbourhood. A study of local (non-party) politics in a Welsh village showed the same stratagems as are employed on the one hand in the wider national setting and on the other in pre-literate communities where the perception of the past is continually revised in the light of the present. Studies providing data relevant to practical problems included those of the family life of old people and widows. A number of publications were devoted to the analysis of social change *per se*, such as the effect of nationalism in Indonesia and industralization in Guatemala. They were particularly concerned with urbanization—the problems that arise when hitherto tribal peoples adopt an urban way of life—and the processes operating in non-western urban societies; *e.g.*, in the African community in the Rhodesian copperbelt and among the Chinese in Singapore. One comparative study, in approach rather different from much contemporary British social anthropology, attempted to define the conditions under which one particular social phenomenon, the millenarian cults in Melanesia, occurred. Social anthropology also tended to look back at its own development; *e.g.*, in evaluating anew the contribution of B. K. Malinowski.

In Britain, the Institute of Race Relations was formed to promote understanding of the relations between different races and peoples; under its auspices a symposium on race and race relations was held at the Royal Anthropological institute. For physical anthropologists the Society for the Study of Human Biology was formed and a symposium on natural selection in man was held. At Section H (Anthropology) of the British Association meeting in Glasgow in 1958, while papers were presented to celebrate the Darwin centenary, the main theme was folk life; at the York meeting in 1959 archaeological and historical topics were discussed. The 33rd International Congress of Americanists met in Costa Rica in 1958, the 12th annual conference of the International Folk Music council at Siraia, Rumania, the International Congress of Folk Tale Research at Kiel in Aug. 1959 and the 4th World Congress of Sociology at Milan in Sept. 1959.

It was pleasing to see the *Anthropologischer Anzeiger* recommence publication after an interval of 15 years. A new international quarterly *Comparative Studies in Society and History* appeared, while from Moscow emanated an imposing new journal of physical anthropology *Sovietskaia Anthropologia*.

Anthropology suffered by the deaths of Paul Rivet, distinguished for his work on ethnography and American linguistics and joint founder of the Musée de l'Homme and l'Insitut d'Ethnologie, and R. H. Lowie, distinguished for his teaching and his field investigations among the American Indians.

Because 1959 was the centenary of the publication of Charles Darwin's *The Origin of Species*, numerous efforts were made during the year to re-examine evolutionary theory, take stock of its current formulation and examine the man most responsible for its original formulation. Anthropologists participated fully in these events. Two major commemorative symposia were held in the United States, the first at the general meeting of the American Philosophical society in Philadelphia in April and the second sponsored by the University of Chicago in November. Papers for the April meeting were published by the society and included the Penrose Memorial lecture by Wilfred Le Gros Clark on "The Crucial Evidence for Human Evolution". Three of the five topics in the Chicago symposium dealt largely with anthropological matters: "Man as a Biological Organism", "The Origin and Nature of Mind" and "Social and Cultural Evolution". A symposium, sponsored by the Linnaean society, was held in London, and a special meeting was held in Singapore—an area from which much of the original evidence for evolution was obtained.

A growing interest in reformulating evolutionary theories of culture had been apparent in recent years, and two works were published in this centenary year. One was Leslie A. White's *The Evolution of Culture*, the first volume of a projected trilogy on the subject. It dealt with evolution in primitive cultures; subsequent volumes were to deal with the evolutionary process in history and with projections into the future. White was awarded the Viking Fund medal in general anthropology for 1959, the highest honour which American anthropology has to offer. The other book was *Man's Way: a Preface to the Understanding of Human Society* by Walter Goldschmidt, which shows the relationship between evolutionary levels and social systems, and the mechanisms of evolutionary change in society.

Anthropologists from all countries continued to investigate native cultures and culture history in all parts of the globe, but perhaps the greatest emphasis, the culmination of a decade or more of increased activity, was devoted to sub-Saharan Africa. Investigations ranged from the earliest known tool-using hominids to the cultural aspects of modern political development. Continuing work on the Australopithecines (African apemen of the Lower Pleistocene) and their association with crude tools in the Union of South Africa engaged the attention of many workers (*see* above).

Much later African historical developments were discussed in two books published during the year. George Peter Murdock analysed the culture history of the continent in his *Africa: Its Peoples and Culture History* and, by examination of archaeological and ethnological data, reconstructed the movement of peoples and cultural elements throughout Africa. Still more recent history, summarizing the evidence for highly developed cultures in sub-Saharan Africa, was presented by Basil Davidson in *Lost Cities of Africa*. (D. F. R.; W. Gt.)

ARABIA: *see* ADEN; BAHRAIN; KUWAIT; MUSCAT AND OMAN; QATAR; SAUDI ARABIA; TRUCIAL SHEIKHDOMS; YEMEN.

ARAB LEAGUE. The League of Arab States aims at co-ordinating the political action and protecting the sovereignty of the Arab countries. Members: Iraq, Jordan, Lebanon, Saudi Arabia, United Arab Republic (Egypt and Syria), Yemen (all founder-members, 1945), Libya (admitted 1953), Sudan (admitted 1956) and Morocco and Tunisia (admitted 1958). Headquarters of league council: Cairo. Secretary-general: Mohammed Abd-ul-Khalek el-Hassuna.

History. During 1959 the internal dissensions in the Arab world—particularly the conflict between the United Arab Republic and Iraq—continued to paralyse the Arab league. At a meeting of the league's political committee, held in Beirut in April, the U.A.R. hoped to obtain a resolution denouncing Communism and its threat to Arab nationalism in terms which would imply condemnation of the new regime in Iraq, but failed to do so. Later in the year, when the league council met in Morocco, Iraq and Tunisia refused to attend, on account of their differences with the U.A.R. All that came out of this meeting was a resolution supporting Algeria's demand for self-determination.   (E. S. A.)

ARCHAEOLOGY. Europe. *Great Britain.* During 1959 S. S. Frere continued the excavations at Verulamium. Two large houses were uncovered, one with a fine mosaic floor depicting a lion carrying a stag's head, which was so far unique in Britain. On Bluehouse hill timber-framed shops burnt down about A.D. 160 were cleared out. Elsewhere at

S. S. Frere (centre), director of the excavations at Verulamium, points out a detail of the 2nd-century mosaic uncovered in 1959.

Verulamium a wood-lined cellar, abandoned about the fourth century A.D., was found to contain iron carpenter's tools and a bronze statuette of Ceres. At Colchester a two-foot high bronze statue of Bacchus dating from the first century A.D. was discovered. On Iona in the Inner Hebrides during the fourth season of excavations, the University of Edinburgh group, under the direction of C. Thomas completed the uncovering of the outline of St. Columba's original monastery, which was surrounded by an earthwork. A number of monastic cells were found, one of which on Tor Abb may have been used by the saint himself. Other, larger buildings were traced from the outline of the sleeper beams. All buildings showed signs of having been burnt down by Norse pirates during the 8th-9th centuries A.D. Another discovery was the " street

of the dead ", an imposing highway running across the island to the royal cemetery, and dated between the 13th and 16th centuries. The Ministry of Works excavations at Nonsuch palace, Epsom, directed by Martin Biddle, uncovered more of the eastern half of the palace. The rubble filling of one pit yielded a number of 17th-century iron cooking utensils. In another there was much fine pottery and also glass wine bottles, tumblers, wine glasses and scent containers of the same period. Some 3,000 copper coins made in mints at Trier, Rome, Lyons, Arles and London formed part of a hoard dating from the 4th century A.D. which was ploughed up near Ipswich. In November the remains of a Roman boat were discovered on a site in Southwark, London.

Austria. During excavations at the ancient town site of Noria, capital of the Celtic state of Noricum, on the Magdalensberg in Carinthia, Professor R. Egger found letters engraved on pottery and tablets, which formed part of an alphabet reading from right to left. The discovery was an important one; it was the first time that a script comparable to the Etruscan or Iberic had been found north of the Alps.

Belgium. Remarkable sculptures from a funerary monument of c. A.D. 150-250 were brought to light at Buzenol, the legendary Montauban. They included reliefs of a river god, mythological figures and agricultural scenes, one of which displayed an ancient mechanical harvester not unlike the modern reaper.

France. A hoard of bronze axes arranged in a circular pattern was found by a ploughman in a field near Loudéac in Brittany. They were of Bronze Age date, c. 1000-800 B.C.

German Federal Republic. At Warendorf in Westphalia, part of an 8th-century Saxon settlement was reconstructed. It included four farms, consisting of ten small buildings grouped around a single central building.

Greece. Reports published in 1959 showed that during the 1958 season at Corinth work continued on the Isthmian sanctuary. In the precinct of Palaimon under the temple foundations, underground passages for a mystery cult were discovered, containing large numbers of votive lamps and bowls. In the precinct of Poseidon, bronze figures of an athlete, a boat and two fine horses' heads were found among the debris of the archaic temple destroyed by fire about

Alexander the Great and Krateros fighting a lion, part of a pebble mosaic floor uncovered during the course of excavations on the site of Pella, the ancient Greek capital of Alexander. Work on this site has been in progress for two years under the direction of P. Petsas.

475 B.C. It was also learnt that during 1958 Professor P. Petsas continued his excavations at Pella, the site of the Macedonian capital of the 4th century B.C. The ground plan of some large-columned buildings with pebble mosaic floors was uncovered, revealing lively designs such as Dionysus riding on a panther, and a lion attacked by swordsmen. The work was carried out in coloured pebbles, with the features outlined by strips of lead. Other finds included tiles stamped with the name of the town and a gold coin of Philip II of Macedonia. Professor C. Blegen continued the excavations at Pylos in 1958, when most of the work was devoted to completing the plan of the palatial buildings. Evidence for the existence of an aqueduct bringing the water supply to the site was found in several places. Further work was carried out at Knossos, Crete, under the direction of S. Hood on the Roman buildings, from which terracotta figurines and a marble statue were obtained. No tablets were found, but there was a large quantity of ivory fragments, which may possibly have come from a workshop. On the mainland an important find of life-size bronze statues was made in a street in Piraeus during excavations for foundations. They were comparable to pieces of the best period of Greek art in the 5th century B.C.

Italy. In Rome Professor G. Jacopi discovered near the basilica of Sta. Croce, a 3rd-century arena, which might well rival the Colosseum in size. Much of the original brick seating and passage ways were in almost perfect condition, and part of the 20-ft. high brick tribune was virtually undamaged. It was thought to be the Varian circus, built in the time of the Emperor Heliogabalus. Thirty bronze tablets inscribed with what appeared to be communal laws of the 4th century B.C. were found in a deposit on the site of the ancient city of Locris in Calabria. In Sicily, reports published in 1959 about the fourth season of excavations (1958) at Serra d'Orlando, the ancient city of Morgantina, under the direction of Professor R. Stillwell told of continued work both on the Hellenistic Agora and on a large building behind the city wall which had not yet been identified. The principal Demeter sanctuary yielded a large number of fine terracotta busts. In the Cittadella area the settlement of the Archaic period produced many terracotta objects, including some large Gorgon antefixes. A few Copper Age shards attested the early occupation of the site.

Spain. A gold treasure probably dating from the late Bronze Age was found by chance while a garden was being enlarged at El Carambolo near Seville. It consisted of two breastplates, and bracelets and seals in granular work. The pieces were of fine workmanship and probably came from Tartessus.

Cyprus. C_{14} tests carried out on material from the Neolithic site of Khirokitia yielded a date in the middle of the sixth millenium B.C. Archaeological dating had previously attributed it to the mid-fourth millenium.

Asia. *Turkey.* It was reported during the year that in 1958 a number of marble reliefs were found by villagers in an old canal at Geyre, the ancient city of Aphrodisias. There were four complete reliefs with almost life-size figures representing personifications of the town, and probably dating from the 2nd century B.C. Also in 1958, a U.S. expedition under the joint direction of Professors George Hanfmann and Henry Detweiler began work at Sardis, with the aim of studying the history of the town from the earliest times. Reports of the first season recorded the finding of a Lydian potter's shop with a dome-like structure which might be a kiln. Shards included part of a large bichrome Lydian jar and an imported Greek piece from Rhodes. In another area, a house of the Roman-early Christian period contained samovar-like heating vessels, two flagons, a large bronze cauldron and an embers shovel with

Christian symbols. On the eastern edge of the city, there was a large apsidal building containing a base with an inscription to the Emperor Lucius Verus. Shards from deep soundings in the river bed near the Artemis temple ranged from the Geometric period to the 6th century B.C.

Israel. At Tell Makmish near Tel Aviv, the Department of Antiquities excavated a Phoenician sanctuary, standing on a small hillock outside the town. The earliest structures belong to the 10th-8th centuries B.C., and upon these Phoenician settlers later built the sanctuary consisting of a main hall and a holy of holies. In the courtyard were plastered basins, an open drain and a stone altar. A large number of votive figurines of terracotta of the Astarte type were found, and also Cypriot stone votive figures of the 5th century B.C.

Iraq. The U.S. expedition under the direction of R. C. Haines completed the uncovering of the Inanna temple at Nippur. The first temple of the series belonged to the early Dynastic period and was repeatedly rebuilt, the last phase belonging to the Parthian period. Many small figurines were obtained from the foundation offerings.

Persia. Professor R. Ghirshmann continued his researches at Choga Zembil and cleared the fourth gate of the Ziggurat. In the gateway the head and feet of a terracotta bull were found, the fragments of the body having already been recovered. It was reconstructed and on the back was found a dedicatory inscription to the god Inshushinak. From the palace rooms two panels of ivory mosaic were recovered depicting the head of a winged deity. Below was a frieze of ibexes standing before a sacred tree. Beneath the floors five monumental tombs were cleared, one of which contained a skeleton laid on a brick couch and the remains of two cremations.

Pakistan. Sir Mortimer Wheeler conducted excavations on the mound of Charsadda near Peshawar, which is known to have been besieged by Alexander the Great. Trial trenches revealed that it had been occupied from the 6th to the 1st centuries B.C., and a number of terracotta figurines and clay sealings were recovered. Air photography also revealed a well-planned Ghandaran city on another mound, on which future work might be undertaken.

China. The well-preserved corpse and effects of a warrior were discovered in the Tsaidam basin in northwestern China. It was buried in a small mound and was clad in a fur coat with light armour fixtures. Beside it were a horse tail, a saddle and bow and arrows. The warrior was believed to have belonged to the Yuan dynasty about 600 years ago.

Africa. *Egypt.* Great impetus was given to archaeological work with the announcement by the government, on a recommendation from Unesco, that it would offer surplus antiquities to the world in exchange for help in excavating, recording and preserving sites in Nubia which would be flooded by the waters of the Nile high dam at Aswan.

Sudan. Professor B. Emery continued his excavations at the great fortress of Buhen. A further section of the fortifications and the well-preserved foundations of the great gate were cleared. The gateway was approached by a drawbridge and the entrance closed by double doors. Both gate and bridge were flanked by spur walls which formed a narrow corridor through which an attacking force would have to enter while exposed to a hail of missiles from above. The fortress was stormed at the end of the Middle Kingdom, and there was much evidence of destruction by fire before its reoccupation by Egyptians of the New Kingdom. In this destruction-level under the new buildings a skeleton of a horse was found buried, dating from the 17th century B.C., 200 years before the horse was supposed to have entered Egypt. In another small room within the main headquarters of the fortress, a quantity of papyri inscribed in Middle Kingdom hieratic, were found deliberately torn up into small fragments. They were probably military despatches.

Tanganyika. Finals plans were drawn up for founding a school of archaeology at Bagamoyo for research into the archaeology and history of east Africa. It would have Treasury support and it was hoped that funds for scholarships would come from commerce and industry.

During his excavations at Olduvai gorge of the pre-Chellean Lower Pleistocene culture which he has named Oldowan, L. S. B. Leakey discovered a skull of fossil man which he considered to be the link between *Australopithecus* and *Paranthropus* and true man (*see* PALAEONTOLOGY).

North America. *Alaska.* On Choris peninsula two large oval houses of the Choris culture, believed to be more than 3,000 years old, were excavated. Lengthy cultural sequences were discovered at Cape Espenberg, Alaska, and at Cape Krusenstern, Northwest Territories. At the latter the fuller sequence ranged from recent Eskimo house sites on the outer beach to a Denbigh flint complex on the highest and earliest beach, with several old Eskimo cultures on intermediate strand lines.

Pacific Coast—Great Basin. The University of Washington continued its archaeological salvage work in the Priest Rapids area on the Columbia river, involving two dams and their reservoirs. A field school group, directed by Robert Greengo, excavating on four sites, established a cultural sequence extending from protohistoric times well back into the prehistoric past.

At the Ice Harbor reservoir of the lower Snake river, a party from the State College of Washington, led by Richard D. Daugherty, discovered, in the lowest levels of their trenches, a new and apparently early stone industry consisting of side-notched projectile points and large, crude scrapers and choppers.

Plains. Richard G. Forbis of the Glenbow foundation in Calgary, Alberta, reported extensive excavations in a large site near Cayley, 50 mi. S. of Calgary. Called the Old Woman's Buffalo Jump, it consists of a vast deposit of bison bones at the base of a cliff over which the Indians, prior to the advent of the horse on the Plains, drove herds of buffalo. Animals killed in the fall were butchered on the spot. The bone deposit, more than 25 ft. deep, produced small side-notched arrowpoints of the late prehistoric period in the upper half, large corner-notched points of the middle period in the lower levels.

Southwest. The University of Illinois field school, directed by John C. McGregor and William J. Beeson, in collaboration with the Museum of Northern Arizona, excavated six large pit houses and a possible ceremonial structure near Flagstaff. This prehistoric village of the Sinagua culture originally consisted of about 20 structures built in late Pueblo I and early Pueblo II times. A late Pueblo ruin near St. Johns, Arizona, comprising more than 50 rooms and two ceremonial chambers or kivas, was explored by Paul S. Martin and John B. Rinaldo of the Chicago Natural History museum. A large quantity of painted pottery was found.

Eastern North America. Archaeological sites in which perishable objects of wood and fibre, and vegetable foods have been preserved are of great rarity in the humid eastern United States. Of unusual interest, therefore, was the discovery of such a site in west-central Pennsylvania, as reported by John Witthoft of the Pennsylvania State museum. Found by amateur archaeologists Melville Corl and John Miller on the Raystown branch of the Juniata river in Huntingdon county, the George Norris site is a large natural shelter beneath a 30-ft. rock overhang.

The occupied area measures about 200 ft. in length. The central portion of the site has remained dry since Indian times, and there, in the upper four to five feet, most of the important finds were made by Witthoft and Edward Stackhouse. This explored zone, which does not reach to bedrock,

yielded at least five culture-bearing soil levels, each separated by a rockfall from the roof, the lowest and oldest found so far yielding pottery and projectile point types of the Early Woodland period. The uppermost horizon consists of a 30-in. refuse deposit left by the Susquehannock Indians, an Iroquoian group of the mid-16th century. This was the richest layer in vegetable remains.

Middle and South America. The University of Pennsylvania museum's 1959 explorations at the Maya city of Tikal, northern Guatemala, under the direction of Edwin M. Shook, made significant contributions to knowledge of the Early and Late Classic periods of this culture. Stele 29, one of the four new carved stone monuments found, bore the oldest hieroglyphic date, equivalent to A.D. 292, yet known for the lowland Maya. Beneath some of the steles and along the centre line of temple mounds, a number of caches of ceremonial offerings were discovered, some accompanying human remains. Among the offerings were hundreds of eccentrically chipped flint and obsidian objects, pigments, seashells and a small, unique, mosaic mask, reputed to be one of the most remarkable art objects ever found in the new world.

(J. D. P. T.; W. A. R. E.)

BIBLIOGRAPHY. J. Desmond Clark, *The Prehistory of Southern Africa* (Harmondsworth, 1959); Annette Laming, *Lascaux* (Harmondsworth, 1959); Sir Cyril Fox, *Life and Death in the Bronze Age* (London, 1959); J. D. Evans, *Malta* (London, 1959); Sir Mortimer Wheeler, *Early India and Pakistan* (London, 1959); J. Edward Kidder, *Japan* (London, 1959); G. Lankester Harding, *The Antiquities of Jordan* (London, 1959); Cheng Te-kun, *Archaeology in China*, vol. 1, *Prehistoric China* (Cambridge, 1959).

ARCHITECTURE. With a few, not always very conspicuous exceptions, the architecture of 1959 was competent, rather than great. This competence was often of an extremely high level, reflecting credit on architecture as a professional discipline, but lacked that final stroke of genius required to give the greatness expected of architecture as an art.

Thorn House, in Upper St. Martin's lane, London, opened on Sept. 7. The 185-ft.-high block supported on 18 columns has a car park beneath it and at ground level a paved garden open to the public.

A view of one façade, with its cantilevered concrete portico, of the Y-shaped secretariat building of Unesco's new permanent headquarters in the Place de Fontenoy, Paris, which were opened in November, 1958. The buildings were designed by a group of architects of international repute and have been decorated by gifts from the governments of member nations, including works by Picasso and Henry Moore.

Unesco. A case in point was the new Unesco headquarters building in Paris, completed so late in 1958 that architectural opinion had no chance to make a proper assessment of it until well into the new year. The opinion among European critics and writers, with very few dissentient voices, was one of disappointment. Designed by a team of distinguished talents—Marcel Breuer (United States), Bernhard Zehrfuss (France) and the engineer Pierluigi Nervi (Italy) and with the guidance of a committee containing some of the greatest names of the century (among whom Walter Gropius was the most active), the final scheme, as executed, consisted predominantly of a tall office block of Y-shaped plan, two of whose wings approximately continued the semicircular plan of the Place de Fontenoy. The third limb of the Y split the rest of the site on the diagonal, with an ingenious conference hall, built of corrugated concrete slabs, on one side and a smaller square office block on the other. Much hard thought had gone into the planning and structure. Distinguished artists, including Picasso and Henry Moore, contributed large works of art. Other architects, including the BBPR group from Italy and Gerrit Rietveld of Holland, worked on the various rooms given or furnished by member governments, but the total effect was generally admitted to be one of too much talent crammed into a design which, in the last analysis, lacked unity and resolution.

Engineering on the Grand Scale. In contrast, the year produced a number of engineer's buildings—or buildings where purely technical considerations were paramount—whose very single-mindedness brought them near to greatness.

Among large buildings for sport, outstanding designs were the *Stadthalle* in Vienna by Roland Rainer, which was the product of a limited competition in which Pierluigi Nervi and Alvar Aalto of Finland had participated, and the Nya Ullevi stadium in Göteborg, Sweden, by Fritz Jaenecke and Sten Samuelsen—the latter building having a remarkable " switchback " roof over the public stands. Commercial structures of the same grandiose order included G. L. Orlandi's group of covered sales areas for the wholesale fruit market in Florence and the immense flattened tripod dome of the C.N.I.T. exhibition hall in the Paris suburb of Puteaux, of which the ubiquitous Nervi had been the original engineer, although the final execution was the work of Jean Prouvé. Two noteworthy Australian structures of the year were another dome, to house the Academy of Science, Canberra, by Grounds, Romberg and Boyd (the last-named, Robin Boyd, had earlier written a shrewd article on the fascination which feats of engineering have for contemporary architects) and the unique tent-like, suspended, acoustic shell for open-air music in a park in Melbourne, designed by Yuncken, Freeman, Freeman, Griffiths and Simpson.

Prestige Office Blocks. Nowhere does sheer professional competence count for more than in the design of large commercial office blocks in densely built cities, and in this field 1959 was a notable year. In Milan the polemics over the gothic silhouette of the *Torre Velasca* had not died away before it was joined on the skyline by two other skyscrapers of " character ". One was the *Torre Galfa* by Melchiorre Bega, a plain rectangle in plan for most of its height, but resolved at the top into a composition of set-backs and over-hangs cantilevered from its central core of lifts and services. The other was the heavily publicized Pirelli tower by Ponti, Fornaroli and Associates, with Nervi—once more—as engineer. This was simpler in silhouette than either the *Torre Galfa* or the *Torre Velasca*, but more subtle in its double-tapered, boat-shaped plan.

In London, the remarkable success of Cecil Elsom's complex group of high and low office blocks in Eastbourne Terrace, Paddington, completed in 1958, was followed by a number of other towers of perfectly plain, rectangular envelope. Conspicuous among them were Thorn house, near Covent Garden, by Basil Spence and Partners, and the Castrol building, in St. Marylebone, by Gollins, Melvin and Ward, with Sir Hugh Casson and Neville Conder. Others were following, under construction or still in the design stage, and the prospect of these tall thin slabs, ten or more storeys higher than their surroundings and spread fairly evenly across the skyline by the workings of town-planning regulations, aroused some alarm, not only from those who doubted the wisdom of admitting such towers to the London scene at all, but also from those who felt that they would be better clustered together in the way that occurs naturally in unplanned cities. Meanwhile, in the German Federal Republic where office building seemed to have settled into an uninspired standard pattern since the end of World War II, there suddenly appeared two unexpectedly well-designed office towers in Düsseldorf. Both were commissioned by big manufacturers of steel tubing who were determined to give their products a showing in the buildings themselves. The results were Paul Schneider-Esleben's exquisitely detailed Mannesmann building, impeccable in the slim rectangularity of its form and the profiling of the members of its glass and metal skin, and the larger Phönix-Rheinrohr building by Hentrich and Petschnigg, also clad in curtain-walling, but in form like three overlapping slabs, each only one room thick.

Collegiate Plans. In England the focus of attention during 1959 was the competition for Churchill college, Cambridge. The organizers selected 21 firms—taken to represent the cream of modern British architects (an assumption that was hotly disputed in some quarters)—whom they invited to submit designs. Twenty did so, and four of these were sent forward to a second stage of the competition for further study and reworking before the final selection was made. What was remarkable about this procedure was not so much the winning design by Richard Sheppard, Robson and Partners—which was precisely of the high professional competence which was the keynote of the year's work—but the fact that the final four designs should have included two by offices that were not only young, but belonged to the extreme modernists. In the subsequent post mortems on the competition it became clear that these two schemes, by Howell, Killick and Partners, and by James Stirling and James Gowan, were widely preferred to the winning one. Henry-Russell Hitchcock, the U.S. art historian, whose book *Architecture, Nineteenth and Twentieth Centuries* was the most important and most controversial British architectural publication of the year, drew attention to the fact that Le Corbusier had just completed an exactly analogous building, which could serve as a standard by which to judge the Churchill college entries. In fact, Le Corbusier was concerned with two collegiate buildings completed in 1959. One of these, the Brazilian hostel in the University of Paris, in which he collaborated with Lucio Costa, was neither a masterpiece nor comparable with the Churchill college problem. The other—the Dominican teaching monastery of La Tourette, near Lyons—was fully comparable. Here, in contrast with the very personal idiom of his previous essay in sacred architecture—the chapel at Ronchamp—Le Corbusier confined himself to the closely specified requirements of the Dominican rule and the claustral tradition. The architecture was simple, in exposed concrete. The three blocks of cells and communal rooms formed three sides of a square court, resembling a medieval cloister; the fourth side was occupied by a bare, plain box of a chapel. It was thought that the result might yet prove to be the year's one undoubted masterpiece.

Canada. The opening of the St. Lawrence seaway in June 1959 forms a convenient opportunity to record the construction of its associated township of Don Mills, even though this was not yet completed. With the exception of " uranium towns " like Elliot Lake, Don Mills was Canada's first and only " new town " on the British pattern. Its early planning was largely the work of Wells Coates, and its detailed execution gave extensive exercise to the office of John B. Parkin Associates. Excellent housing was done by James Murray and Henry Fliess, but this was rivalled in quality by Jerome Markson's housing at Elliot Lake. Indeed, the *Architectural Review's* comparative study of architecture in the four temperate-climate dominions, published in October, suggested that Canada might be about to surpass South Africa in the quantity of good modern architecture being erected, and Australia in the quality of its best work. Buildings which lent support to this forecast included Page and Steele's ingenious block of duplex flats with skip-level access in Regent's Park South, Toronto, the widely praised BC-Electric skyscraper in Vancouver, by Thompson, Berwick and Pratt, the same designers' group of buildings for the Arts faculty at the University of British Columbia, also in Vancouver, Paul Caspary's blocks of flats in Calgary and Toronto, and churches such as Notre Dame du Bel Amour in Cartierville, Montreal, by Roger d'Astons, and the Yorkminster United church, by James Murray. The last-named, a big church seating 500, was situated by a clover-leaf crossing on a transcontinental highway.

United States. The death of Frank Lloyd Wright (*see* OBITUARIES) on April 9, 1959, removed one of the great pioneers of modern architecture. That he continued bold and independent to the very end was attested by the vehemently divergent opinions that greeted the opening in October of the Solomon R. Guggenheim museum in New York City, Wright's most prominent work to be posthumously completed.

Apart from the Guggenheim museum and Wright's synagogue for the Beth Sholom congregation at Elkins Park, Pennsylvania, two of the most significant buildings were Louis Kahn's medical research building for the University of Pennsylvania, not yet fully completed but already virtually a text piece for younger architects in its romantic-appearing but classically ordered handling of great service stacks; and Paul Rudolph's second high school for the Sarasota (Florida) school district, with another vigorous and highly sculptural articulation, this time of hooded-form classrooms in a fresh composition. The year saw no exciting departures in so-called engineering architecture such as the camel-back suspension-roofed Yale hockey rink of the previous year; but Severud-Elstad-Krueger-Associates, the engineers of the rink, were associated with A. G. Odell, Jr., on a civic centre project for Baltimore which included a 13,000-seat auditorium to be roofed with an unusual " folded plate " system.

Meanwhile not all was fresh and new and healthy: for example, the new $25 million Senate office building was roundly attacked as jejune and even illiterate classicism; and the slums continued to grow apace, no impressive slum clearance projects having been completed in the snail-like pace of urban redevelopment. (*See also* BUILDING AND CONSTRUCTION INDUSTRY; HISTORIC BUILDINGS; HOUSING; NEW TOWNS; TOWN AND COUNTRY PLANNING.)

(P. R. BA.; D. HL.)

AREAS AND POPULATIONS. The political entities of the world are listed here with their areas, populations and number of persons per square mile. The latest census or official estimates available are given for each country.

Name of continent and state	Area (in sq.mi.)	Population ('000)	Persons per sq.mi.
WORLD TOTAL .	59,919,893	2,832,554	47·3*
AFRICA . . .	11,725,884	233,594	19·9
Belgian colony and trusteeship .	925,907	17,931	—
British dependencies .	1,937,997	68,725	—
Egypt	386,110	24,020	1,779·8†
Ethiopia (incl. Eritrea) .	456,500	18,000	39·4
French Community countries and French trusteeships . .	4,102,440	42,126	—
Ghana	91,843	4,911	53·5
Guinea	108,455	2,492	23·0
Italian trusteeship (Somalia) .	178,200	1,300	7·3
Liberia	43,000	1,500	34·9
Libya	625,000	1,092	1·7‡
Morocco (incl. places of Spanish sovereignty) . . .	172,556	10,330	59·9
Portuguese overseas territories .	794,959	10,603	—
South Africa, Union of .	472,685	14,673	31·0
South-West Africa (mandate of South Africa) . . .	317,725	554	1·7
Spanish colonies (incl. places of Spanish sovereignty in Morocco)	96,675	450	—
Sudan	967,500	11,037	11·4
Tunisia	48,332	3,850	79·7
ANTARCTICA . . .	6,000,000	—	—
ASIA (excl. of U.S.S.R.) .	10,569,156	1,562,770	147·9
Afghanistan . . .	250,000	12,000	48·0
Bahrain	231	125	541·1
Bhutan	18,000	700	38·9
British dependencies .	195,527	6,808	—
Burma	261,600	20,255	77·4
Cambodia	69,866	4,740	67·8
Ceylon	25,332	9,361	369·5
China (incl. Tibet) .	3,863,000	640,000	165·7
Formosa (Taiwan) . .	13,885	9,851	709·5
India	1,259,797§	397,540§	315·6
Indonesia	575,893	86,900	150·9
Iraq	171,604	6,538	38·1
Israel	7,993	2,016	252·2
Japan	146,690	92,420	630·0
Jordan	37,302	1,578	42·3
Korea {People's Democratic Republic .	46,814	9,345	199·6
{Republic of Korea .	38,452	22,655	589·2
Kuwait	5,990	206	34·4
Laos	91,000	2,000	22·0
Lebanon	4,000	1,525	381·3
Malaya, Federation of .	50,692	6,499	128·2
Mongolia	591,119	1,130	1·9
Muscat and Oman . .	82,000	550	6·7
Nepal	54,000	8,910	165·0
Netherlands New Guinea .	152,100	700	4·6
Pakistan	365,037	85,635	234·6
Persia	634,400	19,723	31·1
Philippines . . .	115,707	23,563	203·6
Portuguese overseas territories .	8,876	1,268	—
Qatar	8,500	40	4·7
Ryukyu Is. (U.S. occupied) .	935	951	1,017·1
Saudi Arabia . . .	618,000	6,036	9·8
Sikkim	2,745	136	49·5
Syria	71,229	4,080	57·3
Thailand (Siam) . .	198,270	21,474	108·3
Trucial Sheikhdoms . .	32,300	80	2·5
Turkey	296,184	25,932	87·6
Vietnam {Democratic Republic .	63,360	13,000	205·2
{National Republic .	65,726	12,000	182·6
Yemen	75,000	4,500	60·0
AUSTRALASIA and OCEANIA .	3,304,910	15,766	4·8
Australia	2,974,581	10,008	3·4‖
Australian dependencies .	183,739	1,837	—
British dependencies .	19,229	583	—
French overseas territories .	9,199	149	—

Name of continent and state	Area (in sq.mi.)	Population ('000)	Persons per sq.mi.
New Hebrides (Anglo-French condominium) . . .	5,700	54	9·5
New Zealand . . .	103,736	2,282	22·0
New Zealand dependencies .	1,322	126	—
United States possessions .	7,404	727	—
EUROPE (excl. of U.S.S.R.) .	1,903,326	418,714	220·0
Albania	11,100	1,507	135·8
Andorra	191	6	31·4
Austria	32,374	7,021	216·9
Belgium	11,779	9,053	768·6
British dependencies .	124	347	—
Bulgaria	42,796	7,722	180·4
Czechoslovakia . .	49,354	13,438	272·3
Denmark (incl. Faeroe Islands) .	17,116	4,565	266·7
Finland (incl. Åland Islands) .	130,119	4,376	33·6
France	212,821	44,788	210·5
Germany {Federal Republic	95,822	54,719	571·0
{Democratic Republic	41,646	17,312	415·7
Greece (incl. islands) .	51,182	8,150	159·2
Hungary	35,911	9,888	275·3
Iceland	39,768	169	4·2
Ireland, Republic of .	26,600	2,853	107·3
Italy	116,290	48,735	419·1
Liechtenstein . . .	61	15	245·9
Luxembourg . . .	999	320	320·3
Monaco	0·6	20	—
Netherlands . . .	12,868	11,186	869·3
Norway (excl. Svalbard) .	125,185	3,526	28·2
Norwegian dependency (Svalbard)	23,641	4	—
Poland	120,359	29,600	245·9
Portugal (incl. Azores and Madeira) . . .	35,415	8,980	253·6
Rumania	91,700	18,059	196·9
San Marino . . .	38	14	368·4
Spain (incl. Canary Islands) .	194,945	29,662	152·2
Sweden	173,622	7,415	42·7
Switzerland . . .	15,944	5,185	325·2
United Kingdom (incl. home dependencies) . . .	94,283	51,681	548·2
Vatican City . . .	0·5	1	—
Yugoslavia . . .	99,271	18,397	185·3
U.S.S.R. . . .	8,598,678	208,826	24·3
NORTH AMERICA . .	9,366,168	259,118	27·7
British dependencies .	21,356	3,425	—
Canada	3,851,113	17,550	4·6
Costa Rica . . .	19,695	1,076	54·6
Cuba	44,218	6,466	146·2
Dominican Republic .	18,681	2,704	144·7
El Salvador . . .	8,260	2,434	294·7
French territory and *départements*	1,206	520	—
Greenland (part of Denmark) .	840,000	27	—
Guatemala . . .	42,042	3,550	84·4
Haiti	10,714	3,424	319·6
Honduras	43,277	1,888	43·6
Mexico	760,373	33,304	43·8
Netherlands Antilles .	371	194	522·9
Nicaragua	57,143	1,378	24·1
Panama (excl. Canal Zone) .	28,753	1,024	35·6
United States (50 states) .	3,615,212	177,726	49·2
United States possessions	3,754	2,428	—
SOUTH AMERICA . .	6,882,615	133,766	19·4
Argentina	1,084,359	20,256	18·9
Bolivia	424,162	3,412	8·1
Brazil	3,288,042	62,725	19·1¶
British dependencies .	87,618	543	—
Chile	286,396	7,298	25·5
Colombia	439,512	13,823	31·5
Ecuador	105,685	4,116	38·9
French Guiana . . .	35,135	30	0·9
Netherlands territory (Surinam) .	54,143	241	4·5
Paraguay	157,047	1,677	10·7
Peru	496,222	10,524	21·2
Uruguay	72,152	2,801	38·8
Venezuela	352,142	6,320	17·9

* In computing the world density the area of Antarctica is omitted. † Density calculated for the cultivated and settled area of the Nile valley, delta and oases, *i.e.*, 13,496 sq.mi. ‡ The country is mainly a desert but there are no data for assessing the cultivated and settled area. § Incl. Kashmir, the incorporation of which is disputed by Pakistan. ‖ The bulk of the population is concentrated in the southeast; more than half of Australia is a desert. ¶ Three-quarters of the population lives in an area along the Atlantic coast, where the principal towns are located.

ARGENTINA. Second largest South American republic, occupying the southeastern part of the continent. Area (excl. claims in Antarctica): 1,084,359 sq.mi. Pop.: (1947 census) 15,893,827; (mid-1958 est.) 20,256,000. The population is overwhelmingly European in origin (mostly Spanish and Italian, with Irish, German, Croat and Polish admixtures); in 1940 about 9% were of mixed blood, the dwindling Indian population being estimated at 262,600; by mid-1953 the total foreign-born population was 2,847,000. Language: Spanish. Religion: mainly Roman Catholic; Jewish 360,000. Chief towns (pop., 1947 census, city proper): Buenos Aires 2,981,043; (1957 est.: 3,680,600); Rosario 467,937; Córdoba 369,886; Avellaneda* 273,839; San Martín* 269,514; Lanus* 244,473; La Plata 207,031; Tucumán 194,166; Santa Fé 168,791; Vicente Lopez* 149,958; Lomas de Zamora* 125,943; Quilmes* 115,113; Mar del Plata 114,729; Bahia Blanca 112,597; Morón* 110,344. President, Arturo Frondizi. Main imports: machinery and vehicles; fuels and lubricants; iron, steel and mill products; textiles, fibres and manufactures. Main exports: meat, wool, hides and skins. Monetary unit: *peso* (free rate, Oct. 1959, *c.* 225·00 pesos = £1 sterling).

* Part of Buenos Aires agglomeration.

History. In Dec. 1958, after U.S. economic experts had approved a stabilization programme for Argentina, loans and credits totalling $329 million were granted by the International Monetary fund, the U.S. government and 11 North American commercial banks. The main features of the programme were: there would no longer be an official rate of exchange: the *peso* would be allowed to fluctuate according to supply and demand; all import controls were to be removed, but imports of non-essentials were to be subject to high surcharges, ranging up to 300%; bank credit was to be permitted only for productive activities; internal price controls were to be cancelled; and the number of government employees was to be reduced. The programme was denounced by nationalists and the trade unions as a surrender to Wall Street.

The austerity measures came into force on Jan. 12, 1959, when the value of the *peso* declined from the previous official rate of 50·40 to the £ to a free rate of 188. By June, the *peso* had fallen to 256 to the £, and the cost of living had risen 70%. Although some wage increases were authorized, the burden of the programme fell heavily on the working-class, and this provoked a long succession of partial and general strikes, which showed that Arturo Frondizi had lost the support of the Peronista workers whose votes had been largely responsible for his election to the presidency. The strikes were ineffectual, as the country was still under a state of siege and the workers in certain industries (notably petroleum and transport) had been " mobilized ", so that they were compelled to resume work, under armed guards, or face trial by military courts for desertion.

Frondizi visited the United States in Jan. 1959. Not only his critics in the armed forces and in opposition political parties, but also many of his own followers, expressed disgust at seeing the president, who had campaigned as a left-wing nationalist and a bitter opponent of " dollar imperialism ", now travelling to Washington, cap in hand.

After his victory in the presidential elections in Feb. 1958, Frondizi had declared that he would not favour any section of the population, but would govern for the nation as a whole. During 1959, however, he gradually gave in to the officers of the army, navy and air force who had overthrown Perón in 1955 and who now refused to concede that Peronistas should be allowed to share in the direction of national affairs. Under successive threats of military *coups d'état* Frondizi, month by month, eliminated from his government and from his circle of advisers such persons as the officers considered to be tainted with Peronismo, or Communism. He remained in office merely because the military leaders of the 1955 revolution had pledged themselves to uphold constitutional government and were reluctant to earn discredit by seizing power again.

On June 25, confronted with yet another military ultimatum, Frondizi brought into his cabinet one of his keenest critics,

Alvaro Alsogaray, a former military engineer and latterly a successful business man. Alsogaray, a champion of free enterprise and an enthusiastic advocate of attracting foreign investment, agreed to become minister of economy on condition that he might simultaneously act as minister of labour, with the object of trying to effect a reconciliation between employers and workers. He accepted the stabilization programme, but insisted on being allowed to use his own methods and his own team of experts in carrying it out. His demands

Alfredo Camarero of Argentina, the 28-yr.-old winner of the 1959 Channel swim sponsored by Billy Butlin, with the trophy.

were granted. The new minister at once announced that he would end the mobilization of workers in the petroleum industry and transport, and when 250,000 metal workers went on strike in August he declared that, although he deplored the strike, it would not be repressed by force, as on previous occasions.

Frondizi and his austerity policy continued to be widely unpopular, but Alsogaray created an atmosphere of greater confidence in business circles. The *peso* strengthened slightly, and foreign companies showed more willingness to invest in Argentina. Although in September the anti-Peronista officers compelled the president to undertake a further purge of his *entourage*, under the threat of civil war, they agreed to Alsogaray's demand for a reduction in the military budget as a part of his drive to cut national expenditure, which was greatly in excess of revenue. (G. P.)

ARMIES OF THE WORLD. Nato. There was a curtailment in the original plans for the location of intermediate-range ballistic missile (IRBM) squadrons in various North Atlantic Treaty organization countries. Four squadrons of Thor missiles (15 missiles in each squadron) were in place in England, while two squadrons of Jupiter missiles were being installed in Italy, and one in Turkey. Plans for locating IRBM squadrons in Greece and western Germany were abandoned. By the end of the year 1959 more than half the 100 squadrons (or battalions) of missiles of all types

Italian alpine troops deploying from a U.S. army helicopter near Monte Simeone, northern Italy, during joint manoeuvres in October.

planned to be completed in 1963 were in place in the Nato countries. Included among these were three groups in the U.S. forces in Germany equipped with the 700-mi.-range Martin Matador, in process of being replaced by the longer-range Martin Mace. There were also three battalions of the 200-mi. Redstone missiles with the U.S. forces. Other Nato forces were being equipped with Matadors and Corporals while the air-to-air Sidewinder missile was also being sent by the United States to Nato forces. A new U.S. anti-aircraft missile, 17 ft. long, 14 in. in diameter, using solid fuel, with a range of 25 mi., was licensed for European manufacture.

A special fact-finding group was established by the president of the United States to study military aid. Under the chairmanship of William Draper, this group recommended, among other things, that the 1,500-mi., solid-fuel Polaris rocket be distributed to Nato powers when ready for operational use in 1960. It also recommended that the United States allocate $10 million for the French wire-controlled SS 10d anti-tank missile, and $43 million for radar-detection and fire-control systems. The Nato forces defending the central sector in Europe consisted of 22 divisions facing a total of 31 Soviet divisions—10 armoured, 10 mechanized, 2 artillery and 9 anti-aircraft.

Major Western Powers. *United States.* The U.S. defence appropriation bill for fiscal year 1959-60 amounted to $39,228,239,000 of which $9,375,805,000 was for the army. The appropriation would support an 870,000-man 14-division army. In making the appropriation the congress placed a specific ban on a proposed cut of the army national guard from 400,000 to 360,000 and also provided funds so that the army reserve need not be cut from 300,000 to 275,000. The funds provided would maintain the army at 14 divisions with the 8 divisions overseas, supported by 8 battlegroups, 18 surface-to-surface and 10 surface-to-air missile battalions. The strategic reserve army corps in the United States—a highly mobile organization for rapid movement to any crisis area in the world—consisted of two airborne and one infantry division, one infantry brigade and one armoured cavalry division. The other units in the United States were principally two infantry and one armoured division, one infantry brigade, one cavalry regiment, three battlegroups and nine battalions.

The president directed that the army turn over all space

activities to the National Aeronautics and Space agency, which would result in the transfer of the Army Ballistic Missile agency. Under the Government Reorganization act, this change could be cancelled by the Congress if it acted within 60 days. Six reserve divisions were reorganized on a " pentomic " basis, each with five battlegroups, one battalion of eight-inch howitzers and one battalion of Honest John rockets. The strength of each of these units was reduced from 17,500 to 13,750 men. The infantry was re-euipped with M14 rifles and M60 machine guns. General Lyman Lemnitzer replaced General Maxwell Taylor as chief of staff of the army.

Overseas the 1st cavalry and 7th infantry divisions remained in Korea. A considerable part of the strength of these units consisted of South Koreans integrated into the organizations. The 7th army remained in western Germany with the 3rd, 8th and 24th infantry, 3rd and 4th armoured divisions, and the 2nd, 11th and 14th cavalry regiments. The 46th artillery group, equipped with Redstone surface-to-surface missiles, was transferred from Fort Sill, Oklahoma, to Germany. A battlegroup of about 12,000 men remained in Berlin, and another battlegroup of 3,000 men in the Panama canal zone.

New equipment delivered to line units or placed into production by the army included a 90-mm. recoilless rifle, 4 ft. long with a weight of 35 lb., which has an effective range of 500 yd. and can be handled by a two-man crew; about 720 M60 tanks, enough to equip two armoured divisions; and 52-ton tanks each with a 105-mm. gun and double the range of previous heavy tanks. Also purchased were 600 M113 armoured personnel carriers (enough to equip three divisions and two armoured cavalry regiments). These are lightweight, amphibious and air-transportable. The heavier M59 armoured personnel carriers were in use by the two armoured divisions in Germany. The signal corps was developing a remote-controlled drone aircraft called the " Snooper " to carry photographic, infra-red, radar and television equipment on reconnaissance missions over enemy areas. The plane, weighing only 1,000 lb., was 15 ft. long and had an 11-ft. wing. It was powered by a reciprocating engine and launched from a mobile trailer with two Arrow II rocket engines, landing by parachute upon return. Experiments were also being conducted with a vehicle which supported itself off the ground by the use of air blasts against the ground. These vehicles would be useful for crossing rough terrain and water, and carrying heavy loads with little power. Also under development was a 60-ft. assault bridge that could be hydraulically put in place in less than two minutes by a truck. For longer river crossings there was a new raft that could carry 12-ton loads on streams with a velocity of up to 8 ft. a second—the Larc, an amphibious vehicle of aluminium, with a capacity of 5 tons on land. It could travel at 5 m.p.h.-10 m.p.h. in water and at 30 m.p.h.-35 m.p.h. on land. The Barc was a larger version.

In the missile field, the Sergeant, a solid-fuel surface-to-surface air-transportable weapon with a range of 100 mi., was replacing the shorter-range liquid-fueled Corporal. The Sergeant also had a new advanced guidance system of drag brakes using fins and vanes. The Lacrosse was delivered to the missile battalion at Fort Sill, Oklahoma.

France. The bulk of the French armed forces remained committed to the war in Algeria. France negotiated for the purchase of the Regulus II missile from the U.S., which had been given up by the U.S. navy in favour of other missiles. On the other hand, France refused to allow U.S. nuclear stockpiles on French soil and would not establish a Nato IRBM base, and gave strong indications that its price for full participation in Nato was the appointment of a French officer as deputy supreme allied commander in Europe.

German Federal Republic. At the start of 1960 the U.S., British, French, Belgian and Dutch forces in western Germany were placed under the Nato status of forces agreement. The council of the Western European union agreed to German manufacture of the surface-to-air Hawk missile (which would be manufactured jointly with France and Italy) and the air-to-air Sidewinder missile, in addition to the anti-tank rocket for which permission had been previously granted. The defence budget was set for the year 1960 at *c.* DM.10,000 million as the army was changing from conventional to multi-purpose weapons. The U.S. delivered to the German armed forces several multi-purpose weapons, including the Honest John, 15-mi.-range artillery rocket, the 50-mi.-range Nike-Hercules anti-aircraft rocket and three wings of the 600-mi.-range Matador winged missile.

Franz Josef Strauss, the minister of defence, announced that western Germany would maintain a ratio of 50% domestic production of weapons and 50% purchased abroad. Production plans included the manufacture of light guns, aircraft, troop carriers, tanks and rockets. A new 30-ton tank was under development in Stuttgart, and the Krupp subsidiary, Flugzeugbau Weser, was manufacturing medium-range military transport aircraft.

The projected strength of the army was dropped from 500,000 to slightly over 300,000, with an ultimate total of 12 combat-ready divisions. Emphasis was placed on bringing the existing divisions to combat readiness by speeding up delivery of weapons, equipment and quartermaster supplies. However, cadres from the original five divisions were used to form the nucleus of the 10th and 11th divisions in 1959. The 12th and last division would be organized early in 1960.

U.S.S.R. Col.-General F. I. Golikov, chief of the political administration in the Ministry of Defence, announced that there would be a greater exchange of positions between political officers and military officers in the armed forces. The political control units were given much greater authority, including a voice in the efficiency ratings given to officers. It was officially announced that by Jan. 1, 1959, a new cut of 300,000 in the strength of the armed forces had been carried out. This was in addition to the cuts of 1,840,000 in 1955-57. About 41,000 troops were withdrawn from Germany and 17,000 from Hungary, probably as a result of reorganization of the units into smaller battle groups. The units in Germany, which had most of the latest equipment, were armed with T54 medium tanks, the new 53-ton heavy tank, and tactical missiles with a 300-mi. range.

Chinese People's Republic. The 1959 budget called for a 16% increase in the defence expenditures with an approximate total of about U.S.$2,300 million directly allocated to the military forces. This represented 11·2% of the budget compared with 12·5% in 1958. Marshal Lin Piao replaced General Peng Teh-huai as minister of defence. Lin, one of China's leading military strategists and tacticians, was a guerrilla fighter against the Japanese during their occupation of China; he studied in the U.S.S.R., and organized and led the crack 4th Field army during the civil war. Simultaneously, Marshal Lo Jui-ching succeeded General Huang Ko-cheng as army chief of staff. Lo was formerly minister of public security and his appointment was interpreted to mean an intensification of discipline, and an emphasis on loyalty and political indoctrination in the army. (*See also* AIR FORCES OF THE WORLD; CENTRAL TREATY ORGANIZATION; COMMONWEALTH ARMIES; MISSILES; NAVIES OF THE WORLD; NORTH ATLANTIC TREATY ORGANIZATION; SOUTHEAST ASIA TREATY ORGANIZATION.)

(L. B. K.)

ART EXHIBITIONS. In Paris, in the autumn of 1958, the Musée Jacquemart-André rescued Pierre Paul Prud'hon from comparative obscurity with the third collective showing of his paintings and drawings since his death in 1822.

" *St. George and the Dragon* " *by Paolo Uccello* (c. *1397-1475*), *a new acquisition by the National gallery, bought for £125,000.*

Meanwhile, in London, art exhibitions were numerous and varied. Donald Hamilton Fraser showed elegant pictures at Gimpel Fils. The Arts Council at its St. James's Square gallery paid pleasing memorial tributes to John Minton and Barnett Freedman in concurrent exhibitions. Contemporary U.S. art was represented in a show at the Cultural Affairs office of the United States Information services, by a Jackson Pollock retrospective at the Whitechapel Art gallery and by Alfred Cohen's paintings at the Ben Uri gallery. At the Tate gallery, the Arts Council's presentation of 92 pictures from the Urvater collection was London's most comprehensive exhibition of surrealism since 1936. Two large pictures, bought for Commonwealth collections, had a brief showing, William Hogarth's " A Midnight Modern Conversation " at Tooth's gallery and Sebastiano Ricci's " Finding of Moses " at Messrs. Colnaghi's, prior to their departure for Canada and Australia respectively.

In Italy, an exhibition of paintings and drawings by Amedeo Modigliani, at the Palazzo Reale, Milan, was held in Nov. 1958, a sequel to the spring showing of his work in Paris. In

Spain, the great Hospicio at Toledo was a wonderful setting for tapestries, pictures and sculpture selected from Spanish collections to commemorate the quatercentenary of Charles V's death and to illustrate his life against the background of 16th-century European culture.

In the new year, 1959, at Burlington house, London, an

" The Defence of Petrograd " by A. A. Deineka, from the Royal Academy's winter exhibition of 13th-20th century Russian art.

eagerly awaited exhibition of Russian art (the first representative collection to be seen in western Europe) proved a disappointment, both in the exhibits and the sad shabbiness of the Royal Academy walls. The 122 pictures ranged from medieval icons to 20th-century social realist paintings. There were beautiful examples of the former, particularly from the 12th-13th-century Novgorod school but, except for Alexander Deineka's " Defence of Petrograd ", the latter were not generally admired. The Arts Council's 1959 exhibitions began at the Tate gallery with a collection of paintings by the German Impressionist, Lovis Corinth, and with a simultaneous showing, at St. James's square, of stained glass, paintings and drawings by Evie Hone. In other exhibitions, early in 1959, Graham Sutherland showed a small group of paintings at Arthur Jeffress' gallery and Anthony Fry's four large pictures of strange ritual dances dominated a mixed show at the Leicester galleries. Additionally, there were notable exhibitions in the provinces. At Nottingham, the University Art gallery showed such endearing favourites as Holman Hunt's " The Hireling Shepherd " and W. F. Yeames's " And When Did You Last See Your Father? " in a nostalgic miscellany of Victorian paintings. At Wakefield, the City Art gallery exhibited works of ten foreign artists who had chosen to live in England. Among them were Oskar Kokoschka, Josef Herman, Jankel Adler and Mark Zulawski, whose January exhibition at Zwemmer's gallery had displayed his considerable powers as a draughtsman.

In Paris, in January, the Galerie Charpentier held the first retrospective exhibition of paintings by Maurice Utrillo since his death in 1955. In the same month, La Maison de la Pensée Française showed 113 paintings executed by Chinese artists between 1850 and 1950. Augmented by a collection of popular prints, the exhibition summed up the dilemma of oriental artists poised between their own traditions and western influences. The compulsion of western influences was vividly apparent in the exhibition of new U.S. painting presented in the same month at the Musée d'Art Moderne. Of the 17 artists chosen to represent the extreme *avant-garde*

of U.S. painting, Jackson Pollock, Willem de Kooning and Mark Rothko were dominant figures. In February, Bernard Buffet showed 19 rather flat pictures of New York at the Galerie David et Garnier and, towards the end of the month, under the joint patronage of Queen Elizabeth II and President Charles de Gaulle, the Musée des Arts Décoratifs du Louvre opened a splendid exhibition of 18th-century English furniture, pictures, china, glass and silver under the general title of " Le siècle d'élégance anglaise ". It consisted of nine rooms arranged chronologically, starting with the comparative austerity of Queen Anne styles and finishing with the fanciful *chinoiseries* of the regency. The exhibits were beautifully presented with notable ingenuity and selected with imaginative discernment.

A remarkable collection from Switzerland, " de Géricault à Matisse ", seen at the Petit Palais in the spring, disclosed the great richness of the Swiss share of 19th- and 20th-century French masterpieces. Meanwhile, in Switzerland, the Berne museum showed 200 17th-century French paintings and drawings.

In the City of London, an exhibition of great interest opened in March at the Goldsmith's hall. It was a superb display of plate and other art treasures from Cambridge colleges and the Fitzwilliam museum. During the following months, the Arts Council showed, at the Tate gallery, the melancholy, sensitive work of Francis Gruber, the Redfern gallery presented the first retrospective exhibition devoted to Christopher Wood since 1938, and the Obelisk gallery displayed pictures by Guy Warren, an Australian painter, in a first one-man show. In May, Zwemmer's gallery showed Professor Carel Weight's beguiling pictures; the Whitechapel Art gallery offered a large retrospective show of Jack Smith's work; Ivon Hitchens' elusive improvisations were on view at the Leicester galleries and the National gallery showed the public its fine acquisition, " St. George and the Dragon " by Paolo Uccello.

At the open-air museum of modern European sculpture at

" Durian Season ", by Chuah Thean Teng, using a batik dyeing technique, from an exhibition at the Commonwealth institute in May.

Middelheim, in Antwerp, an international exhibition opened in May with an especial emphasis on the British entry. The high reputation which British sculpture had enjoyed in Europe for some years was sustained in the work submitted by Henry Moore, Barbara Hepworth (*see* BIOGRAPHIES), Kenneth Armitage, Lynn Chadwick, Reg Butler and Eduardo Paolozzi. In Paris, a great programme of exhibitions began early in the spring. At the Musée Jacquemart-André there were 50 works by Henri de Toulouse-Lautrec. At La Maison de la Pensée Française, an exhibition of tapestries, stained glass and mosaics by Fernand Léger threw light on his virtuosity as a decorator and designer. At the Galerie Charpentier 548 exhibits were on view in an impressive display called " Trésors d'art précolombien " and the Orangerie

" *The Red Funnel, Mousehole, Cornwall* ", *from a retrospective exhibition of works by Christopher Wood at the Redfern gallery.*

presented a large exhibition, " L'Art champenois ", which displayed manuscripts, sculptures and enamels from country churches in Champagne. The brilliant sequence of summer shows included 60 paintings by Claude Monet at the Galerie Durand-Ruel, 50 years of painting by Marc Chagall at the Musée des Arts Décoratifs and 119 paintings by Chaïm Soutine at the Galerie Charpentier. The French provincial museums were not inactive. At Marseilles, the Musée Cantini showed a choice anthology of Picasso's works representing his output from 1901-58. At Nice, the Galeries des Ponchettes, which had mounted an important exhibition of paintings by Kees Van Dongen in the spring, followed it with a retrospective showing of 30 years' painting by Yves Brayer.

Elsewhere in Europe, the Musée de l'Athénée at Geneva held a large commemorative exhibition of paintings, drawings and sculpture by André Derain and the Galerie Beyeler at Zürich revived a 1905 scandal with 49 works by the original Fauvists. In Venice, at the Palazzo Pesaro, a collection of 235 pictures by painters of the *seicento* was a denial that, after the 16th century, Venetian art had lost its creative momentum, while, later in the year, at the Palazzo Grassi, an exhibition called " Vitality in Art " sought to reveal this quality in the works of 30 contemporary artists who belonged to the international *avantgarde*.

In England, during the summer, a loan exhibition of drawings and paintings by T. S. Lowry was to be seen at the Manchester City Art gallery and a group of pictures called " Canaletto in England " at the Guildhall Art gallery in London. In June, a show of Francis Bacon's ominous works at the Hanover gallery was a welcome rarity and Messrs. Wildenstein's exhibition provided a unique opportunity of seeing an outstanding collection of masterpieces on loan from their New York house. The salient feature of the summer was, undoubtedly, " The Romantic Movement ", a double

exhibition which opened simultaneously at the Tate gallery and the Arts Council's gallery in St. James's square. The fifth of a cycle of large exhibitions sponsored by the Council of Europe, its aim, like that of its predecessors, was to stress the wide European, rather than the confined national, character of great artistic movements. The supreme difficulty of containing the diffuse meanings of romanticism within the shape of an exhibition was admirably solved by subtle selection and emphasis. The smaller exhibitions in London included Kurt Schwitter's ingenious collages at Lord's gallery, the Whitechapel Art gallery's retrospective of Kenneth Armitage's ten years' work as a sculptor and a combined show by two Indian artists, Laxman Pai, a painter, and Sada Bakre, a sculptor, at Gallery One. Meanwhile, in Edinburgh, the festival exhibition, " Masterpieces of Czech Art ", was received with moderate enthusiasm.

John Bratby, who had eight huge pictures at the Beaux Arts gallery in February, exhibited more paintings at Zwemmer's gallery in October while Keith Vaughan shared the Leicester galleries with Carl Plate, an Australian. In the same month, London celebrated a " Swiss Fortnight " and the Arts Council honoured the occasion with an exhibition of Swiss art at the Tate gallery under the title " From Hodler to Klee ".

In western Germany, a very big exhibition at Kassel, in July, called " Documenta ", attempted a comprehensive assessment of the trends in art since 1945. In September, the National gallery at Karlsrühe assembled over 300 works by Hans Baldung Grien in the first extensive exhibition of his work since 1935. During the closing months of 1959, Bernard Lorjou showed four enormous canvases at Messrs. Wildenstein's in Paris which, under the title of " Bal des Fols ", hauntingly described the plight of contemporary humanity. The first Paris Biennale opened. This vast assembly of work by artists under 35 from 41 countries was on view at the Musée d'Art Moderne which, during November and December, accommodated a retrospective survey of the work of Max Ernst.

In the United States, in late 1958 and early 1959, a superb group of 150 Dutch drawings ranging from the 15th to the 20th centuries was shown at the National gallery, the Morgan library, the De Young museum in San Francisco, the Cleveland museum and the Art Institute of Chicago through the generosity of the Dutch government. Among the early artists represented were Hieronymus Bosch, Lucas van Leyden and Hercules Seghers; there was also a group of important Rembrandts and among the more modern works were drawings by Van Gogh. Another outstanding exhibition in 1959 concerned a field not often featured by U.S. museums: the Detroit Institute of Arts showed " Decorative Arts of the Italian Renaissance, 1400-1600 ", made up of loans from museums all over the United States and from 25 Italian museums, as well as the Louvre, the Rijksmuseum in Amsterdam and the Victoria and Albert museum in London. About 500 items from what is probably the most outstanding private collection in America (that of Robert Lehman of New York City) were shown in a lavish setting at the Cincinnati Art museum. In this rich collection were paintings, drawings, tapestries, vestments, Venetian glass, enamels, Gothic bronzes and Renaissance jewellery. The Baltimore museum assembled an exhibition of great charm, " The Age of Elegance: the Rococo and Its Effect ". About 450 items represented the 18th-century art of Italy, France, Germany, Austria, England and the American colonies. Paintings by Watteau, Boucher and Fragonard were shown with Beauvais tapestries, Sèvres porcelain and English and colonial furniture. A comprehensive exhibition of the work of Nicolas Poussin was the joint undertaking of the Minneapolis Institute of Arts and the Toledo Museum of Art. This honoured Minneapolis' recent

purchase of "The Death of Germanicus" by Nicolas Poussin.

A group of contemporary American paintings was sent to Moscow for exhibition. Chosen by Franklin Watkins, Theodore Roszak, Lloyd Goodrich and Henry Hope, the group included Ben Shahn, Andrew Wyeth, Ivan Albright, Jack Levine, Willem de Kooning, Jackson Pollock, Robert Motherwell, Peter Blume ("The Eternal City") and Edwin Dickinson ("The Ruins at Daphne"). The Worcester (Massachusetts) Art museum showed "The *Dial* and the *Dial* Collection" honouring the *Dial*, a vigorous monthly magazine featuring contemporary art which was active between 1920 and 1929. More than 200 paintings were shown (including 16 Picassos) as well as drawings, prints, sculpture and documents. Painting and sculpture by 18 Americans were shown at the Whitney Museum of American Art, New York city, chosen by polling the Friends of the Whitney Museum, a group made up largely of collectors. Included in the diversified group were Edward Hopper, William Zorach, Max Weber, Georgia O'Keeffe, Alexander Calder, Mark Tobey, Morris Graves, Philip Custon, David Smith and Seymour Lipton. A major retrospective exhibition of the work of Winslow Homer was shown at the National gallery in Washington, the Metropolitan museum in New York and the Museum of Fine Arts in Boston. Oils, water colours, drawings, prints and illustrations gave a full-scale view of one of America's major artists whose rugged interpretations of the sea are especially memorable. (*See also* ART SALES; DRAWING, ENGRAVING AND ILLUSTRATION.)

(F. W. W.-S.; F. A. Sw.)

See Herbert Read, *A Concise History of Modern Painting* (London, 1959).

ART SALES. Diamonds, furniture, books and stamps, porcelain, armour and, above all, paintings attracted great attention in the world's auction rooms during 1959. Christie's year opened with an appetizer organized with De Beers Consolidated Mines, Ltd. This was an exhibition, "The Ageless Diamond", that attracted long queues to King street. The £4 million-worth of celebrated diamonds were protected by many detectives. The show included Queen Alexandra's diamond tiara, parts of the Cullinan diamond made into a brooch, worn by Queen Mary at her wedding, Marie Antoinette's necklace that helped her to the scaffold, the Eureka diamond (found by a lad and given to a passing pedlar) that caused the diamond rush in 1869, and the Nepal diamond, mined in Golconda four centuries previously. Many important jewel sales followed. One at Sotheby's totalled £164,904, including the Westminster tiara, bought for £110,000. Another at Christie's included a 23·7 carat step-cut diamond ring, sold by Mrs. Michael Wilding for £56,000, the highest price for a single stone ring on the London market.

Among the Westminster paintings "The Adoration of the Magi" by Rubens was the great sensation. For this work (one of the few great old masters still remaining in private hands) Rubens received 920 florins from a Louvain convent which, later suppressed, caused the painting to be sold for 8,400 florins. Three years later, the price fell by 400 florins. At Sotheby's on this June morning in 1959, however, Leonard Koetser bought it for an anonymous client for £275,000, the highest price ever paid for a painting, outbidding a syndicate of four U.S. dealers. The new owner lent the work to the National gallery for two years after Koetser had cleaned it. Other high prices by this bidder at this sale included £24,000, a new Van Goyen record, and £72,000 for an El Greco. In Sotheby's last complete season for all sales (189), pictures fetched £3,108,317 and books £753,648, both world records.

In London, Paris and New York the Impressionists and their successors continued to command great prices. Americans who bequeath their paintings to public galleries escape death duties, which may partly account for high prices. In New York, the Parke-Benet galleries had an all-time record for their last complete season of $10,208,879. In May the Thelma Chrysler Foy collection sold for $2,625,880, displacing the previous record of $2,221,353 for the Lurcy collection in 1957 for similar items. Seventeen Impressionists alone totalled $1,666,440, Walter Chrysler Jr. paying the top price of $255,000 for "Les Filles de Durand Ruel" by Auguste Renoir who, incidentally, painted 6,000 pictures. Near-contemporaries, however, challenged their predecessors for public favour. At Sotheby's Pablo Picasso's "La Belle Hollandaise" achieved a record auction price of £55,000 for a living artist, and Georges Braque's "Femme à la Mandoline" commanded £36,000. A flower painting by I. H. Fantin-Latour reached a new record at £15,000.

Two famous auctioneers use the Galerie Charpentier in Paris. In March and June the Pierre Bonnards and Jean Vuillards of Etienne Ader took pride of place. "Portrait de Madame Marthe Bonnard" by the former fetched Fr.22 million, and "Mme. Hessel et Daniel Nathanson, Villerville", by the latter Fr.20·5 million. Raoul Dufy's popularity was undimmed at Fr.15 million for "Le Tribune des Regates au Havre". In the March sale of Maurice Rheims, apart from two Claude Monets "Argenteuil" (Fr.20·2 million) and "Lavacourt" Fr.20 million, the chief honours went to Picasso's "La Course de Taureaux" for Fr.18·5 million, which was Fr.4 million more than Renoir's "Le Bras d'Argenteuil". Henri Matisse paintings reached Fr.9·1 million and Fr.9 million.

Prices have their little ironies. In the age of the atom bomb, a suit of armour was sold for £3,570, its value having appreciated five times in 20 years, for it was bought in 1939 for £650. It was acquired by the Tower of London. The reward of courage, however, also continued to appreciate. A Victoria Cross group realized £650 at Christie's, equalling their previous year's world record. Music also had its triumph. In June, a Stradivarius fetched £8,190, a new auction record. Stamps had their golden moment. An unused block of British "Penny Blacks", the first stamps used in Britain (1840) fetched £4,400 at Harmers. They were discovered in an old box. Board of Trade figures showed that art imports and exports had increased fourfold in value in Great Britain since 1937-38, and the increase was continuing. (*See also* ART EXHIBITIONS.)

(G. S. Ss.)

ASSOCIATION FOOTBALL. England's supporters were sorely upset by the results of many international matches during 1958-59. A 5-0 victory over the U.S.S.R. at Wembley in Oct. 1958 restored good humour following a 3-3 draw with Northern Ireland in Belfast, and a draw 2-2 with Wales and a 1-0 win against Scotland at Wembley at least meant sharing the home championship with Northern Ireland. Then things went awry. Against an inexperienced and experimental Italian side at Wembley on May 6 the defence sprang leaks and the attack failed to take its chances so that after leading 2-0 England only drew 2-2. Three defeats while on tour by Brazil (2-0), Peru (4-1) and Mexico (2-1) followed with only an 8-1 victory over a raw United States team as compensation. A storm of criticism directed at the competence of the selectors arose from many popular newspapers and their readers. Some of the selections were certainly a little odd, and in a season when England could not find a satisfactory centre-forward and mostly used an inside forward, R. Charlton, there were many who could not understand the omission of B. Clough of Middlesbrough, who with 43 goals was the highest scorer in the Football league. Among the troubles were a lack of first-class ball players, a lack of combination and understanding, and the fact that in May, at the end of the long league season, many players are mentally stale and find it hard to recover zest in strange countries, eating strange food and suffering from long journeys by air and sudden changes of climate. The Football association showed no sign of yielding to popular clamour and dismissing the selectors or coach, and the Football league were unwilling to surrender club players for long periods of special training.

The Football league itself had a notable victory during the close season when it won a copyright action concerning the use of its fixtures by football pool organizers and then received and accepted an offer by the leading pool promotors of £250,000 a year for ten years for their continued use. The league decided not to do anything immediately with this huge sum, which about trebled its income. As a provisional and temporary measure it suspended its 4% levy on member clubs which had brought in about £125,000 a year. The league had already been much encouraged by the first appreciable rise in attendances for ten years. There was no clear reason for this rise as there was no obvious improvement in the general standard of play or accommodation and the weather was not particularly kind.

The league season brought a second successive championship to Wolverhampton Wanderers, and there was no doubt they were the best side. W. Wright, who joined the staff before the war, again captained the team and also brought his record bag of England caps to 105 before he announced his retirement in Aug. 1959. Few professional footballers had won so much affection and respect. The club was, however, unsuccessful in the European cup. At one time it looked as though Manchester United might catch them in the league, for after a bad time in the early autumn the United had a run of 12 matches without defeat. Both teams scored more than 100 league goals, but the better Wolverhampton defence told in the end and they won by six points at 61 to Manchester United's 55. Manchester City escaped relegation from the First division by winning their last game. Aston Villa only drew theirs and were obliged to join Portsmouth in the Second division. They were replaced by Sheffield Wednesday and Fulham, the Wednesday winning their third Second division championship in eight years.

The F.A. Cup competition brought its usual crop of surprises before Nottingham Forest beat Luton Town 2-1 despite losing a man in the first half when they were playing brilliantly and leading 2-0. This was the Forest's first victory in the final since 1898. In the third round they were two goals down to the amateurs of Tooting and Mitcham before earning a replay. Luton had to replay their semi-final with Norwich City, a Third division side which had put out such famous clubs as Manchester United, Cardiff City, Tottenham Hotspur and Sheffield United, before winning 1-0. The F.A. Amateur cup returned north to Crook Town, only a few miles from Bishop Auckland where it had remained for three years before visiting Woking. Crook Town narrowly beat Barnet 3-2 in an exciting final.

In Scotland, Rangers won the league title for the 19th time

Billy Wright, England's captain, is ambushed by young autograph hunters at Stamford Bridge in April as he goes out on to the pitch to train for the match against Scotland. Wright gained his 100th international cap on this occasion—an unequalled record.

J. Welch of Barnet (striped shirt) threatens Crook Town's goal in the F.A. amateur cup final at Wembley on April 18. Crook won 3-2.

and St. Mirren took the Scottish cup. The latter owed much to a U.S.-born forward, G. Baker, who came into an unsuccessful side on Nov. 22 and scored 19 league and 8 cup goals. Aberdeen avoided descent into the Second division for the first time by achieving the near impossible in their last game victory on Rangers' ground. Queen's Park, the famous amateur club, had a sad season, finishing next to bottom in the Second division. (*See* also SPORTING RECORD.) (L. M.)

ASSOCIATIONS: *see* SOCIETIES AND ASSOCIATIONS.

ASTRONOMY. General. Several new instruments and two new radio-astronomical observatories began full-scale operation in 1959. These were the U.S. National Radio Astronomy observatory at Greenbank, West Virginia, dedicated on Oct. 16, 1958, and the California Institute of Technology Radio Astronomy observatory, dedicated on Dec. 19, 1958. On the optical side, the newly completed 120-in. reflector at the Lick observatory was dedicated on July 16, 1959. In fundamental astronomy, work was completed on the AGK 2, a 15-volume catalogue giving photographically determined positions of the 185,187 stars down to visual magnitude 9ᵐ0 north of —2° declination, based on reference stars measured with meridian circles at Hamburg-Bergedorf, Bonn, Pulkovo and elsewhere in 1928-32. The positions of the same stars for 1960, currently being re-measured for the forthcoming AGK 3, would provide a 30-year baseline for the determination of proper motions. The first volume appeared of the unified U.K. *Nautical Almanac* and U.S. *American Ephemeris* (for 1960), now based on Ephemeris time. Ephemeris time (flowing uniformly, as nearly as possible, in accordance with Newton's laws of motion) was currently running some 35 sec. ahead of Universal time (which is affected by irregularities in the rotation of the earth).

Solar System. Early in the year, there was much discussion on the observation by N. A. Kosirev, at the Pulkovo observatory's Crimean station, of a bright eruption in the lunar crater Alphonsus on Nov. 4, 1958. Between 0300 U.T. and 0330 U.T., the outline of the central peak of Alphonsus grew blurred and a short-lived reddish cloud appeared. A spectrum taken with the Crimean observatory 50-in. reflector from 0230 U.T. to 0300 U.T. was weak in the ultra-violet (presumably owing to scattering by dust), while a further spectrum exposed from 0300 U.T. to 0330 U.T. showed emission bands of C_2 and C_3 molecules, somewhat resembling the spectrum of a comet head, and revealing the presence of expelled gases either heated to incandescence or reflecting sunlight by resonance scattering. Observations a fortnight later (when this area was again illuminated by sunlight) revealed no permanent change in the area. A remarkable development in lunar studies was the series of photographs of the invisible side of the moon taken on Oct. 7, 1959, by the third Soviet Lunik and automatically transmitted to the ground 11 days later. Somewhat fewer features appeared than on the visible side, but it was felt that further pictures were needed before firm conclusions could be drawn.

In the afternoon of July 7, 1959, the bright star α Leonis (Regulus) was occulted by the planet Venus. Several observers took advantage of this very rare occurrence to study the structure of the Venusian atmosphere by visual, cinematographic and photoelectric observations, mainly in the Mediterranean area. At the Péridier observatory in southern France, G. de Vaucouleurs and R. Levy found that the light from Regulus diminished for 5 sec. before disappearing completely and inferred an atmospheric scale height of 6 km. between 100 km. and 150 km. above the planet's surface (compared with 8 km. in the earth's atmosphere). William M. Sinton contributed to the question of plant life on Mars by reporting infra-red observations with the coudé spectrograph of the 200-in. Palomar reflector during the planet's 1958 opposition. In the dark areas, Sinton found three infra-red absorption bands near 3·5 microns wave-length, two of which coincide with those produced by organic molecules in terrestrial plants.

Stellar Structure and Evolution. O. J. Eggen and A. R. Sandage examined the effect of the weakness of absorption lines characteristic of Population II stars on their measured colour indices. Using the solar spectrum as a standard, they showed that the removal of absorption lines displaces representative points in the two-colour-index diagram (ultra-violet **U** *minus* blue magnitude **B** plotted against blue **B** *minus* visual magnitude **V**) along a " blanketing line " (analogous to the " reddening line " that indicates the effect of differential absorption by interstellar dust), and that the amount of the displacement along this blanketing line needed to represent a star of the same surface temperature with absorption lines of normal strength could be determined from measurements of the " ultra-violet excess "; *i.e.*, the amount by which the observed **U-B** colour index falls short of the normal value for

This 85-ft. steerable radio telescope was dedicated on Oct. 7 by the University of Michigan. It is the first in the United States.

given **B-V**. Eggen and Sandage showed that when this correction is applied to subdwarfs, which form a sequence below and parallel to the main sequence in the ordinary colour-luminosity diagram, they are shifted into close coincidence with the normal main sequence as defined by the stars in the Hyades. Hence subdwarfs do not form a separate sequence in a diagram in which total energy output (as opposed to luminosity in the visual spectral range) is plotted against effective surface temperature. Their poverty in heavy elements affects the observed colours because of the consequent abnormal faintness of absorption lines, but does not affect the basic structural relation between luminosity and radius (and, presumably, mass); this result is consistent with the dominance of free-free absorption processes, rather than photoelectric absorption, in stellar interiors.

In a further paper, Eggen and Sandage used proper motion and radial velocity data to establish the existence of a nearby moving group of subdwarfs including the variable RR Lyrae, estimating the visual magnitude of the latter at $+0^m8$ (fainter than previously assumed, but consistent with recent statistical-parallax data for RR Lyrae stars in general). This calibration of RR Lyrae star luminosities is important in estimating the distances of globular clusters, many of which are rich in variables of this type. Four other RR Lyrae stars were identified as members of moving groups, leading to a mean absolute magnitude of $+0^m6$. This result confirmed calculations by C. B. Haselgrove and F. Hoyle, leading to the conclusion that the age of the galaxy must exceed 10^{10} years and thus once more approaching Sandage's revised time scale for the expansion of the universe. An application by Eggen of the blanketing correction to the old galactic cluster M 67 and to subgiants in the moving γ Leonis group suggested that M 67 was at least as old as these subgiants, thus removing a difficulty in the theory of the evolution of giants and subgiants away from the main sequence, the brighter stars moving off first. Furthermore, the group parallax of γ Leonis itself, which is a visual binary giant star, enabled Eggen to establish that the sum of the masses of the two components does not exceed $2\cdot7$ times that of the sun, in agreement with the view that they evolved from the main sequence with an initial luminosity much lower than they possess now.

Galactic Structure and Stellar Populations. Frank D. Drake, at the U.S. National Radio Astronomy observatory, traced the galactic centre region simultaneously on 22 cm. and 3·75 cm. wave-lengths and found that the shorter wave-length tracings revealed four separate features, the strongest of which was three minutes of arc away from the centre of the unresolved source found at 22 cm. At the Perkins observatory, Ohio, S. van den Bergh studied the distribution of periods of cepheid variables at various galactic longitudes and showed that short periods (two to six days) predominate in the anticentre direction, while long periods (10 to 30 days) are commonest towards the centre; a similar effect exists in the Magellanic Clouds. Photoelectric measurements of cepheids in six colours by G. E. Kron and S. N. Svolopoulos at the Lick observatory suggested that the long-known fact that galactic cepheids are redder than the Magellanic Cloud cepheids could not be explained by interstellar absorption alone and must be attributed to intrinsic differences.

Cosmology. A new method of estimating the ages and stellar contents of galaxies by spectral classification was developed by W. W. Morgan of the Yerkes observatory and N. U. Mayall of the Lick observatory, who showed that one could distinguish types a, f, g, k (corresponding to stellar spectral types A, F. G, K) and intermediate types and correlate these with morphological features, colours, mass-luminosity ratios and star counts. The use of several of these methods by various astronomers in the examination of galaxies, clusters and the solar neighbourhood led to a more complex picture than the simple division into old (Population II) and young (Population I) systems accepted some years previously. In particular, studies of elliptical galaxies by W. G. Tift, W. A. Baum and A. D. Code suggested that, while the dwarf ellipticals are pure Population II, giant ellipticals are mixed Population II and old Population I (resembling the galactic cluster M 67). (*See also* RADIO, SCIENTIFIC DEVELOPMENTS IN; SPACE EXPLORATION.)

(B. E. J. P.)

BIBLIOGRAPHY. R. H. Baker, *Astronomy*, 7th ed., (Princeton, 1959); R. N. Bracewell (ed.), *Paris Symposium on Radio Astronomy* (Stanford, 1959); S. Flügge (ed.), *Encyclopædia of Physics*, vols. 50-53 (Berlin, 1958-59); E. F. Freundlich, *Celestial Mechanics* (London, 1958); Z. Kopal, *Close Binary Systems* (London, 1959); B. Lehnert (ed.), *Electromagnetic Phenomena in Cosmical Physics* (Cambridge, 1958); H. W. Newton, *The Face of the Sun* (London, 1958); D. J. K. O'Connell (ed.), *Stellar Populations* (Rome, 1958); D. J. K. O'Connell, *The Green Flash, and Other Low Sun Phenomena* (New York, 1958); E. J. Öpik, *Physics of Meteor Flight in the Atmosphere* (New York, 1959); O. Struve and others, *Elementary Astronomy* (Oxford, 1959); G. J. Whitrow, *The Structure and Evolution of the Universe* (London, 1959).

ATHLETICS. Unlike 1958, the pre-Olympic season of 1959 was not dominated by a single athlete. Indeed the Australian mile record holder, H. J. Elliott, achieved little though he did contribute one of the only four sub-four-minute miles of the year.

The two major occasions were the second United States *v.* U.S.S.R. match at Philadelphia on July 18-19 and the third Pan-American games in Chicago the following month. In the former at Franklin field the United States won the men's match by 19 points (127-108) but lost the women's match 40 points to 67. The outstanding performances were those of the coloured Californian, O. R. Norton, who took the two sprints in 10·3 sec. and 20·7 sec. (round a turn) and brought the U.S. sprint relay team home in 39·8 sec.; G. C. Bell's (U.S.) 26 ft. 7 in. long jump; O'Brien's world record shot putt (*see* table in SPORTING RECORD) and the Soviet V. D. Kuznetsov's decathlon of 8,350 points. Notable among the women's performances were the U.S. 200-m. record by L. Williams in 23·4 sec. and the Soviet victories in the high jump (5 ft. 10 in., T. Chenchik), shot putt (55 ft. 6¾ in., T. P. Press), and discus throw (185 ft. 1½ in., N. Ponomareva).

The international match scoring system failed to reflect the United States' immense superiority on the track. The U.S.S.R.'s solid progress was best evidenced in the high jump in which R. Shavlakadze won the four-way tie at 6 ft. 9 in. and by V. Rudenkov, who defeated the Olympic hammer champion H. V. Connolly. The U.S.S.R. maintained its place as the world's second and Europe's number one power, though in the early season in Warsaw on June 27-28 its national team labelled only "Russian Soviet Federated Socialist Republic" was defeated 104 points to 108 by Poland's national team which, in retaliation, was named "West Poland". This incident was one of several examples of strained sporting relations between eastern European countries. The U.S.S.R. rather surprisingly crushed the team of the German Federal Republic in Moscow on Aug. 22-23 by 129 points to 91. In turn the west Germans defeated the Poles (111-101) at Cologne on Sept. 19-20, so the year's European order emerged as 1, U.S.S.R.; 2, German Federal Republic; 3, Poland; 4, Great Britain; 5, France.

For the first time the International Amateur Athletic federation (I.A.A.F.) differentiated between 200 m. and 220 yd. records made on a straight track and those made around a turn. This long overdue reform was justified by the fact that straight furlongs can be run at least two-fifths of a second faster than those round a 180° bend. Legislation on the permissible thickness of shoes used by high jumpers (maximum 13 mm.) was reflected in the fact that none of three Soviet jumpers, who in 1957 cleared heights in excess of seven feet, were able to repeat this. The reduction of the throwing sector from 90° to 60° resulted in fewer foul throws among discus throwers than among hammer throwers. In May the council of the International Amateur Athletic federation fixed, for the first time, qualifying standards for the athletic

C. W. Fairbrother (G.B.) clears 6ft. 8¾in. for 2nd place in the high jump at Rome on Oct. 10. S. Pettersson (Sweden) won at 6ft. 9½in.

events. Though every nation would have the right to enter one competitor, irrespective of standard, in each event, they would only have the right to enter a second and third competitor provided that all reached the standard laid down (*see* table). These are as follows:

Men

100 m.	.	.	.	10·4 sec.	(or 9·5 sec. for 100 yd.)
200 m.	.	.	.	21·3 sec.	(or 21·4 sec. for 220 yd.)
400 m.	.	.	.	47·3 sec.	(or 47·6 sec. for 440 yd.)
800 m.	.	.	1 min. 49·2 sec.	(or 1 min. 49·8 sec. for 880 yd.)
1,500 m.		.	3 min. 45·0 sec.	(or 4 min. 2·0 sec. for 1 mi.)
5,000 m.	.	14 min. 10·0 sec.	(or 13 min. 45·0 sec. for 3 mi.)
10,000 m.	.	29 min. 40·0 sec.	(or 28 min. 45·0 sec. for 6 mi.)
3,000 m. steeplechase	8 min. 55·0 sec.		
110 m. hurdles	.	.	14·4 sec.	(or 14·4 sec. for 120 yd.)
400 m. hurdles	.	.	52·2 sec.	(or 52·5 sec. for 440 yd.)
High jump	.	.	2·05 m.	(or 6 ft. 8¾ in.)
Pole vault	.	.	4·40 m.	(or 14 ft. 5¼ in.)
Long jump	.	.	7·50 m.	(or 24 ft. 7¼ in.)
Hop, step and jump	.	15·60 m.	(or 51 ft. 2 in.)
Shot	.	.	.	17·00 m.	(or 55 ft. 9¼ in.)
Discus	.	.	.	53·00 m.	(or 173 ft. 10½ in.)
Hammer	.	.	62·00 m.	(or 203 ft. 5 in.)
Javelin	.	.	76·50 m.	(or 251 ft. 0 in.)
Decathlon	.	.	6,750 pts.	

Women

100 m.	.	.	.	11·8 sec.	(or 10·9 sec. for 100 yd.)
200 m.	.	.	.	24·3 sec.	(or 24·5 sec. for 220 yd.)
800 m.	.	.	2 min. 12·0 sec.	(or 2 min. 13·0 sec. for 880 yd.)
80 m. hurdles	.	.	11·2 sec.	
High jump	.	.	1·67 m.	(or 5 ft. 5¾ in.)
Long jump	.	.	5·90 m.	(or 19 ft. 4¼ in.)
Shot	.	.	.	14·60 m.	(or 47 ft. 10¾ in.)
Discus	.	.	.	48·0 m.	(or 157 ft. 6 in.)
Javelin	.	.	49·0 m.	(or 160 ft. 9½ in.)

In October it became known from sources in the German Democratic republic that the 32-year old Soviet athlete, V. P. Kuts, who in a short career set up eight world records and captured both the 5,000 m. and 10,000 m. Olympic titles at Melbourne, was in very poor health. Z. Krzyszkowiak, the brilliant 1958 European champion of the same distances, was also in declining form owing to digestive ailments of the kind which afflicted both Kuts and E. Zátopek. (*See* also SPORT-ING RECORD.) (N. McW.)

ATOMIC ENERGY: *see* NUCLEAR ENERGY.

AUSTRALIA, COMMONWEALTH OF.

A realm of the Commonwealth of Nations in the southern hemisphere. Federal cap.: Canberra. Areas and populations of the federated states, Northern Territory and Australian Capital Territory are given in the table below. Cities (apart from the larger state capitals) with pop. of more than 100,000 in 1959: Newcastle, N.S.W. (1958 est.) 192,940, Greater Wollongong, N.S.W. (1958 est.) 112,390. Territories under the administration of the Commonwealth of Australia but not included in it comprise: Papua and the trust territory of New Guinea (*see* PAPUA-NEW GUINEA; TRUST TERRITORIES); Norfolk Island (13·3 sq.mi., pop. [1957 est.] 1,060); the island trust territory of Nauru (8·2 sq.mi., pop. [1954 census] 3,473, [1958 est.] 4,308); Christmas Island (55 sq.mi., pop. [1959 est.] 2,810); Ashmore and Cartier islands, Heard and Macdonald islands (113 sq.mi.); Cocos (Keeling) islands (5 sq.mi., pop. [1958 est.] 600); and the Australian antarctic territory (*c.* 2,362,875 sq.mi.). Language: English. Religion (1954 census): Anglican 3,408,850; Roman Catholic 2,060,986; Methodist 977,933; Presbyterian 870,242; Baptist 127,444; Lutheran 116,178; Church of Christ 80,344; Greek Orthodox 74,760; Congregational 69,452; other Christian 247,485; Jewish 48,439; other non-Christian 6,378; indefinite and no religion 42,140; no reply 855,819. Queen, Elizabeth II; governor-general, Field Marshal Sir William Slim; prime minister, Robert Gordon Menzies. Main imports: motor vehicles and parts, machinery, cotton fabrics, petroleum and products, drugs and chemicals, electrical goods, paper, iron and steel. Main exports: wool, meats, wheat, butter and sugar, hides and skins, ores and concentrates, lead and alloys. Monetary unit: Australian pound (£A125 = £100 sterling, £A45 = U.S. $100).

History. *General.* A demographic milestone was passed in March 1959, with the birth of the ten millionth Australian. The number of births in 1958 (222,504) set a new record, and marked the tenth consecutive annual increase. The number of immigrants arriving that year numbered 109,857, not far below the target of 115,000, but the excess of arrivals over departures was only 64,879. About 100 families, otherwise unqualified for admission, were accepted in response to the International Refugee organization's effort to settle displaced persons. For the first time Spanish immigrants numbered some hundreds. The government increased the target for 1960 to 125,000, expressing confidence that this number could be reached.

Official policy still explicitly favoured the immigration of Britons, to whom still stronger inducements were made. The Belgian, French, Italian and Greek governments agreed to proposals which would facilitate the migration of their nationals to Australia. Two notable visitors to the country—Learie Constantine, the West Indian parliamentarian and former test cricketer, and V. K. Rao, the vice-chancellor of Delhi university—criticized the exclusion of coloured immigrants from Australia.

The early parliamentary session of the year was notable for controversy over increased salaries for members (*see* HOUSES OF PARLIAMENT) and for the passage of the banking legislation first proposed in 1957. The banking legislation separated the country's central bank from its other banking institutions and reconstituted it as the Reserve Bank of Australia. The administration of the established trading and savings banks and the new development bank were vested in the Commonwealth Banking corporation. Warren D. McDonald became the first chairman of the corporation.

Presenting his first budget in August, the treasurer, H. E. Holt, declared that the government had sought to offer incentives to effort and enterprise without threatening the stability of the economy. The major concession was a flat 5% reduction in income tax, while other measures aimed to encourage investment, especially from overseas. Several pension and social service payments were increased and the pharmaceutical benefits scheme was reorganized. On the other hand, postage and telephone rates were raised, provoking strong opposition, particularly from groups which stood to suffer from the new bulk postage costs, and the government subsequently modified some of the details. The opposition attacked the budget as designed to benefit the rich man disproportionately, notably by infringing the principle of progressive taxation. Total government revenue was estimated at £A1,621·3 million and expenditure at £A1,682·3 million.

The attorney-general, Sir Garfield Barwick, introduced a bill for the establishment of a uniform divorce law throughout the country, which brought together the more liberal provisions of the various state codes. The bill evoked criticism from both the Anglican and Roman Catholic Churches. After a lengthy debate it was submitted to a free vote in parliament, and passed with only minor amendments.

The government came under fire from its back-bench supporters on all major issues. Unrest came to a head when Sir Wilfrid Kent Hughes sought unsuccessfully to persuade the Parliamentary Liberal party henceforth to elect cabinet representatives instead of leaving the matter to its leader's discretion. Meanwhile H. V. Evatt survived E. J. Ward's challenge to his leadership of the opposition and the Parliamentary Australian Labour party.

At the annual conference of the Democratic Labour party S. M. Keon attacked sectarian influences which, he alleged, sought to dominate the party. He was subsequently deposed as senior vice-president. The D.L.P. suffered a setback when

the High Court reversed the more important judgments of the Tasmanian Supreme Court in the case of Frank and Dennis Hursey (*see* article on AUSTRALIA in *Britannica Book of the Year 1959*). Members of the D.L.P., the Hurseys had denied the validity of an electoral levy in aid of the A.L.P. imposed by the Tasmanian Waterside Workers' federation. The High Court declared such an impost legitimate.

The Communist party appeared prominently for the first time for some years in connection with a disarmament conference held in Melbourne in November. The government denounced the conference (which numbered J. B. Priestley and Linus Pauling among its participants) as Communist-organized.

The Commonwealth Parliamentary association met in Canberra in November, under the chairmanship of Sir A. McMullin. The delegates included Earl Attlee and Tengku Abdul Rahman, the prime minister of Malaya.

Various celebrations were held to mark the centenary of Queensland. A high light was the tour (extended to Victoria and New South Wales) of Princess Alexandra. Many buildings were opened, local festivals were held and improvement works launched.

Elections were held in New South Wales, Tasmania, South Australia and Western Australia. Only in Western Australia was there a change of government, the D.L.P.'s unusual

Scenes from Princess Alexandra's tour of Australia in August and September: (Left) The princess in the royal barge at Coronation drive, Brisbane. In the course of an eight-mile journey down the winding Brisbane river she took the wheel herself and steered close to the banks lined with cheering crowds. (Top left) Talking with Australian veterans of World War I during a visit to the soldiers' home at Narrabeen, Sydney. (Above) The princess accompanied by the premier of Victoria, H. E. Bolte, at a state reception which was held in her honour in Melbourne on Sept. 17.

strength in this state contributing largely to the defeat of the A.L.P. The new premier, David Brand, had a solid Western Australian background and some ministerial experience. The Tasmanian election was precipitated by the expulsion from the A.L.P. of its treasurer, R. J. Turnbull. Standing as an Independent, he was returned to parliament with a high vote, while the A.L.P. won a narrow victory. The A.L.P.'s victory in New South Wales emphasized the skill of the premier, J. J. Cahill (*see* OBITUARIES), in maintaining unity throughout a period of crisis. His successor, R. J. Heffron, had been minister of education since 1944 and deputy premier since 1952. C. Cutler and R. W. Askin became leaders of the New South Wales Country and Liberal parties respectively.

The South Australian election was uneventful, but later in the year the state was shaken by the case of R. M. Stuart, an aboriginal who was sentenced to death for the murder of a nine-year-old girl. A group of people who believed that Stuart had been wrongfully convicted managed to get his execution postponed several times, and finally a Royal commission was appointed to re-investigate the whole case. Stuart's sentence was remitted to one of life imprisonment. The findings of the commission supported the original verdict and exonerated the police concerned.

The Defence Department of the public service moved from Melbourne to Canberra during the year. A committee under Sir Richard Boyer advised that public service recruitment should become more flexible, and that seniority alone should have no effect on promotion.

The recently appointed archbishop of Sydney, H. R. Gough, became the new Anglican primate. An interesting item of news for Australians was the awarding of a K.C.M.G. to the Roman Catholic archbishop of Brisbane, James Duhig. All Protestant Churches joined in sponsoring the Australian tour of the U.S. evangelist, Billy Graham.

The Economy. For the financial year to June 30, 1959, the gross national product rose from £A5,852 million to £A6,197 million. Half-way through this period the balance of trade was markedly unfavourable, but a strong recovery enabled exports to reach the value of £A813·8 million, £A17·1 million more than the total value of imports. This was achieved despite a fall in wool prices to the lowest level in ten years. The indefinite continuation of such a trend would inevitably become dangerous, but it had so far had remarkably little ill effect. Meanwhile, wool production reached a peak at 1,557 million lb. The same bountiful season was enjoyed by most farm products, the total output being estimated at 8% higher than ever before. The volume and value of meat exports reached a record level. The substantial inflow of foreign capital, the unprecedented number of registrations of new motor cars and the most rapid construction of home units since World War II—all emphasized and contributed to the pervading optimistic spirit. The Federal Arbitration commission gave expression to this confidence when in June it ordered basic wage increases of 15s. a week for men (bringing the minimum wage up to £A14 3s. in Sydney) and 11s. 3d. for women.

There were however some shadows. The cost of living continued to rise appreciably and 63,600 persons were registered as unemployed in July. The deficit on the international balance of payments amounted to £A187 million, reserves having fallen by £A10 million to £A515 million. The hire-purchase debt continued to rise—but less sharply than in 1958—to reach £A360 million on Aug. 31.

The promotion of trade attracted considerable attention. One trade mission toured the African continent, concentrating on the central and eastern territories with some success, while another visited Czechoslovakia and Poland. Canada, the German Federal Republic, The West Indies, Burma and Indonesia were among other countries in which possibilities for expansion were investigated. The second annual review of the Japanese Trade agreement was concluded with satisfaction on both sides. Moves towards economic unification in Europe caused some misgivings.

From Aug. 1 the total import rate allowed by the government rose by £A50 million per annum, and most discrimination against dollar imports was removed. The Tariff Board studied some 250 items with a view to liberalizing the general structure of duties.

The development of the national economy continued steadily. The Manufacturing Industries Advisory council pointed out that in 1958 manufacturing employed 30·3% of the labour force, compared with 18·1% employed by commerce and 13·6% by primary industry. This proportion was higher than the comparable figure in the United States and was certain to increase. A notable event in the industrial field was the release of the British Motor corporation's first Australian car, a four-cylinder Morris saloon, 96% of which was manufactured in Australia. The Malkara missile, designed and produced in Australia, became standard anti-tank equipment in the British army. The production of investment goods increased more rapidly than that of consumer goods—a significant departure from the pattern of the preceding years. An extensive petro-chemical plant was projected for Altona, Victoria, where Australia's first carbon-black factory opened in October. The oil refinery at Kurnell, Sydney, and the aluminium works at Bell bay, Tasmania, were both to be expanded.

Primary industries were not neglected. The Commonwealth Scientific and Industrial Research organization publicized a new wool-dyeing method and a process for imparting drip-dry qualities to woollen fabric. The organization also developed a " bullet " for the treatment of cattle deficient in cobalt and a technique of adding gypsum to irrigation water to facilitate its infiltration into the heavy clay soils of the Riverina district. C. S. Christian, a leading officer of C.S.I.R.O., declared that proper land utilization in the Northern Territory could render 3,000 sq.mi. suitable for prosperous mixed farming. A new section of the organization began research on tropical pastures. The government appointed a committee to inquire into the workings of the dairy industry and allocated £175,000 for wheat research in 1959-60. The Commonwealth Bureau of Mineral Resources continued to be active in the search for further deposits of

State or territory	Capital (with pop. mid-1958 est.)	Area (sq.mi.)	Population* (1954 census)	Population* (March 1959 est.)	Premier (at Dec. 31, 1959)	Ministry
New South Wales . .	Sydney (2,016,620)	309,433	3,423,529	3,745,201	R. J. Heffron	Labour
Victoria . . .	Melbourne (1,726,100)	87,884	2,452,341	2,796,959	H. E. Bolte	Liberal and Country
Queensland . .	Brisbane (555,000)	670,500	1,318,258	1,428,656	G. F. R. Nicklin	Country-Liberal
South Australia .	Adelaide (548,000)	380,070	797,094	914,763	Sir Thomas Playford	Liberal and Country
Western Australia .	Perth (382,000)†	975,920	639,771	714,569	D. Brand	Liberal-Country
Tasmania . . .	Hobart (105,110)	26,215	308,752	343,990	E. E. Reece	Labour
Northern Territory .	Darwin (8,066)	523,620	16,469	19,747	J. C. Archer‡	
Australian Capital Territory	Canberra (39,061)	939§	30,315	44,780		
		2,974,581	8,986,529	10,008,665		

* Excl. full-blooded aborigines (1947) 46,638, but incl. half-caste (1954) 27,179.   † Incl. Fremantle.   ‡ Administrator.   § Incl. 28 sq.mi. at Jervis Bay (federal port, 90 mi. E.N.E. of Canberra).

tin, copper, gold, uranium and bauxite. As ever, the quest for oil was pursued vigorously, but in vain. On April 28 the first power from a major generating station in the Snowy Mountains scheme flowed into the New South Wales electricity system. The main storage dam in the Kiewa (Victoria) hydroelectric complex was completed. Situated 5,338 ft. above sea level, it was the highest dam in the country.

The " Princess of Tasmania " brought new standards of comfort and convenience to the crossing of Bass strait between Melbourne and the northern Tasmanian coast. She accommodated 100 cars, including heavy lorries, and both tourism and industry promised to benefit. After protracted negotiations the federal government guaranteed a loan of £A20 million to Queensland for the reconstruction of the Townsville-Mount Isa railway. Estimated to cost £A30 million in all, the project could become a vital factor in the development of north Queensland.

Business history provided the most dramatic elements in the year's economic activity. Stocks and shares of almost every description enjoyed a remarkable buoyancy. In the week to July 13, there were new trading records on both the Melbourne and Sydney stock exchanges, with calls continuing for hours longer than usual. Most companies reported big profits. The total for General Motors-Holden was £A15,343,107 for the year ended Dec. 31, 1958—the largest ever achieved by an Australian firm—while Broken Hill Proprietory netted £10,214,911. Amalgamations and take-over bids proceeded rapidly, although the biggest move of this nature ever projected in Australia—the purchase of Adelaide Steamship company shares by H. C. Sleigh, Ltd.— fell through. Entrepreneurs in the hotel business, credit-finance corporations, real estate and construction companies were much in the public eye.

External Affairs. Although the broad lines of Australian policy showed no change during 1959 there were nevertheless some interesting developments. The visit of the Indonesian foreign minister, Dr. Subandrio, ended with a declaration by the government that while still recognizing the Netherlands' sovereignty in West New Guinea, it would not object to a Dutch-Indonesian agreement about its transfer. Both the parliamentary A.L.P. and several right-wing spokesmen saw this as a substantial modification of the government's previous attitude and suggested the possibility that a hostile power might become Australia's immediate neighbour.

Diplomatic relations with the U.S.S.R., broken off in 1954 as a consequence of the Petrov affair, were resumed. The missions to Brazil, Belgium and the Republic of Vietnam were raised to embassy level.

The government enthusiastically supported the British prime minister's negotiations for a summit conference. The Australian prime minister, R. G. Menzies, himself canvassed the idea on his world tour, and H. V. Evatt expressed his approval.

The U.N. Economic Commission for Asia and the Far East held its 15th session at Broadbeach, Queensland, in March. The chief issues discussed were the fluctuations in world prices of vital export commodities, the problem of ever-increasing population, the effect on world trade of the European common market and the prospects for expanded industrialization throughout Asia. One specific project which attracted interest was the development of the Mekong river in southeastern Asia, potentially valuable to Laos, Thailand, Cambodia and Vietnam. Australia offered technical aid worth £100,000 for this scheme.

Early in the year international symposia were held at Melbourne and Canberra on various aspects of Antarctic science including meteorology, mapping, biology and radio communication. Australia also participated actively in the Washington conference on the future of Antarctica. The

Queensland's premier, G. F. R. Nicklin, speaking at the opening of the British pavilion at the Queensland centenary exhibition.

government's stated policy was to secure the freedom of scientific research, non-militarization and the suspension of territorial claims.

R. G. Menzies' travels extended to Britain, other major European countries, the United States, Canada, New Zealand, Singapore, Pakistan, India, Malaya and Indonesia. R. G. Casey, the minister for external affairs, also visited several of these countries as well as Thailand, Japan and the Republic of Korea. Visitors to Australia included the British minister of agriculture, John Hare, and the U.S. secretary of defence, Neil McElroy.

Educational and Scientific. The expansion of educational facilities continued steadily. An important event was the establishment of a universities commission under the chairmanship of Sir Leslie Martin. It was to advise the government, particularly on the allocation of finance. The first scholarships under a government scheme to encourage post-graduate research were awarded. Canberra University college was separated from the University of Melbourne but its precise status remained uncertain. Educationists in every field joined together to establish the Australian College of Education.

A National Heart foundation, intended to finance research into heart diseases, was established in February. The Academy of Science appointed a committee for space research under the chairmanship of Professor L. G. H. Huxley, who suggested that satellites could be launched from the Woomera rocket range. Sir John Eccles, the president of the academy, was elected an honorary member of the American Academy of Arts and Sciences. The Commonwealth and Scientific Industrial Research organization suffered a great loss with the death of its chairman, Sir Ian Clunies Ross. His own scientific work (dealing with the control of sheep parasites) was of the highest quality, and he had served many humanist causes with distinction. The new chairman of the C.S.I.R.O. was F. W. G. White, by birth a New Zealander, whose scientific interests included radio physics, biology and wool technology.

The Arts and Entertainment. Randolph Stow won further acclaim with his third novel, *To The Islands*, set on an aboriginal mission station in Western Australia. Another young writer from an outlying state, Christopher Koch, used a Tasmanian background with rare effect in *The Boys In The Island*. Veteran novelists who published work during 1959 included Xavier Herbert (*Seven Emus*), Leonard Mann (*Andrea Caslin*) and Vance Palmer (*The Big Fellow*). Palmer's death (*see* OBITUARIES) prompted recall of the great service given by himself and his wife to Australian letters. Collections of short stories included *Coast to Coast* edited by Dal Stevens, *West Coast Stories* edited by Henrietta Drake-Brockman, *Evening under Lamplight* by David Campbell and *The Little Ghosts* by Ethel Anderson. Among poets whose work appeared in collected editions were David Rowbotham, Ian Mudie, Nan MacDonald and William Hart-Smith. Vincent Buckley edited *Australian Poetry 1958*. Historical studies gained most from *Alexander Maconochie of Norfolk Island* by J. V. Barry, *Catholic Education in Australia* by R. Fogarty, *South West Pacific, First Year* by Dudley McCarthy, *The Generations of Men* by Judith Wright and *The Australian Legend* by Russel Ward. Other notable titles were *The Moral Point of View* by Kurt Baier, *Public Administration in Australia* edited by R. N. Spann, *Catholic Action in Politics* by Tom Truman, *The Development of Australian Trade Union Law* by J. H. Portus and *Aggression and World Order* by Julius Stone. *The Melbourne Critical Review*, *The Australian Journal of Statistics* and *The Journal of Industrial Relations* were learned periodicals which appeared for the first time in 1958-59.

Two important buildings were opened. The Sidney Myer Music Bowl, Melbourne, was a vast aluminium canopy, sheltering a stage and seating more than 2,000. Another 20,000 could gather in the splendid parklands at the rear. The American Institute of Architects described the bowl as " functional, beautiful and dignified . . . a new concept of enclosing space which should have a great influence on the architecture of our time." B. B. Patten of Yuncken, Freeman Brothers, was the chief designer. The headquarters of the Australian Academy of Science at Canberra (architects— Grounds, Romberg and Boyd) was a copper-sheathed dome, wholly surrounded by a moat. The central conference room was executed with a most impressive perfection of detail.

Eight artists styling themselves " The Antipodeans " presented an interesting exhibition in Melbourne. They sought to " defend the place of the image in art against the present fashionable tendencies that seek to abolish it." Thomas Gleghorn and Eric Smith were among other painters who commanded particular attention. Albert Namatjira died in August (*see* OBITUARIES); his watercolours of the Northern

Territory had established a new era of aboriginal art. A competition for three fountains to be built in Sydney attracted many imaginative designs, the major prize being awarded to R. Woodward and P. Taranto.

The visit of an ensemble from the Bolshoi ballet, which included Yuri Kondratov and Rimma Karelskaya, was a great success. Other overseas groups which visited Australia were the Czech Philharmonic orchestra and the Yugoslav " Kola " song-and-dance troup. Concerts were also presented by the U.S. conductor Alfred Wallenstein, the Hungarian pianist Andor Foldes, the Rumanian conductor Constantin Silvestri, the Czech pianist Rudolf Firkusny, the French organist Pierre Cochereau, and the singers Mattiwilda Dobbs, Jan Peerce, Gerald Souzay and Igor Gorin. The success of the Australian Joan Sutherland in the Covent Garden, London, production of *Lucia di Lammermoor* won general acclaim.

The Piccadilly Bushman, produced in Melbourne, demonstrated that Australian playwright Ray Lawler had not exhausted his talent in his famous *Summer of the Seventeenth Doll*. His new work investigated with sympathy and intelligence the perennial theme of the Australian love-hate for Britain. Drama throughout the country continued to be encouraged by the Elizabethan Theatre trust. The trust's outstanding production was Eugene O'Neill's *Long Day's Journey into Night*, while a new Australian venture was J. A. Coburn's *The Bastard Country* (alternatively named *Fire on the Wind*). Long Shakespearian seasons were presented in Melbourne and Sydney by a company under the direction of John Alden.

Visiting popular entertainers included Danny Kaye, Joyce Grenfell and Sabrina. The " Rock 'n' Roll " boom produced a number of talented local exponents including Col Joye, Dig Richards, Johnny Devlin and Johnny Rebb. Television was first broadcast in Brisbane and Adelaide, and plans continued for its diffusion throughout rural areas. The control of this medium by newspaper interests and the high proportion of U.S. material broadcast came under heavy criticism.

Ava Gardner, Gregory Peck and Fred Astaire went to Australia on location for the film *On the Beach*, and Peter Ustinov, Deborah Kerr and Robert Mitchum for *The Sundowners*.

Two striking architectural structures completed in Australia in 1959. (Above) The Academy of Science building, Canberra, a copper-sheathed dome designed by Grounds, Romberg and Boyd, opened on May 7. (Right) The Sidney Myer "music bowl", Melbourne, designed by B. B. Patten and opened on Feb. 12. Its plywood and aluminium canopy is supported by a steel cable slung over two 70-ft. masts.

Sport. The year's sport was rather uneventful, excitement coming mainly from the scoring of unexpected victories by national teams. This applied especially to the test cricketers whose successes were particularly welcome, but were largely the result of abysmal play by the England team. The tour of India and Pakistan promised nothing spectacular. In Pakistan Australia won two tests and drew one.

The return of the Davis cup to Australia compensated for the shock defeat of 1958. The " Kangaroos " (Rugby League footballers) enjoyed a better winter in Europe than was generally expected, having earlier won a series 2-1 against New Zealand. Two Rugby Union tests were lost to Britain, while the Scottish Heart of Midlothian soccer team crumpled the best opposition Australia could produce.

The achievement of Jack Brabham in becoming world champion motor-racing driver brought Australia into prominence in a new field. The Canada Cup professional golf tournament, held in Melbourne, was won by Australia. The government of Victoria legalized off-course betting on horse racing, and an inquiry into this subject in Western Australia produced a considerable amount of evidence of a sensational nature. (*See* also PAPUA-NEW GUINEA; TRUST TERRITORIES.)
(O. M. R.)

AUSTRIA. Republic of central Europe, bounded N. by Germany and Czechoslovakia, E. by Hungary, S. by Yugoslavia and Italy and W. by Switzerland. Area: 32,374 sq.mi. Pop.: (1951 census) 6,900,283; (1957 est.) 6,997,000. Language: German 98%, others 2% (mainly Slovene in Carinthia). Religion (1951): Roman Catholic 89·3%; Protestant 6·2%; Jewish 0·16%; most of the remainder professed no religion at all. Principal towns (pop., 1951 census): Vienna (cap.) 1,744,069; Graz 226,453; Linz 184,685; Salzburg 102,927; Innsbruck 95,055; Klagenfurt 62,782. President, Adolf Schärf; chancellor, Julius Raab. Main imports: coal and coke; machinery and vehicles; grain; cotton; wool. Main exports: iron, steel and manufactures; petroleum and products; machinery and vehicles; pulp, paper and manufactures. Monetary unit: *Schilling* (Sch.72·80 = £1 sterling).

History. The most important event during 1959 in Austrian home affairs was the election for the Nationalrat (parliament) on May 10, followed by very complicated and tiresome negotiations to form the government. In March the two ruling parties, the Volkspartei and the Sozialistische Partei, had decided that they could not satisfactorily settle various important questions, and therefore the writ for elections was issued earlier than was required by the constitution. In the elections the Socialists gained four seats and the Christian Democrats (Volkspartei) lost three seats. The Communists lost their three seats and the right-wing Freiheitliche Partei won eight seats, a gain of two. (*See* ELECTIONS.)

The negotiations to form the new government were extremely difficult because the Socialist party had obtained more votes, but had one seat less than the Christian Democrats. The result seemed to indicate that most of the electorate were more discontented with some Christian Democratic ministers and their appointees than completely satisfied with the Socialist programme. The negotiations lasted ten weeks and on July 14 Julius Raab was again installed as chancellor and the posts of ministers were equally divided between the two main parties. The Socialists gained the Ministry of Foreign Affairs, to which they appointed Bruno Kreisky. But their greatest success was achieved in the field of economics by the dissolution of the Industrie- und Bergbau-verwaltung, the state-owned company formed in 1956 to administer centrally all state-owned industrial and mining enterprises (including the oil industry). This became part of the re-formed Ministry of State Enterprises with the Socialist vice-chancellor, Bruno Pittermann, as its head. Local elections in October showed even a greater loss for the Christian Democratic party.

A test for the new coalition was the budget negotiations for 1960, but finally Reinhard Kamitz, the Christian Democratic minister of finance, pushed his Sch.42,000 million proposal

through, which seemed to safeguard a cautiously favourable business juncture. Economically Austria was stronger than ever before and only in the first quarter of the year was slightly affected by the general recession. The industrial production index stood at 162 in April 1959 (1953 = 100), while the cost of living index rose only to 115 (1953 = 100). Unemployment fell to its lowest figure (77,400 in May 1959), the Schilling was sound and no foreign loan was raised during the year.

Austria was interested in the commercial integration of Europe, but its freedom of movement was limited by the state treaty of 1955. The most important commercial partners of Austria were members of the European common market, but membership in this organization was not compatible with Austrian neutrality. Austria, therefore, decided to join the European Free Trade association of the " Seven ", with the possibility of future multilateral agreements with the common market states.

Vienna was becoming a meeting place for east and west. The International Atomic Energy agency had its headquarters here and the city was also the prospective residence of the international agency planned to control the ban on nuclear test explosions.

Destroyed by floods on Aug. 13: the bridge carrying the Munich-Salzburg-Vienna motorway over the River Salzach at Hellbrunn.

From May 16 to 18, 300,000 " Sudetendeutsche ", who after World War II were forced to leave Czechoslovakia, held in Vienna their tenth annual conference. A resolution demanding annexation of the " Sudentenland " by Germany was adopted. At the end of July the Seventh (Communist) Youth festival took place in Vienna. This was the first time that such a festival had been organized outside eastern Europe and the Austrians boycotted it completely. The Austrian youth organizations, through discussions, exhibitions and personal contact, tried to enlighten the Communist participants and explain to them the ideas and principles of the west. While the whole Austrian press ignored the festival, a daily newspaper in seven different languages supplied the Communists with free and independent information.

The Vienna Symphony orchestra was the first orchestra to give a performance in the Vatican in presence of the Pope. The Vienna Philharmonic orchestra made a world tour lasting a month, during which it played in Tokyo, among other places.

In January Raab visited Japan, Nobosuke Kishi, the Japanese prime minister, returning his visit in July. The United States signed at the end of January a treaty concerning the return of Austrian property in accordance with article 27 of the Austrian state treaty. In October President Schärf visited Moscow.

The fate of the German-speaking population of South Tirol caused Austria much concern during the year. Italy had not fulfilled its obligation to grant them a certain autonomy in the province of Alto Adige but had, on the contrary, fostered immigration with the aim of Italianizing the province. At the 150th anniversary of the Tirolean fight for independence against Napoleon, the Tiroleans in Austria assured their brothers in the south of their sympathy and help. Austria felt bound to remind Italy of its obligations. As all Austria's approaches to the Italian government were in vain, the government called on international organizations. First the attention of the Council of Europe was drawn to the matter and in September the foreign minister asked the United Nations for help. (F. P. M.)

AUTOMATION. Following the announcement of the Soviet seven-year plan there was considerable public discussion of the " British need for automation ", though there were few useful suggestions about how to re-equip British industry in " the most automated and modern fashion ". Later Soviet reports stressed many familiar difficulties about their rather modest programme of installing 1,300 automatic and semi-automatic lines before 1966—the lack of training institutions, of work incentives in automatic factories and of knowledge of the economics of automation, and low capacity in industries making the means to automation.

In 1958 sales of computers in Britain rose from £20 to £30 million. E.M.I. and Ferranti, supported by the National Research Development corporation, did further development work on the high-speed computers Emidec 3400 and Atlas. Sirius, a desk-sized, digital, general purpose computer costing £15,000, appeared and Burroughs introduced a low-cost, versatile record computer designed for banking. The Management Consultants association's pamphlet *Preparing for a Computer* explained the functions and costs of computers and the time and organization involved in securing full benefits from these machines.

Other interesting developments were: Pilkington's new float process for producing sheet glass; the Samcomatic automatic machine for fashioned knitwear; a fully automatic hardboard-manufacturing plant; a flame-cutting machine in which exact drawings were fed into a photo-electric tracing system and cutting torches followed the electronic impulses; The E.M.I.-Wadkin electronically controlled automatic drilling machine for accurately positioning and drilling holes in steel of up to 2-in. diameter at very high speed; a largely automatic process for the large-scale production of hydrogen at I.C.I.; and automatic control of the mastication of crude rubber and the subsequent mixing of ingredients for tyre manufacture at Fort Dunlop. There were more machines designed with automatic cycling and loading so that they could be linked up into a production line as required. The Churchill Gear company installed an assembly line of 25 automatically linked standard machines. Gresham Developments announced a system of process control specially suited to small firms; it was made of relatively inexpensive standard units designed to govern a predetermined sequence of operations (*e.g.*, mixing, heating, conveying and pumping). Kinetic packaging

—so that immediately upon receipt the packages could be loaded directly into the first process—increased, particularly for electrical components, such as resistors and capacitors, for screws, nuts and bolts and for small sub-assemblies. In the United States the Martin company and Bendix Aviation corporation developed a new electronically controlled machine tool to reduce " lead time ". Coded information from a blueprint was put on tape and then " read " into the milling machine that automatically turned out finished, precision-built aircraft and missile structural parts. The new machine would eliminate many weeks of setting up and changing tools. (B. R. W.)

AVIATION, CIVIL. Jet aircraft continued to come into greater use during 1959. Apart from the big transcontinental airliners which linked the chief European capitals with America, the Caravelle medium-range jet liner was put into increasing service on European routes by Air France and Scandinavian Airlines system, and before the end of the year British Overseas Airways corporation's Comets were seen regularly at Bahrain, Bombay, Colombo, Rangoon, Singapore, Hongkong and Tokyo. The Comet was also about to reopen the route between London and Buenos Aires soon after it had been made to link North and South America by Aereolinos Argentinos. Qantas put Boeing 707s on the run between Sydney and San Francisco and extended their operations across the United States and the Atlantic to London.

This greater use of jet transports on scheduled services coincided with a recovery in the rate of traffic increase. By Feb. 1959 all classes of traffic were showing signs of rising sufficiently to offset the lag of the previous year. This was to be explained only in part by the introduction of the jets, for British European airways, which had no jet liners in service, reported a rise in passenger traffic of about 22% in the first nine months compared with the same period of 1958. There was also a marked upward trend in freight which, in several months in Britain, showed an increase of more than 30%. The improvement in business on the North Atlantic route was undoubtedly influenced by the new jet services, on which load factors of 90% were frequently reported. The economy fares continued to attract about four passengers for every one who travelled in other classes. This led the British operators to press for an extension of economy-class travel to other main routes besides the Atlantic. They met heavy opposition from a majority of other national carriers.

Among the principal air lines there was anxiety also about the growth of the independent air operators. These had already begun to break into the main airline business by obtaining permission to run cheap-fare services to colonial territories which fell within the scope of cabotage (*i.e.*, were restricted to domestic carriers) and were not subject to International Air Transport association agreements. They had also greatly developed their part in " packaged " tours. In this system operators were free to offer air travel to tourist agents at any fare they pleased, provided it was not less than half the price paid by the tourist for the whole holiday. This sometimes led to fares little more than half the normal tourist rates. Most of the European airlines were engaged in this class of business but, whereas the independents turned over whole fleets of aircraft to it, major lines like B.E.A. and Alitalia usually set aside a certain number of seats in selected scheduled services for packaged tour business. The bulk of this traffic therefore continued to be carried by the independents, who had an extremely prosperous summer. Although B.O.A.C. was little involved in this kind of traffic, it attributed some of its revenue difficulties to the competition of independent carriers on the cabotage routes. Both it and B.E.A. were faced at the end of the year with government proposals

The Soviet TU 114 Rossiya turbo-prop airliner on arrival at Le Bourget from Moscow on June 19 to take part in the Paris international air show. The Rossiya, which seats 225 passengers, stands unusually high on its undercarriage, and extra steps were needed for disembarkation.

to give more scheduled services to independent operators.

In the year ended March 31, 1959, B.O.A.C. had a deficit of some £5 million, half of it said to be due to losses suffered by its subsidiary and associated companies. Part of the remainder arose from interruptions in services through teething troubles of the Britannia turbo-prop liner and part from the cost of training crews for the opening of services by the Comet 4. Most of the other European companies were able to show a profit although they too had felt the effect of the slowing down in the rate of traffic increase. Since they had added to their capacity on the basis of an expected 14% increase and had further additions to come in 1959, the anxiety which these companies felt at the beginning of the year was understandable.

Winter fog in England also cut seriously into revenue. B.E.A. estimated that the cancellation of some 13% of its services in November-February, together with the loss of possible passengers who distrusted the weather, caused a loss of about £200,000. In the end it showed a profit of £230,000 on its financial year, less than a quarter of that made in the previous year. It had been bringing a new type of Viscount turbo-prop liner into service and had achieved a relatively low utilization rate for it. With the older Viscounts it had obtained 2,400 hr. of use per aircraft, the highest rate recorded by B.E.A. for any type of liner and regarded as highly satisfactory in short-haul work. The summer saw it well on the way to a profitable year, with the prospect of introducing shortly the Vanguard turbo-prop liner and the Comet 4B, both markedly faster than the latest Viscount. B.E.A. was therefore expecting to derive the same sort of benefit from an increase in capacity ton-miles, due to speed, as B.O.A.C. was already beginning to enjoy.

The arrival of the Comet on B.O.A.C. services showed clearly how jets could help to lower costs despite their theoretically higher cost of operation per ton-mile as compared with piston-engine types. Because it could offer more ton-miles per flying hour, the same volume of work could be done by a smaller fleet requiring less maintenance work. However, B.O.A.C. had a disappointment during the summer. It had reckoned on completing its round-the-world service in April by extending its route from San Francisco across the Pacific through Honolulu and Wake Island to Tokyo. An objection by a U.S. operator delayed the granting of rights and the new service was not begun until August. The consequent loss in revenue was said to be nearly £1 million. Against that was to be set the undoubted lift given to revenue wherever the Comet was put into service. The best example was on the North Atlantic route where, in the first six months, B.O.A.C.'s passenger traffic increased by 38% as against an average for all operators on that route of 11%. From April to the end of the summer B.O.A.C. was making a profit of about £100,000 a month.

Signs of truly economic helicopter operation in the near future were to be found in B.E.A.'s decision to order six Rotodynes for delivery probably in 1964. This would be the developed Rotodyne using Rolls-Royce turbo-prop engines, having seats for 60 passengers and cruising at 200 m.p.h. While this decision was being taken there was still no firm plan for a heliport for London; and other British cities were awaiting a lead from the government. A heliport on the south bank of the Thames opposite Chelsea was established in early summer and served throughout the year. A project for another on the same bank, but two miles nearer the centre approved and recommended by the minister of transport, was rejected by the minister of housing and local government, who was later being pressed to revise that decision.

While car ferry services across the English channel continued to develop, an extra airport (the former military airfield at Manston) was brought into use near Margate to deal with ferry passengers who used surface transport for the greater part of their journeys between London and other European capitals. At the same time an independent operator was proposing to use D.C.4s to carry up to 5 cars and 25 passengers from England deep into France—as far as Lyons—so that drivers might complete the journey between London and the Riviera in a day.

TABLE I. U.K. CIVIL AIR TRAFFIC: SCHEDULED SERVICES

	All Services		Domestic		International	
	1957-58*	1958-59	1957-58*	1958-59	1957-58*	1958-59
Mi. flown ('000)	85,670	87,096	13,979	13,348	71,696	73,748
Pass. carried	3,990,746	4,068,636	1,583,711	1,489,901	2,407,035	2,578,735
Pass.-mi. ('000)	2,437,623	2,639,613	314,061	309,124	2,123,562	2,330,490
Freight (short tons)†	115,219	144,556	12,625	8,961	102,594	135,594
Freight ('000 short ton-mi.)†	56,830	59,719	1,787	1,713	55,043	58,005
Mail (short tons)†	11,616	11,805	2,789	2,611	8,827	9,193
Mail ('000 short ton-mi.)†	23,834	24,883	481	449	23,353	24,434

* Final figures, replacing those previously issued. † Incl. weight of vehicles, excess baggage and diplomatic bags.
SOURCE. Ministry of Transport and Civil Aviation.

TABLE II. FINANCIAL RESULTS OF U.K. CORPORATIONS
(Financial Year April 1-March 31)

	B.O.A.C.*		B.E.A.	
	1957-58	1958-59	1957-58	1958-59
Operating rev.	£53,526,375	£58,401,855	£28,340,725	£31,761,313
Operating exp.	53,691,926	57,405,743	26,465,070	30,302,824
Op. profit/loss	—165,551	+996,112	+1,875,655	1,458,489
Non-op. exp. (net)	2,673,799	6,175,532	820,848	1,225,794
Profit/loss for year†	—2,839,350	—5,179,420	+1,054,807	+232,695

* Excl. profit or loss on disposal of assets. † After payment of interest on capital.

Airport development in general was awaiting apparently on policy decisions concerning traffic handling. At Gatwick the long, covered pier for embarking passengers had given full satisfaction for more than a year but, recognizing that this had entailed heavy capital expenditure, the Ministry of Transport was experimenting at London airport with an idea for loading and unloading jet aircraft on an open apron in such a way that no inconvenience from blast would arise. This involved arranging a diamond pattern of standings with one aircraft parked on each of the four sides and with taxiing paths to and from these sides so defined that no aircraft would ever direct its blast at another. On the control side, London airport began in September a preferential system of " climb out " for all aircraft using the Decca navigator. This allowed them to climb away after take-off straight on to course instead of having to pass over prescribed beacons on their way out. Decca was regarded as capable of enabling captains to keep an exact course on the " climb out " path with a maximum error of a quarter of a mile. Tests also began late in the year at an R.A.F. station of a new type of Fido (fog dispersal by heat near runways), which promised to reduce the cost of a landing so aided from some thousands of pounds to £300 at most.

United States and Canada. The United States officially entered the commercial jet age on Oct. 26, 1958, when a scheduled U.S.-flag airline flew a commercial turbo-jet aircraft across the Atlantic. Such aircraft cut flying time by about 40%. The Douglas DC-8s were later added to U.S. air fleets and the Convair 880 was expected to go into service in mid-1960.

In 1959 there were about 110,000 U.S. aircraft in operation. Of these, more than 65,000 belonged to the category of flying known as general aviation, including business, industry, agriculture, air taxi, instruction, geophysical research, survey and patrol, and pleasure use. Military flying involved about 43,000 planes. The remainder was made up of airline aircraft, which numbered approximately 1,900. Of this number, about 300 were turbo-prop or turbo-jet aircraft.

During 1958 the scheduled U.S. airlines operated 4,075 million ton-mi.—the highest number in their history. Mail also reached a new record with a 177-million-ton-mi. haul. Express was up 6% to a new peak of 48,837,000 ton-mi., but freight traffic showed a drop. The number of revenue passengers carried fell from 49,339,000 to 49,075,000. In 1958 the airlines took $2,237,469,000 in operating revenues, spent $2,131,542,000 on operating expenses and realized $52,914,000 in net profit after taxes and interest.

The 13 local service airlines in the United States operated 35,586 mi. of unduplicated route during 1958. The number of cities served increased from 468 to 516, of which 283 received their only air service from the local service lines. Passengers increased from 3,943,000 to 4,265,000 and passenger miles from 747·3 million to 820·2 million.

(Left) An earth mound built by Air India at London airport to muffle engine roar during ground running. (Above) Valve gear of the new underground fuelling system at Frankfurt.

The helicopter airlines carried 228,000 passengers and operated 4,885,000 passenger mi. during 1958, representing gains of 54% and 44%, respectively, over the previous year. Available ton-miles reached a new peak of 1,497,000 in 1958, a gain of 41·8% on 1957. Together, the three helicopter lines served 29 points in greater Los Angeles, Chicago and New York, and operated 22 aircraft over 905 route-mi.

During 1958 the U.S. international airlines flew an all-time record of 5,974·6 million revenue passenger mi., a rise of

The Armstrong Whitworth Argosy freighter-coach aircraft in flight. It is powered by four Rolls Royce Dart turbo-prop engines.

3·9% on the previous year. Cargo ton-miles reached a new record of 128,925,000, an increase of 4·6% over 1957, while mail ton-miles jumped from 57,265,000 in 1957 to 65,825,000 in 1958.

Because of the discontinuance of service by one of the all-cargo lines in 1958, the all-cargo carriers showed a 40·2% drop in mail, a 56·2% drop in express and a 31% decrease in freight. They carried 1·1 million ton-mi. of mail, 700,000 ton-mi. of express and 107 million ton-mi. of freight. Total revenue ton-miles for the all-cargo group declined by 11·3% to $298·7 million.

In Nov. 1958, six airlines joined in an agreement, approved by the Civil Aeronautics board, that allowed limited financial assistance to be given in the event of a strike against any member airline. The payments were to be based on the additional revenue received by the carriers still in operation.

Operating revenues of Canadian air carriers in 1958 rose by 5·3% to $200,146,709, and operating expenses increased by 5·2% to $199,240,633, resulting in a surplus of $906,076. During the year Canadian air carriers flew a total of 95,747,996 mi., transporting 4,021,721 revenue passengers and 222,391,217 lb. of revenue cargo, including mail. There were seven domestic scheduled carriers and approximately 120 non-scheduled carriers in operation during 1958. Early in 1959 Canadian Pacific airlines were licensed by the department of transport to operate a scheduled trans-Canada service, using Britannia turbo-prop aircraft. This ended Trans-Canada airlines' monopoly of that service since its inception in 1937. (*See* also COMMUNICATIONS; JET PROPULSION AND GAS TURBINES.)   (E. C. SD.; S. G. TN.; R. J. L.)

AVIATION, MILITARY: *see* AIR FORCES OF THE WORLD.

BACTERIOLOGY. *The Essence of a Virus.* It had been reported several years earlier that virus particles had been

broken into two components, neither of which could initiate infection, while recombination of the protein and nuclei acid fractions resulted in an agent capable of producing the disease and replicating the natural virus. By 1959 techniques had been developed which yielded purified and relatively refined nucleic acids and methods of handling this material so that nucleic acid could be maintained in an active state.

Frederick L. Schaffer and Carl T. Mattern reported that highly purified ribonucleic acid (RNA) from two strains of polio virus, western and eastern equine encephalitis, and foot and mouth disease would infect experimental animals and, when inoculated in tissue cultures, produce typical alterations in the growing cells (cytopathologic changes) which were characteristic of the native virus. They were able to destroy the infectivity and replicating properties, as had other workers by treating the RNA with the specific enzyme ribonuclease, thus demonstrating the association of these characteristics with the intact ribonucleic acid.

Leroy C. McLaren, John H. Holland and Jerome T. Syverton at the University of Minnesota, Minneapolis, working with the RNA extracted from strains of ECHO 8, Coxsackie A-9 and B-1 as well as Polio I viruses, showed that the purified RNA could infect and replicate in tissue cultures which were completely resistant to the native, intact virus; yet the resultant viruses in all ways resembled the original virus particles.

The importance of the nucleic acid component was made evident in yet another way. Igor Tamm of the Rockefeller institute approached the study of antiviral therapy by investigating the effect of the compounds closely resembling the building blocks required in the formation of virus nucleic acids.

In experiments with mouse pneumonia virus Tamm's compounds lengthened the survival time of experimentally infected mice and inhibited some virus multiplication. As Tamm progressed in his work, he found that by altering slightly the chemical structure of his compound he could increase or decrease its antiviral activity.

Bacterial Elastase. At the autumn meeting of the American Chemical society, Ines Mandl and Betty B. Cohen of the College of Physicians and Surgeons of Columbia university reported the isolation of a protease produced by a species of *Flavobacterium* growing in a partially digested liver medium.

While the bacterial enzyme differed from the pancreatic elastase in several physical properties, its activity upon elastin from various sources was quite comparable. A similar enzyme found in the human pancreas was shown to be reduced in those patients suffering from atherosclerosis, more commonly referred to as hardening of the arteries.

Until this report, elastase had been recovered from hog or beef pancreas in very limited quantities. This practical method of preparation was expected to provide an adequate supply of the enzyme to permit a clinical evaluation of elastase in treating atherosclerosis and other diseases in which connective tissues harden.

Sex Appeal in Yeast. Heterothalic organisms are characterized by mating types; *i.e.*, one type may mate with the other but not with cells of its own type. The two haploid cells of opposite mating type will fuse under conditions proper for contact and a diploid cell will be formed.

In the study of the conditions responsible for attraction and contact little was known. Thomas D. Brock at Western Reserve university, Cleveland, Ohio, demonstrated a protein coat on yeast cells of one strain of *Hansenula wingei* and a polysaccharide on the surface of a complementary strain of the same species. The attraction and the clumping of the two types were directly related to the surface polysaccharide of strain 5 and the protein coat of strain 21. Removal of either surface component greatly reduced attractive and adhesive forces. Brock also showed the chemical forces holding the cells together were hydrogen bonds. (*See also* BIOCHEMISTRY.) (L. J. LE. B.)

BIBLIOGRAPHY. H. Fraenkel-Conrat, *Harvey Lectures* series 53, no. 56 (1959); H. Fraenkel-Conrat and B. Singer, *Bull. Soc. Chem. Biol.* 40, 1717-25 (1958); Leroy McLaren, John H. Holland and Jerome T. Syverton, *Proc. Soc. Ex. Biol.* 100, 843 (1959); Thomas D. Brock, *Science,* 129, 960-961 (1959).

BAGHDAD PACT: *see* CENTRAL TREATY ORGANIZATION.

BAHAMA ISLANDS. British colony; a 760-mi. chain (N.W.-S.E.) comprising about 20 inhabited and 680 uninhabited islands off the Florida coast. Area: 4,404 sq.mi. Pop.: (1953 census) 84,841; (1958 est.) 136,229 with *c.* 83% Negro. Language: English. Religion: Christian. Capital: Nassau (pop. [1958] 50,405), on New Providence island. Administration: governor; executive council; nominated legislative council; elected House of Assembly. Governor, Sir Raynor Arthur. Main imports: machinery, cotton manufactures, foodstuffs. Main exports: lumber, crawfish, salt, tomatoes, pit-props. Currency: sterling with local notes; U.S. and Canadian currencies circulate.

History. During 1959 the legislation passed a General Assembly Election act implementing reforms agreed in 1958 with the secretary of state for the colonies. These provided for unrestricted adult male suffrage, four additional seats in the House of Assembly, constituency boundary changes and other alterations in electoral procedure.

An extensive programme of public works set in hand or completed during the year included a large combined project for electricity generation and water distillation in New Providence to produce 1 million gal. of drinking water a day, a major extension to the Prince George dock in Nassau and the building of a new government high (secondary) school. In the private sector of the economy, the construction and reconstruction of several luxury hotels and other tourist facilities went some way to meet the ever-growing demands of the tourist trade. The year was again a record one for tourism.

On Grand Bahama Island approximately 60 mi. off the Florida coast, the Freeport authority constructed major bunkering facilities to provide the only sterling bunkering in the area north of Trinidad for ocean-going vessels.

(K. M. WY.)

BAHRAIN. British protected Arab Sheikhdom. An archipelago 20 mi. off gulf coast of Saudi Arabia. Area: 231 sq.mi. Pop.: (1958 est.) 125,000, composed of Shia Moslems and Sunnis in roughly equal numbers. Chief towns: Manama (cap. and headquarters of the British political resident, Persian gulf, Sir George Middleton), pop. *c.* 45,000; Muharrek, *c.* 20,000. Sheikh, Sulman bin Hamad el-Khalifah; British political agent, C. A. Gault. Monetary unit: Indian *rupee.* Chief export: petroleum.

History. At the beginning of March 1959 extremely high winds caused some damage to shipping off the coast and to houses inland.

On March 20 a court in St. Helena dismissed a writ of *habeas corpus* for the release of Abd-ul-Rahman el-Baker, the Bahrain nationalist leader imprisoned on the island since 1956. He had been tried and sentenced for plotting to murder the ruler of Bahrain and his British adviser.

BAKING INDUSTRY: *see* BUSINESS REVIEW.

BALANCE OF PAYMENTS. In the period from July 1958 to June 1959 world trade rose from an annual rate of $94,600 million to one of $101,500 million, whereas in the preceding 12 months it had declined from a previous high level of $101,100 million. The period was not only one of recovery; it was notable in that the " dollar gap "—the rest of the world's deficit with the United States—seemed to have disappeared. Indeed, there were signs of a " dollar glut ". Allowing for seasonal variations, Table I shows that the

TABLE I. UNITED STATES BALANCE OF PAYMENTS ($ million)

	1958				1959	
	1st Qtr.	2nd Qtr.	3rd Qtr.	4th Qtr.	1st Qtr.	2nd Qtr.
A. CURRENT ACCOUNT						
1. Exports of goods	4,054	4,191	3,806	4,176	3,798	4,069
2. Exports of services	795	907	986	924	838	939
3. Income from investments abroad	607	699	703	913	635	684
4. Other receipts .	110	123	76	129	110	109
Total receipts .	5,566	5,920	5,571	6,142	5,381	5,801
5. Imports of goods	3,139	3,166	3,124	3,517	3,604	3,885
6. Imports of services	698	955	1,138	817	768	997
7. Income on foreign investments in U.S.	174	150	164	188	180	194
8. Other payments .	64	71	105	65	69	71
9. Military purchases	829	908	841	838	801	821
Total payments	4,904	5,250	5,372	5,425	5,422	5,968
CURRENT BALANCE .	+662	+670	+199	+717	—41	—167
B. CAPITAL ACCOUNT						
10. Remittances to foreigners .	133	127	123	142	140	134
11. Government grants, etc. (net)	429	472	418	474	479	398
12. Government loans, etc. (net)	246	222	332	166	89	314
13. Private loans (net)	642	1,025	451	726	383	611
Capital " outflow "	1,450	1,846	1,324	1,508	1,091	1,457
14. Foreign long-term investment in U.S. .	+13	—15	—26	+52	+75	+165
Capital " inflow " .	+13	—15	—26	+52	+75	+165
CAPITAL BALANCE	—1,437	—1,861	—1,350	—1,456	—1,016	—1,292
CURRENT BALANCE .	+662	+670	+199	+717	—41	—167
Errors and omissions .	+196	+101	+212	—87	+220	+305
Net movement [outflow (+)] of gold and liquid dollar reserves .	+579	+1,090	+939	+826	+837	+1,154

NOTE. The table excludes military grants-in-aid, but includes " offshore " purchases. It excludes payments of subscription to the I.M.F.
SOURCE. U.S. Department of Commerce, *Survey of Current Business.*

result of U.S. international transactions was, by the second quarter of 1959, to add to the world's reserves of gold and dollars at an annual rate of about $4,000 million. With world monetary reserves outside the United States of about $50,000 million, this represented an annual rate of increase of about 8%—more than four times the world's annual production of new gold, excluding the U.S.S.R. Comparing the first half of 1958 with the first half of 1959, the rate of outflow of reserves from the United States had increased by about a quarter, but this did not lead to an equivalent loss of gold by the United States, since foreigners were willing to hold a proportion of their new assets in liquid dollar securities.

It must be noted that even in the second quarter of 1959 only a small portion ($167 million out of $1,154 million) of the movement in reserves was caused by a U.S. deficit on current account; but it is notable that such a deficit had developed from the surplus of $670 million in the corresponding period of 1958. The cause of the change was a slight fall in the value of exports and a considerable rise in the value of imports; the United States failed to take its share of expanding world exports, while buying its share of expanding imports. Important though this trend was, it must not be forgotten that U.S. imports included military purchases totalling about $3,000 million annually—including contracts deliberately placed to supply dollars to the rest of the world; thus the U.S. deficit on current account was not quite what it seemed. The main source of " extra " dollars remained, however, U.S. capital transactions; throughout the period being considered, U.S. capital outflow as recorded was greater than the offsetting loss of reserves. In the second quarter of 1959, for example, U.S. government grants and loans to foreigners accounted for nearly three-quarters of the movement of reserves. Thus the " dollar glut " was largely the result of U.S. government policy.

TABLE II. U.K. BALANCE OF PAYMENTS (£ million)

	1956	1957	1958 Jan.-June	1958 July-Dec.	1959 Jan.-June
A. CURRENT ACCOUNT					
1. Exports of goods .	3,538	3,402	1,721	1,707	1,750
2. Exports of services .	1,049	967	489	512	440
3. Income from investments abroad . .	365	381	169	175	165
Current receipts .	4,952	4,750	2,379	2,394	2,355
4. Imports of goods .	3,569	3,466	1,628	1,702	1,727
5. Imports of services .	880	827	383	417	375
6. Income on foreign investments in U.K. . .	261	265	131	163	111
Current payments .	4,710	4,558	2,142	2,282	2,213
CURRENT BALANCE .	+242	+192	+237	+112	+142
B. CAPITAL ACCOUNT					
7. Net loans to U.K. government* . . .	+59	—70	—23	—37	+3
8. Net loans by U.K. government* . .	+13	+19	+9	+6	+31
9. Other net long-term capital*† . . .	—270	—190	—90	—100	—70
BALANCE ON CAPITAL ACCOUNT*‡ . .	—198	—241	—104	—131	—36
CURRENT BALANCE .	+242	+192	+237	+112	+142
10. NET BALANCE TO BE FINANCED‡ . .	+44	—49	+133	—19	+106
C. MONETARY MOVEMENTS					
11. Change in overseas holding of sterling, etc.‡ .	—194	—21	+24	+57	—42
12. Balancing item (errors and omissions) . .	+163	+112	+130	—41	+31
Change in gold and dollar reserves‡ (= 10+11+12)	+13	+42	+287	—3	+95

* An increase in the ownership of foreign assets by U.K. is shown by a (—); a decrease by a (+). Items 7 and 8 include current repayments of past loans as well as new lending. † Includes private capital. For revisions and interpretations of these figures, see INVESTMENTS ABROAD. ‡ Excludes subscription to International Monetary fund in Feb. 1959.
SOURCE. *United Kingdom Balance of Payments 1956-1959* (Cmnd. 861, H.M.S.O. London, 1959.)

United Kingdom. The United Kingdom had a surplus on current account in both halves of 1958 and in the first half of 1959, as Table II shows. However, although it earned a surplus on current account with the United States of £117 million in the first half of 1959 (compared with a surplus of only £44 million in the corresponding period of 1958), its balance with the rest of the sterling area distinctly worsened in the same period—from a surplus of £242 million to one of only £92 million. Thus the United Kingdom had taken its share of the

increased dollar market, but not of increasing world purchases as a whole. The table shows that, in money terms, U.K. exports of goods and services remained almost constant between 1958 and 1959, while export prices were also constant. Imports in money terms rose by about 6% while import prices fell very slightly; the terms of trade remained steady and Britain took its share of increasing world imports. In consequence, with constant receipts and rising payments, the U.K. balance on current account fell from a surplus of £237 million (probably an underestimate of the surplus actually earned, and representing a substantial downward revision from earlier estimates) to a surplus of £142 million. This was still a healthy balance, but the failure of exports to resume their upward path was somewhat disturbing.

The U.K. capital account showed a slight reduction in net private long-term capital investments abroad, probably because in 1959 there was an increase (perhaps substantial) in U.S. investment in the United Kingdom, accompanied by a slightly smaller increase in investment overseas by U.K. firms and individuals. The change of sign on the governmental loans account reflects some repayments and adjustments of German debt to the United Kingdom.

The financing of the resultant surplus of foreign obligations to the United Kingdom led to an increase in the U.K. gold and dollar reserves from £1,099 million in June 1958 to £1,133 million in June 1959, overseas sterling holdings rising from £3,905 million to £4,071 million. If the effect is excluded of the increased U.K. subscription to the International Monetary fund paid in 1959, reserves would have risen to £1,191 million in June, and overseas sterling holdings would have remained steady at £3,897 million. Since the I.M.F. subscription certainly did not detract from U.K. reserves, it may be said that the United Kingdom's net short-term reserve position improved by some 10%. By November U.K. gold and dollar reserves were down to £1,062 million, but this was more than explained by a repayment (in advance) of a $250 million U.S. loan made in 1957.

Rest of the Sterling Area. The Commonwealth and other countries comprising the rest of the sterling area (R.S.A.) had a current deficit of about £100 million with non-sterling countries in the first half of 1959, compared with a deficit of about £200 million in the corresponding period of 1958; at the same time the R.S.A. deficit in trade with the United Kingdom fell from £242 million to £92 million. The over-all improvement in the R.S.A.'s position was caused by a rise in the volume of exports, the end of the adverse movement in the terms of trade and a fall in imports. R.S.A. exports were £131 million higher in Jan.-June 1959 than in the corresponding period of 1958.

R.S.A. deficits in the first half of 1959 were financed (a) as to £121 million by sales of gold in the United Kingdom and (b) by net borrowing etc. of some £281 million (about £118 million from the United Kingdom). Since these together were more than enough to offset a current deficit of £194 million, there was (allowing for statistical discrepancies) an increase in R.S.A. sterling balances of £126 million in the half year. Some sterling countries thus seemed to be " lending short " to the United Kingdom and " borrowing long " from the United Kingdom and elsewhere. (*See* also EXCHANGE CONTROL AND EXCHANGE RATES; INVESTMENTS ABROAD.)

(M. V. P.)

BALLET: *see* DANCE.

BANKING. With economic re-expansion well under way almost everywhere, 1959 was a year of progress for most banking institutions. Besides materially enlarging traditional types of business, many banks continued the process of exploring the new fields which they had been encouraged to

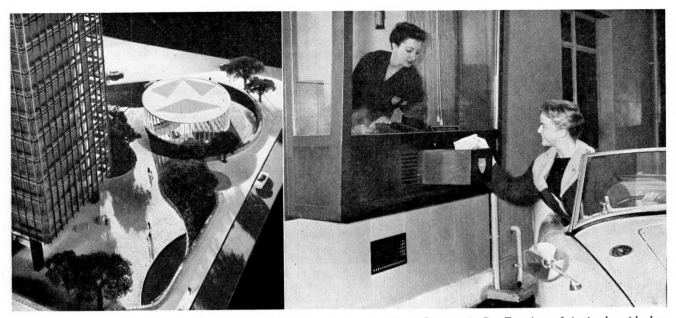

(Left) A model of a branch bank due for completion in 1959 for the American Trust Company in San Francisco. It is circular with glass walls. (Right) Britain's first " drive-in " bank, a branch of the Westminster at Prince's road, Liverpool. The window is bullet-proof.

enter by relaxations of official restrictions on banking operations during 1958. In most countries banks continued to enjoy, until late in the year, much greater freedom from governmental interference with the development of their activities than in the 1945-57 period. But here and there official monetary controls were tightened before the close of the year owing to fears that the fast pace of re-expansion would lead to renewed inflationary stresses.

Interest rate levels being generally much lower than when dear money policies were being widely applied in 1955-58, many classes of banking work were less remunerative than in the preceding years. But most institutions were fully compensated for this by the expansion in the volume of business handled. They also benefited from the fact that their earnings were no longer being eroded in terms of purchasing power by the decline in the value of money, prices in most countries being much nearer stability than at almost any time since the end of World War II. Moreover, with security values rising in response to easier money trends and the rise in the status of many currencies, some substantial capital gains were shown on investment holdings, providing funds for rebuilding the reserves that had been severely depleted earlier in the 1950s by capital losses sustained when interest rates rose steeply.

United Kingdom. The year 1959 was a hardly less exciting one for British banks than the preceding one. The authorities satisfied themselves early on that the measures they had already taken to stimulate spending on consumption and capital investment would be sufficient to keep re-expansion proceeding at an adequate pace. Thus no important new measures to reduce the cost of money or expand the supply of it were taken after the removal in January of almost all remaining restrictions on borrowing by business concerns in the capital market and from the banks for financing capital outlays at home. Bank rate remained at the level of 4% to which, by Nov. 1958, it had been reduced from the 1957 crisis level of 7%, and none of the additional freedom to expand their lending business which the banks had been given in 1958 was withdrawn.

With the rising tempo of industrial and commercial activity combining with the steps the banks had already taken to extend and popularize their services in order to stimulate the demand for loans, the advances of the London clearing banks—which together accounted for about 95% of the country's commercial banking turnover—rose rapidly. They increased by £666 million, or rather less than one-third, in the 12 months to mid-December, when they stood at the record level of £2,935 million. To ensure that liquidity difficulties did not unduly limit the contribution that increased bank lending could make to re-expansion, the authorities so arranged their own financing as to increase official borrowings from the banks against Treasury bills. Even so, most banks found that they had to counter the impact on their liquidity ratios of the rise in advances in part by reducing the amount of their resources employed in other non-liquid assets. Thus the clearing banks' holdings of government securities contracted by £383 million, or about one-fifth, in the period mentioned. The net effect of these and other small changes in assets was to raise deposits by £240 million to £7,439 million, a record figure.

The only important new elaboration of banking services arose from the decision of one of the " big five " clearing banks to introduce fixed-term loans for financing capital development by farmers and small business concerns (traditionally, all lending by U.K. commercial banks is nominally repayable on demand, though in practice they rarely exercise this right). Other banks contented themselves with developing the new types of activity embarked upon in the previous year, engaging in much keener competition with one another as they did so. The rise in the international standing of sterling and the further relaxation of exchange restrictions brought about a marked increase in foreign exchange and other business reaching British banks from abroad.

During the year the leading banks made an investigation into the possibility of improving the money transfer facilities they provided by employing techniques used in continental European giro systems. The government agreed to revise the Truck acts to encourage the use of cheques for making wage payments. The first drive-in banks made their appearance in Britain, while new book-keeping systems making more extensive use of electronic processes were installed by many banks. The report of the Radcliffe committee on the working of the U.K. monetary system found little to criticize in the functioning of the commercial banking system and recommended only a few minor changes. The committee thought that the traditional requirement that the clearing banks' ratio of liquid assets to deposits should never fall below 30%

should be made more explicit, that the Scottish banks should reveal their ratios of cash and liquid assets to deposits at monthly intervals, as the clearing banks already did, and that all other deposit banks should also start publishing monthly figures. The report suggested that the authorities should be prepared at times of stress to influence the banks' credit creation activities by the use of devices to raise the proportion of resources employed in liquid assets beyond 30%, though on the condition that other lending institutions were similarly controlled. In the event of a threat of headlong inflation there could be more precise restrictions on bank lending, hire purchase and capital issues.

Two important eastern banks—the Hong Kong and Shanghai Banking corporation and the Mercantile bank were merged during the year. The fusion of the Commercial Bank of Scotland with the National Bank of Scotland was completed and the merchant banking firm of Philip Hill, Higginson acquired that of Erlangers.

Savings banks benefited from the high level of savings activity in general. The trustee savings banks indicated their intention to introduce a limited cheque service.

Commonwealth. Since economic recovery proceeded fairly slowly in most primary producing countries in 1959 owing to the absence of any marked recovery in the prices of many leading commodities, the increase in banking activity was of a more modest character in most Commonwealth countries than in the more industralized regions of the world. Although the Australian, New Zealand and South African governments were all pursuing easier money policies, the rise in both bank deposits and bank advances was limited to a few per cent. in the year to mid-1959. The increase in banking activity was of a larger order in India and Pakistan, the impact on deposits and advances of official development programmes and economic re-expansion being reinforced by inflationary stresses. However, this latter factor was deprived of its force in Pakistan in the later months of the year as a result of the initial success of the extensive overhaul of economic policies undertaken early in 1959. In Canada official fears that re-expansion would lead to inflation brought about a hardening of monetary policy in the first half of the year, and this slowed down the steep rise in bank advances then in progress. The central bank's handling of the policy change brought some criticism from the commercial banking community.

In South Africa and the Federation of Rhodesia and Nyasaland new discount houses were set up, usually with U.K. assistance, to promote the plan for the creation of a domestic money market. Further steps taken for the same purpose in Australia included the inauguration of an arrangement whereby selected discount houses could rediscount securities with the central bank within certain limits. The Australian government, having at last obtained a majority in both houses of parliament, reintroduced the bill, previously rejected on several occasions by the opposition majority in the Senate, for completing the separation of the central banking and trading banking departments of the Commonwealth bank and giving the authorities power to impose a variable liquidity ratios system on the commercial banks. The central bank set up by the Federation of Malaya to take over responsibility for the currency issue and supervise the activities of the commercial banks came into operation in January. An immediate result was the closing down of Bank of China branches in the country, the authorities exercising their new right to refuse licences to government-controlled foreign banks. India introduced a special " external " rupee note, to replace existing supplies of Indian currency circulating in the Persian gulf area, in order to curb illicit capital exports. New institutions to finance development were set up in Nigeria with U.K. help. In South Africa a number of leading banks extended their direct participation in hire-purchase

finance by acquiring substantial interests in finance houses specializing in this field.

Continental Europe. Re-expansion led to a considerable increase in banking activity in the main commercial countries of western Europe during 1959. But in the German Federal Republic, Switzerland, the Netherlands and Belgium the movement met with official resistance through a tightening of monetary policy. In France restrictions imposed on banking activity at the end of 1958, in connection with the currency stabilization plan, were progressively relaxed. With the franc enjoying a striking recovery as the trading position improved and capital flowed back to the country, the authorities discontinued the practice of periodically borrowing the foreign exchange holdings of the commercial banks. There was an extensive overhaul of the Spanish financial system in connection with the economic stabilization plan which the authorities put into operation in July. The Portuguese government set up a development bank to promote industrialization. The development bank created by the countries of the European Economic community to help the less developed regions within their territories made its first advances. There was an extensive reorganization of the banking system of the U.S.S.R., a number of specialized institutions handing over their functions to the State and Industrial banks.

Far and Middle East. A steep rise in industrial activity in Japan was accompanied by a major expansion in bank business which met with a little official resistance towards the close of the year. The authorities took steps to reform the central bank to enable it to control more effectively the operations of the commercial banks. A number of new banking institutions were set up in Persia with foreign assistance. Iraq left the sterling area but it was stated that it would preserve its close financial links with the United Kingdom. In Syria the banking system was brought into line with that in Egypt. A law was put into effect which debarred banks, including branches of foreign banks, from operating in the country unless 70% of their capital was owned in the United Arab Republic (or 51% if the remainder was owned in other Arab countries).

United States. With recovery from the business recession, tight money was once again the dominant characteristic of the monetary situation. Demands for funds were high. Savings available for lending and investing by the major institutional investors showed some slowing down and competition for the saver's dollar was greatly intensified. The federal reserve system followed a policy of monetary restraint. The U.S. Treasury encountered serious difficulties in debt management, not from further growth in size of the debt but rather from its composition. These developments together brought higher interest rates and lessened availability of funds.

The increase in total mortgage debt on non-farm one- to four-family houses during the year ended Sept. 1959 was $13,800 million compared with an increase of $10,300 million in the calendar year 1958. Late in 1959 lessened availability of mortgage funds was reducing home building activity. Consumer credit showed the largest relative increase between 1958 and 1959; it rose by $6,180 million in the year ending Oct. 1959 compared with an increase of only $300 million in 1958.

In the first six months of the year total commercial and industrial loans by all weekly reporting commercial banks rose by $760 million, compared with a decrease of $1,085 million in the same period of 1958. This was probably mainly due to the need to finance inventory accumulation in anticipation of the steel strike. Between July and Nov. 1959 total commercial and industrial loans rose by $1,530 million compared with an increase of $700 million in the same months of

1958. In this period loans to trade firms, commodity dealers and public utilities were important. The bank prime commercial loan rate was increased to 4½% on May 18, 1959, after having been at 4% since Sept. 11, 1958. A further rise to 5% became effective on Sept. 1, 1959.

Total loans and investments of all commercial banks reached a new peak of $188,200 million on Nov. 11, 1959, the increase of $5,700 million in the preceding 12 months comparing with an increase of $15,100 million in the calendar year 1958. Total commercial bank loans amounted to $108,900 million on Nov. 11, up $12,700 million during the preceding 12 months, but holdings of U.S. government securities had declined by almost $7,000 million and on Nov. 11 amounted to slightly less than $59,000 million. In other words, since the banks were not provided by the federal reserve system with sufficient reserves to meet all demands for credit placed upon them, they met these demands, in part, by selling U.S. government securities. There was a continued decline in the commercial banks' over-all liquidity. On Nov. 11 total loans comprised 57·8% of total loans and investments, a ratio above the previous record in 1957, and the ratio of holdings of U.S. government securities to total loans and investments stood at 31·3%, the lowest proportion since 1945.

The privately held money supply reached a new record of $242,500 million on Nov. 25.

In the 12 months ended June 1959 deposits with mutual savings banks rose by $1,642 million to $34,624 million and assets rose by nearly $2,000 million to $38,560 million. The banks' mortgage holdings rose to 61·9% of their total assets compared with about 60% a year earlier. Holdings of U.S. government securities fell to 19% of total assets. (*See also* ACCOUNTANCY; BANK OF ENGLAND; INTERNATIONAL BANK FOR RECONSTRUCTION AND DEVELOPMENT; INTERNATIONAL MONETARY FUND.)   (C. H. G. T.; J. K. L.; G. W. EY.)

BANK OF ENGLAND.

The important step taken towards the establishment of fully convertible sterling at the close of 1958 by raising the transferable £ circulating in non-sterling countries outside the dollar area to the same status as U.S. account sterling having proved entirely successful, the bank was much less occupied with external financial problems in 1959 than for many years. The sterling markets maintained a firm appearance throughout the year, even the possibility of a change of government as the general election approached failing to weaken confidence to any marked extent. In these circumstances the bank was able to obtain Treasury sanction for a number of further relaxations of exchange control. The ceiling on spendings by British tourists abroad was abolished; the freedom previously given to the authorized banks to arrange forward exchange business in connection with merchandise trade transactions was extended to cover payments; capital investment, dividend payments and other invisible; and the London bullion market was granted permission to undertake all types of forward business in gold.

The bank's principal concern in 1959 was internal economic management, its task being to collaborate with the government in devising official policies which might be expected to continue re-expansion without taxing the country's resources to the point of generating a new inflationary problem. It was soon discovered that no further measures to stimulate business activity would be needed. Nor, with the economy showing no marked tendency to drift into disequilibrium, was it thought necessary to take restraining action by making money dearer or tighter, and bank rate remained at 4%. The bank also had to turn its attention to a number of financial matters of a more specialized character including the modification of new issues control, the implications for the city of the spate

of take-over bids and the need for more supervision of the activities of hire-purchase finance houses and building societies.

With prices remaining stable, the growth of the bank's note circulation was again proceeding at a slower pace than in the period immediately after World War II. The increasing popularity of the new £5 note introduced in 1957 was reflected in a decline in demand for £1 notes.

The report of the Radcliffe committee on the working of the U.K. monetary system included an extensive examination of the bank's work. Its organization and status were found to be generally satisfactory. However, it was suggested that the bank's responsibility for formulating the monetary side of official economic policy should be seen to be more fully shared by government departments—this to be achieved by setting up an advisory committee on monetary policy on which the Treasury and the Board of Trade as well as the bank would be represented and by arranging for bank rate changes to be announced by and on the authority of the chancellor of the exchequer. The report recommended that part-time directors should remain but should not be allowed to take such a large part in discussions on policy decisions as in the past and that the bank should keep the public better informed about its activities. (*See* also BANKING.)

(C. H. G. T.)

BAPTIST CHURCH.

The baptism of believers by immersion is practised in accordance with New Testament custom; churches are organized on a " gathered " or congregational principle, but have always shown a tendency to unite at regional and national levels. The Baptist World alliance, founded in 1905 and with its headquarters in Washington, D.C., with a European secretary in London, had (1958) a membership of more than 22 million, incl. North America, 19·8 million; Europe, 1·5 million; Asia, 718,395; Africa, 279,241; South America, 146,988; Central America and W. Indies, 104,829; Australasia and Oceania, 51,503. Community strength was three or four times as great as membership.

During 1959 the alliance president, T. F. Adams, made a tour of Africa, Europe and South America, attending in the Netherlands the 350th anniversary of the baptism of John

The interior of the new Baptist tabernacle, built on the site of two previous ones near the old Elephant and Castle, London.

Smyth who, when in that country, founded the first English Baptist church. Erik Ruden was appointed European secretary of the alliance and was succeeded by the Rev. Simon Oberg as secretary of the Swedish Baptist union. T. B. McDormand resigned as general secretary of the Baptist Federation of Canada to become executive vice-president of Acadia university. A new Baptist hospital was dedicated in Berlin. The executive of the Baptist World alliance met in Rochester, New York state, and the American Baptist convention dedicated its new 55-ac. site at Valley Forge, Pennsylvania, for the denomination's new headquarters. By the death of F. W. Boreham, whose ministry was in New Zealand and Australia, Baptists lost one of their best-known essayists and preachers.   (F. T. L.)

See E. A. Payne, *Baptist Union: A Short History* (London, 1959); A. Gilmore (ed.), *Christian Baptism* (London, 1959).

BARBADOS: *see* WEST INDIES, THE.

BASUTOLAND: *see* BRITISH SOUTH AFRICAN TERRITORIES.

BECHUANALAND: *see* BRITISH SOUTH AFRICAN TERRITORIES.

BEEKEEPING. No census of beekeepers in Britain was taken in 1958 owing to a decision of the Ministry of Agriculture that in future a census should be made every three years. However, figures compiled from available statistics showed that there had been a small increase in the number of beekeepers and colonies during the year. The report on the working of the Foul Brood Disease of Bees order stated that 12 out of every 1,000 inspected were suffering from brood disease, a slight decrease on 1957, though fewer apiaries were inspected owing to bad weather.

FOUL BROOD DISEASE IN ENGLAND AND WALES, 1957-58

	Apiaries visited	Colonies examined	No. of colonies with foul brood disease	Percentage of infected colonies
1957 .	19,148	73,405	947	1·3
1958 .	16,869	71,549	883	1·2

The excellent weather which prevailed during the summer in the British Isles and on the continent of Europe resulted in good honey crops generally, though in some areas extreme drought in the latter part of the summer greatly reduced the yield and most nectar-bearing plants had an unusually short flowering period. Owing to heavy winter losses due to the weakened state of colonies generally after the poor 1958 season, coupled with severe incidence of *nosema apis* disease, the total honey crop was not unusually large. The crop of heather honey was exceptionally good in most districts.

Owing to heavy infestation of seed crops in Britain with aphis and other insect pests, spraying operations on an unusually wide scale were carried out, often on open blossom, and serious losses of bee colonies were reported particularly in the eastern counties. In an adjournment debate in July in the House of Commons the parliamentary secretary to the Ministry of Agriculture stated that severe losses of bees had been confirmed and that he had called a meeting of spray manufacturers and contractors to consider the position. A further meeting of all interested parties, including the National Farmers' union and beekeeping associations, was held in November.

In Great Britain a special bee husbandry sub-committee of the Agricultural Improvement council, representing all beekeeping interests, was set up to advise the minister on beekeeping matters.

In the United States average honey crops were reported from most areas, while in Australia a further light crop in the 1958-59 season led to reduced overseas exports.   (H. PN.)

See J. Free and C. Butler, *Bumblebees* (London, 1959).

BELGIAN OVERSEAS TERRITORIES. The Belgian overseas territories consist of the Congo in central Africa and the adjacent trust territories of Ruanda & Urundi administered with Congo. Total area: 925,907 sq.mi. Total pop. (1958 est.) 17,931,900. Areas, populations, capital town, status and governors of the separate territories are given in the table. Main exports: copper, zinc, cobalt, gold, silver and diamonds, manganese and uranium ore; palm oil and palm kernels; gum copal; cotton; coffee. Main imports: machinery and manufactures; fuel oil. Monetary unit: Congolese *franc*, at par with the Belgian franc.

History. Important events occurred in the Belgian Congo in 1959. Reforms had been introduced and local elections took place in several centres in 1957 and 1958. The name of the Ministry of the Colonies was changed to the Ministry of the Belgian Congo and of Ruanda-Urundi. A government statement about the future of the Congo was announced when, on Jan. 4, rioting started in Léopoldville, the capital, after the police had dispersed a meeting for which no permission had been requested. On that tragic Sunday police vans were set on fire, cars belonging to Europeans were attacked and damaged, shops, schools, and missions were raided. The following day looting continued, 49 Europeans and 74 Africans were taken to hospital and African troops fired on the crowds to restore order. According to official reports 37 Africans were killed and 12 died afterwards.

A parliamentary commission of enquiry reported on March 28 that human relations had not kept pace with the evolution of some of the African population; segregation was resented and Africans had developed over-sensitiveness; other causes were the economic recession, the influx of natives into overcrowded Léopoldville, large-scale unemployment and young people's remaining idle; the impact of

The 42,000 kw. Zongo I hydroelectric plant on the Inkisi river, Belgian Congo. A second, 110,000 kw. plant was discussed in 1959.

Communist propaganda should not be exaggerated but the influence of the independence given to former territories of French Equatorial Africa was important.

On Jan. 13 King Baudouin in a broadcast and the government in parliament announced reforms leading to independence. Maurice van Hemelrijck, minister of the Congo, paid several visits to the territory and introduced reforms as a prelude to general elections. Freedom of the press, of association and of public meetings was granted. When the minister announced his intention to set up a provisional government several of his colleagues in the cabinet disagreed and he resigned on Sept. 3. He was succeeded by Auguste De Schrijver, a minister of state of the Christian Social party.

De Schrijver said he intended to adopt an economic policy running parallel with the political evolution because the economic aspect had not been sufficiently taken into account.

Prince Albert of Liège, brother of King Baudouin and heir to the Belgian throne, with his bride Donna Paola Ruffo di Calabria in the church of St. Michel and St. Gudule, Brussels, on July 2. The wedding service followed a civil ceremony in the royal palace.

A new time-table for reforms was outlined by the minister on Oct. 16 providing for direct elections for district and rural councils in December by an electorate estimated at more than 3 million male African and Belgian inhabitants of the Congo aged 21 and over. The next stage was the granting to the six provinces of extensive powers over education, public works and other matters and the setting up in March 1960 of provincial councils. Six-tenths of members of provincial councils were to be elected by the members of district and rural councils, three-tenths co-opted by these members and one-tenth nominated from among representative people. The third step was also to be made in 1960, namely the installation of two legislative assemblies, a chamber elected directly or by the district and rural councillors, and a senate elected partly by the provincial councils, and other members being co-opted or chosen by the king. Both houses would be competent to pass bills. A central government would be presided over by the governor-general, the representative of the king.

Pending the elections further clashes resulting from tribal hatred occurred in October mainly in the Kasai district between Lulua and Baluba, the serf tribe.

In November savage events occurred in the trust territory of Ruanda where the Bahutsi serf tribes who make up over 80% of the population had revolted against their giant Watutsi overlords. The last-named launched the local pygmies against the Bahutsi. More than 200 Africans were said to have been killed. A state of emergency was proclaimed in Ruanda on Nov. 12 and 2,000 Belgian-officered African troops and 300 Belgian paratroopers were sent to the area.

At the end of November three African leaders arrived in Brussels to confer with De Schrijver. Joseph Kasavubu,

president of the Abako (Association Culturelle des Ressortissants du Bas Congo), Albert Kalonji, head of the Congo National movement, and M. Gizenga, president of the African Solidarity party, asked the minister to postpone the elections. On Dec. 4 De Schrijver refused and the African leaders declared that their parties would not take part in the elections scheduled to take place throughout the Belgian Congo during December. On Dec. 16, quite unexpectedly, King Baudouin left Brussels for Congo on a fact-finding mission. (M. Ss.; X.)

BELGIUM. Kingdom of western Europe bounded S.W. by France, N. by the Netherlands and E. by Germany and Luxembourg. Area: 11,779 sq.mi. Pop.: (1947 census) 8,512,195; (1958 est.) 9,053,000. Language (1954 est.): Flemish 50%; French 34%; Flemish and French 15%; German 1%. Religion: mainly Roman Catholic. Chief towns (pop., 1954 est.; first figure including suburbs, second figure *commune* only): Brussels (cap.) 976,447 (177,335); Antwerp 795,000 (258,674); Liège 575,000 (154,007); Charleroi 455,000 (25,983); Ghent 450,000 (163,578); Namur 220,000 (31,925); Bruges 201,000 (51,650). Ruler, King Baudouin I. Prime minister, Gaston Eyskens. Main imports: machinery and vehicles, petroleum, wool, cotton. Main exports: iron and steel manufactured goods, machinery and vehicles, nonferrous metals. Monetary unit: Belgian *franc* (B.Fr.140·00 = £1 sterling).

History. During 1959 King Baudouin paid official visits to the United States, Luxembourg and the Netherlands. He also visited Queen Elizabeth II privately at Balmoral and President Heinrich Lübke in Bonn, when he inspected Belgian military units in western Germany. The nation rejoiced when Prince Albert, brother of the king and heir to the throne, married Donna Paola Ruffo di Calabria. King Leopold, father of King Baudouin, who was president of the Belgian National Commission for the Promotion of Science and Research, delivered the report of the commission on the need for a reform of higher education, easier entry into universities

BELGIAN COLONIAL EMPIRE

Country	Area (sq.mi.)	Population (1958 est.)	Capital	Status	Governor
Belgian Congo .	904,991	Africans 13,174,900 Europeans 115,804	Léopoldville (pop.: 350,000, incl. 20,000 Europeans)	Oversea territory	Henri Cornelis, governor-general
Ruanda ⎫ . Urundi ⎭	20,916	Africans 4,630,100 Europeans 7,257 Others 3,863	Usumbura*	⎧ Sultanates, ⎨ Trust territories	J. P. Harroy, governor

* Principal town of Ruanda, Kigali; principal town of Urundi, Kitega.

and into scientific careers. The 83-year-old Queen Elisabeth, the king's grandmother, visited Israel and Yugoslavia. In 20 months she had travelled no fewer than 100 hours by air, probably a world record for one of her age.

Rejoicing alternated with grave concern, mainly about troubles in the Belgian Congo and in the trust territory of Ruanda. A rift in the cabinet over the Congo reforms resulted in September in the resignation of Maurice van Hemelrijck and his succession by Auguste De Schrijver as minister for the affairs of the Congo, Ruanda and Urundi. The country also faced the problem of a coal surplus (7 million tons in stock) and of uneconomic coalmines. Working days were reduced to four and when some pits were closed strikes occurred in the Borinage area and spread through the province of Hainault.

At the end of February an agreement was reached between the government, the employers and the unions over the timing of coalmine closures and arrangements for re-employment of miners. A total of 34 pits was to be closed over a period of three years. In the Ghent area there were demonstrations when textile factories were closed. The general economic recession affected Belgium later than other countries because of considerable works executed for the Brussels exhibition of 1958, but the improvement in 1959 was slower than in other countries. However, the general index of industrial production (1953=100) was estimated at 128·5 for Oct. 1959 against 120·7 in Oct. 1958. Steel production reached record figures (587,000 tons in October). House building was again in progress and there was a recovery in all textile branches. A long-term programme of improvements to railways, roads, canals and ports was drafted. The cost of living index (1953=100) rose to 110·4 in Oct. 1959 against 108·2 in Oct. 1958. As a result wages of civil servants and of workers in various industries and pensions had to be adjusted. Increasing state expenditure forced the government in November to increase postal rates. There was much opposition against other taxation increases which the government intended to introduce and severe cuts in the 1960 budget expenditure were advocated. Reforms in education, the programme for scientific research and especially aid to the Belgian Congo meant an exceptional financial burden only to be eased by reducing military expenditure. In September the period of military service was reduced to one year.

A border dispute dating from the middle ages was settled after the Belgian and Dutch governments decided to submit the case to the International Court of Justice. The dispute concerned the Belgian enclaves in the Baarle Nassau and Baarle Hertog region where an area of about 30 ac. was contested. On June 20, 1959, by 10 votes to 4, the court found that the sovereignty belonged to Belgium. (*See also* INTERNATIONAL COURT OF JUSTICE.)   (M. Ss.)

BERLIN. Capital of the German Reich from 1871 to 1945, Berlin was still in 1959 the largest city of Germany. Area: 341·3 sq.mi. Pop.: (1930 census) 4,321,500; (Dec. 31, 1957, est.) 3,338,516. From June 6, 1945, Berlin was administered by an inter-Allied government authority consisting of the commandants of the four sectors of Berlin. After June 24, 1948, when the Soviet commandant proclaimed the dissolution of the authority, Berlin was in fact divided into two opposing administrations. By Dec. 31, 1959, the three western sectors (area, 185·7 sq.mi.; pop., Dec. 1957 est., 2,226,000) were under the authority of the three following Allied commandants: Great Britain, Maj.-General Rohan Delacombe; United States, Maj.-General Barksdale Hamlett; France, Brig.-General Jean Lacomme. In the Soviet sector (area, 155·6 sq.mi.; pop., Dec. 1957 est., 1,110,009) Col.-General Matvei V. Zakharov was military commander. There were also two rival German city governments and two lord mayors. Willy Brandt was *Oberbürgermeister* of western Berlin appointed by an elected city assembly; Fritz Ebert was *Oberbürgermeister* of the Soviet sector appointed by the Sozialistische Einheitspartei Deutschlands.

History. The Berlin problem continued to absorb the interest of the great powers during 1959. The " problem ",

as such, became acute when N. S. Khrushchev demanded a radical change in the city's status in Nov. 1958. His first proposal was that western Berlin should be denuded of Allied troops and that its communications with the German Federal Republic should be placed under the control of the German Democratic Republic. Khrushchev then suggested that western Berlin, whose three sectors were under the control of the western Powers, should become a " free city ", with a token garrison supplied either by the western powers or the United Nations.

On Nov. 27, 1958, Khrushchev sent notes on the subject of Berlin to the three western powers and also to the German Federal Republic. These notes were answered on Dec. 31, 1958, by the three western powers. They rejected the proposal for a " free city " of western Berlin, upheld the rights of their garrisons to free access to Berlin from western Germany and refused to accept the substitution of eastern German for Soviet authorities on the Berlin-Helmstedt motor road. The western German government sent a similar reply to the Soviet government on Jan. 5, 1959. This reply included the demand that Berlin should be allowed to resume its natural role as the capital of a united Germany; it repudiated Soviet suggestions that western Berlin was being used as a " spy-centre ", and rejected the Soviet plan for creating a " confederation " of two equally entitled German states. On Jan. 7 the Soviet government received a note from the government of the German Democratic Republic expressing wholehearted support for the Soviet proposals for Berlin. This note declared that the presence of Allied garrisons in Berlin was illegal.

On March 8 Khrushchev visited eastern Berlin, after spending four days at the Leipzig trade fair, and on March 9 he stated that western Berlin must become a " free city ", although some Allied troops could continue to be stationed there. On the same day he interviewed Erich Ollenhauer, the chairman of the western German Social Democratic party, and told him that all east-west differences could perfectly well be settled by peaceful means. Ollenhauer admitted later that there was " some disagreement " on important points. He was bitterly criticized in the western German press for visiting Khrushchev while the latter was on eastern German soil and for failing to contest some of Khrushchev's more flagrant assertions about the western powers and the western German regime.

The Berlin problem subsequently became one of the main points discussed, but without any solution being reached, at the two Geneva conferences of the foreign ministers. The Soviet threat to western Berlin was never officially withdrawn, but the Berlin problem was tacitly " put on ice " pending the series of international conferences which were being prepared at the end of 1959. The intention of the western powers to fulfil their obligations and maintain their rights in Berlin were restated during the year by President Dwight D. Eisenhower, Harold Macmillan and other western statesmen.

As was to be expected, there were several incidents in or near Berlin during the year which were directly caused by the Soviet and eastern German desire to put pressure on the city. On Feb. 2 a U.S. military convoy of four lorries was held up by Soviet frontier guards just inside the borders of the German Democratic Republic at Helmstedt. The Soviet guards demanded the right to search the vehicles. This right was refused by the U.S. army drivers, and on Feb. 4 the convoy was allowed to proceed into western Germany only after an energetic protest had been made by the U.S. commandant in western Berlin, Maj.-General Barksdale Hamlett.

Again, on March 27 and April 3, aggressive actions were carried out by Soviet fighters against U.S. transport aircraft flying at roughly 25,000 ft. along one of the Berlin air corridors. The Soviet fighters " buzzed " the U.S. aircraft, and officials of the Soviet office in the Allied air safety centre in Berlin later claimed that these actions were justified, because the Soviet authorities insisted on a 10,000 ft. ceiling for all aircraft using the air corridors. The Soviet case was based on the claim that Soviet military aircraft used the airspace above as well as on either side of the air-corridors and that high flying on the corridors would therefore be dangerous. U.S. transport aircraft continued to fly above 10,000 ft. intermittently, even after this incident.

The next incident was provoked by the eastern German authorities who, on Oct. 6, instructed their agents to hoist the new flag of the German Democratic Republic (hammer and compass superimposed on the old German black, red and gold colours) on stations belonging to the Berlin overhead city railway. Some 70 of these stations were on western Berlin territory, although they were the property of the eastern German Reichsbahn. On Oct. 6 and 7 scuffles took place on some of the stations between western Berlin police, who were under orders to take the flags down, and eastern German railwaymen and " factory guards ", who had been brought in in strength to defend the flags. A score of people were injured, some of them seriously. On Oct. 8 the remaining flags (the western Berlin police removed around 30) were taken down by the eastern Germans.

This flag-hoisting incident took place at the time of the 10th anniversary of the German Democratic Republic. Similar action was forecast for Nov. 7, the 42nd anniversary of the Russian Communist revolution. On Nov. 4 the western commandants warned Col.-General M. V. Zakharov, commander-in-chief of the Soviet forces in eastern Germany, that the Soviet government would be held responsible for any disorders which arose out of a flag-hoisting operation on western Berlin railway stations. On Nov. 7 the new eastern German flag was flown only in eastern Berlin. The eastern German government explained that its plans were changed as it did not intend to be provoked by the massive police-forces of western Berlin.

Another incident was promised, when the eastern German authorities threatened to prevent Otto Dibelius, Lutheran bishop of Berlin and Brandenburg, from preaching the Reformation-Day sermon in the eastern Berlin Marienkirche. This church served as the cathedral of his diocese, since the old eastern Berlin Dom was destroyed by Allied bombing during the war. Dibelius had published a statement that duties to an atheistical Communist state were not compatible with the Christian conscience, but later he explained that obedience to government was not a direct concern of the conscience. Dibelius was allowed to preach his sermon on Nov. 1 to a congregation of 2,000, many of whom assembled outside the church afterwards and cheered the bishop. (*See also* GERMANY.) (T. C. Pe.)

BERMUDA.
British colony, *c.* 300 small islands (*c.* 20 inhabited) *c.* 570 mi. E.S.E. of Cape Hatteras, North Carolina, and 690 mi. from New York. Area: 20·59 sq.mi., incl. 2·3 sq.mi. leased to United States for naval and air bases. Pop.: (1950 census) 37,403, comprising 22,679 coloured and 14,724 white; (1958 est.) 43,480. Language: English. Religion: Christian (*c.* 54% Anglican). Chief towns: Hamilton (cap.) pop. *c.* 3,000; St. George's, *c.* 1,500. Administration: governor; executive council; legislative council; elected House of Assembly. Governors in 1959: Lieut.-General Sir John Woodall and (from Nov. 30) Maj.-General Sir Julian Gascoigne. Colony's chief sources of income: tourists, goods and services to U.S. bases and revenue from locally established " foreign " companies. Main imports: foodstuffs, fuel, clothing, building material, house furnishings, motor vehicles and parts, liquor. Main exports: drugs and essences, cut flowers. Re-exports: bunkering supplies, diamonds, liquor, personal effects, gas cylinders, motor vehicles and parts, household effects. Monetary unit: Bermuda pound (=£1 sterling); U.K. coinage circulates.

History. Government revenue for 1959 was estimated at £3,421,853 and expenditure at £3,406,604. The principal source of revenue was customs which in 1958 brought in £2,548,643. In 1958 there were 129,933 tourists (including a further increase in winter visitors) who again provided a major source of income. During April 28-29 Bermuda was visited by the Duke of Edinburgh. The 350th anniversary of the settlement of Bermuda in 1609 was commemorated in an extensive programme of events, including a visit by British warships, military parades, art exhibitions, plays and pageants and the issue of special commemorative postage stamps. The year marked the end of racial differentiation in cinemas, hotels and restaurants. The construction of a new " Bermudiana " hotel to replace the building gutted by fire in 1958 made rapid progress. (C. S. Ba.)

BETTING AND GAMBLING.
The total amounts staked on various forms of betting in 1958 were: football pools, £85,630,000; greyhound totalizators, £59,600,000; horse totalizators, £27,019,000; Irish hospital sweepstakes, £14,170,000. These figures showed increases of 18% and 11% over the 1957 figures for football pools and Irish hospital sweepstakes respectively, a decrease of 3% for greyhound totalizators and no change for horse totalizators.

Early in November the government introduced a Betting and Gaming bill on lines which had been recommended by the Royal Commission on Betting, Lotteries and Gaming, 1949-51. Part I of the bill dealt with betting. It proposed to remedy the situation under the existing law, which sought (though not with complete effect) to forbid the provision of facilities for cash betting, by bringing off-the-course cash betting into the open and regulating it. This involved: (1) requiring a bookmaker to hold a permit (at an initial fee of £100) from the local justices in England and Wales or the licensing court in Scotland which might be refused if evidence were produced that the applicant was not a fit and proper person to hold a bookmaker's permit; and (2) allowing the establishment of licensed betting offices for betting with bookmakers or the totalizator operated on horse racecourses. Applications for licences for betting offices might be refused by the justices or licensing court on the grounds: (1) that the premises were unsuitable for use as a licensed betting office having regard to their layout, character, condition or location; or (2) that the grant or renewal of a licence would be inexpedient after account was taken of local demand and the numbers of offices available to satisfy it; or (3) that premises for which a renewal of a licence was sought had not been properly conducted. Under the bill, licensed betting offices might not be used for any purpose other than betting; people under 18 would not be admitted; loitering inside or outside would be forbidden; and neither radio nor television might be provided.

Part II of the bill would sweep away all the existing law regarding gaming and make a new start. No game would be unlawful in itself; gaming would only be unlawful if it broke any of three simple rules: (1) the game in itself must be fair as between one player and another (as in whist or bridge) or the gaming must be conducted in a fair manner (*e.g.*, if the game had a banker, all the players must have an equal opportunity of being banker); (2) the money staked by the players must all be repaid to the winners (*i.e.*, there must be no " cut " on the stakes for the benefit of the organizer); and (3) there must be no charge for the right to take part in the gaming. However, clubs were to be exempted from the third rule; amusements with prizes on fairgrounds and at fun fairs would be allowed provided that neither the charge for each " go " nor any money prize exceeded 1*s.*; and similar amusements with prizes would be permitted without restriction at fêtes and bazaars not run for private gain. Gaming machines would be allowed in private premises (such as clubs), provided that the coin operating them was not more than 6*d.* and that they were not operated for private gain.

In the United States, during the fiscal year ending June 30, 1959, 8,500 federal $50 wagering occupational tax stamps were purchased, compared with 8,121 the preceding year; 17,500 premises purchased $250 federal tax stamps for coin-operated gaming devices, compared with 16,771 the previous year. In the first nine months of 1959, 20,139,346 persons attended 44 major horse race tracks in the United States, and $1,577,737,679 passed through the pari-mutuel machines. At the same tracks in 1958, during the corresponding period, the attendance was 20,286,323 and the pari-mutuel total was $1,524,401,749.

Nevada realized $4,185,549 from legalized gambling during the first half of 1959 compared with $3,335,598 in the same period of 1958. For the whole of 1958 Nevada's revenue from gambling was $7,130,911, compared with $6,845,910 during 1957. Legalized bingo began operating in New York on Jan. 1, 1959, and by March 31 the State Lottery Control commission had approved 1,758 requests for licences from organizations. Authorized bingo games took in $4,310,632, and bingo operators paid $92,120 to the state in licence fees and an identical amount to cities, towns and villages in which the games were played.   (H. W. Sy.; V. W. P.)

BHUTAN. Indian-protected princely state in the Himalayas, between India (Assam [S. and E.] and West Bengal [S.W.]), Tibet (N. and N.W.) and Sikkim (W.). Area: c. 18,000 sq.mi. Pop. (1959 est.): 700,000, mainly Bhutanese, Bhotias or Duk-pa of Tibetan origin (Bhot = Tibet); also many Nepalese in the south. Language: a Tibetan dialect. Religion: Duk-pa Buddhism, a crude unreformed Lamaism. Capitals: Punakha (winter), Paro and Tashichodzong (summer). Maharaja, Jigme Dorji Wangchuk. Monetary unit: Indian *rupee* = 1s. 6d.

History. Jawaharlal Nehru, prime minister of India, declared in New Delhi on Aug. 25 that India was responsible for the defence of Bhutan. "We would defend Bhutan against any intrusion", he said in the Rajya Sabha (Council of States). Jigme Dorji, 39-year-old prime minister of Bhutan (a relative of the 32-year-old maharaja, Jigme Dorji Wangchuk), visited New Delhi during the summer. On Sept. 15 he expressed his confidence that the Chinese government did not intend to infringe on Bhutanese territory, although in some of their new maps, he noted, they laid claim to about 200 sq.mi. of Bhutanese land. "People of Bhutan are a little worried", he said, "but not panicky". During his negotiations with the Indian government Jigme Dorji secured a credit of Rs.150 million for the construction of five roads in Bhutan and Rs.700,000 for special economic assistance. (*See* also Sino-Indian Frontier Dispute.)

BIOCHEMISTRY.   **Protein Structure and Function.** Protein molecules are involved in almost all biochemical activities. Only recently has enough been learned about the structure of a few of these molecules to correlate their structure with their biological activity. Because proteins are large molecules, structural problems are considered at various levels of organization. These levels have been designated as the primary, secondary, tertiary and quaternary levels. The greatest progress has been made in determining the primary structure of a number of important proteins. The primary structure refers to the sequence of the amino acid residues in the polypeptide chains of the protein. The complete amino acid of the enzyme ribonuclease was determined in 1959, the first time this had been done for any enzyme.

The term secondary structure has been applied to the arrangement assumed by the amino acids in a single polypeptide chain. Recent work supported the α-helix structure proposed by L. C. Pauling and R. B. Corey. The term tertiary structure refers to the spatial relationship between neighbouring segments of the polypeptide chains of the protein molecule. Since physical studies show that the globular proteins are round, and it is known that they are made up of long polypeptide chains, the tertiary structure of the globular proteins must be complex. Detailed X-ray diffraction studies were made of the protein, myoglobin. These studies culminated in the publication in 1959 of the complete tertiary structure of this molecule. The tertiary structure reveals a molecule composed of a complicated and twisted polypeptide chain. The principles governing the configuration were not apparent at this stage of the analysis and there was no symmetrical scheme which could be proposed for the structure of this molecule.

Although the immediate relevance of the structural arrangement of the molecule to its biological activity was not apparent, workers in the field assumed that the main purpose of the tertiary structure is to obtain a proper arrangement of the side chains of amino acids at a particular site in the protein molecule. For example, the haeme portion of myoglobin has a number of substituted groups arranged around the central haeme ring in a peculiar and unsymmetrical fashion. It was proposed that the tertiary structure of the myoglobin molecule allows interaction between the substituents of the haeme and the side chains of amino acids of the polypeptide chain to produce the configuration necessary for its activity.

The use of the term quaternary structure to describe still another level of organization in protein molecules was more recent than the use of terms previously discussed, and work during 1959 showed that knowledge of this level of organization was extremely important in understanding the biological activity of large molecules and even some of the smaller molecules. For instance, the haemoglobins, which are not excessively large molecules, can be dissociated into sub-units and the number of sub-units which can be formed depends upon the method of dissociation. These studies revealed that the haemoglobin molecule is composed of four different sub-units which are held together in a specific manner. These sub-units are composed of separate polypeptide chains and it was suggested that each of the polypeptide chains contains one of the four haeme groups which are known to exist in haemoglobin.

The existence of sub-units in protein molecules is not restricted to the very large protein molecules. β-lactoglobin, a protein which has a molecular weight of 35,000 was recently shown by X-ray diffraction to consist of two similar sub-units. The much larger molecule, ferritin, whose molecular weight is 747,000, is also built up of sub-units. The X-ray evidence suggested that the molecule contains 24 identical protein sub-units each with a molecular weight of 19,000. These sub-units are apparently arranged to form a spherical shell which contains micelles of ferric hydroxide. It had been known for some time that ferritin serves as a reserve storehouse for iron in the animal. The existence of a hollow protein shell containing iron hydroxide within it would clearly serve this function. These studies showed that protein molecules may not be as large or complicated as was originally thought. The larger molecules in most cases appeared to be made up of identical or at least very similar sub-units.

Congenital Galactosemia.   The disease congenital galactosemia is caused by lack of a single enzyme called galactose-l-phosphate transferase. Recently galactose metabolism was studied in adults with galactosemia. In spite of the lack of the enzyme galactose-l-phosphate transferase, the adult can convert galactose-l-phosphate to glucose and use the glucose for energy purposes. The liver of adults who have this defect contains a newly discovered enzyme called UDP-galactose pyrophosphatase. This enzyme catalyses a reaction between galactose-l-phosphate and a coenzyme called UTP to yield UDP-galactose plus pyrophosphate. The UDP-galactose formed by this reaction is then converted to UDP-glucose which can be used by the animal. The liver of the newborn galactosemic animal is deficient in both galactose-l-phosphate and in the UDP-galactose pyrophosphatase. In the adult animal, however, UDP-galactose pyrophosphatase increases considerably and this appears to be the reason why individuals with congential galactosemia develop their most pronounced symptoms only in infancy. (*See* also PHYSIOLOGY.)

(L. M. K.)

See J. C. Kendrew, " Structure and Function in Myoglobin and other Proteins ", *Fed. Proc. 18*, 740-751 (1959); H. Holzer, " Carbohydrate Metabolism ", *Annu. Rev. Biochem. 28*, 171-222 (1959).

BIOGRAPHIES of some of the outstanding personalities of 1959.

Ayer, Alfred Jules, British philosopher (b. London, Oct. 29, 1910), was in Jan. 1959 appointed Wykeham professor of logic at the University of Oxford. He was educated at Eton and Christ Church, Oxford, and subsequently spent a short time at the University of Vienna. During 1932-35 he was a lecturer in philosophy at Christ Church, and from 1935 a research student there. Joining the army in 1940, he served throughout most of World War II in military intelligence. He returned to Oxford in 1945 as fellow and dean of Wadham college. In the following year he became Grote professor of the philosophy of mind and logic in the University of London, remaining in this post until 1959.

A disciple of the Vienna group of philosophers, A. J. Ayer is one of the leading British exponents of logical positivism, which holds that scientific knowledge is the only kind of factual knowledge and that all traditional metaphysical doctrines are to be rejected as meaningless. His first work, *Language, Truth and Logic* (1936), was followed by *The Foundations of Empirical Knowledge* (1940), *Philosophical Essays* (1954) and *The Problem of Knowledge* (1956). In the course of his career Ayer has lectured at many foreign universities and was during 1948-49 visiting professor at New York university. Since 1952 he has been a fellow of the British Academy. He has become known to the public as a member of the B.B.C. television " Brains Trust ".

Balewa, Alhaji Abubakar Tawafa, Nigerian statesman (b. Tawafa Balewa, Bauchi province, Northern Region, Nigeria, Dec. 1912), was re-appointed prime minister of Nigeria after the federal elections of 1959. A strict Moslem, he was educated at Bavebi Provincial school and Katsina Higher college, being later appointed a teacher at the Bauchi Middle school, of which he eventually became headmaster. In 1945 he went to Britain to take a one-year course at the London University Institute of Education and in 1949 he was made an education officer. He had already turned his attention to politics and in 1947 had been elected to the Northern Region House of Assembly, in addition becoming a member of the central legislative council. In 1948 he went to London as Nigerian delegate to the Commonwealth Parliamentary conference. When the 1951 constitution came into force he was returned as first Bauchi member of the Northern House of Assembly and was also elected to the central House of Representatives. He subsequently joined the Council of Ministers with the portfolio of minister of works, becoming two years later minister of transport. As a result of the constitutional conference of 1957 Balewa was appointed first prime minister of the federation. Confirmed in this office following the victory of his party, the Northern People's congress, in the 1959 elections, he would thus be his country's prime minister when it achieved independence in 1960. Balewa declared after the election that Nigeria would remain in the Commonwealth and would seek closer association with the United States.

Banda, Hastings Kamuzu, Nyasa politician (b. Nyasaland, 1906), as leader of the Nyasaland African National congress became in 1959 the focal point of his country's opposition to the Central African Federation. As a boy he attended a Church of Scotland mission, and has remained a staunch member of the Church of Scotland. He left home at the age of 12 to further his education in South Africa. There he worked for several years as an interpreter on the Rand goldfields, studying in the evenings. Eventually he went to the United States, where he qualified as a doctor at Mecheray Medical college, Nashville, Tennessee. In 1938 he left the United States for Britain and during World War II worked as a general practitioner in Liverpool. Later he established a large practice in Kilburn, London. He began to meet African students, corresponded with political leaders in Nyasaland and was concerned in the creation of the Nyasaland African National congress. When the proposals for the creation of the Central African Federation (The Federation of Rhodesia and Nyasaland) became known, he campaigned unsuccessfully to keep Nyasaland completely under British control. In 1958 the government of the federation put forward its demand for complete independence in 1960, and Banda accepted an offer to take over the active leadership of the N.A.N.C. Later the same year he returned to Nyasaland and in a series of speeches condemned what he alleged was an attempt to impose upon the people of Nyasaland a regime which they did not want. Following the outbreak of disturbances in Nyasaland during Feb.-March 1959 and the subsequent declaration of a state of emergency, the N.A.N.C. was proscribed. Banda was arrested and held in detention in Southern Rhodesia.

Beauvoir, Simone Lucie Ernestine Marie Bertrand de, French philosopher and writer (b. Paris, Jan. 9, 1908), the first volume of whose autobiography *Memoirs of a Dutiful Daughter* appeared in English during 1959. She was brought up in a bourgeois Roman Catholic family and her father was a lawyer. Educated in private schools and at the Sorbonne (Ecole Normale Supérieure), she was runner-up to Jean-Paul Sartre in the *concours d'agrégation,* the higher competitive examination following graduation. During 1931-43 she taught philosophy in various schools in the provinces and then in Paris. In 1943 her first novel, *L'Invitée*, appeared and in the same year she gave up teaching. Together with Sartre, Simone de Beauvoir has been a leading figure in the existentialist movement and has edited its journal *Les Temps modernes.* She is a philosopher in her own right, and it has been said of her that if she had not met Sartre and if existentialism had never existed, she would have invented or discovered it. Her humane and positive version of this philosophy, which pervades all her writings, is most fully expressed in *Pour Une Morale de l'ambiguïté* (1948). Her study of the status of the human female, *Le Deuxième Sexe*, was published in English in 1953. She has travelled widely, *America Day by Day* (1952) containing her outspoken comments on the United States, and *La Longue Marche* (1957) a sympathetic account of modern China. In 1954 she was awarded the Prix Goncourt for her novel *Les Mandarins.* Her chief distinctions as a writer are her lucidity and her fearless self-analysis.

Bergman, (Ernst) Ingmar, Swedish film director and theatrical producer (b. Uppsala, Sweden, July 14, 1918), has made an outstanding contribution to the postwar Swedish cinema. The son of a pastor, he completed his education at Stockholm university. In 1940 he became an assistant producer at the Royal Opera house, Stockholm, and in the same year began work for Svensk Filmindustri as a script-writer and producer. He wrote the script for the film *Frenzy* (1944), the story of a schoolboy terrorized by a sadistic master. During the next few years he directed several films, beginning with *Crisis* (1946), and achieved real stature with *Summer Interlude* (1951), an idyllic story of young love. This was followed by several notable films: *Waiting Women* (1952), *Sawdust and Tinsel* (1953), *A Lesson in Love* (1954) and *Smiles of a Summer Night* (1955)—the last a near masterpiece of comedy. His most ambitious work, *The Seventh Seal* (1957), is set in the 14th century and has close affinities with the medieval morality play. A knight returning from the crusades to a country stricken by the plague meets Death and endeavours to learn from him the purpose of human existence. The idea of loneliness—ever present in this film—is a dominating theme in Bergman's work, and appears in *Wild Strawberries* (1957), in which in a single day an aged professor recalls the events of his life. *Brink of Life* (1958) is a realistic study of the life of women in a hospital maternity ward. *The Face* (1958) takes place in mid-19th century Sweden and portrays a travelling hypnotist and magician who encounters the hostility of sceptically minded men. Although he has achieved an international reputation through the cinema, Bergman has continued to work regularly for the theatre, and in 1959 directed a production of *Faust* in London.

Birkett, William Norman Birkett, Baron, of Ulverston in the county of Lancashire, British judge (b. Ulverston, Lancashire Sept. 6, 1883), acted as independent chairman in the negotiations which ended, on July 31, in the resolution of the six-week long printing industry dispute of 1959. Educated at Barrow-in-Furness and at Emmanuel college, Cambridge, where he was president of the Union society in 1910, he was called to the bar in 1913 and took silk in 1924. As Liberal M.P. he represented East Nottingham during 1923-24 and 1929-31. Appointed a judge of the King's Bench division in 1941, he has been chairman of Buckinghamshire Quarter Sessions since 1946. From 1941 to 1950 he was chairman of the advisory committee for Defence regulation 18B and took part in the Nuremburg trials during 1945-46. From 1950 to 1957 he was a lord justice of appeal. In 1956 Birkett was treasurer of the Inner Temple, and he has been master of the Curriers' company on four occasions since 1936. He was chairman of the 1957 committee of inquiry into telephone-tapping set up as a result of the Marrinan case. His conduct of the 16-day long negotiations in the printing dispute was praised by both sides. Birkett was knighted in 1941 and created a baron in 1958.

Bullock, Alan Louis Charles, British historian (b. Bradford, Yorkshire, Dec. 13, 1914), has become known to the public through his prominent part in the founding of the new Oxford college, St. Catherine's, his study of Adolf Hitler and his television appearances. Educated at Bradford Grammar school and at Wadham college, Oxford, he gained first class honours in classics (1936) and modern history (1938). He held the Bryce studentship at Oxford up to the outbreak of World War II, whereupon he served in the B.B.C. European service until 1945. During 1945-52 he was fellow, dean and tutor in modern history at New college, Oxford. In 1952 he accepted the appointment of censor of St. Catherine's society and has taken an active part in the administrative work of Oxford university, serving on the Hebdomadal council. Also in 1952, his authoritative work, *Hitler, A Study of Tyranny*, was published. He followed this in 1956 with *The Liberal Tradition*, and his biography of Ernest Bevin was to be published early in 1960. Bullock was the driving force behind the plans for the new St. Catherine's college which he conceived one evening during an enforced wait at Reading station. His regular appearances on the B.B.C.'s " Brains Trust " have made him familiar to many and probably helped his remarkably successful efforts to raise money from industrialists for the new college of which he is to be the first master. He is a member of the B.B.C. General Advisory council.

Butler, Richard Austen, British statesman (b. Attock Serai, northern India, Dec. 9, 1902), became chairman of the Conservative party after the 1959 general election, while retaining his previous posts of home secretary and leader of the House of Commons. Educated at Marlborough college and at Pembroke college, Cambridge, where he was president of the Union society in 1924, he has represented Saffron Walden in parliament since 1929. In 1931 he became parliamentary secretary to the secretary of state for India and Burma and later under secretary of state at the India Office. After some years as parliamentary secretary to the Ministry of Labour and under-secretary at the Foreign Office, he was during 1941-45 minister of education and introduced important changes in the educational system. With the Conservative party in opposition, he became chairman of its advisory committee on policy and political education and also of its research department. From 1951 to 1955 he was chancellor of the exchequer and from 1955 lord privy seal and leader of the House of Commons. It was widely supposed that he would succeed Sir Anthony Eden as prime minister after the latter's resignation in 1957. As home secretary from that year he had to deal with a number of issues of wide public interest: the reintroduction of flogging or birching, for which he rejected demands both from his own side of the house and from outside parliament; the publication of the Casement diaries; the implemention of parts of the Wolfenden report in the form of the Street Offences act; the interception of private telephone conversations by the police; and the relationship between the police and the public, into which, on Nov. 18, 1959, he announced an independent inquiry, following a motion of censure on himself arising from the Garrat *v.* Eastward case involving a Metropolitan police officer. On Oct. 21 Butler married Mrs. A. Courtauld, a kinswoman by his first marriage.

Butterfield, Herbert, British historian (b. Oxenhope, Yorkshire, Oct. 7, 1900), was in 1959 elected vice-chancellor of Cambridge university. He was educated at the Trade and Grammar school, Keighley, and at Peterhouse college, Cambridge. During 1924-25 he was Jane Eliza Procter visiting fellow at the University of Princeton, New Jersey. He was a lecturer in history at Peterhouse from 1930 to 1944, when he became professor of modern history at Cambridge. In 1955 he was elected master of Peterhouse. He has written on a variety of subjects, his first book—a study of the historical novel—appearing in 1924. Other works include *The Whig Interpretation of History* (1931), *The Statecraft of Machiavelli* (1940), *George III, Lord North and the People*, *Christianity and History* (both 1949), *History and Human Relations* (1951) and *Christianity, Diplomacy and War* (1953). During 1938-52 he was editor of the *Cambridge University Journal*. He was installed as vice-chancellor at Cambridge in succession to Lord Adrian on Oct. 1.

Castle, Barbara Anne, British politician (b. Chesterfield, Derbyshire, Oct. 6, 1911), was chairman of the Labour party during 1958-59. The daughter of an Inland Revenue inspector, Frank Betts, who was also the editor of a left-wing journal, the *Bradford Pioneer*, she grew up in an atmosphere of intellectual socialism. From Bradford Girls' Grammar school she went up to St. Hugh's college, Oxford, where she played an active part in university political life. At 25, she was the youngest member of St. Pancras borough council. During the war she was an administrative officer with the Ministry of Food until 1944, when she became housing correspondent and, later, director of the advice bureau for the Forces on the *Daily Mirror*. In 1944 she married a fellow-journalist, Ted Castle. Member of parliament for Blackburn from 1945-50, for Blackburn East from 1950-55, and for Blackburn since 1955, she was returned with an increased majority in the general election of Oct. 1959.

Her good looks, red hair, vigorous personality and intelligence, and a flair for publicity inherited, perhaps, from her days in Fleet street, have all contributed to her success. In the Labour governments of 1945-51 she was parliamentary private secretary to the president of the Board of Trade and in 1950 she secured her seat on the party's national executive committee. Within the Labour party she stands to the left, was a Bevanite during the Bevan controversy, and since 1951 has been particularly prominent as a critic of Conservative colonial policy. Remarks which made enemies for her in Kenya and Southern Rhodesia culminated in Sept. 1958 in her criticism of the conduct of British troops in Cyprus. Emerging, apparently unscathed, from the furore which this unleashed in the national press, Barbara Castle succeeded to the chairmanship of the Labour party in Oct. 1958. Her last act in this office was to preside over the party conference at Blackpool on Nov. 28-29, when she spoke strongly against abandoning any socialist principles, saying that "it simply won't wash to say that nationalization is fusty and out of date". At the subsequent election for the national executive she came top of the poll in the constituency section.

Castro, Fidel, Cuban revolutionary leader (b. Mayarí, eastern Cuba, Aug. 13, 1927), became prime minister of Cuba in Feb. 1959. The son of a wealthy sugar planter, Castro studied law at the University of Havana, receiving his doctorate in 1950. Meanwhile he had become attracted to revolutionary activities. Setting up law practice in Havana, he specialized in defending poor litigants without fee. His candidacy for the national legislature came to a swift end with the Fulgencio Batista coup of 1952. On July 26, 1953, with 160 like-minded youths, he began his anti-Batista campaign in Santiago de Cuba. His attack on the army barracks failed, he was captured, sentenced to 15 years' imprisonment but was amnestied in 1955. In exile, first in New York and then in Mexico, he organized and trained a group of fellow exiles in the latter country and returned with a body of 82 armed rebels to his native Oriente province in Cuba on Dec. 2, 1956. His guerrilla talents baffled the regular Cuban army, which tried vainly to capture him and disperse his force of several thousand volunteer irregulars. From his headquarters in the Sierra Maestra, Castro directed a surprisingly effective campaign of harassment and civil terrorism that led finally to complete victory over Batista who fled to the Dominican Republic on Jan. 1, 1959. The "July 26 movement" was victorious. (For the events of 1959 *see* CUBA.)

Chamberlain, Owen, U.S. physicist (b. San Francisco, July 10, 1920), received the 1959 Nobel prize for physics jointly with Emilio Segre, another U.S. physicist. He was educated at Dartmouth college and the University of Chicago, receiving his Ph.D. in 1949. He then became a member of the University of California's faculty at Berkeley where he was an associate professor of physics in 1959. Earlier, Chamberlain had been associated with the Manhattan district atom bomb project and was present at Alamogordo, New Mexico, when the first atom bomb was exploded in 1945. Chamberlain's Nobel award, amounting to half of the total prize of about £15,220, was in recognition of his co-discovery of the existence of the antiproton. Although long certain of the existence of the antiproton, nuclear physicists had never observed it until Chamberlain and Segrè, working with a team of physicists at the University of California's radiation laboratory at Livermore, California, identified the atomic particle in some subatomic matter produced by the laboratory's bevatron. Antiprotons have negative electric charges as opposed to the positive charges of ordinary protons. The two destroy each other upon contact, creating a powerful burst of energy. Chamberlain's and Segrè's discovery was hailed by physicists as a significant step towards man's understanding of the nature of the universe and the elements which compose it.

Dahanayake, Wijayananda, Ceylonese statesman (b. Galle, Ceylon, Oct. 22, 1902), became prime minister on Sept. 26, 1959, following the assassination of S. W. R. D. Bandaranaike. He was educated at the Galle Methodist school, the Anglican St. Thomas's college in Colombo and the government Teachers' Training college near Colombo. He taught in secondary schools and in 1935 began his political career when he was elected to the Galle municipal council. Four years later he became mayor, a post to which he was constantly re-elected. He entered the national legislature in 1944 when he became a member of Ceylon's state council. In the first parliamentary election of 1947 he stood successfully for Galle, retaining this seat in 1952 and 1956. He formed his own political group, the Bhasa Peramuna (Language front), which claimed that Sinhalese should be the country's only official language. When Bandaranaike, from 1951 leader of the Sri Lanka Midahas Pakshaya (Blessed Ceylon Freedom party), formed the Mahajana Eksath Peramuna (People's United front) to contest the 1956 general election, Dahanayake joined him with his group. After the P.U.F. victory in the election, he was appointed minister of education in the Bandaranaike cabinet. When parliament was dissolved on Dec. 4 he resigned from the Sri Lanka party and declared that he would form a new party to contest the election in 1960. A Buddhist, Dahanayake is known as a hard worker and a gifted, witty speaker in both English and Sinhalese.

Dalai Lama (PAMO TSIRING), the 14th Dalai Lama (b. June 6, 1935, near Jyekundo, eastern Tibet), was granted asylum in India in 1959. The son of a peasant Tibetan couple, he was when four years old identified by Lamaist emissaries from Lhasa as the new earthly incarnation of Chenrezi, God of Mercy, the patron deity of Tibet, who on Dec. 17, 1933, departed from the body of the 13th Dalai Lama. Enthroned in the Potala, or chief palace, of Lhasa on Feb. 22, 1940, he became the spiritual and political ruler of Tibet. The Tibetans do not use the name of Dalai Lama, a Mongolian expression meaning "all-embracing lama". They call their ruler Gyalpo Rimpoche (the precious king) or Kundün (the presence). When in Oct. 1950 the Chinese Communist army began its invasion of Tibet, the Dalai Lama fled to Yatung, near Sikkim, and appealed for Indian help. He was advised by Jawaharlal Nehru, the prime minister of India, to reach agreement with China. On May 23, 1951, such an agreement was signed in Peking and on Aug. 17, the Dalai Lama returned to Lhasa and on Oct. 9 Chinese troops occupied the Tibetan capital. In Sept. 1954, the Dalai Lama visited Peking where he was received by the chairman of the Chinese People's Republic Mao Tse-tung. He remained there until March 1955, trying his best to establish Tibetan autonomy which had been guaranteed by the 1951 agreement. However, the constant interference of the Chinese in Tibetan domestic affairs was such that in 1956 a revolt started in eastern Tibet. On March 17, 1959, open battle broke out between Tibetans and Chinese at Lhasa. The Dalai Lama, with his family and his high officials, left the capital and crossed the Indian frontier on March 31, arriving at Tezpur, Assam, on April 18. Three days later he reached Mussoorie, in northern India, which was to be his residence. Nehru visited him on April 20, declaring later that no political activities would be permitted to the Dalai Lama during his exile in India.

Debré, Michel (Jean Pierre), French statesman (b. Paris, Jan. 5, 1912), became in Jan. 1959 the first prime minister of the Fifth French Republic. The son of a prominent doctor, he was born a Jew but was converted to Roman Catholicism. A doctor of law of Paris university, with a diploma of the Ecole des Sciences Politiques, he joined the civil service at the Conseil d'Etat, winning first place in the entrance examination. Shortly before World War II Debré met General Charles de Gaulle and was deeply impressed by him. In 1939 he became a cavalry lieutenant, and eventually joined the French resistance. On the liberation of France de Gaulle commissioned him to prepare a report on administrative reform. He turned to politics, and in 1948, as a member of the Gaullist Rassemblement du Peuple Français, became senator for the Indre-et-Loire *département*. He remained in the Senate for ten years, criticizing tirelessly "the system" and proclaiming the country's need to call back de Gaulle. When on June 1, 1958, the general formed his government, he made Debré minister of justice and asked him to draft the new constitution. He was also elected to the central committee of the new Gaullist party, the Union pour la Nouvelle République. On Jan. 8, 1959, de Gaulle became president of the republic, and he appointed Debré his *premier ministre* (and not *president du conseil des ministres* as the heads of government had up to then been called). On Jan. 16 the National Assembly confirmed this choice by 453 votes to 56 (Socialists and Communists). Debré paid a visit to London (April 13-14) and to Bonn (May 6) for talks with Harold Macmillan and Konrad Adenauer respectively. He visited Algiers three times during 1959, pointing out that Algeria would never be separated from France. On July 7-8 he was present at the meeting of the executive council of the French Community at

A. J. Ayer

Simone de Beauvoir

Barbara Castle

Paul Hoffman

Antananarivo, Madagascar. On Aug. 16 he declared that the French must make themselves heard in order "to avoid being crushed by agreements between very great powers".

Dolci, Danilo, Italian social reformer (b. Trieste, June 28, 1924), whose book on conditions in Sicily, *Inchiesta a Palermo*, was translated into English as *To Feed the Hungry* in 1959. Having studied architecture, he joined Zeno Saltini's community for abandoned children at Nomadelfia. In 1952 he moved to Trappeto, a fishing village in a depressed, bandit-infested part of western Sicily. He built a house and a school and taught children and adults to read, write and enjoy music and the arts. He found poverty, unemployment, ignorance, delinquency, illiteracy and a total lack of confidence in the power of personal effort to improve things. At Trappeto he staged his first hunger strike to draw attention to the fact that in parts of Italy people were dying of starvation. His first book, *Fare presto e bene perché si muore* ("Make Haste, for People are Dying"), described conditions in Trappeto. *Banditti a Partinico* (1955) contrasted the total number of years the inhabitants spent in school (650) with those they spent in prison or banishment (3,000), and pointed out the folly of spending huge sums to police the region instead of investing to develop its resources. *Inchiesta a Palermo* (1956) earned him a literary prize and a trial for pornography. Dolci gradually extended his work to the whole of the Mafia country between Montelupo, Corleone and Palermo. To remind the authorities that the constitution guaranteed the right to work he led a party of unemployed to mend a cart track. His resulting trial attracted general attention. Though he is a firm believer in non-violence, to local authorities he appeared subversive, and the central government withdrew his passport because of his efforts to make Sicilian conditions known abroad. In 1958 he organized a meeting of sociologists and economists in Palermo to discuss a policy of full employment.

Heath, Edward Richard George, British politician (b. Broadstairs, Kent, July 9, 1916), was appointed minister of labour in the reconstruction of the cabinet after the general election of Oct. 1959. The son of a master builder, he was educated at Chatham House Grammer school, Ramsgate, Kent, and at Balliol college, Oxford, where he became president of the J.C.R. He was active in university politics and in 1939 was president of the Oxford union. During World War II he served with the Royal Artillery and rose from the ranks to lieutenant-colonel, a rank which he currently holds in the Honourable Artillery company. In the immediate postwar years he worked at the Ministry of Civil Aviation, but in the general election of Feb. 1950 he won Bexley from Labour by 133 votes. By Oct. 1959 his majority had risen to 8,633. In Feb. 1951 he became an assistant Conservative whip, in May 1952 joint deputy chief whip, in June 1953 deputy chief whip and in Dec. 1955 chief whip. A progressive within the Conservative party and a member of the One Nation group, Heath is generally considered to have been the most powerful Conservative chief whip since the 1930s, being remembered particularly for his successful handling of party discipline during the Suez crisis. During the latter part of the 1955-59 parliament he was known to be among the prime minister's closest advisers and his appointment to ministerial office in Oct. 1959 caused little surprise.

Hepworth, Barbara, British sculptor (b. Wakefield, Yorkshire, Jan. 10, 1903), who was awarded the major prize at the São Paulo biennial exhibition in 1959, is one of the senior of the half-dozen or so contemporary British sculptors whose work has for some years enjoyed a very high reputation in Europe and the Americas. She was educated at Wakefield high school, at Leeds School of Art and at the Royal College of Art, London. In 1924 she went to Italy on a travelling scholarship and stayed there two and a half years, studying in Florence and Rome. Her first exhibition was held in London in 1928. She has been influenced by Constantin Brancusi and Jean Arp and also by the painter Ben Nicholson, who became her second husband in 1933. During the prewar years the Nicholsons were at the centre of an international group of artists and architects working in England, including Piet Mondrian, Walter Gropius and Laszlo Moholy-Nagy, and during this period her sculptures became increasingly abstract and symbolic. In 1950 she was given a one-man exhibition in the British pavilion of the 25th Biennale in Venice, and has exhibited in many other European and North American cities. Examples of Barbara Hepworth's work are owned by the

Tate gallery, London, the Museum of Modern Art, New York, and the national galleries of Australia and Canada. Her bronze *Meridian* a four-ton abstract composition to be erected at State house, a new 16-storey London office building, was cast at a French foundry in Nov. 1959.

Herter, Christian Archibald, U.S. statesman (b. Paris, March 28, 1895), succeeded John Foster Dulles as U.S. secretary of state on April 21, 1959, following Dulles' resignation shortly before his death. Herter graduated from Harvard university and studied architecture for a time before entering the U.S. foreign service in 1916. He was associated with Dulles as an adviser on German reparations at the Versailles peace conference in 1919 and assisted Herbert Hoover in eastern European relief work in 1920. In 1921-24 he was an assistant to Hoover when the latter was secretary of commerce. In 1929 Herter became a lecturer on international relations at Harvard. He was a member of the Massachusetts house of representatives from 1931 to 1934 and speaker in 1939-43. For the next ten years he represented the 10th Massachusetts district in the U.S. House of Representatives, and then became governor of Massachusetts for two terms (1953-57). Herter was appointed under secretary of state in 1957. On becoming secretary of state he had immediately to face the international crisis arising from the U.S.S.R.'s attempt to dislodge the western powers from Berlin, and at the Geneva conference of foreign ministers in May-August he continued his predecessor's firm stand against further Communist political encroachment. In August he accompanied President Dwight D. Eisenhower to Europe for the conference with western European leaders that preceded the visit of Nikita S. Khrushchev to the United States. In November he said that ". . . rules must be devised to temper acute political problems which cannot now be fully solved, and to bring under control the spiralling arms race which those problems goad onward."

Heyrovsky, Jaroslav, Czechoslovak chemist and director of the Polarographic institute of the Czechoslovak Academy of Sciences (b. Prague, Dec. 20, 1890), won the Nobel prize for chemistry of £15,220 in 1959 "for his discovery and development of polarography". He was educated at the University of Prague and at University college, London university, where he worked under Sir William Ramsay and Professor F. G. Donnan and, in 1913, held the post of demonstrator in the chemistry department. After World War I Heyrovsky returned to Prague where at the Charles university he became in turn assistant in the chemistry department (1920), lecturer (1922), assistant professor (1924), and professor of physical chemistry and director of the Physical Chemistry institute (1926-54). The work which led eventually to the discovery of polarography was begun during his student days in London when he investigated the electrode potential of aluminium at the suggestion of Donnan. The polarograph is an instrument for measuring the current which flows when a predetermined potential is applied to two electrodes immersed in the solution being analysed. The first polarographic apparatus was made and described in 1925, but the method did not come into general use until about ten years later. Polarography permits of some determinations which are difficult or impossible to carry out by other means, and the method finds increasing applications both in qualitative and quantitative chemical analysis. Heyrovsky's monograph, *Polarographie*, appeared in 1941, and the importance of his work is shown by the fact that nearly 10,000 papers on the subject had been published by the end of 1959.   (W. J. Bp.)

Hoffman, Paul Gray, U.S. business executive, federal government and United Nations official (b. Chicago, Illinois, April 26, 1891), became the first managing director of the United Nations Special fund in Dec. 1958. After study at the University of Chicago he was a salesman for a Studebaker agency in Los Angeles, later becoming district branch manager for Studebaker in that city. After service in World War I as an artillery officer he bought the Studebaker agency in Los Angeles and in 1925 was appointed vice-president of the Studebaker corporation with headquarters in South Bend, Indiana. In 1933 Hoffman and another officer successfully reorganized the corporation after bankruptcy and he was president from 1935 to 1948. One of the founders of the Committee for Economic Development, Hoffman was chairman of its board of trustees from 1942 to 1948. In 1948 President Harry S. Truman appointed him administrator of the Economic Co-operation administration; he supervised the European Recovery programme (Marshall plan) until his resignation in Sept. 1950. Shortly afterwards he became president of the Ford foundation. Hoffman was one of the earliest supporters of Dwight D. Eisenhower for the Republican presidential nomination in 1952. In Feb. 1953 he resigned as president of the Ford foundation to return to Studebaker as board chairman. When Studebaker merged with the Packard Motor Car company in 1954 Hoffman became board chairman of Studebaker Packard. In 1956 he was a delegate to the U.N. general assembly. As managing director of its Special fund, created to assist underdeveloped nations, in Feb. 1959 Hoffman proposed that foreign aid from contributing nations, both public and private, should be increased to between $60,000 million and $80,000 million for the ensuing decade.

Johansson, Ingemar, Swedish boxer (b. Gothenburg, Sweden, Sept. 22, 1932), in 1959 became the first Swede to win the heavyweight championship of the world and the first European to win this title since Max Schmeling (Germany) beat Jack Sharkey (United States) in 1930. Only two men, Johansson and Rocky Marciano, have won the world title without one defeat as professionals. Johansson won Swedish amateur titles and boxed for his country in the Olympic games at Helsinki in 1952 when along with Ed Sanders (United States), his opponent in the heavyweight final, he was disqualified for " not trying ". On Dec. 5, 1952, he turned professional and by April 15, 1956, had won 14 contests, mostly by knockouts. On Sept. 30, 1956, in his first professional fight outside Sweden, he won the European championship, knocking out Franco Cavicchi (Italy) in 13 rounds at Milan. He defended this title successfully by knocking out Henry Cooper (Britain) in five rounds at Stockholm in 1957 and by forcing Joe Erskine (Britain) to retire in 13 rounds at Gothenburg a year later. After defeating Eddie Machen (United States), the leading contender, in one round at Stockholm in 1958, he went to the United States and in June 1959 won the world title by flooring Floyd Patterson in three rounds at Yankee stadium, New York. This was Johansson's only contest in 1959. Apart from his achievements as a boxer, Johansson has had great success as a businessman and is wealthy and intelligent enough to avoid dependence on a professional boxing career. (F. Br.)

Kornberg, Arthur, U.S. biochemist (b. Brooklyn, New York State, March 3, 1918), shared the 1959 Nobel prize for medicine and physiology with Severo Ochoa (*q.v.*). He was educated at City college, New York, and the University of Rochester from which he received a medical degree in 1941. From 1942 to 1953 he was on the staff of the U.S. Public Health Service, and from 1947 to 1951 he also taught at Washington university, St. Louis, Missouri. Returning there in 1953, he was head of the biochemistry department at the medical school until his resignation in 1959 to assume a similar position at Stanford university. Kornberg's Nobel award cited his and Ochoa's discovery of enzymes that would artificially produce some of the vital substances of life. Specifically, Kornberg was honoured for his discovery of an enzyme that promotes the production of deoxyribonucleic acid (DNA); Ochoa discovered an enzyme that produces ribonucleic acid (RNA). DNA is believed to be the chemical that transmits hereditary characteristics from one generation to another; RNA is considered necessary to the production of protein. Kornberg's research, together with that of Ochoa established the principle that unlinked nucleotides could be made to form spirals by such enzymes if some of the natural product was used to serve as a model. This achievement was considered a significant advance to the understanding of the basic life process. The two scientists divided the prize of £15,220.

Littlewood, Joan, British theatrical producer (b. London), has achieved an international reputation through the quality of her work. Of working-class parentage, she was educated in London and won a scholarship to the Royal Academy of Dramatic Art. In 1934 she moved to Manchester and there worked with the B.B.C. as an actress and as a writer of documentary material. She subsequently formed an amateur, left-wing theatrical group known as the Theatre union, which despite a lack of resources enjoyed considerable success. During World War II for a time she wrote radio scripts. In 1945 the Theatre union was re-formed in Manchester as a new, professional company, Theatre Workshop. For several years this toured both in Britain and on the continent before, in 1953, establishing itself at the Theatre Royal, Stratford, London. Two years later Theatre Workshop was invited to represent Britain at the Paris International Festival of Dramatic Art. The theatre-going public, however, did not become familiar with the work of Joan Littlewood until two plays directed by her—*The Hostage* and *A Taste of Honey*—were transferred from Stratford to the west end early in 1959. Joan Littlewood herself has asserted that she has no interest in the London theatre (for which she developed a dislike at the beginning of her career) and that her intention has been to provide a theatre for ordinary people—a truly " popular " theatre. A striking feature of her productions is the deliberate appeal by the actors to the spectators, who are never allowed to forget that they are watching a play. During 1959 she received two awards: the prize for the best production (*The Hostage*) at the Paris International festival and an Italian award, the Olympic prize for the theatre, for her work as a whole.

Liu Shao-chi, Chinese Communist leader (b. Yinchan, Honan province, 1898), on April 27, 1959, became chairman of the Chinese People's Republic. The son of a rich peasant, he was educated at Changsha high school. He joined the Chinese Communist party (Kungchantang or K.C.T.) in 1921, and was sent to Moscow for training. He took an active part in the revolution of 1924-27 and in May 1925 was elected vice-chairman of the All-China Trades Union federation. He worked in that capacity in Shanghai, Honan province, Canton and Hankow. In 1927 the fifth congress of the K.C.T. elected him to the central committee and in the following year he was given a place on the party's control commission. In Jan. 1931 he was elected a member of the party's Politburo. He took part in the " long march " (1934-36) from Kiangsi to Yenan (Shensi). From here he was sent by Mao Tse-tung to Tientsin as secretary of the northern office of the K.C.T. After the Japanese invasion of China in 1937 Liu became secretary of the Central China office of the K.C.T. In 1941 he was appointed political commissar of the New Fourth army. From 1943 he worked in Yenan as deputy chairman of the National Revolutionary War council and two years later he was re-elected to the Politburo and became secretary of the party. In the central government of the Chinese People's Republic formed in Peking on Oct. 1, 1949, Liu was one of the six vice-chairmen under the chairmanship of Mao. He served also as chairman of the standing committee of the National People's congress, and in April 1959 the N.P.C. elected him chairman of the republic to succeed Mao who remained chairman of the K.C.T.

Lübke, Heinrich, German statesman (b. Enkhausen, Westphalia, Oct. 14, 1894), became second president of the German Federal Republic in 1959. The son of a farmer and shoemaker, he studied agriculture at the Universities of Berlin and Münster. After service in World War I he graduated as a land surveyor in 1921. He was one of the organizers and later director of the Deutsche Bauernschaft, Berlin. As a member of the Catholic Centre party, which he represented in the Prussian Landtag from 1931 to 1933, Lübke was deprived of all his offices by the Nazis, and spent 20 months in prison. In 1945 he was one of the founders of the Westphalian Christian Democratic union. Lübke was elected to the Bundestag in 1949 and re-elected in 1953, when he became federal minister of food and agriculture. On July 1, 1959, in western Berlin, the federal assembly elected him president of the German Federal Republic. In the second ballot he received 526 votes against 386 for Carlo Schmidt, a Social Democrat, and 99 for Max Becker, a Free Democrat. He succeeded Theodor Heuss on Sept. 15.

Maclean, Sir Charles Hector Fitzroy, chief of the clan Maclean and lord lieutenant of Argyll (b. London, May 5, 1916), became chief scout of the British Commonwealth and Empire on Sept. 6 in succession to Lord Rowallan. Educated at Canford school, Dorset, he was commissioned in the Scots Guards and during World War II served with the Guards armoured division in the Normandy campaign. He retired from the army in 1947 with the rank of major. From his own wolf cub days he has maintained a strong interest in scouting. He was county commissioner for Argyllshire from 1953 to 1955, a member of the council of the Boy Scouts association from 1953 and chief commissioner for Scotland from 1954. He became deputy chief scout in Feb. 1959. He is also a member of the Royal Company of Archers (the queen's bodyguard for Scotland) and a justice of the peace, and is actively interested in a large number of societies concerned with ex-service affairs, agriculture and other matters. Maclean lives at Duart castle on the Isle of Mull where he farms Highland cattle and Blackface sheep, in the breeding of which he is keenly interested.

Macmillan, (Maurice) Harold, British statesman (b. London, Feb. 10, 1894). For his career to the end of 1958 see *Britannica Book of the Year 1959*. In Feb. 1959 he and Selwyn Lloyd, the secretary of state for foreign affairs, made a ten-day visit to the U.S.S.R., during which they had exploratory talks with Nikita S. Khrushchev and other Soviet leaders concerning such matters as Germany, disarmament, and greater trade and cultural exchanges between the United Kingdom and the U.S.S.R. On his return Macmillan stressed their mutual agreement " that the great issues which separate east and west must be settled by negotiation ". In March he and Lloyd visited Paris, Bonn, Ottawa and Washington for discussions, particularly on the Berlin problem, other German questions and European security. In June Macmillan toured Lancashire, making speeches in which he explained the government's proposals for the reorganization of the cotton industry. On Aug. 31, during President Dwight D. Eisenhower's visit to the United Kingdom, they made together an historic television broadcast from 10, Downing street, in which they reviewed Anglo-American relations and the problems facing the western world. After the announcement that a general election would take place on Oct. 8, Macmillan explained that he thought people should have the opportunity of deciding who were to represent them in the important international negotiations which lay ahead. During the campaign he made a tour of 2,500 mi. and spoke at 74 meetings attended by 150,000 people. His claim was that the objectives of peace and prosperity were more likely to be attained under a Conservative than a Labour government. He and his party were returned to power with an over-all majority of 100 in the House of Commons.

Maudling, Reginald, British politician (b. Finchley, Middlesex, March 7, 1917), became president of the Board of Trade in Oct. 1959. The son of a consulting actuary, he was educated at Merchant Taylors' school and at Merton college, Oxford, where he obtained a first in greats. In 1940 he was called to the bar. During World War II he was a staff officer in the Royal Air Force and spent some time as private secretary to the minister for air. Having failed to win a seat in the general election of 1945, he was appointed head of the economic section of the Conservative Central office. In 1950 he entered parliament as Conservative member for Barnet and two years later became parliamentary secretary to the Ministry of Civil Aviation. Specializing in economic affairs, and with a quick mind, he was economic secretary to the Treasury from 1953 to 1955, when he became minister of supply and privy councillor. In Jan. 1957 he was appointed paymaster-general and was soon given the additional task of supervising and co-ordinating the government's preparations for negotiations towards the establishment of a European free trade area and of acting as the U.K. representative in them. From Jan. 1958 Maudling assisted the chancellor of the exchequer, Derick Heathcoat Amory, over the whole range of economic affairs. A member of the cabinet since Sept. 1957, he succeeded Sir David Eccles as president of the Board of Trade in the reconstruction of the cabinet after the general election of Oct. 1959. In December he and Amory signed on behalf of the United Kingdom the "outer seven" agreement for a European Free Trade association.

Mboya, Thomas Joseph, Kenya politician (b. Rusinga island, Lake Victoria, Sept. 15, 1930), has become a leading figure in the movement for African independence. A member of the Luo tribe, he is the son of illiterate parents who had been converted to Roman Catholicism. He received his early education at Roman Catholic missions, and subsequently attended school near Nairobi. He began his career in 1951 as a sanitary inspector for the Nairobi city council, but left in 1953 to take up the post of general secretary to the Kenya Local Government Workers' union (later known as the Kenya Federation of Labour). He was also treasurer of the Kenya African union at the time of its proscription the same year. Mboya first came into prominence in March 1955, when, after persuading dockers on strike at Mombasa to return to work, he successfully negotiated a substantial increase in wages on their behalf. Awarded a British Workers' Travel Association scholarship, he left Kenya in Sept. 1955 to study industrial relations at Oxford university for a year. After his return to Kenya he became recognized as one of the country's outstanding political figures. Elected a member of the colony's legislative council in 1957, he refused to take part in the scheme of multiracial government embodied in the Lyttelton constitution, and his declared aim was "undiluted democracy", which meant in effect African rule in Kenya. In 1958 Mboya was elected president of the Nairobi Peoples' convention and later the same year was chairman of the All-African People's conference held in Accra, Ghana. In April 1959 he began an Africa Freedom Fund campaign with a lecture tour in the United States. In December he went to London for private talks with the secretary of state for the colonies, Iain Macleod.

Noel-Baker, Philip John, British statesman and internationalist (b. London, Nov. 1, 1889), advocated international disarmament in the cause of world peace and was awarded the Nobel peace prize (valued at £15,220) in 1959. A member of the Society of Friends, he was educated at Bootham school, York, Haverford college, Pennsylvania, and at King's college, Cambridge. President of the Cambridge Union society in 1912, he also captained the British Olympic Games team. During World War I he served with the Friends' and other ambulance units in France, Belgium and Italy, being decorated for distinguished conduct. After working at the peace conference in 1919 as a member of the British delegation, he joined the secretariat of the League of Nations, where he assisted Fridtjof Nansen in his work for refugees, Lord Robert Cecil at sessions of the assembly and Arthur Henderson, the president, at the Geneva Disarmament conference, 1932-33. In the House of Commons, Noel-Baker represented Coventry (1929-31) and Derby, later Derby South (since 1936). Between 1945 and 1951, he was successively minister of state, secretary of state for air, secretary of state for commonwealth relations and minister of fuel and power. For 40 years, aided by a fluent command of seven languages, he campaigned for peace through international disarmament. *The Arms Race: a Programme for World Disarmament* (1958) was acclaimed as a monumental survey of the whole disarmament problem. (L. R. A.)

Nyerere, Julius Kambarage, Tanganyika politician (b. Butiama, Musoma district, Tanganyika, Feb. 1921), has played an important part in his country's evolution towards independence. The son of a chief and a convert to Roman Catholicism, he was educated at Musoma Village school, St. Mary's Secondary school, Tabora, and at Makerere college in Uganda, where he obtained a diploma in education. After teaching for a few years he went to Edinburgh university and graduated there in 1952. On his return to Tanganyika he took up teaching again. Becoming increasingly interested in politics, he was in 1953 elected president of the Tanganyika African association and in the following year of its successor body the Tanganyika African National union. He visited the United States early in 1955, when he addressed the U.N. Trusteeship council. He paid a second visit in 1956 and went for a third time in 1957, again

appearing before the Trusteeship council. The same year he accepted appointment as a representative member of the Tanganyika legislative council but later resigned. In Sept. 1958 he was elected to the legislative council in Tanganyika's first elections. He was subsequently appointed chairman of the Tanganyika Elected Members organization and, as such, the leading spokesman from the representative side of the legislative council. After the announcement in Dec. 1959 that Tanganyika would be granted internal self-government, it seemed probable that Nyerere would be called upon to form the territory's first African administration.

Ochoa, Severo, naturalized U.S. biochemist (b. Luarea, Spain, Sept. 24, 1905), shared the 1959 Nobel prize for medicine and physiology with Arthur Kornberg (q.v.). He was educated at the University of Madrid where he received a medical degree in 1929. He began his career as a teacher of physiology at the University of Madrid and after spending several years teaching at Heidelberg and at Oxford university, he settled permanently in the U.S. in 1940. Following a year on the medical faculty of Washington university, St. Louis, Missouri, Ochoa joined the staff of the college of medicine of New York university where in 1959 he was chairman of the department of biochemistry. He shared the prize of about £15,220 with his former student for their chemical work on heredity. In announcing the award, the Caroline institute of Stockholm cited Ochoa and Kornberg for their "discoveries of the mechanism in the biological synthesis in ribonucleic acids and deoxyribonucleic acids." Working separately from Kornberg, Ochoa discovered an enzyme that produces ribonucleic acid (RNA). It is believed by biochemists that RNA is essential to the production of protein of which all living tissue is primarily composed. RNA, together with deoxyribonucleic acid (DNA) are the chemical agents that are believed to control heredity. The achievement of Ochoa and Kornberg was considered a significant contribution to the understanding of the life process.

Quasimodo, Salvatore, Italian poet (b. Modica, Sicily, Aug. 20, 1901), received the Nobel prize for literature (valued at £15,220) in 1959. The man who was to become one of the most original Italian poets of the 1950s had a thoroughly technical education, which might explain his enthusiastic awareness of contemporary technological progress in his later poems. After graduating in engineering at the polytechnic in Rome, for ten years he travelled Italy as a member of the state engineering service. In 1935 he settled in Milan, where, as his literary achievements gained recognition, he was appointed professor of Italian literature at the conservatoire. Later he became dramatic critic for a national weekly and a contributor to various reviews. A person of left-wing sympathies, in the 1930s Quasimodo had begun to be known as one of the leading figures of the *ermetismo.* This was a school of poetry which derived from French Symbolism a passionate concern with experimenting in new verse techniques as well as the assumption that unconscious associations of feeling and elusive logical patterns created by unusual links of expression and sound were more important than the conventional meaning of words. At first a disciple of G. Ungaretti and E. Montale, he soon developed a personal style, into the coldly calculated rhythms of which he introduced a touching human note. From *Acque e terre* ("Waters and Land", 1930) to *La terra impareggiabile* ("The Incomparable Earth", 1958), which won the Viareggio prize, Quasimodo's poetry developed coherently out of dry, rhetorical perfection towards deeper understanding of life and dramatic commitment in the struggles of the times. "The ultimate conquest of poetry", he said, "is reality". He has also translated widely from Greek, Latin and English (*e.g.,* Shakespeare's *The Tempest*), with a striking awareness both of the spirit of the texts and of modern sensibility and taste.

Rockefeller, Nelson Aldrich, U.S. state governor and government official (b. Bar Harbor, Maine, July 8, 1908), was elected governor of New York, Nov. 4, 1958, by a margin of almost 600,000 over the Democratic candidate, Averell Harriman. Rockefeller, the second son of John D. Rockefeller, Sr., who founded the family fortune in oil, graduated from Dartmouth college, Hanover, New Hampshire, in 1930. In the early 1930s he helped to develop New York city's Rockefeller centre, of which he became president. From 1935 to 1940 he was a director of Creole Petroleum corporation. Rockefeller's

Reginald Maudling   *Tom Mboya*   *Dame Mary Smieton*   *Right Rev. A. M. Stockwood*

long series of appointments to government office began in 1940 when he became co-ordinator of inter-American affairs, providing economic, social and cultural aid to Latin-American nations. He served in this position until 1944, when he became assistant secretary of state in charge of relations with Latin America. He resigned in 1945 and spent the next few years organizing and directing two private corporations for the economic and social development of Latin America. In 1950-51 he was chairman of President Harry S. Truman's advisory board for international development (the Point Four programme). In 1953-54 Rockefeller was under secretary of health, education and welfare. In 1954-55 he was a special assistant to President Dwight D. Eisenhower to consider " cold war " policies, and still later he was chairman of the president's advisory committee on government organization, from which he resigned in 1958. In Dec. 1959 he declared that he would not stand for the 1960 Republican presidential nomination.

Segrè, Emilio, naturalized U.S. physicist (b. Tivoli, Italy, Feb. 1, 1905), received the 1959 Nobel prize for physics jointly with Owen Chamberlain (*q.v.*). He was educated at the University of Rome, taking his doctor's degree in 1928. Segrè went to the United States in 1938 and became a U.S. citizen in 1944. Before joining the University of California at Berkeley in 1938, Segrè had taught physics at the universities of Rome and Palermo. During most of World War II, he was at Los Alamos, New Mexico, where he was actively associated with the Manhattan District project which exploded the first atom bomb in 1945. In 1946 Segrè again joined the physics faculty of the University of California. Sharing half of the £15,220 award with his co-worker Chamberlain, Segrè was honoured by the Nobel committee for his part in the discovery of the existence of antiprotons. Nuclear physicists had strongly suspected their existence for some time before Segrè and Chamberlain observed them for the first time in some subatomic debris produced by the bevatron at the University of California's radiation laboratory at Livermore, California, in 1955. Although having the mass of ordinary protons, antiprotons carry negative electric charges in contrast to the positive charges of ordinary protons. Upon contact, the two destroy each other, thereby releasing great amounts of energy.

Smieton, Dame Mary Guillan, British civil servant (b. London, Dec. 5, 1902), became in Oct. 1959 the second woman permanent secretary in a British government department. The daughter of the librarian and bursar of a Cambridge college and the granddaughter of a pioneer in industrial welfare, she was educated at Perse school, Cambridge, Wimbledon High school, Bedford college, London university, and Lady Margaret hall, Oxford. She entered the administrative grade of the civil service in 1925 and, after three years in the Public Record office, transferred to the Ministry of Labour. This was the department where she made her career, although in 1938 she was seconded to the Home Office, where she played an important part in organizing the newly formed Women's Voluntary services. Returning to the Ministry of Labour in 1940 she was largely responsible for the mobilization of the women of Britain for war work. She was promoted to the rank of under secretary in 1946, later in the year becoming the first director of personnel in the U.N. secretariat in New York. In 1948 she returned to the ministry to take charge of the employment policy department. Created D.B.E. in 1949, in 1953 she took charge of the safety, health and welfare department. Two years later Dame Mary Smieton was appointed deputy secretary of the ministry in charge of the departments for employment, youth employment and disabled persons, military recruitment and resettlement of ex-regulars. She became the permanent head of the Ministry of Education, in succession to Sir Gilbert Flemming, at the age of 56.

Steele, Tommy (THOMAS HICKS), British entertainer (b. London, Dec. 17, 1936), was the British representative at the Moscow state film festival in Aug. 1959. He began work in 1953 as a cabin boy. A year later, a longish stay in hospital with spinal meningitis gave him the time to learn the guitar and on subsequent transatlantic crossings he gained his first experience as an entertainer. On shore leave he played " Rock 'n' Roll " in Soho coffee bars where, in 1956, he met a young publicity man, John Kennedy. Steele had two weeks' leave and Kennedy undertook to get him launched in show business within this period. By a series of unorthodox publicity stunts Kennedy succeeded, and Steele got a short booking at the Stork club at £20 a week. Thenceforth, success was rapid; within a year he was earning £1,000 a week, his records were prominent on the hit parade (the most famous, " Singing the Blues ", selling over 1 million copies) and two films, *The Tommy Steele Story* and *The Duke Wore Jeans*, added to his fame. By the end of 1958 when he appeared as Buttons in the pantomime *Cinderella* at the London Coliseum he was one of the highest-paid British entertainers in the history of show business.

During 1959 Steele showed that his success was unlikely to be as ephemeral as the medium of " Rock 'n' Roll ", through which he had become established. The " Prince of Rock ", in fact, transformed himself into an all-round entertainer, and although his records no longer enjoyed the automatic success of 1957-58 and only three reached the " Top Twenty ", his engagement book was full. During the year he completed another film, *Tommy the Toreador*, which was released in Dec. 1959, and made a series of appearances on the independent television show *Saturday Spectacular*.

Stockwood, Right Rev. Arthur Mervyn, Anglican bishop (b. Bridgend, Glamorgan, May 27, 1913), was consecrated bishop of Southwark on May 1, 1959. Educated at Kelly college, Tavistock, and at Christ's college and Westcott House Theological college, Cambridge, he was ordained deacon in 1936 and priest in 1937. Until 1955 he was engaged in pastoral work in Bristol as curate and later vicar of St. Matthew, Moorfields, and in 1953 he was appointed an honorary canon of Bristol cathedral. In 1955 he became vicar of Great St. Mary's, Cambridge (the university church), and examining chaplain to the bishops of Manchester and Sodor and Man. In both Bristol and Cambridge he has been a Labour city councillor. In his presidential address to the Southwark diocesan conference in June 1959 the new bishop stated that services should be conducted in accordance with the Book of Common Prayer, and in particular that the order of the Communion service should be that of 1662. Stockwood's intention was to preserve the essential character of the Anglican Church and to exclude " practices . . . contrary to the spirit of the Reformation ". In Aug. 1959 much publicity attached to his acceptance of the resignation of the Rev. R. A. E. Harris, who had conducted services according to the Roman Catholic rite at St. Andrew's Mission church, Carshalton. A reputation for a certain unconventionality was added to by his deprecation of the " 18th-century riding kit rig-out " of a bishop, and by a press photograph of himself wearing a bow-tie.

Suslov, Mikhail Andreevich, Soviet Communist leader (b. Shakhovskoe, Ulyanovsk region, 1902), led a delegation of the Supreme Soviet which in March 1959 visited Britain. The son of a poor peasant, after the Nov. 1917 revolution he worked in the local committee of poor peasants. He joined the Russian Communist party in 1921 and in the same year went to Moscow to study in a " Rabfak " (workers' faculty). He completed his studies in 1924 and then entered the Plekhanov Institute of National Economy. Having graduated in 1928 he continued to study at the Institute of Red Professors and afterwards lectured at Moscow university and at the Industrial academy. In 1931 he was assigned to the control commission of the All-Union Communist party. He was sent in 1937 to Rostov to work as party secretary of the now dissolved Northern Caucasus area. Two years later he became first party secretary of the Stavropol territory. The 18th congress of the All-Union C.P. (1939) elected him to the central auditing commission. In 1941 he became a member of the party's central committee. During World War II he was a member of the War council of the North Caucasian front and chief of staff of the Stavropol partisan detachments. In March 1946 Suslov was appointed to the party's central committee as chief liaison officer with the European Communist parties. He was re-elected to the central committee at the 19th (1952) and 20th (1956) party congresses. Since 1947 he has been a secretary of the central committee of the C.P.S.U. and since July 1955 a member of the party's presidium (former Politburo). From 1949 to 1950 he was editor-in-chief of *Pravda*. A member of the Supreme Soviet of the U.S.S.R., he was elected in 1954 chairman of its foreign affairs committee.

Swart, Charles Robberts, South African statesman (b. Winburg, Orange Free State, Dec. 5, 1894), was in Dec. 1959 appointed governor-general of the Union of South Africa. As a boy he was put in a concentration camp with his mother during the Boer war, and at the age of 20 took part in an attempted rebellion organized by a group of South Africans in protest against their country's participation in World War I. He was educated at the University of Orange Free State, and after lecturing on law for a time went to the United States, where he obtained a diploma in journalism at Columbia university, New York, He subsequently worked as a reporter and also appeared in small parts in several films, once playing the part of a sheriff in a " western ". Returning to South Africa, he entered parliament in 1923 as a supporter of Daniel Malan's Nationalist party. Along with other Nationalists he strongly opposed South Africa's entry into World War II. In 1940 he became leader of the Nationalist party in the Orange Free State and when the party was returned to power in the general election of 1948, Swart was made minister of justice. He was largely responsible for the passing of such controversial measures as the Suppression of Communism act, 1950, which established a statutory definition of Communism and made it a crime. He remained minister of justice until his appointment as governor-general. A tall man of forbidding appearance, he nevertheless has a sense of humour.

Thomson, Roy Herbert, Canadian proprietor of newspapers and radio and television stations (b. Toronto, June 5, 1894), enlarged his U.K. interests in July 1959 by acquiring control of the entire Kemsley Newspapers chain. The son of a barber, after a brief education and a varied number of jobs he started his career in 1929, the year of the great slump. Finding himself in northern Ontario with some wireless sets he could not sell, he borrowed sufficient money to start a radio station to encourage people to buy his sets. It was then that he first appreciated the possibilities of commercial radio, and within a few years he had acquired other stations. He also secured a weekly paper and managed to make it pay in difficult times. In 1944 he bought four papers in southern Ontario, paying for them with bonds and with money raised from the banks. By the end of World War II he had become a wealthy man and by 1959 he owned about 30 papers in North America, supplying them with editorial material in bulk by means of teletype-setting from his head office in Toronto. He had already extended his sphere of operations to the United Kingdom by taking control of Scotsman Publications' newspapers in 1953, going to live in Edinburgh himself soon afterwards; and he started Scottish commercial television in 1957. His acquisition of Kemsley Newspapers gave him control of the *Sunday Times* and three other Sunday papers, together with four dailies and seven evening papers in the provinces. Thomson has said that he has no desire to impose his own views or policy on his paper and that " a prime factor of successful editing is that the editor's own character must emerge through his own paper." In view of the number of Labour supporters in Britain, he would like to see more papers supporting the Labour party.

Touré, Sékou, Guinean statesman (b. Faranah, Guinea, 1922), became in Oct. 1959 the first president of the Republic of Guinea. He is the

Tommy Steele   *Sékou Touré*   *Maj.-General G. P. Vanier*   *Robert Willis*

son of a Malinké farmer and allegedly a great-grandson of Almami Samory Touré who led a revolt against the French until his capture in 1898. As a Moslem, Sékou Touré attended a Koranic school at Kankan. In 1937 he went to Konakry to study at the French technical college, but was soon expelled for fomenting a students' food strike. He became a French colonial treasury clerk, but his real interest was in organizing African workers in trade unions. When after World War II the French tried to send him to a post outside Guinea he resigned and became the head of the Guinea branch of the French Communist-led Confédération Générale du Travail. In May 1945 he founded the Parti Démocratique de Guinée. In the following year he was one of the organizers at Dakar of the first convention of the Union Générale des Travailleurs de l'Afrique Noire. In the same year he visited Paris for the first time, where he met Félix Houphouët-Boigny and other rising political leaders of French Africa. His P.D.G. joined the newly founded Rassemblement Démocratique Africain. As a friendly delegate from the U.G.T.A.N., Sékou was invited to attend Communist trade union congresses in Warsaw and Prague in 1950 and in eastern Berlin in 1952, but by then the U.G.T.A.N. had for fundamental reasons broken with the C.G.T. In 1951 Sékou was elected a member for Guinea to the French National Assembly but his election was declared invalid by the governor. When elected again in 1953 he was allowed to take his seat. In the meantime the P.D.G., of which he was secretary-general, had become the most powerful party in the country. On March 31, 1957, when the first Guinean territorial assembly was elected by universal suffrage, the P.D.G. won all the seats. When Guinea's first African government was formed, Sékou was the obvious choice as its head. On the proclamation of the new French constitution offering immediate independence to any territory which did not wish to accept it, Sékou seized the opportunity, and on Sept. 28, 1958, Guinea rejected the constitution by an overwhelming majority. On Oct. 2 the Republic of Guinea was proclaimed at Konakry, with Sékou Touré as its first president. Between Oct. and Dec. 1959, the new president paid official visits to Washington, London, Bonn, Moscow, Prague and Rabat.

Addressing the U.N. general assembly (Nov. 5) Sékou Touré gave equal credit to the United States and to the U.S.S.R. for aid that they had given in Africa. But he added that if any nation failed to understand the Africans' determination to follow their own aims " they had better abstain from helping Africa ". What Africa sought, he said, was assistance which would make it " free from pressure and exploitation ".

Vanier, George Philias, Canadian soldier and diplomat (b. Montreal, April 23, 1888), on Sept. 15, 1959, became Canada's 19th governor-general. He studied at Loyola college, Montreal, and Laval university, Quebec. He was called to the Quebec bar in 1911. A founder-member of the famous French-Canadian regiment the Royal 22nd, he was wounded twice in World War I, losing his right leg. He returned briefly to civilian life, but with special permission of the military authorities rejoined the army. In 1921-22 he served as an aide to the governor-general, Lord Byng, and in a similar position with Lord Willingdon from 1926 to 1928. He was commanding officer of the Royal 22nd from 1925 to 1928, when he became Canada's military representative with a League of Nations commission. In 1931 Vanier was appointed secretary to the Canadian high commissioner's office in London. He was minister to France 1938-40. During 1940-43 he was a member of the permanent joint board of defence in Ottawa. He was appointed Canadian ambassador to France after the war, remaining in this position until he retired in 1953.

Watkinson, Harold Arthur, British politician (b. Walton-on-Thames, Surrey, Jan. 25, 1910), was appointed minister of defence in Oct. 1959. He was educated at Queen's college, Taunton, and King's college, London. An engineer by profession, he became a director of machine tool and engineering companies and in 1948 was chairman of the Production Efficiency committee for the south of England set up by the Machine Tool Trades association. In World War II he served in the Royal Naval Volunteer reserve, reaching the rank of lieut.-commander. In 1949 Watkinson was adopted as the prospective Conservative candidate for Woking which he won in the 1950 general election. He has since held the seat with increased majorities. In parliament he was recognized as an expert on industrial production

problems and was appointed parliamentary private secretary to the minister of transport and civil aviation. From 1952-55 he served as parliamentary secretary to the Ministry of Labour and National Service and applied himself particularly to problems of employment and industrial efficiency, becoming chairman of several important committees. In Dec. 1955 Watkinson became minister of transport and civil aviation, a post he held until his appointment as minister of defence, thus becoming associated with Britain's hitherto most ambitious road-building programme. He was also concerned with the plans for the modernization of British railways and new types of aircraft for the civil airlines. From Jan. 1957, he has been a member of the cabinet.

Willis, Robert, British trade union leader (b. Sunderland, Feb. 27, 1904), played a prominent part in negotiating a settlement on behalf of the printing trade workers in the six-week dispute in the industry during 1959. Orphaned at an early age, he was brought up by foster parents, and on leaving school was apprenticed as a compositor. In 1930 he went to London and joined the London Society of Compositors and also became a member of the Typographical association. By 1945, he was general secretary of the London Society of Compositors and took a leading part in arranging its amalgamation in 1955 with the Printing Machine Managers Trade society as the London Typographical society. Willis was elected joint secretary of the new organization and finally became sole general secretary in 1956. From 1938 to 1945 he was secretary of the London Trade council and chairman from 1952-59. Willis has visited the International Labour organization (I.L.O.) on several occasions and in 1947 and 1949 went to western Germany on behalf of the T.U.C. He has travelled widely abroad in the course of his trade union duties and in Nov. 1959 visited India and Pakistan on a goodwill mission. After the conclusion of the 1958 Trades Union congress he was unanimously elected chairman of the general council (the first from the printing trade since 1900) and on retirement became a vice-chairman. During the 1959 printing dispute he was a leading spokesman and negotiator for the strikers, helping to gain for them a $4\frac{1}{2}\%$ basic wage rise and a 42-hr. week.

Wolfson, Isaac, British businessman (b. Glasgow, Sept. 17, 1897), was made an honorary fellow of the Royal College of Physicians and an honorary doctor of laws of London university during 1959. Educated at Queen's Park school, Glasgow, he began his career in his father's wholesale business. In 1932 he joined the Great Universal Stores Limited, a Manchester mail-order house, as merchandise controller; two years later he became managing director of the company and in 1946 its chairman. Under his leadership, the trading profit of Great Universal Stores rose from £304,159 in 1934 to £24,569,202 in the year ending March 31, 1959, and the company had grown into a group operating some 2,500 stores, shops and mail-order warehouses in the United Kingdom and the Commonwealth.

Since July 1955, when Wolfson founded a charitable trust known as the Isaac Wolfson foundation to operate mainly in the fields of education, health and youth activities in the United Kingdom and the Commonwealth, he has become almost better known as a philanthropist than as a businessman. By the end of 1959 the foundation had made grants amounting to about £3 million to beneficiaries which included Oxford and London universities, the Westminster Hospital School of Nursing, the British Empire Cancer campaign, the Post-graduate Medical school, the National Playing Fields association and the Royal National Institute for the Blind. The grants made during 1959 included £450,000 for a new building for the Royal College of Physicians; £300,000 for a hall of residence at Glasgow university; £184,000 to the Institute of Psychiatry; and £150,000 to Cambridge university to found an Institute of Criminology. Isaac Wolfson also has many philanthropic interests in Israel, where he is an honorary fellow of the Weizmann Institute of Science and a trustee of the Religious centre, Jerusalem.

BIOLOGY: *see* BACTERIOLOGY; BIOCHEMISTRY; BOTANY; ENDOCRINOLOGY; ENTOMOLOGY; GENETICS; MARINE BIOLOGY; ORNITHOLOGY; PALAEONTOLOGY; PHYSIOLOGY; ZOOLOGY.

BIRDS: *see* ORNITHOLOGY.
BLOOD DISEASES: *see* DISEASES.

BOLIVIA. Land-locked republic in central South America and one of the highest inhabited areas of the world. Area: 424,162 sq.mi. Pop.: (1950 census) 3,019,031; (1959 est.) 3,416,000. Estimated racial distribution: Indian 52%, *mestizo* 28%; white 13%; Negro 0·2%; unspecified 6·8%. Language: Spanish, but the Indians speak Quechua and Aymará. Religion: predominantly Roman Catholic. Chief towns (pop., 1950 census; 1959 est. in brackets): La Paz, the seat of government, 321,073 (409,500); Sucre, the judiciary capital, 40,128; Cochabamba 80,795 (99,099); Oruro 62,975 (77,874). President, Hernan Siles Suazo. Main imports: machinery and manufactures; wheat and foodstuffs. Main exports: tin (68%), tungsten (11%), lead (6%), silver (5%). Monetary unit: *boliviano*, with a selling rate of Bs.25,606 to the £ sterling (Aug. 1958).

History. The year 1959 was among the most difficult in Bolivia's agitated history. The National Revolutionary Movement (M.N.R.) faced its seventh year in power with such multiple problems as a disastrous economic situation, increasing opposition from other parties, grave labour troubles, widespread anti-U.S. demonstrations and a split in its own ranks.

National production which had declined steadily in previous years decreased 64% from Jan. 1958 to Jan. 1959. Exports of minerals, Bolivia's main source of income, dropped from $88·7 million in 1957 to $55·8 million in 1958. Exports in the first five months of 1959 were $26·3 million. Petroleum, the only bright spot in previous years, also declined in late 1958 and early 1959. Constant strikes paralysed the nation. Although the United States supported the Bolivian budget by 32%, total economic bankruptcy was feared.

In March violent anti-U.S. riots broke out in La Paz, Cochabamba and Oruro. These riots were sparked off by a *Time* magazine article appraising the grave economic situation of Bolivia. The article quoted an unauthorized source from the U.S. embassy suggesting the dissolution of Bolivia. Afterwards strikes swept the mines where workers protested against the demands of U.S. aid officials that the commissary subsidies be abolished. At the commissaries the employees purchased goods at below market costs.

On April 19 the aggressive opposition party, the Bolivian Falange (F.S.B.), tried again to overthrow the government by revolution. The attempt failed, but not before widespread bloodshed had occurred and the Falange chief, Oscar Unzaga de la Vega, was assassinated. His death brought sharp criticism from all sectors in Bolivia, but the government tried to create the impression that Unzaga committed suicide or was killed by his own partisans. In June government forces aided by Indian militia crushed a revolt in the city of Santa Cruz.
(C. W. A.)

BOOK PUBLISHING: *see* BUSINESS REVIEW.

BOOK SALES. The 1959 season was notable for the first part of the sale of the Dyson Perrins illuminated manuscripts. This realized a record auction total for any single day's book sale of £326,620. During the previous summer 106 books from the Chatsworth library sold for £109,851 and the hitherto record total of £110,356 was reached as long ago as 1919 at the dispersal of the fabulous Britwell library.

Dyson Perrins bequeathed to the British Museum the *Gorleston Psalter*, an East Anglian manuscript of outstanding importance, and a magnificent eastern manuscript. The British Museum was also able to buy another eight manuscripts from his estate on favourable terms. This did not detract from the superb quality of many of the manuscripts sold and it is not surprising that the record price (£33,000) created in 1929 by the sale of the Bedford *Hours* was passed with £39,000 for the *Helmarshausen Latin Gospels*, a mid-12th-

A 1623 folio edition of Shakespeare's " Comedies, Histories and Tragedies " on show in Stockholm in November prior to its sale.

century German manuscript. The second highest price, £36,500, was realized by a delightful French 13th-century *Aviary and Bestiary*. The third was £33,000 for the *Gradual of St. Catherinenthal* (*c.* 1312). Another notable manuscript *Vidal Maior*, on the Laws of Aragon, and reputed to be the finest Spanish manuscript in England, fetched £28,000. Remarkable prices were also given for the following: the *Warwick Hours and Psalter*, an English 15th-century manuscript, and the *Psalter* of Richard of Canterbury (early 14th century), another English manuscript, realized £18,000 and £13,000 respectively while a Lille manuscript of *The Histories of Thebes* (1469) realized £16,600. An illuminated manuscript equal in importance to those of Dyson Perrins was sold on the previous day. This was the Llangattock *Hours of the Virgin*, attributed to the workshop of William Vrelant of Bruges in the mid-15th century. It contained minatures of great beauty and outstanding artistic quality, and was in its original signed binding. It sold for £32,000.

The price of historical and literary manuscripts maintained their high level. Two manuscripts relating to Admiral Lord Howe and the American War of Independence, instructions sent to him by George III " for restoring peace in North America " (1776) and a secret intelligence report from Lord North to Howe, sold for £1,000 and £950 respectively. The last portion of the André de Coppet collection of manuscripts was also sold bringing the final total for this collection to £196,454.

Among literary manuscripts eight autographed poems by John Chalkhill realized £1,400, 122 letters from Henry James to Elizabeth Robins fetched a surprisingly high price of £2,400, 61 letters from John Ruskin to Lady Waterford sold for £1,050 and Samuel Johnson's touching letter to his goddaughter, Jane Langton, aged seven, written in 1784, brought £1,250. Two early English manuscripts were sold, the

Brudenell codex of Chaucer's *Canterbury Tales* (c. 1450) fetched £15,200 and the Burghley codex of Ranulf Higden's *Polychronicon*, translated by John de Trevisa, (early 15th century) £3,600. The most important musical autograph was a three-page letter of Beethoven's, mentioning his opera *Fidelio*, dated 1804. It sold for £2,200.

Perhaps the most attractive individual book sold during the season was Caxton's *Myrrour of The Worlde* (1481), the first English book designed for illustration. It sold for £14,000 compared with £1,900 in 1938 for the last copy sold. Another exceptional book was a copy of the second folio edition (1542) of Chaucer's *Works* bound in a contemporary binding for Thomas Wotton. This, the only recorded Wotton binding on an important English book, realized £2,800. A collection of five rare legal books printed by Wynken de Worde fetched £2,900. The first edition of Sir Thomas Littleton's *Tenures* and the *Abbreviamentum Statutorum* (1481) bound and printed by Lettou, the only known example in this condition, sold for £8,000, the authorized version of the Bible (1611) for £2,500 and Erasmus' *New Testament* (1516), a presentation copy from Erasmus to John Fisher, for £2,800. A magnificent copy of Spenser's *Faerie Queene* in original vellum fetched the record price of £4,000 and a volume of his poems containing his rare *Prothalamion* (1596) £1,400. Shakespeare's four folios, with some defects, realized £8,500 and a copy of his *Poems* (1640) £1,500.

The late Michael Sadleir's books were noted for their fine condition and among those sold were Jane Austen's *Pride and Prejudice* (1813) for £145, Darwin's *Origin of Species* (1859) for £170, Lewis Carroll's *Alice in Wonderland* (1866) in white presentation vellum for £280 and Thomas Hardy's *Tess of the D'Urbervilles* (1891) for £145. Americana was as much sought after as ever. Jacques Cartier's *A Shorte Narration of the Two Navigations to the Northweaste Partes* (1580) achieved the highest price, £4,200. The last copy sold, in 1922, fetched £910. The Marquess of Exeter's copies of Captain John Smith's *Generall Historie of Virginia* (1627) and W. Faden's *North American Atlas* (1777) each sold for £1,100. Fine flower books sold well, Pierre Redouté's *Roses* (1817-24) and *Choix des plus belles fleurs* (1827) sold for £1,800 and £1,250 respectively, and R. J. Thornton's magnificent *Temple of Flora* (1799-1807) fetched £600, the Exeter copy consisting of only 20 original parts making £420. Two copies of C. Schutz and J. Ziegler's magnificent coloured plate book *Vues de la Ville de Vienne* (1779-98), were sold. One of them with 81 plates realized £750 but the Exeter copy containing only 66 plates fetched £1,200. (C. D. M.)

BORNEO: *see* BRITISH BORNEO; INDONESIA.

BOTANICAL GARDENS. At the Royal Botanic gardens, Kew, the remarkably sunny and hot spring and summer coincided with the celebrations for the bicentenary of the founding of the gardens. On June 2 the queen accompanied by the Duke of Edinburgh attended a garden party and took tea in the recently refurbished Orangery. The queen toured the gardens and inspected the Palm house which was open to the public that evening for the first time since it was closed for repairs in 1952. Meanwhile the Duke of Edinburgh visited the Herbarium to see the large exhibition which stressed the part that Kew had played in promoting botanical science in the previous 200 years. Many distinguished British and overseas botanists were also present and about 1,000 people visited the exhibition during the three days it was open. C. E. Hubbard was appointed deputy director and E. Milne-Redhead deputy keeper of the Herbarium. A rose pergola was built in the Herbaceous ground and new river-water mains were laid through part of the gardens. Because of the extended hot, dry weather these latter were useful in main-

Queen Elizabeth II in the water-lily house at the Royal Botanic gardens, Kew, on July 2, when with the Duke of Edinburgh she attended a garden party to mark the bi-centenary of the inauguration of the gardens. To commemorate her visit the queen planted a walnut tree.

taining a good supply of water to the spray lines which were kept in constant use. A large part of the northeastern corner of the Rock garden was reconstructed with sandstone blocks. On Nov. 5 the new 225 ft. flagpole made from a Douglas fir from British Columbia was erected. A documentary colour film was made of the garden and its activities.

In the Royal Botanic garden, Edinburgh, taxonomic work on the following genera and families was continued during 1959: *Compositae, Gesneriaceae, Labiatae, Oleaceae, Buddleia, Cintractia, Incarvillea* and *Rhododendron.* Treasury sanction was received for the erection of a new herbarium and library and plans for this new building were approved. Propagation houses 1 and 2 were extended and a start made on the construction of the new process buildings. Ten acres adjacent to the garden were purchased to serve as a nursery and experimental garden. At the Botanic gardens, Glasgow, the rebuilding of the Palm house gave opportunity for replanting the central beds and a special feature was made of epiphytic plants on palms, tree stumps and pillars. The orchid collection was much increased and the show-house rebuilt, incorporating a section for the more tropical types. Work began on the reconstruction of the small rock garden, and a rock border for primulas was established.

At Montreal, development of the Botanical garden continued, and there were more than 70,000 sq.ft. under glass, including nine conservatories. Several new species of orchids, begonias and bromeliads were described from the living collections, also a new orchid genus, *Teuscheria*, with three species. The genus was named after H. Teuscher, the curator of the garden.

The area of the National Botanic Gardens of South Africa was increased as a result of the incorporation by bequest of the 400-ac. Harold Porter Botanic reserve at Betty's bay, 60 mi. S.E. of Cape Town. The reserve was founded in 1950 by Harold Porter for growing plants from the winter rainfall area of South Africa. The locality is particularly suitable for growing heaths (*Erica* spp.).

The National Botanic gardens, Lucknow, India, founded in 1953 on the site of an old public park and garden known as Sikander Bagh, continued in 1959 to develop the main functions of the institution, which included the collection, introduction and cultivation of ornamental and economic plants, especially the medicinal and essential oil-bearing ones. There were 38 research workers on the staff and the laboratory building, only completed in 1958, was being equipped and the Herbarium prepared for the incorporation of 60,000 sheets previously housed elsewhere. Of the three botanic gardens in Ceylon the Royal Botanic gardens at Peradeniya are the oldest, having been founded in 1831 for growing exotics, and cover 146 ac. at an altitude of 1,550 ft. The Botanic gardens, Haggala, established in 1861 as a quinine experimental station, are situated at an altitude of 5,581 ft. with a climate in which many temperate plants flourish. The Botanic gardens, Henarathgoda, established in 1876 for the reception of the original rubber trees (*Hevea braziliensis*) sent from Kew, are situated near Colombo at an elevation of 35 ft. The original rubber trees still survived in 1959.

At the Royal Botanic gardens, Melbourne, the National herbarium was renovated and plans were developed to rehouse the specimen folders in new cabinets under a more efficient classification. A complete bibliography of about 600 species of *Acacia* indigenous to Australia was compiled. In New Zealand a sound start was made to the development of the new experimental garden of the Botany division, Department of Scientific and Industrial Research, at Lincoln, near Christchurch. The area of about 20 ac. had roads, paths and a rock garden laid down with the final objective of growing an extensive collection of New Zealand native plants. (*See* also HORTICULTURE.)   (F. N. HR.)

BOTANY.   The nature of the factors controlling the development of plant structures and forms received considerable attention during 1959. U.S. workers at Wisconsin and Cornell were for the first time able to grow whole plants from single cells in pure culture. At Cornell normal carrots, complete with thickened pigmented tap-roots, were grown from cells isolated from cultures of phloem tissue. The relationship between the length of day a plant receives and the nature of its growth was also investigated by many workers. At Belfast the form of the leaf in hemp (*Cannabis sativa*) was varied by changing the day length. The pattern of the main veins of the leaf was affected by the length of day experienced by the plant in the period preceding the laying down of the primordium, while the amount of lamina developed was directly related to the length of day during the subsequent expansion of the primordium. Abnormal crinkled leaves, with the amount of lamina much greater than that normally in association with the vascular framework present, were produced by lengthening the time of illumination after the primordia had appeared.

Considerable advances were made in the study of photosynthesis. At Berkeley, California, workers using suspensions of isolated chloroplasts showed that the " dark " phase (in which the assimilation of carbon dioxide occurs) was associated with the water-soluble chlorophyll-free portion of the chloroplast (the *stroma*), while the " light " phase (in which energy from incident light enters into the system) was dependent upon the pigmented grains (the *grana*). Following separation of these two elements of the chloroplast, the incorporation of the incident energy into the chemical system was studied independently of the synthesis of carbohydrates. Subsequently, D. I. Arnon pointed out that the first products of photosynthesis appear to be adenosine triphosphate and reduced triphosphopyridine nucleotide. This capacity of chloroplasts to use light energy for the formation of pyrophosphate bonds rich in chemical energy (photosynthetic phosphorylation) appears to be a feature common to the photosynthesis of bacteria and green plants. In the Netherlands, C. J. P. Spruit showed that *Chlorella* cultured anaerobically was capable of evolving hydrogen and oxygen simultaneously, even in the presence of carbon dioxide. Numerous other topics concerned with photosynthesis were discussed in a special issue of *Plant Physiology* dedicated to the late Robert Emerson.

The metabolism of nitrogen received much attention. N. W. Pirie, in the *Annual Review of Plant Physiology*, discussed leaf proteins, and the 13th *Symposium* of the Society for Experimental Biology was entirely devoted to a consideration of the utilization of nitrogen by plants. G. E. Fogg described the effect of withholding nitrogen from a simple alga in the exponential phase of growth. Photosynthesis continues (at a declining rate), but the products of photosynthesis, instead of entering into the synthesis of proteins, go to form carbohydrates. Eventually the proportion of nitrogen in the cells falls to a critical value, catabolic changes ensue and the metabolic pattern changes drastically. In the same symposium, V. S. Sokolov described recent work in the U.S.S.R. on the accumulation of alkaloids in plants. The ratio of scopolamine to hyoscyamine in species of *Datura* could be markedly changed by controlling the length of day in which the plants were grown.

In plant genetics, P. C. Mangelsdorf and R. G. Reeves reported a series of previously unknown alleles in maize concerned with the development of the glumes. A series of genotypes produced by repeated backcrossing showed: (a) a decline in the prominence of the tassel and an increase in that of the ear; (b) a progression from a predominantly pistillate to a wholly staminate tassel; and (c) a progressive decrease in the development of the glumes. These changes would reduce the chances of survival in the wild, so if maize evolved along this path from some *Tripsacum*-like ancestor, the evolution is likely to have accompanied domestication. Cytologists continued investigations into the synthesis of deoxyribonucleic acid in meiosis and mitosis. L. F. La Cour and S. R. Pelc showed that in the root meristems of *Vicia faba* (broad bean) colchicine influenced either the synthesis of deoxyribonucleic acid or its subsequent distribution among the sister chromatids. The phenomena of bacterial transformation and transduction were among the subjects discussed at a symposium held in the German Federal Republic. F. Kaudewitz reported that two pseudo-alleles in *Salmonella typhimurium* existed not only in the extreme states of preventing or facilitating the synthesis of histidine, but also in a series of quantitatively intermediate states. A possible explanation of these results was that the increasingly efficient synthesis was correlated with a series of enzymes with slightly different protein molecules.

Among the fungi, investigations into the ballistics of spore discharge in *Sordaria* showed that the eight ascospores tended to cohere in linear arrangement. Breaks, equally likely at any of the seven possible places in the line, often occurred during discharge. Contributions to plant ecology and geography included N. Polunin's *Circumpolar Arctic Flora* and J. J. Barkman's detailed study of the phytosociology of the cryptogamic epiphytes of Europe. R. E. Schultes published a systematic account of the orchids of Trinidad and Tobago and C. Schweinfurth of those of Peru. A survey, edited by C. L. Withner, covered may different aspects of the biology of orchids. (*See also* HORTICULTURE.)   (P. R. B.)

BIBLIOGRAPHY (all 1959, unless otherwise stated). D. I. Arnon, " Conversion of Light into Chemical Energy in Photosynthesis ", *Nature Lond.*, *184*, July 4; L. J. Audus, *Plant Growth Substances*, 2nd ed. (London); J. J. Barkman, *Phytosociology and Ecology of Cryptogamic Epiphytes* (Assen, Netherlands, 1958); N. Bor, *Grasses of India and Ceylon* (London); A. H. Brown (ed.), *Robert Emerson Memorial Issue*, *Plant Physiol.*, *34*, May (Lancaster. Pa.); A. S. Crafts (ed.) *Annu. Rev. Pl. Physiol.*, *10* (Palo Alto, California); L. F. La Cour and S. R. Pelc, " Effect of Colchicine on the Utilization of Thymidine labelled with Tritium during Chromosomal Reproduction ", *Nature London.*, *183*, May 23; Deutsche Gesellschaft für Physiologische Chemie, *Colloquium IX, Chemie der Genetik.* (Berlin); J. and Y. Heslop Harrison, " Studies on Flowering-Plant Growth and Organogenesis ", *Proc. R. Irish Acad.*, *59*, Nov. 1958 (Dublin); J. Hutchinson, *The Families of Flowering Plants*, 2nd ed. (Oxford); C. T. Ingold and S. A. Hadland, " The Ballistics of *Sordaria* ", *New Phytol.*, *58*, April (Oxford); P. C. Mangelsdorf and R. G. Reeves, " The Origin of Corn ", *Bot. Mus.* *Leafl. Harv.*, *18*, Feb.-April (Cambridge, Mass.); N. Polunin, *Circumpolar Arctic Flora* (Oxford); H. K. Porter (ed.), *Utilization of Nitrogen and its Compounds by Plants. Symp. Soc. exp. Biol.*, vol. XIII (Cambridge); W. Ruhland (ed.), *Encyclopedia of Plant Physiology*, vol. XVII, pt. 1 (Berlin); R. E. Schultes, *Orchids of Trinidad and Tobago* (London); C. Schweinfurth, " Orchids of Peru ", *Fieldiana, Bot.*, *30*, March 27 (Chicago); C. J. P. Spruit, " Simultaneous Photoproduction of Hydrogen and Oxygen by *Chlorella* ", *Meded. LandbHoogesch., Wageningen*, *58*, no. 9, 1958; F. C. Steward, M. O. Mapes and K. Mears, " Growth and Organized Development of Cultured Cells ", *Amer. J. Bot.*, *45*, Dec. 1958 (Baltimore); W. B. Turrill (ed.), *Vistas in Botany* (London); C. L. Withner (ed.), *The Orchids* (New York).

BOXING.

The outstanding achievement in 1959 was that of Ingemar Johansson, the Swedish and European heavyweight champion (*see* BIOGRAPHIES), who shocked U.S. and world boxing circles by winning the world title from Floyd Patterson. The experts had given the Swede little chance of dethroning the U.S. holder when they met at the Yankee stadium, New York, but Johansson scored seven knockdowns in the third round and the referee intervened to save the bewildered Patterson from further punishment. Johansson, who became heavyweight champion without one defeat as a professional, was the first Swede to win the world heavyweight championship and joined Max Schmeling (Germany) and Primo Carnera (Italy) as the only European heavyweights to win the world title in this century.

Prior to this Floyd Patterson had successfully defended his world title against Brian London, knocking out the British heavyweight in 11 rounds at Indianapolis. London fought in defiance of the British Boxing Board of Control who disapproved of his taking part in a world title fight only a few months after he had lost his British and Empire championships to Henry Cooper. On his return to Britain, London was fined £1,000 and suspended for six months.

The most remarkable champion was again Archie Moore who, although nearly 46 years old, retained the world's lightheavyweight title by twice knocking out the Canadian Yvon Durelle, the British Empire champion, at Montreal. The two most successful British champions were Dave Charnley (lightweight) from Dartford and Freddie Gilroy (bantam) from Belfast. Both these young southpaw champions won Empire titles and Charnley made an unsuccessful bid for the world lightweight crown of the U.S. champion Joe Brown at Houston, Texas.

Gilroy won the British and Empire bantamweight championships from Peter Keenan whom he stopped in 11 rounds at Belfast. He then became Britain's only European titleholder, outpointing Piero Rollo (Italy) over 15 rounds at Wembley. By winning this third title Gilroy kept intact his unbeaten record after 19 professional fights. Charnley won the Empire lightweight title knocking out Willie Toweel (South Africa) in ten rounds. Another South African, Gawie de Klerk, made an unsuccessful Empire championship bid when he was defeated by the heavyweight

Ingemar Johansson of Sweden watches expectantly for the referee's decision after felling Floyd Patterson for the seventh and last time in the third round of their world heavyweight championship match at the Yankee stadium, in New York, on June 26.

champion, Henry Cooper, in three rounds at Porthcawl.

The United States recognized two world middleweight champions. New York state still regarded Sugar Ray Robinson as champion while the National Boxing association which controlled boxing in most other states declared Robinson's title vacant when he declined to defend his title against Carmen Basilio. The N.B.A. therefore recognized Gene Fullmer, who beat Basilio in 14 rounds, as champion.

Hogan (Kid) Bassey (Nigeria) failed to regain the world featherweight title from Davey Moore at Los Angeles. Moore came to Britain and in a non-title bout beat British featherweight champion Bobby Neill (Scotland) in 2 min. 55 sec. The shortest championship reign was John (Cowboy) McCormack's. The Scot won the British middleweight title from Terry Downes on an eighth-round disqualification at Wembley, but lost it back to Downes 49 days later when Downes stopped him in eight rounds.

Boxing in the United States suffered a setback in 1959 because of investigations by the Kefauver crime committee, grand jury hearings in New York and federal indictments in California based on extortion plots. There were small attendances at matches and low receipts, and New York was replaced as a world boxing centre by Los Angeles. Boxing became more popular in other parts of the United States.

Don Jordan retained his world welterweight title by outpointing Virgil Akins in 15 rounds at St. Louis, Missouri, and again successfully defended it at Portland, Oregon, by outpointing Denny Moyer. Joe Brown, lightweight champion, defended his title on three occasions: he outpointed Johnny Busso in 15 rounds at Houston, Texas, stopped Paolo Rosi in the 9th round at Washington, D.C., and stopped Dave Charnley (England) in 5 rounds at Houston. At Los Angeles Joe Becerra of Mexico knocked out Alphonse Halimi in the eighth round to win the world bantamweight crown. Pascual Perez of Argentina outpointed Kenji Yonekura of Japan in 15 rounds to retain the flyweight championship at Tokyo, and again did so when he knocked out Sada Yaoita of Japan. (*See* also SPORTING RECORD.)   (F. BR.; N. FL.)

See Nat Fleischer, *Fifty Years at Ringside*, (New York, 1958); Peter Wilson, *More Ringside Seats* (London, 1959).

BRAZIL. Largest of the Latin American republics, the United States of Brazil has a common frontier with all South American countries except Ecuador and Chile. Area: 3,288,042 sq.mi. Pop.: (1950 census) 51,944,397; (1958 est.) 62,725,000. About 50% was of European stock; the remainder included mulattoes (26%), Negroes (11%), Indians and *mestizos* (12%), and about 330,000 Asiatics. Language: Portuguese. Religion: predominantly Roman Catholic (93%), with about 1·7 million Protestants of various denominations and 120,000 Jews. Capital, coterminous with the federal district: Rio de Janeiro, pop. (1950 census) 2,303,063 (1956 est.: 2,852,000). Other chief towns (pop., 1956 est.): São Paulo 2,915,894; Recife 660,816; Salvador (Baía) 505,469; Pôrto Alegre 484,796; Belo Horizonte 469,694; Fortaleza 338,867; Belém (Pará) 286,978. President, Juscelino Kubitschek. Main imports: machinery and vehicles; petroleum and products; wheat and flour; iron, steel and manufactures. Main exports: coffee beans, cacao beans, raw cotton. Monetary unit: *cruzeiro* (free rate, Oct. 1959, Cr.$390·00 = £1 sterling).

History. In 1958 Brazil had received considerable financial aid from U.S. banks on the understanding that it would introduce measures to curb inflation. In fact, however, effective anti-inflationary action was not taken. When, early in 1959, President Juscelino Kubitschek sought further loans, officials of the International Monetary fund and U.S. banks demanded assurances that Brazil would now carry out the required reforms in budget management and credit policy and that a realistic exchange rate for the *cruzeiro* would be adopted. Kubitschek declared that the conditions laid down by the foreign bankers were an insult to national pride. He said, moreover, that his government was based on popular consent, and that the proposed austerity programme would cause social unrest. He was confident that the expansion of the Brazilian economy would continue, with or without foreign assistance. This nationalist attitude pleased the Brazilians and was observed with sympathy in other Latin American countries, where the irksome austerity requirements of the I.M.F. had been complied with.

The inflation and the disequilibrium in Brazil's balance of payments did not indicate economic deterioration: on the contrary, they were the result of vigorous economic growth which outstripped resources. Production of motor cars, machinery for heavy industry, steel and many other industrial goods increased. Private foreign investment, notably from the German Federal Republic, continued. World coffee prices were still in decline, but the Brazilians released some of their crops at the reduced prices, thereby augmenting their earnings of foreign currency.

Again and again the public protested against the constant rise in the cost of living and the shortage of staple foods, such as beans and beef, which they attributed to the ineptitude of their rulers. In October the voters of São Paulo showed their dissatisfaction by electing a rhinoceros from the zoo to the municipal council. The rhinoceros (known as Cacareco) headed the poll, but was disqualified.   (G. P.)

See N. P. Macdonald, *The Land and People of Brazil* (London, 1959).

BREWING AND BEER: *see* BUSINESS REVIEW.

BRIDGES. In 1959 intensive research was being made into the commercial production of low-alloy steel of higher quality for use in bridgework, problems of brittle fracture and fatigue as affected by welded connections, and the design of bridges, especially reinforced-concrete skew spans suitable for the new motorways.

Australia. The Narrows highway bridge over the Swan river, Perth, was completed and work began on the new 2,000-ft. Gladesville bridge across the Parramatta river near Sydney, valued at £A2·4 million. The central arch, designed as four hollow box-section ribs with a clear span of 1,000 ft. and carrying a prestressed-concrete roadway 72 ft. wide, would be the world's longest reinforced-concrete span.

Belgium. Work began on a fine cantilever bridge of composite construction with a central span of 360 ft. and two 213-ft. anchor arms over the Meuse at Cheratte near Liège.

Finland. Reinforced-concrete box-girder twin bridges, with spans of 41 m., 52 m. and 41 m. over the river Ii in the north, were completed and work proceeded on the Lempäälä bridge over a canal on the Helsinki-Tampere highway and a bridge with two prestressed-concrete spans of 57 m. at the Åland Islands between Finland and Sweden.

France. The great new Tancarville suspension bridge over the Seine estuary, with the longest main span on the continent (608 m.), was opened in July. The towers were of reinforced concrete and the two main cables, each built of 56 stranded wire ropes of 72 mm. diameter, were anchored to the deck at the centre of the span by special steel collars to increase the aerodynamic stability of the bridge.

German Federal Republic. The new autobahn bridge over the Wupper valley near Wuppertal, with seven spans varying from 44 m. to 72·8 m., had a reinforced-concrete deck slab in composite construction with steel box girders of novel trapeze-shaped section and inclined webs. The Mannheim-Ludwigshafen bridge which was opened over the Rhine had three 91·3-m. spans consisting of four shallow steel box girders and a battledeck roadway. The new Severin bridge, a 302 m. cable-braced span over the Rhine at Cologne was opened in November. This had only one river pier, on which was an A-shaped steel tower over which the cables passed, near the east bank.

Great Britain. New bridges begun over the Thames included a steel arch of 177-ft. span for the Staines bypass and a 270-ft.-

(Left) The new suspension bridge over the Seine estuary at Tancarville, opened in July. *(Right)* The Kingsferry lifting bridge, a new road, rail and pedestrian traffic link between the Isle of Sheppey and the Kent mainland, nearing completion in October.

span welded-steel bridge of eight girders to carry the Slough-Maidenhead bypass. Construction also began on the Tamar suspension bridge, with a span of 1,100 ft., close to I. K. Brunel's famous Saltash bridge. This was to have a 33-ft. wide roadway carried by locked-coil cables passing over reinforced-concrete towers. Bridges opened on the new motorways included seven on the second stage of the Neath bypass in south Wales and the Chiswick flyover on the Great West road. In Scotland good progress was made on the foundations for the Forth Road bridge and on two new three-span prestressed-concrete bridges, the Inverness Town bridge and the Victoria bridge at Perth. On the railways a heavy programme of bridge reconstruction, mostly in steel, was undertaken.

India. The great new double-deck Ganges bridge at Mokameh, comprising 14 spans of 397 ft., was opened for road and rail traffic in June. Work started on a huge new bridge of similar design comprising ten spans of 397 ft. on very deep foundations over the Brahmaputra river to link Amingaon and Pandu. Big concrete bridges opened included the 860-ft. bridge over the Sabarmati river at Rinza and the bridge over the Betwa river in Jhararghat, which comprised 31 continuous and cantilever spans of 67 ft.

Japan. A single-track railway bridge with six welded-steel trusses of 209-ft. span was completed over the Zinzu river and the 1,890-ft. Jōga-shima bridge, with navigation spans of 230 ft., 312 ft. and 230 ft., provided access to Jōga-shima island.

Netherlands. The Gorinchem bridge across the Merwede comprised a single-leaf 30-m. steel bascule, two tied-arch spans of 170 m. with stiffened-steel battledecks and prestressed-concrete approach spans.

New Zealand. The Auckland Harbour bridge, with an over-all length of 3,348 ft., including an 800-ft. navigation span, was opened in May. One of the biggest floating-in operations ever undertaken was the erection of the third span which was 581 ft. long, weighed 1,200 tons and had to be landed on piers 75 ft. above the water.

Nigeria. Construction began on a new road bridge with ten steel spans each of 427 ft. over the river Niger to link Asaba and Onitsha.

Poland. The new double-deck Citadel bridge over the Vistula, comprising six steel spans with an over-all length of 408 m. and a weight of steel of 2,300 tons, was opened to traffic in Warsaw.

South Africa. Work proceeded on three concrete highway

bridges: the 1,297-ft. J. J. Serfontein bridge and the 1,101-ft. bridge at Hopetown over the Orange river; and a bridge with a 300-ft. arch span at Krantz over the Olifants river.

Sweden. The new six-span, all-welded, steel-girder road bridge over the Söderström in Stockholm was opened in June and work continued on a new highway bridge over the Lule river at Harads, Norrbotten, consisting of two steel arches each of 106-m. span.

Switzerland. Reinforced- and prestressed-concrete bridges under construction included the Boudry viaduct (415 m. over-all) which crossed the River Aveuse and had spans up to 41 m.; a new 240-m. bridge of continuous spans over the River Aubonne on the Lausanne-Geneva road; and the Illas bridge which had a central arch of 81·6 m. over a deep gorge in the Saastal in Valais.

U.S.S.R. The new two-level concrete bridge over the Moscow river at Luzhniki which, with its approaches, measured 2,030 m. over-all, carried a 21-m. motor road on the upper deck and interurban railways below. The three tied-arch skew spans of 45 m., 108 m. and 45 m. over the river were erected by an entirely novel method for a prestressed-concrete structure, being assembled in halves longitudinally on the foreshore in large precast units, floated out on barges and landed on the piers.

United States and Canada. Construction was started in 1959 on the Narrows bridge, between Brooklyn and Staten Island, New York state. The bridge would be of the suspension type and would have the longest single span in the world —4,260 ft. The new Carquinez bridge in California, paralleling the original bridge, was completed late in 1958. In 1959, after the older one had been repaired, each bridge carried one-way traffic. They had identical spans—two 500-ft. anchor arms and two 1,100-ft. main cantilever spans, separated by a tower 150 ft. long. The Glen Canyon bridge over the 700-ft.-deep gorge of the Colorado river, joining the states of Arizona and Utah below the Glen Canyon dam, was completed in 1959. The bridge was a two-hinged arch of 1,028-ft. span, 40-ft. width and 165-ft. rise, making it the fourth longest arch in the world. The Roosevelt International bridge, a suspension bridge across the South Cornwall channel of the St. Lawrence river, was completed late in 1958. It had a main span of 900 ft. and two side spans of 450 ft. and carried a two-lane, 27-ft.-wide concrete roadway. The Fort Pitt bridge over the Monongahela river at Pittsburgh, a 750-ft. tied arch of unique construction, was completed in 1959. The tie consisted of a double-deck truss while the arch rib was a slender box member. Each deck carried four lanes of traffic. The suspenders consisted of four parts of 3¼-in. wire ropes.

In Canada the second Narrows bridge, across Burrard inlet in British Columbia, was completed in 1959. It had a total length of 4,240 ft. and included a cantilever span of 1,100 ft. It carried six lanes of traffic and two sidewalks and cost approximately $22 million.   (H. S. S.; D. B. S.)

BRITISH ARMY: *see* COMMONWEALTH ARMIES.

BRITISH BORNEO. Colonies of North Borneo (incl.
Labuan island) and Sarawak, and protected sultanate of Brunei. Language: various indigenous; Chinese; Malay (*lingua franca*). Religion: Moslem; Buddhist; various pagan; many Chinese Christians. Monetary unit: Malayan dollar (=2*s*. 4*d*. sterling). Main imports: rice and other foodstuffs, textiles and apparel, tobacco products, machinery and vehicles, building materials. Main exports: crude oil (Brunei, mainly to Sarawak for refinement) and refined petroleum products, rubber, timber, copra, tobacco.

North Borneo. Area: 29,388 sq.mi. (incl. Labuan 35 sq.mi.). Pop.: (1951 census) 334,141; (1957 est.) 400,836, incl. 268,498 Borneans, 97,248 Chinese, 1,981 Europeans and Eurasians, 33,109 others. Chief towns (pop., 1951 census): Jesselton (cap.) 11,704, Sandakan (port) 14,499, Tawau 4,282, Victoria (Labuan) 2,526. Administration: governor; executive council; legislative council with official majority; and local town and rural boards with unofficial majorities. Governor, Sir Roland Turnbull.

Sarawak. Area: *c.* 47,500 sq.mi. Pop.: (1947 census) 546,385; (1956 est.) 631,431, incl. 197,945 Sea Dayaks (Ibans), 49,175 Land Dayaks, 30,541 other indigenous races, 189,826 Chinese, 155,419 Malays and Melanaus, 2,106 Europeans, 6,419 other non-indigenous races; (1957 est.) 640,000. Chief towns (pop., 1957 est.): Kuching (cap.) *c.* 58,000, Sibu (river port) *c.* 35,000, Miri (oil centre) *c.* 12,500. Administration: governor; supreme (executive) council; Council Negri (legislative council with elected majority); and various local representative councils. Governor, Sir Anthony Abell.

Brunei. Area: 2,226 sq.mi. Pop.: (1947 census) 40,670, incl. Malay 49%, Dayak 3·5%, other indigenous 25·5%, Chinese 19%, other Asian 1·5%, European 1·5%; (1957 est.) 73,000. Chief towns (pop., 1957 est.): Brunei Town (cap.) *c.* 16,000, Seria and Kuala Belait (oilfields) *c.* 26,000. Administration: sultan; British high commissioner; *mentri besar* (chief minister); privy council; executive council presided over by the sultan; legislative council with unofficial majority presided over by the *mentri besar.* Sultan, Omar Ali Saifuddin; high commissioner, D. C. White.

History. A new constitution for Brunei was promulgated by the sultan in Sept. 1959. The former state council was replaced by executive and legislative councils, and the legisla-

The sultan of Brunei, Sir Omar Ali Saifuddin, inspects boy scouts in Brunei Town on the occasion of his birthday, Sept. 23.

tive council would in due course have a popularly elected minority. Provision was also made for the appointment of a *mentri besar* (chief minister) responsible to the sultan. The post of British high commissioner, formerly held by the governor of Sarawak, passed to an officer resident in Brunei, who assumed direct responsibility for defence and external affairs.

During the year legislative committees in Sarawak and North Borneo studied proposals for the closer association of the Borneo territories. In both colonies new local authorities were created, leaving only a small area around Miri in Sarawak and about half of North Borneo without formal local government councils.

The Council Negri of Sarawak adopted for the period 1959-63 a revised development plan giving first priority to the expansion of cash-crop production.

It was announced that the North Borneo government's scheme for sponsored immigration from Hong Kong, aimed at meeting long-term labour requirements, had failed to attract recruits in significant numbers.   (R. P. GN.)

BRITISH COMMONWEALTH: *see* COMMONWEALTH OF NATIONS.

BRITISH COUNCIL. Lord Bridges was appointed
chairman of the council in July 1959, in succession to the late Sir David Kelly. In March the government announced that the demand overseas fully justified yet further expansion of the council's English teaching and other educational services, and in June that they had decided to provide funds also for further expansion of library services generally and to assist the development of library systems in colonial territories. The council took over from the Foreign Office responsibility for British educational and cultural work in the German Federal Republic, opened offices in Ethiopia, Somaliland Protectorate and Bahrein and posted a liaison officer in the office of the U.K. high commissioner in Canada.

At the end of 1959 the council was represented in 39 non-Commonwealth countries and in 30 Commonwealth territories, including Australia, Canada, South Africa, India, Pakistan and Ceylon. The council continued to supply material and services to countries where it was not directly represented. In the United Kingdom it provided services for students and others from overseas through 20 offices and centres and four student residences.

Funds voted by parliament for the financial year 1959-60, after allowing for estimated earnings, totalled £5,308,150, made up of £3,271,100 for work in foreign countries, £1,169,600 for work in the self-governing countries of the Commonwealth, £747,200 for work in the colonies and £120,250 for services mainly for colonial students in the United Kingdom.

During the year to March 31, 1959, courses in English language, literature and British institutions were provided in 22 countries for 56,173 fee-paying adults at the council's centres or by organizations, mainly in Latin America, with which the council was associated. It assisted in 20 countries, 40 schools using English as a language of instruction. Summer schools for teachers of English and others were held in 27 countries. The council published 17 new or revised brochures in the *British Writers* and other series and its usual periodicals. It arranged 101 overseas tours and advisory visits by British experts.

The council dealt with 5,153 visitors to the United Kingdom, the great majority of these visits being financed from international or overseas sources. It awarded 286 postgraduate scholarships and 184 short-term bursaries to overseas students, and through it 20 foreign countries and international bodies awarded 82 scholarships to British students. Under schemes of university interchange 117 university teachers and research workers visited British universities and 98 British university teachers and research workers visited overseas universities. Services to overseas students included meeting 7,487 on arrival, accommodating 450 in British council residences, finding accommodation for 3,525, providing social and cultural activities in British council centres for 9,749 and introduction, vacation and other courses and visits for 14,119.   (A. P. S.)

BRITISH EAST AFRICA: *see* EAST AFRICA HIGH COMMISSION; KENYA; SOMALILAND PROTECTORATE; TANGANYIKA; UGANDA; ZANZIBAR.

BRITISH GUIANA. British colony on northeast of South America between Venezuela (W.), Brazil (S.W. and S.) and Surinam (E.). Area: 83,000 sq.mi. Pop.: (1946 census) 375,701; (1958 est.) 540,620, comprising 258,610 East Indians, 182,710 Negroes, 61,830 mixed, 21,490 Amerindians, 12,540 Europeans (including two-thirds Portuguese) and 3,440 Chinese. Language: English; various East Indian. Religion (1946 census): Christian 60%; Hindu 30%; Moslem 8%. Principal towns (pop., 1958 est.): Greater Georgetown (cap.) 126,550, New Amsterdam 14,120. Administration: governor; executive council; legislative council with elected majority. Governors in 1959: Sir Patrick Renison and (from Dec. 22) Sir Ralph Grey. Leader of the majority party, Cheddi Jagan. Main imports: machinery, fuel oils, flour. Main exports: sugar, bauxite, rice. Monetary unit: British West Indies dollar ($4·80 = £1 sterling); sterling also in circulation.

History. The year 1959 was remarkable for a real movement forward in the political and economic fields. A deputation led by the governor, Sir Patrick Renison, was successful in obtaining for the 1960-64 Development plan the third largest programme of aid granted by the Colonial Office under the new Colonial Development and Welfare act. The minister of trade and industry, Cheddi Jagan, while acknowledging the generosity of the U.K. government, claimed that the amount was not enough for the country's needs, and sought public support for an approach to the U.S.S.R. for a large loan at little or no interest. The opposition and the Trades Union council rejected his request for the formation of a national front on this issue.

The legislature, which had been set up as a constitutional committee by the secretary of state for the colonies in order to revise British Guiana's constitution, took the deliberate decision that it would frame a new constitution for British Guiana behind closed doors and without asking for memoranda from the general public. The opposition promptly created a rival body called a constituent assembly, consisting of politically articulate members of the community, which moved about the countryside taking evidence in public from groups and individuals. At the request of the Colonial Office, the governor published the report of the constitutional committee for public comment.

During the year British Guiana developed further links with Venezuela by means of trade and cultural missions, and also took part in trade talks with Canada and the United Kingdom. The ruling People's Progressive party, suffering from internal dissensions and attempting to push through controversial legislation like the Land Bonds' issue, was particularly interested in " package-deals " with investors on a long-term low interest basis. Austerity measures continued to be enforced and the economy was strengthened by the world recovery of bauxite. (*See* also WEST INDIES, THE.)   (A. J. S.)

BRITISH HONDURAS. British colony in Central America bounded by Mexico (N. and W.), Guatemala (W. and S.), and the Gulf of Honduras and Caribbean sea (E.). Area: 8,867 sq.mi. Pop.: (1946 census) 59,220, incl. 41,053 Creoles, 10,030 Amerindians (Maya); (1957 est.) 85,098. Language: English; Spanish; Indian dialects. Religion: mainly Roman Catholic. Chief towns (pop., 1957 est.): Belize (cap.) 38,500; Stann Creek 3,500. Administration: governor; executive council; legislative assembly with speaker and elected majority. Governor, Sir Colin Thornley. Main imports:

machinery and vehicles, mineral fuels and petroleum products, textile piecegoods, cereals and dairy products. Main exports: timber (mahogany and pitch pine), fruit. Monetary unit: British Honduras dollar ($4 = £1 sterling).

History. In Jan. 1959 the legislative assembly approved a resolution rejecting Guatemala's claim to sovereignty over British Honduras, declaring that the people of British Honduras had no desire to be in any way subject to, or part of Guatemala. This resolution was passed in protest against a Guatemalan government decree which had named 1959 as " the year of recovery " of British Honduras.

A grant of £2 million was given to the colony from Colonial Development and Welfare funds for the five-year period ending 1964. The development plan to be financed by this grant would be discussed in London between a delegation from British Honduras and the Colonial Office. The services of Jack Downie, a Colonial Office economic expert, were made available to help to prepare development plans. To help raise additional funds for local schemes, the government floated a debenture loan of more than £100,000 at 6½%.

Sir Hilary Blood visited British Honduras as constitutional commissioner to review the constitution which had been in force since 1954. He held discussions with all sections of the community and submitted his recommendations for an advanced constitution to the secretary of state for the colonies.

A ten-man expedition from Cambridge university arrived in British Honduras for a year's research work in archaeology, botany, physics, zoology and physiography. (*See* also WEST INDIES, THE.)   (A. L. A.)

BRITISH SOMALILAND: *see* SOMALILAND PROTECTORATE.

BRITISH SOUTH AFRICAN TERRITORIES. Basutoland (colony), an enclave within southeastern South Africa; Bechuanaland Protectorate, north of the Union; and Swaziland (protectorate), between Transvaal and Mozambique. The three are generally referred to as the High Commission Territories in South Africa:

	Area (sq.mi.)	Population (1956 census)	(1958 est.)	Capital (with est. pop.)
Basutoland	11,716	641,674	658,000	Maseru (5,000)
Bechuanaland Prot.	275,006	327,305	334,000	—*
Swaziland	6,705	237,041	260,000	Mbabane (1,600)

* Admin. H.Q. are at Mafeking, Cape province, Union of South Africa.

Pop.: Basuto, Bechuana, Swazi; in Bechuanaland most numerous tribe is Bamangwato, with capital at Serowe (c. 25,000). Europeans (1956): Basutoland 1,926; Bechuanaland 3,177; Swaziland 5,932. Religion: Christian, several denominations; various indigenous. Administration: high commissioner (who is also U.K. high commissioner in the Union of South Africa) responsible to the U.K. secretary of state for Commonwealth relations; resident commissioners. High commissioner, Sir John Maud. Resident commissioners: (Basutoland) A. G. T. Chaplin; (Bechuanaland) M. O. Wray; (Swaziland) B. A. Marwick. Main imports: textile piecegoods, household goods, agricultural equipment. Main exports: asbestos (Swaziland), carcasses (Bechuanaland), wool (Basutoland). All three territories are in customs union with Union of South Africa. Monetary unit: South African pound (= £1 sterling).

History. *Basutoland.* Following discussions with a delegation from Basutoland in London at the end of 1958, the secretary of state for Commonwealth relations, the Earl of Home, agreed that a measure of constitutional reform should take place in the territory. The changes would include: the conversion of the Basuto National council into a legislative council with powers to legislate on everything except external affairs, defence, internal security and certain other matters; the establishment of an executive council; the strengthening of local government; and the creation of a House of Chiefs.

Bechuanaland. In April 1959 the secretary of state for Commonwealth relations informed the high commissioner that he would be happy to consider proposals to establish a legislative council for the protectorate. For this purpose the resident commissioner was requested, after consultation with the Joint Advisory council, to submit proposals to the high commissioner, who would then make recommendations to the secretary of state.

Consignments of Bechuanaland beef were exported to markets in Europe for the first time during 1959.

Swaziland. A special exclusive prospecting licence to prospect for iron ore near Mbabane was issued under the new mining proclamation. (AY. SY.)

BRITISH WEST AFRICA: see GAMBIA; NIGERIA; SIERRA LEONE.

BRITISH WEST INDIES: see WEST INDIES, THE.

BROADCASTING, SOUND. **Programmes.** *Great Britain.* By the autumn of 1959 there were still more than ten million people who had not yet acquired television sets—a massive potential audience for sound programmes. Their numbers, however, had declined from 14 million during the preceding 12 months. On an average evening during 1959 6·7% of the total adult population were still listening to sound programmes. Of those without television receivers, an average of 18·2% were listening, a proportion which had remained steady during the preceding 12 months. During the autumn the B.B.C. announced that, far from planning to reduce sound programmes, it was likely to extend its local sound broadcasting, and would resume its experimental broadcasts in stereophony.

The Third programme maintained its high standards in programmes for the serious listener. Three notable discussions on parliamentary procedure were broadcast early in the year. To commemorate the bicentenary of the death in London of Handel (April 14, 1759) concerts of his choral and orchestral works, chamber music and operas were broadcast throughout the year. Other notable music programmes were: a studio performance of Sergei Prokofiev's *The Fiery Angel*; a Covent Garden performance of *Lucia di Lammermoor*; *Fidelio*; *Le Nozze di Figaro* and *La Cenerentola* from Glyndebourne; *Der Fliegender Holländer* from Bayreuth; and *Die Zauberflöte* from Salzburg. A Third programme promotion of Igor Stravinsky's *Oedipus Rex* was broadcast from the Royal Festival hall. Samuel Beckett's radio play *Embers*, broadcast in June, won a prize in the "Italia" competition in September. James Joyce's *Finnegan's Wake*, adapted for radio by Eric Ewens, was broadcast twice during the year. D. G. Bridson visited Italy and made recordings of his conversations with Ezra Pound, which were broadcast in three weekly programmes of 45 min. each. Recordings made by Prudence Smith in both the English-speaking and French-speaking parts of west Africa were an important element in a series of programmes about west Africa. In a lighter vein was *Not a Drum was Heard: the War Memoirs of General Gland*, broadcast, it was said, because the Third programme was impressed by the success with which other retired military leaders had invaded the territories of journalism, publishing, sound broadcasting and television.

In the Home service a new development in international broadcasting was *Asking the World*, in which an audience in the United Kingdom put questions to and heard answers from speakers in various parts of Europe, the United States and Canada. Thus the audience might be in a boys' school in Kent, and the foreign speakers in Washington, Paris and Stockholm. *Asking the World* successfully established itself during the year and was expected to continue monthly in 1960. Transatlantic music relays were also a new feature. Using the new transatlantic cable, the Boston Symphony orchestra broadcast "live" from Boston and other music relays were

taken from European capitals. The 1959 Reith lectures were given by Professor P. B. Medawar on *The Future of Man*. As the Home service was the main vehicle in sound for current affairs broadcasting, its schedules had frequently to be altered in 1959 in order to cover such events as President Dwight D. Eisenhower's visit to Britain, N. S. Khrushchev's visit to the United States, the royal tour of Canada and the British general election. Adjustments had also to be made as a result of the printing dispute. In the absence of provincial papers, the B.B.C.'s regional home services provided more local news and information, and " journalists without newspapers " took to the air instead of writing in their normal columns.

In Network Three a notable development was the start of a long series of elementary Russian lessons. There was also a series on careers, designed for school-leavers, and a series *Building Matters*, specially planned for the public directly or indirectly interested in building and its affiliated trades and professions.

The Light programme continued to provide broadcasts for relaxation and entertainment from 6.30 A.M. to midnight on weekdays and from 9 A.M. to midnight on Sundays. The schedules included news-in-brief bulletins on an hourly basis, a ten-minute bulletin at 10.30 P.M. and the daily *Radio Newsreel*. The first tour abroad of the B.B.C. Concert orchestra was made to the Netherlands during April 23-29. Public concerts were given at Scheveningen, Nijmegen, Utrecht and Amsterdam, and the orchestra appeared at the annual ceremony for the installation of the " queen of the flowers " at Keukenhof Flower show. Dutch music critics were enthusiastic about the orchestra's versatility and its ability to perform with distinction classical works as well as musical comedy items. In collaboration with the London County council the B.B.C. organized the annual Light Music festival at the Royal Festival hall in June and early July. There were five Saturday evening concerts, in one of which were performed the winning entries in the *New Music for Brass* competition, and in another the final in the *Let the People Sing* competition for amateur choirs.

Commonwealth. During 1959 the Australian Broadcasting commission presented the programme which won the Italia prize (documentary division). This was *The Death of a Wombat* by Ivan Smith with music by George English—a powerful portrayal of the ravages inflicted by an Australian bushfire. The A.B.C. also arranged the annual Commonwealth Christmas day broadcast, hitherto always in the hands of the B.B.C. Wilfrid Thomas was director and narrator. The celebrated comedian-compere, Jack Davey, died at the age of 49. On July 31, 97% of Australian homes had at least one radio receiving set. The 2,265,530 licences then operating represented an increase of 118,992 over the same period of the preceding year.

In the Canadian Broadcasting corporation's " Wednesday Night " winter drama series, an outstanding broadcast was *A Beach of Strangers*, written and produced by a member of the C.B.C. staff, John Reeves. This play later won the Italia prize for drama. Another notable production, early in the year, was W. H. Auden's verse oratorio, *The Age of Anxiety*. During the summer " Wednesday Night " featured a number of operas, symphonies and recitals broadcast from the festivals at Stratford (Ontario), Vancouver and Saskatoon. Later in the year a series of concerts, *Music of To-day*, brought Canadian listeners first performances of contemporary music from all over the world.

Technical and Organizational Developments. The annual output of the B.B.C.'s Home, Light, Third and Network Three programmes, including the home services of the six regional centres, amounted to some 20,000 programme hours. There was a further development in the v.h.f. coverage by the B.B.C. during 1959. The 18 v.h.f. sound broadcasting stations in service were supplemented by new stations at Peterborough, at Orkney (formerly temporary) and at Thrumster. Plans were announced for a new v.h.f. sound station at Dover. The completion of the network of 20 v.h.f. stations meant that 96·4% of the population could receive the Home, Light and Third programmes (with Network Three) on v.h.f., with greatly improved quality and freedom from interference. Plans were also announced for further low-power satellite stations for v.h.f. sound broadcasting, and ten were to be built during the next three years. These new stations would give coverage to about 640,000 more people and improved service to a further 380,000. It was estimated that some 3 million v.h.f. sets were in use in 1959. The extension of v.h.f. transmitters also permitted further developments to be made in area broadcasting. Programmes of news and general local interest were broadcast on the v.h.f. Home service wavelengths to cover smaller areas than the regional news bulletins on the medium wavelengths.

An average of 20 million people used their radio sets each day during 1959. Some 8 million copies of pamphlets to supplement B.B.C. broadcasts to schools were issued. In Sept. 1959, the total number of receiving licences in force was 14,917,893, including 9,718,472 combined sound and television licences.

Moscow citizens crowd around a radio receiver to hear the latest news of Lunik II on its way to the moon, which it reached on Sept. 13.

The B.B.C. made further series of experimental transmissions in stereophonic sound, using medium wave, v.h.f. and television sound transmitters. These test transmissions were made at times of day when the transmitters used were not carrying normal programmes.

A closed-circuit television system was devised to speed the presentation of news items in the B.B.C.'s sound news bulletins. A 14-in. picture monitor in the sound studio could show to the reader or announcer an important news item which might be received in the news room while he was actually broadcasting. Reading from the monitor the announcer could then insert the item at a convenient point in his broadcast.

An example of the progressive application of transistors to broadcasting equipment was the production by B.B.C. engineers of transistorized, portable, sound outside-broadcasting equipment. When this was used by commentators, no technical assistance was necessary.

In the external services of the B.B.C. the broadcasts in Arabic were increased to 12 hr. daily. There was still systematic jamming of B.B.C. transmissions in Russian, Hungarian, Czech, Slovak, Bulgarian, Rumanian, Finnish, Hebrew, German, Persian, Turkish, Polish, Greek, Albanian, Kuoyo and Cantonese. Although jamming of B.B.C. Polish broad-

casts was stopped by the Polish government, these transmissions were still being jammed from sources inside the U.S.S.R. and Czechoslovakia.

The relaying of B.B.C. programmes by local broadcasting stations throughout the world continued to grow. The new service in Swahili was re-broadcast daily in Kenya, Tanganyika and Zanzibar. The General Overseas service was re-broadcast every day by stations in 30 countries and by seven British Forces broadcasting stations. At the same time B.B.C. sound radio programmes in recorded form were distributed by the B.B.C. Transcription service to the extent of some 60,000 records in the year (700 separate programmes). Transcriptions in Arabic were distributed to the middle east. A transcription service for Latin America was revived.

Some 39 members of the B.B.C. staff, both engineers and programme officials, were seconded to Colonial Broadcasting organizations in 1959 and 47 guests from other broadcasting organizations attended B.B.C. staff training courses. The International Radio Consultative committee (C.C.I.R.) held its ninth plenary assembly in Los Angeles in 1959. A convention of the International Telecommunications union met in Geneva to discuss the allocation of bands of frequencies to the various radio services, including broadcasting.

Cyprus Broadcasting corporation started commercial sound broadcasting in April 1959. Progress was made in developing the new Kenya Broadcasting service which came into operation in Oct. 1959. Both the director of broadcasting and the chief engineer were seconded from the B.B.C.

The Sierra Leone Broadcasting service became an independent Department of Broadcasting in Jan. 1959, and the service took over the technical side of broadcasting from the Posts and Telegraphic Departments. In January Radio Malaya assumed responsibility for broadcasting within the federation and Radio Singapore began operations as a government Department of Broadcasting. A new government v.h.f. transmitter was planned for Hong Kong. The new commercial broadcasting station there began operations. Expansion of education by radio was continued in Sarawak. The new Broadcasting service of the British Solomon Islands Protectorate came into operation in 1959. The Jamaican Broadcasting corporation, an independent body, run on semi-commercial lines, began full scale operations.

In Canada a notable event in sound broadcasting in 1959 was the setting up of a small network of privately owned stations in the maritime provinces. The year's major development, however, was the extension of the work of the C.B.C. into the far north.

A strike among producers affected both the sound and vision networks of the C.B.C. early in the year. In June a mass resignation took place in Toronto of staff of the C.B.C.'s Department of Talks and Public Affairs. The staff alleged that the management had been unduly influenced by political pressure in cancelling a daily commentary on parliamentary affairs. The resignations were withdrawn when the programme was reinstated. A parliamentary committee investigated the charges and reported that they had not been proved. (*See* also RADIO, SCIENTIFIC DEVELOPMENTS IN; TELEVISION.)

(G. WR.; O. M. R.; EN. M. T.)

BUDGETS. In 1959 attempts were made in several eastern countries to encourage industry and commerce by reductions in direct taxes or corporation taxes, but at the same time taxes on commodities were raised in order to restrain imports. The same pattern was followed in some western countries, but general tax reductions were made in Great Britain and general tax increases in Canada and South Africa.

Great Britain. In presenting the 1959-60 budget, the chancellor of the exchequer considered that it would be possible for there to be an appreciable increase in production above its current level. He also felt that Britain should play its part in reviving world trade. Accordingly, he gave substantial tax concessions. The standard rate of income tax was cut by 9d. to 7s. 9d., each of the lower rates being cut by 6d., and this concession alone was expected to cost £229 million in a full year. Consumers also benefited from a purchase tax reduction of one-sixth, to 50%, 25% and 12½% on all goods previously chargeable at 60%, 30% and 15% respectively. They were also helped by a reduction of 2d. a pint in the duty on beer. The main changes affecting business concerned initial allowances, which are deducted from depreciation claims in later years, and investment allowances, which are not. The existing initial allowance of 30% on new plant and machinery was replaced by an investment allowance of 20% together with an initial allowance of 10%, and the existing initial allowance of 15% on the construction of industrial buildings was replaced by an investment allowance of 10% together with an initial allowance of 5%. The existing 40% initial allowance on the construction of mining works was replaced by a 20% investment allowance and a 20% initial allowance. New buildings and works in agriculture and forestry became eligible for an investment allowance of 10%. Among other measures, changes were made in the system of liquor licence duties and steps were taken to protect the tax revenue from " bond washing " (the making of a quick and illegitimate profit at the expense of the revenue by the purchase of securities cum-dividend and their sale ex-dividend). In addition, the qualifying age for payments of postwar credits was reduced by two years to 63 for a man and 58 for a woman. Postwar credits were also to be payable in certain cases of hardship, and compound interest at 2½% per annum free of tax was to be paid on credits becoming eligible for payment after Oct. 1, 1959. On balance, the various tax changes were expected to cause a reduction in revenue of £295 million in 1959-60 and about £370 million in a full year. The postwar credit changes were expected to cost £71 million in 1959-60, but only £1 million per annum thereafter.

An " above the line " surplus of £364 million for 1958-59 had been envisaged, but net borrowing of £236 million had been anticipated after allowing for capital as well as current expenditure. The actual " above the line " surplus was £377 million. This was due to a yield from taxation of £41 million more than had been anticipated, and expenditure of £28 million more. The larger " above the line " surplus was accompanied by a " below the line " deficit of £41 million less than had been anticipated. On balance, net borrowing was £182 million. For 1959-60 the chancellor envisaged a rise of £140 million in tax receipts, on the basis of 1958-59 tax rates, and a rather smaller rise in expenditure, with the " above the line " surplus rising to £397 million and net borrowing of £355 million. The 1959-60 budget changes reduced the " above the line " surplus to £102 million, expenditure being estimated at £5,223 million (against actual expenditure of £5,103 million in 1958-59). The " below the line " deficit was expected to rise to £823 million against an actual deficit of £559 million in 1958-59, leaving estimated net borrowing at £721 million.

PERSONAL INCOME TAX, UNITED KINGDOM AND UNITED STATES
(1959 tax rate in £ for married couple with one child)

Income	Tax		Income	Tax	
£	U.K.*	U.S.†	£	U.K.*	U.S.†
500	4	—	3,000	804	464
700	36	—	5,000	1,830	1,106
1,000	114	51	10,000	5,200	3,667
1,500	265	141	20,000	13,825	10,436
2,000	416	240	50,000	40,450	35,867

* Rates are for couple with one child not over 11 years of age. † Federal income tax only.
SOURCE. U.K. Financial Statement; U.S. Treasury Department.

Commonwealth. *Australia.* A budget deficit of £A61 million was expected in 1959-60 compared with an actual

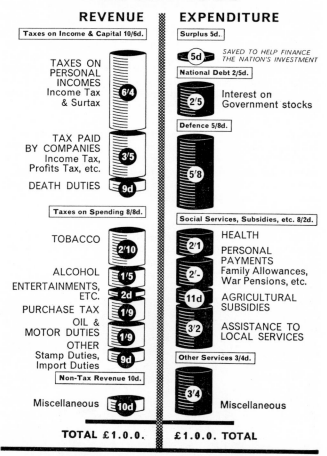

BUDGET 1959

REVENUE

Taxes on Income & Capital 10/6d.

TAXES ON PERSONAL INCOMES Income Tax & Surtax — 6/4

TAX PAID BY COMPANIES Income Tax, Profits Tax, etc. — 3/5
DEATH DUTIES — 9d

Taxes on Spending 8/8d.

TOBACCO — 2/10
ALCOHOL ENTERTAINMENTS, ETC. — 1/5
— 2d
PURCHASE TAX — 1/9
OIL & MOTOR DUTIES — 1/9
OTHER Stamp Duties, Import Duties — 9d

Non-Tax Revenue 10d.

Miscellaneous — 10d

EXPENDITURE

Surplus 5d.

5d — SAVED TO HELP FINANCE THE NATION'S INVESTMENT

National Debt 2/5d.

2/5 — Interest on Government stocks

Defence 5/8d.

5/8

Social Services, Subsidies, etc. 8/2d.

2/1 — HEALTH
2/- — PERSONAL PAYMENTS Family Allowances, War Pensions, etc.
11d — AGRICULTURAL SUBSIDIES
3/2 — ASSISTANCE TO LOCAL SERVICES

Other Services 3/4d.

3/4 — Miscellaneous

TOTAL £1.0.0.   £1.0.0. TOTAL

A chart of the British budget for 1959-60. How the government proposed to collect each £ of revenue and to spend each £ collected.

deficit of £A30 million in 1958-59. The rate of personal income tax was reduced by 1s. in the £A, at a cost of £A20 million in a full year, and concessions were made to help newly established companies and companies engaged in oil exploration. A small reduction was made in the import duty on petrol, but postal, telephone and telegraph charges were increased and a charge was imposed for prescriptions.

Canada. A budget deficit of $430 million was expected in 1959-60 compared with a deficit of about $600 million in 1958-59. Taxes were increased on personal and corporation income and on cigarettes, cigars and spirits. The special income and sales tax for old-age security was also increased. Some changes in deductible medical expenses were proposed and it was announced that import tariffs would be revised for certain items.

Ceylon. The budget for 1959-60 envisaged total expenditure of Rs.1,736 million and total revenue of Rs.1,343 million. New tax proposals, estimated to yield an additional Rs.32 million, included increases in the excise tax on arrack, in import duties on cars, watches and foreign liquors, and in export duties on coconut products. Import duties on certain industrial raw materials and items of equipment were, however, reduced.

India. It was expected that there would be an over-all budget deficit of Rs.2,220 million in 1959-60 compared with an over-all deficit of Rs.2,550 million in 1958-59. Increases were made in various customs and excise duties and an increase of 0·5% was made in the wealth tax on individuals and Hindu undivided families. A slight reduction in the export duty on tea came into effect. No change in personal income tax was made but some exemptions under the new expenditure tax were withdrawn. The wealth tax on companies and the excess dividends tax were abolished. Later in the year, concessions in indirect taxes amounting to Rs.10 million were announced but no changes were made in the direct tax proposals.

New Zealand. The budget provided for tax reductions of £NZ17 million in a full year. Income tax rates were reduced by 20% from Oct. 1, 1959, and the social security tax of 1*s*. 6*d*. in the £NZ on all income was to be separated from income tax from April 1, 1960.

Pakistan. A small budget surplus on current account was expected in 1959-60. Capital expenditure was expected to rise from Rs.1,451 million to Rs.1,497 million, but more attention was to be paid to agricultural development and less to industrial than in the past. Some concessions were made in direct taxes, while most sales, excise and customs taxes were raised. The tax increases were expected to yield Rs.44 million on balance.

South Africa. After taking into account tax increases, the budget surplus in 1959-60 was expected to be £SA37 million, the same as in 1958-59. Subsidies were reduced and payments to pensioners increased. Tax increases were imposed on diesel fuel, beer, cane spirit and gramophone records. Increases were also made in postal and telephone charges and a new duty on rice was introduced. Building societies, hitherto exempt from taxation, would in future have to pay a company tax of 60% on their income from investments.

Europe. *France.* A tax reform bill was presented to the government by the finance minister in May 1959. The main provisions were: the replacement of the two existing income taxes (proportional and progressive) by a single progressive tax to be levied, as far as possible, at the source of income; the abolition of the fiscal privileges of some industries; provision for accelerated amortization by industries vulnerable to foreign competition; reduced estate duties for inheritance in direct line and increased duties for inheritance in indirect line; and a reform of the turnover tax. Some concessions were made, family allowances being raised by 10%.

German Federal Republic. The 1959 budget included provision for expenditure (including capital expenditure) of DM.39,120 million, DM.400 million more than in 1958. It was anticipated that ordinary tax revenue would amount to DM.30,160 million and that DM.3,700 million would be borrowed. Expenditure on defence would probably be less than envisaged in the budget and this would help to balance the budget.

Italy. Expenditure was expected to increase slightly less than revenue in 1959-60 and a budget deficit of L.129,000 million was expected compared with a deficit of L.135,000 million in 1958-59. The deficit had been progressively reduced in recent years, but this policy had been hampered by the need for increases in expenditure to stimulate economic activity and hold down unemployment.

Netherlands. Total expenditure in 1960 was expected to be Fl.9,062 million and total revenue Fl.8,280 million. The expected budget deficit of Fl.782 million compared with an estimated deficit of Fl.1,850 million in 1959. Temporary tax increases imposed in 1958 continued, but some tax relief was granted to unmarried persons.

Norway. Current revenue and expenditure were both expected to rise in 1959-60, and a budget surplus of Kr.705 million was anticipated compared with a surplus of Kr.794 million in 1958-59. Taking capital expenditure into account, an over-all deficit of Kr.230 million was expected. In the budget the tax on undistributed profits was reduced from 8% to 4%, but telephone charges and postal rates were increased.

Sweden. A budget deficit of Kr.599 million on current account was expected in 1959-60 and an over-all deficit of Kr.2,470 million. This compared with an over-all deficit of

Kr.2,219 million in 1958-59. Total revenue was expected to rise by Kr.163 million to Kr.12,896 million and expenditure on current account by Kr.974 million to Kr.13,495 million. Government capital expenditure was expected to increase to Kr.2,731 million. Some time before the 1959-60 budget was announced steps had been taken to alleviate corporate taxes by postponing the introduction of new regulations regarding the valuation of commodity stocks.

United States. In a report issued in Sept. 1959, the Bureau of the Budget reviewed the U.S. budget for the year ending June 30, 1960. Budget receipts were expected to total $79,000 million, a sharp rise from the previous year's revised total of $68,158 million because of the higher level of economic activity. Budget expenditures were estimated at $78,900 million, approximately $1,800 million lower than in 1959. A balanced budget was envisaged for 1959-60, with revenues exceeding expenditures by about $100 million, compared with a deficit of $12,541 million in the previous year.

Of the $79,000 million which the government expected to collect in 1959-60, approximately four-fifths was accounted for by income taxes on individuals and corporations, rates of which were unchanged. Expenditures for the four major national security programmes—the military functions of the Department of Defence, military assistance under the Mutual Security programme, atomic energy, and stockpiling and defence production expansion—were estimated at $45,713 million for 1959-60, or about $700 million less than the actual amount spent in 1958-59. Outlays for these programmes were scheduled to absorb 58% of total budget expenditures in 1959-60. The expansion in major national security programmes from 1949-50 to 1959-60 had accounted for more than four-fifths of the increase of about $39,000 million in total budget expenditures over the period. Budget expenditures for governmental international programmes in 1959-60 were estimated at $2,050 million, a fall of $1,700 million from 1958-59. The drop reflected the inclusion in the 1958-59 total of $1,375 million for the additional U.S. subscription to the International Monetary fund. (*See* also WEALTH AND INCOME, DISTRIBUTION OF.) (A. STN.; C. F. SZ.)

BUILDING AND CONSTRUCTION INDUSTRY.

Although at the beginning of 1959 there were many signs of increased building activity, the bad weather during the early part of the year, combined with the very wet state of the ground, restricted site activity. Once the weather improved, however, the increased scale of building and civil engineering operations was everywhere very noticeable. The large programme of road construction, begun during 1958, was in full progress and this, combined with the acceleration of building activity, produced a load on the industry which many regarded as comparable to the overload of two years previously. British construction work overseas was 5% higher than in the previous year and was at the highest recorded level. There was a substantial increase in the value of new contracts obtained in non-sterling areas.

Output rose significantly above the level for the previous year and there was a corresponding advance in productivity. Equally significant was the fact that prices of building work remained steady at a figure somewhat below their 1957 peak in spite of the increase of 5% in wage rates since then.

There was a small increase in wage rates owing to a rise in the index of retail prices but the trade unions' claim for 4*d*. per hour increase was rejected after arbitration. The trade unions also indicated their intention of pressing for a reduction in the working week from 44 hr. to 40 hr. and the National Joint council appointed a committee to consider the matter. The building trade unions held a conference in May at which delegates considered the effect on the building worker (particularly the skilled craftsman) of the introduction of new materials and techniques. The conference was notable for some sound constructive thinking by many of the representatives but it was clear that leadership of a high order would be needed if the work of the conference was to be followed up effectively in the industry.

TABLE I. CEMENT PRODUCTION* ('000 metric tons)

Countries	1938	1946	1952	1957	1958
United States . .	18,279	28,102	42,394	52,573	52,272
U.S.S.R. . .	5,688	3,373	13,910	28,908	33,360
German Fed. Rep. . .	15,053†	2,328	12,886	19,252	19,404
Japan . . .	5,925	929	7,118	15,176	14,988
France . . .	4,129	3,859	8,833	12,708	13,644
Italy . . .	4,608	2,445	6,906	11,869	12,384
United Kingdom .	7,840	6,679	11,317	12,154	11,856
China . . .	2,293‡	...	2,860	6,700	...
India . . .	1,427§	2,068§	3,594	5,691	6,168
Canada . . .	887	1,890	2,940	5,494	5,712
Poland . . .	1,719	1,339	2,671	4,496	5,040
Spain . . .	...	1,835	2,457	4,483	4,812
Czechoslovakia .	1,182	921	2,209	3,672	4,104
Belgium . . .	3,000	1,890	4,111	4,705	4,056
German Dem. Rep. .	1,936‖	...	2,023	3,460	3,552
Brazil . . .	618	826	1,619	3,376	...
South Africa . .	878	1,180	2,021	2,525	2,724
Mexico . . .	374	738	1,757	2,560	2,544
Sweden . . .	993	1,462	2,116	2,450	2,496
Argentina . .	1,237	...	1,545	2,363	2,472
Rumania . . .	510	315	1,505	2,421	...
Australia¶ . .	866	735	1,257	2,208	2,352
Austria . . .	648	392	1,390	2,129	2,154
Yugoslavia . .	712	696	1,313	1,983	1,968

* Excl. countries with production less than 1·75 million metric tons. † Prewar Germany. ‡ 1942. § Incl. Pakistan. ‖ Present area. ¶ Year ended June 30. SOURCE. U.N. *Statistical Yearbook 1958*; U.N. *Monthly Bulletin of Statistics*.

TABLE II. BUILDING BRICKS PRODUCTION* (million units)

Countries	1938	1946	1952	1957	1958
U.S.S.R. . .	7,586	3,239	14,854	24,000	27,600
United States . .	3,533	4,869	5,889	6,658	6,492
Great Britain . .	7,800	3,450	6,622	6,912	6,432
German Fed. Rep. . .	4,572†	608	4,731	5,498	5,412
France‡ . . .	3,100§	2,094§	3,276	4,334	4,284
Poland . . .	1,848‖	513	1,718	2,492	2,676
Belgium . . .	...	2,081¶	2,166	2,412	2,208
German Dem. Rep. .	2,600**	...	1,759	2,148	2,184

*Excl. countries with production less than 2,000 million units. † 1936, prewar Germany. ‡ Thousand metric tons. § Incl. hollow tiles for floor construction. ‖ 1937, prewar area. ¶ 1947, common bricks only. ** Present area.

Increased efficiency of building continued to be sought mainly in the direction of improved organization. The Joint Committee of Architects, Quantity Surveyors and Builders continued to press for more thorough planning of projects before actual building work was begun and there were signs that contractors were placing more reliance on the careful planning and programming of work. This was reflected in a

Construction of a cavity wall in one unit with hollow perforated clay bricks developed by the Building Research Station, Herts.

notable acceleration in the speed of construction, particularly in the case of important city buildings where contract times averaged little more than half of those customary in the early 1950s. The application of work-study techniques to building operations made some headway and an increasing number of firms showed interest in training staff for this work. Further evidence of these general trends was to be found in the continued widespread interest in management training which advanced a further step in the publication of a report by the Institute of Builders in the latter part of the year. Concern was expressed in the industry that the level of recruitment of craft apprentices had not followed the upward trend of building activity to any significant extent. Proposals were put forward for changes in apprenticeship training arrangements calculated to appeal to employers but there seemed little prospect of early action being taken. The introduction of new techniques, the employment of specialized sub-contractors and the extensive activities of national contractors with no continuing interests in any particular area, all contributed to the difficulty in increasing the recruitment of apprentices although it was generally recognized that no alternative system of training was available.

There was continued criticism of the system of unrestricted tendering for building work as practised by many local authorities and some private building owners and developers. It was widely felt that the number of contractors invited to tender for a contract should be related to the value of the work and the joint committee previously referred to published a code for selective tendering which was generally well received. It was increasingly evident that some large contracting firms were returning to their prewar practice of building development either in the housing or commercial building field. Substantial savings in building costs could be achieved when one organization functioned as client, designer and builder but few firms could command the capital resources necessary to take advantage of these possibilities.

In the field of technical development interest seemed to be centred mainly on rapid erection methods and off-site fabrication. Experiments were reported on the use of large-scale concrete wall sections and developments of clay blocks. Improved performance of internal finishes which could be rapidly assembled from large units was also achieved. In all, the impression given was of an industry in which the accelerated technical advance was causing increasing concern with the problems of training personnel.

Indication of increased public interest in building was to be found in the introduction, in September, of a weekly 30-min. broadcast entitled " Building Matters ". At the general election in October the programmes of both large political parties contained promises involving increases in building activity. The choice lay essentially between a continuance of a system of free endeavour under the Conservatives and a return to planned control had a Labour government come into office. (*See also* ARCHITECTURE; HOUSING.) (D. A. G. R.)

BULGARIA. People's republic in the eastern part of the Balkan peninsula, bounded N. by Rumania, W. by Yugoslavia, S. by Greece and E. by Turkey and the Black sea. Area: 42,796 sq.mi. Pop.: (1956 census) 7,629,254. Language (1947 est.): Bulgarian 88%; Turkish 9·8%. Religion (1947 est.): Orthodox 84%; Moslem 11·5% (of which one-sixth Pomaks, or Moslem Bulgars, remainder Turks); Roman Catholic 0·9%; Gregorian Armenian 0·4%; Jewish 0·3%; Protestant 0·2%. Chief towns (pop., 1956 census): Sofia (cap.) 725,756; Plovdiv 162,518; Varna 119,769; Ruse 83,472; Burgas 72,795; Dimitrovo 59,721; Pleven 57,758; Stara Zagora 55,322. First secretary of the Bulgarian Communist party, Todor Zhivkov; chairman of the presidium of the National Assembly, Dimiter Ganev; chairman of the council of ministers, Anton Yugov. Main imports: machinery and vehicles, petroleum and products, cotton. Main exports: tobacco, foodstuffs. Monetary unit: *lev*; L.19·04 = £1 sterling; tourist rate L.27·28 = £1 sterling.

*(Left) Citizens of Sofia, Bulgaria, buying early editions of newspapers carrying details of the new economic plan announced in January.
(Right) Secondary school pupils receiving instruction in a Gabrovo textile mill from a "hero of Socialist labour".*

History. The year 1959 was chiefly remarkable for the considerable raising of the country's economic aims and the major reorganization of the administration designed to attain the new objectives. The Bulgarian Communist leaders planned a " big leap forward " on the Chinese Communist model, accompanied by many reforms based on the Soviet pattern. The new plan, proposed on Jan. 20 by Todor Zhivkov, first secretary of the Communist party, and approved by the National Assembly in March, included the following aims. The output of steel, which was 211,000 metric tons in 1958, was to be raised to 400,000 tons by 1962 and 900,000 tons by 1965. The output of electric power was to be more than doubled by 1962, when it would be nearly 7,000 million kwh. Compared with 1957, industry as a whole was to double its output by 1962 and more than treble it by 1965. Similarly ambitious goals were set for agriculture, which was to treble its total output by 1965.

The existing territorial administrative division of the country was abolished. In its place 30 administrative economic districts were set up, each responsible for " the whole political, state, economic and cultural life " in its area. This devolution of authority was accompanied by the dissolution of seven national ministries of an economic nature. In April elections were held to appoint officials of the new administrative districts, resulting in a 99·82% vote in favour of the Fatherland front candidates.

In agriculture the machine tractor stations were abolished and the system of compulsory deliveries from farmers replaced by one of contractual purchasing at prices considerably higher than the old fixed prices but still below those paid for farm produce on the free market. By a process of amalgamation the total number of collective farms was reduced from 3,450 to 625, and they were to take over local commercial and manufacturing enterprises associated with agriculture.

A fundamental reform of the educational system had as its declared object " the closer linking of education and the training of youth for productive labour ". The plan envisaged schoolchildren spending as much as a third of their time in active production. Vlko Chervenkov, former leader of the Communist party, was made chairman of a new state council for science.

Diplomatic relations between Bulgaria and the United States were resumed on March 27. They had been broken off on Feb. 21, 1950, when Donald R. Heath, then U.S. minister in Sofia, was said to be implicated in the trial of Traicho Kostov. No public withdrawal of these charges was made. On July 22 the Bulgarian government proposed the conclusion of a 20-year non-aggression treaty with Greece, which did not accept the offer. After visiting Albania in October, Zhivkov visited Moscow in November and was received by N. S. Khrushchev. (*See* also EASTERN EUROPEAN ECONOMIC PLANNING.) (D. F.)

BURMA. Independent federal republic on the eastern side of the Bay of Bengal, between Pakistan and India on the northwest, Tibet on the north and China, Laos and Thailand (Siam) on the east. The republic comprises Burma proper, the Karen, Shan, Kachin and Kayah states, and the Chin special division. Area: 261,600 sq.mi. Pop.: (1941 census) 16,823,798; (1958 est.) 20,255,000. Racially, the peoples of Burma are Mongoloid. Religion: Buddhist (84%), Moslem (4%), Hindu (3·9%), Christian (2·3%). Language: Burmese (66%). Largest indigenous minorities: Karens, Shans, Kachins, Chins, etc. Largest immigrant minorities (1955 est.): Indian 600,000, divided equally between Moslems and Hindus; Chinese 350,000. Chief towns (pop., 1955 est.): Rangoon (cap.) 737,100; Mandalay 182,400; Moulmein 101,700. President of the Union of Burma: U Win Maung; prime minister, General Ne Win. Main imports: manufactured goods. Main exports: rice, cotton, teak. Monetary unit: *kyat* (K.13·33 = £1 sterling).

History. General Ne Win took office as prime minister on Oct. 29, 1958. It was his avowed intention to hold an early general election. During Jan. 1959 a number of organizations voiced the desire that his government should continue in power, because the country was still too disturbed for the holding of elections. This would need suspension of the constitutional requirement that a member of the government who for any period of six months was not a member of parliament must resign. On Feb. 13 Ne Win resigned on the ground that conditions were impossible for free and fair elections, and said he would accept office again only if the constitution were amended. Under threat of reversion to the deadlock from which his assumption of power had delivered the country, parliament amended the constitution as required and unanimously re-elected Ne Win prime minister. Minor changes took place in the cabinet. Preparations began for the holding of elections in April 1960. There were surrenders of insurgents, increases in the strength of the civil and military police, and a marked advance in the pacification of the country.

The process of appointing military officers to the charge of departments and of eliminating political bosses continued, and further steps were taken to combat corruption and inefficiency. On Dec. 1, 1958, the Rangoon municipal corporation was dissolved and Colonel Tun Sein appointed commissioner with an advisory committee of non-politicians. Subsequently Colonel Khin Nyo was placed in charge of the railway, Lieut.-Col. Saw Mya Thein of the customs department and the Rangoon port, and Lieut.-Col. Chit Khine of the labour department. Committees were appointed to investigate alleged corruption and maladministration, pressure was applied to recover advances overdue to be repaid to the State Agricultural Marketing Board, hours of work in government offices were extended and enforced. A drive was instituted to clean up Rangoon, 2,000 government employees being brought out on Sunday mornings to help sweep pavements and streets.

The paddy crop was 1·3 million tons greater than in 1958. Negotiations for export to India failed because the government of India planned to buy more cheaply from China, but Chinese intervention in Tibet so inflamed Indian opinion that the government of India abandoned their plans and placed their orders in Burma at the price originally demanded by the Burmese government. The Cattle Slaughter act was repealed to allow revival of the export of hides and skins. Notice was served upon a number of foreign firms and advisers who were considered to have been responsible for ill-founded and extravagant ventures. A number of new economic undertakings were launched, particularly by the Defence Services institute, an army organization designed to by-pass corrupt or politician-ridden departments. These included shallow-water sea fishing, a shipping service to the far east, and the taking over of banking operations from A. Scott & Co. Ltd. Further foreign aid was promised, $37 million from the U.S. government for the construction of a modern highway between

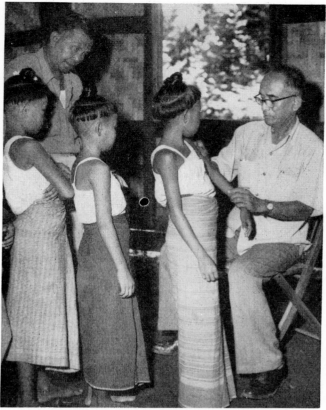

Burmese village children are examined for signs of leprosy, which Unicef is helping to combat. There are 200,000 lepers in Burma.

embassy. Since the Burmese government did not recognize the right of a foreign embassy to grant asylum Kaznacheev was handed over to the Burmese government which refused either to protect or to detain him, but also placed no obstacle in the way of his going whither he would. Accordingly Kaznacheev stepped out into the U.S. ambassador's waiting car which placed him aboard a special U.S. air force plane bound for Manila.   (F. S. V. D.)

BUSINESS REVIEW. The following is an account of some of the principal business and trading activities during 1959. Major basic industries have separate articles, which are: AIRCRAFT MANUFACTURE; BUILDING AND CONSTRUCTION INDUSTRY; COAL; COTTON; ELECTRICAL INDUSTRIES; IRON AND STEEL; MINERAL AND METAL PRODUCTION; MOTOR CYCLE AND CYCLE INDUSTRY; MOTOR INDUSTRY; PETROLEUM; PLASTICS INDUSTRY; PRINTING; RUBBER; TEXTILE INDUSTRY; TIMBER; WOOL.

Baking Industry. Early in 1959 a parliamentary storm broke out over the Baking Industry (Hours of Work) act, 1958, which restricted night work by bakery operatives to a maximum of 26 weeks a year, with not more than 4 weeks consecutively. This had caused considerable hardship to many smaller bakers who were unable to maintain production without night work and had insufficient workers to arrange alternating shifts. Philip C. Goodhart, M.P. for Beckenham, introduced a private member's bill seeking to give the minister of labour power to grant exemptions from the act in cases of proved difficulty. On its second reading in the House of Commons the bill was bitterly opposed by Labour members but was passed by 125 votes to 114, one of the biggest votes ever recorded on a Friday afternoon. However, both sides of the house made it clear that they would favour a solution by negotiation between the master bakers and the Amalgamated Union of Operative Bakers rather than through legislation. During the committee stage it was evident that the bill had little chance of reaching the statute book. Therefore, following an assurance from the minister that the government would introduce an amending bill if the two sides did not reach an agreement, the bill was withdrawn. Subsequently, a national working agreement was made between the National Association of Master Bakers and the union providing, in return for a scale of

The Burmese prime minister, General Ne Win, garlanded on arrival at New Delhi on Oct. 8 on an official visit, with Jawaharlal Nehru.

Rangoon and Mandalay and of modern dormitories and classrooms for the intermediate colleges of the University of Rangoon, and $515,000 from the Ford foundation for various purposes. Price control, relaxation of import licensing and vigorous action against profiteers and hoarders brought down the cost of living, which by March was 12% lower than a year before.

On June 26 Aleksandr Kaznacheev, an employee of the Soviet embassy, sought and was granted asylum in the U.S.

higher wages, a formula allowing assenting members to employ up to four workers regularly on bread baking for five nights a week. The agreement was accepted by the minister of labour as grounds for exempting assenting members from the act under section 9.

The Millers' association announced that in 1958 the downward trend in flour sales, which had continued since World War II, was halted, 20,000 more tons being sold compared with 1957. It was assumed that at least part of this extra usage of flour was reflected in higher bread consumption, which may have been partly due to the intensive television and press advertising campaign for bread run by the millers. In most parts of the country the price of bread remained stable throughout the year.

The two major milling groups, Ranks and Spillers, as well as Allied Bakeries Ltd., continued to buy up private bakery firms although on a lesser scale than in previous years because few of the larger undertakings remained in private hands. In at least two parts of the country, family bakers hit back at the continuous incursion of factory-made bread into their own trade. They set up their own plant bakeries, with financial aid from a firm of millers, with the object of producing plant

Judging loaves in the " British Baker " bread and confectionery competition held at Caxton hall, Westminster, on March 12.

bread on a co-operative basis. Participating bakers bought their supplies of the standard loaf from the factory but continued to bake their own speciality breads. (R. Sᴅ)

Book Publishing. For the general public the most notable event in the British publishing trade during 1959 was the seven-week printing strike (*see* Pʀɪɴᴛɪɴɢ). This delayed publication of many books and resulted in increased costs which were bound in the following months to produce higher published prices. From a long-term point of view, however, it was probable that the government's long-awaited plans to promote book exports in certain areas, announced by the chancellor of the Duchy of Lancaster, Dr. Charles Hill, on June 22, would be of greater significance. These plans provided for the annual expenditure of £500,000 for the following purposes: (1) to overcome shortages of sterling (as in Pakistan); (2) to promote the production of low-priced books (at the probable rate of about 20 titles a year, to be selected under government direction) for sale in countries where commercial prices leave an unsatisfied market (as in India); (3) to enable the British Council to extend its library services; (4) to assist the development of library systems in various colonial territories; and (5) to increase the circulation of periodicals and newspapers in selected areas. While these plans were welcomed by the trade and the press alike, it remained to be seen how much could be achieved on the announced budget.

The book trade's export earnings in 1959 were expected to amount to over £26 million (compared with £23·8 million in 1958), representing 38% of total turnover (37·4% in 1958). Total turnover was expected to be £65 million (£63·6 million in 1958).

The average published price at the end of the year was 21s. 7½d. compared with 19s. 8d. a year earlier. The number of titles published fell because of the printing strike to 20,690 (including 5,522 reprints) compared with 22,143 (5,971 reprints) in 1958. The only increases in titles occurred in children's books (from 2,120 in 1958 to 2,122 in 1959), medical books (from 963 to 1,048), engineering books (from 474 to 588). Fiction fell (4,166 to 3,842). Once again fewer travel books were issued (175 compared with 188) and there were also fewer biographies (465 instead of 577). The publishers who issued most titles during the year (H.M.S.O. excepted) were Oxford University Press, Collins, Hale, Muller, McGraw-Hill, Faber and Hutchinson.

Expenditure on books by schools and public libraries rose slightly (to about £5·25 million and £4·5 million respectively) but hardly more than necessary to meet increased prices. The 1960 figures might show whether, as some educationists feared, fewer rather than more books were being used in schools since the introduction of the block grant system.

The book trade featured in the year's spate of "take-over bids", Odhams Press Ltd. acquiring most of the book-publishing interests of Hulton Press and Newnes and Pearson, and the Daily Mirror acquiring the Amalgamated Press, which became Fleetway Publications.

The Obscene Publications act, 1959, which had had a long and difficult passage, came into force in September. Apart from repealing Lord Campbell's act of 1857, which provided for seizure under warrant, the new act made the offence of obscene publication a statutory offence and not one of common law. It provided, *inter alia*, a " test " for obscenity which took into account the effect of the work as a whole and, " having regard to all relevant circumstances ", the public likely to read it; it provided that the publisher and author might appear before the court to defend a particular work even though they might not be the party summoned; and it provided for the first time that expert opinion might be heard in court as to the literary or other merits of the work. The act, sponsored by Roy H. Jenkins, M.P., was generally recognized as a notable advance.

The Net Book agreement, 1957, which was regarded by the trade as essential to the efficient service of the public, was referred in October to the Restrictive Practices court for examination. The case was to be heard some time during 1960. Meanwhile, the trade had set itself to examine the problems of book distribution which, with some 300,000 separate titles currently in print, were becoming increasingly complex.

A notable event of the year was the large exhibition of British books staged by the British Council at the Lenin library in Moscow in November. This important step towards closer cultural relations between the two countries was heralded by the inauguration in July of the Great Britain-U.S.S.R. association, under the inspiration of Sir Fitzroy H. Maclean, M.P., and Christopher P. Mayhew, M.P. This new body proposed, apart from sponsoring numerous cultural exchanges with the U.S.S.R., to investigate, in the absence of any copyright convention between the two countries, the possibility of some arbitrary arrangement for the payment of royalties on translations.

The International Publishers' association held its 15th congress in Vienna in May, attended by delegates from more than 20 countries. The problems discussed included European integration, instalment-plan bookselling, the book trade in Asia, the development of lifetime reading habits and the free flow of books.

Canadian publishers concentrated their activities during 1959 on a greatly increased programme of exhibitions and displays sponsored by a total of 48 firms which were members of either the Book Publishers' association, Toronto, or La Société des Editeurs Canadiens du Livre Français, Montreal and Quebec City. Of these the largest were an exhibition of 1,300 books (including 550 Canadian publications) shown for 11 weeks at the Stratford festival, and a bilingual Salon du Livre presented in Montreal. In keeping with Canada's new but rapidly increasing interest in typographic design, Canadian books were shown at the International Design conference at Aspen, Colorado, and at the International Book Design exhibition in England. Members of the Australian Book Publishers' association published in the year ended June 30, 1958, 132 new titles (compared with 181 in the previous year) and 178 reprints (compared with 308). Their sales value throughout the world fell from £A971,000 to £A803,000.

In the United States the number of new books and new editions published between Oct. 1958 and the end of Sept. 1959 totalled 14,548. This continued a steady upward trend—12,538 published in the calendar year 1956, 13,142 in 1957 and 13,462 in 1958. Fiction titles for Jan.-Sept. 1959 were 1,898 compared with 1,608 in the similar period in 1958. Other categories showing marked increases in this nine-month period were business with 328 titles (248 in the same period of 1958), education with 290 (236), general literature and criticism with 557 (434), poetry and drama with 344 (296), religion with 760 (663) and technical books with 503 (388). In the 1958 year-end totals the greatest proportionate increases over 1957 totals were evident in the categories of fine arts, technical books, science books and books on sociology and economics. Estimated total sales of books in the United States in 1958, excluding library, school and other institutional sales and exports, amounted to $715 million, or $4·25 *per capita*. (R. E. Bʀ.; J. Kɢ.)

Brewing and Beer. The drag on beer consumption in the United Kingdom, which seemed to be caused by the heavy excise duty, became more evident than ever early in 1959. The output for the 12 months ended March 31, 1959—23,783,833 bulk bbl.—was the lowest since 1937. The wet, cold weather in the summer months of 1958 was partly responsible for the decline, but that the heavy tax was mainly the cause was suggested by the total for the three months January-March when, although the weather was rather less inclement than usual, output was at its lowest since 1955. The yield from the beer duty being in the long view in some jeopardy, it was not surprising that the chancellor of the exchequer, in presenting his budget in April, reduced the duty by 43s. 7d. per bbl., making it 111s. 9¼d. at the minimum strength of 1,030 degrees with the addition, as before, of 6s. 7½d. per degree above that strength. The reduction was a little short of the 2d. a pint which the brewers were asked to take off the price to the customer, but the chancellor terminated monopoly value and introduced new nominal rates of licence duties and club duty, computing the consequent loss of revenue to be 4s. 5d. per bbl., so rounding off all the tax reductions to the equivalent of 2d. a pint. In adjusting wholesale prices, however, brewers in effect took over from retailers part of the load of the old licence duties, and accepted the loss on stocks brewed before the budget and charged at the higher rate of duty but sold to the public at the lower rate. The total cost of this latter concession was estimated at £5 million.

Beer consumption began to recover almost immediately though largely, it was felt, as a result of particularly fine weather which began in the spring and continued without a serious break until the end of October. There was an additional factor, too, in the form of the public houses newly built or improved since building restrictions were largely removed a few years before. Many hundreds of houses had shared in this vast improvement programme and by 1959, as was to be expected, they were beginning to make their influence felt on sales. The total output for the five months ended Aug. 31 was 11·9 million bulk bbl., an increase of about 9% compared with the same period of 1958 and the highest April-August total for ten years.

The revenue in 1958-59 from the customs and excise duties on beer was reported in April to have been £253 million compared with £261 million in the previous year. The budget estimate for 1959-60 was £218 million. In the same report the materials used in brewing were shown to be annually about 9·5 million cwt. of malt and other cereals, 1·5 million cwt. of sugar and 215,000 cwt. of hops.

British brewers' applications for hops of the 1959 crop totalled 187,000 cwt., later increased by 2,769 cwt., and a further 2,705 cwt. were required for export. The average price of the 1958 crop was fixed by the Permanent Joint Hops committee at £27 5s. 6d. per cwt., compared with £27 15s. 6d. for the 1957 crop. The yield in 1959 was satisfactory and harvesting completed more swiftly and easily than any grower could remember. The crop was estimated at 222,768 cwt., compared with 302,640 cwt., from a larger acreage, in 1958. The barley harvest, too, was early and abundant and, for the first time in history, brewers had taken almost all their initial requirements before the end of August.

Canadian consumption was reported to have fallen from 222·3 million gal. in 1957 (13·4 gal. per head compared with the U.K. figure of 17·3 gal.) to 215·9 million gal. (12·7 gal. per head) in 1958. In Ontario the price of draught beer in the beverage rooms was raised in August from 10 cents to 15 cents for a slightly larger glass.

In Australia the federal budget for 1959-60 showed an estimated excise revenue from beer of £A106·5 million (about half the total excise revenue), compared with actual revenue of £A106 million in 1957-58. Consumption in 1958 was estimated almost unchanged at 222·5 million gal., but per capita consumption had fallen from 23·1 gal. to 22·6 gal. New Zealand had the same per capita consumption at 22·6 gal. (these were the highest figures in the world, after Belgium and Luxembourg), but the total rose from 50·4 million gal. to 51·3 million gal. (years ended March 31). The production in that country of dried wort from which beer could be brewed in the home posed a new problem for the government, which was concerned to ensure that the mixture made its due contribution to the national revenue. Between 6 million gal. and 9 million gal. of this home brew were estimated to have been made during the year.

Because of the excise duty, beer in South Africa continued to be more expensive, strength for strength, than wines and spirits, the reason for the higher duty on beer being that the Cape province wine industry tended to produce more wine than could be readily marketed. The rationalization of the brewing industry reached a point at which almost 95% of the beer was under unilateral control. This facilitated a coherent marketing policy and the introduction of new brands, with the result that unusually unfavourable conditions for the industry were being combated with fair success. (X.)

Canning Industry. Although the 3rd International Congress on Canned Foods was held in Rome in 1956, the proceedings in English did not appear until 1959 (Comité International Permanent de la Conserve, Paris). However, the delay did not detract from the value of the work. The texts of the papers and discussions occupied 340 quarto pages and covered current technological problems, containers, machinery, sanitation, bacteriological problems, education and market research, and nutrition. Studies on the rotation of cans as a help towards more rapid processing at higher temperatures continued to interest research engineers and C. Hoogzand and J. A. S. Moerman reported on " end-over-end " rotation (*Conserva*, 1959, 207-213; 235-242). They found that scorching of fluid packs at high temperatures could be avoided using this technique; but also stated that certain more solid packs in which the heat was transferred almost entirely by conduction would also be processed successfully provided that a certain proportion of free space was left in the can. Electrolytic tinplate was being introduced gradually into the food canning industry and a report of the greater susceptibility of this material to rust during shipment and storage appeared (*Industr. Engng. Chem.*, Oct. 1958, 34A). Differentially

coated tinplate was the subject of this report, cans made of such material having a minimum thickness of tin on their outer surface. The most practical way to avoid external rusting appeared to be to wrap the cases or blocks of cases in a moisture-resistant plastic film.

World production of canned fruit in 1957 was 2,588,000 tons according to the Commonwealth Economic committee's annual review *Fruit* (H.M.S.O., London, 1958). At 416,000 tons, Commonwealth production was very similar to that of the previous three years. The United Kingdom's production was low at 77,300 tons, and Australia and South Africa were the Commonwealth's biggest producers during 1957 with 126,000 tons and 90,000 tons respectively. It is noteworthy that U.K. production exceeded that of any other European country and that the combined output of canned fruit from the European common market countries was less than 150,000 tons. Information on the Australian industry in *International Processed Fruits* (vol. iii, 1/1959, 40) revealed that peaches and pears each accounted for 40% of the total fruit canned and that almost the whole quantity was in cans of retail sizes.

UNITED KINGDOM CANNING PACKS
(net weight of contents, in long tons)

	Fruit	Vegetables	Soups	Milk	Meat	Fish
1957 .	77,300	471,200	154,000	182,000	38,000	11,900
1958 .	98,800	508,900	155,000	179,000	46,000	11,300

SOURCE. Min. of Agriculture, Fisheries and Food.

U.K. production of canned fruit in 1958 constituted a new high record, following a bad season in 1957. The packs of strawberries and gooseberries were the largest ever recorded and there was a partial recovery of the output of canned plums. The output of canned vegetables was also greater than in any previous year.

The United States pack (including the states of Hawaii and Alaska) of canned fruits, vegetables, fruit juices, specialities, milk, meat and fish amounted to 675 million cases during the 1958-59 season. This quantity was 13 million cases larger than in 1957-58 and the second highest on record. The top-ranking fruit was again peaches, with a pack of 28·4 million cases. The top-ranking vegetable was tomatoes which, at 29·6 million cases, exceeded the pack of all other canned vegetables. (The pack of canned tomato juice was 32·6 million cases.) Tomatoes were followed in order of magnitude by canned peas, sweet corn, green beans and tomato ketchup, while peaches were followed by pineapple, fruit cocktail, apple sauce and pears. The retail value of all canned foods consumed in the United States in 1958 reached a new record of more than $4,800 million, of which canned vegetables accounted for $1,100 million. (D. D.; H. L. SR.)

Catering Industry. Towards the end of 1959 there were signs that at last real progress was being made towards providing Britain with new and up-to-date tourist hotels. For years past there had been complaints that foreign visitors, especially in the peak holiday months, were unable to obtain the type of hotel accommodation they desired, with the result that many shortened their stay and others bypassed Britain altogether. Up to the end of 1958 not more than two completely new tourist hotels had been built in London since World War II. However, by the end of Nov. 1959 at least three new hotels were under construction in London, to provide eventually nearly 800 of the 3,000 modern hotel bedrooms which the city was said to be lacking. Two of these were being built by American companies (one Canadian) and the third was a joint venture by Watney's, the brewers, and Lyons, the caterers. Several other schemes were pending, including the project for a huge skyscraper hotel in Park lane, London, to be operated by the Hilton Hotel corporation of the United States, and others in provincial cities such as Manchester, Birmingham, and Swansea. These new hotels were not of the traditional pattern. They were streamlined buildings in which conventional design had been deliberately subjugated to the need for economy in space, maintenance and running costs. Often the ground floor was given over to shops, providing valuable all-the-year-round revenue, and the bedrooms were situated in a slim central tower, many storeys high. Bathrooms were placed back to back and ceiling to floor, with a central duct, thus saving plumbing and maintenance.

During the year, existing hotel companies continued to prosper and trading profits were generally higher, as these examples (previous year in brackets) show: Grosvenor House, £584,243 (£484,135); Savoy Hotel Ltd., £817,956 (£781,458); Trust Houses Ltd., £759,907 (£695,729). However, little or no relief from taxation was given by the government despite repeated pleas by leaders of the industry for concessions. Both the main political parties, in their general election campaign, promised if returned to power to consider the reform of the licensing laws. During the year wage rates increased in all sections of the industry and this was reflected in higher prices for restaurant meals.

A major cause of dissension during the year was the question of credit cards, which permit users to sign bills for hotel and restaurant services. Hotels all over Europe objected to paying the commission demanded by promoters of these schemes and a number of large hotel groups retaliated by launching their own credit schemes for regular guests. It appeared likely that the International Hotel association would promote its own credit scheme unless the commercial promoters were willing to transfer their fees from the hotel to the user.

Hotel expansion continued in most European countries, in North and South America and also in the Commonwealth countries. Several big schemes progressed in Africa, and in Australia two large projects were announced—the £3·5 million Chevron hotel in Sydney, due to open with accommodation for 1,000 guests in April 1960, and a new 350-bedroom hotel, costing £4 million, to be built in Melbourne by Pan American airways. Promotion on a big scale was started for the nine hotels owned by the Tourist Hotel Corporation of New Zealand.

In Britain, more training schemes were organized to attract new recruits into the industry, special efforts being directed at the " bulge " in school leavers which was anticipated in 1961-63. Seaside caterers, helped by the prolonged summer weather, had their best season for a decade, but in some resorts hotels were alarmed by the increasing tendency for motorists to camp out or sleep in their cars rather than seek a hotel room. Concern was expressed over the large number of private houses (not subject to hygiene or wages control or to commercial rating assessment) which were letting rooms to holiday makers. In Brighton a test case was brought against one private house as a result of which it was re-assessed as commercial premises.

Hotels in the United States did a gross business of approximately $2,677 million in 1958, but net earnings were 4·69% compared with 4·83% in 1957. This was due to decreases in room, food and beverage sales. Occupancy dropped for the 12th consecutive year, from 71·2% in 1957 to 67% in 1958. Principal sources of income in 1958 were: room sales, 48·8%; food sales, 32·8%; and beverage sales, 12·7%. Cost of food sold was 34·3 cents per dollar sale and cost of beverages sold was 32·1 cents per dollar sale. Labour costs again rose slightly and the average hourly wage of hotel employees was 243% greater than in 1938. Perhaps the outstanding development in the industry was the trend towards building luxurious motor hotels. Some of these structures were several storeys high, but they maintained all the advantages of the wayside hotels, including ease of parking, separate entrances for motorists and a minimum of tipping. In the first eight months of 1959 the American Hotel association reported that $405,183,000 was spent in construction of new hotels, $94,514,000 in construction of new motor hotels and $97,100,000 in modernization of hotels. The most recent U.S. census figures showed that there were 24,738 hotels of all types in the United States. These employed 376,592 people having an annual payroll of $796,955,000 (R. O. B.; C. A. HH.)

Clothing Industry. *Great Britain.* In 1958 total consumer expenditure rose by £751 million (5%) compared with 1957, but expenditure on clothing rose only £1 million. Comparing 1958 with 1951 the increases were 41% in total and 29% for clothing. One factor drawing away expenditure from clothing after the middle of 1958 was the relaxation of restrictions on the hire purchase of durable goods. The industry was able to maintain the volume of its sales, but price increases were smaller than those for other goods and services. However, hire purchase and credit sales began to slow up in the middle of 1959 and clothing expenditure in the first six months showed an increase over the same period of 1958. Advertising and promotion by the industry, which was generally less than for other goods and services, except in the corsetry section, appeared to have done little beyond maintaining demand.

According to the census of distribution carried out by the Board of Trade in respect of 1957, 64,192 women's wear and general clothing shops, including drapery, were responsible for a turnover of £726 million and employed 269,000 persons, while 14,906 men's wear shops had a turnover of £245 million and employed 68,000 persons. (Sales of clothing by department stores are excluded from these figures.) Sales of clothing on credit (where recorded) were 7% of the total. New Board of Trade index numbers for the production of clothing were published in 1959, based on an enlarged survey. For the first half of 1959 they averaged (1954=100): men's and boys' tailored outerwear, 107; women's and girls' tailored outerwear, 106; weatherproof outerwear, 101; dresses, lingerie, infants' wear, etc., 137; overalls and men's shirts and underwear, etc., 116; total, 115.

The development of synthetic fibres continued in 1959 and new finishes and varieties appeared frequently. Texturing, a comparatively new development, continued to exercise the minds of scientists. This process consisted of bulking the yarn from which the fabric was woven or otherwise produced and thus imparted a softer handle to the material, which was not only pleasing but also warmer. An investigation into the possibilities of automation in the clothing industry was planned by the Clothing institute. While the making of collars, pockets, belts and similar small articles had been achieved by semi-automation, the day seemed far distant when cloth could be fed into a machine with a pattern and would appear at the end of the operation as a garment fully sewn and finished. A new invisible zip appeared on the market and extensive production was planned for it.

There was much speculation as to the ultimate benefits to the clothing industry of the European Free Trade association. The decision in Nov. 1959 to remove almost completely the existing restrictions on the import of U.S. goods led the Apparel and Fashion Industry's association to protest at the abruptness of the change. However, although it was felt that this would be detrimental in the short run, the industry remained confident of its ability to meet all competition in the long run.

Commonwealth. The recession which appeared in 1958 and was common to all countries disappeared in 1959 and the clothing industries in the countries of the Commonwealth enjoyed generally better trade. In all the industrial countries production of ready-made clothing continued to expand and to be conducted more efficiently with the constant spread of knowledge of new methods.

United States. The year 1958 was a relatively poor one for all lines of apparel because of generally depressed conditions throughout the country. Sales declined from $9,268 million in 1957 to $8,962 million in 1958. In 1958 about 850,000 workers were employed in the industry, although there were weeks of unemployment as production dropped. However, business conditions improved in 1959 and there was a substantial rise in production. The growing importation of low-priced finished garments from the far east, particularly Japan and Hong Kong, led to bills being introduced into the Senate which were intended to put competition between the United States and other countries on the basis of efficiency rather than labour costs. (A. T. E.; H. A. CN.)

Diamonds. Total diamond sales in the year 1959 broke all records at £91,135,945. This included a record figure of £63,033,187 for gems, while industrial sales, inflated by U.S. stockpiling, reached a record of £28,102,756. The total for 1959 was 39% higher than in 1958.

SALES OF ROUGH DIAMONDS, 1953-59

				Gem	Industrial	Total
1953	.	.	.	£43,336,109	£17,819,832	£61,155,941
1954	.	.	.	45,610,010	16,543,115	62,153,125
1955	.	.	.	50,253,946	24,034,749	74,288,695
1956	.	.	.	50,542,240	24,003,770	74,546,010
1957	.	.	.	52,818,096	23,954,016	76,772,112
1958	.	.	.	49,420,696	16,122,691	65,543,387
1959	.	.	.	63,033,187	28,102,756	91,135,945

De Beers' diamond research laboratory in Johannesburg had carried out intensive research to establish a new natural diamond grit, especially prepared for resinoid bonded grinding wheels. This was claimed to be 40% more efficient than grit previously used and to give diamond drills considerably longer life. De Beers' laboratory also succeeded in manufacturing synthetic industrial diamonds, some of which were bonded into grinding wheels and were undergoing laboratory tests. Reports from the U.S.S.R. stated that several large diamonds had been found in Yakutia, including diamonds of 46·85, 40·4 and 37·35 carats respectively. A 3·65 carat diamond was also found in a diamondiferous crater in Arkansas, United States. The famous Hope diamond was presented by Harry Winston to the Smithsonian institution in Washington.

After the joint purchase of Williamson Diamonds Limited by the Tanganyika government and De Beers, the board was reconstructed to consist of eight directors, four appointed by the government and four by De Beers. De Beers acquired an interest in exclusive diamond prospecting rights in Basutoland obtained by Jack Scott from the paramount chief. While no payable deposit had yet been proved, several Kimberlite occurrences had been investigated. The Sierra Leone Government Diamond office, through which all Sierra Leone's alluvial production was to be exported, was opened on Aug. 5, 1959. Managed on behalf of the government by the Diamond corporation, it was directed by an executive board on which the government had a majority. Since 1954 African diggers in Ghana had been obliged to sell their production through the Accra market. (X.)

Dyestuffs. The needs of the textile industry continued to dictate developments in the dyemaking field. In particular the colouring of the newer synthetic fibres, alone and in an increasing number of combinations with each other and with the older man-made and natural fibres, led to new dyes being added to most of the established ranges. The search for bright blues and greens resulted in the introduction of new reactive dyes, and also a coupling component for azoic combinations, based on the phthalocyanine nucleus. The latter had already provided direct and ingrain dyes, as well as a sulphur and a vat dye in the same colour range, in addition to the original pigments. With vat dyes the particle size and dispersibility of the dye is a determining factor in rate of reduction and suitability for application by pre-pigmentation, particularly by continuous methods, and another range of vat dyes giving still better dispersions but in convenient granular form was introduced. Disperse dyes of improved physical form also appeared. Pigments for resin-bonding continued to attract attention, the emphasis being on binders of improved efficiency and simplified padding and printing compositions.

The reactive dyes continued to increase in importance. New members were added to the ranges based on reactive chlorine atom(s) in a triazine ring structure (Procions, Cibacrons), and a new type based on a reactive vinylsulphone grouping (Remazols) appeared for colouring cellulosie fibres. Methods were developed for colouring still more forms of cellulosic material and recommendations were made for applying Procions and Cibacrons to polyamide fibres, wool and silk. A new range of reactive dyes (Procinyls) was introduced primarily for colouring polyamide fibres. In the initial stage of dyeing they behaved as disperse dyes and thus gave much more level dyeings on continuous filament material than the anionic types, including the water-soluble reactive dyes, but since in the final stage they combined co-valently with the fibre molecules the wet fastness properties of the dyeings were excellent.

Recognition by dyemakers and users in western Europe of the value of an internationally recognized informative label for colour fastness led to the formation in 1956 of the International Association for the Felisol Fastness Label with headquarters in Zürich. By April 1959, membership included 16 dyemakers and 6 national organizations with 179 members together with 12 associates. The Technical committee made selections of dyes, initially only for cellulosic fibres, guaranteed to give colourings having a specified minimum fastness to light, washing and weathering, and pattern cards were issued for these dyes giving minimum permissible depths of colour (if any) and restrictions in use.

A preliminary report based on 323 individual dyes showed a 2% decrease in U.S. production in 1958 compared with 1957 but there were increases in sales (9% by quantity and 8% by value). Vat (30%), sulphur (18%), direct (15%) and acid dyes (8%) accounted for more than 70% of the total production. The U.S. Tariff commission reported that in 1958 2·9 million lb. of fluorescent brightening agents were sold in the United States of which 62% was used in detergents, 24% in the paper industry and 12% in the textile industry, the remaining 2% being used in the plastics industry and for miscellaneous purposes. In O.E.E.C. countries a 10%-11% decrease in production was forecast for 1958. A plant for producing sulphur blacks and optical brightening agents was opened in Bombay. (C. B. Ss.)

Furniture Industry. For the British furniture industry 1959 was a year of opportunity and achievement. The removal of hire purchase restrictions in Sept. 1958 marked the end of the depression dating from their imposition more than three and a half years earlier. Increased activity in the last quarter of 1958 brought both the volume and value of manufacturers' deliveries of domestic furniture during the year above those for 1957, and at the beginning of 1959 orders on hand, at over £10 million, were worth more than twice as much as 12 months previously. The revival continued and, after record production during the first nine months of 1959, the value of orders at the beginning of October was estimated at £13·3 million, compared with £9·5 million at the same time the year before. Prices remained steady.

However, the industry's hopes of increased exports to western Europe were dashed by the breakdown of the O.E.E.C. free trade area negotiations. Neither could manufacturers feel much initial enthusiasm for the subsequent proposal for a free trade association of the " outer seven " since the United Kingdom had been importing more than three times as much furniture from these countries as it had exported to them and it was estimated that this adverse balance would increase rather than diminish under the new arrangements.

In 1959 for the first time, in conjunction with the general assembly of the manufacturers' federation—Union Européenne de l'Ameublement —held annually since its formation in 1950, an international furniture congress was organized at The Hague with a programme of technical papers, discussions and visits. The success of this experiment led to a decision to hold a similar congress in 1960 in London, with " Marketing and Distribution " as the theme, in Italy the following year and in Sweden in 1962. The year 1959 also saw the formation of a federation of national retailers' associations—Fédération Européenne du Négoce de l'Ameublement.

While technical developments in the industry and the widespread use of new methods and materials, especially in finishing processes, had led to many improvements and increased value in its products, the industry had grown steadily more conscious of the need to promote sales to maintain its share of consumer spending in the face of competition from former luxuries which were now within reach of wider sections of the community. Manufacturers' advertising, especially in the press, had greatly increased and in 1958 for the first time surpassed that of retailers. Steps were taken too in promoting schemes of collective publicity, which previously had failed to attract sufficient support in the trade. A modest start was made in 1959 with a public relations campaign, organized under the auspices of the British Furniture Trade Joint Industrial council, based on a series of " furniture fortnights " in five areas spread over the traditionally slack period of April to June. This evoked only moderate response from retailers, whose representative bodies did, however, pledge their full support for one national " furniture fortnight " in May 1960. (D. D. M.)

Fur Trade. The improvement in conditions in the fur trade, first apparent in the autumn of 1958, was maintained throughout 1959. The increase in supplies of ranched mink (8 million skins in 1957-58; 10 million in 1958-59) proved to be slightly less than expected and from the opening of the new raw fur season there appeared to be no fear of over-supply in the minds of buyers. By late spring there was little raw mink left in the hands of the auction houses and by the beginning of autumn dealers' stocks were scarcely sufficient to meet the anticipated needs of their manufacturing customers. This was primarily due to the demand of the cloth-coat trade for mink of all types, so that this one fur dominated the trimming trade as it had dominated the garment trade for so long. The supply of the light brown " mutation " mink, although it exceeded that of the well-known dark or "standard" brown, was still insufficient and led to higher prices than in the previous year. However, prices of the rarer types such as white or gun-metal eased somewhat as a result of increased supply. The extra dark brown type, which had seemed to be losing favour only a few years before, commanded record prices, often exceeding those of wild mink.

The bulk of the persian lamb crop, from South and South-West Africa, Afghanistan and the U.S.S.R., was again sold in London. One of the worst droughts for many years in South-West Africa resulted in reduced quantities and its effects were expected to be felt even more severely in 1960. Taking the year as a whole prices were somewhat higher. The German Federal Republic was the biggest buyer but France bought far less than in previous years.

The waning interest in, and declining prices of, furs other than persian lamb and mink was halted, and most of them made good some of the losses of the previous few years. Interest in the long-haired furs, first noted in 1958, was perceptibly greater; as a result the price of such furs as lynx doubled and red fox trebled during the year, although still not reaching their pre-1939 values. The prices of several other wild furs, although higher, were still too low to divert trappers from more profitable pursuits, and the ever-increasing labour content in the cost of fur garments concentrated the interest of buyers on the better grades of each parcel. Low qualities often became hard to sell at any price.

In spite of the renewed attention paid to fur as a trimming by the fabric coat designers, fashions in fur garments themselves altered little. The full-length fur coat, which had been losing ground to the jacket and stole, gained somewhat in favour; jackets become longer and stole ends shorter. Stoles in fox, reminiscent of the feather boa, were seen, but only in *haute couture* circles and there was no evidence of a return to the once ubiquitous silver fox stole. The public became increasingly conscious of the possibility of acquiring light-weight, supple fur garments and the trade of the need to concentrate on these qualities in its processing development.

A stand at the annual Furniture exhibition at Earls Court, London in January, which typifies the transformation that has taken place at the exhibition in recent years. " Contemporary " design has established new clichés, but much ugliness has disappeared.

Just as mink, followed at some distance by persian lamb, led the fine fur market, so the various sheepskin products, followed at some distance by rabbit, outdistanced the sale of all other furs in the low price categories. With beaver and musquash (both largely produced on preserves) the favourites at medium prices, the trade continued to evolve towards the use of man-controlled products rather than those of wild life. Indeed, a number of fur dyers and manufacturers went further and transferred their skills to entirely man-made products such as pile fabrics imitating fur.

Fur farmers did well, increasing their production by just enough to meet market requirements without causing a glut. Their success attracted the interest of those in several countries not hitherto concerned with the production of fur and experiments were set on foot which might well prove of great ecological interest. Mink farmers outside the United States were much encouraged by the decision in Sept. 1958 of the U.S. Tariff commission to reject the case made out by U.S. farmers for a quota or tariff on the import of raw mink into the United States. By far the greatest part of the European output of mink was sold to the United States so that the consequences of any other decision would have been serious.

In 1959 retail fur sales in the United States reached $350 million to $375 million in garments and at least $75 million in trimmings. The industry was considered to have had its best year of the 1950s. Mink maintained its dominant position, in both the garment and trimming fields, accounting for approximately 65%-70% of garment volume. In trimmings, no fewer than 2 million mink skins were said to have been used for collars and cuffs on coats and sweaters of every description. This represented more than 20% of total world mink production.

(J. G. L.; E. Gᴅ.)

Gas Industry. In Feb. 1959 a converted tanker, renamed " Methane Pioneer ", crossed the Atlantic from the Gulf of Mexico to the Thames estuary, conveying the first load of liquefied natural gas ever to be carried across the seas. This experiment was being conducted under the joint auspices of the Gas council of Great Britain and Constock International Methane Ltd. (Bahamas). The gas was liquefied at a temperature of —258°F., thereby reducing its volume to 1/600th of that occupied in the gaseous state. On arrival at Canvey Island, Essex, the liquid was regasified and conveyed by pipeline to the Romford works of the North Thames Gas board for re-forming. It was then taken into the normal distribution system for supply to consumers in that area. Further trial voyages of a similar nature took place later in the year. There were many parts of the world where vast supplies of natural gas were available with no local demand for them. It was hoped that, if large vessels could be built to carry this gas and long-term contracts for its supply could be negotiated, it would prove cheaper than gas manufactured by the traditional methods of carbonization.

The gas industry was making other efforts to reduce the price of its product. It was hoped that " complete gasification " processes, which could make use of the poorer and cheaper grades of coal, might begin to replace the carbonization processes which required higher grade and more expensive coals. Work proceeded on the construction of a complete gasification plant of the Lurgi type for the Scottish Gas board at Westfield, Fife, where coal was to be obtained from an adjacent open-cast site. Approval had been given in principle for the construction of a similar plant at Coleshill, near Birmingham, for the West Midlands Gas board.

Increasing use of oil for gasification, together with the trial importation of liquid natural gas, caused some criticism, especially from mine-workers and others connected with the coal industry, in view of the declining use of coal for gas manufacture. The peak figure of 28 million tons a year had already declined to less than 24·5 million and it was estimated that in about four years' time the industry's total coal consumption in Britain might be reduced to about 21·5 million tons. The industry, however, made it clear that its aim would continue to be to give the consumer of gas the best possible service at the lowest possible price, and that all its trials, experiments and research were directed towards that end.

At the end of 1959 Sir Harold Smith retired from the chairmanship of the Gas council, a position he had held for eight years. He was succeeded by the deputy chairman, Sir Henry F. H. Jones, the new deputy chairman being W. K. Hutchison, formerly chairman of the South Eastern Gas board.

Capital expenditure during the year ended March 31, 1959, was £46·1 million compared with £55·7 million the year before. Seventy-three of the smaller and less efficient works were closed, leaving 463 manufacturing works in use compared with 1,050 on vesting day (May 1, 1949). The industry had a deficit during the financial year of £1,466,882, this being the first deficit since nationalization. The cumulative surplus for the period from May 1, 1949, to March 31, 1959, was £22·8 million. The number of persons employed in the industry was 132,576 (compared with 136,379 a year earlier) and the number of consumers was 12,923,978 (compared with 12,922,197) of whom 12,177,593 (12,173,735) were domestic consumers. (X.)

Gems. Retail trade in gem-jewellery increased in several countries. There were no marked changes in fashion but some extremely interesting

new designs for jewellery were created in Switzerland. Greater use of coloured gems in smaller sizes was a feature of some continental pieces, larger stones being almost exclusively used for rings. Necklaces of two, three and more strands of cultured pearls in the form of " chokers ", and bracelets of these pearls with huge clasps set with a large centre stone, were also in demand. Among collectors' pieces which were in demand were blue and golden topazes, large green beryls, black opals and demantoid garnets. At auction sales in the United Kingdom sales of gem-jewellery were particularly large and satisfactory prices were obtained. A diamond tiara, containing the so-called Arcot diamonds, fetched £110,000 in London.

The diamond market had another good year (*see* Business Review: *Diamonds*). Prices of rubies, sapphires, ermeralds, opals and aquamarines of good size and quality continued to be high. Supplies of gems from Ceylon and Thailand came through regularly but supplies from Burma, which had been very slack for several years, did not improve. From South America amethyst and agate were plentiful but supplies of fine quality emerald, aquamarine and topaz were limited. Sales of real pearls were not so marked, though prices remained high, and there was no significant change in the cultured pearl market. In the United Kingdom cultured pearls of a non-nucleated type were offered, their shape being extremely baroque and similar to those described previously in the United States. In that country cultured pearls artificially coloured black were marketed. Synthetic emerald, made in the German Federal Republic and similar to the synthetic " Igmerald " produced there after World War II, was reported. There was further production of synthetic ruby in the United States, probably by the use of a hydrothermal method, which was of some significance to the gem trade.

The Canadian Gemmological association was founded and the continued interest in gemmology was marked by the greater number of candidates for the examination of the Gemmological Association of Great Britain. Entries from Finland were especially high. (G. F. A.)

See G. F. H. Smith, *Gemstones*, 13th ed. rev. by F. C. Phillips (London, 1958); B. W. Anderson, *Gem Testing*, 6th ed. (London, 1958); Cavenago-Bignami Moneta, *Gemmologia* (Milan, 1959).

Glass Industry. The 5th International Congress on Glass sponsored by the International Glass commission and the German Glass Technological society took place in Munich from June 29 to July 4. The congress was attended by 800 representatives and 45 technical and scientific papers were delivered apart from 17 lectures on the history and design of glass. Meetings of representatives of the European glass

John Hutton, the designer and engraver of the glass wall of Coventry cathedral, on which will be depicted 66 saints and angels.

industries to discuss common problems took place in Brussels, Düsseldorf and London. Projects announced during the year included new glass works in India (at Durgapur), optical and ophthalmic glass; Turkey, window glass; Iraq, glassware generally; the Philippines, window glass; the Netherlands, flat glass; the German Democratic Republic, flat glass, glass fibres, foam glass and television tubes; and Brazil, glass generally. In the first three cases help was expected to be given by the U.S.S.R. Extensions of glass production in existing works were also reported in many places.

The uses for glass continued to increase, particularly in the electronic field. In the United States the cones of missiles were made of a relatively new material, Pyroceram, best described as a family of crystalline materials made from glass. Expansion also took place in existing uses; for instance, in the United States and elsewhere motor car designs necessitated the greater employment of safety glass and set new problems in processing the glass into new forms. Pilkington Bros. Ltd., of St. Helens, Lancashire, announced a new method of making high-quality flat glass as the result of seven years' intensive research. It was said to be " the most fundamental, revolutionary and important of all the advances in glass making in the present century ". The new glass, called "float" glass, was made by a process which rendered grinding and polishing unnecessary. It involved drawing a continuous ribbon of molten glass from the melting tank and floating the ribbon on the surface of a molten metal at a controlled temperature. Reports were made of the opening of new laboratories and extensions of glass research in England, the United States and elsewhere, both on a national scale and also by individual glass manufacturers. The Corning Museum of Glass in the United States issued the first (annual) volume of the *Journal of Glass Studies*, described as a " scholarly volume . . . to record the art and history of glass making ".   (D. RR.)

Hemp and Jute. World production of hemp and other hard fibres was well maintained in 1959 despite the decline in sales experienced in the previous year. It was thought to exceed 750,000 tons of which sisal constituted about 68%. Consumers, having worked off their accumulated stocks, were back in the markets early in the year and sales were reported to be up by about 5%. By the end of June the Philippines had shipped 423,838 bales compared with 357,454 bales for the same period of 1958. Japanese consumers bought heavily. The crisis in the Italian hemp industry continued and production in the northern area was cut to 1,500 tons and that of the south to about 12,000 tons. Stocks of Italian hemp were reported plentiful at approximately 20,000 tons. Exports of Italian hemp continued to decline.

The new regime in Pakistan took many steps to keep jute production in line with domestic and world requirements. Acreage was controlled, the Jute Marketing corporation was dissolved, smuggling of jute to India was checked and the whole industry reorganized to end labour unrest. During the year there was none of the wild rises and falls in jute prices which earlier did so much to destroy the confidence of consumers. By June, the end of the jute year, Pakistan had available a stock of 6·5 million bales, of which 4·8 million bales were for export. In 1958-59 Pakistan had exported 4·3 million bales. The combined production of both Pakistan and India was not expected to fall short of the previous year's figure of 11 million bales, of which mill consumption would account for: India, 5 million bales; European and other consumers, 4·3 million bales; and Pakistan, 1·5 million bales. The United Kingdom maintained full production at 135,000 tons per annum and increased its purchases of raw jute by almost 20%, other countries which increased purchases being the United States and Belgium. Production of jute goods by the Pakistan mills, which had an estimated annual capacity of 220,000 tons, reached a peak of 20,000 tons in Jan. 1959, but average monthly production was about 17,000 tons. Pakistan aimed at exporting 160,000 tons per annum by the end of 1960.

During 1959 there were threats to India and Pakistan's monopoly in raw jute—from Burma, which hoped to export some 6,000 tons a year, and from Thailand, which had an exportable surplus of 28,000 tons.

In the finished goods section of the industry the most important feature of the year was the unsealing by India of 1·5% of its total loomage in June 1959 and a further 2·5% in August, leaving only 10% of India's capacity idle for the first time since 1956. The additional loomage added about 3,500 tons to the monthly output of sacking. During the year ended June 1959 the production of hessian totalled 412,300 tons compared with 331,600 in the previous year. The corresponding figures for sacking were 345,100 tons and 385,000 tons. Stocks of sacking at the end of July had fallen to 54,200 tons, the lowest figure since Feb. 1958, while hessian stocks had increased to 26,000 tons, the highest recorded since the same month.

Prices for jute goods appreciated quite substantially as the result of relatively low stock figures, an improvement in U.K. and U.S. demand, together with substantial orders from Argentina and China. Significant orders were also received from Burma, Indonesia, Egypt and Australia. For Indian mills generally, the year was one of remunerative trading, the loss of markets to Pakistan being offset by increased domestic demand and by the industrial growth of the underdeveloped countries. On the other hand, output from the European manufacturing centres was estimated to be unchanged at about 368,000 tons. U.K. production was up at about 85,000 tons and Belgian production was maintained at 40,000 tons, but production fell in Italy, France and the German Federal Republic. The downward trend in exports from Europe was arrested with increased shipments from the United Kingdom, Belgium and France. Consumption of jute cloth by the United States was encouraging, but stocks at the end of July 1959 was 271·1 million yd., compared with 228·7 million yd. a year earlier.   (G. Hs.)

Leather. In 1959 there was an almost unprecedented (peacetime) rise in the prices of hides and skins, followed by an almost equally dramatic fall. Signs of the rise were apparent but largely ignored in the latter half of 1958, and when hides began to advance rapidly at the outset of 1959 tanners and manufacturers alike seemed to have been taken by surprise. Between midsummer 1958 and midsummer 1959 hide prices more than doubled after a five-year period of relative stability during which they had remained only about 25% above the 1939 level. The causes were thought to have been a unique combination of reduced supplies and increased demand; there were substantially lower killings in Argentina for the purpose of replenishing cattle stocks, smaller than usual kills in the United States and elsewhere, bigger requirements for footwear consequent upon almost universally rising standards of living, increased buying of hides and leather by the U.S.S.R. and other eastern European countries, and the emergence of Japan as a substantial consumer of hides. Calfskins reacted as violently and goatskins, sheepskins, semi-tanned and other hides and skins followed suit to a lesser extent (although prices of U.K. sheepskins reached unprecedented heights). This was partly in sympathy, partly for special reasons of their own and partly because of transferred demand.

The raw material situation caused several countries to impose or to contemplate emergency export restrictions on raw hides and skins in order to preserve their domestic supplies and led simultaneously to a marked increase in leather prices and a heavy demand for leather of all types for shoes, gloves and other leather goods. Shoe manufacturers sought and used where suitable cheaper grades of upper leather to maintain price tickets as long as possible, but prices of footwear and all other made-up articles using leather tended to rise.

The emphatic continuation of the main trends of 1958, such as clothing leathers, " softee " shoe uppers, aniline finishes and high fashion and promotional colours, indicated an expanding demand for leather quite apart from any need to hedge against rising prices. For many years suède leather clothing had been fashionable in the United States and on the continent of Europe. In 1959 grain leathers began to challenge this lead in clothing while suède clothing became so popular in Britain that " the leather look " became a fashion promotional headline. In leather goods the movement towards leather handbags continued and nappa leathers supplied the need for a relatively cheap leather in gay colours.

To meet the competition of alternative shoe bottom materials, sole leather tanners emphasized quality features such as levelness, flexibility, water and wear resistance and speciality vegetable, chrome and combination tannages. These efforts, combined with an intensified publicity campaign for the all-leather shoe, helped to stem the relative decline in sole leather usage in shoes. No solution was found to the problem of low-cost upper leathers imported from abroad. This concerned both U.K. and U.S. producers and the latter unsuccessfully tried to obtain higher rates of duty on what they claimed to be subsidized imports of calf and kip upper leathers from Europe.

The initial impact of the tariff changes on Jan. 1, 1959, within the European Economic community tended to be counteracted by the market stimulus of rising hide prices. Great Britain, which had been expected to lose most, in fact substantially increased its leather exports.
                    (G. G. R.)

Linen and Flax. By 1959 U.S.S.R. exports of flax to western Europe and other world markets had become an accepted part of the flax trade. The current Soviet plan provided for a 31% increase in flax fibre production between 1958 and 1965. This implied a 1965 figure of 580,000 tons, from which, allowing for the planned increase in Soviet linen production, about 50,000 tons of flax would be available for export. Western European flax sowings were reduced in 1959 to balance the intake of Soviet flax and the world position was similar to that obtaining before World War II, although there was the possibility of further adjustments in France where production substantially exceeded home demand. At the end of 1959 world flax prices rose sharply.

Aided by a strong market for by-products like shive and seed and by subsidization, western European retter-scutchers stabilized their industry by increasing the efficiency of the smaller number of plants operated. This involved further mechanization and re-equipment. They were helped also by the disappearance of flax growing in countries like Ireland which had become dependent on imports to feed their flax-spinning mills. The number of flax-spinning spindles was further reduced in Northern Ireland and continental countries although surplus capacity remained in the finer counts. Outputs did not fall as much as a spindleage, because of substantial re-equipment and two-shift working of most wet ring-spinning frames. The number of looms owned by linen firms also fell, but in this case possibilities of compensating increases in production per loom were limited.

There was some recovery in sales of U.K. linens in the second half of the year. Quantitatively, linen piecegood shipments to the United States were 23·5% higher in the first ten months of 1959 than in the same period of 1958. However, over-all U.K. exports of linen yarn, thread and cloth were, up to the end of Oct. 1959, 30% lower by value than in the same period of 1958.

The costs of linen manufacture were reduced through more efficient operation of wet ring-spinning frames and reduction of the number of operatives in preparing rooms. Blending of flax tow with viscose rayon, polyester fibre and other fibres continued. At the weaving factory stage costs were reduced by automatic or semi-automatic weft winding and by improvement in loom performance through better yarn supplies. Automatic screen printing tables were replacing manually operated ones and big claims were made for a system of printing dress linens after, instead of before, resin treatment.

Irish linen firms continued to invest accumulated funds, or money realized by the sale of assets, in such fields as carpet manufacture, engineering and car distribution. By contrast, the Netherlands man-made fibre group A.K.U. took a financial interest in Novivlas, the co-operatively owned Dutch flax mill producing yarns from rove-boiled unretted flax. (WM. C.)

Man-Made Fibres. A notable economic recovery in the major manufacturing countries was reflected in a general broadening in demand for man-made fibres in 1959. In the United States and Britain particularly, a policy of short-term buying and stock reduction in 1958 gave way to confident forward buying in 1959. Thus statistically the year was expected to show an all-round expansion over 1958. Technical progress continued unabated and, though the fully synthetic fibres of the main groups continued to enhance their reputations and widen their usefulness, there was a growing awakening to the possibilities of improving further the intrinsic merits of fibres based on cellulose—perhaps as competitors with the natural fibres rather than with the polyamides and polyesters. " Recent advances in the chemistry and physical chemistry of cellulose and of the viscose process have resulted in the production of completely new cellulose fibres with a strength (tenacity) of almost three times that of standard viscose rayon (regenerated cellulose), and with a lower water imbibition (almost a half of standard viscose rayon)," said H. A. Thomas, addressing the British Association in September. Indeed, from tyrecord yarns to various types of staple for apparel and general use there seemed to be vast scope for development of popular priced fibres. Cross-linked cellulose fibres were reaching commercial-scale development in the United States and the M. group of viscose fibres with modified cross-section were already on the market in Britain, while an acetylated cellulose fibre had been developed in Japan and its production licensed in several European countries.

WORLD MAN-MADE FIBRE PRODUCTION
(million lb.)

	Production			Capacity	
	1956	1957	1958	1959	1960
Viscose and Acetate					
Viscose yarn (normal and medium tenacity) . .	1,171	2,212	1,085	1,513	1,670
Viscose yarn (high tenacity) .	689	709	612	803	821
Acetate yarn . . .	372	378	379	558	582
Viscose staple and tow .	2,924	3,061	2,826	4,251	4,434
Acetate staple and tow .	93	90	92	169	173
Total	5,249	5,450	4,994	7,294	7,680
Non-cellulose fibres .	793	1,034	1,057	1,679	1,974
Total (all types) . .	6,042	6,484	6,051	8,973	9,654

SOURCE. Textile Economics bureau, New York.

On both sides of the Atlantic secondary acetate fibres supplemented by triacetate, with its extremely useful pleating and other properties, were generally in short supply and fitted in particularly well with a fashion trend towards soft-draping fabrics which looked and felt like silk. Acetate indeed seemed to be regaining some of the ground it had lost to nylon in the warp knitting trade by its increased popularity in the weaving trade. Also, in the form of staple and tow it had gained new-found end uses in cigarette filter tips and insulation materials, a trend noted in previous years but more prominent in 1959.

Protein fibres appeared to have lost ground in the United States, but for specialized end uses they maintained their position relatively well in Britain and Europe generally. Carpets provided the most important British outlet, and a quality injected with a mothproof agent gained ground in conventional carpets when blended with wool to the extent of 20% protein rayon to 80% wool. This resulted in completely mothproof carpets priced lower than those made entirely of wool without mothproof treatment.

Britain appeared to have led the way with polyethylene fibres, now produced in multi-filament as well as mono-filament qualities, and the major outlet for polyethylene yarns lay in the marine cordage and rope trade with specific progress in trawl-nets. It was announced during the year that polypropylene fibres, first developed in Italy, were being produced on a small scale in Britain. They would probably tend to compete with the polyethylene, polyvinyl and polyvinylidene fibres rather than with the polyamides and polyesters. Their main interest lay in the comparatively low cost of the basic polymer.

With the advance of polyesters and polyacrylics the position of nylon (and other polyamides) was particularly interesting, but there was no evidence to suggest that competition from the newer fibres was likely

A new collapsible nylon container for bulk transportation of liquids being tested on the Rhine at Cologne. It is 28 yd. long.

at the current stage of development to result in any slowing down in demand for nylon generally. In the United States there were temporary periods of overproduction of nylon, but in Britain plans for further expansion were in hand. Nylon remained extremely versatile in apparel, household and industrial uses and, though Terylene had advantages for uses requiring high resistance to sunlight and was particularly effective in blend with wool for suitings, the two rival fibres were each making progress in their own fields.

The challenge of the acrylic fibres, two of which were in commercial production in Britain, was probably most likely to be directed towards end uses traditionally concerned with wool; the high-bulk process, resulting in extremely light and lofty, but hardwearing and stable knitted outerwear which was much more washable than wool, remained a major field for enterprise. As there was no parallel process of giving nylon and Terylene controlled, selective shrinkage by heat treatment, the tendency was for these fibres to be developed in modified filament yarn qualities in direct competition with the high-bulk acrylics. Thus good technical progress was being achieved in non-torque, controlled-stretch, bulked nylon and Terylene, which also had many of the properties such as warmth, lightness and stability required for modern knitted outerwear. (P. M. RE.)

See J. Gordon Cook, *A Handbook of Textile Fibres* (Watford, 1959).

Paper and Pulp Industry. Following a record total production in the United Kingdom in 1958 the tempo of activity in the paper- and board-making industry showed little change in 1959. However, rising expenditure on domestic appliances, radio and television sets, wrapped foodstuffs and most classes of consumer goods resulted in increased demand for boards, wrapping and packing papers and processed papers and boards. The reduction from 30% to 15% in the tax on wallpaper, display papers and household paper had some effect on sales, especially of wallpaper. On the other hand, the printing dispute in the summer of 1959 had an unfortunate effect on demand, some mills being closed and others working short time. Total imports decreased slightly although foreign competition in some kinds of paper was very keen. This competition was even more strongly felt in the traditional export markets, where falling demand had been evident for some time. The industry was therefore giving attention to new and potentially valuable markets abroad.

Pulp of all kinds—Scandinavian, Finnish and North American—was available in sufficient quantities, as were esparto grass, waste paper, hemp, jute and most of the industry's other raw materials. The total output of paper and board in the first three-quarters of 1959 was

2,626,000 tons, compared with 2,510,000 tons in the same period of 1958. In the same period (1958 comparisons in brackets) the production of predominantly writing and printing papers, other than newsprint, was 634,000 (642,000) tons, and of packing and wrapping papers and technical papers and boards 1,497,000 (1,403,000) tons. The main increases in production during the year were in packing and wrapping papers and boards. The main decreases were in printing and writing papers.

Import figures for the nine months were: printing and writing papers, other than newsprint, 4,000 (5,000) tons; packing and wrapping papers 253,000 (200,000) tons; boards, including fibre building boards, 325,000 (343,000) tons; and newsprint 362,000 (383,000) tons. In the same period imports of wood pulp were 1,421,000 (1,383,000) tons; of esparto 152,000 (144,000) tons; and of rags 18,000 (13,000) tons.

Total employment in the industry at the end of July 1959 was 99,100 compared with 90,800 in July 1956. Great attention was being given to the development of scientific and technological education in relation to the industry. It was recognized that considerable expenditure would be involved and there was a ready response from the industry. The City and Guilds of London institute continued its excellent work in examinations in paper-making technology, the number of candidates in 1958 being 215 for the intermediate examination, compared with 160 in 1957 and 188 in 1956, and 88 for the final examination, compared with 94 in 1957 and 79 in 1956. Considerable advances were made in the re-equipment of the paper-making technology department of Manchester university, and the introduction of a new experimental machine gave substantial opportunities for technological education. Such institutions as the Heriot-Watt college, Edinburgh, continued to develop the facilities for new entrants to, and existing members of, the industry. The necessity for higher education of a research standard was also receiving the close attention of the industry and it was hoped that by 1970 there would be a substantially larger number of men and women with research degrees in the industry.

A major event was the setting up of the European Free Trade association by Austria, Denmark, Norway, Portugal, Sweden, Switzerland and the United Kingdom (the " outer seven "). The industry, expecting that this would have the effect of canalizing foreign supplies of paper into the United Kingdom, made representations on the subject to parliament.

Some contributions of major importance to paper technology appeared during the year in the *Proceedings* of the Technical section of the British Paper and Board Makers' association, Kenley, Surrey.

(F. H. L. T.)

Pottery and Porcelain. The general pattern of the world trade in domestic pottery remained substantially unaltered in 1959. In the first six months of the year the value of U.K. pottery (tableware) exports was £7,117,323 compared with £7,024,823 in the same period of 1958. The value of exports in 1958 as a whole (45 % of U.K. output) had been 10 % higher than in 1957. The establishment of the European Free Trade association was not expected greatly to affect the U.K. pottery industry as the six countries concerned took only 4 % of total U.K. exports in 1958. Approximately 70 % of U.K. exports of pottery went to other Commonwealth countries in 1958. A British firm gained the premier award for pottery at the 1958 Brussels exhibition.

IMPORTS AND EXPORTS OF POTTERY, 1957
(Values converted to £ sterling)

	Imports £	Exports £
Australia	2,563,000	40,000
Belgium-Luxembourg . . .	2,464,000	377,000
Canada	5,910,000	400,000
Denmark	584,000	884,000
Finland	49,000	146,000
France	633,000	2,522,000
German Fed. Rep. . . .	750,000	12,900,000
Italy	3,496,000	1,850,000
Japan	7,000	18,240,000
Sweden	1,609,000	297,000
United Kingdom . . .	1,360,000	12,908,000*
United States . . .	15,960,000	1,180,000

* U.K. exports for 1958 were £14,200,000.

An increasing proportion of U.S. domestic pottery was being made on the west coast, where tunnel kilns of much smaller cross-section were used. Besides making for more uniform firing this practice offered greater flexibility in production. One of the most efficient U.S. potteries was working continuously on a four-shift basis, mass-producing a very limited range of ware. Extensive handling was a major problem and much thought was being given in U.S. potteries to re-deployment of equipment to facilitate mechanical handling. Interest continued in high-alumina bodies, particularly on account of their exceptional strength. Heat-release transfers were introduced at one U.S. pottery; as their use necessitated heating the ware to 250°F. it was doubtful whether the process would prove economic. Improved methods of packaging were being studied.

In Australia, where the domestic pottery industry meets only a small proportion of the demand, except for artware, the Department of Trade was endeavouring to attract the establishment of factories by foreign firms. A German company, Rosenthal Porzellan A.G., negotiated for control of the Brackenware factory at Blackheath, South Africa. Rosenthal already had factories in Brazil, Chile and Spain, in addition to their main factory in the German Federal Republic, which supplied over half the German pottery exports to South Africa. A pilot-scale pottery in British Guiana was completed; the country has large deposits of suitable clays. Italian production capacity increased by 4 % during 1958, but actual output decreased by 6·5 % as the factories were not working in full capacity.

(A. E. Dᴅ.)

See A. B. Searle and R. W. Grimshaw, The Chemistry and Physics of Clays and other Ceramic Materials, 3rd ed. (London, 1959); A. Hecht, Elektro-Keramik (Berlin, 1959).

Shoe Industry. Trading in 1959 was governed by two over-riding considerations, rising leather prices and exceptionally good weather. The January sales augured well showing an increase over 1958 which was maintained during the year, but clouds in the shape of rising hide and skin prices, increasing imports and falling exports appeared on the horizon. During the first quarter production sagged, while imports surged ahead to total 8·5 million pairs by the end of October, or 70 % over 1958. Retail sales fluctuated from a severe drop in February to a maximum increase of 21 % in May compared with 1958. The rising trend in sales continued, with fine weather during the summer bringing heavy demands for repeat orders. The principal factor over the year was, however, the soaring increase in leather prices during the early months, which caused manufacturers to buy only on replacement values. The prospects of higher shoe prices in the autumn and winter stimulated the forward placing of orders by the retail trade.

Steadier leather prices from July onwards enabled shoemakers to place forward leather commitments and quote firmer prices for the autumn selling season. Summer sales proved excellent and production during the first nine months was up 17 % compared with 1958. The import picture continued to cause concern with a record total entering the country during the year. Hong Kong remained the principal supplier on a quantity basis, with Italy leading on value. Exports made a considerable recovery in the latter half of the year with North America again providing the best market. Trade with Europe also increased with the prospective " outer seven " agreement providing an additional stimulus, whilst the most notable event was possibly the Anglo-Russian trade agreement, arranging for initial exports to that market of footwear to a value of £470,000.

Labour relations remained good, another strike-free year being added to the industry's proud record, while employment continued at a high level with exceptional mid-year production demands creating a labour shortage in some centres. The biennial conference between the operatives' union and the employers' federation was held in November to agree terms and conditions of employment for the ensuing two years. During 1959 there was a contraction of the number of individual manufacturing units but the volume of production was maintained. Trading results published during the latter months reflected the satisfactory production and sales situation.

(B. E. W.)

Silk. During 1959 there were many indications of the revival in the popularity of silk as a fashion fabric, and world production and consumption of silk showed a slight increase over the previous year. The seventh congress of the International Silk association held in Munich reaffirmed the importance of maintaining a stable level of prices by the continuation in Japan of the silk stabilization law. A reorganization of the silk interests in Japan had been effected which was likely to result in the intensification of propaganda for silk throughout the world. It was probable that special measures would be taken to popularize silk in the men's wear trade, in ties, dressing gowns and shirts and also in men's light-weight suitings which had become more popular in recent years.

The recent world recession in textiles did not appear to have affected the world silk industry and the ever-growing range of man-made fibres was not expected to result necessarily in any further diminution in the demand for silk fabrics, particularly in the field of fashion. In the technical field, researches were undertaken to improve the crease resistance of silk without reducing its intrinsic qualities. Research was also being undertaken for " drip dry " silks, although it was thought that since these involved resin finishes the appearance and characteristic texture of silk fabrics might be impaired by such treatment. The establishment of an international trade mark for silk fabrics was being actively pursued and a suitable symbol was registered for this purpose.

(R. R. Cʏ.)

Soaps, Perfumery and Cosmetics. In 1959 the 2nd World Congress on Essential Oils was held at Grasse, Alpes-Maritimes, France, the centre of the flower oils industry, where delegates from most of the western European countries met others from the United States, the U.S.S.R., Bulgaria, Yugoslavia, the German Democratic Republic and India. The science and technology of perfumery were discussed by a Nobel prizewinner and many other distinguished chemists. In June a meeting of scientists in the perfumery and cosmetic fields had taken place in Paris as part of the International Conference of Chemical

Arts. In August the newly formed International Federation of Societies of Cosmetic Chemists met in Brussels to elect Maison G. deNavarre (U.S.) their first president.

In the United Kingdom, purchase tax on perfumery and cosmetics was again lowered, from 60% to 50%. At the U.S. exhibition held in Moscow, Helena Rubinstein was chosen to introduce western cosmetics to Russian women, apparently with great success. She later described Russian fashions in make-up and wrote of research that was being conducted at the Moscow Institute of Medical Cosmetics. Widespread attention was also paid by technologists in the western world to translated accounts, first published in 1959, of what was actually being done in the detergent and perfumery industries of the U.S.S.R. The international interdependence of science in these fields was amusingly illustrated by the fact that a well-known British firm chose in June, as its new director of research, a U.S. chemist of high standing, while in the following month a U.S. firm made exhaustive approaches in the United Kingdom with the object of engaging a chemist of similar calibre.

Blended synthetic detergents in bar form were marketed as toilet soap substitutes during the year. Other successful lines were white and pearly lipsticks, a new lotion for beautifying the feet, a new hair-growth-promoting lotion and several new pressurized spray (aerosol) packs. The New York Academy of Sciences organized a symposium devoted to hair growth and hair regeneration. A highly successful British Congress of Cosmetic Science was held at the Royal College of Surgeons, London, in April. It was attended by cosmetic chemists, dermatologists, physiologists, etc. from all over the world. China rapidly became an important source of supply of perfumery oils of natural origin. Some of these oils were the subject of papers by Horst Schmidt (German Fed. Rep.) and F. V. Wells (England). (F. V. W.)

See W. J. Corlett, *The Economic Development of Detergents* (London, 1958).

Tourist Trade. The year 1959 again showed steady expansion, the natural outcome of gradual changes: increasing liberalization of travel; a greater variety of tourist attractions; faster, cheaper, more comfortable transport; and higher living standards. There were few areas in the world which did not register an increased volume of traffic and, within each area, few sectors of the tourist industry which did not record improved business.

In 1959 a new record was reached in the number of overseas visitors to Britain—1,400,000 compared with 1,258,560 in 1958. The number of U.S. visitors was 350,000 compared with 325,000 in 1958 and there was a large increase in the number of European visitors—approximately 670,000 compared with 600,000 the year before. It was also a record year for British travel abroad, and the abolition of currency restrictions on foreign travel from Nov. 1 augured well for the future. Figures for the first part of the season suggested that the number of British residents having holidays on the continent of Europe would have increased from 2 million in 1958 to 2·2 million in 1959. However, the great majority of British holidaymakers continued to favour British holiday resorts, which probably had the best season on record. The number of staying holidaymakers was slightly greater than the previous year and the exceptionally good weather produced the heaviest volume of day-trippers so far recorded. In many resorts receipts from municipal undertakings, mainly catering for day-trip traffic, showed increases of from 20% to 30%.

More Americans travelled abroad than before and 700,000 went to Europe compared with 637,000 the year before. The number of U.S. passports issued or renewed in 1958 (676,898 compared with 585,994 in 1957) indicated an increased volume of U.S. traffic. It was expected that more passports would have been issued in 1959 than in 1958 and that 1 million would be issued in 1961. The number of passports issued in Canada also increased—from 97,738 in 1957 to 100,594 in 1958. North Atlantic air traffic increased by 20% in the first quarter of 1959 and by 12·5% in the second quarter compared with the same periods of 1958. In the first part of the year tourist traffic to the German Federal Republic, France, Switzerland and Italy increased substantially.

Other factors besides high living standards and the reduction in the real cost of travel had been very important stimulants to the growth of tourism. In Europe, in particular, there had been new moves each year to reduce tiresome frontier formalities. By 1959 it was possible for citizens of most continental countries to visit neighbouring countries with no other document than an identity card (*see* PASSPORTS). Fourteen countries had abolished the *triptyque* for motorists and it was significant that where formalities for motorists were at a minimum there had been the biggest increases in motor traffic. The volume of international car movement in Europe can be shown by these examples: some 800,000 French motorists visited Switzerland in 1957; more than 2 million went to the German Federal Republic; about 400,000 Italian cars entered Switzerland and 100,000 entered Germany.

In general, Britain's tourist industry was offering a greater variety of attractions and services. More local authorities, associations and individuals were realizing the possibilities of their localities and this was shown in the greater scope and variety of exhibitions, festivals and local events. More historic houses and monuments were open to the public. Car-hire companies were expanding their fleets and providing improved services and information for their clients. In 1958 more day tours by coach from London were offered to tourists than before.

INTERNATIONAL TOURIST TRAVEL
Number of Visitors ('000)
(Only countries with more than 100,000 visitors in 1957 are included)

Country of arrival	1950	1955	1956	1957
Italy[1][2] . . .	3,500	6,200	7,000	7,900
United States[3] .	2,964	5,671	5,990	6,402
Canada[4] . .	4,887	5,928	5,904	5,974
German Fed. Rep.[5][6]	1,175	4,038	4,464	4,866
France[1] . .	3,052	4,010	4,305	4,310
Switzerland[1][5] .	1,903	3,704	3,831	4,146
Austria[1][5] . .	857	2,608	3,039	3,412
Belgium[5] . .	213	2,866[6]	3,065[6]	3,407[6][7]
Spain[8] . .	750[1]	2,522	2,728	...
Yugoslavia[5][9] .	40	485	391	1,966
Ireland, Rep. of[10] .	1,250	1,279	1,212	1,952
United Kingdom[11] .	618	1,037	1,107	1,180
Netherlands[5][9] .	368	1,045	1,118	1,167
Norway[1][12] .	534	892	976	1,020
U.S.S.R.[13] .	...	...	486	553
Lebanon . .	68[5]	902[14]	855[14]	542[14]
Luxembourg[5][6] .	...	615	621	538
Sweden[1][15] . .	197	266[16]	318[16][17]	345[16][17]
Morocco . .	144[18]	155[18]	141[18]	286
Denmark[1][14] .	307	424	433	271[19]
Finland[1] . .	66	235	240	252
Portugal[1][20] .	76	202	232	251
Greece[1][12][21] .	33	172	181	222
Bahamas[22] . .	64	132	155	195
Puerto Rico . .	78	135	163	187
South Africa, Union of[23]	79	162	138	153
Egypt[21] . . .	...	150	170	128
Bermuda[12][21] .	68	106	108	116
Poland . . .	...	77	78	116

[1]Excl. own nationals residing abroad. [2]Excl. day excursionists. [3]Excl. arrivals by land from Mexico. [4]Excl. U.S. visitors staying less than 2 days. [5]Data based on hotel records. [6]Number of "tourist nights" divided by average length of stay in 1955 (1·9 days). [7]Yr. ended Sept. 30. [8]Incl. visitors in transit. [9]Tourist arrivals at hotels. [10]Excl. arrivals by private motor car. [11]Incl. Commonwealth visitors but excl. travellers in transit staying less than 3 days and visitors from the Irish Republic. [12]Excl. cruise passengers. [13]Incl. persons travelling for medical treatment, family affairs, religious purposes, delegations, business, sports and in-transit. [14]Data based on police records. [15]Excl. Danish and Norwegian nationals. [16]Excl. Finnish nationals. [17]Excl. Icelandic nationals. [18]Former French zone only. [19]From April 1 excl. visitors from other Scandinavian countries. [20]Incl. arrivals of foreign residents in Portugal; excl. the Azores and Madeira. [21]Excl. visitors in transit. [22]Arrivals in Nassau of " stop-overs " and " transients ". [23]Visitors of European descent only.

SOURCE. British Travel and Holidays Association.

Investment and development in both air and sea transport continued. Side by side with the increase in jet and turbo-prop fleets, there was a heavy increase in charter flights operated by companies which had bought the older equipment of the large air corporations. Many shipping companies also had impressive building programmes. In 1959 there were two notable additions to the North Atlantic fleet—the " Bremen " (Norddeutscher Lloyd) and the " Rotterdam " (Holland-America). The " Pendennis Castle " (Union Castle) made her maiden voyage to South Africa and the " Orcades ", a refitted ship of the Orient line, also made her first voyage. Progress was made in ship-building programmes in 1959 which should result in many important additions to the world's passenger fleets in 1960.

It was expected that in future years more and more people would have the money to visit Britain, but whether they would in fact be able to do so depended to a great extent on the size of the hotel investment and re-equipment programme. It was encouraging to observe that about 100 beds would have been added to London's tourist class accommodation by the end of 1959 and there were at last signs that investors were becoming interested in the need for hotels in London and other centres. (*See also* EMPLOYMENT; INTERNATIONAL TRADE; PRICES; PROFITS AND DIVIDENDS; SHOPS AND DEPARTMENT STORES; STOCKS AND SHARES; TARIFFS AND QUOTAS.) (A. Mo.)

BYELORUSSIA. Republic in the Union of Soviet Socialist Republics, bounded N. by Latvia, E. by Russia, S. by the Ukraine and W. by Poland and Lithuania. Area: 80,154 sq.mi. Pop. (1959 census): 8,060,000. Language: mainly Byelorussian. Religion: mainly Orthodox. Chief towns (pop., 1959 census): Minsk (cap.) 509,000; Gomel 166,000; Vitebsk 148,000; Mogilev 121,000. First secretary of the Byelorussian Communist party, Kiril T. Mazurov; chairman of the presidium of the Supreme Soviet, Vasili I. Kozlov; chairmen of the council of ministers in 1959: Nikolai E. Avkhimovich and (from April 10) Tikhon Ya. Kiselev. Monetary unit: Soviet rouble.

History. Speaking on Jan 3, 1959, in Minsk, on the occasion of the 40th anniversary of the republic, N. S. Khrushchev said that although the Germans had ruined or burned down 209 urban settlements and 9,200 villages, the Byelorussian people had not only rehabilitated their ravaged economy but had by far surpassed the prewar levels of industry. In 1958 the republic's industrial production was 27 times as great as it had been in 1913. Between 1928 and 1958 generation of electric power rose from 39 million kwh. to 2,650 million kwh. Before World War I Byelorussia had no metal-working industry: in 1958 it was producing as much as 12% of the total Soviet tractor output and 11% of the total metal-cutting machine tools.

In agriculture, however, progress was slow and during the previous two years the numbers of livestock had dropped. In 1958 there were only 3,152,000 head of cattle as compared with 3,288,000 in 1956. The number of pigs fell during the same period from 3,486,000 to 2,704,000. These and other shortcomings were the reason why in April N. E. Avkhimovich, the premier, three deputy premiers, the chairman of the State Planning commission, and the ministers of agriculture and trades were dismissed. T. Ya. Kiselev became the new chairman of the council of ministers.

The census of population of Jan. 15, 1959, revealed that Byelorussia had a population of 8,060,000—850,000 less than in Nov. 1939, after the incorporation of the former Polish western Byelorussia. The reduction can be explained by the killing of Jews during the German occupation, transfer of Poles to Poland and Soviet deportations. (K. M. S.)

CABINET MEMBERS.
The following are lists of cabinet members of Great Britain and the other main Commonwealth countries on Dec. 1, 1959:

Great Britain

Post	Name
Prime Minister and First Lord of the Treasury	*Harold Macmillan
Secretary of State for the Home Department	*R. A. Butler
Lord Chancellor	Viscount Kilmuir
Secretary of State for Foreign Affairs	Selwyn Lloyd
Chancellor of the Exchequer	D. Heathcoat Amory
Lord President of the Council and Secretary of State for Commonwealth Relations	The Earl of Home
Secretary of State for Scotland	John Maclay
Lord Privy Seal and Minister for Science	Viscount Hailsham
Minister of Aviation	Duncan Sandys
Secretary of State for the Colonies	Iain Macleod
Minister of Defence	*Harold Watkinson
Minister of Housing and Local Government and Minister for Welsh Affairs	Henry Brooke
Minister of Education	Sir David Eccles
Paymaster-General	Lord Mills
President of the Board of Trade	*Reginald Maudling
Minister of Agriculture, Fisheries and Food	John Hare
Minister of Labour	*Edward Heath
Chancellor of the Duchy of Lancaster	Charles Hill
Minister of Transport	Ernest Marples

Australia

Post	Name
Prime Minister	R. G. Menzies
Minister of Trade	J. McEwen
Treasurer	H. E. Holt
Minister for External Affairs and in charge of Commonwealth Scientific and Industrial Research Organization	R. G. Casey
Vice-President of the Executive Council and Minister for National Development	W. H. Spooner
Minister for Defence	A. G. Townley
Minister for Territories	P. M. C. Hasluck
Minister for Labour and National Service	W. McMahon
Minister for Shipping and Transport and for Civil Aviation	S. D. Paltridge
Postmaster-General	C. W. Davidson
Minister for Immigration	A. R. Downer
Attorney-General	Sir Garfield Barwick

Canada

Post	Name
Prime Minister and President of the Privy Council	J. G. Diefenbaker
Secretary of State for External Affairs	H. C. Green
Minister of Finance and Receiver-General	D. M. Fleming
Minister of Veterans' Affairs	A. J. Brooks
Minister of Transport	George Hees
Solicitor-General	Léon Balcer
Minister of National Defence	G. R. Pearkes
Minister of Trade and Commerce	G. M. Churchill
Minister of Justice and Attorney-General	E. D. Fulton
Minister of National Revenue	G. C. Nowlan
Minister of Agriculture	D. S. Harkness
Minister of Citizenship and Immigration	Ellen L. Fairclough
Minister of Fisheries	J. Angus MacLean
Minister of Labour	Michael Starr
Postmaster-General	W. M. Hamilton
Minister without Portfolio	William J. Browne
Minister of Mines and Technical Surveys	Paul Comtois
Minister of National Health and Welfare	J. W. Monteith
Minister of Northern Affairs and National Resources	F. A. G. Hamilton
Minister of Defence Production	R. J. M. O'Hurley
Secretary of State of Canada	Henri Courtemanche
Associate Minister of National Defence	J. P. A. Sévigny

Ceylon

Post	Name
Prime Minister and Minister of Defence and External Affairs and Education	*W. Dahanayake
Minister of Home Affairs	T. B. Illangaratne
Minister of Health	A. P. Jayasuriya
Minister of Posts, Broadcasting and Information	C. A. S. Marikkar
Minister of Transport and Power	M. Senanayake
Minister of Food, Commerce and Trade	R. G. Senanayake
Minister of Nationalized Services and Shipping	C. Wijesinghe
Minister of Works	H. Abeywickrema
Minister of Labour	M. P. de Zoysa
Minister of Cultural Affairs and Social Services	I. R. P. G. Kalugalla
Minister of Industries and Fisheries	W. J. C. Munasinha
Minister of Justice	J. H. V. S. Jayawickrema
Minister of Finance	M. Mustapha
Minister of Agriculture and Lands	C. P. de Silva
Minister of Local Government and Housing	M. B. W. Mediwake

Ghana

Post	Name
Prime Minister	Kwame Nkrumah
Minister of Finance	K. A. Gbedemah
Minister of Economic Affairs	Kojo Botsio
Minister of Local Government	E. A. Ofori-Atta
Minister of Foreign Affairs	Ako Adjei
Minister of the Interior	A. E. Inkumsah
Minister of Transport and Communications	Krobo Edusei
Minister of Health and Social Welfare	Imoru Egala
Minister of Education and Information	Kofi Baako
Minister of Food and Agriculture	F. Y. Asare
Minister of Works and Housing	E. K. Bensah
Minister of Commerce and Industry	P. K. K. Quaidoo
Minister of State for Guinea Affairs	J. H. Allassani
Minister without Portfolio	N. A. Welbeck
Minister of State responsible, under the Prime Minister, for Defence	C. T. Nylander

* See BIOGRAPHIES.

India

Post	Name
Prime Minister and Minister of External Affairs and of Atomic Energy	Jawaharlal Nehru
Minister of Home Affairs . .	Govind Ballabh Pant
Minister of Finance . . .	Morarji R. Desai
Minister of Railways . .	Jagjivan Ram
Minister of Labour and Employment and Planning	Gulzarilal Nanda
Minister of Commerce and Industry	Lal Bahadur Shastri
Minister of Transport and Communications	S. K. Patil
Minister of Steel, Mines and Fuel .	Swaran Singh
Minister of Works, Housing and Supply	K. C. Reddy
Minister of Food and Agriculture .	Ajit Prasad Jain
Minister of Defence . . .	V. K. Krishna Menon
Minister of Irrigation and Power .	Hafiz Mohammed Ibrahim
Minister of Law	Asoke Kumar Sen

Malaya, Federation of

Post	Name
Prime Minister	Tengku Abdul Rahman Putra
Deputy Prime Minister, Minister of Defence and in charge of the Ministry of Rural Development	Tun Abd-ur-Razak bin Dato Hussein
Minister of External Affairs . .	Dato Ismail bin Dato Abd-ur-Rahman
Minister of Finance . . .	Tan Siew-sin
Minister of Justice . . .	Tun Leong Yew-koh
Minister of Posts, Works and Telecommunications . . .	Dato V. T. Sambanthan
Minister of the Interior . . .	Dato Suleiman bin Dato Abd-ur-Rahman
Minister of Agriculture and Cooperatives	Inche Abd-ul-Aziz bin Ishak
Minister of Transport . . .	Inche Sardon bin Haji Jubir
Minister of Health and Social Welfare	Dato Ong Yoke-lin
Minister of Education . . .	Inche Mohammed Khir bin Johari
Minister of Labour . . .	Inche Bahaman bin Shamsuddin
Minister of Commerce and Industry	Inche Abd-ur-Rahman bin Haji Talib

New Zealand

Post	Name
Prime Minister, Minister of External Affairs and Maori Affairs . .	W. Nash
Deputy Prime Minister, Minister of Agriculture and Lands . .	C. F. Skinner
Minister of Finance . . .	A. H. Nordmeyer
Attorney-General, Minister of Justice and Health	H. G. R. Mason
Minister of Labour, Mines and Immigration	F. Hackett
Minister of Marine, Housing and State Advances . . .	W. A. Fox
Minister of Works and Electricity .	H. Watt
Minister of Forests, Associate to Minister of Maori Affairs .	E. T. Tirikatene
Minister of Defence and Police .	P. G. Connolly
Postmaster-General, Minister of Railways and Telegraphs . .	M. Moohan
Minister of Industries and Commerce, Scientific and Industrial Research	P. N. Holloway
Minister of Education . .	P. O. S. Skoglund
Minister of Social Security, Welfare of Women and Children . .	Mabel Howard
Minister of Transport, Civil Aviation, Island Territories, Tourist and Health Resorts	J. Mathison
Minister of Customs and Broadcasting	R. Boord
Minister of Internal Affairs .	W. T. Anderton

Pakistan

Post	Name
President and Chief Martial Law Administrator, Minister of Defence and Kashmir Affairs . . .	Field Marshal Mohammed Ayub Khan
Minister of Foreign Affairs . .	Manzoor Qadir
Minister of Health and Social Welfare	Lieut.-General W. A. Burki
Minister of Rehabilitation . .	Lieut.-General Azam Khan
Minister of Communications .	F. M. Khan

Post	Name
Minister of Education, Information and Broadcasting . . .	Habib-ur-Rahman
Minister of the Interior . . .	Lieut.-General K. M. Sheikh
Minister of Industries, Works, Irrigation and Power	Abd-ul-Kasim Khan
Minister of Food and Agriculture .	Hafiz-ur-Rahman
Minister of Commerce . . .	Z. A. Bhutto
Minister of Finance . . .	M. Shoaib
Minister of Law	Mohammed Ibrahim

Rhodesia and Nyasaland, Federation of

Post	Name
Prime Minister and Minister of External Affairs . . .	Sir Roy Welensky
Minister of Home Affairs and Power	Sir Malcolm Barrow
Minister of Economic Affairs, Defence and Public Service .	J. M. Caldicott
Minister of Transport . . .	W. H. Eastwood
Minister of Health and Education .	B. D. Goldberg
Minister of Agriculture . . .	J. C. Graylin
Minister of Law	J. M. Greenfield
Minister of Finance . . .	D. MacIntyre
Minister of Commerce and Industry, and Posts	F. S. Owen
Minister of Works . . .	G. W. R. L'Ange

South Africa

Post	Name
Prime Minister	H. F. Verwoerd
Minister of Justice . . .	C. R. Swart
Minister of Lands, Forestry and Public Works	P. O. Sauer
Minister of External Affairs . .	E. H. Louw
Minister of Finance . . .	T. E. Donges
Minister of Defence . . .	F. C. Erasmus
Minister of Transport . . .	B. J. Schoeman
Minister of the Interior . . .	J. F. T. Naude
Minister of Education, Arts and Science, Social Welfare and Pensions	J. J. Serfontein
Minister of Labour and Mines .	J. De Klerk
Minister of Bantu Administration and Development . . .	M. D. C. De Wet Nel
Minister of Agriculture, Technical Services and Water Affairs . .	P. M. K. Le Roux
Minister of Bantu Education . .	W. A. Maree
Minister of Economic Affairs . .	N. Diederichs
Minister of Posts and Telegraphs, and Health	J. A. M. Hertzog
Minister of Agricultural Economics and Marketing	D. C. H. Uys

CAMBODIA. An independent kingdom situated in the southern part of the Indochinese peninsula, on both banks of the Mekong river, bounded W. and N. by Thailand (Siam), N.E. by Laos, E. and S.E. by the Republic of Vietnam and S.W. by the Gulf of Siam. Area: 69,866 sq.mi. Pop.: (1948 est.) 3,748,000; (1958 est.) 4,740,000. Cambodians (Khmers) 76%; national minorities (1958 est.): Chinese 500,000; Vietnamese 350,000; Chama (survivors of the former empire of Champa in southern Vietnam) 70,000; tribesmen, 250,000. Religion: Buddhist. Capital (pop., 1958 est.): Phnom-Penh 400,000. Ruler, King Norodom Suramarit. Prime minister, Prince Norodom Sihanouk. Main exports: rice, rubber. Main imports: machinery and metal products, textiles and mineral products. Monetary unit: *riel* with an exchange rate of R.98·00 = £1 sterling.

History. Cambodia's determined neutralism had caused anxiety and even hostility among its anti-Communist neighbours. In addition, an old territorial dispute between Cambodia and Thailand continued and in Nov. 1958 diplomatic relations between the two countries were severed. Baron Johan Beck-Fries (Sweden), special representative of Dag Hammarskjöld, U.N. secretary-general, was sent at the beginning of Jan. 1959 to Bangkok and Phnom-Penh. As a result of his mediation diplomatic relations were resumed on Feb. 20.

Three days later, however, Prince Norodom Sihanouk, the prime minister, accused Thailand and South Vietnam of plotting to overthrow his government. The chief plotters were: Sam Sary, a right-wing politician, who in July 1958 had been recalled in disgrace from his post as ambassador to London and who later took refuge in Thailand; general Chuon Mohulpich, the deposed governor of Siem-Reap; and

Son Ngoc Thanh, a pro-Thai Vietnamese. Mohulpich, wounded by the government forces, died on March 4.

On Aug. 3 Sihanouk began a three-day visit to South Vietnam, where he had a long talk with President Ngo Dinh Diêm. Not all the differences between the two countries were

Queen Kossamak of Cambodia awaits the arrival of President Rajendra Prasad of India by air on March 15 for his state visit.

resolved but the meeting established a personal basis for subsequent negotiations.

On Aug. 31 King Norodom Suramarit and Queen Kossamak narrowly escaped death from a bomb sent in a parcel, but Prince Norodom Vakrivan, assistant director of the royal household, and a servant were killed.

On Oct. 3, the U.S.S.R. complained to Great Britain about its proposal to dissolve the International Commission for Supervision and Control established by the Geneva conference in 1954. On Nov. 3, after consultation with the Cambodian government, Great Britain proposed that the I.C.S.C. in Cambodia should be amalgamated as an economy measure with the similar commission in Vietnam.

On July 22 Sihanouk opened a motor road linking Phnom-Penh with the new port at Sihanoukville. It was built with U.S. economic aid at a total cost of R.1,197·5 million. Frederick A. Seaton, U.S. secretary of the interior, was present at the ceremony. A five-year (1960-64) development plan was prepared with the aim of increasing national income from R.14,800 million to R.18,900 million or by 28%.

In November and December Sihanouk paid state visits to the United Arab Republic and Yugoslavia.   (K. M. S.)
See Martin F. Herz, *A Short History of Cambodia* (London, 1958).

CAMEROONS: *see* CAMEROUN; NIGERIA; TRUST TERRITORIES.

CAMEROUN. An autonomous state under French trusteeship, bounded west and northwest by the Atlantic ocean and the Cameroons under British trusteeship, east by the Republics of Chad and Central Africa and south by the Republics of Congo and Gabon. Area: 170,231 sq.mi. Pop.: (1936 est.) 2,389,500; (Dec. 1957 est.) 3,187,000, mainly Negro; Europeans (1957) 16,515, mostly French. Religion: animism, some Moslems in the north, 300,000 Christians in the south. Chief towns (pop., 1955 est.): Yaoundé (cap.) 54,000; Douala (main port, 1958) 119,100 (5,900 Europeans). French high commissioner, Xavier Torré. Prime minister, Ahmadou Ahidjo. Main

exports: cocoa, coffee, bananas, timber. Monetary unit: *franc CFA* (Colonies Françaises d'Afrique) = metropolitan Fr.2.

History. On March 13, 1959, at the proposal of France, the U.N. general assembly decided by 56 votes (with 23 abstentions) to end the trusteeship status of Cameroun on Jan. 1, 1960. A referendum would take place in the British Cameroons to decide whether this territory would join Cameroun or the Federation of Nigeria. The premier of the Southern Cameroons, John N. Foncha, paid a visit to Yaoundé on May 12.

Calm returned to Sanaga Maritime, where a U.P.C. (Union des Populations Camerounaises) leader, Mayi Matip, decided to fight the government within the National Assembly. At the end of June and the beginning of July there were outbreaks of violence at Yaoundé causing 14 deaths, including those of 7 Europeans. In Bamiléké territory, near British Cameroons, a campaign of murder against persons of influence and Europeans was continued. Hundreds of deaths were recorded.

André Marie M'Bida, a former prime minister, made common cause with the outlawed U.P.C. The prime minister, Ahidjo, protested against the support given by Ghana and Guinea to this opposition movement led by Félix Moumié.
(HU. DE.)

CANADA. A realm of the Commonwealth of Nations, covering all north America north of the United States except Alaska; a federal union of provinces and centrally administered territories (*see* table). Total pop., incl. Indians and Eskimoes (1956 census) 16,080,791; (Sept. 1959 est.) 17,550,000. Language (1951): English only 66·1%; French only 19·6%; French and English 13·2%; neither French nor English 1·1%. Religion (1951): Roman Catholic 44·7% (incl. Greek rite 1·4%); United Church of Canada (a Methodist-Presbyterian-Congregational federation) 20·5%; Anglican 15%; continuing Presbyterian 5·6%; Baptist 3·7%; Lutheran 3·2%; Greek Orthodox 1·2%; Jewish 1·5%. Chief towns (pop., 1956 census, metropolitan area): Ottawa, Ont. (cap.), 345,460; Montreal (Prov. Quebec) 1,620,758; Toronto 1,358,028; Vancouver (B.C.) 665,017; Winnipeg 409,121; Quebec 309,959; Hamilton (Ont.) 327,831; Edmonton 251,004; Windsor (Ont.) 185,865; Calgary (Alberta) 200,449; Halifax 164,200; London (Ont.) 154,453. Queen, Elizabeth II. Governors-general in 1959: Vincent Massey and (from Sept. 15) Maj.-General George Vanier. Prime minister, J. G. Diefenbaker. Main imports: automobiles and parts, machinery, crude petroleum, electrical apparatus. Main exports: newsprint, wood and wood manufactures, non-ferrous metals and products, wheat. Monetary unit: Canadian dollar. (No fixed rate of exchange. In 1959 the market value fluctuated around C$2·70 = £1; C$0·97 = U.S.$1.)

History. The year 1959 saw further growth in the Canadian economy. Recovery from the mild recession of 1957 continued. Output of goods and services was running about 7% ahead of the previous year, corporation profits approached a record, government outlay reached a new high level and unemployment was down compared with 1958. As a result of the expansion in business activity and the demands of the provincial governments, credit supplies became inadequate and a period of " tight money " and rising interest rates began. The lending rate of the Industrial Development bank rose from 6% to 6½% in March and from 6½% to 7% in late September.

The federal budget was presented on April 9. The deficit for the fiscal year ended March 31, 1959, was in excess of $600 million. A range of new taxes was introduced, with the hope of reducing the deficit to about half that sum in the succeeding 12 months. Six months later, following the recovery in business, it was thought that a balanced budget might be reached by 1960-61.

Reports published in 1959 showed that immigration to Canada in 1958 was maintained at a more normal level, following the exceptionally large inflow in 1957, the total number of immigrants being 124,851, compared with 282,164 the previous year. Italians formed the largest group (28,564), immigrants from Britain the second largest (26,622) and those from the German Federal Republic the third largest (14,449).

In February the government of Ontario announced plans to build a major seaport at Moosonee on James bay, which would provide northern Ontario with shipping facilities. It was stated in the federal House of Commons on Feb. 6 that $17 million would be made available to India out of Canada's Colombo Plan appropriation for the year 1958-59, enabling India to purchase certain essential commodities in Canada.

The Queen greets President Eisenhower and his wife at St. Hubert on June 26, prior to the opening of the St. Lawrence seaway.

Notable events during the year included the six-week tour by Queen Elizabeth II and the Duke of Edinburgh, the formal opening of the St. Lawrence seaway and the beginning of the South Saskatchewan irrigation and power project.

The sudden death on March 17 of Sidney Smith, the minister of external affairs, came as a great shock (*see* OBITUARIES). A former president of the University of Toronto, he had materially strengthened the cabinet of J. G. Diefenbaker, and his value in this key position was already beginning to be widely appreciated. Diefenbaker eventually appointed Howard Green, the minister of public works, to the external affairs portfolio.

The death on Sept. 7 of the premier of Quebec, Maurice Duplessis, brought to a close one of the longest periods of office in Canadian history. His successor was the former minister of youth and welfare, Paul Sauvé. Among the pressing problems tackled by the new premier was the financial plight of Quebec's universities. They were eligible for a share in federal grants, which by September had reached nearly $25 million. However Duplessis had requested the universities not to accept federal grants because he considered these a threat to Quebec's educational independence.

There was controversy in February over the discontinuance of production of the CF-105 Avro Arrow for Canada's aerial defence and the unemployment which resulted. In July the government decided to buy 200 U.S. Lockheed F-104G Starfighter supersonic aircraft, to be produced in Canadian plants, for the Royal Canadian Air Force division serving with Nato in Europe.

Early in the year Atomic Energy of Canada Ltd. announced that a new 10-million volt atom smasher (the first of its kind) had gone into service at Chalk River, Ontario. During the year Canada signed agreements with the United States, Japan and Australia, providing for co-operation in the use of atomic energy.

Just before Christmas, 1958, Diefenbaker returned to Ottawa after a round-the-world tour which had taken him to nearly all the Commonwealth nations. During Feb. 5-7 the lord mayor of western Berlin, Willy Brandt, paid an official visit to Ottawa. On March 18 the British prime minister, Harold Macmillan, arrived in Ottawa for talks with the Canadian government on German reunification, before going on to Washington to discuss the same problem with the president of the United States, Dwight D. Eisenhower. On April 20 the prime minister of Cuba, Fidel Castro (*see* BIOGRAPHIES), paid a short visit to Montreal. On May 20 the Australian prime minister, R. G. Menzies, went to Ottawa for talks.

The royal tour began at Torbay airport, Newfoundland, on June 18, inaugurating a visit which touched on nearly all the larger centres of the ten provinces and the northern territories. On June 26 the St. Lawrence seaway was formally opened in a historic ceremony at St. Lambert, Quebec, by the queen and President Eisenhower. The ceremony marking the official start of construction on the South Saskatchewan project took place on May 27. This project, costing nearly $200 million, would create an artificial lake 140 mi. long, provide irrigation for 1 million ac. and produce a large amount of electricity as well. It was expected that it would be completed in 1965. In August the minister for northern affairs and national resources announced the discovery of oil in the Yukon.

Vincent Massey, the first native-born Canadian governor-general, retired from his post in the autumn and was succeeded by another Canadian, Maj.-General George Vanier, who for many years had been a senior Canadian diplomat (*see* BIOGRAPHIES).

There were five provincial general elections during 1959. In Alberta the Social Credit party led by E. C. Manning was returned in a landslide that saw the opposition virtually

Provinces	Capital	Area (sq.mi.)	Population (1951 census)	Population (1956 census)	Premier (as at Dec. 31, 1959)	Ministry
Alberta	Edmonton	255,285	939,501	1,123,116	E. C. Manning	Social Credit party
British Columbia	Victoria	366,255	1,165,210	1,398,464	W. A. C. Bennett	Social Credit party
Manitoba	Winnipeg	251,030	766,541	850,040	Dufferin Roblin	Progressive Conservative
New Brunswick	Fredericton	27,985	515,697	554,616	H. J. Flemming	Progressive Conservative
Newfoundland and Labrador	St. John's	156,185*	361,416	415,074	Joseph R. Smallwood	Liberal
Nova Scotia	Halifax	21,068	642,584	694,717	R. L. Stanfield	Progressive Conservative
Ontario	Toronto	412,582	4,597,542	5,404,933	L. M. Frost	Progressive Conservative
Prince Edward Island	Charlottetown	2,184	98,429	99,285	Walter Shaw	Progressive Conservative
Quebec	Quebec City	594,860	4,055,681	4,628,378	Paul Sauvé	Union Nationale
Saskatchewan	Regina	251,700	831,728	880,665	T. C. Douglas	Co-op Commonwealth Federation

Territories		Area (sq.mi.)	Population (1951 census)	Population (1956 census)	Commissioner	
Northwest Territories (Districts of Franklin, Keewatin and Mackenzie) —		1,304,903	16,004	19,313	R. G. Robertson	—
Yukon	Whitehorse	207,076	9,096	12,190	Frederick H. Collins	—

Total 3,851,113† 14,009,429‡ 16,080,791

* Newfoundland island 42,734 sq.mi.   † Incl. 301,153 sq.mi. of fresh water.   ‡ Excl. 155,874 Indians and 9,733 Eskimoes.

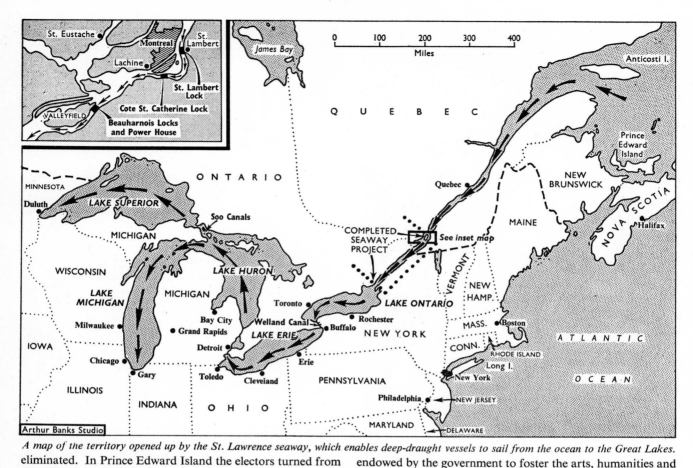

St. Eustache
Montreal
St. Lambert
Lachine
St. Lambert Lock
Cote St. Catherine Lock
VALLEYFIELD
Beauharnois Locks and Power House

Arthur Banks Studio

A map of the territory opened up by the St. Lawrence seaway, which enables deep-draught vessels to sail from the ocean to the Great Lakes.

eliminated. In Prince Edward Island the electors turned from the Liberals, who had been in office for many years, and elected a Progressive Conservative government. In Ontario, the largest and most populous of the provinces (passing the 6 million mark in 1959), the Progressive Conservative government under Leslie Frost came back into power, although with a reduced majority. In Manitoba the Progressive Conservative premier, Dufferin Roblin, secured a clear majority. The general election in Newfoundland was fought on labour issues, and on charges by the premier, Joseph Smallwood, that the Diefenbaker government was refusing to honour the financial terms of confederation. The overwhelming victory of Smallwood's party suggested that he had correctly guessed the sentiments of the electorate when he asked for a dissolution of the legislature.

On the whole it was a favourable year for the Progressive Conservatives, in spite of the Newfoundland victory and the moderate improvement in Liberal fortunes in Alberta. The public opinion polls seemed to indicate some falling off from the peak of popularity of the Diefenbaker government as shown in 1958, but this was not unexpected. Much was made by both major political parties of the by-elections of October, one to fill the seat made vacant by the death of Sidney Smith, and the other to elect a new member for Russell, on the outskirts of Ottawa. Both seats went as before, one to the Progressive Conservatives and one to the Liberals, but the Liberal majority in Russell, made in the face of a great Conservative drive, was sufficiently notable to give the Liberals some encouragement.

The Canadian Broadcasting corporation underwent a major reorganization on its administrative side following a difficult year, marked by strikes and charges of political interference with programmes. Hearings were arranged to permit applications for the establishment of private television stations.

The second annual report of the Canada council, set up and endowed by the government to foster the arts, humanities and social sciences, announced " an upsurge in activity and interest in the arts right across the country ". Among the many projects financed or encouraged by the council were tours of opera companies, dramatic societies and musical groups into regions of Canada, which, because of their isolation, had seldom or never before been given an opportunity to witness such performances. The council also began a policy of assisting in the publication of literary manuscripts of merit.

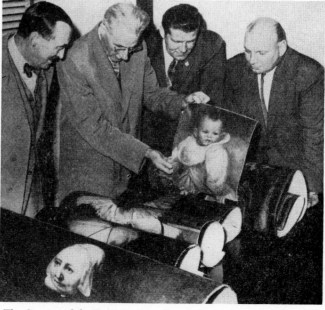

The director of the Toronto Art gallery holds up Renoir's " Claude ", one of six paintings recovered after their theft on Sept. 14.

It was agreed in January that a collection of Polish state art treasures which had been deposited in the Bank of Montreal since 1940 should be returned to Poland. On June 9 appeared the first issue of Canada's only all-Eskimo magazine, *Inuktitut* ("The Eskimo Way"), produced by Eskimoes in their own language.

At the Stratford (Ontario) festival held during June-September there were productions of *Othello* and *As You Like It*, with Irene Worth and Douglas Campbell as the leading players. A special feature of the Montreal festival was the performance of the plays of Molière and Henry de Montherlant by members of the Comédie Française. The Vancouver International festival opened its second annual season in July with a concert devoted to the music of Beethoven, conducted by Herbert von Karajan. (WD. E.; X.)

CANALS AND INLAND WATERWAYS. Great Britain.

The annual report and accounts of the British Transport commission stated that during 1958 total traffic originating on its inland waterways was 9·3 million tons, which was 600,000 tons less than in 1957. The deficit for 1958 on waterways-owning was £642,000 (£285,000 more than in 1957). Despite the decline in canal-borne freight, gross receipts were substantially maintained following an increase in tolls, but working expenses were higher. Carrying operations resulted in a deficit of £196,000 (£28,000 less than in 1957). Further progress was made on the development plan for the major waterways, the revised estimated cost being £6 million, of which £2 million had been spent by the end of 1958. The main work during the year consisted of bank protection and channel widening on the River Weaver, the Gloucester and Sharpness canal, the River Lee, the Grand Union canal and the Yorkshire waterways. The commission put in hand engineering and economic surveys to assess the prospective value of making the Grand Union canal navigable by wide barges between Birmingham and the Port of London. In Feb. 1959 a white paper was published containing the government's proposals following the report of the committee of inquiry into inland waterways issued in 1958. It set out an interim policy for a two-year period during which the navigable canals were to remain under commission ownership and operation and to be maintained at least in their existing condition. An Inlands Waterways Redevelopment Advisory committee was set up to promote and consider schemes for conversion for other uses or abandonment of canals no longer used for transport.

Continental Europe. During 1958 river navigation between Kaliningrad (formerly Königsberg), Frankfurt-on-Oder and Magdeburg was opened for transit across Poland. In connection with the Rhine development programme between Basel and Strasbourg the Vogelgrün-Fourth canal of the Grand Canal d'Alsace was opened for Rhine traffic in March 1959. Development of the Rhine-Main-Danube canal as far as Nürnberg to enable it to take large vessels continued and was expected to be completed by 1970. By the construction of a series of locks the Neckar river had been made navigable as far as Stuttgart, thus joining the capital of Baden-Württemberg by waterway with the Ruhr and the North sea. Deepening of the Dortmund-Ems canal was completed.

The royal yacht " Britannia", with Queen Elizabeth II and President Eisenhower aboard, steams up the St. Lawrence seaway on June 26 to mark the ceremonial opening of the 2,300-mi.-link between the Atlantic and the Great Lakes. The seaway was unofficially opened in April.

In connection with the development of the port of Rotterdam a new canal to relieve the New waterway, constructed 80 years earlier to bypass the tortuous and silted mouth of the river Maas, was to be built to take inland craft and would involve the construction of a number of locks.

Negotiations were started between Finland and the U.S.S.R. concerning the reopening of the Saimaa canal, 6 of the 11 locks of which were in Soviet territory. Under a draft agreement the U.S.S.R. was to repair the canal on its territory and Finland was to be granted a 50-year lease on the canal facilities and also on storage and reloading space in the harbour of Vysotsk, outside Vyborg. Plans were made to broaden the canal, which was only about 25 ft. wide.

Studies were begun on the possibilities of connecting the Danube and the Sava by the construction of a canal, nearly 40 mi. in length, from Vukovar on the Danube to Samac on the Sava, bypassing Belgrade. Construction was expected to take four years and, when finished, the route from Croatia and Bosnia-Herzegovina via the Danube to Hungary and Austria would be shortened by about 250 mi.

North America. The 1,200-mi. St. Lawrence seaway from below Quebec to the head of the Great Lakes was opened for traffic in April 1959 and the official opening by Queen Elizabeth II and President Dwight D. Eisenhower took place in June. The seaway was immediately used to such an extent that traffic bottlenecks occurred. Plans were therefore drawn up to increase the potential capacity of the Welland Ship canal by 25% and work on building some 7,000 ft. of additional tie-up wall was expected to be completed by the opening of the 1960 navigation season at a cost of some £6 million.

Africa and Asia. In 1959 work started in Madagascar on the Pangalanes canal which was to run parallel to the coast and connect the rivers serving the coastline with the port of Tamatava. The United States Development Loan fund granted a loan of $1·75 million to the East Pakistan Inland Water Transportation authority to meet the foreign exchange costs of installing a system of modern navigational aids on waterways in East Pakistan.

In June a contract was signed providing for the widening and deepening of the Suez canal between the Bitter lakes and Suez. Negotiations for substantial development of the canal were opened between the government of the United Arab Republic and the International Bank for Reconstruction and Development.

In China, following extensive surveys, plans were drawn up for the Peking-Canton canal which was to be made the major artery for waterborne transport in central and southern China. With the widening and deepening of the ancient Grand canal in northern and eastern China there would be direct navigation from the Yellow river at Cheng-hsien to Peking. The northern section was to run roughly parallel with the Peking-Canton railway and the southern section from the Yangtze to the Chu Chiang at Canton. A route had also been tentatively fixed for the section linking Lu-shan on the Sha Ho tributary of the Huai Ho in Honan with Cheng-hsien. (*See* also DOCKS AND HARBOURS; PANAMA CANAL ZONE; SUEZ CANAL.)   (E. A. J. D.)

CANCER: *see* DISEASES.
CANNING INDUSTRY: *see* BUSINESS REVIEW.

CAPITAL INVESTMENT. The volume of capital formation in the 1950s was high throughout the world. Probably in every single country or territory more was invested in new buildings, plant, machinery and vehicles than in any other decade and the contrast with the 1930s was indeed remarkable.

The effort made in different countries is indicated by percentages of gross national product devoted to gross fixed capital formation shown in Table I. Despite attempts at standardization, the figures for different countries are not completely comparable. Nevertheless, certain broad differences between countries are beyond doubt. The proportion of national product invested was highest in countries like Australia, Norway or the Belgian Congo which received finance or aid from other countries for industrial development, and was lowest in predominantly non-industrial countries like Ceylon, Egypt or the Philippines. As a general rule, the poorest countries had the lowest proportion of income spent on investment and this applied also to countries not shown in the table, such as India.

TABLE I. GROSS DOMESTIC FIXED CAPITAL FORMATION AS PERCENTAGES OF GROSS NATIONAL PRODUCT

Country	1951	1952	1953	1954	1955	1956	1957
Argentina	22	20	18	18	18	20	22
Australia	30	25	25	27	27	25	26
Austria	21	20	18	21	24	22	22
Belgian Congo	25	30	32	28	27	27	27
Belgium	14	14	15	15	16	16	16
Brazil	18	18	13	14	14	14	13
Burma	12	15	14	18	19	19	19
Canada	22	22	23	23	23	26	28
Ceylon	9	12	10	9	10	10	12
Denmark	17	18	18	19	17	17	17
Ecuador	11	9	11	14	14	14	13
Egypt (U.A.R.)	14	12	10	10	10	9	...
Finland	24	27	25	26	26	28	27
France	17	15	16	16	18	18	19
German Fed. Rep.	19	19	20	21	23	23	22
Ghana	9	11	11	11	12	14	13
Greece	14	13	12	14	14	16	15
Ireland	15	15	14	14	14	14	13
Italy	18	20	19	20	20	21	22
Jamaica	14	13	12	13	15	23	...
Japan	20	20	22	20	19	23	26
Mexico	...	14	13	14	14	15	15
Netherlands	19	19	21	21	23	25	25
New Zealand	20	23	22	23	22	22	23
Norway	24	26	30	30	30	28	28
Peru	23	24	23	21	24	26	...
Philippines	7	6	7	7	7	8	9
South Africa	24	28	27	25	23	21	21
Sweden	18	19	21	21	20	20	20
United Kingdom	13	13	14	14	15	15	15
United States	16	16	16	16	17	18	17
Venezuela	18	21	21	22	21	31	35

SOURCE. U.N. *Yearbook of National Accounts Statistics 1958.*

Figures for the U.S.S.R. and the eastern European countries are not available on a comparable basis, but it can be established that the rate of capital formation was at a very high level, though not as high as in some of the western countries which received capital from abroad.

On the whole, throughout the world there was little fluctuation in the rate of capital accumulation in the 1950s. The greatest contrast with periods before World War II is that the high level of investment was sustained in all industrial areas, instead of capital formation proceeding in fits and starts. Not only in Communist but also in capitalist countries governments made conscious efforts to achieve this.

The percentage figures in Table I hide the fact that the level of the national product as well as the relative price of investment goods varied from country to country. A direct comparison of *per capita* levels of investment is shown for the United States and eight European countries in Table II. The level of investment in Europe as a whole, and in the United Kingdom in particular, was about one-half of that in the United States, but it was much less in Italy and much more in Norway. The gap between the United States and European countries distinctly diminished between 1950 and 1955.

The smallest differences between the United States and European countries were in residential construction and the

TABLE II. INDICES OF PER CAPITA INVESTMENT BY CATEGORY OF INVESTMENT IN 1950 AND 1955
(United States = 100)

	Belgium		Denmark		France		German Fed. Rep.		Italy		Nether-lands		Norway		United Kingdom	
	1950	1955	1950	1955	1950	1955	1950	1955	1950	1955	1950	1955	1950	1955	1950	1955
At U.S. price weights																
Total . . .	60	65	55	52	40	46	42	66	20	32	47	54	78	87	39	49
Producers' durables .	63	89	52	62	39	50	33	59	15	21	41	66	57	74	43	59
Construction . .	58	50	57	47	41	44	49	70	24	38	51	48	95	95	37	43
Residential . .	79	82	65	62	30	61	74	136	20	44	56	54	96	111	52	74
Other . . .	39	29	49	36	50	32	27	24	28	34	46	43	95	85	24	23
At European price weights																
Total . . .	54	61	47	47	37	41	35	54	18	27	42	52	64	74	35	43
Producers' durables .	58	82	47	55	32	42	30	55	13	19	39	62	51	67	36	50
Construction . .	48	40	49	38	43	40	41	54	24	35	45	42	84	81	32	36
Residential . .	79	82	65	62	30	61	74	136	20	44	56	54	96	111	52	74
Other . . .	33	24	40	30	49	32	26	23	27	32	40	38	78	70	23	22

SOURCE. O.E.E.C., *Comparative National Products and Price Levels: a Study of Western Europe and the United States.*

largest in non-residential construction. Residential construction was much cheaper in Europe than in the United States but producers' durables were on the whole more expensive.

In the United States the highest volume of fixed capital formation was reached in 1956, but residential construction was already falling. After no change in the total in 1957 (but with residential construction falling further), there was a sharp decline in 1958. A recovery started in 1959 and with a further rise expected in 1960 the United States would be back at the 1956 volume. In western Europe, on the other hand, the increase in capital formation was continuous but in 1958 and 1959 the rise was only about 2% per annum. In Japan a pattern similar to that of the United States was followed. By contrast, capital formation rose throughout the period by about 10% in the U.S.S.R. and (except in 1957, which was a year of mixed performance) in the eastern European countries.

In the western countries, at various times between 1955 and 1958, governments took restrictive measures (such as raising interest rates) which adversely reacted on investment. But the easing of restrictions begun in 1958 continued, while residential construction was generally encouraged and public investment expanded. The resulting growth of capital formation throughout the world was expected to continue in 1960.

In the United Kingdom investment in manufacturing industry began to decline at the end of 1956. The main element in the investment boom of 1955-56 was the rapid rise in the construction of new factories; the fall in factory building was subsequently the main element in the decline, which persisted in 1959. The lower level of investment in manufacturing was, however, offset by rising investment in the distributive trades and service industries. In the public sector a rapid increase in road building and railway modernization contributed to a rise. The construction of dwellings by local authorities declined steadily from 1953 but on the other hand private building increased; in 1959 the latter more than offset the former. (T. BAR.)

CARIBBEAN COMMISSION.
An advisory body set up in 1946 by France, the Netherlands, Great Britain and the United States in succession to the Anglo-American Caribbean commission to encourage co-operation among the territories in this area and to facilitate research. Two subsidiary bodies set up were the Caribbean Research council and the West Indian conference. The conference assembles every second year and provides a forum at which representatives of the people themselves can discuss social and economic matters. The commission has a secretariat at Port of Spain, Trinidad, and meets twice a year.

History. A conference of regional information officers was held in Surinam during March 14-19, 1959, under the joint sponsorship of the commission and the government of Surinam. In July, the Third Caribbean Fisheries seminar was held in St. Maarten, Netherlands Antilles. In addition, two other meetings were held—one of the preparatory committee and one of the special session of the West Indian conference—to set up a successor organization to the commission. Likely to be known as the Caribbean organization, the new body would bring about a reorganization more in keeping with the constitutional developments which had taken place in the Caribbean since the commission was established. The 28th meeting of the commission took place in St. Thomas, U.S. Virgin Islands, in August. (E. L. C.)

CATERING INDUSTRY: *see* BUSINESS REVIEW.
CATTLE: *see* LIVESTOCK.
CAVE EXPLORATION: *see* SPELEOLOGY.

CENTENARIES.
The following is a selected list of the more important centenaries celebrated throughout the world during 1959:

Great Britain
Jan. 11 Centenary of birth of Lord Curzon of Kedleston, viceroy of India, 1899-1905.
Jan. 15 Bicentenary of opening of British Museum.
Jan. 25 Bicentenary of birth of Robert Burns, Scottish poet.
Jan. 29 Centenary of opening of Wellington college (Sandhurst).
Feb. 2 Centenary of birth of Henry Havelock Ellis, author and psychologist.
Feb. 21 Centenary of birth of George Lansbury, Labour leader and politician.
March 8 Centenary of birth of Kenneth Grahame, author of *The Wind in the Willows.*
March 26 Centenary of birth of A. E. Housman, poet and scholar.
May 2 Centenary of birth of Jerome K. Jerome, author and humorist.
Centenary of ceremonial opening by Prince Albert of I. K. Brunel's bridge over River Tamar at Saltash, Cornwall.

Big Ben, 100 years old on July 1, was first heard on July 11, 1859. A view from beneath the Boadicea statue on the embankment.

May 13* Parade held in honour of centenary of formation of Corps of Commissionaires and inspected by the queen.

May 15* 17/21st Lancers celebrated bicentenary of 17th Lancers.

May 22 Centenary of birth of A. Conan Doyle, novelist and originator of the famous fictional detectives, Sherlock Holmes and Dr. Watson.

May 28 Bicentenary of birth of William Pitt the Younger, statesman.

May 31 Big Ben, Westminster clock, began operation 100 years ago.

June 2* 200th anniversary of Royal Botanical gardens, Kew, celebrated by a garden party attended by the queen.

June 7 Centenary of death of David Cox, watercolour artist.

June 12 Bicentenary of death of William Collins, poet.

June 23* Exhibition opened in London to celebrate bicentenary of production of Wedgwood pottery.

July 13 Centenary of birth of Lord Passfield (Sidney Webb), economist and Fabian.

Aug. 24 Bicentenary of birth of William Wilberforce, the philanthropist who worked for the abolition of slavery. Among places which held special celebrations was his birthplace, Hull.

Sept. 15 Centenary of death of I. K. Brunel, designer and builder of Royal Albert bridge, Saltash, Cornwall, and architect of Great Western railway.

Oct. 12 Centenary of death of Robert Stephenson, engineer.

Nov. 22 Centenary of birth of Cecil J. Sharp, author and musician, and founder of English Folk Dance and Song society.

Nov. 24 Centenary of publication of Charles Darwin's *Origin of Species*.

Dec. 5 Centenary of birth of Lord Jellicoe, admiral of the fleet.

Dec. 8 Centenary of death of Thomas de Quincey, author.

Dec. 18 Centenary of birth of the poet Francis Thompson.

Dec. 28 Centenary of death of Lord Macaulay, historian and poet.

Outside Great Britain

Jan. 27 Memorial service held in Berlin to commemorate birth of Kaiser Wilhelm II.

March 29 Centenary of first publication of the *Irish Times*.

April 14 Bicentenary of death of George Handel, composer. Principal celebrations held in Britain and in his birthplace, Halle, German Democratic Republic.

April 30 Centenary of death of S. T. Aksakov, Russian writer.

May 15 Centenary of birth of Pierre Curie, French physicist.

June 6 Centenary of establishment of Queensland as a colony.

June 11 Centenary of death of Prince Metternich, Austrian statesman.

June 24 Centenary of battle of Solferino in which the Austrians were defeated by the French and Italians.

August 400th anniversary of first European settlement in Florida, United States.

Aug. 1 Celebrations held in Britain and the German Federal Republic to mark bicentenary of battle of Minden in which British and German forces defeated the French.

Aug. 4 Centenary of birth of Knut Hamsun, Norwegian author.

Sept. 13 200th anniversary of capture of Quebec and death of General Sir James Wolfe during the battle.

Oct. 3 Centenary of birth of Eleonora Duse, Italian actress.

Oct. 4 Centenary of death of Karl Baedeker, originator of the Baedeker tourist guide-books.

Oct. 18 Centenary of birth of Henri Bergson, French philosopher.

Nov. 10 Bicentenary of birth of the German poet, Friedrich Schiller.

Nov. 28 Centenary of death of Washington Irving, U.S. author.

Dec. 2 Centenary of birth of Georges Seurat, French painter who took a prominent part in the Neo-Impressionist movement.

* Date of commemoration in 1959. Not exact date of original event.

CENTRAL AFRICAN REPUBLIC (RÉPUBLIQUE CENTRE-AFRICAINE, formerly Ubangi-Shari), a member state of the French Community. Central Africa is bounded N. by the Republic of Chad, E. by Sudan, S. by Belgian Congo and the Republic of Congo, W. by the autonomous republic of Cameroun. Area: 238,224 sq.mi. Pop.: (1950 est.) 1,072,000; (1959 est.) 1,171,000, mainly Negroes, with semi-Hamitic, semi-Negroid pastoralists in the north; Europeans (1959 est.): 9,000. Language: Bantu and Sudanic dialects. Religion: animist with a Moslem minority. Chief towns (pop., 1957 est.): Bangui (cap. 77,000); Bambari; Mobaye; Bangassou. Prime ministers in 1959: Barthélemy Boganda and (from April 30) David Dacko. French high commissioner, Paul Bordier. Chief export: cotton. Monetary unit: *franc CFA.*=metropolitan Fr.2.

History. On Nov. 29, 1958, the republic was proclaimed at Bangui amid great enthusiasm. The territorial assembly adopted a new flag: blue, white, red, green and yellow, with a white star. The constitution was approved on Feb. 10, 1959. The official language was to be French. The prime minister had complete executive power and could dissolve the National Assembly which was to be elected for a period of five years. On March 29 Boganda was killed in an air accident. The first National Assembly of 50 was elected in April. The

Boganda party (Mouvement pour l'Evolution Sociale de l'Afrique Noire) got 91% of the votes cast. David Dacko became prime minister.   (HU. DE.)

CENTRAL TREATY ORGANIZATION (CENTO, formerly BAGHDAD PACT). Defensive alliance of five states originating from the Turco-Iraqi mutual defence treaty signed in Baghdad on Feb. 24, 1955, which was expanded by the adherence of Great Britain (April 4, 1955), Pakistan (Sept. 23, 1955) and Persia (Oct. 11, 1955). On March 5, 1959, the United States concluded in Ankara bilateral defence agreements with Pakistan, Persia and Turkey. On March 24, 1959, Iraq formally withdrew from membership in the Baghdad pact. Headquarters, Ankara. Secretary-general, Mirza Osman Ali Baig (Pakistan).

History. The sixth ministerial council of the treaty organization was held in Karachi, Pakistan, on Jan. 26-28, 1959, and was attended by the prime ministers of Pakistan, Persia and Turkey, by Duncan Sandys, the British minister of defence, and by Loy Henderson, the U.S. deputy under secretary of state. The council was able to announce several important decisions of its economic committee, and disclosed that discussions had taken place about the formation of a common market between the middle east members represented.

Bilateral defence agreements between the United States on the one hand and Pakistan, Persia and Turkey on the other were signed in Ankara on March 5. The United States, though for constitutional reasons unable to become a full member of the treaty organization, thereby undertook, in the case of aggression against Pakistan, Persia or Turkey, to take such action, including the use of armed force, as might be mutually agreed upon, and would in the meantime continue to provide the other party with military and economic aid.

On March 24 Iraq formally withdrew from the treaty organization. The British Foreign Office thereupon stated that the Anglo-Iraqi bilateral agreement of 1955 and the guarantee of British assistance to Iraq if attacked had lapsed, as both arrangements were linked with Iraqi membership of the treaty. Arrangements were made to withdraw the R.A.F. detachment from the air base at Habbaniya, and the withdrawal was completed by the end of May. Nevertheless, it was agreed that the British government should continue to supply the Iraqis with arms of certain types.

With the formal withdrawal of Iraq, the expression Baghdad Pact ceased to be appropriate, and on Aug. 19 it was announced from Ankara that the pact would in future be known as the Central Treaty organization (CENTO).

The first meeting of the council under this name was held in Washington, D.C., on Oct. 7-9. The U.S. delegation described once more the reasons which prevented the United States from assuming full membership, but explained that the commitments which it had assumed by the bilateral agreements of March 1959 were as wide as the Moslem members had assumed to each other by full membership. The U.S. representatives also pointed out that Turkey, Persia and Pakistan had between them received $770 million in economic aid in the preceding two years.   (B. S.-E.)

CEREALS: *see* AGRICULTURE.

CEYLON. A realm of the Commonwealth of Nations; an island S.E. of most southerly point of India. Area: 25,332 sq.mi. Pop.: (1953 census) 8,097,895, incl. 5,616,705 Sinhalese, 884,703 Ceylon Tamils, 511,425 Moors (Ceylon and Indian), 974,098 Indians (mostly Tamils); (1958 est.) 9,361,000. Language: Sinhalese 69%, Tamil 21%. Religion: Buddhist 61%, Hindu 22%, Christian (mainly Roman Catholic) 9%, Moslem 7%. Chief towns (pop., 1953 census): Colombo (cap.) 426,127; Jaffna 77,181; Dehiwala-Mt. Lavinia 80,086; Moratuwa 58,160; Kandy 57,200; Galle 55,848; Kotte 53,862. Queen, Elizabeth II; governor-general, Sir Oliver Goonetilleke; prime ministers in 1959, S. W. R. D. Bandaranaike and (from Sept. 26) W. Dahanayake. Main imports: rice, cereals, petroleum products, sugar. Main exports: tea, rubber, coconut products. Monetary unit: Ceylon *rupee* (Rs.13·33=£1 sterling).

History. In 1959 continuing political instability culminated in the assassination on Sept. 25 of the prime minister, S. W. R. D. Bandaranaike (*see* OBITUARIES), who was shot on the verandah of his bungalow in Colombo by a Buddhist monk and died the next morning. Barely two hours after the shooting an island-wide state of emergency was declared by the governor-general. The universal reaction in Ceylon was one of horror mingled with a profound sense of mourning, manifested in remarkable scenes of public grief, for a man who, whatever his faults as prime minister, was widely recognized as a noble-hearted patriot. Four hours after Bandaranaike died (on Sept. 26) the new prime minister was sworn in. He was W. Dahanayake (*see* BIOGRAPHIES), the minister of education and acting leader of the House of Representatives. The death penalty for murder, suspended in April 1956, was re-introduced, and a stringent press censorship was imposed for three weeks. The state of political unrest and conflict between the parties became more intense and was accompanied by a growing sense of economic insecurity. Parliament was dissolved on Dec. 4 and a general election was to be held in March 1960. Dahanayake resigned from the Sri Lanka Freedom party and said he would form a new party. He and his cabinet were to continue in office as a caretaker government.

Before the shock of these events, notable progress had been made in the sphere of economic aid and technical co-operation with other countries. President Tito visited Ceylon in January and the Yugoslav government offered Rs.70 million to be used over a period of three years for the purchase of capital goods. The first steps were taken towards the setting up of an iron and steel works to be built with technical assistance

Wijayananda Dahanayake, who became prime minister of Ceylon after the assassination of S. W. R. D. Bandaranaike on Sept. 25.

from the U.S.S.R. and financed out of the Rs.140 million credit extended to Ceylon by the Soviet Union. Work was started on the state-owned rubber tyre and tube factory near Colombo, which was being built with Soviet assistance. The rice-rubber agreement with the Chinese People's Republic was renewed on the basis of the purchase of 30,000 tons of rubber by China against 230,000 tons of rice by Ceylon. Agreement

was reached with the United States for the purchase of rice and wheat flour to the value of Rs.40 million, most of which was made available to Ceylon for economic and business development.

Introducing the budget in July the minister of finance, Stanley de Zoysa, said that production in 1958 was higher in many spheres and the terms of trade moved in Ceylon's favour. Income from exports rose by Rs.29 million to Rs.1,711 million and the value of imports fell from Rs.1,805 million in 1957 to Rs.1,717 million in 1958, largely owing to a fall in prices. The trade balance showed a deficit of only Rs.6 million compared with Rs.123 million in 1957, although the over-all balance of payments position continued to be adverse. The production of tea in 1958 increased by 15 million lb. to 413 million lb. and, in spite of a small price decline, the value of tea exports constituted almost exactly two-thirds of the total value of exports. The total expenditure for 1959-60 was estimated at Rs.1,736 million, of which Rs.1,400 million was chargeable to revenue. Revenue under the existing taxes was estimated at Rs.1,342 million, and new taxation to yield an additional Rs.32 million was imposed.

The budget was framed against the background of Ceylon's ten-year development plan, the result of three years' intensive study and research by the National Planning council. This plan, announced in June, provided for a capital investment of Rs.13,601 million, of which the government would contribute 61%, and the balance would be subscribed mainly by private investors. To assist replanting of tea, rubber and coconuts, more than Rs.1,200 million was ear-marked for these three main export industries. A further Rs.2,714 million was to be devoted to industrial development to yield an annual gross output of Rs.910 million and to provide employment for 237,000 people by 1968. The planners envisaged the raising of the national income from Rs.4,742 million to Rs.8,905 million in ten years and the creation of 1·4 million new jobs by 1968. During this period, however, it was calculated that the population of Ceylon would have risen by 3·6 million. Nevertheless, a rise in living standards was expected, with income per head rising by 36% and consumption by 19%.

Labour unrest which at times threatened to cripple the working of the port of Colombo continued until July when the government adopted a firmer attitude towards the trade unions and called out servicemen to keep the port going. Owing to delays in unloading—on one day in June there were 34 ships waiting outside Colombo harbour—the government had been paying large sums in demurrage on food cargoes and, during the first six months of 1959, these amounted to Rs.6 million. Delays in the port resulted in an increase in freight rates to Colombo and added to the injury inflicted on trade and commerce in the island. From July, however, conditions in the port improved, and the output of work per head of the 14,000 labourers in the harbour began to increase.

During 1959 notable steps were taken to improve communications and transport in Ceylon. A ten-year plan for roads was adopted, which would include the construction of 300 mi. of new highways. A new bridge, costing Rs.5 million, was opened over the Kelani river near Colombo. Progress was made with the large-scale programmes to modernize the railways and to build more airports to enable internal air services to be expanded.

As part of a survey to assess the island's mineral resources, a team of scientists from the International Atomic Energy agency decided after a ten-day visit that there was every possibility of finding uranium deposits in Ceylon.

Vidyalankara college, which was founded in 1875 and had become one of the most famous seats of learning for oriental studies and Buddhist culture, achieved university status in July. The University of Ceylon continued to expand and a second faculty of science was added. With the opening of 300 more schools in Ceylon the number of children at school rose to more than 2 million.

With the death of Sir Paul Pieries, at the age of 85, Ceylon lost an outstanding administrator, a public figure of deep learning and culture and a noted scholar. Sir Paul was a civil servant for 40 years, but he was best known as an historian, particularly of the Portuguese period in Ceylon.

One of the seven persons who were charged with conspiracy to murder S. W. R. D. Bandaranaike is escorted from the chief magistrate's court, Colombo, after the hearing.

During the annual Esala Perahera procession in Kandy in August, one of the largest of the temple elephants stampeded and, in the confusion among the massed crowd of spectators, 15 people were killed and 150 injured. The elephant had to be shot. During the 400 years' history of the Perahera ceremony such an incident had never previously occurred. (*See* also COLOMBO PLAN.)   (J. HKN.)

CHAD, REPUBLIC OF (RÉPUBLIQUE DU TCHAD),

a member state of the French Community. Chad is bounded N. by Libya, E. by Sudan, S. by the Republic of Central Africa, and W. by the autonomous Republic of Cameroun, Nigeria and the Republic of Niger. Area: 495,752 sq.mi. Pop.: (1950 est.) 2,241,000; (1959 est.) 2,580,000; semi-Hamitic, semi-Negroid; Europeans (1957 est.) 4,880. Language: Sudanic dialects. Religion: animist 54%, Moslem 46%. Chief towns (1957 est.): Fort Lamy (cap., 44,000); Fort Archambault; Abéché. Prime ministers in 1959: Gabriel Lisette, Gontchomé Sahoulba, Ahmed Koulamallah and (from March 26) François Tombalbaye. French high commissioner, Daniel Houstin. Chief export: cotton. Monetary unit: *franc CFA* = metropolitan Fr.2.

History. On Dec. 9, 1958, the territorial assembly proclaimed itself a constituent one. The constitution was passed on April 1, 1959. Chad was a " republic one and indivisible, secular, democratic and social ". The government was responsible to the National Assembly. The official language was French.

The new republic experienced several political crises. On Feb. 12 the Lisette government was replaced by the Sahoulba government. The latter was succeeded by the Koulamallah government, which was in turn replaced by the Tombalbaye government on March 26.

The first National Assembly was elected on June 2. The Parti Progressiste Tchadien (Lisette) won 57 seats out of 85. A new government was formed: François Tombalbaye became prime minister and Gabriel Lisette deputy prime minister.   (HU. DE.)

CHAMBERS OF COMMERCE.

In 1959 the most important topic for members of chambers of commerce in the international economic field was the proposed European Free Trade association (the " outer seven "), comprising Austria, Denmark, Norway, Portugal, Sweden, Switzerland and the United Kingdom. Chambers welcomed the initiative of the Swedish government in this matter, seeing the proposals as advantageous in themselves, as a means of bridging the gap with the European Economic community, and as a way in which the greater conception of a European free trade area might be achieved. Discussions on this subject with ministers and government officials were numerous, and the links between chamber of commerce organizations in the " seven " were strengthened.

U.K. domestic affairs of concern to industry and commerce were varied. For example, the Association of British Chambers of Commerce undertook jointly with the British Association for the Advancement of Science an inquiry to ascertain opinions on how far the introduction in the United Kingdom of a decimal coinage and the metric system of weights and measures would be beneficial, and to try and estimate the cost of such a change. Learned and professional societies, trade associations and companies were asked to co-operate, and a report would be published during 1960.

At the request of the minister of transport views were submitted to the British Transport commission advising how best British railways might stop the decline in goods traffic and commenting on whether the modernization plan was tuned to industrial and commercial needs. A memorandum was submitted to the minister of transport recommending greater freedom for air transport operators, suggesting that a statutory body should replace the Air Transport Advisory committee and that the Ministry of Civil Aviation should be re-created.

Proposed legislation on which views were expressed by chambers of commerce included the Domicile bills, the Factories bill, the Offices Regulation bill, the Thermal Insulation (Industrial Buildings) bill, the Town and Country Planning bill and the Truck Acts and Wages bill. With regard to the last-named, industry and commerce were in general agreement that if the provisions to pay manual workers by cheque were to be permissive no objections would be raised. Memoranda, or written or oral evidence, were submitted to the Cohen Council on Prices, Productivity and Incomes, to the Weir committee concerning the possibilities of greater co-operation between area gas and electricity boards, to the British Transport commission regarding proposed new harbour charges schemes, to the minister of housing on the control of advertisement regulations and on the report of the Ritson Committee on the Rating of Plant and Machinery.

Maintaining close liaison with the Export Credits Guarantee department chambers of commerce were successful in obtaining a special guarantee to cover confirming house transactions and clarification on other important points affecting British exporters.

The 1959 budget letter to the chancellor of the exchequer suggested that encouragement could be given to re-expansion of the economy, both in home and overseas markets, without undue risk of reviving inflationary pressures. The hope was expressed that capital expenditure by nationalized industries and local authorities would be financed by loans on the market.

International. The International Chamber of Commerce held its 17th biennial congress at Washington, D.C., during

April 20-25, 1959. Delegates numbered 943 from 41 national committees, with 57 from the British National committee. There were 104 observers from other international organizations including the Economic and Social Council of the United Nations (Ecosoc), the General Agreement on Tariffs and Trade (G.A.T.T.), the newly formed Special U.N. Fund for Economic Development (S.U.N.F.E.D.), the International Monetary Fund (I.M.F.), the International Bank for Reconstruction and Development (I.B.R.D.) and the Organization for European Economic Co-operation (O.E.E.C.). The congress formally adopted 58 resolutions and statements (*see* I.C.C. brochure 207, *Statements and Resolutions 1957-59*), based on the work of the preceding two years, many having been published in 1958.

Important subjects covered by resolutions and statements were monetary stability and economic expansion, assistance to underdeveloped countries and measures to attract foreign capital investment to them, avoidance of double taxation and special administrative and policy problems in the European Economic community and the rest of Europe. Other important fields covered were international sea, air and inland transport, commercial law (including patents and trade marks), advertising, marketing, distribution and the organization of international trade fairs and exhibitions.

Economic developments in Europe continued to occupy the attention of the I.C.C., which kept pace with measures taken to implement the treaty of the European Economic community in all aspects affecting private industry and commerce, and in many of the I.C.C.'s technical commissions working parties were specially constituted for the purpose. The I.C.C. continued to press for a wider European agreement on the freeing of trade, and collaborated with Ecosoc, with O.E.E.C. (especially on inland transport matters) and also with G.A.T.T. At the 14th session of the contracting parties to G.A.T.T. in May a recommendation, based on the I.C.C.'s initiative, was adopted, to the effect that governments should avoid any measures in the field of transport insurance which would have a restrictive effect on international trade.

Carlos Mantero (Portugal) became president of the I.C.C. at the congress in April. Israel and the Republic of Korea established national committees. The total membership of 66 countries was 1,416 trade and industrial organizations and more than 6,000 firms.

The latter half of the year was occupied with maintenance of relations with intergovernmental bodies and the inauguration of further studies provided for in the chamber's programme of work for 1959-61.   (A. C. F. H.; C. A. G. S.)

BIBLIOGRAPHY (all I.C.C. brochures, 1959). *General Transport Policy in Europe* (194); *Promotion of Advertising Expenditure Surveys by Class of Media on an Internationally Comparable Basis* (195); *Double Taxation —Settlement of Disputes* (196); *Taxation and the Developing Nations* (197); *Customs Valuation of Imported Goods* (198); *Export Credits* (199); *Attracting Foreign Investment* (200); *Monetary Stability* (201); *Marketing Research Aids Business Judgment* (202); *Who Sees Outdoor Advertising* (203); *How to Reduce Distribution Costs* (204); *Simplification of International Payment Orders* (205): *Education and Training in Advertising* (cr.).

CHANNEL ISLANDS.

Group of islands in the English channel *c.* 10-30 mi. W. of Cherbourg peninsula; the only parts of the Duchy of Normandy remaining to the English crown. Divided politically into two crown dependencies with internal autonomy: (1) the bailiwick of Jersey and (2) the bailiwick of Guernsey and its dependencies. Language: English; French (official in Jersey); Norman French *patios*, with local dialects in country districts. Religion: Anglican (Jersey and Guernsey are each a deanery of the diocese of Winchester); Roman Catholic; Nonconformist denominations. Main imports: fuel, building materials, foodstuffs. Main exports: tomatoes, potatoes (Jersey), flowers, stone (Guernsey), cattle. Currency: sterling with local notes and coinage.

Jersey. Area: 45 sq.mi. Pop.: (1957 est.) 57,000. Capital: St. Helier, pop. (1955 est.) 28,000. Administration: lieut.-governor; bailiff (president of States and royal court); States committees (executive); States (elected legislature). Lieut.-governor, General Sir George Erskine; bailiff, Sir Alexander M. Coutanche.

Guernsey and Dependencies. Total area (incl. Alderney, Great and Little Sark, Brechou, Herm, Jethou, Lihou, etc.): 30 sq.mi. Total pop.: (1957 est.) 40,721. Capital: St. Peter Port, pop. (1955 est.) 18,250. Administration: lieut.-governor; bailiff; States committees; States of Deliberation with elected majority. *Alderney* (3 sq.mi.; pop. [1957 est.] 1,350) has an elected States; *Sark* (2 sq.mi.; pop. [1957 est.] 437) is administered by a hereditary *seigneur* (since 1955 by his widow, the *dame de Sercq*) through its partly elected Court of Chief Pleas. Lieut.-governor of Guernsey and dependencies; Vice-Admiral Sir Geoffrey Robson; bailiff, Sir Ambrose J. Sherwill.

History. On Jan. 2, 1959, an earth tremor lasting several seconds was recorded in Jersey. It was also felt in Guernsey where three glasshouses were demolished. There was another slight tremor in Jersey on March 22.

Exports of broccoli from Jersey in 1958-59 amounted to 7,221 tons, representing a value of between £150,000 and £200,000. In 1959 early potato growers on Jersey experienced the best season for 50 years and 47,397 tons were exported. Prices throughout the season were relatively high and the gross estimated value to growers was £1,790,300.

More tourists than ever before visited the islands during 1959 and record amounts of sunshine were recorded. Drought conditions on Jersey forced the authorities to introduce water rationing towards the end of the summer, and the hot weather brought on the outdoor tomato crops earlier than usual. The same conditions on Guernsey advanced the glasshouse tomatoes, and while the crop was the heaviest since the end of World War II, market returns were low and hundreds of tons were dumped.

Jersey introduced a 40-mi.-an-hour speed limit for the whole island in October as a result of the number of accidents during the year.

Princess Margaret visited Guernsey, Sark, Alderney and Jersey in June. Her principal engagement was on Guernsey where she opened a new secondary school.   (C. T.)

CHEMISTRY.

Physical Chemistry. *Fuel Cells.* In 1959 one of the first public demonstrations of a fuel cell producing useful amounts of energy was given. A cell designed by F. T. Bacon at Cambridge was shown operating a fork lift truck. Fuel cells convert chemical energy directly into electricity, whereas a power station and other forms of generator convert the chemical energy first into heat and then into electricity. In a large power station the operation might be 35% efficient, whereas a fuel cell might have an efficiency of 70% or more. Mobile power sources such as petrol and diesel engines are only about 20% efficient in converting chemical energy into useful work. This efficiency is the most considerable advantage of the fuel cell.

Fuel cells promised to find their first applications as replacements for accumulators because they weighed less for the amount of power delivered. Moreover, the cells can be instantaneously " charged " by the addition of fresh fuel. Since electric vehicles have many advantages over those driven by oil or petrol it was in transport that fuel cells seemed likely to be most widely used. The Bacon cell operated on hydrogen and oxygen which were converted into water. The electrolyte was 27% potassium hydroxide and the electrodes were of porous nickel. The weight of the cell was considerably increased by the large amount of auxiliary equipment that was needed to maintain the pressures of the two gases exactly equal and to discharge the water. Other fuel cells were being developed that operated on hydrocarbon gases. The problems involved in using solid fuels were great.

High Temperature Transistors. Commercial transistors were made from germanium and silicon which limited their operating temperatures to 70°C. and 150°C. respectively. One of the great advantages of transistors was their small size, but the resulting miniaturization of equipment accentuated the difficulties of overheating. Silicon carbide appeared a promising material for use at high temperatures because its energy gap is 3 volts as compared with $1 \cdot 1$ for silicon and $0 \cdot 7$ for germanium. The difficulty was to grow large single crystals of the carbide. Crystals up to 7 mm. long were grown at Stanford Research institute, California. A seed of silicon carbide was mounted above a graphite crucible at 1,500°C. to 1,600°C. containing a solution of silicon carbide in silicon. It was not shown whether the crystals were sufficiently pure to be usable as semiconductors.

Nonwoven Fabrics. Nonwoven fabrics consist of randomly oriented fibres held together by a binder. They ranged from lightweight cotton batts containing some 10% binder up to leather-like materials with 300% binder based on fibre weight. Production rose in the United States from some 15,000 lb. in 1945 to more than 115 million lb. in 1959. About 60% of the fibres used were products of the chemical industry, viscose rayon accounting for about two-thirds of this total. Fillers included polyvinyl acetate, polyvinyl chloride, butadiene-styrene and butadiene-acrylonitrile latexes. Cheaper binders, such as starch and gums, were only used for batting or as preliminary binders because of their poor hand, low wet strength and brittleness. Polyvinyl acetate, which had good flexible strength, was used for towelling and wiping materials, draperies and tape. Polyvinyl chloride conferred good abrasion resistance and formed a stiff, tough fabric. The latex binders provided resiliency and crease resistance. More expensive binders and fibres were only used for special applications such as filters. The most promising outlets for use in manufacture of such nonwoven fabrics were backing for cars, domestic draperies and clothing.

Biradicals. Compounds such as methylene, CH_2, and imine, NH, were widely described as biradicals because they could be formed by the removal of two hydrogen atoms from methane and ammonia respectively. It was uncertain whether they contained two unpaired electrons that would justify their name. Some information on this point was obtained in 1959 when the absorption spectrum of methylene was photographed for the first time.

The biradicals were usually formed by the photolysis of highly reactive compounds such as ketene, diazomethane and hydrazoic acid. Biradicals reacted like the more common monoradicals. Thus, like methyl, methylene extracted hydrogen from alkanes. More remarkable were the insertion reactions whereby methylene added directly to, for example, propane and formed *n*-butane and *iso*-butane without the intervention of monoradicals. Methylene was found to add directly to double bonds yielding cyclopropyl derivatives. The reactions were very exothermic and frequently the cyclopropanes contained sufficient energy to isomerize before they could be deactivated by collisions. Methylene reacted with ethers both by the expected insertion reaction and by displacing an olefin to yield a methyl ether. Again no monoradical species appeared to be involved.

A remarkable feature of the biradicals was the extreme rapidity with which they reacted. Studies in a time-of-flight mass spectrometer showed that methylene reacted with ketene before it had undergone 100 collisions. As ketene was present in many of the reaction systems, this meant that the other reactions were comparably fast. Biradicals were not generally used for large scale preparative purposes because they were expensive to produce and indiscriminate in their reactions. A promising source was the reaction of haloforms, such as chloroform, with potassium alkoxides which yielded dichlorocarbene. As workers became more familiar with the reactions of biradicals, their presence in a large number of reactions was rapidly recognized.

Organic Chemistry. The marked progress made during 1959 is illustrated by describing work under three headings. Important advances were reported in several other of the normal divisions during the year, but in the three topics selected for review points of especial interest arose.

Techniques. Among physical methods of analysis nuclear magnetic resonance spectroscopy (NMR) was applied more widely to problems of structural analysis. This technique was extremely useful in several cases where the well-established infra-red and ultra-violet spectrographic methods could not be applied with certainty. From the nuclear magnetic resonance spectra of the two ethyl β-chlorocrotonates, (I) and (II), R. Morris and his collaborators were able to deduce the geometric configurations of these compounds. The crucial difference between the spectra was that the C-methyl proton resonance occurred at lower field strength in the *cis*-compound (I), this effect being attributed to weak bonding between the hydrogen of the methyl group and the C=O of the ester group.

Conformational equilibria were also investigated by NMR spectroscopy. Previous work, using kinetic methods, had indicated a value of $3 \cdot 4$ for the conformational equilibrium constant of cyclohexyl bromide (III ⇌ IV) in 87% ethanol. The NMR results showed a value of $4 \cdot 8$ for the bromide in chloroform and $1 \cdot 5$ for the pure liquid. E. L. Eliel interpreted these figures as showing that in solvents such as ethanol and chloroform the preference for the adoption of the equatorial conformation (IV) was increased by preferential hydrogen bonding of this form. Further measurements using infra-red analysis supported this view, although the infra-red method did not lead to precise values for the equilibrium constant.

An NMR investigation of allyl magnesium bromide indicated that in this compound there was a rapid equilibrium between the two forms shown in (V). It was noted that the symmetrical bridged structure (VI) and ionic representations such as (VII) were excluded by the experimental results. This work was, however, related specifically to allyl magnesium bromide and could not be taken to show that all Grignard reagents existed as covalent molecules R-Mg-Ha.

Gas-liquid chromatography had been widely used in many divisions of organic chemistry for several years, but most of the work was carried out with liquids of relatively low boiling point. A publication from Glasgow university described a valuable extension of the method whereby compounds with boiling points above 250°C. could be studied. This was made possible by the use of extremely sensitive detectors which enabled the sample size to be appreciably decreased. It was found that a few micrograms of material vaporized rapidly in the gas stream at temperatures 100°-150°C. below the boiling point of the substance. Even hexatriacontane, $C_{36}H_{74}$, was eluted from a column at 230°C. in less than six hours.

Vitamin D_2, and Steroids Derived from Ergosterol. During early work in this field irradiation of ergosterol solutions was found to give the isomeric compounds lumisterol, tachysterol, vitamin D_2 (calciferol) and the suprasterols. It was thought that these compounds were formed in the sequence stated and, although the gross structures of the products were established, little was known about the stereochemical details. Later it was shown that irradiation of an ergosterol solution below 20°C. afforded little vitamin D_2, but that the vitamin was formed in appreciable quantity by warming such an irradiated solution. The ultimate step in the vitamin's formation was therefore a thermal, not a photochemical reaction.

Studies by E. Havinga and L. Velluz established the structure (VIII) for precalciferol, the labile precursor of vitamin

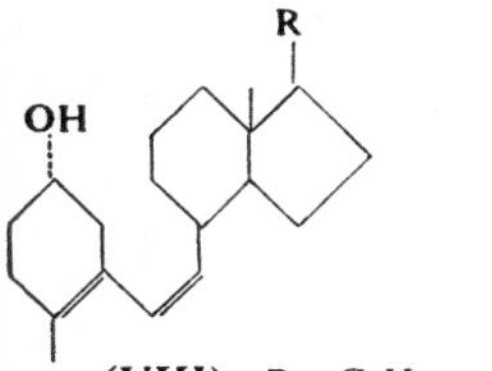

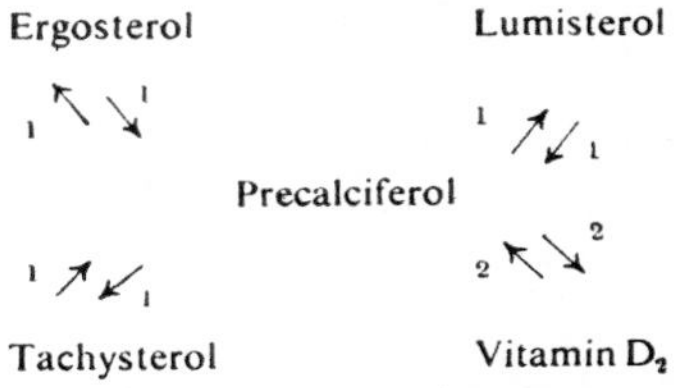

Ergosterol   Lumisterol

Precalciferol

Tachysterol   Vitamin D₂

(VIII); R = C₉H₁₇   (IX); l = irradiation, 2 = heat

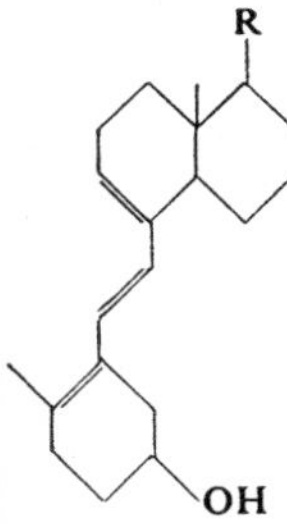

(X) 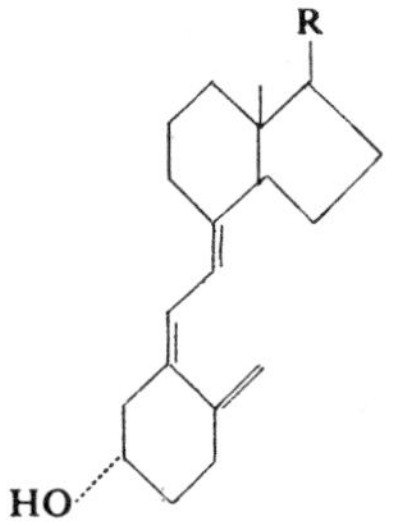   (XI) 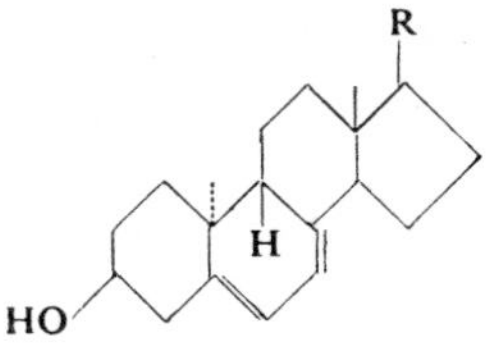   (XII)

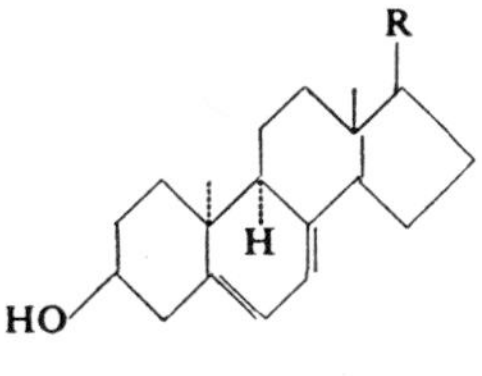

(XIII) 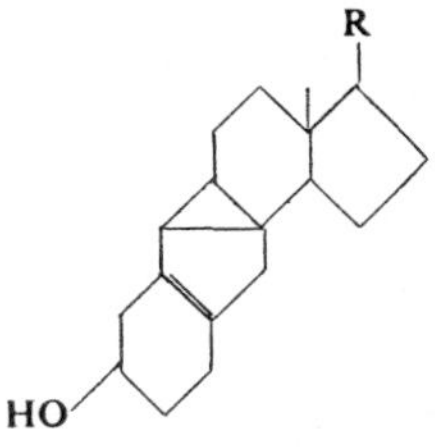   (XIV)

D_2, and the relationships within this group of compounds were expressed by the annexed scheme (IX). Chemical, spectrographic and crystallographic evidence led to structures (X) and (XI) for tachysterol and vitamin D_2 respectively. Decisive new experiments by E. R. H. Jones and his co-workers showed that lumisterol had the 9β-hydrogen orientation (XII): pyrocalciferol thus became the 9α-isomer (XIII). It is interesting to note that this work reversed the structures assigned to lumisterol and pyrocalciferol in 1939. Close examination of the prewar publications showed that there was in fact no sound reason for the structural assignments made at that

time. In the recent investigation of suprasterol-II, culminating in the proposal of structure (XIV), W. G. Dauben and his colleagues used physical methods of analysis to confirm the results from standard chemical degradations.

Configuration and Biogenesis of Alkaloids. Of the many excellent papers which appeared on this subject the contributions by E. Wenkert deserve special mention. Previous work on the yohimbine-type alkaloids (XV) had shown that the D/E rings were *cis*-fused in some compounds and *trans*-fused in others, but no correlations between representatives of the two types had been established. Wenkert provided this missing connection and established that *all* the compounds had the α-configuration at $C_{(15)}$ irrespective of the type of D/E ring junction. From this important result he went on to propose an ingenious theory for the biogenesis of the indole alkaloids.

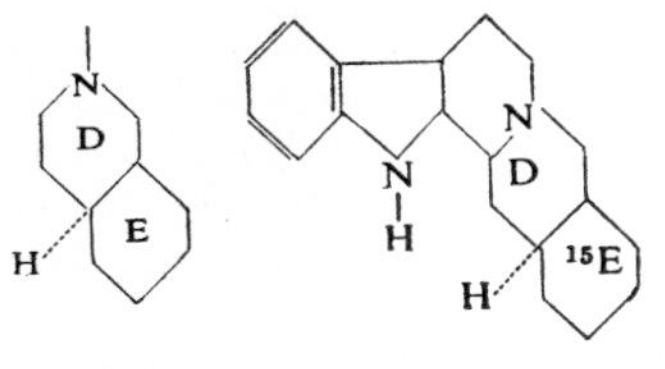

(XV) 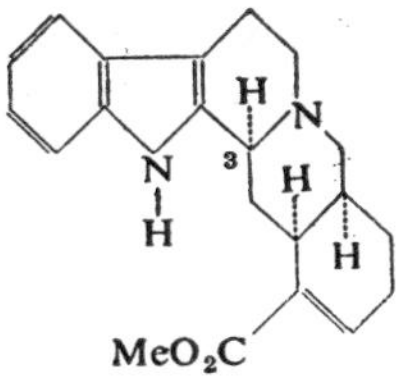   (XVI)

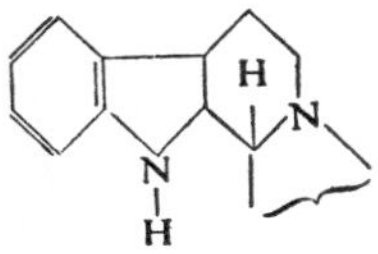

(XVII)

Wenkert also participated in a joint publication from four laboratories in which different groups had been working independently on the stereochemistry of reserpine and deserpidine. This admirable example of co-operation, resulting in one authoritative paper rather than several incomplete publications, established that the two alkaloids were isomeric at $C_{(3)}$ and that reserpine had the α-configuration (XVI) and deserpidine the β-orientation (XVII). (*See* also BIO-CHEMISTRY; NUCLEAR ENERGY.)   (A. F. T.-D.; G. D. M.)

CHILE. Republic occupying the Pacific coast of South America for about 2,600 mi. and having an average width of only 110 mi. Chile is bounded on land N. by Peru and E. by Bolivia and Argentina. Area: 286,396 sq mi. Pop.: (1952 census) 5,930,809; (1958 est.) 7,298,000. The racial composition, largely of European origin, includes *mestizos* (15%) and Indians (4·2%). Language: Spanish. Roman Catholicism is the predominant religion. Chief towns (pop., 1952 census): Santiago (cap.) 1,348,283 (incl. suburbs 1,748,708); Valparaiso 218,829; Concepción 119,887; Viña del Mar 85,281; Antofagasta 62,272. President, Jorge Alessandri Rodriquez. Main imports: machinery, tools and electrical equipment; industrial oils; paints and chemical products; transport material; iron, steel, other metal manufactures; sugar. Main exports: copper, nitrate of soda; wool. Monetary unit: *peso* (free market rate, Oct. 1959) 2,955 pesos = £1 sterling.

History. The year 1959, first in the administration of President Alessandri, saw the domestic financial scene transformed, thanks to public support for official loans and government economic policy based on a balanced budget and avoidance of further inflation. This policy was given definite shape in the *proyecto económico-financiero* approved by Congress on April 6. This law gave the president, for one year, wide special powers to modify banking laws and practice, reorganize the fiscal aspects of the public administration, simplify and co-ordinate taxation, increase customs duties and promote house-building.

Consequences of this law, and previous action of similar nature, were that, despite a heavy budget deficit in 1958, Chile met outstanding obligations promptly for the first time in many years; the dollar shortage disappeared and foreign exchange reserves rose. From January to June bank deposits increased by 34% and advances by 33%—in both cases three times the comparative figures for 1958. Emphasis in bank advances was towards agricultural, industrial and mining production. Financing of foreign travel, speculation and luxury imports was prohibited. Industrial production was 25% higher than in the first half of 1958 and industrial sales rose by 8·5% and rail freight movements by 8·9%.

Foreign support for the government's policies was reflected in the success of a visit by Roberto Vergara Herrera, the finance minister, to the United States and Europe; he obtained loans and credits for a total of $282 million repayable over eight years. The United States provided $132 million, one-sixth of which sum was in the form of industrial equipment; France $50 million, and the German Federal Republic $100 million of which the greater part was to be devoted to modernization of the state railways (which celebrated their centenary on May 27). Foreign capital investments during the year included three by the International Finance corporation —$1·5 million in a food factory, $1 million for a cement plant and an extra $900,000 for a copper smelting project.

This progress was clouded by a rise in the cost of living. At the end of July, when meat and potato prices nearly doubled, it had increased by 27·8% since January. The government pursued a campaign to hold down prices which was supported by manufacturing and retail chemists, textile and footwear manufacturers and the metallurgical industry, who either reduced their prices or undertook not to raise them before the end of the year. Although the rise in living costs led to some labour unrest, including strikes involving steelworkers, coal- and copper-miners, this was less widespread than in recent years. From January to June copper production, at 242,487 metric tons, was up by 65,666 tons on the comparable figure for 1958. In the same period iron ore exports totalled 1·5 million tons, the principal importing countries being the United States, the German Federal Republic, Japan, Argentina and Czechoslovakia. Estimated production of Chile's three sugar-beet plants was 50,000 tons (23% of annual domestic consumption). Nitrate production for the year ended June 30 was estimated at 1,350,000 tons and total output was sold at $30 per ton in the United States and Europe.

The Anglo-Lautaro company announced investments in production and other improvements totalling $9·8 million. The Huachipato national steel plant also announced expansion plans costing $70 million over three years.

Pending conclusion of a multilateral agreement between Chile, Argentina, Brazil, Uruguay, Paraguay and Peru, the trade treaty with Argentina was renewed providing that Argentina should buy 250,000 tons of coal a year and that Chile should also supply semi-worked copper, steel, timber and newsprint in return for cattle, meat, edible oils and other products. Political relations between the two countries were strained in January and September by an exchange of protests over naval activity in waters claimed by both nations in the Beagle channel.   (N. P. MACD.)

CHINA. The most populated and second largest country of the world, China is situated in southeastern Asia. It is bounded N.E. by Korea, N.E., N. and N.W. by the U.S.S.R. and Mongolia, W. by Afghanistan, S.W. by Kashmir, S. by India, Nepal, Sikkim, Bhutan, Burma, Laos and Vietnam. Total estimated area: c. 3,876,900 sq.mi. Pop.: (1953 est.) 592 million; (1957 est.) 640 million. The Chinese proper, or Han people, form 94% of the total population of the people's republic; they speak Chinese, with a number of dialects, the most important being the Mandarin (or *Kuanhua*) which dominates nearly four-fifths of China proper. Religion: Buddhist, Confucian and Taoist.

In 1954 there were 35,320,360 (6%) of national minorities, the strongest group among them being the Turkic tribes of Moslem religion, numbering about 8 million (Uigurs, Kazakhs, Kirghiz, Tungans, etc.). The 2,776,000 Tibetans and the 1,463,000 Mongols speak respectively their own languages, but both are Buddhist-Lamaist. In the southern provinces of Kweichow, Kwangsi and Yunnan live the following minorities: 6,611,000 Chuang; 3,254,000 Yi; 2,511,000 Miao; 1,248,000 Puyi; 570,000 Thai, etc.; all are Buddhist and use their own south-eastern Asian languages, sometimes described as belonging to the Sino-Tibetan family. In the northern provinces of Heilungkiang and Kirin there are 2,419,000 Manchus and 1,120,000 Koreans.

Administratively China was composed at the end of 1959 of 21 provinces (the old 17 of imperial China, 3 Manchurian and Tsinghai), 3 municipalities (Peking, Shanghai and Tientsin) and the 5 following autonomous regions:

Autonomous region	Area (sq.mi.)	Pop. (1954 est.)	Capital
Tibet (q.v.) .	470,000	1,270,000	Lhasa
Inner Mongolia .	328,007	6,100,000	Huhehot (Kweisui)
Ningsia Hui .	...	...	Yinchwan (Ningsia)
Sinkiang-Uigur .	705,769	4,874,000	Urumchi (Tihwa)
Kwangsi Chuang	...	...	Nanning

Chief towns (pop., 1957 est. if not otherwise stated): Peking (cap.) 4,140,000; Shanghai 6,900,000; Tientsin 3,100,000; Wuhan (combining

An aquatic parade of nationalist Chinese marines at the annual naval review before General Chiang Kai-shek at a base in southern Formosa.

Hankow, Wuchang and Hanyang) 1,900,000; Chungking (1953) 1,620,000; Shenyang (Mukden, 1950) 1,551,000; Sian (Siking) 1·3 million; Talien (Dairen, incl. Lushun [Port Arthur], 1950), 1,054,000; Nanking (1950) 1,020,000; Paotow 1,015,000; Nanchang 1,010,000; Harbin 1,000,000; Tsingtao (1948) 884,000; Chengtu (1948) 750,000; Tsinan (1948) 642,000; Chanchung (1940) 544,000; Taiyuan (Yangku, 1956) 500,000; Anshan (1953) 400,000.

During the year 1959 China continued to have two governments:

(1) THE COMMUNIST, formed in Peking on Oct. 1, 1949, with Mao Tse-tung as chairman of the Chinese Communist party; Liu Shao-chi as chairman of the people's republic; Marshal Chu Teh as chairman of the National People's congress and Chou En-lai as chairman of the state council (government)*. Monetary unit: *jenminpiao* or People's Bank dollar with an official exchange rate of PB$6·72 to the £ sterling.

(2) THE NATIONALIST, which in Dec. 1949 was moved to Taipei, Formosa (Taiwan). This large island is separated from China by the 90-mi. wide Straits of Formosa. Area: 13,885 sq.mi., including Pescadores (Penghu) and neighbouring islands. Pop.: (1953 census) 9,438,016, incl. *c.* 650,000 civilian refugees from the mainland; (1958 est.) 9,851,000. Chief towns (pop., 1956 census): Taipei (cap.) 748,510; Kaohsiung 371,225; Tainan 287,797; Taichung 249,946; Keelung 197,029. President of the republic, Generalissimo Chiang Kai-shek; premier, General Chen Cheng. Monetary unit: New Taiwan dollar with an exchange rate (1957) of NT$95·20 to the £1 sterling.

* By the end of 1959 the Communist government was recognized as that of China by the following 33 states: Afghanistan, Albania, Bulgaria, Burma, Cambodia, Ceylon, Czechoslovakia, Denmark, Finland, German Democratic Republic, Guinea, Hungary, India, Indonesia, Iraq, Israel, Korea (Northern), Laos, Mongolia, Nepal, the Netherlands, Norway, Pakistan, Poland, Rumania, Sudan, Sweden, Switzerland, United Arab Republic, United Kingdom, U.S.S.R., Vietnam (Northern) and Yugoslavia.

History. China entered 1959 in a mood of confident but grim sobriety. The high tide of effervescence had markedly diminished. The accounting at the meetings of the party leaders towards the end of 1958 had produced a lengthy and devastating resolution by the central committee in the Wuhan plenum exposing conditions in the communes, and calling for a drastic reorganization. Over-eager zealots and officials who became " dizzy with success and exhibited certain rude attitudes " towards the masses were severely criticized together with those guilty of " the evil of exaggeration about achievements ". The sharp contrast between loudly heralded claims of bumper crops and the iron rations and general shortages depressed everybody.

It was the rumour, which spread like wildfire through the capital, that the chairman of the people's republic Mao Tse-tung was stepping down from his post as head of the state that caused most commotion. Some of the older people in Peking reacted in the way common to their ancestors when some emperor died or a dynasty fell. It was made clear later, in party and other pronouncements, that though Mao had relinquished the post of chairman of the republic, he remained not only head of the party but the most potent personality in the regime. It was widely expected that Chu Teh, the vice-chairman, would succeed to the post and that Mao desired this, but the No. 2 party leader and its principal trainer and organizer, Liu Shao-chi (*see* BIOGRAPHIES), was appointed on April 28, while Marshal Chu Teh took his place as chairman of the National People's congress (N.P.C.).

With these exceptions, almost the entire government was reappointed under Chou En-lai, who had been head of the state council (government) ever since the people's government was formed in 1949. He was the natural leader of the administrators and planners responsible for the running of the government, and it was they who were said to have differed seriously with the methods whereby the ideologists practised their theories in the communes. The stability of the central government was thus once more confirmed and was all the more striking in view of the instability and constant purges and changes in the provincial regimes.

The Wuhan resolution (adopted by the Chinese Communist party on Dec. 10, 1958) revealed the manifold revolutions, right down to the old family system itself, represented by the communes, the disruption of plans threatened by the zealots, and the chaos created both in the communes and in the transport system, to which mass native industrialization was

also a contributor. The central committee declared that " the Communist system of distribution can be put into effect only when there is a great abundance of social products " and that " any attempt to enter Communism by over-reaching ourselves when conditions are not mature is undoubtedly a Utopian concept that cannot possibly succeed."

Communes in cities were deferred and an elaborate process of " tidying up " and consolidation in the communes ordered. Stress was laid on improvement in living and social conditions so that the peasants could have at least eight hours' sleep; the observance of democratic management of the communes despite the military system on which they were organized; and the necessity of obeying the unified policies of the state.

The mass movement for the mining and smelting of iron ore had caused small native-style furnaces to appear like mushrooms all over the countryside. They involved toil, time, energy, resources and manpower out of all proportion to the useful results. Not more than 52% of the output could be used for steel and costs were high, but Chou En-lai told the N.P.C. that in spite of this they answered the needs of the villages and it was an error to despise them. Thousands of the village furnaces were later demolished and larger furnaces concentrated in small numbers, with improved equipment and technique, in more appropriate centres nearest the sources of coal and ore, while simplified coal-washing equipment was mass produced to reduce the sulphur problem.

Five great multi-purpose schemes for harnessing the Yellow river were accelerated. Great plans were announced for developing internal waterways, including the building of numerous canals to link up the great rivers from the Amur in the far north to the Pearl river at Canton. Ambitious canal-building projects progressed in the loess country of the northwest, where a vast area of arid, treeless and waterless land was being transformed. Irrigation canals built 10 to 20 centuries ago, connected with the new Chingtung gorge project on the Yellow river at Ninghsia, were dredged and were watering about 500,000 ac. Navigation between Paotow and Yinchwan was to be possible for ships up to 500 tons.

After the severe and almost continuous " rectification " since June 1957, the intellectuals were again invited to bud in the spring, but they declined to blossom in view of the drastic consequences of former criticism. Vast numbers of books were published and the stage and screen and other cultural media multiplied. But in nearly all instances it was a matter of quantity, not of quality. It was revealed that many noted scholars and writers refused to write, and that even those who did venture to do so shrank back into their shells whenever criticized.

Three academic discussions in succession were held in Peking in May by the Chinese Society of Philosophy, at which problems of logic, the heritage of Chinese philosophy, the philosophy of Lao Tzu—" was he a materialist or an idealist? "—were debated as they used to be centuries ago, with this time Marxist philosophy as the party theorists' reward for permitting this indulgence in the past. In Shanghai all the intellectuals, in their various specialist circles, discussed topics of interest to them. The economists debated commodity production and the law of value in a socialist society; the historians, greatly daring, chose China's most famous villain of stage and statecraft, Tsao Tsao, and by the remarkable correspondence of his time and event with the present day, subtly and indirectly passed their judgment on the regime while discussing events nearly 2,000 years previously. Party ideologists hoped that the discussion on Tsao Tsao would not merely help in a less damning appraisal but would also help the intellectuals to understand the viewpoint of historical materialism and to uphold the Marxist contention that a character in history should be judged from the over-all viewpoint. There were some shrewd and topical thrusts but

(1) Like extras in a Cecil B. deMille production, thousands of Chinese coolies throng about the massive dam being constructed in 1958 as part of the Ming Tombs reservoir project near Peking. (2) A worker in a Shanghai textile printing and dyeing factory cutting material into lengths. The floral pattern shows that the emphasis is not wholly on utility and austerity. (3) At a rural iron works unskilled peasants are given some basic instruction in metallurgy. Much of the pig-iron produced at such works is too inferior for steelmaking. (4) Life in the new China as symbolized by an official artist on the occasion of the tenth anniversary of the Chinese People's Republic on Oct. 1. (5) A 72,500-kw. generator under construction at Harbin in north-east China. It is destined for a power station being built at Hsinnankiang in Chekiang province. The revised 1959 target for electricity production was 39,000 million kw.hr. (6) Rigorous conditions of communal life, admitted by the government, are not reflected in this scene from a commune in Chincheng, Shansi province.

it was asserted that a few academic workers who had refused to study Marxist theory would change their minds. The intellectuals remained a class apart, as always, and while there was decreasing zeal among the zealots, an increasing if silent insistence by the intellectuals on remaining themselves was obvious. Most of them refused to be inveigled from the cloistered life they led among the old classics, to which even the students more and more turned with relief and relish. Nevertheless the tale of a Communist family by Tao Chang (*My Family*) exceeded 1 million copies, while a dozen best-selling novels aggregated 6 million copies.

The principle of mingling manual with mental labour was rigorously continued, and manual work was graded for urban people and students from four days a week for children under nine to two to four months annually for college students.

The increasing preoccupation with the weather, which began when vast areas in north and northeast China suffered a lack of snowfall and spring rain, grew steadily with the constant threat of floods throughout the southern provinces and a persistent plague of locusts in the region along the Yellow river. Wheat was sown and reaped despite the drought, which was partially remedied by water from countless deep wells, but drought is invariably followed by excessive rain in China, and much wheat had just been cut or was still standing when the deluge began. Western China seemed to fare better, but in Kiangsi, Kwangtung and Kwangsi flooding was disastrous despite the maximum measures taken by the party and state officials in mobilizing millions of peasants to guard and raise the dykes, and succour the victims. The deluge in June (which brought 30 in. of rain to Hong Kong in five days) moved northward, flooding the countryside as it moved, so that the greater part of the country south of the Yangtze was seriously affected.

Along the Yangtze and Huai rivers drought followed the torrential rains. In mid-August Peking reported that Communist officials and 50 million peasants were fighting the worst drought in a decade, affecting ten provinces, while at the same time Peking and outskirts suffered severely from torrential rains.

The party press, in a reversal of normal policy, gave much the same banner headlines and constant coverage to the natural disasters as it had done in 1958 to bumper crops, together with appeals to farmers to replant at once and to the urban population to maintain solidarity and help to remedy the shortage of foodstuffs as a result of the floods and drought. Peking described the disaster around the capital as the worst for a century, and called for further mass effort throughout the country to conquer the difficulties and secure good autumn harvests.

At the same time Peking complained that " certain cadres on the economic front had lost ardour and lacked conviction ", and did not even try to overcome difficulties. The reference to this and other " rightist tendencies " was taken to indicate another rectification movement. It was also assumed to be one of the consequences of secret meetings of party leaders about which complete silence was maintained at the time, but which were reported to have debated the state of the communes, the U.S.-Soviet exchanges, about which Peking offered little comment, and the Laos situation. Some of the leaders also toured the communes, and the disaster areas to consider or enforce remedial measures.

National People's Congress. The first session of the second N.P.C. was opened on April 18 by Mao. The People's Political Consultative council, widely representative of bourgeois parties and other collaborating groups, met at the same time. N.P.C. deputies numbered 1,226, of whom 179 were from the national minorities and 150 were women. The P.P.C.C. comprised over 1,000 members. Three former " rightists ", dismissed as ministers (Lo Lung-chi, Chang Po-

chun and Chang Nai-chi), resumed their seats as deputies.

In his report Chou En-lai stressed " the gigantic and all-round leap forward ", the " ignominious defeat " of the Tibetan rebels and the decision to introduce social reforms there. He still hoped that the Dalai Lama " would be able to free himself from the hold of the rebels and return to the motherland ". China, he said, desired an area of peace free from atomic weapons throughout eastern Asia and the Pacific, but would not sit idly by while " Japanese militarism is being revived ", and China was determined to liberate Taiwan (Formosa) and bring about the withdrawal of all U.S. forces from the area.

Li Fu-chun, vice-premier and chairman of the State Planning commission, introduced " a grand and arduous national economic plan for 1959, which was expected to raise the total industrial and agricultural output by 40% compared with 1958. Aims were raised ambitiously. State investment was set at nearly PB$27,000 million, and about 3,700 mi. of new railways were to be built. Referring to the agreement signed by Chou in Moscow in February, he said China would continue to get help from the Soviet Union and other Communist states in the construction of projects.

Li Hsien-nien, vice-premier and minister of finance, reported to the N.P.C. that in 1958 both revenue and expenditure greatly exceeded the original estimates, with state revenue of about PB$40,300 million and a surplus of PB$800 million —" a victory gained in a year's hard battle by the people ". Revenue was up 26% and expenditure up 35% over 1957. Defence allocations totalled PB$4,770 million and repayment of foreign and domestic loans PB$1,140 million.

The budget estimates for 1959 provided for revenue at PB$50,000 million, with which expenditure balanced. The defence allocation would rise to PB$5,376 million.

The N.P.C. abolished the ministries of justice and supervision, appointed 14 vice-chairmen and 100 members of the Council of National Defence, with Liu Shao-chi as chairman, and passed a resolution that Tibet was an " inalienable part of China " and no foreign interference in China's internal affairs could be tolerated.

A Shortened Leap. Following a plenary session of the central committee of the C.C.P., held from Aug. 2 to 16 at Lushan (Kiangsi), a communiqué was issued on Aug. 26 containing an official and painful admission that production in 1958 was much lower than the aims fixed for that year. Considerable reductions in the major production aims for 1959 were announced at the same time. (*See* Table.)

CHINA'S INDUSTRIAL AND AGRICULTURAL PRODUCTION
(In metric tons; electricity in thousands of kwh.)

	1958		1959	
	First Claims	Revised Claims	April Aims	August Aims
Coal	270,000,000	270,000,000	380,000,000	335,000,000
Electricity	27,500,000	27,500,000	40,000,000	39,000,000
Steel	11,080,000	8,000,000*	18,000,000	12,000,000
Grain	375,000,000	250,000,000	525,000,000	275,000,000
Cotton, raw	3,350,000	2,100,000	5,200,000	2,300,000

* Excluding 3 million tons of " steel " produced in the countryside.

Changes in High Command. On Sept. 17 Peking announced that Marshal Lin Piao had succeeded Marshal Peng Teh-huai as defence minister and that General Lo Jui-cheng had been succeeded as minister of public security by General Hsieh Fu-chih. General Lo had been appointed chief of staff of the armed forces. There was much speculation about the significance of these changes, but no official explanation was vouchsafed, and it was likely that the causes were many and complex.

Marshal Lin Piao was commander-in-chief of the people's liberation army which conquered the whole of mainland China in 1948-49, but owing to a breakdown of health he was inactive for many years. His return to health and to official activity was indicated when, in 1958, he was appointed a member of the Politburo. Marshal Peng, whose fame was not enhanced by the failure of the Quemoy operation in 1958, remained a deputy prime minister.

U.S.S.R. and China. Nikita S. Khrushchev, the Soviet prime minister, carried the spotlight of international attention with him from Washington to Peking, where he arrived on Sept. 30 to attend the celebrations of the tenth anniversary of the people's republic. In three separate statements he emphasized the theme of coexistence and peace. It would be wrong, he said, for Communism to test the stability of capitalism by force. " The people would never understand and would never support those who took it into their heads to act in this way," he said. " We on our part must do everything possible to preclude war as a means for settling outstanding questions, which must be settled by negotiations." At the same time he hailed the economic achievements of the U.S.S.R. and China and insisted that the Communist way of life was " sure to win in any peaceful contest with the west."

Khrushchev was the chief guest at the anniversary parade, in which thousands of steel-helmeted men of the three armed services took part, together with troop-carriers and tanks, while overhead roared 45 jet bombers and 100 jet fighters—all made in China. In an order of the day the new defence minister declared: " We shall never invade anyone, nor shall we allow anyone to invade us." But he emphasized China's determination to " liberate " Formosa, with which no foreign power would be allowed to interfere.

Before attending the state banquet in Peking on Oct. 2, Khrushchev and Mao Tse-tung held conversations " in an atmosphere of cordiality and friendship "—as the official Peking news agency put it. Khrushchev was accompanied by A. A. Gromyko and M. A. Suslov (*see* BIOGRAPHIES), and Mao by Chou En-lai, Liu Shao-chi, and Marshals Chu Teh, Lin Piao and Chen Yi (foreign minister).

The absence of the usual joint communiqué encouraged an impression that the Soviet premier had failed to inspire Mao in any major move to relax international tensions. Khrushchev's final speech made no allusion to this, though he referred to Sino-Soviet friendship as " the invincible stronghold of peace ".

Formosa. The Chinese Communist forces opposite Quemoy and Matsu continued to observe the strange rules of one day off and one day on in their shelling, but this, with one retaliatory exception, was strictly limited. There was a virtual standstill there and in the Formosan straits. There was some concern about the economic position of the island, despite the U.S. aid, totalling over US$900 million since 1950. A 46,400-ton tanker was launched on March 6, costing US$75 million. The Tibetan revolt caused some excitement but the Nationalists were disappointed over the Tezpur statement on April 18 (*see* TIBET). The plenary session of the Kuomintang central executive committee on May 15 approved a political programme of 18 points for the return to the mainland. The decision of the International Olympic committee about Formosa's status was deplored as " a great and unjust blow ". Much discussion continued throughout the greater part of the year on the problem posed by the ending of President Chiang Kai-shek's second six-year term in May 1960. (*See* also HONG KONG; SINO-INDIAN FRONTIER DISPUTE.) (W. V. P.)

CHURCH OF ENGLAND: *see* ANGLICAN COMMUNION.
CHURCH OF SCOTLAND: *see* PRESBYTERIAN CHURCHES.
CIGARS AND CIGARETTES: *see* TOBACCO.

CINEMA. **Films of 1959.** As a welcome change from the trend towards fewer, bigger and worse motion pictures, the films of 1959 seemed more numerous and more varied. British cinema programmes also took on a more international air than for many years, owing partly to the increase of so-called " co-productions " and partly to the greater number of films coming from eastern European and Asian countries.

What might be called the film of the year came from France. Jacques Tati's comedy of electronic-age manners, *Mon Oncle*, reached London, laden with the Grand Prix from the 1958 Cannes festival, the New York Critics' award for the same year and a 1959 " Oscar " for the best foreign film. Writer, director and star of his films, Tati took his place beside Chaplin as a creator of international comedy, but he was less emphatically the clown and more concerned with the absurdity of the surrounding human scene. The charm of Tati's relaxed style was threatened only by the indiscipline of a free hand and the temptation to run on too long.

The official 1959 " Oscar " went to a Franco-U.S. co-production, *Gigi*, made into a musical by Alan Jay Lerner and Frederick Loewe. *Gigi* won " Oscars " for its director (V. Minnelli), for colour cinematography and seven more for music, writing and spectacle, including a thoroughly deserved one to Cecil Beaton for costume design.

Acting " Oscars " also honoured the Anglo-U.S. production *Separate Tables* which starred the Americans Rita Hayworth and Burt Lancaster, not quite in their element, and Deborah Kerr in a remarkable character performance. However, the " Oscars " for the best actor and best supporting actress were awarded to David Niven as the army officer and Wendy Hiller as the manageress of the hotel.

The " Oscar " for the best actress went to Susan Hayward for *I Want to Live*. This grim drama of a woman condemned to death for murder and unable to establish her innocence was widely held to be based on an actual case. In spite of the " X " certificate, an episode thought to be too gruesome was cut from the version shown in Britain. A real crime was the inspiration for *Compulsion*, a very taut retelling of the Leopold-Loeb " perfect murder " case. The leading players were Dean Stockwell and Bradford Dillman as the two young murderers and Orson Welles at his most striking as the defence lawyer who is strongly opposed to capital punishment. All three won " best actor " awards at Cannes.

A gratifying award was made at Cannes to the French actress Simone Signoret for her performance in *Room at the Top*, which many considered the best British film of the year. Adapted by Neil Paterson from John Braine's novel of life in a modern industrial town, it was directed by Jack Clayton and starred Laurence Harvey as the caddish young social climber. John Osborne's *Look Back in Anger* was directed for the screen by Tony Richardson, who had also been responsible for the extremely successful stage production at the Royal Court theatre. The transposition was skilfully made by Nigel Kneale, the writer of the screenplay, and the very strong cast benefited especially from the introduction of Claire Bloom as Helena, the " other woman ", and Dame Edith Evans as a character only talked about in the play. Richard Burton brought his strength and intelligence to the part of the aggressive Jimmy Porter.

For British films generally 1959 was a year of modest competence. Within this field one of the most satisfying films was *Tiger Bay*, directed by J. Lee-Thompson from a first-rate script by John Hawkesworth and Shelley Smith. This story of friendship between a small girl and the Polish seaman who kidnaps her was told with sympathy and suspense and outstandingly played by Hayley Mills as the child, John Mills (her father) and a German actor, Horst Buchholz, as the Pole. *Sapphire*, a conventional thriller directed by Basil Dearden, was distinguished both by its sympathetic approach to the colour problem—reflecting, however superficially, a contemporary preoccupation—and by the fine performance of many coloured players. For the rest, British films concentrated on comedy. The Boulting brothers made *Carlton-Browne of the F.O.*, but found it difficult to keep up an even quality in this satire on diplomacy, although Terry-Thomas was well cast in the title role. In *I'm All Right Jack*, they lashed out both at the trade unions and at the management side of industry. Another topical satire was *The Mouse that Roared*, exploiting a breach of relations between the United States and the smallest grand duchy in the world, controversy over the "Q-bomb" and the versatility of Peter Sellers, playing with considerable brilliance three parts—the grand duchess, her prime minister and the envoy to the United States. Decidedly crazy comedy, the film attempted too much, but had long passages of hilarity.

Alec Guinness's version of Joyce Cary's novel *The Horse's Mouth*, directed by Ronald Neame and with paintings by John Bratby, was certainly the most serious comedy of the year. Guinness's own performance as the rapscallion Gulley was a round character study in eccentricity, and the film was further enriched by remarkable performances by Renée Houston and Kay Walsh.

From Hollywood too came welcome signs of a return to comedy. *Houseboat* was a thoroughly amusing, characteristic example of a Cary Grant comedy. The film was notable for the splendidly spirited comedy performance of Sophia Loren. *Auntie Mame*, the wildest of U.S. nostalgic extravaganzas, showed off Rosalind Russell in her original stage part.

A Hole in the Head, starring Frank Sinatra, proved to be an authentic Capra comedy in the old master's best sentimental vein. *The Reluctant Debutante*, drastically adapted by William Douglas-Home from his own stage comedy about London society, made an agreeable trifle. It was directed by Vincente Minnelli and elegantly played by Rex Harrison and Kay Kendall (*see* OBITUARIES). *Ask any Girl* was another trifle made appealing by its delightfully quaint leading lady

Shirley MacLaine. Billy Wilder used his tough, sardonic talent in directing *Some Like it Hot*, a more robust, even coarse, style of comedy, complete with Marilyn Monroe and female impersonations by Tony Curtis and Jack Lemmon.

One Hollywood film which made a deep impression was *The Diary of Anne Frank*, directed by George Stevens. This was due principally to the original story of a young Jewish girl whose diary was found after she had died in a concentration camp. The film, in spite of being based on a play instead of on the actual diary, and casting Millie Perkins, a professional model without acting experience, as Anne Frank, stayed close enough to the real story to impress audiences unfamiliar with it. Rudolph Schildkraut was authentically moving as Anne Frank's father.

Another quasi-documentary film about a crime was the U.S. entry at the Venice festival, Otto Preminger's *Anatomy of a Murder*. This was not based on any known case but on a best-seller by a U.S. Supreme Court justice. It made a brilliant court-room melodrama, with James Stewart as the defence lawyer and Ben Gazzarra as the accused charged with murdering a bartender alleged to have raped his wife.

Fred Zinnemann made *The Nun's Story* into one of the outstanding films of the year largely through impeccable casting. Audrey Hepburn intelligently and poignantly expressed the stress of a young nun trying to make a religious vocation out of her nursing ambitions.

The Inn of the Sixth Happiness, based on the biography of Gladys Aylward, *The Small Woman*, tried to convey the courage and spirit of a woman who saved her wages as a servant in order to travel to China as a missionary, and then with great courage brought a band of children to safety under the noses of the Japanese. The casting of Ingrid Bergman—never less than robust—as "the small woman" was fatal, although she played with genuine warmth. Robert Donat's performance as the aging mandarin was beautifully

(*Top left*) *Jacques Tati in " Mon Oncle ", in which, with his own brand of inconsequential humour, he satirizes contemporary " gracious living ". (Top right) More hazards of the gracious life—from " Auntie Mame ", starring Rosalind Russell. (Bottom left) From " Ashes and Diamonds ", A. Wajda's film of postwar conflict in Poland. (Bottom right) David Niven, Gladys Cooper, Deborah Kerr, Rita Hayworth and Burt Lancaster in " Separate Tables ".*

tender and the more moving on account of the actor's own death soon after.

Foreign language films were much in evidence in 1959. The French representatives ranged from what amounted to a recording of the Comédie Française production of *Le Bourgeois Gentilhomme* to the work of the newest school of young French *cinéastes*. These carried off nearly all the awards at Cannes. The grand prix went to Marcel Camus' *Orfeu Negro*, which transplanted a variation of the Orpheus legend to Brazil and among the negroes at carnival time. The prize for the best direction went to François Truffaut's *Les Quatre Cent Coups*, a beautifully photographed, lyrical story of unhappy childhood. The International Critics' prize was awarded to Alain Resnais' *Hiroshima Mon Amour*, a love story of a French girl and a Japanese man told dually through their different backgrounds. The leading member of this quite vigorous new wave of French talent seemed to be Claude Chabrol. His second film, *Les Cousins* (shown in England before his first, *Le Beau Serge*), was a story of two cousins told in a complex mixture of counterpoint, decidedly brilliant in style and sombre in content. Another sensational success from this group was Louis Malle's *Les Amants*, a candidly erotic episode of illicit love. Most of these French productions were shown at the National Film theatre's third London Film festival, as was another Cannes prize-winner, Luis Bunuel's *Nazarin*, a brilliant, slightly mellower example of his ferocious anti-clericalism. The festival's gala premiere was devoted to *The World of Apu*, the third in Satyajit Ray's Indian trilogy and containing long passages of exquisite beauty and sensibility.

A striking manifestation of the impact of foreign language films in Britain was the sudden vogue for Swedish films and the thoroughness devoted to the work of Ingmar Bergman (*see* BIOGRAPHIES). The showing of *Wild Strawberries*, Bergman's biography of an aged professor (finely played by Victor Sjöström), seemed to set off a whole season of Bergman's films, of which the most interesting were *The Face* and *Journey into Autumn*. Seldom does the public have a chance to survey so large a range of a director's work.

Japanese film production continued to impress—in particular *Living*, which showed an elderly civil servant's discovery that he is dying of cancer. This unlikely subject was treated with beauty, compassion and gaiety. From Poland came a very good selection of films of which Andrzej Wajda's *Ashes and Diamonds* was the finest. Mellower and less savage than the same director's *Kanal*, this was a remarkable attempt to find a reconciliation between the embittered elements of postwar Poland. Equally inspired in its way was the Polish slapstick short film *Two Men and a Wardrobe*.

From Greece came *A Matter of Dignity*, an exceptionally fine drama of a family trying to save its face while under the threat of bankruptcy and of a daughter involved in deeper tragedy. This was another triumph in the series of films directed by Michael Cacoyannis, starring Ella Lambetti and exquisitely photographed by E. Walter Lassally.

Two pictures outside the normal categories made a considerable impact. In the U.S. film *The Savage Eye*, a narrative commentary, the autobiographical venom of a divorcee accompanied a candid camera tour of the blacker spots of Los Angeles. The British *We are the Lambeth Boys* was a sympathetic treatment by Karel Reisz of teddy boys.

At the end of the year France mourned the deaths of Gérard Philipe, leading film hero of the postwar years (*see* OBITUARIES), and of the talented actor Henri Vidal.

Postwar Survey. The record of the cinema from 1945 to 1960 was scrawled across a very wide screen. Like most widescreen images it was not easily held clearly in focus. In the United States, and to a considerable extent in Britain, economic considerations overshadowed the cinema of the 1950s, and it was the problems of holding fast to a shrinking audience rather than the inclinations of its artists which governed Hollywood's policies. In Europe the purest and most influential of the cinema's postwar movements, neo-realism, flourished and dwindled within the decade 1945-55. In the east and in eastern Europe new industries began to develop, while well-established film-producing countries for the first time saw their films making an impact on a world market. A decline in one sector was seen to be balanced by an advance in another. For the prewar film historian, the cinemas of the United States, Europe and the Soviet Union provided material enough. The postwar critic had to keep pace with a more rapidly changing screen.

Hollywood remained the symbolic capital of world film-making, the industrial focal point and the perennial " dream factory ". Although in ten years there was a sizeable decline in production (241 U.S. features released in the United States in 1958 against 366 in 1948), the U.S. product still dominated the screens of the English-speaking and much of the western world. But the old Hollywood of the great production empires belonged to the past. The " divorce decree " of 1948, when a Supreme Court ruling resulted in the separation of ownership of cinema chains from that of studios, made it less immediately imperative for the production centres to maintain a constant flow of films to the cinemas. Increasingly, the pattern became one of smaller, independent units, using the facilities of the major studios, and films were made in New York or overseas as well as in Hollywood itself. These transitions were in part a reaction to the sweeping changes in audience demand. The major discovery of the 1950s was that the cinema-going habit, so easily formed, could equally easily be broken.

During the last year of World War II cinema attendances stood at 85 million a week in the United States and 30 million in Britain. In 1946 the weekly figures were 90 million (a record only equalled in 1930) and 31·4 million. There was then a decline, at first a gradual one, but increasing rapidly with the early 1950s and the advance of television first as a challenge, then as a virtually unbeatable rival. By 1958 U.S. cinema attendances were estimated at something under 42 million a week and British were down to 14·5 million. In 12 years more than half the 1946 audience had melted away, won from the cinemas not only by television but by other leisure activities encouraged by rising living standards. Sociologists could conclude that it was in years of war or depression that the cinema of diversion and escape flourished most effortlessly. In any event, the mixture of caution and nervous daring that characterized much film production policy in the 1950s found its explanation largely in these audience statistics.

Before 1950, alarm bells of another kind had sounded. The un-American activities committee turned its attention to Hollywood in 1947, and the case of the " Hollywood Ten "— the writers, producers and directors cited for contempt of congress—had prolonged and significant repercussions. Shortly after the war, productions dealing with problems of rehabilitation (*The Best Years of Our Lives*), of the United States' racial minorities (*Crossfire*, *Intruder in the Dust*) and of crime and corruption (*Boomerang*, *The Asphalt Jungle*) suggested that Hollywood could set itself new standards of realism; but McCarthyism sent many talents into exile and imposed a conformism that went far beyond politics.

In any case, political pressures only accelerated a process which economic stress would rapidly have accomplished. In the economic crisis companies were inevitably less ready to take risks with controversial subjects. Instead, they risked changing the shape and dimensions of the screen itself. Just as Warner Brothers had turned to sound in the 1920s during a period of financial hazard, so 20th Century-Fox in 1953

Scenes from some noteworthy postwar films: (1) From the Indian " Aparajito ", directed by Satyajit Ray, a prize-winner at the 1957 Venice festival. (2) Victor Mature, Richard Burton and Jean Simmons in " The Robe ", Hollywood's first full-length production in CinemaScope (1953). (3) From " Rashomon ", the Japanese grand prix winner at the Venice festival of 1951, directed by Akira Kurosawa. (4) Carlo Battisti (left) as " Umberto D ", the penniless retired civil servant in Vittorio de Sica's intensely moving neo-realist film of 1952. (5) A tense scene from " Crossfire " (1948), a Hollywood film dealing with anti-semitism in the United States. (6) Orson Welles as Harry Lime in " The Third Man " (1949), Carol Reed's atmospheric film of corruption in occupied Vienna after World War II: one of the most memorable of British postwar films. (7) From Robert Bresson's starkly realistic film of a war-time escape, " Un condamné à mort s'est échappé " (1957).

gambled successfully on the wide screen with *The Robe*, the first CinemaScope feature. The anamorphic lens was in itself nothing new, having been devised by the French scientist Henri Chrétien as early as the 1920s, but no one had previously thought it worth abandoning the traditional 4 to 3 screen ratio for CinemaScope's 2·55 to 1. Once introduced, the revolution, although not total, was widespread. Within five years most of the world's major industries were making a proportion of their pictures in one of the many wide-screen processes, ranging from the triple screen of Cinerama to the 1·85 to 1 ratio of VistaVision. Film-makers and critics who at first resisted the innovation—" the next time I write a poem ", Jean Cocteau said contemptuously, " I'll use a big sheet of paper "—became acclimatized or even enthusiastic. The wide screen, the increased use of colour, the stereophonic sound track —all were assimilated into the cinema's routine equipment.

It was the outsize productions, the so-called Hollywood " blockbusters " of the late 1950s, however, that essentially imposed a new pattern of film-making. Costing anything up to $15 million to make, films such as *The Ten Commandments* and *Ben Hur*, *Around the World in 80 Days* and *Giant*, had to be seen by enormous audiences to make them economic propositions. The producers rightly recognized that the modern audience, turning to television for its routine entertainment, could easily be persuaded into the cinemas by anything sufficiently big, spectacular or unusual. At the same time, fully aware that the under-20s made up the most loyal section of its public, Hollywood launched into an onslaught of horror and science fiction, musicals exploiting the rock 'n' roll fashion and analyses of the problems of blue-jeaned youth in its rebellion against authority. From *Rebel Without a Cause*, and the extravagant appropriation of James Dean as the symbol of his generation, to *I Was a Teenage Frankenstein*, the progression appeared inexorable.

Something of this Hollywood pattern repeated itself in other western countries. The British cinema, with a parallel decline in attendance figures, with cinemas closing (from 4,597 in 1951 to 3,721 in 1959) and with the additional burden of entertainments tax, received some measure of government aid. The main instrument of this was the National Film Finance corporation, founded in 1948 to act as a film bank, advancing loans to independent producers and so keeping alive an important sector of the production industry. Britain's particular problem was that, lacking anything comparable to the enormous U.S. home market, its industry could not afford to compete with the most expensive and profitable types of film except (as in the case of *The Bridge on the River Kwai*) through Anglo-U.S. collaboration. The world reputation of the British feature cinema, at its highest in the postwar years of *Great Expectations*, *Kind Hearts and Coronets* and *The Third Man*, was sustained at a lower level in the 1950s by such classical productions as Sir Laurence Olivier's *Richard III*, by a whole string of performances from Sir Alec Guinness and by some surviving comedies in the Ealing tradition. But Ealing studios were lost to the cinema in 1955, the site being absorbed, almost symbolically, into the expanding television industry. In 1959 the essentially contemporary toughness of *Look Back in Anger* (from John Osborne's play) and *Room at the Top* (from John Braine's novel) signalled the arrival of a new generation.

The truculent mood of 1959, so accurately reflected in these and other films, was a long distance from the atmosphere of 1945; and no movement in the cinema did more to define the sensations of the early postwar years than that which originated in Italy and became known as neo-realism. Luchino Visconti's *Ossessione* (1942) had been its standard-bearer; Roberto Rossellini's *Open City* (1945) and Vittorio de Sica's *Bicycle Thieves* (1948) established the neo-realist image in the public mind. De Sica and his scriptwriter and theorist Cesare Zavattini in *Umberto D* (1951), and Visconti in *La Terra Trema* (1948), explored the characteristic neo-realist themes of loneliness, neglect and economic insecurity, with the clearest sense of where the boundary between the " real " and the " dramatized " might be laid down. Neo-realism was the Italian cinema's response to a liberation which gave artistic freedom while leaving the economic problems and the question of the individual's place in society without a solution. It was a cinema of conscience, and its films looked at life with a resolution which excited cinema enthusiasts all over the world, although the mass popular audience in Italy was left largely unmoved. The neo-realist directors found it more difficult to finance their projects, and the Cinecittà studios in Rome became a fashionable centre for lavish Hollywood productions, increasing the cost of film-making. More significantly, the driving force itself weakened. Elements of self-pity, or a view of the poor as picturesquely victimized, crept into the films. The Italian cinema of these years influenced film-makers everywhere, but by the mid-50s critics had begun to speculate about the possible successors to neo-realism.

By this time, the horizons of world cinema stretched altogether more widely. Partly because the cutting back of Hollywood production left the commercial cinemas with some shortage of material, partly because of the world-wide extension of the film society and film archive movements, films made outside western Europe and the United States had become a great deal more accessible. Japan had always possessed a major cinema industry, expanding between 1948-57 from a production of 123 to well over 400 features a year, but it was not until Akira Kurosawa's *Rashomon* won the Venice Festival grand prix in 1951 that Europe seriously took note of a cinema so remote from its own traditions. Japanese films filtered slowly westwards, enough being seen to indicate the extreme richness of a cinema whose first triumph had seemed to some sceptical western critics merely a victory for oriental exoticism. Similarly, it was at European festivals that the west first encountered a major talent from another important eastern industry, when Satyajit Ray's *Pather Panchali* revealed this young director as the poet of the Indian cinema. With the Soviet cinema breaking loose from Stalinist disciplines, with the Polish Andrzej Wajda emerging as spokesman of his own war-torn generation, and with the appearance of a young Hungarian film school at much the same time as the 1956 October rising, the cinemas of the eastern bloc seemed to have shaken off the authoritarian restrictions which determined their postwar policies. Finally, from Sweden came the most fashionable of all directors of the late 1950s, Ingmar Bergman (*see* BIOGRAPHIES). Film periodicals gave up issues to analyses of his work, testifying to the hold on the world's imagination of an artist whose films (*The Seventh Seal*, *The Face*) revealed him as uniquely preoccupied with the conflict between belief and doubt.

The cinema of the 1950s inevitably reflected the societies that produced it, the tensions of ten uneasy years. In many countries there were also specifically economic problems to be faced, arising to a considerable extent from the increased costs of production. One European solution was co-production on a large scale, most frequently between French and Italian companies, sometimes involving more exotic partnerships. In 1957, for instance, 61 out of a total of 142 French features were made as co-productions. The method was strongly criticized by some French film-makers, who argued that national characteristics were surrendered to economic expediency and a hybrid internationalism. Yet the French cinema preserved its individualist traditions and reputation through the two most significant among its specifically postwar talents: Jacques Tati (*Jour de Fête*, *Mon Oncle*) and Robert Bresson (*Journal d'un Curé de Campagne*, *Un Condamné à Mort s'est Echappé*). Respectively an exuberant comedian and a brilliant film-maker of the most austere severity, they were alike in their unswerving determination to make their own films in their own way.

At the end of the 1950s this determination seemed to be spreading among young film-makers. The documentarists of the Free Cinema movement in Britain, essentially concerned with the everyday world, the " beat generation " explorers of the unconscious in the United States and the young French school with its romantic nihilism had little in common beyond their conviction that the need was for a more individual approach to cinema. These film-makers were in revolt against the past and against a cinema which seemed to have become impersonal and over-industrialized. The danger was that the breach might widen between the mass-medium cinema and the films made by enthusiasts largely for other enthusiasts. The hope was that from these young artists might come a cinema with a greater freedom to interpret the world. What seemed certain in 1959 was that the cinema, having survived the worst of its crises, was in considerably better health than had seemed at all probable five years earlier.

Economic and Organizational Developments. There was an indication in 1959 that the catastrophic decline in cinema attendances in Great Britain was nearly over and that the stabilization point might soon be reached. This point had been variously estimated at from 600 million to 625 million attendances a year—a weekly average of between 11·5 and 12 million. In the last two quarters of 1958 attendances averaged 15·2 million and 12·6 million a week respectively, giving an annual average of 14·5 million—18% below the 1957 figure. This meant that in two years the British cinema had lost about one-third of its already contracting home audience. In the first two quarters of 1959 the attendance figure fell from 12·5 million to 11·8 million a week, and although there was a seasonal drop in the third quarter, it seemed as if the worst might be over.

Concomitant with the decline in attendances was the closure of cinemas. Official figures published in 1959 showed that the total number of cinemas closed each year from 1954 to 1957 were 72, 93, 224 and 216 respectively. For the year 1958 the provisional figure was 261, making a total of 866 closures in five years. On June 30, 1959, there were 3,721 cinemas open in Great Britain.

Because of the difficulties which the cinema was experiencing there was great disappointment when the chancellor of the exchequer failed to make any reduction in entertainments tax in his April budget. Two months later, however, during the debate on the Finance bill, he announced that he proposed to make a change after all. Entertainments tax, which was then running at 13·5% of gross box-office takings, would be reduced by a quarter. In his speech the chancellor stated that the industry was undergoing difficulties arising from other amenities, but that was not an automatic reason for relieving its patrons entirely from taxation. The growth of television was the biggest single factor. It would be unrealistic to suppose that this change in social habits would be reversed by the abolition of entertainments duty. He further declared that the closing of cinemas to date was inevitable and whatever was done more had to close. The one aspect which gave him particular concern was that of the small rural cinemas and cinemas serving small market towns. Many were having difficulty in staying open, and the social implications here were more serious than in large towns.

During the year the policy of " rationalization " was continued. There were many examples of this both in the U.S. and British industries. The major U.S. company Warner Brothers, which had long had a powerful interest in one of the main groups in the British industry, Associated British Picture corporation, joined with A.B.P.C.'s distribution subsidiary, Associated-British Pathé, to form a new company,

Warner Pathé distributors, which handled films from A.B.P.C.'s Elstree studio and Warners' Burbank studio.

Everywhere the tendency was to cut down expenses and amalgamate operations wherever possible. In Britain rationalization made a change in the pattern of the main exhibiting circuits. Previously there had been three main circuits—the Odeon and Gaumont circuits owned by the Rank organization and the A.B.C. circuit owned by A.B.P.C. Then there grew up, for various reasons, an informally organized " fourth circuit ". In Oct. 1958, the Rank organization announced that it proposed to close a number of cinemas and to amalgamate its two circuits into one of about 300 cinemas (*see* article CINEMA in *Britannica Book of the Year 1959*). This it did. The A.B.C. remained the second circuit, and the so-called " fourth circuit " became known as the third circuit. Although it had no centralized booking arrangement, the latter was none the less an operative " main " circuit. It consisted of the important Granada cinemas, some of the large Essoldo group and other cinemas from various of the larger cinema-owning companies.

It had been felt in some quarters that the export of British films, which had been showing a sustained improvement over a period, would be considerably aided by the shortage of U.S. products resulting from Hollywood's concentration on making films for television rather than for the cinema. The time seemed ripe once again for an all-out attack on the U.S. market, which was still large enough to be extremely profitable to British producers if they could establish themselves on a sufficiently broad base. The Rank organization—as it had done once before—took up the challenge. The result was announced in Lord Rank's annual statement in Sept. 1959. He said that the group's efforts to operate a system for distributing its films in the United States had had to be abandoned.

With so much gloom to report in the cinema's affairs it is only fair to redress the balance by stating that 1959 showed that the industry was far from dead. A good film, cleverly publicized and intelligently distributed, still made a handsome profit. What was dead was the old, ritualistic cinema-going habit. (F. B. Lt.; A. P. H.; D. Cw.)

BIBLIOGRAPHY. J. L. Anderson and D. Richie, *The Japanese Film: Art and Industry* (Vermont, 1959); R. Griffith and A. Mayer, *The Movies* (New York, 1957); Arthur Knight, *The Liveliest Art* (New York, 1957); Jay Leyda, *Kino* (London, 1959); Political and Economic Planning, *The British Film Industry* (London, 1952, with a supplement published in 1958); P. Rotha and R. Griffith, *The Film Till Now* (London, 1949).

CIVIL AVIATION: *see* AVIATION, CIVIL.

CIVIL DEFENCE.

In its white paper *Progress of the Five Year Defence Plan* (Cmnd. 662) the government reaffirmed the policy of maintaining the role of civil defence and the regional and local framework. Operational planning was further developed, particularly as regards the settlement of boundaries down to the lower levels of control. Essential communications were strengthened. The rescue and warden sections of the Civil Defence corps were reorganized to improve their operational effectiveness. More protected accommodation was constructed for the warning and monitoring organization. Further supplies of radiac instruments were added to the stockpile. Advice was issued to industry about fire precautions in war and the advance preparations required. The prospective end of compulsory national service made it necessary to disband the Mobile Defence corps, but the territorial army began more specialized training in civil defence.

Training of volunteers, instructors and officers continued in full swing at the local authorities' training centres and at Home Office establishments—the Staff college, the three Civil

Defence schools, the Air-Raid Warning school and the two Fire Service training centres; the latter, having ceased to train national servicemen in fire-fighting at the end of 1958, were extensively used for training regular and auxiliary firemen in the use of emergency fire-fighting equipment. Frequent exercises were held; some were on a very large scale, including a warning and monitoring exercise in which units at widely separated centres took part. In training and exercises generally, special attention was given to radiological hazards. The first national competition for units of the Civil Defence corps and the Industrial Civil Defence service was held; Queen Elizabeth the Queen Mother presented the trophy to Bristol, the winning team. The Duke of Gloucester attended a tourney held by the North-West region at Manchester in which 2,000 volunteers took part; the Women's Voluntary Service for Civil Defence celebrated its 21st anniversary.

On Oct. 31, 1959, the strength of the Civil Defence corps in England, Scotland and Wales stood at 379,014, and that of the Auxiliary Fire service at about 19,000. The industrial Civil Defence service numbered about 195,000.

Information on civil defence planning, training and organization was exchanged between the United Kingdom and other Commonwealth countries, in several of which well-established civil defence organizations continued to make steady progress.   (S. C. Kn.)

Civil service typists who took part in a march from Whitehall to the Treasury on Aug. 6 in protest against proposed pay cuts.

A demonstration of emergency cooking on an oven built from debris, staged by civil defence workers outside St. Paul's cathedral.

CIVIL SERVICE.   Civil Service Pay Research Unit.

The Royal Commission on the Civil Service recommended in 1955 that the pay of civil servants should be determined by fair comparison with the current remuneration of persons outside the civil service engaged on comparable work, account being taken of other conditions of service, and that the necessary facts about pay and conditions in outside employment should be collected by a body not concerned with the negotiations of pay claims. The Pay Research unit set up for this purpose produced a number of reports during 1959, which were the subject of negotiation during the year, including those on six executive and three administrative grades, on the technical class, on typists, messengers and cleaners. Negotiations on the clerical class report of 1958

resulted in a reference to the Civil Service Arbitration tribunal in Feb. 1959. Up to Sept. 1959 the pay of about three-quarters of the non-industrial civil service had come under review on the basis of pay research reports.

Advisory Committee on the Pay of the Higher Civil Service. The royal commission recommended that an advisory committee should be set up to exercise a general oversight of the remuneration of the higher civil service; *i.e.*, staff above the level of principal and equivalent grades. This committee, set up under the chairmanship of Lord Coleraine in 1957, undertook in the second half of 1958 the first general review of higher civil service pay since that carried out by the royal commission itself. It reported to the prime minister in Jan. 1959. Its recommendations for increases ranging from approximately 10% to 20% in higher civil service pay, with effect from Feb. 1, 1959, were accepted and implemented, the rate for the permanent secretary of a major government department in London becoming £7,000 per annum. The higher rates among those with which the committee were concerned had not been increased since April 1, 1956.

Civil Service Recruitment. In order to widen the field from which civil servants are recruited the upper age limit for the executive class competition was raised from 19·5 years to 24 years. For the clerical class it was raised from 18 to 20 except in certain areas of shortage where there was recruitment at any age between 16 and 60.

Civil Service Numbers. On Oct. 1, 1959, there were 638,299 non-industrial civil servants, as compared with 632,316 a year previously.   (N. C. B.)

See (all published London, 1959) Brian Chapman, *The Profession of Government*; Charles Dixon, *The Civil Service*; Charles H. Sisson, *The Spirit of British Administration*.

CLASSICAL STUDIES.

The third international congress of classical studies was held in London from Aug. 31 to Sept. 5, 1959, and was attended by over 600 delegates, half of whom came from overseas. The centenaries of R. Bentley and A. E. Housman were celebrated by exhibitions at the congress. In April the Classical association held its annual four-day meeting at Hull, where the presidential address was given by Sir Cyril Hinshelwood, president of the Royal Society. This address, "Classics among the intellectual disciplines", was later used as the basic paper for discussion by the International Council for Philosophy and Humanistic Studies at its meeting at Ann Arbor, Michigan.

The year 1959 was made memorable by the publication of

a newly discovered play of Menander, the *Dyskolos* (" Misanthrope "). The papyrus was edited by Victor Martin of Geneva and published with full photographs of the text and translations by the Bodmer library (Cologny-Geneva). Copies became generally available in March. The text is carelessly written and raises many problems of correction. Emendations have already been published in the *Bulletin of the Institute of Classical Studies*, *VI* (London) by E. G. Turner (ed.), T. B. L. Webster, E. W. Handley and others, and by H. Lloyd-Jones and others at Oxford in the *Classical Review*, *LXXIII* (n.s.*IX*), 2. During the year the play was broadcast in the B.B.C. Third programme.

A whole number of *Athenaeum* (Pavia) was devoted to papers read at the 2nd international colloquium of Minoan-Mycenaean studies (see *Britannica Books of the Year*, *1953-59*) and several sessions at the international congress in London were also devoted to these problems. The Olive Oil tablets of Pylos were published by E. L. Bennett in a supplement to *Minos* (Salamanca) and text from the palace of Nestor excavations of 1957 by C. W. Blegen and Mabel Lang in *American Journal of Archaeology*, 62 (Princeton). The personal names were treated by O. Landau in *Studia graeca et latina Gotoburgensia*.

The deaths of A. W. Gomme, J. A. K. Thompson, N. W. DeWitt, Kathleen Freeman, J. J. R. Bridge, F. J. Kinchin Smith and W. B. Anderson (*see* OBITUARIES) were a great loss to classical studies.   (L. J. D. R.)

Important books of 1959 (or late 1958) included: (from Oxford) E. Löfstedt, *Roman Literary Portraits* (trans. P. M. Fraser); N. G. L. Hammond, *History of Greece*; L. A. Moritz, *Grain-Mills and Flour in Classical Antiquity*; R. Storrs, *Ad Pyrrham*; W. V. Clausen, *Persius and Juvenal*; (from Cambridge) M. L. Clarke, *Classical Education in Britain, 1500-1900*; A. G. Woodhead, *Greek Inscriptions*; (published in London) G. Luck, *Latin Love Elegy*; E. C. Woodcock, *New Latin Syntax*; Gisela Richter, *Handbook of Greek Art*; S. Sambursky, *Physics of the Stoics*. The following are also of note: A. C. Moorhouse, *Studies in the Greek Negatives* (Cardiff); R. E. Smith, *Service in the Post-Marian Roman Army* (Manchester); S. M. Adams, *Sophocles the Playwright* (Toronto); G. M. Kirkwood, *A Study of Sophoclean Drama* (Cornell); C. H. Whitman, *Homer and the Heroic Tradition* (Harvard); J. C. Kamerbeek, *Trachiniae* (Leiden); and W. Lenz, *Tibullus* (Leiden). Further volumes completed the Chicago translation of Euripides, A. S. Pease's *De Natura Deorum* of Cicero (Harvard) and J. M. Edmonds' *Fragments of Attic Comedy* (Leiden). E. V. Rieu translated the *Argonautica* of Apollonius for Penguin books (Harmondsworth).

CLOTHING INDUSTRY: *see* BUSINESS REVIEW.

COAL. The end of 1958 followed the expected pattern with the National Coal board's stocks of coal reaching nearly 20 million tons (about 11 million tons more than at the end of 1957), despite a reduction in output of nearly 8 million tons for the full year. The main reasons for the reduction in demand were given as increased fuel efficiency, increased use of fuel oil, lower industrial production and loss of exports. The number of men employed was 22,600 fewer than at the start of 1958 and productivity was the highest ever recorded. The financial result for 1958 was a loss of £3·5 million, a better figure than had been forecast.

Staffing, Labour and Recruitment. It was announced in Jan. 1959 that clerical staff would be reduced by 2,500 resulting in an annual saving of £2 million. Two results of the changes in the fuel economy of the country were the appointment by the National Coal board of fuel technologist-salesmen to work in the marketing department and the creation of a new department for process development under J. Bronowski. At the same time an advisory committee was set up by the minister of power to study the processing of coal and its use as a chemical rather than a solid fuel. The recruitment of adult labour had been halted in 1958 and this policy was continued. The greatest difficulty was to find places for the men rendered redundant by closing 36 collieries,

TABLE I. WORLD PRODUCTION OF COAL*
(Million metric tons)

	1954	1955	1956	1957	1958
WORLD	1,473·63	1,593·30	1,681·92	1,728·40	2,081·80†
U.S.S.R.	243·68	276·64	303·95	328·44	496·80‡
United States	379·15	442·41	477·09	467·60	385·03
China	79·93	93·60	105·92	123·90	270·00‡
Great Britain	227·69	225·18	225·57	227·22	219·26
German Fed. Rep.	129·07	131·81	135·62	134·38	132·58
Poland	91·62	94·48	95·15	94·10	94·98
France	54·41	55·34	55·13	56·80	57·72
Japan	42·72	42·42	46·56	52·26	49·81
India	37·47	38·84	39·91	44·20	46·07
South Africa	29·32	32·15	33·60	34·77	37·08
Belgium	29·25	29·92	29·46	29·09	27·06
Czechoslovakia	21·61	22·14	23·41	24·18	25·81
Australia	20·08	19·58	19·58	20·13	20·66
Saar	16·82	17·33	17·09	16·46	16·43
Spain	12·40	12·43	12·85	13·93	14·44
Netherlands	12·07	11·90	11·84	11·38	11·88
Canada	11·61	11·36	11·41	9·93	8·54
Turkey	3·69	3·50	3·72	3·97	4·07
Southern Rhodesia	2·75	3·32	3·55	3·85	3·54
Formosa (Taiwan)	2·11	2·36	2·53	2·92	3·18
Korea, South	0·89	1·31	1·82	2·44	2·67
Hungary	2·44	2·69	2·37	2·28	2·63
German Dem. Rep.	2·65	2·68	2·74	2·75	2·50
Brazil	2·06	2·27	2·23	2·12	...
Chile	2·03	2·06	2·28	2·10	...
Colombia	1·50	1·80	1·90	...	...
Mexico	1·31	1·34	1·41	1·42	1·48
Yugoslavia	0·99	1·13	1·23	1·23	1·21

* Only countries with a yearly production exceeding 1 million tons of anthracite and bituminous coal are specified.   † Incl. coal equivalent of brown coal and lignite.   ‡ Incl. lignite.
SOURCE. U.N. *Statistical Yearbook 1958*; U.N. *Monthly Bulletin of Statistics*.

TABLE II. WORLD PRODUCTION OF LIGNITE*
(Million metric tons)

	1954	1955	1956	1957	1958
WORLD	496·40	537·60	567·50	595·00	...
German Dem. Rep.	181·91	200·61	205·87	212·60	214·97
U.S.S.R.	103·43	114·62	125·23	134·92	...
German Fed. Rep.†	87·93	90·48	95·36	97·15	93·49
Czechoslovakia	37·86	40·75	46·30	51·02	56·83
Hungary	19·10	19·62	18·22	18·92	21·61
Yugoslavia	12·68	14·07	15·87	16·78	17·88
Bulgaria	8·63	9·76	10·45	11·50	12·35
Australia	9·48	10·27	10·73	10·91	11·83
Poland	5·91	6·05	6·18	5·95	7·54
Austria	6·29	6·62	6·73	6·88	6·49
Spain	1·76	1·83	1·94	2·52	2·65
France	1·91	2·05	2·25	2·29	2·32
United States	2·58	2·87	2·61	2·37	2·21
Canada	1·92	2·08	2·12	2·04	2·04
New Zealand	1·81	1·80	1·86	1·81	1·88
Turkey‡	1·09	1·19	1·32	1·73	1·74
Japan	1·44	1·37	1·55	1·66	1·58

* Only countries with a yearly production exceeding 1 million tons of lignite or brown coal are specified. The thermal equivalent of lignite, expressed in tons of lignite per ton of coal, is approximately as follows: German Dem. Rep. 4·5, Czechoslovakia 1·7, other countries 3. † Excl. *pechkohle* (production between 1 and 2 million tons yearly). ‡ State-owned mines only (about 80% of total production).
SOURCE. U.N. *Statistical Yearbook 1958*; U.N. *Monthly Bulletin of Statistics*.

TABLE III. MANPOWER AND PRODUCTIVITY IN BRITISH COALMINES

	Total deep-mined output (million tons)	Total manpower	Over-all output (tons per manshift)
1955	210·2	704,000	1·225
1956	209·9	703,000	1·232
1957	210·1	710,000	1·231
1958	201·5	698,800	1·264
1959*	165·3	669,100	1·326

* First 44 weeks.
SOURCE. Ministry of Power weekly statistics.

TABLE IV. COAL OUTPUT PER MANSHIFT (metric tons)

	Underground		Over-all	
	June 1958	June 1959	June 1958	June 1959
Belgium	1·167	1·255	0·846	0·998
France	1·710	1·725	1·146	1·159
German Fed. Rep.				
(Saar)	1·805	1·853	1·165	1·244
(other)	1·644	1·885	1·268	1·455
United Kingdom	1·638	1·720	1·283	1·352

SOURCE. O.E.E.C. Coal committee.

mainly in Wales and Scotland. These closures brought objections from all areas, with parliamentary lobbying and mass demonstrations in January when some mines were closed. Benefits were offered to men who were willing to leave their own areas to work in the newer coalfields. Early in the year the National Union of Mineworkers asked the National Coal board for a shorter working week of 35 hours and an extra week's holiday per year without reduction in wages. This claim was rejected as it would have cost £70 million per year which the industry could not afford.

Wages, Output and Prices. There were no major changes in national wage agreements during 1959, but earnings were lower in the industry due to the operation of the five-day week and the general slackening in production. There were also no changes in prices for inland consumption apart from an extension of the period when the cheaper summer prices operated. Bunker coal prices were reduced by 10s.-20s. per ton in an effort to encourage sales. Coal exports were running at approximately 80% of the 1958 average. The over-all coal stocks position was somewhat alleviated early in the year, but by April they had begun to accumulate until at the end of October there were some 35 million tons held by the National Coal board and 16 million tons by large consumers. This was partly due to the large amount of small sizes produced, and during the year the board continued its efforts to encourage increases in the percentage of large coal mined. The N.U.M. suggested the complete winding up of open-cast production but the board refused in view of the high cost of breaking contracts, the profitability of the method and the large sizes of coal produced. Government assistance was sought in

restricting conversion to fuel oil but little success was forthcoming except that two power stations were to continue coal firing for a further 12 months. A new revision of the plan for coal was published in October. It was announced that 240 pits would be closed before 1965 and that annual production would be between 200 and 215 million tons and not 240 as was estimated in 1956. The process would be one of concentration, with the outputs of the North-Eastern and East Midlands divisions expected to rise.

Technical Progress. This was affected in many ways by the new " contraction economy " of the industry. Two new collieries in Scotland and two in south Wales had their development postponed, while the mechanization drive was now aimed at efficiency rather than bulk production (as was indicated at the annual conference of colliery managers at Harrogate in July). Another casualty in the economy campaign was the Mechanization centre at Sheffield. This was closed in the autumn as it was felt that the new area central workshops could undertake its functions at a much lower cost. Several tunnelling records were achieved at Agecroft, Lancashire, where 105 yd. were driven and completed in seven days, and in south Wales, while a new British shaft-sinking record of 90 yd. in four weeks was set up at Parkside colliery, Lancashire. Research on tunnelling and shaft sinking continued at the N.C.B. research stations at Isleworth, Middlesex, and Bretby, Derbyshire. Shaft sinking was started at a new £10·5 million colliery at Kellingley, Yorkshire, and sinking continued at Wolstanton, Staffordshire. Shafts were completed at Cotgrave, Nottinghamshire, and at Agecroft. It was announced that Thorne colliery, Yorkshire, which had been

One of the vast coal dumps in the Buxton, Derbyshire, area. After tipping, the lorry loads are levelled by a bulldozer in preparation for further deliveries. Undistributed stocks throughout the country amounted to about 20 million tons in March, when this picture was taken.

closed since 1957 for shaft repairs, would not re-open until 1962. The first large-scale coal-mining trolley locomotive system in Britain was put into service at Silverwood colliery, Yorkshire, during the year. The progress in mechanization was indicated by a remarkable exhibition of mining machinery held by British manufacturers in London in July. The wide range of equipment on view showed the great progress made in this field over the previous ten years. The gasification project at Newman Spinney, near Chesterfield, Derbyshire, was scheduled to be discontinued owing to lack of success after many years' work. Thus far only small-scale utilization had been obtained.

Safety. Falls of roof and sides continued to be the principal cause of fatal accidents underground and scarcely a week passed without a death from this source. Such accidents do not normally involve public inquiries, but the very serious fire at Aucheingeich colliery, Lanarkshire, where 47 men were killed, and the explosion at Walton colliery, Yorkshire, where five men were killed, did receive great publicity in the press. Two further explosions in Yorkshire collieries resulted in the death of two men at Hemsworth collieries and three men at St. John's colliery. Another explosion at Bockershaw colliery caused the death of five miners engaged in sealing-off operations following a heating. The year generally, however, was a good one from the safety aspect and steady progress was made.

It was announced in parliament that the National Coal board had paid out £100,000 in compensation for damage due to surface subsidence since nationalization.

Commonwealth. In Canada the coal industry was in very reduced circumstances, the 1958 production being the lowest since 1911 and some 1·75 million tons less than in 1957. Most of the decrease was in the bituminous fields of Alberta and British Columbia. Owing to discontinuous working, productivity was also reduced during 1958. The general decline of the Alberta coalfields was due to incursions by oil and natural gas. A ray of hope was the re-opening of the market in Japan which could assist these western coalfields. The Indian coal industry had a relatively successful year in 1958 but, even so, the increase in output of 4% was much less than the previous year. The main difficulty was in importing machinery. In New Zealand the coal industry was awaiting the development of a local steel industry and during the year announcements regarding the development of the titanium-iron beach sand raised hopes in this direction. The Australian coal industry had a good year with increased production of bituminous and brown coal. The export trade was revived and increased efficiency and mechanization enabled the over-all output per manshift to be increased to over four tons. The African coalfields continued to develop slowly and there was an increase in production of over 2 million tons for the whole continent during 1958, mostly from South Africa. (*See also* EUROPEAN COAL AND STEEL COMMUNITY.) (J. T. W.)

BIBLIOGRAPHY. E. J. Pryor, *Economics for the Mining Engineer* (London, 1958); A. Nelson, *Methods of Working* (Wigan, 1958); D. Le Jeune, *Mining Machinery and Transport* (London, 1959); *Second Symposium on Coal Preparation* (Leeds, 1959); *European Congress on Ground Movement* (Leeds, 1959).

COCOA: *see* FOODSTUFFS.
COFFEE: *see* FOODSTUFFS.

COLOMBIA. Republic in northwestern South America adjoining the isthmus of Panama. Colombia is the only South American country with both Caribbean and Pacific coast lines. Area: 439,512 sq.mi. Pop.: (1951 census) 11,548,172; (1959 est.) 13,823,600. About 58% of the population is classified as mixed blood, 35% as white, 2% as Indian and 5% as Negro. Language: Spanish. Religion: predominantly Roman Catholic. Chief towns (metropolitan area, pop., 1959 est.): Bogotá (cap.) 1,124,770; Medellín 578,940; Cali 545,410; Barranquilla 411,330; Bucaramanga 184,680; Cartagena 167,980;

Manizales 161,000; Ibagué 133,380; Cúcuta 131,410. President, Alberto Lleras Camargo. Main imports: machinery and manufactured goods. Main exports: coffee (83%), petroleum (13%). Monetary unit: *peso* with a free market rate of 22·60 to the £ sterling (July 1959).

History. Under the National Front government headed by Lleras Camargo the internal situation of Colombia continued to improve in 1959. The National Front had won the support of most of the population, including the political parties, armed forces, commercial and industrial associations, labour unions and churches. It continued to function effectively through constant interparty consultation and the designation of bipartisan committees to work out conflicts of interest. The most common difficulty was related to parity of the parties in public employment and offices. Restoration of political institutions was completed by Nov. 1, 1958, when elected municipal councils resumed their functions for the first time since 1949, except in 74 municipalities in which councillors of only one party were elected. Interparty understanding on the alternation of the presidency between the Liberals and Conservatives became a constitutional amendment in Sept. 1959.

The former dictator Gen. Gustavo Rojas Pinilla returned on Oct. 11, 1958, to defend his record. On Nov. 19 he was ordered to be tried before the Senate. On Dec. 3 the government forestalled a pro-Rojas uprising, and restored the state of siege from Dec. 4, 1958, to Jan. 12, 1959. Rojas was convicted for violating the constitution and laws, and for acts unworthy of a president. He was sentenced on April 1 to permanent loss of political rights, pensions and military rank.

Colombia's economic situation improved under an austerity programme and inflation was checked. Foreign commercial debts were being reduced, production and employment in agriculture and industry increased; the peso grew stronger; participation in international coffee marketing pacts stabilized the price of Colombia's coffee, the source of most of the nation's foreign exchange. Labour organization was being encouraged, and labour-management relations were maintained on a fairly good basis by hard-working Ministry of Labour conciliators. (R. L. G.)

COLOMBO PLAN. In Jan. 1950 the Colombo conference of Commonwealth foreign ministers set up the Consultative Committee for South and Southeast Asia to find means of improving economic conditions in the area. In Nov. 1950 the committee published a report, later known as the Colombo plan, which analysed the development programmes drawn up by the individual countries for the period 1951-57. The plan came into operation on July 1, 1951. The founder members of the consultative committee were Australia, Canada, Ceylon, India, New Zealand, Pakistan and the United Kingdom, including the U.K. territories in southeast Asia. The United States, Cambodia and the Republic of (South) Vietnam joined the committee in 1951; Burma and Nepal in 1952; Indonesia in 1953; Japan, Philippines and Thailand in 1954; and Laos in 1955. The Federation of Malaya became a member in its own right in 1957, and Singapore was admitted to full membership at the 1959 meeting.

In Dec. 1958 it was announced that under the Colombo plan an engineering institute would be established at Delhi with British assistance. The 11th meeting of the consultative committee was held at Jogjakarta, Indonesia, during Nov. 11-14, 1959, and its eighth annual report was published soon afterwards. The committee decided that the Colombo plan should be continued for five years after 1961 on the understanding that the period of a further extension should be considered at the 1964 meeting. Indications were noted of a growth in *per capita* income in the area as a whole. Inflationary pressures, however, tended to persist, with some continuing strain in the internal economies of the countries. Particular reference was made to the urgent problem of an increasing population in the area. Confidence was expressed that the continuation of the Colombo plan would bring renewed vigour to the tasks ahead. (A. E. Ps.)

COMMENT OF THE YEAR. Birth Rate.

Dr. Arnold Toynbee appealed at the World Food and Agriculture organization conference in Rome for a world-wide conversion to birth control to prevent famine: " We may select the most desirable crops and livestock and raise them on the soils best suited to them; we may cultivate the sea, as the Japanese have begun to do. But sooner or later food production will reach its limit. Then, if the population is still increasing, famine will do the execution that was done in the past by famine, pestilence and war combined . . . We must consciously try to establish an equilibrium or, sooner or later, famine will stalk abroad again.

" The control of the birth rate is a religious issue in the sense that it raises the question: What is the true end of man? Is it to populate the earth with the maximum number of human beings that can be kept alive simultaneously by the world's maximum food supply? Or is it to enable human beings to lead the best kind of life that the spiritual limitations of human nature allow? The first of these possible objectives seems irrational. What matters, surely, is not that the surface of this planet should hold say 4,000 million instead of 3,000 million living human beings—what matters is that living human beings, whatever their number, shall develop the highest capacities of their nature.

" And if this is the true end of man, what we should aim at is the optimum size of population for this purpose in the economic and social circumstances of each successive generation . . . The good life that is to be the criterion of the optimum size of population means a good life for individuals in the setting of the family, but this objective is far removed from the objective of maximum numbers for their own sake."

Britain. Max Beloff, Gladstone professor of government and public administration at a Liberal summer school at Oxford, described Britain as a " police state ". " There are more controls and it is more difficult to get in and more difficult to get out of than almost any other country. The Home Office stands as a perpetual and solitary sentinel over the rights of Englishmen—as it defines them . . . The impression we give is that the rest of the world is madly keen to come and settle illegally in this country."

Communication. Dr. John Lockwood, master of Birkbeck college, University of London, asked medical students to use simple English: " Go to the meeting of a committee and what does one hear: often raw slices of maundering, repetitive, ungrammatical, formless jargon. Look at the agenda of many academic committees, at the letters and documents from government departments, from advertisers and candidates— diffuse, tedious and turgid. Too many people will not take the trouble to keep to a brief, terse, controlled style and to cut out the unnecessary and falsely impressive. On the clarity of your words may hang at the worst a life, at the best a speedy or complete recovery."

Hints to politicians who appear on television were given in London by Ed Murrow, the U.S. television commentator: " I have the feeling that in both our countries the politicians are unduly fascinated by the mechanics of this new method of communication—a little too inclined to make political television a competition between film cutters and producers, rather than a competition of ideas and convictions. There is, I suggest, no substitute for the man who has at least a mild fire in his belly, and is able to pierce that screen with his own conviction." Politicians, he believed, should not be permitted to control television. " Let them use it; let them be as persuasive as they may be. But do not allow them to use this instrument to prevent today's minority from becoming tomorrow's majority."

International Affairs. Wasteful duplication of effort for the sake of national prestige and petty pride was deplored by Sir Miles Thomas when he addressed the American Chamber of Commerce in London: " I am increasingly distressed by what I might call technical me-tooism, which demands that when you launch a satellite we must launch a satellite, which demands that when you make a new bomb we must duplicate it, and when you design a rocket we must design a bigger one. Speaking plainly I believe it is essential that instead of ' me too ' we should say ' we two ' and say it together as a co-operative project."

Speaking as guest of honour at a Foyles literary luncheon in London to mark the publication of *On My Own*, Mrs. Eleanor Roosevelt referred to the importance of the uncommitted nations of the world: " I think the struggle that we in

Eleanor Roosevelt speaking at a Foyles literary luncheon in London on April 6 to mark the publication of her book " On My Own ".

the United States are least aware of, and are meeting least well, is the struggle to win the uncommitted peoples of the world through understanding their problems on the economic and cultural fronts. I think that you as a people have a great advantage over us because you have been concerned about the world for a far longer period of time than our people have. We have been so busy developing our country that we have given very little thought to the world as a whole. Today I can quite understand why there is flowing out to many of these peoples the feeling that the Soviets know more about them and can help them meet their needs better than we can."

On a visit to Australia Lord Attlee said that the conception of the national state must give way to a confederation of states in which some sovereign power was ceded to a wider power. " At present what we have to give up is the right to make war. We want to abolish all national armaments, keeping only the minimum required for internal security, and to substitute an international force which will be available when there are minor difficulties." The progress of invention " has rendered national defence entirely obsolete—because there is no defence today." If all the energy, power and wealth which was spent on armaments could be devoted to peaceful purposes the standards of half the world that was still living on the borderline of starvation would be raised. " I am devoting such amount of energy as I have at the end of my life to advocating this idea. It is not enough to persuade statesmen. We have also got to persuade people."

Nuclear Weapons. Lieut.-General Sir John Cowley, controller of munitions at the Ministry of Supply, in a lecture at the Royal United Service institution, referred to the policy of nuclear deterrence: " Unless we bring the nuclear deterrent into play we are bound to be beaten, and if we do bring it into play we are bound to commit suicide. Britain's limited resources therefore should be concentrated " in other directions than in producing weapons which are only useful because of their threat, and which can only be threatened in very exceptional circumstances . . . In 100 years the mid-20th century will be regarded as a nightmare period when mankind seriously considered destroying itself as a preferable alternative to reconciling two differing political views. Is it right for the population of a country to choose complete destruction rather than some other alternative, however unpleasant? "

At Edmonton, Canada, Dr. Linus Pauling, the chemist and Nobel prizewinner, declared that about 1·5 million people would die from the effects of nuclear weapons exploded in the past 14 years. " The national leader who orders nuclear bomb tests started again with our knowledge, our certainty, will be committing an act of criminal folly, showing contempt for the people." For each new bomb exploded, 15,000 to 30,000 persons would die of cancer and the same number from genetic effects. " The maximum fall-out from the bombs exploded so far will fall around 1967, then peter out. But it will continue falling for the next 100 years."

(S. M. F.)

COMMONWEALTH AIR FORCES. Royal Air
Force. The air estimates for 1959-60 amounted to £491·8 million (allowing for the receipt of £2 million from the Federal German government) compared with £467·1 million for 1958-59 (allowing for the receipt of £7·5 million from Germany). Of the total sum, 42·5% represented the cost of personnel, and the expected expenditure on aircraft and stores was £213·9 million, an increase of £17·1 million, chiefly owing to higher expenditure on guided missiles.

In his memorandum covering the estimates, the secretary of state referred to the continued build-up of Bomber command with Victors and Vulcans and said that the V-force had reached a high degree of efficiency. The state of readiness was such that the average time between the receipt of orders by the crews in the crew-room and the time of take-off was now only 6 min. The test launching of the full-scale version of the stand-off bomb was expected to begin during the year. This bomb had a built-in guidance system to enable the aircraft to release it and turn away before the bomb exploded. The small reconnaissance force of Valiants was to be re-equipped with Mark II Victors, a single one of which could cover an area as large as the Mediterranean in one radar reconnaissance sortie. A number of Valiants were to be assigned to the Nato European command to replace the Canberra B6s in a tactical role. They, like the Canberras, would be based in the United Kingdom. Fighter command was shortly being equipped with Lightnings, which would be fitted for flight refuelling to improve their capacity for overseas reinforcement. As regards missiles, the first Thor squadron had been formed and Javelin squadrons would be equipped with Firestreak during the year. Transport command had been increased and the first of the Britannia 253s on order was expected shortly. This aircraft was designed to carry a load of 16 tons over 4,100 mi. at 400 m.p.h. It could carry 115 fully equipped troops in comfort. Work already being performed by the command included the airlift of 32,000 troops in the far east and 12,000 transport sorties in the Arabian peninsula.

Hawker Hunters of No. 111 squadron, R.A.F., rehearsing their " bombshell " manoeuvre for the Farnborough air show in September.

Following the abolition of Home command, Flying Training command took over responsibility for the Air Training corps (A.T.C.), with 39,000 cadets, and the 17 university air squadrons. Under the Flying Scholarship scheme for cadets, 2,310 members of the A.T.C. and the Combined Cadet force had, by the end of 1958, been taught to fly light aircraft and of these about 1,000 had subsequently entered the R.A.F. It was announced that the Royal Observer corps numbered 15,615 men and women volunteers. No. 90 Signals group became a separate Signals command, with headquarters at Medmenham. The first commander-in-chief was Air Vice Marshal L. Dalton-Morris.

During 1958-59 R.A.F. aircraft flew nearly 1,800 hr. in over 150 air-sea rescue incidents, while mountain rescue teams were called out 29 times.

The appointment of Air Chief Marshal Sir Thomas Pike as chief of the air staff in succession to Marshal of the R.A.F. Sir Dermot Boyle, with effect from Jan. 1, 1960, was announced.

Royal Australian Air Force. Progress was made towards the formation of a flying wing of the Australian army, which was moving towards the control of its own flying activities on similar lines to the Army Air corps in the United Kingdom. The R.A.A.F. contingent of the Commonwealth Strategic reserve was completed. Consisting of 44 jet fighters and bombers, the force would be permanently based at Butterworth airfield in Malaya. The extension of the Woomera rocket range into Western Australia to a total length of 1,250 mi. was begun. The new area was to be known as Talgarno. A decision was taken to appoint suitably qualified women as officers of the R.A.A.F. accountant branch.

Royal Canadian Air Force. In January the R.C.A.F. Air Transport command assumed responsibility for all the regular units within the Tactical Air command. Before the end of 1958 the Nato aircrew training scheme which had been operating since 1950 was officially closed at Winnipeg, though some aircrew from Nato countries continued to receive training in the dominion, while the operational training of west German pilots on Canadian Sabre 6s was being carried out at Oldenburg, German Federal Republic. As a corollary to the suspension of work on the supersonic interceptor CF-105 Avro Arrow, it was proposed that Canada would install the Bomarc guided missile and increase radar coverage in the Northwest Territories, the cost being shared with the United States.

Royal New Zealand Air Force. The R.N.Z.A.F. contribution to the Commonwealth Strategic reserve in Malaya was completed. It consisted of No. 75 (Bomber) squadron and No. 41 (Transport) squadron. Up to Dec. 31, 1958, No. 41 squadron had flown over 2 million mi. and carried 50 million lb. of freight in Malaya.

Royal Rhodesian Air Force. Eighteen Canberra strike-reconnaissance aircraft purchased for the R.R.A.F. were flown out to Rhodesia early in 1959 by Rhodesian pilots, who had been under training with the R.A.F. at Bassingbourn.

Pakistan Air Force. Air Marshal Asghar Khan, commander-in-chief of the P.A.F., was appointed the Pakistan military adviser to Seato. A staff college for the P.A.F. was established at Karachi and Air Commodore C. B. E. Burt-Andrews of the R.A.F. was appointed the first commandant. (*See also* AIR FORCES OF THE WORLD.) (D. CR.)

COMMONWEALTH ARMIES.

British Army. The year 1959 saw the completion of the first part of the plan, initiated in 1957, for the reduction in the number of regiments in the army. Twelve armoured and 24 infantry regiments had been amalgamated and 18 artillery regiments disbanded. The second, and final, part of the plan for reduction was due for completion by the end of 1962. The strength of the

A Thunderbird guided missile is prepared for firing at the army School of Anti-Aircraft Artillery at Manorbier, south Wales.

reduced regular army was to be 180,000—not 165,000 as originally intended. Frequent changes of location, due to reductions in the garrison of Cyprus and operational requirements, make it impossible to state the exact deployment of army units.

Europe (*United Kingdom, German Federal Republic and Berlin*). The strength of the British Army of the Rhine, including the Berlin garrison (one brigade group), remained at about 60,000. The headquarters of B.A.O.R. was set up as a separate entity from the Nato headquarters, Northern Army group. The first British contribution to the tactical atomic strength of Nato forces was made in March 1959, when a guided weapon regiment, equipped with Corporal missiles, joined B.A.O.R. Training was based mainly on a study of the tactics of the new brigade group organization. Much new equipment was issued to units in Germany, including Saladin armoured cars, Ferret scout cars and the Mobat anti-tank gun. The strategic reserve in the United Kingdom was considerably strengthened by the withdrawal of troops from Cyprus. The territorial army took over certain civil defence duties from the Mobile Defence corps and selected territorial units were to attend Civil Defence camps every four years. In November it was announced that confinement to barracks (C.B.) would be abolished as a punishment, and would be replaced by " restriction of privileges ".

Middle East and Eastern Mediterranean. The political agreement on Cyprus in Feb. 1959 brought terrorist activities to an end. This enabled British forces to be reduced to the level necessary to fulfil Nato and other outside responsibilities. Conditions in the middle east were comparatively quiet and fewer British forces were deployed in the area than for some years. There were some internal troubles and frontier incidents in Aden, necessitating the continuance of the reinforced British garrison and an increase in the strength of the Aden Protectorate Levies to four battalions.

Malaya and Singapore. Conditions in Malaya were greatly improved. Due to the combined efforts of the Malayan army and the overseas Commonwealth land forces stationed there, the terrorists were reduced to about 700 and in many areas the emergency restrictions were removed. The granting of independence to Singapore and the victory of the Peoples Action party in the elections of June 1959 were not expected to make any difference to British forces on the island, who continued to be responsible for the defence of the Singapore base.

Local Forces. In many parts of the world locally raised forces assisted, or replaced, British troops. They included units of the King's African Rifles, the Somaliland Scouts, the Trucial Oman Scouts and others. In a special position, and forming part of the British army, was the Brigade of Gurkhas, which provided part of the garrisons of Hong Kong and Malaya.

Manpower. On April 1, 1959, the strength of the U.K.-enlisted portion of the British army was about 304,000 (174,000 regulars, 124,000 national servicemen and 6,000 women). By April 1, 1960, this figure was expected to fall to about 266,000. In 1958, 33,287 regular male recruits joined and, as a high proportion enlisted for six years or more, this represented 203,164 man-years. Figures for 1959 were not quite so encouraging (*e.g.*, 2,165 in June as compared with 2,736 in June 1958). There seemed little doubt, however, that sufficient volunteer long-service regular recruits would be forthcoming by 1962, when the last national serviceman would have left the army.

Finance. The army estimates for 1959-60 (after deducting appropriations in aid) amounted to £431,350,100 compared with £431,400,100 (including the supplementary estimate of July 1958) for 1958-59. In spite of reductions in strengths and

The relieving guard arriving at Buckingham palace on Sept. 1, armed for the first time with the new semi-automatic rifle.

many economies, the increasing costs of weapons and equipment prevented any considerable saving in army expenditure.

Appointment. In Sept. 1958 General Sir Francis Festing was appointed in succession to Field Marshal Sir Gerald Templer as chief of the Imperial General Staff and first military member of the Army council.

Commonwealth Armies. *Canada.* The army took over responsibility for certain aspects of national survival in the event of the country being attacked with nuclear weapons or seriously affected by radioactive fall-out. Canada continued to provide the commander and a strong contingent of the United Nations Emergency force in the middle east.

New Zealand. With the abolition of national service in May 1958 plans were made, and were in course of implementation, to reorganize the regular army. It was to be approximately doubled in strength and would include a static force and an operational brigade group (the latter to include a battalion stationed in Malaya). The territorial force was to remain as previously organized, but came on a voluntary basis on April 1, 1959.

South Africa. The army remained a small cadre of regular officers, non-commissioned officers and men (the Permanent force). Part-time service was given by personnel of the Citizen force and Commando units, the latter being mainly for internal security purposes. F. C. Erasmus, the minister of defence, stated in parliament early in 1959 that the government had in mind the early reorganization of the defence forces, based on fewer but bigger units, better strategic location of units, mobility and modern technique.

Federation of Malaya. The army of the newly formed federation (together with the navy, air force and non-regular forces) was brought under the Armed Forces council for everything except operations. By agreement, the United Kingdom was to keep in Malaya such forces as were considered to be necessary and these, together with the federation's own forces, were to come under the operational command of the senior U.K. officer.

No major changes took place during 1959 in the armies of other Commonwealth countries. (*See also* ARMIES OF THE WORLD.) (C. N. B.)

See *Progress of the Five-Year Defence Plan,* Cmnd. 662; *Defence Statistics 1959-60,* Cmnd. 661; *Memorandum of the Secretary of State for War Relating to the Army Estimates 1959-60,* Cmnd. 669. (All H.M.S.O., 1959.)

COMMONWEALTH NAVIES. Royal Navy. Although contraction of the navy continued, the net estimates for 1959-60 (at £371 million) showed an increase of £31 million over those originally voted for 1958-59. Manpower was progressively reduced by a further 4,000, the reduction in officers being proportionately rather greater than that in ratings. Civilians employed were also reduced by about 8,000 during the year. The increased expenditure was mainly on the construction of new ships and the provision of equipment, which outweighed the savings on personnel and the economies so far achieved by closing certain dockyards and shore establishments.

The trials of the cruiser H.M.S. " Tiger " were successfully completed and she joined the operational fleet. H.M.S. " Hermes ", the last of the light fleet carriers, began her trials at the close of the year, her construction having been delayed to enable her to be fitted with steam catapults, fully angled flight deck and the latest radar. H.M.S. " Ark Royal " rejoined the fleet after an extensive refit and H.M.S. " Eagle " was taken in hand for the fitting of steam catapults, a deck edge lift and improved radar. Meanwhile, experience with H.M.S. " Victorious " confirmed the superiority of her radar and aircraft direction equipment over any other corresponding equipment. The 12 " Blackwood " class A/S frigates and nearly all of the two other classes of A/S and A/A frigates having already joined the fleet, only one frigate was completed during the year. Three submarines of the new " Porpoise " class joined the fleet, together with four minesweepers.

Orders were placed for four guided-missile destroyers of the County class, namely " Devonshire ", " Hampshire ", " Kent " and " London ", and the keels of the first two were laid down in March. Designs of these vessels were larger than the current types of fleet escorts. They were to have novel machinery combining steam and gas turbines, which would enable them to get under way instantly in emergency. They were to be armed with the Seaslug guided missile and would also carry the shorter-range Seacat, for close air defence, and an anti-submarine helicopter. However, the outstanding event of the year was the laying down in June of H.M.S. "Dreadnought", the Royal Navy's first nuclear submarine. The machinery for this vessel was being made in the United States and was similar to that of the latest U.S. submarines. Work was also started on a special graving dock for nuclear submarines.

Little change in the disposition of the fleet, or in the conditions of service of officers and men, took place during the year. The proportion of men who re-engaged for pension rose to virtually prewar levels, and the national service intake was reduced to about 500. Changes were made in the academic standards required for entry into the Royal Naval Cadet college at Dartmouth, with the object of ensuring an adequate knowledge of mathematics and physics. It was also decided to revert to the old practice of sending midshipmen to sea with the fleet before completing their professional instruction.

Admiral of the Fleet Lord Mountbatten was succeeded as first sea lord by Admiral Sir Charles Lambe, the latter being succeeded as commander-in-chief Mediterranean by Admiral Sir Alexander Bingley.

There was no major Nato exercise in 1959, but valuable training exercises were conducted, including one in which H.M.S. "Victorious" gave an excellent account of herself. A large-scale submarine exercise was also held in which H.M.S. "Adamant" and eight submarines joined forces of the U.S., Canadian and Netherlands navies in the western Atlantic. The Royal Navy performed an arduous and delicate task in furnishing a patrol for the protection of British trawlers fishing in the vicinity of Iceland (*see* FISHERIES).

Royal Australian Navy. Vice-Admiral H. M. Burrell relieved Vice-Admiral Sir Roy Dowling as chief of naval staff. Two more "Daring" class destroyers, "Vendetta" and "Vampire", were completed and joined the fleet.

Royal Canadian Navy. The postwar building programme of 82 vessels, including a carrier and 14 Canadian-designed and -built destroyer escorts, was completed. A further six improved destroyer escorts and a tanker/supply ship were projected.

Royal Ceylon Navy. A further "Algerine" class minesweeper, "Parakrame", was transferred to Ceylon.

Royal East African Navy. This was reinforced by one inshore minesweeper as a gift from the Royal Navy to replace H.M.E.A.S. "Rosalind".

Royal Malayan Navy. Four inshore minesweepers were added to the Malayan navy during the year.

Royal New Zealand Navy. The Type 12 frigates "Otago" and "Taranaki", currently under construction in the United Kingdom, were expected to be completed and join the fleet in 1960.

Royal Nigerian Navy. The Nigerian Naval force was granted the new title of Royal Nigerian Navy in July and H.M.N.S.

H.M.S. "Eagle" heading into the wind in the Channel off Weymouth on April 29, with the Queen, the Duke of Edinburgh and the Prince of Wales aboard. During a four-hour visit the prince took a brief turn at the helm while the ship steamed at 25 knots on a swinging course.

On board H.M.S. "Vigilant", a frigate of the Royal Navy's Dartmouth Training Squadron, during an anti-submarine exercise.

"Nigeria" (formerly the ocean minesweeper "Hare") and one S.D.M.L. were transferred to Nigeria in the same month.

Ghana Navy. This force was being established and two inshore minesweepers were being purchased from the United Kingdom.

Indian Navy. One Type 41, three Type 14 and two Type 12 A/S frigates completed building in the United Kingdom and joined the Indian navy. The new aircraft carrier "Vikrant" was expected to be completed early in 1961.

Pakistan Navy. Rear-Admiral A. R. Khan relieved Vice-Admiral H. M. S. Choudri as chief of naval staff. The Type 16 frigates "Tippu Sultan" and "Tughrill" completed conversion in the United Kingdom and joined the Pakistan navy.

South African Navy. The South African navy took part in exercises with the Royal Navy and the Portuguese navy during the year. (*See* also NAVIES OF THE WORLD.)   (J. H. HT.)

COMMONWEALTH OF NATIONS, the com-
munity of independent nations and dependent or semi-dependent territories bound together by allegiance to the British crown or by recognition of the British sovereign as head of the Commonwealth. The Commonwealth comprises: (i) the United Kingdom of Great Britain and Northern Ireland and its colonies and other dependencies; (ii) six other realms or kingdoms in each of which the British monarch is sovereign—Australia, Canada, New Zealand, South Africa and their dependencies, and Ghana and Ceylon, which decided that they would eventually become republics within the Commonwealth; (iii) India, a republic recognizing the British sovereign as head of the Commonwealth; (iv) the Federation of Malaya, a kingdom recognizing the British sovereign as head of the Commonwealth; and (v) Pakistan, a federal republic, recognizing the British sovereign as head of the Commonwealth.

The Commonwealth of Nations covers about one-quarter of the area of the world and contains about one-quarter of its population.

Developments in 1959: the Independent Countries. The year was notable for an expansion of Commonwealth interests, while the opening of the St. Lawrence seaway provided opportunities for increased consultation with the United States. The most extensive royal tour of the year was made

by the Duke of Edinburgh, who paid the first royal visit to the Solomon Islands and the Gilbert and Ellice Islands in the course of his journey round the Commonwealth, which also included Singapore, Sarawak, Brunei, Hong Kong, the Bahama Islands and Bermuda. Queen Elizabeth the Queen Mother visited Kenya and central Africa and Princess Alexandra made a tour of Australia, calling at Fiji on the way there. Queen Elizabeth II was unable to follow her Canadian tour by a visit to Ghana, but the Duke of Edinburgh went there in her stead.

A Colonial Welfare and Development act made available £95 million and provided for exchequer loans of up to £100 million. A white paper published on March 2 estimated that an additional £1·5 million would be needed for overseas information services, while, as a result of the Commonwealth Education conference held in July, £10 million was to be spent on co-operative measures, particularly the training of teachers and technical education. An Overseas Research council was established to further scientific development, and the United Kingdom was to contribute about half the cost of a new £80 million round-the-world Commonwealth cable system. The Commonwealth Economic Consultative council met in September for a general exchange of views, as did the first informal, inter-service Commonwealth Defence conference, which discussed problems of defence in a nuclear age.

In Canada the joint opening of the St. Lawrence seaway by the queen and President Dwight D. Eisenhower was followed by a six-week royal tour, the longest undertaken by a reigning monarch. The 2,300-mi. seaway, built by Canada and the United States in co-operation, ranked as the world's greatest inland navigation system and a rich source of hydro-electric power. Consideration was also given to the development of Canada's northlands in order to establish arctic air bases and exploit metal, oil and gas deposits. By the end of 1958 exploration permits covering 76 million ac. were issued and in 1959 applications for permits in the arctic archipelago covered an equal area. The Canadian government also established a C$100 million ten-year "roads to resources" programme, to give access to these underdeveloped areas, and work on the polar ports—Tuktoyaktuk, Copper Mine, Rankin and Frobisher—went ahead.

In March Australia celebrated the announcement that its population had reached 10 million after 171 years of British settlement. The increase of 2 million in the preceding ten years was due largely to immigrants, half of whom were British. It was announced at the end of the year that Viscount Dunrossil was to be governor-general of Australia in succession to Field Marshal Sir William Slim.

In New Zealand in May the 3,500-ft. Auckland Harbour bridge was opened, and after discussion with the British government on butter, meat and fruit exports in relation to foreign dumping, the New Zealand government signed a trade agreement in August. In September the Samoa Amendment bill was introduced in parliament. This provided for the establishment of cabinet government for the trusteeship territory of Western Samoa as a step towards independence in 1961.

In the Union of South Africa legislation was passed in June to promote self-governing Bantu homelands and abolish Bantu representation in parliament. The trial of South Africans on a charge of high treason before the Special Criminal Court in Pretoria continued throughout 1959. The court refused an application by the crown for leave to appeal against the quashing of the indictment against 61 of the accused. The trial of the other 30 was resumed in August. The governor-general of South Africa, E. J. Jansen, died in November (*see* OBITUARIES). He was succeeded by C. R. Swart, formerly minister of justice (*see* BIOGRAPHIES).

Following the outbreak of disturbances in Nyasaland a

TABLE I. REALMS AND MEMBER-NATIONS OF THE COMMONWEALTH WITH THEIR DEPENDENCIES*

Country	Area (sq.mi.)	Population (latest estimate)	Capital	Status	Governors-general, etc., and prime ministers (as at Dec. 31, 1959)
GREAT BRITAIN AND NORTHERN IRELAND, UNITED KINGDOM OF	94,283†	51,681,000†	London	kingdom	Prime minister, Harold Macmillan
AUSTRALIA, COMMONWEALTH OF	2,974,581	10,008,665	Canberra	kingdom; federation of states	Governor-general, Field Marshal Sir William Slim Prime minister, R. G. Menzies
PAPUA-NEW GUINEA	183,540	1,828,418	Port Moresby	external territory & trust territory	Administrator, Brig. D. M. Cleland
NORFOLK ISLAND	13	1,060	—	external territory	Administrator, Brig. H. B. Norman
NAURU	8	4,303	—	trust territory	Administrator, J. P. White
OTHER ISLANDS	178	3,219	—	external territories	
ANTARCTIC TERRITORY	c. 2,472,000	—	—	external territory	
CANADA	3,851,113	17,550,000	Ottawa	kingdom; federation of provinces	Governor-general, Maj.-Gen. George Vanier Prime minister, J. G. Diefenbaker
CEYLON	25,332	9,361,000	Colombo	kingdom	Governor-general, Sir Oliver Goonetilleke Prime minister, W. Dahanayake
GHANA	91,843	4,911,000	Accra	kingdom	Governor-general, Lord Listowel Prime minister, Kwame Nkrumah
INDIA	1,259,797‡	397,540,000‡	New Delhi	republic; union of states	President, Rajendra Prasad Prime minister, Jawaharlal Nehru
MALAYA, FEDERATION OF	50,692	6,499,000	Kuala Lumpur	kingdom; federation of states	Yang di-Pertuan Agong, Tuanku Abdul Rahman Prime minister, Tengku Abdul Rahman Putra
NEW ZEALAND	103,736	2,282,000	Wellington	kingdom	Governor-general, Lord Cobham Prime minister, Walter Nash
WESTERN SAMOA	1,130	102,195	Apia	trust territory	High commissioner, G. R. Powles
OTHER ISLANDS	192	23,350	—	external territories	
ROSS DEPENDENCY	c. 175,000	—	—	external territory	
PAKISTAN	365,037	85,635,000	Karachi	federal republic	President (with supreme powers) General Mohammed Ayub Khan
SOUTH AFRICA, UNION OF	472,685	14,673,000	Pretoria Cape Town Bloemfontein	kingdom; union of provinces	Governor-general, C. R. Swart§ Prime minister, H. F. Verwoerd
SOUTH-WEST AFRICA	317,725	554,000	Windhoek	mandated territory	Administrator, D. T. du P. Viljoen
PRINCE EDWARD AND MARION ISLANDS	103	—	—	external territory	

* Excl. U.K. dependencies: see Table II. † Incl. for census purposes Isle of Man and Channel Islands, not part of legislative area of U.K.; see also Table II. ‡ Incl. Kashmir, the incorporation of which is disputed by Pakistan. §Designate

TABLE II. UNITED KINGDOM DEPENDENCIES

Country	Area (sq.mi.)	Population (latest est. in '000s)	Capital	Status	Rulers, governors, prime ministers, etc. (as at Dec. 31, 1959)
EUROPE					
CHANNEL ISLANDS:					
JERSEY	45	57	St. Helier	crown dependency	Lieut.-gov., General Sir George Erskine
GUERNSEY AND DEPENDENCIES	30	41	St. Peter Port	crown dependency	Lieut.-gov., Vice-Admiral Sir Geoffrey Robson
GIBRALTAR	2	25	—	colony	Governor, General Sir Charles Keightley
MALTA (incl. Gozo and Comino)	122	322	Valletta	self-governing colony	Governor, Admiral Sir Guy Grantham
MAN, ISLE OF	220	55	Douglas	crown dependency	Lieut.-gov., Sir Ambrose D.Flux Dundas
ASIA					
ADEN (incl. dependencies)	c. 112,000	800	Aden	colony and protectorate	Governor, Sir William Luce
BRITISH BORNEO:					
NORTH BORNEO	29,388	401	Jesselton	colony	Governor, Sir Roland Turnbull
SARAWAK	c. 47,500	640	Kuching	colony	Governor, Sir Alexander Waddell*
BRUNEI	2,226	73	Brunei	protected sultanate	Sultan, Omar Ali Saifuddin
CYPRUS	3,572	549	Nicosia	colony	Governor, Sir HughFoot
HONG KONG	391	2,478	Victoria	colony	Governor, Sir Robert Black
MALDIVE ISLANDS (Maldivia)	115	82	Malé	protected sultanate	Sultan, Mohammed Farid Didi Prime minister, Ibrahim Nasir
SINGAPORE	225	1,515	Singapore	self-governing colony	Yang di-Pertuan Negara, Inche Yusof bin Ishak Prime minister, Lee Kuan Yew
AFRICA					
BRITISH SOUTH AFRICAN TERRITORIES (*High Commission Territories*)			—		High commissioner, Sir John Maud
BASUTOLAND	11,716	658	Maseru	colony	Resident commissioner, A. G. T. Chaplin
BECHUANALAND PROTECTORATE	275,006	334	—	protectorate	Resident commissioner, M. O. Wray
SWAZILAND	6,705	260	Mbabane	protectorate	Resident commissioner, B. A. Marwick
GAMBIA	4,003	285	Bathurst	colony and protectorate	Governor, Sir Edward Windley
KENYA	224,960	6,351	Nairobi	colony and protectorate	Governor, Sir Patrick Renison
MAURITIUS (incl. dependencies)	809	623	Port Louis	colony	Governor, Sir Colville Deverell
NIGERIA, FEDERATION OF (incl. Cameroons trust)	373,250	34,634	Lagos	fed. of 3 regions and 2 federal territories	Governor-general, Sir James Robertson Federal prime minister, Alhaji Abubakar Tafawa Balewa
RHODESIA AND NYASALAND, FEDERATION OF	487,652	7,650	Salisbury	fed. of 2 protectorates and a self-gov. colony	Governor-general, Lord Dalhousie Federal prime minister, Sir RoyWelensky
NORTHERN RHODESIA	288,137	2,262	Lusaka	protectorate	Governor, Sir Evelyn Hone
NYASALAND	49,178	2,706	Zomba	protectorate	Governor, Sir Robert Armitage
SOUTHERN RHODESIA	150,337	2,480	Salisbury	self-governing colony	Governor, H. V. Gibbs Prime minister, Sir Edgar Whitehead
ST. HELENA (incl. dependencies)	126	5	Jamestown	colony	Governor, R. E. Alford
SEYCHELLES	156	42	Victoria	colony	Governor, Sir John Thorp
SIERRA LEONE	27,925	2,260	Freetown	colony and protectorate	Governor, Sir Maurice Dorman Premier, Sir Milton Margai
SOMALILAND PROTECTORATE	c. 68,000	650	Hargeisa	protectorate	Governor, Sir Douglas Hall
TANGANYIKA	362,688	8,906	Dar es Salaam	trust territory	Governor, Sir Richard Turnbull
UGANDA	93,981	5,767	Entebbe	protectorate	Governor, Sir Frederick Crawford
ZANZIBAR (incl. Pemba)	1,020	299	Zanzibar	protected sultanate	Sultan, Seyyid Sir Khalifa bin Harub Resident, Sir George Mooring
AMERICA					
BAHAMA ISLANDS	4,404	136	Nassau	colony	Governor, Sir Raynor Arthur
BERMUDA	21	43	Hamilton	colony	Governor, Maj.-General Sir Julian Gascoigne
BRITISH GUIANA	83,000	541	Georgetown	colony	Governor, Sir Ralph Grey Leader of the majority party, Cheddi Jagan
BRITISH HONDURAS	8,867	85	Belize	colony	Governor, Sir Colin Thornley
FALKLAND ISLANDS (excl. dependencies)	4,618	2	Stanley	colony	Governor, E. P. Arrowsmith
VIRGIN ISLANDS, BRITISH	c. 59	8	Road Town	colony	Administrator, G. P. Allsebrook
WEST INDIES, THE	8,005	3,153	Port of Spain	fed. of colonies	Governor-general, Lord Hailes Federal prime minister, Sir Grantley Adams
BARBADOS	166	237	Bridgetown	colony	Governor, Sir Robert Arundell Premier, H. G. H. Cummins
JAMAICA (incl. Cayman Islands and Turks and Caicos Islands)	4,677	1,667	Kingston	colony	Governor, Sir Kenneth Blackburne Chief minister, Norman Manley
LEEWARD ISLANDS	356	130	St. John's	colony	Governor, Sir Alexander Williams
TRINIDAD AND TOBAGO	1,980	789	Port of Spain	colony	Governor, Sir Edward Beetham Chief minister, Eric Williams
WINDWARD ISLANDS	826	330	St. George's	colony	Acting governor, H. L. Lindo
AUSTRALASIA					
FIJI (incl. Pitcairn)	7,055	368	Suva	colony	Governor, Sir Kenneth Maddocks
TONGA	269	58	Nuku'alofa	protected kingdom	Queen, Salote Tupou Premier, Crown Prince Tungi
PACIFIC IS. (*W. Pacific High Commission, excl. New Hebrides*)	11,905	156	Honiara	colony and protectorate	High commissioner, Sir John Gutch
NEW HEBRIDES	c. 5,700	54	Vila	Anglo-French condominium	British resident commissioner, J. S. Rennie

* Designate.

state of emergency was declared in Southern Rhodesia on Feb. 26. The Southern Rhodesian government subsequently introduced special legislation to implement the emergency regulations. In July it was announced that a 26-man commission would be appointed to assemble facts about the Federation of Rhodesia and Nyasaland for the 1960 constitutional conference. Of the 13 members drawn from central Africa, five would be Africans. The United Kingdom would supply 11 members and the Commonwealth 2. Progress on the Kariba dam was well ahead of schedule in 1959, and construction continued on the Southern Rhodesian Kyle dam, which formed part of a £3 million irrigation scheme.

In Ghana the three-man commission appointed to inquire into an alleged plot to assassinate the prime minister, Kwame Nkrumah, and other cabinet ministers and overthrow the government by force issued a majority report finding the existence of a plot but no evidence to show that the leader of the opposition, K. A. Busia, was involved in it. A government white paper published in June asserted that the opposition party was in fact implicated and proposed wide security legislation. Busia left the country and accepted an academic post in Europe. The agreement for a union between Ghana and Guinea, signed in Accra at the end of 1958, was elaborated in a joint declaration from Konakry in May, which envisaged a union of independent African states. The relationship of Guinea to the Commonwealth remained obscure.

The August general elections in the Federation of Malaya resulted in a conclusive victory for Tengku Abdul Rahman Putra's Alliance party, which aimed at maintaining racial partnership and religious toleration in the federation.

In Pakistan the government of President Mohammed Ayub Khan tackled the major problem of growing enough food for the country. A £10 million loan for economic development was granted by Britain, while one of Canada's major contributions under the Colombo plan was the C$36 million Warsak hydroelectric project, to be completed in 1960. This would irrigate 120,000 ac. of waste land and supply energy for industry in West Pakistan. Ayub Khan's meeting on Sept. 1 with the Indian prime minister, Jawaharlal Nehru, was hailed as a step towards better relations between India and Pakistan and an augury of success for the Indus Waters scheme.

Relations between India and China, which became strained at the time of the Tibetan rising in March and the subsequent flight of the Dalai Lama to India, deteriorated sharply following the occupation by Chinese troops of outposts on Indian territory in the Northeast Frontier Agency and Ladakh (*see* Sino-Indian Frontier Dispute). In June there was an outbreak of disorder in the Communist-governed state of Kerala and the central government intervened in order to proclaim president's rule.

Events in Ceylon were overshadowed by the assassination on Sept. 25 of the prime minister, S. W. R. D. Bandaranaike (*see* Obituaries). When in May his coalition government began to disintegrate Bandaranaike had resigned, formed a government based solely on his own party and had begun to prepare constitutional reforms. The new prime minister, W. Dahanayake (*see* Biographies), retained the post of minister of education and took over the portfolios of defence and foreign affairs.

United Kingdom Dependencies. One of the outstanding events of the year was the signing in Feb. 1959 of the London agreement under which Cyprus was to become an independent republic in 1960. In March the Northern Region of Nigeria duly attained self-government and the Duke and Duchess of Gloucester attended the official celebrations in May. In November the Northern Cameroons voted by a large majority to remain under British trusteeship in preference to joining an independent Nigeria in 1960. The first elections to the Somaliland legislature were held in March. The secretary of state for the colonies, A. T. Lennox-Boyd, announced in February in the course of a visit to the protectorate that the legislature would have an unofficial majority by the end of 1960. It was stated in July that a ministerial system would be introduced in the protectorate in 1960.

In 1959 there were constitutional advances in both Northern Rhodesia and Nyasaland. In Northern Rhodesia in March more power passed to the unofficial members of the legislative council (including Africans). In Nyasaland, after the disturbances in February and March and the commission of inquiry which followed them, interim constitutional changes giving more representation to Africans took place in August. The east African territories all had constitutional changes. Those in Uganda announced in Nov. 1958 were of a minor nature. The country had considerable trouble during 1959, principally over the boycott of non-African goods. In Kenya, also with a constitutional conference in prospect, there was much political shuffling and the announcement of a new status for the White Highlands had a mixed reception from both Africans and Europeans. The ending of the seven-year-old state of emergency in November was an event of considerable importance. Tanganyika's common-roll elections held in Sept. 1958 and Feb. 1959 were followed on July 1 by the appointment of a Council of Ministers including one unofficial member from each of the three races. In Zanzibar the sultan approved changes involving an increase in electors, in representative members in the executive council and elected members in the legislative council.

Other constitutional changes were announced or came into effect in Basutoland (Dec. 1958), Barbados (March 1959), Mauritius (March 1959), Gambia (Sept. 1959), British Virgin Islands (July 1959), Trinidad and Tobago (July 1959), Leeward and Windward Islands (June 1959) and Jamaica, Cayman Islands and Turks and Caicos Islands (May 1959). The sultan of Brunei approved the new constitution for his country in Sept. 1959. It was also announced that Brunei would have its own high commissioner and that the governor of Sarawak would cease to hold that office. The state of Singapore came into being after elections in May and in November adopted a new flag. Aden's new constitution came into force in January. Six of the rulers of the Aden Protectorate formed themselves into the Federation of South Arabian Amirates and entered into new treaty relations with Britain in February. A seventh state joined later in the year.

Malta was the one exception to the story of political advance, and interim arrangements for administration by the governor were introduced in April.

The resignation of Lennox-Boyd after the British general election in October brought to an end a notable term of office. In parliament he had taken part in more debates on colonial affairs than any previous holder of his office, and several of the fiercest were in 1959, particularly those on the Hola camp tragedy in Kenya—which aroused widespread feeling in Britain—and on central Africa. Moreover, colonial affairs took up an increasing amount of parliamentary time.

During 1958-59 Colonial Development and Welfare expenditure was £17·8 million and grants-in-aid and payments for specific purposes nearly £24·25 million. Loans on the London market were about £8 million. Capital expenditure approved by the Colonial Development corporation was nearly £3·6 million, of which more than £2 million was for new schemes. The total revenue of the dependencies for 1958 was about £478 million. There were 11,193 colonial students in the United Kingdom and the Republic of Ireland at the end of 1958, 1,270 more than in 1957.   (M. Mr.; W. H. Is.)

COMMUNICATIONS

(Statistics are for the latest year available, 1958, unless otherwise stated. All figures are in thousands, unless otherwise stated.)

Country	Area (sq.km.)	Railways Route length (km.)	Railways Pass. traffic (million pass.-km.)	Railways Goods traffic (million net ton-km.)	Roads Total length (1957) (km.)	Roads Motor vehicles (1957) Passenger	Roads Motor vehicles (1957) Commercial	Merchant Shipping Gross registered tonnage	Merchant Shipping No. of vessels (units)	Civil Air Passengers carried (pass.-km.)	Civil Air km. flown (1957)	Civil Air Freight carried incl. mail (ton-km.)	Radio Receiving Sets (1957)	Telephones (Jan. 1, 1958)
Europe														
Austria	83·8	5·9	6,187[1]	6,819[1]	31·8	233·2	69·9	—	—	...	...	...	1,838	592·2
Belgium	30·5	6·7[2]	9,057[1]	5,889[1]	93·0[3]	615·6	158·3	601	199	1,198,056	35,188	34,596	2,307	987·0
Bulgaria	111·5	5·5	3,088	5,243	25·4	7·0	16·8	...	...	27,821[2]	2,331[1]	450[2]	399[4]	120·3[2]
Czechoslovakia	127·9	13·4	18,682	38,476	120·9[4]	115·0	79·6	...	...	135,000	7,657	4,612	3,055	790·0
Denmark	43·0	4·4	3,267[1]	1,324[1]	58·4[3]	279·8	117·5	2,035	751	508,668	15,004	11,232	1,551	951·0
Finland	337·0	4·4	2,215	4,076	66·3	139·2[3]	58·5[3]	755	347	177,348	9,959	2,268	1,121	524·6
France	551·2	39·6[1 2]	32,310[1]	52,880[1]	1,156·0	3,972·0	1,371·0	4,338	1,307	4,122,372	102,413	118,404	10,881	3,498·9
German Dem. Rep.[6]	107·4	16·1[2]	21,399	30,101	47·7	110·0	119·0	...	...	...	...	...	5,306[4]	534·0[2]
German Fed. Rep.[6]	248·0	36·1	38,782	56,640	132·9[7]	2,637·0	669·0	4,077	2,379	664,248	15,970	17,388	14,634	4,731·9
Greece	132·6	2·6[2]	...	363	47·2[4]	24·7[4]	28·1[4]	1,611	397	140,112	5,020	2,064	545	153·8
Hungary	93·0	8·9	11,889	10,242	63·7[4]	16·0	32·5	—	—	22,000	...	...	1,587[4]	347·7[2]
Ireland, Rep. of	70·3	4·0	...	357	81·8	140·2	45·3	137	81	185,916	6,209	2,424	477	129·6
Italy	301·2	21·6	25,597[1]	13,073[1]	181·0	1,238·0	405·0	4,900	1,300	759,360	21,468	13,716	6,759	2,750·6
Netherlands	32·5	3·2[2]	7,466	3,124	13·1[8]	375·7	131·0	4,600	1,966	1,986,132	64,784	80,376	3,128	1,318·3
Norway	323·9	4·4	1,711[1 9]	1,372[1 9]	49·5[3]	153·0	94·5	9,385	2,624	565,956	18,584	12,084	985	646·5[2 9]
Poland	311·7	27·0	38,085	57,192	284·9	61·9	99·5	458	202	101,015	6,720	2,503	4,028	405·8
Portugal	92·2	3·6[2]	1,933	738	29·0[10]	116·0[10]	45·4[10]	552	320	161,604	7,643	2,604	596	304·9
Rumania	237·5	10·2	13,323[1]	16,120[2]	109·5[11]	8·0	19·2	...	...	...	...	...	1,499	164·3
Spain	503·5	18·2[2]	8,730[1]	8,614[1]	120·8[4]	181·0	126·8	1,607	1,314	609,564	21,315	6,240	2,105	1,339·7
Sweden	449·7	15·8	5,240[1]	9,512[1]	148·6[7]	863·0	111·0	3,303	1,218	849,276	26,418	19,560	2,695	2,409·8
Switzerland	41·3	5·1[4]	6,912[1]	3,236[1]	50·5	347·0	65·2	98	23	1,014,576	28,796	27,156	1,308	1,385·1
United Kingdom	244·0	31·9	34,963[12]	30,129[12]	328·4	4,205·0	1,296·0	20,286	5,417	4,139,436	133,969	120,468	14,654[13]	7,354·7[5]
U.S.S.R.	22,403·0	121·2	154,400	1,295,000	1,506·0	415·0[4]	2,885·0[4]	2,966	1,390	...	...	...	34,888	3,558·0
Yugoslavia	255·8	11·8[2]	8,716	13,032	82·3	21·6	38·2	439	200	58,944	3,084	768	890	198·1
Asia														
Burma	678·0	3·0	1,065	630[14]	41·0[8]	17·5	17·6	...	...	40,260[2]	2,700	792[2]	15[15]	8·0
Cambodia	172·5	0·4	76	58	3·6	5·7	4·7	...	...	...	...	...	7[4]	2·8
Ceylon	65·6	1·4[2]	1,419	264	18·2	18·2	24·2	...	...	45,708	2,055	1,440	164[1]	30·0
China	9,761·0	28·0[2]	...	...	180·0	20·0[8]	101·0[8]	540	257	...	...	...	...	255·0[16]
India	3,281·8	55·9[2]	...	70,620[8]	532·9	203·2[4]	181·4[4]	674	230	866,004	37,812	40,836	1,076[4]	334·7[5 7]
Indonesia	1,491·6	7·4[2]	5,515	1,068	75·0[11]	73·2[4]	62·9[4]	119	183	280,116[2]	14,469	5,436	500[8]	84·8
Iraq	444·4	1·7	658[5]	908[5]	19·3[8]	25·9	14·4	...	...	48,084	2,382	576	66[11]	47·1
Israel	20·7	0·4	349	201	3·5[3]	17·4[4]	22·1[4]	206	44	278,076	4,774	5,592	354	80·0
Japan	369·7	27·6	106,208	44,725[1 5]	144·6[1 5]	218·5	419·5	5,465	2,413	686,304	17,628	14,580	14,440	3,886·3[5 7]
Korea (South)	96·9	2·9	4,172	2,449	40·7[8]	9·7	17·5	...	...	...	...	...	181[4]	55·9
Malaya, Fed. of	131·3	2·1[1 7]	588	389[17]	10·6	72·9	25·5	...	...	...	...	...	...	61·7
Pakistan	299·4	11·3	...	6,684[8]	97·0[4]	31·8	21·0	128	51	228,924	7,065	6,516	109[8]	57·6
Persia	1,630·0	3·4	1,535	1,452	34·1[4]	49·9[8]	31·1[8]	...	...	36,724[2]	2,678	945[2]	184[18]	64·6
Philippines	299·4	1·1	707	186	35·2[8]	65·8[4]	68·5[4]	123	87	187,284	10,184	4,164	217[11]	73·8
Syria	184·5	1·1	42	89	10·0[8]	8·7	14·3	...	...	...	...	...	50[18]	37·2
Thailand	514·0	3·5[2]	1,965	1,082	7·4[4]	33·2	32·5	—	—	50,208	4,373	876	108[11]	13·9
Turkey	777·0	7·8[2]	5,107	5,038	55·0[8]	33·4[4]	43·0[4]	596	288	163,224	7,028	1,356	1,083	203·5
Vietnam, Rep. of	170·8	1·3[2]	427	84	14·0	22·9	13·1	...	...	...	...	...	21[16]	12·7
Africa														
Algeria	2,381·7	4·4[2]	654	1,594	68·7	126·1	63·9	...	...	...	...	...	407	153·3
Belgian Congo (incl. Ruanda Urundi)	2,399·1	5·1[2]	371	2,215	152·8	36·4	25·5	...	...	...	...	...	17[8]	22·4
Egypt	1,000·0	5·7[2]	...	...	24·1[11]	75·0	29·7	129	69	101,352	3,270	1,572	850[4]	180·9
French Equat. Africa	2,523·0	0·5	52	156	28·0	8·4	14·8	...	...	...	...	...	10[19]	6·7
French West Africa	4,634·0	4·1[2]	508	598	69·8[8]	34·3	46·5	...	...	...	...	...	50[19]	28·1
Ghana	237·9	1·0	242	300	53·7[8]	13·4[4]	14·9[4]	...	...	...	...	...	31[4]	17·1
British E. Africa	1,765·8	5·4	...	2,856	89·1	89·7	23·9	...	...	...	...	...	45[4 20]	57·0
Morocco	443·7	1·9	587	1,557	47·9[8]	125·2[4 21]	52·8[4 21]	...	...	...	...	...	431[21]	126·3[22]
Nigeria	878·4	2·9	595	2,259[5]	59·6	20·2	19·9	...	...	...	...	...	70	26·5[2 3]
Rhodesia and Nyasaland, Fed. of	1,263·0	5·2	...	5,978	85·0	96·0	37·5	...	...	135,744	8,274	1,572	44[8 2]	84·3
South Africa, Union of	1,223·4	21·7[2]	...	27,160[5]	338·1[4]	690·0	197·0	194	143	427,332	13,291	10,272	794	828·4
Tunisia	125·2	2·1[2]	276	965	9·1	37·8	...	...	...	...	...	...	108	34·6
N. America														
Canada	9,974·4	70·7	4,013	96,831	865·4	3,375·0	1,015·0	1,516	1,096	3,231,552	95,309	49,668	9,050[4]	4,816·1
Costa Rica	50·9	0·3	...	...	3·0[8]	11·3	9·6	510	144	...	...	...	50[11]	12·4
Guatemala	108·9	1·2	...	234	8·1[4]	19·9	9·5	...	...	...	...	...	36[11]	11·7
Honduras	112·1	1·3	...	...	2·5	3·2	3·8	338	89	...	...	...	30[4]	4·7
Mexico	1,969·3	23·4[2]	2,554[1]	10,131[1]	43·5[8]	320·4[4]	261·1[4]	162	70	1,754,580[2]	69,320	57,744[2]	2,500[8]	413·0
Nicaragua	148·0	0·5	...	36	4·5	7·8	5·7	...	...	5,020[2]	1,225	760[2]	30[11]	6·3
Panama	74·5	0·2	...	...	2·2	14·9	7·1	4,358	602	...	...	...	95[8]	23·0
Salvador, El	20·0	0·8	...	...	8·0	15·1	5·6	...	...	...	...	...	21[11]	11·3
United States	7,828·0	336·5	37,500	805,236[25]	5,559·5	55,906·0	11,229·0	25,590	4,301	50,692,044	1,570,958	1,133,412	150,000[4]	63,620·9
S. America														
Argentina	2,778·4	46·0	15,884[2]	14,352[2]	146·9[4]	364·5	318·8	1,029	356	528,924	22,535	8,712	2,900[19]	1,181·1
Bolivia	1,098·6	2·7	...	...	22·8[8]	13·5	22·0	—	—	33,350[2]	3,666	2,552[2]	200[4]	23·2
Brazil	8,513·8	37·0[2]	12,712[4]	10,375[4]	467·4	396·0	389·0	911	409	2,289,496[2]	130,517	109,189[2]	3,500[11]	869·8
Chile	741·8	8·4	1,529	2,146	64·4[4]	53·4	54·8	231	102	386,664	15,189	9,552	650[11]	160·3
Colombia	1,138·4	3·0	658	706	29·2	83·6[3]	73·8[3]	...	...	631,824	38,350	51,612	500[18]	222·9
Ecuador	270·7	1·3	112[4]	100[4]	8·0	5·2	16·5	...	...	...	...	...	100[4]	22·0
Paraguay	406·8	1·1	39[2]	18	6·9	4·0	3·0	...	...	...	...	...	80[19]	8·2
Peru	1,285·2	2·7[2]	320[2]	524[2]	39·1	64·4	54·5	108	54	109,820[2]	6,765	6,405[2]	500[18]	79·2
Uruguay	186·9	3·1	...	...	41·6	83·0	58·5	72	38	...	...	...	500[4]	128·9
Venezuela	912·1	0·7	5	8	24·2	222·0[3]	153·6[3]	233	99	359,952	22,528	15,900	218[16]	139·8
Oceania														
Australia	7,704·2	42·5	...	11,093[1 9]	847·5	1,565·0	707·0	631	353	2,183,388	88,747	78,204	2,138	1,873·8
New Zealand	268·0	5·6	...	1,896[5 7]	90·3	465·7[3]	125·4[2]	256	162	377,448	15,402	11,412	531[2]	605·2[8 7]

[1] State system only. [2] 1957. [3] 1958. [4] 1956. [5] Year ended March. [6] Excl. Berlin. [7] 1959. [8] 1955. [9] Year ended June. [10] Excl. the Azores and Madeira Islands. [11] 1954. [12] Excl. N. Ireland. [13] Incl. 7,761,000 combined sound-television licences. [14] Year ended September. [15] 1952. [16] 1951. [17] Incl. Singapore. [18] 1950. [19] 1953. [20] Excl. Uganda. [21] Former French zone. [22] Former French and Spanish zones. [23] Incl. Cameroons. [24] Excl. S. Rhodesia (24,000 in 1951). [25] Class I railways.

SOURCES. *Lloyd's Register, Statistical Tables* (London, 1958); U.N. *Statistical Yearbook 1958*; U.N. *Monthly Bulletin of Statistics*; U.N. *Annual Bulletin of Transport Statistics for Europe*; official published statistics of the different countries.

COMMUNIST MOVEMENT. The Communist movement achieved a state of relative stability in 1959. There was no serious dissension between the Communist Party of the Soviet Union and the ruling parties of eastern Europe, though there was a certain uneasiness apparent in relations between Moscow and Peking towards the end of the year. The dispute between the orthodox Communists and Marshal Josip Broz Tito's supporters in Yugoslavia remained unresolved but was conducted in relatively mild terms. Communism registered no gains as a political force in western Europe, but the influence of Communists on events in the middle east, Africa and South America was more apparent.

The relative quiescence of the Communist movement appeared to derive from the new tactics imposed by Nikita Khrushchev in the field of foreign affairs and confirmed at the 21st congress of the C.P.S.U. in Feb. 1959. Although belief in the ultimate triumph of Communism over capitalism remained basic to the Communist movement, Khrushchev decreed that the victory would not be achieved by an all-out assault on capitalism but in the course of peaceful competition with capitalism, in which the superiority of the Communist system, especially in economic respects, would be demonstrated to the world. Appeals to rally the forces of the working people of the world to overthrow the " Anglo-American imperialists " were replaced by appeals for friendship between Moscow and Washington as the key to world peace. The visits of Anastas Mikoyan, Frol Kozlov and finally of Khrushchev himself to the United States were practical expressions of the new line. By the end of the year the effect of this revision of Marxism on a world scale was only beginning to be felt.

Though the Chinese Communists formally conceded leadership of world Communism to the C.P.S.U., there were indications that they did not always frame their policies to accord with Soviet wishes. Their forceful seizure of power in Tibet and their incursions into Indian territory did not assist Khrushchev's policy of *détente* with the United States. His warning, on arrival in Peking in October, that Communists should not allow themselves to be led by the strength of their " camp " to test the stability of the capitalist system by force was regarded as an admonition to the Chinese leaders, who later gave formal support to the new line in Soviet policy.

Though relations between the U.S.S.R. and Yugoslavia remained correct on the governmental plane, and diplomatic and economic relations were maintained, there was no improvement in relations between the C.P.S.U. and the League of Communists of Yugoslavia. Albania and Bulgaria continued to conduct a propaganda war against Tito's regime.

Important steps were taken towards the closer integration of the economies of the countries of eastern Europe and the U.S.S.R. At a meeting of the Council for Mutual Economic Aid in Tirana in May decisions were taken co-ordinating economic plans for the period 1959-65. The programme provided for a substantial increase in the output of coal and steel in the whole area, the establishment of a common electric power supply and the construction of an oil pipeline from the U.S.S.R. to eastern Europe. A " division of labour " between the various countries was also agreed, by which each country's major function in the bloc was laid down.

The Communist parties of western Europe registered no gains in 1959, though the French Communists slightly improved their position in the municipal elections in March. The Communist Party of Great Britain put up 18 candidates and received 30,897 of a total of 27,863,338 votes cast in the general election on Oct. 8. Communism remained insignificant as a political force in North America.

Communist parties continued to be suppressed in the majority of countries of the middle east, including the United Arab Republic, but with the notable exception of Iraq. The influence of Communism generally in the area suffered a setback with the deterioration in relations between Moscow and Cairo. But this was compensated for by the greatly increased part played by the Communists in Iraq. After an unsuccessful campaign to secure participation for itself in the government of Brigadier Abd-ul-Karim Kassem, the Iraqi Communist party moderated its demands and reconciled itself to conducting political activity through the various " front " organizations. Meanwhile relations between the U.S.S.R. and Kassem improved throughout the year and much economic aid was provided by the Soviet government.

The issue of Communist influence in India was thrown into relief by the Indian government's dismissal of the Communist government which had won power in Kerala in 1957. This action was taken by Jawaharlal Nehru on the grounds that the Communists had lost the backing of a majority of the population in the state. It was placed under presidential rule by a decree of July 31 which was endorsed by an overwhelming majority of the Indian parliament, the Communist party finding it possible to gather 38 votes in opposition. Serious

MEMBERSHIP OF THE COMMUNIST PARTIES*
(First date, the year of party's foundation; second date, year of latest estimate of party's membership)

A. Countries of the Communist Bloc

China (1921; 1958)	12,500,000	Poland (1918; 1959)	1,072,932
U.S.S.R. (1903; 1959)	8,239,000	Rumania (1921; 1958)	865,000
Czechoslovakia		Bulgaria (1919; 1958)	484,255
(1921; 1958)	1,422,199	Hungary (1918; 1959)	437,950
German Dem. Rep.		North Vietnam	
(1946; 1956)	1,427,000	(1930; 1957)	460,000
North Korea		Albania (1941; 1957)	c. 50,000
(1925; 1958)	1,181,195	Mongolia (1921; 1958)	42,896

B. Other European Countries

Austria (1918; 1958)	50,000	Ireland, Republic of	
Belgium (1921; 1958)	12,000	(?; 1959)	c. 100
Denmark (1921; 1958)	10,000	Italy (1921; 1959)	c.1,787,338
Finland (1918; 1958)	30,000	Luxemburg (1921; 1958)	500
France (1920; 1958)	c. 200,000	Netherlands (1918; 1959)	c. 15,000
German Fed. Rep.		Norway (1922; 1959)	5,000
(1948; 1958)†	c. 10,000	Portugal (1921; 1958)†	9,000
Great Britain (1920; 1959)	26,749	Spain (1921; 1958)†	5,000
Greece (1920?; 1958)†	c. 20,000	Sweden (1921; 1959)	c. 25,000
Iceland (1930; 1958)	c. 1,000	Switzerland (1921; 1958)	6,000
		Yugoslavia (1919; 1957)	755,066

C. Countries of the Far East and Southeast Asia

Burma (1939; 1957)	8,000	Laos (1957; 1958)	c. 15,000
Cambodia (1950; 1957)	c. 1,000	Malaya (1930; 1957)†	c. 5,000
Ceylon (1943; 1958)	c. 2,000	Nepal (1951; 1957)†	c. 3,000
India (1921; 1959)	300,000	Pakistan (1948; 1957)†	c. 3,000
Indonesia (1920; 1959)	1,500,000	Philippines (1930; 1958)	3,000
Japan (1922; 1958)	50,000	Thailand (?; 1957)†	5,000

D. Countries of the Middle East

Iraq (1932; 1958)	5,000	Sudan (1956; 1959)	c. 1,000
Israel (1921; 1957)	2,000	Turkey (1920; 1957)†	2,000
Jordan (1951; 1958)	2,000	United Arab Republic:	
Lebanon (1930; 1958)†	8,000	Egypt (1920; 1958)†	c. 8,000
Persia (1920; 1958)†	c. 8,000	Syria (1930; 1958)†	c. 10,000

E. Countries of North America

United States (1921; 1958)†	7,000	Canada (1922; 1958)	6,000

F. Countries of Australasia

Australia (1920; 1958)	5,000	New Zealand (1924; 1958)	c. 1,000

G. Countries of Latin America

Argentina (1920; 1957)	75,000	Haiti (1930; 1958)†	200
Bolivia (1949; 1957)	5,000	Honduras (1920; 1958)†	400
Brazil (1921; 1958)†	60,000	Mexico (1919; 1958)	7,000
Chile (1921; 1958)	45,000	Nicaragua (?; 1958)†	200
Colombia (1926; 1959)†	c. 5,000	Panama (1930; 1959)†	250
Costa Rica (1930; 1959)†	300	Paraguay (1928; 1959)†	400
Cuba (1925; 1959)	12,000	Peru (1928; 1957)†	6,000
Ecuador (1928; 1957)	1,000	Uruguay (1920; 1958)	4,000
El Salvador (1925; 1958)	500	Venezuela (1931; 1959)	20,000
Guatemala (1924; 1958)†	1,000		

* Including candidate members. † The Communist party is banned.

divisions occurred in the party over the attitude to be taken towards the Chinese encroachment on Indian territory.

Though Communism was not a political force in Africa, the year saw a notable increase in African issues by Communist leaders. An Association of Friendship with the Peoples of Africa was set up in Moscow in April. Communist propaganda regularly encouraged African peoples to fight for " national liberation ". Many delegations, mostly commercial, visited Ghana and Guinea from Communist capitals. The Afro-Asian Youth conference held in Cairo in February was under strong Communist influence, but was not an entire success for its organizers, who were unable to suppress criticism of the Communist attitude to nationalism.

The principal Communist " front " activity was the organization of the World Youth festival in Vienna in July. It was the first time such an event had been outside the Communist countries, and it resulted in interesting contacts with non-Communist youth. Its main propaganda effect was thought to have been on the young people of Asia and Africa who attended.

The 10th anniversary session of the World Peace council took place in Stockholm in May and was attended by some 350 delegates. It issued an appeal for the cessation of nuclear tests and the calling of a summit meeting. A statement on the German problem was issued, closely following the line taken by the Soviet government, and the council expressed its support for the " oppressed African peoples ". Professor J. D. Bernal was made chairman of the presidential committee, formed to replace the presidency, which had been vacant since the death of Prof. J. F. Joliot-Curie.

The fifth conference against atomic and nuclear bombs was held in Hiroshima in August. It was attended by delegates from 25 countries and six international organizations, mostly Communist. There were protests against the Communist bias shown by the Japanese organizers of the conference.

At the 21st congress of the C.P.S.U. in Moscow in February Nikita Khrushchev claimed that there were then Communist parties in 83 countries and that their membership exceeded 33 million. (There were 43 parties with a total of some 4 million members on the eve of World War II.) Of this total 28 million members belonged to the Communist parties in power in the Soviet sphere, of which the Chinese party claimed over 12 million and the C.P.S.U. over 8 million members. The 70 parties of the Non-Communist world thus accounted for about 5 million members, of whom the only " mass " parties, the French, Italian and Indonesian, accounted for about 3·5 million members. (*See* also EASTERN EUROPEAN ECONOMIC PLANNING; ELECTIONS; POLITICAL PARTIES, EUROPEAN; U.S.S.R.) (D. F.)

COMORO ARCHIPELAGO (TERRITOIRE DES COMORES),

an overseas territory of the French Republic consisting of four islands (Grande Comore, Anjouan, Moheli, Mayotte) lying in the Indian ocean between Africa and the northern tip of Madagascar. Area: 849 sq.mi. Pop.: (1950 est.) 168,890; (1958 est.) 181,288, of mixed Negro and Arab blood, with some Malagasy elements. Language: Comorean, akin to Swahili. Religion: Moslem. Capital: Moroni (pop., 6,488), on the Grande Comore island. High administrator: George Arnaud. Chief exports: vanilla, copra, scent ingredients. Monetary unit: *franc CFA* =metropolitan Fr.2.

History. A new territorial assembly was elected on March 9, 1959. On April 26 Ahmed Abdallah was elected a member of the French Senate. From Nov. 30, 1958, Said Mohammed Sheikh and Prince Said Ibrahim Abdallah (president of the assembly) were members of the French National Assembly. Mohammed Ahmed served under the high administrator as deputy prime minister.

On July 9 General Charles de Gaulle went to Moroni, where he was received by Jacques Soustelle, minister-delegate to the prime minister's office, who was visiting the four islands. (HU. DE.)

CONGO, REPUBLIC OF (RÉPUBLIQUE DU CONGO,

formerly Moyen-Congo), a member state of the French Community, Congo is bounded N.E. by the Republic of Gabon, N. by the autonomous Republic of Cameroun and by the Central African Republic, E. and S.E. by the Belgian Congo, S. by the Portuguese Congo (Cabinda), and W. by the Atlantic ocean. Area: 132,046 sq.mi. Pop. (1950 est.) 684,000; (1959 est.) 765,000; mainly Bantu Negroes; Europeans (1957 est.) 10,424. Language: Bantu dialects. Religion: animist with a strong Christian minority. Chief towns (pop. 1957 est.): Brazzaville (cap., 99,000); Pointe-Noire (38,000); Franceville; Dolisie. President of republic, Abbé Fulbert Youlou. French high commissioner, Guy Georgy. Chief exports: timber, palm kernels, palm oil. Monetary unit: *franc CFA* =metropolitan Fr.2.

History. The Republic of Congo was proclaimed on Nov. 28, 1958, by the territorial assembly. Fulbert Youlou, appointed head of the government, transferred the capital from Pointe-Noire to Brazzaville. The constitution was adopted by his supporters (Union Démocratique de Défense des Intérêts Africains) on Feb. 21, the opposition (Mouvement Socialiste Africain) having retired. The constitution provided for an assembly which would invest the prime minister. The power to initiate legislation was shared between the assembly and the government.

During a riot on Feb. 18, members of the M'Boshi tribe, supporters of Jacques Opangault, the leader of the opposition, and the Balali, supporters of Youlou, attacked one another. There were 120 killed and 200 wounded. Opangault was arrested. On Sept. 28, while some followers of the André Matsoua (d. 1942) sect, which refused to pay taxes, were being moved to a new locality, 35 died from suffocation.

At the elections held on June 15, the supporters of Youlou obtained 64% of the votes cast and 49 seats out of a total of 61. Youlou was re-elected prime minister, and Opangault was set free. A flag was adopted: green, yellow and red in vertical stripes. On Nov. 21 Youlou proclaimed himself president of the Republic of Congo. (HU. DE.)

CONGREGATIONAL CHURCHES.

The Congregational churches, stemming from the Separatists, Puritans and Independents of the 16th and 17th centuries, emphasize the local

Marjorie Inkster, a former psychiatric social worker, who was appointed assistant minister at the City Temple, London, in March.

gathered community meeting under the lordship of Christ as the true Christian church, though they associate together at different levels for many common purposes. World membership (1959), c. 2·3 million, incl. 370,000 in Great Britain.

The outstanding event of 1959 was the decision to set up eight commissions to study and report on the total life and witness of the Congregational churches of England and Wales. The matters for review were: the nature of Christian unity and its challenge to the churches; the relation of the churches to one another and to the Congregational union; the preparation of a statement of faith for the use of the churches; the effectiveness of the life and witness of the local church in the contemporary world; the elimination of superfluous churches and the establishment of new causes; the nature of the church's missionary obligation and the relationship between the union and the London Missionary society; the nature of the ministry and the meaning of ordination; and the more effective moral influence of the churches on the life of local communities and of the nation.

At the assembly meetings in May B. J. Hartwell, a lawyer, took office as chairman of the union. The Rev. Dr. J. Trevor Davies of Bournemouth was elected his successor for the following year.

A number of changes took place in the staff of the union during the year. Edith Rawlings, women's secretary, who died in office, was succeeded by Dorothy J. Biggs. The Rev. John White, home churches secretary, was appointed a moderator and was replaced by the Rev. Douglas Smith. Harold Simpson retired after a long period of service as financial secretary.

At the end of 1958 the *Congregational Quarterly* ceased publication after a life of 36 years. The Rev. William Hodgkins replaced Dr. Erik Routley as editor of the *Congregational Monthly*.

In the United States, during 1958, 103,663 members were added to the membership of the local churches. Gifts of benevolences during that year totalled $10,155,582 and local church expenditures amounted to $57,533,522. The total value of local church property of the denomination was $606,294,174. Forty-one new church buildings were completed and dedicated during 1958 and a two-year campaign was begun to raise $7·5 million for Christian higher education —a fund to provide a Christian ministry in the interest of higher education both in the United States and throughout the foreign mission fields. The United Church of Christ, which had been formed in Cleveland, Ohio, on June 25, 1957, by the action of the General Council of the Congregational Christian Churches with the Evangelical and Reformed Church, was in process of preparing and adopting a constitution and of co-ordinating and unifying the programme of the uniting communions. (R. F. G. C.; F. Ho.)

CONGRESS, U.S. The first session of the 86th congress convened on Jan. 7, 1959, and ended on Sept. 15. It was notable as the first congress to seat senators and a representative from the state of Alaska. As a result of the elections of the previous November the Democrats enjoyed a massive majority in both houses. In the Senate there were 64 Democrats and 34 Republicans; in the House of Representatives 283 Democrats and 153 Republicans. The principal officers in the Senate were: Richard M. Nixon, president; Lyndon B. Johnson, majority leader; Mike Mansfield, majority whip; Everett M. Dirksen, minority leader; and Thomas H. Kuchel, minority whip. Those in the House were: Sam Rayburn, speaker (for the ninth time, a record); John W. McCormack, majority leader; Charles A. Halleck (who defeated his predecessor, Joseph W. Martin, in a dramatic contest), minority leader. There were no important changes in committee chairmanships. The filibuster rule was modified—in response to a liberal "revolt"—to enable debate to be terminated by a vote of two-thirds of senators present and voting instead of, as previously, two-thirds of the entire membership.

In his State of the Union message on Jan. 9 President Dwight D. Eisenhower emphasized the need for thrift and a balanced budget and in his budget message on Jan. 19 envisaged receipts of $77,100 million to meet expenditures of $77,000 million, $3,900 less than was spent in the previous year.

Johnson and Rayburn were surprisingly successful in the dual task of holding together their Democratic majorities and in getting along with a Republican executive. By its Easter adjournment congress had made more progress than usual and had passed bills granting Hawaii statehood and extending selective service for four years. Subsequently, however, relations between legislature and executive worsened. The Senate criticized the presidential nomination of Mrs. Clare Luce as ambassador to Brazil and later rejected that of Lewis L. Strauss as secretary of commerce. The president vetoed a housing bill as "excessive"; congress eventually passed one he found acceptable. Both with the White House and within congress there was much disagreement over the "toughness" appropriate to a new law designed to control abuses in trade unions. As finally passed the measure was a compromise, reluctantly accepted by the A.F.L.-C.I.O. and detested by the Teamsters at which it was especially aimed. Stimulated by the findings of Senator John F. Kennedy's investigating committee, the bill restricted "blackmail" picketing and secondary boycotts and provided a "bill of rights" for union members. Presidential pressure forced congress to pass a measure raising the petrol tax by 1 cent a gal., but the president's veto of an $800 million public works bill designed to provide politically useful local benefits was overridden by 280 to 121 votes in the House and 72 to 23 in the Senate. (In all, in the year, 19 bills were successfully vetoed by the president.) Congress also successfully insisted on its own estimate of what should be spent on foreign aid— $3,200 million, in place of the $4,400 million asked for by the president. On several important issues congress took no action. It refused to increase the interest rate payable on long-term bonds, to provide federal aid for schools or to pass any legislation to protect negroes in the exercise of their civil rights.

In September the first Congressional Distinguished Service awards were given to Senators Hubert H. Humphrey and John J. Williams, former congressman and now senator, Kenneth B. Keating and Congressman Carl Vinson, chosen by the American Political Science association. Such awards were first suggested by Senator William Benton, whose William Benton foundation had underwritten the programme, and were to be given every two years. (H. G. N.)

CONSERVATIVE PARTY. The policy on which the Conservative party contested the general election of Oct. 8, 1959, was laid down in the party manifesto *The Next Five Years*; its theme was peace and prosperity. The result of the election was that the Conservative government obtained a majority of 106 over the Labour party, and a majority of 100 over all other parties, compared with majorities of 60 and 54 respectively in the previous House of Commons. This was the first occasion since the Reform act of 1832 that a political party had won three consecutive general elections, twice increasing its majority while continuously in office.

With the confirmation of a Conservative government in office for a third term, Harold Macmillan, the prime minister, remodelled his cabinet. (*See* CABINET MEMBERS.) Both Alan Lennox Boyd, secretary of state for the colonies, and Geoffrey Lloyd, minister of education, resigned from the cabinet; newcomers were Edward Heath and Ernest Marples. Eight ministers retained the offices they held in the previous government. The Ministry of Transport and Civil Aviation was divided. Edward Heath was succeeded as government chief whip by Martin Redmayne. R. A. Butler also succeeded Viscount Hailsham as chairman of the Conservative Party organization, and Sir Toby Low became deputy chairman *vice* Lord Poole.

Preceding the election two main publicity and propaganda factors were press advertising and a nation-wide poster campaign. The party organization concentrated on building up its constituency, ward and polling district branches, stressing the importance of the postal vote. This was reflected in two publications issued by the organization department entitled respectively *Branch Lines* and *Guide to Postal Voting*. An instructional film showing the working of a district committee room during an election was produced and widely used. Important election publications included: *The Campaign Guide, 1959* and *Supplement*; *All the Answers*; *How Conservatives have helped the British People* (9th edition); and *Daily Notes* (16 issues).

In the local government elections the Conservative party had a net gain of 321 seats.

The Young Conservative and Unionist organization held a national rally at the Royal Festival hall in April, attended by over 4,000 members, and addressed by the prime minister. The national leadership training scheme for new officers was enlarged and at the general election 62 Young Conservatives stood as parliamentary candidates, of whom 9 were elected. Peter Walker was re-elected as chairman of the national advisory committee in March.

Conservative Political centre publications included *Minds Matter*; *The Health Services*; *Reform of Purchase Tax*; *Achievement in Agriculture*; *Tomorrow Our Responsibility*; *Some Reflections on British Foreign Policy*; *The Responsible Society*; *Everyman a Capitalist*; *The Missile Years*; *The Challenge of Leisure*; *Work for Wales*; and *Willingly to School*. (*See* also ELECTIONS; GENERAL ELECTION.)   (R. Ss.)

COSTA RICA. Central American republic between Nicaragua and Panama. Area: 19,695 sq.mi. Pop.: (1950 census) 800,875; (1958 est.) 1,076,337; classified as about 80% white, 17% mixed, 2% Negro and 1% other. Language: Spanish. Religion: predominantly Roman Catholic. Capital: San José (pop., 1958 est.) 102,297. President, Mario Echandi Jiménez. Main exports: bananas, coffee, cacao. Monetary unit: *colón* with a free exchange rate of C.18·50 to the £ sterling.

History. Costa Rican political events in 1959 indicated a moderating of the party divisions caused by the presidential election in 1958. Echandi's National Union party held only 10 of the 45 seats in the Legislative Assembly and had to rely upon the varying support of third and fourth parties to offset some of the strength of José Figueres' National Liberation party with its 20 seats. Echandi vetoed 18 bills passed since his election in Feb. 1958, while the assembly succeeded in overriding the veto once only. That body accused Echandi of being too neutral over the matter of dictatorship in Latin America and by a narrow vote censured him for attending formal ceremonies with the president of Nicaragua.

Much optimism developed from Costa Rica's success in obtaining international loans for the expansion and diversification of its economy. The Export-Import Bank of Washington granted $5,540,000 to help complete the last 90 mi. of the Inter-American highway in southern Costa Rica. The International Bank for Reconstruction and Development authorized $3·5 million for the importation of capital goods to aid the government's loan programme in agriculture and light industry.

Costa Rica extended diplomatic recognition to the revolutionary government of Fidel Castro in Cuba in Jan. 1959. Later, however, Castro attacked Figueres for declaring that there was Communist influence in Cuba.   (T. L. K.)

COST OF LIVING. The upward drift in the cost of living which had persisted in most countries from 1955 had ended in many of them by the middle of 1959. In 1958 world prices of many raw materials had fallen as demand for them ceased to expand; this was when world industrial production stopped growing. The slackening of demand and reduced raw material prices were followed by almost stationary wholesale prices for manufactured products. There was, however, a further time lag of approximately one year before retail prices neared stability. The normal time lag was probably increased by the moderate extent of the world recession and its nature. The recession was primarily in investment, with wage rates and consumption expenditure being well maintained, or even increased, in most countries. Late in 1959 the stability in retail prices was still being maintained despite a recovery in demand and a resumed growth in world industrial output. There seemed to be prospects, perhaps for the first time since the end of World War II, of a continuation of stable prices. The accumulated demands for peace-time products had at last been met, the acute shortages following the war were over and the capacity for further production had been increased after the war-time destruction. The stability was not, this time, a reaction from a short period of rapid price rises such as had accompanied the Korean war of 1951. The relationships between raw material, wholesale and retail prices looked reasonable and further changes could not be anticipated. There was no marked disequilibrium.

Generalizations, however, are never fully correct. The stability covered North America, most of Europe, some of the Commonwealth countries and a few other countries such as Japan and Israel. In other countries the upward drift of about 3% per year continued, while in a few, especially in South America, the upward trend was too marked to be called a drift. Thus there were obviously some world influences at work and, superimposed thereon, national influences.

United Kingdom. The achievement of near stability was welcomed especially in the United Kingdom as it followed a period when the cost of living tended to drift upwards slightly more than in competitor countries. The fall in world prices of raw materials had special significance for the United Kingdom as a large importer. In addition there had been the credit and hire purchase restrictions of the autumn of 1957, but these, in conjunction with world recession, had seemed to be holding back prices at a cost of potential production which was too great to be continued. Thus from the autumn

TABLE I. RETAIL PRICES, UNITED KINGDOM (Jan. 1956 = 100)

	1957 Oct.	1958 Oct.	1959 Jan.	1959 April	1959 July	1959 Oct.
All food	104·7	108·1	109·8	108·6	107·4	107·4
Bread, cereals	119	118	119	119	119	119
Meat, bacon	99	108	110	107	107	107
Fish	110	114	117	112	109	114
Butter, margarine, etc.	88	78	87	84	92	100
Milk, cheese, eggs	110	114	110	106	103	110
Tea, coffee, etc.	102	100	100	101	101	100
Sugar, preserves	100	103	104	105	105	105
Vegetables	101	115	125	128	114	104
Fruit	111	99	102	107	112	99
Other food	103	104	104	104	103	103
Alcoholic drink	105·7	105·8	105·9	97·8	98·1	98·0
Tobacco	107·8	107·8	107·8	107·8	107·8	108·2
Housing	114·1	123·8	125·8	127·1	128·5	128·8
Fuel and light	109·9	110·9	116·6	117·0	111·1	112·2
Durable household goods	101·2	100·0	100·1	98·1	97·9	97·8
Clothing	102·9	102·8	102·2	102·3	102.4	102·9
Transport	111·6	112·7	113·4	114·3	114·7	115·0
Miscellaneous goods	111·1	113·5	113·6	113·0	113·8	113·8
Services	113·7	115·2	114·8	115·6	116·4	116·8
All items	107·1	109·4	110·4	109·5	109·0	109·2

SOURCE. *Ministry of Labour Gazette.*

of 1958 the restrictions were progressively removed, with bank rate being reduced in steps from 7% to 4%, banks lending far more freely to customers and restrictions on hire purchase removed. Production, which had increased little since 1955, started to grow again—with no obvious adverse effects upon prices. Indeed, so far as industrial products were concerned the increased activity enabled the new equipment to be worked more fully and hence more efficiently, thus helping to keep prices down. It was, however, not yet certain whether the upward drift that had continued since 1935 had been completely ended. There were some disappointing features in the recorded details of retail price changes. Food was, in October, slightly cheaper than a year before, and comparison over shorter periods than a year can be very misleading because of seasonal variations. Here an important factor was an increase in the prices of fats; since butter, mainly imported, had recovered somewhat from a very low level, the increase was not surprising. Alcoholic drink was cheaper by 7% and housing dearer by 5%, the former

entirely the result of government action in reducing customs and excise duties, the latter mainly, but not entirely, a continuation of the effects of removal of rent restrictions. The average expenditure per household on alcoholic drink is not much less than on housing (rent, rates, etc.). Durable household goods became about 2% cheaper in the year, this being due to reductions in purchase tax. For the rest the drift, though slight, was still unmistakably upward and especially so for items incorporating a large proportion of U.K. labour and other resources. The upward drift, still averaging some 1% per year, existed in services, transport, and fuel and light, though clothing showed little change.

Other Countries. Interest attached to those countries which were exceptional in not achieving stability in their cost of living. In most of Europe the general pattern was of stability or of a 1% rise compared with a 3% rise in the preceding year. A recorded rise of some 2% or 3% in the year tended to confirm a continuance of the old drift in such countries as Greece, Portugal and Finland. Rises of 9% in Spain, 6% in Paris and 5% in Reykjavik suggested real failures to adhere to the prevailing pattern. Within the Commonwealth stability seemed to have been achieved in Canada, Ceylon and Kenya, while in Pakistan prices were recorded as having fallen. By contrast the upward drift continued in Australia, South Africa, the Rhodesias and Jamaica. There were increases of more than 3% in New Zealand, Cyprus and Ghana. In other areas the continuation of a rising cost of living was far more common, with prices doubling in Argentina, increasing by over one-third in Chile and Brazil and by 8% in Peru. Outside South America there were increases of 15% in Persia and 9% in Algeria, but there was stability in Japan, Burma and Formosa. (*See also* NATIONAL INCOME; PRICES; WAGES AND HOURS; WEALTH AND INCOME, DISTRIBUTION OF.) (H. S. B.)

TABLE II. RETAIL PRICES IN SELECTED COUNTRIES (1953=100)

	1957 (average)	1958 Sept.	1958 Dec.	1959 March	1959 June	1959 Sept.*
United States						
Food	102	107	105	104	105	105
All items	105	108	108	108	108	109
United Kingdom						
Food	119	119	123	121	122	119
All items	116	119	121	121	120	119
Other Europe						
Austria (Vienna)	113	115	115	115	...	...
Belgium	107	108	109	109	110	110
Denmark	116	118	119	...	...	...
Finland	120	128	128	128	129	130
France (Paris)	106	123	124	128	128	129
German Fed. Rep.	106	109	110	110	111	112
Greece (Athens)	129	131	132	133	133	135
Iceland (Reykjavik)	121	130	140	129	129	129
Italy	110	114	113	112	112	113
Netherlands	114	116	117	115	117	120
Norway	112	120	120	119	120	121
Portugal	104	105	107	108	103	107
Spain	123	143	148	149	151	150
Sweden	113	119	119	119	119	121
Switzerland	105	108	108	106	106	107
Yugoslavia	121	122	126	127	125	128
Commonwealth						
Australia†	113	115	116	117	118	119
Canada	106	109	109	109	109	110
Ceylon (Colombo)	101	103	103	103	105	103
Cyprus	127	135	132	138	134	135
Ghana (Accra)	109	110	109	116	114	107
India	104	114	112	110	115	117
Jamaica (Kingston)	103	108	109	110	114	114
Kenya (Nairobi)	116	118	117	117	118	118
New Zealand†	113	121	122	122	122	124
Pakistan (Karachi)	106	114	100	103	104	110
Northern Rhodesia	115	118	118	120	120	120
Southern Rhodesia	108	113	113	115	116	116
Singapore	94	91	92	92	91	91
South Africa	110	115	115	115	116	115
Tanganyika	110	112	114	114	114	114
Other Areas						
Algeria (Algiers)	106	120	124	129	128	131
Argentina (Buenos Aires)	165	235	275	379	482	525
Brazil (São Paulo)	206	243	265	302	315	344
Burma (Rangoon)	119	122	102	97	98	100
Chile (Santiago)	627	791	843	953	1,043	1,126
Formosa (Taipei)	133	137	135	...	...	...
Israel	135	143	140	140	140	140
Japan	109	109	109	109	109	111
Lebanon (Beirut)	109	...	115	118	118	117
Mexico (Mexico City)	135	151	155	152	155	154
Morocco (Casablanca)	113	113	121	121	113	113
Persia	139	139	147	161	165	...
Peru (Lima)	125	138	139	143	149	161

* Or latest available. † Average of quarters ending in month shown.
SOURCE. U.N. *Monthly Bulletin of Statistics.*

COTTON. A further marked contraction in international trade in cotton goods took place during the early part of 1959, but as the year progressed a more healthy tone pervaded the markets and in the later stages demand became insistent. During the 1958-59 season prices of raw cotton declined to the lowest levels for several years, and the use of the raw material was curtailed in many countries where spinning mills found difficulty in securing orders. On a statistical basis the season marked a turning point in the world cotton situation after stocks had been reduced to the smallest carry-over total since 1953. Output and consumption during the 12 months were roughly in balance and the long liquidation of the surplus of cotton formerly built up was halted. Acreage controls in the United States were relaxed for the new season and the early estimates of a U.S. crop approaching 14·8 million bales in 1959 brought fears of a return of rising stocks. World stocks at the beginning of the 1958-59 season had been 18·4 million bales, a reduction of 2 million bales compared with the previous season. By the end of 1958-59 stocks remained unchanged since, although the acreage harvested in 1958 in the United States was the smallest for 80 years, this was more than offset by a rise in the average yield to nearly one bale per ac., while in other countries the area harvested set new records. Meanwhile, in most of the consuming areas there was a lack of confidence in prices and customers were reluctant to extend their purchases. It was not until the early summer that a change took place and business began to broaden. Aggregate world consumption of raw cotton in the 1958-59 season was estimated at less than 28 million bales compared with 28·5 million bales in the previous season and the postwar peak of 29·6 million bales in 1956-57.

Great Britain. 1959 was an eventful year for cotton traders, starting with the abandonment of the price regulation schemes in spinning and doubling, due to the adverse verdict of the Restrictive Practices court, and ending with a government-sponsored reorganization plan which involved the scrapping of more than 13 million spinning and doubling spindles and over 100,000 looms. Sharp cuts in yarn prices followed the ending of the spinners' agreement and created much confusion in the market. Further difficulties arose in connection with the redundancy programme, as many mills decided to withdraw from the industry, receiving compensation for their scrapped machinery. The government plan also provided for a five-year re-equipment scheme, offering a 25% subsidy towards the cost. Arrangements were made to put an upper limit on the quantity of cloth and garments imported from Hong Kong, India and Pakistan for retention in the home market. Voluntary agreements with each country set a ceiling on annual arrivals for the next three years. Activity in the Liverpool futures market remained narrow and price changes were rare. U.S. 1-in. middling spot cotton began the year at 23·65d., there being a reduction to 22·25d. in March. A recovery followed to 23·35d. in June, with 22·70d. posted early in November. Sudan Sakel C6 quotation was 27·50d. in January, rising to 29·75d. in November. Sudan Lambert 6 opened the year at 27·00d., the November figure being 30·05d.

United States. An improvement in activity preceded the revival encountered in the rest of the world. Yarn output in the second quarter of the year was 16% higher than in the same period of 1958. The average margin between raw cotton and cloth prices widened steadily and in July was at its highest level since 1956. A campaign was launched to restrict imports of made-up goods from all foreign sources. (*See* also TEXTILE INDUSTRY.)   (A. TL.)

COUNCIL OF EUROPE. An institution of consultative character founded on May 5, 1949, in London, and inaugurated on Aug. 10 of the same year at Strasbourg. It consists of a committee of ministers (composed of the foreign ministers of member countries) and a consultative assembly (delegations from the several parliaments), the former providing for the development of co-operation between governments, the latter a means through which the aspirations of the European peoples may be formulated and expressed. Every member government was to " accept the principles of the rule of law and of the enjoyment by all persons within its jurisdiction of human rights and fundamental freedoms." From 1949 the following countries were full members: Belgium, Denmark, France, Greece, Republic of Ireland, Italy, Luxembourg, Netherlands, Norway, Sweden, Turkey and the United Kingdom. Iceland joined on March 7, 1950, and Austria on April 16, 1956. The German Federal Republic became an associate member in 1950 (full member on May 2, 1951). From May 13, 1950, until Dec. 31, 1956, the Saar was also an associate member, sending its representatives to the consultative assembly only. Headquarters, Strasbourg; president of the assembly (elected April 21, 1959), John Edwards (Britain); secretary-general (elected May 2, 1957), Lodovico Benvenuti.

History. The year 1959 saw the completion of the first decade of the council's existence. In Strasbourg the anniversary ceremonies in May were arranged to coincide with the opening of the 11th session of the consultative assembly, and the occasion was marked by the solemn induction of the European Court of Human Rights, whose 15 judges had been elected at the previous part-session in January. With European economic integration very much in the melting-pot, however, owing to the collapse of the negotiations on a free trade area, the mood was necessarily restrained. In April, and again in September, the assembly approved a joint recommendation of its political and economic committees reaffirming the determination of the governments to bring about eventually a multi-lateral association between the European Economic community (the six) and the other member countries of O.E.E.C. and calling specifically for the signature of declarations of intent to that effect by March 31, 1960. The September recommendation was made with specific reference to the new Stockholm agreement of the outer seven (Austria, Denmark, Norway, Portugal, Sweden, Switzerland and the United Kingdom).

Appropriately the ministers, however conscious they might be that the council's role was now chiefly one of marking time, supplied a political counterpart to these aspirations towards economic integration. Their resolution of April 20 on the revival of European co-operation at the 15-power level confirmed the vocation of the council to constitute the general framework of European policy, underlined the progress made by the conclusion of European conventions and the habit of consultation induced and developed by the Strasbourg meetings, welcomed especially the imminent completion of the European Social charter and reiterated the council's intention to rationalize the European institutions in the light of ten years' experience.

In this connection, following a lead from the Belgian foreign minister, Pierre Wigny, the ministers acted on the initial recommendations of a special committee composed of senior officials of the 15 countries. They demanded, on the one hand, that representatives of Portugal and Switzerland should be invited to attend regularly whenever O.E.E.C.

H. Macmillan speaking in London on May 4, when the tenth anniversary of the Council of Europe was celebrated. Seated (l. to r.): Lord Kilmuir; P. Wigny, Belgian foreign minister; J. Edwards, president of the assembly; and the secretary general, L. Benvenuti.

reports or other economic questions were under discussion by the assembly—which would thus take on the character of a *de facto* parliamentary organ for O.E.E.C.—and, on the other hand, that the council of the seven-power W.E.U. (Western European union) should arrange for a transfer of social and cultural matters to the 15-power organization.

In January the assembly staged a notable political debate on the problem of Berlin. Speakers included Willy Brandt, the chief burgomaster of the city, as well as the foreign minister of the German Federal Republic, Heinrich von Brentano.

Outside the political field the chief event of the year was the ministers' signature of a further batch of the European conventions already mentioned above. Those signed in April related to the compulsory insurance against civil liability for motor vehicles, mutual assistance in criminal matters and the abolition of visas for refugees. In Dec. 1958 the subjects had been the exchange of television films and of " therapeutic substances of human origin ". The last-named, providing in effect a European blood-bank, was designed to meet an urgent need which had been high-lighted at the time of the flood disasters in Holland in 1953 when a high proportion of gifts of blood-products had been found to be unusable. (*See* also EUROPEAN COAL AND STEEL COMMUNITY.)

(W. H. CTR.)

See A. H. Robertson, *European Institutions* (London, 1959); P.E.P., *European Organisations* (London, 1959); George Watson, *The British Constitution and Europe* (Leyden, 1959).

COUNTRY LIFE.

It was difficult to find any excuses for the truly deplorable summer of 1958, although some had attributed it to the testing of various atomic devices; whereas the summer of 1959 was such that people had to go back a long way in their memories to remember a parallel. For many it was the finest since 1921.

It is true that in many agricultural areas the prolonged drought had most unfortunate results, especially in such light-land districts as East Anglia. But, on the other hand, in Northumberland, the combination of almost record-breaking sunshine figures and just enough rainfall undoubtedly produced yields of corn crops never expected by even the most optimistic farmers. Wheat frequently topped the 2-ton per acre mark, a yield unheard of 20 years before, and a 16-ac. field of spring barley gave 45 cwts. to the acre.

A raingauge situated six mi. N.E. of Alnwick, Northumberland, gave a reading to the end of October of 13·64 in., compared with the average for the period of 20·68 in.; these figures probably have a greater impact when it is remembered that the 7 in. deficiency represents no less a rainfall than 700 tons per acre. Later in the year heavy and prolonged rain helped to make up for this scarcity, the raingauge registering 3·86 in. for November compared with an average of 2·31 in. for the month.

Sportsmen naturally expected that the wonderful summer would suit grouse admirably but in fact this was by no means true. The unfortunate combination of lack of heather seed, due to the very poor summer of 1958, together with a very late growth of young spring heather shoots, caused an extremely heavy mortality in old birds; some died at laying-time, and others actually on the nest from starvation. These conditions were prevalent in eastern Scotland, while many moors in northern England failed owing to lack of water for the young broods.

In several districts, also, partridges failed when, presumably, everything should have been in their favour. This may be attributed, at least partially, to the lack of both rainfall and dew, for the drought was not conducive to much insect life, and for the chicks there was no dew to replace juices normally obtained from the insects devoured. On the other hand, wild pheasants had probably not done so well for many years.

Sacks of newly-picked Kentish hops being carried into oast houses at the end of August. The picking began earlier than usual.

One remarkable feature of 1959 was the astonishing growth of late autumn grass, as a result of fogs, October rainfall and mild temperatures. Lawns needed the motor-mower in November, which is rare in northeastern England.

The lack of any rainfall or prolonged wet grass suited the hares just as well as it did the wild pheasants; and it must have been many years since so large a proportion of leverets reached maturity. Many areas would have to arrange hare drives if crops were not to be badly attacked in the summer of 1960. Many parts of Britain received a second and, in some cases, a third visit of myxomatosis, usually of the virulent as distinct from the attenuated strain. These out-breaks assisted agriculture to no small extent and probably afforded that breathing-space so much required before the rapidly growing number of rabbit clearance societies really get into their stride.

As the ranks of skilled bird-watchers grow steadily in number year by year, it is natural that rare species come to light; but 1959 will surely go down historically as the year in which the osprey returned. At the third attempt, and due to the untiring efforts of many willing helpers, a pair of these magnificent birds was enabled to rear its three young ones safely in the highlands. It is much to be hoped that, not only will the process be repeated, but that in time the power of public opinion will be so strongly weighted against the ranks of the collector and the dealer in rare eggs that such elaborate arrangements to safeguard Britain's once-common species will no longer be necessary. Two rarities turned up in Northumberland in May: a black stork and a woodchat shrike.

In 1959 wild fruits and berries were local and sporadic, as compared with the almost universally lavish crops of the preceding year. Crab-apples were rare; some whitethorns were covered with haws, but many were unadorned; acorns and beechmast were very irregular; and some Spanish chestnuts in Gloucestershire shed a mass of nuts, with no squirrels of either variety to devour them.

The extremely low state of most rivers held up the passage of salmon and sea trout almost completely until the arrival of the late autumn rains, and many tidal reaches were a heaving mass of fish awaiting the arrival of fresh water to help them reach the redds. This, needless to say, benefited the nets as distinct from the rods, and the Tweed Salmon company announced an income of more than £109,000, with a tax-free dividend of 20%; the former, at least, must have been near their record. After a hopeful and considerable improvement in herring drift-fishing from the Buchan ports of Peterhead and Fraserburgh, the almost complete failure of the East Anglian voyage must have come as a bitter disappointment to crews and curers alike.

With the well-ripened wood of every species of tree as a result of the prolonged sunshine of 1959, lavish fruit crops, both wild and cultivated, could be confidently expected should the weather at blossom-time be at all reasonable. (*See* also AGRICULTURE; BEEKEEPING; FIELD SPORTS; ORNITHOLOGY; WILD LIFE CONSERVATION.) (J. MU. C.)

CRICKET. An M.C.C. team under P. B. H. May, with M. C. Cowdrey as vice-captain, toured Australia in the winter of 1958-59, and was decisively defeated 4-0, with one match drawn. The new Australian side, enthusiastically led by R. Benaud, won the first two tests at Brisbane and Melbourne by eight wickets each, had the better of a draw at Sydney, won the rubber with a ten-wicket victory at Adelaide, and confirmed its superiority with another easy win at Melbourne by nine wickets. England, who had not lost a rubber since 1950-51, never recovered from a bad start. Beset by injuries to leading batsmen and faced by several bowlers whose actions were questionable, they followed a policy of cautious defence which contrasted sadly with Australia's more positive approach. They were outclassed in fielding and throwing and went down to demoralized defeat, despite winning the toss in the first four tests.

Australia's most consistent and prolific batsman was C. C. McDonald, who scored two centuries. In support were R. N. Harvey, who played one superb innings of 167, and the outstanding discovery of the season, N. O'Neill, who never failed till the rubber was won. He made a century on his first appearance against the Englishmen and showed the skill and temperament to be one of the great players in cricket history. The Australian bowling was based on the unusual combination of two fast left-handers, A. K. Davidson and

I. Meckiff, supported in the last two tests by the veteran R. R. Lindwall, and a young giant, G. Rorke, whose tremendous speed was accentuated by a pronounced drag. Both he and Meckiff were markedly inaccurate and appeared to throw or jerk. Benaud, who took 31 wickets with his leg-breaks and googlies, proved an ideal contrast.

May and Cowdrey, with one century apiece, literally carried the English batting and both played superbly. Their chief supporters were T. W. Graveney and T. E. Bailey, the latter once more being pressed into service as an opener, owing to injuries to C. A. Milton and W. Watson. The biggest disappointment was the total failure of P. E. Richardson till the rubber was lost. The fast bowlers J. B. Statham, F. S. Trueman, P. J. Loader and F. H. Tyson worked hard, but they rarely had a large England score behind them when they bowled, and the slow wickets early in the tour militated against them. J. C. Laker proved himself again a great off-spinner, but G. A. R. Lock was terribly expensive, and Bailey, after the first test, was scarcely a force.

In the first test England were perhaps unlucky to win the toss, but in neither innings did they attack some mediocre bowling. The Australians, still mindful of the 1956 disasters in England, secured a lead of only 52 against fine bowling by Loader, Bailey and Laker. In the second innings Bailey, sent in at number three to defend, batted for seven and a half hours for 68. Cowdrey and Graveney were victims of unlucky decisions and when the dreary innings ended, Australia hit off the runs for two wickets, O'Neill, with 71 not out, supplying the only positive batting of the match. Davidson virtually won the second match for Australia by taking three wickets in his second over. A great century by May (113) partially saved England, but Harvey's 167 gave Australia the lead, despite fine bowling by Statham (7 for 57). England then collapsed for 87 against Meckiff (6 for 37) and Davidson, and Australia won easily. England's batting failed again at Sydney, this time against Benaud (5 for 83), and Australia built up a long lead by consistent batting down to number eight (Davidson 71). Thanks to Cowdrey (100 not out) and May (92) England then put up their best performance of the series, 287 for 7 declared, and the game was tamely drawn.

With the rubber now at stake, May, winning his fourth toss, gambled desperately by putting Australia in on a perfect pitch. A first wicket partnership of 171 between McDonald (170) and J. W. Burke (66) virtually settled the issue. Australia made 476, and England, despite 84 from Cowdrey, had to

C. A. Milton, who with K. Taylor opened the batting for England in the first Test match with India at Trent bridge on June 4, plays to Surendra Nath, who later bowled him for 9 runs. India lost by an innings and 59 runs, and their defeat was repeated in the remaining four Tests.

Yorkshire, the county champions. (Left to right, back): G. Alcock (masseur); J. Birkenshaw; W. B. Stott; M. Ryan; D. Wilson; J. G. Binks; K. Taylor; D. E. V. Padgett; C. Turner (scorer). (Front): F. S. Trueman; D. B. Close; J. R. Burnet (captain); J. V. Wilson; R. Illingworth.

follow on 236 behind. More consistent batting in the second innings just avoided the innings defeat, but Australia won by ten wickets. In the final game, Australia confirmed their superiority with another easy win after sending England in first. The fragile batting again failed and McDonald made another century. England could do little better in the second innings against the speed of Davidson, Lindwall and Rorke, and the spin of Benaud, and Australia emerged winners.

This was a heavy season for India. During the English winter, they were at home to the West Indies and lost the series 3-0, with two drawn. The Indian batsmen, unused to fast bowling, were easy victims for W. Hall and R. Gilchrist, and their bowlers could rarely curb such great batsmen as G. Sobers, R. F. Butcher, R. Kanhai, J. Solomon, J. K. Holt and O. G. Smith, who aggregated nine centuries in the tests. Only S. P. Gupte, with leg-breaks and googlies, consistently worried them, and he was grossly overworked. Most of the leading Indian batsmen played at least one good innings, but only C. G. Borde made a century.

A revised and rather younger team then toured England, under D. K. Gaekwad, and lost all five tests by overwhelming margins. The English selectors, bent on rebuilding, called on 21 players, and only Cowdrey, Trueman and K. Barrington played in all five tests. After the rubber had been won, May dropped out owing to illness, whilst Statham and A. E. Moss missed two tests through injury. The major successes as batsmen were M. J. K. Smith and Barrington at numbers four and five, and G. Pullar, who clinched his position as a convert to number one with a maiden century at Old Trafford. Three different pairs of opening batsmen were tried. R. Illingworth, with off-breaks and sound batting, emerged as a genuine all-rounder, and for the first time for several years, England fielded a leg-spinner in T. Greenhough. In the fast bowling department, H. J. Rhodes showed real speed, but a tendency to injury. The long reign of T. G. Evans as England's wicket-keeper in 91 tests ended at Lord's and R. Swetman, his deputy in Australia, succeeded him.

Despite a glorious summer of hot sunshine and firm wickets, the Indians were outclassed. The fast bowlers ripped through their defences, and Greenhough proved a good contrast. Their approach to batting was tentative and defence-minded, though they certainly suffered from a long series of injuries to leading batsmen. V. L. Manjrekar, the best player of fast bowling, did not play after the second test, and N. J. Con-

tractor, C. G. Borde, D. K. Gaekwad and P. R. Umrigar all missed one test. In contrast, A. A. Baig, an undergraduate at Oxford, joined the team in mid-July and scored a charming and high-class century in his first test—at Old Trafford. The bowlers, with the exception of Gupte, were young and inexperienced, but the opening pair, Surendra Nath and R. B. Desai, showed great promise and worried all the batsmen. Gupte took the most wickets, but was ineffective against the best players. The fielding was often lackadaisical, and the team suffered from a lack of firm tactical direction on the field.

The appeal to captains and players for a more positive approach, allied to a golden summer, produced the most exciting struggle for the County championship for many years. Surrey, seven times champions, made a bad start, and the other counties kept beating each other. Early in July, Yorkshire went to the top, followed by Warwickshire, Derbyshire and Middlesex, with Surrey seventh, and Gloucestershire tenth. By the end of July Surrey were top, with Warwickshire, Yorkshire, Hampshire and Gloucestershire close behind, and the championship was wide open. Gradually Derbyshire, Hampshire and Glamorganshire found the pace too hot and first Warwickshire, then Gloucestershire, headed the table. Finally, on Sept. 1, Yorkshire beat Sussex by five wickets in a tremendous finish and reached an unassailable position whilst Surrey were having the worst of a draw against Middlesex.

Yorkshire, with a young side, owed most to their captain, J. R. Burnet, for inculcating team spirit and the will to win, to the big advance as an all-rounder of Illingworth and, as a batsman, of D. E. V. Padgett, to the continued promise of W. B. Stott and K. Taylor as opening batsmen, to the fiery hostility of Trueman, well supported by the in-swing of R. K. Platt, and to some good all-round performances by D. B. Close. Surrey, at full strength, were probably still the best side, but May was unable to play for most of the season and Laker, Lock and Loader were less effective. Barrington made great strides as a batsman, and J. H. Edrich had a phenomenal start to his career as a left-handed opening batsman. A. V. Bedser was a most successful captain, but age told against his team in a hot summer. For Warwickshire, Smith had a tremendous season with the bat (3,245 runs) and T. W. Cartwright showed much promise as an all-rounder. In December, Yorkshire broke with tradition and appointed their first professional captain, J. V. Wilson, since about 1885. (*See* also SPORTING RECORD.)   (A. R. A.)

CRIME.   A Postwar Survey. It is generally taken for granted that practically everywhere in the world there has been a very considerable postwar increase in crime, especially in juvenile and adolescent delinquency. In view of the well-known unreliability of criminal statistics in general and of their total inadequacy in a number of countries, this impression cannot be verified; nor would international comparisons make any sense without the most intimate knowledge of the details relating to criminal statistics, criminal law and procedure, the court systems and the socio-cultural background in each individual country. The following is a brief survey of the situation in England and Wales.

According to *Criminal Statistics*, England and Wales, 1958 (H.M.S.O. Cmnd. 803), which is the most recently published volume, indictable offences known to the police numbered 472,489 in 1946, 545,562 in 1957 and 626,509 in 1958. Persons found guilty of such offences numbered 107,809 in 1946 and 146,714 in 1958. It will be seen that the increase has been less than 50%. Persons found guilty of non-indictable offences numbered 536,013 in 1946 and 846,542 in 1958, an increase of slightly over 50%, largely due to the rise in traffic offenders from 260,350 in 1946 (although there were 475,124 in 1938) to 596,587 in 1958. These over-all figures are less meaningful, however, than those for individual offences, age groups and the sexes. While the number of persons found guilty of larceny rose from 69,127 in 1946 to 87,966 in 1958, of breaking and entering from 20,874 to 28,834, of sex offences from 3,331 to 5,423, that of violence against the person rose from 2,172 to 7,895. On the other hand, cases of murder of persons aged one year and over numbered 113 in 1946 and 114 in 1958, of which latter figure 27 were listed as capital murder and 87 as non-capital murder. However, as pointed out in *Criminal Statistics*, 1958, because of the passing of the Homicide act, 1957, the figures before and after its coming into operation are not strictly comparable, but even so it can be said that there is no evidence so far for an increase in murder as a result of the abolition of capital punishment for certain categories of this crime. The over-all sex ratio for indictable offences, which was six male offenders to one female in 1946, was 7·5 to 1 in 1958, but this, too, varied greatly according to type of offence and age group.

Turning now to age groups, the figures of indictable offences per 100,000 of population in the age group concerned have remained the same for boys aged 8 to under 14, but have risen for boys aged 14 to under 17 from 1,638 in 1946 to 2,274 in 1958, for adolescents aged 17 to under 21 from 1,076 to 1,974, for men aged 21 to under 30 from 652 to 1,070. The other changes are insignificant. For females too, the greatest increases have occurred in the age groups 14 to under 17, from 162 to 227, and 17 to under 21, from 173 to 221. An interesting fact is that the figures given for young adult males aged 21 to under 30 differ strikingly from those in certain other countries; *e.g.*, the United States and the German Federal Republic, in that they are far surpassed by those for adolescents and still more by those for boys aged 14 to under 17. For offences against the person the rise was, in absolute figures, for persons aged 14 to under 17 from 110 in 1946 to 787 in 1958, for ages 17 to under 21 from 285 to 2,084, for ages 21 to under 30 from 823 to 2,585. It is the group 17 to under 21, therefore, where the increase in crime of violence has been most conspicuous, although the absolute figures for an estimated population in this age group of over a million males and far over a million females (whose share in this type of offence is, of course, negligible) may not appear quite as alarming as sometimes believed. It is also pertinent to add that the most serious rise has taken place only since 1954 and, in particular, after 1956, when the corresponding figures were 767 and 1,248, a fact which makes it appear unlikely that the rise has been due to the limitations in the use of imprisonment

for persons under 21 years of age introduced by section 17 of the Criminal Justice act, 1948.

In spite of the weaknessess of criminal statistics it can hardly be doubted that considerable increases in crime actually occurred after the war, although they may not always be accurately reflected in the official figures. The " dark numbers " of criminal statistics vary greatly according to the type of crime, the difficulties which its detection presents to the police, the attitude of the public towards its penalization and other factors. The proportion of unknown offences is likely to be higher; *e.g.*, in the case of procuring criminal abortion (where offences known to police declined from 286 in 1946 to 140 in 1958), housebreaking and most sexual offences, especially of the homosexual type, than for murder; higher for offences committed by adults than for those of children. According to information published by the Wolfenden report, homosexual offences known to the police increased from 2,331 in 1946 to 6,644 in 1955 (5,471 in 1958); convictions for prostitution offences from 4,393 in 1946 to 11,878 in 1955 (19,536 in 1958). The report comments rightly that " it does not necessarily follow from these figures that there has been an increase either in homosexuality or in homosexual behaviour; still less can these figures be regarded as an infallible measure of any increase which may have occurred during that period " and it also stresses that " sexual matters are more openly talked about today than they were in the days of our parents and grandparents." On the question whether this readiness to discuss the subject openly has led to a more understanding public attitude and a more willing acceptance of the legislative proposals of the Wolfenden report, whatever little evidence exists seems to be conflicting, and the government still holds that because of insufficient public support for those proposals legislative changes would be premature. On the other hand, the Street Offences act, 1959, has carried into effect the mainly negative and repressive recommendations of the Wolfenden report on

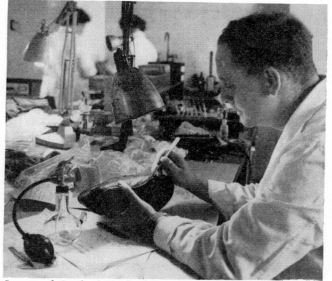

In one of Scotland Yard's fully-equipped laboratories a biologist examines the shoe of a suspect in a case of housebreaking.

prostitution, although in the light of the heated discussions following its publication it may be doubted whether they were truly representative of public opinion on the subject.

In the case of another offence, attempted suicide (offences known to the police being 3,406 in 1946 and 5,060 in 1958), public opinion has moved strongly towards the view that such offenders are more in need of sympathetic understanding and possibly specialized treatment than of penal action and that, consequently, the law should be amended " to provide that attempted suicide (excluding attempted suicide pacts, etc.) should no longer be a criminal offence as such ", but only where it occurs in a public place and/or in circumstances which cause alarm and annoyance " (report of joint committee of British Medical association and Magistrates' association, 1958).

Considering the causes of the postwar increases, it is clear that no single factor can be blamed in isolation. Wartime conditions and initial postwar shortages, which must have severely affected the childhood of many of the present teen-agers and young adults, may be partly, but not exclusively, responsible. The place of poverty as a major factor has now been taken by frustrated emotional drives and social ambitions. If such frustrations are coupled with severe housing problems and sexual jealousy they lead to racial disturbances of the recent London (Notting Hill) and Nottingham type. Mass rioting and vandalism of a non-racial kind by teddy boys and their counterparts abroad can be explained partly as symptoms of pubertal difficulties, faults in education and lack of acceptable leisure interests. Bank robberies and similar highly organized types of professional crime as well as " white collar " crimes require in the first place sociological rather than individual-psychological interpretations, although the latter are also indispensable to explain the individual case.

BIBLIOGRAPHY. Hermann Mannheim, *Social Aspects of Crime in England Between the Wars* (Part I on criminal statistics) (London, 1940), *Criminal Justice and Social Reconstruction* (London, 1946), *Group Problems in Crime and Punishment*, Chap. 5 (London, 1955), " Criminal Law and Penology " in *Law and Opinion in the 20th Century*, ed. by Morris Ginsberg (London, 1959); Lord Pakenham, *The Causes of Crime* (London, 1958); Barbara Wootton, *Social Science and Social Pathology* (London, 1959); *Report of the Committee on Homosexual Offences and Prostitution* (H.M.S.O., Cmnd. 247, London, 1957); *Penal Practice in a Changing Society*, (H.M.S.O., Cmnd. 645, London, 1959); *Criminal Statistics, England and Wales, 1946* and *1958* (H.M.S.O., Cmd. 7428 and Cmnd. 803, London); *Street Offences Act, 1959.*

Statistics for 1958. *England and Wales.* In 1958 the rise continued in the total number of indictable offences known to the police. The total figure of 628,509 was 14·8% higher than in 1957 and 31% higher than in 1945. The over-all number of persons found guilty in 1958 of offences of all kinds was 993,445, of whom 146,714 were found guilty of indictable offences, 846,542 of non-indictable offences and 189 of offences against the Defence regulations. The last three figures were, respectively, up 12·1%, up 15·4% and down 33·7% compared with 1957. Traffic offences (dealt with summarily) accounted for 60·1% of the total found guilty in 1958 of offences of all kinds. The next largest groups were larceny (8·9%), drunkenness and other offences against the intoxicating liquor laws (6·9%) and breaking and entering (2·9%).

Judging by the statistics of convictions the increase in crime, as in 1957, was much more rapid among juveniles over 14 and young men and women than among younger children or older men and women. The most serious proportionate increases, compared with 1957, were in robbery (39%), breaking and entering (24%), malicious injury to property (18%), receiving (15%), frauds and false pretences (14%) and violence against the person (12%).

United States. In 1958 fundamental changes in the tabulation of Uniform Crime reports were designed by the Federal Bureau of Investigation to improve the quality of the crime index, to sharpen the distinction between rural and urban crime, to provide a more up-to-date population base for crime rates and to improve the accuracy of crime estimates for non-reporting areas. In 1958, on the basis of the new index, the crime rate in the metropolitan areas was nearly three times as great as in the rural areas; in other cities it was half as great again as the rural rate. The rural areas' crime rate was not so markedly favourable however in crimes against persons. Their murder and non-negligent manslaughter rate was higher than

those of either metropolitan areas or " other cities "; their rape and aggravated assault rates were also higher than those for " other cities ". In the country as a whole between 1957 and 1958 the crime rate increased in all categories except murder and non-negligent manslaughter, which remained unchanged. In 1958 two-thirds of those arrested for car theft were under 18; nearly half of those arrested for burglary and

Guenther Fritz Podola (hooded) is taken from the London hotel where he was arrested on July 16th for the murder of a police officer.

for larceny were under this age. Nearly a third of all persons arrested for all offences were under 25. The number of persons under 18 who were arrested increased 8·1% in 1958, whereas the total of arrests for all ages increased by only 2·5%.

Some Cases in 1959. On Sept. 24 Guenther Fritz Podola, a 30-year-old Canadian photographer of German extraction, was convicted in the Central Criminal court of the capital murder of Detective-sergeant Raymond William Purdy by shooting him through the heart with a revolver at point-blank range in South Kensington, London, on July 13. His counsel having declared that Podola was suffering from hysterical amnesia, Mr. Justice Edmund Davies directed that it was for the defence to establish that he was insane so as to be unfit to stand his trial. After nine days a jury decided that Podola was sane and fit to be tried. During the subsequent two-day trial, with a new jury sworn, Podola persisted in his plea of amnesia. The home secretary took the unusual step of referring the case himself to the Court of Criminal Appeal, where however the appeal was rejected. Permission to appeal to the House of Lords having been refused, Podola was executed at Wandsworth prison on Nov. 5.

On Sept. 30 Donald Brian Hume, a 39-year-old British subject, was convicted and sentenced at Winterthur, Switzerland, to hard labour for life for shooting a taxi-driver dead after robbing a Zürich bank and wounding a cashier. During the trial Hume admitted that he had killed Stanley Setty, a British car dealer, out of jealousy, sawing off his limbs and making them into parcels later dropped from an aircraft. In 1950 Hume had been found not guilty of the murder of Setty but guilty of being an accessory after the fact, and in 1958 he had been released from a British prison after serving two-thirds of his sentence.

On April 9 Attilio Messina, a 49-year-old antique dealer, pleaded guilty to charges of procuring Edna Kallman to become a common prostitute in 1949 and of living on the earnings of prostitution for ten years. In sentencing him at the Central Criminal court to four years' imprisonment, and recommending deportation, Sir Gerald Dodson, the recorder, said " . . . you have made a sumptuous but a revolting form of living from the suffering bodies of women you trapped or seduced and reduced to a form of slavery . . . You have caused great suffering; it is only right and just that you also should suffer."

During the weekend of Oct. 10-11 jewellery and cash valued at more than £200,000 were stolen from four branches of the Goldsmiths' and Silversmiths' association in London. The thieves first forced an entrance to the Dover street branch and forced open the safe. Then, apparently, they made a tour of the other shops using keys to unlock most of the doors and all the safes. A reward of £10,000 was offered for information leading to the recovery of the jewellery, and towards the end of the year two men were arrested in connection with the case.

In Canada, on Sept. 14, thieves broke into the Toronto Art gallery and stole six old masters—including " Izaac Abrahamsz. Massa " by Frans Hals, " Elevation of the Cross " by Peter Paul Rubens and " The Harvest Waggon " by Gainsborough—valued at about $650,000 (£234,000). Early in October, after an intense search on both sides of the Canadian-United States border, the Toronto police received an anonymous phone call which led them to find the paintings in a garage in the city.

In the United States four white youths were sentenced in Tallahassee, Florida, to life imprisonment for the rape of a 19-year-old Negro college girl on May 2. The judge said that they were fortunate that the jury had recommended mercy. (*See* also JUVENILE DELINQUENCY.)

(H. MM.; O. W. W.; X.)

CUBA. Island republic in the Caribbean sea. Area (incl. the Isle of Pines and other minor islands and keys): 44,218 sq.mi. Pop. (1953 census): 5,829,029, incl. 149,327 foreigners (74,561 Spaniards); (1958 est.) 6,466,000. Racial distribution officially calculated at 72·8% white (about one-third of this group is mulatto), 12·4% Afro-American, 14·5% mixed and 0·3% Asiatic (largely Chinese). Language: Spanish. Religion: predominantly Roman Catholic. Chief cities (pop., 1953 census): Havana (cap.) 785,455; Marianao (a Havana suburb) 219,278; Santiago de Cuba 163,237; Camagüey 110,388; Santa Clara 77,378. Presidents in 1959: Maj.-General Fulgencio Batista, Manuel Urrutia Lleo (from Jan. 2) and Osvaldo Dorticos Torrado (from July 17); prime minister, Fidel Castro. Main imports: machinery and manufactured goods. Main exports: sugar and molasses (85%), tobacco and products (6%). Monetary unit: *peso* at par with the U.S. dollar.

History. In the closing weeks of 1958, the support of President Fulgencio Batista seemed to melt away, even though much of the army remained loyal in spite of the lack of sufficient munitions which the government had experienced after the United States imposed an embargo upon the export of arms to Cuba. The phantom guerrilla force operating since 1956 in the mountains of eastern Cuba became a victorious army, fighting pitched battles with ample modern equipment acquired from some foreign source. Batista relinquished the presidency on Jan. 1, 1959, and flew to the Dominican Republic. On Aug. 20, Batista flew to Portugal, having secured permission to live in Madeira.

When Batista handed over his powers to the commander-in-chief, General Eulogio Cantillo, the latter established a provisional government. The rebel leader, Fidel Castro, refused to deal with this government, and two days later his first column entered Havana under the command of Ernesto Guevara, a Communist medical student of Argentine birth, long associated with Castro in his Cuban, Central American and Colombian adventures. A new provisional government was established on Jan. 2, with Manuel Urrutia Lleo as president and Castro as prime minister.

Arrests and executions began at once throughout Cuba. One of the first acts of the new regime was to confer upon Guevara the status of a native-born Cuban, so as to make him eligible for any post, and during the year Guevara presided over military prisons, directed courts martial, and made extensive tours of Asia, north Africa and the U.S.S.R.

Although the programme repeatedly announced by Castro had emphasized the urgency of an immediate, honest election of congress, as soon as he was in power he indicated that elections could wait. Triumphant visits to neighbouring

countries were arranged. He flew to Caracas, Venezuela, for a few days and made sweeping prophecies of the early realization of a proletarian revolution throughout the Americas. The United States was becoming critical of the Castro regime, so, on the strength of an invitation from a group of newspapermen, Castro went to Washington, D.C., where he called on the secretary of state and congressional committees.

Financial help from the United States was not forthcoming and Castro turned to expropriation, heavier taxation and exchange control. A programme of expropriation of all landholdings exceeding 1,000 ac., regardless of the owner's nationality, was included in an agrarian reform decree promulgated on June 4, 1959, as part of the Cuban constitution. The United States protested on June 11. Five members of the Cuban cabinet resigned the next day. Cuba replied that the law was a final and sovereign decision and its conditions would not be modified.

Dissension in his administration because of the clash with the United States led Castro to tender his resignation as prime minister on July 17; he declared that he could not work with President Urrutia. A proletarian demonstration to demand Castro's return gave him a popular endorsement in his resistance to what he called " foreign imperialism ". Urrutia was forced to resign and was placed under arrest, being replaced the same day by Osvaldo Dorticos Torrado.

Many defections occurred during the year, including the chief of the air force, Major Pedro Luis Diaz Lanz. By

Fidel Castro, surrounded by his followers, addressing a crowd during a halt in his victorious march to Havana in January.

October, genuine uprisings were occurring sporadically in Pinar del Rio, the westernmost province of Cuba, as well as in the central provinces.

Throughout 1959, the economic condition of Cuba rapidly deteriorated. Unemployment rose and construction under private auspices declined. The fall in world prices of sugar, tobacco, cacao and other Cuban products made matters still worse. (C. McG.; X.)

CURAÇAO: *see* NETHERLANDS OVERSEAS TERRITORIES.

CYPRUS. British island colony and strategic base in the eastern Mediterranean, about 40 mi. S. of coast of Turkey. Area: 3,572 sq.mi. Pop.: (1946 census) 450,114; (1958 est.) 549,000 (Greeks, 78·8%; Turks, 17·5%). More than 10% of pop. can speak English; knowledge of English is spreading rapidly. Chief towns (pop., 1958 est.): Nicosia (cap.) 50,900; Limassol 38,000; Famagusta 27,900; Larnaca 18,500. Administration: governor (with special powers under emergency regulation, 1955); executive council; joint council (executive council and transitional committee sitting together, presided over by governor). Governor, Sir Hugh Foot. Main imports: cereals and wheat, timber, mineral fuels and lubricants, machinery and transport equipment, textiles and clothing. Main exports: fruit, non-ferrous ores and concentrates, copper ores. Monetary unit: Cyprus pound (=£1 sterling).

History. In Feb. 1959 a conference was held at Zürich between the Greek and Turkish prime ministers and foreign ministers, which led to the conclusion of a compromise agreement on Cyprus. A second conference which took place in London the same month and was attended by all parties to the dispute—representatives of the Greek and Turkish communities in the island being invited to share in the negotiations—confirmed and elaborated the solution outlined at Zürich.

Cyprus was to become a republic under a Greek Cypriot president and a Turkish Cypriot vice-president elected by universal suffrage for periods of five years. A council of ministers (seven Greek and three Turkish) would assist them in the exercise of the executive power. Legislative authority was to reside in a House of Representatives chosen by universal suffrage and drawn in the proportion of 70% from the Greek Cypriot and 30% from the Turkish Cypriot communities. The London agreement also envisaged the creation of separate communal chambers, one for each of the two dominant communities in the island, these chambers having the right to impose on their respective populations taxes intended to meet the cost of communal projects and needs.

Other clauses in the agreement concerned the structure and composition of the civil service, the armed forces, the judicial system and, in addition, the separate municipalities which, as an experiment for a period of six years, the Turkish Cypriots would be allowed to establish in five of the chief towns in Cyprus. It was laid down in the London agreement that in future Cyprus should not be united either wholly or in part with another state nor be subject to partition. A pact guaranteeing the independence, the territorial integrity and the constitution of Cyprus was to be signed between Great Britain, Greece, Turkey and Cyprus. The Cypriot and Turkish republics, together with Greece, would also enter into a joint military alliance. It was further enjoined that both these treaties should have in relation to Cyprus a constitutional status and force. Great Britain retained full sovereignty over two areas in Cyprus, and the Republic of Cyprus was to provide facilities which would permit Great Britain to develop and use these areas as military bases. The London conference also agreed that the transfer of power in Cyprus should be completed not later than Feb. 19, 1960.

On March 27, 1959, Archbishop Makarios and Fazil Küçük, the leader of the Turkish Cypriots, announced the formation of a council of ministers, which, acting in conjunction with the British governor, would constitute in effect a provisional government of Cyprus until the attainment of full independence. Joint committees for the preparation of the basic treaties and for the drafting of a constitution met, the one in London on March 23 and the other in Nicosia on April 13. The British government stated in June that over a period of years it would contribute a substantial measure of financial aid to Cyprus. Makarios and Küçük, with the approval of the council of ministers, declared in July that Cyprus intended to remain within the sterling area for at least ten years after the achievement of independence.

Archbishop Makarios acknowledges the jubilant welcome given to him by thousands of excited Greek Cypriots on the way from Nicosia airport to the capital on March 1, when he returned to Cyprus after three years of exile, following agreement in London on the island's future.

After holding talks at Rhodes in October to resolve differences of opinion between himself and Makarios, the former Eoka leader, General Georgios Grivas, gave the archbishop a pledge of full support. On Dec. 14 Makarios was elected first president of the Republic of Cyprus. (V. J. P.)

See W. Byford-Jones, *Grivas and the Story of EOKA* (London, 1959).

CZECHOSLOVAKIA.
People's republic of central Europe, bounded W. and N.W. by Germany, N. and N.E. by Poland, E. by the U.S.S.R. and S. by Hungary and Austria. Area: 49,354 sq.mi. (incl. autonomous Slovakia, 18,902 sq.mi.). Pop. (April 1958 est.): 13,437,793 (incl. Slovakia 3,881,816). Nationality (1957): Czech 66·5%; Slovak 27·8%; German 1·2%; Hungarian 3·0%; Ukrainian 0·6%; Polish 0·6%. Religion (1930 census): Roman Catholic (Latin rite) 73·5%; Protestant (all denominations) 7·7%; Czechoslovak Church 5·4%; Greek Catholic 4%; Greek Orthodox 1%; Jewish 2·4%; atheist 5·8%. Chief towns (pop. Jan. 1958): Prague (cap.) 984,772; Brno 309,313; Bratislava 252,046; Ostrava 227,287; Plzeň 135,282; Košice 81,047. First secretary of the Communist Party of Czechoslovakia and president of the republic, Antonín Novotný; chairman of the council of ministers, Vilem Široký. Main imports: iron ore, cotton, wool, petroleum and products. Main exports: machinery and manufactured goods. Monetary unit: *koruna* (official exchange rate Kč.20·00 =£1 sterling; tourist rate Kč.61·71 =£1 sterling).

History. Economic rather than political problems were to the fore in 1959. Industrial output continued to expand, and in February it was announced that it had risen by over 11% in 1958, bringing that year's production of bituminous coal to 25·8 million metric tons, of steel to 5·5 million tons, and of machine tools to 22,000 tons. Cash wages rose by only 2·2% but the situation of the wage-earners was improved in March by price reductions of 10%-20% on certain essential foodstuffs and articles of clothing and some manufactured goods. Family allowances were raised for the admitted purpose of increasing the birth rate. The lower rates of pensions for old and disabled people were raised, though "former entrepreneurs and representatives of the capitalist system" were expressly excluded from these benefits. The need for ever greater production in industry was repeatedly stressed, and in February a special Technical Development committee was set up under the direction of Václav Ozkuý, former minister of precision engineering. Otakar Šimunek was made deputy premier and chairman of the reorganized State Planning commission. In November Antonín Novotný revealed plans for sweeping reform of the regional people's committees (organs of local government) to accord more closely with the country's economic divisions.

Agricultural production increased by only 3·4% in 1958, and this was given as the reason for continuing high food prices. In January it was decided to follow the Soviet example and sell off most of the machinery in the machine-tractor stations to the farming co-operatives, though the stations themselves were not dissolved. At a co-operative farming congress in March Antonín Novotný, first secretary of the Communist party, forecast that agriculture would be completely collectivized by 1961. At the end of May it was said that only 143 new co-operatives had been formed in the first quarter of the year, bringing the total up to 12,283, embracing 74·7% of the country's arable land. With other forms of state-owned farms included, this meant that 79% of the land was in the "socialist sector". In June the party central committee announced that compulsory deliveries of farm produce would be abolished and a new unified system of prices introduced at about 15% above the 1958 level. The cost of machinery and other services sold to farms was reduced but taxes were raised and some state subsidies reduced. These measures were expected to bring about the planned 40% increase of farm output by 1965. Lubomir Strougal was appointed minister of agriculture in March.

The private practice of medicine was reported to have been brought to an end by the beginning of the year. In April a reform of the education system on Soviet lines introduced a compulsory 9-year secondary system and provided for more practical training in industry and agriculture in later school life. The 3rd congress of the Czechoslovak Youth league (ČSM) in Dec. 1958 revealed that the membership of 1,161,129 was only 44,000 above the 1955 figure.

The conference of the Writers' union in March and the congress of Socialist Culture in June were both occasions for the reaffirmation of political control over creative artists. Two literary journals, *Nový Život* and *Květen*, which had shown signs of independence, were suspended. A successful novel by Josef Skvorecký, *The Cowards*, which dealt with postwar events in an unheroic manner, was banned. There were numerous trials, with heavy sentences imposed, of

In a Prague shop window a notice gives details of price reductions, on some foodstuffs and other goods, which took effect on March 8.

priests, private traders, suspected spies, thieves and embezzlers of "socialist property" and of many critics of the Communist system.

Czechoslovak foreign trade continued to expand, primarily with the U.S.S.R. and its allied countries. Nearly half of the exports were of machinery and nearly half the imports were of raw materials. Czechoslovakia's position as the main supplier of engineering products in the Soviet bloc was confirmed in May at the meeting in Albania of the Council for Mutual Economic Aid. But the government also showed much interest in trade with countries of the middle east and Africa. Agreements were concluded with the United Arab Republic, Iraq, Ethiopia, Ghana and Guinea. A Czechoslovak cultural institute was established in Cairo. (*See also* EASTERN EUROPEAN ECONOMIC PLANNING.) (D. F.)

DAHOMEY, REPUBLIC OF
(RÉPUBLIQUE DU DAHOMEY), a member state of the French Community. Dahomey is bounded W. by the autonomous Republic of Togo, N. by the Republics of Upper Volta and Niger, E. by Nigeria and S. by the Atlantic ocean. Area: 44,710 sq.mi. Pop.: (1945 est.) 1,458,000; (1959 est.) 1,720,000; mainly Dahomi Negroes, and many allied tribes; also Peul (Fula) and Hausa communities in the north and Yoruba in the south; Europeans 1,200. Language: many local dialects. Religion: animist, with Moslem and Christian minorities. Chief towns (pop., 1956 est.): Porto Novo (cap., 31,500), Cotonou (56,200), Abomey (18,900), Ouidah (14,000). Prime minister, Hubert Maga. French high commissioner, René Tirant. Chief exports: palm kernels, palm oil, groundnuts. Monetary unit: *franc CFA*=metropolitan Fr.2.

History. The republican constitution was passed unanimously by the territorial assembly at Cotonou, on Feb. 14,

1959. The official language was to be French. The prime minister, elected by the assembly, had executive power; he was responsible to the assembly. A tribunal of state was instituted.

At the general election to the first National Assembly on April 2 the Parti Républicain du Dahomey, the party of the prime minister Sourou Migan Apithy, won 37 out of a total of 70 seats. The Union Démocratique Dahoméenne (leader Justin Ahomadegbé) obtained 11 seats and the Rassemblement Démocratique Dahoméen (leader Hubert Maga, representing the tribes of the interior) 22 seats. As the two opposition parties polled 234,311 votes and the government party only 144,038—disorders followed. On May 22 Maga became prime minister. Ahomadegbé had been elected president of the assembly. In September Apithy, influenced by the example of Guinea, declared himself in favour of independence. Dahomey adhered to the Sahel-Bénin *entente* (*see* IVORY COAST).

An agreement was concluded with France for the construction in four years of the port of Cotonou, providing for a yearly traffic of up to 300,000 metric tons. (HU. DE.)

DAIRY FARMING AND DAIRY PRODUCE.

The U.K. dairy herd was a little smaller in 1959 than in 1958, the combined total of dairy cows in milk and in calf having fallen by 33,000. A rise of 62,000 in the number of heifers in calf, however, suggested that the decline in the dairy herd was being checked and even reversed.

TABLE I. COWS AND HEIFERS IN THE UNITED KINGDOM ('000 head)

Year	Dairy cows and heifers in milk*	Dairy cows in calf*	Heifers in calf	Beef cows†	Total
1957 .	. 2,678	459	835	764	4,736
1958 .	. 2,699	450	765	741	4,655
1959‡ .	. 2,662	454	827	755	4,698

* Includes beef cattle in Northern Ireland. † Great Britain only. ‡ Provisional figures.
SOURCE. Ministry of Agriculture.

In the first nine months of 1959 sales of milk fell by 87 million gal. (5%) compared with the same period of the previous year. This was partly because of the fall in the number of dairy cows, but the main reason was the drop in yields due to the unfavourable weather. As there was a rise of 14 million gal. in liquid consumption the quantity available for sale on the lower-priced manufacturing market fell by 101 million gal. The government decided that no increase in the guaranteed price was justified, since it considered that production was still too high. However, owing to the higher proportion of milk sold for liquid consumption, the Milk Marketing board was able to fix provisional prices for 1959-60 which were 1¼d. a gallon above those quoted for the previous year. The premium paid for T.T. milk was raised from 3d. to 4d. a gallon from October onwards. In order to increase the total production of Channel Island milk and even out its supply over the winter and summer, the premium was raised by an average of about 2d. per gallon during the winter months.

The number of cows artificially inseminated in England and Wales in 1958-59 represented 61% of the breeding herd. A rise in the proportion of dairy-type inseminations (from 52·3% to 54·9%) and a slight fall in the percentage from beef bulls (from 35·6% to 34·8%) suggested that the tendency for beef production to expand at the expense of dairying had been checked. Inseminations from dual-purpose bulls continued to fall and formed only 10·3% of the total.

Figures published during the year threw an interesting light on trends in the structure of the dairy farming industry. A fall of 20,000 in the number of milk producers between 1954 and 1959 was largely due to the difficulties of many small producers and the increased attractions of other branches of farming. The number of producers fell especially in eastern and south-

A milking parlour at Glebe farm, near Leamington Spa, in which one man can milk, feed and manage a 50-cow herd in six and a half hours.

eastern areas, dairying becoming rather more confined to traditional grassland dairying areas. Rising costs of distribution were responsible for a fall in the number of producer-retailers from over 60,000 in 1939 to less than 14,000 in 1959.

Representatives from over 40 countries attended the International Dairy congress in London; nearly 400 scientific and technical papers were discussed.

In New Zealand, with favourable weather during the 1958-59 season, milk production was only slightly below the record level of 1957-58, despite a fall in dairy cow numbers. Butter production reached a record level, but the decline in cheese production, which had been checked in the previous season, was resumed and output fell by 12%. The season in Australia was very good and milk production was expected to be about 7% above that of the previous year, although it remained below the record level of 1955-56. Butter and cheese production increased considerably.

TABLE II. BUTTER AND CHEESE OUTPUT IN NEW ZEALAND AND AUSTRALIA ('000 tons)

Season (July-June)	New Zealand		Australia	
	Butter	Cheese	Butter	Cheese
1956-57	201·3	94·6	189·8	45·2
1957-58	218·1	96·6	172·6*	34·9*
1958-59	221·3	85·0	190·0†	40·0†

* Provisional figures. † Forecast estimate.
SOURCES. *The Dairy Situation* (Bureau of Agricultural Economics, Canberra, May 1959); *Intelligence Bulletin* (Commonwealth Economic Committee, London, Sept. 1959).

Both New Zealand and Australia benefited considerably from the higher prices for butter and cheese in the United Kingdom—by far their most important market—due to a fall both in U.K. production and in its supplies from the continent of Europe. The restrictions that Britain had imposed on butter imports from a number of European countries were removed in Aug. 1958, but prices continued to rise. At the end of Oct. 1959 the price of New Zealand finest butter on the London market was 61% higher than a year earlier. The increase in cheese prices occurred mainly in the later months of 1958, after which they remained fairly steady. At the end of Oct. 1959 New Zealand finest white cheese was 15% higher than in Oct. 1958.

For the third year in succession dairy cow numbers in Canada fell slightly. Butter production in the first nine months of 1959 fell by 4% compared with the same period of the previous year. Cheddar cheese output, on the other hand, was 11% higher.

Taking the Commonwealth as a whole, the market for dairy produce improved appreciably during 1959. (*See* also LIVE-STOCK; VEGETABLE OILS AND ANIMAL FATS.) (O. T. W. P.)

See E. L. Crossley, ed., *The United Kingdom Dairy Industry* (London, 1959).

DANCE. Ballet.

The year 1959 was more interesting than 1958: it revealed a growing split between the taste of the critics and the constant balletgoers on the one hand, and the general public on the other. The first had become eager for novelty, while the latter, especially in the provinces, were firmly wedded to the classics. The " regulars ", who had been accustomed to the rapid changes and excitements of the formative period of the national ballet, sometimes failed to appreciate the rise in the general level of technique during this time of consolidation.

The ballet of the year was undoubtedly John Cranko's *Antigone*, a free adaptation of Sophocles' tragedy, presented by the Royal ballet at Covent Garden on Oct. 20. The *décor* and costumes by the Mexican, Rufino Tamayo, plunged one immediately into the atmosphere of tragedy and violence and, though modern in design, gave the feeling of antiquity. They were perfectly matched by the Greek composer Nikis Theodorakis' exciting score, a model of writing for narrative ballet. Cranko's choreography was superbly taut with none of the clever insertions that have so often disfigured his work, nor of the pseudo-Greek movement so much a *cliché* in ballet. Cranko had absorbed the style and reinterpreted it in the same manner as Tamayo and Theodorakis. The company as a whole revealed its ability to act, with outstanding performances by Svetlana Beriosova as Antigone, Michael Somes as Creon, and David Blair and Gary Burne as the warring brothers.

Andrée Howard's *La Belle Dame sans Merci*, first performed by the Edinburgh Festival ballet in 1958, was adopted by the Royal ballet and received its Covent Garden première on Sept. 2. Donald MacLeary, a 22-yr.-old dancer from Inverness, gave a dignified performance as the palely loitering knight, but the choreography was dull and attenuated and only Alexander Goehr's music captured the romantic atmosphere.

Jerome Robbins' Ballets U.S.A. enjoyed an outstanding success, first at Edinburgh and then for a short season in London. Its programme consisted of four ballets, all with choreography by Robbins, interpreted by a small and extremely efficient company especially trained for this repertoire. The most effective ballet was a new interpretation of *L'Après-midi d'un Faune*, set in a dance studio, the dancers being a white girl and a coloured boy. This was not only a work of great beauty, more in harmony with the music than the Nijinsky ballet, but deeply moving in its implications. The remaining ballets in an idiom made familiar by *Interplay*, *Fancy Free* and *West Side Story*, had little direct bearing on the main ballet tradition and were in some respects already dated, though many critics saw in them the much longed for novelties and wrote of a choreographic renewal. There could be no doubt as to their theatrical quality or the precision with which they were performed.

Festival Ballet's *Summer Morning*, the much heralded Noel Coward ballet given on the occasion of this company's tenth anniversary, was a serious disappointment. It turned out to be nothing but an expanded scene from a Cochran revue of the 1920s. Jack Carter's choreography was slick, but had no trace of humanity.

The Ballet Rambert presented two new ballets for their May season at Sadler's Wells. The first was *Hazana*, with music by Carlos Surinach and *décor* by Ralph Koltai, and a choreography by Norman Morrice which developed the promise shown in *The Brothers*. *Hazana* told a story of the conflict between religion and materialism in a central American town. The choreographer's sincerity and his direct approach to his subject led to a climax at the same time dramatic and physical. The other novelty, *La Reja*, to harpsichord sonatas by Scarlatti, with *décor* by Carl Toms and choreography by John Cranko, was set in Spain. Although there was much beauty in the grouping and the *décor*, the dancing was without real interest and the general result monotonous. This, the oldest British company, had gained fresh vitality, and the dancing of a newcomer, Lucette

(*Left*) Susana and José, Spanish dancers who appeared at Sadler's Wells theatre for a short season in May. (*Right*) Svetlana Beriosova and her new partner, 22-yr.-old Donald MacLeary, at Covent Garden on the eve of their first appearance together, in " Swan Lake ", on Aug. 20.

Aldous, especially in *demi-caractère* roles, made a great impact.

Ludmilla Tcherina presented her Theatre Ballet at the Cambridge theatre for a short season from March 19, but in spite of the collaboration of Nikis Theodorakis in two ballets *Les Amants de Teruel* and *Gunpowder Flash* and of some striking *décor*, the season failed through lack of any real choreographic interest.

Roland Petit's three-act ballet *Cyrano de Bergerac* (Adelphi theatre, Nov. 18) was a partial success. Indeed in some respects it was a triumph over material that did not lend itself to choreography. The famous balcony scene, for instance, was magnificently translated into dance terms, and there were some remarkable war scenes in the great French tradition of Callot. The main failure lay in a cabaret-type divertissement, in the realization of Roxane, which was far too modern in conception, and in a poor score by Marius Constant, devoid of any romanticism where romanticism was of the essence. The great triumph was in Petit's own role of Cyrano, surely one of the greatest male roles in ballet. St. Laurent's costumes were elegant but little more; Basarte's decors were truly in the spirit of Rostand.

In the New Year's honours list, 1959, Michael Somes was awarded the C.B.E. During the year, the deaths occurred of Lydia Kyasht, Catherine Devilliers and Carlotta Mossetti, all of whom made their names in the pre-Diaghileff ballet; Deirdre Dixon, soloist of the Royal ballet; Gordon Hamilton, formerly of the Sadler's Wells and Roland Petit companies and latterly *maître de ballet* of the Vienna opera; Doris Humphrey, a pioneer of the modern American dance; and of the German historian Curt Sachs.

Folk Dance. Two special anniversaries were celebrated in 1959, both connected with Cecil Sharp, founder of the English Folk Dance society: the centenary of his birth on Nov. 22, and the 60th anniversary of his meeting, on Boxing day, 1899, with William Kimber, Morris dancer and concertina player, from which, when the Morris dancers of Headington, Oxford, first caught Sharp's attention, grew an interest in and revival of folk dancing that by the 1950s was world wide.

Large crowds in July attended the 13th International Eisteddfod at Llangollen, which owing to its very success and popularity seemed in danger of losing the happy informality of earlier meetings. The winning team in the folk dance section was the Hungarian Folk Dance group from London, closely followed by the Bondeungdomslaget "Ervingen" of Bergen, Norway, and the St. Aloysius School of Irish Dancing, Hebburn, Co. Durham.

Of the various tours of folk dance groups, the most noteworthy was perhaps that of the Georgian State Dance company of the U.S.S.R. which came to England in November. For the leader Iliko Sukhishvili, this was a return visit, for he had brought a group of Georgian folk dancers to London for the big International Folk Dance festival of 1935. Part of the company also visited the United States.

The International Folk Music council met in Rumania from Aug. 12 to Aug. 22, by invitation of the Rumanian Folklore institute and the national commission for Unesco. After a conference at Sinaia, the 100 delegates, from 26 countries, moved to Bucharest to see a festival of folk dance groups from various regions.

Ballroom Dancing. Throughout the year "Rock 'n' Roll", as well as Cha-Cha-Cha, remained popular in the dancehalls. The ever-increasing popularity of ballroom dancing resulted in crowded floors in spite of more and more dancehalls becoming available. This led to a strong demand for a style of dancing which could be quickly learned and danced in the minimum of space. A form of dancing known as "Rhythm-Rock" grew in popularity during the last few months of the year, powerfully aided by its presentation, together with lessons, on B.B.C. television.

The four "standard dances", waltz, foxtrot, quickstep and tango, remained the firm choice of the more serious dancers and a record number of people passed medal tests in these during the year. There was a great increase in the number of entrants in junior championships (restricted to dancers in the 12-16 age-group) and also a considerable increase in the

Desmond Ellison and Brenda Winslade, winners of the 1959 world professional ballroom dancing championship, held in London.

number of formation teams participating in competitions both in Modern-style dancing and in Old Time. In the various countries of the Commonwealth the English style continued to gain in popularity. It also made some progress in the United States, where hitherto it had been little danced.

The principal competition results during the year were: "Star" professional championship (London), Sonny Binick and Sally Brock; "Star" amateur championship (London), Eric Donaldson and Edna Barnett; World professional championship (London), Desmond Ellison and Brenda Winslade; World amateur championship (London), Peter Eggleton and Diana Gradwell. British professional old time championship (Blackpool), Jack Rigby and Florence Newbegin; British amateur old time championship (Blackpool), Bill and Betty Elsdon; International professional championship (London), Harry Smith-Hampshire and Doreen Casey; International amateur championship (London), Michael Houseman and Valerie Waite. (A. L. HL.; S. E. J.; V. SR.)

DEFENCE POLICY. In 1959 there was no development in British official defence policy comparable in importance with either the changes in the structure of the forces announced in 1957 or the modifications of the central defence organization promulgated in 1958. The most notable development was in the policy of the Labour party in relation to the manufacture of the atom and hydrogen bombs. The practical importance of the idea of the so-called "non-nuclear club", as formulated by Hugh Gaitskell and adopted by the party's national executive committee, depended, first, on whether a Labour government was to take office in the near future and, secondly, if so, on what degree of support the idea commanded outside the United Kingdom. It was significant, in any case, as being the first formulation on behalf of a major political party of any position between, on the one hand, a complete (however reluctant) acceptance of nuclear weapons and, on the other, their complete rejection. While during the year international talks on disarmament continued and a suspension of nuclear tests was in force, the formulation of the Labour party's policy designed to limit the manufacture of nuclear weapons to the United States and the U.S.S.R. satisfied, as an objective, both those who primarily feared a nuclear arms race and those who saw the great danger in the spread of limited wars and the best insurance against it the concentration, by all members of the western alliance except the United States, upon strength in conventional weapons and forces. It may have appeased to some extent those who conscientiously objected to the manufacture of nuclear weapons since, if an agreement such as that envisaged were to be reached, it would debar the United Kingdom from itself manufacturing or using nuclear or thermonuclear weapons, though not from relying upon their use by the United States. The idea received a measure of sympathetic interest from the Socialist parties of western Europe, but it was difficult in the prevailing circumstances to envisage the possibility of France, at least, agreeing to any arrangement that would debar it from becoming a nuclear power.

The 1959 white paper, *Progress of the Defence Plan* (Cmnd. 662), summarized the government's defence policy in familiar phrases. " Britain," it said, " in co-operation with other members of the Commonwealth and with her allies in Nato, Seato and the Baghdad Pact, must continue to play her part in the collective defence of the free world. She must also continue to provide protection for her colonies and other overseas territories "; and it proceeded to recite the announcement in 1957 of the five-year defence plan. The white paper also summarized the progress made in implementing this plan. Substantial headway was being made with modernizing existing ships and bringing new ones into service, and the fleet air arm was receiving new types of aircraft. (*See* COMMONWEALTH NAVIES.)

The keynote of the passage in the white paper on the re-equipment of the army was in the sentence that " present plans provide for the extensive re-equipment of the Army, so that the smaller, but more highly trained, all-regular force of the future may operate with maximum efficiency." The equipment of the army with F.N. rifles and Sterling submachine guns, and equipment of two artillery regiments with the Corporal guided missile were among the developments mentioned. (*See* COMMONWEALTH ARMIES.) Similarly, in the Royal Air Force, the expansion of the carrying capacity of Transport command was announced, as part of the policy of increasing the mobility of the forces. Britannias were coming into service for long-range movement and so releasing Hastings aircraft for use in the tactical role. An increase in the number of tactical freighters suitable for dropping parachutists was another measure announced with the same object. (*See* COMMONWEALTH AIR FORCES.)

The contraction of the manpower of the forces had proceeded in accordance with the policy laid down, so that half of the reduction from about 700,000 (1957) to about 400,000 (1962) was achieved by April 1959. The figure for expenditure on defence, given in the defence estimates for 1959-60, represented an increase of approximately £20 million.

Problems similar to those facing the United Kingdom, though in different forms and degrees, confronted the other countries of the Commonwealth. In Canada the threat of the intercontinental ballistic missile led to changes in the pattern of defence production, and " intensive study " (in the words of the minister of national defence, G. R. Pearkes) was taking place as to the equipment of the army with new

weapons, and equally as to air detection and defence. In Australia a considerable programme of scientific research, largely in collaboration with the United Kingdom, was continued. In New Zealand the basis of recruitment was changed by the National Service Registration act, 1958, which among other things repealed the Military Training act, 1949, and substituted for the universal and compulsory military training prescribed by that measure a system of registration, coupled with medical examination, but without obligation to serve, for all males of the age of 18; the responsibility to serve in the reserves of all those already members of them was retained. This measure was strongly opposed by the leader of the opposition on the ground that it would not suffice to meet overseas commitments. (W. T. Ws.)

DENMARK. Constitutional monarchy of north central Europe composed of the peninsula of Jutland and 100 inhabited islands, the largest being Zealand (Själland) and Fyn (Fünen). Area, excl. Faeroe Islands and Greenland (*qq.v.*): 16,576 sq.mi. Pop.: (1955 census) 4,448,401; (1959 est.) 4,541,000. Language: Danish. Religion: Lutheran, with small Roman Catholic and Jewish minorities. Chief towns (pop., 1958 est.): Copenhagen (cap. incl. Frederiksberg and Gentofte) 942,058; Aarhus 118,205; Odense 109,136; Aalborg 85,318; Esbjerg 53,013. Ruler, King Frederik IX; prime minister, Hans Christian Svane Hansen, Main imports: coal, petroleum and products, machinery and vehicles, textiles, iron and steel, mill products. Main exports: dairy and meat products, machinery. Monetary unit: *krone*, pl. *kroner* (Kr.19·34 =£1 sterling).

History. When the European Economic community (common market) came into effect on Jan. 1, 1959, Denmark

Albert Schweitzer (left) with Niels Bohr at a dinner given in Schweitzer's honour by the Danish foreign minister in September.

negotiated an agreement with the German Federal Republic, which secured the export of beef, oxen, eggs and cheese to the German market to the same extent as hitherto. The agreement also contained a Danish promise that the import of German industrial goods would be increased. Some reduction of duties was also negotiated, but it was clear that in the long run the Netherlands, as a member of the E.E.C., would be in a better competitive position on the German market than Denmark, and some of the Danish agricultural organizations demanded Denmark's adhesion to the common

The King and Queen of Denmark (on left) at the consecration of the new Danish Seamen's church at Stepney, London, on April 19.

market. The Danish smallholders, however, being the main producers of Danish butter and bacon, of which the chief part was exported to Great Britain, feared the loss of the British market should Denmark become a member of the E.E.C. Most of the Danish industries were against Danish membership of the common market, and so were the trade unions. Moreover many Danes opposed a Danish participation in the common market because they considered that collaboration with Scandinavia and Great Britain was more important for the country.

When the plans for a European Free Trade association, comprising Great Britain, Sweden, Norway, Austria, Switzerland, Portugal and Denmark, came up and were discussed at the Stockholm meeting in June 1959, the Danish government decided to send Jens Otto Krag, the minister of foreign affairs, and Karl Skytte, the minister of agriculture, to London to discuss the problems of Danish agricultural exports to Great Britain. They negotiated an agreement securing the lifting of the British duty on Danish bacon, canned cream, blue cheese and some canned meat products; Denmark, on the other hand, would import more British goods. Afterwards the Danish government approved in principle the plans for the seven countries' Free Trade association. A resolution to that effect was passed in the Folketing on July 15, with 86 votes in favour (Social Democrats, Radicals and the Retsforbundet), 6 votes against (Communists and the representative of the German minority) and 73 abstentions (Conservatives and Agrarians).

From Dec. 29, 1958, unrestricted external convertibility of the Danish krone came into effect, in line with the currencies of the other member countries of the European Payments union. Capital movements, however, remained restricted. The accumulated surplus of foreign exchange made the restoration of external convertibility possible, and the convertibility did not affect the surplus, which rose steadily during the following months and amounted to Kr.1,740 million on Oct. 15. Investments, industrial and agricultural production, and exports rose considerably, so that the increase of home sales of all goods by *c.* 10% did not cause inflationary tendencies. In the summer the activity of the building trades

reached the highest level since World War II. As manpower was short and wages began to rise, government investments were cut, and on Sept. 18 the National Bank raised its discount rate from 4½% to 5%.

On April 1 a new Housing act was promulgated. It replaced government loans by government guaranties. Its effect was that most of the new houses were being built by private firms and not by building societies financed by government loans.

The Danish Communist party split in Nov. 1958, when Aksel Larsen, its chairman and leader in the Folketing, was expelled, after having been denounced for Titoist revisionism. In March 1959 he registered the Socialist People's party, with himself as leader and single member in the Folketing. (*See* also FAEROE ISLANDS; GREENLAND.) (H. LN.)

DENTISTRY. The increasing incidence of dental disease, particularly in countries which were adopting the mode of life of western civilization, was causing grave concern, and in 1959 some events indicative of this took place.

In February, the World Health organization held a Second Dental Health seminar at Adelaide, Australia, to discuss prevention and control of dental disease, the evaluation of existing services, and the principles concerned in recording dental conditions and planning a dental health service. Later in the year W.H.O. published the report of a study group on dental health services for children, held in Brussels in 1958. In May the British Dental association published a memorandum on the dental health of children.

The International Dental federation prepared a survey showing how far the principles of fluoridation of domestic water supplies were applied throughout the world, but only in the United States and in Canada was this done to any degree approaching a national scale. Further work was reported on the effects upon teeth of the use of high-speed drills and although much remained to be learned about this method there was no evidence to show that lasting damage to the pulpal tissue could not be avoided.

Any radioactive strontium which is incorporated in the calcified tissues of a developing tooth will remain, except for movement by ionic exchange and, therefore, the burden will be related to the fall-out during the period of calcification. The period during which portions of a given tooth from an individual of known age were calcified can be assessed with sufficient accuracy for a reliable estimation of fall-out to be made. The Medical Research council of Great Britain therefore started an investigation on these lines.

In August 12 students from the dental school at the Hebrew University of Jerusalem received their diplomas in the first graduation ceremony for dental students to be held there.

The necessity of increased research into the cause of dental diseases was beginning to be realized: in Great Britain a department of dental science was opened at the Royal College of Surgeons of England and, in Bethesda, United States, a $4 million building was begun, scheduled to open in 1960. (L. J. G.)

BIBLIOGRAPHY (all 1959). G. C. Dickson, *Orthodontics in General Dental Practice* (London); T. W. Frost, *Hypnosis in General Dental Practice* (London); J. H. Scott and A. D. Dixon, *Anatomy for Students of Dentistry* (Edinburgh); J. Adriani, *Fundamentals of General Anaesthesia for Students and Practitioners of Dentistry* (Oxford); N. A. Shore, *Occlusal Equilibration and Temporomandibular Joint Dysfunction* (Philadelphia); J. Osborne and G. A. Lammie, *Partial Dentures*, 2nd ed. (Oxford); M. A. Rushton and B. E. D. Cooke, *Oral Histopathology* (Edinburgh).

DIAMONDS: *see* BUSINESS REVIEW.

DISASTERS.

During 1959 loss of life and property in disasters included the following:

Air

Jan. 8   All ten persons aboard U.S. airliner lost when it crashed on a mountain near Kingsport, Tennessee.

Jan. 11   Lufthansa Constellation airliner crashed at Rio de Janeiro international airport, Brazil; 36 killed.

Jan. 11   Anchorage, Alaska. U.S. air force Globemaster crashed on glacier, killing all nine aboard.

Jan. 16   Curtis airliner of Austral company crashed into sea near Mar del Plata, Argentina, during rainstorm; 50 killed.

Feb. 3   American Airlines Electra turbo-prop airliner crashed in East river, near La Guardia airport, New York; 65 killed.

Feb. 17   Viscount airliner of Turkish Airlines bound for Gatwick airport crashed near Rusper, Surrey, killing 14 including several Turkish government members. Adnan Menderes, the Turkish prime minister, was among the survivors.

March 5   Managua, Nicaragua. Viscount crashed at Las Mercedes airport; 13 killed.

March 29   Indian Airlines Dakota crashed near Hailakandi, Assam, killing all 24 aboard.

April 12   Portuguese military Dakota crashed in sea near Lisbon; all 11 aboard killed.

April 17   Mexican airliner crashed in northern Mexico, killing all 26 aboard.

April 29   Spanish airliner of Iberia Airlines crashed near Valdemeca, Spain; 27 reported killed.

May 12   Capital Airlines Viscount turbo-prop exploded in mid-air over Maryland, killing all 31 aboard.

June 26   Super-Constellation airliner of Trans World Airlines crashed after being struck by lightning during violent thunderstorm near Milan, Italy; all 68 on board killed.

June 30   Ishikawa City, Okinawa. Eighteen people killed when wreckage of U.S. air force jet fighter which exploded in mid-air fell on houses and a school; pilot escaped safely.

Aug. 19   Transair Dakota crashed in Montseny mountains, near Barcelona, Spain; all 32 aboard, mainly students, killed.

Sept. 24   Bordeaux, France. French DC.7 airliner crashed; 54 killed, including the Cameroun minister of health.

Sept. 29   U.S. Electra airliner exploded in mid-air near Waco, Texas, killing all 34 aboard.

Oct. 29   Olympic Airways Dakota crashed in mountains near Kakosalessi, Greece, killing all 18 on board.

Oct. 30   Dakota of Piedmont Airlines crashed in the Blue Ridge mountains near Waynesboro, Virginia, United States; 26 killed.

Nov. 16   U.S. National Airlines DC.7B airliner crashed in Gulf of Mexico; 42 killed.

Fires and Explosions

Jan. 6   Istanbul, Turkey. An explosion in a printing office reported to have killed 23 and seriously injured may others.

Jan. 8   Boswell, Oklahoma, United States. Fire in a farmhouse killed 16 members of a Negro family.

Jan. 27   A mother and her five sons died in a fire at their Kidderminster, Worcestershire, home.

Feb. 21   Crystal City, Texas, United States. Mother and seven children died in a fire which destroyed their home.

Feb. 23   Utashinai, Japan. Fourteen miners reported killed in an underground explosion.

March 5   Little Rock, Arkansas, United States. A fire in a school for delinquent Negro boys killed 21.

March 17   Cross Hill, South Carolina, United States. A fire in a wooden house killed 11.

April 13   Dagupan, Luzon, Philippines. Thirty-four people reported killed when a demolition bomb exploded.

April 22   Wakefield, Yorkshire. Explosion at Walton colliery killed five miners.

May 29   Merlebach, France. An underground explosion killed 18 miners and injured 35 others.

June 5   Bombay, India. A warehouse explosion killed 11 and injured 7.

June 23   A fire which swept a wooden hotel at Stalheim, Norway, killed 24 tourists.

July 1   Sixteen prisoners died in prison camp fire in eastern Finland.

July 3   Twelve reported killed in an oil pipeline explosion near Bernet, southeastern Mexico.

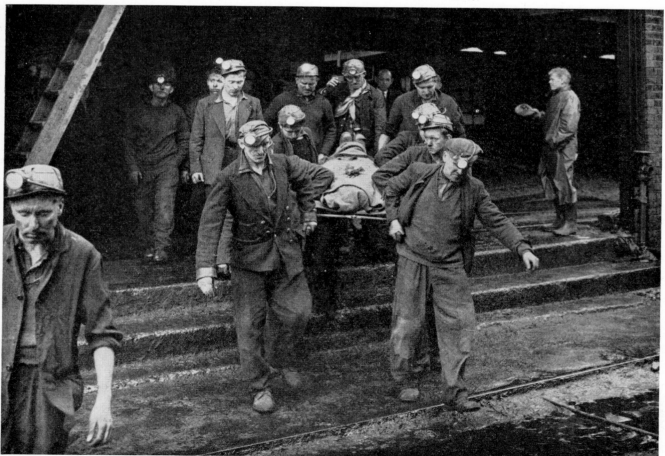

The first victim of the disaster at Parc colliery in the Rhondda valley on April 10 is brought to the pithead. Four men lost their lives when several hundred tons of rubble fell in the middle of the coalface. One of the four was brought to the surface alive but died in hospital.

Aug. 1 A forest fire in the Aurès mountains, Algeria, killed 48 French soldiers.

Sept. 2 Seville province, Spain. After an explosion in a coal mine 16 miners were reported dead.

Sept. 18 Chryston, Lanarkshire. Fire in Aucheingeich colliery caused deaths of 47 miners.

Nov. 20 Yokohama, Japan. An explosion at an explosives plant killed 78 and injured more than 1,000.

Nov. 25 A fire in the coal mine at Matravideki, near Gyöngyös, Hungary, killed 31 miners.

Dec. 13 Dortmund, German Federal Republic. Thirty-six killed in a fire which destroyed two houses following a gas-leak explosion.

Marine

Jan. 30 After hitting an iceberg off Cape Farewell, Greenland, the Danish motor-vessel " Hans Hedtoft " disappeared without trace with the loss of all 95 aboard.

May 8 Egyptian pleasure steamer sank on the Nile near Cairo with the reported loss of 119 people.

May 12 Wewak, New Guinea. Explosion in the coaster " Busama " killed 13.

July 8 An explosion in a Danish pleasure boat on Haderslev lake, south Jutland, caused the deaths of 55.

Aug. 11 Twenty-five Indonesians reported drowned when a sailing boak sank off the Borneo coast.

Oct. 4 Pielisjärvi lake, Finland. A collision in fog between two motor vessels killed 15.

Nov. 24 All 15 aboard the coaster " Holmglen " were reported lost when it foundered off Timaru, South Island, New Zealand.

Dec. 14 Trawler from Fleetwood, Lancashire, presumed sunk with loss of all 19 aboard in gales off Islay, Scotland.

Miscellaneous

Jan. 9 At least 132 lost their lives when the Vega de Tera dam burst and engulfed Ribadelago village, Zamora province, Spain.

Jan. 22 Ten reported killed when a house in Alexandria, Egypt, collapsed during a storm.

Jan. 25 When a cinema roof collapsed at Kutchukyali, near Istanbul, Turkey, 33 were killed.

Feb. 22 Southern Rhodesia. Seventeen workmen killed by falling down a shaft while working on the Kariba dam.

March 9 Monterrey, Mexico. After drinking industrial alcohol from a leaking railway tank, 26 were reported to have died.

July 17 Pusan, Republic of Korea. Sudden rainstorm caused thousands of spectators at open-air show to stampede for shelter; 48 died.

Aug. 19 Kandy, Ceylon. In the stampede which followed a frightened elephant's running amuck during a pageant, 14 were killed.

Aug. 23 Bhakra dam, India. Flooding of the galleries and body of this dam caused ten deaths.

Sept. 16 Barletta, Italy. Five-storey block of flats collapsed killing 58.

Dec. 2 French Riviera. Breaking of the Malpasset dam killed 323 in Fréjus and St. Raphaël.

Natural

Jan. 6 Deaths of 63 people in eastern United States attributed directly or indirectly to a cold wave.

Jan. 20-25 At least 115 people died in severe floods in the north-eastern United States.

April 2 About 500 reported dead as result of flooding in Madagascar which followed torrential rain and five cyclones.

April 12-19 More than 35,000 people were rendered homeless in Uruguay and neighbouring parts of Argentina and Brazil by flooding of the Rivers Plate and Uruguay.

May 24 Severe flooding in Natal and East Griqualand following previous torrential rain reported to have killed 60.

June 15 Hong Kong. Following four days of torrential rain, floods killed 43.

July Flooding in West Pakistan killed 67.

July 20 India. More than 130 people reported to have died in severe flooding in Jammu and Kashmir during earlier part of the month.

Aug. 10 It was estimated that 493 people died, 543 were missing and more than 100,000 made homeless in the worst floods for 60 years in central and south Formosa.

Aug. 11 Eleven people reported killed and 17 missing following a typhoon on Japan's eastern coast.

Aug. 14 Nine people reported dead in widespread floods in Austria during preceding few days.

Aug. 14 Japan's seventh typhoon of 1959 which struck the southwest coast killed more than 140 and injured many others.

Aug. 15 Hungchun, Formosa. Earthquake killed 16 people and rendered more than 6,000 homeless.

Aug. 23 In Fukien province, Chinese People's Republic, 1,716 people were reported killed or missing following a typhoon.

Aug. 26 Earthquake in eastern Mexico killed between 20 and 40 people, and caused severe damage.

Sept. 7 Flooding during previous weekend in central and southern Italy killed at least 11.

Sept. 16 Many drowned and more than 250,000 rendered homeless in floods north of Bombay, India.

Sept. 17 Japan. Fifteen persons reported killed and many others missing following a typhoon.

Sept. 26 Typhoon struck central Japan, particularly Nagoya, killing at least 4,000 people and causing serious losses to nearly 1 million.

Oct. 4 Derna, Cyrenaica. Fifteen people reported killed and many injured by floods following a cloudburst.

Oct. 4 Three days of heavy rain rendered about 6,000 homeless and killed 5 in Oklahoma, United States.

Oct. 17 Typhoon at Okinawa caused at least 45 deaths.

Oct. 25 At least 17 killed by earthquake shocks in eastern Turkey.

Oct. 28 Typhoon which struck Pacific coast of Mexico during previous weekend devastated the port of Manzanillo, and killed at least 1,500 and injured many others.

Railways

May 28 West Java, Indonesia. Express train overturned between Bandjar and Bandung, killing at least 91.

June 28 Georgia, United States. Line of tank wagons carrying butane gas exploded after derailment at Maldrin, near Savannah; 25 believed killed and 75 injured.

July 6 Near Sivas, Turkey. Head-on collision between two trains; ten killed and eight seriously injured.

Aug. 27 Banja Luka, Yugoslavia. Twelve killed when a Zagreb-Sarajevo train was derailed.

Roads

Feb. 6 Near Guadalajara, Mexico. Collision between bus and lorry; 12 killed and several injured.

March 5 Eastern Cape, South Africa. Bus plunged over cliff near Matatiele, killing 15 and injuring 30.

March 6 East Griqualand, South Africa. Bus plunged down cutting in mountains; 15 killed and 30 injured.

April 7 Mexico. Ten reported killed and nine seriously injured when bus plunged into a gorge on Mexico City-Laredo road.

June 20 Near Lauffen-am-Neckar, German Federal Republic. Collision between express train and bus at a level-crossing; 37 killed at once and others critically injured.

Aug. 24 Dahanu, India. Bus plunged into flooded ravine, drowning 30.

Sept. 2 Luzon, Philippines. Seven reported killed and 25 seriously injured when a collision occurred between a bus and a truck near Tuguegarao.

Oct. 2 Poland. Collision between a lorry and an express train at a level-crossing at Dąbrówka, near Warsaw, killed 19.

Nov. 23 Bavaria, German Federal Republic. Nine killed and 15 seriously injured in a collision between a bus and a lorry near Amberg.

DISEASES.

DISEASES. The following is an account of some of the more important diseases and of developments in their treatment during 1959.

Allergic Diseases. A considerable advance was made during 1959 in the detection and determination of various substances which are released in tissues as a result of antigen-antibody union. In addition to histamine, which had long been known to be one of these substances, other substances attracted a good deal of interest, especially acetylcholine, serotonin and bradykinin.

Almost any organ of the body can act as a shock tissue in allergy. The shock tissue is the locale of antigen-antibody union giving rise to allergic manifestations. Not infrequently, this tissue or organ may not only act as a locale for the reaction, but may take an integral part in the reaction; in other words, it becomes antigenic itself. It was shown experimentally that it is possible to sensitize animals to their own organs by injection with extracts of these organs. Thus, the corresponding organ in the animal may become affected. This process may involve the thyroid, the testes or the kidney. There is a clinical counterpart to this condition. Certain disorders of the thyroid gland may be due to an acquired antigenicity on the part of the thyroid.

These phenomena are referred to as auto-immune diseases, conditions which are brought on as a result of an immunologic process during the course of which antibodies are formed to tissue or an organ and these antibodies unite with the tissue or organ producing pathological lesions and, therefore, clinical disease. The formed elements of the blood may also become involved in this process. Thus, agranulocytosis and neutropenia (involvement of the white blood cells) may be due to drug allergy which causes the white cells to become antigenic and produce antibodies against them. Then the antibodies unite with the white blood cells in the presence of the same drug to lead to their destruction.　　　(L. H. C.)

Blood, Diseases of the. The transplantation of blood from one human to another is a commonplace procedure. The red blood cells will survive for the same length of time in the recipient as they would have done within the donor's own circulation, providing the persons, even if of different families or different races, have compatible blood groups. This survival is probably attributable to a special characteristic of red blood cells: they do not have nuclei. However, if one tries to transplant blood-producing cells; *i.e.*, bone marrow cells which contain nuclei, the transplanted cells are rejected. This is due to the development of transplantation antibodies.

In animal experiments, attempts were made to modify, or even destroy, the rejection potentiality by total body radiation, a large and ordinarily fatal dose of X-rays being given. The radiation destroys the marrow, and at the same time destroys the ability to reject further marrow. Animals given lethal radiation were protected experimentally by marrow injections and the transplanted marrow " took ". Mice with leukaemia, when given total body radiation, survived and the leukaemia was destroyed. These experiments aroused considerable interest because of their possible use in treating human disease.

If marrow is removed from an individual and then reinjected into the same individual, it is an " autologous " marrow transfusion. It will naturally " take " without the necessity of using various methods for stopping the rejection phenomenon. This method might be useful under several sets of circumstances. If an individual; *e.g.*, an atomic scientist, should have some of his marrow stored in a functioning " marrow bank ", this could be utilized if the scientist were accidentally radiated and suffered bone marrow injury. If an individual required a massive dose of a chemical or radiation and his marrow was reasonably normal, the marrow could be removed beforehand, and then given soon after the administration of the dose. This technique was under trial in several clinics for the treatment of severe or apparently hopeless cancer, Hodgkin's disease or lymphosarcoma. If an individual who had leukaemia developed a complete " remission " (*i.e.*, showed no evidence of his disease either in blood or marrow), some of his marrow might be removed and stored at —80°C. for later use, upon the inevitable return of the leukaemic process. At that time, it might be possible to give drastic treatment for leukaemia safely, because of the availability of good marrow which would " take ". This method, too, was under trial.　　　(W. Dк.)

Cancer. Numerous contributions were made during 1959 in the field of carcinogenesis, raising important fundamental questions as to what extent the process of cancer causation is direct or indirect and the role to be attributed to viruses. A review of the current position of experimental cancer research was made by J. Furth (*Cancer Res.*, 19, 241-258), and the implications of indirect mechanisms of induction were considered by H. S. Kaplan (*Cancer Res.*, 19, 791-803). Important publications were O. Neubauer's *Bibliography of Cancer Produced by Pure Chemical Compounds* (London, 1959), H. F. Blum's *Carcinogenesis by Ultra Violet Light* (Princeton, 1959) and R. E. Eckardt's *Industrial Carcinogens* (New York, 1959). A symposium on the experimental aspects of carcinogenesis was held at Rehovot, Israel, under the auspices of the

Weizmann Institute of Science (the proceedings to be published in the *Acta Un. int. contra Cancrum*). To the long list of carcinogens already known, an interesting addition was made through the discovery by H. G. Richmond (*Brit. med. J.*, 1959, i, 947-949; *see also* A. Haddow and E. S. Horning, *J. nat. Cancer Inst.*, 24, in press) of the carcinogenicity of an iron-dextran complex, thus stimulating renewed attention to the function of metals in tumour induction and growth.

The subject of the tumour and leukaemia viruses was reviewed by L. Dmochowski (*Bact. Rev.*, 23, 18-40) and by L. Gross (*Lancet*, 1959, i, 891). A new development was the demonstration of such viruses in leukaemias induced by ionizing radiation (*see* L. Gross, B. Roswit, E. R. Mada, Y. Dreyfuss and L. A. Moore, *Cancer Res.*, 19, 316-320). As yet, although studies had only begun, there had appeared no example of a causative virus in cancer in man. While most of the findings relating to animal tumours and leukaemias appeared to be increasingly accepted, there were marked differences as to the significance to be attributed to them, especially in relation to natural infective causation. A more genetical interpretation was given by C. D. Darlington in a valuable discussion of plasmagene theory and cancer genesis during a symposium under the auspices of the University of Texas and the M. D. Anderson hospital at Houston, Texas. On the observational side, progress continued in the study of virus-like particles in the tissues of mice with induced leukaemia (*e.g.*, W. Bernhard and L. Gross, *C. R. Acad. Sci.*, 248, 160-163).

Many further studies were made, both statistical and experimental (*see* E. L. Wynder, *Brit. med. J.*, 1959, i, 317-322, and J. Cornfield, W. Haenszel, E. C. Hammond, A. M. Lilienfeld, M. B. Shimkin and E. L. Wynder, *J. nat. Cancer Inst.*, 22, 173-203), of the relationship between the smoking habit and lung cancer (the incidence of which continued to increase). A bibliography of the constituents of tobacco smoke was provided by the Tobacco Manufacturers' Standing committee (Research Paper No. 3, ed., H. R. Bentley and E. G. N. Berry, 1959). Sir Ronald Fisher continued to press his view that genetical constitution exerts a considerable influence (*Smoking: The Cancer Controversy*, Edinburgh, 1959), but again nothing appeared during the year to diminish the far more likely explanation that cigarette smoking is responsible for a large part of the incidence of cancer of the lung. The additional role of bronchitis and atmospheric pollution was again considered by P. Stocks (*Brit. med. J.*, 1959, i, 74-79).

Many papers given at the VIIth International Cancer congress in 1958 were published in the *Acta Un. int. contra Cancrum* (1959, 15), providing a useful conspectus of recent and current developments. Among general works may be mentioned those by D. M. Wallace (ed.) on *Tumours of the Bladder* (Edinburgh, 1959), G. T. Pack and I. M. Ariel (ed.) on *Treatment of Cancer and Allied Diseases* (vol. i, London, 1959), Dorothy S. Russell and L. J. Rubinstein on the *Pathology of Tumours of the Nervous System* (London, 1959) and P. Denoix on *Les cancers humains* (Paris, 1959).　　　(A. Hw.)

Ear, Nose and Throat Diseases. By 1959 rapid advances were being made in the surgical treatment of impaired hearing. The surgical procedures all dealt with conductive hearing loss, the type in which normal mechanisms for conduction are interfered with as a result of a perforated ear drum (from injury or infection), scarring produced by long continued drainage from the middle ear, or due to new bone formation (otosclerosis) which prevents the footplate of the stapes (the stirrup-like bone) from moving freely in the oval window, thereby impeding transmission of sound waves to the inner ear and thence to the auditory centres in the brain. These conditions are approached surgically through the outer ear canal.

Julius Lempart reviewed the development of modern ear surgery from its earliest beginnings in the 18th century. Lempert's procedure of fenestration created a window in the lateral semi-circular canal, replacing the one occupied by the footplate of the stirrup, through which airborne sound could pass to the inner ear (cochlea) and permitting the affected ear to hear the ordinary conversational voice. The results were reported as approximately 80% successful. A chief drawback is that the operation leaves a large surgical cavity which requires a lifetime of periodic re-checks and attention.

An effort was made by Abner M. Fuchs to delineate the common cold illnesses which are caused by a host of agents—viral, bacterial and allergic. Advances in virus studies made possible the identification and classification of a new family of viruses with the generic name of adenoviruses. These viruses cause an influenza-like illness with inflammation of the mucous membranes of the respiratory and ocular systems. At least 25 serologically distinct human and simian viruses in the adenovirus group had been isolated.

Physicians effectively control cold symptoms due to allergy by elimination or avoidance of the offending substances, and by specific immunotherapy and antihistamine therapy. Bacterial infections are controlled with chemotherapeutic agents. However, there appears to be no specific method which will affect the course of the non-febrile running-nose type of simple cold or the febrile influenza-like viral colds, except possibly by the promotion of good health habits, increasing general resistance to infection and symptomatic management. An effective vaccine against serotypes 3, 4 and 7 of the adenoviruses was developed and much effort was being expended to develop a polyvalent vaccine for the entire group of adenoviruses which were responsible for a large segment of febrile respiratory illnesses. (F. L. LR.)

Eye Diseases. When the drainage mechanism of the eye becomes clogged by debris or by adhesions of inflammatory character, it often causes the intra-ocular pressure to rise beyond the tolerance for natural function. Abnormally high intra-ocular pressure is known as glaucoma. It was estimated that there were 800,000 cases of undiscovered glaucoma in the United States in 1959, and that 12% of the blindness was due to glaucoma. Where natural outflow of fluid from the eye cannot be restored by medicines or surgery, an artificial drainage can be established by making a fistula in the sclera. However, many of the operations are not permanently successful because the fistula tends to close. New methods of ophthalmic surgical technique employ plastic tubes or polyethylene for drainage in glaucoma cases that require the fistulizing type of operation. The polyethylene tubes are not irritating and when properly placed they provide adequate drainage and normalize intra-ocular pressure.

Medical treatment of glaucoma was greatly aided by the discovery of additional drugs after the introduction of Diamox (acetazolamide) by Becker in 1954. There was almost universal agreement among ophthalmologists that acetazolamide does lower the intra-ocular pressure both in normal and glaucomatous eyes and that it is a useful adjunct in the treatment of glaucoma. Many patients with chronic simple glaucoma, previously uncontrolled by maximal medical therapy, had normal intra-ocular pressures for three to four years after treatment with a combination of acetazolamide plus miotic therapy. The long-term medication with acetazolamide did not suppress the aqueous flow irreversibly and after discontinuation of acetazolamide the intra-ocular pressure went up again in these patients. In 1959, several other drugs known as carbonic anhydrase inhibitors appeared and were under investigation. None of them surpassed acetazolamide in its effect on intra-ocular pressure and clinical usefulness, but when one of them failed to lower ocular tension or had many annoying side effects, others were available. (W. L. BE.)

Gastric and Intestinal Diseases. The origin of canker sores of the mouth (aphthous stomatitis) remained obscure in 1959. Food (such as shellfish, pork, chocolate and walnuts), viral infection, endocrine and emotional disturbances had all been implicated. Citric and acetic acids applied locally provided a useful test of citrus fruits as possible causes.

Many approaches became available for diagnosing bleeding from the digestive tract, a difficult problem. These included intravenous injection of radioactive iron which is incorporated into the red blood cells; a new test for haemoglobin in the faeces; the use of fluorescein intravenously; the swallowing of radioactive tape to locate the site of bleeding; and careful operative inspection of the digestive tract with illuminated instruments (endoscopes). Decreased local temperature of the stomach via ice-water lavage, or by cooling through a thin-walled balloon introduced into the stomach, reduced acid-pepsin production, retarded digestion and thereby controlled bleeding from peptic ulcer. Emotional problems were important in the symptomatology of the ulcer patient, and, if not managed effectively, caused recurrent distress despite medical or surgical treatment.

The incidence of stomach cancer was increased in people with pernicious anaemia, as a consequence of inflammation and regeneration. The biological nature of the tumour, and its tendency to grow slowly or rapidly, determined the outcome of surgery. Exploratory abdominal operations revealed lymphoblastoma, tuberculous peritonitis and chronic granulomatous inflammation as causes of persistent obscure fever.

Inflammation of the small intestine (regional enteritis) caused fever, abdominal cramps, weight loss, diarrhoea and obstruction. Surgery was required for complications and good health was possible despite extensive removal of bowel. Nevertheless, recurrences were frequent. Medical treatment was effective in uncomplicated cases.

Excessive fat in the faeces (steatorrhoea) accompanied diseases of the small bowel, poor function of the pancreas, disorders of the liver and biliary tract and severe diabetes, and occasionally appeared after the use of antibiotics (neomycin). Newly developed tubes facilitated the removal of tissue from the small bowel for diagnostic study. A unique illness, intestinal lipodystrophy, affected chiefly middle-aged men, and was characterized by fatty diarrhoea, migratory polyarthritis and weight loss. Diagnosis was established by microscopic examination of lymph nodes, which showed large cells with special staining properties.

Newer X-ray methods revealed an increasing number of tumours of the small intestine; bleeding and intermittent obstruction were common symptoms. Intestinal polyposis, a hereditary condition, was associated with blackish-purple pigmentation in and around the mouth. A special tumour (carcinoid) composed of argentaffin cells, on extending to liver and lymph nodes, produced the chemicals serotonin and histamine responsible for skin flushes, abdominal cramps and diarrhoea. Associated findings were asthma and disorders of the heart. Diagnosis was aided by the identification of a chemical, 5-hydroxyindoleacetic acid, in urine. Surgical removal was the only treatment. Carcinoids were also found in the appendix and the bronchus of the lungs.

Arthritis, including ankylosing spondylitis of the spine, frequently accompanied ulcerative colitis; other concomitants found were abnormal blood proteins and liver cirrhosis. Medical treatment was helpful in most cases of ulcerative colitis. Rectal installation of adrenal steroids (hydrocortisone hemisuccinate and methyl prednisolone) by enema decreased the inflammation and facilitated healing, especially in mild or moderate cases. The beneficial effect seemed to be chiefly a local action, although with certain compounds partial systemic absorption occurred. In patients with uncontrollable haemorrhage, fulminating disease, perforation, unresponsiveness to medical treatment, possible cancer and disabling anorectal complications, surgical treatment was required. Young women could undergo such operations without subsequent inability to bear children.

Liver disease produced many biochemical disorders; some of these were utilized to evaluate liver function, identify the type and degree of hepatic injury, and predict the course of illness. Practical tests included bromsulphalein retention, serum bilirubin, estimates of plasma prothrombin after administration of vitamin K and measurements of various serum enzymes, including cholinesterase, transaminase and alkaline phosphatase. Injection of radio-opaque material into the spleen under local or general anaesthesia was used to detect obstructions and by-passes in the circulation (percutaneous splenoportography). Inspection of the interior of the abdomen (peritoneoscopy) and removal of tissue from the liver by a needle were additional diagnostic aids. A 15-year survey in the United States indicated little chance of serum hepatitis occurring in patients receiving pooled plasma stored for six months at room temperature in a fluid state. Immunological mechanisms appeared to be involved in the progression of acute to chronic hepatitis among women.

For inflammation of the pancreas accompanying inflammation of the gall bladder, operations which removed stones in the bile ducts and facilitated drainage of bile were very helpful. Over-eating and excessive intakes of alcohol, by stimulating secretion of pancreatic juice, were important causes. Chronic relapsing pancreatitis originated in various ways. Hence, no single treatment was uniformly effective; operations chiefly relieved obstruction to the flow of pancreatic juice. (J. B. Kr.)

Heart Diseases. In 1959 the attack on congenital cardiovascular defects continued to make increasing use of some type of pump which allowed an attack on the heart and adjacent vessels with the heart open and under direct vision. In general the techniques were simpler and the equipment needed to achieve the bypass of the heart and monitor the resulting body changes was less complex than at first seemed necessary. It was found that too long a period of standstill of the heart was accompanied by irreversible metabolic changes involving particularly the storage and use of glycogen, a sugar, and that the heart, while capable of resuming its beat, might function with decided impairment if arrested too long.

One area of particular concern in congenital heart disease had been the presence, in some patients with an increased flow of blood to the lungs, of an increase in pressure in the blood-vessel (pulmonary artery) leading from the right side of the heart to the lungs. In some cases where this increased flow was due to a shunt of blood through a defect between the two receiving chambers (atria) of the heart, closure of the defect was followed in a period of months by a significant drop in pressure in the pulmonary artery. However, this evidence of reversibility of high blood pressure in the lung did not necessarily apply to all cases with this finding. In some, this elevation in pressure had been shown to be independent of blood-flow, and attack by surgery often proved difficult or disastrous. The relationship of fats to the blood-flow through the coronary arteries was investigated. T. J. Regan showed that when the level of fats in the blood was high, the blood-flow through the coronary arteries was decreased and the removal of oxygen by the heart muscle was diminished. Other investigations suggested that patients with coronary heart disease did not remove fatty substances from the blood as rapidly as normal persons; following a fatty meal, the fatty substances in the blood rose to a higher and more sustained level than in normal persons. Other studies indicated that epinephrine and norepinephrine, which are released by a portion of the adrenal glands in response to

urgent demand by the body, also tend to cause an elevation of the fat levels in the blood as does acute emotion itself. The conclusion that " stress " was the cause of coronary heart disease did not yet receive widespread support despite these findings, and no quantitative measure of stress was yet available. (O. Pl.)

Respiratory Diseases. No real advance was made during 1959 towards the prevention or effective treatment of lung cancer and chronic bronchitis which remained the two major problems in respiratory disease. The role of cigarette smoking in the production of both these conditions received further emphasis in the medical and lay press but the continued rise in the sale of tobacco suggested that the general public was not paying serious attention to the many warnings issued by the medical profession.

In the treatment of ventilatory insufficiency and respiratory acidosis secondary to chronic bronchitis and emphysema the value of tracheostomy became firmly established. Artificial positive pressure respiration also proved effective in selected cases. There was declining favour for the belief that many or indeed most cases of sarcoidosis have a tuberculous basis. Evidence was presented during the year to suggest that " exposure of a susceptible host to pine pollen " might be one of the ways in which sarcoidosis is produced.

Serious anxiety persisted throughout 1959 over the prevalence of staphylococcal respiratory cross-infection in hospitals and restrictions in the use of wide-spectrum antibiotics were advocated by some authorities. Two new antibiotics, vancomycin and ristocetin, became available for the treatment of staphylococcal pneumonia or other infections due to organisms resistant to the standard antibiotics. Vancomycin and ristocetin, being effective only when given by the intravenous route, are for that reason less liable to be abused than erythromycin and its predecessors, and the widespread emergence of staphylococci resistant to these antibiotics is thus less likely to occur.

Prolonged corticosteroid therapy continued to be used with caution during the year in cases of chronic asthma resisting simpler measures. Triamcinolone did not, as had been expected, displace prednisone and prednisolone as the drug of choice because of reports of severe muscle weakness occurring with the newer preparation. The efficacy of dexamethazone, the newest steroid, in the treatment of chronic asthma had not been finally assessed at the end of 1959. In the diagnostic field the pleural biopsy punch designed by L. D. Abrams (1958) was found to be of considerable value in determining precisely the cause of pleural effusions.

(I. W. B. G.)

Rheumatic Diseases. During 1959, search was continued for the specific changes in connective tissues of the human organism which permit the development of arthritis. The role of mechanical factors in producing disorders of connective tissue was also being studied.

Localization of arthritis is often determined by trauma. Joints which have been subjected to injuries and to excessive use are often sites of severe arthritic changes. Reactions of fibrous tissues to trauma are determined by the chemical nature of the surrounding medium. The presence of small amounts of nucleic acid or of other polysaccharides in the surrounding medium causes fibrous tissue to disintegrate rapidly when subjected to grinding. A line for research was the determination of what chemical features of connective tissues might set the stage for traumatic and degenerative arthritis.

Another important question was the mechanism by which tissues become calcified or lose calcium from previously well-calcified areas. Researches during 1959 showed that the initiation of calcification results from the process of heterogeneous nucleation of apatite crystals in the presence of a highly specific stereochemical configuration in crystal structures of native-type collagen fibrils. Calcification can apparently proceed in the organism only when the basic molecules of collagen are packed in a specific manner. Thus any disorder of fibrous tissues which would result in abnormal orientation of basic molecules would cause disturbance of calcification.

The ability to initiate mineralization or calcification is not specific for the fibrous tissues or collagen of bone; in fact a variety of reconstituted native-type collagen tissues which are normally not calcified can be caused to take on calcium. All collagenous tissues are apparently capable of becoming calcified, but under normal circumstances this calcification is inhibited by specific inhibitors. These inhibitors are believed to be acid mucopolysaccharides or polymers of these compounds. Accurate delineation of the nature of calcification inhibitors could provide powerful tools with which to bring about the dissolution and disappearance of abnormal calcium deposits.

Another interesting development concerned the nature of changes which take place in human cartilages with advancing years. The data were significant because of their relevance to the most frequent variety of crippling human arthritis, namely osteoarthritis, which is encountered with increasing frequency as aging progresses. Studies showed that the ratio of chondroitin sulphate to dry weight of cartilage decreases at a constant rate with increasing age. The ratio of keratosulphate to dry weight of cartilage increases to maturity and then remains constant. The ratio of keratosulphate to total polysaccharide increases from zero at birth to the ratio of one to one when an individual reaches the age of 70. Further, it was found that chondroitin sulphate present in the newborn is notably different in chemical characteristics from the chondroitin sulphate of adults. These data indicated that the aging of cartilage involves a process of continuous chemical differentiation rather than one of degeneration. (E. F. RG.)

Skin Diseases. The most significant development of 1959 in dermatology was the introduction of griseofulvin, an orally administered antibiotic agent for the treatment of certain common superficial fungus infections of the skin, hair and nails. It was the first useful systemically administered agent to be introduced, and the early reports of its effectiveness were most heartening.

Griseofulvin, a product of several penicillia, was isolated by British investigators in 1939 and was used to treat fungus diseases of lettuce and tomatoes, then of laboratory animals and cattle, and 20 years later, of human beings. The British used it in topical form and found it ineffective. Harvey Blank, in the United States, suggested that it could be administered systemically in man and he reported his results late in 1958. He found that it was quickly effective in ringworm of the scalp, in difficult-to-cure ringworm of the nails, in notoriously resistant infections of the skin and nails due to the organism *Tinea rubrum*, and in athlete's foot and similar conditions. Like bacterial antibiotics, it appeared to exert an effect upon certain organisms only, so that proper laboratory investigations were necessary before instituting treatment. Yeast infections (moniliasis), such as those due to *Blastomycosis dermatitidis*, the disease caused by *Tinea versicolor* and the deep mycotic infections were not helped. A few instances of toxic reactions were noted, such as hives, headache, rash, and gastro-intestinal discomfort, but these were transitory and readily controlled by lowering the dosage of the drug.

The drug promised exciting possibilities for further study. However, much had yet to be learned about the possibility of delayed toxic effects, the results from long-term usage, the encouragement of resistant strains of fungi, the precise mode of action of the drug, its specificity, optimum dosage, its effect upon concurrent diseases and, as with all new potent agents, the results from its misuse. (H. RA.)

Tropical Diseases. Intensive search for new drugs for the treatment of leprosy continued, much work being done on the effects of combining drugs of known efficacy. Diethyldithiolisophthalate (Etisul., E.T.I.P.), a new drug for use by widespread inunction, was shown to lack toxicity and to be of value in the early stages of treatment, inducing a rapid fall in the bacterial index and leading to accelerated resolution. When used in combination with drugs such as D.D.S. or Ciba 1906, administered orally, resolution was rapid and uniform and no sign of drug resistance was detected. E.T.I.P. produced a most offensive odour but this could be partially neutralized by deodorant aerosol sprays. (T. F. Davey, *Leprosy Rev.*, 30, 3, 1959.)

The outstanding importance of disorders of nutrition in tropical pathology was emphasized in widely differing fields. G. L. Money surveyed the incidence of neuropathies caused by the administration of isoniazid to ambulant tuberculosis patients in Ibadan, Nigeria. The high incidence of severe neurological damage compared with that occurring in patients in socially advanced countries, the relief of symptoms on withdrawing isoniazid and the economic difficulty in providing adequate nutrition for the vast majority of tuberculosis patients in the tropics pointed to the need for the routine provision of cheap vitamin B supplements when high dosages of isoniazid (given in Europe and the United States with no untoward results) were administered to indigenous peoples in the tropics (*Lancet*, 7095, July, 1959).

The importance of good general nutrition in the prevention of illness in the presence of adverse factors was stressed by K. R. Hill in the case of vomiting sickness of Jamaica; a severe and frequently fatal disease shown by Sir Harold Scott to be associated with the ingestion of Ackee, a tropical fruit. Two compounds, hypoglycin A and B, were isolated at the University College of the West Indies. These extracts from Ackee fruit produced in experimental animals the lowering of the blood sugar content found in vomiting sickness in man. It was noted that the toxicity of hypoglycin A was much enhanced by starving the rats or by giving them a deficient diet. This might be significant in view of the fact that the disease occurred commonly in poor, badly nourished children and was not seen amongst the well-to-do even if they ate Ackee fruit.

In studies in Jamaica of hepatic veno occlusive disease (V.O.D.), a condition of cirrhosis of the liver with ascites, Hill concluded that the blockage of the venous system within the liver was due to the action of the pyrrolizidine group of alkaloids found in bush tea made from *Crotolaria retusa*. Similar conditions were known to occur in field animals in Britain and in many parts of the world after eating species of *Senecio* (ragwort, etc.). K. Rhodes pointed out that human sufferers from V.O.D. invariably had a background of protein deficiency. It was probable that, although a toxic factor was responsible for V.O.D., accessory factors determined the severity and prognosis of the disease in an individual and that the most important determining factor was dietetic. (*Trans. R. Soc. trop. Med. Hyg.* 53, no. 3, 1959.)

Colonial Office reports noted considerable advances in knowledge of trypanosomiasis, especially in tsetse fly control. Dieldren emulsion had been valuable in controlling tsetse flies in Northern Rhodesia and Dieldrex 15 appeared to have eliminated the fly *Glossina palpalis* from 300 mi. of two river systems. The study of preferred hosts of various species of tsetse fly continued. *G. longipennis* preferred to feed on the blood of the rhinoceros, *G. tabaniformis* on the red river hog and porcupine, and *G. longipalpis* on the bushbuck. On the shores of Lake Victoria the more deadly *Trypanosoma rhodesiense* continued to replace *T. gambiense* in the same places and occupations. Advances were made in the experimental use of tsetse flies. The difficulty of infecting *G. palpalis* was reduced by feeding on the first day of life. Studies of the local reaction at the site of the bite indicated that the trypanosomes multiplied there and changed into the blood forms (*Colonial Research Report: Tsetse Fly and Trypanosomiasis Committee*, Nov. 1958 [Cmnd. 591]). D. H. H. Robertson reported unfavourable reactions with nitrofurazone in the treatment of trypanosomiasis. Polyneuritis with profound weakness and low blood pressure occurred. If given early thiamine produced rapid improvement.

The joint W.H.O./F.A.O. expert committee on zoonoses (those diseases which are naturally transmitted between vertebrate animals and man) published its second report. It pointed out that more than 100 zoonoses were now recognized and drew attention to the fact that domestic animal reservoirs of zoonoses were the sources of the greatest danger to man since he was in closest contact with such animals. Even in temperate climates such conditions as ringworm and cat scratch fever might be caused by pets. The possibility of infection by tuberculosis from dogs, cats and monkeys must be borne in mind. The ornithoses, particularly psittacosis—the typhoid-like disease carried by birds of the parrot family—must always be taken into account. The increased recognition of Q fever in man and animals in all parts of the world pointed

to the need for further research in the mode of transmission of the rickettsial organism involved—*Rickettsia burneti*. In the original Australian investigation, transmission to man involved a tick and a bandicoot but it had been discovered that many wild animals, particularly rodents and migrant birds, were infected and that migrant birds were responsible for carrying the disease from one country to another. There was great need for careful co-ordinated investigation of the ecology of both wild and domestic animal reservoirs of disease.

P. C. C. Garnham and D. J. Lewis recently showed that bay sore, an ulceration of the ear lobes occurring in British Honduras among the *chicleros* (men who enter the forests during the rains to collect the raw material for chewing-gum) was caused by a subspecies of *Leishmania braziliensis* transmitted by a sandfly in the forests where, owing to the paucity of human beings, the infection must be maintained by an animal carrier, as yet unknown. (*Trans. R. Soc. trop. Med. Hyg.* 53, no 1, Jan. 1959.)　(G. R. McR.)

Tuberculosis. Progress continued to be made during 1959 in combating this disease. In the preventive field, improvements in the standards of living and hygiene, the isolation of infectious cases and active measures such as vaccination were still all important. Mass radiography remained the best method of finding undetected infectious cases. Fear of the

EUROPEAN MORTALITY FROM TUBERCULOSIS (ALL FORMS) AND FROM TUBERCULOSIS OF THE RESPIRATORY SYSTEM, 1952-57
Actual number of deaths (A) and crude rates per 100,000 population (B)

Country			All forms						Respiratory system					
			1952	1953	1954	1955	1956	1957	1952	1953	1954	1955	1956	1957
Austria	.	A.	3,184	2,373	2,405	2,197	2,049	1,918	2,694	2,054	2,044	1,900	1,757	1,711
		B.	45·8	34·1	34·5	31·5	29·3	27·4	38·8	29·5	29·3	27·2	25·2	24·5
Belgium	.	A.	2,339	2,505	2,325	2,237	2,039	...	1,975	2,222	2,057	2,020	1,847	...
		B.	26·8	28·5	26·4	25·2	22·8	...	22·6	25·3	23·3	22·8	20·7	...
Denmark	.	A.	472	383	341	278	227	219	421	339	310	227	191	191
		B.	10·9	8·8	7·7	6·3	5·1	4·9	9·7	7·8	7·0	5·1	4·3	4·2
Finland	.	A.	2,359	1,848	1,697	1,773	1,636	1,649	2,075	1,684	1,551	1,653	1,518	1,564
		B.	57·7	44·6	40·4	41·8	38·1	38·0	50·7	40·7	37·0	39·0	35·4	36·1
France	.	A.	18,652	15,691	13,963	13,535	12,419	11,902	15,525	13,411	12,072	11,923	11,022	10,632
		B.	43·8	36·8	32·4	31·3	28·5	27·0	36·5	31·4	28·0	27·6	25·3	24·1
German Democratic Rep.	.	A.	8,826	5,737	4,887	4,572	4,219	...	7,594	4,886	4,282	4,052	3,774	...
		B.	48·2	31·6	27·1	25·2	23·8	...	41·4	26·9	23·7	25·2	21·3	...
German Federal Republic	.	A.	13,281	10,594	10,110	10,039	9,694	9,412	11,186	9,127	8,843	8,892	8,649	8,570
		B.	27·4	21·6	20·4	20·1	19·5	18·7	23·1	18·6	17·9	17·8	17·4	17·0
Hungary	.	A.	6,109	4,243	3,511	3,330	3,441	3,375	...	...	3,040	2,897	3,085	3,036
		B.	64·3	44·3	36·2	34·0	35·0	34·4	...	...	31·4	29·5	31·4	30·9
Iceland	.	A.	20	14	10	4	13	7	13	8	10	2	10	7
		B.	13·5	9·3	6·3	2·5	8·1	4·3	8·8	5·3	6·3	1·3	6·2	4·3
Ireland	·	A.	1,579	1,187	1,005	889	689	696	1,207	911	797	729	562	583
		B.	53·5	40·3	34·3	30·5	23·8	24·1	40·9	31·0	27·2	25·1	19·4	20·2
Italy	.	A.	13,017	11,125	10,961	10,921	10,710	9,965	10,205	9,192	9,214	9,295	9,267	8,736
		B.	27·7	23·6	23·0	22·7	22·2	20·6	21·8	19·5	19·3	19·3	19·2	18·1
Luxembourg	.	A.	72	52	36	56	36	47	56	44	30	43	31	38
		B.	23·9	17·1	11·8	18·1	11·5	15·0	18·6	14·5	9·8	13·9	9·9	12·1
Netherlands	.	A.	1,278	966	798	717	596	515	991	747	656	587	487	425
		B.	12·3	9·2	7·5	6·7	5·5	4·7	9·5	7·1	6·2	5·5	4·5	3·9
Norway	.	A.	667	539	520	434	354	...	561	453	441	371	314	...
		B.	20·0	16·0	15·3	12·7	10·2	...	16·9	13·5	13·0	10·8	9·1	...
Portugal	.	A.	8,279	5,408	5,348	5,518	5,587	5,200	6,671	4,347	4,395	4,598	4,787	4,497
		B.	96·8	62·7	61·5	63·0	62·3	58·4	78·0	50·4	50·6	52·5	54·2	50·5
Spain	.	A.	15,971	11,533	10,802	10,255	9,704	...	12,388	9,014	8,702	8,318	8,021	...
		B.	56·4	40·4	37·6	35·4	33·2	...	43·8	31·6	30·3	28·7	27·5	...
Sweden	.	A.	1,233	1,022	935	775	703	...	1,089	909	834	693	631	...
		B.	17·3	14·3	13·0	10·7	9·6	8·8*	15·3	12·7	11·6	9·5	8·6	7·8*
Switzerland	.	A.	1,224	1,143	1,090	1,042	975	...	947	910	864	844	792	...
		B.	25·4	23·4	22·1	20·8	19·3	17·6*	19·7	18·7	17·5	16·9	15·7	14·4*
U.K.: *England and Wales*	.	A.	10,585	8,902	7,897	6,492	5,375	4,783	9,335	7,913	7,069	5,837	4,853	4,249
		B.	24·1	20·2	17·8	14·6	12·0	10·6	21·2	17·9	16·0	13·1	10·8	9·4
Northern Ireland	.	A.	410	316	251	211	164	175	325	257	196	180	147	150
		B.	29·8	22·8	18·1	15·1	11·7	12·5	23·6	18·6	14·1	12·9	10·5	10·7
Scotland	.	A.	1,612	1,341	1,128	982	801	723	1,409	1,159	1,010	860	715	664
		B.	31·5	26·2	22·0	19·1	15·6	14·0	27·5	22·6	19·7	16·8	13·9	12·9
Yugoslavia	.	A.	2,699	1,819	2,592	2,826	2,806	...	2,180	1,499	2,129	2,398	2,426	...
		B.	74·7	48·5	67·9	55·8	54·1	...	60·4	40·0	55·8	47·4	46·8	...

* Approximate or preliminary figure.

discovery of disease was the most important cause of non-attendance for a mass X-ray and it was shown that home visiting increased the response in people over middle-age by as much as 30% to 40%. Doubts about the use of B.C.G. (bacille Calmette-Guérin) vaccination continued to be raised. It was claimed that a high degree of tuberculosis eradication had been achieved with little or no use of B.C.G. in such places as Iceland, Hawaii and the Netherlands, and that mass vaccination in areas of low prevalence of tuberculosis would destroy the usefulness of the tuberculin skin test as a case-finding technique. However, a second report by the British Medical Research council gave incontrovertible evidence that B.C.G. vaccination decreased the incidence of tuberculosis. Over a five-year period the annual incidence of tuberculosis in vaccinated children was 0·38 per 1,000 compared with 2·29 per 1,000 in those who had not been vaccinated, a reduction of 83%.

In the treatment of the disease, isoniazid remained the ideal drug as it was cheap and effective and was taken by mouth. To prevent the development of isoniazid-resistant organisms, either streptomycin or para-aminosalicylic acid (P.A.S.) were used in addition. Both these drugs had disadvantages, especially when used by out-patients in the more under-developed countries. Streptomycin was unsatisfactory for self-administration as it had to be given by injection and the gastro-intestinal symptoms caused by P.A.S. had resulted in half the patients discontinuing the drug. Search continued for a more satisfactory drug to be given in conjunction with isoniazid. A trial of diaminodiphenylsulphone (D.D.S.) was carried out in east Africa. This drug, which was cheap and nontoxic, had already been used for leprosy. Unfortunately, it failed to prevent the development of isoniazid-resistant organisms in about 40% of patients after six months' treatment. Further trials, both with experimental tuberculosis and in humans, were being carried out with thiocarbanidin and alpha-ethyl-thioisonicotinamide. The latter drug had a high incidence of gastro-intestinal irritation, but further reports were awaited. For table *see* page 170.   (G. W. St.)

Venereal Diseases. The report of the Ministry of Health on the state of public health in England and Wales for 1958 and the first six months of 1959 showed that the decrease in the incidence of syphilis, although small, had been maintained; from 786 (Jan. 1957-June 1958) to 748 (Jan. 1958-June 1959). On the other hand there had been a further steep rise in the number of cases of acute gonorrhoea (in both sexes) and non-gonococcal urethritis attending venereal disease clinics.

INCIDENCE OF VENEREAL DISEASES IN ENGLAND AND WALES

	1958			1959 (*first 6 months only*)		
	Male	Female	Total	Male	Female	Total
Early Syphilis (primary and secondary)	427	84	511	189	48	237
Gonorrhoea	22,507	5,508	28,015	11,567	2,902	14,469
Non-gonococcal urethritis (males only)	17,536	—	17,536	11,250	—	11,250
Other conditions requiring treatment	14,456	12,130	26,586	7,384	6,043	13,427
Other conditions not requiring treatment	21,541	8,879	30,420	11,274	4,756	16,030

Returns from the clinics showed that the increase in the incidence of gonorrhoea and non-gonococcal urethritis had occurred in many parts of the country and that it had been particularly marked in London and in some provincial towns. The trend had been downward in a few urban areas such as Tyneside where immigrants had not so far penetrated to any great extent. The recent immigration of coloured members of the Commonwealth (it was reported in parliament to be 190,000 in Great Britain) was mainly responsible for the increase in the incidence of gonorrhoea. Ambrose King considered that the rise was partly due to the emergence of strains of gonococci resistant to penicillin. Nevertheless, many cases described as resistant to penicillin had been due to re-infection and not relapse.

It was alarming to note that an increased proportion of persons committed to prison were suffering from gonorrhoea. Many girls under the age of 18 attended V.D. clinics and in Holloway women's prison 50% of the teen-age prostitutes were found to be infected. It will be seen that gonorrhoea continued to be the main menace (it was also so in other European countries and the United States) and if the disease continued to increase at the 1959 rate the ministry report maintained that it was hard to believe that there would not also be a rise in the incidence of syphilis.

F. Albertazzi of the University of Turin gave intra-muscularly 100,000 units of sodium penicillin to 17 hospitalized sero-negative cases of primary syphilis. Herxheimer reactions (inflammatory reactions in the tissues) with rise in temperature were observed in all cases. Serological tests became positive after varying intervals of time (in six patients 48 hours following the injection). Albertazzi maintained that the Herxheimer produced by a small dose of penicillin could be a valuable diagnostic aid in sero-negative primary syphilis.

No advances had been made on the aetiology of non-gonococcal urethritis in men, but it was interesting to note that B. R. Jones, L. H. Collier and C. H. Smith had isolated a virus from a baby with inclusion conjunctivitis and from a woman suffering from inclusion cervicitis—two diseases closely allied to non-gonococcal urethritis in men.

                                                          (A. H. H.)

In the fiscal year ending June 30, 1959, state health departments in the United States reported a total of 359,670 cases of venereal disease. Included in this total were 119,981 cases of syphilis, 237,318 cases of gonorrhea, 1,574 cases of chancroid, 332 cases of granuloma inguinale and 436 cases of lymphogranuloma inguinale. During the year 8,178 cases of primary and secondary syphilis were reported, an increase of 22·7% over the number of infectious syphilis cases reported for the preceding year. This increase was of great concern because there had been a consistently significant decline reported in this stage of syphilis from 1947 to 1954, after which it stabilized at between 6,500 and 6,800 cases per year. The trend of gonorrhea incidence was similar to the syphilis pattern in that increases were reported among whites and non-whites of both sexes, and by both private physicians and clinics. However, it was conservatively estimated that a minimum of 1 million cases of gonorrhea actually occur annually in the United States, but many thousands of cases are not reported. (*See* also SURGERY; MEDICINE.)   (W. J. BN.)

See F. Albertazzi, *Minerva dermat.*, **33**, 265 (1958); B. R. Jones, L. H. Collier and C. H. Smith, *Lancet*, *1*, 902 (1959); A. J. King, *Lancet*, *1*, 651 (1958).

DOCKS AND HARBOURS. Great Britain. The annual report of the British Transport commission for 1958 showed a fall in both gross and net receipts from the nationalized docks, harbours and wharves. Gross receipts at £21 million were £750,000 less and net receipts at £2·2 million were down £26,000, before reckoning central charges. Although rates were twice increased during the year, a reduction in gross expenses made possible by a fall in traffics and from economies was insufficient to meet higher costs, caused mainly by increased wages. Inward traffic fell by 1·4 million tons (nearly 5%) and outward by 4·9 million tons (nearly 14%), the decline in coal movements again being largely responsible.

National Dock Labour Board. The annual report of the board recorded an average total of 74,132 workers registered throughout 1958 of whom 64,451 were on the live register, compared with 76,691 and 67,611 in 1957. Employment continued to decline until the closing month of the year when an increase took place which continued into 1959. Operating costs rose by £558,000 to £5,998,000. Management fund income fell short of expenditure by £826,000 and in Nov. 1958 the basic levy was raised from 12% to 13·5%.

United Kingdom Ports. The annual report of the Port of London authority for the year ended March 31, 1959, stated that despite a serious interruption of port operations due to an unofficial strike the net registered tonnage of shipping entering and leaving the port reached a new high record totalling 80,450,000 tons, 5·2 million tons greater than for 1957-58. Tonnage of goods passing through the port declined by nearly 3·5 million tons on the record tonnage established in 1957-58. Passengers embarking and disembarking increased to 83,000 and 110,000 from 72,000 and 108,000 respectively. Most of the authority's charges were increased from Jan. 1, 1959. Works completed included the construction of a dam across the inner-end of Royal Victoria docks (western entrance); new gates and replacement of the upper jetty at Gallions Upper Entrance (Barge) dock, Royal Albert dock; and the final stage of the construction of new sheds at Millwall docks. Work continuing included the overhaul of St. Katherine dock; the permanent closing of the Wapping lock entrance, which neared completion; construction of a new bridge over the Canada-Greenland passage; improvements to the Surrey lock entrance at Surrey Commercial docks; and construction of a new No. 4 berth at Royal Victoria docks. The Thames Navigation service came into operation in May as an aid to navigation by means of radio-telephony and radar at continuously manned operations buildings and through two remote out-stations.

The first oil terminal in Europe capable of the continuous handling of fully loaded tankers up to 100,000 tons was opened at Finnart, Dunbartonshire, in June 1959. Progress continued at Milford Haven, where the £6·5 million British Petroleum terminal capable of receiving 100,000-ton tankers was scheduled for completion in mid-1960, and work continued on the Esso Petroleum jetty and on the ore terminal

for the Steel Company of Wales. Plans were announced by Regent Oil for a terminal at Queen Alexandra dock, Cardiff, and Mobil Oil started construction of a £1 million ocean-fed terminal at Ellesmere Port, Cheshire.

In May 1959, the princess royal opened the new £1·75 million Riverside quay at Hull where new works included a quay on the south side of Albert docks, transit sheds and passenger buildings. Work also started there on a £1 million scheme for the replacement of No. 1 jetty and a new branch jetty at Salt End, and in Oct. 1959 the British Transport commission passed a £4·75 million scheme of improvements at the King George dock. At Southampton a modern passenger terminal in the New docks and new transit sheds in Empress dock were authorized. The first stage of the £1·25 million programme for the modernization of the docks at Garston was completed and improvements at Kings Lynn approved. Improvements to piers and buildings and the modernization of cargo handling facilities were carried out at Holyhead docks. In June 1959 the Duke of Edinburgh dry dock at Swansea was opened and construction of a new entrance jetty was completed. At Newport a bulk dry-cargo discharging berth came into operation and a similar one was under construction at Barry. In May 1959 the commission announced further schemes of improvement and modernization at the south Wales ports of Newport, Cardiff, Penarth, Barry, Port Talbot and Swansea to cost £1,125,000. Plans were made for a new dry dock costing £4,350,000 to be built with Treasury assistance at Greenock. A new oil-loading terminal was completed at Whitegate, Cork.

Europe. The construction of Europort (the extension of the port of Rotterdam) made considerable progress during the year, and the first tanker berths were planned for completion in 1961. The new port area covered 9,000 ac. between the mouth of the river Meuse and the New Waterway opposite the Hook of Holland. Progress was made in the ten-year development plan at Antwerp: a new dry dock for tankers of up to 40,000 tons came into use in June 1959, and the construction of the extended quay for bulk cargo and of a new pier was completed. Completion of the 5th harbour dock was scheduled for early 1960, when work on the 6th harbour

The 42,000-ton tanker "British Duchess" at British Petroleum's new oil jetty at Finnart, Loch Long, Scotland, which was officially opened on June 9. The jetty, connected by pipeline to the company's refinery at Grangemouth, can accommodate tankers of 100,000 tons d.w.

SHIPPING MOVEMENTS IN MAJOR BRITISH PORTS* (thousand tons net)

| | Foreign Trade | | | | | | | Coasting Trade | | | | | |
| | Arrivals | | | Departures | | | | Arrivals | | | Departures | | |
Port	1938	1957	1958	1938	1957	1958	Port	1938	1957	1958	1938	1957	1958
London . .	22,521	26,064	28,622	20,418	25,195	27,560	London . .	8,256	10,747	10,062	10,686	11,640	11,595
Southampton .	11,519	16,162	18,280	11,579	15,963	18,260	Belfast . .	4,003	5,884	5,819	4,229	5,923	5,867
Liverpool . .	14,637	15,151	15,307	13,522	14,575	15,142	Southampton .	1,950	4,207	5,085	1,935	4,302	4,915
Manchester (incl.							Cowes . .	2,983	4,224	4,312	2,976	4,222	4,306
Runcorn) .	3,536	6,083	6,588	2,896	5,363	5,994	Tyne ports .	4,115	4,554	4,366	2,893	3,601	3,857
Glasgow . .	4,902	5,090	5,308	4,907	5,342	5,509	Liverpool .	2,991	3,329	3,328	4,326	3,865	3,774
Dover . .	3,779	4,861	5,270	3,782	4,837	5,218	Portsmouth .	2,451	2,796	2,821	2,468	2,855	2,808
Hull . .	5,421	4,220	4,445	4,750	3,907	4,115	Blyth . .	2,033	2,242	2,244	1,714	2,117	2,136
Bristol . .	2,937	3,518	4,384	2,318	3,253	4,076	Glasgow .	1,672	2,118	2,255	1,528	1,862	1,919
Tyne ports .	5,015	3,598	3,313	6,225	4,425	4,051	Sunderland .	2,169	2,038	1,816	1,850	1,965	1,792
Harwich . .	2,724	3,444	3,514	2,724	3,444	3,473	Swansea .	1,271	1,784	1,724	428	1,262	1,306

* With cargo and in ballast including foreign trade vessels moving in ballast, on completing discharge, to other U.K. ports for loading.
SOURCE. *Board of Trade Journal.*

dock and new lock near Zandvliest was due to begin. At Bremen the new Klockner harbour with seven berths, and at Wilhelmshaven a new oil jetty capable of taking tankers of up to 60,000 tons were finished. At Helsinki a harbour for the handling of oil imports was being established at Laajasalo. Work started on the new deep-water wharf in Grand harbour, Valletta, in connection with the modernization of Malta's port facilities. Completion of the scheme, which includes two new quays, was scheduled for autumn 1960 and British government loans of £6 million were agreed in Sept. 1959 towards the capital cost of converting the dockyard to civilian use.

Asia. In Japan, a five-year development plan to improve the major ports of Yokohama, Nagoya, Kobe and Osaka got under way. A deep-water terminal for the Basrah Petroleum company to the south of Iraq's oil port of Fao was projected at a cost of £16 million. Plans by the United Arab Republic for improvements in Syria included a 4,000-ft. breakwater and a quay to accommodate ocean-going ships at Latakia and a harbour and oil terminal at Tartus. The handling capacity of the port at Karachi reached 4 million tons in 1959 and a 30% increase was planned. At Singapore the Queen's dock, catering for large oil tankers, came into service.

Africa. At Mombasa two of the four deep-water berths being built to accommodate ocean-going vessels came into operation and completion of the other two was expected during 1960. A new wharf and an oil jetty were finished at Dar es Salaam and work on two new berths started at Beira. Plans were drawn for a £2 million new ocean terminal at Durban to be completed within two years, while in Nigeria works to cost £7,650,000 at the mouth of the Escravos river were undertaken to enable deep-water shipping to enter the delta ports. Completion of extensions at the Port Harcourt wharf was expected in 1960. In Oct. 1959 at Tema, Ghana, the first stage of development of the harbour providing four deep-water berths and costing £13 million neared completion. The Colonial Development and Welfare fund granted in Oct. 1959 £540,000 towards the cost of improvements to Port Louis harbour, Mauritius.

Australasia. At Port Kembla, New South Wales, the 1,100-ft. wharf constructed for the Australian Iron and Steel company was brought into use and work continued on the inner harbour scheduled for completion in 1960. The first stage of the Kuching Port development scheme in Sarawak was begun and it was anticipated that the new port would be ready in 1960. Wharves had also been built and improved at Sebuyan, Singga, Marudi, Trusan and in North Borneo. At Honolulu work started on a new passenger-freight terminal due for completion in 1961; in the Gilbert and Ellice Islands reconstruction of Betio harbour and Bairiki anchorage continued with further grants from the Colonial Development and Welfare fund; and in the British Solomon Islands good progress was made with the new wharf at Honiara.

North America. In April the new Pier 1 in the Fulton terminal area of the Brooklyn port authority, the third of ten new piers to be completed under the Port of New York authority's $85 million water-front development programme, was opened. Work on improvements began at Los Angeles and at Wilmington, North Carolina, and new facilities came into service at Baton Rouge, Louisiana. In Alaska, the construction began of a 20-ac. terminal at Anchorage with dock accommodation for cargo-carrying ships. Plans were made projecting a sub-Arctic outlet to the ocean for Ontario at Moosonee on the Moose river, and for the building of a deep-water wharf on a 90-ac. site in Vancouver to provide an outlet to the sea for the Canadian railways. With the opening of the St. Lawrence seaway many improvements were made to the inland lake ports.

Latin America. The World bank granted a loan to Ecuador of $13 million for construction of a new port at Guayaquil, and one of $6·5 million for expansion to the port of Callao, Peru, including construction of five new berths. This formed part of a scheme for the expenditure of $119 million during 1959-71 on the provision of 30 new berths and the reconstruction of 32 existing ones. At Salaverry the first development stage in the construction of the largest port in northern Peru was completed with a breakwater 1,300 m. long and three groynes 400 m. long. Plans for the second stage were well advanced. At Rio de Janiero a new deep-water quay was under construction.

Caribbean. Work began on a programme of jetty and other harbour works in Nevis, Montserrat and the Virgin Islands. At Freeport, Grand Bahama, the deep-water harbour came into operation as a free port. Construction of a new pier at St. George's, Grenada, was finished during 1959, and progress was made with the deep-water harbour at Bridgetown, Barbados. (*See* also CANALS AND INLAND WATERWAYS.)

(E. A. J. D.)

DOMINICAN REPUBLIC. West Indian republic covering the eastern two-thirds of the island of Hispaniola or Haiti. Area: 18,681 sq.mi. Pop.: (1950 census) 2,135,872; (1957 est.) 2,703,656. Racial distribution is estimated at 13% white, 68% *mestizo* and mulatto and 19% Negro. Language: Spanish. Religion: Roman Catholic. Capital: Ciudad Trujillo, pop. (1957 est.) 294,830. President, Héctor Trujillo y Molina. Main imports: machinery and manufactures. Main exports: sugar (45%), coffee (23%), cacao (13%). Monetary unit: *peso* at par with the U.S. dollar.

History. Héctor Trujillo was president throughout 1959. His brother, General Rafael Leonidas Trujillo, continued to occupy the post of commander-in-chief of the armed forces. In no previous year had General Trujillo so serious a challenge to his rule as during 1959 when an invasion of about 400 Dominican exiles, based on Cuba, occurred in June. Three separate landings took place, but none was successful and all of the invading forces were killed. Retaliatory action against Cuba was taken in early July, and diplomatic relations with that country were severed. Threats of an expedition from the

(Left) One of Nigel Lambourne's illustrations for the Folio society's " Short Stories " of Guy de Maupassant. (Centre) " Yeux Clos ", a lithograph by Odilon Redon from an Arts Council exhibition in April. (Right) From " Cat's Tales ", written and illustrated by Lynton Lamb.

Dominican Republic against Cuba and a demand, made by Cuba and Venezuela, that the Dominican Republic be expelled from the Organization of American States led to a special meeting (Aug. 12-17) at Santiago de Chile of the 21 foreign ministers of the American republics. The meeting resolved against intervention in the internal affairs of any country and condemned foreign activities designed to overthrow constituted governments. Expressions deprecating the continued existence of authoritarian regimes in Latin America were also incorporated in the final record of the meeting.

Economic stability prevailed in 1959, despite weakness in the prices of sugar and coffee; the exports of both products were expected to fall below the volume level of 1958.

(C. McG.)

DRAWING, ENGRAVING AND ILLUSTRATION.

If contemporary drawings were little in evidence during 1958-59, exhibitions of drawings by masters of the past were diverse and frequent. George Stubbs's anatomical drawings, which were discovered in Worcester, Massachusetts, in 1957, were shown in London at the end of 1958. In Paris, during 1959, the Cabinet des Dessins du Louvre presented two categories of drawings by Peter Paul Rubens; the first exemplified his copies of Italian masters, the second, his brilliantly realized personal studies. In London, during 1959, interesting exhibitions of old master drawings included 15th-18th-century Italian drawings at the Victoria and Albert museum, Italian, French, Dutch and English drawings at Messrs. Colnaghi's gallery and 17th-century Italian drawings at the Fitzwilliam museum, Cambridge. In France, the Musée de Montauban showed immaculate drawings by J. D. Ingres. In Venice, the Fondazione Cini arranged an exhibition of accomplished drawings and *pensieri* by Giovanni Antonio Pellegrini. A wholly remarkable display was the British Museum's unheralded " Seven Centuries of Portrait Drawing in Europe ". This glittering assembly of rare and beautiful drawings included life-sized heads by Albrecht Dürer, self-portraits by Raphael, Rembrandt, Nicolas Poussin, Gianlorenzo Bernini and studies by Gentile Bellini, Goya and Watteau.

Colour woodcuts and lino-cuts were shown in London at the end of 1958 in the fifth Giles Bequest exhibition and Michael Rothenstein, at Zwemmer's gallery, displayed inventive exploitations of colour lino-cutting. In 1959, a London exhibition of Polish graphic art contained a particularly impressive group of woodcuts.

In the field of engraving, the high light of 1959 was a collection of Jacques Villon's prints at the Bibliothèque Nationale in Paris in an exhibition which firmly established his status as one of the great engravers of all time. In London, S. W. Hayter and Ru van Rossem showed sets of colour etchings at the St. George's gallery. Both revealed masterly technical accomplishment.

Lithography in Great Britain was represented by an exhibition in Athens in Dec. 1958, while at the same time in London Michael Ayrton showed a series of colour lithographs, " The Greek Suite ", at the St. George's gallery. In 1959 the Arts Council provided an opportunity of seeing, in London, the strange and imaginative lithographs of Odilon Redon and, in Paris, the Maison de la Pensée Française devised a curious and intriguing display of 100 lithographic posters by such artists as Henri de Toulouse-Lautrec, Pablo Picasso, Georges Braque and Jean Cocteau.

Among outstanding examples of book illustration in 1959 were Raymond Hawthorn's two-colour wood-engravings for *The Struggle for Greece* translated from Herodotus, and Nigel Lambourne's powerful line and tint drawings for Guy de Maupassant's *Short Stories*. Notable illustrations for children's books included Edward Ardizzone's drawings for *Nicholas and the Fast Moving Diesel* and Lynton Lamb's pictures for *Cat's Tales*. (*See* also ART EXHIBITIONS; ART SALES.)

(F. W. W.-S.)

See (both London, 1959) Julian S. Held, *Rubens: Selected Drawings*; Jules Heller, *Printmaking Today*.

DRESS: *see* FASHION AND DRESS.
DRUGS AND DRUG TRAFFIC: *see* NARCOTICS.
DYESTUFFS: *see* BUSINESS REVIEW.
EAR, NOSE AND THROAT DISEASES: *see* DISEASES.

EAST AFRICA HIGH COMMISSION.

The commission, established in 1948 to replace the East African Governors' conference, administers defence, taxation, transport and certain other aspects of economy and development common to Kenya, Tanganyika and Uganda (*qq.v.*). It also performs services for Zanzibar and for certain other governments. It can legislate on these matters, with the advice and consent of a central legislative assembly. Constitution: the commission itself (the governors of the three territories); east Africa central legislative assembly with unofficial majority representing the three territories and racial groups. Headquarters: Nairobi, Kenya. Chairman of the high commission, Sir Patrick Renison, governor of Kenya. Administrators in 1959: Sir Bruce Hutt and (from Sept. 9) E. B. David.

History. In fulfilment of the hope expressed by the secretary of state for the colonies, A. T. Lennox-Boyd, at the East African Governors' conference in Sept. 1957, a further conference (presided over by Lennox-Boyd) was held in Britain in Jan. 1959, which was attended by the governors of Kenya, Uganda and Tanganyika and by the British resident in Zanzibar. Among the subjects discussed were the effects upon colonial policy of the rapidly growing political and economic forces in east Africa.

The report of the working party on higher education in east Africa, under the chairmanship of J. F. Lockwood, vice-chancellor of London university, was published in February. Its major recommendation was that a university of east Africa should be created not later than 1966 with constituent colleges in Kenya and Tanganyika, in addition to the existing Makerere college in Uganda. The east African governments' comments on the report were to be published at a later date. (*See* also KENYA; TANGANYIKA; UGANDA.)   (K. I.)

EASTERN EUROPEAN ECONOMIC PLANNING.
Tenth Anniversary of the Council for Mutual Economic Aid. In Jan. 1949 an economic conference of the representatives of Bulgaria, Czechoslovakia, Hungary, Poland, Rumania and the U.S.S.R. was held in Moscow. The participating countries discussed the problem of organizing greater economic co-operation in order to promote the rapid development of their national economies. For this purpose the conference decided to create the Council for Mutual Economic Aid. In Feb. 1950 Albania was admitted to the Council and in Oct. 1950 the German Democratic Republic. The 10th anniversary of the C.M.E.A. was celebrated in all the countries of the area by public meetings and press articles. The results which had been obtained were impressive enough. Between 1950 and 1958 Albanian industrial production increased 450%, that of Bulgaria 290%, of Czechoslovakia 230%, of the German Democratic Republic 240%, of Hungary 230%, of Poland 280%, of Rumania 270% and of the U.S.S.R. 250%.

During the period 1950-58 the combined extraction of coal (calculated in terms of hard coal) in all eight countries rose from 364 million metric tons (including 212 million tons in the U.S.S.R.) to 665 million tons (including 425 million tons in the U.S.S.R.)—an increase of 83% for the whole area and of 100% for the U.S.S.R. alone.

The combined generation of electricity rose from 117,860 million kwh. (including 91,200 million kwh. in the U.S.S.R.) to 327,300 million kwh. (including 233,000 million kwh. in the U.S.S.R.)—an increase of 177% for all the area and of 156% for the U.S.S.R. alone.

The total production of crude steel in the area was 34,979,000 tons in 1950 (of which 27,329,000 tons in the U.S.S.R.), while in 1958 it reached 71,854,000 tons (including 54·9 million tons in the U.S.S.R.)—a total increase of 105% and of 100% for the U.S.S.R. alone.

Combined production of cement during the same period rose from 18 million tons (including 10·2 million tons in the U.S.S.R.) to 50·9 million tons—an increase of 183% for the whole area and of 226% for the U.S.S.R. alone.

The total foreign trade turnover of the eight member states in 1958 was two and a half times greater than in 1950. The corresponding increases for the countries taken separately were: Albania increased its foreign trade with the remaining countries of the area by 270%; Bulgaria by 170%; Czechoslovakia by about 100%; the German Democratic Republic by about 300%; Hungary by about 100%; Poland by 70%; Rumania by nearly 100% and the U.S.S.R. by 170%.

From 1956 observers from the Chinese People's Republic attended the meetings of the C.M.E.A.; from 1957 they were joined by observers from the People's Democratic Republic of Korea and from 1958 by those from the Mongolian People's Republic and the Democratic Republic of Vietnam.

TABLE I. SOVIET SEVEN-YEAR PLAN, 1959-65
(In this and following tables figures are in thousands of metric tons unless otherwise stated)

	1940	1958	1959 (est.)	1965 (Plan)
Coal (incl. lignite) . .	165,000	496,000	507,000	600,000
Crude petroleum . .	31,100	113,000	127,000	235,000
Natural gas (million cu.m.) .	3,388	29,800	34,800	150,000
Electricity (million kwh.) .	48,300	233,000	260,000	510,000
Iron ore (45% metal content) .	29,900	88,800	94,000	155,000
Pit iron . . .	14,902	39,600	42,400	67,500
Crude steel . . .	18,317	54,900	59,200	88,500
Cement . . .	5,675	33,300	38,100	78,000
Sulphuric acid . .	1,587	4,800	4,900	...
Mineral fertilizers (gross) .	3,238	12,400	12,700	36,000
Diesel and electric locomotives	14	1,056	1,400	2,265
Motor vehicles (units) .	145,400	511,000	489,000	800,000

TABLE II. POLISH FIVE-YEAR PLANS, 1956-60 AND 1961-65

	1938*	1958	1960 (Plan)	1965 (Plan)
Coal	38,104	94,981	105,000	113,500
Brown coal . . .	10	7,541	11,850	27,000
Crude petroleum . .	507	175	...	...
Electricity (million kwh.) .	3,977	23,946	25,340	45,000
Pig iron . . .	880	3,864	4,780	...
Crude steel . . .	1,441	5,631	6,540	9,000
Cement . . .	1,719	5,041	4,520	10,000
Sulphuric acid . .	181	573	560	1,060
Artificial fertilizers† . .	88	381	298	840
Motor vehicles (units) .	—	21,740	...	71,100
Ocean shipping (dead weight tons)	—	175,000	...	440,000

* In pre-1939 frontiers.   † In terms of pure components.

TABLE III. CZECHOSLOVAK FIVE-YEAR PLANS, 1956-60 AND 1961-65

	1937	1958	1960 (Plan)	1965 (Plan)
Coal	16,672	25,812	29,300	36,000
Brown coal and lignite .	17,895	56,838	57,800	77,000
Electricity (million kwh.) .	4,115	19,620	25,340	38,000
Pig iron . . .	1,675	3,774	4,780	7,040
Crude steel . . .	2,301	5,510	6,540	9,700
Cement . . .	1,273	4,110	4,520	7,000
Sulphuric acid . .	166	463	560	...
Artificial fertilizers* .	75	225	298	840
Motor vehicles . .	...	58,556	...	...

* In terms of pure components.

TABLE IV. GERMAN D.R. FIVE-YEAR PLANS, 1956-60 AND 1961-65

	1936	1958	1960 (Plan)	1965 (Plan)
Coal . . .	3,523	2,903	2,900	...
Brown coal . . .	101,056	214,970	260,000	278,000
Electricity (million kwh.) .	14,000	34,874	44,000	...
Pig iron . . .	202	1,775	2,250	2,150
Crude steel . . .	1,199	3,043	3,500	4,630
Potash salt . . .	953	1,650	2,200	...
Cement . . .	1,686	3,558	5,200	...
Sulphuric acid . .	301	531	725	...
Artificial fertilizers* .	261	456	535	900
Motor vehicles . .	79,910	53,640	...	150,000

* In terms of pure components.

The C.M.E.A. was conceived from its beginning as a supranational planning board, an accounting office and a high authority, but during the first eight years of its existence foreign trade had been used as the main instrument of planning. The eighth plenary meeting of the C.M.E.A. held in Warsaw from June 18 to 22, 1957, was the turning point in the council's activity. Co-ordinated long-term national plans were to determine the principles on which the division of labour was to be carried out in the area. An Economic commission of the C.M.E.A. was formed in Moscow in Oct. 1957, as well as 13 specialized committees, each dealing with a separate branch of industry.

The Prague Meeting. From Dec. 11 to 13, 1958, the tenth meeting of the C.M.E.A. was held in Prague. Decisions were taken envisaging practical measures for more thorough

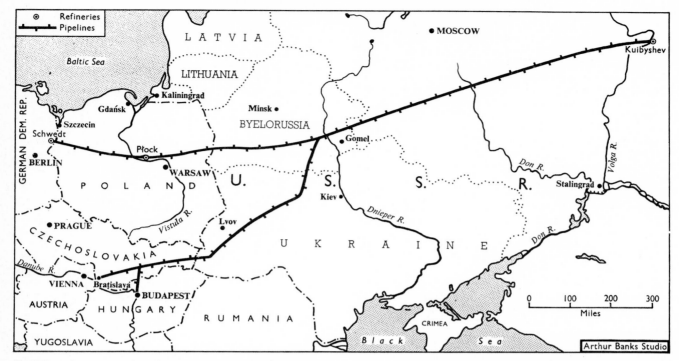

In 1959 work was started on the construction of a pipe-line which was to pump crude petroleum from the oil-bearing regions of the U.S.S.R. to various eastern European countries. The map shows the route to be followed by the pipe-line when completed.

specialization and co-operation in the chemical and iron and steel industries which would help to carry out more effectively the long-term development plans of the member countries. In connection with a greater volume of deliveries of Soviet crude petroleum to the European people's democracies, the council decided to construct a trunk oil pipeline to carry oil from the U.S.S.R. to Poland, the German Democratic Republic, Hungary and Czechoslovakia (*see* below). A permanent commission for economic, scientific and technical co-operation in the consumer goods and food industries was also set up.

The Tirana Meeting. The 11th meeting of the C.M.E.A. was held in Tirana, Albania, from May 13 to 16, 1959. The council examined a number of reports and proposals on questions of economic relations between member countries following from their long-term development plans for major industries for the period ending in 1965.

The priority expansion of coking coal resources in the European people's democracies was discussed. These countries planned to increase the production of coking coal by 53·5% by 1965, with a general growth in coal extraction by 21%. For example, the output of coking coal was to rise by 60% in Czechoslovakia, by 50% in Poland and several times in Bulgaria. A shortage of coking coal in Rumania, Hungary and the German Democratic Republic over a number of years had resulted in a certain strain in meeting the requirements of the iron and steel and chemical industries. Co-ordinated measures for further developing the coal industry and also the substantial deliveries of coking coal envisaged from the U.S.S.R. would make it possible to meet growing requirements.

The meeting examined also the question of raising the output of ferrous metals and expanding the raw material facilities of the iron and steel industry. It was intended to increase considerably the production of pig iron, steel, rolled metal and pipes in 1959-65. By 1965 output of pig iron would go up by 80%, compared with 1958, steel and rolled metal by 70% and steel tubes by nearly 90%. The expansion of iron ore extraction envisaged by the Soviet seven-year plan 1959-65 would make it possible for the U.S.S.R., apart from

meeting home requirements, nearly to double its deliveries to the European people's democracies.

It was planned to build in 1959-64 power transmission lines of voltages of 220 kilovolts and more between the power grids of the German Democratic Republic, Poland, Czechoslovakia and Hungary; between Hungary and the west Ukrainian power system of the U.S.S.R.; and between Poland and the Kaliningrad (former Königsberg) power system of the U.S.S.R.

The meeting paid great attention to examining recommendations of the permanent committee for co-operating in engineering. It approved the committee's recommendations on specializing the production of mining and rolling equipment, of special machine-tools for the ball-bearing industry, oil-drilling equipment and loading machines. For example, light-section rolling mills were to be manufactured mainly in the German Democratic Republic and in Poland, and large-section mills chiefly in the U.S.S.R. and Czechoslovakia. Oil-drilling units and equipment for oil refineries and oil-chemical industry were to be produced in the U.S.S.R. and Rumania; multiple-bucket excavators for open-cast mining in the German Democratic Republic and Czechoslovakia; single-bucket excavators in the U.S.S.R. Special advanced types of machine-tools for the ball-bearing industry were to be produced as follows: 40 types in the German Democratic Republic, 12 types in Poland, 55 types in the U.S.S.R. and 10 in Czechoslovakia.

It was expected that the specialization of production approved by the Tirana meeting would help to reduce the cost of construction and the manufacture of engineering goods, to increase bulk production, to raise the technical level and the quality of machines and equipment and to ensure the full satisfaction of the member countries' needs in these machines and equipment. The 11th meeting of the C.M.E.A. also recommended that co-operation should be expanded between the member countries in sharing the latest achievements of science and know-how to promote the more rapid introduction of advanced techniques.

With the growth of production and the rise in the living

standards of the member nations, and the further expansion of the division of labour between them, it was expected that the trade turnover among these countries would greatly increase. Bilateral talks on reciprocal deliveries of basic items during the period up to 1965, held in accordance with the council's recommendations, called for an increase of approximately 70% in trade turnover compared with 1958. This was a lesser rate of expansion than during the period 1950-58 when, for instance, the turnover of the Soviet foreign trade rose from Rb.13,000 million (of which 57·4% with the eastern European people's democracies) to Rb.34,600 million (73·7% with eastern Europe). In several countries the foreign trade with the other member countries of the C.M.E.A. was to expand more slowly than the rise in national product. In Poland, for example, the foreign trade turnover was to rise by 46%, while the increase in domestic production was to expand by 60%. In Czechoslovakia the corresponding figures were 58% and 75%.

The Sofia Meeting. The 12th meeting of the C.M.E.A. took place in Sofia, Bulgaria, from Dec. 10 to 14. The council approved the charter of the C.M.E.A. A convention on diplomatic immunity of the council officials was signed.

Giant Pipeline to Carry Soviet Oil Westwards. Plans for a 2,700-mi. underground pipeline to carry Soviet crude petroleum from the U.S.S.R. to Poland, Czechoslovakia, Hungary

Table V. Hungarian Five-Year Plans, 1956-60 and 1961-65

	1938	1958	1960 (Plan)	1965 (Plan)
Coal	1,042	2,628}	29,400	28,000
Brown coal and lignite . .	8,318	21,612}		
Crude petroleum . . .	43	828	1,900	1,750
Electricity (million kwh.)	1,399	6,480	8,350	10,700
Pig iron	335	1,100	1,410	1,600
Crude steel . . .	647	1,627	2,240	2,400
Bauxite	540	917*	1,600	...
Aluminium . . .	1·3	39·5	...	55
Cement	343	1,302	1,860	2,400
Nitrogenous fertilizers . .	...	153†	...	600
Sulphuric acid . . .	40	115*	200	...

* 1957.   † In terms of pure components.

Table VI. Rumanian Five-Year Plan, 1956-60

	1938	1955	1958	1960 (Plan)
Coal	345	172}	7,387	29,400
Brown coal and lignite . .	2,478	5,912}		
Crude petroleum . . .	6,594	10,555	11,336	13,600
Methane gas (million cu.m.) .	301	3,972	5,075	10,100
Electricity (million kwh.)	1,130	4,340	6,184	8,000
Pig iron	133	570	737	1,160
Crude steel . . .	284	766	932	1,700
Cement	510	1,991	2,687	3,600
Sulphuric acid . . .	44	92	...	210
Motor vehicles (lorries) .	—	3,053	6,842	...
Tractors (units) . . .	—	3,500	7,003	...

Table VII. Bulgarian Five-Year Plan, 1958-62

	1939	1955	1958	1962 (Plan)
Coal and anthracite . .	166	293}	12,730	19,215
Brown coal and lignite .	2,049	9,758}		
Crude petroleum . . .	—	150	285*	...
Electricity (million kwh.)	266	2,073	3,024	5,000
Pig iron	—	9	56*	205
Crude steel . . .	6	74	211	353
Cement	225	812	934	1,760
Sulphuric acid . . .	—	19	64	290

* 1957.

Table VIII. Albanian Industrial Production

	1938	1950	1957	1958
Coal	3·7	40·9	238	256
Crude petroleum . . .	108	132	490	403
Electricity (million kwh.)	9·3	21·4	125·0	149·7
Chrome ore . . .	7·0	52·2	167·3	201·3
Copper ore . . .	—	14·2	56·0	87·5
Iron ore . . .	—	...	...	88·2
Cement	9·0	15·9	70·2	77·6

and the German Democratic Republic were announced in Moscow in August. The pipeline, of an annual capacity likely to be about 15 million tons, would start near Kuibyshev on the Volga river, a city lying about 150 mi. west of the rich Bashkirian oilfields. The pipeline would run through the central regions of European Russia to southern Byelorussia, cross the Dnieper west of Gomel and then divide into two main branches. The northern branch, supplying oil to Poland and the German Democratic Republic, would pass north of Warsaw and cross the Vistula near Płock, where an oil refinery with an initial annual capacity of 2 million tons (rising later to more than 4 million tons) was being built. The pipeline would continue westwards and cross the Oder south of Szczecin ending at the new German refinery with a similar capacity, already in construction at Schwedt. The southern branch would run through the western Ukraine, cross the Carpathians and continue westwards across southern Slovakia to Lučenec, where it would divide again: one branch going to Budapest to feed a proposed refinery of about 1 million tons annual capacity, and another to Bratislava, where a refinery of nearly that capacity was already in operation. From Bratislava the pipeline was likely to be continued by way of Brno to feed refineries in Bohemia at Pardubice, Kolin and Kralupy.

Over 20 pumping stations would be built along the pipeline route, all operations being fully automatic. Each country would build the pipeline sections passing through its own territory at its own expense, and would have full ownership of the completed sections. The pipeline was expected to be completed by 1963. It was estimated that it would carry sufficient petroleum to meet in full the requirements of the four above-mentioned countries. Gas obtained in oil refineries would provide raw material for the development of the chemical industries in those countries.   (K. M. S.)

See Jan Wszelaki, *Communist Economic Strategy: The Role of East-Central Europe* (Washington, 1959); E. Birke & R. Neumann, *Die Sowjetisierung Ost-Mitteleuropas 1945-1957* (Frankfurt-on-Main, 1959).

EASTERN ORTHODOX CHURCHES: *see* ORTHODOX EASTERN CHURCHES.

ECUADOR. Republic on the west coast of South America, straddling the equator, bounded N. and E. by Colombia and E. and S. by Peru. Area: 105,685 sq.mi. (including the Galápagos Islands, 3,028 sq.mi.). Pop.: (1950 census) 3,202,757; (1958 est.) 4,116,451; *c.* 39% Indians, 41% *mestizos* (mixed blood), 10% whites and 10% Negroes. Language: Spanish, but Indians speak Quechua and Jibaro. Religion: mainly Roman Catholic. Chief towns (pop., 1959 est.): Quito (cap.) 267,700; Guayaquil (the main port) 410,000; Cuenca 66,800. President, Camilo Ponce Enríquez. Main imports: machinery and manufactures. Main exports: bananas (32%), coffee (25%), cacao (20%), rice (10%), *toquilla* or "Panama" hats (4%). Monetary unit: *sucre* with a free rate of S.47·50 to the £ sterling.

History. During the closing months of 1958 a conflict developed between the municipal government of the port of Guayaquil and the provincial council of Guayas. There were charges of inefficiency and there was evidence that municipal services had suffered. The mayor and some of the councillors were considered "disqualified" from service, but they refused to relinquish their posts. Meanwhile, city workers went on strike. General unrest, which stemmed from conditions of poverty in parts of the city, unsettled labour conditions along the coastal area and poor health conditions, provided an atmosphere of uncertainty and tenseness. Soon after the council of state made it possible for the mayor to resume his office, the city found itself in the midst of a dock strike. The national government intervened by calling the strike illegal and moving armed forces into the customs buildings. The strikers were then joined by the banana and petroleum workers who called the intervention unconstitutional, and sympathy strikes followed in other cities.

The immediate cause of a strike in April by textile workers in Quito was a reduction of the daily working hours from eight to six. But behind the strike lay a long-standing complaint against the smuggling of low-priced Colombian goods into the country, an operation apparently encouraged by the high costs of Ecuadorian manufactures resulting from inefficient and antiquated equipment. The walkout ended when assurance was given the workers that the six-hour day would be temporary.

In the economic field, Ecuador continued to make progress. It attracted foreign business and investment in 1959, possibly to a greater degree than in any previous period. Foreign reserves remained at satisfactory levels and the export of bananas, the principal export commodity, increased during the year. (A. E. TR.)

EDUCATION. **Selection for Secondary Education.** In several countries modifications were made in existing practice during 1959. More English local authorities announced plans for abolishing the " 11-plus " examination; at Newcastle upon Tyne in Oct. 1958 the university representatives on the city's education committee resigned in protest against its proposal to introduce a system of comprehensive secondary schools. Teachers in New South Wales, Australia, approved in Sept. 1958 proposals made in an official survey of the state's secondary education that entry tests be abolished and that there be a non-selective high school in every district; later, parents' organizations opposed the proposals. In Norway an education bill proposing the lengthening of compulsory schooling from seven to nine years, and envisaging comprehensive schools covering the entire age-range, led to disputes about how pupils should be allocated to different courses during the later years. In Denmark reforms passed by parliament in June 1958 and coming into force in 1959 included abolition of the " 11-plus " examination and the introduction of seven-year comprehensive primary schools with differentiated instruction in English, German and mathematics during the last two years. France, on the contrary, determined to expand from 1960 the " 11-plus " by adding to it aptitude tests.

School Reform. In Sept. 1958 N. S. Khrushchev elaborated his proposal to reduce the Soviet ten-year school course to one of seven or eight years, after which most pupils would go directly into productive work, with day-release and evening classes for continued study. A few ten-year schools would be retained for especially gifted children. Bulgaria promptly remodelled its educational system along similar lines. Czechoslovakia, on the other hand, increased by 1 year the course in some of its 8- and 11-year schools. In Sept. 1958 the Italian government produced an ambitious ten-year plan designed to provide, at a cost of 1,386,000 million lire (£792 million), places for an additional 2 million pupils and 700,000 teachers, with free education in all state schools. In May 1959 the Belgian government enacted measures to make primary and secondary education free, raise the school-leaving age from 14 to 15, earmark 2,300 million francs (£16·3 million) for building new schools and offer a 60% subsidy for equipping new municipal and provincial schools. While refusing to subsidize the building of " free " (private) schools, the government agreed to compensate them for the abolition of fees and to increase the subsidy for teachers' salaries. In Jan. 1959 a law radically revising the French system was published; this included the raising of the school-leaving age from 14 to 16 and the provision of five alternative forms of secondary education. The reforms, which became operative immediately, affected all children entering school in Oct. 1959 and later, and would thus be fully implemented by 1969.

In Dec. 1958 the British government announced a secondary school building programme costing £300 million for England

In the gymnasium of East Bergholt secondary modern school, which accommodates 300 children from within five miles of the village.

and Wales and £100 million for Scotland over the years 1960-65, designed to ensure that " every child shall be able to travel along the educational road as far as his ability and perseverance can carry him." The first part of the report of the Central Advisory Council for Education (England) was published in Dec. 1959. Its main recommendations were: school-leaving age should be raised from 15 to 16 between 1966 and 1969: compulsory part-time education should be introduced for all 16- and 17-year-olds not already receiving full-time education; two school-leaving dates each year (Easter and July) should be substituted for the present three (Easter, July and Christmas); experiments should be undertaken with external examinations on a local or regional basis below the level of the G.C.E. for pupils in secondary modern schools.

In July 1959 the B.B.C., having judged its experimental television service to schools begun in Sept. 1957 to be successful, announced that from Sept. 1960 the service would be doubled. Simultaneously, Associated Rediffusion (independent television) announced its intention to expand its school service, begun in May 1957.

In June 1959 the first candidates sat the examinations for the " Baccalauréat Européen " established in 1957 for pupils of the European Coal and Steel community's international school at Luxembourg. This baccalauréate is accepted as an entrance qualification by all the universities in the six countries forming the community: Belgium, France, the German Federal Republic, Italy, Luxembourg and the Netherlands.

Supply of Teachers. All the independent countries and 17 colonial territories were represented at a Commonwealth Education conference held at Oxford in July 1959. Resolving that " Education must for the future be accepted as a matter

(Education and population statistics refer to 1957, unless otherwise stated)

Country	Est. pop. ('000)	Compulsory education period (1958)	Primary			Secondary			Vocational			Teacher Training Students
			Schools	Pupils ('000)	Teachers	Schools	Pupils ('000)	Teachers	Schools	Pupils ('000)	Teachers	
Europe												
Austria	6,997	6-14	5,236	716·0	25,165	193	84·2	4,485[1]	186	45·3	4,395	5,473
Belgium	8,989	6-14	9,047	945·5	34,095[2]	891[3]	161·9	8,204[4]	2,532[3]	147·1	...	20,462
Bulgaria[3]	7,601	7-15	6,444	965·8	39,563	359	163·4	7,450	278	79·4	4,722	8,989
Czechoslovakia	13,353	6-14	12,092	1,670·3	73,458	413	341·0	5,131	717	196·9	...	17,749
Denmark	4,500	7-14	3,050	514·6	15,317	612	158·0	9,940	335	66·6	...	5,645
Finland	4,336	7-15	11,852[5]	622·3	25,212	422	161·9	8,168	520	45·3	4,689	5,367
France	44,091	6-14	88,038[6]	6,861·4	192,273[7]	2,484	1,064·5	43,059	1,507[1]	327·9[3]	22,676[3 7]	21,303[3]
German D. Rep.	17,517	6-14	10,098	1,738·2	73,727	373	91·3	5,807	307	115·8[8]	6,368	
German F.Rep.[9 10]	52,150	6-14(15)[11 12]	30,794	4,941·3	169,665	2,526	1,101·9	62,181	6,548[13]	2,353·7[13]	72,553[13]	18,464[13]
Gibraltar[9]	25	5-15	18	3·6	113	8	1·7	81	—	—	—	—
Greece	8,096	6-14	9,722	936·7	20,832	553[14]	212·5[14]	7,431[14]	245	38·8	...	2,507
Hungary	9,815	6-14	6,291	1,259·0	53,667	449[15]	159·4	8,055	...	...	...	
Ireland, Rep. of	2,885	6-14	4,869	488·2	13,402	480	62·4	4,739	816	90·4	2,606	1,452
Italy	48,480	6-14	43,761	4,827·6	183,628	3,306[5]	674·0[5]	60,319[5]	2,533	518·3	43,360	111,754
Malta[4 9]	322	6-14	113	55·5	1,971[3]	6	2·6	143[3]	10	1·4	35[3]	201[3]
Netherlands	11,021	7-15	7,832	1,520·0	43,613	1,471	332·0	17,204	1,714	406·1	22,376[3]	17,179
Norway	3,494	7-14	5,092	432·1	14,321[3]	298	53·5	2,941[3]	557[3]	51·5[3]	7,613[3 16]	2,421
Poland	28,234	7-14	24,502	3,924·2	119,791	824	195·1	11,431	3,673	412·6	31,500	
Portugal	8,909	7-13	16,678	841·9	23,383	380	76·6	4,919	251	65·0	...	2,777
Rumania[3]	17,829	7-14[17]	15,683	1,819·0	90,914[18]	448	156·3[8]	...	628	124·0	8,023	5,689
Spain[3]	29,203	6-12	85,440	3,454·6	88,529	1,137	328·0	18,835	403	134·6	7,744	28,551
Sweden	7,367	7-14	7,986	830·2	41,942	395	199·4	13,129	583	125·8	...	3,523
Switzerland	5,117	6-14(15)[12] 7-14(15)	3,011[19]	557·4	16,429	837[19]	126·0	4,065	119[19]	21·9	...	...
United Kingdom[9]	51,680	5-15	31,449[20 21]	5,735·6[20 21]	198,494[20 21]	7,091[5 15]	2,818·6[5 15]	137,647[5]	1,271[14 22 23]	282·4[16 22 23]	3,209[23]	22,948[24]
U.S.S.R.	205,000	7-17(15)[25]	214,200[18]	30,625·0[18]	1,859,000[18]				3,500	1,941·0	...	
Yugoslavia	18,005	7-15	14,257[9]	2,316·0[9]	71,803[9]	2,466	598·6	28,602	1,103	174·4	14,846	20,930
Asia												
Burma[9]	20,255	6-11	10,751	1,374·1	32,983[13]	693	228·0	6,374[13]	9	1·8	...	2,418
Ceylon	9,165	5-16	6,483[26]	1,506·9	55,410[18]	636	326·2	...	8[2]	...	...	2,807[3]
China[3]	621,225	—	510,000	53,100·0	...	5,000	4,473·0	...	...	...	...	280,203[2]
India[3]	387,350	6(5)-10(11, 12)[12 17]	278,138	24,528·3	691,249	32,568	6,809·7	338,188	5,685	334·7	...	104,714
Indonesia[3]	83 200	8-14	33,112	7,409·4	143,864	4,299[5]	636·7[5]	39,668[5]	635[1]	91·7[1]	7,060[1]	163,191[1]
Iraq	6,538	6-12[17]	2,223[14]	465·0[14]	14,480[14]	245[5]	70·3[5]	3,572[5]	14	2·9	194[3]	6,681
Israel	1,937	5-14	1,157	310·6	13,178	184[14 22]	24·3[14 22]	2,418[14 22]	82	12·3	1,116	4,174
Japan	90,900	6-15	26,988	12,956·3	351,533	16,607	7,145·3	291,332	2,604	917·9	...	19,579[8]
Jordan	1,527	7-12	1,331[18]	214·6	8,019[18]	...	50·9	...	10	0·8	90	1,061
Korea (S)	22,303	6-12	4,922	3,794·3	44,285[2]	1,383	602·1	...	391	128·7	...	21,410
Lebanon[2]	1,425	—	2,039	176·7	6,756	92	4·7	2,322	33	1·4	...	205
Malaya, Fed. of[9]	6,499	—	5,358[18]	1,163·4[18]	39,256[18]	...	...	...	71	11·4	250	3,184[13]
Pakistan	84,450	6-11[17]	42,503	4,040·3	...	5,675	1,278·4	...	37[1]	9·6[1]	...	6,930[27]
Persia[2]	18,347	7-13	6,623	824·0	30,735	767	142·1	6,336	729	13·7	...	3,266
Philippines[2]	21,849	7-14	26,576	4,156·0	88,514	1,907[5]	820·2[5]	25,613	416	33·0	...	39,000[1]
Syria	4,082	6-11	3,014	375·7	11,232	286	61·8	4,046	15	2·7	234	1,231
Thailand	21,076	8-15[17]	21,231[3]	3,195·6	90,721	1,480[3]	377·5	12,945	194[1]	63·2	3,160	10,670
Turkey	25,500	6-14	20,773	2,279·2	48,826	598	228·7	6,426[3]	379	101·8	3,827	18,576
Africa												
Algeria[9]	10,143	6-14	2,141[6]	498·2[6]	12,917[4 6 18]	48[4]	43·1[4]	1,308[4]	...	22·7	688[7]	890
Belgian Congo	13,124	—	28,485	1,576·0	55,041	131	9·5	...	457	20·5	...	16,091
Egypt	24,026	6-12	7,440	2,089·7	55,041	950	387·6	23,735	169	63·1	4,465	28,397
Ghana	4,763	—	3,751	468·0	15,249	1,191[5]	139·7	4,733	46	5·2[16]	271[16]	3,940
Kenya[9]	6,351	—	4,692	652·9	15,193	80	15·1	971	31	3·1	278	3,821
Libya	1,136	—	502	96·8	3,061	53	6·9	525	8	0·7	87	1,568
Morocco	10,115	—	...	615·8[16]	...	...	33·1	...	15[28]	6·1[28]	...	232[1 29]
Nigeria	34,600	—	14,084	2,540·0[8]	70,782	300	88·0[9]	1,958	26	3·5[9]	332	24,760[9]
Rhod. & Nyasaland, Fed. of[30]	7,450	7-15[31 32]	7,219	778·0	18,960	37	3·4	236	63	3·5	221[32]	2,166
South Africa, Union of[2]	13,668	7-16(15)[12 31]	10,504[6 18]	1,974·5[6 18]	59,509[6 18]	...	...	...	69	70·3[16]	...	13,170
Tanganyika	8,760	—	2,783	374·2	6,755	399	45·5	2,138	10[33]	1·2[33]	91[33]	2,216[33]
Tunisia	3,815	—	1,671	303·1	6,996[34]	82	31·9	405[1]	69	12·8	865	667[35]
Uganda[9]	5,767	—	5,290	468·7	15,469	288	29·2	1,231	96	4·3	476	4,147
North America												
Canada[3]	16,081	6-16[12]	32,359[1 15 18]	3,369·9[15 18]	129,960[15 18]	...	...	...	31	7·0	207	14,337[1]
Costa Rica	1,033	7-14	1,461	168·0	6,677	41	15·7	1,079				3,000
Guatemala	3,451	7-14	3,670	249·8	8,796	79	14·8	1,598[36]	95	10·5	1,230	2,797
Honduras	1,769	7-15	2,415	147·4	4,472	50[3 15 36]	10·0[3 15 36]	1,319[3 15 36]				
Mexico[1]	31,426	6-14	28,417	4,106·2	88,931	769[5]	117·3[5]	14,309[5]	606	83·3	12,117	30,753
Nicaragua[1]	1,204	7-12	1,931	80·6	3,446	39	3·7	462	34[37]	4·0[37]	175[37]	389
Panama[3]	940	7-15	1,151	141·3	4,495	103	27·3	1,245	67[2]	8·6[2]	473[2]	1,386[2]
Salvador, El	2,350	7-14	2,291	245·2	7,868	313	26·3	1,716	5	0·9	111	1,772
United States[3]	168,337	7-16[12]	117,210	28,221·4	1,298,906[18]	30,061	7,711·6	...	66,383[19 38]	3,413·2[38]	78,707[38]	294,688
South America												
Argentina[1]	18,754	6-14	16,189	2,565·2	109,669	459	102·7	15,948	1,340	216·3	25,542	86,009
Bolivia[3]	3,235	7-14	640	159·7	6,938	130	31·2	...	...	...	...	5,009
Brazil	61,268	7-12	80,178	5,406·3	171,822	2,937	667·6	44,602	1,521	161·9	17,892	73,948
Br. Guiana[9]	533	6-14	316	111·7	2,757	10	4·6	157	3	2·3	31	58
Chile[3]	6,944	7-15	6,886	1,011·4	24,979	389	125·4	7,785	112[1 39]	31·0[1]	...	6,284[1]
Colombia	13,227	7-11	16,695	1,381·3	35,327	787	107·6	8,787	547	43·0	4,312	16,392
Ecuador[3]	3,800	6-14	4,170	419·6	10,891[2]	300	40·5	2,672[2]	64[2]	12·1[2]	985[2]	4,558[2]
Paraguay	1,638	7-14[17]	2,040	287·0	9,927	134	16·9	2,148	...	0·6	53	2,523[19]
Peru[3]	9,651	7-16	12,163	1,101·2	28,965	348	92·1	6,366	217	34·0	3,319	3,463
Uruguay[3]	2,650	6-14[17]	1,803	243·6	7,005	196[13]	47·5[13]	4,540[13]	...	14·7[2]	...	301[2]
Venezuela	6,134	7-13	6,791	677·2	20,221	264[3 15]	44·4[3 15]	3,359[3 15]	...	...	...	4,305[2]
Oceania												
Australia[3]	9,428	6-14(15, 16)[12]	9,738[20]	1,774·8[20]	62,045[20]	...	...	...	164	178·5[1]	8,364	11,426
New Zealand[40]	2,229	7-15	2,458[5]	412·4[5]	12,312[5]	302	71·7	2,716[4]	36	17·5	969	4,014

[1] 1954. [2] 1955. [3] 1956. [4] Official schools only. [5] Incl. intermediate. [6] Incl. pre-primary. [7] Excl. private schools. [8] Incl. correspondence and part-time pupils. [9] 1958. [10] Incl. Saar but excl. Berlin. [11] And 15-18 part-time. [12] Varies with province, state or canton. [13] 1957. [14] Incl. night schools. [15] Incl. technical. [16] Incl. part-time. [17] Not universally in force. [18] Incl. secondary. [19] 1953. [20] Incl. all-age schools. [21] Excl. independent schools in Scotland and N. Ireland. [22] Incl. continuation schools. [23] Scotland and N. Ireland only: further education centres and, in Scotland, 13 central institutions of higher education, incl. art schools. [24] New admissions only (16,947) in England and Wales. [25] In urban areas only. [26] Excl. 179 *pirivenas* with 6,688 pupils. [27] 1951. [28] Secondary technical only. [29] Former French protectorate. [30] S. Rhodesian figures are for 1954-55. [31] Not for Africans. [32] Excl. Nyasaland. [33] African only. [34] Excl. private Catholic schools. [35] Secondary only. [36] Incl. teacher training. [37] Commercial schools only. [38] Excl. higher professional schools. [39] Excl. agricultural schools. [40] Excl. correspondence schools.

of common concern for the Commonwealth," the conference made proposals for improving the supply and training of teachers for the less developed territories.

That the world shortage of teachers showed little sign of improvement was the burden of an International Labour organization report presented in Oct. 1958 to a 22-nation conference at Geneva. The English minister of education, Geoffrey Lloyd, had already announced a £15 million building programme to provide 12,000 additional places in training colleges by 1962; in June 1959 he announced that a further 4,000 places would be provided by 1964. These

The last pupil sits an examination in the St. Bernard's hall of Mercers' school, Holborn, London, closed in July after 600 years.

additions would bring the total number of places to 40,000 and allow as large an output of teachers from the three-year training course, due to start in Sept. 1960, as from the existing two-year course.

Teachers' Salaries. Trouble arose in England at the end of 1958 when the National Union of Teachers rejected an agreement for a 5% salary increase made by the Burnham committee, the statutory negotiating body for teachers' salaries. Lloyd refused a request of the teachers' panel of the committee to intervene, but on being asked again suggested that the committee should meet " to review the working of the existing report without preconceived ideas on either side about the outcome." In Jan. 1959 the 5% increase was accepted by the teachers after agreement by the Burnham committee to start negotiations for a new salary scale. During the course of these negotiations the minister informed the local authorities' panel that he would not approve a basic minimum salary above £510 per annum. However, in June the Burnham committee recommended a scale starting at £520 per annum for men. In July the minister approved this scale, having decided not to press his objection to the higher starting salary in view of the fact that the committee had recommended that the new scales remain in force for at least two and a half years from Oct. 1959.

Church and State. The perennially controversial issue of state aid to church schools flared up again in France in 1959. In May the *Association de Parents d'Elèves de l'Enseignement Libre*, formed to press the case for state aid to " free " (mainly Roman Catholic) schools, mustered 40,000 supporters at its first congress, including 50 deputies. The association, which claimed to have 780,000 members, decided

to hold its hand until July in view of the fact that the prime minister, M. Debré, had promised that the government would then introduce new legislation. The government bill was passed in the National Assembly on Dec. 24 by 427 votes to 71. It provided for aid (which might cost between £20 million and £50 million a year) to " free " schools in return for a measure of state control. A day before the vote André Boulloche, minister of education (a Socialist), resigned in protest against the government's concessions to the Roman Catholic majority in the assembly. On Dec. 30 the Senate passed the bill by 173 votes to 99.

In Sept. 1958 W. Gomułka told the Roman Catholic Church in Poland that, while religious instruction could continue as an optional subject in schools (as agreed in 1956), he would not countenance the introduction of other religious practices or of uncertificated teachers of religion. In South Africa the secretary for Bantu education, F. J. de Villiers, announced in March 1959 that Roman Catholic and other mission schools for Africans would be granted indefinite registration provided they were not in " white " areas.

In May 1959 the New Zealand Educational institute (teachers' association) decided by a large majority that they did not object to religious instruction in state schools, but that this should be given only by accredited instructors—normally ministers of religion—and not by teachers. Religious instruction should be given only between 9 and 9.30 a.m. or 11.30 and 12 noon, not, as was happening in many schools, at any time.

In July 1959 the British parliament passed an Education act raising, from 1960, government grants for capital expenditure to voluntary aided and special agreement schools from 50% to 75%. The act was a consequence of the government's five-year plan to improve secondary education. The increase was expected to be worth £30 million to the churches over the following 15-20 years.

Language Problems. Difficulties presented by the spread of English led the Ford foundation in 1959 to offer over $600,000 to improve the teaching of English as a foreign language, especially in Asia and Africa. The Nuffield foundation, which in 1956 gave £20,000 to the government of Uttar

The restored chapel of Eton college, showing the new fan vault designed by Sir W. Holford, which replaces a wooden roof of 1699.

At the Whitechapel Art gallery rooms have been set aside where children may themselves paint after looking at selected pictures.

against the continued detention of their headmaster, arrested the previous July as an Eoka suspect. A school strike and public demonstrations by Slovenes resident in the Austrian province of Carinthia resulted from attempts by the Austrian government in 1958 and 1959 to restrict bilingual instruction in Carinthian schools. Rumours in Delhi in March 1959 that children had died after " poisonous injections in the neck " caused a panic which almost emptied many schools. This subsided when the city corporation suspended all anti-diphtheria injections.

Miscellanea. In accordance with the Local Government act, 1958, percentage grants from the government to local authorities for public education in England and Wales ceased in March 1959. From April general (block) grants in aid of all local authority expenditure began. Those announced for the years 1959-60 and 1960-61 were £393 million and £414 million respectively, being 55·5% and 55·6% of the estimated total expenditure by local authorities. The superseded percentage grants were estimated to represent in 1958-59 56·4% of expenditure. Public education normally absorbs 85% of local authority expenditure.

In Oct. 1958 the western German minister for all-German questions, E. Lemmer, appealed to teachers and doctors in eastern Germany to remain there as long as possible. In Aug. alone 619 teachers made their way to western Germany.

Following successful exchange visits of British and Soviet teachers in training in 1957-58 further exchanges were arranged. Courses for teachers of Russian and English, in Devon and Moscow respectively, were also drawn up.

In Nov. 1958 the non-European teachers' associations in South Africa established a federation to defend common interests. In June 1959 the minister for Bantu education in South Africa, W. A. Maree, rejected a parliamentary request that a committee of inquiry should investigate the possibility of giving African children better school meals. The business of his department, he said, was to instruct the children, not feed them, and his policy was to abolish school meals.

The death occurred in July 1959 of Lady Ewing, who with her husband Sir Alexander Ewing built up the unique Department of the Education of the Deaf at Manchester university and pioneered notable advances in the ascertainment and training of deaf children.

United States. The U.S. Office of Education estimated in August that total student enrolment for the year 1959-60 would reach a record of 46,480,000. It stated that in Oct. 1958 89·2% of all young persons aged 14-17 were studying in high schools and colleges, as compared with 81·8% a decade earlier, and that there was expected to be a shortage of 195,000 qualified teachers in 1959-60. In January the National Science foundation made an award of $480,000 to 12 colleges and universities to improve the teaching of arithmetic and science in the elementary schools. It also allocated $1·6 million in federal funds towards the summer training programmes to encourage science studies among high-school students. It was reported in August that 400 high schools would be teaching Russian in the autumn, in comparison with 16 offering it a year earlier, when the U.S.S.R. sent up the first sputnik. By September there were 34 educational television stations, about two-thirds of which were showing programmes exclusively for elementary and secondary schools.

In October, according to a survey by the Southern Education Reporting service, there were 762 integrated school districts among 2,880 bi-racial districts in 17 southern states and the District of Columbia. A total of 518,357 Negro children were attending elementary and secondary schools with 2,486,988 white children in what were described as " integrated situations ". This meant that one out of every six Negro children attending a southern school was in a

Pradesh (India) to establish an English teaching institute in Allahabad, announced in 1959 the grant of a further £20,000 over three years. Encouraged by this experiment, the government of India had opened in Nov. 1958, with aid from the Ford foundation, a Central Institute of English at Hyderabad. In Pakistan a language unit was established at the University of the Punjab in Lahore. The British Council aided all three projects with staff and equipment. In Thailand H. C. Burrow, a Unesco officer, started in 1958 what is believed to be the first English radio course for schoolchildren in Asia. In June 1959 the first course in Malay for qualified teachers organized by the new Singapore government was opened; this was in pursuance of the government's policy to make Malay the national language. Of the 1,080 teachers enrolled 797 were serving in schools where English was the medium of instruction. The government of Northern Rhodesia announced in Oct. 1958 a language bonus scheme designed to encourage resident Europeans to learn African languages.

Disputes and Disorders. Nonviolent opposition to the Communist government of Kerala in India, led by the Roman Catholic Church and the Nair Services society, made the government's Education act of 1957 (*see* EDUCATION in *Britannica Book of the Year 1959*) the chief point of attack. It prevented the schools from re-opening in June 1959 and brought Jawaharlal Nehru to Kerala. He advised the government to withdraw the clauses in the act relating to the appointment of teachers in private schools.

In Oct. 1958 the 143 pupils of the Nyasaland government's African secondary school were expelled for demonstrating against an African teacher whom they alleged to be a policeman. In Oct. and Nov. there were serious disorders at the South African government's Zulu training school at Amanzimtoti near Durban (formerly Adams college). Discrimination against Africans by the Afrikaans-speaking staff was alleged by the students. Greek Cypriot schoolgirls in Nicosia stayed away from school in Jan. 1959 in protest desegregated atmosphere, although only about 211,000 Negroes were in the same classes with white pupils.

At the beginning of the autumn term 3,258,556 students were in attendance at higher institutions, with the freshman class showing an increase of 7% over the previous year. A report by the Office of Education in July disclosed that tuition costs in colleges and universities had increased by 33·5% during the preceding four years. In September the Council for Financial Aid to Education reported that business and industry had given $136 million to higher institutions, a 23·5% rise over the amount given in 1956. A total of 47,245 students from 131 foreign nations and areas were enrolled in U.S. colleges and universities during 1958-59, an increase of almost 4,000 on the previous year, and 10,213 U.S. students attended foreign universities during 1957-58, a decrease of 2,600 from 1956-57. (*See* also FURTHER EDUCATION; LIBRARIES; UNITED NATIONS EDUCATIONAL, SCIENTIFIC AND CULTURAL ORGANIZATION; UNIVERSITIES AND COLLEGES.)

(H. C. D.; W. W. BN.)

See H. T. Himmelweit, A. N. Oppenheim and P. Vince, *Television and the Child* (London, 1958).

EGYPT: *see* UNITED ARAB REPUBLIC.
EIRE: *see* IRELAND, REPUBLIC OF.

ELECTIONS. During 1959 general elections were held in 11 sovereign countries. The results are given below.

Commonwealth of Nations. *Malaya, Federation of.* On Aug. 19, about 1,591,000 citizens of the Federation of Malaya, or about 73% of the total electorate, went to the polls to elect their first 104-member House of Representatives. The results were as follows:

Parties	Seats
Alliance Party of Malaya (Tengku Abdul Rahman)*	74
Pan-Malayan Islamic party (Burhanuddin el-Helmy)	13
Socialist front (Ahmed Boestaman)	8
People's Progressive party (D. R. Seenivasagam)	4
Others	5

* The Alliance's members were: United Malays' National organization with 69 candidates; Malayan Chinese association with 31 candidates; and Malayan Indian congress with 4 candidates.

United Kingdom. On Oct. 8, the Conservative party won its third consecutive general election. At these three elections the nation voted as follows:

	1951	1955	1959
Total electorate	34,553,197	34,855,907	35,389,029
Number of voters	28,602,323	26,760,661	27,863,338
% of those who went to the polls	82·9	76·8	78·7
Conservatives	13,724,418	13,311,938	13,730,849
% of the total votes cast	48·0	49·8	49·3
Liberals	730,551	722,395	1,661,262
% of the total votes cast	2·5	2·7	6·0
Labour	13,948,385	12,405,246	12,151,395
% of the total votes cast	48·7	46·3	43·6

The composition of the House of Commons, compared with the four previous postwar elections (with the numbers of candidates in brackets), was as follows:

Parties	1945		1950		1951		1955		1959	
Conservative*	213	(624)	298	(621)	321	(617)	345	(624)	365	(625)
Liberal	12	(307)	9	(475)	6	(109)	6	(110)	6	(217)
Labour	393	(604)	315	(617)	295	(617)	277	(617)	258	(621)
Communist	2	(21)	—	(100)	—	(10)	—	(17)	—	(18)
Other†	20	(127)	3	(55)	3	(23)	2	(41)	1	(55)
	640	(1,683)	625	(1,868)	625	(1,376)	630	(1,409)	630	(1,536)

* Including National Liberals, etc.
† Independents, Sinn Fein, Plaid Cymru and Scottish Nationalists.

In 1959, 56 Liberal candidates lost their deposits, as did 17 Communist candidates, 14 Welsh Nationalists (out of 20), 7 Sinn Feiners (out of 12) and 3 Scottish Nationalists (out of 5). Out of a total of 34,912 votes cast in Kensington North, Sir Oswald Mosley, leader of the Union movement, received only 2,821 votes and he lost his deposit. (*See* also GENERAL ELECTION.)

Europe. *Austria.* The general election for the fifth 165-member Nationalrat since World War II took place on May 10. Its results, compared with those of 1956, were as follows:

An old peasant couple arrive at a polling station to cast their votes for a new Sicilian regional assembly in the election of June 7.

	1956			1959		
Parties	Votes	%	Seats	Votes	%	Seats
Austrian People's (Ö.V.P.)	1,999,986	46·0	82	1,927,690	42·0	79
Socialist (S.P.Ö.)	1,873,295	43·0	74	1,953,566	46·0	78
Freedom (F.P.Ö.)*	283,749	6·5	6	335,949	9·0	8
Communist	192,438	4·5	3	142,598	3·0	—

* The Freitheitliche Partei Österreichs is a neo-Nazi movement.

France. The first Senate of the Fifth Republic was elected on April 26. On that day 108,266 electors (deputies, councillors of the 90 metropolitan *départements* and delegates of the municipal councils) voted for 255 senators. On the same day 12 senators were elected in the four overseas *départements* and five overseas territories of the French Republic. Senatorial elections in Algeria and Sahara took place on May 31. The composition of the new Senate, compared with the previous one, known as the Council of the Republic and completed by half on June 19, 1955, was as follows:

Parties or Groups	1955	1959
Conservatives (right-wing Independents)	} 83	{ 73
Peasants		{ 20
Gaullists*	46	44
Mouvement Républicain Populaire	24	34
Overseas Independents	14	—
Gauche Démocratique (Radicals)	74	58
Socialists	56	51
Communists	14	14
Others	9	13
	320	307

* Groupe des Républicains Sociaux in the old Senate and Union pour la Nouvelle République in the new one.

Iceland. There were two general elections during 1959: on June 28 Icelanders elected a 52-member Althing and approved a new electoral law changing the constituencies; on Oct. 25-26 they elected a new 60-member Althing under the new law. The system of proportional representation remained unchanged. The results of the two elections were as follows:

	June 28, 1959			Oct. 25-26, 1959		
Parties	Votes	%	Seats	Votes	%	Seats
Independence (Conservative)	36,029	42·6	20	33,798	39·7	24
Progressive (Farmers')	23,062	27·3	19	21,884	25·7	17
Social Democratic	10,472	12·4	6	12,910	15·2	9
Communist	12,929	15·3	7	13,621	16·0	10
National Defence (anti-U.S.)	2,137	2·4	—	2,882	3·4	—

On both occasions about 90% of the electorate went to the polls.

Luxembourg. On Feb. 1 a new 52-member Chambre des Députés was elected. The results, as compared with those of the three previous elections, were as follows:

Parties	1948*	1951	1954	1959
Social Christian	22	21	26	21
Democratic (Liberal)	9	8	6	11
Socialist	14	19	17	17
Communist	5	4	3	3

* In 1948 there were only 51 members and the total included 1 Independent.

The Netherlands. A general election was held on March 12 for a new Second Chamber (Tweede Kamer) of the States General. The distribution of votes and seats, as compared with the results of the 1956 election, was as follows:

Parties	1956			1959		
	Votes	%	Seats	Votes	%	Seats
Political Reform*	129,572	2·3	3	129,621	2·1	3
Anti-Revolutionary*	567,517	9·9	15	562,996	9·4	14
Christian Historical*	482,848	8·3	13	486,204	8·1	12
Catholic People's	1,815,242	31·9	49	1,895,222	31·6	49
Freedom (Liberal)	502,325	8·8	13	732,952	12·2	19
Labour	1,871,990	32·8	50	1,821,677	30·4	48
Communist	272,167	4·8	7	144,371†	2·4	3
Pacifist Socialist	—	—	—	110,174	1·8	2

* Protestant parties of Conservative tendency. † There was also a Dissident Communist party which obtained 34,917 votes but no seat.

Out of an electorate of about 6·5 million 5,998,859 (92·3%) went to the polls. The membership of the Second Chamber had been increased in 1956 from 100 to 150.

Switzerland. On Oct. 25 a new 196-member National Council (Nationalrat or Conseil National) was elected. The composition of the new council, compared with three previous ones, was as follows:

Parties	1947*	1951	1955	1959
Catholic Conservative	44	48	47	47
Liberal Conservative	7	5	5	5
Peasants, Artisans and Middle Class	21	23	22	23
Radical Democratic (Freisinnig-Dem. Partei)	52	51	50	51
Independent (Landesring der Unabhängigen)	8	10	10	10
Democratic	5	4	4	4
Social Democratic	48	49	53	51
Communist (Partei der Arbeit)	7	5	4	3
Others	2	1	1	2†

* In 1947 there were 194 members. † Both represent the Evangelische Volkspartei.

Africa. Tunisia. On Nov. 8, the first National Assembly of independent Tunisia was elected. Out of an electorate of 1,099,577, 91·4% went to the polls. Habib Bourguiba's government party, the Neo-Destour, won all the 90 seats. Bourguiba himself received 1,005,769 votes and was proclaimed first popularly elected president of the Tunisian Republic. On March 25, 1956, when the Constituent Assembly was elected, 83·7% of the electorate voted and Bourguiba's National front won all the 90 seats. When the republic was proclaimed, the Constituent Assembly unanimously, on July 25, 1957, elected Bourguiba president.

Asia. Israel. On Nov. 3 the fourth 120-member Knesset (parliament) was elected. The results, compared with those of 1955, were as follows:

Parties	1955		1959	
	Votes	Seats	Votes	Seats
Heruth (Nationalist)	107,190	15	130,515	17
Religious {Hapoel Hamizrahi	77,936	11	95,581	12
parties {Agudat Israel	39,836	6	45,569	6
General Zionist	87,099	13	59,700	8
Progressive (Liberal)	37,661	5	44,889	6
MAPAI (Mifleget Poalei Eretz Israel)*	274,735	40	370,585	47
MAPAM (Mifleget Poalei Menuhedet)†	62,401	9	69,468	9
Ahdut Ha'avodah‡	69,475	10	58,043	7
Communist	38,492	6	27,374	3
Arab parties affiliated with MAPAI	37,777	5	33,353	5

* Mapai is the right-wing Socialist party led by David Ben Gurion. † A centre Socialist party. ‡ A left-wing Socialist party.

Of the 1,216,000 electors, 969,337 (79·7%) recorded their votes.

Japan. On June 2 half of the 250-member House of Councillors (Upper Chamber) were elected for six years. The composition of the new house, compared with the previous one, was as follows:

Parties	1956	1959*
Ryokufu-kai (Green Breeze Society, Nationalist)	31	11
Liberal Democratic (Conservative)	122	133
Independents	15	18
Social Democratic	80	84
Communist	2	3

* There was one vacancy.

(K. M. S.)

ELECTRICAL INDUSTRIES. The Trend of Development.

With the British nuclear power programme still being actively followed, major manufacturing efforts were devoted to it in 1959. Nevertheless, the absence of any world-wide demand for large and costly nuclear generating stations tended to deflect some of the development towards smaller nuclear plants suited to under-developed areas and to ship propulsion. New materials of construction suitable for nuclear power plants were being developed. Other forms of power plant for isolated areas were also receiving attention. For the home market, much work was done on equipment for railway electrification. The demand for domestic electric appliances increased significantly and there were some notable advances in public lighting, in control systems and in electronic devices such as digital computers.

Commonwealth Electrical Industries. The increasing efforts towards industrial development, in some parts of the Commonwealth, accompanied by the continued demand for electrification, encouraged further manufacturing expansion. In Canada a disconnecting switch with a maximum rating of 400 kv., 1,800 B.I.L. (Basic Insulation Level), the largest ever built in North America, was developed for the Chute des Passes hydroelectric project. Atomic Energy of Canada awarded, to a Canadian manufacturer, a contract for the design, study and development of a nuclear power station suitable for the Arctic. To reduce transmission maintenance costs, helicopters were being successfully used in Ontario for patrolling overhead lines, for spraying to control vegetation and for lifting equipment. In India good progress was being made in the manufacture of transformers, and electric furnaces were being used in steel production. A new cable factory was being set up and a new works making heavy-duty industrial low-voltage distribution gear was opened at Madras. In Australia two cable-making firms were amalgamated and in South Africa six cable-manufacturing plants were capable of meeting most of the union's demands.

U.S. Electrical Industries. During 1959 U.S. manufacturers delivered 14,000 Mw. of turbine generators. Of this total about 12,400 Mw. was delivered to U.S. electric power systems and the remainder was delivered to U.S. industrial plants and foreign companies. Steam turbine generators accounted for more than 12,400 Mw. of the units delivered during 1959, the remainder being hydraulic turbines. Deliveries of power transformers had reached a record 72,078 Mva. during 1957. Shipments during 1958, amounting to 47,199 Mva., were only 60% as much. Shipments during 1959 showed a further decline to 34,000 Mva. The first commercial generation of electric energy from nuclear sources had taken place during 1957. By mid-1959 more than 1,400 Mw. of new atomic generating plant was under construction or in planning. The list of commercial atomic power reactors included 17 major units, and construction was well under way on five of these units by the end of 1959. However, there was evidence that conventional energy sources (coal, oil and gas) would continue to supply electric power in the United States for many years.

Generating Plant. Good progress was made in the construction of the nuclear power stations in Britain, but the small number of foreign orders led to the suggestion that the number of constructional consortia might be reduced from five to three by effecting group combinations. A conference on thermo-nuclear fission was held in London in April. Fifteen British companies were engaged in design and research work on nuclear power plant for ships. One completed design was for a plant giving 55 Mw. of thermal power and 20,000 shaft h.p. It would use slightly enriched uranium with stainless steel canning and carbon dioxide cooling and its cost would be about £2 million. The first reactor and two turbo-generators at Chapelcross, a station similar to Calder Hall, were commissioned in May. Constructional work started on the Loch Awe pumped-storage project, involving three power stations with a total capacity of 450 Mw. The Finlarig hydroelectric scheme had a 30-Mw. Pelton turbine operating under a head of 1,244 ft. Two interesting new developments in plant of smaller capacity were a 1-Mw. mobile gas-turbine plant made for the U.S.S.R., burning oil or natural gas and designed for operation in air temperatures down to —40°C., and a 3-Mw. gas-turbine unit, remotely controlled, for use under peak-load conditions and for emergency in isolated areas. A new type of three-phase, self-excited, brushless alternator for use on British aircraft had a capacity of 22·5 kva. and operated at 200 v., 400 cycles per sec.

Transmission and Distribution Equipment. The emphasis was on equipment for bulk transmission of power, at high voltages, needed for developments in Britain and abroad. Transformers, switchgear and cables increased in capacity. The Central Electricity Generating board ordered two 310-Mva., three-phase, double-wound transformers stepping up the generated voltage to 295 kv.; they were water-cooled and had on-load tap-change gear. Digital computers were being used for the design of transformer cores and windings. The first installation of 275-kv. oil-filled cables was completed at the Drakelow B station. Multi-cored irradiated polythene cables were made for a British rocket research station, the completed cables being passed through an electronic beam from a 2,000-Mv. Van de Graaff electrostatic particle accelerator. A non-profit-making organization for the testing and certification of electric cables was established.

Utilization. The £150 million scheme for electrification of the main London-Liverpool railway line was advanced by two or three years and large orders for equipment resulted. One group of these, worth £11 million, was for 2,000-h.p. and 1,365-h.p. diesel-electric locomotives, and another was for 95 mi. of cables worth £290,000. Auto-electric control of movements in a shunting yard was a new feature. Electrogyro locomotives, each having a flywheel with a storage capacity of 9 kwh., proved suitable for use in coal-mines. The National Coal board placed an order for a 1,750-h.p. mine winder having a D.C. motor fed from a three-phase, 11,000-v. supply through a 1,085-kw., 750-v. mercury-arc converter equipment.

There was a rapid increase in the use of domestic electric equipment. Sales by the area electricity boards during the year ending July 31, 1959, showed the following increases compared with the previous year: cookers, 41·6%; immersion water heaters, 19·8%; storage water heaters, 29·7%; washing machines, 107·2%; and refrigerators, helped by the exceptionally good summer, 150%. New types of refrigerators, spin driers and electric heaters were introduced and another new development was a vacuum cleaner operated from a 12-v. battery.

A new 7·5-Mw. distribution scheme at a food factory near Wigan had seven substations connected by two 6·6-kv. ring mains. Over 500,000 sq.yd. of main lines and marshalling yards at Crewe were floodlit by a new installation using twelve 150-ft. towers. The use of electricity in horticulture advanced and there was much interest in complete environmental control in greenhouses.

Research and Development. Good progress in nuclear research was made and several new experimental reactors were under construction. Under the international project Dragon, initiated by the O.E.E.C. European Nuclear Energy agency, an experimental high-temperature reactor at Winfrith heath, generating several megawatts of power, was to form the basis of the five-year joint research programme for Great Britain, Euratom, Austria, Denmark, Norway, Sweden and Switzerland. In Britain the Central Electricity Generating board announced the establishment of a new £1 million nuclear research centre near its Berkeley nuclear station. A chair of nuclear engineering was founded at Manchester university where a new £1 million digital computer, 100 times faster than the fastest currently made in Europe, was being built.

A new cable-testing laboratory for development testing up to very high operating voltages was commissioned; this had a 3,200-kv. impulse generator. The importance of corrosion was recognized by the formation of a British Association of Corrosion Engineers and there was a conference on corrosion arising from the use of heavy mineral fuel oils in boilers. A new insulating material, of ceramic-plastic compound, capable of operating at 1,550°F., was introduced and the Electrical Research association developed automatic equipment for

F. T. Bacon watches a test of the hydrogen-oxygen fuel cell developed by him for the National Research Development corporation.

carrying out the international test for tracking of insulation.

A British manufacturer developed, for quantity production at a low cost, a new 1,100-h.p. diesel-electric locomotive as a general purpose unit particularly suited to overseas requirements. A new battery-powered electric tractor, to propel a total load of 9 tons, was developed. Demonstration of the hydrogen-oxygen fuel cell showed that this was reaching the stage of practical application as a source of electricity and a method of energy storage. The Electrical Research association's wind power research, in conjunction with the Isle of Man Electricity board, included the experimental operation of a 25-kw. aerogenerator connected to a network.

Trade. The total value of U.K. exports of electrical equipment and apparatus in the first seven months of 1959 was £136 million compared with £131 million for the corresponding period of 1958. The increase was largely in radio exports. However, the most striking increase was for cable exports to the United States, the value rising from £0·3 million to £3·4 million, while total exports of electrical goods to the United States were more than doubled. South Africa (£11·5 million) continued to be the best customer, followed by India (£11·3 million), Australia (£10·1 million), the United States (£9·6 million) and Canada (£7·2 million).

Negotiations for Britain to supply Japan's first nuclear power station, at Tokai Mura, were concluded. It was to have a net electrical output of 150 Mw. and to cost about £20 million. An important contract with Poland, worth £2·75 million, was for 20 electric locomotives and overhead line equipment. The first 330-kv. oil-filled cable made by a British manufacturer was installed in Australia at the T.1 (Tumut river) station of the Snowy Mountains Hydro-Electric authority. For the Auckland (N.Z.) Power board, 110-kv., three-core impregnated pressure cables were being supplied. Among transformer orders was one for two 100-Mva. auto-transformers for the Komati power station in South Africa. The first of six 111-Mva. alternators for Kariba, Rhodesia, was successfully tested, as was one of five 200-Mw. turbo-alternator sets for the High Marnham station in Britain. (*See* also ELECTRONICS; RADIO, SCIENTIFIC DEVELOPMENT IN; TELEVISION.)   (E. W. G.; AR. MO.)

ELECTRIC POWER. The year 1959 was marked by steady progress in the construction of large power schemes started in previous years rather than by many new projects of exceptional size. Potential users of nuclear generating plant were studying its economy, as applied to their own circumstances, and the integration of such plant with hydroelectric and thermal stations having different characteristics. Exploitation of hydropower and cheap coal resources was still considered essential. Progress towards reduction of construction costs for nuclear plant was rather slow and there was some embarrassment, especially in Britain, due to an unexpected coal surplus.

United Kingdom. Sales of energy by the electricity boards in England and Wales in the year ending March 31, 1959, increased by 7·5% to 78,098 million units. The average price rose by 0·021d. to 1·554d. per unit and the number of consumers rose by 315,699 to 15·2 million. Progress in rural electrification was indicated by the fact that, at March 31, 1959, 76·9% of all farms had been connected. The surplus for the year was £27·3 million. Fuel consumed (previous year in brackets) included 41·7 (44·6) million tons of coal and 3·12 (0·91) million tons of oil. The average thermal efficiency of the steam power stations rose by 0·59% to 26·10%, with a highest value of 33·04% at Castle Donington station. New generating capacity of 1,124 Mw. brought the total installed capacity of the Central Electricity Generating board to 25,409 Mw. in 238 stations. There was an increase of 200 route mi. in the 275-kv. super-grid system.

For future generation a three-fuel economy—nuclear, coal and oil—was planned. The construction programme for 1959-64 included 12,300 Mw. of plant with 25 entirely new stations. Five of these were nuclear stations—Bradwell, Berkeley, Hinkley Point, Trawsfynydd (450 Mw.-500 Mw.) and Dungeness (550 Mw.) for which consent was granted in July. Application was made for another (650-Mw.) nuclear station at Sizewell, Suffolk. The 300-Mw. pumped-storage scheme at Festiniog was under construction and a 3·75-Mw. pilot power station, employing underground gasification of coal, was completed in 1958 but uncertain economic prospects of the method caused cessation of the trials in 1959.

The North of Scotland Hydro-Electric board had another difficult operating year because rainfall was 14% below the average in the catchment areas. The net loss for the year ending Dec. 31, 1958, was £112,238. However, in the 15 years since the board's formation it had developed over a quarter of the usable water power resources in the highlands and supplied electricity to over 90% of the population in its area. In the last year the number of consumers rose by 9,997 to a total of 374,199. Nearly 84 Mw. of new hydroelectric plant was brought into commission to make a total of 813 Mw.; water power produced 80% of the 2,043 million units generated. The average price rose from 1·5755d. per unit to 1·6821d., while the generating costs per unit were: hydro-electric, 0·7267d.; steam, 1·0539d.; and diesel, 1·7789d. Energy consumption averaged 3,600 units per consumer and, for farms only, 8,900 units.

Sales of electrical energy by the South of Scotland Electricity board rose by 7·7% to nearly 6 million units in the year ended Dec. 31, 1958, but its operating surplus fell to £67,901. The number of new consumers was 24,838, making a total of 1,321,488, and the average price was 1·474d. per unit. The first Scottish 120-Mw. generating set was commissioned; the total installed capacity rose to 1,658 Mw. and the first length of 275-kv. transmission line was put in service. Good progress was made on the construction of the 360-Mw. Hunterston nuclear station.

The gross revenue of the Electricity Board for Northern Ireland in 1958 rose by £476,000 to £4,946,000. Of the total of 561 million units sold, at an average price of 2·09d. per unit, 12·53% was to farm consumers.

Commonwealth. *Canada.* During 1958 a record amount of new hydroelectric generating capacity, over 1,800 Mw., was installed while a further 1,500 Mw. was being installed in 1959. Major installations were at the Robert H. Saunders-St. Lawrence station, where nine units totalling 500 Mw. were commissioned, and at the Bersimis I station in Quebec, where three units totalling 350 Mw. were installed. At the end of 1958 the total Canadian generating capacity was 20,140 Mw. and the annual energy generated was 96,744 million units. A 132-Mw. thermal station at Saskatoon (later to be increased to 264 Mw.) was opened by Queen Elizabeth II in July 1959. A proposal was made for the construction of a tidal power scheme, at a cost of $300 million, on the Bay of Fundy.

Australia. The total installed capacity of generating plant had risen to 4,950 Mw. by the end of 1958, while the energy generated in that year was 20,448 million units. In Victoria, sales of energy rose by 8·4%, the average consumption per domestic consumer being 2,363 units; a 1,200-Mw. thermal station was planned. An increased government subsidy for rural electrification in New South Wales, where 78·8% of the farms were already connected, was to increase the total to 95%. The first of four 80-Mw. generating sets in the T.1. (Tumut river) station of the Snowy Mountains Hydro-Electric authority, and the 330-kv. transmission line connecting the scheme with the New South Wales grid, were commissioned in May 1959. The total installation of 320 Mw. at T.1. was to be completed by the end of 1959. Sales of electrical energy in Tasmania for the year 1957-58 increased by 6·3% to over 2,000 million units.

New Zealand. It was planned to increase the installed capacity of hydroelectric generating plant to 2,100 Mw. by

A giant gantry lifts a temporary roof from one of the reactors on the site of the Hinkley Point nuclear power station, Somerset.

TABLE I. WORLD PRODUCTION OF ELECTRICAL ENERGY*
(million kwh.)

	1954	1955	1956	1957	1958
WORLD† . .	1,360,400	1,535,000	1,677,900	1,781,300	1,863,300
United States .	544,645	629,010	684,804	715,706	724,008
U.S.S.R. . .	150,695	170,225	191,653	209,480	232,800
Great Britain .	86,349	94,076	101,165	105,536	98,508‡
Canada . .	73,976	82,816	85,800	90,249	96,744
German Fed. Rep.	68,521	76,542	85,074	91,773	94,212
Japan§ . .	60,076	65,193	73 582	81,303	80,280
France . .	45,570	49,627	53,829	57,433	61,800
Italy . .	35,574	38,124	40,592	42,715	44,304
German Dem. Rep.	26,044	28,695	31,182	32,735	34,872
Sweden . .	23,957	24,721	26,631	28,972	30,420
China . .	11,001	12,278	16,593	19,000	27,500
Norway . .	21,780	22,682	23,750	25,840	27,180
Poland . .	15,469	17,751	19,495	21,155	23,940
Australia‖ .	13,707	15,202	16,675	18,289	20,448
Union of S. Afr.¶	14,636	16,351	17,659	18,947	20,052
Czechoslovakia .	13,610	15,013	16,591	17,720	19,620
Switzerland** .	13,180	15,448	14,895	15,894	16,872
Spain†† . .	10,480	11,922	13,673	14,523	15,468
Brazil . .	11,871	13,350	15,447	...	...
Netherlands .	10,588	11,188	12,448	13,367	13,848
India . .	9,669	10,877	11,972	10,872‡	12,372‡
Belgium . .	10,339	10,948	11,847	12,611	12,516
Austria . .	9,847	10,751	11,718	12,463	11,040‡

* Only countries with an output exceeding 10,000 million kwh. in 1958 are specified; total output; *i.e.*, including that by industrial establishments generating primarily for own use, if not otherwise stated. † Excl. N. Korea and some small producers. ‡ Production by enterprises generating primarily for public use. § Years beginning April 1. ‖ Years ended June 30. ¶ Approximately 95% of total production. ** Years ended Sept. 30. †† Incl. Canary islands and N. African possessions.
SOURCE. U.N. *Statistical Yearbook 1958*; U.N. *Monthly Bulletin of Statistics.*

TABLE II. CONSUMPTION, PRODUCTION AND EXCHANGE OF ELECTRICAL ENERGY IN SELECTED EUROPEAN COUNTRIES IN 1958*

	Total annual consumption (million units)	Thermal production (%)	Hydro production (%)	Generation by industry (%)	Net international exchange† (%)
Austria . .	12,000	24	76	23	11 (E)
Belgium . .	12,500	96	4	44	0
Czechoslovakia .	18,000	87	13	29	1 (E)
Denmark . .	4,400	100	0	8	11 (I)
Finland . .	7,800	18	82	39	—
France . .	59,500	44	56	27	1 (I)
German F. R. (Saar)	2,700	99	1	83	11 (E)
German F.R. (other)	92,600	86	14	39	3 (I)
Hungary . .	6,700	94	6	14	5 (I)
Italy . .	44,400	16	84	14·5	0·3 (I)
Luxembourg .	1,238	100	0	100	1 (I)
Netherlands .	13,300	100	0	23	2 (I)
Norway . .	27,500	0·5	99·5	47	—
Poland . .	22,800	97	3	24	1 (I)
Spain . .	15,400	32	68	5	0
Sweden . .	30,000	5	95	0	3 (E)
Switzerland .	16,100	0·5	99·5	19	13 (E)
United Kingdom .	108,500	97	3	12	—
Yugoslavia . .	7,100	43	57	11	3 (E)

* The last four columns are all expressed as percentages of total annual consumption. They add up to more than 100% since generation by industry and net international exchanges are also included in thermal and hydro production. Figures are estimated where data for the complete year ended March 31, 1959, were not available.
† (E)—net export and (I)—net import.
SOURCE. U.N. *Quarterly Bulletin of Electric Energy Statistics for Europe.*

1965. The energy produced in 1958 was 5,644 million units—the same as in 1957. Power rationing was necessary in the North Island but this ceased in the spring of 1959. A new survey of the hydroelectric resources was being made in the North Island and the possibilities of tidal power were being considered.

Other Commonwealth Countries. At the end of 1958, installed capacities of generating plant (with the annual production of electrical energy in brackets) were: India, 4,250 Mw. (15,022 million units); Pakistan, 530 Mw. (1,500 million units); Federation of Rhodesia and Nyasaland, 816 Mw. (2,450 million units); Union of South Africa, 3,975 Mw. (20,052 million units). With the commissioning of a 40-Mw. generating set at the Panchet station, the total installation of the Damodar Valley corporation, in India, rose to 254 Mw. A rural electrification scheme for 300 villages in West

Pakistan was started and agreement was reached on a 30-Mw. power station to use Sylhet natural gas. In Rhodesia, site investigations were being made for the second stage of the Kariba project and hydrological surveys for the Kafue scheme. In 1958 the Uganda Electricity board increased its sales of energy by 22% to a total of over 278 million units. Production of electrical energy in Ghana in 1958 was 312 million units. In Nigeria, consumption for the ten months ending Jan. 31, 1959, showed a 28% increase. In Jamaica, plans were made for a grid system to cover the whole island. Sales of electricity in Malaya increased by 15·6% in the year ending Aug. 31, 1958. Bermuda had a total installed capacity of 21·6 Mw. and an annual consumption of 3,100 units per domestic consumer.

Europe. Growing industrial activity in Europe, accompanied by the spread of rural electrification, had necessitated the installation of more thermal generating plant and the development of new hydroelectric schemes. International exchanges of energy greatly improved the integration of these two power sources. The supply position is shown in Table II.

U.S.S.R. The outstanding features continued to be the building of new large hydroelectric stations, with individual total capacities of 2,000 Mw. or over, and the extensions to the transmission networks operating at 400 kv. or 500 kv. The basis of rural electrification was changing from local power stations to the main network. In 1958 the total production rose to 233,000 million units of which 20% was hydroelectric.

United States. Electric utility generating plants in the United States under the control of the Federal Power commission produced a total of 679,880,183,000 kw.hr. during the year ended June 30, 1959. This amount was 7·7% above the utility output for the year ended June 30, 1958. Combined utility and industrial production in the year ended June 30, 1959, reached 765,160,280,000 kw.hr., 7·6% above 1958.

Total installed capacity of utility generating plants on June 30, 1959, was 150,222,443 kw., including the net addition of 15,890,690 kw., or 11·8% in the 12-month period ended on that date. Industrial generating capacity was 18,152,501 kw. on June 30, 1959, while the nation's total utility and industrial generating capacity reached 168,374,944 kw. on the same date. (E. W. G.; J. K. K.)

ELECTRONICS. An indication of the advance of electronics in the modern world can be given by the ever-increasing number of applications to everyday life. By 1959 the electronic computer was used as an aid in any business in which large quantities of information or statistics had to be collected and analysed on a systematic basis. The spectacular advances that were being made in the exploration of space by the use of rockets and artificial earth satellites were becoming more and more dependent on the electronic instruments in the satellites and at the ground stations associated with them. The interest in this field was demonstrated by the number of conferences and symposia held to discuss the technical progress already achieved and future possibilities.

In May an International Transistor convention and exhibition was held in London, some 2,000 delegates being present, of whom about 400 were from 26 overseas countries. The papers presented reviewed the progress made in developing more efficient semiconducting materials for transistors and their application to line communication systems, the circuit elements of measuring instruments and computers. The technology of the design and manufacture of the various devices was discussed in detail, and the theoretical papers showed how much was still imperfectly understood about the inter-atomic reactions that are the basis of semiconductor operation. On the practical side, the progress made was in the development of, on the one hand, the robust devices capable of switching currents of hundreds of amperes and, on the other, the more delicate items for use at very high radio frequencies of hundreds of megacycles per second. A new class of semiconductor devices was contemplated as a result of experiments on crystals of cadmium sulphide through which steady current densities of several amperes per square centimetre had been obtained with the application of only a few volts.

The use of solar batteries to supply the electrical power for radio transmission from earth satellites had clearly become a practical attainment, since at least one such body had been using this arrangement for more than a year, and its signals were now only heard when it was in sunlight. A similar application was to be the use of a series of silicon batteries to serve a telephone repeater station needing a supply of 4·5 w. In a location in Japan where this was required, an investigation as to the number of sunny days resulted in a plan for the generation of ten times the power normally consumed, the surplus being stored in nickel-cadmium batteries. It was expected that this station would work for many years relying entirely upon solar power.

An interesting device which was shown at another exhibition in London comprised the combination of a silicon resistor having a positive temperature coefficient of 0·77% per degree centigrade in series with a thermistor with a negative temperature coefficient. By using a thermistor with a time constant which was short compared with that of the resistor, an unstable condition resulted when connected to a direct current supply and the combination oscillated at a very low frequency. Apart from the rapidly increasing use of transistors in broadcast receivers at very high frequencies as well as in the lower bands, a variable-capacity germanium diode had been developed for use as an automatic frequency control in such receivers. At a conference held at Cambridge the scientific uses of television were discussed. Two possible methods of assisting the astronomer in his difficult problem of examining optically faint celestial bodies through the partially transparent layer of the earth's atmosphere were examined. In one of these an image orthicon pick-up tube was used at the telescope followed by standard television technique. This had resulted in a gain of several times in light sensitivity. Secondly, and more speculatively, there was the possibility of placing a television camera in an artificial earth satellite travelling above the atmosphere. A slow rate of scan and narrow bandwidth could be used for recording the television signals, for subsequent replaying on command. Towards the end of the year this technique was used successfully by the U.S.S.R. for photographing the remote side of the moon, and transmitting pictures of it to the earth.

W. L. Wilcock with the electronic picture multiplier developed by himself and D. L. Emberson at the Imperial College of Science, London. It increases the brightness of dull pictures 50,000 times and will have uses in astronomy, nuclear physics and radiography.

Automatic handling of bank accounts, a method of electrostatic photography of the earth from satellites, a radar system for military use that could detect a moving person at a distance of several miles, a new electronic amplifier called the " tunnel diode " and a device for using a microscope with ultraviolet light were among the many electronic developments of 1959 in the United States.

Electronic banking began operating in California for the Bank of America. Electronic Recording Method of Accounting (ERMA) keeps books for up to 220,000 accounts. The system employs a computer and a character reader which can read directly, from a cheque or deposit slip, data imprinted in a magnetic ink. These are recorded in figures of special stylized form standardized by the American Banking association. In addition to the amount of the transaction, the system gives such information as the issuing bank's number, a routing symbol and the account number. These data are read off in much the same way as sound is reproduced from a magnetic tape. Engineers estimated that ERMA could read, sort and post 33,000 accounts per hour, compared with about 245 per hour that an experienced bookkeeper could post.

An electrostatic photography process which could photograph the earth from satellites was developed in laboratory form by scientists of the Radio Corporation of America. The image is recorded by electrical charges on a tape made of thin layers of conductive, photosensitive and insulating materials on a transparent base. In use, the film is flooded with electrons and thus given a uniform negative electrical charge. When it is exposed to light in a camera, electrons are driven off in proportion to the light intensity. This leaves an invisible image of electrical charges which lasts for weeks. When the image is to be sent to the ground from a satellite, the exposed tape passes before an electron scanning beam which reads off the electrical charge pattern and produces television signals.

A new supersensitive radar detector, developed jointly by the U.S. army signal research and development laboratory and the Hazeltine corporation, can detect a crawling soldier two miles away. The entire installation may be transported

by helicopter or on a special two-wheeled trailer. The antenna is mounted in a 5-ft. plastic bubble on a 25-ft. pole and connected to the controls and displays in a special shelter, which may be some distance away. Each type of target produces a characteristic sound and an experienced operator can tell the difference between a jeep or a walking soldier, and even distinguish between a man and a woman.

An electronic aid to medicine, announced during the year, was an attachment for a microscope to make visible the magnified image of a specimen illuminated with invisible ultraviolet radiation. This was the ultrascope, designed by R. G. Stoudenheimer of the electron tube division of the Radio Corporation of America at Lancaster, Pennsylvania. Ultraviolet rays pass through the object being examined and are focused by the objective lens on the faceplate of the ultrascope tube. On its inner surface is a photosensitive material which converts the ultraviolet image into a corresponding electron pattern. When this is focused by electron lenses on a fluorescent viewing screen at the other end of the tube, it is converted to a visible image in a yellow-green light.

Another new device, the tunnel diode, performs all the functions of a standard low-power transistor. In addition, it can handle other tasks of which the transistor is incapable. The tunnel diode is even smaller than the transistor—in fact, it is dwarfed by the head of a common pin—and has still lower power requirements, operating on only 1/1,000,000 w. One of its important features is negative resistance. When electricity flows in a copper wire, an increase in the voltage causes an increase in the current. In a tunnel diode an increased voltage may decrease the current, and because of this it can act as an amplifier, for the signal is not absorbed, but is increased.

Another new development, that might lead to " transistorized " tubes, was announced at the Westinghouse Research laboratories in Pittsburgh, Pennsylvania. W. J. Choyke and Lyle Patrick found that silicon carbide, which is used (under the trade name of Carborundum) as an abrasive in grinding wheels, emits electrons when it is excited electrically. These electrons come from tiny spots that glow with blue light and are unaccompanied by heat. Westinghouse engineers suggested that a highly efficient tube might be made by replacing the hot filament in the usual electron tube with a cool silicon carbide cathode or electron emitter. By thus removing a serious limitation of conventional tubes, they might better be able to compete with transistors in future applications. (*See* also NUCLEAR ENERGY; RADIO, SCIENTIFIC DEVELOPMENTS IN; TELECOMMUNICATIONS.)

(R.L.S.-R.; J. STO.)

EL SALVADOR: *see* SALVADOR, EL.
EMIGRATION: *see* IMMIGRATION AND EMIGRATION.

EMPLOYMENT. The recession in business activity that had been induced by the counter-inflatory measures taken by the authorities in most of the industrial countries during 1957 gave way in 1959 to a strong upward trend in output and consumption. However, the demand for labour did not reach inflationary levels during the year and the prices of manufactured commodities remained relatively stable.

In Great Britain, in January, unemployment reached its maximum level at any time since 1945, but thereafter the number of unemployed registered by the Ministry of Labour fell steadily. By September the proportion of persons out of work had fallen from the peak figure of 2·8% to 1·9%. By the autumn of 1959 there were signs in certain industries, notably building and construction, in the metropolitan area, that the demand for labour had again reached a point at which employers were willing to countenance special payments above the recognized rates to obtain labour.

The problem of structural unemployment arising in areas heavily dependent on single industries again figured prominently in discussions of employment policy. Soon after the general election in October the government brought before the new parliament a bill to provide more power to encourage new industries to be started in areas with an above-average level of unemployment.

During the year there was much discussion of the adequacy of existing statistics of unemployment. It was alleged by H. A. Turner of Manchester university in an important article in the *Manchester School* (May 1) that, for several reasons, the methods currently used by the Ministry of Labour to obtain its figures did not give an adequate picture of the true level of unemployment. The number of unemployed counted by the ministry was the number registered at the employment exchanges as out of work. But it was likely that many of the classes of workers who were not entitled to unemployment benefit did not register for work when they were unemployed. These classes included the majority of married women workers who had opted out of the insurance scheme, workers drawing their retirement pension who were again seeking work and contributors who for one reason or another were disqualified from benefits. Some indication of the possible size of the difference that could arise if the count were on a different basis might be obtained from a comparison of the number of people who were returned as " out of work " by the census of 1951. This figure was 445,000. At that time the number of registered unemployed was less than 250,000. From an examination of the figures, Turner's conclusion was that many workers failed to register with the employment exchange because they preferred to seek jobs through private channels rather than through the official machinery.

Differences in methods of counting the numbers of persons out of work might be highly significant in making international comparisons of unemployment. For example, the method currently used by the U.S. authorities was that of sample survey of some 35,000 households. Only those actively seeking work were enumerated, but this method did mean that persons such as married women who did not register as unemployed were counted. It was suggested that if the same methods had been used in Britain as in the United States the average percentage figure of unemployment during the postwar years would probably have been doubled.

Unemployment and under-employment continued to be problems of major importance in most of the underdeveloped tropical countries in the world. Unfortunately the pace of economic development in these territories, though extremely rapid by any earlier standards, was at best no more than

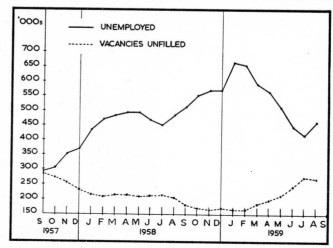

The chart shows the number of unemployed compared with the number of vacancies unfilled in the United Kingdom during 1957-59.

keeping up with the growth of population. In most of the countries concerned the population was actually growing faster than jobs were being created. The effect of this situation was to encourage emigration from underdeveloped areas to countries with higher levels of employment. Since 1950 many thousands of West Indians had come to Britain. These migrants had in the main been absorbed into the British labour force without undue difficulty. It is worthy of note that the number of immigrants from the West Indies fell off sharply in 1958 as unemployment rose in Britain and job opportunities, especially in Jamaica and Trinidad, expanded with the development of a minor industrial and tourist boom. During 1958 and 1959 an increasing number of migrants arrived in Britain from India and Pakistan and it was estimated that the total number living in Britain was 100,000 compared with 120,000 West Indians already resident in the country. The flow of immigrants was expected to continue, but would probably not raise the labour force by an annual net figure in excess of 30,000 during the next decade. (B. C. R.)

ENDOCRINOLOGY.

Clarification of the means of hormonal transport through the blood stream opened new approaches to the understanding of hormonal utilization. During 1959 several new endocrine preparations became available, one of which was an agent that was far more anabolic than androgenic. Many studies dealt with the role of enzymes in the mechanism of hormonal action.

Pineal Gland. Renewed interest in the pineal gland resulted in contributions that warranted the reclassification of this enigmatic structure as an endocrine gland. During the year evidence indicated that extracts of the pineal stimulate aldosterone secretion. The purified fraction, named glomerulotropin, seemed specifically and selectively to stimulate aldosterone secretion. This was the first time that steroidogenic activity had been determined for extracts obtained from pineal tissue. The importance of this observation was that hitherto aldosterone secretion had been considered autonomous, independent of pituitary activity, and not dependent on any trophic or stimulating substance from a higher centre.

Pituitary Gland. Pituitary tumours which secrete only thyroid-stimulating hormone (TSH) were produced in mice through radiation effects on the thyroid gland. Mice with transplantable TSH-producing tumours were studied in which plasma levels of the hormone were found to be 1,000 times that of the normal mouse. The content of TSH in the tumour was 2,000 times that of mouse pituitary. In spite of the heavy concentration of TSH in these tumours, no exophthalmic factor (EF) was found. Hitherto, in the preparation of TSH extract, it was difficult to separate completely EF and luteinizing hormone (LH) contaminants, and such extracts administered to experimental animals induced both exophthalmos and thyroid enlargement. However, with the new evidence, it could be said that EF and TSH, though closely allied in thyrotoxicosis in man (Graves' disease) are, at least in mice and cattle, separate entities. Through the aid of chromatography on cellulose ion exchanges it was possible to prepare a bovine TSH which is so purified that it does not contain EF or LH.

Adrenal Glands. Cushing's syndrome, a metabolic state resulting from overproduction by the adrenal cortex of glucocorticoids such as hydrocortisone (cortisol), frequently presents difficulties in diagnosis. A new test was devised which enables the clinician to distinguish between patients with the disease and those in whom the syndrome is simulated. The test utilized the suppressive action of such agents as dexamethasone on urinary output of 17-hydroxycorticoids. In contrast to healthy controls, all Cushing's patients resisted its suppressive action at low dosage. At higher dosage levels, however, the suppressive agents aided in differentiating patients with adrenocortical hyperfunction from those with tumour, for the latter patients were particularly resistant to even larger doses of dexamethasone or similar drugs.

Diabetes. A new test for identifying potential diabetics was reported. The test uses cortisone for heightening sensitivity to the standard glucose tolerance test. Persons predisposed to diabetes mellitus cannot compensate for cortisone's ability to increase the formation of glucose in the liver and decrease its utilization in the rest of the body. The test predicts with considerable accuracy the possibility of a " pre-diabetic state " in man and helps to locate potential diabetics. It was able to uncover a large number of potential diabetic patients, particularly among the relatives of known diabetics who probably would not have been discovered by the standard test.

Gonodal Hormones. The successful delivery of a full-term infant by a pseudo-hermaphrodite with congenital adrenal hyperplasia finally took place. Endocrinologists interested in this field had hopefully awaited this event. Previously, one such patient was reported to have become pregnant twice but aborted each time before the stage of viability of the foetus was reached. Several years earlier it was shown that female pseudo-hermaphrodites, when given cortisone-like hormones, would have a lowering of 17-ketosteroids with lessening of their virilization, and the appearance of feminine characteristics such as menstruation and ovulation would occur with considerable regularity. The first successful termination of pregnancy occurred in a female pseudo-hermaphrodite in whom therapy was started at the age of 16, conception taking place $4\frac{1}{2}$ years after the start of cortisone therapy. A healthy female infant was born. Cortisone medication was continued throughout the pregnancy without untoward effects upon the mother or the offspring. (*See also* BIOCHEMISTRY; PHYSIOLOGY.) (R. B. GT.)

ENGINEERING TECHNIQUES.

In 1959 engineering designers turned increasingly to computers to aid them in their calculations. This trend was particularly noticeable in branches of engineering where the designer must weigh the influence of a large number of parameters as, for example, in aeronautical work. A typical example in electrical engineering was the design of power transformers. A British firm found that it was practicable to programme an automatic digital computer so that, by feeding in the specification for the transformer on tape, a preliminary design was prepared " with the accuracy of a very experienced designer but in a very much shorter time ".

Considerable interest was aroused among designers and users of gears by news of the Novikov system of gearing which was being developed in the U.S.S.R. It differed from conventional involute-form gears in that the teeth had profiles based on circular arcs. Reports indicated that for certain applications this design offered advantages over involute gears. In the transmissions of vehicles, dissatisfaction had long been expressed with the traditional gearbox, whether of the manually-controlled or automatic type. Engineers had always hankered after a transmission which would provide a drive of infinitely variable ratio between bottom gear and top gear. Several new hydrostatic drives, designed to provide this feature, were announced during the year. Typically, a pump driven by the vehicle's engine supplied oil under pressure to hydraulic motors connected to the road wheels. Another old idea in hydraulics which seemed to show new promise in commercial application was the hydraulic transport of solids. Solid particles suspended in a liquid could be borne along a pipeline. Experiments showed that widely varying solid/liquid mixtures could be transported in this way.

Increased emphasis was placed on the use of wind tunnels in the aerodynamic design of motor cars. Preliminary studies extending over two years by the Motor Industry Research

Inside the echo-free chamber at the National Engineering laboratory, Glasgow, designed for research into noise-reduction.

association in England had determined the most suitable apparatus for such research, and it was decided to build two special wind tunnels for this work. The object was not only to reduce aerodynamic drag (and thereby increase maximum speeds) but also to examine related problems such as the access of air to brakes for cooling purposes, stability of the vehicle when struck by winds at various angles, and the flow of air for engine cooling, to the engine intake, and for ventilating and air conditioning.

New techniques were developed for reducing the noise of machines and mechanisms. Just as public opinion had earlier provoked action to reduce pollution of the atmosphere, so there was increasing awareness of the need to stop the crescendo of noise from all kinds of machines. New research apparatus was brought into use to enable designers to isolate the sources of noise and subsequently modify designs. An anechoic (echo-free) chamber for noise research was inaugurated at the National Engineering laboratory, Glasgow.

Outstanding among the newer engineering techniques of transport and propulsion were flexible barges, vertical take-off aircraft and the Hovercraft (*see* AIRCRAFT MANUFACTURE). The flexible barge idea, first propounded three years earlier at the time of the Suez conflict, had matured by 1959 to the point where Dracones (as they were named in Britain) were used commercially for transporting petroleum products from Fawley oil refinery. Dracones were made of nylon fabric coated with special types of synthetic rubbers and each could carry 10,000 gal. of cargo.

Though prime movers are the oldest and most fundamental type of machine in engineering, the year showed that it was still possible for new ideas to spring up. Brief, preliminary details of the design of a new form of rotary-piston engine were released towards the end of 1959. The inventor,

Felix Wankel, was associated with a German firm and a U.S. firm in the development of the engine. It was said to have only two moving parts and to permit high rotative speeds and lightweight construction.

The free-piston engine, which had caused worldwide interest in previous years, was further developed, particularly for large installations. A large chemical firm in England installed a bank of free-piston units for compression duty in a new petrochemical plant. Experiments were undertaken also to provide engines suitable for road vehicles.

A new engineering technique for producing electrical power direct, without the need to go through the traditional boiler, engine and generator stages, became practical during the year. More than 12 years' work by a team at Cambridge culminated in a practical fuel cell with an output of 5 kw. at 24 v. Applications envisaged ranged from fork-lift trucks to space vehicles. A U.S. firm manufacturing the fuel cells under licence supplied some to the U.S. air force. Large-scale research into thermoelectric power (of which this fuel cell was an important result) was carried out at many centres in the United States, Britain and other industrial countries.

Another important development in the technique of generating power was the introduction of a multi-fuel internal-combustion engine. Such an engine was designed to meet the military requirements of the War Office. Ideally, the army preferred diesel engines because of their low fuel consumption and the consequent reduction in the amount of fuel transported in the field. If, however, diesel fuel was not available in certain circumstances, the army wanted to be able to use petrol or gas-turbine fuel in the same engines. The technical difficulties were successfully overcome and several manufacturers produced their own engines of this type.

Apart from the continued widespread development of plastics and their engineering applications, " glass-ceramics " (a comparatively new range of materials) were studied for their engineering potentialities. These materials are made from glass by a process of controlled crystallization. Among their useful properties are unusually high strength and extremely smooth wear characteristics. They can be polished to an optical surface and resist high temperatures in terms both of strength and of oxidation. They resist chemical attack and are lighter and harder than most metals. Among the applications regarded as promising were: for precision gauges, for the beds of special machine tools and for bearings.

In the field of engineering production tools, the sixth European Machine Tool exhibition, held in Paris during September, afforded ample evidence of the continued trend towards automation and other improved forms of control, and higher degrees of precision.

A remarkable case of successfully cutting very thick steel was reported. A slab of forged steel plate 1,580 mm. (approximately 5 ft.) deep was flame-cut using oxy-propane gas. Propane was selected because it is a " slow burning " gas and because its low flame velocity inhibits flashback. It also tends to produce the long flame needed for cutting very thick materials. Difficulties which had been experienced when propane was tried ten years earlier were overcome by using special nozzles developed by an English firm.

In the foundry, mechanization was advanced by the introduction of a " packaged foundry ". Its design was based on the fact that foundry work consists essentially of three interlocked cycles of operation: (1) the box cycle, from empty boxes through moulding, pouring, cooling and shake-out to the return of the box to the machine; (2) the metal cycle, from melting through casting and dressing to the return of scrap for melting; and (3) the sand cycle, from shake-out through reconditioning, moulding and pouring to return to shake-out. The heart of the system was an automatic moulding machine built on machine tool principles.

In civil engineering a noteworthy development was the special interest in the use of models in the analysis of structures. A symposium was held by the Institution of Civil Engineers and an international conference was held in Madrid. For many engineering structures, particularly some of the new and striking architectural forms, design calculations had been based on questionable assumptions, or no theoretical treatment at all was available. In such cases scale models were a great help to the designer. It was argued that many designs of structures would benefit if authorities would accept model analyses from reputable laboratories as they normally accepted calculations. Among the structures which had been designed with the help of models were the Hammersmith fly-over, a factory roof at Bedford, Clifton bridge at Nottingham and the proposed Medway bridge.

As a method of joining the components of a civil engineering structure, high-strength bolts gained prominence and a conference on the subject was held by the Institution of Structural Engineers. The British Standards institution issued a standard on " friction grip " bolts of this type and planned to issue recommendations on the use of the bolts later.

An old civil engineering technique, pile driving, came in for some improvements. By vibrating the pile while it was being driven, increased speeds, possibly up to five times, were reported. Research work was also planned on a device to apply a pulsating vertical load to the pile head, phased to reinforce the travelling stress wave in the pile.

Steel stanchions are often encased in concrete. Previously, British designers were not permitted to assume that the concrete casing contributed to the load-carrying capacity. A new British Standard permitted this and tests showed that, as a result, savings of about 30% in the amount of steel used could be expected. (*See* also MACHINERY AND MACHINE TOOLS.) (F. B. R.)

ENGLAND: *see* GREAT BRITAIN AND NORTHERN IRELAND, UNITED KINGDOM OF.

ENGLISH LITERATURE. General.

It might be taken as a sign of growing internationalism that the more noteworthy publications of 1959 tended to cross frontiers and extend horizons. Insularity had never been less evident. Authors were either reaching out towards the people, flavours and affairs of other countries, or returning from these countries with their own weight of experience to be welcomed and interpreted. A mean or common multiple of the various kinds of books could only be described, Polonius-fashion, as personal-political, geographico-historico-exploratory, deductive, penetrative and hortatory. Needless to say, not all examples contained all ingredients but possibly one did, skimming them with a lightly elegant touch that left no bruises. This was *A Passage to England* by Nirad Chaudhuri, a Hindu visitor whose familiarity with western culture was equalled by his independent outlook and his easy command of a gracious, flexible English. The genial irony in some of his comments was offset by a comparison that revealed as much about Hindu customs as about his reactions to English ones.

From Italy Fosco Maraini came, in Eric Mosbacher's fine translation, to discourse on a complex nation in *Meeting with Japan*. From experience of the country's beauties and brutalities he conducted a broad inquiry into Japanese art, religion, architecture, mental attitudes and social conditions —an inquiry none the less acceptable for admitting a personal element. In Europe one tourist spot—Sicily—was unflinchingly laid bare by Danilo Dolci (*see* BIOGRAPHIES) in *To Feed the Hungry* and by Gavin Maxwell in *The Ten Pains of Death*. The Italian social worker and the British inquirer—the one writing with art, the other with journalistic skill—reached the same verdict on conditions of abject poverty and mis-

government that appalled the civilized reader. A situation fresh in the memory if not without obscurity was clarified by Flora Lewis in *The Polish Volcano*, which traced the sequence of events in Poland leading to its defiance of Soviet domination in 1956. Peter Fleming's *The Siege at Peking* gave the first fully documented, detached and frequently sardonic narrative of the " Boxer " attack on the foreign legations, unveiling some incredible behaviour on both sides. Without any pretence of handling main-line history E. Arnot Robertson slipped off westwards to examine the papers of the Jamaica prize court. The odd, forgotten facts and personal moments drawn from these records made *The Spanish Town Papers* unique for its revitalizing of old maritime hazards.

Again, the memoirs of three women writers were interpenetrated by leading influences from overseas. In *The Flame Trees of Thika* Elspeth Huxley vividly and informatively recalled a childhood spent in British East Africa. E. M. Butler's diverting *Paper Boats* proved the compatibility of high spirits with scholarship. With a more romantic vision Mary Lutyens beautifully and delicately recaptured her girlhood adoration for an Indian youth in the theosophists' circle. *To Be Young* was a haunted, unforgettable evocation of charmed episodes in India and at home. But the classic of personal traffic—the word classic is not lightly used—came from Wilfred Thesiger, whose *Arabian Sands* enshrined a lifetime's love and exploration of the desert and its people.

Biographers in search of subjects flocked to the continent, and particularly to France. From among their royal, theatrical and literary subjects Marcel Proust stood out, or rather he was planted with exactitude by George G. Painter in the social circle that provided *A la Recherche du temps perdu* with its synthetic portraits. *Marcel Proust: a Biography* made its point successfully against the school of criticism that divorces literature from life. Moving to Italy, Anthony Rhodes gave a rich, exuberant and finally merciless portrayal of Gabriele D'Annunzio, whose bombast was suggested in the title, *The Poet as Superman*.

All this broadening of horizons did not divert attention from indigenous figures, especially those whose repute was international. James Pope-Hennessy discharged his official

Edith, Osbert and (standing) Sacheverell Sitwell on the occasion of the publication of the last-named's " Journey to the Ends of Time ".

responsibility with good judgment in making of *Queen Mary* a queenly portrait without minimizing the human, womanly features, of the background of a restricted court life in a faded era. With *Northcliffe*, Reginald Pound and Geoffrey Harmsworth succeeded in almost the opposite task of pricking an immense balloon of power and dictatorship while mapping its dizzy flights. In his long and supremely readable *Havelock Ellis: a Biography*, Arthur Calder-Marshall had evidently worked with head and heart to appreciate and convey his subject's psycho-sexual outlook. Yet his book was more a narrative of Ellis' life than an account of his thought and writings, which were critically discussed by John Stewart Collis in *An Artist of Life*. Another instalment of a monumental undertaking arrived in vol. iii and iv of the *Collected Letters of Samuel Taylor Coleridge 1807–1819*, edited with consummate care and patience by Earl Leslie Griggs. For the details of the poet's biography no better work could be desired, but on the sources and quality of his inspired poems J. B. Beer offered some keen and scholarly theories in *Coleridge the Visionary*.

Two further literary giants faced illuminating criticism, in Barbara Hardy's *The Novels of George Eliot: a Study in Form* and Kathleen Williams' *Jonathan Swift and the Age of Compromise*. The long-neglected youngest Brontë sister was suddenly set upon by two independent biographers. Ada Harrison's *Anne Brontë: her Life and Work*, with a critical section by Derek Stanford, was soon followed by Winifred Gérin's ampler biographical study, *Anne Brontë*. Finally, frontiers were crossed again in a mammoth work of reference, *The Oxford Companion to French Literature*, compiled and edited by Sir Paul Harvey and Janet E. Heseltine.

Biography. Christopher Hassall, *Edward Marsh*; Evelyn Waugh, *The Life of Ronald Knox*; V. Sackville-West, *Daughter of France*; Sir Thomas Beecham, *Frederick Delius*; Christopher St. John, *Ethel Smyth*; Robert Rhodes James, *Lord Randolph Churchill*; Michael Brecher, *Nehru: a Political Biography*; Ernest Mortimer, *Blaise Pascal*; Joanna Richardson, *Sarah Bernhardt*; John Connell, *Auchinleck*; Peter Green, *Kenneth Grahame*.

Memoirs and Letters. Sacheverell Sitwell, *Journey to the Ends of Time*, vol. i; Bertrand Russell, *My Philosophical Development*; Lord Woolton, *Memoirs*; Field Marshal Sir William Slim, *Unofficial History*; James Kirkup, *Sorrows, Passions and Alarms*.

Literary Criticism. Herbert J. Hunt, *Balzac's Comédie Humaine*; Helen Gardner, *The Business of Criticism*; S. A. Vahid, *Iqbal: his Art and Thought*; Bernard Blackstone, *The Consecrated Urn*.

Travel. Arland Ussher, *Spanish Mercy*; Freya Stark, *Riding to the Tigris*; Thomas Pakenham, *The Mountains of Rasselas*; Fitzroy Maclean, *Back to Bokhara*; Rupert Croft-Cooke, *The Quest for Quixote*; Percy A. Scholes (ed.), *Dr. Burney's Musical Tours in Europe*.

History, Politics, Sociology. W. G. Hoskins, *Local History in England*; Asa Briggs, *The Age of Improvement, 1783–1867*; Denis Mack Smith, *Italy: a Modern History*; James Cameron, *1914*; David Divine, *The Nine Days of Dunkirk*; Sir Leonard Woolley, *History Unearthed*; Max Beloff, *The Great Powers*; A. C. B. Lovell, *The Individual and the Universe*; Aldous Huxley, *Brave New World Revisited*; Rosalind Haywood, *The Sixth Sense; an Enquiry into Extra-Sensory Perception*; Barbara Wootton, *Social Science and Social Pathology*; Bertrand Russell, *Wisdom of the West*; Colin Wilson, *The Age of Defeat*.

Fiction. For the English novel 1959 proved a strangely interesting year. With so many leading authors failing to publish anything, several younger writers of promise were given their chance. The most notable figure was undoubtedly Pamela Hansford Johnson, whose two novels, both appearing in a single year, would entitle her to first place in any summary. The first, *The Unspeakable Skipton*, was a brilliant and farcical satire, revolving round a corvine sponger-artist living (and partly living) on his wits in Bruges—a city familiar to readers of Pamela Hansford Johnson's previous books. This was a *tour-de-force* of wit and high spirits with an undertone of melancholy, beautifully rendered. Her second novel, *The Humbler Creation*, had a Kensington vicar as its hero. It was a poignant study in the author's earlier manner and a fine addition to the large body of her published work. She had never enjoyed the full recognition which her work deserved, but with the appearance of these two books she had at last come into her own.

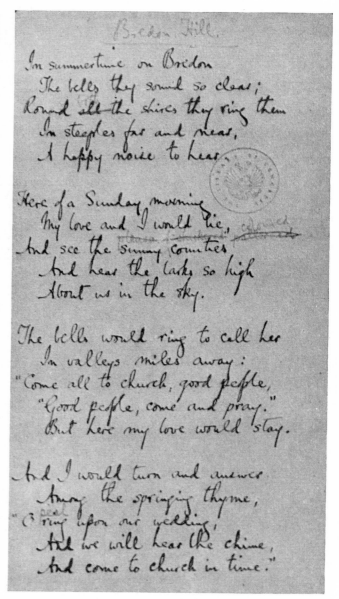

In September this fair copy of the original manuscript of A. E. Housman's " Bredon Hill " was shown in public for the first time.

Bruce Marshall and Walter Allen both brought out new novels in 1959. Allen's *All in a Lifetime*, his first novel since *Dead Man Over All* (1950), told the story of a British Labour leader looking back on his life from the vantage-ground of old age. As with everything that Allen writes, it was a distinguished piece of narrative, although his admirers may have wished that the debt to Joyce Cary had not, in this case, been quite so apparent. Marshall's *A Thread of Scarlet*, the tale of a Scots priest who became cardinal of Scotland, was well up to his old standard of competence and confirmed him as one of the most readable of contemporary English middlebrow novelists.

In *Free Fall* William Golding managed to be every whit as harrowing, although not perhaps so effective as usual. In *Memento Mori*, a grisly comedy set in the aged women's ward of a general hospital, Muriel Spark added immensely to her reputation, proving herself a crisp and witty stylist with a depth of feeling that one had not before suspected.

The political novel, a rare occurrence in contemporary fiction, made an unexpected appearance early in the year, with the publication of Wilfred Fienburgh's *No Love for Johnnie*. Fienburgh, a well-known Labour M.P., was killed in a car crash shortly before the book appeared, and the novel seemed to have been his posthumous comment on political life in Britain, especially inside the House of Commons. Its revealing frankness drew an outburst of fury upon the head of the dead man, but to the average reader the novel seemed a not unfair description of the kind of thing that goes on at Westminster. Although the narrative was highly contrived, the book was a vivid and an extremely talented piece of reporting. Another novel with a political theme was Paul Johnson's *Left of Centre*, set in Paris in 1958.

A newcomer, Simon Raven, two of whose novels, *The Feathers of Death* and *Brother Cain*, appeared during the year, seemed to most of the critics to be a writer of quite unusual talent and one whose gifts, if they could be matured, might well carry him to great heights in his profession. His first book was a study of military life in a colony—obviously Kenya—centred on a homosexual relationship between a subaltern and a young soldier whom he befriends. Raven dealt with the situation and the tragedy that followed in a moving and morally exploratory manner that showed great craftsmanship and a fine feeling for building up tension. His second novel, while immensely effective in an Ian Fleming-ish manner, was altogether inferior, although it, too, had insights remarkable in such a young writer. Despite more specious claims, Raven remained one of the discoveries of the year. If he could maintain his impetus and get rid of his silver fork pretensions—a certain mannered snobbishness and a preference for high life—he would surely go as far as any of his contemporaries.

Other notable works appearing during the year included Alan Sillitoe's collection of short stories, *The Loneliness of the Long Distance Runner*, Ivy Compton Burnett's *A Heritage and its History* and Roy Fuller's *The Ruined Boys*.

Poetry. If 1959 was undistinguished for new poetry of outstanding merit, it was, at least, remarkable for the opportunities it afforded young and unknown poets of presenting their work to the public, either in separate volumes or in anthologies sponsored by publishers and cultural or commercial organizations. Few of the well-known poets produced a collection during the year.

Among a surprising number of poets who had their first volumes published were Laurence Lerner, a South African living in Belfast, Rex Taylor, formerly a Lancashire quarryman, James Harrison, James Michie and Patricia Beer. In his *Domestic Interior* Lerner seemed to have made a too deliberate attempt to conform to the fashionable trend towards excessive restraint, so that his work often lacked tension, but when his material was taken direct from personal experience, as in the African section, he displayed an individual talent. Less mature in outlook and somewhat indebted to Edward Thomas, Taylor failed to make the most of his gifts for accurate observation in his pastoral *Poems*. Harrison (*Catchment Area*) and Michie (*Possible Laughter*) provided a striking contrast: while the former expressed a contemplative turn of mind in a quiet, almost casual tone, the latter attacked the problems of his generation with the sharper weapons of irony and wit. The most exciting of them all was Patricia Beer, whose *Loss of the Magyar* appropriately became the spring choice of the Poetry Book society. Her delight in language and her originality, combined with careful craftsmanship, made her the " discovery " of the year. Edwin Brock aroused wide interest with *An Attempt at Exorcism*, in which he celebrated a working-class environment without sentimentalizing his experience.

Goodbye Earth, by I. A. Richards, was an interesting first volume of a rather different order, since it appeared not at the beginning but at a rather later stage of the author's distinguished career as a critic of poetry. Another unusual

Alan Sillitoe　　　　*Patricia Beer*

collection was *New Poets 1959* which, edited by Edwin Muir (*see* Obituaries), introduced the work of Iain Crichton Smith, Karen Gershon and Christopher Levenson. Although possessing little in common, these three young poets all showed promise of future development, but Smith exhibited the widest range and the liveliest imagination. Christopher Logue's *Songs* served merely to reinforce his growing reputation as an exponent of " poster poems " and political rhetoric, although his work undoubtedly had refreshing vitality.

Of the established poets Anne Ridler again attracted considerable attention by her skilful handling of intimate personal relationships in *A Matter of Life and Death*, and Louis MacNeice successfully demonstrated the whole range and quality of his shorter pieces in *Eighty-Five Poems*, which he had chosen from his earlier volumes. The 1959 (and fourth) version of *Collected Poems* by Robert Graves revealed the hand of the master craftsman, although informed more by Graves's personality than by any comprehensive philosophy, while *A Book of South African Verse*, selected by Guy Butler, proved to be the best anthology of South African poetry in English yet to be published. (*See* also English Research Studies; Historical Studies.) (S. Nn; Jn. Rd.; Hd. S.)

ENGLISH RESEARCH STUDIES. The year 1959 was remarkable chiefly for the amount of biographical material published and for several excellent editions, both of major and minor works. Among critical studies A. G. Brodeur's *The Art of Beowulf* stood out for its attempt to present *Beowulf* from a purely artistic standpoint. C. L. Barber's *Shakespeare's Festive Comedy* presented the comedies in a new light by relating them to traditional rites and pastimes. Kathleen Williams' *Jonathan Swift and the Age of Compromise* was a work of intelligent revaluation, comparable with that of Irvin Ehrenpreis' *The Personality of Jonathan Swift*. *Coleridge the Visionary*, by J. B. Beer, traced Coleridge's intellectual and religious development and offered new interpretations of some of the poems. *John Keats: a Reassessment*, edited by Kenneth Muir, was a collection of essays by various hands, covering a variety of topics and providing a fresh evaluation of Keats both as poet and as critic. Several new works on Dickens appeared, outstanding among them being J. Hillis Miller's *Charles Dickens: the World of his Novels*, published at the end of 1958. Adopting a new critical approach, the writer argued that the dominating theme of several of the major novels is that of the search for selfhood. The study of George Eliot also flourished; new works included Barbara Hardy's *The Novels of George Eliot*, dealing mainly with her sense of form, and Reva J. Stump's *Movement and Vision in George Eliot's Novels*, which was concerned with her imagery.

Biographical material included R. C. Bald's interesting study, *Donne and the Drurys*; the first volume of *The Correspondence of Edmund Burke*, edited by Thomas W. Copeland, covering the period of Burke's youth; *The Diaries, Prayers, and Annals of Dr. Johnson*, edited by E. L. McAdam, Jr., with Donald and Mary Hyde; volumes iii (1807-14) and iv (1815-19) of *The Collected Letters of Samuel Taylor Coleridge*, edited by E. L. Griggs, which afforded further insight into Coleridge's peculiar difficulties; the third and last volume of *The Diaries of John Ruskin*, selected and edited by Joan Evans and J. H. Whitehouse; an enlarged edition of Humphry House's *The Journals and Papers of Gerard Manley Hopkins*, completed by Graham Storey; and Joseph Conrad's *Letters to William Blackwood and David S. Meldrum*, edited by William Blackburn.

Among important texts Jackson J. Campbell's edition of *The Advent Lyrics of the Exeter Book* must be mentioned. The Arden Shakespeare continued its excellent series with editions of *Timon of Athens* by H. J. Oliver and of *All's Well that Ends Well* by G. K. Hunter. *The Literary Works of Matthew Prior*, edited by H. Bunker Wright and Monroe K. Spears, made a welcome appearance, as did the first critical edition of Burke's *Enquiry into the Sublime and Beautiful* (1958), by J. G. Boulton, which provided much useful information about the sources of Burke's ideas and their influence. Another important event was the publication of Ernest de Selincourt's edition of Wordsworth's *The Prelude*, revised by Helen Darbishire. In his masterly edition of *The Sermons and Devotional Writings of Gerard Manley Hopkins*, Christopher Devlin provided an indispensable text for the study of Hopkins, together with an invaluable commentary on it. Minor works of interest included *The Old English Apollonius of Tyre*, edited by Peter Goolden; *The Sonnets of William Alabaster*, edited by G. M. Story and H. Gardner, which provided the first complete text of this Elizabethan recusant and early metaphysical poet; and an edition of three little-known Elizabethan plays, *Edward III*, *Mucedorus* and *Midas*, by J. Winny.   (J. Gy.)

ENTOMOLOGY.

Insect Endocrinology. New information was obtained on the corpus allatum and its secretion, the " juvenile hormone ". The most striking property of this secretion is to induce the moulting insect to retain its larval characters, but it is also required by most adult insects during ovary maturation. The silkmoths, which develop their eggs precociously, are exceptional in this respect, although histological and other studies showed that they also had active corpora allata. Following this lead C. M. Williams discovered that the fat body of the adult cecropia silkmoth contained considerable accumulations of hormone which, after ether extraction, appeared as a yellow oil. The active principle is highly stable and may be a steroid.

When active extracts were injected into cecropia pupae, the latter moulted to a second pupal stage. But a more delicate bioassay was developed by H. A. Schneiderman and L. I. Gilbert who took advantage of the known sensitivity of regenerating tissues to the hormone. The test extract was blended with wax and spread over a small window cut in the pupal cuticle. When the pupa moulted to the adult, juvenile hormone activity was revealed by the small island of pupal cuticle. By this means hormone activity was recorded, not only in insect material, but in extracts made from many other classes of invertebrates, including the Hydrozoa, Annelida, Holothuroidea and Decapoda. C. M. Williams, L. V. Moorhead and J. F. Pulis also discovered that a variety of mammalian organs such as thymus, bone marrow, placenta, ovary and adrenal cortex yielded active extracts. The functional significance in mammals was unknown.

It is well established that moulting in insects is initiated by a neurohormone elaborated by neurosecretory cells in the brain; and that this in turn activates the prothoracic glands whose function is to secrete the true moult-inducing hormone, ecdysone. The demonstration that implanted corpora allata could also cause moulting, even in brainless insects, was therefore surprising. According to M. Ichikawa and J. Nishiitsutsuji, who worked with the silkmoth *Philosamia cynthia*, the corpora allata may store neurosecretory material which has passed down nerves from the brain. However, Gilbert and Schneiderman also induced moulting with extracts apparently free of ecdysone. They suggested that the juvenile hormone might have biochemical affinities with the brain neurohormone.

The juvenile hormone was also shown by M. Lüscher to be of great importance in controlling the development of polymorphic forms in the termite *Kalotermes flavicollis*. The larvae, which are the main " workers " of the colony, have several potentialities: they may remain as larvae after moulting or they may moult into supplementary reproductives or soldiers. Their fate depends on the timing of the endocrine events. It was found that a static larval moult resulted if ecdysone secretion (and moulting) coincided with a low level of juvenile hormone activity. On the other hand, when the corpora allata hypertrophied some days before the prothoracic glands, they moulted to soldiers; and when both hormones were secreted simultaneously they became supplementary reproductives. In the termite colony supplementary reproductives arise when the colony is deprived of a fertile queen; and in the same way soldiers appear if the colony is deficient in these forms. It has been accepted that such individuals produce substances (as yet unidentified) which are transmitted through the alimentary canal to other members of the colony. These have the remarkable function of controlling the endocrine " programme " of the larva. Biologically active substances of this kind have been termed " pheromones " by P. Karlson and M. Lüscher.

Pheromones. P. Karlson and A. Butenandt, in reviewing this field, pointed out that pheromones share some of the properties of hormones, particularly in their rather highly specific action and their activity in minute concentrations. On the other hand, they are liberated externally and their function is in communication between different individuals of the same species. Other examples quoted by these authors include the queen substance of bees, the odours used by bees for " marking " flowers and the sexual attractants of lepidoptera, cockroaches and other insects.

Insect Tissue Culture. The successful cultivation of insect cells and organs in artificial culture media might be expected to yield much valuable information in the study of embryology, morphogenesis, nutrition, pathology, etc. In discussing recent progress in this field M. F. Day and T. D. C. Grace pointed out that empirical solutions based on vertebrate culture media have invariably failed. Some special difficulties are probably associated with insect material, for example, the lack of bulk tissue and therefore the absence of " feeder " cells; the possible interference with respiration in the absence of a tracheal system; the presence of a selectively permeable membrane around all organs. Nevertheless, the greatest obstacle was undoubtedly the lack of information about the composition of insect blood.

Recent work by G. R. and S. S. Wyatt on the biochemistry of silkworm haemolymph confirmed that great differences separate insect and vertebrate blood. They recorded a totally different ionic balance, there was a remarkably high amino acid and organic phosphate content in the former and the energy source was not glucose but trehalose. Synthetic media based on these analyses permitted cells derived from the ovary wall to survive and undergo mitosis. But continuous subculturing still proved unattainable.

The Rôle of Glycerol in Cold Hardiness. The protective action of glycerol on vertebrate tissues at low temperatures has attracted considerable attention. The demonstration that this substance also occurs abundantly in overwintering insects was therefore noteworthy. H. Chino observed that glycogen in the silkworm egg was converted quantitatively into glycerol and sorbitol before diapause set in, and was resynthesized after the termination of this state. R. W. Salt discovered that the wasp parasite *Bracon cephi* showed true cold-hardening; *i.e.*, the freezing and undercooling points fell as the insect was chilled. The fully cold-adapted insect contained up to 10% of glycerol and survived temperatures below —40°C. He concluded that the function of this and other solutes of low molecular weight was not only to prevent freezing but also to protect the larvae even if freezing should take place.

Clothes Moths and Mothproofing. Keratin, the main structural protein of wool, hair and feathers, owes its great resistance to the presence of disulphide bridges which bind together neighbouring polypeptide chains. Only a few

An adult cecropia silkmoth. In 1959 this species was the subject of experiments on the properties of the " juvenile hormone ".

animals—all of them insects—have evolved means of utilizing this potential food source. They include the clothes moths (Tineidae), the " carpet beetles " (Dermestidae) and the chewing lice of birds (Mallophaga). The unique process of digestion in these species was discussed in 1958 by D. F. Waterhouse. The digestive mechanism has been found to depend on their ability to maintain very strong reducing conditions in the midgut. After reduction, the cystine linkage in the keratin molecule can be attacked by proteolytic enzymes. The poor tracheal supply to the midgut probably assists in maintaining these conditions.

Although conventional insecticides, as well as certain colourless dyestuffs, have been shown to be efficient mothproofing agents, a more novel approach has been to render the keratin itself either toxic or resistant to digestion. If reduced wool is re-oxidized in the presence of metallic salts, metal ions are incorporated in the molecule which are subsequently released on digestion by the moth. Unfortunately the metals are rapidly converted to their sulphides which are relatively harmless. Another line of attack has been to increase the stability of wool by re-oxidation in the presence of certain chemicals such as aliphatic halides. A considerable increase in resistance to moth damage has been achieved by this means. (A. D. Ls.)

BIBLIOGRAPHY (all 1959 unless otherwise stated). F. L. Campbell (ed.), *Physiology of Insect Development*, the Developmental Biology Conference (Chicago); R. Christophers, *Aëdes aegypti* (L.), *the Yellow Fever Mosquito* (Cambridge); M. F. Day and T. D. C. Grace, " Culture of Insect Tissues ", *Ann. Rev. Ent.*, **4**, 17; E. M. Du Porte, *Manual of Insect Morphology* (New York); L. I. Gilbert and H. A. Schneiderman, " Prothoracic Gland Stimulation by Juvenile Hormone Extracts of Insects ", *Nature, Lond.* **184**, 171; M. Ichikawa and J. Nishiitsutsuji-Uwo, " Studies on the Role of the Corpus Allatum in the Eri-silkworm, *Philosamia cynthia ricini* ", *Biol. Bull.* **116**, 88; P. Karlson and A. Butenandt, " Pheromones (Ectohormones) in Insects ", *Ann. Rev. Ent.*, **4**, 39; P. Karlson and M. Lüscher, " Pheromones: a New Term for a Class of Biologically Active Substances ", *Nature, Lond.*, **183**, 55; M. Lüscher, " Über die Entstehung der Soldaten bei Termiten ", *Rev. Suisse Zool.*, **65**, 373 (1958); R. W. Salt, " Role of Glycerol in the Cold-Hardening of *Bracon cephi* (Gahan) ", *Canad. J. Zool.*, **37**, 59; H. A. Schneiderman and L. I. Gilbert, " Substances with Juvenile Hormone Activity in Crustacea and in Other Invertebrates ", *Biol. Bull.*, **115**, 530; E. A. Steinhaus, (ed.), *Journal of Insect Pathology*, vol. 1; D. F. Waterhouse, *Wool Digestion and Mothproofing* (New York, 1958); C. M. Williams, " The Juvenile Hormone-I ", *Biol. Bull.*, **116**, 323; C. M. Williams, L. V. Moorhead and J. F. Pulis, " Juvenile Hormone in Thymus, Human Placenta and Other Mammalian Organs ", *Nature, Lond.*, **183**, 405.

EPIDEMICS.

EPIDEMICS. The epidemiological reporting service of the World Health organization continued in 1959 to give up-to-date information on the world-wide prevalence of disease. Daily radio broadcasts from Geneva and from a network of stations in the middle and far east and weekly printed publications from headquarters in Geneva and from Washington, Alexandria and Singapore disseminated the information provided by member governments. Some of the Communist countries did not supply reports.

The first six diseases are the quarantinable diseases of the International Sanitary regulations.

Plague. Late in 1958 sporadic cases occurred in the Belgian Congo (eastern province), Madagascar (Tananarive province) and Brazil (Baia state). The downward trend of plague incidence observed during recent years continued in 1959. In Asia the incidence was mainly in southern India (states of Mysore, Madras and Uttar Pradesh), in Burma (Mandalay and Magwe divisions) and in Persia where the focus which started in 1958 in Kurdistan was active. In South America sporadic cases were notified from Brazil, Ecuador and Peru. Single cases of sylvatic origin were reported in the United States from California (Mono and Tuolumne counties) and New Mexico (Bernalillo county).

Cholera. After an absence of ten years cholera was present towards the end of 1958 in West Pakistan (Lahore, Dadu and Sukkur states and in the city of Karachi). No further cases occurred in 1959. The focus which started in 1958 in Thailand continued with widespread incidence over most of the country. There was no recurrence in Nepal. Cholera remained widespread in India (Andhra Pradesh, Assam, Bihar, Bombay, Madhya Pradesh, Madras, Mysore, Orissa, Punjab and West Bengal states) and East Pakistan (Chalna, Dacca and Chittagong states), but the incidence was below the high level reached in 1958.

Yellow Fever. Angola (north of 10°S. latitude), Belgian Congo (north of 10°S. latitude), Gambia, Ghana, Federation of Nigeria, Sierra Leone and Sudan (south of 12°N. latitude) were regarded as endemic areas. Sporadic cases were reported in Africa from Ghana (Accra district), Nigeria (Northern region) and Belgian Congo (eastern province). In South America single cases were reported from Colombia (Caldas, Santander and Antioquia departments), Peru (Loreto department) and Trinidad and Tobago (southern division).

Smallpox. In Asia sharp outbreaks occurred in Singapore (April, May and June) and Thailand (Pattani province in July after sporadic cases only had been reported in previous years). Outbreaks also occurred in Kuwait, Qatar, Saudi Arabia, Iraq and Persia. Endemicity continued in India, East and West Pakistan and Burma. Scattered cases occurred in Indonesia with an epidemic in Celebes. There was a single case in the U.S.S.R. (Surkhan-Darya region). In Africa there was a low endemic level in French Equatorial Africa, French West Africa, Nigeria (concentrations in Sokoto and Bornu provinces), the Federation of Rhodesia and Nyasaland, Uganda, Tanganyika, Togo, Portuguese Guinea and Liberia. Single scattered cases occurred in Ghana, Sierra Leone and the United Arab Republic (Cairo in June and July). Widespread endemicity existed in Ethiopia and the Belgian Congo and was present in Kenya and Bechuanaland. In America foci were present in Brazil, Colombia, Ecuador, Argentina and Bolivia. In Dec. 1958 and Jan. 1959 18 cases occurred in the German Federal Republic (Heidelberg). A single case occurred in England (Liverpool in March).

Louse-borne Typhus and Relapsing Fever. In Asia endemicity continued in Persia and Afghanistan. An outbreak of typhus occurred in Korea (Seoul city). In Africa high scattered endemicity of both diseases occurred in Ethiopia, with low scattered incidence in Libya, the United Arab Republic, Algeria, Tunisia and the Union of South Africa. In

Europe cases were reported from Bulgaria and Yugoslavia and in America from Mexico, Colombia, Ecuador and Bolivia.

Poliomyelitis. The year 1959 was not characterized by a generally high incidence.

Influenza. During the winter of 1958 there was little evidence of any widespread epidemic in any area of the northern hemisphere. In 1959 influenza was mostly of a sporadic character with localized epidemics and outbreaks reported were not so severe as those of the pandemic of 1957-58. (*See* also BACTERIOLOGY.)   (L. H. M.)

ERITREA: *see* ETHIOPIA.

ETCHING: *see* DRAWING, ENGRAVING AND ILLUSTRATION.

ETHIOPIA. Independent empire of northeastern Africa, including (from Sept. 15, 1952) the autonomous province of Eritrea, bounded W. by the Sudan, N.E. by the Red sea and French Somaliland and (British) Somaliland Protectorate, and S.E. and S. by (Italian) Somalia trust territory and Kenya. Area: *c.* 456,500 sq.mi., incl. Eritrea 47,800 sq.mi. Pop. (1957 est., no census ever taken): 18,000,000, incl. Eritrea 1,000,000. Language: Amharic, official language; also Galla, Tigrinya, Tigré, Somali, etc. Religion: Christian monophysite (in communion with the Egyptian Coptic church); also Moslem. Chief towns (1956 est.): Addis Ababa (cap.) 400,000; Asmara 120,000; Dessié 53,000; Harar 40,000; Diré-Dawa 30,000. Ruler, Emperor Hailé Selassié I; deputy prime minister, Tshafe Tenan Aklilu Haptewold. Main imports: cotton goods, vehicles and machinery, petroleum and products. Main exports: coffee, hides and skins, cereals and pulses, oilseeds. Monetary unit: Ethiopian dollar (Eth. $7·08 = £1 sterling).

History. President Tito paid a second visit to Ethiopia in Feb. 1959, and the king and queen of Greece made a state visit in March, but the most important event politically was the extensive tour made abroad by the emperor. During June, July and August he visited the United Arab Republic, the U.S.S.R. (14 days), Czechoslovakia, Belgium, France, Portugal, Germany and Yugoslavia (his second visit). In consequence, agreements providing for financial and economic assistance were signed with the U.S.S.R. (including a low-interest loan of Rb.400 million), Czechoslovakia and Yugoslavia. After his return the emperor broadcast exhortations to the people to take full advantage of the credit, expertise and finance thus obtained by investing their money and labour in implementing the five-year plan. An agreement for technical and economic co-operation was also signed with the German Federal Republic.

The U.N. Economic Commission for Africa, with headquarters at Addis Ababa, held its inaugural session in January. After speeches by the emperor and Dag Hammarskjöld, U.N. secretary-general, a comprehensive programme of work was approved. The commission was active throughout the year. Africa Freedom Day was elaborately observed.

Diplomatic storms blew up over the Somali territories and sharp notes were sent to the United Kingdom, the United States and Italy protesting against their alleged support of the conception of Greater Somalia which would embrace an area of Ethiopian territory. No progress was made towards settling the Ethiopia-Somalia boundary dispute. Trygve Lie, former U.N. secretary-general, was appointed under U.N. arrangements as an independent arbiter.

The long-standing rift between the Coptic Churches of Ethiopia and Egypt was healed in June. After official visits were exchanged, the head of the former (Archbishop Basilios) was elevated to the status of patriarch.

Because of locusts and drought, near-famine conditions prevailed in parts of Eritrea and the northern provinces. Gifts of grain for distribution were made by the United States (46,500 tons) and the U.S.S.R. (2,000 tons) and local relief services were organized. Further locust infestation occurred during the year.

The economic situation showed some deterioration mainly due to the fall in the world price of coffee. Some measures aimed at restricting imports and conserving foreign exchange were introduced in the autumn.

A German company was granted the oil concession abandoned by the Sinclair company. New schemes of development were introduced and highways, bridges, airport and telecommunication construction continued on a substantial scale. Education facilities continued to expand.

The Eritrean legislature abolished the state flag in favour of the Ethiopian flag and also adopted the Ethiopian penal code.   (F. E. S.)

EUROPE, COUNCIL OF: *see* COUNCIL OF EUROPE.

EUROPEAN ATOMIC ENERGY COMMUNITY. An organization of six western European powers (Belgium, France, the German Federal Republic, Italy, the Netherlands and Luxembourg) set up by a treaty signed in Rome on March 25, 1957, which came into effect on Jan. 1, 1958. The aim of the community (Euratom) is to promote the speedy growth of nuclear industries for peaceful purposes in the member states by the establishment of a common market for nuclear materials, by the development of research and the spreading of technical knowledge, by facilitating investments, by ensuring a regular supply of ores and nuclear fuels, by guaranteeing the appropriate controls and establishing uniform health standards. The community as such owns special fissionable materials; and the supply of these and ores and other source materials is handled through a community supply agency. The other institutions of the community resemble those of the European Coal and Steel community and the European Economic community: an independent executive of five members (the commission), a council of ministers, a consultative and technical committee and, in common with the other two communities, a parliamentary assembly and a court of justice. Provisional headquarters, Brussels. President of the commission, E. Hirsch (France).

On Jan. 1, 1959, a common market for nuclear products was introduced by the community. All customs duties and quantitative restrictions were abolished between member states, and a common nuclear customs tariff was introduced. Reactor parts and spare parts were included, but the duty of 10% on them was waived for three years. A control, accounting and inspection system was introduced to ensure that nuclear material destined for peaceful uses was not diverted to other ends.

A major step forward with the community's research programme was taken on July 22 when an agreement was signed with the Italian government for the gradual transference to Euratom of the research centre of Ispra (Italy). Euratom announced that the major part of its research programme, including work on power reactor technology, instrumentation and documentation, would be undertaken there in the period 1959-62. Research contracts were placed with other centres for work on radiobiology, plutonium and controlled nuclear fusion. A study on the application of nuclear power to marine propulsion was announced.

The first three research contracts under the Euratom-United States agreement, to a value of $315,000, were awarded; and on Aug. 17 the Export-Import bank, Washington, D.C., announced a loan of $135 million to help finance the joint power programme. The date for the presentation of firm proposals for participation in this was postponed from Sept. 1 to Oct. 20, when five projects were presented. Only one was complete in all details, however, and talks on a further extension of the timetable were undertaken between Euratom and the U.S. authorities.

On Feb. 4 an agreement for co-operation was signed between the United Kingdom and Euratom. Good progress was made by a joint working group set up under this agreement and at the first meeting of the ministerial committee held in London on Dec. 4 it was announced that close collaboration between the two sides would be established in fusion research. Proposals for co-operation in work on fast breeder reactors and the advanced gas-cooled reactor were also to be pursued. Euratom also agreed to share with the United Kingdom the major cost of an experimental gas-cooled reactor to be built, under the auspices of the

O.E.E.C. Nuclear Energy agency, at Winfrith heath, Dorset.

An agreement with Canada, signed in October, provided for a joint programme of research and development on heavy water reactors, and a framework co-operation agreement with Brazil was also negotiated. (*See* also EUROPEAN ECONOMIC COMMUNITY.) (RY. P.)

See *Second General Report on the Activities of the Community, Sept. 1958-March 1959* (Brussels, 1959).

EUROPEAN COAL AND STEEL COMMUNITY.

An organization of six western European powers (France, the German Federal Republic, Italy, Belgium, the Netherlands and Luxembourg) to establish and maintain a common market in coal, steel, iron ore and scrap, and by doing so to increase efficiency in coal and steel industries and raise the standard of living among coal- and steel-workers of the member countries. The idea of this organization was mooted by Robert Schuman, the French foreign minister, on May 9, 1950, as a step towards a united Europe. The treaty creating the community was signed in Paris on April 18, 1951, and ratified on July 25, 1952. The executive organ, called the High authority, which has certain supranational powers, is composed of nine members. The consent of a council of ministers must be obtained for certain of its decisions; others are discussed during their preparation with a consultative committee representing producers, consumers and workers. The community shares with the European Economic community (common market) and the European Atomic Energy community (Euratom) a parliamentary assembly and a court of justice. Provisional seat of the High authority, Luxembourg. Presidents of the High authority in 1959; Paul Finet (Belgium) and—from Sept. 16—Piero Malvestiti (Italy).

A serious coal crisis dominated the affairs of the Community during the year 1959. In January undistributed stocks of coal and coke amounted to 22·5 million metric tons, with a further 20·5 million tons held in stock by consumers. By April 1 stocks reached nearly 50 million tons. Consumption continued to fall in the first part of the year partly because of the recession and more particularly the growing competition from other sources of energy, especially oil. To meet the crisis the High authority urged recourse to direct action provided for in the community treaty. It proposed a programme of import cuts, production quotas, freezing of stocks and special financial aid to miners affected by unemployment or short-time working. The unanimous agreement of the council of ministers of the community was however required for this programme, and this was not obtained. On May 14 the High authority's plan was rejected, France, the German Federal Republic and Italy voting against it.

EUROPEAN COAL AND STEEL COMMUNITY PRODUCTION
(Million metric tons)

	Coal			Steel		
	1957	1958	1959*	1957	1958	1959*
German Fed. Rep.	134·38	132·58	141·3	24·51	22·79	29·4
Saar	16·46	16·43		3·47	3·46	
France	56·80	57·72	57·7	14·10	14·60	15·2
Italy	0·92	0·72	0·7	6·78	6·28	6·8
Belgium	29·09	27·06	22·6	6·28	6·01	6·3
Netherlands	11·38	11·88	12·0	1·19	1·44	1·7
Luxembourg	—	—	—	3·49	3·38	3·7
Total	249·03	246·39	234·3	59·82	57·96	63·1

* Estimates.

Thereafter the High authority's principal concern was to take measures to deal with the Belgian coal situation, which was the most critical. Approval for emergency aid totalling $5 million to supplement unemployment allowances was obtained; a new price list for Belgian coal was sanctioned; a cut in coal imports into Belgium was called for; and work intensified on a comprehensive reorganization scheme for the whole Belgian coal industry. The High authority protested to the Belgian government in September against certain restrictions it imposed on the export and import of coal; following discussions in Brussels the High authority obtained assurances that measures for the reorganization of the Belgian coal market would be submitted to it before they were applied.

The High authority's term of office came officially to an end on Feb. 10, and one of its members, Franz Bluecher, (German Federal Republic) died on March 26, but the vacancy was not filled until the general renewal which took place on Sept. 16. Piero Malvestiti (Italy), formerly vice-president of the European Economic community, became president of the High authority, and P.-O. Lapie (France) and Fritz Hellwig (German Federal Republic) joined as members. Paul Finet (Belgium), formerly president, returned as the co-opted member.

In his first policy speech before the community's parliament that month, Malvestiti replied to suggestions (made by the French foreign minister) that the time had come to reduce the powers of the High authority and at the same time create a single community to deal with energy problems. He insisted on the need to keep the community's powers intact, and said that the High authority, much concerned about the need for a co-ordinated energy policy, would take the initiative in this field. At the same time the new president announced that the High authority would seek a minor revision of the treaty to allow for the continuance of readaptation aid to miners.

Unlike coal, the steel industry of the community was little affected by the recession, and production during the year reached an all-time record of 63·1 million metric tons. (*See* also EUROPEAN ATOMIC ENERGY COMMUNITY; EUROPEAN ECONOMIC COMMUNITY.) (RY. P.)

See William Diebold, Jr., *The Schuman Plan* (New York, 1959); *Seventh General Report* (High Authority, Luxembourg, Feb. 1959).

EUROPEAN ECONOMIC COMMUNITY.

An organization of six western European powers (Belgium, France, the German Federal Republic, Italy, the Netherlands and Luxembourg) set up by a treaty signed in Rome on March 25, 1957, which came into effect on Jan. 1, 1958. Its aim is to replace the existing national economies of member states by a single common market, through the gradual abolition (over a period of 12-15 years) of internal tariffs and quotas, the establishment of a common external tariff, and the progressive freeing of national restrictions on the movement of labour, capital and services within the community. Common policies are also to be established for agriculture and transport; a common social fund will help workers whose jobs are threatened; and an investment bank will make loans to develop less favoured regions. For a trial period of five years the overseas territories of the members are associated with the common market, and will have access to a special development fund of $581·25 million. The institutions follow the pattern of the other European communities: an independent nine-man commission, a council of ministers, a consultative economic and social committee, a parliamentary assembly and a court of justice (the last two being common to all three communities). Provisional headquarters, Brussels. President of the commission, Walter Hallstein (German Federal Republic).

On Jan. 1, one year after the entry into force of the treaty establishing the community, the first measures were taken to reduce tariffs and enlarge quotas on goods moving between the six member states. All tariffs (other than those on goods covered by the European Coal and Steel community and European Atomic Energy community) were reduced by 10%. Bilateral quotas were globalized and enlarged in their total value by 20%: quotas equivalent to a minimum of 3% of the national output were established for those products where previously small or nil quotas had been in force. The commission reported that the technical difficulties of these operations had been successfully overcome. There was a marked and vigorous response on the part of all sections of industry to these measures foreshadowing the gradual establishment of a full common market. There was also a marked rise in foreign—and especially United States—investment in the member countries. During the year industrial production recovered strongly and for the community as a whole was 5·5% higher than in 1958.

Much of the activity of the commission was devoted to preparatory work for further stages of the common market. In March the commission reported that the major part of the preliminary draft of the common external tariff had been completed; and negotiations continued for the fixing of the

" Look what I made out of the spare wheel "—a cartoon by Low which appeared in the " Manchester Guardian " on June 17.

common tariff on outstanding items included in List G in the Rome treaty for which agreement was still required. Agreement was reached on the application of articles 85 and 86 of the treaty (concerning rules of competition). Work continued on proposals for a co-ordinated transport policy, and the commission's proposals for a common agricultural policy were published. Draft regulations to govern the application of the social fund (for vocational retraining and industrial reconversion) were approved by the commission and submitted to the council of ministers. Measures to extend the benefits of social security schemes for migrant workers came into force in January and preparatory work continued on measures designed to implement the treaty's provisions concerning freedom of movement of workers within the community.

Within the framework of the commission's policy for the development of the less-favoured regions of the community (on which discussions with representatives of the member governments were held), the investment bank began its operations and announced on March 18 four loans totalling $24 million, three of them for industrial development in southern Italy.

The overseas development fund also began its operations: on Jan. 31 it had already received 91 requests for aid. Up to Sept. 30 a total of $19·4 million was made available in the form of non-repayable loans for 36 approved projects.

One major development in the external relations of the community was its decision to take advantage of the United

States offer to negotiate tariff reductions during the 1960 session of G.A.T.T. (General Agreement on Tariffs and Trade). As regards the community's relations with the other countries of O.E.E.C. (Organization for European Economic Co-operation), the commission published its first memorandum (the " Hallstein report ") on Feb. 26. It observed that there had been " very widely differing points of view " about the objective of the free trade area talks, and that agreement on essential conditions from the community's point of view had not been reached. While pledging the community to a liberal trade policy, the memorandum concluded that although an eventual multilateral association with the other O.E.E.C. countries was desirable there was no immediate prospect of achieving it. The commission therefore proposed an annual increase of 20% in quotas within O.E.E.C., and an effort to reduce tariffs in G.A.T.T.

A special committee consisting of representatives of the commission and the six member states was set up by the community's council of ministers on March 17 to consider this memorandum. In September, however, the commission presented a second memorandum which stated that no agreement on the fundamental questions of a multilateral association had been reached. It again proposed a series of liberal measures to deal with immediate problems. On the basis of these proposals the council of ministers decided on Nov. 24 that the quota increases to be granted between member states on Jan. 1, 1960, would be extended to all members of G.A.T.T. and would not be subject to reciprocity. Member states would also be at liberty to extend to non-member countries the tariff reductions due on July 1, 1960, as long as such reductions did not lower tariffs beyond the level of the agreed common external tariff. The council also approved the commission's proposals for a contact committee composed of community countries and other members of O.E.E.C. to deal with any immediate difficulties which might arise in trade between them. It also declared its readiness to participate in regular consultations with the United States, Canada, the United Kingdom and other European countries on aid policy to underdeveloped countries and cyclical trade policy. The principle of a speeding-up of the transition period was also accepted.

In the meantime seven of the other O.E.E.C. countries— Austria, Denmark, Norway, Portugal, Sweden, Switzerland and the United Kingdom—announced on July 21, after a ministerial meeting at Stockholm, their intention of creating a European Free Trade association (E.F.T.A.). An agreement on this was signed on Nov. 20. It provided for the removal of trade barriers on industrial products between members (on a timetable equivalent to that of the common market itself), and special arrangements for increased trade in agricultural and marine products. The members of the " outer seven " also expressed their readiness to undertake new negotiations with the " six ". The creation of a bridge between the two groups, though much discussed, remained problematical.

In the middle of the year both Greece and Turkey— members of neither group—applied for association with E.E.C. The community's council of ministers having agreed, negotiations for a customs union between E.E.C. and these two countries then began with the commission in September. (*See* also COUNCIL OF EUROPE; EUROPEAN ATOMIC ENERGY COMMUNITY; EUROPEAN COAL AND STEEL COMMUNITY; ORGANIZATION FOR EUROPEAN ECONOMIC CO-OPERATION.)   (RY. P.)

BIBLIOGRAPHY. *Second General Report on the activities of the Community, Sept. 18, 1958-March 20, 1959* (Brussels, 1959); *First Memorandum from the Commission . . . concerning . . . a European Economic Association* (Brussels, 1959); *Second Memorandum* (Brussels, 1959); *Stockholm Draft Plan for a European Free Trade Assocaition* (London, 1959); Miriam Camps, *The European Free Trade Association* (London, 1959); *Tariffs and Trade in Western Europe*, P.E.P. study (London, 1959); *European Free Trade Area, Text of Convention and other Documents* (London, 1959).

THE COMMON MARKET AND THE " OUTER SEVEN "
Trade in all goods in 1957, in millions of U.S. dollars (c.i.f.)

Exports from / Exports to	U.K.	Denmark	Norway	Sweden	Austria	Switz.	Portugal	E.F.T.A. total	E.E.C.
United Kingdom	—	321	179	439	26	103	48	1,116	1,376
Denmark .	331	—	48	122	7	23	4	535	490
Norway .	222	40	—	206	6	16	3	493	397
Sweden .	336	100	89	—	16	47	7	595	955
Austria .	47	6	7	14	—	55	2	131	586
Switzerland .	105	16	8	31	49	—	4	213	1,130
Portugal .	66	2	5	12	4	15	—	104	185
E.F.T.A. total .	1,107	485	336	824	108	259	68	3,187	5,119
E.E.C. .	1,284	342	227	787	456	577	68	3,741	7,030

SOURCE. O.E.E.C., *The Network of Intra-European Trade* (Paris, 1957).

EXCHANGE CONTROL AND EXCHANGE RATES. During the last quarter of 1958 and the first threequarters of 1959 the terms of trade remained favourable to the more highly industrialized countries, and the international financial position of Europe in particular showed further marked improvement. By contrast, most of the raw material producing countries continued to experience difficulties, brought on by the low prices obtainable for their products abroad and often aggravated by inflation at home.

Throughout 1958 Europe's gold and dollar reserves increased, reflecting in part the return of confidence in its currencies, and exchange controls were gradually relaxed. On Dec. 27, 1958, when the United Kingdom and most of the leading trading countries of Europe declared their currencies freely convertible for current transactions by non-residents, the European Payments union procedure whereby outstanding balances between member countries could be settled up to 25% by credit was replaced by a multilateral clearing system in which all such settlements were to be made in gold or dollars. At the same time, however, a European fund was established with a capital of $600 million to make short-term credits to members on an *ad hoc* basis to help them overcome temporary balance of payments difficulties in such a way as to avoid imposing restrictions on trade and payments. The international liquidity position was further reinforced in Sept. 1959 by a general 50% increase in quotas in the International Monetary fund, which resulted in a corresponding increase in the ability of member countries to purchase foreign exchange from the fund.

United States. As Europe's reserve position improved, there was a continued outflow of gold from the United States. U.S. reserves fell from $20,870 million in Sept. 1958 to $19,580 million in Sept. 1959, and from the end of 1957 the drop amounted to more than $3,000 million. It reflected a fall in U.S. exports while imports were stable and foreign aid remained at a high level—larger in fact than the surplus in current commercial transactions. Although U.S. reserves still represented about 18 months' imports, the continuing gold outflow also led to rumours—vigorously denied by the U.S. authorities—that the United States might increase the dollar price of gold.

Canada. Except for brief periods the Canadian dollar remained strong, despite an increase in imports. In Sept. 1959 it commanded a premium of 5% over the U.S. dollar. This strength reflected the continued inflow of foreign capital, both short- and long-term, partly in response to interest rates which rose even more steeply in Canada than in the United States. The rise in the Treasury bill rate from 1·54% in Sept. 1958 to 5·64% a year later was particularly striking.

Sterling Area. Sterling continued to be strong in the latter part of 1958 and in 1959, the gold and dollar reserves of the sterling area amounting to $2,974 million at the end of Nov. 1959. The U.K. monetary authorities therefore continued their policy of loosening restrictions on the use of sterling, the most noteworthy measure being the declaration on Dec. 27, 1958, that sterling obtained in current account transactions by non-residents would be fully convertible. By this move the former U.S., Canadian, transferable and registered accounts were unified into a single class of "external accounts". This meant the disappearance of the transferable sterling rate, which for some time had been supported by the authorities at a level only very slightly below the official rate. In the new conditions sterling remained above the par value of $2·80, except for a time in December.

Further steps were taken to make sterling more widely usable. In February more liberal provisions were introduced with respect to the transfer of legacies abroad, the maximum

for emigrant remittances to the dollar area was increased to £5,000 and permission was given to London banks to engage in arbitrage transactions in foreign bank notes. In March facilities for forward foreign exchange transactions were broadened and the amount of sterling bank-notes that travellers might legally take out of the United Kingdom was increased from £10 to £20, this being further increased to £50 in November. In June restrictions were further relaxed on dollar imports and in November most of the remaining controls on dollar imports were removed.

Most of the other members of the sterling area took steps in line with the United Kingdom to ease restrictions on transactions with the dollar area. Since their currencies were already fully convertible into sterling they now became freely convertible into dollars for current account transactions by non-residents.

However, certain primary-producing countries in the sterling area continued to experience special difficulties. In India heavy development expenditures and unfavourable market conditions for exports caused the foreign exchange holdings of the reserve bank to fall to their lowest postwar level of $621 million in July 1959 and led the authorities to maintain strict control over imports and oblige exporters to surrender their foreign exchange earnings without delay. The position of Pakistan was even more difficult. In Jan. 1959 control of all foreign exchange earnings was centralized in the state bank, and the government introduced a scheme to promote minor exports, by permitting exporters of these to retain 20% or 40% of their earnings. Import restrictions, so severe that there was substantial industrial unemployment through lack of materials and spare parts, were maintained. As a result of these measures foreign exchange holdings improved somewhat in the first eight months of 1959. In June Iraq ceased to be a member of the sterling area and announced its intention to diversify its currency reserves and foreign balances, previously held in sterling.

French Franc Area. In 1959 there was a strong improvement in the international economic situation of France. Official gold and foreign exchange reserves rose from $965 million in Dec. 1958 to $1,875 million in Aug. 1959. On Dec. 27, 1958, the franc was made fully convertible for current account transactions by non-residents (except residents of countries with which France maintained bilateral payments arrangements). At the same time the par value of

Three of the new, or "heavy", French francs, each equivalent to 100 old francs. They were due to enter circulation on Jan. 1, 1960.

the franc was reduced from 420 to 493·706 per U.S. dollar; the proportion of earnings which exporters were allowed to retain was reduced from 20% to 15%; the 10% rebate allowed on certain tourist expenditures was abolished; and the 3% tax on foreign exchange purchased by French residents travelling abroad was removed. In May the restrictions on dealings in foreign bank-notes were ended, and the "parallel" or free exchange rate for the U.S. dollar fell below the official rate for the first time in 20 years. It was announced that before the end of 1959 the existing franc would be replaced by a "heavy franc", with the exchange taking place in the ratio of 100 old francs to 1 new franc.

Most of the overseas members of the franc area followed the devaluation of the franc, but Morocco introduced a new currency, the *dirham*, equivalent to 100 French francs, and Tunisia the *dinar*, equivalent to 1,000 French francs.

Other Western European Countries. At the end of 1958, and following the lead of the United Kingdom, the monetary authorities of Austria, Belgium and Luxembourg, Denmark, Finland, the German Federal Republic, Italy, the Netherlands, Norway, Portugal and Sweden declared their currencies convertible for current account transactions by non-residents. Greece took a similar step in May 1959. In most cases residents of countries with which bilateral payments agreements were in force were excepted from these facilities. In the case of Germany, the declaration of convertibility was followed in January by the elimination of virtually all remaining restrictions applicable to transactions on current account, by residents as well as non-residents. Restrictions on exports of capital were removed entirely and those on imports of capital relaxed. The only restrictions on the latter that remained were designed to check any inflow of short-term speculative money. In Spain the peseta was devalued from the previous principal rate of 42 to one of 60 per U.S. dollar in July, and the various other rates were abolished.

After various western European countries had declared their currencies convertible, the exchange rate of the Swiss franc (previously the only convertible European currency) weakened slightly. Fewer foreign funds flowed to Switzerland as other financial centres became more active, and there was an increased outflow of Swiss capital. (*See also* BALANCE OF PAYMENTS; INTERNATIONAL MONETARY FUND.) (A. STE.)

EXHIBITIONS: *see* ART EXHIBITIONS; FAIRS, SHOWS AND EXHIBITIONS.

EXPLORATION AND DISCOVERY.

With the continued reduction in the areas on the earth's surface which have never been visited by civilized man the tendency for expeditions to be organized on a smaller, more personal scale continued. During 1959 no expedition of the calibre of the Everest or Trans-Antarctic expeditions was in the field. Among the objectives of expeditions scientific investigation was at least as important as individual adventure, but this was not new. It was true when James Cook sailed to the Pacific to observe the transit of Venus in 1769, and it was true before that.

Full scientific results of expeditions do not become available immediately on their return; indeed, field work is the first, and often the least protracted stage in investigations, so it is legitimate to include among the discoveries of the year the newly published conclusions of the Norwegian-British-Swedish expedition of 1949-52 and of other Antarctic expeditions. These were largely in the field of glaciology. Charles Swithinbank, who had worked at Maudheim, showed that the extent of the ice shelves protruding from the Antarctic coastline is largely governed by the anchorage provided in bays in the coast or in the inland ice sheet and by locally grounded areas, without which the ice would break up and float out to

sea. He also discussed evidence which showed that although at some time in the past the ice sheet had been thicker it was not thinning any further. This was confirmed by Malcolm Mellor who made a close comparison of maps and aerial photographs of the coast of Mac-Robertson Land, in an entirely different part of Antarctica from Maudheim. He found that although the snouts of glaciers lengthen seawards and the accumulated ice does not break off for several years, some glaciers had advanced and others had been cut back so that during a period of 20 years there was no general advance or retreat of the ice edge.

Current field work in the Antarctic included an exploration of the Bellingshausen sea area, a survey of Victoria Land and glaciological investigations in Marie Byrd Land, all supported by the United States, in addition to continued activity centred on the Australian bases at Mawson, Davis and Wilkes station (the last a U.S. Geophysical Year station which was handed over to Australia), and by the Falkland Islands Dependencies survey.

Two mountain ranges and a plain concealed under the ice-cap near Pionerskaya, the Soviet station in east Antarc-

The base camp of the women's expedition to Cho Oyu in the Himalayas. Two members of the party lost their lives.

tica, were named after the Soviet scientists Golitsyn, Amburstev and Schmidt. In November the 12 nations involved in International Geophysical co-operation in Antarctica negotiated a treaty providing for free scientific investigations and the "freezing" of all territorial claims.

In spite of a most discouraging report by Alfred Gregory, who led a reconnaissance in 1958, a party of six, supported by four experienced Sherpas, attempted to climb Ama Dablam (22,494 ft.) in Nepal. The party, led by Emlyn Jones, established their base camp on April 17 at the foot of their chosen route, a spur leading up to the north ridge. This spur presented a climb of about 3,000 ft. almost entirely on rock.

Camp 1 was pitched on a restricted site approximately half way up this spur and camp 2, which was occupied on May 5, was placed at the junction of the spur and the ridge. Between camps 2 and 3 the ridge was of rock and its principal features were two great rock towers which had to be bypassed on their eastern flank on very loose and unpleasant ground. From camp 3 Mike Harris and George Fraser set out on May 18 carrying the equipment for a light camp which they placed that night somewhere near the top of the rock ridge. The following day they tackled the ice ridge ahead of them and must have put a camp that night out of sight of those below. On May 20 they were seen to be going strongly up what appeared to be the final obstacles guarding the comparatively easy slopes immediately below the summit, and went out of sight over the top of an ice tower about 8.30 A.M. When they had not returned two days later it could only be concluded that they had met with an accident. No trace of them could be found. It is possible that they reached the summit and died on the descent.

Disaster also overtook a seven-man expedition led by Keith Warburton to an unnamed 25,540-ft. peak in the Batura Mustagh region of the Karakoram. Two members remained at base camp to carry out glaciological observations when their companions set out with 28 days provisions to try to reach the summit. Not long after their departure there were several days of extremely bad weather and although no anxiety about their fate was entertained at the time they did not return, and in spite of a widespread search they were not found. In November almost the whole of an expedition of three Japanese and 31 Nepalis, including porters, was reported missing on Gauri Sankar (23,440 ft.). They returned safely in the following month, but were robbed by bandits. This year of Himalayan disasters also witnessed the loss of two members, including the leader Claude Kogan (see OBITUARIES), of a 12-woman expedition to Cho Oyu (26,750 ft.).

In addition to the expeditions led by Emlyn Jones and Keith Warburton the Royal Geographical society supported a number of others including one from Imperial College of Science and Technology (London university) to carry out underwater studies of marine flora and fauna in the Azores, and another from Cambridge university to make a speleological investigation of water resources of the limestone plateau of Jebel el Akhdar in Cyrenaica. The society supported a large number of expeditions, the majority of them sponsored by exploration clubs of the British universities.

Scientific research into land use in northern Australia led to the discovery that 3,000 sq.mi. in the Northern Territory were sufficiently fertile to be suitable for mixed farming, particularly for growing peanuts and producing fat cattle, instead of the store cattle for fattening elsewhere which had previously been characteristic of the region.

Carbon-14 tests on specimens of animal and plant life found 35 mi. south of Regina enabled Robert Nero of the Saskatchewan Museum of Natural History to say that dense forest covered the Canadian prairies up to 9,500 years ago. (See also ANTARCTICA; SPELEOLOGY.) (A. M. F.)

See Norwegian-British-Swedish Antarctic Expedition, 1949-52, Scientific Results, vols. 3, 4, 5, Glaciology (Norsk Polarinstitutt, Oslo, 1957-59); M. Mellor, " Variations of the Ice Margins in East Antarctica ", Geogr. J. 125: 230-35 (1959).

The U.S. navy's bathyscaphe "Trieste", designed by August Piccard, being loaded at San Diego, California, for shipment to the Marianas Islands. It was hoped to reach with it the bottom of the Marianas trench, the deepest known place on the earth's surface.

EXPORTS AND IMPORTS, U.K. The table below shows the movement of U.K. exports and imports during 1956-59. Values throughout are in £ million.

	Exports					Imports				
	1956	1957	1958	1958 9 months	1959 9 months	1956	1957	1958	1958 9 months	1959 9 months
By Area										
DOLLAR AREA . . .	519·6	552·0	559·2	408·6	489·5	850·8	963·6	786·0	572·5	577·0
Canada . . .	177·6	195·6	188·4	140·2	148·9	348·0	320·4	308·4	227·9	223·5
United States . .	242·4	243·6	272·4	192·8	267·3	406·8	481·2	350·4	244·4	246·1
Latin America . .	76·8	86·4	81·6	62·4	61·8	91·2	154·8	121·2	95·5	102·5
NON-DOLLAR										
Latin America .	57·6	78·0	69·6	51·8	52·3	180·0	190·8	174·0	132·6	145·9
NON-STERLING, O.E.E.C.* .	867·6	907·2	843·6	630·9	663·4	1,000·8	1,017·6	1,011·6	744·3	785·5
Belgium-Luxembourg .	69·6	78·0	60·0	46·4	44·4	75·6	61·2	58·8	42·8	42·0
Denmark, Faeroe Islands and Greenland	82·8	86·4	78·0	57·9	64·1	122·4	114·0	115·2	83·5	99·2
France . . .	87·6	87·6	70·8	54·1	57·6	111·6	110·4	100·8	77·3	73·4
German Federal Republic .	91·2	104·4†	122·4†	89·8†	100·8†	110·4	124·8†	135·6‡	101·0†	103·0†
Netherlands . .	118·8	117·6	97·2	72·7	83·2	136·8	132·0	159·6	116·9	120·5
Sweden . . .	105·6	110·4	104·4	76·9	78·0	145·2	157·2	134·4	99·6	93·2
Other* . . .	312·0	322·8	310·8	233·1	235·3	298·8	318·2	307·2	223·2	254·2
STERLING AREA . .	1,387·2	1,436·4	1,392·0	1,039·6	970·7	1,470·0	1,512·0	1,356·0	1,008·1	1,068·6
United Kingdom Colonies .	302·4	298·8	295·2	216·6	224·3	282·0	302·4	266·4	200·8	220·7
Australia . . .	238·8	235·2	235·2	179·4	159·7	236·4	248·4	199·2	137·6	165·7
New Zealand . .	127·2	140·4	128·4	96·3	66·4	196·8	183·6	160·8	124·6	141·7
Ceylon . . .	26·0	25·8	28·0	19·7	23·7	39·1	40·8	46·4	34·7	29·2
India . . .	168·0	175·2	158·4	115·5	124·0	141·6	157·2	139·2	94·4	95·2
Pakistan . .	32·8	34·6	29·0	21·0	24·3	22·8	25·7	19·8	12·7	17·8
Union of S. Africa .	153·6	172·8	186·0	142·6	110·8	91·2	92·4	90·0	69·4	67·0
Republic of Ireland .	103·2	102·0	109·2	83·1	77·6	90·0	109·2	108·0	82·6	75·2
Other . . .	235·2	251·6	222·6	165·4	159·9	370·1	352·3	326·2	251·3	256·1
SOVIET EASTERN EUROPE .	43·2	56·4	45·6	30·4	42·3	98·4	109·2	102·0	73·4	82·6
REST OF WORLD . .	262·8	260·5	261·6	194·9	207·0	259·2	248·4	320·4	234·5	248·3
TOTAL. . . .	3,138}‡ 3,139}	3,291	3,172	2,356	2,425	3,859}‡ 3,860}	4,042	3,750}‡ 3,751}	2,765}‡ 2,766}	2,908
By Commodity										
FOOD, BEVERAGES, TOBACCO .	178·1	201·1	188·4	136·0	133·9	1,435·6	1,479·0	1,493·0	1,084·9	1,110·7
Meat§ . .	4·2	5·6	5·6	4·4	3·4	292·2	307·6	313·9	232·9	237·7
Dairy products‖ . .	6·1	9·0	7·8	6·1	4·7	169·4	139·9	136·0	95·7	133·9
Cereals§ . . .	16·2	10·1	13·2	7·9	9·9	235·0	213·9	226·9	169·9	178·5
Fruit and vegetables .	7·7	8·1	8·0	4·8	5·5	221·0	213·1	249·4	195·8	183·4
Beverages§ (incl. spices)	70·3	74·8	78·5	55·9	60·3	196·0	223·7	228·3	161·6	149·0
Other food¶ . .	50·3	71·9	53·6	40·2	36·1	241·3	295·2	251·5	174·7	180·4
Tobacco§ . .	23·3	21·9	21·6	16·7	13·9	80·6	85·5	87·0	54·3	47·7
BASIC MATERIALS . .	176·6	183·3	140·2	103·6	112·3	1,137·8	1,185·4	907·0	686·7	675·7
Coal** . .	60·8	60·5	31·4	23·4	16·8	43·3	25·5	7·1	5·9	1·3
Metal ores and scrap .	2·4	2·0	4·9	2·0	12·0	182·1	205·2	137·8	109·8	86·1
Oils and oil seeds .	9·7	7·7	6·5	4·7	6·3	112·5	117·1	95·2	71·7	86·7
Wool . . .	68·5	78·5	65·3	50·1	50·6	187·4	205·3	145·4	104·9	122·1
Cotton . . .	2·1	1·8	1·7	1·2	1·1	104·2	108·4	71·7	59·3	48·7
Other textile fibres and waste	11·5	12·2	9·9	7·2	9·0	31·6	40·0	30·0	20·0	24·5
Timber and pulp . .	2·2	2·4	2·4	1·7	1·7	267·5	278·6	238·1	175·8	174·6
Rubber (incl. synthetic) .	1·6	1·5	1·6	1·1	1·9	88·5	84·2	75·9	60·0	45·5
MANUFACTURED GOODS†† .	2,698·5	2,823·3	2,764·0	2,063·0	2,126·4	1,272·4	1,363·0	1,335·1	983·6	1,110·5
Chemical manufactures .	243·1	265·9	261·5	194·3	213·7	107·3	114·7	120·1	88·2	98·1
Woollen manufactures .	89·8	95·1	79·9	61·6	61·3	8·7	10·9	10·8	7·6	6·8
Cotton manufactures .	88·6	88·4	71·1	54·9	46·0	25·8	33·4	32·4	23·1	30·4
Synthetic fibre manufactures .	31·8	32·9	27·9	21·7	19·8	10·9	13·7	12·6	9·9	6·8
Miscellaneous textiles .	84·1	84·2	75·3	56·3	54·7	30·0	30·9	29·4	20·9	25·0
Iron and steel . .	172·2	212·3	186·5	136·7	134·3	105·1	78·6	45·8	39·2	27·6
Metal and metal manufactures	268·1	263·5	244·1	177·7	190·8	238·1	210·7	192·9	142·9	163·2
Machinery . . .	502·9	559·8	566·0	426·3	458·2	110·2	124·6	136·5	100·9	120·9
Electrical machinery and appliances . .	215·6	226·0	221·9	163·9	170·9	23·5	26·6	29·4	21·1	28·6
Railway vehicles . .	45·2	41·9	46·3	33·9	28·3	1·8	1·7	1·3	0·9	0·9
Road vehicles and aircraft .	366·6	397·8	449·8	344·4	360·6	21·8	26·2	22·0	16·5	23·5
Ships and boats . .	93·8	79·3	63·1	42·3	36·8	6·1	10·8	20·9	15·8	9·8
Petroleum products†† .	98·7	90·0	99·6	74·2	69·5	370·4	440·2	433·7	314·5	354·3
PARCEL POST (and live animals not for food) . . .	85·4	82·7	79·0	53·5	52·6	14·2	14·8	15·5	10·7	10·9

NOTES. Only selected items appear under main commodity headings. * Incl. dependencies. † Incl. Saar. ‡ Total for lower portion of table has been based on different estimates. § Incl. products and preparations. ‖ Incl. honey. ¶ Incl. sugar and sugar preparations; live animals chiefly for food; feedingstuff for animals and food waste; fish and fish preparations. ** Incl. coke and other manufactured fuel. †† Incl. crude petroleum.
SOURCE. Board of Trade; *Accounts relating to Trade and Navigation of the United Kingdom* (H.M.S.O.).

" Why not arms for Russia, too? After all, it will only infuriate the rest of the people we want to please . . ."—a cartoon by Cummings which appeared in the " Daily Express " on May 15.

EYE DISEASES: *see* DISEASES.

FAEROE ISLANDS. (FAERÖERNE). Self-governing part of the kingdom of Denmark in the north Atlantic situated between Iceland and the Shetland Islands, about 200 mi. N.W. of the latter. Area: 540 sq.mi.; there are 21 islands of which 18 are inhabited. Pop.: (1950 census) 31,664; (1955 census) 32,456. Language: Faeroese, akin to Icelandic rather than to Danish. Religion: Lutheran. Capital, Thorshavn, on the island of Stromo, pop. (1955) 6,067. Governor-general, C. A. Vagn-Hansen. Currency: Danish.

History. After gaining three seats at the Lagting (Diet) election on Nov. 8, 1958, Peter Mohr Dam, the leader of the Social Democrats, became chief minister of the local government on Jan. 9, 1959. The outgoing chief minister, Kristian Djurhus (Sambands Party) became his deputy. Niels Winther Poulsen (Selvstyre Party) also joined the government.

On Feb. 24 the Lagting approved an Anglo-Danish agreement on Faeroese fishing limits. The agreement would remain in force for three years, subject to one year's notice of termination by either side. It fixed a 6-mi. limit within which British trawlers were forbidden to fish; between this limit and a 12-mi. limit some areas were closed to British fishing for certain periods of the year.

Improved old age pensions were enacted in May, and Danish State loans and guarantees of bank-loans for constructing Faeroese fishing vessels were increased. (H. LN.)

FAIRS, SHOWS AND EXHIBITIONS. The Royal Agricultural society took a further step towards acquiring a permanent show ground. Following the successful policy of the Great Yorkshire and Three Counties shows, the " Royal " had found that in recent years the cost of moving to a new site each year could no longer be justified on economic grounds. In October the society advertised for a site of from 350 ac. to 500 ac. in the triangle between Warwick, Nottingham and Chester. In recent years, the " Royal " at Woollaton park, Nottingham, in 1955, was one of the most successful shows; in that year the attendance was 185,527 and the profit £2,447. In 1958 at Whitchurch airport, Bristol, the attendance was only 87,727. The 1960 and 1961 shows were planned to be held on the same site at Cambridge, and it was hoped that a permanent site would be acquired for use in 1962. The 1959 show was held at Kidlington, near Oxford; the attendance was 94,341, an increase of 6,614 over 1958, but considerably below 1955.

In October, the report was published of a committee of the Federation of British Industries which had been set up following a request in 1957 by the president of the board of trade for advice on future policy regarding exhibitions in Britain. The committee recommended the building of a new exhibition centre in central London, to supplement or take the place of Earls Court or Olympia. It was estimated that the building would cost £10 million, that the minimum size should be 500,000 sq.ft., and that one of the essential requirements would be adequate parking facilities. The report found that the present exhibition facilities in London had insufficient solid floor space and the committee suggested that north or south Kensington would be the most suitable district for the new centre. A possibility would be the construction of a new building over the railway lines at Olympia.

The two principal autumn exhibitions once again clashed in 1959, but even so attracted large crowds. The Motor show (Earls Court, Oct. 21-31) was heralded by considerable advance publicity because of the introduction of many new models—particularly in the small car range. The attendance was poor for the first few days, and the final total of 560,313 was the third largest in the history of the Motor show. The other major autumn exhibition, the Dairy show (Olympia, Oct. 27-30) attracted nearly 11,000 more visitors than in 1958 (1959, 88,433; 1958, 77,641).

An exhibition of Wedgwood pottery was opened at the Victoria and Albert museum on June 22, 1959, to mark the firm's bicentenary.

The Ideal Home exhibition (Olympia, March 4-29), the largest annual exhibition in the British Isles, was again attended by over 1 million visitors (1,229,977 in 1959) about 100,000 below the peak of 1957. (A. J. KD.)

FALKLAND ISLANDS.

British colony (East and West Falkland and adjacent islands) and dependencies in the South Atlantic. Dependencies: (1) South Georgia (1,600 sq.mi., whaling industry centre), with South Orkney (240 sq.mi.) and South Sandwich (130 sq.mi.); and (2) South Shetland (1,800 sq.mi.) and Graham Land (on Antarctic mainland). Pop. of dependencies: c. 1,200 in summer, c. 700 in winter. Area of colony: 4,618 sq.mi. Pop.: (1953 census) 2,230; (1958 est.) 2,253 mainly of British descent and Protestant. Only town, Stanley, pop. (1953 census) 1,135. Distances: colony, c. 480 mi. N.E. of Cape Horn; South Georgia, c. 800 mi. E. of colony; South Orkney and South Sandwich c. 450 mi. S.W. and S.E. respectively of South Georgia; South Shetland c. 500 mi. S. of colony. Administration: governor; executive council; legislative council with elected minority. Governor, E. P. Arrowsmith. Chief imports: foodstuffs, fuels and lubricants, oils and fats, machinery and transport equipment. Chief exports: whale products, wool, seal oil. Currency: sterling with local notes.

History. At the end of Dec. 1958 the Falkland Islands Dependencies survey took over the base at Halley bay (Coats' Land) established by the Royal Society in 1956 as part of the British contribution to the International Geophysical Year. An intensive programme of meteorological and other research work was carried out there during 1959.

The research ships "John Biscoe" and "Shackleton" returned from their annual relief voyages to the dependencies on June 12 and June 25 respectively. The 1958-59 Antarctic season was one of the worst ever recorded, and the "John Biscoe" experienced extremely difficult ice conditions on her return, although she arrived without serious damage.

The "Shackleton" sailed again on Oct. 5 taking with her to Stanley the relieving parties for the dependencies and also two youths who were participants in the Voluntary Service Overseas scheme. These young men were to work as auxiliary teachers on farms in the Falkland Islands for a year. (W. H. Is.)

FASHION AND DRESS.

Following the complete disappearance from the field of fashion of the sack and its unhappy offspring during the first half of 1958, designers were engaged during the second half of that year and the whole of 1959 in what may be called the battle of the waistline. The high "empire" line was the outstanding (but by no means universally accepted) feature of 1958-59 winter styles. By the spring, however, waists had come down to normal (with some high-waisted effects) and the plain or pleated shirtwaist dress, launched in the *haute couture* spring collections, proved to be the best-seller throughout the long, fine summer of 1959. The high fashion shirtwaist had a gently fitted waist and a moderately full skirt, quickly vulgarized by the ready-to-wear trade into strangled waists and ultra-full, ultra-short skirts swaying out over layers of stiffened petticoats. With this summer "uniform", a variant of which was the fitted, low-cut top and swinging skirts, went low-cut court shoes in bright colours and a curious high-built, tousled hair-style imitating that of the French film actress, Brigitte Bardot.

The over-enthusiastic welcome given to the new-found waistline and facile shirtwaist styles by the ready-to-wear business had the effect of making high fashion veer away from the fully engaged waist; and by the time the autumn and winter collections came round it was obvious that a more mature mood was developing. For high fashion the shirtwaist had danced for but one summer. In its place came a longer, straighter silhouette often marked at a slightly lowered waistline by gentle pouching over fabric or leather belts. A variant of this was the straight dress brought in at the true waist by very wide, soft leather belts—a style that Balenciaga had been sponsoring for some time. (The sharp reaction to ready-to-wear styles based on previous *haute couture* collections gave rise to serious anxiety in all branches of the fashion trade, the probability of arbitrary change every six months offering little or no guarantee of continuity in trend or of rational evolution.)

Skirts, for most of the year, remained short; but later, with the feeling for more mature styles, they lengthened to about 3-4 in. below the knee-cap. Jackets had shown a tendency to lengthen since the spring when the house of Dior and other leading creators seemed to be making their way back to a more classic tailoring of suits. By winter, basques had dropped to wrist- and even knuckle-length; but high fashion was always tending away from the classic approach and towards a long, straight, often low-belted and sometimes bloused jacket with a tunic look to it—a feeling that was repeated in straight, fractional-length, low-belted coats worn over straight, matching dresses. If there was a retrospective influence at work it was that of the slack, soft, transition period that preceded the true low waist of the middle '20s.

Balenciaga, too, had shown signs of a longer jacket line, while Balmain was sponsoring a frankly long (wrist-knuckle) classic jacket with softly tailored classic revers. This gave rise in the autumn of 1959 to a wide choice of suit styling, but the general tendency was towards longer basques, low belting and, in some cases, a casual, indirect approach to classic treatments. The three-quarter sleeve was still the generally accepted length but a new "bracelet" length was noticed. Shoulders had tended to widen throughout the period, but by cut and effect, not by build-out. Since the spring the standaway neckline for daytime had shown some signs of waning and by winter most collars on suit jackets and coats fitted up closely to the sides of the throat. Important fur collars appeared on suit and ensemble jackets.

Coats still favoured the easy, straight line. They were often informally belted and armholes remained widely comfortable. Fractional-length tunic-type coats were favoured towards the end of the year. Collars were softly treated and generous—versions of the shawl collar designed to give an impression of shoulder width. Macfarlanes and other types of cape-coats showed up for winter, as did some softly fitted coats of the redingote type—a possible pointer to future styles. Following the 1958 lead by Balenciaga and Givenchy there was a general feeling for reversible coats. For formal late afternoon and evening the tent-shaped coat in plain or printed silk continued its popularity. Early in the year, and indeed into summer, fabrics had been highly textured following the mood launched in the previous autumn. But already there were signs of a return to more classic patterns (twills and surahs were favoured for shirtwaists) and by autumn there was a marked tendency towards more controlled surfaces. " Soft but not shaggy " was the keynote. Plaids and checks were to the fore. The return to more classic tailoring had brought with it also a feeling for more tightly woven woollens and worsteds. Double-faced patterns destined for reversible coats were prominent. In silks a marked trend towards rich, full and soft-handle classics had succeeded the " rustic " and slubbed patterns of the preceding 12 months. Failles, crêpes, taffetas, plain and warp-printed satins were all favoured for formal winter wear. Brocades, brochés, lamés and cut-velvet satins brought richness and glamour to the evening scene.

The beige ranges (with some greys) had been popular for the winter of 1958-59 (also the mauve to violet ranges); but the autumn of 1959 saw a darkening of the beige ranges to deeper spice and tortoise-shell shades, and brown had become extremely important for evening as well as day. Slate-grey, violet, maroon, bronze, olive, the fuchsia mixtures, black and white mixtures and a bright red also stood out. Round-the-clock black had swung back into fashion.

The newest trend to emerge in evening styles was the ankle-length dress and the suit: slim, ankle- or floor-length sheath, often belted, with its own matching jacket. The short, belted or unbelted sheath or chemise dress, or a princess version of the same style, was by autumn replacing the *bouffant* style.

Buttons played an important part in fashion throughout the year, in the latter part becoming extremely large but sparingly used. Pearl, braiding, jewels and embossed metals were favourite materials. Shoes still favoured the arrow-pointed toe, low uppers and high or medium heels. Gay or extremely light colours remained in vogue throughout the spring and summer. Since the advent of the hatless craze

(which continued unabated in 1959) the tendency to replace the buying of hats by the buying of pretty but fragile, short-lived shoes had been accentuated. Highly popular throughout the year was the coarse-knit mohair pullover or cardigan, usually in pastel colours. Full-length hand-knit coats were also much in demand.

Hair-styles—apart from the " Brigitte Bardot mane " favoured by teenagers—tended to stream-line sophistication with a feeling, as the year advanced, to narrow height given by a chignon known as the " bomb ". Millinery was conditioned by this style: chignon-covering toques, deep cloches, forward-tilted pillboxes, tambourine shapes, etc. The fashion for wigs and switches continued and ready-to-wear models (often in nylon) appeared in the stores.

In the drip-dry, minimum-iron field of dress fabrics 1959 saw the blending of Terylene and cotton, a mixture for which non-iron properties were claimed. Printed Terylene also came on the market for the first time.

Men's Fashion. The flare line silhouette for men, introduced in 1958, continued to influence styling in Savile row in 1959, but it was considerably modified. The rather longer jackets of town suits accentuated the waistline, and the higher single-button fastening contributed to the longer look. Slender lapels and narrow sleeves were a feature of most jackets. Trousers, too, were cut narrow with a slight flare at the bottoms. Fronts generally were unpleated at the waist. A tendency in three-piece suits to relate the waistcoat material to that of the jacket and trousers, rather than have an exact match, provided a touch of novelty. An example was jacket and trousers in a grey hairline pattern with red block stripes running through, worn with a waistcoat in which the red was omitted and the hairlines ran horizontally instead of in the more usual perpendicular formation. In another outfit the plain grey of the waistcoat matched that in the grey and blue striped material used for the jacket and trousers. Double-breasted waistcoats with bold lapels were styled with single-breasted jackets and often featured six buttons on either side, placed in pairs, as opposed to the more usual three-a-side.

In cloths, stripes of various type were favoured to give

(*Left*) " *Coup d'essai* ", a black and red woollen afternoon dress with a black matching collarless coat shown in the autumn and winter collection of Dior of Paris. (*Centre*) A model displays the deep pleated cape collar which was the feature of a black pure wool cocktail dress, entitled " *Merry Widow* ", from the autumn and winter collection of Marcus of London. (*Right*) Shown by Norman Hartnell in August, this three-tiered dress and coat of tobacco brown satin faced with mohair, worn with a scarf and hat of natural blue fox, marked a trend away from the more highly textured fabrics which had been launched during the previous autumn.

suits a two-tone effect. Copper bronze, for example, was teamed with black. The former shade was also favoured for country or week-end suits. One informal ensemble was designed with a bronze striped cheviot cloth for jacket and trousers and a waistcoat of bronze-shade worsted gaberdine. The jacket was flared and the slanted, flapped side pockets were placed low. The generally more colourful appearance of country suits, which separated them sharply from those designed for town, was part of a concerted effort on the part of the tailors to stop the drift to suits which could be worn both in town and at week-ends. The Men's Fashion council's latest attempt to bring colour into evening wear was a dinner jacket in russet grey with maroon spots, lined with red satin. Collar and lapels were faced with black satin. (*See also* BUSINESS REVIEW: *Clothing Industry*.)   (P. H.; R. J. MY.)

FATS: *see* VEGETABLE OILS AND ANIMAL FATS.

FERTILIZERS. The rate of increase in world consumption of fertilizers showed no sign of falling off in 1958-59, increases of 7% for nitrogen (N), 3% for phosphoric acid (P_2O_5) and 6% for potash (K_2O) being forecast, compared with 1957-58.

TABLE I. ESTIMATED WORLD CONSUMPTION OF FERTILIZERS*
(in '000 metric tons of plant food)

	1957-58			1958-59		
	N	P_2O_5	K_2O	N	P_2O_5	K_2O
WORLD	7,257	8,099	6,749	7,766	8,343	7,139
Europe	3,293	4,175	4,221	3,474	4,322	4,369
North and Central America	2,272	2,259	1,764	2,482	2,283	1,974
South America	132	159	91	133	159	91
Asia	1,267	557	552	1,374	591	574
Africa	254	305	73	262	322	82
Oceania	39	644	48	41	666	49

* Excluding U.S.S.R., China and People's Democratic Republic of Korea. The figures do not include ground mineral phosphate applied directly to the land, amounting to about 500,000 metric tons, nearly all of which was used in Europe and North America.
SOURCE. F.A.O. *Annual Review of World Production and Consumption of Fertilizers, 1958.*

Erection of new fertilizer plants and enlargement of existing ones were reported from many countries and it seemed likely that for several years to come increased demands would be more than adequately covered by increased production. Europe and North America together produced and consumed between 80% and 90% of the total world supplies of fertilizers. Urea, a soluble nitrogenous compound (46% N), which is used as such and in the manufacture of concentrated and liquid fertilizers, was produced in greater quantity and many countries reported plans for extending their manufacturing capacity. Consumption of urea in 1958-59 amounted to 312,000 metric tons of nitrogen, almost 5% of the world's fertilizer nitrogen.

In the United Kingdom, consumption of all three types of fertilizer increased, especially nitrogen (10%) and potash (7%). There was a small increase (about 1%) in the use of phosphatic fertilizers, in contrast with the recent tendency to decline.

TABLE II. CONSUMPTION OF FERTILIZERS IN THE UNITED KINGDOM
(in tons of plant food)

	N	P_2O_5	K_2O
1939-40	77,100	195,500	85,000
1945-46	164,600	358,700	123,000
1956-57	302,000	369,600	337,500
1957-58	309,800	365,800	348,100
1958-59	340,300	369,700	375,400

SOURCE. Ministry of Agriculture estimates.

The subsidy paid to farmers on fertilizer purchases was expected to amount to about £28 million for 1958-59, an increase of about £3 million on 1957-58. Small reductions in the prices of some home-produced nitrogenous fertilizers were announced in July. Otherwise, fertilizer prices altered little. No change was made in the method of fertilizer subsidy payments, but the contribution per ton on sulphate of ammonia went up by 1s. 6d. as the guaranteed nitrogen content was raised from 20·8% to 21·0%.

TABLE III. FERTILIZER PRICES IN THE UNITED KINGDOM

	July 1958		July 1959	
	Price[1]	Subsidy	Price[1]	Subsidy
	£ s. d.	£ s. d.	£ s. d.	£ s. d.
Nitrate of soda[2]	28 0 0	7 12 0	26 10 0	7 12 0
Sulphate of ammonia[3]	20 8 0	9 18 0	20 0 6	9 19 6
Nitro-chalk[4]	18 10 0	7 7 6	24 0 0	9 19 6
Nitra-shell[5]	24 8 6	9 14 9	26 5 0	10 18 6
Muriate of potash[6]	19 5 0	none	19 13 0	none
Sulphate of potash[7]	19 17 0	none	20 5 0	none
Kaynitro[8]	—	—	26 17 6	7 12 0
Basic slag[9]	7 10 0	3 6 0	7 10 0	3 6 0
Superphosphate[10]	14 8 6	6 15 0	14 8 6	6 15 0
Ground mineral phosphate[11]	11 17 0	5 16 0	11 17 0	5 16 0
Compound[12]	30 5 0	10 3 4	30 7 6	10 3 4

[1] Price per ton for six-ton lots, before subsidy. [2] 16% N. [3] 20·6% N in 1958, 21% N in 1959. [4] 15·5% N in 1958, 21% N in 1959. [5] 20·5% N in 1958, 23% N in 1959. [6] 60% K_2O. [7] 48% K_2O in 1958, 50% K_2O in 1959. [8] 16% N, 16% K_2O. [9] 15% P_2O_5. [10] 18% P_2O_5. [11] 29% P_2O_5. [12] 12% N, 12% P_2O_5, 18% K_2O.
SOURCE. *Farmer and Stock Breeder*, Aug. 11, 1959.

A richer grade of Nitro-chalk (21% N) was introduced and the nitrogen content of Nitra-shell was raised to 23%. These two fertilizers are formulated from ammonium nitrate and chalk or limestone. A modification which was marketed was Magnesium Nitra-shell (20·5% N, 7% Mg O). This product made from dolomitic limestone, provided, in addition to nitrogen, a slow-acting source of magnesium, which is an essential plant food. A new compound fertilizer, Kaynitro (16% N, 16% K_2O), which incorporated ammonium nitrate, ammonium sulphate and muriate of potash, was also introduced. It is of value where phosphate is not needed, as where basic slag is extensively used. Compound fertilizers supplying all three major plant foods were used more widely and more concentrated types were available as ammonium nitrate (35% N) in part superseded ammonium sulphate (21% N).

Two new nitrogen fixing plants were completed in the United Kingdom, one of Shell Chemicals on the Thames estuary and the other of Imperial Chemical Industries at Billingham. Employing partial oxidation of petroleum fractions to provide the hydrogen required for ammonia synthesis, they were the first of their kind in the country. Together they were designed to fix some 110,000 tons of atmospheric nitrogen per annum, equivalent to one-third of the nitrogenous fertilizers currently used in the United Kingdom. In Scotland, bulk delivery of granular fertilizers for direct application was introduced by Scottish Agricultural Industries and proved very economical in time, labour and cost.

O.E.E.C. examined the use/efficiency pattern of fertilizers in the farming economy of participating countries (*Economic Optimum Fertilizer Use*, 1959) and made estimates of the optimum dressings required for a series of crops. The figures suggested that the fertilizers used in the United Kingdom in 1956-57 represented only 51% of the optimum for nitrogen, 80% for phosphoric acid and 56% for potash. Even in countries where fertilizer use was high there appeared to be considerable scope for an increase in the application of nitrogen.   (M. S. SH.)

FESTIVALS. The number of festivals continued to grow throughout Europe in 1959. New festivals were established in Norway, Sweden and Portugal and local festivals were organized in many provincial towns, particularly in England, France, Germany and Italy.

The tercentenary of the birth of Purcell and the bicentenary of the death of Handel were commemorated by a Purcell-Handel festival in London at which many of their neglected works were revived, including the operas *Rodelinda, Semele* and *Samson* of Handel and Purcell's *The Tempest*. Other operas of Handel were given at festivals at his birthplace at Halle, at Munich, Helsinki and Perugia, and at the Florence festival which also gave Purcell's *Dido and Aeneas*. The 150th anniversary of Haydn's death brought performances of

Lady Barbirolli (centre) playing in an overture for vacuum cleaners at the Society for the Enjoyment of Music's festival at Buxton in May.

his opera *Il Mondo della Luna* at the Holland festival and also at Salzburg and Aix-en-Provence. Orchestral and choral works of Haydn were given at the Vienna festival.

At the festivals of international standing Salzburg gave, in addition to operas of Mozart and Richard Strauss, first performances of Heimo Erbse's *Julietta* and Fritz Hochwälder's mystery play, *Donnerstag*. Venice, at its 22nd festival of contemporary music, gave three one-act operas by Gino Negri, Luciano Berio and Alberto Bruni Tedeschi, and at Edinburgh there were performances by the Stockholm Opera of K. B. Blomdahl's *Aniara* and Alban Berg's *Wozzeck*. New productions were given of Wagner's *Der Fliegende Holländer* at Bayreuth, of Strauss's *Ariadne auf Naxos* at Munich and of Strauss's *Der Rosenkavalier* and Beethoven's *Fidelio* at Glyndebourne. At Bonn, Beethoven's birthplace, the new Beethoven concert hall was inaugurated with performances of the nine symphonies by Volker Wagenheim, Joseph Keilberth and Georg Szell. At the Holland festival Otto Klemperer conducted Wagner's *Tristan und Isolde* with Martha Mödl and Ramon Vinay. At the second Vancouver festival Herbert von Karajan and Bruno Walter conducted works of Beethoven and Mozart, and the soloists included Elisabeth Schwarzkopf and Kerstin Meyer. At the Stratford (Ontario) festival in Canada Offenbach's *Orpheus in the Underworld* was given with Martial Singher and Irene Jordan.

Programmes of several festivals were the creation of a single personality, notably the Yehudi Menuhin festival at Gstaad in Switzerland. At the Pablo Casals festival at Prades, France, chamber works of Bach, Mozart and Beethoven were given, and in Casals' honour a concert was arranged of the works of Monteverdi. At the Festival of Two Worlds at Spoleto, Italy, organized by Gian Carlo Menotti, Donizetti's opera *Il Duca d'Alba* was revived and the modern opera was Sergei Prokofiev's *Angel of Fire*. Three one-act plays by Jack Dunphy, William Inge and Tennessee Williams were given at this festival which also included sketches by W. H. Auden, Tennessee Williams and Jean Cocteau and a Shakespeare recital by Sir John Gielgud. At the festival organized by Benjamin Britten at Aldeburgh, Suffolk, Britten's *The Rape of Lucretia* and Dylan Thomas's *Under Milkwood* were given and unknown catches and rounds by Purcell, the sophisticated texts of which had precluded their performance in modern times, were sung by the English Opera group.

New works by Pierre Boulez and others were heard at the annual festival, given in 1959 in Rome, of the International Society for Contemporary Music. At the third Warsaw festival of contemporary music new works were given by Luigi Nono, Pierre Boulez, Witold Szalonke, Henryk Górecki and others. Berlin brought first performances of works by H. F. Hartig, G. Klebe and V. Vlogel, and festivals of contemporary music were also held at Cheltenham and Darmstadt.

At Bordeaux a programme of orchestral music was given to commemorate the 30th anniversary of the death of Sergei Diaghilev, and an art exhibition was held to illustrate the discovery of light by artists ranging from the primitives to the Impressionists. At Bergen in Norway, Kurt Weill's *Die Dreigroschenoper* was given and also Strindberg's *The Dance of Death* and Ibsen's *Ghosts*. Athens gave orchestral concerts and ballets, and staged tragedies by Aeschylus, Euripides and Aristophanes with music by contemporary Greek composers. At the Monaco festival concerts by the orchestra of the Paris Opéra were given at the palace of Prince Rainier. At Granada recitals by Andrés Segovia, Victoria de los Angeles and others were heard in the palace of Charles V, and ballets were given in the gardens of the Generalife. A cycle of orchestral works by Sibelius was given at the Helsinki festival at which Hugo von Hofmannsthal's *Jedermann* was heard with Sibelius's incidental music. At Perugia Léonide Massine provided the choreography for a sacred spectacle, *Laudes Envagelii*, by V. Bucchi, in the church of S. Agostino, and concerts by the Vienna chamber choir and the orchestra of the Polish radio were given at the Palazzo dei Priori. (*See* also MUSIC.) (E. L.)

FIELD SPORTS. *Hunting.* Of the shire packs the Cottesmore started well and finished brilliantly, the hounds killing an average number of foxes. Sport with the Pytchley was above average, despite interruption by the snow, ice and fog experienced throughout Britain during the winter of 1958-59. The Quorn, in contrast, had a disappointing season, the more regretted since it was the last for George Barker, huntsman since 1929. Fog marred the first part of the season and scent throughout was poor. The Duke of Beaufort's enjoyed sport above the average before Christmas, then came the hard weather, followed by poorer scent. In the north, the Middleton and Middleton East had their best season since the war, including a 12-mi. point from Howsham, Yorkshire; in the south and west, the Portman had consistently good sport, the Berkeley had an open season and the Heythrop killed well over 100 brace. In Wales, Sir Watkin Williams

The Brighton and Storrington foot beagles out on Oct. 14 at Wolstonbury hill, near Brighton, with their master, Sir F. Samuelson.

Wynn's enjoyed consistently good sport after a moderate start when scent was poor on wet ground.

Of the harehunting packs the Newcastle and District maintained a good average with some outstanding days and the Old Berkeley had a memorable three-mi. point when hounds killed their hare in 60 min. The otterhunting season in the south was spoilt by lack of water, but towards the end some good hunts were recorded.

Shooting. No year since World War II, and few in living memory, proved more favourable than 1959 for the breeding of game birds. In mid-June keepers on grouse moors, partridge manors and pheasant shoots all reported that the weather had been ideal and signs of disease rare. When shooting began pheasants were plentiful, partridges more numerous than for many years, but grouse proved unexpectedly disappointing. What birds there were had grown well and were healthy, but numbers were few where heavy stocks had been reported. The re-appearance of grouse late in the season on moors earlier found to be almost empty led to suggestions that the prolonged hot weather had caused a movement to high ground. Conservation schemes, and insistence on the proper sporting code, both instigated by the Wildfowlers' Association of Great Britain and Ireland, led to better duck-shooting. Concern was again felt for the future status of wild geese, most of which breed in Arctic Russia.

Fishing. The year 1959 will be remembered because of the frustrations it brought to fishermen all over the country. The continuous drought and consequently lower and staler rivers produced a disappointing and, at times, disastrous season. Some smaller streams and spawning redds dried up and many salmon parr died; main rivers were often reduced to comparative trickles. Early-run salmon, which travelled well upstream, became trapped in warm, de-oxygenated pools and later fish remained in the estuaries—easy catches for the nets. Fishing virtually ceased by midsummer. Even the sea-trout were at times reluctant to run, although conditions for night fishing for them were often ideal.

Disease and severe pollution were less than expected, but no doubt was left of the dangers inherent in increased water abstraction and drainage. Trout fishermen fared better than the salmon fishers and the chalk streams, benefiting from the rains of 1958, remained in fairly good order, though lower than normal. The handicap lay more in the bright hot sun, cloudless skies and clear water. Except at evening rise it was nymph rather than dry-fly which was successful for those who could use it. On the rain-fed streams of the north and west conditions, and often sport, matched those on the salmon rivers, although there was usually the advantage of a rise to

fly. Fishing on the trout lakes varied and at least two used as reservoirs—Ladybower (Derbyshire) and Vyrnwy (Montgomeryshire)—dried out. (*See also* ANGLING.)   (W. Ss.)

FIJI. British colony, *c.* 322 islands (*c.* 106 inhabited) in the Pacific, *c.* 1,100 mi. N. of Auckland, New Zealand. Total area: 7,055 sq.mi., incl. main islands Viti Levu (4,011 sq.mi.) and Vanua Levu (2,137 sq.mi.), and Rotuma dependency (18 sq.mi.), *c.* 400 mi. to N. of Viti Levu. Pop.: (1956 census) 345,737, incl. Fijians 148,134, Rotumans 4,422, other Pacific islanders 5,320, Indians 169,403, Europeans 6,402, part-Europeans 7,810, Chinese and part-Chinese 4,155, others 91; (1958 est.) 374,284. Religion (1956 census): Fijians, 86% Methodist, 12% Roman Catholic; Indians, 81% Hindu, 15% Moslem. Capital: Suva, on Viti Levu, pop. (1956 census) 37,371. Administration: governor; executive council; legislative council with unofficial minority variously elected and nominated. Governor, Sir Kenneth Maddocks. Main imports: cereal products, fish and other foodstuffs, cotton fabrics and apparel, mineral fuels and petroleum products, iron and steel, machinery and vehicles. Main domestic exports: sugar, gold, manganese, coconut products, bananas. Monetary unit: Fijian pound (£F111 =£100 sterling).

The governor of Fiji is also governor of Pitcairn *ex officio*, and is responsible for the general exercise of British protection of Tonga (*q.v.*).

Pitcairn. British colony by settlement, situated in Pacific ocean midway between New Zealand and South America. Area: 2 sq.mi. Pop. (1959 est.) 131 Anglo-Polynesians descended from " Bounty " mutineers. Dependencies: uninhabited islands of Oeno, Henderson, and Ducie (total area 17 sq.mi.). Religion: Seventh-Day Adventist. Administration: chief magistrate, executive committee and island council, all popularly elected annually. Chief magistrate: John Christian. Monetary unit: Fijian pound.

History. During July-Sept. 1959 a commission of inquiry, headed by Sir Alan Burns, collected data in Fiji with the object of recommending a course for the colony's future economic development. It was expected that the commission's report would be published early in 1960.

In June the governor made public the findings and proposals of Professor O. H. K. Spate concerning the economic circumstances of the Fijians. One of the main points of the Spate report was that conservative chiefs, entrenched in power by the government, had inhibited individual enterprise, while failing to adapt the Fijian communal system to meet modern economic needs.

Rioting occurred on Dec. 9 in Suva when police banned an address by a leader of a trade union which had called a strike of oil workers. Some damage was done and a dusk-to-dawn curfew was imposed.

The outstanding feature of the year's development programme was the emphasis given to tourism and transport. Runways to accommodate jet airliners were completed at Nadi airfield, a two-year wharf-construction project was begun at Lautoka and legislation was enacted to promote the expansion of the hotel industry.   (R. P. GN.)

See O. H. K. Spate, *The Fijian People: Economic Problems and Prospects* (Suva, 1959).

The governor of Fiji, Sir Kenneth Maddocks, and Lady Maddocks are borne ashore on Lakemba, an outlying island of the Tongan group, which they visited in May. Later, at Nuku'alofa, the Tongan capital, the 1958 treaty of friendship between Britain and Tonga was ratified.

FINLAND. Republic of northeastern Europe bounded N. by Norway, E. by the U.S.S.R., S. by the Gulf of Finland and W. by the Gulf of Bothnia and Sweden. Area: 130,119 sq.mi., including Ahvenanmaa or Åland Islands (581 sq.mi.) and inland waters (12,189 sq.mi.). Pop.: (1950 census) 4,043,538; (1959 est.) 4,412,631. Language (1950): Finnish 91·26%; Swedish 8·55%; Lappish and other 0·19%. Religion: Lutheran 96%; Orthodox 1·8%. Chief towns (pop., 1950 census): Helsinki (Helsingfors, cap.) 369,380; Turku (Åbo) 101,824; Tampere (Tammerfors) 101,143. President, Urho Kaleva Kekkonen. Prime ministers in 1959: Karl August Fagerholm, and (from Jan. 13) Väinö Johannes Sukselainen. Main imports: machinery and vehicles; textiles, iron, steel and manufactures; coal, petroleum and products. Main exports: wood and manufactures, wood pulp, paper and products. Monetary unit: *markka* (F.Mk.896·00 = £1 sterling).

History. At the beginning of 1959 relations between Finland and the U.S.S.R. were clouded, and Finland was without a government. The previous prime minister, the Social-Democrat Karl August Fagerholm, had resigned early in December, partly as a result of Soviet disapproval; the subsequent crisis lasted 40 days. The skies lightened a little in mid-January, when the Agrarian V. J. Sukselainen formed a minority government, consisting of members of his own party, with Ralf Törngren as minister for foreign affairs. Törngren, although a member of the Swedish Party, entered the government as a " professional minister ". Sukselainen's government commanded only 48 of the 200 votes in parliament.

The outlook improved considerably when, later in January, President Kekkonen returned from a visit to Leningrad with N. S. Khrushchev's assurances of peaceful co-operation with Finland. These assurances, nevertheless, seemed to be offered only to an Agrarian-ruled Finland, for in May, Khrushchev, in an interview published in *Pravda*, once again accused the Social-Democratic leaders, and in particular the veteran Väinö Tanner (who had, in 1946, been imprisoned as a " war criminal " at Soviet instigation) of working against good relations with the Soviet Union.

When Sukselainen took office, it had been assumed that an attempt would eventually be made to broaden the base of the government, experience having shown that political stability could best be assured by an Agrarian-Social Democratic coalition. But the Soviet attitude discouraged such an attempt.

In external trade relations, too, the Finns felt the U.S.S.R. looking over their shoulders. Finland was able to participate freely and fully in the discussions preparatory to the formation of a Nordic Customs union. But when this plan was dropped, the question of joining the " outer seven " raised difficult problems. On the one hand, Finland feared, if it remained outside the " seven ", a loss to Sweden and Norway of some trade with the west; on the other hand, reports of the possibility of Finland joining the " seven " met with immediate disapproval in the Soviet press.

On Oct. 22-28, Helsinki received a visit from A. I. Mikoyan, the Soviet deputy prime minister, who came with the foreign trade minister, N. S. Patolichev, to open the Soviet industrial fair and to be present at the signing of the Russo-Finnish trade agreement for 1961-65. Mikoyan spoke obliquely against economic groupings, but refused to comment when asked for his views on the possibility of Finland joining the " outer seven ". The Finnish government decided to investigate the possibility of securing some of the rights of the " seven ", without joining the group as a full member.

According to the provisions of the new five-year agreement, signed on Oct. 23, trade between Finland and the Soviet Union would remain in the years 1961-65 at about the same level as during the years 1956-60, reaching a total turnover of Rb.6,120 million. In the period 1956-58, 17% to 19% of Finland's exports went to the U.S.S.R., while 14% to 18% of its imports came from the U.S.S.R. The Soviet Union again undertook to balance the difference between exports and imports by paying Finland Rb.40 million a year in transferable currency. (W. HL.)

FIRE SERVICE. At the end of 1958 local authority fire brigades in England and Wales contained 19,932 whole-time and 14,154 part-time men (including whole-time men who had undertaken retained obligations) and about 600 women. In Scotland the whole-time personnel of the 11 brigades consisted of 1,998 men and 87 women. In addition there were 2,595 part-time men. Thus the increased recruitment for fire brigades continued and showed no sign of abating during 1959.

During 1958, fire brigades in England and Wales attended approximately 90,380 fires (excluding chimney fires) and helped in the rescue of some 280 persons from dangerous situations. In the course of their duties 3 firemen were killed and 280 injured. During the same period fire brigades in Scotland attended 10,223 fires and rescued 34 persons. One fireman died on the way to a fire and one during firefighting operations. One fireman was seriously injured.

In March 1959, a fire at a department store and shops at Ilford was estimated to have resulted in a loss of more than

At the height of the extensive fire at Ilford on the night of March 16-17, when a block more than 100 yards square was burnt out.

£1 million. The fire causing the largest financial loss of the year occurred in May, 1959, at a Leicestershire firm of engineers. Damage was estimated at £3 million.

The Fire Services act, 1959, received the royal assent on July 9, 1959. This act embodies the result of a review of central controls over the fire service which was instituted as a result of the passage of the Local Government act, 1959 (which substituted, in respect of fire services and other services operated by local authorities, the payment by the Exchequer of a general grant, fixed in advance, for the payment of a 25% grant on actual expenditure). In general, the purpose of the 1959 act is to give fire authorities a greater measure of freedom while at the same time retaining in the hands of the secretary of state the " key " controls considered essential for the maintenance of efficiency. The act also contains some provisions regarding pensions. The Factories act, 1959, is also of special interest as it provides for the transfer to fire authorities of responsibility for the certification of means of escape from fire in factories. It also makes provision for the inspection of factories by an officer of a fire brigade, at the request of one of H.M. inspectors of factories. (K. A. L. P.)

FISHERIES. World Production. The world catch of fish, crustaceans and molluscs in 1958 increased by about 9% over the preceeding year. The total, as estimated by the Food and Agriculture organization (F.A.O.) of the United Nations, was 33,720,000 tons live weight, over 3 million tons more than 1957 and almost 13 million tons above the corresponding estimates for the years 1938 and 1948, just before and after World War II. As the table shows, 21% of the total was composed of herrings, sardines, anchovies, and other clupeids; over 13% were cods, hakes and haddocks; and 16% were freshwater fishes (more than double the weight caught before World War II). In all these groups, and others, catches were by 1958 well above the 1938 level, but this was still not the case for salmons, trouts, smelts, and other salmonids which formed a valuable, though not a quantitatively important group.

Asians contributed 50% of the world total; European fishermen (excluding those from the U.S.S.R.) more than 22%; and North Americans about 10%. The U.S.S.R. reported catches amounting to over 8% of the total. Africa, where some spectacular developments took place, contributed some 5%. The great bulk of the catches was still made and landed in the northern temperate zone. Seven countries each caught more than 1 million tons in 1958 and accounted for nearly 60% of the world total. Japan had by far the greatest sea fish catch, nearly 5·5 million tons in 1958, a goal which had been previously set for 1960. The United States, the Chinese People's Republic and the U.S.S.R. each caught between 2 and 3 million tons of sea fish in 1958, while Canada, Norway, the United Kingdom and India each produced about 1 million tons. Korea, one of the great pre-war producers with a catch of 1·8 million tons in 1938, produced less than 500,000 tons. Thirty-two countries had catches between 100,000 and 1,000,000 tons each—in the aggregate 31% of the world total. The remaining catch (about 9%) was contri-

(million metric tons, live weight)

	1938	1948	1955	1956	1957	1958*
WORLD GRAND TOTAL .	20·47	19·09	28·20	29·79	30·60	33·72
By groups of species						
Freshwater fishes . .	2·30	1·79	2·97	3·03	3·51	5·28
Salmons, trouts, smelts, etc. .	0·85	0·47	0·71	0·72	0·71	0·70
Flounders, halibuts, soles, etc. .	0·33	0·48	0·60	0·66	0·66	0·76
Cods, hakes, haddocks, etc. .	3·20	3·50	4·67	4·92	4·47	4·33
Herrings, sardines, anchovies, etc. .	5·34	4·81	6·41	7·02	7·23	7·10
Tunas, bonitos, mackerels, etc. .	0·92	0·93	1·54	1·71	1·83	1·96
Mullets, jacks, sea-basses, etc. .	0·86	1·13	2·86	2·99	3·20	3·49
Sharks, rays, etc. .	0·23	0·35	0·29	0·31	0·31	0·32
Unsorted and unidentified fishes	4·26	3·57	5·00	5·21	5·22	6·51
Crustaceans . .	0·49	0·53	0·78	0·83	0·82	0·75
Molluscs . .	1·14	1·28	1·88	1·89	2·04	2·01
Aquatic animals† .	0·06	0·07	0·08	0·08	0·07	0·07
Aquatic plants . .	0·49	0·18	0·41	0·42	0·51	0·44
By regions						
Africa . . .	0·54	0·83	1·69	1·80	1·91	1·93
America, North . .	3·15	3·62	3·89	4·29	3·95	3·90
America, South . .	0·24	0·45	0·80	0·86	1·11	1·38
Asia	9·35	6·49	11·59	12·02	13·30	16·27
Europe . . .	5·55	6·12	7·62	8·08	7·66	7·49
Oceania . . .	0·09	0·09	0·11	0·12	0·13	0·13
U.S.S.R. . . .	1·55	1·49	2·50	2·62	2·54	2·62

* Includes an estimated catch for the Chinese People's Republic of 3 million metric tons of freshwater fishes and 3 million metric tons of unsorted and unidentified fishes, compared with a 1957 catch of 1·18 million metric tons of freshwater fishes and 1·77 million metric tons of unsorted and unidentified fishes. † Not elsewhere specified.
SOURCE. F.A.O. *Yearbook of Fishery Statistics, 1958.*

buted by a very large number of small producers. The Chinese People's Republic appeared to be the leading freshwater fish producer.

In 1958 about half the total catch was marketed in fresh or frozen form. About a quarter of the total was cured; *i.e.*, dried, smoked, salted, marinated or similarly processed; about 14% was used for reduction to fishmeal and oil, 9% was canned and the small remainder used for other purposes.

A comparison with earlier years showed that the proportion of fish marketed fresh remained stable with a continuing increase in that frozen. There was also an increase in salted and dried fish, particularly of herring, sardines and anchovies. The amount of frozen crustaceans and molluscs increased as did the canning of these forms. On the other hand production of fish meal and solubles declined slightly over the previous year mainly due to failure of the herring fishery in the North sea.

In Dec. 1959, the British Trawlers' federation said that financial aid and guarantees would be sought from the British government to meet the expected threat of increased imports of cheap fish from the other members of the European free trade area.

International Law. Disputes over fishing rights between states and the breadth of the territorial sea continued to attract the uneasy attention of the fishing world. The four conventions formulated by the United Nations Conference on the Law of the Sea which was held in the spring of 1958 still awaited the 20 ratifications that would bring them into force. Those directly affecting fisheries: the Convention on Fishing and Conservation of the Living Resources of the High Seas, the Convention on the Continental Shelf (see *Britannica Book of the Year 1959*) and the Convention on the Territorial Sea and the Contiguous Zone had received none as at Oct. 30, 1959. Indeed the whole question of the seaward limits of territorial waters proved to be so contentious and difficult that the United Nations decided to call another conference on this subject to be held in Geneva in the spring of 1960.

The United Kingdom ratified the North East Atlantic Fisheries convention on Aug. 27, 1959, being the first state to do so. This convention is designed to supplement one currently in effect: the Convention on the Regulation of the Meshes of Fishing Nets and the Size Limits of Fish, 1946,

The Fleetwood trawler " Lord Montgomery " is brought into Vestmannaeyjar harbour in April by an Icelandic coastguard crew.

and goes a good deal further to meet the necessity for conservation of the high seas fishery of that area. Such measures included, *inter alia*, closed seasons and areas, and transplantation of organisms. The new convention required ratification of all signatory states before it entered into force, but if by April 1, 1960, not less than seven states had ratified, they might agree among themselves to bring the convention into force. The states concerned were Belgium, Denmark, France, the German Federal Republic, Iceland, the Republic of Ireland, Netherlands, Norway, Poland, Portugal, Spain, Sweden, U.S.S.R. and the United Kingdom.

International Organizations and Commissions. World fisheries continued to be served by many international commissions and treaty bodies. Many of these had as their object the regulation of fish catching in the interest of maximizing continuous yield. Others, such as the International Council for the Exploration of the Sea, the Food and Agriculture organization, the Indo-Pacific Fisheries council, and the General Fisheries Council for the Mediterranean continued to aid the development of scientific knowledge upon which regulation could be based.

Technical aid continued to be given to many countries where fisheries were underdeveloped by the F.A.O. and bilaterally by the United States, Norway and the Colombo plan countries. The countries so helped were mainly in east Asia, Africa, Latin America and the middle east, and included such subjects as surveys of potential fisheries resources, mechanization of fishing boats, processing, marketing and distribution, and studies related to fisheries economics. Africa, with its newly emerging independent territories and states was calling more and more on the services of the United Nations and specialized agencies. The United Nations have established an economic commission for Africa whose headquarters is in Addis Ababa, Ethiopia, and the F.A.O. an African regional office at Accra, Ghana. Much emphasis continued to be placed upon training and education of government administrators and fisheries operatives, as well as on the principles and role of fisheries co-operatives.

Research and Development. The trend towards the use of factory ships, which not only catch fish by improved methods, but which also preserve it by freezing and canning as well as making stock feed out of fish that would otherwise be wasted, continued to increase during the year, especially in the countries of eastern Europe. Fears were expressed as to whether the known fisheries in the high seas could maintain their abundance under this new intensive method of harvesting. This gave rise to the search for new fisheries; *e.g.*, the west coast of Africa, and intensification of biological research, particularly on the population dynamics of exploited fisheries populations. Much of this latter work was conducted co-operatively between nations through existing fisheries treaty bodies and fisheries commissions which laid plans for future work.

In addition to the more productive methods of factory ships, a relatively new method of catching herring by trawls from the bottom of the sea, as opposed to catching them by drift nets or seines on the surface, showed increases. Here again, the attention of fisheries biologists was turned to the effect of this new method of exploitation upon the maintenance of the stock of herring and this was another problem requiring an intensification of international effort. A new method for the study of fish in their natural environment was reported by the U.S.S.R., which was said to be using submarines with specially built observation compartments for this purpose. Japan also produced designs for submarines dependent upon atomic power, intended for fishing purposes.

Attention of fisheries technologists continued to be turned towards the production of flavourless fish flour for use as a

Fishermen from Shizuoka, Japan, struggling to haul aboard their boats part of a large catch of dolphins—a Japanese delicacy.

protein concentrate to blend with other carbohydrate foods. It was used in making bread with consequent protein enrichment and was undeteeted at the level of 10% when used in school lunch programmes. Nutritionists found these flours very useful in raising standards of diets of children, especially in underdeveloped countries.

Inland fisheries claimed a good deal of attention during the year. The fact that these fisheries are subject to ownership made it possible for the owners to reap the rewards of cultivation and husbandry. Much work on inland fisheries management continued to be done by governments and research institutes, in both developed and underdeveloped countries. The initial stages of plans to use water impounded primarily for irrigation purposes also for the purpose of producing fish crops in, for example, the United Arab Republic and Ethiopia, were in the process of development.   (D. B. F.)

FOOD AND AGRICULTURE ORGANIZATION.

This was established on Oct. 16, 1945, with the signing of its constitution at Quebec, as a specialized agency of the United Nations, to promote food production and distribution and raise nutritional standards throughout the world. The organization collects, analyses and disseminates basic information on food, hunger and malnutrition problems, provides direct technical assistance to member governments on request and promotes action towards solving food and agriculture problems. The 77 full members and 9 associate members of F.A.O. at the end of 1959 are given in the table (*see* p. 212).

F.A.O. is governed by a biennial conference, a council of 25 member nations and a staff headed by a director-general. Headquarters, Rome; director-general, Binay Ranjan Sen (India).

Developments in 1959. World food production in 1958-59 reached a record level (4% up on 1957-58) and by mid-1959 food surpluses had increased by 10%, North America holding 80% of the surplus stocks. These growing surpluses, the unfavourable terms of trade for agricultural exporters, the need for adjustments in national agricultural policies and a tendency toward regional arrangements were features of the world commodity situation during the year. An F.A.O. expert panel reported on price support and stabilization measures and suggested 25 guiding principles to mitigate their harmful effects on consumption and to reduce surpluses.

Considerable attention was paid by governments to F.A.O.'s "Freedom From Hunger" campaign. With world population growing—it rose by 1·7% in less-developed areas and by 1·2% in developed areas during the year—there was an urgent need for more and better food, higher agricultural incomes and better distribution of food and purchasing power. Efforts were to be made to educate the public throughout the world on the hunger problem. There were supporting plans for national and international action, such as developing food reserves, creating fertilizer pools and promoting better use of land and the use of better seeds. The campaign would culminate in a World Food congress in 1963.

MEMBER-STATES OF F.A.O., DEC. 31, 1959

Afghanistan	Finland	Lebanon	†Rhodesia and
Argentina	France	Liberia	Nyasaland, Fed. of
Australia	†Gabon	Libya	Saudi Arabia
Austria	*German Fed.	Luxembourg	†Senegal
Belgium	Rep.	†Madagascar	†Somalia
Bolivia	Ghana	Malaya	Spain
Brazil	Greece	Mexico	Sudan
Burma	Guatemala	Morocco	Sweden
Cambodia	*Guinea	Nepal	*Switzerland
Canada	Haiti	Netherlands	Thailand
Ceylon	Honduras	New Zealand	†Togo
†Chad	Iceland	Nicaragua	Tunisia
Chile	India	†Nigeria, Fed. of	Turkey
Colombia	Indonesia	Norway	Un. of S. Afr.
Costa Rica	Iraq	Pakistan	United Arab Rep.
Cuba	Ireland, Rep. of	Panama	United Kingdom
†Cyprus	Israel	Paraguay	United States
Denmark	Italy	Persia	Uruguay
Dominican Rep.	Japan	Peru	Venezuela
Ecuador	Jordan	Philippines	*Vietnam, South
El Salvador	*Korea, South	Poland	Yemen
Ethiopia	Laos	Portugal	Yugoslavia

* Not a member of the United Nations. † Associate member, not a member of the United Nations.

An international training course on radio isotope techniques in agricultural research was jointly organized at Cornell university, United States, and a European seminar on the training of agricultural advisory services on agricultural aspects of environment contamination was held at Cambridge university. The World Seed campaign, aimed at stimulating national efforts for the better use of seed by farmers, was being supported by a number of international, regional and national organizations. The Mediterranean Development project, concerned with arable and grazing lands, forests and irrigation of 18 countries in the region, was expected to lead to national pilot projects. Preparations continued for the 1960 World Census on Agriculture.

The Second World Fishing Boat congress, attended by about 300 participants from 35 countries, was held at F.A.O. headquarters in April 1959. Other developments included an F.A.O.-I.L.O. Technical Meeting on Fishery Co-operatives, a Training Centre in Fisheries Statistics for the Mediterranean, African and middle east regions, an Expert Meeting on Fisheries Statistics in the North Atlantic and the World Scientific Meeting on the Biology of Sardines and Related Species.

Under the Expanded Technical Assistance programme there were over 400 experts at work in 72 countries in mid-1959, with a total of 2,030 completed assignments. Over 220 technical assistance programme fellowships were scheduled for 1959, 1,746 having been awarded since the programme began. A budget of $18,980,050 was approved for 1960-61. In addition the F.A.O. would receive $8,004,686 for carrying out the Expanded Technical Assistance programme in 1960.

Publications during 1959 included: *The State of Food and Agriculture*; Commodity Reports on *Rice, Dairy Products* and *Olive Oil*; *National Grain Policies*; Forestry and Fisheries *Yearbooks*; *World Bibliography of Food and Agriculture Marketing* and *Marketing Guides* on (1) general problems, (2) fruits and vegetables, (3) eggs and poultry.   (F. A. O.)

FOOD RESEARCH: *see* NUTRITION.

FOODSTUFFS. Cocoa.

World cocoa production recovered in 1958-59 to 870,000 tons, the result of large crops in Ghana and Nigeria and some revival in Ivory Coast. Output remained steady in Brazil but fell in the Dominican Republic. Indications were that the west African crop in 1959-60 would show a further increase. Production figures (in '000 long tons) were:

				1956-57	1957-58	1958-59	1959-60 (prelim.)
Ghana	.	.	.	264	207	256	261
Brazil .	.	.	.	158	160	160	170
Nigeria	.	.	.	135	81	140	130
French Africa		.	.	138	118	124	138
Others.	.	.	.	185	184	190	201
Total	.	.	.	880	750	870	900

SOURCE. Messrs. Gill and Duffus *et al.*

As a contribution to the second development plan Ghana producers accepted a reduction for five years in the producer price from £134 8s. 0d. a ton to £112, starting with the 1959 mid-crop. In Nigeria the price in the Western Region (the most important producing area) remained at £150 a ton in 1958-59, but was increased to £160 in 1959-60. Trade in cocoa beans showed some recovery in 1959. Among Commonwealth countries shipments from Ghana during Jan.-Sept., at 201,000 tons, were one-third greater than a year earlier, while those from Nigeria more than doubled during Jan.-June. Elsewhere, consignments from Brazil during January-June, at 32,000 tons, were one-fifth more than a year earlier while Ivory Coast shipments showed a marked increase. Imports into the United States during Jan.-Sept. totalled 160,000 tons, against 198,000 tons in the full year 1958, while the United Kingdom took some 76,000 tons during Jan.-Oct., compared with 91,000 tons in the whole of 1958. Market prices for cocoa remained steady during the first half of 1959, at a level below that of 1958 (the price of Ghana cocoa in June at 37 cents a lb. in New York and 298s. a cwt. in London was some 25% lower), but some decline became subsequently apparent with the reports of large new crops. World consumption in 1959 was believed to have shown some recovery, although not to the record level reached in 1957.   (E. O. G.)

Coffee. World coffee production in 1958-59 was estimated at 71 million long cwt., 6 million cwt. more than in 1957-58, while a further increase in 1959-60 to 80 million cwt. was forecast. The expansion was mainly in Brazil, where the plantings made during the time of high prices were maturing, but east Africa also showed an increase. There was a further slight decline in exports of coffee in 1958, but during the first months of 1959 consignments from both Brazil and Colombia were markedly higher than a year earlier. Estimates of output (in million long cwt.) were as follows:

				1957-58	1958-59	1959-60 (prelim.)
Brazil .	.	.	.	29·5	35·4	41·3
Colombia	.	.	.	9·2	9·1	9·4
Other Latin America		.	.	12·3	11·7	13·4
British East Africa		.	.	2·6	2·7	2·9
Other Africa	.	.	.	8·4	9·1	9·6
World total (incl. others)		.	.	64·9	70·9	79·6

SOURCE. U.S. Dept. of Agriculture.

Exports from Latin America rose slightly from 30·8 million cwt. in 1957 to 31·1 million cwt. in 1958. Shipments from Brazil, however, fell from 16·9 million cwt. to 15·2 million cwt. Nearly two-thirds of the Latin American total went to the United States and 30% to Europe (including 10% to the German Federal Republic). Exports from Africa also rose slightly to 10·7 million cwt. Imports from all sources into the United States declined from 24·7 million cwt. in 1957 to 23·8 million cwt. in 1958, while those into continental Europe rose from 15·1 million cwt. to 16·0 million cwt. (of which the European Economic community accounted for 10·4 million cwt.). U.K. imports, which in 1958 had fallen slightly to 870,000 cwt. (63% from east Africa) amounted to 855,000 cwt. during Jan.-Oct., 1959. Latin American countries, which had agreed to limit their exports during 1959, entered into a one-year coffee-marketing agreement with the French Community, Cameroons and Portuguese Africa, fixing a total marketing quota for the year beginning Oct. 1, 1959, at 38·6 million cwt.   (E. O. G.)

Fruit. In 1959 reports from all over the world indicated that orchard fruit production would continue to increase. There were many examples of expansion in citrus-growing, particularly oranges. Orange exports from the western Mediterranean countries were 18%, and from Israel 37%, higher than in 1958. Global apple production was also going to increase in the next decade. After a quarter of a century of decline, the trend in U.S. production was turning upwards. Observers said that both China and the U.S.S.R. were making big strides in technology and that planting-up was on a large scale in both countries.

Exporters of fruit were already alarmed, not so much at the level of prices of fruit, but at the prospect for prices if current trends in the markets continued and became intensified. Many small trade delegations went abroad on goodwill or exploratory visits to importing or potential importing countries. Commonwealth fruit producers met in London and agreed to curtail deliveries of summer apples.

United Kingdom. Some falling off from the record production of 1958 was inevitable, but 1959 crops were surprisingly good, and the exceptionally fine summer was not wholly responsible for this. Production of dessert apples and pears was above the total for 1957, being sustained by the crop from young orchards. Features of the year were an excess production of the early apple Worcester Pearmain, a local glut of plums in the Evesham district and the comparative failure of the cherry crop. In some orchards, bulk harvesting—a technique employed in New Zealand of transporting the fruit in large, shallow boxes—was tried out, and there was further progress in the direct supply of retailers from packing stations in the fruit growing areas.

Fruitgrowers expected to be able to share in the grants which would probably be allocated to the horticultural industry as a whole. These would be available for five years and would total £7·5 million. In its first annual report the Horticultural Marketing Advisory council laid stress on the need to minimize wastage in distribution. Its proposals for a permanent council, to be financed by the industry after two years instead of by public funds, did not receive support from all sections of the industry.

Imports of fruit were higher than for many years. More oranges were received—largely from Brazil—and more bananas from the Windward Islands, where production was still expanding, but in addition to these staple items there were much larger deliveries of melons and peaches. In the second half of the year slightly more generous quotas for many items from dollar areas came into operation. The new (with the old) limits were: canned fruit other than citrus, apple and pineapple £3·2 million (£2·2 million); fresh citrus, £1,150,000 (£1,050,000); dried fruit, £3·2 million (£2·75 million). Import totals (to Aug. 31) were above those of 1958. Citrus imports increased by 20% to 365,000 tons (sweet oranges, 290,000; grapefruit 34,000). Bananas increased by 11% to 230,000 tons and apples by 6% to 180,000 tons. More grapefruit and apples of U.S. origin were received.

British Commonwealth. Tree fruit crops in Canada were lighter than in the previous year. Official estimates were (in million bu.): apples, 15·4; peaches, 2·5; pears, 1·2; plums and prunes, 0·57. Apple production was low in British Columbia but high in Nova Scotia. South Africa's citrus exports to the United Kingdom were relatively high, and early in the season some citrus was sent to Canada to make good the lack of supplies from Florida. Markets other than the United Kingdom tended to become more important. There was a further rise in the freight rate to the United Kingdom for citrus, but that for deciduous fruit was reduced. Refrigerated storage was a feature of deciduous growers' plans for progress. In Australia new-type faster packing machinery was introduced, and shipments of apples were made in half-ton bulk bins, which effectively reduced the amount of bruising previously experienced. Deliveries to the United Kingdom totalled 3·6 million cases—as many as in 1958, but less than the amount originally intended. In New Zealand an apple crop of 3·7 million bu. was harvested—half of it from the Nelson district. Apples were sent to the United Kingdom, France and the western areas of the United States. Some did not keep well, and prices were occasionally uneconomic.

United States. The estimated production of the nine most important tree fruits totalled 15·8 million tons—below the 1958 level, but higher than the recent average. Although 1959 was a late season, conditions in the western states were favourable, and there was an abundant harvest of deciduous fruit in California. There was also a general recovery in citrus yields and a mild resurgence in apple yields.

The rate of expansion in citrus production in Florida was slowing down, but it was still the source of two-thirds of supplies. In 1959, the crop of early and mid-season varieties was no better than in 1958, but the late (Valencia) crop was 14% higher. Citrus production in California returned to normal, but prolonged dry weather accentuated the small-fruit problem with which many growers were faced. (R. R. W. F.)

TABLE I. ESTIMATED GROSS PRODUCTION OF TOP FRUIT, ENGLAND AND WALES, 1958 AND 1959 ('000 imperial tons)

	1958	1959		1958	1959
Dessert apples .	276	248	Plums .	71	97
Culinary apples	339	258	Cherries	34	15
Cider apples .	79	56		—	—
Table pears .	82	65	Total .	881	739

SOURCE. Ministry of Agriculture, Fisheries and Food.

TABLE II. ESTIMATED COMMERCIAL PRODUCTION OF TOP FRUIT, UNITED STATES, 1958 AND 1959 ('000 short tons)

	1958	1959		1958	1959
Apples .	2,491	2,374	Oranges* .	4,414	5,619
Pears .	648	769	Grapefruit* .	1,427	1,704
Peaches .	1,360	1,452	Lemons and limes*	640	682
Plums (fresh) .	67	108	Cherries (all) .	186	219
Grapes (all) .	2,996	3,129			
			Total .	14,229	16,056

* Crop from bloom set in 1958.
SOURCE. U.S. Dept. of Agriculture.

Meat. Greatly increased supplies of lamb and mutton, beef hardly keeping pace with demand and towards the end of the year a scarcity of pig supplies—all contributed to lack of balance in types of meat marketed during 1959. Moreover, the long, hot, dry summer brought home-produced meat on to the market earlier than expected, and cut back demand, particularly for stewing meats.

The number of sheep and lambs in England and Wales, at more than 18 million, was the highest on record since 1932. In Scotland the total exceeded 8·25 million and showed a considerable increase on the previous record year of 1939. Northern Ireland had for the first time more than 1 million. New Zealand, the biggest exporter to the United Kingdom, had a sheep population of more than 46 million, 3·75 million more than in the previous year. This glut meant that compared with 1958 prices fell substantially. In wholesale values they dropped by as much and more than a shilling a pound, and for a considerable period the government subsidy to the home producer exceeded the prices realized in the live auctions. Also for some weeks New Zealand cold lambs fetched more on wholesale dead markets than the home-produced ones. To some extent this could be explained by the adverse effect of the extremely warm weather on the condition of home-produced lambs, but the fact remained that a consistently good marketing policy, providing a standardized commodity over many years, had helped New Zealand during a difficult period.

Publicity over lamb prices revealed some criticism by producers of the prices charged retail to consumers. The butchers' reply to this was that there was a limit to the amount of lamb and mutton consumers would take (in the first six months of 1959 consumption rose by less than 4%) and, in addition, the hot weather created far greater wastage. Moreover the high costs of retailing had to be met mainly from this item, with beef and pork costly at the source and retail margins diminished.

Beef continued firm in price, and supplies fell short of demand, mainly because the Argentine slaughterings had made inroads into breeding stock. With big increases in prices home consumption in Argentina dropped, thus releasing more supplies for export, but it was expected that exports to the United Kingdom would be considerably short of the 255,000 tons sent in the year 1958. Australia sent more beef to the United Kingdom, but supplies were diverted from this source and from New Zealand by a strong market in the United States, which, however, was expected to ease in 1960. A new source of supply was Southern Rhodesia, and although in the aggregate the quantity was small, it was significant that in the first six months of 1959 Southern Rhodesia earned twice as much as in the whole of 1958 from its beef exports, of which the United Kingdom took 75%. New Zealand beef exports showed a marked decline. Generally there was a greater amount of " plain " beef on offer, doubtless a reflection of efforts to increase production from dairy herds at home. The demand for lean beef continued, and Argentina showed every indication of catering for this by reorganizing its production policies.

The pig market displayed marked instability. Producers followed government action in the annual price review by cutting back numbers. Bacon factories ran short as meat manufacturers encroached on their supplies, and prices hardened. For the first time since subsidies were introduced during the free market, in one week during the autumn of 1959 none was paid on pigs by the government because the live market returns exceeded the minimum at which a guarantee was available. (*See also* LIVESTOCK.) (R. J. LH.)

MEAT OUTPUT IN MAJOR PRODUCING COUNTRIES ('000 metric tons)

Beef and Veal	Prewar	1956	1957	1958
United States .	3,617·0*	7,086·0†	6,924·0†	6,392·4†
Brazil .	953·3*	1,278·0	1,319·0	...
Argentina .	1,608·0‡	1,508·4†	1,292·4†	...
France .	883·0‡	1,015·2	987·6	972·0
Australia .	540·0§	753·6	813·6	862·8
German Fed. Rep.	756·0‖	741·6	824·4	853·2
United Kingdom .	625·0¶	811·2†	835·2†	825·6†
Canada .	333·0*	454·8	489·6	460·8
Italy .	320·0‡	352·8	360·0	379·2
Mutton and Lamb				
Australia .	321·0§	350·4	400·8	451·2
New Zealand**	247·0††	344·4	339·6	...
United States .	395·0*	331·2†	315·6†	306·0†
United Kingdom .	206·0¶	205·2†	202·8†	193·2†
France .	99·0‡	80·4	86·4	80·4
Argentina .	186·0‡	84·0†	72·0†	...
Pig Meat				
United States .	3,328·0*	4,674·0†	4,345·2†	4,364·4†
German Fed. Rep.	985·0‖	1,173·6	1,261·2	1,322·4
Poland .	...	580·8	692·4	800·4
United Kingdom .	410·0¶	640·8†	657·6†	714·0†
France .	678·0‡	642·0	660·0	664·8
Denmark .	310·0*	500·4	544·8	552·0

* 1935–39 average. † Commercial production; *i.e.*, excl. farm slaughter, etc.
‡ 1934–38 average. § 1934/35–1938/39 average. ‖ 1936/37–1938/39 average. ¶ 1938. ¶ 1936/37–1938/39 average. ** Year ended Sept. 30 (June 30 prewar). †† 1937–39 average.
SOURCE. F.A.O. *Monthly Bulletin.*

Spices. Pepper production in India in 1958–59, at 512,000 cwt. (112 lb.), was some 20,000 cwt. lighter than in the preceding season, while the cultivated area showed a slight decrease. Exports during January–June fell from 151,649 cwt. in 1958 to 84,198 cwt., the proportion going to the United States rising from 19% to 27%, but that to the U.S.S.R. falling from 50% to 14%. Indonesian shipments during 1958 had fallen to 245,000 cwt., while a further decline was indicated in 1959. The average value of black pepper imported in June 1959 into the United States, the principal world market, showed little change, at 23 cents a lb., from a year earlier. Clove production in Zanzibar fell from a record figure of 483,896 cwt. in 1957-58 to 140,921 cwt. in 1958-59. Exports declined from 222,034 cwt. to 165,626 cwt. in the same season, the proportion going to Indonesia rising from 53% to 63% and that to India falling from 24% to 14%. The average monthly price for fair quality cloves on the local market eased from 118·25s. in July 1958 to 110s. in June 1959.

Ginger output in India declined from 304,000 cwt. in 1957-58 to 268,000 cwt. in 1958-59. Exports during January-June fell from 72,695 cwt. in 1958 to 35,675 cwt. Consignments of ginger from Jamaica during Jan.-June 1959 totalled 11,999 cwt. as against 11,804 cwt. in the corresponding period of the previous year. Shipments from Nigeria during January-June rose from 12,908 cwt. in 1958 to 21,807 cwt., while those from Sierra Leone during January-June, at 17,252 cwt., were 7,708 cwt. heavier than in 1958. Consignments of nutmegs and mace from Grenada during 1958 increased from 5,000 cwt. to 15,000 cwt., but those from Indonesia fell from 58,000 cwt. to 37,000 cwt. Jamaican exports of pimento during January-June fell from 10,300 cwt. in 1958 to 2,733 cwt. The output of chillies in India, the largest producer, fell in 1958-59 from 7,240,000 cwt. to 6,640,000 cwt. Exports during January-June fell from 62,455 cwt. to 15,088 cwt. in 1959. Ceylonese cinnamon exports totalled 17,741 cwt. in Jan.-May 1959, as against 17,635 cwt. in the corresponding period of 1958. Exports of cardamoms from India, the major world source, rose in January-June from 15,022 cwt. in 1958 to 16,282 cwt. (J. R. D.)

Sugar. Output of centrifugal sugar continued to expand in 1958-59, rising from 42·1 million long tons to a new record figure of 45·5 million long tons. New high levels were recorded of 26·5 million long tons for cane sugar and 19 million long tons for beet.

Final U.S. supply quotas for 1958 totalled 9,230,000 short tons. The initial quotas of 9·2 million short tons set for 1959 were increased to 9·3 million short tons in September. Cuban exports during January-May fell to 1,771,678 long tons (of which 1,265,273 tons went to the

One of the exhibits in the 1959 lord mayor's show, held in November, which took agriculture as its theme.

United States), as against 2,610,952 long tons (1,630,760 tons to the United States) in the corresponding period of 1958. Shipments from The West Indies and British Guiana during January-April, mainly to the United Kingdom and Canada, increased from 358,518 long tons to 360,980 long tons.

U.K. imports during January-August totalled 1,670,710 long tons, compared with 1,757,833 long tons a year earlier, while exports of refined sugar declined from 376,632 long tons to 365,829 long tons. It was announced in Dec. 1959 that the Commonwealth Sugar agreement had been extended for a further year to 1966. The " negotiated price " for 1960 was reduced from £45 2s. 0d. a ton to £44 8s. 10d. a ton, while the " negotiated price quotas " were increased by 3% (over-all agreement quotas " remained unchanged). The working of the system for determining the negotiated price was reviewed and confirmed, and an arrangement was made to restrain prices during 1961-63.

A new five-year International Sugar agreement came into operation in Jan. 1959. It provided for an increase in the minimum stocks held by exporting members from 10% to 12·5% of basic export tonnages, while exporting members of the Commonwealth Sugar agreement gave an undertaking to hold stocks of not less than 50,000 long tons for export to the free market at the call of the International Sugar council.

WORLD PRODUCTION AND EXPORTS OF SUGAR
('000 long tons)

	Production* 1958-59	Production* 1959-60†	Exports 1958	Exports 1959‡
Cane				
Cuba	5,893	5,600	5,436	2,874
United States and territories .	2,171	2,393	1,307	1,001
British Commonwealth .	10,588	10,210	3,367	1,620
Other western hemisphere .	8,457	8,247	2,020	1,162
Other Asia .	3,089	3,122	1,803	1,262
Beet				
Europe (incl. U.S.S.R.) .	16,444	15,666	1,233	524
World total .	50,485	49,200	15,542	8,467

* Including non-centrifugal. † Est. ‡ January-July only.
SOURCE. Commonwealth Economic Committee *et al.*

Uncertainty concerning Cuba's sugar policy and the marketing of a large beet crop in Europe depressed prices at the end of Jan. 1959 to below 3·25 cents, and a cut of 2·5% in export quotas automatically came into force early in February. Later that month the International Sugar council made a further reduction of 5% and withheld 10% of export tonnages. Prices continued to fall to a low point of 2·82 cents early in April. In June the council applied the maximum quota reduction of 20% for countries with a basic export tonnage of at least 50,000 tons and 10% for others, but a renewed decline in prices followed, to 2·55 cents at the end of July. Purchasing by the U.S.S.R. and the decision by the council in August to allow a carry-over into 1960 of up to 10% of basic export quotas led to some recovery. (J. R. D.)

Tea. World tea production in 1959 promised to reach some 1,605 million lb., slightly below the level of the preceding year, as a result of the fall in output in southern India. Exports were somewhat below those of the previous year, since the fall in consignments from India and Indonesia was not made good by the expansion in Ceylon and east Africa. Gross imports into the United Kingdom, which represented about one-half of world imports, fell from 342 million lb. in Jan.-Aug. 1958 to 299 million lb., while re-exports rose from 20 million lb. to 28 million lb. The U.S. offtake during January-July increased from 63 million lb. in 1958 to 68 million lb. Australia took 29 million lb. during Jan.-June 1959, as against 26 million lb. a year earlier, supplies from Ceylon remaining at around 67%. Canadian imports in January-May declined from 20 million lb. to 19 million lb.

ESTIMATES OF WORLD TEA PRODUCTION AND TRADE (EXCL. CHINA)
(in million lb.)

	Production 1957	Production 1958	Production 1959*	Exports 1957	Exports 1958	Exports 1959†
India . . .	685	716	710	444	506	228
Ceylon . .	398	413	410	368	411	259
Pakistan . .	46	56	55	10	13	1
Japan . .	160	164	160	24	17	10
Indonesia . .	105	103	93	79	76	47
Formosa . .	34	30	30	26	26	16
Other countries .	121	131	147	124	143	75
Total . .	1,549	1,613	1,605	1,075	1,192	636

* Provisional. † 8 months.
SOURCE. International Tea Committee and Commonwealth Economic Committee.

The scarcity of good quality tea was reflected in a hardening of quotations at the London auctions during the first four months of 1959, but prices declined thereafter until the arrival in August of the northern Indian crop which fetched good prices. The market declined during the closing months of the year. The over-all average price rose from 4s. in January to 4s. 8d. at the end of April, and then fell to 3s. 9d. in July. It rose sharply to 5s. 8d. in September, but had fallen to 4s. 9d. by early December. The Ceylon export duty of 70 cents per lb. was replaced in June by a uniform rate of 35 cents per lb. with an additional *ad valorem* levy on quality tea of 50% of the excess over 85 cents per lb. realized, subject to a maximum of 70 cents. The Indian export duty was reduced in March 1959 from 26 n.p. to 24 n.p. per lb. The export duty of 6 annas per lb. was retained in Pakistan. (J. R. D.)

Vegetables. Drought conditions, of a severity rarely experienced in many western European countries, affected the 1959 vegetable harvest in the United Kingdom. Glut conditions were widespread for such sun-loving crops as tomatoes, but in the case of root crops, greens and salads, constant hot sunshine and lack of any real rainfall for weeks on end led to serious yield reductions. It was in any event an anxious time for producers, with the balance clearly in favour of those with regular means of irrigation. By the end of September, the Ministry of Agriculture's observers were expecting winter vegetable shortages. Tomato prices fell to an uneconomic level at the peak season, affecting British, Dutch and Channel Island growers. On the other hand, with the exception of aphis, pests were fairly easily controlled, and disease attacks were mild. There was very little potato blight and the quality of tubers was good, although the yield was lighter. Conditions also suited onions in all respects except weight of crop.

From the consumers' standpoint serious shortages were unlikely, as there would undoubtedly be adequate supplies of processed vegetables

AREA AND PRODUCTION OF MAJOR VEGETABLE CROPS, UNITED KINGDOM, 1958-59

	Acreage ('000)	Tons ('000)		Acreage ('000)	Tons ('000)
Asparagus .	1·4	1·3	Cauliflower .	16·6	143·1
Beans, broad	9·6	44·1	Onions, bulb .	1·9	27·1
Beans, runner	9·5	50·3	Onions, salad .	1·4	13·5
Beans, dwarf	3·9	9·0	Parsnips .	3·8	47·3
Beetroot .	7·5	91·4	Peas, green .	28·7	80·0
Broccoli .	15·1	109·2	Peas, dry .	56·4	33·8
Cabbage .	43·6	375·7	Peas, processing .	62·8	54·4
Carrots .	31·4	360·7	Sprouts .	48·9	157·9
Celery .	5·7	106·5	Turnips and swedes	4·5	110·0

SOURCE. Ministry of Agriculture, Fisheries and Food.

(not necessarily from the 1959 crop) to offset any scarcity of fresh vegetables. The season served to emphasize the wisdom of the processing industry in its endeavours to secure sufficient produce for its needs regardless of local weather conditions. One large international group took the precaution, during the winter of 1958, of shipping an entire harvesting and processing plant from Britain to New Zealand, as a safeguard against the failure of the British harvest. In retrospect, this ambitious project proved prophetic, and a widespread adoption of the plan seemed highly probable.

Produce pre-packaging continued to grow steadily on a world-wide basis, involving a wide range of vegetable crops. An initial international conference and exhibition, sponsored by O.E.E.C. and organized in London by the Ministry of Agriculture, drew delegates from the majority of member-countries of O.E.E.C., and emphasized the rapid strides being made in this type of marketing.

O.E.E.C. through its productivity agency also began trans-European marketing tests, aimed at establishing the best methods for the transport of produce throughout Europe and investigating the merits of different containers. These tests, which were to be extended in their scope, involved the transportation of broccoli from Italy to England and other northern European centres.

In Britain a major development in the autumn was the announcement by the Tomato and Cucumber Marketing board that it intended to acquire additional marketing powers, enabling compulsory grading to be introduced in 1961. There was to be a year's trial period with the proposed grades during 1960. The object of this move was to place the grading of U.K. produce on a par with imported produce from the continent of Europe and, to this end, O.E.E.C. grades as commonly used in most European countries, were to be adopted.   (V. A. J. W.)

FOOTBALL: *see* ASSOCIATION FOOTBALL; RUGBY FOOTBALL.

FORAGE CROPS: *see* AGRICULTURE.

FORESTRY. A very wet winter in most parts of England and Wales during 1958-59 seriously delayed both timber extraction and planting operations. In the hot, dry summer of 1959 forest fires were numerous, but improvements in fire-fighting equipment and in radio communication reduced the actual damage done. Much damage in young plantations by rabbits and hares was recorded from several regions, and it was found that myxomatosis could no longer be relied upon to keep down the rabbit population.

A considerable increase in the value of agricultural and forest land in England and Wales became evident during the year, chiefly due to the purchase of both good and derelict woodlands and vacant land for afforestation by several large new financial syndicates. The importance of determining the best use of land, whether for forestry, agriculture, industrial or recreational purposes, was one of the main themes of a conference held at Oxford in June and attended by prominent forestry and agricultural representatives and soil scientists from many parts of the Commonwealth.

Increased demands for water supplies for industrial and other purposes having arisen in many countries, a scientific investigation into the influence of various forest crops on catchment area yields was inaugurated. This project included the study of the effects of various types of vegetation and forests on erosion and floods in areas with different kinds of basic soils and geological formation. A Forest Tree Seed association for England and Wales was formed which enabled members to collaborate in collecting and processing seed from genetically selected and certified parent trees. It was also to deal with the rearing of nursery stock from the selected seed.

Commonwealth. In Canada, analysis of the causes of forest fires over a period of ten years showed that tobacco smoking was the greatest, lightning the second and camp fires third. The worst months for fires were May and August and over $20 million were spent annually on fire protection. In British Columbia a large Sikorsky helicopter was chartered for

During 1959 the Forestry commission began to pay special attention to the task of afforestation in the uplands of Wales. Students, including one from Uganda, are here seen learning how to point fencing staves at Gwydyr Forestry school, Capel Curig, North Wales.

transporting to forest fires up to 12 men with equipment. The cost at about £200 per flying hour was considered to be well covered by the value of the timber saved. A Douglas fir tree, 370 years old and 255 ft. high, was given to Britain by the Forest Industries of British Columbia. Claimed to be the world's tallest wooden flagpole, it was floated up the Thames and erected in Kew Royal Botanic gardens. The extraction of white pine logs, weighing up to 5 tons, from forests near the summit of a mountain range near Vancouver, formerly considered to be economically inaccessible, was successfully carried out by a Swiss logging team with a new type of Wyssen Skyline crane.

In British Honduras a record 1,175 ac. of new plantations were established, chiefly of pine and mahogany. Thirteen thousand acres of natural pine forest were placed under intensive management and special fire protection. The areas of balsa forest under regeneration were also considerably extended. In Trinidad an additional area of 37,600 ac. was proclaimed as a government forest reserve, bringing the total area reserved for permanent forests to a quarter of the whole country.

The extension in Western Nigeria of the areas of high forest under controlled regeneration and exploitation continued, the area of each annual coupe being about 34 sq.mi. The total area of forest under regeneration was over 270,000 ac., of which only about 3% was planted artificially. In the Southern Cameroons timber trees were planted in combination with local farming operations, bananas being planted between the tree species. The East African railways in Kenya started tests with impregnated locally grown *Pinus radiata* and also a number of indigenous hardwoods. Increased demands for railway sleepers for Rhodesia and Nyasaland led to trials of suitable timber species in both Tanganyika and Kenya. In Northern Rhodesia, where the copper mines had for many years needed very large supplies of timber, both for fuel and mine-timbering, a stock-taking of the remaining timber reserves was started. The afforestation of plateau land in Nyasaland with exotic softwood species was continued and government plantations covered an area of over 20,000 ac. The reserved areas of indigenous forest were also increased, reaching a total of over 3,000 sq.mi. or nearly 9% of the whole protectorate. A large modern departmental sawmill at Blantyre was extended by the addition of seasoning kilns which enabled the production of high quality sawn timber.

The sabotage of government property in Cyprus early in the year held up forestry operations. Over 100 outbreaks of fire destroyed 7 sq.mi. of forest. A large government sawmill was also destroyed by fire, but labour conditions later improved and forestry work was resumed.

Europe. An important six-year plan for state afforestation was launched in Portugal over an area of 100,000 ha. This was supplemented by the supply of seeds and plants and free technical assistance to private landowners wherever afforestation was considered to be indispensable for soil conservation. The climate of Portugal is particularly suited to fast-growing conifers. In Italy the rehabilitation of mountain territories received particular attention, and financial aid on a large scale was given for land reclamation and afforestation. In Greenland, where attempts at afforestation with Canadian and Norwegian conifers had failed, new trials were made with Siberian dwarf larch. Forty thousand trees were planted after intensive soil preparation which included the importation of humus from other countries. A national nature reserve was established in the Pfälzer Wald in the German Federal Republic, an area of 645 sq.mi. making it probably the largest forested reserve in Europe. In Norway trials were made with new types of tractors, power-saws, barking machines and cableways. In Finland improvements were also sought in the better organization and uses of forest labour, particularly the methods of payment, housing conditions and other amenities.

United States. In 1959 the secretary of agriculture presented to congress a programme calling for intensified management and development of the 181 million ac. of public forest lands administered by the forest service. Tree planting in the United States covered a total of 1,568,708 ac. in 1958. This was an increase of nearly 400,000 ac. over 1957, more than double the acreage planted in 1953 and three times the 1950 planting. Of the 1958 plantings, 86% were on private lands.

The forest service reported that forest fire losses in 1958 were the lowest on record. The area burned in the United States (exclusive of Alaska) was 3,280,000 ac. compared with an annual average for the preceding five years of more than 9 million ac. Organized protection by federal, state and private agencies in 1958 covered 614,134,000 ac. of public and private forest lands, but about 36 million ac. still lacked systematic protection. More than half of the total acreage burned during the year was on these unprotected lands. (*See* also TIMBER.)

(A. H. LD.; J. L. V. C.)

BIBLIOGRAPHY. R. D. Meikle, *British Trees and Shrubs* (London, 1958); H. M. Steven and A. Carlisle, *The Native Pinewoods of Scotland* (London, 1959); R. C. Haw, *The Conservation of Natural Resources* (London, 1959); W. E. Hiley, *Conifers: South African Methods of Cultivation* (London, 1959); H. C. Dawkins, *The Management of Natural Tropical Forest in Uganda* (Oxford, 1959); A. Pavari, " Forest Influences ", *Unasylva*, 13, 1 (Rome, 1959).

FORMOSA: *see* CHINA.

FRANCE. Republic of western Europe bounded N. by the English channel, N.E. by Belgium and Luxembourg, E. by Germany and Switzerland, S.E. by Italy, S. by the Mediterranean sea, S.W. by Spain and W. by the Atlantic ocean. Area: 212,821 sq.mi., including the Mediterranean island of Corsica (3,367 sq.mi.), but excluding the overseas *départements* of Algeria, French Guiana, Guadeloupe, Martinique and Réunion (*qq.v.*). Pop.: (1954 census) 42,843,520; (Jan. 1, 1959, est.) 44,788,000. Language: French is almost universally spoken but there are also other regional languages or dialects: German in Alsace and part of Lorraine; Breton in Brittany; Flemish in the northern corner of the Nord *département*; Provençal in the Alpes Maritimes, Basses-Alpes, Var and Bouches-du-Rhône *départements*; Catalan in Roussillon (Pyrénées-Orientales); Basque south of Bayonne; and Italian in Corsica. Religion: mainly Roman Catholic with *c.* 700,000 Protestants and more than 230,000 Jews. Chief towns (pop., 1954 census, first figure administrative area, second figure with suburbs): Paris (cap.) 2,830,160 (4,790,200); Marseilles 649,720; Lyons 466,000 (644,960); Bordeaux 255,340 (410,020); Lille 192,220 (356,420); Roubaix 110,540 (267,720); Rouen 118,040 (267,100); Toulouse 266,400; Nice 247,620; Nantes 240,180; Strasbourg 196,940 (234,740); 17 towns with a pop. of from 100,000 to 200,000. Presidents of the republic in 1959: René Coty and (from Jan. 8) General Charles de Gaulle. Prime ministers in 1959: General Charles de Gaulle and (from Jan. 8) Michel Debré (*see* BIOGRAPHIES). Main imports: machinery and vehicles; iron, steel and manufactures; coal, petroleum and products; cotton and wool. Main exports: machinery and vehicles, textiles, wine, dairy products, fruit and vegetables. Monetary unit: *franc* (Fr.1,377·00 = £1 sterling).

History. *Home Affairs.* During 1959 the setting up of the institutions of the Fifth Republic continued. On Jan. 8 General Charles de Gaulle was officially installed as president of the Republic and of the Community and he appointed Michel Debré to be prime minister. The latter immediately formed his cabinet, which consisted of 27 members, 6 of whom were not deputies. The extraordinary session of parliament opened on Jan. 15. In the message which he addressed to both houses the head of state mentioned Algeria, where a political solution, he said, " could only be achieved through universal suffrage ". The prime minister outlined his government's general policy and declared that the offer for the cessation of hostilities made to the F.L.N. (Front de la Libération Nationale) on Oct. 23 was still open. On Jan. 16 the National Assembly gave the government a vote of confidence by 453 votes to 56 and 29 abstentions. The Socialists were in opposition.

The Assembly then voted on its provisional rules of procedure. The distribution of seats among the various parties was as follows: U.N.R. (Union pour la Nouvelle République) 206; Independents 117; deputies from Algeria 66; M.R.P. (Mouvement Républicain Populaire) and associates 64; Socialists 47; non-registered (mainly Radicals) 40; Republican Centre (Radicals supporting André Morice) 12; Communists 10; others 14. There were in all 576 deputies. The extraordinary session ended on Jan. 30. No legislative work had been carried out, this having been left to the government which was invested with special powers which did not expire until Feb. 5.

Before the opening of the ordinary session which was due to take place on April 28, municipal elections were held on March 8 and 15. These were marked by a distinct gain for the Communists, and while the Socialists maintained their positions, the U.N.R. lost ground. In Algeria where the elections took place during April 19-25 there were numerous abstentions (40% in many places, 56% in Algiers). The Moslems were confused. The " activists ", who questioned the policy of de Gaulle, brought pressure to bear on the Europeans.

The elections to the Senate took place on April 26 and resulted in the formation of a body similar in composition to the Senate of the Fourth Republic. The U.N.R., which had been so strong in the parliamentary elections in Nov. 1958, had lost its impetus. The Conservatives and M.R.P. made some headway, while the Radicals and the Socialists lost ground slightly (*see* ELECTIONS). On March 5 the Constitutional Council was installed (nine ordinary councillors and two extraordinary councillors, the former presidents of the republic, Vincent Auriol and René Coty). On Feb. 3-4 the executive council of the Community was set up, comprising 12 heads of African governments, the French prime minister and 8 ministers concerned with the Community's affairs.

While the Fifth Republic was being organized with both old and new type assemblies, de Gaulle was giving a new significance to the office of head of state. During Feb. 14-18 he made his first official trip to the southwestern part of the country, a triumphant occasion with, however, some hostile demonstrations. During April 16-18 he made a second journey to the Nivernais, the Bourbonnais and Burgundy, and in May he visited Berry, Orléans and Touraine (May 7-9). During June 5-7 he went to Auvergne, and later (Sept. 24-27) to the north and the Pas-de-Calais. Finally during Nov. 18-22 he visited Alsace.

During July 2-11 the president of the republic went to Madagascar and to Réunion. He presided over the executive council of the Community at Tananarive (July 7-8), and on his return to Paris, on July 15, he officially opened at the Palais du Luxembourg the first session of the Senate of the Community.

De Gaulle was the sole initiator of the domestic and foreign policy of France, and through the medium of his press conferences he addressed himself directly to French and to international opinion. In particular, during a conference held at the Elysée palace on March 25, he put forward the idea of a " fraternal organization " which would help the underdeveloped countries to benefit from a proportion of the wealth of economically strong countries.

On April 28 the first ordinary session of the new parliament began. On April 30 the National Assembly approved unanimously (with the exception of the Communists) the statement by the minister for foreign affairs on foreign policy and on the Geneva conference arranged for May 11. Debré was engaged in a lengthy dispute with a large number of deputies over the question of whether voting should or should not take place after oral questions had been put to the government by deputies. The discussion continued throughout the month of May. Debré was strongly opposed to the idea of a vote, which seemed to him to be a revival of interpellation, which had been abolished by the new constitution. Finally on June 3 he got his own way by 487 votes to 91, and on July 1 the Constitutional Council consolidated its success by doing away with the right of deputies to propose resolutions inviting the government to pursue a particular course of action. He interpreted the constitution in its strictest sense. The Senate too was not allowed to vote on oral questions. But opposition to the government in the Senate took on a

President de Gaulle with the newly formed French cabinet, which he received in the Elysée palace on Jan. 11. On his right is the prime minister, M. Debré, and on his left J. Soustelle, minister-delegate. A. Pinay, minister of finance, is on the left of the front row.

determined character and the political *malaise* was intensified by the resignation of two ministers, Jean Berthoin (Radical, interior) and Roger Houdet (Independent, agriculture), who chose to remain senators rather than to stay in Debré's cabinet (May 27). They were replaced by Pierre Châtenet and Henri Rochereau respectively.

After the elections to the Senate in Algeria (May 31) in which the moderates were successful, a great debate began in the National Assembly on June 4 concerning Algeria and the passing of two government measures, unifying the budgets and banknotes of metropolitan France and Algeria. The government carried the measures on June 11 by 466 votes to 57. Georges Bidault declared himself in favour of the views of the " federalists "—in other words for the policy of " Algérie française ". In the Senate on June 26, following interruptions in which the views of the " federalists " were freely put forward, the government had 155 votes against 67, with 80 abstentions. Parliament recessed from July 27 to Oct. 6.

The Algerian drama continued to occupy the centre of the political stage. On Aug. 27 de Gaulle went to Algeria in order to examine the military situation. On Sept. 16 he made a declaration of great importance: he recognized the right of the Algerians to self-determination and announced that a referendum would take place four years after the country had been pacified. This declaration had repercussions in Algeria, Tunisia and Morocco. There was a possibility that Habib Bourguiba, the president of Tunisia, might act as mediator between France and the " provisional government of the Algerian republic " which issued its reply on Sept. 28, noting the promise of self-determination and asking implicitly to be recognized as the political organization of the F.L.N.

Parliament began work again on Oct. 6, and on Oct. 13 Debré made a statement of general policy. He commented upon the declaration of Sept. 16 on Algeria. He was received rather coldly in both the Assembly and the Senate. Many deputies from Algeria did not take part in the debate. Finally, on Oct. 16, the government obtained 441 votes against 23 with 28 abstentions; 56 deputies did not record their vote. There was some dissension within the U.N.R. and nine so-called " May 13 " deputies were expelled from the party by its political committee. While on Oct. 30 the National Assembly was voting on the plan for fiscal reform and at the beginning of November was examining the budget for 1960, there was an attempt at political subversion aimed at removing Debré from office, and official investigations were made in

" activist " circles in Paris and in the provinces. The atmosphere of conspiracy was made still thicker by the apparent attempt on the life of a former minister, François Mitterand.

On Oct. 28 de Gaulle addressed a message to the civil servants and armed forces in Algeria, reminding them that the Debré government had his complete confidence in carrying out the definite steps in policy laid down on Sept. 16. Moreover, Marshal Alphonse Juin was requested not to take part in any political discussions.

On Nov. 10 de Gaulle announced in his press conference that if the representatives of the " Algerian organization of the exterior " decide to come to France they would be received by " the personalities properly qualified ". As the " provisional government of the Algerian republic " appointed as negotiators the five insurgent leaders, headed by Ahmed Ben Bella, detained by the French, de Gaulle refused on Nov. 20 to talk to such spokesmen but declared his readiness to negotiate a cease-fire with " those who are fighting ". (*See* also UNITED NATIONS.)

At the beginning of December more than 300 people in the towns of Fréjus and St. Raphaël lost their lives following the collapse of the Malpasset dam.

Foreign Policy. During 1959 France displayed intense diplomatic activity, an indication of its new position in Europe and in the world at large. The conflict over western Berlin provoked by the threats of N. S. Khrushchev was examined on Feb. 6 during the meeting between de Gaulle, Maurice Couve de Murville, the foreign minister, and John Foster Dulles. On March 4 de Gaulle received Konrad Adenauer, the federal German chancellor, in Paris. During March 9-10 he was visited by Harold Macmillan who talked to him about his trip to Moscow. During conversations with Antonio Segni and Giuseppe Pella on March 19-20, de Gaulle brought Italy into the east-west negotiations, and on March 18 he had declared in an address to his partners in Nato that France must " keep a certain amount of freedom in the employment of its military forces in general and its naval forces in particular."

France took part with a certain amount of scepticism in the foreign ministers' conference which began at Geneva on May 11 and finished on Aug. 5 (after a break lasting from June 20 to July 13). As a preliminary to this conference at Geneva, Debré and Couve de Murville had conferred in London on April 13 with Macmillan and Selwyn Lloyd.

(*Left*) *Watched by a young boy with a few belongings saved from his wrecked home, troops search among mud-covered debris in Fréjus, southern France, after the Malpasset dam disaster in December.* (*Right*) *French government officials view the shattered dam.*

During June 23-28 de Gaulle made a stay in Italy on the occasion of the centenary of Solferino and the war of 1859. Then during Sept. 2-3 he received President Dwight D. Eisenhower in Paris at the time of a crisis in the relations with Great Britain and the United States, mainly caused by a speech by Debré on Aug. 16.

During the last six months of the year the various disputes between Paris, London and Washington continued. In opposition to British-U.S. opinion, France kept to its decision to explode an atomic bomb in the Sahara. After Khrushchev's visit to the United States in October de Gaulle invited the head of the government of the U.S.S.R. to visit France at the beginning of 1960. On the other hand, while agreeing to Dec. 19 as the date of the meeting of the heads of government

The French atomic centre at Marcoule, showing the reactor which on April 22 began to supply electricity for public consumption.

of the western powers to prepare for the future meeting with Khrushchev, he endeavoured to postpone the " summit " conference which Macmillan had wanted to hold as soon as possible after the Eisenhower-Khrushchev conversations at Camp David.

In December the heads of government of Britain, France, the German Federal Republic and the United States met in Paris for the " western summit " conference. (*See* SUMMIT CONFERENCE, APPROACHES TO.)

The Economic and Social Position. During the year there was an improvement in the French economic situation. Industry was expanding, the deficit in overseas trade was being reduced and the franc was consolidating its standing internationally. The reports issued by Antoine Pinay, the minister of finance, and by the governor of the Bank of France (at the end of July) were relatively optimistic. This was also the case with a parliamentary report on the budget estimates for 1960, which spoke of " the austere road to prosperity " and of the necessity of fighting " inflation, the only thing which could bring about the failure of the government's economic policy."

Drought, however, caused some shortage in food supplies in the country. The price of many commodities increased and, chiefly at the end of the year, there was considerable unrest among trade unions. Several unions demonstrated in support of an increase in wages. The guaranteed minimum wage had to be raised twice and the price of bread went up by one franc from Aug. 3. In November the government endeavoured, by importing foodstuffs and cutting down manufactured products, to forestall fresh rises in prices and to check any attempt at a strike in the country. In December the rise in prices was stopped by a variety of measures favouring the consumers, but social unrest persisted. On Dec. 2 civil servants organized a one-day strike. (*See also* FRENCH COMMUNITY; FRENCH LITERATURE; PARIS.) (A. PR.)

FRENCH COMMUNITY (LA COMMUNAUTÉ). With the promulgation on October 5, 1958, of the constitution of the Fifth Republic, the French Community comprises: (1) The French Republic including the 18 overseas *départements* (Algeria [12], Sahara [2], Martinique, Guadeloupe, Réunion and Guiana) and 5 overseas territories; (2) 12 other member states. The organs of the Community are: the president of the French republic who is also the president of the Community; an executive council consisting of the heads of government of each member state and the ministers responsible to the Community for common affairs; a Senate formed of delegates of the National Assemblies of the member states; and an Arbitration Court. Total area of the Community, excluding France proper and the New Hebrides (Dec. 1959 est.): 4,147,980 sq.mi.; total population (1959 est.): *c.* 42,825,000. Certain essential information on the component parts of the Community is given in the table. (*See* also separate articles.)

History. On Dec. 21, 1958, General Charles de Gaulle was elected president of the republic. In France he obtained 78·5% of the votes cast, in the overseas *départements* 81%, in Sahara 97%, in the overseas territories 95% and in the States of the Community 96·7%. In the Michel Debré government (Jan. 8, 1959) Jacques Soustelle (U.N.R.) became minister-delegate for the overseas *départements*, the overseas territories and Sahara; Robert Lecourt (M.R.P.) became minister of state responsible for the trusteeship territories. The other functions of the former Ministry for Overseas France were shared among the technical ministries. An Algerian woman, Sid Cara, became secretary of state for Moslem affairs. Raymond Janot, a member of the Conseil d'Etat, was appointed secretary-general of the Community.

The former French West Africa (with the exception of Guinea which had become independent) was divided up into the following states: Mauritania, Soudan, Senegal, Ivory Coast, Upper Volta, Dahomey and Niger. The former French Equatorial Africa was split up into four states: the Central African Republic (formerly Ubangi-Shari), Gabon, Congo (formerly Middle Congo) and Chad. Madagascar became a republic. Each of the republics adopted a constitution and some of them created national flags. The other territories (Saint-Pierre and Miquelon, French Somaliland, Comoro archipelago, New Caledonia and French Polynesia) chose to retain the *status quo*.

The executive council of the Community, composed of the president, the prime ministers of the states and ministers dealing with joint Community affairs, met several times. Firstly, in Paris on Feb. 4-5, 1959, it decided that the Senate of the Community would have one member for every 300,000 people, or 284 members, of which 186 would represent the French Republic with its overseas *départements* and territories, and 98 the other states. Four committees were created to deal with common technical matters. The official language of the Community was to be French; its motto " Liberty, Equality, Fraternity "; its national anthem the " Marseillaise "; its flag the red, white and blue tricolour. There would be one army for the whole Community. Secondly, in Paris, on March 2-3, agreement was reached about the posts to be allocated in the French diplomatic service to officials from the various states. Thirdly, in Paris, on May 4-5, decisions were taken about the handing over of overseas wireless stations. Fourthly, at Tananarive (Madagascar), on July 7-8, the council presided over by General de Gaulle, decided that the states would be associated with the French delegations at the United Nations and could become members of other international organizations. The problems of the diplomatic service and of defence were examined. The problems of dual citizenship (of the member-state and of the Community) were studied. Fifthly, in Paris, on Sept. 11, it was agreed that the Community would have an evolutive character and that a certain diversity in status could be considered for the various states. Sixthly, there was a meeting at Dakar (Senegal), on Dec. 11-14.

Divergent views led to opposition between Félix Houphouët-Boigny, the prime minister of Ivory Coast, who favoured an

FRENCH COMMUNITY

President of the French Republic and of the Community, General Charles de Gaulle

A. MEMBER STATES

Country	Area (sq. mi.)	Population*	Capital	Status	Prime ministers	High commissioners
FRANCE	212,821	44,788,000	Paris	Republic	Michel Debré	—
MAURITANIA	364,092	625,000	Nouakchott	Republic	Mokhtar Ould Daddah	Pierre Anthonioz
SENEGAL	81,081	2,300,000	Dakar	Republic	Mamadou Dia	Pierre Lamy
SOUDAN	460,308	3,700,000	Bamako	Republic	Modibo Keita	Jean Sicurani
VOLTA	121,892	3,500,000	Ouagadougou	Republic	Maurice Yamégo	Paul Masson
NIGER	470,656	2,500,000	Niamey	Republic	Hamani Diori	Jean Colombani
IVORY COAST	123,359	3,100,000	Abidjan	Republic	Félix Houphouët-Boigny	Yves Guéna
DAHOMEY	44,710	1,720,000	Porto Novo	Republic	Hubert Maga	René Tirant
GABON	103,089	411,000	Libreville	Republic	Léon M'Ba	Jean Risterucci
CONGO	132,046	765,000	Brazzaville	Republic	Fulbert Youlou	Guy Georgy
CENTRAL AFRICA	238,224	1,171,000	Bangui	Republic	David Dacko	Paul Bordier
CHAD	495,752	2,580,000	Fort Lamy	Republic	François Tombalbaye	Daniel Houstin
MADAGASCAR	228,000	5,065,000	Antananarivo	Republic	Philibert Tsiranana	André Soucadaux†

B. OVERSEAS DÉPARTEMENTS OF THE FRENCH REPUBLIC

Country	Area (sq. mi.)	Population*	Capital	Status	Administrators
ALGERIA	117,760	9,875,000	Algiers	12 départements	Delegate-general, Paul Delouvrier
SAHARA	803,860	501,000	—	2 départements	Administrator, Jacques Soustelle‡
RÉUNION	970	310,000	Saint-Denis	département	Prefect, Jean Perreau-Pradier
FRENCH GUIANA	35,135	30,000	Cayenne	département	Prefect, André Dubois-Chabert
GUADELOUPE	686	255,000	Basse-Terre	département	Prefect, Jean-Pierre Abeille
MARTINIQUE	427	260,000	Fort-de-France	département	Prefect, Jean Parsi

C. OVERSEAS TERRITORIES OF THE FRENCH REPUBLIC

Country	Area (sq. mi.)	Population*	Capital	Status	Governors
FRENCH SOMALILAND	8,378	63,700§	Jibuti	Overseas territory	Governor, Jacques Compain
COMORO ARCHIPELAGO	849	181,288¶	Moroni	Overseas territory	High administrator, Georges Arnaud
SOUTHERN OCEAN AND ANTARCTIC LANDS	152,720	150	—	A section of Antarctica and a group of islands	Administrator, Pierre Roland‡
SAINT-PIERRE AND MIQUELON	93	4,900	Saint-Pierre	Overseas territory	Administrator, Jean Louis Pont
NEW CALEDONIA	7,654	72,478‖	Nouméa	Overseas territory	High commissioner for the Pacific ocean and governor, Laurent Péchoux
FRENCH POLYNESIA	1,545	77,000‖	Papeete	Overseas territory	Governor, Pierre Sicaud
NEW HEBRIDES	5,700	53,000	Vila	Franco-British condominium	French resident, Benjamin Favreau

* 1959 estimates if not otherwise stated.   † High commissioner-general.   ‡ Administrator resides in Paris.   § 1955 est.   ¶ 1958 est.   ‖ 1957 est.

organic federation, and Modibo Keita, the prime minister of the Soudan republic, who preferred a confederation on the model of the British Commonwealth of Nations. Senegal and Soudan formed the Federation of Mali (*q.v.*), Ivory Coast, together with Upper Volta, Dahomey and Niger, created a Sahel-Bénin *entente*. Two agreements were reached on customs unions: one among the states of the former French West Africa, and another among the states of the former French Equatorial Africa.

The Senate of the Community, composed of members of the National Assemblies of the states nominated by these assemblies, was installed by General de Gaulle on July 15. Two days later it set up its political groups and its office. A Guianese, Gaston Monnerville, the president of the French Senate, was elected president. Houphouët-Boigny, Philibert Tsiranana (prime minister of Madagascar), Gabriel Lisette (deputy prime minister of Chad) and Léopold Senghor (president of the National Assembly of Senegal) were appointed minister-councillors to the French Republic to deal with matters concerning the Community.

The members of the Court of Arbitration of the Community were appointed. A meeting of ministers of justice of the different states agreed upon a certain number of general principles, the control of the Court of Cassation and the French Conseil d'Etat over the juridical powers of the states and the possibility of appeal at the level of the Community.

The war continued in Algeria, with some progress by French forces in Ouarsenis and Kabylia. General de Gaulle, in his speech of Sept. 16, put forward a possible solution which made provision for a referendum in the 12 Algerian *départements* four years after a cease-fire.

On Sept. 25, after a two-day conference at Dakar, the Federation of Mali announced its intention of asking for independence, but wished to retain some ties with the Community. Addressing on Dec. 13 the Mali federal assembly, de Gaulle announced acceptance of the federation's wish to become independent in 1960.   (HU. DE.)

FRENCH EQUATORIAL AFRICA. Despite the appeals of Barthélemy Boganda for the setting up of one large central African state, at the end of 1958 French Equatorial Africa split up into four states: the Central African Republic (formerly Ubangi-Shari) and the republics of Chad, Congo and Gabon (*qq.v.*). A high commissioner for the whole group was to remain in office until Jan. 1, 1960. All the republics formed part of the French Community.

Two conferences brought the prime ministers of the states together to discuss a customs union. Agreement was reached in Paris on Jan. 17, 1959, on the free circulation of merchandise and capital, and on the creation of a common public office for administration of railways and navigable waterways, and another for posts and telecommunications. Provision was made for economic and fiscal co-operation and also for a permanent secretariat. The prime ministers were to meet twice a year.   (HU. DE.)

FRENCH GUIANA, French overseas *département* on the N.E. coast of South America bounded E. and S. by Brazil and W. by Surinam. Area, incl. territory of Inini: 35,135 sq.mi. Pop.: (1954 census) 27,863, incl. 2,380 natives of Inini; (1959 est.) 30,000. The coastal lowland population is creole French or Negro; Europeans *c.* 1,500; Inini, aboriginal Indians. Religion: mainly Roman Catholic. Capital and chief port, Cayenne, pop. (1954 est.) 13,346. Prefect, André Dubois-Chabert. Main exports: gold, timber. Monetary unit: metropolitan *franc*.

History. At the senatorial election on April 26, Guéril (U.N.R., Gaullist) was elected, defeating Robert Vignon (Socialist), formerly prefect of Guiana.

Prospecting for gold was resumed, with 699 kg. mined in 1958, compared with less than 200 kg. the year before. The Société Guyanaise des Bauxites was created, with the participation of Kaiser Aluminum Co. and the Guianese Mining bureau.   (HU. DE.)

FRENCH LITERATURE.

In 1959 literary production remained just as plentiful as in the preceding years and the novel continued to be the dominant literary form. However, one of the year's most notable books was a work of nonfiction, François Mauriac's *Mémoires intérieurs*, which one eminent critic rightly described as " a wealth of ideas ", in order to emphasize the variety and the richness of the subjects treated by the writer. It contained evocations of childhood and youth, intimate reminiscences about dead friends and pages of criticism on Racine, Charles Baudelaire, Arthur Rimbaud, Balzac, Marcel Proust, André Gide and others. In the words of Emile Henriot, Mauriac's colleague at the Académie Française, the *Mémoires intérieurs* was " François Mauriac's finest, most powerful, most substantial and truest work ".

Among other writers of the older generation Georges Duhamel set down his recollections as a man and as a writer in *Travail, ô mon seul repos*, André Maurois wrote a remarkable biography of Sir Alexander Fleming and Henri Bordeaux published the fifth volume of his memoirs, entitled *Douleur et gloire de Verdun*. Pierre Benoît published a new novel, *Flamarens*. Henry Troyat began a new romantic series under the title of *La Lumière des justes* with an historical novel, *Les Compagnons de coquelicot*, which recounted the adventures of a young Russian lieutenant in Paris in 1814. Roger Peyrefitte —never afraid of shocking the public—drew in *L'Exilé de Capri* (set at the beginning of the century) the portrait of a homosexual, Jacques d'Adelsward-Fersen. Following his magnificent historical novel on the flight of Napoleon from the island of Elba, *La Semaine sainte*, Louis Aragon wrote *Elsa*, a collection of fine love poems dedicated to his wife Elsa Triolet.

The two novels of 1959 which attracted particular attention were *Lolita*, the French version of Vladimir Nabokov's book, and *Aimez-vous Brahms*, Françoise Sagan's fourth novel, considered by critics a more mature work than the previous ones, in which she displayed her sensibility and her knowledge of the human heart. Among the many other books published during the year, the following were the most important: *Le Ciel de la fenêtre* by Jacques Chardonne; *Double Chance* by Alexandre Arnoux; *Le Pont des sorts* by Joseph Peyré; *Les Belles Croisades* by Jules Roy; *L'Eau profonde* by Philippe Diolé; *Routes de l'aventure* by Maurice Génevoix; *Feu de braise* by André Pieyre de Mandiargues; *L'Expérience* by Albert Palle; *Le Grand Mal* by Jean Forton; *La Grande Idée* by Jacques Perry; *Zazie dans le métro* by Raymond Queneau; *La Vaisselle des évêques* by Georges Borgeaud; *L'Homme de sang* by José Luis de Vilallonga; and *Terre paradis* by Paul Colin. Works by women writers worthy of mention in this brief honours list were: *Roses à crédit* by Elsa Triolet; *Planetarium* by Nathalie Sarraute; *Soleils d'hiver* by Martine Cadieu; *Migraine* by Louise de Vilmorin; and *Le Tour du monde d'une femme seule* by Agnès Chabrier.

The year saw the publication of the first volume of Jules Michelet's *Journal*, the last volume of the *Journal des Goncourt*, the 12th volume of the *Correspondance générale de Mérimée*, the full text of H. F. Amiel's *Journal intime* for the year 1866, *Mémoires inédits* of Alfred de Vigny, edited by Jean Sangnier, *Lettres de Colette à Marguerite Moreno*, *Lettres de P. J. Toulet et d'Emile Henriot*, *Lettres inédites de George Sand et de Pauline Viardot* and *Correspondance de Stéphane Mallarmé (1862-1871)*. Among the most noteworthy studies in literary history were: *L'Ame sensible* by Jean Dutourd (on

Françoise Sagan adopts an ironical pose before the hearing of her appeal against a careless driving conviction at Corbeil.

Stendhal); *Mérimée* by Robert Baschet; *Benjamin Constant muscadin* by Henri Guillemin; *Léon-Paul Fargue* by Edmée de la Rochefoucauld; and *Saint-Exupéry* by Marcel Migeo.

Several anthologies also appeared: *Trésor de la poésie universelle* by Roger Caillois and Jean-Clarence Lambert; *Anthologie des poétes de la N.R.F.* (new edition with a preface by Paul Valéry); *De L'Amour au voyage, anthologie thématique de la poésie française* by Max-Pol Fouchet; and finally the 21st and last volume of the *Encyclopédie française*.

The centenary of the deaths of Alexis de Tocqueville and Marceline Desbordes-Valmore and of the birth of Henri Bergson were commemorated. Among those who died during the year were the poet René Arcos, the novelists Jean de la Varende, Henri Pourrat and Francis de Miomandre, and the critic Robert Kemp. (*See also* LITERARY PRIZES.) (A. PR.)

FRENCH SOMALILAND: *see* SOMALILAND, FRENCH.

FRENCH SOUTHERN OCEAN AND ANTARCTIC LANDS

(TERRES AUSTRALES ET ANTARCTIQUES FRANÇAISES), a group of islands in the southern part of the Indian ocean including a section of Antarctica. A special administration for these lands was created by a decree of Sept. 18, 1956, with an administrator residing in Paris. The following lands are included: two volcanic islands, Saint-Paul (2·7 sq.mi.) and Nouvelle-Amsterdam (16 sq.mi.); Kerguelen island with many adjacent islands (c. 2·700 sq.mi. in all); the small volcanic Crozet islands; and Adélie land in Antarctica (c. 150,000 sq.mi.). Total area: c. 152,720 sq.mi. Pop. (1959 est.): 150. Administrator, Pierre Roland.

History. Scientific research continued within the framework of International Geophysical Co-operation. Relieving parties took over in the islands in March 1959 and in Adélie land in December.

At Kerguelen helicopters were brought in to prospect in the eastern regions which were still little known. At the seal factory the carcasses of 500 animals produced 500 metric tons of oil and seal flour.

The setting up of a meteorological station on the Crozet islands was being planned. A geodesic mission was to survey the coast of Adélie land. By Dec. 15, 1958, an expedition had penetrated about 300 mi. into the interior.   (HU. DE.)

FRENCH WEST AFRICA.

At the end of 1958 French West Africa (with the exception of Guinea which had become independent) was divided into seven republics, corresponding to the former territories. Mauritania, the Soudan, the republics of Senegal, Ivory Coast, Upper Volta, Dahomey and Niger (qq.v.). All belonged to the French Community.

At the conference held at Bamako (Dec. 30, 1958), the delegates from Senegal, Soudan, Upper Volta and Dahomey decided to form a federation. On Jan. 17, 1959, the Federation of Mali (q.v.) was proclaimed, with a government, a parliament and federal institutions. Upper Volta and Dahomey subsequently withdrew from the federation in order to join the " Sahel-Bénin entente " with Ivory Coast and Niger.

The local political parties allied themselves either with the Rassemblement Démocratique Africain (Félix Houphouët-Boigny) or with the Parti de la Fédération Africaine (Léopold Sedar Senghor), which advocated African unity.

French West Africa ceased to exist on Jan. 21, 1959. Agreements were concluded among the states for the sharing of common property and the setting up of a customs union.   (HU. DE.)

FRIENDS, THE RELIGIOUS SOCIETY OF.

Founded during the 17th century, the Society of Friends places special emphasis on the immediate access of the individual, and of the worshipping group or church, to the presence and guidance of God. From this central tenet springs its mode of worship in silence, without pre-arranged direction. During this silence anyone present may minister vocally. Long practice of this informal mode of worship has developed a tradition of restraint which renders a Quaker meeting, both in its silence and in its vocal passages, quite unlike other modes of Christian expression. World membership (Jan. 1, 1959): c. 200,000, incl. 118,000 in the United States, 29,000 in Kenya, 21,643 (incl. children) in Great Britain and 2,000 (incl. children) in Ireland.

The year opened with several Friends serving short prison sentences as a result of individual participation in non-violent protest by trespass at a nuclear rocket site in Norfolk. Quaker peace witness continued in corporate support of the Campaign for Nuclear Disarmament, and in corporate sponsorship (with Christian Action) of a great meeting of Christian witness against nuclear war, at the Albert hall (May 25). Friends conducted a special project in Austria for World Refugee Year. In November revisions to Christian Discipline, the Quaker handbook on Christian faith and practice, were approved.

Well-known Friends who died towards the end of 1958 or

The new Quaker meeting house at Hitchin, Herts., designed by Paul Mauger. It stands on piers above a 200-yr.-old burial ground.

during 1959 included Reginald Reynolds, Barbara Duncan Harris, Edward Bernstein, Laurence Housman, Gerard Hoffnung (see OBITUARIES), Cyril Barnard, David Evans, Eleanor Morland Shewell, Mignon Castle, George Percy Harris, Geoffrey Maw, Dorothea Wood, Eleanor Crosfield, Ida M. Whitworth and Marjorie Gullan.   (B. CA.)

BIBLIOGRAPHY. Anne Vernon, A Quaker Business Man: The Life of Joseph Rowntree, 1832-1925 (London, 1958); John Sykes, The Quakers: A New Look at Their Place in Society (London, 1958); Otelia Cromwell, Lucretia Mott (Oxford, 1959); Elizabeth Gray Vining, Friend of Life: The Biography of Rufus M. Jones (London, 1959); Richard K. Ullmann, Between God and History: The Human Situation Exemplified in Quaker Thought and Practice (London, 1959); Harold Loukes, The Castle and the Field: An Essay in the Psychology of Religion (London, 1959).

FRUIT: see FOODSTUFFS.

FURNITURE INDUSTRY: see BUSINESS REVIEW.

FURTHER EDUCATION.

The main emphasis in 1959 was on the expansion of vocational education. In April the British government announced a £54 million capital investment programme for technical education in England and Wales in 1961-64. It was proposed to give in 1963-64 priority to buildings for commercial education, whose large development was advocated by the McMeeking report, published in March. The National Council for Technological Awards in England and Wales reported that in March there were 2,518 students reading for the diploma in technology, almost double the figure of the previous year. In May the council announced the creation of a College of Technologists, membership of which constitutes a qualification higher than the diploma. In April the value of the Whitworth foundation fellowships, England's premier award in engineering, was doubled to provide from 1960 three fellowships annually of £1,000 with allowances. In June the new Industrial Training council accepted a £75,000 government grant for expanding apprenticeship and other training schemes. The grant was conditional upon industry raising the same amount.

International co-operation aided several Asian projects. In 1958 the New Zealand government, under the Colombo plan, made a grant to Ceylon to equip two junior technical schools. In Jan. 1959 the Duke of Edinburgh laid the foundation stone of a new engineering institute near Delhi, established jointly by the British and Indian governments and British industry. The institute would provide for 800-900 undergraduate and 100 post-graduate students. In May Paul Hoffman, managing director of the United Nations Special fund, announced that the fund would give $850,000 over three years to establish in India a vocational training institute for training up to 800 craftsmen a year. The Japanese Federation of Machinery Industries proposed to open in 1959, with the co-operation of the Indian and Malayan governments respectively, technical centres in West Bengal and Kuala Lumpur. The first girls' secretarial school in the Sudan was opened in 1959 in the Khartoum Technical institute.

Adult Education. In Oct. 1958 the minimum age of entry into Swedish folk high schools was raised by law from 17 to 18 (girls not till 1962) and the minimum length of a year's course was increased from 21 to 30 weeks. State grants for current expenditure were increased and subsidies of up to 75% for new buildings made available. It was announced in July 1959 that the Beit and Dulverton trusts had given nearly £40,000 towards the establishment of two multiracial colleges of citizenship for adults in Rhodesia and Kenya. Independent governing bodies for the colleges were set up and a site secured near Salisbury for the Rhodesian one. Half of the West Nigerian government's television service, due to begin full transmission in Sept. 1959, consisted of educational programmes for schools and adult education.

During the year the Sudan government closed down the Sudanese Workers' Educational association and confiscated its assets. It had been founded in 1957 with the aid of Unesco, the International Labour organization and the International Federation of Workers' Educational Associations. (*See* also UNIVERSITIES AND COLLEGES.)   (H. C. D.)

FUR TRADE: *see* BUSINESS REVIEW.

GABON, REPUBLIC OF (RÉPUBLIQUE GABONAISE),

a member state of the French Community. Gabon is bounded N. by Spanish Guinea and the autonomous republic of Cameroun, E. and S. by the Republic of Congo and W. by the Atlantic ocean. Area: 103,089 sq.mi. Pop.: (1950 est.) 409,000; (1959 est.) 411,000; mainly Bantu Negroes; Europeans (1956 est.) 3,981. Language: Bantu dialects. Religion: animist, with a strong Christian minority. Chief towns (pop., 1957 est.): Libreville (cap. 19,000); Port Gentil; Mayoumba; Lambaréné. Prime minister: Léon M'Ba. French high commissioner, Jean Risterucci. Chief exports: timber, palm kernels, palm oil. Monetary unit: *franc CFA* = metropolitan Fr.2.

History. The Republic of Gabon was proclaimed on Nov. 28, 1958, and the constitution was passed unanimously by the territorial assembly on Feb. 20, 1959. The official language was to be French. The assembly invested the prime minister, who held executive power. After two ministerial crises he could dissolve the assembly.

A Société des Mines de Fer de Mekambo was set up with French, German, Dutch and U.S. companies (Bethlehem Steel had 50% of the shares). Plans were made for a railway 700 km. in length and for the draining of the estuary of the Gabon. The stratum lying in the northeast contained about 500 million metric tons of 60% iron ore. On June 30 a $35 million loan was granted by the International Bank for Reconstruction and Development for exploitation of manganese deposits in the Franceville area by the Compagnie Minière de l'Ogoué.   (HU. DE.)

GAMBIA.

British colony and protectorate on the west coast of Africa surrounded by the Republic of Senegal. Area: 4,003 sq.mi., incl. protectorate 3,974 sq.mi. Pop.: colony (1951 census) 27,297; protectorate (1952 census) 250,160. Colony and protectorate, (1957 est.) 285,000. Language: many tribal dialects; Hausa. Religion: mainly Moslem, some pagan; c. 5,000 Christians in Bathurst. Capital: Bathurst, pop. (1951 census) 19,602, (1957 est.) 21,000. Administration: governor; executive council, including departmental ministers; legislative council with speaker and elected majority. Governor, Sir Edward Windley. Main imports: machinery and metal manufactures, cotton piecegoods, rice, kola nuts. Main export: groundnuts. Monetary unit: West African shilling (=1s. sterling).

History. In June 1959 the secretary of state for the colonies, A. T. Lennox-Boyd, visited Gambia and expressed confidence that the British government would agree to constitutional arrangements consistent with Gambia's needs in time to allow elections to be held in May 1960. The arrangements foreshadowed were announced in September. Universal adult suffrage would be extended to include the whole territory. The representation of the protectorate in the legislative council would be increased from 7 to 20 members, of whom 8 would be elected by chiefs and 12 by the electorate. The colony would retain seven directly elected members and the council would continue to include five *ex officio* and official members and two nominated unofficial members. The total membership of the council would be increased from 21 to 34. The number of ministers in the executive council would be increased to not more than six, of whom not less than three were to have portfolios. The four *ex officio* members would remain with the governor, who would retain his reserve powers and final responsibility for good government.   (W. H. Is.)

GAMBLING: *see* BETTING AND GAMBLING.
GAS INDUSTRY: *see* BUSINESS REVIEW.
GASTRIC AND INTESTINAL DISEASES: *see* DISEASES.

GAS TURBINES: *see* JET PROPULSION AND GAS TURBINES.
GEMS: *see* BUSINESS REVIEW.

GENERAL ELECTION.

The British general election that took place on Oct. 8, 1959, created a precedent in British political history. Never before under the modern party system had one party—in this case, the Conservatives—won a third general election in succession with an increased majority each time. The Conservatives, who had been defeated in 1945, returned to office in 1951 with a majority of 17 over all other parties. In 1955 their majority rose to 60, and in 1959 to 100.

The Conservatives' strength rose from 345 in 1955 to 365 in 1959; Labour's fell from 277 to 258; and the Liberals' remained static at 6. In 1955, two Sinn Feiners were elected in Northern Ireland completing the total of 630 members of the House of Commons. Later they were replaced by Ulster Unionists to swell the Conservative majority. In 1959 no minority groups secured any seats although Communists, Welsh Nationalists, Sinn Feiners, Scottish Nationalists and others contested the election.

The relative standing of the three principal parties immediately before and during the election campaign did not provide conclusive evidence of the size of the ultimate Conservative majority. The election campaign, throughout its course, was something of a puzzle. When Harold Macmillan, the prime minister, announced on Sept. 8 that the election would be held a month later, the signs were that the public decisively favoured the Conservatives. As the campaign went on, Labour made sufficient headway to reduce the Conservatives' lead until, shortly before polling day, the declared supporters of each side were equal. This position was inconclusive for three reasons: many electors would not reveal their voting intentions either to party canvassers or opinion pollsters; the effect of 217 Liberal candidatures upon those of the Conservative and Labour parties was difficult to estimate; and opinion might change in the last few days of the campaign. The poll showed that there had been a national swing of 1·5% to the Conservatives, although in some areas—notably Scotland and Lancashire—there was a slight swing to Labour. Electors who had not declared themselves before polling day tended to vote Conservative on Oct. 8, and there was a shift of support from Labour to the Liberals.

So slight a movement of opinion gave the Conservatives a majority of 100, but in fact the combined Labour and Liberal vote was greater than that of the Conservatives by 0·3%. The anti-Labour vote (Conservative and Liberal combined) was, however, 11·5% higher than the Labour vote. The Conservatives entered the election campaign with the prophecy that, if they beat Labour for the third time in succession, Labour in Britain would be dead.

The Conservatives took " Peace and Prosperity " as their election slogan, and Macmillan launched his campaign in a period of exceptional calm both at home and abroad. This sharpened the point of the two " simple " questions which the Conservatives asked the electors in their manifesto:

Do you want to go ahead on the lines which have brought prosperity at home? Do you want your present leaders to represent you abroad?

During the election campaign the economic omens were favourable—production good, reserves sound, unemployment down. Abroad, Nikita Khrushchev was visiting President Dwight D. Eisenhower in the United States—only a week or two after Eisenhower had visited Macmillan in Britain. Macmillan told the electors that if he and Selwyn Lloyd, the foreign secretary, had not gone to Moscow earlier in the year and broken the ice that had frozen east-west relations,

Two cartoons showing the importance which the political parties attached to the floating voter in the general election—(left) by Vicky in the " New Statesman " on July 4 and (right) " The bright side's the right side " by Emwood in the " Daily Mail " on Oct. 6.

Khrushchev and the President could scarcely have met in the United States. At the moment when the election date was announced, Hugh Gaitskell, leader of the Labour party, and Aneurin Bevan, Labour's " shadow " foreign secretary, were themselves in Moscow. They saw Khrushchev just before he left Moscow for the United States.

Although Macmillan in his election tour spoke frequently and fully about foreign affairs, Conservative propaganda dwelt on prosperity and claimed that all sections of the community were sharing in it. Before the election Macmillan had reiterated the phrase: " You've never had it so good ". Labour attacked this claim in the first paragraphs of its manifesto, " Britain Belongs to You ". The contrast between the extremes of wealth and poverty, said Labour, was sharper

now than it had been eight years ago when Labour left office. On the one hand were the business men with tax-free expenses, speculators with tax-free capital gains, retiring directors with tax-free redundancy payments; on the other hand were the widowed mothers with children, the chronic sick, the unemployed, the old age pensioners. To reduce the gap between the " haves " and " have nots " Labour proposed to raise at once the old age pension by 10s. a week, to introduce an elaborate state superannuation scheme, to increase the rate of municipal house-building, to curb expenses and to tax capital gains. Labour's campaign also relied heavily on criticism of the government's foreign policy at the time of Suez, and of its colonial administration particularly in Nyasaland and at the Hola detention camp in Kenya. Labour demanded an end to

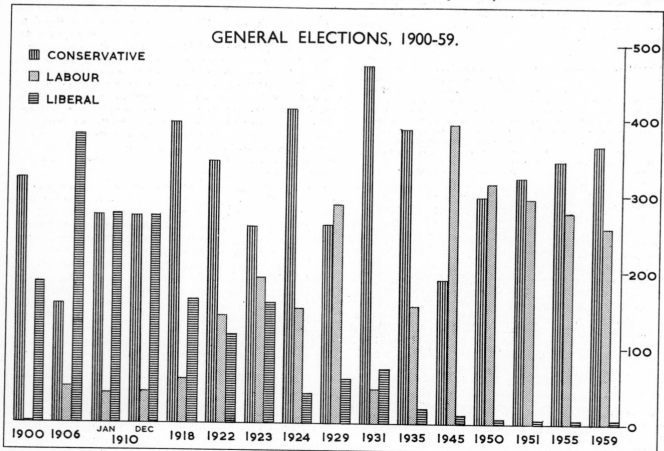

The chart shows the number of seats won by each of the three main political parties at every British general election since 1900. In 1959 the newly elected House of Commons consisted of 630 members.

(*1*) *The prime minister, Harold Macmillan, answers a question at Bury during his election tour of Lancashire towns.* (*2*) *The leader of the Labour party, Hugh Gaitskell, seen at an election meeting at Wandsworth with Pat Llewellyn Davies, the Labour candidate for Wandsworth Central, who was subsequently defeated by her Conservative opponent, Michael Hughes-Young.* (*3*) *The leader of the Liberal party, Jo Grimond, arriving by helicopter in Manchester, where he was to speak in support of a Liberal candidate.* (*4*) *Election posters being prepared for dispatch at the Labour party headquarters in London.* (*5*) *On the eve of polling day ballot boxes are carried out of St. Pancras town hall to be distributed among various polling stations in the Holborn district.*

(*6*) *Women going to record their votes in the waiting room at Beaulieu Road railway station, Hampshire, which was set up as a polling centre to serve people living in a remote part of the New Forest.* (*7*) *The scene at St. Pancras town hall as the votes are being counted.* (*8*) *Later, Geoffrey Johnson Smith, who won Holborn and St. Pancras South for the Conservatives by a narrow margin, is congratulated by the Labour candidate, Lena Jeger.* (*9*) *Jeremy Thorpe (right), elected Liberal M.P. for North Devon with a majority of 362 votes, shakes hands with the Conservative candidate, James Lindsay. The Labour candidate, Geoffrey Pitt, is in the centre.*

(*Left*) " *I didn't think it was such a bad speech as all that, Grandma* "—Giles in the " *Daily Express* " on Oct. 1. (*Right*) " *The nutshell king* "—*a comment by Franklin on the Liberal party's ambitions, which appeared in the* " *Daily Mirror* " *on April 21.*

all nuclear arms tests and a check on the spread of nuclear arms to countries which hitherto had lacked them.

The Conservatives' main purpose during the campaign was to force the electors to estimate the cost of Labour's social programme and to conclude that Labour's finance was irresponsible. Labour replied that their projects could be financed out of increased production and by " catching the tax-dodgers ". In an effort to counter the effects of the Conservatives' attack on Labour's finance, Gaitskell announced during the election campaign that a Labour government would not increase income tax in time of peace. He announced, too, that a Labour government would remove purchase tax from essential household goods. These declarations stiffened the Conservatives' demand to know what other taxes would be raised in compensation. Labour pledged itself to re-nationalize that section of the steel industry which the Conservatives restored to private ownership after 1951 and to re-nationalize long-distance commercial road haulage which the Conservatives had also restored to private ownership. Neither the Conservatives nor the Liberals would contemplate any more nationalization.

Both Macmillan and Gaitskell made strong personal impacts on the public not only by speaking tours throughout the country but by television broadcasts. But for the stimulus of Gaitskell's campaigning, and the skill with which Labour's headquarters team caught the public's attention, the result of the election might have been even worse for Labour. The party's policies lacked the power to attract the uncommitted voters who had contributed so heavily to Labour's success in 1945.

This was the first election that the Liberals had fought under the leadership of Jo Grimond, whose long-term purpose was to substitute his party for Labour as the alternative to the Conservatives. The Liberal manifesto, " People Count ", asserted individual judgment against the power of party machines and individual partnership in industry against both Socialism and the " boss-employee " relationship.

The Liberals were as critical as Labour of the government's management of foreign and colonial affairs. They ran twice as many candidates as they had done in 1955; they polled 1,661,262 votes and increased their share of the total poll by $3 \cdot 2\%$ compared with 1955; but they failed to increase their representation in parliament. It was a disappointing result for the Liberals and, as they were quick to point out, was another instance of the unrepresentative nature of the British electoral system. (*See also* ELECTIONS.)   (J. F. BD.)

GENETICS. Human Chromosome Abnormalities. Chromosome number and shape can be readily determined only during the short period of cell division called metaphase. Even in a

tissue in which active division is going on, only very few cells will be at this stage and the difficulty of obtaining sufficient numbers of human cells of the right type for cytological examination prevented, until recently, any large scale cytological study of man. Techniques were recently developed, however, for growing human cells in artificial culture media and handling them in much the same way as bacteria, and cytological studies consequently became a practical proposition. The first discovery was that human cells normally have 46 chromosomes, not 48 as had previously been claimed. In 1959 C. E. Ford, P. A. Jacobs, J. H. Tjio, T. T. Puck and others went further with a cytological study of a number of individuals suffering from developmental abnormalities. Some 18 mongoloid imbeciles were examined and all were found to have 47 chromosomes; there were three representatives of one of the smallest chromosomes in the human set instead of the normal pair. More interesting were chromosome counts of individuals with characteristic types of abnormality in sexual development. Individuals exhibiting Turner's syndrome are predominantly female in appearance, but have abortive ovaries. A number of patients with this abnormality were found to have only 45 chromosomes. One of the sex-determining chromosomes was missing, these individuals having the constitution XO instead of XX as in normal females. Individuals with Kleinerfelter's syndrome are predominantly male in appearance, but have abortive testes. Patients with this abnormality were found to have 47 chromosomes. The extra chromosome was again one of the sex chromosomes and these individuals had the constitution XXY instead of XY as in normal males.

A most interesting feature of these results was that they showed that the mechanism of sex determination in man was quite different from that in the fruit fly *Drosophila*, the only other animal in which the mechanism had been well worked out. In *Drosophila*, as in man, females were known to have two identical sex chromosomes and males two morphologically different sex chromosomes. It was well known, however, that the Y chromosome played only a passive role, the sex of the fly being dependent on the number of X chromosomes in relation to the number of other chromosomes. Thus a fly with two X chromosomes was female, a fly with one was male. Consequently flies with the constitution XXY were females and flies with the constitution XO were males. In man, on the other hand, it was now clear that the Y chromosome played a positive male-determining role since XXY individuals were males and XO individuals females. That the role of the Y chromosome in man might be characteristic of mammals in general was suggested by the observation of W. J. Welshons and L. B. Russell that XO mice were also anatomically female.

The origin of these chromosomal abnormalities in man was not determined but a number of authors pointed out that occasional failure of the chromosomes to sort out equally between the two daughter cells during cell divisions involved in the formation of eggs and sperm would produce such abnormalities, and such failures were well known in other organisms. They were known to occur more frequently in aging cells and this suggested an explanation for the fact that the frequency of mongoloid infants increased with the age of the mother at the time of conception. There was no corresponding correlation with the age of the father and this suggested that sperm with abnormal chromosome numbers were non-functional.

DNA Duplication. Deoxyribonucleic acid (DNA), the carrier of genetic information in most organisms (*see* GENETICS in *Britannica Book of the Year 1959*), was known to consist of a large number of small molecules attached end to end to form a chain. These molecules were normally of four kinds which differed according to whether they contained the bases adenine, guanine, thymine or cytosine. A gene consisted of a length of DNA several thousand bases long and the properties of genes were thought to be determined by the sequence of these bases. An important question was how a molecule of DNA was able to make an exact copy of itself with an identical base sequence when a cell divided, so that two daughter cells could inherit identical genes from the parent cell.

In a series of outstanding experiments A. Kornberg achieved for the first time the synthesis of DNA. He discovered an enzyme system in bacteria that was able to catalyze the synthesis of DNA when added to a mixture containing derivatives of the four bases. An additional requirement was that a small amount of DNA must be added to the reaction mixture as a primer. This was in accordance with the currently accepted view that DNA was not synthesized *de novo* but required the presence of existing DNA to act as a pattern or template. More striking was the observation that the amount of the different bases withdrawn from the reaction mixture to make new DNA was proportional not to their relative concentrations, but to the proportion of each type in the primer. This was also in accordance with the hypothesis that the base sequence of newly synthesized DNA was determined by that in the pattern or template DNA. Kornberg's synthesis of DNA provided the nearest approach yet made to the synthesis of living material in the test tube.

(R. H. Pd.)

GEOGRAPHY.

GEOGRAPHY. The year 1959 was the centenary of the death of two men, Alexander von Humboldt and Karl Ritter, who have been called " the founders of modern geography ". Appropriate celebrations were held and tributes paid, notably in Berlin during May. The 80th birthday of Professor Emeritus Eva G. R. Taylor on June 22, 1959, was marked by an appeal for the endowment of an annual lecture in the branches of knowledge (including the history of geographical ideas and discovery and of nautical science) to which she had made, and was still making, important contributions. Professor S. W. Wooldridge was elected a fellow of the Royal Society.

The Royal Geographical society's Patron's medal for 1959 was awarded to Commander W. R. Anderson, commander of the U.S. submarine " Nautilus " which made the first voyage under the north pole in Aug. 1958. The Founder's medal was given to Sir Raymond Priestley, a member of Shackleton's expedition of 1907-9 and of Scott's expedition of 1910-13, and British observer with the United States Antarctic expedition of 1958-59. G. Seligman, president of the British Glaciological society, was awarded the Victoria medal for his contributions to glaciological research. The American Geographical society awarded the Cullum Geographical medal to C. W. Thornthwaite, the distinguished climatologist, and Sir Vivian Fuchs received the Hubbard medal, the National Geographic society's highest distinction, for his leadership of the Commonwealth Trans-Antarctic expedition and for the crossing of the south pole a year previously. Lord Nathan continued as president of the Royal Geographical society. The Earl of Wemyss and March succeeded Douglas Allen as president of the Royal Scottish Geographical society for the next three years.

The Institute of British Geographers met in Cambridge under the presidency of Professor E. G. Bowen of University college, Aberystwyth. His address, " Le pays de Galles ", a study of the interrelationship of systematic geographical phenomena in Wales, was published in the institute's *Transactions and Papers, 1959, 26* (London, 1959). The Geographical association's conference, held in London, had agricultural geography as its theme and the subject of Professor R. O. Buchanan's presidential address was " Some Reflections on Agricultural Geography ". The association's spring meeting was held in Leicester. York was the meeting place for the annual meeting of the British Association in September. Professor K. C. Edwards of the University of Nottingham, president of section E (Geography), discussed trends in urban expansion in his presidential address. Further progress with the plans for the 19th international congress to be held in Stockholm in July and Aug. 1960 under the auspices of the International Geographical union was reported. Negotiations also continued during the year for the establishment of an international cartographic organization in close association with the International Geographical union.

The Second Coastal Geography conference, held in Baton Rouge, Louisiana, in April was attended by 60 specialists, and a joint seminar of British and Polish geographers took place in Warsaw during September at the invitation of the Polish government. Collaboration between geography and medicine to co-ordinate research in the geography of disease was strongly urged by A. Leslie Banks, professor of human ecology in the University of Cambridge, in a paper read in January (*Geogr. J., 125*, 199-216, 1959). The American Geographical society published the first of its studies in medical geography, Dr. Jacques M. May's *The Ecology of Human Disease* (New York, 1959).

Deaths included those of Homer Leroy Shantz, Charles Camsell and Augustine Courtauld (*see* OBITUARIES).

The following noteworthy books were published:

J. A. Taylor and R. A. Yates, *British Weather in Maps* (London, 1958); A. A. Miller and M. Parry, *Everyday Meteorology* (London, 1958); A. Guilcher, *Coastal and Submarine Morphology*, Eng. trans. by B. W. Sparks and R. H. W. Kneese (London, 1958); and J. Beaujeu Garnier, *Géographie de la population*, tome ii (Paris, 1958); T. W. Freeman, *The Conurbations of Great Britain* (Manchester, 1959); J. M. Lambert, J. N. Jennings and others, *The Origin of the Broads: a Re-examination of the Problem in the Light of New Evidence* (Royal Geographical society research memoir, no. 3, London, 1959); W. B. Fisher and H. Bowen-Jones, *Spain: a Geographical Background* (London, 1958); F. J. Monkhouse, *A Regional Geography of Western Europe* (London, 1959); T. L. Hills, *The St. Lawrence Seaway* (London, 1959); E. Higbee, *American Agriculture: Geography, Resources Conservation,* (New York, 1958); E. A. Boateng, *A Geography of Ghana* (Cambridge, 1959); B. W. Hodder, *Man in Malaya* (London, 1959); and N. Ahmad, *An Economic Geography of East Pakistan* (London, 1958). The American Geographical society published " Geographic Study of Mountain Glaciation in the Northern Hemisphere " in nine volumes with an atlas. The Hakluyt society issued two volumes (Cambridge, 1959), *The Troublesome Voyage of Captain Edward Fenton, 1582-83*, edited by E. G. R. Taylor, and *The Tragic History of the Sea, 1589-1622*, edited by C. R. Boxer.

Atlases and Maps. A notable addition to the national atlases of the world was the National Atlas of India, edited by S. P. Chatterjee, which appeared in a preliminary Hindi edition (Dehra Dun, 1957). Books and atlases published included P. D. A. Harvey and H. Thorpe's *The Printed Maps of Warwickshire, 1576-1900* (Warwick, 1959); a new edition of Williams Rees' *An Historical Atlas of Wales from Early to Modern Times* (London, 1959); R. A. Skelton's *Explorers' Maps:*

Chapters in the Cartographic Record of Geographical Discovery (London, 1958); and the fifth volume of *A List of Geographical Atlases in the Library of Congress* (Washington, 1958), containing records of most atlases published between 1920 and 1955.

The Royal Geographical society and the Bodleian library, Oxford, collaborated in the production of *The Map of Great Britain circa A.D. 1360, known as the Gough Map* (Oxford, 1958) with an accompanying text by E. J. S. Parsons and a paper by Sir Frank Stenton. Of the countless modern maps issued, a few only can be mentioned: among British Ordnance survey productions, another 1:63,360 tourist sheet (Lorn-Lochaber), the first of the new second series of half-inch maps (Birmingham) and a special sheet of Wales and the Marches at a scale of 1:250,000; a new 1:100,000 map series of the Aden Protectorate with a three-dimensional effect of relief and a set of 1:25,000 land-use maps of the Gambia (both published by the British Directorate of Overseas surveys); the first of a series of detailed 1:6,366 land-use maps of rural Singapore (Singapore Improvement trust and Department of Geography, University of Malaya); and a 1:10,000,000 vegetation map of Africa south of the Tropic of Cancer (Oxford, 1959), for the Association pour l'Etude Taxonomique de la Flore d'Afrique Tropicale, with an explanatory memoir by R. W. J. Keay. (*See* also ANTARCTICA; EXPLORATION AND DISCOVERY.)　　　　　　　　　　(R. W. SL.)

GEOLOGY. Books.

During 1959 increasing interest in the history of geology was shown by publications such as James Hutton's *Theory of the Earth* (New York, 1959), first published in 1795, and a translation of Nicolaus Steno's *Earliest Geological Treatise* (1667) by A. Garboe (London, 1959). For the first time in English a convenient summary of the theories of Otto Schmidt was available in *The Origin of the Earth* (London, 1959). New textbooks included B. F. Howell's *Introduction to Geophysics* (New York, 1959); J. A. Jacobs, R. D. Russell and J. T. Wilson's *Physics and Geology* (Toronto, 1959); W. W. Moorhouse's *Study of Rocks in Thin Section* (New York, 1959); F. Rinne's *La Science des Roches* (Paris, 1959); and P. C. Badgley's *Structural Methods for the Exploration Geologist* (New York, 1959).

New editions of the following well-known works also appeared: Sir Harold Jeffreys' *The Earth*, 4th ed. (London, 1959); J. Gilluly, A. C. Waters and A. D. Woodford's *Principles of Geology*, 2nd ed. (New York, 1959); and F. E. Zuener's *The Pleistocene Period*, 2nd ed. (London, 1959). In applied geology new editions of the following appeared: *Geologia Applicata all' Ingegneria* by A. Desio, 2nd ed. (Milan, 1959); a symposium *Subsurface Geology in Petroleum Exploration* by J. D. Haun and L. W. LeRoy (Colorado, 1958); and *Geology for Engineers* by J. M. Trefethan, 2nd ed. (New York, 1959).

Oceans and Continents. The geology of the oceans claimed increasing attention during 1959 as plans were made for more ships to follow a variety of investigations. Rapid advances in accurate sounding began to yield results which, for the North Atlantic at least, gave a picture of the ocean floor in considerable detail. One feature of the Atlantic basin was a contrast between the great irregularity of most of the floor and the extremely flat abyssal plains in the main bordering the continents, and with evidence of contemporary deposition by turbidity currents. Another feature which had long attracted attention was the mid-Atlantic ridge and the resolution of modern sounding profiles suggested a median rift structure throughout the length of a massive ridge trench complex. It was propounded that basalts had filled a median fissure suggesting an intermittent widening of the Atlantic ocean, possibly coupled with compression structures (B. C. Heezen *et al.*, "The Floors of the Oceans: I. North Atlantic", *Spec. Pap. geol. Soc. Amer.*, 65, 1959).

The long suspected complexity of the ocean floor and continental shelves was illustrated with more precision than hitherto by the impressive seismic investigations off the east coast of the United States. One of a series of papers (J. B. Hersey *et al.*, "Geophysical Investigation of the Continental Margin Between Cape Henry, Virginia and Jacksonville, Florida", *Bull. geol. Soc. Amer.*, 70, 437-466, 1959) described 40 seismic profiles from which two new features emerged: (1) geosynclines near the edge of the continental shelf showed that thick sedimentation had developed well away from the present shore; (2) the Blake plateau appeared to be a volcanic region with islands compensated at depth by a root of intermediate density material depressing the " Moho ". Speculation as to the history of this uplift suggested the familiar idea of an asthenolith or undation.

In *Continental Drift* (Hobart, 1958), a number of papers given in a symposium convened by S. W. Carey in 1956 were published. Successive symposia on the history of the continents had appeared from time to time reflecting the changing fashions of thought. Hitherto somewhat indeterminate bio-geographical considerations had played a large part and the drift argument really rested on the reassembly of the fragments of Gondwanaland, especially to account for the late Palaeozoic glaciation. A paper by Irving summarized the critical new evidence from palaeomagnetism and the principal contribution, by Carey, summarized his views by a synthesis of tectonic deformation which combined to give a detailed pattern of continental reassembly. Key points in this theory were the straightening of curved mountain belts (oroclines), their stretching (orotaths), and the opening of the crust by parallel sliding (rhombochasm) and rotation (sphenochasm). For the first time substantial parts of the hypothesis were dealt with in sufficient detail to be tested by direct geological evidence.

A notable development on a small scale arose out of the discovery of unexpectedly high fluid pressure in deep wells in the Texas-Louisiana and other areas. From this it was deduced that rapid deposition in geosynclines may trap sufficient water to lead to tectonic instability and sliding. Indeed, the long-standing problem of how to account for large-scale, low-angle thrusting seemed at last solved, in that a thrust slice resting on a high-pressure interstitial fluid may move readily because of the very low coefficient of friction resulting from the fluid support. The fluid trapped within the pore spaces of the geosynclinal sediments gives a mechanism which might be likened to that of the Hovercraft (M. K. Hubbert and W. W. Rubey, "The Role of Fluid Pressure in Mechanics of Overthrust Faulting", *Bull. geol. Soc. Amer.*, 70, 115-206, 1959).

On a still smaller scale progress was made in the study of the relation of small-scale structures to deformation processes, and one representative of a large number of local studies was by B. Engels "Die kleintektonische Arbeitsweise unter besonderer Berücksichtigung ihrer Anwendung im deutschen Paläozoikum" (*Geotektonische Forschungen*, Stuttgart, 1959).

Stratigraphy. What promised to be one of the most comprehensive stratigraphical works yet to appear, *Handbuch der stratigraphischen Geologie*, edited by F. Lotze, was launched in 1958-59 with the publication in Stuttgart of the two parts of vol. III on the Tertiary. Part 1 by A. Papp dealt mainly with the marine successions throughout the world, summarizing much of the new work on Foraminifera and correlating it with the molluscan and other evidence. Part 2 by P. Thening was concerned with vertebrates and was largely a parallel treatment of continental geology.

In the U.S.S.R. the Tertiary system with special reference to the southern Caucasus was reviewed by V. P. Zhizhchenko in his *Printsipy Stratigrafii . . . (Principles of the Stratigraphy and Unification of the Cainozoic Scheme*, Moscow, 1958).

Regional Geology. Amongst the most notable regional syntheses which became available during the year were: P. B. King's *The Evolution of North America* (Princeton, New Jersey, 1959); *Geologicheskoe Stroenie S.S.S.R.* (*The Geological Formation of the U.S.S.R.*), edited by N. A. Belyavski, A. P. Markovski *et al.* (Moscow, 1958). Vol. I, *Stratigrafie* (*Stratigraphy*), was edited by N. K. Ovechkin and contains an appendix of maps, vol. II, *Magmatizm*, was edited by U. I.

Polovinkina and vol. III, *Tektonika*, by L. I. Kyasny, with a geological map in two sheets scale 1:7,500,000 and a geomorphological map scale 1:15,000,000. *Regional Stratigraphical Tables of China, Academia Sinica* (Peking, 1956-58), divided the country into 119 areas in each of which the stratigraphical succession, with principal fossils, was listed and also a number of references. In 1959 a complementary volume appeared reviewing the stratigraphy of China in a series of palaeogeographical maps. Other valuable regional reviews included: D. Andrusov's *Geológia Československých Karpát* (Bratislava, 1958); J. L. Hough's *Geology of the Great Lakes* (Urbana, 1958); J. T. Kingman's " A Tectonic History of New Zealand " in *N.Z. Jn. Geol. Geophys.*, 2, 1-55, 1959; and J. R. H. McWhae *et al.*, *The Stratigraphy of Western Australia* (Melbourne, 1958). A new series of four miles to one inch geological maps was initiated on Australia. (*See* also MINERALOGY; OCEANOGRAPHY; PALAEONTOLOGY; SEISMOLOGY.) (W. B. HD.)

GERMAN LITERATURE.

During 1959 posthumous works were again important. Karl Wolfskehl's *Zehn Jahre Exil: Briefe aus Neuseeland 1938-1948* was a moving testimony to the spiritual anguish and courage of a distinguished poet who had been in contact, virtually by correspondence only, with the world of friendship and literature to which he once belonged. *Sfaira der Alte*, the last full-scale work by Alfred Mombert, was a cycle of visionary verse, while Arno Nadel's *Der weissagende Dionysos* was a volume of mainly erotic hymns.

Well-known living authors contributed a number of interesting novels and prose tales. Heinrich Böll, in *Billard um Halb Zehn*, was trying his hand, perhaps somewhat controversially, at the experimental novel in order to illuminate contemporary life. In his collection *Gib Acht in Domokosch*, Gerd Gaiser, another experimentalist, included some striking short stories. His *Sizilianische Notizen* was a sensitive record of his observations during a journey to Sicily. Ina Seidel depicted the rise and fall of Nazism and its effect on a group of people in her novel *Michaela: Aufzeichnungen des Jürgen Brook*. Werner Bergengrün, in two collections of prose tales, *Zorn, Zeit und Ewigkeit* and *Bärengeschichten*, continued to explore the grotesque and mysterious aspects of life. In *Fastnachtsbeichte*, Carl Zuckmayer applied his experience as a successful dramatist to the genre of prose fiction; this work was a carefully planned and well-knit composition noteworthy for its strikingly dramatic situations. Rudolf Hagelstange's novel *Spielball der Götter* was a fictitious account of the life of Paris during the siege of Troy; it was characterized by a sensitivity of language to be expected from a fine lyric poet. *Das Lied der Muschel*, his prose account of a journey to the islands of the Aegean, also came to life through his poetic use of the German language. Uwe Johnson's first novel, *Mutmassungen über Jacob*, was a symbolic analysis of contemporary Germany which singled him out as a writer of considerable promise. Other significant novels were: Stefan Andres, *Der graue Regenbogen*, Hans Bender, *Wunschkost*, Günther Grass, *Die Blechtrommel*, Ruth Rehmann, *Illusionen*.

Some important works of non-fiction prose were also published. The most moving was perhaps Stefan Escher's *Das Jahr in Pusan* in which the author recorded, in diary form, impressions of the life and work of a physician during a year in Korea. In *An der Zeitmauer* Ernst Jünger, on the other hand, analysed general cosmological and historical problems. The bicentenary of Schiller's birth called forth two standard works: Benno von Wiese's *Friedrich Schiller*, a monumental account of his whole life and work, and Gerhart Storz's *Der Dichter Friedrich Schiller*, a searching analysis of his dramatic and poetic work. Emil Staiger completed his masterly monograph on Goethe by the publication of the third volume, *Goethe 1814-1832*. Other works of note were: Hannah Arendt, *Rachel Varnhagen* (a biography), Friedrich Heer, *Die Dritte Macht* (historical), Peter Demetz, *Marx, Engels und die Dichter* and Heimito von Doderer, *Grundlagen und Funktion des Romans* (literary history).

In lyric poetry, Paul Celan confirmed his place as one of the leading poets by his volume of verse *Sprachgitter*. Lyrical poetry of interest was found in the work of two Austrian poets, Christine Lavant, *Spindel im Mond*, and Max Roden, *Neue Gedichte*, as well as in Peter Rühmkorf's *Irdisches Vergnügen in g*. It had, however, been a disappointing year for drama, for in that field there appeared to have been no outstanding new publication. (H. S. R.)

GERMANY.

Country of central Europe, bounded N. by the North sea, Denmark and the Baltic sea, E. by Poland, S. by Czechoslovakia, Austria and Switzerland, and W. by France, Luxembourg, Belgium and the Netherlands. From 1949 Germany was partitioned into two republics with a special provisional regime for Berlin (*q.v.*). Areas and populations of the two states and Berlin are as follows:

	Area (sq.mi.)	Population (1950 census)	(Dec. 1958 est.)
German Federal Republic .	95,636*	48,640,400*	52,492,500*
Western Berlin . . .	186	2,147,000	2,226,000
	95,822	50,787,400	54,718,500
German Democratic Republic	41,490	17,199,100	16,202,000
Eastern Berlin . .	156	1,189,100	1,110,000
	41,646	18,388,200	17,312,000
Total	137,468	69,175,600	72,030,500

* Including the Saar.

Language: German, with small admixture of Lusatian (260,000 in the Kottbus-Bautzen area), Polish (150,000, mainly in Westphalia) and Danish (120,000). Religion: (1938 est.) Protestant 62·7%; Roman Catholic 32·5%; Jewish 0·7%; other 4·1%; (1950 census, Federal Republic) Protestant 50·7%, Roman Catholic 45·2%; (1950 census, Democratic Republic) Protestant 81·3%, Roman Catholic 11%.

GERMAN FEDERAL REPUBLIC. Chief cities (with population over 200,000, Dec. 31, 1957, est.): Bonn (cap.) 140,761; Hamburg 1,772,400; Munich 983,200; Cologne 727,500; Essen 708,200; Düsseldorf 668,400; Frankfurt 633,500; Dortmund 617,900; Stuttgart 610,500; Hanover 547,000; Bremen 521,600; Duisburg 485,000; Nuremberg 430,000; Wuppertal 409,500; Gelsenkirchen 381,100; Bochum 351,200; Mannheim 291,500; Kiel 258,800; Wiesbaden 247,700; Oberhausen 246,600; Brunswick 242,300; Lübeck 229,900; Karlsruhe 226,000; Augsburg 201,700; 27 cities from 100,000 to 200,000. Presidents of the republic in 1959: Theodor Heuss and (from Sept. 15) Heinrich Lübke (*see* BIOGRAPHIES); federal chancellor, Konrad Adenauer. Main imports: processed foodstuffs, raw materials, petroleum and products. Main exports: finished and semi-finished manufactured goods, coal. Monetary unit: *Deutsche Mark* (DM.11·76 = £1 sterling).

GERMAN DEMOCRATIC REPUBLIC*. Capital, eastern Berlin. Chief cities (with pop. over 100,000; Dec. 31, 1957, est.): Leipzig 598,909; Dresden 491,714; Karl-Marxstadt (formerly Chemnitz) 286,016; Halle 280,614; Magdeburg 258,447; Erfurt 184,819; Rostock 149,301; Zwickau 129,953; Potsdam 115,934. First secretary of the Socialist (Communist) Unity Party of Germany, Walter Ulbricht; president of the republic, Wilhelm Pieck; chairman of the council of ministers, Otto Grotewohl. Monetary unit: *Deutsche Mark (Ost)*, officially at par with the DM. (West); actually in western Berlin, in Nov. 1959, the exchange rate was DM. (West) 1·00 = DM. (Ost) 4·05.

* By the end of 1959 the German Democratic Republic was recognized by the following 13 states: Albania, Bulgaria, Chinese People's Republic, Czechoslovakia, Iraq, Hungary, the People's Democratic Republic of Korea, Mongolia, Poland, Rumania, U.S.S.R., the Democratic Republic of Vietnam and Yugoslavia. *De facto* trade relations at governmental level were established with the following eight states: Burma, Finland, Great Britain, India, Lebanon, Sudan, United Arab Republic and Yemen.

History. *General.* The close interlinking of the Berlin and the broader German problems, and intermittent Soviet pressure for solutions of both favourable to the Communist *bloc* meant that the question of Germany's future was almost continually in the news during 1959. This principal question was, apart from the foreign ministers' deliberations in Geneva, the subject of a number of letters which passed between governments and was the reason for several visits paid by statesmen to each other's countries during the year.

Willy Brandt, the burgomaster of western Berlin, with Konrad Adenauer, the federal German chancellor, who entertained him at the Schaumburg palace, Bonn, on March 11. They discussed the Berlin question and Brandt's visit to the Far East, the United States and Canada.

The western notes of Dec. 31, 1958, rejecting the Soviet proposals of Nov. 27 for a solution of the German question, brought another Soviet rejoinder on Jan. 10, 1959. In this note the U.S.S.R. called for the recognition of the Oder-Neisse line as Germany's eastern frontier, for the signing of a German peace treaty prior to German reunification, and—if necessary—the signing of peace treaties with both German states individually. The eastern German government immediately welcomed these proposals; for the western government Konrad Adenauer stated on Jan. 12 that the only answer would be an " unequivocal no ".

On Feb. 7 and 8 John Foster Dulles, the U.S. secretary of state, visited Bonn. A short statement at the end of the visit explained that there had been full agreement between the two statesmen over a rejection of the Soviet plan for a " confederation " of two German states, over the maintenance of western rights and garrisons in Berlin and over the general need to make no concessions to the U.S.S.R. without securing " counter-concessions ".

On March 4 Adenauer visited General Charles de Gaulle and had a long private talk with him at Marly-le-Roi. The Berlin and German problems were discussed. On March 12 and 13 Harold Macmillan and Selwyn Lloyd went to Bonn for the same purpose. Talks were conducted in a cordial atmosphere and there was a measure of general agreement over Berlin, the German question as a whole and European security requirements. No agreement, however, was reached over Macmillan's plan for a limited zone in central Europe, in which armaments would be restricted, controlled and equalized. Adenauer did not like this plan, on the ground that it could involve discrimination against western Germany and crystallize the political *status quo* in Europe. Nor was the federal chancellor impressed by Macmillan's suggestion that progress in the field of disarmament should be accompanied by political progress towards the solution of the Berlin and German problems. Instead, Adenauer favoured steps towards general, controlled disarmament, which would be sought quite independently of the Berlin and German problems.

On Aug. 26 President Dwight D. Eisenhower arrived in Bonn, leaving the next day for London. At a press conference on Aug. 27 the president said that there should be a " western summit " meeting before the " real " summit with N. S. Khrushchev took place. He said that he did not believe anybody wanted a World War III and he repeated previous assurances given to the German Federal Republic.

Khrushchev had in the meantime, on Aug. 18, sent a letter to Adenauer. The chancellor answered this letter on Aug. 30 in a conciliatory spirit. He denied that there was any spirit of revenge in western Germany as a result of a lost war, and stated that Communism and Socialism should be recognized as " forms of economic development which encourage progress ". He again urged general, controlled disarmament. On the next day he carried this temporary spirit of conciliation a stage further by sending a message to the Polish people on the 20th anniversary of the German invasion of Poland. This drew a sharp retort from the Polish prime minister, Józef Cyrankiewicz, who accused Adenauer of trying to drive a wedge between the Polish and Russian peoples.

On Oct. 2 Adenauer received a personal assurance from President Eisenhower that U.S. policies, particularly with regard to Berlin, had not altered in any way. On Nov. 17 Adenauer arrived for a three-day visit in London, and on Dec. 1 he visited General de Gaulle in Paris. The purpose of both journeys was to bring more unified thinking into the western alliance, prior to summit talks. Both visits were stated by the German federal government to have been successful. Existing Anglo-German differences were cleared up in London, and Adenauer took note of the British desire to secure a close and good working arrangement between the European Economic community and the European Free Trade association led by the United Kingdom. Minor differences between Adenauer and de Gaulle on the subject of Nato organization and armament were stated, after the Paris meeting, to be " not serious ". From Dec. 19 to 21 Adenauer was again in Paris to take part in the western " summit " conference. (*See* also SUMMIT CONFERENCE, APPROACHES TO.)

German Federal Republic. The main political events in the internal affairs of the German Federal Republic in 1959 were the decision of Adenauer, the chancellor, to stand for the presidency, his subsequent revision of this decision and the disputes within the Christian Democratic party (C.D.U.)

which this caused. Adenauer made his first decision on April 7, when he accepted the C.D.U. candidature for the presidency which had already, on March 3, been turned down by his minister of economics, Ludwig Erhard. On April 8 Adenauer broadcast to the German people, telling them that his decision was " deeply considered and correct ", since it would " ensure the continuity of our policies for years to come ". At the same time Adenauer made accusations of " wire-pullers " being at work in Great Britain, with the results that attacks were being made there on the Federal Republic and on him personally. The chancellor gave no explanation, then or later, as to who the " wire-pullers " were. He stated, too, that the " Macmillan plan " for a zone of limited and equalized armaments was " imprecise ". Letters which passed between him and Macmillan were not published.

On June 5 Adenauer announced to the C.D.U. parliamentary party that he had changed his earlier decision and would not stand for the presidency. His official reasons were that Dulles had died in the meantime and that he was needed at the head of the government in the existing difficult world situation. It was no secret, however, that Adenauer had quarrelled with the majority of his party over the choice of a new chancellor. He himself wanted Franz Etzel, minister of finance, while the party wanted Erhard. In addition, Adenauer had discovered that the powers of a federal president were strictly circumscribed, and were not open to new and more liberal interpretation.

On June 7 Erhard, who was in Washington, said in a television interview that Adenauer's decision was to be regretted. On June 9 he denied Adenauer's suggestion that he was " less firm on foreign policy issues than the chancellor himself ", and stated " I will fight ". On June 10 Adenauer declared that he had intended no disparagement of his minister, but on June 17 he repeated in an interview previous remarks that Erhard did not know enough about foreign affairs. A further clash between the two men was only resolved on June 22 and 23 by an exchange of letters. The C.D.U. had meanwhile

Children of Frankfurt-on-Main playing among the fountains of the " spray field " constructed for them in the municipal forest.

the U.S. and French newspapers in which he accused Great Britain of a weak foreign policy and of supporting military disengagement in Europe. Subsequently Adenauer indicated his determination to remain chancellor until 1961, and to seek re-election then for a fourth term in office.

On July 1, in western Berlin, Lübke was elected by the Federal Assembly. On the first count Lübke, who was the candidate of the C.D.U., received 517 votes. His Social Democratic and Free Democratic opponents, Carlo Schmid and Max Becker, received 385 and 104 votes respectively. Since there were 25 abstentions and 8 delegates were not present, Lübke did not gain an absolute majority of the votes, but on the second count he was successful with 526 votes (Schmid 386, Becker 99). He succeeded Theodor Heuss, who on Sept. 12 had completed the second of two five-year terms in office.

The next most important political event was the publication, on March 19, of the Social Democratic party plan for Germany. The plan envisaged a three-stage reunification of Germany: by east-west all-German discussion, the planning of economic reunification and the arranging of a national referendum, and the election of an all-German parliament. The plan called, too, for step-by-step disarmament in Europe, a nuclear-free zone, the phased withdrawal of foreign troops from German soil and the organization of a European security system. The plan was tabled immediately after the return from Moscow of two party members, Carlo Schmid and Fritz Erler. Khrushchev had told them that " Nobody wants German reunification at this moment—nobody at all ".

The only other political events of importance were the formation of a new government in the Saar under Franz Roeder (the previous prime minister, Hans Reinert, was killed in a car accident), the Saar's economic reunion with Germany on July 5, and *Länder* elections in Lower Saxony and the Rhine-Palatinate in April, and in Bremen in October. The first two showed small C.D.U. gains, while at Bremen there was a big swing to the Social Democrats. Concern was caused in December by manifestations of anti-Semitism.

Steady economic progress was made in 1959 and unemployment fell in September to 187,000—its lowest since World

Some of the 50-60 thousand western German miners who visited Bonn on Sept. 25 to demonstrate against conditions in the industry.

hurriedly adopted, on June 15, Heinrich Lübke as presidential candidate. The sequel of the anger which had been aroused in Adenauer by the incident was a series of interviews given to

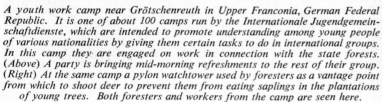
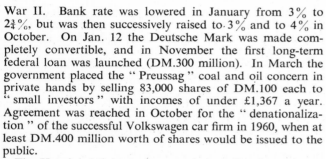

A youth work camp near Grötschenreuth in Upper Franconia, German Federal Republic. It is one of about 100 camps run by the Internationale Jugendgemeinschaftdienste, which are intended to promote understanding among young people of various nationalities by giving them certain tasks to do in international groups. In this camp they are engaged on work in connection with the state forests. (Above) A party is bringing mid-morning refreshments to the rest of their group. (Right) At the same camp a pylon watchtower used by foresters as a vantage point from which to shoot deer to prevent them from eating saplings in the plantations of young trees. Both foresters and workers from the camp are seen here.

War II. Bank rate was lowered in January from 3% to 2¾%, but was then successively raised to 3% and to 4% in October. On Jan. 12 the Deutsche Mark was made completely convertible, and in November the first long-term federal loan was launched (DM.300 million). In March the government placed the " Preussag " coal and oil concern in private hands by selling 83,000 shares of DM.100 each to " small investors " with incomes of under £1,367 a year. Agreement was reached in October for the " denationalization " of the successful Volkswagen car firm in 1960, when at least DM.400 million worth of shares would be issued to the public.

The Housing Ministry announced that all refugee camps would be closed by 1961 and that the housing shortage should end by 1963, while the Ministry of Transport launched a DM.8,000 million five-year road-building programme. A credit of DM.25 million was granted to Sudan in January for economic development and German interest was stirred by the statement in Bonn of Sir David Eccles, on April 24, that Anglo-German trade had doubled since 1953 and that German economic co-operation would be welcomed in the Commonwealth. On Sept. 30 old-age pensions were increased by an average of 6%. The government's only worrying economic problem was the glut of unsold coal. Imports of coal were cut on Jan. 30 and the decision was taken to close down a dozen uneconomic coalpits. A seven-man commission was set up to decide the fate of Alfried Krupp's coal and steel interests. These assets should, under a six-year-old agreement, have been sold by Jan. 31, 1959. The commission, which had a Swiss chairman, three Allied and three German members, had made no recommendation by the end of 1959.

German Democratic Republic. The history of the German Democratic Republic in 1959 was one of rigorously maintained political despotism and of marked economic progress. The eastern German regime continued to treat the Federal Republic with violent animosity and to provide substance for the Soviet theory and plans for a " two-state Germany ". It was for this reason that the regime sent an official delegation

to the Geneva conferences, headed by the foreign minister, Lothar Bolz. The western German delegation, on the other hand, was led by Wilhelm Grewe, and the federal foreign minister, Heinrich von Brentano, was present only as an " observer ". The eastern German regime also instructed General Heinz Hoffmann, the director-general of the armed forces of the German Democratic Republic, to hold a press conference in Geneva at which he accused the Federal Republic of preparing for militarist aggression.

The biggest political event of the eastern German year was the visit to Leipzig and Berlin of N. S. Khrushchev from March 4 to 10. On March 4 he addressed a huge crowd at the Leipzig trade fair. On the next day he stated that the proposed transfer of powers of control to eastern Germans in Berlin and on the Berlin-Helmstedt *Autobahn* would not take place on May 27 if negotiations among the great powers were under way by then. On March 8 Khrushchev told an All-German Workers' conference that it was vital to secure a German peace treaty and a guarantee of Germany's existing frontiers. German reunification, he declared, " could be left to history to complete ".

The execution of Soviet policies for Germany was keenly supported by the eastern German regime. Throughout the year the deputy prime minister, Walter Ulbricht, invariably acted as spokesman for his government. On Jan. 18 he declared at a plenary meeting of the central committee of the Socialist Unity Party (S.E.D.) that Allied garrisons should be first reduced and then entirely withdrawn from western Berlin. There was no eastern German intention of threatening western Berlin's communications, but the western powers should " respect the authority of the German Democratic Republic ". Ulbricht proposed the formation of an All-German council of 100 members, which would devise measures for a drawing-together of the two German states.

On Jan. 21 Ulbricht told the Volkskammer that Germany's frontiers were final and unalterable. On Feb. 9 he announced that the Soviet Union would sign a separate peace treaty with his government, failing positive proposals by the western powers for a settlement of the German question. On April 8 the eastern German government sent a letter to Adenauer proposing joint action by the two German delegations at the coming Geneva conference. (A roughly similar letter was sent five days earlier to the western German Social Democratic party by the central committee of the S.E.D. It asked for joint action in fighting German militarism, preventing nuclear armament and working for a German peace treaty.) On May 24 Ulbricht offered an east-west all-German non-aggression pact. It would provide for a nuclear-free all-Germany, for the limitation of both German armies to about 100,000 men, for the phased withdrawal of all Allied troops from German soil and for the conversion of western Berlin into a " free city ". Ulbricht repeated these proposals on Sept. 20, in a five-point programme for " relaxing political tension ". None of his proposals met with any response from the Federal Republic or the other western powers.

In order to boost eastern German prestige Otto Grotewohl, the prime minister, led a 26-man delegation which visited African and Asian countries in January. The first result of this tour was the semi-official recognition won from the United Arab Republic, which allowed eastern German representatives in Cairo and Damascus to call themselves consuls. A cultural and scientific agreement was signed with Iraq on April 1. Trade agreements with both Iraq and Guinea had been signed at the end of 1958. Eastern German prestige was enhanced by the discontinuance of payment of all occupation costs to the Soviet Union on Jan. 1. In 1958 DM.600 million had been paid.

In January Ulbricht announced plans for doubling chemical production by 1965; DM.9,000 million were to be invested in this single industry during the next six years.

A ceremony was held in eastern Berlin in September to mark the inauguration of the new flag of the German Democratic Republic.

On Jan. 26 the Chamber of Foreign Trade of the German Democratic Republic concluded an agreement with the Federation of British Industries for the exchange of goods to the value of £7 million in each direction during 1959. The British government pointed out that this agreement in no way involved political recognition.

On Sept. 22 Walter Ulbricht made sweeping promises of the economic benefits which the seven-year plan (ending in 1965) would bring. Consumer goods were to increase by 68%, real wages by 60% to 65% and pensions by 55%. Prices would be brought down and working hours reduced. The housing shortage would be ended in two years time.

Political repression continued during 1959, and in the first six months 74,000 people fled to western Germany. One of the few people who moved in the opposite direction was the nuclear scientist, Klaus Fuchs, who emigrated to Dresden after his release from a British gaol. On April 17, five Dresden students, all between the ages of 18 and 21, were sentenced to a total of 38 years in gaol. (*See also* BERLIN; EASTERN EUROPEAN ECONOMIC PLANNING.) (T. C. PE.)

BIBLIOGRAPHY (all 1959). H. G. Alexander, *Zwischen Bonn und London* (Düsseldorf); H. Mau and H. Krausnick, *German History, 1933-45* (London); F. Schlamm, *Grenzen des deutschen Wunders* (Bonn); Göttinger Arbeitskreis, *Das östliche Deutschland* (Würzburg).

GHANA. A realm of the Commonwealth of Nations on west coast of Africa, bounded W., N., and E. by the Republics of Ivory Coast and Upper Volta and by Togo. Total area: 91,843 sq.mi. Total pop.: (1948 census) 4,118,450; (mid-1959 est.) 4,911,000. Cap.: Accra. Areas and populations of geographical regions are as follows:

	Area (sq.mi.)	Population (mid-1959 est.)	Chief town (with 1959 pop.)
Southern Ghana and Volta Region	29,781	2,700,000	Accra 210,000 (excl. suburbs)
Ashanti . . .	24,379	1,024,000	Kumasi 100,000
Northern Ghana .	37,683	1,187,000	Tamale 19,000

Official language: English. More than 60 Sudanic tongues are also spoken. Religion: pagan; Moslem and Christian minorities. Other important towns, with 1959 pop.: Sekondi-Takoradi 55,000; Cape Coast 26,550; Koforidua 20,500; Ho 7,000. Queen, Elizabeth II; governor-general, the Earl of Listowel; prime minister, Kwame Nkrumah. Main imports: manufactured consumer goods and constructional materials. Main exports: cocoa, gold, manganese ore, timber, diamonds. Monetary unit: Ghana pound (£G1 = £1 sterling).

History. During 1959 the government's chief domestic tasks continued to be the process of nation-building and the establishment of itself as the sole source of authority.

On Jan. 23 the government appointed a three-man commission of inquiry, under the chairmanship of Mr. Justice Granville Sharp, to investigate allegations that members of the opposition had conspired together to bring about the assassination of the prime minister, Kwame Nkrumah, and overthrow the government by force. The commission started its lengthy hearings on Feb. 9, and published its findings on May 22. The majority report held that a conspiracy to assassinate Nkrumah and to carry out a *coup d'état* did in fact exist, but exonerated the leader of the opposition, K. A. Busia. Granville Sharp himself submitted a minority report, maintaining that the existence of the conspiracy was not proved.

Brigadier A. J. Turner, the national organizer of the Builders' brigade, resigned on May 8 in protest against the proposed dismissal of three European officers of the brigade, but withdrew his resignation after talks with Nkrumah. After Turner's death on Oct. 4 the brigade was taken over by John Tettegah, hitherto secretary-general of the Trades Union congress.

The *Sunday Times* representative in Accra, Russel Howe, was deported on June 3 on the grounds of alleged misreporting. At the Sekyere West by-election on June 9, which resulted in a gain for the Convention People's party, 38 persons, including members of the Builders' brigade, were arrested after clashes.

Busia, who had been sued for libel by the attorney-general, left the country in mid-June, and subsequently accepted two academic posts in the Netherlands.

On June 24 the government issued a white paper on the Granville Sharp report, in which it announced its intention to tighten up the law on offences against the state.

The opposition United party won the Anlo South by-election on July 2, after an orderly campaign, and at the Tumu by-election on July 23 Imoru Egala (C.P.P.), formerly chairman of the Cocoa Marketing board, was returned unopposed.

On Aug. 6 the government announced its intention to withdraw government agents from the districts and to replace them with political district commissioners.

Mechanical drawing at a Ghana technical school. The 1959-64 development plan allocates £1·5 million to technical education.

On Oct. 6 the C.P.P. candidate won in the Wenchi West by-election, in which gross irregularities were alleged by the U.P. Two C.P.P. supporters were killed. Despite this, opposition activity gradually declined as the year drew on.

During 1959 Nkrumah paid official visits to India, the United Arab Republic, the Federation of Nigeria, Guinea, Liberia and the United Kingdom. His foreign policy continued to be one of opposing colonialism, particularly in Africa, retaining Ghana's leadership of the independent African states and affirming the solidarity of the Afro-Asian bloc at the United Nations. He received visits from the secretary of state for Commonwealth relations, and Hugh Gaitskell. In a major policy speech delivered on Dec. 16 Nkrumah announced that Ghana would become a republic in 1960.

Ghana's armed forces were strengthened during the year by the setting up of a navy and an air force, both trained by Israelis, and by the separation of the Ghana army from the Royal West African Frontier force. The appointment of the first three Ghanaian lieut.-colonels was announced on July 10.

Despite the fall in the world cocoa price, the economy continued to prosper throughout the year. However, the announcement of the second five-year development plan, to begin on July 1, was an act of faith in foreign investment, since it involved a total expenditure of £242,386,000 on general development and £100 million on the construction of hydro-electric works, at a time when the government's easily realizable reserves were only about £90 million. As a gesture towards financing the plan, ministers accepted a salary cut of 10% while M.P.s, after voting themselves a salary increase of £240 per annum (to £1,200 per annum), cut their own salaries by 10%. In spite of protests from many farmers, the United Ghana Farmers' council announced that until the completion of the development plan they would accept from the Cocoa Marketing board a price of £3 a load (60 lb.), instead of the previous fixed price of £3 12s. As a result, drastic action had to be taken to prevent the smuggling of cocoa into French territories. The final estimate for the 1958-59 cocoa crop was 245,000 tons.

Opening his fifth budget on July 2, the minister of finance, K. A. Gbedemah, announced that he was budgeting for a surplus of £440,000 on a recurrent expenditure of £53 million. Total recurrent and development expenditures for 1959-60 were estimated at more than £90 million. Budgetary changes included increased postage and electricity charges, and increased duties on beer, wines, timber, jewellery, tyres, sports equipment and roofing materials. Gbedemah also announced a favourable trade balance in 1958-59 of £10·8

million and an increase in Ghana's International Monetary fund quota from $15 million to $35 million.

The U.K. trade mission, which visited Ghana in March, issued its report on Sept. 21, stating that there were increased opportunities for trade, but that British interests would have to be both imaginative and very competitive if they were to maintain their position.

On Aug. 16 the German Federal Republic offered to invest £16·5 million in development in Ghana.

Throughout most of the year lavish preparations were made for a visit by Queen Elizabeth II, in November. On Aug. 7 Nkrumah announced that the queen's visit had been postponed as she was expecting a child. He subsequently flew to Britain and met the queen at Balmoral, being appointed a member of the Privy Council during his visit. The Duke of Edinburgh undertook a short tour of Ghana in November, and received an enthusiastic welcome. During his stay he visited Tema harbour, which was nearing completion, and inaugurated the Ghana Academy of Learning.

The deaths occurred in 1959 of Sir Emmanuel Charles Quist, the first speaker of the National Assembly (March 1), and of George Padmore, the prime minister's adviser on African affairs.   (J. H. P.)

GIBRALTAR. British fortress colony, city and port, on a peninsula from S.W. coast of Spain at western entrance to Mediterranean. Area: 2·25 sq.mi. (incl. reclamation). Pop., excl. armed forces: (1951 census) 22,848, (1957 est.) 25,403, mainly of Italian origin. Language: English and Spanish. Religion: mainly Roman Catholic. Administration: governor; executive council; legislative council with elected majority. Governor, General Sir Charles Keightley. Currency: sterling with local notes.

History. Two parties and five independent candidates contested the election to the legislative council, which was held on Sept. 23, 1959. Three members of an established Labour party, one of a new party based on the Transport and General Workers' union and three independents, including Gibraltar's first woman candidate, were successful. Under new constitutional changes the life of the legislature was extended from three to five years. A chief member was appointed, and all the unofficial members were given titles and departmental responsibilities.

Trade and tourism continued to flourish. Port improvements costing nearly £1 million were completed, as a result of which ships could in future bunker and water, and discharge passengers and cargo alongside. Housing remained the colony's biggest problem, and with the help of a grant of £550,000 from Britain a five-year plan to build another 750 low-rental flats was prepared.   (J. D. Bs.)

GILBERT AND ELLICE ISLANDS: see Pacific Islands, British.
GLASS INDUSTRY: see Business Review.
GŌA: see Portuguese Overseas Territories.

GOLF. The golfing season of 1959 was disappointing from the British viewpoint. Both matches against the United States were lost and the Commonwealth domination of the open championship continued with the victory of a young South African, G. Player. There were great hopes that the British Isles team might win the Walker Cup match for the first time since 1938 but all four foursomes were lost. In the singles J. B. Carr beat the U.S. captain, C. R. Coe, R. R. Jack comfortably defeated W. J. Patton and A. E. Shepperson recovered magnificently after being four down to T. D. Aaron. The British team's starting and finishing were poor; there was a tendency to play defensively in the foursomes, and in moments of pressure the U.S. putting was superior.

The United States regained the Ryder cup by winning the

match at Palm Desert 8½-3½. The British made a splendid showing in the foursomes. P. Alliss and C. O'Connor played excellent golf in beating D. Ford and A. Wall, and D. C. Thomas and H. Weetman halved with the formidable partnership of S. J. Snead and C. Middlecoff. The British were never in sight of getting the 4½ singles points necessary to retain the cup against some commanding U.S. golf. E. C. Brown gained his fourth consecutive singles victory by beating Middlecoff 4 and 3, a remarkable record. N. V. Drew made a brave recovery to halve with D. Ford, and Alliss, who halved with J. Hebert, was the only British player to emerge undefeated from the match.

South Africa won the Commonwealth tournament at Johannesburg, defeating Great Britain, Canada and New Zealand, but losing to Australia, the holders. Britain should have finished second alone but surprisingly lost 1½-7½ to New Zealand and came second jointly with Australia and New Zealand.

Six members of the U.S. Walker Cup team competed in the amateur championship at St. George's, Sandwich, and two reached the final where D. Beman beat W. Hyndman 3 and 2, after defeating G. Wolstenholme, the only British player to reach the semi-final. Beman, a slightly built young man of 21, played superbly all the week. His driving on fast, narrow fairways was particularly fine and his putting almost infallible.

Amateur golf again showed signs of great improvement. R. R. Jack played supremely well in his first open championship and finished fourth, only four strokes behind Player. Wolstenholme and M. F. Bonallack, who had played the match of the year in the final of the English championship, finished high in the order. Carr, after a 64 in one qualifying round, also qualified for the last day's play. Moreover, he achieved a memorable performance in the Masters at Portmarnock where he finished second to O'Connor in a field which included all the leading professionals. The amateurs also played splendidly in losing 5½-9½ against the professionals whom they had beaten the previous year.

Several young professionals made their mark during the season. Drew won a tournament, played himself into the Ryder Cup team and became the first British golfer to play in both Walker and Ryder Cup matches. D. Snell won the most surprising victory of the year when he beat Weetman, the holder, by 3 and 2 in the final of the match play championship. P. J. Butler, another promising young golfer, also won his first major event. Only a week after helping D. J. Rees to win the Sherwood Forest foursomes D. Smalldon was killed in a road accident. For some years he had been one of the most accomplished of the younger players. B. J. Hunt, Weetman, Rees and O'Connor were the most consistent of the senior professionals and Rees, who won three events, seemed to have lost none of his skill or intense enthusiasm at the age of 46.

Miss E. Price won the women's championship, after having lost six previous national finals, and a week later the first women's Commonwealth tournament was held at St. Andrews. Britain beat Australia, Canada, New Zealand and South Africa mainly because of the splendid golf of Mrs. R. Smith and Miss J. Robertson. Britain also easily beat the Continent of Europe in October. Many promising young players excelled during the summer, notably the 20-year-old Miss R. Porter who beat Mrs. Smith in the final of the English championship at Aldeburgh in July.

In the United States A. Wall, G. Littler and M. Souchak were the most successful in tournaments. W. Casper, by a phenomenal display of putting, won the open championship. R. Rosburg, the runner-up, won the Professional Golfers' Association championship. Coe, defending his title of amateur champion, was only beaten on the last green of the final by J. Nicklaus, the youngest member of the Walker Cup team. Miss M. Wright successfully defended her open title, but women's professional golf was dominated by Miss B. Rawls, who set new records by winning ten tournaments and over $26,000 in prize money. (*See* also SPORTING RECORD.)

(P. A. W.-T.)

J. Tudor-Davies putting on the fourth green at Worplesdon in the final of the open mixed foursomes on Oct. 15. He and his partner, Mrs. I. Goldschmid of Italy (a former Italian ladies champion), were beaten four and three by the Scottish pair Miss J. S. Robertson and I. Wright.

GOVERNMENT DEPARTMENTS. The following were the chief officers of the more important public departments in Great Britain on Dec. 1, 1959.

Admiralty, Board of
First Lord . . . . . Lord Carrington
Civil Lord . . . . C. I. Orr-Ewing
Permanent Secretary . . . Sir John Lang

Agriculture, Fisheries and Food, Ministry of
Minister . . . . . John Hare
Parliamentary Secretaries . . Earl Waldegrave
Joseph Godber
Permanent Secretary . . Sir John Winnifrith

Air Ministry
Secretary of State . . . George Ward
Parliamentary Under Secretary . W. J. Taylor
Permanent Under Secretary . Sir Maurice Dean

Aviation, Ministry of
Minister . . . . . Duncan Sandys
Parliamentary Secretary . . Geoffrey Rippon
Permanent Secretary . . . Sir William Strath

Cabinet Office
Secretary of the Cabinet . . Sir Norman Brook

Civil Service Commission
First Commissioner . . . Sir George Mallaby

Colonial Office
Secretary of State . . . Iain Macleod
Minister of State . . . Earl of Perth
Parliamentary Under Secretary . Julian Amery
Permanent Under Secretary . Sir Hilton Poynton

Commonwealth Relations Office
Secretary of State . . . Earl of Home
Parliamentary Under Secretary . R. H. M. Thompson
Permanent Under Secretary . Sir Alexander Clutterbuck

Customs and Excise, Board of
Chairman . . . . Sir James Crombie

Defence, Ministry of
Minister . . . . . *Harold Watkinson
Permanent Secretary . . Sir Edward Playfair

Development Commission
Chairman . . . . Countess of Albermarle

Duchy of Lancaster, Office of the
Chancellor . . . . Charles Hill

Education, Ministry of
Minister . . . . . Sir David Eccles
Parliamentary Secretary . . Kenneth Thompson
Permanent Secretary . . *Dame Mary Smieton

Exchequer and Audit Department
Comptroller and Auditor-General . Sir Edmund Compton

Foreign Office
Secretary of State . . . Selwyn Lloyd
Ministers of State . . . David Ormsby-Gore
John Profumo
Parliamentary Under Secretaries . Marquess of Lansdowne
R. A. Allan
Permanent Under Secretary . Sir Frederick Hoyer Millar

Forestry Commission
Chairman . . . . Earl of Radnor

General Register Office
Registrar-General . . . E. M. T. Firth

Health, Ministry of
Minister . . . . . Derek Walker-Smith
Parliamentary Secretary . . Edith Pitt
Permanent Secretary . . Sir John Hawton

Health, Welsh Board of
Chairman . . . . K. H. Hodges

Home Office
Secretary of State . . . *R. A. Butler
Parliamentary Under Secretaries . David Renton
Dennis Vosper
Permanent Under Secretary . Sir Charles C. Cunningham

Housing and Local Government, Ministry of
Minister and Minister for Welsh Affairs Henry Brooke
Minister of State for Welsh Affairs Lord Brecon
Parliamentary Secretary . . Sir Keith Joseph
Permanent Secretary . . Dame Evelyn Sharp

Information, Central Office of
Director-General . . . T. Fife Clark

Inland Revenue, Board of
Chairman . . . . Sir Alexander Johnston

Labour, Ministry of
Minister . . . . . *Edward Heath
Parliamentary Secretary . . P. J. M. Thomas
Permanent Secretary . . Sir Laurence Helsby

Law Officers' Department
Attorney-General . . . Sir R. Manningham-Buller
Solicitor-General . . . Sir Jocelyn Simon

Lord Advocate's Department
Lord Advocate . . . W. R. Milligan
Solicitor-General . . . William Grant

Lord Chancellor's Department
Lord Chancellor . . . Viscount Kilmuir
Permanent Secretary . . Sir George Coldstream

Lord Privy Seal
Lord Privy Seal and Minister for Science Viscount Hailsham

National Debt Office
Comptroller-General . . . G. D. Kirwan

Paymaster-General's Office
Paymaster-General . . . Lord Mills

Pensions and National Insurance, Ministry of
Minister . . . . . John Boyd-Carpenter
Parliamentary Secretaries . . Patricia Hornsby-Smith
W. M. F. Vane
Permanent Secretary . . Sir Eric Bowyer

Post Office
Postmaster-General . . . Reginald Bevins
Assistant Postmaster-General . Mervyn Pike
Director-General . . . Sir Gordon Radley

Power, Ministry of
Minister . . . . . R. F. Wood
Parliamentary Secretary . . J. C. George
Secretary . . . . Sir Dennis Proctor

Prison Commission
Chairman . . . . Sir Lionel Fox

Privy Council Office
Lord President . . . . Earl of Home
Clerk . . . . . W. G. Agnew

Public Prosecutions, Department of the Director of
Director . . . . . Sir Theobald Mathew

Public Record Office
Keeper of the Records . . Sir David Evans
Deputy Keeper . . . H. C. Johnson

Royal Mint
Master . . . . . D. Heathcoat Amory
Deputy Master and Comptroller . J. H. James

Scientific and Industrial Research, Department of
Secretary . . . . Sir Harry Melville

Scottish Office
Secretary of State . . . John Maclay
Minister of State . . . Lord Craigton
Parliamentary Under Secretaries . Niall Macpherson
Thomas Galbraith
Gilmour Leburn
Permanent Under Secretary . Sir William Murrie

Stationery Office
Controller . . . . Sir John Simpson

Trade, Board of
President . . . . *Reginald Maudling
Minister of State . . . F. J. Erroll
Parliamentary Secretary . . John Rodgers
Permanent Secretary . . Sir Richard Powell

Transport, Ministry of
Minister . . . . . Ernest Marples
Parliamentary Secretaries . . Lord Chesham
John Hay
Permanent Secretary . . L. J. Dunnett

Treasury
Prime Minister and First Lord . *Harold Macmillan
Chancellor of the Exchequer . D. Heathcoat Amory
Economic Secretary . . . A. P. L. Barber
Financial Secretary . . . Sir Edward Boyle
Parliamentary Secretary . . Martin Redmayne
Permanent Secretaries . . Sir Norman Brook
Sir Frank Lee

War Office
Secretary of State . . . Christopher Soames
Parliamentary Under Secretary and
Financial Secretary . . . Hugh Fraser
Permanent Under Secretary . R. G. K. Way

Works, Ministry of
Minister . . . . . Lord John Hope
Parliamentary Secretary . . Harmar Nicholls
Permanent Secretary . . Sir Edward Muir

GRAIN CROPS: *see* AGRICULTURE.

GREAT BRITAIN AND NORTHERN IRELAND, UNITED KINGDOM OF.

Kingdom of northwestern Europe, comprising the main island of Great Britain (kingdom of England, principality of Wales and kingdom of Scotland) and the six northeastern counties of Ireland, together with many small islands. It is a constitutional monarchy, with a sovereign and a parliament of two houses: the House of Lords, which on Oct. 28, 1959, consisted of 4 royal dukes, 22 dukes, 27 marquesses, 132 earls, 106 viscounts, 26 lords spiritual, 564 barons; and the House of Commons, 629 members (including the speaker) elected by universal suffrage. Areas and population of the component parts and home dependencies of the United Kingdom are as follows:

	Area (sq.mi.)	Population (1931 census)	(1951 census)
England	50,329	37,794,003	41,159,213
Wales (*q.v.*) . . .	8,016	2,158,374	2,598,675
Scotland (*q.v.*) . . .	30,404	4,842,980	5,096,415
Isle of Man (*q.v.*) . .	221	49,308	55,253
Channel Islands (*q.v.*)* .	75	93,205	102,776
Great Britain . .	89,045	44,937,870	49,012,332
Northern Ireland (*q.v.*) .	5,459	1,279,745‡	1,370,921
United Kingdom . .	94,504	46,217,615	50,383,253‡

* Not part of legislative territory of United Kingdom, but included in it for census purposes.   † 1937 census.   ‡ 1958 est. 51,681,000.

Language: English is almost universally spoken, but in Wales (1951 census) 1·7% of the population spoke Welsh only and 28·9% spoke both languages; in Scotland (1951 census) 2,652 spoke Gaelic only and 91,630 spoke both languages; in the Isle of Man 528 spoke English and Manx. Queen, Elizabeth II (*see* ROYAL FAMILY); prime minister, Harold Macmillan (*see* BIOGRAPHIES).

Main imports: petroleum and products; meat and meat preparations; non-ferrous metals; timber and pulp; cereals and cereal preparations; fruit and vegetables; sugar; tea; wool. Main exports: machinery and electrical machinery and apparatus; road and rail vehicles, ships and aircraft; iron, steel and manufactures; chemicals; woollen and cotton yarn and manufactures. Monetary unit: pound sterling (£1 = U.S. $2·80).

TABLE I. PRINCIPAL CITIES OF THE UNITED KINGDOM

	1931 census	1951 census		1931 census	1951 census
London (Greater) .	8,215,673	8,348,023	Bristol . .	403,948	442,994
			Nottingham .	276,189	306,055
London (County and City) .	4,397,003	3,347,982	Hull (Kingston-upon-Hull) .	313,649	299,105
Birmingham .	1,002,603	1,112,685	Bradford .	298,692	292,403
Glasgow .	1,093,337	1,089,767	Newcastle upon		
Liverpool .	856,072	788,659	Tyne .	286,255	291,724
Manchester .	766,331	703,082	Leicester .	257,718	285,181
Sheffield .	518,257	512,850	Stoke-on-Trent	276,639	275,115
Leeds .	482,827	505,219	Coventry .	178,126	258,245
Edinburgh .	439,010	466,761	Cardiff .	226,937	243,632
Belfast .	438,086*	443,680	Portsmouth .	252,421	233,545
			Plymouth .	213,038	208,012

* 1937 census.

TABLE II. UNITED KINGDOM: MEMBERSHIP OF MAIN RELIGIOUS GROUPS, 1957 ESTIMATES (in thousands)

	England	Wales	Scotland	N. Ireland	Total
Anglican* . .	26,771†	200‡	106§	353‖	27,430
Roman Catholic .	3,227	116	757	476	4,576
Presbyterian . .	71	154	1,308¶	133**	1,666
Methodist . .	680	39	14	75††	808
Congregational .	218‡‡	118§§	35	2	373
Baptist . . .	204	97	20	5	326
Jewish*** . .	384	4	15	2	405

* Established Church of England, disestablished Church in Wales, Episcopal Church in Scotland, Church of Ireland.   † Baptized members.   ‡ Easter communicants.   § Persons "definitely attached".   ‖ 1951 census.   ¶ Established Church of Scotland, other small Scottish Presbyterian bodies being excluded.   ** All Ireland.   †† All Ireland, 1951 census.   ‡‡ Incl. North Wales and South Wales English.   §§ Figure is for Union of Welsh Independents, mainly in Wales.   *** Towns and cities only, latest estimate.

NOTE. In England, Presbyterians, Methodists (incl. indep. Methodists and Reform union), Baptists, Congregationalists (incl. Countess of Huntingdon's Connection chapels) and Moravians (1957: 2,911 communicants) are linked by Free Church Federal council. Other important Christian bodies were (1957 U.K. figures); the Brethren 146,300; Unitarian and Free Christian Churches 28,000; United Free Church of Scotland 24,856; Church of Jesus Christ of Latter Day Saints 9,460; Lutheran Council of Great Britain 11,710; Salvation Army 6,118 (officers); Friends (Quakers) 21,343; Seventh-Day Adventists 7,863; Independent Methodists 7,594; Wesleyan Reform union 6,294; Churches of Christ in Great Britain and Northern Ireland 9,500.

History. *Politics.* On Jan. 16, 1959, J. D. Profumo was appointed minister of state, Foreign Office, following the

President Eisenhower gave a dinner for his war-time associates at the U.S. ambassador's home in London on Sept. 1. Seated with him are Sir Winston Churchill and Lord Alexander. Also present are Lords Montgomery, Alanbrooke, Portal, Tedder and Ismay, and H. Macmillan.

resignation of Commander Alan Noble. Profumo was succeeded as parliamentary under secretary of state, Foreign Office, by R. A. Allan. C. I. Orr-Ewing succeeded Allan as parliamentary and financial secretary, Admiralty.

During the year the principal of a firm of management consultants, Colin Hurry, conducted a survey of public opinion on nationalization in marginal constituencies. The results tended to show that the electorate was opposed to further nationalization. There was a pronounced swing in favour of the Conservatives in the municipal elections which were held in May.

The continued decrease in unemployment, the increase in average earnings, the improvement in the balance of payments position and the desirability that the British people should have the opportunity of deciding who should represent them at the coming " summit " talks—these were among the factors that induced the prime minister, Harold Macmillan, to decide upon a general election on Oct. 8.

The election resulted in a victory for the Conservatives, who increased their over-all majority to 100. The final state of the parties was as follows: Conservatives and allies 365, Labour and allies 258, Liberals 6, Independents 1 (*see* ELECTIONS; GENERAL ELECTION).

The composition of the new Macmillan government was announced on Oct. 14. Selwyn Lloyd and Derick Heathcoat Amory retained their posts as secretary of state for foreign affairs and chancellor of the exchequer respectively. Among the more important changes were the appointment of Iain Macleod as secretary of state for the colonies in place of A. T. Lennox-Boyd who had resigned, and of Edward Heath (*see* BIOGRAPHIES), formerly the Conservative chief whip, as

minister of labour. Harold Watkinson became minister of defence (*see* BIOGRAPHIES), Ernest Marples minister of transport and Duncan Sandys minister of aviation. R. A. Butler, the new chairman of the Conservative party, remained secretary of state, Home Office, but relinquished the post of lord privy seal (*see* BIOGRAPHIES). This was taken over by Lord Hailsham, who was also to act as minister for science and technology.

Herbert Morrison retired from the House of Commons and accepted a life peerage as Lord Morrison of Lambeth. Four new life peerages were conferred in January, the recipients being Sir Eric James, high master of Manchester Grammar school, Sir Edwin Plowden, chairman of the United Kingdom Atomic Energy authority, Professor Lionel Robbins, professor of economics in the University of London and Sir Hartley Shawcross. All were made barons.

W. S. Morrison resigned as speaker of the House of Commons and was raised to the peerage as Lord Dunrossil. It was subsequently learnt that he was to succeed Field Marshal Sir William Slim as governor-general of Australia. The new speaker was Sir Harry Hylton-Foster.

Foreign Affairs. One of the main features of the government's foreign policy during 1959 was its attempt to establish a better understanding with the U.S.S.R. In pursuit of this aim the prime minister, accompanied by the foreign secretary, visited the Soviet Union during February-March. On his return Macmillan summed up the visit as " a voyage of discovery which had its moments of uncertainty as well as its moments of hope and satisfaction."

It was announced in February that the Cyprus dispute had been settled. A white paper published in London on Feb. 23, disclosed that the Greek Cypriot majority would in effect

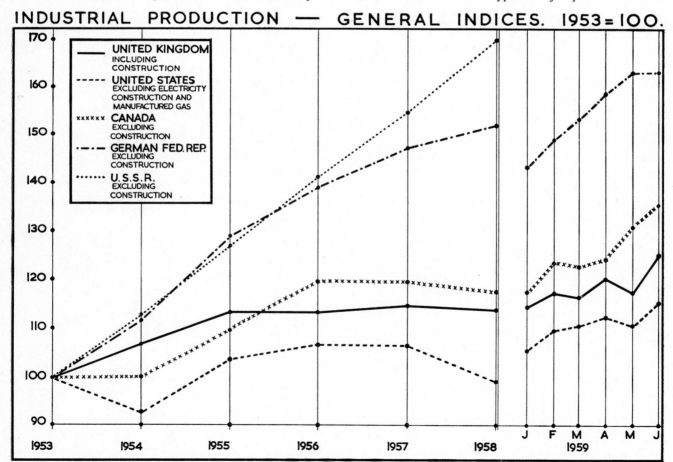

INDUSTRIAL PRODUCTION — GENERAL INDICES. 1953 = 100.

The chart shows the general indices of industrial production of some of the major industrial countries for the years 1953-59. The indices do not measure the actual levels of output, but indicate the relative rates of growth in output in each country.

Traffic at a standstill on the Great West road at the end of the Whitsun holiday. Some 500,000 vehicles were returning to London at the rate of about 35,000 an hour. Four-mile long traffic jams were common and through some towns jams extended from six to eight miles.

govern the island. The traditional character and culture of the Turkish Cypriot community would, however, be fully protected. Turkey and Greece were to be given a share in the defence of the status and security of the island, and Britain would retain control of certain areas to be used as bases.

Riots broke out in Malta in February when notices of dismissal were served on 6,000 out of the 12,000 workers employed in the Valletta dockyard. The south Wales ship-repairing firm, which was taking over the dockyard from the Admiralty, offered employment to all those discharged.

Disturbances in Nyasaland in February led to the declaration of a state of emergency. It was reported that on March 3 26 Africans had been killed in riots, and the secretary of state for the colonies informed the House of Commons that the Nyasaland African National congress planned to carry out widespread acts of violence including the murder of Europeans.

A commission of inquiry under the chairmanship of Mr. Justice Devlin investigated the disturbances. The commission's report, published in July, vindicated the resort to emergency powers by the governor of Nyasaland, but did not accept the view that there was a widespread murder plot. The report also questioned the accuracy of other statements made in the government's white paper which appeared in March.

Great concern was expressed in Britain when it was reported that an inquest on 11 Mau Mau detainees, who had died at Hola camp in Kenya, revealed that they had been beaten.

Early in the year agreement was reached between Britain and the United Arab Republic over problems arising from the Suez conflict in 1956. Diplomatic relations were resumed on Dec. 1.

During his trip to Europe in August the president of the United States, Dwight D. Eisenhower, met Macmillan in London and also went to Balmoral to visit Queen Elizabeth II.

During the year there were continued skirmishes between British fishing trawlers, escorted by warships, and Icelandic gun boats in the disputed areas of Iceland's coastal waters.

Financial and Economic. In his 1959 budget the chancellor of the exchequer gave considerable encouragement to industrial expansion, conceding £295 million in tax reliefs for the current year and £360 million in a full financial year. The standard rate of income tax was reduced from 8s. in the £ to 7s. 9d. Concessions were also announced regarding postwar credits, with repayment for men at 63 instead of 65, and a grant of $2\frac{1}{2}\%$ interest on remaining credits from Oct. 1959.

Changes in national assistance were announced on June 15 by the minister of pensions and national insurance, A. T. Boyd-Carpenter. The new rates came into effect on Sept. 7, and were expected in a full year to cost £32 million.

Take-over bids for the transfer of ownership of breweries, stores and newspapers, involving millions of pounds, were much in the news during the year, eventually reaching a climax when negotiations for the transfer of the Ely brewery, Cardiff, were abandoned. The failure of a building society led to proposals for strengthening the law relating to building societies. The Issuing Houses association also published a code of conduct for take-over bids.

The nationalized industries, with the exception of electricity and the post office, did not fare well in 1958. British Overseas Airways corporation and associated companies lost £5,179,420, compared with £2,839,350 in 1957. The Gas council recorded its first deficit in 1958, the loss being £1,466,882. By way of contrast the Electricity council returned a record surplus of £27·3 million in 1958, and in the same year the post office made a profit of £8·25 million.

In 1958 the National Coal board disclosed a net loss of £3·5 million compared with £5·3 million in 1957, bringing the accumulated deficit to £32·6 million.

The total deficit of the British Transport commission for 1958 was £88,975,734, nearly £25 million more than in 1957. All fares on British Railways and some in the London Transport executive region were raised on Nov. 1, but cheaper rates for off-peak travel in the London area were announced.

It was stated during the year that in 1958 the number of

motor cars made in Britain was 1,051,551—the first time that the million mark had been exceeded in a single year.

In Nov. 1958 the number of unemployed had reached 536,000 and by Feb. 1959, the figures had increased to 620,000. In March, however, the government was able to announce that the number of unemployed had fallen during the month by 58,000. The figure for April was 531,000, and the reduction in numbers continued during the summer months. However, by mid-November the figures had begun to increase.

Restrictions on the amount of foreign currency that anyone in Britain could obtain for travel abroad were withdrawn. The amount of sterling currency which individuals were permitted to take abroad was increased from £20 to £50.

General. The queen, accompanied by the Duke of Edinburgh, visited Canada for the opening of the St. Lawrence seaway in June. It was announced on Aug. 7, shortly after the queen's return to Britain that she was expecting a baby early in the new year, and would undertake no further public engagements. She was therefore unable to visit Ghana in November as had been previously arranged, and the Duke of Edinburgh went there alone. Earlier in the year he had visited Burma, Pakistan, India, Singapore, North Borneo, Sarawak, Hong Kong and the Pacific Islands.

Other notable visits abroad by members of the royal family included those of Queen Elizabeth the Queen Mother to Nairobi in February, of Princess Margaret to Lisbon in June and of Princess Alexandra to Australia in September.

A printing strike began in June, involving more than 100,000 workers in some 4,000 printing firms and about 1,000 provincial and London suburban newspapers. With the exception of those offices which maintained an emergency service by

" *Notice how all of a sudden they stop giving us ' You-don't-get-summers-like-we-had-when-we-were-boys '.*"—*a cartoon by Giles which appeared in the " Daily Express " on July 9.*

obtaining volunteer labour or complying with the unions' demands, all the provincial press closed down until August, when work was resumed on terms arrived at during negotiations under the chairmanship of Lord Birkett (*see* BIOGRAPHIES).

In June the firm of Saunders-Roe Ltd. demonstrated its Hovercraft, a machine which could fly or hover nine inches above ground or sea level at a speed of 25 knots.

In his annual report in July, the commissioner of the metropolitan police, Sir Joseph Simpson, referred to a new peak of crime.

The remarkably dry, warm and sunny summer months gave most parts of the country better weather than in any year since 1911. By September many regions were experiencing drought conditions.

There was increased traffic on the roads and a heavy accident toll. Britain's first motorway—the M.1—running between London and Birmingham, was opened on Nov. 2.

The government announced on Dec. 16 that it would set up a committee to look into the powers of disciplinary tribunals to compel evidence. This followed the action of Reading police who had listened to a telephone conversation and handed over a report to the General Medical council.

Sport. John Michael Hawthorn (*see* OBITUARIES) was killed when his car crashed on the Guildford by-pass on Jan. 22. He was world champion motor driver in 1958, and had announced his retirement from racing.

On Feb. 5, Australia beat England in the fourth test match at Adelaide and thus regained the Ashes. Yorkshire won the County Cricket championship for the first time since 1949. Gloucestershire were runners-up.

The Grand National (March 21) was won by J. E. Bigg's Oxo, ridden by M. Scudamore. Only 4 horses out of 34 starters finished the course. The Derby was run at Epsom on June 3, and resulted in a victory for Sir Humphrey de Trafford's Parthia, trained by C. Boyd-Rochfort and ridden by W. H. Carr.

The 105th university boat race, held on March 28, was won by Oxford by six lengths in a time of 18 min. 52 sec. Donald Campbell created a new world record speed in his motorboat " Bluebird " on May 13, crossing Coniston water at an average speed of 260·35 m.p.h.

The Wimbledon tennis tournament ended on July 4, with Maria Bueno (Brazil) and A. Olmedo (Peru) as the individual champions.

The British Lions rugby team ended its tour of Australia and New Zealand on Sept. 20, with a belated victory over the All Blacks in the final test, after losing the three previous matches. In Australia they had won both international matches. They played in all 31 matches, won 25 and lost the remainder.

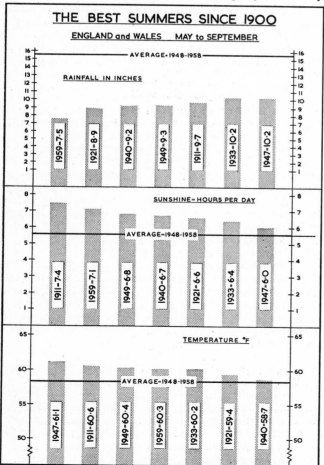

THE BEST SUMMERS SINCE 1900

ENGLAND and WALES   MAY to SEPTEMBER

AVERAGE·1948-1958

RAINFALL IN INCHES

| 1959-7·5 | 1921-8·9 | 1940-9·2 | 1949-9·3 | 1911-9·7 | 1933-10·2 | 1947-10·2 |

SUNSHINE = HOURS PER DAY

AVERAGE-1948-1958

| 1911-7·4 | 1959-7·1 | 1949-6·8 | 1940-6·7 | 1921-6·6 | 1933-6·4 | 1947-6·0 |

TEMPERATURE °F

AVERAGE-1948-1958

| 1947-61·1 | 1911-60·6 | 1949-60·4 | 1959-60·3 | 1933-60·2 | 1921-59·4 | 1940-58·7 |

The United States regained the Ryder cup (golf) from Britain on Nov. 7. (*See* also CHANNEL ISLANDS; COMMONWEALTH OF NATIONS; GOVERNMENT DEPARTMENTS; MAN, ISLE OF; NORTHERN IRELAND; SCOTLAND; WALES.) (E. T. Ss.)

GREECE. Kingdom in the southern part of the Balkan peninsula. Area: 51,182 sq.mi.; the mainland accounts for 41,328 sq.mi.; the islands, of which the largest is Crete (3,255 sq.mi.), for 9,854 sq.mi. Pop.: (1951 census) 7,632,801; (1958 est.) 8,150,000. Language (1951): Greek 95·6%; Turkish 2·4%; Slavonic 0·8%; Macedo-Rumanian 0·5%; Albanian 0·3%. Religion (1951): Greek Orthodox 97·9%; Roman Catholic 0·4%; Moslem 1·5%; Jewish 0·08%. Chief towns (1951 census, municipal area only): Athens (cap.) 565,084*; Piraeus 186,014; Salonika (Thessaloniki) 217,049; Patras 79,014; Volos 65,090; Iraklion 51,144. Ruler, King Paul I; prime minister, Konstantinos Karamanlis. Main imports: machinery and vehicles, manufactured goods, coal, petroleum and products. Main exports: tobacco, currants and raisins, olives and olive oil, wines, iron ore, pyrites, bauxite. Monetary unit: *drachma* (Dr.84·00 = £1 sterling).

* The population of Greater Athens, which included the populations of Piraeus and suburbs, was 1,378,586.

History. *Home Politics.* Municipal elections held on April 5 showed a drop of about 15% in left-wing strength as compared with the voting at the parliamentary elections of May 1958. On Jan. 5 Panayotis Kanellopoulos left the opposition benches and joined the government as deputy premier; and the fragmentation of the Liberal (opposition) party continued with the secession of its joint leader Georgios Papandreou who formed the Liberal Democratic party on April 25.

The Athens Permanent Court Martial sentenced on July 23 Manolis Glezos to five years' imprisonment, four years' exile and eight years' loss of all civil rights. He was found guilty of aiding Communist spies in Greece.

The emergence of the Eoka leader Georgios Grivas as an aspirant to political leadership introduced a new, and as yet incalculable, element into the Greek political scene, though the response to the general's preliminary bids for public support was not very enthusiastic.

Defence. The question whether medium-range missile bases should be established on Greek territory continued to be a subject of political controversy and heated public discussion. On June 4 the Greek government rejected a Soviet proposal for the setting up of a " nuclear-free zone " in the Balkans on the grounds that such a plan aimed at weakening the defensive power of the west; and several Rumanian approaches

proposing a " Balkan summit meeting " were also rebuffed as a propaganda stunt and impracticable in view of the non-existence of the indispensable pre-requisites for such a meeting.

Foreign Affairs. The discussion of the Cyprus question by the U.N. general assembly resulted in the adoption on Dec. 5, 1958, of a compromise resolution urging the interested parties to persevere in their efforts towards " a peaceful, democratic and just solution "—a hope which materialized in the form of a meeting in Zürich on Feb. 5-11 between the Greek and Turkish premiers and foreign ministers, who agreed to establish an independent Republic of Cyprus by Feb. 1960. The London agreement of Feb. 19, to which Greece, Turkey, Great Britain and the leaders of the Greek and Turkish communities in Cyprus were signatories, formalized this decision, and parliament endorsed the government's policy on Feb. 28 by a vote of 170 to 118.

The restoration of cordial relations with Italy was taken a step further by a state visit to Rome on May 19-22, in the course of which King Paul and Queen Frederika were received by the pope. Amintore Fanfani, the Italian premier, visited Athens on Jan. 10 for discussions regarding the balance of $15 million war reparations due to Greece, which the Greek government agreed to utilize for the importation of capital goods from Italy. Konstantinos Karamanlis, the Greek premier, accompanied by Evangelos Averoff, the foreign minister, visited Italy on Nov. 9 for further talks on Greco-Italian economic relations and a review of the international situation.

President Tito visited Greece on March 2-5 and met Greek leaders at Rhodes. This visit was followed by one from Koča Popović, the Yugoslav foreign minister, on June 16 and the setting up of a mixed Greco-Yugoslav commission which led to the signature of a number of agreements regulating various outstanding questions affecting economic, technical, cultural, legal and transport matters. These visits were returned by Kanellopoulos on Sept. 6-12 for an exchange of views in Belgrade regarding further extension of Greco-Yugoslav commercial and economic co-operation.

The Cyprus settlement initiated a progressive improvement of relations with Turkey, and on May 7-12 Karamanlis and Averoff visited Turkey for a reaffirmation of joint adherence

The arrival of Colonel Grivas at Athens airport on March 17, after four and a half years as the leader of Eoka in Cyprus. After being welcomed by the Greek primate and the foreign minister he made a triumphal progress along the eight-mile route to the city.

to the Zürich and London agreements on Cyprus. A Greco-Turkish commission was appointed to make recommendations on various questions at issue between the two countries regarding the Turkish minority in Thrace, the Greek minority in Istanbul, the position of the oecumenical patriarchate in Turkey and fishing rights in narrow waters in the Aegean.

On May 15 the Greek government called on Bulgaria to begin payment of war reparations of $45 million awarded to Greece under the Bulgarian peace treaty.

The government tabled on Nov. 24 a parliamentary motion of confidence. The vote took place on Nov. 30 at the close of a general debate on economic and foreign policies. There were 170 votes for the government and 117 against.

On Dec. 14-15 President Dwight D. Eisenhower visited Athens. Addressing the Greek Chamber of Deputies he paid tribute to Karamanlis and his government who produced a remarkable record of achievement.

Economic. Limited convertibility of the drachma was introduced on May 25. Greece's application to join the European Economic community was approved by the council of the E.E.C. on July 26, and discussions took place subsequently in Brussels and Athens to decide on the form and extent of Greece's association.

A five-year capital investments plan was announced on April 28 covering expenditure of some $1,000 million and aimed at creating employment for nearly 400,000 people and raising the average per capita income from $275 to $370.

Several more ships were registered under the Greek flag during the year, bringing the total tonnage of the Greek merchant fleet to 2·8 million gross tons.   (S. L. H.)

See (all London) Patrick Leigh Fermor, *Mani* (1958); Patrick Anderson, *First Steps in Greece* (1959); Geoffrey Chandler, *The Divided Land* (1959).

GREENLAND.

GREENLAND. Large island (840,000 sq.mi., more than four-fifths covered by an ice cap), part of the kingdom of Denmark, in the north Atlantic ocean, N.W. of Iceland. Pop. (1956 est.) 28,298, distributed in settlements along the west coast, except for 2,046 on the east coast and 455 on the north (Thule); 2,121 Europeans (mostly Danes), the rest native Greenlanders (Eskimoes). Language: Danish and Eskimo. Religion: Lutheran. Capital, Godthaab (second governor's seat, Godhavn). Governor-general, Poul Hugo Lundsteen. Main exports: fish and fish products, whale blubber, cryolite. Currency: Danish.

History. On May 28, 1959, the Danish Folketing passed an act, authorizing the minister for Greenland to invest Kr.57 million during a five-year period in Greenland in plants for fish canning and fish freezing, in power plants and water

Part of a camp constructed below the surface of the Greenland ice cap by U.S. army personnel to house polar research scientists.

supplies, and in improved port facilities supplying Jakobshavn, Holsteinsborg, Sukkertoppen and Frederikshaab with piers for oceangoing vessels.

In August Faeroese fishermen got extended fishing rights in Greenland waters and were allowed to land their catches at Greenland ports.

On Jan. 30 the motorship " Hans Hedtoft ", the flagship of the state-owned Royal Greenland Trading company, collided with an iceberg about 30 mi. southeast of Cape Farewell, while she was returning from Julienehaab to Copenhagen on the second half of her maiden voyage; she foundered with the loss of all her 55 passengers and her crew of 39. Among the passengers was Augo Lynge, one of the two Greenland members in the Danish Folketing (he was succeeded in the Folketing by Nicolaj Rosing). On Feb. 3 a commission was set up to consider the question of sailing conditions on the Denmark-Greenland route in the winter months. In September the commission recommended continued sailing during the winter months on condition that rescue services in Greenland were improved.   (H. Ln.)

GUADELOUPE, French overseas *département* in the Lesser Antilles: two main and five smaller islands. Total area: 686 sq.mi. Pop.: (1954 census) 229,120; (1959 est.) 255,000; mainly coloured (Negro or mixed). Language: French and creole French. Religion: Roman Catholic. Chief towns (pop., 1954 census): Basse-Terre (cap.) 11,837; Pointe-à-Pitre 26,160. Prefect, Jean-Pierre Abeille. Main exports: sugar, bananas, rum. Currency: metropolitan *franc*.

History. At the municipal elections held in March the U.N.R. (Gaullists) captured eight town councils, the Independents 6, the left-wing Socialists 6, the Communists 5, the Socialists 4 and the Radicals 4. Basse-Terre, the capital, had a Socialist town council. Lucien Bernier and Torribien, both Socialists, were elected senators on April 26. (Hu. De.)

GUATEMALA. Central American republic bounded W. and N. by Mexico, E. by British Honduras, the Caribbean sea, Honduras and El Salvador and S. by the Pacific ocean. Area: 42,042 sq.mi. Pop.: (1950 census) 2,790,868; (1958 est.) 3,545,901; 66% pure Indian descending from Maya or Quiché strains, 33% mixed Indian and Spanish (*ladinos*) and Indian and Negro blood, and 1% white. Language: Spanish, but many speak only Indian dialects (numbering at least 18). Religion: predominantly Roman Catholic. Chief towns (pop., 1950 census; 1957 est. in brackets): Guatemala City (cap.) 284,276 (355,254); Quezaltenango 27,672 (33,726); Puerto Barrios 15,155 (19,268). President, Miguel Ydígoras Fuentes. Main imports: machinery and manufactured goods. Main exports: coffee (77%); bananas (17%). Monetary unit: *quetzal*, at par with the U.S. dollar.

History. An incident off the coast of Guatemala on the closing day of 1958 led, on Jan. 23, 1959, to a break in diplomatic relations with Mexico. Laying claim to 12 mi. of territorial waters, the government of Guatemala ordered the bombing and sinking of shipping craft operating within the proclaimed limits. When several Mexican shrimp boats were bombed on Dec. 31, 1958, by Guatemalan air force planes several fishermen were killed and a number wounded. Mexico, though not contesting the right of Guatemala to arrest and punish foreigners who might have been fishing in Guatemalan waters, challenged the right to any open attack resulting in the loss of life. Guatemala refused to consider the Mexican government's proposal that the issue be placed before the International Court of Justice. But through mediation initiated by the Chilean ambassador to Mexico diplomatic relations were renewed on Sept. 15, 1959.

In March, President Ydígoras made the charge that a plot was under way in Mexico to invade Guatemala. In May, reports caused the government to sound an alert to prepare for four armed boats which had left Cuba supposedly to invade Guatemala. In the midst of these events, Ydígoras stated that the political and economic control of British Honduras was a definite aim of his administration.

The economic programme, presented by Ydígoras early in

the year, called for economy and austerity throughout 1959. With imports rising faster than exports and a consequent decline in exchange reserves, the government, for the first time since World War II, decreed quantitative import restrictions for items not considered essential. (A. E. TR.)

GUIANA, BRITISH: see BRITISH GUIANA.
GUIANA, DUTCH (Surinam): see NETHERLANDS OVERSEAS TERRITORIES.
GUIANA, FRENCH: see FRENCH GUIANA.

GUINEA. An independent republic on west coast of Africa, proclaimed on Oct. 2, 1958, bounded N. by Portuguese Guinea and Senegal, N.E. by Sudan, E. by Ivory Coast and S. by Liberia and Sierra Leone. Area: 108,455 sq.mi. Pop. (1957 est.): 2,492,000, mainly Negro; the most important tribes are the Fula, Malinké and Soussou; Europeans 8,700, mostly French. Religion: Moslem, animist, Christian. Chief towns (pop. 1957 est.): Konakry (cap.) 65,000; Kankan 24,600. President of the republic, Sékou Touré (see BIOGRAPHIES). Main exports: coffee, bananas, palm kernels, iron ore, bauxite. Monetary unit: Guinean *franc* =French Fr.2.

History. On Jan. 7, 1959, a Franco-Guinean agreement was signed in Paris on the following points: (1) Guinea would remain in the franc area, with its own currency; (2) there would be co-ordination in matters of foreign policy; (3) France would be able to give assistance in the form of trained personnel, help in the training of Guinean civil servants, send out study missions and represent Guinea in countries where it had no representatives of its own; (4) students from Guinea would have access to French universities on the same footing as French students. On Jan. 15 the French government recognized Guinea as an independent state and announced that a *chargé d'affaires* was to be sent to Konakry.

From April 23 to May 12 Kwame Nkrumah, the prime minister of Ghana, visited Guinea. A union, not legally defined, was agreed upon between Ghana and Guinea. The two leaders presented this as the nucleus of a Union of Independent African States. From July 14 to 19 Sékou Touré and Kwame Nkrumah visited William Tubman, president of Liberia, at Monrovia. In a joint declaration the three leaders announced that a conference would be held in 1960 to discuss the possibility of an African Commonwealth of Nations.

Ghana was the first state to help Guinea in its financial difficulties and offered a loan of £10 million. On Aug. 24 a Soviet-Guinean agreement was signed in Moscow by A. I. Mikoyan, Soviet deputy prime minister, and Saifoulaye Diallo, president of the National Assembly of Guinea. The agreement provided for a Soviet loan of Rb.140 million (£12·5 million) redeemable in 12 years at 2·5%. The credit was to cover the cost of economic and technical assistance for building industrial establishments, developing agriculture and laying roads.

All the political groups of the republic formed a single Parti Démocratique de Guinée of which Sékou Touré became secretary-general. It was decided to form a small army. When the United States failed to respond to an appeal for a shipment of arms, Czechoslovakia rushed forward to fill the gap. In March and April three ships unloaded rifles, machine guns, light artillery and armoured cars at Konakry.

Towards the end of the year Sékou Touré was invited to visit the United States and Great Britain. He arrived in Washington on Oct. 26, and was met at the airport by Richard M. Nixon, the vice-president. He had an hour's talk with President Dwight D. Eisenhower and Christian Herter, the secretary of state. After visiting Chicago and Los Angeles on Nov. 5 he addressed the U.N. general assembly. Africa, he said, would not be " taken in tow " either by the west or by the U.S.S.R.

On Nov. 10 Sékou Touré arrived in London. He was welcomed at the airport by Harold Macmillan, the prime minister, and Selwyn Lloyd, the secretary of state for foreign affairs. The following day the queen received Sékou Touré and his wife.

From Nov. 15 to 18 President Touré was the guest of the German Federal Republic, from Nov. 19 to 27—of the U.S.S.R., from Nov. 28 to Nov. 30—of Czechoslovakia, and from Dec. 1 to 4—of Morocco. (HU. DE.; X.)

GYNAECOLOGY AND OBSTETRICS. The effect of abdominal decompression on the first stage of labour was described by O. S. Heyns (*J. Obstet. Gynaec., Brit. Emp.*, 66, 220, 1959). He placed each of 100 primiparous women during early labour into a plastic bag of laminated polyvinyl chloride with an airtight plastic zip built to contain the trunk up to the part of the thorax just above the base of the breasts. A rigid cage made of steel rods or fibre glass was placed inside the bag over the abdomen and thorax with the patient sitting in a semi-reclining canvas chair. The arms and legs were left free outside the bag. The bag was connected to a 70 litre per min. suction pump and decompression was carried out during uterine contractions, being controlled by the patient herself by means of a valve. A partial vacuum at pressures of 50 mm. to 100 mm. of mercury (one to two lb. per sq.in.) below atmospheric was produced over the abdomen and lower thorax because they were underneath the incompressible cage. Heyns found that 84 of the 100 women were delivered within ten hours of beginning decompression and 64 within six hours. The most striking effect, however, was the remarkable relief from pain. When the two factors of duration of labour and pain relief were taken together analysis of the cases showed the results were: excellent, 62%; very good, 24%; satisfactory, 12%; and failure 2%. Heyns explained the good effect on labour of abdominal decompression. He pointed out that the uterus works at its best mechanical advantage when it can adopt a spherical shape. Normally the tense and muscular abdominal wall prevents the uterus from becoming spherical unless the abdomen is made to bulge forward by decompression.

Ruth Graham and J. B. Graham reported in 1953 (*Cancer, N.Y.*, 6, 215) that in cases of carcinoma of the cervix there were certain changes in the non-cancerous basal cells of the vagina which could be used to indicate a good response to irradiation. These changes they called the " sensitization response " or SR. In 100 patients the five-year survival rate in those with a good response was 66% and in those with a poor response it was only 18%. R. L. Lanier and W. T. Wikle (*Radiology*, 72, 217, 1959) were unable, however, to find any correlation between the results of treating 96 patients since 1950 and the SR. G. G. Herman, H. E. Hughes and S. B. Gusberg (*Surg. Gynec. Obstet.*, 108, 463, 1959) found the SR in women without cancer and thought that it was an index of endogenous oestrogen secretion, being high in postmenopausal women and in patients who had had their ovaries removed.

The committee under the chairmanship of the Earl of Cranbrook, appointed to review the maternity services in England and Wales and to make recommendations, issued its report (report of the Maternity Services committee, H.M.S.O., 1959). They were not able to recommend changing the tripartite structure of the maternity services whereby the pregnant woman may be seen at different times in her pregnancy by the consultant in hospital, the local authority midwife and the general practitioner. T. B. FitzGerald (*Lancet,1*, 404, 1959) described a unified system in which all confinements took place either in hospital in charge of the consultant or in well-equipped maternity homes supervised by the general practitioner. All abnormal patients were booked for hospital confinement and all normal patients due to be confined in a maternity home were seen by the consultant early in pregnancy and again at the 36th week; the normal mother and baby were discharged home 48 hr. after delivery to be nursed there by midwives who rotated through the hospital and maternity homes. The Cranbrook committee recommended instead the setting up of local liaison committees for the professional members of the three branches to discuss clinical and administrative problems. They also recommended that hospital accommodation should be provided for 70% of all deliveries, with normally a ten-day stay in hospital and antenatal beds for 20%-25% of all pregnant women. Only general practitioners who had completed six months residential work under a consultant would be on the obstetric list and thus entitled to a fee for maternity services.

(T. L. T. L.)

BIBLIOGRAPHY (all 1959). S. J. Behrman and J. R. G. Gosling, *Fundamentals of Gynaecology* (Oxford); A. W. Bourne, *Synopsis of Obstetrics and Gynaecology*, 12th ed. (London); R. J. Crossen, *Synopsis of Gynaecology*, 5th ed. (London); I. Donald *Practical Obstetrics Problems*, 2nd ed. (London); Sir E. Holland and A. W. Bourne, *British Obstetrics and Gynaecological Practice*, 2nd ed. (London); F. Musgrove, *Lecture Notes on Obstetrics* (London); C. A. Smith, *Physiology of the Newborn Infant*, 3rd ed. (Oxford); H. Speert, *Obstetric and Gynecologic Milestones* (New York); W. R. Winterton, *Aids to Gynaecology*, 11th ed. (London); *Yearbook of Obstetrics and Gynecology, 1958-59* (Chicago).

HAITI. West Indian republic forming the western third of the island of Haiti or Hispaniola. Area: 10,714 sq.mi. Pop.: (1950 census) 3,097,220; (1958 est.) 3,424,000, of whom 95% are Negro and the remainder—the ruling class—almost exclusively mulatto. Language: French and creole French. Religion: Roman Catholic, but voodooism is practised in rural areas. Chief towns (pop., 1950 census): Port-au-Prince (cap.) 142,840; Cap Haitien 24,975. President, François Duvalier. Main imports: machinery and manufactures. Main exports: coffee (66%), sisal (13%), sugar (6%). Monetary unit: *gourde* (official exchange rate G.14·00=£ sterling).

History. Grave disorder prevailed during 1959 in many parts of the republic, aggravated by opposition leaders, many of them in exile, as well as by agents of Cuba and the Dominican Republic. In the middle of August, an invasion of southwestern Haiti was attempted by a small band of Cubans, Venezuelans and Haitian exiles; according to the government, it had been organized by Louis Dejoie, a former Haitian senator, then in Venezuela. Within a week most of the invaders had been killed or captured. Cuba and Haiti broke off diplomatic relations on Aug. 29. But almost at once a sharp conflict broke out between the Haitian government and the Roman Catholic clergy, comprising mainly French citizens. The government ordered the expulsion of two priests. Mgr. François Poirier, the archbishop, protested. The government ordered his arrest, then immediately suspended, but did not cancel, the order. In an attempt to settle the crisis without losing face, the president, in a broadcast on Sept. 22 reviewing his administration on the second anniversary of his inauguration, confined his reference to the controversy with the clergy to a vague complaint of priests who aroused public opinion against the government.

The economic situation of Haiti went from bad to worse. In addition to the low prices of coffee and sugar, and poor crops generally, the northwestern peninsula was afflicted with a prolonged and severe drought, and several hundred people died of starvation.

The United States lent a total of more than $10 million for general and special purposes during 1959, in an effort to hold the Haitian economy together. The balance of payments was decidedly unfavourable, exceeding $8 million by the beginning of October.

(C. McG.)

HARBOURS: *see* Docks and Harbours.

HAUTE VOLTA: *see* Volta, Republic of.

HAWAII. The 50th state admitted to the United States consists of eight large islands and numerous islets in the Pacific. From southeast to northwest the islands are Hawaii (4,021 sq.mi.), Kahoolawe, Maui, Lanai, Molokai, Oahu, Kauai and Niihau; stretching northward beyond Niihau for more than 1,100 mi. is an archipelago of rocks, reefs and shoals which includes Midway. Total area: 6,435 sq.mi. Pop.: (1950 census) 499,794; (1959 est.) 597,910; cosmopolitan, the Japanese and Caucasian (white) groups being the largest. Principal town: Honolulu, on Oahu island (cap., pop., mid-1958, 307,204). Governor, William F. Quinn.

The Hawaiian flag, which includes the union jack (Hawaii was discovered by Capt. James Cook), displayed by an enthusiastic group.

History. After nearly 60 years as an incorporated, organized territory of the United States, Hawaii achieved statehood in 1959. The bill providing for Hawaii's admission as the 50th state of the Union was passed by the U.S. congress on March 12, 1959, and was signed by President Dwight D. Eisenhower on March 18. The official proclamation of admission was issued by the president on Aug. 21.

The general election on July 28, 1959, resulted in the election of Hawaii's first voting members of congress. William F. Quinn, the last appointed governor of Hawaii, was the first elected governor.

In 1959 the state legislature, which henceforth would meet in annual session, was composed of a Senate of 14 Republicans and 11 Democrats and a House of Representatives of 33 Democrats and 18 Republicans.

During 1959, a jet service to and from Hawaii both east and west was inaugurated by Japan Air Lines, Pan American Airlines and Quantas Airlines, reducing the time from the mainland to Honolulu to less than five hours. (W. F. Q.)

HEADS OF STATE: *see* Sovereigns, Presidents and Rulers.

HEART DISEASES: *see* Diseases.

HISTORICAL STUDIES. Great Britain contributed in full measure to large-scale undertakings: early 1959 saw the completion of the *Cambridge History of the British Empire* (8 vol., Cambridge) with the appearance of vol. iii, dealing with the still unfamiliar period 1870-1921, while at the opposite extreme of local topography the Victoria county history produced no fewer than six new volumes during the year, the most important being the attractive and authoritative account of the *University and City of Cambridge* (Oxford). Another reference work of permanent value was given wider circulation by an edition in English of the *Dictionary of Welsh Biography down to 1940* (Oxford). A further volume, in the Oxford History of England, was May McKisack on *The Fourteenth Century*, 1307-1399 (Oxford). Dom David Knowles completed his close examination of *The Religious*

Orders in England with a final volume on *The Tudor Age* (Cambridge).

For ancient history perhaps the most significant British contribution was a concise *Study of Greek Inscriptions* (Cambridge), by A. G. Woodhead. P. Argenti added three more massive volumes to his study of one Greek island: *The Occupation of Chios by the Genoese and their Administration of the Island, 1346-1566* (Cambridge). In the co-operative French version of the *Histoire de l'Eglise* a new stage was reached with a survey of *Institutions ecclésiastiques de la Chrétienté médiévale* (Paris), by G. Le Bras. A single French scholar, R. Boutruche, began a detailed analysis of *Seigneurie et féodalité* with a first volume on *Le Premier Age des liens d'homme à homme* (Paris). Another well-known writer, B. A. Pocquet du Haut-Jussé, examined *La France gouvernée par Jean Sans-Peur* (Paris), with particular reference to the expenditure of the *receveur-général du royaume*. German scholars were also active in the medieval scene, the most considerable work being the first two volumes of *Erforschung des Mittelalters* (Berlin), by P. Lehman. A German emigré, H. Holborn, produced in the United States two impressive volumes on *The Reformation* (New York), as part of a general *History of Modern Germany*. From Switzerland came a new general account, *Schweizer Geschichte* (Zürich) by P. Dürrenmatt and a quatercentenary tribute, *L'Université de Genève, 1559-1959* (Geneva), by P. G. Geisendorf. Italian scholarship was represented by a fine biography, *Il Doge Nicolo Contarini* (Venice) and by the first volume of Mario Toscano's *Lezioni di storia dei trattati e politica internazionale* (Turin), dealing especially with the publication by governments of diplomatic correspondence, which began with the printing of the Anglo-Spanish treaty of 1604 by order of James I. A young French professor, F. Crouzet, made a fresh approach to a vital subject in *L'Économie britannique et le Blocus continental, 1806-1813* (2 vol., Paris). British scholars added to knowledge of French history by studies of *The Crowd in the French Revolution* (Oxford), by G. Rudé, and of *The Government and the Newspaper Press in France, 1814-1881* (Oxford), by Irene Collins. A reasonable German view of a perennial subject was *Bismarck und Napoleon III* (Cologne), by H. Geuss, who surveyed relations between Prussia and France from 1851 to 1871.

For modern British history one of the most interesting monographs was Garrett Mattingly's colourful account of *The Defeat of the Spanish Armada* (London). Another American scholar, W. K. Jordan, added considerably to knowledge of the period with his study of *Philanthropy in England, 1480-1660* (London). There were two further volumes in the series *English Historical Documents* (London), one for the period 1714-1783, edited by D. B. Horn and Mary Ransome, the other for 1783-1832, edited by A. Aspinall and Anthony Smith. Asa Briggs edited a variety of *Chartist Studies* (London). A highly-praised monograph was H. J. Hanham's *Elections and Party Management: Politics in the Time of Disraeli and Gladstone* (London). For the overseas empire E. E. Rich began putting together the studies of a lifetime in *The History of the Hudson's Bay Company*, vol. i, 1670-1763 (London). The bicentenary of the battle of Quebec produced a number of studies, notably by B. Connell on *The Plains of Abraham* (London) and by C. Hibbert on *Wolfe at Quebec* (London). D. Creighton summarized *The Story of Canada* (Toronto) in masterly fashion. Much light on Africa was thrown by I. Schapera's edition of *David Livingstone: Family Letters*, 1841-56 (London), and by *The Diaries of Lord Lugard* (3 vols., London), ed. by Margery Perham and Mary Bull. Among the numerous works on American history and historiography may be singled out an appraisal of *Henry Adams: the Middle Years* (Cambridge, Massachusetts), by E. Samuels. For the far east there was Sir George Sansom's

Queen Victoria giving every indication of being amused in a photograph from the pictorial biography by H. and A. Gernsheim.

definitive *History of Japan* (3 vols., London). In the middle east Sir John Glubb summed up a lifetime's experience in a fair-minded account of *Britain and the Arabs* (London). Under the title *Fear God and Dread Nought* (London), A. J. Marder brought to a conclusion his three-volume edition of the correspondence of Lord Fisher of Kilverstone, revealing the clash of naval policies between the fiery admiral and Winston Churchill in World War I. B. H. Liddell Hart linked the two world wars in his detailed account of *The Tanks* (2 vols., London). Numerous volumes came out in the various series of official war histories, of especial interest being vol. xii of the *History of United States Naval Operations in World War II*, in which S. E. Morison carried the story down to the decisive battle of Leyte. In the United Kingdom Civil series W. N. Medlicott completed his account of *The Economic Blockade*, vol. ii (London). Facts about the later stages of the European war were put together by R. Aron in *L'Histoire de la Libération de la France, juin 1944-mai 1945* (Paris). The American Historical Association committee for the study of war documents issued *A Catalogue of Files and Microfilms of the German Foreign Ministry Archives, 1867-1920*. This was likely to prove an invaluable aid to the study of the captured German documents about to be returned to western Germany. (*See* also ENGLISH LITERATURE.)   (A. T. Me.)

HISTORIC BUILDINGS. The sixth annual report of the Historic Buildings Council for England, published in May, 1959, stated that in view of the funds then available to the council some retrenchment in its work would be necessary. For the next few years the council would be obliged to reduce the number of recommendations for grants to below the level reached in 1958 and more rigorous standards would have to be applied. The annual provision for expenditure had now reached £425,000, of which £350,000 had been allocated to England and this was proving insufficient. The report also discussed the importance of preserving buildings of outstanding group-value and the report of the Scottish council touched on the same theme. The Welsh council thought that the peak of their work had probably been passed and many of the most important buildings in Wales had been dealt with in the five years of the council's existence.

The three councils, which advise the minister of works on the allocation of grants to buildings of outstanding importance, recommended 132 grants during 1959. Among the buildings assisted were the following: Pembridge castle, Herefordshire, a small 13th-century moated border castle; the Court house, East Meon, Hampshire; Berkeley castle, Gloucestershire; the late medieval Moot hall at Hexham, Northumberland; Ordsall hall, Salford, Lancashire, a large, 15th-century timber-framed house; Chilham castle, Kent, an early 17th-century house which has an early medieval castle adjoining; Sir John Moore's Grammar school, Appleby Magna, Leicestershire; Castle Howard, Yorkshire, Sir John Vanbrugh's splendid early 18th-century palace; Prior Park, Bath, by John Wood the elder; Ditchley, Oxfordshire, the large early 18th-century mansion by James Gibbs; and Milton Abbey school, Milton Abbas, Dorset, the most ambitious of the domestic works of Sir William Chambers. In Wales, Powis castle, Welshpool, Montgomeryshire and the 16th-century Plas Mawr, Conway, Caernarvonshire, were among those assisted, and in Scotland, Robert Adam's Newliston, West Lothian, and Sir Robert Bruce's Prestonfield house, Edinburgh, were included in the lists.

The Historic Churches Preservation trust in its sixth annual report (for 1958) announced grants to 195 churches and chapels totalling £50,539 and interest-free loans to 13 other churches amounting to £7,350. This brought the total amount voted by the end of 1958 to £377,779 and the number of churches which had received grants to 884.

In Dec. 1958, a commission was appointed by the archbishops of Canterbury and York to consider the problem of redundant churches which had a claim to be preserved on grounds of historic and architectural interest. The commission under the chairmanship of Lord Bridges would make recommendations on the procedure for dealing with such cases and the financial problems involved.

In May the Oxford Historic Buildings trust announced in a first report that £1,808,854 had been contributed to the appeal by the end of 1958. Thus the appeal, launched in June 1957, had reached its target but it was found when work started in some of the buildings that a much greater degree of decay existed than had been expected and, as a result, an even larger sum would be needed if the work of repair was to be satisfactorily undertaken. At Cambridge the repair of the Gate of Honour at Gonville and Caius college was completed. In London the centenary was celebrated of All Saints', Margaret street. This church, designed by William Butterfield and considered to be one of his finest works, had been recently restored at a cost of nearly £30,000. At Eton, the college chapel, founded by Henry VI, was given a new stone vault designed by Sir William Holford to replace a timber roof, dating from 1699, which had been ruined by death watch beetle. The Pilgrim trust made a further grant towards work on the chapel and in its 28th annual report (for 1958) announced grants totalling £81,261 for the preservation of historic buildings, both secular and ecclesiastical. At Greenwich the cleaning of the Thornhill ceiling in the great hall of Greenwich hospital was completed and at Kew, the Orangery, designed by Sir William Chambers, and Decimus Burton's Palm house, were both re-opened after repair.

The National Buildings record in its 18th annual report (for 1958-59) reported some diminution in the number of large and important country houses threatened with demolition, though smaller buildings of historic and architectural interest were still considered very vulnerable. Among the buildings

demolished during 1959 were Holyrood house, Spalding, Lincolnshire, an early Tudor timber-framed building with a Georgian brick front; Shavington hall, Shropshire, a house of 1685 with additions by Norman Shaw; and 3, St. James's street south, Bath, a fine early 18th-century town house probably designed by William Killigrew.   (O. J. W.)

BIBLIOGRAPHY (all London, 1959). N. Pevsner, *The Buildings of England* series, *The West Riding of Yorkshire*; K. Downes, *Hawksmoor*; T. S. R. Boase, *The Oxford History of English Art*, vol. 10, *English Art 1800-1870*; The Royal Commission on Historical Monuments, *The City of Cambridge*, 2 vols.

HOCKEY.

England had a distinctly lean season in 1958-59. They retained the international championship, which is restricted to the four home countries, but not the triple crown. That was lost on a glorious afternoon at Sunderland by a combination of deplorably bad shooting by England and an inspired Scottish defence. The result, 1-1, gave Scotland their only point in the championship for they were beaten by both Ireland and Wales, who in turn were beaten by England. The victory over Ireland at Belfast that nearly slipped through England's fingers and the final defeat by the Netherlands in the first international played at Hurlingham park, London, produced further evidence of a decline. Here again the inability of the England forwards to press home their attacks robbed the team of due reward for the control they exerted much of the time in midfield.

This limitation of scoring power was emphasized by a goalless draw in the first England trial and in the University match. The final of the county championship was also dominated by defence, Middlesex beating Gloucestershire 2-1 only in the closing minutes of a stirring contest. The same trend was apparent in August when the England team made an out-of-season trip to Poznań and drew their first international with Poland 1-1. The British Hockey board took a preliminary step in preparation for the Olympic tournament at Rome in 1960 when they turned out an experimental Great Britain team against Belgium at Hove in April and lost 0-1. Later a somewhat experimental British party of 16 took part in an international tournament in Munich (Oct. 11-18) where it drew 1-1 with India, lost 1-4 to Belgium, lost 1-3 to Germany, beat Denmark 2-0, beat Switzerland 2-0 and drew with Spain 3-3.

An incident during the women's international hockey match held at Wembley in March, in which England beat South Africa 4-1.

The women's hockey associations of the four home countries had an exceptionally heavy programme of international fixtures, arising from the 15-nation International Federation of Women's Hockey associations (I.F.W.H.A.) tournament held in Amsterdam from April 24 to May 7 and from visits to Britain by the Australian, New Zealand and South African teams, among others, *en route* to Amsterdam. The England team came out of their strenuous list of engagements against all the leading countries with a splendid record judged even by their own high standard. In the home internationals they won their three matches with considerable ease. In the I.F.W.H.A. tournament they won six matches out of six. In all they played 11 matches and won 10, with a total of 51 goals to 9 against. They drew one match against Australia at Folkestone 1-1, but, in a return game at Amsterdam, England won by 3 goals to 2. (*See* also SPORTING RECORD.)   (R. L. HS.)

HOLLAND: *see* NETHERLANDS.

HONDURAS. Republic of Central America, bounded W.
by Guatemala, S. by El Salvador, the Pacific and Nicaragua and N. by the Caribbean. Area: 43,277 sq.mi. Pop.: (1950 census) 1,505,465; (1959 est.) 1,887,569, *c.* 87% *mestizo*, but incl. *c.* 35,000 tribal Indians and *c.* 25,000 Negroes. Language: Spanish; Indian dialects. Religion: Roman Catholic. Capital, Tegucigalpa (pop. 1950): 72,385. President of the republic, Ramón Villeda Morales. Main imports: machinery and manufactures. Main exports: bananas (37%), coffee (26%), timber (10%). Monetary unit: *lempira* (5·60 to the £1 sterling).

History. In Jan. 1959 the possibility of a full-scale revolt appeared imminent as Honduran rebels were reportedly gathering on the Nicaraguan side of the border in preparation for an invasion aimed at overthrowing the government. The authorities claimed that Nicaragua was harbouring enemies of Honduras, and was permitting them to operate a clandestine radio within its territory. A joint military delegation of the two countries, after visiting the border, reported the presence of armed rebels in the Zopotille area of Nicaragua, the government of which promised to arrest and disarm any rebel forces gathered within its territory.

During February a revolt, presumably instigated by Colonel Armando Velásquez Cerrato who had been identified with a number of previous abortive efforts, failed to overthrow the government. The ambassadors of Honduras and Nicaragua to the Organization of American States signed an agreement in Washington, D.C., which provided that the territory of neither country was to be used as a base for attack on the other. (*See* NICARAGUA.) Within a month Honduras was again claiming that Nicaragua was allowing rebels to cross the frontier. With feeling running high, in July Velásquez Cerrato attempted another coup to overthrow Villeda Morales. However, the armed forces and the party members formed a united front behind the government, and the effort collapsed.

The new labour code, passed by the congress in May, was approved by the president over the strong opposition of many employer groups. The principal opposition was directed against the provision which entitled the worker to full pay during illness, even though contracted off the job, for periods up to eight months.

Despite the political turmoil throughout much of the year, the government took steps to improve and diversify agriculture. A loan of $600,000 by the U.S. Export-Import bank was used to finance the purchase of pure-bred cattle.   (A. E. TR.)

HONDURAS, BRITISH: *see* BRITISH HONDURAS.

HONG KONG. British colony on S.E. coast of China
consisting of Hong Kong island and ceded territory of Kowloon, etc., and the New Territories (the rest of Kowloon peninsula and numerous islands, leased from China in 1898 for 99 yr.). Total area: 391 sq.mi.; colony 36 sq.mi. (H.K. island 32 sq.mi., Stonecutter's Island 1 sq.mi., ceded territory of Kowloon 3 sq.mi.); New Territories 355 sq.mi. (incl. Lan Tao island 58 sq.mi.). Total pop.: (1931 census) 849,751; (1958 est.) 2,748,000, incl. *c.* 15,000 permanently resident European British subjects from United Kingdom and Commonwealth. Language: Chinese (Cantonese); *c.* 5% speak English. Chief towns: Victoria (cap.), pop. *c.* 1 million; Kowloon, *c.* 900,000. Administration: governor; executive council; legislative council with official majority. Governor, Sir Robert Black. Hong Kong free port has large entrepôt

The Duke of Edinburgh receiving an address of welcome from a Chinese delegation during his visit to Hong Kong in March.

trade. Main local exports: cotton yarn and manufactures. Monetary unit: Hong Kong dollar ($1 = 1*s.* 3*d.* sterling).

History. During March 6-8, 1959, the Duke of Edinburgh visited Hong Kong as part of his world tour. In June more than 30 in. of rain fell in five days, disrupting communications and causing some 50 deaths and heavy damage. A special committee on housing reporting at the end of 1958 urged the creation of several satellite towns outside the urban areas, and the drafting of a ten-year plan of development. In his budget speech the governor, Sir Robert Black, reported favourably on the colony's economic position. Exports were higher than ever, prices, profits and dividends were lower, and although the tonnage of imports was greater, their value was lower. The capital value of nonrecurrent public works in hand was $1,000 million, of which the new Shek Pik reservoir scheme on Lan Tao accounted for $220 million. New buildings put up by private enterprise in 1958 reached the record value of $240 million. Additional places were found for 62,000 primary schoolchildren and for 10,000 in secondary schools.

Preparations were being made during the year to form a federation of all Hong Kong industries. The government appointed a three-man commission to advise on the form and extent of the control to be exercised over the two electricity companies in the colony.

Revenue for the year 1958-59 exceeded $600 million for the first time, while expenditure was $577 million.

The total trade for 1958 amounted to $7,582 million. Imports were down by $555 million to $4,593 million and exports were just under $3,000 million. Exports of Hong Kong products rose to $1,260 million.   (W. V. P.)

HONOURS. The following is a list of the most important
honours conferred by Queen Elizabeth II during 1959.

Viscounts

MORRISON, W. S., Q.C., M.P.	STUART, J. G., M.P.

Barons

DUGDALE, Major Sir Thomas L., M.P.	ROBBINS, Prof. L. C.*
FORSTER, Sir John, Q.C.	ROOTES, Sir William E.
JAMES, Sir Eric J. F.*	SHAWCROSS, Sir Hartley W.*
MACANDREW, Sir Charles G.	SPENS, Sir (W.) Patrick, Q.C., M.P.
MORRISON, H. S., M.P.*	TURNER, Sir James
PLOWDEN, Sir Edwin N.*	

Baroness

HORSBRUGH, Dame Florence, M.P.*

Baronets

BIBBY, Major Sir (A.) Harold	OAKSHOTT, H. D., M.P.
GILLETT, Sir (S.) Harold	PICKTHORN, K. W. M., M.P.
LLEWELLYN, Colonel Sir (R.) Godfrey	PLATT, Prof. R.

*Life peer.

Alhaji Ahmadu, sardauna of Sokoto, premier of Nigeria's Northern Region, leaving for Buckingham palace to be knighted.

Privy Councillors

BEVINS, J. R., M.P.
CARRINGTON, Peter Alexander Rupert, Baron
COBBOLD, C. F.
DUNDEE, Henry James Scrymgeour-Wedderburn, Earl
HARMAN, Sir Charles E.
HILBERY, Sir (G.) Malcolm
HOPE, Lord John (Adrian), M.P.

HORNSBY-SMITH, (M.) Patricia, M.P.
MCBRIDE, Sir Philip A. M.
NKRUMAH, Kwame
REDMAYNE, M., M.P.
ST. ALDWYN, Michael John, Earl
TOUCHE, Sir Gordon C., M.P.
WOOD, Hon. R. F., M.P.

Order of Merit

ALEXANDER OF TUNIS, Harold Rupert Leofric George Alexander, Field Marshal Earl

Companions of Honour

BEAZLEY, Prof. Sir John D.
CLARK, Sir Kenneth M.

NASH, W.

Knights Bachelor

BAIRAMIAN, V. R.
BAIRD, Prof. D.
GRATTAN-BELLEW, A. J.
BLACK, C. W., M.P.
BRIDGLAND, A. V.
BURKE, A. F.
BURNE, L. C.
CADZOW, N. J. K.
CLEARY, T. P.
COLES, E. B.
COOPER, W. J.
CRAWFORD, J. G.
CUST, Col. L. G. A.
DUMAS, R. J.
DUNPHIE, Maj.-General C. A. L.
DUTHIE, W. S., M.P.
EWING, Prof. A. W. G.
GAMAGE, L. C.
GERMAN, R. E.
JOHNSON-GILBERT, I. A.
GILLETT, S.
GILLIES, A.
GOMES, S. E.
GOTHARD, C. F.
GRIME, H. R.
GUINNESS, A.

GUNNING, O. P.
HARROD, H. R. F.
HAYGARTH, Col. J. H.
HAYWARD, Alderman I. J.
HEYSEN, H.
HODGE, Prof. W. V. D.
HOLLAND, E. M., Q.C.
HULL, H.
HURD, A. R., M.P.
HUTCHISON, J. D.
JAMES, D. J.
JENOUR, A. M. C.
JOHNSTON, G.
KIRKWOOD, R. L. M.
LAING, J. W.
LEWIS, Prof. A. J.
LINSTEAD, R. P.
LLOYD, R. O.
LOGAN, D. W.
LYLE, I. D.
MCCARTHUR, G. S.
MCGOVERN, P. S.
MACGREGOR, C. M.
MCKEE, Major W. C.
MAHONEY, J. A.
MARGAI, M. A. S.

MASTERMAN, J. C.
MILNE, J. A.
MITCHELL, J.
MORROW, A. W.
MURRAY, Brig. G. D. K.
NORTH, A. K.
SMYTH-OSBOURNE, Air Commodore H. P.
PACKER, D. F. H.
PRIOR-PALMER, Brig. O. T., M.P.
PATERSON, G. M.
PEARSON, J. R.
PEEL, Capt. F. R. J.
PEPPIATT, L. E.
PODE, E. J.
POLLEN, Capt. W. M. H.
POLLOCK, G., Q.C.
POPE, S. B.
PRESTON, K. H.
PUGH, J. A.
PYM, Major C. E.
REDGRAVE, M. S.
ROBINSON, V. L.
ROPNER, R. D.

RUGG, Alderman E. P.
SHEEHY, C.
SIMON, J. E. S., Q.C., M.P.
SMITH, T. E. B.
SMITH, W. P.
SMITHERS, A. T.
SPENCER, K. T.
SPENCER, S.*
SYKES, W. E.
SYME, Prof. R.
SYMONETTE, R. T.
TANGE, A. H.
TERRELL, Capt. T. A. R.
THOMAS, F. W.
THOMSON, Prof. A. R.
THOMSON, J. B.
THORP, J. K. R.
TROUT, H. L.
WALKER, W. G. N.
WARD, Alderman W.
WARREN, M. L.
WILKINSON, T. C. S.
WOOD, W. W.
YATES, T.

Order of the Bath

G.C.B.

DAVIS, Admiral Sir William W.
MILLS, Air Chief Marshal Sir George H.

STOCKWELL, General Sir Hugh C.
WARD, General Sir Dudley

K.C.B.

BINGLEY, Vice-Admiral A. N. C.
BOWER, Lieut.-Gen. Sir Roger H.
CHESHIRE, Acting Air Marshal W. G.
CROSS, Acting Air Marshal K. B. B.
DALTON, Vice-Admiral N. E.
GOODMAN, V. M. R.
KOELLE, Vice-Admiral H. P.

MACDONALD, Acting Air Marshal W. M. L.
MERTON, Air Vice-Marshal W. H.
POETT, Lieut.-General J. H. N.
PROCTOR, P. D.
STRATH, W.
WATSON, Vice-Admiral R. D.
WEST, Lieut.-General M. M. A. R.
WINNIFRITH, A. J. D.

Order of St. Michael and St. George

G.C.M.G.

BENSON, Sir Arthur E. T.
CACCIA, Sir Harold A.
LEE, Sir Frank G.

RAISMAN, Sir Abraham J.
SELKIRK, George Nigel Douglas-Hamilton, Earl of

K.C.M.G.

ARROWSMITH, E. P.
BUSK, D. L.
CLUTTON, G. L.
COSGROVE, R.
DUHIG, Most Rev. J.
GREY, Sir Ralph F. A.
JOHNSTON, C. H.
MORLAND, O. C.
MORLEY, A. F.
NOBLE, Commander A. H. P., M.P.

WILLIAM-POWLETT, Vice-Admiral Sir Peveril B. R. W.
SCOTT, Maj.-General W. A.
SHUCKBURGH, C. A. E.
THOROLD, G. F.
WADDELL, A. N. A.
WALKER, J.
WELENSKY, Sir (Roland) Roy
WOODALL, Lieut.-General Sir John D.
WOLFF, A. A.

Order of the British Empire

G.B.E.

BALFOUR, Sir John
KEMSLEY, James Gomer, Viscount
PALMER, Sir William

PARHAM, Admiral Sir Frederick R.
PELLY, Air Chief Marshal Sir Claude B. R.

D.B.E.

BROOKEBOROUGH, Cynthia Maria, Viscountess
BUCKLEY, Hon. Ruth B.

COLVIN, Brig. Mary K. B.
WEST, Rebecca (Mrs. Cecily Andrews)

K.B.E.

AHMADU, Alhaji
ALLISON, Sir (W.) John
ANDERSON, J.
ASHTON, H., M.P.
AXON, A. E.
BASSETT, W. E.
BRACKENRIDGE, A.
BRUNT, Prof. Sir David
CHILTON, Acting Air Marshal C. E.

COLLINGWOOD, Lieut.-Gen. R. G.
COTTON, Prof. C. A.
DALTON-MORRIS, Air Vice-Marshal L.
DIXON, Air Vice-Marshal F. W. P.
GARDNER, G. W. H.
GARRETT, Lieut.-General A. R.
HENDERSON, J. T.
INGLIS, Vice-Admiral J. C.
JACKMAN, Air Marshal H. D.

* *See* OBITUARIES.

HORSE RACING.

In National Hunt racing in 1958-59 Fare Time won the Champion hurdle easily, and Roddy Owen the Cheltenham Gold cup from Linwell and Lochroe. Lochroe had previously beaten Roddy Owen by a head in the King George VI steeplechase over the easier Kempton Park course. Taxidermist just beat the mare Kerstin in the Hennessy Gold cup at Sandown park. The Triumph hurdle, for four-year-olds at Hurst Park, went to Amazon's Choice. Oxo won the Grand National steeplechase in a thrilling race by 1½ lengths from Wyndburgh and Mr. What, the previous year's winner. T. Brookshaw on Wyndburgh rode the last eight fences without irons in an exemplary fashion, after a stirrup leather had broken. This rider had a fine season and became the leading National Hunt jockey for the first time.

On the flat the splendid summer of 1959 brought hard going for the greater part of the season. As a result fields were often small and the racing mediocre. Horses who required soft going had little chance once the spring was over, and the Cesarewitch in mid-October produced an unusually small field of 17, a number of candidates having dropped out because they could not be given enough preliminary work.

The three-year-old fillies were better than the colts. Among them Prince Aly Khan's Petite Etoile, a grey filly by Petition out of Star of Iran, showed herself to be outstanding, certainly the best since Meld (1955) and possibly the best of the century. She won the One Thousand guineas, the Oaks, the Sussex stakes, the Yorkshire Oaks and the Champion stakes, Rosalba in the guineas being the only horse to get her off the bit. The Chanteur filly Cantelo from whom she cantered home in the Oaks by five lengths won the Ribblesdale stakes at Royal Ascot and went on to smash the colts in a fast-run St. Leger. Petite Etoile proved herself to be an unexpectedly strong stayer possessing devastating speed, who could have taken on any horse at any distance at weight for age. Her owner, whose prize winnings in England she helped to raise to a record sum of more than £100,000 (altogether in England, France and Ireland his season's winnings had reached a record of more than £250,000), announced that she would be kept in training in 1960. Her trainer N. Murless also topped his record of winnings with £145,726, and her own winnings of £55,487 were a record for a filly. Rosalba won the Coronation stakes at Royal Ascot and ran gamely to win the Queen Elizabeth II stakes at Ascot in September.

Of the three-year-old colts, Parthia was a worthy winner of the Derby, and it was a pity that an incomplete recovery from coughing prevented his running at his best in the St. Leger, his only defeat. Prince Aly Khan's Taboun from France took the Two Thousand guineas in style but afterwards trained off. Fidalgo ran second in both the Derby and the St. Leger, and won the Irish Derby. Prince Aly Khan's Saint Crespin, not at his best when fourth in the Derby, won the Eclipse stakes for France and later, at Longchamp, the rich Prix de l'Arc de Triomphe. The Pinza colt Pindari won the King Edward VII stakes at Royal Ascot and the Great Voltigeur stakes at York and ran third in the St. Leger.

Alcide among the older horses lost the Gold cup at Royal Ascot to the French-trained Wallaby II but took his revenge with a well-deserved victory in the King George VI and Queen Elizabeth stakes. Primera, a horse who required to be saved as long as possible for a sharp final burst of speed and with whom L. Piggott developed an understanding, won the Ebor handicap at York in a brilliant season. The grey Malton sprinter Right Boy reasserted his claim to be the champion sprinter and swept past his opponents in a series of victories for the second year in succession at Royal Ascot, Newmarket, Goodwood and York. In his last race before retirement, Right Boy went down in glory at Doncaster when he failed by ¾ length to give 32 lb. to New Issue, the champion sprinter of Malaya. Queen Elizabeth II's Agreement won the Chester cup and the Doncaster cup, and her Above Suspicion the St. James's Palace stakes at Royal Ascot. Queen Elizabeth the Queen Mother's Bali Ha'i III, a present from New Zealand, won Royal Ascot's Queen Alexandra stakes. Faultless Speech won the Royal Hunt cup and the

Petite Etoile, ridden by Lester Piggott, wins the Champion stakes for Aly Khan at Newmarket on Oct. 17. Half a length behind are Barclay (G. Bougoure), second in the three-horse field, and, nearest the rails, Javelot (F. Palmer). Petite Etoile won £55,487 in the season.

William Hill Gold cup at Redcar. The good colt Aggressor won at Sandown park, took Goodwood's Chesterfield cup and won the Cumberland Lodge stakes at Ascot.

Paddy's Sister from Ireland with her victories in the Queen Mary stakes at Royal Ascot, the Gimcrack stakes and the Champagne stakes and Aly Khan's Venture II from France with his in the Imperial Produce stakes and the Middle Park stakes were the outstanding two-year-old filly and colt; after them, the colt Sing Sing and the filly Queensberry were fast. The northern-trained colt Newbus, who won the Chesham stakes at Royal Ascot, made a gallant effort to get to Paddy's Sister in the Champagne stakes.

D. Smith was champion jockey again, and Piggott had his most solidly successful season. The Australian jockey G. Moore, riding for Aly Khan mainly in France, had a very successful first season in Europe and won many valuable races. The deaths occurred of the brilliant jockey E. Mercer (*see* OBITUARIES) in a fall at Ascot and of the well-known trainers G. Colling and P. Thrale.

Features of the season were the trial at Newmarket of the recording of the running of races by film cameras (already in general use in the United States and on certain occasions in France) and the experiment, from Aug. 7, of introducing a final forfeit stage only three days before a race. By inducing owners and trainers to make up their minds three days before a race and avoid a heavier forfeit, this would, it was hoped, cut down the large number of " probables " who did not run and thus save considerable expense in the printing of Tote tickets and race programmes. Not without importance, it would mean the virtual elimination of " surprise " runners (" probables " who were not expected to run but nevertheless did so), who had been a long-standing grievance with off-the-course punters as the imagined source of part of their ruin. Before the close of the year a Betting bill was laid before parliament; one of its objects was to legalize cash betting off the racecourse (*see* BETTING AND GAMBLING).

Australia's greatest horse race, the Melbourne cup, was won at Flemington by the Queensland horse MacDougal, ridden by Pat Glennon, with Nether Gold and White Hills behind him. (*See* also SPORTING RECORD.)   (R. M. G.)

HORTICULTURE.

In contrast with the cold, wet conditions of 1958, in 1959 most districts in Britain had the hottest, driest summer for many years. By August severe drought was affecting most fruit and vegetable crops in England and Wales, except where equipment was available for irrigation, and the experience of many growers during the year further stimulated the rapidly increasing interest in irrigation.

Production Areas. There was another small drop in the acreage of glasshouses, and a fall of 100 ac. in tomatoes showed a continuing trend away from what had traditionally been the mainstay of the glasshouse industry. Vegetables increased by about 3% to 436,000 ac., mainly owing to greater interest in peas grown for canning and in carrots and celery.

Techniques. The main technical developments were in bulk harvesting of apples—a method introduced from New Zealand, aerial spraying of fruit and potatoes against diseases and pests, the growing use of mist propagation, mobile glasshouses of several patterns and the use of polythene film for lining glasshouses to reduce heat losses in winter.

Diseases and Pests. The most serious development was the incidence of fire blight, a bacterial disease of pears new to Britain, which was first noticed in 1957 and had spread to several thousand trees in Essex and Kent in 1959. The disease, which had been proving very destructive to orchards in the United States and New Zealand, was made notifiable under a parliamentary order, and drastic measures were taken

The use of a hydro-cooling plant such as this keeps leaf vegetables fresh-looking during the marketing period in hot weather.

to eradicate affected trees wherever they were found. Growers pressed unsuccessfully for a scheme of compensation for trees destroyed under the order. Endeavours to clean up stocks of chrysanthemums, strawberries, raspberries and fruit trees, by introducing virus-free plants through the nuclear stocks scheme and the nursery trade, began to show results, with spectacular increases in yields where improved stocks of the first three crops were planted.

Marketing. There was much discussion about the setting up of a permanent Horticultural Marketing council to collect, analyse and distribute information on supply, demand and prices of horticultural produce, to promote research into consumer habits and preferences, and to study technical aspects of packing and marketing. It was proposed that the council should ultimately be financed by the industry, possibly by a compulsory levy on sales, but support from public funds was sought to meet costs in the first two years. The proposals did not meet with universal approval from growers, but two voluntary specialist advertising organizations were set up. A voluntary scheme for advertising apples also made a useful start in face of a difficult marketing situation caused by the great increase in production from trees which were planted after World War II. It was decided that the increased supplies would necessitate rationalized marketing, better publicity and more adequate storage facilities to prevent short-term gluts. In the glasshouse industry a group of dissatisfied growers failed to secure the abolition of the Tomato and Cucumber Marketing board, the only official horticultural producer organization. Because of a bad glut of tomatoes, brought on by the summer heat, the board for the first time used its powers of control by restricting the sale of small and low-grade fruit. The pre-packing of fresh fruit and vegetables continued to increase, although the emphasis was again on ware potatoes. More than 8,000 tons of washed and dry-brushed potatoes were pre-packed weekly at the height of the 1958-59 season. Increasing quantities of tomatoes, apples, salad and vegetable packs, cauliflowers, brussel sprouts and root crops were also pre-packed to keep pace with the rapid increase in the number of self-service shops. Ambitious plans were announced for the redeployment of Covent Garden market.

Policy. The minister of agriculture announced a £7·5 million scheme for assisting the horticultural industry to improve its efficiency, especially in the presentation and marketing of horticultural produce, and to encourage the activities of producer co-operative organizations. It was the first time that the latter became eligible for help from public funds. Regarding tariffs, the Board of Trade announced in March a 50% increase in the duty levied on many imported flowers, a decision widely welcomed by flower growers, but the board was unable to agree to an application by the National Farmers' union for a more general increase in tariffs on other horticultural products, notably tomatoes, new potatoes and lettuce. There was increasing dissatisfaction in the industry with the tariff position and, indeed, a growing feeling that the time had come to look for other forms of protection against competition from abroad.

Education and Research. Following recommendations made by the de la Warr committee, the Ministry of Education took over responsibility for agricultural and horticultural education from the Ministry of Agriculture. The Lee Valley Experimental Horticulture station at Hoddesdon was inaugurated; it was to work on problems of glasshouse production.

Developments in Commonwealth Countries. In Canada there was rapid development in the processing of horticultural products, including " sparkling cider ", new blends of fruit juices based on apple juice, vacuum packing of apple slices and new potato products. Apples from the heavy crop of 1958 were stored so successfully in " controlled atmospheres " that some were in competition with early varieties of the 1959 crop. A division of horticulture was formed in the Indian Agricultural Research institute to further the production and preservation of fruits as well as to encourage ornamental gardening. Horticulture in New Zealand saw the rapid development of a number of new techniques, including the method of bulk harvesting of apples which created the liveliest interest in other fruit-growing countries, including Australia, Britain and Canada. (*See* also BOTANICAL GARDENS; BOTANY; MARKET GARDENING.) (J. P. HN.)

BIBLIOGRAPHY (all published 1959, unless otherwise stated). D. Akenhead, *Horticulture in the British Commonwealth—an Outline 1958*, Tech. Comm. 26, Commonwealth Bureau of Hort. and Plantation Crops (Commonwealth Agric. Bur.); S. A. Searle and L. P. Smith, *Weatherwise Gardening* (Blandford, 1958); British Weed Control Council, *Weed Control Handbook* (Oxford, 1958); G. E. Tidbury, *The Bulk Harvesting of Orchard Fruit* (Commonwealth Agric. Bur.); R. L. Smyth, *The Distribution of Fruit and Vegetables* (London); *Report of the Committee on Further Education for Agriculture provided by Local Education Authorities*, Cmnd. 614 (H.M.S.O., 1958); W. B. Turrill, *Royal Botanic Gardens, Kew* (London).

HOSPITALS.

International. The 11th congress organized by the International Hospital federation was held in Edinburgh in June 1959, attended by 800 participants from 44 countries. Dr. Romain de Cock (Belgium) was elected to succeed Avv. L. Colombo (Italy) as president of the federation. The theme chosen for discussion was " Efficiency Methods in the Hospital " and a report of the proceedings was published later in the year.

The *First Report on the World Health Situation 1954-1956* published by World Health organization (Geneva, 1959) provided an extensive review of various aspects of public health work in many countries. It stated that the general tendency was towards increasing control and supervision of hospitals in local, provincial or national governments and, although it was doubtful whether the number of hospital beds was a good index of social progress, the serious gap between

needs and their fulfilment was only too obvious in many lands. A Conference on Hospital Statistics and their Application in Health Administration was sponsored by the W.H.O. regional office for Europe in Geneva in Nov. 1958. *The Cost of Medical Care* published by the International Labour organization (Geneva, 1959) surveyed the cost of social security medical care services of 15 countries.

Great Britain. The cost of the hospital service in Great Britain for 1958-59, including a supplementary estimate, was £445·9 million (compared with £410·0 million for the previous year). The estimated cost of £466·7 million for 1959-60 included an allocation of £25·3 million, the largest yet made, for capital improvements and new building projects.

Under the Mental Health act, 1959, provision was made for a complete reform of the law on mental health. The two main objectives were to encourage those suffering from any form of mental illness or disability to seek treatment promptly and voluntarily, and to ensure adequate restraint and safeguards where patients had to be compulsorily treated and detained. The act provided for the establishment of Mental Health Review tribunals to consider applications for discharge from hospitals from patients or from patients' relatives on their behalf. (*See* also PSYCHIATRY.)

The *Report of the Ministry of Health, 1958* (H.M.S.O., London, 1959) included a survey of the hospital and specialist services over the previous ten years. In that time about £105 million had been spent on hospital capital development, and of the share made available to regional hospital boards (£86 million) about one-quarter had been used for mental and mental deficiency hospitals. The volume of work undertaken had increased by about one-third and had been achieved with the use of only about 6% more beds. The alteration in the percentage allocation of beds reflected the changing pattern of care provided.

TABLE I. PERCENTAGE ALLOCATION OF BEDS IN NATIONAL HEALTH SERVICE HOSPITALS IN ENGLAND AND WALES

	1949	1958
Total: all departments	100·0	100·0
General medicine	7·1	7·1
Infectious diseases	4·6	1·7
Diseases of the chest	6·0*	5·1
Dermatology	0·3	0·5
Other medical departments	0·4	0·3
Total: medical departments	18·4	14·7
Chronic sick and geriatrics	11·5	12·0
General surgery	6·8	7·1
Ear, nose and throat	1·1	1·5
Traumatic/orthopaedic	2·5	3·6
Ophthalmology	0·7	0·9
Thoracic surgery	0·3	0·5
Other surgical departments	0·7	1·2
Total: surgical departments	12·1	14·8
Gynaecology	1·5	2·0
Obstetrics	3·7†	3·7
Mental disorder	41·8	44·3
Pre-convalescent	0·3	1·0
Convalescent	1·1	0·6
General practitioner beds	1·6	2·1
Private pay beds	1·4	1·2
Others	6·6‡	3·6

* Includes some beds for the treatment of non-respiratory tuberculosis now classified under the specialist department responsible. † Includes some beds now classified as general practitioner beds. ‡ Includes a small number of geriatric beds.
SOURCE. *Report of the Ministry of Health, 1958* (H.M.S.O., London, 1959).

Costing returns for hospitals in the national health service in England and Wales for the year ended March 31, 1958, were published by the Ministry of Health in two volumes. Volume I concerned some 200 large hospitals, chiefly acute or mainly acute hospitals operating the main scheme, and included detailed departmental costs as well as a comprehensive summary of the full in-patient cost per week. Volume II

The first stage of the Princess Margaret hospital, Swindon, which was opened on Oct. 25. It comprises out-patient, casualty, physiotherapy and pathology departments and an orthopaedic ward. When later stages have been completed the hospital will have 600 beds.

related to approximately 2,000 hospitals operating a modified form of costing limited to the principal direct expenses of certain departments. These informative returns were a great improvement on those established for earlier years.

TABLE II. COSTING RETURNS FOR NATIONAL HEALTH SERVICE HOSPITALS IN ENGLAND AND WALES FOR YEAR ENDED MARCH 31, 1958

(1) *Hospitals Administered by Regional Hospital Boards and Hospital Management Committees*

	(a)*			(b)†		
	£	s.	d.	£	s.	d.
‡Acute:						
‡ 1-50 beds	21	3	1	40	12	11
51-100 beds	23	17	3	44	1	1
101-300 beds	23	14	7	46	6	0
301-900 beds	21	13	3	49	18	4
Over 900 beds	15	10	10	42	10	6
‡Acute: all hospitals	22	12	5	46	6	0
‡Mainly acute	19	5	10	56	11	11
‡Partly acute	15	19	9	63	13	6
Mainly long-stay	13	8	0		...	
Long-stay	9	6	1		...	
Chronic	9	9	5		...	
Pre-convalescent	13	14	6	33	4	0
Convalescent	9	19	0	25	0	11
Rehabilitation	10	3	8	45	15	5
Isolation	26	4	9		...	
‡Maternity	23	2	4	36	3	1
Mental illness	6	8	11		...	
Mental deficiency	6	2	1		...	
‡Orthopaedic	18	2	2		...	
Tuberculosis and chest	16	14	3		...	
Tuberculosis, chest and isolation	20	11	8		...	
‡Children's (acute)	22	12	0	47	9	1
‡Eye	20	15	10	38	15	0

(2) *Hospitals Administered by Boards of Governors of Teaching Hospitals*

	(a)			(b)		
	£	s.	d.	£	s.	d.
Acute:						
(i) London	33	4	2	77	12	10
(ii) Provinces	27	10	1	52	7	9

* Column (a) represents the net in-patient cost per week. † Column (b) represents the net in-patient cost per case. ‡ These figures should be compared with those of previous years with particular caution in view of the new departmental costing schemes which came into operation on April 1, 1957, for the hospital types concerned contain a considerable proportion of hospitals with significant numbers of out-patient attendances.
SOURCE. *National Health Service: Hospital Costing Returns, 1957-58*, vol. i and ii (H.M.S.O., London, 1958 and 1959).

Commonwealth. The Canadian federal government maintained its financial support of the hospital construction programmes, including an expansion of rehabilitation services. The Australian government began negotiations with registered medical benefit funds to introduce considerably higher government and fund benefits for major surgery and certain other medical services; the new scheme, due to come into operation on Jan. 1, 1960, would involve a small increase in the contributions of insured persons. Under the New Zealand Hospitals act, 1957, the 39 hospital boards were now trustees for the annual government expenditure of some £23 million, and as part of a substantial hospital works programme particular attention was to be given to out-patients and psychiatric services. Throughout the colonies a growing appreciation of the curative services provided by hospitals, clinics and dispensaries led to a further increase in attendances; this demand was met, in part at least, by the substantial programme of reconstruction and expansion of hospitals and clinics. Fifteen new health centres were completed in Kenya and five in Cyprus.

United States. Increased utilization and increased services continued in 1959 to characterize hospitals in the continental United States. Hospital admissions, which had been rising steadily for ten years, again increased by more than 3% over the preceding year. Admissions for 1958 reported to the American Hospital association totalled 23,697,157. By far the greatest number of admissions, 15,825,136, were to voluntary short-term hospitals. Hospitals operated by state or local government units had 4,762,780 admissions, while federal hospitals and proprietary hospitals each had about 1·5 million admissions. The 6,786 hospitals listed by the American Hospital association reported 1,572,036 beds and an average daily census of 1,322,938 in 1958.

On June 30, 1959, of the total of 4,625 projects authorized under the Hill-Burton programme, 3,167 were completed and in operation, 1,206 were under construction and 252 initially approved. A total of 894 projects was started in 1957 and 1958, representing a total cost of $837,271,175, of which the federal share was $268,389,549.

Hospitals in the continental United States in 1958 employed 1,464,829 full-time staff, an average of 111 per 100 patients.

In 1958 there was an increase of 9·8% in health insurance benefits over 1957, while the number of persons covered by health insurance increased by more than 1·5 million.

(W. E. HL.; E. L. CY.)

HOUSEWIFERY. The year 1959 saw a continued effort towards greater convenience and functional aptness in domestic equipment, allied to aesthetic appeal. Manufacturers' growing awareness of the importance of good design and colour was clearly demonstrated at the International Plastics exhibition at Olympia, where consumer products from 11 countries were displayed, many of the exhibits (particularly the German and Scandinavian ones) showing a new and satisfying aesthetic value.

In the kitchen the main trend was towards still greater compactness in furniture and equipment. A table with fitted shelves under the top and a swivel stool came on the market; and, for family use, a kitchen-dining-table with four swivel, fold-away stools. Black and white ("magpie") schemes predominated in the 1959 kitchen, providing a good background for the bright colours of the vitreous-enamelled ware shown at the Hardware fair. (Judgelite put out a range of saucepans of vitreous-enamelled aluminium providing a depth of colour hitherto not available on that ground; also a new vitreous-enamelled aluminium tile which, it was claimed, could be bent, punched and cut with shears.) The nylon sink unit produced in Germany in 1958 was made available in Britain.

In refrigeration the tendency was again towards "fit-in-anywhere" models with "table" tops. A new "tray" top refrigerator (Electrolux) also put in an appearance. Further trends were towards all-plastic linings and plastic-coated shelves. The desire of British housewives for combined home freezer and refrigerator units was met by a tendency towards larger ice-making compartments in standard models, while Prestcold put out a luxury model comprising three separate temperature zones: moist, chill and freezer. An interim U.K. report showed a 60% increase in refrigerator sales compared with 1958.

In electric cookers the 1958 trend towards U.S. and

Electric cookers with separately-sited oven and hot-plate units allow the architect greater freedom in kitchen-planning.

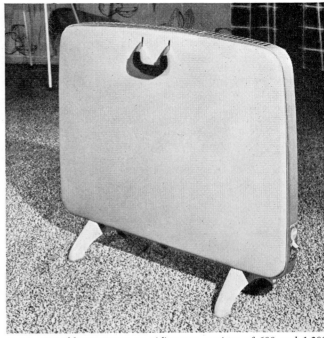

A new portable convector providing two settings of 600 and 1,200 watts. Convectors give an evenly-distributed warmth.

Canadian "built-in" wall ovens and separately sited surface units was fully confirmed and the first British model on these lines (the Tricity) was made available. In gas cookers the newest improvement was Flavel's "swing-down" oven roof, designed (by a woman) for ease in cleaning.

The popularity of electric under-floor heating grew apace, special "off-peak" tariffs making it attractive to local government housing estates. The British Electrical Development association gave the average running costs of an "all-electric" home for four people as £68 a year, including under-floor heating. A new development in thermostats was the Plug-stat, a plug top which could be fitted to any fixed or portable heating appliance.

In the bathroom, an *avant-garde* feeling was towards U.S. styles: gay, steam-proof, often floral papers, coloured fittings and all-over nylon carpeting. A new product, Carpetiles, 12-in. nylon carpet squares that could be stuck down, came on the market; also a plastic stair-carpeting that could be stuck down. To the Shire (Lynx) silent plastic lavatory cistern was added a low (29-in.) pottery pan suite designed to go under windows. A reinforced polyester resin bath was shown at the Plastics fair.

A new-comer to bathroom and bedroom was the Formica-faced Vanitory unit comprising wash-basin and dressing-table. At the Arts Ménagers exhibition (Paris) the "referendum flat", incorporating the ideas of a million women, confirmed the growing resistance of housewives to the open-plan tendency in modern architecture. In the "Britannia Mews" flats at the Ideal Homes exhibition a constructive effort was made to eliminate some of the routine maintenance of conventional housing; window frames faced with I.C.I.'s P.V.C. coating (Welvic) were guaranteed not to require painting or maintenance. Nylon was used to provide self-lubricating slides and bearings. A plastic-fortified wall-paper (Lintex) was also shown at the Ideal Homes exhibition. A new pattern telephone instrument chosen by the G.P.O. (the first model was offered to Queen Elizabeth II) was in I.C.I.'s thermoplastic material Diakon, available in a range of colours.

New gadgets included: polystrene furniture feet in a range of colours and sizes; all-plastic furniture legs in a variety of styles and colours for the home carpenter; a space-saving wall scale in high-density polythene; an insulating bag (Insulex) lined with glass fibre for frozen-food shopping; and a Scandinavian invention made available in Britain (Freezella) consisting of a small plastic " cushion " which, when frozen, remained cold for a number of hours—also for carrying home frozen foods, ice-creams etc. Food developments included poultry and joints which could be cooked without removing the wrapping and bread that could be baked similarly.

The trend in the decoration and furnishing of homes was towards more muted wall colours as backgrounds to colourful furnishings such as deep lilac, turquoise and olive. The mauve, violet and purple ranges had swept New York after the launching of these colours in the spring Paris fashion collections but, though British decorators liked and used them, they were slow to touch the popular markets. The Town and Country Colours exhibition, however, showed developments of this trend in Medici wine and alpine violet, often used with yellows, pinks, turquoise and blues, in deeply textured woven fabrics. Kingfisher and peacock tended to richer, deeper tones. Cedar green, dahlia red and grey continued to be popular for carpets in combination with nasturtium, bamboo shoot and azalea orange.   (P. H.)

HOUSING. United Kingdom. During the first nine months of 1959, 178,431 permanent dwellings were completed in England and Wales, compared with 176,504 for the same period of 1958. Of these 74,110 were built by public authorities and 104,321 by private builders. Private builders, whose output had overtaken that of public authorities by 1958, continued to maintain their higher completion rate throughout 1959. By Sept. 30, 1959, 3,314,459 new permanent houses and flats had been completed in Great Britain since the war, 2,346,232 in England and Wales and 968,227 in Scotland.

The total production for England and Wales for 1958 was 241,523, representing a rather more significant reduction on the 1957 figure than the 1957 total showed compared with 1956. On the credit side, the Ministry of Housing and Local Government claimed to have achieved in 1958 the government's target of moving 200,000 people a year from slums. In England and Wales just over 55,000 houses were demolished or closed during 1958, and 12,800 in Scotland. Slum clearance continued to gather momentum in England and Wales during 1959, and by Sept. 30 a total of 291,800 dwellings had been demolished or cleared and 899,684 people rehoused since the end of World War II. The £22 1s.-a-year subsidy for 60 years was still payable by the exchequer for each house built by a local authority to replace a slum house. Subsidy was also payable for houses built to rehouse families from central areas in new or expanded towns, and the London County council reported in September that 1,599 families had been moved to a dozen country towns under arrangements in pursuance of the Town Development act, 1952. The council planned to provide homes and employment for a further 28,500 families over the following 15 years, and development schemes were also being promoted by other cities and conurbations.

The 18-storey blocks of flats which form part of the L.C.C.'s Brandon estate, Southwark, tower up behind a group of temporary prefabricated dwellings due for demolition with the occupation of the new flats early in 1960. The estate will have a shopping centre and library.

Local authorities were also being encouraged by means of a subsidy to promote housing for small households, many of which were households of one or two old people. They were receiving £10 a year for 60 years in respect of one-bedroom dwellings. By the third quarter of 1959, 25% of all new local authority dwellings were in this category. During the year a number of schemes for old people based on the ministry's handbook *Flatlets for Old People* reached completion. Such schemes contained some shared amenities, and the welfare authority was able to contribute towards any services provided, such as a warden's flat and a bell system for summoning help in case of need, if the services enabled old people who might otherwise have needed care in a communal home to live independently. There was also a wide variety of experiments in designing dwellings for the old.

The most important new legislation during the year was the House Purchase and Housing act, 1959. Part I of the act provided powers to make exchequer funds available to building societies to enable them to make more and bigger loans for the purchase or improvement of houses built before 1919 and valued at not more than £2,500 (£3,000 in the Metropolitan Police district or the City of London). The act came into force on June 14, and by the autumn more than 54 building societies had come into the scheme. The Building Societies association, whose members had increased their rate of interest on mortgages to 6%, recommended a new rate of 5½%. Part I of the act also allowed local authorities to make loans of up to 100% of the value of any house to be owner-occupied, this being an extension of existing powers. To enable large houses to be purchased for conversion, the act removed the previous limit of £5,000 on the value of any property upon which a local authority could make a loan.

The second part of the act introduced a new system of standard grants for the provision of standard amenities to improve old dwellings with a 15-year life. These grants were made available as of right for five standard improvements as follows: (1) a fixed bath or shower in a bathroom, £25; (2) a wash-hand basin, £5; (3) a hot water supply, £75; (4) a water closet in or contiguous to the dwelling, £40; and (5) satisfactory facilities for storing food, £10. The actual grant payable was to be one-half of the cost of the work, subject to a maximum of £155, which was to be reduced by the amounts listed above if these amenities already existed. After improvement the dwelling had to be equipped with all five amenities and, if a hot water supply was provided, it had to be connected to a sink as well as to the bath or shower and wash-hand basin. No application for grant could be entertained if the dwelling concerned was provided after 1944, except where a conversion of a building completed before the end of 1944 was carried out before the end of 1958. The earlier scheme for larger grants for more extensive improvements to houses with a 30-year life remained in force, but in this case grants were given at the discretion of the local authority. The act applied to Scotland with some adjustment to meet local conditions. Booklets were issued by the Ministry of Housing and Local Government and by the Department of Health for Scotland drawing attention to the facilities available under the act and showing some ways of providing standard amenities in typical old houses.

A short act, the Landlord and Tenant (Furniture and Fittings) act, 1959, came into force at the end of August, strengthening the law relating to the charging of excessive prices for furniture and fittings as a condition of an agreement for a tenancy. Such premiums were illegal and the new act made it an offence to offer such articles at an unreasonably high price or to fail to furnish a proper inventory. It also gave powers to local authorities to inspect the premises and institute proceedings.

In Dec. 1958 a new handbook was published by the ministry, *Flats and Houses, 1958*. This contained studies of the planning and costs of high-density housing schemes consisting of houses, four-storey maisonettes and high blocks of maisonettes and flats. Comparisons were made of schemes at different densities and containing different proportions of dwellings in low and high blocks. In Feb. 1959 another important publication, the report of the management sub-committee of the Central Housing Advisory committee (C.H.A.C.), *Councils and their Houses*, was published, its recommendations being brought to the attention of local authorities by the ministry. It dealt with the management and maintenance of local authority houses and the functions of housing managers. Its recommendations included the organization of all management functions, such as letting, rent collection, maintenance and the social aspects of housing work, under one principal officer responsible to one committee wherever possible, and arrangements to ensure close co-ordination between managers and officers responsible for house construction and repair. Another sub-committee of the C.H.A.C. was appointed to examine housing standards and to make recommendations, and this sub-committee began collecting evidence from local authorities, private enterprise and professional and other interests concerned with house design.

In Northern Ireland, by employing all suitable agencies, it had been possible by the end of September to build 80,000 houses since the war, thus housing over a quarter of the population in accommodation built to postwar standards. After a drop in production in 1957-58 resulting from high interest rates and unfavourable economic conditions, an extra subsidy of £15 per house, granted for houses placed on contract between April and Dec. 1958, led to higher completion figures during the following year. Following the fall in interest rates, the extra subsidy for 1959 was only £7 per house. The Northern Ireland Housing trust had recently placed a contract for two 11-storey blocks in Belfast, and construction started during the summer of 1959. This would be the first time that high blocks of flats had been built in Northern Ireland.

Continental Europe. House production in 1958 showed a fairly general decline compared with the previous year, except in some eastern European countries and in France, Greece, Portugal and Spain, which had all previously had a rather low output of new dwellings per thousand inhabitants. The U.S.S.R. had by far the highest proportional output with 12·9 per thousand, the next highest output being in the German Federal Republic, with 9·4. Yugoslavia, Spain and Portugal were still completing fewer than four dwellings per thousand inhabitants.

During 1958 there was a tendency for building costs to stabilize and in a few countries even to decline—a change from the almost steady rise in costs since the war. The abatement of the general postwar housing shortage in Europe was leading everywhere to a redirection of housing policy towards slum clearance and urban renewal. This was reflected in the calling of a United Nations seminar during 1959 to discuss urban renewal.

Commonwealth. In the older dominions the emphasis continued to be on home ownership, although some slum clearance work was being carried out; *e.g.*, in some of the bigger and older towns in Canada. The Ontario Department of Planning and Development and the Central Mortgage and Housing Corporation of Canada were also conducting a study, arising out of concern with problems of blighted urban areas, to produce minimum standards. In the Union of South Africa extensive building was being undertaken to house de-tribalized African workers in segregated communities.

Throughout the underdeveloped areas, housing activity was gathering momentum and departments in such areas,

An 11-storey block of flats nearing completion on the L.C.C.'s Alton street site in east London, an extension of the Lansbury estate. Some 600 dwellings will be provided on this site, giving accommodation to small and large families and to old people living alone.

many of which had been established only during the previous decade, were endeavouring to meet the housing needs which were growing out of urbanization and industrialization. An international technical conference on housing and urbanization was held in Nairobi, Kenya, in 1959, British territories being well represented. The recent establishment of a Ministry of Housing in Kenya showed the importance attached to the subject. The first stage of a Nairobi housing project to house 25,000 Africans was completed and progress was also being made in smaller towns with loans from the Central Housing board. In Aug. 1959 the minister opened a low-density housing estate based on the tenant-purchase principle. This scheme, designed for the rising African middle-class householder, provided for freehold plots of 0·25 ac. and bungalows of different types and sizes. In Nigeria the Lagos Executive Development board made progress with its 70-ac. clearance and redevelopment project in the central area. The African Housing department of Uganda had established a training scheme for African estate management staff. Although much of their work was in the few large towns in the protectorate, smaller towns were developing, and a conference was held for members of African local governments or district councils as well as central government members and officers to discuss urban development problems.

In Hong Kong, where the housing shortage was probably more acute than anywhere else in the Commonwealth, the housing authority was building high flats at exceptionally high densities. The Resettlement department had rehoused more

than 273,000 squatters by the end of 1958. In Barbados the housing authority established in 1956 made progress with the construction of houses for letting, while assistance to house building, improvement and repairs was given by means of favourable loans. (*See* also ARCHITECTURE; BUILDING AND CONSTRUCTION INDUSTRY; NEW TOWNS; TOWN AND COUNTRY PLANNING.) (M. C. BR.)

HUNGARY. People's republic of southeastern Europe bounded W. by Austria, N. by Czechoslovakia, N.E. by the U.S.S.R., E. by Rumania and S. by Yugoslavia. Area: 35,911 sq.mi. Pop.: (1949 census) 9,204,799; (mid-1959 est.) 9,900,000. Ethnic composition (1956 est.): Hungarian 97%; German 2·2%; Slovak 0·1%; Rumanian 0·1%. Religion (1956 est.): Roman Catholic 67%; Protestant 27·3%; Greek Catholic 2·5%; Jewish 1·5%. Chief towns (pop., 1957 est.): Budapest (cap., with suburbs) 1,850,000; Miskolc 150,000; Debrecen 130,000; Pécs 110,000; Szeged 100,000; Györ 68,000; Kecskemét 67,000; Nyiregyháza 56,000; Hódmezövásárhely 54,000; Békéscsaba 50,000. First secretary of the Hungarian Socialist Workers' (Communist) party, János Kádár; chairman of the presidential council of the national assembly, István Dobi; chairman of the council of ministers, Ferenc Münnich. Main imports: iron ore, cotton, machinery, timber, fertilizers. Main exports: livestock, grain, vegetables, wine, machine tools. Monetary unit: *forint* (official exchange rate F.34·20 = £1 sterling; tourist rate F.66·00 = £1 sterling).

History. Three weeks after the 1958 election (Nov. 16) the central committee of the Hungarian Communist party discussed economic and agricultural policy and stated that the political and economic situation made it "possible to quicken the pace of development in collective farming". Until the beginning of 1959 experiments in collective farming had proved unsuccessful, but the campaign which started in mid-January had by the end of March gained spectacular results compared with the results of former years. (*See* Table.)

COLLECTIVIZATION OF AGRICULTURE IN HUNGARY

Year	Collectivized arable land	No. of collective farms	No. of collectivized holdings
Dec. 1952	22·6%	5,110	369,203
Dec. 1956	8·5%	2,089	119,315
Dec. 1958	13·5%	3,507	168,920
June 1959	35·6%	5,187	...

In the first six months of 1959 one-half of Hungary's 13 million ac. of arable land was socialized, 4,580,000 ac. in collective farms and the remainder in state farms and collective pastures. It was reported that 1,680 new collective farms with 2,964,000 ac. had been formed.

Propagandists, organizers, rural officials and factory agitators literally occupied the villages and refused to move until the peasants had signed the applications to join the collective farms. Pressure was coupled with promises of rent for the land and compensation for the equipment contributed, tax exemptions, free health service, family allowances and old age pensions. " The rapid advance of Socialist transformation caused a certain amount of confusion ", admitted the party monthly, and to meet the new requirements the U.S.S.R. agreed in April to deliver 12,000 agricultural machines. Fundamentally the drive for collectivization was a return to the policy of the Rákosi period which led to the 1956 revolution.

The trend to put back the clock was already manifest in an article by Kádár, published on Jan. 1, 1959, emphasizing that the main political party line had not changed even after 1956. In industry, however, the regime kept to a more realistic planning than its predecessors. The report of the Central Statistical office stated in January that the state industry had exceeded its target only by 4% in the first year of the present three-year plan (1958-60), a revision of the former five-year plan (1956-60).

Pressure continued to be exerted on the churches and the intelligentsia. The bishops took the oath of loyalty in April 1959, a measure originally decreed in 1951. The Writers' association—banned after the 1956 revolution—was re-formed on Sept. 25, but neither the great populist writers (Gyula Illyés, László Németh, Áron Tamási) nor the best writers within the party (Milán Fust, J. J. Tersánszky) figured in the presidium of the association. Western intervention on behalf of the gaoled Communist writers (Tibor Déri and others) remained unsuccessful and the prosecution of people who had taken part in the revolution went on: István Bibó's life sentence was made public in the last days of 1958; the intellectuals arrested in Oct. 1958

(Ferenc Méney and Sándor Fekete) received prison sentences.

The principle of the Rákosi era, reiterated by Kádár in 1959, that " the criterion of proletarian internationalism is our relationship with the Soviet Union " was again closely observed; 1,000 new Soviet-Hungarian Friendship societies were formed; Soviet " polytechnical " methods were introduced to 551 secondary and 68 high schools. Students were sent to those Communist countries which had been less affected by liberalization (3,000 to the German Democratic Republic, 1,000 to Czechoslovakia, but only 200 to Poland).

In foreign policy Kádár strengthened his ties with Czechoslovakia (he visited Prague during Feb. 18-21). A delegation led by Ferenc Münnich visited China; N. S. Khrushchev, on his way back from Albania (June 4-6), called on his " splendid friend " Kádár in Budapest. Towards the end of September the party issued directives for the November party congress. According to these the international *détente* offered favourable conditions in Hungary " to lay a firm foundation to Socialism and build strongly on it ", and a new five-year plan should increase industrial production by 65%-70% by 1965.

The reimposed rigidity was mitigated by some concessions: passports were issued more freely, tourism to Hungary was encouraged and the standard of living raised. Visitors to and from Hungary spoke of a working compromise between government and people, hatred for everything Russian, disappointment in the west and the national self-confidence gained in 1956 unaltered.

The seventh congress of the Hungarian Socialist Workers' (Communist) party was held in Budapest from Nov. 30 to Dec. 5. There were 674 voting and 63 non-voting delegates. Kádár said in his report that the party had 402,456 full members and 35,500 candidates; 60% of members were of working class origin and 14% of peasant origin. This compared with 810,227 members and 54,380 candidates in May 1954. After the Oct. 1956 revolution the membership dropped to about 100,000.

In his report Kádár dealt with the 1956 revolution. Two factors, according to him, played an important part in those events: first, the " mistakes " of Mátyás Rákosi; second, the " unprecedented treachery " of Imre Nagy. He also said that Soviet troops were in Hungary " exclusively for international reasons " and they would stay as long as the international situation made it necessary.

On Dec. 1 the congress was addressed by N. S. Khrushchev. He described Kádár as " a true son of the Hungarian people ". He, too, spoke of " serious mistakes " of Rákosi who " undermined the party's guiding role and weakened the dictatorship of the proletariat ". The lesson of the "counter-revolutionary revolt " in Hungary was that the enemies of socialism were not abandoning their plans for smashing the Socialist camp and were " looking for weak links in it ". Khrushchev was more outspoken the following day when, speaking at a Budapest factory, he admitted that " some comrades " in the Kremlin had had doubts about intervening in the Oct. 1956 revolt. But others were confident that they had to help their class brothers.

After the congress Kádár accompanied Khrushchev to Uzhgorod, in Soviet Transcarpathian Ukraine. In a speech on Dec. 7 he admitted that he had been there " about three years ago " to ask the Soviet people " for brotherly help " against the counter-revolution.

Béla Kovács, a Smallholders' party leader, and József Révai, a trusted lieutenant of Mátyás Rákosi, died on June 21 and Aug. 4, 1959, respectively (*see* OBITUARIES). (*See* also EASTERN EUROPEAN ECONOMIC PLANNING.) (Z. L. SZ.; X.)

BIBLIOGRAPHY (all London, 1959). Tibor Meray, *Thirteen Days that Shook the Kremlin*; T. Aczel and T. Meray, *The Revolt of the Intellectuals*; George Mikes, *The A.V.O.: a Study in Infamy*; *The Truth about the Nagy Affair*.

N. Khrushchev with János Kádár (right), first secretary of the Hungarian Socialist Workers' party, in Budapest on June 4.

ICELAND. Island and republic of the northern Atlantic. Area: 39,768 sq.mi. Pop.: (1950 census) 144,263; (1958 est.) 169,000. Language: Icelandic, closely akin to Old Norse. Religion: Lutheran. Capital: Reykjavik (pop. 1957) 67,589. President of the republic, Asgeir Asgeirsson. Prime ministers in 1959: Emil Jónsson and (from Nov. 20) Olafur Thors. Main imports: fuel oil, petrol, coal, cement, salt. Main exports: fish and fish products. Monetary unit: *króna*, pl. *krónur* (Kr. 45·60 = £1 sterling; tourist exchange rate, Kr.70·00 = £1 sterling).

History. The general election on June 28, 1959, resulted in considerable gains for the Progressive (Farmers') party, which almost doubled its vote (receiving 27·3%, compared with 15·62% on June 24, 1956), and a slight advance by the Independence (Conservative) party. The Social Democrats and the Communists lost respectively about 30% and 25% of their vote. Emil Jónsson of the Social Democratic minority government continued in office with the support of the Independence party, as no administration based on a majority could be formed. Jónsson's government was a caretaker government, and the newly elected Althing had only to deal with constitutional reform proposals, including an increase in the members of parliament from 52 to 60, and changes in the electoral system introducing eight multi-member constituencies providing together 49 seats to which 11 supplementary seats would be added from the parties' national lists.

On Oct. 25-26 a new Althing was elected. As a result the vote of the Independence party fell from 42·6% to 39·7% and that of the Progressives from 27·3% to 25·7%. Their losses meant gains by the Social Democrats whose vote between June and October rose from 12·4% to 15·2%, and by the Communists who improved theirs from 15·3% to 16%. But neither of the two leftist parties was able to regain

"*She was annoying me*". An Icelandic interpretation of an incident in the fisheries dispute, reproduced in "*The Times*" of May 14.

all the ground lost in the previous election in June. (*See* ELECTIONS.)

On Nov. 20, after the resignation of the Jónsson cabinet, Olafur Thors, leader of the Independence party, formed a new government. (H. LN.)

IMMIGRATION AND EMIGRATION. The decline in emigration from the United Kingdom to non-European countries which characterized 1958 continued during 1959 though the rate of decline was falling. Those leaving by the long sea routes totalled 54,800 during the first six months of 1959 against 61,200 in the same period of 1958. Of these 48,100 went to Commonwealth countries. Reduced emigration to Canada was again mainly responsible for the decline; during the first half of the year those entering Canada from Britain totalled 10,817 against 16,292 in the same period of

Admitted to Britain after being held, with others, for suspected passport irregularities, this aged Indian rests on his baggage.

1958. By contrast, emigration to Australia was higher in the first six months (23,300 compared with 21,500 during the same period of 1958). In the first six months the total numbers leaving by the long sea routes destined for Commonwealth countries and the United States were 53,800, of whom 51,200 were Commonwealth citizens, and of these 48,100 went to Commonwealth countries and 5,700 to the United States compared with 52,100 and 8,100 in the corresponding period of 1958.

During 1958, whereas emigration by sea from the United Kingdom fell by nearly one-third, almost entirely due to the sharp fall in movement to Canada, immigration into the United Kingdom was about 8% higher than in 1957. Of the 113,000 emigrating, 105,000 were Commonwealth citizens and of these 93,800 went to Commonwealth countries. Australia took 37,400, Canada 16,000, New Zealand 10,800, South Africa 5,300 and the Federation of Rhodesia and Nyasaland 4,200. Foreign countries attracted a total of 17,900 from the United Kingdom, 15,600 going to the United States, of whom 9,700 were Commonwealth citizens. Although family groups continued to constitute the majority leaving the United Kingdom, there was an increase in the proportion of unmarried persons emigrating. The largest occupational group was the professional and managerial one, with the clerical and non-industrial group the next largest.

During 1958 the decline in immigration into the United Kingdom from the Commonwealth experienced in 1957 was halted. A total of 55,300 Commonwealth citizens arrived by sea to take up permanent residence in the United Kingdom, about 4,300 more than in 1957. From Canada came 11,900 and from Australia 8,500. Official estimates of immigrants coming by all routes in 1958 were 6,200 from India, 5,000 from Pakistan and 15,000 from the Caribbean area, but measures taken during the year by the respective governments had the desired effect of bringing about a decline in the figures in 1959. During the first six months only 1,600 arrived from India and 5,400 from the Caribbean area, while for Pakistan it was estimated that there was a small net outward movement of its citizens. Some 3,000 West Indians were also estimated to have returned to their countries. (E. A. J. D.)

Countries of emigration	Argentina[1]	Australia	Belgium	Brazil[1]	Canada	Denmark[2][3]	Israel[2]	Netherlands[4]	New Zealand[5]	Rhodesia and Nyasaland, Fed. of	Sweden	South Africa, Union of[6]	United Kingdom Com'nwealth citizens[7]	Aliens[8]	United States[9]
ALL COUNTRIES	20,058	109,857	47,124	49,839	124,851	21,901	71,224	67,747	24,852	16,951	22,097	14,673	60,966	66,835	260,686
AFRICA	69	...	4,612[10]	116	1,355	321	25,716	2,282	...	6,920	201	4,275	9,644	...	2,631
Tunisia, Morocco Algeria	25	...	...	13	669	...	12,478	...	...	...	...	...	8[11]	...	...
Union of South Africa	...	379	...	19	367	...	75	955	182	6,323	71	—	3,172	...	...
NORTH AMERICA	653[12]	...	3,256[12]	2,057[13]	10,974[13]	3,430[12]	1,295[12]	5,330[12][14]	...	220[13]	2,052[12]	323[12]	...	...	52,522[13]
Canada	22	1,430	1,264	104	104	585	34	1,875	749	48	285	107	11,932	...	23,082
Mexico	...	...	...	23	...	...	...	...	...	...	18	...	...	104[13]	23,061
United States	341	2,111	1,449	1,905	10,846	1,281	226	2,123	694	169	1,523	157	3,944	19,813	—
SOUTH AMERICA	...	...	...	696	2,168	...	...	...	...	8	...	...	1,288[13]	470	9,792
Argentina	—	...	...	317	...	49	653	...	...	3	54	17	...	84	...
Brazil	55	...	...	—	...	81	...	...	...	1	56	10	...	88	...
WEST INDIES	...	...	...	...	1,192	...	...	3,808[15]	...	12	4	...	7,438	...	12,218
ASIA	...	4,985	817	9,336	4,450	384[16]	4,309	39,567	...	548	260	159	15,164	...	24,312
Arab States	48	...	...	1,048	312[17]	...	145[18]	...	...	...	...	...	66[19]	517[19]	...
China	10	749	...	530	894	...	...	...	...	5	16	...	26[20]	17	...
India	11	1,021[21]	...	11[22]	426[21]	...	...	...	180	387	68	14[21]	6,114[21]	...	...
Indonesia	...	466	...	11	...	...	...	37,576	...	...	22	20	34	75	...
Israel	72	...	...	1,036	531	...	—	...	...	46	19	40	8	282	...
Japan	226	...	...	6,586	199	...	...	...	...	1	35	...	58	209	...
Malaya	...	2,749[23]	...	...	...	...	...	...	...	34[23]	...	31	5,466	...	...
Philippines	...	...	...	1	...	...	...	...	...	...	...	...	20	...	...
EUROPE	18,872	90,379	38,239	36,358	102,034	17,346	38,551	12,387	...	9,132	19,483	9,662	124[24]	43,723	158,023
Austria	43	3,178		71	4,544	169	33	...		86	562	89	2	1,437	2,355
Belgium	11	...	—	52[25]	1,832[26]	82	...	60		4	73	70	—	340[25]	...
Bulgaria	11	...		6	...	...	...	24		...	10	...	...	11	2,813
Czechoslovakia	...	...	736	7	42	...	...	...		17	3,661	71	—	2,193	...
Denmark	10	507		31	1,746	—	...	...		...	7,645	7	—	616	...
Finland	...	...		28	1,177	231	...	...		...	...	...	...	...	...
France	111	...	6,312	457	2,727	608	259	...		23	182	45	8	3,616	4,487
Germany	230	6,120	3,639	825	13,888	1,761	63	31		97	2,688	1,245	26	12,742	31,422
Greece	232	5,023	...	831	5,190	27	31	...		57	84	196	2	406	4,507
Hungary	202	1,185	...	162	2,362	817	7,383	...		10	1,180	9	...	303	...
Ireland, Rep. of	...	...	...	23	1,226	18	...	47		299	12	133	...	...	7,371
Italy	8,503	14,468	11,841	4,819	27,043	240	47	51		442	282	971	—	8,420	16,251
Netherlands	98	7,163	3,676	329	7,420	171	51	...	1,464	554	182	1,941	—	2,224	4,005
Norway	...	...		16	482	3,739	...	...		11	1,752	36	4[26]	1,195	2,484
Poland	175	...	708	195	2,292	49	29,580	...		7	228	104	8[27]	492	8,301
Portugal	764	...	...	21,928	1,938	24	...	679		119	16	...	—	375	20
Rumania	32	...		10	...	...	...	...		...	5	...	44[29]	2,887	...
Spain	7,764	...	3,381[28]	5,768	318	104	...	...		17	128	...	—	1,287	2,079
Sweden	24	...		113	442	5,620	...	...		10	...	32	—	...	...
Switzerland	47	...	979	184	1,024	432	...	...		33	246	194	2	4,777	...
Un. Kingdom	207	44,062[30]	1,486[30]	409	24,777	2,103	217	...	13,189	7,313	342	4,450	—	...	20,954
Yugoslavia	383	1,718	936	92	984	178	24	...		33	106	...	...	293	4,349
OCEANIA	18	...	57	...						111	80	254	11,416	...	870[31]
Australia	3	...		13	1,898	169	30[31]	2,023	4,485	80	73	193	8,528	...	...
New Zealand	3	3,310		...	446	...	...	345	...	28	6	51	2,788	...	...
Pacific Islands	...	1,849	...	...	...	...	...	2,005[32]	1,620[33]	3[34]	...	10	100	...	...
U.S.S.R.	21	...	143	2	18	22	1,309	...	...		18	...	...	14	...
UNSPECIFIED	58	5,414[35]	...	1,261	316	270	14	2,289	...		...	—	14	1,622	318

NOTE. — indicates nil; ... indicates number unknown. The figures shown are for 1958, unless otherwise stated. Migrants are normally classified by country of last residence, not by race or nationality (except as indicated). Residence of one year or longer is considered permanent. [1] By nationality. [2] 1957. [3] Incl. 16,331 Danish subjects. [4] Incl. 58,337 Dutch subjects. [5] Year ended March 31, 1959. [6] Whites only. [7] Immigrants travelling direct by sea from ports outside Europe and the Mediterranean. [8] Immigrants according to nationality admitted for 12 months or more. [9] Year ended June 30, 1959. [10] Of whom 4,050 from the Belgian Congo. [11] French Africa. [12] Incl. Central and South America. [13] Incl. Central America. [14] Excl. Surinam. [15] Incl. Surinam. [16] Incl. Turkey (19). [17] Lebanon. [18] Iraq. [19] Persia. [20] Formosa. [21] Incl. Pakistan and Ceylon. [22] Incl. Pakistan. [23] Incl. Singapore. [24] Incl. Channel Is., Malta and Cyprus. [25] Incl. Luxembourg. [26] Incl. Svalbard. [27] Incl. Azores. [28] Incl. Portugal. [29] Incl. Balearic Is. [30] Incl. Republic of Ireland. [31] Incl. New Zealand. [32] Netherlands New Guinea. [33] Commonwealth countries only. [34] Fiji and New Guinea. [35] Of whom 2,321 from Commonwealth countries and 846 from Egypt.

SOURCE. Institut National de Statistique, Brussels; New Zealand House, London; Rhodesia House, London; British Board of Trade and Home Office; U.S. Department of Justice, Immigration and Naturalization Service; official published statistics of the different countries.

INDIA. Republican member of the Commonwealth of Nations in southern Asia: a union of 14 states, with 6 centrally administered territories. Populations (1951 census) and areas (revised) as from Nov. 1, 1956 (States Reorganization act), are given in the table. Constitution of union government: president and vice-president; prime minister and council of ministers; Rajya Sabha (upper house) of 250 members (12 nominated by the president; the rest elected by the elected members of the state legislatures); Lok Sabha (lower house) of 520 members elected by universal adult suffrage, with allocation of seats for each state and for scheduled castes and tribes; Supreme Court of eight judges. President, Rajendra Prasad; prime minister, Jawaharlal Nehru. The states have provincial autonomy with governor, ministry and elected assembly (bi-cameral legislature in some states). Centrally administered territories are the responsibility of the president and government of the republic, with local administrators. Language in India falls into two main groups. (1) *Indo-Aryan* or northern, incl. Hindi (spoken by 46% of the population and incl. Urdu, Hindustani and Punjabi, as it was impossible to show these four languages as separate percentages in the 1951 census), Bengali (8%), Marathi (8%) and Gujarati (5%). (2) *Dravidian* or southern, incl. Telugu (10%), Tamil (8%), Kannada (Kanarese) (4·5%) and Malayalam (4%). English is used for all official purposes but is eventually to be replaced by Hindi in the Devanagari script. Religion: Hindu (c. 85%), Moslem (c. 10%), Christian (c. 2%) and Sikh (c. 2%); Jain, Buddhist, Parsee, Jewish, etc. Union capital, New Delhi; pop. (1951 census) 276,314. Chief towns other than provincial capitals (pop., 1951 census): Ahmedabad 793,813; Kanpur 705,383; Poona 588,545; Nagpur 449,099; Howrah 433,630; Agra 375,665; Madurai 361,781; Banaras 355,777; Allahabad 332,295; Amritsar 325,747; Indore 310,859. Main imports: cereals, mineral fuels, machinery and transport equipment, chemicals, raw cotton, textile yarn and fabrics, iron and steel, motor vehicles. Main exports: tea, manufactured jute, manufactured cotton, non-ferrous ores and concentrates. Monetary unit: *rupee* (Rs.13·33 =£1 sterling).

History. *Foreign Affairs.* The year 1959 was dominated by India's relations with its neighbours Pakistan and the Chinese People's Republic. The shooting down on April 10 of an Indian military jet aeroplane, which had inadvertently flown over the territory of Pakistan, aroused considerable feeling in both countries, but thereafter relations improved.

States	Area (sq.mi.)	Population	Capital (with pop., 1951)
Andhra Pradesh	106,052	31,260,133	Hyderabad (1,085,722)
Assam . . .	84,899	9,043,707	Shillong (53,756)
Bihar . . .	67,198	38,783,778	Patna (283,479)
Bombay . .	191,038	48,265,221	Bombay (2,839,270*)
Jammu and Kashmir†	86,024	4,410,000‡	Srinagar (207,787§)
Kerala . . .	15,003	13,549,118	Trivandrum (186,931)
Madhya Pradesh .	171,210	26,071,637	Bhopal (102,233)
Madras . . .	50,132	29,974,936	Madras (1,416,056)
Mysore . . .	74,122	19,401,193	Bangalore (788,977)
Orissa . . .	60,162	14,645,946	Cuttack (102,505)
Punjab . . .	47,084	16,134,890	Chandigarh (...)
Rajasthan . .	132,150	15,970,774	Jaipur (291,130)
Uttar Pradesh .	113,452	63,215,742	Lucknow (496,861)
West Bengal . .	33,928	26,302,386	Calcutta (4,578,071‖)
Total . .	1,232,434	357,029,461	
Centrally administered territories			
Andaman and Nicobar Islands	3,215	30,971	Port Blair (17,671)
Delhi . . .	573	1,744,072	Delhi (1,384,211)
Himachal Pradesh .	10,880	1,109,466	Simla (46,150)
Laccadive, Minicoy and Amindivi Islands	11	21,035	—
Manipur . .	8,628	577,635	Imphal (133,606)
Tripura . . .	4,036	639,029	Argartala (42,595)
Total . .	27,343	4,122,208	
Grand Total . .	1,259,797	361,151,669¶	

* Greater Bombay. † Inclusion of Jammu and Kashmir in India disputed by Pakistan; the question of its status remained in 1959 as one of the U.N. Security council's unsettled problems. ‡ 1951 est. § 1941 census. ‖ Greater Calcutta. ¶ 1958 est., 397,540,000.

A cartoon by Low published in the " Guardian " on Sept. 2.

On April 17 an interim agreement on the distribution of the Indus canal waters was concluded. On Sept. 1 the president of Pakistan, Mohammed Ayub Khan, stopped at Delhi for a few hours on his way to East Pakistan, and had a cordial meeting with the Indian prime minister, Jawaharlal Nehru. Early in October the Pakistan minister for the interior visited Delhi, and an agreement was reached on the border problems between India and East Pakistan.

Relations with China, on the other hand, rapidly worsened. The Chinese government objected to the grant by India of asylum to the ruler of Tibet, the Dalai Lama, who on March 31 crossed the Indian border. He was followed by a large number of Tibetan refugees. The Chinese government accused India of permitting anti-Chinese activities at Kalimpong and allowing the Dalai Lama himself to indulge in political activity. There was continuous harassment by the Chinese of Indian nationals in Tibet.

However, differences between India and China came to a head with a dispute about two sections of the 2,500-mi. border between India and Tibet—one lying to the northwest and the other to the northeast—neither of which had ever been properly demarcated on the ground (*see* SINO-INDIAN FRONTIER DISPUTE). In 1959 China for the first time explicitly repudiated what had been accepted as the traditional boundary between India and Tibet. On Sept. 8 in a letter to Nehru, the Chinese prime minister, Chou En-lai, brought forward various arguments to support his contention that the whole question of the boundary between the two countries was an open one. In his reply of Sept. 26 Nehru made it clear that

The Dalai Lama (centre) is welcomed to India after his flight from Lhasa in March by representatives of the Indian government. Later, at Tezpur, Assam, he issued a statement denying that he had been abducted to India, as claimed by Chou En-lai, the Chinese prime minister.

A scene from Midnapore, West Bengal, where serious flooding occurred in October. Nearly a million people were rendered homeless.

there could be no question of discussing the whole northern boundary which had been settled for centuries. As the border terrain made physical demarcation on the ground impossible in many places, it was likely that minor border rectification would be required, and the government of India was willing to hold discussions for such a purpose. However, any such discussions would have to be on the basis that the frontier was, on the whole, well known and beyond dispute.

Since 1954, as the white paper published by the Indian government in September showed, there had been numerous instances of border infiltration by Chinese troops, and in 1959 there were some grave incidents. In July Chinese patrols camped at Khurnak in Ladakh (the Indian frontier district). On Aug. 7 they occupied Khinzemane, and on Aug. 26 they overran, after an exchange of fire, the Indian outpost of Longju, both places well within Indian territory. Despite repeated protests Chinese forces remained in possession of Longju. On Oct. 21 an Indian patrol near the Kongka pass, almost 50 mi. inside Ladakh, encountered Chinese troops, who had taken up a fortified position on a hill top. In the ensuing clash the Indian party suffered heavy casualties. Feelings ran high in India. On Nov. 7 Chou En-lai wrote to Nehru, proposing that both sides withdraw their troops 12·5 mi. from the positions they had taken up. Civilian and administrative personnel were, however, to remain. He also proposed that the two prime ministers should meet as soon as possible.

Among the visitors to India during the year were President Tito of Yugoslavia, the Duke of Edinburgh, the prime ministers of Ghana, Afghanistan and Mongolia, and the secretary-general of the United Nations. Nehru visited Nepal in June, and Afghanistan and Persia in October. The president of the United States, Dwight D. Eisenhower, paid a five-day visit to India from Dec. 9-13.

Home Affairs. In June C. Rajagopalachari, the former governor-general of India, formed a Conservative party in opposition to Nehru's ruling Congress party. This new group, known as the Swatantra (Freedom) party, was mainly opposed to the Congress programme of joint co-operative farming, by which land would be used for joint cultivation, the farmers continuing to keep their property rights and getting a share from the net proceeds in proportion to the amount of land they owned.

In the first half of the year, opposition to the Communist government in Kerala brought administration there almost

to a standstill. On July 31 the state government was dismissed by the central government and president's rule was established pending a general election.

Economic Affairs. The harvest in 1959-60 was good, but floods in most parts of northern India caused considerable destruction.

The momentum of industrial development was maintained. In February the first blast furnace of the steel plant at Rourkela went into operation, and the steel plant at Bhilai was inaugurated. In March, the coke-oven plant at Durgapur was formally opened. On May 1 the bridge over the Ganges near Hathidah was opened to traffic. The only setback in industrial progress was the flooding of the hoist chamber in the Bhakra-Nangal dam in August.

Substantial loans were received from both the United States and the U.S.S.R. during the year. In March the United States made available to the Indian government more than £75 million, representing the sale proceeds of agricultural commodities, and lying to the credit of the United States. In September the Soviet government granted

The scene at a Bombay suburban railway station on Aug. 14, when there was a mass demonstration against irregular services.

a loan of £135 million to help the Indian government to implement its third five-year plan. (*See* also KASHMIR; POLITICAL PARTIES, COMMONWEALTH.) (S. GL.)

See M. Brecher, *Nehru* (London, 1959); H. Venkatarubbiah, *Indian Economy since Independence* (Bombay, 1958); G. W. Overstreet and M. Windmiller, *Communism in India* (Berkeley, California, 1958).

INDOCHINA: see CAMBODIA; LAOS; VIETNAM.

INDONESIA.
Asian republic consisting of three groups of islands: (1) Major Sunda Islands (Java, Sumatra, Borneo, Celebes); (2) Lesser Sunda Islands (Bali, Lombok, Sumba, Sumbawa, Flores, part of Timor); (3) Molucca archipelago (Halmaheira, Ceram, Ambon, etc.). Area: 575,893 sq.mi. Pop. (mid-1958 est.): 86,900,000. Large indigenous groups on Java (where two-thirds of the total population live): Javanese, Sundanese, Madurese (incl. the inhabitants of the island of Madura) and Jakartans; on Sumatra: Menangkabaus, Achinese and Bataks; on the Lesser Sunda Islands: Balinese; on Celebes: Buginese. Non-indigenous groups: Chinese 3,000,000, Europeans (mainly Dutch) 60,000. Language: as well as the Indonesia official language (Bahasa Indonesia), an adaptation of Malay, 25 major languages and c. 250 dialects are spoken. Religion: Moslem (Shafi'i) c. 80%; Christian 4·3%; Buddhist 3%; Hindu 2·2%. Chief towns (pop., 1951 est.): Djakarta (cap.) 2,800,000; Surabaya 1,100,000; Bandung 800,000; Semarang 530,000; Surakarta 306,000; Medan 260,000; Jogjakarta 246,000. President of the republic and (from July 10) head of government, Ahmed Sukarno; first minister, Djuanda Kartawidjaya. Main imports: textiles, rice, chemicals and products, machinery. Main exports: rubber, petroleum and products, tin, copra. Monetary unit: *rupiah* (official exchange rate [from Aug. 25, 1959] Rp.126·45 = £1 sterling).

History. During the year 1959 President Sukarno enacted his concept of "guided democracy". Sweeping monetary measures introduced in August did little to improve the country's economic position. In foreign policy the most significant development was the U.S. reassessment of Indonesian neutralism: Sukarno's "guided democracy" appeared in Washington as limiting Communist activities and increasing the influence of the army. Although large-scale revolts collapsed in the previous year, many outlying areas in Sumatra, Celebes and other islands remained in rebel hands. During the year 13,354 Indonesians were killed in various rebellions; the figure included c. 7,500 rebels.

Presidential System Introduced. In a speech broadcast from Jogjakarta on Feb. 20, Sukarno called on the nation to return to the 1945 constitution as the best means of implementing "guided democracy". The president announced that he would seek quick enactment of two bills: one would reduce the number of political parties and the other would revise the electoral law to permit representatives of functional groups in parliament. The members of parliament would be partly elected and partly appointed. Earlier on the same day Djuanda, the prime minister, said in Djakarta that the cabinet favoured the reinstatement of the 1945 constitution. That constitution, promulgated when Nationalists led by Sukarno and the former Vice-President Mohammed Hatta declared Indonesia independent of Dutch rule, gave the president strong executive powers.

On April 22, in his address to the Constituent Assembly in Bandung, Sukarno formally requested the re-adoption of the 1945 constitution. The following day he left the country for an extensive tour abroad. He visited Turkey, Poland, Sweden, Denmark, the U.S.S.R., Italy (where he was received, on May 14, by Pope John XXIII), Portugal, Brazil, Argentina, Mexico, Japan, North Vietnam and Cambodia. He returned to Djakarta on June 29.

In the meantime the Constituent Assembly (elected in 1955) failed to reach a two-thirds majority on the government's proposal for the re-enactment of the 1945 constitution. The parties in favour of the proposal were, among others, the Nationalists, the Protestants, the Catholics, the Socialists and the Communists. It was opposed by all the Moslem parties who demanded the inclusion in the constitution of the Djakarta charter of June 22, 1945, with its safeguards for the

Flooding on the outskirts of Djakarta, Indonesia, early in the year gave these children the opportunity for a swim in the street.

Moslems, while the government wanted the adoption of the constitution in its original form, as proclaimed on Aug. 17, 1945. Article 29 stated:

"The state shall be based upon the faith in the Divine Omnipotence. The state guarantees the freedom of each inhabitant to profess his own religion and to perform his religious duties according to his faith and belief."

Immediately after the third inconclusive vote Lieut.-General Abdulharis Nasution, chief of staff of the Indonesian army, with the full knowledge and consent of the government, banned all political activities in the country. On July 5 President Sukarno promulgated a decree dissolving the Constituent Assembly and re-enacting the 1945 constitution. The decree also announced the formation of a provisional People's Consultative Congress composed of members of the House of Representatives (elected in 1955, together with the Constituent Assembly) and representatives of the regions and "functional groups".

On July 9 Sukarno announced a ten-member non-party cabinet with himself as prime minister, Djuanda as first minister and minister of finance, and Lieut.-General Nasution as minister of defence and of people's security. The following day he was sworn in under the 1945 constitution and then installed the cabinet, the 18th government in 14 years. On July 12 Sukarno announced the names of 25 deputy ministers, all non-party men or no longer affiliated to political parties. There were two army officers in the inner cabinet and seven among the deputy ministers. In addition, the air force and navy chiefs of staff were *ex officio* ministers. On July 22 the House of Representatives approved by acclamation the decree of July 5. However, the spokesman of the Masjumi (Madjelis Sjuro Muslimin Indonesia or Council of Indonesian Moslem Organizations) denounced the presidential decree as "an act of force". On Dec. 16, as the state of war was to expire, Sukarno extended it indefinitely with the difference that all authority was centred in his hands.

From Sept. 7 to 15 the Indonesian Communist party held in Djakarta its sixth congress. Dipa Nusantara Aidit, its first secretary, was in favour of continuing to co-operate with Sukarno and his guided democracy. This line, although criticized by Mohammed Lukman, deputy secretary, was adopted by the congress. At the close of the congress Sukarno emphasized in an address the necessity of maintaining the projected People's Consultative Congress as a permanent institution.

Economic Position. On Aug. 24 Sukarno introduced drastic measures to put the country's currency on a sounder basis. All 500 and 1,000 rupiah notes in circulation were devalued to 10% of their face value, but notes ranging from one rupiah to Rp.100 were unaffected; 90% of the money above Rp.25,000 in every bank account was frozen. It was believed that the Rp. 32,300 million in circulation (including Rp. 9,670 million in bank deposits) were reduced to about Rp.17,000 million. During the previous 18 months the government had put about Rp.12,000 million into circulation to meet increasing expenditure, the most important part of which was the cost of the campaign against anti-Sukarno rebels in 1958 which was believed to be Rp.17,000 million. Total state revenues in 1960 were estimated at Rp.44,039 million and expenditure at Rp.45,961 million.

The official rupiah rates of Rp.11·40 to the U.S. dollar and Rp.31·90 to the pound sterling, that had been in effect since Feb. 1952, were abolished and new rates were introduced: Rp.45·00 to the $ and Rp.126·45 to the £. But by the beginning of October black market operators were offering Rp.140 to the $ and Rp.390 to the £.

Subandrio, the Indonesian foreign minister, said in an interview on July 29 that Indonesia was planning to approach the United States for a $300 million development loan. He added that during its 27 months in office the Djuanda government had obtained $450 million in foreign credits: half from the United States and half from the Socialist countries, including $117·5 million from the U.S.S.R. and $50 million from the Chinese People's Republic.

Foreign Relations. Subandrio visited Canberra from Feb. 10 to 15. He had discussions both with R. G. Menzies, the Australian prime minister, and Richard G. Casey, the minister for external affairs. An agreed statement said: "There was a full explanation of the considerations which have led each country to a different view in connection with West New Guinea, with Australia recognizing the principle of self-determination." The statement added that the dispute between the Netherlands and Indonesia "was one to be settled by peaceful means". On Dec. 1, Menzies arrived in Djakarta for a week's visit. He invited Sukarno to visit Australia.

Tension developed towards the end of the year between Indonesia and Communist China over the economic restrictions the Djakarta government imposed on foreign traders in rural areas. Most of these businesses were shops and they were mainly owned by some 300,000 Chinese. By Dec. 31, 1959, they had either to close or to move to the cities. Huang Chen, the Chinese ambassador, had on Nov. 17 a 90-min. talk with Subandrio and complained that the Indonesian government were fostering an "anti-Chinese movement". It was believed that out of 3 million Chinese in Indonesia less than one-fifth were Indonesian citizens.

On Dec. 9, Chen Yi, Chinese foreign minister, sent to Subandrio a stiff note protesting against the "most cruel treatment" of the Chinese residents in Indonesia. With studied courtesy but not without anger Subandrio rejected on Dec. 11 the Chinese protest.

The Armed Forces and the Rebels. On Jan. 31 Lieut.-General Nasution said in Djakarta that it would take years to suppress rebel activities in outlying areas of Indonesia. At the end of the year it was estimated that in certain areas of Sumatra, Java, Celebes and Halmaheira there were altogether about 28 rebel battalions, including 15 belonging to the Dar-ul-Islam movement and 13 still obeying the orders of the colonels who had joined the "revolutionary government" of Sjafruddin Prawiranegara.

Air Vice-Marshal Suryadarma, commander of the air force, objected to serving under Lieut.-General Nasution as minister of defence. His politics were reputed to be as much inclined to the left as Nasution's inclined to the right. On July 17 Suryadarma was appointed head of the joint chiefs of staff. The following day Vice-Admiral Subyakto, commander of the navy, was relieved of his post and replaced by Colonel Raden Eddy Martadinata.

At the beginning of the year it was announced that Britain had granted export licences for 18 Fairey Gannet patrol aircraft for the Indonesian forces and that the United States had agreed to equip 20 Indonesian army battalions with small arms. This made a "painful" impression in Dutch government quarters. In April six Yugoslav-built destroyers were transferred to the Indonesian navy at Tandjung Priok. (K. M. S.)

See Louis Fischer, *The Story of Indonesia* (London, 1959).

INDUSTRIAL DESIGN. From the point of view of individual designs 1959 was not especially distinguished. No single design appeared of the proportions of, say, the moulded glass-fibre chair of 1948 by the U.S. designer Charles Eames, which signalled a new concept of chair fabrication. On the other hand, 1959 did witness a further increase in the number of industrially designed products available and in industry's and the public's awareness of the designer's role. This represented a continuation of a trend that had been developing throughout the 1950s. A large part of the credit for this widened interest was due to the various design societies and organizations in different countries which had staged exhibitions, awards, competitions, lectures, etc., with the aim of educating the public to the importance of industrial design. For example, in Great Britain the Council of Industrial Design put on its third annual exhibition "Designs of the Year" in 1959 and for the first time presented the Duke of Edinburgh's Award for Elegance. Similar awards were made, for example, by the Canadian National Industrial Design council and in the 1959 Japanese Industrial Design competition. Also in 1959 the Institute of Design, Chicago, organized a poll called the "100 Best Designs of Modern Times", and Svensk Form (Swedish Design centre) opened in Stockholm.

Undoubtedly activities of this kind had intensified public interest but at the same time they had been received by some critics with a certain amount of misgiving, particularly the awards. This was primarily because the standards adopted by the organizers seemed unnecessarily narrow and ultimately restricting to designers themselves. The definition of design that most of the organizations subscribed to and publicized could fairly be called orthodox. That is, they tended to see the problem of the industrial designer as one of maintaining a certain aesthetic standard for articles manufactured by machine processes, and to do this they had accepted a theory which had its origins in the period between the aftermath of the industrial revolution at the end of the 19th century and the first few years of the Weimar Bauhaus (founded in 1919). This theory, in addition to vindicating machine production, demands that "form follows function". In other words, the appearance of a product should be determined by a consideration of its function, the materials of which it is composed and the processes by which it is made. In spite of the references to function in this theory it is concerned essentially with aesthetics, or more exactly with "pure form", which means simply that a product, say, a teapot has something of the formal qualities of abstract sculpture allied to the function of containing and pouring liquid. When, in 1959, a product was described as "well-designed" or even just "industrially designed" these qualities were automatically imputed to it.

It is evident from this that, by the end of the 1950s, design practice was heavily influenced by theory, and another symptom of the same condition was the readiness of designers to meet at conferences to discuss their profession and its problems.

In 1959 the ninth annual International Design conference was held at Aspen, Colorado, where designers, educators and several scientists met to discuss the " image in communication ", and in Stockholm the International Council of Societies of Industrial Design held a convention with delegates from 18 countries. The international character of these conferences was being extended to the practice of design itself, one example being the range of cars produced by the British Motor corporation for which the Italian car designer Pinin Farina acted as consultant; the Austin A40 which appeared in 1959 was typical of the range.

The orthodox definition of design, which covers most of the points mentioned so far, had at least one advantage in that it was producing actual designs. On the other hand, the most significant moves in industrial design in the latter half of the 1950s had no products to show for themselves. These new moves were basically attempts to study function in a much more rigorous and inclusive sense, taking into account irrational factors in a consumer's behaviour as well as making the most subtle adaptations of a tool to suit the human being who uses it. This new study of function involved the science of ergonomics, which, briefly defined, is the study of man in relation to his working environment. Ergonomics utilizes experimental psychology, physiology, anatomy and statistics, and out of it was arising an approach to design best summed up by the term " logical design methods " (a roughly analogous study in the United States was called " human engineering "). The Hochschule für Gestaltung (school of design) at Ulm, German Federal Republic, founded in 1955, and in 1959 under the chairmanship of Tomás Maldonado, was teaching industrial design by logical methods and calling upon such comparatively new studies as information theory, mathematical logic and topology to do so. Unlike the orthodox theory of design, Ulm rejected the idea that design is basically an art and Maldonado suggested that, in the future, " use " value would replace " aesthetic " value as a criterion for evaluation.

It should be emphasized that, by the end of the 1950s, logical methods of design were only beginning and that, even at Ulm, they had not yet produced a definitive design. However, this approach to industrial design was almost certain to replace the intuitive method of the orthodox theory in spite of the many questions that remained to be answered.

The following are some of the international magazines dealing wholly or in part with industrial design: *Design* (London), the organ of the Council of Industrial Design, including articles on ergonomics; *Industrial Design* (New York), with a bias towards technological subjects; *Stile Industria* (Milan), including pictorial reviews of products; *Form* (Stockholm), the organ of Svenska Slöjdföreningen (Swedish Society of Arts and Crafts and Design); *Ergonomics* (London), the journal of the Ergonomics Research society, essentially a technical publication. (R. Cn.)

INDUSTRIAL HEALTH. The annual report for 1958 of the chief inspector of factories was again presented as two short reports, one on the general work of his department and one on industrial health. The new form, which had first been introduced the year before, had been received favourably by industry and the press. Fatal accidents in factories rose from 651 in 1957 to 665 in 1958, but total reported accidents fell from 174,713 to 167,697, thus continuing the downward trend; the 1958 figure was the lowest since 1935. Handling goods (26·9%), power-driven machinery (15·7%) and persons falling (14·3%) remained the chief causes. Electricity stations and 2,746 factories made returns of accident statistics. In these the accident frequency rate—the number of lost-time accidents per 100,000 man-hours worked—increased slightly in certain industries between 1957 and 1958 (*e.g.*, from 1·71 to 2·37 in agricultural machinery), but decreased in others (*e.g.*, from 2·64 to 2·23 in iron and steel) and there was an over-all reduction from 1·625 to 1·568. The lowest rate was in clothing and footwear (0·43) and the highest in coke-ovens and manufactured fuel (3·51). By contrast there was a rise in accidents in building operations and works of engineering construction. To stimulate preventive measures the chief inspector was to publish a triennial report on safety and health in building and civil engineering industries.

Previous to 1958 the figures for persons " reportably injured " in coalmines included minor injuries caused by dangerous occurrences. To give a more accurate picture of serious bodily injury these minor injuries were thenceforth to be excluded. In 1958 there were 327 fatal accidents in coalmines, the lowest number ever recorded. Serious injuries increased from 1,604 in 1957 to 1,752 in 1958; falls of ground accounted for nearly 40% and haulage and transport for 28%.

	ACCIDENTS IN BUILDING AND ENGINEERING			
	Building Operations		*Engineering Construction*	
	All accidents	Fatal	All accidents	Fatal
1957 . . .	14,568	156	1,924	31
1958 . . .	15,017	207	2,329	51

SOURCE. *Annual Report of H.M. Chief Inspector of Factories for 1958* (H.M.S.O., London, 1959).

Towards the prevention and mitigation of burning accidents the Board of Trade issued regulations, including standards for non-inflammable textile fabrics. Ship-breaking was again the main cause of lead poisoning in industry. No case of lead poisoning occurred in the pottery industry between 1954 and 1957, owing to the replacement of raw lead by low-solubility lead glazes. However, the need for constant vigilance was underlined in 1958 by two cases arising in processes involving the use of fluxes containing about 20% soluble lead; calcium disodium versenate proved effective in treatment of the disease.

Of the 13 fatal cases of epitheliomatous ulceration due to mineral oil the scrotum was the site in 10. Often this disease does not appear until years after the workman has left the causative industry and perhaps is no longer under periodical medical inspection at work. It should be impressed on these workers that they should immediately seek advice for any skin sore, as early diagnosis is essential to effective treatment. No evidence of malignant change was noted among 205 cases of chrome ulceration. Chapter iii of the Report on Industrial Health for 1958 was devoted to a review of current knowledge of occupational cancer. Industrial dermatitis continued to be a leading cause of disablement. The Institute of Occupational Health, Helsinki, reported that of over 3,000 consultations at the occupational diseases clinic, 73% were skin cases. The Atomic Energy authority carried out a major review of their health and safety organization. In addition to control of radiation hazards particular attention was directed to the risks arising from beryllium metal powder and oxide. At the 43rd session of the International Labour organization the protection of workers against radiation was discussed (I.L.O., *Report VI* (1) and (2), Geneva, 1959).

Of 2,216 deaths certified as due to pneumoconiosis, coalmining accounted for 1,715 and manufacture of pottery 85. New cases of pneumoconiosis among coalminers in 1958 totalled 2,902 against 3,756 in 1957. A scheme for the radiographic examination of all coalminers at five-yearly intervals began at the end of 1958. Owing to the discovery of hitherto undetected cases pneumoconiosis certifications were expected to increase during the next few years but this would not indicate increased prevalence. Several reports, particularly from the United States, focused attention and research on amorphous, non-crystalline silica as a cause of simple and progressive massive fibrosis of the lungs. An international scientific conference on pneumoconiosis, organized by the

South African Council for Scientific and Industrial Research, was held at Johannesburg in February. The report of the proceedings and recommendations was in the press. A comprehensive report on industrial anthrax in Great Britain from 1895–1957 was published in November (Cmnd. 846, H.M.S.O., London).

The I.L.O. continued to consider the organization of occupational health services and India and New Zealand were extending such services. In Great Britain advance towards the extension of medical services in industry by the government was foreshadowed by the investigations of the Industrial Health Advisory committee, the Factories act, 1959, and the Labour party's health policy statement, *Members One of Another*. The importance of environmental hygiene, supported by hygiene laboratories, was stressed. (*See* also ACCIDENTS.) (A. MN.)

See *Industrial Health: a Survey of the Pottery Industry in Stoke-on-Trent* (H.M.S.O., London, 1959); Donald Hunter, *Health in Industry* (Harmondsworth, 1959); *The Annals of Occupational Hygiene* (Pergamon Press, London).

INDUSTRIAL RELATIONS: *see* EMPLOYMENT; STRIKES; TRADE UNIONS; WAGES AND HOURS.

INSECTS: *see* ENTOMOLOGY.

INSURANCE. Trading results published in Great Britain during 1959 referred to home and overseas operations in 1958. During this year the recession in the United States, the decline in commodity prices and the slower tempo of industrial progress in other important areas resulting from the need to contain inflation had some effect upon world-wide premium income, but this nevertheless reached a new high level. Fire profits showed an encouraging improvement compared with the particularly unfavourable underwriting results in 1957, but accident underwriting—dominated by a continuing unfavourable experience on the motor account—followed the unprofitable pattern of the two preceding years. Premium development on marine account was much more difficult in 1958 than formerly. The continued contraction of international trade resulted in the laying-up of about 8% of the world shipping tonnage, with a consequent sharp fall in the level of insured values and a substantial return of premiums. On the cargo side, the smaller volume and lower value of goods and commodities led to lower premium rates and keen competition among insurers for the available business.

Despite British insurance companies' adverse underwriting results in the United States their dollar investment earnings left them with a net positive dollar balance in 1958.

The table below, based on published results, records the 1958 performance of 22 major companies.

TABLE I. FIRE, ACCIDENT AND GENERAL INSURANCE 1958 (£'000)

Year	Premiums	Claims	Profit and loss credit	% of Premiums
Fire				
1956 . . .	222,210	111,135	3,288	1·5
1957 . . .	230,678	119,698	1,855	0·8
1958 . . .	234,747	117,460	6,440	2·7
Accident and General				
1956 · · ·	333,421	202,681	— 3,244	— 1·0
1957 . . .	373,179	225,775	— 4,014	— 1·1
1958 . . .	398,328	246,919	— 2,761	— 0·7

TABLE II. MARINE INSURANCE 1958 (£'000)

Year	Premiums	Profit and loss credit	Fund	% of Premiums
1956 . . .	44,720	4,094	70,133	156·4
1957 . . .	51,637	3,560	75,960	147·1
1958 . . .	51,161	2,364	76,121	148·8

Record new business and increased bonuses marked the favourable progress of life assurance in 1958. In the ordinary section, new sums assured amounted to about £1,655 million, as against £1,375 million in 1957—an increase of 20%, following an increase of 10% in 1957 over 1956. In the industrial ("home service") section, new sums assured written in 1958 by eight leading companies at £262·5 million were higher than the previous year by £10,973,000, an increase of 4·4%. Industrial life premiums were 4·3% up on the year. The average sum assured per policy issued worked out at £63, against £63·9 in 1957, £61·2 in 1956 and £57·7 in 1955.

Despite greater hesitancy in the field of industrial pensions in 1959, resulting from the extension of the state plan, many new assurance schemes were arranged during the year and an additional substantial new business total was written in the form of increased benefits under existing schemes. Policies of a short-term nature in connection with gifts *inter vivos* and policies providing for estate duty payments continued in demand, while an increased interest was shown in life assurance for use with house purchase loans. The profit-earning capacity of the life offices was reflected in bigger bonus distributions. Many offices distributed bonuses on a higher scale than at any time in their history. Taken as a whole, life assurance in 1959 remained buoyant and reached a high production level.

The new 1959 National Insurance act introduced graded pensions related to individual earnings, and there were provisions for the contracting out of the state scheme where an existing private scheme provided sufficiently favourable benefits. The changes, to take effect in 1961, would doubtless affect the future trend of the business of the life offices, but the precise nature and extent of their impact could not yet be envisaged.

Difficulties encountered by insurers during 1956 and 1957 in fire and accident underwriting were less acute in 1959, but the general problems of intense competition for business, inadequate premium rates, increasing claims costs, and high acquisition charges remained unresolved. The many large fires in the United Kingdom included one at the Rolls-Royce works at Leicester, with an estimated loss of £3 million, a fire at Rootes motor works in Coventry, with an estimated loss of £3·5 million, and a fire at the Avro works, Chadderton, Lancs., where the loss was variously estimated to be between £1 million and £5 million. In the overseas field a number of serious fires together with losses under extended coverage again resulted in heavy costs for insurance companies.

Accident and general insurance increased both in volume and revenue total. With growing road congestion and ever-increasing repair costs for motor cars, increases in the rate of motor premiums which were effective in 1959 failed to satisfy the profit need. Crime figures in general were mounting and a rise in loss ratios on the burglary account was inevitable. Other categories of accident insurance, including employers' liability and personal accident business, were transacted with a reasonable profit margin. Marine underwriting accounts closed at end of 1959 produced only a meagre over-all surplus.

With industrial and scientific expansion demanding world-wide insurance cover for risk accumulations of immense proportions, sheer size in underwriting units was becoming a first essential. In 1959 there was a considerable degree of administrative reorganization and a series of insurance company mergers took place.

In the United States, at the end of 1959, 115 million persons owned more than $530,000 million of legal reserve life insurance. In the previous ten years average family ownership of life insurance had more than doubled and the number of policyholders had increased by nearly 30 million. New life insurance purchased in 1959 reached a record $68,000 million and legal reserve life insurance companies paid families nearly $8,000 million in life insurance benefits. In Canada, ownership of legal reserve life insurance reached a peak of more than $40,000 million at the end of 1959, nearly three times the amount which was purchased ten years earlier.

Business written by U.S. property insurance companies in 1958 increased by about 5% and the year closed with a combined loss and expense ratio of 99·4%. The first half of 1959 produced a loss ratio of 62·3% and an expense ratio of 35·9%, giving a combined ratio of 98·2%, and there was a 7% increase in premiums over the first half of 1958. Straight fire insurance premiums advanced about $30,000 million in 1958 to reach a total of $1,360 million, but the package policies continued to be the leaders in the development of property insurance. In 1958 409 companies reported $280 million in premiums on the homeowners' forms of insurance, and 285 companies produced a premium volume of $27 million on the commercial multiple-peril forms of insurance. Ocean marine insurance was up about $193 million. (P. Ss.; H. J. J.; L. J. A.)

INTERNATIONAL BANK FOR RECONSTRUCTION AND DEVELOPMENT.
The articles of agreement establishing the bank were drawn up by the U.N. Monetary and Financial conference which met at Bretton Woods, New Hampshire, United States, in July 1944. The bank came into existence on Dec. 27, 1945. The authorized capital, originally $10,000 million, was raised to $21,000 million in 1959 and it was expected that, when all the new subscriptions became effective, its subscribed capital would amount to about $19,000 million. The total of its outstanding loans and guarantees was not to exceed its subscribed capital, reserves and surplus. Loans made or guaranteed by the bank were to be for specific projects or for programmes of reconstruction or development. For a list of member states, *see* INTERNATIONAL MONETARY FUND.

The bank is controlled by the board of governors appointed by the members; and by the board of 14 executive directors, of whom five are appointed by the five members with the largest number of shares (U.S., U.K., China [Nat.], France, India) and nine elected by the governors of the other members. The president is elected by the executive directors. Headquarters, Washington, D.C.; president, Eugene R. Black (U.S.).

History. On Sept. 15, 1959, the bank's authorized capital was increased from $10,000 million to $21,000 million. Most member governments were doubling their capital subscriptions, but Canada, the German Federal Republic, Japan and 14 other countries were making further additions. Upon completion of the new subscriptions about one-tenth of the bank's capital would be paid in. The bank would be able to call on the remaining nine-tenths if it should ever need additional funds to pay off what it had borrowed from other investors through the sale of its bonds and notes. The major part of the bank's capital, in effect, constituted a guarantee of its obligations; and the result of increasing the bank's subscribed capital was an increase in its ability to borrow.

In 1959, in negotiating the settlement between the United Kingdom and the United Arab Republic of the financial claims arising out of the Suez conflict, the bank brought the two parties together on the basis of a compromise acceptable to both sides. Marked progress was also made in the efforts the bank had been carrying on since 1952 to help India and Pakistan to settle their dispute over the sharing of the waters of the Indus basin.

In the year ending June 30, 1959, the bank made 30 loans totalling the equivalent of $703,125,000. Half the new loans, $354 million, were made in Asia. The balance was made up of $136·5 million in Latin America, $110·6 million in Africa and $102 million in Europe. Three of the year's loans—in the Republic of Gabon, Malaya and Sudan—were in countries where the bank had not previously lent. Electric power development accounted for $294 million of the total. These power loans would, among other things, assist the installation of almost 2·5 million kw. of new generating capacity in 11 member countries. Transportation accounted for $257·2 million. The bulk was lent for railway improvements, including $85 million for the Indian railways and $36·6 million for an extended railway expansion programme in South Africa. The two road loans of the year included the largest loan the bank had yet made for this purpose: $72 million for large-scale development of Persia's road system.

Loans for industry totalled $149 million. The Japanese steel industry benefited from loans totalling $65 million. In Finland the manufacture of chemical pulp and newsprint was being assisted by a loan of $37 million. In Italy bank lending would give further impetus to the development of new chemical industries in Sicily. Another loan, of $35 million, would make possible the mining and transportation of manganese ore from large deposits in the Republic of Gabon. The only loan made directly for agriculture was of $3·5 million to the Central Bank of Costa Rica to finance the import of equipment for farming and for light industry.

Net earnings of the international bank, exclusive of receipts from loan commissions, were a record $46 million, and disbursements reached a record of $583 million. Sales of parts of bank loans amounted to $148 million, exceeding the previous record of $99 million reached in 1955. On the other hand, the bank borrowed only $432 million in 1958-59 compared with $650 million in 1957-58. On June, 30, 1959, the bank's total reserves had reached $420 million, an increase of $70 million during the financial year. Although gross income for the year, excluding loan commissions, increased by almost 25%, net earnings increased by only 10%, mainly because of the bank's increasing reliance on borrowed funds, for which it must pay market rates of interest, rather than on subscribed capital which is available interest-free. Repayments to the bank amounted to $45 million and borrowers repaid $64 million on maturities of their loans which had been sold by the bank to other investors. Total principal repayments were thus 38% above those of the previous year. By May the interest rate on new bank loans had risen to 6%, compared with 5% in July 1958. The bank financed 46% of the year's disbursements by drawing currencies other than dollars.

The bank continued to provide technical advice and assistance to its members through general survey missions, the stationing of resident representatives and the provision of experts to assist in more specialized fields of development. At the end of the year the report of the general survey mission to Thailand had been submitted to the government, the report of the mission to Libya was in preparation and a general survey mission to Tanganyika had begun its field work. Members of the bank's staff also helped to organize or operate development banks in Paraguay, Peru, Formosa, Persia and India. The Economic Development institute, a staff college for senior officials of the bank's less-developed member-countries, held its fourth course during the year, and the bank's training programme for more junior officials from member-countries completed its 12th year. (E. R. Bk.)

INTERNATIONAL COURT OF JUSTICE.
The principal judicial organ of the United Nations composed of independent judges. Its statute is based on that of the Permanent Court of International Justice created in 1920 under the auspices of the League of Nations. All members of the United Nations are *ipso facto* parties to the statute of the I.C.J. A non-member state may become a party to the statute on conditions to be determined in each case by the general assembly upon the recommendation of the Security council. The I.C.J. is composed of 15 members elected for nine years by the general assembly and the Security council, voting independently, by an absolute majority in both bodies. The seat of the I.C.J. is at The Hague. On Dec. 31, 1959, the following judges were members of the I.C.J. (figures in brackets denote the year of expiry of office; all terms expire Feb. 5 of the year designated):

Helge Klaested, Norway (1961), president
Muhammad Zafrulla Khan, Pakistan (1961), vice-president
Green H. Hackworth, U.S. (1961)
Abd-ul-Hamid Badawi, Egypt (1967)
Enrique C. Armand-Ugon, Uruguay (1961)
Jules Basdevant, France (1964)
Roberto Córdova, Mexico (1964)

Fedor Ivanovich Kozhevnikov, U.S.S.R. (1961)
Sir Hersch Lauterpacht, U.K. (1964)
Lucio Moreno Quintana, Argentina (1964)
Sir Percy Spender, Australia (1967)
Ioannis Spiropoulos, Greece (1967)
Bohdan Winiarski, Poland (1967)
V. K. Wellington Koo, Nationalist China (1967)

During the course of 1959 the court disposed of the following cases:

Case Concerning the Aerial Incident of Sept. 4, 1954. (U.S. *v.* U.S.S.R.). By order dated Dec. 9, 1958, the case was removed from the list since the U.S.S.R. refused to accept the court's jurisdiction.

Interhandel Case (Switzerland *v.* U.S.A.). The matter arose from the seizure of the assets of the General Aniline and Film corporation by the United States during World War II. Switzerland sought their restitution on the ground that the sequestered property belonged to Interhandel, a Swiss national, whose connection with I. G. Farbenindustrie terminated in 1940. The United States objected (*inter alia*) that local remedies had not been exhausted. The court, by a judgment dated March 21, 1959, upheld this objection and dismissed the case.

Case Concerning the Aerial Incident of July 27, 1955 (Israel *v.* Bulgaria). By a judgment dated May 26, 1951, the court refused jurisdiction over the dispute. To establish such jurisdiction over Bulgaria, Israel relied on a Bulgarian declaration of 1921 accepting the compulsory jurisdiction of the Permanent Court of International Justice, on Article 36(5) of the statute of the court and on the admission of Bulgaria to the United Nations in Dec. 1958. The court held that Article 36(5) was ineffective to transfer jurisdiction from the Permanent Court to the International Court in respect of states not signatory to the San Francisco charter and states not party to the statute before the Permanent Court lapsed on April 18, 1946.

Case Concerning the Sovereignty over certain Frontier Land (Belgium *v.* Netherlands). By judgment dated June 20, 1959, the court found for Belgium. The case concerned the interpretation of the boundary convention of 1843 in respect of two small plots of land whose position was equivocal. The Dutch claim to sovereignty based on Belgian acquiescence in the exercise of acts of sovereignty over the plots was dismissed on the facts.

Cases instituted in preceding years continued save for that concerning the aerial incident of July 27, 1955 (U.K. *v.* Bulgaria) which was discontinued by consent.

The following proceedings were instituted during the period Dec. 1958-Dec. 1959: *Case Concerning the Compagnie du Port, des Quais et des Entrepôts de Beyrouth and the Société Radio-Orient (France v. Lebanon); Case Concerning the Aerial Incident of Nov. 7, 1954 (U.S. v. U.S.S.R.); Request for an Advisory Opinion on the Constitution of the Maritime Safety Committee.* (*See* also INTERNATIONAL LAW.) (H. A. P. F.)

INTERNATIONAL GEOPHYSICAL CO-OPERATION.

After the official ending on Dec. 31st, 1958, of the observational phase of the International Geophysical Year (I.G.Y.), much remained to be done to enable science to reap the full benefit from the vast mass of data accumulated during the 18 months through which the observations extended.

The special committee appointed by the International Council of Scientific Unions (I.C.S.U.) to formulate the programmes of observation for the I.G.Y. was disbanded on June 30, 1959, and the office of the secretariat in Brussels was closed on Oct. 31, 1959. The bureau and executive board of the I.C.S.U. had had under continuous consideration the steps to be taken for the termination of the I.G.Y. and for the continuation of international co-operation in geophysical research. There was a general feeling among many of the participating countries that the observations should not be abruptly ended at the end of 1958 but that international co-operation in geophysics should continue for a further period, though not on the same intensive scale. There were various reasons why such a continuation was desirable. First, some countries came into the enterprise at a rather late stage, and some of the special instrumental equipment designed specifically for certain portions of the programme was not available by the time the observations began. Secondly, so many of the problems that arise in various branches of geophysics require for their solution observations in all parts of the globe; observations extending over a longer period than 18 months would assist in their elucidation. Thirdly, there were special reasons for the continuation over a period of several years of certain portions of the programme, particularly in Antarctic research, oceanic research and space research.

The sun viewed from a rocket at a height of 123 miles. A photograph obtained on March 13 by the U.S. Naval Research laboratory.

The I.C.S.U. decided that the continuation of research in these three fields should be entrusted to special committees appointed for the purpose, and that the observational and data-collecting activities in the geophysical sciences should be continued during 1959 on the same general plan as in 1957-58, each participating country being free to decide at what level and in what disciplines it would continue observations. This continuation of observational programmes was designated the International Geophysical Co-operation (I.G.C.) 1959.

Antarctic Research. Before the I.G.Y. began, very little was known about the great Antarctic continent which, covered as it is with a vast ice mass, is of particular significance for many problems in geophysics. During the I.G.Y., 57 stations were established in Antarctica by 12 nations, some on the fringe of the continent, some deep in its interior. There was a widespread feeling, not only that the continuation of Antarctic research for a considerably longer period was inherently desirable, but also that the effort and very heavy expenditure entailed in setting up well-equipped observing stations should not be lost. The I.C.S.U. accordingly appointed a Special Committee for Antarctic Research, charged with furthering the co-ordination of scientific activity in Antarctica, with a view to framing a scientific programme of circumpolar scope and significance. This committee secured the co-operation of all the nations that participated in Antarctic observations during the I.G.Y., with the addition of Poland.

A few stations were closed in 1959; a few were transferred from one country to another; one new station was established. Observing programmes were formulated in meteorology, the ionosphere, auroral physics, geomagnetism, cosmic rays, geology, glaciology, geomorphology, cartography, seismology, gravity, vulcanology, oceanography, marine biology and physiology. The activities in the Antarctic during at least the next two years were to be maintained at about the same level as during the I.G.Y.

Oceanic Research. The oceans cover about seven-tenths of the earth's surface and in a great many respects man's knowledge about them was very incomplete at the end of the 1950s. It had been said that the topography of the surface of the Moon was better known than that of the ocean floor. Not a great deal was known about currents in the oceans below the surface, about the interchange between the deep

Explorer VII, the U.S. satellite launched into orbit from Cape Canaveral, Florida, on Oct. 13, shown partly disassembled. The launching was the last connected with the International Geophysical Year, and was planned to provide data for studies of the earth's weather.

water and surface waters, about the balance between carbon dioxide in the oceans and in the atmosphere, and about the effects of the winds on the circulation of the oceans, etc.

The I.C.S.U. therefore established also a Special Committee on Oceanic Research. This committee made specific recommendations about the continuation of the I.G.Y. oceanographic research and was planning a large-scale international co-operative attack on the scientific problems of the Indian ocean, to be carried out in 1962-63. Not only was the Indian ocean the one about which least was known, but it had a special interest and offered fruitful scope for research because of its two monsoon periods with the changing direction of the winds. Whereas the other oceans are open both to the north and south, the Indian ocean is closed at its northern end. The effect of changing winds on the currents and density layering could thus best be studied. Marine biologists were much interested in the high and varying productivity of different parts of the Arabian sea, where there were shifting populations of important food fishes and frequent catastrophic mass mortalities of fish. These problems were of great economic importance, for the rapid growth in world population meant that mankind would have to depend to an increasing extent upon the harvest of the sea for food supplies.

Space Research. The launching of artificial satellites by the U.S.S.R. and the United States, to supplement the information obtained from instrumented rockets, had opened up a new field of scientific investigation with tremendous potentialities. The launching of satellites was followed by the launching of moon-probes and developments were certain to follow rapidly during the next few years. The I.C.S.U.

appointed a Special Committee on Space Research, whose main purpose was to provide the world scientific community with the means whereby it might exploit the possibilities of satellites and space-probes of all kinds for scientific purposes, and exchange the resulting data on a co-operative basis. This committee, on which all countries with satellite and/or rocket programmes were represented, was concerned only with fundamental scientific research. It was not to concern itself with such technological problems as propulsion, construction of rockets, their guidance and control.

Availability of Data. The data obtained from the continued international co-operation in geophysics were to be stored at the three world data centres set up for the I.G.Y., so that they could be made available to scientists. As the I.G.Y. data would inevitably provide the material for most geophysical researches and investigations for several decades, the work of the data centres was expected to be very heavy. Certain basic data, relating for instance to solar activity, meteorology, geomagnetism, the ionosphere, the aurora and airglow, and cosmic rays, were therefore to be made more readily available by publication in some two dozen or more separate volumes of the *Annals of the I.G.Y.* This would greatly stimulate the analysis and discussion of the material and the investigation of correlations and relationships between the data in different disciplines. Eventually a complete bibliography of the I.G.Y. would be published.

Inter-Union Geophysical Committee. Because of the necessity for adequately terminating the work of the I.G.Y. and the I.G.C. 1959, and the merits of continual international and inter-disciplinary scientific co-operation in the fields of geophysics and related sciences, the I.C.S.U. delegated to the

International Union for Geodesy and Geophysics the authority to establish a committee, to be known by the short title of Inter-Union Geophysical committee. The objects of this committee were: first, to ensure the fullest possible exploitation of the I.G.Y. and I.G.C. 1959 data; and secondly to elaborate plans and to co-ordinate activities for the furtherance of inter-disciplinary co-operation in geophysics and related sciences in the light of experiences gained in the I.G.Y. and I.G.C. 1959. The membership of this committee was selected so that the various interested scientific disciplines were represented on it and so that there was adequate regional representation.

One special project which the Inter-Union Geophysical committee would organize was a World Magnetic survey. The use of aircraft equipped with special magnetometers, and of surface vessels with special equipment, would enable the oceans to be adequately surveyed, while satellites would provide information about the earth's magnetic field at great heights. The observations for such a survey would best be made at a time of minimum solar activity, when large magnetic disturbances would be relatively infrequent. This survey would accordingly be planned to take place at the time of the next solar minimum, which was expected to occur in 1964 or 1965. (See also ANTARCTICA; SPACE EXPLORATION.) (H. S. Js.)

INTERNATIONAL LABOUR ORGANIZATION, THE.

Established on April 11, 1919, as an autonomous institution associated with the League of Nations. Its original constitution was adopted as part XIII of the Treaty of Versailles and formed part of other treaties of peace. The original members of the I.L.O. were the original members of the league, and, later, membership in the league carried with it, but was not necessary for, membership of the organization. An agreement defining the I.L.O. as a specialized agency of the United Nations came into force on Dec. 14, 1946. Thereafter new members were admitted into the I.L.O. if they were members of the United Nations; otherwise they required a two-thirds vote of the delegates of the general conference including two-thirds of the votes cast by government delegates. The following 78 states were members of the I.L.O. at the end of 1959:

Afghanistan	Dominican Rep.	Japan	Rumania
Albania	Ecuador	Jordan	Spain
Argentina	El Salvador	Lebanon	Sudan
Australia	Ethiopia	Liberia	Sweden
Austria	Finland	Libya	*Switzerland
Belgium	France	Luxembourg	Thailand
Bolivia	*German Fed. Rep.	Malaya	Tunisia
Brazil	Ghana	Mexico	Turkey
Bulgaria	Greece	Morocco	Ukraine
Burma	Guatemala	Netherlands	Union of S. Afr.
Byelorussia	Haiti	New Zealand	U.S.S.R.
Canada	Honduras	Nicaragua	United Arab Rep.
Ceylon	Hungary	Norway	United Kingdom
Chile	Iceland	Pakistan	United States
China (Formosa)	India	Panama	Uruguay
Colombia	Indonesia	Persia	Venezuela
Costa Rica	Iraq	Peru	*Vietnam, South
Cuba	Ireland, Rep. of	Philippines	Yugoslavia
Czechoslovakia	Israel	Poland	
Denmark	Italy	Portugal	

* Not a member of the United Nations. On the other hand Cambodia, Guinea, Laos, Nepal, Paraguay, Saudi Arabia and Yemen, although members of the United Nations, do not belong to I.L.O.

The organs of the I.L.O. are the general conference, the governing body and the International Labour office, which is controlled by the governing body. Headquarters, Geneva; director-general, David A. Morse (United States).

History. In 1959 the International Labour organization celebrated its 40th anniversary. Governments throughout the world marked the anniversary with celebrations, and the 43rd general conference of the I.L.O., held during June at Geneva, observed the occasion with a solemn sitting.

More than 900 delegates, advisers and observers from 75 countries and 11 territories attended the conference, at which approximately 170 speakers, including more than a score of labour ministers, discussed the report of the director-general. The report dealt with current problems and trends in employ-

A demonstration of mechanical handling of radioactive materials. Such industrial safety techniques are a concern of I.L.O.

ment and unemployment, in social problems of economic development, and in institutions and social problems. The conference adopted four new international instruments: three conventions dealing with, respectively, minimum age of employment for fishermen, medical examination of fishermen and articles of agreement of fishermen, and a recommendation concerning the occupational health services in places of employment.

Among significant events at the conference was the admission of employer delegates from eastern European nations to technical committees of the conference. These delegates, seated by decision of an impartial board appointed by the conference, had not previously taken part in the work of technical committees as voting members.

In January the I.L.O. opened its fifth field office, at Lagos, Nigeria, to serve the African continent. Other field offices were in Bangalore, India (for Asia); Istanbul (for the near and middle east); Lima (for South America), and Mexico (for Central America, Mexico and the Caribbean). (DD. A. M.)

INTERNATIONAL LAW.

During 1959 John B. Howard of the Ford foundation noted (University of Chicago, *Law Review*, summer 1959, p. 577 ff.) the "considerable measure of common accord" that international law, in its widest sense, was changing its content because of changes in the fields both of technology and of ideology, because of the emergence of new legal problems arising from the increasing number of transnational transactions and because of the shift in the intellectual outlook of international jurists arising from these circumstances. This shift was illustrated in such books as C. W. Jenks's *The Common Law of Mankind* (London, 1958), foreseeing the development of a universal law applicable to individuals as well as to states through comparison of the legal systems in all parts of the world; Sir Hersch Lauterpacht's *The Development of International Law by the International Court* (London, 1958), emphasizing the constructive activity of the court in giving practical effect to generally accepted legal maxims, in applying treaties attributing jural status to individuals and international organizations as well as states, and in reconciling states' sovereignty to the rule of law by practical accommodations; Percy E. Corbett's *Law in Diplomacy* (Princeton, 1959), indicating the practical accommodations of international law to the political interests of governments; and Alejandro Alvarez's *Le Droit International Nouveau* (Paris, 1959), emphasizing the development of " a social international law " to regulate the increasing interdependence of states. International lawyers were, according to Howard, increasingly departing from the positivism of the 19th century and recognizing that, while natural scientists must conceive of an order which is to be discovered, jurists in a dynamic society must conceive of an order which is continuously created. Thus a sharp distinction between law-as-it-is and law-as-it-ought-to-be appeared impossible. Law, as Justice Benjamin Cardozo pointed out, is a continuous process of becoming, and this was especially true of international law in the rapidly changing international society of the 20th century.

Rights and Duties of States. The House of Lords reversed the decision of the Court of Appeals in allowing the high commissioner of Pakistan in London to sue the Westminster bank for a sum of money given to him in trust by the Nizam of Hyderabad. The bank claimed that such a suit would be, in effect, against the Nizam and was barred by the principal of sovereign immunities in national courts, but the House of Lords held that the action for money to which Pakistan and its agent had title was not directly against the Nizam, although the latter might have an equitable interest. It distinguished between a proceeding in which a foreign sovereign was sought to be made a party and a proceeding in which the subject matter was property in which the foreign sovereign claimed an interest. In the latter case, the immunity depended upon whether the prosecution of the claim so affected the interest of the foreign sovereign as to amount to a suit against him (*Rahimtoola* v. *Nizam of Hyderabad and another* [1958] A.C. 379).

The problem of the distribution of the waters of international rivers attracted much attention during 1959. Jurists and governments had generally agreed that some principle of equitable distribution of such waters among states in an international river basin was required by international law, but the extent to which the interests of prior users and the interests of those with great future needs should be reconciled was uncertain. The duty to negotiate in good faith and the value of international procedures to balance such interests was generally recognized (*Am. J. Int. Law 53*, 30, 650). The arbitral award in the *Lake Lanoux* case between France and Spain held that France could not be prevented from utilizing waters in its territory flowing into Spain if due consideration was given to Spanish interests either by supplying waters or paying compensation (*Am. J. Int. Law 53*, 157).

India and Pakistan accepted an apportionment of the Indus river system proposed by the International Bank for Reconstruction and Development. The general subject of international rivers was actively considered by the International Law association and the Institute of International Law.

Nuclear Energy, Outer Space and Polar Regions. The International Atomic Energy agency established its headquarters at Vienna and entered into an agreement with Austria in 1958 establishing immunities from local jurisdiction. The agreement in general followed that of other specialized agencies with the governments in whose territory they had their headquarters but went further in extending privileges and immunities to nongovernmental organizations accredited to the agency (*British Year Book of International Law* [*B.Y.I.L.*] 1958, p. 391). A recent study of this agency's activities indicated a policy of the states providing fissionable materials and atomic isotopes, especially the United States, to operate through bilateral agreements and thus to restrict the scope and effectiveness of the agency's operations (*Com-*

mission to Study the Organization of Peace, 11th Report 1959, p. 17, 217).

Juristic discussion and diplomatic initiatives manifested both an increased interest in the legal regulation of the polar areas and an opinion favourable to their internationalization in some form (Robert D. Hayton, *Am. J. Int. Law 52*, 764). Equally insistent was the demand for adequate international regulation of the high seas and the bed of the sea beyond national domain, and a clear definition of the limits of the national domain. An international conference was called for the spring of 1960 to deal with aspects of this problem on which agreement failed in the Geneva conference of 1958.

Treaties. A convention on the Recognition and Enforcement of Foreign Arbitral awards adopted by a United Nations conference among representatives of 45 states went into effect on June 7, 1959, having been ratified by Israel, Morocco and the United Arab Republic. This convention contributed to the solution of the important problem of maintaining arbitral clauses in concession-contracts made by corporations with foreign governments. While the United States did not participate in the making of this convention, it appeared that it might relax the opposition it had maintained since 1953 towards international legislation by general treaty, at least in this case (G. W. Haight, *The Arbitration Journal*, 14, 73).

War and Aggression. The United Nations had not reached agreement on a definition of aggression, but jurists continued to discuss the question. Some believed that it would be unjust to prevent forcible self-help unless international procedures for assuring just settlement of disputes were firmly established, and they therefore questioned the desirability of defining aggression (Julius Stone, *Aggression and World Order*, Berkeley, 1958). Others believed, with Charles De Visscher, that under current conditions " peace will serve justice better than justice will serve peace " (*Theory and Reality in Public International Law*, Princeton, 1957, p. 328) and that consequently a realization of the U.N. charter policy of preventing aggression by collective security should be pursued, with its implication that the concept of aggression should be clearly defined (Leo Gross, *B.Y.I.L.* 1958, p. 421 ff.). Contributions towards such a definition were made by studies of the generally accepted justifications for the use of force in international relations—self-defence (D. W. Bowett, *B.Y.I.L.* 1958, p. 429), invitation by the country in whose territory force is used (Q. Wright, *Am. J. Int. Law 53*, 112) and the authority of the United Nations as manifested by general assembly resolutions.

On the latter point, Sir Gerald Fitzmaurice, legal adviser of the British Foreign Office, commenting on the international law applied by the International Court of Justice, asserted that: " an Assembly resolution may sometimes, irrespective of strict legality, operate indirectly to authorize, or at any rate to permit certain things to occur with impunity " (*B.Y.I.L.* 1958, p. 5). This seemed to imply that military intervention in pursuance of a general assembly resolution should not itself be regarded as aggression. This approach to a definition suggested that all uses of armed force in international relations in which these justifications could not be successfully urged were to be regarded as aggression. The issue was placed in proper perspective by Hans Kelsen in his authoritative study of *Collective Security under International Law* (Naval War College, International Law Studies, 1954, 1957, p. 58 ff.) which distinguished the legal from the technical and political usages of the term.

War was said to exist against a Nato state within the meaning of a charter party during the Suez invasion by Great Britain and France in 1956 (*Navas Corporation* v. *The Ulysses II*, 161 F. Supp. 932, 1958).

International Adjudication. The European Court of Human Rights was established during the year with Lord McNair, former president of the International Court of Justice, as president, thus completing the structure for the protection of human rights in western Europe initiated by the Council of Europe at the Rome conference in 1953, when the European Human Rights convenant was signed by 15 states. Besides defining human rights this covenant provided for a commission to investigate alleged violations of human rights on individual petition or petition by states, and for adjudication of the legal issues on the initiation of the commission or a state. Individuals were not to have direct access to the court.

The International Court of Justice during the year decided that Sweden did not violate a treaty with the Netherlands in providing for the protective custody of a Dutch child in its territory in accordance with its national law. In the *Interhandel* case between Switzerland and the United States, concerning the taking by the United States of assets of this Swiss corporation on the grounds that they were enemy (German) property, it held that it was not competent because local remedies had not been exhausted. The court also began hearings on the merits of the Portuguese claim of access to the enclaves of Dadrá and Nagar-Aveli, north of Bombay in India (*Am. J. Int. Law 53*, 301, 319, 436, 671).

Belgium, Finland, Turkey and Japan renewed declarations under the optional clause of the International Court of Justice statute for five years. Great Britain did so with extensive reservations and the right of termination on notice, and Sudan did so with a reservation on the U.S. model, excluding cases which it considered within its domestic jurisdiction.

The problem of reservations to such declarations was the subject of much comment during the year. The American Society of International Law in April, the Institute of International Law in September and the Committee on International and Comparative Law of the American Bar association in October, passed resolutions urging withdrawal of destructive reservations such as the Connally reservation, approved by the U.S. senate in 1946, providing for self interpretation of domestic jurisdiction. In the *Interhandel* case certain members of the International Court questioned the validity of such reservations because of the provision of the statute authorizing the court to decide its own jurisdiction. The U.S. attorney-general, William P. Rogers, and President Dwight D. Eisenhower urged withdrawal of the Connally reservation. The Special Committee on World Peace through Law of the American Bar association supported this position and during the year held five conferences on The Rule of Law among Nations. A resolution was introduced in the U.S. senate by Senator Hubert Humphrey of Minnesota to eliminate the Connally reservation.

Codification. At its tenth meeting at Geneva from April to July 1958 the U.N. International Law commission completed a draft convention on arbitral procedure and discussed a preliminary draft on diplomatic intercourse and immunities. At its 11th session in 1959 it gave preliminary consideration to drafts on consular intercourse and immunities, treaties and the responsibility of states for injuries to aliens. It listened to a report of the Harvard Research in International Law on the latter topic (*Am. J. Int. Law 53*, 230).

International Law Meetings. The American Society of International Law met in Washington, D.C., from April 30 to May 2, 1959, and discussed the broad problems of reconciling diverse systems of public order. Attention was given to the need of universality, and the peculiarities of the Islamic, Latin American and other regional systems. The allocation of resources, human rights, international trade, the expropriation of concessions, treaties and intervention during civil strife were also discussed (*Am. J. Int. Law 53*, 668).

The Academy of International Law met at The Hague in July and Aug. 1959 with more than 500 students of 44 nationalities. Lectures were given on fisheries, space law, the strengthening of international law, human rights, rights of states, the International bank and the competence of the U.N. general assembly, as well as on several questions of private international law.

The Institute of International Law met in Neuchâtel, Switzerland, in Sept. 1959 and passed resolutions on the strengthening of the International Court of Justice and the enforcement of foreign arbitral awards. The law of war, with a special reference to the influence upon it of general treaties making aggressive war illegal, was deferred for further study. The International Commission of Jurists met at Delhi in Jan. 1959 and examined the meaning of the rule of law in various civilizations. The International Law association at a meeting of the executive council in London in May 1959 elected Lord McNair chairman. The new British Institute of International and Comparative Law was incorporated in Nov. 1958, the chairman of the board of governors being Lord Denning. (*See* also INTERNATIONAL COURT OF JUSTICE.)   (Q. W.)

INTERNATIONAL MONETARY FUND. The fund was established on Dec. 27, 1945, as a result of the U.N. Monetary and Financial conference held at Bretton Woods, New Hampshire, United States, in July 1944. By Dec. 31, 1959, the following 68 states, with an aggregate quota of $12,662 million, were members:

Afghanistan	Ecuador	Italy	Peru
Argentina	El Salvador	Japan	Philippines
Australia	Ethiopia	Jordan	Saudi Arabia
Austria	Finland	*Korea, South	South Africa
Belgium	France	Lebanon	Spain
Bolivia	*German Fed. Rep.	Libya	Sudan
Brazil	Ghana	Luxembourg	Sweden
Burma	Greece	Malaya	Thailand
Canada	Guatemala	Mexico	Tunisia
Ceylon	Haiti	Morocco	Turkey
Chile	Honduras	Netherlands	United Arab Rep.
China (Formosa)	Iceland	Nicaragua	United Kingdom
Colombia	India	Norway	United States
Costa Rica	Indonesia	Pakistan	Uruguay
Cuba	Iraq	Panama	Venezuela
Denmark	Ireland, Rep. of	Paraguay	*Vietnam, South
Dominican Rep.	Israel	Persia	Yugoslavia

* Not a member of the United Nations.

The I.M.F., while an independent organization, was brought into relationship with the United Nations by the agreement of April 15, 1948. Headquarters, Washington, D.C.; managing director and chairman of the board of executive directors in 1958, Per Jacobsson (Sweden).

History. The applications for membership of Laos and Portugal were approved during the 14th annual meeting in Sept. 1959, but the formalities of membership remained to be completed. The quota of the Philippines was increased on Jan. 30, 1959, from $15 million to $50 million.

A general increase in quotas was initiated at the annual meeting of the governors of the fund held in New Delhi, India, in Oct. 1958. The executive directors subsequently submitted to the governors a report that recommended a general 50% increase in quotas and, in view of relative economic growth and other considerations, higher proportional increases for 17 countries. Countries with small quotas have an opportunity to increase their quotas up to certain stated amounts beyond 50%, and under specified conditions a member might increase its quota by instalments. On Sept. 30, 1959, 42 members of the fund, representing 84% of the fund's quotas as of Jan. 31, 1959, had consented to increases in their quotas by amounts ranging from 50% to 100%; the increase in the German quota exceeded 100%. On Jan. 31, 1959, the fund's assets amounted to the equivalent of $9,200 million and, under the recommended increases, its assets would be enlarged by the equivalent of $5,800 million.

Assets of the fund as of Sept. 30, 1959, were $12,821·6 million, including $2,451·9 million in gold, $9,514·5 million in national currencies (including $2,040 million in U.S. dollars) and $848·8 million in subscriptions receivable from member countries.

In the 12-month period ending Sept. 30, 1959, purchases from the fund were not at the high level of the two previous years, but ten countries drew U.S. dollars, French francs and pounds sterling in an amount equivalent to U.S.$139·8 million.

During the same 12 months, repayments to the fund reached a record level because of the improved reserve positions of several members, and because the repayments to which some members had committed themselves became due. Nineteen countries repurchased amounts of their currencies with gold and dollars totalling $453,722,665, bringing the total repurchases since the beginning of fund operations to $1,781 million, of which $370·4 million was paid in gold and $1,410·7 million in U.S. dollars.

Initial par values had been agreed between the fund and all but 13 of its members. During the year initial par values were agreed with Ghana, Ghanaian pounds 0·357143 per U.S. dollar, Nov. 5, 1958; Spain, Spanish pesetas 60 per U.S.

dollar, July 17, 1959; and Libya, Libyan pounds 0·357143 per U.S. dollar, Aug. 12, 1959. A new par value for the French franc of 493·706 per U.S. dollar was agreed on Dec. 29, 1958.

The fund's net income of $20,494,308 for the fiscal year ended April 30, 1959, was transferred to a general reserve, raising this reserve to $25,584,387. The fund's investment income amounted to $4,108,526 and was transferred to the special reserve account, bringing the total to $6,939,086 as of April 30, 1959. In July 1959 the executive board approved an increase in the fund's investment programme from $200 million to $500 million by a gradual increase of the fund's holdings of U.S. securities up to the latter amount through the sale of gold.

At the 14th annual meeting held in Washington, D.C., Sept. 28-Oct. 2, 1959, the board of governors of the fund accepted the *Annual Report* of the executive directors for the fiscal year ended April 30, 1959. The report stated that the

INTERNATIONAL TRADE
(F.o.b. value in millions of U.S. dollars)   *World Exports by Origin*

Exports from	World*	North America		Latin America		Continental western Europe	Dependencies of continental western Europe	Morocco and Tunisia	Other Europe†	Eastern Europe	
		United States	Canada	Dollar area	Non-dollar area					U.S.S.R.	Other‡
WORLD*	105,112·5	12,870·2	4,703·3	4,775·2	3,363·8	29,548·9	3,509·5	622·7	2,288·6	3,961·7	5,594·5
UNITED STATES:	17,703·9	—	3,337·1	2,930·0	1,121·4	3,193·4	212·0	48·3	365·7	3·1	105·1
CANADA:	5,082·3	3,021·1	—	142·4	47·5	559·9	10·8	1·2	9·6	19·5	3·7
LATIN AMERICAN DOLLAR AREA:	5,059·5	2,640·4	118·4	145·2	214·4	674·2	599·4	14·5	60·3	18·3	1·5
Colombia	454·0	318·0	5·5	4·2	6·5	75·2	24·4	—	4·1	1·8	—
LATIN AMERICAN NON-DOLLAR AREA:	3,044·3	944·0	21·7	48·9	344·6	930·9	26·8	8·1	73·6	21·3	84·3
Argentina	993·9	127·6	5·2	13·4	115·9	380·3	4·3	—	16·7	9·2	38·8
Brazil	1,243·0	534·4	13·6	3·3	143·0	321·5	22·4	7·2	36·1	—	38·7
CONTINENTAL WESTERN EUROPE:	30,072·4	2,255·9	304·4	974·1	965·1	14,496·6	2,139·9	422·2	903·2	317·1	730·6
Belgium-Luxembourg	3,045·7	286·7	34·4	80·0	92·8	1,716·6	144·5	12·6	49·6	17·7	44·5
France	5,121·4	303·9	42·5	93·3	119·2	1,630·2	1,595·3	293·1	141·9	75·7	69·7
German Federal Republic‖	8,808·5	642·9	104·3	341·0	364·1	4,654·7	89·9	28·1	306·0	72·2	205·2
Netherlands	3,217·8	181·1	25·2	86·1	46·4	1,791·0	112·5	15·3	62·1	10·8	40·8
Italy	2,533·1	246·2	30·1	159·8	110·6	1,070·2	32·4	38·3	94·1	31·0	56·8
FRENCH OVERSEAS TERRITORIES:	1,278·4	57·4	1·7	0·4	0·1	1,014·6	71·0	33·8	4·6	4·4	2·4
OTHER OVERSEAS TERRITORIES OF CONT. WESTERN EUROPE:	1,514·4	395·9	41·9	65·3	110·9	470·8	47·9	3·2	14·7	0·6	0·2
Belgian Congo	392·1	56·2	0·3	0·4	0·4	257·2	6·2	0·5	0·3	—	—
STERLING AREA:	20,803·7	1,965·3	741·6	291·3	321·6	4,606·1	274·3	34·8	297·9	198·8	189·6
United Kingdom	8,906·5	770·3	526·7	228·9	193·4	2,142·8	142·6	21·8	198·3	66·3	59·9
Iceland and Ireland	418·5	28·8	2·3	0·8	1·0	39·9	0·1	0·1	7·2	10·8	12·8
Australia, New Zealand, South Africa, Fed. Rhodesia-Nyasaland	3,711·6	293·4	49·9	14·6	11·8	695·2	47·7	0·6	18·6	7·4	54·5
Australia	1,653·8	93·8	29·8	9·7	1·1	324·3	9·3	—	11·2	—	40·1
South Africa	997·0	71·5	6·9	3·1	2·6	186·9	29·8	0·4	4·6	5·1	2·3
Far east independent	2,051·0	260·0	47·8	15·8	30·2	239·8	11·4	4·8	12·9	69·2	27·3
Ceylon	346·8	28·3	16·2	2·0	2·7	35·0	1·3	2·8	0·9	4·1	1·1
India	1,201·0	195·8	31·0	13·2	25·6	99·1	7·9	1·7	4·0	49·3	13·2
Middle east	2,119·6	210·9	13·0	0·4	48·0	823·2	23·4	6·4	32·3	—	1·1
Other sterling area	3,596·5	401·9	101·9	31·2	37·2	665·2	49·1	1·1	28·6	45·1	34·0
Hong Kong	523·0	62·6	9·0	10·9	0·3	29·0	18·8	—			
Malaya (incl. Singapore)	1,217·4	124·0	19·7	17·2	24·1	207·1	6·3	1·0	18·1	44·8	32·0
U.S.S.R.‖:	4,200·0	17·0	3·0	0·5	14·0	350·0	3·0	1·0	190·0	—	2,400·0
OTHER EASTERN EUROPE‡‖:	5,880·0	46·0	9·0	12·0	70·0	925·0	1·5	3·8	179·0	2,130·0	1,540·0
CHINA:	1,800·0	0·1	5·6	1·5	1·0	118·0	4·0	18·0	6·0	910·0	250·0
OTHER EUROPE†:	1,701·7	112·3	7·8	28·4	51·6	667·4	19·0	12·8	19·1	171·9	144·5
Finland	774·6	35·7	0·6	5·0	30·5	273·8	3·5	1·4	9·9	133·7	50·7
Yugoslavia	441·7	33·1	0·6	0·2	4·1	186·4	2·9	1·2	2·6	36·6	87·0
MOROCCO AND TUNISIA:	484·9	9·8	0·2	0·5	1·0	357·4	45·7	2·5	11·7	1·0	7·5
MIDDLE EAST NON-STERLING:	2,471·5	162·3	32·4	3·2	14·3	668·1	31·5	5·8	118·4	121·0	129·4
Egypt	479·7	9·4	0·3	—	0·7	81·5	—	0·5	31·2	83·7	98·6
JAPAN**:	2,876·6	691·5	76·3	117·5	85·2	210·9	16·8	5·5	9·6	15·5	4·9
REST OF FAR EAST:	1,924·0	509·1	2·0	13·8	1·0	271·1	4·8	6·2	2·2	29·2	0·8
Indonesia	755·4	131·4	0·1	2·6	0·1	96·8	0·4	—	0·2	11·2	0·7

FOOTNOTES. * The figures for total exports include certain exports which, because their regions of destination could not be determined, are not included elsewhere in the table, which therefore does not add up. † Spain, Finland and Yugoslavia. ‡ Albania, Bulgaria, Czechoslovakia, Hungary, Poland, Rumania and the German Democratic Republic. § Where exports to Formosa (Taiwan) could not be distinguished from exports to mainland China they are shown as exports to China. ‖ Excludes trade with the German Democratic Republic. ¶ Conversions have been made at 4 roubles to the U.S. dollar. ** Totals include ships exported to Liberia.

establishment of external or non-resident convertibility of the major European currencies in Dec. 1958 was perhaps the most notable step since the end of World War II towards establishing a truly multilateral system of payments. Inflationary pressures had been largely eliminated and the western European countries were able to achieve the monetary conditions necessary for a strong balance of payments position. For the first time since World War II, world industrial production was lower than in the previous year. The volume of world trade fell from 1957 to 1958 by much the same proportion as world industrial production. The value of world exports in 1958 was 5% less than in 1957, and more than half of this decline reflected a fall in prices.　　　　(F. A. Sᴅ.)

INVESTMENTS ABROAD.

The latest full figures for investments overseas relate to 1957. For the United States there have long been available statistics showing both direct investments (foreign physical assets owned by U.S. residents) and portfolio investments (the book value of foreign bonds and shares owned by U.S. residents). Table I gives the latest information on these holdings. But for the United Kingdom, and indeed most other countries, the information is much more sketchy.

TABLE I.　U.S. Pʀɪᴠᴀᴛᴇ Iɴᴠᴇsᴛᴍᴇɴᴛs Aʙʀᴏᴀᴅ
($ million at year ends)

	1950	1955	1957	1958
Book value of direct investments	11,788	19,313	25,252	27,075
Portfolio investments	4,333	5,481	5,919	...

Sᴏᴜʀᴄᴇ.　U.N., *The International Flow of Private Capital, 1956-58* (1959). U.S. Department of Commerce, *Survey of Current Business.*

United Kingdom. Until 1959 virtually the only figures available were those published annually by the Bank of England. These showed total U.K. foreign investments to be only about £2,100 million at the end of 1957 (virtually unchanged since end of 1956), but these figures were known to be a gross underestimate of both direct and portfolio investment. The Radcliffe committee inquiries led in 1959 to the publication

and Destination, 1958

(F.o.b. value in millions of U.S. dollars)

Middle East (non-sterling area)	Sterling area							China§	Other far east		Exports ← to
	Total	United Kingdom	Iceland and Ireland	Australia, New Zealand, South Africa, Fed. Rhodesia-Nyasaland	Far east independent	Middle east	Other		Japan	Other§	Exports from ↓
2,416·4	21,823·9	9,451·1	560·0	4,177·4	2,830·1	1,042·8	3,762·5	1,738·7	2,569·7	2,612·6	WORLD*
382·2	2,224·3	820·4	42·3	492·9	453·4	120·6	294·7	—	831·7	822·8	Uɴɪᴛᴇᴅ Sᴛᴀᴛᴇs
13·1	1,112·5	805·6	9·1	126·2	104·9	1·3	65·4	7·3	108·8	23·6	.Cᴀɴᴀᴅᴀ
8·4	387·7	295·1	6·6	8·8	5·0	5·1	67·1	4·7	163·0	5·6	. Lᴀᴛɪɴ Aᴍᴇʀɪᴄᴀɴ Dᴏʟʟᴀʀ Aʀᴇᴀ
—	11·8	7·8		0·1	—		3·9		1·2	1·2	. Colombia
											Lᴀᴛɪɴ Aᴍᴇʀɪᴄᴀɴ Nᴏɴ-Dᴏʟʟᴀʀ
18·3	440·9	399·2	10·4	12·4	8·9	0·5	9·5	7·9	59·1	12·3	. . . . . AREA
1·1	256·6	238·6	7·8	3·2	2·2	0·2	4·8	0·4	24·9	3·7	. . . . . Argentina
12·2	72·3	53·6	1·8	6·7	5·2	0·5	4·5	7·5	24·5	6·8	. . . . . Brazil
855·6	4,485·6	2,310·4	100·7	680·1	652·0	245·0	497·4	375·8	176·4	426·2	Cᴏɴᴛɪɴᴇɴᴛᴀʟ Wᴇsᴛᴇʀɴ Eᴜʀᴏᴘᴇ
70·9	366·2	173·8	11·6	54·9	54·3	27·6	44·0	52·1	18·2	25·8	. . . Belgium-Luxembourg
118·3	465·6	250·6	8·5	55·7	76·3	22·0	52·5	44·4	16·2	94·7	. . . . . France
331·9	1,214·8	347·9	29·8	276·9	339·2	78·7	142·3	162·4	83·1	141·3	. German Federal Republic‖
68·7	635·9	382·9	17·3	65·4	30·4	25·8	114·1	11·9	13·1	61·6	. . . . . Netherlands
123·9	402·4	173·2	4·1	58·7	60·8	52·7	52·9	32·6	8·0	56·5	. . . . . Italy
3·6	51·5	31·7	0·8	2·4	0·4	—	16·2	—	15·4	1·6	Fʀᴇɴᴄʜ Oᴠᴇʀsᴇᴀs Tᴇʀʀɪᴛᴏʀɪᴇs
											Oᴛʜᴇʀ Oᴠᴇʀsᴇᴀs Tᴇʀʀɪᴛᴏʀɪᴇs ᴏғ
7·0	260·7	150·4	5·6	28·3	21·5	0·3	54·6	5·0	9·6	4·0	Cᴏɴᴛ. Wᴇsᴛᴇʀɴ Eᴜʀᴏᴘᴇ
1·6	53·8	38·1	—	9·9	2·3	—	3·5	—	0·4	0·8	. . . . . Belgian Congo
479·4	9,520·0	3,507·7	337·3	2,460·4	1,002·6	401·7	1,810·3	213·9	704·9	547·5	. . . . Sᴛᴇʀʟɪɴɢ Aʀᴇᴀ
304·2	3,999·7	—	314·2	1,684·0	639·0	249·8	1,112·7	74·8	54·3	89·7	. . . . United Kingdom
0·8	312·0	304·1		0·8	0·9	—	5·7		0·2	0·4	. . . . Iceland and Ireland
											Australia, New Zealand, South Africa, Fed. Rhodesia-Nyasaland
13·9	2,003·1	1,350·5	4·8	362·5	60·5	10·4	214·4	30·1	235·6	30·7	. . . . . Australia
5·0	843·5	491·2	4·5	141·6	40·7	8·9	156·6	27·2	205·3	23·6	. . . . . South Africa
8·9	490·0	296·1	0·1	151·2	2·1	1·5	39·0	1·5	13·5	4·9	. . . Far east independent
90·0	1,029·6	532·2	12·4	128·2	175·6	59·1	122·1	40·1	113·6	49·9	. . . . . Ceylon
18·3	202·7	118·7	1·6	49·7	10·0	19·0	3·7	16·3	7·8	1·0	. . . . . India
66·9	605·3	342·1	9·6	62·5	69·4	35·0	86·7	7·7	55·6	24·1	. . . Middle east
57·1	639·0	390·3	1·5	100·6	30·8	65·8	50·0	0·1	112·8	43·3	. . . Other sterling area
13·4	1,537·6	930·6	3·9	184·3	95·8	16·6	306·4	68·8	188·0	333·5	. . . Hong Kong
0·1	210·6	68·8	—	23·7	10·9	9·0	98·2	27·3	21·0	124·0	. Malaya (incl. Singapore)
4·6	365·2	166·3	0·1	69·6	47·5	4·3	77·4	38·1	115·0	196·4	
150·0	255·0	160·0	11·0	2·0	80·0	1·0	1·0	610·0	14·0	25·0	. . . U.S.S.R.¶
150·0	235·0	140·0	16·0	16·0	46·0	8·0	9·0	355·0	2·0	45·0	.Oᴛʜᴇʀ Eᴀsᴛᴇʀɴ Eᴜʀᴏᴘᴇ‡¶
30·0	290·0	47·0	0·7	13·0	45·0	0·3	184·0	—	61·0	40·0	. . . CHINA
64·3	341·9	279·5	11·7	14·2	23·6	2·5	10·4	13·1	10·7	5·8	. . Oᴛʜᴇʀ Eᴜʀᴏᴘᴇ†
17·0	199·4	167·5	9·1	11·7	7·8	0·5	2·8	8·4	1·2	1·4	. . . . . Finland
25·2	51·4	34·7	—	0·1	12·6	1·8	2·2	4·6	—	0·4	. . . . . Yugoslavia
1·5	36·9	25·7	1·4	4·4	0·3	1·3	3·8	2·8	2·0	2·5	. . Mᴏʀᴏᴄᴄᴏ ᴀɴᴅ Tᴜɴɪsɪᴀ
131·9	793·3	245·8	0·4	154·9	148·9	192·5	50·8	42·5	170·7	42·6	Mɪᴅᴅʟᴇ Eᴀsᴛ Nᴏɴ-Sᴛᴇʀʟɪɴɢ
37·9	48·1	20·6	—	2·0	18·3	6·7	0·5	34·7	30·1	21·2	. . . . . Egypt
91·6	758·6	98·0	5·9	110·5	187·3	53·3	303·6	56·1	—	494·6	. . . JAPAN**
29·5	630·8	130·1	0·1	50·6	47·0	12·4	390·6	45·1	239·7	115·9	Rᴇsᴛ ᴏғ Fᴀʀ Eᴀsᴛ
0·4	382·1	93·8	0·1	48·1	17·3	—	222·8	39·3	27·4	43·3	. . . . . Indonesia

Gᴇɴᴇʀᴀʟ Nᴏᴛᴇ.　The symbol — indicates less than $50,000 *or* not applicable.　The data for most countries represent the official export figures, converted to U.S. dollars.　Where official figures were not available, estimates, based on imports reported by partner countries and on other subsidiary data, were used.　The figures of total exports from and to the U.S.S.R., other eastern Europe and China are not comparable with those given in *Britannica Book of the Year 1959*, since no recent data were then available on the trade of these countries with one another.

Sᴏᴜʀᴄᴇ.　U.N. *Monthly Bulletin of Statistics.*

of new information on the current flow of funds (*see* below) which themselves make the bank's figures seem meaningless, and also produced an estimate of the private portfolio of dollar securities held in the United Kingdom—$4,000 million at market prices—much greater than the bank's figures would suggest (*Committee on the Working of the Monetary System, Report*, Cmnd. 827, H.M.S.O., London, 1959). For a useful comparison between the United States and the United Kingdom (which together accounted for by far the major portion of current investment abroad) it is necessary, therefore, to examine the annual additions to the stocks of investments—the flow of funds.

Table II shows the activities of the United States and the United Kingdom between 1952 and 1957. It can be seen that the outflow was considerable from both countries, but that, reasonably enough in view of differences in national income, etc., the U.S. figures were usually larger by a factor of nearly three. The Radcliffe committee in fact voiced some doubts as to the wisdom, from the point of view of the United Kingdom, of such large investment abroad; perhaps the resources could be more profitably used at home.

TABLE II. UNITED KINGDOM AND UNITED STATES: OUTFLOW OF NEW FUNDS AND REINVESTED PROFITS FOR DIRECT INVESTMENT, 1952-57
($ million)

	1952	1954	1956	1957
*United Kingdom**				
Private funds	672	896	1,176	1,092
Government loans . .	64	73	59	84
United States†				
Private funds	1,726	1,308	2,813	3,089
Government loans . .	...	...	190	380

* Estimates are extremely uncertain and are minimum estimates; the true figures are probably much higher. † Figures exclude very substantial government grants.
SOURCE. U.N., *The International Flow of Private Capital, 1956-58* (1959); *Committee on the Working of the Monetary System, Report*, Cmnd. 827 (H.M.S.O., London, 1959).

The U.K. figures in Table II are gross; *i.e.*, they reflect transactions in one direction only. In fact, during this period there was very considerable foreign (largely U.S.) investment in the United Kingdom. In the period 1952-58 gross private investment outwards from the United Kingdom was over £2,300 million, while foreign investment inwards was about £900 million, leaving a figure for net U.K. investment abroad of only £1,400 million (these and subsequent figures come from information given by the U.K. Treasury). Thus Table II overestimates the extent of net acquisition of foreign assets by the United Kingdom, although (within the limits of accuracy of the figures) it reflects correctly the contribution of U.K. investors to foreign developments.

Direction of U.K. Investment. Of a total (recorded) U.K. gross foreign private investment of £2,300 million between 1952 and 1958, £1,453 million went to the rest of the sterling area (R.S.A.), while of the remainder perhaps nearly £250 million went to Canada; thus about 70% of U.K. private investment funds flowed to the Commonwealth and associated territories.

The United Kingdom, then, invested abroad about £330 million gross a year between 1952 and 1958, and was itself a gross borrower of about £130 million a year. Borrowings and lendings by the United Kingdom outside the sterling area were roughly in balance, thus U.K. net investment was directed very largely to the sterling area. Its investment of £120 million a year in the dollar area and elsewhere was largely direct investment, very often connected with export trade, and it was offset by U.S. investment in the United Kingdom of nearly £100 million a year. However, it must be remembered that unofficial transactions might well have been so large that the United Kingdom was nevertheless a net investor even outside the sterling area.

Investment in the Commonwealth. Although published statistics are very inadequate, some estimates can be made of the distribution of the £250 million a year that the United Kingdom was investing in the Commonwealth and sterling area. The colonial territories took perhaps between £40 million and £50 million a year (half their total inflow of private capital; the other half coming from non-Commonwealth sources); the Federation of Rhodesia and Nyasaland about £25 million a year; Canada £45 million a year; Australia and New Zealand together £60 million a year; and the rest went to India, South Africa, etc.

It may be noted that the United Kingdom appears to have been the biggest foreign investor in both India, where in 1956 it owned £305 million out of total foreign-owned assets of £380 million, and South Africa.

Australia was a net recipient of foreign investment funds in the 1950s; in the four years ending 1958 private and official loans to Australia averaged about £A90 million a year, of which perhaps half came from the United Kingdom. New Zealand received about £NZ30 million net per year.

Income from Investments. The Bank of England figure for interest and dividends earned on U.K. overseas investments in 1957 was £218·8 million; but this figure refers only to the small portfolio of securities of which the bank took official cognizance. The Treasury figures in Table III (which excludes

TABLE III. U.K. GROSS EARNINGS FROM OVERSEAS INVESTMENTS, 1956-59*
(£ million)

	1956	1957	1958	1959†
From rest of sterling area . .	237	225	207	209
From dollar area . . .	81	83	83	80
From O.E.E.C. countries . .	28	28	28	28
Other	35	29	26	21
Total	381	365	344	338

* Private and government accounts combined. † An estimate based on actual figures for Jan.-June 1959.
SOURCE. *U.K. Balance of Payments 1956-1959*. Cmnd. 861 (H.M.S.O., London, 1959).

shipping and oil companies) purport to include " so far as possible " profits retained overseas for reinvestment; there is reason to believe, however, that coverage of reinvestment is not complete. Even so, the contrast with the bank's figure is striking.

Between 1956 and 1959 nearly two-thirds of U.K. investment income came from the R.S.A.; and it was seen above that about the same proportion of U.K. current lending went to the R.S.A.; nevertheless, the steady flow of investment income from the dollar area to the United Kingdom was quite large—equal, in 1958, to 8% of total U.K. current account receipts from the dollar area.

It may be noted that, during the period 1956-59, the United Kingdom's total earnings from past investments were, in aggregate, about equal to the total outflow of new funds for investments; the United Kingdom was " ploughing back " earnings at the rate of about 100%. The United States, in the same period, was investing less than its investment income, attaining a " 100% plough-back " only in 1957. The contrast is heightened by the fact that the United Kingdom was paying, during the period, investment income to foreigners equal to 75% of its own gross receipts.

Contrast with Internal Investment. The United Kingdom, by 1959, was investing abroad at a rate equal to more than 20% of its net capital formation at home. Yet while home investment had frequently been limited (by monetary policy, etc.) for balance of payments reasons, comparable restrictions do not seem to have been so effectively applied on investment abroad. Irrespective of the relative merits of home and foreign investment, the new figures available place the history of the 1950s in a somewhat new light.

United States. After reaching a peak of $3,175 million in 1957, private capital outflows from the United States declined to $2,844 million in 1958 and there was a further decline in the first half of 1959. Whereas in 1958 a sharp cutback in direct investment flows was offset by larger portfolio investments, especially in the first half of the year, in 1959 direct investments were expanding more rapidly while purchases of foreign bonds and lending by banks declined because of the relatively high interest rates prevailing in the United States. Nevertheless, the combined rate of outflow, together with reinvested foreign earnings and some gains in the market values of foreign securities, brought the value of U.S. private foreign investments to $40,800 million by the beginning of 1959. Earnings of U.S. private foreign investments declined by about 10% in 1958 to $3,370 million, with most of the drop attributable to lower earnings of petroleum enterprises.

In the first half of 1959 the net outflow of direct investment capital from the United States was about $630 million and the total for the year seemed likely to exceed the $1,094 million recorded in 1958. In both 1958 and 1959 the petroleum industry found that it was developing available supplies at a faster rate than demand, and also faced rising taxes and costs in producing areas. These factors reduced earnings and also brought some rescheduling of investment programmes. However, significant new discoveries of reserves in north Africa and Canada, and major programmes for expanding refineries and pipelines in Europe, appeared certain to keep investment expenditures high. By the beginning of 1959 this industry had foreign holdings with a book value of $9,681 million, an increase of about $700 million over the previous year. U.S. manufacturing companies also continued to expand their foreign production facilities. Investments in this field increased by about $600 million in 1958, bringing the total to $8,485 million. Mining companies also were planning large outlays to develop new sources for iron ore, bauxite and other minerals.

The pace of investment by U.S. companies in Canada slackened somewhat in 1958, in line with some reduction in general economic activity in that country. About $600 million was added to direct investments in 1958. U.S. companies had increased their holdings in Latin America by a record of $1,266 million in 1957, but the increase in 1958 was down to $405 million and the outlook in 1959 did not indicate any substantial improvement.

As economic activity in most countries of western Europe began to expand in early 1959, the flow of capital from U.S. companies increased significantly. U.S. direct investments in the area in the first half of 1959 appeared to have equalled the amount for the entire year 1958 (about $400 million). U.S. direct investments in France increased by $70 million in 1958 and a great variety of projects was reported in 1959, including U.S. participation in a $100 million pipeline to carry crude oil produced in north Africa and the middle east from Marseilles to northeast France and into the German Federal Republic. Nearly $80 million was added to U.S. direct investments in the German Federal Republic in 1958 and Italy received more than $30 million. U.S. direct investments in the United Kingdom expanded at a somewhat slower rate in 1958 than in the previous two years, but turned upwards strongly in 1959. Aluminium companies accounted for two major transactions, with the Reynolds Metals company acquiring a controlling interest in the British Aluminium company, while the Aluminum Company of America formed a joint company with Imperial Chemical Industries to manufacture aluminium products.

U.S. investors added a further $100 million to their stake in middle east petroleum resources in 1958, as production rose sharply. Substantial sums continued to be invested in 1959 to improve production facilities, although earnings were adversely affected by lower prices and governments in the area continued to exert pressure for a larger share of earnings.

Investments in north Africa expanded rapidly as very large petroleum reserves were being explored and developed. About $130 million was added to U.S. direct investments in the far east in 1958, with more than half the total going to Australia. The flow to Australia continued high in 1959, with new projects including a $50 million petrochemical industry in which the Standard-Vacuum Oil company and the Union Carbide corporation were to join with Australian firms.

The U.S. government subscribed an additional $1,375 million to the International Monetary fund in 1959 and its commitments to the International Bank for Reconstruction and Development were increased by $3,175 million. An International Development association was suggested for the purpose of making loans largely repayable in currencies of the borrowers, and the United States agreed to participate in the proposed Inter-American Development bank. The Development Loan fund was entering into sizable operations in 1959, and the Export-Import bank began to lend local currencies acquired under surplus disposal programmes to foreign subsidiaries of U.S. companies.

Although foreign investors placed only about $24 million of new capital in long-term investments in the United States in 1958, foreign holdings of corporate stocks rose by more than $2,000 million through price increases. Foreign holdings of liquid dollar assets rose by about $1,000 million in 1958, even though foreign countries used $2,294 million to purchase gold in the U.S. (*See* also BALANCE OF PAYMENTS.)

(M. V. P. ; S. PR.)

IRAN: *see* PERSIA.

IRAQ. Arab republic, bounded N.W. by Syria, N. by Turkey, E. by Persia, S.E. by Kuwait and the Persian gulf, S. by Saudi Arabia and W. by Jordan. Area: 171,604 sq.mi., incl. 91,019 sq.mi. in the 14 settled *liwas* (provinces). Pop.: (1947 census revised, *liwas* only) 4,816,185; (1957 census) 6,538,109. Language: Arabic 77%; Kurdish 15%; others 8%. Religion: Moslem 94%; Christian 3%. Chief towns (pop., 1957 census): Baghdad (cap.) 656,399; Mosul 179,646; Basra 164,623. Prime minister, Brigadier Abd-ul-Karim Kassem. Main imports: iron and steel goods, electrical machinery, motor vehicles and parts, sugar, tea, artificial silk piecegoods. Main export: crude oil. Monetary unit: *dinar* (=£1 sterling).

History. The year 1959 was characterized by Brigadier Abd-ul-Karim Kassem's attempt to steer a middle course both internally and externally—internally, by curbing the opposing forces of Communism and pro-Egyptian Arab nationalism, which had been struggling to obtain control of the new regime, and externally, by pursuing a policy of neutrality. In the first half of the year, he struck openly at the nationalists. The cabinet was reshuffled so as to exclude all those with nationalist sympathies, and their chief representative in the army, Colonel Abd-ul-Salam Aref (who had collaborated with Kassem in carrying out the revolution of July 14, 1958, and had been for some time deputy prime minister), was tried on a charge of treason and sentenced to death. The quarrel with the United Arab Republic became extremely bitter, and inside Iraq the Communists seemed to be gaining the upper hand. Early in March, the nationalists, acting through a section of the army in Mosul led by Colonel Abd-ul-Wahhab Shawwaf, rose in revolt against the government. The rebellion, which apparently received some support from the U.A.R., was unsuccessful, and its leaders were tried and executed. This encouraged the Communists, who shortly afterwards murdered a number of their opponents at Kirkuk. Kassem then began to deal severely with the Communists, many of whom were rounded up and imprisoned. Those implicated in the Kirkuk massacre were put on trial, some being sentenced to death. The Communist leaders made a public confession of their " error " in taking matters too much into their own hands and affirmed their loyalty to Kassem and the republic. The apparent drift of Iraq towards Communism was thus halted, and Kassem's control of the internal situation seemed, for the time being at least, to be firmly established. He, moreover, still refused to admit any Communists into his cabinet on the grounds that political parties were banned and could not therefore be represented in the government.

In its determination to achieve complete independence from the west and extricate itself from all the commitments of the former regime, Iraq relinquished its membership of the Baghdad pact in March. This led to the withdrawal of R.A.F. personnel from their base at Habbaniya. In June Iraq left the sterling area. However, relations with the Iraq Petroleum company (representing the major western commercial interest in the country) continued, despite certain restrictions, to be friendly, and there was no indication that the Iraqi government intended as yet to nationalize the oil industry. Iraq also asked for, and received in June, a delivery of arms from Britain. Later, talks were initiated with a view to concluding a cultural agreement between the two countries, which would provide for the training of Iraqi teachers in Great Britain. Yet the contracts of some British engineering firms carrying out development work in Iraq were terminated, and Soviet personnel were called in to complete the enterprises concerned, and to help Iraq generally with its economic development. An agreement was concluded with the U.S.S.R., whereby the latter undertook to provide Iraq with a credit of £50 million and supply a large number of technicians. The Development board set up under the previous regime was replaced by a Ministry of Planning.

In early October an attempt was made on Kassem's life, but he escaped with minor injuries. Many arrests were made, but the assailants were not identified, although the Iraqi press said that they were pro-Egyptian nationalists. (E. S. A.)

See Caractacus, *Revolution in Iraq* (London, 1959).

IRELAND, NORTHERN: *see* NORTHERN IRELAND.

IRELAND, REPUBLIC OF. Republic having *c.* 85% of the area (south, centre and northwest; 26 of the 32 counties) and *c.* 67% of the population of the whole of Ireland. Area: 26,600 sq.mi. Pop.: (1951 census) 2,960,593; (1956 census) 2,898,264; (1957 est.) 2,853,000. Language: English *c.* 76%, Erse (Gaelic) *c.* 24%. Religion (1946 census): Roman Catholic 94·2%; Anglican 4·2%; Presbyterian 0·8%; Methodist 0·3%; Jewish 0·1%. Chief towns (pop., 1956 census): Dublin (cap.) 539,476; Cork 80,011; Limerick 50,886. Presidents in 1959: Seán T. O'Kelly (Seán T. Ó. Ceallaigh) and (from June 25) Éamon de Valera. Prime ministers in 1959: Éamon de Valera and (from June 23) Seán F. Lemass. Main imports: machinery and vehicles, foodstuffs, petroleum products. Main exports: livestock, food, beverages, wool and hair. Monetary unit: Irish pound (=£1 sterling).

History. At the end of 1958 an autumn session of the Dail was held as usual. Its deliberations were restricted to one main subject, a government bill to change the electoral system from proportional representation based on the single transferable vote and multi-member constituencies, to single-member divisions and single nontransferable votes. The government expected to get the measure through all stages in both Dail and Senate before Christmas. However, the opposition parties opposed the bill strongly and it became necessary to recall the deputies immediately after Christmas in order to deal with its final stages. There was further strenuous opposition, but the measure was eventually adopted by the Dail and sent to the Senate.

After several weeks of debate the upper house rejected the bill by one vote. This could only delay the bill since the government and the Dail refused to accept its rejection. At the expiry of the period prescribed by the constitution it would automatically become an act of parliament, but as it involved an amendment to the constitution it had to be submitted to a referendum.

A presidential election took place in 1959. The outgoing president, Seán T. O'Kelly, having served two terms was ineligible for re-election. The Fianna Fail party nominated the prime minister, Éamon de Valera, as candidate. Fine Gael, the principal opposition party, nominated General Seán McEoin, who had been minister for defence in the previous coalition government.

The government decided to hold the presidential election and the referendum on the same day. The opposition groups strongly objected to this on the grounds that many electors would be confused about the issues involved. May 19 was chosen as polling day. There were approximately 1·8 million names on the electoral lists and about 50% of the electorate voted. De Valera was elected president by a majority of 120,000 over his opponent. The bill to change the electoral system was defeated by 486,989 votes to 453,229.

De Valera immediately resigned office as prime minister and was formally installed as president on June 22. Seán F. Lemass, vice-premier and minister for industry and commerce, was elected prime minister by the Dail. He appointed John Lynch, minister for education, to follow him as minister for industry and commerce. Erskine Childers, the minister for lands, became minister for transport and power. Seán MacEntee, the minister for health, was appointed vice-premier.

In the earlier part of the year there was a notable falling off of hostile raids in Northern Ireland organized within the territory of the Republic of Ireland and the government of the republic released most of the persons interned on suspicion of engagement in illegal activities. The summer was quiet but there were some disturbing incidents in early autumn.

The monthly trade returns showed a progressive increase of the adverse balance on visible external trade which by September had reached £61 million. As far as invisible trade was concerned, substantial amounts accrued from tourist traffic, interest on external investments, emigrant remittances and other sources on which the country relied to balance the over-all trading account. The bulk of both visible and invisible trading was as usual transacted with Britain and Northern Ireland. Revenue returns for the fiscal year ended March 31, 1959, showed a slight excess of receipts over expenditure. The budget submitted for the ensuing year was based on the assumption that revenue would be at least equally buoyant and would yield a modest credit balance allowing for a reduction of income tax as well as tax concessions on the profits of industries engaged in export trade. Generally speaking, the budget was favourably received by

Mgr. Riberi (centre), *the new papal nuncio to the Irish republic, with F. Aiken the foreign minister, and the archbishop of Dublin.*

the business and industrial sections of the community. The principal criticism directed against it in the Dail and in some banking circles was that its equilibrium was obtained by a certain amount of book-keeping manipulation. It was argued that on the expenditure side certain current charges were treated as capital outlay and that on the revenue side non-recurrent payments which should be regarded as capital were classified as income. The criticism was also heard in relation to the accounts for 1958-59. Chief revenue heads were income and property taxes and customs and excise duties.

After agriculture, tourism again proved to be the most important source of invisible earnings in balancing the visible external trade deficit. All through the season from April to October the weather favoured holiday-making and many foreign visitors went to the recognized resorts. There were fewer arrivals by air at Shannon, particularly of the kind of people who would generally spend a few days in Ireland before or after visiting the continent of Europe.

The twin problems of unemployment and emigration remained unsolved. Fewer names were on the unemployed registers than in previous years, but it was not known to what extent this was due to emigration. Emigration which declined in 1958 compared with 1957 again reached the average per annum since the end of World War II. Emigration was most marked in the rural areas. This was not a new experience, but had been the pattern of Irish emigration for many years.

(D. J. R.)

IRON AND STEEL. The two main influences on iron and steel production in 1959 were the recovery from the economic recession of the previous year, which brought an increase in demand for the products of the industry, and the prolonged steel strike in the United States, which cut production drastically in the largest steel producing country of the world. As an example of the former may be cited the trend of industrial output in the six countries of the European Coal and Steel community which rose by 9% in 1956 and by 7% in 1957, but which, in 1958, rose by only 3%, and in the first quarter of 1959, 2%. In the last quarter output rose again by 7%. During 1959, there was in consequence a material rise in the demand for steel in the six countries, and steel output rose to 62·5 million tons—7% above 1958. The same trend was noticed in other producing countries, including the United States in the first half of the year. Demand from importing countries also rose in response to economic recovery and there was a substantial increase in exports from western Europe and Japan.

Despite this upward trend in demand and production world production, at some 285 million tons, was still below the 1957 peak, though it rose by some 18 million tons (7%) above 1958. This rather mediocre result, in the face of renewed economic expansion, was due to the long and bitter dispute between steel employers and unions in the United States where production in the first half year, at 57·5 million tons, was a record, but, in the second half year amounted to only 15 million tons. World capacity in 1959 was some 370 million tons—an increase of 30 million tons over 1958.

This enormous gap, 85 million tons, between output and capacity, was to a large extent a reflection of the loss of some 40 million tons of output in the United States. The remainder was chiefly accounted for by the under-utilization of plant in the main producing countries in the earlier part of the year. By the end of the year, the Japanese steel industry was at full stretch and west European producers were making fairly full use of their capacity. Indeed, signs of renewed tension in the steel market were making an appearance at the end of the year, particularly in overseas markets. Importing countries, for whom the market had eased considerably in the previous 18 months, were caught somewhat unprepared by the resur-

TABLE I. WORLD PRODUCTION OF IRON ORE*
('000 metric tons)

	Metal Content	1938	1956	1957	1958
U.S.S.R.	(60%)	27,800	78,000	84,240	88,800
United States†	(50%)	28,908	99,420	107,856	69,048
France	(35%)	33,048	52,692	57,768	59,460
Sweden	(60%)	13,932	18,948	19,920	18,600
Venezuela	(65%)	—	11,100	15,384	15,480
United Kingdom	(30%)	12,084	16,500	17,172	14,868‡
Canada§	(55%)	...	20,280	20,232	14,112
German Fed. Rep.	(30%)	10,080‖	12,216	13,140	12,636
Luxembourg	(30%)	5,136	7,596	7,848	6,636
India	(65%)	2,784	4,980	5,160	5,796
Spain	(50%)	2,544	4,404	5,232	4,908
Brazil	(70%)	368¶	4,080	3,996	...
Austria	(30%)	2,664	3,252	3,492	3,408
Malaya	(60%)	1,642	2,484	3,024	2,844
Czechoslovakia	(30%)	1,750	2,544	2,808	2,796
Peru	(60%)	—	2,688	3,576	2,592
Chile	(60%)	1,608	2,664	2,700	...
Australia**	...	1,509	2,584	2,505	...
Algeria	(55%)	3,060	2,580	2,796	2,304
Union of S. Africa	(60-65%)	504	2,064	2,076	2,208
Poland‡‡	(34%)	947	1,968	1,992	2,172
Japan††	(55%)	841	1,908	2,244	2,004
Yugoslavia	(50%)	607	1,728	1,872	1,992
Norway	(65%)	1,355	1,550	1,548	1,765§§
Morocco	(55%)	1,604	1,668	1,872	1,536
German Dem. Rep.‖	(30%)	...	1,756	1,478	1,506
Sierra Leone	(60%)	876	1,332	1,344	1,440¶
Italy	(50%)	1,006	1,687	1,588	1,291
Tunisia	(55%)	771	1,169	1,175	1,104
Philippines	(55%)	920	1,440	1,346	1,099

* Only countries with a yearly marketable extraction exceeding 1·1 million tons are specified. † Excl. manganiferous iron ores. ‡ Year of 53 weeks. §§ Shipments. ‖ Gross production. ¶ Exports. ** Incl. iron sand. ‡‡ Incl. pyrites. §§ Incl. ferro-titanium (9% of total in 1957).
SOURCE. U.N. *Statistical Yearbook 1958*; U.N. *Monthly Bulletin of Statistics.*

TABLE II. WORLD PRODUCTION OF PIG IRON AND FERRO-ALLOYS*
('000 metric tons)

	1938	1956	1957	1958
WORLD	82,500	201,077	211,200	186,500†
United States	19,475	70,461	73,409	52,416‡
U.S.S.R.§	14,652	35,754	37,038	39,000
German Fed. Rep.	15,180	17,692	18,470	16,752
United Kingdom	6,869	13,406	14,512‖	13,188‖¶
France	6,056	11,640	12,077	12,144
Japan	2,677	6,264	7,134	7,692
Belgium	2,426	5,761	5,588	5,520
China (People's Rep.)	900**	4,777	5,500	...
Poland‖	880	3,506	3,682	3,864
Czechoslovakia§	1,323	3,282	3,563	3,768
Luxembourg	1,551	3,316	3,368	3,288
Saar	2,411	3,031	3,168	3,108
Canada	774	3,455	3,582	2,880
Australia††§	945	1,942	2,132	2,280
Italy	928	1,994	2,205	2,172
India	1,577‡‡	1,989	1,942	2,148
Austria	554	1,738	1,962	1,824
German Dem. Rep.	200§§	1,574	1,663§	1,776§
Union of S. Africa	294	1,357	1,419	1,583
Spain	442	944	999	1,342
Sweden	714	1,411	1,545	1,298§
Hungary	335	768	836	1,100
Netherlands	267	662	701	913
Yugoslavia	116	647	737	780
Rumania	133	583	686	...
Norway	174	452	557	508
Mexico§	98	409	414‖	478‖
Chile§	—	368	382	306
Turkey	—	216	218	230

* Only countries with a yearly production exceeding 200,000 tons are specified. † Excl. China. ‡ Excl. production in electric furnaces. § Excl. ferro-alloys. ‖ Excl. production in electric furnaces of ferro-alloys. ¶ Year of 53 weeks. ** Manchuria only. †† Year ended May 31. ‡‡ Excl. direct castings. §§ 1936.
SOURCE. U.N. *Statistical Yearbook 1958*; U.N. *Monthly Bulletin of Statistics.*

gence of home demand in producing countries and by the intractable nature of the U.S. industrial dispute, which both deprived them of a source of imports and gave them a new competitor in the quest for supplies. In the home markets of the main producing countries too, signs of strain were developing at the end of the year. Over the previous 18 months, consumers had gradually adjusted their stocks downwards as industrial activity slackened and as producers'

H. Peake, chairman of the Steel Company of Wales, lights up the new £7 million blast furnace at the company's Margam works on May 8. One of the three biggest in the world, the furnace is 248 ft. high with a hearth diameter of 31 ft. Its capacity will be 10,000 tons of pig iron weekly.

delivery dates shortened. The reversal of these trends increased their need for steel both for use and for stock. For sheet steel, in particular, demand was especially strong. Not only had the motor industry, one of the main users of sheet, continued to expand despite the recession, but the industries which recovered quickest and which were increasing fastest—those making durable consumer goods—were also major users of sheet.

The renewal of tension was manifested in a lengthening of delivery dates and, mainly in export markets, a tendency for prices to rise. The continental export price for merchant bars, for example, rose from $82 per ton in January to $104 in July and $110 in November. Delivery dates lengthened from a few weeks to several months.

United States. General industrial activity and steel consumption were at much higher levels in the first six months of 1959 than in the corresponding period of 1958. Nevertheless, steel deliveries were at even higher levels, nearly 70% higher than in 1958, reaching a peak in June. This rate of delivery reflected the urgency with which consumers were buying for stock in anticipation of a strike following the mid-year wage negotiations between the employers and the trade unions. Their expectations were fulfilled and by August steel output was cut to a mere trickle by U.S. standards. Production was resumed, but at a much lower rate than earlier in the year, only in November, when the steelworkers were ordered back to work by the government under the Taft-Hartley act, for a period of 80 days. So prolonged a stoppage had not been expected and left steel consumers critically short of steel in spite of their precautions in the first half of the year. Work was resumed in November with no settlement of the dispute

in sight and with relations between employers and labour even worse than when the strike began in July.

United Kingdom. By contrast, steel production in Britain continued to fall, in comparison with the previous year, until the second quarter of 1959. In the third quarter, it was 12% higher than in the same period of 1958 (though still lower than in 1957), and in the last quarter it increased to record levels. For the year as a whole it reached 20·3 million tons—nearly 1·75 million tons less than in 1957, but 1·5 million tons more than in 1958. Steel consumption, which had also fallen continuously since 1957, began to increase by mid-year, though the fall in stocks continued well into the third quarter. Exports of iron and steel rose during the year, though by less than 10% and were still well below the tonnages recorded in 1957. Exports to the Commonwealth, in particular, were the lowest for many years. The main increases were to the United States, Argentina, western Europe and the far east. Imports declined, despite an increase in sheets for the motor trade, which accounted for well over half of the total trade.

Western Europe. In the European Coal and Steel community (E.C.S.C.), steel output in the second quarter rose by 1·5 million tons. Despite the holiday period, it again rose slightly in the third quarter. In the fourth it increased by over 1·5 million tons. Output for the year, at 62·5 million tons, was over 2·5 million tons higher than the previous peak reached in 1957. This recovery was due in part to a marked rise in industrial activity, which had levelled off in 1958, and to the reversal of the de-stocking movement begun in 1957 when consumers became aware that their needs were not increasing as fast as hitherto and that they could obtain quicker delivery than before. Export demand also made a

TABLE III. WORLD PRODUCTION OF STEEL*
('000 metric tons)

	1938	1956	1957	1958
WORLD	110,185	282,665	291,540	292,444
United States	28,805	104,522	102,253	77,244
U.S.S.R.	18,057	48,698	51,039	55,200
German Fed. Rep.	17,904	23,189	24,507	22,788
United Kingdom	10,565	20,990	22,047	19,884†
France	6,221	13,398	14,098	14,604
Japan	6,472	11,106	12,570	12,120
China (People's Rep.)	485	4,465	5,240	8,000
Italy	2,323	5,908	6,787	6,276
Belgium	2,279	6,382	6,276	6,012
Poland	1,441	5,014	5,304	5,628
Czechoslovakia	1,873	4,882	5,166	5,508
Canada	1,174	4,809	4,570	3,936
Saar	2,573	3,374	3,466	3,456
Luxembourg	1,437	3,456	3,493	3,384
German Dem. Rep.	2,179	2,740‡	2,894‡	3,048‡
Australia§	1,199	2,357‡	2,819‡	2,616‡
Sweden	987	2,425	2,511	2,400
Austria	673	2,078	2,509	2,388
India	982	1,766	1,742	1,848
Union of S. Africa	300	1,605	1,737	1,836
Hungary	647	1,416	1,375	1,632
Brazil‖	92	1,375	1,597	...
Spain	574	1,243‡	1,345‡	1,560‡
Netherlands	57	1,050	1,185	1,438
Yugoslavia	230	887	1,049	1,120
Mexico	142	591‡	687‡	989‡¶
Rumania	284	779	864	...

* Only countries with a yearly production exceeding 250,000 tons are specified.
† Year of 53 weeks. ‡ Excl. castings. § Year ended May 31. ‖ Excl. alloy steels.
¶ Not comparable with previous years.
SOURCE. U.N. *Statistical Yearbook 1958*; U.N. *Monthly Bulletin of Statistics*.

contribution to this result. Exports increased by 11% during the year, being particularly high in the second and third quarters. For the year as a whole, the E.C.S.C. exported 22% of its output of steel to countries outside—a higher percentage than in 1958. Home prices in the E.C.S.C. countries tended to rise during the year. Devaluation at the end of 1958 had been followed by a rise in French steel prices, though the final price in terms of currencies other than the franc was lowered. This had a depressing effect on prices throughout the common market, particularly as the recession in the steel market left producers with an incentive to increase their sales abroad. The price alignment rules of the E.C.S.C. then operated to reduce the effective price at which a large volume of community steel was sold. With the recovery in demand, price alignment gradually disappeared and one or two producers raised their actual list prices. Steel production in Austria and Sweden, the only other producers of any size in western Europe, increased by 2% and 9% respectively. There were no raw material difficulties in the way of increased production, though towards the end of the year signs of a tightening in the market for scrap were becoming apparent.

U.S.S.R., China and Eastern Europe. Soviet steel production in 1958 was 54·9 million tons, an increase of nearly 4 million tons over the previous year. A similar increase in 1959 brought output up to 59 million tons. Under the current seven-year plan, this rate of increase was to be stepped up to over 5 million tons a year, to reach the target of 91 million tons in 1965. The U.S.S.R. was, by 1959, an exporter of a substantial volume of steel—over 1·5 million tons in 1957—but little of this went to countries outside eastern Europe. Occasionally supplies of cheap Soviet pig-iron caused some disquiet in western European producing countries. The other countries of eastern Europe together produced some 18·5 million tons—1 million tons in excess of 1958. China, which claimed an output of 11 million tons in 1958 under the impulse of the " great leap forward ", admitted in 1959 that the " backyard blast-furnace " movement had produced largely unusable material and had choked the transport system of the country. Real production in 1958 was therefore only about 8 million tons and might have been increased in 1959 to 11 million tons, compared with the 18 million forecast.

Commonwealth. Recovery in the Canadian steel industry, which had suffered from labour troubles and the effects of the recession in 1958, brought an increase in output of over 1 million tons compared with the bare 4 million tons produced in the previous year. Output in the other Commonwealth producing countries (Australia, India and South Africa) also increased. In total, the dominions produced nearly 13 million tons, compared with less than 11 million tons in 1958. It was estimated that steel capacity in these four countries would have grown to 30 million tons by 1965, of which 13 million tons would be in India. In India, pig-iron production at the three new integrated steelworks, built in association with the U.S.S.R., the German Federal Republic and Great Britain respectively, began in 1959 and there was, in consequence, some increase in pig-iron output. Steel production on an appreciable scale, however, was not expected to begin until 1960. (*See* also EUROPEAN COAL AND STEEL COMMUNITY; METALLURGY; MINERAL AND METAL PRODUCTION.) (F. P. W.)

ISLAM. (Arabic " submission "; *i.e.*, to the will of God) is the name which all Moslems give to their religion; it claims to be a divine revelation communicated to the world through Mohammed who was the last of a succession of inspired prophets. Its doctrine and practice are based upon the Word of God, the Koran and the sayings and manner of life (*sunna*) of Mohammed. Islam has no formal supra-national organization and it is divided into many sects. The Sunnites form by far the largest number: by 1958 about 340 million out of a total of 400 million; Shiites in 1958 numbered about 35 million. The main Moslem states are Pakistan, Indonesia, Turkey, the United Arab Republic, Persia, Afghanistan, Sudan, Morocco, Saudi Arabia, Iraq, Tunisia, Yemen, Lebanon, Jordan, Libya, Albania, the Federation of Mali and the Islamic Republic of Mauritania. There are important Moslem minorities in India, the U.S.S.R., China, Malaya, Nigeria, Guinea, Somaliland, Philippines, Yugoslavia, Bulgaria and Greece.

In the Moslem world in 1959 the emphasis was still on education. In Pakistan there was an increase of 103,114 in

The Mosque of the Dome of the Rock, Jerusalem, one of the holiest shrines of Isalm, the restoration of which was begun in 1959.

the number of primary school students, and the increase in the school attendance of girls in all branches of education was very noticeable. A special Educational commission was set up to reorganize the educational system. A Central Islamic Research institute was being set up to co-ordinate Islamic studies, history and culture, and a third Islamic academy was to be set up in Dacca, East Pakistan. In July 1959 work started on the Urdu edition of the *Encyclopedia of Islam*. A noted interpreter of Islamic culture, Khalifa Abd-ul-Hakim, died in 1959. His works include *Islamic Ideology*, *Fikr-i-Iqbal* (in Urdu) and *Tashbihaat-i-Rumi*. Professor Ahmed Shah Bokhari, the director of the U.N. department of public information, died in Dec. 1958. Three Pakistani abstract artists, Ahmed Parvez, Sufiuddin Ahmed and A. J. Shemza, held successful one-man shows at the New Vision Centre gallery in London. Professor Abdus Salam of the Imperial College of Science and Technology, London, was jointly awarded the Adam prize for his paper on " Invariance Properties in Elementary Particles Physics ".

In the United Arab Republic in 1958-59 there were 1,424,627 boys and 860,364 girls in Egyptian primary schools, an increase of 121,984 boys and 77,403 girls. There were 77,347 university students in Egypt and 5,000 in Syria. The Popular Arts centre of the Ministry of Culture and National Guidance published a new magazine, in Arabic, French and English, on world folklore. The General Cultural administration of the ministry was undertaking the publication of a young people's encyclopaedia and encyclopaedias of biography and geography. In Sudan the education budget was reduced by 3% and the opening of the Teachers' college and the Institute of Education scheduled for July 1959 was postponed through lack of funds, but during 1958-59 an additional 100,000 boys and girls were receiving education and nearly 40 new primary schools were built. There were 964 students in Khartoum university, an increase of 114.

In the summer holidays of 1959 an intensive anti-illiteracy campaign was carried out in Iraq by the government backed by the teachers and advanced students. A medical school was opened in Mosul and an Oil institute in Baghdad. A faculty of modern languages was added to Baghdad university.

In May the Moroccan minister of education stated that 527,635 children between the ages of 6 and 12, out of a total of 1,827,000, were at school; in three years of independence 322,952 children had been afforded primary education. In Tunisia a new university was opened in Nov. 1959. The figures for primary education in 1958-59 showed a rise of 52,554 to 320,362, and in secondary education there was a rise of 2,279 to 10,831. There were 874 students in teachers' training colleges (an increase of 145) and the number of students in receipt of higher education rose by 347 to 2,606. Tunisia introduced a ten-year plan to increase the number of children between 6 and 14 in schools to 836,925 and the number of teachers to 14,917. In 1959 the number of children at school in Algeria was increased from 700,000 to 860,000.

In Persia the number of students in Tehran and provincial universities rose by 1,733 to 14,439 and the number of students studying abroad from 4,681 to 11,742. Twice as many books were distributed to students in 1958-59 as in 1957-58 and 376,347 adults attended literary courses. In Turkey in 1958-59, 2,414,977 boys and girls were in primary schools, an increase of 125,977 over the previous year. Between Oct. 1958 and June 1959, 1,478 performances of 45 different plays were given in nine Turkish cities. The state theatre had nine separate companies.

In Afghanistan the number of students at Kabul university rose from 1,295 in 1958 to 1,505 in 1959. The fourth volume of the *Afghan Encyclopedia* and the third volume of the *Geographical Encyclopedia of Afghanistan* were published. Twenty-seven regular and 175 elementary schools were

opened, and 1 million textbooks were specially printed abroad under 25 different titles. One hundred doctors graduated from the medical school of the University of Indonesia in 1958-59. In the previous six years the foreign staff of the Indonesian universities had been halved and the Indonesian staff increased by over 1,000. (*See also* ARAB LEAGUE.) (G. H. N. B.)

BIBLIOGRAPHY (all 1959). S. F. Mahmud, *The Story of Islam* (Oxford); Nevill Barbour (ed.), *A Survey of North West Africa* (Oxford); A. J. Arberry, *The Romance of the Rubaiyat* (London); Rom Landau, *The Philosophy of Ibn 'Araby* (London); Ziya Gökalp, *Turkish Nationalism and Western Civilization* (London).

ISLE OF MAN: *see* MAN, ISLE OF.

ISRAEL. A republic, proclaimed on May 14, 1948, bounded N. by Lebanon, E. by Syria and Jordan, S. by Egypt and W. by the Mediterranean. Area: 7,993 sq.mi. Pop.: (Nov. 1948 census) 782,000, incl. 713,000 Jews; (Oct. 1958) 2,016,110, incl. 1,800,000 Jews. Religion (1957 est.): mainly Jewish but there were 141,000 Moslems: 18,000 Druzes and 45,000 Christians. Chief towns (pop., 1959 est.), Jerusalem (cap., Israeli part only) 156,000; Jaffa-Tel Aviv 380,000; Haifa 170,000. President of the republic, Isaac Ben-Zvi; prime minister, David Ben-Gurion. Main imports, foodstuffs; wood, iron, steel and manufactures; machinery; crude oil. Main exports: cement, citrus fruits, diamonds (cut and polished), textiles and apparel, fruit juice, artificial teeth. Monetary unit: Israeli *pound* (tourist exchange rate [Sept. 1959] I£6·06 = £1 sterling).

History. After the excitements of the 10th anniversary celebrations of 1958, it was not surprising that 1959 appeared at first as something of an anti-climax. In the event, it happened otherwise. In many ways, it turned out to be possibly the most significant year in domestic affairs since the state was established in 1948. In the course of it there emerged the successor generation to the leaders of 1948; at the same time the oriental Jewish communities, which comprise more than half the population, appeared for the first time as a powerful political factor in deciding the future government of the country.

It was this silent struggle of the successor generation which dominated politics on the home front, and as the year wore on this struggle became increasingly less silent. This trend from old political thinking to the new was concentrated on three men: on the former chief-of-staff who commanded the successful Sinai operations against Egypt in 1956, General Moshe Dayan, who had left the army in 1958 in order to devote himself to politics; on the former Israeli ambassador in Washington, Abba Eban, who left the diplomatic service in May 1959 in order to contest a seat in parliament; and on

A stretch of the new road linking the important Israeli towns of Beersheba and Eilat, which was opened early in the year.

David Ben-Gurion, the prime minister of Israel, chatting with a group of participants in the international seminar of youth leaders which he formally opened in Tel Aviv on March 12. The seminar was held under the auspices of the International Union of Socialist Youth.

the former director-general of the Ministry of Defence, Shimon Peres, one of the principal architects of Israel's close collaboration with France, who resigned from the civil service in June 1959 to contest the elections. Dayan and Eban were in their middle forties, Peres ten years younger. All three were very popular, but not popular enough to make any serious impact on the firmly-established party hierarchy of Mapai, the Israeli Labour party. They had, however, an invaluable asset on their side which turned the scales. They enjoyed the support of the prime minister and leader of the party, David Ben-Gurion. Thus, when the party lists were prepared for Knesset membership (elections are based on proportional representation), all three newcomers figured prominently among the candidates for the safe seats.

However, the old guard of Mapai did not take kindly to this intrusion, and a severe tussle inside the party followed in an attempt to restrain the consolidation of these new forces. The elections for the Israeli Federation of Labour, the Histadrut, the over-all governing body of the trades unions, was conducted largely by the old guard and both Ben-Gurion and the so-called " new thinkers " remained largely in the background. The result was not reassuring for Mapai. Its proportion of votes declined from $57 \cdot 7\%$ to $55 \cdot 7\%$ while that of all other left-wing parties (except the Communists) increased by $3 \cdot 5\%$. The result did not affect Mapai's over-all control, but it was taken as warning that Mapai's prospects in the general election scheduled for later in the year were none too good.

The pendulum continued to swing against Mapai as the election came nearer. The attempt to force a Danish freighter carrying a cargo of Israeli cement for Ceylon through the Suez canal misfired when the " Inge Toft " was stopped in the canal on May 23. Then during the first two weeks of

July there were disorders and rioting by oriental Jews in the slums of Haifa and in Beersheba. Mapai, as the party in power, was blamed for the conditions which had produced the trouble. In yet a third instance the party also came in for much criticism. The much-publicized mass immigration of Jews—100,000 had been expected during the year—had petered out. The Rumanian government had seemingly changed its regulations after representations to the Soviet leaders by the Arab governments. After February, this immigration had been reduced to a trickle. The handling of the publicity and diplomacy was blamed on the Jewish agency and the government, and in both Mapai was the dominant factor.

When the prospects of the party were at their lowest and even optimists expected a considerable loss of seats, if not the party's dominant position, the prime minister intervened. A tremendous nation-wide campaign was organized for a period of ten weeks, designed to give a new image to Israel's Labour party. The new men, together with Ben-Gurion, Mrs. Golda Meir, the foreign minister, and her predecessor, Moshe Sharett, took over the campaign, addressing themselves to the nation. Ben-Gurion spoke to some 300,000 people at great mass meetings; Sharett and Mrs. Meir each addressed some 60 meetings, but the test was the attempt to break into the oriental Jewish quarters, to capture the floating vote and to turn Mapai from a purely class party into a national party. The party was considerably helped in this by the unexpectedly popular reaction which showed itself after the sudden cabinet crisis at the end of June over the publication of news that the Ministry of Defence had sold arms and munitions to the German Federal government.

The public shared the premier's satisfaction and not the critics' disgust. But yet another factor, hardly noticeable in official reports or statistics, was beginning to make itself felt

A Bedouin woman squats with her children in the market place of Beersheba, whose camel market is a meeting place for these people.

in the country. The economy was booming. Inflation (except in property) had been kept within bounds, the shops were full, unemployment had been reduced to relatively unimportant sectors, huge sums had come into the country as part of western German restitution to individual victims of Nazism, and this money was largely invested in building and business. Agriculture had reached a point where all the needs of the home market could be met from domestic sources while new categories of exports were being opened up such as melons and tropical fruits. An air of well-being hung over the country and it affected the workers, merchants and industrialists alike. Pinhas Sapir at the Ministry of Trade and Industry had pressed the industrialization and capitalization of business with almost reckless abandon, but it had paid off. Israel was more prosperous than it had ever been.

All this told when the country went to the polls on Nov. 3. The unexpected happened. In terms of proportional representation, there was something like a landslide towards Mapai. The party gained almost 100,000 more votes from all sections of the population; some of the largest gains were in the well-to-do quarters of Jerusalem and Tel Aviv. The final results were as follows (in brackets the number of seats obtained in 1955): Mapai 47 (40); Mapai Arab lists 5 (5); Herut (Nationalists) 17 (15); Religious parties 18 (17); General Zionists 8 (13); Progressives 6 (5); Mapam, a left Socialist party 9 (9); Ahdut Ha'avoda, a left-wing but more activist Socialist party 7 (10); Communists 3 (6). (*See* also ELECTIONS.)

The result was significant. It showed that the trend was towards the clearly defined parties of the centre and away from extremes. True, Herut won two seats but they had expected to win ten; Ahdut Ha'avoda had run a smear campaign against Ben-Gurion and had lost, and the Arab voters deserted the Communists. There had been 24 lists but none of the communal or separatist lists polled the 1% necessary for one candidate.

On Dec. 16, after six weeks of negotiations, Ben-Gurion presented his new government to the Knesset. Mapai was the dominating partner in the five-party coalition. Ben-Gurion remained defence minister and Mrs. Meir foreign minister. Eban was appointed minister without portfolio and Dayan minister of agriculture. Peres became deputy minister of defence. Sapir remained at the Ministry of Trade and Industry and Levy Eshkol was appointed minister of finance. On Dec. 17 Ben-Gurion won a vote of confidence by 78 to 33. (*See* also JEWRY.)   (J. KE.)

ITALIAN LITERATURE. The main literary events of 1959 were two novels different in style and subject matter—Giuseppe Tomasi di Lampedusa's *Il gattopardo* and Pier Paolo Pasolini's *Una vita violenta*—which caused a division of opinion over the awarding of the Strega prize (which went to *Il gattopardo*) and provided a topic of discussion in intellectual circles. Both works were notable for their stark realism, thus illustrating the basic unity underlying the disconcerting variety of contemporary Italian literature.

In his novel, published five years after his death, Lampedusa, who was a Sicilian nobleman, paints a sympathetic, satirical picture of the 19th-century Sicilian aristocracy. The plot centres on Prince Fabrizio Salina, whose family coat of arms —a leopard—gives the story its title. Awareness of the present has its influence on the recapture of the past in this novel, where noblemen with the manners of Spanish grandees and shady clerics are contrasted with thrifty tradesmen and rugged labourers. The conflict between youth and age set against the background of a slowly changing social and political structure, acquires a deeper meaning, becoming almost a fatal necessity.

In *Una vita violenta* Pasolini, a leading young north Italian writer of middle-class origins living in Rome, tells the story of a gang of boys in the squalid city slums. He writes in a mood of cold detachment, stressing the disguised bitterness of his social protest. His work is imbued with a fatalism similar to that in Lampedusa's novel.

Other notable works of fiction were Alberto Moravia's *Nuovi racconti romani*, an addition to his previous collection of stories dealing with the picaresque characters to be found among the Roman working class; Domenico Rea's *Una vampata di Rossore*, which satirizes the tendency of some southern Italians to exploit their physical attractiveness to women in order to keep them in bondage; and Goffredo

Salvatore Quasimodo, the Italian poet, originally an engineer, who was awarded the 1959 Nobel prize for literature.

Parise's *Amore e fervore*, the story of a provincial clerk, which ridicules the prejudices of the inhabitants of a small town.

The chief Marzotto prize was awarded to Riccardo Bacchelli for his historical novel *I tre schiavi di Giulio Cesare*. Other awards went to *Il taglio del bosco*, a collection of stories by Carlo Cassola and *Il canto del destino*, a book of poems by Giorgio Vigolo. Prizes were also given for the best plays of the year—Giorgio Prosperi's *La congiura* and Giuseppe Dessi's *La giustizia*.

During 1959 the deaths occurred of the leading *avante-garde* poet Vincenzo Cardarelli, the historian Carlo Antoni and the sociologist Luigi Sturzo (*see* OBITUARIES). The award of the Nobel prize for literature to Salvatore Quasimodo (*see* BIOGRAPHIES) was particularly welcome, as he was the first Italian since Luigi Pirandello to receive an international literary award.   (F. MI.)

ITALIAN SOMALILAND: *see* SOMALIA.

ITALY. A republic of southern Europe, bounded on land N.W. by France, N. by Switzerland and Austria and N.E. by Yugoslavia. The country includes the whole of the Apennine peninsula, the large Mediterranean islands of Sicily and Sardinia and a number of smaller islands. Area: 116,290 sq.mi. Pop.: (1951 census) 46,737,629; (1958 est.) 48,735,000. Language: mainly Italian, but in Venezia Trindentina there are *c.* 210,000 German-speaking Tirolese and *c.* 10,000 speaking Rhaeto-Romance dialects; in the area east of Udine there are *c.* 11,200 Slovenes and the population of Val d'Aosta (*c.* 6,600) is French-speaking. Religion: mainly Roman Catholic (99·6%). Chief towns (pop. 1955 est.): Rome (cap.) 1,750,707; Milan 1,305,407; Naples 1,059,121; Turin 783,119; Genoa 711,515; Palermo 528,125; Florence 392,635; Bologna 364,064; Venice 327,743; Catania 320,951; Bari 287,683; Trieste 270,919; Messina 231,620; 14 towns with a pop. of from 100,000 to 200,000. President, Giovanni Gronchi. Prime ministers in 1959: Amintore Fanfani and (from Feb. 15) Antonio Segni. Main imports: petroleum and products, cotton, coal and coke, grain, wool. Main exports: machinery and vehicles, fruit and vegetables, wine, artificial fibres and manufactures, cotton and manufactures. Monetary unit: *lira* (L.1,750 = £1 sterling).

History. Politically the year 1959 began with the congress of the left-wing Italian Socialist party (P.S.I.) from Jan. 15 to 18 in Naples. Its leader, Pietro Nenni, against the wishes of the party officials, succeeded in carrying a motion in favour of the party's autonomy which implied its liberation at last from Communist control. This had a disintegrating effect upon the more moderate Italian Social Democratic party (P.S.D.I.) and, since the latter was represented in Amintore Fanfani's cabinet, upon the government as well. The Social Democratic minister of labour, Ezio Vigorelli, resigned on Jan. 22 because if Nenni became independent of the Communists, Vigorelli preferred him as Socialist leader to the right-wing leader of the P.S.D.I., Giuseppe Saragat. The result was that Fanfani, whose majorities in the parliament had been dwindling, was obliged to resign too. On Feb. 15 a new cabinet was formed under a former prime minister and colleague of Fanfani, Antonio Segni.

Although Giovanni Gronchi, the president of the republic, made clear his disapproval, Segni accepted support from more conservative elements than would have countenanced Fanfani, and formed a one-party Christian Democratic government supported by the parties to the right, with Giuseppe Pella as foreign minister. On Feb. 27 the Chamber of Deputies passed a vote of confidence in its favour by 333

Part of a completed section of the " Autostrada del Sole " south of Sperlonga, where it follows the rocky coastline of the Gulf of Gaeta. Eventually the new " highway to the sun " will traverse central Italy from Milan to Naples via Bologna, Florence and Rome.

votes to 248; in the Senate (March 6) the favourable votes were 143 to 97 against. The epilogue to this change was spoken at the meeting of the Christian Democratic party council held from March 14 to 17 when Fanfani was deposed as secretary-general in favour of Aldo Moro.

Meanwhile on Feb. 8, in preparation for their hoped-for fusion with Nenni, Vigorelli and his friends formed a new Socialist group called the Movimento Unitario di Iniziativa Socialista; the P.S.I., however, made great difficulties for them. And it was noticed with interest that in October a group of former Communists headed by Eugenio Reale, at one time Italian ambassador in Warsaw, preferred to join Saragat's Social Democrats.

In the spring political interest was focused upon the regional elections due to take place in the Val d'Aosta on May 17. On April 13 the new Pope John XXIII made a public pronouncement condemning any party which co-operated with the Communists. This seemed to have the opposite effect from that which the Vatican intended: 91% of the electors in the Val d'Aosta went to the polls; of these 48% voted for the parties favourable to the government, and 52% for the autonomist Union Valdôtaine, the P.S.I. and the Communists. Since the government had chosen to abolish proportional representation in favour of a majority system this meant that there were in the new Aostan chamber 15 autonomists, 7 supporters of Nenni and 3 of Vigorelli opposed by 4 Christian Democrats, 4 Independents, 1 Liberal and 1 follower of Saragat: the regional administration was then formed of autonomists and left-wing Socialists.

On June 7 there followed elections for the parliament of autonomous Sicily, which since the previous October had been in a state of ferment. The result of the voting showed that the Marxist parties had made very substantial gains on the last regional election of 1955 and had nearly maintained the position they had won in the general election of 1958. Silvio Milazzo now campaigned as leader of his Christian Social group which had split away from the Christian Demo-

The tax inspector's lot was not a happy one at Marigliano, Italy, after discontented farmers sacked his offices in September.

crats. The result was 34 seats in a chamber of 90 went to the Christian Democrats, 21 to the Communists, 11 to Nenni and 9 to Milazzo; the neo-Fascist M.S.I. picked up a little (9 seats, gaining 1), but the other smaller parties lost. After all kinds of false alarms, on July 28 Milazzo was re-elected prime minister of Sicily by a majority of two with the support of the Communists and of Nenni's Socialists, and in defiance of both Christian Democratic headquarters in Rome and of the pope. A Sicilian government was then elected consisting of four members of Milazzo's Christian Social union and four dissidents from other parties. It should be remembered that Milazzo's breakaway had begun in collaboration with the right. He now depended on the extreme left which, though not represented in his cabinet, slipped into a number of administrative positions.

On May 31 and June 7 elections were also held in a number of communes in Italy; on the whole the Christian Democrats did fairly well although the deadlock between the centre and leftist parties in Ravenna obstinately remained. Further local elections which were to have been held in the autumn were postponed.

On Oct. 23 the Christian Democrats opened their national congress in Florence. Tribute was paid to Don Luigi Sturzo (*see* OBITUARIES), the founder of their parent party, the Popolari, who had died on Aug. 8. After unusually violent debates an attempt from the left wing to reassert the authority of Fanfani was defeated when 68 supporters of Segni were elected to the party executive as against 46 followers of Fanfani. This was to have been expected. Indeed, during the year extreme rightist influence had asserted itself openly if spasmodically in the country as a whole; an example was the refusal for the first time of the municipal authorities of Rome to celebrate the anniversary of the liberation of the capital by the Allies on June 4, 1944.

It was a stormy year in the world of labour too. The workers were determined to obtain a larger share of the growing national product and to resist the usual periodic dismissals by uneconomic concerns. On Jan. 9, 350 workmen dismissed by the Galileo concern in Florence occupied one of its factories from which the police evicted them after some violence on Jan. 27. Similar events occurred in other towns, the Communists explaining them as caused by German competition made possible by the common market. There were a number of strikes, notably the seamen's strike which lasted for 40 days, ending on July 23 with a 9% increase in wages; bank employees received a rise of only 6% after a 16-day strike in June. It was officially stated in October that during the first seven months of 1959 about 65·3 million

On the eve of talks with President Eisenhower in Paris on Sept. 3: A. Segni (left) and G. Pella, prime and foreign ministers of Italy.

working hours had been lost as compared with 20·6 million during the same period in 1958. In October itself there was a miners' strike. A metal- and machine-workers' strike ended on Oct. 23 with an increase of wages by 5·5%.

While the Communist-dominated General Confederation of Labour (C.G.I.L.) admitted to a loss of 400,000 members in 1958, in 1959 it seemed slightly to revive, and the Christian Democratic trade unions (C.I.S.L.) appeared to have come to a standstill; they had been weakened by a break-away in the big Fiat concern of the group which called itself " Liberi Lavoratori Democratici " and which on April 7 came out at the head of the poll in the Fiat shop-steward elections. When on Oct. 18 elections were held in the big chemical concern of Montecatini, however, the C.G.I.L. lost 2 seats and the C.I.S.L., gaining 2, came out top.

After the economic hitch caused by the recession in the United States in 1958, Italian industry and trade on the whole developed favourably, though ship-building, for instance, for which the state was indirectly responsible, ran at a loss. Foreign trade increased, particularly with the German Federal Republic and France, but also with the United States and with the Communist states (including Yugoslavia) and Finland. Italy's foreign trade deficit, which had not diminished as much as had been expected in 1958, was further reduced in 1959.

Since the new Segni government had come into being in protest against the policy of increasing the nationalized sector of industry which Fanfani, backed by President Gronchi and Enrico Mattei, had favoured, there was much talk after February of denationalization. Several ministers, however, after a few months in office, reproached private capitalists with their unwillingness to invest in industry. They stressed the need for private initiative and state enterprise at the same time, and in August it was arranged that the big banks controlled by I.R.I. (the Italian state investment agency) should increase their capital. In July, moreover, when Mattei was openly attacked in parliament for using E.N.I. (Ente Nazionale Idrocarburi) funds, i.e., government money, to finance the paper Il Giorno, which pursued a leftist policy, Mario Ferrari Aggradi, the minister for state investment, defended Mattei. He pointed to the latter's recent achievement, the discovery two months earlier of methane gas at Ferrandina in Lucania, the poorest region of southern Italy. This discovery might, indeed, be regarded as a major contribution to the development of the south after so much of north Italian industry had become based upon the gas discovered and conveyed by E.N.I. In connection with the projecting of four atomic energy plants to which E.N.I. also contributed, on April 13 a centre for nuclear research was opened at Ispra on Lake Maggiore.

At about the same time the U.S.S.R. uttered one of its major threats to Italy over the transference of United States rocket bases on to its territory: the transference continued, however, during 1959, mainly involving the training of Italians in the use of nuclear apparatus. When Pella succeeded Fanfani as foreign minister he emphasized Italian fidelity to Nato. Under-currents, chiefly of a commercial nature, continued to impel Italy into a certain patronage of the Arab countries whose potentialities Mattei was ever eager to help develop. This occasionally made Italian relations with France uneasy. Further, as the end of its successful trusteeship in Somalia approached, Italy, to a certain extent instinctively, displayed itself as the western power with the most understanding for the new, backward Asian and African nations.

Italy's relations with Austria proved more difficult during 1959 because of the discontent of the South Tirolese or German-speaking population in the province of Alto Adige. The housing decrees issued by Giuseppe Togni, the minister of public works under both Fanfani and Segni, were resented

Specimens of the Murano glassware which was the Italian president's wedding gift to Crown Prince Akihito of Japan and his bride.

by the South Tirolese as a violation of their provincial autonomy and as favouring Italians at their expense. Their leaders went to Vienna early in February to consult the Austrian government. Since the general election was due in Austria in May, all the political parties there took up the popular South Tirolese cause. Although the Italian government made administrative concessions in the summer, on Sept. 21, the new Austrian foreign minister, Bruno Kreisky, felt obliged to refer to the South Tirol at some length when he addressed the United Nations.

From Dec. 4 to 6 President Dwight D. Eisenhower paid an official visit to Rome.   (E. WI.)

See Denis Mack Smith, A History of Modern Italy (London, 1959).

IVORY COAST, REPUBLIC OF (RÉPUBLIQUE DE CÔTE D'IVOIRE), a member state of the French Community. Ivory Coast is bounded W. by the republics of Liberia and Guinea, N. by the republics of Soudan and Upper Volta, E. by the realm Ghana and S. by the Atlantic ocean. Area: 123,359 sq.mi. Pop.: (1951 est.) 2,169,600; (1959 est.) 3,100,000; Negroes of Kru, Agni (Ashanti), Baulé, Senufo and Dioula and other tribes. Language: many local dialects. Religion: animist and Moslem; Christian minorities. Chief towns (pop., 1958 est.): Abidjan (cap., 160,000, incl. 8,000 Europeans); Bouaké (30,700); Grand-Bassam (12,000). Prime minister, Félix Houphouët-Boigny. French high commissioner, Yves Guéna. Chief exports: coffee, cocoa, bananas, timber. Monetary unit: *franc CFA* = metropolitan Fr.2.

History. The Republic of Ivory Coast was proclaimed on Dec. 4, 1958. The constitution was approved on March 26, 1959. At the parliamentary elections held on April 12, the Rassemblement Démocratique Africain won all the seats. Europeans had 18 seats out of a total of 100. On May 1 Félix Houphouët-Boigny became prime minister.

Ivory Coast created a Sahel-Bénin *entente*, together with Upper Volta, Niger and Dahomey. The *entente* would have a complete customs union and a common fund of capital on which each country could draw.

At the R.D.A. congress held at Abidjan on Sept. 4, Houphouët-Boigny called pan-Africanism the "condemnation of Africa to misery and anarchy ". The trade unions formed the Union des Travailleurs de Côte d' Ivoire which detached itself from the U.G.T.A.N. (Union Générale des Travailleurs d'Afrique Noire).

The king of Samwi (near Ghana), who demanded independence, was arrested. A strike of civil servants ended after 184 had been dismissed.

A vein of manganese was discovered on the coast, near Grand Lahou. (HU. DE.)

JAMAICA: *see* WEST INDIES, THE.

JAPAN. Island nation in the western Pacific consisting of the following four main groups of islands:

Honshu (with 382 adjacent small islands)	.	.	.	88,919 sq.mi.
Shikoku (with 167 islands)	.	.	.	7,248 sq.mi.
Kyushu (with 373 small islands)	.	.	.	16,247 sq.mi.
Hokkaido (with 68 small islands)	.	.	.	34,276 sq.mi.
		Total	.	146,690 sq.mi.

Pop.: (1955 census) 89,275,529; (1959 est.) 92,420,000. Language: Japanese. Religion: Buddhist, Shintoist and Christian (in 1933 there were 191,000 Roman Catholics and 249,000 members of other denominations). Chief towns (1955 census): Tokyo (cap.) 6,969,104; Osaka 2,547,316; Nagoya 1,336,780; Kyoto 1,204,084; Yokohama 1,143,687; Kobe 979,305. Emperor, Hirohito; prime minister, Nobusuke Kishi. Chief imports: raw materials and fuels (60%), foodstuffs (25%). Chief exports: manufactured goods (77%). Monetary unit: *yen* (Y.1,010 = £1 sterling).

History. *Foreign Relations.* Japan's relations with the United States during 1959 were dominated by the issue of revision of the U.S.-Japan security agreement, which had been signed along with the peace treaty on Sept. 8, 1951. Both in official parleys with the U.S. ambassador, which had begun in Oct. 1958, and in unofficial conversations between the government and the ruling Liberal-Democratic party, one of the most important points was the question whether Okinawa and the Bonins, not yet returned to Japanese jurisdiction, should be included in the treaty area.

Meanwhile, on March 30 the government was jolted when the Tokyo district court based its acquittal of seven trespassers on a U.S. air base upon the assertion that the security treaty and its related special criminal law were unconstitutional. Not only art. IX of the constitution (which forswears armed forces as instruments of national policy forever), but also more basically the whole structure of treaty-constitutional relations, became subject to review.

Japan's reappraisal of relations with the United States also affected its negotiations with the U.S.S.R. In Dec. 1958 A. A. Gromyko, the Soviet foreign minister, had urged Japan to follow " a policy of neutrality ", a suggestion promptly rejected by Aiichiro Fujiyama, the foreign minister. On Jan. 27 N. S. Khrushchev, Soviet prime minister, followed with a proposal for a denuclearized zone in the far east and Pacific areas; on May 4 another note urged neutrality and requested Japan's views on denuclearization. On May 15 Japan formally disclaimed neutralism and stated that prohibition of nuclear weapons must be considered part of the general disarmament problem.

Japan continued without official contact with the Chinese People's Republic. In March 1959 a nine-man Socialist-party mission, led by Inejiro Asanuma, the party's secretary-general, left Japan for Peking. There Asanuma called for closer ties with the people's republic; co-operation in the denuclearization of, and withdrawal of foreign troops from, Asia; abrogation of the Tokyo-Taipei treaty; and Asian economic co-operation built round China and Japan. However, Chou En-lai, head of the Chinese government, insisted that trade was inseparable from politics, and that government-to-government negotiations would be necessary to adjust commercial relations.

During 1959 protracted negotiations with South Korea for normal treaty relationships faced a crisis when, on Feb. 13,

Survivors searching for possessions in a street of Handa, central Japan, after the typhoon " Vera " had laid waste large areas in and around the industrial town of Nagoya on Sept. 26-27. The typhoon was the worst ever recorded and rendered nearly 1 million homeless.

(Right) Crown Prince Akihito of Japan and his bride, Crown Princess Michiko, divested of the heavy ceremonial robes in which they were married, pose for photographers in western dress after the wedding. (Above) Princess Suga, the Japanese emperor's youngest daughter, with her fiancé, Hisanaga Shimazu, who is a cousin of the empress. Their engagement was announced in March.

the Japanese cabinet approved Fujiyama's scheme to repatriate North Koreans. There were about 600,000 Koreans in Japan, and it was estimated that about 117,000 desired to return to North Korea. South Korea immediately protested, terminated diplomatic negotiations and threatened to sever trade relations with Japan. Nevertheless, Japan asked the International Committee of the Red Cross to verify the individual Korean's wishes. On Aug. 12, South Korea offered to reopen normalization talks " without attaching any conditions ", but its unilateral declaration prohibiting fishing behind the so-called Rhee line continued to block normal relations. Meanwhile, on Aug. 11 in Geneva the Red Cross decided to assist in Japan's proposed repatriation of North Koreans; and on Aug. 13 in Calcutta, Red Cross delegates from Japan and North Korea signed a repatriation agreement.

Domestic Affairs. In Nov. 1958, the Imperial Household council announced the engagement of Crown Prince Akihito to Miss Michiko Shoda, a commoner. The marriage on April 10, 1959, was marked by the largest national celebration since the end of World War II.

Parliamentary proceedings during the year were troubled by questions of Japan's defence policy and by party disputes over related security measures. Since Oct. 1957, the National Public Safety commission had been studying a draft Police Duties law. In Oct. 1958, Kishi argued that social unrest germinated by mass violence proved the need for a revised law. The Socialist opposition accused the government of trying to enlarge police powers (along with revision of the security treaty with the U.S.), thereby opening the way for revival of a police state. On Nov. 4, 1958, parliamentary proceedings were thrown into complete confusion as the Liberal-Democratic party unilaterally announced a 30-day extension of the session to pass the police bill, and the Socialists tried forcibly to keep the House of Representatives from operating. Finally on Nov. 22, Kishi, as president of the Liberal-Democratic party, and Mosaburo Suzuki, chairman of the Socialist party, solved the impasse. The Police Duties law was shelved and the House of Representatives did not meet again during the extended session. The 31st regular parliament opened on Dec. 10, 1958, but trouble immediately began over the election of a speaker and deputy speaker.

When parliament reopened on Jan. 26, 1959, Kishi was attacked by the Socialists, who demanded termination, rather than revision, of the U.S. security treaty.

In February both parties were occupied in the House of Representatives with the explosive issue of prohibition of nuclear weapons for Japan. After Kishi himself said that he was against nuclear armament of the self-defence forces, and would not permit U.S. forces to bring such arms into Japan, Socialists pressed the Liberal-Democrats to co-sponsor a resolution to this effect. Parliament closed its session on May 2, after passing 163 laws, including the Defence Agency Establishment law revision providing a 12,000-man increase in self-defence personnel.

On June 2 half of the House of Councillors (Upper Chamber) were elected (*see* ELECTIONS).

The third reconstruction of the Kishi cabinet (June 19) brought in all new appointees, except for Fujiyama, the foreign minister, and Eisaku Sato, the finance minister.

On Sept. 26-27, central Japan staggered under the impact of typhoon " Vera ", the worst in recorded history; more than 1,300 persons were reported dead, 1,200 were missing, 5,600 injured and almost 1 million were homeless. The industrial town of Nagoya was hardest hit. (A. B.)

JET PROPULSION AND GAS TURBINES.
Great Britain. The several forms of flight propulsion made marked progress during 1959 but, in general, industrial gas turbine activity remained subdued.

Turbo-Jets. Bristol and Armstrong Siddeley, integrated as Bristol-Siddeley, announced a new range of turbo-fan engines designed for high thrust with good fuel economy and low weight. The first example exhibited was the BE.58 with a 46-in.-diameter fan intake and over 1·5:1 by-pass ratio. Maximum sea-level static thrust was 14,500 lb., specific fuel consumption 0·57 lb./lb. thrust/hr. and dry weight 2,600 lb. A military version, BE.53, was in development but no details were released.

Olympus double compound turbo-jets continued in production for Vulcan bombers. The 200 series, rated at 17,000 lb. m.s.l.s.t., weighed 3,600 lb., was 36½ in. in diameter and 296 in. long. Reheat thrust was 24,000 lb. Higher-rated engines in development were reported to give 33,000 lb. with reheat. Olympus turbo-jets were chosen for the new TSR.2 military aircraft. Several Orpheus variants were in production. B.Or.12 (6,810 lb. m.s.l.s.t.) in development for supersonic interceptors was flight-tested. With " simplified " reheat it gave 8,170 lb. thrust for take-off. Capable of supplying a considerable flow of compressed air for wing boundary layer control, the de Havilland Gyron Junior turbo-jet was in development based on D.GJ.1 (7,000 lb. m.s.l.s.t.). Two Gyron Juniors powered the Blackburn NA-39 naval aircraft and D.GJ.10 (10,000 lb. m.s.l.s.t. and 14,000 lb. thrust with reheat) was chosen for the Bristol T.188 research aeroplane.

The production of Rolls-Royce single-shaft Avons in quantity continued, a total of over 6,600 having been delivered and more than 2·5 million hr. flown. Latest military version exhibited was RB-146 rated at 13,220 lb. m.s.l.s.t. The civil RA-29 (10,500 lb. m.s.l.s.t.), as used in Comet 4, was approved for 1,300 hr. between overhauls. Conway two-shaft by-pass engines, in manufacture for Victor B-2 bombers, were uprated to 17,500 lb. m.s.l.s.t. for VC-10, Boeing 707 and D.C.8 airliners. Designed to give 14,300 lb. m.s.l.s.t., the RB-141 two-shaft by-pass turbo-jet, with air-cooled turbine blades, ran initial tests. A scaled-down version, the RB-163 (10,100 lb. m.s.l.s.t.) was intended for the revised DH-121 airliner. The RB-108 (2,010 lb. m.s.l.s.t.) high thrust/weight ratio (approx. 10 : 1) turbo-jet was demonstrated in SC.1 experimental V.T.O.L. aircraft. Air jets supplied by a fan driven by a piston engine supported and propelled the Saunders Roe SR-N1 Hovercraft.

Ram-Jets. A sectioned Bristol-Siddeley Thor BT.1 ram-jet, which powered early Bloodhound surface-to-air missiles, was exhibited. The outer sheet metal casing, 16 in. in diameter and 96 in. long, supported an inner streamlined body by three struts. The inner body contained the air/fuel ratio control unit. Air which entered the annular intake at supersonic speed was slowed down and thereby compressed by shock waves. The airflow then passed through an annular duct which contained fuel injectors, igniters and flame stabilizers. A ram-jet of this size should develop 16,000 lb. thrust at Mach 3. Bristol were engaged on ram-jets of larger size. A compression-ignition ram-jet was proposed for flight speeds around Mach 3 to 4 where existing ram-jets give place to rockets. The basic principles included the introduction of fuel into the airstream before compression, duct compression by inclined shock waves and ignition by the heat of compression.

Jet Propulsion Rocket Motors. Details were published of the Gamma 201 kerosene/H.T.P. rocket motor which propelled the Black Knight re-entry research vehicle. This four-chambered controllable motor developed by Bristol-Siddeley gave 16,400 lb. thrust at sea level and nearly 19,000 lb. in the upper atmosphere. The over-all diameter was 36 in., length 38 in. and weight about 700 lb. The de Havilland Double Spectre kerosene/H.T.P. motor, with variable thrust between 800 lb. and 16,000 lb., was used for the initial flight tests of the Avro Blue Steel air-to-surface missile. For accelerated take-off and for target propulsion, Napier Scorpion was offered in single-, double- or triple-chambered forms, each chamber giving 2,000 lb. thrust. Rolls-Royce tested a rocket engine for a long-range ballistic missile but no details were released.

Turbo-Props. Rolls-Royce Dart engines in service had ratings between 1,600 and 1,900 s.h.p. These two-stage centrifugal-compressor type turbo-props had accumulated over 8 million hr. flying and reached approved overhaul life of 2,300 hr. The Dart 540 was in development towards 2,500 s.h.p. Tyne engines, with high (over 13 : 1) pressure ratio, double-compound, axial compressors, rated at 4,985 max. equivalent horsepower, powered the first Vanguard airliners

The Dowty Turbocraft, a new water-jet propelled motor launch capable of 35 m.p.h., demonstrates an about-turn at full speed.

for B.E.A. Higher-rated versions, R.Ty.11 (5,525 m.e.h.p.) and R.Ty.12 (5,730 m.e.h.p.) were in development for Canadian CL.44 and Britannic 3 military transports. A special variant was chosen for the Rotodyne helicopter.

The Napier Eland N.El.6 (3,500 m.e.h.p.) became the first turbo-prop to obtain the full airworthiness certification under the new Anglo-U.S. regulations and entered passenger service in Convair 540 aircraft of Allegheny Airlines. Eland variants powered prototype Rotodyne and Westminster helicopters. The Gazelle free-power turbine engine was in production for Bristol 192 and Wessex helicopters. The maximum ratings were 1,650 s.h.p. (5 min. limit) and 1,450 s.h.p. (60 min. limit) respectively. De Havilland introduced the Gnome D.Ge.1 British-built version of the U.S. GE.T.58 axial-compressor type turbo-shaft engine. Offered at 1,000 s.h.p. for helicopter installations, early engines were flight-tested in Whirlwind and SR-P531. The Gnome P.1000, a turbo-prop version for fixed-wing aircraft, was exhibited. Blackburn A.129 axial-cum-centrifugal-compressor type gas turbine, in development towards 970 s.h.p., was also flight-tested in helicopters.

Power-Generating, Industrial, Marine and Locomotive Gas Turbines. An English Electric EM.27.P 2,250-kw. two-shaft, open-cycle, gas-turbo alternator was installed for stand-by duty at the Ashford Common, Middlesex, pumping station of the Metropolitan Water board. A similar gas turbine, to drive a five-stage centrifugal compressor, was incorporated in a new butadiene extraction plant at the Fawley refinery, Hampshire. Fired by gas drawn from an ethylene recovery unit, this gas turbine gave continuous rated output of 2,625 h.p. at 7,500 r.p.m. Batch production of EM.85 8,000-s.h.p. open-cycle gas turbines continued. These 6 : 1 pressure ratio axial-compressor machines had independent two-stage compressor and power turbines, a single combustion chamber and operated at 790°C. turbine inlet temperature.

Sales of Ruston and Hornsby Mark TA 1,260 h.p. open-cycle gas turbines reached over 100, largely for oil-field operation. This continued to be the most successful British industrial gas turbine production line. A 1,000-kw. mobile gas turbine-driven generating plant was delivered to the U.S.S.R. for use on railway construction sites or for emergency duty. Mounted on a specially constructed twin-bogie chassis, a Mark TA gas turbine capable of running on either fuel oil or natural gas drove a 1,250-kva. alternator through gearing. The complete wagon weighed 65 tons and was 66 ft. long.

H.M.S. " Brave Borderer ", first R.N. fast patrol boat with

Bristol-Siddeley Marine Proteus gas turbines, achieved over 50 knots during preliminary sea trials. Published ratings were 3,800 h.p. maximum $\frac{1}{2}$ hour power and 3,000 h.p. continuous, the weight being 2,900 lb. The South Western Electricity board installed two Proteus-powered 3,000-kw. turbo-generator sets for peak-load duties. Diesel fuel consumption was 0·575 lb./s.h.p./hr. Each self-contained set was automatically controlled with remote push-button starting. Notwithstanding successful operating experience of their gas turbo-alternator sets for shipborne emergency power generation, Allens decided to discontinue gas turbine work. Perkins, makers of diesel engines, formed the Perkins Gas Turbines, Ltd., to manufacture, under licence, a range of industrial gas turbines from 50 h.p. to 1,500 h.p., designed and developed by Solar Aircraft of San Diego, California.

Through reorganization, the gas turbine activities of Metropolitan-Vickers and British Thomson-Houston were combined within Associated Electrical Industries. M-V, L.51.C, 4,000-kw. natural gas-burning turbo-alternator sets continued in manufacture for use in oil-fields. M-V marine gas turbines were installed in a " Tribal " class frigate. This was the first ship to have combined steam and gas turbine machinery for main propulsion: the steam turbines for cruising and the gas turbines for quick starts and for boost power for high speeds. The 12,000-ton Shell tanker " Auris ", propelled by a single B.T-H. 5,500-h.p. open-cycle, two-shaft, recuperative, intercooled gas turbine ran sea trials. Thermal economy equalled that of a steam turbine and was less than that of a diesel. This assessment, coupled with high capital cost, decided Shell against the installation of gas turbine propulsion machinery in their other ships.

Blackburns offered a compact 200-kw. set driven by a 325-h.p. Turmo free-power, turbine type engine. Its fuel consumption was 375 lb./hr. The A129, rated at 700 s.h.p. for industrial purposes, was in development. A vehicle-mounted Palouste air-bleed gas turbine capable of delivering 2·0 lb./sec. of air at 38·5 p.s.i.g. was exhibited. A Palouste with an additional compressor to give the same air flow at 70 p.s.i.g. was also available. Rover marketed a mobile power trolley in which a 60-h.p. production 1S/60 gas turbine supplied either 0·875 lb./sec. of air at 33 p.s.i.g. or 9-kw. D.C. power. Budworth offered two sizes of small gas turbine, the 45/60-h.p. Brill and the 500-h.p. Basilisk, both capable of delivering either shaft power or low-pressure air. In the latter version, the Basilisk was rated at 2·5 lb./sec. at 60 p.s.i.g. The Standard gas turbine was also available in two forms either to give 250 s.h.p. or 2·0 lb./sec. air at 40 p.s.i.g. and at 200°C. The single-shaft, centrifugal-compressor type engine had two reverse-flow combustion chambers and inward-flow radial turbine.

Commonwealth. The cancellation of Canadian government orders for the Avro Arrow fighter caused Orenda Engines, Ltd., to terminate development of the Iroquois turbo-jet. Subsequently, Orenda obtained an $80 million order for the U.S.-designed GE.J79 (15,000 lb. m.s.l.s.t. with reheat) turbojets for the Canadian-built Lockheed Starfighter aircraft. The repair and overhaul of Orenda (7,000 lb. m.s.l.s.t.) turbo-jets for CF-100 fighters continued and adaptations of Orenda for industrial purposes were in hand. The Canadian Pratt and Whitney bench-tested a new turbo-shaft engine, PT6, rated at 500 s.h.p. The quoted weight was 225 lb. with a 6,000-r.p.m. output shaft and 250 lb. with reduction gear and 2,400-r.p.m. propeller shaft. The Australian Aircraft corporation continued its production of Avon engines for the new line of Sabre fighters for the R.A.A.F. and Hindustan Aircraft proceeded with preparations for the production of Orpheus turbo-jets.

Europe. In Belgium Fabrique Nationale were in production with Rolls-Royce Avon 10,000-lb. thrust turbo-jets, Marcel

Dassault in France manufactured 3,200-lb. thrust Farandole turbo-jets and Hispano Suiza passed a 150-hr. type test with 3,300-lb. thrust turbo-jets. Société Nationale d'Equipements et de Constructions Mécaniques pour l'Aviation (S.N.E.C.M.A.) put four turbo-jets into production: 8,160 lb. thrust ATAR E5, and afterburner version, 9,700-lbt. ATAR G3, 9,700-lbt. ATAR 8 and afterburner version, and 1,300-lbt. ATAR 9. S.N.E.C.M.A. received a licence to manufacture Bristol Orpheus. In addition to two turbo-jet, two turbo-shaft and one turbo-compressor models in production, Turbo-méca were developing 550-lbt. and 1,540-lbt., turbo-jet engines, and two turbo-shaft engines of 354 s.h.p. and 716 s.h.p. In the German Democratic Republic, Vereinigung Volkseigener Betriebe Flugzeugbau were in small production of 6,950-lbt. turbo-jets. In the German Federal Republic Heinkel tested new turbo-jets in 14,300-lbt. and 19,800-lbt. afterburner versions. Engine departments of Heinkel and Junkers were amalgamated to develop engines of all types. In Italy Fiat continued development of the 5,950-lbt. turbo-jet and of the 550-air-h.p. turbo-compressor, while Svenska Flygmotor in Sweden produced Rolls-Royce Avon 11,250-lbt. turbo-jets. Nuclear-powered aircraft developments in Europe included work by Hispano Suiza and S.N.E.C.M.A. in France.

STAL at Västervik, Sweden, began tests on a 40-Mw. gas turbine for use with heavy oil at the maximum inlet temperature of 700°C.; the set being designed for peak load and the synchronous condenser for power factor correction. Brown Boveri in Switzerland outlined uses of their gas turbines in integrated power chemical plants throughout the world, citing Houdry plants, nitric acid and sulphite liquor oxidation. Six German escort vessels under construction in the yard of Stulcken Sohn, of 1,700 tons each with twin screw propulsion, were fitted with two 3,000-b.h.p. 900-r.p.m. MAN Vee type diesels for cruising. The addition of two Brown Boveri 13,000-h.p. gas turbines at 6,500 r.p.m. gave a total available power of 38,000 h.p. In Czechoslovakia, Brno engineering works tested a 1,000-kw. gas turbine designed to burn methane and were constructing 6,000- and 12,000-kw. sets. Skoda at Plzeň announced that they were running on a combined steam/gas turbine set of 4·4 Mw. which gave an over-all efficiency of 28%. A similar 50-Mw. set with 35% thermal efficiency was also projected.

United States. Developments continued with ram-jets, rocket-jets and gas turbines. Allison put in production a 4,050-e.h.p. turbo-prop in one civil and two military versions in addition to a 14,000-lbt. turbo-jet with an afterburner and a 5,200-lbt. turbo-jet for guided missiles; under development were 250-s.h.p. turbo-props with turbo-jet version and civil and military 5,500-e.h.p. turbo-props, as well as a high Mach No. turbo-jet designed to use high-energy fuel. Continental Aviation and Engineering corporation was in full production with a 920-lbt. turbo-jet for target drones and with high-thrust missile engines, as well as a turbo-compressor of 190 air h.p. A turbo-jet of 2,000 lbt. was under development and early testing by Fairchild Engines. General Electric produced an 11,000-lbt. commercial engine, with an afterburner military version at 15,000 lbt., and developed a 15,000-lbt. turbo-fan; other developments of General Electric were tests of a 2,000-lbt. turbo-jet, a 1,024-h.p. turbo-shaft in small production, also a 25,000-lbt. engine for use with high-energy fuel and for nuclear energy development. Lycoming reported the production of a 825-s.h.p. engine for helicopter use and of a turbo-prop of 1,005 e.h.p. They were also ready to produce a 1,670-e.h.p. engine and its helicopter version at 1,850 s.h.p. Marquardt Aircraft announced the manufacture of a 10,000-lbt. ram-jet with higher powers under development, besides a nuclear-powered ram-jet. Pratt and Whitney's latest productions were military turbo-jets of 7,250 lbt. without and 17,000 lbt. and 26,000 lbt. with afterburner. In civil versions the two latter gave 13,500 and 17,000 lbt. respectively. Pratt and Whitney developments included 2,900-lbt. turbo-jets for commercial aircraft and the high-energy, fuel-fired 30,000-lbt. engine, in addition to the 25,000-lbt. nuclear reactor engine. Westinghouse produced a 3,400-lbt. turbo-jet and were testing a 6,500-lbt. turbo-jet. A 4,500-lbt. engine with an afterburner was produced by Wright.

The development of the following nuclear-powered engines continued: G.E. open-cycle turbo-jet and the Pratt and Whitney closed-cycle turbo-jet, both of which had a 25,000 lb. thrust. Test facilities were used on the G.E. cycle with a nuclear reactor, while other facilities at Connecticut and Wright Air Development became available. Nuclear power plants for ram-jets and rockets were also under development.

The use of ground power units and of mobile turbo-starters increased: K.L.M. ordered 18 of the former with 1,000 hr. life between overhauls equivalent to 3,000 start-ups and 16 of the latter for aircraft use. Mayagüez, Puerto Rica, installed 40,000 kw. on a twin-shaft $2 \times 20,000$-kw. Brown Boveri set with a maintenance cost of one-third that of a steam plant. Westinghouse improved the position of gas turbines in the petrochemical industry with four plants providing compressed air at 10-12 p.s.i. at 1,000°F. for butadiene production with a total of 12,000 hr. operation; two plants in Japan totalling 16,900 hr. and two in Sumatra 11,000 hr., all at 3,000 h.p. each; also one plant in Cuba of 3,000 h.p. for 5,500 hr.; and one 12,000-h.p. machine under development. General Electric with 32 machines in the field on gas line pumping totalled 1 million hr. operation. The cost of gas turbine operation compared with reciprocating engine gave a saving of 30% made up as follows: 25% labour, 4% maintenance, 4% oil and 2% in volume, less 1% in fuel. Eight more sets of 5,000 h.p. were ordered by El Paso. Ford announced new developments in a 160-h.p. lorry with 810°C. maximum turbine inlet temperature, with a reliable heat exchanger. The cost of a turbine wheel of small size was solved by a process involving the extrusion of a turbine wheel hub around the turbine blade roots.

U.S.S.R. Five turbo-jets were in production: 12,000-lbt. Lulko, 15,400-lbt. Zubets for commercial aircraft and, for military use, 19,800-lbt. MIK, 15,000-lbt. MIK with afterburners and a 7,500-lbt. Klimov with an afterburner. Turbo-props in production were the 4,400-e.h.p. Kuznetsov and 13,000-e.h.p. NK for both civil and military planes. A 4,500-s.h.p. turbo-shaft engine for helicopter use was also in production. No information was received on nuclear power aircraft developments. Nevski Engineering works of Leningrad provided a mobile 4,000-kw. set on three railcars: one car contained the turbine, one the electrical equipment and one a workshop and crew living quarters; diesel oil or mazout was specified for a top inlet temperature of 700°C. Elektrosila works in Leningrad reported that tests had been completed on the water cooling of components of a 3,000-kw. set and plans for the construction of a 165-Mw. set with forced hydrogen cooling of rotor and water cooling of stator were made. Design was started on a 50,000-kw. gas turbine for the Kirov building plant in Kharkov and the national seven-year plan included gas turbine installations of from 100 Mw. to 300 Mw. (*See* also AIRCRAFT MANUFACTURE; AIR FORCES OF THE WORLD; AVIATION, CIVIL.)   (R. H. SL.; C. G. C.)

BIBLIOGRAPHY (all London 1959). A. W. Morley, " Notes on Air Breathing Engines for Supersonic Flight ", *Royal Aeronautical Society Journal*, 63, 577 (Jan.); A. C. Lovesey, " The Art of Developing Aero-Engines ", *Royal Aeronautical Society Journal*, 63, 584 (Aug.); " British Aero Engines ", *Flight*, 76, 2634 (Sept.); " British Gas Turbine installed in New Petrochemicals Plant ", *Oil Eng.*, 27, 310 (June).

JEWRY. World total of Jews (1959), c. 12,169,300, including 6,176,730 in America, 3,452,350 in Europe, 1,915,000 in Asia, 560,750 in Africa and 64,500 in Australasia. The four largest Jewish com-

munities were: United States, 5·25 million; U.S.S.R., c. 2 million; Israel, 1,780,000; Great Britain, 450,000.

Religious and Communal Life. The chief rabbinate of Israel convened a special session of the Supreme Religious council to discuss the suppression of religious practices in the U.S.S.R. and eastern Europe. A testimonial fund was raised in honour of Dr. Isaac Herzog, chief rabbi of Israel, to celebrate his 70th year; he died shortly afterwards. The board of directors of the Claims conference in New York allocated $10 million to

Daniel Barenboim, the young Israeli pianist, rehearsing with William Steinberg for his concert at the Festival Hall on Feb. 5.

Jewish communities, organizations and institutions in 30 countries. A foundation of $350,000 established by Baron Edmond de Rothschild made grants to Jewish communities in France for educational and religious purposes. The Warsaw municipality agreed to spend Zł.200,000 on the resiting of the ghetto fighters' memorial. The Jewish State Museum of Prague had the names of over 70,000 Jewish victims of Nazi persecution in Czechoslovakia painted on the walls of an ancient synagogue, which was converted into a museum. The centenary of the birth of the Jewish novelist and humorist, Sholem Aleichem, was celebrated in all Jewish communities. Refugees in England who had been in camps were resettled among the Jewish communities in London and the provinces. The 11th international conference of the World Union for Progressive Judaism was held in London and the plenary assembly of the World Jewish congress in Stockholm. About 200,000 Jews throughout the world were assisted by the American Joint Distribution committee. Fifteen scrolls of the Law and the Ark were reduced to ashes and thousands of pounds of damage were caused by a fire at a synagogue in Liverpool.

Political. The 3,000 British Jews forced to leave Egypt claimed over £30 million as compensation. In Libya a decree ordered the sequestration of all money and property of Jews. Austria agreed to establish a fund of $6 million as compensation to victims of Nazism. The Federal German government agreed to pay the Bnai Brith organization 10 million marks as compensation for destruction of its property. During his visit to Moscow Harold Macmillan conveyed informally to his hosts " the interest felt among British Jews in the position of the Russian Jewish community." The pope appointed Eliahu Sasson, Israel's ambassador to Italy, as a Knight of the Grand Cross of St. Sylvester. Dr. Stella Klein-Low was the first Jewish woman to become a member of the Austrian parliament.

Anti-Semitism. Anti-Semitic incidents continued disturbingly in the German Federal Republic. Bavaria was a centre of anti-Semitic groups composed of Hungarian emigrants, German neo-Nazis and Fascists, who formed an international league. Dr. Otto Schweinsberger, chief prosecutor of Hesse, was arrested on the charge of having repeatedly insulted Jews. In Hamburg an injunction was granted to the Central Council of German Jews restraining the dissemination of a defamatory anti-Jewish pamphlet. The Federal German government passed a law imposing imprisonment for incitement to racial or religious hatred or defamation. Gustav Sorge and Wilhelm Schubert, former Nazi guards, were sentenced to hard labour for life for the murder of 67 persons in Sachsenhausen concentration camp. Wilhelm Unkelbach was similarly sentenced for murdering 30 Jews in Częstochowa. At the end of the year the leader of the Cologne branch of the extreme right-wing Deutsche Reichspartei was arrested and charged in connection with the desecration of a synagogue on Christmas Eve. In Czechoslovakia two former members of the Hungarian Arrow guard were sentenced to death for activities against Jews during World War II. In the same country 26 Zionists were sentenced to a total of 264 years imprisonment. Erich Koch, war-time Nazi governor of the Ukraine, was sentenced to death in Warsaw for complicity in many murders. In the United States a group of negroes calling themselves " Moslems " conducted anti-Semitic propaganda. Extreme right-wing Hungarian journalists in London published an anti-Semitic journal. An anti-Semitic group, formed under the name of the French National party, was dissolved by the French government.

Contributions to National Life. For educational grants by the Isaac Wolfson foundation and Jack Cotton, *see* UNIVERSITIES AND COLLEGES. Sir A. Jeremy Raisman was appointed G.C.M.G. and Sir Roy Welensky, prime minister of the Federation of Rhodesia and Nyasaland, K.C.M.G. In the U.S.S.R., of 230,000 government scientific research workers, 24,000 were Jews. Prof. Max Oppenheim was re-elected vice-chancellor of the University of Malaya for five years. Prof. René Cassin was appointed French representative in the European Court of Human Rights. In Britain Dr. Max Sorsby was appointed a member of the General Optical council.

Migration. The emigration of Jews from the U.S.S.R. to Poland was reduced to a trickle, leaving 40,000-50,000. The continued exodus from Rumania to Israel was curtailed under pressure from the United Arab Republic. About 1,000 Jews were flown from Austria to Israel. Twenty-six Moroccan Jewish emigrants who had been arrested by the Moroccan authorities at Oudjda were conditionally released. (*See* also ISRAEL.) (I. C.)

See *American Jewish Year-Book* (Philadelphia, 1959); *Jewish Year-Book* (London, 1959).

JORDAN. Arab kingdom bounded W. by Israel, N. by Syria, E. by Iraq and S.E. by Saudi Arabia. Area (incl. Arab Palestine): 37,302 sq.mi. Pop. (1958 est.): 1,578,000 (745,786 [1953 est.] in west Jordan [Arab Palestine]). Capital: Amman, pop. (1954 est.) 202,213. Language: mainly Arabic. Religion: Moslem (chiefly Sunni); Christian *c.* 8% (mainly Arab-speaking Greek Orthodox). King, Hussein I. Prime ministers in 1959: Samir Rifai and (from May 5) Hazzaa Majali. Main imports: foodstuffs, cotton and silk fabrics, vehicles, iron and steel manufactures. Main exports: vegetables, fruit, fertilizers and olive oil. Monetary unit: Jordan *dinar* (=£1 sterling).

History. On the whole the situation in Jordan was far less disturbed during 1959 than in the previous year. This remarkable change from a state of acute tension to one of comparative normality was due to several factors, both internal and external. Internally, King Hussein emerged from the 1958 crisis with enhanced prestige and popularity, owing to the personal courage and resolution he had displayed. Externally, the apparent drift of Iraq towards Communism in the early months of 1959 and President Gamal Abd-ul-Nasser's open attack on Communists throughout the Arab world, favoured the king, weakened the opposition (which contained many Communist elements) and even brought about a certain improvement in the relations between Jordan and the United Arab Republic.

By March the king felt so confident about the situation in Jordan that both he and his prime minister, Samir Rifai, were able to leave the country on a visit to the United States and Britain, in the course of which the two conferred with members of the U.S. and British governments. During their absence there was a round-up of Communists in Jordan, about 30 persons being arrested, but the prevailing tranquillity in the country was undisturbed.

On May 5, shortly after the king's return to Jordan, Samir Rifai resigned as prime minister, on the grounds that he needed a rest and that the crisis which had led him to accept office two years earlier had passed, leaving the country at peace and confidence between the throne and the people re-established. The retiring prime minister also announced that he had obtained from London and Washington promises of financial assistance which would ensure Jordan's economic stability. The king appointed the court minister, Hazzaa Majali, to succeed Rifai as prime minister. Majali had

The speaker of the Jordan parliament, Mostafa Khalife, reading his reply to the speech from the throne to King Hussein on Oct. 12.

championed the Baghdad pact in 1955, but on his appointment as prime minister he made it clear that the pact was a thing of the past, and both he and the king promised that Jordan would stay out of all foreign alliances.

On May 23, Major-General Sadiq Share'i, deputy chief of staff of the Jordan army, was arrested, together with a number of other officers, on a charge of plotting to seize power while the king was abroad. The plot, it was stated, had been discovered by the king before he left Jordan, and he had foiled it by taking Share'i with him on his tour. The accused officers were put on trial in August, the prosecution alleging that the plot was connected with the Iraqi revolution. The trial ended in mid-October when Share'i and two other officers were sentenced to death.

In June, following a frontier dispute, the U.A.R. closed its Syrian border with Jordan. The matter was brought before the United Nations by the Jordan government, but the border was re-opened before the affair had developed any further. In December, King Hussein paid a second visit to Britain.
(E. S. A.)

JUVENILE DELINQUENCY.
The upward trend in juvenile delinquency observable since 1955 continued in 1958, linked with a further general increase in criminal activity. As over the whole period, the statistics showed a higher rate of increase for all age-groups under 21 than for adults. Of all those convicted of indictable offences 35% were boys and girls under 17, and 51% were under 21. This was apparently the first time since World War II that more than half of those found guilty of indictable offences were under 21. Again, this was not simply due to an increase in the size of the juvenile population, since when the figures are corrected for change in the size of population they still show a rather higher rate of increase among those under 21 than among adults.

Among those under 21, the 8-14-year group showed a slight fall in the share of all indictable offences, from 19·3% in 1957 to 19·1% in 1958, but the 14-17-year group showed a 1% increase and the 17-21-year group an increase of 1·7%. The percentage variations compared with 1957 for different types of crime (see table) show a marked tendency towards an increase in violence among juveniles.

PERCENTAGE CHANGES IN CONVICTIONS FOR INDICTABLE OFFENCES, BY AGE GROUPS, 1958 COMPARED WITH 1957*

	8-14	14-17	17-21	Total(all ages)
Larceny	+10 (20)	+16 (16)	+20 (15)	+9
Breaking and entering	+12 (27)	+28 (22)	+40 (19)	+24
Receiving	+30 (17)	+24 (16)	+26 (11)	+15
Sexual offences	+3 (6)	—9 (14)	+18 (15)	—4
Violence against the person	+37 (3)	+37 (10)	+27 (26)	+12
Robbery	+74 (12)	+24 (10)	+52 (34)	+39

* The figures in brackets are percentages representing each age-group's share in all convictions for offences of each type.
SOURCE: *Criminal Statistics, England and Wales, 1958.* Cmnd. 803 (H.M.S.O., London, 1959).

Girls under 14 show a notably higher proportional increase over the 1957 figures for convictions of indictable offences taken as a whole than do boys. But the difference narrows in the 14-17-year group and is reversed in those over 17.

A government white paper, *Penal Practice in a Changing Society: Aspects of Future Development, England and Wales* (Cmnd. 645), published in February, mentioned plans to increase the provision of detention centres. Currently, two of the four centres were for boys of 14-17, but it was not specified for which age-groups the new centres would be designed. Any further proposals for the treatment of juvenile offenders were specifically postponed to await the report of the Ingleby committee (see JUVENILE DELINQUENCY in *Britannica Book of the Year 1959*).

Public concern at the increase in crimes of violence among young people was expressed by the passing in May of a private members's bill, making illegal both the manufacture of " flick " and " gravity " knives and dealings in them.

During the weekend of Aug. 28-30 there were serious disturbances at the approved school at Carlton, Bedfordshire. The trouble culminated in a mass walk-out by about 80 boys, after some damage had been done to the school and its farm. In October-November an independent inquiry was held into the disturbances by Victor Durand, Q.C., who was to submit his report to the Home Office. The approved school system currently handled some 8,000 children in schools provided and run by local authorities and voluntary bodies, under Home Office inspection. (*See* also CRIME; YOUTH EMPLOYMENT.)   (R. A. BZ.)

JUVENILE EMPLOYMENT: *see* YOUTH EMPLOYMENT.

KASHMIR (JAMMU AND KASHMIR). Country in Indian sub-continent, bounded W. and S.W. by West Pakistan, N. and E. by Wakhan salient of Afghanistan (dividing Kashmir from U.S.S.R. by 35 mi.) and China (Sinkiang and Tibet autonomous regions), and S. by India (Punjab state and Himachal Pradesh territory). Area (incl. Gilgit frontier agency): 84,471 sq.mi. Pop.: (1941 census) 4,021,616; (1950 est.) 4,370,000. Language: Kashmiri, akin to Punjabi. Religion: Moslem 75%; Hindu 20% (mainly in Jammu district). Partitioned *de facto* into two states: Indian-controlled east and south of 1948 cease-fire line; Pakistan-controlled north and west of it.
INDIAN-CONTROLLED KASHMIR. Chief towns (pop., 1941 census): Srinagar (cap.) 207,787; Jammu (winter cap.) 42,794. *Sadr-i-riyasat* (elected state president), Yuvraj Karan Singh; prime minister, Bakshi Ghulam Mohammed. Chief exports: forest products; cottage manufactures. Monetary unit: Indian *rupee*.
AZAD (" FREE ") KASHMIR (PAKISTAN-CONTROLLED). Cap.: Muzaffarabad. President of government, K. H. Khurshid. Monetary unit: Pakistan *rupee*.

History. The year 1959 brought no change in the situation of this disputed state, New Delhi refusing a plebiscite and regarding Jammu and Kashmir as part of the Republic of India, while Karachi was continuing to claim the state because of its Moslem majority.

In March, a Soviet government delegation, led by A. A. Andreev and Nuritdin Mukhitdinov, visited Indian-controlled Kashmir. In a speech at Srinagar Mukhitdinov repeated a statement made by N. S. Khrushchev in Oct. 1955, namely that Kashmir was part of India. In April Yuvraj Karan Singh, president of Indian-controlled Kashmir, paid an official visit to the U.S.S.R. Sheikh Mohammed Abdullah, former prime minister of Kashmir, remained in an Indian prison, facing trial on charges of criminal conspiracy.

On Sept. 1, General Ayub Khan, president of Pakistan, informally met Jawaharlal Nehru, prime minister of India, at the Palam airport near New Delhi. The joint communiqué said that the outstanding issues between the two countries " should in the mutual interest be settled in accordance with justice and fair play ".

On May 1, K. H. Khurshid replaced Mohammed Ibrahim Khan as president of " Azad " Kashmir. In July he opened at Muzaffarabad a newspaper editors' conference which adopted a resolution reiterating that the future of Jammu and Kashmir should be determined by a free plebiscite.

During the year the Chinese People's Republic claimed that quite a considerable section of the province of Ladakh, populated by Tibetans, belonged to China. (*See* also SINO-INDIAN FRONTIER DISPUTE.)   (X.)

KENYA. British colony and protectorate in east Africa bounded N. by Sudan and Ethiopia, E. by Somaliland Protectorate and the Indian ocean, S. by Tanganyika and W. by Uganda. The protectorate—the leased mainland dominions of the sultan of Zanzibar—is a ten-mile-wide coastal strip between the Tanganyika border and Kipini, together with the Lamu archipelago. Total area of Kenya: 224,960 sq.mi., incl. 5,170 sq.mi. of inland water. Total pop.: (1948 census)

5,405,966, incl. 29,660 Europeans, 97,687 Indians and Goans and 24,174 Arabs; (1958 est.) 6,351,000. Main tribes (1948 census): Kikuyu 19·5%, Luo 14·4%, Baluhya 12·5%, Kamba 11·7%, Meru 6·2%, Nyika 5·6%. Language: Bantu and Nilotic; Swahili as *lingua franca*. Religion: Africans mainly pagan; *c.* 800,000 Christians; the Moslem religion flourishes in coastal, urban and some northern communities. Principal towns (pop., 1948 census): Nairobi (cap.), 118,976, (1957 est.) 221,700; Mombasa, 84,746; just over 50% Africans in each city. Administration: governor; council of ministers; legislative council, partly elected and partly nominated, with a speaker appointed by the governor; council of state. Governors in 1959: Sir Evelyn Baring and (from Oct. 23) Sir Patrick Renison. Main imports: machinery and vehicles, mineral fuels, food products. Main exports: coffee, tea, sisal, hides and skins. Monetary unit: east African shilling (20*s.* = £1 sterling).

History. At the beginning of 1959 Rawson Macharia, one of the prosecution witnesses at the trial of Jomo Kenyatta in 1952, was charged with swearing a false affidavit to the effect that he and six other witnesses had been procured and suborned by the crown to give false evidence against Kenyatta. The trial, which opened in Nairobi, was adjourned to Kitale in the interests of security when Kenyatta himself and five other convicts were called to give evidence. After a hearing lasting 29 days Macharia was found guilty and sentenced to 21 months' imprisonment. An appeal against the sentence was dismissed.

In the meantime a more serious event had caught public attention. Eleven Mau Mau detainees at the Hola camp were found after a post-mortem examination to have died of violence. At the inquest on the dead men it was revealed that they had been beaten in an attempt to compel them to work, apparently with the intention of putting into effect a plan drafted by a senior prisons officer to deal with detainees who had proved intractable. The findings of the coroner gave rise to numerous questions in the British House of Commons, and the governor of Kenya appointed a tribunal to consider disciplinary charges against the commandant and deputy commandant of the camp. The composition of the tribunal, which consisted of three civil servants of the Kenya government, was severely criticized by opposition members of the British parliament. In June a motion of censure was moved in parliament against the secretary of state for the colonies, A. T. Lennox-Boyd, for his failure to take immediate steps to set up a public inquiry to ascertain where responsibility for the use of unlawful violence should be placed. The charges against the prison officers, it was argued, prevented

A member of the Arab community is presented to Queen Elizabeth the Queen Mother in Mombasa during her tour of Kenya in February.

a full inquiry into the issue of who was responsible at a higher level for taking decisions which had made the use of violence possible.

In February Lennox-Boyd announced a further grant of £800,000 and an interest free loan of the same amount to help Kenya finance its recurrent expenditure arising from the emergency during the financial year 1959-60. It was also agreed with the Kenya government that this would be the last year in which the British government would be asked to provide financial assistance for this purpose.

In February, also, Queen Elizabeth the Queen Mother visited Kenya as part of her tour of east Africa. In spite of a threat by certain sections of the African population to boycott her visit she was received everywhere by enthusiastic crowds.

Early in April Michael Blundell announced his resignation as minister of agriculture in order to assume the leadership of a group comprising elected, specially elected and nominated members of the legislative council, of all races, with the title of the New Kenya group. Simultaneously another group consisting of African, Indian, Moslem and Arab elected members and one European elected member formed itself into the Kenya National party. In policy statements both groups stressed the need to end racialism in Kenya and to provide equal opportunities for all.

In October an important sessional paper on land tenure and control outside native land units was tabled in the legislative council. Its most striking proposal was that in future the main consideration governing the ownership or occupation of land in the "white highlands" would be sound farming, not race. Inevitably the white paper aroused lively criticism from Europeans. An equally important announcement to the effect that the seven-year-old emergency would be brought to an end at the end of the year was made in November by the new governor, Sir Patrick Renison. Earlier the same month it had also been announced that provisional arrangements were being made to hold a conference on the Kenya constitution in London in Jan. 1960. The secretary of state for the colonies, Iain Macleod,

Kikuyu on the Hola settlement, Kenya: the man on the left farms four acres on his own account. His helper is still under detention.

arrived in Nairobi on Dec. 13 to hold talks with members of the government and political leaders.

There was an increase in racial tension between Africans and Asians at the end of the year following the murder of an Asian family, and disturbances were reported in Nairobi. (*See also* EAST AFRICA HIGH COMMISSION.)   (K. I.)

KOREA (CHOSON, " Country of Morning Calm ") is situated on a peninsula extending from Manchuria southward 600 mi. between the Yellow sea and the Sea of Japan; for 11 mi. it borders the U.S.S.R.; the rest of the boundary is with China. Total area: 85,226 sq.mi. Total pop.: (1944 census) 25,120,174; (1959 est.) 30,718,000. The parallel of lat. 30° N. separates South Korea (44 % of total area, 74 % of population) from North Korea. Religion: Buddhist, Confucian and Tonghak (Chutokyo), a unique eclectic religion; in 1959 there were about 1,582,000 Christians, including 262,000 Roman Catholics.

REPUBLIC OF KOREA (south).   Area: 38,452 sq.mi.   Pop.: (1955 census) 21,526,374; (1959 est.) 22,746,000.   Chief towns (pop., 1959 est.): Seoul (cap.) 1,700,000; Pusan 840,000; Taegu (1955) 489,000; Inchon (1955) 318,000.   President of the republic, Syngman Rhee (Li Syn Man).   Chief imports: foodstuffs.   Chief exports: raw materials. Monetary unit: South Korean *hwan* (official exchange rate: 1,400 = £1 sterling).

PEOPLE'S DEMOCRATIC REPUBLIC OF KOREA (north).   Area: 46,814 sq.mi.   Pop. (1959 est.): 7,972,000.   Capital: Pyongyang (Pkhenian), pop. (1955 est.) 500,000.   Chairman of the central committee of the Workers' (Communist) Party of Korea, commander-in-chief and chairman of the council of ministers, Marshal Kim Ir Sen (Kim Il Sung); chairman of the presidium of the Supreme People's Assembly, Tsoi Yen Gen.   Monetary unit: North Korean *won* (official exchange rate: 33·60 = £1 sterling).

History.   *General.*   On Dec. 9, 1959, the U.N. general assembly once more called on the " Communist authorities " to agree to the creation of a " unified, independent and democratic Korea " by means of " genuinely free elections ".   It also maintained in existence the U.N. Commission for the Unification and Rehabilitation of Korea.   The vote was 54 to 9, with 17 abstentions, the opposing votes being cast by the Communist countries.

On Oct. 26, Nam Ir, deputy chairman of the council of ministers of North Korea, proposed a union with South Korea through nation-wide elections to be preceded by the withdrawal of all foreign troops.   The government of South Korea not only opposed the withdrawal of U.S. troops, but also a general election throughout Korea.   According to Chung Whan Cho, foreign minister of South Korea, all that was necessary for reunification was the free election of 100 North Korean deputies who would sit in the existing South Korean 233-seat House of Representatives (elected on May 2, 1958).

On April 22, President Dwight D. Eisenhower appointed General George H. Decker, commander of the U.S. forces in Korea, vice chief of staff of the army.   Decker's successor was General Carter B. Magruder.   The U.S. army comprised two divisions (1st cavalry and 7th infantry).   About half the 14,000 men in each were Koreans known as " Katusa " (Koreans attached to the U.S. army).   Of the other troops sent to Korea only the Turkish brigade and a Thai unit remained.

There were 611,085 Koreans in Japan who had been brought there as forced labourers during World War II.   The majority of them were now desperately poor.   It was estimated that about 160,000 wanted to return to North Korea and Japan would gladly get rid of them.   But Syngman Rhee, president of South Korea, claiming that his administration was the only legal government of Korea, protested against such " provocation ".   In February the Japanese government asked the International Committee of the Red Cross to supervise the repatriation in order to ensure that the return was voluntary. After six months of negotiations an agreement was signed in Calcutta, India, on Aug. 13, between the Red Cross societies of Japan and North Korea under which Koreans residing in Japan who " by their freely expressed will " wished to be repatriated to North Korea would be permitted to do so.   The South Korean government opposed this agreement and retali-

ated by severing trade relations with Japan.   On Dec. 14, with a great display of organized enthusiasm, the first group of about 1,000 Koreans sailed in two Soviet ships from Niigata for the North Korean port of Chongjin.

On Dec. 30 it was announced in Moscow that two days earlier a South Korean patrol vessel had fired on the Soviet hydrographic ship " Ungo," at a point 30 mi. off the eastern coast of the People's Republic of Korea and 36 mi. northeast of the South Korean frontier.   One member of the Soviet crew was killed and four injured.   The South Korean authorities strongly denied this attack and suggested that a North Korean ship apparently mistook the Soviet vessel for a South Korean one.

Republic of Korea.   Two laws, enacted by the House of Representatives on Dec. 24, 1958, caused bitter political controversy.   The laws were passed after the forcible ejection of the opposition Democratic party members who barricaded themselves in the assembly in an attempt to stop the bills.   The two laws were voted by the Liberal (pro-Rhee) party majority alone.   One law imposed severe penalties, including death, for disseminating false statements or criticism of the government that would assist an enemy.   The other law gave the central government the power to appoint mayors of cities and villages in place of elections to those offices.

On May 1, 1959, the second largest newspaper in the republic, the *Kyunghyang Shinmun*, with a circulation of 250,000 and which supported the Democratic party, was closed for " seditious comment ".   On July 31 Cho Bong Am, former leader of the outlawed Progressive party, was hanged in Seoul on charges of attempting to overthrow the government in collaboration with the North Korean authorities.   He opposed Rhee in the 1952 and 1956 presidential elections.

Lieut.-General Song Yo Chan in February was appointed chief of staff in succession to General Paik Sun Yup (appointed in 1957).   Song started a campaign against corruption in the army: three major-generals and three brigadiers were dismissed from active service.

People's Republic of Korea.   The five-year (1957-61) development plan was said to be progressing satisfactorily.   On April 17, an *Izvestia* correspondent reported from Pyongyang that the 1958 industrial production was 5·7 times higher than that before World War II.   In the first half of 1959 coal production was 45 % higher and iron ore output 65 % higher than in the same period of 1958 (*see* TABLE).   Despite severe drought the 1958 grain crop amounted to 3·7 million tons compared with 3·2 million tons in 1957.   The aim in 1965 was 7 million tons.

INDUSTRIAL PRODUCTION IN NORTH KOREA
(In thousands of metric tons; electricity in millions of kwh.)

	1956	1957	1958	1961 (Plan)	1965 (Plan)
Coal	3,900	4,500	6,822	9,500	25,000
Electricity	5,100	6,265	7,631	9,700	20,000
Pig iron	189	246	320	700	4,000
Steel	191	254	365	670	3,250
Cement	597	812	1,244	2,000	5,000
Chemical fertilizers	196	312	457	630	1,750

In December, however, the central committee of the North Korean Labour (Communist) party decided to revise radically the five-year plan which was obviously too ambitious in the field of heavy industry.   In order to eliminate " tensions created in some sectors of national economy " it was decided to improve housing construction and raise agricultural production.

On Feb. 12, 1959, a new currency was introduced: the new *won* was exchanged for 100 old *wons*; wages and prices were converted accordingly.

On Oct. 25, Nam Ir was relieved of his post as foreign minister, retaining that of deputy chairman of the council of ministers.   Pak Sung Chur was appointed foreign minister.

On March 17 a Soviet-Korean agreement was signed in Moscow: the U.S.S.R. was to give North Korea technical assistance totalling about Rb.500 million.

In April and May Tsoi Yen Gen, chairman of the presidium of the Supreme People's Assembly, visited the U.S.S.R., the German Democratic Republic, Poland and Czechoslovakia. In October North Korea was visited by Antonín Novotný, president of Czechoslovakia, and Aleksander Zawadzki, chairman of the Polish council of state.   (K. M. S.)

KUWAIT.
British-protected Arab sheikhdom on northwest coast of the Persian gulf. Area: 5,990 sq.mi. Pop.: (1957 census) 206,177. Cap. Kuwait, pop. *c.* 25,000. Sheikh, Abdullah es-Salim es-Sabah. British political agent, A. S. Halford. Chief export: petroleum. Monetary unit: Indian rupee.

History. Alarm was caused in Kuwait in the early part of 1959 by the growth of Communist influence in Iraq, and there were reports of an impending Communist coup in Kuwait itself, engineered by Iraqi Communists, who were alleged to be smuggling arms into the country. The Kuwait security authorities arrested some Communist suspects and deported a number of Iraqis and Palestinians who had been living in Kuwait.   (E. S. A.)

LABOUR PARTY.
The total membership of the party, as recorded in the 1959 annual report, was 6,542,186, a decrease of 40,363 on the previous year. Of this total, 5,627,690 were trade-union-affiliated members, 888,955 individual members and 25,541 Co-operative- and Socialist-society-affiliated members.

The party was largely preoccupied during the year with preparations for the general election, which took place on Oct. 8. Labour contested 621 of the 630 seats and secured 258 seats in the new House of Commons after a loss of 28 seats and a gain of 5. The total Labour poll was 12,151,395, representing 43·6% of the votes cast. In Nov. 1958 the party had launched a pre-election " Into Action " campaign with the publication of *The Future Labour Offers You*, which outlined all the party policy documents in popular form. Separate conferences were held in London for trade union representatives, M.P.s and candidates, and agents, followed by demonstrations and conferences in all parts of the country. A special Campaign committee was set up by the National Executive committee to direct the campaign and make pre-election arrangements.

Three policy statements were issued during the year by the national executive. These were: *Members One of Another*, dealing with the health service; *Leisure for Living*, covering all leisure activities; and *Forward With Labour*, the party's policy for Wales. In addition there was a statement on the future of the new towns, and the Youth commission set up by the party issued its first report under the title *The Younger Generation*.

At the end of August, Hugh Gaitskell and Aneurin Bevan visited the U.S.S.R. and had talks with Nikita S. Khrushchev. Gaitskell said that there was some tough argument but there were four points of agreement. First, the U.S.S.R. wanted an agreement on nuclear tests; second, there was agreement on the dangers of the spread of nuclear weapons; third, the U.S.S.R., like Labour, favoured a European zone of controlled disarmament; and fourth, there was ground for a temporary agreement on Berlin. The visit had to be curtailed owing to the announcement of the general election.

During the year there were seven parliamentary by-elections, none of which brought any change of representation. Six seats were vacant when parliament was dissolved. In the local elections in April and May, which in 1959 included the metropolitan boroughs, Labour gained 176 seats and lost 498, a net loss of 322 seats; this compared with a net gain of 325 seats in the same elections in 1956.

The party's annual conference, due to be held in early October, had to be cancelled because of the general election. In its place an abbreviated special conference was held at Blackpool on Nov. 28-29. One of the main functions of this conference was the election of the new National Executive committee. The National Executive then elected George Brinham as chairman of the party for the year, and Richard Crossman as vice-chairman. The secretary of the party was Morgan Phillips. Hugh Gaitskell was re-elected leader of the Parliamentary Labour party, and Aneurin Bevan was elected deputy leader. On the resignation of James Griffiths, Bevan was also re-elected treasurer.

In the voting for the Labour Parliamentary committee (" shadow cabinet ") earlier in November the following retained their seats: Harold Wilson, James Callaghan, Sir Frank Soskice, Alfred Robens, Anthony Greenwood, Thomas Fraser, George Brown, P. Gordon Walker and G. R. Mitchison. New members elected were: F. Lee, F. Willey and Denis Healey. (*See also* GENERAL ELECTION.)   (A. W. Bx.)

LAOS.
A land-locked kingdom situated in the Indochinese peninsula, bounded N. by China, N.E. by the Democratic Republic of Vietnam, E. by the Republic of Vietnam and S. by Cambodia. Area: *c.* 91,000 sq.mi. Pop. (1959 est., no census ever taken): over 2 million*. The Laotians (66%) are Thais and speak a Thai dialect. The primitive Meo and Kha peoples, of the northern and southern hilly regions respectively, constitute the largest minority groups. Religion: Buddhist. Chief towns (pop., 1959 est.): Vientiane (administrative cap.) 160,000; Luang-Prabang (royal cap.) 15,000. Rulers in 1959: King Sisavang Vong and (from Nov. 3) King Savang Vatthana. Prime minister, Phui Sananikone. Main exports: coffee, tin ore. Monetary unit: *kip*, with an exchange rate of K.225 to £1 sterling.

* Some estimates place the population between 2·5 million and 3 million. There are also varying estimates of the size of the country.

History. On Jan. 24, 1959, Phui Sananikone, the prime minister, formed a new government under the exceptional powers granted him by the National Assembly for a period of 12 months in order to meet the " new and very grave situation " facing the country. The general election, due to be held in the summer, was postponed. The new cabinet contained three army officers, six members of the Phui's Lao People's Rally and one independent.

The new government proclaimed a policy of hostility to

the Neo Lao Hak Sat (Patriotic Front of Laos) headed by Prince Suvanna Vong, former leader of the Pathet Lao (Free Lao) pro-Communist movement, but since his agreement with the former premier, Prince Suvanna Phuma (his half-brother), the leader of a 21-member group in the 59-member National Assembly.

Opposing also the neutralist trends in Laos, Phui announced on Feb. 11 that his government had no further use for the International Commission for Supervision and Control in Laos (I.C.S.C.L.) set up under the Geneva agreements of July 20, 1954, that ended the Indochina war. Phui added that his government henceforth would recognize the United Nations as the sole arbitration body for disputes in the area.

One of the points of agreement reached between the two half-brothers was that the Pathet Lao units would be merged into the Laotian army. Instead of merger by agreement, General Uan Rathikone, chief of staff of the Laotian army, ordered that the Pathet Lao units were to surrender their arms. One battalion was disarmed in May, north of Luang Prabang, but another fled northeast into the jungle where it was later joined by some guerrilla fighters.

Laos is a country without railways, with very few roads and a few grass strip airfields. The terrain and the climate is unsuitable for any large-scale military operations but ideal for guerrilla warfare. Such warfare started in the summer in the north and on July 28 Prince Suvanna Vong and several of his supporters were arrested by the government. They were to be tried on charges of conspiracy but at the end of October the trial was postponed indefinitely.

In the meantime guerrilla activity continued and the Democratic (Communist) Republic of Vietnam was charged with military and political aggression against Laos, while the governments of Peking and Hanoi accused the Vientiane government of having provoked a civil war and violated the Geneva agreement which had stipulated that Laos was not to join military alliances or permit foreign bases.

China and North Vietnam asked for the recall of the I.C.S.C.L. (dormant since July 19, 1958), in which Canada, India and Poland were represented. The U.S.S.R. and India also favoured it. Great Britain and Canada regarded the commission's work as done and thought it should be left to the Laotian government to decide whether they wanted it. Instead Laos appealed on Sept. 4 to the U.N. Security council for the " dispatch of an emergency force to halt the aggression and prevent it from spreading ".

On Sept. 7 the council, by 10 votes to one (the U.S.S.R.) decided to set up a sub-committee and instructed it to conduct in Laos " such inquiries as it may determine necessary, and to report to the Security council as soon as possible ".

The sub-committee, under the chairmanship of Shinichi Shibusawa (Japan), and with Brig.-General Heriberto Ahrens (Argentine), Lodovico Baratieri di San Pietro (Italy) and Habib Bourguiba Jr. (Tunisia) as members, arrived at Vientiane on Sept. 15. On Nov. 5 it presented its report to the Security council. The sub-committee found no evidence

After their wedding in Luang-Prabang on Aug. 10, Princess Dala, the grand-daughter of King Sisavang Vong of Laos (who died on Oct. 29), and her bridegroom Prince Si Suphanuvong, the director of Laotian civil aviation, leave the royal palace under the shade of parasols.

A sentry stands guard above a Laotian army post in Northern Laos during the guerrilla warfare between government forces and rebels of the Pathet Lao pro-Communist movement. Laos alleged intervention by North Vietnamese forces, but this was not proved.

of aggression by the North Vietnam government but added that "it would appear that various degrees and kinds of support have been accorded to hostile elements from sources on the North Vietnamese side of the border."

On Nov. 8 Dag Hammarskjöld, U.N. Secretary-general, accepted an invitation from the government of Laos to visit that country. Arkadi Sobolev, Soviet chief delegate to the U.N. Security council, warned him in a letter on Nov. 9 that in the opinion of the Soviet government it was only the "urgent resumption of the activities of the I.C.S.C.L. that was necessary for the normalization of the situation in Laos."

At the beginning of December a split occurred in the ruling Lao People's Rally. As the mandate of the National Assembly was expiring on Dec. 25, the prime minister decided to hold a general election on April 3, 1960, but insisted that the existing assembly should retain its powers until the next was elected. A young reform group known as the Committee for the Defence of National Interests, and represented in the cabinet by three ministers (including Brig. Phumi Nosavan, defence minister), protested against such "anticonstitutional" procedure. They wanted an immediate election. All the three were dismissed by Phui Sananikone on Dec. 15, but army commanders replied by a show of strength in the streets of Vientiane. On Dec. 31 Phui resigned and the "security of the country" was temporarily placed under the control of three army officers: General Sutone Pathamma Vong, commander-in-chief; General Uan Rathikone, chief of staff, and Brigadier Phumi Nosavan, inspector general of the armed forces. It was a *coup d'état* but in Laotian style: *en famille*, no bloodshed.

King Sisavang Vong (born in 1885) died at Luang Prabang on Oct. 29 (*see* OBITUARIES). He had been ill for some time and on Aug. 21 named his eldest son, Prince Savang Vatthana, as regent of the kingdom. On Nov. 3 Savang was proclaimed king. (K. M. S.)

LAW AND LEGISLATION. United Kingdom Statute
Law. The Mental Health act, which in its main proposals gave effect to the recommendations of the Royal Commission on Mental Illness and Mental Deficiency, was undoubtedly the most important legislative achievement of the 1958-59 session. The general approach was to lay greater emphasis on medical treatment and to shift the emphasis away both from the old definitions and, in abolishing the old procedure of certifying patients as insane, from the quasi-judicial elements involved in the decision to segregate a patient and deprive him of control over his own affairs. Details of the act were as follows:

Section 1 repealed the Lunacy and Mental Treatment acts, 1890 to 1930, and the Mental Deficiency acts, 1913 to 1938, subject to certain transitional provisions. Section 2 abolished the board of control and

transferred its rights, liabilities and obligations to the minister of health. Section 3 provided that there should be a mental health review tribunal for every area for which there was a regional hospital board under the National Health Service act, 1946, for the purpose of dealing with applications and references by and in respect of patients under this act. Section 4 provided the definitions of "mental disorder", "severe subnormality", "subnormality" and "psychopathic disorder". Section 5 provided for the informal admission of patients; section 6 enlarged the duties of local health authorities, especially in relation to the provision of residential accommodation; and section 7 empowered the minister of health to make regulations as to the conduct of premises where accommodation or facilities for training were provided. Sections 8 and 9 defined the functions of welfare and children authorities, and sections 11-13 made provision for the care and training of child patients in lieu of their education. Sections 14-24 made provision for mental nursing homes, residential homes, etc.; also their registration, the regulations to be made for them by the minister of health and their inspection.

Sections 25-59 dealt with the crucially important questions of the compulsory admission of patients to hospitals and to guardianship, and their discharge. Section 25 laid down that a patient might be admitted to a hospital, and there detained for a period of 28 days in pursuance of an application for admission signed by two medical practitioners, who must state (a) that the patient was suffering from mental disorder of a nature or degree which warranted his detention in hospital for at least a limited period, and (b) that he ought to be so detained in the interests of his own health or safety or with a view to the protection of other persons. The patient might not be detained for more than 28 days unless he had become liable to detention by a subsequent application. Section 26 dealt with applications for admission for treatment, as distinct from admission for observation. Here too there had to be a written application signed by two medical practitioners, the grounds here being (a) that the patient was suffering from mental disorder being (i) in the case of a patient of any age, mental illness or severe subnormality; (ii) in the case of a patient under 21, psychopathic disorder or subnormality, the disorder being of a nature or degree which warranted the detention of the patient in a hospital for medical treatment under this section; and (b) that it was necessary in the interests of the patient's health or safety or for the protection of other persons that the patient should be so detained. Section 27 provided that an application for the admission of a patient should be made either by his nearest relative or by a mental welfare officer. A later section, 54, enacted that it was the duty of a mental welfare officer to apply for the admission of a patient to hospital or to guardianship where he was satisfied that such an application ought to be made. Section 33 laid down the procedure for reception into guardianship: the person named as guardian might be either a local health authority or any individual person (including the applicant himself). Section 34 defined the effect of a duly made guardianship application and section 35 authorized the minister of health to make regulations as to the exercise by guardians of their powers. Sections 47 and 48 prescribed the procedure and the requisite conditions for discharge, and section 57 authorized the minister of health to refer to the mental health review tribunal any case he thought fit.

Sections 60-80 dealt with the admission of patients concerned in criminal proceedings and the transfer of patients under sentence; Part VI of the act with the removal and return of patients within the United Kingdom; and Part VII with " special hospitals ", the minister having the duty to provide " such institutions as appear to him to be necessary for persons . . . who . . . require treatment under conditions of special security on account of their dangerous, violent or criminal propensities." Part VIII laid down the constitution, functions and procedure of the court of protection for the management of the property and affairs of patients. Part IX dealt with a number of miscellaneous and general provisions, the most important of which were section 123, which prescribed the conditions under which a mental health review tribunal must discharge a patient and conferred upon it a discretion to do so in any case; and section 147, which was the definitions section.

Second in importance to the Mental Health act were the Obscene Publications act, the Street Offences act and the Legitimacy act. The first of these, a private member's bill, embodied, in section 1, the classic judicial definition of obscenity with important amplifications: " an article shall be deemed to be obscene if its effect . . . is, taken as a whole, such as to tend to deprave and corrupt persons who are likely, having regard to all relevant circumstances, to read, see or hear the matter contained or embodied in it "; it was plainly of great importance that the effect of the article was to be " taken as a whole " and that regard must be had to " all relevant circumstances ".

Sub-section (3) of section 1 enacted that for the purpose of the act a person published an article who " (a) distributes, circulates, sells, lets on hire, gives or lends it, or who offers it for sale or letting on hire; or (b) in the case of an article containing or embodying matter to be looked at for a record, shows, plays or projects it "; but paragraph (b) was not to apply either to cinematograph exhibitions in private houses to which the public were not admitted or to anything done in the course of television or sound broadcasting. Section 2 provided the penalties: on summary conviction a fine not exceeding £100 or imprisonment for not more than six months, and on conviction or indictment a fine (unlimited in amount) or imprisonment for a term not exceeding three years, or both. Summary proceedings might be taken only within a year from the commission of the offence and a prosecution on indictment was not to be commenced more than two years after that date. Among other provisions, section 3 empowered a justice to issue a search warrant if

" *Vera, why you have to ask a man the way in Curzon-street I shall never know.*" *A cartoon by Giles in the " Daily Express " on May 7.*

satisfied by information on oath that there was reasonable ground for suspecting that obscene articles were kept for publication or gain on any premises or stall or vehicle specified in the information.

The Street Offences act was designed to give effect to the recommendations as to prostitution of the interdepartmental committee on the law relating to homosexual offences and prostitution presided over by Sir John Wolfenden, and proved a highly controversial measure in its passage through parliament. It brought the law on this matter on to the same basis for the whole of England and Wales. Section 1 (1) made it an offence for a common prostitute to loiter or solicit in a public place for the purpose of prostitution. (This was criticized both because it eliminated the previous requirement that annoyance to the passers-by should be proved and because it contained the reference to the common prostitute.) Sub-section (2) provided for increased penalties:

(a) a fine not exceeding £10 for the first offence (as against a previous maximum of £2 however often the offence was repeated); (b) after one previous conviction, a fine not exceeding £25; and (c) after more than one previous conviction, a fine not exceeding £25 or imprisonment for not more than a month, or both.

Section 2 provided that a woman cautioned by a constable that if she persisted in her conduct it might result in her being charged with an offence under section 1, might within 14 days apply to a magistrate's court for an order directing that there was to be no entry in respect of that caution in any record maintained by the police. Section 3 increased the maximum fines under the Refreshment Houses act, 1860, for allowing prostitutes to be in night cafés and certain other classes of premises. Section 4 increased the maximum penalty for living on the earnings of prostitution from two to seven years' imprisonment.

The Legitimacy act proved another controversial measure. Again a private member's bill, its main provision, in section 1, was to repeal sub-section (2) of section 1 of the Legitimacy act, 1926, with the result that a child might now be legitimated after the marriage of his parents even though there was some obstacle in law to their being married at the time of his birth.

Section 2 provided that the child of a void marriage should be treated as legitimate if at the time of the act of intercourse resulting in the birth (or at the date of the celebration of the marriage, if later) both or either of the parents reasonably believed that the marriage was valid; this provision applied only where the father's domicile was in England at the material time. Section 3 made it possible for the father of an illegitimate child to have legal custody or guardianship over it, and section 4 for a married woman to apply for an affiliation order provided that she was single at the time of the birth.

Of the other measures enacted, the Adoption act, 1958, provided the codification of this branch of the law promised in the debate on the Children act enacted in the previous session. The Malta (Letters Patent) act, one of the few measures of any constitutional importance, provided that the Malta (Constitution) Letters Patent, 1947, should have effect as though there were thereby reserved to the crown full power, by order in council or by further letters patent, to revoke or amend all or any of the provisions of the 1947 letters patent—in effect the constitution of Malta.

The Family Allowances and National Insurance act provided, by section 1, for the determination of claims and questions under the Family Allowances act, 1945, to be made by insurance officers or local tribunals subject to appeal to the national insurance commissioner. Section 2 provided for appeals under the Industrial Injuries act from any decision of a medical appeal tribunal to the industrial injuries commissioner on the ground that the decision was erroneous in point of law. The Emergency Laws (Repeal) act carried one step further the piecemeal repeal of the provisions of the Emergency Powers (Defence) act, 1939, and the Supplies and Services (Transitional Powers) act, 1945. The effect of the Representation of the People (Amendment) act was that it was no longer an illegal practice to use more than a limited number of vehicles at a parliamentary election. The House Purchase and Housing act authorized exchequer advances to, and the deposit of trust funds with, building societies for the purposes of house purchase; and also authorized local authorities to make grants up to a total of £155 for the provision of certain standard amenities. Another measure concerned largely with house property was the Rating and Valuation act, which effected a further postponement, from 1961 to 1963, of the date for the entry into force of the new valuation list for rating purposes under Part III of the Local Government act, 1948. The main provisions of the Landlord and Tenant (Furniture and Fittings) act were:

(1) to impose a penalty of a fine not exceeding £100 for attempts to obtain from prospective tenants of rent-controlled premises excessive prices for furniture and fittings; (2) to authorize local authorities to enter premises and inspect the furniture where there were reasonable grounds for suspecting that an offence under this act had been committed; and (3) to impose penalties for obstructing an inspection carried out under a magistrate's warrant.

Two measures concerned with the maintenance of public order were the Metropolitan Magistrates act, which increased the number of metropolitan magistrates from 27 to 35 and empowered the receiver for the metropolitan police district to provide premises for probation purposes; and the Restriction of Offensive Weapons act, which prohibited the manu-. facture, sale, hire, offering for sale or hire, or the lending or giving, of types of knives known as " flick knives " and " gravity knives ".

Two measures of interest for their effect on private rights were the Rights of Light act and the Fatal Accidents act. The effect of the former was to ensure that rights of light should not be acquired solely by virtue of demolition or war damage that took place between 1939 and 1945. The effects of the latter were:

(1) to extend the classes of persons for whose benefit or by whom an action might be brought under the Fatal Accidents acts; and (2) to provide that in assessing damages under the Fatal Accidents acts or under the Carriage by Air act, 1952, there should not be taken into account any insurance money, benefit, pension or gratuity which had been or would or might be paid as a result of the death.

Other measures worth mention were the Nuclear Installations (Licensing and Insurance) act; the Cotton Industry act; the Pensions Increase act; the National Assistance act (authorizing the Ministry of Pensions and National Insurance to increase the amounts of assets to be disregarded for the purpose of payments of national assistance); the Education act (enlarging the powers of the minister of education to make contributions, grants and loans in respect of aided schools and special agreement schools); the New Towns act (providing, amongst other things, for the dissolution of development corporations that had achieved or substantially achieved their purposes, and establishing the New Towns commission to acquire and develop their property); the Wages Council act (authorizing the minister of labour in specified circumstances to establish wages councils); and the Factories act (containing a series of detailed provision supplementing, strengthening and extending the provisions of the Factories act, 1937, in relation to safety regulations and welfare).

Commonwealth Statute Law. *Australia.* A Judges Pension bill was enacted, increasing pensions from 40% to 50% of a judge's salary, and from 20% to 25% for judges' widows, and reducing the period of service qualifying for the maximum pension from 15 to 10 years provided that the judge on retirement had reached the age of 60. Another important measure was the Nationality and Citizenship act, which erased from the principal act all discrimination between naturalized Australians and people born in Australia, except that, where a person was convicted of obtaining naturalization by means of a false statement or by the concealment of a material circumstance, the minister was empowered to deprive him of Australian citizenship if he was satisfied that it would be contrary to the public interest for him to continue to be an Australian citizen. The four Banking bills to give effect to the government's reform of Commonwealth banking institutions were passed through all stages in both houses.

Ceylon. Late in 1958 the Tamil Language (Special Pro-

vision) act was passed. Its main purpose was to provide for instruction in, and the use of, Tamil subject to the position of Sinhalese as the official language. In 1959 the Public Security (Amendment) act was passed, giving the government additional emergency powers. A Parliamentary Elections (Amendment) act was also passed, the most important provision of which lowered the qualifying age for the franchise from 21 to 18. It also provided for the issue of identity cards (to prevent impersonation) and regulated such matters as deposits by candidates and the use of vehicles to take electors to the poll.

Ghana. The Constitution (Repeal of Restrictions) act, which was passed at the end of 1958, repealed the provisions of the order in council which laid down the special procedures for passing bills designed to alter the constitution. Also in December there was passed the Industrial Relations act, which conferred legal recognition on the Trade Union congress and prescribed a compulsory conciliation procedure. Early in 1959 there were enacted the Constitution (Amendment) act, whose main effects were (1) to regulate the appointment of judges, parliamentary secretaries and civil servants, and (2) to abolish the regional assemblies; and the National Assembly Disqualification act, which disqualified members of parliament detained under the Preventive Detention act, 1958, and those who were habitually absent from meetings of the house or who publicly declared their intention to boycott such meetings.

New Zealand. The National Service Registration act, 1958, repealed the Military Training act, and substituted compulsory registration and submission to medical examination for young men of 18 instead of compulsory military training; the responsibility for service in the reserves was retained for those to whom it previously applied. Some controversy was aroused by the Customs Act (Amendment) act, anti-dumping legislation being criticized by the opposition on the ground that the wide powers taken by the executive would enable the government to discriminate against British textiles whether or not dumping practices had been used; but the government denied that there was any material extension of its powers.

Rhodesia and Nyasaland, Federation of. The Immunities and Privileges Amendment act made it a punishable offence for proprietors of hotels, restaurants or entertainments and managers of business premises to refuse admission or to refuse to serve, or sell goods, on grounds of race alone, to members of the diplomatic and consular corps who were carrying cards of identity issued by the federal government; and provided that anyone charged should, unless he proved the contrary, be deemed to have acted on grounds of race alone.

South Africa. Late in 1958 an Electoral Law Amendment act was passed, lowering the qualifying age for the franchise from 21 to 18. A South Africa Act Further Amendment act was also passed providing for the enlargement of the cabinet by two members and for the appointment of not more than eight deputy ministers who would not be members of the cabinet. In 1959 a Promotion of Bantu Self-Government act was passed, providing for the abolition of native representation in parliament and empowering the governor-general to transfer his legislative powers to the Bantu territorial authorities. Other measures included an Extension of University Education act, intended to provide for separate universities for the non-white population, and a Decimal Coinage act, substituting two coinage units, the rand (equivalent in value to 10s.) and the cent (one-hundredth of the rand) for pounds, shillings and pence.

United Kingdom Case Law. Perhaps the most interesting case, from the point of view of the removal of an old doubt, reported in 1959, was Diplock J.'s decision in *Fowler* v. *Lanning* (1959 2 W.L.R. 241). The defendant in this case had injured the plaintiff by accidentally shooting him at a shooting party. The form which the argument of the case took was that the statement of claim baldly averred the fact of the shooting without alleging that the shooting was either intentional (which it was common ground it was not) or negligent. The judge in the course of his judgment disposed of the argument that negligence was not a necessary ingredient of an action for unintentional trespass and held that the burden of establishing negligence rested on the plaintiff.

A decision of the House of Lords of considerable importance in view of the contemporary multiplicity of law reports was that in *Qualcast (Wolverhampton) Ltd.* v. *Haynes* (1959 2 W.L.R. 510). In this case a workman was suing his employers for negligence. The county court judge who tried the action decided it in favour of the plaintiff on the footing that he was bound to do so by the authority of previous decisions where the facts had been similar, but that left to himself he would not have found any negligence. The House of Lords ruled that these decisions, being on questions of fact and not questions of law, were not binding on the judge and reversed his decision and that of the court of appeal.

In re Yarn Spinners' Agreement was one of the most interesting and important of the decisions of the Restrictive Practices court. As they had usually done, the court rejected all the arguments of benefit to the public alleged on behalf of the Yarn Spinners' association to flow from its minimum price scheme; but it held that the removal of the restriction would be likely to have serious and persistent effect on the general level of employment in the 11 areas selected by the association for the purposes of its case. None the less, the court decided that whereas the adverse effects on employment of ending the scheme would be localized, the detriments of retaining it were felt nationally; and they accordingly declared the scheme to be contrary to the public interest.

Solicitors' Practice. *Conveyancing.* The chief land registrar in his report showed an increase in the work of the registration of title department, which followed the reduction in stamp duty in Aug. 1958. The main increase came from London and Middlesex and it was thought this was due to a large extent to the Rent act, 1957. It was considered that the House Purchase and Housing act, 1959, would have a similar or greater effect. The increase in first registrations was 45% while first dealings showed an increase of 9·6%, both of which were record figures.

Legal Aid and Advice Act, 1949. The lord chancellor made alterations in the Assessment of Resources regulations and advised the Law society that he would during 1960 amend the financial limits in the act so that more applicants would be entitled to legal aid certificates. After nearly 10 years it was found that about 87% of all types of cases and 78% of Queen's Bench cases were successful. Having regard to this experience the Joint Committee of the Law Society and Bar Council considered that the time had arrived for the payment of costs of successful unassisted persons out of the Legal Aid fund.

Companies. The report for 1958 showed 22,370 new companies registered, which was 46% more than the average for the previous five years. The total number of companies at the end of 1958 was 345,674, of which 329,314 were private companies.

Bankruptcy. According to the annual report for 1958 there was an increase of 189 Receiving and Administration orders, the total being 2,250, but there was a decrease of 37 in deeds of arrangements, the number being 276.

United States Case Law. There was unusual interest in the work of the U.S. Supreme Court in the 1958-59 term, because it had been predicted that the appointment of Justice Potter Stewart would tip the balance of the court in favour of a position more responsive to the needs of the government and less concerned with the liberties of individuals. In the event,

Lord Chief Justice Parker arrives at Westminster abbey for the service to inaugurate the Michaelmas law sittings on Oct. 1.

Justice Stewart's decision in *Brown* v. *United States*, 79 S. Ct. 539, seemed restrictive of the right of a witness to invoke the privilege against self-incrimination, but his decision in *Kingsley Int. Pictures* v. *Regents of the University of the State of New York* represented a sharp attack on the right of a state to censor motion pictures.

Among cases involving the regulation of business, in *Safeway Stores Inc.* v. *Oklahoma Retail Grocers' Assocation,* 79 S. Ct. 1196, the court was asked to pass upon certain aspects of trading stamps. The Oklahoma Retail Grocers' association brought an action against Safeway stores to enjoin it from selling some of its goods below cost in violation of an Oklahoma statute. Safeway replied that the statute permitted it to meet the allegedly illegal competition of stores using trading stamps. The Oklahoma court found that trading stamps were not to be reckoned into the price; that, therefore, the competitors were not selling below cost; and that Safeway had no defence to the charges. Appealed to, the Supreme Court sustained the Oklahoma court. In a unanimous decision the court said that Oklahoma had not discriminated against Safeway in favour of stores using trading stamps because " . . . the number of stamps varies directly with the total cost of goods purchased. Safeway's price cutting, however, was selective. This difference is vital in the context of the act . . . The selling of selected goods at a loss in order to lure customers into the store is deemed not only a destructive means of competition, but it also plays on the gullibility of customers by leading them to expect . . . that a store which offered such an amazing bargain was full of other such bargains. Clearly . . . selective price cuts tend to perpetuate this abuse whereas the use of trading stamps does not."

Perhaps the most important civil rights case was *Lassiter* v. *Northampton County Board of Elections*, 79 S. Ct. 985, holding that a literacy test as a prerequisite to registration as a voter was not necessarily unconstitutional. The appellant, a Negro citizen of North Carolina, sued to have the literacy test for voters prescribed by the state declared unconstitutional. Failing in the state courts, he appealed to the Supreme Court, which held unanimously against the appellant. " The states have long been held to have broad powers to determine the conditions under which the right of suffrage may be exercised ... The ability to read and write ... indicates some relation to standards designed to promote intelligent use of the ballot. Literacy and illiteracy are neutral on race, creed, colour and sex .... Of course a literacy test, fair on its face, may be employed to perpetuate that discrimination which the Fifteenth Amendment was designed to uproot. No such influence is charged here .... The present requirement, applicable to members of all races, is that the prospective voter ' be able to read and write any section of the Constitution of North Carolina in the English language.' That seems to us to be one fair way of determining whether a person is literate, not a calculated scheme to lay springs for the citizen." (*See* also INTERNATIONAL COURT OF JUSTICE; INTERNATIONAL LAW.)

(W. T. Ws.; C. L. W. C.; W. D. Hd.)

LAWN TENNIS. In the men's game there was no general change during 1959 in the dominance, strongly marked since 1946, of players from Australia and the United States.

There was, however, a fluctuation of fortune between these two nations. At the end of Dec. 1958 the United States, contrary to expectations, won back the Davis cup from Australia to establish itself as champion nation. A narrow 3-2 win was achieved in Brisbane mainly by the efforts of Alejandro Olmedo. Olmedo won both his singles and, with Hamilton Richardson, the doubles. Shortly after this tie the two leading Australians, Ashley Cooper and Malcolm Anderson, both of whom lost to Olmedo, became professionals, together with another Australian Mervyn Rose. Olmedo went on to win the Australian national singles title and in 1959 was outstanding in the Wimbledon championship where he took the men's singles title with ease.

The supremacy of the United States did not last long. At the end of August, Australia successfully challenged the United States at Forest Hills, New York, and regained the Davis cup by 3-2. Neale Fraser equalled Olmedo's performance of 1958 by winning both his singles and, with Roy Emerson, the doubles. Olmedo, playing less well than before, won a singles against Rodney Laver, the Wimbledon runner-up, but could not otherwise hold the Australians. A few days later Fraser won the U.S. national singles title at Forest Hills, repeating in the final the victory he had against Olmedo in the Davis cup. The major honours of the year were thus shared between Fraser and Olmedo. The latter, a Peruvian, marked

(*Below*) *A. Olmedo, a member of the U.S. Davis cup team, in play against R. Laver (Australia) in the final of the men's singles on the centre court at Wimbledon on July 3. Olmedo, a Peruvian, won 6-4, 6-3, 6-4.* (*Right*) *Maria Bueno (Brazil) in the final of the women's singles at Wimbledon on July 4, when she beat Darlene Hard (U.S.) 6-4, 6-3.*

his rapid rise to fame by becoming a professional at the end of the year.

In Europe there were signs of a decline in the strength of most nations except Italy and Spain. The latter reached the zone final in the Davis cup and notably beat Great Britain in the semi-final. Italy won the zone for the second year running and for the sixth time since 1946. Its continued power was stressed in the major hard court meeting of the world, the French championships in Paris, where the men's singles was won by Nicola Pietrangeli and the men's doubles by Pietrangeli and Orlando Sirola. This was the first success by Italian players in any of the four major individual championships—Australia, France, Wimbledon and the United States.

The winning Australian Davis cup team and the presidents of the Australian and U.S. lawn tennis associations, with the trophy.

The women's game was dominated by the 20-year-old Miss Maria Bueno of Brazil. Though never consistent in performance at lesser events, she played brilliantly to win the women's singles at Wimbledon and was equally supreme at Forest Hills in taking the U.S. title. She proved one of the most penetrating servers and volleyers ever seen in the women's game and broke the long succession of U.S. winners in the women's singles at both Wimbledon and Forest Hills, the last non-U.S. winner at Wimbledon being in 1937 and the last at Forest Hills in 1930.

Fraser was notably successful in three events in the U.S. championships taking not only the singles but the doubles with Emerson and the mixed doubles with Margaret du Pont. This was Mrs. du Pont's 24th U.S. title, her first being the women's doubles with Sarah Palfrey Cooke in 1941. The outstanding woman player of 1958, the coloured U.S. player, Althea Gibson, did not defend any of her titles. She came from retirement only to win the lawn tennis event in the Pan American games held in Chicago in August. The United States, however, reasserted its old supremacy over Great Britain in the Wightman cup contest when, at Sewickley, near Pittsburgh, it avenged by 4-3 the defeat at Wimbledon the year before. An outstanding performer on the U.S. side was the ambidextrous Californian Beverly Fleitz who, nevertheless, did not do well at Wimbledon and did not take part in the U.S. championships. In the autumn Althea Gibson joined the professional ranks.

From Great Britain, Christine Truman had much success. Though Angela Mortimer proved too good for her in the final of the British hard court championships at Bournemouth, she won the women's singles in the Italian championships in Rome and shortly afterwards gained the French women's title. She lost in an early round at Wimbledon but reached the final of

the U.S. championships before losing to Miss Bueno.

For the first time players from the U.S.S.R. competed in the championship events at Wimbledon. Comparatively inexperienced, they were unsuccessful but one of their number, Thomas Leius, from Tallinn, Estonia, won the junior invitation event for boys.

Among professionals the supreme rivalry was between the U.S. player Pancho Gonzales and the Australian Lew Hoad. Under the sponsorship of Jack Kramer, these two men and Ken Rosewall, Frank Sedgman, Tony Trabert, Cooper, Anderson, Rose and others played in many parts of the world at a higher standard than the amateurs but without creating the same competitive interest. The difficulties of amateurism again occupied the annual general meeting of the International Lawn Tennis federation in Dublin and the rule limiting expenses to 150 days abroad in any year, passed only 12 months before, was amended to 210 days. A special committee was again constituted to examine the problems and to bring new proposals to the 1960 meeting. (*See also* SPORTING RECORD.) (L. O. T.)

LEATHER: *see* BUSINESS REVIEW.

LEBANON. Arab republic bounded W. by Mediterranean, N. and E. by Syria and S. and S.E. by Israel. Area: *c.* 4,000 sq.mi. Pop.: (1957 est.) 1,525,000. Language: Arabic 90%; French, Armenian, Greek, etc., also spoken. Religion: Christian *c.* 50% (more than half are Maronites, in communion with Rome); Moslem *c.* 45%. Chief towns (pop., 1957 est.): Beirut (cap.) 500,000; Tripoli 100,000, Zahlé 33,000; Saida 22,000. President of the republic, General Fuad Shehab; prime minister, Rashid Karameh. Main imports: gold and precious metals, livestock, cereals, textiles, iron, steel and manufactures. Main exports: gold and precious metals, fruit, vegetables, textile raw materials. Monetary unit: Lebanese pound (£L16·13 = £1 sterling).

History. The hopes entertained of a return to normal conditions in 1959 under the coalition government of Rashid Karameh were not entirely fulfilled. Although the situation bordering on civil war had been brought to an end, tension continued throughout the year, accompanied by occasional acts of violence, the most serious of which was the murder, on a public occasion, of a former leading supporter of the Camille Shamun regime by a crowd belonging to the rival faction. In the autumn the government was on the point of dissolution, following the resignation of Raymond Edde, one of its two Christian members. Karameh himself wanted to resign, but President Fuad Shehab asked the ministers to remain at their posts for the time being, until an alternative government could be formed.

On March 25 a meeting took place, on the Lebanese border, between the president of the United Arab Republic, Gamal Abd-ul-Nasser, and President Shehab. The initiative for this meeting had come from the Lebanese government, whose main concern was to improve relations between Lebanon and Syria. There had been friction between the two countries for years, and during the internal disturbances in Lebanon in 1958, President Shamun had openly accused Syria (after its incorporation in the United Arab Republic) of smuggling volunteers and arms across the border to help the nationalist opposition. Nasser's attack on Communists throughout the Arab world probably encouraged the Lebanese government to hope for better relations between Lebanon and the U.A.R., and Nasser, for his part, was anxious to secure Lebanese support for his anti-Communist policy. In an official statement issued after the meeting the two presidents affirmed their keenness to foster brotherly ties and the promotion of mutual co-operation in all that might lead to a strengthening of their independence and sovereignty. They also stated that they would seek to solve outstanding economic problems.

Ten days before this meeting, both the Soviet information office in Beirut and the house of a Lebanese Communist leader had been severely damaged by explosives. (E. S. A.)

LEEWARD ISLANDS: *see* WEST INDIES, THE.
LEGISLATION: *see* LAW AND LEGISLATION.

LESSER EASTERN CHURCHES. The lesser eastern Churches are those ancient Churches of the east which divided from the rest of Christendom at the Council of Chalcedon (451). The Armenian Church numbers about 3·4 million, including 2·7 million in the U.S.S.R.; the Coptic Church, about 10·7 million, including the Ethiopic Church, *c.* 9 million; the Syrian Orthodox (Jacobite) Church, about 134,000, including 80,000 in Iraq, plus 450,000 in S. India; the Church of the East (Assyrian), about 75,000 including 20,000 in Persia. The last of these is considered to be Nestorian and the others Monophysite.

In Dec. 1958 the split in the Syrian Orthodox (Jacobite) Church in South India was ended after almost half a century when the Syrian Orthodox Church of Malabar (Catholicos party) and the Malankara Jacobite Syrian Church (Patriarchal party) became reconciled, following a decision in the Supreme Court in favour of the Catholicos party. The Church of Malabar agreed to acknowledge the spiritual authority of the Syrian Orthodox patriarch in Homs while the patriarch agreed to accept the catholicos as head of an autonomous Syrian Orthodox Church in South India.

Seven members of the Armenian Brotherhood of St. James in Jerusalem were threatened with having to leave Jordan in Dec. 1958 until the minister of the interior finally gave permission for their residence permits to be renewed. Tiran Nersoyan, the patriarch elect, was still refused permission to return to Jordan. A new cathedral was consecrated in April

Kyrillos VI, the 116th patriarch of the Coptic Orthodox Church of Egypt, who was chosen by " holy selection " in Cairo on April 19.

for the Church of the East (Assyrian) community in Baghdad. The ceremony was attended by General Abd-ul-Karim Kassem, a Moslem, who wished to demonstrate that the interim constitution in Iraq forbade any religious or racial discrimination.

Kyrillos VI was elected 116th patriarch of the Coptic Orthodox Church of Egypt in April. Neither the Ethiopian Church nor the Ethiopian government was represented at his enthronement in May, but the rift between the two Churches was healed in June when Anba Kyrillos VI consecrated Anba Basilios as first patriarch of the Ethiopian Church, which hitherto had merely been allowed to have its own metropolitan. Although the Coptic patriarch of Alexandria must be an Egyptian subject, a concession was made whereby Ethiopian representatives would in future take part in elections to the patriarchal see of Alexandria. (*See also* ORTHODOX EASTERN CHURCHES.) (J. R. SE.)

LIBERAL PARTY. After nine months of intense preparation, the Liberal party put 217 candidates into the field in the general election, against 110 in 1955. They drew greatly increased votes in a large majority of the constituencies they contested—an average of 17·4% compared with 15·4% in 1955—but emerged with no more than the number of seats they held when the last parliament ended.

The winning of Devon North from the Conservatives by Jeremy Thorpe, a 31-year-old barrister and ex-president of the Oxford union, was the only gain, and that was counterbalanced by Mark Bonham Carter's loss to the Conservatives of the Torrington seat he won from them in a by-election in 1958.

Despite gaining 6% of the total poll, Liberals won less than 1% of the seats. The increase of 938,867 votes (from 722,395 in 1955 to 1,661,262) brought them only one seat above the 1955 total—the equivalent of their 1958 by-election success. Each seat cost 276,877 Liberal votes, against 37,671 for each Conservative seat and 47,098 for each Labour one.

Nevertheless the election marked a stage in the achievement of their leader Jo Grimond's reiterated aim of displacing the Labour party as the radical opposition to the Conservatives, and continued the rise in Liberal support in all parts of the country which by-elections in England and Scotland had maintained earlier in the year. For the first time many votes were demonstrably taken from Labour.

The manifesto theme was " People Count ". Liberals joined Labour in severe criticism of the government's Suez attack and colonial administration in Cyprus and Africa. Repudiating nationalization, they offered co-ownership, with tax-reforms as the initial instrument. Their only promises were cuts in income and purchase tax, old age pensions increased at once to £3 a week and abolition of schedule A tax on owner-occupied houses. Opposition to Britain's independent manufacture of nuclear weapons continued.

As the election had postponed the annual assembly, Sir Arthur Comyns Carr remained president till the November council meeting when Harold Glanville succeeded him. After the election, Grimond repeated his appeals to radicals of all parties to join in building a powerful new opposition to Conservatism. (*See also* ELECTIONS; POLITICAL PARTIES, EUROPEAN.) (R. A. SH.)

See Joseph Grimond, *The Liberal Future* (London, 1959).

LIBERIA. Republic on the west coast of Africa, bounded N.W. by British colony of Sierra Leone, N. by Guinea and E. by the Republic of Ivory Coast. Area: *c.* 43,000 sq.mi. Pop. (no census taken, 1959 est.): 1,500,000, all Negroes. English is the official language; the tribal languages are divided into some 28 dialects which stem from Sudanic and Arabic language roots. Liberia grants religious freedom to all denominations: nearly all Christian churches have had missions in Liberia for many years. Capital, Monrovia (pop. 1955 est.) 45,000. President (inaugurated in Jan. 1944), William Vacanarat Shadrach Tubman. Main imports: machinery and manufactures. Main exports: rubber (65%), iron ore (20%), diamonds (6%), palm kernels (3%). Monetary unit: *U.S. dollar.*

History. President W. V. S. Tubman was re-elected for the fourth time on May 5, 1959. Announcement was made in Sept. 1959 of a defence agreement between the United States and Liberia pledging consultation on U.S. military aid to Liberia in the event of aggression or threat of aggression against it.

Liberia continued to play a more significant part in inter-African affairs during 1959. Early in the year the Liberian government proposed the formation of a loosely connected organization of independent African nations. Diplomatic relations between Guinea and Liberia were established. Eight nations met in Monrovia for the 14th session of the Commission for Technical Assistance South of the Sahara. In June the leaders of Liberia, Guinea and Ghana met in Monrovia, where Kwame Nkrumah, the prime minister of Ghana, proposed an African union in which each member nation would cede substantial sovereignty to a federal organization, but a final decision was deferred until 1960.

Liberia continued to advance economically during 1959. In February the taxes on the profits of the Firestone Rubber company's plantation lands were raised from 25% to 35%. The Seven Stars Line, a branch of the Israeli ZIM Line, initiated ship service between Liberia and the United States.

(D. R. Pn.)

LIBRARIES. International.

Automation and mechanization were among the main topics under consideration during 1959, and the linking of libraries with the aid of teleprinters was further developed. In April 1957, the Delft Technical University library had become the first scientific library in Europe to be equipped with a telex installation, and G. Schuurmans Stekhoven (*Library Association Record*, 61, 6, June) described the working of telex and the linking of 26 libraries in the Netherlands to the international telex network.

The Dewey decimal classification went into a 16th edition (2 vol., New York, 1958). Used in the majority of public libraries of the English-speaking world, it was designed for a general collection, and would remain popular with this type of library for lack of a better scheme. Owing to the rigidity of the main classes it was impossible to maintain the revision of all subjects to serve the requirements of specialists, but it was proposed to publish continuous revisions in the form of bulletins.

The first international congress of the Galpin society, the fifth international congress of Music Libraries and the third general assembly of the International Association of Music Libraries were held jointly from June 29 to July 4 at King's college, Cambridge. The Fédération Internationale de Documentation held its 25th conference in Warsaw during Sept. 17-26, and the conference of the International Federation of Library associations was also held there during Sept. 14-19.

Great Britain. The most discussed item was the Roberts' report, published by the Ministry of Education as *The Structure of the Public Library Service in England and Wales* (Cmnd. 660, H.M.S.O., London). This recommended that the Ministry of Education should have oversight of the public library service and power to enforce the discharge by the public library authority of its statutory duty, that parish councils should cease to be library authorities and that the minister should review the services provided by library authorities and withdraw these powers where this was considered necessary. It further proposed that a minimum annual expenditure on books should be laid down and that the system of library co-operation should be extended. Higher priority should be given to capital expenditure on premises and equipment for public libraries and a new Public Libraries act should be passed, giving effect to these recommendations and consolidating existing legislation.

British public library statistics for 1958-59 issued in November showed that at least 33,438 service points and 235 mobile libraries were in operation, with a total stock of 71 million volumes, and a full-time staff of 13,199. Book expenditure was £4,550,000, and the total cost of the service

was £18,773,033 or 7s. 4d. per head of population. Lending library issues were 397 million, or 8 per head.

The annual conference of the Library association was held at Torquay in September under the presidency of Earl Attlee, sessions being devoted to co-operation between municipal and county library systems, public library costs and statistics, the future of county libraries and the public library in education. The annual lecture was delivered by W. F. Oakeshott, and the Library Association Carnegie medal for an outstanding children's book of 1958 was awarded to Ann Philippa Pearce for *Tom's Midnight Garden* (O.U.P.). The association published a *Guide to Reference Books* (London), edited by A. J. Walford, an invaluable source book. Two of the association's officers retired after many years' service—P. S. J. Welsford, the secretary, and D. C. Henrik Jones, the librarian and information officer.

The new headquarters of Aslib in Belgrave square, London, was opened in January by Lord Hailsham, and the association held its annual conference at Scarborough in October. Sessions were devoted to technical information in industry, and Japanese sources of scientific and technical information, with a discussion on documentary reproduction. The new Sheffield University library was opened in May, with room for about 1 million volumes and seating accommodation for more than 400.

Commonwealth. Recent developments in the special libraries of India were outlined by B. Agard Evans and G. B. Ghosh (*Aslib Proceedings*, 11, 6, June). The Geological Survey of India library, Calcutta (founded 1850), had a stock of about 180,000 volumes, with five branch libraries in the states of Madras, Andhra Pradesh, Uttar Pradesh, Bombay and Kashmir. Founded in 1945, the Tata Institute of Fundamental Research had a library of 11,200 volumes devoted to physics, mathematics and electronics, and housed a depository collection of nearly 40,000 reports of the Atomic Energy commissions of the United States, the United Kingdom, Canada and France. More than 260,000 map sheets and about 68,000 volumes were housed in the Indian Statistical Institute library, Calcutta, and the Central Water and Power Commission library, New Delhi (established 1931), had 53,000 books, 40,000 volumes of periodicals, and 10,000 maps, plans and other items. The Indian Agricultural Research Institute library, founded at Pusa in 1905 and moved to New Delhi in 1936, had more than 142,000 volumes, and the Indian Council of Agricultural Research, New Delhi (founded 1930), stocked about 80,000 volumes. Functioning as the national central library of information serving engineers and architects throughout India, the National Building Organization library, New Delhi (founded 1954), contained 10,000 books and pamphlets.

Public library services in Singapore were described by L. M. Harrod (*Library Association Record*, 61, 9, September). In 1823 a subscription library called the Singapore library was opened at the Raffles institution, and later became the Raffles museum and library. The government took over financial responsibility in 1874, and new buildings were erected between 1887 and 1916. In 1945, after the Japanese occupation, the library became the official depository for publications printed in Singapore, and in 1950 a children's library was provided. A law was passed in 1958 making the collection the Raffles National library, Singapore, and it ceased to be a subscription library. Branch libraries were opened and mobile libraries employed, the emphasis being on books for children. Serving a population of nearly 1·5 million, 75% of whom were Chinese, the library had a stock of about 150,000 volumes, including books in Chinese, Malay and Tamil.

R. F. Kennedy described the development of library services over the previous 40 years in the Union of South Africa (*Library World*, 60, February). Many started as subscription libraries and were still in the pioneering stage. Johannesburg took over the local library in 1924, Pretoria in 1933, Durban in 1937 and Bloemfontein in 1946. The State library at Pretoria was the centre for inter-library lending and also a copyright depository, as was the South African Public library, Cape Town, which had become a national reference library and bibliographical centre. Four provincial councils had established libraries in the previous few years, and the Transvaal Provincial library with a stock of almost 1 million books served 80 town and village libraries, with 460 depots.

The Unesco public library pilot project in the Eastern Region of Nigeria was described by S. H. Horrocks (*Unesco Bulletin for Libraries*, 13, 1, January), and the general problems of public library development in Nigeria were outlined by Kalu Okorie (*Library World*, 60, March). The Northern Region had a library service in 1952 under the Education Department, with a regional library at Kaduna. The Eastern Region had a public library under a Library board at Enugu, the capital, with divisional libraries based on townships at Port Harcourt, Aba, Onitsha, Akakaliki and Calabar, with mobile libraries, a book box service and postal services where required. The Ministry of Education was responsible for the library service in the Western Region, and a temporary library service was inaugurated at Ibadan in 1959, a new regional library headquarters being planned. There was no real library service in the Southern Cameroons, but in Lagos there was the Lagos Municipal library (1946), the Lagos library, the Anglo-Nigerian Art Centre library and the United States Information Service library (1951). Staffing difficulties, financial problems, apathy concerning the lack of library services, low standards of literacy and poor communications were among the problems faced, and the results of the pilot project in the Eastern Region of Nigeria were awaited with interest.

Libraries and scientific progress in west Africa were studied by H. Anthony Rydings (*WALA News: Bulletin of the West African Library Association*, 3, 3, June), and Wilfred J. Plumbe (*ibid.*) surveyed new library developments in Asia and Africa, excluding west Africa. Progress since World War II in Indonesia, Malaya, the Philippines, Hong Kong, Thailand, Burma, India, Sudan and east and central Africa was described.

Other Countries. The resources of the technical libraries of western Europe were outlined by Robert E. Betts (*American Documentation*, 10, 1, January). He surveyed the principal libraries of many large towns, giving details of their development and stocks. L'Ecole Nationale des Ponts et Chaussées, Paris (founded 1747), stocked 150,000 volumes; the Eidgenössische Technische Hochschule, Zürich (1854), possessed 300,000 books and 2 million patents; the Deutsches Museum, Munich, contained 330,000 volumes and 15,000 mss.; the Technische Hogeschool, Delft (1842), had 250,000 volumes; and the Danmarks Tekniske Bibliotek, Copenhagen, stocked 130,000 books.

Several Finnish research libraries had been provided with new buildings in the previous few years, and these were described, with plans and photographs, by J. Vallinkoski and others (*Libri*, 9, 1). Helsinki University library, the national library of Finland, was rehoused, the previous main building having been completed in 1844, with an extension in 1906. Turku University library was opened to the public in 1922, and the new library was completed in 1954, two new buildings being added to it in 1958. The library contained 450,000 volumes. Åbo Akademi (1918), which had a new building completed in 1957, possessed a stock of more than 400,000 volumes and 27 departmental libraries. The Student Union library, University of Helsinki, opened in 1858, was totally independent of the university, and was prominent among scientific libraries in Finland. The stock of 170,000 books

The new Deutsche Bibliothek in Frankfurt, German Federal Republic, which was opened by President Heuss in April. For works in German only, it will eventually house some 560,000 volumes.

was housed in a building completed in 1955. The University College of Jyväskylä, founded in 1912 (one of the four Finnish libraries collecting national literature and the central library for pedagogical research in Finland), with a stock of about 325,000 volumes, was also rehoused.

Etienne Didier described the " bibliotrain " (*Unesco Bulletin for Libraries*, 13, 2-3, February-March), a railway library carriage which was first put into service in France in April 1957. It provided a book service for about 12,000 railwaymen and their families, and operated independently on its 33-day tour, covering 1,500 mi. The reading room contained some 7,000 books, tables and chairs, and both reference books and periodicals were also provided.

The Krupskaya State Library institute, Leningrad, celebrated its 40th anniversary in Dec. 1958, having trained more than 9,000 librarians during its lifetime. During the school year 1958-59, 3,564 students took courses at the institute, the work of which was outlined by N. Skrypnev (*Unesco Bulletin for Libraries*, 13, 4, April).

Libraries in China were described by Chi Cheng (*Libri*, 9, 2). According to 1936 statistics there were 5,196 libraries in the country, but in 1943 only 940 were left. By the end of June 1958, there were 490 public libraries under the Ministry of Culture, 2,657 in the cultural clubs, 25,419 under the labour unions and 288,326 in the rural areas. In addition there were 235 collegiate libraries under the Ministry of Education and 101 under the Chinese Academy of Science (these latter contained 267 million volumes), as well as numerous school libraries and libraries of official organizations. Peking library had 5,660,000 volumes, the public libraries housed 42·7 million books, the institutes of higher learning stocked 44 million and the labour union libraries about 23 million. Peking university and Wuhan university conducted courses on library science.

In the United States, at budget time, attacks were made on two library books. One, in Alabama, a children's story called *The Rabbits' Wedding* in which a black rabbit married a white rabbit, was described as propaganda for interracial marriages. The objection to the other, in Wisconsin, a Russian folk-tale called *My Mother is the Most Beautiful Woman in the World*, was because of its charming illustrations of life on a collective farm. As a result of the attacks both books were put on closed shelves. A survey revealed that nearly a third of the libraries in California had permanently discarded some controversial books and that most of the rest sometimes chose not to buy such books.

The 28 accredited library schools in the United States and Canada placed 1,138 graduates in initial positions in 1959, but there was still a shortage of librarians, and enrolments in the schools remained low. Salary scales were rising but the average starting salary for librarians of $4,683 did not equal that paid to school teachers with comparable qualifications. The three large library systems of New York found themselves with 150 vacancies in 953 professional positions, recruitment at a standstill and resignations increasing.

The Massachusetts Institute of Technology concluded an agreement to exchange scientific publications with libraries in the U.S.S.R. The University of Texas library purchased the celebrated Bibliotheca Parsonia, consisting of 40,000 books and several thousand manuscripts. There were two notable additions, totalling more than 500 letters and documents, to the Library of Congress collection of the papers of Chester A. Arthur, the 21st president of the United States. A significant proportion of the presidential papers in the Harry S. Truman library was opened to researchers, and Averell Harriman, former governor of New York, gave 500,000 of his public and private papers to Syracuse university.

Congress appropriated $6 million for the Federal Library services for 1959-60. The new $2·5 million library building of the University of Alaska was opened and the Louisiana State university dedicated a new $3·5 million, air-conditioned library building.   (J. L. T.; H. W. Wr.)

See R. L. Collinson, *Indexes and Indexing*, 2nd ed. (London, 1959); L. M. Harrod, *The Librarians' Glossary*, 2nd ed. (London, 1959); S. R. Ranganathan, *Library Administration*, 2nd ed. (Bombay, 1959).

LIBYA. A federal kingdom in North Africa, bounded N. by the Mediterranean, W. by Tunisia and Algeria, S. by the republics of Niger and Chad, and E. by Sudan and Egypt. Area: *c.* 625,000 sq.mi. Pop.: (1954 census): 1,091,800 including Tripolitania 746,200, Cyrenaica 291,100 and Fezzan 54,500; Berbers, with Arab admixture; Italians, about 45,000 (all in Tripolitania); small Greek, Maltese and Jewish communities. Language: Arabic. Religion: mainly Moslem.

Oil was struck in the Libyan desert in 1959. Here prospectors are using a mobile drilling rig to secure themselves a water supply.

Capitals (pop., 1958): Tripoli 172,200 (incl. 131,415 Libyans), Benghazi 70,533. King, Mohammed Idris I el-Mahdi es-Senussi. Prime minister, Abd-ul-Majid Kubar. Main imports: manufactures, foodstuffs, fuel. Main exports: esparto, groundnuts, tunny. Monetary unit: Libyan pound (=£1 sterling).

History. The event of the year 1959 was the oil find in the Jebel Zelten area, about 100 mi. from the coast and 200 mi. south of Benghazi. The No. 1 well, where oil was struck in June, had a flow of 17,500 barrels a day; the flow in well No. 2 was said to be 15,000 barrels a day. This discovery encouraged hopes that worthwhile oilfields existed.

The main sources of the country's revenue continued to be the British yearly grant of £3·75 million and the U.S. yearly rental of $4 million for the use of Wheelus air base near Tripoli. In July it was rumoured that Libya had asked for the rental to be increased to $40 million.

The British garrisons in Libya were reduced and at the end of the year they comprised two infantry battalions, at Tripoli and Benghazi, and the armoured cars of the 2nd Royal Tank regiment at Homs, west of Tripoli.

LIECHTENSTEIN. Independent principality between Switzerland and Austria, united with Switzerland by monetary and customs union. Area: 61·4 sq.mi. Pop. (Dec. 1, 1955, census): 14,757, including 2,866 foreigners (1,078 Swiss, 959 Austrians, 565 Germans, etc.). Language: German. Religion: Roman Catholic. Capital, Vaduz, pop. (1955) 3,031. Sovereign prince, Franz-Josef II; minister-president (appointed Sept. 3, 1945), Alexander Frick. Currency: Swiss.

History. The chief event of the year was the meeting at Vaduz, on Oct. 23, of a " baby summit " meeting of the four smallest sovereign states of Europe. Andorra was represented by Casimir Arajol, Liechtenstein by Baron Eduard von Falz-Fein and Gebhard Banzer, Monaco by Gabriel Ollivier and San Marino by Emanuele Noel. There was also an observer from the Vatican City State. The delegates discussed matters of common interest; *i.e.*, the sale of postage stamps and tourism. The representative of Monaco proposed that the membership of the group should be extended to Luxembourg. The representative of Liechtenstein objected because Luxembourg, with its population of 320,000, was far too big. It was decided, however, to invite Luxembourg. " We have reached agreement and this is more than can be said for other conferences I could name," the Monaco representative reported at a press conference.

LIFE-BOAT SERVICE: *see* Shipping, Merchant Marine.

LINEN AND FLAX: *see* Business Review.

LITERARY PRIZES. The Nobel prize for literature was awarded to Salvatore Quasimodo (*see* Biographies).

Great Britain. Among the principal literary awards made in 1959 were: James Tait Black memorial prizes for 1959 to Joyce Hemlow for *The History of Fanny Burney* (biography) and Angus Wilson for *The Middle Age of Mrs. Eliot* (fiction); Arts Council poetry prize to Roy Fuller for *Brutus's Orchard* (1957) and Thom Gunn for *The Sense of Movement* (1957): Authors' Club award to Alan Sillitoe for *Saturday Night and Sunday Morning* (1958); Foyle Prize for Poetry to John Betjeman for *Collected Poems* (1958); Guinness poetry awards to W. H. Auden for *Goodbye to the Messogiorno*, Robert Lowell for *Skunk Hour*, Edwin Muir (*see* Obituaries) for *Impersonal Calamity*, Edith Sitwell for *La Bella Bona Roba*, plus a special award to William Plomer for *A Young Jackdaw*; Library Association Carnegie medal to Ann Philippa Pearce for *Tom's Midnight Garden* (1958); W. H. Smith and Son literary award of £1,000 to Patrick White for *Voss* (1957); John Llewelyn Rhys memorial prize to Dan Jacobson for *A Long Way from London* (1958).

France. Among the main literary prizes awarded in 1959 were: Grand Prix de Poésie de l'Académie Française to

Tristan Klingsor for his work as a whole; GRAND PRIX DE LITTÉRATURE DE L'ACADÉMIE FRANÇAISE to Thierry Maulnier for his work as a whole; PRIX DU ROMAN DE L'ACADÉMIE FRANÇAISE to Gabriel d'Aubarède for *La Foi de notre enfance*; GRAND PRIX NATIONAL DES LETTRES to Saint-John Perse for his poetry; PRIX ALBERT LONDRES, reserved for a journalist, to J. M. Théolleyre; PRIX GONCOURT to André Schwartz-Bart for *Le Dernier des justes*; PRIX FÉMINA to Bernard Privat for *Au Pied du mur*; PRIX MÉDICIS to Claude Mauriac for *Le Dîner en ville*; PRIX INTERALLIÉ to Antoine Blondin for *Un Singe en hiver*; PRIX THÉOPHRASTE RENAUDOT to Albert Palle for *L'Expérience*.

United States. The principal prizes awarded during 1959 and the latter months of 1958 were: ACADEMY OF AMERICAN POETS AWARD, to Robinson Jeffers (1958), Louise Bogan (1959); Lamont Poetry selection, to Donald Justice for *Summer Anniversaries*. AMERICAN ACADEMY OF ARTS AND LETTERS AND NATIONAL INSTITUTE, gold medal for drama to Arthur Miller, Rosenthal award of $1,000 to Frederick Buechner for *The Return of Ansel Gibbs*, Award of Merit medal and $1,000 to Aldous Huxley, Marjorie Peabody Waite award of $1,000 to Leon Hartl, Prix de Rome fellowships to Harold Brodkey and Edmund Keeley. AMERICAN POLITICAL SCIENCE ASSOCIATION, Woodrow Wilson Foundation award of $1,000 for the best book on government and democracy jointly to Christian Bay for *The Structure of Freedom* and to James S. Coleman for *Nigeria: Background to Nationalism*. ANISFIELD-WOLF AWARDS, $1,000 each for books on race relations, administered by the *Saturday Review*, to Martin Luther King, Jr., for *Stride Toward Freedom*, and to George Eaton Simpson and J. Milton Yinger for *Racial and Cultural Minorities*. BANCROFT PRIZES, $3,000 each for the two best books on American history, diplomacy or international relations, to Daniel Boorstin for *The Americans: the Colonial Experience*, and to Ernest Samuels for *Henry Adams: the Middle Years*. PULITZER PRIZES, $500 each to Robert Lewis Taylor for *The Travels of Jaimie McPheeters* (fiction), to Arthur Walworth for *Woodrow Wilson* (biography), to Leonard D. White for *The Republican Era: 1869-1901* (history), written with the assistance of Jean Schneider, to Stanley Kunitz for *Selected Poems, 1928-1958*, to Archibald MacLeish for *J.B.* (drama). (X.; A. PR.; OA. S.)

LITERATURE: *see* AMERICAN LITERATURE; ENGLISH LITERATURE; FRENCH LITERATURE; GERMAN LITERATURE; ITALIAN LITERATURE; LITERARY PRIZES; SOVIET LITERATURE; SPANISH LITERATURE.

LIVESTOCK. The trends towards specialized production, emphasis on meat and modification of breed characters—for example, by the introduction of polling—which were marked features of the livestock situation in 1958, continued in 1959. Superimposed on them, however, were other trends towards greater intensification of production and fuller exploitation of the capacity of ruminant stock (cattle and sheep) to convert the relatively cheap nutrients derived from grassland into products for human consumption. Techniques for growing more and better grass and for the conservation of surplus grass for feeding during periods of seasonal shortage, especially winter, had become so well developed and widely adopted that stock farmers were now seeking more efficient methods of using grazing and preserved grass as the major sources of stock feed. In relation to this general development, more attention was being devoted in scientific studies to the recognition and treatment of subclinical conditions and parasitism, which depress production, and to the more precise definition of nutritional requirements. Of special relevance to the last, work on the physiology of the rumen and on digestion in ruminants made notable progress during the year.

At the Exford, Somerset, sheep fair in September, E. du Cann (right), Conservative candidate for Taunton, talks to shepherds.

Towards intensifying production, the general aim appeared to have been to introduce new methods of stock husbandry or to modify old ones so that more productive stock could be kept per unit area of land and managed with less of ever more costly labour. The year 1959 may well come to be regarded as a peak year of practical experiment, or trial and error, in the wide field of animal husbandry, especially through the application of methods proved successful in one form of production to others. In some cases this had set the stage for marked expansion; for example, intensive systems of rearing

LIVESTOCK NUMBERS (million head)						
Cattle	1938-39	1953-54	1954-55	1955-56	1956-57	1957-58
India . .	137·9*	...	...	158·7	...	...
United States†	66·0	95·7	96·6	96·8	94·5	94·0
Brazil .	40·7	57·6	61·4	63·6	66·7	69·5
U.S.S.R. .	54·5‡	55·8	56·7	58·8	61·4	66·7
China . .	...	43·3	44·8	45·3	...	...
Argentina .	33·2§	43·6	...	46·9	44·2	...
Pakistan .	24·4	31·1	31·1	31·1	31·1	31·1
Mexico .	11·6*	...	20·5	22·8	...	...
Ethiopia .	...	...	...	...	...	20·0
France .	15·6	16·9	17·3	17·6	17·7	17·9
Australia.	12·9	15·6	15·8	16·5	17·3	16·9
Colombia .	9·0	11·0	...	12·5	13·4	...
Turkey .	9·3	10·8	10·9	11·1	11·5	12·1
German Fed.Rep.	12·2	11·6	11·5	11·6	11·8	11·9
South Africa	11·9	11·6	11·7	11·8	...	...
United Kingdom†	8·9	10·7	10·7	10·9	10·9	11·0
Canada† .	8·2	9·4	9·7	10·0	10·4	10·3
Sheep						
Australia.	111·1	126·9	130·8	139·1	149·8	149·3
U.S.S.R. .	79·9‡	99·8	99·0	103·3	108·2	120·2
China .	22·9†	48·1	50·4	53·4	...	...
Argentina .	43·9§	46·8	...	45·2	45·7	...
India .	41·5*	...	...	39·2	...	...
New Zealand .	29·2‖	38·0	39·1	40·2	42·4	...
South Africa	38·3	37·1	37·0	37·5	...	...
United States† .	51·6	31·4	31·6	31·3	30·8	31·3
Turkey .	25·2	27·3	26·8	26·4	28·0	29·2
United Kingdom†	26·9	22·9	22·9	23·6	24·8	26·2
Uruguay .	17·9§	25·7	24·5	23·3	...	...
Pigs						
China .	78·5§	101·7	87·9	84·0	...	...
U.S.S.R. .	27·5‡	47·6	51·1	52·2	56·5	...
United States† .	50·0	45·1	50·5	55·2	51·7	51·6
Brazil .	21·8	32·7	35·6	38·6	41·4	44·2
German Fed.Rep.	12·3	12·4	14·5	14·6	14·4	15·4
Poland .	7·5	9·8	10·9	11·6	12·3	12·0
Mexico .	5·1*	7·5	9·7	9·6	...	...
German Dem.Rep.	5·7	8·2	8·4	9·0	8·3	8·3
France .	7·1	7·3	7·6	7·7	7·8	8·1
United Kingdom†	4·4	6·3	5·8	5·5	6·0	6·6

* 1940. † On agricultural holdings. ‡ 1941. § 1937. ‖ 1936-37.
SOURCE. F.A.O. *Year Book of Agricultural Statistics* and *Monthly Bulletin of Agricultural Economics and Statistics*.

and managing hens for egg production had been widely and simply adapted for raising and quickly finishing broilers and turkeys, with the result that specialized auxiliary enterprises had been developed on many farms. Moreover, improved methods of preservation and storage (*e.g.*, by deep freezing) enabled " out of season " production to be practised. Again, the self-feeding of pigs having proved simple and labour saving in practice, the same principle of allowing the stock to get their own feed rather than to have it taken and rationed to them had come to be applied to dairy cows and beef cattle using silage. Further instances of such transfer or modification of husbandry methods that had become prominent were the so-called " creep feeding " of lambs, whereby they could graze and receive supplementary feeds away from their dams and make better growth, and the extension of " early-weaning " systems to dairy and beef calves in which specially prepared milk substitutes and balanced concentrates were used to encourage early growth without feeding relatively large amounts of liquid milk over a long period, and thus to reduce rearing costs.

The exploitation of such methods was related also to the general tendency to speed up the development of meat animals towards slaughter at earlier ages and lighter carcass weights, in spite of the conflict between financial return per carcass at heavier weights and quality of meat or suitability to consumer preference at lighter weights. Efficiency of food conversion had become recognized as being as important in the young meat animal growing to slaughter stage as in the adult dairy cow. Performance testing of meat animals increased markedly during the year and included, as a prominent feature, this aspect of production.

Notwithstanding the wide adoption of improved husbandry and feeding techniques, the vulnerability of livestock industries to untoward conditions was well shown during 1959 in the effects of the summer drought in Europe, which immediately lowered milk yields, and thus the supplies of liquid and processed milk. The longer-term effects in reduced winter feed supplies for dairy and other stock had already become felt by the end of the year. On the other hand, rains ended the drought which had earlier affected some pastoral areas in Australia, and with wool holding its strong position as a main textile fibre the sheep industry in that country regained its buoyancy. Even as a by-product of mutton and lamb production, wool further established itself as an important source of income to flockmasters. (*See* also DAIRY FARMING AND DAIRY PRODUCE; POULTRY; VETERINARY MEDICINE.)

(J. E. N.)

LOCAL GOVERNMENT.

The Local Government act, 1958, had its first impact on the finances of local authorities during 1959. An order was made in Nov. 1958, fixing the general grant payable to local authorities for the financial years 1959-60 and 1960-61 at £393 million and £414 million respectively. This was to replace a number of specific percentage grants. The Fire Service act, 1959, also gave effect to the government's stated policy in the 1958 act of a general relaxation of control over the functions of local authorities. It abolished the secretary of state's powers to regulate pay and other conditions of service (except discipline) in the fire service and relaxed certain other controls. The 1958 act also authorized county district councils having populations of not less than 60,000 to apply for permission to submit schemes under which they would exercise functions in relation to health and welfare or education by delegation from the county council. By Nov. 1959 approval had been given for the submission of 11 schemes in respect of health and welfare and four for education.

A new Rating and Valuation act postponed until 1963 the new rating valuation lists due to come into operation in 1961, giving the Valuation Office of the Board of Inland Revenue more time to make new valuations of all house property. The act also repealed the power of local authorities to propose alterations to the valuation list.

The report of the Committee on the Rating of Charities, under the chairmanship of Sir Fred Pritchard (Cmnd. 831), recommended that charities should continue to enjoy special privileges and should receive a mandatory relief of 50% of the rates chargeable. Local authorities should have discretion to grant relief to charities not entitled to mandatory relief, and additional relief to those so entitled. The committee recommended compulsory registration of all charities in rateable occupation of land.

The committee set up in 1957 to review the structure of the public library service in England and Wales, under the chairmanship of Sir Sydney Roberts, reported in February (Cmnd. 660). They recommended that the library service should come under the general supervision of the minister of education and be assisted by advisory bodies. Outside London, counties and county boroughs would be the library authorities, although non-county boroughs and urban districts which could satisfy the minister that they were capable of providing an efficient library service would be entitled to exercise library functions.

The Mental Health act, 1959, repealed the Lunacy and Mental Treatment acts, 1890 to 1930, and the Mental Deficiency acts, 1913 to 1938, introduced a new terminology for the classification of mental patients and brought certification to an end. It also provided for a simplification of admission procedures and the extension of community care, including local authority guardianship and local authority hostels and residential accommodation for those who did not need hospital accommodation. Two important reports affecting the social services were presented to the minister of health during the year. The first, by a committee under the chairmanship of the Earl of Cranbrook, considered the maternity services. No substantial alteration was proposed to the basic tripartite structure of maternity services provided by hospitals, local health authorities and general practitioners. The committee recommended the establishment of local maternity liaison committees and clinical meetings. Local health authorities were asked to continue to maintain an efficient domiciliary midwifery service and to pay particular attention to health education, mothercraft instruction for expectant mothers, priority dental treatment and the home help service. The second report, by a committee under the chairmanship of Miss E. L. Younghusband, inquired into the proper field of work and the recruitment and training of social workers in the local authorities' health and welfare services. It proposed a reorganization of training and advocated three grades of trained social worker with a new National Council for Social Work Training to sponsor and promote this object.

Compensation for compulsory purchase by local authorities was restored to a " market value " basis by the Town and Country Planning act, 1959. This also provided for the removal of ministerial consent to a number of local authority land transactions, for the implementation of recommendations of the Committee on Administrative Tribunals and Enquiries (Cmnd. 218), particularly as to rights of appeal to the High Court in relation to action taken under the planning acts, and notification to owners of applications for planning permission. It also gave a right to an owner-occupier of property affected by " planning blight " to require the public authority concerned to purchase his property forthwith at a price unaffected by the scheme.

In January the Committee on the Consolidation of Highway Law, under the chairmanship of the Marquess of Reading, presented its report (Cmnd. 630). Its task was to consider which of the enactments relating to highways, etc., should be consolidated and what minor amendments could be included in a consolidation bill. A consolidation act was subsequently passed and came into effect on Jan. 1, 1960.

Following a resolution in the House of Lords accepting the principle that pending further inquiry county council bills should not confer on any other authority or persons functions in which the county council had no interest, a joint committee of both houses of parliament was appointed to consider the extent to which proposed private bill enactments which would alter the powers or duties of persons other than the promoter should be allowed. The joint committee's report (H.L.176: H.C.262) emphasized the need for general legislation at regular intervals conferring powers applicable either to local authorities generally or to particular classes of local authority. On the main issue the view was expressed that, subject to certain safeguards, no objection on grounds of principle need in future be raised to bills promoted by county councils containing clauses to confer powers on other authorities in the county in any local government matter. (*See* also Housing; Town and Country Planning.) (G. H. Bl.)

LONDON. Capital of the United Kingdom of Great Britain and Northern Ireland and the centre of the Commonwealth of Nations. The term " London " is used here to describe three areas: (i) the City, the ancient heart of London, which for some purposes functions as a county; (ii) the administrative county, comprising the City and the county proper (which consists of 28 metropolitan boroughs); and (iii) Greater London, embracing the City, the county proper and the suburbs as far as the borders of the Metropolitan police

area; *i.e.* including Middlesex and parts of Essex, Kent, Surrey and Hertfordshire. *City.* Area 1·05 sq.mi.; night pop. (1951 census) 5,268. Lord Mayors in 1959, Sir Harold Gillett and (from Nov. 8) Sir Edmund Stockdale. *County.* Area (incl. City) 116·95 sq.mi.; pop. (1951) 3,348,336, (1958 est.) 3,225,000. Lord lieutenant, Lord Alexander of Tunis; chairman of London County council, Sidney J. Barton. *Greater London.* Area *c.* 722 sq.mi.; pop. (1951) 8,348,023.

London's year was transformed and dominated by the splendid summer which caused the citizens to change their habits in many ways. Ice manufacturers and vendors of light summer suits for men were engulfed in new business on a scale that is possible only once in a decade. The parks were full all day, every day, for weeks on end, some aspects of which did not escape the notice of Billy Graham, the U.S. evangelist, who commented on their resemblance to a bedroom due to the behaviour of many couples. The open air theatre in Regent's park had a successful season and the weather made it possible for the *Daily Mail* competition for the fastest journey from Marble Arch to the Arc de Triomphe, Paris, to succeed beyond expectations. It was not just a publicity stunt, but provided evidence that it might prove possible to reduce the travelling time between the two city centres by something like an hour.

After many years the last stretches of the Cromwell road extension were finished and opened, the Chiswick flyover completed and the westward exit from central London shortened by as much as 15 min. Reports from London Transport and from the commissioner for Metropolitan police repeated more emphatically the warning that London was about to throttle itself with its own traffic. A short

The helicopter station on the south bank of the Thames at Battersea, which was opened on April 23. London's first specially designed " heliport ", it is a commercial venture by a firm of helicopter manufacturers, and can accommodate the largest existing machines.

(Left) A sentry box is moved on Oct. 17 when, after incidents arising from the importunity of sightseers, the Buckingham palace guard withdrew to positions of greater safety. (Right) The old Elephant and Castle tavern sign is taken away during demolition of the area.

stretch of road in the City, with car parks underneath, an extension of parking meters from Mayfair into Marylebone and a multi-floor garage behind Oxford street were the main palliatives presented during the year. The first signs that the public transport system was shrinking under the impact of "private" motoring appeared, so that Londoners might, within a decade, anticipate being in the same position as New Yorkers so far as bus services were concerned—paying high prices for constantly curtailed services. Just before Christmas the first large-scale attempt to regulate car parking in the main shopping area was made.

Several sawn-off "skyscrapers" of 14 to 17 storeys were completed and opened, but the 25-storey Shell-Mex building on the south bank was still unfinished though the towering framework had become a feature of the skyline. On Oct. 24 the new north block of the British Museum (Natural History)

at South Kensington, designed by W. Kendall, was opened by the museum trustees. The brilliantly designed Mermaid theatre, opened in the summer, immediately became popular.

The splendid summer would have provided a memorable setting for great processions or public occasions, but the only one was the visit of President Eisenhower which brought cheering Londoners into the streets in much larger numbers than anybody had calculated. The spectacle of the guardsmen doing their drill outside Buckingham palace was marred by the provision of new automatic weapons with which they could no longer mesmerize the spectators by their glittering precision. To prevent a continuation of the various types of petty annoyances to which they had so long been subjected by members of the public, the guards were moved in the autumn to new positions inside the palace railings. (G. F.)

The new block at the British Museum (Natural History), South Kensington, opened on Oct. 24. It lies behind the main building.

LUTHERANS.
The Lutheran Churches are those which adopt the Augsburg confession as a confessional document. Estimated world membership in 1959: 70·1 million.

Two Scandinavian primates who had been leading figures in the oecumenical movement died in 1959—Bishop Eivind Berggrav, who had been primate of Norway from 1937 to 1950, and Dr. Yngve Brilioth, primate of Sweden from 1950 to 1958 (*see* OBITUARIES). After the government of the German Democratic Republic had set up an office in Stalinstadt to promote atheist ceremonies for baptisms, marriages and burials, the synod of the Evangelical Church in eastern Germany met in February to take measures to stiffen Christian opposition. Bishop Johannes Jänicke, reporting increased pressure against the church in Saxony, revealed that 700 pastorates from a total of 1,700 were vacant and that the number of confirmation candidates had been halved. In July there were reports of new campaigns by the Rumanian and Hungarian governments against confirmation in the Lutheran Church. Sigurbjorn Einarsson, formerly a professor of theology at Reykjavik university, was consecrated in June as bishop of Iceland. His election marked a decline of the influence held previously in the Icelandic Church by Lutheran clergy with Spiritualist tendencies. The new diocese of Helsinki, with a population of 450,000, was established in July by the Finnish Lutheran Church, having been separated from the diocese of Tampere, and Bishop Martti Simojoki of Mikkeli was elected as its first bishop. In August Archbishop Gunnar Hultgren of Sweden was elected a member of the central committee of the World Council of Churches.

(J. R. Se.)

LUXEMBOURG. Independent grand duchy in western Europe bounded S. by France, N.W. by Belgium and N.E. by Germany. Area: 999 sq.mi. Pop.: (Dec. 31, 1947 census) 290,992; (Dec. 1958 est.) 320,000. Languages: *Letzeburgesch*, a German dialect, and French (official). Religion: Roman Catholic 98%. Capital, Luxembourg, pop. (Jan. 1958) 70,158. Sovereign, Grand Duchess Charlotte; prime ministers in 1959, Pierre Frieden and (from March 7) Pierre Werner. Main imports: manufactured goods and foodstuffs. Main export: steel. Monetary unit: Luxembourg *franc* (= Belgian franc).

History. A general election was held on Feb. 1, 1959, the Liberals almost doubling their representation at the expense of the Social Christians. Their seats rose from 6 to 11, while the Social Christians dropped from 26 to 21. The Socialists were unchanged at 17 and the Communists at 3. (*See* also ELECTIONS.)

Pierre Frieden, the prime minister and a Social Christian leader, died on Feb. 23. He was succeeded by Pierre Werner, another Social Christian, who on March 7 formed a coalition government with the Liberals. Joseph Bech, former foreign minister, was elected speaker of the Chamber of Deputies.

On June 16 King Baudouin of Belgium paid an official visit to Luxembourg.

MACHINERY AND MACHINE TOOLS. On the whole, the value of production in various branches of the machine-building industry was well sustained during the early months of 1959. As Table I shows, there was a further substantial advance in agricultural machinery, and the total for the first half corresponded to an annual rate of £181·4 million, whereas the figure for the year 1956 was £102·5 million. For civil engineering contractors' plant, the rate of output was substantially the same as for 1958 and 1956, and somewhat lower than in 1957. Makers of internal combustion engines achieved an average output of £4,368,000 during the first four months of 1959, which was very slightly higher than the figure for the corresponding period of 1958. For accounting and similar machinery the average production for the four months was £2,719,000 compared with £2,481,000 for the full year 1958. For conveyors and elevators, however, the average (for five months) fell to £1,979,000 from the 1958 (full year) figure of £2,149,000. In addition there was a further and particularly unwelcome fall in machine tool deliveries, as shown in Table I. At the same time there was a decline in the value of orders in hand from £54,384,000 at the end of Dec. 1958, to £50,653,000 at the end of May 1959. This latter figure, however, represented a slight increase on the total for the end of April, so that in May, for the first time for many months, new orders exceeded deliveries.

During the first seven months of 1959, exports of machinery (other than electric) had an aggregate value of £364 million,

A drilling machine controlled by a tape-fed electronic system providing automatic positioning to within limits of 0·001 in.

compared with £340 million for the corresponding period of 1958. The former figure represented an annual rate of £624 million, whereas the actual total for 1958 was £566 million. Despite the further rise in the value of exports during the first seven months of 1959, the tonnage was again lower, a trend which had persisted over a period of at least three years. It seemed probable that this was attributable only partly to rising prices, and that the proportion of more intricate machinery, which necessarily had a higher ton-value, was increasing. The growing importance of the part which the machine-building industry was playing in the overseas trade of the country was shown by the fact that during the period Jan.-July 1959, exports of machinery (other than electric) accounted for 22·2% of the total value of exports of manufactured goods and for 18·9% of all exports. Machine tool exports, however, did not contribute to the general expansion, and following the substantial fall in 1958 there was a further decline in the first half of 1959. For this period the monthly average was only £1·84 million, corresponding to an annual rate of £22·1 million, whereas for 1958 the total was £24·2 million and for 1957, £28·1 million.

It was estimated that during the first five months of 1959 deliveries to the home market of British-built and imported machine tools totalled only £29·7 million, corresponding to an annual rate of £71·3 million, whereas the aggregates for 1958 and 1957 were £77·4 million and £91·8 million respectively.

The most significant developments in the machine tool field were associated with systems for automatic positioning and continuous control of movements, which were evidently destined to be of great practical importance in the near future. For one new system the measuring elements comprised a fixed bar and a non-rotating, moving sleeve, both of which had multiple helical conductors, and this arrangement was claimed to permit a setting accuracy of 0·0001 in. Another well-established system, involving the use of diffraction gratings, was modified and improved with the result that the maximum machining period controlled by a 3,600-ft.-long magnetic tape was increased from 40 min. to 190 min. A universal boring and surfacing machine which was built and equipped for automatic positioning had a capacity for workpieces weighing up to approximately five tons. The arrangement provided for locating the spindle head, table and saddle, either in accordance with the settings of control dials or from punched cards.

In the United States there was much development in techniques of cutting metal, partly because of the need for

TABLE I. VALUES OF PRODUCTION OF SOME TYPES OF MACHINERY
(monthly averages in £'000)

	Civil engineering contractors' plant	Agricultural (incl. tractors)	Machine tools
1955	3,134	9,458	6,282
1956	3,515	8,542	7,123
1957	3,696	10,842	7,936
1958	3,562	11,850	6,993
1959	3,555 (6 mo.)	15,100 (6 mo.)	6,551 (6 mo.)

TABLE II. EXPORTS OF MACHINERY AND MACHINE TOOLS

	All machinery (other than electric)	Machine tools
1957	561,087	28,092
1958	565,977	24,222
1958 (7 mo.)	340,403	14,711
1959 (7 mo.)	363,758	12,849

machining the so-called super-alloys. Along with the attempts of the aircraft and missiles industries to fabricate high-temperature alloy steels, the motor industry was trying to machine silicon aluminium. Electrolytic grinding had already become a fairly common method for certain specialized applications. Electrical-discharge machining was another process (first applied as a metal-cutting method in the U.S.S.R.) which made considerable headway. The metal-removal rates by this process were expected to be stepped up considerably as a result of new research work. Chemical milling is an ingenious way of removing metal. At first aluminium and titanium were milled by this process, and later stainless steel was chemically milled. The technique was being applied to motor car parts such as sculptured wheel rims. The chemical milling and electrical-discharge processes were combined in what is called electrochemical milling, which yields faster removal rates than can be obtained by the electrical-discharge process alone. Progress was being made in ultrasonic machining, a method which removes metal by using a fine abrasive and an ultrasonic head which introduces high-speed vibrations into the tool. This method is selected mostly for hard, brittle, non-conductive material which would tend to break under conventional machining processes. The ray gun process of removing metal was one of the newest techniques. In this process an X-ray is concentrated into a beam that vaporizes the metal. Thus holes can be drilled to incredibly small, precise sizes.

Another innovation in the United States was the plasma-jet process which ionizes material into plasma. The plasma is then fed into a beam through a jacket, the exterior of which is cooled. The effect is to make the beam hotter and hotter as it passes through the jacket, the temperature reaching 25,000°F. to 30,000°F. This process was being used for flame-cutting; it gave a more precise surface than with conventional flame-cutting. Liquid-jet machining was perhaps the newest development of all. It was observed that when aeroplanes fly at supersonic or ultrasonic speeds, raindrops machine the surfaces of the wings. With that fact in mind, artificial liquid-jet pressures and speeds were created for drilling holes.

In the field of metal-forming machine tools, as contrasted with metal-cutting machines, technical developments in the United States were striking. New concepts of the plastic flow of metal emerged. Cold extrusion was one of the results. For example, a carefully sawn or sheared slug of steel is put into a die and by extrusion a finished part, including gear teeth, is produced. This complicated part is made in one press operations instead of several intricate machining operations. Explosive forming was the latest method of achieving plastic flow of metal. A metal blank is put over a die opening and a container filled with water is set above the die. An explosive is then put in the water and detonated. Instantaneously the energy released by the detonation causes the water to form the metal blank to the shape of the die cavity. (*See* also AUTOMATION; ELECTRONICS; ENGINEERING TECHNIQUES.)

(C. H. BU.; B. FY.)

MADAGASCAR (RÉPUBLIQUE MALGACHE), a member state of the French community. Madagascar is an island (fourth largest in the world) off S.E. coast of Africa. Area (with dependencies; *c.* 228,000 sq.mi. Pop.: (1950 est.) 4,181,810; (1959 est.) 5,065,000; many indigenous racial and tribal groups, the Merina (Hova) being the most numerous (24%). Europeans (1959 est.): French 69,908. Other foreigners 25,800 (mostly Indians and Chinese). Language: Malagasy, related to the Malayo-Polynesian group. Religion: Christian and pagan. Chief towns (pop., 1959 est.): Antananarivo or Tananarive (cap.) 202,000; Majunga 50,400; Tamatave 40,000; Diego-Suarez 38,200; Fianarantsoa 34,800. President of the republic, Philibert Tsiranana. French high commissioner general, André Soucadaux. Chief exports: coffee, rice, preserved meat, tobacco, perfume plants, copra. Monetary unit: *franc CFA* = metropolitan Fr.2.

History. At the end of March 1959 five cyclones in succession devastated the eastern coast and a part of the plateau. The towns of Mananara, Mandritsara and Port-Bergé were destroyed, roads and railways blocked, and the plains of Antananarivo and the Alaotra flooded. There were *c.* 500 deaths and 83,230 made homeless. In several regions the rice harvests were lost; and numerous coffee, vanilla and clove plantations were destroyed. Help came from all parts of France but for a month Antananarivo was linked to the coast only by air.

The constitution was almost unanimously approved by the Malagasy National Assembly on April 24. The president of the republic was head of the government; he was elected for seven years by the assemblies together with delegates from the provinces. The Legislative Assembly was to be elected by universal suffrage. The Senate comprised 6 elected members, each from 6 provinces and 12 appointed by the government to represent social and cultural groups. The president had the power to dissolve the assembly. An Upper Council was to supervise the working of the institutions. Each province had an elected general council and secretary of state delegated by the government. Rural communes were created, covering the entire territory.

On May 1 Philibert Tsiranana was elected president of the republic and took the oath at Mahamasina where kings were formerly consecrated. He recalled that he was " the son of a peasant and once a herdsman ".

A split occurred in the Malagasy Independence Congress party (A.K.F.M.) which was partially Communist-controlled. Alexis Bezaka, the former minister, decided to co-operate with the government. At the municipal elections, which took place on Oct. 12, the A.K.F.M. was victorious at Antananarivo and Diego Suarez, Bezaka's party at Tamatave and the P.S.D. (Social Democratic party, led by Tsiranana) in most of the other 24 urban communes and 739 rural communes.

The executive council of the Community met at Antananarivo on July 7-8 under the presidency of General Charles de Gaulle.

(HU. DE.)

Hungry and homeless after catastrophic cyclones and flooding in March, Malagasy queue for food at a French rescue centre.

MAGAZINES: *see* NEWSPAPERS AND MAGAZINES.

MALAYA, FEDERATION OF.   A realm of the Commonwealth of Nations comprising the states of Johore, Kedah, Kelantan, Malacca, Negri Sembilan, Pahang, Penang, Perak, Selangor, Trengganu and Perlis.   Area: 50,692 sq.mi.   Pop.: (1947 census) 4,908,086; (1957 census) 6,276,915; (1958 est.) 6,499,000. Pop. includes Malays and Malaysians *c.* 49%, Chinese *c.* 37·5%, Indians and Pakistanis *c.* 12%.   Religion: Malays are Moslem, Indians mainly Hindu, Chinese Buddhist, Confucian and Taoist.   Chief towns (pop., 1957 census): Kuala Lumpur (Selangor; federal cap.) 315,040; George-town (Penang) 234,855; Ipoh (Perak) 125,855; Klang (Selangor) 75,687; Malacca 69,865; Taiping (Perak) 48,199; Johore Bahru 74,495; Seremban (Negri Sembilan) 52,038.   Head of state, with title of Yang di-Pertuan Agong (paramount ruler): Tuanku Abdul Rahman.   Prime ministers in 1959: Tengku Abdul Rahman Putra, (from Feb. 9) Tun Abdul Razak and (from Aug. 21) Tengku Abdul Rahman Putra.   Main imports: textiles, foodstuffs, machinery and transport equipment.   Main exports: rubber, tin, timber, coconut oil, palm oil, ore.   Monetary unit: Malayan dollar (=2*s*. 4*d*. sterling).

History.   A memorable date in the history of the two-year-old independent Federation of Malaya was Sept. 12 when the first parliament was officially inaugurated by the paramount ruler, Tuanku Abdul Rahman.   On Aug. 18 a general elec-tion for the 104 seats in the Dewan Ra'ayat (lower house) had been held.   In these elections the Alliance party led by Tengku Abdul Rahman Putra won 74 seats against 13 secured by the Pan Malayan Islamic party, 8 by the Socialist front, 4 by the Peoples Progressive party and 5 by Independents.

Earlier in the year elections for the 11 state governments were held.   First results suggested that the hold of the Alliance party was being strongly maintained, but results from the two east coast states of Kelantan and Trengganu showed a sweeping victory for the Pan Malayan Islamic party, which campaigned on strongly religious lines.

The P.M.I.P.'s successes in the state elections were repeated at the general election, and in both Trengganu and Kelantan parliamentary and local control was almost entirely in their hands.   The increase in the strength of the P.M.I.P. came as a great shock to the ruling Alliance party.

At the general election the Socialist front had some success in certain urban areas, but did not gain as much ground as some observers had thought possible.   The People's Progres-sive party won votes in Perak state, where it had laid emphasis on the language and educational grievances of non-Malays.

A few months before the general election the prime minister, Tengku Abdul Rahman, retired temporarily in favour of his deputy, Tun Abdul Razak, the minister of defence.   After resting for a time Tengku Abdul Rahman began campaigning throughout the country.   The day after the result of the general election was declared he returned as prime minister.

He subsequently stated that increasing attention would be paid to rural areas, particularly on the east coast where, he indicated, there was still great ignorance among many people and where the introduction of religion into politics had damaged the Alliance party and its continued emphasis on inter-communalism.

Relations with Singapore continued to be friendly, but despite continued reference by Singapore political leaders to the desirability of a union between the two countries there were no indications that this was any closer.   In fact evidence was generally to the contrary, with such significant develop-ments as the splitting of radio services into two divisions: Radio Malaya (in Kuala Lumpur) and Radio Singapore.

When the new cabinet was announced there were few notable changes.   The most important decision was the announcement by the prime minister that he himself would take control of rural development.   By the end of the year several schemes for land development had already been started and many more were planned.

The campaign against Communist terrorism continued. At the end of 1959 there were some 200 terrorists left, virtually

Tengku Abdul Rahman, prime minister of the Federation of Malaya for the second time, signs the oath of office on Aug. 21.

all of them confined to the jungle area along the Malayan-Thailand border.   No incidents of any importance occurred during the year and with the exception of one small area of Pahang state the whole country, apart from the border area, was declared " white ".   Warnings were however still given against the danger of subversion.

Gangsters in secret societies continued to be a social menace, and the government used its powers of detention and restricted residence in order to curb their activities.

At the end of the year there were near boom conditions in the rubber industry, on which some 2 million Malayans directly or indirectly depended for a living.   Prices rose to the highest point since the Korean war, and such evidence as was available indicated that despite the increase in synthetic production there would be a continuing demand for natural rubber for at least the next decade.   This spurred the govern-ment into renewed efforts to hasten the replanting of small-holders' plots of land, since without measures of this sort it was felt that the industry would be unable either to compete with synthetic rubber in price or to fulfil world requirements.

Restrictions on tin production were eased to some extent but the industry was still far below maximum output.   There were renewed calls from leaders in the industry for greater freedom for prospecting and acquisition of tin-bearing land.

There was a continual flow of capital to Malaya and the tax free " holiday " offered to pioneer industries attracted growing attention from overseas.   By the end of the year some 50 new factories had been started or planned at Petaling Jaya, the satellite town six miles from Kuala Lumpur.

Work was started during the year on the Cameron High-lands Hydroelectric scheme for which a loan of M.$100 million had been provided by the International Bank for Reconstruc-tion and Development.   A start was to be made early in 1960 on the Klang Straits Development scheme, which would give vastly increased harbour and dockyard facilities at Port Swettenham, 35 mi. from Kuala Lumpur.

The paramount ruler paid a state visit to Brunei during the year, and was due to make a visit to India and Pakistan in October but he was taken ill and arrangements were cancelled. In November the prime minister visited Australia where he opened Malaya's new chancery building and had talks with the Australian prime minister, R. G. Menzies, and other ministers. Menzies paid a return visit to Malaya in December.

While maintaining good relations with fellow members of the Commonwealth and with its Asian neighbours Malaya took an independent line in the United Nations, and together with the Republic of Ireland, sponsored a resolution deploring Chinese action in Tibet. Its delegates also spoke out against *apartheid* in South Africa and discussed the Algerian situation.

The year generally was a prosperous one for the country, but much remained to be done. The natural increase in population was one of the highest in the world, and the necessity of finding work for a rapidly growing urban population and also of taking measures to counter considerable under-employment was becoming more urgent. There were also increasing demands for housing and for better hospital and educational facilities.   (F. M. H.)

MALDIVE ISLANDS (MALDIVIA).

British-protected sultanate; a chain of some 2,000 coral islands (c. 220 inhabited) in 17 groups of low islets in the Indian ocean, stretching about 470 mi. northwards from just N. of the equator and lying 400 mi. S.W. of Colombo, Ceylon. Total area: 115 sq.mi. Pop.: (1931 census) 79,281; (1956 census) 81,950; apparently of Indo-Aryan stock akin to Sinhalese, with Dravidian, Semitic and Negro admixture. Language: Maldivian, akin to Elu or old Sinhalese. Religion: Moslem, Sunni sect. Capital: Malé (pop., c. 8,000) on Sultan's or Malé Island. Administration: elected sultan; prime minister and cabinet; elected subjects' council or Majlis. Sultan, Amin Mohammed Farid Didji; prime minister, Ibrahim Nasir. Main imports: rice, flour. Main exports: fresh and dried fish. Monetary unit: Maldivian *rupee* (1 M.R. =[nominal value] 1s. 6d.).

History. Early in 1959 a revolt took place in the southern atolls of the Maldive Islands, and a " United Suvadive Islands " government, headed by Abdullah Afif Didi, was set up. The rebels, who declared that they had revolted against the tyranny of the Maldivian regime, claimed control of Fua Mulaku Island, Huvadu Atoll and Addu Atoll (of which Gan Island with its R.A.F. staging post formed part). In March the British government sent a ship carrying supplies of food to the southern atolls, which had been stricken by famine.

Pakistanis and natives of the neighbouring Maldive Islands at work on oil installations for the new R.A.F. base on Gan Island.

The Maldivian government subsequently denounced the importing of foodstuffs into the islands by Britain as interference in its internal affairs. The British government rejected allegations made by the Maldivian government that a British officer serving with the R.A.F. on Gan Island had been primarily responsible for the revolt on the southern islands. The Maldivian government later suspended negotiations which it had been conducting in Colombo with the British high commissioner in Ceylon. These negotiations had centred on the Maldivian demand for independence in exchange for Britain's right to an air base on Gan Island.

At the beginning of April it was reported that Maldivian government forces had attempted a seaborne attack on the rebel-held Fua Mulaku Island. It was announced that same month that H. A. Arthington-Davy was to succeed Major W. W. A. Phillips as adviser on Maldivian affairs with the R.A.F. on Gan Island. Later, news was received that certain of the islands which had rebelled earlier in the year had surrendered to the Maldivian government. At the beginning of August in a note to the Maldivian government the British government expressed regret at the serious loss of life during operations by armed parties under the authority of the Maldivian government against the inhabitants of Huvadu Atoll. It further declared that it would take measures to safeguard its installations and personnel on Gan Island, should there be a repetition of these events in Addu Atoll. The British government also offered to mediate between the Maldivian government and the rebels. Later the same month a company of British soldiers was flown to Gan Island, but was withdrawn following a protest by the Maldivian government. The latter rejected the British offer of mediation and also refused to send a delegation to London (as had been earlier agreed) to re-open negotiations on the future status of the Maldive Islands. At the end of the year the R.A.F. base on Gan Island was ready for service.   (X.)

MALI, FEDERATION OF.

Mali is the name of a Negro Moslem empire that existed from the 11th to the 17th century in an area situated on the upper and middle Niger. At an assembly held at Dakar on Jan. 17, 1959, this name was suggested for a federation grouping Senegal, Soudan, Upper Volta and Dahomey. Later the two last-named refused to join. Modibo Keita, prime minister of Soudan, is the head of the federal government, and Léopold Senghor president of the federal assembly. (*See* SENEGAL, REPUBLIC OF; SOUDAN, REPUBLIC OF.)

MALTA.

British colony and strategic base; a group of three Mediterranean islands and three uninhabited islets, c. 60 mi. S. of Sicily. Area of main islands; Malta 94·9 sq.mi.; Gozo 25·9 sq.mi.; Comino 1·1 sq.mi. Total pop.: (1948 census) 305,991; (1957 census) 319,656; (1958 est.) 322,000. Language: Maltese (of Arabic origin, with heavy overlay of Siculo-Italian); English and Italian also spoken. Official languages: Maltese and English. Religion: Roman Catholic. Principal towns (pop., 1957 census): Valletta (cap.) 18,175, excl. suburbs; Sliema 23,381; Pawla and Tarxien 19,097; Hamrun 17,139; Birkirkara 17,076. Administration: governor; executive council, comprising three *ex officio*, three nominated official and four nominated unofficial members, presided over by the governor. Governors in 1959: Sir Robert Laycock and (from June 8) Admiral Sir Guy Grantham. Most necessities are imported. Main exports: scrap metal, manufactured goods, potatoes. Currency: Maltese 20s. and 10s. notes at par with sterling; U.K. coin.

History. In Feb. 1959 the U.K. House of Commons debated and approved a bill that restored to the crown the prerogative power to revoke the constitution of 1947 which had granted self-government to Malta. The state of emergency proclaimed in 1958 continued until April 15 when the 1947 constitution was revoked and the Malta (Constitution) Order in Council, 1959, came into force. Malta thus reverted to the status of a crown colony. The governor was given full legislative and executive powers. He was to be assisted by an executive

An unusual aerial view of Marsamxett harbour, Valletta, with Sliema on the right, taken from an aircraft of the Queen's flight flying north in a reserved altitude channel. Valletta itself, with the Grand harbour out of sight to the south, is in the lower left-hand corner.

council consisting of *ex officio* and nominated members, but he was not bound by its advice.

Political parties and constituted bodies in Malta protested vigorously against the suspension of responsible government. The Labour, Nationalist and Democratic Nationalist parties gave instructions to their members not to accept nomination to the executive council. The Labour party called for independence, while the Nationalist and Democratic Nationalist parties continued to press for dominion status. The Progressive Constitutional party envisaged a royal state of Malta. The U.K. government declared that its aim was to restore representative government as soon as possible.

In March the Broadcasting board set up by the governor in Sept. 1958 inaugurated regular party political broadcasts over the local rediffusion system. Only two parties, the Democratic Nationalist party and the Progressive Constitutional party, agreed to participate.

Important changes were effected in the island's economy. In March the naval dockyard was transferred to C. H. Bailey Ltd., a Welsh ship-repairing firm. When the date of the transfer was made known, disturbances broke out in the dockyard causing damage to property. The Malta government placed the main responsibility for these incidents on the " disruptive agitation " carried on by the leader of the Labour party, Dominic Mintoff, and his supporters. Some arrests were made and several people were sentenced to terms of imprisonment.

In April an Aids to Industries ordinance was promulgated. It provided for exemption from income tax for ten years and relief from customs duty. The budget for 1959-60 announced an estimated revenue of £10·75 million and expenditure of £17·25 million. The deficit was to be made good by the U.K. government. Later, taxes were increased on some imported goods, car licences and income. This measure was strongly opposed by all political parties who protested against what they considered to be taxation without representation.

In August the secretary of state for the colonies, A. T. Lennox-Boyd, gave his final approval to a five-year plan for a capital development programme. The aim of the plan was to attract new industries, develop tourism and carry out capital works in order to strengthen the economic position of the island. The British government undertook to make available for this purpose £29 million, partly on loan and

partly by way of a grant. It was proposed to raise a further loan of £3 million from Malta's own resources. The main items of the plan were development of water resources, port modernization, direct aid to industries, including capital grants, and the conversion of the dockyard from naval to commercial use. The plan also covered the extension of public services and the furthering of agriculture, fisheries, education and housing.

Lennox-Boyd's successor, Iain Macleod, paid a brief visit to the island in December and held talks with various political leaders.

The British Petroleum Exploration company gave up its licence to search for oil, after drilling a test well almost 10,000 ft. in depth without satisfactory results.

On Sept. 30 the U.S. flag was hauled down for the last time at Hal Far airport, when U.S. navy aircraft and personnel stationed there were transferred to Sicily.

The 1959 World Underwater Fishing championships, held in Malta in August, were won by Spain.　　　　(A. G.)

MAN, ISLE OF. Island in the Irish sea, dependency of the British crown with internal autonomy. Area: 220 sq.mi. Pop.: (1951 census) 55,253; (1958 est.) 55,000. Language: English. In 1951 355 also spoke Manx, the Celtic language most closely related to Scottish Gaelic. Religion: slight majority are Nonconformist; Manx church (Anglican) constitutes a diocese (Sodor and Man) of province of York, but has its own convocation and canon law. Chief towns (pop., 1956 est.): Douglas (cap.) 20,361; Ramsey 4,621. Administration: lieutenant-governor; executive council (advisory body); legislative council (*ex officio*, appointed and indirectly elected members); popularly elected House of Keys. Legislative council and Keys consider legislation separately but combine as Tynwald court (where two houses vote separately) to transact executive business and to sign bills. Lieut.-governors in 1959, Sir Ambrose D. Flux Dundas and (from Sept. 14) Sir Roland Garvey. Currency: sterling.

History. During 1959 only eight Acts of Tynwald were promulgated, including the Copyright act and the Income Tax act, the latter providing relief in respect of retirement and purchased annuities. The chief political event of the year was the submission of the report of the commission on constitutional reform in the government of the island. The report would in due course be put before the Tynwald. Among the many suggested changes in the constitution was a proposal that if a bill should be passed by the House of Keys and refused by the legislative council in two successive sessions, it should become law on being passed a third time by the House of Keys. A second recommendation was that a finance board should be set up to assist the governor in financial and budgetary matters. The commission also suggested that only the senior deemster should be a member of the legislative council, that the governor should cease to attend council meetings except on special occasions and that the deemster should normally preside over the council. The commission further proposed that the speaker should not be compelled to record his vote in the House of Keys or the Tynwald, that the executive council should be elected differently and that a permanent civil service commission should be set up.

Budgetary revenue from all sources amounted to £3,520,502, including £2,335,280 from customs duties and purchase tax. Expenditure was £3,719,049. (E. H. S.)

MAN-MADE FIBRE: see BUSINESS REVIEW.

MARINE BIOLOGY. During 1959 the first International Congress of Oceanography was held in New York. This underlined the increasing attention being paid to the study of the sea and the need to co-ordinate and extend the many and widely different aspects of marine science. Many marine biological subjects were covered by the congress, including primary production in the sea, the distribution of marine animals and the evolution of the deep-sea fauna. In 1959 also the reports of the Symposium on the Classification of Brackish Waters which was held at Venice in 1958 were published. In the previous few years special studies had been made of the biological conditions in estuaries in widely separated areas including South Africa, Australia and the United States. In 1959 reports were made on the ecology of lagoons on the west African coast and special attention was paid to the factors governing the distribution and behaviour of the cephalochordate *Branchiostoma nigeriense*.

Accurate figures for the swimming speeds of a number of fish became available. The maximum speeds for gadoid fish, such as cod, haddock and whiting, and for herring were about 4½ m.p.h., while for fast swimmers, such as sea trout and mackerel, they were approximately 7 m.p.h. At these speeds the distance swum by a fish before exhaustion was about 45 yd. to 65 yd. for gadoids, 115 yd. for mackerel, 240 yd. for sea trout, while the herring could keep up a speed of about 4 m.p.h. for 275 yd.

Prior to its departure from the rivers to its breeding area in the central north Atlantic the European eel undergoes certain changes. Its yellow coloration changes to silver, its eye enlarges and its pupil becomes relatively even greater. It was shown that concurrently with these changes the retinal pigment alters from the purplish-coloured rhodopsin of freshwater fish to the golden coloured chrysopsin typical of deepsea fish. The maximum absorption of the retina is thus shifted 33μ towards the shorter wave-lengths and the eye becomes more efficient at collecting and absorbing the light present in deep water. These changes, which fit the eel for its new environment, take place before the fish leave freshwater. A seasonal cycle in thyroid activity was also demonstrated in adult and immature cod. Activity coincides with the period of maturation of the gonads; i.e., during the time of the spawning migration.

Physiological differences were shown in the same invertebrate from widely separated regions. For instance, the small plankton copepod *Acartia* had a higher metabolic rate under similar conditions at Southampton, England, than the same species in Long Island sound, United States. Even more striking was an endocrinological difference in the proportions of moulting hormones present in prawns living at Plymouth, England, from those in prawns at Roscoff, France. The problem concerning the occurrence of green coloration in

the gut of the luminescent worm *Chaetopterus* was finally settled after first being named " chaetopterin " 60 years ago. It was found to be composed of phaeophorbides A and B, breakdown products of chlorophyll, which must be derived from the detritus on which the worm feeds. It was proved definitely that it was not a symbiont. It was shown that the tubes of Pogonophora are chitinous; it had previously been suggested that these were cellulose. Radioactive calcium was used to study the physiology of skeleton formation in reef-building corals. Calcium deposition was much reduced in darkness and in animals from which the zooxanthellae were removed. It was suggested that the rate of calcification may be dependent on removal of carbonic acid by the symbiotic plant cells.

A new family of polychaete annelids was found in fossil form from near the base of the Cambrian in South Australia. These have lateral extensions in the head region resembling those of the living planktonic worm *Tomopteris* suggestive of the primitive head shield in trilobites.

The electron microscope continued to prove its value in the elucidation of fine structure in marine organisms. Especially interesting were a number of observations made on the detailed structure of coelenterate nematocysts. These showed that earlier generalized accounts of their form and evagination were essentially correct, but gave new information on the finer details of the capsule wall and operculum, and on the cnidocil. (*See also* FISHERIES; OCEANOGRAPHY; ZOOLOGY.)

(F. S. R.)

BIBLIOGRAPHY. A. M. Keen, *Sea Shells of Tropical West America* (Stanford, Calif., 1958); H. B. Moore, *Marine Ecology* (London, 1958); J. E. Morton, *Molluscs* (London, 1958); C. Ray and E. Ciampi, *The Underwater Guide to Marine Life* (London 1958); V. B. Scheffer, *Seals, Sea Lions and Walruses* (London, 1958); H. Barnes, *Oceanography and Marine Biology* (London, 1959); D. B. Carlisle and F. G. W. Knowles, *Endocrine Control in Crustaceans* (Cambridge, 1959); B. W. Halstead, *Dangerous Marine Animals* (Cambridge, Maryland, 1959); A. Hardy, *The Open Sea, pt. II, Fish and Fisheries* (London, 1959).

MARKET GARDENING. One of the outstanding features of market gardening in 1959 was the continued development, in suitable areas throughout the world, of the growing of all-the-year-round chrysanthemums. Events entirely discredited the early opposition from the markets, whose representatives firmly declared that there would be no demand for chrysanthemums out of season. By rigid observation of precision growing methods blooms could be produced practically to a day at any period of the year. The flowers proved long lasting and the demand for them was keen. In addition, the production of young all-the-year-round chrysanthemum plants was becoming a specialist activity on a factory scale at large nurseries in the United States and Britain, with an output totalling many millions a year.

Economic conditions were causing a gradual reduction of heated glasshouse acreages in many growing areas, although in the Netherlands there was some expansion, with the development of a new glasshouse district around Emmen on the northeastern border, to cater for markets in the German Federal Republic. A striking feature of this project was the adoption of a method of co-operative heating, whereby all glasshouses over a wide area were heated by a central system feeding lagged underground pipes, which ran from holding to holding.

In Britain the area of heated glasshouses declined by 69 ac. during the year, notably in the Lea valley and Clyde valley districts. On the other hand, growers continued with the cautious expansion of intensive forms of cultivation involving the use of unheated glass, including frames, cloches and Dutch light houses. The total area of all glasshouses in 1959 was 685 ac., compared with 658 ac. the previous year.

A nursery in Sussex equipped for all-the-year-round growing of chrysanthemums on the batch system. In the early spring both shade and artificial light are required. The shade cloths over the beds and the curtains to screen the lighted areas from other plants can be seen.

The trend towards contract-growing of soft fruit continued in most of Europe, with a rising output from the Balkan countries and Poland. British fruitgrowers found themselves in difficulties, with long-term prices tending to weaken because of the increased supplies of continental pulp available. Under these conditions the processing industries showed no inclination to allow for higher farm-production costs in Britain. Cider-fruit growing in England had already been badly affected by this new economic factor and strawberry-growers, in particular, were afraid of suffering the same fate. The fresh fruit market was unable to absorb the entire output at profitable rates and a healthy outlet in the processing industries remained vital.

There was no marked reduction in the damage caused to horticultural crops by the drift from hormone sprays applied

ESTIMATED SOFT FRUIT PRODUCTION, ENGLAND AND WALES, 1958 AND 1959

	1958		1959	
	Acreage	Gross Production (tons)	Acreage	Gross Production (tons)
Strawberries . . .	16,712	28,700	16,136	35,800
Raspberries . .	2,452	3,900	2,440	4,000
Currants, black . .	12,347	21,200	13,044	16,100
Currants, red and white .	747	1,500	735	1,300
Gooseberries . .	5,429	15,900	5,518	11,500
Loganberries and blackberries	1,203	1,900	1,421	2,700
Total	38,890	73,110	39,294	71,400

SOURCE. Ministry of Agriculture, Fisheries and Food.

as agricultural weedkillers, which was rapidly becoming a great international problem. It was of particular concern since even minute traces of hormone preparations were sufficient to mar many specialist horticultural crops, tomatoes being particularly sensitive. Although this question was not necessarily related to spraying from aircraft, it was one of the problems discussed at the first international conference on agricultural aviation, called by O.E.E.C. and held in Britain in September. No ready solution was found but it was emphasized that any failure to take the problem seriously might ultimately lead to a ban on the use of some hormone specifics. The conference also considered various aspects of the use of aircraft for horticultural purposes, notably orchard and plantation spraying, and the opinion was expressed that

optimum efficiency might call for the eventual production of a new type of aircraft for this particular work. Another possibility for the near future was the development of pilotless planes operated by remote control. (*See* also FOODSTUFFS; HORTICULTURE.)   (V. A. J. W.)

MARTINIQUE. French overseas island *département* in the Lesser Antilles. Area: 427 sq.mi. Pop.: (1954 census) 239,130; (1959 est.) 260,000; mainly coloured (Negro or mixed). Language; French and creole French. Religion: Roman Catholic. Capital: Fort-de-France, pop. (1954 census) 60,648. Prefect, Jacques Boissier. Main exports: sugar, rum, bananas. Currency: metropolitan *franc*.

History. The municipal elections held on March 8-15, 1959, resulted in the return of 262 Socialists, 262 Progressives (the party led by Aimé Césaire, a former Communist), 94 Communists, 67 Radicals, 66 Gaullists (Union pour la Nouvelle République) and 27 others of various parties.

On April 26, Paul Symphor (Socialist) and M. Marianne (Progressive) were elected senators.

Overpopulation and unemployment had been for years the main cause of social unrest in the island. On Dec. 20 serious three-day rioting took place in the streets of Fort-de-France In clashes between the police and demonstrators three civilians were killed and a dozen injured.   (HU. DE.)

MATHEMATICS: ARTICLE CARRIED IN ALTERNATE YEARS.

MAURITANIA, ISLAMIC REPUBLIC OF
(RÉPUBLIQUE ISLAMIQUE DE MAURITANIE), a member state of the French Community. Mauritania is bounded N. by Spanish West Africa and the Algerian Saharan *département* of Saoura, E. and S. by the Republic of Soudan, S. by the Republic of Senegal and W. by the Atlantic ocean. Area: 364,092 sq.mi. Pop.: (1945 est.) 497,000: (1959 est.) 625,000, mainly Moorish with strong Negro admixture. Language: Arabic. Religion: Moslem. Chief towns: Nouakchott (cap.), Port Etienne, Atar, Tidjikja, Kaédi. Prime minister, Mokhtar Ould Daddah. French high commissioner, Pierre Anthonioz. Monetary unit: *franc CFA* = metropolitan Fr.2.

History. The Islamic Republic of Mauritania, a member of the Community, was proclaimed at Nouakchott on Nov. 28, 1958, and the constitution received approval by the territorial assembly on March 25, 1959.

At the elections of the first National Assembly held on May 24, the Parti du Regroupement Mauritanien won all the seats. Mokhtar Ould Daddah was unanimously re-elected prime minister. On June 1 Mauritania concluded a customs union with the Federation of Mali.

The future of Mauritania depended on a range of hills rising from the desert near Fort Gouraud. It was estimated that these hills contain at least 125 million tons of haematite ore of 66% iron content. An international consortium of British, French, Italian and German capital was planning the exploitation of these reserves. A large mining town would be built near Fort Gouraud and a railway would carry the ore to Port Etienne, which would be considerably enlarged. The whole cost of the operations was estimated at Fr.60,000 million.　　　　　　　　　　　　　　　　　　　　(HU. DE.)

MAURITIUS. British colony in the Indian ocean, about 500 mi. E. of Madagascar, with island dependencies, of which the largest is Rodrigues, about 365 mi. N.E. of Mauritius. Area: Mauritius 720 sq.mi.; Rodrigues 42 sq.mi.; other dependencies (Chagos archipelago incl. Diego Garcia, Agalega and Cargodus Carajos or St. Brandon groups) 47 sq.mi. Pop.: Mauritius (1952 census) 501,471; (1958 est.) 605,000, incl. *c.* 68% Indo-Mauritians (Indian immigrants and their descendants); Rodrigues (1952 census) 13,333, (1957 est.) 16,535, mostly of African descent; Diego Garcia and other dependencies (1952 census) 1,752, (1957 est.) 1,767. Languages: English and French (official); creole French and Hindi widely used. Religion: Indo-Mauritians mainly Hindu; others mainly Roman Catholic. Chief towns (pop., 1957 est.): Port Louis (cap.) 82,900; Beau-Bassin-Rose Hill 33,600; Curepipe 26,250; Mathurin (Rodrigues). Administration: governor; executive council; legislative council with elected majority. Governors in 1959, Sir Robert Scott and (from Nov. 2) Sir Colville Deverell. Main imports: rice and flour, machinery and transport, textiles, mineral fuels. Main exports: sugar, molasses. Monetary unit: Mauritius *rupee* (Re.1 = 1*s.* 6*d.* sterling).

History. The £16 million development programme, initiated in 1958, continued to make satisfactory progress during 1959. The first elections under universal adult suffrage were held on March 9. The mainly Hindu Labour party gained 23 out of

A sugar cane train in Mauritius. Sugar is the mainstay of the island's economy: the annual value of exports is about £23 million.

40 seats, but voting did not follow a rigidly communal pattern. The Moslem Committee of Action made an electoral pact with the Labour party and five of the six successful Independent candidates were Labour party sympathizers. In view of the rapid increase in population it was clearly necessary that there should be a thorough investigation of the island's sources of wealth. In November, therefore, it was announced

that at the request of the ministers of the Mauritius government, the secretary of state for the colonies, Iain Macleod, had agreed to appoint a mission from Britain to carry out an economic survey early in 1960.　　　　　　　　　(K. I.)

MEDICINE. In 1959 the United States had its worst recurrence of poliomyelitis since the introduction of the Salk vaccine four years previously. The disease did not reach the epidemic proportions of the pre-vaccination era, but a disturbing feature was that some 15% to 20% of the paralytic cases had had at least three injections of Salk vaccine. Paralytic poliomyelitis in persons vaccinated with the recommended three doses of the formalin-inactivated virus had already been observed and earlier in the year Jonas Salk had reviewed (*J. Amer. med. Ass.*, *169*, 1,829) current immunization practices with killed vaccines and the premises on which they were based. His survey of some 2,700 vaccinated schoolchildren showed that 9·1% had no detectable antibody to type 1 virus, 0·5% had none to type 2 and 18·7% had none to type 3. The evidence suggested that the low levels for types 1 and 3 were not due to waned immunity but to failure to induce immunity in the first place. Salk's data indicated that when vaccines of relatively high potency were used for primary and booster doses the immunity response was high and there was little or no decline in antibody levels. He concluded, therefore, that the use of Salk-type vaccines of less than optimal potency could be the reason for the occurrence of paralytic poliomyelitis in vaccinated persons. His solution was that multiple doses of weak vaccine were unreliable and that vaccine of a potency such as could be expected to give protection in two doses given at an interval of 2 to 6 weeks should be used, with a third dose 7 to 12 months later to prolong immunity.

Meanwhile the rival claims of living attenuated poliomyelitis virus vaccines gained ground. They were easier to make and easier and cheaper to administer in large quantities. By virtue of their oral administration the attenuated viruses had the advantage of following the path of a natural infection, and for this reason they were likely to stimulate a local immunity in the intestinal wall, which many virologists believed to occur in natural exposure to infection, in addition to stimulating antibody production in the circulation. The Salk-type vaccine, while erecting a barrier between the point of entry of invading viruses and the vital nerve centres, probably did nothing to prevent their multiplication in the intestine. This meant that Salk-vaccinated persons, though protected themselves, could be hosts to, and excrete, virulent viruses dangerous to other, unvaccinated persons. The importance, then, of live attenuated vaccines was that they could prevent the epidemic spread of virulent strains of virus from host to host. In short, they could break the chain of infection. Furthermore, living attenuated vaccine viruses could pass by natural means from person to person, thus conferring on their recipients an immunity similar to that granted to those to whom they were originally fed. Nor, it was believed, need a living attenuated virus vaccine necessarily be type specific in order to confer immunity.

The crux of the debate on the merits of live poliomyelitis vaccines centred on their safety. Could the attenuated strains in the live vaccine be guaranteed to remain avirulent in spite of passage through a series of human intestines? It was generally agreed that, to be usable, a living attenuated virus must be incapable of recovering its power to paralyse. Unfortunately, all virologists who had studied the matter, including A. B. Sabin, had found that attenuated viruses possessed rather more neurotropism after human passage than before. The tests applied, however, were stringent, and consisted in injecting the viruses directly into the immediate vicinity of the spinal cords of monkeys. Sabin believed that

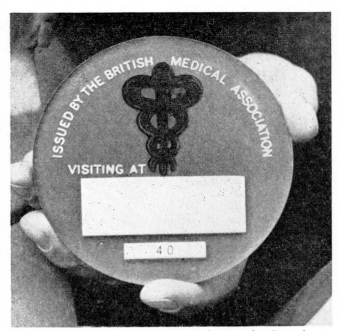

The British Medical association's car badge, issued in December to doctors living in the restricted parking area of central London.

his attenuated strains had permanently lost the power to invade and spread in the human central nervous system by natural pathways and, contrary to more conservative opinion, but in agreement with an expert committee of the World Health organization (*Wld Hlth Org. tech. Rep. Ser.*, No. 145, 1958, Geneva), he thought that large-scale trials of live vaccines were justified. One such trial was carried out in an epidemic of poliomyelitis which occurred in Singapore during the last months of 1958 and the beginning of 1959. It was reported by J. H. Hale and E. S. Monteiro and their colleagues in the *British Medical Journal* (1, 1,541). The epidemic was caused by a type 1 strain of virus. Eleven weeks after the appearance of the first cases an attenuated living vaccine of type 2 virus provided by Sabin was offered. One of the reasons for choosing a type 2 vaccine was to test the belief that it would interfere with the establishment of the type 1 virus, and that it would also promote heterologous protection against it. Nearly 200,000 children received a dose of the vaccine and among them 16 cases of paralytic poliomyelitis occurred. Among the 300,000 children who were not vaccinated there were 179 paralytic cases. Much more information was required before these results could be properly interpreted, but it was evident that the type 2 vaccine gave substantial protection against a type 1 infection. On the all-important question of safety, the immediate evidence suggested that the vaccine was harmless to those who were fed it and, with one possible exception, to those who were infected from them with the vaccine virus. However, a thorough follow-up surveillance of the subsequent behaviour of the attenuated type 2 virus liberated in the population by the vaccine would be needed for reliable information on its safety. Besides the Sabin vaccine experimental quantities of live vaccines had been prepared by H. Koprowski and H. R. Cox. Successful trials of these were reported at a conference in Washington arranged by the Pan-American Health organization and W.H.O.

The incidence of coronary-artery disease continued its upward trend. Deaths from it in Britain in 1958, the latest year for which figures were available, numbered 84,048 (52,089 males and 31,959 females). This represented a rate of 1·86 per thousand population. Little progress was made, however, in ascertaining the causes of the disease, which

predisposed to thrombosis and consequent devitalization (infarction) of portions of the heart muscle. There was strong cumulative evidence, from statistics of the incidence of coronary thrombosis in various countries and groups of people, of an association between coronary disease and a high consumption of animal fats. For this reason some workers urged that as a preventive measure diets should contain more unsaturated fatty acids from vegetable oils and less saturated fatty acids from animal fats. Others contested this conclusion. In favour of the first view, of all the possible aetiological factors none could be so closely related to the pathological, metabolic and epidemiological features of coronary disease as the nature of the dietary fat intake. Anti-coagulant drugs were already well established as a life-saving measure in the treatment of acute myocardial infarctions, but the value of long-term administration of these drugs in preventing recurrent attacks was unproven. To obtain some reliable information on the subject, a working party of the British Medical Research council studied the progress of 383 selected patients who had survived at least one month after a myocardial infarction, one-half of whom were given an effective continuing dose of anticoagulant and the remainder, as controls, were given an ineffective dose. Various difficulties in selecting the patients somewhat limited the conclusions which could be drawn from the results (*Brit. med. J.*, 1, 803), but some interesting findings emerged. In men, long-term anticoagulant therapy reduced the mortality during the first three months of its administration, but not significantly thereafter. In men, anticoagulants reduced the incidence of further infarction throughout the two years of the study, and in those under the age of 55 infarction recurred at only one-fifth of the rate observed in the control group, while over that age the reinfarction rate was halved. There was no evidence that continued anticoagulant therapy was of benefit to women patients, and this difference between the sexes remained unexplained. The main, and confident, conclusion from the trial was that men under the age of 55 who suffered a myocardial infarction could be expected to benefit from the

A Melrose " heart-lung " machine at the International Hospital and Medical Services exhibition which opened in London on May 25.

continuation of anticoagulant therapy for six months after the infarct. This undoubtedly foreshadowed a change in therapeutic policy.

The dream of being able to replace diseased, worn out tissues with living spare parts came a step nearer reality in 1959. This advance resulted from a not altogether chance overlapping of research into radiation effects with that of research into tissue-transplantation immunity. It had been generally accepted that grafts of living cells exchanged between unrelated members of a species were destroyed by an antagonistic immune response—the homograft reaction—by the recipient. For special reasons transfusions of blood and transplants of bone, cartilage and artery were exceptions to this rule. In addition to these exceptions the host's immune system did not function if it was defective owing to immaturity (as in the foetus), disease (agammaglobulinaemia) or damage. It had been discovered that doses of whole-body radiation damaged the immune mechanism and that doses high enough to suppress completely the immune reaction also destroyed bone-marrow to a fatal degree. With doses in this range therefore marrow replacement became not only essential to recovery but also possible. This possibility of replacing diseased marrow with living transplants of healthy marrow stimulated a number of clinicians independently to consider high dosage whole-body radiation followed by marrow transplant as a treatment for the hitherto incurable disease leukaemia. Many practical difficulties had to be overcome, but preliminary clinical trials with leukaemic subjects were carried out by, among others, J. W. Ferrebee and his colleagues (*Blood*, **4**, 1). A few patients survived for several months but unequivocal evidence of a permanent " take " of the transplanted cells was still awaited.   (J. G. T.)

MENTAL DISEASES: *see* PSYCHIATRY.

METALLURGY.

The year 1959 contained some notable conferences and discussions. Theoretical work on the fracture of metals, which had been very active, culminated in an international seminar on " The Atomic Mechanisms of Fracture " at Swampscott, Massachusetts, in April. Following the pioneer work of G. I. Taylor, E. Orowan and M. Polanyi in 1934, it had been recognized that the mechanical properties of metals are determined by the existence of local imperfections in the arrangement of the atoms. These are called " dislocations ". But for them, engineering structures could have had an elegance quite unknown at the end of the 1950s because they could have been designed in metals about 1,000 times stronger. Metal " whiskers " with strengths approaching such high values could be made, but there did not appear to be a great deal of hope of bridging the gap between these and a usable form. At Swampscott it was clear that there was now considerable understanding of the normal fracture of metals under tension in terms of the coalescence of these dislocations to form a crack. It was suggested that the dangerous brittle fractures arose if the cracks produced by this coalescence attained such a size that they could propagate through the metal. The atomic processes in the other methods of fracture-fatigue (by an alternating stress less than the tensile fracture stress) or creep (by gradual deformation under stress at high temperatures) were considerably less well understood.

Catastrophic brittle fracture, particularly of welded mild steel structures, was the subject of another conference organized by the Admiralty at Cambridge in October. This was concerned with the macroscopic, as distinct from the atomic, aspects of the problem and with finding out what had been achieved since the first Admiralty conference held in Cambridge in 1945 at the height of the brittle fracture scare touched off by ship failures during World War II. It was clear that the official bodies in the shipbuilding, oil and chemical engineering industries were now facing up to the increased cost associated with the use of mild steel of improved resistance to brittleness. The steps adopted for improvement involved increased manganese and reduced carbon contents, with manganese/carbon ratios as high as ten, fine grain size by control of finishing temperature or by normalizing, and even the acceptance of full deoxidation with aluminium. There had also been considerable advance in the recognition and elimination of design features that promoted brittle fracture. Nevertheless, there remained a great deal unknown about the macroscopic mechanics of fracture propagation and about the utilization of this in design.

A tremendous step forward in the understanding of metals had been taken by P. B. Hirsch, R. W. Horne and M. J. Whelan and by W. Bollmann in 1956 when they showed that the atomic dislocations (referred to above) became directly visible in photographs of thin metallic films taken in a high-resolution electron microscope by transmission of the electrons through the film. This had initiated a great burst of activity which was reviewed in a symposium held by the Institute of Metals in London in Nov. 1959. Perhaps the most impressive feature was the way in which the previous purely theoretical deductions about dislocation behaviour were directly confirmed. One of the new things that the technique showed was the important effect on strength of the entanglement of dislocations into networks by complex interactions among themselves.

Very active interest continued in the application of oxygen to steelmaking and half the annual general meeting of the Iron and Steel institute in London was devoted to this. The Linz-Donawitz process, which simply blows oxygen into molten iron in a stationary vessel, continued to find favour for low-phosphorus irons and practical experience was reported with the injection of lime into the oxygen to refine higher phosphorus contents. There appeared however to be a strong challenge from the Kaldo process in which oxygen is blown into a rotating reaction vessel. The accurate control, the range of iron compositions that can be used and the heat economy arising from combustion of the carbon monoxide within the reaction vessel were points advanced in its favour.

Another paper at the same meeting by R. Durrer and G. Heintz of Switzerland reported a further challenge to open-hearth steelmaking. This was from the electric-arc process. Normally this started from scrap, but the paper showed that direct refining of liquid iron could be achieved at a cost competitive with the open hearth at least under Swiss conditions.

Very great interest also continued to centre on the vacuum degassing of molten steels (particularly for hydrogen removal to prevent the " hair-line " cracking of alloy forgings on cooling), and on the vacuum melting of special steels in either the induction furnace or the consumable-electrode-arc furnace to give a cleaner, sounder product mainly for aircraft and other important uses. A special discussion on these topics was arranged by the British Iron and Steel institute. Because of reduced forging troubles, it was stated that the saving on degassed steel was about five times the cost of the treatment. In the recently developed vacuum-arc furnace, the consumable electrode is melted by the arc and falls onto, and solidifies in, the other electrode—a water-cooled copper crucible. Larger amounts can be melted than in the induction furnace and the production of eight-ton ingots was reported. The directional solidification gave a particularly good ingot structure.

Developments in the United States. A pilot steel plant was planned, to employ a successful laboratory process using iron powder reduced from high-grade ore. The powder passes between rolls to form into a sheetlike compact, which is then heated in a reducing atmosphere to weld the particles together; the compact is hot-rolled to eliminate porosity and then finished in the conventional way. Such a plant would cost much less than a conventional steel plant of equal capacity.

One pound of samarium was contracted for to investigate the properties of this rare-earth metal. A method was developed for extracting 4f-type rare-earth metals from bastnasite ore from a large deposit in California. Plutonium fuel elements were successfully produced and used in existing nuclear reactors, and a plutonium recycle reactor was under construction.

Molybdenum, as well as tungsten, chromium, columbium and tantalum, and even rarer metals, such as rhenium, were being investigated for use at temperatures above 2,000°F. After many years of development, ductile high-purity chromium became available in quantity. A method of melting and casting complex shapes of molybdenum was developed, using an electron furnace for melting. Electron heating equipment became available for welding large parts.

A small plasma torch, using highly ionized gas for heating to a temperature up to 30,000°F., became available for working refractory materials. Thus large complex shapes could be built up of high-melting-point metals, and many materials could be given refractory coatings. The solar furnace also found use in research at temperatures up to 5,000°F. as a source of heat without contamination of high-purity specimens.

The undesirable effects gases have in metals resulted in constantly increasing use of vacuum melting, annealing, welding and even forming. A vacuum pouring device was developed which permits melting in a conventional furnace and then pouring into the evacuated ingot mould through a special ladle that maintains a gastight seal during pouring. The small stream of metal falling into a vacuum is broken into droplets and efficiently degassed. As in Britain, high-energy-rate or explosive forming saw rapid development in 1959. (N. J. P.; D. F. C.)

METAL PRODUCTION: *see* MINERAL AND METAL PRODUCTION.

METEOROLOGY. The following notable awards were made during 1959: the World Meteorological organization's gold medal and prize to Prof. J. Bjerknes for his outstanding contributions to synoptic meteorology; the American Meteorological society's award for applied meteorology to Prof. C.-G. Rossby, posthumously; the Royal Meteorological society's Symons gold medal to Sir Graham Sutton for his outstanding work on atmospheric diffusion and micrometeorology; the Lenin prize to Prof. M. I. Budyko for his contributions to the study of the heat balance of the atmosphere; and the Napier Shaw Memorial prize of the Royal Meteorological society to Prof. S. K. Runcorn for an essay on " Climatic Variation ".

A substantial effort in geophysical observation on a global scale was continued during the year as an extension of the International Geophysical Year (I.G.Y.) 1957-58. Some highlights of the latter began to appear; *e.g.*, an auroral display observed in Samoa on Aug. 1, 1958, proved to have been man-made by a high-level atomic explosion in about the same latitude of the northern hemisphere as Samoa is in the southern hemisphere; a surface temperature of —124°F. (—87°C.) observed 400 mi. from the south pole on Aug. 17, 1958, was the lowest on record; and it was established that there was about 40% more ice on the earth than earlier supposed, most of it in Antarctica where a maximum depth of ice of 14,000 ft. overlying rock at 8,200 ft. below sea level was recorded 100 mi. E. of Byrd station. The major dividends of the I.G.Y. effort in meteorology could not however be expected to appear until time had elapsed for substantial analysis. A world record height for a balloon, of 146,000 ft. (28 mi.), was achieved in a meteorological sounding from New Jersey on Feb. 11, 1959.

Observations on the change with time of the orbits of artificial earth satellites led to the discovery that the density of the very high atmosphere was materially greater than earlier supposed. The exploitation of artificial satellites for global observations of weather and for measurements of the radiation absorbed from the solar beam and emitted by the earth and its atmosphere—these radiations determine the evolution of the atmosphere—remained for the future.

Northwestern Europe experienced the most sustained, brilliant summer for many decades but meteorologists were not yet able to show how this arose out of antecedent events.

Its detailed study in relation to world weather, simultaneous and earlier, might however provide useful empirical evidence on long-term weather sequences.

Among international conferences on meteorology held during the year, those on winds in the ionosphere (Cornell, July), on radiation and ozone (Oxford, July) and on tropical meteorology (Nairobi, December) were particularly notable. Regarding the first of these conferences, winds, including turbulence, in the ionosphere, are important in the study of radio propagation by means of this layer. The motions of the layer may arise from a general motion of the air in which the ions and electrons are embedded (*i.e.*, a wind) or from a drift of electron clouds through the medium as a result of the earth's magnetic field. The exploitation of the ionosphere for radio propagation depends on an understanding of the two processes. Regarding the second conference, the radiation reaching the earth from the sun and escaping from the earth to space are both affected by the ozone in the atmosphere, giving point to their joint discussion. Again, ozone is a valuable tracer of certain upper-level atmospheric motions arising from the distribution of temperature in the atmosphere and the latter is in part controlled by the radiation streams passing through the atmosphere. This study formed another part of the Oxford conference.

Weather: Sept. 1958–Aug. 1959. *British Isles.* Wet weather, a feature of the late spring and summer of 1958, continued during September. On Sept. 5 a tornado moved across Sussex into Kent, accompanied by strong winds and torrential rain, with hailstones as large as tennis balls at Horsham. Anticyclonic weather prevailed during the latter half of October and also towards the end of November. October and November were milder, drier and duller than usual. Foggy weather persisted during the last week of November and during much of the period Dec. 15-25. The year 1958 ranked as rather cooler, duller and wetter than usual, with a wet and thundery summer, although the early spring and late autumn were dry.

January, the sunniest January of the 20th century, was cold with some wet periods. Fog was widespread during Jan. 13-16 and during the last week of the month. February ranked as the driest February over England and Wales since that of 1891. The last few days of the month were particularly mild

The familiar " Air Ministry roof " of London meteorological bulletins was moved across Kingsway to this new location in August.

and sunny. March brought mild and rather dull weather, with rainfall about average. April continued the changeable and mild weather, being remarkably free from air frost and wetter than usual.

Dry, warm and sunny weather prevailed during the four months May to August, although Scotland recorded more than average rainfall and only average sunshine during June and July. The anticyclonic weather brought a pressure of 1,042·9 millibars on June 13, the highest ever recorded in the British Isles in June. Maximum temperatures reached about 95°F. on July 5 in parts of Norfolk and Lincolnshire. Thunderstorms occurred locally, mainly on July 11 and July 27 and again on Aug. 10, when 5·06 in. fell near Porlock, Somerset. These four months of 1959 gave better weather in most parts of England and Wales than in any year since 1911. The last year with more sunshine in these four months over England and Wales was 1911, although over Scotland sunnier weather occurred as recently as 1955. The general rainfall

TABLE I. MONTHLY RAINFALL AND TEMPERATURE: BRITISH ISLES

		1958					1959						
		July	Aug.	Sept.	Oct.	Nov.	Dec.	Jan.	Feb.	March	April	May	June
Fort William	(1)	3·27	5·39	5·10	10·39	2·44	5·65	3·00	6·20	6·23	6·00	1·44	6·57
	(2)	−2·06	−0·58	−1·91	+1·16	−5·44	−3·03	−6·95	−0·96	+1·14	+1·22	−2·54	+2·03
	(3)	58·3	58·9	58·3	50·5	44·7	39·7	33·9	39·8	44·5	47·4	55·0	56·5
	(4)	+0·8	+1·5	+4·5	+1·9	+1·5	−1·0	−5·6	+0·1	+2·4	+1·8	+4·7	+1·7
Edinburgh. (Royal Observatory)	(1)	6·47	3·11	2·29	0·93	1·08	3·99	0·90	0·53	0·39	1·87	0·41	1·99
	(2)	+3·44	−0·04	−0·26	−1·90	−1·34	+1·88	−1·55	−1·15	−1·21	+0·25	−1·80	+0·11
	(3)	57·7	58·1	57·7	51·0	44·1	39·5	34·1	40·3	43·9	47·5	50·8	56·1
	(4)	−0·8	+0·5	+3·6	+2·6	+1·3	−0·6	−4·6	+1·5	+2·6	+3·0	+1·7	+1·2
Renfrew	(1)	4·77	3·63	3·17	3·31	1·69	4·62	1·27	1·35	1·65	2·78	1·09	2·83
	(2)	+1·67	+0·30	−0·40	−1·39	−2·43	+0·43	−3·39	−1·84	−0·86	+0·46	−1·54	+0·42
	(3)	59·5	58·7	58·6	51·0	44·1	38·3	32·9	39·9	44·7	47·3	54·7	57·5
	(4)	+0·7	+0·7	+4·6	+2·6	+2·1	−1·3	−5·5	+0·6	+2·8	+1·9	+4·3	+1·9
Weymouth	(1)	2·33	2·53	4·32	3·30	3·63	4·64	4·53	0·33	3·55	1·94	0·83	0·79
	(2)	+0·17	+0·35	+1·82	+0·07	−0·12	+1·15	+1·34	−1·99	+1·53	+0·14	−1·12	−0·66
	(3)	61·7	61·6	61·5	55·3	46·8	44·1	40·8	42·1	47·3	50·8	56·3	60·6
	(4)	−0·5	−1·0	+2·0	+1·5	−0·6	+0·6	−1·9	−0·4	+2·5	+2·2	+2·6	+1·5
Liverpool. (Bidston)	(1)	3·35	4·47	4·93	2·93	1·71	3·62	3·14	0·48	1·15	2·41	1·97	2·93
	(2)	+0·58	+1·34	+2·30	−0·08	−1·07	+0·99	+0·58	−1·45	−0·49	+0·72	−0·29	+0·95
	(3)	59·7	60·1	59·1	51·7	45·5	41·3	36·7	41·1	45·3	48·4	55·6	58·5
	(4)	−0·7	+0·2	+2·7	+1·3	+1·1	+0·1	−3·3	+1·1	+2·5	+1·6	+3·5	+1·3
Bristol. (Long Ashton)	(1)	1·99	3·07	5·47	3·18	2·42	3·66	3·93	0·33	2·74	2·87	1·68	1·74
	(2)	−1·14	−0·50	+2·26	−0·79	−1·23	+0·15	+0·47	−2·22	+0·50	+0·62	−0·86	−0·39
	(3)	61·2	61·1	59·5	52·6	44·4	41·9	37·5	40·1	46·0	49·7	55·5	59·3
	(4)	−0·5	−0·1	+2·2	+1·5	−0·3	+0·7	−3·0	−0·5	+2·2	+1·9	+2·5	+0·7
Llandudno	(1)	3·26	1·80	6·10	2·48	1·97	2·41	4·65	0·15	0·77	3·35	1·37	1·03
	(2)	+1·19	−0·74	+3·38	−0·75	−0·88	−0·50	+1·71	−2·02	−1·09	+1·66	−0·70	−0·76
	(3)	59·6	60·1	60·0	52·9	47·3	43·1	40·1	43·9	46·7	48·8	54·7	58·5
	(4)	−0·9	−0·5	+2·4	+0·5	+0·6	−0·6	−2·6	+1·8	+2·3	+1·2	+2·6	+1·3
Aldergrove	(1)	3·92	2·79	4·07	2·05	1·62	4·24	1·97	1·23	2·58	1·97	0·96	1·59
	(2)	+0·87	−0·50	+1·05	−1·55	−1·57	+0·70	−1·71	−1·16	+0·57	−0·22	−1·50	−0·66
	(3)	58·6	57·9	57·5	50·7	45·6	39·5	35·0	42·9	44·9	46·8	53·3	57·3
	(4)	+0·3	+0·1	+3·1	+1·6	+2·3	−1·2	−4·7	+2·7	+2·3	+1·2	+3·0	+1·7
Berwick-on-Tweed	(1)	3·47	4·38	2·25	1·34	0·69	3·13	1·47	0·23	0·52	2·05	0·33	1·41
	(2)	+1·05	+1·68	+0·25	−1·08	−1·55	+1·43	−0·56	−1·26	−0·99	+0·70	−1·42	−0·27
	(3)	57·3	57·8	56·0	51·1	42·3	39·5	34·5	39·5	43·9	47·0	48·9	55·4
	(4)	−0·6	+0·7	+2·1	+2·4	−0·7	−0·9	−4·3	+0·2	+2·3	+2·4	+0·7	+1·4
York.	(1)	2·87	2·33	2·41	1·37	0·70	3·41	2·21	0·27	0·99	3·09	0·45	1·42
	(2)	+0·39	−0·24	+0·33	−0·84	−1·66	+1·38	−0·13	−1·41	−0·44	+1·39	−1·52	−0·43
	(3)	60·9	61·7	59·1	51·5	42·9	40·1	33·7	40·5	44·9	49·9	55·0	59·9
	(4)	−1·0	+0·9	+2·4	+1·4	−0·5	+0·2	−5·2	+0·9	+2·1	+2·9	+2·7	+1·8
Cambridge	(1)	3·24	2·36	2·66	1·82	1·59	2·55	2·77	0·11	2·46	1·66	0·44	1·91
	(2)	+0·82	+0·46	+0·62	−0·14	−0·49	+0·90	+0·82	−1·27	+1·16	−0·11	−1·36	+0·44
	(3)	62·1	62·1	60·2	52·3	43·5	40·5	34·3	39·6	45·5	49·9	54·2	60·7
	(4)	−0·5	+0·3	+2·6	+1·9	0·0	+1·0	−4·6	+0·1	+2·6	+2·4	+1·1	+1·9
Felixstowe	(1)	2·09	2·62	2·40	1·87	0·96	3·25	1·56	0·15	0·86	1·56	0·28	0·81
	(2)	+0·27	+0·78	+0·60	−0·28	−1·36	+1·27	−0·43	−1·25	−0·41	−0·03	−1·12	−0·53
	(3)	62·4	62·9	61·5	54·3	46·7	42·8	36·7	38·8	44·9	49·7	53·5	60·4
	(4)	−0·5	0·0	+2·1	+1·6	+1·4	+2·1	−2·8	−0·9	+2·4	+2·6	+1·1	+1·6
Birmingham	(1)	3·41	2·72	3·92	2·48	1·97	3·33	3·67	0·19	1·75	3·88	1·06	0·93
	(2)	+0·55	−0·04	+1·43	−0·41	−1·19	+0·63	+0·69	−2·02	−0·12	+1·58	−1·52	−0·97
	(3)	60·7	60·8	58·9	51·1	44·1	40·3	36·3	39·7	45·0	48·9	55·1	59·5
	(4)	−0·6	+0·3	+2·3	+1·1	+0·7	+0·4	−2·6	+0·5	+2·3	+2·1	+2·9	+1·7
Oxford	(1)	2·50	2·65	3·17	2·85	3·03	3·32	3·70	0·08	3·40	2·05	1·01	0·99
	(2)	+0·17	+0·39	+0·97	+0·35	+0·44	+1·04	+1·34	−1·71	+1·73	+0·15	−1·02	−0·70
	(3)	61·9	61·7	59·9	52·3	44·1	41·1	35·9	39·5	45·9	50·5	55·5	60·7
	(4)	−0·9	−0·4	+2·0	+1·5	0·0	+0·8	−3·6	−0·6	+2·3	+2·5	+2·0	+1·6
Cardiff	(1)	3·42	5·69	7·01	4·70	2·46	4·55	4·78	0·45	3·28	3·19	1·20	1·97
	(2)	−0·01	+1·82	+3·33	+0·20	−1·93	+0·20	+0·20	−2·55	+0·74	+0·63	−1·72	−0·31
	(3)	61·3	61·2	59·7	53·2	45·1	41·1	37·6	40·3	45·9	49·9	56·0	60·0
	(4)	−0·1	+0·1	+2·2	+1·9	0·0	−0·5	−3·0	−0·4	+2·1	+2·1	+3·0	+1·5
London. (Kew Observatory)	(1)	2·62	3·27	3·97	2·02	1·89	2·97	2·13	0·09	1·56	2·04	0·53	0·60
	(2)	+0·18	+1·03	+1·99	−0·23	−0·60	+0·91	−0·01	−1·46	+0·10	+0·23	−1·28	−1·12
	(3)	63·3	62·5	60·9	53·3	45·6	42·5	37·1	40·5	46·7	50·9	56·0	61·9
	(4)	−1·2	−0·2	+2·4	+1·7	+1·3	+1·1	−4·2	−0·6	+2·8	+3·2	+1·5	+2·0
Penzance	(1)	3·29	5·78	5·74	3·50	3·28	6·50	7·10	0·40	3·94	3·06	1·60	1·00
	(2)	+0·55	+2·83	+2·59	−0·86	−1·62	+1·66	+2·09	−3·10	+0·77	+0·55	−0·84	−0·96
	(3)	60·3	60·9	60·5	54·9	49·3	46·1	44·3	46·3	48·5	50·5	55·4	59·5
	(4)	−1·2	−0·8	+1·4	+0·7	0·0	−0·1	−1·2	+1·2	+1·5	+0·9	+1·5	+0·7

(1) Total monthly rainfall (in.); (2) deviation of (1) from normal (in.); (3) average monthly temperature (°F.); (4) deviation of (3) from normal (°F.). The normals for rainfall are for the period 1916–50; normals for temperature are for the period 1921–50. SOURCE. Meteorological office, Air Ministry, London.

over England and Wales amounted only to 7·2 in., comparable with that during the similar periods in the dry years 1921 and 1911, the earlier years 1887 and 1870 alone giving smaller amounts.

Europe. Sept. 1958 was generally warm except in the U.S.S.R. A stormy period from late September to mid-October, with flooding in France and some breaches in the Dutch sea dykes, was followed by remarkably calm, fair weather later in the autumn. October and November ranked as mild over most of Europe, especially in Scandinavia, where

TABLE II. MONTHLY RAINFALL AND TEMPERATURE: WORLD

Location		1958 July	Aug.	Sept.	Oct.	Nov.	Dec.	1959 Jan.	Feb.	March	April	May	June
Toronto Lat. 43° 41′N. Long. 79° 38′W. (578 ft. above mean sea level)	(1)	2·4	2·8	3·1	1·2	2·8	1·2	2·8	2·8	2·4	2·4	1·6	0·8
	(2)a	−0·9	−0·3	+0·4	−1·3	+0·4	−1·1	0·0	+0·6	+0·1	−0·4	−1·2	−2·0
	(3)	69·4	67·8	60·4	48·6	38·8	19·8	18·9	19·2	27·7	43·5	57·2	67·3
	(4)a	+1·2	+1·8	+1·0	+1·3	+2·8	−4·3	−0·5	+0·9	−1·8	+2·0	+4·1	+4·9
San Francisco Lat. 37° 37′N. Long. 122° 23′W. (18 ft.)	(1)	0·0	0·0	0·0	0·1	0·2	1·6	3·9	4·7	0·4	0·4	0·0	0·0
	(2)b	0·0	0·0	−0·5	−0·8	−1·9	−1·9	+0·1	+0·6	−2·5	−0·7	−0·6	−0·2
	(3)	65·1	67·3	69·4	63·3	57·2	55·2	53·4	53·2	57·9	59·7	59·2	61·5
	(4)b	+6·5	+8·1	+7·5	+2·1	+0·4	+4·1	+3·8	+0·1	+3·6	+3·8	+2·5	+3·0
Washington Lat. 38° 51′N. Long. 77° 02′W. (65 ft.)	(1)	7·1	6·3	2·8	2·4	2·0	1·6	2·4	1·6	2·4	3·9	2·8	5·5
	(2)a	+2·6	+1·9	−0·5	−0·4	−0·2	−1·7	−0·9	−1·0	−0·9	+0·4	−0·3	+1·3
	(3)	79·3	75·6	69·3	59·4	50·2	33·1	35·1	39·0	45·4	58·6	70·0	76·1
	(4)a	+2·7	+1·3	+0·6	+2·0	+4·2	−3·2	+0·8	+3·9	+0·4	+4·6	+6·0	+4·1
Buenos Aires Lat. 34° 35′S. Long. 58° 29′W. (82 ft.)	(1)	2·8	...	...	...	...	...	...	...	...	...	...	1·6
	(2)a	+0·7	...	...	...	...	...	...	...	...	...	...	−0·3
	(3)	60·3	...	...	...	...	...	...	...	...	...	...	46·9
	(4)	+11·0	...	...	...	...	...	...	...	...	...	...	−2·9
Reykjavik Lat. 64° 08′N. Long. 21° 57′W. (59 ft.)	(1)	0·4	0·8	2·4	4·3	8·3	2·0	1·6	6·3	4·7	2·0	2·0	2·4
	(2)c	−1·5	−1·2	−1·1	+0·9	+4·6	−1·5	−2·3	+3·0	+2·0	−0·4	+0·1	+0·5
	(3)	53·6	50·4	52·5	43·2	40·6	32·5	25·2	36·1	38·3	36·3	45·7	47·8
	(4)d	+2·0	−0·1	+7·0	+4·0	+6·8	+2·5	−4·6	+6·3	+7·2	0·0	+2·9	−0·8
Stockholm Lat. 59° 21′N. Long. 17° 57′E. (33 ft.)	(1)	2·8	3·1	2·0	1·6	1·6	2·4	3·5	0·4	1·2	2·4	0·4	1·2
	(2)a	0·0	0·0	−0·1	−0·5	−0·3	+0·5	+2·0	−0·7	+0·1	+0·9	−1·2	−0·7
	(3)	61·9	59·4	55·8	48·0	40·6	30·0	25·3	33·4	37·2	42·4	51·1	59·5
	(4)a	−0·5	0·0	+3·6	+4·5	+5·7	+0·3	−2·2	+6·1	+5·9	+3·9	+2·5	+2·7
Brussels Lat. 50° 48′N. Long. 04° 21′E. (328 ft.)	(1)	3·9	3·1	2·4	3·9	1·6	2·8	3·9	0·4	3·1	2·4	0·4	1·6
	(2)a	+0·4	+0·1	−0·2	+0·9	−1·5	−0·4	+1·3	−1·6	+0·7	−0·1	−2·1	−1·0
	(3)	62·8	63·1	61·2	51·4	41·4	40·5	35·4	35·2	46·4	50·9	57·6	62·2
	(4)a	+0·6	+1·6	+4·0	+1·4	0·0	+2·6	−1·5	−2·4	+4·5	+4·1	+2·6	+3·4
Hamburg Lat. 53° 38′N. Long. 10° 00′E. (54 ft.)	(1)	4·9	3·9	2·7	3·7	0·7	1·7	2·4	0·2	0·7	1·6	0·8	0·8
	(2)a	+1·5	+0·4	+0·3	+1·3	−1·6	−0·8	0·0	−1·7	−1·2	−0·5	−1·4	−1·7
	(3)	61·5	61·7	58·6	50·7	40·3	38·1	32·7	32·5	43·3	49·1	54·5	60·4
	(4)a	−0·2	+1·8	+3·7	+3·4	+1·3	+3·0	−0·6	−0·9	+5·0	+4·9	+1·1	+1·9
Lisbon Lat. 38° 43′N. Long. 09° 09′W. (253 ft.)	(1)	0·0	1·6	0·0	...	1·2	9·1	5·1	...	...	2·8	3·5	0·0
	(2)a	−0·2	+1·5	−1·1	...	−2·9	+5·8	+2·5	...	...	+1·0	+2·2	−0·7
	(3)	70·3	70·0	68·7	...	57·7	54·7	55·0	...	...	58·5	63·5	67·6
	(4)a	0·0	−1·6	−0·2	...	+1·2	+2·0	+3·9	...	...	+0·9	+1·4	+0·7
Malta Lat. 35° 51′N. Long. 14° 29′E. (261 ft.)	(1)	0·0	0·0	0·0	0·4	1·6	9·1	3·9	1·2	1·6	0·4	2·8	1·2
	(2)e	0·0	−0·1	−0·8	−0·6	+5·0	+0·6	−2·1	−0·9	−1·3	+1·9	+0·8	−0·1
	(3)	77·7	81·1	75·5	70·3	63·3	59·6	53·5	53·7	58·1	59·7	65·5	72·0
	(4)e	−0·1	+2·5	−0·1	−0·2	−0·4	+2·2	−1·0	−0·8	+1·3	−0·2	+0·1	−0·5
Cairo Lat. 30° 08′N. Long. 31° 24′E. (223 ft.)	(1)	0·0	0·0	0·0	0·0	0·0	0·0	0·1	0·4	0·0	0·1	0·0	0·0
	(2)f	0·0	0·0	0·0	0·0	0·0	−0·1	−0·2	−0·1	+0·2	−0·2	0·0	0·0
	(3)	82·6	82·9	78·1	73·8	67·3	61·9	57·2	53·4	61·3	70·0	76·8	80·6
	(4)f	+0·7	+1·2	+0·6	+0·9	+1·6	+4·7	+3·1	−2·9	0·0	+1·6	+1·2	+0·4
Cape Town Lat. 33° 58′S. Long. 18° 36′E. (162 ft.)	(1)	0·4	2·8	1·2	1·2	0·8	0·0	0·4	0·4	1·2	4·3	6·7	0·8
	(2)e	−2·5	0·0	−0·7	+0·3	0·0	−0·4	0·0	−0·1	+0·8	+3·0	+4·5	−2·5
	(3)	53·4	54·5	55·9	59·2	62·6	69·4	67·1	68·9	65·3	59·9	55·6	53·8
	(4)g	−0·3	+0·2	−0·4	−0·7	−1·4	+2·7	−1·2	−0·2	−1·2	−3·1	−1·7	−0·9
Tokyo Lat. 35° 41′N. Long. 139° 46′E. (20 ft.)	(1)	7·8	3·1	26·5	10·9	3·3	3·9	2·3	4·5	3·7	6·2	8·0	4·7
	(2)h	+2·2	−4·0	+16·4	+3·0	−0·2	+1·7	0·0	+1·5	−0·6	+0·9	+2·1	−2·0
	(3)	76·8	78·4	73·6	60·8	52·0	46·2	38·7	45·0	48·0	59·5	65·3	68·5
	(4)h	+1·6	+0·7	+2·4	0·0	+1·3	+4·8	+1·3	+6·0	+3·9	+5·0	+3·4	0·0
Aden Lat. 12° 50′N. Long. 45° 01′E. (12 ft.)	(1)	0·1	...	0·0	0·0	0·0	0·1	1·2	0·1	0·0	0·0	0·0	0·0
	(2)a	+0·1	...	−0·1	−0·2	0·0	0·0	+0·8	0·0	−0·2	−0·2	−0·1	−0·1
	(3)	90·1	...	90·5	84·9	79·9	79·9	78·7	79·2	81·0	82·5	88·3	91·2
	(4)a	+2·0	...	+2·6	+1·0	0·0	+2·6	+2·4	+2·2	+1·6	−0·5	+1·0	+1·5
Calcutta Lat. 22° 32′N. Long. 88° 20′E. (20 ft.)	(1)	13·4	7·1	10·6	2·8	0·8	0·0	0·8	0·4	0·4	3·1	4·3	13·8
	(2)a	−0·5	−6·3	+1·5	−1·6	+0·1	−0·2	+0·4	−0·7	−1·1	+1·0	−0·8	+1·8
	(3)	84·7	84·7	84·7	83·7	77·5	71·1	69·8	72·5	83·3	88·2	88·7	85·8
	(4)a	+0·3	+0·9	+0·5	+1·8	+3·4	+3·8	+2·5	+0·7	+2·5	+2·2	+2·0	0·0
Colombo Lat. 06° 54′N. Long. 79° 52′E. (23 ft.)	(1)	1·5	3·1	1·9	14·0	10·6	6·4	1·7	2·7	0·5	18·4	12·1	12·3
	(2)i	−2·9	−0·1	−2·9	−0·3	−1·2	+1·3	−1·6	+0·8	−3·8	+8·7	+1·2	+5·0
	(3)	82·5	81·1	81·9	80·6	79·5	80·3	80·3	80·0	81·8	82·1	82·0	80·9
	(4)i	+1·4	0·0	+0·8	+0·2	−0·6	+0·8	+0·8	−0·4	−0·1	−0·7	−0·8	−0·8
Sydney Lat. 33° 52′S. Long. 151° 12′E. (138 ft.)	(1)	1·5	3·5	1·2	2·4	0·8	5·9	6·3	7·9	5·5	1·6	2·4	4·3
	(2)e	−3·7	+1·1	−1·6	−0·4	−1·8	+2·3	+2·4	+4·8	+1·1	−1·6	−0·3	+0·6
	(3)	54·7	57·7	57·9	64·6	70·2	69·4	72·5	72·9	71·6	66·6	59·4	56·3
	(4)e	+0·6	+1·8	−2·2	+0·7	+3·1	−0·6	+0·7	+0·8	+1·8	+1·7	−0·3	+0·9
Wellington Lat. 41° 17′S. Long. 174° 46′E. (391 ft.)	(1)	2·0	2·0	2·0	2·8	0·8	5·1	3·5	2·0	2·8	2·8	10·2	1·6
	(2)j	−3·5	−3·6	−2·1	−1·7	−2·2	+0·7	+0·5	−2·3	0·0	−1·2	+5·7	−2·7
	(3)	46·0	48·4	50·5	56·5	57·4	61·2	63·7	61·9	60·6	57·0	48·2	47·7
	(4)k	−2·0	−0·2	−1·1	+2·2	+0·6	+0·9	+1·3	−0·7	0·0	0·0	−4·7	−1·8

(1) Total monthly rainfall (in.); (2) deviation of (1) from normal (in.); (3) average monthly temperature (°F.); (4) deviation of (3) from normal (°F.). Periods of the normals are indicated as follows: a 1901-30; b 1906-35; c 1876-1925; d 1873-1920; e 1911-40; f 1909-45; g 1932-40; h 1897-1926; i 1869-1920; j 1916-45; k 1864-1923. SOURCE. Meteorological office, Air Ministry, London.

mean temperatures were 6°C. above normal in some places. Nevertheless snow came early to the Alps, blocking some passes around Oct. 20, most being blocked finally by mid-November. The first avalanche warning (Oct. 23) was the earliest for 20 years. The Alpine winter was not cold, but the snow gave a good winter sports season ending (rather early) in prolonged sunshine in February.

The winter was very rough in Spain and Portugal, some months having up to four times the normal rainfall and heavy snows in the mountains. Violent gales affected Portugal in December. There were long periods of drought in the eastern Mediterranean and very little winter snow in the Ukraine. The winter was mild in central and eastern Europe, especially the U.S.S.R. Over Scandinavia, Britain and the northern seas most of December and January was decidedly cold. The severe weather was brought by repeated outbreaks of very cold northerly winds. Unusually extensive sea ice developed but seems to have broken up in late January when a Danish steamer foundered after striking unexpected ice off Cape Farewell, Greenland. In places north of Iceland the severest conditions for about 40 years were reported.

The change of weather in late January ended the winter in many places, being followed by a succession of warm months. Persistent anticyclones over Britain and central Europe produced a completely rainless February in many places—a rare phenomenon. Over the dry soil, exceptional warmth was attained at the end of February both in England and the Ukraine. The spring was generally warm and very forward. Mostly dry, warm weather continued throughout the summer over northern Europe. In eastern Norway the drought was exceptional. The northwestern coasts however had a wet summer as did eastern central Europe, floods causing damage in Austria. In northern waters the summer brought south exceptionally extensive polar pack ice.

Commonwealth. The 1957 monsoon had produced the greatest annual rainfall so far recorded anywhere: 670 in. at Mawsyhram in the Khasi hills, Assam, near Cherrapunji. This was nearly twice the normal rainfall for that district, believed to be the wettest in the world. The 1958 monsoon was heavy in northwestern India and Pakistan; in Assam it was about normal.

Australia had no serious summer droughts in 1958-59. The autumn was wet in eastern Australia and New Zealand. Auckland was struck by a hurricane in March. The cyclone season was also severe in the southern Indian ocean, though Madagascar was more affected than Mauritius. Heavy rains caused flooding in Natal in May. In west Africa the winter dry season was prolonged, the intertropical front being unusually far south.

The 1958-59 winter was severe in eastern and central Canada. The St. Lawrence ice was the worst for 25 years. Winnipeg had its longest recorded spell (97 days) with no thaw. Nevertheless March saw considerable warming, with Chinook winds in Alberta. Queen Elizabeth II's visit in July 1959 was attended by heat waves all across Canada.

(P. A. Sd.; J. Ge.; H. H. Lb.)

BIBLIOGRAPHY. L. J. Battan, *Radar Meteorology* (Chicago, 1959); C. H. B. Priestley, *Turbulent Transfer in the Lower Atmosphere* (Chicago, 1959); S. Petterssen, *Introduction to Meteorology*, 2nd ed. (New York, 1958); H. R. Byers, *General Meteorology*, 3rd ed. (New York, 1959); F. N. Frenkiel and P. A. Sheppard (eds.), *Atmospheric Diffusion and Air Pollution* (London, 1959); H. S. W. Massey and R. L. F. Boyd, *The Upper Atmosphere* (London, 1959).

METHODIST CHURCH.

An Evangelical Protestant Church emphasizing the doctrines of assurance, conversion and fellowship in Christian service, owing its origin to John Wesley and others in the early 18th century. World membership (1957): *c.* 18·5 million adults in full membership; *c.* 40 million adherents; *c.* 60,000 ordained ministers.

The annual conference, at Bristol, in July 1959 stressed the city's close association with the beginnings of Methodism.

Differences of race, colour and language were overcome by the fellowship in which representatives of the Churches in Ireland, The West Indies, New Zealand and South Africa joined with the nationals from India and west Africa, and with U.S. Methodist leaders who visited the conference. During the year an official statement expressed the belief that " man is not wresting from an unwilling God the secrets of His universe, but is being led by His Spirit to new discovery and fuller knowledge." Special appeals were made for a return to regular habits of worship, and for active co-operation with the World Council of Churches and with the Free Church Federal council in their efforts to gain a more intimate knowledge of the beliefs and practice of various Christian communions. Ampler accommodation was provided in the Methodist Homes for the Aged and in the National Childrens' home. Important pronouncements were made on road safety, penal reform and gambling.

The number of members and communicants in Great Britain was 736,781, with 4,534 ministers and supernumeraries. Overseas districts had 243,621 members, an increase of 7,922. There were 22,806 fully accredited local preachers in Great Britain and 664,560 Sunday school scholars. Membership of youth organizations and youth clubs totalled about 100,000. The Rev. Edward Rogers was designated president of the conference to be held in 1960, and George Thomas vice-president. In Ireland there were 31,864 members, 317 ministers, 393 local preachers, 2,041 Sunday school teachers and 15,725 scholars. A scheme was approved to deal with the situation in the sparsely populated Sligo district, in co-operation with the Presbyterian Church. The new Youth Community centre in Belfast, for university students and student nurses, was named Aldersgate house. The Rev. R. Ernest Kerr was appointed president of the Irish conference.

The 76th annual conference of the Methodist Church in South Africa met in Pietermaritzburg under the presidency of the Rev. C. Edgar Wilkinson. A Planning commission was appointed to administer finance and secure funds for the building of new churches for African, Indian and Coloured people ejected through the Group Areas act. The Church reaffirmed its belief in " the multi-racial character of Christ's Kingdom ". An increase of 11,000 members was reported and 43 candidates for the ministry were accepted, including 24 non-Europeans. In New Zealand and Australia visits from representative Methodists in Britain strengthened the bonds with the mother country. There was some success in the use of planes, helicopters and radio to overcome the distances between scattered groups and the cities, where gains from recent evangelistic crusades were consolidated. (L. F. C.)

MEXICO. Federal republic of North America lying between the United States on the north and Guatemala and British Honduras on the south. Area: 760,373 sq.mi. Pop.: (1950 census) 25,791,017; (1959 est.) 33,304,000; about 55% *mestizo*, 29% Indian and 15% of pure European origin. Language: Spanish, with an estimated 3·6% (1950) speaking Indian tongues only. Chief towns (pop. 1950 census, 1958 est. in brackets): Mexico City (cap.) 2,234,795 (3,448,218); Guadalajara 377,015 (444,139); Monterrey 333,422 (426,573); Puebla 211,331 (252,803); 11 towns with a pop. from 200,000 to 100,000. President, Adolfo López Mateos. Main imports: machinery and apparatus, chemicals, cereals. Main exports: cotton, coffee, lead, copper, petroleum and products. Monetary unit: *peso* (34·90 pesos = £ sterling).

History. The new administration of President López started its six-year term on Dec. 1, 1958, with a substantial budget deficit inherited from the previous regime. Informed observers said the deficit was traceable largely to inefficient operation of such nationalized properties as the National Railways of Mexico and Petroleos Mexicanos.

In January the administration announced the largest budget in Mexican history for the calendar year: 9,375 million

President López of Mexico acknowledges the cheers of the crowd at the time of the dispute with Guatemala over fishing limits.

pesos. This was increased in July when López approved a rise to 9,750 million pesos.

Following an incident on Dec. 13, 1958, in which Guatemalan aircraft attacked Mexican fishing boats allegedly fishing in Guatemalan waters, Mexico broke off diplomatic relations with Guatemala. Three Mexican fishermen were killed and 14 injured, and a number of vessels were badly damaged. Restoration of relations with Guatemala was announced by López in Sept. 1959. (*See also* GUATEMALA.)

Strife in Mexican railway unions in February and March led to the arrest of Demetrio Vallejo, Communist leader of the 60,000-member National Railway Workers union and a few hundred other union leaders and members. They were charged with subversion.

The presidents of Mexico and the United States exchanged visits during 1959. In February, President Dwight D. Eisenhower went to Acapulco at the invitation of López. The president of Mexico repaid the courtesy the following October, visiting Washington, Chicago and New York. López also visited Canada on the same tour.

During his United States tour, López spoke before the Organization of American States and the United Nations general assembly. In a blunt statement before the O.A.S., he asserted that the organization's work had not measured up to Latin America's expectations. He said the O.A.S.'s economic efforts " have not satisfied the legitimate aspirations of our peoples nor the confidence they have placed in our organization." He said that practical action was needed to deal with the crisis brought about by the unbalance in distribution of wealth in the western hemisphere. Prosperity and democracy go hand in hand, he remarked.

On May 8, Antonio Ortiz Mena, minister of finance, told a bankers' convention at Torreón that Mexico's rapidly increasing population offered opportunity for both public and private investments to improve the nation's standard of living.

In October a hurricane hit the west-coast states of Colima and Jalisco, with winds which reached a velocity of 146 mi. per hr. The storm levelled banana and coconut plantations along a 400-mi. stretch of the coast and left widespread destruction and death in its path. Five ships were sunk in the harbour of Manzanillo by the blow, and floods caused by torrential rains borne by the storm virtually destroyed many villages. Though an official count of the dead had not been released, authorities believed it would exceed 1,000.

(C. D. HE.)

MIDDLE EAST DEFENCE TREATY: *see* CENTRAL TREATY ORGANIZATION.

MINERAL AND METAL PRODUCTION. The year 1958 was one of readjustment throughout the mineral and metal producing industries. Although production of many non-metallic minerals was increased, most metals continued the downward trend started in mid-1957 and only aluminium, mercury, uranium and the precious metals showed increases. At the beginning of 1958 all major metals were in over-supply and suffered from precipitous price falls.

The weakness was due in the first place to the decline in industrial activity in the United States, but it was not so much reduced consumption that brought large surpluses; the virtual cessation of stockpile purchases, which had gone far beyond the requirements of changed military strategy, and the completion of many government-aided mining projects started in the post-Korean war period left production capacity far in excess of demand. Persistent sales of some metals (notably aluminium, tin and zinc) by the U.S.S.R. caused further weakness in world markets. Output restrictions, in some cases severe, and the closing of many mines gradually corrected the surpluses, helped by some recovery in demand following the end of the business recession. The U.S.S.R. agreed to limit its exports of aluminium and tin. The copper surplus changed gradually to threatened shortage as a result of strikes at several leading production centres.

There was a decrease in exploration and development; nevertheless the long-term outlook remained expansionist. It was considered that, quite apart from the capital investment required to maintain existing levels of mining production, additional new investment at the rate of over £2,000 million per annum would be needed to meet long-term rising consumption trends. With its domestic mining industry noticeably on the decline, the rate of U.S. investment in foreign metal mining had increased considerably in scale and intensity and was believed to be not far short of that of the whole of the rest of the world. Viewed against this background the recession of 1957 and 1958, though embarrassing to all producers, appeared to be purely temporary. Even so the prospect for the following two or three years was generally one of continuing excess capacity, with the necessity for keeping some in reserve until consumption could catch up with the over-rapid expansion in production facilities.

Aluminium. World production of aluminium increased by 4% in 1958 to a new record of 3,470,000 tons, including an estimated 540,000 tons in the U.S.S.R. The increase came mainly from Canada, the U.S.S.R. and western Europe. In the United States, the largest producer, output fell by 5% to 1,398,000 tons through reduced demand and competition from European metal. Although several plants were closed in the United States capacity was increased by 333,000 tons to a total of 1,972,500 tons. World production capacity was estimated to be 4,452,000 tons rising to 5,630,000 tons by 1960. Canada produced 545,000 tons in 1958. Canadian British Aluminium brought its second unit into operation but Aluminium Ltd. operated below capacity and suspended construction on new plant at Kitimat. Production in western Europe began to level off. Competition from Soviet supplies persisted and anti-dumping action was sought, but not taken, against shipments to Britain. Thereafter shipments declined steadily and in October the Soviet authorities announced the limitation of further such shipments to 16,500 tons per annum. A growing application of aluminium in transport and building construction partly offset declines in other uses and important inroads were made into the electrical field. An upward trend of consumption later in 1958 led to the reopening of some U.S. plants.

Beryllium. Although interest in beryllium continued to grow, production dropped sharply to 6,200 tons in 1958. Mozambique, Argentina, Belgian Congo, Brazil and India in that order remained the largest producers. U.S. consumption rose to 5,500 tons, mainly as a result of greater production of beryllium metal. The United States Atomic Energy commission reduced its annual purchase contracts by two-thirds and interest in beryllium shifted from nuclear to space-age applications. Imperial Chemical Industries announced that it was establishing the first plant in Europe for the fabrication of beryllium in wrought forms, to begin production in 1959.

Cadmium. World production of cadmium had been rising considerably since World War II in response to rapidly growing demand. In 1958 it fell by 6% to 5,880 tons, mainly because of lower production of lead and zinc ores from which it is obtained as a by-product. U.S. production of cadmium from domestic and imported zinc ores and flue dusts fell to 4,320 tons, but many smaller countries showed increases and production of cadmium metal was begun in Mexico.

Cobalt. World production of cobalt fell in 1958 for the second consecutive year and was 8% lower at 13,100 tons, through voluntary output restrictions and losses from copper strikes in Canada and Northern Rhodesia. Nevertheless, the new plants at Sherritt Gordon mines (Canada) and Chibuluma mines (Northern Rhodesia) increased their output and approached capacity working. The Union Minière de Haut Katanga continued construction of a new 4,000-ton-per-annum hydro-metallurgical plant at Kolwezi in the Belgian Congo. A new 2,000-ton-per-annum nickel-cobalt plant at Moa bay, Cuba, was expected to be in production by mid-1959.

Copper. In early 1958 the copper industry continued to suffer from overproduction, unsold stocks and low prices (about £160 per ton at the end of February). Most major producers had curtailed production by 10% or more and by the spring the trend of prices was reversed, helped by an increase in U.S. demand. Lengthy strikes in Chile, Northern Rhodesia, Canada and the United States, which lost some 122,000 tons of production, more than corrected the oversupply, and a threatened shortage in the autumn took the price to nearly £260 per ton. In the event world mine production fell by only 4% to 3,340,000 tons (including an estimated 420,000 tons in the U.S.S.R.), though production was lower in almost every country. The excise tax of 1·7 cents per lb. on copper imports was reimposed in the United States after seven years' suspension. However, both U.K. and U.S. export controls on copper were relaxed and the U.S.S.R. bought substantial quantities later in the year. The Board of Trade announced the intended disposal of the 47,500 tons of copper remaining in the U.K. stockpile. It was estimated that mine production capacity in the non-Communist world would rise by 25% to some 3,570,000 tons per annum by 1962. The increase was expected to come mainly from the Southern Peru Copper corporation, from the El Salvador mine in Chile and from new mines in Northern Rhodesia and the Belgian Congo.

Gold. Being influenced more by monetary than by industrial considerations, gold was one of the few metals to show an increase in production in 1958. World production rose for the fifth consecutive year to a total of 40·4 million oz., including an estimated 10 million oz. in the U.S.S.R. The increase was mainly due to continued expansion in South Africa, particularly the new mines of the Orange Free State,

where output rose to a record of 17·7 million oz. Other important producing countries showing increases were Canada, where the Emergency Gold Mining Assistance act was extended to 1960, and Ghana, where subsidies were considered for marginal producers. U.S. gold stocks declined by $2,251 million during 1958, reflecting the reversal in the balance of payments with the United Kingdom and western

These gold-miners broke the world record when they sank a shaft at Vaal Reefs, Transvaal, from 1,132 ft. to 2,054 ft. in 30 days.

Europe. Sales of Soviet gold were again reported towards the end of 1958 and were estimated to have been some 6 million oz. (7·5 million oz. in 1957).

Lead. Under the influence of low prices, poor demand and the virtual cessation of U.S. government stockpile purchases and barter transactions, world mine production fell in 1958 for the first time for 12 years and was 4% lower at 2,240,000 tons. Voluntary output restrictions in many countries continued from 1957 and many high-cost mines were closed, particularly in the United States, where output declined by 21% to 238,700 tons. Australia, the largest producer, showed only a 2% decline to 326,000 tons owing to expansion by Mount Isa mines. Mexican production fell by 6% to 198,700 tons but Canada showed a slight increase to 165,300 tons. Production in the U.S.S.R. was estimated to have been about 295,000 tons. Stocks accumulated in the United States as surplus foreign production continued to pour in. This led to demands for protection and on Oct. 1 import quota restrictions were imposed. A meeting of interested countries organized by the United Nations in September suggested that exporting countries should consider regulating their exports. These announcements stimulated some buying but the market soon became inactive again.

Manganese. Manganese suffered in 1958 from the overproduction and excess stocks of the previous year. World production fell by 8% to 10,708,500 tons, but demand remained poor and stocks increased to approximately 2 million tons. The U.S.S.R. remained the largest producer, accounting for an estimated 5,281,000 tons, nearly half the total. India was the largest non-Communist producer but output fell sharply to 1,229,000 tons, the centralization of ore sales and quotas for individual mines having turned buyers to other sources for supplies. India's first ferro-manganese plant began operating as part of a programme to compete with mines being developed and expanded elsewhere. South Africa produced 834,000 tons and was virtually the only country to show an increase; much of this ore was retained for use in uranium recovery. In Brazil the Amapa mine approached peak capacity but total Brazilian production fell to 684,100 tons. Development of immense deposits was continued in Gabon, with production scheduled for 1961. In early 1959 the U.S. government sold the 265,000-ton low-grade Mexican ore stockpile.

Nickel. Nickel was abundant in 1958 for the first time for ten years. World production fell by 26% to 173,000 tons, including an estimated 49,000 tons in the U.S.S.R., but the diversion of U.S. government stockpile deliveries to industry at a time of falling consumption brought over-supply. The International Nickel Company of Canada, the world's largest producer, reduced its output in three successive cuts with the result that Canadian production fell by 25% to 125,760 tons; nevertheless development continued at the company's new Thompson mine in Manitoba. Production in Cuba fell to 17,660 tons, partly owing to internal disorders. World production capacity, excluding the U.S.S.R., rose to 234,400 tons in 1958 and was expected to reach 290,200 tons by 1961. The German Democratic Republic's nickel smelter at St. Egidien, Saxony, was nearing completion and Czechoslovakia announced plans for constructing a nickel plant to treat Albanian ores.

Tin. World mine production fell by 25% to 152,000 tons in 1958. The main producing countries, all showing decreases, were: Indonesia, 23,201 tons; Malaya, 34,458 tons; China (estimate), 23,000 tons; Bolivia, 17,731 tons; Belgian Congo, 11,163 tons. Sales of Soviet tin in western Europe increased to over 17,000 tons (6,820 tons in 1957). The International Tin council strove to achieve balanced supply and stable prices by buffer stock buying at a floor price of £730 per ton and by limiting exports of its member countries. Partly through heavy offerings of Soviet metal, however, the buffer stock reached its maximum in the early spring and a supplementary special fund was created. Import controls on Soviet tin were imposed by several countries, particularly the United Kingdom and the Netherlands, but in Jan. 1959 were lifted when the U.S.S.R. announced its intention of limiting 1959 exports to non-Communist countries to 13,500 tons. Rising consumption and improved demand in 1959 brought liquidation of most of the International Tin council's stocks and export quotas were raised on two occasions.

Titanium. Most titanium producers continued to suffer from the drastic cut in U.S. government military requirements made in mid-1957. By mid-1958 U.S. production of titanium sponge had dropped to 10% of capacity and, although some improvement followed, U.S. production for the year totalled only 4,096 tons (15,401 tons in 1957). Some 2,320 tons were delivered against old contracts to the General Services administration, which held 19,850 tons in stock at the end of 1958. In the United Kingdom production of titanium metal by Imperial Chemical Industries was believed to be running below the plant capacity of 1,800 tons per annum, and production in Japan fell as exports to the United States contracted. Sharp price reductions and the development of new alloys brought increased commercial use of titanium in late 1958 and in 1959 but total demand remained low. A long wait was forecast before producers could hope to obtain a market sufficient to support the capacity built up to meet U.S. military requirements.

Tungsten. Tungsten mining continued the decline that had followed the suspension of U.S. government purchases in Dec. 1956. Although world production of concentrates (60%WO$_3$) fell by only 15% in 1958, to 56,590 tons, the decline was severe in most non-Communist countries. Faced with a market price of only about one-half the cost of production, most producers suspended or curtailed operations. China was the largest producer with an estimated output of 20,000 tons and production in the U.S.S.R. was believed to be about 7,400 tons. Some Chinese and Soviet metal found limited markets in western Europe. U.S. production dropped to 3,380 tons (less than one-quarter of the 1956 output) and Bolivia's exports fell by 20% to 3,450 tons. Brazil, the one remaining country shipping to the U.S. government stockpile, showed only a modest decline to 2,320 tons. By the end of 1958 production was below consumption and some increase in demand lifted prices, but large stocks remained for disposal.

Uranium. The year 1958 was good for uranium producers, who were shielded from the general decline by long-term contracts at guaranteed prices. World production of uranium

The Mary Kathleen mine in northwestern Queensland, which produces uranium oxide for the U.K. Atomic Energy authority.

concentrates rose sharply to approximately 31,190 tons, the main producing countries being: Canada, 12,050 tons; United States, 10,980 tons; South Africa, 5,510 tons; Belgian Congo, 760 tons; France, 730 tons; and Australia, 625 tons. Canadian production climbed steadily and approached the expected maximum rate of 13,400 tons per annum as newly completed mills reached capacity. U.S. production was expected to reach 16,000 tons in 1959 and to continue at this level until 1966; production started at four new mines and at eight new mills. South African output reached the ceiling of 5,500 tons imposed by the Combined Development agency but potential production was believed to be much higher. It was estimated that by 1960 the world would have 1·5 million kw. of nuclear power capacity needing 1,280 tons of uranium metal to stock the reactors and 356 tons per annum for refuelling. By 1965 there would be 15·3 million kw. capacity requiring an initial 14,700 tons and an annual refuelling of 4,000 tons. With markets guaranteed until 1966 the outlook for uranium remained good; nevertheless, producers were searching for new markets in anticipation of keen competition to come in later years.

(*Continued on page 330*)

MINERAL AND METAL PRODUCTION

(Metric tons unless otherwise specified; th. indicates thousands, and m. millions of units)

World Mineral and

Country	Aluminium (th.)	Bauxite (th.)	Antimony*	Arsenic†	Asbestos (th.)	Barytes (th.)	Chromite (th.)	Coal (m.)	High temperature coke (m.)	Medium temperature coke (m.)	Copper (in ore) (th.)	Copper (smelter) (th.)	Felspar (th.)	Fluorspar (th.)	Gold (th. oz.)	Graphite (th.)	Gypsum (th.)	Iron ore (th.)
N. & C. America																		
Canada	586·0	—	420	1,021	839·4	182·6	—	10·60	3·01	0·06e	314·6	299·2	16·1	56·0e	4,537	—	3,606·2	14,387
United States	1,420·2	1,331·7	640	10,440	39·9	441·2	130·4	391·56	48·63	0·17[6]	888·4	969·8	477·3	289·9	1,759	—	8,709·2	69,038
Mexico	—	—	2,747	3,094	—	190·0e	—	1·47	0·60	(p)	65·0	60·9	—	222·2	332	19·6	P	970e
Central America	—	—	—	—	—	—	1·0e	—	—	—	—	—	—	—	249	—	15·1	5
West Indies	—	6,098·4	—	—	—	8·5	75·1e	—	—	—	13·0	—	—	—	(p)	—	726·4	180
Other N. American	—	—	—	—	—	—	—	(p)	—	—	—	—	—	—	—	—	—	—
South America																		
Argentina	—	—	—	(p)	(p)	17·0e	—	0·26	—	0·06e	—	—	5·0e	8·0e	7e	0·5e	150·0e	140
Bolivia	—	—	5,278	—	—	—	—	—	—	—	2·9	—	—	—	19	—	—	—
Brazil	9·5e	41·5	—	100e	1·5	56·8	2·6	2·20	0·51	—	1·3	—	P	—	140?	0·8e	110·0e	5,240e
British Guiana	—	1,611·3	—	—	—	—	—	—	—	—	—	—	—	—	18	—	—	—
Chile	—	—	—	—	—	1·0e	—	1·82	0·40e	0·09	462·2	437·4	0·8e	—	71	—	70·0e	3,759
Colombia	—	—	—	—	—	13·0	—	2·20	0·30	—	—	—	—	—	372	—	60·0	552
Ecuador	—	—	—	—	—	—	—	0·17	(p)	—	—	—	—	—	19	—	(p)	—
Peru	—	—	791	20e	—	106·9	—	—	—	—	49·8	38·4	—	—	133	—	63·9	2,591
Venezuela	—	—	—	—	8·3	—	—	(p)	—	—	—	—	0·3	—	76	—	—	15,485
Other S. American	—	2,988·0	—	—	—	—	—	—	—	0·03	—	—	—	—	24	—	—	—
Europe																		
Austria	56·9	23·6	466	(p)	—	4·3	—	6·64	1·60	0·33	2·4	9·5	2·7	—	P	21·2	542·0	3,411
Belgium	—	—	—	400e	—	—	—	27·06	6·91	(p)	(p)	—	—	(p)	—	—	—	124
Bulgaria	—	—	1,600?	—	1·0e	—	P	12·73	(p)	—	8·0?	6·0?	P	—	P	—	P	300e
Czechoslovakia	26·4	—	—	(p)	(p)	(p)	—	78·40	7·40e	2·66?	—	—	P	—	P	P	211·0e	2,760e
Finland	—	—	(p)	7·2	—	—	—	—	—	0·13	28·9	30·7	13·4	—	28	—	(p)	215
France	169·1	1,816·8	—	5,600e	18·6	65·0e	—	60·04	12·47	1·60	1·0	—	70·0e	90·0e	30e	—	3,500·0e	59,455
German Fed. Rep.	136·8	5·0e	—	186	—	371·1	—	228·84	43·58	5·56	1·0	268·2	190·5	117·9	4e	10·9	1,022·0	17,988
Greece	—	800·0	—	10	—	150·0	25·0	0·98	—	0·03	—	—	—	—	6	—	25·0	300
Hungary	39·5	1,053·0	(p)	(p)	—	—	—	24·24	0·37e	0·45	—	—	—	—	—	—	—	305
Italy	64·1	299·0	118	1,000e	35·9	93·2	—	1·54	3·36	0·81	1·0	0·6e	56·1	140·0	6	4·0	670·0e	1,283
Luxembourg	—	—	—	—	—	—	—	—	—	0·04	—	—	—	—	—	—	—	6,638
Netherlands	—	—	—	—	—	—	—	12·14	4·08	0·56	—	—	—	—	—	—	—	—
Norway	121·6	—	—	—	—	—	—	—	—	0·06	15·0	17·5	50·0e	—	—	4·5	—	1,554
Poland	22·6e	—	—	—	—	11·2e	—	102·52	10·10	1·00e	8·0e	17·4	—	—	—	—	350·0e	2,150e
Portugal	—	—	10[7]	800e	(p)	(p)	—	0·72	—	0·04	1·1e	—	1·2e	—	14e	—	65·0e	217
Rumania	10·2?	20·0?	—	—	(p)	—	P	7·39	0·56	P	—	—	P	—	P	—	P	700e
Spain	16·0e	6·0	215	—	—	26·8	—	17·09	2·01	0·27	7·5	5·0	6·0	103·0e	11	0·5e	1,055·0e	4,908
Sweden	15·4	—	—	10,000e	—	—	—	0·32	0·10	0·62e	19·4	20·2	44·4	2·9	100e	1·0e	—	13,394
Switzerland	31·2	—	—	—	—	—	—	(p)	—	0·51e	—	—	—	—	—	—	90·0	78e
United Kingdom	26·8	—	—	(p)	—	64·3	—	219·29	18·75	11·44	—	—	—	—	—	—	4,055·2	14,848
Yugoslavia	21·7	733·0	1,665	—	5·4	137·0	113·6	20·19	1·03	0·03	33·7	33·7	14·0e	78·6	60e	0·9	85·0e	1,997
Other European	34·0e	—	—	P	—	35·2	201·3	238·48	0·53	10·11	26·8	30·0	—	65·0	—	—	325·5	1,594
U.S.S.R.	550?	2,750?	P	P	500?	120?	800?	496	50·90	P	425?	425?	P	165?	10,000?	45?	3,000?	88,800?
Africa																		
Algeria	—	—	1,003	—	—	43·0	—	0·15	—	0·10e	0·4	—	—	—	—	—	76·0e	2,315
Angola	—	—	—	—	—	—	—	—	—	—	3·0	1·4	—	—	(p)	—	10·0e	287
Belgian Congo	—	—	—	—	—	—	—	0·29	—	—	237·7	237·7	—	—	354	—	10·0e	—
Ethiopia	—	—	—	—	—	—	—	—	—	—	—	—	—	—	—	—	—	—
French Africa	31·5	330·0	—	—	—	—	—	—	—	—	—	—	—	—	36	—	—	415
Ghana	—	210·4	—	—	—	—	—	—	—	—	—	—	—	—	853	—	—	—
Kenya	—	—	—	—	—	—	—	—	—	—	—	—	—	—	29	0·7	—	—
Madagascar	—	—	—	(p)	—	—	—	—	—	—	—	—	—	—	8	13·0e	11·1	—
Morocco	—	—	—	—	—	42·7	—	0·51	—	—	1·1	—	—	—	—	—	25·0e	250e
Nigeria	—	—	—	—	—	—	—	0·94	—	—	—	—	—	—	(p)	—	—	—
N. Rhodesia	—	—	—	—	—	—	—	—	—	—	400·1	381·0	—	—	4	—	—	—
Sierra Leone	—	—	—	—	—	—	11·4	—	—	—	—	—	—	—	—	—	—	1,443
South Africa	—	—	7,170	—	159·1	2·5	631·5	37·09	1·77	0·08	49·5	48·4	7·8	43·8	17,666	0·8	231·9	2,212
S. Rhodesia	—	—	137	620	115·3	(p)	561·4	3·54	—	0·22e	7·6	—	0·5	(p)	555	—	—	144
S.-W. Africa	—	—	—	—	—	—	—	—	—	—	28·1	—	—	(p)	—	—	—	—
Spanish Morocco	—	—	183	—	—	—	—	—	—	—	—	—	—	—	—	—	—	1,290e
Tanganyika	—	—	—	—	—	—	—	—	—	—	1·6	—	—	—	—	—	—	—
Tunisia	—	—	—	—	—	—	—	—	—	—	—	—	—	—	56	—	9·4	1,103
U.A.R. (Egypt)	—	—	—	—	—	(p)	(p)	—	—	0·03e	—	—	—	—	—	—	15·0e	250e
Uganda	—	—	—	—	—	—	—	—	—	—	11·0	—	—	—	3e	—	1,000·0e	—
Other African	—	5·0e	—	—	24·6	(p)	—	0·25	—	—	0·4	—	—	—	9	—	1·7	2,254
Asia																		
Burma	—	—	80	—	—	(p)	—	—	—	—	(p)	—	—	—	(p)	—	—	(p)
China	27·2?	—	15,000?	(p)	35?	(p)	—	270·00	18·00?	P	15·0?	15·0?	(p)	150?	P	P	350?	30,000?
Cyprus	—	—	—	—	13·3	—	12·0	—	—	—	33·2	—	—	—	—	—	—	—
Formosa (Taiwan)	8·6	—	—	(p)	—	—	—	3·18	0·19	0·08	1·5	1·7	—	—	21	—	10·1	—
India	8·3	116·4	—	—	1·5e	14·0e	61·4	46·06	3·07	1·96	8·3	8·0	6·0e	—	170	0·8	801·7	6,003
Indonesia	—	343·9	—	—	—	—	—	0·60	—	—	—	—	—	—	P	—	—	—
Israel	—	—	—	—	—	—	—	—	—	—	—	—	—	—	—	—	50·0?	—
Japan	84·6	—	290	1,400e	10·1	14·9	41·8	50·84	5·91	2·96	80·8	103·4	45·0e	5·3	259	3·6	477·1	2,035
Korea	(p)	—	—	—	(p)	(p)	—	9·55	0·43	—	0·5	0·8	—	1·6	73	94·2	(p)	261
Malaya	—	266·6	—	—	—	—	—	(p)	—	0·02	—	—	—	—	—	—	—	2,840
Pakistan	—	2·0	—	—	—	—	24·4	0·61	—	—	(p)	—	—	—	—	—	67·2	—
Persia	—	—	40[6]	—	—	—	25·0	0·17	—	—	(p)	—	—	—	—	—	—	—
Philippines	—	—	—	—	—	5·0e	416·3	0·11	—	—	47·0	—	(p)	—	—	—	500?	1,099
Thailand	—	—	—	—	—	—	—	0·13	—	—	—	—	—	—	423	P	1·5	—
Turkey	—	—	1,530	—	—	5·5	475·0e	10·38	0·54	0·11	22·5	22·5	—	(p)	—	—	9·3	947
Vietnam, North	—	—	—	—	—	—	—	1·10	—	—	—	—	2·0e	—	—	—	—	—
Vietnam, South	—	—	—	—	—	—	—	(p)	—	0·07e	—	—	—	—	—	—	—	—
Other Asian	—	138·5	—	—	—	—	—	(p)	—	0·03	—	—	—	—	1·68	9·1	403·1e	3,628
Australasia																		
Australia	11·1	5·0e	700e	—	14·5e	7·4	(p)	32·56	2·34	0·90	74·6	65·6	7·4	—	1,099	—	510·0e	3,988
New Caledonia	—	—	—	—	—	—	47·4	—	(p)	—	—	—	—	—	—	—	—	295
New Zealand	—	—	—	(p)	—	—	—	2·76	(p)	0·07e	—	—	2·0e	—	25	—	—	—
Other Australasian	—	—	—	—	—	—	—	0·10	—	—	—	—	—	—	131	—	—	—
World Total	3,530	21,000	40,000	36,000	1,830	2,300	3,680	2,436	254·25	46·57	3,390	3,570	1,040	1,600	40,400	305	33,435	403,453

NOTE. e indicates an estimate; (p) a small production, unknown in amount or less than the minimum base of the table; P a larger but unknown production; * metal content of ore; † white arsenic; ‡ 60% WO₃ basis; [6], [7], indicate data for 1956 and 1957, respectively, where 1958 figures are lacking.

The production of certain other minerals and metals was as follows ('000 metric tons).—*Diatomite* (main countries): U.S., 334·2; Denmark, 57·2; German F.R., 102·2e; France, 78·0e; U.K., 23·0e; Guatemala, 19·2; Italy, 27·0e; Spain, 12·0e; Algeria, 27·0. *Ilmenite:* U.S., 511·0; Canada, 151·3; Australia, 64·1e; India, 314·0; Norway, 211·9; Finland, 106·5; Malaya, 76·0; French Africa, 32·8; S. Africa, 28·9; Japan, 3·5; Brazil, 5·2; U.A.R. (Egypt), 3·4e; Thailand, 1·0e; Mexico, Portugal, (p). *Nickel:* Canada, 127·8; West Indies, 17·9; U.S., 10·7; New Caledonia, 12·0e; S. Africa, 3·5; Brazil, Finland, Greece, Burma, French Africa, (p); U.S.S.R., P. *Potash* (K₂O equiv. of salts produced): U.S., 1,948·3; France, 1,463·0e; German F.R., 1,716·0; Spain, 214·0e; Chile, 10·0e; Israel, 72·6e; Japan, China, Ethiopia, Italy, Korea, Poland, (p); U.S.S.R., P. THE FOLLOWING ARE IN METRIC TONS—*Beryllium:* Australia, 270e; Brazil, 806; Argentina, 1,000e; India, 544; Belgian Congo, 1,000e; Mozambique, 1,029; S. Rhodesia, 302; S.-W. Africa, 224; U.S., 420; S. Africa, 419; Portugal, 40e; Madagascar, 70e; Uganda, 75; Kenya, N. Rhodesia, U.S.S.R., (p). *Bismuth:* Canada, 207; Mexico, 190; Argentina, 27; Bolivia, 40e; Peru, 406; France, 50e; Spain, 50e; Sweden, 50; Yugoslavia, 77; Japan, 65e; Korea, 90; Mozambique, S.-W. Africa, Uganda, S. Africa, Australia, Brazil, German F.R., China, U.S.S.R., P. *Cadmium:* U.S., 4,388;

MINERAL AND METAL PRODUCTION

Metal Production in 1958   (Metric tons unless otherwise specified; th. indicates thousands, and m. millions of units)

Pig iron (th.)	Steel (th.)	Lead (in ore) (th.)	Lead (smelter) (th.)	Crude magnesite (th.)	Manganese ore (th.)	Nitrogen (th.)	Petroleum (m. bbl.)	Phosphate rock (th.)	Pyrites (th.)	Salt (th.)	Silver (th. oz.)	Sulphur (th. long tons)	Tin (in ore) (long tons)	Tin (smelter) (long tons)	Tungsten (conc.) ‡	Zinc (in ore) (th.)	Zinc (smelter) (th.)	Country
																		N. & C. America
2,877	3,942	167·9	122·3	P	—	375	165·52	—	1,690·7	2,142	31,088	—	—	321	—	522	384·8	228·7	Canada
53,403	77,342	242·6	425·8	447·2	293·1	3,100	2,448·87	15,117·9	989·6	19,877	36,800	4,645·6	544	1,564[7]	3,436	373·8	708·7	United States
496	1,038	201·9	198·0	P	170·0e	—	95·53	—	240e	—	47,590	1,236·9	—	371e	(p)	224·1	57·5	Mexico
—	—	11·0	—	P	1·8	80	37·70	—	—	122	3,485	—	—	—	—	11·8	—	Central America
—	—	(p)	—	—	68·7	—	86·8	—	25·4	261	325	—	—	—	—	6·2	—	West Indies
—	—	8·5e	—	—	—	—	—	—	—	—	—	—	—	—	—	—	—	Other N. American
																		South America
29	244e	30·0	32·0	—	10·0e	—	35·83	—	—	327	1,543	30·0e	47e	39[7]	1,002	36·3	15·4	Argentina
—	—	22·8	95·9	—	—	—	3·44	—	—	(p)	6,051	(p)	17,731	659	3,508	14·2	—	Bolivia
1,400e	1,517	6·0e	6·0e	2·7	695·0	—	19·92	125·0	(p)	800e	326	—	180e	1,401[7]	2,355	—	—	Brazil
—	—	—	—	—	—	—	—	—	—	—	—	—	—	—	—	—	—	British Guiana
370	390	2·6	(p)	—	38·2	200	5·57	90·0e	—	50e	1,776	24·0	—	—	—	1·2	—	Chile
149	118	—	—	—	—	—	47·95	—	—	283	105	6·7	—	—	—	—	—	Colombia
—	—	—	—	—	—	—	3·11	—	—	21	48	21·2	—	—	—	—	—	Ecuador
—	—	121·5	64·1	—	2·9	—	18·73	160·0e	—	108	24,158	—	—	—	888	129·1	29·1	Peru
—	—	—	—	—	8·2	—	950·80	—	14·2	88	—	—	—	—	—	—	—	Venezuela
—	—	—	—	—	—	—	—	—	—	—	—	—	—	—	—	—	—	Other S. American
																		Europe
1,818	2,393	5·5	12·5	1,221·2	—	163	19·55	—	—	515	—	—	—	—	132	5·9	10·6	Austria
5,519	6,011	—	95·9	—	—	310	—	18·0	—	—	—	—	—	8,723	—	—	214·8	Belgium
56e	211	70·7e	26·0	150·0e	80·0e	35	2·21	—	P	60e	P	—	—	—	—	50·0?	8·2	Bulgaria
3,720e	5,532	6·0?	9·0	P	(p)	75	1·00	—	P	160e	1,608	—	200e	—	360	47·0	P	Czechoslovakia
101	188	2·3	—	—	—	33	—	—	255·0	—	561	—	(p)	—	1,020	14·7	149·9	Finland
12,136	14,606	12·3	70·6	—	—	630	10·00	75·0e	375·9	3,519	670	—	—	—	—	—	—	France
16,656	22,785	60·9	134·3	—	—	1,345	32·13	—	565·9	3,564	2,112	—	—	701e	—	85·2	133·2	German Fed. Rep.
—	113	14·0	3·3	70·0	20·0	—	—	—	150·4	95	96	3·0e	—	—	—	18·3	—	Greece
1,100e	1,627	—	—	—	120·0e	25	6·33	—	—	P	64	—	—	—	(p)	136·8	71·4	Hungary
2,166	6,271	56·0	48·0	5·9	43·4	545	10·46	—	1,513·9	1,610	1,334	158·7	—	(p)	—	136·8	71·4	Italy
3,285	3,379	—	—	—	—	—	—	—	—	—	—	—	—	—	—	—	—	Luxembourg
913	1,438	—	—	—	—	415	11·31	—	—	795	—	—	—	17,098	—	—	26·6	Netherlands
508	366	2·1	—	(p)	—	250	—	—	787·4	—	64	—	—	—	—	8·4	45·1	Norway
3,760e	5,628	35·7	35·7	17·0e	—	210	1·30	(p)	210·3e	1,300e	129	50	—	—	—	140·0?	163·0?	Poland
—	—	1·5e	0·9e	—	5·0e	35	—	—	598·5	850e	50	—	1,245	1,267	1,867	—	—	Portugal
737	932	12·0	12·0?	200·0e	—	—	84·49	—	176·8e	850e	643	—	—	—	—	—	—	Rumania
1,373	1,573	67·4	68·4	57·0	37·9	65	—	—	1,765·9	1,829	1,645	3·7e	240e	459e	923	82·9	24·3	Spain
1,254	2,407	42·3	33·1	—	(p)	50	—	—	334·3	—	2,900	—	—	—	522	64·8	—	Sweden
34	232	—	—	—	—	25	—	—	—	125	—	—	—	—	—	—	—	Switzerland
13,201	19,884	4·1	4·0?	—	—	545	0·58	—	4·1e	5,007	27	—	1,087	32,551	100?	60·0	75·8	United Kingdom
780	1,136	89·8	84·3	223·2	4·0e	33	3·27	—	331·2	157e	3,752	—	—	—	600e	100?	31·2	Yugoslavia
4,938	6,801	6·4e	30·0	P	—	352	2·69	—	150·4	1,764	4,500	—	720e	600e	P	P	—	Other European
39,600?	54,900?	300?	310?	P	5,366	P	834·23	6,000?	P	6,500?	25,000	P	13,500?	13,500?	7,500?	365?	365?	U.S.S.R.
																		Africa
—	—	9·7	—	—	—	—	3·42	565·0	24·4	120e	55e	—	—	—	—	31·8	—	Algeria
—	—	—	—	—	34·9	—	0·36	—	—	69	—	—	—	—	—	—	—	Angola
(p)	—	—	—	—	331·1	—	—	—	—	(p)	4,533	15e	11,163	2,644	1,345	114·0	53·4	Belgian Congo
—	—	—	—	—	—	—	—	—	—	15e	—	—	—	—	—	—	—	Ethiopia
—	—	3·3	33·1	—	—	—	3·55	105·9	—	10	—	—	132	—	—	—	—	French Africa
—	—	—	—	—	520·8	—	—	—	—	22e	46	—	—	—	—	—	—	Ghana
—	—	—	(p)	—	—	—	—	(p)	—	19	44	—	—	—	—	—	—	Kenya
—	—	—	—	—	—	—	—	(p)	—	(p)	—	—	(p)	—	—	—	—	Madagascar
—	—	92·9	—	—	410·1	—	0·56	6,335·8	18·3	61	2,411	—	(p)	(p)	—	49·9	—	Morocco
—	—	(p)	—	—	—	—	1·97	—	—	(p)	(p)	—	6,200	—	—	—	—	Nigeria
—	—	12·9	12·9	—	45·3	—	—	—	(p)	—	556	—	—	—	—	34·5	30·7	N. Rhodesia
—	—	—	—	—	—	—	—	—	—	—	—	—	—	—	—	—	—	Sierra Leone
1,583	1,832	(p)	—	72·8	847·4	45	—	216·5	500·9	219	1,795	—	1,416	900	62	—	—	South Africa
80e	60	—	—	—	2·3	—	—	58·9	—	87	265	—	534	503	93	—	—	S. Rhodesia
—	—	76·0	—	—	93·5	—	—	—	—	12e	1,720	—	161	—	—	40·6	—	S.-W. Africa
—	—	5·8	—	(p)	—	—	—	—	—	30	19	—	19	—	—	—	—	Spanish Morocco
—	—	22·5	28·6	—	—	—	—	—	—	160	135	—	—	—	4·1	—	—	Tanganyika
—	—	—	(p)	—	—	—	—	2,278·5	(p)	450e	—	—	—	—	—	—	—	Tunisia
—	100	(p)	—	—	5·0e	30	22·11	600·0e	—	160	—	—	—	—	—	28	—	U.A.R. (Egypt)
—	—	(p)	—	—	—	—	—	0·6	—	10e	(p)	—	35	—	—	—	—	Uganda
—	20	1·2	—	—	11·3	18	17·1	—	—	235	44	—	22	—	—	P	—	Other African
																		Asia
—	—	18·7	17·8	—	1·3	—	3·45	—	—	111	1,961	—	1,200e	—	1,512	11·0	—	Burma
9,500e	8,000	25·0?	16·0?	P	550·0?	180	6·00?	500?	P	10,400?	510	(p)	23,000?	23,000?	20,000?	P	22·0?	China
—	—	—	—	—	—	—	—	—	1,022·1	(p)	P	—	—	—	—	—	—	Cyprus
17	60	—	—	—	—	70	(p)	—	32·5	444	52	6·2	—	—	—	3·9	—	Formosa (Taiwan)
2,167	1,842	4·0	3·4	100·6	1,249·7	130	3·45	14·8	(p)	4,135	110	—	—	—	600e	—	—	India
(p)	—	—	—	—	43·9	—	118·72	(p)	—	275	—	—	23,201	600e	—	—	—	Indonesia
—	—	—	—	—	—	10	0·64	250·0e	—	34	—	—	—	—	—	—	—	Israel
7,705	12,118	36·5	38·5	—	276·2	950	2·56	3,193·4	(p)	1,058	6,728	177·2	1,104	1,307	772	141·2	141·0	Japan
393e	365e	17·0	17·0?	P	(p)	70	—	(p)	(p)	436	248	P	—	—	4,000	35·0e	—	Korea
—	—	—	—	—	—	10	—	—	—	359	—	—	38,458	45,336	52	—	—	Malaya
—	—	17·0	1·0	—	2·0	—	2·27	—	—	300e	—	—	—	—	—	9·0	—	Pakistan
—	—	1·3	—	—	22·3	9	301·36	—	19·3	140	498	1·3e	—	—	—	—	—	Persia
—	66	(p)	—	—	—	—	—	—	8·3	300?	—	—	—	—	—	1·0	—	Philippines
(p)	(p)	3·0	1·5e	(p)	30·2	—	2·40	81·3	—	488	(p)	12·6	7,728	—	658	1·9e	—	Thailand
228	160	—	—	—	—	10	—	—	—	97	—	—	301	—	—	—	—	Turkey
—	—	—	—	—	—	—	—	—	—	—	—	—	—	—	—	—	—	Vietnam, North
—	—	1·2	—	—	125·6e	18	1,293·57	644·2	—	340	320	—	301	—	3,327	P	—	Vietnam, South
—	20	—	—	—	—	—	—	—	—	—	—	—	—	—	—	—	—	Other Asian
																		Australasia
2,293	3,106	332·3	252·6	68·7	56·5	24	—	10·0e	232·7	440?	16,250	—	1,914	2,220	1,452	267·1	116·6	Australia
—	—	—	—	—	—	—	—	—	—	21	—	—	(p)	—	—	(p)	—	New Caledonia
—	—	(p)	(p)	—	—	—	1·85	—	—	—	50	—	—	—	—	—	—	New Zealand
—	—	—	—	—	—	—	—	1,902·9	—	—	—	—	—	—	—	—	—	Other Australasian
196,350	270,700	2,280	2,250	5,400	11,843	10,452	6,617·66	35,400	17,933	73,400	236,800	6,500	152,400	159,700	57,600	3,040	2,730	*World Total*

Canada, 835; Austria, 16; Belgium, 675e; Belgian Congo, 488; France, 177; German F.R., 319; Guatemala, 40e; Italy, 204; Japan, 441; Mexico, 769; Netherlands, 16; Norway, 109; Peru, 50; Poland, 254; N. Rhodesia, 17; S.-W. Africa, 1,219; Spain, 8; U.S.S.R., 470e? U.K., 126; Yugoslavia, 20; Australia, 358. **Cobalt:** U.S., 1,825; Canada, 1,144; Belgian Congo, 6,501; Morocco, 926; N. Rhodesia, 1,609; Australia, 12; New Caledonia, 130; Finland, (p). **Magnesium:** U.S., 27,302; Canada, 5,271; France, 1,735; Italy, 3,800e; Norway, 9,277; U.S.S.R., 40,000e; U.K., 2,375e? Japan, 400e; German F.R., 190; Poland, 150e; China, (p). **Vanadium:** U.S., 2,749; S.-W. Africa, 395; S. Africa, 287; Finland, 390; Argentina, Angola, (p). **Platinum Group Metals** ('000 oz.): U.S., 14·3; Canada, 295·3; Colombia, 16·0; S. Africa, 305·0e? U.S.S.R., 250·0?; Japan, Belgian Congo, Ethiopia, Sierra Leone, Australia, New Guinea, (p). **Diamonds** ('000 carats): Angola, 400; Belgian Congo, 15,900; French Africa, 220; Ghana, 1,900; Liberia, 500; Sierra Leone, 900; S.-W. Africa, 60; Tanganyika, 290; S. Africa, 1,610; Brazil, 150; British Guiana, 20; Venezuela, 75; India, Borneo, Australia, U.S.S.R., (p). **Mercury** (flasks of 76 lb.): U.S., 38,067; Italy, 58,712; Spain, 55,000e; Mexico, 22,568; Yugoslavia, 12,270; Japan, 10,298; Philippines, 3,321; Turkey, 928; Chile, 600e; Peru, 1,978; Czechoslovakia, 725; Bolivia, Colombia, Tunisia, (p); U.S.S.R., China, P.

Source. U.S. Bureau of Mines.

WORLD PRODUCTION OF PRINCIPAL MINERALS AND METALS
(Thousand long tons, gross weight, unless otherwise stated)

	1954	1955	1956	1957	1958
Metals and metallic ores					
Aluminium	2,770	3,090	3,320	3,330	3,470
Antimony ores[1]*	39·35	46·25	47·25	45·25	39·35
Arsenic, white*	33·46	40·35	42·32	38·38	35·43
Bauxite	15,900	17,500	18,500	20,100	20,700
Beryllium[2]	6·90	7·90	11·50	10·60	6·20
Bismuth	1·65	1·95	2·55	2·45	2·15
Cadmium[1]	7·20	8·25	9·00	9·40	8·85
Chromite	3,310	3,590	4,080	4,580	3,620
Cobalt	12·90	13·10	14·30	14·20	13·10
Columbite ⎱ Tantalite ⎰	4·28	5·15	4·00	3·08	2·23
Copper, mine[1]	2,780	3,050	3,380	3,480	3,340
Copper, smelter	2,930	3,240	3,570	3,630	3,510
Gold[3]	35,000	36,000	38,400	39,600	40,400
Iron ore	301,000	363,000	388,000	423,000	397,000
Pig iron[4]	156,200	189,500	198,100	208,200	193,300
Lead, mine[1]	2,030	2,170	2,210	2,330	2,240
Lead, smelter	1,980	2,000	2,150	2,240	2,210
Lithium minerals	92	85	103	109	86
Magnesium	116	118	126	138	90
Manganese ore	9,000	9,800	10,600	11,600	10,700
Mercury[5]	180	185	220	245	248
Molybdenum	31·50	33·50	31·40	34·10	25·20
Nickel[1]*	172	192	207	231	170
Platinum group[6]	940	1,080	1,100	1,310	880
Selenium[7]	1,402	1,622	1,923	1,940	1,630
Silver[3]	214,400	224,000	225,000	230,100	236,800
Steel	220,400	265,700	279,100	287,500	266,400
Strontium*	4·16	7·26	15·64	11·60	11·70
Tellurium[7]	106	192	241	287	214
Tin, mine	189	197	199	200	152
Tin, refined	197	198	200	195	160
Titanium, ilmenite	1,103	1,255	1,600	1,761	1,528
Titanium, rutile	51	68	109	139	92
Titanium metal	5·33	8·50	17·04	19·98	7·02
Tungsten[8]	69·88	73·52	73·62	67·02	56·69
Uranium[9]*	—	—	15·00	22·00	31·19
Vanadium[1]*	3·45	3·57	3·78	3·83	3·78
Zinc, mine[1]	2,620	2,860	3,050	3,130	2,990
Zinc, slab zinc	2,410	2,650	2,790	2,880	2,690
Zirconium[10]	60	76	115	144	87
Non-metallic minerals					
Asbestos	1,495	1,735	1,760	1,845	1,800
Barytes	2,100	2,400	2,800	3,100	2,300
Cement (hydraulic)	191,900	214,600	232,700	243,000	258,800
Corundum	8·86	6·89	9·84	8·86	9·84
Diamonds, indust.[11]	16,800	17,500	18,300	20,800	22,000
Diatomite	650	690	680	690	750
Felspar*	930	1,050	1,090	1,040	1,020
Fluorspar	1,210	1,380	1,680	1,710	1,570
Graphite	170	270	250	360	300
Gypsum	27,500	31,600	32,500	32,700	32,900
Magnesite, crude	4,000	4,100	4,800	4,900	5,300
Mica	128	143	138	143	143
Nitrogen*	7,190	7,900	8,430	9,440	10,287
Phosphate rock	30,000	30,200	33,900	32,600	34,800
Potash[12]	6,500	7,200	7,500	7,800	7,900
Pyrites	15,000	16,500	17,700	17,800	17,700
Salt	59,500	63,600	67,100	69,900	72,200
Talc, pyrophyllite and soapstone	1,400	1,600	1,700	1,800	1,800
Sulphur, native	6,300	7,000	8,000	7,300	6,500
Vermiculite*	216	234	227	222	212
Fuels					
Lignite[13]	487	527	557	585	605
Bituminous coal and anthracite[13]	1,453	1,573	1,662	1,713	1,793
Coke[13]	253	285	300	309	296
Fuel briquettes	96,900	102,400	106,000	107,800	104,300
Natural gas[14]	265,000	282,000	310,000	329,000	...
Peat*	8,000	9,000	9,000	9,000	7,000
Petroleum, crude[15]	5,017	5,626	6,125	6,451	6,618
Carbon black†	0·76	0·92	0·98	1·00	0·93

* Excl. allowance for U.S.S.R. † Excl. allowance for Canada. [1] Metal content. [2] Concentrates. [3] '000 troy oz. [4] Incl. ferro-alloys. [5] '000 flasks. [6] Pt. Pd, Ir, Os, Rh, Ru. [7] '000 lb. [8] Concentrates of 60% WO_3. [9] U_3O_8. [10] Zircon content. [11] '000 carats. [12] K_2O equivalent. [13] Million tons. [14] Million cu.m. [15] Million bbl. SOURCE. Mainly U.S. Bureau of Mines.

Zinc. Zinc followed much the same pattern in 1958 as its sister metal lead—over-supply, the cessation of U.S. government purchases, U.S. import quotas and U.N. recommendations on the limitation of exports. Sales of Soviet zinc were maintained at a high level. Being less dependent than lead on government support, however, the zinc-producing industry was able to adjust more quickly to the changed conditions. The reduction in output was greater than for lead and the autumn market recovery was more marked and heralded 12 months of rising prices. World mine production in 1958 fell by 4·5% to 2,990,000 tons, while smelter production was nearly 7% lower at 2,690,000 tons. Mine production actually rose in Canada (378,670 tons), Japan (138,960 tons), Poland (137,800 tons), Italy (133,850 tons) and many smaller producing countries and most Communist countries were believed to have increased their output. In the United States, however, production fell by 22% to 367,470 tons and there were sharp declines in Australia (262,910 tons), Mexico (220,560 tons) and Peru (127,020 tons). By the end of 1958 production and consumption were roughly in balance; consumption showed a rising tendency but surplus capacity remained to meet any marked increase in demand. Meanwhile it was considered that once the current phase was passed rising consumption over the following 15 years would require an increase of about 1·5 million tons in world mine production. (*See* also COAL; EUROPEAN COAL AND STEEL COMMUNITY; IRON AND STEEL; METALLURGY; PETROLEUM.) (P. E. G.)

MINERALOGY. In the field of experimental synthesis new data on rock-forming and ore minerals were obtained. The determination of the phase relations and mix crystal compositions in the synthetic system FeS-ZnS made it possible to use the iron content of sphalerites deposited in equilibrium with pyrrhotite in geologic thermometry. This thermometer had been applied in more than 100 ore deposits. In a hydrothermal investigation of amphiboles the stability fields for tremolite, pargasite and magnesian riebeckite were determined and phase diagrams for these amphiboles provided [P. H. Abelson (ed.), *Researches in Geochemistry*, 301-335, 377-396 (New York, 1959)]. A calcium analogue of chondrodite—calciochondrodite—was prepared hydrothermally from tricalcium silicate (*Amer. Min.*, 43, 818-823). New chemical, optical and X-ray data were obtained for dumortierite and the formula revised to (Al, Fe)$_7$BSi$_3O_{18}$ without (OH) (*Mineral. Mag.*, 31, 901-907). A synthetic analogue of braunite was prepared in the form of a Mn_2O_3 solid solution ranging from Mn_2O_3 as one end member to a silica content of at least 40 weight per cent SiO_2, Si^{+4} substituting for Mn^{+4} in the Mn_2O_3 lattice (*Amer. J. Sci.*, 257, 297-315). In phase equilibrium studies in the subsolvus region of the system $NaAlSiO_4$-$NaAlSi_3O_8$-H_2O, analcites with a wide range of solid solution were synthesized, the water content of the analcites varying linearly with variation in silica (*Amer. Min.*, 44, 300-313). An olivine-spinel type inversion was established in the iron olivine fayalite, with a transition temperature of 600°C. at 38,000 bars pressure (*ibid.*, 44, 659-661).

The crystal structures of the following minerals were determined: inyoite (CaB$_3O_3$(OH)$_5$.4H$_2$O) shown to contain isolated [B$_3O_3$(OH)$_5$]$^{.2}$ polyions formed by two BO$_4$ tetrahedra sharing corners and one BO$_3$ triangle linking the two tetrahedra (*Acta Cryst.*, 12, 162-171); pyroxmangite [(Mn, Fe, Mg)SiO$_3$] showing chains of SiO$_4$ tetrahedra parallel to [001] with seven tetrahedra in the identity period of the chain (*ibid.*, 12, 177-181); protoenstatite (MgSiO$_3$), a fully extended SiO$_3$ chain structure but with one of the magnesium atoms showing an irregular co-ordination which was held to account for the instability of the compound at low temperatures (*ibid.*, 12, 515-519); coesite, the dense high-pressure form of silica, monoclinic, with a new tetrahedral network of four rings showing some resemblance to the alumina-silica network of the feldspars.

Among new minerals described were cornubite ($Cu_5(AsO_4)_2(OH)_4$), monoclinic, dimorphous with cornwallite, from Cornwall (*Mineral. Mag.*, 32, 1-5); delhayelite, orthorhombic, a complex Ca, Na, K aluminium silicate from a melilite nephelinite from the Belgian Congo (*ibid.*, 32, 6-9); delrioite ($CaO.SrO.V_2O_5.3H_2O$) from Colorado (*Amer. Min.*, 44, 261-264) and ningyoite, a new orthorhombic uranous phosphate from Japan with formula close to $Ca U(PO_4)_2.2H_2O$ but containing rare earths (*ibid.*, 44, 633-650).   (C. E. T.)

BIBLIOGRAPHY. E. W. Heinrich, *Mineralogy and Geology of Radioactive Raw Materials* (New York, 1958); W. Eitel, *Structural Conversions in Crystalline Systems and their Importance for Geological Problems*, Geological Society of America, Special Paper 66 (New York, 1958); P. F. Kerr, *Optical Mineralogy*, 3rd ed. (New York, 1959); C. M. Riley, *Our Mineral Resources* (New York, 1959).

MISSILES. Information on guided weapons programmes outside the United States was published in increasing quantities during 1959. Anxiety to sell developed missiles to allies changed the British policy of silence; more also became known about the French, Swedish, Japanese, Italian and Swiss programmes. Knowledge of Soviet missiles still rested largely on conjecture, a few announcements of tests, the 1957 anniversary parade and the satellite programme. Nevertheless, interest outside the United States centred on the Soviet ballistic missile programme because it was of the first importance for the world balance of power. A growing series of bombardment weapons for use on the battlefield had been obvious for some years, but range had been growing and it was generally assumed during 1959 with a ballistic missile of at least 1,200-mi. range. The multi-stage intercontinental rocket which was tested in Aug. 1957 was considered to be in series production and some western observers believed it to be in service. The moon rockets showed the excellence of its guidance. In general, the intelligence appreciation was that operational numbers would be able to hit the United States in 1962. An official Soviet booklet said that production of intercontinental missiles was successfully under way; and Nikita S. Khrushchev said that the U.S.S.R. had a missile with 8,700-mi. range, which made Americans wonder if they were being threatened across every border rather than exclusively from the north. Soviet progress in surface-to-air (anti-aircraft) missiles was almost as important to the east-west balance and certainly as little known. The day that these weapons, especially with atomic warheads, could keep bombers from important bases, the U.S. and British bomber forces could no longer claim to be deterrents. The surface-to-air weapon shown in 1957 (generally called the M-2) seemed to have been in extended production and Khrushchev's statements indicated great confidence in his air defence command.

Great Britain made substantial progress on a number of missiles during the year. It became known that the Blue Streak ballistic missile was much closer to the United States' intercontinental Atlas and Titan weapons than to the intermediate Thor and Jupiter. Its range was generally conceded to be about 2,500 mi., though it might turn out to be substantially more than this with the lighter U.S. warheads which were made available under new legislation. The British programme concentrated heavily in its early days on the destruction of aircraft, and operational surface-to-air missiles progressed steadily during 1959. A second R.A.F. Bloodhound base became operational, Thunderbird regiments were formed in the army and four County-class ships to carry Seaslugs were laid down. Later versions were being designed with nuclear warheads. In addition, the Firestreak air-to-air missile went into service in the new R.A.F. and R.N. all-weather fighters—the Javelin and Sea Vixen—and was under

development in an advanced version which would be more flexible in service. One important new British missile was announced during the year—the surface-to-surface solid-fuel weapon Blue Water, which English Electric was developing for the army. This was designed to replace the Corporal missile, a U.S. weapon which had been adopted for training but was not well suited to battlefield conditions. The Australian Malkara anti-tank missile was adopted as a short-range weapon for the army against two competing British private ventures and the well-tested French SS-10 and SS-11. The larger anti-tank weapon being developed by Fairey Aviation was cancelled. The future of Bomber command was increasingly linked to the Blue Steel air-to-surface missile, under development by A. V. Roe, which would free its aircraft from having to approach close to defended targets.

The French had an interesting array of defensive missiles and announced their decision to develop a ballistic missile with a nuclear warhead to be in service by 1970. The SS-10 and SS-11 gave the French army the protection against tanks it required, but the Parca and R.422 anti-aircraft missiles were not apparently an adequate defence against aircraft. A U.S. system, the Hawk, appeared to be the choice and would be built by a consortium of France, the German Federal Republic, Belgium, Italy and the Netherlands. Another group led by the German Federal Republic, but not including France, was planning to build the U.S. Sidewinder air-to-air missile. One unusual project which might have considerable possibilities was the B.B.10 air-to-surface weapon which transmitted pictures to the aircraft from which it was launched and controlled.

Swedish missiles, like Swedish aeroplanes, were being developed in small numbers to the highest international standards. Even so, the services were not adopting them unless they were the best. It had been expected that the air-to-air Robot 321A would be used in the Draken fighter, but the Sidewinder was chosen. Equally, the British Bloodhound was chosen as a first-generation surface-to-air weapon. Robot 304, however, was put into production for the attack wings of the Royal Swedish Air Force, and the claim that this was the first powered and guided bomb to reach squadron service anywhere was probably correct.

In Switzerland two ground-to-air weapons and one anti-tank weapon had been developed, giving the defence ministry extra backing for its historic defensive policy. Italy had announced one air-to-air weapon and two surface-to-air weapons and Japan was developing two air-to-air missiles and one anti-tank missile.

In the United States significant progress was made in 1959 with the big strategic ballistic missiles, Atlas and Titan, which were capable of carrying thermonuclear warheads a quarter of the way round the globe. The Titan was successful in its first four test flights, although not in the fifth. Only the first stage of this two-stage missile was tested. Early in the year the Atlas was plagued by a series of unidentified failures, but subsequently four successful flights were made and Atlas was pronounced operational by the air force in September. The first flight test of the operational ablation nose cone was conducted successfully in October. Early in 1960 President Dwight D. Eisenhower announced that in 14 recent test launchings, at ranges of more than 5,000 mi., Atlas had been striking on an average within 2 mi. of the target. During 1959 the programme leading to a second-generation intercontinental ballistic missile, known as Minuteman, was in the component development stage. In contrast with Atlas and Titan, the Minuteman employed a lighter warhead and used solid, instead of liquid, propellant rocket engines. It was designed for an extremely fast reaction time and was to be fired from underground concrete emplacements. Because of the somewhat lower performance and higher weight of the solid propellent system, Minuteman would use three powered stages. It was believed that solid propellent engines would be improved to the point where their better handling characteristics and greater readiness would lead to their replacing liquid engines for most military purposes. This trend was also seen in the intermediate-range ballistic missiles (I.R.B.M.). The liquid-propelled Thor and Jupiter both became operational during the year. The navy's Polaris, the first I.R.B.M. to use solid propellents, was successfully fired both from the shore and from a surface ship, and three nuclear-powered submarines designed specifically to deploy Polaris missiles were launched.

Among smaller U.S. missiles, a new programme was initiated by the air force for an air-launched stand-off missile. The army announced the development of the Shillelagh, a new, lightweight, surface-to-surface missile for close support of troops, and the Redeye, a portable, shoulder-fired missile designed to enable troops to destroy low-flying strafing or bombing aircraft. The army also broke with precedent by initiating procurement of the French Nord SS-10 and SS-11 anti-tank guided missiles.

The only complete ballistic missile defence system under active development in the United States was the army's Nike-Zeus. There was considerable controversy as to whether this constituted an adequate system. In comparison with enemy aircraft, ballistic missile warheads are generally very small and enter very high and very fast, creating a difficult detection problem. Moreover, an enemy could produce, at little expense, large numbers of very light decoys which would be practically indistinguishable from actual warheads. An early warning system using giant radar installations was being installed along the Arctic circle and considerable sums of money were being spent in the search for a really effective defence system. (*See* also COMMONWEALTH ARMIES; COMMONWEALTH AIR FORCES; COMMONWEALTH NAVIES.)

(D. L. B.; R. C. T.)

MONACO. Sovereign principality on the Mediterranean coast, 9 mi. E. of Nice, bounded on all land sides by the French *département* of Alpes Maritimes, and united to France by customs union. Area: 0·578 sq.mi. Pop.: (1946 census) 19,242; (1956 census) 20,422, incl. 2,696 Monegasques, 11,209 French, 4,490 Italians and 655 British; wholly divided between the three communes Monaco-Ville, Monte Carlo and La Condamine. Language: French. Religion: Roman Catholic. Sovereign, Prince Rainier III; ministers of state in 1959: Henri Soum and (from Feb. 1) Emile Pelletier. Monetary unit (small denominations only): Monegasque franc (= French franc).

History. On Jan. 29, 1959, Prince Rainier III suspended the Monegasque 1911 constitution. He did so, he explained, because of the " continuously hostile attitude " of the 18-member National Council elected in Jan. 1958. He dissolved the National Council and appointed an eight-member delegation to help him to administer the principality. He also announced his intention to bring in various reforms, including women's franchise.

Rainier's action followed the council's attempts to withhold money from him by refusing to approve the budget unless they were granted more power. Joseph Simon, president of the dissolved council, claimed that Rainier had brought about a *coup d'état*. " My husband ", commented Princess Grace, " is no dictator. He is working in the interest of the people." On Sept. 14, the *Bulletin Officiel de la Principauté de Monaco* stated that in the event of the prince's death his wife would be the regent until his son Albert (b. March 14, 1958) came of age.

On Jan. 30, Emile Pelletier, former minister of the interior in the de Gaulle cabinet, was appointed by Rainier minister of state to succeed Henri Soum. This post, equivalent to that of prime minister, must, in accordance with Franco-Monegasque treaty arrangements, always be held by a Frenchman.

Princess Caroline and Prince Albert of Monaco out in Paris, where they were on a visit with their parents in October.

On Oct. 12 Prince Rainier and Princess Grace paid a state visit to Paris and on Nov. 4 to Rome. They were also received by Pope John XXIII. On May 5 it was announced that ex-king Farouk of Egypt had become a subject of the principality. As a Monegasque he would enjoy a tax-free life.

On Dec. 13, Aristoteles Onassis, the Greek-born shipowner (naturalized Argentinian), revealed that for several months he had " more than 500,000 shares " of the *Société des Bains de Mer de Monaco*, the company which owns the Monte Carlo casino, its best hotels and the opera house. Until then it was believed that Onassis owned 420,000 of one million shares of Fr. 500 each.   (X.)

MONGOLIA. People's republic of eastern Asia*, bounded N. by the U.S.S.R. and E., S. and S.W. by China. Area (1954 Soviet est.): 591,119 sq.mi. Pop. (no census ever taken): (1925 est.) 651,700; (1957 est.) 1,130,000. Language: Mongol. Religion: Lamaistic Buddhism. Capital: Ulan Bator, pop. (1957 est.) 120,000. First secretary of the Mongolian People's Revolutionary (Communist) party and chairman of the council of ministers, Yumzhagiin Tsedenbal; chairman of the presidium of the Great People's Khural, Zhamsarangiin Sambu. Monetary unit: *tugrik* (=Soviet *rouble*).

* By the end of 1958 Mongolia was recognized by the following 15 states: Albania, Bulgaria, Burma, China, Czechoslovakia, Germany (Eastern), Hungary, India, Indonesia, Korea (North), Poland, Rumania, U.S.S.R., Vietnam (North) and Yugoslavia.

History. On March 30, 1959, many important leaders in Mongolia were victims of a purge within the Mongolian People's Revolutionary (Communist) party. This was the outcome of a four-day session of the party's central committee. Dashiin Damba, already demoted in Nov. 1958 from the post of first to that of second secretary, was dismissed from the Politburo, together with three other full members (B. Damdin, D. Lamchin and Ch. Surenzhav) and two alternate members. Surenzhav also ceased to be chairman of the Great People's Khural (National Assembly). All those in disgrace were accused of insincerity towards the party, lack of principles, profound ideological backwardness, conservatism, inertia and arrogance. They had probably resisted the collectivization of the raising of livestock.

L. Tsende, the newly elected party second secretary, presented to the Politburo a report on the revision of the three-year (1958-60) development plan adopted by the 13th congress of the M.P.R.P.: the increase in livestock (estimated at 24 million head in 1959) and the increase in virgin land under cultivation were the more important changes approved by the central committee. The revised plan stipulated that by

1961 about 800,000 ha. of the virgin land must be under cultivation, so that the 1961 harvest could cover all national needs in grain—a revolutionary step in a country where people traditionally have lived by their animals and despised all agricultural work.

At Sain-Shand, in the Middle Gobi *aimak* (province), extraction of crude petroleum began during the year. In July it was announced at Ulan Bator that 97% of the livestock farms belonged to large co-operatives.

Yu. Tsedenbal, the party's first secretary and prime minister, visited N. S. Khrushchev at Yalta (Aug. 20), paid an official visit to India (Sept. 10-16) and had a talk with Chou En-lai in Peking (Oct. 3). (K. M. S.)

MONUMENTS AND MEMORIALS.
Among the more notable monuments and memorials unveiled during 1959 were the following:

Memorial to King George VI
May 25   The new King George VI Memorial Youth hostel at Holland house, London, was opened by the queen.

War Memorials
April 1   General Francisco Franco inaugurated the vast new Spanish civil war memorial in the Valley of the Fallen, about 30 mi. north of Madrid.

May 3   Sir Anthony Eden unveiled a plaque on the war memorial of the Queen's Westminster Rifles, commemorating those members of the regiment killed in World War II.

Oct. 5   Prince Albert of the Belgians unveiled a memorial to the Belgian resistance movement in World War II at Louvain, Belgium.

Nov. 15   The submarine war memorial on the Victoria embankment, London, which was altered to commemorate the 82 submarines lost in World War II, was unveiled by Rear Admiral B. W. Taylor.

Literary
April 19   Evelyn Waugh unveiled a bronze head of Mgr. Ronald Knox by Arthur Pollen in Trinity college library, Oxford. The work was financed by the Knox Memorial fund.

April 22   A statue of Lord Byron in the Borghese gardens, Rome, was unveiled by Queen Elizabeth the Queen Mother.

Miscellaneous
April 14   A 100-ft. memorial bell tower on Capitol hill, Washington, was dedicated to Senator Robert A. Taft.

May 27   A memorial plaque to Admiral Sir Francis Beaufort, inventor of the Beaufort scale, was unveiled in London by F. N. Beaufort-Palmer, his great-grandson.

June 27   The international friendship monument at the Moses-Saunders power dam on the Canadian-U.S. border, 70 ft. above the St. Lawrence seaway, was unveiled by the queen in the presence of the vice-president of the United States, Richard M. Nixon.

July 13   A memorial to Dame Christabel Pankhurst, which was added to the statue of her mother, Mrs. Emmeline Pankhurst, was unveiled in Victoria Tower gardens, London, by Lord Kilmuir.

Sept. 12   Otto Grotewohl, prime minister of the German Democratic Republic, unveiled a monument to the 92,000 women who died in the Ravensbrück concentration camp during World War II. The camp itself was re-opened as a national memorial.

Oct. 17   Lady Baden-Powell laid the foundation-stone of the Baden-Powell memorial house in South Kensington, London. A centenary edition of Lord Baden-Powell's book, *Scouting for Boys*, was placed beneath it.

Oct. 28   A statue in memory of Sir Walter Raleigh, the explorer, was unveiled in Whitehall, London, by the U.S. ambassador in London, J. H. Whitney.

Lady Astor, the first woman in Britain to become a member of parliament, speaking at the unveiling in London on July 13 of a memorial to Dame Christabel Pankhurst, the suffragette leader. Seated (left to right) are Lord Attlee, Mrs. V. L. Pandit, Lord Kilmuir, Dame Vera L. Mathews, Lord Pethwick-Lawrence and Lady Mountbatten. (Inset) The bronze relief forming part of the memorial.

MOROCCO. Independent kingdom of northwest Africa, with both Mediterranean and Atlantic coastlines, divided until the end of 1955 into French protectorate, the Spanish protectorate (*see* also SPANISH OVERSEAS TERRITORIES) and the international zone of Tangier. Area and populations:

	Area (sq.mi.)	Population (1952 est.)
Former French protectorate . . .	153,870	8,004,000*
Former Spanish protectorate (both zones) .	17,631	1,132,000†
Places of Spanish sovereignty‡ . . .	823	188,000
Tangier	232	162,000
Total	172,556	9,486,000

* Incl. 362,814 Europeans and 199,156 Jews. † 1950 est. ‡ Alhucemas Ceuta, Chafarinas, Melilla, Peñon de Veles and the Ifni territory.

Pop. (1958 est.): 10,330,000, mostly Arabs and Berbers who are Moslem and speak Arabic (64%) or Berber (22%) or are bilingual (14%). Chief towns (pop., 1952 est.; Europeans in brackets): Rabat (cap.) 156,000 (41,000); Casablanca 700,000 (135,000); Marrakesh 215,000 (12,000); Fez 180,000 (15,000); Tangier 162,000 (40,000); Meknès 140,000 (21,000); Tetuan 94,000. King (Melek), Mohammed V ben Yusuf. Prime minister, Mulay Abdallah Ibrahim. Main exports: phosphates, iron ore, barley, lead, dried fish, citrus fruit. Monetary unit: *dirham* (14·17 dirhams =£1 sterling).

History. On Jan. 26, 1959, the Istiklal party split between the supporters of Mehdi Ben Barka (left-wing) and those of Allal el-Fassi (traditionalists). Ben Barka's party, which won the adherence of several members of the Parti Démocratique de l'Indépendance, took the name Union Nationale des Forces Populaires (U.N.F.P.). It gave its support to the government of Mulay Abdallah Ibrahim.

On Feb. 2, Addi ou-Bihi, formerly governor of Tafilatet, who had rebelled in Jan. 1957 against the Istiklal government, was condemned to death with seven of his followers (four of them *in absentia*). Six of the accused were sentenced to life imprisonment and 20 to terms of imprisonment up to 20 yr.

The king made several trips abroad: in February to Corsica and Madagascar, in July to France. He took back to Corsica in his aircraft company sergeant-major Ignace Cacciaguerra, who had been captured by the army of liberation in Feb. 1957. In the autumn the king also made official tours to the Rif and to southern Morocco.

French officials serving in Morocco (481 in all) signed an appeal for negotiations in Algeria; five were recalled or dismissed by the French government. Horma Ould Babana, a former Mauritanian deputy, who favoured the union of his country with Morocco, was appointed Moroccan ambassador to Libya.

Proceedings were started for the expropriation of lands on which French colonists had been settled. On Aug. 1 bandits captured a mixed Franco-Moroccan boundary commission in the Ich region, to the west of Colomb-Béchar. The members of the commission were released after a few days. These events aroused considerable feeling both in the French government and press.

The town of Fedala took the king's name and called itself Mohammedia. When the Arab league met at Casablanca on Sept. 2, Tunisia and Iraq did not attend, but the " provisional government of the Algerian republic " was represented. The king opened the meeting declaring: " The victory of Algeria will complete the freedom of Moghreb." The league decided to intervene in the United Nations against the " war of extermination " in Algeria.

An agreement was signed with Enrico Mattei, the head of Ente Nazionale Idrocarburi, for the construction of an Italo-Moroccan petrol refinery.

A new Moroccan Central bank (Banque du Maroc) was set up on July 1, 1959. It assumed the sole right to issue notes. On Oct. 17 the Moroccan franc was devalued by 20·44%. A new national currency, the *dirham*, worth 100 Moroccan new francs, was introduced. At the same time Morocco established control of monetary transfers with France and other countries of the franc zone. Abd-ur-Rahim Bouabid,

The King of Morocco (right) receives Ferhat Abbas, the Algerian rebel prime minister, to discuss de Gaulle's offer of Sept. 16.

minister of national economy, described these measures as part of the government programme to " liberate " the Moroccan economy from dependence on France.

Another measure aimed at the protection of the dirham against currency speculators was the decision to put an end to the special status of Tangier. The government decided to integrate Tangier economically with the rest of the country.

Between Jan. and the end of Sept. 1959 Spain reduced its forces in the former northern zone from 60,000 to 11,000. At the end of September only 5,000 Spanish foreign legionaries remained near Tetuan. France still had at the end of the year about 25,000 men of its air and naval forces on Moroccan territory.

The U.S. government announced on Oct. 30 its intention to withdraw the U.S. forces from Morocco, that is, from the three major air bases (Nouaseur, Sidi Slimane and Benguerir), from the auxiliary base at Boulhaut and from the naval base at Port-Lyautey. Discussions on this subject started in 1957 when King Mohammed visited President Dwight D. Eisenhower in Washington, D.C. A U.S. aid agreement signed in Washington on June 30 provided $40 million to replace French aid for Morocco's development programme. On Dec. 22 President Eisenhower visited King Mohammed at Casablanca. (HU. DE.; X.)

MOTOR CYCLE AND CYCLE INDUSTRY.

The year 1959 was one of record sales in Britain of motor cycles, including scooters and mopeds, both British and imported. Total sales reached 350,000—more than twice the 1958 figure. The increase was brought about mainly by the removal of hire-purchase control in Sept. 1958, which began to take full effect in 1959, assisted by the reduction in the purchase tax on motor cycles by 5% to 25% in April 1959. Deliveries to the home market of British motor cycles and scooters rose to more than 100,000 during the year. Besides the B.S.A.-Sunbeam and Triumph four-stroke scooters, there were 11 other makers, all using Villiers two-stroke engines. The Raleigh moped introduced in late 1958 gained rapidly in popularity. By July 1959 British moped deliveries were being made at the rate of 120,000 a year, mostly to the home market, contributions to this soaring trade being made by the Phillips and Norman organizations, which were able to offer single-, two- and three-speed models. The 5% reduction in purchase tax was too small to have any significant effect on home cycle sales, but the long, dry summer coupled with a £10,000 advertising campaign by the cycle industry and trade helped sales to reach nearly 1 million in 1959, 14% more than in 1958.

Exports of motor cycles began to rise in 1959 from the lowered business of 1958. A total of 32,339 machines was exported in the first nine months, their value with engines and parts being estimated at £5,352,000, compared with 28,038 machines valued at £5,070,000 in the same period of 1958. The 1959 figure included about 4,000 mopeds and 1,000 scooters, indicating that British models had already entered the export market strongly despite competition from Italy, the German Federal Republic, France and Austria. Britain had become virtually the only country in the world exporting orthodox motor cycles. Exports of cycles and parts in 1959 did not reach the level of the previous year, but the figure of £1·25 million for sales abroad nevertheless confirmed Britain as the world's leading exporter of cycles, for it accounted for half the world's trade in cycles.

The total number of motor cycles registered in Britain reached a record 1·75 million in 1959, including about 375,000 mopeds and 250,000 scooters. While the total amount of cycle traffic was estimated at 60% of the 1938 figure of between 10 million and 12 million, usage of juvenile bicycles and tricycles rose to an estimated figure of 3 million.

The Earls Court motor cycle and cycle show having become biennial, the next one was to take place between Nov. 12 and 19, 1960. However, several firms took steps to bring their models before agents in comparable ways in 1959, notably Triumph motor cycles and Elswick-Hopper cycles, mopeds and scooters. Motor-cycle design continued along the lines established during the previous three years. The most remarkable postwar twin two-stroke design, the Ariel Leader, was modified and lightened to form an additional model, the Ariel Arrow, of sporting appearance and performance. Fibreglass enclosure was adopted by other firms, notably on the Bond scooter. (H. Bfe.)

MOTOR INDUSTRY.
" The motor car industry has been the main pace maker of the industrial boom during the last twelve months." Thus, aptly, the *Financial Times*, in a leading article, summarized impressions of the outstanding performance of British car makers in 1959. Production set new records and exceeded all expectations. The output of passenger cars in April reached a peak of 25,116 per week, compared with a previous peak of 21,574 per week in May 1958 and an average throughout the year 1958 of 19,841 per week. Total output of cars in the first nine months of the year was 827,394, an increase of 5·6% over the output of 782,996 units in the first nine months of 1958. Production had naturally tailed off somewhat in the summer months but it was up to a record 27,589 per week in October.

Commercial vehicle output also increased sharply in 1959, with demand stimulated by the abolition of purchase tax on commercial vehicle chassis in the April budget. In September production reached a new record of 8,449 vehicles per week, compared with a previous peak of 7,925 per week in June 1959 and an average of 5,903 per week throughout 1958. Total output of commercial vehicles in the first nine months was 265,073, an increase of 15·4% over the output of 229,674 in the same period of 1958.

Despite the rapid rate of expansion, the leading car manufacturers publicly expressed confidence that the boom would continue well into the future. In October a deputy managing director of the British Motor corporation (B.M.C.) said that the group's target was 1 million cars per year within two years compared with a current rate of about 670,000 per year. The newly formed Standard-Triumph International said that by the end of November, that is within three months of the sale of the tractor interests of the group to Massey-Ferguson, car output was expected to have replaced the loss of 70,000 units previously represented by tractor output. The group was spending £1·5 million on a new assembly hall designed to

raise output to at least 185,000 a year in 1960. Ford Motors' confidence in the future was shown by proposals to spend a further £45 million following the completion, during 1959, of the previous £70 million plan. Similarly the Rootes group announced its intention of spending £10 million on expansion over the next year or so. Over-all, therefore, the industry was looking to increased production in 1960 and it was estimated that total output of cars might rise, in peak periods, to an annual rate of 1·6 million.

Some outside observers, at least, expressed doubts about the British motor industry's ability to maintain the projected rate of expansion. Overhanging the whole situation was the still unresolved future of European trade relations. On the positive side, however, three things became increasingly clear during 1959. First, the opening of the new motorway, M.1, and the Hammersmith flyover promised a new era in the development of Britain's road programme. Secondly, in a prosperous democracy, car ownership was coming more and more to be regarded as an essential part of modern life. Thirdly, the industry continued to do outstandingly well in export markets (*see* below).

Production in the other major European manufacturing countries was also expanding in 1959. In the German Federal Republic 1,077,932 cars were produced in the first nine months of 1959, compared with 960,262 in the first nine months of 1958. Similarly, west German commercial vehicle production was 157,688 in the first nine months compared with 137,721 in the same period of 1958. Thus west German car (but not commercial vehicle) production considerably exceeded U.K. production although the British industry's plans, if successful, would enable it to catch up in 1960. France, the next largest producer, manufactured 812,470 cars in Jan.-Sept. 1959 against 679,192 in Jan.-Sept. 1958, and 109,471 commercial vehicles against 140,438. France's car production was thus slightly below that of the U.K. and commercial vehicle production was considerably below. Italy's car production increased to 332,801 in the first three-quarters of 1959 compared with 280,370 in the first three-quarters of 1958, but commercial vehicle production was down to 20,073 compared with 26,012.

In the United States production was estimated to be running at about 6·3 million cars per year compared with an actual 4,258,000 in 1958. Towards the end of the year, however, the effects of the prolonged strike in the steel industry were being felt and it seemed probable that part of the production scheduled for the last quarter of 1959 might have to be carried over into 1960. The U.S. industry, like that in the United Kingdom, was looking to expansion, with the 1960 output forecast at 6·5 million. Furthermore, the chairman of General Motors forecast that by 1965 a normal motor industry output for the year might be 7 million cars. Two fundamental changes were taking place in the U.S. market. First, imports of foreign cars were increasing rapidly and it seemed likely that the year's total would exceed 600,000, or 12 times the 1955 level of imports. Secondly, there was a great upsurge in the demand for the smaller home-produced car in the $2,000 range. These cars, with engines of from 80 h.p. to 100 h.p., were large by most European standards but were " small " in relation to the more expensive ranges of U.S. production. Output by the " big three " (Chrysler, Ford and General Motors) of smaller cars, so defined, amounted to about 250,000 in 1959 but was expected to be between 750,000 and 1 million in 1960. It seemed that U.S. manufacturers were backing the smaller car range to meet growing imports of foreign cars and their spokesmen forecast that such imports would fall by as much as 16% in 1960. Importers, on the other hand, by no means shared this opinion, and were developing service facilities in expectation of a still expanding market. Not the least interesting aspect

TABLE I. MOTOR VEHICLE PRODUCTION (thousands)

	1938		1957		1958	
	Pass- enger cars	Com- mercial vehicles	Pass- enger cars	Com- mercial vehicles	Pass- enger cars	Com- mercial vehicles
United States .	2,019·6	488·8	6,113·3	1,107·2	4,257·6	877·2
German Fed. Rep.	274·8*	63·5*	959·0	252·8	1,180·8	313·9
United Kingdom	341·0	103·8	860·8	288·3	1,051·6†	312·8†
France . .	182·4	45·0	723·8	204·1	924·2	203·5
U.S.S.R. . .	27·0	182·4‡	113·6	381·9§	122·4	388·8§
Italy . .	59·0	11·8	318·5	33·9	369·0	34·8
Canada . .	123·8	42·3	340·0	71·5	297·0	58·4
Japan . .	1·8	22·6	47·1	134·9	50·4	137·3
World‖ . .	3,050·0	1,017·0	9,700·0	2,650·0	8,540·4	2,478·8

* Prewar Germany. † Year of 53 weeks. ‡ Excl. buses and wheeled tractors.
§ Excl. tractors. ‖ Approximate figures only, and excl. China mainland.
SOURCE. U.N. *Statistical Yearbook 1958*; U.N. *Monthly Bulletin of Statistics*.

TABLE II. MOTOR VEHICLE EXPORTS (thousands)

	1938		1957		1958	
	Pass- enger cars	Com- mercial vehicles	Pass- enger cars	Com- mercial vehicles	Pass- enger cars	Com- mercial vehicles
German Fed. Rep.	65·1*	13·0*	502·2	82·0	630·5	102·9
United Kingdom	68·3	15·5	426·3	123·3	486·8	112·6
France . .	19·3	4·5	218·6	33·4	320·1	39·2
United States .	161·6	115·6	142·0	194·0	121·8	147·7
Italy . .	18·3	2·0	111·0	8·2	161·1	8·1
Canada . .	40·3	17·4	16·2	3·9	13·4	3·0

* Prewar Germany.
SOURCE. The Society of Motor Manufacturers and Traders.

of the struggle was the support given by the " big three " to the sales drives, in the United States, of their European affiliates. Competition of course remained intense, with Ford apparently gaining ground. Of total new registrations of " big three " products, Ford's share rose to 33·4% in the first half of 1959, compared with 30·5% in 1958 and 32·5% in 1957. General Motors' share was 53·5% in the first half of 1959, which was the same as the 1958 figure, although the 1957 figure had been no more than 48·0%. By contrast, Chrysler was definitely losing ground with no more than 13·1% of total " big three " registrations in Jan.-June 1959, compared with 16·0% in 1958 and 19·5% in 1957.

Exports. The British motor industry achieved new export records in 1959 by shipping nearly half of its output overseas. It was thus firmly established as the United Kingdom's biggest exporting industry with the year's total overseas earnings forecast at about £540 million. This figure was approximately one-sixth of total U.K. exports. Furthermore, the fact that the United Kingdom balanced its visible trade with the United States for the first time for nearly 100 years was largely due to the sales drive of the car companies. In the first nine months of the year 412,558 cars or 49·8% of total production were exported. Of these, 162,381 or 19·6% of total output went to the United States and 132,428 or 16% of output to Commonwealth countries. By contrast, total car sales overseas in the first nine months of 1958 had been 374,499, of which 109,045 or 13·7% of total output had gone to the United States and 142,229 or 17·9% of output to the Commonwealth countries. Thus the United States took over, for the first time, from the Commonwealth, traditionally the British industry's largest market.

It is of special importance that sales to other Commonwealth countries actually declined. Indeed only Canada, which took £23 million worth of U.K. cars in Jan.-Sept. 1959, compared with £13·9 million in Jan.-Sept. 1958, showed appreciable expansion. In Australia, the next largest Commonwealth market, quota control and rapid expansion by local manufacturers were increasingly felt and the value of exports thereto dropped to £4 million in the first three-quarters of 1959 compared with £6·7 million in the same period of 1958. In New Zealand and South Africa, in both

of which import controls were in operation, U.K. car sales were sharply down. Moreover, in both these countries a high level of car ownership had been reached which militated against further rapid growth in sales.

Good as the U.K. export performance was, the west German motor industry did even better. Total west German car exports in Jan.-June 1959 were 366,000 compared with 310,000 in the first half of 1958. In terms of percentage increase France excelled both countries with exports of 251,000 cars compared with 166,000 for the same period of 1958, and Italy also showed a big proportionate increase with sales of 109,000 compared with 81,000.

Against this competition U.K. car salesmen found it hard to maintain sales. Indeed, total disposals in Europe fell to 76,993 or 9·3% of total output in the first nine months of 1959 compared with 77,267 or 9·7% in the corresponding period of 1958. European markets, apparently ripe for further expansion, promised to be a most challenging field in 1960.

Design and Engineering Developments. The most significant trend was the emphasis on smaller cars from European and U.S. manufacturers. In the United States Ford with the Falcon, Chrysler with the Valiant and Chevrolet with the Corvair produced compact cars in an effort to counter European imports. These three cars were not small by European standards, being comparable with the British Ford Zephyr and the Vauxhall Cresta.

Ford and Chrysler adopted an orthodox layout of front engine in unit with the gear-box, and a live axle at the rear suspended on half-elliptical springs. Corvair went for the unorthodox, probably influenced by the success of small European cars. They adopted an air-cooled flat-six engine at the rear which demanded the use of independent rear suspension. As on all rear-engine cars this meant that the front luggage locker was small by U.S. standards. Much space was taken up by the spare wheel and the petrol-combustion heater —necessary for passenger comfort, as an air-cooled engine is inefficient in this respect in very cold climates. Automatic transmissions on orthodox three-speed manual gear-box were optionally available on each of these three new cars. The Valiant used an A.C. generator with a rectifier to convert the current to D.C., the advantage being high outputs at idling speeds.

In Britain Standard-Triumph introduced the Triumph Herald, which had a separate chassis frame, from which routine greasing had been eliminated, bodywork built up in separate sections for easy replacement and repair, and independent suspension front and rear.

To meet competition from the small European cars B.M.C. produced a new 850 in Austin Seven and Mini-Minor form. It had front-wheel drive, achieved by placing the engine transversely in the chassis, and the gear-box was housed in the sump, using a common oil with the engine. Independent suspension, utilizing rubber springs, was used for all four wheels, and although the car stood only waist high four adults could be carried in comfort.

Ford of Dagenham struck a new styling note with the Anglia, which had an unusual reverse-angle rear window to increase head-room. The new overhead-valve 997-c.c. engine had a cylinder bore very much larger than the length of the stroke and, for the first time on any British Ford car, a four-speed gear-box was fitted.

Three new British vee-8 engines were produced: the 6·23-litre Rolls-Royce, fitted to the " S " series car and the new Phantom V, and two by Daimler, the 2·54-litre in the SP250 sports car and the 4·56-litre for the Majestic Major.

A general view of the motor show at Earls Court during the press preview on the eve of its opening by the prime minister on Oct. 21.

An outstanding tyre development came from Pirelli. The treads were separate from the carcase and could be replaced when worn, or changed to suit winter and summer road conditions.   (W. HAN.; H. MY.)

MOTOR RACING. For the first time since the beginning of the drivers' world championship, points were scored in the Grand Prix of the United States at Sebring as well as in selected European Grands Prix and the Indianapolis track race in the United States. This put the championship in doubt until the very end of the racing season. Stirling Moss started the year very badly and an early lead on points was secured by Tony Brooks driving as No. 1 driver in the Ferrari team. However, this was later surpassed by the Australian Jack Brabham, driving a Cooper, who won the championship.

The leading road races were contested between cars complying with the former maximum engine-size limit of 2,500 c.c., non-supercharged, with less important events for cars of up to 1,500 c.c., these being designated Formula One and Formula Two, respectively. British Cooper cars were outstanding in both categories. The first Grand Prix of 1959 finished with only two cars really in the running, Brabham winning at Monaco from a Ferrari driven by Brooks. This was proof that the Coventry-Climax-engined Cooper, although less powerful than the Dino 246 Ferrari, was a match for the Italian car on twisting circuits. However, as the season progressed it was evident that the little Cooper in full 2½-litre form was also as fast as the bigger cars. At Zandvoort Moss made the fastest lap in a Cooper-Climax before retiring with gearbox failure, the Swedish driver J. Bonnier winning in a British B.R.M. from Brabham's Cooper.

Moss elected to drive a B.R.M. in the Grand Prix of Europe held over the exceedingly fast circuit at Reims but he failed to complete the course and in tropical heat the Ferraris were victorious, Brooks and the U.S. driver Phil Hill finishing first and second, ahead of Brabham's Cooper. Britain held its Grand Prix at Aintree and here Moss in a B.R.M. was unable to catch Brabham's Cooper, while a young New Zealander, Bruce McLaren, drove very well to finish a close third. This race was notable for the appearance of two Aston Martin Grand Prix cars which were entered on behalf of the millionaire industrialist David Brown, and which had made a promising début at Silverstone earlier in the year. At Aintree the Aston Martin driven by R. Salvadori was placed sixth but C. Shelby's retired with magneto trouble. Vanwalls, victorious in 1958, were absent from the circuits—due to their owner's ill-health—except in this Aintree race, when Brooks appeared in one but put up a disappointing performance.

The German Grand Prix moved from Nürburg to a track with a steeply banked corner at one end, at Avus, where the French champion Jean Behra was killed when his Porsche skidded in the rain (*see* OBITUARIES). Ferrari dominated the race, in the order Brooks, D. Gurney, Hill. Tyres played an important part in the Italian Grand Prix at Monza and Moss drove with discretion to win for Cooper, in a car prepared by R. R. C. Walker's team, Hill's Ferrari stopping for a wheel change. The Casablanca Grand Prix was cancelled. The season ended with the U.S. Grand Prix at Sebring, Florida, which was won by McLaren in a Cooper-Climax. M. Trintignant, also in a Cooper-Climax, came second and Brook's Ferrari third. Brabham's Cooper-Climax ran out of fuel but he pushed it over the line to finish fourth, by which time his world driving championship was in any case safe.

Britain took the Sports Car championship, Aston Martin winning the T.T. at Goodwood after Moss had taken over the second car of this team, his own car being burnt out while refuelling. Aston Martin had won the 24-hr. sports car race at Le Mans and the 1,000-km. race over the Nürburgring, which gained them valuable points.

Club racing thrived in England and small meetings at Silverstone attracted entries which in one instance totalled 200 cars. At Goodwood the *Motor Sport* Brooklands Memorial trophy was again contested on points and was won by C. de Selincourt, who used Triumph, Lotus and Lola sports cars.

Monza abandoned its terrifying track race between U.S. and European drivers but in the United States the Indianapolis track race over a distance of 500 mi. was held, traditionally, on May 30 and won by R. Ward in a Leader Card Special at 135·86 m.p.h. after three stops for new tyres.

Continental rallies continued to attract excellent entries.

Jack Brabham, followed by Stirling Moss, both in Cooper-Climaxes, lead the field round the first corner of the International Gold cup race at Oulton Park, Cheshire, on Sept. 26. Moss passed Brabham after five laps and won the 55-lap race at an average speed of 96·29 m.p.h.

The winter marathon to Monte Carlo was won by P. Col-telloni and P. Alexandre in a Citroen ID19, with Jaguar capturing the team prize. A Fiat Abarth headed the list of award winners in the Sestriere rally in Italy; K. Kling's diesel Mercedes-Benz won the Algiers-Cape rally; the very tough Liège-Rome-Liège high-speed rally which had 97 starters but only 14 finishers went to a Porsche; and the more gentle Scottish rally was won by R. W. Dalglish in a Triumph.

The racing world mourned the loss of Mike Hawthorn, who was killed in a road accident on Jan. 22, six weeks after he had announced his retirement from racing, and of Ivor Bueb, who died after a crash on the Auvergne circuit in July (*see* OBITUARIES). (*See* also SPORTING RECORD.) (W. C. B.)

MOTOR TRANSPORT. The Conservative victory in the general election of 1959 removed the possibility of re-nationalization from the haulage section of the motor trans-port industry for a number of years at least and, in the view of many observers, removed it permanently. The industry was thus stabilized into a relatively small publicly owned sector and a large privately owned sector.

The total number of vans and lorries in use in the United Kingdom, as indicated by current licences, remained more or less static at slightly more than 1·2 million. Vehicles in public ownership amounted to about 57,000, including some 25,000 additional trailers for articulated vehicles. Of these, British Road services had approximately 16,000 motor vehicles (with 5,400 additional trailers) of which 6,500 were heavy carriers of over eight tons capacity and a further 5,800 were medium-heavy vehicles of four tons to six tons capacity. British rail-ways were operating about 4,800 rigid motors, 4,100 of which were below four tons capacity, and about 10,500 articulated units plus 19,000 trailers, most of which again were below four tons capacity. The Carter Paterson and smalls delivery service of British Road services, which was offered for sale as a whole under the Transport act, 1953, remained unsold and appeared likely to stay in public ownership.

In the privately owned sector the number of " C " licences (issued to firms and individuals for the exclusive transport of their own goods) increased further to 1,099,282 at the end of 1958, compared with 1,070,201 at the end of 1957 and 733,044 at the end of 1950. As far as commercial hauliers were con-cerned, " A " licences declined slightly to 91,008 at the end of 1958 compared with 92,019 a year earlier, while " A " contract licences increased slightly to 26,495 from 24,548 and " B " licences increased to 72,573 from 70,691. It was clear that the removal of purchase tax on motor vehicle chassis in the 1959 budget encouraged the renewal of haulage fleets, and new registrations of vans and lorries rose to a new peak of 18,000 per month in July.

Motor transport statistics are notoriously inadequate but the publication by the Ministry of Transport, in July 1959, of a report entitled *The Transport of Goods by Road* threw interesting light on competition between road and railway. Based on samples made in 1958, the pamphlet estimated the annual road contribution to inland transport at 23,100 million ton-mi. compared with 18,800 million ton-mi. in 1952, the year of the most recent previous sample. By con-trast the rail contribution was put at 18,300 million ton-mi. in 1958 compared with 22,400 in 1952. Over the six-year interval it appeared that the road percentage of inland goods transport had increased from 46% to 56%, while the railways' percent-age had fallen from 54% to 44%.

The report also estimated that, with a ton-milage of approximately 513 million during the sample week, " A " and " B " licence-holders were responsible for about 275 million ton-mi. and " C " licence holders for about 238 million ton-mi. In addition to the swing from rail to road

transport the report also showed an increasing tendency towards the use of heavy vehicles. The number of vehicles of unladen weight of three tons to five tons increased by one-third between 1952 and 1958 and those over five tons by two-fifths. Holders of " A " licences (commercial hauliers plying freely for hire and not under contract) carried 35% of the total ton-milage. Of this two-fifths was in very heavy vehicles of average capacity 13·7 tons, 98% of which were diesel-powered.

The report also analysed the quantities of goods carried by road during the sample week. Building and civil engineers were shown as the main generators of road traffic, accounting for 6,612,000 tons weekly, or approximately one-third of the total. The second most important group was foodstuffs, groceries and farm products and requirements, which totalled 4,355,000 tons, and next came the coal and coke group with 2,581,000 tons. The figures also showed that the railways had suffered particularly from the loss of coal, iron ore and steel traffic to the roads during the six years between the two samples.

On the passenger transport side, municipal bus fleets had remained almost static at nearly 17,000 since 1952. On the other hand the average size had increased and designers were making more efficient use of available space by mounting engines amidships and below floor level. Even so, the use of buses was declining. In the first three-quarters of 1959 passen-ger journeys originating in the London Transport system aver-aged 43·2 million per week compared with an average of 49·0 million in 1957 and 50·0 million in 1956. (The 1958 figure of 39·5 million journeys per week was, of course, abnormally low due to prolonged strikes.) In the first half of the year the estimated total of passenger journeys on buses and coaches, other than London Transport, was down to 5,005 million, compared with 5,015 million in the first half of 1958. The annual total for 1958 was 10,194 million compared with 10,287 million in 1957 and 10,697 million in 1956.

Reasons for the declining use of buses were the increase in delivery services, mobile shops, the stay-at-home attractions of television and, above all, the increase in private ownership of cars. Wages were generally high, unemployment low and hire purchase conditions easy in 1959. Furthermore, the leading car manufacturers were competing intensely in the popular markets. The number of licences current for motor cars rose steadily and reached a new peak of 4,875,000 in August compared with 4,549,000 in the autumn of 1958 and 4,187,000 in the autumn of 1957. The increasing popularity of scooters also took traffic away from public transport and motor cycle licences reached a peak at 1,655,000 in Aug. 1959 compared with 1,520,000 in the autumn of 1958 and 1,471,000 in 1957.

Congestion on the roads continued to increase with a total vehicle population of 8,366,000 in Aug. 1959 compared with 7,904,000 in 1958 and 3,094,000 in 1938. Even so, the opening of the London-Birmingham motorway, M.1, promised to be the beginning of a new age for motor transport and there were new approaches to metropolitan traffic problems such as the Hammersmith flyover and the large-scale restricted parking plan for central London.

A survey published by *The American Automobile* showed that for the first time on record the increase in the bus and lorry population outside the United States exceeded the United States' own increase. The world total motor vehicle population was estimated to have increased by 5·3% to 112,724,000 in the year ending Jan. 1, 1959. In western European countries the total vehicle population was estimated to have increased by about 10% to 21,987,000. By contrast the same survey estimated, on the evidence available, that the total motor vehicle population of the U.S.S.R., China, Albania, Bulgaria, Czechoslovakia, the German Democratic

(Left) A new British double-deck motor coach for long distance travel. It will carry a hostess and steward. (Above) This articulated trolleybus for 200 passengers began service in Moscow in June.

Republic, Hungary, Poland, Rumania and Yugoslavia was no more than 4,505,700, of which about 3,500,000 were estimated to be lorries. In Africa and the surrounding islands, according to the same source, motor transport was expanding almost as rapidly as in western Europe. The total vehicle population was estimated at 2,323,000 units, an increase of 9·4% over the 1958 estimate, and of this total 732,000 were lorries. The survey estimated that the motor vehicle population of the African continent had more than doubled during the 1950s.

The trucking industry of the United States recorded during 1959 the best year in its history. Total operating revenues for the nearly 18,000 interstate motor carriers regulated by the Interstate Commerce commission, which had hovered at $6,200 million in 1957 and 1958, were expected to exceed that amount by 15% by the close of the year. These revenues do not include the hundreds of millions of dollars worth of services by the larger number of private and for-hire carriers not under federal economic regulation. Reports for class I and class II interstate carriers during the first half of 1959 showed the most favourable ratios of operating expenses to revenues for several years—95·7 and 93·4 for the first and second quarters, respectively. Reports from about 400 truck terminals in 34 selected metropolitan areas showed an average gain of 15% in weekly truck tonnages for the first 39 weeks of 1959, but the later weeks were expected to show a smaller increase. Private and commercial truck registrations reached 11 million in 1959, an increase of 3·5% on the year before. The industry provided employment for more than 7 million persons. (*See also* ROADS.)   (W. HAN.; B. A. GH.)

MOZAMBIQUE: *see* PORTUGUESE OVERSEAS TERRITORIES.

MUSCAT AND OMAN. Sultanate in close treaty relationship with Great Britain, occupying regions extending N.W. and S.W. from most easterly point of Arabia, together with an enclave in Trucial territory stretching southward for *c.* 45 mi. from Cape Musandam. Total area: *c.* 82.000 sq.mi. Pop.: (1957 est.), 550,000, incl. many Baluchis, Pakistanis and Negroes in chief towns and on coast. Chief towns (with est. pop.): Muscat (cap.), 5,500; Matrah, 8,500. Sultan, Said bin Taimur. Main imports: rice, cotton piecegoods. Main exports: dates, fish and fish products. Monetary units: Indian *rupee* (official); Maria Theresa dollar (commonly used); local copper and nickel coins (*baizas*).

History. In Jan. 1959 the British force which had gone to the aid of the sultan of Muscat at his request finally defeated the Omani " liberation army " led by Ghalib bin Ali, the imam of Oman, and his brother Talib. The imam fled to the United Arab Republic.

In the last days of Dec. 1958, the United States had signed a treaty of " amity, economic relations and consular rights " with the sultan of Muscat. It was emphasized that the treaty was a normal commercial one with no political significance, and that the United States was not taking sides in the internal rebellion in the sultanate.

Ghalib declared in Cairo on Aug. 2, 1959, that he considered himself the president of an independent republic of Oman and that he would continue his revolt against the sultan of Muscat and Oman. He further stated that British troops had destroyed 32 Omani villages and killed 25,000 Omanis in their effort to end the rebellion. His assertions were described by the Foreign Office as " ludicrous ".

(E. S. A.)

MUSIC. Review of 1959. Composers, particularly of the younger generation, were extremely active organizing large-scale festivals of contemporary music. The principal centres devoted to experimental works were Rome, Berlin, Donaueschingen, Warsaw, Cheltenham and Dartington, Devon. On the whole the style of the new music was abstract and intellectualized, refuting principles of tonality and experimenting with serial techniques, electronic music or with combinations of small orchestras independently conducted. Anton von Webern continued to exert the widest influence, and other important composers were Pierre Boulez and Luigi Nono. Iaian Hamilton's *Sinfonia* for two orchestras, given at the Edinburgh festival, was a British example of this trend, and others were Nono's *La Victoire de Guernica*, inspired by the picture by Pablo Picasso, heard at Munich, and Henri Pousseur's *Rimes pour différentes sources sonores*, using electronically recorded music, and Luciano Berio's *Allelujah II*, for multiple instrumental groups, heard at Donaueschingen. Polish, Swedish and Japanese composers were among the many nationalities represented in this movement which had its principal support in Germany and Italy. Though works by these and other composers were broadcast from radio stations, practical considerations in regard to resources as well as the experimental nature of the inspiration in these works made it

unlikely for many of them to be adopted in the general concert repertory.

New symphonies on more conventional lines by William Alwyn, Alan Rawsthorne and Humphrey Searle were heard in London. John Joubert's piano concerto was given at Manchester, and Ernest Ansermet conducted the first English performance, broadcast by the B.B.C., of the opera *The Tempest* by the Swiss composer, Frank Martin, earlier given at Vienna, Zürich and New York. New chamber works included Robert Simpson's *Variations on a Theme of Haydn* for piano and Elizabeth Maconchy's *Variations on a Theme from Job* for cello. Hans Werner Henze's ballet *Undine*, first performed in London at the end of 1958, was successfully revived in Munich. Belonging to the style of the beginning of the 20th century, the piano concerto, *The Forgotten Rite* and several of the songs and chamber works by John Ireland, who celebrated his 80th birthday, were given in London where, also, Jascha Horenstein conducted Gustav Mahler's seldom-heard *Eighth Symphony* (the " Symphony of a Thousand "). At the end of 1958 the oratorio *Yunus Emre* by the Turkish composer Ahmed Adnan Saygun was given in New York under the auspices of the United Nations, and the suite from Alban Berg's opera *Lulu* was first performed at Sydney, Australia. George Kraus, Ian Johnston and Noel Nickson were among the Australian composers whose works were heard at Sydney.

Anniversaries. In many countries in Europe and in the United States celebrations were organized to commemorate the bicentenary of the death of Handel. A great tribute was paid at his birthplace, Halle, in the German Democratic Republic, where four of his operas were revived, *Admetos, Giulio Cesare, Ariodante* and *Porus*, as well as his lesser-known oratorios *The Triumph of Time and Truth, Judas Maccabeus, Belshazzar* and *L'Allegro ed il Penseroso*. At Hamburg *Belshazzar* was given in opera form in an inspiring production by Joachim Herz, Munich staged the opera *Deidamia*, conducted by Meinrhad van Zallinger, and Göttingen produced *Ariodante*. The main U.S. contribution to the Handel celebrations was the New York City centre's production of the opera *Ezio*. At the end of 1958 La Scala, Milan, mounted the oratorio *Hercules*, with Fedora Barbieri as Dejania and Elizabeth Schwarzkopf as Jole. In London Joan Sutherland sang in the Covent Garden production of *Samson* and in *Rodelinda* at Sadler's Wells, where there was also a production of *Semele*. A substantial number of Handel's vast output of operas and oratorios were thus revived, some of them for the first time since his lifetime. The tercentenary of the birth of Purcell was marked by many performances of his chamber and religious works as well as of some of his lesser-known incidental scores for plays, chiefly in London. Purcell's opera *Dido and Aeneas* was given at Hampton court. An exhibition of manuscripts and other documents relating to Handel and Purcell was held at the British Museum. The centenary of the

death of Ludwig Spohr was marked by a concert in London of his chamber works. The bicentenary of the death of the Swedish composer J. H. Roman was marked at the end of 1958 by the publication of archives of Swedish music, *Monumenta Musicae Svecicae*, dedicated to Roman's memory, and by performances of his orchestral works. Further celebrations marking the centenary of the birth of Puccini at the end of 1958 included a broadcast of his opera *Le Villi* by the B.B.C., and a production of *Turandot* at La Scala, Milan, conducted by Antonio Votto with Birgit Nillson in the title role.

Opera. The operatic repertory was vastly enlarged by revivals of 18th-, 19th- and 20th-century works, indicating an eclectic taste among opera-goers and a widening historical outlook. On the whole the international scene was flourishing, with the main opera houses vying with each other for novel productions and the vogue for opera encouraged by the issue of many fine commercial recordings. The revival of Cherubini's *Medea* at Covent Garden, in a setting by the Greek producer Alexis Minotis, and conducted by Nicola Rescigno, allowed Maria Menghini Callas to display her supreme gifts as an operatic actress, commanding in both gesture and characterization. At Covent Garden, too, the Australian soprano Joan Sutherland achieved a brilliant triumph in her impassioned rendering of the mad scene in Donizetti's *Lucia di Lammermoor*, tastefully produced by Franco Zeffirelli and conducted by Tullio Serafin. The part of Lucia was later successfully sung at Covent Garden by Mattiwilda Dobbs. At Sadler's Wells Dvořák's *Rusalka* was revived with Joan Hammond in the title role. Other operas revived at Sadler's Wells included the triple bill of one-act operas, Béla Bartók's *Duke Bluebeard's Castle*, Gian-Carlo Menotti's *The Telephone* and Ralph Vaughan Williams' *Riders to the Sea*. Among modern operas, first British performances were given at Sadler's Wells of Luigi Dallapiccola's *Il Prigionero*, based on a tale by Villiers de l'Isle Adam, and Carl Orff's comic opera *Die Kluge*, illustrating Italian and German trends. At the Royal Festival hall in London the Virtuosi di Roma gave concert performances of 18th-century operas including Cimarosa's *Il Maestro di Capella* and Galuppi's *Il Filosofo di Campagna*. A revival of Wagner's *Parsifal* at Covent Garden was produced by Herbert Graf with Karl Liebl as Parsifal and conducted by Rudolf Kempe. Wagner's *Der Ring der Nibelungen* was conducted by Franz von Konwitschny, who made a successful debut at Covent

Garden. At the end of 1958 Mussorgsky's *Boris Godunov* was given in Russian at Covent Garden with Boris Christoff in the title role and conducted by Rafael Kubelik. The Paris Opéra revived its sumptuous production of Rameau's *Les Indes Galantes*, one of the most rewarding of the 18th-century revivals, and the Paris Opéra-Comique gave the first performance of Francis Poulenc's *La Voix Humaine*, a one-act work for a single character, taken by the soprano Denise Duval, on the monodrama by Jean Cocteau. Haydn's satirical opera *Il Mondo della Luna*, revived in a version by H. C. Robbins Landon, was the main attraction at three of the European festivals. At the end of 1958 La Scala, Milan, staged an elaborate production of Rossini's *Mosè* with Giulietta Simionato as Sinaide and conducted by Gianandrea Gavazzeni, and later revived Verdi's *Ernani* under Gavazzeni with Nicola Rossi-Lemeni as Silva. Rossi-Lemeni also took the part of Don Quixote in a revival of Manuel de Falla's *El Retablo del Maese Pedro* at the Piccola Scala in Milan. in Rome the Teatro della Cometa was opened as one of several small theatres in Italy for the production of intimate 18th-century opera. Sesto Bruscantini and Adriana Martino took the leading parts there in Cimarosa's *Le Trame Deluse*.

At the Metropolitan Opera in New York an outstanding performance was given of Verdi's *Don Carlos*, conducted by Fausto Cleva with Cesare Siepi as Philip II, Leonie Rysaneck as Elisabetta and Blanche Thebom as Eboli. Karl Böhm conducted an authoritative performance of Alban Berg's *Wozzeck*, also at the Metropolitan. New American operas given at the New York City centre included Hugo Weisgall's *Six Characters in Search of an Author*, based on the play of Luigi Pirandello, Norman dello Joio's *The Triumph of Saint Joan*, on a libretto by the composer, and Robert Ward's *He Who Gets Slapped*. *Aniara*, a new opera based on a fantasy of space travel, by the Swedish composer Karl Birger Blomdahl, was given at Stockholm and at the Edinburgh festival. One of the most original of 20th-century operas, Arnold Schoenberg's *Moses und Aaron*, earlier given at Zürich, was enthusiastically received at its first performance in Germany at the Berlin festival. At Brno, Czechoslovakia, the first production outside the U.S.S.R. was given of Serghei Prokofiev's revolutionary opera *Semyon Kotko*, conducted by Vaclav Nosek, and at Ljubljana, Yugoslavia, the first performance was given of an imaginative opera *Crne Maske* (" The Black Masks ") by Marij Kogoj, a pupil of Schoenberg. In Moscow the operetta *Moskva Cheremushki* (the name of a housing estate), by Dmitri Shostakovich showed this composer in a lighter style, and the Bolshoi theatre in Moscow mounted a new production of Rimsky-Korsakov's *Tsar Sultan*.

Publications. At the end of 1958 Wolfgang Boetticher published in German an authoritative study of the Renaissance composer Orlando di Lasso. Also in 1958 Donald Mitchell published the well-documented study *Gustav Mahler: The Early Years*, Willi Apel an exhaustive survey of Gregorian chant, and F. H. Harrison opened new fields of research in his study *Music in Medieval Britain*. Winton Dean's *Handel's Dramatic Oratorios and Masques* (London, 1959) threw an important new light on the whole of Handel's background and his work. *Bizet and his World* (London, 1959) by Mina Curtiss revealed unpublished correspondence of the period. Christopher St. John's *Ethel Smyth* (London, 1959) was a sensitively drawn character study. *Conversations with Igor Stravinsky* by Igor Stravinsky and Robert Craft (London, 1959) was principally devoted to aesthetic assessments.

Deaths. Musicians who died during the year were the Swiss-born composer Ernest Bloch, the Czech-born composer Bohuslav Martinu, the English composer Haydn Wood (for all these *see* OBITUARIES), the Finnish composer Yrjö Kilpinen, the American composer George Antheil and the Australian composers Hubert Clifford and Robert Dally-

Scarlett. Other musicians who died were the British critics Ernest Newman and Eric Blom, the Polish-born harpsichordist Wanda Landowska, the Russian-born pianist Lev Pouishnoff, the Austrian conductor Rudolf Moralt, the Dutch conductor Eduard van Beinum, the Canadian tenor Edward Johnson (for all these *see* OBITUARIES), the British violinist May Harrison, the German-born musicologist Curt Sachs, and the Rumanian musicologist Constantin Brailoiu.

Postwar Survey. The most important development in music since 1945 has been the widespread adoption, throughout Europe and America, of the twelve-note or serial method of composition devised by Arnold Schoenberg about 1923 to replace the traditional system of major and minor keys, which he had abandoned. For many years the method was taken up only by a few pupils of Schoenberg (notably Alban Berg and Anton Webern), and their music, like his, encountered strong resistance both from the public and from the majority of musicians. In comparison with, say, Béla Bartók and Igor Stravinsky, they have still not had much popular success with audiences (though Berg has come near it), but since World War II their method of composition has been adopted by, or has influenced, a large number of composers in almost every country.

The youngest generation, led by Pierre Boulez in France, Luigi Nono in Italy and Karlheinz Stockhausen in Germany, have been inspired not so much by Schoenberg himself as by his more radical disciple Webern, whose methods have been the starting-point for their own still more radical experiments, in which continuity of melodic line and of instrumental texture is almost entirely abandoned. In Great Britain Peter Maxwell Davies and Iaian Hamilton, in his most recent works, have been outstanding among those who use this technique.

Older composers have been more cautious, and many of them have modified Schoenberg's technique in various ways, partly in an attempt to make their music more " accessible " than his to the average listener. Among the composers of this group are Luigi Dallapiccola in Italy, Frank Martin in Switzerland, Wolfgang Fortner in Germany, Elisabeth Lutyens in England, the late Fartein Valen in Norway, Roberto Gerhard, a Catalan composer of Swiss origin living in England, and Sándor Veress, an Hungarian living in Switzerland. Peter Racine Fricker in England, although younger than any of these, might also be grouped with them on these grounds.

Most of the composers so far mentioned have used serial technique fairly consistently in a considerable number of major works. In addition there are many composers of more conservative inclination who, although they have not felt able to adopt the technique completely, have in some way been influenced by it, and have toyed with it, or made experiments of varying importance with it—a remarkable testimony to the potency of the idea. Prominent among these composers are Benjamin Britten and Sir William Walton in England, Francis Poulenc and Olivier Messiaen in France and Aaron Copland in the United States. Even Dmitri Shostakovich in the U.S.S.R., where the technique was long condemned as an extreme example of western decadence, contrived to smuggle a short twelve-note statement into his *Third String Quartet*. Similar twelve-note passages and themes appear also in the later works of some contemporaries of Schoenberg who were never associated with him—notably Ernest Bloch and Bartók. Much more striking and important however is the serialism in the late works of Stravinsky, who at the age of 70, immediately after the success of what was probably his greatest work in his older, " neo-classical " style, the opera *The Rake's Progress* (1951), suddenly began to use serial technique. Like his youngest contemporaries he was influenced not so much by Schoenberg directly as by Webern, whose concise, transparent-textured music would obviously be the more congenial to him. Stravinsky's " conversion " to serial technique, and the series of late masterpieces that he has

Igor Stravinsky in Copenhagen during his visit in May to receive the Sonning prize and to conduct the Royal theatre orchestra.

produced with it (among them the *Septet*, the *In Memoriam Dylan Thomas*, parts of the ballet *Agon* and the religious works *Canticum Sacrum* and *Threni*) have done more than anything composed by any of his juniors to persuade conservative musicians and the public of the validity of this technique. His use of it is as different from Webern's as from Schoenberg's, and the unmistakably Stravinskian sound and character of these late works have shown decisively that in the hands of genius the serial method, contrary to what was often said of it in earlier years, allows as many differences of style and expression as any other method of composition.

While these works by Stravinsky have met with immediate popular success, those of Schoenberg and Webern are still having to battle for acceptance by performers and the public. Only now that Schoenberg's newly invented method of composition has been vindicated by its almost universal adoption, and the inevitable revolution in compositional technique that he prophesied has come about, has it become possible to make a natural response to and assessment of his work, unclouded by irrelevant disputes or reservations about his technique. An important step towards the popularization of his music has been the performance of his most ambitious work, the unfinished but effectively complete opera *Moses und Aron* (first heard some years after his death in a concert version at Hamburg, and since staged at Zürich and Berlin), which has won over many who were formerly hostile to or unconvinced by his music.

Of the composers who have not accepted serial technique, the most prominent and the most vehemently opposed to it is Paul Hindemith, whose reputation however has faded slightly since his adventurous early works. In his generation Darius Milhaud, Arthur Honegger, Serghei Prokofiev and Carl Orff also remained indifferent to the new technique, and among the best-known younger composers Britten and Shostakovich, although not indifferent to it, have generally preferred to use

more traditional techniques. There are of course also very many other composers in every country who continue to write in a more conventional way, but their number is steadily decreasing, and very few of them have made any international impression.

In England the postwar musical scene has been dominated by Vaughan Williams and Britten. In 1947 Vaughan Williams, then already well past 70, completed his *Sixth Symphony*, and in the remaining 11 years of his life composed three more, and numerous other major works. Britten has devoted himself since World War II chiefly to opera. His first mature work in this form, *Peter Grimes* (an earlier one, *Paul Bunyan*, written and produced in the United States, has never been published) was first performed at the Sadler's Wells theatre in London in 1945, immediately after the end of World War II. It was quickly followed by *The Rape of Lucretia*, a chamber opera for a small group of singers and players. Since then Britten has composed several other operas of both kinds, one of which, *Gloriana*, based on the life of Queen Elizabeth I of England was commissioned to celebrate the coronation of Queen Elizabeth II in 1953. Britten's great success in this field has led to a strong revival of interest in opera on the part of British composers, and works in this form by Walton (*Troilus and Cressida*), Michael Tippett (*The Midsummer Marriage*), Sir Arthur Bliss (*The Olympians*), Lennox Berkeley (*Nelson*), Arthur Benjamin (*A Tale of Two Cities*) and Vaughan Williams (*The Pilgrim's Progress*), have been staged in London.

A renewed British interest in opera has also led to an attempt since 1946 by the Royal Opera house in London (Covent Garden) to establish and build up a national opera company. Excellent progress has been made towards this end, although there have been faint signs recently of a neglect of this policy in favour of the more frequent engagement of foreign guest performers and the singing of works in their original language instead of English. One of the problems has been that of finding and retaining a musical director of distinction and authority—a problem which older-established opera houses in other countries (among them Hamburg and Vienna) have also experienced, owing to the ease of international travel, which makes it possible for the best-known conductors, producers and singers to work entirely freelance. A more stable but more modest national opera company in London exists at the Sadler's Wells theatre. In 1958 this company absorbed most of the members of the former Carl Rosa Opera company, which collapsed when its subsidy from the Arts Council of Great Britain was withdrawn. This was part of a general re-organization of opera in Britain, with increased subsidies for the Royal Opera house and Sadler's Wells. The long-term effect or effectiveness of these changes had still to be seen in 1959. Opera is not taking root easily in Britain, and there appeared to be little hope for many years to come of establishing an opera house outside London.

England has not been alone in its operatic troubles. Financial crises have been experienced at the Paris Opéra and even in some of the most famous Italian houses. The need for vast subsidies for this expensive art is accepted most readily in the German-speaking countries where many opera houses damaged or destroyed during World War II have been restored or replaced (notably at Vienna, Berlin, Hamburg and Cologne). In England the most important postwar building for music has been the Royal Festival hall, opened in 1951 for the Festival of Britain. This has replaced the old Queen's hall, destroyed by bombing, as the main orchestral concert hall in London.

A remarkable feature of postwar musical life has been the great increase in the number of summer music festivals all over Europe. Many of these serve a commercial as much as a cultural purpose, and are subsidized by government or municipality in order to attract tourists. Among the outstanding and most popular ones are those at Aix-en-Provence, Bayreuth, Berlin, Edinburgh, Florence (Maggio Musicale), the Netherlands, Munich, Prague, Salzburg, Vienna and Warsaw. In addition there are the annual festivals of the International Society for Contemporary Music, held in a different country each year, and several other festivals devoted to contemporary music, notably at Venice, Darmstadt and Donaueschingen. In England there is the Cheltenham Festival of British Contemporary Music, founded in 1945, where every programme includes at least one first performance.

The commercial use of the long-playing (microgroove) gramophone record and of tape-recording is another new major feature of musical life since World War II. It has made much more music accessible to listeners all over the world who are not within easy reach of a concert hall. Besides innumerable different versions of all the popular orchestral and operatic classics, and most of the classical repertoire of songs and chamber music, there are many recordings of less familiar works of every kind. from vocal music of the middle ages to the complete works of Webern. Developments in recording and related techniques have also attracted some modern composers to experiment with the creation of works entirely or mainly by these means—electronic music and *musique concrète*. Several radio stations in the German Federal Republic, Italy and France have special studios for this work.

In the field of musical scholarship much has been done to reveal more fully the music of the 18th and earlier centuries. As a result of these researches many performers have become convinced of the necessity of presenting early music as authentically as possible, and several old instruments have been restored to general use, principally the harpsichord, but also the recorder, the various viols, and the lute, as well as the countertenor. Only the castrato seems unlikely to come back. Music before Haydn is now rarely performed without a proper continuo part, and in keyboard music it is becoming as common to hear the harpsichord as the piano. Whereas Bach, Handel and Scarlatti used to be the earliest composers well-known to most listeners, today Purcell, Vivaldi and Monteverdi can almost be called popular, and scholars are digging still deeper into the past. There has also been a marked revival of interest in Italian opera of the early 19th century.

Important publications of music and books on music have been very numerous, and for this reason mention here is confined to two important new dictionaries—the completely revised and largely new fifth edition of *Grove's Dictionary of Music and Musicians*, in nine volumes, edited by Eric Blom (London, 1954) and *Die Musik in Geschichte und Gegenwart*, edited by Friedrich Blume, still in course of publication in 1959 (Kassel, 1949-).

Recorded Music. Stereophonic recording continued to advance during 1959. Equipment improved and received wide publicity at the audio fair in London. Most of the records issued by Decca, E.M.I. and D.G.G. (Deutsche-Grammophon Gesellschaft) appeared in both stereophonic and single-channel form. Wagner's *Das Rheingold* (Decca) caused something of a sensation in its stereophonic form—the performance, balance and realism of the records outshone most representations of the work in the opera house.

The record companies realized more and more the need for cheaper issues. H.M.V. began a " Concert Classics " series, which included popular orchestral works performed by well-known artists; Decca expanded their Ace of Clubs repertory; D.G.G. brought out interesting records on their cheaper Heliodor label; and Philips started an Evergreen series. Most of these discs were about half the usual price, as were the record club issues, which continued to flourish.

Among the standard lists there were many adventurous choices. Serghei Prokofiev's *First Symphony* was conducted by Sir Eugene Goossens on Pye and his *Fourth Symphony* was given by the U.S.S.R. State Radio Symphony orchestra under Gennady Rozdestvensky (Parlophone). The same composer's *First Piano Concerto* was performed by Mindru Katz on Pye, his *Second Violin Concerto* by David Oistrakh (Columbia) and his *Sinfonia Concertante* for cello by Mstislav Rostropovic (H.M.V.). The American composer Charles Ives was represented by his *Third Symphony* and *Three Places in New England*, given by the Eastman-Rochester orchestra, conducted by Howard Hanson (Mercury). The Eastman Symphonic Wind ensemble performed chamber music by Richard Strauss, Darius Milhaud, Arnold Schoenberg, Paul Hindemith and Igor Stravinsky (Mercury). Some little-known operas from Czechoslovakia were recorded for the first time on Supraphon: Smetana's *The Two Widows*, Leoš Janáček's *The Cunning Little Vixen* and Eugen Suchon's *The Whirlpool*.

Another operatic first recording was Richard Strauss's *Capriccio*, conducted by Wolfgang Sawallisch (Columbia). Outstanding among other operatic issues were Benjamin Britten's *Peter Grimes* (Decca); Act one of Wagner's *Die Walküre* (Decca); *Cavalleria Rusticana* (R.C.A.); *Eugene Onegin*, recorded by the Bolshoi Opera company (Parlophone); and Puccini's *Gianni Schicci*, with Tito Gobbi (H.M.V.). Maria Callas, Joan Sutherland, Teresa Berganza, Mark Reizen (in scenes from *Boris Godunov* and *Prince Igor*) and Elizabeth Schwarzkopf all recorded excellent operatic recitals.

Among discs of well-known orchestral works, the best were Sir Thomas Beecham's two records with the French National Radio Symphony orchestra of César Franck's *Symphony in D Minor* and Berlioz's *Symphonie Fantastique* (H.M.V.); Mendelssohn's music for *Midsummer Night's Dream*, directed by Peter Maag (Decca); Tchaikovsky's *Fifth Symphony* played by the Boston Symphony orchestra under Pierre Monteux (R.C.A.); and *Also Sprach Zarathrusta* by the Vienna Philharmonic under Herbert von Karajan, in magnificent stereophonic sound (Decca).

The finest concerto discs were William Walton's *Cello Concerto*, with Gregor Piatigorsky (R.C.A.); Brahms's *Violin Concerto*, with Henryk Szeryng (R.C.A.); Grieg's *Piano Concerto* and Liszt's *Second Piano Concerto*, by György Cziffra (H.M.V.). A second complete recording of the *Brandenburg Concertos* was made by the Stuttgart Chamber orchestra (Decca).

The ninth volume of H.M.V.'s *History of Music in Sound* was devoted to 19th-century opera and lieder, the tenth volume to 20th-century works. Reissues on R.C.A.'s Camden label included such famous names of the past as Giovanni Martinelli, Rosa Ponselle, Lotte Lehmann and Serge Rachmaninov. The same company reissued many of Arturo Toscanini's recordings.

Boris Christoff attempted, successfully, the Herculean task of singing all Mussorgsky's songs; Dietrich Fischer-Dieskau made a complete recording of Wolf's Mörike *lieder* and D.G.G. issued an uncut version of Bach's *St. Matthew Passion*, conducted by Karl Richter.

Popular Music. With *My Fair Lady* continuing its run at the Drury Lane theatre, the writers Alan Jay Lerner and Frederick Loewe shook the town once again with the musical film *Gigi*. The long-playing record made by the screen cast Leslie Caron, Maurice Chevalier, Louis Jordain and Hermione Gingold challenged the supremacy of the earlier disc on the film's first week of showing in London. While *Gigi* did not produce any individual song hits, it was a masterly musical score, and with *Paint your Wagon* and *Brigadoon* already to their credit, Lerner and Loewe were widely tipped to don the mantle of those masters of the musical play, Rodgers and Hammerstein. No new musical from Rodgers and Hammerstein themselves was seen in Britain during the year, but the film of their *South Pacific* entered its second year at the

Dominion theatre, and the long-playing disc of the show, taken from the sound track of the film, created a record in itself, by topping the long-playing Hit Parade for 52 weeks in succession.

The biggest rise to fame of any individual " pop " recording star was that of Russ Conway, who at the end of 1958 joined the Billy Cotton T.V. Wakey Wakey show in a special piano solo spot. He helped to create top viewing figures for the Cotton programme, and with his own compositions " Side Saddle ", " Roulette " and " China Tea ", and a couple of best-selling L.P.s to his credit, Russ Conway joined the favoured few at the top of the Hit Parade. Although Elvis Presley had to serve his time with the United States army, his sponsors made sure that he left a number of discs ready to market before he went overseas, and he maintained his position as the king of " Rock 'n' Roll " with *A Fool such as I,* and *I Need your Love Tonight.*

The tragic death of Buddy Holly gave a chance to other " Rock 'n' Roll " youngsters, although Holly's last record " It doesn't Matter any More " topped the Parade several months after his death. Newcomers in this field were Cliff Richard, Lloyd Price, Bobby Darin and England's own Anthony Newley, who became a top pop singer by accident. A rising film star, Newley had to interpret the part of a night club singer in one film. The suggestion that the songs be dubbed by a leading well-known vocalist was turned down by Newley, who surprised the film producers (and the public) with his own renderings of " I've Waited so Long " and " Personality ".

An attempt to bring down the price of long-playing records by the Pye company saw them group a dozen of their best-known artistes, including Lonnie Donegan and Petula Clark, on one record called " Curtain Up ". At the cut price at which it was offered, the dealers regarded it as an advertising stunt to sell more Pye records and in this it was successful. This move by Pye started a price war, and with L.P.s being offered at 21s., the " Golden Guinea " and Decca's " Ace of Clubs " series entered into keen competition. At the beginning of the year the sale of records dropped some 21% on previous comparable figures in 1958 but there were signs by the end of the year of some improvement, chiefly due to the cut in prices, and more closely knit propaganda for the big selling artistes.

Sales of sheet music fell to an all-time low, but music albums, giving good value for money, continued to thrive. To combat the loss of royalties from sheet music, songwriters and publishers received increased income from broadcast and general fees through the Performing Right society from both B.B.C. and I.T.A. networks. (*See* also FESTIVALS.)

(E. L.; Cn. Mn.; A. G. F. C. B.; H. W. D.)

NARCOTICS. The United Kingdom report on dangerous drugs for the year 1958, which was forwarded to the United Nations in the summer of 1959, showed that the number of convictions for dangerous drugs offences had risen from 90 in 1957 to 148; this is about the number of convictions usually recorded (compare this figure with the 169 convictions in 1955 and 151 in 1956). During 1959 there were 212 convictions for dangerous drugs offences of all kinds. Of the 212 persons convicted 123, or 58%, were Africans, Asiatics or West Indians. In 164 cases the drug concerned was cannabis (Indian hemp) and natives of the areas mentioned above account for 100, or 61%, of the offences. There was only a small increase in the number of seizures of cannabis but the total amount involved was the highest ever recorded; about nine-tenths was confiscated on vessels plying between United Kingdom ports and Rangoon, Burma.

The number of known addicts rose from 359 in 1957 to 442 in 1958; the number of known addicts in 1959 was 446

A contraband consignment of Indian hemp, said to be worth £150,000 found on board the cargo vessel " Yoma " at Liverpool in August.

of whom more than half were women and about one-sixth doctors, dentists or nurses. Morphine was used by 201 addicts and diacetylmorphine (commonly known as heroin) was used by 59. Of the synthetic drugs only pethidine (121) and methadone (55) were used to a significant extent by addicts.

In 1959 the United Kingdom referred to the World Health organization of the United Nations two new synthetic drugs which had been developed and which were considered to be capable of producing the same harmful effects as morphine and cocaine if improperly used. A statutory instrument made on Dec. 21, 1959, which came into operation on Jan. 1, 1960, brought these drugs (benzethidine and furethidine) and four other drugs (dimenoxadole, norcodeine, normorphine and phenazocine) under control in conformity with the international obligations of the United Kingdom.

International. At the 14th session of the U.N. Narcotics commission, held in Geneva from April 27 to May 15, 1959, governments were requested to provide prompt provisional control of new narcotic drugs having powerful analgesic or antitussive properties, pending findings by the World Health organization regarding the drugs' addiction-producing liabilities. The World Health organization was invited to revise the list of exempted narcotic preparations, to be limited to those generally used in current medical practice which could be safely exempted from most control measures, for inclusion in the Single Convention on Narcotic Drugs. The World Health organization was requested to prepare a report on the use of cannabis for the extraction of useful drugs, especially anti-biotics, preferably in time for the 15th session of the commission, and specifically for use in the plenipotentiary conference to adopt the Single convention, so that the extraction of useful drugs from cannabis could be permitted under that convention.

The secretary-general, in co-operation with the International Civil Aviation organization, the World Health organization and the International Criminal Police organization, was asked to prepare and distribute to governments, in time for action at the 15th session of the commission, essential standards to control the use of narcotic drugs in first-aid kits on board aircraft engaged in international flights. All governments which had not yet done so were requested to adhere to the 1948 protocol, and all governments of opium-producing countries were urged to adhere to the International Opium protocol of 1953 so that it could come into force. Caution was advised in the publicity given to new analgesic drugs by manufacturers, journalists, or on radio or television to prevent claims that these drugs were not addiction-producing.

Total seizures of narcotic drugs reported for 1958 were considerably less than for 1957, although the reverse was true in the United States, the chief target of illicit heroin traffic. The largest seizures of raw and prepared opium were made in Asia, particularly in Burma-China-Thailand border areas of clandestine cultivation. Persia also had much illicit traffic in opium. The clandestine manufacture and smuggling of morphine and heroin from Asia to other parts of the world continued. The United States seized much heroin smuggled from Hong Kong and Japan. The concern of the commission about cocaine traffic was shown by its request to the secretary-general to send reports of the cocaine discussion, held during the 14th session of the commission, to the governments of several South American countries, urging full co-operation by all countries to reduce this traffic. Heavy traffic in cannabis continued, mostly in the far east, Africa, United States, Central and South America. Very large seizures were made in several countries because of vigorous enforcement measures and Mexico continued to co-operate with the United States to check illicit traffic.   (E. H. Gn.; H. J. A.)

NATIONAL INCOME.

The year 1958 saw a slowing down and in some countries a reversal of the growth in the money value of national income which had been the experience of almost all countries in recent years. Estimates available for a few countries indicate a return to a more rapid growth in national income in the first half of 1959.

Table I shows estimates of net national income for a number of countries for which fairly up-to-date information on a broadly comparable basis was available late in 1959. National income measures aggregate earnings of all kinds (e.g., wages, profits and interest) accruing to normal residents from their participation in economic activity at home and abroad; and net national income is calculated by making a deduction for the consumption of fixed capital. These estimates do not provide a satisfactory basis for comparing the level of incomes in various countries but may be used in comparing the year-to-year development in different countries.

In the United States the money value of national income fell by 1% in 1958 compared with an increase of 5% in 1957. Canada, however, experienced an increase of 3% which was somewhat greater than in the previous year (2%). In Europe the United Kingdom's national income increased by 4% compared with a 6% increase in the previous year, and in the German Federal Republic there was an increase of 6% as against 8% in 1957. Other European countries to experience the decrease in the rate of growth in the money value of national income were Denmark 3% (7% in 1957), the Netherlands 3% (9%), Sweden 3% (8%), Austria 6% (10%) and Spain 15% (23%). In Belgium and Norway the national income decreased by 1% and 3% in 1958 compared with increases of 8% and 5% respectively in 1957. In France, however, national income increased by 13% as against 11% in 1957, while Italy showed the same growth (7%) as had prevailed in 1957. Among Commonwealth countries Australia's national income increased by 6% compared to a decline of 1% in the previous year, while New Zealand showed a growth of 3% (5% in 1957). Large increases in national income in money terms were again experienced by most countries in South America: in Argentina 42% (25%

TABLE I. NET NATIONAL INCOME, 1956-58*

	1956	1957	1958	% increase 1958 over 1957
Argentina (P. '000 million) .	151	189	268	42
Australia (£A million) . .	4,685	4,653	4,931	6
Austria (Sch. '000 million) .	89	98	104	6
Belgium (B.Fr. '000 million) .	431	464	458	—1
Brazil (Cr. '000 million) .	724	852	977	15
Burma (million kyats) . .	4,336	4,450	...	...
Canada (C.$ million) . .	23,401	23,942	24,759	3
Ceylon (Rs. million) . .	4,847	5,067	...	...
Chile (P. '000 million) .	1,295	1,766	2,315	31
Cuba (P. million) . .	2,034	2,321	2,140	—8
Denmark (Kr. million) . .	25,405	27,072	27,880	3
France (Fr. '000 million) .	14,112	15,727	17,761	13
German Fed. Rep. (DM. '000 million) . . .	148	160	169	6
India (Rs. '000 million) .	113	114	...	...
Ireland, Rep. of (£ million) .	439	458	468	2
Israel (£I million) . .	2,113	2,598	2,943	13
Italy (L. '000 million) . .	11,469	12,319	13,126	7
Netherlands (million guilder)	26,650	29,170	30,180	3
New Zealand (£NZ million) .	883	930	962	3
Norway (Kr. million) . .	21,676	22,805	22,095	—3
Philippines (P. million) . .	8,414	8,818	9,232	5
Spain (P. '000 million) . .	311	383	439	15
Sweden (Kr. million)* .	44,883	48,612	50,209	3
Switzerland (Fr. million) .	25,800	27,280	28,300	4
United Kingdom (£ million) .	16,606	17,598	18,252	4
United States ($ '000 million)	346	364	361	—1
Venezuela (B. million) . .	13,665	15,612	17,600	13

* Figures are for net national income except in the case of Sweden, where they are gross; i.e., only the Swedish figures include provision for the consumption of fixed capital.

SOURCE. U.N. *Monthly Bulletin of Statistics*; O.E.E.C. *General Statistics Bulletin*; I.M.F. *International Financial Statistics*.

TABLE II. DISPOSAL OF GROSS NATIONAL PRODUCT

	Year	% private con- sumption	% govt. current expenditure	% gross domestic capital formation	% export surplus
Canada . .	1938	73·6	9·9	15·0	2·1
	1957	62·7	14·0	27·6	—4·3
	1958	64·5	14·2	24·4	—3·1
Denmark .	1938	76·6	9·3	12·6	1·5
	1957	67·1	12·8	19·1	0·9
	1958	67·1	13·6	16·5	2·9
France . .	1938	74·0	13·0	14·0	—1·0
	1957	67·0	15·3	19·8	—2·0
	1958	66·3	14·5	20·2	—1·0
German Federal Rep.	1936	60·5	20·8	18·7	—
	1957	58·7	13·4	24·0	4·0
	1958	58·5	13·5	24·0	4·0
Italy . .	1938	66·9	16·3	17·3	—0·5
	1957	66·6	12·2	22·4	—1·2
	1958	65·5	12·5	21·3	0·7
Netherlands .	1938	74·4	11·4	11·2	3·0
	1957	58·2	15·0	28·3	—1·5
	1958	58·1	14·4	23·2	4·4
Norway . .	1938	69·7	9·9	18·9	1·5
	1957	57·8	12·2	29·6	0·4
	1958	60·6	13·0	30·9	—4·6
Sweden .	1938-9	70·2	10·4	18·7	0·7
	1957	60·0	17·6	22·6	—0·1
	1958	61·4	18·1	20·9	—0·4
United Kingdom .	1938	76·3	13·5	11·3	—1·1
	1957	64·7	16·9	16·9	1·6
	1958	65·4	16·9	15·4	2·3
United States .	1938	75·1	11·4	12·0	1·5
	1957	63·1	18·0	17·6	1·3
	1958	65·0	18·8	15·8	0·5

SOURCE: O.E.E.C. *Statistics of National Product and Expenditure, no. 2, 1938 and 1947 to 1955* and *General Statistics Bulletins*.

in 1957), Brazil 15% (17%), Chile 31% (36%) and Venezuela 13% (14%).

In almost all countries prices continued to rise in 1958 so that the increases in incomes were even smaller when measured in real terms. Available estimates showed that real income decreased in the United States, Belgium, the Republic of Ireland and Norway between 1957 and 1958, while in Canada, Sweden and the United Kingdom the growth in real national income was less than 1%. The general level of prices increased by 11% in France in 1958, 3% in the German Federal Republic, 2% in Italy and 1% in the Netherlands. In Australia and New Zealand the cost of living increased during 1958 by 2% and 4% respectively. In South America the cost of living increased by 32% in Argentina, 15% in Brazil, 20% in Chile and 5% in Venezuela.

In the first half of 1959 the gross national product of the United States was some 10% higher in money terms and 9% higher in real terms than in the same period in 1958. The corresponding figures for Canada were estimated to be 8% and 7%. The United Kingdom national product in the first half of 1959 was estimated to be about 3% higher in money terms and 2% higher in real terms than in the same period of 1958.

Table II shows how gross national product was devoted to the various end-uses. Although there were no major changes in the structure of final demand during 1958, government current expenditure accounted for a somewhat greater proportion of national product in nearly all countries, while a smaller part of available resources was devoted to capital formation. The share of private consumption remained relatively stable and for some countries the export surplus accounted for a larger share of national product. (*See* also CAPITAL INVESTMENT; COST OF LIVING; PRICES; PROFITS AND DIVIDENDS; WEALTH AND INCOME, DISTRIBUTION OF.) (M. GT.)

BIBLIOGRAPHY. M. Malinvaud, *Initiation à la Comptabilité Nationale* (Paris, 1958); D. Paige and G. Bombach, *A Comparison of National Output and Productivity of the United Kingdom and the United States* (O.E.E.C., Paris, 1959); P. Studenski, *The Income of Nations. Theory, Measurement, and Analysis: Past and Present* (New York, 1958); Studies in Income and Wealth, vol. XXII, *A Critique of the United States Income and Product Accounts* (Princeton, 1958).

NATIONAL PARKS. England and Wales.

No new national parks were established during 1959. Progress was made by the park planning authorities in constructing new car parks and lay-bys, signposting roads leading into the parks, clearing derelict sites and providing information centres for visitors. Three further areas of outstanding natural beauty were established: the Shropshire hills (300 sq.mi.), 400 sq.mi. of the Dorset coast and hinterland and about 40 sq.mi. of the Malvern hills.

Australia. *New South Wales.* Two new national parks, the Blue mountains and Brisbane Water national parks, were established during 1959. The Blue Mountains park (155,000 ac.) is situated in the central Blue mountains, between the towns of Glenbrook and Mount Victoria, and is noted for its bracing climate and magnificent scenery. The Brisbane Water park (15,000 ac.) lies north of the Hawkesbury river in the Woy Woy district. It provides excellent views of the Hawkesbury river, Broken bay and Brisbane water.

Queensland. One new national park of 740 ac. was proclaimed in the parish of Hull, embracing Bicton hill and part of the Walter Hill range. A total of 253 national parks were in existence in 1959 with an area of 838,134 ac. The number of people who visited the parks during 1959 was 550,000.

South Australia. During the year 400,000 persons visited the Belair national park. An interesting addition to the attractions of the park was a 20-ac. wild life enclosure which was being stocked with kangaroos, wallabies and emus.

Western Australia. Two further areas were earmarked as national parks. These were an area of 127 ac. at Greenmount in the Darling range, about 16 mi. from Perth; and an area of 3,430 ac. along the eastern banks of the Chapman and Blackwood rivers in the extreme south western corner of the state.

Canada. A record total of 4,959,110 people visited the national parks and national historic parks during the year. An extensive construction programme to improve park highways continued. The Trans-Canada highway from Banff national park to Yoho national park was completed and opened to traffic. The province of Prince Edward island joined the list of provinces with national historic parks by the establishment of Fort Amherst, or Fort La Joie, a 207-ac. site near Charlottetown.

Kenya. The well-known "Treetops" tree-house in the Aberdare national park continued to be popular with visitors and a large number of elephant, rhino and buffalo were observed at night from this vantage point. A road was constructed over the moorlands of this national park and at one point reaches a height of 10,524 ft., giving magnificent scenic views.

Northern Rhodesia. The Kafue national park, the only national park proclaimed in Northern Rhodesia, covered an

The village of Abbotsbury, Dorset, lying in a fold of the hills midway between Weymouth and Bridport, is included in the " area of outstanding natural beauty ", 400 square miles in extent, established in August by an order of the National Parks commission.

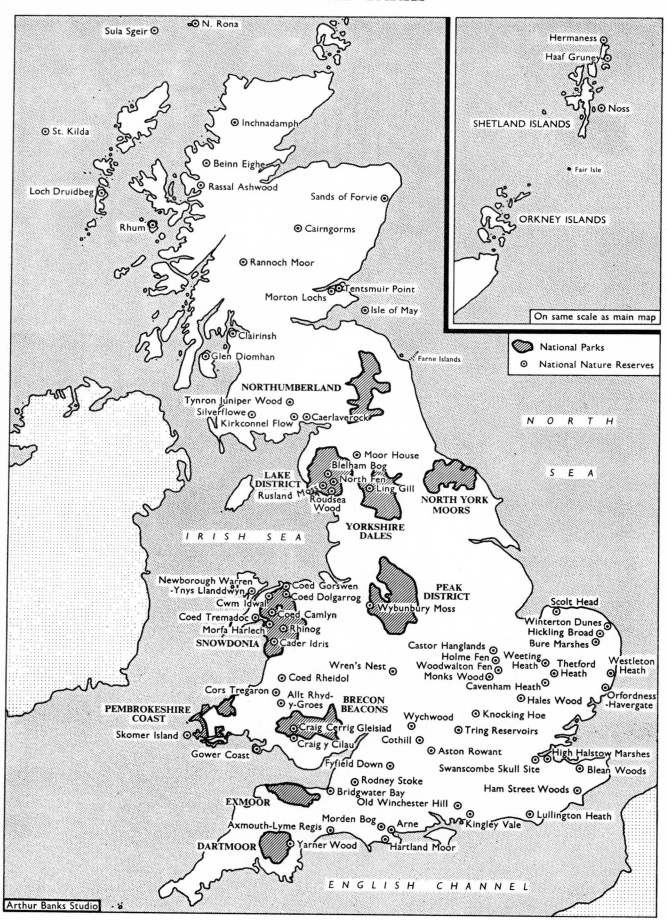

Sula Sgeir ⊙
⊙ N. Rona
Inchnadamph ⊙
⊙ St. Kilda
Beinn Eighe ⊙
Rassal Ashwood ⊙
Sands of Forvie ⊙
Loch Druidbeg ⊙
Rhum ⊙
Cairngorms ⊙
Rannoch Moor ⊙
Morton Lochs ⊙ ⊙ Tentsmuir Point
⊙ Isle of May
Clairinsh ⊙
Glen Diomhan ⊙
Farne Islands

NORTHUMBERLAND
Tynron Juniper Wood ⊙
Silverflowe ⊙
Kirkconnel Flow ⊙ ⊙ Caerlaverock

⊙ Moor House
Blelham Bog
LAKE DISTRICT ⊙ North Fen
Rusland Moss ⊙ ⊙ Ling Gill
⊙ Roudsea Wood
NORTH YORK MOORS
YORKSHIRE DALES

IRISH SEA

PEAK DISTRICT
Wybunbury Moss ⊙

Newborough Warren ⊙ Coed Gorswen
-Ynys Llanddwyn ⊙ Coed Dolgarrog
Cwm Idwal ⊙
Coed Tremadoc ⊙ ⊙ Coed Camlyn
Morfa Harlech ⊙ ⊙ Rhinog
SNOWDONIA ⊙ Cader Idris
Wren's Nest ⊙
Castor Hanglands ⊙
Holme Fen ⊙ Weeting ⊙ Thetford
Woodwalton Fen ⊙ Heath ⊙ Heath
Monks Wood ⊙
Cavenham Heath ⊙
⊙ Coed Rheidol

Cors Tregaron ⊙
PEMBROKESHIRE COAST
Allt Rhyd-y-Groes ⊙ **BRECON BEACONS**
Skomer Island ⊙ Craig Cerrig Gleisiad ⊙
Craig y Cilau ⊙
Gower Coast ⊙
Fyfield Down ⊙
Rodney Stoke ⊙
⊙ Bridgwater Bay
EXMOOR
Axmouth-Lyme Regis ⊙ Morden Bog ⊙ ⊙ Arne
DARTMOOR ⊙ Yarner Wood
Hartland Moor

Wychwood ⊙
Cothill ⊙
⊙ Knocking Hoe
⊙ Tring Reservoirs
⊙ Aston Rowant
Swanscombe Skull Site
Old Winchester Hill ⊙
⊙ Kingley Vale

Scolt Head ⊙
Winterton Dunes ⊙
Hickling Broad ⊙
Bure Marshes ⊙
Westleton Heath ⊙
⊙ Orfordness-Havergate
⊙ Hales Wood
High Halstow Marshes ⊙
Blean Woods ⊙
Ham Street Woods ⊙
Lullington Heath ⊙

NORTH SEA

⊘ **National Parks**
⊙ **National Nature Reserves**

ENGLISH CHANNEL

SHETLAND ISLANDS
Hermaness ⊙
Haaf Gruney ⊙
⊙ Noss
Fair Isle ·
ORKNEY ISLANDS
On same scale as main map

Arthur Banks Studio

area of 8,650 sq.mi. in the Kafue River basin, stretching for 250 mi. from Kasempa district in the north to Kalomo district in the south. An attractive feature is the beautiful river (after which it is named) which flows through the park and along its border for 160 mi.

Rhodesia and Nyasaland. A further national park was established at Sebakwe, near Que Que, Southern Rhodesia, with an area of 6,200 ac. The total number of people who visited the parks in 1959 was 500,000.

South Africa. A new park, named the Bontebok national park, was established at Swellendam. During 1959 140,000 people visited the national parks, which included 122,000 visitors to the Kruger national park.

Tanganyika. Arrangements were being made for the establishment of two new national parks: the Lake Manyara park of 100 sq.mi. and the Ngurdoto Crater park of two square miles.

United States. Mission " 66 ", the long-range park conservation programme initiated by the U.S. National Park service in 1956, moved steadily forward in 1959 by improving facilities and services in the various units of the national park system, while at the same time keeping intact their scenic and historic treasures. The programme's major objective was to provide a national park system adequately equipped and staffed to care for an anticipated 80 million visitors annually. The total of visitors in 1959 was approximately 62 million, nearly double the 1949 total.

Significant progress was made, under the Mission " 66 " programme, towards developing a national inventory of existing parks and recreation areas, and their facilities, and of potential areas suitable for administration at federal, state and local levels of government.

Early in 1959, the National Park service issued a report recommending the establishment of a 30,000-ac. national seashore park on Cape Cod, Massachusetts, to include a 40-mi. stretch of outer beach from Provincetown to the tip of Nauset beach. (*See* also WILD LIFE CONSERVATION.)

(H. M. As.; C. L. WI.)

NATIONAL TRUST. The year 1959 was primarily one of consolidation. Fewer properties were acquired than in immediately preceding years, which enabled the trust to give special consideration to the maintenance and improvement of properties already in its ownership. In particular a large-scale programme was undertaken, costing some £100,000, for the improvement of farms and cottages, and for extensive repairs to historic buildings. On Sept. 1 membership stood at 83,000, an increase of 9,000 over the total at the beginning of the year. A photographic exhibition at Charing Cross Underground station featuring properties belonging to the trust within the area covered by the London Transport executive's services resulted alone in the enrolment of more than 1,000 new members. Free legacies and donations amounted to nearly £100,000, but the annual accounts showed a deficit of some £120,000, mainly owing to the improvement programme undertaken.

Benthall hall, Shropshire, which was given with the more important contents by Mrs. J. Hoyer Benthall and endowed by Sir Edward Benthall, was the only house to come into the care of the trust during the year. A 16th-century stone house, Benthall hall was considerably altered inside in the early 17th century when an interesting staircase and the oak panelling and decorated plaster ceilings were added.

Among the open spaces given to the trust by benefactors were Pencarrow head, south Cornwall; an area of 264 ac. of

A map showing the distribution of national parks and national nature reserves throughout England, Scotland and Wales.

A drawing room at Waddesdon manor, Bucks., opened to the public on July 1. The manor was acquired by the National Trust in 1957.

cliff and farmland; Rosemergy, north Cornwall, where 55 ac. of cliffland overlooking the Brandys rock, Porthmoina cove and Bosigran head were given as a memorial to his father by Nicholas Thomas in addition to covenants protecting a further 208 ac. of farm and moorland adjoining; and 18 ac. at Gunwalloe, Cornwall which completed the trust's ownership of the whole of the Towans.

Properties transferred under the National Land Fund scheme included 100 ac., mainly in the Valency valley, near Boscastle on the northeast coast of Cornwall, and St. Anthony in Roseland, Cornwall; an area of 433 ac. of coast farmland surrounding the hamlet of Bohortha. In Worcestershire, 364 ac. of the Clent hills, including Clent hill and Walton Hill common, were given by Worcestershire County council, the Feeny trustees and Bromsgrove Rural District council. (*See* also HISTORIC BUILDINGS.) (D. H. McC.)

NAVIES OF THE WORLD. At the end of 1959 there were three great navies, those of the United States, the U.S.S.R. and the United Kingdom. Other major fleets were those of France and Italy, followed by those of the Netherlands, Sweden, Spain, Turkey, Canada, Australia, Argentina, Brazil and Chile. There were also 56 lesser navies. The strengths in ships, of and above the escort categories, of the navies of the world were as shown in Table I.

Among the naval events of the year were: On March 17, 1959, the nuclear powered submarine " Skate " surfaced at the North Pole and completed a 12-day sub-Polar cruise. On April 3 the giant U.S. attack aircraft carrier " Independence ", the fourth unit of the " Forrestal " class, the largest aircraft carriers in the world, was completed.

For ten days in April Nato exercise " Medflex Guard " involved every destroyer and frigate of the British Mediterranean fleet and most of the ships of the other Nato powers in the Mediterranean. On April 9 fire damaged the Royal Navy's largest aircraft carrier " Ark Royal " in Devonport dockyard and injured a dozen men. The biggest Seato maritime exercise yet held began on April 14 when three naval task forces sailed from Singapore and 40 ships from five of the Seato nations (Australia, France, New Zealand, United Kingdom and United States) took part under the over-all command of the flag officer commanding the Australian fleet.

The nuclear powered submarine U.S.S. " Skipjack ", commissioned on April 15, made the highest speed ever attained by a submarine on trials. On May 15 the world's first nuclear-powered frigate, the U.S.S. " Bainbridge ", as big as a light cruiser and armed with guided missiles, was laid down at Quincy, Massachusetts. On June 9 the world's first nuclear-powered fleet ballistic missile submarine, the U.S.S. " George Washington ", was launched at Groton, Connecticut.

On June 12 the Royal Navy's first nuclear-powered submarine " Dreadnought " was laid down at Barrow-in-Furness by Admiral of the Fleet Prince Philip, Duke of Edinburgh.

Warships of the Royal Navy, the Royal Canadian Navy and U.S. navy escorted the Royal yacht " Britannia " at the ceremonies attending the opening of the St. Lawrence seaway by Queen Elizabeth II and President Eisenhower on June 26.

On July 14 the U.S.S. " Long Beach ", the first nuclear-powered surface fighting ship in the world, the first surface ship to be armed with a main battery of guided missiles and engined by a nuclear propulsion plant, and the first ship to be designed and constructed from the keel up as a cruiser for the United States since the end of World War II, was launched at Quincy, Massachusetts. The world's largest submarine, the U.S.S. " Triton ", the first submarine to be engined with two atomic reactors instead of one, and the U.S. navy's first nuclear-powered radar picket submarine, designed to serve as an " early warning " station for the Supreme Allied Atlantic command, was completed in August at Groton, Connecticut. The U.S. large aircraft carrier " Wasp " returned on Aug. 19 from anti-submarine manoeuvres in the Atlantic with two men dead and 20 injured from an explosion in the hangar.

On Sept. 15 the newly completed large Soviet icebreaker " Lenin ", the world's first nuclear-powered surface ship,

The U.S. nuclear-powered submarine " Skipjack " making fast at Portland on Aug. 14, on arrival for a four-day visit to Britain.

TABLE I.   NAVIES OF THE WORLD (Dec. 1959)

	Heavy aircraft carriers	Large aircraft carriers	Light aircraft carriers	Escort carriers	Battleships	Cruisers	Destroyers	Frigates and escort vessels	Submarines
UNITED STATES	7	24	7	40	10	53	379	365	196
U.S.S.R.	—	—	—	—	—	32	180	300	500
UNITED KINGDOM	—	3	6	—	1	12	55	102	54
FRANCE	—	—	4	1	2	5	19	57	20
ITALY	—	—	—	—	—	3	8	40	6
NETHERLANDS	—	—	1	—	—	2	12	20	5
SWEDEN	—	—	—	—	—	3	12	11	25
SPAIN	—	—	—	—	—	5	14	27	6
TURKEY	—	—	—	—	—	1	12	—	10
CANADA	—	—	1	—	—	—	9	34	—
AUSTRALIA	—	—	2	—	—	1	7	17	—
ARGENTINA	—	—	1	—	—	5	9	11	2
BRAZIL	—	—	1	—	—	2	15	8	5
CHILE	—	—	—	—	—	2	4	6	2
INDIA	—	—	1	—	—	2	3	10	—
CHINA (P.'s Rep.)	—	—	—	—	—	2	5	32	20
NEW ZEALAND	—	—	—	—	—	2	—	8	—
GREECE	—	—	—	—	—	1	4	14	2
PAKISTAN	—	—	—	—	—	1	6	7	—
PERU	—	—	—	—	—	2	—	6	8
JAPAN	—	—	—	—	—	—	14	24	2
NORWAY	—	—	—	—	—	—	5	7	8
PORTUGAL	—	—	—	—	—	—	5	13	3
CHINA (Nat.)	—	—	—	—	—	—	11	19	—
GERMAN FED. REP.	—	—	—	—	—	—	6	7	2
RUMANIA	—	—	—	—	—	—	4	5	6
UNITED ARAB REP.	—	—	—	—	—	—	4	4	10
VENEZUELA	—	—	—	—	—	—	3	9	—
POLAND	—	—	—	—	—	—	4	—	7
THAILAND	—	—	—	—	—	—	—	5	—
DOMINICAN REP.	—	—	—	—	—	—	2	8	—
SOUTH AFRICA	—	—	—	—	—	—	2	4	—
ISRAEL	—	—	—	—	—	—	2	2	2
COLOMBIA	—	—	—	—	—	—	4	3	—
YUGOSLAVIA	—	—	—	—	—	—	3	4	1
DENMARK	—	—	—	—	—	—	—	12	3
INDONESIA	—	—	—	—	—	—	1	7	—
GERMAN DEM. REP.	—	—	—	—	—	—	—	6	4
MEXICO	—	—	—	—	—	—	—	8	—
KOREA (South)	—	—	—	—	—	—	—	6	—

Other naval forces with four or fewer escort vessels were those of Cuba, Belgium, Rep. of Ireland, Korea (North), Persia, Uruguay, Ecuador and Burma. Minor warships were possessed by Bulgaria, Cambodia, Ceylon, El Salvador, Ethiopia, Finland, Ghana, Guatemala, Haiti, Honduras, Hungary, Iceland, Iraq, Lebanon, Liberia, Malaya, Nigeria, Panama, Paraguay, Philippines, Syria and Vietnam (South).

sailed into the Baltic on her maiden voyage. On Sept. 21, during his visit to the United States, N. S. Khrushchev casually told the captain of the U.S. coast guard cutter " Gresham ", on a trip round San Francisco bay, that the U.S.S.R. was cutting its number of cruisers by 90%.

On Oct. 20 the U.S. navy announced that the " Nautilus ", the world's first nuclear-powered submarine, had been sabotaged while having a new core fitted to her reactor at Portsmouth, New Hampshire. The U.S.S. " Halibut ", the first guided missile nuclear-powered submarine, and the first submarine ever designed from the keel up as a guided missile carrier, was completed at Mare Island naval shipyard at the end of the year.

U.S. Naval Strength. The new nuclear-powered attack aircraft carrier " Enterprise ", of 75,700 tons, was nearing the launching stage. Two giant aircraft carriers of 60,000 tons were being built, the " Kitty Hawk " and " Constellation ", of the class of which the " Forrestal ", " Ranger ", " Saratoga " and " Independence " were the forerunners. The large attack aircraft carrier " Coral Sea ", of 51,000 tons, was being extensively reconstructed and modernized. The new amphibious assault ship " Iwo Jima " (helicopter carrier), of 15,000 tons, was laid down, and a sister ship was projected. The heavy cruiser " Albany ", of 13,700 tons, was being converted into a guided-missile cruiser. Ten nuclear-powered

*(Left) Soviet sailors man an anti-aircraft gun on board a frigate during manoeuvres in the Black sea on Feb. 23—Soviet army and navy day.
(Right) The Bréguet 1050 " Alizé " anti-submarine aircraft with which the new French carriers " Clemenceau " and " Foch " will be equipped.*

submarines were in commission. Twenty-three guided-missile destroyer leaders (frigates), 18 guided-missile destroyers, a nuclear-powered destroyer, 2 destroyer escorts and 29 more nuclear-powered submarines were under construction or projected. In addition to the ships enumerated in Table I, there were 324 minesweepers and minelayers, 23 escorts, 88 patrol vessels, 466 amphibious craft, 745 auxiliaries and 1,574 service craft. The U.S. navy comprised a total of 4,300 vessels at the end of 1959, of which 864 were active (389 warships, 475 support ships and 100 naval reserve training ships) and 1,511 were in reserve (not including service craft).

U.S.S.R. There was a considerable increase in Soviet naval activity on the high seas during 1959. The Soviet navy was cutting down its cruiser strength and concentrating instead on the building of submarines, torpedo boats, minesweepers and guard boats. In addition to the categories enumerated in Table I, there were 1,000 mine-sweepers, 125 patrol vessels,

500 motor torpedo boats, 120 landing craft and 160 fleet auxiliaries.

Great Britain. The new aircraft carrier " Hermes " was completed. The aircraft carrier " Leviathan " was still suspended. The large aircraft carriers " Ark Royal " and " Eagle " were being reconstructed and modernized. The aircraft carrier " Bulwark " was being converted into a commando carrier. The new cruiser " Tiger " was completed and the construction of the cruisers " Blake " and " Lion " neared completion. Four guided-missile destroyers and seven general-purpose frigates were under construction or projected. Fifteen new frigates of the anti-aircraft, aircraft-direction and anti-submarine types were being built. Thirteen new submarines, including the nuclear-powered " Dreadnought ", were under construction and others projected. Warships other than those shown in Table I included 3 fast minelayers, 2 netlayers, 28 ocean minesweepers, 10 coastal minelayers, 104 coastal

TABLE II. MODERN TYPES OF WARSHIPS

Category	Name or class	Date of completion	Country	Tons displacement	Main armament guns	Torpedo tubes	Aircraft	Shaft horse power	Knots speed
HEAVY AIRCRAFT CARRIERS	" Independence "	1959	U.S.	60,000	8 5-in.	—	100	260,000	35
	" Coral Sea "	1947	U.S.	51,000	10 5-in.	—	137	212,000	33
FLEET AIRCRAFT CARRIERS	" Ark Royal "	1955	U.K.	36,800	16 4·5-in.	—	110	152,000	31½
	" Oriskany "	1950	U.S.	33,100	8 5-in.	—	100	150,000	33
LIGHT AIRCRAFT CARRIERS	" Hermes "	1959	U.K.	22,500	10 40 mm.	—	45	76,000	29½
	" Wright "	1947	U.S.	14,500	40 40 mm.	—	50	120,000	33
	" La Fayette "	1943	France	11,000	26 40 mm.	—	45	100,000	32
BATTLESHIPS	" Missouri "	1944	U.S.	45,000	9 16-in.	—	—	212,000	33
	" Vanguard "	1946	U.K.	44,500	8 15-in.	—	—	130,000	30
	" Jean Bart "	1949	France	38,750	8 15-in.	—	—	150,000	30
LARGE CRUISERS	" Alaska "	1944	U.S.	27,500	9 12-in.	—	—	150,000	33
HEAVY CRUISERS	" Salem "	1949	U.S.	17,000	9 8-in.	—	—	120,000	33
	" Zhdanov "	1956	U.S.S.R.	15,450	12 6-in.	10 21-in.	—	130,000	34½
	" Roanoke "	1948	U.S.	14,500	12 6-in.	—	—	120,000	32
	" De Ruyter "	1953	Netherlands	9,735	8 6-in.	—	—	85,000	32
LIGHT CRUISERS	" Tiger "	1959	U.K.	9,550	4 6-in.	—	—	75,500	31½
	" Colbert "	1958	France	8,500	16 5-in.	—	—	86,000	32
	" Göta Lejon "	1947	Sweden	8,000	7 6-in.	6 21-in.	—	100,000	33
	" Wilkinson "	1954	U.S.	3,700	2 5-in.	4 21-in.	—	80,000	35
	" Tartu "	1958	France	2,750	6 5-in.	6 21·7-in.	—	63,000	34
	" Diana "	1954	U.K.	2,610	6 4·5-in.	10 21-in.	—	54,000	34¾
LEADERS AND DESTROYERS	" Morton "	1958	U.S.	2,850	3 5-in.	4 21-in.	—	70,000	35
	" Alamein "	1948	U.K.	2,400	5 4·5-in.	10 21-in.	—	50,000	31
	" Kotlin "	1957	U.S.S.R.	3,000	4 4-in.	10 21-in.	—	90,000	38
	" Halland "	1955	Sweden	2,600	4 4·7-in.	8 21-in.	—	50,000	35
	" Blackpool "	1958	U.K.	2,200	2 4·5-in.	12 21-in.	—	30,000	30
FRIGATES	" Leopard "	1958	U.K.	1,920	4 4·5-in.	—	—	16,000	25
	" L'Agenais "	1958	France	1,295	6 2·25-in.	12 21·7-in.	—	20,000	27
	" Triton "	1959	U.S.	5,900	(radar picket)		—	...	30
	" Skipjack "	1958	U.S.	2,850	—	6 21-in.	—	...	25
	" Growler "	1958	U.S.	2,174	(guided missiles)		—	...	20
SUBMARINES	" Z 60 "	1958	U.S.S.R.	2 250	2 2·5-in.	8 21-in.	—	...	22½
	" Porpoise "	1958	U.K.	1,700	—	8 21-in.	—	...	18
	" Dauphin "	1957	France	1,200	—	8 21·7-in.	—	...	16

minesweepers, 85 inshore minesweepers, 13 motor torpedo boats, 30 coastal craft, 21 trawlers, 33 landing ships, 80 landing craft, 68 boom defence vessels, 7 surveying vessels, 88 fleet support ships and many miscellaneous ships and auxiliaries.

France. The new aircraft carrier " Clemenceau " was preparing for service and her sister ship " Foch " was in an advanced stage of construction. A helicopter carrier was projected. A new anti-submarine destroyer was under construction; 3 new frigates were completed and 9 were under construction, and 16 submarines were being built or were projected.

Italy. A light cruiser was being converted to carry guided missiles. Three guided-missile escort cruisers, two guided-missile destroyers, six frigates and four submarines were under construction or projected.

Netherlands. Four submarines were being built or projected and 16 inshore minesweepers were in various stages of construction.

Sweden. Nine submarines, five motor torpedo boats and six coastal minesweepers were being built or projected.

Turkey. Four large destroyers were acquired from Great Britain where they had been refitted.

Canada. The seven new destroyer escorts of the " Restigouche " class were completed and a new batch of six were under construction.

Australia. The " Parramatta ", second of four " Whitby " class fast anti-submarine frigates, was launched.

Peru. The cruisers " Newfoundland " and " Ceylon " were purchased from Great Britain and renamed. (*See* also COMMONWEALTH NAVIES.)   (R. V. B. B.)

See Raymond V. B. Blackman, *Jane's Fighting Ships, 1959-60*, 62nd ed. (London, 1959).

NEPAL. Himalayan kingdom between India and Tibet. Area: *c.* 54,000 sq.mi. Pop. (1954 census) 8,431,537; (1958 est.) 8,910,000. Aboriginal stock is Mongolian, with Hindu admixture. Language: Gorkhalis (Gurkhas) speak Parbatia, of Sanskrit origin; Bothias use Tibetan; Newars, from southern India, speak Gubhajius, resembling Tibetan but with many Sanskrit words. Religion: Buddhism overlaid with Hinduism. Capital (pop., 1954 est.): Kathmandu 110,000. King, Mahendra Bir Bikram; prime minister, Bisheshwar Prasad Koirala. Main imports: textiles and footwear, cigarettes, salt, fuels, sugar, metal manufactures and machinery, cement. Main exports: food grains, timber, oil seeds, *ghee* (clarified butter), potatoes, medicinal herbs, hides, cattle. Monetary unit: Nepalese *rupee* = Indian rupee.

History. On Feb. 12, 1959, King Mahendra promulgated his country's first democratic constitution. It was drafted by a committee of seven assisted by Sir Ivor Jennings. It provides for a two-house parliament: a 109-seat House of Representatives (Pratinidhi Sabha) and a 36-member Upper House (Maha Sabha). While the former is elected by all Nepalese citizens over 21, 18 members of the latter are elected by the lower house and 18 nominated by the king.

Elections to the House of Representatives started on Feb. 18 and ended on April 3. The Nepali Congress party (moderately Socialist) led by B. P. Koirala won 74 out of 109 seats. The rightist Gurkha Parishad (Rana family party) obtained 19 seats, the United Democratic party (led by K. I. Singh, who was himself defeated) 5, the Nepali Communist party (leader, Pushpa Lal) 4, others 7.

On May 27 the king swore in the first fully elected Nepali government headed by B. P. Koirala. It had 8 ministers and 11 deputy ministers. On July 22 the Senate was sworn in and two days later the king opened the first session of parliament in Nepali history.

On June 11, Jawaharlal Nehru arrived in Kathmandu to meet the king and the prime minister. According to responsible sources the king, disturbed by events in Tibet, was contemplating applying for membership of Seato. Nehru

In Kathmandu the " monsoon devil " performs his farewell dance during the carnival at the end of the monsoon season in September.

advised against such a step. When Nehru announced on Sept. 27 in the Indian parliament that any attack on Nepal would be regarded as aggression against India, Koirala said the following day to a British press representative: " We are at peace with everybody, so there is no occasion for us to ask aid from anyone."

A Soviet-Nepali agreement was signed at Kathmandu on April 24 under which Nepal would receive Rb.30 million (£2·7 million) for technical aid. General Subarna Shamsher, the finance minister, on Aug. 10 gave details of the Nepali budget of N.Rs.248,958,000 (about £12,447,900). He said that the United States would contribute N.Rs.63,540,000 and India N.Rs.40,183,000. (*See* also SINO-INDIAN FRONTIER DISPUTE.)   (X.)

NETHERLANDS. Kingdom of northwest Europe, bounded N. and W. by the North sea, E. by Germany and S. by Belgium. Area: 12,868 sq.mi. (not including waterways and sheets of water larger than 185 ac.). Pop.: (1947 census) 9,625,499; (mid-1959) 11,346,180. Language: Dutch. Religion (1947): Roman Catholic 38·50%; Dutch Reformed 31·03%; Reformed Churches 7·93%; non-church members 17·04%. Chief towns, pop. (mid-1959): Amsterdam (official capital), 870,973; Rotterdam 731,848; The Hague (seat of the government) 606,270; Utrecht 252,892; Haarlem 169,122; Eindhoven 164,588; Groningen 143,874; Tilburg 135,752; Nijmegen 128,251; Arnhem 123,710; Enschede 122,921; Breda 106,381; Apeldoorn 102,031; Hilversum 100,629. Ruler, Queen Juliana. Prime ministers in 1959: Louis Beel and (from May 19) Jan Eduard De Quay. Main imports: coal; petroleum and products; machinery and vehicles; ores, iron, steel and manufactures; textile fibres and manufactures; cereals and seeds. Main exports: cattle and meat; dairy produce incl. eggs; vegetables and seed potatoes; metal and manufactures; machinery and electrical apparatus; textile fabrics; petroleum and products. Monetary unit: *guilder* or *florin* (Fl.10·64 = £1 sterling).

History. The caretaker cabinet under the leadership of Louis Beel, which was formed after the crisis of Dec. 1958, dissolved the Lower Chamber. A general election took place on March 12, 1959. The 150 seats were divided as follows (previous strength in brackets): Catholic People's party 49 (49); Labour party 48 (50); Anti-Revolutionary party 14 (15); Liberals 19 (13); Christian-Historical union 12 (13); Political Reform party 3 (3); Communists 3 (7); Pacifist Socialists 2 (0). (*See* also ELECTIONS.) The party with the biggest gain, the

Liberal party, consolidated its successes in the provincial elections of 1958, while the Labour party recovered partly from its losses at that time. The loss of four seats by the Communist party was due to the serious internal discord amongst its leaders which had already led to a split in the party in 1958.

As usual, the formation of a new cabinet progressed slowly and with difficulties. From the start of the discussions the Labour party wished to co-operate only if a stronger tie between government and parties would be established with regard to the programme and composition of the cabinet; *i.e.*, stronger than was deemed desirable by the non-Socialist parties. As a result the Socialists were no longer included in the discussions.

Jan De Quay, of the Catholic People's party, who had been asked to form a new cabinet, met with great difficulties concerning the allocation of portfolios among the participating parties. On May 19 the new cabinet was sworn in with the following membership: 6 Catholics, 3 Liberals, 2 Anti-Revolutionaries and 2 Christian-Historicals. For the first time since 1945 the Socialists went into opposition.

In a government statement made in the Lower Chamber on May 26, the new government announced that in broad outline the policy of the previous government would be continued but that more attention would be given to private initiative, especially with regard to housing. Rents would be increased by 20% as from Jan. 1, 1960, and the consumer subsidy on milk would be decreased. To this end a general wage compensation to a total of 4% would be granted. Apart from this, a more differentiated wage structure, within the framework of the general wage control and to be effected by changing the collective labour agreements, would be allowed in as far as wage increases could be paid out of increased productivity without causing an increase in prices.

During the parliamentary debate on the government statement the Chamber demanded a further explanation of the policy with regard to rents, wages and consumer subsidies. In a debate from July 14 to 17, the government made concessions with regard to the date at which the measures would come into force: these were postponed until April 1960. Opposition motions to grant priority to wage increases over rent increases and subsidy decreases were rejected. Fearing inflation the cabinet then issued strict directives for control of the wage increases; these directives were opposed by the trade unions who claimed that, apart from the general wage increase of 4%, too little room was provided for a differentiated wage

The charming little Drakestein castle near Soestdijk palace, bought by Queen Juliana of the Netherlands for Princess Beatrix.

The statue of Albert Plesman, the founder of the famous Dutch airline, K.L.M., unveiled by his grandson in The Hague on Oct. 7.

revision. However, in a further parliamentary debate on Oct. 4, the government persisted in its policy.

The state budget for 1960, presented on Sept. 15, showed a marked improvement compared with the 1959 budget; the estimated deficit for 1960—Fl.951 million—was half the estimated deficit for 1959. As the whole of the estimated 1960 deficit would be caused by intended capital investments, it would be covered by issuing loans. The improvement of economic activity during 1959 was greater than had originally been anticipated. However, increased imports went hand in hand with increased exports in order to supplement stocks which had decreased during previous years. The balance of payments should therefore show an estimated surplus of about Fl.550 million less than in 1958 when it was Fl.1,694 million. The gold and currency reserves of De Nederlandse Bank increased, due partly to the sale of securities to foreign countries. The relaxation in the money and capital markets, which had already begun in 1958, showed in the lowering of the bank rate from 3½% to 3% on Nov. 15, 1958, and from 3% to 2¾% on Jan. 21, 1959. A government loan of Fl.400 million, which was issued in Jan. 1959, was over-subscribed many times. In 1958 the national savings amounted to 19·7% of the national income (1950: 11·6%). Although demand for manpower increased during 1959, no great tension occurred on the labour market by the end of the year; the business world reacted cautiously to the improvement in the economic situation, this caution being reflected in investments.

Parliament accepted unanimously an act relating to a general widows and orphans insurance. By this act, which came into effect on Oct. 1, a temporary or permanent benefit was granted to widows and orphans. The fight against the housing shortage was continued and *c.* 80,000 dwellings were built during 1959. Proposals were laid before parliament for extension of all sectors of education, especially in view of the ever increasing industrialization. As a result of the rapid increase in the number of television sets (estimated at 580,000 at the end of 1959) a government plan was published to increase gradually television broadcasting time from 15 hr. per week in 1959 to 30 hr. in 1963. (M. RJ.)

NETHERLANDS OVERSEAS TERRITORIES.

Netherlands Guiana or Surinam and the Netherlands Antilles are with Holland equal components of the kingdom of the Netherlands. Each of the countries has internal autonomy and its own legislature. The fourth part of the kingdom, Netherlands New Guinea, is a non-self-governing territory. Total area (Surinam, Netherlands Antilles and Netherlands New Guinea): c. 206,615 sq.mi.; total pop. (1958 est.) 1,143,000.

Surinam (NETHERLANDS GUIANA). A self-governing part of the kingdom of the Netherlands lying in northeastern South America between French Guiana to the E. and British Guiana to the W. Area: 54,143 sq.mi. Pop.: (1950 est.) 221,300; (1958 est.) 241,000. The population composition in 1950 was as follows: 47·5% of African or aboriginal descent; 31·4% were either born in India or descended from persons born there; 17·8% Indonesian; 1·2% Chinese; 1·3% European (mainly from the Netherlands); 0·8% from various other origins. The official language is Dutch, but other languages and dialects are widely used. Capital, Paramaribo, pop. (1958 est.) 105,000. Governor, J. van Tilburg; prime minister, S. D. Emanuels. Main export: bauxite (82%). Monetary unit: *Surinam florin* (S.Fl.5·28 =£1 sterling).

History. S. D. Emanuels' cabinet, backed by a three-party coalition which held 17 of 21 seats in the Legislative Assembly, continued in 1959 its policy of extending the economic foundations of the country and reducing its dependence on the export of its most important product, bauxite. Provision was made for the building of two highways, one connecting Nieuw Nickerie in the extreme west to Albina in the extreme east of the country's coastal regions and another one from the capital Paramaribo south to Godo. The first of these highways was being built; the plan of the second was announced. These highways would open up part of the inland jungle, the mineral wealth of which was to be explored.

Netherlands Antilles. A self-governing part of the kingdom of the Netherlands, the state consists of six islands in the Caribbean. Total area: 371 sq.mi. Total pop. (1958 est.) 194,057. The three Leeward Islands consist of Curaçao (173 sq.mi., pop. 126,103), Aruba (69 sq.mi., pop. 58,486) and Bonaire (95 sq.mi., pop. 5,775). These three are about 40 mi. from the coast of Venezuela. Northeast of them, in the Windward Islands (east of Puerto Rico), are St. Martin (17 sq.mi., the northern part constitutes a French colony; pop. 1,537), St. Eustatius (12 sq.mi.; pop., 1,086) and Saba (5 sq.mi.; pop. 1,070). The official language is Dutch, but a local *patois* (known as *papiamento*) of diverse origin is equally widespread. Religion: mainly Roman Catholic. Willemstad on Curaçao is the capital; pop. (1955 est.) 49,248. Governor, A. B. Speekenbrink. Prime minister, Ephraim Jonckheer. Main import: crude petroleum. Main exports: petroleum products. Monetary unit: *Curaçao florin* (C.Fl.5·28 =£1 sterling).

History. The cabinet, originally backed by 12 of the 22 members of the Legislative Assembly, extended its support in this representative body to 14 members by attracting two more ministers. On May 25, 1959, elections were held for the legislative councils in each of the six islands. About 90% of the voters went to the polls. The results showed only minor differences from those of the *Staten* elections in the previous year, except that the Catholic party at Curaçao lost 25% of its support.

After the elections the new councils had to nominate their deputies in the executive body of their respective islands. In the preceding four-year period the executive body of the island of Curaçao consisted of members of each of the four parties represented in the legislative council. For the new period, however, the Democratic party and the Catholic party holding between them 11 out of 21 seats in the council, decided to keep the two other parties out. They did not succeed because one of the Democratic members in the council refused to take part. He joined the other two parties with a newly established party of his own. With the majority of 11 seats now on their side, this new three-party combination nominated an executive body of its own. Two months later however the wheel turned again when one of the members of the three-party combination went over to the Democratic party. Of the members of the executive body (elected for the full period of four years) all but one refused to retire. As a result of all this shuffling and reshuffling the island government found itself in a situation of confusion and frustration.

The Dutch expedition which climbed the 15,376-ft.-high Juliana Top in the Sterren Gebergte, Netherlands New Guinea, in 1959.

Netherlands New Guinea. The western part of New Guinea in the western Pacific, with adjacent smaller islands. Area: c. 152,100 sq.mi. Pop. (1958 est.) 700,000 (of whom c. 360,000 are in districts under regular administration), mainly Papuans but incl. c. 17,000 Europeans and 18,000 Asians. Principal town: Hollandia (cap.), pop. (1958 est.) c. 16,000. Governor: P. J. Platteel. Main export: crude petroleum. Monetary unit: New Guinea *florin* (at par with the Dutch florin).

History. Between 1950 and 1958 the area under regular administration was increased from 48·6 to 101·9 sq.mi. The exports of native produce were in 1958 twice the weight and three times the value of 1950 exports. The export of copra rose from 2,844 to 5,651 tons. The cultivation of cocoa by the Papuans, introduced a few years previously, proved to be successful. The number of medical doctors rose from 19 in 1950 to 80 in 1958. In July 1959 the construction of a large modern hospital at Hollandia, with extended facilities for the training of medical personnel was completed.

During the 1950-58 period the number of schools and special courses increased from 652 to 1,205, the number of teachers from 952 to 1,940 and the number of pupils from 31,395 to 53,012.

In 1959 a regional community for the Schouten Islands was set up. Preparations were made for the election of the members of the council for this community.   (H. G. H.; X.)

NEW GUINEA: *see* NETHERLANDS OVERSEAS TERRITORIES; PAPUA-NEW GUINEA; TRUST TERRITORIES.

NEW HEBRIDES.

Anglo-French condominium, the British element of which is within the jurisdiction of the western Pacific high commission (*see* PACIFIC ISLANDS, BRITISH); group of c. 30 islands and many islets, about 500 mi. W. of Fiji. Area: c. 5,700 sq.mi. Pop. (1957 est.): native 49,304, mostly Melanesians; non-native 4,584, incl. 599 under British jurisdiction and 3,985 under French jurisdiction. Religion: pagan; Christian minorities. Capital: Vila (pop. c. 2,000) on Efate I. Resident commissioners: British, J. S. Rennie; French, B. M. Favreau. Main imports: rice and other foodstuffs, hardware and machinery, fuels, textiles. Main exports: copra, cocoa, coffee, fish. Currency: sterling, Australian, French (250 New Hebridean francs = £1 sterling).

History. During the fiscal year 1958-59 an Anglo-French economic development programme was inaugurated, with emphasis on the improvement of communications and the promotion of native co-operatives and cash-crop production. The Compagnie Française des Phosphates de l'Océanie proceeded in 1959 to test and develop the manganese deposits discovered by its geologists on Efate Island.

The first stage of the World Health organization's anti-yaws campaign was completed.

Native membership of the advisory council was increased to parity with European membership.

On Dec. 28 Vila was struck by a cyclone which caused widespread destruction, and it was subsequently reported that all women and children were to be evacuated from the town. (R. P. Gn.)

NEWSPAPERS AND MAGAZINES. The provincial and local newspapers and periodicals were hard hit by the printing strike in 1959 (*see* PRINTING). A parallel dispute in the printing ink industry threatened the national dailies with a stoppage, but this was averted by an agreed importation of ink and the nationals had only to reduce the number of their pages. Eighty-seven morning and evening provincial newspapers and over 1,000 local weeklies as well as magazines and periodicals were brought to a standstill. Some of the newspapers produced abbreviated or occasional editions; three Bristol papers combined volunteer labour and issued an eight-page newspaper, *News of the West*; and in at least one place the town crier's help was enlisted to announce important local news. Several periodicals were printed abroad, although some foreign printers refused such " tainted " work. During the printing strike there were several instances of local councils refusing to admit to meetings journalists working for the emergency editions of local newspapers. Under the existing law the press had a statutory right, with proper exceptions, to attend open council meetings, but this right did not extend to committee meetings and it was found easy for a council to resolve itself into committee in order to exclude the press.

Several major " take-over bids " were made in the newspaper and periodical field during 1959. In what was described as the biggest newspaper deal since World War II, Roy Thomson, Canadian newspaper owner and head of Scotsman Publications' newspapers, acquired control of the entire Kemsley Newspapers chain. This comprised four Sunday newspapers including the *Sunday Times*, four provincial dailies and seven provincial evening papers. Lord Kemsley relinquished the position of editor-in-chief of the *Sunday Times*, and he and members of his family resigned from the board on the take-over, Kemsley Newspapers becoming Thomson Newspapers. The *News of the World* group made two bids for the ordinary share capital of George Newnes, publishers of more than 50 magazines and periodicals including *Country Life*, *Woman's Own*, *Woman's Day* and *Amateur Gardening*, but eventually Odhams Press' counterbid of about £12·3 million was accepted by 96·4% of the holders. In a £1·8 million share transaction Odhams also acquired Hulton Press, whose publications included *Housewife*, four children's newspapers, the *Studio* and *Lilliput*. Amalgamated Press, already acquired by the *Daily Mirror-Sunday Pictorial* group, disposed of its shares in Condé Nast, the U.S. publishing firm, for £1·8 million, and changed its name to Fleetway Publications.

The year saw the voluntary winding-up of the Newsprint Supply company. This company, of which the shares were held by nine London national newspapers, two representatives of the Newspaper society and one representative of the Scottish Newspaper Proprietors' association, was established in 1940 and was responsible during the war and the postwar years for the supply and equitable distribution, and the regulation of consumption, of newsprint.

According to a survey published by the Institute of Practitioners in Advertising, the gross readership of Sunday newspapers was 81·2 million, more than 53 million of which was accounted for by the *News of the World*, the *Sunday Pictorial*, the *People* and the *Empire News*. The combined readership of the *Sunday Times* and the *Observer* was 4·4 million. The same survey gave the average daily readership for the national newspapers as nearly 50 million, the *Daily Mirror* and the

FRANKLIN

" Hey there ! Put him down at once ". A " Daily Mirror " comment on " The Times' " report on June 1 of Selwyn Lloyd's " possible transfer " from the Foreign Office.

Daily Express accounting for over half the total. The Newspaper society's regional readership survey among housewives revealed that more than four out of five housewives read their local newspapers. In towns where local evening newspapers were published they were read by 82% of housewives, and in weekly newspaper centres outside the large cities 83% of housewives read local weeklies.

On June 1, 1959, *The Times* published a speculative article by its political correspondent on the future of the foreign secretary, Selwyn Lloyd. This article had wide repercussions, especially at Geneva where Lloyd was attending a conference of foreign ministers. Following this incident, Emrys Hughes introduced into the House of Commons The Times Newspaper Nationalization bill, but on the day it was down for second reading the house was counted out and the bill was not proceeded with. The *Manchester Guardian* dropped the word " Manchester " from its title and became *The Guardian*. The newspaper stated that this implied no change of policy but merely acknowledged an accomplished fact, for nearly two-thirds of the paper's circulation now lay outside the Manchester area. The *Daily Telegraph* and the *Sunday Times* both adopted a new type-face, the Linotype Jubilee, claimed to be the only original newspaper text-face designed in Britain since The Times roman in 1932.

Lord Astor resigned the chairmanship of The Times Publishing company and his son Gavin Astor was elected to succeed him. Lord Astor retained the office of chief proprietor with John Walter and remained a member of the board. C. V. Wintour succeeded P. Elland as editor of the *Evening Standard* on the latter's appointment to be chairman and managing director of the Evening Standard, Ltd. R. J. Edwards became managing editor of the *Daily Express*, and Arthur Christiansen resigned the post of editorial director of that paper. Arthur Wareham relinquished the editorship of the *Daily Mail*; his place was taken by William Hardcastle, whose post as editor of the *Sunday Dispatch* was filled by Herbert Gunn. Arthur Crook became editor of *The Times Literary Supplement* on the resignation of Alan Pryce-Jones; Leonard Skevington was made editor of *Time and Tide* on the resignation of Anthony Lejeune; and Selwyn Powell became editor of the *Geographical Magazine*, succeeding Michael Huxley who had founded the magazine in 1935. W. A. Cole followed Sir Christopher Chancellor as general manager of Reuters. The Statesman and Nation Publishing company appointed Gerald Gardiner as chairman on the death of Prof. G. D. H. Cole (*see* OBITUARIES). Deaths reported in

BRITISH PRESS PICTURES OF THE YEAR

The pictures on these facing pages received awards in the 12th annual " British Press Pictures of the Year " competition sponsored by " Encyclopædia Britannica " and the Institute of British Photographers. The awards were presented by Dame Margot Fonteyn at a reception at the Savoy hotel on Dec. 14. The number of entrants, 294, was the highest ever, and included 42 overseas photographers. As usual, the competition was organized in seven categories, for each of which there was a separate panel of judges. Eight of the entrants won awards for the first time. Rosemary Mathews of Keystone Press Agency became the first woman to win an award in the present categories. She gained the 2nd prize in the Sequence category. Of the 19 awards made, 14 were won by newspaper photographers.

PORTFOLIO. (Right) 1st prize, " Far From Home " one of ten pictures by Terence Fincher of the " Daily Herald ", who was awarded the Hector McNeil Trophy and the title of " British Press Photographer of the Year " for the second time. The 2nd prize in this category was won by Victor Blackman of the " Daily Express ", exhibiting for the third time. Tony Eyles of the " Daily Herald " and Peter Keen of the " Observer " were both honourably mentioned.

FEATURE. (Above, left) 1st prize, " Clowning together " by John Hawken of the " Western Mail ", Cardiff, who was exhibiting for the second time. He was one of the three provincial newspaper photographers who received awards. The 2nd prize in the Feature category was won by Harry Benson of the " Daily Express ". This was the third occasion on which his pictures were selected for exhibition.

ROYAL. (Above, right) Robert Haswell of the " Daily Express " won this category with his picture of Princess Alexandra entitled " Will you be my Valentine?". He won the News category in 1956 G. S. Finlayson of " The Guardian " was awarded the 2nd prize in the Royal category, while Steve Brodie of the " Sunday Dispatch " and Chris Ware of Keystone Press Agency both received honourable mentions.

NEWS. (Left) 1st prize, " Baton Charge " by Laurie Bloomfield of the " Natal Daily News ", showing police attempting to disperse African women rioters in the shanty township of Cato Manor. This was one of three awards won by South African photographers (the other two went to Ian Berry of " Drum " magazine). It was the first occasion on which Bloomfield had pictures selected for exhibition.

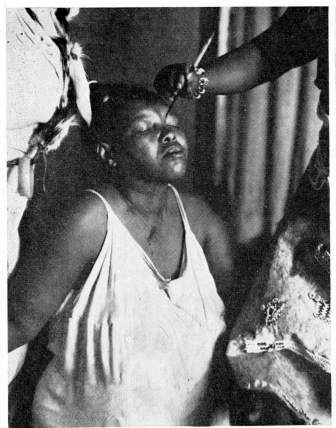

SEQUENCE. (Above, left) One of a sequence of 13 pictures entitled " City Witchdoctor " which won the 1st prize for Ian Berry of " Drum " magazine, South Africa. The sequence shows a woman witchdoctor practising her art in an African suburb of Johannesburg. Berry, exhibiting for the first time, was also honourably mentioned, and became the first entrant to win two awards in one category in one year.

SPORT. (Above, right) 1st prize, " Going into Orbit? " by C. Thomas of the Manchester " Evening Chronicle ". The 2nd prize in this category was also won by a Manchester photographer, W. Bradley of the Manchester " News Chronicle ". It was the first time either had pictures selected for exhibition.

(Above) " Crash Horror ", a picture taken by Colin Fletcher of Southern News Pictures for the " Daily Mirror ", won the 2nd prize in the News category. It shows the accident in a motor cycle race at the Crystal Palace, London, on March 30, in which two riders were killed. This was Fletcher's first exhibition.

(Right) " The Stars Look Down ", by Victor Blackman of the " Daily Express ", who won the 2nd prize in the Portfolio category: Vivien Leigh, Noel Coward, Lauren Bacall and Kay Kendall after a visit to the theatre.

In the COLOUR category (not illustrated) the 1st prize was shared by Walter Lockeyear of P.A.-Reuter Photos and Barnet Saidman of the " News Chronicle ". Saidman was the winner of this category in 1954 and 1958.

The Manchester Guardian.

Manchester: Printed and Published by J. GARNETT, No. 29, Market-street.

No. 1.   SATURDAY, MAY 5, 1821.   PRICE SEVEN-PENCE.

The Manchester Guardian

No. 33,032   SATURDAY, SEPTEMBER 27, 1952   Price Threepence

MANCHESTER GUARDIAN

No. 35,188   WEDNESDAY AUGUST 19 1959   Price 3d

THE GUARDIAN

No. 35,192   Manchester, Monday August 24, 1959   Price 3d

On Aug. 24 the " Manchester Guardian " became " The Guardian ", a change in keeping with its status as a national rather than a provincial newspaper. Above are shown the four chief masthead styles used by the paper (with minor variations) since its foundation in 1821.

1959 included those of Sir Frank Brown of *The Times*; two other *Times* men, W. Thomson Hill, since 1943 a regular contributor on archaeological matters, and R. D. Charques, a distinguished literary critic and an authority on Russian history; two eminent music critics, Ernest Newman and Eric Blom; H. E. Wortham, " Peterborough " of the *Daily Telegraph* since 1934; H. F. Harvey, editor of the *Birmingham Mail* from 1907 to 1944; Collin Brooks, who was for 12 years editor of *Truth*; and Stefan Litauer, a well-known Polish journalist (*see* OBITUARIES).

New weeklies appearing in 1959 included *John O'London's Weekly*, under different management from the journal of that name which ceased publication in 1954; *Scope*, intended to help ambitious young men and women in business and industry; and *Television Today*, sponsored by the *Stage*. New quarterlies included the *Commonwealth Socialist Review*, sponsored by the Labour party, and *Critical Quarterly*, a medium for academic critics. An appeal was made for annual subscriptions from all colleges to save the *Oxford Magazine*, founded in 1882. Publications which ceased to appear included three weeklies published by Amalgamated Press: *Home Chat* (founded in 1895), *Everybody's* (1925) and *TV Mirror* (1953). Other casualties were the *Sketch*, the illustrated fortnightly first published in 1893, and, surely a sign of the times, the weekly *Pawnbrokers' Gazette and Trade Circular*.

Commonwealth. The Commonwealth Press union, with a membership of nearly 600, celebrated its golden jubilee. Its report once again drew attention to several cases of infringement of the liberty of the press and mentioned that representations to the governments responsible had in many cases met with success.

In Nyasaland a group of Europeans launched a new monthly magazine, *Tsopano*, aiming to be " a true and genuine medium for the expression of African opinion ". The trustees of the weekly journal *Central African Examiner* resigned in order that the paper might be run on conventional commercial lines, but it was emphasized that the journal would continue to give general support to the concept of federation. The minister of education and information in Ghana stated that prosecutions in regard to offences against the new Constitution (Amendment) act could only be taken by the attorney-general on the instructions of the prime minister, who had made it clear that he was very jealous of the freedom of the press, and the act would not be used to interfere with legitimate press freedom. The government had

decided that no prosecutions under the act would be initiated against any staff correspondent of any newspaper or news agency. It had been stated earlier that no British newspaper maintained a staff correspondent in Ghana. Most papers had correspondents whom they paid on the basis of material printed and, since sensational news was more likely to be printed, these correspondents tended to send what they knew would be published. Two of Kenya's political weeklies, the *Independent*, a right-wing review, and *Uhuru* (" Freedom "), owned by the Nairobi People's Convention party, were proscribed because they persisted in publishing material which stimulated race hatred and might result in violence if not checked.

In South Africa the estimated circulation of English dailies was 731,559 and of Afrikaans dailies 165,922. English weekly and Sunday publications had a total sale of 1,060,621 and Afrikaans 668,090. A statement by the minister of external affairs, complaining of distorted reports of South African affairs appearing in the overseas press and suggesting that it might become necessary to take action against offending foreign newspaper correspondents who were not South African nationals, was answered by a special meeting of British, U.S., French and other foreign correspondents who affirmed that they would continue to maintain the internationally accepted standard of journalism and would take no part in South African politics.

The rivalry between the two Sydney, Australia, newspapers, the *Daily Telegraph* and *Sydney Morning Herald*, led to a legal action. In an effort to win some of the long list of small advertisements appearing in the *Sydney Morning Herald*, the *Daily Telegraph* inserted advertisements copied from the *Herald* into its own columns and claimed them as a free service. The *Telegraph* was trapped into copying fictitious advertisements which had been printed deliberately in the *Herald* columns. The judge, however, after stating that the conduct of the defendant company left a great deal to be desired, dismissed the case, having come to the conclusion that, since there had been a substantial departure from the *Herald* form, this was not strictly copying. Controversy in Canberra over increases in ministers' and members' salaries was stimulated by bitter criticisms in newspapers. R. G. Menzies, the prime minister, attacked the press, specifically the *Melbourne Herald* and the *Sydney Morning Herald*, for a " great campaign to lower the prestige of parliament and correspondingly to increase the authority of the press ", to which the editor of the *Sydney Morning Herald* replied: " A newspaper has a duty to assess the merits of government policies and to criticize them freely if its editor believes they are damaging to the public interest."

Canada had 100 daily newspapers, all local in distribution and approaching 4 million in total circulation. The Victoria *Daily Colonist* celebrated its centenary (Dec. 1958). Founded as a weekly, it had become a daily in 1860 and was the oldest daily newspaper in Canada west of Winnipeg. The Conservative *Ottawa Journal* was bought by Victor Sifton, owner of the Liberal *Winnipeg Free Press*. An announcement said that the *Ottawa Journal* would continue as an " independent Conservative " newspaper.

In 1958 there were signs that the newspaper-reading habit was spreading among the people of India. Over 300 daily newspapers, in English, Hindi and all the other principal languages of India, sold a total of 3·5 million copies daily to a population of some 370 million. Because of an Indian government decision, made to encourage the development of Indian news agencies, that communications facilities should be given to foreign news agencies only through an Indian news agency with whom they had entered into an agreement, three out of the four international news agencies distributing world news in India were compelled to suspend their service. Owing to its long-standing arrangement with the one remaining Indian news agency, Press Trust of India, Reuters enjoyed a monopoly in the Indian market.

An ordinance was issued in Pakistan providing for the banning of publication and distribution of newspapers containing " matters likely to endanger the defence, external affairs or security of Pakistan ". The ordinance gave the government authority to remove from control or management the owner, director or any other person in a newspaper establishment. The new powers would, the government stated, permit continuity of publication while ensuring that " the policy of the newspaper concerned is not determined by foreign influence ". Almost immediately an official administrator was appointed to take over the Lahore company, Progressive Papers, Ltd., which published the *Pakistan Times*, two Urdu dailies, *Improz* published in Lahore and Karachi, and *Lailo Nahar*, a Lahore weekly, on the ground that these newspapers were producing material and documents which were " likely to endanger the security of Pakistan ". The editors of the newspapers were replaced and the *Pakistan Times* in its first leading article under the new order disavowed its previous policies. The shares of the company were ordered to be seized and sold by auction.

A severe censorship was temporarily imposed on the newspapers of Ceylon in October after the murder of the prime minister, S. W. R. D. Bandaranaike.

In Singapore threats against the press were contained in pre-election declarations by the leader of the (eventually successful) People's Action party, Lee Kuan Yew. Referring to newspapers which tried to "sour-up " relations between the Federation of Malaya and Singapore, Lee said " any editor or reporter who goes along this line will be taken in under the P.P.S.O. (Preservation of Public Security ordinance). We shall put him in and keep him in." Later a special observer from the International Press institute came to the conclusion that, while there was still a potential danger to the freedom of the press in Singapore, the threats were an electoral incident and might have been exaggerated. Before the election the *Straits Times* had moved its main centre of publication from Singapore to Kuala Lumpur within the federation.

Europe and International. More than 200 journalists from 29 countries attended the Eighth General assembly of the International Press institute held in west Berlin. It was stated that the necessary qualifications for membership of the I.P.I.,

which represented 500 newspapers in 38 countries, were the absence of censorship and the existence of an opposition press. The I.P.I. published a report of a two-year survey entitled *The Press in Authoritarian Countries* covering such countries as Spain and Egypt and many in South America, as well as those in eastern Europe. The survey revealed evidence in many authoritarian countries of the aspirations of journalists to a greater freedom of expression and a greater degree of truthfulness in news.

The price of French newspapers was raised from Fr.20 to Fr.25 because of increased costs. A new morning newspaper, *Paris-Jour*, in tabloid form, took the place of *Paris-Journal*. When newspapers were excluded from the formal inauguration of the French Constitutional council, at which the state-controlled press services were represented, protests were made against the attitude of the new regime to the press. It was stated that the regime had been reluctant to grant the facilities to which journalists felt themselves entitled. *L'Express* and *France-Observateur*, both weekly left-wing newspapers, had issues seized for publishing offending articles on Algeria. The sale and circulation of *L'Express* were banned in military camps and quarters. There came into force in France a new penal code, one of the main features of which was to restrict the considerable liberty hitherto allowed to the press in reporting judicial proceedings. It laid down that police, magistrates and counsel could no longer hold " press conferences " about their inquiries before a matter came to court, and made a newspaper liable to penalties if it criticized a court decision.

According to figures from German sources, the Federal Republic had 5,630 newspapers and periodicals, 10% of which were published in west Berlin, while the Democratic Republic had 492, of which 64% were published in east Berlin. A foundation was established to ensure the independence of the *Frankfurter Allgemeine Zeitung*, one of western Germany's leading newspapers. The aims of the foundation were to preserve the newspaper from governmental, party political, economic or personal influence. Concern was caused in the Federal Republic over the involuntary retirement of Fritz Sänger, the editor-in-chief and general manager of the German Press agency. Dr. Sänger was a member of the Social Democratic party, and the agency's supervisory board which decided to dispense with his services was largely composed of supporters of anti-Socialist parties.

About 100 newspapers were published in Italy, with a total circulation of not more than 4 million. According to a survey by the Italian Central Institute of Statistics, in half of Italy's families no daily newspaper, magazine or book was read from one year's end to another. Only 22% of families took a daily newspaper and only 19% read both a daily and a periodical.

Pravda published its 15,000th issue and claimed that its circulation had reached 6 million. A new anti-religious monthly, *Nauka i Religiya* (" Science and Religion ") made its appearance in the U.S.S.R. A. F. Adzhubey, son-in-law of Nikita S. Khrushchev, was appointed editor of *Izvestia*.

The persecution of the press in Turkey continued. Official figures showed that, between 1950 and 1958, 2,324 trials of newspapermen had taken place, 811 newspapermen being sent to prison. The prime minister proposed an amnesty for journalists in prison, but neither this nor a modification in the press law materialized, and new trials leading to prison sentences were held during 1959. The opposition organ *Ulus* was again suppressed for three months and *Vatan* was suspended for one month.

United States. The combined daily copy circulation for 1,750 dailies stood at 58,604,942 for the six-month period ending March 31, 1959. The circulation of 554 Sunday papers reached 49,043,905. These totals may be compared with a daily circulation of 57,418,311 and a Sunday circulation of 46,954,686 in 1958. Newspaper advertising volume, which dropped by 2·8% in 1958, was running 7·3% ahead in the first nine months of 1959, according to Media Records. At that level, the 1959 total in the annual *Printers' Ink* advertising volume estimates would be more than $3,400 million. National advertising in newspapers, which declined by 5% in 1958, was running 7% higher in 1959 (at a level of $820 million), according to *Printers' Ink*. Such figures would set new records for the U.S. newspaper industry.

In Jan. 1959 John S. Knight sold the controlling interest in the *Chicago Daily News* to Field Enterprises, Inc., headed by Marshall Field, Jr., owner of the *Chicago Sun-Times*. This $24 million transaction gave Field both morning and evening papers to compete with the *Chicago Daily Tribune* and its evening affiliate, the *Chicago American*. The Knight newspaper group purchased the *Charlotte News* (North Carolina) in April to gain control of both of that city's newspapers and restore the group's holdings to five dailies. The trend towards consolidation of newspaper properties was accelerated by the Scripps-Howard group, which was involved in a newspaper merger in San Francisco in Aug. 1959 and one in Columbus, Ohio, in November. Altogether, the disappearance of daily newspapers brought the number of U.S. cities with competing dailies down to 65 (4·5% of the 1,450 cities with dailies).

A year after the merger of United Press and the International News Service, the new United Press International reported that it had 5,900 clients in 85 countries. The Associated Press figure was approximately 7,100 in 80 countries. Listings in the *Editor and Publisher International Yearbook* for 1959 showed that the A.P. was servicing 45% of U.S. dailies on a one-agency basis and the U.P.I. 30%, while 25% received both services.

There were spurts in the circulations of major mass magazines in 1959, which was also a record year for magazine advertising revenues. Joining *Life*, *Look* and the *Saturday Evening Post* at circulations exceeding 6 million by the close of 1959 were the *Ladies' Home Journal* and *McCall's*. *Reader's Digest*, with a circulation of more than 12 million in the United States and 11 million overseas, remained the leader. Other major circulations included *TV Guide*, with more than 7 million, and *Everywoman's Family Circle Magazine* with 5 million sales in the supermarkets. *Better Homes and Gardens* moved up to 4,850,000 copies and *Good Housekeeping* to 4·3 million. *Time*, the leading news magazine, advanced to a circulation of 2,450,000. Circulation increases for 170 leading magazines averaged 4·2% for the first six months of 1959. *Printers' Ink* predicted that national advertising volume in magazines would reach the record level of $850 million in 1959, 11% higher than the 1958 recession level.

Samuel Newhouse, owner of 13 daily newspapers and seven radio and television stations, became a magazine publisher in April when he bought a controlling interest in Condé Nast Publications, publishers of *Vogue*, *House and Garden*, *Glamour* and *Bride's Magazine*. In August he added eight Street and Smith magazines, headed by *Charm*, *Mademoiselle* and *Living for Young Homemakers*. *Charm* was then merged with *Glamour*. Newhouse's investment in the magazines totalled nearly $10 million.   (D. Hn.; E. Ey.)

Bibliography. Majid Nizami, *The Press in Pakistan* (Lahore, 1958); Reginald Pound and Geoffrey Harmsworth, *Northcliffe* (London, 1959); G. H. Scholefield, *Newspapers in New Zealand* (Wellington, 1958); Elizabeth Wiskemann, *A Great Swiss Newspaper: The Story of the Neue Zürcher Zeitung* (London, 1959); Political and Economic Planning, *The Work of Newspaper Trusts* (London, 1959); International Press Institute, *The Press in Authoritarian Countries* (Zürich, 1959).

Corrigendum. In the article Newspapers and Magazines in the *Britannica Book of the Year 1959* (p. 355, line 28), it was stated in error that the *Morning News* is the only English-language daily in Pakistan. There are in fact 12 English-language dailies in Pakistan.

NEWS STORIES. Travel, of one sort or another, was the great headline theme of the year in which the Russians got to the moon and also to Washington, and Ernest Marples sent London motorists speeding off to Birmingham along the new motorway. **Roads,** at home, were news all the time. In January the recently opened Preston bypass was put out of action by frost, and, though Harold Watkinson, then minister of transport, seemed to think that people were making too much fuss since only 1% of the road surface was affected, this was enough to close the road to traffic for over a month. Near the year's end the way in which motorists started to use M.1, the new motorway, alarmed Marples, the new minister, but they steadied down later and Queen Elizabeth II and the Duke of Edinburgh celebrated their 12th wedding anniversary by going for a drive on it. M.1 was soon " blooded ", as some of the papers said, with its first fatalities, and road accidents mounted everywhere. Among the victims of speed was **Mike Hawthorn,** who had just retired from racing at the age of 29 after declining to take part in the Monte Carlo rally because it was too dangerous. He was on his way in a Jaguar, along

Dr. Barbara Moore, 348 miles behind her and 25 miles ahead to London, swings along the hard high road south of Welwyn on Dec. 24. Later in the day she arrived at Marble arch.

a wet road, to judge a competition in aid of the Invalid Tricycle association. Motorists stopped and laid flowers at the spot where he crashed. The travelling year drew to its close with a number of foot-slogging feats, and the first of a series of **marching records** was achieved by a royal marine who marched 110 mi. in 36½ hr. Late on Christmas Eve Dr. Barbara Moore, aged 57, reached Marble arch after a 373-mi. march from Edinburgh to London which took her 7½ days.

The Russians sought to get farther faster and they succeeded. In mid-September the front pages were black with the news that an 860-lb. sphere containing instruments had struck the **moon** somewhere in the region of Mare Tranquillitatis, and the astonishing accuracy of this piece of cosmic marksmanship may have justified a remark by the head of the Moscow Astronomic institute that " a couple of moon flights like this one and we will be ready for perfectly safe manned space trips ". Various preliminary steps were reported. The Russians launched two dogs and a rabbit to a great height and claimed that they had brought them safely back to earth. The Americans sent up two monkeys, named Able and Baker, 300 mi. into space at 10,000 m.p.h., and though they were said to be in excellent shape when they got back, and held a press conference, one of them died on the operating table when a recording instrument was removed. A U.S. satellite vehicle with four mice aboard re-entered the earth's atmosphere and burned up. In October a Russian rocket was sent round the moon and, during several crucial days, brought about a total eclipse of the British general election. The front-page sensation finally produced was not a story but a picture—the picture of the far, unknown side of the moon. Exposed films were processed automatically in the rocket and relayed by radio to ground stations in the U.S.S.R.

Top politicians travelled a great deal though still on the earth's surface or within its atmosphere. Harold Macmillan, in a white sheepskin hat, went to Moscow in February and met Nikita Khrushchev—not, as he told him, to negotiate on particular matters but to try to get a better understanding. (" Something of a reconnaissance " was what the prime minister called it in parliament.) This made big news in the United States as well as in Britain, as did other visits by heads of state. In August President Eisenhower visited Britain. Khrushchev visited the United States in September and found it beginning to recover from the stunning effect of the Soviet moon-marksmanship. Yet a **summit** conference between the heads of state did not seem to be materializing in 1959 despite Macmillan's indiscreet election remark that it looked likely to happen " within a few days ". That was in October, and weeks later the opposition in the new parliament taunted him with this over-optimism as the summit appeared to be clouding again.

Less official travellers also hit the headlines. **Field Marshal Lord Montgomery** was much in the news during the year with some heavily publicized indiscretions of his own about Americans, Labour voters and others, and in May he fixed up a private summit with Khrushchev. " I had two very long, interesting talks ", he was reported as saying. " I then did a lot of thinking and I have come back." There was also **Lord Malvern,** formerly prime minister of the Federation of Rhodesia and Nyasaland, who flew in to the House of Lords to make his contribution to the complexities of race relations in Africa by saying, virtually, that all Africans were liars.

An impressive domestic journey was made by the **Aldermaston marchers.** Some 4,000 campaigners for nuclear disarmament set out for London, about 50 mi. away, *via* Reading and Slough. Songs, guitars and accordions cheered them on their way and the marchers swelled to an estimated 15,000 as they crossed London to Trafalgar square. " Well done ", some Londoners shouted. " You ought to have your heads tested ", others called.

At Nottingham there was a long dispute between **Capt. Athelstan Popkess,** the chief constable, and the Labour-controlled watch committee of the city council. Two council members who went on a trip to the German Democratic Republic had their activities investigated and as a result the chief constable was suspended from duty for 32 days because, it was said, he refused to tell the watch committee about investigations into corporation matters and had shown a " lack of impartiality ". It was after the home secretary had asked the watch committee to reconsider its decision that Popkess was reinstated. The Conservative minority on the council maintained throughout that the chief constable did his duty properly.

Prostitutes were in the public eye through going out of it. The Street Offences bill became law in August and drove them off the streets. Known prostitutes could now be arrested for loitering only and this aroused some strong criticism in the House of Commons and also from a number of peers, who called the new measure " a shocking bill " and " a pimp's benefit ". All the newspapers at once sent their investigators to the midnight streets and they reported that London and the other great cities were, at least on the surface, changed places.

Two men were hanged for **killing policemen,** Ronald Henry Marwood being the first since the Homicide act of 1957 retained this type of murder as a capital offence. There were

demonstrations outside the prison. Later in the summer the Podola case caused a sensation, in particular through the circumstances of Guenther Fritz Podola's arrest after shooting a detective—there were questions in the Commons about his handling by the police—and his unavailing plea of lost memory at the trial.

Neil Moss, an Oxford undergraduate, was trapped in a Derbyshire pothole in March and died after 46 hr. The attempts at rescue were described as " marvellous ". A team of 30 volunteers got busy soon after it became known that the youth was trapped in a crevice 1,000 ft. below ground in a recently discovered part of the Peak cavern. Altogether ten times as many took part, most of them volunteer potholers from all over Britain. Finally a remaining party of 21 had to give up their attempt to recover the body and the tunnel was blocked up.

Questions were asked in the Commons about two young men, one well-known and the other obscure. **Terry Dene,** the " Rock 'n' Roll " singer, found his brief army career so trying that he was taken to hospital after what was described as an " emotional crisis " and finally discharged for psychiatric reasons after an effective service of one day. **John Waters,** a boy of 15 who complained of being assaulted by the police at Thurso, finally had a tribunal to look into his case and this was hailed as a victory for determined parliamentary back-benchers.

(N. S.)

NEW TOWNS. The deliberate creation of a new town is no new phenomenon in human history. Within the last 200 years a number of new towns have been built for specific purposes, mainly as capital cities. Typical of these are Washington, Canberra and New Delhi. All new towns of this kind were built by the respective governments. Similarly, after World War II, a number of countries, particularly the U.S.S.R., Poland and Czechoslovakia, began to build new towns for the purpose of carrying on specific industries and housing their workers.

In the United Kingdom, in the first half of the 20th century, two new towns were successfully established by private enterprise—Letchworth and Welwyn Garden City in Hertfordshire. The purpose of each of these was to attract industry and population away from London and to create good, healthy living conditions in relatively rural surroundings. Until the New Towns act, 1946, however, no country had undertaken the erection of new towns on a systematic and comparatively large scale. Britons may justifiably take pride in the fact that in this respect they were pioneers. Although, by 1960, the idea of new towns was generally accepted and they were regarded as among the most notable British postwar achievements, this was not the case in the beginning. Strong and

The Episcopal church at East Kilbride, Lanarkshire, a new town which will relieve housing and industrial congestion in Glasgow.

Houses at Newton Aycliffe, Co. Durham, a residential township being developed in conjunction with an adjoining industrial estate. It lies alongside the Great North road, outside the Durham coalfields and on the fringe of the lovely countryside of Teesdale.

even violent objections were raised by a number of the local inhabitants of Stevenage, Hertfordshire, Crawley, Sussex, and other proposed new towns. In two cases the development of the towns was held up pending High Court proceedings against the minister responsible. The chief objections were to bringing large numbers of Londoners into what were at the time relatively small country towns and completely changing their character. Other objections were to the acquisition of land which would be necessitated and to the then existing basis of compensation. By 1960 there were 15 new towns in the United Kingdom in various stages of completion, the most advanced—Crawley, Harlow, Essex, and Hemel Hempstead, Hertfordshire—being within close reach of their agreed population of some 60,000 to 80,000, and the most recent, Cumbernauld, Dunbartonshire, being virtually at the beginning. A number had had their target figure increased and were rapidly reaching the higher target, the largest being Basildon, Essex.

These new towns fall into several groups. The majority, and especially those in the neighbourhood of London, were started expressly to relieve congestion of population and industry in London and to prevent its indefinite growth. The same applies to East Kilbride, Lanarkshire, and Cumbernauld in relation to Glasgow. Other new towns—such as Corby, Northamptonshire, Cwmbran, Monmouthshire, Newton Aycliffe, Co. Durham, Hatfield, Hertfordshire—were initiated to provide good living conditions close to their work for workers in existing industrial areas—the steel works of Corby, the heavy industries of Cwmbran, the large number of light industries at Aycliffe and the great aircraft works near Hatfield. Peterlee, Co. Durham, and Glenrothes, Fifeshire, fall into another category, being intended to provide improved living conditions for those engaged in the mining industry in the vicinity and, in addition, to make alternative employment available for those unable or unwilling to work in the mines and for female workers.

The development of new towns followed a consistent pattern as laid down in the New Towns act. A development corporation set up by the minister concerned was responsible to him for the building of the town and for engaging the necessary administrative and technical staff. Finance was provided by the Treasury, which exercised what some thought to be a too rigid control. The plan of the town was prepared in advance, usually after a public inquiry. Each of the towns was being built on the neighbourhood system, a town with a population of 60,000 being generally divided into some eight or nine neighbourhoods. There was relatively little difficulty in what had been regarded as the most difficult of all the problems

facing the new towns, namely, that of synchronizing the availability of housing and industry. Industry was reasonably diversified. On the whole, but with some notable exceptions, such as in a few cases school accommodation, the provision of essential services kept pace with general development of the town. Shops appeared; first the essential shops in the neighbourhoods and then the main shopping area in the centre. Public buildings, churches, schools, etc., were going up and in most cases the towns were likely to be completed within the period of 15 years from their inception as originally contemplated. A number of the industrial areas and many of the new schools and churches were remarkable in their design and architectural attractiveness. Financially, the results were likely to be good and, in due course, as one would expect, they would become an asset to the community.

So much can be said in praise of the new towns. On the other hand, certain defects emerged. It had been the intention of the promoters of the New Towns act that the new towns would become centres of experiment and pioneering in the way of living. It had been hoped that there would be a considerable amount of freedom given to the corporations to indulge their ideas architecturally and socially and to experiment in new ways of town development. They had each appointed eminent architects responsible for the whole scheme as well as other architects to carry out work in the different neighbourhoods. It was thought that, at the very best, the number of new towns within the foreseeable future would not exceed about 20. The total population would be a microcosm of the population of the country and, since most of the United Kingdom's existing towns would require redevelopment over, say, the following 75 years, the new towns were expected to play a valuable part in leading the way to new ideas of development in all populated areas in the country. Unfortunately, by 1960, this had not happened as much as had been hoped. Whether it was a lack of imagination on the part of the architects and development corporations, or whether it was frustration by the ministry whose natural inclination was towards orthodoxy and uniformity, the fact remained that it was, generally speaking, difficult to distinguish one new town from another, one neighbourhood in a new town from another and, indeed, most of the new towns from any normal large housing estate built by a local authority. There was a uniformity in design and general appearance about them all which made for dullness and monotony. There was nothing comparable with, for example the civic centre of Coventry or of Plymouth, both of which had been built since World War II. There were, of course, exceptions. The centres of some of the

The Town square, Stevenage, showing an arcade of shops and, on the left, the base of the clock tower. There is no through traffic.

new towns were really exciting and could well be emulated by other towns requiring development in the future—a good deal of statuary and other ornamental features had been provided. Stevenage and Crawley were especially to be commended in this respect, but beyond these exceptionally fine general features and some rather fine architecture in the industrial zone of Crawley no buildings of outstanding architectural merit had emerged by 1960. However, many people thought, with some justification, that there was not enough homeliness about the new towns. The streets were too wide and un-urban so that the houses gave an impression of remoteness and un-neighbourliness, and the continuity of houses was not sufficiently broken up. Then there was not enough variety about the housing so as to create really balanced communities, even though a limited number of better type houses had been built by private enterprise for sale. Perhaps Harlow and Bracknell, Berkshire, among the new towns had made the best attempts to deal with this question—in the case of Harlow by the erection of a number of high, attractive blocks of flats.

There were numerous complaints that there was not enough for young people to do in the evenings. This was, of course, not confined to new towns, but new towns had provided an opportunity for new thought and new ideas in this matter and very little seemed to have emerged. It is admittedly difficult to get people coming from different parts of a large city to settle down together quickly as neighbours and to develop some kind of social life. This process would have been very greatly assisted if more facilities had been given for meeting and for creating the right environment in which the populations of the new towns could be integrated. This is not to suggest that no thought had been given to the matter and nothing done. The criticism was that not enough had been done. It was recognized that " spoon-feeding " the population was not a good thing. They had to be prepared to do things for themselves, but they needed help and somebody to take the initiative. The faults may have been partly due to the requirement of the New Towns act that the new town must pay, which may have been taken too literally. The intention had been that it should pay after all necessary facilities had been provided. The difficulty about the new towns was that many of them had failed to provide the right kind of leadership. It might have been a good thing to have deliberately

introduced families for the express purpose of providing this kind of leadership. The churches did a great deal, but the business men whose industries were located in the new town, the schoolmasters and the professional men were singularly backward in taking a lead. Possibly this resulted from the failure to provide sufficient housing suitable for such persons within the new towns. In 1960 it was a fact that many of the people engaged in administration of the new towns, in their industries, schools or professions, and who carried on their daily work there, deliberately went outside to live.

Very little indeed had been done by way of research into the social needs of the newcomers to the new towns. The corporations had been far too ready to accept traditional ideas of development such as the division into neighbourhood units and a single industrial zone. In the beginning, the ministry appointed an officer to carry out research into the best methods of providing for these needs, but the development corporations showed little enthusiasm for, or even interest in, research and the office was discontinued.

In a survey of this kind it is natural that criticisms loom larger than praise. It is essential however to have a sense of proportion. In 1960 these towns were new and had hardly had time to settle down. They could not be compared with existing towns which had been established for centuries and had developed gradually. It is an almost impossible task to create synthetically, within a very short time, all the characteristics of long-established towns. There was a need for patience, but the task would never be achieved unless the authorities faced fairly and frankly the difficulties existing in the new towns already building and realized what was wrong, with a determination gradually to put things right.

On the whole, by 1960, the general view was that the new towns had completely justified themselves. They represented one of Britain's most remarkable postwar achievements. People came to visit them from all over the world and expressed great admiration for what was being done, and

The first pour from a steel furnace at Crawley, Sussex, a town of 50,000 inhabitants developed from three scattered communities.

many countries desired to emulate Britain. Indeed, with such success and universal praise, many people wondered why additional new towns were not being provided to meet the needs of congested towns such as Manchester, Liverpool and Birmingham. As long as the authorities did not become complacent about the new towns, resting on their laurels, Britain had something of which it could well be proud.

(Ls. Sn.)

NEW YORK.
The largest city in the United States and third largest in the world (after London and Tokyo). Area: c. 315 sq.mi. Pop.: (1950 census) 7,891,957, (mid-1958 est.) 8,010,000.

New York city experienced an unusually active year of business and industrial construction. More new office space was to be completed in 1959 than in any other year in the city's history. Sixteen skyscrapers were in the final stages of construction, compared with 11 in 1958. Largest of the new structures was the 10-storey Produce Exchange building; others included the 28-storey Corning Glass building and 27-storey buildings on Third avenue and Wall street.

President Dwight D. Eisenhower laid the foundation stone on May 15, 1959, of the Lincoln Centre for the Performing Arts. When completed, the centre would include a new Metropolitan Opera house, a library-museum, a school of music, a dance and operetta theatre, a repertory drama theatre and a Philharmonic hall, the first unit which would be built. This was part of a slum clearance project, the largest ever undertaken in the United States, which would also have about 5,000 middle-income apartments, a 20-storey co-operative apartment building, new Red Cross headquarters and Fordham university's midtown centre. The project was to be completed in 1963.

To accommodate the increase in vehicular traffic, New York was undertaking a vast arterial highway building programme, including the Verrazano-Narrows bridge, construction of which began in Aug. 1959. This bridge would link Brooklyn with Staten Island and was planned for completion in 1965. It was to be 2·7 mi. long and would bring together the parkways of Long Island, Westchester and New England with the arterial systems of New Jersey and other western and southern

The Guggenheim museum in New York. It was opened in October, six months after the death of its architect, Frank Lloyd Wright.

cities. Another bridge under construction was the Throgs Neck bridge connecting Queens and the Bronx across the East river, to be completed in 1961. Work on the second, or lower, deck, a six-lane roadway, of the George Washington bridge began in June 1959.

Housing continued to be a principal concern. A Fair Housing Practices law, the first such legislation in the United States, was put into effect; it prohibited discrimination in the renting of private housing. In 1959 more than 37,000 dwellings were added to the city's housing. Of 23 slum clearance projects approved, four were completed and fully occupied. In addition to slum clearance, New York city was undertaking an extensive urban renewal programme. The first area to undergo such a development was on Manhattan's west side.

In an effort to halt the growing rise in juvenile crime occurring in the city, the administration undertook a campaign to co-ordinate the work of the public and private agencies that dealt with young people. Particular efforts were made to ensure that facilities serving youngsters were made available in the summer months when youth crime rates were at their highest.

(R. F. W.)

NEW ZEALAND.
A realm of the Commonwealth of Nations in the south Pacific, New Zealand proper comprises the large North and South Islands, and Stewart, Chatham and other minor islands. Dependencies: (i) island territories (Tokelau Islands, Niue Island and Cook and associated islands); (ii) Ross (antarctic) Dependency; (iii) Western Samoa (trust territory). Area: New Zealand proper 103,736 sq.mi.; island territories 192 sq.mi.; Ross Dependency c. 175,000 sq.mi.; W. Samoa 1,130 sq.mi. Pop.: New Zealand proper (1956 census) 2,174,062; (1958 est.) 2,282,000, incl. c. 147,000 Maoris; Tokelau Islands (1958 est.) 1,690; Niue Island (1958 est.) 4,735; Cook Islands (1958 est.) 16,925; W. Samoa (1958 est.) 102,195. New Zealand lies about 1,200 mi. E. of Australia, 6,000 mi. W. of South America and 12,000 mi. distant from London. Language: English; Maori (a Polynesian language). Religion: Christian (1956 census: Anglican 35·5%, Presbyterian 21·8%, Roman Catholic 14·1%, Methodist 7·3%, Baptist 1·5%). Chief cities (1956 census, urban area only): Wellington (cap.) 138,297 (excl. Hutt); Auckland 381,063; Christchurch 193,367; Dunedin 99,370; Hutt 86,053. Queen, Elizabeth II; governor-general, Lord Cobham; prime minister, Walter Nash. Main imports: machinery, motor vehicles, metal manufactures, petrol, textiles. Main exports: wool, dairy products, meat. Monetary unit: New Zealand pound (=£1 sterling).

History. In 1959 New Zealand's economy returned to a more buoyant state. Whereas in the previous year the overseas price for butter had fallen disastrously, leading to the imposition of licensing for many imports, a steady rise in overseas prices for New Zealand dairy products now took place. This was mainly due to the extremely dry summer in Europe which caused dairy production in European countries to fall. A near record output of butterfat in New Zealand was an added advantage. Sales of dairy products in countries in the dollar area also rose to about $8·5 million.

However, a record production of lamb (17·5 million carcasses being exported) dulled the U.K. market, and prices at Smithfield were the lowest for ten years. Beef prices remained firm. A further record production of wool (54 million lb. weight) was also followed by the lowest average price for ten years—37d. per lb.

In spite of these setbacks the improved financial situation enabled the government to release many import items from licensing control and cut the taxes on beer, tobacco and alcohol which it had applied to meet the emergency. By the end of the year New Zealand's overseas exchange transactions showed a surplus of £41 million compared with a deficit of £30 million in the previous year. The budget, announced in July, remitted £17 million in taxes in a full year. Most of the remission was on income tax. Taxation for the year for consolidated fund and social security purposes was estimated at £280·4 million, a slight fall on the previous year, while total taxation was estimated to produce £300·75 million. Ordinary income tax was reduced by 20% with a maximum rebate of £30 to any one person. To encourage overseas investment, companies not carrying on business in New Zealand could be taxed at the rate applying in the country of residence if this were lower than in New Zealand.

A comprehensive programme of public works was begun, emphasis being placed on hydroelectrical development. A

The new Auckland harbour road bridge, which was opened by the governor-general of New Zealand on May 30. The bridge, which links the business and residential quarters of the city, cost about £7 million to build and is expected to produce an annual toll revenue of £500,000.

decision was made to proceed with a £7 million scheme at Aratiatia, an £8 million project on the Rangitaiki river and to provide funds for much-needed harbour development. The second stage of the Wairakei geothermal scheme was also approved. A further interesting economic development was the establishment of an iron and steel industry in New Zealand, with the provision of facilities for smelting scrap metal at Auckland. The paper-making industry's potential increased when a second paper machine was installed at Kinleith by New Zealand Forest Products, Ltd. The Tasman Pulp and Paper company also installed a second machine and increased their share capital from £6 million to £8 million. The Bowater company became associated with the Tasman company, which envisaged further large-scale expansion. It was also announced that an oil refinery with an initial capacity of 2 million tons a year was to be built with government support by a consortium of the oil companies operating in New Zealand.

High-lights of the year were the opening of the Auckland Harbour bridge (which had cost £7 million) and the new Wellington airport. The former was a magnificent feat of precision engineering, and the construction of the airport involved intensive work on levelling hills and reclamation of land from the sea.

In July the governor-general, Lord Cobham, paid an official visit to the island territories including Tonga, the Cook group, Western Samoa and Fiji. The biggest international conference ever to take place in New Zealand—the fifth council meeting of Seato—was held in Wellington in March. This was preceded in January by an unofficial conference on Commonwealth relations held at Palmerston North.

In October Western Samoa was granted self-government in internal matters. In future the administration would rest with a cabinet responsible to the local legislative assembly, with provision for review of decisions by a council of state. The New Zealand prime minister, Walter Nash, said that his country would continue to take care of the defence of Samoa if necessary.

In February Nash paid a goodwill visit to Japan for talks with the Japanese prime minister and members of his government. In November he attended the meeting of Anzus in Washington, before journeying on to London for private talks with the British prime minister, Harold Macmillan. Nash returned to New Zealand by way of Indonesia, where he attended a Colombo Plan conference, and supported an extension of the scheme. New Zealand's contribution so far under this plan had been £9 million. It had provided aid by sending experts in various scientific, engineering and educational fields to assist in planning projects in the various Colombo Plan countries and had made provision for the training of Asian students in educational institutions in New Zealand. New Zealand, with special interests in the Antarctic, was represented at the 12-nation conference on Antarctica held in Washington.

The Indonesian foreign minister, Dr. Subandrio, visited New Zealand in February and held friendly talks with the government.

On the domestic front the government set up a committee of inquiry into university education and Sir David Hughes Parry accepted the chairmanship. An interesting report accepting the principle of a decimal coinage was tabled, the work of a committee set up in 1957. The Marlborough district held its centennial celebrations.

A notable religious event was the visit of the U.S. evangelist, Billy Graham, and meetings held by him at the main centres of population were attended by many thousands of people. In August the primate of New Zealand, Archbishop R. H. Owen, announced his impending retirement.

Among those who died during the year were the former New Zealand high commissioner in London, Sir William Jordan, the M.P. for Hamilton, Dame Hilda Ross, and Sir James Elliott, well-known in medical circles.

The major youth event of the year was the Pan-Pacific Scout jamboree at Auckland, which helped in the task of promoting better relations and understanding among nations.

In sport, the main items of interest during the year were the visit of "The Lions" (the British Isles Rugby football team), an M.C.C. eleven and a Costa Rican soccer team. Tremendous interest was aroused by the Rugby football, particularly in the test matches in which the rubber was won by New Zealand. The M.C.C., following its tour of Australia, beat New Zealand at Christchurch, and the second test at Auckland was abandoned because of heavy rain. Stirling Moss won the sixth New Zealand Grand Prix before 80,000 people at Ardmore, near Auckland, in January. In the same month New Zealand gained a notable yachting victory, winning the Inter-Dominion Silastic trophy for 12-ft. yachts. New Zealand's top golfing honour, the Open championship, was won by P. W. Thomson, of Australia. An interesting new feature was New Zealand's rise into world class in women's badminton, the New Zealand team beating Australia in the Uber cup-tie, to enter the world zone final in the United States in Feb. 1960.　　(A. T. Cl.)

NICARAGUA.

Republic in Central America, situated between Honduras (N.) and Costa Rica (S.) with a coastline of over 300 mi. on the Atlantic and over 200 mi. on the Pacific. Area: 57,143 sq.mi. (incl. 3,475 sq.mi. of water). Pop.: (1950 census) 1,057,023; (1957 est.) 1,377,600. The population of the eastern half is mainly Indian or Negro, and of the western part is of mixed Spanish and Indian extraction, with some of pure Spanish descent. Language: Spanish. Religion: Roman Catholic. Cap., Managua (pop., 1950 census; 1958 est. in brackets): 109,352 (173,024); León 30,544 (44,226). President, Luis Somoza Debayle. Main imports: machinery and manufactures. Main exports: coffee, cotton, gold and timber. Monetary unit: *córdoba* with an official exchange rate of C.19·75 = £1 sterling.

History. In the wake of invasion rumours, street demonstrations and acts of violence which were features of the political scene in Nicaragua during the first five months of 1959, there followed in rapid succession the government's declaration on May 30 of a state of siege; a general strike on June 1 in Managua against the government, which halted most of the capital's commercial activity for nearly a week; Somoza's immediate retaliatory suspension of all import licences; the arrival from Costa Rica on May 31 and June 1 of two plane-loads of rebel invasion troops; Nicaragua's appeal on June 3 to the provisions of the Rio treaty of 1947 by requesting the council of the Organization of American States to convoke the organ of consultation; and the complete triumph of Somoza over both invaders and strikers.

Both external and internal forces influenced the course of events leading up to the crisis of early June. Prior to the agreement signed in Washington by the Nicaraguan and Honduran representatives on the council of the Organization of American States (*see* Honduras), Nicaragua had denied the Honduran charge that the Somoza government was giving aid to Honduran rebels in Nicaraguan territory. Recent developments in Cuba and Venezuela and formal statements issued by

Franco Chamorro, cousin of Pedro Joaquín Chamorro, a leader of the abortive Nicaraguan invasion, with a rebel patrol on June 3.

sympathizers in these countries encouraged demonstrations in the Nicaraguan capital against the Somoza dictatorship.

In the midst of these events, Enrique Lacayo Farfán, the exiled opposition leader, suggested that the O.A.S. should investigate the presence in Nicaragua of 25 Dominican pilots and 15 Dominican aircraft. After considering the report of its special committee relative to the circumstances prompting Nicaragua's appeal of June 3, the council of the O.A.S. concluded that there was no basis for action.　　(A. E. Tr.)

NIGERIA, FEDERATION OF.

British dependent country in west Africa, bounded W., N. and E. by French African territories and S. by the Atlantic. It is administered as a federation which is divided into the semi-autonomous Western, Eastern and Northern Regions, the Southern Cameroons and the federal capital territory of Lagos. The territory of the Cameroons was included as an integral part of Nigeria in 1946 in accordance with a trusteeship agreement. The northern portion is administered as part of the Northern Region, while the southern portion is administered separately as quasi-federal territory. Total area of the federation: 373,250 sq.mi. Total pop.: (1958 est.) 34,634,000. Tribal groups (1952-53 censuses): Hausa (17·7%) and Hausa-speaking Fulani (9·7%), mainly in Northern Region; Ibo (15·8%), mainly in Eastern Region and Southern Cameroons; Yoruba (14·5%), mainly in Western Region. Religion: Moslem (north); pagan (south; Christianity widespread among the educated). Pop. of Lagos (federal cap.): (1958 est.) 337,000. Administration: governor-general; council of ministers, comprising the governor-general as president, the prime minister and not less than ten other ministers; House of Representatives with speaker and elected majority. Governor-general, Sir James Roberston (who is also high commissioner for the Southern Cameroons); federal prime minister, Alhaji Abubakar Tafawa Balewa (*see* Biographies). Main imports: machinery and motor vehicles, cotton piecegoods. Main exports: groundnuts, palm kernels and oil. Monetary unit: Nigerian pound (=£1 sterling); West African shilling circulates.

Western Region. Area: 45,376 sq.mi. Pop.: (1952 census) 6,087,917; (1957 est.) 6,613,000. Chief towns (pop. 1952 census): Ibadan (cap.) 459,196; Ogbomosho 139,535; Oshogbo 122,728; Ife 110,790; Iwo 100,006. Administration: governor; premier; executive council presided over by the premier; House of Chiefs; House of Assembly with elected majority. Governor, Sir John Rankine; premier, Chief Obafemi Awolowo.

Eastern Region. Area: 29,484 sq.mi. Pop.: (1953 census) 7,217,829; (1957 est.) 7,782,000. Chief towns: Enugu (cap.), pop. (1953 census) 62,764; Onitsha, pop. (1953 est.) 77,000. Administration: governor; premier; executive council presided over by the premier; elected House of Assembly. Governor, Sir Robert Stapledon; premier, Nnamdi Azikiwe.

Northern Region. Area: 281,782 sq.mi. (incl. 17,500 sq.mi. of Cameroons trust territory). Pop.: (1952 census) 16,840,479; (1957 est.) 18,465,000. Chief towns (pop. 1952 census): Kaduna (cap.) 38,794; Kano 130,173. Administration: governor; executive council presided over by the premier; House of Chiefs; Council of Chiefs; House of Assembly with elected majority. Governor, Sir Gawain Bell; premier, Alhaji Ahmadu, the sardauna (sultan) of Sokoto.

Southern Cameroons. Area: 16,581 sq.mi. Pop.: (1953 census) 753,358; (1957 est.) 811,000. Capital, Buea, pop. (1953 census) 3,009. Administration: commissioner; executive council with unofficial majority (one of whose members is premier) presided over by the commissioner; House of Assembly with elected majority. (Provision has been made for the setting up of a House of Chiefs, which will be a deliberative not a legislative body.) Commissioner, J. O. Field; premiers in 1959, E. M. R. Endeley and (from Feb. 1) J. N. Foncha.

History. On Feb. 11, 1959, the federal minister of finance, Chief Festus Okotie-Eboh, presented the last budget before independence, describing it as a "budget of responsibility". Revenue for 1959-60 was estimated at £83·9 million, of which £46·9 million would be for federal expenditure; £4 million would go to the development fund, and current expenditure would be £39 million. The development programme for 1955-62 was estimated at more than £148 million of which £36 million had been spent. Taking into account the regional development programmes there was a total gap of £58·1 million between federal resources and the balance of planned expenditure. In May the federal government launched a 5%-6% £2 million internal loan, which was over-subscribed. In July the British government agreed to make £15 million available towards federal and regional development programmes, which provided for £153 million to be spent during

1958-62. Of this £105 million was being raised from local resources, about £6 million from Colonial Development and Welfare funds and £10 million as a loan from the International Bank for Reconstruction and Development. The new loan towards the balance of £32 million would consist of an exchequer loan of £3 million and a Commonwealth assistance loan of £12 million.

In his speech from the throne at the opening of the fifth session of the House of Representatives the governor-general, Sir James Robertson, described the progress of " Nigerianization " of the public service which was being pursued by all possible means. In 1959 40 officers would have been trained to represent Nigeria overseas.

The British, Nigerian and U.S. governments jointly sponsored a commission on higher education under Sir Eric Ashby, to investigate Nigeria's needs in sixth form and higher education over the next 20 years and to recommend how these could be met.

By September the Shell-B.P. Petroleum Development Company (Nigeria), Ltd., had reached a production rate of 14,000 barrels a day. An agreement for 30 years was signed in June between the federal government and the company providing for a 50-50 share of the profits, sanctioned by a federal act. The government's share of the profits included royalties of 12·5% on the value of the oil produced.

At the end of 1958 a Nigerian national shipping line was established with an authorized capital of £2 million. Palm line and Elder Dempster lines were technical partners with the federal government in this venture and would train Nigerians as navigating and engineering officers and for other sea-going and managerial duties.

Richard Costain Ltd. were given an £8 million contract to construct a six-mile breakwater and a separate island breakwater in Benin bight to protect a dredged channel off the mouth of the Escravos river, which would allow ships with a draught of 20 ft. to enter the river to reach the delta ports.

In March 1959 the Trades Union Congress of Nigeria was formed to replace the All-Nigeria Trades Union federation and the Nigerian Trades Union council.

Following the federal elections held in December, in which the Northern People's congress emerged as the largest single party, a coalition government was formed between the N.P.C. and the National Council of Nigeria and the Cameroons.

Western Region. The regional budget for 1959-60 estimated current expenditure at £14·7 million and capital expenditure at £14·9 million. The government spent £31 million under the five-year development plan for 1955-59. More than 1,000 mi. of road had been tarred and many towns provided with water and electricity. Towards the end of the year the government launched the first educational and commercial television service in Africa.

Eastern Region. The budget for 1959-60 provided for the expenditure of £19·2 million of which £12·9 million was on current account and the remainder for development. The five-year development programme for 1958-62 would cost £16·6 million altogether. The premier, Nnamdi Azikiwe, gave further details of the new university which it was proposed to build at Nsukka, where 600 ac. of land had been acquired, and stated that £2 million was already available.

Northern Region. The region attained self-government within the federation on March 15. The Duke and Duchess of Gloucester attended the official celebrations in May. In February the House of Assembly and the House of Chiefs accepted unanimously the government's proposals on the report of a panel of jurists concerning the organization of the legal and judicial systems. The report recommended a criminal code based on that of Sudan as a means of avoiding conflict between the three systems of criminal law currently in force in the Northern Region. The regional budget for 1959-60 provided for current expenditure of £15 million and capital expenditure of £8 million.

Southern Cameroons. In the general election held on Jan. 24 the Kamerun National Democratic party won 14 of the 26 seats, and the allied Kamerun National congress and the Kamerun People's party the other 12. The K.N.D.P. leader, J. N. Foncha, succeeded E. M. R. Endeley, leader of the K.N.C., as premier. The main issue was whether the Southern

(*Left*) *An object of interest to the guard of honour's mascot, a crane, the Duke of Gloucester arrives at Kaduna on May 13 for the Northern Nigerian self-government celebrations.* (*Right*) *C. R. Niven* (*in rear*), *the British speaker, replaced under self-government by Alhaji Gwandu.*

Cameroons should secede from the federation or continue to associate with it as an autonomous region. The K.N.D.P. favoured secession. In March the U.N. general assembly adopted a resolution that a plebiscite should be held between Dec. 1959 and April 1960 to ascertain the wishes of the people of the Southern Cameroons. (W. H. Is.)

NIGER, REPUBLIC OF (RÉPUBLIQUE DU NIGER).

A member state of the French Community, Niger is bounded N. by the Algerian Saharan *département* of Oasis and also by Libya, E. by the Republic of Chad, S. by Nigeria and the Republic of Dahomey, W. by the republics of Upper Volta and Soudan. Area: 470,656 sq.mi. Pop.: (1945 est.) 2,168,000; (1959 est.) 2,500,000; mainly Tuareg in the north and Negroes in the south (Jerman, Hausa). Language: many Sudanic dialects. Religion: Moslem, animist, Christian minorities. Chief towns (pop., 1959 est.): Niamey (cap., 40,000); Zinder (13,000); Birni N'Koni; Maradi; Agadès. Prime minister, Hamani Diori. French high commissioner, Jean Colombani. Chief exports: groundnuts. Monetary unit: *franc CFA* =metropolitan Fr.2.

History. The Republic of Niger was proclaimed on Dec. 19, 1958. The constitution was approved by the territorial assembly on Feb. 25, 1959. The prime minister, elected by the assembly, could only be removed from office at the end of three years. Hamani Diori remained prime minister.

Niger joined the Sahel-Bénin *entente* (*see* IVORY COAST). It reached an agreement with France over the Saharan regions, where the Organisation Commune des Régions Sahariennes was to be responsible for hydraulic engineering, communications and research. (HU. DE.)

NOBEL PRIZES.

The value of each prize awarded in 1959 was 220,678 Swedish *kronor* (about £15,220). The peace prize went to a British member of parliament, Philip Noel-Baker, and that for literature to the Sicilian poet Salvatore Quasimodo. The prize for chemistry was awarded to Prof. Jaroslav Heyrovský, for his discovery and development of the polarographic method of analysis, and the physics prize was shared by Dr. Emilio Segré and Dr. Owen Chamberlain, for their discovery of the anti-proton. The prize for medicine was shared by Prof. Severo Ochoa and Prof. Arthur Kornberg, for their discoveries of the mechanisms in the biological synthesis of ribonucleic acid and deoxyribonucleic acid. For further information concerning these prizewinners, *see* BIOGRAPHIES.

NORTH ATLANTIC TREATY ORGANIZATION

(NATO). The North Atlantic treaty, in which the signatories pledged themselves to joint resistance in case of aggression against one of them and a co-operative defence effort in time of peace, was signed on April 4, 1949, by 12 North Atlantic and European nations: Belgium, Canada, Denmark, France, Iceland, Italy, Luxembourg, the Netherlands, Norway, Portugal, the United Kingdom and the United States. In 1951 Greece and Turkey and in 1955 the German Federal Republic joined Nato. After the outbreak of the Korean war in 1950 and the following rearmament of the United States and its allies, Nato established a chain of joint military commands covering northern, central and southern Europe, the Mediterranean and the Atlantic.

MILITARY ORGANIZATION

Shape (supreme headquarters, Allied powers, Europe) Rocquencourt, near Paris: SACEUR (supreme Allied commander, Europe), General Lauris Norstad (U.S.); deputies, General Sir Richard Gale (U.K.), Admiral Pierre Barjot (France) and General Leon W. Johnson (U.S.); chief of staff, General James Edward Moore (U.S.); deputy chiefs of staff, Lieut.-General André Beauffre (France), Lieut.-General Friedrich Albert Foertsch (German Fed. Rep.) and Air Marshal Clarence Rupert Dunlap (Canada).

(A) **European Command:** 1. *Northern Europe* (Oslo, Kolsås): commander-in-chief, Lieut.-General Sir Horatius Murray (U.K.); commander of Allied land forces in Norway, Oslo, Major-General R. Ø. R. Dahl; commander of Allied land forces in Denmark, Copenhagen, Lieut.-General Viggo Hjalf; commander of Allied air forces, Sandwik, Norway, Major-General Norman D. Sillin (U.S.); commander of Allied naval forces, Vice-Admiral Arthur Reid Pedder (U.K.).

2. *Central Europe* (Fontainebleau): commander-in-chief, General Jean-Etienne Valluy (France); commander of Allied land forces, General

Hans Speidel (German Fed. Rep.); commander of Allied air forces, Air Chief Marshal Sir Harry Broadhurst (U.K.); commander of Allied naval forces, Vice-Admiral Henrik Bos (Netherlands). Northern army group (Mönchen-Gladbach): commander, Lieut.-General Sir Dudley Ward (U.K.). Central army group (Heidelberg): commander, Lieut.-General Clyde D. Eddleman (U.S.); this army group includes the French forces under the command of General Jacques Allard.

3. *Southern Europe* (Naples, Camp Bagnoli): commander-in-chief, Admiral Charles R. Brown (U.S.); commander of Allied air forces, Lieut.-General Richard C. Lindsay (U.S.); commander of Allied land forces in Italy, Verona, Lieut.-General Aurelio Guy (Italy); commander of Allied land forces in Greece and Turkey (Izmir), Maj.-General Paul D. Harkins (U.S.); commander of the naval striking and support forces (U.S. 6th fleet), Vice-Admiral George W. Anderson (U.S.).

4. *Mediterranean Command* (Malta): commander-in-chief, Admiral Sir Alexander Bingley (U.K.).

(B) **Atlantic Command;** SACLANT (supreme Allied commander, Atlantic), Norfolk, Virginia: Admiral Jerauld Wright (U.S.).

There is also a North Atlantic council sitting in Paris composed of permanent delegates of the 15 member countries. Secretary-general: Paul-Henri Spaak (Belgium).

History. Nato celebrated its tenth anniversary in 1959 during a period of renewed tension in Europe over Berlin. This remained an important preoccupation during the year, though diplomatic activity spread steadily upwards to the level of heads of government. The Nato council meeting on Dec. 15-17 at foreign and defence ministers' level was held immediately before the meeting of western heads of government. It maintained and symbolized the newly established practice that the Nato council must be informed of all important diplomatic activity and consulted on matters of direct interest such as Europe and disarmament.

The council with its permanent representatives took an important part in a number of negotiations. In particular, it participated in the settlement in principle of the Cyprus dispute which affected three members—Great Britain, Greece and Turkey. It was less successful in the Anglo-Icelandic fisheries conflict, but it heard a dispassionate and full elaboration of the position of both sides.

The expansion of the council's activities and the whole scope of the alliance was once more urged by parliamentarians, journalists and scholars at an Atlantic congress which was held in London in June. Its object was to reconsider the position after ten years of Nato. A report said that the time was ripe for the building of an Atlantic community.

The relations between France and Nato were throughout the year, in the words of Paul-Henri Spaak, the secretary-general, the main internal problem of the alliance. In the

The new Nato building at the Porte Dauphine in Paris. Although not yet completed it was in use by the end of 1959.

early months of the Fifth Republic it became clear that General Charles de Gaulle desired the creation of a system of consultation and co-ordination with the United Kingdom and the United States to decide on a common and unified policy towards the world beyond Europe. Within Nato he wanted full support in Algeria, freer sharing of nuclear weapons information and a more important place in the command structure. Few if any of these were acceptable to France's principal allies and de Gaulle let it be known that his government would accept no further obligations towards the alliance until it had reasonable satisfaction. This conflict emerged clearly at the Atlantic congress, where General Pierre Billotte put forward the resolution that " Atlantic defence should be the application in the area of the alliance of a common strategy conceived and directed on a world scale." The British and Americans opposed it sharply and received general support—a public demonstration of what was evidently going on in private.

This debate led to one of the few clear examples of a difference between members affecting the military defence of western Europe. The French government informed General Lauris Norstad that it would not make any new commitments to the alliance while its general political requirements remained unfulfilled. It made it clear that the stock-piling of U.S. nuclear bombs in France for the use of the squadrons of F-100C fighter-bombers of the U.S. air force would be considered to be a further commitment. After discussions, General Norstad let it be known in June that he proposed to move the squadrons out. During the rest of the year about 225 aircraft were moved steadily into the German Federal Republic and the United Kingdom.

Otherwise, the progress of M.C.70, the defence plan which was adopted in Dec. 1957, was continuous. The number of divisions at the disposal of Shape rose steadily as the western German Bundeswehr brought its seventh division up to full strength and got well advanced with three more. (*See* table.) British reductions, which had caused so much difficulty in the preceding year, stopped at the 55,000 level which had been tentatively proposed, as a better balance of payments position developed. Air power and artillery were considerably increased by the growth of tactical atomic weapons. The training of Nato forces from several countries in the handling of U.S. missiles for these weapons was extended.

The proposal to begin the production of a family of weapons in Europe with the co-operation of the U.S. government made some headway. In particular, two missile programmes for the production under licence of established U.S. anti-aircraft weapons were announced. The first was for the Hawk, a surface-fired missile, which was to be produced jointly by the French, German, Italian, Belgian and French governments. The project was placed under the direction of the Société Européene de Téléguidage, a corporation registered under French law and created by one important company from each of the five countries. Later Denmark, the German Federal Republic, Greece, the Netherlands, Norway and Turkey joined in producing the Sidewinder, which is fired from interceptor aircraft.

NATO ORDER OF BATTLE (Dec. 1959)

LAND FORCES. *Northern Europe:* 2 Norwegian and 2 Danish brigade groups. *Central Europe:* 7 German, 5 U.S., 3 British, 2 French, 2 Belgian and 2 Dutch divisions; 1 Canadian brigade group. *Southern Europe:* 7 Italian divisions and 1 U.S. regimental combat team in Italy; 5 Greek divisions; 12 Turkish divisions.

AIR FORCES: 5,000 aircraft based on 219 airfields and grouped in four allied tactical air forces; strategic air forces under U.S. and British command.

STRATEGIC ROCKETS (under U.S. bilateral arrangements): 4 launching sites in Great Britain, 2 in Italy (not completed), 1 in Turkey (planned).

NAVIES: Committed to Saclant, 450 surface ships, 150 submarines.

A contingent of German sailors in the parade held at Mainz in April to mark the tenth anniversary of the founding of Nato.

The military forces of the alliance carried out a large number of exercises in the course of the year, mainly directed towards improving standardized procedures. It became more widely agreed, in particular by Great Britain, that air defence as a national responsibility in Europe was unrealistic. A clear decision to put it under joint command was not, however, taken. Under the infrastructure programme much money was still being spent on pipelines, the early warning radar chain and very advanced communications, for which large contracts were let in Great Britain and France. This continued expenditure on basic military works on a voluntary basis remained one of the most evident signs of the seriousness with which governments regarded the defence objectives of the alliance. (*See* also U.S. FOREIGN AID; WESTERN EUROPEAN UNION.)　　　　　　　　　　　　(D. L. B.)

NORTHERN IRELAND. Part of the United Kingdom, but with limited local autonomy; comprises *c.* 60% of former province of Ulster, viz., Counties Antrim, Armagh, Down, Fermanagh, Londonderry and Tyrone. Area: 5,459 sq.mi. Pop.: (1951 census) 1,370,921; (1957 est.) 1,402,000. Language: English. For main religion groups *see* GREAT BRITAIN AND NORTHERN IRELAND, UNITED KINGDOM OF. Chief towns (pop. 1958 est.): Belfast (cap.) 436,200; Londonderry 51,500; Newtownabbey 30,930; Bangor 22,610. Administration: governor; prime minister and ministry; Senate comprising 24 elected and 2 *ex officio* members; elected House of Commons of 52; N. Ireland is represented in U.K. House of Commons by 12 members. Governor, Lord Wakehurst; prime minister, Viscount Brookeborough of Colebrooke. Main imports: cotton goods; machinery; coal; tobacco. Main exports: linen and rayon manufactures; manufactured cotton goods; livestock; ships; machinery; farm produce. Currency: sterling.

History. The campaign of violence directed against Northern Ireland by raiders operating from within the territory of the Republic of Ireland diminished during 1959, but outrages nevertheless continued. Political commentators saw in this campaign, begun in 1956, one of the major causes of a remarkably complete victory for the Ulster Unionist party in the U.K. general election of Oct. 1959. The party won all 12 Northern Ireland seats with a strong majority in every case, including the two constituencies of Mid-Ulster and of Fermanagh and Tyrone, won by Sinn Fein in the general election of 1955. Sinn Fein contested all 12 seats, the Northern Ireland Labour party contested 3 Belfast seats, and there was 1 Independent Labour candidate and 1 Liberal. Total voting was as follows: Unionists 445,013; Sinn Fein 63,415; Northern Ireland Labour 44,370; Independent Labour 20,062; and

One of the competitors in the world ploughing championship which was held at Armoy, Co. Antrim, Northern Ireland, in October.

Liberal 3,253. In December A. B. D. Faulkner succeeded W. W. B. Topping as minister of home affairs.

The year saw a change for the better in the economic position. The textile recession, at its worst in 1958, had improved. Unemployment figures in textile industries, which had been more than 10,000 in the summer of 1958, fell to 3,219 in Aug. 1959. By Sept. 1959, the number of persons employed in Northern Ireland as a whole was 15,000 greater than a year before.

The 1958 output of the Belfast shipyard was the highest in the United Kingdom, amounting to 102,678 gross tons. Work continued in 1959 on the 45,000-ton passenger liner " Canberra ", the largest and fastest since the " Queen " liners. The 20,000-ton passenger liner " Amazon " was launched in July by Princess Margaret. The Belfast aircraft factory secured an order for the construction of the new Britannic III long-range freighter. Nevertheless redundancy caused the dismissal of a number of aircraft workers during the year.

In farming the trend towards increasing specialization in livestock continued. Sheep passed the 1 million mark for the

During a visit to Northern Ireland in May the Duke of Edinburgh unveiled a plaque at the plant of Chemstrand Ltd. at Coleraine.

first time. Pigs reached a new record of 843,350. Cattle were just under 1 million and poultry almost 12 million.

Total trade in 1958 was £621,679,000, the value of exports being £293,718,000 and of imports £327,961,000.

A change in trade union affiliation took place in 1959. In February a new Irish Congress of Trade Unions was approved by separate conferences held in Dublin by the Congress of Irish Unions and the Irish Trades Union congress. The I.T.U.C. had consisted largely of British-based unions. The headquarters of the new I.C.T.U. was to be in Dublin, with a committee for Northern Ireland. The I.T.U.C. and C.I.U. were wound up in July, and the first congress of the new body was held in Dublin in September.

Queen's university, Belfast, celebrated the 50th anniversary of its charter in April. Large new buildings were opened by the Duke of Edinburgh. Professor Michael Grant, professor of humanity at Edinburgh university, was appointed to succeed Sir Eric Ashby as vice-chancellor.

A feature of social change in Belfast, which was becoming more marked in 1959, was the extensive rehousing and a withdrawal of population from the county borough to new residential areas in Down and Antrim, including the satellite town of Newtownabbey. For the first time population figures for the city were falling, the 1958 estimated total for Belfast county borough being 436,200 compared with 443,671 at the 1951 census.   (H. SN.)

NORTHERN RHODESIA: *see* RHODESIA AND NYASALAND, FEDERATION OF.

NORWAY. Constitutional monarchy of northern Europe, bounded N. by the Arctic ocean, E. by the U.S.S.R., Finland and Sweden and S. and W. by the North sea. Area (excl. Svalbard archipelago*): 125,185 sq.mi. Pop.: (1950 census) 3,278,546; (1958 est.) 3,526,000. Languages: Norwegian and Lappish (*c.* 20,000). Religion: Lutheran. Chief towns (pop. Jan. 1, 1957, administrative area): Oslo (cap.) 455,113; Bergen 114,723; Trondheim 58,742; Stavanger 52,599. Ruler, King Olav V; prime minister, Einar Gerhardsen. Main imports: textiles, machinery, ships, coal, petroleum and products. Main exports: pulp and paper; fish and products; non-ferrous metals and manufactures. Monetary unit: *krone*, pl. *kroner* (Kr.20·00 = £1 sterling).
   * Svalbard archipelago (Spitsbergen and Bear Island): area, 23,641 sq.mi. The population, largely miners, shifts seasonally; in 1957 it was estimated at 1,530 Norwegians and 2,746 Russians.

History. The municipal elections in Oct. 1959 were hard-fought, with national issues to the fore, but produced no significant swing in political affiliations. With an over-all increase in votes cast, all parties except the Communists could claim increased electoral support. The Labour party—in power nationally with an over-all majority in the Storting (parliament) ever since 1945—claimed the result as a vote of confidence in its administration.

The opposition parties were on the offensive on two issues relating to foreign affairs. First, the government was strongly criticized for permitting the export of ammunition to Cuba during the civil war early in the year. The ammunition came from a state-owned factory, and opposition critics declared that the government had allowed local employment considerations to take precedence over prudence. From the government's point of view the position was not improved when it was discovered that the ammunition was U.S.-financed under the military aid programme. The government promised not to export ammunition in future to countries involved in civil war. It refused however to accept the opposition view that the minister of defence (the main scapegoat) should resign.

The opposition parties were also strongly critical of the government's decision to invite N. S. Khrushchev, the Soviet prime minister, to Norway in August. Eventually the visit was postponed indefinitely on the initiative of Khrushchev who referred to the unfavourable comments in newspapers in Scandinavia.

(*Top left*) *After a landslide at Øverhalla, northern Norway, in May, two occupants of this half-submerged house were swept out to sea with it and drowned.* (*Bottom left*) *The passing-out parade of the 1957-59 class—Crown Prince Harald's—of the military college, at Akershus fortress, Oslo.* (*Above*) *King Olav* (*second from left*) *inspects the new nuclear reactor at Halden.*

Plans for setting up a Scandinavian common market, which the government had been studying for several years despite opposition from business circles, were shelved with the materialization of the European Free Trade association of the " outer seven ". On the whole, Norwegian business welcomed E.F.T.A. although a European free trade area including the six common market countries would have been preferred. A good deal of disappointment was expressed when Arne Skaug, minister of trade, failed in London to persuade the British government to accept frozen fish as a free trade commodity. Nils Lysø, minister of fisheries, declared that Norway might have to reconsider the question of participation in E.F.T.A., but at subsequent multilateral discussions at Saltsjøbaden, Sweden, Great Britain did after all conditionally admit frozen fish on the duty-free list.

Production and trade generally recovered well from the temporary recession which Norway shared with other countries in 1958. The exceptionally dry summer, however, produced problems as winter approached because of the low water level in hydroelectric storage basins. Power cuts were introduced and production had to be scaled down in certain industries.

The economic improvement generally only slightly affected the low level of freight rates which had begun in 1958 and which had caused the lay-up of a considerable quantity of merchant shipping. However, towards the end of the year a number of idle ships were fixed at economic rates. In the course of the year the merchant fleet took delivery of more than a million tons of new vessels ordered in earlier boom years. Much of the new tonnage entered profitable time-charters fixed in advance when freights were high, and in spite of the slack market it was anticipated that shipping earnings would make a large contribution to Norway's foreign exchange income.

Tourism too showed expansion with the total number of visitors estimated at about 1·5 million—a new record.

To attract more foreign capital to Norway, the government appointed Trygve Lie as " ambassador extraordinary " to inform business abroad about investment possibilities. With not more than a quarter of Norway's cheap water power resources harnessed, it was believed that scope for industrial expansion was considerable, and that foreign capital could help to speed up power development and industrialization. A significant innovation was the reduction of the working week from 48 to 45 hr. The reduction was approved by the Storting on the understanding that total output would remain undiminished.

King Olav formally inaugurated the Halden boiling heavy water reactor on Oct. 10. It was designed and built by Norwegian nuclear scientists and engineers. Being the first of its kind in the world, it aroused considerable international interest, and an agreement was negotiated whereby nuclear physicists of a number of countries would operate the reactor jointly for a three-year term.   (O. F. K.)

NUCLEAR ENERGY. The year 1959 was characterized by a recession in the commercial prospects of nuclear power, together with rather greater hopes for an agreement on the ending of nuclear weapons tests. Growing surpluses of coal in Europe, improvements in conventional power stations and the continuing rapid rate of development of nuclear power station design served to delay decisions on the building of new nuclear stations. Many manufacturers turned also to ship propulsion as a promising field of application, and some types of reactors were said to be economically suitable for very large ships. So far as was known, no tests of nuclear weapons took place during the year, while some progress was made in discussions on ways of ensuring their complete abolition,

Materials. The output of uranium in processed concentrates was estimated at 35,000 tons in 1959. A large proportion of this, some 15,000 tons to 20,000 tons of metal per year, was still being used for military purposes. In general the supply of uranium exceeded the demand and there were indications that prices would be lower but for previous agreements. A price of about $8 per lb. was reported for concentrates produced in South Africa, while uranium metal was offered to the International Atomic Energy agency (I.A.E.A.) at $54·34 per kg. by the United States and at $34·00 per kg. by Belgium. Canada offered it free of charge and 3,000 kg. was resold to Japan at $35·50 per kg. A further indication that uranium was becoming an ordinary commercial commodity was the publication of sales figures by the South African mining companies.

A new £12 million factory for producing reactor fuel elements was put into operation by the United Kingdom Atomic Energy authority (U.K.A.E.A.) at Springfields, Lancashire. India and Japan produced their first ingots of uranium metal. France announced plans for a diffusion plant. The production of nuclear-grade beryllium metal was increased and the first plant in Europe for the manufacture of wrought beryllium was opened in Birmingham. A new type of steel was reported, containing titanium, with less cobalt and manganese than usual and consequently smaller neutron absorption.

Research and Development. Indicative of ever-growing activity were the new research centres for the U.K.A.E.A. at Winfrith, Dorset, and for the French Atomic Energy commission at Grenoble. The 5-Mw. reactor Merlin, the first privately owned research reactor in the United Kingdom, went into operation. Another company produced Britain's first training and research reactor, based on a U.S. design exhibited with great success at the 1958 conference in Geneva. The first research reactor in Italy was put into operation. Later, the first private research reactor on the continent of Europe was put into operation by a group of companies in northern Italy. The first reactor in Africa was commissioned at Lovanium university, Léopoldville, Belgian Congo, and the first in Central America in Puerto Rico. A research reactor was also put into operation at the newly named Hahn-Meitner institute in western Berlin. In the United Kingdom, the Central Electricity Generating board (C.E.G.B.) started work on a £1 million research laboratory for applied physical and engineering research in nuclear power.

In the field of more basic research, " tandem " accelerators, producing particles of twice the energy of the electrostatic generator, were operated at a number of establishments. The 50-Mev proton linear accelerator came into use at the National Institute for Research in Nuclear Science, Harwell. Experiments with a hydrogen bubble chamber and the Bevatron at the University of California proved the existence of the " neutral xi " particle.

Direct production of electricity from nuclear energy was achieved experimentally in the United States by means of a caesium plasma surrounding uranium carbide. Progress in the field of controlled fusion reactions was steady but unspectacular. An international conference was held in London in April. The U.K.A.E.A. decided to set up a new establishment at Culham, Oxfordshire, for all work in this field, and new apparatus was to be constructed to investigate sources of instability in Zeta (*see* ZETA in *Britannica Book of the Year 1959*).

Experimental Reactors. The world's first boiling heavy-water reactor began operating at Halden, Norway, with a thermal output of 5 Mw. used to produce process steam. In England, the zero-energy system, Zenith, for the 10-Mw. high-temperature gas-cooled reactor, Dragon, was commissioned. Like the Halden reactor, Dragon would be a collaborative project of the O.E.E.C. countries. The U.S. Atomic Energy commission ordered a 40-Mw. power station using a similar reactor. It also invited co-operation in the construction and operation of small pressurized-water power plants, producing 16·5 Mw. of electricity, or 22 Mw. with superheaters. The organic-moderated reactor was to be developed in Canada for use in the Arctic.

In the German Federal Republic, a 15-Mw. " pebble-bed " reactor was to be built, in which the core would consist of a large number of graphite balls containing uranium inserts. A reactor using boiling sulphur as coolant was studied in the United States. After much delay the fast breeder reactor at Dounreay, Scotland, was started up.

Electricity Generation. Scotland's first nuclear generating station, of 140-Mw. output, began operating at Chapelcross. The French station at Marcoule began feeding power to the grid. In the United States the 180-Mw. boiling-water power station was completed at Dresden, Tennessee. Work was begun on a 500-Mw. station for the C.E.G.B. at Trawsfynydd, Wales, as well as on the British-designed station at Latina, Italy. A number of new sites were also investigated for future power stations in the United Kingdom. The sites at Sizewell, Sussex, and Dungeness, Kent, were approved, the latter arousing particularly intense opposition.

The cost of electricity from nuclear stations was estimated at from 0·65d. to 0·70d. per unit, compared with from 0·50d. to 0·65d. for up-to-date coal-fired stations, while the capital cost of nuclear stations was greater by a factor of three. The slower growth in the use of nuclear power and the heavy expense involved were causing some concern in the British nuclear industry, little or no profit being expected on current contracts. Various solutions to the problem were discussed, and four of the five large consortia joined in two

The charge floor of No. 1 reactor at Chapelcross nuclear power station, Dumfriesshire, showing the charge and discharge machines for loading and unloading the fuel elements. There are four reactors in all, identical with those at the Calder Hall station.

pairs to tender for the next C.E.G.B. stations. The Select Committee on Estimates urged the increasing use of industry for researched sponsored by the U.K.A.E.A.

On the continent of Europe the Euratom programme was cut drastically and it was expected that only 2,100 Mw. capacity would be installed by 1965, instead of the 15,000 Mw. previously planned. The U.S. Export-Import bank granted a credit of $135 million at $4\frac{1}{2}\%$ interest towards the cost of U.S.-built stations for Euratom, but detailed plans were slow in being put forward. Euratom signed agreements with the United Kingdom and Canada for collaboration in nuclear power development. Japan ordered a 150-Mw. power station, specially designed to resist earthquakes, from one of the British consortia. India announced plans for its first power station, of 250 Mw., to cost £32·25 million. Among plans in the United States was a proposal for nuclear power stations at each of its four Antarctic bases within three years.

Nuclear Propulsion. The Soviet nuclear icebreaker " Lenin " started its maiden voyage. In the United States a 14,000-ton cruiser and the passenger-cargo ship " Savannah " were launched, as well as a number of submarines. The keel was laid of the Royal Navy's first nuclear submarine " Dreadnought ", which would be equipped with a U.S. reactor and follow the same new design principles as the U.S. submarine " Skipjack ". The latter was of " dolphin " shape and was controlled in much the same way as an aircraft. In April it went deeper and faster than previously known for a submarine—below 400 ft. and over 20 knots.

British companies submitted plans for marine reactors to an Admiralty committee, In addition to pressurized-water and boiling-water reactors, a steam-cooled heavy water, a high-temperature gas-cooled, an organic-moderated and an advanced type of gas-cooled graphite-moderated reactor were proposed. Costs were claimed to be comparable with those of conventional engines for very large oil tankers and passenger liners, although shipping companies did not seem to be convinced. Euratom decided to study nuclear power for ships. Plans for a small tanker were advanced in the German Federal Republic. A 3,000-ton fishing vessel was designed in Japan.

It was rumoured that a nuclear-powered aeroplane had actually flown in the U.S.S.R., and in the United States projects for two aircraft, two rockets and two auxiliary power units were said to be in hand.

Radiation. Late in 1958 the Brookhaven Medical Research centre was opened in the United States for comprehensive studies on the medical applications of nuclear energy. A London hospital planned a new branch solely for work with radiation and radio-isotopes. Ten more linear accelerators were planned, to make radiation treatment available conveniently in any part of Britain.

A conference on the application of large radiation sources to industrial processes was organized by the I.A.E.A., and the U.K.A.E.A. built a pilot plant for the irradiation of commercial products—the first of its kind in the world. Designed to operate automatically 24 hr. a day, it was loaded initially with 150,000 curies of cobalt-60.

In the United States a single piece of radio-cobalt with an initial activity of 2,794 curies was put into use. New types of linear accelerators were produced, particularly for radiography of space vehicles and rocket propellents. The Brookhaven reactor was used to enhance the appearance and value of poor-quality diamonds. High-energy protons were used in Sweden in the treatment of mental depression.

A thermoelectric generator giving 5 w. initially, with a half-life of 138 days, was produced in the United States. Among other equipment a back-scatter γ-ray counter was developed for the routine inspection of railway sleepers.

Work in progress at Arish Mell, Dorset, on the sea section of the effluent pipeline from the Winfrith U.K.A.E.A. establishment.

The successful transfusion of bone marrow in the case of five Yugoslav scientists suffering from severe overexposure to radiation indicated a possible cure for otherwise hopeless cases of leukaemia (*see* PHYSIOLOGY). In London a foetal-bone-marrow " bank " was established.

A number of experimental results during the year pointed to the possibility that the danger from man-made sources of radiation was rather less than previously thought, but many scientists remained unconvinced. Radioactive waste disposal was much discussed. In the United Kingdom some cases of carelessness with radioactive sources led to demands for more stringent controls. A meeting of the World Health organization urged more research on radiation and its dangers, although a W.H.O. committee on medical supervision in radiation work considered that, basically, radiation hazards should be treated in the same way as any other industrial danger.

Weapons. Following declarations by the United States, the U.S.S.R. and the United Kingdom, made in the autumn of 1958 and renewed after the initial 12-month period, no tests of nuclear weapons were carried out during 1959. France, however, announced its intention of carrying out tests in the Sahara, probably early in 1960. The United States revealed that three tests in Sept. 1958 had been 300 mi. above the earth. An artificial band of radiation had been produced which caused aurorae in the same latitude of each hemisphere and interference with long-range radar. At the same time much useful data on the earth's magnetism was obtained. Also among the last U.S. tests were very small weapons down to about the equivalent of 1 ton of T.N.T.

At the beginning of the year the levels of radioactivity in air and water in Europe were several times higher than normal, apparently owing to the extensive Soviet tests towards the end of 1958, but in October they were reported to have dropped again by about 90%. Although a U.K. report gave the levels of strontium-90 in food products as well below the possible danger level, the Joint Congressional Committee on Atomic Energy in the United States warned that if tests were resumed on the same scale as in 1958 a hazard to the world's population could result. Another report by the committee gave an estimate of 50 million dead in a limited nuclear attack (less than 300 bombs) on the United States.

Nuclear Disarmament. Although the ten-nation conference on the prevention of surprise attack was adjourned indefinitely at the end of 1958, the talks between the United States, the United Kingdom and the U.S.S.R. on a treaty to end nuclear weapons tests continued at intervals throughout 1959.

Supporters of the Campaign for Nuclear Disarmament at the beginning of their 50-mi. march from Aldermaston to London in March.
They are led by Benn Levy, the dramatist, Sir Richard Acland and Canon L. J. Collins. In the second file (wearing hat) is Jaquetta Hawkes.

The main difficulty centred on an effective inspection system. It was agreed that it should be possible to detect any test explosion in the earth's atmosphere or in outer space, using a network of ground control posts supplemented by earth satellites, but controversy remained over the detection of small underground test explosions which could be confused with earthquakes. Argument was concentrated on such subjects as the application of the " veto" to control-committee decisions, the nationalities of the staffs of control posts and the precise basis for the inspection of a certain quota of doubtful earth-tremor recordings.

The Republic of Ireland tabled a motion for the United Nations to limit the possession of nuclear weapons to countries already having them. In the United Kingdom the idea of a " non-nuclear club " was widely debated and eventually adopted by the Liberal party, Labour party and the Trades Union congress. This idea involved the renunciation of nuclear weapons by all nations except the United States and the U.S.S.R. Public opposition to nuclear weapons seemed to be growing throughout the world and there was widespread unrest in Africa at the French proposal to conduct tests.

The enlarged U.N. disarmament commission (all 82 member states) met for the first time in September and voted unanimously to establish a ten-nation working committee. After suggesting during the year the establishment of " nuclear-free " zones in the Pacific and the Balkans, Nikita Khrushchev proposed before the U.N. general assembly complete disarmament by all states within four years.

Legislation and Commerce. The O.E.E.C. convention on nuclear safeguards came into force, based on inspection of plant and maintenance of accounts of fissile material. Third-party insurance against nuclear risks was also made compulsory in O.E.E.C. countries. In the United Kingdom the Nuclear Installations (Licensing and Insurance) act, 1959, became law. Among its provisions, this specified licensing of every nuclear reactor and also compulsory insurance.

Commercial insurance pools were set up in most European countries, with further co-operation and exchanges of information. In England the Joint Marine Atomic Energy committee was formed to study the insurance of nuclear-powered ships.

The I.A.E.A. sent teams of technical experts to a number of countries. The number of its research fellowships awarded exceeded 600; and the building of new laboratories started at its headquarters, Vienna. However, the agency's services in the fields of safety standards and control of fissile materials were still largely disregarded by independent national arrangements. (*See also* EUROPEAN ATOMIC ENERGY COMMUNITY; PHYSICS.)   (A. G. HR.)

BIBLIOGRAPHY. *Proceedings of the 2nd United Nations Conference on the Peaceful Uses of Atomic Energy* (Geneva, 1959); European Council for Nuclear Research, *Proceedings of the International Conference on High Energy Accelerators and Instrumentation* (Geneva, 1959); A. M. Weinberg and E. P. Wigner, *The Physical Theory of Neutron Chain Reactors* (Cambridge, 1959); *Who's Who in Atoms* (London, 1959).

NUTRITION. Pantothenic Acid Deficiency.

Nutritionists had assumed that pantothenic acid was necessary for the maintenance of health in man. Spontaneous deficiencies, however, had not occurred or had not been recognized because of the abundance of pantothenic acid in natural foods. Even in very poor diets, other vitamin deficiencies seemed to be limiting factors before pantothenic acid deficiencies caused definite trouble.

Six volunteers participated in a study conducted by R. E. Hodges and his associates which attempted to produce pantothenic acid deficiency in man by tube feeding purified diets, low in pantothenic acid together with metabolic antagonists to pantothenic acid. (*J. Clin. Invest.*, 37, 1642-57, 1958.) Tube feeding of a normal hospital diet, which was emulsified in a blender, was done to detect any psychic or physical effect of the procedure itself for the first three weeks of the study. The six men were paired in three groups. One pair, the deficient pair, received the basic diet, adequate in all respects but devoid of pantothenic acid. At the end of this deficient period, 4,000 mg. of pantothenic acid was given daily. Another pair, the antagonist pair, received the same formula but, in addition, they received 750 mg. of a pantothenic acid antagonist. Later some of the signs and symptoms of deficiency began to diminish spontaneously, so the dose of the antagonist was increased to 1,000 mg. daily. At the end of the deficient period the antagonist was continued while 4,000 mg. of pantothenic acid daily was added. The remaining " control " pair received the basic formula supplemented by 20 mg. of pantothenic acid daily, together with all other essential vitamins and minerals given to the other subjects.

During the deficient period, the antagonist pair gradually developed deficiency symptoms. A little later the two men in the deficient group began to note similar complaints. The signs of deficiency included: serious personality changes with irritability, restlessness, quarrelsomeness, malaise, sleep disturbances, excessive fatigue, neurological disturbances such as numbness of the hands, paresthesias (a sensation as of pricking, tingling or creeping on the skin), muscle cramps and a peculiar gait. Physical examinations revealed few objective findings other than transient increase of the tendon reflexes and faulty co-ordination associated with tremor. The most constant, annoying and persistent complaints, fatigue, headache and weakness, usually occurred simultaneously. Administration of pantothenic acid was followed by improvement of the paresthesias and muscle weakness, but fatigue and some degree of irritability persisted.

Gastro-intestinal bacteria could quite possibly have produced some pantothenic acid and limited the extent of deficiency observed. The degree of the deficiency probably was relatively minor since many biochemical reactions which require coenzymes containing pantothenic acid continued unchanged.

Hypervitaminosis A. Very high doses of vitamin A when given to pregnant rats influence the development of the foetus. The abnormalities resulting from an overdose of vitamin A include anencephalia (absence of brain), anophthalmos (absence of the eyes) or large, open, protruding eyes, spina bifida (absence of the arches in the spinal column), cleft palate, malformations of the extremities, labial fissures and cataracts.

F. M. Deuschle and co-workers produced a variety of such congenital defects in rats by the administration of a single dose of vitamin A (75,000 to 150,000 I.U.) on the 9th, 10th or 11th day of pregnancy. (*J. Dent. Res.*, **38**, 149-55, 1959.) On the basis of present knowledge, no correlation could be drawn from animal research concerning pregnancy in women. However, the striking nature of the defects and the relative ease with which they could be produced (and the fact that any vitamin A taken in excess of the body's needs is stored) suggested cautious use of large and repeated doses of vitamin A during early pregnancy. (M. B. McC.; F. J. Se.)

NYASALAND: *see* Rhodesia and Nyasaland, Federation of.

OBITUARIES. The following is a selected list of prominent men and women who died during 1959:

Adams, Marcus Algernon, British photographer (b. Southampton, May 16, 1875—d. North Stoke, Oxfordshire, April 9), gained his reputation by his studies of children and was photographer to the royal family for more than 30 years. The son of a previous court photographer, he was educated at York House school, University college, Reading, and in Paris. He began photography in 1889 and in 1926 opened a children's studio in London which soon became famous. He had a particular faculty for photographing children, making them behave naturally in his studio. The last royal photograph Adams took, two years before his retirement in 1957, was of Princess Anne.

Alexandra Victoria Alberta Edwina Louise, Princess Arthur of Connaught, Duchess of Fife (b. Richmond, Surrey, May 17, 1891—d. London, Feb. 26), was a granddaughter of King Edward VII. The eldest daughter of Princess Louise Dagmar (the Princess Royal) and the Duke of Fife, she was granted the title of princess and the style of Highness in 1905. Seven years later she succeeded to the titles Duchess of Fife and Countess of Macduff upon the death of her father. On Oct. 15, 1913, she married Prince Arthur, the only son of the Duke of Connaught. Endowed with a practical nature, Princess Arthur took very seriously her chosen career of nursing: she worked in hospitals throughout World War I, was sister in charge of a casualty clearing station during World War II, and was matron of the Fife Nursing home, which she founded, between 1939 and 1949. During 1920-23 she was in South Africa where her husband was governor-general and in 1939, 1943 and 1944, during absences abroad of King George VI, she was a councillor of state.

Anderson, Sir Kenneth Arthur Noel, British general (b. Bombay, India, Dec. 25, 1891—d. Gibraltar, April 29), commanded the 1st army in north Africa in 1942-43 and was governor of Gibraltar from 1947 until his retirement in 1952. Educated at Charterhouse and Sandhurst, he was commissioned in the Seaforth Highlanders in 1911. He served in India and, during World War I, in France, where he was badly wounded and won the M.C., and in Palestine with Allenby. After further service in India in 1938 he was given command of the 11th Infantry brigade, which he took to France at the outbreak of World War II. During the Dunkirk evacuation he led the 3rd Division and was promoted major-general and awarded the C.B. In Aug. 1942 Anderson was appointed to the command of the 1st army, which bore the brunt of the fighting in Algeria and Tunisia during Operation " Torch ", the campaign which, in conjunction with the 8th army's drive from El Alamein, brought about the complete defeat of Axis forces in north Africa. On his return to England in 1943 Anderson was knighted. Later commands included that of East Africa (1945-46). His term of office as governor of Gibraltar was twice extended and during it the constitutional reforms of 1950 were introduced.

Anderson, Maxwell, U.S. dramatist (b. Atlantic, Pennsylvania, Dec. 15, 1888—d. Stamford, Connecticut, Feb. 28), the author of many successful plays, effectively introduced verse drama into the contemporary U.S. theatre. The son of a Baptist minister, he graduated from the University of North Dakota in 1911. During his early years he held a number of jobs, including those of schoolteacher and journalist. In 1918 he went to New York to take up the post of dramatic critic of the *New Republic*, later working for the *New York Globe* and the *New York World*. In 1923 he produced *The White Desert* a tragedy in blank verse, which attracted some favourable attention from critics. In the following year a realistic war play *What Price Glory*, written in collaboration with Lawrence Stallings, proved very popular. Anderson now devoted all his energies to writing plays and his next success was *Saturday's Children* (1927). His verse drama *Elizabeth the Queen* (1930), which had an historical subject, was widely acclaimed and he subsequently used the poetic form in several of his plays, of which *Winterset* (1935), based on the Sacco-Vanzetti trial, is perhaps the best. Among his other works were a political satire *Both Your Houses* (1933), which won a Pulitzer prize, *The Star Wagon* (1937), *Key Largo* (1939), *The Eve of St. Mark* (1942), *Storm Operation* (1946) and *The Bad Seed* (1954). Some of his plays were made into films.

Anderson, William Blair, Scottish scholar (b. Aberdeen, July 28, 1877—d. Cambridge, Dec. 9), was a recognized authority on Latin poetry of the silver age. Educated at Robert Gordon's college, Aberdeen, and at the University of Aberdeen, he graduated in 1898 with first class honours in classics and then entered Trinity college, Cambridge. Here he obtained first classes in both parts of the classical tripos and the Browne medal for Greek epigram. Then followed between 1901 and 1913 various posts in the universities of Aberdeen, Manchester and Kingston, Ontario. In 1913 he returned to Manchester to help R. S. Conway as professor of imperial Latin, succeeding in 1929 to the Hulme chair of Latin. When A. E. Housman died in 1936, Anderson was appointed his successor as Kennedy professor of Latin at Cambridge. One of the greatest Latin scholars in England, he unfortunately published little of his researches but gave unstinted attention to his students.

Astor, (William) Vincent, U.S. businessman and philanthropist (b. New York, Nov. 15, 1891—d. New York, Feb. 3), was at the time of his death head of the U.S. branch of the famous Astor family. He was reported to have substantially increased his inheritance of $87 million. Like his forebears, he made New York city real estate his principal commercial interest. Unlike many of them, however, he was a liberal in politics and an early, although temporary, supporter of the New Deal. He sold many of his tenement holdings to the New York city housing authority for nominal cash payments. Astor also owned *Newsweek* magazine. Childless in three marriages, he left the bulk of his fortune to charities.

Aynesworth, Allan (Edward Abbot-Anderson), British actor (b. Sandhurst, Berkshire, April 14, 1864—d. Camberley, Surrey, Aug. 21), had a long and distinguished career in comedy parts. The son of a general, he completed his education in France, where he studied French acting technique. He subsequently appeared in various plays on the London stage, including A. W. Pinero's *The Ironmaster*, but first achieved real success with his creation of the role of Algernon Moncrieff in *The Importance of Being Earnest* (1895). He went on to give notable performances in many plays and was also an actor manager. He ended his theatrical career in 1938 after appearing in Laurence Housman's *Victoria Regina*.

Baedeker, Hans, German publisher (b. Leipzig, July 29, 1874—d. Leipzig, March 15), was the grandson of Karl Baedeker, the founder of the firm famous for its guidebooks. He was the son of Fritz Baedeker who in 1872 transferred the business from Koblenz to Leipzig. He studied at the universities of Edinburgh, Geneva and Rome, joining the firm in 1899. World War I and postwar inflation almost interrupted the firm's activity. During World War II a concentrated bombing of Leipzig in 1943 destroyed the Baedeker building. After the war the firm started publishing in western Germany and although Baedeker remained in Leipzig he continued to keep in close touch with its affairs.

Baer, Max(imilian Adelbert), U.S. boxer and film actor (b. Omaha, Nebraska, Feb. 11, 1909—d. Hollywood, California, Nov. 21), was world heavyweight champion for a year in 1934-35, defeating Primo Carnera by a technical knockout in the 11th round on June 14, 1934, and losing to James Braddock when he was outpointed over 15 rounds on June 13, 1935. Perhaps his greatest win was over Max Schmeling of Germany in ten rounds in 1933. Baer had one of the hardest right-hand punches of any heavyweight and in a fight in 1930 his opponent Frankie Campbell failed to recover consciousness. It is probable that from that time Baer would not punch his full weight and he certainly seldom took his boxing seriously, becoming known as the " Clown Prince of Boxing ". After he finally retired from the ring in 1941 he appeared in films (one of which was *The Prizefighter and the Lady* with Myrna Loy), in music halls and on television.

Bairnsfather, Bruce, British artist and journalist (b. Murree, India [now Pakistan], July 1888—d. Norton, Worcestershire, Sept. 29), will be remembered chiefly for his remarkable humorous drawings of trench life in World War I. He became a captain in the Royal Warwickshire regiment in 1915. His series of drawings, " Fragments from France ", which were sent to *The Bystander* from the front, portrayed the humorous side of a grim war. They and the characters in them, particularly Old Bill with his heavy drooping moustache and bulbous nose, caught the public fancy and led to further ventures in the same vein. Bairnsfather's play, *The Better 'Ole,* written in collaboration, derived its name from the famous caption to a drawing of two miserable soldiers beleaguered in a shell hole—" Well, if yer knows of a better 'ole, go to it ".

Bandaranaike, Solomon West Ridgeway Dias, Ceylonese statesman (b. Colombo, Jan. 8, 1899—d. Colombo, Sept. 26), whose electoral victory in 1956 was revolutionary in its effect. He was the son of a rich landowner, and was educated at Christ Church, Oxford. Called to the bar at the Inner Temple in 1925, he soon afterwards returned to Ceylon where he entered politics and renounced Christianity to become a Buddhist. In 1931 he entered the newly formed state council. In 1947, as a prominent member of the United National party, he was elected to the new House of Representatives and appointed minister of health and local government. Having resigned from the government and from the U.N.P. in 1951, he was returned in 1952 as founder of the Sri Lanka (Blessed Ceylon) Freedom party. He became the leader of the opposition. Four years later he formed the People's United front, a political alliance of four leftist parties which won the election, and he became prime minister on April 12, 1956. The P.U.F. advocated a neutralist foreign policy and a Sinhalese Buddhist nationalism at home. By amicable agreement the British bases on the island were relinquished in 1957 and Ceylon remained a realm of the Commonwealth of Nations. The attempt to introduce Sinhalese as the country's official language led to serious riots. In 1959 the country's economy began to falter and in May a split occurred in the P.U.F., depriving Bandaranaike of a parliamentary majority. Steering a complicated course to retain power, he alienated some of his former supporters. He was shot on Sept. 25 and died the following day. A Buddhist monk (*thero*), Taldune Somarama, was later arrested.

Barrymore, Ethel, U.S. actress (b. Philadelphia, Pennsylvania, Aug, 15, 1879—d. Hollywood, California, June 18), with her brothers Lionel (1878-1954) and John (1882-1942), formed the famous " royal family " of the U.S. theatre. Her grandparents were the well-known John Drews of the 19th-century stage; her uncle was the younger John Drew (1853-1927); and her father was Maurice Barrymore (1847-1905), a popular romantic player of his time. She made her first appearance in 1894 in *The Rivals,* and her first leading part was in *Captain Jinks of the Horse Marines* some six years later. She subsequently appeared in numerous Broadway productions, films and television plays, but acted only once with both her brothers—in the picture *Rasputin and the Empress* (1934). In 1944 she won an Academy award for her supporting role in the film *None but the Lonely Heart.*

Bateman, James, British painter and wood-engraver (b. Kendal, Westmorland, March 22, 1893—d. London, August 2), made his reputation chiefly as a painter of cattle. After he had started as a sculptor, wounds suffered in World War I caused him to take up oil painting instead. He studied at the Royal College of Art and the Slade school. " Cows in the Rickyard ", exhibited at the Royal Academy in 1931, was his first popular success and was compared by the critics with paintings of the Italian Renaissance. Thereafter he concentrated on the depiction of cattle, either as part of his landscapes, as in " Woodland and Cattle " (1932), or at market, as in " Commotion in the Cattle Ring " (1936, Tate gallery). An A.R.A. from 1935, Bateman became R.A. in 1942.

Bechet, Sidney, U.S. jazz musician (b. New Orleans, May 14, 1897—d. Grigny, nr. Paris, May 14), was widely known as " the poet of jazz ". The son of a Negro shoemaker, he began playing the clarinet at the age of eight and had played with several well-known New Orleans bands by the time he was 18, including that of Bunk Johnson. About the time of his first European tour in 1919 he began playing the soprano saxophone, which he preferred to the clarinet for its greater volume. He returned to Europe in 1925 and stayed for five years. He is said to have killed another coloured musician in a brawl and was in prison in Paris for a year. In 1928 he joined Noble Sissle's band in Paris, went back to America with it in 1930 and continued to play with Sissle until 1938. With the revival in popularity of traditional, New Orleans jazz after World War II, Bechet regained a pre-eminent position in the jazz world. He spent the last ten years

of his life in France, making only occasional visits to the United States. Though Bechet was a self-taught player and his fingering eccentric, his technique with both clarinet and soprano saxophone was formidable and his style characterized by forcefulness and rich, vibrant playing. Bechet was also a composer and at the time of his death the Chris Barber recording of his " Petite Fleur " was a best-seller in England and had sold more than a million copies.

Behra, Jean, French racing motorist (b. Nice, Feb. 16, 1921—d. Berlin, Aug. 1), was a leading international driver, and was motor-racing champion of France in 1956 and 1957. Previously, from 1947 until 1952, he had been the French motor-cycling champion. He drove successively for the Gordini, Maserati, Porsche and Ferrari teams, and in 1957 he took the B.R.M. to victory in the Caen Grand Prix and in the *Daily Express* international trophy race at Silverstone. Although he won many grand prix and sports car events, bad luck often robbed him of a victory which seemed to be his, and he was never placed higher than fourth in the world championship. He had several serious accidents, and was killed when his Porsche crashed in a sports car race on the Avus track, Berlin.

Berenson, Bernard, Russian-born U.S. art historian (b. Buividžiai, near Vilnius, Lithuania, June 26, 1865—d. Florence, Italy, Oct. 6), had for long been the doyen of world art experts and a legendary figure even in much wider circles. His villa, I Tatti, at Settignano, was a centre of pilgrimage for scholar and student alike. Of Jewish parentage, he was taken in boyhood to the United States, where his family settled at Boston, Massachusetts. After studying at Boston university, he went on to Harvard and later to Oxford, Berlin and Paris. He switched his attention from literature to art and gradually established himself as a leading authority on Italian Renaissance painting, making his first important contribution in 1896 and 1897 with the publication of the second and third of four essays, *Florentine Painters of the Renaissance* and *Central Italian Painters of the Renaissance,* afterwards incorporated (with the other two) in one volume entitled *The Italian Painters of the Renaissance* (1932, rev. ed. 1952). These, together with his pioneer study *The Drawings of the Florentine Painters* (1903, rev. ed. 1938), formed the hard core of his research. Despite these achievements Berenson was not satisfied with expertise alone, and in *Sketch for a Self-Portrait* (1949) expressed a regret that he had not written more about aesthetics and the philosophical aspects of life and art. His interests and knowledge ranged far beyond his chosen field. He was widely read in the literature of some eight languages in the original and of many others in translation. A scholar of inflexible standards, he revised many of his previous opinions in the light of subsequent research. Converted to Roman Catholicism early in life, he lived and thought as an heir of the best humanist traditions, and his library was among the richest of its kind.

(D. L. Fr.)

Berggrav, Eivind Josef, Norwegian bishop (b. Stavanger, Norway, Oct. 25, 1884—d. Oslo, Jan. 14), as primate of Norway took a leading part in his country's resistance movement during World War II. The son of a Lutheran bishop, he was educated at the University of Oslo and began his career as a schoolteacher. He also took up journalism, becoming in 1909 the editor of the periodical *Kirke og Kultur,* a position he retained for nearly 50 years. In 1919 he was ordained a pastor and after holding various appointments, including that of prison chaplain, he was in 1928 consecrated bishop of Hallogoland, a diocese covering northern Norway and Spitzbergen. He became bishop of Oslo in 1937 and subsequently made strenuous efforts through the medium of the World Alliance for Friendship to avert the threat of world war. After the German occupation of Norway in 1940 his firm stand on Christian principles against totalitarianism made him a focal point of opposition. Arrested in 1942, he was taken to Bredtvedt concentration camp on a charge of high treason. Later released and put under house arrest, he nevertheless continued to be actively concerned in the resistance to the Germans. After the war he played a leading role in the oecumenical movement and was one of the joint presidents of the World Council of Churches during 1948-54.

Beveridge, Lady Janet, British educational administrator (b. Dundee, Nov. 26, 1876—d. Hexham, April 25), was secretary and acting dean of the London School of Economics from 1919 to 1938, during the directorship of Sir William (later Lord) Beveridge, who became her second husband in 1942. She contributed a weekly article on London university to the *Sunday Times* for many years and was the author of *Beveridge and His Plan* (1954).

Bloch, Ernest, Swiss-born U.S. composer (b. Geneva, July 24, 1880—d. Portland, Oregon, July 15), introduced distinctive Jewish themes into much of his music. Of Jewish parentage, he was educated at Geneva and Brussels, where he studied at the conservatoire under Eugène Ysaÿe and François Rasse, and completed his musical training at Frankfurt-on-Main and Munich. His early works included a symphony in C sharp minor and an opera, *Macbeth,* both of which attracted some attention. In 1916 he went to the United States as the conductor for the dancer Maud Allen. While there he was invited to conduct a performance of his *Three Jewish Poems* and a concert of his works was subsequently held. He was successively director of the Cleveland Institute of Music (1920-25) and the San Francisco conservatory (1925-30). In this period he produced some of his best chamber music, as well as the *America* rhapsody and the *Helvetia* symphony. During his subsequent stay in Europe he had some success, particularly in Italy (his *Sacred Service* [1933] was first performed in Turin) and in England, where interest in his music led to the forming of an Ernest Bloch society. After his return to the United States before World War II he continued composing, and the works of his later years included a piano concerto, several string quartets and a *sinfonia breve.*

Blom, Eric Walter, British musicologist and critic (b. Berne, Switzerland, Aug. 20, 1888—d. London, April 11), edited the fifth edition of

Grove's *Dictionary of Music and Musicians* (1954). Having begun his career by writing programme notes for Henry Wood's Queen's hall concerts, in 1923 he became London music critic for the *Manchester Guardian*, moving, eight years later, to the *Birmingham Post*, where he remained until 1946. From 1949 he was music critic for the *Observer*, for which he wrote regularly until his death—his last article, on Handel, appearing on April 12, 1959. In addition to his journalistic activities, Blom was continually engaged in sound scholarly work of which his edition of Grove, the most complete and thorough-going revision since 1889, was the crowning achievement. Earlier he had edited the *Everyman's Dictionary of Music* (1947, rev. ed. 1954) and the biographical " Master Musicians " series, in which he himself contributed the volume on his favourite composer, *Mozart* (1935). He also translated several important works from German, French and Italian, was editor of the periodical *Music and Letters* during 1937-50 and from 1954, and contributed to the *Encyclopædia Britannica*. In 1955 he was awarded the C.B.E. and honoured by a D.Litt. from Birmingham university.

Brilioth, Yngve Torgny, Swedish Lutheran prelate (b. Västra Ed, Sweden, July 12, 1891—d. Uppsala, April 27), was until his retirement in 1958 primate of Sweden and archbishop of Uppsala. He was keenly interested in oecumenical affairs and frequently visited England in this connection, being presented with the Lambeth cross in 1942. His book *The Anglican Revival* showed his deep understanding of the Church of England.

Brooks, William Collin, British author and journalist (b. Southport, Dec. 22, 1893—d. London, April 6), whose prolific writings covered widely differing subjects, was from 1940 until 1953 chairman and editor of *Truth*. Educated at Christ Church hall, Southport, he entered journalism after World War I, during which he served with the Machine Gun corps and won the M.C. He was literary editor and leader writer of the *Liverpool Courier* (1920-23), assistant editor of the *Yorkshire Post* (1923-28) and of the *Financial News* (1928-33). During the course of a long association with the first Lord Rothermere, whom he accompanied on many of his rearmament missions during 1936-40, Brooks became city editor and later editor of the *Sunday Dispatch*. Besides numerous books on politics and finance he produced more than 20 novels and two volumes of verse. He was also a skilled broadcaster. His editorship of *Truth* was marked by attempts in 1941 to suppress its publication.

Brown, Sir Frank Herbert, British journalist (b. Wisbech, Cambridgeshire, March 13, 1868—d. London, Feb. 14), had an exceptionally wide knowledge of affairs in the Indian sub-continent. The son of a Baptist minister, he gained his first journalistic experience with the *Cambridgeshire Times*. He went to India in the 1890s and became assistant editor of the *Bombay Gazette* and later editor of the *Indian Daily Telegraph* at Lucknow. Returning to England after seven years, he worked first as a free-lance for various English and Indian journals and as the London correspondent of the *Times of India*. In 1929 Brown joined the staff of *The Times*, to which he had contributed regularly for many years. Though his personal experience of India was confined to a period during which the passions of nationalism were still subdued, and life and journalism were more leisurely than they were to become, he spared no efforts to keep his knowledge up-to-date. He was honorary secretary of the East India association (1927-54), and was for many years on the executive committee of the Pakistan society. He contributed a number of articles to the *Encyclopædia Britannica*, and was part author of *Political India* (1932) and *British Commonwealth—a Family of Nations* (1952). He was knighted in 1937.

Bueb, Ivor, British racing motorist (b. London, June 6, 1923—d. Clermont Ferrand, France, Aug. 1), was an outstanding driver of sports cars who twice won the Le Mans 24-hr. race, on the first occasion as co-driver with J. M. Hawthorn in the tragic race of 1955 during which 83 people were killed. Bueb died of injuries received when his Cooper Borgward crashed during a race on the Auvergne circuit.

Burnett, Sir Robert Lindsay, Scottish admiral (b. Old Deer, Aberdeenshire, July 22, 1887—d. London, July 2), is best remembered for his share in the sinking of the German battle cruiser " Scharnhorst " in 1943. Educated at Bedford school and at Eastman's, Southsea, he entered the Royal Navy in 1902 and became a destroyer commander in World War I. An outstanding specialist in physical and recreational training, in 1933-35 he was director of physical training and sports. In 1942 he twice won distinction in the defence of convoys to north Russia, being first made a C.B. and then awarded the D.S.O. On Boxing Day, 1943, as commander of the Tenth Cruiser squadron, he played an outstanding part in the operations which led to the destruction of the " Scharnhorst " and the saving of another Soviet convoy. For this he was knighted. He was commander-in-chief at Plymouth from 1947 to 1950, when he retired and was advanced to G.B.E.

Butler, Eliza Marian, British scholar (b. Bardsea, Lancashire, Dec. 29, 1885—d. London, Nov. 30), a professor emeritus of Cambridge university, she had a long and distinguished academic career. She was educated at Hanover, Paris, Cheltenham and Cambridge and began her career as an assistant lecturer in German at Newnham college, Cambridge. During World War I she served with the Scottish Women's hospitals in Russia and Macedonia. Returning to Newnham in 1920, she eventually became director of studies in modern languages there. In 1936 she was appointed professor of German at Manchester university, remaining in this position until 1945 when she returned to Cambridge as Schröder professor of German, a post she held until her retirement in 1951. Her first work, *The Saint-Simonian Religion*, was published in 1926. Her later works include *The Tyranny of Greece over Germany* (1935), *Rainer Maria Rilke* (1940) and her reminiscences, *Paper Boats* (1959). Up to the time of her death she was a contributor to the *Encyclopædia Britannica*.

Cahill, John Joseph, Australian politician (b. Sydney, Jan. 21, 1891—d. Sydney, Oct. 22), was premier of New South Wales from 1952 until his death. Of Irish parentage, he was educated at the Patrician Brothers' college, Sydney, and entered the New South Wales Railway department at the age of 15, where he started work as an apprentice fitter. He became interested in trade union affairs and was sacked when emergency powers were used to break the transport strike of 1917. After holding a succession of engineering jobs, he entered the New South Wales parliament in 1925 as a Labour M.P. He was a government whip from 1930 to 1932, losing his seat in the latter year. He was elected to parliament again in 1935, and after the return to power of the Labour party in 1941, he was appointed minister of works. In 1949 he became deputy premier, and in 1952 premier. When in 1954 the Australian Labour party was split by internal dissension, Cahill's shrewd political instincts enabled him to save the New South Wales Labour party from the disasters which swept Labour governments from office in Queensland and Victoria. In the state election held in March 1959 he again led his party to victory.

Caracciola, Rudolf, German racing motorist (b. Remagen, Jan 30, 1901—d. Kassel, Sept. 28), was one of the most skilful and successful drivers of the inter-war period, when he shared with other near-legendary figures such as Nuvolari, Varzi and Chiron a fame equal to that of, say, Nurmi or Dempsey in other fields of sport. Caracciola began racing in 1922 and retired after an accident in 1952. Though in the early 1930s he drove for Alfa Romeo, his name was throughout his career linked with that of Mercedes-Benz, whose team he led to victory in *grandes épreuves* and sports car events all over Europe. He won more than 100 races, of which 20 were grands prix. He was a disciplined driver whose skill was built on sound technical knowledge, and who was never involved in an accident off the race track.

Carpenter, Spencer Cecil, English clergyman (b. London, Nov. 3, 1877—d. Exeter, Aug. 19), was a distinguished historian, writer and preacher on religious affairs. From University College school, London, he entered Caius college, Cambridge, where he gained a second class in the Classical tripos, a first in the Theological tripos and the Carus Greek Testament prize. After ordination in 1902, he held a succession of ecclesiastical posts of increasing importance. He was examining chaplain to the bishop of Southwark from 1916-22 and to the bishop of Manchester from 1927-31. In 1930 he was appointed master of the Temple, a post he retained until he became dean of Exeter in 1935. He retired in 1950. Carpenter wrote several historical and theological works of note, his *Church and People 1789-1889* (1933) becoming the standard work on the history of religion in England in the 19th century. Some of his books, such as his Pelican *Christianity*, were popular with the public at large and he wrote in a style that had wide appeal. He wrote many newspaper articles and was an outstanding preacher who was not afraid to deal with temporal questions.

Catto, Thomas Sivewright Catto, 1st Baron, of Cairncatto, British businessman and banker (b. Newcastle upon Tyne, March 15, 1879—d. Holmbury St. Mary, Surrey, Sept. 23), was governor of the Bank of England during its period of transition from private to public ownership. Born into a merchant family, he was educated at Peterhead academy and at Heaton school (Rutherford college), Newcastle. Entering a shipping office at 16, by the time he was 27 he had become assistant general manager for Europe and the middle east of the merchant house of MacAndrews and Forbes. In 1909 he went to the United States as vice-president of his company's American house. In 1919 he became head of the great merchant house of Andrew Yule and Co., Calcutta, and for the next 12 years was an eminent figure in the commercial life of India. A baronet since 1921, he was made a baron in 1936 for his services to India. Having earlier become a director of the merchant banking firm of Morgan Grenfell and Co., in 1940 he joined the board of the Bank of England, but he was soon asked to give up all business appointments to become unpaid financial adviser to the chancellor of the exchequer. In 1944 he succeeded Montagu Norman as governor of the Bank of England, which was already regarded as an intrument of government policy, and in 1946 Lord Catto handled the delicate negotations with the Labour government concerning the nationalization of the bank. Three years later he was able to retire in the knowledge that its independence and form of organization were substantially unchanged.

Chandler, Raymond Thornton, U.S. author (b. Chicago, Illinois, July 23, 1888—d. La Jolla, California, March 26), was an outstanding detective story writer of his day and the co-founder (with Dashiel Hammett) of the " tough " school of crime fiction. Chandler was only nine when his Quaker parents divorced and his Anglo-Irish mother took him to England. After being educated at Dulwich college and privately in France and Germany, his early and not altogether successful efforts at teaching and journalism were interrupted by World War I, with service in the Canadian army and in the Royal Flying corps. Subsequently he returned to the United States where he had a mixed career, with a predominance of free-lance journalism until, in 1939, he published his first novel, *The Big Sleep*. Its success was followed by that of *Farewell, My Lovely* (1940), *The High Window* (1942), *The Lady in the Lake* (1943), *The Little Sister* (1949), *The Simple Act of Murder* (1950) and *The Long Goodbye* (1954).

Set in California, Chandler's novels had as their central character the private detective, Philip Marlowe—an archetypal figure who, with Dashiel Hammett's Sam Spade, provided the model for the "private eye " of modern crime fiction. Marlowe was a crusading knight who lived amid the corruption and squalor of " a world gone wrong ", but always emerged triumphant: a modern exemplification of the victory of good over evil. Chandler's view of his hero, the shock effect of his tough situations, and the mastery of his laconic irony and incisive observations were the ingredients of his success, together with his creed that " the crime . . . is not half so important as its effects on the characters . . . the reactions of the people to the crime are what makes the story ".

Cherry-Garrard, Apsley George Benet, British polar explorer (b. Bedford, Jan. 2, 1886—d. London, May 18), achieved fame as a member of Captain R. F. Scott's last expedition to the south pole and through his book, " The Worst Journey in the World " which described the expedition. Educated at Winchester and Oxford university, he owed his selection for the expedition to E. A. Wilson. During the expedition he formed an intense friendship with Wilson and H. R. Bowers and shared several perilous adventures with them. When Scott pushed on to the pole with his two friends, Cherry-Garrard stayed behind at base and eventually was the only officer available to take supplies to One-Ton depot for Scott's return journey. In later years, he needlessly blamed himself for not endeavouring to look for Scott's party, becoming so obsessed with the disaster which resulted in the death of his friends that it affected his health.

Clapham, Charles, English music-hall and radio comedian (b. London, Jan. 30, 1894—d. St. Leonards-on-Sea, Sussex, July), was the " funny man " of the successful Clapham and Dwyer partnership—Dwyer being the " straight man ". The two began their act in 1926 and performed together for 14 years until Dwyer retired in 1940. In the tradition of cross-talk acts much of the humour derived from the contrast in their appearance and utterance. Clapham, slight and wispy in his " toff's " get-up of white tie and monocle, was all but unintelligible in the confused inconsequence of his patter; Dwyer on the other hand was burly, resonant-voiced and " sensible ".

Cole, George Douglas Howard, British political thinker (b. London, Sept. 25, 1889—d. London, Jan. 14), was a prominent Socialist intellectual and writer who throughout his life combined the tenure of important academic posts with the propagation, often by language of a militant character, of advanced and sometimes unorthodox political and social opinions. He was educated at St. Paul's school and at Balliol college, Oxford. In 1912 he obtained a prize fellowship at Magdalen college, in 1913 he published his first book, *The World of Labour*, and on the outbreak of World War I he was teaching philosophy at Armstrong college, Newcastle upon Tyne. A pacifist, he became during the war an official of the Amalgamated Society of Engineers and of the Labour Research bureau, and helped to prepare the Labour case in a number of industrial disputes. During this period he wrote *The Payment of Wages* (1918), a recognized classic in its sphere. After the war Cole returned to teaching and writing as his main occupations. For a time he devoted himself to adult education and then, in 1925, returned to Oxford as a fellow and tutor of University college and as university reader in economics. Later he became a fellow of Nuffield college. He was a frequent contributor to the *New Statesman* and a prolific writer, his books including *William Cobbett* (1925); *A Short History of the British Working Class Movement* (rev. ed., 1948); *The Intelligent Man's Guide through World Chaos* (1932); and *A History of Socialist Thought* (4 vol., 1953-59). He also contributed to the *Encyclopædia Britannica*. Cole was first and foremost a teacher and he had an exquisitely clear literary style, so that his writings, however controversial, made as a rule no great demands on the intellectual powers of his readers. His most important contribution to politics was the lead he gave in furthering research designed to frame up-to-date and coherent policies for the Labour party after the *débâcle* of 1931. When war came in 1939 he was no longer a pacifist and before taking up the chair of social and political theory at Oxford in 1944 he worked in the Ministry of Labour and National Service. From 1939-46 and 1948-50 he was chairman of the Fabian society and from 1952 its president. (W. T. Ws.)

Cornwallis, Sir Kinahan, British administrator and official (b. Feb. 19, 1883—d. North Warnborough, Basingstoke, June 3), played a notable part in the development of modern Iraq. He was educated at Haileybury and at University college, Oxford, where he won distinction as an athlete. In 1906 he joined the Sudan civil service where he remained until 1914, when he was transferred to the Egyptian civil service. Two years later he was appointed director of the Arab bureau and was subsequently attached to the British army in Syria as a political officer. At this time he became acquainted with the Amir Faysal of Syria, with whom he was to be associated for many years. In 1920 Cornwallis was entrusted with the task of offering Faysal the throne of Iraq and later escorted him on his journey to his new kingdom where, during 1921-35, Cornwallis occupied an important position as adviser to the ministry of the interior. In 1941 he was recalled to become ambassador to Iraq in the critical period following the pro-Axis *coup d'état* in that country and eventually arranged the surrender terms of the defeated Iraqi army. After his retirement in 1945 he was for a time chairman of the Middle East committee of the Foreign Office. He was created a G.C.M.G. in 1943.

Costello, Lou (Louis Francis Cristillo), U.S. comedian (b. Paterson, New Jersey, March 6, 1908—d. Beverly Hills, California, March 3), began in show business as a dialect comedian and gained international fame as a member of the radio and film team of Abbott and Costello, in which he played the comic foil for Bud Abbott in the classic slapstick manner. Perhaps their most famous act was " Who's on First? ", a baseball dialogue of puns and mixups that they repeated several thousand times on the stage and in night clubs. Abbott and Costello first achieved fame on the radio in the Kate Smith show and then appeared in the musical *Streets of Paris* in 1939-40. Among their films were *Buck Privates*, *Rio Rita*, *Lost in a Harem* and *Abbott and Costello in Hollywood*.

Courtauld, Augustine, British Arctic explorer (b. Bocking, Essex, Aug. 26, 1904—d. London, March 3), achieved fame by his bravery and resourcefulness in manning single-handed an ice-cap station in east Greenland for more than five months of the winter of 1930-31 although completely snowed-up with only the ventilation shaft showing. Relief came eventually in May 1931 when his fuel was almost exhausted. This exploit was part of the British Arctic Air Route expedition to Greenland which sought to study meteorological conditions preparatory to the establishment of an air route to Canada. Courtauld had previously participated, when in his early twenties, in expeditions to Greenland in 1926 and 1929. In the latter, led by Sir James Wordie, he was one of those who reached the summit of the 11,000-ft. Petermann peak. The son of Samuel Courtauld, a director of Courtaulds Ltd., he received his education at Charterhouse and Trinity college, Cambridge. During World War II he served in the Royal Navy and afterwards was a deputy lieutenant for Essex, a justice of the peace and a county councillor. In 1953 he was appointed high sheriff of Essex. His autobiography is entitled *Man the Ropes* and he also compiled a polar anthology.

Craster, Sir (Herbert Henry) Edmund, British librarian (b. Dorking, Surrey, Nov. 5, 1879—d. March 21), was Bodley's librarian at Oxford from 1931 to 1945. The son of Edmund Craster of Beadnell hall, Northumberland, he was educated at Clifton college and at Balliol college, Oxford. As editor of the *History of Northumberland* between 1904 and 1914 he was responsible for vols. viii-x of that massive work and his experience as a scholar was of great value to him in his work at the Bodleian, the staff of which he joined in 1912. Appointed keeper of the western manuscripts in 1927, four years later he became Bodley's librarian and it was during his long tenure of this office that the great extension of the Bodleian was carried out. He was knighted in 1945 and used his retirement to write a *History of the Bodleian Library, 1845-1945*, published in 1952.

DeMille, Cecil Blount, pioneer U.S. film producer and director (b. Ashfield, Massachusetts, Aug. 12, 1881—d. Hollywood, California, Jan. 21), brought to the screen spectacular and costly presentations of biblical and classical stories. Educated at the Pennsylvania Military academy and at the New York Academy of Dramatic Art, he began his career as an actor and playwright before entering the motion picture industry in association with Samuel Goldwyn and Jesse Lasky. Their first picture, *The Squaw Man* (1913), was one of the earliest feature films ever made. DeMille went on to produce numerous films over a period of many years, including *The Ten Commandments* (1923), *The King of Kings* (1926), *The Sign of the Cross* (1932), *Cleopatra* (1934) and *The Crusades* (1935). He dismissed the criticism of those who deplored his productions as garish and inartistic with the rejoinder that public acceptance was a good artistic goal. One or two of his films, based on episodes in U.S. history, notably *The Plainsman* (1936) and *Union Pacific* (1938), were more favourably received by the critics. In later years he returned to biblical themes with such films as *Samson and Delilah* (1949) and a new version of *The Ten Commandments* (1956).

De Nicola, Enrico, Italian statesman (b. Naples, Nov. 9, 1877—d. Naples, Oct. 1), became first president of the Italian Republic in June 1946. After graduating in law, he started work as a journalist, turning later to politics. As a Liberal he was elected deputy in 1909, 1913, 1919 and 1921. He served as under secretary of state for the colonies in the Giolitti cabinet (Nov. 1913-March 1914) and under secretary of state for the treasury in the Orlando cabinet (Jan.-June 1919). On June 26, 1920, he was elected speaker of the Chamber of Deputies, holding this office until Jan. 25, 1924. Although Neapolitan by birth, he had the qualities of moderation and impartiality, and he would not come to terms with the Fascists. He was elected in 1924 to the first Fascist Chamber of Deputies, but he never appeared at Montecitorio; nominated senator in 1929, he refused to take his seat. He returned to his law practice, only taking an interest in politics again after the fall of Fascism. On June 28, 1946, he was elected by the Constituent Assembly (396 votes out of 501) provisional head of state. In 1947 he was asked to continue in this office until May 11, 1948, when the new constitution ended his term of office. In Jan. 1956 he was nominated senator for life.

Dukes, Ashley, British dramatist, critic and producer (b. Bridgwater, Somerset, May 29, 1885—d. London, May 4), made an outstanding contribution to the British theatre, in particular as a translator and adaptor of foreign plays. The son of a clergyman, he was educated at Silcoates school and at Manchester university, where he took a degree in science. He was already greatly interested in the theatre, and after a short period as a university lecturer, followed by a post-graduate course at Munich, he began writing articles on the theatre. During World War I he served with the Machine Gun corps and afterwards continued to work as a dramatic critic for some years. His first play, *Civil War*, was produced by the Stage society in 1910, and he subsequently wrote several others, of which the best known is *The Man with a Load of Mischief* (1924). He also adapted many plays from French and German. In 1933 with his wife Marie Rambert, the founder of the Ballet Rambert, he opened the Mercury theatre, in which the plays of T. S. Eliot and Ronald Duncan were performed with notable success. A man of cosmopolitan outlook, Dukes was twice British delegate of the Critics' circle at the International Congress of Critics and after World War II was theatre and music adviser to the British section of the Control Commission for Germany. He was still active in his later years and *The Broken Jug*, which he adapted from the German, was staged in 1958.

Duleepsinhji, (Prince) Kumar Shri, Indian cricketer (b. Nawanagar state, June 25, 1905—d. Bombay, India, Dec. 5), achieved great distinction as a batsman for Sussex and England. The nephew of the Indian cricketer K. S. Ranjitsinhji, he was educated at Cheltenham college and Clare college, Cambridge. An outstanding batsman at school, he soon made his mark at Cambridge and was awarded his blue in 1925. In 1926 he qualified for Sussex and scored runs very freely. The following year, he became seriously ill, but returned from Switzerland in 1928 with his health restored and played again with even greater success. In first-class cricket he made more than 2,500 runs in each season from 1929 to 1931, including many centuries. As captain of Sussex, he scored 333 against Northamptonshire and a century and a double century in the same match against Kent. In 1930, he played his first test match for England, against Australia, and scored a magnificient 173. Unfortunately, his career was all too brief and in 1932 tuberculosis forced him to retire in the following year.

In 1949, Duleepsinhji joined the Indian foreign service and became Indian high commissioner in Australia and New Zealand. Returning to India in 1953, he was appointed in 1954 chairman of the public service commission in Saurashtra state.

Dulles, John Foster, U.S. statesman (b. Washington, D.C., Feb. 25, 1888—d. Washington, D.C., May 24), in 1953 became secretary of state in the Republican administration of President Dwight D. Eisenhower. His first experience in diplomacy was as a secretary at the second Hague peace conference in 1907. The following year he graduated from Princeton university, then studied at the Sorbonne in Paris and at George Washington university law school. He was admitted to the New York state bar and established a practice in 1911 which he built up principally on his knowledge of international law. He was an adviser on German reparations at the Paris peace conference in 1919; earlier he had negotiated agreements with Central American nations for the military security of the Panama canal in World War I. In the late 1930s he became a political associate of Thomas E. Dewey and was Dewey's principal adviser on foreign affairs in the unsuccessful Republican presidential campaigns of 1944 and 1948. Franklin D. Roosevelt chose Dulles as senior adviser to the U.S. delegation at the United Nations organizing conference in San Francisco in 1945. He attracted Democratic attention and became one of the sponsors of the U.S. bipartisan policy in foreign affairs. In the Harry S. Truman administration Dulles drafted and negotiated the Allied-Japanese peace treaty of 1951. As secretary of state from Jan. 21, 1953, to April 15, 1959, Dulles' principal aim was to prevent the spread of Communism. His determination not to yield to Soviet or Chinese threats was widely and often violently attacked in the United States and abroad as " too inflexible " and " too stubborn ".

Three of the more serious crises came in Dulles' last year of office. In the summer of 1958, following an Iraqi revolution, Dulles decided that U.S. troops should land in Lebanon. Later that year, in the face of a massive artillery bombardment of the Nationalist Chinese islands of Quemoy and Matsu, Dulles said that the U.S. would help to repel any invasion from the mainland of the offshore islands. The third crisis coincided with Dulles' last illness—the Soviet threat to declare the German Democratic Republic a sovereign nation and thus to imperil west Berlin. Dulles was actively planning the position the United States would take at the Geneva conference of foreign ministers on the Berlin crisis when he had to announce his resignation (April 15, 1959) after his physicians had diagnosed incurable cancer. He died within six weeks and was given an official funeral at Washington.

Always a somewhat controversial figure, Dulles was probably most severely criticized when an article in *Life* (Jan. 1956), inspired by him, stated that " the ability to get to the verge (of war) without getting into war is the necessary art . . . if you are scared to go to the brink, you are lost."

Edwards, (Lewis) John, British politician (b. Aylesbury, Buckinghamshire, May 27, 1904—d. Strasbourg, France, Nov. 23), became in April 1959 the first British president of the consultative assembly of the Council of Europe. The son of a railwayman, he was educated at Aylesbury Grammar school and for a time studied theology at the Community of the Resurrection, Mirfield. He took a degree in economics at Leeds university and later had various appointments as a lecturer in economics. In 1938 he was elected general secretary of the Post Office Engineering union. He became Labour M.P. for one of the Blackburn constituencies in the 1945 general election and two years later was appointed parliamentary secretary to the Ministry of Health. He was unsuccessful in the 1950 general election but shortly afterwards won Brighouse and Spenborough in a by-election, becoming economic secretary to the Treasury in Oct. 1950. With the Labour party in opposition Edwards devoted most of his attention to the cause of European union. He became a delegate to the Council of Europe in 1955 and vice-president in 1957. He was also chairman of the budget committee of Western European union and chairman of the executive committee of Political and Economic Planning.

Epstein, Sir Jacob, U.S.-born British sculptor (b. New York city, Nov. 10, 1880—d. London, Aug. 19), whose major works never failed to arouse violent controversy among critics and the general public, was nevertheless accepted as the outstanding sculptor of his generation, though he remained virtually uninfluenced by the trends of 20th-century art. His parents were Russian-Polish Jews who had emigrated to the United States and as a youth he studied drawing, painting and modelling in a New York art school. In 1902 he went to Paris and for a time attended the Ecole des Beaux-Arts. Then, in 1905, he moved to London, where, apart from short intervals, he spent the rest of his life. Controversy over his work began with the unveiling, in 1908, of his first important commission, a group of 18 figures on the new headquarters of the British Medical association

Sir Jacob Epstein, who died on Aug. 19, photographed in his London studio surrounded by some of his works. On the right is his massive Christ figure in Subiaco stone, " Ecce Homo ", which, completed in 1933, was the subject of renewed controversy shortly before his death.

in the Strand (later Rhodesia house). These were described by a police officer as " rude ", though Bishop Lang (later archbishop of Canterbury) observed " nothing unusual " in them. Epstein's monumental carvings, deriving from the primitive sculpture of the middle east and Africa, embodied for the uninformed all the objectionable features of " modern art ", but it was probably the basic realism and the underlying humanity of even his most violent stylizations that offended the susceptibilities of so many. Among the offended was Stanley Baldwin—if his muttered " My God! " on unveiling *Rima* in Hyde park is not apocryphal. *Rima*, a memorial to W. H. Hudson, was disfigured on several occasions, and later works such as *Genesis* (1931), *Ecce Homo* (1933), *Adam* (1939) and *Jacob and the Angel* (1940) fared little better. The last-named was bought by a showman and exhibited in an Oxford street amusement arcade.

As a modeller and portrait sculptor Epstein was pre-eminent, and his fame may rest more securely on the many vividly penetrating bronzes of leading figures of his day than on the carvings. His subjects included Albert Einstein, Ramsay MacDonald, Joseph Conrad, Lord Beaverbrook, Chaim Weizmann, George Bernard Shaw, Yehudi Menuhin and Vaughan Williams. Modelled works on a larger scale were the bronze *Virgin and Child* (1953) in Cavendish square and the aluminium *Christ in Majesty* (1957) for Llandaff cathedral, both of which strengthened the view that his genius found its best expression in a plastic medium rather than in stone. At the time of his death he was engaged on a bust of Princess Margaret, his first royal sitter, and a group, to be cast in bronze, for the Bowater building in Knightsbridge. He was knighted in 1954.

Flynn, Errol (Leslie), Australian-born U.S. film actor (b. Hobart, Tasmania, June 20, 1909—d. Vancouver, Canada, Oct. 14), was one of the most handsomely paid players of his time. His father, Professor T. Thompson-Flynn, is an authority on ocean life. Before he started his acting career with a Northampton repertory company Flynn had been a policeman, coconut plantation overseer, sailor and gold miner. He went to Hollywood in 1935 where he was usually cast as a swashbuckling adventurer. He made his first big hit in *Captain Blood*, and later pictures included *Robin Hood*, *Gentleman Jim*, *Crossed Swords*, *The Sea Hawk*, *Adventures of Don Juan* and *Objective Burma*. More recently he received much praise for his performance as the dissolute Englishman in the film version of Ernest Hemingway's *The Sun Also Rises*. In his private life Flynn continued to enact the parts he created on the screen. He joined Fidel Castro's forces in Cuba at the beginning of 1959 and was wounded. He published three books, including his autobiographies *Beam Ends* and *My Wicked, Wicked Ways*.

Fothergill, (Charles) Philip, British politician (b. Earlsheaton, Yorkshire, Feb. 23, 1906—d. Dewsbury, Yorkshire, Jan. 31), was a prominent member of the Liberal party. Born of Yorkshire radical, nonconformist, wool-manufacturing stock, he was trained for the textile industry, joining the firm of Oldroyd and Son, of which his father was a director. In 1938 he founded his own business. During World War II much of his time was spent in Scotland where he was hon. regional welfare officer and deputy transport commissioner. He was a member of the National executive of the Liberal party for many years and its chairman during 1947-49 and 1952-54. Between 1950 and 1952 he was president of the party, between 1952 and 1955 vice-president, and from 1954 joint treasurer. Shrewd, witty and a forceful speaker on a platform, Fothergill, perhaps more than any other single person, kept the party alive in a most unpromising period of its history. He unsuccessfully contested three parliamentary seats as a Liberal. A victim to gout, he was a staunch temperance worker, being president of the United Kingdom alliance.

Gibb, Sir Claude Dixon, British engineer (b. Queenstown, South Australia, June 29, 1898—d. Newark, New Jersey, Jan. 15), achieved international recognition for his ability in applying science to the progress of mechanized engineering. Educated at the South Australian School of Mines and Adelaide university, he graduated in engineering. During World War I he served in the Australian Flying corps, after which he accepted an appointment under Sir Robert Chapman at Adelaide university, but in 1923 went to Britain to gain more experience. He joined C. A. Parsons and Company Ltd., as a fitter and by 1929 rose to be chief engineer and a director. Until World War II he was engaged in steam turbine research, and then successively occupied several important posts in war munitions production with considerable success. He rejoined Parsons as chairman and managing director in 1945 and played a leading part in the firm's postwar development and in the formation of the Nuclear Power Plant company in 1958. A pioneer in the development of commercial nuclear power, he became chairman of the new company. In 1945 he was knighted and created a K.B.E. in 1956.

Gomme, Arnold Wycombe, British scholar (b. London, Nov. 16, 1886—d. Aylesbury, Jan. 18), was professor of Greek at the University of Glasgow between 1946 and 1957. The son of Sir Lawrence Gomme, he was educated at Merchant Taylor's school and Trinity college, Cambridge, and obtained his first academic post as an assistant lecturer in classics at Liverpool university. Shortly afterwards he moved to Glasgow, where he held the posts of assistant lecturer and lecturer in Greek and Greek history, and reader in ancient history before attaining the professorial chair. He was editor of the *Hellenic Journal* in 1951, Sather professor at the University of California in 1951-52, president of the Hellenic society in 1956 and president of the Scottish Classical association in 1956-57. His life's work was on Thucydides, the first volume of a projected four-volume *Historical Commentary on Thucydides* appearing in 1945 and two more in 1956.

Goodhart-Rendel, Harry Stuart, British architect and critic (b. Cambridge, May 29, 1887—d. London, June 21), was perhaps most successful in designing and restoring churches. Educated at Eton and Trinity college, Cambridge, he practised as an architect from 1910. He became Slade professor of fine art at Oxford (1933-36) and president of the Royal Institute of British Architects (1937-39). His church designs include those for St. Wilfrid's, Brighton, and Prinknash Abbey church which, when completed, was to have an unusual circular central tower. His best-known secular work is Hay's wharf, near London bridge. A noted critic of the arts and an accomplished musician, Goodhart-Rendel was a governor of Sadler's Wells and vice-president of the Royal Academy of Music. His most important publication is *English Architecture since the Regency* (1953).

Grahame-White, Claude, English aviator (b. Bursledon, Hampshire, Aug. 21, 1879—d. Nice, France, Aug. 19), was an outstanding pioneer of aviation. Educated at Crondall House school, Surrey, and Bedford school, he started his career in the engineering side of his uncle's woollen business. After working as steward of a large estate in Sussex, he went in 1906 on safari in Africa. Back in England he entered the motor business and raced at Brooklands. In 1909, Louis Blériot's cross-channel flight inspired him to take up flying which he learnt in France, obtaining his certificate from the French Aero club in 1910 (the first Englishman to do so). The same year he opened a British flying school at Pau, France, and it was then that he captured everyone's imagination by bravely, but unsuccessfully, attempting to win the *Daily Mail's* £10,000 prize for the first flight from London to Manchester. He made two efforts, on one occasion flying part of the way at night, but on both flights got no farther than Lichfield and the Frenchman, Louis Paulhan, won the prize. Nevertheless, Grahame-White was awarded the French Aero club's gold medal and during the next two years he won several prizes and set up new air records in Britain and the United States. During World War I, while serving in the Royal Naval Air Service, he participated in an air raid on enemy-occupied Belgium, but in Aug. 1915 the government put him on constructional work at Hendon airport. For several years after the war he continued his manufacturing interests, but then retired to watch eagerly the fulfilment of his prophecies on the importance of flying.

Greg, Sir Walter Wilson, British scholar (b. Wimbledon, Surrey, July 9, 1875—d. Midhurst, Sussex, March 4), was an authority on the bibliography and paleography of Elizabethan drama. A son of the economist Walter Wilson Greg, he was educated at Harrow and at Trinity college, Cambridge, and was originally intended to become editor of *The Economist*, a family concern. However, he soon began to apply himself to the textual study of Elizabethan drama, publishing *A List of English Plays* in 1900 and editing Henslowe's diary and papers between 1904 and 1908. In 1906 he was made general editor of the Malone society, a post which he occupied until 1939, becoming president of the Bibliographical society in 1930, Clark lecturer at Trinity college, Cambridge, in 1938, and James P. R. Lyell reader in bibliography at Oxford in 1954. He was knighted in 1950. His published works include *Pastoral Poetry and Pastoral Drama* (1906); *A Bibliography of the English Printed Drama in the Restoration* (2 vol., 1939-51); *The Editorial Problem in Shakespeare* (1942); and *Some Aspects and Problems of London Publishing between 1550 and 1650* (1956); and he edited Marlowe's *Dr. Faustus* (1950) and *Jonson's Masque of Gipsies* (1952).

Grock (Adrien Wettach), Swiss clown (b. Loveresse, near Reconvilier, Switzerland, Jan. 10, 1880—d. Imperia, Italy, July 14), elevated pantomime to an art. The son of a watchmaker, at the age of seven he saw his first circus and decided to be a clown. His dream became a reality, but before he had established himself as Grock he had to earn his living as a jack of all trades. He became famous before World War I and appeared in Berlin at a command performance for William II. " Why, you are even better known than I am," said the Kaiser. " Why shouldn't I be? I'm funnier ", replied Grock. His brand of humour failed in the United States, where he appeared in 1918, but in London he was an immediate success. However, because of a dispute over fees and income tax, he left Britain in 1924 never to return. He continued to tour the continent always giving the same act—pathos mingled with comedy. He would appear on the stage funnily dressed and start a series of adventures with his tiny violin (removed from gigantic case) or with a piano (which he pushed towards the stool). He was a good musician, and also an acrobat. His act was enlivened by a dialogue with the ringmaster. *Sans blague* (or *unmöglich*, or " no kidding "), he would say with perplexity when listening to a truism. He amassed a great deal of money, lost some of it in unhappy speculations, but lived comfortably after his farewell performance in 1954 in Hamburg. He wrote *Die Memoiren des Königs der Clowns* (1956), translated into English as *Grock, King of Clowns* (1957).

Grosz, George, German-born caricaturist (b. Berlin, July 26, 1893—d. Berlin, July 5), studied painting at the Dresden academy (1909-11), and later took part in the Dada movement. He began to satirize the army, the Junker caste and during World War I attacked Kaiser William II personally. A warrant was issued for his arrest but he went into hiding. He was arrested some time later because one of his paintings represented crucified Christ with a gas mask. He was sentenced to be shot for sacrilege, but was paroled and sent to the front. After the war, profoundly disillusioned, he drew cartoons castigating militarists, profiteers, priests and prostitutes. In 1927, because his cartoons were " wounding the susceptibilities of normal people ", he and his two publishers were fined 500 marks each. Early in 1933 he emigrated to New York where he became a teacher at arts schools and in due course became naturalized as a U.S. citizen. He returned to Berlin in June 1958. His autobiography, *Ein grosser Nein und ein Kleines Ja*, was published in 1955.

Gwenn, Edmund, English film actor (b. London, Sept. 26, 1877—d. Hollywood, United States, Sept. 6), had a reputation as a character actor in both Britain and the United States. Educated at St. Olave's and King's college, London, he went on the stage and excelled in portraying coarse and noisy personalities. From these he graduated to more sophisticated roles at the Court theatre where he created

" Grock " (Adrien Wettach)   *Lord Halifax*   *General George Marshall*   *Gérard Philipe*

many small parts in plays by George Bernard Shaw, Harley Granville-Barker and John Galsworthy. His film career began in the 1920s and before going to Hollywood in 1935 he played Jess Oakroyd in *The Good Companions*. He usually appeared in genial roles and his portrayal of Santa Claus in *Miracle on 34th Street* won him an Oscar in 1948.

Hale, Sonnie (JOHN ROBERT HALE-MONRO), British actor (b. London, May 1, 1902—d. London, June 9), was a clever and versatile light comedian in musical comedy. He came from a theatrical family, his father being well-known in pantomime and musical comedy and his sister as a comedienne. On finishing his education at Beaumont college, Old Windsor, he decided to follow them on the stage. His first appearance was at the London Pavilion in 1921 in the chorus of *Fun of the Fayre*. Within a decade he had scored a great success in such shows as *One Dam Thing After Another*, *This Year of Grace* and *Evergreen*. In the early 1930s he virtually gave up the stage to devote himself to playing in and directing films with considerable success. Hale reappeared on the stage in 1939 and, in 1940, played in his own comedy, *Come Out and Play*, but it was in pantomime that he re-established himself. When he died he was about to appear in the West End production of his own play, *The French Mistress*.

Halifax, Edward Frederick Lindley Wood, 1st Earl of, British statesman (b. Powderham castle, Devon, April 16, 1881—d. Garrowby hall, near York, Dec. 23), was viceroy of India from 1925 to 1931 and secretary of state for foreign affairs during 1938-40. The fourth son of the 2nd Viscount Halifax, who was well known as a leader of the Anglo-Catholic movement, he was educated at Eton and at Christ Church, Oxford, being elected a fellow of All Souls, Oxford, in 1903. He entered parliament in 1910 as Conservative member for Ripon and during World War I served for a time with the Yorkshire Dragoons in France. In 1921 he was appointed parliamentary under-secretary for the colonies and in the following year became president of the Board of Education, holding this post until 1924. During 1924-25 he was minister of agriculture. His first major appointment was as viceroy of India (1926-31), and he served in India during a period of great nationalist ferment in which Gandhi played a leading part. Halifax himself was deeply religious and this enabled him to recognize and respond to the element of mysticism in Gandhi's nature. On his return from India he again became president of the Board of Education (1932-35). He was then successively lord privy seal (1935-37) and lord president of the council (1937-38). The most controversial period of Halifax's career followed his appointment as foreign secretary in Feb. 1938, after Anthony Eden's resignation from the Chamberlain government. Halifax had previously been politically close to Neville Chamberlain and his acceptance of the Foreign Office meant that he identified himself with Chamberlain's policy of " appeasement " towards Nazi Germany. In Nov. 1937 he had visited Adolf Hitler and Hermann Goering while attending a hunting exhibition in Berlin as master of the Middleton foxhounds. In Jan. 1939 he accompanied Chamberlain on a visit to Benito Mussolini and Count Galeazzo Ciano in Rome. When Winston Churchill became prime minister in May 1940, Halifax remained at the Foreign Office for seven months, but at the end of that year he went to Washington as British ambassador, remaining in this post until May 1946. In 1934 he had succeeded his father as 3rd Viscount Halifax and in 1944 he was created 1st Earl of Halifax in recognition of his valuable work for the Allied cause in the United States. In 1957 he published a volume of memoirs, *Fulness of Days*. (J. F. BD.)

Harwood, Harold Marsh, British playwright (b. Eccles, Lancashire, March 29, 1874—d. London, April 20), was the author of numerous successful light plays over a period of some 30 years. They included *Please Help Emily* (1916), *The Grain of Mustard Seed* (1920) and *The Old Folks at Home* (1933). He frequently collaborated with his wife, F. Tennyson Jesse, who died in 1958.

Hatoyama, Ichiro, Japanese statesman (b. Tokyo, Jan. 1, 1883—d. Tokyo, March 7), achieved his life's ambition at 71 by serving as prime minister for two years. In 1915 he was elected a Conservative member of the Lower Chamber and was continually re-elected until 1942. He was chief cabinet secretary (1927-29) and minister of education (1931-34). During World War II he retired to his country home, emerging in 1945 as one of the organizers of the Liberal party. On April 4, 1946, he was elected to the House of Representatives and expected to form the new government, but General D. Macarthur

forbade him to take his seat because in a book published in 1937 he had praised Hitler and Mussolini. Vindicated in 1951, he became prime minister on Dec. 9, 1954, resigning on Dec. 20, 1956, because of failing health.

Hawthorn, John Michael, British motor-racing driver (b. Mexborough, Yorkshire, April 10, 1929—d. near Onslow, Surrey, Jan. 22), became world champion racing motorist in 1958. He was killed in a road accident some six weeks after announcing his retirement from Grand Prix racing. Hawthorn began racing at 21 with Riley sports cars and two years later, driving a Cooper Bristol, he won the Chichester cup at Goodwood and was placed high in numerous British and continental races. In 1953, driving for Ferrari, he won the French Grand Prix from Juan Fangio at Reims, and the following year he won the Spanish and came second in the British, German and Italian Grands Prix. During 1955-56 he drove for Vanwall, Jaguar and B.R.M., and in 1955, in a Jaguar, he won the tragic Le Mans 24-hr. race during which some 80 spectators were killed. With the B.R.M. he had no success, for the car broke down at every meeting. In 1957 he rejoined Ferrari and was highly placed in four Grands Prix and the Nürburg 1,000-km. sports car race. Following many successes in 1958 his second placing in the Moroccan Grand Prix in October won for him the title of world champion. Well liked among his fellow drivers, Hawthorn was a popular figure at international meetings. A tall, well-built man, he fitted into a *monoposte* cockpit rather as an egg sits in its cup, and was easily recognized by his characteristic crouch over the wheel.

Heal, Sir Ambrose, British furniture designer and manufacturer (b. Sept. 3, 1872—d. Beaconsfield, Nov. 15), was for 40 years the head of the family business founded by his great-grandfather in 1810, which has been situated in Tottenham Court road, London, since 1840. Educated at Marlborough college and privately, he was apprenticed to a cabinet maker at Warwick before joining the business under his father in 1893. Influenced by members of the Art Workers guild, such as W. R. Lethaby, S. Surage and C. F. A. Voysey, whom he met through his cousin Cecil Brewer, the architect, he began to design furniture which in the simplicity of its lines contrasted strongly with the elaborate reproduction pieces of the day, and relied for its effect on the display of fine woods undisguised by heavy polishes. In 1900 he won an award at the Paris exhibition for a bedroom suite, and in 1906 he became a member of the Arts and Crafts society. After his father's death he became chairman of the firm, and was responsible for the expansion of its activities from mattress-making to the sale of every description of household goods. With the passing of the years Heals became an accepted venue for all interested in well-designed furniture, textiles and pottery. A founder-member of the Design and Industries association, he was knighted in 1933 for his services to industrial art. He was keenly interested in calligraphy, on which he published a book, *The English Writing-Masters and Their Copy-books, 1570-1800* (1931).

Heilbron, Sir Ian, Scottish chemist (b. Glasgow, Nov. 6, 1886—d. Sept. 14), was celebrated for his outstanding work in organic chemistry, particularly on natural products. He received most of his education in Glasgow, and after leaving its university he took a Ph.D. degree at Leipzig university. His highly successful academic career was interrupted by service in World War I, following which he successively occupied the chairs of organic chemistry at Liverpool (1920-33), Manchester (1933-38) and the Imperial College of Science and Technology, London (1938-49). From 1949-57 he was director of the Brewing Industry Research foundation and directed much research in the field of synthetic organic chemistry. He also made valuable contributions at this time to the chemistry of vitamins A and D_2, and penicillin. From 1939 he was an adviser to the government and was awarded a knighthood in 1946. He received many academic honours.

Hitchcock, Sir Eldred Frederick, British industrialist (b. London, Dec. 9, 1887—d. Tanga, Tanganyika, April 6), played a leading part in the development of Tanganyika sisal. He was educated at Burford grammar school and at Oxford university, subsequently becoming secretary of Toynbee hall. During World War I he was employed as a government wool statistician, eventually being appointed deputy director of wool textiles at the War Office. After a short period as warden of Toynbee hall he turned to business, eventually becoming connected with a firm which was concerned with the growing of sisal in Africa. Later he settled in Tanganyika, where he soon achieved an important position in the sisal industry. During World War II it was largely due to his efforts that the production of sisal was vastly expanded so that it became the country's chief export. In 1949 he formed the Tanganyika Sisal Marketing association and by the end of the 1950s Tanganyika was the world's largest producer of sisal. Hitchcock was engaged in many other activities and notably made great efforts to establish better working conditions for his African employees. He was a strong advocate of a multi-racial society and was for a time a member of the Tanganyika legislative council. Created a C.B.E. in 1920, he was knighted in 1955.

Hoffnung, Gerard, British artist and musician (b. London, March 22, 1925—d. London, Sept. 28), endeared himself to many both as a cartoonist and as the creator of a remarkable symphony orchestra. Educated at Highgate school and at the Harrow School of Art, he was for a time a schoolmaster. He later became a freelance artist, illustrating books and contributing humorous drawings to *Punch* and other magazines. He published several books of musical cartoons for which his extensive knowledge of music provided a source of inspiration. His cartoons came to life when in 1956 he arranged a festival performed by the Hoffnung Symphony orchestra, with an unusual collection of musical instruments including three vacuum cleaners. A Quaker and a man of deep humanity, he included among his many activities that of prison visitor.

Housman, Laurence, British writer and artist (b. Bromsgrove, Worcestershire, July 18, 1865—d. Glastonbury, Somerset, Feb. 20), reached his widest public with a series of plays about the Victorian era, of which the most successful was *Victoria Regina* (1934). His prolific and varied production covered a period of some 60 years. One of a family of seven, and a younger brother of the poet A. E. Housman, he studied art in London, and among his earliest works as an artist were illustrations for Christina Rossetti's *Goblin Market*. His first writings were fairy tales and poems which he illustrated himself. In 1900 he published anonymously *An Englishwoman's Love Letters*. This was widely read and, though later deprecated by Housman himself, achieved a considerable success. There followed numerous books of verse, stories, novels and plays. His first play, *Bethlehem*, was privately produced by Gordon Craig in 1902, but, like many of his dramatic works, was for some years withheld by censorship from public performance. *Prunella* (1906), a charming fantasy in which Harley Granville-Barker collaborated, escaped this fate. It was not however until 1922 that Housman again became prominent, with the publication of the first of three collections entitled *Little Plays of St. Francis*. In the same year appeared the Victorian historical piece *Angels and Ministers*, and in 1922 *Dethronements*. These preceded the many one-act Victorian "palace-plays" and the full-length *Victoria Regina*, which was staged in the United States with great success before it was licensed by the lord chamberlain in 1937. The note of satire which in varying degrees pervaded much of his writing was dominant in the novel *Trimblerigg* (1924), of which Lloyd George was the thinly disguised butt. An individualist without allegiance to any literary movement, Housman described himself as "a rabid pacifist and internationalist".

Ilchester, Giles Stephen Holland Fox-Strangways, 6th Earl (b. London, May 31, 1874—d. London, Oct. 29), was known as a distinguished authority on English politics and social life in the 18th century. The eldest son of the 5th Earl of Ilchester, from Eton he went up to Christ Church, Oxford, but did not take his degree. During World War I he was a king's messenger, receiving for his services the O.B.E. and the Legion of Honour. His family were related to Henry Fox, the 1st Lord Holland, and Charles James Fox, the statesman. His first publication was *The Life and Letters of Lady Sarah Lennox* (1901), and he edited the 3rd Lord Holland's *Further Memoirs of the Whig Party* and the *Journals of Elizabeth, Lady Holland* (1908). *Henry Fox, His Family and Relations* was published in 1920. On the death of his father in 1905 he had become the owner of one of London's largest historic houses, Holland house, whose story he told in *The Home of the Hollands, 1605 to 1820* (1937) and *Chronicles of Holland House, 1820 to 1900* (1937). After World War II, during which the house was badly damaged, he edited *Letters of Lady Holland to her Son* (1946) and *Lord Hervey and his Friends 1726-1738* (1950). Among his many other activities he was a trustee, and from 1941 chairman, of the National Portrait gallery, a trustee of the British Museum, president of the London library during 1940-52 and chairman of the Royal Commission on Historical Buildings, 1943-57. In 1943 he became president of the Walpole society. Lord Ilchester had been a member of the Jockey club since 1907 and was senior steward in 1939, although he did not have much success as an owner.

Ironside, William Edmund Ironside, 1st Baron, of Archangel and of Ironside in the County of Aberdeen, Scottish soldier (b. Ironside, Aberdeenshire, May 6, 1880—d. London, Sept. 22), commanded the Allied expeditionary forces in northern Russia after the revolution. The son of an army surgeon-major, he was educated at Tonbridge school and the Royal Military academy, Woolwich, serving in the artillery during the Boer war. In Jan. 1918 he became commandant of the Small Arms school in France and during the final German offensive he commanded the 99th infantry brigade. Promoted brigadier-general, he was appointed in Oct. 1918 to command the Allied expeditionary forces based on Archangel, northern Russia, with the task of helping the new Russian government to ward off the Germans. The struggle against the Bolsheviks, however, became his main preoccupation and following a series of mutinies in his own forces he was obliged to withdraw from Archangel and Murmansk in Oct. 1919. After varied service during the inter-war years he was promoted lieut.-general in 1931 and general in 1935 and held important appointments in Cairo, Gibraltar and Poland. When World War II began, Ironside became chief of the imperial general staff and arranged the dispatch of the expeditionary force to France. After the evacuation of British forces from Dunkirk, he was succeeded as C.I.G.S. by Sir John Dill in May 1940. In July 1940, he was promoted field marshal and was created a baron in 1941.

Ismail, Sir Mirza Muhammed, Indian statesman (b. Bangalore, India, Oct. 23, 1883—d. Bangalore, Jan. 5), gave outstanding service as prime minister of Mysore during 1926-41. Educated at the Central college, Bangalore, and at Madras university, he subsequently entered the Mysore state service, becoming in 1906 assistant secretary to the maharaja. Appointed private secretary in 1922, he assumed in 1926 the duties of dewan (prime minister) for a period of five years, but was twice reappointed. During his long term of office the great improvements which he made in the administration of Mysore won him wide recognition. In the 1930s he was a delegate to the Indian Round Table conference and also to the Joint Parliamentary Committee on Indian Reforms. Soon after relinquishing his post in Mysore in 1941 he was appointed prime minister of Jaipur, remaining in this position until 1946. In that year he accepted the invitation of the Nizam of Hyderabad to become prime minister of his state, but resigned the following year. He was knighted in 1930 and was created a K.C.I.E. in 1936.

Jansen, Ernest George, South African statesman (b. near Dundee, Natal, Aug. 7, 1881—d. Pretoria, Nov. 25), was governor-general of the Union of South Africa from 1951 until the time of his death. Educated privately and at Ladysmith and Durban, he studied law and was admitted as an attorney in 1906. He subsequently practised at the bar in Pietermaritzburg. Joining the Nationalist party in 1915, he was elected to parliament in 1921 as member for Vryheid, a constituency he was to represent for 22 years. When the government of General James Hertzog came into power in 1924, Jansen was appointed speaker and held this office continuously until 1943, except for four years between 1929 and 1933. Considered by many to be the best speaker the South African House of Assembly had ever had, Jansen was noted for his impartiality and dignity on all occasions. Having lost his seat in the 1943 election, he became for a short time editor of *New Era*, an English language Nationalist weekly. Returned to parliament at a by-election in 1946, he was given the portfolio of native affairs when D. F. Malan (*see* OBITUARIES) formed a government following the Nationalist victory in the general election of 1948. Three years later Jansen was appointed governor-general, a post he was to hold with distinction during a difficult period in his country's history. A shy man with an austere manner, he had a high sense of public duty.

Jayakar, Mukund Ramrao, Indian lawyer and politician (b. 1873?—d. Bombay, March 10), for many years played an important part in his country's affairs. He was educated at Elphinstone High school and college, Bombay, and subsequently studied law at Lincoln's Inn. On his return to India he began practising as a barrister in the Bombay High Court. In 1923 he became a member of the Bombay legislative council. Three years later he was elected to the central legislative assembly and from 1927 to 1930 he was leader of the National party in the assembly. In 1937 he was appointed a judge of the Federal Court. During 1948-56 he was vice-chancellor of Poona university.

Jenkins, Claude, British scholar (b. West Bromwich, Staffordshire, May 26, 1877—d. Tunbridge Wells, Jan. 17), had been regius professor of ecclesiastical history at Oxford and canon of Christ Church since 1934. He was educated at King Edward's school, Birmingham, and gained an open classical exhibition at New college, Oxford. After ordination in 1904, he became curate at St. Martin-in-the-Fields and, the following year, lecturer in ecclesiastical history at King's college, London, where from 1918-34 he was professor. At Oxford he was widely known as a university "character", easily recognizable by his rigid adherence to old-fashioned ecclesiastical garb, a costume he varied only during vacations at Tunbridge Wells. Among his many diverse interests—he once claimed to have been a member of more than 50 committees simultaneously—membership of the Oxford Union society held, perhaps, first claim on his affections; he had been a member of the society for more than 60 years and its senior librarian since 1939.

Jordan, (Heinrich Ernst) Karl, German-born British entomologist (b. Almstedt, near Hildesheim, Germany, Dec. 7, 1861—d. Hemel Hempstead, Hertfordshire, Jan. 12), made outstanding contributions to entomology which were recognized on his 94th birthday by the publication in his honour of a special volume of the transactions of the Royal Entomological Society of London. The son of a small farmer, Jordan was helped into the high school at Hildesheim by a prosperous uncle. In 1886 he graduated from Göttingen university with the highest honours in botany and zoology, and later joined the grammar school at Münden, remaining there until 1892 when he was appointed to the staff of the School of Agriculture, Hildesheim. At Münden he met Ernst Hartert, the newly appointed director of the Zoological museum at Tring, Hertfordshire. In 1893 he was invited to Tring and undertook the immense task of arranging and classifying the huge collection of insects which Lord Rothschild had accumulated. For the greater part of his life he worked there, first as curator of entomology (1893-1939) and finally as director of the museum (1930-39). He produced an astonishing volume of scientific papers on biological variation and entomology. Most of these were concerned with the taxonomy and evolution of beetles, flies, butterflies and moths. Karl Jordan's sympathies were international and he initiated the very successful International Congresses of Entomology, the first of which was held in Brussels in 1910. He also served as president of the International Commission on Zoological Nomenclature and of the Royal Entomological society (1929).

Jordan, Sir William Joseph, New Zealand politician (b. Ramsgate, May 19, 1879—d. Auckland, April 8), was high commissioner for New Zealand in London from 1936 to 1951. He left school at the age of 13 and after a variety of jobs joined the Metropolitan police.

In 1904 he emigrated to New Zealand and took part in the formation of the Labour party there. From 1922 until 1936 he was a member of the New Zealand parliament. His appointment to the high commissionership in London followed the rise to power of his party in 1935. He became president of the council of the League of Nations in 1938 and represented his country at various international conferences. In 1946 he became a member of the Privy Council and was created K.C.M.G. in 1952.

Kassner, Rudolf, Austrian writer (b. Gross-Pawlowitz, Moravia, Sept. 11, 1873—d. Sierre, Switzerland, April 1), is perhaps best known for his philosophical works. Educated in Vienna and Berlin, he travelled widely, making the acquaintance of men of letters in various countries. In 1945 his *Der Zauberer* won him the Schiller prize. In 1953 he was awarded the Prize of the Austrian State for his life's work.

Kelly, Sir David, British diplomat (b. Adelaide, South Australia, Sept. 14, 1891—d. Inch, Wexford, Republic of Ireland, March 27), was British ambassador to the U.S.S.R. and an authoritative commentator on Soviet affairs after his retirement. He was the son of an Ulster Protestant but he was converted to Roman Catholicism. After brilliant studies at St. Paul's school and Magdalen college, Oxford, he secured a nomination to the Foreign Office in 1914 but, as World War I had broken out, he joined the army and served in France, mainly in intelligence. In 1919 he entered the diplomatic service and served in South and Central America, Europe and the Foreign Office. In 1934 he was appointed counsellor at the Cairo residency and four years later he became head of the Egyptian department at the Foreign Office. Kelly was appointed minister in Bern in 1939 and in 1942 he was knighted and promoted ambassador in Buenos Aires. He held similar appointments in Ankara (1946) and Moscow (1949), retiring in 1951.

In 1929 Kelly had married, as his second wife, the Comtesse de Jourda de Vaux. During his ambassadorship in Turkey he and his wife travelled throughout the country and played a prominent part in maintaining satisfactory Anglo-Turkish relations in the difficult postwar years. Even during his appointment to Moscow during the Stalinist period Kelly and his wife saw much of the U.S.S.R. and Lady Kelly wrote two descriptive books. In his autobiography, *The Ruling Few* (1952), he described the function of a diplomat. He formulated his views on Christian conservative humanism in *The Hungry Sheep* (1955). In his articles and lectures he emphasized the importance of the Atlantic alliance and the closest possible collaboration with the United States.

Kendall, Kay, British actress (b. May 21, 1927—d. London, Sept. 6), graduated from the chorus line of revues and variety shows to the front rank of screen comediennes, though her reputation rested on only three or four films. She belonged to a theatrical family—her grandmother was the well-known Edwardian ballad singer Marie Kendall —and her first public appearance was at the London Palladium at the age of 12. During World War II she toured in revue and with E.N.S.A. and played a number of small film parts. However, her film career suffered a setback through the failure of the British musical *London Town* (1946), in which she played opposite Sid Field. After some years in repertory and revue she returned to the screen and in 1953 had her first great success in *Genevieve*. In Hollywood she made *Les Girls* (1957) and *The Reluctant Debutante* (1958). Her last film, *Once More With Feeling*, was completed shortly before her death.

Ketelbey, Albert William, English composer (b. Birmingham, Aug. 9, 1875—d. Cowes, Isle of Wight, Nov. 26), was well known to the public through his light musical compositions. Educated at Fitzroy college, London, he studied at Trinity College of Music where he won every medal and prize. At 22 he was director of a London west end theatre and later worked as André Charlot's musical director at the Vaudeville. On the continent, he frequently appeared as a guest conductor of well-known orchestras. An accomplished composer in many fields of music, he was sensitive to atmosphere and this is apparent in those of his works which achieved most popularity: *In a Monastery Garden* and *In a Persian Market*.

Knipper-Chekhova, Olga Leonardovna, Russian actress (b. Glazov, U.S.S.R., 1870—d. Moscow, March 22), was the widow of the writer Anton Chekhov. Of German extraction, the daughter of an engineer, she studied at the dramatic school of the Moscow Philharmonic society and in 1898 became a founder-member of the Moscow Art theatre. She quickly achieved distinction in the plays of Anton Chekhov, creating the roles of Arkadina (*The Seagull*, 1898), Elena (*Uncle Vanya*, 1899), Masha (*The Three Sisters*, 1901), Anna Petrovna (*Ivanov*, 1904) and Ranevska (*The Cherry Orchard*, 1904). In 1901 she married Chekhov and continued with her career. During 1919-24 she played in the United States and in various European countries, and until her death remained in close touch with the theatre.

Knowles, Guy John Fenton, British art collector (b. London, July 1, 1879—d. Dorking, April 8), was during his life and by the terms of his will one of the principal benefactors of the Fitzwilliam museum, Cambridge. Educated at Rugby and at Trinity college, Cambridge, he followed the profession of engineer until World War I, during which he served as an artillery officer. After the war he took over the management of his family's estates, and from 1921 to 1949 he was supervisor of the copyright agency acting for Cambridge University library, the Bodleian, the National Library of Scotland and Trinity college, Dublin. His love of the arts received early encouragement from his parents. As a boy he was taught drawing and sculpture by Alphonse Legros, works by whom formed part of his varied collection of paintings, drawings, bronzes and other works of art, the whole of which he bequeathed to the Fitzwilliam museum.

Kogan, Claude, French mountaineer (b. Paris, 1919—d. Cho Oyu, Nepalese Himalayas, October), was the leader of the international all-women climbing expedition which left Kathmandu on Aug. 21, with the object of reaching for the first time the 26,750-ft. summit of Cho Oyu, the eighth highest mountain in the world. A designer and manufacturer of swimming suits by profession, she had acquired in less than a decade a reputation as the leading woman mountaineer of her time. She had taken part in expeditions to the Andes, to Greenland and to the Caucasus, and on two previous occasions to the Himalayas, where in 1954, with the Swiss climber Raymond Lambert, she attempted the ascent of Cho Oyu for the first time, reaching to within 2,000 ft. of the summit. Mme. Kogan died during a blizzard, with Claudine van der Stratten, a Belgian member of the expedition, and a Sherpa guide, Angnorbu, some time after the three had started out, on Oct. 1, to set up a fourth camp at 23,000 ft. The blizzard raged for more than a week, and on Oct. 10 a search party of other members of the expedition found no trace of the lost climbers.

Kovács, Béla, Hungarian Smallholders' party leader (b. in a village of the county of Báranya, 1908—d. Pécs, June 21), was one of the toughest opponents of Communism. The son of a peasant, he became after World War II secretary general of the Independent Smallholders' party founded by Ferenc Nagy, and was instrumental in the party's electoral victory of Nov. 4, 1945 (245 seats out of a total of 409). Kovács was appointed minister of agriculture in Ferenc Nagy's cabinet. Because he attempted to squeeze the Communists out of the government, he became their main enemy; backed by the Soviet occupation authorities, they forced him to resign. When parliament refused to waive his immunity, Lieut.-General V. P. Sviridov, Soviet president of the Allied Control commission, ordered his arrest on Feb. 25, 1947, accusing him of "organizing espionage against the Soviet forces". He was deported to the U.S.S.R. and imprisoned there for almost nine years. Physically broken, he was released in Jan. 1956 and returned to Hungary. On Nov. 2, 1956, during the October rising, he was given the post of minister of state in the Imre Nagy cabinet. When the rising had been crushed, Kovács returned to Pécs. At first he refused to collaborate with János Kádár, but on Nov. 16, 1958, he was elected to the House of Representatives as a candidate of the Patriotic People's front.

Kramer, Gustav, German biologist (b. Mannheim, March 11, 1910—d. while climbing, in Calabria, Italy, April 19), was a world authority on bird migration, especially the problems of navigation and orientation. His outstanding achievements were his demonstration that migrating birds orientate by means of the sun combined with a definite time sense, and his work on the means by which birds "home" from unfamiliar localities. Most of his postwar work was done at the Max-Planck-Institut at Wilhelmshaven, but just before his death he was appointed director of the new Max-Planck-Institut für Verhaltensphysiologie at Tübingen.

Krause, Frederick Edward Traugott, South African judge (b. Bloemfontein district, Orange Free State, Aug. 29, 1868—d. Pretoria, Transvaal, Aug. 23), was judge president of the Orange Free State during 1933-38. Of German parentage, he was educated at Bloemfontein, Stellenbosch and the universities of Amsterdam and Cambridge. Appointed first state prosecutor and acting attorney-general of the Witwatersrand in 1896, he became on the outbreak of the Boer War military governor of Johannesburg, and in this capacity surrendered the town to Lord Roberts. Tried in Britain on a charge of high treason, Krause was eventually sentenced to two years' imprisonment for attempted incitement to murder. After the war he resumed his career and in 1923 became a judge of the Supreme Court of South Africa, holding this post until his appointment as judge president.

Krauss, Werner, German-born Austrian actor (b. Gestungshausen, near Coburg, Germany, June 23, 1884—d. Vienna, Oct. 20). He made his first appearance in 1904 at the provincial theatre at Guben. After World War I he had established himself in classical roles, and later was a leading actor in the Expressionist movement in Berlin. Krauss appeared in many silent films, *The Cabinet of Dr. Caligari* being the best-known. He continued to appear on the stage and, under the Nazi regime, became vice-president of the "Reich Theatre chamber". His remarkably evil portrayal of the title role in the Nazi film version of *Jew Süss*, first exhibited in Berlin in Sept. 1940, was closely followed by the systematic extermination of the Jews by the Nazis. After World War II, he acquired (in 1948) Austrian nationality and became a member of the Vienna Burgtheater company.

Krzhizhanovski, Gleb Maksimilianovich, Russian power engineer (b. Samara [now Kuibyshev], Jan. 24, 1872—d. Moscow, March 31), a pioneer of the electrification of the U.S.S.R., joined the Russian Social Democratic (later Communist) party in 1893 when he was a student at the St. Petersburg Technological institute. Two years later he was arrested and in 1897 was deported for three years to Siberia. On his return he continued both his studies and revolutionary activities. In 1903 he was elected a member of the central committee of the R.S.D.W.P. In 1920 Lenin appointed him head of the State Commission for the Electrification of Russia (GOELRO). From 1921 to 1930 he was chairman of the State Planning committee. In subsequent years he worked in a number of government institutions. From 1924 to 1939 he was a member of the central committee of the Communist Party of the Soviet Union. Krzhizhanovski was a vice-president of the Academy of Sciences of the U.S.S.R. from 1929 to 1939 and up to the time of his death he was head of the academy's Institute of Power Engineering. He played a considerable part in planning, designing and building the principal Soviet power stations.

Landowska, Wanda, Polish musician (b. Warsaw, July 5, 1877—d. Lakeville, Connecticut, United States, Aug. 16), is chiefly remembered for her revival of the harpsichord. She studied at the Warsaw conservatoire and at Berlin, and later went to Paris. She was already known as a pianist when in 1903 she gave her first public harpsichord performance, thereafter devoting herself almost entirely to this instrument. She was the first modern musician to play the continuo part in Bach's *St. Matthew Passion* on a harpsichord. In 1925 she founded her École de Musique Ancienne at Saint-Leu-la Fôret, near Paris, which she had to abandon in 1940 after the German invasion of France. She subsequently went to live in the United States. An authority on early keyboard music, Wanda Landowska made many fine recordings of works by Bach, including *The Chromatic Fantasia and Fugue*, *The Goldberg Variations* and the 48.

Lane, Lupino (HENRY GEORGE LUPINO), British actor manager (b. London, June 16, 1892—d. London, Nov. 10), a comedian in the best tradition of Cockney humour, belonged to a theatrical family which can trace its origins back to the reign of James I. He first appeared in public at the age of four in a benefit performance for Vesta Tilley. Seven years later he was billed at the London Pavilion as " Nipper " Lane, and by his early twenties, after touring in variety, was appearing in west end successes such as *Watch Your Step*, *Follow the Crowd*, *Extra Special* and *Afgar*. The latter took him to New York on the first of many visits, and his popularity in the United States was increased by his film work, begun in 1913. One of the films in which he appeared was *The Love Parade*, with Maurice Chevalier. Lupino Lane's many stage successes of the 1920s and 1930s (*The League of Notions*, *Turned Up*, *Hearts and Diamonds*, *The One Girl*, *Twenty to One* and others) culminated in his production at the Victoria Palace in 1937 of *Me and My Girl*, in which he launched *The Lambeth Walk* and appeared for 1,550 consecutive performances.

Lanza, Mario (ALFRED ARNOLD COLOZZA), U.S. singer and actor (b. New York, Jan, 31, 1921—d. Rome, Oct. 7), was the immensely popular star of a number of musical films of the 1950s, including in particular *The Great Caruso*, *Because You're Mine* and *Serenade*. Born of Italian parents, he had from boyhood a great admiration for Caruso, whose records his father collected. He worked for a time as a piano mover, then studied at the Berkshire, Massachusetts, school of Music and in 1942 made a successful debut at the county music festival. After three years' military service he continued his musical career with concerts, recordings, radio performances and, in 1949, his first film, *That Midnight Kiss*. During later years increasing weight interfered with his film work and caused disputes with his studio, as over *The Student Prince*, in which Edmund Purdom eventually took over the name part from him, though Lanza's voice remained on the sound track. Although he had a well-balanced and powerful tenor voice which might have been successful on the operatic stage, he tended to pay more attention to force and volume than to finesse.

Layton, Eleanor Dorothea Layton, Baroness (b. London, Oct. 4, 1887—d. March 18), was throughout her life active in public affairs. She was educated at Prior's Field and at Newnham college, Cambridge, and in 1910 married Walter (later Lord) Layton. In her youth she took part in the movement for women's suffrage and her keen interest in politics led her to join the Liberal party, with which she was to be associated for many years. An enthusiast for the work of the League of Nations, she became in 1925 a member of the executive committee of the League of Nations union. She was concerned with the foundation of the Women's Advisory Council on Indian Affairs, of which she was appointed chairman in 1941.

Lady Layton's wide range of interests included vigorous support for the campaign for family allowances during the 1920s. She was one of those responsible for the care of Basque children evacuated to Britain during the Spanish civil war, and also helped to provide relief for Chinese refugees during the Sino-Japanese war. After World War II she was for some time a member of the executive of the United Nations association. From 1947 to 1949 she was president of the Women's National Liberal federation.

Litauer, Stefan, Polish diplomat and journalist (b. Łódź, May 31, 1892—d. London, April 23), one of the best known of foreign correspondents in London, studied law and history at the universities of Paris, Heidelberg and Erlangen. In 1917 he entered the newly created Polish Foreign Office, later serving in the Polish diplomatic mission in Kharkov, and in Moscow. During 1928-29 he was assistant director of the press department. In 1929 Litauer began his long term as London correspondent of the PAT (Polish Telegraphic agency). From 1936 to 1941 he was the president of the Foreign Press association in London. He was dismissed in 1944 by the London government-in-exile and decided to go back to Poland. In 1945 he served for a few months as chargé d'affaires in Washington. Recalled to Warsaw, he was appointed in 1947 Polish minister to Canberra, but the Australian government refused to give its *agrément*. He returned to journalism and became a popular radio commentator. In 1958 he was appointed London correspondent of *Życie Warszawy*, a Warsaw daily newspaper.

Londonderry, Edith Helen, Dowager Marchioness of (b. Dec. 3, 1879—d. Mount Stewart, County Down, April 23), for more than a quarter of a century had much influence as a political hostess. She was the elder daughter of the first Viscount Chaplin, and her childhood and youth were spent in the Scottish and London homes of her maternal grandparents, the duke and duchess of Sutherland. In 1899 she married Viscount Castlereagh, later the seventh marquess of Londonderry. During World War I she founded and directed the Women's Legion and also organized an officers' hospital in Londonderry house. For this work she became, in 1917, the first woman to receive the military D.B.E. During the postwar years she entertained many of the leading political figures of the day at Londonderry house, at Mount Stewart in Northern Ireland and at Wynyard park, Co. Durham. She wrote a number of books, among them *Henry Chaplin: A Memoir* (1926); *The Magic Inkpot* (1928); *Retrospect* (1938) and *Frances Anne* (1958).

McLaglen, Victor, British-born U.S. film actor (b. Tunbridge Wells, Dec. 11, 1886—d. Newport Beach, California, Nov. 7), had his first notable film starring role as Captain Flagg in *What Price Glory* (1926), then won world acclaim in John Ford's *The Informer* (1935), in which he played Gypo Nolan, a drunkard who betrays his Irish fellow-revolutionaries to the British. McLaglen appeared in some 150 pictures, other notable ones being *The Lost Patrol* (1934) and *The Quiet Man* (1952). A clergyman's son, at the age of 14 he ran away from home to fight in the Boer war, and became regimental boxing champion before his family found him. Before going to Hollywood in 1924 he had been an Australian gold prospector, a professional wrestler and boxer (he had lasted six rounds against Jack Johnson, the world champion) and British army officer in World War I.

Malan, Daniel François, South African statesman (b. Riebeck West, Cape Province, May 22, 1874—d. Stellenbosch, Feb. 7), as prime minister of the Union of South Africa during 1948-54 was responsible for putting into practice the doctrine of *apartheid*. He was educated at Victoria college, Stellenbosch, and at the University of Utrecht, where he obtained the degree of doctor of theology. On his return to South Africa he was for some time a minister in the Reformed Church. In 1915 he relinquished this position in order to become editor of *Die Burger*, the newspaper founded by the Nationalist movement, and shortly afterwards was appointed chairman of the newly formed Nationalist party in Cape Province. In 1917 he was elected to parliament, and when in 1924 J. B. M. Hertzog became prime minister Malan was given the post of minister of the interior, public health and education, which he held until 1933. Withdrawing his support from Hertzog after the latter formed a coalition with J. C. Smuts, Malan led a section of the Nationalist party into opposition. On the outbreak of World War II he advocated a policy of neutrality and after assuming the leadership of the reunited Nationalist party remained strongly opposed to South African participation in the war. He also belonged to a society called the *Afrikaner Broederbond*, many of whose members expressed pro-Nazi sympathies. In 1948 following the victory of the Nationalist party in the general election he became prime minister and minister for foreign affairs. His declared aim was to maintain the predominant position of the white race and during his term of office he took steps to bring about the complete segregation of whites and non-whites in South Africa and to limit the franchise to whites only. Ill health obliged him to retire in 1954.

Markham, Violet Rosa (MRS. J. CARRUTHERS), British administrator and social worker (b. Brimington, Derbyshire, Oct. 3, 1872—d. Wittersham, Kent, Feb. 2), served on many public inquiries and committees and was deputy chairman of the Assistance board, 1937-46. The youngest daughter of Charles Markham, the coalowner, and a granddaughter (on the distaff side) of Sir Joseph Paxton, the designer of the Crystal palace, she was educated privately. Initiated into the problems of local government and administration at her family home in Chesterfield, she became a member of the executive committee of the National Relief fund after the outbreak of World War I and the deputy director of the women's section of the National Service department in 1917. Also in 1917, she was one of the first to be received into the newly established Companionship of Honour. Although she had opposed the prewar agitation for female suffrage, in 1918 she stood, unsuccessfully, as a Liberal in the general election.

During the inter-war years, work with the Industrial court, as the representative of the Canadian government on the governing body of the International Labour Office at Geneva, in local government at Chesterfield, and with the Assistance board, kept Violet Markham in the forefront of public life. Nor did her activities diminish during World War II: from 1939 she was a member of the Home Office Aliens Advisory committee and in 1942 chairman of the government committee to report on welfare and amenities in women's services. In later years she published two volumes of memoirs and reminiscences, *Return Passage* (1953) and *Friendship's Harvest* (1956). Her earlier publications included a biography of her grandfather, *Paxton and the Bachelor Duke* (1935).

Marshall, George Catlett, U.S. soldier and statesman (b. Uniontown, Pennsylvania, Dec. 31, 1880—d. Washington, D.C., Oct. 16), was chief of staff of the U.S. army during 1939-45 and was awarded the Nobel prize for peace in 1953. A graduate of Virginia Military institute (1901), Marshall was commissioned as a second lieutenant in 1902. In World War I he was chief of operations of the 1st U.S. army with the American Expeditionary forces in France, and later chief of staff of the 8th army corps. He was aide-de-camp to General John J. Pershing from 1919 to 1924 and was stationed in China from 1924 to 1927. In World War II Marshall subordinated all U.S. military operations to those aimed at the defeat of Germany—a policy that led him into direct conflict with General Douglas MacArthur and others who believed that the Pacific theatre of war merited equal effort. Marshall also had disagreements with the British chiefs of staff, who had a poor opinion of him as a strategist. He was raised to the rank of five-star general of the army in Dec. 1944. He resigned as chief of staff in Nov. 1945 but in the same month President Harry S. Truman sent him as special presidential envoy to China with the rank of ambassador in an unsuccessful effort to merge the rival Chinese Nationalist and Communist armies and so bring the Chinese civil war to an end. In Jan. 1946 Marshall became U.S. secretary of state. In June 1947 he advanced a plan for the economic recovery of Europe with U.S. financial aid. This proposal, soon known familiarly as the Marshall plan, was put into effect in April 1948 when the United States, through its economic co-operation administration, began financial support of the west European economy. Marshall resigned as secretary of state in Jan. 1949 but was again a member of the cabinet as secretary of defence in 1950-51 during the Korean war, when his high sense of duty and moral courage contrasted with the attacks that Senator Joseph McCarthy directed against him. It was probably largely through Marshall's influence that President Truman decided to recall General MacArthur from Korea.

Marshall, Sir Guy Anstruther Knox, British entomologist (b. Amritsar, Punjab, India, Dec. 20, 1871—d. London, April 8), was a leading authority on the Curculionidae, or Weevils. He developed his entomological interests while working in Southern Rhodesia between 1895 and 1906, publishing many valuable observations on his return to Britain. When in 1909 the Entomological Research committee (Tropical Africa) was formed by the government, Marshall became scientific secretary. By 1913 the committee was so successful that it was expanded in scope and called the Imperial Bureau (now Commonwealth Institute) of Entomology and he was appointed director, retiring in 1942. Marshall was elected to the Royal Society in 1923 and was knighted in 1930.

Martinů, Bohuslav, Czech composer (b. Polička, Bohemia, Dec. 8, 1890—d. Liestal, Switzerland, Aug. 28), was a prolific composer of orchestral, chamber, operatic, ballet and choral music, besides works for solo instruments. The son of a shoemaker, from the age of six he studied the violin, later entering the Prague conservatory and joining the Czech Philharmonic orchestra. Having shown talent as a composer—in 1922 his ballet *Istar* was produced by the National theatre—from 1923 he studied the technique of composition under Albert Roussel in Paris, where he was to remain until 1940. His first international success was his *Second String Quartet*, performed at the Siena festival of 1928. However, despite frequent commissions (as for the radio opera *Half Time*, inspired by football), his financial position remained difficult and his important *Concerto Grosso* was written in an attic. It was first performed by the Boston Symphony orchestra after Martinů and his wife had fled to the United States. There he composed, among other works, his four symphonies and his short *Memorial to Lidice*. In 1946 he returned to the Prague conservatory as professor of composition. Although Martinů's work varied greatly in quality, at his best he was a composer of great vitality, charm and originality.

Mathews, Dame Vera Laughton, British woman naval officer (b. London, Sept. 25, 1888—d. London, Sept. 25), was director of the Women's Royal Naval service throughout World War II. The daughter of Sir John Laughton, a naval historian, she volunteered for the W.R.N.S. as soon as it was formed in 1917 and within six months had reached a rank equivalent to lieut.-commander. Later she played a prominent part in the Girl Guide movement. As director of the re-formed W.R.N.S. from 1939 to 1946 she gained the affection of both officers and ratings and was created D.B.E. in 1945. After retirement her many posts included that of adviser on women's affairs to the Gas council.

Mayerl, Billy (WILLIAM JOSEPH MAYERL), British pianist (b. London, May 31, 1902—d. Beaconsfield, Buckinghamshire, March 25), became well known through the radio. He was unable to continue his studies at the Trinity College of Music through financial difficulties and he worked as a pianist in a cinema. By the time he was 18 he had joined the Savoy Havana band. For many years he was a popular broadcaster. Among the pieces he wrote for the piano perhaps " Marigold " is the best-known.

Mercer, Emanuel, English jockey (b. 1930—d. Ascot, Berkshire, Sept. 26), had just ridden 100 winners in 1959 when he was thrown and killed before the start of a race at Ascot heath. " Manny " had his first big success when he won the Lincolnshire handicap on Jockey Treble in 1947 riding at 6 st. and went on to become one of the most popular leading riders of the English turf. He was retained by G. Colling's stable and continued to ride for it when, on the death of his master in 1959, it was transferred to J. Oxley. In 1955 Mercer had married Susan, the daughter of the trainer and former leading jockey H. Wragg.

Mollison, James Allan, British aviator (b. Glasgow, April 19, 1905—d. London, Oct. 30), made many record-breaking long-distance flights in light aircraft during the 1930s. Educated at Glasgow and Edinburgh academies, he served as an officer in the Royal Air Force in 1923-28 and then became a pilot of Australian National airways. A fine navigator as well as pilot, in 1931 he flew a Gypsy Moth from Darwin to England in the record time of 8 days 18 hr. 25 min. In 1932, in a Puss Moth, he established a record time of 4 days 17 hr. 5 min. between England and Cape Town, and in the same year he made the first solo westward flight across the Atlantic, using another Puss Moth; this was also the first crossing of the North Atlantic in a light aircraft. In 1933, in the same plane, he undertook the first flight from England to South America, making a 2,000 mi. crossing of the South Atlantic in the record time of 17 hr. 40 min., and for this he was awarded the Britannia trophy. In 1934 he and his first wife, Amy Johnson, together set up an England-India record of 22 hr. in a DH Comet. During World War II, as a member of the Air Transport auxiliary, Mollison ferried more than 1,000 aircraft from the United States to Britain.

Muir, Edwin, Scottish poet, critic and translator (b. Deerness, Orkney, May 15, 1887—d. Cambridge, Jan. 3), received his widest recognition in the last decade of his life. The son of a crofter and the youngest of six children, he was educated in Kirkwall until in 1902 the family migrated to Glasgow, where the remainder of his youth and his early manhood were spent as a clerk. His marriage in 1919 to Willa Anderson marked the beginning of his literary career. After a period in London, he and his wife lived for some years in various European countries. The critical works *Latitudes* (1924) and *Transition* (1927), products of these years, were notable for outspoken praise of D. H. Lawrence. Other books of criticism were *The Structure of the Novel* (1927) and *Essays on Literature and Society* (1949). Of greater influence than his criticism or his early poems were the translations of the novels of Franz Kafka, done in collaboration with his wife. These appeared during the 1930s and were almost entirely responsible for establishing Kafka's reputation in Britain. Muir's full stature as a poet first became apparent with *The Voyage* (1946) and *The Labyrinth* (1949). These were followed by *Collected Poems* (1952) and *One Foot in Eden* (1956), while new poems which appeared in periodicals until the last months of his life all added to his reputation. He was honoured by many universities in Britain and abroad and in 1953 was created a C.B.E.

Muir, Sir Robert, Scottish pathologist and bacteriologist (b. Hawick, Scotland, July 5, 1864—d. Edinburgh, March 30), was one of the great pathologists of his generation. Educated at Hawick academy and Edinburgh university, he gained a gold medal in 1890 and became lecturer on bacteriology at Edinburgh in 1892. From then on he held various teaching posts in the universities of Edinburgh and St. Andrews until his appointment as professor of pathology at Glasgow, a post he held until his retirement in 1936. Muir was best known as a teacher and author of standard textbooks on bacteriology and pathology, but he specialized chiefly in immunology and published his *Studies on Immunity* in 1909. For many years a member of the Medical Research council, he was elected a fellow of the Royal Society in 1911 and was awarded a royal medal for his research on immunity in 1929. His knighthood followed in 1934.

Munnings, Sir Alfred (James), English painter (b. Mendham Mill, Suffolk, Oct. 8, 1878—d. Dedham, Essex, July 17), was renowned for his paintings of horses and country life, both of which he loved from his boyhood. When he left Framlingham college he was apprenticed to a Norwich firm of lithographers, studying in the evenings at the Norwich School of Art. In 1898 he set up his own studio in Mendham and had two paintings accepted by the Royal Academy. Soon afterwards, he lost an eye in an accident, but before long he was back at work, moving about the countryside and depicting the rural scene on his canvases. A good sale enabled him to study in Paris and then in 1904 he moved to a farmhouse near Norwich, actively participating in rural life, especially hunting, in addition to his artistic work. Pictures of hunting and horse racing, with a glistening, open-air freshness, won him the public eye and he held his first exhibition at the Leicester galleries, London, in 1913. After World War I he lived at Dedham, Essex, and continued to enjoy success at various exhibitions. He was elected an R.A. in 1925 and president in 1944, when he was also knighted. He retired from the presidency in 1949, the year when he made at the Royal Academy banquet one of his celebrated attacks on surrealist tendencies in modern art, prompted by his dislike for any work of art which he thought failed to represent accurately things as they appeared in nature.

Namatjira, Albert, Australian aboriginal artist (b. Hermannsburg, Northern Territory, July 28, 1902—d. Alice Springs, Northern Territory, Aug. 8), became one of Australia's best-known painters. A member of the Aranda tribe, he was educated at Hermannsburg mission and worked for most of his life as a stockman, station hand and camelman. After World War I he met Rex Battarbee, the Australian artist, who was on a painting expedition in central Australia. Battarbee's skill fascinated Namatjira and he offered to work for him as a camelman in exchange for tuition. Battarbee detected his latent talent, and under his guidance Namatjira rapidly progressed and showed a good sense of form and colour. Following exhibitions in Melbourne and Sydney, he achieved widespread fame.

Newman, Ernest, British critic and author (b. Liverpool, Nov. 30, 1868—d. Tadworth, Surrey, July 7), was generally recognized as an outstanding authority on music. Educated at Liverpool college and Liverpool university, he was prevented by poor health from joining the civil service, and went into business, at the same time engaging in literary work. His first books *Gluck and the Opera* (1895) and *A Study of Wagner* (1899) revealed a keen critical insight and attracted favourable attention. A collection of his journalistic articles published in 1906 under the title *Musical Studies* showed an equally high standard. In 1903 at the invitation of Granville Bantock he joined the staff of the Midland Institute school of music at Birmingham. Two years later he resigned in order to become music critic to the *Manchester Guardian*. In 1906 he left in order to take up a similar post with the *Birmingham Daily Post*, where he remained until 1919. After a brief period with the *Observer*, in 1920 he became music critic to the *Sunday Times*, a position he was to hold until the end of 1958. His weekly articles in this newspaper won him a high reputation, and were enjoyed by the music lover and the general reader alike. Newman made a special study of Wagner: apart from early works on this composer he also published *Wagner as Man and Artist* (1914; rev. ed. 1926) and *The Life of Richard Wagner* (4 vol., 1933-47). His last book *More Opera Nights* appeared in 1954.

O'Connor, Una, Irish actress (b. Belfast, Oct. 23, 1893—d. New York, Feb. 4), was in her later years best known for the character parts she played in Hollywood films. Educated in Ireland and in London, she studied at the Abbey Theatre school in Dublin, and first appeared professionally at the Abbey in 1911 in *The Showing Up of Blanco Posnet*. Thereafter she appeared continually on both sides of the Atlantic, in *Damaged Goods*, *Paddy the Next Best Thing*, *The Man Who was Thursday*, *The Passing of the Third Floor Back* and many other plays. Among her favourite parts were the waitress in *The Fake* (1924-25) and Mrs. Jones in *The Silver Box* (1928). In 1931 she achieved probably the greatest success of her stage career as Ellen Bridges, the housemaid in Noel Coward's *Cavalcade*, and it was to play the same part in the film version of *Cavalcade* that she first went to Hollywood in 1932. From then on she was mainly occupied in film-making, and it was not until 1945 that she reappeared on the stage, in New York, in *The Ryan Girl*. Her subsequent stage appearances were mostly in New York, and she also took part in U.S. radio and television programmes.

Palmer, (Edward) Vance, Australian writer (b. Bundaberg, Queensland, Aug. 28, 1885—d. Melbourne, July 15), was the author of a number of novels of Australian life of which the underlying theme is the interaction of character and environment. Before World War I Palmer worked in London for some years as a free-lance journalist, and in 1915 he published *The World of Men*, sketches which drew on his personal experience of life on a Queensland cattle station. His first novel, *Cronulla*, appeared in 1924. Among later books *The Passage* (1930) and *Golconda* (1948) stand out. Palmer was chairman of the advisory board of the Australian Literary fund, 1947-53.

Parker, Charles Warrington Leonard, English cricketer (b. Prestbury, Gloucestershire, Oct. 14, 1884—d. Cranleigh, Surrey, July 11), was an outstanding bowler who took 3,278 wickets in first-class cricket during his long career. His county debut was for Gloucestershire in 1905, but he did not command a regular place in the side until 1908. Despite many fine performances, he only once played for England—against Australia at Manchester in 1921. A rather faster than average slow left-hander, he was particularly effective on his home wickets at Bristol and Cheltenham. In his benefit match against Yorkshire at Bristol he struck the wicket with five consecutive balls, though the second was a no-ball.

Pavelić, Ante, Croatian nationalist (b. in the Lika region of Croatia, July 17, 1889—d. Madrid, Dec. 28), was the premier of the Nazi-Fascist-sponsored independent Croat state during World War II. The son of a railwayman, he studied at Zagreb university and later practiced law at Zagreb. After World War I, when the Kingdom of Serbs, Croats and Slovenes was created, Pavelić was elected in Nov. 1920 to its Constituent Assembly and formed a Croatian separatist group. When King Alexander changed the name of the country to Yugoslavia and assumed all powers in Jan. 1929, Pavelić fled to Vienna where he formed the *Ustaša*, a Croatian terrorist organization pledged to fight for an independent Croatia. In the same year a Belgrade court martial sentenced him to death *in absentia*. Advised and financed by Fascist Italy, he organized the assassination of King Alexander in Marseilles (Oct. 9, 1934). He was again sentenced to death by a French court but took refuge in Italy. On April 10, 1941, Hitler and Mussolini presented the Croatian *poglavnik* (leader) with an " independent " state of Croatia. A ruthless cold-blooded man, he was responsible for killing several hundred thousands of orthodox Serbs and Jews. When Germany capitulated, he fled to Italy and later to Argentina. On April 10, 1957, he escaped assassination by an unknown man. Six days later Yugoslavia asked Argentina for his extradition. (A similar request in 1951 had been rejected by Juan Perón.) Pavelić, however, escaped once more, this time to Spain.

Pepler, Sir George (Lionel), British planning consultant (b. Croydon, Surrey, Feb. 24, 1882—d. London, April 13), was a leading authority on town and country planning. Educated at Bootham and Leys schools, he began his career as a surveyor and planner in 1903 in partnership with Ernest Allen. They specialized in planning garden-city type towns and villages and established a successful practice. One of the founders of the Town Planning institute, Pepler subsequently took a keen interest in its work and was for many years an external examiner. In 1914 he joined the civil service as town planning inspector and remained as technical head of planning from 1919 until he retired in 1946. Between the world wars he did much to persuade local government authorities of the wisdom of, and necessity for, planning development. Besides performing other public service, he was chairman of the Inter-Allied Committee for Physical Planning and Reconstruction, 1942-45, and was knighted in 1948.

Philipe (PHILIP), Gérard (Albert), French actor (b. Cannes, Dec. 4, 1922—d. Paris, Nov. 25), who combined charm and good looks with outstanding acting ability. After studying at the Institution Stanislav in Cannes, and the Conservatoire d'Art Dramatique in Paris, he began acting in 1942 and although his international reputation rests on his film work he never abandoned the stage, his chief roles being in *Ruy Blas*, *The Prince of Homburg*, *Caligula* and *Le Cid*, mainly for the Théâtre National Populaire, for which he also acted as producer. In one of his first films, *L'Idiot*, his sensitive portrayal of Prince Mishkin made a deep impression. When he was only 23 he gave a subtle performance in *Le Diable au Corps* as the schoolboy involved in a love affair with an older woman. In England he is perhaps best remembered for his parts in *La Ronde*, *La Beauté du Diable*, *Les Belles de Nuit* and *Les Grandes Manoeuvres*. His last film was Roger Vadim's *Les Liaisons Dangereuses*.

Pigou, Arthur Cecil, British economist (b. Ryde, Nov. 18, 1877—d. Cambridge, March 7), was for 35 years professor of political economy at Cambridge. Educated at Harrow and at King's college, Cambridge, where he became a fellow in 1902, he was elected, at the age of 31, to the chair of political economy in succession to Alfred Marshall, whose favourite pupil he had been. His reputation as an economist rested mainly on his numerous published works, of which *The Economics of Welfare* (1920), a revision of the earlier *Wealth and Welfare*, proved the most important. Other significant books included *Industrial Fluctuations* (1927), *Public Finance* (1928) and *Employment and Equilibrium* (1941). Occasional works, such as *Socialism versus Capitalism* (1937) and *Income* (1945), exhibited the lucidity at a popular level which was found in his lectures, but in general his fondness for mathematical formulae restricted his readership to professional economists. In public life he was a member of the Committee on the Currency and Foreign Exchanges (1918-19), the Royal Commission on the Income Tax (1919-20) and the Committee on the Currency and Bank of England Note Issues (1924-25), and he was also a frequent correspondent of *The Times*.

Pirow, Oswald, South African lawyer and politician (b. Transvaal, 1880?—d. Pretoria, Oct. 11), was until the time of his death the chief counsel for the prosecution at the South African treason trial. The son of an immigrant German doctor, he studied law and was called to the bar by the Middle Temple, London, in 1913. After his return to South Africa he established a successful practice in Pretoria. Entering parliament in 1924, he was appointed minister of justice in the Hertzog cabinet in 1929, becoming minister of defence in 1933. Three years later he went to London to discuss with the British government the defence of South Africa in the event of war. During a second visit to Europe in 1938 he had talks with Hitler and Mussolini.

When in 1939 South Africa declared war on Germany, he resigned his office and became associated with the extreme wing of the Nationalist party. Pirow's political philosophy—the " New Order ", which was outlined in an issue of *Vaterland* in Oct. 1940, bore a close resemblance to Nazi doctrines. Although at the beginning of 1957 he had announced his intention of retiring from the bar he later accepted a brief as prosecutor of the 150 people who were in December of that year charged with treason.

Pouishnoff (Puishnov), Lev Nikolaevich, Russian-born pianist (b. Odessa, Oct. 11, 1891—d. London, May 28), won much distinction as a pianist. He was educated at Kiev and studied at the St. Petersburg conservatory (1907-10), where he won the gold medal and Rubinstein prize. He left the U.S.S.R. in 1920, intending to settle in Paris, but found his way to London and obtained British citizenship in 1931. During the 1920s he established his name by a series of highly successful concerts in London and the United States. In 1934 he made an extensive tour of Australasia and followed this by various world tours. A popular artist at the Henry Wood Promenade concerts, he celebrated the 50th anniversary of his first public appearance at a concert in the Albert hall in 1946. Apart from his distinguished performances of classical works, he also composed several orchestral and vocal works, and piano pieces.

Prideaux, Sir (Joseph) Francis (Engledue), British psychiatrist and medical administrator (b. Wellington, Somerset, March 13, 1884—d. London, Nov. 15), was a leading authority on the treatment and rehabilitation of nervous disorders. Educated at Epsom college and University College hospital, he qualified as M.R.C.S., L.R.C.P., in 1908. His first post was with the Brompton Hospital for Consumption, after which he joined the colonial service and was medical officer in Fiji from 1909-16. Returning to Britain in 1916, he was commissioned in the R.A.M.C., and became engaged in the study, treatment and rehabilitation of nervous disorders, especially those grouped under " shell shock ". After World War I he was called in by the Ministry of Pensions to help with the enormous number of cases of nervous disorders resulting from the war. This he did with much success. Concerned more with achieving practical results than with theoretical conceptions, he upheld the value of occupational therapy as a means of rehabilitation. With the approach of World War II, he undertook research which provided the basis for the ministry's war policy and in Oct. 1939 was appointed director of medical services. He was then successively deputy D.G.M.S. (1942) and D.G.M.S. (Sept. 1947). He retired from the Ministry of Pensions in 1949 and was knighted the same year.

Révai, József, Hungarian Communist leader (b. Budapest, 1898—d. Budapest, Aug. 4), was one of the founders of the Hungarian Communist party in 1919. The son of a Jewish shopkeeper named Rosenfeld, he graduated from the Budapest Commercial academy. During the short-lived Hungarian Communist government of Bela Kun (March 21-Aug. 1, 1919) Révai edited *Vörös Ujság*, the Communist daily newspaper. Afterwards he fled to Vienna and Moscow, returning to Budapest with a false passport in Jan. 1931 to replace Pál Földes (arrested four months before) as leader of the Communist underground, but was soon arrested and sentenced to three years' imprisonment. From 1935 he worked in the Comintern central office in Moscow. He returned to Hungary early in 1945 and became a member of the Politburo of the Hungarian Workers' (Communist) party. He also edited *Szabad Nép*, the party's central organ until his appointment as minister of popular enlightenment in 1949. In June 1953, after Stalin's death, he was dropped from the Politburo and in July from the government. When in July 1956 Ernö Gerö succeeded Mátyás Rákosi as the party's secretary-general, Révai was re-elected to the Politburo, but after the Oct. 1956 revolution he again disappeared from the political scene. In 1957 he became a member of the editorial board of *Társadalmi Szemle*, the party's political monthly.

Richardson, Sir Owen (Willans), British physicist and Nobel prize-winner (b. Dewsbury, Yorkshire, April 26, 1879—d. Alton, Hampshire, Feb. 15), was best remembered for his discovery of the fundamental law of physics controlling the motion of electrons from hot bodies known as the Richardson law. He made this subject peculiarly his own and gave it the name " thermionics ". Richardson was educated at Batley Grammar school and at Trinity college, Cambridge, where he became a fellow. He was professor of physics at Princeton university, 1906-13, and Wheatstone professor of physics at King's college, London, 1914-24. He was then appointed a Yarrow research professor by the Royal Society and director of research in physics at King's college, a post he held until 1944. In 1931, Richardson was elected F.R.S. and he was knighted in 1939. He was awarded the Nobel prize for physics in 1928 and wrote the standard works: *The Electron Theory of Matter* (1914) and *The Emission of Electricity from Hot Bodies* (1916). A kind and generous man who confined himself largely to his scientific work, he was extremely modest and consequently little known to the world at large.

Riseley, Frank Lorymer, British lawn tennis player (b. Clifton, Bristol, July 6, 1877—d. Newton Abbot, Feb. 6), achieved distinction in the formative period of modern lawn tennis in the early years of the 20th century when the skill of the brothers H. L. and R. F. Doherty did much to shape the game. His doubles partnership with another west of England player, S. H. Smith, was famous and they were the only pair to beat the Doherty brothers at the height of their career, in 1902 and 1906, in the challenge round of the men's doubles in the Wimbledon championships. Riseley was also notable in singles matches and won the Wimbledon All Comers' Men's Singles in 1903, 1904 and 1906. In 1904 he played singles for Britain in the Davis cup. Eighteen years later, in 1922, he again joined the British Davis Cup team, partnering A. R. F. Kingscote against Italy. In 1924, in his 47th year, he and J. D. P. Wheatley won the men's doubles in the British Hard Court championships at Torquay. He was an honorary life vice-president of the Lawn Tennis association, with which governing body he was first associated as councillor in 1906. (L. O. T.)

Rohmer, Sax (ARTHUR H. SARSFIELD WARD), British writer (b. Birmingham, 1888—d. London, June 1), was the author of the Dr. Fu Manchu mystery stories. Interested in the orient from boyhood, he attempted unsuccessfully to secure a civil service appointment in the middle east before turning to journalism. Dr. Fu Manchu was created in 1913 and Rohmer immediately became famous. Thereafter an enormous number of novels and stories about this oriental gangster flowed from his pen. Fu Manchu, twice resurrected by his creator from the dead, was the same throughout all his adventures—villainous, inscrutable and unscrupulous and, until he weakened in his last years and started fighting the Communists, always out for personal power. Rohmer's books were translated into 25 languages and were frequently adapted for the cinema and television screens.

Saavedra Lamas, Carlos, Argentine statesman (b. Buenos Aires, Nov. 1, 1878—d. Buenos Aires, May 5), won the 1936 Nobel peace prize for his part in ending the Chaco war which simmered between Paraguay and Bolivia during 1928-35. The treaty of non-aggression and conciliation signed in Rio de Janeiro in Oct. 1933 by 32 American states was mainly a result of his initiative. He was Argentina's minister of foreign affairs (1932-38) and president of the League of Nations assembly (1936).

Siegfried, André, French political writer, geographer and economist (b. Le Havre, April 21, 1875—d. Paris, March 29), well-known interpreter of modern French, British and American history, was the son of Jules Siegfried, a prominent Protestant Republican of Alsatian origin. Having completed studies at the University of Paris, he travelled round the world in 1900-02. His attempts in 1902, 1906 and 1910 to be elected to the Chamber of Deputies were unsuccessful. In 1911 he was appointed professor of economic geography at the École Libre des Sciences Politiques. In 1920 he became director of the economic section of the League of Nations department at the Quai d'Orsay and attended many international conferences. He left the Ministry of Foreign Affairs in 1922, continuing to teach, to travel and to write. By then he had already published six books of which *Le Canada, les deux races* (1906) was a success. In 1924 appeared *L'Angleterre d'aujourd'hui* and three years later *Les États-Unis d'aujourd'hui*—both promptly translated into English, both models of comprehensive and unbiased analysis. His *Tableau des partis en France* (1930) was a penetrating if somewhat optimistic exposition of French politics. In *La Crise britannique au XXe siècle* (1931), *Le Canada, puissance internationale* (1947) and *America at Mid-Century* (1955) Siegfried continued his study of the English-speaking world. In all he wrote some 30 books, *Suez, Panama et les routes maritimes mondiales* (1940) and *La Suisse démocratie témoin* (1948) being worthy of mention. In 1932 he was elected a member of the Académie des Sciences Morales et Politiques and in Oct. 1944 of the Académie Française. During World War II he restricted his public activities and did not wish to be associated with the Vichy government. After the war he joined the board of *Le Figaro* to which he contributed until his death. He will be remembered as a master of French political science, a distinguished writer and a brilliant talker.

Sisavang Vong, king of Laos (b. Luang Prabang, 1885—d. Luang Prabang, Oct. 29), was the son of Zakarine, the 11th king of Luang Prabang. Belonging to a Buddhist dynasty founded in 1707 by King Kitsarat, Sisavang Vong was educated in Paris at the École Coloniale where he acquired a liking for the French way of life. In spite of his European education he had 13 wives and about 50 children, 14 of his sons being drowned in a canoe accident. On the death of his father in 1904 he acceded to the throne. He remained loyal to the French during the Japanese occupation and was deposed for a few months in 1946 by the pro-Thai Lao-Issara movement. When the French returned to Laos, they restored him not only as king of Luang Prabang but of all Laos; *i.e.*, the territory which had been ruled by King Kitsarat. In April 1953 the Communist Vietminh forces invaded Laos and Sisavang Vong asked France for support. The Vietminh forces, with dissident Laotian units, retreated to the north and on Oct. 25 a Franco-Laotian treaty was signed: France recognized Laos as an independent state; Laos pledged itself to remain a member of the French Union. As a result of the Geneva agreements (July 21, 1954) and the transformation of the French

Union into a Community, all constitutional ties between Laos and France lapsed. During the last few years of his life Sisavang Vong was crippled by arthritis and left most of the royal functions to the crown prince, Savang Vatthana, his eldest son, who succeeded him.

Smith, Sir Matthew (Arnold Bracy), English painter (b. Halifax, Yorkshire, Oct. 22, 1879—d. London, Sept. 28), was a great colourist with an international reputation. He was educated at Giggleswick, Yorkshire, eventually studying at the Manchester School of Art and the Slade school. In his late twenties he went to France, working for a time in Henri Matisse's school in Paris, where he became acquainted with Fauvist art. Here he acquired his love of brilliant colour and began contributing to the London Group exhibitions. He continued to paint in the Fauvist spirit during his army service in World War I and in the immediate postwar years, producing some fine landscapes. After 1920 he retained a London studio, but worked mostly in France, painting nudes and landscapes in richly splendid colour schemes dominated by brilliant crimsons and greens, orange and peacock blue. His one-man exhibition in the Mayor gallery, London, in 1926, was a major success and was followed at regular intervals by others which demonstrated the maturity of his work. In 1938 23 of his paintings were shown at the Venice Biennale and 26 more in 1950. He was created a C.B.E. in 1949 and was knighted in 1954.

Smith, Sidney Earle, Canadian politician and administrator (b. Port Hood, Nova Scotia, March 9, 1897—d. Ottawa, March 17), after a notable academic career became in 1957 secretary of state for external affairs in the Canadian government. He was educated at Port Hood academy and King's college, Windsor, Novia Scotia, and during World War I served with the Canadian Expeditionary force. After the war he studied at Dalhousie university and at Harvard, subsequently obtaining a lectureship at the Dalhousie Law school. In 1934 he was appointed president of the University of Manitoba and in 1945 president of the University of Toronto. Although he had not held any political office before his appointment as secretary of state Smith took an active interest in public affairs.

Spencer, Sir Stanley, English painter (b. Cookham, Berkshire, June 30, 1891—d. Taplow, Buckinghamshire, Dec. 14), was, above all, a distinguished painter of religious subjects. The seventh son of William Spencer, organist at Cookham church and teacher of music, he was educated at the village school and at Maidenhead Technical institute and then, with financial help from his eldest brother William, was able to satisfy his artistic ambitions by studying at the Slade School of Art. His bent for religious pictures, in which biblical characters were dressed in contemporary clothes, soon became evident—as in " The Visitation " (1913). In World War I he served in the Royal Army Medical corps in Macedonia and the most important of his subsequent war pictures was " Travoys arriving with Wounded ", commissioned for the Imperial War museum. His great " Christ carrying the Cross " appeared in 1920, but he did not become known to the general public until he painted his first " Resurrection " (1927), representing the dead rising from their tombs in Cookham churchyard. His major work, and indeed one of the greatest British works of the 20th century, was the decoration of the oratory of All Souls, Burghclere, Hampshire, commissioned by Mr. and Mrs. J. L. Behrend. These paintings, " Resurrection of the Soldiers " over the altar and scenes of army life on the side walls, were completed in 1932. Spencer's work also included closely observed and highly finished landscapes and humorous comments on the absurdity of human behaviour. Elected an associate of the Royal Academy in 1932, he resigned three years later because he had been asked to withdraw two of the pictures which he proposed to exhibit in the summer exhibition. However, he was re-elected as a royal academician in 1950, the year when he was appointed C.B.E. In 1950, also, he completed his second " Resurrection ", this time representing a cemetery near Glasgow, whither he had been sent in 1940 as an official war artist to record the activities of Clydeside. In his later years Spencer exhibited a series of paintings on the theme of Christ preaching at Cookham regatta, and in 1955 a retrospective exhibition of his work was held at the Tate gallery. Although his paintings had never found universal favour, there was nevertheless general recognition of his power in representation. He painted with a Pre-Raphaelite attention to

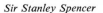

Sir Stanley Spencer   *Viscount Templewood*   *Frank Lloyd Wright*

detail, but the distortion of his figures contributed to the sense of urgency and rhythm of his larger compositions. His great achievement was to express timeless religious ideas through 20th-century, and usually parochial, symbols, with a strong autobiographical element. In 1959, after a lifetime of controversy, he was awarded a knighthood.

Stenning, John Frederick, English scholar (b. London, Feb. 14, 1868—d. Oxford, Nov. 10), was warden of Wadham college, Oxford, from 1927 to 1938. He went from Merchant Taylors' school to Wadham, where he obtained a second in theology and a first in oriental languages and won a number of scholarships. Being elected to a senior demyship at Magdalen college in 1893, he was able to travel to the east with Arthur Cowley to examine Semitic manuscripts in the Sinaitic monasteries. He subsequently contributed to and helped to edit *Anecdota Oxoniensia*, vol. i, pt. ix, and also contributed to the 11th and 14th editions of the *Encyclopædia Britannica*. In 1898 he was elected a fellow of Wadham and turned his attention to teaching oriental languages. He was successively dean, senior tutor and estates bursar of his college. He also lectured on the Old Testament and was reader in Aramaic from 1909 to 1927. Even after becoming warden of Wadham Stenning continued to teach and this left him with a decreasing amount of time for his painstaking and accurate research work. A great patron of plays and an epicure, he made friends among a generation of undergraduates who included the men later to become Lord Birkenhead and Sir John Simon.

Sturges, (Edmund) Preston (Biden), U.S. playwright and film writer, director and producer (b. Chicago, Illinois, Aug. 29, 1898—d. New York city, Aug. 6), won the 1940 motion picture academy award for original screen writing with his *The Great McGinty*, which he also directed. Sturges began writing stage plays in 1928; the best-known was *Strictly Dishonorable* (1929). His first original screenplay was *Haywire Hotel* (1937) and in the 1940s he had much success as a writer-director of comedies of social satire including *Christmas in July* (1940), *Sullivan's Travels* (1942) and *Hail the Conquering Hero* (1944). His best film of this period was probably the sophisticated comedy *The Lady Eve* (1941). In 1954 Sturges settled in Paris where he directed *The Notebooks of Major Thompson*.

Sturzo, Don Luigi, Italian political thinker (b. Caltagirone, Sicily, Nov. 26, 1871—d. Rome, Aug. 8), was the principal founder in 1919 of the Partito Popolare Italiano from which the modern Partito Democratico Cristiano derives. He was ordained priest on May 19, 1894, at Catania, obtained in 1898 a degree in divinity at the Gregorian university in Rome and from 1899 to 1903 was professor at the Caltagirone seminary. In 1899 he was elected town councillor of his native city, of which he was later mayor for 15 years. He became the leader of the Christian Democratic movement, then politically limited to municipal and provincial contests. When after World War I the papal boycott of united Italy had been lifted, Sturzo formed the Popular party on a national basis. At the Nov. 1919 general election the *popolari* gained 101 seats in the Chamber of Deputies, increasing their strength two years later to 107. As a priest, Sturzo was kept out of parliament, but as the party's political secretary he played an important part behind the scenes. When Benito Mussolini staged his *coup d'état* on Oct. 30, 1922, Sturzo wanted the party to oppose Fascism, but two *popolari* joined the first Mussolini cabinet. Under Fascist attacks and some pressure from the Vatican, Sturzo resigned in 1923 from his party office and was succeeded by Alcide De Gasperi. At the 1924 general election, in which all opposition parties had been reduced by electoral law to one-third, the *popolari* obtained only 46 seats. After the murder of Giacomo Matteotti the *popolari*, with the entire opposition, withdrew from parliament. Pope Pius XI ordered Sturzo to leave politics. Profoundly disappointed, he left Italy in Oct. 1924. After a long exile in Paris, London and New York, he returned to Italy in Nov. 1946 and was again active in politics until the general election of April 1948 when the Christian Democrats won an absolute majority in the first parliament of the Italian Republic. As a national figure, surrounded with universal respect, in Sept. 1952 he was nominated a senator for life. He published many books, some of them translated into English: *Italy and Fascismo* (London, 1926), *Spiritual Problems of Our Times* (New York, 1945) and *Nationalism and Internationalism* (New York, 1946).

Sullivan, Alexander Martin, British lawyer (b. 1871—d. Beckenham, Kent, Jan. 10), was the last of the serjeants-at-law, a title applied to the highest form of counsel in England until 1877 and in Ireland until 1922. Sullivan took silk in Ireland in 1908 and during the earlier part of his professional life he practised mostly in that country. His defence of Sir Roger Casement in 1916, however, brought him to the forefront in England and he remained in that position for many years, practising in a wide range of cases but perhaps achieving most prominence in libel actions. He took silk in England in 1919 and in 1920 was made a serjeant-at-law in Ireland. A ready rather than a profound lawyer, he was a most effective cross-examiner and his rather long white beard gave him in his later years a presence which was both imposing and intimidating. In 1952 he published his reminiscences entitled *The Last Serjeant*. (W. T. Ws.)

Templewood, Samuel John Gurney Hoare, 1st Viscount, of Chelsea, British statesman and diplomatist (b. London, Feb. 24, 1880—d. London, May 7), gave many years of devoted service to his country. He was educated at Harrow and New college, Oxford. Subsequently entering politics, he was in 1910 elected Conservative M.P. for Chelsea, a constituency he was to represent for many years. In World War I he joined military intelligence and spent some time in Russia. Returning to parliament after the war, he became in 1922 secretary of state for air, a position he held almost continuously until 1929. During his tenure of office he took measures to build up the R.A.F. as an effective defence force. In 1931 he was appointed secretary for India in the National government and later in the face of much opposition successfully steered the India act through parliament. In 1935 he became secretary of state for foreign affairs and in the same year negotiated with the French prime minister Pierre Laval an agreement on a series of proposals, which were intended as a basis for the settlement of the conflict between Italy and Abyssinia. However, it appeared to many people that these proposals offered too many concessions to Italy and the British government was severely criticized on all sides. Templewood (then Sir Samuel Hoare) resigned, but returned to office in 1936 as first lord of the Admiralty. Becoming home secretary the following year, he began work on civil defence. In May 1940 he was appointed ambassador to Spain and held this post with great distinction during a particularly difficult period in Anglo-Spanish relations. After his resignation in 1944 he was raised to the peerage. He was now able to devote himself to penal reform, a subject which had long concerned him, and he became known as a strong opponent of capital punishment. He was the author of several books and his many interests included tennis and skating.

Tizard, Sir Henry (Thomas), British scientist (b. Gillingham, Kent Aug. 23, 1885—d. Fareham, Hampshire, Oct. 9), is best remembered for his important administrative work in applying scientific research to problems of defence. He was educated at Westminster school and Magdalen college, Oxford, graduating with first-class honours in chemistry in 1908. In 1909, he studied in Berlin, but ill-health forced his return before he had taken his Ph.D. He then worked at the Davy Faraday laboratory at the Royal institution, before election in 1911 to a fellowship at Oriel college, Oxford. In 1914 he attended the British Association meeting in Australia, travelling out with Lord Rutherford, for whom he acquired great admiration. When World War I started he returned to Britain and was eventually placed in charge of scientific work at the aeroplane-testing station at Martlesham Heath. Here he worked under Bertram Hopkinson, who also greatly influenced him. In 1920 Tizard accepted the post of assistant secretary of the Department of Scientific and Industrial Research, succeeding to the secretaryship in 1927. From 1929 to 1942 he was rector of the Imperial College of Science and Technology and was able to combine his duties with service on important government committees. In expectation of World War II, he helped to build up the Air Ministry's scientific organization which successfully influenced the outcome of the battle of Britain. He joined the Air council in 1942 and in July the same year was elected president of Magdalen college, Oxford. In 1946 he resigned in order to chair the government's new committees on defence research and scientific policy, retiring in March 1952. Tizard was knighted in 1937.

Tsankov, Aleksandr, Bulgarian statesman (b. Oriakhovo, 1879—d. Belgrano, Buenos Aires, Argentina, July 17), studied law at Sofia university, where in 1910 he became professor of economics. In 1922 he became the leader of a secret group called Naroden Zgovor (National Concord), drawn from the right-wing intelligentsia and former army officers, which aimed at overthrowing the democratically elected Agrarian (or Peasant) party government headed by Aleksandr Stamboliski. The *coup d'état* succeeded on June 9, 1923, and three days later Stamboliski was murdered. Tsankov became prime minister until he was replaced by Andrei Liapchev on Jan. 3, 1936. His tenure of office coincided with one of the most tragic periods in modern Bulgaria's history. During the disturbance that broke out after Stamboliski's overthrow thousands of lives were lost. On Sept. 9, 1944, after the Soviet troops had occupied Bulgaria, Tsankov formed in Austria, under German auspices, a Bulgarian government-in-exile, but in May 1945 he surrendered to the U.S. forces and for several months was interned in Austria. Later he was released and emigrated to South America.

Tsereteli, Irakli Georgievich, Georgian politician (b. Tbilisi [Tiflis], 1882—d. New York, May 21), one of the leaders of the *menshevik* wing of the Russian Social Democratic party and a member of the Republican Kerenski government of 1917, was the son of Georgi Efimovieh Tsereteli, a prominent Georgian progressive writer and politician. Elected to the second Duma (1907), he was leader of the Social-Democratic parliamentary group and was a brilliant and effective speaker. Arrested in June 1907 after the Duma's dissolution he was deported to Siberia. After the March 1917 revolution he returned to Petrograd (now Leningrad) and became one of the most resolute opponents of the *bolshevik* wing of the party. From 1919 to 1921 he was a member of the Georgian Zhordania government. In Feb. 1921, after Georgia had been occupied by the Red army, he went abroad, first to Paris and in 1940 to New York.

Tshekedi Khama, African statesman (b. Serowe, Sept. 1906—d. London, June 10), was a former regent of the Bamangwato tribe in Bechuanaland. A son of the Bamangwato chief, Khama the Great, he was educated at the Church of Scotland college, Lovedale, Cape Province, and at Fort Hare Native college, where he was still a student when, in 1926, he was made regent for his four-year-old nephew Seretse. During his long regency he introduced many reforms, the most notable of which were the introduction of communal granaries to safeguard against the hardships of crop failures, and the provision of secondary education. A fierce fighter for the rights of his people, it was this quality which first brought him into prominence when, in 1933, he ordered corporal punishment for a white man guilty of immoral conduct with African women. Marines were dispatched by the British government and Tshekedi was deposed. Public outcry in Britain led to his prompt restoration and he bore no bitterness for his treatment, giving ample proof of his loyalty during World War II. In the postwar years, the affairs of the Bamangwato were clouded by the dispute within the tribe over Seretse Khama's marriage to Ruth Williams and the British government's intervention led to the banishment of both Tshekedi and Seretse. Permitted to return to Bechuanaland in 1956, Tshekedi played an important role in the affairs of the Bamangwato council in his last years.

Tshekedi Khama was unique in that while maintaining a strong insistence on the rights and dignity of the African people he managed to avoid the extremes of complete acceptance or rejection when confronted with the values of western civilization. He was widely respected both in Africa and in Britain: General J. C. Smuts called him the greatest African he had ever known.

Van Beinum, Eduard (Alexander), Dutch musician (b. Arnhem, Sept. 3, 1901—d. Amsterdam, April 13), was principal conductor of the Amsterdam Concertgebouw orchestra from 1943 until his death. He first studied the violin and at the age of 16 was playing the viola in the Arnhem orchestra. He later studied at the Amsterdam conservatory and gained his first important post in 1927 when he was appointed conductor of the Haarlem orchestra. Four years later he became deputy conductor of the Concertgebouw orchestra, and in 1938 he shared the duties of first conductor with Willem Mengelberg and Bruno Walter. After the liberation of the Netherlands and the dismissal of Mengelberg, Van Beinum became sole principal conductor. Though less of a virtuoso than his predecessor, Van Beinum soon won international renown for his thorough musicianship and the high level of performance to which he raised the Concertgebouw. In 1949-50 he undertook a season as conductor of the London Philharmonic orchestra. Van Beinum gave special attention to the compositions of Bruckner and Mahler, and was responsible for the introduction of several of their works into the regular concert repertory. He was also a devoted interpreter of Brahms, one of whose symphonies he was actually rehearsing with the Concertgebouw at the time of his death.

Villa-Lobos, Heitor, Brazilian composer (b. Rio de Janeiro, March 5, 1887—d. Rio de Janeiro, Nov. 17), who found his greatest inspiration in the traditional music of his country, was probably the most prolific composer of his time. Though his talents were early discovered and encouraged by his father, his formal musical education was slight. He supplemented it by consorting with the *chorões*, the popular street musicians of Rio de Janeiro, and later by travelling throughout Brazil, earning a living by playing the 'cello, absorbing the folk music of the different districts and composing numerous songs and guitar pieces. Of his later composition, astonishing in its compass, two important groups of work are the *Chôros* and the *Bachianas Brasileiras*, the latter reflecting his early and enduring devotion to Bach. Other, later influences were Wagner, Puccini and, as a result of his friendship with Arthur Rubinstein, Claude Debussy. On his first visit to Europe in 1923 he was also much influenced by Maurice Ravel. Villa-Lobos gave much time and enthusiasm to musical education: in 1936 he represented Brazil at the Prague congress of education and in 1942 he opened his own conservatory in Rio de Janeiro. In 1948 and 1949 he visited London to conduct the B.B.C. symphony orchestra, on the last occasion in the first performance of his seventh symphony.

Williams, Sir Evan, Welsh mining industrialist (b. Llwyn Gwern, Pontardulais, Carmarthenshire, July 2, 1871—d. Glyndwr, Pontardulais, Feb. 3), was acknowledged one of the greatest authorities on the mining industry in Britain. The eldest son of a local mineowner, he received his education at Christ college, Brecon, and Clare college, Cambridge, then returned to Carmarthenshire to devote himself to mining interests. This he did in a whole-hearted manner, concerning himself with all aspects and learning every duty, both below and above ground. Early in his career he joined the South Wales Coalowners' association, eventually becoming its chairman. In 1919 he became the youngest-ever president of the Mining Association of Great Britain, an office which he held for 25 years. During the industrial unrest which followed World War I he was generally acclaimed for the conciliatory part he played, especially as a representative of the employers on the 1919 Coal commission. He was created a baronet in 1935.

Wilson, Charles Thomson Rees, Scottish physicist (b. Glencorse, near Edinburgh, Feb. 14, 1869—d. Carlops, Peebles-shire, Nov. 15), is remembered as the inventor of the cloud chamber. The son of a sheep farmer, he received his education at Owens college, Manchester, where he studied biology, and Sidney Sussex college, Cambridge. Here he changed to physics, graduated in 1892 and eventually joined the research staff of the Cavendish laboratory, Cambridge. In 1894, he spent his vacation as a holiday relief observer at the meteorological observatory on Ben Nevis and was impressed by the remarkable optical phenomena seen when the sun shines on the clouds, which he resolved to reproduce in the laboratory. This led him to design the cloud chamber and when in 1896 he passed X-rays through it, he was able to demonstrate conclusively that the condensation nuclei of the dense vapour formed in the dust-free air were charged atoms (ions). The possibility of making visible the tracks of these ions then occurred to him and in 1911 he succeeded in producing a cloud chamber which revealed the ion tracks as thread-like trails of minute water drops. The Wilson cloud chamber paved the way for much important research in nuclear physics and gained its inventor a share in the 1927 Nobel prize for physics. Elected a fellow of the Royal Society in 1900, Wilson became a lecturer at Cambridge in 1901, Jacksonian professor of natural philosophy in 1925 (retiring in 1934) and had many honours conferred upon him.

Windaus, Adolf, German chemist (b. Berlin, Dec. 25, 1876—d. Göttingen, June 9), was awarded the Nobel prize for chemistry in 1928 for research on the constitution of sterins and their connection with the vitamins of D-group. He taught at the universities of Freiburg-im-Breisgau and Innsbruck. In 1915 he became professor and head of the chemical institute at the University of Göttingen. His chief work is *Abbau- und Aufbauversuche im Gebiet der Sterine* (1922).

Wood, Haydn, British composer and musician (b. Slaithwaite, Huddersfield, Yorkshire, March 25, 1882—d. London, March 11), whose sentimental ballads made him famous. After studying the violin at the Royal College of Music, London, and later in Brussels, he established his reputation on a world tour with Madame Marie Albani. He began writing popular ballads for his wife, Dorothy Court, producing over 200. Among the most successful were "Roses of Picardy", "Bird of Love Divine" and "Love's Garden of Roses". Wood was also successful as a composer of serious and entertainment music, writing a violin and a piano concerto, orchestral pieces and suites. He won a Cobbett prize with a string quartet.

Woodward, Right Rev. Clifford Salisbury, Anglican prelate (b. Reigate, Surrey, Aug. 12, 1878—d. Dulcote, Somerset, April 14), was bishop of Bristol from 1933 to 1946 and thereafter of Gloucester until 1953. The son of a clergyman, he was educated at Marlborough school and at Jesus college and Wycliffe hall, Oxford. After his ordination in 1902 he spent many years, apart from a period as chaplain of Wadham college, Oxford, in the diocese of Southwark, where he found much to occupy his interest in social conditions and particularly in the housing problems of the day. After World War I he became vicar of St. Peter's, Cranley Gardens, and was later made a canon of Westminster and rector of St. John the Evangelist, Smith square (1926-33). Woodward was a man of moderate views. He described himself as "left-centre" in politics, from which he held that churchmen could not be aloof.

Wright, Frank Lloyd, U.S. architect (b. Spring Green, Wisconsin, June 8, 1869—d. Phoenix, Arizona, April 9), was the greatest architect the North American continent has yet produced. He had enjoyed, in effect, two brilliant careers of architectural mastery and international acclaim, separated by a period—roughly from 1915 to 1935—when his reputation was at a somewhat lower ebb. The first period may be taken to begin in 1887, when he moved to Chicago from his native Wisconsin, entered the office of his "beloved master", Louis Sullivan, and then branched out on his own in the early '90s. From then until his journey to Europe in 1909, he designed some 60 houses, including the world-famous Robie house, and other buildings such as Unity temple and the Larkin office block in Buffalo, in which were seen the first harbingers of the new architecture of the 20th century. The bold rectangular forms, overhanging roofs and interpenetrating internal spaces, culminating in the Midway Gardens, Chicago, of 1914, were a primer in which modern architects learned a new language of design.

The next decade was a bleak one for Wright, overshadowed by personal tragedy and not much relieved by the success of his earthquake-proof Imperial hotel in Tokyo. But from this low point his situation recovered until, in the mid '30s, the vigorously expressed appreciation of refugee European architects arriving in the United States coincided with a purely domestic re-discovery of him. A series of brilliantly original works such as the Johnson office building in Racine, Wisconsin, the Kauffmann house at Bear Run, built over a waterfall, and his own desert retreat, Taliesin West, in Arizona, revived his reputation and re-established him as one of the two or three great architects of the world. This second period saw its culmination in the Price tower at Bartlesville, a realization of a long-nurtured, ever-frustrated, skyscraper dream, and the remarkable descending spiral of the Guggenheim museum in New York, which was on the point of completion when he died. (P. R. BA.)

Young, George Malcolm, British humanist and scholar (b. Charlton, Kent, April 29, 1882—d. Goring-on-Thames, Oxfordshire, Nov. 18), had interests ranging from history and archaeology to art and education, but will be remembered best as an historian of the Victorian age. Educated at St. Paul's school and Balliol college, Oxford, where he took a first in classical moderations and a second in greats, he became a fellow of All Souls in 1905. Three years later he joined the Board of Education and in 1911 he became the first secretary of the Standing Advisory Committee for University Grants. In 1917 he was appointed joint secretary of the short-lived Ministry of Reconstruction. He left the civil service in the 1920s to give his time to literature, but his first book, *Gibbon*, was not published until he was almost 50. In 1934 there appeared *Early Victorian England*, two volumes of essays which he had edited, and he then expanded his own editorial essay as *Victorian England: the Portrait of an Age* (1936), which is a remarkable and very readable piece of historical interpretation. He was now a regular contributor to weekly newspapers and reviews. He republished his essays and addresses in *Daylight and Champaign* (1937), *Today and Yesterday* (1948) and *Last Essays* (1950). His *Stanley Baldwin* (1952) won the James Tait Black Memorial prize, but his criticisms of the former prime minister were not accepted by everybody. He also shared in the editing of *English Historical Documents, 1833-1874* (1957). In 1937 Young had become a trustee of the National Portrait gallery, in 1938 a member of the Standing Committee on Museums and Galleries, in 1947 a trustee of the British Museum and in 1948 a member of the Historical Manuscripts commission. In his later years he had been re-elected to a fellowship at All Souls, where his love of, and distinction in, conversation made him thoroughly at home.

OBSTETRICS: *see* GYNAECOLOGY AND OBSTETRICS.

OCEANOGRAPHY. Some results of the International Geophysical Year appeared in 1959 and an International Congress of Oceanography was held in the United Nations building in New York from Aug. 30-Sept. 11, 1959, where all aspects of oceanographical work were considered, including most of the following. E. Lisitzin found that sea-level data for the North Atlantic ocean indicate a half-yearly variation in the subtropical regions and an exchange amounting to about 5 cm. between the subpolar and subtropical regions, the subpolar region being lowest in summer and highest in winter. J. G. Pattullo summarized new information and showed that the changes in the South Pacific ocean are less than those in the North Pacific ocean. She also found that seasonal variations are greater near the continents than in the middle of the ocean. W. G. Van Dorn gave new information about the propagation and decay of long waves and estimated the energy put into the North Pacific ocean by an earthquake on March 9, 1957, as 10^{22} ergs.

J. C. Swallow and L. V. Worthington described a detailed study of the deep countercurrent below the Gulf stream off South Carolina, correcting calculations based on the Geostrophic equation with measurements of the drift of deep floats. The average transport in the countercurrent was 5×10^6 m³/sec., and that in the Florida current at the surface ten times as much. H. Lacombe and J. C. Lizeray showed that the flow of water through the Straits of Gibraltar is largely determined by the changes in atmospheric pressure over the western Mediterranean sea. R. Frassetto made a thermal survey of the strait using a continuously recording thermistor chain. The temperature structure was remarkably complex: short-period oscillations of isotherms had vertical ranges as much as 80 m. J. A. Knauss described new measurements of the strong eastward subsurface current below the equator in the Pacific ocean. Velocities up to three knots were recorded. The current is symmetrical about the equator and appears to be kept there by the difference in the effect of the earth's rotation between the two hemispheres.

J. F. T. Saur, L. E. Eber and O. E. Sette prepared a historical series of monthly sea-surface temperature charts of the North Pacific ocean and showed that the unusually high surface temperature and mean sea-level observed along the western seaboard of North America during the past few years were paralleled by unusually cold conditions on the other side of the ocean. V. N. Stepanov made new calculations of the thermal balance of the oceans. G. H. Jung calculated the heat transport by currents across 40°N. in the Atlantic ocean. J. Fonselius, N. W. Rakestraw and others described recent studies of the carbon dioxide content of the oceans and atmosphere and the exchanges between them. Variations in the surface water are much greater than those in the air just above it, and it is clear that the interchange is a very slow process. U.S. and Soviet scientists collected much new information about the topography of the bottom and the nature of the sediments in the Arctic ocean. G. Dietrich showed a sharp change in the character of the mid-Atlantic ridge north of 53°N. H. Charnock summarized a discussion on turbidity currents, which included some theoretical justification.   (G. E. R. D.)

OIL: *see* PETROLEUM.
OILS AND FATS: *see* VEGETABLE OILS AND ANIMAL FATS.

ORGANIZATION FOR EUROPEAN ECONOMIC CO-OPERATION.

This organization was created on April 16, 1948, following the offer of Marshall aid to Europe, to elaborate and execute a joint recovery programme, and to promote the economic revival and integration of Europe. Its original 16 members were Austria, Belgium, Denmark, France, Greece, Iceland, Republic of Ireland, Italy, Luxembourg, the Netherlands, Norway, Portugal, Sweden, Switzerland, Turkey and the United Kingdom. The German Federal Republic became a member in Oct. 1949, and Spain in July 1959. The supreme body of the O.E.E.C. is the council. There is an executive committee, a number of subsidiary committees and a secretariat with headquarters in Paris. Canada and the United States are associate members; Yugoslavia, a member for agriculture, otherwise has observer status. Secretary-General: René Sergent (France).

The free trade area negotiations, suspended in Dec. 1958, were not resumed in 1959, and though the idea of an eventual association between the European Economic community (the six), the European Free Trade association (the " outer seven ") and the remaining five countries of O.E.E.C.—which from July 1959 included Spain—were still very much to the fore, any such solution remained dependent on political rather than on technical factors. In the absence of such an agreement for trade, the organization decided that further efforts were required in the economic sphere to ensure the continuation of the healthy expansion of Europe's economy (which had been marked during 1959) by frequent consultation and confrontation of policies between the member countries. It was therefore decided that the Economic Policy committee should meet three times yearly on the highest level.

After the European Monetary agreement replaced the former European Payments union at the end of 1958, loans from the European fund established under E.M.A. were granted to Greece, Spain and Turkey. Under the terms of the agreement, these loans were to be repaid within two years.

Progress was made during 1959 towards the transformation of the European Productivity agency into an operational branch of the organization dealing with economic development. Among its sections would be the Office for Scientific and Technical Personnel and one dealing with aid to the developing areas.

During the year, a convention for third party liability of operators for damage caused by nuclear accidents was prepared by experts of the O.E.E.C. European Nuclear Energy agency and was expected to be signed shortly. The E.N.E.A. convention for security control came into operation in July. Of the agency's joint undertakings, the Halden boiling heavy water reactor, in Norway, was opened in September, and an agreement between the United Kingdom, five other O.E.E.C. countries and the Euratom commission for the joint construction of an experimental high-temperature reactor at Winfrith heath, England, was signed in March. (*See* also EUROPEAN ECONOMIC COMMUNITY.)   (E. P. T.)

ORNITHOLOGY.

The chief event of 1959 was the centenary celebrations of the British Ornithologists' union in March. These, appropriately, were held in Cambridge where just over 100 years ago " eleven gentlemen attached to the

Three young ospreys, the first to be bred in the British Isles for 40 years, and one of the parent birds at Loch Garten, Scotland.

study of ornithology " met in the rooms of Professor Alfred Newton and agreed to form the union. From this small beginning, the union had grown to its current membership of more than 1,000 in 67 countries. This meeting was attended by 260 members and guests who heard many of the world's leading ornithologists review past achievements and describe current work and theories.

The journal of the B.O.U., *The Ibis*, also celebrated its centenary and the special centenary celebrations issue of July was undoubtedly the outstanding publication of the year. Among the many papers included was one by E. Mayr on the trends of avian systematics and another, by N. Tinbergen, reviewed the problems connected with behaviour characteristics as used in taxonomics. W. H. Thorpe evaluated current work on the learning ability of birds and R. A. Hinde dealt with motivation. David Lack discussed current theories on the migration of land birds across the sea and Gustav Kramer described his latest experiments on orientation. A jubilee in 1959 was that of 50 years of bird-ringing (banding) in Britain, and in his paper in the same issue Robert Spencer surveyed the work accomplished and suggested that future work be concentrated on special projects. Population-density problems were discussed by H. N. Southern in relation to food and mortality, and by V. C. Wynne-Edwards in relation to social behaviour. There were also papers on the attachment of pied flycatchers (*Muscicapa hypoleuca*) to nest-sites by Bruce Campbell and on population problems concerning the house sparrow (*Passer domesticus*) by D. Summers-Smith. Another section dealt with breeding biology and physiology.

The tragic death of Gustav Kramer (*see* OBITUARIES) soon after attending the B.O.U. centenary celebrations was a great loss to ornithology.

Interest in bird-watching continued to grow with migration being one of the most popular subjects of study. An increasing number of observation stations were being manned and a new journal, *Bird Migration*, was launched by the British Trust for Ornithology with reports and analyses of the main spring and autumn movements.

The use of radar as a new technique for the study of migration was being made in Britain by W. G. Harper and David Lack. In *British Birds* (*52*, 258-267), Lack gave a history of bird detection by radar, explained photographs of bird echoes under different conditions and discussed the main ornithological findings. In another paper (*Ibis, 101*, 209-234), he gave a detailed account of migration studies over the North sea off the Norfolk coast. Through radar, large movements were found to be most frequent in March, April and November. The main movements were found to be to the east between January and May, to the west in June and July, and to the west or southwest during the rest of the year. Other regular migration patterns were found to be dependent on the weather. The chief additions to existing knowledge (based on visual evidence) were of huge eastward emigrations in spring; the arrivals from the northwest, presumably direct from Scandinavia, in late autumn; and the presumed redetermined movements eastwards after wind-drifted arrivals. A paper by Harper (*Ibis, 101*, 201-208) described the unusual radar echoes attributable to the roosting movements of large flocks of birds and to departures from roosts on migration flight. The most striking were attributable to the starling (*Sturnus vulgaris*). Radar also demonstrated that there is a much more rapid break-up of flocks on migration at night than by day.

The successful breeding of the osprey (*Pandion haliaëtus*) in Scotland was a triumph for the protectionists. Following an unsuccessful attempt to breed in 1958, when the nest was robbed by an egg collector, the birds returned again to the same area in 1959. The Royal Society for the Protection of Birds had made thorough preparations for their return and

from the moment of their arrival a 24-hr. a day watch was maintained on the nest. Directly the eggs hatched, the bold decision was taken to hold a press conference and arrangements were made for the public to see the birds. An observation point was established about 200 yd. from the nest and a first-class view of the young birds in the nest was obtainable through high-powered binoculars. The full story is given in *Bird Notes* (*28*, 494-500) and so successful were these arrangements that more than 14,000 people visited the site without disturbing the birds which successfully reared three young—the first ospreys to have been definitely reared in the British Isles for more than 40 years. (*See* also WILD LIFE CONSERVATION; ZOOLOGY.) (D. R. WN.)

ORTHODOX EASTERN CHURCHES.

Often referred to as the Greek Church, the official title is the Holy Orthodox Catholic Apostolic Eastern Church, which is a confederation of independent (autocephalous) Churches. The oecumenical patriarch of Constantinople (from Nov. 1, 1948, Athenagoras I, 268th holder of this title) has jurisdiction over the Greek Orthodox in Turkey (mainly in Istanbul and district), and is *primus inter pares* among the heads of the other Orthodox Churches. At the end of 1959 there were 13 autocephalous Orthodox Churches, all in Europe and the near east, and a number of smaller autonomous Churches. The total number of the Orthodox is thought to be about 180 million, including 95 million in the U.S.S.R.

History. A crisis arose in the Church of Greece in April 1959 when there was sharp divergence between the archbishop of Athens and seven members of the Holy Synod over the

Part of the Church of the Holy Sepulchre, Jerusalem. Restoration began in 1959 after agreement among the religious communities.

election and translation of metropolitans. The government intervened and proposed action forbidding translation except to three major sees. Although it was hoped that constitutional reforms would be passed at the October meeting of the synod, a large majority voted in favour of permitting the translation of metropolitans.

In June the Macedonian Orthodox Church, which had been set up irregularly by a convention of Macedonian clergy and laity in Oct. 1958, was recognized by the Serbian Orthodox bishops as autonomous. While the Macedonian Orthodox Church recognized the Serbian patriarch as its patriarch and president of its council and its representatives were to conjoin with Serbian electors in the election of a new patriarch, the administration of the two branches of the Church was to be separate.

The meeting of the central committee of the World Council of Churches in Rhodes in August was marked by the reluctance on the part of the Orthodox delegates to accept the proposed integration with the International Missionary council. For the first time observers were present from the Russian Orthodox Church. At this meeting Archbishop Jakovos, who earlier in the year had been translated from Melita on his election as archbishop of North and South America, was elected a vice-president of the World Council of Churches in place of the late Archbishop Michael. Informal contact was made between Orthodox participants and Roman Catholics who had gone as observers.

In May 1959 interest had been aroused by the official visit of King Paul and Queen Frederika of the Hellenes to the Vatican on the occasion of their stay in Rome as the guests of the president of Italy. The policy of the Vatican towards the Orthodox Church had been the subject of considerable speculation from the time of the new pope's reference in January to the calling of an oecumenical council subsequently announced for 1962, and of the visit of the papal nuncio in Istanbul to the oecumenical patriarch and the preceding visit by Archbishop Jakovos of North and South America to the pope.

In the Patriarchate of Alexandria the breach between the Patriarch Christoforos and the Holy Synod was healed at the end of 1958. As an immediate result five new bishops proposed by the patriarch were elected by the synod. (*See* also LESSER EASTERN CHURCHES.)   (J. R. SE.)

ORTHOPAEDICS.

The Back. David L. Filtzer and Henry T. Bahnson drew attention to vascular obstruction as a cause of backache and crural pain. In a group of 60 patients with proved aortoiliac obstruction 13 complained of backache. The back symptoms in six were relieved by re-establishment of the circulation. They emphasized the importance of palpation of the femoral and peripheral pulses in the orthopaedic examination of patients with low back symptoms. (*J. Bone Jt. Surg.*, *41*B, no. 2, p.244.)

Peripheral Nerve Injuries. George Bonney evaluated the recovery in 19 patients with brachial plexus lesions who had been observed for 24 months or longer. Each patient recovered normal or useful power in the trapezius, rhomboids and serratus anterior muscles. Useful power was recovered in the pectoralis major by 12 patients, in the biceps and triceps by 6 patients and in one or more of the wrist and finger flexors by 5. Recovery in the deltoid and lateral rotators of the shoulder was uncommon, and was absent in the extensors of the wrist and fingers and the intrinsics of the hand. He found that recovery could begin after degeneration which had lasted for more than 24 months. The two factors chiefly responsible for the poor prognosis in these lesions were the tearing apart of nerves distal to the intervertebral foramina and the avulsion of roots from the spinal cord. Severe pain and the presence of a Horner's syndrome were evidence of a severe injury. Operative exploration was found to be of little value in determining the prognosis. Bonney found that axon reflexes were valuable in distinguishing between post-ganglionic and pre-ganglionic lesions. A normal axon reflex response in an area of skin affected by a degenerative lesion of the brachial plexus meant that the lesion of the nerve supplying that area was proximal to the posterior root ganglion. (*Ibid.*, *41*B, no. 1, p.4.)

The Foot. F. C. Dwyer described a new surgical approach

to the treatment of pes cavus. The operation consisted in a subcutaneous division of the contracted plantar fascia and correction of the varus deformity of the heel by osteotomy of the os calcis with removal of a wedge from its lateral aspect. He regarded the operation as a prophylactic procedure which should be performed before there was gross structural deformity and while active growth was still taking place. (*Ibid.*, *41*B, no. 1, p.80.)

The Hand. J. Vernon Luck recognized three pathological stages in Dupuytren's fasciitis: the proliferative, the involutional (contracting) and the residual. In the proliferative stage one or more nodules composed of fibroblasts formed in the palmar fascia. In the involutional stage stress on the fascia proximal to the nodule led to the formation of a cord of thickened fascia by reactive hypertrophy. He maintained that contraction took place in the nodule only and not in the cord. The degree of flexion contracture of the fingers depended on the situation of the nodules: it was severe when the nodules lay in the distal portion of the palm or in the fingers, slight when the nodules were in the proximal portion of the palm. The speed of involution and of flexor contracture was variable. In the residual stage the nodule disappeared, leaving an area of puckered skin and a proximal fibrous cord, and the deformity of the affected fingers was arrested. Treatment depended upon the stage of the disease. During the involutional stage Luck advised excision of the nodule and subcutaneous division of the proximal cords. In the residual stage he advocated multiple subcutaneous division of the thickened cords and considered that radical excision of the palmar fascia was unnecessary. (*Ibid.*, *41*A, no. 4, p.635.)
                                                            (J. S. BR.)

PACIFIC ISLANDS, BRITISH.

Territories administered by the high commissioner, western Pacific.

		Area (sq.mi.)	Population*
British Solomon Islands Protectorate†	.	11,500	114,300
Gilbert and Ellice Islands Colony‡	.	369	42,000
Central and Southern Line Islands§	.	36	—
		11,905	156,300

* 1959 est. † Incl. Guadalcanal, San Cristobal, Malaita, Santa Isabel, Choiseul, New Georgia, Santa Cruz, Lord Howe (Ontong Java), Reef and Duff groups and Mitre Island. ‡ Incl. Phoenix and Northern Line Islands and Ocean Island; Phoenix Is. include Canton, an Anglo-U.S. condominium with international airport, and Line Is. include Christmas Island with nuclear testing station. § Comprising Flint, Caroline, Vostock, Malden and Starbuck Islands.

British interests in the New Hebrides (*q.v.*), an Anglo-French condominium, are also administered by the western Pacific high commissioner.

Populations: Melanesians predominate in Solomons, Micronesians in Gilbert and Ellice Is. Headquarters: Honiara (pop. *c.* 2,750), on Guadalcanal. Administration: high commissioner, who administers Solomons directly; resident commissioners in Gilbert and Ellice Is. and New Hebrides. High commissioner, Sir John Gutch; resident commissioner, Gilbert and Ellice Is., M. L. Bernacchi. Main imports: basic foodstuffs, fuels, machinery, cotton piecegoods, tobacco. Main exports: copra; phosphate of lime (Ocean Island); trochus shell (Solomons). Currency: Australian.

History. Substantial progress was made in 1959 towards the development of a cocoa industry in the Solomons. The project, backed by Colonial Development and Welfare funds, entailed in its initial stage the building of a road system to open up large tracts of land on the island of Malaita. The discovery of valuable stands of commercial timber in the Solomons further widened the scope for economic diversification in a territory long dependent on copra for most of its export trade.

The mass treatment of yaws, a campaign sponsored by the United Nations in co-operation with local administrations, was completed in all territories.

A major advance in the field of education was the opening of a teachers' and vocational training college at Honiara.

The Solomon Islands' first census, based on sampling techniques, was conducted in November.   (R. P. GN.)

PACIFIC ISLANDS, FRENCH.

Two French overseas territories and the Anglo-French condominium of the New Hebrides (*q.v.*). Areas and populations are:

	Area (sq.mi.)	Pop. (1957 est.)
New Caledonia and dependencies . .	7,654	72,478
French Polynesia	1,545	77,000

Population, *New Caledonia* proper (6,533 sq.mi.) and the dependencies: Melanesian with Polynesian admixtures; Europeans 24,882, mostly French; Vietnamese 4,468; Indonesians 3,260. Seat of high commissioner: Nouméa, pop. (1957 est.) 22,238. High commissioner for the Pacific ocean and governor of New Caledonia, Laurent Péchoux.

French Polynesia consists of the Society Islands (the largest of which is Tahiti), the Marquesas, Tuamotu and other smaller islands. Pop.: Polynesian, majority Christian; Europeans (1957 est.) 1,600, mainly French; Chinese 7,000. Seat of governor: Papeete, on Tahiti, pop. (1957) 17,247. Governor, Pierre Sicaud.

Main exports: nickel, chrome, phosphates, copra. Monetary unit: *franc CFP* (Colonies Françaises du Pacifique) = metropolitan Fr.5·50 (Fr.CFP 250·00 = £1).

History. *New Caledonia.* In the elections to the territorial assembly held on Dec. 8, 1958, the Union Calédonienne (Europeans and Melanesians) maintained its majority. At the municipal elections of March 8, 1959, the Rassemblement Calédonien (right-wing) was victorious, as it was also at the senatorial elections on April 26 when Henri Lafleur was elected. But at the parliamentary by-election (May 24), the leader of the Union Calédonienne, M. Lenormand, was re-elected with an enormous majority, even at Nouméa.

On Sept. 11 Jacques Soustelle, minister-delegate to the prime minister's office, inaugurated the dam at Yaté, which was to help the nickel industry. The creation of a port and town at Nepoui, on the northeastern coast, was approved by the territorial assembly.

Polynesia. An enactment of Dec. 27, 1958, gave the country a new status, in response to the wishes of the territorial assembly. The executive council was presided over by the governor and comprised five members elected by the assembly.

The Parti de l'Union (pro-French) defeated the Parti de Puvanaa (autonomist) in all the elections: executive councils, town council (May 8) and senatorial election (April 26, Gérald Coppenrath elected senator). At the end of September Soustelle visited Tahiti and other Society Islands.

(Hu. De.)

PACIFIC ISLANDS, U.S.

Under this heading are grouped the possessions and trust territory of the United States in the Pacific. Monetary unit: U.S. *dollar*.

American Samoa. A U.S. territory consisting of the islands of Tutuila, Tau, Olosega, Ofu, Aunuu and Swain and the coral atoll, Rose island, 2,200 mi. S. of the Hawaiian islands. Total area: 76 sq.mi. Pop.: (1956 census) 20,154 (*c.* 85% on Tutuila). Religion: 80% Protestant. Language: Samoan. Capital, Pago Pago, on Tutuila, pop. (1956) 1,600. Governor, Peter T. Coleman. Main export: canned tuna fish.

Guam. Southernmost island of the Marianas, unincorporated U.S. territory. Area: 206 sq.mi. Pop.: (1958 est.) 38,578, excluding 27,529 U.S. military personnel and 5,975 contract labourers from the Philippines. Guamanians are Chamorros. Religion: mainly Roman Catholic. Capital: Agana, pop. (1956) 1,023. Governor (acting), Marcellus G. Boss. Main export: scrap metal.

Marshall, Caroline and Marianas Islands. These constitute the U.S. trust territory of the Pacific Islands. It contains *c.* 2,141 islands in 96 groups, of which 64 are inhabited. Total land area: 687 sq.mi. Pop.: (mid-1958 est., excl. U.S. military personnel) 70,594 (*c.* 66% live on the six principal groups, Saipan, the Palaus, Yap, Truk, Ponape and Majuro). Languages: 11 are spoken, incl. English and Japanese. Religion: mainly Christian. High commissioner, Delmas H. Nucker. Main exports: copra, phosphate rock.

History. Elections for the Samoan legislature were held in Nov. 1958 and the sixth legislature convened in the spring of 1959. In Nov. 1958 Fred A. Seaton, U.S. secretary of the interior, approved a statement of objectives and policies for American Samoa. The two basic objectives were to provide for the orderly and progressive development of the people towards self-government and to assist the people to attain the maximum possible self-support.

At the Guam election held in Nov. 1958, the Popular party maintained its control of the legislature; members of that party were again elected to fill all 21 seats.

In 1959 Guam served as the headquarters of the government of the trust territory of the Pacific Islands and of the U.S. air force's Strategic Air command in the Pacific.

The seven administrative districts of the Marshall, Caroline and Marianas trust territory in 1958 were Saipan (under U.S. navy administration except for the island of Rota), Rota, Palau, Truk, Ponape, Yap and Marshall Islands. Although plans existed for creating a territorial legislature, it had not by 1959 been considered feasible to implement them in view of such problems as the absence of a national political consciousness. There were 102 municipalities in the trust territory. By June 1958, 12 of these municipalities had received formal charters which permitted some degree of self-government. Most of the municipalities were expected to be so chartered within the next five years. (S. Nr.)

PACIFIC ISLANDS UNDER TRUSTEESHIP:
see Trust Territories.

PAINTING: *see* Art Exhibitions.

PAKISTAN.

A member of the Commonwealth of Nations; a federal republic, comprising two provinces. East Pakistan, with *c.* 56% of the population, is in the northeastern part of the subcontinent, 850 mi. by air from West Pakistan in the northwest. Karachi, the federal capital, geographically in West Pakistan, is administered as a separate area. Total area: 365,037 sq.mi., incl. port and territory of Gwadur (*c.* 300 sq.mi.). Total pop.: (1951 census) 75,842,165; (1958 est.) 85,635,000. Area of West Pakistan: 310,236 sq.mi. (incl. small areas in Karachi not part of West Pakistan province but reserved to the federal government and excl. Kashmir [*q.v.*] under dispute between India and Pakistan). Pop.: (1951 census) 33,779,555; (1958 est.) 37,396,000. Area of East Pakistan: 54,501 sq.mi. Pop.: (1951 census) 42,062,610; (1956 est.) 46,500,000. Language: Urdu (principal language and widely understood), Punjabi, Sindhi, Pushto, Balochi and Gujarati in West Pakistan; Bengali (principal) in East Pakistan; English used for many official purposes and higher education. Religion (1951 census): Moslem 85·5%; Hindu 12·9%; Christian 0·7%; Buddhist, Parsee and other minorities. Chief towns (pop. 1951 census): Karachi 1,126,417, (1957 est.) *c.* 1,500,000; Lahore (cap. of West Pakistan) 849,476; Dacca (cap. of East Pakistan) 411,279; Chittagong 294,046; Hyderabad 241,801; Rawalpindi 237,219; Multan 190,122; Lyallpur 179,144; Sialkot 167,543; Peshawar 151,776; Gujranwala 120,860; Quetta 83,392. President of the republic (with supreme powers), Field Marshal Mohammed Ayub Khan. Main imports: machinery, oils, drugs and medicines, cotton yarn and piecegoods, vehicles, iron and steel. Main exports: raw jute, cotton and wool, tea, raw hides and skins, fish. Monetary unit: Pakistan *rupee* (Rs.13·33 = £1 sterling).

History. Throughout 1959 the government which had assumed power in Oct. 1958 continued its extensive reform of every branch of national life. Executive and legislative authority was vested in a cabinet appointed by President Mohammed Ayub Khan, consisting of three soldiers and eight civilians (four from West Pakistan and four from East Pakistan), to whom were later added the governors of West and of East Pakistan as regular members. Although martial law continued in operation, it was used to strengthen, not to weaken, the authority of the civil administration, the entire machinery of which functioned as usual. Public confidence in the new regime grew rapidly when it became clear that all the members of the cabinet were experts in the affairs of the departments assigned to them and that, under the lead of the president, they were determined to secure the national interest through efficient conduct of public affairs. The first care of the new government was to restore the structure of law and order. Vigorous measures were employed to suppress the black market in food and in imported goods, with the result that prices fell. Drastic steps were taken to stop the smuggling of gold and of foodstuffs. Tax evasions were dealt with by allowing an amnesty to those who made declarations of what they owed by a certain date. More than Rs.20 million of

President Mohammed Ayub Khan of Pakistan examines maps on the site of the new federal capital to be built near Rawalpindi.

illicit gold, and more than Rs.1,000 million of tax arrears, were recovered for the Treasury. Administrative reorganization, which took the form of simplification of procedure, drastic reduction of cadres by weeding out corrupt, incompetent and superfluous officials, and the institution of strict codes of discipline for public servants, saved something like Rs.28 million. These measures were all part of the introduction of a strict system of Treasury supervision over every branch of national expenditure, which was something new in the history of Pakistan.

During 1959 intelligent and forceful control transformed the financial outlook. Foreign reserves in sterling and dollars rose from Rs.420 million to Rs.780 million. In place of a balance of payments deficit of Rs.336 million there was a surplus of Rs.34·6 million. The index of industrial production rose by 11·8 points to 167·2 (1954 = 100). The restoration of confidence in the country's finances was reflected both in an increase in foreign investment and by the oversubscription in one day of a Rs.15 million development loan for East Pakistan in September. Financial stability enabled the second Five Year plan (1960-1965) to be based on lines which frankly recognized the necessity of maintaining a minimum rate of growth in East as well as in West Pakistan—a conclusion which envisaged the net transfer of both domestic and foreign resources to East Pakistan to correct the disparity in development in that region. This recognition illustrated the avowed determination of the new regime to secure for East Pakistan a partnership of complete equality and parity with West Pakistan.

Side by side with this administrative and financial reorganization the government carried through a number of important reforms involving delicate and complex issues which its predecessors had hesitated to tackle. It evolved a standardized procedure. When a problem was recognized as important, a small expert committee was appointed by the president to examine it, with a strict time-limit. As soon as the report was received, it was given first place on the cabinet agenda; and within a matter of days, a decision was taken and final orders were issued. By this means during the year land reform, refugee resettlement, arbitral determination of industrial disputes, reform of the educational, health and social services, the institution of a new system of "basic

democracies", as well as proposals for the simplification and cheapening of judicial procedure, were all put in hand.

The most radical step taken in 1959 concerned land reform. The great estates in West Pakistan, over which landlords had ruled with almost feudal powers, were broken up and distributed among tenants, the former owners being compensated by interest-bearing bonds. No one could possess more than 1,000 ac. of non-irrigated or 500 ac. of irrigated land—maximum holdings fixed deliberately on the high side in order to make agriculture a worth-while occupation. Occupancy tenants became full owners. Six million ac. in excess of the maximum holdings, together with land reclaimed by the state in colonization areas, was distributed to the cultivators. Tenants everywhere were given security. An embargo was placed on rent-enhancement and upon all exactions of labour and service from tenants. Standing land commissions were appointed to enforce these reforms with the full authority of the state. The land reforms were by no means wholly economic in their effects. While they set the agricultural industry on a sound footing, they also broke the political influence of the great landowning interests, whose "lobby" in the former federal and provincial legislatures fostered corruption in public life and contributed actively to the chronic political instability which had afflicted Pakistan almost from its creation as a state.

Similar energy marked the measures to clean up Karachi and to remove the slums which housed thousands of refugees in deplorable conditions. Being unmoved by fear of offending potential voters, the government dealt firmly with all efforts at obstruction. Public health regulations were enforced, epidemics were stamped out at their inception and the water supply was improved. A large new town at Korangi, outside Karachi, with adequate accommodation, good communications, hospitals, schools and community kitchens, drew off 40,000 refugees.

The unsatisfactory aspects of Karachi, a commercial city of recent foundation, as a federal capital induced the new government to investigate the possibilities of alternative sites. After thorough examination a commission recommended the construction of a new federal capital on the Patwar plateau near Rawalpindi. The government endorsed the finding, and the move of departments to temporary accommodation in Rawalpindi, pending the building of the new capital, began towards

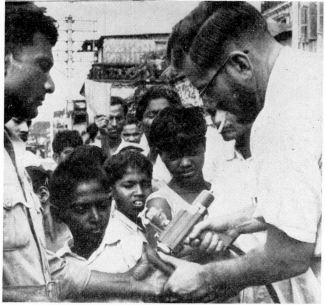

A member of a U.S. medical team inoculating children in Dacca, East Pakistan, during the severe cholera epidemic in October.

the end of the year. It was announced that for the convenience of the diplomatic corps the Foreign Ministry would remain for some time in Karachi.

The government was in form a military dictatorship without constitutional limitations. Towards the end of the year, however, the president took the first step towards constitutional development by creating a tier of elected assemblies based on adult suffrage, to exercise authority in villages and city wards, in subdivisions, in districts, in groups of districts and eventually in both regions of the country. These " basic democracies " were intended to form the foundation of a new constitution, the requirements of which were already being examined.

Since the regime came into power expressly to reform internal conditions, and with no desire to alter existing foreign relations, few changes took place in this sphere. Ties with the Commonwealth remained strong and friendship with the United States, Persia and Turkey was maintained. On the initiative of the president, who met the Indian prime minister, Jawaharlal Nehru, in Delhi in September, relations with India notably improved. A procedure was laid down for obviating border friction in East Pakistan, substantial progress was made in composing financial disputes and the quarrel over the Indus Basin water resources was resolved. Of the disputes which long embittered Indo-Pakistani relations, only the Kashmir problem remained unsolved. However, the continued U.S. aid to Pakistan in the form of arms and munitions aroused criticism in India. The new strength of Pakistan's internal situation was reflected by fresh trade and financial agreements with Britain and the German Federal Republic. During Dec. 7-8 the president of the United States, Dwight D. Eisenhower, paid an official visit to Karachi. (L. F. R. W.)

PALAEONTOLOGY.

Several outstanding discoveries were made during 1959. In the first Louis S. B. Leakey and his wife gave further evidence of their remarkable skill in locating hominid ancestors. In 1948, Mrs. Leakey discovered the major part of a skull of *Proconsul*, the only known Miocene ape, in Kenya. On July 17, 1959, while working in the Olduvai gorge, Tanganyika, Mrs. Leakey discovered the upper jaw and palate and other bones of a new kind of fossil

L. S. B. Leakey with the 600,000-yr.-old " Nutcracker man's " skull discovered by his wife at Olduvai, Tanganyika, on July 17.

man. Details of the discovery were made clear by Dr. Leakey in Sept. 1959, and it appeared that a considerable portion of the skull—though in fragments—had been found, and that reconstruction could therefore be made. The remains appeared to be those of a young man of 16 to 18 years of age and are remarkable for their size. The teeth, especially the molars,

are enormous and show that their owner lived mainly upon vegetables and nuts, competing with the giant baboons of the time. This new anthropoid, which has been described as intermediate between the South African apemen, *Paranthropus* and *Australopithecus*, and modern man, has been named " nutcracker man " and, more scientifically, *Zinjanthropus boisei* (Zinj is the ancient name for East Africa). The remains are of Lower Pleistocene age, approximately 600,000 years old, and thus the oldest tool-making man known. It was also announced that a lower jaw of Peking man, *Pithecanthropus pekinensis*, had been found near the original site, not far from Peking. Further details were awaited.

Work on the mammals included an important paper, published by the Geological Survey of India, in which M. R. Sahni reviewed, and provided a new classification for, the Indian Deinotheres. These were large Proboscideans, with down-turned lower tusks, that ranged over Europe, Africa and Asia during the late Tertiary times, from Miocene to Pleistocene. Sahni also described a new species, *Deinotherium orlovii*, a rare event with these animals.

The outstanding vertebrate event of the year was the publication of the discovery of the third *Archaeopteryx*. Previously, only two specimens had been found of this remarkable fossil bird, known only from the Middle Kimeridgian (Upper Jurassic) of Solnhofen, German Federal Republic. The first, discovered in 1861 near Pappenheim, was purchased by the British Museum and named *Archaeopteryx lithographica*. The second specimen, discovered in 1877 in a locality of the same deposit about 10 miles away from the previous discovery, went to the Berlin Natural History museum. It was named *Archaeopteryx siemensi*. The unique systematic position of these specimens, almost intermediate between reptiles and birds, has caused them to be much investigated. Modern opinion is that they are both of the same species; *A. lithographica*, the London specimen, being an adult and the Berlin example a younger bird. In 1956, a third skeleton, less complete than either but with an excellent series of arm and leg bones, was quarried, but its significance was not apparently realized until 1958. The detailed scientific account, fully illustrated, by Florian Heller, was published in 1959 (*Erlanger Geologische Abhandlungen*, 31, 1-25). The new specimen was obtained in the same locality as the London specimen 95 years earlier, but from about 20 ft. higher in the series, so it is many years younger in absolute age than its predecessor. Yet its bones are the same size as in the older specimen and the most careful examination reveals no difference of any significance.

Among the invertebrates, much valuable work was accomplished by European palaeontologists. L. Sarv dealt with the Devonian ostracods of Estonia. Cretaceous cephalopods of Poland were described by Stefan Cieśliński, while the Polish Carboniferous cephalopods, brachiopods and echinoids were investigated by Halina Zakowa. Devonian spirifer brachiopods of Czechoslovakia were monographed by Vladimir Havliček.

Palaeobotany. Further advances were made in the study of *Glossopteris* in two important publications by Edna P. Plumstead (*Trans. & Proc. Geol. Soc. S. Afr.*, 1xi, 51-94). She not only described the fructifications and provided a provisional classification upon them but also analysed the habit of growth of these ancient plants. She decided that they were arid, woody plants of tree-like appearance and that they had the leaves, flowers and fruits growing from short stalks on the woody stem and also at the end of the stem and branches. She regarded the Glossopterids as a new experiment in Palaeozoic times. Other Palaeozoic plants, this time in Germany, were described by Rudolf Daber. He dealt with the Carboniferous (Visean) flora in the deep borings from Doberlug Kirchhain.

(W. E. Sn.)

PANAMA. Republic of Central America adjoining South America and bisected by the Canal Zone (leased to the U.S.). Area: 28,753 sq.mi. Pop.: (1950 census) 805,285; (1959 est.) 1,024,000. Both area and population are exclusive of the Canal Zone. The racial composition includes Europeans (11%), native Indians (9%), Negroes (14%), *mestizos* or mixed (65%), the rest being Asiatics. Language: Spanish. Religion: Roman Catholic 93%, Protestant 6%. Chief towns (pop. 1950; 1958 est. in brackets): Panama City on the Pacific coast (cap.), 127,874 (238,980); Colón, on the Atlantic coast, 52,204 (64,430). President, Ernesto de la Guardia. Main imports: machinery and manufactures. Main exports: bananas (58%), fresh shrimp (28%), cacao (4%). Monetary unit: *balboa* at par with the U.S. dollar.

History. Sporadic disorders occurred in Jan., March and April 1959. The most publicized of these occurrences was the alleged conspiracy led by Roberto Arias, son of a former president. Arias' wife, the ballerina Dame Margot Fonteyn, was arrested on April 20 on suspicion of revolutionary activity and expelled from Panama. Her husband eluded capture and left Panama by means of a safe conduct from the Brazilian embassy.

On April 26 a band of invaders, said to number 80 men, seized Nombre de Dios on Panama's Caribbean coast, and was reported to be intent on capturing Porto Bello and ultimately on overthrowing the government. Three members of the band who were captured indicated that Arias was their leader and Cuba their point of departure. Fidel Castro, the prime minister of Cuba, denied any connection with them and said that no other armed bands would leave Cuba.

On April 28 the United States and 19 other American republics pledged their aid to repel the invaders. An investigating committee of five members was appointed, and a sea and air patrol to which the United States, Colombia and Ecuador contributed was instituted to provide protection. The investigating committee conferred with the invaders and appeared to have induced their surrender. They were taken into custody by the national guard and sent back to Cuba for trial.

The observation of Panama's Independence day, Nov. 3, was marked by a display of anti-United States feeling. Groups of men, said to have been students, tried to march into the Canal Zone to plant the Panamanian flag there. (A. R. W.)

PANAMA CANAL ZONE. A United States military reservation comprising a ten-mile strip across the Isthmus of Panama, leased for the protection and administration of the Panama canal. Area: 558 sq.mi., incl. 186 sq.mi. of fresh water. Pop., incl. military personnel (1950 census): 52,822; (1958 est.) 57,000. Administrative centre: Balboa Heights. Governor: Maj.-General William E. Potter.

CANAL TRANSITS, CARGO AND TOLLS

Item	1938	1957	1958	1959
Transits	5,524	8,579	9,187	9,718
Cargo (mtr. tons)	27,386,000	49,703,000	48,125,000	51,153,000
Tolls	$23,170,000	$38,444,000	$41,796,000	$45,529,000

History. Oceangoing traffic through the canal in 1959 was marked by a record number of vessels requiring daylight passage or one-way navigation in Gaillard cut, causing transit delays and reducing capacity. Traffic studies indicated that transit demands would become critical in 1971, thus emphasizing the necessity for an early decision on proposals for major canal operational improvements and capacity increase, which since 1957 had been under consideration by the United States congress. An important navigational improvement started in 1959 was the widening and deepening of Gaillard cut.

U.S.-Panamanian relations were complicated by continued agitation by Panamanians to gain jurisdiction of the canal from the United States. In spite of this, the United States continued to fulfil the 1955 U.S.-Panama treaty obligations, among them being the construction of the Thatcher ferry site bridge across the canal's Pacific entrance. (M. DuV.)

PAPER AND PULP INDUSTRY: *see* BUSINESS REVIEW.

PAPUA-NEW GUINEA. Territory of Papua and trust territory of New Guinea occupying S.E. and N.E. quarters respectively of the island of New Guinea, administered with adjacent islands as one area by Australia. Areas and populations are given in the table.

AREA AND POPULATIONS OF PAPUA-NEW GUINEA

	Area*(sq.mi.)	Population (*mid-1958 est.*) Indigenous	Non-Indig.†
Papua‡	90,540	478,595	8,555
New Guinea§	93,000	1,326,195	15,073
	183,540	1,804,790	23,628

* Approximate. † *c.* 78% European, 12% Asian, 10% other races. ‡ Incl. d'Entrecasteaux, Louisade and Trobriand (with Woodlark) islands (total area *c.* 3,000 sq.mi.). § Incl. adjacent minor islands, Bismarck archipelago (incl. New Britain 14,600 sq.mi., New Ireland 3,340 sq.mi., New Hanover 460 sq.mi., Admiralty Is. 800 sq.mi.) and northeastern Solomon Is. (incl. Bougainville, 3,880 sq.mi., Buka 220 sq.mi.).

Native pop.: Papuan and (especially in Bismarcks, Solomons and coastal New Guinea) Melanesian; Negritò, Micronesian and Polynesian minorities. Religion: pagan with Christian minorities. Administration: administrator; executive council; legislative council with partly elected unofficial minority. Capital of joint administration: Port Moresby (pop. [mid-1958 est.] 18,226). Administrator, Brigadier D. M. Cleland. Main imports: foodstuffs, textile goods, machinery, hardware, fuels and chemicals, tobacco products. Main exports: coconut products and shell; rubber (Papua); gold, cocoa, coffee and timber products (New Guinea). Currency: Australian.

History. With copra prices at their highest levels since 1951 and with larger outputs of cocoa and coffee, the territory's export earnings reached the record total of £16·3 million for the fiscal year ended June 30, 1959. An encouraging feature of this development was the marked increase of cash-crop production by native growers.

The search for oil was continued in 1959 with greater financial backing, the confidence of investors having been stimulated by the strike made in Nov. 1958. Further investigations were made of proposals for the hydroelectric development of the Purari river (Papua).

Legislation was enacted to introduce a graduated income tax in place of export taxes. The European elected members of the legislative council resigned their seats in protest against the measure.

The fourth South Pacific conference, representing dependent peoples of Oceania, was held at Rabaul (New Britain) in April and May. The conference discussed social, economic and medical problems of general concern to member territories. (R. P. GN.)

PARAGUAY. South American republic bounded N. and E. by Brazil, S. by Argentina and W. by Bolivia. Area: 157,047 sq.mi. Pop.: (1950 census) 1,408,400; (1958 est.) 1,677,000. Homogeneous mixture of Spanish and Guarani (with some Portuguese and Italian). Language: Spanish; Guarani is secondary and recessive. Religion: Roman Catholic. Capital (pop., 1950 census), Asunción 201,340. President, General Alfredo Stroessner. Main imports: cotton cloth, motor vehicles, farm implements, tin plate, wheat, petroleum products. Main exports: cotton, timber, quebracho extract, corned beef, hides, tobacco, essential oils, oranges. Monetary unit: *guarani* (G.318·00 = £1 sterling).

History. During 1959, differences between the Paraguayan army and the governing Colorado party created special problems for President Stroessner who, in response to an army ultimatum, took over personal control of the government late in February. The president found himself impelled to respond to developments abroad as his opponents capitalized on the overthrow of Fulgencio Batista in Cuba and on the criticism of the Stroessner regime by members of the Inter-American Press association.

When Edgar Insfran, the minister of the interior, placed the blame for the government's troubles on the Liberal party and subjected its members to a campaign of sharp repression, a powerful section of the army turned against the Colorado party and demanded that the president should re-establish a constitutional system. On April 28, the president decreed the end of the state of siege which had existed since 1947, but this lasted only until May 30 when the congress was dissolved after a vote by its members censuring the government for undue severity in handling a student demonstration. The state of siege was restored, and the government announced that elections for a new congress would be held in 60 days and that members of the opposition party would be able to seek election. Opposition to Stroessner's rule grew stronger as efforts got under way to form a coalition of all opposition forces with a view to ousting the existing regime.

In the meantime, the president extended the state of siege for another 60 days and called for elections in Feb. 1960 to elect a new Chamber of Deputies. Political uneasiness continued to increase, especially after the government's order early in September closing the southern border against activities of Paraguayan exiles based in Argentina.

In mid-December incursions by Paraguayan exile commandos against Stroessner's regime plunged the country into a new period of repression. The rebellion was apparently organized by Liberal and Febrerista politicians. (The Febrerista party, a leftist one, was led by Colonel Rafael Franco, a provisional president in 1936-37.) The rebels tried to invade the country from Argentina and Brazil. Their commander was Arnaldo Valdovinos, a Febrerista, who had shortly before spent a month in Cuba and also visited Venezuela. Many opposition leaders, among others Justo Pastor Benitez, a Liberal, and Carlo Caballero Gatti, a Febrerista, were arrested in Asunción. The rebellion was crushed with great severity. (A. E. Tr.; X.)

PARIS. Capital and largest town of France. Pop. (Jan. 1, 1959): 3,020,000. The "Paris region", a new administrative area, had a pop. of 7,980,000. Presidents of the municipal council in 1959: Jean-Louis Vigier and (from March 23) Pierre Devraigne.

The new president of the municipal council, a member of the Union pour la Nouvelle République (the Gaullist political party which was victorious at the 1958 parliamentary elections), was elected at the first ballot, by 40 votes against 30 to M. Bossus, the candidate of the extreme left; the Socialists abstained.

The summer session of the municipal council opened in June. It was concerned with the housing shortage—still very acute—and arrangements were made for the repair of houses, an operation made all the more necessary by the fact that 86% of Paris houses had been built before 1915.

The municipal council studied measures intended to check

President de Gaulle and his wife at a reception for the diplomatic corps at the Elysée palace. On the president's left is Mme. Debré.

the growth of the capital and set up a fund to help in the planning of green spaces. Protests were raised at the plan to do away with the trees in the Boulevard Raspail and also against new building work which threatened to destroy the beauty of certain districts. The movement of traffic was becoming increasingly difficult and after the " blue zone " (where parking was prohibited) had been done away with in August, it had to be hastily re-established to avoid congestion in the centre of the city. There was continued discussion about the modernization of the street lighting on the main boulevards and the transfer of the Halles Centrales (the produce market) to a new site.

Schools (both primary and secondary) re-opened on Sept. 15, two weeks earlier than usual. Owing to the considerable increase in the number of children attending school, some difficulties were encountered and in several schools and *lycées* the re-opening was delayed. However a big effort was being made in the building of new schools and the Parisian region was to have eight new *lycées*.

At Porte Dauphine the Nato building was completed and work was begun on the new Palais de la Radio. As every year in June, the shops in the Rue du Faubourg Saint-Honoré had their fortnight's window display on a common theme. This time they paid homage to the " French novels of all periods ", from the *Roman de la Rose* to contemporary works. (A. Pr.)

PARLIAMENT, HOUSES OF. Great Britain. Both Houses resumed on Jan. 20, 1959. By the beginning of the summer adjournment on July 30, 77 bills (55 of them government measures) had reached the statute book. Of these, the following had been foreshadowed in the queen's speech at the opening of the session: Agriculture (Small Farmers) (enacted Feb. 19); House Purchase and Housing (May 14); National Insurance (July 9); and Mental Health (July 29).

On the domestic front, a private member's bill—the Legitimacy bill—introduced by John Parker, had a chequered career. Its principal clause sought to make possible, on the subsequent marriage of the parents, the legitimization of a child originally born illegitimately because one (or both) of the parents was not free to marry at the time, and it was passed by the Commons on May 8. On July 2 the House of Lords struck out this principal clause, but on July 21 reinstated it. The Obscene Publications bill, another private member's measure, introduced by Roy Jenkins as an attempt to clarify the law on obscenity, was enacted on July 29.

One of the more controversial government measures was the Street Offences bill, which received a second reading in the Commons on Jan. 29 and was finally enacted on July 16. It gave legislative effect to certain recommendations of the Wolfenden Committee on Homosexual Offences and Prostitution, and was debated on second reading in the Lords on May 5. The National Insurance bill, which offered to certain categories of workpeople a system of graduated pensions in addition to the state retirement benefit, was opposed by the Labour party for failing " to provide for a fully comprehensive national superannuation scheme ".

As a result of representations from Sir David Robertson, a tribunal of inquiry was set up under the Tribunals of Inquiry (Evidence) act, 1921, to investigate the allegation that John Waters was assaulted by the police at Thurso on Dec. 7, 1957. The report was published in April and debated by the Lords on May 14.

The principal provisions of the budget introduced on April 7 were: a reduction of the standard rate of income tax by 9d. to 7s. 9d., with corresponding reductions in the reduced rates; arrangements for the accelerated repayment of postwar credits; and a reduction of the beer duty. Increased

(Left) Sir Harry Hylton-Foster, speaker of the House of Commons from Oct. 20. (Right) M. Redmayne, the new government chief whip.

rates of national assistance were foreshadowed in proceedings on June 15 and June 24 in the Commons, and in the bill enacted on July 9, and pension increases were granted to retired public servants under the Pensions (Increase) act enacted on the same day. The report of the select committee on House of Commons procedure was published in February and debated on July 13. Two matters which gave rise to repeated concern were the general level of unemployment during the winter months (full debate in the Commons on April 30 and in the Lords on March 11) and the accumulation of excessive stocks of coal (full debates in the Commons on Feb. 6, May 4 and July 23, and in the Lords on July 15). Other measures passed included the Education bill (July 29), embodying broad agreement on the question of denominational schools, and the bill to encourage reorganization in the cotton industry (July 9).

Overseas events included an attempted settlement of the Cyprus dispute (announced in both Houses on Feb. 19) and the temporary revocation of the constitution of Malta (Commons, Feb. 2 and Feb. 16; Lords, Feb. 19). African affairs were especially prominent. At the end of February John Stonehouse was declared a prohibited immigrant by the government of the Federation of Rhodesia and Nyasaland. The matter was discussed in the Commons during March 2-4, and Stonehouse made a personal statement there on March 13. Disturbances in Nyasaland led to the appointment on March 24 of a commission of inquiry under the chairmanship of Mr. Justice Devlin. The deaths of 11 men in the Hola detention camp, Kenya, were discussed in the Commons on June 16 and July 27 and in the Lords on July 29. The report of the Devlin commission, published on July 24, was debated in the Commons on July 28 and in the Lords on July 29. In the meantime (July 21-22) the Commons had discussed the advisory commission which was to study the future of central Africa.

Parliament was dissolved on Sept. 18, and polling in the general election took place on Oct. 8. The government, which at the dissolution had a majority of 54 over the Labour and Liberal parties combined (6 seats being vacant), was returned with an absolute majority of 100 (*see* GENERAL ELECTION). Parliament re-assembled on Oct. 20, when Sir Harry Hylton-Foster was elected speaker of the House of Commons in place of W. S. Morrison, who had retired.

The queen's speech, read by royal commission on Oct. 27, foreshadowed legislation in 14 bills, including betting reform, relief of local unemployment, airline licensing and payment of wages by cheque. On Nov. 30 Sir Winston Churchill spoke in the Commons for the first time since March 31, 1955. He acknowledged the compliments of the House on his 85th birthday. Both Houses adjourned for Christmas on Dec. 17.

Australia. In 1959 members of the federal parliament received substantial increases in salary, ranging from a basic £A400 to £A3,250 for the prime minister. The move provoked strong criticism from various newspapers notably from the *Sydney Morning Herald*. In reply the prime minister, R. G. Menzies, alleged that sections of the press were seeking to usurp the functions of government. The Parliamentary Privilege committee absolved H. G. Pierce from charges of corruption.

An interesting situation arose in Tasmania when R. J. Turnbull refused to resign from the cabinet following his expulsion from the Parliamentary Labour party. He was finally dismissed by the administrator, acting on the premier's advice. The Supreme Court of South Australia ruled that women had the right to sit in that state's Legislative council. The general elections in South Australia resulted in the return of one woman to the Council and another to the Assembly, both being the first to achieve such distinction. Arrangements for the abolition of the Legislative Council of New South Wales continued during the year.

Canada. The new session of parliament was opened on Jan. 15 by the governor-general, Vincent Massey. In his speech from the throne he forecast action on the following matters: a House committee to review broadcasting policy; a bill of rights; a national energy board; amendments to the Export Credits Insurance act; and the strengthening of the provisions in the Criminal act concerning obscene publications.

The same day the prime minister, J. G. Diefenbaker, announced three new appointments to the Senate.

Ghana. In February the government published the Constitution (Amendment) bill, which sought to make changes in the constitution dealing with the appointment of parliamentary secretaries, civil servants and members of the judiciary. The bill also proposed to make the government responsible for dealing with offences against the state, which had hitherto been the concern of the attorney-general.

On Feb. 28 the death occurred of the speaker of the National Assembly, Sir Emmanuel Quist.

In March the government introduced legislation designed to frustrate the boycott of sittings of the Assembly by opposition members.

At the end of May a Ghanaian parliamentary delegation arrived in Britain for a three weeks' visit at the invitation of the U.K. branch of the Commonwealth Parliamentary association.

In June the increase in members' salaries of £20 a month was announced. In July the government stated that it would create ten seats in the National Assembly exclusively for women.

South Africa, Union of. The representation of Africans in both houses of parliament was abolished by a new measure that would come into operation at the end of the 1960 parliamentary session. This change affected three members of the House of Assembly and four senators—all Europeans who had been periodically elected since 1937 by special African constituencies. This government measure was opposed by the United party and also by one Nationalist member of the Assembly from South-West Africa, J. D. du P. Basson, who was consequently expelled from his party.

The prime minister, H. F. Verwoerd, announced that the Senate would be reformed in 1960. The number of seats would be reduced from 89 to 50, and the principle of proportional representation would be restored in order to allow provincial minorities to win places.

Twelve members resigned from the United party to form

a new Progressive party, but in spite of some criticism they refused to resign their seats in the Assembly. (*See* also CABINET MEMBERS; ELECTIONS; POLITICAL PARTIES, COMMONWEALTH.)   (E. C. T.; O. M. R.; X.; J. LN.)

PASSPORTS. As a result of decisions taken by members of the Council of Europe and of the Organization for European Economic Co-operation (or in some cases because of independent arrangements), by 1959 many restrictions on travel within Europe had been relaxed. Visas had been entirely abolished for nationals of one member country visiting another. Passports were no longer necessary for entry and a stay of up to three months in the following cases:

For Austrians visiting Belgium, France, the German Federal Republic, Greece, Italy, Luxembourg, Netherlands and Switzerland; Belgians visiting Austria, France, German Fed. Rep., Greece, Italy, Luxembourg, Netherlands and Switzerland; British visiting the Republic of Ireland; Danes visiting Iceland, Norway and Sweden; French visiting Austria, Belgium, German Fed. Rep., Greece, Italy, Luxembourg, Netherlands and Switzerland; west Germans visiting Austria, Belgium, France, Greece, Italy, Luxembourg, Netherlands and Switzerland; Icelanders visiting Denmark, Norway and Sweden; Irish visiting the United Kingdom; Italians visiting Austria, Belgium, France, German Fed. Rep. and Greece; Luxembourgers visiting Austria, Belgium, France, German Fed. Rep., Greece, Netherlands and Switzerland; Dutch visiting Austria Belgium, France, German Fed. Rep., Luxembourg and Switzerland; Norwegians visiting Denmark, Iceland and Sweden; Swedes visiting Denmark, Iceland and Norway; and Swiss visiting Austria, Belgium, France, German Fed. Rep., Luxembourg and Netherlands.

Although British travellers required passports for visits to all west European countries except the Republic of Ireland, and passports were required for all visits in the opposite direction, it must be remembered that even travellers who did not need passports for visits between other European countries were in many cases required to carry their normal identity documents. *Carnets de passage* were no longer needed by any west European nationals, but an international insurance card was required by car-drivers of member countries visiting Austria, Belgium, Denmark, France, the German Federal Republic, Greece, Italy, Luxembourg, Netherlands, Norway, Sweden and Switzerland. The relaxation of restrictions already referred to represented a first phase in the continuing efforts to bring about the total abolition of travel documents for citizens of the member countries of the Council of Europe and of the O.E.E.C.   (X.)

PERSIA (IRAN). Independent kingdom of western Asia, bounded E. by Pakistan and Afghanistan, N. by the U.S.S.R., W. by Turkey and Iraq and S. by the Persian gulf and Arabian sea. Area: *c.* 634,400 sq.mi. Pop.: (1956 census) 18,944,821; (1958 est.) 19,723,000. Language: mainly Persian, but Turkic and Armenian in the N.W., Kurd in the W., Arabic in the S. and Pushtu in the E. Religion: Moslem, mainly Shia, but the Kurds (850,000) are Sunni; Christian (there are *c.* 110,000 Gregorian Armenians, 10,000 Catholic Armenians and 40,000 Nestorians); Jewish 40,000; and Zoroastrian *c.* 13,000. Chief towns (1956): Tehran (cap.) 1,513,164; Tabriz 290,195; Isfahan 254,876; Meshed 242,165; Abadan 226,103; Shiraz 169,088; Kermanshah 125,181; Ahwaz 119,828; Resht 109,493; Hamadan 100,029. Ruler, Shahanshah Mohammed Riza Shah Pahlavi; prime minister, Manuchehr Ikbal. Main exports: petroleum and products, cotton, rugs, fruit, caviar. Monetary unit: *rial* (R.214·00 = £1 sterling).

History. At a meeting of the Baghdad pact in July 1958 the United States had announced that though not formally joining the pact it would conclude bilateral defence agreements with each of the Moslem members. At first the Soviet government tried by propaganda to prevent the Persians from agreeing to this. Then it changed its tactics, and in an *aide-mémoire* of Jan. 16, 1959, declared that it was ready to join with the other powers in guaranteeing the security and integrity of the middle east countries, and that it was ready to exchange views on this suggestion with the Persian government. To this end a Soviet delegation led by Vladimir Semyonov, Soviet deputy foreign minister, arrived in Tehran on Jan. 29, but after a few days discussions were abruptly broken off, and the Soviet delegation left Persia on Feb. 11.

The Shah of Persia and his bride, Farah Diba, after their wedding on Dec. 21 in the Hall of Mirrors of the Marble palace, Tehran.

The Soviet government thereupon accused the Persians of wrecking the negotiations by refusing to sign a non-aggression treaty which the Persians had themselves proposed. The Persian version was given by Ali Hekmat, the foreign minister, in the Majlis on Feb. 15. He said that the non-aggression treaty was proposed, not by the Persian government, but by the U.S.S.R., and that the Soviet terms were that Persia should withdraw from the Baghdad pact (later renamed Central Treaty organization), should refrain from concluding a defence agreement with the United States and should permit no U.S. military bases to be established on Persian territory. The Persian foreign minister added that the government had accepted all these terms except the requirement that they should leave Cento.

The breakdown of the negotiations was followed by a further outburst of anti-Persian propaganda from the U.S.S.R., notwithstanding which discussions between Persia and the United States continued. Agreement was finally reached and the bilateral defence agreement was signed in Ankara on March 5, simultaneously with similar agreements between the United States on the one hand and Turkey and Pakistan on the other.

From May 5 to 7 the shah paid a state visit to the United Kingdom accompanied by Ali Hekmat. Addressing a press conference on May 8 he said that bitter experience in two world wars had shown that Persia could not live in isolation. Accordingly Persia rejected the idea of " cruising in neutral gear ", and was determined to remain a member of the Central Treaty organization from natural and lawful motives of self-preservation. However, he added, it would never grant military bases to any foreign power.

In home affairs, the principal development was the continuation of the shah's attempts to modernize the country. With this in view, on Oct. 15, 1958, two important bills were introduced by the government and approved by the Majlis. One abolished the feudal practice whereby peasants paid their landlords in kind or by giving them their labour. The other required that all civil and military officials should disclose their wealth and the source of their income, including that of their wives, and compelled them to sell all their holdings in organizations which did business with the government. The shah, commenting on these measures in the first press conference given by a Persian ruler, said that the decrees formed part of a programme designed to convert Persia into a model state of social justice and orderly government; and that they would be enforced by a new imperial inspection service. In June 1959 there were a few changes in the cabinet, including

(Left) Persian women, with their children, at one of the many thousand evening schools to combat adult illiteracy. (Right) The prospect of army life has reduced the young man on the right to tears. He was rounded up in Tehran with other military service defaulters.

the replacement of Ali Hekmat as foreign minister by Abbas Aran.

In the economic field, prices were kept reasonably stable, and the gold and foreign currency reserves were maintained. Production of crude oil by the international consortium increased from 34·8 million tons in 1957 to 39·8 million tons in 1958. There were important developments in the sphere of banking. In Aug. 1959 it was announced that the International Bank for Reconstruction and Development had approved a loan to Persia of $5·2 million, bringing the total lent to Persia by this bank to over $150 million. The new loan was to be made available to the Industrial and Mining Development Bank of Iran, formed with a capital of $5·3 million by private investors in Persia, the United States, Great Britain, France, Belgium, the German Federal Republic, the Netherlands and Italy, with the object of stimulating industrial development in Persia by making medium and long-term loans and investing in share capital.

On Dec. 14 President Dwight D. Eisenhower paid a six-hour visit to Tehran. A joint communiqué said that in a two-hour talk with the shah Eisenhower expressed " the admiration of the people of the United States for the brave stand of the Persian people and government in face of outside pressure ". Eisenhower also addressed the Persian parliament.

On Dec. 21 the shah married in Tehran Farah Diba, the daughter of an army captain. He had been married twice before: in 1939 to Princess Fawziah, sister of King Farouk of Egypt, whom he divorced in 1948, and in 1951 to Soraya Isfandiari, daughter of a Persian diplomat, whom he divorced in 1958. In both cases the reason was that no son had been born of the marriage.   (B. S.-E.)

PERU. South American republic, bounded N. by Ecuador and Colombia, E. by Brazil and Bolivia, S. by Chile and W. by the Pacific. Area: 496,222 sq.mi., incl. islands. Pop.: (1950 census) 8,405,000; (1959 est.) 10,524,000; c. 52% whites and *mestizos*; 46% Indians; some Asiatic and Negro elements. Religion: Roman Catholic. Language: Spanish; Indians speak only Quichua or Aymará. Chief towns (pop., 1958 est.); Lima (cap.) 1,186,212; Callao 129,365; Arequipa 121,896; Cuzco 68,483. President, Manuel Prado y Ugarteche. Main imports: machinery, apparatus, vehicles, metal and manufactures, cereals, chemicals, textiles. Main exports: cotton, sugar, petroleum. Monetary unit: *sol* (S.74·50 = £1 sterling).

History. A trade deficit of $45 million in 1958, and continued low prices for exports resulting in a net foreign exchange deficit of $5·3 million in Jan. 1959 led to a serious deterioration in the internal economic situation. Restrictions on dollar transactions caused a decline in dollar deposits, and limitation of imports to essentials and renewal of U.S. stabilization credits of $35 million did not prevent the net foreign exchange deficit reaching $20 million by June 30, when it was estimated that the national accounts, showing a 27·75% rise in expenditure over 1958, would close with a deficit of approximately 1,000 million soles.

Internal differences over the economic situation led the government to resign on July 5. It was replaced by an administration headed by Pedro Beltran, owner of the newspaper *La Prensa*, critic of previous financial policies and advocate of austerity in public expenditure and lower taxation. Assuming the finance portfolio he declared that henceforth expenditure would not exceed revenue, and that the increased production for higher living standards would need domestic and foreign investment obtainable only if the currency were sound. Among his first acts were withdrawal of the meat subsidy and doubling of retail prices of oil products to encourage domestic production; this, amounting to only half domestic consumption, had been declining.

The year was again marked by labour unrest, with some rioting which led to suspension of constitutional guarantees for varying periods. In September the International Bank for Reconstruction and Development cancelled a $15 million loan for railway improvement granted in 1958 because the Peruvian government had been unable to fulfil certain conditions attached to it. However, the International Finance corporation announced a further $1·4 million investment in Peruvian industry, and U.S., French, Italian, and Japanese capital shared in development of domestic production in dairy products, stockings, chemical fertilizers, cement and motorcycles.   (N. P. MACD.)

PETROLEUM. Crude oil prices started to fall in Texas early in 1959 and Venezuelan and Caribbean crude followed suit. British Petroleum, chief marketing company in the Persian gulf, later made a uniform cut of 18 cents per bbl. of all grades. By the end of June 7·3 million deadweight tons

	1955	1956	1957	1958
WORLD	773,766	840,963	885,740	906,300
North America				
United States	335,744	353,698	353,630	330,936
Canada	17,492	23,241	24,536	22,368
Central and South America				
Venezuela	115,169	131,521	148,378	139,116
Mexico	12,793	12,972	12,630	13,548
Colombia	5,493	6,104	6,339	6,480
Trinidad	3,563	4,139	4,875	5,340
Argentina	4,365	4,437	4,858	5,100
Peru	2,302	2,543	2,553	2,520
Other countries*	1,438	1,898	2,773	3,199
Middle East and N. Africa				
Kuwait	54,756	54,982	57,286	70,212
Saudi Arabia	47,042	48,201	48,361	49,476
Persia	17,070	26,481	35,129	39,996
Iraq	32,705	31,322	21,876	35,664
Qatar	5,438	5,877	6,611	8,220
Egypt	1,821	1,723	2,362	3,168
Bahrein	1,502	1,506	1,599	2,028
Other countries†	614	719	687	1,154
Far East				
Indonesia	11,736	12,732	15,468	16,104
Brunei and Sarawak	5,320	5,709	5,593	5,208‡
Other countries§	1,000	904	1,063	820
Western Europe				
German Fed. Rep.	3,147	3,506	3,960	4,428
Austria	3,665	3,427	3,186	2,832
Netherlands	1,024	1,097	1,523	1,621
Italy	204	569	1,257	1,535
Other countries‖	1,294	1,703	1,968	1,852
Communist Bloc				
U.S.S.R.	70,793	83,806	98,340	112,800
Rumania	10,556	10,920	11,184	11,340
China	966	1,163	1,440	2,500
Hungary	1,601	1,202	675	828
Other countries¶	470	936	1,097	315

* Cuba, Bolivia, Brazil, Chile, Ecuador; Cuba excluded in 1957 and 1958; Bolivia and Ecuador excluded in 1958. † Algeria, Morocco, Pakistan, Turkey. ‡ Brunei only. § Burma, Japan and (except in 1958) Netherlands New Guinea. ‖ France, Yugoslavia and (except in 1958) Great Britain. ¶ Albania, Bulgaria, Czechoslovakia, Poland; Albania excluded in 1955 and 1958; Bulgaria excluded in 1958.
SOURCE. U.N. *Statistical Yearbook*, 1958; U.N. *Monthly Bulletin of Statistics*.

of tankers were laid up, about one-eighth of the world total, due to the industry's mistaken forecasts of oil consumption.

In 1959 the industry entered into its second 100 years of existence as measured from the sinking of Edwin Drake's first successful well in Pennsylvania, a circumstance which resulted in the appearance of much comparative data, appraisal of progress and speculation about its future. Published figures gave world oil production as having increased from 20 million tons in 1900 to over 906 million tons in 1958. Similar spectacular increases were shown in the consumption of petroleum products; but only 3% of the world's shipping

was oil-fired in 1914 while in 1958 only 7% was not. It was estimated that by the early 1970s world consumption of oil and natural gas would have doubled and over half the energy the world needed would be derived from these materials. At the beginning of 1959 " proven reserves " (that portion of the total known to be available for commercial exploitation) were over 37,000 million tons—about 40 years' supply at current usage rates. Among characteristic trends during the previous few years were noted the increasing demand for paraffin-type aircraft fuels—for example the Comet 4 burned 1,000 gal. per hr. and the Boeing 707 nearly double that amount, consuming 65 tons on a transatlantic crossing—the consequent reduction in the demand for high-octane spirit causing refiners to produce super-grade motor fuel in the expensive plant so released. Again, the petro-chemical industry, that comparative newcomer of the 1930s, had grown to the extent that some three-quarters of all organic chemicals in the United States were made from petroleum. Some problems still remained unsolved: the economic extraction of shale oil and the recovery of the oil in the Athabaska (Canada) tar sands whose potential yield was estimated at a possible 300,000 million bbl.

United Kingdom. Refinery output showed a 15% increase in 1958 compared with 1956 (1957 was an abnormal year due to the Suez conflict) while in the same period home consumption rose from 23 million tons to 31 million tons a year. With refinery expansions completed production was well in advance of needs and, it was believed, would be so for some considerable time to come. Early in 1959 the first shipment of liquid methane gas was received from the United States (*see* BUSINESS REVIEW: *Gas Industry*). This first 2,000 tons was enough to satisfy the domestic needs of 40,000 people for a year and was equivalent to 200,000 tons of coal. Waste gas from the refineries at Fawley, Isle of Grain, Coryton and Petrochemicals (Manchester) was also being used by the local gas boards and it was reported that Whitby (Yorkshire) would draw on natural gas supplies from neighbouring moors in 1960.

France. The bulk of the estimated 1959 investment in the industry (Fr.250,000 million) was earmarked for the development of the Sahara oil fields. The completion by 1960 of the 400-mi. pipeline terminating at the Algerian port of Bougie was expected to raise the annual output of the Hassi Messaoud field from 8 million tons to an eventual 14 million tons. Preliminary work was started on another 24-in. line, running 450 mi. from Edjelé to the Tunisian coastline near Gabès.

Middle East. A project discussed at the first Arab oil congress held in the spring was a pipeline to link the three

(Left) An oil worker at Nevis, Alberta, draws a longbow to shoot a flaming arrow at an extinguished waste gas outlet. (Centre) A mobile oil drilling platform built in Britain for use off Borneo. (Right) Drilling near Kimmeridge, Dorset, where oil was found in March.

principal states. Branches from Saudi Arabia, Kuwait and Iraq would join and run to the Mediterranean coast at Tripoli, Lebanon, or Baniyas, Syria. A 40-in. line running over 1,000 mi. with an annual capacity of 40 million tons was envisaged.

United States and Canada. The United States had become responsible for over half the world's consumption of oil and imports reached a figure of some 600 million barrels a year. Mandatory controls on imported crude oil were imposed in March. In Canada, exploration concessions were obtained for areas such as the Mackenzie River delta and as far north as Axel Heiberg island and Ellesmere island on the fringe of the polar region. Georg Tugendhat examined the existence of enormous oil reserves in Canada—a politically stable country —in relation to imports into the United Kingdom. Were Canadian exports of oil to the United Kingdom to become a commercial proposition the Canadian oil industry could develop at a rate currently impossible.

Venezuela. The country became the largest exporter of oil in the world, its principal customers being the United States, Canada and the United Kingdom. By raising income tax rates the government was able to increase its share of the profits of foreign oil concessions from the previous 50% to 60% and, with other taxes and royalties, was able to take as much as 65%. (E. G. E.)

See R. J. Hengstebeck, Petroleum Processing (London, 1959); Henry Longhurst, Adventure in Oil: The Story of BP (London, 1959).

PHARMACY. The action of a drug may need to be modified to produce a more rapid effect, a more prolonged action or an action without any side effects. At the British Pharmaceutical conference held in Bournemouth in 1959, Andrew Wilson pointed out (*Pharm. J. 2*, 191) that parenteral injection gave the fastest response (of 496 new products introduced in the United States in 1957, 52 were for injection); more use could be made of sublingual administration; a relatively water-insoluble form of drug would delay its absorption; the gastric mucosa acted as a lipoid barrier which selectively permitted passive diffusion of the un-ionized lipid-soluble form; *e.g.*, aspirin and barbiturates, but prevented the diffusion of the lipid-insoluble ionic form; *e.g.*, quinine, ephedrine and amidopyrine. A new approach was the use of such compounds as β-diethyl-aminoethyl diphenylpropylacetate (SKF525-A), 2:4-dichloro-6-phenyl-phenoxyethyl diethylamine (Lilly 18947) and *iso*propyl-2-*iso*nicotinyl hydrazine (iproniazid, Marsilid), which, with little or no action themselves, prolonged the action of some drugs by inhibiting the enzyme systems in liver microsomes that inactivated them.

The storage of medicinal preparations was discussed at the 19th International Congress of Pharmaceutical Sciences in Zürich. Hydrolysis, oxidation and racemization were the most frequent causes of decomposition and factors which

played an important part were temperature, *p*H, oxygen concentration, catalysts, decarboxylation (as with *para*-amino-salicylic acid) and the presence of enzymes or bacteria (S.A. Schou, *Pharm. Acta Helvet.*, 34, 398).

A working party of the Medical Research council on standards of steam sterilization in hospitals reported (*Lancet*, 1, 425) that there was a widespread lack of understanding of the technical requirements involved and that, until routine supervision was insisted upon, patients in many hospitals would continue to be exposed to the unnecessary hazard of infection caused by the use of imperfectly sterilized articles. At a symposium at Brighton on " The Operation of Sterilising Autoclaves ", J. H. Bowie recommended that all forms of instrument, bottle, bedpan and basin boiler in hospitals be replaced by rapid high pressure sterilizers with a vacuum-drying arrangement. Ethylene oxide in a concentration of 1,000 mg./litre at 20°C. was found (*Pharm. J.*, 2, 232) to penetrate plastic and polyethylene containers and satisfactorily to sterilize their contents; *e.g.*, experimentally contaminated sodium chloride solution, as well as penicillin solution and buffered (*p*H 5 to 7) solution of thiamine hydrochloride without any significant decomposition of the solutions.

A new edition of the British Pharmaceutical Codex, and supplements to the British Veterinary Codex and to the International Pharmacopoeia, were published. (W. K. F.)

PHILATELY. The year 1959 was marked by one event which not only received wide publicity in the stamp press throughout the world but also was reported at length in the national dailies of the Republic of Ireland and Great Britain. This was the collapse of Shanahans Stamp Auctions Ltd., of Dun Laoghaire, which went into liquidation, by order of the High Court, on June 8. According to a statement made by

Some of the new stamps issued during 1959. Apart from the three in the centre of the top row all are from Commonwealth countries or British colonies. (Bottom right) The St. Lawrence seaway commemorative stamp.

the liquidator, the creditors, numbering some 15,000 investors, faced a loss of about £1·25 million. On May 30 the four directors were arrested. The hearing and adjudicating on claims by the examiner was fixed for Jan. 27, 1960.

International exhibitions of the first importance took place at Hamburg and Palermo, to both of which Queen Elizabeth II sent a portion of the royal collection. In Britain Stampex, the annual national show, was held in March, instead of January as hitherto, resulting in vastly improved attendance. The task of organizing the London International exhibition 1960 and Unipex, the South African show in Johannesburg, was pressed forward. Warsaw also announced an exhibition and the queen consented to take part.

The British Post Office took another step forward in its policy of mechanization; from October every address in the City of Norwich was coded. For example NOR22K might represent " Green Street, Norwich, Norfolk ". The machinery installed impresses covers with an appropriate combination of fluorescent dots, and they in turn react on a second machine which sorts the letters into their code boxes.

When Queen Elizabeth II opened the St. Lawrence seaway, both Canada and the United States simultaneously issued a commemorative stamp of the same design. On Aug. 20 a supply of the Canadian issue (5c.), purchased in Winnipeg, was found to have the central blue panel inverted in relation to the red inscriptions. This was the first occasion on which any such error had occurred among Canadian stamps. At a London auction in December a specimen realized £380.

Several important sales took place in the London auction rooms. Among these may be mentioned the late Marquess of Bute's collection of war stamps which realized £85,000 (Robson Lowe), and the John Lek " German States " and Hurlock " Barbados and Trinidad " (H. R. Harmer).

As might be expected the International Geophysical Year resulted in a number of commemorative issues, the designs of which, in some cases, were distinctly strange. Two of these, from the German Democratic Republic, 20pf. and 25pf., were intended to represent cosmic rays and oceanography respectively. (C. W. B. H.)

BIBLIOGRAPHY (all published 1959). S. D. Tchilinghirian and W. S. E. Stephen, *Stamps of the Russian Empire Used Abroad*, part IV (Aberlour); Royal Sydney Philatelic Club, *The Cook Islands to 1919* (Melbourne); C. W. Wickersham, *Early Stamps of Venezuela* (New York); D. R. Martin, *Pakistan Overprints 1948-9* (London); W. R. Forrester-Wood, *Stamps and Postal History of Sarawak* (London).

PHILIPPINES.

PHILIPPINES. Island republic lying about 500 mi. off the southeast coast of Asia; an archipelago of 7,107 islands, the largest being Luzon (40,814 sq.mi.) and Mindanao (39,906 sq.mi.). Total area: 115,707 sq.mi. Pop.: (1948 census) 19,234,182; (1959 est.) 24,718,000. Languages spoken (1948 census): English 7,156,420; Spanish 345,111; and about 87 tongues and dialects; Tagalog, spoken by c. 7·5 million, was declared the national language. Religion (1948): Roman Catholic 15,941,422; Aglipayan (Independent Christian) 1,456,114; Protestant 444,491; Moslem 791,817; pagan 353,842. Chief towns (pop., 1954 est.): Manila (cap., incl. suburbs) 1,450,000 (1959 est. 1,850,000); Cebu 182,000 (1959 est., 205,201); Iloilo 121,000; Bacolod 115,000. President, Carlos P. García. Main imports: cotton and manufactures (13%), petroleum and products (8%), metals and machinery, motor cars, rayon and manufactures, cereals and products, dairy products. Main exports: copra (29%), sugar (24%), abacá (9·4%), metals, timber, coconut oil, canned pineapple. Monetary unit: *peso* (P.5·62½ =£1 sterling).

History. President García had originally pledged his administration to continue close co-operation with the United States, but the year 1959 was marked by rising criticism of the United States by the government who pressed the United States on four basic issues: increasing U.S. military aid to the Philippines; the pattern of tariffs and other taxes mutually applicable to the two countries; U.S. military bases and the Status of Forces agreement, covering legal jurisdiction over U.S. military personnel in the islands; and a large group of financial claims against the United States. In September the United States paid certain of the claims, but rejected most of them as invalid. In October the United States agreed to relinquish all bases except Clark Field air force base, Sangley Point naval air station (Cavite), Subic Bay naval base, Camp John Hay recreational station near Baguio in the north Luzon mountains and three lesser stations. The latter action relieved tensions, but the rejection of financial claims and the continuance of other problems left matters over which antagonistic elements in the Philippines could provoke difficulty.

Political opposition to García, on the issues of corruption and Anti-Americanism, brought about the union of the Liberal and Progressive parties, in June, under the Liberal banner, led by the Liberal party leader, Vice-President Diosdado Macapagal.

Weather during the early part of the year was good, so that bumper yields occurred during the 1958-59 crop year. (J. E. S.)

PHILOSOPHY. The year 1958 saw the death of G. E. Moore, perhaps the most influential of native-born British philosophers in the century (*see* OBITUARIES in *Britannica Book of the Year 1959*). Moore took up the subject at a time when its dominant characteristic was large-scale speculation rather than close argument; by insisting on stating philosophical theses in terms which were crystal-clear and on distinguishing carefully between views which were superficially similar but fundamentally different he did more than any man to reverse this state of affairs. The overthrow of the powerful philosophy of absolute idealism, fashionable at the beginning of Moore's career, was the joint work of Moore and Bertrand Russell; of the two Moore made far less impact on the general public, but considerably more on his fellow professionals, especially in the later years of his life. A number of his papers, notably his " A Defence of Common Sense " (1925), as well as his early book *Principia Ethica* (1903), were repeatedly discussed in the journals and elsewhere, and new pronouncements from him were eagerly studied right up to his death. Overshadowed as he was towards the end of his career by Ludwig Wittgenstein, he nevertheless shared with the latter in shaping the conception of philosophy most prevalent in Britain in the mid-20th century. Wittgenstein himself admired him for his extraordinary tenacity and integrity when working at philosophical questions, and it seemed likely at the time of his death that these qualities would long command respect for him, whatever the ultimate verdict on his achievement.

The philosophical revolution in which Moore played so large a part was the subject of much lively discussion in 1958 and 1959. There were some, such as G. R. G. Mure in his *Retreat from Truth*, who deplored it altogether. Others, including Russell himself and, in a different way, Ernest Gellner, author of *Words and Things*, a large-scale study of linguistic philosophy, thought of it as a revolution which had gone wrong, degenerating from something constructive and forward-looking into a futile classification of linguistic usages with no ultimate object. It was noteworthy that this low estimate of " Oxford " philosophy, as it was often called, was shared by some of Wittgenstein's own disciples, including his literary executor G. E. M. Anscombe. The genesis and a justification of the orthodox Oxford conception of philosophy were admirably sketched by G. J. Warnock in his *English Philosophy since 1900*. But there was evidence that Warnock's confidence in the correctness and fruitfulness of the local ways of doing philosophy was not shared by all his Oxford colleagues. P. F. Strawson's subtly argued *Individuals* broke with accepted ways of thought not only in its method, which showed the influence of Kant as much as that of Wittgenstein, but also in the problems it raised; its sub-title, " an essay in descriptive metaphysics ", was startling in itself. S. Hampshire's *Thought and Action*, a study of a number of issues in general philosophy and ethics, was another book to open up new ground. Firmly based in the linguistic tradition, it nevertheless displayed a speculative freedom and informality of argument which suggested at times that the philosophical clock was being turned back about half a century. But its conclusions were nearer to some of the characteristic theses of existentialism than to the doctrines of F. H. Bradley or T. H. Green, with whom some reviewers compared the author.

The publication of a further instalment of Wittgenstein's literary remains, with the promise of more to come, stimulated still more interest in that extraordinary man's philosophical development. His enigmatic *Tractatus* won particular attention. Miss Anscombe, in her tantalizingly brief *Introduction* to that work, suggested convincingly that it was a profound mistake to connect it, as so many of its first readers did, with the European empiricist tradition: its problems originated in the logic of Gottlob Frege, and were often more clearly continuous with those discussed in Greek philosophy than with the questions raised by Hume. It was noteworthy during 1958-59 that a number of the younger philosophers showed, under Wittgenstein's influence, signs of a distinctly cool attitude to the British empiricists; this was true in particular of P. T. Geach in his short book *Mental Acts*. There was some tendency for these philosophers to form a distinct group of their own, a group whose members were distinguished by their strong interest in formal logic as well as their antipathy to the philosophical establishment. It may or may not be significant that several of the best-known members of the group were Roman Catholics.

In moral philosophy there was much criticism of the evaluative descriptive dichotomy set up by R. M. Hare in his influential work *The Language of Morals* (1952). A more wide-ranging attack on Hare and other moralists recently in fashion was delivered by Miss Anscombe in an article in *Philosophy* (Jan. 1958), in the course of which she maintained that moral philosophy could not be expected to advance in the prevailing state of confusion about the concepts of philosophical psychology. Her own work on *Intention* was put forward as a first attempt to clear up some of this confusion.

In the field of philosophical logic the most notable publication was that of the Finnish professor G. H. von Wright, whose *Logical Studies* afforded an admirable combination of close argument, mastery of technical detail and lucidity. The long-awaited English translation of K. R. Popper's *Logic of Scientific Discovery* finally made its appearance in 1959. Apart from the works on recent thought already referred to there was little of interest written on the history of philosophy, except for J. N. Findlay's study of Hegel, which was a singularly sympathetic and perceptive account, and a surprising one to come from a philosopher whose sympathies for the Moore-Russell revolution had never been in doubt.

(W. H. W.)

BIBLIOGRAPHY. *Logic and Scientific Method.* S. E. Toulmin, *The Uses of Argument* (London, 1958); E. Nagel and J. Newman, *Gödel's Proof* (New York, 1958); N. R. Hanson, *Patterns of Discovery* (London, 1958).
Metaphysics and General Philosophy. L. Wittgenstein, *The Blue and Brown Books* (Oxford, 1958); G. E. Moore, *Philosophical Papers* (London, 1959); N. Malcolm, *Dreaming* (London, 1959); R. J. Hirst, *The Problems of Perception* (London, 1959).
Ethics, Politics, Religion. A. Farrer, *The Freedom of the Will* (London, 1958); B. Mayo, *Ethics and the Moral Life* (London, 1958); P. Winch, *The Idea of a Social Science* (London, 1958); A. C. Ewing, *Second Thoughts on Moral Philosophy* (London, 1959); K. Baier, *The Moral Point of View* (Ithaca, 1958); H. D. Lewis, *Our Experience of God* (London, 1959); I. Berlin, *Two Concepts of Liberty* (London, 1959).
History of Philosophy. F. Copleston, *A History of Philosophy,* vol. 4 and 5 (London, 1959); T. D. Weldon, *An Introduction to Kant's Critique of Pure Reason,* 2nd ed. (London, 1958); B. Russell, *My Philosophical Development* (London, 1959); A. R. White, *G. E. Moore: a Critical Exposition* (Oxford, 1958); Richard Wollheim, *F. H. Bradley* (Harmondsworth, 1959).

PHOTOGRAPHY

PHOTOGRAPHY. During 1959 trends towards further simplifications of camera manipulation continued and the virtual disappearance of all sizes of negative other than the 35 mm. (24 mm. × 36 mm.) and 2¼-in. square (6 cm. × 6 cm.) was practically complete. The 4 in. × 5 in. and the continental size of 9 cm. × 12 cm. still remained the most popular in the press field although many press photographers also carried a 35-mm. camera as an auxiliary.

The increasing popularity of the 35-mm. camera was undoubtedly due to the fact that with this size colour transparencies of high quality could be made at prices which compared very favourably with the cost of a black-and-white print while projectors to take the resultant 2 in. × 2 in. transparencies were available for under £10. Colour was thus bringing into the market a new public which hitherto had not bothered to take photographs but now found itself able to take and project really good colour transparencies with the minimum of effort.

With this hitherto unreached field to exploit the manufacturers were trying to make the handling of the camera as simple as possible and many of the designs which were new at the 1958 Photokina exhibition at Cologne had become obsolescent. One of the biggest practical improvements to cameras in the previous few years had been the introduction of what is generally termed a " bright line " finder. With this the field of view to be seen through the finder window is larger than that taken on the film, the actual field photographed being outlined by a clearly illuminated white line which leaves no uncertainty as to where the edge of the picture will come. This is a great boon to photographers who have to wear glasses.

In 1959 the built-in photoelectric exposure meter had been on the market for two or three years, but when its readings had to be manually transferred to the diaphragm ring and shutter-speed scale it had no real advantage other than portability over the separate meter and indeed some disadvantages such as the fact that if it went wrong the whole camera needed to be sent to the repairer. However, if, as in the more advanced cameras, the photoelectric meter adjustments were mechanically coupled to the shutter camera manipulation was greatly simplified and as a result an increasing number of cameras were being provided with such mechanism. Progress in this connection had been greatly facilitated by the introduction of the " Prontormat " shutter by the German firm of Gautier of Calmbach who shared with the Deckel company virtually the whole of the German shutter business and a good deal of that of other countries.

The Prontormat shutter, for use in cameras having a built-in photoelectric exposure meter coupled to the shutter mechanism.

Deckel, who made the " Compur " shutter, had also brought out its equivalent. Slight variations occurred between different makes of camera in the use of the coupled exposure meter but generally by turning a knob or ring a moving pointer in the exposure meter window was made to coincide with a fixed pointer, and when this was done the shutter was correctly set for the particular exposure required. In a number of cameras the two indicators appear together in the same window as the viewfinder.

While there had been no big advances in the lens field mention must be made of the new Voigtländer " Zoomar "

The Voigtländer Bessamatic 35-mm. reflex camera, fitted with the firm's new Zoomar f.2·8 lens of 36 mm. to 82 mm. focal length.

f.2·8 lens which had a continuously variable focal length from 36 mm. to 82 mm. The basic focal length was 36 mm. which suited wide-angle shots and the lens mount was engraved with figures denoting lengths of 36 mm., 40 mm., 50 mm., 60 mm., 70 mm. and 82 mm., although all intermediate focal lengths could also be obtained. The maximum lens aperture in all cases was f.2·8 but the diaphragm could be closed down to f.22. An ingenious arrangement enabled the focusing to be done at the full f.2·8 aperture although on pressing the shutter release the lens stopped down automatically to a pre-set figure. Thus the image being focused was always brightly illuminated. The lens was at first fitted only to the Voigtländer Bessamatic, a single-lens reflex camera, but it was to be available later to other single-lens reflex cameras, the only type of camera to which such a lens could be conveniently fitted.

Many of the later novelties in camera design were shown at the British Photo fair held at Olympia in May. Towards the end of the show the British importers were able to demonstrate to the press a new Rolleiflex camera of unusual design. Many owners of twin-lens reflex cameras often wish that their instruments were fitted with interchangeable lenses so that long focal lengths could be used for special work such as portraiture. This new camera was fitted with a pair of 13·5 cm. focus objectives (5⅜ in.) which made it particularly suitable for studio portraiture and also for many specialized purposes. It was not by any means a " general purpose " camera and for close-up work it was necessary to use special supplementary lenses which were fitted on a hinged mount. The depth of focus was so small with such lenses that the problem of keeping the film absolutely flat for accurate focusing was a most serious problem. For this reason, in the new Rolleiflex camera, the film was held completely flat by being pressed on to an optically worked glass plate.

The Japanese camera industry was forging ahead rapidly and was proving a formidable competitor to the Germans in world markets, particularly in the United States. The Japanese lens industry, which made its own optical glass, was establishing a high reputation for its output particularly with the very large apertures of f.1·5 and over. Comparatively few Japanese cameras, which were made in all the popular sizes and designs, reached the British market owing to the very small import quota but in the United States the Japanese imports were mounting steadily and were fast approaching the German dimensions.

Few, if any, novelties appeared in slide projectors although intense competition brought prices down rapidly. Automatic slide changers which obviated the tedious work of picking up, inserting and taking out individual slides, were increasingly coming into use and more efficient projection from the optical point of view resulted from the introduction of new and smaller types of bulb with built-in reflectors. Fan cooling of condensers and slides had become standard in all the higher-powered projectors, a number of which were fitted with extractor fans which drew the air down through the instrument instead of blowing it upwards.

There was a steady increase in the popularity of colour prints on paper, made from colour negatives from which, if necessary, black-and-white prints could also be produced. " Kodacolor " negative material and the professional grade known as " Ektacolor ", which had been on the market in the United States for some years, were being manufactured in Britain and were available in all the popular sizes, including 35 mm., while " Pakolor " colour negative and paper was also of British manufacture. Other colour negative and paper print materials were " Agfacolor ", " Gevacolor " and " Ray-color ". The great majority of colour negatives and prints were of course made by commercial houses but the amateur could if he wished obtain his material himself and make either contact prints or enlargements. The special colour printing paper originally called " Kodak Type C " but later known as " Ektacolor " paper, was being made in Britain and was used very successfully by a number of pictorialists for exhibition prints in colour, tending to displace for pictorial work the previously popular trichrome carbro and dye transfer processes both of which required the preparation of the separation negative and a very high degree of skill. In the colour sections of the exhibitions of the London Salon of Photography and the Autumn exhibition of the royal photographic society it was noticeable that " Tripack " colour prints by such processes as " Agfacolor ", " Kodacolor " and " Ektacolor " had largely replaced the previously popular methods. Colour transparencies, however, remained the most popular form of amateur colour photography and excellent paper prints could be made from them. (*See also* CINEMA; TELEVISION; X-RAY AND RADIOLOGY.) (P. W. H.)

PHYSICS. Colour Perception. Experiments by E. H. Land (*Proc. nat. Acad. Sci. Wash.*, 45, 115; 636; *Sci. Amer.*, 200, 84) on the perception of a wide range of colours arising from only two stimuli caused widespread interest. Conventional colour reproduction uses three: usually red, green and blue " primary " lights. While a link with three separately localized receptors in the eye has never been established, and colour measurements are expressed in terms of three abstractions called X, Y and Z (which, indeed, lose even this identity in the matrix juggling of colour television transmission), it was generally held that the three attributes of colour—hue, saturation, intensity—must need three separate pieces of information to specify them somehow. Land first repeated an old, but not well-known, experiment using white light and red light. Then, with two transparencies (" long " taken in red light, " short " in green light) he found satisfying colour reproduction with almost any two monochromatic illuminants, provided only that the longer wavelength lit the " long " picture—though this condition reversed at the violet end of the spectrum. The two illuminants needed only to be about 100 angstrom units (say, 1/40 of the visible spectrum range) apart in wavelength.

In a world of monochromatic illuminants and pigments, full colour perception might be enjoyed from a very narrow spread of wavelengths. This implied that the assessment of contrasts fluctuating in a random manner over a wide field, rather than response to wavelength, might be the basis of colour vision; the experiments indicated a double assessment, first of the intensity of each signal with respect to the maximum available, and then a balance between " long " and " short ". The idea of two information channels as opposed to three is not in itself new. About 150 years ago the poet Goethe regarded colour as " the interplay of light and darkness ", and some experiments by the Goethe foundation at Clent, Worcestershire, show that this, properly applied, would give a working recipe for colour reproduction. The physiologist Ragnar Granit in the 1930s observed two distinct types of electrical impulse from nerve fibres in the living eye, which he interpreted as " dominator " (giving white sensation) and " modulator " (giving colour sensation by some kind of code signal). Colour television effectively works on about two and a half, since one of its three signals is inoperative for fine detail. The next step proposed by Land was to experiment further using three stimuli, in order to discover what additional information a third channel actually conveyed.

Plasma. The properties of plasma—a fully ionized gas which is an assembly of equal numbers of positive ions and free electrons—were exploited in several ingenious ways. In plasma, a motion of fluid is also an electric current which sets up a magnetic field; motion of a magnetic field H carries with it fluid " attached to the lines of force ", for in a perfect conductor there can be no relative motion of field and medium since this would set up an infinite induced current, and plasma is almost a perfect conductor. Thus, changes in H propagate mechanical waves (Alfvén waves) which can be likened to transverse waves on the lines of force which behave as loaded cords. The velocity of propagation is usually low, being proportional to $Hn^{-\frac{1}{2}}$ where n is the ion density. D. F. Jephcott (*Nature, Lond.*, June 13, 1959) observed Alfvén waves in ionized helium and argon, travelling at about 20 cm. per sec., at " discharge-tube " pressure; much greater speeds occur under natural ionosphere conditions. " Attached " is a loose term, for ions and electrons can execute helical paths about lines of force with frequency $He/2\pi m$; and on moving into a region of greater H describe tighter helices, increase rotational energy at the expense of translational energy and eventually stop and reverse direction. This is essentially the " magnetic mirror " or " magnetic bottle " principle of containment in thermonuclear work. The possibility of extracting thermonuclear energy from a hot plasma by reversible Carnot-cycle means using electromagnetic pumping was discussed by R. J. Bickerton and J. D. Jukes. The removal of hot electrons from such a plasma in exchange for cold electrons from the single electrode of a unipolar arc (A. E. Robson and P. C. Thonemann) was another suggested method for extracting energy directly. Finally, A. von Engel discussed the use of plasma as a space-vehicle propellent: high-speed (10^6 cm. per sec.) ion jets, equivalent to currents of 100-1,000 amp., would give reasonable thrust; electrostatic drag on the vehicle would have to be neutralized and he further suggested that a space-ship might make its own rarefied plasma by collision with neutral atoms, and that this might be propulsively directed by magnetic fields produced by the craft.

The Van Allen Radiation Belt. Information about the radiation belt, or belts, obtained from rockets and satellites, unravelled to show a zone in which a radiation comprising chiefly fast-moving electrons was spiralling about the earth's magnetic lines of force, and trapped as in a magnetic bottle, at an altitude of 1,000-2,000 km. Aurora, and lower-level radiation, were attributed to particles released from the trap. Energies were about 1 MeV, fluxes 10^6-10^7 per sq.cm. per sec. per unit solid angle, and the total number of particles about 10^{27}—an amazingly small quantity, about 1,000 moles, comparable in order with the number released by a single nuclear explosion. T. Gold (*Nature, Lond.*, Feb. 7, 1959) suggested that beta-decay $(n\rightarrow p+e+\nu)$ of neutrons from the earth would be inadequate as a source and that the particles were trapped from the outer regions of the sun's corona; P. J. Kellog said that the solar corona itself might have a magnetic bottle of its own from which the particles transferred. He also discussed the possible release of particles from the earth's belt by high-altitude explosion. Injected particles from the explosion would bottle-shuttle along the force-lines, followed on their first trip by the slower Alfvén wave. This wave disturbance would release some *natural* radiation, but not injected particles, and a few such explosions (possibly also a single one) might stock up the belt far beyond its natural content. The low-level (possibly 100 mi.) explosion at Johnston island (16°N, 170°W) on Aug. 1, 1958, gave aurora and magnetic disturbances at the magnetic conjugate Apia (14°S, 175°W), and though this was below the Van Allen region it gave some idea of what might be expected higher up.

Elementary Particles. Few surprises remain, and the expected neutral Ξ particle, of mass 2,582 m_e, decaying to Λ° and π°, was reported in March 1959, bringing the *known* total up to 30. During the year, a new classification and vocabulary appeared, in terms of statistical class (*Bose-Einstein or Fermi-Dirac*) and mass, viz.

Bosons, indistinguishable as individuals:
   Photon, γ
   Mesons: pions π°, π^-, and $\pi+$; kaons K°, $\bar{K}^\circ$, $K+$, and K^-
Fermions, distinguishable and obeying the exclusion principle:
   Leptons: neutrino ν, $\bar{\nu}$;
   electrons e^-, $e+$;
   muons, μ^-, $\mu+$; although current literature still used the term μ- meson frequently.
   Baryons: (a) nucleons: neutrons n°, $\bar{n}^\circ$; protons $p+$, p^-.
            (b) hyperons: Λ°, $\bar{\Lambda}^\circ$; Σ^-, Σ°, $\Sigma+$;
                          Ξ^-, Ξ°, and possible Ξ antiparticles.

Leptons are allotted a "lepton number", $+1$ for particle, -1 for antiparticle; baryons similarly a "baryon number" $+1$ or -1.

Possible reactions conserve lepton and baryon number, the abstract " isotopic spin " and, for strong nuclear-force reactions, " strangeness number " and " parity "; weak interactions may conserve only the first three. O. R. Frisch in June 1959 suggested that these 30 will not, like the chemical elements, be found eventually to be subdivisible, but may appear as the solutions of " a monstrous world equation ".

Gravitational Waves and Elementary Particles. H. Bondi in vol. XXII, p. 99, of the Physical society's *Reports on Progress in Physics*, 1959, and more fully in *Proc. roy. Soc.* (Ser. A), June 1959, discussed the possibility of gravitational waves. This matter is important for two reasons. First, if such waves exist, then they should, like electromagnetic waves, be quantized; that means that quantum mechanics should be applicable to gravitational as well as to electromagnetic fields. Secondly, there are among the elementary particles only three kinds of electric charge, positive, negative and zero; and only one size—the electronic charge $1\cdot6\times10^{-19}$ coulombs—so far as is known. But masses range from the zero rest-mass of the neutrino to the 2,582 m_e of the heaviest hyperon. Why should charge be so well organized and mass so untidy? The general theory of relativity, or Einstein's principle of equivalence, is generally held to postulate that inertia-mass and gravitational-mass are one and the same, and it seems likely that further progress towards Frisch's "monstrous equation" may come from the gravitational side, since mass provides a major unsolved problem. Bondi presented the case for the plausibility of gravitational waves in non-mathematical form in his Physical society article; the Coulomb field due to a static charge is accompanied by electromagnetic waves if it accelerates, so the inverse-square gravitational field of a static mass might be accompanied by gravitational waves on acceleration. But no means can at present be visualized for putting the matter to experimental test, though it seems likely from the importance of the subject that efforts to achieve the apparently impossible may have been considered.

Einstein's principle of equivalence does not help to identify the concept mass; on the contrary, it really disposes of the concept of gravitation as a force, and indeed this does disappear and become a property of space if the right kind of geometrical space is considered. Bondi said that the principle is "void of all physical meaning, and simply a mathematical challenge". He mentioned the theory of J. A. Wheeler, in which an empty space carrying electromagnetic and gravitational waves develops singularities that collect up energy and so behave like charges and masses; with the comment that, though elegant, it had not so far helped the theory of elementary particles.

In Sept. 1959 M. F. C. Allais reported results of a long series of pendulum experiments, revealing periodic gravity anomalies which he attributed to "a new kind of field". In the same month accounts appeared of the theory of the Soviet astronomer, N. Kozyrev, that the passage of time (at about 700 km. per sec.) generates energy and can lead to mechanical forces on rotating bodies.

"Contemporary Physics". A new British periodical, *Contemporary Physics: A Journal of Interpretation and Review*, was launched in Oct. 1959 by the publishers of the *Philosophical Magazine*. Described in a foreword to the first issue by the president of the Royal Society, Sir Cyril Hinshelwood, as a journal in which experts would endeavour to present the whole field in perspective to a wider circle of scientific colleagues, its purpose was to record and review progress in physical science at a relatively elementary level within the capacity of the ordinary scientific worker. (*See also* ASTRONOMY; ELECTRONICS; NUCLEAR ENERGY; RADIO, SCIENTIFIC DEVELOPMENTS IN.) (G. R. N.)

PHYSIOLOGY.
During 1959 an increasing number of original papers were published. While research into basic ideas was maintained on a world-wide basis, the continued expansion in the applied fields concerning space and climatic physiology was equally sustained.

From the Curie hospital in Paris came reports (*Rev. Franç. Etud. Clin. Biol.*, 4, 210-238, 1959) on six subjects, five males and one female, who were accidently exposed to acute neutron and gamma radiation from a nuclear reactor. An evaluation of the dosage of radiation to which they had been exposed was made by determining the content of the sodium-24 isotope in their bodies. One received a supralethal dose, later confirmed at autopsy, four received lethal doses and one a sublethal dose. They all showed an initial phase of radiation shock marked by asthenia, psychical depression, anorexia, vomiting, sweating and parasthesias in the upper limbs. A latent period of two to three weeks followed in which loss of weight, profuse sweating, insomnia, erythema and depilation were prominent. In the fourth, fifth or sixth week a crisis accompanied with high fever, anorexia, nausea and nocturnal sweats occurred. Within 30 days of the irradiation the red cell count of five of the subjects fell to $1 \cdot 3—3 \cdot 5$ millions per cu.mm., the white cells practically to zero and the platelets to less than 28,000 per cu.mm., and all showed marked purpuric symptoms. A transfusion of human bone marrow cells was made in the fifth week and was followed by an immediate simultaneous increase in reticulocytes, granulocytes and platelets. Within 60 days the formed elements of the blood, except for the lymphocytes, had reached normal values in four subjects. The sixth subject with a sublethal exposure was not transfused and made a spontaneous but slow recovery. The subject with the supralethal exposure had in the fifth week a progressive melaena, haemoptysis and haematemesis from which he died on the 32nd day. At autopsy a generalized purpura of the gastro-intestinal tract, pulmonary infarctions and renal petechiae were found although the haematological response to bone marrow transfusion had been immediate and marked. From an examination of the characteristics of the blood cells it appeared that the "grafted" bone marrow cells actively proliferated for at least a month after transfusion.

Rushmer and his colleagues (*Circulation*, 7, 602-627, 1959) have examined the performance of the canine left ventricle during spontaneous treadmill exercise, under anaesthesia, artificial respiration, thorocotomy and infusion of blood or catechol amines. Simultaneous recordings of changes in diameter, effective pressure, heart rate, "power", stroke "work", accumulated work per unit of time and rate of change of pressure were made. Experimentally induced increased venous return, reduced peripheral resistance by arteriovenous shunts or intravenous infusion of adrenaline or noradrenaline did not mimic the effects obtained in spontaneous exercise, where the response appeared to be predominantly an increased heart rate with little change in stroke volume. Many observations in trained dogs indicated even in the succeeding cardiac cycle, initiation of the cardiovascular responses observed in exercise by the central nervous system; *e.g.*, starting of the treadmill. Stimulation of the periventricular grey matter in the hypothalamus reproduced more precisely the left ventricular response to exercise than any other experimental procedure.

The effect on the heart rate in "athletic" men between 56-68 years of age of performing muscular work up to maximal loads on a bicycle ergometer was studied by Åstrand and his colleagues in Philadelphia (*J. appl. Physiol.*, 14, 562-566, 1959). With one exception the heart rate did not rise beyond 165 per min. The maximal oxygen intake averaged $2 \cdot 24$ litres per min. and blood lactic acid 83 mg. per 100 mm. Breathing oxygen did not raise the maximal heart rate.

The intake and expenditure of energy over a period of time in an adult are normally almost equal, usually due to adjustment of the food ingested. Bilateral lesions in the ventromedial hypothalamic nuclei in the rat cause hyperphagia and obesity. From Cambridge came an account (*J. Physiol.*, 145, 336-352, 1959) of the effect of such lesions on one of a pair of inbred parabiotic rats. Parabiosis was performed in litter mates of the same sex before four weeks of age. Of 39 pairs, 32 survived to young adults, the hypothalamic lesions in one of the pair were made after the maximum growth spurt and caused hyperphagia and obesity in all such animals. The parabiotic partners became thin. Some died, others were killed when moribund, two were subjected to hypothalamic lesions and became hyperphagic; one of these animals ate so avidly as soon as food was offered that it choked and died the next day. It was suggested that these experiments may be evidence for a feedback control of food intake to the hypothalamic controlling centres.

From Leningrad came a study (*Sechenov J. Physiol.*, 45, 22-28, 1959) of the individual activity of the parotid glands in six adult women following unilateral or symmetrical stimulation of the mouth by irrigation, followed by swallowing. Unilateral stimulation always provoked bilateral secretion and unless there was a marked functional inequality the ipsilateral gland was the more active. The secretory activity of a gland varied according to the prevailing chewing habits.

The pineal body is a small mass which rests on the mesencephalon between the two thalami. It is attached by a short stalk to the habenular and posterior commissures. A small recess of the third ventricle extends into the stalk. Its morphology varies widely in different species. In a few cases, all males of 3 to 16 years, pineal tumours had been reported in association with macrogenitosomia praecox—a precocious development both of the body and of the sex organs. Altschule and his colleagues (*Amer. J. Physiol.*, *197*, 108-110, 1959) extended their work on the rat. Pinealectomy was performed in 26 day-old female rats. Twenty-eight days later the rats were killed and the weights of the ovaries, adrenals and pituitaries compared with intact rats or pinealectomized rats treated intraperitoneally with protein-free bovine pineal extract and sham-operated rats. Pinealectomy caused ovarian and pituitary hypertrophy but the bovine extract reversed these effects. In the intact animal the extract caused a decrease in the weight of the ovaries, adrenals and pituitary. (C. C. N. V.)

PIGS: *see* LIVESTOCK.

PLASTICS INDUSTRY. World output of plastics increased rapidly during 1959, maintaining the vigorous progress of earlier years. This progress is borne out by the production figures given in the accompanying table. With the recovery from the industrial recession of 1958 business activity increased, but world prices for plastic raw materials continued to fall slowly as the industry became increasingly competitive. The planned removal of tariff barriers between the seven members of the new European Free Trade association was expected to result in improved trade between them in plastic materials to the partial exclusion of imports from non-member countries.

Thermoplastics maintained healthy progress, development being most marked in the field of polyolefines, although the early promise of the low-pressure processes for polythene manufacture was not realized. By contrast, polythene made by the high-pressure process continued to make spectacular progress and there was every indication that the future for this material would remain bright. During the year progress was made in the construction of new high-pressure polythene plants, or the expansion of existing capacity, in many countries. Manufacture started for the first time in India and in the Netherlands. There was continued evidence that the U.S.S.R., Rumania, China and the German Democratic Republic were taking active measures to install polythene-manufacturing facilities. Future planned capacity throughout the non-Communist world for all types of polythene appeared to have increased to about 1·5 million tons a year of which roughly three-quarters were to be made by the high-pressure process.

Plans continued to be pressed ahead for the production of isotactic polypropylene, and further manufacturers in the United Kingdom and the United States made known their intentions of producing this new material. First signs became evident of a possible future trend towards the conversion of existing plants, originally designed for low-pressure polythene, to produce polypropylene.

In the over-all field of the chemistry of polyolefines attention was directed towards the copolymerization of ethylene with propylene or other monomers.

The expansion of polyvinyl chloride (P.V.C.) production facilities slowed in most countries owing to the existence of

Laying a flexible water main of polyvinyl chloride in Northwich, Cheshire, to combat high corrosion and soil subsidence.

excess capacity in some of the main producing centres. New plans were announced, however, for manufacture in Australia and Turkey, while a new plant was brought into production in China. Although capacity for P.V.C. manufacture still exceeded that for polythene production, output of the latter exceeded that of P.V.C. for the first time.

The construction of plants for the manufacture of polycarbonates proceeded during the year in the German Federal Republic, the United States and Japan, while in the United States the completion of a plant to manufacture a polymer based on formaldehyde was announced.

In the United Kingdom construction began on a new plant to produce polyester film, while additional capacity for a similar product was in course of installation in the United States.

Exploratory studies began on the utilization of Saharan oil for the manufacture of plastics based on petroleum chemicals in Algeria. In general, the trend of the previous decade towards the increased use of petroleum derivatives for plastics manufacture throughout the world continued to be one of the factors having a strong influence on the course of development in the industry. As a result, several countries with a hitherto underdeveloped industry began to consider domestic manufacture within the framework of petrochemicals production.

Of the many and varied uses for plastics materials the most vigorous advance was still being maintained in packaging applications of all kinds. The widespread development of the self-service store necessitated the prepackaging of more foods

PRODUCTION OF PLASTICS AND SYNTHETIC RESINS
('000 tons)

	1954	1955	1956	1957	1958
United States . .	1,265	1,560	1,840	2,030	2,040*
German Federal Republic	338	426	505	589	645†
United Kingdom .	250	325	338	400	411‡
Japan . . .	94	102	219	240	320§
France . . .	78	95	130	156	197‖
Italy . . .	57	80	144	149¶	180¶**

* *Chemical Week*, Jan. 10, 1959. † *Chemische Industrie*, May 1959. ‡ *Annual Abstract of Statistics 1958*. § *Plastic Industry News*, April 1959. ‖ *Industrie des Plastiques Modernes*, June 1959. ¶ Not strictly comparable with previous figures owing to revised classification, according to which 1956 production would be c. 115,000 tons. ** *Chemistry and Industry*, May 16, 1959.

such as vegetables and meat for retail sale. With bigger production of packaging film came diversification to meet the specialized needs of different sections of the market. The principle of choosing a film made from a particular polymer for a particular application—such as the use of polyvinylidene chloride film for its superior barrier properties or of polyethylene terephthalate film for electrical purposes—was already well established, but even within the single field of polythene film there was a trend towards specialized types for different applications. Three particular types were noteworthy: a film of the greatest toughness for industrial use and for the pre-packaging of vegetables and similar produce; a film of high transparency and adequate strength for the packaging of soft goods; and a film of the thinnest possible gauge as a replacement for paper in the dry-cleaning trade (in the United States in particular it was becoming the custom to return clothing after cleaning in a tailored envelope of thin polythene film rather than in the traditional paper package).

The progress of plastics in the packaging field, however, was not confined to the use of films, and an increasing variety of bottles, containers and aerosol dispensers was made.

Among fabrication processes for larger articles advances were noted in the technique of forming very large products in heated hollow moulds. This technique was used with polythene for the manufacture of a variety of large containers, such as bins for use in factories, and also for small boats. Thus polythene became the second plastic material used for boat building, the first being the already well-established fibre-glass laminates.

Decorative plastic laminates were finding increasing use in the manufacture of furniture, and for particular applications, such as sink units, the use of acrylic sheet was also of growing importance.

In the field of communications the advantages stemming from the installation of the polythene-insulated transatlantic telephone cable were remarkably demonstrated by the comparatively speedy transmission with its aid of television pictures during the visit of Queen Elizabeth II to Canada. Future developments in this field were foreshadowed by the announcement of a plan for a round-the-world cable linking various countries of the Commonwealth.   (J. G.; W. J. S.)

POLAND. People's republic of eastern Europe bounded E. by the U.S.S.R., S. by Czechoslovakia, W. by the German Democratic Republic and N. by the Baltic sea. Area: 120,359 sq.mi. Pop. (1950 census) 24,976,926; (Dec. 31, 1959 est.) 29,527,000. National minorities (1959 est.): Ukrainians 200,000; Byelorussians 120,000; Jews 50,000; Slovaks 15,000; Lithuanians 10,000; Germans 7,000. Religion: predominantly Roman Catholic, but (1958 est.) there were c. 400,000 Orthodox and 120,000 Lutherans. Chief towns (pop. 1958 est.): Warsaw 1,088,000; Łódź 696,000; Cracow 461,000; Wrocław 410,000; Poznań 392,000; Gdańsk 272,000; Szczecin 254,000; Bydgoszcz 224,000; Katowice 209,000; 12 other towns with a population of over 100,000. First Secretary of the Polish United Workers' (Communist) party, Władysław Gomułka; chairman of the council of state, Aleksander Zawadzki; chairman of the council of ministers, Józef Cyrankiewicz. Main imports: machinery; raw materials (iron ore, cotton, wool); petroleum and products. Main exports: coal, finished and semi-finished manufactured goods; meat and dairy produce. Monetary unit: złoty, in foreign trade at par with the Soviet rouble (Zł.11·20 =£1 sterling); tourist rate: Zł.67·20 =£1 sterling.

History. The year 1959 was economically one of slight recess and in home politics somewhat troubled. In spite of some signs to the contrary, there were no fundamental departures from the policies inaugurated by Władysław Gomułka in Oct. 1956.

Communist Party Congress. During March 10-19, 1959, the third congress of the Polish United Workers' (Communist) party was held in Warsaw. On Jan. 1, 1959, the party numbered 1,072,932 full members and candidates compared with 1,296,938 at the time of the second congress (March 1952). The reduction of party membership was mainly the

W. *Gomułka and J. Cyrankiewicz,* the Polish leaders, caricatured in *" Trybuna Ludu ",* the Polish Communist party newspaper.

result of the 1958 " verification ". In his six-hour report to the congress Gomułka said that the party leadership was not disturbed by the loss in numbers because it meant a cleansing from ideologically embarrassing " revisionist " and " dogmatic " elements. But he was worried by the fact that the percentage of workers among the party members was only 41·8% (6·5% less than in 1954), and that the peasant membership had fallen during the same period from 13·1% to 12·2%. The congress elected a new central committee of 77 full and 63 alternate members. Fourteen prominent " dogmatists " (or Stalinists) were dropped and only two were re-elected. The new central committee retained the nine members of the Politburo, the high command of the party, and added three more, all Gomułka's supporters (Zenon Kliszko, General Marian Spychalski and Edward Gierek).

Economic Position. Reporting to the party congress, Gomułka was optimistic about the steady growth of industrial production and national income. Between 1946 and 1958 the country's urban population had risen by 5·5 million while the rural population had fallen by 500,000. The numbers employed in agriculture had remained basically the same but those employed outside agriculture had risen from 3·2 million to 6·6 million and in industry alone the increase had been from 1·2 million to 2·9 million. Workers' and employees' real wages rose between 1955 and 1958 by 24·8%, reaching on the average Zł.1,462 per month. The congress gave its approval to the directives for the new five-year development plan 1961-65. It was planned that industrial production would rise by 50% compared with the provisions for 1960 and by 80% compared with those for 1958.

But agricultural production was lagging. In 1958 the four main cereal crops amounted to 13·5 million tons, similar to the 1957 harvest, yielding 14·8 quintals per ha. Gomułka said that between 1959 and 1965 it was planned to increase agricultural production by 30%. To achieve this it was necessary to raise the yield of grain per hectare from 14·8 to 17·5 quintals and that of potatoes from 120 to 160 q. per ha. It was also necessary to increase the number of cattle from 8·2 million to 11 million head; *i.e.*, from 40 to 54 head for every 100 ha. of agricultural land. Edward Ochab, a member of the Politburo, pointed out that while in Bulgaria 95% of arable land was collectivized, in Czechoslovakia this proportion reached 75% and in Rumania 65%, in Poland only 18% of arable land belonged to the " socialized sector " (of which 12·5% belonged to 5,621 state farms). In other words 82% of arable land belonged to 3,632,800 individual farmers of whom some 2·3 million owned 5 ha. or less. Ochab insisted that with agriculture in such a condition it was impossible to guarantee a steady growth of production. But the party would not accept the advice of " dogmatists " who would like to accelerate the development of producers' co-operatives, using coercive " administrative methods ". The peasant masses would only gradually become mature enough to accept the advantage of large-scale farming.

The Polish anomaly of private agriculture in a state with centrally-planned economy was one explanation of the meat shortage that became serious in the second half of the year. Another was the bad planning in the state farms which were permitted to reduce the numbers of their livestock. Still another was poor potato and other fodder crops caused by drought. Finally, as the government allowed the prices of potatoes to rise while holding down the price of meat, the peasants found it more profitable to sell potatoes than to feed their pigs. As a result the party had to take the unpopular decision, announced by Gomułka on Oct. 17 at the plenary session of the central committee, to increase the price of meat animal fats and meat products by 25% on the average. Accordingly, wages lost 3% to 4% of their real value.

Government Changes. In order to tighten controls over economy, on Oct. 27 Gomułka transferred Ochab from the Ministry of Agriculture to the party secretariat where he replaced Jerzy Morawski. Mieczysław Jagielski, from 1957 under secretary of state in the Ministry of Agriculture, was appointed minister. Eugeniusz Szyr and Julian Tokarski, who had been prominent planners before Oct. 1956, were appointed vice-chairmen of the council of ministers, while Tadeusz Gede, former deputy premier and from Nov. 1956 ambassador to Moscow, became first deputy chairman of the State Planning commission. At the same time Władysław Bieńkowski ceased to be minister of education and was succeeded by Wacław Tułodziecki; this change, however, did not mean any revision of policy.

Presenting on Nov. 25 the 1960 budget to the Sejm (Zł.195,000 million in revenue and Zł.193,300 million in expenditure), Cyrankiewicz, the prime minister, insisted that the appointment of two new deputy premiers should not be regarded as an abandonment of the road the government had chosen. " On the contrary, they are steps along this road ", he said.

The Church and the State. " We do not want war with the Church, but the Church must be only a Church, it must confine itself to matters of religion," said Gomułka on March 10. Speaking on Aug. 26, at Częstochowa, to a crowd of about 100,000 pilgrims, Cardinal Stefan Wyszyński, the primate of Poland, said that the Church had no intention of " provoking any effervescence or starting any political struggle among the people." He added that " Governments come and go, but the family and the Church remain."

The cardinal did not refer to any specific issues between the Church and the state. There was for instance, a decision of the minister of finance (Feb. 25) concerning income tax and land tax to be paid by the Church. There was a letter of the minister of local government (April 23) claiming that Church property in the formerly German western provinces belonged to the state. In May there was a government's reminder that members of the clergy were henceforward liable to military service. There was a letter of June 5 in which Jerzy Sztachelski, minister of state for Church affairs, informed Mgr. Zygmunt Choromański, bishop of Warsaw and secretary of the Polish hierarchy, that the government was asking for the resignation or removal of Mgr. Czesław Kaczmarek, the bishop of Kielce. Mgr. Kaczmarek was accused of anti-state propaganda. Only the pope has the power to remove a bishop from his diocese, but on Aug. 19 John XXIII addressed a letter to Mgr. Kaczmarek sending him his fatherly love and expressing the hope that the conflict would be happily settled. In spite of all these menacing signs nothing irreparable happened between the Church and the state. The *modus vivendi* established in Dec. 1956 continued.

Foreign Affairs. In his report of March 10 to the party congress Gomułka devoted a considerable place to the problem of Poland's western frontier on the Oder and Neisse rivers.

" No sensible person (he said), let alone statesman, should have had any doubt whatever that the confirmation of Poland's western boundary in a future peace treaty with Germany, as stipulated in the Potsdam agreement, was a pure formality. Almost 14 years have passed since the signing of the Potsdam agreement. During that time Poland has rehabilitated these lands from war devastation and re-settled them with millions of Poles repatriated from the Soviet Union and brought from other regions of Poland; millions of Polish children have been born in these lands and a new Polish generation is growing up there. Yet, so far, the governments of the western signatories of the Potsdam agreement have not said a single official word, nor made a single attempt to contradict the various statements made publicly and officially by Chancellor Adenauer of the German Federal Republic and his ministers demanding the revision of the Polish-German boundary on the Oder and Neisse rivers. How is this to be explained? "

On March 25 one western statesman, General Charles de Gaulle, replied indirectly to Gomułka's questions. The president of the French Republic, not a signatory of the Potsdam agreement, declared himself for the re-unification of the two German republics on condition that the German people " would not question the present German frontiers in the west and in the east, in the north and in the south." On Oct. 13, speaking in the French National Assembly, Michel Debré, the prime minister, declared that France was " for the respect of all frontiers, including that which was usually described as the Oder-Neisse line."

N. S. Khrushchev, first secretary of the Communist Party

The Polish Ministry of Agriculture in Warsaw. In the background on the right is the tower of the Palace of Science and Culture.

While in Warsaw in June, John Armitage, London editor of the "Encyclopædia Britannica", had talks with the staff of the new Polish Encyclopaedia. (L. to r.) A. Windholz, B. Stachoń, Mrs. A. Kossuth, J. Armitage, Mrs. L. Majzner, L. Marszałek (editor), Miss J. Stobniak and W. Olendzki.

of the Soviet Union and prime minister of the U.S.S.R., visited Poland from July 14 to July 23. Speaking in Szczecin on July 17 he said: " Wrocław, Gdańsk and Szczecin are Polish towns and they will remain Polish for ever."

At the end of 1959 the Polish population of the new western territories amounted to 7·5 million, including 2·6 million born there since 1945.

Returning from Moscow, Richard M. Nixon, vice-president of the United States, arrived in Warsaw on Aug. 2 for a three-day visit, the people receiving him enthusiastically. On Aug. 3 Nixon had a five-hour talk with Gomułka who brought up the problems for which he held the United States responsible: the western refusal to recognize Polish sovereignty over former German territories, the increased military strength of the German Federal Republic and the rejection of the Rapacki plan for a central European zone free from nuclear arms.

On June 10 the United States granted Poland credits and aid totalling $50 million. Together with loans and aid given in 1957 and 1958, U.S. credits to Poland amounted to $243 million. In 1958 Polish exports to the United States amounted to $29,683,000 while Polish imports from the United States reached the record figure of $104,630,000.

Polish exports to the United Kingdom rose in 1958 by 5% reaching £23·3 million. In the period Jan.-Aug. 1959 the value of these exports rose by 47% compared with the same period of 1958. Deliveries of British goods to Poland in the first eight months of 1959 amounted to £11·4 million, almost twice as much as in the corresponding period of 1958. In August a group of British M.P.s, headed by Peter Thorneycroft and Emmanuel Shinwell, attended the Inter-Parliamentary conference in Warsaw. On Oct. 9, H.M.S. " Tiger ", a modern cruiser of the Royal Navy, arrived in Gdynia on a four-day visit.

On Dec. 13 the U.N. general assembly elected Poland to a non-permanent seat of the Security council.

On Feb. 3, after almost 20 years of exile, a part of the Polish national treasures, deposited in Canada in 1940, returned to Poland. Apart from jewellery, armour and ancient scrolls they included the coronation sword of the Polish Piast kings, the first Gutenberg bible and manuscripts of Chopin's music. But another part of the treasure, including a large number of priceless Arras tapestries from the Wawel royal castle in Cracow, were still in the cellars of the Quebec Provincial museum. Maurice Duplessis, the provincial premier, refused to return them to Poland. (*See also* EASTERN EUROPEAN ECONOMIC PLANNING; ROMAN CATHOLIC CHURCH; UNITED NATIONS.)   (K. M. S.)

BIBLIOGRAPHY. Christine Hotchkiss, *Home to Poland* (New York, 1958); M. K. Dziewanowski, *The Communist Party of Poland* (Cambridge, Massachusetts, 1959); Frank Gibney, *The Frozen Revolution; Poland: A Study in Communist Decay* (New York, 1959); K. S. Karol, *Visa for Poland* (London, 1959); Stefan Korboński, *Warsaw in Chains* (London, 1959); Flora Lewis, *The Polish Volcano* (London, 1959).

POLICE. England and Wales. The year 1959 was one in which increases in the volume of crime and of road traffic imposed a substantial additional burden on the police. To offset this burden, the police forces of England and Wales increased in numbers over the year and at the end of 1959 the number of policemen was 70,155 and policewomen 2,338. Some part of the increase in strength stemmed from the improvement of the situation in Cyprus, following which the police officers serving there in support of the local police began to return to their home forces. Despite the over-all increase in strength, there was continuing difficulty in attracting and retaining an adequate number of recruits of good standard in the cities and large towns. The increase in the mechanization of the police and in their use of radio only partly offset the effects of the shortage of manpower.

There were no major changes in police conditions of service. During the year the Police Council for Great Britain reached agreement on claims for increases in rates of refreshment, subsistence and lodging allowances, and in the pay of station sergeants of the Metropolitan police; for changes in the basis of calculation of overtime payment and of overtime incurred on casual escort duty; and for a revision of the scale of issue of uniform. Agreement was also reached on new scales of pay, to take effect from April 25, 1958, for chief officers of police; these were consequential on pay increases from that date which had previously been granted to the lower ranks of the police service.

The Police Federation act, 1959, removed the restrictions placed by the Police act, 1919, on the dates of elections and annual meetings of the Police federation, which is the representative organization for police officers up to and including the rank of chief inspector. The annual conference which would otherwise have been held in Nov. 1959, was consequently postponed until 1960.

A new development in the field of criminal investigation was the establishment at the headquarters of the Cardiff city police of a regional criminal record office to serve police forces in Wales, and of a similar office at the headquarters of the Durham constabulary to serve forces in northeastern England. This made a total of eight such offices in addition to the Criminal Record office at New Scotland yard, each containing records relating to criminals who have some connection with the region. These offices were established to facilitate crime detection by enabling detectives in the field to consult quickly the records of criminals and crimes committed in the region. A further object was to make it possible to reduce the number

(Left) A City of London police constable, touring north America for the British Travel and Holiday association, is shown New York by a U.S. colleague. (Right) The entrance to the new police station at Ampthill, Beds. Within, air-conditioned cells have hot and cold water.

of records to be kept by individual forces and so to enable detectives to devote more of their time to actual investigation.

In view of the increased number of police forces making use of dogs for police work and the shortage of suitable dogs in Great Britain, the Metropolitan police decided to import a limited number of dogs from the continent and breed from them. In this way the breeding and general standards of police dogs in this country would gradually be improved. Steps were also being taken to improve the training of dogs and their handlers.

The decision of the Nottingham Watch committee to suspend from duty the chief constable of the city, Capt. Athelstan Popkess, following his refusal on grounds of principle to furnish them with a report for which they had asked, led to much controversy and the intervention of the home secretary. The Watch committee subsequently lifted the suspension.

On Dec. 16, a royal commission was appointed with Sir Henry Willink as chairman to review the constitutional position of the police and police administration, and in particular:

the constitution and functions of local police authorities; the status and accountability of members of police forces including chief officers of police; the relationship of the police with the public and the means of ensuring that complaints by the public against the police are effectively dealt with; and the broad principles which should govern the remuneration of the constable, having regard to the nature and extent of police duties and responsibilities and the need to attract and retain an adequate number of recruits with the proper qualifications.

Scotland. The strength of the 33 Scottish forces rose from 8,226 men and 248 women at the beginning of Jan. 1959, to 8,366 men and 268 women in October, and the authorized establishments increased by 63 men and 8 policewomen. Recruits comprised 546 men and 49 women, compared with 521 and 35 respectively in the first ten months of 1958. Vacancies fell from 524 to 407 for men and from 30 to 15 for women. Police cadets increased from 154 to 156. On Oct. 31 the special constabulary numbered 7,915 (including 141 women), but was still substantially below establishment.

Initial training courses for recruits and second-year refresher courses continued at the junior division of the Scottish Police college. At the senior division in Tulliallan castle two six-month courses for sergeants and four three-month courses for inspectors were held. A new extension at Tulliallan was expected to be completed in mid-1960, thus providing permanent accommodation for the junior division.

About 4,600 policemen occupied houses provided by police authorities. Some 3,100 houses have been built since World War II and about 250 were under construction at the end of 1959. Progress was made in building new stations and modernizing existing stations.

Commonwealth. At the end of 1958, the number of full-time policemen in Australia totalled 13,044 and policewomen 165, excluding trainees, reserves and native trackers. In Canada, on Nov. 1, 1958, the Royal Canadian Mounted police numbered 7,001, provincial police in Ontario and Quebec totalled *c.* 2,550 in 1956, and municipal police 10,757 in 1955. Full-time policemen in New Zealand on March 31, 1959, numbered 2,389, and policewomen 48. In South Africa there were 21,808 policemen and women on Sept. 30, 1956, including 10,939 whites, 9,737 natives, 840 coloured and 292 Indians.

United States. During the 1950s the increase in crime frequency in the United States was four times more rapid than the increase of population, and during 1958 it was five times more rapid. There was no evidence of growing police inefficiency that could explain the rapidly increasing crime rate and neither could it be accounted for by a sudden decrease in police strength. In fact, the number of police department employees per 1,000 inhabitants increased from 1·7 in 1951 to 1·8 in 1958. The increases were found principally in cities over 500,000 inhabitants (from 2·2 to 2·4 employees per 1,000 population) and in cities of less than 10,000 population (from 1·2 to 1·3).

During the 1950s police standards were raised in a number of respects. By 1959 the formal educational background of the police was higher than at any other time in U.S. history; the police were participating in more extensive and continuous in-service training, and they were better equipped with communications and transport, and with scientific crime detection equipment than ever before. These developments should have increased police effectiveness, but in spite of them the crime rate continued to rise. (*See* also CRIME; JUVENILE DELINQUENCY; PRISONS.)

(W. H. C.; J. AN.; X.; O. W. W.)

POLITICAL PARTIES, BRITISH: *see* CONSERVATIVE PARTY; LABOUR PARTY; LIBERAL PARTY.

POLITICAL PARTIES, COMMONWEALTH.

Under this heading are recorded the activities in 1959 of the main political parties in the sovereign countries of the Commonwealth of Nations, with the exception of the parties of the United Kingdom to which special entries are devoted.

Conservative. On Oct. 14 quinquennial regional elections were held in the four provinces of the Union of South Africa. The result was disappointing for the ruling Nationalist party led by Hendrik F. Verwoerd, the prime minister. The Nationalists had two advantages: the opposition United party was split and the extension of the franchise to 18-year-olds had secured the enrolment of 130,000 new voters. Yet they received in all four provinces only 305,778 votes against a total anti-government poll of 322,827. Making a cautious allowance for the distribution of votes in the uncontested seats, the *Cape Times* calculated that if there had been contests in all constituencies the distribution of votes would have been: Nationalists 593,800; United party 598,500; others 27,900. The Nationalists retained their control of the provincial councils in Transvaal (although with a reduced majority), in Orange Free State and in the Cape province, while the United party continued to control Natal.

" Conservative " is a suspect word in India, but a party with a Conservative programme was founded on Aug. 2 in Bombay. It was called Swatantra (" Self Acting " or Freedom) party and its leader was Chakravarti Rajagopalachari. The aging " old fox of Madras ", who was Gandhi's chief confidant after Nehru, and had helped to build the Congress party, said at the Bombay convention that the Swatantra party would " act as a timely brake on the ideological extremism of India's rulers ". It seemed certain that the Nagpur resolution of the Congress party (*see* below) prompted Rajagopalachari to launch his venture. The founders of the new party believed that " democracy and a free economy were as closely linked as dictatorship and state ownership ". N. G. Ranga, a member of the Lok Sabha (People's Assembly), who had recently resigned from the Congress party, was elected chairman of the new party. Among its principal sponsors were: M. R. Masani, a former member of the All-India Congress committee; M. A. Venkata Rao, an active member of the Jan Sangh (People's Rally, a right-wing party); Bhailalbhai Patel, former vice-chancellor of the Vallabh Vidyanagar university (Anand); and V. P. Menon, a former governor of Orissa.

Liberal. On Nov. 13, 1959, at a congress in Johannesburg attended by 400 delegates, the Progressive party, a truly Liberal party in the European sense of the word, was formally established in the Union of South Africa. Any person over the age of 18 who supported the party's principles would be considered for membership. The party based itself on the following six principles:

(1) Maintenance of western civilization, protection of fundamental human rights and safeguarding of the dignity and worth of the human being, irrespective of race, colour or creed.

(2) No citizen of the Union of South Africa to be debarred on grounds of race, religion, language, or sex from making the contribution to the national life of which he or she may be capable.

(3) Recognition that in South Africa there is one nation which embraces various groups differing in race, religion, language and traditions; that each group is essential to protection of these things and to its share in the government; and that understanding, tolerance and good will must be fostered among the different groups.

(4) Maintenance of the rule of law.

(5) Promotion of social progress and improvement of living standards through energetic development of a modern economy based on free enterprise whereby the national resources of men and materials can be fully used.

(6) Promotion of friendly relations with other countries, particularly members of the Commonwealth and those who share the heritage of western civilization.

Jan van Aswegen Steytler, born in 1910, the son of a farmer and Boer War veteran, was elected leader of the new party; Harry G. Lawrence was elected chairman and parliamentary leader. The party had 12 members in the House of Assembly, all former members of the United party formed during World War II by Field Marshal Jan C. Smuts and led since 1951 by Sir de Villiers Graaff. Prominent among the 12 " rebels " were Sidney Waterson, Ray Swart, Clive van Ryneveld, Zac De Beer, John Cope, Colin Eglin, Professor I. S. Fourie and

TABLE I. CONSERVATIVE PARLIAMENTARY REPRESENTATION IN THE COMMONWEALTH

(Figures in parenthesis in this and following tables are those of the preceding election)

Country	Party's official name	Date of last election	Votes obtained	% of total votes	Party's seats	Total no. of seats
AUSTRALIA	Australian Country party	Nov. 22, 1958	... (332,906)	... (7·6)	19 (18)	124
CANADA	Progressive-Conservative party	March 31, 1958	3,738,522 (2,378,632)	53·6 (38·6)	208 (113)	265
CEYLON	United National party	April 5-10, 1956	737,447 (990,475)	... ...	8 (54)	95
NEW ZEALAND	National party	Nov. 30, 1957	511,699 (481,056)	44·1 (43·7)	39 (43)	80
SOUTH AFRICA	{National party	April 16, 1958	{ 642,069 (600,446)	55·3 (49·2)	103 (94)}	163 (159)
	United party}		{ 503,639 (576,074)	43·4 (47·2)	53 (57)}	

TABLE II. LIBERAL PARLIAMENTARY REPRESENTATION IN THE COMMONWEALTH

Country	Party's official name	Date of last election	Votes obtained	% of total votes	Party's seats	Total no. of seats
AUSTRALIA	Liberal Party of Australia	Nov. 22, 1958	... (1,753,602)	... (40·0)	58 (57)	124
CANADA	Liberal party	March 31, 1958	2,316,322 (2,509,998)	33·3 (40·7)	49 (106)	265
CEYLON	People's United front*	April 5-10, 1956	1,045,725 (378,104)	... ...	51 (10)	95
INDIA	Indian National Congress	Feb. 24-March 14, 1957	57,278,612 (47,528,911)	48·1 (44·0)	369 (332)	494 (489)

* Mahajana Eksath Peramuna, a coalition of Sri Lanka Midahas Pakshaya (Blessed Ceylon Freedom party) and two other groups.

TABLE III. LABOUR PARLIAMENTARY REPRESENTATION IN THE COMMONWEALTH

Country	Party's official name	Date of last election	Votes obtained	% of total votes	Party's seats	Total no. of seats
AUSTRALIA	Australian Labour party	Nov. 22, 1958	1,912,222 (1,958,592)	42·0 (44·7)	45 (48)	124
CANADA	Co-operative Commonwealth fed.	March 31, 1958	671,736 (676,868)	9·7 (10·9)	8 (25)	265
INDIA	Praja-Socialist party	Feb. 24-March 14, 1957	11,642,726 (17,285,126*)	9·8 (16·3)	21 (21)	494 (489)
NEW ZEALAND	Labour party	Nov. 30, 1957	559,096 (484,634)	48·2 (44·1)	41 (37)	80
SOUTH AFRICA	South African Labour party	April 16, 1958	2,670 (39,157)	0·2 (3·5)	0 (4)	613 (159)

* At the previous election (from Oct. 25, 1951, to Feb. 21, 1952) there was a coalition of the Socialist and Kisan Mazdur Praja (Peasants' and Workers' party). The Praja-Socialist party was the result of their fusion.

NOTE. No special table for the Communist parliamentary representation in the Commonwealth was necessary as only in India was the Communist party a political force. At the 1957 general election it obtained 12,068,452 (10·15%) votes and gained 27 seats, compared with 4,712,009 (4·45%) votes and 23 seats at the 1951-52 election.

Mrs. Helen Suzman. Harry Oppenheimer, the mining magnate and former M.P., also resigned from the United party and announced his general sympathy with the Progressives. The new party opposed the Nationalist party policy of creating " Bantustans " or separate African regions. It remained to be seen how much electoral support the Progressives could command among the notoriously Conservative white electorate. To be labelled " Liberal " was politically derogatory in South Africa.

The Liberal government of the Canadian province of Newfoundland, led by Joseph R. Smallwood, was returned to power in an election on Aug. 20. The Liberals won 31 of the 36 seats of the provincial legislature. It was their fourth successive victory since Newfoundland became part of Canada in 1949.

Labour. The Australian Labour party led by Herbert V. Evatt was in 1954 in power in every state except South Australia. It lost Victoria in 1955 and Queensland in 1957. At the state election on March 21, 1959, it also lost Western Australia. Its majority in New South Wales was cut to two seats and in Tasmania to one.

A meeting of some 300 delegates of the Canadian Labour congress (the equivalent of the British T.U.C.) and of the Co-operative Commonwealth federation (the equivalent of the British Labour party) was held in Winnipeg at the end of August. It planned to organize a new Canadian left-wing party which would be fully prepared to fight the next general election due in 1962 or 1963. Stanley Knowles, former vice president of the C.C.F. and now vice president of the C.L.C., predicted that Canada would follow the British rather than the U.S. political pattern with trade unions throwing their support behind the new party. Although the Winnipeg meeting did not formulate in detail the new party policy it seemed certain that the old C.L.C. nationalization programme would be toned down, although a report on public ownership favoured nationalization of the Canadian banks. The new party would also back long-term planning.

The 61st annual convention of the Indian Congress party was held at Nagpur from Jan 9 to 11. About 10,000 delegates representing 8 million members were present. It adopted by an overwhelming show of hands a resolution committing the party to a programme of bigger and bolder economic planning. The goal it set was " a democratic and Socialist society." The resolution, prepared and defended by Jawaharlal Nehru, the prime minister and party leader, satisfied neither the left nor the right wing of the party. Among others, it recommended " joint co-operative farming " and a state monopoly in the wholesale trade in food grains. U. N. Dhebar, who had been president of the party since 1954, resigned. He was succeeded by Mrs. Indira Gandhi, Nehru's daughter.

(K. M. S.)

POLITICAL PARTIES, EUROPEAN.

Under this heading are recorded the national and international activities in 1959 of the main political parties of Europe. For the Communist parties *see* COMMUNIST MOVEMENT.

Conservative. Because of the electoral system, by which members of the French Senate are elected by 108,266 electors (deputies, councillors of the *départements* and delegates of the municipal councils), right-wing Independents slightly increased their strength in the elections of April 26. Out of a total of 307 senators, they obtained 73 seats. On Nov. 26, the central committee of the Centre National des Indépendants et Paysans elected its new executive committee (bureau). Senator Roger Duchet was re-elected secretary-general.

The new Gaullist party, the Union pour la Nouvelle République, held from Nov. 13 to 15 its first national congress in Bordeaux. A deep though officially unavowed split appeared among the 1,800 delegates. The congress was marked by the sharp rivalry between Jacques Soustelle, minister-delegate for Sahara and champion of Algerian integration or *francisation* (rejected by General Charles de Gaulle in his statement of Sept. 16), and Albin Chalandon, the young left-of-centre secretary-general of the party, an opponent of old-fashioned conservatism, and supporter of the *association* formula which de Gaulle favoured. The party unity was saved for the time being by a resolution calling " for a close union between metropolitan France and Algeria in freedom, equality and fraternity ". A new central committee was elected composed of 12 ministers, 19 deputies, 6 senators and 25 *militants*. Michel Debré, the prime minister, was *de jure* party leader. As Chalandon refused to continue as secretary-general, he was succeeded by Senator Jacques Richard.

In Italy, the two monarchist parties, the Partito Monarchico Nazionale (led by Alfredo Covelli) and the Partito Monarchico Popolare (led by Achille Lauro), which split in 1954, decided on April 11, 1959, to merge again under the name of Partito Democratico Italiano. The decision was reached after talks in Paris with ex-King Umberto. The reunited party had 24 seats in the Chamber of Deputies and 7 in the Senate. It supported the government of Antonio Segni.

Peasant. The 3rd congress of the Polish United Peasant party was held in Warsaw from Nov. 27 to 30. Addressing the 995 delegates, Stefan Ignar, chairman of the party's supreme committee, reported that membership was 233,000 compared with 210,000 at the time of the 2nd congress in March 1956. He defined the U.P.P. as a " Socialist-type " party. As such it encouraged Polish peasants to join voluntarily " agricultural circles " or, better still, to form new producers' co-operatives, because only through collective efforts would Polish peasantry be able to produce more food for the rapidly growing urban population. Józef Ożga-Michalski, deputy chairman of the supreme committee, stated that in 4,700 villages where party basic organizations existed there were so far no agricultural circles. The congress was also addressed by Władysław Gomułka, first secretary of the Polish United Workers' (Communist) party, who said that the existing 22,000 agricultural circles grouping together 600,000 peasant farms were a sufficient basis to start co-operative mechanization of Polish agriculture and modernization of farming methods. Fraternal delegates from the Bulgarian, Czechoslovak and German Democratic Peasant parties also spoke. The congress elected a new supreme committee which nominated a new presidium. Ignar was re-elected chairman and Józef Ożga-Michalski, Bolesław Podedworny and Czesław Wycech deputy chairmen.

The 6th congress of the International Peasant union, grouping representatives of the 12 Peasant parties of eastern Europe in exile, assembled in Washington, D.C., from May 30 to 31. Stanisław Mikołajczyk (Poland) was re-elected president and Georgi M. Dimitrov (Bulgaria) secretary-general of the I.P.U.

Christian Democratic. The 7th congress of the Italian Partito Democratico Cristiano was held in Florence from Oct. 23 to 28. Seven hundred and four delegates, representing 1·6 million card-holding members, were present. Two main conflicting ideologies divided the party: a left-wing tendency towards an *iniziativa democratica*, that is a political alliance of Christian Democrats and Socialists, and a right-wing trend looking for political allies on the right. Amintore Fanfani was the leader of the former group and at the beginning of the year seemed to be the unchallenged leader of the party, but a section of his supporters, led by Antonio Segni, decided to support the conservative wing. Fanfani had to resign (Jan. 26) and was succeeded as prime minister by Segni. He also resigned as the party's secretary-general and on March 17 a supporter of Segni, Aldo Mori, was elected to that post by the

112-man national council. In Florence, however, open split was avoided. The membership of the national council was brought up to 144. Segni was able to count on three-fifths of the national council membership. But while Fanfani could rely on the remaining two-fifths, the Segni majority was composed of the centre group and of at least three right-wing groups led respectively by Giulio Andreotti (who led the so-called *primavera* faction), and by Giuseppe Pella and Mario Scelba. The congress re-elected Mori as party secretary-general.

On Nov. 19 the new national council met in Rome to elect a 20-man party executive committee. Fanfani and four of his supporters joined the executive. Of these Adone Zoli was re-elected chairman of the executive, while Renato Branzi was re-elected administrative secretary. Another *fanfanista*, Ettore Bernabei, was made deputy editor of *Il Popolo*, the party daily newspaper, of which he was previously the editor.

In the Austrian general election the People's (Christian Democratic) party saw its popular vote reduced from 46% to 42% and the number of its seats from 82 to 79 in a 165-member parliament.

On May 28-30 the 13th congress of the Nouvelles Equipes Internationales was held at Freiburg, German Federal Republic. About 400 parliamentarian and political leaders of 15 western European countries were present, as well as delegates of Polish, Czechoslovak, Hungarian and Rumanian Christian Democratic groups in exile. Auguste De Schrijver (Belgium) and Paul Coste-Floret (France) were re-elected respectively president and secretary-general of the organization.

Liberal. The western German Free Democratic party continued in opposition to the Christian Democratic union. In the *Länder* elections in Lower Saxony (April 19, 1959), Rhineland-Palatinate (April 19) and Bremen (Oct. 11) the F.D.P.'s percentage of the vote fell from 7·9%, 12·7% and 8·6% to 5·2%, 9·7% and 7·1% respectively.

Divisions within the French Radical ranks between Mendesistes and " anti-Mendesistes " grew deeper during the year 1959. In the Senate elections (April 26), the various Radical sections were reduced from 74 to 58.

In Luxembourg (Feb. 1) the Liberals increased their parliamentary strength from 6 to 11 in the elections of Feb. 1, against 21 members of the Christian Social party and 17 Socialists.

The Netherlands' Liberals (Party for Freedom in Democracy) increased (March 12) their seats from 13 to 19, with 230,627 additional votes.

In Switzerland the Radicals in the elections of Oct. 25 gained equal strength (51) with the Socialists in the National Council (Lower House).

The Liberal International's ninth congress met at Gardone, Italy (Oct. 1-4). The programme (a free economy in a free society) was approved, together with a resolution supporting the World Refugee Year. Approval was also given to the special working party's proposals for bringing the members of the European Economic community and the European Free

TABLE I. CONSERVATIVE PARLIAMENTARY REPRESENTATION IN EUROPE*
(Figures in brackets in this and following table are those of the preceding election)

Country	Party corresponding to Conservative	Date of last election	Votes obtained	% of total votes	Conservatives' seats	Total no. of seats
DENMARK . .	Konservative Folkepartiet	May 14, 1957	383,918 (364,960)	16·6 (16·8)	30 (30)	175
FINLAND . .	Kansallinin Kokoomus Poulue	July 6-7, 1958	288,327 (239,412)	15·61 (12·8)	29 (24)	200
FRANCE . .	Gaullists† / Conservatives‡	Nov. 23-30, 1958	3,603,958 (948,854) / 4,092,600 (3,086,414)	17·6 (4·4) / 19·9 (14·3)	188 (16) / 132 (95)	465 (541)
GERMAN FED. REP.	Deutsche Partei / Gesamtdeutscher Block§	Sept. 15, 1957	1,007,286 (896,128) / 1,374,066 (1,616,953)	3·4 (3·3) / 4·6 (5·9)	17 (15) / 0 (27)	497 (487)
GREAT BRITAIN .	Conservative party	Oct. 8, 1959	13,730,849 (13,311,938)	49·3 (49·8)	365 (345)	630
GREECE .	National Radical union	May 11, 1958	1,578,513 (1,595,946)	41·2 (47·4)	172 (165)	300
ICELAND .	Sjálfstaedis Flokkurin	Oct. 25-26, 1959	33,798 (36,029)	39·7 (42·6)	24 (20)	60 (52)
ITALY . . .	Partito Monarchico Italiano	May 25-26, 1958	1,436,916‖ (1,856,661)	4·8 (6·9)	25 (40)	596 (590)
NETHERLANDS	Anti-Revolutionaire Partij / Christelijk Historische Unie	March 12, 1959	562,996 (567,517) / 486,204 (482,848)	9·4 (9·9) / 8·1 (8·3)	14 (15) / 12 (13)	150
NORWAY .	Høyre	Oct. 7, 1957	300,306 (325,885)	16·9 (16·6)	29 (27)	150
SWEDEN .	Högerpartiet	June 1, 1958	693,747 (663,693)	18·7 (17·1)	45 (42)	231
SWITZERLAND .	Liberal Conservative party	Oct. 25, 1959	... ...	... ...	5 (5)	196
TURKEY . .	Cumhuriyet Halk Partisi / Cumhuriyetçi Millet Partisi	Oct. 27, 1957	3,689,000 (3,193,471) / 793,000 (480,249)	40·1 (35·1) / 8·6 (5·3)	178 (31) / 4 (5)	610 (541)

* Only self-avowed or well-defined Conservative parties of European countries having a parliamentary system and free election are included. Neo-Nazi and Neo-Fascist parties, like the German Reichspartei, Austrian Freiheitliche Partei, the Movimento Sociale Italiano or the French Poujade movement are not listed. † Union pour la Nouvelle République. ‡ An electoral alliance of Independents and Peasants. § The Refugee party. ‖ Total for the National and Popular Monarchist parties.

TABLE II. PEASANTS' PARLIAMENTARY REPRESENTATION IN WESTERN EUROPE*

Country	Party corresponding to a Peasant party	Date of last election	Votes obtained	% of total vote	Peasants' seats	Total no. of seats
DENMARK . .	Venstre	May 14, 1957	578,500 (499,656)	25·0 (23·1)	45 (42)	175
FINLAND . .	Maalaisliitto	July 6-7, 1958	445,536 (470,063)	23·06 (24·10)	48 (53)	200
ICELAND .	Framsoknarflokkurin	Oct. 25-26, 1959	21,854 (23,062)	25·7 (27·3)	17 (19)	60 (52)
NORWAY .	Bondepartiet	Oct. 7, 1957	154,392 (156,315)	8·7 (8·4)	15 (14)	150
SWEDEN .	Bondeförbundet	June 1, 1958	480,892 (366,612)	13·0 (9·5)	32 (19)	231
SWITZERLAND .	Peasants' and Artisans' party	Oct. 25, 1959	... ...	... ...	23 (22)	196

* At the 1946, 1951, 1956 and 1958 elections the French Peasant party went to the polls in an alliance with the Independents (Conservatives).

TABLE III. CHRISTIAN DEMOCRATIC PARLIAMENTARY REPRESENTATION IN EUROPE

Country	Party corresponding to Christian Democratic	Date of last election	Votes obtained	% of total votes	C.D.'s seats	Total no. of seats.
AUSTRIA . .	Österreichische Volkspartei	May 10, 1959	1,927,690 (1,999,986)	42·0 (46·0)	79 (82)	165
BELGIUM . .	Parti Social-Chrétien	June 1, 1958	2,464,924 (2,123,408)	46·50 (41·98)	104 (96)	212
FRANCE . .	Mouvement Républicain Populaire*	Nov. 23-30, 1958	2,378,788 (2,374,221)	11·6 (11·0)	57 (71)	465 (541)
GERMAN FED. REP.	Christlich-Demokratische Union	Sept. 15, 1957	13,008,399 (12,433,981)	50·2 (45·2)	270 (243)	497 (487)
ITALY . . .	Partito Democratico Cristiano	May 25-26, 1958	12,520,207 (10,884,508)	42·4 (40·0)	273 (264)	596 (590)
LUXEMBOURG .	Parti Social-Chrétien	Feb. 1, 1959	... ...	... ...	21 (26)	52
NETHERLANDS .	Katholieke Volkspartij	March 12, 1959	1,895,222 (1,815,242)	31·6 (31·9)	49 (49)	150
NORWAY .	Christian People's party	Oct. 7, 1957	182,162 (186,090)	10·2 (10·4)	12 (14)	150
SWITZERLAND .	Catholic Conservative party	Oct. 25, 1959	... ...	... ...	47 (47)	196

* The 1958 figures include the votes and seats obtained by Georges Bidault's Démocratie Chrétienne de France.

TABLE IV. LIBERAL PARLIAMENTARY REPRESENTATION IN EUROPE

Country	Party corresponding to Liberal	Date of last election	Votes obtained	% of total votes	Liberals' seats	Total no. of seats
BELGIUM	Parti Libéral	June 1, 1958	585,620 (661,932)	11·05 (12·15)	21 (25)	212
DENMARK	Radikale Venstre*	May 14, 1957	179,568 (169,295)	7·8 (7·8)	14 (14)	175
FINLAND	Kansanpuolue	July 6-7, 1958	113,691 (148,438)	5·90 (7·88)	8 (13)	200
FRANCE	Radicals†	Nov. 23-30, 1958	2,347,989 (2,876,398)	11·5 (13·3)	35 (74)	465 (541)
GERMAN FED. REP.	Freie Demokratische Partei	Sept. 15, 1957	2,307,135 (2,629,163)	7·7 (9·5)	41 (48)	497 (487)
GREAT BRITAIN	Liberal party‡	Oct. 8, 1959	1,661,262 (722,395)	6·0 (2·7)	6 (6)	630
GREECE	Liberal party	May 11, 1958	793,831 ...	20·7 ...	36 (65)	300
ITALY	Partito Liberale Italiano	May 25-26, 1958	1,047,081 (815,681)	3·5 (3·0)	17 (13)	596 (590)
LUXEMBOURG	Parti Libéral	Feb. 1, 1959	... ...	... ...	11 (6)	52
NETHERLANDS	Volkspartij vor Vrijheid	March 12, 1959	732,952 (502,325)	12·2 (8·8)	19 (13)	150
NORWAY	Venstre	Oct. 7, 1957	170,372 (176,778)	9·6 (9·9)	15 (15)	150
SWEDEN	Folkpartiet	June 1, 1958	669,763 (923,564)	18·0 (23·8)	38 (58)	231
SWITZERLAND	{Freisinnig-Demokratische Partei / Parti Démocratique}	Oct. 25, 1959	... ...	... ...	{51 (50) / 4 (4)}	196
TURKEY	Demokrat Partisi	Oct. 27, 1957	4,000,000 (5,313,695)	48·0 (58·4)	424 (503)	610 (541)

* There is also the Retsforbundet or Justice party, sometimes described as right-wing liberal, which in May 1957 polled 122,629 votes (5·3% of the total) and obtained 9 seats. † The Parti Républicain Radical et Radical-Socialiste, the Rassemblement des Gauches Républicaines and two dissident groups. ‡ In 1959 the Liberal party presented 217 candidates compared with 110 in 1955.

TABLE V. SOCIALIST PARLIAMENTARY REPRESENTATION IN WESTERN EUROPE

Country	Party's official name	Date of last election	Votes obtained	% of total votes	Socialists' seats	Total no. of seats
AUSTRIA	Sozialistische Partei Österreichs	May 10, 1959	1,953,566 (1,873,295)	46·0 (43·0)	78 (74)	165
BELGIUM	Parti Socialiste Belge	June 1, 1958	1,897,303 (2,000,241)	35·79 (37·34)	84 (86)	212
DENMARK	Socialdemokratiet	May 14, 1957	910,862 (894,913)	39·4 (41·3)	70 (74)	175
FINLAND	Socialidemokraattinen Poulue	July 6-7, 1958	445,591* (511,043)	23·11 (26·25)	48 (54)	200
FRANCE	Parti Socialiste (S.F.I.O.†)	Nov. 23-30, 1958	3,167,354 (3,180,656)	15·5 (14·8)	40 (88)	465 (541)
GERMAN FED. REP.	Soz.-dem. Partei Deutschlands	Sept. 15, 1957	9,495,571 (7,944,943)	31·8 (28·8)	169 (151)	497 (487)
GREAT BRITAIN	Labour Party	Oct. 8, 1959	12,151,395 (12,405,246)	43·6 (46·4)	258 (277)	630
ICELAND	Althýduflokkur	Oct. 25-26, 1959	12,910 (10,472)	15·2 (12·4)	9 (6)	60 (52)
IRELAND, REP. OF	Labour party	March 5, 1957	111,748 (161,034)	... ...	12 (19)	147
ITALY	{Partito Soc.-Dem. Italiano / Partito Socialista Italiano}	May 25-26, 1958	{1,345,447 (1,223,870) / 4,206,726 (3,440,222)}	{4·5 (4·5) / 14·2 (12·7)}	{22 (19) / 84 (75)}	596 (590)
LUXEMBOURG	Parti Ouvrier Socialiste	Feb. 1, 1959	... ...	... ...	17 (17)	52
NETHERLANDS	Partij van de Arbeid	March 12, 1959	1,821,677 (1,871,990)	30·4 (32·8)	48 (50)	150
NORWAY	De Norske Arbeiderparti	Oct. 7, 1957	860,624 (827,491)	48·3 (46·6)	78 (77)	150
SWEDEN	Soc.-Dem. Arbetarepartiet	June 1, 1958	1,738,765 (1,729,463)	46·9 (44·6)	111 (106)	231
SWITZERLAND	Sozial-Demokratische Partei‡	Oct. 25, 1959	... ...	... ...	51 (53)	196

* Excluding 33,555 votes and 3 seats obtained by the Independent Socialist party. † S.F.I.O. stands for Section Française de l'Internationale Ouvrière. ‡ Fr. Parti Socialiste Suisse, It. Partito Socialista Svizzero.

TABLE VI. COMMUNIST PARLIAMENTARY REPRESENTATION IN WESTERN EUROPE

Country	Party's official name	Date of last election	Votes obtained	% of total votes	Communists' seats	Total no. of seats
AUSTRIA	Kommunistische Partei Österreichs	May 10, 1959	142,598 (192,438)	3·0 (4·5)	0 (3)	165
BELGIUM	Parti Communiste Belge	June 1, 1958	100,113 (184,108)	1·98 (3·57)	2 (4)	212
DENMARK	Danmarks Kommunistiske Parti	May 14, 1957	73,310 (93,824)	3·2 (4·3)	6 (8)	175
FINLAND	S.K.D.L.*	July 6-7, 1958	445,832 (417,276)	23·17 (21·59)	50 (43)	200
FRANCE	Parti Communiste Français	Nov. 23-30, 1958	3,882,204 (5,532,631)	18·9 (25·7)	10 (145)	465 (541)
GERMAN FED. REP.	Komm. Partei Deutschlands†	Sept. 15, 1957	— (607,413)	— (2·2)	0 (0)	497 (487)
GREAT BRITAIN	Communist Party of Great Britain‡	Oct. 8, 1959	30,897 (33,144)	0·11 (0·12)	0 (0)	630
GREECE	Enosis Dimokratikis Aristeras§	May 11, 1958	934,842 ...	24·3 ...	79 (18)	300
ICELAND	S.A.S.||	Oct. 25-26, 1959	13,621 (12,929)	16·0 (15·3)	10 (7)	60 (52)
ITALY	Partito Communista Italiano	May 25-26, 1958	6,704,454 (6,122,638)	22·7 (22·6)	140 (143)	596 (590)
LUXEMBOURG	Parti Communiste Luxembourgeois	Feb. 1, 1959	... ...	... ...	3 (3)	52
NETHERLANDS	Communistische Partij Nederland	March 12, 1959	144,371 (272,167)	2·4 (4·8)	3 (4)	150
NORWAY	Norges Kommunistiske Parti	Oct. 7, 1957	59,920 (89,882)	3·3 (5·1)	1 (3)	150
SWEDEN	Sveriges Kommunistiska Parti	June 1, 1958	127,675 (194,016)	3·4 (5·0)	5 (6)	231
SWITZERLAND	Partei der Arbeit¶	Oct. 25, 1959	... ...	... ...	3 (3)	196

* Suomen Kansan Demokraatinen Liitto or Finland's People's Democratic league (Communists and fellow-travellers). † Name used only in western Germany; the K.P.D. was banned on Aug. 17, 1956, and did not participate in the 1957 election. ‡ There were in 1959 18 Communist candidates, 17 of them losing their deposits. § E.D.A., or Union of the Democratic Left, is a cover name for the banned K.K.E. (Kommunistikon Komma Ellados). || Sameingarflokkur Althýda Socialistaflokkurin or United People's Socialist party. ¶ Fr. Parti du Travail, It. Partito del Lavoro.

Trade association into a liberal economic grouping. Nineteen countries were represented, and plans were made for increasing direct political action by the Liberal International and for extending its work to areas where, as yet, no Liberal movement existed. Salvador de Madariaga continued to serve as president of honour and Giovanni Malagodi as president.

Socialist. In Dec. 1958 the Icelandic Social Democrats broke their coalition with the Independence (Conservative) party but agreed to form a minority caretaker government to undertake electoral amendment of the constitution. The process required two general elections. At the first, on June 28, 1959, Social Democratic strength dropped from 8 to 6 in a house of 52 seats. At the second, on Oct. 25-26, it rose from 6 to 9 in a reconstituted house of 60 seats. The Social Democratic poll increased by 2·8%. They formed a new coalition government with the Independence party.

In Feb. 1959 the Italian Social Democrats ended their coalition government with the Christian Democrats who formed a minority government.

The Luxembourg Socialists retained their 17 seats in the Feb. 1 election but were replaced by the Liberals in the coalition government.

The Dutch Labour party obtained 48 seats in the March 12 election, a loss of two. It refused to resume coalition with the Catholics (49 seats) who formed a coalition with the Liberals (19 seats).

Austrian Socialist strength rose from 74 to 78 in the May 10 general election. The party remained in coalition with the People's party (79 seats).

At the Swiss election on Oct. 25 Socialists and Radicals

A view of the platform during the sixth congress of the Socialist International, held in Hamburg, western Germany, on July 14-17.

tied with 51 seats each, the Socialists losing two seats and their former position as the strongest party.

The western German Social Democrats registered considerable gains in regional elections. In Lower Saxony (April 19) their strength rose from 57 to 65 seats and their popular vote from 35·2% to 39·5%. On Oct. 11, they captured nine new seats in Bremen where, with 61 seats out of 100, they obtained an absolute majority.

In France there were no indications of reunification between the official Socialist party and the Autonomous Socialist party (formed in Sept. 1958 after disagreements over support for de Gaulle in the constitutional referendum). (*See* also COMMUNIST MOVEMENT; ELECTIONS.) (K.M.S.; D.MN.; J.F.CK.)

POLITICAL SECURITY.

Under this heading are grouped summaries of legislation, official rules and major incidents relating to espionage and counter-espionage.

U.S.S.R.-United States. A report published on Jan. 4, 1959, by the U.S. House of Representatives Committee on Un-American Activities, said that the Soviet spy network in the United States operated " largely through diplomatic cover ". The report gave a warning against the " dangerous tendency " to underestimate the threat Soviet spying presented to the United States' security. It recommended an immediate review of all laws and policies governing the admission of foreign diplomats and also a study of possible grounds for revoking diplomatic status.

The Times Washington correspondent reported on Oct. 6 a " joke " made by N. S. Khrushchev during his tour of the United States. When Allen W. Dulles, director of the U.S. Central Intelligence agency, was introduced to him, Khrushchev said that they both were reading the same reports, sometimes from the same people. Khrushchev suggested that they should pool their intelligence networks so that they " don't have to pay twice for the same information ".

On Oct. 16, Russell A. Langelle, the U.S. embassy security officer, was forcibly abducted in a Moscow street and subjected to blackmail and threats of violence. When he refused to converse with his captors he was released. The following day Edward L. Freers, U.S. chargé d'affaires, delivered a strong protest against such a " flagrant violation of diplomatic immunity ". At the time of delivery of the note, the deputy chief of the U.S. section at the Ministry of Foreign Affairs of the U.S.S.R. stated to Freers that " competent " Soviet authorities had informed the ministry Langelle had used his stay in the Soviet Union to carry out intelligence work not compatible with his diplomatic status and that the Soviet government considered Langelle's further stay in the U.S.S.R. undesirable. On Oct. 19 a Soviet statement said that Langelle was caught " red-handed " giving Rb.20,000 for espionage purposes to a Soviet citizen aboard a Moscow bus. On the same day Langelle left Moscow. At a news conference held in Washington, on Oct. 26, Langelle said that his job at the U.S. embassy was not to collect any kind of intelligence on the Soviet Union. " There had been many situations," he added, " in which I, as security officer, managed to thwart and circumvent some of their (*i.e.*, Soviet) activities." When asked to elaborate, Langelle replied: " This unfortunately gets into the realm of sensitive activities and security matters, which I prefer not to discuss."

It was believed that General Ivan A. Serov, who on Dec. 8, 1958, had ceased to be chairman of the State Security committee of the council of ministers of the U.S.S.R., was the new head of Soviet military intelligence.

U.S.S.R.-Latin America. On March 31, 1959, the Mexican government ordered the expulsion of Captain Nikolai V. Aksenov, military attaché, and Nikolai M. Remizov, second secretary of the Soviet embassy. Mexico had complained that their behaviour was " not consistent with the democratic regime that Mexico observed ". The government stated that the two diplomats were involved in a national railway strike.

On April 7 the Argentine government ordered four Soviet diplomats to leave the country within 48 hours. They were Nikolai Belov, counsellor of the Soviet embassy in Buenos Aires, Dimitri Diakonov, first secretary, Konstantin Monakhov, cultural attaché, and Vasili Ivashov, commercial attaché. At the same time Alexei Marin, cultural attaché of the Rumanian embassy, was also expelled. This followed a Communist riot on April 3, when a group of 800 tradeunionists withstood security forces for six hours, causing damage estimated at £350,000. The diplomats were said to have intervened " directly and personally " in organizing the riot.

The Two German Republics. On Jan. 22, 1959, a highly unusual refugee from the German Democratic Republic was introduced to German and foreign press correspondents in Bonn—Lieut.-Colonel Siegfried Dombrowski, former deputy chief of the G.D.R. military intelligence or *Verwaltung für Koordinierung* in the eastern German Ministry of Defence. According to Dombrowski, this department worked under supervision of four Soviet army colonels. He named them as Petrov (real name Musatov), Loginov (real name Igonin), Makhumov and Dimitrov. Two other security organizations were the Ministry of State Security and a special department in the Ministry of the Interior. These three networks employed about 60,000 agents and about 12,500 of them worked in western Europe.

On May 16 Captain Max Heim, an official of the eastern German Ministry of State Security, escaped to western Germany. According to Heim, the number of eastern German agents working in the Federal Republic alone amounted to 10,000, including some 2,000 or 3,000 who lived there. At the end of May many arrests of these agents in the Federal Republic were announced in Bonn. Some of the arrested were members of the Christian Democratic union, the party in power in western Germany.

Otto John, former head of the Bundesamt für Verfassungsschutz (Federal Office for the Protection of the Constitution), was refused permission to land at Dover on Feb. 9, 1959. He was described at the Home Office as an undesirable alien.

Klaus Fuchs left London on June 23 to fly to eastern Berlin. He was released from Wakefield prison after serving nine years of a 14-year prison sentence for passing to the U.S.S.R. Britain's nuclear secrets. A German Communist, he had fled to Great Britain from Nazi Germany and took British nationality. He had been chief of the theoretical physics branch of the Atomic Research establishment at Harwell. He was granted citizenship in the German Democratic Republic and his appointment as deputy director of the Central Institute for Atomic Physics was announced in Leipzig at the end of August.

Klaus Fuchs (right) boards an aircraft for eastern Germany at London airport on June 23, the day after his release from prison.

Great Britain-Egypt. James Swinburn, sentenced in June 1957 to a five-year term of imprisonment for being the head of a " dangerous espionage ring of the British intelligence ", was amnestied after serving three years. He arrived in London from Cairo by air on Sept. 22. James Zarb, a Maltese, who received ten years, was still in prison. When Swinburn was asked by reporters if there was any foundation for the charges made against him at the Cairo trial in June 1957, he replied: " That is not a thing on which I am prepared to make any comment."

Czechoslovakia. On Nov. 4, 1959, it was announced in Washington, D.C., that Lieut.-Colonel František Tišler, military attaché at the Czechoslovak embassy there, had asked for asylum in the United States. This was granted.

Poland. Lincoln White, U.S. State Department press officer, confirmed on Nov. 23 that Colonel Paweł Monat, who up to May 1958 had been Polish military attaché in Washington, had applied for asylum in the United States for himself and his family. Recalled from Washington to Warsaw, Monat was believed to be in charge of co-ordinating the work of Polish military attachés all over the world. In mid-1959 he left with his family for a holiday in Yugoslavia, stopped in Vienna and disappeared. His defection embarrassed Władysław Gomułka who in November decided to recall from Prague Brig.-General Kazimierz Witaszewski, a member of the central committee of the Polish United Workers' (Communist) party, and appoint him deputy chief of staff in charge of military intelligence.   (X.)

See Nikolai Khokhlov, *In the Name of Conscience* (New York, 1959); Boris Morros, *My Ten Years as a Counterspy* (London, 1959); Harry H. Ransom, *Central Intelligence and National Security* (New York, 1959).

POPULATIONS: *see* AREAS AND POPULATIONS.

PORTUGAL. Republic of southwestern Europe, forming part of the Iberian peninsula and bounded E. and N. by Spain. Area: 35,415 sq.mi., including Azores (888 sq.mi.) and Madeira (302 sq.mi.). Pop.: (1950 census) 8,441,312, incl. Azores (317,409) and Madeira (266,990); (1958 est.) 8,980,000. Language: Portuguese. Religion: Roman Catholic. Chief towns (pop., 1950 census): Lisbon (cap.) 790,434; Oporto 284,842; Setúbal 44,030; Coimbra 42,640; Funchal (Madeira) 37,215. President of the republic, Rear-Admiral Américo Deus Rodrigues Tomás. Prime minister, António de Oliveira Salazar. Main imports: machinery and vehicles; coal, petroleum and products; steel mill products; raw cotton; wheat. Main exports: cork and manufactures; fish, canned and in brine; cotton fabrics; wine. Monetary unit: *escudo* (Esc.80·00 = £1 sterling).

History. The political climate of the country, adversely affected in 1958 by General Humberto Delgado's disturbing, though unsuccessful, candidature in the presidential election, continued unsettled in 1959. It was notable that both Monarchists and Catholics were among the outspoken critics of the Salazar regime. Although Delgado himself sought asylum in Brazil on April 20, his uninhibited election campaign with its threat to replace Salazar appeared to have heartened the forces of opposition and to have given rise to what was described by the government as a plot to " alter public order ". An official announcement on May 7 by Arnaldo Schultz, minister of the interior, said that the plot had been crushed when 22 civilians and 9 members of the armed forces were arrested. Summing up the history of the plot, the minister stated that " as well as Communist inspiration there was the influence of political fanaticism created by the so-called opposition during the electoral campaign."

In the context of the 1958 election the most significant among a number of amendments to the 1933 constitution approved by the National Assembly on June 18, 1959, was one providing for the election of the president of the republic by an electoral college in place of the former system of election by popular vote. The electoral college would consist of members of the National Assembly and the Corporative Chamber, municipal representatives of each metropolitan district and representatives of the legislative or governing councils of the overseas provinces. Another amendment increased the membership of the National Assembly from 120 to 130.

The public accounts for the year 1958 showed a surplus of Esc.57·18 million; it was the largest for five years, exceeding the estimated surplus by nearly Esc.44 million. For 1959 revenue was estimated at Esc.9,519·6 million, on which a small surplus of Esc.1·8 million only was forecast. The most important change in the composition of revenue was a rise in direct taxes of some Esc.237 million, representing 30% of the total estimated increase over 1958. As a consequence of this change direct and indirect taxation were to be more nearly equalized at Esc.2,281·8 million and Esc.2,448 million respectively.

The second six-year development plan (1959-64) came into force on Jan. 1, 1959, and the budgetary resources allocated to its execution in 1959 amounted to Esc.1,000 million, while the total estimated investments for the year were given as Esc.5,300 million.

Plans were announced for considerable expansion of Lisbon airport to handle latest types of jet passenger planes, including the construction of an additional runway of some 11,300 ft.; and for the simultaneous construction of two new airports at Madeira and Porto Santo islands. The first stage of the Lisbon underground railway was opened, and a motor industry was established by government licence for the manufacture of cars, lorries and tractors. The licence provided that 20% of the component materials of all vehicles manufactured in the first year of the industry's activity should be of national origin, and that this figure should reach 60% by the end of the sixth year. Tenders were invited for the building of a bridge across the river Tagus linking the centre of Lisbon with the rapidly

A huge statue of Christ, surmounting a 90-ft.-high tower, nearing completion in Lisbon. A lift ascends to the head of the statue.

growing suburb of Almada on the south side of the river.

A British trade fair was held in Lisbon during May and June, in the course of which Princess Margaret visited Portugal. Other important visitors in 1959 included the Emperor Haile Selassie I of Ethiopia and President Ahmed Sukarno of Indonesia. (F. B. H.)

See (all London, 1959) C. R. Boxer, ed., *Tragic History of the Sea*; Gilbert Renault, *The Caravels of Christ*; James L. Taylor, *A Portuguese-English Dictionary*.

PORTUGUESE OVERSEAS TERRITORIES.

Under this heading are grouped the Portuguese possessions in Africa and Asia. Their total area is approximately 803,805 sq.mi., and the total population (1950 census) 11,837,064. Areas, populations, capital towns and governors of the territories are given in the table.

History. Of the total projected investments of Esc.5,300 million in the first year of Portugal's second development plan (1959-64) Esc.1,277·5 million was earmarked for the overseas territories. Approximately one-half of this would be devoted to road, railway and port construction and improvement. In the African provinces of Angola and Mozambique work was continued on widening of the railway gauge, realignment of tracks and construction of extension lines linking up with the neighbouring territories of the Belgian Congo and Rhodesia.

Among the most important of the hydroelectric undertakings in process of construction in the African territories was that at Cambambe on the Cuanza river in Angola, where it was reported that some Esc.164 million had already been spent on preliminary buildings, purchase of equipment and excavation works which included the drilling and removal of over 30,000 cu. metres of rock. The ultimate potential of this undertaking was given as 3,000 million kwh., said to equal the total estimated output of all other Angolan hydroelectric systems already completed or in process of construction.

An incident considered by some observers to be not altogether unrelated to the political unrest in the motherland occurred in Portuguese Guinea in August when what was described in an official statement as a "strike and mutiny" of native port workers at Bissau was put down with severity. The official statement declared that public order and the prestige of authority would be defended by all possible means, and added the government's regret at the number of victims resulting from "repressive steps promptly taken in a manner adequate to the intention of the mutineers' attacks". It did not, however, give the number of casualties.

Addressing the U.N. general assembly in October, José Vasco Garin, Portuguese ambassador to the United States, once more declared his country's refusal to submit reports to the Trusteeship council on its overseas provinces. Nor, he added, would Portugal acknowledge any international statute which sought to discriminate between the different parts of the national territories, the independence of which was clearly established by the independence of the Portuguese nation itself.

In September the second phase of Portugal's case against India over its right of access to the enclaves of Dadra and Nagar-Aveli opened at the Hague International Court of Justice. On the eve of the opening India submitted to the United Nations a note in which it was stated that while it accepted the compulsory jurisdiction of the International Court it did so with certain reservations, one being that such jurisdiction was not applicable to disputes with the government of any state with which, at the time of an application to the Court, the government of India had no diplomatic relations. For Portugal it was held that since the present case was first referred to the Court in Dec. 1955, when diplomatic relations still existed between the two states, it was not affected by the Indian reservation. It was expected that the hearing of the case would continue until towards the end of

	PORTUGUESE OVERSEAS TERRITORIES			
Country	*Area* (sq.mi.)	*Population** (1950 census)	*Capital* (pop. 1950 census)	*Governor*
AFRICA				
Angola	481,351	4,145,266 (Eur. 78,826)	Luanda 158,882	†Colonel Horácio José de Sá Viana Rebelo
Cape Verde Islands .	1,557	148,331 (Eur. 2,909)	Praia 9,980	Major Silvino Silvério Marques
Guinea	13,948	510,577 (Eur. 2,263)	Bissau 18,309	Cmdr. António Augusto Peixoto Correia
São Tomé and Principe Is. .	372	60,159 (Eur. 1,152)	São Tomé 7,813	Manuel Marques de Abrantes Amaral
Mozambique . . .	297,731	5,738,911 (Eur. 48,213)	Lourenço Marques 93,516	†Cmdr. Pedro Correia de Barros
ASIA				
India‡ . . .	1,538	637,591 (Eur. 892)	Nova Gôa (Pangim) 31,950	†Brig. Manuel António Vassalo e Silva
Macao	6·2	187,772 (Eur. 2,719)	Macao 166,544	Major Jaime Silvério Marques
Timor	7,332	442,378 (Eur. 568)	Dili 43,589	Major Filipe José Temudo Barata

*Europeans are included in the territorial totals. † Governor-general. ‡ Comprises Gôa (1,390 sq.mi.), Damão (134 sq.mi.) and Diu (14 sq.mi.).

the year, after which the Court would adjourn and announce its findings some weeks later.

It was announced that during 1959 the 11 municipalities of Gôa would together spend some Esc.13·2 million on local works, a great part of it on road construction, conservation and repair. A small part of this expenditure was expected to be covered by government subsidies, but in the main the burden would be borne by municipal and other local authorities.　　　　　　　　　　　　(F. B. H.)

POST OFFICE. The total value of post office transactions with the public in the United Kingdom during the year ended March 31, 1959, was £5,825 million, an increase of £726 million on the figure for the previous 12 months.

Postal. The number of letters and letter packets, etc., posted during 1958-59 was estimated to have been 9,700 million compared with 9,600 million in 1957-58. The number of parcels handled during the year was 243,354,000 compared with 247,421,000 in 1957-58.

Telegraphs. The number of telegrams handled during the year ended March 31, 1959, was 34,625,000 including 14,086,000 inland telegrams and 20,539,000 overseas telegrams and radio telegrams with ships at sea, compared with 37,161,000 during 1957-58 (15,233,000 inland and 21,928,000 overseas and radio telegrams). The 12 coast radio stations in the United Kingdom exchanged 13,485,107 words (832,714 telegrams) with ships at sea during the year ended March 31, 1959. The stations dealt with 666 messages requesting medical services, 1,044 messages concerned with ships in distress and 20 concerned with aircraft in distress. In addition, 1,734 navigation warnings and 10,219 weather bulletins and gale warnings were broadcast while 304 direction-finder bearings were given to ships.

Telephones. On March 31, 1959, the telephone system of the United Kingdom comprised 4,982 automatic and 1,027 manual local exchanges serving more than 7,532,000 telephones. There were more than 73,000 public call offices. New telephone kiosks totalled 1,161. The number of local telephone calls handled during the year was 3,700 million, an increase of 0·79% on the previous year; inland trunk calls increased by 4·04% to 340 million. At the end of the year, the number of trunk lines in use over 25 mi. radial distance was 24,404.

Outgoing calls to European countries totalled 2,474,844, an increase of 10·2% on the previous year's figure of about 2,245,500. The number of telephone calls to countries outside Europe increased by 13·9%, totalling 234,894, against 206,100 in the previous year. Short-range radiotelephone calls between ships and telephone subscribers ashore, through the coast stations, numbered 105,126.

Savings Bank. Deposits for the year ended March 31, 1959, amounted to £454,261,000, an increase of £785,000 on the previous year; the number of separate accounts was 22,644,718. On Dec. 31, 1958, the amount due to depositors was £1,645,569,000. In the year ended March 31, 1959, 17,194,000 savings certificate documents were issued.

Staff. In March 1959, post office staff numbered 349,352 (part-time staff counted as half), with a salary and wage bill of £250,803,000 for the financial year. (*See* also TELE-COMMUNICATIONS.)　　　　　　　　　　　(G.P.O.)

(Top) An " automatic post office " introduced by the French postal service. Stamps, postal orders and change can be obtained from it and it also houses a telephone and a letter box. (Centre) Transparent telephone booths installed in a post office at Mannheim, western Germany. It was hoped they would help to discourage prolonged conversations. (Bottom) Sorting mail in one of the new post office vans which entered service in the western region of British railways, between London and Penzance, in October.

POTTERY AND PORCELAIN: *see* BUSINESS REVIEW.

POULTRY. The threatening effects of over-production of eggs was the outstanding and somewhat disturbing feature of 1959. In the white paper accompanying the government's annual price review of agricultural products the industry was reprimanded for over-expansion of laying flocks and the consequent drain on exchequer support to implement the guaranteed price of eggs. That price, in fact, was reduced by 1*d.* a dozen, the third successive year in which eggs had been treated in this way.

The warning to halt the expansion of egg-laying flocks was not heeded and, despite the Egg Marketing board's attempts to increase the consumption of eggs, supplies outstripped demand. Increasing quantities of eggs had to be withdrawn from normal trading channels to be processed for subsequent marketing as frozen eggs. In addition, the chairman of the board circularized over 400,000 registered producers, advising a brake on the further expansion of laying birds. A more equitable balance between supply and demand was a problem yet to be solved. It was being tackled and the industry's leaders were wisely bearing in mind that should producers be forced to reduce the size of their laying flocks to the point where available supplies of eggs were insufficient to meet the needs of the home market, the gap would be closed by the importation of foreign produce and the structure of self-sufficiency built up consequently gravely endangered.

The remarkable expansion in poultry produced for table consumption continued, although there were periods during the year when the profit margins to producers shrank to such an extent that serious misgivings were expressed by those who had invested capital in this class of intensive poultry keeping. Nevertheless, it was estimated that the production of these fast-growing broilers had increased from 3 million four years ago to some 70 million annually by 1959. Expansion was expected to continue. One well-informed estimate of future prospects had put production in 1965 at 220 million birds. Further advances were made in the design of the specialized type of accommodation currently in use for housing these young table chickens (which must reach a market weight of 3 lb. in ten weeks). The units employed in 1959 were windowless and the point had been reached where the birds were reared under completely intensive conditions. Ventilation and lighting were automatically controlled and the management routine was devised to ensure that food intake was not dissipated in unproductive exercising by the birds.

Towards the end of the year fowl pest again became a major issue. There had been sporadic outbreaks calling for temporary restrictions on the movement of poultry in small areas, but the number of outbreaks rose steeply in November. Compensation paid by the exchequer against the compulsory slaughter of birds falling prey to this notifiable disease, already in the region of £650,000 annually at the time of the intensified November outbreaks, looked like reaching alarming proportions as the year closed. The fear was expressed that the official slaughter policy, which had hitherto been regarded as the best hope of eradicating fowl pest in Britain, might have to be abandoned as being too costly to maintain. Should such a decision be reached, restrictions on the importation of poultry from those overseas countries where the disease is endemic would be removed and the way would be left open for the importation of large quantities of table poultry and breeding stock, thus disrupting the expectations of those who had invested large sums of money building up home production.

In Commonwealth countries, as elsewhere in the world, modern intensive methods of producing eggs and table poultry continued at a rapid rate. In Canada, as in the United States, table poultry producers expressed disatisfaction with market returns, while in New Zealand registered poultry keepers requested their Poultry board to review the conditions under which they were required to operate. By these representations it was hoped to secure a guaranteed price for eggs.

The provisional poultry population of England and Wales was estimated at 78,993,000, as compared with 71,521,000 in the previous year. The 1959 figure represented 73,944,000 fowls, 1,011,000 ducks, 379,000 geese and 3,659,000 turkeys. (*See* also VETERINARY MEDICINE.) (C. G. MY.)

PRESBYTERIAN CHURCHES. Reformed Churches holding the Presbyterian order. The total membership was estimated to be 45 million in 1959. Almost all these Churches of the Geneva Reformed tradition are united in a free association, the World Alliance of Reformed Presbyterian Churches, founded in 1875.

During 1959 certain events directed Presbyterians all over the world to think of their common origin in the Reformation that was inspired and guided by John Calvin and the other Geneva reformers. In May the National synod of the Reformed Church of France celebrated the 400th anniversary of its first meeting in Paris. The centre of these celebrations was the historic church of the Oratoire, next to the Louvre museum, and delegations from many Churches in the old world and the new joined in paying honour to the Huguenots, the first to organize their Church nation-wide according to the Presbyterian pattern. In Geneva Presbyterians celebrated the 400th anniversary of the University of Geneva, which had its origin in the college that Calvin founded. Scholars from all parts of the world were there to pay tribute to one of the great scholars of his time, whose active interest in education was bequeathed to the Churches of the order he inspired.

But while the Presbyterian Churches were thus reminded of their past, there was evidence even in the gatherings in Paris and Geneva themselves that the traditions they had inherited quickened awareness of the present. For example, the French synod issued statements on Marxism and on the vexed question of Algeria, characteristic of a denomination which had always laid stress on the cultivation of the Christian conscience. On a broader stage the specific role of the Church in the modern world was the theme of the 18th General council of the world alliance held in July and August in São Paulo, Brazil. Attended by about 400 representatives

The Right Rev. R. H. W. Shepherd (left) succeeds the Very Rev. J. A. Fraser (right) as moderator of the Church of Scotland.

of 78 Churches from 53 countries, it was the largest of all the General councils held in the history of this alliance and was also the first to be held in South America. The Presbyterian Church of Brazil, reputed to be the fastest-growing member of the whole Presbyterian family, held its 100th anniversary in Rio de Janeiro immediately after the close of the General council. In the space of a century this Church had grown to more than 300,000 adult communicants of the many races and nationalities that had mingled to make up the Brazilian nation. It enjoyed complete liberty and had earned great public respect in the country on account of the high level of character and integrity found among its members.

In the United States the leaders of the United Presbyterian Church, which had a membership of 3·2 million, made a forthright statement during the controversy over the rights of coloured children to enter public (state) schools. They expressed deep concern that Negroes were " discriminated against, oppressed and denied rights that are morally and legally theirs ".

In Canada most of the Protestants were organized in the United Church and the Presbyterian Church, both belonging to the denomination, though the first and larger was the outcome of a union with Methodist and Congregational Churches. Both had been growing rapidly though they were stretched to cope with the growth of the population. The same was true of the Churches in Australia and New Zealand. In Australia especially, where natural growth was supplemented by large-scale immigration, all the Presbyterian Churches in the several states (combined in the Presbyterian Church of Australia) were much concerned to expand their resources to meet the increasing opportunity. This had stimulated them to lay special stress on stewardship. Their success in organizing a vigorous movement to raise urgently needed funds had resulted in quickening the spiritual pulse of congregations and inculcating a deeper and stronger sense of Christian responsibility. As a result they faced the challenge of the times with a buoyancy that might well have been the envy of older Churches elsewhere. Under the impulse of the New Life movement in New Zealand, a comparatively small country, 77 new parishes had been instituted during the past decade.

In Great Britain the negotiations on church unity between Presbyterians and Anglicans came to a standstill when the General assembly of the Church of Scotland rejected the proposals contained in the Joint Report on Relations between Anglican and Presbyterian Churches, but left the door open for the continuance of conversations on certain specific subjects which that report was felt to have bypassed. At the same time conversations on union were begun with the Congregational Churches, perhaps more hopefully, considering that unions of Presbyterians and Congregationalists had already taken place in other countries. During the year the Presbyterian Church of England decided that women should be allowed to become ministers.

(A. Kg.)

PRICES.

In 1959 the picture generally was one of price stability—for raw materials, for manufactured output and for retail sales of goods and services. This contrasted with the picture in 1958 when raw material prices had recently fallen, prices for manufactured output were stable and the slow upward drift of retail prices continued. The course of world prices in 1959 was not, however, a passive stability. It should be considered in relation to events in 1958, when there had been a sharp decline in U.S. industrial activity followed by a very rapid recovery; in other countries the decline had been less marked and the recovery slower and later. Reversing the usual order of events, raw material prices had probably fallen before the decline in industrial output. Throughout 1958 manufacturers had the advantages

TABLE I. COMMODITY PRICES

	1958		1959			
	Aug.	Nov.	Feb.	May	Aug.	Nov.
*World prices** (1952 = 100)						
All items	87	90	87	91	88	91
Food	92	90	85	85	83	83
Fibres	79	74	74	82	81	82
Metals	71	78	77	78	80	83
Other	109	125	121	132	119	132
*British commodity prices**						
Tea, Ceylon† . .	53	56	53	71	52	63
Wool, tops, 64's† . .	106	95	92	113	114	109
Copper, electro‡ .	205	238	236	235	234	234
Lead, soft‡ . .	70	76	70	72	73	73
Zinc, g.o.b.‡ . .	63	77	74	77	87	95
Tin, cash‡ . .	730	758	771	784	793	798
Rubber, R.S.S. spot† .	23$\frac{7}{16}$	25$\frac{11}{16}$	25$\frac{3}{16}$	30$\frac{7}{16}$	31$\frac{13}{16}$	38$\frac{3}{8}$
American commodity prices §						
Wheat, No. 1, Canadian‖	165	164	171	168	166	165
Cocoa, Accra beans¶ .	47·3	44·3	36·5	37·8	37·7	34·1
Coffee, Santos No. 4¶ .	46·2	44·2	39·6	37·0	36·5	36·8
Sugar, f.o.b. Cuba¶	3·47	3·43	3·10	2·93	2·81	2·96
Cotton, middling 15/16″¶	36·4	36·2	35·7	36·3	33·2	32·8
Copra, c.i.f. Pacific** .	190	239	257	266	215	225
Petroleum, crude††	357	351	336	325	322	...

* Mid-month. † *d.* per lb. ‡ £ per ton. § Monthly averages. ‖ In store Fort William, Canadian cent per 60 lb. ¶ Cent per lb. ** $ per ton. †† South Arabian, c.i.f., cent per barrel.
Source. *Economist,* U.N. *Monthly Bulletin of Statistics* and U.K. *Monthly Digest of Statistics.*

TABLE II. IMPORT, EXPORT AND WHOLESALE PRICES, UNITED KINGDOM

	1958		1959			
	Aug.	Nov.	Feb.	May	Aug.	Nov.
Import and export prices			(average 1954 = 100)			
Imports, all items . .	99	99	98	97	98	101
Food, beverages, tobacco	97	100	98	96	97	102
Basic materials . .	94	91	91	91	94	96
Fuels . . .	112	111	110	103	101	102
Manufactures . .	102	104	102	104	104	107
Exports, all items . .	110	109	109	109	108	111
Metals . . .	119	117	117	116	113	113
Engineering products .	116	116	116	117	117	121
Textiles . . .	101	97	99	97	95	97
Other manufactures .	105	104	106	105	106	106
Terms of trade* . .	90	91	90	89	91	91
Wholesale prices						
For manufacturing . .	101·0	101·5	101·8	101·4	101·8	102·6
Basic materials . .	97·2	97·9	98·2	98·1	98·5	99·4
Fuels . . .	129·8	128·6	128·7	126·9	126·8	126·6
Manufactured output† .	111·1	111·5	111·7	111·3	111·4	111·7
Food products . .	105·1	106·5	107·2	106·2	106·9	107·7
Iron and steel . .	129·6	129·6	129·7	129·7	128·3	128·6
Chemicals . . .	105·0	105·8	106·3	107·4	106·0	106·6
Clothing and footwear .	105·3	105·0	104·5	104·9	105·3	106·0
Other textiles . .	97·7	96·5	95·0	95·5	95·9	97·6
Furniture . . .	109·7	109·8	109·8	109·4	109·7	109·6
Electrical appliances .	104·1	104·2	104·9	104·4	103·9	103·5
Retail prices and wages						
Retail prices‡ . .	116·7	118·0	118·6	117·3	117·5	118·3
Wage rates in manufacturing industry‡ . .	124·4	126·7	126·8	127·3	127·6	128·1

* Ratio of import to export prices, a fall indicating a favourable movement. † Output for the home market. ‡ Linked back to 1954 for purposes of comparison.
Source. *Board of Trade Journal* and *Ministry of Labour Gazette.*

of reduced raw material prices and the urge of reduced activity to encourage price reductions, but with a continued rise in wages all that happened was the achievement of stable prices after several years of increase. What was striking, however, was that in 1959, when demand had risen again and industrial activity increased to above its previous level, prices did not immediately rise, but remained stable.

Even world prices of basic materials, normally the most volatile of prices, changed little, in the aggregate, with the revival of industrial demand. This was partly because some of the raw materials for manufacturing were being produced subject to controls. Output could be restricted to limit the price fall and expanded again when demand rose without much effect upon prices. But this was not the whole picture. Table I shows that although the over-all index was stable in the year there was a decline in food prices and a rise in other prices. The changes were quite marked; in November food prices were 8% lower than a year before, metals were 6% higher, fibres 11% higher and other commodities 6% higher. In August British prices were dearer by 7·5% for wool, 14% for copper, 38% for zinc, 8·5% for tin, 13·5% for rubber and 4% for lead. By contrast, the American prices quoted for cocoa, coffee and sugar were all cheaper. With increased demand the raw materials for manufacturing were in fact dearer though some of them, such as wool, copper, lead and zinc, were not yet dear by the standards of recent years. Tin, quite effectively controlled, had always held its price well and the price of rubber, towards the end of 1959, had recovered to a level higher than the average for the previous few years.

United Kingdom. In the year ending Nov. 1959 U.K. import and export prices both rose by about 2%. Nevertheless, compared with 1954, import prices had been stable while export prices had risen. There had been a fall in import prices of basic materials while imported fuels and manufactured goods had risen slightly. But even among manufactures the type imported had risen in price very much less than the type exported, though manufactured textiles had, in fact, fallen in price. These figures illustrate some of the advantages gained in the previous few years by manufacturing countries relative to primary producers. In 1959 the terms of trade were such that a given volume of U.K. exports could pay for a volume of imports increased by 10% compared with 1954.

" *Hey mate! Where the 'ell's Downin' street?* " *Fear of lower prices caused British bacon producers to oppose the Anglo-Danish tariff agreement of July 8: Thelwell in the " News Chronicle ".*

TABLE III. WHOLESALE PRICES IN SELECTED COUNTRIES*
(1953 = 100)

	1958			1959		
	June	Sept.	Dec.	March	June	Sept.
United States						
Raw materials	102	99	98	100	99	97
All items	108	108	108	109	109	109
Europe						
Austria .	110	110	112	113	114	115†
Belgium .	101	100	100	100	101	102†
Denmark .	105	105	105	105	106	105†
France .	121	120	121	125	124	127
German Fed. Rep. .	106	106	105	105	105	105†
Greece .	126	128	127	129	131	131†
Italy .	102	100	99	97	97	97†
Netherlands .	104	102	107	105	105	105†
Norway.	111	112	111	111	111	112
Portugal .	102	99	100	99	98	...
Spain .	146	148	152	151	147	...
Sweden .	107	107	107	106	107	108
Switzerland .	102	101	100	100	99	100
Turkey .	192	206	217	221	...	...
United Kingdom:						
Basic materials .	101	100	101	101	101	102
Finished goods .	111	111	112	112	111	111
Commonwealth						
Australia‡ .	106	107	104	109	108	110†
Canada .	103	103	104	105	105	105†
India .	107	112	107	109	111	112
New Zealand .	106	111	112	...	...	...
South Africa .	106	108	107	105	107	107†
Other areas						
Algeria .	120	116	124	130	...	...
Brazil .	212	231	245	281	293	...
Chile .	799	867	872	985	1,053	...
Colombia .	172	174	177	181	190	...
Egypt .	118	116	116	118	118	...
Israel .	152	156	152	152	152	...
Japan .	98	97	97	98	98	100
Lebanon (Beirut) .	...	...	103	102	103	...
Mexico (Mexico City)	143	140	144	144	143	...
Morocco (Casablanca)	108	113	115	112	110	110†
Persia (Tehran) .	118	119	121	125	120	...
Peru (Lima) .	148	150	151	156	159	...
Syria (Damascus) .	97	95	96	100	102	101
Thailand (Bangkok) .	122	135	127	117	112	...
Tunisia .	114	118	114	112	109	...

* General wholesale price index numbers unless otherwise specified. † Aug. 1959
‡ Domestic goods.
SOURCE. U.N. *Monthly Bulletin of Statistics.*

Table II shows that basic materials for U.K. manufacturing industry moved in much the same way as import prices, being cheaper in 1959 than in 1954 but slightly dearer in the last year. Manufactured output for the home market, like exports, was about 10% dearer than in 1954, and again both changed little in the last year. It should be noticed that fuels used by manufacturing industry (primarily home-produced coal) and wage rates in manufacturing industry had both risen, from 1954, far more than prices of manufactured output, while retail prices had risen more than wholesale prices. Thus the recent stability of wholesale and retail prices had been achieved primarily because of cheaper imports and in spite of the rise in home costs. However, although 1954 was the last period of near stability in prices it was also one of reaction from the high prices of the Korean boom which itself followed closely upon the devaluation of sterling in Sept. 1949. Comparison with the period immediately before devaluation shows that in 1959 prices of both raw materials and manufactured products were about 40% higher, and so were consumer prices generally. (The retail price index increased rather more than 40%, but this was because it was more heavily weighted with " essential " goods which in 1949 were controlled and subsidized far more extensively than in 1959.) This suggests that the price changes that followed devaluation had worked themselves out, but certainly the United Kingdom was not in the same economic disequilibrium as in 1949. By 1959 it had succeeded in doubling its 1939 volume of exports and its balance of payments remained good. The increased activity which followed the lowering of bank rate, extension of bank advances and removal of hire purchase restrictions was not leading to higher prices, but an issue of the Oct. 1959 election was how much further encouragement could be given to industry without causing a rise in prices.

Other Countries. Table III shows that in the year ending in mid-1959 there was very little movement in wholesale prices in the United States and in European countries. These " general " index numbers of wholesale prices, which include manufactured products as well as basic raw materials, present a picture of price stability, and in economies which were once again expanding. The increased demand was still being met by increased output rather than by its alternative, rising prices. The situation had not yet become inflationary. Any increases in raw material prices and in labour costs could still be absorbed by the increased efficiency of recently installed equipment, better organization and by equipment working nearer to capacity. (In the United States the almost complete stoppage of the steel industry for four months from mid-July saved that industry from problems of limiting output from a capacity which had become too large for expected demand and hence might have had price repercussions.) However, in France wholesale prices rose by some 4% in the year, a continuation of the steady inflation of the previous few years which put French prices 25% above their 1953 level when most European countries showed increases of less than 10%. The latest increase may have been partly due to the general devaluation of the franc at the end of Dec. 1958, following partial devaluation in 1957; the total 1957-58 devaluation was one of 41%, a devaluation very similar to that of sterling in 1949. Such devaluations are a result of internal prices rising more than elsewhere and a cause of further increases because of dearer imports. In Spain, too, the continued chronic inflation raised prices by 6% in the last year and put them 50% above the 1953 level.

In Commonwealth countries the near stability of 1958 was followed by a tendency for the upward drift to be resumed, starting in New Zealand in the second half of 1958 and in Australia early in 1959. In India the position was more difficult to assess as a rise in the middle of 1958 was followed by price reductions. In Canada the resumption of the upward drift amounted to only 2% in the year. In most South American countries price increases continued at a substantial rate. After some months without figures for Lebanon during disturbances the resumed series showed only small increases. Stability existed in Japan, with prices below the 1953 level, and in Israel, with prices 50% above that level. In Egypt and Tunisia prices were approximately stable, but in Algeria, with devaluation similar to that of France, prices rose more than in France. (*See* also COST OF LIVING; NATIONAL INCOME; WAGES AND HOURS; WEALTH AND INCOME, DISTRIBUTION OF.) (H. S. B.)

PRINTING. During 1959 the British printing industry suffered the worst labour dispute in its history—a seven-week stoppage of work affecting all main groups except the national newspapers. It was estimated that it cost the printing trade unions more than £3 million in strike pay and some £6 million in lost wages. It cost employers more than £10 million, not counting the loss of advertising revenue for provincial newspapers and magazines which ceased publication.

In January the unions had demanded a 40-hr. week and a 10% increase in wage rates for 250,000 workers. The demands were rejected on the grounds that they were economically impracticable. The employers suggested instead a conference to consider ways and means of reducing costs and increasing productivity. If by those means it were found possible to improve the economic position of the industry the unions' claims might be reconsidered. The unions, refusing to submit the dispute to arbitration, applied a ban on overtime, instructed their members to withdraw from incentive schemes and considered strike action. The employers then offered a 42½-hr. week and a 2·5% wage increase, conditional on the acceptance of a 22-clause document dealing with labour supply, demarcation, productivity and new processes. This offer was rejected and the unions began to apply sanctions. The employers retaliated by employing union members on a day-to-day basis only. This in its turn prompted a union counter-move—an instruction to their members to stop work. Over 100,000 workers were involved in about 4,000 printing firms and 1,000 provincial and London suburban newspapers, as well as magazines and periodicals.

The dispute was complicated by a parallel one in the printing ink industry over similar claims. The national newspapers, which were not directly involved in the dispute, found that they might have to close down because of the drying up of ink supplies, but the problem was solved by the importation of ink from France with union approval.

Eventually the unions agreed to meet the employers under the independent chairmanship of Lord Birkett. After two weeks of lengthy meetings a settlement was agreed—a 4·5% pay rise and a 42-hr. week, conditional on union acceptance of a number of measures designed to improve productivity and efficiency. There was a return to work in early August.

In June just before the British stoppage, Icelandic printers struck work for a 15% wage increase. After nine days the printers won their demands.

The main trade event of the year was the printing, publishing and map-making exhibition in Milan in October, when not only printing and allied machinery was on show, but also exhibits reviewing cultural and artistic activities connected with the industry.

The British Printing and Kindred Trades federation published a report on the visit of a delegation to the U.S.S.R. in 1958. The general conclusion was that the British printing industry, so far as technical development, methods of production and processes were concerned, had little to learn from the Soviet printing industry. The Soviet industry was content to adopt methods already well tried in the western world and had not yet taken advantage of all developments that were now common practice in British printing firms. However, a report published by the Printing, Packaging and Allied Trades association claimed that output from the Soviet printing industry had increased five-fold in the period 1941 to 1955 and that the country produced a little more than one-fifth of the world's books each year.

In May the first case-bound Monophoto film-set book was published, entitled *The Toy*. It was set on film by Filmset Limited of Crawley and printed by offset lithography by Straker Brothers of London. Demonstrating the flexibility of this new method of setting, the body matter of a book called *State Barges on the Thames* was set on Monophoto equipment, again by Filmset Limited of Crawley, and the film sent by post to the Netherlands where the whole book was printed by photo-lithography by De Jong and Co. of Hilversum. Earlier in the year the first commercial publication of any kind set on the Monophoto had been published; it was a pamphlet for the Conservative Political centre. Another technical development was the construction, by Strachan and Henshaw, for the book printers Butler and Tanner of the first British reel-fed perfector printing machine to work from thin flexible plates—possibly made of nylon. By its use it was hoped to produce books at prices more competitive with those produced abroad.

A nylon printing plate, already commonplace in the United States, was also developed by the German Printing Research institute for rotary letterpress printing. Although the Stempel typefoundry of Frankfurt-on-Main had been the principal owner of the famous Klingspor foundry since 1950, it was not until 1959 that it included selected Klingspor types in its casting programme. This ensured that the tradition of the distinguished typefounder, Karl Klingspor, was continued. Nepal and Cambodia received their first mechanical typesetting machines from the Monotype corporation and the corporation reported that it was working on the development of special type faces which could be mechanically set for Malaya and Thailand.

The biggest event of the year in the United States was a graphic arts exposition held in New York at which both domestic and foreign manufacturers exhibited machines developed in the previous few years. Many new models were shown for the first time. It was the largest display of printing equipment in the United States in the decade.

Making their appearance for the first time in the United States were wrap-around plates for the letterpress field and specially designed presses which would accommodate them. The wrap-around plate method permits direct-to-paper

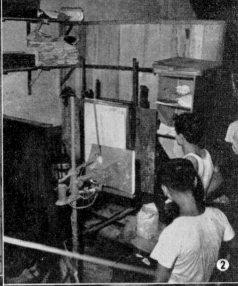

The pictures on this page show stages in the production of a pirated edition of the "Encyclopædia Britannica" in Formosa. Piracy of English books in the far east is nothing new and is part of the bigger problem of goods being sold under bogus trade marks. Formosa has not previously been involved, but as it is not a member of the world copyright association, it is difficult for foreign publishers to obtain redress. During 1959 two Formosan firms circulated catalogues throughout the far east offering British and U.S. educational, scientific and technical books at a sixth to a tenth of their prices in Britain. These books are printed by photo-lithography, a method that saves the costs of compositors, typesetters and proof readers. Cheap labour and a local supply of paper further lessen printing costs. One of the main markets is Hong Kong, where book piracy, formerly prevalent, has been checked in recent years.

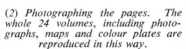

(1) Pages of the "Encyclopædia Britannica" taken from a volume of an original set are placed in order ready for photographing.

(2) Photographing the pages. The whole 24 volumes, including photographs, maps and colour plates are reproduced in this way.

(3) Developing the plate glass negative from which the lithographic plate will be produced.

(4) The printing process. Much of the equipment is believed to have been purchased from Switzerland with a government loan.

(5) A young girl sewing pages together in one of the final stages in the production of the pirated edition of the "Encyclopædia Britannica".

(6) Sets of the completed encyclopaedia stacked ready for distribution. They will probably be sent out to purchasers by post.

printing from original plates with a relief only one-third as deep as that required for conventional letterpress, and thin enough to be fastened around a rotary cylinder like an offset plate. A variety of commercial and carton printing could be produced by this method, including halftones, some types of line work and multicolour jobs on various paper and board stocks. Plates had been made on magnesium, zinc and copper, but a photopolymer plate was being developed from a light-sensitive plastic material. This is placed in contact with a high-contrast photographic negative, exposed to an ultra-violet light source and the unexposed portions washed out. The plate is mounted on a steel support and is then ready for the press.

There was much evidence in the United States that the web offset process could be used for producing newspapers, but it appeared that in the immediate future the process would be confined to newspapers with small circulations and limited manpower resources. The process permits a newspaper to use a large number of illustrations without increased cost, as well as some of the economical cold type methods. Much of the copy is set by automatic-justifying electric typewriters; headlines and display copy are set by photolettering machines.

One U.S. metropolitan newspaper found, after an exhaustive comparison of the setting of copy on photographic typesetting machines and on hot metal machines, that the over-all reduction in time using photocomposition had been more than 25%. This led to a complete conversion of its retail display advertising composition to the new typesetting process.

There was also continued progress in applying electronic principles to printing and related operations in the United States. A new development was the introduction of the Scan-A-Color colour separator designed for producing three or four colour-continuous tone separations, fully colour corrected in one hour or less. The machine produces negative or positive separations on films with predetermined densities and with the proper amount of undercolour removed. It scans colour transparencies or any reflection copy that can be wrapped around the copy cylinder.

One U.S. typesetting company used electronic punched-card equipment for obtaining a report of the chargeable hours and production for the preceding day and night in each department of the plant. The equipment also showed the time reported by each worker and provided an accurate cost summary for every job produced.   (J. C. Mn.; E. H. O.)

PRISONS.   The outstanding event of the year was the publication of the white paper " Penal Practice in a Changing Society " (Cmnd. 645), which discussed the growth of crime, the weapons of which society disposes against crime, the need for more knowledge of its causes and a more accurate measurement of the success of various forms of treatment and the development of penal methods. Under the last heading the task of the prisons, and particularly of the local prisons, was discussed against the background of continued overcrowding and shortage of suitable work, leading to the conclusion that " the prison commissioners are faced with a building programme of formidable dimensions and great urgency." A detailed building programme including over 30 new establishments of all kinds was drawn up.

Meanwhile the population of the commissioners' establishments rose from about 26,000 at the end of 1958 to nearly 27,000. Numbers sleeping three in a cell in local prisons exceeded 6,400. This situation was not relieved by any additional accommodation, mainly owing to increasing reluctance by local planning authorities to give planning clearance for sites without public inquiries into local objections.

In furtherance of the new building programme, the new

Mrs. J. E. Kelley, who was appointed governor of Holloway women's prison, London, in October, in succession to Lady Taylor.

buildings item in the prisons estimates 1959-60 was increased from about £1 million to £3 million. A Design and Development group was set up to reconsider prison planning and design so as to meet contemporary needs with maximum efficiency and economy, and produced revolutionary designs for future prisons.

It was likely that the level of prison population would be lowered by two statutes which came into force in 1959. The Maintenance Orders act, 1958, which provided for the attachment of wages of men defaulting on maintenance orders, was followed by a significant fall in the numbers committed to prison for default. The First Offenders act, 1958, imposed restrictions on the imprisonment of first offenders of or over the age of 21 similar to those imposed by section 17(2) and (3) of the Criminal Justice act, 1948, for offenders under 21.

While the number of young offenders committed to prison and borstal continued to increase, the population of the borstals was stabilized at about 4,500 and overcrowding was remedied by the reduction towards about 16 months in the average period of training for boys and the extra accommodation acquired late in 1958. The former step related to that " radical reconsideration of the principles of treatment for young offenders " which led the prison commissioners in 1958 to place before the Advisory Council on the Treatment of Offenders proposals which were in substance approved in the council's report " The Treatment of Young Offenders ", published in Oct. 1959. The main conclusions of the report were that sentences of imprisonment up to six months should be replaced by sentences of three or six months in detention centres, to be followed by a period of one year's statutory after-care; that for those for whom a court considers a period of detention between six months and two years is required. there should be one sentence only, which would be an indeterminate sentence with a minimum of six months and a maximum of two years, along the lines of the present borstal sentence, to be followed by two years statutory after-care.

In the treatment of adult prisoners, there was continued development of group-counselling and inmate participation, and the Norwich system spread to all the small local prisons and some of the larger. To improve the employment situation, a distinguished industrialist was appointed as voluntary industrial adviser to the commissioners and, in some large towns with local prisons, committees of industrialists, trade unionists and other interested persons were set up to help find more work for the prisons. Twenty-four new workshops were built and, at some prisons, farms were bought to provide outside work. The earnings scheme was completely recast: piece-rates were abolished, the first week's earnings were credited in advance and the maximum was raised to 6s. per week. The dietary scales were also improved, the meat ration being doubled.

In Scotland the number in custody reached a peak of 2,987 in May—93% above the 1938 level. For the first time prisoners were placed three in a cell. The total so accommodated at one time exceeded 300 but fell sharply later owing to the provision of additional cells and a decrease in the number of committals. During the year an additional open borstal institution was acquired, a mental observation ward opened at Barlinnie prison and a psychiatric unit, both for treatment and research projects, set up at Edinburgh prison. (L. W. F.)

PROFITS AND DIVIDENDS.

It was not until the second half of 1959 that the published profits of British industrial companies began to reflect a recovery from the period of virtual stagnation dating back to 1957. Profits figures published in the closing months of 1958 continued to reflect the flattening out of the preceding period and there was a marginal downward movement during the first half of 1959. A halt was called in July and the following months witnessed a reversal of the movement. This pattern was not, however, reflected in dividends, which, partly for technical reasons, showed throughout 1959 a perceptible advance on those of 1958.

Figures published by the *Financial Times*, relating to 1,736 companies reporting during the first six months of 1959, showed that aggregate trading profits were 2% below the comparative figure for 1958, with equity earnings down by 2·7%. The figures for June, the last month of the period, conformed with that picture, trading profits and earnings being down by 1·9% and 1·3% respectively, yet net ordinary dividends were now up by 7·1%, partly in reflection of the lower tax rate. (Prior to that reduction the average increase in dividends had been running at about 4%.) The figures for July showed increases (compared with July 1958) of 10% in trading profits and 11·6% in earnings, and this improvement was later maintained. Thus trading profits for the first 11 months of 1959 were fractionally higher than in the same period of 1958 in respect of a grand total of 2,922 companies, and 1·5% higher in respect of 2,457 industrial companies. Dividends for the same period showed an increase of 12%, of which it was calculated that about half was due to the tax alteration.

Thus 1959, after a slow start, ultimately began to reflect the end of the credit restrictions and the stringent financial policy which had hampered all sections of British industry throughout most of 1958, as well as a recovery in the general economy. However, owing to the incidence of accounting dates and the time lag before the publication of accounts, the industrial results announced in 1959 often covered only a brief period of improved trading conditions, the full benefits of which might not be reflected until 1960.

As always, the results of the various industrial groups varied widely. Textile companies, with profits showing a decline of 27%, and shipping groups (23% lower) showed the most severe set-backs, while profits of companies in the entertainment industry increased by 38%, in household goods by 21% and in the motor industry by 13%. Outside the range of industrial companies, oil companies experienced

a temporary upset in the supply-demand equilibrium and the profits of 19 companies announced in the first eight months of 1959 showed a decline of 5%. The full force of the 1957-58 setback in certain commodity prices was reflected in the early results of several producers but the partial recovery in copper, lead and zinc prices saw a reversal late in the year; the fall of 26% in the profits of metal producers, reflecting the Australian and Rhodesian economies, was reduced to a mere 1·75% later. Malaya, Ceylon and India, however, all benefited from the substantial improvements in rubber and tea prices. The former came too late to leave a substantial impact on the profits of producing companies announced in 1959, yet the latter was reflected, while the dividends of both groups, which normally distribute liberally from earnings, were appreciably higher. South Africa, too, benefited from the development of its younger gold mines, whose growth the previous year left an impression on 1959 profits and dividends; while similar concerns in Ghana met with corresponding success.

In short, 1959 saw the end of the marginal downward trend in profits which began the previous year and it eventually reflected the upturn in the economic and financial conditions in the United Kingdom as well as a selective improvement in certain sectors of the world economy. (*See also* NATIONAL INCOME; STOCKS AND SHARES.) (B. P. W.)

PSYCHIATRY.

The most important event in the field of psychiatry in Great Britain was the passing of the Mental Health bill in July 1959. Based on the recommendations in the *Report of the Royal Commission on the Law Relating to Mental Illness and Mental Deficiency 1954-57* (see *Britannica Book of the Year 1958*), the bill aimed at combining the requirements of modern treatment with safeguards for the liberty of the subject and the protection of the community. It initiated a reorientation of the mental health services away from institutional care towards care in the community. This new emphasis on the social aspects of psychiatry was not confined to Britain. It was well illustrated by two publications by the World Health organization, *Social Psychiatry and Community Attitudes* and *Mental Health Problems of Ageing and the Aged* (*Tech. Rep. Wld Hlth Org.* 177 and 171, 1959). The term " social psychiatry " referred to " the preventive and curative measures which are directed towards the fitting of the individual for a satisfactory and useful life in terms of his own social environment." This definition included both the task of fitting the mentally ill into the community and the provision of social conditions useful for the prevention and cure of mental disorder. Industrialization and concomitant social changes had led to a growing tendency to segregate the mentally ill from the rest of the community, even if they were no danger to themselves or others. This rejection of the mentally ill often delayed recovery and made return to normal life more difficult. Psychiatrists recognized that they could help their patients more effectively by removing the barriers which separated them from the community. The open-door principle was adopted in an increasing number of mental hospitals. The " day hospital ", where patients were treated during the day only, without leaving their homes, proved of great value both therapeutically and economically. Social isolation was found to be one of the factors contributing to mental illness. It could sometimes be successfully combated with the help of therapeutic social clubs. However, it was realized that if society wanted to benefit from the advances of modern psychiatry a change in the attitude of the community towards the mentally ill was essential. In several university centres " attitude research " projects were undertaken. It was hoped that these studies would lead to more rational and helpful attitudes towards the mentally ill than had existed previously among lay persons. Rejection of the mentally ill was found to be associated with strong prejudices against other human groups because they belonged to another sex, race, religion, nation, etc. It was recognized that the community could not be expected to adopt a more liberal attitude to the mentally ill unless psychiatric patients were received and treated in hospital as far as possible like patients suffering from physical illness. The removal of all but the absolutely necessary restrictions by the new Mental Health act was expected to initiate a profound change in the approach to mental illness among the general population.

The growing proportion of old people in the population, which was mainly due to the successful treatment of infectious diseases affecting the younger age groups, led to an increase in the number of aged mental invalids. The second of the above-mentioned reports dealt with the problems arising from this situation which presented a challenge to the mental health services. The relationship between age and hospital admission was illustrated by some figures of first-admission rates to mental hospitals in the United States. Per 100,000 population, these figures were 76·3 in the age group 25-34, 93·0 in the age group 35-54; and 236·1 for those over 65. The number of persons of 65 or over in the United States had increased approximately fourfold between 1904 and 1950, but the number of first mental hospital admissions in this age group had increased ninefold. There was no indication that the incidence of mental illness had increased; the excessive demand on the mental hospital services was probably due to social factors. Suicide was in all countries much more frequent among the aged than among other age groups. This was due partly to the frequency of social isolation but also to physical illness and penury. Retirement forced upon healthy old people was another contributory cause of mental disorder. Heredity, too, was shown to play a part in the mental illnesses of old age. Contrary to the belief commonly held, a considerable proportion of mental disorders of old age proved curable, at least for a time. This applied particularly to the depressive illness of old age which responded to the same methods as similar conditions occurring in younger age groups. A drastic reorientation of the geriatric mental health services was recommended. It was proposed that the emphasis be placed on community care and hostel accommodation rather than on conventional mental hospital care. The latter was required only for a minority of elderly patients. Such a geriatric mental health service was put into effect in Amsterdam, where about 10% of the population of 1 million was over 65. It was estimated that about 8,000 of them would have to be cared for by the mental health services, but that only a fraction of this number would require permanent hospitalization. This was an entirely new approach to the treatment of the aged mentally sick, who in most places had had to spend the end of their lives as hospital inmates.

Intensive research continued in most fields of psychiatry, especially in psycho-pharmacology; i.e., the study of the effect of drugs on mental states. The most important new drug was an antidepressant, Tofranil ($C_{19} H_{25} Cl N_2$), synthesized in Switzerland, which was structurally related to the " tranquillizer " promazine. No final estimation of its therapeutic value was arrived at, but there was general agreement that it was useful in the treatment of depressive states. It was expected to supplement rather than to replace electroconvulsive therapy. The effect of Tofranil formed one of the chief topics of the McGill University Conference on Depressions and Allied States (Canad. Psychiat. Ass. J. 4, special supplement, 1959).

A further decrease was reported in the number of persons under care in mental hospitals in England and Wales; they numbered 138,124 at the end of 1958, as compared with 146,952 a year earlier. The decline was greater than in any previous year. (E. SL.)

PSYCHOLOGY. In the field of general psychology there was, in the late 1950s, a marked revival of interest in cognitive processes as distinct from emotional or motivational processes, and particularly in the higher mental processes, as distinct from conditioning and the simpler forms of learning. In The Psychology of Perception (London, 1957), D. W. Hamlyn criticized in some detail the current theories of different psychological schools. He emphasized, rather as the Herbartian apperceptionists formerly did, the great complexity of the mind's own contributions to the interpretation of sensory stimuli, and contended that an essential prerequisite for the experimental study of perception is a sound philosophical analysis of the concept. S. H. Bartley, in Principles of Perception (New York, 1958), summarized the results of the more recent researches carried out on the subject, with a view to deducing the fundamental principles to which any general theory must conform; the work of the Gestaltists was given less prominence than usual, but the part played by social and motivational factors was clearly brought out. D. E. Broadbent's Perception and Communication (London, 1958) summarized recent research carried out at Cambridge and put forward the view that a perceptual system may be regarded as a communication channel of limited capacity with its approach guarded by a " filter ". He claimed that the main features of his hypothesis could be embodied in an entirely mechanical model and was to that extent scientifically validated. He contrasted his own conception with the oversimplified stimulus-and-reaction theory adopted by the behaviourist school, and his own method of validation with that of the psychological investigators who pinned their faith to hypothetico-deductive procedures. No attempt was made to use information theory quantitatively, but the experiments reported threw considerable light on problems of auditory perception —particularly multi-channel listening, the effects of noise and the perception of speech.

Sir Frederic Bartlett, in a very readable work on Thinking (London, 1958), attempted " to put thinking in its place as a natural development from earlier forms of skilled bodily behaviour ", and described in non-technical terms a series of experiments carried out with university students and designed more especially to demonstrate the analogies between the simpler kinds of skills and the higher types of conceptional processes. D. Wheeler, in a long article on " The Development of Reasoning in School Children " (Brit. J. statist. Psychol., 11, 137), reported the results of group and individual tests applied to children of various ages. The increasingly complex types of reasoning achieved in the average child as he matures from year to year were described with technical precision in the language of modern logic and with the aid of symbolic notation, and the conclusions drawn were carefully checked by statistical analysis. The evidence confirmed the hypothesis that there is a special factor for reasoning ability (over and above the influence of general intelligence) and that this in turn can be subdivided into a number of group factors. Ian Hunter continued his studies of problem-solving in children and young adults by series of experiments on the solution of anagrams. The results revealed a fairly regular sequence of phases and the importance of implicit as well as explicit processes of reasoning (Brit. J. Psychol., 50, 193).

In education the problem of the inheritability of intelligence still attracted considerable attention. In the new journal Educational Research (London, 1959) P. E. Vernon and others discussed the theory of mental testing with particular reference to general and special abilities, innate or acquired. F. W. Warburton and J. Conway criticized in some detail the view of A. H. Halsey and J. E. Floud that " measured intelligence is largely an acquired characteristic " and that class-differences in intelligence are due solely to environmental conditions

(*Brit. J. educ. Psychol.*, 28, 290). Conway described a mathematical model (suggested by the earlier work of Sir Ronald Fisher and C. D. Darlington) showing how the multi-factorial theory of inheritance and the known facts of social mobility would in the course of six or seven centuries lead to a distribution of intelligence similar to that reflected in the class-averages obtained with current tests (*Brit. J. statist. Psychol.*, 12, 1, London, 1959).

Dealing with problems at the other end of the age-scale, A. T. Welford summarized investigations recently carried out at Cambridge on the psychology of old age and urged the need for research on "attitudinal qualities" (*Ageing and Human Skill*, London, 1958). In a symposium on aging (*Bull. Brit. Psychol. Soc.*, London, 1959) a number of other investigators reported inquiries into various aspects of the problem, particularly with reference to the occupational implications. Extra-sensory perception once again became the centre of controversy as a result of the striking series of experiments carried out on telepathy in children by S. G. Soal and H. T. Bowden (*The Mind Readers*, London, 1959). The results so far obtained in the various branches of para-normal psychology were reviewed by Rosalind Heywood in a work largely based on a systematic and critical survey of investigations undertaken since its inception by the Society for Psychical Research (*The Sixth Sense*, London, 1959). In a suggestive study, *Human Potentialities* (New York, 1958), Gardner Murphy emphasized the importance of "unrecognized new fields, such as parapsychology"—still largely unknown to or ignored by academic psychologists—and contended that they "point to unrealized capacities whose meaning is at present all too dim". Viewing man as an organism still evolving, he attempted to show how, by the exercise of intelligence and conscious choice, man may be able to "transcend his biological and cultural heritage, and so open up a way for the freer expression of his virtually unlimited potentialities." (C. L. B.)

PUERTO RICO.
United States commonwealth in the West Indies. Area: 3,435 sq.mi. Pop.: (1950 census) 2,210,703; (1959 est.) 2,340,000. Language: Spanish and English. Religion: predominantly Roman Catholic. Capital: San Juan, pop. (1950 census) 224,767. Governor, Luis Muñoz Marín. Main exports: sugar, molasses, rum, leaf tobacco. Monetary unit: U.S. *dollar*.

History. Among the legislative actions of 1959 was the approval of a law establishing an election fund and regulating contributions to political parties in Puerto Rico. By this act, each main political party could draw annually up to $75,000 from the fund. In election years, the parties could use the unspent balances from previous years, plus an amount not over $150,000 for each party. Voluntary contributions to political parties would be limited to $200 per donor per year.

With the help of the government, 564 new factories were established from 1948 to the end of June 1959. This represented 46,383 new industrial jobs with an annual payroll of $78 million for an estimated net yearly income of $129 million to the Puerto Rican economy. (C. Os.)

QATAR.
British-protected Arab sheikhdom in Persian gulf. Area: 8,500 sq.mi. Pop.: (1958 est.) 40,000. Cap.: Doha (or Bida). Sheikh, Ali bin Abdullah-el-Thani; British political agent, J. S. R. Duncan. Monetary unit: Indian *rupee*. Chief export: petroleum.

History. A delegation from Qatar attended the first Arab Oil congress, which met in Cairo during April 16-23, 1959.

Preliminary surveys and estimates were made for the improvement of the port of Doha, but the cost was too high to allow work to be undertaken for the time being.

Oil production continued at the rate of about 8 million tons a year. Doha airport was being rapidly developed, and by the end of the year a hotel for transit passengers and other visitors was nearing completion.

RADIO, SCIENTIFIC DEVELOPMENTS IN.
The year 1959 was outstanding in the field of radio progress, not only for the steady development of communications of all types, but also for the use of radio for the control of artificial earth satellites and for obtaining information from the instruments carried in these satellites to measure all kinds of radiation in outer space. In addition, the conference of the International Telecommunications union, which was held at Geneva during the last four months of the year, had to revise the International Radio Regulations drawn up at the Atlantic City conference in 1947, and to take note of the need for specific frequency allocations for the scientific requirements of radio astronomy and space research. In preparation for this meeting, the union's technical advisory body on radio matters, the International Consultative Committee on Radio-communications (C.C.I.R.), held a plenary assembly in Los Angeles, United States, in April.

Radio Communications in Tropical Regions. Among other matters discussed at this meeting of the C.C.I.R. was that of the propagation of radio waves by way of the ionosphere. This is of particular importance to tropical broadcasting, for which high-frequency waves are much more effective than medium waves on account of the very high level of atmospheric noise present in most tropical regions. Past studies had shown that the usual methods of computing the field strength of sky wave signals were considerably in error in low latitudes. In a report entitled *The Calculation of the Median Sky Wave Field Strength in Tropical Regions* (D.S.I.R. Radio Research Special Report no. 27, H.M.S.O., London, 1959), by W. R. Piggott of the Radio Research station, Slough, this subject was reviewed with the aid of an analysis of the problem of identifying the most effective type of reflection for particular circumstances. As the report showed, some of the difficulties in interpreting the results of field-strength measurements in low latitudes had been due to changes in the dominant mode of ionospheric propagation, and the consequent variation in the attenuation of the waves and the angle of elevation at which they arrived at the receiver. The rate of advance of knowledge of this subject depends upon the continual interplay of practical observations with theory, and the publication of this report was expected to encourage radio research workers who operated in low latitudes to investigate their

A radar scanner, part of a new scheme to improve navigation on the Thames introduced by the Port of London authority in May.

wave propagation phenomena in a great deal more detail.

Mobile Radio and Television. From the earliest days of radio development, there was full appreciation of its advantages for communication with mobile stations, whether these were land vehicles, ships or aircraft. The application of radio to mobile vehicles on land was taken a step further during the year, when the first public radio-telephone service for motorists was opened in Lancashire. This enabled motorists in their cars to make and receive calls to and from telephone subscribers anywhere in Britain.

During the year, also, the temporary arrangements for the linking of the television systems of western Europe, which had been working for five years, were put on a more satisfactory engineering basis. The General Post Office opened a new permanent station near Dover as the terminal for the cross-channel radio link with the corresponding station near Calais. This link operated on a frequency of 4,000 Mc./sec. and the stations were equipped with the most modern television equipment, in addition to the provision of 600 new telephone channels. Both space and frequency diversity techniques were used to minimize the signal fading which had been experienced on the cross-channel link. The modulation signals, whether for television or telephony, were applied to a klystron oscillator followed by a travelling wave tube amplifier, and then by a waveguide feeder to the aerial. The output from the transmitter was 5 w., but this power was concentrated into a narrow beam by a parabolic reflector 10 ft. in diameter, mounted on a tower 200 ft. high, giving optical or line-of-sight transmission to the receiving station. The introduction of this new link would result in greater reliability and better quality Eurovision pictures.

Radio and Space Exploration. Radio played an outstanding part in rocket and satellite techniques, since it provided the necessary communication by which the scientific observations made in the vehicle were transmitted to the investigator on the earth. Radio was also used to supplement optical observation to determine the position of rockets and satellites when observations on phenomena such as solar radiation and cosmic rays were sent by telemetry to the receiving station on the earth.

One outstanding example of the use of radio during the year was in connection with the second moon rocket launched by the U.S.S.R. in September. Observations were made with the radio telescope at Jodrell Bank on the evenings of Sept. 12-13, during which signals were received on frequencies of 183·6 Mc./sec. and 19·992 Mc./sec. The precise value of the latter frequency was measured on Sept. 12 and found to vary uniformly (between 20 hr. 30 min. and 22 hr. 30 min. U.T.) at a rate of 4 c./sec. per hour. The rate expected from the earth's rotation alone was about 6 c./sec. per hour; thus the rocket was at that time being slightly retarded by the earth's gravitational attraction. On the following evening, Sept. 13, the frequency was found to be decreasing more rapidly, first at about 10 c./sec. per hour and then rising rapidly to more than ten times this value. The measured values of frequency changes were in agreement with those to be expected from the acceleration of an object moving directly towards the centre of the moon. The signals on both frequencies ceased abruptly and simultaneously at 21 hr. 02 min. 23 sec. U.T. on Sept. 13. At precisely this time, which was c. 1 min. 30 sec. after the predicted time of impact, at least two optical astronomers in England saw a minute pin-point of light and a kind of dark ring as though dust had been disturbed near the centre of the moon. It was estimated from the radio telescope observations that the velocity of impact was c. 3 km./sec. ± 0·5 km./sec.

This achievement was followed a few weeks later by the launching of Lunik III, which went into an orbit round the moon and the earth. The outstanding event on this occasion was the control by radio of the satellite when it was some 30,000 mi. beyond the moon, so that the end containing a camera was so orientated as to face the side of the moon remote from the earth. For a period of c. 40 min., two cameras of different apertures took photographs on 35-mm. film, one recording the whole disc, while the other took detailed pictures of various parts of the surface. While the satellite continued in its orbit round the moon and back towards the earth, the film was automatically processed, special protection against cosmic radiation being provided to avoid fogging. The final stage was carried out when the satellite was still nearly 300,000 mi. from the earth; on the receipt of a command signal the pictures were transmitted by radio to the earth receiving station. Thus for the first time man was given a view of the far side of the moon, and the pictures obtained would provide material for study and increased knowledge of the earth's only natural satellite.

The Ionosphere and the International Geophysical Year. During the International Geophysical Year (I.G.Y.), which terminated on Dec. 31, 1958, some 160 observatories throughout the world concentrated on a joint study of the characteristics of the ionosphere as measured by radio waves at vertical incidence. These soundings resulted in more than 1 million tables of measurements and photographic records. The assimilation of this vast accumulation of data would take many years, but a few examples were already available of the new knowledge being produced by this work.

In the first place, the vertical distribution of the electron density in the ionospheric layers was already better understood. This would enable better forecasts to be given of the optimum frequencies to be used for radio communications and, in particular, of the most appropriate angles at which to transmit the waves for reception at various distances. Secondly, during the I.G.Y., solar activity was considerably higher than it had been for the previous 200 years; as a consequence, the ionization and hence the critical penetration frequencies of the ionospheric layers reached unprecedented levels. This new information was unique and might not be repeated for very many years to come. The detailed results were being analysed, and the increased knowledge so obtained would be applied to new and more accurate methods of predicting the best frequencies for communications in the future.

A third major outcome of the I.G.Y. activities in radio science was the result of studying the drift of clouds of ionization in the upper atmosphere. In temperate and tropical latitudes it had been found that there are diurnal changes in the horizontal direction of these drifts as well as vertical movements. In some cases there was evidence of a long-term variation with the solar cycle period of about 11 years. The importance of such movements of ionization became particularly evident in the results obtained at the Halley Bay observatory in Antarctica during the I.G.Y. Here it was found that the electron density in the ionosphere at noon was greater in midwinter than in midsummer, although in the former case the solar radiation was entirely absent day and night, whereas in the summer the sun never sets. It is clear that, in this case, the behaviour of the ionosphere must be almost entirely determined by movements or drifts of ionization and not by direct solar influence.

(R. L. S.-R.)

RADIOLOGY: *see* X-RAY AND RADIOLOGY.

RAILWAYS. Great Britain. The modernization plan for British railways was in full progress in 1959 with the virtual ending of steam locomotive building and the spread of diesel traction to nearly all areas. Diesel locomotives numbered over 1,200 and the diesel railcar fleet approached 2,500, with further large deliveries awaited. Electric multiple-unit trains totalled nearly 5,300 vehicles, far exceeding the number in

(*Left*) *The view from the control tower at the Temple Mills marshalling yard at Stratford in east London, which was brought into service during the year.* (*Right*) *Inside the control tower an operator supervises the movement of trucks in the yard.*

any other country. Diesel and electric repair and maintenance depots came into service at many centres including Stratford, Tyseley near Birmingham and Stoke-on-Trent.

Main-line electrification, with the large-scale capital expenditure involved, was slower to complete, but newly electrified sections were inaugurated in the Colchester and Crewe areas, and also important extensions of the Southern region's existing network to Ramsgate and Dover. Progress was made with the conversion to electric traction of the London-Tilbury-Southend route, which involved major reconstruction at Barking. Other important civil engineering works completed were the three new tunnels at Hadley Wood on the east coast main line to Scotland, thus eliminating a double-track bottleneck, and the new passenger stations at Banbury and Barrow-in-Furness. A diesel repair depot at Bristol constructed of laminated timber and plywood was a novel development, as also a fully automatic train-washing plant at St. Leonard's-on-Sea.

Resignalling at Newcastle upon Tyne, with 10 mi. of line controlled from one cabin, equipped with 641 route switches, was concluded. It controlled one of the most complex sets of junctions in Britain with over 850 trains handled on a summer Saturday. Temple Mills marshalling yard at Stratford was brought into service and progress was made with the new Margam yard in south Wales. At Peterborough a large new freight station was inaugurated, also a centralized stores depot. Considerable milages were relaid with long-welded rails, and certain main lines were equipped with the automatic warning system repeating lineside signals within the locomotive cab. Tests were conducted with automatic couplings and many thousands of freight vehicles were equipped with vacuum brakes. Trials were made with sliding-roof wagons and heavy traffics (grain, cement, flour, sugar) carried in bulk wagons with automatic discharge. The container fleet, of many types, exceeded 47,000 units and a fast overnight container service was inaugurated between London and Glasgow.

Railbuses were tried out on light traffic lines and a fast Pullman service, known as the " Master Cutler ", operated between London (King's Cross) and Sheffield. The " Bristolian's " schedule for the 118·5 mi. between London (Paddington) and Bristol was reduced to 100 min. in either direction; it was normally diesel-hauled. A major closure was that of the Midland and Great Northern lines in Norfolk and

among smaller examples was that of the Ross-on-Wye - Monmouth-Chepstow route, Monmouth becoming a county town without a rail service. Financial results of British railways for 1958 revealed the very serious loss of nearly £90 million after payment of interest charges.

Continental Europe. In France continued priority was given to main-line electrification and the vital traffic artery between Lille and Paris was converted throughout to electric traction with accelerated services; passengers could telephone from the trains to any subscriber in Europe. Station reconstruction was completed at Calais, Amiens and Angers. Tests were conducted with wireless control of diesel locomotives in marshalling yards and many miles were laid with long lengths of welded rail, mostly on concrete sleepers. Sleeping-car services were extended and operating efficiency increased, but revenues suffered from railwaymen's strikes and the financial deficit remained heavy. Belgian National railways electrified their Namur-Charleroi and Gembloux-Jemeppe sections and further electrification was proposed though some schemes were postponed. Passenger services were withdrawn from several routes. Netherlands railways opened a new station in Rotterdam after five years of construction work.

In the German Federal Republic reconstruction of the famous four-track Hohenzollern bridge at Cologne was completed; few railway bridges in the world carried more trains per day. Electrified milage rose to 2,150, the complete programme envisaged being 5,200 mi. Thus considerable acceleration was made possible over the Rhine route between Cologne and Basel. However, 73% of all traffic was still handled by steam locomotives. No less than 12% of mechanical signals on the west German railways had been replaced by modern colour-light signals and the administration retained its pre-eminence in the development of specialized wagons; two new designs were of self-discharge and so-called " portal " wagons, a new term.

Austrian Federal railways continued electrification of the Semmering and Selzthal routes and inaugurated the Trans-Alpin electric multiple-unit express over the Arlberg route between Vienna and Zürich. In Italy progress was remarkable, with ever-extending electrification, notably the sections Venice-Trieste and Messina-Catania. A new design of 4,000-h.p. electric locomotive entered service, as also a new train-ferry for the Strait of Messina service. Strikes at times paralysed the railways. Swiss Federal railways electrified the Nieder-weningen branch, thus almost completing the electrification of their system, and double-tracking was continued in the Sargans, Biel and Zug areas. Zürich suburban services were greatly improved and a new train-ferry for Lake Constance entered service. Spanish National railways extended centralized traffic control (C.T.C.) by a further 190 mi. and completed the new Zamora-Corunna line. The 4·5-mi. La Engaña tunnel was finished and cafeteria-cars proved popular.

Throughout western Europe the Trans-Europ expresses were extended and the *wagon-lits* carried in a year over 2 million sleeping-car passengers—an all-time record. Scandinavian progress included the opening of Norway's Nordland line to Fauske and the inauguration of a train-ferry to Denmark, where a new train-ferry entered service on the Great Belt. Sweden finished doubling the Stockholm-Göteborg line, a programme started in 1937; C.T.C. was extended and long milages laid with concrete sleepers. Finnish railways placed heavy main-line diesels in service and Poland introduced express railcars between Warsaw, Berlin, Poznan and Brest (U.S.S.R.). Electrified services in the German Democratic Republic were reintroduced at Leipzig, and in Czechoslovakia steam locomotive production ceased, being replaced by diesel-hydraulic and diesel-electric types. Hungary completed reconstruction of Györ station, operated express tourist trains to Lake Balaton and introduced a light-weight dining-car, many coaches and diesel locomotives. Concrete sleepers were laid extensively and record passenger traffics handled. In Yugoslavia modernization progressed, including the laying of long-welded rails, the entry into service of 3,000-h.p. electric locomotives and the introduction of fast railcar schedules between Belgrade, Sarajevo and Ljubljana.

Asia. Both the Soviet and Turkish railways link Europe with Asia. Turkish railways pressed forward with C.T.C. and the U.S.S.R. inaugurated through service between Moscow and Tehran *via* Dzhul'fa, Persian railways having reached Tabriz and converted the Tabriz-Dzhul'fa section to standard gauge; Dzhul'fa was thus the only gauge-changing station. In the U.S.S.R. certain Moscow-Peking trans-Siberian expresses were diverted *via* Ulan-Ude, instead of Harbin, and electrified milage, which totalled 3,545 in 1957, was expected to reach 8,500 by 1960. French-built 6,000-h.p. electric locomotives entered service. Many 3,000-h.p. diesel-electric locomotives were introduced; current plans provided for dieselization of 43,500 mi. Large-scale railway construction continued in the Chinese People's Republic, including the opening of the new 700-mi. line between Lan-Chou and Pao-T'ou and the completed doubling of the Hankow-Peking route. At Canton a new bridge over the Chu Chiang was finished, as also the Nan-Ping-Foochow line. A new 380-mi. line, commenced in 1939, linked Kwei-Yang with Liu-Chou, located on the main line from Peking to Vietnam. Electrification made progress but steam locomotives were still being constructed at Tsingtao and diesels at Dairen.

In Japan the underground railways in Tokyo were extended and the National railways improved their services by the new electric multiple-unit luxury train " Kodama " (" Echo ") between Tokyo and Osaka, providing telephone communication with public exchanges. The new " Azakaze " (" Morning Breeze ") express covered the 733 mi. between Tokyo and Fukuoka in 17 hr. 10 min. Indian developments included further electrification in the Calcutta area, progress with the vital Khandwa-Hingoli line linking the metre-gauge systems of northern and southern India and the steady growth of rolling stock construction, including steam locomotives, coaches and wagons; diesels, however, had still to be imported. In Pakistan progress was represented by further dieselization with many additional coaches and wagons, the latter produced near Lahore; while in Ceylon, in spite of financial difficulties, more diesels were introduced. Malayan traffic fell grievously but stainless-steel railcars, built in Australia, reduced operating costs.

Africa. South African railways are the largest railway concern in Africa with 12,650 route mi. of which nearly 1,000 mi. were electrified by 1959. Financially successful, with ever-growing suburban traffic totalling almost 240 million passengers annually, they extended the electrified network (*e.g.*, between Vereeniging and Kroonstad) and received some of

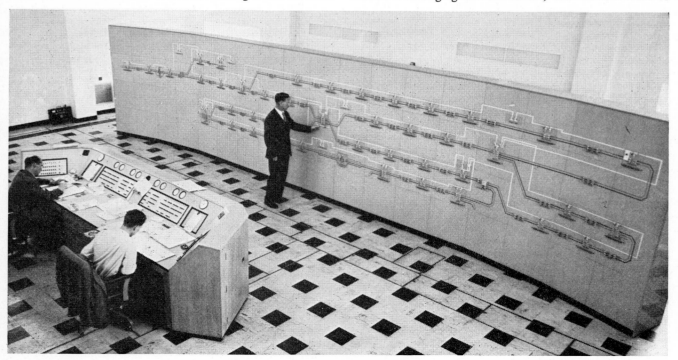

During the year further progress was made in the electrification of the Southern region of British railways. The scene in the region's supervisory control room at Canterbury, where power supplies are distributed to the Gillingham, Ramsgate and Dover sections.

the 135 electric locomotives on order from Britain. Orders were placed for 115 U.S.-type diesel-electric locomotives, the union being one of the last countries to turn away from steam traction, which was expected to be in use there for many years. Diesel-hydraulic locomotives also arrived from Germany and over 400 new passenger coaches were being built in the union by an Australian company. Widening progressed on several main lines and capacity was increased on the Johannesburg-Durban route. The working of the 580-mi. Vryburg-Bulawayo link with Rhodesia was taken over by Rhodesia railways, which had long owned it, and this administration increased its C.T.C. milage, introduced further diesel as well as Garratt steam locomotives and additional passenger coaches. A fast freight service was started between Bulawayo and Salisbury. In east Africa the Masasi extension was completed and the Jinja cut-off commenced, but electrification was postponed. New milage was opened in Sudan to Nyala. Extensive construction was started in Nigeria and contracts were placed for a 200-mi. railway in French Equatorial Africa. Congo traffics fell seriously but further sections were equipped with C.T.C. Algerian State railways changed their title to French National Railways of Algeria, thus reflecting their link with French National railways.

North America. *Canada.* The two great railway systems, Canadian National and Canadian Pacific, continued steady replacement of steam by diesel traction. Following the C.P.R.'s lead the C.N.R. reached agreement with its employees on the manning of diesel locomotives in freight and yard service. This agreement made the provision of firemen on such services unnecessary and was in line with European practice; it was expected to have important reactions in the United States. Freight train schedules between Montreal and Vancouver were accelerated and pick-a-back (trailers on flat-cars) service extended to the Atlantic and Pacific coasts. Light-weight aluminium refrigerator-cars entered service on the C.N.R. and cafeteria-cars gained in popularity. Construction continued in Quebec of the new line between St. Félicien and Chibougamau, and reconstruction of Mount Royal tunnel was begun. The C.P.R. regrouped its lines into four regions and the provincially owned Ontario Northland railway inaugurated stainless-steel coaches. Pacific Great Eastern railway lines were extended to Fort Saint John and linked with Northern Alberta railways at Dawson Creek; this railway, owned by British Columbia, used micro-waves for its communications.

United States. After a promising start toward recovery from the 1958 recession in the first six months of 1959, U.S. railroads suffered severe declines in traffic, earnings and employment during the last half of the year, largely as a result of the prolonged steel strike. The end of the year was also clouded by the unresolved dispute between rail management and employee organizations over wage rates and working rules.

Declines in carloadings during the second half of 1959 wiped out about half the gains made in the first half. Total carloadings on the class I railroads in 1959 were 31,304,000 compared with 30,206,000 in 1958. Measured in tons hauled one mile, revenue freight traffic increased from 552,000 million ton-miles in 1958 to an estimated 573,000 million in 1959, a gain of 4% on the previous year. Travel by rail declined in 1959 to 22,250 million passenger-miles, the lowest figure since 1938.

Total operating revenues in 1959 were $9,860 million, an increase of $296 million above 1958, but a decline of $631 million below 1957. Freight service produced $8,340 million in revenue, while passenger, mail and express service brought in $1,105 million, and all other revenues amounted to $415 million.

Total operating expenses were $7,715 million. Net railway operating income, after payment of operating expenses and

taxes but before interest, rentals and other fixed charges, amounted to $760 million, compared with $762 million in 1958. The rate of return on investment after depreciation earned was 2·76%, the same as in 1958 and lower than for any other year since 1946.

Net income after charges (the amount available for dividends, capital improvements and reserves) totalled $570 million in 1959, $32 million less than in 1958 and the lowest figure for any year since 1946.

For the year as a whole, employment averaged 820,000 compared with 841,000 for 1958. Payrolls totalled $5,065 million in 1959, bringing the average earnings of employees above $6,000 per annum for the first time. Straight time hourly earnings of employees averaged $2·70.

In 1959 railroads spent an estimated $850 million for capital improvements in plants and equipment, an increase of $112 million on 1958, but less than the amount spent in all but two years of the preceding decade.

New records in freight train loading and speed were again set in 1959, with average loads per train of 1,440 tons, an average speed of 19·5 miles an hour and a transportation output per freight train hour of 62,000 gross ton-miles, nearly 50% more than a decade earlier.

South America. Except for the nationalization of the 215-mi. Antioquia railway in Colombia, which virtually completed national ownership of railways in that country, and the extension of diesel traction on the Southern railway of Peru, where U.S.-built units were employed, railway developments of interest in South America were confined to Brazil and, to a lesser extent, Argentina. Argentine State railways suffered greatly from labour disputes and the financial situation deteriorated, revenues being only one-third of expenditures forecast for 1959. Contracts were placed for an extension of the Buenos Aires underground railways and plans completed for electrification of General Roca railway between Buenos Aires and La Plata. A Fiat subsidiary was to construct new rolling stock in Argentina and an Italian group was to build diesel locomotives.

Brazil's phenomenal railway development included new electric multiple-unit trains, built in Japan, on the Sorocabana railway and extension of diesel traction on the Central of Brazil. Nearly 200 U.S.-built diesels entered service and new stainless-steel passenger coaches were ordered. Diesel maintenance shops were completed and several sections were converted to electric traction, as on the Leste and Mineira lines. The Noroeste and Central lines were improved and the Rio Grande do Sul was incorporated in the Federal railway network which, however, incurred a heavy financial deficit.

Australasia. Victorian railways continued construction of the new standard-gauge line to the New South Wales border at Wodonga, a scheme costing £11 million, so important to the two railways concerned. Single-class travel was introduced on the Melbourne suburban services and C.T.C. on Glen Waverley section, while further diesel locomotives were ordered. In New South Wales further suburban lines were electrified, including completion to Gosford; Enfield locomotive depot, servicing 60 electric and 100 diesel units, was finished and new stainless-steel electric trains were introduced. On Queensland railways diesel traction permitted widespread accelerated services; bridge construction continued actively, but improvements to the Mount Isa line hung fire. South Australia completed regauging in the Naracoorte area but no progress was recorded with the Port Pirie-Cockburn (New South Wales border) scheme, which was vital to Australian rail communications. In Western Australia C.T.C. was installed between Pinjarra and Armadale, new cool-storage vans were introduced and the interstate container service was developed, involving the trans-Australian section of Commonwealth railways, which continued to be the sole Australian railway system more than covering its interest charges. In New Zealand progress included the addition of diesels, new refrigerator-vans, reconstruction of bridges and extension of C.T.C. A train-ferry service across Cook strait was planned. (*See* also COMMUNICATIONS.) (C. E. R. S.; R. S. H.)

RED CROSS.

RED CROSS. In 1959 the 100th anniversary of the birth of the Red Cross idea was observed in various ways by Red Cross, Red Crescent and Red Lion and Sun societies throughout the world. On June 27 representatives of 40 national societies gathered at Solferino, Italy, for the dedication of a memorial on the battlefield where Jean Henri Dunant launched the Red Cross movement.

The League of Red Cross Societies, in collaboration with the Tunisian and Moroccan Red Crescent societies, undertook in 1959 to feed and clothe 120,000 Algerian refugees in Tunisia and 100,000 in Morocco, a total increase of 100,000 over 1958. The league also provided assistance to victims of floods in Argentina, Austria, Bolivia, Brazil, Ethiopia, India, Indonesia, the Republic of Korea, Madagascar, Pakistan, Paraguay, Poland, Sudan, Tunisia and Uruguay.

The question of the repatriation of some 600,000 Koreans residing in Japan was referred to the International Committee of the Red Cross by the Japanese Red Cross at the request of the Japanese government. After negotiations extending over six months in Geneva between representatives of the Red Cross societies of Japan and the People's Democratic Republic of Korea, with observers from the Red Cross society of the Republic of Korea, it was agreed that the repatriation of the estimated 160,000 Koreans in Japan who wished to return to north Korea would be facilitated by the Red Cross societies of the two countries under observation of the international committee. Similar negotiations took place in Burma between the Red Cross societies of Thailand and the Democratic Republic of Vietnam, with observers from the international committee, for the repatriation of approximately 50,000 north Vietnamese from Thailand.

The International Committee of the Red Cross continued its inspection of internment camps in Algeria and Cuba and acted as a neutral intermediary in Indonesia and in various Caribbean conflicts. (H. W. DG.)

REFUGEES: A POSTWAR SURVEY.

REFUGEES: A POSTWAR SURVEY. Throughout history wars of conquest, revolutions and racial and religious persecutions have created refugee problems, but those of the mid-20th century were on an unprecedented scale. The large numbers involved, the complexities of modern life, a high population density in many areas and a heightened sense of nationalism combined to form a series of intractable problems, but these were eased by an increasing readiness to join in international action to help refugees.

It has been estimated that more than 70 million people were forcibly uprooted as a result of World War II and that by 1959 a further 40 million had become refugees (*see* Table I). A serious problem of the immediate postwar years was created by the 1 million refugees and displaced persons in Germany, Austria and Italy (including Russians, Balts, Poles, Czechoslovaks, Hungarians, Bulgars and Rumanians) who were unwilling to return to their homelands, despite pressure from their governments. The largest group of European refugees were the 13 million ethnic Germans who fled or were expelled from Poland, Czechoslovakia, Yugoslavia and Hungary, 9 million to western Germany and 4 million to eastern Germany. In addition to this problem and that of the non-German refugees, the west German government also accepted about 3 million German refugees from eastern Germany and this movement was continuing throughout 1959.

Other large postwar movements of refugees in Europe were the expulsion to Turkey of 350,000 Bulgarians of Turkish

Otto Frank, father of Anne Frank, at a ceremony near Wuppertal, W. Germany, to mark the founding of the Anne Frank refugee village.

ethnic origin, the transfer to Finland of 400,000 Karelians after the Karelian isthmus was ceded to the U.S.S.R. by the 1947 peace treaty and the flight of 179,000 Hungarians to Austria and Yugoslavia in late 1956 and early 1957 after the Hungarian rising.

At the end of World War II there were about 450,000 refugees of Jewish origin in Europe. In 1948 the new Jewish state of Israel was proclaimed and many refugees were included among the large numbers of Jewish immigrants accepted in Israel after that date (*see* Table II). However, the establishment of Israel and the fighting which preceded it produced considerably more than 1 million Arab refugees, notably in Jordan, Syria, Lebanon and the Gaza strip. Thereafter a persistent excess of births over deaths added considerably to the Arab refugee problem. In the year ended June 30, 1959, this excess, plus new registrations, amounted to

TABLE I. REFUGEES, 1946–59: ALL CATEGORIES

Europe . . .	17,965,000	including 16,400,000 Germans.
Asia		
Jordan . . .	596,000	Arabs from Palestine.
Egypt (including Gaza strip) .	249,000	Arabs from Palestine.
Lebanon . . .	132,000	Arabs from Palestine.
Syria . .	111,000	Arabs from Palestine.
Kuwait . .	25,000	Arabs from Palestine.
Saudi Arabia .	12,000	Arabs from Palestine.
Iraq . . .	12,000	Arabs from Palestine.
Pakistan . .	7,000,000	from India.
India . .	8,500,000	from Pakistan.
Hong Kong .	1,000,000	from China.
Macao . .	40,000	from China.
Formosa . .	600,000	from China.
South Korea .	3,000,000	from north Korea.
Vietnam . .	900,000	from north of 17th parallel.
India and Nepal .	20,000	from Tibet.
Total . .	22,197,000	
Africa		
Tunisia . .	125,000	from Algeria.
Morocco . .	100,000	from Algeria.
Ghana . .	5,000	from French Ivory Coast.
Total . .	230,000	
WORLD TOTAL	40,392,000	

34,280. The areas where the Arab refugees were mainly congregated could not support the total populations and the refugees remained substantially dependent on international assistance.

The 15·5 million refugees shown in Table I against India and Pakistan were uprooted in the period immediately following the creation of the new independent states of those names in 1947. It is estimated that in 1959 about 2·5 million in each territory still remained in need of assistance, but in each case the government had accepted these refugees as its own problem and had not appealed for international assistance. Three major refugee problems in Asia were directly or indirectly connected with the establishment and increasing influence of Communist China: the influx of 1 million Chinese refugees into Hong Kong, 600,000 into Formosa and others into Macao; the flight of 3 million north Koreans to the south during the Korean war (1950-53) and the transfer of 900,000 Vietnamese from the north to the south after the division of their country in 1954.

In 1957 and 1958 a serious refugee problem developed when some 200,000 Algerians entered Tunisia and Morocco. In Jan. 1959 it was reported that about 5,000 Ghanaian refugees of the Ewe tribe had fled from the French Ivory Coast after the rioting there in Oct. 1958. In March 1959 the subjugation of Tibet by China and the flight of the Dalai Lama to India resulted in an influx of refugees into Nepal and India.

International Agencies. Between Dec. 1945 and the end of June 1947 the United Nations Relief and Rehabilitation administration (U.N.R.R.A.), which had been created in 1943, arranged the repatriation of about 1 million displaced persons. In 1948 the functions of U.N.R.R.A. and the Intergovernmental Committee on Refugees were taken over by the International Refugee organization (I.R.O.). By the time I.R.O. was wound up in 1951 it had arranged the resettlement of about 1,038,000 refugees at a cost of nearly $430 million, but 1,440,000 refugees remained under its mandate. In 1949 the general assembly of the United Nations had established the Office of the United Nations High Commissioner for Refugees (U.N.H.C.R.) to provide international protection after the I.R.O. ceased operations. The statute of the U.N.H.C.R. was approved in 1950 and his office, an integral part of the United Nations organization, operated under a mandate later extended to the end of 1963. The office's administrative expenses were to be borne by United Nations funds, but assistance and resettlement costs had to be met from voluntary contributions.

At the end of Dec. 1958 there remained about 160,000 unsettled refugees under the U.N.H.C.R.'s mandate in Europe, of whom some 32,000 were living in official camps maintained by the host governments. By the end of 1959 this group had been reduced to 110,000, of whom 20,000 were living in official camps. In 1958 the U.N.H.C.R. brought into operation a programme for clearing all the official camps, with the object of resettling all who had spent more than ten years as refugees. The programme included vocational training, placing in jobs, initial financial help in settlement and the provision of low-cost housing. For those unable to provide for themselves—the old, the disabled and the chronically sick —plans were prepared to provide care and security in decent surroundings. The cost of these projects was to be shared between the host governments and the high commissioner's funds, the former providing in some cases as much as two-thirds of the cost. The high commissioner's programme provided for the closure of all official camps in Europe by the end of 1960 if adequate funds could be made available, but by the end of 1959 this was still not assured. In addition to the camp clearance programme, U.N.H.C.R.'s budget for 1960 included provision for the expenditure of $20 million on the resettlement of refugees living outside the official camps.

TABLE II. REFUGEES STILL REQUIRING INTERNATIONAL ASSISTANCE OR REMAINING UNDER THE MANDATE OF THE U.N. HIGH COMMISSIONER, DEC. 31, 1959

	Total including settled refugees	Refugees still unsettled or requiring assistance
First and Second Asylum Countries		
Austria	56,000	32,000
Belgium	69,600	1,000
France	280,000	36,000
German Fed. Rep. . . .	217,000	49,000
Greece	15,000	10,000
Italy	20,000	10,500
Netherlands . . .	13,000	—
Hong Kong (White Russians) .	10,000	10,000
Norway	4,500	—
Sweden	30,000	—
Switzerland . . .	20,000	—
United Kingdom . . .	220,000	—
Total Europeans . .	955,100	148,500
Hong Kong (Chinese) .	1,000,000	1,000,000
Macao (Chinese) . . .	40,000	40,000
Jordan, Lebanon, United Arab Republic, Iraq, Saudi Arabia and Kuwait (Arabs) .	1,149,000	990,181*
Vietnam	900,000	900,000
India and Nepal (Tibetans) .	20,000	20,000
Total Asians . .	3,109,000	2,950,181
Tunisia and Morocco .	225,000	225,000
Ghana	5,000	5,000
Total Africans . .	230,000	230,000
Resettlement Countries		
United States . .	483,000	
Canada . . .	240,000	
Australia . . .	235,000	
Israel . . .	170,000	
Brazil . . .	42,000	
Argentina . . .	35,000	
Venezuela . . .	20,000	
Chile . . .	7,500	
New Zealand . . .	6,500	
Union of South Africa .	2,500	
Uruguay . . .	2,000	
Colombia . . .	1,500	
Others . . .	137,000	
WORLD TOTAL . .	5,676,100	3,328,681

* Actual number registered with and receiving help from U.N.R.W.A. on June 30, 1959.

In handling the refugee problem, the U.N.H.C.R. was acting in partnership with local and international voluntary agencies, the social services of the countries concerned and the Intergovernmental Committee for European Migration.

The United Nations general assembly, in Sept. 1948, established as a temporary measure the United Nations Relief for Palestine Refugees organization. This was superseded in May 1950 by the United Nations Relief and Works Agency for Palestine Refugees in the Near East (U.N.R.W.A.), which was made responsible for rehabilitation as well as relief. U.N.R.W.A. was financed by voluntary contributions in cash and in kind from governments. It organized relief work, such as the provision of food and shelter, and welfare and educational services and, on a smaller scale, rehabilitation work such as vocational training, land settlement and the encouragement of small industries. In 1959 nearly 40% of the Arab refugees lived in U.N.R.W.A. camps and a programme was in hand to replace all tents there with simple huts. U.N.R.W.A. was assisted by 33 international and local voluntary organizations. Up to the end of 1958 supporting governments had contributed $278·2 million. In 1959 U.N.R.W.A. operated on a budget of $37·1 million. Its mandate was due to expire on June 30, 1960, but a preliminary expenditure budget of $38·7 million had been prepared for operations to be carried out during 1960.

Assistance to Korean refugees was given from July 1, 1950, by the body known later as the Korean Civil Assistance command. On Dec. 1, 1950, the United Nations general assembly approved the creation of the United Nations Korean Reconstruction agency (U.N.K.R.A.) to plan and assist in the reconstruction of Korea. Its operations ceased on June 30, 1958, by which time its revenue from governments had amounted to $148·5 million.

World Refugee Year. On Dec. 5, 1958, the general assembly of the United Nations approved a resolution, sponsored by Great Britain and nine other nations, calling for a World Refugee Year, with the object of focusing interest on the refugee problem and encouraging additional financial contributions from all sources and additional opportunities for permanent solutions. A World Refugee Year secretariat was established at Geneva. By the end of 1959, 63 countries had agreed to participate and to encourage the formation of special national committees. The World Refugee Year was launched in the United Kingdom on June 1, 1959, and this was quickly followed in other countries.

The hope of the intergovernmental refugee organizations, the governments concerned and the voluntary refugee agencies was that the World Refugee Year would result in an improved flow of funds from governments and the general public and in a relaxation of restrictions preventing the entry of refugees for permanent settlement. By the end of 1959 there was evidence that this hope would be justified in all respects.

(HD. SW.)

RESPIRATORY DISEASES: *see* DISEASES.

RÉUNION.
French overseas island *département* in the Indian ocean. Area: 970 sq.mi. Pop.: (1954 census) 274,370; (1959 est.) 310,000; French creoles, Negroes, Mulattoes, Indians and Chinese. Language: French and creole French. Religion: Roman Catholic. Capital, Saint-Denis; pop. (1954 census) 41,863. Prefect, Jean Perreau-Pradier. Main exports: sugar, rum. Monetary unit: *franc CFA* = metropolitan Fr.2.

History. At the municipal elections of March 8-15 the Gaullists (Union pour la Nouvelle République) won 211 seats, the Independents (right-wing) 235, the Communists 27 and various other parties 57. At Saint-Denis the Gaullist-Socialist alliance won with 7,300 votes against 6,700 for the Communists. On April 26 Georges Repiquet (U.N.R.) was re-elected senator. At the parliamentary by-election on May 24, M. Valère (U.N.R.) was elected deputy. The Communists alleged that these elections were fraudulent.

President Charles de Gaulle visited Saint-Denis during July 9-10, accompanied by Jacques Soustelle, minister-delegate to the prime minister's office. (HU. DE.)

RHEUMATIC DISEASES: *see* DISEASES.

RHODESIA AND NYASALAND, FEDERATION OF.
Federation of three British central African countries: Northern Rhodesia, protectorate (N. of River Zambesi); Nyasaland, protectorate (E. of N. Rhodesia); and Southern Rhodesia, self-governing colony (S. of Zambesi). The federation is bounded N. by Tanganyika and the Belgian Congo, E. by Mozambique, S. by Bechuanaland and the Union of South Africa and W. by Angola. Area: 487,652 sq.mi. Pop.: (1958 est.) 7,650,000, incl. Asians and Coloureds. Language: English, tribal dialects and (in S. Rhodesia) Afrikaans. Religion: Moslem, Christian, pagan. Federal capital, Salisbury, Southern Rhodesia. Administration: governor-general; prime minister and other ministers with assigned functions; federal assembly with speaker and elected majority; African Affairs board (standing committee of federal assembly representing African interests and scrutinizing relevant bills); the three component countries retain prefederation legislative structure. Governor-general, Lord Dalhousie; federal prime minister, Sir Roy Welensky. Main imports: textile piecegoods and apparel, machinery, motor vehicles, motor spirits. Main exports: copper, tobacco, gold, asbestos, tea, chrome ore. Monetary unit: Central African pound (=£1 sterling). Southern Rhodesian currency is also legal tender.

Northern Rhodesia. Area: 288,137 sq.mi., incl. 3,000 sq.mi. of lakes. Pop.: (1956 census) Europeans, 64,800; Asians, 5,400; Coloureds, 1,550. African pop.: (1957 est.) 2,190,000. Chief towns (total pop., African, 1956 est., European pop. in brackets, 1956 census): Lusaka (cap.) 60,000 (9,400); Kitwe 73,000 (9,700); Ndola 57,500 (6,800); Luanshya 52,366 (6,000); Broken Hill 40,000 (4,200); Mufulira 53,358 (5,600); Chingola 32,984 (4,600). Administration: governor; executive council; legislative council with unofficial majority (mainly elected Europeans). Governors in 1959: Sir Arthur Benson and (from April 23) Sir Evelyn Hone.

Nyasaland. Area: 49,178 sq.mi., incl. 12,398 sq.mi. of lakes. Pop.: (1956 census) Europeans, 6,700; Asians, 8,510; Coloureds, 1,200. African pop.: (1958 est.) 2,690,000. Chief towns: Zomba (cap.), pop. c. 6,600; Blantyre-Limbe c. 24,000. Administration: governor; executive council; legislative council with official majority. Governor, Sir Robert Armitage.

Southern Rhodesia. Area: 150,337 sq.mi. Pop.: (1956 census) Europeans, 176,300; Asians and Coloureds, 13,206. African pop.: (1957 est.) 2,290,000. Chief towns: Salisbury (cap.), pop. (1956 est.) African 125,000, European (1956 census) 62,000; Bulawayo, African 94,000, European (1956 census) 41,000. Administration: governor; prime minister; executive council (cabinet); elected legislative assembly. Governor, Vice-Admiral Sir Peveril William-Powlett; prime minister, Sir Edgar Whitehead.

History. In Nyasaland the first three months of 1959 were troubled by acts of violence. Disturbances took place in Zomba in the third week of January after a mass meeting of the Nyasaland African congress. Further demonstrations followed a few days later in Blantyre and Limbe when an emergency conference of delegates of the congress, summoned by the congress leader, Dr. Hastings Banda (*see* BIOGRAPHIES), was held in Blantyre. Other acts of violence in a number of widely separated areas during February resulted in a request from the governor, Sir Robert Armitage, for troops of the King's African Rifles to be moved from Lusaka in Northern Rhodesia to Nyasaland, and European troops were also sent from Southern Rhodesia as a precautionary measure. Still the disturbances continued and in the early hours of March 3 Armitage declared a state of emergency and outlawed the congress. On the same day Banda and other congress members were arrested and deported to another part of the federation.

In the first 24 hr. of the emergency 26 Africans were killed when security forces fired on demonstrators in different parts of the protectorate. The declaration of an emergency in Nyasaland had been preceded five days earlier by a similar

Detainees at Kanjedza prison camp, Nyasaland. In September a commission of inquiry began investigating conditions at the camp.

(Left) Rescue operations to save animals trapped by rising waters following the creation of an artificial lake above the Kariba dam. On the right is the governor of S. Rhodesia. (Right) An aerial view of the dam, which was nearing completion at the end of 1959.

move in Southern Rhodesia, where the Southern Rhodesia African National congress, the Nyasaland African congress, the Zambia National congress and the Northern Rhodesia African National congress had been banned as illegal organizations. The announcement of the Nyasaland emergency, however, was quickly taken up in the U.K. House of Commons, where opposition members had already severely criticized the government for its apparent acquiescence in the federal government's declaration that a British Labour M.P., John Stonehouse, was a prohibited immigrant in central Africa. An opposition offer to co-operate in the appointment of a parliamentary commission to visit Nyasaland as soon as possible in order to investigate the background to the disturbances was rejected by the government, which argued that the next step should be for the minister of state, Lord Perth, to go to Nyasaland when the governor thought the time appropriate. On March 13, after further shootings and arrests in areas which had previously been undisturbed, some Conservative M.P.s also pressed the secretary of state for the colonies, A. T. Lennox-Boyd, to appoint a commission of inquiry but Lennox-Boyd urged his party to remain patient.

Ten days later the U.K. government published as a white paper a dispatch sent by Armitage to Lennox-Boyd on March 18. In it the governor traced the activities of the Nyasaland African congress leading to a secret meeting on Jan. 25 at which, Armitage claimed, congress leaders arranged for demonstrations to take place, to be followed, in the event of Banda's arrest, by a campaign of violence involving the assassination of the governor and other senior administrative officers. Events in February, the white paper continued, had provided evidence that the early stages of the congress plan were already under way, and that only the summoning of reinforcements and the declaration of an emergency had prevented the full-scale implementation of the plan.

On the following day (March 24) it was announced that a commission of inquiry under the chairmanship of Mr. Justice Devlin had at last been appointed. However, the commission's report which was published towards the end of July aroused very mixed feelings, for, while vindicating the Nyasa-

land governor's resort to emergency powers it rejected the claim that a widespread murder plot had existed and challenged the accuracy of a number of other statements contained in the white paper published in March. The U.K. parliament then found itself in a paradoxical situation in which the government introduced a motion advocating the acceptance of only some of the views contained in the commission's report, while the opposition unsuccessfully moved an amendment in favour of accepting the complete report. The whole sequence of events stimulated lively comment throughout the United Kingdom, not least in Scotland, since the Church of Scotland through its missionary activities had had a long tradition of association with Nyasaland. Emphasis was laid on the fact that in spite of the alleged murder plot no European lives had been lost, while security forces had killed more than 50 African rioters and demonstrators. By the middle of the year, however, only isolated incidents were taking place in Nyasaland. Nevertheless, the protectorate continued to hold public attention and there was continued criticism of the Central African Federation in Britain.

In Southern Rhodesia a series of bills was introduced into the parliament in the earlier part of the year with the object of outlawing permanently the African National Congress movement. A Preventive Detention bill aroused particular criticism, and women wearing black sashes stood at the entrance to the parliament building in silent protest against it. The bill, under the terms of which persons detained for known or suspected subversive activities might be detained indefinitely at the governor's pleasure and without any recourse to the courts, was subsequently withdrawn. It was later replaced by another rather less rigorous bill which, however, aroused objections from church leaders in Southern Rhodesia and from the Salisbury Bar association.

It was, therefore, against this stormy background that preparations began for the review of the constitution to take place in 1960. In April the secretary of state for Commonwealth relations, Lord Home, visited Rhodesia for preliminary discussions, and in July the federal prime minister, Sir Roy Welensky, flew to Britain where he met members of the

Lady William-Powlett, wife of the governor of S. Rhodesia, talks to an African schoolteacher at a native " indaba " or meeting.

government and also the opposition leader, Hugh Gaitskell. While in Britain Welensky stated that he was agreeable to the proposal to appoint a commission to visit the federation in order to obtain information in advance of the 1960 discussions, and he added that, if necessary, he was prepared to accept the inclusion in the commission of members from other parts of the Commonwealth, who had had experience of a federal state. On July 21 the British prime minister, Harold Macmillan, announced that a 26-man commission would in fact be appointed on which the United Kingdom would have 11 members, the Commonwealth 2 and central Africa 13. Of the last group five would be Africans and none would be members of either the governments or legislatures of their respective countries. It was later announced that Lord Monckton would be chairman of the commission.

In both Northern Rhodesia and Nyasaland constitutional changes took place in the course of the year. After the legislative council elections in Northern Rhodesia in March the first two Africans were appointed as ministers. Of the 22 elected seats in the legislature Welensky's United Federal party won 13, but failed to obtain an over-all majority, since the council consisted of 8 appointed members in addition to the elected members. One of the two Africans chosen as ministers was a member of the United Federal party, but the other was an Independent. The four elected European ministers were all members of the party. The United Federal party had feared some loss of African support, partly because of a belief that the party was paying only lip service to the idea of racial partnership. The formation of a new party, the Central African party, by R. S. Garfield Todd and Sir John Moffat, was also expected to result in some loss of support for the United Federal party, as the new group had as its declared object the construction of a united nation comprising all races on the basis of equality of opportunity in political, economic and social fields.

It was announced in August that the number of Africans on the representative side of the Nyasaland legislative council was to be increased from five to seven thus giving Africans a majority over the six official members representing Europeans and Asians on that side of the house. The government side, however, succeeded in retaining its majority. It was further stated that two African members would for the first time be appointed to the Nyasaland executive council.

The fall in the price of copper combined with the fear that the events in the federation would have a discouraging effect upon capital investment from overseas, led to a decision that the federal government's development plan for 1959-63 would have to be based upon a lower rate of expenditure than had been proposed in the existing plan which covered the period 1957-61.   (K. I.)

ROADS. Europe. In most European countries at the end of the 1950s there were more vehicles being licensed each year, with greater congestion on the roads and a greater pressure from public opinion for more roads.

In 1959 in Britain the Great North road was being modernized throughout its length. Of the 220 mi. between London and Newcastle upon Tyne, 60 mi. of dual carriageway were completed and 60 mi. under construction. Stilton had been bypassed and work was proceeding on bypasses at Biggleswade, Stamford and Doncaster. Bypasses were nearly completed at many other towns notorious as the scene of traffic congestion, notably Maidenhead on the London-Bath road and Maidstone on the road from London to towns on the Kent coast. Work involving new bridges over the Thames was proceeding on ring roads at Oxford.

The motorway M.1, from London to Birmingham, was completed and work started on the major viaducts needed to carry its extension to Penrith over the River Mersey and the Manchester Ship canal. A second section of 86 mi. of the London-Yorkshire motorway was planned to join M.1 near Rugby and link it with the bypass at Doncaster on the Great North road. Easier access from central London to London airport was provided by a flyover at Chiswick, and the provision of dual carriageways and a 4-mi. stretch of motorway were being planned to link central London to the motorways running north. A road tunnel was completed under the Thames between Dartford and Purfleet. When ready for traffic in 1962 it would link together the projected North and South Orbital roads which would form a ring round London at some 15 mi. from its centre. The linking of these great trunk highways by urban motorways with the centres of the towns they served raised problems which would be studied by special groups in the larger cities in co-operation with the Ministry of Transport. To help the flow of traffic the ministry was also making an experiment with " clearways "; *i.e.*, sections of

A section of M.1, the London-Birmingham motorway, which was officially opened to traffic by the minister of transport on Nov. 2.

" Things to come ? " A cartoon by Brockbank which appeared in an October issue of the " Highway Times ", a periodical published by the Roads Campaign council. The council represents various organizations concerned with the improvement of the British road system.

trunk road on which parking was forbidden. Work began on a road bridge over the Firth of Forth to replace the existing ferry. The minister's report on the roads in England and Wales for the year ended March 31, 1959, showed that payments for major improvements and new construction rose to £44,024,000 compared with £23,416,000 in 1957-58.

In France a new road bridge over the Seine at Tancarville linked lower Normandy with eastern Brittany and shortened the journey from Le Havre to Deauville by 60 mi. A motorway was planned from Tancarville to Marseilles *via* Paris and Lyons, with a northern spur from Paris to Lille and Valenciennes. In Belgium construction began on motorways from Antwerp to Liège and from Brussels to Namur.

In Italy the motor road linking Genoa with Milan was nearing completion. It formed part of the plan for a direct express road link between Genoa and Amsterdam. The new " motorway of the sun " was also under construction. It would link Milan with Naples *via* Bologna, Florence and Rome. There were plans to continue it over the Brenner pass to Munich and Warsaw, with a branch from Rome *via* Venice to Vienna, Budapest and Belgrade. Some 65 mi. southwards from Milan were already open to traffic, and some 30 mi. of motorway was already in operation between Budapest and Györ which would form part of the ultimate link with Vienna. Work was proceeding on the 7·5-mi. tunnel under Mont Blanc between Aosta and Chamonix, to be completed in 1963. It would reduce the distance by road between Paris and Milan by 190 mi. In the German Federal Republic the network pattern of motor roads was being completed with sections running north and south to provide " Europa " highways from Hamburg to Basel and Vienna.

A new road through the Vale of Tempe and skirting Mount Olympus was under construction in Greece. It would reduce by 80 mi. the distance by road from Athens to Salonika. In the U.S.S.R. a new " tourist road " was opened, running from the Finnish border to Moscow *via* Leningrad. Work was in hand on the first of Czechoslovakia's " super highways ", which would link Prague with the country's eastern border. Of the 750 mi. planned some 120 mi. had been completed. In Yugoslavia a highway following the Adriatic coast was completed and the main highway linking the coast with the Rumanian border *via* Belgrade was extensively modernized.

Some sections had been completed of a 25-mi. six-lane ring road round Berlin, and an overhead road 1,000 yd. long had been built at Ludwigshafen to carry traffic over the centre of the city. An inner ring road was being planned for Stockholm and an outer ring dual carriageway with a diameter of some

20 mi. was planned for Moscow. In Austria the Gross Glockner road was being widened to 20 ft. throughout its length and extensive car parks were being provided at sites offering panoramic views.

Africa. In Libya a new road over 700 mi. long was planned to link the coastal towns with the Fezzan. Some £4 million was to be spent in Kenya in reconstructing a group of trunk roads with a bituminous surfacing. A road linking Uganda to the Belgian Congo was completed. In Nigeria a 1-mi.-long bridge over the Niger was under construction at Onitsha and 50 other road bridges were to be modernized. The closing of the Kariba dam reduced the width of the Zambesi, enabling road communications between Nyasaland and Southern Rhodesia to be maintained in the rainy season. A road had been built across Gambia between Dakar and Konakry (including a bridge across the River Gambia) and progress had been made in the building of the trunk road from Dakar to St.-Louis, Senegal.

About £10 million was to be spent on building a ring road and other express ways to ease traffic congestion in Cape Town. Plans were in hand to make the central trunk road from the Cape of Good Hope to Nairobi usable in all weathers.

Mobile police at Southend experimenting with new apparatus to detect vehicles making excessive and unnecessary noise.

Asia. Over £60 million were to be spent in Persia on a trunk road linking the Caspian sea with the head of the Persian gulf and on other main trunk roads in the western provinces; the International Bank for Reconstruction and Development was to lend £24 million for the work. Persia's main road links with both Turkey and Pakistan were also to be improved. An all-weather link between India and Kashmir was provided by the opening of the 1·5-mi. Jawahar tunnel. One lane was in operation, replacing the old road over the Banihal pass which was blocked by snow in winter. The Economic Commission for the Far East was considering plans for a Trans-Asian highway 5,000 mi. long. A new highway was to be constructed from Bangkok to Sara Buri in Thailand with the help of more than £4 million from the United States. Very large programmes of road construction were being put in hand in northwestern and southwestern China so that lorries could replace pack animals for transport in these remote areas. Work began on two express highways in the neighbourhood of Bombay, one to the north and the other to the east towards Poona.

Australasia. A " Commonwealth " plan was put forward to spend some £720 million throughout Australia on roads and bridges during the succeeding five years. A ring road and other improvements were being planned for Melbourne to cost £20 million.

United States. It was estimated that a record $10,504 million was spent during 1959 for highways and streets, in capital improvement, maintenance, highway police, administration and interest on highway debt. Construction expenditures alone amounted to $5,750 million. Capital expenditure (including right-of-way costs) for the improvement of about 39,000 mi. of principal highways amounted to $5,487 million and capital expenditure on about 93,000 mi. of local roads and streets amounted to $1,453 million. All roads and streets, improved and unimproved, in the United States totalled 3,477,000 mi.

The Federal-Aid Highway act of 1958 had provided $3,400 million of federal aid to the states for the year ending June 30,

1960. This was the largest federal-aid apportionment for highways ever made—more than the sum of all authorizations made during the first 24 years of federal aid for highways, from 1917 to 1940. It included $2,500 million for the national system of inter-state and defence highways (a $300 million increase over the previous fiscal year) and $900 million for primary, secondary and urban highways. Of the latter amount, 45% was for the federal-aid primary system, 30% for the secondary system and 25% for urban highways. In these three categories the requirement that the states match the federal grant dollar for dollar was continued. For the inter-state system the 90% federal, 10% state, matching basis was continued. Of the total 1959-60 apportionment, the largest share, $302 million, went to California. The second largest apportionment, $198 million, went to Ohio. New York state, with $180 million, was third.

In the year ended June 30, 1959, actual commitments of federal funds totalled $3,223 million, including $2,284 million for inter-state highways and $939 million for the primary, secondary and urban systems. Work completed during the fiscal year on the inter-state system cost $1,325 million, of which $1,039 million was federal aid. Much of the year's expenditure involved preliminary engineering and right-of-way purchases, but construction contracts were completed on 2,290 mi. Completions on all classes of federal and federal-aid projects during the fiscal year accounted for the improvement of 32,828 mi. of roads and streets at a cost of $3,275 million, including $2,095 million of federal funds. About 12% of the federal-aid roads built during the year were multi-lane expressways, which were helping to relieve traffic congestion in cities and along major traffic routes.

The Inter-American Highway. By the end of 1959, 72% of the highway from Laredo, Texas, to Panama City, Mexico, was paved and and another 24% was usable the year round. It was possible to travel by road at all times from Laredo to San Isidro, Costa Rica, a distance of 2,725 mi. The next 150 mi. to Concepción, a few miles beyond the Panama border, though under construction, were still impassable. (*See* also Communications.)   (W. H. G.; X.)

ROMAN CATHOLIC CHURCH.

The Roman Catholic church is governed by a hierarchy of bishops with the pope (bishop of Rome) at its head. Under him patriarchs, archbishops and other great prelates are possessed of various local jurisdictions over the bishops of their respective provinces. On Dec. 31, 1959, there were in all 2,128 Roman Catholic jurisdictions in the world, namely 10 residential patriarchates, 1,704 residential archbishoprics and bishoprics, 86 abbacies and prelatures *nullius*, 11 apostolic administrations, 16 prelatures of oriental rites, 175 vicariates apostolic, 120 prefectures apostolic and 6 missions *sui iuris*. The Church teaches that the authority of all these varied jurisdictions must be sought in the authority given by Our Lord Himself and recorded in the Gospels. Estimated world numbers of Roman Catholics of all rites (June 30, 1959): 527,643,000, incl. 37·5 million in the United States and 4·5 million in the United Kingdom. There were in the world about 416,000 churches, 177,000 parishes, 260,000 diocesan clergy and 120,000 regular clergy of various orders.

History. Pope John XXIII announced on Jan. 25, 1959, when he had been pope for only 12 weeks, his decision to convene the 21st general or oecumenical council in the history of the Church and a diocesan synod in Rome which would serve as a model for others throughout the Latin Church, as well as to complete as soon as possible the code of canon law for the eastern Church and to bring that for the western Church under revision. Within six months eight commissions had virtually completed the preparations for the Roman synod, and on the feast of Christ the King the pope announced that this would meet on Jan. 25, 1960.

The 21st General Council. The general council, however, was a much more complicated matter, and as the year advanced it became clear that this would take longer to prepare than some had at first supposed and that initial

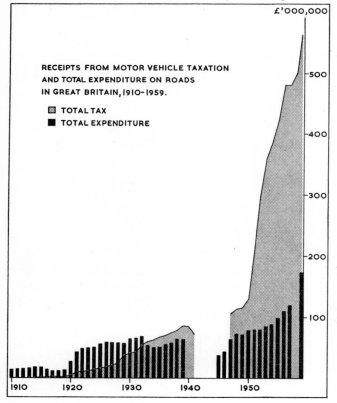

RECEIPTS FROM MOTOR VEHICLE TAXATION AND TOTAL EXPENDITURE ON ROADS IN GREAT BRITAIN, 1910-1959.

▨ TOTAL TAX
■ TOTAL EXPENDITURE

£'000,000

The ordination of a young priest. The ceremony took place at All Saints Roman Catholic church, Ferryhill, Co. Durham.

speculation about its agenda had been misleading. The date chosen for the announcement, the last day of the annual octave of prayer for Christian unity, and the pope's own phrase about " an invitation to the separated communities to seek for unity ", with other indications, suggested that the council would in some direct fashion seek the reconciliation of the separated Eastern Churches with the Holy See. The pope's Christmas message had included a reference to the Orthodox Churches, and there was a cordial reply from the patriarch of Constantinople. On March 18 an Orthodox bishop was received by a reigning pope for the first time for 350 years; he was the Metropolitan Iakovos, newly appointed to be the representative of the patriarch of Constantinople in the New World. In May the king of the Hellenes became the first ruler of Greece to call on a pope since the last of the Byzantine emperors did so on his way to the council of Florence.

Five unofficial Roman Catholic observers were present when the World Council of Churches met, with Orthodox participation, on the island of Rhodes during August. A premature announcement was then made of an informal meeting of Roman Catholic and Protestant theologians to take place at Venice during 1960, but delicate matters had been too quickly and too publicly broached, and in October it was announced that the Venice meeting would not take place, and that a meeting of Roman Catholic and Protestant theologians that was to have begun in Assisi on Oct. 26 had been cancelled.

At one of the press conferences that were a novel feature of the new pontificate Cardinal Domenico Tardini, as chairman of the preparatory commission for the general council, said on Oct. 30 that it would not meet before 1963, and perhaps not until 1965. It would be called the second council of the Vatican. No special invitations would be sent to Churches not in communion with the Holy See, although representatives of these would be welcome as observers; the council, being " a family affair of the Church ", could not include negotiations with any individuals or groups not in communion with the Holy See. Some 2,700 bishops all over the world had been invited to submit their views on the agenda, and about 1,700 had already done so; the Roman Catholic universities were also being consulted. Cardinal Tardini emphasized that the council would not condemn persons or ideas; its purpose was, by strengthening the faith of Roman Catholics, renewing *mores* and reforming ecclesiastical discipline, to present the Roman Catholic Church in all its splendour, so attracting men to it and promoting Christian unity by that means.

France. On June 11 the pope had personally informed Cardinal Maurice Feltin, the archbishop of Paris, of the decision of the Holy Office not to grant the request of the French bishops, as earlier conveyed to the Holy See by Cardinal Feltin, that " priest-workers " should be allowed to resume full-time work in the factories. At the same time the

Holy Office recommended that secular institutes, of laymen bound by religious vows, should undertake a special apostolate among the French working class. These decisions, and the reasons for them, were formally set forth in a letter which Cardinal Giuseppe Pizzardo, the secretary of the Holy Office (who resigned in October), addressed to Cardinal Feltin on July 3. The letter was intended to be private, as the rejected request had been, but *Le Monde* obtained a copy and published the text on Sept. 13, to the grave embarrassment of the French bishops.

Italy. In Italy the pope gave new statutes to Catholic Action, decentralizing it and making it dependent upon the bishops' conference, as in France and Germany, and no longer directly upon the Holy See. Professor Luigi Gedda was not reappointed to be its president, being succeeded by Professor Agostino Maltarello, and in the light of several passages in papal addresses the change gave the impression that Catholic Action would be less concerned in future with political opposition to the Communists and, by implication, support for the Christian Democrats. Yet a ruling of the Holy Office on April 4 reaffirmed that Catholics could in no way co-operate with Communists; it appeared to be directed mainly against Silvio Milazzo, the rebel Christian Democrat in coalition with the Communists in Sicily. (*See* also ITALY.)

Germany. The rarely exhibited Holy Coat of Trier was venerated by nearly 2 million pilgrims between July 19 and Sept. 20. The validity of the concordat of 1933 between the Holy See and Germany, upheld in principle by a judgment of the western German constitutional court at Karlsruhe in 1957, was denied by the prime minister of Hesse at the beginning of August, when he administered the oath of civil allegiance taken by the new bishop of Fulda, Mgr. Adolf Bolte; and the Rhineland and Westphalian bishops criticized a ruling of the Constitutional Court given in the same month which seemed to undermine the authority of the father of a family.

The bishop of the eastern German diocese of Meissen, Mgr. Otto Spülbeck, preaching at the close of the annual meeting of the German bishops at Fulda, condemned not only Communism in eastern but also materialism in western Germany. In eastern Germany the pressure on the Church increased considerably, with Cardinal Julius Döpfner, the bishop of Berlin, more and more under Communist attack.

Poland. In Poland, too, it was a year of increasing pressure, despite the gesture made by the new pope in declining to

Pope John seen in audience at the Vatican with the archbishop of St. Andrews and Edinburgh (left) and the archbishop of Glasgow.

accept the credentials of Kazimierz Papée, the émigré ambassador who had long represented the Polish government-in-exile at the Holy See. (The pope had similarly declined in the case of the émigré Lithuanian minister at the Holy See.)

Cardinal Domenico Tardini, as secretary of state at the Vatican, wrote at the beginning of the year to all the bishops of Poland reminding them that their quinquennial *ad limina* visits to Rome were due in 1959, but the Polish government allowed only three of them to go. They were Mgr. Eugeniusz Baziak, archbishop of Cracow, Mgr. Franciszek Barda, bishop of Przemyśl, and Mgr. Paweł Zakrzewski, bishop of Płock. They were received by the pope on Dec. 7. (*See* also POLAND.)

Other Countries. Several bishops from Yugoslavia, including the archbishop of Belgrade, were able to visit Rome for the first time since the end of the war. In September the provincial prime minister of Croatia intimated that Cardinal Alojzije Stepinac would be allowed to return to Zagreb on the expiry of the 16-year sentence passed on him in 1946; hitherto the Yugoslav government had declined to envisage this possibility.

In March the Hungarian government closed the Budapest theological seminary after allegations of political nonconformity on the part of its students. On April 6 the same government claimed the right to fill any episcopal office after it had been vacant for 90 days and any other ecclesiastical office after 60 days; four appointments were subsequently made in Hungary by the Holy See—the first at least since the rising of 1956—when administrators were appointed to four sees, including Cardinal József Mindszenty's, although only one of these was vacant through death.

Cardinal Gregorius Petrus XV Agagianian, pro-prefect of the Congregation of Propaganda, having been present in the Philippines in Dec. 1958 at the first conference of far eastern bishops, made an extended far eastern tour between February and April.

The bishops of the Union of South Africa spoke frequently against racialist measures there. The erection of the hierarchy in Northern Rhodesia and Nyasaland was announced on May 17, and the bishops of those territories, with those of Southern Rhodesia, together representing the Church in the federation, addressed a public warning to the prime minister of the Federation of Rhodesia and Nyasaland on Oct. 14, speaking of " the very great degree of opposition to federation " and drawing a contrast between " the ideal of (racial) partnership so greatly

publicized and the practice of it in all three territories ".

An important meeting of representatives of the hierarchies of the New World—the United States, Canada and Latin America—was held in Washington from Nov. 2 to 5 under the chairmanship of Cardinal Richard J. Cushing, archbishop of Boston, primarily to discuss the future of the Church in Latin America. Archbishop Antonio Samore, secretary both of Extraordinary Ecclesiastical Affairs at the Vatican and of the Pontifical Commission for Latin America, was present.

A pastoral letter signed by the cardinal patriarch of Lisbon and all the Portuguese bishops, read throughout Portugal on Jan. 18, described the relationship of the Church to the regime of Antonio Salazar. The bishop of Oporto, a critic of the regime, left Portugal during the summer for an unknown destination, and his auxiliary bishop was appointed to administer the diocese.

An auxiliary to the Latin patriarch of Jerusalem, appointed in September, became the first bishop of the Latin rite in the state of Israel. Archbishop Martin Lucas took up residence in Stockholm during the summer as the first permanent apostolic visitor for the Scandinavian countries. Dom Benno Gut, abbot of Einsiedeln, Switzerland, was elected in September to be abbot-primate of the Benedictine confederation for the next 12 years. (*See* also VATICAN CITY STATE.) (M. DK.)

ROOT CROPS: *see* AGRICULTURE.

ROWING. The European championships were held on the River Saône, Mâcon, France, the occasion being marked by the official opening of the French Centre Nautique National by Maurice Herzog, high commissioner for youth and sport. Once more the German Federal Republic carried off the chief honours, winning the eights, coxed fours, and coxswainless and coxed pairs, and finishing second in the coxswainless fours and single sculls. Nevertheless the challenge to their supremacy seemed stronger than in 1958. The U.S.S.R. won both sculling events, though it must be added that S. A. Mackenzie, the Australian holder of the single sculls title, had

Oxford leading Cambridge in the boat race as the crews approach Hammersmith bridge. Oxford won by six lengths in 18 min. 52 sec.

left hospital after an operation only a week or two before the regatta. The remaining event, the coxswainless fours, was won by Switzerland. Great Britain sent, numerically, its strongest team to date. It was thought that they would reach at least four finals, but in the end they could do no better than a fourth place in the coxswainless pairs.

At home the chief feature of the rowing season was the revival of Oxford university. In spite of a much publicized mutiny in Oct. 1958, when several leading oarsmen tried to form a rival university crew, Oxford, coached throughout by Gp. Capt. H. R. A. Edwards, won the university boat race by a handsome margin. With three changes this crew entered at Henley regatta under the title of Oxford University Isis Boat club. This was the first occasion for exactly 100 years that a British university crew had entered for the Grand Challenge cup. Although criticized before the regatta they lost to Harvard, the winners, in the semi-final, by only half a length, after a desperate struggle. A second Isis crew lost to the Harvard lightweights, winners of the Thames cup, by an even narrower margin of a canvas. A composite four from St. Edmund hall and Lincoln college, containing three of the so-called Oxford mutineers, won the Stewards' cup, and a Hertford College pair won the Silver goblets. Cambridge provided both finalists in the Ladies' cup and the Visitors' cup. The Australian S. A. Mackenzie retained the Diamonds and became the first sculler to achieve the double by also winning the Double sculls in partnership with C. G. V. Davidge.

After Henley Oxford sent a university crew to Japan where they won one and were narrowly beaten in two of their engagements. This was considered a satisfactory result in view of the unaccustomed conditions in which they were racing. A Cambridge crew made a protracted tour of South African rowing centres and returned unbeaten in any of their main engagements.

Of the regattas following Henley, the *News of the World* regatta on the Serpentine, Hyde park, was outstandingly successful. This fixture, started in 1953 as a publicity venture and regarded by oarsmen as an end-of-season diversion, had by 1959 achieved a position of importance in the rowing calendar. Not only had it helped to bring rowing to the notice of Londoners, but with a course accommodating four crews it provided useful experience of racing under international conditions, although only over a half-mile distance.

The exceptionally fine summer brought crowds to the river and nearly every regatta was well attended. The general standard seemed rather higher than in the previous few years and the number of school crews competing in open regattas continued to rise. During the year the Amateur Rowing association set up a special committee to study the problem of providing a 2,000 m. course which would fulfil the requirements of international competition. (*See* also SPORTING RECORD.) (R. D. B.)

See (both 1959) Colin Porter, *Rowing to Win* (London); A. S. Irvine (ed.), *British Rowing Almanack* (London).

ROYAL AIR FORCE: *see* COMMONWEALTH AIR FORCES.

ROYAL FAMILY. World tours, one of them (the 15,000 mi. tour of Canada) ending with the news of the queen's expected child, dominated the royal year. The first was the Duke of Edinburgh's 14-week visit to the Commonwealth territories in Asia and the Pacific, starting at Delhi where the duke was surprised to find himself landing in fog. His main interests, in India and Pakistan alike, were technical; he paid more attention to the Bhakra dam than the Taj Mahal. He was a great success with the city crowds as well as in the more orthodox haunts of Calcutta clubland, and at Singapore he met an embarrassing situation with the right

The Shah of Persia, who paid a state visit to Britain in May, helps the Queen to alight from her carriage at Buckingham palace.

disarming note when students, disappointed that his official programme passed them by, solaced themselves by building a dummy duke. The tour extended to North Borneo (where he saw a display of blowpipe marksmanship by jungle warriors), Hong Kong, the Pacific Islands, the Bahamas and Bermuda.

After only a short interval at home, the duke set off again with the queen for Canada, her oldest dominion beyond the seas, on the longest tour ever made there by a British sovereign. They flew to Newfoundland in mid-June. All the bells were ringing in Quebec. Montreal gave the queen a tickertape welcome and also a silver bowl to mark the opening of the St. Lawrence seaway, and she made a television broadcast at Ottawa to celebrate Dominion day. The royal pair stepped on U.S. soil to look at Chicago before going on west to the Rocky mountains and finally to the Yukon. Here the queen was ill with an upset stomach and she cancelled a day's arrangements.

On her return from Canada it was announced that the queen was expecting her third child early in the new year, and it emerged that she had been anxious not to say anything earlier that would cause the curtailing of her Canadian tour. One of the first people to be given the news was Kwame Nkrumah, the prime minister of Ghana, where a tour was planned for later in the year and now had to be put off with the queen's other engagements. Yet Ghana's preparations to welcome royalty were able to proceed, for the Duke of Edinburgh visited the new country mainly to see something of its economic achievements.

The Canadian visit raised issues which, in an increasingly informal era, were bound to be heard more of. Some U.S. papers reported that there was a marked coolness in the public mood, and though this was by no means borne out by the British accounts there was, nevertheless, a good deal of complaint that the tour was over-organized. The Duke of Edinburgh, the least pompous of men, did his best to preserve the humanities. Sometimes he was, for a royal figure, startlingly frank, as when he spoke of the effect of the Canadian high standard of living on the national *embonpoint*. He was also forthright on the subject of photographers, his relationship with whom, in one mood and another, was a feature of the year. "I have the reputation," he was reported as saying, "of being nasty to photographers. I never object

(Left) Queen Elizabeth the Queen Mother and Princess Margaret leaving the British embassy in Rome to attend a dinner given in their honour. (Right) The prime minister of Ghana, Kwame Nkrumah, walking with the royal family during his visit to Balmoral in August.

to a photographer doing his job, but when he pokes a long lens through my keyhole then I am bloody nasty." He was not going to have his privacy assailed. This was certainly refreshing language, far from the stiff protocol of which critics complained, though just where royal privacy begins and ends was not defined.

There was some mild trouble at Exeter university where the students complained of too much formality in the plans for a visit by Princess Margaret. Also in Wales, where resignations followed the queen's invitation to the 1960 national Eisteddfod because this, it was objected, would violate the "all-Welsh language rule". There was criticism in Lisbon about Princess Margaret's visit in June, again on the grounds that officialdom was not anxious to help the princess in her desire to meet the people. She had an affectionate welcome, so far as this was possible, from the Portuguese crowds. She also had tea with her third cousin, the pretender to the Spanish throne, and the pretender to the French throne looked in too.

At the same time that the duke was in the Pacific, Queen Elizabeth the Queen Mother was on a three-weeks tour of Kenya and Uganda. She received a great welcome at Nairobi, was greeted by the chanting crews of Arab dhows at Mombasa, was hailed as a rainmaker by the weather-afflicted Masai tribesmen, watched big game from the Treetops hotel at Nyeri, flew to the Mountains of the Moon, and learned one morning that a thunderflash had been used to drive away an elephant which wandered into the camp where she slept.

The Queen Mother and Princess Margaret went to Rome in the spring for a week's private visit which nevertheless involved a good deal of tussling with the ubiquitous cameramen. They met Pope John XXIII in private audience, and the Queen Mother later unveiled a statue of Lord Byron while the princess went sightseeing along the Appian way.

Princess Alexandra established herself as a front page personality in her own right. She went in the spring with her mother, the Duchess of Kent, on a tour of Latin America. They were the first royal visitors since 1931. This time, as if to demonstrate the unreasonableness of the critics, it was complained in some quarters that the atmosphere of the tour was too relaxed and that there should have been more pomp

and circumstance. The royal visitors evidently enjoyed the informality with which Mexico met them, as well as the honours accorded them at Valparaiso, and the Grand Cross of Diamonds of the Order of the Sun they received at Lima.

There was no doubting the triumph of Princess Alexandra's tour of Australia in the late summer. She was wildly cheered in the " outback ", watched some rough-riding said to be the best rough-riding the world can offer, sat on the governor of Queensland's top hat, and was mobbed by students at Sydney. Often the crowds threatened to get out of hand, and officialdom had some nerve-shaking moments, but the princess showed such unaffected enjoyment of almost everything that happened that when the crowds shouted " Come back, Alex ", their heart was in the invitation. " I must come back ", was her answer at Melbourne, " I have loved it all ".

Nigeria was visited in June by the Duke and Duchess of Gloucester, to launch Northern Nigeria's celebrations of self-government. At home one of the queen's chief pleasures was to receive President Eisenhower at Balmoral. She drove him round the estate in a shooting brake, and he met the duke and the royal children on the shores of a loch which Queen Victoria liked to visit, and where they all had a picnic together.

The royal children did not figure much in the news, except when Princess Anne joined the brownies and had chickenpox, the Prince of Wales steered the carrier H.M.S. "Eagle" and had influenza, and the police put a bigger guard round Cheam, his preparatory school, as a defence against photographers.

Princess Arthur of Connaught, a granddaughter of King Edward VII and Queen Alexandra, died in February (*see* OBITUARIES). In the same month the prime minister announced that the queen had offered to place Marlborough house, one of her palaces, at the government's disposal for Commonwealth meetings in London. Traditionally it was the home either of the Queen Mother or of the heir to the throne, and Harold Macmillan added, when he told the House of Commons, that no doubt a future parliament would want to see that the Prince of Wales had a " home of his own ". (N. S.)

ROYAL NAVY: *see* COMMONWEALTH NAVIES.
RUANDA AND URUNDI: *see* BELGIAN OVERSEAS TERRITORIES; TRUST TERRITORIES.

RUBBER. Supply and Demand. Total production in 1958 was 1,955,000 tons of natural rubber and 1,250,000 tons of synthetic rubber, excluding production in Communist countries. The estimated production for 1959 was 2,075,000 tons of natural rubber and 1,625,000 tons of synthetic rubber. During 1959 the market price of good-quality smoked sheet steadily climbed from a little over 2s. 0d. per lb. to a little over 3s. 0d. per lb. Throughout this period the price of general purpose synthetic rubber remained constant at 1s. 10d. per lb.

Total consumption of natural rubber in 1958, including about 430,000 tons imported into Communist countries, was 1,982,500 tons and consumption of synthetic rubber, excluding that produced in Communist countries was 1,247,500 tons. In 1959 estimated consumption of natural rubber was 2,125,000 tons and of synthetic rubber 1,550,000 tons.

TABLE I. RATIO OF SYNTHETIC TO TOTAL RUBBER CONSUMPTION, 1958-59

Year	Continental Europe	United Kingdom	United States
1958	27·3	26·4	64·5
1959*	30·7	30·2	65·9

* Estimate.

The difference in the ratios for the three areas shown in the above table is largely explained by the proportion of passenger car tyres manufactured (synthetic rubber) to heavy duty tyres manufactured (natural rubber).

TABLE II. NATURAL RUBBER PRODUCTION* ('000 metric tons)

	1938	1948	1952	1956	1957	1958
WORLD	925·0	1,545·0	1,815·0	1,915·0	1,930·0	1,986·0
Malaya†	365·3	709·4	593·6	636·0	647·8	674·4
Indonesia	322·3	439·3	762·5	697·7‡	695·5‡	612·0
Thailand‡	42·3	97·4	99·4	135·7	135·1	139·7
Cambodia and Vietnam (South)	61·0	44·6	64·1	102·3	101·4	105·2
Ceylon	50·8	96·5	98·0	96·9	99·7	102·0
Liberia‡	3·0	24·9	35·9	39·0	38·8	43·0
Nigeria‡	3·2	8·1	18·6	38·7	40·6	41·8
Sarawak	17·8	40·3	32·4	41·4	41·6	39·6
Belgian Congo‡	1·2	5·0	16·8	32·5	34·3	35·0
India	12·7	15·7	20·2	23·8	24·1	24·5
N. Borneo and Brunei‡	11·0	22·5	21·2	21·6	21·3	21·6
Brazil§	13·7	20·5	26·9	24·1	24·3	20·6
Burma‡	6·8	9·2	14·1	12·6	12·8	10·8
Papua and New Guinea‡	1·2	1·4	2·2	3·9	3·8	4·6
Cameroun‡	1·8	2·8	2·5	3·0	3·1	…

* Main producing countries; including rubber content of latex but excluding reclaimed rubber. † Incl. Singapore. ‡ Net exports. § Gross weight in 1938; thereafter, dry weight.

SOURCE. U.N. *Statistical Yearbook 1958*; U.N. *Monthly Bulletin of Statistics*.

In October the U.K. government announced that it would dispose of its strategic stockpile of natural rubber amounting to 100,000 tons. Sales would be made on a graduated price basis involving limited sales at prices over 2s. 6½d. per lb. and no sales at prices under 2s. 1¼d. per lb. About the same time the U.S. government gave notice to congress that it was proposing to dispose of 470,000 tons of stockpile rubber over a period of nine years. Included in this rubber was 40,000-50,000 tons which had deteriorated and for the immediate sale of which congressional permission had been granted.

Developments in Natural Rubber. About 2,000 tons of superior processing rubber were consumed in 1959—the first year in which it was marketed on a commercial scale. Superior processing rubber is prepared by mixing four parts of fresh latex with one part of vulcanized latex and then coagulating the mixture and sheeting and drying the coagulum in the usual way. As its name implies this new type of rubber facilitates manufacturing processes, particularly those involving sheeting and extruding operations.

Nearly 60,000 tons of technically classified natural rubber was produced in 1959, about the same as in previous years. This is rubber which has been tested in an approved laboratory in the country of origin and found to vulcanize at a rate within prescribed limits.

Among the new developments of which particulars were announced was the preparation of a superior processing " masterbatch "—rubber containing a high proportion of vulcanized particles and which is suitable for mixing with standard grades to produce superior processing properties. Another development was a simple way of chemically modifying rubber by treating it at a high temperature with sulphur dioxide so as to induce partial isomerization and obtain a type of rubber resistant to crystallization at low temperatures. This rubber can be used at arctic temperatures without becoming hard and brittle.

Replanting (about 125,000 ac.) and new planting (about 25,000 ac.) mostly with high-yielding budded stock was continued in Malaya in 1959. The injection of trees with yield stimulants such as dichlor- and trichlorphenoxy acetic acid was partly responsible for a 20% increase in the yield of unselected seedlings over a period of five years.

It was claimed that there had been a 20% increase in yield in 12 months on estates in the Republics of Vietnam and Cambodia following the application of injection treatments combined with the application of fertilizers based on assessment of requirements from leaf and latex analyses, but the increase was not as yet reflected in published production statistics.

Developments in Synthetic Rubber. A number of existing plants were extended and a start made in the erection of plants for the combined production in the United States of 70,000 tons per annum of *cis*-polyisoprene and polybutadiene. The former is chemically identical with the hydrocarbon in natural rubber and can replace it for all purposes. The latter is more

In 1959 the Dunlop Rubber company was manufacturing collapsible containers made of rubber reinforced with nylon for the carrying and storage of liquids in bulk. These containers were being used by civil engineering firms. Above is a 10,000-gal. tank for static storage.

resilient than natural rubber and in this respect differs from other synthetic rubbers which are inferior to natural rubber.

It was also reported that a factory was to be erected in Italy to produce some 60,000 tons of propylene-ethylene copolymer. It was claimed that this would cost less and offer better resistance to abrasion compared with other synthetics. Work was started on establishing an oil refinery in Melbourne, Australia, to include the production of 30,000 tons per annum of butadiene for the manufacture of synthetic rubber.

Latex. Despite competition from polyurethane foams, particularly the polyether variety, there was an appreciable increase in the consumption of both preserved natural and synthetic latices amounting to about 5% for natural and 25% for synthetic. Many firms were marketing latex in which the bulk of the ammonia was replaced by other bactericides such as boric acid, zinc dimethyl dithiocarbamate and salts of ethylene diamine tetra-acetic acid. Previously natural latex was preserved almost wholly with about 0·7% ammonia.

(Ge. M.)

RUGBY FOOTBALL. Rugby Union. The 1958-59 season was notable for France's achievement in winning the unofficial international championship outright for the first time. Once more the French team owed a great deal to an outstanding captain, L. Mias, a second row forward who had led it to a draw and a victory against South Africa in 1958. He turned a set of fast and heavy forwards into a devastating unit and the whole side played fine attacking football in beating Scotland and Wales in Paris. Mias was unfit to play

against England and without him the forwards at once began to play as individuals. Even so, had the backs taken their chances they would have beaten instead of drawn with a most disappointing England team that never got going behind the scrum and scored only three penalty goals in four games. Yet England had two good wings in P. B. Jackson and P. H. Thompson and a brilliant young stand-off half in A. B. W. Risman, Salford-born son of a famous Welsh Rugby league captain, A. J. Risman. Ireland had the next best side under the lively leadership of A. R. Dawson, a hooker. As usual, Ireland beat Scotland at Murrayfield and, after being a little unlucky to lose narrowly to England and Wales, defeated the French when they had already made sure of the championship and had clearly relaxed. The Welsh were too erratic and the Scots again poor behind the scrum. Warwickshire deservedly retained the county title, but the most improved side was Durham which won the Northern group for the first time for 27 years and lost to Gloucestershire only after a replay. Cambridge were much too clever and fast for Oxford in an open university game.

During the season the president of the Rugby Football union took great interest in junior games and repeatedly urged clubs and county unions to organize colts teams for boys between 15 and 18 who had left school. The Midlands and the Southwestern counties had long been pioneers in this work and good progress was made during the season in Lancashire and Kent. The R.F.U. itself decided to back financially the English Schools R.F.U., which since World War II had done much work encouraging schools to adopt

A dramatic moment during the game between the British Lions rugby union team and the Victoria fifteen, which was held at Olympic park, Melbourne, on May 23. The British team won by 53 points to 18 in this the first match of their tour of Australia and New Zealand.

Rugby Union as an alternative to Association football. It was decided that in future one schools international with Wales at under 15 or under 18 years of age should be played at Twickenham annually.

Although the home British international sides had not been very impressive the team picked to represent the British Isles in Australia and New Zealand settled down almost at once into a brilliant attacking machine and attracted record crowds in both countries. R. E. G. Jeeps, who had been a great success in South Africa four years before but had been dropped by England's selectors, made a perfect partner to Risman, and Jackson, M. Price (Wales), D. Hewitt (Ireland) and A. J. O'Reilly (Ireland) were a fast and clever three-quarter line brilliantly supported in attack by K. J. F. Scotland (Scotland) from full back. Forwards from all four countries soon got together under Dawson's leadership—R. H. Williams, W. J. Faull and H. Morgan, of Wales, H. F. McLeod, of Scotland, and R. W. D. Marques, of England, perhaps being outstanding. Distinguished New Zealand provincial sides like Taranaki, the Ranfurly shield holders, Wellington and Auckland were routed, but Otago kept their record of beating touring sides from South Africa and Britain. Both international matches with Australia were won easily and but for six penalty goals by D. B. Clarke, the New Zealand full back, in the first test (lost 17-18) and a late try and conversion by him in the second (lost 8-11 with a much weakened team owing to injuries) New Zealand might have lost a series to Britain at home for the first time. As it was, they lost the last test by 6-9, but won the third decisively by 22-8.

Rugby League. The same clubs again dominated the Northern Rugby league and, as on the whole they were the richer clubs and thus able to attract players by unrestricted bonuses, they seemed likely to continue their sway. In Lancashire, St. Helens, Wigan, Oldham and a revived Swinton finished first, second, fourth and sixth in the Northern league. St. Helens became the first club to score more than 1,000 points in ordinary league games with 1,005, and in the league semi-final and final beat Oldham 42-4 and Hunslet 44-22. Wigan, who had been surprised at home 22-11 by Hunslet in their league semi-final, retained the Challenge cup by beating Hull 30-13. (*See also* SPORTING RECORD.) (L. M.)

RUMANIA. People's republic of southeastern Europe, bounded N. and N.E. by the U.S.S.R., E. by the Black sea, S. by Bulgaria and W. by Yugoslavia and Hungary. Area: 91,700 sq.mi. Pop.: (1956 census) 17,489,450; (1959 est.) 18,059,000. Language (1956 census): Rumanian 85·7%; Hungarian 1,653,700 (9%); German 395,374 (2·2%); Ukrainian 68,252; Russian 54,029; Yiddish 34,337 (but 146,264 declared themselves Jewish). Religion (1947 est.): Orthodox 81%; Greek Catholic 9%; Roman Catholic 7%; others 3%. Chief towns (pop., 1956 census): Bucharest (Bucureşti, cap.) 1,236,908 (1959 est., 1,286,000); Cluj 154,723; Timişoara 142,257; Braşov (Stalin) 123,834; Ploeşti 114,544; Iaşi (Jassy) 112,977; Arad 106,460; Brăila 102,491; Constanţa 99,676. First secretary of the Rumanian Workers' (Communist) party, Gheorghe Gheorghiu-Dej; chairman of the presidium of the Grand National Assembly, Ion Gheorghe Maurer; chairman of the council of ministers, Chivu Stoica. Main imports: machinery and vehicles, cotton. Main exports: petroleum and products, bread grain. Monetary unit: *leu*, pl. *lei* (official exchange rate L.16·80 =£1 sterling; tourist rate L.34·39 =£1 sterling).

History. The year 1959 was largely uneventful, taken up mainly with minor administrative and economic reforms. In April the government claimed that industrial output had risen in 1958 by nearly 10% over 1957 and that the year had seen the introduction into service of three new steel furnaces, two new rolling mills, three chemical plants and extensions of oil refining capacity.

In July the government announced a general increase in wages and salaries of all state employees, which it claimed would raise the real incomes of workers, technicians and clerks by more than 30% over the 1955 level and improve

Watching demonstrations marking the 15th anniversary of the liberation of Rumania by the Soviet army are (l. to r.) the Soviet marshal I. S. Konev, I. G. Maurer, Chivu Stoica and G. Gheorghiu-Dej.

considerably the lot of the lower-paid workers. At the same time changes in the social insurance system increased old-age pensions by over 60% and sickness benefits by nearly 50%. In August prices on a wide variety of goods, mostly in the more expensive or luxury categories, were appreciably reduced, and the system of credit sales of consumer goods was extended.

On April 13 the government was reshuffled. Emil Bodnaraş was replaced as minister of transport and telecommunications by Dimitru Şimulescu; Stefan Voitec was replaced as minister of consumer goods by Alexandru Sencovici; Gherasim Popa was replaced as minister of heavy industry by Carol Loncear. The three replaced ministers remained deputy premiers. On Aug. 12 Gheorghe Radulescu took Marcel Popescu's post as minister of commerce.

The situation in agriculture was not as satisfactory as in industry, mainly because of the poor harvest in 1958. Grain production for that year was only 7·3 million tons, compared with over 11 million tons in the exceptional harvest of 1957. The process of drawing farmers into the collective farms continued, and the total area of collectivized land increased by about 20% in 1958.

An intensive drive to increase the area of land and number of peasant households in the " Socialist sector " of agriculture was conducted in the latter part of 1958 and the beginning of 1959: 214,000 families were said to have joined collective farms during the first three months of the year, compared with only 47,000 in 1958. It was reported in May that the state-controlled sector of agriculture comprised 9·4 million ha., or 65% of the arable land.

An event which attracted widespread attention in the world press was the resumption of the issue of exit permits to Rumanian Jews. The flow of Jews through Vienna on their way to Israel began in Oct. 1958 and continued until March, during which time a total of about 12,000 were thought to have reached Israel. This influx of population into Israel evoked protests from the Arab states, which may have caused the eventual cessation of emigration. The official Rumanian explanation of the unexpected change of policy towards Jews was that, acting on humanitarian grounds, the authorities had decided to permit Jews with relatives in Israel to be reunited with their families. There was other evidence during the year of a milder treatment of the Jewish minority which, with nearly 200,000 members, was still the largest in any eastern European country.

On Aug. 23, on the 15th anniversary of the entry of Soviet troops into Rumania, the government declared an amnesty which annulled or reduced prison sentences imposed for all except the most serious offences. The authorities organized a vigorous campaign against various offences concerning state property which involved theft and embezzlement. N. S. Khrushchev paid an informal visit to Rumania in October for talks with party leaders.

In August the Rumanian government concluded a commercial agreement with Sweden, thus resuming trade between the two countries, which had been at a standstill for 15 years. Sweden undertook to supply various raw materials in exchange for machinery and high-grade steel. Compensation for Swedish property confiscated by the Rumanian government was to be met by a proportion of Rumanian exports. A Rumanian trade delegation visited Great Britain to discuss expansion of trade and settlement of compensation claims, but little progress was made. (*See* also EASTERN EUROPEAN ECONOMIC PLANNING.) (D. F.)

RUSSIA: *see* UNION OF SOVIET SOCIALIST REPUBLICS.
RUSSIAN LITERATURE: *see* SOVIET LITERATURE.

SAHARA, FRENCH. The group of African territories in the French Community forming part of the desert region. Area: *c.* 1,544,000 sq.mi., including the two Algerian Saharan *départements* (Saoura and Oasis) and the northern parts of the Republics of Soudan, Niger and Chad. Pop. (1959 est.): *c.* 1,200,000; Moors in the west, Arabs in the north, Touareg in the centre, Teda in the east. The Organisation Commune des Régions Sahariennes is administered directly from Paris. Minister-delegate, Jacques Soustelle.

History. Algerian Sahara was divided into two *départements*: (1) *Oasis*, capital Laghouat (temporarily, until transfer to Ouargla), with three subdivisions: Laghouat, Ouargla and Touggourt; (2) *Saoura*, capital Colomb-Béchar, with two subdivisions: Colomb-Béchar and Adrar. Each *département* had an elected general council; the *communes* (of which there were 93) each had an elected municipal council. Sahara sent three deputies and two senators to the French parliament.

The Organisation Commune des Régions Sahariennes (O.C.R.S.) was reorganized. It was to be responsible for the economic and social development of the two *départements*, but could broaden its field of action. Agreements were concluded with the Republic of Niger and the Republic of Chad: the O.C.R.S. gave increased assistance in matters of hydraulic engineering, communications and research in the Saharan territory of the two republics.

A new oilfield was discovered at El-Gassi, south west of Hassi-Messaoud. The 24-in. pipeline from Hassi-Messaoud to Bougie was completed (413 mi.) and inaugurated on Dec. 5 by the French prime minister, Michel Debré. The Edjelé-Gabès pipeline was under construction. It was expected that total oil production would be 1·5 million metric tons in 1959, 10 million metric tons in 1960 and 50 million metric tons a year from 1965.

Natural gas from Hassi-R'mel, the annual production of which would reach 25,000 million cu.m., would be sold at a very low price in Algeria (3·50 francs a cu.m.) in order to encourage industrial development. The roads from Ghardaïa to El-Goléa and from Ghardaïa to Ouargla were completed. The building of the new towns Ouargla III and Hassi-Messaoud was begun. Forty new schools were set up and 60 doctors assigned to duties in Sahara. Total investments reached Fr.122,000 million. (HU. DE.)

SAINT HELENA. British colony in the South Atlantic, about 1,200 mi. from southwest coast of Africa, with dependencies of Ascension (34 sq.mi.; pop. [1958 est.] 326) and the Tristan da Cunha group (total area 45 sq.mi.; only Edinburgh settlement on Tristan da Cunha [38 sq.mi.] inhabited; pop. [1958 est.] 257). Colony area: 47·3 sq.mi. Pop.: (1958 est.) 4,802, mainly of mixed European and African descent. Language: English. Religion: Christian (90% Anglican). Capital: Jamestown, pop. (1956 census) 1,568. Administration: governor; executive council; advisory council; (Tristan da Cunha)

administrator and island council with elected majority. Governor, R. E. Alford; administrator (Tristan), P. A. Day. Main imports: foodstuffs, cotton piecegoods, machinery and motor vehicles, hardware. Main exports: phormium flax fibre, tow, rope, twine. Currency: sterling; S. African currency circulates.

History. In April 1959 the wages and salaries of lower-grade workers in the colony were revised and later certain staple items of diet were considerably subsidized. (In the previous year the colony's first trade union, the St. Helena General Workers' union, had been founded.) In May the colony celebrated the tercentenary of its foundation, the occasion being marked by the issue of three commemorative stamps. A three-day celebration of the tercentenary was held in November. (G. A. L.)

SAINT-PIERRE AND MIQUELON. French overseas territory consisting of three small islands off the south coast of Newfoundland. Area: 93 sq.mi. Pop.: (1945 census) 4,354; (1959 est.) 4,900. Language: French. Religion: Roman Catholic. Chief town: Saint-Pierre, pop. (1945) 3,636. Governor, Jean Louis Pont. Main export: dried cod. Monetary unit: *franc CFA* = metropolitan Fr.2.

History. At the municipal elections of March 8, 1959, the outgoing councillors were re-elected at Saint-Pierre and the single list at Miquelon. Henri Claireaux (Mouvement Républicain Populaire) was elected senator on April 26 and M. Lorelli, Gaullist (Union pour la Nouvelle République), was elected deputy on May 27.

A direct telephone line with France was opened.

(HU. DE.)

SALVADOR, EL. Republic on the west coast of Central America. Area: 8,260 sq.mi. Pop.: (1950 census) 1,855,917; (1958 est.) 2,434,430. Aboriginal and mixed races, *ladinos* and *mestizos*, constitute the bulk of the population. Language: Spanish. Religion: Roman Catholic. Capital: San Salvador, pop. (1950 census) 161,951; (1958 est.) 221,708. President, Lieut.-Colonel José María Lemus. Main imports: manufactures and machinery. Main exports: coffee (85%), cotton (7%). Monetary unit: *colón* (C.7·04 = £ sterling).

History. Although no urgent political problems confronted El Salvador at the beginning of 1959, the country's economy had been seriously affected during 1958 by the decline in coffee and cotton prices. Since exports of coffee and cotton normally account for about two-thirds of the country's foreign exchange, the gold reserves fell.

With the return of President Lemus from the United States late in March there was an increase in the requests from foreign firms interested in establishing themselves in El Salvador. Before the end of the year, plans under way or in execution included the establishment of a fertilizer plant near Acajutla, a sugar refinery near Apopa, a paint factory near Ilopango and a dried milk plant to supply the eastern part of the country.

By its ratification of the Multilateral Treaty of Central American Free Trade and Economic Integration, the National Assembly made it possible in January for the treaty to go into effect. It became valid upon ratification by three countries, the first two being Guatemala and Nicaragua. (A. E. TR.)

SALVATION ARMY. A religious and philanthropic body, distinguished from other Christian denominations by its quasi-military organization. It adopts a simple order of worship which excludes the usual sacraments. The Army's activities extends to 86 countries and are carried on in 17,126 evangelical centres, 2,259 social institutions and agencies apart from day schools. Its full-time officers number 25,835 apart from local officers (voluntary) and thousands of "soldiers". A detailed annual report is published.

During 1959 the Salvation Army in Great Britain was engaged in a "Mission to the Family" launched in January by the lord mayor of London at a reception at the Caxton hall. Intensive efforts were made to stress the importance of family life in the community and the significance of religious observances in the home.

In June the Danforth (Toronto) Citadel Songster brigade composed of 80 members—one of the largest and best known choral groups in Canada—toured Britain. An enthusiastic reception at the Royal Albert hall, crowded for the occasion, was their first engagement in an itinerary which included the leading cities.

General Wilfred Kitching, the international leader, made Salvation Army history when, during an extensive tour of centres in the United States, he visited Mexico, becoming the first head of the organization to do so since operations were started in that country in 1937. The Salvation Army was honoured by Queen Elizabeth II when, following the opening of the St. Lawrence seaway, she visited the Salvation Army Eventide home in Toronto. This newly erected building, called the Isabel and Arthur Meighen lodge after the donors, accommodated 166 old people and cost $1 million.

A new development was the opening of a people's high school in Stockholm to provide advanced specialized education for young people. In Great Britain summer music camps for young people proved increasingly popular.

New publications included a biography of the late Albin Peyron, for many years head of the Armée du Salut, by M. Forisson, and a biography of British Bandmaster George Marshall by Archibald Wiggins, under the title *Triumph of Faith*. (A. C.)

SAMOA, AMERICAN: *see* PACIFIC ISLANDS, U.S.
SAMOA, WESTERN: *see* NEW ZEALAND; TRUST TERRITORIES.

SAN MARINO.
Small republic in central Italy (with which it has a customs union), entirely surrounded by the province of Emilia and situated on the slopes of Monte Titano, 14 mi. S.W. of Rimini. Area 38 sq.mi. Pop. (1957 est.): 14,000. Language: Italian. Religion: Roman Catholic. San Marino is governed by two *capitani reggenti* appointed every six months by a Grand and General Council elected by universal suffrage every four years. Currency (small denominations only): Sammarinese *lira* (= Italian *lira*).

History. On Sept. 13, 1959, the anti-Communist parties scored a clear victory in the general election. The results are given in the table.

Primo Marani (left) and Giordano Giacomini, former captains regent of San Marino, who were sentenced to imprisonment on Oct. 8.

	Parties	Votes	%	Seats
Government	Christian Democratic . .	2,811	44·22	27
	Social Democratic . .	1,015	15·97	9
Opposition	Left-wing Socialist . .	878	13·81	8
	Communist . .	1,653	26·00	16
	Total	6,357		60

The Christian Democrats and the Social Democrats were thus assured of an absolute majority in the Grand and General Council. The electorate was in all 8,426 strong, including 3,401 residents, 4,112 Sammarinese living in Europe (mainly Italy) and 913 outside Europe.

On Feb. 16 James D. Zellerbach, the U.S. ambassador to Italy, visited San Marino and announced that U.S. economic aid of $850,000 would be paid shortly. On May 16 the two *capitani reggenti* paid an official visit to Giovanni Gronchi, president of the Italian Republic, and two days later they were received by Pope John XXIII.

On Oct. 8 the two *capitani reggenti* in office at the time of the 1957 *coup d'état*, Primo Marani (Communist) and Giordano Giacomini (Left-wing Socialist), were sentenced to 15 years of imprisonment. They were accused of an attempt against the security of the state. Three other leftists were sentenced to 12 years and two to 5 years. All decided to appeal. (X.)

SAUDI ARABIA.
Arab kingdom covering four-fifths of the Arabian peninsula. Area: *c.* 618,000 sq.mi. (incl. uninhabited Rub-al-Khali desert of *c.* 193,000 sq.mi.). Pop.: (1956 est., no census ever taken) 6,036,000. Religion: Moslem. Chief towns (pop., 1956 est.): Riyadh (cap.) 150,000; Mecca 200,000; Jidda 160,000; Hufuf 100,000; Buraida 50,000; Medina 50,000. King, Saud ibn Abd-ul-Aziz; prime minister and viceroy of Hejaz, Amir Faysal, crown prince and brother to King Saud. Main imports: textile piecegoods, foodstuffs (tea, coffee, sugar, rice and other cereals), machinery and vehicles, chemicals, building materials. Main export: oil. Monetary unit: *riyal* (*c.* 10¼ riyals =£1 sterling).

History. The year 1959 was, on the surface at least, a quiet one in Saudi Arabia. The dispute with Britain over the Buraimi oasis remained unsettled, and in January King Saud told the U.N. secretary-general, Dag Hammarskjöld, that his country would bring the matter before the United Nations. Mecca radio reporting this, which took place while Hammarskjöld was paying a visit to Saudi Arabia, complained that Britain in the past had shown " aggressive intentions ", and had occupied the oasis by force of arms after an agreement had been reached to take the question to the International Court of Justice. However, no action had been taken in the matter by the end of the year.

Despite the outstanding difference there were indications during the year that diplomatic relations between Saudi Arabia and Britain might be restored, particularly after relations between Britain and the United Arab Republic had been resumed.

At the Arab Oil congress held in Cairo in April, the Saudi Arabian view that the " 50-50 principle " should be extended to all sections of the oil industry was one of the major questions discussed. (E. S. A.)

SCOTLAND.
A kingdom forming part of the United Kingdom of Great Britain and Northern Ireland (*q.v.* for linguistic and religious data). Area: 30,404 sq.mi. Pop.: (1951 census) 5,096,415; (1958 est.) 5,169,000. Chief towns (pop., 1951 census): Edinburgh (cap.) 466,761; Glasgow 1,089,767; Aberdeen 182,729; Dundee 177,340. Scotland has its own legal system, and the secretary of state for Scotland, a United Kingdom minister, is responsible for the agriculture, education, health and home departments and shares responsibility for certain services organized on a United Kingdom basis; he is assisted by a minister of state and three under secretaries of state. Secretary of state, John Maclay; minister of state, Lord Craigton. Main Scottish contributions to U.K. economy: iron and steel manufactures, shipbuilding, coal, woollen manufactures, whisky, fisheries. Scottish banks issue their own sterling notes.

History. Nothing displayed more clearly the distinctive

A road widening scheme under way near Gruinard, Ross. Many roads in the north of Scotland are too narrow for two lines of traffic.

status, outlook and experience of Scotland than the result of the general election of 1959. Although the result was a victory for the Conservatives, Scotland inflicted upon them a net loss of three marginal seats in returning 38 Labour members to parliament, the largest representation which that party had enjoyed in Scotland for 30 years. Some minor considerations helped to bring about this result, but the chief factor, admitted by all parties, was dismay that the economic condition of Scotland had not improved as much as that of Britain as a whole. The government gave particular attention to the problem for most of the year and, although by November a substantial improvement seemed to be in progress, the unemployment figures for that month still showed a total of

91,444 on the registered list, or 4·3% of the insured population, against the over-all British figure of 2%. The Scottish Council (Development and Industry), calculating that the country required to provide 12,000 new jobs every year, set up a committee of inquiry into the problems of Scottish industry, and in other ways it was clear that a most determined attempt was being made to discover why it was not possible to attain full employment in Scotland.

The year had opened in an atmosphere of economic gloom with an unemployment figure of 116,510, the highest for 19 years. Anxiety in the Clyde and east coast shipbuilding yards persisted throughout 1959 for, while there were a number of orders placed, their effect on order books was offset by cancellations. Firms building smaller types of freighters and cargo-liners were brought to closing point, the final pay-off being delayed by one or two timely orders. Where shipbuilding suffered, so did the dependent industries. The government extended the economic aid available in development areas under the Distribution of Industry (Industrial Finance) act, 1958, to more parts of Scotland. "Advance" factories were to be built at Coatbridge to encourage industrialists to start production.

The greatest fillip to industrial expansion was the approval of the construction of a steel strip mill at Ravenscraig, Motherwell, an undertaking planned to employ 1,700 men and to cost £47 million. There was expansion in the clothing industry, and a Motherwell firm making mining machinery opened a new plant at Glenrothes. At Dumfries a plant which had closed after the unsuccessful development of a man-made fibre was re-opened and equipped for the manufacture of polyester film, a new plastic material of great strength, the cost of equipment being about £2·5 million. In the border country, where the tweed and woollen industries found it hard to satisfy their labour requirements, a U.S. precision tool company started production. There was further U.S. investment in Scotland's whisky-distilling industry. To deal with increasing oil imports, a deep-water ocean tanker berth was opened at Finnart on Loch Long. In coal mining, the pit closures announced at the end of 1958 were carried out in 1959, and more were announced. At Chapelcross, Dumfriesshire, the Atomic Energy authority's new nuclear power

A view of the Chapelcross nuclear power station near Annan, Dumfriesshire, which was officially opened on May 2. The first such station to start operating in Scotland, it has four reactors of the Calder Hall type. Construction was begun in October 1955.

Waiting for news of their menfolk at Auckeingeich colliery, Chryston, Lanarkshire, where 47 miners died in a fire on Sept. 18.

station began to operate. At Kincardine-on-Forth, a new conventional power station was put into service. The Scottish Industries exhibition, held in Glasgow, was generally considered a success.

Prospects of new employment in the highlands came with the formation of a company hoping to build a large pulp mill, perhaps at Fort William. The North of Scotland Hydro-Electric board had started on the Strathfarrar and Kilmorack scheme and also the Awe scheme, a pumped storage development. The year ended with a rush of industrial novelty. The fast-breeder reactor at Dounreay became critical and started to produce energy. Swiss and German firms showed an interest in manufacturing in Scotland. A Clyde shipbuilding firm, actively engaged in the study of nuclear propulsion units, announced that it had selected eight systems for further detailed study. New projects were afoot in such deserving towns as Wick (Caithness), Greenock (Renfrewshire), Glenrothes (Morayshire), Cumnock (Ayrshire), Dumbarton and the former military port Cairn Ryan (Wigtownshire). The Pressed Steel company arranged to build motor car bodies at their Linwood (Renfrewshire) factory, and hopes were developing of a full-scale motor car industry.

By Oct. 1, 1959, Scottish agriculturalists had achieved the complete eradication of bovine tuberculosis from all dairy and beef herds. One of the driest summers in memory added about 250,000 lambs to the sheep population, affecting markets. Beef cattle prices were high, and for many weeks of the year there was no need for a government subsidy to guarantee the price. In heavy land areas where moisture was retained in the ground there were record crops of cereals. The year also saw a world record price paid at a collective auction sale for a bull—25,000 guineas bid at Perth by a U.S. breeder for the Aberdeen Angus champion bred on a border farm. In 1959 the hill farmers also won a fight they started with the government in 1958 over the proposed abolition of the marginal agricultural production grants, considered to be the most effective means of making the uplands productive again. The government agreed to extend the scheme for a further three years.

The Scottish Tourist board, receiving a government grant of £45,000 over three years for highland development, selected Badenoch and east Sutherland as the areas for its first experiments. (A. M. DT.)

SEISMOLOGY.

In 1959 the earth was quiet and few losses of life by earthquake were reported. But seismologists were very active indeed, stimulated by the knowledge that in any world-wide system of control of nuclear weapons the detection of secret underground explosions would depend on them. They were conscious of the fact that they were not yet able to distinguish with certainty between the pattern of seismograph records of a normal earthquake and that of an underground explosion.

In the United States, the special assistant to the president appointed in Dec. 1958 a Panel on Seismic Improvement, consisting of 14 experts. This panel reported at the end of March, recommending great increases in all fields of research in seismology. Recommendations included the introduction of standard modern equipment of high precision into a widespread network of seismological stations, with many new stations in regions hitherto inadequately covered. They also included special local studies by mobile teams, the use of large arrays of (up to 100) seismographs, extensive field studies of artificial explosions of up to five kilotons, systematic solutions of theoretical problems using modern computers and research into methods of processing the data supplied in enormous quantity by manned and unmanned seismic stations. The ultimate objective was stated as the establishment of a system which could identify any seismic event within the earth's crust as a normal earthquake or an artificial explosion, and do this with certainty and speed.

It was clear that the U.S.S.R. was already carrying out an intensive exploration of local crustal structure by geophysical means. Moreover, the general assembly of the Academy of Sciences of the U.S.S.R. listed, as one of the 30 main objectives of Soviet scientific research, "complex geophysical investigations of the structure and evolution of the earth ".

The National Academy of Sciences of the United States appointed a special committee to undertake *Project Mohole,* the boring of a hole through the crust of the earth to the Mohorovicic discontinuity (Moho). Since seismologists had already shown that the Moho rises nearer to the earth's surface under oceans than under continents, a region 200 mi. north of Puerto Rico in the Atlantic was chosen for feasibility studies.

The European Seismological commission met at Alicante, Spain, in October. Important reports concerned progress in assembling material for a seismotectonic map of Europe. At this meeting, the director of the International Seismological summary (I.S.S.), R. Stoneley, described the recent enormous increase in the number of observations reported to the I.S.S.—an increase which raised severe problems of selection and publication of data. (*See* also OCEANOGRAPHY.) (E. R. LA.)

SENEGAL, REPUBLIC OF (RÉPUBLIQUE DU SÉNÉGAL).

A member state of the French Community, Senegal is bounded N. by the Republic of Mauritania, E. by the Republic of Soudan, S. by the independent Republic of Guinea and by Portuguese Guinea and W. by the Atlantic ocean. The British colony of Gambia forms an enclave in the territory of Senegal. Area: 81,081 sq.mi. Pop.: (1945 est.) 1,895,000; (1959 est.) 2,300,000, mainly Negro. Language: Ouolof, Peul (Fula) and other Negro dialects. Religion: Moslem, animist, Christian minorities. Chief towns (pop., 1957 est.): Dakar (cap., 234,000, incl. 34,000 Europeans), Rufisque (50,000), Kaolak (47,000), Saint-Louis (40,000), Thiès (39,000), Ziguinchor (23,000). Prime minister, Mamadou Dia. French high commissioner, Pierre Lamy. Chief exports: groundnuts, groundnut oil, oil cake, phosphates. Monetary unit: *franc CFA* =metropolitan Fr.2.

History. The Republic of Senegal, proclaimed on Nov. 25, 1958, joined the Federation of Mali, while retaining its National Assembly, presided over by Léopold Senghor, and its council of ministers, of which Mamadou Dia was president. At the elections to the National Assembly held on March 22, 1959, the Union Progressiste Sénégalaise (a branch of the Parti Fédéraliste Africain) won all 80 seats. Some

954,500 votes were cast (85% of the electorate). This overwhelming victory was due to the relative majority system.

A section of the Senegalese trade unions broke away from the Union Générale des Travailleurs de l'Afrique Noire. Mamadou Dia made a trip to Gambia and considered the possibility of a union between this country and Senegal. " Senegambia ", he declared, " is a reality ". (*See* also MALI, FEDERATION OF.)   (HU. DE.)

SEYCHELLES. British colony and dependencies; 92 islands in the Indian ocean about 970 mi. E. of Zanzibar. Area: 156·25 sq.mi. (Mahé 55·5 sq.mi.). Pop.: (1947 census) 34,632; (1958 est.) 41,901; Negro, creole, Indian, European, Chinese. Language: English; French creole *patois*. Religion: Christian (*c.* 66% Roman Catholic). Capital: Victoria (Mahé I.), pop. *c.* 10,000. Administration: governor; executive council; legislative council with equal official and unofficial (partly elected) membership. Governor, Sir John Thorp. Main imports: rice and other foodstuffs, cotton piecegoods. Main exports: copra, cinnamon oil and bark, guano. Monetary unit: Seychelles *rupee* (= 1*s.* 6*d.* sterling).

History. In the June 1959 honours list the governor, J. K. R. Thorp, was awarded a knighthood. Earlier the same month it was announced that G. F. Garratt, a former director of tourism in Cyprus, had been appointed director of tourism in the Seychelles. In November details were given of a £2·5 million development programme for the Seychelles, for which the British government had allotted £1 million from Colonial Development and Welfare funds. The scheme, worked out by the Seychelles government, included the development of roads, electricity, water supply and telephone services. Plans were also made for a hotel and tourist industry.

SHEEP: *see* LIVESTOCK.

SHIPPING, MERCHANT MARINE. Although there was a turn for the better in the general volume of international seaborne trade during 1959, the recovery in economic activity was not sufficient to relieve the shipping industry of its depression. Dry-cargo tramp shipping freight rates (as illustrated in Table I) remained at depressed levels and oil tanker freight rates remained similarly depressed. Throughout most of the year about 6 million tons deadweight of dry-cargo tramps and much the same amount of tanker tonnage was laid up for want of employment. Despite a marked increase in the rate of scrapping, this failed to offset the rate of delivery from the shipyards of new ships which had been contracted for in earlier boom years. The delivery of new dry-cargo vessels began to run down, but not so the delivery of new tankers. Demand for tanker tonnage being severely restricted by the decision of the U.S. government to restrict oil imports from overseas, tankers heavily encroached on what is normally regarded as the dry-cargo tramps' field, namely the carriage of grain, for which tankers can be readily adapted. Furthermore, much of the grain trade, one of the principal sources of employment for tramps, was removed from the international commercial market by U.S. legislation which restricted at least 50% of government-sponsored cargoes (such as the " disposal of surplus " grain cargoes) to U.S.-flag ships, regardless of the cost.

Many cargo liner conferences experienced increasing competition from " outsiders " (non-conference vessels attempting to take over business by offering lower rates) and in some cases additional inducements in the way of special rebates had to be offered to prevent business being lost, but on the whole there were few instances of rate cutting and no " freight wars " appeared to develop. On balance there came a halt to the increase in ship operating costs, mainly as a result of decreases in the cost of bunkers. The number of passengers travelling by sea remained at a high level, despite the growing competition of air transport at lower fare levels, but international competition for ocean passenger traffic increased. Although

At Kilcobben cove, the Lizard, Cornwall, material used in building a new lifeboat station has to be brought down a steep cliff.

the French " Ile de France " was broken up in Japan and three Arosa line vessels went out of business, the new Dutch liner " Rotterdam " (38,645 tons gross) and the newly converted German liner " Bremen " (32,336 tons gross, formerly the French " Pasteur ") entered service on the north Atlantic; and three newly converted Dutch liners (the " Willem Ruys ", " Oranje " and " Johan van Oldenbaarnevelt ") were introduced into the Australian and round-the-world passenger services, fitted with stabilizers and air-conditioning. British liners engaged in the same trades were also put through a reconditioning programme which involved improved amenities

TABLE I. TRAMP SHIPPING FREIGHT INDICES, 1959
(1952 = 100)

Month	Voyage rates	Time charter rates	Month	Voyage rates	Time charter rates
Jan.	70·3	53·1	July	69·7	52·3
Feb.	68·2	50·6	Aug.	69·6	55·5
March	65·1	53·6	Sept.	71·0	55·4
April	68·6	52·8	Oct.	80·4	58·4
May	64·6	56·7	Nov.	83·1	63·4
June	69·2	50·2	Dec.	82·5	65·6

SOURCE. Chamber of Shipping of the United Kingdom.

TABLE II. MERCHANT FLEETS OF THE WORLD, DEC. 31, 1958*

Country	Number of vessels	Gross tonnage ('000)	Country	Number of vessels	Gross tonnage ('000)
Unites States†	3,061	24,247	German Fed. Rep.	866	3,866
United Kingdom	2,522	18,655	Sweden	584	3,276
Liberia	1,020	11,253	U.S.S.R.	774	2,789
Norway	1,288	9,503	Commonwealth	614	2,761
Japan	870	5,282	Denmark	357	1,924
Italy	718	4,775	Greece	289	1,776
Panama	546	4,340	Spain	314	1,272
France	624	4,212	Finland	224	687
Netherlands	580	4,140	Other	1,715	7,556
			Total	16,966	112,314

* Excl. specialized ships and Great Lakes vessels. † Including 15,035,000 tons government-owned.
SOURCE. The American Bureau of Shipping.

The new Dutch liner, "Rotterdam", the flagship of the Holland-America line, arriving at Southampton on her maiden voyage to New York with Crown Princess Beatrix on board.

and the installation of air-conditioning. The British troopship "Empire Orwell" (formerly the German "Pretoria") was specially reconditioned and fitted out for the carriage of Moslem pilgrims between Indonesia and Jidda, Saudi Arabia, under the name "Gunung Djati". Negotiations were started between the Cunard line and the British government concerning financial aid towards the eventual replacement of the "Queen Elizabeth" and "Queen Mary".

The opening of the St. Lawrence seaway to ocean navigation for the first time was a historic feature of the year. Although some teething troubles were experienced, involving a certain amount of congestion, the increase of traffic over the route was substantial. Another historic event was the first assembly of the Intergovernmental Maritime Consultative organization (a U.N. agency) in London, which was also the venue of the conventions of the Baltic and International Maritime conference and the International Marine Insurance union.

Shipbuilding. The output of completed ships from the world's shipyards during 1959 remained at much the same level as in the previous year, but there was a marked decline in the volume of new work started (*see* Table III). This was the result of the almost complete cessation of new orders for dry-cargo tramps and tankers resulting from the severe decline in the level of freight rates in the previous two years. The rise in shipbuilding prices came to an abrupt halt in most countries and quotations for such business as was available became very keen. Total shipbuilding capacity, however, continued to increase, as expansion and modernization schemes started in earlier years began to take effect. A large new shipyard was inaugurated in Rotterdam and new berths and other improvements came into operation in the United Kingdom, Sweden and elsewhere. In Sweden a new building dock capable of constructing tankers of 100,000 tons deadweight came into use and work began on the building of an entirely new shipyard capable of constructing two vessels of this size simultaneously, by unorthodox methods. Work started also on the expansion of building facilities in Norway and Denmark.

Launchings of note during the year included that of the U.S. nuclear-propelled cargo and passenger liner "Savannah" in New York on July 21. The largest passenger liners launched came from the United Kingdom—the "Oriana" (40,000 tons gross), designed for service between Europe, Australasia and North America across the Pacific; the "Windsor Castle (38,000 tons gross), the largest vessel yet built for the South African service; and the "Amazon" (20,000 tons gross), the first of a series of three designed for service between Europe and South America.

The largest ship yet built in the Netherlands was the passenger liner "Rotterdam" (38,645 tons gross), a vessel unconventional in appearance and concept. The largest vessel so far built in Sweden was the 68,000-ton deadweight tanker "W. Alton Jones", built for a U.S. oil company. The largest

cargo ship in the world, however, was the tanker "Universe Apollo", a vessel of 104,520 tons deadweight built in a U.S.-operated shipyard in Japan. This ship had an over-all length of 950 ft. and a width of 135 ft., being capable of carrying 1,021,000 bbl. of oil. The "Oriental Giant" (67,800 tons deadweight), which came from a Japanese-operated yard, was the largest vessel to be built, engined, owned, operated and manned entirely by Asiatics. The largest ship believed to have been built so far in the U.S.S.R. was the whaling factory ship "Sovietskaya Ukraina", with a displacement of 44,000 tons and accommodation for a complement of 650 men. The U.S.S.R. also put into service the first non-military nuclear-powered vessel, the powerful icebreaker "Lenin". Cargo liners of some note were the British vessels "Manchester

A section of the new ship hydrodynamics laboratory (with its reflection in the water) at Feltham, Middlesex, opened on Oct. 19.

TABLE III. SHIPBUILDING TRENDS (YEARS ENDED JUNE 1958 AND 1959)

('000 tons gross)

United Kingdom	1958	1959	Change (+ or —)
Commenced	1,545	1,169	—376
Launched	1,422	1,417	—5
Completed	1,347	1,472	+125
Under construction . .	2,295	2,033	—262
Other Countries			
Commenced	8,351	7,209	—1,142
Launched	7,597	7,631	+34
Completed	7,384	7,445	+61
Under construction . .	7,838	7,705	—133

SOURCE. Lloyd's Register of Shipping.

TABLE IV. MERCHANT SHIPS UNDER CONSTRUCTION, JUNE 30, 1959

Country	Number of vessels	Gross tonnage	Country	Number of vessels	Gross tonnage
United Kingdom	280	2,033,745	Norway .	54	313,497
Japan . .	150	1,169,764	Spain .	122	269,317
German Fed. Rep.	172	990,454	Denmark .	32	250,095
Italy . .	90	902,422	Commonwealth	57	224,662
Netherlands .	148	790,877	Belgium .	21	203,079
Sweden . .	65	768,968	Yugoslavia .	26	199,518
United States .	47	648,806	Finland .	41	101,086
France .	55	548,990	Other* .	92	323,756
			Total .	1,452	9,739,036

* Excl. China. U.S.S.R.
SOURCE. Lloyd's Register of Shipping.

Miller " (9,200 tons deadweight), specially designed for service on the St. Lawrence Seaway route, with a speed in excess of 16 knots, and unorthodox in many ways, including the suppression of the funnel; and the " Benloyal ", specially designed for service in the far east, having a capacity of 10,926 tons deadweight and a speed of 19 knots from a steam turbine developing 14,000 shaft h.p. Specialized ships of interest were the English Channel car ferry " Maid of Kent " and the Danish train ferry " Prinsesse Benedikte ", both fitted with transverse bow thrust units.

In October a new £2 million ship hydrodynamics laboratory was opened at Feltham, Middlesex. Its main task was to be the improvement of hull form and propeller efficiency.

Life-boat Service. Although in the main the weather in 1959 was exceptionally good, there was no diminution of the demands made on life-boat crews around the coasts of the British Isles. In fact the summer was the busiest in the whole history of the life-boat service. Between April 1 and Sept. 30 life-boats were launched on service 547 times. Although many of the calls were to yachts and other pleasure craft, the tendency for life-boats to be called out on service to vessels of all kinds in the summer months had been growing steadily in recent years. Throughout the autumn and early winter there were gales of exceptional severity.

The Eighth International Life-boat conference took place at Bremen in June. Delegates from 17 nations attended and among the life-boats on show was a new 52-ft. Barnett boat completed in 1959, afterwards stationed at Ballycottin. It was agreed that the next conference, which was to take place in 1963, should be held in Great Britain.

A major task of construction was started in 1959 when work began on the building of a new life-boat station at Kilcobben cove in Cornwall. This would allow a life-boat of the largest type to be stationed there. To enable the station to be built the Royal National Life-boat institution had to place a contract for constructional work to the value of £70,000. Six new life-boats were completed during the year and went to their stations. In addition to the Ballycottin life-boat there were three life-boats of the 47-ft. class which were stationed at Dunbar, Islay and Newhaven, and two of the 42-ft. class stationed at Aldeburgh and Walmer.

At the annual general meeting of the Royal National Life-boat institution in March six medals for gallantry were awarded. Three were for a service by the St. Ives life-boat when four people who had been marooned in a cave were rescued; two were for a service by the Lerwick life-boat, which rescued the only three survivors of a Soviet trawler; and one was for a service by the Barrow life-boat in taking a sick man off a lightvessel. It was reported that the institution's total payments in 1958 had amounted to £977,794. Receipts, all of which came from voluntary contributions, amounted to £1,118,684.

Coxswain Richard Evans of Moelfre, Anglesey, became the first man to win the institution's highest award for gallantry—the gold medal—for ten years. The award was made for the rescue of the crew of the coaster " Hindlea " on Oct. 27.

On Dec. 8 the Broughty ferry life-boat capsized when going to the assistance of a lightvessel which had broken adrift. The crew of eight lost their lives. This was the first time that an R.N.L.I. life-boat had capsized for five years. (*See also* COMMUNICATIONS.)   (P. D.; P. HH.)

SHOE INDUSTRY: *see* BUSINESS REVIEW.

SHOPS AND DEPARTMENT STORES. After the moderate economic recession in most countries in 1958 retail trade showed a substantial recovery during 1959. In the United Kingdom retail sales were on average 5% higher than in the previous year. The removal of all hire-purchase restrictions late in 1958 and the reduction of purchase tax and

At the entrance to Aberdeen harbour the tow rope between the tug " Danny " and the Faeroese trawler " Fame " breaks. The " Fame ", whose steering gear had been damaged during a severe gale, had been towed nearly 200 mi. from Shetland through rough seas without mishap.

Marks and Spencer's store in Middlesbrough, converted during 1958-59 from 10,000 sq. ft. on two floors to 18,000 sq.ft on one.

income tax in the 1959 budget gave a strong stimulus to retail sales. In particular the trade in household goods was affected, rising by more than 20% above the 1958 level. The trend of more than average rate of expansion by the multiple organizations continued.

In the United States, after a poor year in 1958, retail sales rose sharply in 1959 to a level more than 7% above that of the previous year. Similar trends were evident in most western European countries.

In nearly all countries prices were stable, showing only slight increases, so that the rise in sales which was achieved represented a real increase in the volume of merchandise sold. In most countries 1959 was another record year for retailers.

In the United Kingdom the use of mobile shops spread and more than 3% of all the food trade of the country was done by them. The majority were operated by the co-operative societies. Sales through automatic vending machines grew sufficiently to be significant and many new producers entered this field in the United Kingdom. Big increases were also shown in the United States and in some European countries. Mail order sales grew rapidly in the United Kingdom but seemed to have reached a peak in the United States. Self-service developments were a feature in several countries. The

growth here was particularly marked in the United Kingdom and in France, where the increase in trade was big enough to justify the formation of a self-service institute.

Supermarkets continued to be built, Debenhams of London entering this field for the first time at Croydon. New supermarkets were also opened at Antwerp and Liège in Belgium, at Aarhus in Denmark and in Moscow. In Italy the first furniture supermarket was opened in Bologna.

In many countries price cutting, under the stress of growing competition, was prominent. In France this took place in the food trades through the Leclerc chain of more than 60 shops. By buying direct from manufacturers these shops were able to sell their merchandise at wholesale prices. This action had the approval of the French government.

The efforts of the independent shopkeepers to meet the challenge of the multiples continued. Co-operative buying organizations and voluntary chains were becoming international and by the end of 1959 covered most of western Europe.

Electronic computers continued to be brought into use for merchandise control by a number of retailers in the United States, the United Kingdom and western Europe.

Traffic congestion and high costs encouraged the move away from the main shopping centres. Suburban shopping centres were built in France (Paris, Nancy and Bordeaux), in Australia (Brisbane and Melbourne) and in the United States (Milwaukee and Detroit). (J. Bx.)

SHOW JUMPING AND HORSE TRIALS.

British prestige abroad was maintained at the highest level during 1959 and the policy of the International Affairs committee to give international experience to as many horses and riders as possible fulfilled the hopes of its instigators. Ann Townsend in her first full year of international competition jumping won the Coupe Carven at Lisbon, Madrid and Paris. Britain won the Nations cup at Madrid, at Dublin (for the second year in succession), and at Le Zoute and Rotterdam. The European Ladies championship at Rotterdam went to Ann Townsend and Bandit, and in Paris Piero d'Inzeo became European champion. The British team won the European Junior championship for the fourth year in succession, and the individual honour was shared between G. Castellini of

A view of the Ascot Jumping show, promoted by the Duke and Duchess of Norfolk, which opened its four-day run on the race course on April 22. There were rings for each of the three grades of horse. The Grade A championship was won by L. Vendyback's Topper VI, ridden by F. Welch.

Italy on Venturo and Lady Sarah Fitzalan-Howard on Oorskiet.

The 1959 season of horse trials gave Mrs. John Waddington (Miss Sheila Willcox) her third successive win at the Badminton three-day event. Later in the year, the European championships were held at Harewood, and Britain was beaten into second place by the western German team with the narrowest margin ever recorded. The Individual championship went to Captain Hans Schwarzenbach of Switzerland with Burn Trout. A British team competed also in the French National championships at Fontainebleau, and Captain M. Cavenagh with Landfall was first in the individual placings. Leading Horse of the Year was Major D. Allhusen's Laurien.

The famous show-jumper, Foxhunter, died at the end of the year. Lieut.-Col. H. Llewellyn and Foxhunter were members of the British Olympic team in 1952 when it won the only gold medal for Britain. (*See also* HORSE RACING; SPORTING RECORD.)   (S. WN.)

SHOWS: *see* FAIRS, SHOWS AND EXHIBITIONS.
SIAM: *see* THAILAND.

SIERRA LEONE. British colony and protectorate on the west coast of Africa, bounded N. and E. by Guinea and S.E. by Liberia. Area: colony 256 sq.mi.; protectorate 27,669 sq.mi. Pop. (1958 est.): colony, 130,000; protectorate 2,130,000. Language: tribal dialects, Hausa. Religion: colony mainly Christian; protectorate, pagan with Moslem minority. Chief towns: Freetown (cap.), pop. (1956 est.) 77,420; Bo, pop. *c.* 15,600. Administration: governor; executive council comprising prime minister and not less than seven other ministers drawn from elected side of House of Representatives and presided over by the governor; House of Representatives with elected majority. Governor, Sir Maurice Dorman; premier, Sir Milton Margai. Main imports: textile manufactures and apparel, iron and steel manufactures (incl. machinery) and electrical apparatus, basic foodstuffs and alcoholic beverages. Main exports: oil kernels, iron ore, diamonds, coffee. Monetary unit: West African shilling (= 1s. sterling).

History. On April 3, 1959, for the first time, a Sierra Leone minister of finance presented the budget to the House of Representatives. The total revenue, including £988,217 from Colonial Development and Welfare funds, was estimated at about £12,019,000 and provided a surplus over expenditure of some £200,000. In May the minister of works and housing stated that the Guma Valley dam, which was to provide adequate water for Freetown and the area around it and also a hydroelectric scheme, should be ready in about five years. It was already augmenting the water supply by 250,000 gal. a day.

President William Tubman of Liberia and his wife paid a state visit to Sierra Leone in June and had a cordial welcome. Both Tubman and the governor, Sir Maurice Dorman, spoke of co-operation between their countries, and Dorman proposed an international highway linking the two countries and interstate collaboration in health measures on the frontier. In July the secretary of state for the colonies, A. T. Lennox-Boyd, visited Sierra Leone and said that constitutional talks with a Sierra Leone delegation would be held early in 1960. The premier, Sir Milton Margai, stated that his government would ask for independence in 1961.

The situation in Kono where there was widespread illicit diamond mining continued to give anxiety. Taking vigorous action the police gradually regained the initiative, and thousands of people were arrested for illicit mining and for being in the area without a permit. In January new legislation was brought in to tighten controls, reduce anomalies in the supervision of strangers and facilitate drastic action in protection of the country's economy and the working of the alluvial mining scheme. In August the governor opened the new Government Diamond Mining office. This was to be in future the sole legitimate exporter of African-won diamonds.

    (W. H. Is.)

SIKKIM. Indian-protected state, bounded N. by Tibet, E. by Bhutan, S. by India and W. by Nepal. Area: 2,745 sq.mi. Pop. (1951 census): 135,646, mostly Nepalese (Gurkha) but including Bhotias of Tibetan extraction (*c.* 12%) and Lepchas or Rongpa (*c.* 15%) of Indochinese origin. State religion: Lamaistic Buddhism, but most of the Nepalese are Hindu. Capital, Gangtok (pop., 7,000). Maharaja, Tashi Namgyal. Dewan (chief minister), J. S. Lall. Currency: Indian *rupee.*

History. Replying on Aug. 25, 1959, to a question in the Rajya Sabha (Council of States), Jawaharlal Nehru, prime minister of India, said that Sikkim would be defended against any intrusion. On Sept. 5 the Maharaj Kumar, the heir apparent, said in a press interview: " So far as we are aware, the Chinese have not crossed our borders. Our frontiers are well defined and they have been accepted for years." (*See also* SINO-INDIAN FRONTIER DISPUTE.)   (X.)

SINGAPORE. British internally self-governing colony; an island off southern end of Malay peninsula. Area: Singapore and adjacent islets 224·5 sq.mi. Pop.: (1957 census), 1,445,928, incl. (approx.) 73% Chinese, 13% Malays, 8% Indians; (1958 est.) 1,515,000. Capital: Singapore City, pop.: (1956 est.) 916,760. Administration: yang di-pertuan negara; cabinet presided over by the prime minister; elected Legislative Assembly presided over by a speaker. Heads of state (yang di-pertuan negara) in 1959: Sir William Goode and (from Dec. 3) Inche Yusof bin Ishak. Chief ministers in 1959: Lim Yew Hock and (from June 2 with title of prime minister) Lee Kuan Yew. Singapore is chief port for Malaya. Monetary unit, Malayan *dollar* (= 2s. 4d. sterling).

The U.K. commissioner for Singapore and southeast Asia, with responsibility for the co-ordination of policy in the Federation of Malaya, Singapore, Sarawak, North Borneo and Brunei, has his headquarters in Singapore. Commissioner, the Earl of Selkirk.

History. On May 30, 1959, general elections were held to the first Legislative Assembly under the new constitution establishing a State of Singapore with full internal self-government. Under this constitution responsibility for external affairs and defence remained with the U.K. government, which was also represented, together with Singapore and the Federation of Malaya, on an Internal Security council.

Altogether 13 parties and 35 independent candidates contested the 51 single-member constituencies. The left-wing People's Action party had 51 candidates, the Singapore People's alliance 37 and the Liberal Socialists 30. The election campaign was marked by two features: the failure of the moderate parties—the S.P.A. and the Liberal Socialists —to agree on a common front against the P.A.P.; and the P.A.P.'s allegation that the minister for education, Chew Swee Kee, had received financial aid for political purposes from overseas.

Voting was compulsory. The P.A.P., led by Lee Kuan Yew, won 43 of the 51 seats and polled 281,891 of the 527,919 votes cast by an electorate of 589,797. The S.P.A., led by the outgoing chief minister, Lim Yew Hock, won four seats, the United Malays' National organization won three seats and one Independent was returned.

Before accepting office as prime minister Lee Kuan Yew insisted that eight members of his party detained by the previous government under the Preservation of Public Security ordinance should be released. The governor, Sir William Goode, agreed to this. On June 3 the governor proclaimed the new constitution to be in force and the same day was sworn in as the first yang di-pertuan negara (head of state).

On July 1 the first session of the new Legislative Assembly was formally opened. The ultimate aims of the new government were stated to be union with the Federation of Malaya and the evolution of a Socialist society. The government proposed to encourage industry while maintaining Singapore's entrepôt trade. It promised free transfer of profits and capital, and also a wide range of reforms including revision of marriage laws, making polygamy illegal for all except Moslems.

(Top left) Women queueing outside a polling station in Singapore to cast their votes in the general election on May 30. (Top right) Lee Kuan Yew, leader of the victorious People's Action party and the new prime minister, is chaired by supporters. (Right) Volunteer workers of the National Construction corps, formed to reclaim seafront waste land for recreation grounds and parks.

In its first month of office the government removed "Rock 'n' Roll" music from its radio programmes, banned juke boxes and "yellow culture" publications and tightened censorship against films deemed to glorify colonialism or denigrate Asians.

To balance the budget the government cut the allowances of civil servants, saving $12 million a year. In September the finance minister flew to London to ask the U.K. government to bear the entire cost of local defence forces (approximately $10 million a year) and also to pay for airport development ($14 million). Two months later the finance minister announced that the government had proposed to the Federation of Malaya a common market on the basis of an agreed list of tariff-free local manufactures.

In October the government introduced legislation extending the life of the Preservation of Public Security ordinance for five years. It amended this ordinance (first introduced in 1955) to abolish the appellate tribunal of three judges, substituting an advisory committee, and also widened the definition of subversion to embrace not merely Communist activity, but activity on behalf of foreign powers.

On Dec. 3 Inche Yusof bin Ishak, chairman of the Public Services commission and a former newspaper editor, was made Singapore's first Malayan-born yang di-pertuan negara.

Trade was uncertain during the year. Total trade for the first half of 1959 was $2,787 million compared with $2,960 million for the first half of 1958, a decline of 6%. In the first nine months exports to Indonesia totalled $107·5 million compared with $276·2 million for the corresponding period in 1958. This decline was due mainly to import restrictions introduced by the Indonesians during the year. (L. S. Y.)

SINO-INDIAN FRONTIER DISPUTE.
The frontier between China and the Indian subcontinent stretches roughly along the crest of the Himalayas with two exceptions: in the northwest it turns northwards, crosses the Sutlej and Indus valleys, reaches the Kun-Lun range and then turns west towards a point where the frontiers of Kashmir, Afghanistan and the Sinkiang-Uigur autonomous region of China meet; in the east it crosses the Brahmaputra, turns to the southeast and to the point where the frontiers of India, China and Burma meet. This frontier runs for *c.* 2,500 mi. To describe this line as a Sino-Indian border is not entirely correct, because it comprises *c.* 670 mi. of the northern and eastern frontier of Kashmir—a disputed territory between Pakistan and India. Field Marshal Ayub Khan, president of Pakistan, said in Rawalpindi on Nov. 23, 1959, that Ladakh was Pakistan territory and that Pakistan would not recognize any arrangement between India and China concerning this part of Kashmir. The frontier described above also includes *c.* 650 mi. of the northern frontier of the independent state of Nepal.

Legal Position. No single treaty ever defined the whole length of the Sino-Indian frontier. Certain sections of it remained traditional but undefined; others are delimited by international agreements; others still are in dispute.

(1) The *c.* 370-mi.-long frontier between Kashmir and the Sinkiang-Uigur autonomous region of China is undefined. According to Indian maps it runs partly along the rivers Karakash and Raskemdarya (or Yarkand). Sinkiang ("New Territory"), or Chinese Turkistan, is a comparatively recent

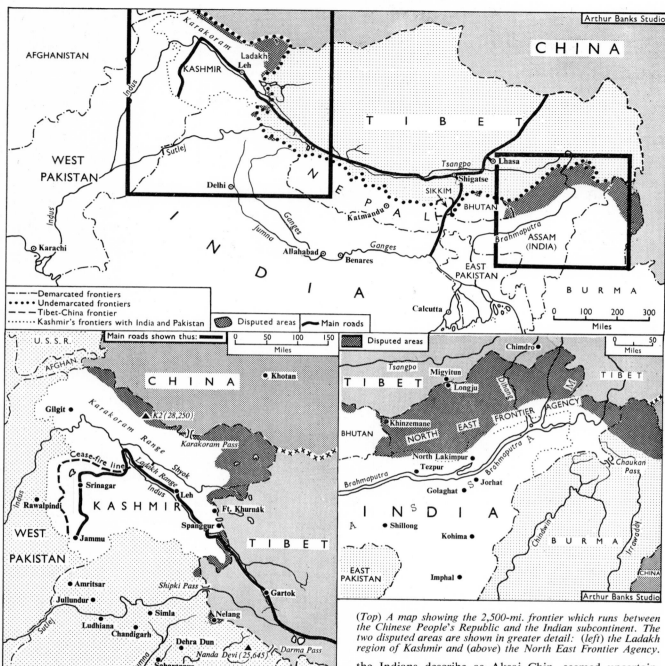

(Top) A map showing the 2,500-mi. frontier which runs between the Chinese People's Republic and the Indian subcontinent. The two disputed areas are shown in greater detail: (left) the Ladakh region of Kashmir and (above) the North East Frontier Agency.

the Indians describe as Aksai Chin, seemed uncertain. According to Chinese maps c. 8,000 sq.mi. of Ladakh belongs to China.

(2) The c. 280-mi.-long frontier between Tibet and the Indian territory of Himachal Pradesh as well as the states of Punjab and Uttar Pradesh was never demarcated. The boundaries marked on Indian and Chinese maps differ here to a much lesser degree than in the case of Ladakh. For instance, the Indians claim that the plain of Barahoti (Wu-Je in Chinese), north of the Niti pass, belongs to India, while the Chinese consider that the Niti pass itself is in Chinese territory.

(3) No dispute exists concerning the Nepali-Tibetan frontier. It was first fixed in the Nepali-Tibetan peace treaty of 1854 and again in the Anglo-Tibetan peace treaty of Sept. 7, 1904, that followed Sir Francis Younghusband's military expedition to Lhasa. The Imperial Chinese government adhered to this treaty on April 27, 1906. Along this frontier

Chinese conquest: it became a province of China in 1884.

The c. 300-mi.-long eastern frontier of Kashmir (or rather of Ladakh, its eastern part) borders Tibet. At the beginning of the 19th century Ladakh was an ethnically Tibetan principality subject to Lhasa. In 1841, Gulab Singh, the maharaja of Jammu and Kashmir, invaded Tibet. With Chinese assistance the invaders were driven back, but according to a treaty concluded in 1842 between Gulab Singh, the Lama Guru of Lhasa and a representative of the emperor of China, Ladakh became part of the Jammu and Kashmir state. The frontier, however, was never delimited. In particular the sovereignty over a large salient protruding eastwards, which stand many of the highest peaks of the Himalayas, including Mount Everest.

(4) The relatively short (*c.* 100-mi.) Sikkimese-Tibetan frontier was clearly defined in the Sino-British convention signed in Calcutta on March 17, 1890, by H. C. K. Petty Fitzmaurice, Marquess of Lansdowne, the viceroy of India, and Sheng Tai, plenipotentiary of the Chinese empire. The convention was ratified on Aug. 27 of the same year. It says:

" The boundary of Sikkim and Tibet should be the crest of the mountain range separating the waters flowing into the Sikkim Teesta and its affluents from the waters flowing into the Tibetan Mochu and northwards into other rivers of Tibet."

In 1895 the Sikkimese-Tibetan frontier was jointly demarcated on the terrain.

(5) The Bhutanese-Tibetan frontier, *c.* 250 mi. long, is undefined. The majority of the population of Bhutan is ethnically Tibetan.

(6) Finally, the *c.* 550-mi.-long frontier separating the Indian North East Frontier agency and Tibet is in dispute. It is known as the McMahon line because it was recorded on a map at the tripartite conference which opened at Simla in Oct. 1913, Great Britain being represented by Sir Henry McMahon, the secretary in the Indian Foreign Department, and by Sir Charles Bell, Britain's adviser in Tibetan affairs, Tibet by the *lön-chen* (chief minister) Shatra and China by Yi Van-chen. The convention was initialled on April 27, 1914. It stipulated that Tibet would be divided into inner or eastern (Chinese province) and outer or western (autonomous, but under Chinese suzerainty). It traced the frontier between Tibet and northeastern India along the crest of the high Himalayas. However, two days later the Chinese Republican government disavowed its plenipotentiary and refused to sign the convention. According to the Peking government the traditional frontier runs here roughly 50 mi. to the south of the McMahon line. A territory of *c.* 35,000 sq.mi. is in dispute.

Alleged Provocations. As long ago as 1956 or 1957 the Chinese moved into eastern Ladakh to complete a road linking Khotan in the Sinkiang-Uigur autonomous region with Gartok in Tibet. This road, a remarkable feat of engineering, crosses Ladakh from a point near Haji-Liangar in the north to a point near Jilganang lake—a distance of some 112 mi. The Indian government learned about this when the road was completed. On Oct. 18, 1958, it protested against the construction of a road through " Indian territory ". On

Nov. 1 the Chinese government said that the road ran through " Chinese territory ". In the autumn of 1959 the Indian government sent a 60-man police force into the Chinese-occupied Aksai Chin plateau (lying at *c.* 17,000 ft. above sea level). The force was stopped by the Chinese on Oct. 21 near a place called Hot Springs, 45 mi. west of the Lanak pass, situated on the frontier as India conceives it. In a clash with the Chinese nine Indians were killed and ten captured. A strong protest was lodged by Delhi against this " aggression ", but on Oct. 22 China made a counter-charge of armed provocation by Indian troops " unlawfully intruding into Chinese territory ". On Nov. 13 the Indians taken prisoner and the bodies of the killed were handed over by the Chinese to an Indian police party at Hot Springs.

On Aug. 26 another incident occurred in the North East Frontier agency. A Chinese force had crossed the McMahon line and captured the Longju outpost situated three or four mi. south of the line. There was no bloodshed.

Proposals for Settlement. Jawaharlal Nehru, the prime minister of India, made many statements on the dispute and frontier incidents. Speaking in the Lok Sabha (People's Assembly) on Aug. 28, 1959, he cautioned the house against being alarmist or panicky. The government were concerned; they were prepared to face any eventuality, but would always be ready to settle certain cases by negotiation.

" So far ", he said, " as chunks of Indian territories which were indicated by a sweep of the Chinese brush on their maps as Chinese territories, no question of any negotiation arose."

Nehru also declared that any aggression against Bhutan and Sikkim would be considered as " aggression against India ". On Nov. 27 he gave a similar pledge to Nepal. Speaking on Oct. 4 at a mass meeting in Bombay he repeated that India was prepared to hold negotiations on minor adjustments of the Sino-Indian frontier, " but there can never be a question of surrendering the Himalayas ". On Nov. 1, at a mass meeting in Delhi, Nehru said: " If any country thinks we are a weak race it is mistaken. China may be big, but so is India." He rejected, however, the advice of his critics to enter into a military alliance with any country.

During the year many notes dealing with the territorial dispute were exchanged between Delhi and Peking. On Nov. 7, Chou En-lai, chairman of the Chinese state council (government), said in a letter to Nehru that " the most important duty facing the two governments was:

(*Left*) Part of a demonstration organized in New Delhi by the Jan Sangh party in protest against alleged violations of the Indian frontier by Chinese troops. (*Right*) A caravan of Bhotian traders using sheep as pack animals, returning to India from Gartok in western Tibet.

" to take effective steps speedily and without hesitation to earnestly improve the disquieting situation on the border between the two countries and work for the complete elimination of the possibility of any border clash in the future."

Chou proposed a mutual 12·5-mi. withdrawal of troops both from " the so-called McMahon line " and from the line " up to which each side exercises actual control in the west " (i.e., in Ladakh).

Replying on Nov. 16, Nehru offered the creation of a large neutral zone in Ladakh: the Chinese would withdraw to the east of the line India considers as the international frontier; the Indians would withdraw to the west of the line China describes on its maps as the international boundary. The Chinese would also withdraw from Longju which the Indians would not reoccupy.

Chou answered on Dec. 18 suggesting a meeting with Nehru on Dec. 26 anywhere in China or in Rangoon, Burma. Three days later Nehru informed Chou that he was always ready to meet him and discuss the frontier dispute but he did not see how an agreement of principles could be reached " when there was such complete disagreement about facts ".

On Dec. 26 Chou, replying to Nehru's note, repeated China's desire for a settlement through negotiations: " The Chinese government is desirous at all times (Chou wrote) of maintaining friendship with the Indian government and people, and, on the boundary question, of holding discussions with the Indian government calmly and amicably . . . In view of the fact that the Sino-Indian boundary question is rather complex and that it would be extremely difficult to bring about a settlement through the exchange of letters, the Chinese government has always maintained that face-to-face talks should be held speedily between the representatives of the two governments, first of all between the prime ministers of the two countries, so as more effectively to exchange views and reach agreement."

A strong argument for the Indian case was that for about a century the Sino-Indian frontier had remained de facto unchanged. While the Chinese may have been justified in asking for a precise delimitation of undefined frontiers, it was not anticipated that they would make an issue of it in 1959. (K. M. S.)

BIBLIOGRAPHY. Blue Book on Anglo-Tibetan Relations (London, 1910); Further Papers Relating to Tibet, Cmd. 5240 (London, 1910); Sir Charles Bell, Tibet, Past and Present (Oxford, 1924); Government of India, Notes, Memoranda and Letters Exchanged and Agreements Signed between the Governments of India and China, pt. 1 (1954-59), p. 2 (Sept.-Nov. 1959) (New Delhi, 1959).

SKIN DISEASES: see DISEASES.
SOAPS, PERFUMERY AND COSMETICS: see BUSINESS REVIEW.

SOCIAL SERVICES. General. United Kingdom. In 1959 a new national insurance scheme introduced a measure of graduated contributions and retirement pensions relating to employees' earnings. As from April 1961 there would be a minimum contribution by employees and employers covering all employees' earnings up to £9 a week—for the flat-rate pensions and benefits. Those earning more than £9 a week, and their employers, would also pay a graduated contribution —a percentage of earnings over £9 and up to £15 a week—and thus qualify for a graduated addition to their retirement pension. Members of occupational pension schemes connected with their employment could be contracted out of the graduated part of the national insurance retirement pensions scheme if their occupational scheme was financially sound and provided pension rights equivalent to the maximum under the graduated part of the state scheme. These equivalent pension rights had to be preserved on change of employment. Contracted-out employees, and their employers, would pay flat-rate contributions to qualify for the current flat-rate pensions and benefits. Provision was made for increasing contributions at four five-yearly intervals during the following 20 years if this should prove necessary to meet the cost of pensions.

The minimum contribution as compared with the previous contribution was to be as follows:

	Men		Women	
	Minimum contribution	Previous contribution	Minimum contribution	Previous contribution
	s.　d.	s.　d.	s.　d.	s.　d.
Employee	8　4	9　11	7　2	8　0
Employer	7　0	8　3	6　4	6　9
Total	15　4	18　2	13　6	14　9

The graduated contribution was to be 8½% on the range of earnings between £9 and £15 a week, divided equally between the employer and the employee, and would be the same for men and women. The graduated contribution would vary from a total minimum of 1s. 8d. where the weekly earnings were between £9 and £10, up to a maximum of 10s. 2d. where the earnings were £15 or more. The following are examples of how the new scheme would work for people of various ages and different levels of earnings:

Level of weekly earnings	Total weekly contributions	Age at entry	Total weekly retirement pension at 65	
			Single men	Married men
	s.　d.		£　s.	£　s.
£10 . .	17　0	30	2　15	4　5
£12 . .	20　4	42	3　0	4　10
£14 . .	23　10	50	3　1	4　11
£15 . .	25　6	57	2　17	4　7

People who postponed retirement beyond the age of 65 (60 for women) would be able to continue to earn pension for the time when they did retire or when they reached the age of 70 (65 for women) whether retired or not. Until then they would, if they were earning more than £9 a week, continue to pay graduated contributions, which would count for graduated pension. In addition, the graduated part of the pension which they would have drawn if they had retired at age 65 (60 for women) could be treated as if it were a graduated contribution paid by the contributor and the employer.

During 1959 the only major alteration in the national insurance scheme taking immediate effect was the amendment of the earnings rules for retirement and widows' pensions. These pensions were not to be reduced unless net earnings were more than £3 a week instead of £2 10s. as previously. For widowed mothers the net amount was raised from £3 to £4 a week. Sixpence was deducted from the pension for every shilling earned between £3 and £4 a week and 1s. for each shilling earned over £4 a week by a pensioner other than a widowed mother. In her case similar deductions were made in respect of earnings between £4 and £5 and over £5 respectively. There were also changes in administrative procedure. The responsibility for determining claims to family allowances was transferred from the minister of pensions and national insurance to an independent insurance officer, with right to appeal to a local tribunal and, ultimately, to the national insurance commissioner.

National assistance rates were increased from 45s. to 50s. a week for a single householder and from 76s. to 85s. a week for a married couple, plus the usual rent allowance. The arrangement whereby an earning member of the household was assumed to be contributing towards the general expenses was terminated. The amount of capital and certain types of income which might be disregarded in deciding the amount of an allowance was liberalized. It was estimated that the additional cost to the exchequer of these alterations would be £32 million in a full year.

Effect was given to the European interim agreement on social security schemes relating to old age, invalidity, survivors' and family allowances, and to a protocol supplementing that agreement, made between member governments of the Council of Europe in 1953. Further reciprocal provision was made as to family allowances, and reciprocity in social security was extended to Denmark; previously the arrangement only applied to industrial injuries benefit.

The report of the Ministry of Pensions and National Insurance for 1958 showed that new claims for sickness benefit totalled nearly 8 million. This figure was higher than in any year since the scheme started (1948) except for 1952 and 1957 (when there were serious epidemics). About 881,000 new retirement pensions came into payment and at the end of 1958 there were in all 5,330,000 retirement pensioners. The increase was mainly due to the coming into the scheme of late entrants who did not qualify for pension until ten years after the start of the national insurance scheme. About 52% of the men and 28·5% of the women awarded pension during 1958 had earned supplements by continuing at work after pensionable age. Changes were made in the procedure for the appointment and administration of local tribunals and it was required that they should normally hear appeals in public.

The report of the National Assistance board for 1958 showed that at the end of the year 1,649,000 allowances were being made. Altogether about 1 million pensioners were being assisted and 47% of the recipients were receiving discretionary allowances, in addition to the ordinary scale, for such items as special diet, laundry, exceptional fuel requirements or domestic help. The total expenditure of the board in respect of allowances was at the rate of £119 million a year. Of the 1,649,000 beneficiaries at the end of 1958, 68% were receiving supplementations of national insurance benefits (retirement pensions, 54·2%; sickness or industrial injury benefit, 6·5%; widow's benefit, 3·2%; and unemployment benefit, 4·0%). Persons receiving supplementations of non-contributory old age pensions were 7·8% of the total and persons not in receipt of such pensions or national insurance benefits formed 24·3% of the total.

Other European Countries. In France a supplementary scheme of assistance for the unemployed was brought into operation. Workers who were unemployed could receive an allowance which in total reached 88·5% of the lowest wage. There were also improvements in the general social security scheme, and rates of contributions were increased. In the Netherlands the rate of benefit for disability due to accidents was increased and old age pensions were increased to take account of the rise in the wages index. Improvements were also made in widows' and orphans' pensions. In Italy general improvements were made in the sickness insurances scheme, in Switzerland in the tuberculosis insurance scheme and in Sweden in the old age pensions scheme. In Belgium the sickness and invalidity insurance schemes were improved and in the German Federal Republic there were increases in the rates of pension for old age, widows and invalids. In Yugoslavia the basic amounts used for calculating pensions were increased by an average of 8%. Alterations in the administrative procedure were made in Czechoslovakia. The district or regional people's council was required to elect social security committees to act as executive bodies. These committees would determine benefits and services within limits laid down by the State Social Security office in agreement with the central Trade Unions council. Improvements were brought about in the general scheme.

Commonwealth. In New Zealand arrangements were made for a family benefit to be paid in cash, or to the credit of the Post Office Savings bank account of the mother, or to the commissioner of inland revenue to meet the income-tax payments of the mother or father. Provision was also made to assist parents with the purchase of home properties. This was by the capitalization of the family benefit in respect of one or more children from the age of one year up to the age of 16, provided that the total of the advance or advances in the case of any one family was not less than £200 or more than £1,000. A counselling and advice service was established, an officer in each of the districts of registrars of social security being designated for the purpose. Beneficiaries, as well as other members of the community, were invited to discuss with these officers those problems which were difficult of solution unaided. Although a large number of the inquiries were related to the work of the Special Security department, the balance covered a wide range of subjects. A superannuation benefit of £110 had been payable in New Zealand, without a means test, to all persons over 65. This was increased to £156 a year from April 1, 1959, and to £208 from March 30, 1960. The superannuation benefit would then be equivalent to the rate of age benefit, which it would substantially replace, thus providing a standard benefit free of means test. Another alteration was the lifting of all restrictions on the personal earnings of blind pensioners. Social security expenditure was financed by a levy of 1s. 6d. in the pound on all income together with a subsidy from the exchequer.

In Australia age, invalid and widows' pensions were increased by 6s. a week to £A3 16s. 0d. a week in the case of the first two benefits and £A3 6s. 0d. for widows. The hospital insurance scheme came into full operation in Canada, financed partly by the provinces and partly by federal grants-in-aid.

A new law in Ceylon provided old age pensions for all workers not employed by the government, and an increased allocation of Rs.2 million was made by the government to extend public assistance to a larger number of people. In India a general security plan was under active consideration and in Jamaica an old age pension and superannuation scheme came into force under which a pension authority was established to prepare and submit to the minister responsible old age pensions or other superannuation schemes.

United States. The ceiling for the earnings taken into account for contributions and benefits purposes was raised and increases were made bringing benefits approximately into line with price changes since benefit was last increased; contributions were also increased. Benefit was for the first time available to the dependants of a person receiving disability insurance benefit. The president reconstituted the Federal Council on Aging by making it representative of all the government departments and other interests concerned.

The annual report of the Department of Social Security showed that at the end of 1958 there were 12·4 million persons receiving benefit under the various social security schemes and 6·7 million being aided under the various public assistance schemes. Some 2·5 million persons were receiving old age assistance. Federal, state and local funds provided $3,250 million for assistance payments during 1957-58, amounting to $18·73 for every person in the nation.

The budget for 1959-60 provided for $2,100 million for social security administration of all kinds, representing 2·7% of the total administrative budget. For the third time provision was made for grants for training and studies in the field of social security totalling $1·8 million.

Other Countries. In Japan a new act came into operation consolidating unemployment insurance legislation. The daily rate of benefit varied according to the wage class to which each worker was assigned and was equal to 60% of the wage up to a maximum of Y.300. The scheme was financed partly by equal contributions from the employer and employee and partly by the state. There was also a review of the national insurance health scheme, making it universal.

In Argentina a sickness insurance scheme was introduced for the first time, administered by a new social security organization.

International. A panel of world experts, meeting at Geneva under the auspices of the International Labour organization, devoted special attention to the possibility of establishing an international instrument on social security for migrant workers and the study of a draft instrument concerning the equality of treatment of nationals and non-nationals in the field of social security. The progress made in the development of social security statistics and possible future programmes in the national and international fields of statistics were also discussed.

Voluntary Social Services. In Britain the National Council of Social Service extended its work of providing for easier contact and co-operation between the various national voluntary organizations among themselves and with the statutory bodies, both at the centre and, by means of local groups, throughout the country. An important part of its work lay in the international field. Its youth department arranged an interchange of young people with the U.S.S.R. and Poland as well as with other countries. The international department co-operated with the British Council in arranging programmes for social workers and students from many parts of the world and with the United Nations Technical Assistance office in the exchange of social workers between different countries. More was done by the National Old People's Welfare council, with its 1,600 local committees, in the training of voluntary workers, including the start of courses for committee members. In attempting to help to meet the housing needs of the elderly there were extensions in boarding out schemes in both urban and rural areas. The citizens advice bureaux continued their work and were used to an increased extent for the dissemination of information and for dealing with difficulties arising from new legislation. Bureaux on the British pattern were established in Israel and Jamaica and were under consideration in Japan and Rhodesia.

In Pakistan Rs.550,000 was made available by the government to the National Council of Social Welfare for making grants to 96 voluntary social welfare organizations throughout the country. In Malaya a welfare council was formed with representatives of all voluntary societies operating throughout the federation. Its funds were mainly derived from grants by the Social and Welfare Services Lotteries board. The Social Welfare department was co-ordinated with the voluntary welfare bodies.

National conferences of social work, allied to the International Conference of Social Work, were held in Burma, the German Federal Republic, India, Japan, Pakistan, the United States and Yugoslavia. An international conference was held at Strasbourg of representatives of 15 European countries.

Child Welfare. The publication of the report of the Working Party on Social Workers in Local Authority Health and Welfare Services was a timely reminder of the need for proper training and increased recruitment of social workers in the health and welfare field. Although this report was not concerned with the child care service, the needs of this service were very similar and the serious shortage of trained personnel was the subject of a special conference of the Association of Children's Officers in London during October.

The Adoption act, 1958, came into force on April 1, 1959, and its effects were considered at another conference in London in October. One practical difficulty was the need for the medical examination before placing to be made after a child was six weeks old. This requirement might well be honoured more in the breach than in the observance.

Child migration to Australia was debated in the House of Commons on Feb. 9, when Nigel Fisher said that one of the principal aims of child migration was to rescue the children of broken homes and bad environments and give them the opportunity of a happy, hopeful future in the Commonwealth; there was no lack of money but a lack of children. Local authorities were criticized for seldom considering migration for children in care. The report of the fact-finding mission which had gone to Australia in 1956 was regarded as prejudiced and having put a brake on child migration. C. J. M. Alport, under secretary of state for commonwealth relations,

did not regard child migration primarily as a solution for social problems and indicated that social changes had altered the pattern of child migration. He stated that the improvements recommended by the mission had been carried out and that the new pattern of child migration fitted in with modern ideas on child care. The discussion did not reveal the serious limitations imposed upon migration of children in care by lack of parental consent and the conditions of the Australian immigration authorities. Indeed, in one large city in Britain none of the intake of more than 600 in six months could have been accepted for immigration into Australia.

The results of the first official research work in child care were published in *Children in Care and the Recruitment of Foster Parents* (S.S. 249, 1959). The inquiry was carried out for the Home Office by P. G. Gray and Elizabeth Parr of the social survey division of the Central Office of Information, between Nov. 1956 and March 1957. Its object was to collect information about the characteristics of existing foster parents, their backgrounds and interests, and to produce information for the guidance of the Home Office and local authorities in their attempts to find more foster parents.

The Mental Health act, 1959, which was not brought into force immediately, contained provisions for the use of children's homes and the making of " fit person " orders by juvenile courts in respect of children and young persons needing treatment.

The Legitimacy act, 1959, came into force on Oct. 29 and had a bearing on the work of children's departments in connection with advice to parents on the legitimation of children in care.   (Jo. Ms.; I. H. D. B.)
See Jean Heywood, *Children in Care* (London, 1959).

SOCIETIES AND ASSOCIATIONS.
The following is a list of selected British societies and associations with date of foundation, chief activities of the year July 1958—June 1959, officers and headquarters address.

Royal Societies

Royal Aeronautical Society. Founded 1866 (prefix Royal granted 1918 and Charter of Incorporation 1949). *Events of the Year.* In Dec. 1958 the council agreed to the formation, within the society, of groups to cover small specialized fields of aeronautics; by June 1959 the Man-Powered Aircraft group and the Agricultural Aviation group had been formed. The name of the Guided Flight section had been changed to the " Astronautics and Guided Flight section ". The Fourth Air Transport course was held at Oriel college, Oxford, March 31-April 21, 1959. In May 1959 an appeal was launched for funds to build a lecture theatre at the rear of the society's offices. *Officers:* president, Peter G. Masefield (1959-60); secretary, A. M. Ballantyne. *Headquarters Address:* 4, Hamilton place, London, W.1. There are 28 branches in the United Kingdom, one overseas branch, in Singapore, and 3 divisions in the Commonwealth, each with its own branches.

Royal Agricultural Society of England. Founded in 1838 (royal charter granted 1840). *Events of the Year.* In July 1959 the Royal Show, attended by the Duke and Duchess of Gloucester and the Princess Royal, was held at Oxford. *Officers:* president (1959), Lord Digby; secretary, Alec Hobson. *Headquarters Address:* 35, Belgrave square, London, S.W.1.

Royal Anthropological Institute. Founded in 1843, as the Ethnological society. *Events of the Year.* The Huxley Memorial lecture for 1958 was delivered by Prof. Sir Wilfrid Le Gros Clark on " Bones of Contention ". *Officers:* president, Dr. Audrey I. Richards; hon. secretary, Dr. Marian W. Smith. *Headquarters Address:* 21, Bedford square, London, W.C.1. There are about 20 affiliated institutions in Great Britain and overseas.

Royal Archaeological Institute. Founded in 1843. *Events of the Year.* The 1959 summer meeting was held at Brighton. Papers read during the session, in the rooms of the Society of Antiquaries, Burlington house, London, ranged from " The Problem of Water in Roman Tripolitania " by Mrs. Olwen Brogan and " Two Late Medieval Houses: Acton Burnell and Tretower " by C. A. Ralegh Radford to " The Furniture Trade in Paris in the Eighteenth Century " by F. J. B. Watson. Vol. cxiv of the *Archaeological Journal* was published in April 1959. *Officers:* president, Prof. W. F. Grimes; hon. secretary, S. D. T. Spittle. *Headquarters Address:* c/o The London Museum, Kensington palace, London, W.8.

Royal Astronomical Society. Founded in 1820. *Events of the Year.* The Gold medal was awarded to Dr. R. A. Lyttleton and the Eddington medal to Dr. J. S. Hey. *Officers:* president, Prof. R. O. Redman; secretaries, Prof. H. Bondi, Dr. M. W. Ovenden. *Headquarters Address:* Burlington house, London, W.1.

Royal Automobile Club. Founded in 1897. *Events of the Year.* On

Nov. 12, 1958, the first award of the R.A.C. diamond jubilee trophy was made to Sir Vivian Fuchs for his journey across Antarctica. Further extensions were made to the club's radio rescue and road patrols services. A junior driver scheme was launched in March 1959 to instruct young people to drive. A conference of delegates from Commonwealth motoring organizations was convened in London on June 10, 1959. *Officers:* chairman, Wilfrid Andrews; director, associate section, Capt. (E) W. Gregson. *Headquarters Address:* 83 and 85, Pall Mall, London, S.W.1. There are 16 county offices.

Royal Forestry Society of England and Wales. Founded in 1822, as the English Arboricultural society (prefix Royal granted, 1905). *Events of the Year.* In 1958, the society made its annual summer excursion to King's Lynn, Norfolk. Examinations were held for the woodmen's and foresters' certificates, and for the certificate and diploma in arboriculture. *Officers:* president, Langshaw Rowland; secretary, P. S. Leathart. *Headquarters Address:* 49, Russell square, London, W.C.1. There are 18 divisions, including two divisions each broken up into three county branches, and one division covering Northern Ireland.

Royal Geographical Society. Founded in 1830. *Events of the Year.* The society supported with grants and other help 23 exploratory and research expeditions. A committee of geographers and medical men was established to sponsor research in the geography of disease. *Officers:* president, the Rt. Hon. Lord Nathan; director and secretary, L. P. Kirwan. *Headquarters Address:* 1, Kensington Gore, London, S.W.7.

Royal Horticultural Society. Founded in 1804. *Events of the Year.* The society held 23 shows in its halls in Vincent square and Greycoat street, Westminster. In addition, the society held the Chelsea show in the grounds of the Royal hospital (May 27-29). Trials of flowers, vegetables and fruit were also carried out at the society's gardens at Wisley, Surrey. *Officers:* president, the Hon. Sir David Bowes Lyon; secretary, A. Simmonds. *Headquarters Address:* 80, Vincent square, London, S.W.1.

Royal Institute of International Affairs. Founded in 1920 to encourage and facilitate the study of international relations. The institute is unofficial and non-political. *Events of the Year.* Forty-three general meetings were held, as well as 37 private discussion meetings, 4 courses for the armed services and 1 for oil companies and other corporate subscribers with kindred interests. All Chatham house publications are handled by the O.U.P. Eleven new books, three revised editions, and five new and three revised mimeographed memoranda were published under the institute's auspices. *Officers:* chairman of the council, Lord Strang; director-general, the Hon. C. M. Woodhouse. *Headquarters Address:* Chatham house, 10, St. James's square, London, S.W.1. There is a branch in Scotland, a group in Manchester, and affiliated institutes in Canada, Australia, New Zealand, South Africa and Pakistan.

Royal Institution of Great Britain. Founded in 1799 for the promotion of science and the diffusion and extension of useful knowledge. *Events of the Year.* The 129th course of Christmas juvenile lectures on "The International Geophysical Year" was delivered by J. A. Ratcliffe, J. M. Stagg, Dr. R. L. F. Boyd, Sir Graham Sutton, Dr. G. E. R. Deacon and G. de Q. Robin. Twenty-four evening discourses, mainly on scientific subjects, were given, and lectures on physics, chemistry and biology for schoolchildren in London and the home counties were held throughout the year, some 20,000 children attending. Three "Research Afternoons" for school-teachers were again arranged to help teachers in keeping up to date with developments in new fields of research. *Officers:* president, Lord Brabazon of Tara; secretary, Sir Harold Spencer Jones. *Headquarters Address:* 21, Albemarle street, London, W.1.

Royal Numismatic Society. Founded in 1836, as the Numismatic Society of London (royal charter granted, 1904). *Officers:* president, Christopher Blunt; secretary, Dr. John Walker. *Headquarters Address:* Department of Coins and Medals, British Museum, London, W.C.1. The society's library is at the Warburg institute, Woburn square, London, W.C.1. Monthly meetings (Oct.-June) are held for the reading of papers and exhibition of rare coins and medals.

Royal Philatelic Society. Founded in 1869, as the Philatelic society, London (prefix Royal granted, 1906; use of royal arms granted, 1924). Meetings of members (who must be amateur collectors) are held fortnightly (Oct.-June). The society will pronounce opinion on any pre-1914 stamp of catalogue status. *Events of the Year.* A display of war rarities from the royal collection was held by permission of Queen Elizabeth II, followed by fortnightly displays of important general and specialized collections by members. *Officers:* president, W. Ewart Gerrish; hon. secretary, L. J. Gilbert-Lodge. *Headquarters Address:* 41, Devonshire place, London, W.1.

Royal Philharmonic Society. Founded 1813. *Events of the Year.* Six concerts were given in the Royal Festival hall. R.P.S. composition prizes were awarded to David Dorward of the Royal Academy of Music and Alan Ridout of the Royal College of Music. The Kathleen Ferrier Memorial scholarships, administered by the society, were given to Elizabeth Vaughan and Victor Godfrey. Sir Thomas Beecham's association with the society was honoured by the purchase of a bronze portrait now on display at the Royal Festival hall. *Officers:* hon. secretary, Leslie Regan. *Headquarters Address:* 4, St. James's square, London, S.W.1.

Royal Photographic Society. Founded in 1853, as the Photographic Society of London (prefix Royal granted, 1894). *Events of the Year.* Three major exhibitions of applied, nature and pictorial photography were held. Special subjects covered by the house monthly exhibitions were French photography, one-man show by José Ortiz Echague (Spain), photo-journalism, and work accepted for the society's associateship and fellowship. *Officers:* president, Miss Margaret Harker; secretary, L. E. Hallett. *Headquarters Address:* 16, Princes gate, London, S.W.7. There are over 1,000 affiliated societies in Great Britain and overseas.

Royal Society, The, properly The Royal Society of London for the Promotion of Natural Knowledge. Founded in 1660. *Events of the Year.* Considerable attention was given to the preparation of a space research programme and the society appointed a British National Committee on Space Research. To further international co-operation the society also appointed a National Committee on Antarctic Research. *Officers:* president, Sir Cyril Hinshelwood; secretaries, Prof. Sir George Lindor Brown, Prof. Sir William Hodge; foreign secretary, Dr. H. G. Thornton. *Headquarters Address:* Burlington house, London, W.1.

Royal Society for the Protection of Birds. Founded 1889 (royal charter granted, 1904). *Events of the Year.* Two new films made by the society, *Island of Birds* and *Reed Warblers*, received their first showing at the Royal Festival hall. Another film, *Highland Birds*, was shown in more than 100 places in Britain. The society organized the day and night guard which enabled a pair of ospreys to nest successfully in Scotland (*see* ORNITHOLOGY). *Officers:* president, the Rt. Hon. Lord Forester; secretary, P. E. Brown. *Headquarters Address:* 25, Eccleston square, London, S.W.7. Scottish office 21, Regent terrace, Edinburgh, 7.

Societies With Branches

Allotments and Gardens Society, National. Founded in 1930 to safeguard the interests of allotment holders, home gardeners and village producers. *Events of the Year.* At the annual conference, held at Brighton, the recreational value of allotment gardens was stressed. Long-term security of tenure was the objective of the society and to this end the government was asked to define its policy towards domestic food producers. *Officers:* president, vacant (following death of Viscount Hudson of Pewsey); secretary, W. France. *Headquarters Address:* Drayton house, Gordon street, London, W.C.1. There are some 4,000 affiliated associations, many of which are grouped into nearly 200 county, area and district bodies.

Automobile Association. Founded in 1905. *Events of the Year.* During the year the association helped some 410,000 members in breakdowns, over 161,500 of them by radio-controlled vehicles. More than a million individual routes were prepared for journeys in Britain and some 182,000 for journeys abroad. *Officers:* president, the Duke of Edinburgh; chairman, Lord Brentford; secretary-general, K. L. Kelly. *Headquarters Address:* Fanum house, Leicester square, London, W.C.2. There are 32 area offices in Great Britain and Ireland, one in Jersey, one in Paris and also offices in all the principal British, Irish and European ports and airports handling motor traffic.

Book League, National. Founded in 1924, as the National Book council, to stimulate the fullest use and enjoyment of books, with a special interest in the reading habits of children. *Events of the Year.* At headquarters: rare book exhibitions on "The Motor Car", and on "Life in London"; the second Antiquarian Book fair; exhibitions of books for children; lectures and discussion meetings. Outside London: the School Library exhibition and subject exhibitions of current books shown at conferences, schools and libraries; Leicester Festival of Books for Youth. *Officers:* president, Sir William Haley; director and secretary, J. E. Morpurgo. *Address:* 7, Albemarle street, London, W.1. There is a Scottish committee.

Boys' Clubs, National Association of. Founded in 1925 (incorporated by royal charter). *Events of the Year.* There were residental training courses for full-time and part-time leaders and helpers, for senior boys' club members and for boys about to enter industry. There were ten arts festivals, a summer school in drama, and national football, boxing and cross-country running competitions. The association's 34th annual conference took place at Leicester in July 1959. The association continued the Duke of Edinburgh's Award scheme which was first launched in Sept. 1956. Boy members raised £44,630 during their annual club week in Oct. 1958. *Officers:* president, the Duke of Gloucester; chairman, Admiral the Hon. Sir Guy Russell; secretary, R. E. Goodwin. *Headquarters Address:* 17, Bedford square, London, W.C.1. Constituent organizations include Scottish, Welsh and Northern Ireland associations and Association for Jewish Youth, all clubs in which are affiliated *en bloc* through the constituent organization. Similarly with the federations of boys' clubs in London, Bristol, Liverpool, Manchester, Birmingham and Southampton. There are also 25 county associations and 7 local councils in England.

British Legion. Founded in 1921 (incorporated by royal charter, 1925), to unite ex-service personnel and former members of the Merchant navy who served during wartime in operational waters and to safeguard their interests. *Events of the Year.* The 1958 Poppy Day appeal resulted in a collection of £1,037,000. The legion led a deputation, representing 31 ex-service organizations, to the minister of pensions and national insurance, which resulted in improved pensions for elderly war widows. *Officers:* president, Maj.-General Sir Richard Howard-Vyse; general secretary, Capt. D. E. Coffer. *Headquarters Address:* 49, Pall Mall, London, S.W.1. There are 5,090 branches (65 overseas) administered through 9 areas and 66 counties.

Classical Association. Founded in 1903, to support the claim of classical studies to an eminent place in the national education. *Events of the Year.* In addition to arranging lectures and courses and organizing prize competitions in schools for reading Latin and Greek aloud, the association held a 4-day meeting at the University of Hull, at which the presidential address was read by Prof. Sir Cyril Hinshelwood. *Officers:* president, Prof. T. B. L. Webster; secretaries, Prof. L. J. D. Richardson (Cardiff) and T. W. Melluish (London). *Headquarters Address:* 1, Howell's crescent, Llandaff, Glam., and 31-34, Gordon square, London, W.C.1. There are 29 branches directly attached on a regional basis.

Drama League, British. Founded in 1919 to assist the development of the art of the theatre. *Events of the Year.* The Junior Drama league membership more than doubled and members were enrolled from all parts of the country. The first Junior Drama League summer school was held in Chichester, and B.B.C. television featured the junior branch in a New Year's day broadcast. Adult summer schools were held at Chichester and Alnwick. The National Drama festival was won by Northern Ireland. The annual conference on "Repertory and Civic Theatres" was held in Birmingham. To celebrate the league's 40th anniversary a booklet *The British Drama League 1919-1959* was published and a luncheon was given at the Café Royal. Two U.S. university drama groups toured the country under league auspices. *Officers:* president, the Viscount Esher; chairman, Ivor Brown; administrator, Peter Carpenter. *Headquarters Address:* 9-10, Fitzroy square, London, W.1.

Engineers (Incorporated), Society of. Founded in 1854. *Events of the Year.* The president's Gold medal was awarded to C. E. Tharratt for his paper "The Saunders Roe Pulse Jet Engine" and the Simms' Gold medal to Frank Parfett for his paper "Trends in the Development of Office Machinery". The Churchill Gold medal was awarded to Sir John Cockcroft for his work in connection with thermonuclear developments in the United Kingdom during the past two years. *Officers:* president, I. C. Cocking; hon. secretary, V. S. Wigmore; secretary, Miss A. R. Cook. *Headquarters Address:* Abbey house, Victoria street, London, S.W.1. There is an Australian division, and also Southeast Asia and Pacific zone branches.

Fabian Society. Founded in 1884, with the aim of establishing "a society in which equality of opportunity will be assured and the economic power and privileges of individuals and classes abolished." The society is mainly engaged on research into economic, social and political problems, both in Great Britain and in the international and colonial fields. *Events of the Year.* Schools, lectures, meetings and conferences were held. One book, *New Fabian Colonial Essays*, 14 pamphlets and three regular periodicals were published. *Officers:* chairman, Mrs. Eirene White, M.P.; general secretary, W. T. Rodgers. *Headquarters Address:* 11, Dartmouth street, London, S.W.1. More than 80 local Fabian societies, affiliated to the national society, but largely autonomous, are organized on a regional basis through voluntary helpers.

Folk Dance and Song Society, English. Folk Song society founded 1898; Folk Dance society, 1911; amalgamated 1932. *Events of the Year.* The Folk Music Festival concert in Oct. 1958 brought together folk musicians, instrumentalists and singers from all over the country, and the English Folk Dance and Song Society festival at the Royal Albert hall in Jan. 1959 brought together many folk dancers and singers. *Officers:* acting president, Lord Verulam; director, Douglas Kennedy; secretary, Commander J. A. Elwin, R.N. *Headquarters Address:* Cecil Sharp house, 2, Regent's Park road, London, N.W.1. There are 45 districts and over 600 groups, mainly on a county plan. Affiliated societies abroad include the Country Dance society (U.S.).

Historical Association. Founded in 1906. *Events of the Year.* The association's publications appeared regularly throughout the year. The branches carried out programmes of lectures and excursions to places of historical interest. The association held its 53rd annual general meeting at Norwich in April 1959. A summer school was held at Hull. *Officers:* president, Prof. R. F. Treharne; secretary, H. A. T. Simmonds. *Headquarters Address:* 59a, Kennington Park road, London, S.E.11. There are over 80 branches and affiliated societies.

Interplanetary Society, British. Founded in 1933 to promote the development of interplanetary exploration and communication by the study of rocket engineering, astronomy and other associated sciences. *Events of the Year.* In 1959 the society was host to the delegates of the 10th International Astronautical congress which had a record attendance of more than 700 scientists and engineers from 22 countries. During this congress, the society organized the 2nd Colloquium on

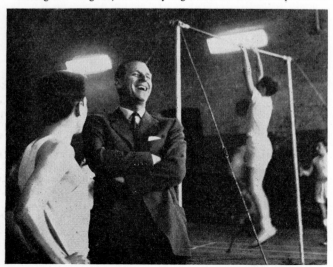

Evidently much amused, the Duke of Edinburgh in the gymnasium of a boys' club in Manchester, which he visited at the end of October.

the Law of Outer Space at Lincoln's Inn. The society also organized a British Spaceflight symposium designed to encourage a combined programme on the part of the United Kingdom and many Commonwealth countries. The society's optical tracking network is now directed as part of the Moonwatch network of the Smithsonian Astrophysical observatory. *Officers:* chairman, Dr. L. R. Shepherd; secretary, L. J. Carter. *Headquarters Address:* 12, Bessborough gardens, London, S.W.1. There are three established branches in England, one in Scotland, and a further three provisional branches in England and one in Washington, D.C., United States.

Mathematical Association. Founded in 1871, as the Association for the Improvement of Geometrical Teaching. The association runs a bureau for the solution of problems, and a library accommodated in the University of Leicester. *Events of the Year.* The annual general meeting was held at Southampton in April, when papers read included the presidential address on "What is Mathematics? New Answers to an old Question", descriptions of the university's digital computer and of the Southampton Port Operation and Information service, and a discussion of the association's newly published report on mathematics in secondary modern schools. *Officers:* president, Miss L. D. Adams; secretary, F. W. Kellaway. *Headquarters Address:* Gordon house, 29, Gordon square, London, W.C.1. There are 22 affiliated branches in Great Britain and overseas; membership reached a new record exceeding 3,600.

Medical Association, British. Founded in 1832, "to promote the medical and allied sciences, and to maintain the honour and interests of the medical profession." *Events of the Year.* The annual meeting of the association was held in 1959 in Edinburgh in conjunction with the Canadian Medical association, and a full programme of clinical and scientific events was arranged. *Officers:* president, the Duke of Edinburgh; secretary, Dr. D. P. Stevenson. *Headquarters Address:* British Medical Association house, Tavistock square, London, W.C.1. There are some 200 divisions, grouped in about 50 branches, in Great Britain, and some 50 branches overseas. The B.M.A. is affiliated to the Canadian, South African, Indian and Ceylon Medical associations.

Mixed Clubs and Girls' Clubs, National Association of. Founded in 1861. Non-uniformed and interdenominational; mainly concerned with young people of 14 to 20 years. The association has national holiday and conference houses in England, Scotland and Wales, and the Devonshire Street club which offers accommodation to members on holiday and those passing through London. *Events of the Year.* There was a further expansion of long-term training for leaders and members. New experiments included a young people's "Players' Tour" to the German Federal Republic, a girls' group visit to a Dominion conference in Canada and the development of some new projects along informal lines—such as coffee bars—in various parts of the United Kingdom. *Officers:* joint presidents, the Duchess of Buccleuch and Queensberry and Sir John Hunt; chairman of council, Sir John Wolfenden; general secretary, Miss E. L. Sewell. *Headquarters Address:* 30-32, Devonshire street, London, W.1. There are three divisional associations in Scotland, Wales and Northern Ireland and 34 local associations in England. Fully affiliated clubs number 2,411 and membership 156,156.

Model Aeronautical Engineers, Society of. Founded in 1909, as the Kite and Model Aircraft association; present title adopted, 1923. *Events of the Year.* The society celebrated its golden jubilee. It organized the 1958 World championships at the College of Aeronautics, Cranfield, during August: Bond Baker (Australia) won the Wakefield cup for rubber-powered models and Erno Frigyes (Hungary) the Victor Tatin cup for power models. Hungary also won both team awards. Scotland, the original donors, won the United Kingdom Challenge cup for the first time. Dick Edmonds (Britain) won the Team Racing contest at the Control Line championships held in conjunction with the Brussels exhibition, Britain being placed second in the over-all results. The Indoor Nationals took place in Manchester during Feb. 1959 and the British Nationals attracted a record entry to R.A.F. Scampton, Lincolnshire, at Whitsun. *Officers:* patron, the Duke of Edinburgh; president, Lord Brabazon of Tara; chairman, A. F. Houlberg; secretary, S. D. Taylor. *Headquarters Address:* Londonderry house, 19, Park lane, London, W.1. Nearly 500 clubs in the United Kingdom are affiliated.

P.E.N. Founded in 1921. International P.E.N. (poets, playwrights, editors, essayists, novelists, with translators also eligible for membership) is a world association of writers existing to promote and maintain friendship and intellectual co-operation among writers in the interests of freedom of artistic expression and international goodwill. P.E.N. administers the P.E.N. Fund for Exiled Writers (previously known as the Fund for Intellectual Freedom). Publishes, with Unesco's assistance, the quarterly bilingual French-English *P.E.N. Bulletin of Selected Books* which reviews books in lesser-known languages, and *P.E.N. News*, both from London. *Events of the Year.* Philippine Writers' conference, Baguio, Dec. 1958; Round Table conference, Paris, Sept. 1958; 30th International congress, Frankfurt-on-Main, July, 1959; election of two new international vice-presidents, André Chamson and Erich Kästner. *Officers:* International president, Alberto Moravia; president of English centre, Alan Pryce-Jones; general secretary, David Carver. *Headquarters Address:* 62-63, Glebe place, London, S.W.3. There are over 60 autonomous centres.

Red Cross Society, British. First active in 1870. *Events of the Year.* Celebrated, together with Red Cross societies throughout the world, the centenary of the birth of the Red Cross idea at the battle of Solferino, 1859. Announced in July 1959 the introduction of short home nursing courses, as it is felt that there should be someone in every home with a knowledge of basic nursing principles. Relief for victims of natural disasters sent to Sudan, South America, India and Pakistan. *Officers:* patron and president, Queen Elizabeth II;

secretary-general, F. H. D. Pritchard. *Headquarters Address:* 14, Grosvenor crescent, London, S.W.1. There is a branch in every British county as well as in British territories overseas.

Rotary International in Great Britain and Ireland. The first Rotary club met in 1905 in Chicago. After the formation in 1911 of clubs in other countries, the organization became international, adopting the above name in 1922. Its aims, as an organization of business and professional men, are to further the ideal of service to others. *Officers:* president, H. B. Shaw; secretary, R. W. Wordley. *Headquarters Address:* Tavistock house (South), Tavistock square, London, W.C.1. There are 10,121 Rotary clubs (868 in Great Britain and Ireland) throughout the world, all member-clubs of Rotary International.

St. John Ambulance Association. Founded in 1877. *Events of the Year.* A total of 95,201 certificates was issued in 1958 and more than 158,000 adults and children were examined in various subjects during the year, in England. There was increasing interest in first aid, especially in industry. The association, in conjunction with the St. Andrew's Ambulance association and the British Red Cross society, published a joint manual on first aid and on nursing. Expansion continued overseas and flourished particularly in east Africa, Ceylon, Malaya and Hong Kong. *Officers:* director-general, H. F. Parshall; secretary, Lieut.-Col. J. E. F. Gueritz. *Headquarters Address:* 10, Grosvenor crescent, London, S.W.1. There are centres in most major towns in England and Northern Ireland, and in most of the colonies. Work in the Commonwealth is under the control of the Priories of the Order of St. John, except in India and Pakistan, which have their own associations.

Soroptimist Clubs of Great Britain and Ireland, Federation of. Started in the United States in 1921 (first club in Great Britain, 1923) to encourage and promote high ethical standards in business and professional life, active interest in public welfare, and international goodwill and understanding through friendship among representative women of different nations. *Events of the Year.* Financial aid was given to refugees in Camp Spittal, Austria, and to Elizabeth house, a play-centre for children in London. Several homes for elderly people were opened by individual clubs. A contribution was also made to assist flood victims in Madagascar. *Officers:* president, Miss K. M. Halpin. *Headquarters Address:* 63, Bayswater road, London, W.2.

Toc H. A movement founded in 1919, as the outcome of British comradeship in World War I, at Talbot house in Flanders, to transmit ideals of Christian fellowship expressed in voluntary service (incorporated by royal charter, 1922). *Events of the Year.* A two-year "Keynotes" operation was launched, local branches concentrating their service on 2 out of 12 practical projects of nationwide importance. A training centre for young men was opened near Broadway, Worcestershire. Plans were made to move Toc H headquarters in 1960 from Westminster to a building near the guild church of All Hallows by the Tower of London. *Officers:* patron, Queen Elizabeth II; presidents include the Archbishop of Canterbury, the Earl of Halifax, Lord Rowallan and Sir William Hamilton Fyfe; founder-padre, Rev. Dr. P. B. Clayton; secretary, R. R. Calkin. *Headquarters Address:* 47, Francis street, London, S.W.1. There are 1,200 branches of Toc H and 600 of Toc H Women's association in Great Britain and overseas.

Townswomen's Guilds, National Union of. Founded in 1929 to encourage the education of women to enable them as citizens to make their best contribution towards the common good. *Events of the Year.* In Aug. 1958, a party of 300 members participated in a music and drama study tour to the Salzburg Music festival. In Nov. 1958, a National Social Studies conference was held in St. Pancras town hall, at which eminent speakers discussed various approaches to world peace: educational, scientific, legal, nutritional and parliamentary. In March 1959, the movement was responsible for putting on an arts and crafts feature at the Ideal Homes exhibition at Olympia. At the National Council meeting, held in Blackpool in May 1959, the guest speaker was David Renton, parliamentary under secretary of state, Home Office. *Officers:* chairman, Mrs. M. Courtney; national general secretary, Mrs. L. F. Norman. *Headquarters Address:* 2, Cromwell place, London, S.W.7. There are 2,174 affiliated guilds, grouped in 101 federations in England, Scotland and Wales.

Women's Institutes, National Federation of. Founded in 1917 to improve and develop conditions of rural life. *Events of the Year.* Handicrafts exhibition at the Victoria and Albert museum, London, representing the work of women's institutes throughout the whole federation. *Officers:* chairman, Lady Dyer; secretary, Miss Alison King. *Headquarters Address:* 39, Eccleston street, London, S.W.1. There are 8,449 institutes and 61 county federations by affiliation.

Workers' Educational Association. Founded in 1903, to stimulate and satisfy the demand of workers for education. *Events of the Year.* The W.E.A. held more than 5,400 classes, attended by more than 88,000 students. *Officers:* president, Asa Briggs; secretary, Harry Nutt. *Headquarters Address:* Temple house, 27, Portman square, London, W.1. There are 996 branches, organized in 21 autonomous districts in Great Britain and Northern Ireland.

Young Farmers' Clubs, National Federation of. Founded in 1932 (first club formed 1921). *Events of the Year.* In October a special general meeting accepted a plan of reorganization, and the constitutions of the clubs, county federations and the national federation were subsequently amended by the annual general meeting the following May. There was increased support for courses and conferences, and also for proficiency tests, particularly in farmhouse and home-craft subjects. Twenty-nine members took part in nationally sponsored exchange visits with the United States, Canada, New Zealand, Southern Rhodesia, Israel and Finland, and 58 visitors were received from countries abroad, including the U.S.S.R. As part of the reorganization plan all members now receive a copy of the *Young Farmer.* *Officers:* president, the Duke of Norfolk; secretary, K. R. Savage. *Headquarters Address:* 55, Gower street, London, W.C.1. There are 1,517 clubs in England and Wales with a total membership of 65,702.

Young Men's Christian Associations (Incorporated), National Council of. The first Y.M.C.A. was founded in 1844 (the National council, 1882). The Y.M.C.A. aims to further the development of the intellectual, social, physical and spiritual well-being of young men and boys. *Events of the Year.* In addition to the normal activities of local Y.M.C.A.s, eight holiday centres and two national camps for boys were held. Centres served members of the armed forces at home and abroad. Special residential centres trained boys for careers in agriculture and at sea; courses of general education were provided for young people from industry; and 12 special hostels were maintained for engineering apprentices and industrial workers. Six new residential clubs were opened. *Officers:* president, the Earl of Romney; secretary, N. S. Tucker. *Headquarters Address:* 112, Great Russell street, London, W.C.1. There are 367 local Y.M.C.A.s in England, Wales, Northern Ireland and the Republic of Ireland affiliated to the National council through 19 divisional councils, and the National council directly operates a further 100 centres engaged in activities listed above. There is a separate National council for Scotland.

Young Women's Christian Association of Great Britain, The. Founded in 1855. It aims to serve the community without distinction of race, nationality or religion and its policy is directed by full members who accept its Christian basis. *Events of the Year.* With the completion of the new hostel at Coventry, opened by Princess Alexandra in November, all blitzed hostels were replaced. The Duchess of Gloucester opened a new mixed hostel, Gloucester house, at Stockton-on-Tees; and Y.W.C.A. house, which provides flats and bed-sitting rooms for business women between the ages of 30 and 40, as well as office accommodation and club facilities, was completed in Birmingham. Work for H.M. forces continued in Cyprus and the German Federal Republic, and British staff served abroad in Y.W.C.A.s in Australia, Austria, Kenya, Nigeria and Uganda. *Officers:* president, the Lady Priscilla Aird; secretary, Miss Ruth Walder. *Headquarters Address:* National offices, Bedford house, 108, Baker street, London, W.1. There are approximately 300 branches, co-ordinated regionally but directly connected to the national association.

Youth Hostels Association (England and Wales). Founded in 1930. *Events of the Year.* Outstanding was the opening in May of the King George VI Memorial hostel in Holland park, London, by Queen Elizabeth II, accompanied by the Duke of Edinburgh. The hostel comprises the restored east wing of the historic Holland house and new buildings designed by Sir Hugh Casson and Neville Conder. Earlier in the year the queen became patron of the association. A noteworthy visitor was the 85-year-old founder of youth hostelling, Richard Schirrmann, who opened the world's first hostel in Germany in 1909. National Youth Hostels week, held in May, again enabled thousands of parents, teachers and youth leaders to inspect a youth hostel for themselves. *Officers:* president, P. J. Clarke; secretary, H. L. Knapp. *Headquarters Address:* National office, St. Albans, Hertfordshire. There are 19 regional groups, which administer the hostels in their areas, under the control of regional councils elected by members.

Societies Without Branches

Adoption Society, National. Founded in 1918. The society is a voluntary body registered under the Adoption of Children (Regulation) act, 1939, for the legal adoption of infants and young children by families. Children assisted are mostly illegitimate, or may be orphaned or the children of broken marriages. It is not the policy to adopt a legitimate child who has parents. The effect of an adoption is legally to transfer all parental rights to the adopting parents whose identity is not disclosed to the mother. Adopters must be married couples, the wife not more than 40 years of age and in good health. More than 10,809 children have been legally adopted through the society, which adopted 140 children in 1958. The work is supported by voluntary contributions and no fees are charged. *Officers:* president, the Lady Gweneth Cavendish; chairman, the Countess of Bessborough; secretary, Mrs. Barbara Jeyes. *Headquarters Address:* 47A, Manchester street, London, W.1.

Antiquaries of London, Society of. Founded in 1707 (royal charter, 1751). *Events of the Year.* The society sponsored renewed excavations at Verulamium, publishing the preliminary results in the *Antiquaries Journal*, and participated in a number of other activities at home and abroad including the establishment of the Cirencester Excavation committee for investigating the Roman city of Corinium. *Officers:* president, Dr. Joan Evans; director, Prof. I. A. Richmond; secretary, A. R. Dufty. *Headquarters Address:* Burlington house, London, W.1. Membership consists of fellows, elected by ballot (there were 1,032 in 1959).

British Association for the Advancement of Science. Founded in 1831. *Events of the Year.* The annual conference was held at York during Sept. 2-9, 1959, and was presided over by Sir James Gray. *Secretary:* Sir George Allen. *Headquarters Address:* 18, Adam street, London, W.C.2. Membership is open to all interested in science.

Contemporary Arts, Institute of. Founded in 1947. *Events of the Year.* Exhibitions included work by E. L. T. Mesens, John McHale, Gwyther Irwin, Lucio Fontana, Jean Fautrier, Roberto Crippa, Giani Dova, Jacques Clemente and Adolph Gottlieb. Theme exhibition, "The Developing Process—New Aspects in Art Teaching", was arranged by Victor Pasmore, Harry Thubron and Richard Hamilton. In many lectures and discussions, speakers included J. D. Bernal, Robert Beloof, Arthur Mizener, Kenneth Rexroth, Kenneth Allsop, Elizabeth Chetwynde, Robert Conquest, John

Lehmann, Alan Pryce-Jones and Wayland Young. Other activities (which covered all the arts) included concerts, lectures on jazz, poetry and play readings and films. *Officers:* president, Sir Herbert Read; chairman, Roland Penrose; secretary, Julie Lawson. *Headquarters Address:* 17-18, Dover street, London, W.1.

English Association. Founded in 1906, to promote the knowledge and appreciation of the English language and of English literature, and to uphold the standard of English writing and speech. *Events of the Year.* Lecturers included Carl Bode, Christopher Hassall, Sir John Wolfenden, Roy Moore, G. P. Gooch, Arthur Brown and Hugh Sykes Davies. *Officers:* president, Sir Maurice Bowra; chairman of committee, Inst. Rear-Admiral Sir Arthur Hall; secretary, Mrs. E. M. Fielding. *Headquarters Address:* 8, Cromwell place, London, S.W.7.

Eugenics Society. Founded in 1907, to study the influences, social and genetical, that may modify the distribution and appearance of inborn human qualities; to formulate and support policies for developing these qualities to the utmost advantage; to promote research upon eugenic problems; to foster a responsible attitude to parenthood; and to guide public opinion in these matters. *Events of the Year.* The society published *West Indian Immigration,* the first in a series of broadsheets to be issued occasionally on topics of eugenic interest. An autonomous council, the A.I.D. Investigation council, promoted by the society early in 1958, began its work within the following terms of reference: to review the present status and future potentialities of human artificial insemination genetically, medically, legally and socially. Publication of *The Eugenics Review* continued. *Officers:* president, Sir Julian Huxley; secretary, Dr. G. C. L. Bertram. *Headquarters Address:* 69, Eccleston square, London, S.W.1.

Film Institute, British. Founded in 1933, to encourage the development of the art of the film, to promote its use as a record of contemporary life and manners, to foster public appreciation and study of it, to co-operate with other bodies working in the same field. *Events of the Year.* Films on the art and history of the cinema continued to be lent from the distribution library; the education department provided lectures in all aspects of film, and extensive use was made of the institute's information centre and book library. In May, a one-week forum, "The Visual Persuaders", was held at the National Film theatre. The institute carries television material and offers lectures and courses on television subjects. *Officers:* chairman of the board of governors, Sylvester Gates; director, James Quinn; secretary, Stanley Reed. *Headquarters Address:* 164, Shaftesbury avenue, London, W.C.2. Both individual and corporate membership terms are available.

Folk-Lore Society. Founded in 1878. The oldest society in the world for the study of folklore. *Events of the Year.* The society's journal *Folklore* entered upon its 70th volume and during the winter and spring a series of lectures was held. *Officers:* president, Sir Arthur Waugh; hon. secretary, C. S. Mundy. *Headquarters Address:* c/o University college, Gower street, London, W.C.1.

Linnean Society of London. Founded in 1788, for the cultivation of the science of natural history in all its branches. *Events of the Year.* In July 1959 the 18th-century herbarium of the great Swedish naturalist, Linnaeus, was recorded on Microfiches in collaboration with the International Documentation centre, Stockholm, Sweden. *Officers:* president, Prof. C. F. A. Pantin; treasurer, Earl of Cranbrook; secretaries, Dr. C. R. Metcalfe (botany), H. R. Hewer (zoology), Dr. J. Smart (editorial); general secretary, T. O'Grady. *Headquarters Address:* Burlington house, London, W.1.

Ornithologists' Union, British. Founded in 1858. *Events of the Year.* The union celebrated its centenary in March 1959 with a three-day symposium conference on "Progress and Prospects in Ornithology" at the University of Cambridge, under the patronage of the Duke of Edinburgh (*see* ORNITHOLOGY). A centenary banquet was held at the Fishmongers' Guildhall in London on March 23, which was attended by leading scientists from many countries. Godman-Salvin medals were awarded to Sir Landsborough Thomson and Dr. David Lack for distinguished ornithological work. Union gold medals were presented to W. B. Alexander, the Rev. E. A. Armstrong, Dr. D. Bannerman, Miss E. V. Baxter, A. W. Boyd and Peter Scott. *Officers:* president, Dr. W. H. Thorpe; hon. secretary, Guy Mountfort. The union publishes a quarterly journal *The Ibis. Headquarters Address:* c/o British Museum (Natural History), London, S.W.7.

Philological Society. Founded in 1842. *Officers:* president, Prof. L. R. Palmer; hon. secretaries, N. C. Scott (School of Oriental and African Studies, London university) and Prof. W. S. Allen. *Headquarters Address:* University college, London, W.C.1.

Physical Society. Founded in 1874. *Events of the Year.* The following conferences were held: on "Discharge Physics", Swansea, Sept. 1958; on "Cosmic Rays", Durham, Sept. 1958; on "Interfacial Phenomena", Cambridge, Dec. 1958; on "Problems of Collective Motion", Birmingham, Jan. 1959; on "Nuclear Physics", Oxford, April 1959; on "Co-operative Phenomena and Phase Transitions", Newcastle upon Tyne, July 1959. The annual exhibition of scientific instruments and apparatus was held in the spring, and associated with it was the annual craftsmanship and draughtsmanship competition for apprentices and learners. *Officers:* president, J. A. Ratcliffe; secretary-editor, Miss A. C. Stickland. *Headquarters Address:* 1, Lowther gardens, Prince Consort road, London, S.W.7.

Psychical Research, Society for. Founded in 1882. *Events of the Year.* The society published a study, entitled *F. W. H. Myers's Posthumous Message,* throwing fresh light on the history of the sealed envelope left by Frederick Myers, to be opened after his death (*Proc. Soc. psych. Res., Lond.,* 52, part 187, 1958). Work continued on the inquiry into spontaneous psychic experiences. *Officers:* president, Prof. C. D. Broad; secretary-general, Mrs. Beale; secretary (research), Miss Green. *Headquarters Address:* 1, Adam and Eve mews, London, W.8.

Zoological Society of London. Founded in 1826. For *Events of the Year* see ZOOLOGICAL GARDENS. *Officers:* president, Sir Landsborough Thomson; secretary, Sir Solly Zuckerman; scientific director, Dr. L. Harrison Matthews. *Headquarters Address:* Regent's park, London. N.W.1.

SOCIOLOGY.

In Sept. 1959 the fourth World Congress of Sociology was held at Milan and Stresa, Italy, under the auspices of the International Sociological association. More than 1,000 participants from 50 countries attended the congress, the theme of which was "Society and Sociological Knowledge". At the congress, Prof. T. H. Marshall was elected president of the association.

The most interesting new development in Britain was the establishment of a new chair and Institute of Criminology at Cambridge university under a generous grant from the Nuffield foundation. The first holder of the chair was Prof. L. Radzinowicz. In the British Sociological association, Lady Wootton's place as chairman was taken by Prof. R. M. Titmuss. During the year there were several books and papers concerned with the subject of the industrial society. C. P. Snow's Rede lecture "The Two Cultures and the Industrial Revolution" dealt with current educational problems and was widely discussed. P. F. Drucker's *Landmarks of Tomorrow* assessed social problems posed by industrial change; F. Steinberg's *The Military and Industrial Revolution of Our Time* put together a variety of data from leading industrial societies, and R. Dahrendorf's *Class and Class Conflict in Industrial Society* was an important contribution to the theory of social classes in modern society. M. Ginsberg edited a volume of lectures, *Law and Opinion in England in the 20th Century,* in which leading experts, including several sociologists, attempted to bring E. J. S. Dicey's 19th-century classic up to date.

From a British writer, D. Mitchell, came a short but useful introductory textbook, *Sociology: the Study of Social Systems.* From the United States came two large panoramic surveys of the various fields of contemporary interest, *Sociology Today,* edited by R. K. Merton and others, and *Contemporary Sociology,* edited by J. Rouček. The latter work contained a shrewd and learned appraisal from D. G. Macrae of the history and progress of sociological studies in Britain. Both works contained useful bibliography and reference material. Also from the United States came a small volume of essays edited by D. Lerner, *The Human Meaning of the Social Sciences,* in which the contributions of N. Glazer and E. A. Shils were of special interest and importance.

A stimulating commentary on the hazards of social explanation (with special reference to the explanation of criminal behaviour) came from Lady Wootton, whose *Social Science and Social Pathology* ranged vigorously over the logical and practical problems of social therapy. Insights into several related problems of social therapy and administration came in the Younghusband committee report on social workers in the local authority health and welfare services.

After the racial disturbances in London in the autumn of 1958 a heightened interest came to be taken in the social analysis of race relations, especially in the United Kingdom context. An important book, *White and Coloured,* by M. Banton, set out a sociological diagnosis. In London the recently established Institute of Race Relations announced the forthcoming publication of its new journal *Race* which would act as a forum for scholarly work in this field. In a related field, the study of minority groups, 1959 saw the publication of the first number of *The Jewish Journal of Sociology,* edited by M. Ginsberg for the World Jewish congress.   (S. J. G.)

SOIL CONSERVATION.

It was apparent during 1959 that recognition of soil and water conservation as a key to both economic and social welfare was having an important influence on planning for the maintenance of the stability of nations. Co-operation almost on a world-wide scale was carried on to study and exchange ideas and plans for solving land problems. In all instances, methods which might contribute to a safe and permanent agriculture with larger per acre yields and better standards of living were reasons stressed for the trend toward co-ordination of conservation programmes.

The device of handling total conservation by applying all soil, water and vegetative treatments to small watersheds as units was studied by 32 conservation leaders from 19 countries in a watershed management seminar and tour in the United States from August to October under sponsorship of the Food and Agriculture organization of the United Nations.

Another feature of world co-operation involved the need, especially in Asian and African countries, for conservation methods of preparing so-called wasteland for agricultural use. This applied to semi-arid steppes, brushland and humid forest land.

America. A major accomplishment of the year in the United States was the completion of survey work in connection with the national inventory of soil and water conservation needs, started in 1956. Plans were made to release the data and descriptive material to the public during the period 1960-62, in reports for each of the 50 states, including all counties, and Puerto Rico and the Virgin Islands, and finally in a national inventory summary. The inventory would include data on present uses of all U.S. lands; a projection of expected changes based on land capabilities by 1975; needs for conservation treatments on both irrigated and non-irrigated cropland, pasture and range lands, forest and woodland, and lands in miscellaneous uses, such as urban, industrial and others; and an inventory of watersheds and their needs for special treatments for flood prevention and water storage, in addition to conventional soil and water conservation of farm, range and forest lands.

A co-operative project for the evaluation of natural resources, started in 1954 and involving Brazil, Argentina, Uruguay and Chile, and sponsored by the Organization of American States, was proving valuable as an impetus to soil-conservation programmes in the southern half of South America. Soil surveys and mapping were completed in Brazil. Soil and erosion surveys had been made in several large areas of Argentina where conservation work was most urgent and more detailed surveys were started by scientists connected with state experimental stations. Chile had completed soil surveys and published one soil map for the whole country, while in Uruguay, surveys were under way for the preparation of a combined soil- and land-classification map of all the country's land. All soil data of the vast region were made available to soil conservationists for use in conservation planning.

Europe. In France very detailed studies on the serious erosion in the lower Rhône valley were reported. Heavy runoff was revealed as the main cause of the decline of plant growth, with low yields and the frequent death of cultivated plants before maturity. The need for drastic changes in land use and for combined conservation treatments was recommended as urgent if the land were to be saved from ruin.

In Greece the hydrogeonomy service was established as an agency of the Ministry of Agriculture to carry out a country-wide soil- and water-conservation programme through research and technical assistance to farmers.

Unusually rapid progress had been made in Spain since that country's soil-conservation service came into being in 1956. In three years the service had organized and trained technical personnel for 16 brigades to work with farmers; 57 farmer committees were working with service personnel in as many watershed projects; 240,000 ac. had been terraced and 417,000 ac. had been given complete conservation treatment.

The re-afforestation work of the country was being closely co-ordinated with the soil-conservation programme, with about 300,000 ac. of new forest plantings a year. The land re-afforested was principally former cultivated or grazed land too eroded or poor to be of use to local farmers.

U.S.S.R. On-the-ground studies by United States soil-conservation scientists revealed that certain modern conservation methods were being integrated into the agriculture of the Soviet Union. Soil surveys, land use classifications and farm planning based on soil maps were found to be firmly established as fundamental to production on the country's 90,000 collective- and state-farm units. These methods were also being used in a large programme to extend agriculture to new areas of Siberia and northern Kazakhstan, southern valleys requiring irrigation and other lands where drainage was essential.

Asia. In Ceylon, erosion-control practices were being rapidly adopted. Broad-based terraces, contour strip cropping and contour tillage were incorporated in all settlement schemes. Tea and rubber plantings on steep slopes were being made on contour benches and small earth dams for storing irrigation water were becoming common. Special efforts were made to halt shifting cultivation through regulation of permits, grouping and close supervision in order to induce cultivators to enter into settlement schemes practising a soil- and water-conservation agriculture. A million acres in the dry zone were found to be irrigable and to provide water the Irrigation department was restoring reservoirs built in the days of the Sinhalese kings, enlarging and improving existing facilities and providing new reservoirs or tanks.

The central soil-conservation organization of Pakistan was experimenting with various methods of dealing with land improvement and conservation of both soil and water in connection with projected land reforms and redistribution of acreages. A soil conservation project, well established in the Rawalpindi division, was developing and adapting conservation practices for use on both irrigated and un-irrigated farms of small and medium sizes. (DD. A. W.)

SOLOMON ISLANDS: *see* TRUST TERRITORIES.
SOLOMON ISLANDS PROTECTORATE: *see* PACIFIC ISLANDS, BRITISH.

SOMALIA. Italian trust territory in east Africa, bounded S.E. by the Indian ocean, W. by Kenya and N.W. by Somaliland Protectorate and Ethiopia. Area: 178,200 sq.mi. Pop.: (Dec. 1958 est.) 1,300,000, incl. 30,000 Arabs, 1,000 Indians, 4,669 Italians and 139 other Europeans. Chief Somali tribal groups: Darot, Hawlya, Rahaniun, Dighil, Dirr and Tunni (nomadic or semi-nomadic pastoralists). Religion: Sunni (Shafi) Moslem. Capital, Mogadishu, pop. (1953) 63,300, including 3,592 Italians. Administrator, Enrico Anzilotti; prime minister, Abdullahi Issa. Monetary unit: *somalo* (=1s. sterling).

History. On Dec. 5, 1959, the U.N. general assembly unanimously decided that on July 1, 1960, five months in advance of the original U.N. timetable, Somalia would become independent. The news was received with great jubilation at Mogadishu as the U.N. general assembly decision was in agreement with the wishes of the Somali Legislative Assembly, expressed on Aug. 25.

The Legislative Assembly was elected on March 4 and 8, 1959. Out of 90 seats, the pro-western Somali Youth league obtained 81. The S.Y.L. and its leader, Abdullahi Issa, provided on the whole an efficient government.

At the request of the 1958 general assembly King Olav V of Norway had appointed Trygve Lie independent commissioner for the settlement of the disputed frontier between Somalia and Ethiopia. His report proposed the establishment of a three-man arbitration tribunal to survey border questions and to make a final settlement that both sides could accept. Ethiopia and Italy agreed to establish this body. Miloš

Radojković (Yugoslavia) was nominated by Ethiopia, Plinos Bolla (Switzerland) by Italy, and Erik Castrén (Finland) was the joint choice of the two other members. (X.)

SOMALILAND, FRENCH (CÔTE FRANÇAISE DES SOMALIS).

An overseas territory of the French Republic in the Gulf of Aden, bounded N., N.W. and S.W. by Ethiopia and S.E. by Somaliland Protectorate. Area: 8,378 sq.mi. Pop.: (1955 est.) 63,700, incl. 28,000 Somalis, 25,000 Danakils, 6,000 Arabs, 3,132 Europeans; (1959 est.) 67,000. Capital, Jibuti (Djibouti), pop. 31,855. Governor, Jacques Compain. Main imports: petroleum products and coal. Main exports: salt from Jibuti; coffee, hides and skins from Ethiopia. Monetary unit: *Jibuti franc* = metropolitan Fr. 2·30 (J. Fr.600 = £1).

History. On May 27, 1959, Hassan Gouled was elected deputy to the French National Assembly and on April 26 Mohammed Kamil was elected senator. Ahmed Dini became deputy prime minister.

On July 3 General Charles de Gaulle visited Jibuti. He warned the partisans of the " Greater Somalia " movement, led by the former prime minister, Mohammed Harbi (who fled to Mogadishu), that France intended to stay in Jibuti and would not abdicate its responsibilities. (HU. DE.)

SOMALILAND PROTECTORATE.

British protectorate in east Africa bounded N. by Gulf of Aden and French Somaliland, W. and S. by Ethiopia and E. by Somalia. Area: c. 68,000 sq.mi. Est. pop. (no complete census ever taken) 650,000, mainly nomadic, of northeastern Hamitic stock with Arab, etc., admixture. Language: Galla derivative with Arabic admixture. Religion: Moslem (Sunni). Chief towns: Hargeisa (cap.) pop. c. 30,000 (c. 40,000 max. in cold season); Berbera (port) c. 7,500 permanent (c. 30,000 max., cold season). Administration: governor; executive council; legislative council with official majority. Governors in 1959: Sir Theodore Pike and (from July 13) Sir Douglas Hall. Main imports: cotton manufactures, foodstuffs, cigarettes and tobacco, motor spirits. Main exports: livestock, hides and skins. Monetary unit: East African shilling (20s. = £1 sterling).

History. The political atmosphere in the protectorate greatly improved after a statement made at Hargeisa in Feb. 1959 by the secretary of state for the colonies, A. T. Lennox-Boyd, promising rapid constitutional development, a ministerial system and an unofficial majority in the legislative council following fresh elections in 1960. If after Somalia attained independence the legislative council wished to discuss the idea of union with that country, talks would be arranged. In March, 13 elected members were added to the legislative council. Later seven ministerial posts were created. The rains came late in 1959, and for a time drought conditions prevailed, with accompanying grazing shortages.

The annual government accounts showed revenue at £1,165,249. A deficit of £628,082 was met by a grant from the U.K. government. (F. E. S.)

SOUDAN, REPUBLIC OF (RÉPUBLIQUE SOUDANAISE).

A member state of the French Community, Soudan is bounded N. by the French Saharan *départements* of Saoura and Oasis, E. and S.E. by the Republic of Niger, S. by the Republics of Upper Volta and Ivory Coast, S.W. by the independent Republic of Guinea and W. by the Republic of Senegal. Area: 460,308 sq.mi. Pop.: (1945 est.) 3,797,000; (1959 est.) 3,700,000; white African nomads and Negroes. Language: French; Bambara, Songhaï and other Sudanic dialects. Religion: Moslem 55%, animist 44%, small Christian minorities. Chief towns (pop., 1957 est.): Bamako (cap., 69,000), Kayes (30,000), Ségou (21,000), Mopti (13,000), Timbuktu (7,000). Prime minister, Modibo Keita. French high commissioner, Jean Sicurani. Chief exports: groundnuts, rice, livestock. Monetary unit: *franc CFA* = metropolitan Fr.2.

History. The Republic of Soudan was proclaimed on Nov. 24, 1958. At the election of its first National Assembly held on March 10, 1959, the Union Soudanaise, a section of the Parti Fédéraliste Africain, won all the seats. Keita became prime minister and Jean-Marie Koné deputy prime minister. The Parti du Regroupement Soudanais (led by Hammadou Dicko) and other non-government parties were dissolved. Soudan joined the Federation of Mali (*q.v.*), of which Modibo Keita became president. Common administrative authorities

were set up: finance, customs, economic affairs, information, security, labour, education, health and public works. (*See* also MALI, FEDERATION OF.) (HU. DE.)

SOUTH AFRICA, UNION OF.

A realm of the Commonwealth of Nations, extending from the southernmost point of the African continent northward to the Limpopo, Molopo and western Orange rivers. The mandated territory of South-West Africa is administered by South Africa. Total pop.: Union (1959 est.) 14,673,000 (3,067,000 Whites, 9,751,000 Africans, 1,405,000 Coloureds, 450,000 Asians); S.-W. Africa (1959 est.) 554,000. Official languages (1951 census, Europeans only): 73% spoke Afrikaans and English, 15·3% English only, 11·4% Afrikaans only; Africans, generally Bantu (Xhosa, Zulu, Swazi, etc.). Adherence to the most important religious groups was as follows:

	European (%; 1951 census)	Non-European (%; 1946 census)
Dutch Reformed . . .	53·2	6·2
Anglican	15·8	8·2
Methodist	8·3	12·1
Roman Catholic . . .	5·4	4·8

Also: Europeans: 4·1% Jewish, 3·8% Presbyterian; Coloureds: 10·8% Congregational; Africans: 9·7% members of native separatist churches, 5% Lutherans; Asians: 63·2% Hindu, 21·5% Moslem. Of non-Europeans, 51% were Christian.

Provinces	Area (sq.mi.)	Population (1951 census)	Capital (total and European pop., 1957 est.)
Cape of Good Hope	277,113*	4,426,726	Cape Town (709,200; 280,000)
Natal . . .	35,284	2,415,318	Pietermaritzburg (88,200; 37,600)
Orange Free State .	49,838	1,016,570	Bloemfontein (141,600; 62,400)
Transvaal .	110,450	4,809,145	Pretoria (335,300; 176,000)
Total . .	472,685†	12,667,759‡	
South-West Africa .	317,725	414,601§	Windhoek (28,500; 15,000)

* Incl. Walvis Bay (374 sq.mi.), an enclave of Cape province administered by South-West Africa. † Excl. Marion Island (c. 85 sq.mi.) and Prince Edward Island (c. 18 sq.mi.), subantarctic dependencies. ‡ European 20·9%, African 67·5%, Asian 2·9% (mainly in Natal), Coloured (mixed) 8·7% (mainly in Cape). § Incl. 48,588 Europeans.

Cape Town is the seat of the legislature, Pretoria that of the government and Bloemfontein is the judiciary capital. Other principal towns (total pop. and European pop., 1956 est.): Johannesburg (1,006,500; 387,800); Durban (591,300; 172 800); Port Elizabeth, (231,400; 92,500); Germiston (205,900; 91,200); Springs (127,900; 38,000); East London (103,700; 47,900). Queen, Elizabeth II; governor-general, E. G. Jansen; prime minister, H. F. Verwoerd. Main imports: textile piecegoods, motor cars and parts. Main exports: wool, atomic energy material, diamonds, fruit. Monetary unit: South African pound (= £1 sterling).

History. *Politics.* The most significant political event of 1959 was the formation of the new Progressive party. In August, at the end of the United party's national congress, 12 prominent members led by Jan Steytler and H. G. Lawrence, resigned on the grounds that the United party's policy towards Africans had become too conservative. In particular, they objected to its decision that it would oppose extension of the native reserves if the new areas purchased by the government were to be regarded as part of the future " Bantustans " or separate African regions. The Progressives held a national congress in November in order to formulate their own policies. (*See* also POLITICAL PARTIES, COMMONWEALTH.)

The elections to the four provincial councils held in October resulted in little change, apart from revealing a measure of support for the Progressives in Natal.

New legislation included the controversial act to exclude non-white students from the three open universities of the Witwatersrand, Cape Town and Natal. Strong protests against this measure were heard at home and abroad, and the opposition fought against it in parliament. The government sought to justify the step taken by building two new African tribal colleges, one at Turfloop in the northern Transvaal and the other at Ngoya in Zululand. It was also planning one near Cape Town for the Cape Coloured people.

A bill was passed enabling extensive regional and local self-government on tribal lines to be introduced into the African

Field Marshal Lord Montgomery with a group of school-children in Pretoria during his visit to South Africa at the end of the year.

areas—the so-called Bantustan plan—and the first Bantu territorial authorities were formally established in the Transkei and in the Transvaal under the ruling chiefs. In conjunction with this administrative development the special representation of Africans in parliament was abolished (*see* PARLIAMENT, HOUSES OF).

Late in 1958 four new ministers entered the cabinet— Nicolaas Diederichs as minister of economic affairs, Albert Hertzog as minister of health and of posts and telegraphs, Willem Adriaan Maree as minister of Bantu education and D. C. H. Uys as minister of agricultural economics and marketing. The last two appointments involved the creation of new portfolios as a result of the growth of the departments concerned with Bantu administration and with European agriculture. Four deputy ministers were appointed to assist ministers whose functions covered a wide field, namely, interior, labour and mines, education and Bantu administration. T. E. Donges became minister of finance and M. D. C. De Wet Nel minister of Bantu administration (formerly called native affairs).

During the year the deaths occurred of the governor-general, E. G. Jansen (*see* OBITUARIES) and of the former prime minister, D. F. Malan (*see* OBITUARIES).

Race Relations. As a form of protest against the government's policy, the African National congress advocated a boycott of the industrial products of certain firms said to be controlled by supporters of the Nationalist party. This boycott was believed to be one reason why the fruit-canning industry found itself facing financial difficulties.

Apprehension was expressed at the possible effect on the union's export trade of the movement to boycott South African goods, which started in Jamaica and spread to other parts of The West Indies, to east and west Africa and subsequently to Britain.

The president of the African National congress, ex-Chief Albert J. Luthuli, was banished to his home district of Groutville, Natal, after he had addressed well-attended meetings in Cape Town and elsewhere. He was also prohibited by law from attending any kind of meeting. A similar order was applied to Oliver Tambo and Duma Nokwe, both leading figures in the congress, and also to Ronald Segal, editor of the international quarterly journal *Africa South*, published in Cape Town. Henry Barzilay, a free-lance journalist and tele-

vision reporter of British nationality, was expelled from the Union. Hans Beukes, a Coloured student from South-West Africa, made his way to London after his passport was withdrawn when he was about to go to Norway to take up a university scholarship there. He later appeared in New York before a U.N. committee investigating conditions in South-West Africa.

There were widespread disturbances among Africans in various parts of Natal where property, especially official buildings, was damaged by rioters. In Durban discontent was reported to be caused by the removal of African women from the municipal area, by police raids in search of illicit liquor brewing and by economic hardships. In the rural areas the enforcement of measures for the prevention of disease among cattle and other agricultural restrictions led to riots. As a result, hundreds of Africans, the majority of whom were women, were prosecuted and imprisoned. The government complained that the press abroad had grossly exaggerated the nature and significance of the disturbances.

Publicity was given to the bad conditions under which farm labourers were forced to work in the eastern Transvaal. A Johannesburg attorney, Joel Carlson, revealed these conditions in a whole series of cases brought before the Supreme Court in *habeas corpus* proceedings. The applicants in these cases were Africans who had been arrested in urban areas for minor breaches of the pass laws, and who alleged that they were induced under pressure to accept farm employment as an alternative to imprisonment. After the Supreme Court had ordered the release of a number of labourers, the government instituted an inquiry into the system under which farmers were supplied with labour through the agency of the Department of Bantu Administration and the police.

There was public controversy over the maintenance of the colour bar in sports teams visiting (or going abroad from) South Africa. A proposed tour of the union by a cricket team from The West Indies was abandoned. The question of whether New Zealand would include Maoris in its cricket team was also raised.

The treason trial, which had begun in Dec. 1956, continued after the special court had quashed the indictment against 61 of the accused. There remained 30 accused. The technical ground for the court's decision was that the accused had not been given sufficient particulars of the conspiracy they were alleged to have organized to overthrow the government. The appellate division of the Supreme Court declined at this stage to consider certain legal issues arising from the trial. The chief prosecuting counsel, Oswald Pirow, died suddenly (*see* OBITUARIES).

Economics. The budget, introduced in March 1959, showed that total expenditure for the ensuing year was estimated at about £289 million and total revenue at £317 million. After certain adjustments a surplus of £10 million was expected for the past year and a similar one for the current year. The budget provided for old-age pensions to be increased and for a slight rise in the income-tax rebate allowed for children. The price of bread, beer and rice would increase and so would the cost of diesel oil, cane spirit and gramophone records, as a result of new taxation and subsidy proposals. Building societies and life insurance companies were to pay a new tax. Concessions were made to gold mines and to industries. In an authoritative survey of the economic state of the union, the governor of the South African Reserve bank, M. H. De Kock, estimated that the national income was just under £2,000 million, the rate of its growth having substantially decreased. He reported, however, that in 1958-59 there had been a net inflow into the union of private capital amounting to £28 million, in contrast to the net outflow of £21 million in the previous year. This favourable turn took place despite the continued net outflow of South African funds for

(Top) A general view of Cato Manor, the shanty town lying just outside Durban, which was the scene of rioting in September, following attempts by police to destroy illicit liquor stills. The police, who were attacked by an angry crowd, opened fire causing several casualties. (Bottom left) A group of African women who had been arrested on charges of creating disturbances at municipal beer halls, waiting outside the Durban courts. (Bottom right) An African policeman carries out a search for illicit liquor underneath a dwelling in Cato Manor.

investment in the Federation of Rhodesia and Nyasaland and certain other African territories. This resumed flow of capital was attributed to renewed foreign interest in South African equities, particularly gold-mining shares.

Although some uncertain elements in the internal economic situation remained, there were indications that the downward trend in the growth of economic activity had been arrested. The country began to feel the benefit of increased demand and higher prices for some of its export products, such as wool, hides, and skins, diamonds, copper and platinum. There were, however, weak spots in certain sections of agriculture and industry. In association with the Land bank the government applied a major scheme to assist more than 4,000 white farmers to rehabilitate themselves after crop failures. About £40 million was advanced by way of loans.

An agreement was concluded in New York whereby the government borrowed $10 million from the Chase Manhattan bank for three years at 5% interest.

A five-year nuclear research programme was approved, the cost (£800,000 a year) to be shared by the government, and the mining and iron and steel corporations. Legislation was passed to establish decimal coinage in 1961. The new gold coin, called a " rand ", would be the main unit, worth ten shillings and divided into 100 cents. To study and facilitate the transition, an official board was set up which would also supervise the compilation of a nation-wide register of all calculating and slot machines and other devices which would have to be scrapped or converted to the new system.

(J. Ln.)

See E. H. Brookes and J. B. Macaulay, *Civil Liberty in South Africa* (Capetown, 1958).

SOUTHEAST ASIA TREATY ORGANIZATION

(Seato). The Southeast Asia collective defence treaty was signed on Sept. 6, 1954, at Manila (Philippines), by Australia, France, New Zealand, Pakistan, the Philippines, Thailand, the United Kingdom and the United States. The signatories pledged themselves to " act to meet the common danger " in the event of armed external aggression against one of them in the treaty area (*i.e.*, south of lat. 21° 30′ N.) or against Cambodia, Laos and the Republic of Vietnam, in the latter case the consent of the governments concerned being necessary for any action on the respective territories, and to confer immediately in the event of internal aggression against any party or any other state in the treaty area. Headquarters, Bangkok. Secretary-general, Nai Pote Sarasin (Thailand).

History. The fifth meeting of the council of ministers of Seato was held in Wellington, New Zealand, during April 8-10, 1959, under the chairmanship of Walter Nash, the prime minister. Among those who attended were Duncan Sandys, British minister of defence, C. Douglas Dillon, U.S. under secretary of state for economic affairs, and Louis Jacquinot, French minister of state.

The council approved the reports of the military advisers and their recommendations for future activities; it reaffirmed the necessity for continued planning of defensive measures against possible aggression directed at the treaty area. During the year Brigadier L. W. Thornton, New Zealand, assumed the post of chief of the Seato military planning office.

The Thai, Filipino and Pakistani delegates made an effort to establish a Seato supreme commander and military headquarters on Shape lines, but this was considered premature by other members.

The council approved budget estimates for the year 1959-60 of $896,860, covering the costs of civil and military headquarters and various programmes which had been undertaken by the organization. (K. M. S.)

SOUTHERN RHODESIA: *see* RHODESIA AND NYASALAND, FEDERATION OF.

SOUTH-WEST AFRICA: *see* SOUTH AFRICA, UNION OF; TRUST TERRITORIES.

SOVEREIGNS, PRESIDENTS AND RULERS.

The following is a list of the names of those holding chief positions in their countries as on Dec. 31, 1959:

Country	Name and Office	Accession
AFGHANISTAN	Mohammed Zahir Shah, king	1933
	Mohammed Daud Khan, prime minister	1953
ALBANIA	Enver Hoxha, first secretary of the Albanian Workers' (Communist) party	1954
	Haxhi Leshi, chairman of the presidium of the People's Assembly	1953
	Mehmet Shehu, chairman of the council of ministers	1954
ARGENTINA	Arturo Frondizi, president	1958
AUSTRALIA	Elizabeth II, queen	1952
	Field Marshal Sir William Slim, governor-general	1953
	Robert Gordon Menzies, prime minister	1949
AUSTRIA	Adolf Schärf, president	1957
	Julius Raab, chancellor	1953
BELGIUM	Baudouin I, king	1951
	Gaston Eyskens, prime minister	1958
BOLIVIA	Hernán Siles Suazo, president	1956
BRAZIL	Juscelino Kubitschek, president	1956
BULGARIA	Todor Zhivkov, first secretary of the Bulgarian Communist party	1954
	Dimiter Ganev, chairman of the presidium of the National Assembly	1958
	Anton Yugov, chairman of the council of ministers	1956
BURMA	U Win Maung, president	1957
	General Ne Win, prime minister	1958
CAMBODIA	Norodom Suramarit, king	1955
	Prince Norodom Sihanouk, prime minister	1958
CANADA	Elizabeth II, queen	1952
	*Maj.-General George Vanier, governor-general	1959
	John George Diefenbaker, prime minister	1957
CEYLON	Elizabeth II, queen	1952
	Sir Oliver Goonetilleke, governor-general	1954
	*Wijayananda Dahanayake, prime minister	1959
CHILE	Jorge Alessandri, president	1958
CHINA — People's Republic (Communist)	*Liu Shao-chi, chairman of the people's republic	1959
	Mao Tse-tung, chairman of the Chinese Communist party	1949
	Chou En-lai, chairman of the state administrative council	1949
CHINA — Republic (Nationalist)	Chiang Kai-shek, president	1943
	General Chen Cheng, prime minister	1958
COLOMBIA	Alberto Lleras Camargo, president	1958
COSTA RICA	Mario Echandi Jiménez, president	1958
CUBA	Osvaldo Dorticós Torrado, president	1959
	*Fidel Castro, prime minister	1959
CZECHOSLOVAKIA	Antonín Novotný, first secretary of the Communist Party of Czechoslovakia (1953) and president	1957
	Vilem Široký, chairman of the council of ministers	1953
DENMARK	Frederick IX, king	1947
	Hans Christian Svane Hansen, prime minister	1955
DOMINICAN REP.	General Héctor Trujillo y Molina, president	1952
ECUADOR	Camilo Ponce Enríquez, president	1956
ETHIOPIA	Hailé Selassié I, emperor	1930
	Tshafe Tezaz Aklilu Haptewold, deputy prime minister	1957
FINLAND	Urho Kaleva Kekkonen, president	1956
	Vieno Johannes Sukselainen, prime minister	1959
FRANCE	General Charles de Gaulle, president	1959
	*Michel Debré, prime minister	1959

Country	Name and Office	Accession
GERMANY — Federal Republic	*Heinrich Lübke, federal president	1959
	Konrad Adenauer, federal chancellor	1949
GERMANY — Democratic Republic	Walter Ulbricht, first secretary of the Socialist (Communist) Unity Party of Germany	1946
	Wilhelm Pieck, president	1949
	Otto Grotewohl, chairman of the council of ministers	1949
GHANA	Elizabeth II, queen	1957
	Earl of Listowel, governor-general	1957
	Kwame Nkrumah, prime minister	1957
GREAT BRITAIN	Elizabeth II, queen	1952
	*Harold Macmillan, prime minister	1957
GREECE	Paul I, king	1947
	Konstantinos Karamanlis, prime minister	1955
GUATEMALA	Miguel Ydigoras Fuentes, president	1958
GUINEA	*Sékou Touré, president	1958
HAITI	François Duvalier, president	1957
HONDURAS	Ramón Villeda Morales	1958
HUNGARY	János Kádár, first secretary of the Hungarian Socialist Workers' (Communist) party	1956
	István Dobi, chairman of the presidential council of the National Assembly	1952
	Ferenc Münnich, chairman of the council of ministers	1958
ICELAND	Asgeir Asgeirsson, president	1952
	Olafur Thors, prime minister	1959
INDIA	Rajendra Prasad, president	1950
	Jawaharlal Nehru, prime minister	1947
INDONESIA	Ahmed Sukarno, president	1949
	Djuanda Kartawidjaya, prime minister	1957
IRAQ	Abd-ul-Karim el-Kassem, prime minister	1959
IRELAND	Eamon de Valera, president	1959
	Sean F. Lemass, prime minister	1959
ISRAEL	Isaac Ben-Zvi, president	1952
	David Ben-Gurion, prime minister	1955
ITALY	Giovanni Gronchi, president	1955
	Antonio Segni, prime minister	1959
JAPAN	Hirohito, emperor	1926
	Nobusuke Kishi, prime minister	1957
JORDAN	Hussein I, king	1952
	Hazzaa Majali, prime minister	1959
KOREA — Republic of Korea	Syngman Rhee, president	1948
KOREA — People's Democratic Republic	Marshal Kim Ir Sen, chairman of the Korean Workers' (Communist) party and chairman of the council of ministers	1948
	Tsoi Yen Gen, chairman of the presidium of the Supreme People's Assembly	1958
LAOS	Savang Vatthana, king	1959
	Phui Sananikone, prime minister	1958
LEBANON	General Fuad Shehab, president	1958
	Rashid Karameh, prime minister	1958
LIBERIA	William V. S. Tubman, president	1944
LIBYA	Idris I, king	1951
	Abd-ul-Majid Kubar, prime minister	1957
LIECHTENSTEIN	Franz-Josef II, sovereign prince	1938
	Alexander Frick, minister-president	1945
LUXEMBOURG	Charlotte, grand duchess	1919
	Pierre Werner, prime minister	1959
MALAYA	Tuanku Abdul Rahman, king	1957
	Tengku Abdul Rahman Putra, prime minister	1957
MEXICO	Adolfo López Mateos, president	1958
MONACO	Rainier III, sovereign prince	1949
	Emile Pelletier, minister of state	1959
MONGOLIA	Yumzhagiin Tsedenbal, first secretary of the Mongolian People's Revolutionary (Communist) party (1958) and chairman of the council of ministers	1952
	Zhamsarangiin Sambu, chairman of the presidium of the Great People's Khural	1954
MOROCCO	Mohammed V ben Yusef, king	1955
	Mulay Abdallah Ibrahim, prime minister	1958
MUSCAT AND OMAN	Said bin Taimur, sultan	1932
NEPAL	Mahendra Bir Bikram, king	1955
	Bisheshwar Prasad Koirala, prime minister	1959
NETHERLANDS	Juliana, queen	1948
	Jan Eduard De Quay, prime minister	1959
NEW ZEALAND	Elizabeth II, queen	1952
	Lord Cobham, governor-general	1957
	Walter Nash, prime minister	1957
NICARAGUA	Luis Somoza Debayle, president	1956
NORWAY	Olav V, king	1957
	Einar Gerhardsen, prime minister	1955
PAKISTAN	Field-Marshal Mohammed Ayub Khan, president	1958
PANAMA	Ernesto de la Guardia, president	1956
PARAGUAY	General Alfredo Stroessner, president	1954
PERSIA	Mohammed Riza Shah Pahlavi, shah	1941
	Manuchehr Ikbal, prime minister	1957
PERU	Manuel Prado y Ugarteche, president	1956
PHILIPPINES	Carlos P. Garcia, president	1957
POLAND	Władysław Gomułka, first secretary of the Polish United Worker's (Communist) party	1956
	Aleksander Zawadzki, chairman of the council of state	1952
	Józef Cyrankiewicz, chairman of the council of ministers	1954
PORTUGAL	Rear-Admiral Américo Deus Rodrigues Tomas, president	1958
	António de Oliveira Salazar, prime minister	1932
RHODESIA AND NYASALAND, FEDERATION OF	Elizabeth II, queen	1952
	Lord Dalhousie, governor-general	1957
	Sir Roy Welensky, prime minister	1956
RUMANIA	Gheorghe Gheorghiu-Dej, first secretary of the Rumanian Workers' (Communist) party	1945
	Ion Gheorghe Maurer, chairman of the presidium of the National Assembly	1958
	Chivu Stoica, chairman of the council of ministers	1955
SALVADOR, EL	Lieut.-Col. José María Lemus, president	1956
SAUDI ARABIA	Saud ibn Abd-ul-Aziz, king	1953
	Amir Faysal, prime minister	1954
SOUTH AFRICA	Elizabeth II, queen	1952
	*†Charles Robberts Swart, governor-general	1959
	Hendrik Frensch Verwoerd, prime minister	1958

* *See* BIOGRAPHIES. † Designate.

Country	Name and Office	Accession
SPAIN . .	. General Francisco Franco, chief of state and president of the council of ministers	1939
SUDAN . .	. General Ibrahim Abboud, prime minister . . .	1958
SWEDEN .	. Gustaf VI Adolf, king	1950
	Tage Fritiof Erlander, prime minister . . .	1946
SWITZERLAND.	. Giuseppe Lepori, president of the federal council	1959
THAILAND .	. Phumiphon Adulyadet, king	1946
	Field-Marshal Sarit Thanarat, prime minister .	1958
TUNISIA .	. Habib Bourguiba, president	1957
TURKEY	{ Celâl Bayar, president	1950
	{ Adnan Menderes, prime minister	1950
UNION OF SOVIET SOCIALIST REPUBLICS .	Nikita Sergeevich Khrushchev, first secretary of the Communist Party of the Soviet Union (1953) and chairman of the council of ministers . . .	1958
	Marshal Klimenty Efremovich Voroshilov, chairman of the presidium of the Supreme Soviet . .	1953
UNITED ARAB REPUBLIC .	. Gamal Abd-ul-Nasser, president	1958
UNITED STATES	. Dwight D. Eisenhower, president	1953
URUGUAY .	. Martín R. Etchegoyen, president of the governing national council	1959
VATICAN CITY	. John XXIII, pope	1958
VENEZUELA .	. Rómulo Betancourt, president	1958
VIETNAM	{ Republic of Vietnam { Ngo Dinh Diem, president	1955
	{ Democratic Republic of Vietnam { Ho Chi Minh, first secretary of the Lao Dong (Communist) party and president .	1954
YEMEN . .	. Ahmed ibn Yahya ibn Mohammed Hamid ed-Din, imam (king)	1948
YUGOSLAVIA .	. Marshal Tito (Josip Broz), president of the republic and chairman of the federal executive council .	1953

SOVIET LITERATURE. The most important event of 1959 was the third Congress of Soviet Writers held in the Kremlin during May 18-24. The main report, by the first secretary of the union, the poet Aleksei Surkov, once more condemned tendencies hostile to socialist realism and denounced the conduct of Boris Pasternak as " treacherous and unworthy of a Soviet writer ". However the trend towards a certain liberalization and towards the pardoning of past errors had several defenders and was even strengthened by N. S. Khrushchev himself, who on May 22 made a brilliant extempore speech before the congress. He called for indulgence towards the " deviationists ", even towards Vladimir Dudintsev, the author of the novel *Not by Bread Alone*, which had created a sensation. The congress naturally reminded its members of their duty to remain faithful to the system of socialist realism and to maintain the closest contact between literature and contemporary life. Soviet writers were mobilized to celebrate the seven-year plan and its heroes. The congress accepted the resignation of Surkov, who had been the object of sharp criticism, and elected as first secretary of the union the well-known novelist Konstantin Fedin. It also appointed the writer S. Smirnov to be editor of *Literaturnaya Gazeta*. After the congress many writers left Moscow for the provinces, to see the places where work forming part of the seven-year plan was in progress, and a group from *Literaturnaya Gazeta* visited Siberia, in particular the area of reclaimed land, during the summer months. As for Boris Pasternak, attacks against him ceased, and it was possible that under the new leadership of Konstantin Fedin he might be reinstated in the Union of Soviet Writers.

The 1959 Lenin prizes were awarded, as usual, on April 22. Among the prize-winners there were only two writers. First, the dramatist Nikolai Pogodin, who was the author of a trilogy dedicated to Lenin: *Chelovek s ruzhyom* (" The Man With a Gun "), *Kremlevskie kuranty* (" The Kremlin Chimes") and *Tretyaya pateticheskaya* (" The Pathetic Third "); and secondly the Kazakh writer Mukhtar Auezov, whose novel *Abai* was devoted to the life of the people of Kazakhstan and their national hero Abai Kunanbaev. In honouring a non-Russian author, the selection committee showed its regard for the other national literatures of the U.S.S.R.

Soviet literary circles considered it a great honour that Khrushchev, the leader of the Communist party and of the government, visited the novelist Mikhail Sholokhov at his Cossack *stanitsa* on the Don and that Sholokhov accompanied him as official delegate when Khrushchev went to the United States in September. Khrushchev thus honoured the

author of *Quiet Flows the Don* as the first great writer of the U.S.S.R.

Several well-known writers died during 1959: the dramatist Boris Lavrenev; the poet and critic Vissarion Sayanov; and Ivan Novikov, the author of historical novels. In addition the death occurred of the great actress of the Moscow Arts theatre, Olga Knipper, the widow of Anton Chekhov (*see* OBITUARIES).   (A. PR.)

SOVIET UNION: *see* UNION OF SOVIET SOCIALIST REPUBLICS.

SPACE EXPLORATION. Moon Rockets. On Jan. 2, 1959, at about 21 hr. U.T., Soviet engineers launched a moon probe weighing 3,245 lb. with a 795-lb. instrument package (Lunik I, or " Mechta ") which released a conspicuous yellow cloud of sodium vapour at a height of 70,000 mi., passed within 4,000 mi. of the Moon's surface and sped on to form an artificial planet, circling the Sun with an orbital period of 445 days, a mean distance of 107 million miles and an eccentricity of 0·15. It was expected to approach the vicinity of the Earth again after 5½ years. While some artificial meteors launched from an Aerobee rocket 50 mi. above New Mexico on Oct. 17, 1957, had possibly escaped into solar orbits, it seemed more likely that these minute bodies had been stopped by the atmosphere, so that Lunik I was actually the first artificial planet. On March 3, 1959, Pioneer IV was launched from Cape Canaveral, Florida, and passed within 37,000 mi. of the Moon, forming a second artificial planet with a period of 392 days. This conical, 13·4-lb. instrument package, probably accompanied by its fourth-stage Sergeant launching rocket, was tracked on 960·05 Mc. signals from a 0·18-w. transmitter out to 410,000 mi.

Lunik II, an 860-lb., gas-filled sphere, was launched from the U.S.S.R. on Sept. 12 with remarkable accuracy, hitting the Moon at 21 hr. 02 min. 23 sec. U.T. on Sept. 13 and landing an unbreakable pennant, probably near the crater Hyginus, seven minutes of arc northwest of the centre of the lunar disk, where a short-lived, bright pin point was reported by some visual observers. Radio signals received at Jodrell Bank, Manchester, on 183·6 Mc. and 19·992 Mc. showed that this body accelerated smoothly during the last hour to the impact velocity of 3 km. per sec., so that it seemed unlikely that any guiding rockets had been released during this period.

Lunik III, weighing 613 lb., was launched on Oct. 4 and passed round the Moon during the succeeding fortnight, becoming an earth satellite with a very elongated orbit. On Oct. 7 this remarkable " automatic space station " orientated

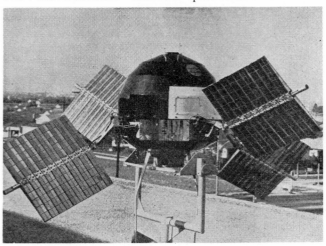

The U.S. " paddlewheel " satellite, put into orbit by a Thor-Able rocket on Aug. 7. Its instruments are operated by solar energy.

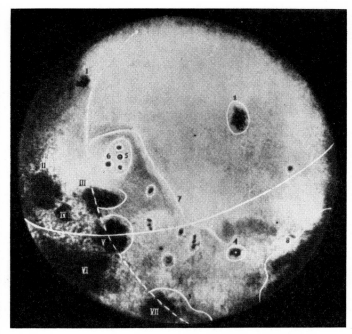

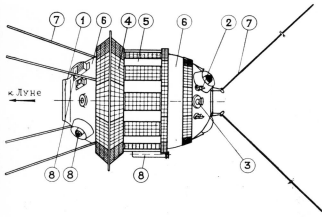

(*Left*) *The Moon's hidden face as photographed by Lunik III on Oct. 7.* (*Right*) *A diagram of Lunik III:* (*1*) *camera window;* (*2*) *orientation motor;* (*3*) *solar monitor;* (*4*) *solar cells;* (*5*) *thermo-regulation shutters;* (*6*) *thermo-screens;* (*7*) *aerials;* (*8*) *research equipment.*

itself with one end pointing to the Sun and the other pointing to the Moon (which was five days old as seen from the Earth and exactly full as seen from the Lunik) and took photographs of the mainly invisible hemisphere with two cameras on 35 mm. film. These were transmitted back by television several days later and published on Oct. 27. In addition to familiar features visible from the Earth that appeared at the edge of the composite picture, several new craters and mountain ranges were recorded, but these were much fewer in number than on the visible side. This result might perhaps be related to the fact that the Moon has a slight bulge towards the Earth, but owing to the possibilities of over-exposure and low contrast on the side directly illuminated by sunlight, it was felt that more pictures would be needed in order to draw firm conclusions.

Scientific Results. The most important scientific discovery that had resulted from space research by the end of 1959 remained the Van Allen particle belt. Results from Pioneers III and IV reported by J. A. Van Allen and Louis A. Frank of Iowa State university showed that there are actually two zones of high particle density: an inner ring with a vertical thickness of about 2,000 km. and a horizontal width of 4,000 km. with its centre line running round the geomagnetic equator at a height of 3,000 km.; and an outer ring of crescent-shaped cross-section (concave towards the Earth) extending from three to four earth-radii in distance from the centre of the Earth and from 60°N. to 60°S. in magnetic latitude. Both

zones, evidently consisting of electrically charged particles of solar origin trapped by the geomagnetic field, appeared to be fairly permanent. The outer zone was found to consist of protons and electrons of comparatively low energy, which penetrate to lower altitudes near the magnetic poles to cause aurorae when the Sun is active. The inner zone, less affected by ordinary solar activity, appeared to consist of high-energy decay products of cosmic rays. The hypothesis of charged particles trapped in thin horizontal layers by the Earth's magnetic field had received an interesting confirmation during three high-altitude nuclear explosions over the south Atlantic on Aug. 27, Aug. 30 and Sept. 6, 1958, monitored by Explorer IV (1958 ϵ), the last of which had produced a brilliant red aurora over the Azores. The analysis by S. N. Vernov and others of measurements carried out with the Lunik instruments generally confirmed Van Allen's results. An analysis of the magnetic data by Van Allen showed no lunar effect, suggesting that the Moon's magnetic moment must be less than that of the Earth. The Soviet workers found the geomagnetic field to be unexpectedly low between heights of 14,000 km. and 21,000 km., confirming the suggestion of S. Dolginov and N. Pushkov that there is a westward-flowing ring current on the inner edge of the outer particle belt.

Considerable advances in geodesy resulted from the analysis of the satellite orbits. From observations of Vanguard I (1958 β), R. Jastrow, J. A. O'Keefe, Ann Eckels and R. K. Squires found the Earth to be very slightly pear-shaped, with the

	Name*					Date of launching	Perigee height (mi.)	Apogee height (mi.)	Weight (lb.)	Time in orbit	Achievements
α1.	Vanguard II	.	.	.	.	Feb. 17	348	2,064	22	about 10 yrs.	Meteorology: scanning Earth and cloud radiation.
β	Discoverer I	.	.	.	.	Feb. 28	?	?	1,600	1 week ?	?
γ	Discoverer II	.	.	.	.	April 13	156	232	1,600	13 days	Stabilized horizontal orientation; ignition by ground signals.
δ2.	Explorer VI	.	.	.	.	Aug. 7	153	26,397	142	2 years	" Paddle wheels " receiving solar power (50 w.); ground-controlled measurements; digital data storage.
ϵ	Discoverer V	.	.	.	.	Aug. 13	135	457	1,600	46 days	Instrument packages jettisoned according to plan, but not recovered.
ζ	Discoverer VI	.	.	.	.	Aug. 19	131	528	1,600	about 2 months	
η	Vanguard III	.	.	.	.	Sept. 18	315	2,300	100	35 years	Physical measurements.
θ	Explorer VII	.	.	.	.	Oct. 13	330	710	92	about 50 years	Radiation measurements.
ι	Discoverer VII	.	.	.	.	Nov. 7	?	?	?	?	Further unsuccessful recovery test.

SELECTED DATA FOR U.S. ARTIFICIAL SATELLITES LAUNCHED IN 1959

* Greek letters indicate order of launching. Numerals indicate order of brightness of the various components of each satellite.

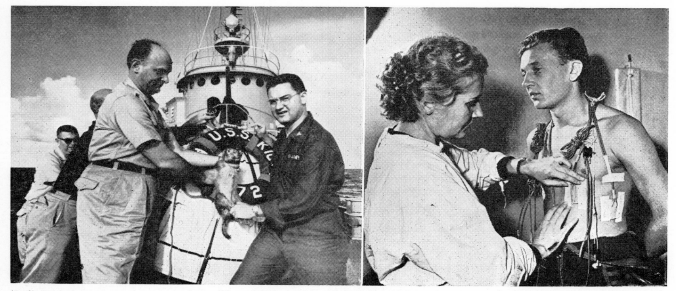

(Left) Back from space: the two monkeys Able and Baker safely retrieved from the Pacific after reaching a height of 300 miles in a U.S. Jupiter missile on May 28. (Right) Preparing for space: meters are fixed to a subject prior to tests in a Soviet altitude chamber.

narrow end at the north pole, the greatest departure from the spheroidal shape being 15 m. This suggests that the Earth's crust and mantle are strong enough to withstand appreciable shearing stresses. Sudden and simultaneous fluctuations in the periods of 1958 β and Sputnik III (1958 δ) were interpreted by L. G. Jacchia as a consequence of density changes in the atmosphere due to solar activity; the changes were well correlated with the 27-day solar rotation period and with radio bursts. By means of a concave diffraction grating mounted on an Aerobee Hi rocket launched to a height of 123 mi. from White Sands, New Mexico, on March 13, 1959, J. D. Purcell and R. Tousey of the U.S. Naval Research laboratory obtained numerous spectroheliograms of the Sun's disk in the Lyman α line of hydrogen (λ 1216 Å). The pattern resembled that shown at the same time by the K line of ionized calcium (λ 3934 Å), but with a coarser structure. A spectrogram taken on the same flight revealed strong emission lines in the far ultra-violet caused by hydrogen and by carbon, silicon and oxygen in various stages of ionization, and weaker lines caused by neutral and ionized helium and nitrogen, neutral sulphur and 9-times ionized magnesium. Radiation in the Lyman continuum of hydrogen (below 912 Å) was also detected. From the absorption of Lyman α radiation at various heights, it appeared that this emission line causes ionization in the D region of the ionosphere, some 50 mi. above the Earth, which is strongly affected by intense solar flares. (*See* also INTERNATIONAL GEOPHYSICAL CO-OPERATION.) (B. E. J. P.)

BIBLIOGRAPHY. L. V. Berkner *et al.* (eds.), *Manual on Rockets and Satellites* (London and New York, 1958); N. E. Howard, *Handbook for Observing the Satellites* (New York, 1958); H. S. W. Massey and R. L. F. Boyd, *The Upper Atmosphere* (London, 1958); Homer E. Newell, Jr., *Sounding Rockets* (New York, 1959); A. Shternfeld, *Soviet Space Science* (New York, 1959).

SPAIN. Country of southwestern Europe, bounded N. by the Bay of Biscay and France, W. by the Atlantic and Portugal, and S. and E. by the Mediterranean. Area 194,945 sq.mi., including Balearic (1,936 sq.mi.) and Canary (2,804 sq.mi.) islands. Pop.: (1950 census) 27,976,755, including Balearic (422,089) and Canary (793,328) islands; (mid-1958 est.) 29,661,813. Language: mainly Spanish (Castilian) but Catalan, Galician and Basque are also spoken. Religion: Roman Catholic; Protestants, *c.* 25,000. Chief towns (pop., Dec. 1956 est.): Madrid (cap.) 1,879,037; Barcelona 1,431,753; Valencia 516,556; Seville 412,307; Malaga 280,200; Saragossa 281,866; Bilbao 257,160; Murcia 237,556; 16 towns with a population from 100,000 to 200,000. Chief of state, president of the council of ministers and commander-in-chief, General Francisco Franco Bahamonde. Main imports: machinery and vehicles, manufactured goods, petroleum and products, textiles. Main exports: oranges, wine, vegetables, iron ore. Monetary unit: *peseta* (official rate [from July 20, 1959] P.168·00 = £1 sterling).

History. *The Stabilization Plan.* The outstanding event in 1959 was the announcement on July 20 of the Spanish government's important stabilization plan following Spain's admission as the 18th full member of the Organization for European Economic Co-operation. (Spain had become an associate member in 1958.) This step was approved at a cabinet meeting held in the Pardo palace, General Franco presiding, at which Alberto Ullastres Calvo, minister of commerce, gave a detailed report of his talks in Washington, New York and Paris. At these talks the plan for stabilizing Spain's economy was promised the support of the O.E.E.C., the International Monetary fund, the U.S. government and also private banks in the United States. Foreign aid, amounting to $375 million, was placed at the disposal of the Spanish government to back up its stabilization plan. A substantial devaluation of the peseta was an important move in connection with the stabilization plan. Spain's currency, which had been officially pegged at P.117·60 to the £ sterling, was quoted at 168. The dollar, formerly at P.42·00, was devalued to P.60·00. The Spanish government was committed to stringent measures against inflation and a gradual return to a liberalized economy in line with other European countries.

Foreign Relations. In April, Adnan Menderes, prime minister of Turkey, accompanied by Fatin Rüştü Zorlu, the foreign minister, went to Madrid for four days at the invitation of Franco. A treaty of friendship between the two countries was signed on April 16.

Another important visitor to Spain in April was Thomas S. Gates, U.S. secretary of the navy. After a cordial meeting with Admiral Felipe José Abárzazu y Oliva, the Spanish minister of the navy, Gates went on a tour of inspection of U.S. air and naval bases. (The U.S. naval installations at Cartagena, built at a cost of some $10 million, were inaugurated on Jan. 16.)

The visit in May of Samuel Waugh, president of the Export-Import bank of Washington, was also significant. He went to study Spain's economic problems in general and to confer with members of the Spanish government, bankers and businessmen. His arrival in Madrid followed upon that of representatives of the O.E.E.C. and the International Monetary fund.

Fernando Maria Castiella y Maíz, the foreign minister,

went to London to see President Dwight D. Eisenhower on Aug. 31. He delivered a letter to the president from Franco inviting him to visit Madrid whenever it might be convenient. On Sept. 1 Castiella was also received by Harold Macmillan, the prime minister, and Selwyn Lloyd, secretary of state for foreign affairs. On Sept. 5 Castiella was received in Paris by President Charles de Gaulle.

In October Castiella met Maurice Couve de Murville, French foreign minister, on an island in the Bidassoa river at the Franco-Spanish border, to join in celebrating the tercentenary of the Pyrenees peace treaty, which in 1659 ended a long struggle between Spain and France.

In November Castiella went to Bonn to have talks with Konrad Adenauer, the chancellor, Ludwig Erhard, minister for economic affairs, and Heinrich von Brentano, the foreign minister. The possibility of establishing closer economic and cultural relations between Spain and the German Federal Republic was studied.

On Dec. 21 President Dwight D. Eisenhower arrived in Madrid on a short official visit. He was enthusiastically cheered by huge crowds in the streets of the Spanish capital, when he drove with Franco in an open car from the Torrejón air base to the Moncloa palace. The next morning a two-hour discussion took place between Eisenhower and Franco at the Pardo palace. On leaving Spain on Dec. 22 Eisenhower said that not only the friendship but also the active co-operation between the United States and Spain would become increasingly stronger.

Home Affairs. On April 1 Spain's vast war memorial, built by order of Franco to the dead of the civil war, was officially opened by the *caudillo* in the Valle de los Caídos (Valley of the Fallen), not far from the Escorial, and about 25 mi. northwest of Madrid. Present at the ceremony were the government, the Cortes, the council of the kingdom, two cardinals and bishops from all parts of Spain, as well as military and civil authorities. Two days before the remains of José Antonio Primo de Rivera, the founder of the Falange party, were transferred from his tomb in the Escorial monastery to the mausoleum in the Valley of the Fallen.

Franco made several speeches during the year in which he outlined the progress achieved during his more than 20 years in power. He specially referred to the stabilization plan which, he stated, marked an important stage in the development of the regime. He admitted there were problems, but with the co-operation of all, the *caudillo* was confident they would be satisfactorily solved.

Monarchists and underground elements were active during 1959. The distribution of clandestinely printed leaflets was steadily carried on. The police rounded up many people during the year, but in spite of stiff sentences the circulation of illegal propaganda attacking the Franco regime continued. An attempted 24-hr. " national peaceful strike " was called for June 18 but there was no noticeable response. Many allegedly involved were detained all over Spain. On Sept. 26, the Madrid Supreme Military Tribunal sentenced Simon Sanchez Montero and Luis Lucio Lobato, described as Communists, to terms of 20 and 14 years' imprisonment, respectively.

Don Juan Carlos, son of Don Juan, count of Barcelona, the pretender to the Spanish throne, made his first public appearance on May 3 in a military parade in Madrid which marked the 20th anniversary of Franco's victory in the civil war. The young prince, with fixed bayonet, was warmly cheered as he marched smartly with other cadets of the Air academy at which he was studying. In the same month another young prince, son of the Carlists' candidate for the throne, Xavier of Bourbon-Parma, assembled with a large crowd in Navarra to promote the restoration of a Carlist monarch.

A group of 90 Liberal Monarchists, Franco's opponents and members of the Union Española (founded in 1957) met on Jan. 29 at a dinner in a Madrid hotel. As all parties were illegal except the Falange, Joaquín Satrustegui, the union's founder, who denounced the " illegal " Franco government, was fined P.50,000.

Young Liberal Catholics announced on May 14 in Madrid the formation of a clandestine Christian Democratic party. In June the police arrested 17 of its organizers including Julio Cerón Ayuso, who had in 1957 joined the Spanish diplomatic service. On Dec. 28 the Supreme Military Tribunal sentenced Cerón to eight years' imprisonment. The 16 other accused received sentences of from one to four years.

Franco inaugurated several new dams and various important land development and irrigation schemes in different parts of the country. In the last months of 1959 increasing unemployment, a steady rise in the cost of living and inadequate wages were three of the main problems which caused much public concern. The government's stabilization plan came under criticism as it was thought to be responsible for these problems. The Ministry of Labour published a decree in November which provided special unemployment benefits for Spaniards thrown out of work. This unemployment pay would amount to 75% of their basic wage for a period not exceeding six months.

The most sensational event of the year was the publication in the *Official Bulletin* on March 9 of a list of 369 Spaniards fined a total of P.117 million for currency offences. All had deposits in a Swiss bank which had not been declared to the Foreign Exchange institute in Madrid.

On Jan. 9, 1959, disaster came to the small village of Ribadelago to the north of Zamora, following the bursting

The new " Torre de Madrid ", claimed to be the highest concrete structure in the world, seen from below the statue of Don Quixote.

of a dam during the night when the inhabitants were asleep. In about ten minutes 125 of the village's 150 primitive dwellings had been washed away; 132 of its 500 inhabitants lost their lives. (X.)

SPANISH LITERATURE.

Spain continued to be one of the few countries where verse and the essay were more successful and even more popular than serious fiction. Most people remained either semi-literate or satisfied with the comic books the censorship allowed to flood the kiosks in lieu of a free press, but a minority consumed a substantial fare of philosophy and poetry. Relatively more books of essays were published in Spain than in any other country. Typical were such uncompromising books as José Ferrater Mora's *Ortega y Gasset*, an analysis of that great thinker's evolution. The Spanish edition was an amplification of a book originally written in English by Ferrater and published in Britain and the United States in 1957. Also by the same writer was *La filosofía en el mundo de hoy*. Américo Castro's first book to be published in Spain since the civil war was his *Origen, ser y existir de los españoles*, a collection of essays on how the Spaniards became what they peculiarly are and made their " historiable " history. Pedro Laín Entralgo published *La curación por la palabra*, an examination of the word (*logos*) as therapeutic agent, and of Greek approximations to psychosomatic medicine. *Monodiálogos de Don Miguel de Unamuno*, by Eduardo Ortega y Gasset (exiled brother of José), containing valuable memoirs of Unamuno in exile, was published in New York. Camilo José Cela issued his first *Memorias*.

While brilliant youth elsewhere was dedicated to fiction and romance on the one hand and to science on the other, the outstanding writer to appear in Spain in 1959 was Alberto Gil Novales (b. 1930), who documented the decadence of Spain during the previous three centuries in a series of fascinating sketches entitled (after Ortega) *Las pequeñas Atlántidas*. Written in a style as subjective as that of a Latin Carlyle, uncontaminated by pale " objectivity ", the book stood up for the tragic valour and value of Spain in continuous decline.

The Premio de la Crítica awards were given to Blas de Otero in poetry for a collection of his work, *Ancia*; to Ana María Matute in fiction for *Los hijos muertos*, an account of the civil war seen from the losing side; and to Eugenio de Nora for his *La novela española contemporánea*, a comprehensive survey of the novel from 1898 to 1927. A work of impressionist biography, *Grandes tipos*, by the vigorous Catalan writer Josep Plá, included an imaginative chapter on the great architect Antoni Gaudí. The literary magazine *Papeles de Son Armadans*, which issued an important commemorative number, with essays on all phases of the work of Gaudí, published as a book Gabriel Celaya's *Cantata en Aleixandre*, verse variations on themes by the classic Vicente Aleixandre. The literary world mourned the death of the poet Manuel Altolaguirre, who had been living abroad since the civil war, and of the two great Catalan poets of the first half of the century, Josep Maria López-Picó and Carles Riba. (*See also* SPAIN.) (A. KN.)

SPANISH OVERSEAS TERRITORIES.

Under this heading are grouped the Spanish possessions in Africa as they stood at the end of 1959. Their total area is estimated at 96,675 sq.mi., and their total population at 480,000. Areas, populations and chief towns are given in the table. The population of the places of Spanish sovereignty in Morocco and of Spanish West Africa is Arab, Berber and Spanish. The population of Spanish Guinea is mainly Negro, with 1,900 whites in continental Guinea and 2,850 on the islands. The governor of Spanish Guinea resides at Santa Isabel (population 21,500), on Fernando Po.

History. A period of calm marked relations between Spain and Morocco during 1959. This was a relief after the tense situation in 1958 produced by attacks of Moroccan troops on Spanish west African possessions which led to serious engage-

SPANISH TERRITORIES	Area (sq.mi.)	Population (1959 est.)	Chief towns
PLACES OF SPANISH SOVEREIGNTY IN MOROCCO			
Ceuta, Melilla, Alhucemas, Chafarinas and Peñon de Velez	82	175,000	—
SPANISH WEST AFRICA			
Province of Ifni . . .	741	45,000	Sidi Ifni
Province of Sahara . . .	85,000	50,000	Aaiun
SPANISH GUINEA			
Continental Guinea (Rio Muni) .	10,039	165,000	Bata
Fernando Po and small islands .	813	45,000	Santa Isabel

ments in Ifni and the Sahara with many casualties. There were, however, various questions still outstanding between the Madrid and Rabat governments, including the delicate one of the delimitation of frontiers in southern Morocco. During 1959 a mixed Hispano-Moroccan commission met several times to discuss these problems.

In April, Mulay Abdallah Ibrahim, prime minister of Morocco, on his way to Rabat from Beirut after attending a meeting of the Arab league, stopped in Madrid to meet General Francisco Franco. The object was to deliver a cordial message of friendship from King Mohammed V and to discuss outstanding questions between the two countries. The Moroccan prime minister admitted there were problems, but between Spain and Morocco there was a close understanding which would help them to overcome any difficulties.

Several officials of the Rabat government accompanied Mulay Abdallah Ibrahim during his talks with the *caudillo* and also with Fernando Maria Castiella y Maíz, the Spanish foreign minister. Among questions discussed was the Moroccan government's request for the withdrawal of all Spanish troops from northern Morocco, the former Spanish protectorate, with its capital at Tetuan, which was incorporated in the new independent Morocco under the Hispano-Moroccan agreement of April 7, 1956.

A new juridical status for Spanish Guinea was approved by the Cortes on July 28. The old colony of Guinea was converted into two provinces with the names of Fernando Po and Rio Muni, subject to the same laws and legislation as provinces in metropolitan Spain. This change in status thus ended the " colonizing phase ", it was stated in the Cortes.

The establishment of the new provinces of Fernando Po and Rio Muni followed upon the 1958 decree creating the new provinces of Ifni and Sahara.

Good crops were again reported of coffee, cocoa, bananas and tobacco, four commodities of much importance for Spain's economy. (X.)

SPELEOLOGY.

The most interesting developments during 1959 were in the study of radioactive carbon from caves. H. W. Franke and his colleagues in Austria demonstrated the importance of C^{13} in cave formations as well as C^{14} and dated individual speleothems at more than 30,000 years old. Similar results were obtained by the U.S. workers, W. S. Broeker and E. A. Olson, who also investigated the proportion of C^{14} in contemporary deposits to assess the reliability of this method of dating. G. Atansiu of Japan discussed the effect of C^{14} upon the ionization of cave air. More conventional meteorological studies came from Cueva Grande, Caguanes, Cuba, by A. N. Jeminez and Carlsbad, Lehmann and Wind caves, United States. Hydrological work at Mole creek, Tasmania, by J. N. Jennings and Marjorie Sweeting established the first case of underground and watershed breaching in Australia.

A petrified waterfall in the depths of the Llangattock caves, Monmouthshire, photographed for the first time in August. The camera and equipment were sealed in a tin to negotiate narrow clefts and icy pools during a four-mile underground journey.

Cave bats also figured prominently, movements of ringed individuals being reported from Missouri (275 mi.) and from Spain (175 mi.). Two new blind millipedes, *Cambala captiosa* and *Speodesmus bicornourus*, were described from Texas, and were associated with a rare beetle, *Comstockia subterrania*, previously only known from female specimens. The Moulis subterranean laboratory, France, produced a film " Faune Cavernicole " dealing with various aspects of cave life.

Cave art studies were equally productive, with a review of the whole field by Professor Paolo Graziosi of Florence and a monograph on the cave of Trois Frères by Abbé Breuil and H. Begouin. Tom Harrisson found other paintings in the Niah caves, whose deposits produced the first definite succession of prehistoric cultures in Borneo. Royal Air Force cavers made an important find of Neolithic pottery in a cave at Aghirda, Cyprus, while in England A. Sutcliffe discovered a skull of the rare northern lynx in a cave at Paignton Zoological gardens, Devon.

There were few outstanding new discoveries of caves reported, though R. Vergnes (Switzerland) continued to

An R.A.F. doctor talks to reporters after many hours in Peak cavern, Derbyshire, during attempts to rescue Neil Moss in March.

explore new ground in Guatemala and a Cambridge university expedition visited Libya to investigate deep caves in relation to groundwater studies. Concern was felt in many countries regarding the destruction of caves and their contents. In the United States negotiations were proceeding to acquire caves for permanent preservation and in Britain a new nature reserve at Craig y Cilau, Breconshire, containing the cave Agen Allwedd, was declared. This cave was of considerable scientific interest because of selenite crystals and calcite formations to be found there.

David Priestman, Neil Moss and J. F. Wallington lost their lives in cave accidents in England. Neil Moss was trapped in Peak cavern and died from carbon dioxide poisoning after a 44-hr. attempt to save him. R. H. Peters was awarded the George medal for his part in this rescue operation and L. B. Salmon and J. A. Thompson the British Empire medal. J. Aspin (Britain) reviewed the present state of knowledge of histoplasmosis contracted in caves and further investigations into this disease were carried on in Mexico and the United States. In the latter country William R. Halliday also studied **cave** dust pneumonitis.

Apart from national meetings there were two specialized symposia, the first in Vienna (Oct. 16-17) on karstic morphology and hydrology, and the second in Chicago (Dec. 28) on speciation in cavernicoles and the origin and development of caves.

(G. T. Wк.)

SPICES: *see* FOODSTUFFS.

SPIRITS. The following table shows the estimated consumption of potable spirits in various countries, in terms of litres (50% alcoholic contents) per capita. One litre = 0·88 imp. quart. (No reference is made in this table to the consumption of wine or beer.)

	1935-37*	1955	1956	1957
Sweden	5·50†	5·50	6·30	5·50
France	4·70	...	...	...
United States	3·21	4·05	4·28	4·43
Switzerland‡	2·88§	3·02‖	...	...
Norway	1·95	2·63¶	2·64¶	2·66¶
Netherlands	1·50	2·33	2·58	...
Italy	0·40	2·60	1·60	1·80
German Fed. Rep.	1·12**	1·30	1·46	1·60
Finland	1·56††	1·55	1·45	1·45
Belgium‡‡	1·19	1·35	1·34	1·39
United Kingdom	1·10	1·07	1·07	1·15
Denmark	0·90	0·90	1·00	1·00

* Yearly average. † 1939. ‡ 40% alcoholic content. § 1933-38 average. ‖ 1950-55 average. ¶ As sold. ** Prewar Germany. †† 1937. ‡‡ With Luxembourg.

SPORTING RECORD. The summary below covers the principal sports and games for the season 1958-59 or the calendar year 1959, as appropriate. There are, in addition, more detailed separate articles on the most widley followed sports to which cross-reference is made after the appropriate sections below.

ARCHERY. Grand National Archery society, Marley, Kennington, Ashford, Kent. Secretary, C. B. Edwards.

British Championships. Gentlemen, Double York round: R. Hall, 1,731 pts.; F. W. Bing, 1,660; D. Charsley-Thomas, 1,657. Ladies, Double Hereford round: Mrs. L. Fowler, 1,745 pts.; Miss J. Warner, 1,674; Miss M. S. D. Weeks, 1,614.

World Championships. Gentlemen, Double FITA round: J. Caspers (U.S.), 2,247 pts.; R. Kadlec (U.S.), 2,203; J. Neely (U.S.), 2,184. Ladies, Double FITA round: Miss A. Corby (U.S.), 2,023 pts.; Mrs. S. Johansson (Sweden), 1,933; Mrs. L. Shine (U.S.), 1,913.

ASSOCIATION FOOTBALL. Football association, 22, Lancaster gate, London, W.2. President, the Duke of Gloucester; chairman, A. Drewry; secretary, Sir Stanley Rous.

International Football (involving British teams): Spain 6, Northern Ireland 2; England 5, U.S.S.R. 0; Scotland 3, German Federal Republic 2; England 2, Italy 2; Brazil 2, England 0; Peru 4, England 1; Mexico 2, England 1; United States 1, England 8.

International Championship (British): Ireland 3, England 3; Wales 0, Scotland 3; Scotland 2, Ireland 2; England 2, Wales 2; England 1, Scotland 0; Ireland 4, Wales 1.

INTERNATIONAL CHAMPIONSHIP

	P.	W.	D.	L.	Goals For	Agst.	Pts.
Ireland	3	1	2	0	9	6	4
England	3	1	2	0	6	5	4
Scotland	3	1	1	1	5	3	3
Wales	3	0	1	2	3	9	1

British Professional Football. Football Association cup. Semi-finals: Luton 1, Norwich City 0 (after draw 1-1); Aston Villa 0, Nottingham Forest 1. Final: Nottingham Forest 2, Luton Town 1. Scottish cup: St. Mirren 3, Aberdeen 1. Scottish League cup: Hearts of Midlothian 5, Partick Thistle 1.

FOOTBALL LEAGUE AND SCOTTISH LEAGUE: FIRST AND LAST TEAMS IN EACH OF PRINCIPAL LEAGUES

Football League: Division I

	P.	W.	D.	L.	Goals For	Agst.	Pts.
Wolverhampton Wanderers	42	28	5	9	110	49	61
Manchester United	42	24	7	11	103	66	55
Aston Villa	42	11	8	23	58	87	30
Portsmouth	42	6	9	27	64	112	21

Football League: Division II							
Sheffield Wednesday .	.	42	28	6	8	106	48	62
Fulham .	. .	42	27	6	9	96	61	60
Grimsby Town	. .	42	9	10	23	62	90	28
Barnsley .	. .	42	10	7	25	55	91	27
Football League: Divison III							
Plymouth Argyle	.	46	23	16	7	89	59	62
Hull City .	.	46	26	9	11	90	55	61
Stockport County	. .	46	13	10	23	65	78	36
Doncaster Rovers	. .	46	14	5	27	50	90	33
Notts County .	. .	46	8	13	25	55	96	29
Rochdale .	. .	46	8	12	26	37	79	28
Football League: Divison IV							
Port Vale .	. .	46	26	12	8	110	58	64
Coventry City .	.	46	24	12	10	84	47	60
York City .	.	46	21	18	7	73	52	60
Shrewsbury Town	.	46	24	10	12	101	63	58
Barrow .	. .	46	9	10	27	51	104	28
Southport .	. .	46	7	12	27	41	86	26
Scottish League: Division I							
Rangers .	. .	34	21	5	8	92	51	50
Hearts .	. .	34	21	7	6	92	51	48
Falkirk .	. .	34	10	17	7	58	79	27
Queen of the South .	.	34	6	22	6	38	101	18
Scottish League: Division II							
Ayr United .	. .	36	28	4	4	115	48	60
Arbroath .	. .	36	23	8	5	86	59	51
Queen's Park .	. .	36	9	21	6	53	80	24
Montrose .	. .	36	6	24	6	49	96	18

British Amateur Football. F.A. Amateur cup: Crook Town 3, Barnet 2. University match: Cambridge 6, Oxford 2. (*See also* ASSOCIATION FOOTBALL.)

ATHLETICS. Amateur Athletic association, 54, Torrington place, London, W.C.1. President, Marquess of Exeter; hon. secretary,

E. H. L. Clynes. Women's Amateur Athletic association. President, Lady Marjorie Reed; hon. secretary, Mrs. M. E. Amies (Toft Lodge, St. Catherine's road, Broxbourne, Herts.).

International Matches. Poland bt. Great Britain (at the White City), *men*, 106-99 pts., *women*, 54-52. German Fed. Rep. bt. Great Britain (at the White City), *men*, 117-95, *women*, 51-64. U.S.S.R. bt. Great Britain (in Moscow), *men*, 129-95, *women*, 76-41. Great Britain bt. Finland (at Helsinki), 126-104.

A.A.A. Championships. 100 yd., P. H. Radford (Birchfield H.), 9·7 sec.; 220 yd., D. H. Jones (Woodford Green), 21·7 sec.; 440 yd., J. D. Wrighton (Southgate), 47·5 sec.; 880 yd., B. S. Hewson (Mitcham), 1 min. 52·0 sec.; 1 mi., K. Wood (Sheffield), 4 min. 8·1 sec.; 3 mi., M. B. S. Tulloh (Portsmouth), 13 min. 31·2 sec.; 6 mi., S. E. Eldon (Windsor and Eton), 28 min. 12·4 sec.; 10 mi., F. Norris (Bolton United), 48 min. 32·4 sec.; marathon, L. J. C. Fleming-Smith (Rotherham), 2 hr. 30 min. 11 sec.; 2-mi. walk, K. J. Matthews (R. Sutton Coldfield), 13 min. 19·4 sec.*; 7-mi. walk, K. J. Matthews (R. Sutton Coldfield), 50 min. 28·8 sec.; 4×110-yd. relay, Thames Valley Harriers, 42·1 sec.; 4×440-yd. relay, Birchfield Harriers, 3 min. 16·0 sec.; 120-yd. hurdles, V. C. Matthews (L.A.C.), 14·5 sec.; 220-yd. hurdles, J. Metcalf (Achilles C.), 23·8 sec.; 440-yd. hurdles, C. E. Goudge (Bolton United), 52·7 sec.; high jump, C. W. Fairbrother (Victoria Park), 6 ft. 7 in.; pole vault, A. Ditta (Pakistan), 13 ft. 6 in.; long jump, D. J. Whyte (Dundee Hawkhill), 23 ft. 9 in.; hop, step and jump, J. E. C. Whall (Blackheath), 49 ft. 2¾ in.†; weight, A. Rowe (Doncaster), 58 ft. 10¾ in.*; discus, M. R. Lindsay (Queen's Park), 175 ft. 7½ in.; hammer, M. J. Ellis (Thames Valley), 201 ft. 0½ in.; javelin, C. G. Smith (Thames Valley), 229 ft. 4½ in.; decathlon, C. J. Andrews (Army), 5,517 pts.; tug of war (100 st.), Hawker Aircraft; tug of war (catchweight), Wood Treatment (Bosley).

* Championship best performance.   † English native record.

Oxford university bt. Cambridge university, 90 pts. to 45.

Cross-Country Running. International Cross-Country union; English Cross-Country union, hon. secretary, G. L. N. Dunn, " Woodlin ", Stapleford, Cambridge.

International Championship. (9 mi. at National stadium, Lisbon, Portugal!): 1, F. Norris (Eng.), 2, F. D. Sando (Eng.), 3, S. Beddiaf (Fr.); team placings: 1, England. 2, France, 3, Belgium.

English Senior Championship. 1, F. Norris, 2, F. D. Sando, 3, M. R. Maynard; team placings: 1, Sheffield Utd. H. & A.C., 2, Derby & City A.C., 3, South London H. (*See also* ATHLETICS).

WORLD ATHLETICS RECORDS IMPROVED OR EQUALLED IN 1959

Event	Name and Nationality	Place	Date	Performance
100 yd.	W. G. Woodhouse (U.S.)	Abilene, Texas	May 5	9·3 sec.
	O. R. Norton (U.S.)	Fresno, California	May 9	9·3 sec.
	R. Cook (U.S.)	Modesto, California	May 30	9·3 sec.
100 m.	O. R. Norton (U.S.)	San Jose, California	April 18	10·1 sec.
200 m. (turn)*	O. R. Norton (U.S.)	Gothenburg	Aug. 4	20·6 sec.
	O. R. Norton (U.S.)	Chicago, Illinois	Aug. 31	20·6 sec.
220 yd. (turn)*	O. R. Norton (U.S.)	San Jose, California	May 2	20·6 sec.
1,000 m.	D. J. R. Waern (Sweden)	Gävle, Sweden	Aug. 10	2 min. 18·0 sec.
	D. J. R. Waern (Sweden)	Karlstad, Sweden	Aug. 21	2 min. 17·8 sec.
120-yd. hurdles	M. Lauer (German Fed. Rep.)	Zürich	July 7	13·2 sec.
110-m. hurdles	M. Lauer (German Fed. Rep.)	Zürich	July 7	13·2 sec.
200-m. hurdles (turn)	H. W. Jones (U.S.)	Lincoln, Nebraska	June 13	22·5 sec.
	M. Lauer (German Fed. Rep.)	Zürich	July 7	22·5 sec.
220-yd. hurdles (turn)	H. W. Jones (U.S.)	Lincoln, Nebraska	June 13	22·5 sec.
Hop, step and jump	O. Fedoseyev (U.S.S.R.)	Nalchik, U.S.S.R.	May 3	54 ft. 9½ in.
	D. C. Long (U.S.)	Santa Barbara, California	March 28	63 ft. 2 in.
Shot putt	W. P. O'Brien (U.S.)	Philadelphia, Pennsylvania	July 18	63 ft. 2½ in.
	W. P. O'Brien (U.S.)	Albuquerque, New Mexico	Aug. 1	63 ft. 4 in.
Discus throw	E. Piątkowski (Poland)	Warsaw	June 14	196 ft. 6¾ in.
Javelin throw	A. A. Cantello (U.S.)	Compton, California	June 5	282 ft. 3½ in.
Decathlon	V. D. Kuznetsov (U.S.S.R.)	Moscow	May 16/17	8,357 pts.
4 × 110-yd. relay	Texas university (W. Wilson, S. E. Southern, H. Gainey, R. Alspaugh)	Modesto, California	May 30	39·6 sec.
4 × 1-mile relay	Australia (D. Wilson, A. G. Thomas, J. M. Murray, H. J. Elliott)	Melbourne	March 21	16 min. 25·6 sec.
	Honved club, Budapest, Hungary (L. Kovács, B. Szekeres, S. Iharos, I. Rózsavölgyi)	Budapest	Sept. 29	16 min. 25·2 sec.

N.B. D. C. Long (U.S.) achieved 63 ft. 7 in. in a seventh trial at Los Angeles on May 2 and W. P. O'Brien 63 ft. 8 in. at Pomona, California, on June 16 in a meeting that was not *bona fide* competition.

Women

Event	Name and Nationality	Place	Date	Performance
60 m.	G. M. Popova (U.S.S.R.)	Nalchik, U.S.S.R.	April 19	7·3 sec.
	N. Polyakova (U.S.S.R.)	Nalchik, U.S.S.R.	April 19	7·3 sec.
400 m.	M. L. Itkina (U.S.S.R.)	Krasnodar, U.S.S.R.	Sept. 12	53·4 sec.
440 yd.	B. Cuthbert (Australia)	Sydney	Jan. 17	55·6 sec.
	M. A. M. Chamberlain (New Zealand)	Sydney	March 14	55·6 sec.
	B. Cuthbert (Australia)	Sydney	March 21	54·3 sec.
	M. L. Itkina (U.S.S.R.)	Krasnodar, U.S.S.R.	Sept. 12	53·7 sec.
High jump	I. Balas .	Bucharest	Sept. 20	6 ft. 0¼ in.
Shot putt	T. P. Press (U.S.S.R.)	Nalchik, U.S.S.R.	April 26	56 ft. 7 in.
Pentathlon	I. P. Press (U.S.S.R.)	Krasnodar, U.S.S.R.	Sept. 15	4,880 pts.

*Inaugural records.

BADMINTON. The International Badminton federation, 4, Madeira avenue, Bromley, Kent. President, A. C. J. van Vossen; secretary, H. A. E. Scheele. The Badminton Association of England, 4, Madeira avenue, Bromley, Kent. President, Brigadier R. Bruce Hay; secretary, H. A. E. Scheele.

All-England Championships. Men's singles: Tan Joe Hok (Indonesia). Ladies' singles: Miss H. M. Ward (England). Men's doubles: Lim Say Hup and Teh Kew San (Malaya). Ladies' doubles: Mrs. W. C. E. Rogers and Mrs. E. J. Timperley (England). Mixed doubles: P. E. Nielson and Mrs. Inge Birgit Hansen (Denmark).

Other National Championships. Irish championships: m.s., C. T. Coates; *l.s.,* Miss H. M. Ward; *m.d.,* A. D. Jordan and R. J. Lockwood; *l.d.,* Mrs. W. C. E. Rogers and Mrs. E. J. Timperley; *mxd.d.,* A. D. Jordan and Mrs, E. J. Timperley (all of England). *Scottish championships: m.s.,* R. S. McCoig; *l.s.,* Miss W. Tyre; *m.d.,* A. W. Horden and D. Ross; *l.d.,* Miss W. Tyre and Miss M. A. McIntosh; *mxd.d.,* R. S. McCoig and Miss W. Tyre (all of Scotland). *Welsh championships: m.s.,* H. T. Findlay; *l.s.,* Miss H. M. Ward; *m.d.,* A. D. Jordan and H. T. Findlay; *l.d.,* Miss H. M. Ward and Mrs. P. E. Broad; *mxd.d.,* H. T. Findlay and Miss H. M. Ward (all of England). *American championships: m.s.,* Tan Joe Hok (Indonesia); *l.s.,* Miss J. M. Devlin (U.S.); *m.d.,* Lim Say Hup and Teh Kew San (Malaya); *l.d.,* Miss S. F. Devlin and Miss J. M. Devlin (U.S.); *mxd.d.,* M. Roche and Miss J. M. Devlin (U.S.). *Canadian championships: m.s.,* Tan Joe Hok (Indonesia); *l.s.,* Miss J. M. Devlin (U.S.); *m.d.,* Lim Say Hup and Teh Kew San (Malaya); *l.d.,* Miss S. F. Devlin and Miss J. M. Devlin (U.S.); *mxd.d.,* D. P. Davis and Miss J. M. Devlin (U.S.).

International Fixtures. England bt. Scotland, 9-0; bt. Ireland, 9-0; lost to Denmark, 0-7; bt. Sweden, 4-3. Scotland bt. Ireland, 7-2. Denmark bt. Sweden, 6-1. Sweden bt. South Africa, 3 tests to 2: 5-6, 8-3, 7-4, 5-6, 6-5 (in South Africa). Australia bt. New Zealand, 11-3. *Inter-county Championship* final: Surrey (holder) bt. Cheshire, 12-3.

BILLIARDS AND SNOOKER. Billiards Association and Control council, Maxwell house, 11, Arundel street, London, W.C.2. President, Earl of Mexborough; chairman, W. E. Chappell.

English Amateur championships: billiards, L. Driffield (3,803) bt. H. Beetham (2,792); snooker, M. Owen bt. A. Barnett by 11 frames to 5. Professional Snooker tournament: Fred Davis, r.-u. Joe Davis. *Scottish Amateur championships:* billiards, W. Ramage, r.-u. W. Taylor; snooker, J. Phillips, r.-u. E. Sinclair. *Welsh Amateur championships:* billiards, J. Ford, r.-u. E. Marks; snooker, J. R. Price, r.-u. M. Berni. *Northern Ireland Amateur championships:* billiards, W. Hanna, r.-u. W. Dennison; snooker, W. Hanna, r.-u. W. Seeds. *Women's Amateur championships:* billiards, E. Morland-Smith, r.-u. R. Craven; snooker, Rita Holmes, r.-u. M. Hazeldine.

BOWLS. English Bowling association, 2, Roseford road, Cambridge. President, A. J. Alsop; secretary, Edward Sussum.

Internationals. England won the *News of the World* trophy, beating Ireland, Scotland and Wales at Cardiff.

National Championships. Singles, K. Coulson (Croydon, Surrey), r.-u. G. T. Flemming (Middlesbrough Albert Park, Yorks.); pairs, F. J. Harris and M. J. Brayley (Paddington, London), r.-u. R. Harris and D. J. Bryant (Clevedon, Somerset); triples, G. E. Worrell, F. I. Smith and G. W. Scott (Hatfield, Herts.), r.-u. E. S. Hayes, H. Lewry and P. A. Line (Banister Park, Hants.); rink, E. Goodchild, J. Paton, W. Clark and E. Barnard (Princes Risborough, Bucks.), r.-u. F. H. Tonkin, T. H. Tonkin, J. Blewett and J. F. Stafford (Penlee, Cornwall).

BOXING. The British Boxing Board of Control, Ramillies buildings, Hills place, London, W.1. President, J. Onslow Fane; general secretary, E. J. Waltham.

World Champions. Heavyweight, Ingemar Johansson (Sweden); light heavy, Archie Moore (U.S.); middle, Gene Fullmer (U.S.) (recognized by National Boxing association), Sugar Ray Robinson (U.S.) (recognized by New York State); welter, Don Jordan (U.S.); light, Joe Brown (U.S.); feather, Davey Moore (U.S.); bantam, Joe Becerra (Mexico); fly, Pascual Perez (Argentina).

European Champions. Heavyweight, vacant; light heavy, Eric Schoeppner (German Fed. Rep.); middle, Gustav Scholz (German Fed. Rep.); welter, Duilio Loi (Italy); light, vacant; feather, Gracieux Lamperti (France); bantam, Freddie Gilroy (Ireland); fly, Risto Luukkonen (Finland).

British Champions. Heavyweight, Henry Cooper; light heavy, vacant; middle, Terry Downes; welter, Tommy Molloy; light, Dave Charnley; feather, Bobby Neill; bantam, Freddie Gilroy; fly, Frankie Jones.

British Empire Champions. Heavyweight, Henry Cooper (Britain); light heavy, Yvon Durelle (Canada); middle, Dick Tiger (Nigeria); welter, George Barnes (Australia); light, Dave Charnley (Britain); feather, Percy Lewis (Trinidad); bantam, Freddie Gilroy (Ireland); fly, Dennis Adams (South Africa).

Amateur: A.B.A. Champions. Heavyweight, D. Thomas; light heavy, J. Ould; middle, F. Elderfield; light middle, S. Pearson; welter, J. McGrail; light welter, R. Kane; light, P. Warwick; feather, G. Judge; bantam, D. Weller; fly, M. Gushlow.

Amateur Internationals. Scotland 5, England 5 (Glasgow); England 6, Ireland 4 (London); France 7, England 3 (Toulouse); Scotland 8, Norway 2 (Glasgow); Scotland 3, U.S.S.R. 7 (Glasgow); England 8,

German Dem. Rep. 2 (London); England 4, German Dem. Rep. 6 (Brighton).

University Match. Cambridge bt. Oxford by 6 bouts to 3. (For results of other individual contests, *see* BOXING.)

CANOEING. British Canoe union; 3, The Drive, Radlett, Herts. President, Dr. M. Gillies; hon. secretary, J. W. Dudderidge.

Canoe Racing. British Senior Championships. Kayak singles (men): 500 m., E. Szörenyi (Birmingham); 1,000 m., R. Rhodes (Royal). Kayak pairs: 500 m., E. Szörenyi and F. Wagner (Birmingham); 1,000 m., R. Rhodes and R. Lowery (Royal/Richmond). Kayak singles (women): 500 m., M. Chandler (Richmond).

British Junior Championships. Kayak singles: 500 m., 1,000 m., 10,000 m., B. Pratt (Royal). Kayak pairs: 500 m. and 10,000 m., B. Pratt and A. Young (Royal/Richmond); 1,000 m., D. Woolley and J. Harris (Birmingham).

European Championships (at Duisburg). Kayak singles (men): 500 m., S. Kaplaniak (Poland); (women) 500 m., S. Kislova (U.S.S.R.); 1,000 m., Szöllösi (Hungary); 10,000 m., F. Hatlacsky (Hungary); relay race 4× 500 m., P. Lange, Schulze, H. Schneider, M. Miltenberger (German Fed. Rep.). Kayak pairs (men): 500 m., Szente and G. Meszáros (Hungary); (women): 500 m., Kislova and A. Seredina (U.S.S.R.); 1,000 m., Szente and Meszáros (Hungary); 10,000 m., Szöllösi and J. Petroscy (Hungary). Kayak fours: 1,000 m., W. Lange, D. Krause, S. Rossberg, G. Perleberg (German Dem. Rep.); 10,000 m., M. Scheur, G. Lietzi, H. Hell, T. Kleine (German Dem. Rep.). Canadian singles, 1,000 m., S. Ismailciuc (Rumania); 10,000 m., J. Párti (Hungary); Canadian pairs, 1,000 m., Domotor and J. Hunics (Hungary); 10,000 m., S. Oshchepkov and V. Silaev (U.S.S.R.).

Slalom. British Slalom Championships. British champion: I. Carmichael (Twickenham).

World Slalom Championships (at Geneva). Class F.1 (men): individual: P. Farrant (Britain); team: German Dem. Rep. Class F.1 (women): individual: H. Urbaniak (German Dem. Rep.); team: German Dem. Rep. Class C.1: individual: V. Jirasek (Czechoslovakia); team: Czechoslovakia. Class C.2: individual: Friedrich and Kleinert (German Dem. Rep.); team: German Dem. Rep. Class C.2 (mixed): Behrend and Market (German Dem. Rep.).

World Championship in Wild Water Racing (at Treignac, France). Class F.1 (men): T. Prijon (German Fed. Rep.). Class F.1 (women): R. Biesinger (German Fed. Rep.). Class C.1 M. Schubert (German Dem. Rep.). Class C.2 Dransart and Turlier (France). Class C.2 (mixed): M. and Mme Malicet (France).

CHESS. British Chess federation, 5, Clifford road, Hounslow, Middlesex. President, Sir Leonard Swinnerton Dyer; secretary, A. F. Stammwitz.

World Championship. Team: U.S.S.R. retained the world title at Munich with 34½ out of 44, followed by Yugoslavia and Argentina. England finished 11th out of 34 countries. Junior: C. Bielicki (Argentina); David Rumens (England) finished third.

C. Bielicki of Argentina (left), winner of the junior world chess championship, is congratulated by David Rumens (G.B.)

Major Tournament Winners. Hastings: W. Uhlmann (German Dem. Rep.). Mar del Plata: M. Najdorf (Argentina) and L. Pachman (Czechoslovakia). Zürich: M. Tal (U.S.S.R.).

British Tournaments. At York, H. Golombek, M. J. Haygarth and J. Penrose tied for the British championship. Bognor: D. V. Mardle and E. Gereben. Ilford: C. Kottnauer. Whitby: D. Janosevic (Yugoslavia). Cambridge university drew with Oxford university 3½-3½. Counties championship: Lancashire bt. Middlesex 8-4. National Club championship: Cheltenham bt. Leicester 5-1.

CONTRACT BRIDGE. British Bridge league, 19, Hertford street, London, W.1. Chairman, G. L. Butler; secretary, A. Truscott. English Bridge union, 12, Frant road, Tunbridge Wells, Kent. Chairman, R. F. Corwen; secretary, Mrs. A. L. Fleming.

Italy won a three-cornered match for the world championship. The United States was second and Argentina third.

European championship: 1. Italy, 2. France, 3. Great Britain, 4. Sweden. British team: J. T. Reese, B. Schapiro, K. W. Konstam, A. Meredith, J. Lazarus, B. Franks, J. Tarlo (non-playing captain). Ladies championship: 1. Great Britain, 2. Belgium, 3. France. British team: Mrs. R. Markus, Mrs. M. Whitaker, Mrs. F. Gordon, Mrs. A. L. Fleming, Mrs. G. E. Higginson, Mrs. M. Edwards, E. Leader-Williams (non-playing captain).

Gold cup: J. Lazarus, B. Franks, S. Blaser, I. Morris, F. Farrington. Waddington cup for masters pairs: J. T. Reese and B. Schapiro.

CRICKET. Marylebone Cricket club, Lord's Cricket ground, London, N.W.8. President, H. S. Altham; secretary, R. Aird.

Test Matches. *England* v. *Australia.* At Brisbane: England 134 and 198, Australia 186 and 147 for 2; Australia won by 8 wickets. At Melbourne: England 259 and 87, Australia 308 and 42 for 2; Australia won by 8 wickets. At Sydney: England 219 and 287 for 7 (dec.), Australia 357 and 54 for 2; match drawn. At Adelaide: Australia 476 and 36 for 0, England 240 and 270; Australia won by 10 wickets. At Melbourne, England 205 and 214, Australia 351 and 70 for 1; Australia won by 9 wickets. *England* v. *India.* At Nottingham: England 422, India 206 and 157; England won by an innings and 59 runs. At Lord's: England 226 and 108 for 2, India 168 and 165; England won by 8 wickets. At Leeds: England 483 for 8 (dec.), India 161 and 149; England won by an innings and 173 runs. At Manchester: England 490 and 265 for 8 (dec.), India 208 and 376; England won by 171 runs. At the Oval: England 361, India 140 and 194; England won by an innings and 27 runs.

Other Matches. Players 396 and 16 for 0, Gentlemen 293 and 115; Players won by 10 wickets. Oxford university 217 and 238, Cambridge university 174 and 196; Oxford won by 85 runs. (*See also* CRICKET.)

LEADING FIRST-CLASS AVERAGES FOR THE 1959 SEASON
Batting

	Inns.	N.O.	R.	Highest	Av.
M. J. K. Smith	67	11	3,245	200*	57·94
Watson, W.	50	10	2,212	173	55·30
Pullar, G.	55	7	2,647	161	55·14
Barrington, K. F.	52	6	2,499	186	54·32
Wight, P. B.	39	3	1,930	222*	53·61
Edrich, J. H.	45	11	1,799	126	52·91
Parks, J. M.	56	11	2,313	157*	51·40
M. C. Cowdrey	44	4	2,008	250	50·20
Parkhouse, W. G. A.	49	3	2,243	154	48·76
Horton, H.	59	8	2,428	140*	47·60
P. B. H. May.	16	2	663	143	47·35
T. E. Bailey.	55	12	2,011	146	46·76
R. Subba Row	46	5	1,917	183*	46·75
Illingworth, R.	50	13	1,726	162	46·64
E. R. Dexter.	53	8	2,055	127	45·66
D. J. Insole.	50	5	2,045	180	45·44
Horton, M. J.	58	3	2,468	212	44·87
D. B. Carr.	60	8	2,292	156*	44·07
J. Aitchison.	8	1	301	190*	43·00
Graveney, T. W.	30	5	1,062	155*	42·48

* Not out.

Bowling

	O.	M.	R.	W.	Av.
Statham, J. B.	997·4	267	2,087	139	15·01
Allen, D. A.	635·5	286	1,322	84	15·73
Sydenham, D. A. D.	174·4	41	399	25	15·96
J. J. Warr	804·5	218	1,793	109	16·49
Jackson, H. L.	1,168·5	349	2,461	140	17·57
Thompson, R. G.	789·1	204	1,743	97	17·96
McConnon, J. E.	799·1	202	2,059	113	18·22
Mortimore, J. B.	1,091·3	472	2,066	113	18·28
Cook, C.	932·4	405	1,850	101	18·31
Moss, A. E.	785·5	228	1,796	96	18·70
Loader, P. J.	829·1	163	2,196	115	19·09
Trueman, F. S.	1,072·4	269	2,730	140	19·50
Tyson, F. H.	702·5	180	1,726	88	19·61
Suttle, K. G.	81·0	13	237	12	19·75
Hitchcock, R. E.	153·4	50	374	18	20·77

INDIA AVERAGES
(Played 33. Won 6. Lost 11. Drawn 16.)
Batting

	Inns.	N.O.	R.	Highest	Av.
V. L. Manjrekar	14	3	755	204*	68·63
P. R. Umrigar	38	5	1,826	252*	55·33
D. K. Gaekwad	38	4	1,174	176	34·52
A. G. Kripal Singh	29	3	879	187	33·80
A. A. Baig	23	2	673	116	32·04
N. J. Contractor	40	2	1,183	114	31·13
P. Roy	47	5	1,207	155	28·73
A. L. Apte	34	2	881	165	27·53
C. G. Borde	46	7	1,060	90	27·17
J. M. Ghorpade	37	2	833	70	23·80
R. G. Nadkarni	41	1	945	80	23·62
M. L. Jaisimha	39	4	824	83*	23·54
N. S. Tamhane	20	2	275	34	15·27
P. G. Joshi	29	3	336	72	12·92
R. Surendra Nath	34	13	226	27	10·76
V. M. Muddiah	13	6	71	46*	10·14
R. B. Desai	29	12	158	23	9·29

* Not out.

Bowling

	O.	M.	R.	W.	Av.
C. G. Borde	512·3	119	1,485	72	20·62
S. P. Gupte	901·2	231	2,526	95	26·58
R. G. Nadkarni	729·5	286	1,563	55	28·41
R. Surendra Nath	901·4	274	2,260	79	28·60
V. M. Muddiah	309·1	82	884	30	29·46
P. R. Umrigar	368·0	87	875	24	36·45
R. B. Desai	600·4	125	1,864	45	41·42
M. L. Jaisimha	402·1	66	1,450	29	50·00
A. G. Kripal Singh	193·0	42	568	10	56·80
J. M. Ghorpade	42·0	6	172	2	86·00

1959 COUNTY CHAMPIONSHIP FINAL POSITIONS

| | | | | | | First innings lead in match | | | |
| | | | | | | No. | | Bonus | |
Points awarded .	P.	W.	L.	D.	T.	dec.	L.	D.	pts.	Pts.
	—	12	—	—	6		2	2	2	—
1. Yorkshire .	28	14	7	7	0	0	0	5	26	204
2. Gloucestershire	28	12	11	4	1	0	1	3	28	186
3. Surrey .	28	12	5	11	0	0	0	8	26	186
4. Warwickshire .	28	13	10	5	0	0	2	1	22	184
5. Lancashire .	28	12	7	9	0	0	1	5	28	184
6. Glamorgan .	28	12	8	7	0	1	3	4	20	178
7. Derbyshire .	28	12	6	10	0	0	3	2	20	174
8. Hampshire .	28	11	10	7	0	0	1	4	26	168
9. Essex .	28	11	7	9	1	0	0	4	22	168
10. Middlesex .	28	10	9	9	0	0	3	3	24	157
11. Northamptonshire.	28	8	10	10	0	0	4	9	24	146
12. Somerset .	28	8	13	7	0	0	4	3	20	130
13. Kent .	28	8	12	8	0	0	2	5	18	128
14. Worcestershire .	28	6	8	13	0	0	1	7	18	106
15. Sussex .	28	6	11	10	0	1	3	3	18	102
16. Leicestershire .	28	5	16	7	0	0	0	2	8	72
17. Nottinghamshire .	28	4	14	9	0	1	1	3	6	62

Middlesex's record includes one point for tie on first innings in match lost.

CROQUET. The Croquet association, The Hurlingham club, London, S.W.6. President, Sir Compton Mackenzie; chairman of the council, Brig. A. E. Stokes-Roberts; secretary, Mrs. V. C. Gasson.

Men's championship, J. W. Solomon; women's championship, Mrs. E. Rotherham; mixed doubles championship, Dr. W. R. D. Wiggins and Mrs. E. Rotherham; open championship, J. W. Solomon; doubles, E. P. C. Cotter and J. W. Solomon.

President's cup, J. W. Solomon. Ladies Field cup, Miss E. J. Warwick. All England handicap winner, N. F. Blackwood (Brighton).

CYCLING. British Cycling federation, 21, Blackfriars road, London, S.E.21. Road Time Trials council; secretary, S. A. Amey, 21, Little Crabtree, Crawley, Sussex.

International Road Races. *World Road Championships.* Professional: 1. A. Darrigade (France), 2. M. Gismondi (Italy), 3. N. Fore (Belgium), 4. T. Simpson (G.B.). Amateur: 1. G. Shur (German Dem. Rep.), 2. E. Maliepaard (Netherlands), 3. H. Goosens (Belgium). Women: 1. Y. Reynders (Belgium), 2. R. Vissac (France). Tour de France: F. Bahamontes (Spain). B. Robinson (G.B.) won the 20th stage by more than 20 min., the biggest post-war victory margin in any stage.

World Track Championships. Professional sprint: A. Maspes (Italy). Amateur sprint: A. Gasporella (Italy). Women's sprint: G. Ermolaeva (U.S.S.R.). Professional pursuit: R. Riviere (France). Amateur pursuit: R. Altig (German Fed. Rep.). Women's pursuit: B. Burton (G.B.). Professional motor-paced: G. Timoner (Spain). Amateur motor-paced: A. Van Hovwelingen (Netherlands).

Road Time Trials Council National Champions. *Men.* 25 mi., G. Ian (Notts Wh.) 56 min. 3 sec.; 50 mi., M. Ward (Haverhill Wh.) 1 hr. 57 min. 22 sec.; 100 mi., R. C. Booty (Ericsson Wh.) 4 hr. 4 min. 25 sec.; 12 hr., P. Beswick (Manchester Vic. Wh.) 263·05 mi.; 24 hr., R. Coukham (Rutland C.C.) 469·17 mi.; hill-climb, G. Rhodes (Huddersfield Wh.). British Best All-rounder, B. F. Wiltcher (Zeus R.C.). *Women.* 25 mi., B. Burton (Morley C.C.) 1 hr. 3 min. 44 sec.; 50 mi., B. Burton (Morley C.C.) 2 hr. 6 min. 38 sec.; 100 mi., B. Burton (Morley C.C.) 4 hr. 20 min. 4 sec. British Best All-rounder, B. Burton (Morley C.C.).

Road Time Trials Council Competition Records (as at Dec. 31, 1959). *Men.* 25 mi., R. A. Engers (Barnet C.C.) 55 min. 11 sec.; 30 mi., R. G. A. Jowers (Twickenham C.C.) 1 hr. 7 min. 30 sec.; 50 mi., B. F. Wiltcher (Zeus R.C.) 1 hr. 53 min. 56 sec.; 100 mi., R. C. Booty (Ericsson Wh.) 3 hr. 58 min. 28 sec.; 12 hr., O. G. Blower (Leicestershire R.C.) 271·8 mi.; 24 hr., D. H. White (Swindon Wh.) 484·75 mi. *Women.* 25 mi., B. Burton (Morley C.C.) 1 hr. 1 min. 27 sec.; 50 mi., B. Burton (Morley C.C.) 2 hr. 6 min. 38 sec.; 100 mi., B. Burton (Morley C.C.) 4 hr. 20 min. 4 sec.; 12 hr., B. Burton (Morley C.C.) 250·37 mi.

B.C.F. National Hard Track Champions. *Men.* Sprint, L. Binch (Notts Castle Bi.C.); 10 mi., D. Skene (Byways R.C.C.); 1,000 m. tandem, D. Handley (Polytechnic C.C.) and P. Carter (Kentish Wh.); 4,000 m. individual pursuit: N. Sheil (Melling Wh.); 4,000 m. team pursuit: Clarence Wh. *Women.* Sprint, J. Dunn (Middx. Clarion); 3,000 m. pursuit, D. Johnson (Skipton C.C.).

Other Events. Tour of Britain: W. Bradley (Southport R.C.C.). B.C.F. amateur road championship: W. Baty (Tyne Velo R.C.). B.C.F. independent-professional road championship: R. Coe (Elswick-Hopper Cycles). Isle of Man amateur international: J. F. Hinds (Southern Roads C.C.). Isle of Man Premier professional race: S. Elliott (Ireland).

FENCING. Amateur Fencing association, 1a, Tenterden street, Hanover square, London, W.1. President, C.-L. de Beaumont; hon. secretary, Mrs. M. A. Glen Haig.

British Championships. Ladies' foil, Miss M. Stafford; men's foil, H. W. F. Hoskyns; épée, A. L. N. Jay; sabre, M. J. Amberg. Team championships: ladies' foil, London F.C.; men's foil, Salle Paul; épée, Lansdowne club; sabre, Army F.U. International cups: ladies' foil (C.-L. de Beaumont cup), Miss G. M. Sheen; men's foil (Coronation cup), H. W. F. Hoskyns; épée (Miller-Hallett cup), J. Simpson; sabre (Corble cup), D. D. Stringer. Junior championships: ladies' foil, Miss

Kamuti (left), Hungarian winner of the foils contest in the students games at Turin in August, in a bout with Ryumin (U.S.S.R.).

J. Browne; men's foil, G. B. Leckie; épée, G. B. Filmer; sabre, G. Talkington.

World Championships. Ladies' foil teams, Hungary; men's foil teams, U.S.S.R.; épée teams, Hungary; sabre teams, Poland; ladies' foil individual, E. Efimova (U.S.S.R.); men's foil individual, A. L. N. Jay (G.B.); épée individual, B. Khabarov (U.S.S.R.); sabre individual, R. Karpati (Hungary).

FIVES. Rugby Fives association, 109, Ridgeway drive, Bromley, Kent. President, John Armitage; hon. secretary, R. A. Colville. The Eton Fives association, 31, Gresham street, London, E.C.2. President, R. G. De Quetteville; hon. secretary, P. C. Curtis.

Rugby Fives. Open championships: singles (Jesters' Club cup), J. N. H. Smith bt. E. Marsh, 15-4, 15-11; doubles (Cyriax cup), J. F. Pretlove and D. R. W. Silk bt. D. E. Gardner and S. Holt, 15-10, 8-15, 15-9.

Scottish championships: singles (Cuthbertson quaich), D. E. Gardner bt. A. I. F. Mackenzie, 15-8, 15-4; doubles (Scottish doubles cup), D. E. Gardner and S. Holt bt. A. I. F. Mackenzie and J. MacNaughton,

8-15, 15-6, 15-5. University match: Cambridge bt. Oxford 270-195.

Schools: singles (Jesters' cup), J. T. Watkinson bt. S. V. Bevan, 11-3, 11-2; doubles (Mappin cup), Blundells bt. Whitgift, 11-4, 11-9. West of England Schools' tournament: singles, J. T. Watkinson bt. G. B. Todd, 11-4, 6-11, 11-5; doubles, Bristol G.S. bt. Blundells, 11-0, 11-7.

Eton Fives. Amateur championship (Kinnaird cup): D. J. S. Guilford and M. J. Shorthand-Jones; r.-u. D. R. S. Saunders and M. L. Y. Ainsworth. Public Schools championship: Aldenham (D. R. Barker and U. Mohammadu); r.-u. Eton. University match: Cambridge.

GLIDING. International governing body: Fédération Aéronautique Internationale, 6, rue Galilée, Paris (XVI). President, Miss J. Cochran; director-general, H. R. Gillman. Gliding commission: President, A. Gehriger; secretary, R. Cartier. British national governing body: British Gliding association, 19, Park lane, London, W.1. President, Viscount Kemsley; chairman, P. A. Wills; secretary, Miss A. E. Russell.

British National Championships—from Lasham, Hants (May 9-18). The more experienced pilots competed in League I. Champion, G. H. Stephenson (Skylark III), 490 pts.; 2, and inter-services champion, Commander H. C. N. Goodhart (Skylark III), 475 pts.; 3, D. H. G. Ince (Olympia 419X), 452 pts. League II: 1, Mrs. R. Harwood, B. Masters, H. Mettam (Skylark III), 464 pts. Inter-Services Team contest: R.A.F.

U.S. National Soaring Competitions—at Elmira, New York State. 1. R. H. Johnson (Weihe).

French Championships—at St. Yan. 1, M. Labar (Bréguet 901).

German Championships—at Forchheim. Open class: 1, E. G. Haase (HKS 3); standard class: 1, H. Huth (Ka-6).

Netherlands Championships—at Terlet. 1, P. A. Wills (G.B.) (Skylark III).

Italian Championships—at Rieti. 1, L. Brigliadori (Urendo).

British National Aerobatic Championships—at Dunstable (Sept. 20). 1, Flight Lieut. B. B. Sharman (Olympia 419).

Victor Boin International Distance Challenge—at Gosselies, Belgium. 1, D. H. G. Ince (G.B.) (Olympia 419X).

During the British championships (May 10), Cdr. H. C. N. Goodhart flew 360 mi. from Lasham to his declared goal at Portmoak, Scotland; this was at the time not only the best distance, goal and speed over 500 km. flight recorded in the United Kingdom, but the British national best in the first two respects. But on June 6, in France, Lieut-Commander G. A. J. Goodhart (his brother) achieved a new British distance mark by covering 384 mi. (Fontainebleau-Pau), flying a Bréguet Fauvette. Also on May 10, Mrs. A. Burns, flying the same type of sailplane as H. C. N. Goodhart (Slingsby Skylark III), flew 282 mi. from Lasham to Bellingham, Northumberland—a British women's distance record. Mrs. A. Welch set up a British women's goal record of 221 mi. in France on Aug. 4.

GOLF. Royal and Ancient club, St. Andrews, Fifeshire, Scotland. Captain, Lord Morton of Henryton; secretary, Brigadier E. Brickman. English Golf union, 34, Aldridge avenue, Edgware, Middlesex. President, W. I. Boulton; secretary, Captain W. G. L. Folkard. Ladies' Golf union, Sandilands, Sandwich bay, Kent. Secretary, Miss M. Thornton.

Principal British and Irish Events. Open championship, G. Player (South Africa); Amateur championship, D. Beman (U.S.); Women's championship, Miss E. Price; English championship, G. Wolstenholme; English Women's championship, Miss R. Porter; English Open Stroke Play championship, D. Sewell; Scottish championship, F. W. G. Deighton; Scottish Ladies' championship, Miss J. Robertson; Irish championship, T. Craddock; Irish Open Amateur championship, J. Duncan; Irish Women's championship, Miss P. Garvey; Welsh championship, H. C. Squirrell; Welsh Women's championship, Miss P. Roberts.

Professional Events. P.G.A. championship, D. J. Rees; Dunlop masters, C. O'Connor; *News of the World* Match Play championship, D. Snell; Daks tournament, C. O'Connor; Dunlop tournament, P. Alliss; Spalding tournament, E. Lester and H. Henning; Swallow-Penfold tournament, P. J. Butler; *Yorkshire Evening News* tournament, N. V. Drew; Sherwood Forest foursomes; D. J. Rees and D. Smalldon.

European Championships. Belgian open, not held; Dutch open, P. Sewgolum (S.A.); French open, D. Thomas (G.B.); German open, K. Bousfield (G.B.); Italian open, P. W. Thomson (Aus.); Portuguese open, S. Miguel (Spain); Spanish open, P. W. Thomson (Aus.); Swiss open, D. J. Rees (G.B.).

Principal United States Events. Open championship, W. Casper; Amateur championship, J. Nicklaus; Women's Open championship, Miss M. Wright; Women's Amateur championship, Miss B. McIntire; Masters tournament, A. Wall; P.G.A. championship, R. Rosburg. (*See also* GOLF.)

GREYHOUND RACING. National Greyhound Racing club, 11, Albemarle street, London, W.1. Senior steward, Marquess of Carisbrooke; secretary, Lieut.-Col. W. T. Forsdike.

Principal Race Winners. Greyhound Derby, Mile Bush Pride; Scottish Derby, Mile Bush Pride; Irish Derby, Sir Frederick; Welsh Derby, Mile Bush Pride; Laurels, Mighty Hassan; St. Leger, Wincot

Clifford; Select Stakes, Mile Bush Pride; Grand National, Prince Poppit; Scurry Cup, Gorey Airways; Gold Collar, Dunstown Warrior; Cloth of Gold, Coolkill Racket; 1,000 Guineas, Town Prince.

GYMNASTICS. Amateur Gymnastic association, 2, Ormesby way, Kenton, Harrow, Middlesex. President, the Earl of Gainsborough; hon. secretary, F. Edmonds.

Men's Individual Championship. W. Stuart, 114·5 pts.; R. Gradley, 113·6 pts.; P. Starling, 107·4 pts. *Women's Individual Championship.* G. Lingard, 223·7 pts.; M. Neale, 216·9 pts.; P. Perks, 213·0 pts. *International Matches* (mixed). Sweden 184·3 pts.; G.B. 182 pts.; England 102·2 pts.; Wales 101·4 pts.

HOCKEY. Men: Hockey association: president, S. H. Saville; hon. secretary, W. Comben Longstaff, 24, St. Mary Axe, London, E.C.3. Women: All-England Women's Hockey association, 24, John street, Bedford row, London, W.C.1. President, Miss M. J. Lodge; secretary, Mrs. M. Macdonald.

Men. International championship results: Ireland 1, Wales 0; Wales 0, England 5; Scotland 1, Ireland 3; England 1, Scotland 1; Ireland 1, England 2; Wales 2, Scotland 0.

International Championship Summary

						Goals	
	P.	W.	D.	L.	For	Agst.
England	3	2	1	0	8	2
Ireland	3	2	0	1	5	3
Wales	3	1	0	2	2	6
Scotland	3	0	1	2	2	6

Other internationals: Scotland 2, Belgium 1; Gt. Britain 0, Belgium 1; England 0, Holland 3. Representative matches: Irish Schools 2, Scottish Schools 1; English Schools 1, Irish Schools 2.

County Championship. Semi-finals: Gloucestershire 4, Lancashire 2; Middlesex 7, Staffordshire 0. Final: Gloucestershire 1, Middlesex 2.

The Divisions

					Goals	
	P.	W.	D.	L.	For	Agst.
South .	2	2	0	0	9	5
Services .	2	2	0	0	7	4
Midlands	2	1	0	1	7	7
North .	1	0	0	1	4	5
East .	1	0	0	1	1	4
West .	2	0	0	2	1	4

Services Championship

					Goals	
	P.	W.	D.	L.	For	Agst.
R.A.F. .	2	2	0	0	6	1
Army .	2	1	0	1	6	3
R. Navy	2	0	0	2	0	8

In the University match Oxford and Cambridge drew 0-0.

Women. Home international matches: England 8, Ireland 2; Wales 3, Scotland 0; Scotland 0, England 7; Wales 0, Ireland 2; Ireland 6, Scotland 2; England 6, Wales 1. Other internationals: England 4, S. Africa 1; Scotland 2, S. Africa 2; England 1, Australia 1; Ireland 1, S. Africa 2; Ireland 3, New Zealand 1.

International Summary

					Goals	
	P.	W.	D.	L.	For	Agst.
England	3	3	0	0	21	3
Ireland	3	2	0	1	10	10
Wales .	3	1	0	2	4	8
Scotland	3	0	0	3	2	16

Territorial Records

					Goals	
	P.	W.	D.	L.	For	Agst.
Midlands	4	4	0	0	13	7
North .	4	2	1	1	6	5
West .	4	2	0	2	7	7
South .	4	1	1	2	9	9
East .	4	0	0	4	4	11

(*See* also Hockey.)

HORSE RACING. Flat racing: Jockey club. Senior stewards, Duke of Roxburghe; secretary, E. W. Weatherby. Steeplechasing and hurdling: National Hunt committee. Senior steward, John Rogerson; secretary, Messrs. Weatherby and Sons, 15, Cavendish square, London, W.1., who act for both bodies.

Classic Races. All 3-yr.-olds, carrying 9 st. Two Thousand guineas (£15,341, 1 mi.): Taboun (owned by Prince Aly Khan, trained by A. Head, in France, ridden by G. Moore, betting 5-2 against), 2. Masham, 3. Carnoustie; 3 lengths, neck. One Thousand guineas (£13,254, 1 mi.): Petite Etoile (o. Aly Khan, t. N. Murless, r. D. Smith, 8-1), 2. Rosalba, 3. Paraguana; 1 l., 4 l. Derby (£36,078, 1½ mi.): Parthia (o. Sir H. de Trafford, t. C. Boyd-Rochfort, r. W. H. Carr, 10-1), 2. Fidalgo, 3. Shantung; 1½ l., 1½ l. Oaks (£21,155, 1½ mi.): Petite Etoile (as above, r. L. Piggott, 11-2), 2. Cantelo, 3. Rose of Medina; 3 l., 5 l. St. Leger (£28,636, 1 mi. 6 f. 132 yd.): Cantelo (o. W. Hill, t. C. F. Elsey, r. E. Hide, 100-7), 2. Fidalgo, 3. Pindari; 1½ l., 3 l.

Some Weight-for-Age and Handicap Races. Lincolnshire handicap (£3,299, 1 mi.): Marshal Pil, 5 yr., 7 st. 13 lb. (o. S. C. Lip, t. S. Hall, r. P. Robinson, 15-2), 2. Precious Heather, Chalk Stream; ¾ l., dead heat. Ascot Gold cup (£10,950, 2½ mi.): Wallaby II, 4 yr., 9 st. (o. Baron G. de Waldner, t. P. Carter, in France, r. F. Palmer, 9-4), 2. Alcide, 3. French Beige; short head, ¾ l. King George VI and Queen Elizabeth stakes (£23,642, 1½ mi.): Alcide, 4 yr., 9 st. 7 lb. (o. Sir H. de Trafford, t. Boyd-Rochfort, r. Carr, 2-1), 2. Gladness, 3. Balbo; 2 l., ¾ l. Cesarewitch stakes (£3,854, 2¼ mi.): Come to Daddy, 4 yr., 7 st. 8 lb. (o. T. H. Farr, t. W. Lyde, r. D. Smith, 6-1), 2. Seascape, 3. Bali Ha'i III; 5 l., 1½ l. Cambridgeshire stakes (£4,071, 1 mi. 1 f.): Rexequus, 3 yr., 8 st. 7 lb. (o. J. N. Adam, t. G. Boyd, r. N. Stirk, 25-1), 2. Anthelion, 3. Thames Trader; ½ l., hd.

Leading Owners, Breeders, Trainers, Sires and Jockeys. Leading

owners: Aly Khan, £100,668 (13 races by 7 horses); Sir H. de Trafford, £68,681 (8 by 3); Queen Elizabeth II, £38,154 (8 by 3). Leading breeders: Aly Khan and the late Aga Khan, £100,668 (13 by 7); Sir H. de Trafford, £70,750 (12 by 6); Sezincourt stud, £40,541 (12 by 6). Leading trainers: Murless, £145,726 (63 by 32); Boyd-Rochfort, £109,406 (34 by 19); Elsey, £67,824 (60 by 33). Leading sires: Petition, £75,921 (44 by 21); Alycidon, £60,258 (40 by 21); Persian Gulf, £60,068 (27 by 15). Leading jockeys: D. Smith (first 157, second 140, third 114, mounts 828); A. Breasley (150, 101, 83, 554); Piggott (142, 96, 85, 559).

Racing Abroad. The French Derby (Prix du Jockey Club) was won by Herbager and the Prix de l'Arc de Triomphe by Saint Crespin III. The Irish Derby was won by Fidalgo. In the United States the Kentucky Derby was won by Tomy Lee and the Washington International by Bald Eagle (U.S.) from Midnight Sun (France) and Tudor Era (U.S.).

National Hunt. Champion hurdle (£4,587, 2 mi. 125 yd.): Fare Time, 6 yr., 12 st. (o. G. C. Judd, t. H. Price, r. F. Winter, 13-2), 2. Ivy Green, 3. Prudent King; 4 l., 1 l. Cheltenham Gold cup steeplechase (£5,363, 3 mi. 2 f. 130 yd.): Roddy Owen, 10 yr., 12 st. (o. Lord Fingall, t. D. J. Morgan, in Ireland, r. H. Beasley, 5-1), 2. Linwell, 3. Lochroe; 3 l., 10 l. Grand National steeplechase (£13,646, 4. mi 856 yd.): Oxo, 8 yr., 10 st. 13 lb. (o. J. E. B. Bigg, t. W. Stephenson, r. M. Scudamore, 8-1), 2. Wyndburgh, 3. Mr. What; 1½ l., 8 l. (*See* also Horse Racing.)

ICE HOCKEY. British Ice Hockey association, Empire house, 175, Piccadilly, London, W.1. President, Air Vice-Marshal Sir Victor Tait; secretary, J. F. Ahearne.

Great Britain. Autumn cup: 1. Brighton Tigers, 2. Murrayfield Royals, 3. Paisley Pirates. British league: 1. Paisley Pirates, 2. Wembley Lions, 3. Brighton Tigers. Southampton tournament: 1. Southampton Vikings, 2. Glasgow Flyers. Northern Amateur tournament: 1. Durham Wasps, 2. Whitley Bees.

World and European Championships—Oslo: 1. Canada, 2. U.S.S.R., 3. Czechoslovakia, 4. United States, 5. Sweden, 6. Finland.

ICE SKATING. National Skating Association of Great Britain, Charterhouse, London, E.C.1. President, Major K. M. Beaumont; secretary, E. G. Coggins.

World Championships. Figures: men, D. Jenkins (U.S.); ladies, Miss C. Heiss (U.S.); pairs, Miss B. Wagner and R. Paul (Canada). Dance: Miss D. D. Denny and C. J. L. Jones (G.B.). Speed: men, J. Jarvinen (Finland); ladies, Miss T. Rylova (U.S.S.R.).

European Championships. Figures: men, D. Divin (Czechoslovakia); ladies, Miss H. Walter (Austria); pairs, Miss M. Kilius and H. Bäumler (Ger. Fed. Rep.). Dance: Miss D. D. Denny and C. J. L. Jones. Speed: men, K. Johannesen (Norway).

British Amateur Championships. Figures: men, D. W. Clements; ladies, Miss P. A. Pauley; pairs, Miss J. Coates and A. Holles. Dance: Miss D. D. Denny and C. J. L. Jones. Speed (indoor): ¼ mi., J. T. Dymock, 42·5 sec.; ½ mi., A. Hunt, 1 min. 24·6 sec.; 1 mi., Dymock, 3 min. 19·4 sec.; 3 mi. relay, Birmingham M.I.R.C., 8 min. 8·10 sec.

LACROSSE. English Lacrosse union, 92, Chelmsford road, London, N.14. President, J. Winkley Heaword; hon. secretary, K. O. Peachey. All England Ladies Lacrosse association, 7, Rowhill mansions, Rowhill road, London, E.5. President, Miss R. L. Moresby White; hon. secretary, Mrs. Dorothy Stokes.

Men. North bt. South, Kent bt. Middlesex, Lancashire bt. Cheshire, Cambridge university bt. Oxford university. In the English Club championships Heaton Mersey bt. Cambridge university.

Flag competition winners. North: senior, Heaton Mersey; junior, Offerton. South: senior, Cambridge university; intermediate, Purley II; junior, Kenton Juniors.

Ladies. International matches: England bt. Ireland, Scotland and Wales. Territorial matches: East bt. South, North and Midlands; West bt. East, Midlands and South; North bt. West and South; South bt. Midlands; Midlands bt. North. Club and College tournament: Bedford C.P.E. and Reigate L.L.C. drew in the final. Schools' tournaments: Wycombe Abbey bt. Malvern; Westonbirt bt. Moreton hall; Benenden bt. Queen Anne's.

LAWN TENNIS. Lawn Tennis association, Palliser road, London, W.14. President, Duke of Devonshire; secretary, S. B. Reay.

Australian Championships. Men's singles: A. Olmedo (U.S.) bt. N. A. Fraser (Aus.) 3-1; Women's singles: Mrs. S. J. Reitano (Aus.) bt. Miss E. Schuurman (S. Africa) 2-0; Men's doubles: R. Mark and R. Laver (Aus.) bt. R. N. Howe and D. Candy (Aus.) 3-0; Women's doubles: Miss S. Reynolds and Miss Schuurman (S. Africa) bt. Miss L. Coghlan and Mrs. Reitano (Aus.) 2-0; Mixed doubles: Mark and Miss Reynolds bt. Laver and Miss Schuurman 2-1.

British Hard Court Championships. *m.s.,* L. A. Gerrard (N.Z.) bt. W. A. Knight (G.B.) 3-2; *w.s.,* Miss A. Mortimer (G.B.) bt. Miss C. C. Truman (G.B.) 2-1; *m.d.,* G. L. Forbes and A. Segal (S. Africa) bt. Knight and J. A. Pickard (G.B.) 3-0; *w.d.,* Miss Mortimer and Miss P. E. Ward (G.B.) bt. Miss S. J. Bloomer and Miss Truman (G.B.) 2-0; *mxd.d.,* Knight and Miss Bloomer walked over M. G. Davies (G.B.) and Miss Truman.

French Championships. *m.s.,* N. Pietrangeli (Italy) bt. I. C. Vermaak (S. Africa) 3-1; *w.s.,* Miss C. C. Truman (G.B.) bt. Mrs. S. Körmözsy

Donald Campbell taking his jet-propelled craft " Bluebird " out to the course on Coniston Water, Lancashire, on May 14, when he raised his own world water speed record of 248·62 m.p.h. to 260·35 m.p.h. This was his fifth successful record bid within four years.

(Hungary) 2-0; *m.d.*, Pietrangeli and O. Sirola (Italy) bt. R. Emerson and N. A. Fraser (Aus.) 3-0; *w.d.*, Miss S. Reynolds and Miss R. Schuurman (S. Africa) bt. Miss Y. Ramirez and Miss R. M. Reyes (Mexico) 2-1; *mxd.d.*, W. A. Knight (G.B.) and Miss Ramirez bt. R. Laver (Aus.) and Miss Schuurman 2-0.

Wimbledon Championships. *m.s.*, A. Olmedo (U.S.) bt. R. Laver (Aus.) 3-0; *w.s.*, Miss M. E. Bueno (Brazil) bt. Miss D. R. Hard (U.S.) 2-0; *m.d.*, R. Emerson and N. A. Fraser (Aus.) bt. Laver and R. Mark (Aus.) 3-1; *w.d.*, Miss J. Arth and Miss Hard (U.S.) bt. Mrs. J. G. Fleitz (U.S.) and Miss C. C. Truman (G.B.) 2-1; *mxd.d.*, Laver and Miss Hard bt. Fraser and Miss Bueno 2-0.

U.S. National Championships. *m.s.*, N. A. Fraser (Aus.) bt. A. Olmedo (U.S.) 3-1; *w.s.*, Miss M. E. Bueno (Brazil) bt. Miss C. C. Truman (G.B.) 2-0; *m.d.*, R. Emerson and Fraser (Aus.) bt. E. Buchholz and Olmedo (U.S.) 3-2; *w.d.*, Miss J. Arth and Miss D. R. Hard (U.S.) bt. Miss Bueno and Miss S. Moore (U.S.) 2-0; *mxd.d.*, Fraser and Mrs. W. du Pont (U.S.) bt. R. Mark (Aus.) and Miss J. Hopps (U.S.) 2-1.

University Match. Oxford bt. Cambridge 11-9.

International. Wightman cup: U.S. won 4-3 (U.S., Mrs. J. G. Fleitz, Miss D. R. Hard, Miss S. Moore, Miss J. Arth, Miss J. Hopps; G.B., Miss C. C. Truman, Miss A. Mortimer, Miss A. S. Haydon, Mrs. C. Brasher). Davis cup, European zone: semi-final, Spain bt. Great Britain 3-2, Italy bt. France 4-1; final, Italy bt. Spain 4-1. American zone: semi-final, Australia bt. Canada 5-0, Cuba walked over Argentina; final, Australia bt. Cuba 5-0. Eastern zone: final, India bt. Philippines 4-1. Inter-zone ties: Australia bt. Italy 4-1, Australia bt. India 4-1. Challenge round: Australia bt. U.S. 3-2. *(See also LAWN TENNIS.)*

MOTOR-BOAT RACING. Marine Motoring association, Forbes house, Halkin street, London, S.W.1. President, Earl Howe; hon. secretary, S. E. Clark.

British National Meetings. *Outboard Hydroplane Championships,* Class *A* (Gosfield, Essex, June 13): 1. Mrs. Christine Crisp (Essex H.R.C.); 2. Miss M. Field (British H.R.C.); 3. R. Pluck (E.H.R.C.). Class *B* (Birmingham, July 12): 1. R. Uden (E.H.R.C.); 2. L. Gage (E.H.R.C.); 3. T. Williams (B.H.R.C.). Class *C* (Birmingham, Sept. 20): 1. R. Allen (Midlands H.C.); 2. E. H. Crisp (E.H.R.C.); 3. J. Broadhurst (M.H.C.). Class *D* (Bedfont, Sept. 5): 1. H. Kemp-Place (E.H.R.C.); 2. E. H. Crisp (E.H.R.C.); 3. F. A. Richards (E.H.R.C.). Class *X* (Bristol, June 21): 1. L. G. Melly (Lancashire H.R.C.); 2. J. Allen (E.H.R.C.); 3. E. Duckworth (M.H.C.).

Inboard Speedboat Championships: Lady Brecknock trophy (Poole, July 26): 1. P. Gush (E.S.C.); 2. S. C. Wheelton (E.S.C.); 3. V. Labrum (S.S.H. and S.C.).

100-mi. Outboard Utility Runabout Championship: Duchess of York trophy (Poole, Sept. 23): 1. R. May (L.M.B.R.C.); 2. E. Platt (S.S.H. and S.C.); 3. J. Merryfield (S.S.H. and S.C.).

Speed Records: On May 14 at Coniston water, Donald Campbell raised his own world unrestricted water speed record for jet boats to 260·35 statute m.p.h. in his turbo-propelled hydroplane " Bluebird ". On July 25 at Lake Windermere, Norman Buckley in his Jaguar-engined " Miss Windermere III " established a new world 1,200-kg. class speed record of 120·63 statute m.p.h.

MOTOR CYCLING. Auto-Cycle union, 83, Pall Mall, London, S.W.1. President, Lord Brabazon of Tara; secretary, K. Shierson.

International Grands Prix. *French G.P.:* 350 c.c., J. Surtees (M.V.), 73·32 m.p.h.; 500 c.c., Surtees (M.V.), 74·76; sidecar, F. Scheidegger (B.M.W.), 64·38. *Isle of Man T.T.:* 125 c.c., T. Provini (M.V.), 74·60; 250 c.c., Provini (M.V.), 77·77; 350 c.c., Surtees (M.V.), 95·38; 500 c.c., Surtees (M.V.), 87·94; sidecar, W. Schneider (B.M.W.), 72·69. *German G.P.:* 125 c.c., C. Ubbiali (M.V.), 97·76; 250 c.c., Ubbiali (M.V.), 109·65; 350 c.c., Surtees (M.V.); 110·31; 500 c.c., Surtees (M.V.), 123·46; sidecar, F. Camathias (B.M.W.), 104·97. *Dutch T.T.:* 125 c.c., Ubbiali (M.V.), 76·67; 250 c.c., Provini (M.V.), 81·62;

500 c.c., Surtees (M.V.), 84·86; sidecar, Camathias (B.M.W.), 74·51. *Belgian G.P.:* 125 c.c., Ubbiali (M.V.), 98·75; 500 c.c., Surtees (M.V.), 119·26; sidecar, Schneider (B.M.W.), 100·72. *Swedish G.P.:* 125 c.c., Provini (M.V.), 82·53; 250 c.c., G. Hocking (M.Z.), 87·00; 350 c.c., Surtees (M.V.), 82·53. *Ulster G.P.:* 125 c.c., S. M. B. Hailwood (Ducati), 81·92; 250 c.c., Hocking (M.Z.), 89·26; 350 c.c., Surtees (M.V.), 91·32; 500 c.c., Surtees (M.V.), 95·28. *Italian G.P.:* 125 c.c., E. Degner (M.Z.), 96·09; 250 c.c., Ubbiali (M.V.), 107·46; 350 c.c., Surtees (M.V.), 107·08; 500 c.c., Surtees (M.V.), 115·16. *World Champions 1959:* 125 c.c., Ubbiali; 250 c.c., Ubbiali; 350 c.c., Surtees; 500 c.c., Surtees; sidecar, Schneider. *British Championship Result:* 125 c.c., Hailwood (Ducati); 250 c.c., Hailwood (Mondial); 350 c.c., A. King (A.J.S.); 500 c.c., Hailwood (Norton); sidecar, P. V. Harris (B.M.W.). *A.-C.U. Road Racing Stars:* 125 c.c., Hailwood; 250 c.c., Hailwood; 350 c.c., Hailwood; 500 c.c., Hailwood; sidecar, Harris.

Trials. *International Six Days' Trial* (Czechoslovakia): trophy, Czechoslovakia; silver vase, Czechoslovakia. *British Experts Trial:* solo, S. H. Miller (Ariel); sidecar, F. Wilkins (Ariel). *A.-C.U. Trials Drivers Stars:* solo, Miller; sidecar, A. Pulman (Matchless).

Scrambles. *Moto Cross des Nations* (Belgium): Great Britain. *British Moto Cross G.P.,* J. V. Smith (B.S.A.). *World Moto Cross Champion:* S. Lundin (Monark). *European Moto Cross Champion:* R. Tibblin (Husqvarna). *A.-C.U. Scramble Drivers' Star:* A. Lampkin (B.S.A.).

MOTOR RACING. Royal Automobile club, Pall Mall, London, S.W.1. Chairman, Wilfred Andrews; secretary, Commander D. P. Little.

International Grands Prix. Monaco: J. Brabham (Cooper-Climax), 107·361 k.p.h.; 2. T. Brooks (Ferrari); 3. M. Trintignant (Cooper-Climax). Zandvoort: J. Bonnier (B.R.M.), 150·406 k.p.h.; 2. Brabham (Cooper-Climax); 3. M. Gregory (Cooper-Climax). Reims: Brooks (Ferrari Dino V6), 205·079 k.p.h.; 2. P. Hill (Ferrari); 3. Brabham (Cooper-Climax). British (Aintree): Brabham (Cooper-Climax), 144·65 k.p.h.; 2. S. Moss (B.R.M.); 3. B. McLaren (Cooper-Climax). Avus: Brooks (Ferrari), 230·7 k.p.h.; 2. D. Gurney (Ferrari); 3. Hill (Ferrari). Portuguese: Moss (Cooper-Climax), 153·396 k.p.h.; 2. Gregory (Cooper-Climax); 3. Gurney (Ferrari). Monza: Moss (Cooper-Climax), 200·177 k.p.h.; 2. Hill (Ferrari); 3. Brabham (Cooper-Climax). Sebring: McLaren (Cooper-Climax); 2. Trintignant (Cooper-Climax); 3. Brooks (Ferrari).

International Sports Car Races. Nürburgring 1,000 k.: S. Moss and J. Fairman (Aston Martin), 132·8 k.p.h.; 2. O. Gendebien and P. Hill (Ferrari); 3. T. Brooks and J. Behra (Ferrari). Targa Florio: E. Barth and W. Seidel (Porsche), 91·310 k.p.h.; 2. E. Mahle, P. Strahle and H. Linge (Porsche); 3. A. Pucci and H. von Hanstein (Porsche). Le Mans 24-hr.: R. Salvadori and C. Shelby (Aston Martin), 181·163 k.p.h.; 2. M. Trintignant and P. Frère (Aston Martin); 3. " Benrlys " and L. Dernier (Ferrari). Tourist trophy (Goodwood): S. Moss, Shelby and Fairman (Aston Martin), 89·41 m.p.h.; 2. W. von Trips and J. Bonnier (Porsche); 3. T. Brooks, Gendebien, G. Cabianca and C. Allison (Ferrari).

Important British Races. Aintree 200: Behra (Ferrari), 88·76 m.p.h.; 2. Brooks (Ferrari); 3. B. McLaren (Cooper). Empire trophy: J. Russell (Cooper), 76·93 m.p.h.; 2. A. Marsh (Cooper); 3. I. Bueb (Cooper). International trophy: Brabham (Cooper), 102·73 m.p.h.; 2. Salvadori (Aston Martin); 3. R. Flockhart (B.R.M.). Oulton Park Gold Cup race: S. Moss (Cooper), 96·29 m.p.h.; 2. Brabham (Cooper); 3. C. Bristow (Cooper). *(See also MOTOR RACING.)*

NETBALL. All England Netball association. President, Miss D. M. Wilkie; hon. secretary, Miss E. L. Sanders, 44, Oakfield road, London, E.5.

Inter-County Tournament. Quarter-finals: Lancashire 6, Kent 15; Bedfordshire 5, Warwickshire 15; Middlesex 16, Birmingham 11;

Surrey 18, Essex 8. Semi-finals: Warwickshire 15, Middlesex 10; Kent 7, Surrey 13. Final: Surrey 10, Warwickshire 9.

International Matches. England 45, Northern Ireland 4; England 42, Scotland 12; England 43, Wales 5; Northern Ireland 12, Scotland 28; Northern Ireland 16, Wales 13; Scotland 24, Wales 16.

First test: England 34, South Africa 18. Second test: England 35, South Africa 23. Final test: England 26, South Africa 24.

POLO. Hurlingham Polo association, 53, Victoria street, London, S.W.1. Chairman, Viscount Cowdray; hon. secretary, Brigadier J. R. C. Gannon; assistant secretary, Lieut.-Col. A. F. Logan.

Tournament Results. Cowdray Park Gold cup (O): Casarejo bt. Cowdray Park 7-6. Midhurst Town cup (HG): Centaurs bt. Brewhurst (rec. ½) 8-3½. Smith-Ryland cup (HG): Windsor Park (rec. 1½) bt. Cowdray Park 9½-7. Duke of Sutherland cup (HG): Cowdray Park (rec. ½) bt. Silver Leys 7½-2. Cowdray Park cup (HG): Centaurs (rec. ½) bt. Cowdray Park 8½-4. Royal Windsor cup (MG): Cowdray Park (rec. ½) bt. Centaurs 6½-5. Smith's Lawn cup (MG): Silver Leys (rec. 1) bt. Cheshire 4-3. County cup (MG): Jersey Lilies bt. Cheshire 6-5. Junior County cup (MG): Jersey Lilies bt. Hertfordshire 6-5. Harrison cup (MG): Centaurs bt. Brewhurst (rec. ½) 6-3½. Cheltenham cup (MG): Jericho Priory bt. Cheshire Forest 5-2. Bluejackets cup (LG): Jericho Priory bt. Rhinefield (rec. ½) 4-3½. Inter-regimental cup (O): Royal Wiltshire Yeomanry bt. Royal Horse Guards 5-3. Captains' and Subalterns' cup (O): Queen's Own Hussars bt. Royal Horse Guards 5-4. Inter-university match (O): Cambridge bt. Oxford 4-1. Whitbread cup and Grooms' prize (LG): Windsor (rec. 1½) bt. Kirtlington Park 4½-1.

NOTE: Tournaments are graded according to the aggregate handicaps of teams engaged, as follows: "high goal" (HG) 20-13, "medium goal" (MG) 12-6, "low goal" (LG) 4-0, "open" (O) handicaps ignored.

RACKETS. Tennis and Rackets association, The Queen's club, West Kensington, London, W.14. President, Marquess of Salisbury; chairman of executive committee, Kenneth O. Hunter; hon. secretary, Col. N. S. Renny.

The open rackets singles championship of Great Britain was won by J. R. Thompson, who beat R. M. K. Gracey by 3 games to 1. Thompson also retained the amateur singles championship, beating J. M. G. Tildesley by 3 games to 2, and thus achieved his fifth success in six years. The amateur doubles was held by D. S. Milford and Thompson who defeated Tildesley and C. J. Swallow by 4 games to 2. In the Noel Bruce cup the Old Tonbridgians gained their fourth success running, beating the Old Rugbean pair Milford and P. Kershaw by 4 games to 1. The army singles championship was won by Lieut. M. W. Bolton (R.E.) and the doubles by the Royal Engineers (Lieut-. Col. M. D. Maclagan and Bolton). In the university match Oxford beat Cambridge. The public schools championship was won by Winchester (Nawab of Pataudi and C. E. M. Snell) and the H. K. Foster cup by J. L. Cuthbertson (Rugby).

RIFLE SHOOTING. National Rifle association, Bisley camp, Brookwood, Surrey. President, the Duke of Gloucester; chairman, Lord Tedder; secretary, Capt. E. K. Le Mesurier.

Bisley Meeting. *Individual Events.* The Queen's prize was won by Lieut. L. W. Mallabar (City R.C.) with a score of 276 out of a possible 300; Duke of Gloucester competition, Armr./Sgt. F. S. French (late Herts Yeo.) with 74 out of 75; St. George's challenge vase, W. L. V. Price (Lond. Univ. R.C.) with 141 out of 150; Grand Aggregate, Major S. Armour (Royal Marines) with 570 out of 615. *Team Events.* The Rajah of Kolapore Imperial challenge cup was won by the mother country with a score of 1,127 out of 1,200; Mackinnon challenge cup, England 1,002 out of 1,200; National challenge trophy, England, 1,961 out of 2,100; Ashburton challenge shield (schools championship), St. Lawrence college, 517 out of 560.

Small-Bore. National Small-bore Rifle association, Codrington house, 113, Southwark street, London, S.E.1. President, Field Marshal Sir Claude Auchinleck; secretary, A. J. Palmer.

Internationals. The Lord Dewar trophy (v. United States and British Dominion countries) was won by Great Britain. The Lord Wakefield trophy, County, State and Provinces match v. Sweden, was won by Great Britain. *Counties of the U.K., States and Provinces of Dominion Countries.* B.S.A. cup, Canterbury (New Zealand). *County Championships.* Queen Alexandra cup, Kent. County cup, Warwickshire. Minor Counties cup, Dundee and Angus. *Empire Cities Match.* Christchurch (New Zealand). *British Club Team Championships.* (Long Range): City of Birmingham. (Short Range): Burroughes and Watts cup (teams of four): Salisbury; *News of the World* cup (teams of six): Lensbury and Britannic house; Mackworth Praed cup (teams of eight): Lensbury and Britannic house. *Individual Championships.* British Long-Range championship for the Earl Roberts cup, A. D. Skinner (City of Birmingham); British Short-Range championship for the *News of the World* cup, M. P. Singleton (University of London); English Long-Range championship for the Royal Society of St. George cup, R. W. Edwards (East Bristol); English Short-Range championship for the Royal Society of St. George cup, M. P. Singleton (University of London); Scottish Long-Range championship for the Earl Haig Memorial cup, W. B. Smillie (Falkirk Lord Roberts); Scottish Short-Range championship for the *Daily Record* cup, D. Ross (Glen Tanar); Northern Ireland Long-Range championship for the Northern Ireland cup, M. Dickson (Co. Londonderry XB); Northern Ireland Short-Range championship for the Amertex cup, C. F. Metson (Ballymena); Welsh Long-Range championship for the *Western Mail and Echo* cup, J. G. Ellis (Lensbury and Britannic house); Welsh Short-Range championship for the *Western Mail and Echo* cup, D. G. F. Steward (Swansea); Women's British Long-Range championship for the Flowers trophy, Mrs. J. J. McKenzie (Dundee and Strathmore); Women's British Short-Range championship for the W.R.A. Championship rose bowl, Miss M. A. Armstrong (Dunfermline).

ROWING. Amateur Rowing association, The Tower, The Terrace, Barnes, London, S.W.13. Chairman, G. O. Nickalls; hon. secretary, J. H. Page.

European Championships. Eights: German Fed. Rep. 5 min. 51·71 sec., Czechoslovakia 6 min. 01·04 sec., U.S.S.R. 6 min. 02·09 sec. Coxswainless fours: Switzerland 6 min. 21·03 sec., German Fed. Rep. 6 min. 21·82 sec., Czechoslovakia 6 min. 22·66 sec. Coxed fours: German Fed. Rep. 6 min. 25·97 sec., Netherlands 6 min. 32·89 sec., Sweden 6 min. 37·80 sec. Coxswainless pairs: German Fed. Rep. 6 min. 44·73 sec., U.S.S.R. 6 min. 45·35 sec., Austria 6 min. 54·74 sec. Coxed pairs: German Fed. Rep. 7 min. 16·40 sec., Italy 7 min. 19·33 sec., Rumania 7 min. 23·98 sec. Double sculls: U.S.S.R. 6 min. 29·49 sec., Czechoslovakia 6 min. 30·17 sec., Netherlands 6 min. 35·10 sec. Single sculls: U.S.S.R. 6 min. 58·89 sec., German Fed. Rep. 7 min. 03·61 sec., Poland 7 min. 08·86 sec.

Universities. University Boat race: Oxford bt. Cambridge by 6 lengths in 18 min. 52 sec. Eights week (Oxford): St. Edmund hall, Christ Church, Merton. May races (Cambridge): Lady Margaret, Jesus, Emmanuel.

Henley Royal Regatta. Grand Challenge cup: Harvard university (U.S.) bt. Thames R.C., 2¾ lengths, 6 min. 57 sec. Ladies' Challenge plate: Lady Margaret B.C., Cambridge bt. Emmanuel college, Cambridge, 1⅓ lengths, 7 min. 13 sec. Thames Challenge cup: Harvard university (U.S.) bt. University of London, 2½ lengths, 7 min. 13 sec. Princess Elizabeth Challenge cup: St. Edward's school bt. Oundle school, ⅓ length, 7 min. 15 sec. Stewards' Challenge cup: St. Edmund hall and Lincoln college, Oxford, bt. Moto Guzzi (Italy) easily, 7 min. 39 sec. Visitors' Challenge cup: Pembroke college, Cambridge, bt. Lady Margaret B.C., Cambridge, 1 length, 7 min. 50 sec. Wyfold Challenge cup: Molesey B.C. bt. Walton R.C., easily, 7 min. 45 sec. Silver goblets: R. B. Norton and H. H. Scurfield (Hertford college, Oxford) bt. J. M. Beresford and C. F. Porter (London R.C.) easily, 8 min. 20 sec. Double sculls: C. G. V. Davidge and S. A. Mackenzie (Leander club) bt. G. C. Justicz and N. Birkmyre (Birmingham R.C. and Ariel R.C.), 2¾ lengths, 7 min. 55 sec. Diamond Challenge sculls: S. A. Mackenzie (Sydney R.C., Australia) bt. H. L. Parker (Vesper B.C., Philadelphia) easily, 8 min. 39 sec.

Other Thames Regattas. Head of the River race: Barn Cottage B.C., Isis B.C. (Oxford), Goldie B.C. (Cambridge). Wingfield sculls (Amateur Sculling championship of Great Britain): J. M. Russell (London R.C.), G. C. Justicz (Birmingham R.C.), G. W. Baker (Marlow R.C.). Scullers' Head of the River race: M. A. Spracklen (Marlow R.C.), G. C. Justicz (Birmingham R.C.), N. Birkmyre (Ariel R.C.). Doggett's coat and badge: G. L. Saunders (Erith), R. F. Taylor (Romford), B. T. Gould (Poplar). (*See* also ROWING.)

RUGBY FOOTBALL. Rugby Football union, Whitton road, Twickenham, Middlesex. President, Wing Commander J. Lawson; secretary, Lieut.-Col. F. D. Prentice. Rugby League, 180, Chapeltown road, Leeds, 7. President, the Earl of Derby; secretary, W. Fallowfield.

Rugby Union. *International Results:* England 3, Scotland 3; England 3, Ireland 0; England 0, Wales 5; England 3, France 3; Scotland 3, Ireland 8; Scotland 6, Wales 5; Scotland 0, France 9; Wales 8, Ireland 6; Ireland 9, France 5; France 11, Wales 3.

RUGBY UNION INTERNATIONAL TABLE

	P.	W.	D.	L.	Points For	Points Agst.	Pts.
France	4	2	1	1	28	15	5
Ireland	4	2	0	2	23	19	4
Wales	4	2	0	2	21	23	4
England	4	1	2	1	9	11	4
Scotland	4	1	1	2	12	25	3

County Championship Final: Warwickshire bt. Gloucestershire, 14-9. *University Match:* Cambridge bt. Oxford, 17-6.

Rugby League. *Representative Games.* Great Britain 8, Australia 25; Great Britain 25, Australia 18; Great Britain 40, Australia 17; Rugby League XIII 8, France 26; France 25, Wales 13; Great Britain 50, France 15; France 24, Great Britain 15.

Home Championships. Rugby League challenge cup, Wigan 30, Hull 13; Northern Rugby League championship, St. Helens 44, Hunslet 22; Yorkshire Rugby League cup, Leeds 24, Wakefield Trinity 20; Lancashire Rugby League cup, Oldham 12, St. Helens 2; Yorkshire league, Wakefield Trinity, runners-up Hunslet; Lancashire league, Wigan, runners-up St. Helens. (*See* also RUGBY FOOTBALL.)

SHOW JUMPING. British Show Jumping association, 16, Bedford square, London, W.C.1. Secretary-general: Captain G. H. S. Webber.

International Horse Show. King George V cup, H. Wiley (U.S.) on Nautical; Queen Elizabeth II cup, Miss A. Clement on Nico. *Daily*

Mail cup, H. Wiley (U.S.) on Nautical. Prince of Wales' cup, United States.

European International Junior Championship. G. Castellini (Italy) on Ventuno; Lady Sarah Fitzalan-Howard (G.B.) on Oorskiet.

European Junior Team Championship. Great Britain, team: M. Cresswell on Tally-ho, B. Coakes on Catriona, Miss J. Kidd on Manka, Lady Sarah Fitzalan-Howard on Oorskiet.

Horse of the Year Show. Leading Jumper of the Year, H. Smith on Farmer's Boy; Leading Junior Jumper of the Year, D. Hughes on Blueflake; Victor Ludorum *Sunday Graphic* cup, Miss Anne Townsend on Bandit IV.

National Championships. National Adult Champion, Alan Oliver on John Gilpin; Ladies National champion, Miss Pat Smythe on Mr. Pollard; National Junior champion, P. Oliver on Kangaroo. (*See also* SHOW JUMPING AND HORSE TRIALS.)

SKIING. Ski Club of Great Britain, 118, Eaton square, London, S.W.1. President, Air Chief Marshal the Hon. Sir Ralph Cochrane; general secretary, Mrs. S. G. Tennant; members' secretary, Mrs. G. E. Turner.

British Ski Championships. Men, G. Pitchford. Ladies, C. Petre. Juniors: boys, P. Norman; girls, T. Heald. Cross-country, Lieut. J. Moore.

Alpine World Ski Championships (Badgastein 1957-58). Men: downhill, Toni Sailer (Austria); slalom, Josl Rieder (Austria); giant slalom, Toni Sailer; combined, Toni Sailer. Ladies: downhill, L. Wheeler (Canada); slalom, I. Bjøorhbakken (Norway); giant slalom, L. Wheeler; combined, F. Danzer (Switz.).

World Cross Country Ski Championships (Lahti 1957-58). 50 km., Jernberg (Sweden); 40 km. relay, Sweden; 15 km., Hakulinen (Finland); nordic combination, Korhonen (Finland).

Arlberg Kandahar (Garmisch-Partenkirchen). Men, K. Schranz (Arlberg). Ladies, A. Heggtveit (Ottawa).

Duke of Kent cup: N. Gardner (G.B.). *Duchess of Kent cup:* T. Legat (Austria). *Lowlanders downhill:* J. Hotermans (Belgium). *Lowlanders cross country:* T. Maule (G.B.). *Roberts of Kandahar:* R. Skepper (Canada).

SPEEDWAY RACING. Speedway Control board, 68, Brewer street, London, W.1. Chairman, Lieut.-Col. R. Vernon C. Brook; manager, Major W. W. Fearnley.

World Champion, Ronnie Moore (Wimbledon and New Zealand); British match race champion, Peter Craven (Belle Vue); National league, Wimbledon; National trophy, Wimbledon; Tom Farndon trophy, Peter Craven (Belle Vue); Test matches, England bt. Australasia 2 matches to 1.

SQUASH RACKETS. The Squash Rackets association, 25 Haymarket, London, S.W.1. President, Capt. J. E. Palmer-Tomkinson; secretary, J. H. Horry.

British Results. Amateur championship: N. H. R. A. Broomfield bt. M. Amin (Egypt) 3-1. Open championship: Azam Khan (Pakistan) bt. Mohibullah Khan (Pakistan) 3-0. Professional championship of the British Isles: Azam Khan bt. Nasrullah Khan 3-0. Professional championship of the United Kingdom: J. H. Giles (holder) bt. W. J. Moss 3-1 and 3-0. Inter-county championship: Surrey bt. Essex 5-0. Women's championship: Miss J. R. M. Morgan bt. Mrs. H. Mackintosh 3-0. University match: Cambridge bt. Oxford 3-2. International matches: England bt. Scotland 5-0, bt. Ireland 5-0, bt. Wales 5-0. Scotland bt. Ireland 5-0, bt. Wales 3-2, bt. Egypt 3-2. Wales bt. Ireland 4-1.

Other National Championships. Australia, B. Stuart. Belgium, D. Medway (Eng.). Canada, J. Smith-Chapman. Denmark, P. Gerlow. India, Lieut. K. S. Jain. Ireland, D. M. Pratt. Kenya, W. R. L. Addison. New Zealand, J. Cheadle (Australia). Sweden, R. Jonasson. Scotland: amateur, I. Amin (Egypt); open, Mohibullah Khan (Pakistan). South Africa, N. H. R. A. Broomfield (Eng.). United States: amateur, B. Heckscher; open, J. D. Mateer. Wales, R. S. Bourne.

SWIMMING. Amateur Swimming Associations of Great Britain, 12, Weir street, Blackburn. Hon. secretary, R. Hodgson.

A.S.A. National Championships. *Men.* Swimming: 110 yd. free-style, I. Black (Robert Gordon, Aberdeen), 58 sec.; 220 yd. free-style, Black, 2 min. 6 sec.; 440 yd. free-style, Black, 4 min. 32·9 sec.; 880 yd. free-style, R. Campion (Stoke Newington), 10 min. 13·5 sec.*; 1,760 yd. free-style, Campion, 20 min. 48·2 sec.*; 110 yd. back-stroke, G. Sykes (Coventry), 1 min. 5·5 sec.; 220 yd. breast-stroke, G. Rowlinson (Bolton), 2 min. 48·5 sec.; 220 yd. butterfly, Black, 2 min. 22·7 sec.; 4×110 yd. free-style relay, York, 4 min. 2·6 sec.; 4×110 yd. medley relay, Stoke Newington, 4 min. 38 sec. Diving: highboard, B. Phelps (Highgate) 148·61 pts.; springboard, P. Squires (Highgate), 150·39 pts.; 1 m. springboard, K. Collin (Isleworth), 132·53 pts.; high plain, Squires, 67·01 pts.

Women. Swimming: 110 yd. free-style, N. Steward (Hornchurch), 1 min. 5·2 sec.; 220 yd. free-style, Steward, 2 min. 25·6 sec.; 440 yd. free-style, Steward, 5 min. 12·9 sec.; 110 yd. back-stroke, M. Edwards (Heston), 1 min. 12·5 sec.; 220 yd. breast-stroke, A. Lonsbrough (Huddersfield), 2 min. 54 sec.; 110 yd. butterfly, S. Watt (Thistle, Aberdeen), 1 min. 13·9 sec.; 4×110 yd. free-style relay, Beckenham Ladies, 4 min. 45·3 sec.; 4×110 yd. medley relay, Heston 5 min.

12·4 sec. Diving: highboard, P. A. Long (Ilford), 81·71 pts.; springboard, M. J. Watson (Bournemouth), 128·48 pts.; 1 m. springboard, N. Thomas (Isleworth), 106·85 pts.; high plain, E. Ferris (Mermaid), 61·13 pts.

Boys. Swimming: 110 yd. free-style, C. Hansard (Swansea), 1 min. 0·5 secs; 220 yd. free-style, P. Hammond (Sheffield English Steel), 2 min. 16·9 sec.; 110 yd. back-stroke, R. Thomas (Bristol City), 1 min. 10·2 sec.; 110 yd. breast-stroke, C. C. Wilkinson (Stockport), 1 min. 18·2 sec.; 110 yd. butterfly, T. Glenville (Hull Olympic), 1 min. 8·3 sec. Diving: B. Phelps (Highgate), 89·47 pts.

Girls. Swimming: 110 yd. free-style, M. Toms (Beckenham Ladies), 1 min. 6·5 sec.; 220 yd. free-style, J. Samuel (Surrey Ladies), 2 min. 25·9 sec.; 110 yd. back-stroke, C. Hussey (Nottingham), 1 min. 16 sec.; 110 yd. breast-stroke, C. Barber (Heston), 1 min. 24·8 sec.; 110 yd. butterfly, P. Baines (Ilford) 1 min. 17·6 sec. Diving: M. Watson (Bournemouth Dolphins), 82·87 pts.

* English native record.

University Match. Cambridge bt. Oxford 47-39 pts.

International Contests. Great Britain bt. German Dem. Rep., 99-69 pts. (swimming); German Dem. Rep. bt. Great Britain, 29-15 pts. (diving); Netherlands bt. Great Britain, 112-89 pts. (swimming and water polo); Great Britain bt. Hungary, 113-72 pts. (swimming); England lost to German Dem. Rep., 20-21 pts. (diving); Great Britain bt. German Fed. Rep., 141-99 pts. (swimming, diving and water polo); Italy lost to Great Britain and to Sweden, 138-170-150 pts. (swimming and diving); England bt. Scotland and Wales, 38-29-17 pts. (swimming—Bologna trophy). Netherlands bt. Great Britain, 93-92 pts. (swimming). In an eight-nation diving contest in Moscow, B. Phelps (G.B.) won the men's highboard event with 153·03 pts. Water Polo: England bt. Scotland, 16-2.

English Channel. Alfredo Camarero (Argentina) won the Butlin's Holiday camps race when he swam from France to England in 11 hr. 48 mins. 26 secs. This was just over 1 hr. slower than the record for this crossing set up by Hassan Abdul Benim (Egypt) in 1950. Greta Anderson (United States, formerly Denmark), the outright winner in 1957 and 1958, was the first woman home in 15 hr. 25 mins.

TABLE TENNIS. English Table Tennis association, 217, Grand buildings, Trafalgar square, London, W.C.2. President, the Hon. Ivor Montagu; chairman, A. K. Vint; secretary, D. P. Lowen.

World Championships (at Dortmund). Men's team, Japan; women's team, Japan; men's singles, Jung Kuo-tuan (Chinese P.R.) bt. F. Sido (Hun.) 3-1; men's doubles, T. Murakami and T. Murakami (Jap.) bt. L. Stipek and V. Vyhnanovsky (Cz) 3-2; women's singles, K. Matsuzaki (Jap.) bt. F. Eguthi (Jap.) 3-1; women's doubles, T. Nanba and K. Yamaizumi (Jap.) bt. F. Eguchi and K. Matsuzaki (Jap.) 3-0; mixed doubles, I. Ogimura and F. Eguchi (Jap.) bt. T. Murakami and K. Matsuzaki (Jap.) 3-0.

English Championships. m.s., I. Ogimura; m.d., I. Ogimura and T. Murakami; w.s., F. Eguchi; w.d., F. Eguchi and T. Matsuzaki; mxd.d., T. Murakami and K. Matsuzaki; junior (boys') singles, M. Ness; junior (girls') singles, Yool Ja Hwang.

International Matches. Senior: (m) W.ch., England won 7 lost 2, lost to Sweden (a.) 3-5, bt. Netherlands (a.) 4-1, lost to Czechoslovakia (a.) 3-5, bt. German Dem. Rep. (a.) 5-0, lost to France (a.) 2-5; (w.) W.ch., England won 7 lost 1, bt. Czechoslovakia (a.) 3-2, bt. Netherlands (a.) 4-1, bt. France (h.) 6-3; (mxd.) England bt. Ireland (h.) 10-0, bt. Netherlands (h.) 8-2, bt. Wales (h.) 9-1, bt. United States (h.) 8-1, 5-3, drew (h.) 4-4; Junior: (mxd.) bt. Scotland (h.) 9-0, bt. France (h.) 8-0, bt. German Fed. Rep. (h.) 5-3, lost (h.) 2-6; bt. Wales (h.) 9-0.

TENNIS (*see* RACKETS). The amateur singles championship was won by D. J. Warburg who beat J. D. Whatman by 3 sets to 2. The doubles championship was won by Lord Aberdare and Whatman, who defeated P. Kershaw and M. M. Jones. P. Kershaw won the Gold Racket (M.C.C. prize) and the Silver Racket was won by D. J. Warburg. In the university match Cambridge beat Oxford and in the Henry Leaf cup (Public Schools Old Boys) Rugby defeated Harrow. In a match for the World's Open Tennis championship played in New York in Feb. 1959, N. R. Knox (U.S.) beat A. Johnson (holder) by 7 sets to 2.

YACHTING. Royal Yachting association, 171, Victoria street, London, S.W.1. President, Duke of Edinburgh; secretary, F. P. Usborne. Royal Ocean Racing club, 20, St. James's place, S.W.1. Admiral, M. D. Wyatt; commodore, A. V. Sainsbury; secretary, A. H. Paul. Royal Cruising club; commodore, Nigel Warington Smyth; hon. secretary, D. C. L. Cree, Pinehurst, Aviary road, Pyrford, Surrey.

Principal Race Results. Britannia cup (Cowes, Aug. 4), "Zwerver" (W. N. H. Van der Vorm, Netherlands). New York Yacht club challenge cup (Cowes, Aug. 6), "Misty Dream" (T. G. Clarke). Fastnet cup: "Anitra" (S. Hansen, Sweden). Admiral's cup: British team consisting of "Griffin II", "Myth of Malham" and "Ramrod". R.O.R.C. points championship: class I, "Ramrod", "Carina", "Lutine"; class II, "Myth of Malham", "Griffin II", "Clair de Lune"; class III, "Meon Maid II" and "Pym" (equal points), "Danegeld"; inter-club championship: R.N.S.A., Portsmouth.

International 6-m. Class. One Ton cup (Poole bay, Aug. 12-18), " Maybe VIII " (sailed by C. H. de Nordenskjöld, Sweden). *International Dragon Class.* Edinburgh cup (Cowes, July 25-29), " Apollyon " (B. B. Banks). *International Flying Dutchman Class.* National championship (Whitstable, July 3-5), " Pandora " (A. Jardine). *International 14-ft. Dinghy Class.* Prince of Wales cup (Lowestoft, July 16), " Hamble Baby " (sailed by C. Currey). *International Finn Class.* National championship (Littlehampton, June 10-12), " Mickey Finn " (V. Stratton). *International Cadet Class.* *Yachting World* trophy (Burnham-on-Crouch, Aug. 18-21), " Castar " (J. Rogge, Belgium).

National Flying Fifteen Class. Championship (Plymouth, Sep. 7-11), " Silver Fox " (G. H. Goodson). *National Merlin/Rocket Class.* Championship (Whitstable, June 21-26), " Restless III " (B. Southcott). *National 12-ft. Dinghy Class.* Sir William Burton trophy (Weymouth, Sep. 2), " Extravagance " (J. Oakley). *National Firefly Class.* Sir Ralph Gore cup (Plymouth, Aug. 26), " Sue Tue " (M. Cocksedge). *Y.W. Hornet Class.* World championship (Plymouth, Sept. 8-12), " Lunka-bunk " (Beecher Moore). (*See also* YACHTING.) (*See also* AIR RACES AND RECORDS; ANGLING; BETTING AND GAMBLING; FIELD SPORTS.)

STEEL: *see* IRON AND STEEL.

STOCKS AND SHARES. For investors in equity shares in the United Kingdom the year 1959, like its predecessor, was a very profitable one. Prices of most stock market securities advanced steadily throughout the year and in many cases surpassed their previous peaks by quite substantial margins. The general pattern of industrial share price movements was illustrated by the performance of the *Financial Times* industrial ordinary share index (reflecting the market behaviour of 30 leading British industrial companies). This stood at 225·5 at the end of 1958, having risen by a full 46% from its low point of 154·4 recorded in Feb. 1958 and passed its previous peak of 223·9 (July 1955). Many people wondered if the pace was too swift to last, but the advance continued almost without interruption. By Dec. 31, 1959, the index had reached 338·4, an increase of a further 50%.

Initially, the continuation of the advance in 1959 was prompted by indications of a strong recovery in the British economy. The reversal of governmental policy towards the end of 1958, which saw a period of severe credit restriction replaced by successive reductions in purchase tax and the abolition of hire purchase restrictions, gradually began to be reflected in booming retail trade figures; and, although published profits of companies engaged in the consumer trade did not reflect the improved conditions immediately, stock exchange prices moved ahead in anticipation. Also, there was evidence of a more liberal dividend policy from most British companies, assisted by the reduction in income tax from 8s. 6d. to 7s. 9d., and this trend combined with cheaper interest rates elsewhere to force up prices of equity shares.

Nevertheless, the yields on British shares remained sufficiently high by comparison with those on other European and U.S. stocks to attract buyers from those countries into British markets, and the demand from abroad became sufficiently strong to lend further stimulus to the upward movement of leading British shares. Side by side with this unprecedented weight of foreign demand came an increase in the number of unit trusts and investment trusts, and buying from this source too was unusually large. All this left its impact on markets which seldom saw much selling by the investing public, who found no economic reason for parting with equity shareholdings.

These were the main factors serving to push share prices well above their previous peaks in the months which preceded the general election; and by August the *Financial Times* index had reached the 250 mark. At this point, however, the approach of the election came more to the fore as a factor affecting market sentiment, and in the following two months there was uncertainty as to the possible repercussions on the stock exchange and on capital investment of a Labour government. Once a specific date, Oct. 8, was settled for the election,

however, markets became firmer again and when the outcome became clear the index jumped by 16 points in a single day, easily a record advance. The gains then scored were further consolidated and improved in subsequent weeks.

The more specific implications of the election result added to the number of especially favoured groups. Outstanding among them were steel shares, which had remained very depressed in the previous three years because of the fear of renationalization of the companies concerned. This group began to improve before the election, but their advance then was insignificant compared with the wild upward surge with which they greeted the Conservative victory. Television shares and the insurance and property sections of the market also responded well to the elimination, for a period at least, of the possibility of a Labour government.

Apart from these specialized interests, hire-purchase shares were among the star performers during the year, reflecting the removal of all restrictions on hire purchase the previous autumn and the big increase in the national hire purchase debt. Many of the groups directly connected with the retail trades also mirrored the boom in this section of the economy, notably the motors and stores sections. To a lesser degree, shares of companies engaged in the building and construction trades reflected the upswing in demand for their services. For the rest, the accompanying table shows how the various broad groups performed in 1959.

The period after the election also saw some quite significant appreciation in the prices of several commodity shares, yields on which became relatively more attractive as the returns on

The Stock Exchange settling room. During the period of the general election a record amount of business was transacted.

recognized industrial shares became progressively lower. Among the best performers throughout the year were rubber shares, which initially reflected the improvement in the price of the raw material and later enjoyed a revision of investment rating, the double figure yields traditionally offered by this class of security being felt to be disproportionately high compared with the degree of risk involved. Similar considerations prompted rises in tin, lead-zinc and copper shares, particularly the first, all three classes being assisted by an improvement in the respective commodity positions during the year. Gold shares as a class were not outstanding. The *Financial Times* gold mines index touched 94·8 in June 1959 but slipped back to 89·2 by Dec. 31; some individual shares, however, did very much better than this, particularly those of the young mines which began to announce unexpectedly good results. Once again oil shares failed to recapture their glamour of three years earlier, and lack of

" This stuff tastes as if somebody's done a merger with the Water Board." A cartoon by Emmwood in the " Daily Mail " of June 5.

investment interest combined with the uncertainty of the supply-demand equilibrium to hold prices almost unchanged until the year-end. Fixed interest stocks, including gilt-edged securities, met with a similar lack of interest in a market which was searching for " growth " prospects.

Quite apart from the general advance in markets, a considerable number of " artificial " upward movements was seen in share prices as a result of an unusually heavy crop of take-over bids made during 1959, for in many cases the terms of such offers were pitched at a level offering an appreciable premium on the market prices previously ruling. That there were more situations of this sort in 1959 than in previous years owed something to the growing economic necessity for integration in several major industries in order to combat rising operating costs as well as to the desire to eliminate competition. In some cases also take-over bids were

Accompanied by his son, Hugh Fraser crosses the road to enter Harrods department store of which he gained control in September.

occasioned by the belief on the part of the bidders that the assets of the company subject to the bid could be put to more effective, or even alternative, uses if backed by bigger resources or better management. On several occasions offers led to counter-bids which pushed share prices even higher, and there was sometimes a protracted struggle for control. Outstanding examples were Harrods, for which offers were made by Debenhams, United Draperies and House of Fraser before the latter finally acquired control at a price almost double that at which Harrods' shares opened the year, and Thomas and Evans, the mineral water manufacturing group, for which Beechams struggled successfully with Schweppes. Other important take-over bids, apart from those in the newspaper world (*see* NEWSPAPERS AND MAGAZINES), were offers for Canadian Eagle by Royal Dutch Shell; for British Aluminium by Tube Investments; for North Central Wagon by the National Provincial Bank; and for Watney Mann by Sears Holdings. The first three were successful, while the fourth offer was eventually withdrawn.

GROUP PRICE MOVEMENTS OF ORDINARY SHARES IN THE UNITED KINGDOM, 1959*	Jan 1, 1959	Oct. 31, 1959	Rise %
Steels	99·5†	203·5†	104
Motors	210·6	385·1	83
Tins	119·6	203·7	70
Stores	287·9	463·7	61
Newspapers	180·7‡	288·8‡	60
Rubbers	129·1	205·2	59
Breweries	157·3	246·0	56
Building materials	192·8	289·7	50
Insurance	130·8‡	195·4‡	50
Machine Tools	120·7‡	178·8‡	48
Investment Trusts	143·5‡	210·5‡	47
Plastics	156·2	229·1	47
Textiles	149·8	217·8	45
Chemicals	265·7	375·9	42
Banks	151·6‡	210·9‡	39
Lead-Zincs	164·0	227·7	39
Tobaccos	134·8	180·1	34
" Financial Times " Industrial Ordinary Index	225·5	302·6	34
Foods	241·4	297·0	23
Coppers	271·6	330·9	22
Teas	88·6	106·8	21
Radio and TV	322·8	391·9	21
Papers	77·4§	92·0§	19
Engineering	220·7	256·6	16
Oils	458·8	514·4	12
Electricals	146·4	160·8	10
Rubber manufacturing	194·5	214·8	10
Shipbuilding	301·8	327·4	8
" Financial Times " Government Securities Index	84·7	87·5	3
Shipping	212·5	216·0	2
" Financial Times " Gold Mines Index	86·0	87·4	1
Aircraft	154·7	147·0	—5

* 1949 = 100 except where indicated. † 1955 = 100. ‡ 1957 = 100. § 1956 = 100.
SOURCE. *Financial Times.*

The United States stock market averages advanced very modestly in 1959 despite record-breaking displays of strength in most significant economic indicators (*e.g.*, corporate profits were nearly 40% higher by the middle of the year compared with a year earlier). Standard and Poor's composite index of 500 common stocks (1941-43 = 10), which had climbed steadily throughout 1958 from an average of 41·12 in January to an average of 53·49 in December (a gain of 30%), was only able to advance to a peak of 59·74 in July 1959 before settling back at lower levels. The industrial index followed a similar pattern, achieving a record of 64·23 in July. During the first nine months of 1959 the high and low averages for utilities were 45·15 and 42·58, while the corresponding figures for rails were 36·86 and 33·78.

The yields on 200 common stocks in the United States, according to Moody's index, declined to the lowest levels in many years. At 3·18% in July 1959 they were well below the yields on high-grade corporate bonds and most U.S. government bonds. The volume of trading on all registered exchanges in the United States during 1959 was the highest for 29 years. During the first six months the volume on the New York stock exchange rose to 443 million shares, an increase of nearly 50% over the first half of 1958.

U.S. government bonds maturing in five years or more, which had been selling well above par in the first half of 1958, fell progressively during the last half of 1958 and most of 1959. By Sept. 1959 Standard and Poor's index had fallen to the lowest-ever figure of 85·27. In a period of tight money, a statutory ceiling of 4·25% on interest rates for long-term government bonds resulted in a vigorous swing to shorter-term issues which, in some instances, sold to yield as much as 5%. Corporate bonds, as measured by Standard and Poor's index, also fell below the levels of the previous year. The highest-grade bonds sold well below par during the first nine months of 1959. In September a figure of 93·0 was reached, the lowest average price for such securities in many years. Yields were more than 4% for long-term government bonds by May 1959 and 4·35% was reached in September. Corporate yields averaged 4·25% in September. In that month the Federal Reserve board rediscount rate, at 4%, was the highest for 27 years and prime rates of 5% at commercial banks set a 28-year record.

During the first six months of 1959 there were 51 stocks which split on a basis of two-for-one or better among the listings on the New York stock exchange. This was the highest figure since 1956 and compared with only five in 1958 and 26 in 1957. A significant number of new securities was admitted to trading on the exchange during the year. By Aug. 1959 the number of shares listed on the "Big Board" was 5,510 million, an increase of 8·5% over the number listed at the beginning of the year.

A seat on the New York stock exchange sold for $157,000 in June 1959, the highest price for 23 years. In Sept. 1959 there were 1,366 seats and 659 member firms. (*See* also PROFITS AND DIVIDENDS.)   (B. P. W.; I. PR.)

STRIKES. In the United Kingdom, during the first nine months of 1959, the number of strikes which occurred, 1,597, was well below the figure of 2,067 in the comparable period of 1958. But the number of working days lost rose to 4,866,000 as against 3,201,000 in the first nine months of 1958.

	Number of strikes	Working days lost
Coal mining	1,000	292,000
Building and contracting . . .	137	91,000
Shipbuilding and ship repairing . .	60	268,000
Vehicles	110	415,000
Paper and printing	4	3,504,000
Engineering	80	67,000
Transport	61	36,000

The largest number of stoppages again occurred in the coal industry but the number was no less than 500 fewer than the year before. It is difficult to account for this other than by the fact that coal was a commodity in over-abundant supply. The industry was faced with the need to reduce its labour force and this fact probably had an important bearing on the readiness of mining employees to strike.

The major strike of the year occurred in the printing industry (*see* PRINTING). This stoppage resulted in the loss of almost 3·5 million man-days and was only settled after the Trades Union congress had been called in to attempt to break the deadlock. The method found to bring the parties together was the novel one of inviting Lord Birkett to act as an independent chairman " to advise, guide and control the discussions to achieve a negotiated settlement." Lord Birkett's role went beyond the normal duties of a conciliator, but did not go so far as that of an independent arbitrator. His

" *You will appreciate, Lucille, that the possibility of my paper round packing up calls for somewhat rigid economy.*" *A cartoon by Giles which appeared in the " Daily Express " on July 2.*

function was a combination of conciliation and arbitration, with power to suggest a binding solution if the two sides found themselves unable to agree on a point of substance. This idea aroused considerable interest as a method of achieving the settlement of a stubborn dispute in which the two sides were unable to arrive at an agreed solution, but were unwilling to entrust a decision to an outsider acting in the comparatively isolated role of impartial arbitrator deciding on the merits of a dispute merely after hearing the case stated by the parties. It was possible that this method of resolving intractable industrial disputes would be resorted to again in the future.

The aspect of the strike situation which aroused most comment during the year was the number of unofficial disputes that occurred, particularly in the motor industry. At one stage in October no less than seven unofficial strikes were under way at the same time. Concern at the readiness of certain shop stewards to call out on strike members of unions in breach of agreements and without the sanction of union executives was voiced at the annual meeting of the T.U.C. The resolution proposed by the Engineer Surveyors' association, calling upon the general council of the T.U.C. to instruct member unions " to examine their structure and to define clearly the function of their officers and shop stewards," was rejected. But in asking the delegates to reject this suggestion the council undertook to examine the whole problem on a broader basis, and it was announced in October that the trade union side of the National Joint Advisory Council to the Minister of Labour would act as a commmittee of inquiry into the problem. However, when a *questionnaire* was sent to all affiliated unions towards the end of the year there was some opposition to the inquiry.

During 1959 there was also a number of demarcation disputes, such as that at Cammell Laird's Birkenhead shipyard, where 1,750 boilermakers went on strike for eight weeks and another 2,600 workers were laid off because the Boilermakers' society and the Shipwrights' association had failed to agree on which men should mark chalk lines on steel plates.

In Sept. 1958, after discussions with both the T.U.C. and the British Employers' confederation, the minister of labour had announced that the order-in-council upon which the Industrial Disputes tribunal was based would be allowed to lapse. This decision was strongly opposed by the T.U.C. which was in favour of maintaining the order on the grounds that it provided: (a) an opportunity to unions to seek redress in sections of employment where they were not recognized and where the strike weapon was not used; (b) a means of obtaining a decision without a joint agreed reference where negotiations had failed; and (c) a way of preventing unfair competition by enforcing widely agreed conditions of work

(Left) Strike-bound lorries at the works of the British Oxygen company, Wembley. (Right) Gondolas lying idle at San Marco landing stage in Venice, following a strike by gondoliers in protest against a proposal to carry out canal dredging work during the tourist season.

upon employers who were not parties to a national agreement. After further consultations with the minister and discussion with the B.E.C., it was eventually agreed that the Industrial Court, which had been in existence as a permanent court of arbitration since 1919, should be empowered to make legally enforceable awards to prevent the undercutting of collective agreements. Thus in cases where a collective agreement covering the major part of an industry was not being observed by a minority of employers it would be possible to bring the employer before the court and obtain an award compelling him to observe the terms and conditions established by agreement for the majority.

WORKING DAYS LOST AND WORKERS DIRECTLY INVOLVED IN STRIKES
IN THE UNITED KINGDOM (1939–59)

Year	No. of stoppages beginning in year	No. of workers directly involved in stoppages* (Beginning in year) '000s	(In progress in year) '000s	Aggregate no. of working days lost in year in stoppages (In progress in year) '000s
1939	940	246	337	1,356
1940	922	225	299	940
1941	1,251	297	361	1,079
1942	1,303	349	457	1,527
1943	1,785	454	559	1,808
1944	2,194	716	826	3,714
1945	2,293	447	532	2,835
1946	2,205	405	529	2,158
1947	1,721	489	623	2,433
1948	1,759	324	426	1,944
1949	1,426	313	434	1,807
1950	1,339	269	303	1,389
1951	1,719	336	379	1,694
1952	1,714	303	416	1,792
1953	1,746	1,329	1,374	2,184
1954	1,989	402	450	2,457
1955	2,424	599	671	3,794
1956	2,643	463	507	2,083
1957	2,855	1,276	1,359	8,415
1958	2,629	455	524	3,462
1959	2,073	...	644	5,250

* Workers involved in more than one stoppage in any year are counted more than once in the year's total. Workers involved in a stoppage beginning in one year and continuing into another are counted in both years in the column showing the number of workers involved in stoppages in progress.
SOURCE. *Ministry of Labour Gazette* (H.M.S.O., London, Jan. 1960).

In the United States more than 85% of the country's basic steel capacity was shut down on July 15, 1959, when the steelworkers and the employers failed to reach a decision to extend their collective-bargaining agreements. About 500,000 steelworkers were directly involved, but before the strike was over an additional 200,000 employees were laid off as an indirect result. Eventually the government obtained an injunction, under the Taft-Hartley act, requiring the Steelworkers' union to terminate the strike. Execution of the injunction was delayed until Nov. 7, when the Supreme Court ruled that it was constitutional. Thus the longest nation-wide steel strike in U.S. history (116 days) was halted. An injunction under the same act also brought to an end after eight days a strike by about 70,000 longshoremen on the Atlantic and Gulf of Mexico coasts. Between 1957 and 1958 the number of work stoppages had increased only slightly, from 3,673 to 3,694, but the number of workers involved in stoppages increased by about 48% (from 1,390,000 to 2,060,000) and the number of man-days idle by about 45% (from 16·5 million to 23·9 million). The number of man-days lost represented 0·22% of the total estimated working time of all workers in 1958, compared with 0·14% in 1957.

In order to avoid causing difficulties for the revolutionary government of Fidel Castro, the Cuban trade union movements decided that no strikes should take place for a period of six months. Elsewhere in Latin America there was less disposition to avoid stoppages. There were serious strikes in Argentina, encouraged by supporters of General Juan Perón, which resulted in clashes with the police. Perhaps the most unusual strike during the period under review was the world-wide boycott called for by the International Transport Workers' federation against ships flying flags of convenience, in which, it was alleged, seamen were employed at low wages and in bad conditions. The boycott lasted during Dec. 1–4, 1958, and was most successful in U.S. ports where dockworkers refused to handle these ships. (B. C. R.; S. A. LN.)

SUDAN. Republic in northeast Africa, bounded N. by Egypt, E. by the Red sea, Eritrea and Ethopia, S. by Kenya, Uganda and Belgian Congo, W. by the Central African Republic and the Republic of Chad and N.W. by Libya. Area: 967,500 sq.mi. Pop.: (1956 census) 10,262,506; (1958 est.) 11,037,000. Language: English, Arabic, and various Nilotic and Negro tribal dialects in the south. Religion: in the six northern provinces the Sudanese, a Negro-Hamite race, are almost entirely Sunni Moslem; in the three southern provinces, containing one-quarter of the country's population, the Negroes are mainly pagan, but one-fifth of them is Christian. Chief towns (pop., 1956 census): Khartoum (cap.) 93,103, Khartoum North 39,082 and Omdurman 113,551—the three towns constituting one agglomeration divided by the two Niles joining here; Port Sudan 47,562. President of the Supreme Military Council and prime minister, General Ibrahim Abboud. Main imports: cotton piecegoods, metals and products, machinery, sugar. Main export: cotton. Monetary unit: Sudanese pound = Egyptian pound (£1 sterling = £E.0·97¼–0·97¾).

History. The military dictatorship which was established in Sudan in Nov. 1958 under the leadership of General Ibrahim Abboud, was challenged from within the army itself early in 1959. The Supreme Military Council of 12 which had ruled the country for five months was dissolved by General Abboud in March, and reconstituted to include two brigadiers

(Mohieddin Ahmed Abdullah and Abd-ur-Rahim Shennan), who had gone to Khartoum from the provinces at the head of their troops. Competition for promotion and political power among the officers themselves was the motive behind this reshuffle, and the crisis passed off as uneventfully as that of the previous November. However, trouble flared up again in May, when more officers led their troops into the capital from the provinces. They complained that the government

On the White Nile near Khartoum, water hyacinths, whose rapid growth was affecting navigation, are sprayed with chemicals.

was not sufficiently effective, and their aim was apparently to replace it with a more homogeneous and active body.

The officers involved, together with the brigadiers who had been ministers since March, were arrested and tried for mutiny and conspiracy to overthrow the regime. At the same time a number of civilians were arrested, and members of the Communist party (a negligible force in Sudan) were rounded up and sent to a detention camp. The trial of the officers ended in September, many of them being convicted and sentenced to long terms of imprisonment.

Economically, the situation began to improve in 1959, largely as a result of resumed cotton sales, and although there remained an acute shortage of imported goods, the restrictions on certain categories of imports were eased. In the autumn, however, there was a serious food shortage in southern Sudan, causing a near famine. Free foreign exchange reserves, which had reached the extremely low level of £S4 million by the end of 1958, rose to £S9 million by July 1959. Credits supplied by the British and Federal German governments were being used for the construction of a power station at the Sennar dam on the Blue Nile. Fresh negotiations with the United Arab Republic were opened in October for a division of the Nile waters, and resulted in an agreement concluded in November, according to which the Sudan would receive (once the Aswan High dam started storing water) one-third of the total annual flow (18,500 million cu.m.), instead of its present share of one-twelfth (4,000 million cu.m.). At the same time a trade agreement was concluded with the U.A.R. for an exchange of goods to the value of £5 million. Other developments in the economic field were the receipt of a loan from Yugoslavia, and the concession given to an Italian company for oil exploration.

Sayed Abd-ur-Rahman el-Mahdi, 74-year-old political and religious leader, died at Khartoum on March 24.

On Dec. 2 two army officers and three former officers were executed at Khartoum after being convicted by a court martial of an attempted mutiny at the Infantry school at Omdurman on Nov. 10.   (E. S. A.)

SUEZ CANAL. An artificial waterway 101 mi. long, with a minimum depth of 40 ft., and a width of from 195 ft. to 245 ft. (265 ft.-360 ft. on curves), connecting Port Said on the Mediterranean sea with Suez on the Red sea. The canal enables shipping between Europe and the east to avoid the long passage around Africa. The average time of transit through the canal is a little over 11 hr. The *Compagnie Universelle du Canal Maritime de Suez* was founded by Ferdinand de Lesseps, who obtained the concession from the sultan of Turkey. The canal was opened in 1869. In 1956 the Egyptian government nationalized the canal, appointing Colonel Mahmud Yunis chairman and managing director of the new Egyptian Suez Canal authority.

History. Throughout the year 1959, traffic through the canal proceeded without incident, except in the case of shipping in which Israel was interested. On Feb. 26, the Liberian vessel " Capetan Manolis " with potash and fruit juice consigned from Haifa to Singapore was detained at Port Said. On March 13, the German vessel " Lealott " with cement consigned from Haifa to Malaya and the Philippines was halted at Port Said. On March 25th the Greek ship " Nikolaos Kairis " with a cargo of cement and steel scrap from Haifa to Hong Kong was also detained. In all three cases the cargo was impounded and the ship allowed to proceed. The Israeli government protested to the U.N. Security council that these incidents violated the Suez Canal convention and a Security council resolution of Sept. 1, 1951, calling on the Egyptians to end all restrictions on the passage of goods and ships through the canal, wherever bound. The United Arab Republic case was that there was still a state of war between Israel and the Arab countries, and that Israel therefore had no right to ship goods through the canal, even in vessels flying non-Israeli flags. In defiance of the Israeli protest, the U.A.R. authorities on May 21 detained the Danish vessel " Inge Toft " and placed it in custody in Port Said when its captain refused to unload the cargo of potash and cement the ship was taking from Israel to Hong Kong and Japan. On June 30, President Abd-ul-Nasser said that the United Arab Republic would not allow ships chartered by Israel or flying the Israeli flag to use the Suez canal, and on Aug. 31 the Israeli government made a further protest to the Security council against this policy.

On Jan. 1, 1959, the United Arab Republic duly paid to the former Suez Canal company the first instalment of the compensation agreed upon, which was passed on to the shareholders by the company in the form of Fr.500 and five shares in a company called the Société d'Investissements Mobiliers

Members of a youth labour camp at Ismailia, Egypt, who were taking part in operations to widen the Suez canal.

for every one share held in the old Suez Canal company. In June it was announced that the British government had accepted an offer of £1·8 million from a London syndicate for the shares it had so received in the Société d'Investissements Mobiliers in respect of its holding in the former Suez Canal company.

On Dec. 22, in Washington, a $56·5 million loan agreement was signed by Eugene Black, president of the International Bank for Reconstruction and Development, Mustafa Kamel, ambassador of the U.A.R., and Colonel Mahmud Yunis, chairman of the board and managing director of the Suez Canal authority. The loan would enable the canal to be deepened, widened and generally improved. By 1961 the canal should be able to take ships with a draught of 37 ft. instead of the current maximum of 35 ft.; this would mean a difference between 36,000 tons deadweight and 46,000 tons. Port Said harbour would also be deepened and improved. The cost of the whole work was estimated at $108 million, the rest of the sum to be met by the canal authority from its own resources. (*See* also ISRAEL; UNITED ARAB REPUBLIC.)

(B. S.-E.)

SUGAR: *see* FOODSTUFFS.

SUMMIT CONFERENCE, APPROACHES TO.
The year 1959 opened in an atmosphere of considerable tension over Berlin, caused by Soviet statements, in the previous November, which the western powers regarded as a threat to terminate western rights in the city by unilateral action within six months. In this atmosphere, it seemed unlikely that the west would agree to a " summit " conference (or meeting of heads of government), although in the spring of 1958 they had tried, unsuccessfully, to agree with the U.S.S.R. on the agenda for such a conference.

On New Year's eve (Dec. 31, 1958) the western powers had addressed notes to the U.S.S.R., rejecting Soviet demands of Nov. 27 for a change in the status of western Berlin, but stating their willingness to enter into discussions with the Soviet government, in any appropriate forum, on any proposals " genuinely designed to ensure the reunification of Germany in freedom ". On Jan. 10, 1959, the Soviet government, replying to these western notes, proposed a peace conference to discuss a peace treaty with Germany (of which a Soviet draft was submitted) and also Berlin. The note added that the Soviet government would agree to an exchange of views with the western powers in advance of the peace conference provided that the German Democratic government and the Federal German government also participated.

This latter suggestion slightly eased tension. Later in January, Harold Macmillan, the British prime minister, said in the House of Commons, in reply to a question about prospects for a summit meeting, that recent exchanges with the U.S.S.R. had shown a desire for negotiation on both sides. On Feb. 16, the western powers replied to the U.S.S.R., reserving their rights in Berlin and proposing a conference of foreign ministers of the U.S.S.R., France, Great Britain and the United States, to deal with the problem of Germany " in all its aspects and implications as raised in the recent exchange of notes ".

Five days later, Macmillan flew to Moscow with Selwyn Lloyd, the foreign secretary, for exploratory talks with Nikita S. Khrushchev. At first, the atmosphere at the talks was said to be relatively good, but on Feb. 24 Khrushchev, without forewarning his British guests, declared in a blunt public speech that the western proposal for a foreign ministers' meeting was only intended to waste time and to bring discussions into a quagmire with no way out. Instead, he said he wanted a summit meeting to discuss a German peace treaty and Berlin.

In spite of this setback Macmillan persisted in stating the western view to Khrushchev, and on March 2 the Soviet government addressed notes to the western powers, advocating a summit conference but consenting to the western proposal for a foreign ministers' meeting " if the governments of the western powers are not yet prepared to take part in a meeting at the summit ". The note added that Poland and Czechoslovakia should also take part.

Macmillan had therefore convinced Khrushchev of the need for a foreign ministers' conference, at least as a pre-condition for a summit. On the other hand, Macmillan left Moscow convinced that real business could only be done at a summit, since in the U.S.S.R. it was only Khrushchev's word which counted. In the following months, there was a certain difference on this point between Macmillan and other western statesmen who—especially President Charles de Gaulle and Konrad Adenauer—were more sceptical about the advantages of a summit. Macmillan was accused in a number of western newspapers of pressing for a summit as an election stunt, in preparation for the general election in the autumn.

Meanwhile agreement was quickly reached between the western powers and the U.S.S.R. on the date and place of the foreign ministers' conference, which began in Geneva on May 11 and lasted, with a recess from June 20 until July 13, until Aug. 5, when it ended inconclusively. Western and eastern German representatives took part in plenary meetings, though an argument between the U.S.S.R. and the three western powers over their exact status remained unresolved throughout. Andrei A. Gromyko, the Soviet foreign minister, proposed that Poland and Czechoslovakia should attend, but did not press his proposal in the face of western opposition.

Before the conference opened, Great Britain had stated, in a note to the U.S.S.R. of March 26, that " as soon as developments in the foreign ministers' meeting warrant holding a summit conference ", the British government would be glad to participate in such a conference. A parallel U.S. note used the word " justify " instead of " warrant ". During the foreign ministers' conference, this verbal difference turned out to have some substance. The U.S. government, as President Dwight D. Eisenhower said at a press conference on July 29, did not consider that enough progress had been made to justify a summit. The British government held that enough progress had been made to move straight on to a summit, where final decisions could be reached.

This rift, however, never became serious, largely, perhaps, because before the foreign ministers' meeting closed, Eisenhower had announced his invitation to Khrushchev to visit the United States. Khrushchev's visit, and his talks with Eisenhower at Camp David, were a turning point. In a joint communiqué on Sept. 27, the two statesmen said that, subject to the approval of the other parties, negotiation on " the specific Berlin question " should be reopened. On the same day, Khrushchev said at a press conference that he considered that conditions for calling a summit conference were already ripe. Eisenhower said at a press conference on Sept. 28 that many of the objections to a summit which he had previously held had been removed by his talks with Khrushchev. He made it clear that he considered that the Soviet threat to Berlin had been lifted.

Discussions about arrangements for a summit were then delayed, first by the British election campaign, then by de Gaulle's opposition to any haste. Macmillan and Eisenhower were understood to be in favour of a summit in early December. On Oct. 21, however, de Gaulle authorized a statement by the French government welcoming in principle the project of a summit, but stressing the need for much preparatory work. In consequence, the statement said, the earliest time for a summit meeting would be in the following spring. Two days later it was announced that de Gaulle had invited

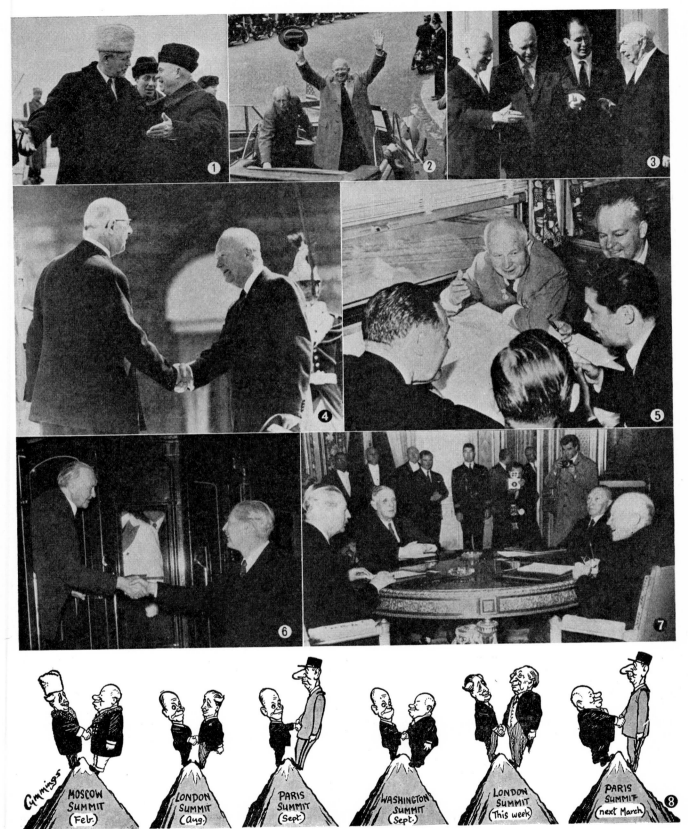

(1) N. Khrushchev greets H. Macmillan at Moscow airport on Feb. 21. (2) President Eisenhower with H. Macmillan in London on Aug. 31.
(3) The U.S. president in Bonn on Aug. 27 with President Heuss (right) and his successor, H. Lübke (left); (4) Presidents de Gaulle and
Eisenhower before their talks at the Elysée palace, Paris, on Sept. 2. (5) On a train journey during his U.S. tour in September, N. Khrushchev
chats through an interpreter with Henry Cabot Lodge (left). (6) K. Adenauer, the western German chancellor, takes leave of H. Macmillan on
Nov. 19 after his visit to London.   (7) The western leaders at the opening of their conference in Paris on Dec. 19-21.   (8) " So much fuss
about THE Summit ! As if they hadn't enough summits around already !"—Cummings in the " Daily Express " on Nov. 16.

" High, higher, highest ".   Steps to the summit as seen by H. E. Köhler in the " Frankfurter Allgemeine Zeitung " of Aug. 12.

Khrushchev to visit Paris, and it was made clear that the French president would not go to the summit until after this visit. It was later announced that Khrushchev's visit would take place from March 15 to 27, 1960: this meant that the summit could not take place until April at the earliest.

Meanwhile, an offer by Eisenhower to visit Europe at the end of October was not taken up by de Gaulle. Instead, it was agreed that the western heads of government should examine the subjects to be discussed at the summit. Eisenhower, Macmillan, de Gaulle and Adenauer met in Paris from Dec. 19 to 21 to discuss questions relating to a summit conference. On Dec. 21, the British, U.S. and French ambassadors in Moscow handed invitations to Khrushchev to a summit conference on April 27 in Paris. The ambassadors were also instructed to explain that in the western view this might be the first of a series of summits, and that among subjects to be discussed should be disarmament, Germany, including Berlin, and east-west relations. The four western heads of government also agreed among themselves to set up working parties to prepare western positions on the main subjects likely to come up at the summit conference.

On Dec. 25 the Soviet government replied to the western powers. The date of April 27 was inconvenient to Khrushchev because of his need to be in Moscow for the annual May Day celebration. He proposed April 21 or May 4. The western powers then suggested May 16 and on Dec. 29 Khrushchev wrote to Eisenhower, Macmillan and de Gaulle accepting the new date.   (EH. M. B.)

SURGERY. Surgical progress continued along the usual lines in 1959. Operations which had been popular became obsolete; others were modified in the light of wider experience which had resulted in increasing safety of the procedure; new diagnostic or therapeutic weapons became dovetailed into the existing procedure as their sphere of usefulness became

known. Simple mastectomy for pain in the breast was an example of a procedure at one time commonly performed but now practically never, since the realization that the symptoms were, in the main, psychogenic. The indications for thoraco-lumbar sympathectomy for hypertension, introduced some 15 years before and very widely performed for a time, had gradually disappeared, not so much because it was valueless, but because of a rise of medical therapy by hexamethonium compounds, rauwolfia and other drugs.

While there were now established satisfactory techniques for the exposure and removal of most of the organs and parts of the body, much work continued to be devoted to determining the indications for the various operations, particularly where the underlying pathology of the disease was unknown and the treatment therefore empirical; e.g., in the case of peptic ulcer of hypertension, and where the limitations of massive ablations such as total pancreatectomy and total gastrectomy in palliation and cure, became obvious. Bilateral total adrenalectomy for advanced carcinoma of the breast was still being widely practised with a relatively small proportion of dramatic successes, which could not yet be predicted beforehand. The rise and decline of new operations, which seemed inseparable from surgical progress, continued to be dictated by the collective experiences of progressive enthusiasts, tempered by the more conservative minds, and always disproportionately influenced by the vocal members of the profession.

The technique of surgical ablations appeared to have reached its peak, but intensive study was being undertaken in animals and man with the aid of techniques of tissue culture, radiotherapy and endocrinology, to advance knowledge of tissue transplantation. The problem of homografting (grafting of tissue from another animal of the same species) was being clarified and occasionally overcome in the experimental animal. Many different variables were found to be significant; e.g., age (tolerance of homografted tissue is great in the embryo and newborn), genetic relationship (success is most likely in grafts performed between siblings) and dosage of the graft. M. F. A. Woodruff (J. roy. coll. Surg., ed., 3, 19, 1957), reviewed this work. It had been shown that the mechanism by which homo-transplants were destroyed was immunological and was conveyed by the cells of the host; and that the agent could be destroyed by certain treatments such as heating to 50°C., repeated freezing and thawing, and freeze-drying. The host's reaction could be reduced temporarily by the administration of cortisone, or by total body irradiation, and by the injection of antigen (a few million cells of the donor), before birth in the case of a mouse, or within two weeks after birth, in a rat. It was hoped that these methods might be adapted for use in the treatment of leukaemia in humans and, in fact, J. W. Ferrebee (Am. J. M. Sc., 235, 369, 1958) had achieved this experimentally in the dog. After splenectomy and prolonged administration of ACTH to reduce the lymphoid tissue and immune responses, it received a lethal dose of total body irradiation and was then successfully transfused with a graft consisting of a large amount of prepared and stored marrow cells. Similar researches were being undertaken in relation to skin and endocrine homografts, which appeared to be capable of survival.

Besides corneal homografts, which had long been in successful clinical use, homo-transplantation was used in arterial replacement and for temporary skin cover in burns. In three instances, the whole kidney had been transplanted between identical twins. Hetero-transplants were less suitable, but it seemed possible that hetero-transplants of cornea might one day be used. Skin homografts were already of limited value in the primary resurfacing of serious burns where sufficient donor skin could not be obtained from the patient. It was known that such homografts would survive about two weeks

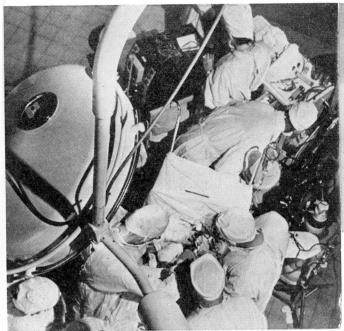

(Left) Members of the team of British heart specialists which visited the U.S.S.R. in May performing a " hole-in-the-heart " operation on a young Russian girl, using the Melrose " heart-lung " machine, at the Moscow Institute of Thoracic Surgery. Soviet doctors assisted. (Above) After the successful operation: (left to right) D. Melrose, S. Kolesnikov and W. Cleland, leader of the British team.

and that a second crop of similar homograft would be destroyed by an immunological reaction within a few days. An alternative method of resurfacing large raw areas was the use of a suspension of particles, each containing 10-100 cells and prepared by an electric kitchen mixer (J. S. Najarian, *et al.*, *Surg. 42*, 218, 1957), which had been found highly successful in rabbits. G. Carmsdale and his co-authors compared (*J. Bone Jt. Surg.*, *41A*, 887, 1959) some hundreds of cases of autogenous and homogenous bone grafts and found the failure rate approximately doubled (20%-30%) with the use of homogenous grafts.

The methods available for the reconstruction of the hip joint were again under evaluation. Reviewing this subject in his presidential address, J. S. Batchelor (*Proc. R. soc. Med.*, *52*, 335, 1959) described surgery of the arthritic hip as a baffling problem, in which the Judet and Crawford Adams arthroplastics had virtually disappeared and only the Smith-Petersen method had survived. There was a tendency to return to the older and better established procedures: arthrodesis, displacement osteotomy and pseudarthrosis. However, the Committee for the Study of Femoral Head Prostheses (*J. Bone Jt. Surg.*, *41A*, 883, 1959) found that 80% of 500 surgeons who participated in a questionnaire were still using prostheses and that there had been a most striking change towards long, intramedullary pegs of stainless steel, whereas nylon prostheses had been virtually abandoned because of breakage and wear. The procedure was principally used for sub-capital fractures, particularly those complicated by aseptic necrosis or non-union and those in the elderly. Cases classified as " good " or " excellent " numbered 60%, but there was a considerable operative mortality and morbidity from sepsis and fracture of the prosthesis. The principle of compression-arthrodesis introduced by J. Charnley and partly derived from a study of the influence of distraction in delaying union of fractures, had been widely accepted with an improvement in surgical results and speeds of union. Much study was being devoted to surgical methods in the relief of spastics by attention to the problems of the urinary bladder and operations on bones, joints and nerves, and in the technique and equipment of rehabilitation. (R. L.)

SURINAM: *see* Netherlands Overseas Territories.
SWAZILAND: *see* British South African Territories.

SWEDEN. Constitutional monarchy of northern Europe, lying on the eastern side of the Scandinavian peninsula, bounded N.E. by Finland, E. and S. by the Baltic sea, S.W. by the strait of Öresund and the Kattegat and W. and N.W. by Norway. Area (incl. inland water): 173,577 sq.mi. Pop.: (1950 census) 7,044,039; (1959 est.) 7,436,066. Language: Swedish, with some Finnish (about 30,000) and Lappish (4,140 in 1945) in the north. Religion: predominantly Lutheran: in 1950 there were, however, 303,000 Protestant dissenters of various denominations, 16,000 Roman Catholics and 6,700 Jews. Chief towns (pop., Jan. 1959): Stockholm (cap.) 804,910 (with suburbs *c.* 1,100,000); Gothenburg (Göteborg) 397,205; Malmö 221,700. Ruler, King Gustaf VI Adolf; prime minister, Tage Fritiof Erlander. Main imports: machinery and vehicles; coal, petroleum and other mineral products; base metals and manufactures; textile fibres and manufactures; vegetable products; chemical products. Main exports: wood, wood pulp and manufactures; machinery, vehicles and ships; iron ore; iron, steel and manufactures. Monetary unit: *krona*, pl. *kronor* (Kr.14·48 =£1 sterling).

History. *Home Affairs.* On May 14, 1959, the question that had dominated politics for three years was decided, at least for the time being, when the lower chamber of the Riksdag passed the Social Democratic government's pensions bill (presented on Feb. 27) by 115 votes to 114. The exact balance between government supporters and opposition was upset by the abstention of Ture Königson, a Liberal shipbuilding worker from Gothenburg. The scheme, a landmark in the history of social reform, and regarded as a crowning achievement by the Social Democratic party, which celebrated its 70th anniversary in April, provided at the age of 67 for a pension of 65% of the pensioner's income during his 15 best-paid years, tied to the cost-of-living index. The additional pension needed to make up the existing basic old age pension to the 65% would be financed by employers' contributions alone; these would be 3% on wages in excess of Kr.4,000 (up to Kr.30,000) when the system started operating in 1960, increasing gradually to a maximum which it was estimated would never exceed 10% of the total wages bill. Substantially the same as the Social Democrats' original plan, the new law retained the compulsory element, but employed persons might contract out of the scheme collectively through their organizations provided the latter arranged alternative superannuation; self-employed persons, who would pay their own contributions, might also withdraw.

The Conservatives declared their determination to have the law repealed; but the pensions controversy was replaced by the problem of balancing the budget as the chief political issue. When Gunnar Sträng, the minister of finance, presented the 1959-60 budget on Jan. 12, he was severely criticized for failing to show how a deficit he himself estimated at Kr.500 million—Kr.1,000 million was to be met. He left this to the Riksdag to decide later. During the summer an all-party parliamentary committee produced, unexpectedly, a unanimous report recommending various long-term budget economies. Meanwhile, to cover the deficit in current (1959-60) expenditure (Kr.13,591 million), Sträng proposed a general sales tax of 4%. This was vigorously opposed, although only the Conservatives pressed for drastic cuts in the credits already voted, but was passed on Dec. 1 in a joint vote of the Riksdag's two chambers by 185 votes to 178; the 7 Communists, loath to be accused of bringing down a Socialist government, abstained.

After exceptionally hard negotiations between the Federation of Trade Unions (L.O.) and the Employers' association (S.A.F.) a general agreement, directly concerning 650,000 wage earners and in practice affecting nearly 3 million employees, was reached on March 4. Valid for one year only, it provided for an increase of 2% in hourly wages and 1½% in piece rates, while those with fixed weekly or monthly wages and working shorter hours as a result of the new 46-hr. week were to receive their wages uncut.

In 1958 both exports (Kr.10,807 million) and imports (Kr.12,200 million) had declined, although car and ship exports—as well as car imports—had risen. Unemployment, the highest since the war, and the failure to increase production in 1958, caused anxiety at the beginning of 1959, but expanding markets for the country's most important exports greatly increased building activity (often state-supported) and industrial investment were among developments that led to a new rise in production. Employment at first lagged behind but by the early autumn the demand for labour had increased in nearly all industries. Renewed inflation became the problem instead, and stricter credit policies began to be applied.

National Defence. Slightly increased defence appropriations (Kr.2,827 million; *i.e.*, over 20% of state expenditure) were voted by parliament without much questioning. The public debate on whether Sweden should possess atomic weapons was continued, however, with great intensity. In Nov. 1958 the government had rejected the commander-in-chief's demand for a special grant for nuclear weapon research; in May 1959 a similar proposal by the Conservatives and some Liberals was defeated in parliament. The government also refused in February to consider the purchase of nuclear charges abroad. Yet, Per Edvin Sköld, the former defence

Carl Sandburg (left), the U.S. poet, with the present owners of the homestead at Appuna, Sweden, which his mother left in 1874.

and finance minister, a Social Democrat, published a book in March recommending the acquisition of atomic weapons.

Foreign Affairs. In Dec. 1958 an agreement to increase trade over the following three years was concluded with the U.S.S.R. Sweden's deliveries would include machinery and complete pulp, paper and chemical plant, while with other minerals, and chemicals, the U.S.S.R. would supply a large proportion of Sweden's requirements of oil and oil products.

On Oct. 14, 1958, Östen Undén, the foreign minister, had condemned the Soviet Union's resumption of nuclear weapon tests. Nevertheless, in Feb. 1959, the government's invitation to Nikita Khrushchev, prime minister of the U.S.S.R., to visit Sweden in the autumn was accepted. In fact the invitation was a renewal of an old one withdrawn after the events of 1956 in Hungary. However, Jarl Hjalmarson, the Conservative leader, Bertil Ohlin, the Liberal leader, and newspapers such as *Dagens Nyheter* now found it highly objectionable and hypocritical to welcome the Soviet prime minister. Tage Erlander, the prime minister, and Undén defended in the Riksdag (in March) the Khrushchev visit as a valuable opportunity to discuss questions of mutual interest and show the Soviet leader something of Swedish life.

When the Soviet idea of a nuclear-free Baltic region was urged by Khrushchev in Riga in June, Undén commented in a speech on June 26: "I dare not believe that the Soviet government is prepared to ban nuclear weapons in a considerable zone of its own territory . . ." On July 19 Khrushchev caused a sensation by cancelling his visit. He justified his action by reference to the anti-Soviet campaign being conducted in Sweden, and even blamed the government for not checking it—a demand for interference with the free expression of opinion that was received with indignation. But speculation that the real explanation was Soviet disappointment at the Swedish rejection of Khrushchev's Baltic plan was possibly supported by the Soviet note's insistence that a mere protocol visit, without definite political significance, would have no meaning.

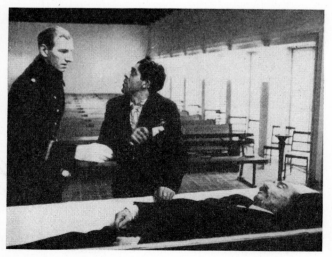

" He needs it, officer "—a prize-winning Swedish press photograph. A constable restrains the son of a gipsy chief who died at Karlstad from putting a bottle of beer in his father's coffin.

The government broke with tradition and caused political bitterness by excluding Hjalmarson from the Swedish delegation to the United Nations. On Sept. 30, at the U.N. general assembly in New York, Undén adopted a reserved attitude to Khrushchev's disarmament plan, but suggested that U.N. experts should examine proposals, such as the Rapacki plan, for nuclear-free zones; he hoped that the existing *de facto* ban on nuclear weapon tests would also be respected by nations which had not yet produced their own weapons. He repeated his view that the Peking government should represent China at the United Nations, expressed Swedish concern at the "curious anachronism" of South Africa's race policy and criticized the unwillingness of Communist regimes to submit to the jurisdiction of the International Court of Justice.

The plans for a free trade area of the "outer seven" were strongly supported in Sweden, which took a leading part in the various discussions in Stockholm, but they led to an indefinite postponement of the long-debated Nordic customs union. The seventh session of the Nordic council in Stockholm (November) was marked by the bitter disappointment of many delegates on this account, and by concern for Finland, which would be left in isolation by the new economic constellation.

Miscellaneous. Yngve Brilioth, former primate of Sweden, died on April 27 (*see* OBITUARIES). The 150th anniversary of the "instrument of government", the oldest written constitution in force in Europe, was celebrated at the royal palace in Stockholm on May 30. Television continued to expand rapidly; by June 1 there was one television set per 18·6 persons, compared with one per 84·3 in 1957. The warship "Vasa", which sank in Stockholm's harbour on her maiden voyage in 1628, was moved inshore to a depth of eight fathoms in August and September. She was to be raised intact in 1960. The first country in the world to offer to receive refugees suffering from tuberculosis (1950), Sweden welcomed 100 more in this category, together with their families, in 1959.

(P. A. B. G.)

BIBLIOGRAPHY. O. Fritiof Ander, *The Building of Modern Sweden* (Rock Island, Illinois, 1958); J. A. Lauwerys, ed., *Scandinavian Democracy* (Copenhagen, 1958); Gunnar Heckscher, *The Swedish Constitution 1809-1959* (Stockholm, 1959); Raymond E. Lindgren, *Norway-Sweden: Union, Disunion and Scandinavian Integration* (Princeton, 1959).

SWITZERLAND. Republican confederation of 22 cantons (three of which have half-cantons) in west central Europe, bounded W. by France, N. by Germany, E. by Austria and Liechtenstein and S. by Italy. Area: 15,944 sq.mi. Pop.: (1950 census) 4,714,992; (1959 est.) 5,243,000. Language (1950): German 72·1%; French 20·3%; Italian 5·9%; Romansh 1·0%. Religion (1950): Protestant 56·3%; Roman Catholic 41·6%; Jewish 0·4%; other 1·7%. Chief towns (pop., 1959): Berne (cap.) 163,000; Zürich 436,475; Basel 200,000; Geneva 172,000; Lausanne 121,000. President of the federal council for 1960, Max Petitpierre. Main imports: machinery and vehicles; coal, petroleum and products; steel mill products. Main exports: watches, clocks and parts; machinery; shoes; textiles; chemicals and related products. Monetary unit: *franc* (Fr.S.12·10 = £1 sterling).

History. Within the framework of its neutrality as established in international and constitutional law, Switzerland during 1959 continued to pursue its policy of active interest in, and co-operation with, numerous international and European efforts towards political, economic and cultural development. Thus, at the beginning of the year, a Swiss consortium of banks offered a new loan of the International Bank for Reconstruction and Development for subscription in Switzerland; the federal council (government) decreed liberalization of payments with some European countries in connection with the replacement of the European Payments union by the European monetary agreement; active co-operation was given—as an alternative to joining the European Economic community —to the "outer seven" (European Free Trade association); and the federal council requested the Federal Assembly to

appropriate a substantial contribution to the United Nations programme for technical assistance to underdeveloped countries.

In the early summer, Geneva was host to a four-power foreign ministers conference. Also in the international field, the International Court of Justice rejected the Swiss government's claim against the United States for restitution of the "Interhandel" company, stating that it had no jurisdiction in the case. Early in the year, the Swiss government donated a committee room to the Unesco building in Paris. Later, the government and people of Switzerland contributed to the relief and rehabilitation of refugees in connection with the World Refugee Year. On the other hand, the federal council refused an eastern German women's organization's request to convene an international women's congress at Lausanne for

The first tank to be designed and built in Switzerland for the Swiss army was demonstrated at Thun in October. The main armament consists of a 90 mm. gun.

the purpose of opposing the projected atomic arms for Switzerland. Along the same lines, the parliament took cognizance of a Communist initiative aiming at prohibiting atomic arms; the federal council was expected to draw up a report on this question with a view to a future referendum.

Developments in domestic politics and economics included discussion in the parliament and in the press of a proposed federal law for the regulation of cartel agreements and free competition; of a Socialist initiative for the introduction of the legislative referendum, in addition to the constitutional referendum already practised; of a revision of the old age insurance and pensions system; of a draft federal law to introduce disability insurance; of a draft law regarding the development of atomic energy for peaceful uses and the control of nuclear radiation; of a petition, put forward by youth groups, for Swiss membership in the Council of Europe; of a trade-union initiative to shorten the work week to 44 hours; of a federal law on the development and maintenance of the national highways; of a pipeline project to carry oil from Genoa to the lower Valais and from there, perhaps, all the way to southern Germany.

In an extraordinary session parliament adopted a new customs tariff to replace the outdated tariff of 1921. Although the new tariff would increase average import duties from the present 4·5% to something above 5%—and was expected to raise living costs by about 1%—it might well be classified as one of the most liberal tariffs in existence.

A government proposal to amend the constitution so as to give women the vote in federal questions and elections was rejected on Feb. 1 in a referendum by 654,924 to 323,306 votes and by all the cantons excepting Geneva, Vaud and Neuchâtel. On the same day, Vaud, the first canton to enfranchise women, also decided by 33,671 to 32,805 to grant women the vote in cantonal questions. On Sept. 27 the male electors of the canton Neuchâtel took a similar decision by 11,240 votes to 9,738. Later in the year, the male electorate voted 380,345 to 230,616 in favour of a new article in the constitution providing for civil defence. In the parliamentary elections held on Oct. 25, the Radicals, the Peasants and the Evangelicals (Protestants) won one mandate each, while the Socialists lost two and the Communists one; the other parties, including the Conservatives (Catholics) and the " Landesring ", remained unchanged. (*See* also ELECTIONS.) On the whole, the stability of the Swiss political scene was once more confirmed.

On Dec. 17 the Federal Assembly—the two chambers in joint session—elected four new ministers and re-elected three others. The government was composed of two Conservatives, two Radicals, two Socialists and one Peasant. Max Petitpierre was re-elected president of the federal council for the third time.

Other developments of interest included the defeat on July 5, by 16,345 to 15,163 votes, in a plebiscite held in the Jura region of the canton of Berne, of a proposal to make this area a separate canton; the observance of the centennial of the battle of Solferino and the role played in it by the Genevese Henri Dunant, originator of the Swiss and International Red Cross organizations; the celebration of the 400th anniversary of the University of Geneva; also, the foundation in Berne of a Swiss association of scientists and industrialists engaged in developing atomic energy for peaceful uses. (M. SK.)

SYRIA: *see* UNITED ARAB REPUBLIC.

TANGANYIKA. British trust territory in east Africa bounded N. by Uganda and Kenya, E. by the Indian ocean, S. by Mozambique and Nyasaland and W. by Northern Rhodesia and Belgian Congo. Area: 362,688 sq.mi., incl. 19,982 sq.mi. inland water. Pop.: (1957 census) 8,788,466, incl. 65,830 Indians, 20,690 Europeans and 19,175 Arabs; (1958 est.) 8,906,000. Language: tribal; Swahili (the *lingua franca*). Religion: animist; many Moslems in coastal areas and up-country trading settlements; African Christians (1949) 1,069,285 (70% Roman Catholic). Chief towns: Dar es Salaam (cap.), pop. (1957 census) 107,709; Tanga (1952 census) 22,136. Administration: governor; council of ministers; executive council; legislative council with speaker and official majority. Governor, Sir Richard Turnbull. Main imports: textiles, machinery and vehicles, metal goods. Main exports: sisal, coffee, cotton, hides and skins, diamonds. Monetary unit: East African shilling (= 1s. sterling).

History. On Feb. 1, 1959, the governor, Sir Richard Turnbull, announced that since Tanganyika was entering upon a period in which it was unlikely to be able to maintain the existing level of public services from its own revenues, the British government had accepted the obligation to assist the territory in meeting its financial difficulties. Later in the same month elections took place for the remaining representative seats in the legislative council. Twelve candidates were returned unopposed and, as in the first half of the election held in 1958, all 15 successful candidates, African, Asian and European, were supported by the Tanganyika African National union. During the March meeting of the legislative council important constitutional changes were announced. These took effect on July 1, when the number of ministers was increased from 9 to 12, of whom 5 were unofficial. The 12 then formed a council of ministers to carry out the advisory duties hitherto performed by the executive council. There was still an official majority in both the legislature and the executive, but the acceptance of the new proposals by the 30 elected members meant that elected councillors now took part in the formulation of policy.

Following upon the elections a committee under the chairmanship of Sir Richard Ramage and with wide terms of reference began its inquiries with a view to making recommendations for further constitutional developments. Far-reaching changes in the constitution based on the committee's

Sir Richard Turnbull (third from left), governor of Tanganyika, on a visit to the oil drilling site at Mandawa.

report were announced by the governor in December. In 1960 Tanganyika was to be granted responsible government with an elected majority both in the council of ministers and in the legislative council. The governor also stated that a general election for the new constitution would be held in 1960. The news was received by Africans with great enthusiasm.

However, progress in the constitutional field was to some extent overshadowed by the concern felt over the country's economic problems. This was not lessened by a suit brought against the Tanganyika government for general and special damages exceeding £820,000 for an alleged breach of agreement in connection with an important sugar project, which was to have been undertaken by Sir J. L. Hulett and Sons. As the governor pointed out in October, however, any economic development in the territory would inevitably depend to a large extent upon the recommendations of a survey mission conducted by the International Bank for Reconstruction and Development. Already, in August, the T.A.N.U. leader, Julius Nyerere (*see* BIOGRAPHIES), had attempted to dispel some of the doubts of potential foreign investors regarding the security of their capital in a self-governing Tanganyika by giving assurances at a press conference in London. While stressing the desire of Tanganyika Africans to secure self-government as soon as possible Nyerere declared that they were fully conscious of their needs and that they were anxious to attract foreign capital to their country and would welcome foreigners with special knowledge and skills.

As a result of a visit to east Africa by the archaeologist, Sir Mortimer Wheeler, it was announced in August that a school of history and archaeology was to be established in Tanganyika with branches in Uganda and Kenya. (*See* also EAST AFRICA HIGH COMMISSION.) (K. I.)

TARIFFS AND QUOTAS. In 1958-59 there were three main developments in the pattern of restrictions on world trade. First, the European Economic community (E.E.C.) came into effect; agreement was reached by the " outer seven " countries on the establishment of a free trade association; and further progress was made in the establishment of the Central American Free Trade area. Secondly, many European countries found greater ease in balancing their current accounts with the dollar area, and this enabled them to reduce their discriminatory restrictions on imports from the United States. Thirdly, several countries, including the United Kingdom, Denmark, Norway, Sweden, Guatemala and El Salvador, adopted new standard tariff structures in accordance with the so-called Brussels nomenclature (*i.e.*, the nomenclature sponsored by the Customs Co-operation council since 1950) or, in the case of the Latin American countries, with the Nomenclatura Arancelaria Uniforme Centroamericana. The importance of this change lay in the opportunities it presented for future comparisons of and reciprocal reductions in tariff levels.

The tendency of these three moves was towards a greater freeing of trade, which doubtless contributed to the determination of G.A.T.T. (the General Agreement on Tariffs and Trade) to initiate a further round of tariff reductions in Sept. 1960.

The single most important change was undoubtedly the reduction, as from Jan. 1, 1959, by 10% of many duties on trade between the six members of the E.E.C. (Belgium, Netherlands, Luxembourg, Italy, France and the German Federal Republic) and the accompanying increase in import quotas; to some extent this reduction was applied to industrial goods imported from other G.A.T.T. countries. Towards the end of 1959 the " outer seven " countries (Austria, Denmark, Norway, Portugal, Sweden, Switzerland and the United Kingdom) reached final agreement on the establishment of a European Free Trade association. Under this agreement, tariffs on trade between member countries in a large range of industrial products were to be reduced initially by 20% on July 1, 1960.

There were, however, some offsetting forces acting to increase tariffs and trade restrictions. The recession in the United States and western Europe and the consequential fall in world prices of primary products had induced, during 1957-58, balance of payments difficulties for many countries. In consequence, some of them, notably New Zealand, were compelled to impose or maintain quantitative restrictions. Even so, most of these countries participated in the general move towards making their restrictions non-discriminatory. Another restrictionist force during 1958 was exerted by the world-wide problems of textile industries. Specific textile tariffs were imposed by many countries during 1958.

Quite apart from these general forces there were a number of small unconnected changes, mostly towards freer trade. Among these were an agreement by India, New Zealand, and France to accord some degree of " most favoured nation " treatment to Japan. Some countries (Ecuador, Nicaragua, Venezuela and others) reduced tariffs on raw materials in order to help in the development of domestic industries. Also, some increase in duty-free trade on a preferential basis was negotiated between New Zealand and the United Kingdom.

A number of peripheral changes may be recorded. Several countries, such as Finland, Guatemala and India, introduced new regulations for the more stringent enforcement of " marks of origin " on imported goods. In export promotion, the G.A.T.T. annual report (*International Trade, 1957-58*, Geneva, 1959) noted intensified competition among sellers and consequential resort to export subsidies by, for example, Iceland and Mexico.

The establishment of *de facto* convertibility of sterling, the French franc, the western German Deutsche Mark and the other principal European currencies in Dec. 1958 removed many of the reasons for the maintenance of discriminatory import restrictions. However, the general level of tariffs is not necessarily influenced by such moves. The chief sources of future, as of current, reductions in the general level of tariffs would therefore be negotiations within G.A.T.T., future developments in the various free trade areas and the construction of new regional agreements of the same sort. (*See* also EUROPEAN ECONOMIC COMMUNITY; EXCHANGE CONTROL AND EXCHANGE RATES.) (M. V. P.)

TASMANIA: *see* AUSTRALIA, COMMONWEALTH OF.
TAXATION: *see* BUDGETS.
TEA: *see* FOODSTUFFS.

TELECOMMUNICATIONS. **International Developments.** Apart from the annual session of the administrative council, the major occupation of the International Telecommunication union during the earlier part of 1959 was the preparation for the Ordinary Administrative Radio conference and for the Plenipotentiary conference.

More than 5,500 proposals were submitted to the Radio conference which was held in Geneva during Aug.-Dec. 1959. Its main task was to revise the Radio Regulations and the Additional Radio Regulations adopted at Atlantic City, New Jersey, in 1947.

The Plenipotentiary conference was held in Geneva during October-December for the purpose of drawing up a new Telecommunication convention to replace the one signed at Buenos Aires in 1952.

The ninth plenary assembly of the International Radio Consultative committee (C.C.I.R.) was held in Los Angeles, California, during April 1-29.

Study groups, sub-groups and working parties of the International Telegraph and Telephone Consultative committee (C.C.I.T.T.) were held during 1959 in Geneva, Tokyo, Paris and Munich to discuss telegraph and telephone engineering, operating and tariff problems referred to the committee for consideration.

During the year, the I.T.U. continued to take part in the Expanded Programme of Technical Assistance and collaborated in the implementation of telecommunication projects.

Cable and Wireless Telegraphs. Several important steps were taken during 1959 towards the organization of the projected 33,000-mi. round-the-world Commonwealth co-axial telephone cable. This project had been adopted by the Commonwealth Trade and Economic conference at Montreal in Sept., 1958, on the assumption that capital contribution towards the cost, estimated at £80 million, would be forthcoming from all Commonwealth countries.

In Aug. 1959 it was announced in London that Cable and Wireless Ltd. had been made responsible on behalf of the U.K. government for financing, laying and maintaining the U.K. share in the cable, which was expected to be approximately one-half.

As part of this arrangement there was to be a working partnership between Cable and Wireless Ltd. and the Post Office, in which the Post Office had been assigned main responsibility for designing and engineering the telephone cables so far as the United Kingdom was concerned. For its part the company would contribute, in addition to finance, its world-wide organization of stations and cable ships, and would ensure integration of the new network with its submarine telegraph cable system and other overseas telecommunications facilities. The partnership arrangement provided also for establishing a joint Submarine Cable and Development unit to serve both the company and the Post Office. Engineers of the company would form part of it and the company would share in the cost.

The next major development took place in Sydney on Sept. 28 when the Australian prime minister, R. G. Menzies, opened a Pacific conference, at which 32 delegates from the United Kingdom, Canada, New Zealand and Australia met to consider arrangements for the laying of the trans-Pacific section of the round-the-world cable. The U.K. delegation of ten members included five representatives of Cable and Wireless Ltd. On Oct. 20 it was announced that the delegates had reached full agreement on recommendations to be put to their governments for the laying of a submarine co-axial cable, with submerged repeaters incorporated, from Australia *via* New Zealand to the west coast of Canada, connecting with the trans-Canadian landlines and the existing and proposed trans-Atlantic systems between Canada and the United Kingdom. The decisions of the governments had not been announced by the end of the year.

Meanwhile, Cable and Wireless Ltd. in conjunction with the Canadian Overseas Telecommunications corporation had, during the year, placed orders for manufacture of all the major items of equipment required for the laying in the summer of 1961 of the first section of the round-the-world cable—the trans-Atlantic section to link Newfoundland and Scotland. The orders included manufacture of 552 nautical miles of shallow-water cable and 1,635 nautical miles of deep-sea cable at a total cost of £3,050,000, and construction of 92 submerged two-way repeaters and 11 equalizers costing an additional £1·8 million. In the autumn of 1958, the Canadian Overseas Telecommunication corporation had placed a £900,000 order for the cable and repeaters needed to link Newfoundland with the Canadian mainland.

Towards the end of 1958, Cable and Wireless Ltd. had announced its intention of disposing of one of their older cable ships and replacing another by a new diesel-electric, cable-repair vessel costing a little more than £1 million and capable of handling the latest types of coaxial cable with submerged repeaters, as well as conventional telegraph cable. The ship was to be of 4,000 tons gross, with an over-all length of 367 ft. and a breadth of 47·5 ft. She was to have a cable capacity of about 21,000 cu.ft. and a maximum speed of 15 knots, and was to be fully air-conditioned. The keel was to be laid in Feb. 1960, and the ship to be commissioned a year later. The company also announced their intention of progressively replacing three more of their fleet of seven cable ships by larger ships, capable of handling telephone and telegraph cable and repeaters.

The directors in their annual report for the year ended March 31, 1959, said that it had become apparent that future years would see the step-by-step replacement of sections of the existing telegraph cable system, either by high-capacity telephone cables or by multi-channel radio links. Normal provision for depreciation of the cable system had been increased by £200,000. A provision of £371,500 had been made for premature obsolescence of part of the cable system and, in addition, a special provision of £250,000 had been made to write off certain cables.

A plan for development and expansion of the inter-island and overseas telecommunications system of the federation of The West Indies at a cost of £735,000, subsequently revised to £920,000, was announced by Cable and Wireless (West Indies) Ltd. in August. It provided for: the installation of a tropospheric scatter radio link between Trinidad and Barbados designed to give adequate capacity for telegraph, telex and telephone services; a new transmitting station and a new central telegraph office in Jamaica to give improved telecommunications services between Jamaica and the United States, Trinidad, Barbados and British Honduras; telex links with Trinidad and Barbados and thus with the United Kingdom and the international network; a very high frequency (v.h.f.) radio network between all the Leeward and Windward Islands on which the company had branches, to give a minimum of three telephone channels on each link; and improved equipment generally throughout the system in the federation. These installations were to be completed by March 31, 1961. Telex was to be introduced on completion of the new installations.

During the year Cable and Wireless Ltd. established telex services between Singapore, Malaya, Hong Kong and the Philippine Islands and the United Kingdom. Extensions *via* the United Kingdom were made available to numerous other

countries. Direct telex links from Singapore to Hong Kong and Japan, and from Hong King to the Philippine Islands, Japan and Australia were opened. Lagos, Nigeria, was also linked with the United Kingdom by telex.

Direct radio telephone services were opened between Bahrain and Beirut, Aden and Addis Ababa, Nairobi and Addis Ababa, Nairobi and Khartoum, Mauritius and Nairobi, Sierra Leone and Dakar, Barbados and Caracas, Hong Kong and Karachi, and Suva and Wellington. Phototelegraphy services were established between Accra (Ghana) and Lagos and also between Cyprus and Greece.

The new wireless transmitting station at Aden was completed and plans were announced for construction of a complementary receiving station.

The total overseas telegraph traffic carried over Cable and Wireless Ltd.'s system during the year ended March 31, 1959, was 423 million words—approximately the same as in the previous year. The directors in their annual report said that this figure was considered satisfactory in view of the large number of private circuits leased to users, the growth of telex and intensified competition from other international telegraph undertakings. Radio-telephone traffic at 2,103,000 paid minutes showed an increase of 15% over the previous year. The directors reported that the service was expanding steadily and that the growth of traffic might be expected to continue.

The total overseas telegraph traffic carried on the Commonwealth system as a whole during the year ended March 31, 1959, was 734 million words—a decrease of 0·94% compared with the previous year.

U.K. Post Office Telegraphs. Following a recommendation made by an independent advisory committee on the inland telegraph service in 1958, the range of de-luxe greetings telegrams was extended during 1959. A de-luxe birthday telegram was introduced in May and an alternative de-luxe wedding design was introduced in June. Two contrasting designs of baby greetings telegram were introduced in October and golden envelopes for standard greetings telegrams were re-introduced in November. There were no other changes in telegraph facilities and charges for inland telegrams remained unchanged at the tariff which was introduced in 1954. During the year ended Aug. 31, 1959, 21,620,152 telegrams were delivered.

The inland telex service continued to expand. Conversion of the service to automatic working, which began in 1958, continued during 1959. About 40% of the network had been automatized by the end of the year. There were 5,376 telex subscribers at Aug. 31, 1959. The telex service was available to 44 overseas countries, the last extension being to Bulgaria in Aug. 1959.

U.K. Post Office Telephones. On March 31, 1959, the number of telephones (including extensions) was 7,532,461, an increase of 171,282 during the year. During the 12 months to Sept. 30, 1959, the number of applications for telephone connections was approximately 428,000, 81,000 more than in the previous 12 months. During the same period 390,000 exchange connections were made, and at Sept. 30, 1959, 1,132,000 customers were sharing lines.

Subscriber trunk dialling facilities, introduced in Bristol in Dec. 1958, were extended to call office users there when the first of the new " pay-on-answer " coin boxes were installed on Sept. 5, 1959. Charges were in units of 3*d.* compared with units of 2*d.* for subscribers, and the coin boxes were adapted to take 3*d.*, 6*d.* and 1*s.* pieces. Coins could not be inserted until the person called answered and the caller heard the " pay tone "—a series of rapid pips. Extension of subscriber trunk dialling facilities to other parts of the country was in progress.

In July the Post Office announced that a telephone answering set would be available later in the year. This instrument was developed to answer telephone calls in the subscribers' absence by means of a recorded message giving the subscriber's telephone number and name, an explanation of the subscriber's absence and/or his expected time of return, and an alternative number at which he might be called, or at which messages might be left.

On Oct. 28 the Post Office opened the South Lancashire

A motorist makes use of the South Lancashire Radiophone Service, the first car radio-telephone system in Great Britain.

Radiophone service, the first car telephone system to be set up in Britain. Subscribers who fitted their vehicles with suitable v.h.f. radio equipment and were within range of the two main radio stations could make telephone calls to, and receive them from, any telephone in the British Isles. This was an experimental scheme and the radio coverage was in 1959 limited to the southern half of Lancashire, the Wirral and north Cheshire.

In the year ended March 31, 1959, 5·5 million telephone calls were exchanged with other countries, an increase of 600,000 over the previous year. The overseas telephone system was extended by opening service with three more countries. Calls between the United Kingdom and North America over the transatlantic telephone cable increased by 17% during the year.

Commonwealth Telecommunications. The external telecommunications of most Commonwealth countries are subject to the oversight of the Commonwealth Telecommunications board. This body, with its headquarters in London, was incorporated by the Commonwealth Telegraphs act, 1949, following the Commonwealth Telegraphs agreement, 1948, between the governments of the United Kingdom, Canada, Australia, New Zealand, the Union of South Africa, India and Southern Rhodesia. Ceylon was admitted on June 1, 1951. On the establishment in 1953 of the Federation of Rhodesia and Nyasaland, it was agreed that the federation should take the place of Southern Rhodesia.

The board consists of a chairman appointed jointly by the partner governments, one member appointed by each partner government and an additional member appointed by the United Kingdom government to represent Commonwealth and colonial territories not directly represented by other members. Its primary function is to advise the partner governments and their national bodies; *i.e.*, the nationalized telecommunications undertakings in the territories of the partner governments on matters relating to their external telecommunication systems. The members are resident in the United Kingdom and each member has an office at the board's headquarters in London. Meetings of the board are normally held in London but are also required to be arranged from time to time in the territories of the other partner governments.

The board publishes a report each year and the latest edition shows that the Commonwealth is served by a network of approximately 145,000 nautical miles of telegraph or telephone-type cables. Maintenance, repair and any other necessary cable work is carried out by 12 cable ships stationed in various parts of the world. There is also a widespread radio network, with radio transmitting and receiving stations providing services throughout the day.

As a result of the Commonwealth Telecommunications conference held in London in the spring of 1958 and the subsequent Commonwealth Trade and Economic conference in Montreal in the autumn of that year, a plan for the adoption of a round-the-world Commonwealth coaxial cable was approved. (See *Cable and Wireless Telegraphs* above.)

United States Telegraphs. Increased automation in the operation of the telegraph system in the United States was a feature of the telegraph industry's progress in 1959. Progress in mechanization and consequent improvement in operations, was achieved in main and branch telegraph offices, trunk lines, customers' "tie-lines" and private wire systems leased to government and industry.

New robot printers which received messages automatically in page form and mechanically ejected them for final handling displaced former tape operation in key message centres, resulting in faster and more efficient message handling. Installation of automatic switching equipment was converting the offices at New York, Chicago and Washington, D.C., to push-button operation on all incoming messages. These would be transmitted automatically to branch offices and customers having teleprinter "tie-lines". These customers would be connected directly into the high-speed national network and would transmit their messages directly over it.

Western Union inaugurated an automatic customer-to-customer telegraph exchange service in 1959 between subscribers in the United States. Direct telex service, inaugurated between New York and Canadian cities in 1958, was extended to Chicago in Feb. 1959 and to San Francisco and Los Angeles later in the year. The network was being extended to many other cities in the United States, and was connected with a similar system in Canada. (I.T.U.; G.H.I.; G.P.O.; W.P.MA.)

TELEVISION. Programmes. A real event—the general election—supplied the outstanding single feature in 1959. Television made a night of it with results coming in until 3 A.M. and the service resuming before breakfast. Here the B.B.C., with its experience and with the imperturbable Richard Dimbleby in command of the commentators, proved more effective than ITV. The B.B.C. lost several television personalities to parliament—Christopher Chataway, Geoffrey Johnson Smith and Woodrow Wyatt, but gained from ITV the unsuccessful parliamentary candidates Robin Day and Ludovic Kennedy.

Another event which made television history was the London visit of the U.S. president, Dwight D. Eisenhower. The unscripted discussion of world affairs between the president and the prime minister, Harold Macmillan, at no. 10 Downing street, was televised as informally as possible by both services. Granada was characteristically quick to follow up this novelty immediately with *Flash Focus*, an instantaneous commentary-discussion by three U.S. correspondents.

B.B.C. and ITV output became increasingly difficult to distinguish in a year of hard-slogging, tit-for-tat matching of programme for programme—often to the extent of a clash in time as in the Tuesday evening plays and in the religious programmes broadcast on Sunday evening at 7 P.M. ITV's *About Religion* was preceded by *Sunday Break*, a curious hotch-potch of "Rock 'n' Roll" and religion for teenagers.

The producers of this programme claimed it had greatly increased the viewing public for the religious programme which followed. ITV's religious programmes generally tended to show greater variety both in the denominations represented and also in form. But one of the B.B.C.'s most notable programmes—not in the regular religious transmissions—was

The top of a new television transmitter tower which was under construction at Dortmund, German Federal Republic, during 1959.

Out of this World, a visit to a Carmelite convent in Wales, compered by Hywel Davies.

In 1959 many favourites established their position more firmly, as was shown by the number of familiar titles such as *What's My Line*, *Sunday Night at the Palladium*, *Emergency— Ward 10* and *Hancock's Half-hour*. Any list of programmes is

a temptation to pair off B.B.C. and ITV: *Panorama*, the B.B.C.'s authoritative "window on the world", and ITV's *This Week*; David Attenborough's *Zoo Quest* (B.B.C.) and Granada's *Zoo Time* (children's television but obviously due for promotion); Patrick Moore's *The Sky at Night* (B.B.C.) and ITV's *It Can Happen Tomorrow*. On B.B.C. Sir Gerald Kelly conducted a series of talks on *Five Great Painters*, beginning with Goya, while on ITV Sir Kenneth Clark's series of *Five Revolutionary Painters* also began with Goya. In *Face to Face* (B.B.C.) John Freeman interviewed C. G. Jung soon after Ludovic Kennedy's *Profile* of Sigmund Freud on ITV. Freeman was named TV personality of the year.

ITV showed a greater flexibility in organizing *ad hoc* specialities such as Associated-Rediffusion's *Battleground* (a documentary of the Spanish civil war) or *Israel's Rise*, a first-rate picture of the new Jewish state.

Only the B.B.C.'s *Monitor* seemed beyond competition, although under the editorship of Alan Pryce-Jones A.B.C.'s *The Bookman* gained ground fast. The B.B.C.'s *Monitor*, *Tonight* and *Panorama*, which took nearly all the television awards given by the guild of producers and directors in 1958, found no single challenger from ITV. It took the combined efforts of the ITV companies to counter the B.B.C.'s *Tonight* with half a dozen short programmes—Granada's political *Who Goes Next* or *We Want an Answer*, Scottish Television's pictorial *This Wonderful World*, compiled by John Grierson, I.T.N.'s *Roving Report* and Associated Television's *Right to Reply*, in which William Clark (formerly of the B.B.C. *Press Conference*) interviewed such personages as Aneurin Bevan, John Foster Dulles, Dag Hammarskjöld and Selwyn Lloyd.

In drama 1959 was a year of cautious débuts by the great. Dame Peggy Ashcroft chose to give her first performance in a television play for the B.B.C., *Shadow of Heroes*, Robert Ardrey's drama about Hungary under Communist rule. (Sir Laurence Olivier had made his television début at the end of Nov. 1958 in a most notable production of Henrik Ibsen's *John Gabriel Borkman* on ITV.) Sir John Gielgud also made his first appearance on television, in N. C. Hunter's *A Day by the Sea*, followed by Sir Michael Redgrave in the same author's *A Place in the Sun* (both on ITV).

Other memorable plays, presented by the B.B.C., were Bertold Brecht's *Mother Courage*, starring Flora Robson in the title role, and *The Porokohawa Tree* by Bruce Mason, a play about Maori problems in New Zealand, with an impressive performance by the half-Maori actress, Hira Tallfrey.

For ITV, more important than any player's début was the advent as television dramatist of the writer Angus Wilson whose *After the Show* was accomplished, original and widely hailed for its promise of attracting authors to the medium.

A highly praised B.B.C. production was the Spanish poet Garcia Lorca's *Blood Wedding*, with a powerful performance by the Greek actress Katina Paxinou. ITV's *Odd Man In* was a thoroughly entertaining English bedroom farce which revealed Donald Sinden as a delightful comedian. *The Mark of the Warrior* (also ITV) gave Robert Harris one of his finest parts in a remarkable production by Peter Graham Scott. Harris shone again against the senior common room background of ITV's *The Face of Treason*.

One preoccupation of many ITV productions was the colour problem. Ted Willis's *Hot Summer Night* was an effective play, with John Slater and Ruth Dunning as the parents and Andrée Melly as the daughter in love with a coloured man. Lloyd Reckord who played this part appeared again in a play which dared to handle the colour problem with gaiety, *A Trick of the Sun*.

A shortage of serious music probably reflected public taste. However, the B.B.C. occasionally gave celebrity concerts, Granada offered an evening with Sir Thomas Beecham and there were also such programmes as *Music for You* (B.B.C.),

Gala (Associated-Rediffusion) and *Chelsea at Nine* (Granada).

The B.B.C. continued occasional ventures into opera, including a production by Rudolph Cartier of Verdi's *Otello*, with Charles Holland, a Negro tenor with a fine presence in the title role, while ITV at Christmas presented the first part of Benjamin Britten's *The Turn of the Screw*. Perhaps the most delightful musical programme of the year was imported from the United States, *An Evening with Fred Astaire*.

Westerns, mostly of inferior quality, seemed to fill every free minute until an hour-long all-star programme, *The Western*, was put on to dignify if not justify the surfeit. In serials a difference was evident between the B.B.C.'s standard classics—Anthony Trollope's *The Eustace Diamonds*, Charles Dickens's *Bleak House*, Sir Walter Scott's *Redgauntlet*, H. G. Wells's *Love and Mr. Lewisham*—and ITV's contemporary thrills and horror.

A new manifestation was the exercise of patronage by ITV. Granada sponsored the British Association lectures on science for sixth forms.

The B.B.C. could pride itself on two fine films, Richard Cawston's *This is the B.B.C.* and Denis Mitchell's international award winner *Morning in the Streets*.

Among the regular television programmes shown in the United States in 1959 westerns and mysteries were the most prominent. There were relatively few quiz programmes. Sir Laurence Olivier won the acclaim of critics in Somerset Maugham's *The Moon and Sixpence* in Oct. 1959, as did Ingrid Bergman in Henry James's *The Turn of the Screw* the same month. Shakespeare's *The Tempest*, Maxwell Anderson's *Winterset* and Ibsen's *A Doll's House* were among other dramatic productions. World news received extensive coverage on television, in particular the visit to the United States of the Soviet prime minister, N. S. Khrushchev.

Technical and Organizational Developments. *Great Britain.* In addition to the 23 B.B.C. television stations in operation—Peterborough came into service in the autumn of 1959—plans were announced in 1959 for building 14 low-power satellite television stations to extend television coverage to sparsely-populated and mountainous areas, to bring another 200,000 people within range of B.B.C. television and to give improved service to a further 940,000.

The B.B.C. continued to contribute to the work of the Television Advisory committee and its technical subcommittee and made available to these bodies the results of research by B.B.C. engineers, especially with regard to colour television and the possible use for television broadcasting of the higher-frequency bands (Bands 4 and 5) and of the 625-line standard.

The B.B.C. successfully developed and introduced the transmission of television news films by transatlantic telephone cable. The first pictures transmitted from London to Canada and the United States were of the departure of Queen Elizabeth II to Canada in June 1959. They were screened in North America 2¼ hr. after the pictures were taken in London. Similarly, the B.B.C. showed to British viewers, within a few hours, the arrival of the queen in Newfoundland. The pictures were also seen by viewers in France over the Eurovision link.

The B.B.C. announced in the summer that in Sept. 1960 the television service for schools would be increased from five to ten broadcasts a week and that telerecorded repeats of all programmes would also be broadcast.

The exchange of television programmes between Great Britain and the other countries in the Eurovision network was improved in the summer with the opening of new permanent cross-channel links, operated jointly by the British Post Office and the French Postes, Télégraphes et Téléphones.

Eurovision programme exchanges were shared by 16 television services in 12 countries. In addition, Eurovision pro-

Edward R. Murrow, the U.S. television commentator, who lectured on "Television and Politics" at the Guildhall, London, on Oct. 19.

grammes were distributed over the networks of Finland, Yugoslavia and Hungary. There was also progress in arranging for the Norwegian Broadcasting corporation to be connected to the network for special occasions.

The Programme, Legal and Technical committees of the Eurovision Broadcasting union met in London in 1959.

Experimental work began in the external services of the B.B.C. on a course of "English by Television" for overseas stations.

The B.B.C. Television service introduced during the year, for experimental trial, a remotely controlled television camera, developed by the B.B.C. Engineering division, located in the All Souls' television interview studio, near Broadcasting house, London. The camera action, which included pan, tilt, focus, zoom and iris, was controlled from a studio at Alexandra palace, six miles away.

There were further developments in the use of television magnetic tape recording (video-tape).

In 1959 the B.B.C. Television Transcription unit distributed abroad more than 150 films and more than 500 telerecordings of B.B.C. programmes.

Adaptations of B.B.C. television programmes and the provision of sound tracks in foreign languages in order to distribute these programmes in countries beyond the Commonwealth and the United States were studied and the B.B.C. proceeded with an experimental development in this field.

A specially designed base for outside television broadcasts was opened in January by the B.B.C. at East Kilbride in Scotland.

The Independent Television authority opened three new stations during 1959, one in northeast England (in January), one in East Anglia and one in Ulster (both in October). The programmes for these stations were provided by Tyne Tees Television Ltd., Anglia Television Ltd. and Ulster Television Ltd. respectively. With their opening, about 93% of the population of the United Kingdom was within range of the authority's transmissions.

Towards the end of the year, test transmissions began from a new station near Dover which would serve southeast England and which was expected to begin programme transmissions early in 1960. Instead of appointing an independent programme company for this station, the authority extended the sphere of operation of Southern Television Ltd., which was already acting as programme company for southern England. It remained the authority's intention, however, to continue to appoint independent companies wherever it was practicable

"'I think it's a lovely Budget', said an average housewife. 'Any Government that brings electric irons down from £5 to £4 17s. 1d. certainly gets my vote'". Giles in the "Daily Express", April 9.

to do so and, consequently, in Dec. 1959 Westward Television Ltd. were appointed as programme contractors in southwest England. This area would be served by two transmitters, one in Devon near Axminster and one in Cornwall near Launceston. They were expected to open in 1961 and to serve a population of about 1·25 million in the southwest.

At the end of 1959 the number of sets able to receive I.T.A. broadcasts exceeded 8·5 million. The average evening audience was estimated to be about 13 million.

I.T.A. COVERAGE AT THE END OF 1959

Area	Station name and opening date	Effective radiated power (vision in kw.)	Population covered (in millions)	Number of homes able to receive I.T.A.
London	Croydon (Sept. 22, 1955)	120	12·3	2,300,000
Midlands	Lichfield (Staffs.) (Feb. 17, 1956)	200	6·4	1,300,000
Northern	Winter Hill (Lancs.) (May 3, 1956)	100		
	Emley Moor (Yorks.) (Nov. 3, 1956)	200 (directional)	12·2	2,450,000
Scotland	Black Hill (Lanark) (Aug. 31, 1957)	475 (directional)	3·6	650,000
South Wales and West of England	St. Hilary (Glam.) (Jan. 14, 1958)	200	3·2	540,000
Southern England	Chillerton Down (I.O.W.) (Aug. 30, 1958)	100 (directional)	2·8	430,000
Northeast England	Burnhope (Co. Durham) (Jan. 15, 1959)	100 (directional)	2·7	470,000
East Anglia	Mendlesham (Suffolk) (Oct. 27, 1959)	200 (directional)	2·0	250,000
Northern Ireland	Black Mountain (Co. Antrim) (Oct. 31, 1959)	100 (directional)	1·1	125,000
	Totals		46·3	8,515,000

Other Countries. In May 1959 the *Financial Times* reported that more than 240 million people in 32 countries were reached by television advertising, transmitted either from their own stations or from those in neighbouring countries.

The first commercial television group in Africa, which began test transmissions from transmitters at Ibadan and Abafon in Nigeria in the autumn of 1959, was operated on a joint basis by the government of the Western Region of Nigeria and Overseas Rediffusion.

The Nippon Educational Television company began Japan's first regular commercial service of cultural and educational programmes in 1959. Some 80% of the programmes were sponsored.

The first television broadcast was made in May 1959 from a new commercial station in Beirut by the Lebanese Television company.

In the Republic of Ireland the minister of posts and telegraphs announced in August that sponsored television was to be controlled and operated by a public authority.

In May 1959 it was estimated that there were 49·3 million television sets in use in the United States, and that 86·3% of all U.S. homes were equipped with television, more than 4·4 million homes having more than one set. Television production for the full year 1958 totalled 4,920,428 sets compared with 6,339,345 in 1957. The number of sets produced during Jan.-Aug. 1959 was 3,680,250 compared with 2,950,455 in the same period of 1958. During the 12 months ended Oct. 31, 1959, the total number of authorized or operating television stations fell from 672 to 669. The number of noncommercial educational television stations increased from 33 to 43 between Oct. 1958 and Oct. 1959. The total revenue of television networks and stations amounted to $1,030 million in 1958, as against $943·2 million the previous year.

Two major issues affected television broadcasting in the United States in 1959. One was the so-called " quiz scandal ", in which several participants in television big-money contests testified before a congressional subcommittee on legislative oversight that they had been " coached "—furnished with questions or answers or otherwise assisted—before their appearances on quiz programmes. The other was an amendment of the " equal-time " law so as to permit networks and stations to cover news items concerning political candidates without being required to give an equal amount of time to all competing candidates. (*See* also RADIO, SCIENTIFIC DEVELOPMENTS IN; PHOTOGRAPHY.)

(F. B. Lt.; En. M. T.; A. W. Pl.; S. Tf.; R. W. Cr.)

TEXTILE INDUSTRY. In the United Kingdom, the over-all situation throughout 1959 revealed the full extent of the uncertainties penetrating every section of the industry. In Lancashire, production of yarn and cloth was distinctly lower and the total of idle spindles and looms had reached alarming figures. Grave concern in responsible quarters and frequent requests to the government finally resulted in a textile pact between the United Kingdom and Hong Kong, beginning on Feb. 1, whereby Hong Kong voluntarily agreed to limit exports of cotton piece-goods for retention in the United Kingdom to 115 million sq.yd. a year for the following three years. Although the agreement did not include cotton yarns, it was felt that this aspect of the problem should also have been dealt with. Probably for the first time in history, the imports of cotton yarns and cloths into the United Kingdom exceeded the country's exports. This decision by Hong Kong was later reflected in a slightly better tone in the United Kingdom spinning and weaving sections and it was hoped that India would follow this lead and agree to some limitation in its exports to Britain.

The most notable and controversial event in the United Kingdom cotton industry was the scrapping and re-equipment plan put forward by the government, details of which were given in the Cotton Industry act, 1959 (*see* COTTON).

Earlier in the year a decision of the Restrictive Practices court virtually ended the agreement operated by the Yarn Spinners association in Lancashire concerning minimum prices for cotton yarns. The court were satisfied that considerable export business had been lost—not so much in yarn as in goods—from the rigidity of the scheme and the refusal of the spinners to make even the smallest concession. This investigation undoubtedly resulted in more spinning firms deciding to close permanently but it was better to face the position realistically than tolerate indefinitely the chaotic conditions of the previous few years.

In the woollen and worsted sections of the industry raw material supplies, prices and production of yarns and cloth were, in general, satisfactory. The decision of the U.S. government to re-negotiate the wool cloth tariff quota was especially gratifying, although any anticipated changes resulting from these negotiations were unlikely to operate before 1961. Stocks

WORLD TEXTILE PRODUCTION

I. COTTON YARN ('000 metric tons)
(Only countries with a yearly production exceeding 90,000 tons)

	1938	1948	1957	1958
U.S.S.R.	566·0	568·0	...	...
India	591·0[1]	657·0	807·0	764·4
Japan	555·0	125·0	517·0	439·2
German Fed. Rep.	276·0[2]	119·0	418·0	392·4
France	250·0	224·0	313·0	308·4
United Kingdom	476·0	409·0	330·0	280·8
Italy	139·0	178·0	173·0	162·0
Pakistan	...	...	143·8	156·6
Poland	64·3[3]	82·0	123·4	134·5[4]
Argentina	24·4	70·0	96·7	...

II. WOVEN COTTON FABRICS
(a) In thousand metric tons (only countries with a yearly production exceeding 70,000 tons are included)

	1938	1948	1957	1958
German Fed. Rep.	222·0[5]	76·0	287·0	273·6
France	183·0	181·0[6]	214·0	222·0
Italy	94·0	113·0	117·0	114·5

(b) In million metres (only countries with a yearly production exceeding 220,000 metres are included)

	1938	1948	1957	1958
United States	7,578[7]	8,815	8,722	8,208
U.S.S.R.	3,460	3,150	5,600	5,760
India	3,904[1]	3,950	4,862	4,500
Japan[8]	2,757	773·0	3,212	2,640
United Kingdom	3,328[9]	1,768	1,489	1,284
Brazil	846·0	1,142[10]	...	...
Poland	325·0[9]	351·0	580·0	608·4
Pakistan	...	81·0	482·0	526·8
Czechoslovakia	377·0	280·0	386·0	420·0
Egypt (U.A.R.)	65·0[4]	156·0[4]	442·0	294·0[4]
Canada	195·0	268·0	261·0[11]	244·8[11]

III. WOOL YARN ('000 metric tons)
(Only countries with a yearly production exceeding 25,000 tons)

	1938	1948	1957	1958
United States	270·0[7]	362·0	298·0[12]	284·4[12]
United Kingdom	212·0	228·0	244·0	224·4
U.S.S.R.	80·0	82·0	...	...
France	118·0	132·0	154·0	134·4
German Fed. Rep.	177·2[3]	38·3	240·0	106·3
Japan	53·7	11·0	116·0	90·8
Poland	34·2[9]	32·7	54·7	...
Belgium	25·8	34·1	47·1	38·0
German Dem. Rep.	...	9·8[13]	20·9	25·8

IV. WOVEN WOOLLEN FABRICS
(a) In thousand metric tons (only countries with a yearly production exceeding 8,000 tons are included)

	1938	1948	1957	1958
France	79·8	84·9	81·4	...
German Fed. Rep.	64·8[4]	25·6	74·8	...
Belgium	15·6	19·4	30·0	...
Sweden	9·8	14·2	11·1	...

(b) In million metres (only countries with a yearly production exceeding 30 million metres are included)

	1938	1948	1957	1958
United Kingdom	290·0[9]	347·0[8]	330·0[8]	...
U.S.S.R.	113·0	124·0	282·0	...
United States	340·0[7]	455·0	266·0	...
Japan[8]	222·0	21·0	206·0	...
Poland	38·0[9]	42·0	76·0	78·1
Czechoslovakia	...	42·1	38·2	42·6
Yugoslavia[8]	12·4[7]	28·7	33·6	...

V. RAYON AND ACETATE FILAMENT YARN ('000 metric tons)
(only countries with a yearly production exceeding 35,000 tons)

	1938	1948	1957	1958
United States	117·0	388·0	324·0	288·0
U.S.S.R.[14]	11·0	11·0	149·0	...
United Kingdom[15]	46·0	67·0	106·0	86·9
Japan	97·0	16·2	121·6	84·8
German Fed. Rep.	65·8[8]	30·0	71·9	64·9
Italy	46·0	47·7	68·2	61·6
France	28·0	43·6	57·9	56·3

VI. RAYON AND ACETATE STAPLE FIBRE ('000 metric tons)
(Only countries with a yearly production exceeding 30,000 tons)

	1938	1948	1957	1958
Japan	148·0	16·0	317·0	241·7
United States	14·0	122·0	193·0	146·4[16]
German Fed. Rep.	161·0[3]	73·0	167·0	138·6
United Kingdom[17]	15·0	39·0	119·0	104·6
Italy	73·5	17·9	77·6	75·8
France	4·9	30·2	62·4	69·7
Austria	4·5[7]	9·8	46·5	46·3
Poland	4·0[3]	10·8	41·4	42·2
Czechoslovakia	0·3	18·0	32·9	39·7
Spain	...	9·3	34·2	32·8

[1] Incl. Pakistan. [2] 1936 (in present frontiers). [3] In 1938 frontiers. [4] About 70% of total production. [5] In present frontiers. [6] 1949. [7] 1939. [8] Million square metres. [9] 1937. [10] 1946. [11] Shipments. [12] Fibres consumed. [13] 1950. [14] Incl. staple and other synthetic yarns. [15] Incl. other synthetic yarns and fibres. [16] Rayon staple only. [17] Incl. other synthetic fibres.

SOURCE. U.N. *Statistical Yearbook 1958*: U.N. *Monthly Bulletin of Statistics*.

of wool in the United Kingdom were maintained at satisfactory levels and machinery activity remained good. The position in the linen and jute industries gave rise to grave concern as the proportion of idle machinery was disquieting. Prinex Ltd. (a subsidiary of Courtaulds Ltd.) and a Soviet importing organization concluded major contracts for complete plants and technical processes for the manufacture of viscose rayon tyre cord, acetate yarn and acrylic staple; the cost was in the region of £15 million. However, a British textile combine, headed by Platt Brothers Ltd., were beaten for another Soviet £10 million order for a textile plant by a U.S. consortium, despite offering a much lower price and credit terms.

There was no lack of new developments in research, new machines and processes. Experiments on a wool card proved that fitting the fancy roller in a different position resulted in a decrease in the end-to-end variation across the machine, fewer end breakages in spinning and higher yarn strength. In weaving, a new British automatic silk and rayon loom was equipped with power reversing motion, starting handles at both sides and pedal-operated shuttle ejectors. Developments in shuttleless looms included new models of a Swedish loom in which the weft was projected through the warp shed by a jet of air at 420 parts per million. A Czech loom operating on somewhat similar principles employed a jet of water to get the weft across the loom. Both models attracted much attention in weaving circles throughout the world.

Developments in knitting technology included a new high speed warp knitting machine capable of running at 400 courses per min., and a new multi-gauge fully-fashioned outerwear knitting machine had a fixed speed of 60 courses per min. Another progressive step in fully-fashioned knitting was the combination on one machine of welt turning and rib transfer into one automatic mechanism. In spinning, a new, narrow-width ringframe for worsteds, synthetics and blends had needle-bearing front rollers and a draft range from 5 to 20. Capable of cutting layers of fabrics 2½ in. to 3 in. thick, a new pattern-cutting machine simplified this operation considerably. An improved automatic cloth finishing press appeared, also a compactly designed air-spin drier which could be placed in any position in cloth finishing operations.

Total world production of wool, cotton, flax and silk was lower but production of jute, sisal, hemp and man-made fibres was higher. On the continent, yarn and cloth production was lower in France, the German Federal Republic, Belgium and the Netherlands. In India, total textile production was maintained at high levels and production increased in Australia. (*See also* COTTON; WOOL.) (A. DR.)

THAILAND (SIAM). Kingdom of southeastern Asia bounded W. and N.W. by Burma, N.E. and E. by Laos and Cambodia and S. by Malaya. Area: 198,270 sq.mi. Pop.: (1947 census) 17,442,689; (1959 est.) 21,881,000 including ethnic Chinese (1955 est.) 2,315,000. Language: Thai (Siamese). State religion: Buddhism. Malay-speaking Moslems 3%. Capital (pop., 1947 census): Bangkok 1,173,549. Ruler, King Phumiphon Adulyadet; prime minister, Field-Marshal Sarit Thanarat. Main imports: machinery and vehicles; textiles; foods; chemicals; petroleum and plant. Main exports: rice, rubber, tin. Monetary unit: *baht* (B.58·15 = £1 sterling).

History. From Oct. 20, 1958, when Field-Marshal Sarit Thanarat assumed personal control, administration was carried on by permanent government officials under the direction of a Revolutionary committee headed by the field-marshal. On Jan. 28, 1959, an interim constitution was promulgated setting up a Constituent Assembly (240 appointed members) with powers to legislate and to draft a new permanent constitution. A council of 15 ministers, including Sarit Thanarat as prime minister, was formed on Feb. 9.

The new government affirmed adherence to the principles of the U.N. charter and acceptance of commitments under Seato. Firm action was to be taken against Communist

With King Phumiphon Adulyadet, Princess Alexandra visits the temple of the Emerald Buddha, Bangkok, during her stay in Thailand.

subversion. (In July, after a much-publicized inquiry, a Thai national, found guilty of printing and distributing Communist propaganda, was executed.) Policy declarations indicated a swing in the direction of economic nationalism. The goal was to be greater self-sufficiency for Thailand through the promotion of industry and the improvement of agriculture and communications. Educational policy was to be co-ordinated. Regulations to prohibit opium smoking were enforced.

The newly formed Economic Advisory committee announced improved conditions for investment of private foreign capital including guarantees against expropriation and state-organized competition. Under the promotion scheme an agreement for the production of pharmaceuticals by a U.S. and a Danish company was signed on June 26. On Sept. 2 the council of ministers approved a contract with a U.S. company, Eastern Petroleum, to build an oil refinery near Bangkok to supplement the one under construction at the newly discovered small oilfield at Fang. The government obtained advantageous terms whereby they would take four-fifths of profits and assume ownership after 10 years.

The immediate economic situation continued to cause anxiety particularly in the export sector. Rice exports for the first five months declined below 1958 levels in quantity and value by 26% and 27% respectively. Rice sold to main customers (Hong Kong, Singapore and Malaya) showed a decrease of 18% but orders for the remainder of the year, from these and other countries, were high. Gold and foreign exchange reserves remained at a satisfactory level and

increased prices for rubber and the improved prospects for tin aided the export revenue position. A general increase in import duties of 10% above existing rates was announced on June 5.

Foreign affairs were dominated by worsening relations with Cambodia dating from the latter's recognition of the Chinese People's Republic in July 1958. The immediate dispute concerned the frontier temple of Wat Phra Viharn claimed by Cambodia on the basis of its interpretation of frontier surveys conducted during the French administration. On Jan. 6 Baron Johann Beck-Friis, appointed by the U.N. secretary-general, began discussions with the parties to the dispute. Diplomatic relations, broken by Cambodia on Dec. 1, 1958, were resumed on Feb. 20. In July the Thai and Cambodian foreign ministers signed a joint communiqué declaring the intention of each country to refrain from threatening the security of the other. Tension rose again in October when it was disclosed in Bangkok that Cambodia might make a specific territorial claim against Thailand before the International Court of Justice. (*See* also CAMBODIA.)

Thailand participated in Seato consultations over the Laotian crisis, and the Thai foreign minister spoke at the U.N. general assembly in favour of establishing long-term U.N. observation in Laos. Goodwill visits at ministerial level were exchanged with Burma, Laos, Malaya and south Vietnam.

(E. H. S. S.)

THEATRE. Great Britain. Introducing the 14th annual report of the Arts Council, Sir W. E. Williams, the secretary general, said in Oct. 1959: " It would be ironic if, at a time when the National Theatre project was gaining favour, the decision to build that institution were to coincide with the mass burial of provincial theatres." The expression " mass burial " might to some have seemed pessimistic. But its pessimism was born out by facts. More provincial theatres, both repertory and commercial, closed down in 1959 than in any other year since World War II. Many towns lost their only theatres—usually to builders of offices—and far too seldom showed either shame or indignation at the loss. For example the big and prosperous city of Leicester had no active playhouse of any sort throughout the year, and Margate had to close its famous old theatre (though not without some public protest). In the provinces—as the secretary general also pointed out—it was the hard core of playgoers, the " steadies " who could formerly be relied upon to attend every new production, who stayed away. The lure of the television set by the fireside was apparently the potent and prevailing reason. The exceptionally fine spring and the unusually long and hot summer were also, of course, blamed for a marked decline of interest in the living theatre.

In London—which means, of course, central London with only the Royal Court in Sloane square (the English Stage company busily continuing), the Theatre Royal at Stratford, E. (Theatre workshop) and the Lyric theatre, Hammersmith, active outside the crowded core—the theatre continued healthily as usual. Indeed these three " outside " theatres and the Arts Theatre club (which is in the very heart of theatre-land) should be given first consideration in 1959 since all four made striking efforts to discover and encourage new and hitherto unknown young playwrights. The acknowledged leader of this young group, John Osborne, had a severe set-back with a musical satire on the press called *The World of Paul Slickey.* Some people assumed that the press was stung into giving this elaborate production severe notices. But all these and more stayed away in large numbers, and the piece was genuinely devoid of real attack, wit, charm or any other vivid necessary quality. It lasted only a week or two, and the author comforted himself in helping to make films of his more acceptable plays.

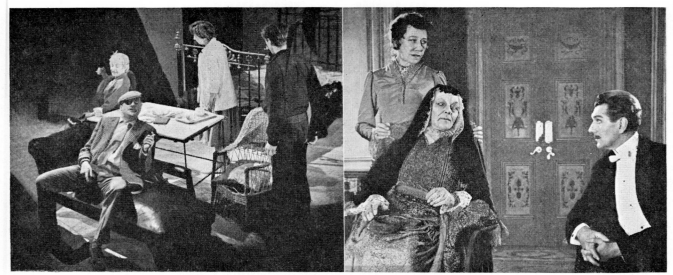

(Left) Nigel Davenport (seated) and (from l. to r.) Avis Bunnage, Frances Cuka and Murray Melvin in a scene from " A Taste of Honey ". (Right) Flora Robson, Beatrix Lehmann and Sir Michael Redgrave in " The Aspern Papers ", an adaptation of Henry James's novel.

Vastly more successful were two products of Theatre workshop which were triumphantly transplanted to the west end—Shelagh Delaney's acrid study of low life in Salford, *A Taste of Honey*, and Brendan Behan's violent, rhapsodic, musical, intensely Irish *The Hostage*. The latter had undoubtedly flecks and flickers of genius, and suggested that Behan could possibly inherit the mantle of Sean O'Casey. But the latter veteran, far from showing any sign of bequeathing his mantle, gave out that in his old age at Torquay he was completing two new plays, and he sent an old one, *Cock-a-Doodle Dandy*, to the Royal Court theatre via the Edinburgh festival (where it proved to be the only new theatrical production of any vitality and salt). Another success in the east end, later transferred to the west end, Wolf Mankowitz's *Make Me an Offer*, suggested that songs and dances were likely to take a prominent part in the new order of playwriting. Indeed at the year's beginning Peter Brook, one of the best and most original directors in the European theatre, prophesied that " more and more music is going to be heard in the theatre and more and more respectable actors will be bursting into song." Bertolt Brecht's influence may be seen in this. It was remarkably exemplified in *The Hostage* and some other new plays.

The chief discoveries at Hammersmith, all showing marked promise, were John Mortimer, Alun Owen and Harold Pinter; and at Sloane square, all showing some achievement, Arnold Wesker, John Arden and Willis Hall. The last-named's play of World War II, *The Long and the Short and the Tall*, was transferred to the west end and had a genuine success. Wesker's play about agricultural life in Norfolk, *Roots*, did much less well, though it was critically acclaimed for breaking new ground; *i.e.*, the soil of the field as distinct from that of the suburban garden. Arden's anti-war play, *Serjeant Musgrave's Dance*, had a very remarkable and memorable last act; but the whole play took much too long to reach its point. It was received with an extraordinary divergence of critical opinion. It had one breath-takingly good performance by Ian Bannen as the sergeant in rebellion against war. No less breath-taking was the acting of Patrick McGoohan as the fanatical hero of Ibsen's great and neglected *Brand* which was courageously and quite sensationally revived at Hammersmith. Some remarked what an object-lesson was the irruption of Ibsen among all these apprentices and beginners in playwriting. It was like a great old master of the pianoforte playing masterful Brahms to some pupils who were averse to practising their scales before tackling even minor pieces.

In the west end itself the most successful younger dramatist was Peter Shaffer whose *Five Finger Exercise* was still running in 1960. Maturer dramatists like Graham Greene and Hugh Williams had resounding successes with *The Complaisant Lover* and *The Grass is Greener*—one a grave and responsible tragic-comedy, the other a truly light one. As distinguished as anything else in the season was a superbly effective dramatization of Henry James's *The Aspern Papers* in which Flora Robson, Beatrix Lehmann, and Michael Redgrave (whose knighthood gave general pleasure) all excelled themselves.

In May a brand-new theatre was opened by Bernard Miles in Blackfriars on the north bank of the Thames. This was the Mermaid, and the first production, *Lock Up Your Daughters*, an adaptation of an old play by Henry Fielding (again with music), was an instantaneous success. The opening of the reconstructed Queen's theatre in Shaftesbury avenue was also welcomed. The first programme, lasting three weeks, consisted solely of Sir John Gielgud's " The Ages of Man ", a marvellously sustained and delivered series of excerpts showing Britain's finest Shakespearian actor's astonishing range between Lear and Hotspur, Leontes and Benedick, Wolsey and Richard II, Oberon and Prospero, Hamlet and The Sonnets.

Shakespeare was splendidly celebrated also at Stratford-on-Avon in what was rather shakily described as " the 100th

Seen from beneath Blackfriars bridge, the new Mermaid theatre which was opened at the end of May by the Lord Mayor of London.

season ". Charles Laughton appeared as Bottom and Lear, Paul Robeson as Othello, Dame Edith Evans as the old countess in *All's Well that Ends Well* and as Volumnia in *Coriolanus*, and Sir Laurence Olivier as Coriolanus himself, another of the year's superlative performances. Shakespeare at the Old Vic in London stepped back—for the first time for several years—to give place to some other world-dramatists including Molière, Ibsen, Shelley, Congreve, Sir Arthur Pinero and Oscar Wilde.

In the world of musical comedy, following on the great and continued success of *My Fair Lady* (which derives directly from Shaw's *Pygmalion*) there were much less fortunate musical versions of Ronald Firbank's *Valmouth* and of Voltaire's *Candide*. On the other hand, a quite outstanding musical drama of gangster warfare set in New York today but closely following the Romeo and Juliet tragedy, *West Side Story*, was an immense and lasting success. It seemed probable that both this and *My Fair Lady* would survive well into 1960.

Continental Europe. In April 1959 André Malraux, the French minister of cultural affairs, announced his projects for the reform of the French state-subsidized theatres, including the separation of the two playhouses of the Comédie Française, the Salle Richelieu and the Salle Luxembourg, the reopening of the former royal theatre at Versailles for public performances and the creation of two new experimental national theatres, one to be in the hands of Jean Vilar, director of the Théâtre National Populaire, a company headed by Vilar and Gérard Philipe (*see* OBITUARIES), and the other to be managed by the novelist Albert Camus. Claude de Boisanger, a diplomat, was appointed administrator of the Comédie Française (the former Salle Richelieu) and Jean-Louis Barrault was made director of the Salle Luxembourg which was renamed the Théâtre de France.

In the autumn the Comédie Française offered new productions of Molière's *L'Ecole des femmes*, Sophocles' *Antigone* and revivals of Henry de Montherlant's *Port-Royal* and Jean Giraudoux's *Electre*. Barrault, installing his own company at the Théâtre de France, opened his season with Paul Claudel's *Tête d'Or*, written in 1889, its author's first play but never before performed. To its production Barrault brought his characteristic energy and enthusiasm but, despite its academic interest, *Tête d'Or* proved heavy and dull.

Jean Vilar's experimental theatre fared less well, opening, as it did, with a very bad first play by a novice, *Le Crapaud-buffle* by Armand Gatti, but at the Théâtre National Populaire Vilar presented imaginative productions of Shakespeare's *Midsummer Night's Dream* and *The Tempest* and Corneille's tragedy *Attila*.

During 1959 many leading French dramatists were represented by new plays. There were three new plays by Jean Anouilh: *L'Hurluberlu* (a satirical comedy about a retired general who seeks to seize political power), *La Petite Molière*, a rather sentimental biography about the great dramatist, and *Becket*, an ironic study of the unhappy friendship of Thomas à Becket and Henry II, one of Anouilh's cleverest theatre pieces, which profited from an ingenious production staged by himself.

Jean-Paul Sartre came forward with a staggering, four-hour drama, *Les Séquestrés d'Altona*, a windy and harrowing tragedy about a former Nazi who meditates wrong-doing and conscience after World War II. Albert Camus dramatized Dostoevski's novel *The Possessed*, Michel de Saint-Pierre dramatized his own novel about a famous novelist and his son who is also a writer, *Les Ecrivains*, and Jean Genêt contributed a weird, poetic fantasy about some West Indian Negroes standing trial for a ritualistic murder in *Les Nègres*.

The Théâtre des Nations festival (running from March until July) at the Sarah Bernhardt theatre brought to Paris the London Theatre workshop in Brendan Behan's *The Hostage*,

the Theatre of Malmö, Sweden, in Ingmar Bergman's *Saga*, the Dublin Gate theatre in George Bernard Shaw's *Saint Joan*, the Pushkin theatre of Leningrad in *The Optimistic Tragedy*, the Arts theatre of London in *Nighttown*, a dramatization of a chapter from James Joyce's *Ulysses*, the Jerome Robbins *Export: Jazz* ballets from the United States, the Gino Cervi company of Rome in Pirandello's last play, *Gods of the Mountains*, and *The Merry Wives of Windsor*, the Morelli-Stoppa company of Milan in Diego Fabbri's *Figli d'arte*, the Schauspielhaus of Bochum, German Federal Republic, in *Julius Caesar* and operatic and dance companies from many lands.

There was much activity but few new plays of note in either western Germany or Austria during 1959. Perhaps the most important event was the premiere of Brecht's *Schweik* which planted Jaroslav Hašek's obedient and comic private in the midst of World War II. It was first presented at Frankfurt in June and later in Berlin during the Theatre festival there (Sept. 26-Oct. 6). Other events of the Berlin festival were Gustav Gründgens' production of part II of Goethe's *Faust*, the Schloss Park's production of Anouilh's *L'Hurluberlu*, the Renaissance theatre's production of Hilty's *Dear Liar* and the German premiere of Tennessee Williams' latest play *Sweet Bird of Youth*. The Burgtheater of Vienna offered Eugene O'Neill's *A Touch of a Poet* as a new production, the Vienna Akademie Pirandello's *Six Characters in Search of an Author* and the Vienna Josefstadt an American dramatization of the Japanese film *Rashomon*.

Commonwealth. In Canada the Stratford Shakespearian festival, under the artistic direction of Michael Langham, enjoyed its most successful season. Playing *Othello* and *As You Like It* in July and August, the festival attracted an attendance of 166,180 for 99 performances, 78% of house capacity for the whole season.

The growth, in both quantity and quality, of the French-language theatre in Canada during the past five years had been a cultural phenomenon of interesting proportions, and 1959 was a boom season in all ways. Four thoroughly successful French theatres active in Montreal during 1959—Comédie Canadienne, Théâtre du Nouveau Monde, Théâtre du Rideau Vert and La Poudrière—made full demands upon available theatre talent. The little theatres throughout Canada had another successful season. Vancouver's International festival, during July and August, included a notable Canadian premiere production of Schiller's *Mary Stuart*, directed by John Reich.

The Elizabethan Theatre trust continued to foster drama throughout Australia. Its most ambitious production was Eugene O'Neill's *Long Day's Journey into Night*. Ray Lawler's *The Piccadilly Bushman* was produced in Melbourne. It dealt with the Australians' attitude to Britain. The first full-time school of acting in the southern hemisphere, the National Institute of Dramatic Art, opened in Sydney in February. It was set up by the Australian Broadcasting commission, the Elizabethan Theatre trust and Sydney university.

United States. The theatrical season of 1958-59 showed the American stage successfully engaged in two usually unrelated areas of interest. *J. B.*, a version of the Job story by Archibald MacLeish, was an unexpectedly successful " poetic drama ", while *A Raisin in the Sun*, a picture of Negro family life in urban surroundings, by the 28-year-old Negress Lorraine Hansberry, was an authentic " social drama ". *J. B.*, originally staged by Curtis Canfield at the Yale School of Drama the season before, was restaged for Broadway by Elia Kazan with an expressive multiple set by Boris Aronson and with an effective cast, including Pat Hingle, Raymond Massey and Christopher Plummer. Without offering a version of the Book of Job that could satisfy the orthodox of any religion and without achieving a completely convincing resolution of the dramatic action, this verse drama lifted Broadway out of the rut of prosaic triviality. MacLeish was awarded the Pulitzer prize for *J. B.* and its partisans acclaimed the play as one of the most significant of the century.

A Raisin in the Sun was a play in common prose flavoured with colloquialisms and humour. Revolving mainly round the chaotic rebellion of a young Negro chauffeur, vividly impersonated by Sidney Poitier, against his circumstances, and the comic confusions of his intellectually ambitious sister, the play was mainly held together by the widowed mother of the family, a woman of notable strength of character, played by Claudia McNeil. Combining effective elements of character conflict with vivid features of social reality, the play proved to be an appealing as well as vital piece of social realism. It won the New York Drama Critics Circle award.

A tendency to revive the faltering social drama appeared in other stage productions as well. An affirmation of the ideals of religious tolerance was especially marked in *A Majority of One*, a comedy by Leonard Spigelgass in which Gertrude Berg and Sir Cedric Hardwicke enacted the roles of a Jewish widow and a Japanese gentleman who overcome the barriers of their respective backgrounds. Even *Sweet Bird of Youth*, Tennessee Williams' essentially private drama, added a social problem to his sardonic treatment of the monstrous personalities of a fading Hollywood star and her gigolo, impersonated by Geraldine Page and Paul Newman respectively. Frustration, with its attendant confusions and turbulence, remained a favourite theme in the American theatre, and two of the most powerful plays of the season by two of the foremost American writers dealt with it. One was William Faulkner's *Requiem for a Nun*, a dramatization of his novel prepared by him with the assistance of the star actress of the production, Ruth Ford. It had considerable power even if it repelled rather than attracted audiences.

Not less powerful but distinctly more appealing was the Harold Clurman production of Eugene O'Neill's posthumous drama *A Touch of the Poet* in which Helen Hayes, Kim Stanley and Eric Portman distinguished themselves. It was the only play O'Neill left in completed form from the cycle of 11 plays on which he had worked irregularly during the last 20 years of his life. It proved an impressive character drama set in the early part of the 19th century.

With the usual collection of musicals, among which *Destry Rides Again* was the most vigorous and Ethel Merman's new vehicle *Gypsy* was the most incisive, Broadway playgoing continued to be lively and visually attractive along familiar lines. Visual gratification of a higher order also appeared on the stage in an excellent production of *Rashomon*, a play by Fay and Michael Kanin based on the Japanese stories of Ryunosuke Akutagawa, with superb settings by the British scene designer Oliver Messel. But *Rashomon* was more noteworthy for its exotic action and its treatment of the question of evil and falsehood in the world. Its theatrical excitement was steeped in reflection, and the philosophical overtones of the work allied it with the serious works of a season that expressed disillusionment or at best only a qualified confidence in the human situation.

Postwar Survey. As an art, as a business and as a social institution the British theatre has lived through remarkable changes since the end of World War II. The stage annals of the past 15 years are a glittering complex of both triumphs and disasters. As J. B. Priestley has said, the theatre is " at once worse off and better off than ever before ".

One fact of outstanding significance is the drastic reduction of the nation's theatrical housing. Over 100 stages were lost to the living theatre after 1954, and the casualty list grows longer every year. By 1960 only some 170 full-time stages remained outside London. At the same time there was, in marked contrast with other European countries, a notable tardiness in reconstruction and an almost complete paralysis of new building. Not until 13 years after the war was a new professional playhouse opened in Britain. This elimination of the theatre's capital assets helped to produce, among other results, the virtual obliteration of the music-hall and the decline of theatrical touring. Touring had already been affected between the wars by the competition of the cinema, but as late as 1950 there were still as many as 140 companies " on the road " in a given month. By the same month in 1959 only a third of that number were on tour. In 1945 theatres were still graded as number one, two and three dates, but by 1960 little was left of the touring circuits outside the number one strongholds in a handful of leading cities. Many towns were completely deprived of any professional theatre. One result was a great increase in centralization: in the nation's theatrical life London in 1960 loomed larger than ever before in the past century.

In analysing the disappearing theatre, the chief blame was often attributed to the state's levy of an entertainments tax. Yet the repeal of that tax in 1957 did little to halt the destruction of the nation's stages. Other factors were more decisive. First, there was the steep rise in urban land-values, and the eagerness of public and private bodies—largely unrestricted by legislation—to develop theatre-sites in more profitable ways. Then there was the chronic deficiency of private capital for refurbishing old buildings, let alone erecting new ones, and the relative reluctance of public enterprise to assume responsibility for the theatre in the role that German local authorities had long taken for granted. Difficulties of survival were intensified by the steep rise in costs, and the resistance of audiences to any corresponding increase in the price of playgoing. Since stalls were established in London some 80 years ago their average price has doubled, but the average cost of entertaining the playgoer has risen by about 700%. More obviously, the withering away of the theatre reflected the competition of television for both artists and audiences. The total of viewers soared from 20,000 in 1947 to over 30 million by 1960, and whatever long-term benefits TV might bring by introducing drama to a vast audience, its immediate impact on the live theatre was often disastrous. The change in the theatre's fortunes was also closely linked with the changes in patterns of leisure and spending. Thus, the drama lost some of its old middle-class patronage without winning the working-class audience from which it had long been insulated; and all classes, schooled in the cinema and TV, learned to demand more than many of Britain's theatres could supply.

This tale of woe may suggest that the theatre was being supplanted by the new mass entertainments. Yet against this dark picture must be set the postwar achievements of the British stage and the transformation of its national status. One prime fact was the incorporation by royal charter in 1946 of the Arts Council of Great Britain, a new public body—financed by the Treasury but free from ministerial control—stemming from the wartime Council for the Encouragement of Music and the Arts. Charged with the task of preserving and improving standards of performance in the arts, its annual budget rose from £398,000 in 1947-48 to £1,218,000 in 1959-60. For the first time in the history of the British people the theatre was officially recognized and subsidized by the state. Although the budget was meagre compared with those of other European countries, the Arts council helped not only to rescue many of Britain's best organizations from destruction in the economic blizzard, but also to recruit new audiences, new patrons and new talent. Another milestone was the assumption of control by a public trust of the Theatre Royal, Covent Garden, and its metamorphosis into a national theatre of opera and ballet which won world-wide fame. (Over half the Arts council's 1959-60 budget was devoted to this Royal Opera house and its Sadler's Wells satellite.) Yet another very significant event was the Local Government act

Some of the outstanding postwar productions of the theatre in Britain. (Top left) " The Love of Four Colonels " with (from l. to r.) Allan Gifford, Colin Gordon, Theodore Bikel, Eugène Deckers, Moira Lister and Peter Ustinov. (Top right) Denholm Elliott and Margaret Leighton in T. S. Eliot's " The Confidential Clerk ". (Bottom left) Sir Laurence Olivier, Vivien Leigh and Alan Webb in " Titus Andronicus ". (Bottom right) Kenneth Haigh and Mary Ure in John Osborne's " Look Back in Anger ".

of 1948, which gave local authorities the right to spend on the arts the product of up to a 6d. rate in England and Wales (in Scotland the maximum was fixed at 4⅘d.). The first British theatre built out of public funds (and the first new one erected for 20 years) was constructed in 1958 by the Coventry corporation, and in 1959 Nottingham announced a similar project. Such civic theatres offer new hope to the provincial " repertories ", which have served for years as the theatre's training-ground. Their expansion—there were nearly three times as many in 1960 as in 1930—helped in part to counterbalance the disappearance of the touring system, yet nearly all survived only most precariously under enormous difficulties. Another epoch-making step was taken by parliament in 1948 when the National Theatre act was passed, permitting the conditional grant of up to £1 million for the erection of a national theatre on a Thames-side site.

In London there were clear signs that the theatre, in many ways, was much better off than before the war. There was a vast new public for farce in the capital (its temple was the Whitehall theatre, where the programme was changed only three times in ten years); for thrillers (Agatha Christie's *The Mousetrap* had been running by 1960 for seven years); and for musicals, especially from Broadway (the historic Theatre Royal, Drury lane, was kept alive by such American triumphs as *Oklahoma* and *My Fair Lady*). Many distinguished plays were staged which could never have survived in the between-wars west end. The quality and prestige of the London stage generally advanced beyond the prewar level, and dramatists enjoyed a wider freedom of expression as the lord chamberlain progressively relaxed his censorship of plays. In spite of the uncertainty, waste and chaos of the system within which its artists were obliged to work, there was a rich wealth of assorted native talent in the British theatre of 1945-60, apart from the galaxy of foreign authors who proved so popular and influential, like Arthur Miller, Tennessee Williams and Jean Anouilh.

The general trend in writing, acting and directing was a movement away from the codes and conventions of genteel naturalism which dominated the stage between the wars. In language, decor, subject, social range and dramatic form attempts were made to break down the barriers between speech, song and dance, between the social classes, between the audience and the actors. In the 1940s—influenced, perhaps, by the austerity of the world outside—this movement veered towards a twopence-coloured theatre of fantasy, fancy dress and poetry. Revivals were frequent; new plays were set in period frames; and the star scene-designers, such as Cecil Beaton and Oliver Messel, acquired new power in the theatre. The dazzling word-play of Christopher Fry's verse-comedy became a box-office success (notably in *The Lady's Not For Burning*, 1948, and *Venus Observed*, 1950) and the demand for a more colourful and eloquent theatre was reflected in the success both of the American musicals and of Shakespeare, especially in the lavish productions of the Memorial theatre at Stratford-on-Avon. This playhouse emerged from relative obscurity to become a national institution, drawing over a third of a million people a year—three times as many as in prewar days. The vogue of Shakespearean spectaculars persisted throughout the period, but although a revival of the modern verse-drama was predicted in the early 1950s, there was no sign of it by 1960. The theatre was moving then in a different direction: towards a harsher contemporary realism in language, setting and theme—away from the enchanted ballroom, as it were, to the barrack-room and the kitchen-sink. The pace was set by a group of didactic young playwrights sponsored by the English Stage company, whose precarious regime at the Royal Court theatre—launched in 1956—had a far-reaching influence on the theatre at large. The most important were two brilliant writers: John Osborne (*Look Back in Anger*, 1956, and *The Entertainer*, 1957) and Arnold Wesker (*Chicken Soup and Barley*, 1958, *Roots* and *The Kitchen*, 1959). Among other outstanding young dramatists in the theatre of this period were John Whiting (*Saints' Day*, 1951, and *Marching Song*, 1954); John Arden (*Live Like Pigs*, 1958, and *Serjeant Musgrave's Dance*, 1959); Brendan Behan (*The Hostage*, 1958); and Peter Ustinov (*The Moment of Truth*, 1951, *No Sign of the Dove*, 1953, and *The Love of Four Colonels*, 1951). J. B. Priestley also experimented in various dramatic forms, although his most successful play in this period, *The Linden Tree* (1947), was set firmly within the conventions of naturalism. The abiding power of those conventions was illustrated in the progress of two eminent playwrights, T. S. Eliot and Graham Greene. Eliot attempted to accommodate his religious, poetic drama with current theatrical forms in *The Cocktail Party* (1949), *The Confidential Clerk* (1953) and *The Elder Statesman* (1958). With each succeeding work the camouflage became more complete, and the result less distinguishable from the secular prose stereotype. In Greene's *The Living Room* (1953) and *The Potting Shed* (1958) his religious outlook was unconcealed, but in *The Complaisant Lover* (1959) Greene, like Eliot before him, cloaked it most skilfully inside the shell of a farcical comedy. Perhaps the most successful exponents of more orthodox playmaking were N. C. Hunter, whose neo-Chekhovian *Waters of the Moon* (1951) and *A Day by the Sea* (1953) ran for years in London, and Terence Rattigan, the master-craftsman of *The Winslow Boy* (1946), *The Browning Version* (1948), *The Deep Blue Sea* (1952) and *Separate Tables* (1954).

The trend of British acting between 1945 and 1960 was, like the trend of the drama, a movement away from mannered understatement and stiff-upper-lippery towards, in one direction, a more richly expressive, rhetorical style and, in another

direction, a more truthful realism of behaviour. In spite of the cinema's competition—some actors, such as Sir Alec Guinness and Jack Hawkins, were seen all too seldom on the stage—a great company of players was intermittently on view, in a wide variety of styles. Many actors who were already at the head of their profession in 1945 extended their range still further in plays ancient and modern (Dame Edith Evans, Dame Sybil Thorndike, Dame Peggy Ashcroft, Sir Laurence Olivier, Sir John Gielgud, Sir Michael Redgrave, Sir Ralph Richardson and many more), while bright new talents emerged to carry on the traditions of the stage (Dorothy Tutin, Joan Plowright, Margaret Leighton, Richard Burton, Paul Rogers, Paul Scofield and so on down a long, illustrious roll-call). Leading players sometimes found opportunity in new plays (thus, Gielgud in *The Lady's Not For Burning* and *The Potting Shed*, Olivier in *Venus Observed* and *The Entertainer*), but their greatest work was achieved in the greatest roles—those created by Shakespeare. Here, too, was the supreme opportunity for such directors as Peter Brook and Peter Hall, who emerged after the war as portents of a new theatrical era.

In the rest of Europe the destruction of the war was rapidly made good, and in both eastern and western Europe governments invested heavily in protecting and promoting the theatre. New actors were trained, new audiences mobilized, new playhouses built; yet, except in France, there was a persistent dearth of significant new drama, and theatres throughout Europe filled their repertoires with the classics (Shakespeare's perennial influence was once again strikingly apparent) and with the contemporary work of English, French, and American authors. In Germany, the most notable figure was Bertolt Brecht, who died in 1956. This brilliant poet, satirist and propagandist of the " epic theatre " and the " alienation effect ", long exiled from his homeland, founded in 1949—with the support of the Communist government of eastern Germany—a theatrical organization, the Berliner ensemble, which had a considerable impact on the western stage. Brecht's most important plays (such as *Mother Courage and her Children* and *Galileo*) were written before 1945, but the Berliner ensemble—which survived Brecht's death—focused attention on his work's significance in the general revolt against the naturalist theatre. In France an important and successful experiment was made to check the virtual liquidation of the theatre outside Paris. In 1947 the government established five provincial dramatic centres, which injected new life into the theatre at large and supplemented the four national institutions in Paris. Another state-aided organization which won international renown was the Théâtre National Populaire after Jean Vilar became its director in 1951. With its Parisian headquarters in the Palais de Chaillot, its annual festivals at Avignon and its frequent tours, the T.N.P. recruited a large new audience for the classics (staged on Brechtian lines). Outstanding among other actor-directors was Jean-Louis Barrault, whose company was based for ten years on the Marigny, which he made one of the world's great theatres. Here he staged some of the treasury of modern French drama poured out since the war, by such internationally famous authors as Jean Anouilh, Jean-Paul Sartre, Eugène Ionesco, Marcel Aymé, Henry de Montherlant, Samuel Beckett, Jean Giraudoux, Armand Salacrou.

In the Commonwealth, the drama won new prestige and popularity, and several dominions moved towards establishing their own national theatres. In 1947 the South African government subsidized the formation of two " national theatre " companies (English and Afrikaans), to tour the main cities. In Canada, long destitute of live theatre, a pioneering new playhouse was opened at Stratford, Ontario, in 1953 for the performance of Shakespeare in near-Elizabethan conditions. Under the direction of Tyrone Guthrie it achieved a remarkable success. In Australia the Elizabethan Theatre trust was founded in 1955 with state help, to promote the cause of the Australian stage, and since then one local playwright—Ray Lawler—has emerged as an international figure. (A. H. D.; T. Q. C.; WR. B. H.; J. W. G.; RD. F.)

BIBLIOGRAPHY. Kenneth Tynan, *He that Plays the King* (London, 1950); Richard Findlater, *The Unholy Trade* (London, 1952); Harold Hobson, *The French Theatre of Today* (London, 1953); Harold Hobson (ed.), *International Theatre Annual* (London, 1956 onwards); the annual reports of the Arts Council of Great Britain (London, 1946 onwards).

THEOLOGICAL STUDIES: ARTICLE CARRIED IN ALTERNATE YEARS.

TIBET. Country of central Asia, N. and N.E. of the Himalayas, having autonomous status within the Chinese People's Republic. Area: *c*. 470,000 sq.mi. Pop. (1953 est.): 1,270,000. Language: Tibetan. Religion: Lamaistic Buddhism. Capital, Lhasa, pop. *c*. 50,000. Ruler, the Ling Erh (" divine child ") Pamo Tsiring, the 14th Dalai Lama. Monetary unit: Chinese *yuan*.

History. The revolt of the Kham tribesmen in eastern Tibet spread to Lhasa in March 1959 and led to the flight of the Dalai Lama and prominent members of his cabinet to India, the dismissal by the Chinese government of the so-called Tibetan local government, and the transfer of its functions to the Preparatory Committee for Autonomy. Peking had previously formally announced the deferment of all " democratic reforms " until 1962.

When the Chinese high command on March 10 summoned the Dalai Lama to go alone to their headquarters for an official entertainment, it was assumed that he would be kept there as hostage or taken to Peking for the National People's congress. A great crowd of people were in the city at the time because of the annual festival and they physically prevented the Dalai Lama from leaving the Norbulingka summer palace. A document signed by the cabinet and the leading lamas denounced the 1951 agreement.

The city was in a state of ferment, and when the Chinese sent in reinforcements and fired two or three mortar shells into the environs of the palace the Dalai Lama, members of his

kashag (government), and his family, escaped on March 17 and made their way through difficult routes to Tezpur, in Assam. In a statement issued there on April 18 the Dalai Lama said categorically that he came to India of his own free will and not under duress, as Peking alleged.

" It has always been accepted that the Tibetan people are different from the Han people of China," said the Tezpur statement, " . . . In 1951, under pressure of the Chinese government, a 17-point agreement was made between China and Tibet. In that agreement the suzerainty of China was accepted, as there was no alternative. But even in the agreement it was stated that Tibet would enjoy full autonomy . . . In fact, after the occupation of Tibet by the Chinese armies, the Tibetan government did not enjoy any measure of autonomy, even in internal matters, and the Chinese government exercised full powers in Tibetan affairs."

On April 20 Jawaharlal Nehru, the prime minister of India, told the Upper House that while the Dalai Lama would be free to carry on his religious activities in India, political activities could not be carried on " from one country against another ".

When the Dalai Lama had reached India, the Peking state council announced the defeat of the rebellion and said that plans for the political, economic and cultural reforms could now continue unhindered. A massive campaign of propaganda, lasting many weeks, followed, with vehement attacks daily on " Indian expansionists ". This campaign changed its tone after the dignified and massive rebuke administered by Nehru in the Indian parliament on April 27, when he disclosed that the Indian government had conveyed to the Chinese government " its deep feeling of regret " that charges should have been made over the Tibetan issue which were " both unbecoming and devoid of substance ", more especially in the speeches delivered in the current session of the National People's congress in Peking. He hoped nothing would be said or done to endanger the friendly relations of the two countries, which were so important for the peace of Asia and the world.

The Panchen Lama returned to Lhasa on June 16 to announce that feudal serfdom would be abolished and other reforms would be introduced while the suppression of the rebellion would continue. On June 20 the Dalai Lama, at

The Dalai Lama, mounted on a white horse, crossing the Zsagola pass in southern Tibet with his entourage during his flight to India. He reached the Indian frontier about 26 mi. to the north of Towang on March 31, having covered some 300 mi. since leaving Lhasa on March 17.

his residence in Mussoorie, called for India's support of Tibet's cause, saying he would welcome a meeting between the Chinese and Indian prime ministers. He referred to the Chinese " reign of terror " in Tibet and called for the creation of a Greater Tibet to incorporate the Chinese provinces of Amdo and Kham, which formerly were part of Tibet.

The statement by the Dalai Lama that, wherever he and his government were, they were recognized as the rightful government by the Tibetan people, elicited the statement from an official Indian spokesman that the Indian government did not recognize any separated government of Tibet, and there was therefore no question of a Tibetan government under the Dalai Lama functioning in India.

Against India's advice, the Dalai Lama decided to ask the United Nations to act as a mediator between Communist China and Tibet. He sent to New York his brother, Gyalo Thondup, styled as the " foreign minister of the Tibetan government in exile ", who succeeded in securing the help of the Irish and Malayan delegations to the U.N. general assembly. The two delegations requested that the question of Tibet should be added to the agenda of the current session. The assembly's steering committee recommended on Oct. 9 a full debate on the charges relating to Communist China's suppression of human rights in Tibet. The committee voted 11 to 5 with 4 abstentions. On Oct. 12, by a vote of 43 to 11, with 25 abstentions, the general assembly decided to debate the charges. The 11 countries voting against included the Communist group of 9 plus Yugoslavia and Indonesia. The United States supported the resolution, while Great Britain and India abstained. The debate, which lasted two days, ended on Oct. 21 by passing a resolution deploring recent events in Tibet and calling for respect for the fundamental human rights of the Tibetan peoples. The voting was 45 in favour and 9 against, with 26 abstentions, including Yugoslavia and Indonesia. (*See* also SINO-INDIAN FRONTIER DISPUTE.) (W. V. P.; X.)

TIMBER.

TIMBER. The U.K. softwood market was over-stocked in the autumn of 1958 and, in the spring of 1959, was further weakened by the U.S.S.R.'s action in making two price cuts. This left Swedish and Finnish sellers with a difficult opening market, particularly in lower quality wood. However, offerings from the U.S.S.R. were readily absorbed and, aided by an upsurge of trade in the United Kingdom, the Swedes and Finns were able to place substantial quantities upon the European market by midsummer, as will be seen from the figures given below. Prices, however, showed an over-all drop of from £3 to £5 per standard, according to quality, and Baltic sellers complained that they had made little, if any, profit on their season's operations.

Sweden's total sales for export for the first six months of 1959 amounted to approximately 700,000 standards compared with 500,000 standards during the same period of 1958. Assuming that Sweden's total export potential amounted to some 900,000 standards, then 80% had been sold by midsummer. In relation to the above figures, the A/B Statens Skogindustrier (State Timber organization) produced approximately 120,000 standards. Owing to diminishing coal markets in a number of European countries, the Swedish pitprop output remained at approximately the low level of 300,000 cu.m., to which it fell in 1958. Television sorting of lumber had passed the experimental stage, and was being installed at the log-sorting centre of Sandslan, Sweden. Using a closed circuit, the operator sits in a comfortable cabin and watches the owners' marks on the ends of the floated logs on his television screen. By pressing a button he passes the logs by a robot system to the various booms reserved for different owners. The centenary of the grouping of the Swedish royal forests into the Domanstyrelsen was celebrated in September

and attended by, among others, Binay Ranjan Sen, director-general of the Food and Agriculture organization, and the director of the division of forestry and forest products, F.A.O.

In Finland, by the end of June, export sales reached approximately 800,000 standards, about 250,000 standards more than in 1958; *i.e.*, roughly 90% of the year's potential export of sawn goods had been sold. In 1959 sawn timber, wood pulp, pulp, paper board and other products amounted to over 75% of Finland's total export trade.

By midsummer the U.S.S.R. had virtually disposed of its season's offerings on the same scale as in 1958. The picture

Huge rafts on the Volga river, near Yaroslavl, carrying timber from the north of Russia to the treeless south.

in the smaller exporting countries, such as Norway, Poland, Rumania and Yugoslavia, followed the same pattern. All disposed of their export surpluses but complained at the prices received for their goods. The revival of trade in the United Kingdom, particularly in the constructional sector, was confirmed by the first half-year's visible consumption of 707,131 standards compared with 646,820 standards for the same period in 1958. The United Kingdom's imports of plywood from Finland, Sweden, the U.S.S.R. and the German Federal Republic amounted to approximately 200,000 cu.m., for the first six months of 1959. The establishment of the European Free Trade association by the " outer seven " countries (outside the European common market) was expected to affect considerably the Baltic market for sawn goods and timber products. Its effects were already being closely studied in the countries concerned.

In the first half of 1959, 160,000 standards of softwoods were sold by Canada to the United Kingdom, a drop of some 10% compared with the preceding year. On the other hand, sales of Douglas fir plywood showed a considerable increase. Unfortunately midsummer found the British Columbia timber industry in the grip of a strike. Canadian lumber exporters were already finding it difficult to compete with their European competitors and this labour dispute further weakened their position. The Canadian Wood Development council planned to spend $270,000, based on 5 cents per 1,000 ft. of lumber production, to promote the sale of timber at home and abroad during 1960. A notable loss to timber circles in British Columbia was the death of Mr. Justice Sloan, who did valuable work in investigating the industry in the province.

The European hardwood market remained stable. Yugoslav producers sold practically all their beech at firm prices. Following the devaluation of the franc, the price for French oak and beech fell by 5%-10%, but export figures remained steady. Rumania entered into beech contracts, while Austria, Bulgaria and Czechoslovakia all made their customary contributions to the beech market.

Fluctuating freights unsettled c.i.f. prices in the west African market, shipowners offering rebates of 10%-30% on their tariffs at various times of the year. Nevertheless, the prices of such typical timbers as obeche, wawa, mahogany and walnut were firm, with a tendency to rise towards the end of the year. Nigeria for the first seven months of the year exported to the United Kingdom 3,766,426 cu.ft. of logs and Ghana contributed 2,495,976 cu.ft. for the same period. Afrormosia lumber remained firm, but some weakness developed in iroko, both in logs and lumber, owing to overproduction. The Ghana timber trade, both in logs and lumber, was affected by a severe drought lasting from Nov. 1958 to May 1959. Restrictions on water consumption had to be imposed to such an extent that the movement of logs by rail was seriously affected. All steam-powered railway engines were concentrated in Northern Ghana, where water was still available, while diesel engines were used for the southern portion of the run to Takoradi. Delivery of contracts was seriously delayed and this undoubtedly helped to establish a firm market. The Ghana Ministry of Commerce and Industry set up a committee under the chairmanship of E. R. A. de Unger to examine the organization for the purchase, sale and export of timber. A contract for the initial work on a giant breakwater at Forcados to protect the ports in the Niger delta had been placed, and its successful completion would enhance the value of these ports as timber exporting centres. In the far east freights from Thailand rose to a more normal level and this had the effect of keeping the c.i.f. quotations for teak and yang firm; under similar influences the price of Malayan keruing hardened. The Sarawak government maintained its quota control of ramin exports and prices were steady.

In the United Kingdom, plans for the more efficient marketing of home-grown timber came to fruition by the establishment of a Woodland Owners' association to take care of both the growing and selling of forest crops, while the Federated Home Timber association set up the Home Grown Timber Marketing corporation to handle part of the home-grown sawn and pitwood production on a co-operative basis.

A preliminary estimate of lumber production in the United States in 1958 placed the total at 33,579 million bd.ft. This estimate, based on information supplied by the National Lumber Manufacturers' association, was reported to the secretary of commerce by his Lumber Survey committee. The production figure for 1958 showed a decrease of more than 1,000 million bd.ft. from the revised estimate for the preceding year, and of more than 4,600 million bd.ft. from 1956. The 1958 total included 27,001 million bd.ft. of softwood (coniferous) lumber and 6,578 million bd.ft. of hardwood lumber (broad-leaved species).

Exports of lumber from the United States in 1958 amounted to 727 million bd.ft., according to Department of Commerce reports. This was a drop of over 84 million bd.ft. from 1957 exports. Of the 1958 total, 540 million bd.ft. was softwood lumber. Imports of lumber in 1958 were 3,392 million bd.ft., compared with 2,959 million bd.ft. in 1957. The 1958 total included 3,155 million bd.ft. of softwood lumber, mostly from Canada. The wholesale lumber price index fell from an average of 119·7 for 1957 to 118·0 for 1958. During the first half of 1959 lumber prices rose. By June 1959, the index figure was 130·4, close to the high point of 130·6 in April

1956. It dropped slightly in July to 129·8. (*See also* FORESTRY.)   (B. L.; C. E. R.)

TIMOR: *see* PORTUGUESE OVERSEAS TERRITORIES.

TOBACCO. World production of leaf (outside China) in 1959, was estimated at about 6·8 million lb., somewhat above that in 1958, but below the record figure in 1956. The U.S. crop totalled 1,800 million lb., 64 million lb. more than in 1958, but 376 million lb. less than in 1956. In the Commonwealth, production in the Federation of Rhodesia and Nyasaland reached the record figure of 231 million lb., 37 million lb. more than in 1958; flue-cured in the Rhodesias totalled 193 million lb. The Union of South Africa produced 67 million lb., only 2 million lb. below the record crop of 1958. Indian production rose to 589 million lb. and that in Pakistan to 218 million lb. The crop in Canada was estimated at 156 million lb., 41 million lb. less than in 1958, as a result of reduced acreage and unfavourable weather.

Shipments from the United States during Jan.-Oct. 1959 totalled 359 million lb. (20 million lb. less than a year earlier); consignments in the fiscal year 1958-59 included 40 million lb. sold for foreign currencies under surplus disposal programmes. Shipments to the United Kingdom in Jan.-Oct. 1959 totalled 113 million lb. (13·0 million lb. less than a year earlier) while 53 million lb. went to the German Federal Republic. Exports from the Federation of Rhodesia and Nyasaland in 1959 reached a record of 176 million lb., 33 million lb. more than a year earlier, consignments to the United Kingdom rising by 17 million lb. to 91 million lb.

Imports into the United Kingdom during the year 1959 totalled 301 million lb., 15 million lb. less than a year earlier.

U.K. IMPORTS OF TOBACCO (million lb.)

From	1956	1957	1958	1959
Rhodesia and Nyasaland .	84	80	75	87
Canada . . .	22	26	23	30
India . . .	40	36	45	37
United States . .	160	168	164	140
Total (incl. others) .	318	319	316	301

SOURCE. Commonwealth Economic Committee.

Gross U.K. clearance from bond in the first 11 months of 1959 was 289 million lb. and withdrawals for domestic consumption 235 million lb., the Commonwealth share of the latter reaching about one half. Stocks fell to 517 million lb. at the end of November, 15 million lb. less than a year earlier. The full duty on tobacco imports continued unchanged at 61s. 2d. per lb. and the retail price of most cigarettes continued at 3s. 11d. for 20. Expenditure on tobacco products in the United Kingdom in Jan.-Sept. 1959 reached £787 million, £19 million more than a year earlier.

At the Federation of Rhodesia and Nyasaland auctions tobacco averaged lower prices for most types than in 1958, although prices for superior grades were well maintained; the seasonal average for Rhodesian flue-cured of 34·4d. per lb. was 2·0d. less than in 1958, while Nyasaland fire-cured declined by 4·1d. to 11·5d. In the United States, however, the flue-cured crop averaged 57·7 cents per lb. as against 57·8 cents in 1958.   (E. O. G.)

TOGO. An autonomous republic under French trusteeship, bounded W. by Ghana, N. by the Republic of Upper Volta, E. by the Republic of Dahomey and S. by the Atlantic ocean. Area: 20,463 sq.mi. Pop.: (1936 est.) 781,000; (1957 est.) 1,093,000, mainly Negro; European (1955 est.) 1,277, mostly French. Religion: animism, with a strong Moslem minority and many Christians. Capital (pop., 1958 est.): Lomé 65,000, including 1,000 Europeans. French high commissioner, Georges Spénale. Prime minister, Sylvanus Olympio. Main exports: coffee, cocoa. Monetary unit: *franc CFA* = metropolitan Fr.2.

History. The resignation of M. Santos, the minister of justice, led to a split in the government party, the Comité d'Unité Togolaise, and the "Juvento" (a group of young people) broke away. The elections to the regional and municipal councils saw the victory of the C.U.T., the "Juvento" obtaining only a few votes.

Sociétés Publiques d'Action Rurale (public companies for rural development) were created. Positions in them were filled by election, and they had a technical director appointed by the government. They were under the supervision of the regional administrator.

In agreement with France, the U.N. general assembly decided on Dec. 5, 1959, that Togo would become completely independent on April 27, 1960. The government drew up a plan for a port at Lomé, which would cost Fr. CFA 7,000 million. (HU. DE.)

TOGOLAND: *see* GHANA; TOGO; TRUST TERRITORIES.

TONGA (FRIENDLY ISLANDS). Kingdom under British protection, which is exercised through the governor of Fiji and a local British representative. Three main island groups: Vava'u, Ha'apai and Tongatapu. Total area: 269 sq.mi. (Tongatapu I. 99·2 sq.mi.). Pop.: (end 1957 est.) 57,920, mainly Tongans, racially and linguistically Polynesian with Melanesian admixture. Religion: Christian (77% belonging to three Methodist bodies, incl. 50% to established Free Wesleyan Church). Capital: Nuku'alofa (pop. [1956 census] 9,202) on Tongatapu I. Administration: sovereign; premier; British commissioner; privy council (cabinet); legislative assembly with popularly elected minority. Queen, Salote Tupou; premier, Crown Prince Tungi. British agent and consul (from May 25, 1959, entitled commissioner and consul): A. C. Reid, (from March 14) Q. V. L. Weston, (from Oct. 6) A. C. Reid and (from Nov. 9) E. J. Coode. Main imports: textile products, processed foodstuffs, hardware and machinery, fuels, tobacco products. Main exports: copra, bananas. Monetary unit: Tongan pound (= Australian pound); Australian, U.K., N.Z. and Fijian coin circulates.

History. Having successfully established its new shipping service on a profit-making basis, in 1959 the government took up the development of a commercial fishing industry. A programme to train Tongans in Japanese fishing methods was begun, and the premier, Crown Prince Tungi, visited Japan to negotiate for an appropriate vessel.

During the year work proceeded on the building and equipping of Tonga's first broadcasting station.

The renewed treaty of friendship with Great Britain came into effect in May. (R. P. GN.)

TOURIST TRADE: *see* BUSINESS REVIEW.

TOWN AND COUNTRY PLANNING. The year 1959 saw a resumption of the upward trend of building construction of all kinds and thus progress towards the fulfilment of many plans. At the same time, even more difficult and numerous problems of land use arose than before.

The most important event in planning administration was the coming into operation of the Town and Country Planning act, 1959. The main provision of this measure was the payment of compensation at market value for land bought by public authorities under compulsory powers. The value was assessed having regard to the development proposed by the acquiring authority as well as to any other development for which planning permission had been given or could reasonably have been expected if the land was not being bought by a public authority. The act did not, however, alter the basis of compensation when permission was refused. A remedy was also provided for those owner-occupiers who wished to sell their property but could not do so, except at a reduced price, because it was shown in a plan as subject to future acquisition; they could require the authority to buy it at the full market value. This applied to all residential property, other property with a net annual value for rating purposes not exceeding £250 and that part of any farmland which was directly affected. Some recommendations of the "Franks" committee, which were not incorporated in the Tribunals and Inquiries act, 1958, were also implemented in this act. An appeal on points

of law arising out of planning decisions was for the courts to decide and the lord chancellor could, after consulting the Council on Tribunals, make rules of procedure for public inquiries.

During the year there was steady progress in the building of new towns, some of which were now nearing completion. In view of this the New Towns act, 1959, provided for a commission to take over from the Development corporations when each town had been substantially completed. The annual reports of the Development corporations published in the autumn revealed growing concern with the needs of the exceptional proportion of young people among the inhabitants. The reports also recorded considerable progress (and world-wide interest) in the complex problems of building the town centres.

The National Parks commission designated the Dorset coast, the Shropshire hills, the Malvern hills and parts of Cornwall as "areas of outstanding natural beauty" within the meaning of the National Parks act, 1949. These orders were confirmed by the minister of housing and local government and the effect, besides attracting exchequer grants, was to put additional emphasis on the need for preserving these areas. The commission also designated a proposed long-distance footpath along the south coast of Devon.

The government made clear in parliament its firm adherence to the policy of restricting the outward expansion of certain towns by "green belts" in which there was a clear presumption against any new building. There was a public inquiry in July about a proposed green belt around Southampton and Portsmouth. Within this area there had been proposals, subsequently withdrawn, for building a large oil refinery at Warsash, on the Solent, where there was an increasing amount of sailing for recreation. This was yet another outstanding example of the conflict between important industrial projects and the preservation of areas for amenity or recreation.

There was considerable emphasis at conferences of planning organizations, in press articles and in exhibitions on the need for urban renewal. The minister of housing and local government himself urged that now the task of rebuilding the devastated areas was almost completed the next step was the far more difficult one of gradual renewal of the outworn parts of towns. Published proposals showed that some local authorities were applying themselves to this task.

During November there was a public inquiry concerning a proposal of the Cambridge County and City councils to rebuild an area close to the centre of the city for a pedestrian shopping precinct, offices, an hotel and an underground car park. The proposal was opposed by the university and by two colleges on the grounds that the area should have a civic and cultural, rather than commercial, character and that it would merely add to and not relieve the congestion in the centre of the city.

There was much building activity in London and the skyline changed as more and more new buildings appeared of much greater height than hitherto. Proposals were published for a new building, 170 ft. high, on a site on the north side of Piccadilly circus. The blank end walls of this building were to be covered with illuminated advertisements and there would be a crane on the top for changing them. These proposals aroused strong criticism in parliament and the minister directed that the application for planning permission should be referred to him for decision. A public inquiry began in December.

Planning in Great Britain and, indeed, throughout the world suffered a great loss in the death in April of Sir George Pepler (*see* OBITUARIES). For more than 30 years he was the chief technical officer of the ministry concerned with town and country planning. His loss would be keenly felt, particularly in the many overseas countries where his guidance on town planning problems was repeatedly sought.

Town and country planning in the Commonwealth countries and U.K. dependencies continued to develop largely on U.K. patterns adjusted to meet local circumstances. An important event was the second international conference on urban problems which took place in Nairobi, Kenya. Planning in Mauritius, Hong Kong and the Bahamas had been further strengthened by the appointment of additional planning officers, and several Ghanaians and Malayans trained in Britain had now returned to take up practice in their respective countries. Desmond Heap, comptroller and solicitor of the Corporation of the City of London, visited Trinidad to advise the government on the revision of town planning legislation. The Town Planning institute had more than 520 overseas members and at the annual summer school, held under its auspices, 19 countries were represented. (*See* also HOUSING; NEW TOWNS; NATIONAL PARKS.)　　　　　　(E. G. S. E.)

TRADE UNIONS. United Kingdom. In 1959 the Trades Union congress reported that its affiliated membership had fallen from 8,337,325 in 1957-58 to 8,176,252 in 1958-59. The membership of registered trade unions was lower by 188,000 and the figure for all trade unions showed a fall from 9·8 million at the end of 1957 to 9·6 million at the end of 1958. This was much the largest fall in membership since 1934. It was difficult to say whether the downturn was the beginning of a new trend or whether it merely reflected the rise in unemployment from less than 2% to almost 3% in 1958.

The report of the Chief Registrar of Friendly Societies for the year 1958 showed that trade unions were still not covering their outgoings by the amount which they received from members. The difference between contribution income and total expenditure had been made good for a number of years past by the income received from investments, which amounted to no less than 13·2% of the total income of trade unions in 1958. Average annual trade union subscriptions had been raised from £2 per member in 1950 to £2 15s. 3d. in 1958. This increase had, however, done no more than keep pace with the rising cost of union administration. Unless unions could halt this trend they would be compelled to make further substantial increases in the level of contributions. The executive committees of most organizations were reluctant to sanction such increases, since these were unpopular with members and might contribute to a further decline in numbers.

The most important event during 1959 from the point of view of many unions was the general election. The T.U.C. and the unions affiliated to the Labour party made a larger effort, both in terms of their financial contributions and the advocacy of their leaders, to bring about the defeat of the Conservatives than at any time since 1945. The amount contributed to the funds of the Labour party and spent in other respects on political activities had risen in 1958 to £707,000, almost exactly double the amount spent in 1945. In the event, 93 candidates sponsored by the trade unions, compared with 96 in the previous house, were elected as Labour members of the House of Commons. In November the Conservative party issued a statement calling upon all their supporters in the trade unions to contract out of paying the political levy on the grounds that the 125 unions with political funds used them in the main for the benefit of the Labour party. The " contracting out " membership of the trade unions had reached 922,000, or 11·9%, in 1958. The Conservative party believed that the number of trade unionists who voted in their favour in the 1959 election was in excess of 3 million and they hoped that by giving publicity to the right of union members to contract out of the political levy they would succeed in weakening the ties between the unions and the Labour party.

Among the many issues dealt with at the annual meeting of the Trades Union congress—held at Blackpool from Sept. 7 to 11—one which aroused important questions concerned allegations made against the Electrical Trades union. The general council of the T.U.C. had sought to discover whether there was any foundation in fact for the many newspaper articles and letters in the press accusing the leaders of the E.T.U. of using undemocratic methods to secure the return of officers who were members of the Communist party. The replies of the executive committee of the E.T.U., which held that the charges were without substance, were not acceptable to the general council. The council considered that the E.T.U. should have brought an action in the courts against the newspapers publishing the allegations, since the charges made were bringing the entire trade union movement into disrepute. The E.T.U. maintained that the courts were biassed against the unions and that the press would report any action unfavourably to the union, but it would be prepared to take legal action if the T.U.C. would foot the bill. The general council rejected this reply and invited the full executive council of the E.T.U. to meet its finance and general purposes committee to discuss the matters at issue. The E.T.U. refused, holding that if there was need for the full executive council of the E.T.U. to be present the meeting should be with the general council as a whole, and that in any case the E.T.U. executive council had other important commitments to fulfil on the date suggested. The general council of the T.U.C. stated that " both the timing and the content of this letter is further and, indeed, conclusive evidence that the majority of the present leadership of the E.T.U. is more concerned to evade than to deal adequately with the questions." The general council therefore decided not to continue the discussions.

In accordance with a resolution passed in the 1958 meeting, the general council prepared a comprehensive statement of its views on the economic situation. This lengthy document, presented to the 1959 congress, criticized the government for permitting machines and men to stand idle in order to prevent prices from rising. The report admitted that the policy of the government had succeeded in checking the inflation which had threatened, but it was felt that more vigorous steps ought to be taken to stimulate demand so as to utilize fully the industrial capacity available. The authors were of the opinion that, in order to secure this increase in demand, the government should reinforce its previous measures by raising pensions and unemployment benefit and by expanding investment in industry, schools, hospitals and slum clearance. The report concluded with the observation that " preoccupation with the problems of full employment has far too often been allowed to obscure the opportunities that full employment offers. It is—for a time—easier to remain inactive than to operate positive expansionary policies, and to meet and overcome any problems they may bring . . . Neither the Trade Union Movement nor the British people can be satisfied with the aims or the results of the Government's policies. A further attempt must be made. It may in some ways be a more difficult task, but it will be the more rewarding one of getting Britain's men and machines back to useful work."

In the field of collective bargaining the unions shifted their attention from wage increases to securing a reduction of the standard working week to 40 hr. The last case to go to the Industrial Disputes tribunal before it was finally wound up was a claim by the Confederation of Shipbuilding and Engineering Unions on behalf of some 3 million workers that basic hours should be reduced from 44 to 40 per week. The tribunal decided, however, that it could not find in favour of the claim and the unions were left to pursue their objective by other means. Towards the end of the year slight reductions in hours of work in the chemical industry, the electricity

Representatives of the trade unions involved in the 1959 printing dispute at a meeting on July 1. The chairman was W. A. Morrison (third from left) of the Printing, Bookbinding and Paper Workers' union. On his left is G. G. Eastwood (Printing and Kindred Trades federation).

supply industry, parts of the motor industry and in agriculture were interpreted by most observers as foreshadowing a general reduction in hours during the next few years.

In December the general council of the T.U.C. decided to ask all trade unionists to express their personal revulsion against the racial policies of the South African government by boycotting South African goods during March 1960.

International and Commonwealth. It was reported by the International Confederation of Free Trade Unions (I.C.F.T.U.) that aid had been rendered from the International Solidarity fund to assist trade union organizations in Peru, Trinidad, Cameroun, Indonesia, Barbados and Cyprus.

Attention was called by the general council of the T.U.C. to the difficulties that could arise as a result of differences in approach to the assistance of unions in underdeveloped territories. In the general council's view African unions had been encouraged to subordinate their trade union functions to the political objective of pan-Africanism. The council believed that the policy of the American Federation of Labour-Congress of Industrial Organizations (A.F.L.-C.I.O.), which was directed towards building African unionism from the top downwards, was not likely to lead to the sound development of unions. The first task should be to strengthen individual trade unions so as to ensure that they were firmly established, before national and regional bodies were promoted. At the sixth congress of the I.C.F.T.U., in Brussels in December, T.U.C. delegates took grave exception to an attack on British colonial policy made by George Meany, president of the A.F.L.-C.I.O. The clash of opinion threatened to disrupt the organization of the I.C.F.T.U. and the congress appointed a sub-committee to thrash out the issues in dispute.

Considerable attention was paid by the general council of the T.U.C. to the adoption by British colonial territories of essential services legislation. The council conveyed its concern at the existing legislation and suggested to the colonial secretary that an examination should be made of the services scheduled as essential, the form of protection required for those services, the type of machinery for the voluntary settlement of disputes that existed in those services, the extent to which there was provision for compulsory arbitration and the implications of the legislation from the point of view of the right to strike. The colonial secretary replied that he was undertaking an inquiry and would appoint a committee to

advise on the problem when full information as to the current position was received from the colonies.

The problem of the regulation of trade union organization in Kenya, Uganda and Tanganyika continued to give rise to difficulties. In each of these territories the formation of inter-territorial unions was banned. An I.C.F.T.U. mission sent to east Africa and Northern Rhodesia in 1958 reported that, while the existing legislation did not seriously hamper the activities of unions, it did contain objectionable features and it imposed a heavy administrative burden on unions at an early stage of their development. One observation by the mission which aroused considerable criticism was that the character of the trade union ordinances in operation in these territories tended to force trade unions into the pattern existing in the United Kingdom. It was pointed out by the general council of the T.U.C. that since the law allowed the formation of different types of unions there was no limitation on their development.

In Dec. 1958 the parliament of Ghana passed the much discussed Industrial Relations act, which was designed to bring the unions under state control. The act made provision for changes in the organization of the Trades Union congress and for the certification of unions in relation to their collective bargaining functions.

The Indian National Trades Union congress held its tenth annual convention at Dibrugarh in Assam in Feb. 1959. It was attended by 1,500 delegates, including fraternal delegates from many other countries and international organizations.

Legislation adopted in British Columbia early in the year was the most stringent and restrictive, in a general sense, which Canada had ever seen. It prohibited picketing, except at the employer's place of business and by members of the striking union only, and outlawed support from the members of other unions. Unless the contrary was shown, the illegal action of any union member was presumed to be done, authorized or concurred in by the trade union. The legislation also made unions legal entities, with the right to prosecute and be prosecuted.

Among international labour organizations the international trade secretariats were, at the end of the 1950s, perhaps the least well known, though they were among the oldest of international institutions. The newest of these secretariats was the Plantation Workers' International federation

(P.W.I.F., founded 1957). Its headquarters were in Brussels and it had field representatives and organizers in India, Tanganyika, Kenya, Mauritius, the British Cameroons, New York and Trinidad. The P.W.I.F. had close working arrangements with the I.C.F.T.U. and also with the International Landworkers' federation, with which it hoped to amalgamate in the near future. The P.W.I.F. was endeavouring to bring about the establishment of trade union organization in many areas where it did not already exist. One of its successes in 1959 was the founding of a union catering for sisal workers in Tanganyika, of whom there were estimated to be 20,000. The federation had also arranged a recruiting and organizing campaign in Kenya, Cameroun, The West Indies and in Asian countries.

Trade unions in Europe were much concerned with problems raised by the progress of economic integration. Following the discussions among the governments of the " outer seven " countries which were not members of the European Economic community, the trade union federations held a conference to discuss the implications of this development. Representatives of only six countries were present at this gathering, however, since the seventh, Portugal, was not regarded as having a free trade union movement and was not invited. In a statement issued at the conclusion of the talks the unions welcomed the hope of the governments that the proposed free trade area would provide a bridge towards the achievement of a wider economic association in Europe as a whole. They found the references in the free trade area plan to the need for continued economic expansion particularly satisfactory. The unions, it was insisted, should be given representation on an equal footing with employers on any institutions that might be established under the plan. Unions should have the right to place items they thought important on the agenda of any such agencies and should have access to the council of ministers, the governing body and the secretariat. The union representatives urged that the plan should guarantee to workers freedom of association and the right to bargain collectively.

United States. As a result of disclosures by the McClellan committee, which indicated that racketeering elements had gained control over some unions, congress enacted the first major labour law since the Taft-Hartley act of 1947. The Labour-Management Reporting and Disclosure act provided for the disclosure of union finances and made specific provisions to safeguard union treasuries. Members were guaranteed the right to freedom of speech and assembly in connection with union affairs and freedom from discriminatory disciplinary proceedings, and the right to elect officers by secret ballot. Amendments to the Taft-Hartley act included additional restrictions upon secondary boycotts and picketing practices.

At the third convention of the A.F.L.-C.I.O. in September in San Francisco a major decision was the agreement to submit inter-union disputes to compulsory arbitration. The problem of jurisdictional rivalry among the craft and industrial affiliates of the federation had been a major one since the A.F.L.-C.I.O. was founded in 1955. The convention also approved the petition by the International Longshoremen's association to affiliate with the federation. The I.L.A. had been expelled from the A.F.L. in 1953 on charges that its leaders were corrupt. Towards the end of 1959 John L. Lewis, aged 79, announced that he would resign the presidency of the United Mineworkers' union. He was to be succeeded by the vice-president, Thomas Kennedy, aged 72.

Affiliated membership of the A.F.L.-C.I.O. amounted in 1959 to 14,092,000, while the total membership of all labour unions was 17,024,000. (*See* also INTERNATIONAL LABOUR ORGANIZATION.) (B. C. R.; N. S. D.; S. A. LN.)

TRINIDAD AND TOBAGO: *see* WEST INDIES, THE.
TROPICAL DISEASES: *see* DISEASES.

TRUCIAL SHEIKHDOMS (or T. OMAN, T. COAST). British-protected Arab sheikhdoms on Persian gulf, comprising Abu Dhabi, Ajman, Dubai, Fujairah, Ras el-Khaimah, Sharjah, and Umm el-Kawain sheikhdoms. Total area: *c*. 32,300 sq.mi. Total pop: *c*. 80,000. Chief towns: Dubai (chief port and British political agent's h.q.), pop. *c*. 30,000; Sharjah; Abu Dhabi (port). British political agent, D. F. Hawley. Monetary unit: Indian *rupee*.

The ruler of Dubai, Sheikh Rashid bin Said el-Maktum, accompanied by his two sons, paid a visit to Britain in June. During his stay he had a meeting with the minister of state for foreign affairs, J. D. Profumo, and was entertained to luncheon by the directors of the British Bank of the Middle East. (*See* also MUSCAT AND OMAN.)

TRUST TERRITORIES. Former German colonies and islands which became mandated territories after World War I and trust territories after World War II; South-West Africa, which remained mandated; and the former Italian Somaliland (now Somalia) which became a trust territory under Italian administration on April 1, 1950. Total area: 1,218,827 sq.mi. Total pop.: *c*. 22,700,000. Certain essential information is given in the table.

TRUST AND MANDATED TERRITORIES

	Area (sq.mi.)	Population	Administering authority
South-West Africa*	317,725	539,000 (1958 est.)	South Africa
Togo (Fr.) . .	20,463	1,092,889 (1958 est.)	France
Cameroons (Br.) .	34,080	1,560,000 (1958 est.)	U.K.
Cameroun (Fr.) .	170,231	3,223,517 (1958 est.)	France
Tanganyika . .	362,688	8,785,613 (1957 census)	U.K.
Ruanda-Urundi .	20,540	4,641,209 (1958 est.)	Belgium
New Guinea† .	93,000	1,341,268 (1958 est.)	Australia
Western Samoa .	1,130	102,860 (1958 est.)	New Zealand
Nauru . .	8	4,308 (1958 est.)	Australia
Pacific Islands‡ .	687	67,000 (1957 est.)	United States
Somalia . .	198,275	1,333,531 (1958 est.)	Italy

* Mandated territory. † Northeast New Guinea, Bismarck archipelago, certain of Solomon Islands. ‡ Marshall, Marianas and Caroline; former Japanese mandated territories.

History. In 1959 the task of setting dates for independence or self-government for the trust territories, in consultation with the respective administering authorities, kept the Trusteeship council and its visiting missions working at full stretch. The general assembly took the unusual course of resuming its adjourned 13th session to consider exclusively the special problems of the Cameroons.

The Trusteeship council, which opened its 23rd session on Jan. 30, went into recess for the duration of the general assembly's " African session " (Feb. 20-March 13). Both bodies had before them reports from the visiting mission which had been studying the situation in the Cameroons on the spot. In Cameroun all the main political groups clearly wanted reunification of the two territories. The British Cameroons, however, seemed to be " two separate entities ". The northern population appeared to wish to become a part of the Northern Region of the Federation of Nigeria. In the south, one group favoured a self-governing association with Nigeria, while another preferred union with Cameroun. After the indecisive election held in the Southern Cameroons on Jan. 24, the mission, in an addendum to its report, suggested that it might be necessary to hold a plebiscite at some appropriate date.

The Trusteeship council recommended that the trusteeship agreement for Cameroun should be ended but, with regard to the British Cameroons, merely asked the general assembly to take " appropriate action ". The issues were considered at 36 meetings of the assembly's trusteeship committee. Finally, in plenary session, it was unanimously agreed that the trusteeship agreement for Cameroun should be terminated when the territory attained independence on Jan. 1, 1960. By a vote of 56-0, with 24 abstentions, the assembly further proposed that separate plebiscites should be held under U.N. supervision in the two parts of the British Cameroons. In the north, the people voted on Nov. 9, 1959, by 67,879 to 41,113, to remain under the trusteeship system indefinitely, rather than join the Northern Region of Nigeria. The framing of questions to be put to the people in the Southern Cameroons was held over until the general assembly's next session.

The Trusteeship council continued to sit until March 20, considering progress reports on conditions in Tanganyika, Ruanda-Urundi and Togo. Major attention was devoted to Tanganyika, where the U.K. representative, J. Fletcher-Cooke, was able to report considerable progress in nearly all fields except finance. He suggested ways in which the territory's development might be assisted by the newly formed U.N. Economic Commission for Africa (E.C.A.).

At its 24th session (June 2–Aug. 6), the Trusteeship council reviewed political, economic, social and educational conditions in four Pacific and three African territories. Western Samoa claimed a major share of attention. During the spring, a U.N. visiting mission to the territory had endorsed a timetable for future constitutional developments, designed to lead to self-government or independence at the end of 1961. It was agreed that a plebiscite should be held in May 1961 to ascertain the exact wishes of the population. The New Zealand representative gave the council his government's assurance that Samoa's independence would be complete and unqualified.

The French representative formally announced April 27, 1960, as the date when Togo would become an independent state. Previously the general assembly had approved plans for independence, but no actual date had been fixed.

During the debate on Italian-administered Somalia, the council was advised by the administering authority that final plans for the transfer of power to the Somali government had been put before the U.N. advisory council for the territory. Italy promised to note the suggestion that new elections in the territory should be held after independence on Dec. 2, 1960. Subsequently the date for independence was changed to July 1, 1960.

U.N. efforts to hasten a settlement of the frontier dispute between Somalia and Ethiopia resulted in both parties inviting the king of Norway to nominate an independent person to assist in defining the terms of reference of the arbitration tribunal. Trygve Lie, the former U.N. secretary-general, accepted the task. (L. R. A.)

See (all New York, 1959) Trusteeship Council, *Report to General Assembly on 23rd and 24th sessions,* and *Official Records;* Visiting Missions, *Reports on the Cameroons under U.K. administration* and *Western Samoa; Special Questionnaire for the Trust Territory of New Guinea.*

TUBERCULOSIS: *see* DISEASES.

TUNISIA.
Independent republic in north Africa between Algeria (W.) and Libya (E.). Area: 48,332 sq.mi. Pop.: (Feb. 1, 1956, census) 3,782,480; 89·5% Moslem and Arabic-speaking (Arabs and Berbers), but incl. 255,332 Europeans (180,450 French and 69,909 Italians) and 57,786 Jews; (1958 est.) 3,850,000. Chief towns (pop., 1958 est.): Tunis (cap.) 678,000; Sfax 65,000; Susa 48,000; Bizerta 44,000; Kairuan 34,000. President, Habib Bourguiba. Main exports: wine, olive oil, wheat, cement, iron ore, phosphate rock, lead. Currency: Tunisian *dinar* (D.1·178 = £1 sterling).

History. The new constitution was promulgated on June 1, 1959. Certain principles were set forth in the preamble: a republican regime, the Islamic religion, the Arab language, the unity of Greater Moghreb, the Arab community, co-operation with the people of Africa. The National Assembly was to be elected by universal suffrage and secret ballot for a period of five years, at the same time as the president of the republic. All citizens were equal before the law; all beliefs and creeds could be freely practised. The liberty of the individual was guaranteed within the limits of the law, as well as the right of property. The president of the republic had to be a

Irrigation and drainage work in progress in the Medjerda valley, Tunisia, where F.A.O. is assisting a rice-growing project.

Moslem; he could not be re-elected more than three times; he was head of the army; he would set his seal to all legislative documents, could demand a second reading for acts of parliament and had the right of free pardon. A Council of State and an Audit Court were set up. A revision of the constitution could be asked for by the president or by one-third of the members of the National Assembly. The second National Assembly of independent Tunisia was elected on Nov. 8. Habib Bourguiba was proclaimed the first popularly elected president. He received 1,005,769 votes (91·4% of the electorate). (*See* ELECTIONS.)

Relations with France went through a difficult stage in February. Nine French post office technicians and five French embassy employees were arrested on Feb. 10 and charged with espionage; one of them, Pierre-Michel Gondolo, committed suicide. All French employees were dismissed from the postal services on Feb. 11. Bourguiba laid claim to Bizerta and a part of the Sahara. But there was an immediate lessening of tension. An agreement on technical and cultural co-operation was concluded on April 15; French civil servants employed in Tunisia would be partially paid by France. About 1,700 French civil servants including 1,100 teachers remained in Tunisia.

On Aug. 20 the discontinuance of the Franco-Tunisian customs union was announced. It was replaced by economic and financial agreements on Sept. 6. Tunisia remained in the franc area with drawing rights of $15 million. Certain French foods, textiles and chemicals would be duty-free or would be given preferential tariffs. Tunisia would be able to export to France 750,000 hl. of wine duty-free and 500,000 hl. at half the normal tariff. France would buy 150,000 tons of wheat in Tunisia at the price of French wheat (above the world price).

On July 19 Bourguiba was received in the Vatican by Pope John XXIII. He had earlier conferred with Giovanni Gronchi, president of the Italian republic, and Giuseppe Pella, the foreign minister.

On July 22 Bourguiba issued a warning to Algerian insurgents who had taken refuge in Tunisia, in order to ensure " respect for Tunisian sovereignty ". On Sept. 17, he declared himself favourably disposed towards President Charles de Gaulle's proposals (of Sept. 16) for a referendum in Algeria and urged the " provisional government of the Algerian Republic " to begin negotiations immediately.

On Dec. 17 President Dwight D. Eisenhower met Bourguiba at La Marsa, near Tunis. The two presidents made a wide survey of the international situation. They agreed that the fact that a solution had not yet been found in Algeria was " a cause of grave concern ". They also agreed that the achievement of self-determination by the people of Africa and Asia was " one of the main events of our age ".

(Hu. De.; X.)

TUNNELS. The Jawahar tunnel between Jammu and Kashmir states, India, was opened to westbound road traffic in Dec. 1958. The tunnel was 1½ mi. long and situated 7,250 ft. above sea level. The single carriageway was 10 ft. 6 in. wide with a footpath on one side. The tunnel was designed for a peak traffic of 250 vehicles per hour.

Work continued in 1959 on the construction of seven penstock tunnels, each 1,000-1,300 ft. long, at Oahe dam, South Dakota (*see* TUNNELS in *Britannica Book of the Year*

Inside the new Mont Blanc tunnel, which will provide an Alpine road link between France and Italy open all the year round.

1957), using mechanical diggers of 29 ft. 6 in. diameter capable of maintaining a rate of advance of 5 ft. per hour. The diggers were propelled by rams bearing against steel supports erected in advance of a concrete lining.

In Britain work progressed on two road tunnels: the Dartford to Purfleet tunnel, which was joined in May 1959, and the Clyde tunnel, where the first shield, for the 29 ft. 6 in. internal diameter tunnel, was driven off in Oct. 1959. During the year authority was received for work to proceed on a second Blackwall tunnel under the River Thames, a Tyne tunnel and a second Clyde tunnel.

At the 1959 congress of the Permanent International Association of Road Congresses held at Rio de Janeiro, a report was presented by a committee convened from engineers representing Belgium, France, Great Britain, the Netherlands, Italy and Switzerland. This report was concerned with the standards of road tunnels and the experience in operating road tunnels in these countries. The greater part of the report concerned standards of ventilation and the results of investigations in the several countries on this subject.

The use of a mobile platform for the construction of a tunnel on the sea-bed was demonstrated during the construction of a 12-ft. diameter sewer extending about six miles out to sea at Los Angeles, United States, in depths of up to 200 ft. of water. The pipes were assembled in a dock in lengths of 192 ft. and floated out to the platform by means of a pontoon. After being slung beneath the platform, the pipes were then

lowered by winch into position and attached to the last completed length, making use of a diver and underwater television cameras. On completion of each length, the 275 ft.-long legs of the platform were retracted and the platform floated to its next position and again lifted clear of the sea on its legs.

(H. D. M.)

TURKEY. Republic in the southeastern Balkans and Asia Minor, bounded W. by the Aegean sea, N.W. by Greece and Bulgaria, N. by the Black sea, N.E. by the U.S.S.R., E. by Persia and S. by Iraq, Syria and the Mediterranean. Area: 296,184 sq.mi., incl. 9,256 sq.mi. in Europe. Pop.: (1955 census) 24,121,778; (1958 est.) 25,932,000. Language (1955): Turkish 90·4%; Kurdish 1,504,482 (6·2%); Arabic 346,404; Circassian 90,738; Greek 81,799; Georgian (Lazian) 80,639; Armenian 46,934; Bulgarian 31,846; Jewish (Spaniol) 29,207. Religion (1955): Moslem 99%; Christian (all denominations) 213,572; Jewish 40,585. Chief towns (pop., 1955 census): Ankara (cap.) 453,151; Istanbul 1,214,616; Izmir 286,310; Adana 172,465; Bursa 131,336; Eskişehir 122,755; 11 towns with a population from 50,000 to 100,000. President of the republic, Celâl Bayar; prime minister, Adnan Menderes. Main imports: machinery and vehicles; iron, steel and manufactures; cotton yarn and fabrics; petroleum. Main exports: raw cotton, tobacco, fruit and nuts, wheat; chrome, copper and iron ore. Monetary unit: Turkish pound or *lira* (£1 sterling = £T.25·20).

History. *Home Politics.* In the course of 1959 the strife between the political parties in Turkey remained full of bitterness. While the National-Peasant party fell more and more into the background, the ruling Democratic party and the opposition Republican People's party (which each received about one-half of the votes at the general election of Oct. 27, 1957) failed to find a solution for their fundamental differences of opinion and personal hatreds.

The government passed measures restricting freedom of assembly and of the press, with the alleged purpose of reconciling freedom with order and safeguarding ministers against defamation in the press. It carefully abstained, however, from taking the last steps leading to a dictatorship. On the other hand, the opposition parties and the independent press disregarded the restrictions, considered by them unconstitutional, and accepted the risks of using the rights of discussion in a democratic way.

At the beginning of May, a draft of a " press peace agreement " was discussed between Adnan Menderes, the prime minister, and six leading newspaper publishers on the following terms: (1) amnesty for press offences; (2) abolition of all restrictive laws; (3) self-control of the press; (4) abandonment of all government interference in the supply of newsprint and advertising; (5) contact between the government and the press through frequent high-level press conferences; (6) the press should feel free, if it wished, to divide space reserved for party politics in the proportion of 40% to the government party and 60% to the opposition. Six leading newspapers formed a committee for exerting self-control and showed that they intended to play their part, but the government failed to carry out the agreement as the government party extremists, who derived their influence from the strained relations with the opposition and the press, destroyed the favourable climate.

A stone-throwing attack at Uşak on Ismet Inönü, the opposition leader, and threatening action against him by some Democratic party agitators in Istanbul, were interpreted by the opposition as a planned attempt against his life. The People's party deputies continually asked for a parliamentary inquiry and, when the discussion of their motion was postponed again and again, they refused to take their seats for a period.

In face of the general desire for internal peace and the dislike of party strife, the moderates in both parties came into conflict with the extremists. The moderates of the government Democratic party decided to put forward a rival candidate for the position of speaker as a way of manifesting their disapproval of the government policy. The rival candidate to Refik Koraltan, for nine years speaker of the Grand National

Assembly and one of the four original founders of the Democratic party, was Sidki Yircali, a deputy of Balikeşir and a former minister of industry. In spite of the strong pressure of the party leadership the rival candidate received 121 votes against 213 for Refik Koraltan, with 5 abstentions (68 deputies were absent).

The distribution of seats in parliament was in 1959 as follows: Democratic party 407 (including 2 Independents); Republican People's party 178; the National-Peasant party 3; vacancies 22. This suggested that the moderate elements of the government party could form a majority with the opposition. The opposition People's party executive council readily accepted the resignation of Kasim Gülek, an ambitious extremist, and replaced him by Ismail Rüştü Aksal, a former minister of finance, who was known to place patriotic aims above party interests.

External Affairs. The Zürich agreement between Turkey and Greece of Feb. 11 and the London agreement of Feb. 19 seemed to have settled the Cyprus conflict, which had created much bitterness between Great Britain, Turkey and Greece and at one time seriously threatened Nato. The agreements which followed a period of confidential discussions were accepted on all sides with relief. (*See* Cyprus.)

The United States, although not a full member of the Cento (Central Treaty organization) group of powers, signed on March 5 separate mutual defence agreements with Turkey, Pakistan and Persia. On Oct. 7-9 the Cento ministerial council met in Washington, D.C. Menderes attended it and also had a talk with President Dwight D. Eisenhower on the international situation. According to an official announcement in the United States and Turkey, the latter agreed that a Jupiter guided missile squadron should be based on its territory.

On Dec. 6 President Eisenhower arrived in Ankara where hundreds of thousands of cheering Turks gave him a welcome that he described as the most stupendous he had ever seen. After conferring with President Celâl Bayar, Menderes and Fatin Rüştü Zorlu, the foreign minister, he departed the following day. A joint communiqué reaffirmed the alliance and partnership of the two countries in Nato and Cento and stressed the importance of raising the living standard of the Turkish people in order to enable Turkey to assume adequately the responsibilities which its geographical position imposed upon it.

Economic Position. The struggle against inflation was not a complete success in 1959. However, the black market for essential goods completely disappeared, and many articles became available on the regular market. To ease the situation for scarce goods facilities including importing without a foreign exchange permit were extended. Printing of banknotes ceased to be considered a source of revenue and the amount in circulation was stabilized around £T.3,300 million. The state industries that used to cover their deficit by loans from the Central bank were forced to increase their prices and to produce in a more rational way. Although the indiscrimate curtailing of credits made the government unpopular and caused difficulties, the anti-inflationary aim was never forgotten.

In consideration of these efforts, the Organization for European Economic Co-operation, the U.S. government and the International Monetary fund reached an agreement with Turkey on July 31 on a financial stabilization plan, $356 million being advanced to Turkey. The outstanding Turkish commercial debts up to $442 million were to be consolidated, to be followed later by bilateral agreements.

With its rapidly increasing population (3% per year), lack of equipment and backwardness in rational methods of work, Turkey had still many problems to solve, but developments in 1959 had brought the country into a better mood to face them squarely. (*See* Central Treaty Organization; United States Foreign Aid.) (A. E. Y.)

UBANGI-SHARI: *see* Central African Republic.

UGANDA. British protectorate in east Africa, bounded N. by Sudan, E. by Kenya, S. by Tanganyika and Ruanda-Urundi, and W. by the Belgian Congo. Area: 93,981 sq.mi., incl. 13,689 sq.mi. of inland water. Pop.: (1948 census) 4,958,520; (1958 est.) 5,767,000, incl. *c.* 9,000 Europeans, *c.* 56,000 Indians and Goans and *c.* 2,000 Arabs. Languages: Bantu (Luganda), Nilotic, Nilo-hamitic and Sudanian; Swahili as *lingua franca*. Religion: pagan, Moslem; *c.* 1,250,000 Christians. Chief towns: Entebbe (cap.), pop. *c.* 11,000; Kampala (cap. of Buganda) *c.* 60,000. Administration: governor; executive council; legislative council with representative minority. Administration in kingdom of Buganda (area 25,631 sq.mi.; pop. [1948 census] 1,323,627): African constitutional monarch (kabaka); chief minister (katikkiro) and five other ministers; indirectly elected council (Great Lukiiko). Governor, Sir Frederick Crawford; kabaka of Buganda, Mutesa II; British resident, C. A. L. Richards. Main Uganda imports: machinery and vehicles, textile manufactures, metal manufactures. Main exports: cotton, coffee. Monetary unit: East African shilling (20*s.* = £1 sterling).

History. Michael Kintu was re-elected katikkiro (chief minister) by the new Great Lukiiko (council) of Buganda in Jan. 1959. The Lukiiko then went on to endorse the decision of its predecessor to press for the termination of British protection and of the agreements existing between Buganda and Britain. Arising out of this recommendation discussions

A pilot plant at Lake Edward, Uganda, capable of drying fish in 24 hr.-36 hr.; the traditional method is sun drying.

began between the governor and a committee representing the Lukiiko in September with a view to a possible revision of the agreements, but no progress was made.

Early in February the governor, Sir Frederick Crawford, announced the composition of a committee to advise on the form of elections to the legislative council to be introduced in 1961. The committee, which consisted almost entirely of members of the existing legislative council, spent several months touring the country to collect the views of the people on its terms of reference. Since there were no representatives of Buganda in the legislative council the kabaka's government was afforded an opportunity to nominate members to the committee. When the offer was rejected the governor himself nominated two members to the committee to serve as representatives of Buganda. An interesting feature of the views presented to the committee was the unanimous rejection by the Indian community of any claim to special representation in the legislature.

The visit of Queen Elizabeth the Queen Mother to the protectorate in February was greeted with universal enthusiasm. Among other functions, in her capacity as chancellor of London university she formally opened the new library at Makerere college, the university college of east Africa.

In March there began in Buganda a boycott of non-African business concerns which was to last for the rest of the year and which resulted in numerous acts of violence and intimidation. The boycott spread throughout the kingdom and several districts were declared disturbed areas. Attempts to win support in other provinces, however, were unsuccessful. The organizers of the boycott adopted the title of the Uganda National movement and when the movement was proscribed by the governor in May it was immediately re-formed as the Uganda Freedom movement. The new society was at once proscribed but again re-emerged as the Uganda Freedom convention. Six of the leaders were arrested on May 30 and were subsequently deported to the northern province. In spite of stricter legislation and appeals by members of the kabaka's government, the acts of intimidation continued, and for a few days in September the flow of food supplies into Kampala for the African population virtually ceased until the intervention of the protectorate and kabaka's governments restored the situation to normal. The loss in revenue to the protectorate government because of the boycott was particularly serious in a year when it was expected that expenditure would exceed income. The governor therefore announced a reduction of £250,000 in the grant to the Buganda government.

In May the Court of Appeal for Eastern Africa dismissed the appeal of the katikkiro of Buganda against the Uganda High Court's decision to reject his claim that he was absolved from responsibility for arranging elections to the legislative council in Buganda. He had argued that the appointment of a speaker meant that the council was no longer the body referred to in the Buganda agreement of 1955. On learning of his defeat the katikkiro decided to carry his appeal to the Privy Council so that Buganda continued to be unrepresented in the legislative council except by nominations to the government side.

Once again during the year elected members of the legislative council urged the government to speed up the process of " africanizing " the civil service in order to bring forward the date of self-government. (*See* also EAST AFRICA HIGH COMMISSION.) (K. I.)

UKRAINE.

Republic in the Union of Soviet Socialist Republics, bounded N. by Byelorussia, N.E. and E. by Russia, S. by the Black sea and W. by the Moldavian S.S.R., Rumania, Hungary, Czechoslovakia and Poland. Area (incl. Crimea): 232,618 sq.mi. Pop. (1959 census): 41,893,000. Language (1940 est.): Ukrainian 66%; Russian 17%; Polish 6%; Yiddish 7·5%. Religion (1940 est.): Orthodox 75%; Roman Catholic 15%; Jewish 7·5%. Chief towns (pop., 1959 census): Kiev or Kyiv (cap.) 1,102,000; Kharkov 930,000; Stalino 701,000; Odessa 667,000; Dniepropetrovsk 658,000; Zaporozhye 435,000; Lviv (Lwów) 410,000; Krivoi Rog 386,000; Makeevka 358,000. First secretary of the Ukrainian Communist party, Nikolai V. Podgorny; chairman of the presidium of the Supreme Soviet, Demyan S. Korotchenko; chairman of the council of ministers, Nikifor T. Kalchenko. Monetary unit: Soviet *rouble*.

History. Speaking in Moscow on Dec. 22, 1959, at the meeting of the central committee of the Communist Party of the Soviet Union, Nikolai V. Podgorny, first secretary of the Ukrainian Communist party, said that, in spite of adverse weather, better techniques and better utilization of machinery had produced a crop of 15·7 quintals of grain per hectare from an area of 17·4 million ha. This suggested that the Ukrainian grain harvest in 1959 amounted to 27·3 million metric tons, about one-fifth of the Soviet total. However, a crop of 15·7 q. per ha. was not impressive: it was larger than the Soviet average (13·7 q.) but only two-thirds of that of the German Democratic Republic. At the beginning of 1958 Ukrainian livestock amounted to 15·1 million head of cattle (22% of the Soviet total) and 13·9 million pigs (30% of the Soviet total). Industrial production of the republic was already

CONTRIBUTION OF THE UKRAINE TO SOVIET INDUSTRIAL PRODUCTION (in thousands of metric tons; electricity in millions of kwh.; textiles in thousands of metres; with percentages of the total Soviet output in brackets)

	1913*	1928	1957
Coal† . . .	22,796 (78)	24,800 (70)	152,300 (33)
Electricity .	452 (24)	1,300 (26)	39,500 (19)
Iron ore . .	... ...	4,700 ...	47,100 (56)
Pig iron . .	2,892 (69)	2,400 (73)	18,500 (50)
Steel . .	2,442 (58)	2,400 (58)	19,600 (38)
Cement . .	269 (18)	297 (16)	5,594 (19)
Artificial fertilizers .	36 (52)	57 (42)	3,305 (28)
Sugar . .	1,107 (82)	1,041 (81)	3,045 (68)
Tractors (units) .	—	200 (15)	74,100 (36)
Lorries . .	—	—	22,700 (6)
Cotton fabrics .	4,700 (1·8)	2,000 (0·8)	60,800 (1·1.)
Woollen fabrics .	... ...	2,000 (2·3)	14,000 (5)

* Present territory.　† Including lignite.

in 1957 about 20 times higher than in 1913 (*see* Table).

On Dec. 4, 1959, the new Kremenchug hydroelectric power station on the Dnieper supplied its first current to industry. Only one turbo-generator, with a capacity of 57,200 kw., went into operation and a second was being completed. The station would reach a capacity of 625,000 kw. when operating at full load and would produce yearly 2,500 million kwh. The Kremenchug dam would improve the work of the power stations situated lower down the river, including the Dnieper station already operating, and those of Dnieprodzerzhinsk and Kakhovka nearing completion. It would also improve navigation conditions on the Dnieper enabling sea-going vessels to sail up the river as far as the town of Kanev, 500 mi. from the river mouth and only 66 mi. south of Kiev.

Progress in education continued. In 1957-58 there were 5,864,000 pupils in primary and secondary schools (5,437,700 in 1940-41), 359,300 pupils in 590 vocational schools and 367,200 students in 138 institutions of higher education (196,800 students in 1940-41).

It was estimated that in 1959 the Ukrainians formed about 80% of the republic's population; *i.e.*, some 34 million; about 9 million Ukrainians lived in other Soviet republics and about 1·8 million outside the U.S.S.R., including up to 900,000 in the United States, 450,000 in Canada and 140,000 in western Europe (25,000 in Great Britain).

Stepan Bandera (b. Uhryniv Stary, Jan. 1, 1909), leader of the Organization of Ukrainian Nationalists, died under mysterious circumstances in Munich on Oct. 15. According to German police he was poisoned by potassium cyanide. The council of the O.U.N. elected Stepan Lenkavski as his successor. (K. M. S.)

UNEMPLOYMENT: *see* EMPLOYMENT.

UNION OF SOVIET SOCIALIST REPUBLICS.

Federation of Soviet Socialist republics, a state covering parts of eastern Europe and of northern and central Asia. Area: (1939) 8,173,557 sq.mi.; (1946) 8,598,678 sq.mi., incl. 1,969,110 sq.mi. (23%) in Europe. Pop.: (1939 census) 170,467,572; (Jan. 1959 census) 208,826,000. Nationalities (1956 est.): Russians *c.* 52·3% of pop.; Ukrainians 18·3%; Byelorussians 3·5%; the strongest non-Slavonic groups were the Turkic (11·3%) and Finno-Ugrian (2·7%) peoples. Religion: Russians, Ukrainians, Byelorussians and Rumanians (Moldavians) are Orthodox; Lithuanians and Poles are Roman Catholic (2·3%); Latvians, Estonians, Germans and Finns are mainly Lutheran; there are about 5 million Protestants of all denominations; 2,763,000 Georgians have their own autocephalous Christian Orthodox Church; 2,662,000 Armenians are Christian; Jews were estimated (1956) at 1,902,000; the indigenous inhabitants of Azerbaijan, the five central Asian Soviet Socialist republics and many autonomous republics (Tatar, Bashkir, Dagestan, etc.) are Moslem (number, 1956 est., 24·5 million); Buryats and Kalmyks are Lamaist Buddhist (*c.* 500,000). Chief towns (pop., 1959 census): Moscow (cap., excluding suburbs) 5,032,000; Leningrad 2,888,000 (incl. suburbs, 3,300,000); Kiev 1,102,000; Baku 636,000 (incl. suburbs, 968,000); Gorki 942,000; Kharkov 930,000; Tashkent 911,000; Novosibirsk 887,000; Kuibyshev 806,000; Sverdlovsk 777,000; Stalino 701,000; Tbilisi 694,000; Chelyabinsk 688,000; Odessa 667,000; Dnepropetrovsk 658,000; Kazan 643,000; Perm 628,000; Riga 605,000; Rostov 597,000; Stalingrad 591,000; Saratov 581,000; Omsk 579,000;

Ufa 546,000; Minsk 509,000; Erevan 509,000; 18 towns with a pop. from 300,000 to 500,000 and 29 towns from 200,000 to 300,000. First secretary of the Communist Party of the Soviet Union and chairman of the council of ministers, Nikita S. Khrushchev; chairman of the presidium of the Supreme Soviet of the U.S.S.R., Marshal Klimenty E. Voroshilov. Monetary unit: *rouble* (Rb.11·20 = £1 sterling; tourist rate, Rb.28·00 = £1 sterling).

Girl representatives of the 15 Soviet republics carry their national flags during the Revolution Day parade in Moscow on Nov. 7.

History. The most important developments in 1959 were in the field of foreign rather than domestic affairs. The visit of N. S. Khrushchev to the United States in September was the symbol of a new attitude to east-west relations and marked the beginning of a *détente* in Soviet-U.S. relations. It also served to emphasize the extent of Khrushchev's command of the situation at home, where the main attention was on the tasks involved in the new seven-year development plan (1959-65). The most spectacular achievement of the year was the photographing of the far side of the moon from a rocket. Towards the end of the year there were some signs of differences with the Chinese Communist leaders on foreign affairs.

Home Politics. The major event of the year was the 21st congress of the Communist Party of the Soviet Union (Jan. 27-Feb. 5). It was an extraordinary congress; *i.e.*, it was called earlier than the party's constitution demanded, and

was therefore not required to elect a new central committee. Its nominal purpose was to approve the new seven-year plan. But its actual function was to acknowledge Khrushchev's personal victory in the struggle for the succession to Joseph Stalin. He dominated the congress and made the principal report. There were many strongly worded denunciations of the defeated G. M. Malenkov-V. M. Molotov opposition group for their alleged obstruction of policies initiated by Khrushchev. No changes were made in the party presidium. It appeared during the congress and later in the year that Khrushchev's closest collaborators in the direction of affairs were A. I. Mikoyan, who seemed to be mainly concerned with foreign affairs, and A. I. Kirichenko, who was responsible for the home front.

The congress approved unanimously Khrushchev's report on the seven-year plan, the purely economic aspects of which are discussed below. Its political significance was that it would create the " material and technical basis of Communism ", bring Soviet industrial output within measurable distance of that of the United States, and ensure the victory of the Communist states in economic competition with the capitalist world. Khrushchev said that by about 1970 the Soviet Union might occupy first place in the world " both in absolute volume of production and in production per head of the population ". The ultimate victory of the " Socialist camp ", led by the Soviet Union, would be assisted by the inherent weaknesses of the capitalist system and the attractive force exerted by Soviet economic and social achievements on the peoples of less advanced countries. This prospect of victory in peaceful competition with the west provided the theoretical basis for the policy of *détente* with the United States.

On Dec. 26, 1958, after long discussion in legal circles, the Supreme Soviet approved some important juridical reforms, which were embodied in documents re-defining the principles of criminal legislation, of the nature of crimes against the state and of the structure of the courts and court procedure. The principal changes introduced were: (i) the age of criminal responsibility was raised from 14 to 16 years; (ii) the maximum sentence of imprisonment was reduced from 25 to 15 years; (iii) denunciation as an " enemy of the people ", deprivation of franchise and expulsion from the U.S.S.R. were abolished as penalties; (iv) the definition of an accomplice and an accessory before or after the fact was made more precise; and (v) the graver political crimes were given a more precise definition. Among the procedural changes the more important were: (i) a reduction of the relative importance of confessions as evidence and an extension of the rights of defence counsel during investigation and trial; (ii) a provision that

TABLE I. UNION OF SOVIET SOCIALIST REPUBLICS

Republic	Capital	Area (sq.mi.)	Population (1959 census)	First Secretary of the Communist party	Chairman of the Presidium of the Supreme Soviet	Chairman of Council of Ministers
Russian S.F.S.R.	Moscow	6,592,443*	117,494,000	N. S. Khrushchev	N. Organov	D. S. Polyanski
Ukraine (*q.v.*)	Kyiv (Kiev)	232,618	41,893,000	N. V. Podgorny	D. S. Korotchenko	N. T. Kalchenko
Kazakhstan	Alma-Ata	1,063,242	9,301,000	N. I. Belyaev	Zh. A. Tashenev	D. A. Kunaev
Uzbekistan	Tashkent	157,336	8,113,000	Sh. R. Rashidov	Mrs. Ya. S. Nasriddinova	A. A. Alimov
Byelorussia (*q.v.*)	Minsk	80,154	8,060,000	K. T. Mazurov	V. I. Kozlov	T. Ya. Kiselev
Georgia	Tbilisi (Tiflis)	29,488	4,049,000	V. P. Mzhavanadze	G. S. Dzotsenidze	G. D. Dzhavakhishvili
Azerbaijan	Baku	33,089	3,700,000	V. Yu. Akhundov	S. M. Dzhafarov	M. A. Iskenderov
Moldavia	Chişinau (Kishynev)	13,050	2,880,000	Z. T. Serdyuk	I. S. Kodiţa	A. Diordiţa
Lithuania	Vilnius (Wilno)	25,174	2,713,000	A. J. Sniečkus	J. I. Paleckis	M. J. Šumauskas
Latvia	Riga	24,903	2,094,000	A. J. Pelše	J. E. Kalnberzinš	J. V. Peive
Kirghizia	Frunze	76,023	2,063,000	I. R. Razzakov	Turabai Kulatov	K. D. Dikambaev
Tajikistan	Stalinabad	55,058	1,982,000	T. U. Uldzhabaev	M. Rakhmatov	N. Dodkhudoev
Armenia	Erivan	11,506	1,768,000	S. A. Tovmassian	Sh. M. Arushanian	A. E. Kochinian
Turkmenistan	Ashkhabad	187,181	1,520,000	Dzh. D. Karaev	A. S. Saryev	B. O. Ovezov
Estonia	Tallinn (Reval)	17,413	1,196,000	I. G. Käbin	J. H. Eichfeld	A. A. Müürisepp
		8,598,678	208,826,000			

* Excluding the Crimea, from Feb. 19, 1954, part of the Ukraine, but including Karelia, which on July 16, 1956, was included in the Russian S.F.S.R.
SOURCE. Areas are taken from the *Bolshaya Sovietskaya Entsiklopedia: S.S.S.R.* (Moscow, 1948). The names of first secretaries, chairmen of the presidia and of the councils of ministers are as at Dec. 31, 1959.

In the grounds of the Kremlin, A. I. Mikoyan (centre), a member of the presidium of the Communist Party of the Soviet Union, jokes with A. I. Kirichenko (third from right), another member, and N. S. Khrushchev (second from right) at the 21st party congress on Jan. 31.

the burden of proving the guilt of an accused person lies on the prosecution; (iii) certain limitations placed on the powers of the investigating authorities; and (iv) abolition of the practice of trial and conviction by " analogy ".

The problem of improving the maintenance of public order was the subject of a decree issued by the party and government in March. It drew attention to the need for greater public support for the efforts of the police and it proposed to draw ordinary citizens into the work of maintaining order. This took the form of groups of people, drawn mainly from the ranks of the Communist party, Komsomol (Communist Youth union) and trade unions, who were to patrol the streets and deal with cases of hooliganism. The practice was also introduced of handing people charged with relatively minor offences and breaches of discipline over for public trial by their workmates and neighbours.

In March Aleksei N. Kosygin replaced Iosif I. Kuzmin as chairman of the State Planning commission (Gosplan). Kuzmin was made chairman of a newly formed Scientific Economic council which was charged with co-ordinating scientific research in the service of the Soviet economic plan. Two new state committees of the council of ministers were set up: one to deal with automation and engineering, with Anatoli Kostousov as chairman, and another for professional and technical education, headed by Kh. I. Zelenko. In January the Ministry of Electric Power Stations was reorganized into a Ministry of Electric Power Construction, with I. T. Novikov as minister responsible for speeding the expansion of the Soviet power network. Sergei Kurashov, former R.S.F.S.R. minister of health, replaced Maria D. Kovrygina as health minister in the all-union government.

Economic Affairs. The central aim of the new seven-year plan was to raise Soviet gross industrial production by 80% by the year 1965. The targets for that year in certain basic commodities, with the output reached in 1958 given in brackets, were agreed as follows: pig iron *c.* 67·5 million metric tons (39·6 million); steel *c.* 88·5 million tons (54·9 million); coal *c.* 600 million tons (496 million); crude petroleum 235 million tons (113 million); electric power *c.* 510,000

million kwh. (233,000 million). These objectives represented a somewhat slower rate of growth than had originally been decreed at the 20th party congress in Feb. 1956. Particular stress was to be laid on the expansion of the chemical industry, for the increased production of synthetic fibres, plastics, synthetic resins and artificial fertilizers, on the share of oil and natural gas in the country's fuel output and on completing the power supply network. The plan provided for the accelerated industrial development of the eastern territories of the U.S.S.R., which were expected to be responsible by 1965 for nearly half the country's industrial production.

The plan pursued the traditional Soviet economic policy of priority for the expansion of the capital goods industries, which were to expand in the seven years by 85%, compared with the 62% expansion expected of the industries catering for consumers' needs. Nevertheless, efforts to satisfy the increasing demand for consumer goods were the subject of much publicity throughout the year. The plan was to make possible a 40% increase in real incomes, provide for the general introduction of a 40-hr. working week by 1962 and allot capital for the construction of 22 million new homes.

For agriculture the plan decreed a 70% gross increase in production, with a gross grain harvest of between 164 million and 180 million tons. It required increases of cotton production by at least 35%, of sugar beet by at least 80%, and of fruit, meat and milk by 100%.

The increase in the grain harvest was said to be the essential precondition for increased output in the other branches of farming. It was to be achieved by raising the average yield, through the greater use of artificial fertilizers and machinery, and the more efficient organization of agricultural processes. Khrushchev devoted much attention to this question and to the future structure of collective farming at the June and December plenary sessions of the central committee. But, despite the increased attention to and investment in agriculture, 1959 was a disappointing year. Widespread drought in the main grain-producing regions reduced the gross harvest from the record figure of nearly 140 million tons in 1958 to less than 115 million tons.

The first census of population for 20 years was conducted on Jan. 15 and the preliminary results were published on May 10. The figures revealed that the total population was only 208,826,000, or only 18·1 million more than at the census of 1939. It was estimated by western authorities that this figure was about 45 million less than it would have been if World War II had not occurred, and that approximately half the 20 million Soviet citizens who served in the armed forces in that war were killed. Some of the more striking facts emerging from the census were: that there were 20 million more women than men in the U.S.S.R.; that the urban population had increased since 1939 by 39·4 million to 99·8 million, or 48% of the total; that there were 123 cities with populations of more than 100,000 and 25 with more than 500,000; that the greatest increases of population had taken place in the Urals (32%), western Siberia (24%), eastern Siberia (34%), the far eastern areas (70%), and central Asia and Kazakhstan (38%); and that the population was increasing at the rate of about 3·5 million a year.

Military and Scientific Affairs. No important changes in the personnel or structure of the armed forces were made public. The military leaders declared on several occasions their allegiance to the Communist party and their approval of Khrushchev's policies. The traditional parades continued to minimize the military aspect of Soviet power, although the Soviet people were assured that the forces were well provided with the latest weapons to defend them in case of aggression.

Scientific and military institutions continued to devote great resources to space research. On Jan. 2 they launched a rocket which passed near the moon on Jan. 4 and then went into orbit round the sun, of which it became the first artificial " planet ". In July the authorities claimed that two dogs and a rabbit had been sent to an unspecified height in the nose cone of a rocket and had been brought safely back to earth. On Sept. 14 a rocket was landed on the surface of the moon. In October a rocket was made to pass round the moon and photograph for the first time the side not visible from the earth. These achievements were taken to indicate that Soviet engineering and technology were still in advance of the American in the field of space research.

Foreign Affairs. The year was notable for Khrushchev's personal assumption of the conduct of foreign affairs and the change brought about on his initiative in Soviet-U.S. relations. The " ultimatum " over the status of western Berlin with which the Soviet government presented the western powers on Nov. 27, 1958, led to intensive diplomatic exchanges in the early months of 1959 and to the calling of a conference of foreign ministers in Geneva in May. Though negotiations proceeded in a friendly atmosphere, the Soviet position remained inflexible and no substantial progress was made. At one point Khrushchev went out of his way to make it clear that A. A. Gromyko, the Soviet foreign minister, was bound entirely by his (Khrushchev's) instructions. The implication was that, if the Soviet side were prepared to make any concessions, they would be made only by Khrushchev personally, and that for this a meeting of heads of government was necessary. The foreign ministers' conference was suspended and in August it was announced that an exchange of visits between Khrushchev and President Dwight D. Eisenhower would take place. The situation in Berlin remained unchanged.

Meanwhile a number of other important steps had been taken which brought about an appreciable improvement in the relations between the Soviet Union and the United States. In January A. I. Mikoyan, first deputy premier, visited the United States on what was described as an " unofficial " visit, in the course of which, however, he had talks with President Eisenhower and John Foster Dulles, the secretary of state, as well as meeting representatives of some of the more influential sections of U.S. public opinion. At the end of June the other first deputy premier, Frol R. Kozlov, visited the United States to open a Soviet exhibition of science, technology and culture in New York. He visited and spoke in a number of other cities. In July Richard M. Nixon, the U.S. vice-president, visited the Soviet Union to open a U.S. exhibition in Moscow, tour the provinces and have talks with Soviet leaders. The exhibition, which depicted the life of ordinary people in the United States, attracted great attention throughout the period it was open in Moscow.

A further step calculated to ease east-west tensions was the visit to the Soviet Union in February of Harold Macmillan,

The " Rocket ", a novel Soviet craft with underwater " wings " that can develop speeds of up to 40 knots, seen on the Volga river. In the background is part of the great industrial city of Gorki.

the British prime minister, and Selwyn Lloyd, the foreign secretary. They had talks with Khrushchev and other Soviet leaders and visited Kiev and Leningrad, but did not arrive at any notable agreements on major international issues. Other British visitors to Moscow were Field Marshal Lord Montgomery in January and Labour party leaders Hugh Gaitskell and Aneurin Bevan in September.

In May Khrushchev, accompanied by Marshal Rodion Ya. Malinovski, minister of defence, paid an official visit to Albania, where he protested at the establishment of missile bases in Italy and Greece and threatened that the U.S.S.R. might erect similar bases in Albania or Bulgaria in retaliation. The visit resulted in an increase of Soviet financial aid to Albania. On his way back to Moscow Khrushchev stopped for two days in Budapest. In July he paid an official visit to Poland, making an extensive tour of the country. In his speeches he reaffirmed Soviet support for the permanence of Poland's current western frontiers on the Oder and Neisse rivers, for the conclusion of a non-aggression treaty between Nato and Warsaw treaty powers and for the creation of zones free of nuclear weapons in central Europe, the Baltic and the Balkans. In October Khrushchev spent a week " resting " in Rumania.

A visit by Khrushchev to Sweden, Norway, Denmark and Finland planned for August did not take place. In July the Soviet government informed the Scandinavian governments that it took exception to the hostile attitude to his visit taken up by certain public figures and organizations in Scandinavia and that it had decided therefore that the visit was not opportune. Khrushchev said: " We are a proud people. If they spit in my face, why should I go to a country whose people take up such an attitude to me? " It was noted subsequently, however, that Khrushchev's visit to the United States would in any case have made the Scandinavian trip difficult to accomplish.

Khrushchev arrived in Washington on Sept. 15, accompanied by his wife, several members of his family and a large company of officials. Since he had announced his assumption, for the purposes of the visit, of the function of head of state, he was accorded the appropriate welcome. In a fortnight's stay he had long talks with President Eisenhower, visited many of the main cities and addressed many different audiences. The burden of his message was the imperative need for peace and friendship between the two great nuclear powers, who alone had it in their power to destroy or preserve the peace of the world. The practical outcome of the visit was the formal withdrawal of any ultimatum over the Berlin issue and agreement to the holding of a summit meeting. While in the United States Khrushchev addressed the U.N. general assembly (Sept. 18) and put forward a plan for complete and universal disarmament.

Immediately after his return from the United States Khrushchev flew to Peking for the celebrations marking the 10th anniversary of the founding of the Chinese People's Republic. In a speech on arrival he spoke of the dangers involved in " testing by force the stability of the capitalist system ". This was taken to signify Soviet disapproval of the Chinese army's invasion of Indian territory. Caught between the demands of friendship with the two great states, China and India, the Soviet government had for the first time to refuse its full support to the Chinese Communists. The Chinese in their turn, while giving formal approval to Khrushchev's peace proposals and his visit to the United States, continued to utter sentiments at variance with the Soviet view of the general strategy of Communism.

Soviet policy towards the uncommitted nations of the middle east, Africa and Asia showed a tendency towards greater caution than in previous years. Interest in the areas was unabated, but support was limited to modest financial aid.

Cultural Relations. A new agreement on Anglo-Soviet relations in the scientific, technological, educational and cultural fields was signed in London on Dec. 1. Amongst the exchanges provided for in the agreement, which would run up to April 1, 1961, were the following: exchange of scientists; of specialists in industry, transport and construction; of agricultural research workers; of professors (12 from British and Soviet universities respectively), postgraduate students, teachers and medical specialists. The agreement also provided for visits of theatrical and ballet companies, symphony orchestras, etc. An exhibition of British art would be held in Moscow and Leningrad in return for the exhibition of Russian and Soviet art held in London in Jan. 1959.

A similar agreement had been signed in Moscow on Nov. 21 between Llewellyn E. Thompson, the U.S. ambassador, and Georgi A. Zukov, chairman of the Soviet State Committee for Cultural Relations with Foreign Countries. Exchange of undergraduates and postgraduate students, teachers and scientists in 1961-62 would not exceed 85 persons in each direction. (*See* also COMMUNIST MOVEMENT; EASTERN EUROPEAN ECONOMIC PLANNING.) (D. F.)

UNITARIAN CHURCH. The Unitarian Church stresses the One-ness of God, the leadership of Jesus and the divinity of man, and asserts the need for freedom of reason and conscience in the search for religious truth, unfettered by authority or tradition. World membership (1959): *c.* 230,000, incl. *c.* 140,000 in North America and Great Britain. None of the Unitarian organizations engages in missionary activity.

The 1959 annual meetings were held in Leeds. The Anniversary preacher was the Rev. W. Waddington. The Essex Hall lecture, on " Mass Communications and the Spirit of Man ", was delivered by the Rev. C. O. Rhodes, former editor of the *Church of England Newspaper.* The Rev. A. W. Vallance was elected president. New minimum stipend scales were adopted providing for £440 per annum on entering the ministry, rising by varying annual increments to not less than £700; all to be in addition to a manse, rent and rates free, small expense allowance and national insurance and pension contributions.

The newly formed publicity department began a national advertising campaign and as a result received inquiries averaging 60 a week; a number of the inquirers joined local churches.

The Unitarian Young People's league celebrated in September the 25th anniversary of its foundation with a special week-end at the Unitarian holiday centre at Great Hucklow, Derbyshire.

The secretary, the Rev. John Kielty, delivered the Minns lectures in Boston in May and, in conjunction with the I.A.R.F. (International Association for Liberal Christianity and Religious Freedom), executive meetings in Frankfurt, visited the Liberal Religious groups in Brussels, Cologne, Frankfurt and Offenbach. The Rev. Margaret Barr expanded her work in her Kharang (Assam) rural centre by an extension of the main school building and the erection of a new clinic and dispensary. There were two qualified midwives and three girl trainees who also operated a nearby sub-centre.

(J. KY.)

See Mortimer Rowe, *The Story of Essex Hall* (London, 1959).

UNITED ARAB REPUBLIC. Union of republics of Egypt and Syria. Total area: 457,339 sq.mi. Total pop.: (1957 est.) 28,108,000. Cap.: Cairo. Supreme power is vested in the president of the republic, who appoints both the executive (Council of the Republic) and the legislature (Council of the Nation). There are two regional executive councils, one for each country, whose members are also appointed by the president. President of the republic, Gamal Abd-ul-Nasser. Vice-presidents (also members of the Council of the Republic), Abd-ul-Latif el-Boghdadi (Egypt), Abd-ul-Hakim Amer (Egypt), Akram el-Hourani (Syria).

Egypt. Arab republic of northeast Africa, bounded N. by the

Archaeologists and their helpers under the great rock front of a temple of Rameses II, dedicated to the goddess Hathor, 175 mi. south of Aswan on the Nile. Unesco is trying to save historic temples threatened by flooding as a result of the Aswan High Dam scheme.

Mediterranean, S. by Sudan, E. by Israel and the Red sea, W. by Libya. Area: 386,110 sq.mi. Pop.: (1947 census) 19,031,840; (1957 est.) 24,020,000. Language: 97% Arabic, with minorities speaking Greek, Italian, Armenian, etc. Religion (1947 census): Moslem (mainly Sunni) 91·46%; Christian (mainly Coptic) 7·89%; Jewish 0·34%. Chief towns (pop., 1947 census): Cairo (cap.) 2,090,654, (1953 est.) 2,447,000; Alexandria 919,024, (1953 est.) 1,105,000; Port Said 177,703; Tanta 139,926; Mehalla el-Kubra 115,758; Suez 107,244; Mansura 101,965. President of the regional executive council, Nur ed-Din Tarraf. Main imports: machinery and vehicles, foodstuffs, chemicals, mineral fuels, textiles, metals and manufactures. Main exports: cotton, rice. Monetary unit: Egyptian *pound* (£E 0·97¼-0·97¾ = £1 sterling).

Syria. Arab republic of southwest Asia, bounded W. by the Mediterranean and Lebanon, N.W. and N. by Turkey, E. and S.E. by Iraq, S. by Jordan and S.W. by Israel. Area: 71,229 sq.mi. Pop.: (1957 est.) 4,080,000. Language: Arabic (86%); also Kurdish, Armenian, Turkish, Circassian. Religion (1954 est.): Moslem (mainly Sunni) 86·3%; Christian 12·8%. Chief towns (pop., 1955 est.): Damascus (cap.) 408,774; Aleppo 407,613; Hama 167,507; Homs 132,637. President of the regional executive council, Nur ed-Din Kuhala. Main imports: fuels and oils, machinery and vehicles, silk and artificial silk, iron and steel. Main exports: cotton, grains, wool. Monetary unit: Syrian *pound* (£Syr. 6·13-6·19 = £1 sterling).

History. Internally, 1959 began with something of a crisis in the relations between Egypt and Syria, which had been steadily worsening since the formation of the United Arab Republic in the previous year. Syrian resentment at the union with Egypt was first openly expressed by the exiled Syrian Communist leader, Khaled Baqdash, who advocated greater independence for his country. Many of his views were later repeated in representations made to President Gamal Abd-ul-Nasser by the Syrian business community, whose leaders complained that Syria's commercial interests (which had suffered severely during the previous year) were not receiving sufficient attention from Egypt, and had been grievously prejudiced by a number of restrictions imposed since the union. Moreover, a drought in the country had destroyed almost all the barley crop and most of the wheat, as well as 10% of the cotton crop, and it was estimated that these and other setbacks had caused Syria a loss of about £20 million

in foreign currency. The land reform law and the proposal to unify the Egyptian and Syrian currencies aggravated the crisis, and capital was steadily flowing out of Syria. In spite of all this, the Syrian business community had no real wish to leave the union, since, in their eyes, the alternative might well be Communism. When Nasser received their complaints sympathetically, and at the same time struck vigorously at the Syrian Communists, the crisis passed. Plans for speeding up the economic development of Syria with Soviet aid also helped to improve the situation. It was decided to proceed with the Muzerib dam project in southern Syria, the U.S.S.R. supplying the necessary equipment and machinery. In October Field Marshal Abd-ul-Hakim, the Egyptian commander-in-chief of the U.A.R. armed forces, was appointed by Nasser as his proconsul in Syria.

The attack which Nasser launched against the Communists in Syria was soon to develop into a general conflict between Arab nationalism and Communism. Nasser became increasingly hostile to the new regime in Iraq, particularly after the abortive rising in Mosul in northern Iraq early in March and the apparent growth of the Iraqi Communists' influence on the course of events in their country. He accused Communists throughout the Arab world of trying to destroy the unity of Arab nationalism, and of acting at the instigation of foreign powers. This led to a crisis in the relations between the U.A.R. and the U.S.S.R. However, after an exchange of letters between the Soviet prime minister, N. S. Khrushchev, and Nasser in February and April, the tension eased, on the understanding that the U.S.S.R. did not wish to interfere in internal Arab affairs and had not abandoned its friendly attitude towards the U.A.R. In September an agreement was signed between the two countries, whereby the U.S.S.R. was to provide technical assistance and equipment for the building of the Aswan High dam, which it had already agreed to finance in 1958 with an initial credit of £33 million.

The first Afro-Asian Youth conference met in Cairo in February. Girls carry maps of Palestine with the words " Palestine is Arab ".

Relations between the U.A.R. and the west began to improve in January, when the financial agreement between Egypt and Britain (ending the dispute dating from the nationalization of the Suez canal in 1956) was initialled. The agreement was finally signed on the last day of February. Britain agreed to release Egypt's frozen sterling balances in London (amounting to about £90 million), and Egypt agreed to repeal the laws sequestering British property in Egypt, and to pay £27·5 million as compensation for nationalized British property that would not be returned to its former owners. Diplomatic relations between the two countries were eventually resumed on Dec. 1.

During the year progress was made in the revival of cultural relations between the U.A.R. on the one hand, and Britain and the United States on the other. An agreement was signed in September between the U.A.R. and the United States for an exchange of students and teachers under the Fulbright programme. At the same time the U.A.R. asked for more places in British universities for Egyptian and Syrian students (of whom 400 continued to study in Britain throughout the period following the Suez conflict), and for British help in higher technical education in Egypt.

Relations between Egypt and Sudan also improved in 1959, and an agreement was finally concluded on the division of the Nile waters before work began on the Aswan High dam; a general trade agreement was also signed. The dispute between the U.A.R. and Jordan was also less acute during 1959.

A new development was the bitter quarrel that flared up in September between the U.A.R. and the Chinese People's Republic as a result of a speech made in Peking by Khaled Baqdash, in the presence of a U.A.R. delegation, violently denouncing Nasser's policies. The delegation was promptly recalled to Cairo.

It was announced in Cairo on Dec. 30 that four Syrian ministers, all members of the Ba'ath Socialist party, had resigned. They included Akram el-Hourani, a vice-president of the U.A.R. (*See* also SUDAN; SUEZ CANAL.)

(E. S. A.)

UNITED KINGDOM: *see* GREAT BRITAIN AND NORTHERN IRELAND, UNITED KINGDOM OF.

UNITED NATIONS. An association of equal and sovereign states, founded on Oct. 24, 1945, to maintain international peace and security, develop friendly relations among nations and achieve international co-operation. The following 82 states were members of the United Nations on Dec. 31, 1959:

Afghanistan	Dominican Rep.	Jordan	Poland
Albania	Ecuador	Laos	Portugal
Argentina	El Salvador	Lebanon	Rumania
Australia	Ethiopia	Liberia	Saudi Arabia
Austria	Finland	Libya	Spain
Belgium	France	Luxembourg	Sweden
Bolivia	Ghana	Malaya	Sudan
Brazil	Greece	Mexico	Thailand
Bulgaria	Guatemala	Morocco	Tunisia
Burma	Guinea	Nepal	Turkey
Byelorussia	Haiti	Netherlands	Ukraine
Cambodia	Honduras	New Zealand	Union of S. Africa
Canada	Hungary	Nicaragua	U.S.S.R.
Ceylon	Iceland	Norway	United Arab Rep.
Chile	India	Pakistan	United Kingdom
China (Nat.)	Indonesia	Panama	United States
Colombia	Iraq	Paraguay	Uruguay
Costa Rica	Ireland, Rep. of	Persia	Venezuela
Cuba	Israel	Peru	Yemen
Czechoslovakia	Italy	Philippines	Yugoslavia
Denmark	Japan		

The principal organs of the United Nations are: the general assembly, the Security council, the Economic and Social council, the Trusteeship council, the International Court of Justice (*q.v.*) and the secretariat. Headquarters, New York; secretary-general, Dag Hammarskjöld (Sweden).

History. The year 1959 witnessed a steady increase in the " quiet " diplomacy advocated by the secretary-general, Dag Hammarskjöld. More problems and issues appeared to be undergoing diplomatic treatment outside the United Nations, including armaments control and regulation, Cyprus, Kashmir, Antarctica and an international development authority.

Membership. On Sept. 22, 1959, by 44 votes to 29, with 9 abstentions, the general assembly again decided not to consider the question of Chinese representation.

Organization and Meetings. The 13th session of the general assembly, after adjourning on Dec. 13, 1958, resumed from Feb. 20 to March 13, 1959, to consider problems concerning the Cameroons. The 14th session, with 53 foreign ministers present, convened on Sept. 15, 1959, and elected as president Víctor Andrés Belaúnde of Peru. The Security council, by the middle of Nov. 1959, had met only six times during the preceding 12 months; twice each to discuss Israel and Jordan, and Laos, and once each to approve the council's annual report and elect a judge of the International Court of Justice. The Economic and Social council held resumed portions of its 26th session on Oct. 23 and Dec. 10-11, 1958. Under the presidency of Daniel Cosio Villegas (Mexico) the 27th session met in Mexico City from April 7 to 24, 1959, and the 28th session in Geneva, from June 30 to July 31, 1959. Under the presidency of Max H. Dorsinville (Haiti), the Trusteeship council held its 23rd session from Jan. 30 to March 20 and its 24th session from June 2 to Aug. 6, 1959.

Elections were held in the general assembly on Oct. 12, 1959, for three non-permanent seats on the Security council. Ceylon and Ecuador, by 72 and 77 votes respectively, were elected on the first ballot to succeed Canada and Panama for two-year terms beginning on Jan. 1, 1960. However, between Oct. 12 and Dec. 11, the general assembly held 51 ballots—a record—without providing either Poland or Turkey with the required majority of two-thirds to succeed Japan. On Dec. 11, in both the 50th and 51st ballots, Poland led by 41 votes to Turkey's 37. Finally, during Dec. 12-13, a compromise was reached: Poland and Turkey would share the two-year term, but this was not to be regarded as a change in the eastern European stand on the equitable geographical distribution of non-permanent seats. Henry Cabot Lodge, U.S. representative, assured all concerned, in plenary session, that in the future the U.S. delegation would " not discriminate against any area or against any nation, including eastern Europe ". On this understanding Poland received 71 votes in the 52nd and conclusive ballot.

The membership of the Trusteeship council for 1960 presented an unusual problem because of the diminishing number of trust territories and because art. 86 of the U.N. charter requires that the membership of the council shall be evenly balanced between states which administer trust territories and those which do not. French Togo and Cameroun were scheduled for full independence in 1960, at which time France would cease to be an administrator of a trust territory. The members of the council who would still administer territories would be: New Zealand, the United Kingdom, the United States, Australia and Belgium. The nonadministering states would be: China, France, the U.S.S.R., Haiti, India,

Vijaya Lakshmi Pandit, Indian high commissioner in London, with G. S. Pathak, an Indian delegate to the U.N. general assembly.

Burma, Paraguay and the United Arab Republic. On Dec. 13 the 14th general assembly contented itself with electing Bolivia to succeed Haiti and re-electing India, both for three-year terms of office.

Finances. A financial crisis developed during 1959, primarily because of two related factors: delay in payment of assessments and refusal to pay for the costs of the U.N. Emergency force (U.N.E.F.). The situation came to a head in June when the secretary-general had to borrow $2 million from special accounts in order to finance the normal operations of the U.N. Over the years the secretary-general had been short of funds late in the spring because the two largest contributors did not complete their remittances until after July 1 (the United States in July and the U.S.S.R. in the autumn) and because China continued to be one year behind in payments. Therefore the secretary-general in 1958 asked for an increase in the working capital fund from $22·5 million to $30 million, but on Dec. 13, 1958, the general assembly agreed to raise the fund only to $23·5 million. On May 31, 1959, arrears in payment of assessments totalled $46,279,000 out of $49,359,240 due. A month later the working capital fund was down to less than $1 million. The crisis in 1959 came about not only because of late payments by China, the U.S.S.R. and the United States, but because 25 members had refused to make any payments, and 12 had made only token payments, on their assessments

towards the cost of maintaining U.N.E.F.; $22·5 million of $55·2 million due had not been paid on May 31, 1959.

The failure of governments to pay their assessments for U.N.E.F., after a general assembly decision that all members should do so, raised a serious question as to whether members intended to respect the obligations contained in art. 17 of the U.N. charter. Unless there was some significant change, the secretary-general estimated that it might be necessary to borrow money in Feb. or March 1960 in order to carry on the work of the United Nations, and so again requested an increase of the working capital fund to $30 million.

Armaments Regulation. During 1959 discussion of the problem of regulation of armaments was, for all practical purposes, conducted outside the United Nations. On Nov. 4, 1958, the general assembly approved several resolutions on the subject, chief of which was one enlarging the Disarmament commission to include all members of the United Nations. On Sept. 7, 1959, the " Big Four " powers requested the secretary-general to convene the commission, which met on Sept. 10 and unanimously welcomed the 10-nation disarmament committee established by the " Big Four " at Geneva (Canada, France, Great Britain, Italy and the United States on one side and Bulgaria, Czechoslovakia, Poland, Rumania and the U.S.S.R. on the other), but with the recognition that ultimate responsibility for general disarmament was vested in the United Nations. On Sept. 18 Nikita Khrushchev, the Soviet premier, proposed to the general assembly a system of complete and universal disarmament. A resolution, transmitting to the ten-nation disarmament committee the Khrushchev proposal and all other major proposals, was sponsored by all members of the general assembly.

United Nations Emergency Force. Virtually unbroken quiet prevailed during 1959 in the Gaza strip, on the Israeli-Egyptian border and at Sharm el-Sheikh, where the U.N.E.F. of approximately 5,400 men was stationed. The withdrawal of the Colombian battalion in the autumn of 1958 was compensated for by increases in the contingents from the seven states that continued to supply forces: Brazil, Canada, Denmark, India, Norway, Sweden and Yugoslavia. The failure of states to pay their assessments towards the cost of U.N.E.F. was a cause of concern. In 1956 the members of the general assembly had decided (by a vote of 62 to 8, with 7 abstentions) that the costs of U.N.E.F. should be borne by all members of the organization in accordance with the scale of assessments for the regular budget. On Dec. 13, 1958, the vote on financing U.N.E.F. for 1960 was 42 to 9, with 27 abstentions.

It was announced on Dec. 4, 1959, that Lieut.-General E. L. M. Burns (Canada) had resigned as commander of U.N.E.F. The general assembly appointed Major-General Prem Singh Gyani (India) to succeed him.

Suez Canal. The United Arab Republic continued to close the canal to shipping to and from Israel, contending that it had the right to do so as a belligerent. Both sides presented their case to the general assembly on Sept. 24, 1959. During the year the secretary-general negotiated with the governments of the United Arab Republic and Israel, but apparently without result. (*See* also SUEZ CANAL.)

Algeria. A draft resolution recognizing the right of the Algerian people to independence, and urging the two parties concerned to negotiate with a view to reaching a solution, was defeated by the 13th general assembly on Dec. 13, 1958, by a vote of 35 in favour to 18 against, with 28 abstentions. The item was included on the agenda of the 14th general assembly in 1959, at the request of 25 members who contended that there had been " no indication of improvement " in the situation. This submission, however, was made prior to President Charles de Gaulle's statement of Sept. 16, 1959, concerning French policy towards Algeria.

On Dec. 13 the general assembly decided not to intervene

in the question of Algeria and failed to adopt a compromise resolution moved by Pakistan on behalf of the Afro-Asian group. This would have called for informal talks between France and the Algerian nationalists directed towards a peaceful solution on the basis of the right to self-determination. The vote was 39 in favour, 22 against, with 20 abstentions. The United States abstained and Great Britain voted against.

Tibet. On Sept. 9, 1959, the Dalai Lama cabled the secretary-general asking that the general assembly should consider charges of aggression by the Chinese People's Republic against Tibet. (*See* also TIBET.)

Hungary. On Dec. 12, 1958, the 13th general assembly (by a vote of 54 to 10, with 15 abstentions) adopted a resolution deploring the continued repression in Hungary of human rights, denounced the execution of Imre Nagy and Pál Maléter, again called upon the Soviet Union and the authorities in Hungary to desist from repressive measures against the Hungarian people, and appointed Sir Leslie Munro (New Zealand) to represent the United Nations and report on significant developments relating to the implementation of general assembly resolutions on Hungary.

On Dec. 9, Munro asked the general assembly to " deplore " the failure of the U.S.S.R. and Hungary to honour previous U.N. resolutions on the Hungarian situation. These resolutions called on the U.S.S.R. to withdraw its troops from Hungary and sought admission of a U.N. representative to survey the situation after the 1956 revolt. The resolution, charging Munro to " continue his efforts ", was adopted by 53 votes to 10, with 17 abstentions.

Special Fund for Economic Development. When the governing board of the fund met from May 26 to 28, 1959, Paul G. Hoffman, the managing director (*see* BIOGRAPHIES), reported that 75 governments had made requests totalling $81 million and that $26 million was available towards the first year's goal of $66 million. By Nov. 1959 the available funds had been increased to $32 million.

Technical Assistance. The expanding programme of technical assistance completed its 10th year after having spent $245 million in 140 countries and territories, including the provision of 8,000 experts and 14,000 fellowships. By 1959 there were 85 countries supporting the programme.

U.N. Children's Fund. Children in 105 countries were assisted by 368 projects that cost about $27 million in 1959. In its efforts to improve children's nutrition, Unicef found it necessary to devote more attention to such problems as community development, social services and the improvement of training for primary school teachers.

Refugees. A concerted world-wide attack on the problem of refugees was recommended by the general assembly on Dec. 5, 1958, when it approved a United Kingdom proposal for a World Refugee Year to begin on June 1, 1959. The purpose of the year was to focus attention on the problem and to encourage additional contributions for its solution. The U.N. high commissioner for refugees, Auguste R. Lindt, reported on June 15 that the population of the refugee camps had been reduced by 17% during the first four months of 1959. By September, 54 governments had pledged support of one kind or another to the refugee year, including a special contribution of $1,630,000 by the United States. (*See* REFUGEES.)

The Trusteeship System. During the year, important steps were taken that were expected to lead to complete independence for Cameroun, Togo and Somalia during 1960, and Western Samoa in 1961. The resumed 13th general assembly, on March 13, 1959, agreed that the trusteeship agreement for Cameroun should be terminated on Jan. 1, 1960, and that the new state should be recommended for membership in the United Nations. The 14th general assembly agreed on Dec. 5 that Togo would achieve independence on April 27, 1960, and that Somalia would achieve independence on July 1, 1960.

The Trusteeship council's visiting mission to Western Samoa (March 25-April 17, 1959) received a tentative timetable for the independence of that territory. The government of New Zealand suggested that a U.N.-supervised plebiscite be held in 1961, and that the general assembly in 1961 might terminate the trusteeship agreement.

Members of the War Resisters league demonstrating outside the United Nations headquarters in New York on Dec. 1. They urged that conscientious objectors in all countries should be given recognition in the U.N. charter of human rights.

On Nov. 9, 1959, the people of the northern area of British Cameroons decided by a vote of 67,879 to 41,113 that they wished to remain under the trusteeship system for an unspecified time, rather than join Nigeria, which was to become independent in 1960. (*See* also TRUST TERRITORIES.)

Specialized Agencies. During 1959 the following organizations were in operation:

Food and Agriculture Organization (q.v.). International Atomic Energy Agency (IAEA): headquarters in Vienna, Austria; director-general Sterling Cole, 69 members. *Intergovernmental Maritime Consultative Organization (IMCO):* headquarters in London; secretary-general Ove Nielsen, 35 members. *International Finance Corporation (IFC):* headquarters in Washington, D.C.; director-general Robert L. Garner, 52 members. *International Bank for Reconstruction and Development (q.v.). International Labour Organization (q.v.). International Monetary Fund (q.v.). International Civil Aviation Organization (ICAO):* headquarters in Montreal, Canada; secretary-general Ronald M. Macdonnell, 74 members. *International Telecommunications Union (ITU):* headquarters in Geneva; acting secretary-general Gerald C. Ross, 96 members. *U.N. Educational, Scientific and Cultural Organization (q.v.). Universal Postal Union (UPU):* headquarters in Berne, Switzerland; director of the international bureau Fritz Hess, 100 members. *World Health Organization (q.v.). World Meteorological Organization (WMO):* headquarters in Geneva; secretary-general David A. Davies, 102 members.

(*See* also KOREA; LAOS.) (W. CN.)

UNITED NATIONS EDUCATIONAL, SCIENTIFIC AND CULTURAL ORGANIZATION was

established on Nov. 4, 1946, when the instruments of acceptance of 20 out of 44 signatories of its constitution of Nov. 16, 1945, had been deposited with the U.K. government. The 81 states which were members of Unesco at the end of 1959, as well as 6 associate members, are given in the table.

The organs of Unesco are a general conference meeting every two years in November, an executive board of the representatives of 24 member states elected in rotation for four years and a secretariat. Headquarters, Paris; director-general, Vittorino Veronese (Italy).

MEMBER-STATES OF UNESCO, DEC. 31, 1959

Afghanistan	Ecuador	Laos	Rumania
Albania	El Salvador	Lebanon	Saudi Arabia
Argentina	Ethiopia	Liberia	*†Sierra Leone
Australia	Finland	Libya	*†Singapore
Austria	France	Luxembourg	*†Somalia
Belgium	*German Fed.	Malaya	Spain
Bolivia	Rep.	Mexico	Sudan
Brazil	Ghana	*Monaco	Sweden
Bulgaria	Greece	Morocco	*Switzerland
Burma	Guatemala	Nepal	Thailand
Byelorussia	Haiti	Netherlands	Tunisia
Canada	Honduras	New Zealand	Turkey
Cambodia	Hungary	Nicaragua	Ukraine
Ceylon	India	*†Nigeria	U.S.S.R.
Chile	Indonesia	Norway	United Arab Rep.
China (Nat.)	Iraq	Pakistan	United Kingdom
Colombia	Israel	Panama	United States
Costa Rica	Italy	Paraguay	Uruguay
Cuba	Japan	Persia	Venezuela
Czechoslovakia	Jordan	Peru	*Vietnam, Rep. of
Denmark	*Korea, Rep. of	Philippines	*†West Indies, The
Dominican Rep.	*†Kuwait	Poland	Yugoslavia

* Not a member of United Nations. † Associate member.

History. The executive board held two sessions in 1959, in June and November. Its chairman for 1959-60 was Sir Ben Bowen Thomas (U.K.). The staff at headquarters in Paris at the close of 1959 totalled 1,046 drawn from 57 countries. In addition 283 experts from 51 countries were on field assignments in 58 countries and territories throughout the world. The budget for the year 1959 was $12,807,377.

Three " major projects " (the achievement of universal free and compulsory education in Latin America, the study of scientific problems of the arid zones and mutual appreciation of eastern and western cultural values) stood out as long-term undertakings on which special efforts and finance were concentrated. An international conference on information processing, held in Paris in June, attracted considerable attention, as did a congress of oceanography held in New York in September.

Unesco also participates, to the extent of some $4,290,000 (or 16% of a total field budget), in the U.N. expanded programme of technical assistance. The technical advice provided by Unesco to the governments and administrations which request it falls mostly in the fields of education, science and mass communication. To supplement this U.N. programme, which is confined to projects serving the end of economic development, Unesco operates out of its own resources a parallel programme of participation in the activities of member states under which, again on request from national authorities, it sends out experts.

A new feature of the year 1959 was the launching of the U.N. special fund for economic development. This differed from the technical assistance programme in that it concentrated on a small number of large-scale undertakings such as the creation of technological institutes, faculties and schools, surveys of mineral or agricultural resources in given areas with a view to their development, etc. Members of the United Nations had by the end of 1959 contributed or pledged more than $60 million to this new fund and here again Unesco was a participant, having been given responsibility for expenditures (over the next five years) of some $7 million for eight projects which included technical faculties in the University of the Middle East in Turkey, a new faculty of engineering in the University College of The West Indies, power engineering research in India, an Institute of Higher Technology in Libya and a Polytechnic institute in Persia.

At its November session the Executive board authorized the director-general to launch a world-wide appeal for saving the ancient monuments of Nubia (a region of the Nile valley

While in London in April the director-general of Unesco, Vittorino Veronese (right), met the minister of education, Geoffrey Lloyd.

divided between the U.A.R. and Sudan) threatened by the proposed high dam at Aswan.

In the field of international legislation 31 states at the end of 1959 were parties to the agreement on the importation of educational, scientific and cultural materials, 31 also to the universal copyright convention and 29 to the convention for the protection of cultural property in the event of armed conflict. The two 1958 conventions on the international exchange of publications were before national authorities for consideration, together with recommendations on international principles applicable to archaeological excavations, international competitions in architecture and town planning and the international standardization of educational statistics. Work was in hand on the drafting of international instruments concerning the prevention of discrimination in education, the protection of certain rights of performers, recorders and broadcasters (" neighbouring " rights to copyright) and on the most effective way of making museums available to everyone.

The circulation of the popular monthly, *Unesco Courier*, published in English, French, Russian and Spanish, exceeded 200,000 in 1959.   (C. M. B.)

UNITED STATES FOREIGN AID.

U.S. foreign aid in 1959 largely followed the pattern of recent years. However, several developments foreshadowed changes of some importance. During the year there was much discussion of the emphasis, organization and methods needed to make foreign aid an effective instrument of continuing U.S. policy.

Policy Developments. Military aid and its relation to economic aid were examined by the president's committee to study the U.S. Military Assistance programme in four reports filed between March and Aug. 1959. Appointed in Nov. 1958, under the chairmanship of William H. Draper, Jr., the committee recommended an increase of $400 million in military aid appropriations, primarily to avoid a decline in deliveries to Nato countries in future years. It opposed any major decrease in military aid to underdeveloped countries as a whole (while leaving the way open for reductions in some cases and increases in others) and urged an increase in economic aid to those countries beginning in 1960-61. The committee took the view that the two kinds of aid, though in many ways complementary, should not be regarded as competing for public funds, since different standards determined the need for each. Because military aid could no longer be regarded as temporary, the Draper committee recommended that in order to avoid the need for two separate legislative actions each year, congress should provide continuing authorization for military aid and that the annual appropriations should be included in the budget of the Department of Defence. That department would also be given responsibility for the administration of military aid, under the foreign policy direction of the State Department.

Shortly before the Draper committee was appointed, Democratic members of the Senate foreign relations committee wrote to the president suggesting that too much military aid was being given to underdeveloped countries. Similar views were frequently expressed during 1959. In congress, military aid to Latin America was sharply but unsuccessfully attacked on the ground that it supported dictatorships. The president did not ask for the additional appropriations recommended by the Draper committee, but there were indications that he would do so in his next budget requests. The Mutual Security act of 1959, passed by congress in June, provided authorization for military aid funds for the fiscal years 1960-61 and 1961-62, without specifying amounts.

The Development Loan fund, which began operations in 1958, was at the centre of some of the debate about long-term policies concerning economic aid. The funds from the previous year having proved inadequate, the Development Loan fund was given a supplementary appropriation of $150 million in May 1959 (the administration had asked for $225 million). When the programme for 1959-60 was being discussed, the Senate foreign relations committee recommended that the Development Loan fund be authorized to borrow $1,000 million a year for five years from the Treasury, thus avoiding the need for annual appropriations. The administration, which had made a similar proposal in 1957, opposed this innovation and asked for a one-year authorization of $700 million. The Senate avoided a vote on the issue of Treasury financing, because of constitutional complications, but authorized the appropriation of a sum of $2,000 million over two years, $750 million of it for the fiscal year 1959-60. In conference these two figures were reduced to $1,800 million and $700 million, respectively, and in the event the appropriation bill carried only $550 million for 1959-60.

The preference for loans over grants apparent in recent

years was emphasized in the congressional debates of 1959. The act passed by congress called on the president to present plans for the reduction and eventual elimination of grant aid, " wherever practicable ".

When the extension of the Agricultural Trade Development and Assistance act was being discussed, Senator H. H. Humphrey proposed a substantial enlargement of the programme for using surplus farm products as a means of providing foreign aid. The Senate foreign relations committee supported some of his suggestions in a modified form, but the law that was adopted maintained the authorization at its existing level of $1,500 million per year for two years (plus $300 million per year for emergency relief). When he signed the bill the president criticized a new provision authorizing him to contract to supply agricultural products to foreign countries for 10 years, to be paid for over 20 years.

The interest of the United States in the possibility of Europe's providing a larger share of the aid for underdeveloped countries was enhanced by the sharp increase in the deficit on current account in the U.S. balance of payments during 1958 and 1959. Gold left the country and short-term indebtedness to foreign countries increased. The leading countries of western Europe, which were also enjoying unprecedented levels of prosperity, were the main gainers. Although the United States was no longer giving economic aid to these countries on any appreciable scale, they had the benefit of military aid, their central banks accumulated dollars as the result of U.S. military expenditures abroad, and their exporters earned dollars by selling goods to underdeveloped countries receiving economic aid from the United States.

Possible means of adjustment were discussed in the United States, but by late 1959 only two major steps had been taken that affected aid policy. One was the strong recommendation to European countries to provide more development aid. This was followed, in December, at the Nato ministerial council in Paris, by a proposal from the United States, the United Kingdom, France and the German Federal Republic that there should be set up a new economic council, composed of representatives of the European Economic community, the European Free Trade association and North America, not only to harmonize economic relations between them but also to co-ordinate economic aid to the underdeveloped nations.

The other U.S. move was the introduction of some restrictions on the use of funds provided by the Development Loan fund and the International Co-operation administration. On Oct. 20 the managing director of the Development Loan fund said that, since other industrialized countries could provide credit for the export of their capital goods, the Development Loan fund would " place primary emphasis on the financing of goods and services of U.S. origin ". Later a similar policy was announced for the International Co-operation administration.

The Export-Import Bank of Washington had long advanced money almost exclusively for the purchase of U.S. goods, but the new steps " tying " other aid funds were sharply criticized. There was disagreement as to what effect the new measures would have on the U.S. balance of payments and on the policies of other countries. At the end of the year no authoritative indication had been given as to how permanent the changes in U.S. policy were likely to be.

The Use of Aid in 1958-59. Tables I and II show the amounts of U.S. foreign aid actually used in 1958-59 and earlier years. Total aid was less than in the previous year but was at about the level of 1956-57. Grants declined slightly in amount but continued to provide the largest part of aid. Purely military grants were at the lowest level since 1951-52 and accounted for a smaller share of aid than in recent years. The use of credits increased in relative importance. Credits were drawn on to the extent of $1,276 million in 1958-59,

TABLE I. FOREIGN GRANTS AND CREDITS OF THE UNITED STATES GOVERNMENT, 1946-59
(Millions of dollars; fiscal years, ending June 30)

	July 1, 1945-June 30, 1959	1957	1958	1959
Total aid	71,000	4,700	4,900	4,600
Net grants	56,900	4,000	3,900	3,800
Net credits	12,000	—199	616	608
Net short-term aid	2,100	858	325	170
Western Europe and dependent areas				
Total aid	39,200	1,500	1,162	706
Net grants	30,300	1,500	994	866
Net credits	8,200	—255	153	—130
Net short-term aid	719	308	15	—30
Middle East, Africa and South Asia				
Total aid	10,000	1,100	1,358	1,539
Net grants	7,800	770	971	1,172
Net credits	1,300	—22	144	195
Net short-term aid	905	355	242	173
Other Asia and Pacific				
Total aid	16,300	1,700	1,740	1,505
Net grants	15,400	1,500	1,665	1,464
Net credits	700	54	90	62
Net short-term aid	240	163	—15	—21
Latin America				
Total aid	2,600	231	410	615
Net grants	1,100	167	191	159
Net credits	1,400	32	214	462
Net short-term aid	122	32	5	—6

NOTES. Figures refer to actual use of aid *i.e.*, the equivalent dollar value of the actual transfers of goods, services or cash (dollars or foreign currencies) to foreign accounts by U.S. government agencies.

Net grants = gross grants minus reverse grants, returns on grants and grants converted to credits. Gross grants for the total postwar period were $61,000 million.

Net credits = new credits and grants converted to credits minus repayment of principal (but not interest) of previous credits. New credits for the total postwar period were $15,500 million.

Net short-term aid = net short-term claims acquired by the U.S. government under agricultural sales programmes, less short-term liabilities for currencies advanced by foreign governments pending delivery of agricultural commodities. When foreign currencies obtained by the U.S. government in this fashion are lent or given away as part of an aid programme, they cease to be "short-term aid" and are included in the totals for grants or credits. The figures for 1957, 1958 and 1959 show the net short-term assistance resulting from the transactions in each year. The total for the postwar period shows the balance as of June 30, 1959.

Greece and Turkey are included in the middle east. South Asia includes Afghanistan, Ceylon, India and Pakistan.

SOURCE. U.S. Department of Commerce, Office of Business Economics, *Foreign Grants and Credits by the United States Government.*

TABLE II. MILITARY AND ECONOMIC AID PROVIDED BY THE UNITED STATES GOVERNMENT, 1946-59
(Millions of dollars; fiscal years, ending June 30)

	July 1, 1945-June 30, 1959	1957	1958	1959
World				
Military grants	24,500	2,300	2,400	2,200
Other aid	46,500	2,366	2,489	2,409
Western Europe and dependent areas				
Military grants	13,500	1,200	799	722
Other aid	25,700	340	363	—17
Middle East, Africa and South Asia				
Military grants	3,800	392	622	554
Other aid	6,100	711	735	986
Other Asia and Pacific				
Military grants	6,500	626	877	810
Other aid	9,800	1,058	863	695
Latin America				
Military grants	458	72	73	50
Other aid	2,200	159	337	565

NOTES. Figures are net. "Other aid" includes cash payments made to help other governments support their military efforts and also supplies, such as food and clothing, that went directly to troops. It also includes short-term assistance extended under agricultural sales programmes.

SOURCE. U.S. Department of Commerce, Office of Business Economics, *Foreign Grants and Credits by the United States Government.*

compared with $1,135 million in 1957-58 and $440 million in 1956-57. (The figures in the tables show these totals minus repayment of principal on past loans.) Nearly one-third of the new credits used in 1958-59 came from foreign currency obtained by the U.S. government by the sale of surplus agricultural products. Another $300 million of these funds was used to provide aid in the form of grants. The $170 million shown as "net short-term aid" in Table I represents the increase in foreign currencies held by the United States

and not used for U.S. expenditures or lent or granted to foreign governments or private interests. Though this figure was smaller than in previous years, the sum received from the sale of surplus farm products in 1958-59 was about $990 million compared with about $930 million the year before. By the end of 1958-59 the United States was holding more than $2,000 million in unused foreign balances obtained in this way.

The absolute and relative importance of aid to western Europe and its dependencies declined sharply in 1958-59 compared with previous years. A drop in new credits combined with increased repayment of old debts to create a net flow of funds to the United States in this category, a condition that had existed in 1955-56 and 1956-57 but not in 1957-58 when funds were advanced to France and Great Britain after the Suez conflict. A major ingredient in this shift was western Germany's advance repayment of five years' amortization on a loan made in 1952-53. The largest increase in the use of net credits and in new credits as well came in Latin America, largely as a result of increased Export-Import bank commitments during 1957-58. The countries of the far east, southern Asia, the middle east (including Greece and Turkey) and the Pacific retained the position of central importance they had had for several years. Almost two-thirds of U.S. military assistance went to those areas. They also received three-quarters of the nonmilitary grant aid, mostly in the form of defence support to countries also receiving military aid. Their share of credits was smaller, but some, notably India, were major recipients of Development Loan fund loans.

India received more nonmilitary aid from the United States than did any other country in 1958-59. More than two-thirds was in the form of the accumulation of rupee balances resulting from the delivery of agricultural products. South Korea, south Vietnam, Turkey, Pakistan and Formosa, the main recipients of defence support aid, were also among the ten countries receiving the most U.S. assistance, as they had been for several years. Spain and Yugoslavia received more aid than in the year before while Poland received somewhat less but remained one of the first ten. Thanks to large Export-Import bank loans, Brazil became the fourth most important recipient of U.S. aid during the year.

The complexity of the United States aid programme was indicated by the differences from country to country. Though Polish leaders became more openly critical of the United States than they had been, a new, but smaller, aid agreement was signed. The new government in Iraq cancelled its military and economic aid agreements (but continued technical assistance). Aid to Egypt was resumed in 1958 and 1959 for the first time since the Suez conflict. Arms were provided to Indonesia, reversing previous policy, and an economic development loan was arranged. Burma, which had for some years refused most aid, announced its willingness to accept a grant. Spain, in addition to receiving increased amounts of U.S. aid, was able to get assistance from the International Monetary fund, the Organization for European Economic Co-operation and private U.S. banks as part of a general programme to stabilize its currency and liberalize its foreign trade.

The Future. In his budget for the fiscal year 1959-60, the president asked for just over $3,900 million in foreign aid funds, of which $1,600 million was to go for military aid, $835 million in defence support, $700 million to the Development Loan fund, and the rest in various other forms of aid, including special and contingency funds and technical assistance. The bill that passed both houses on July 22 authorized aid totalling just under $3,600 million (of which $1,400 million was for military aid, $751 million for defence support and $700 million for the Defence Loan fund). The appropriation bill passed in mid-September reduced this sum by $330 million, of which $150 million was cut from the Development Loan fund, $100 million from military aid, $50 million from defence support and $30 million from technical assistance.

The total appropriated for 1959-60 was $3,226 million compared with $3,298 million for 1958-59. The main reduction was in military assistance and defence support, while the Development Loan fund received an amount equal to the previous year's appropriation of $400 million plus the supplementary $150 million provided in the spring of 1959.

In the course of 1958-59 the United States committed itself to lend nearly $2,000 million, one-third more than during the previous year. The Development Loan fund and loans from the proceeds of agriculture sales each provided about one-quarter while most of the rest took the form of Export-Import bank loans. Increasingly the United States was stressing the need for other advanced countries to participate more actively in the aid process. These overtures found a certain response abroad where the concept of aid to underdeveloped countries was increasingly spoken of as a primary political task, a basis for increased co-operation within the free world, and possibly even something to be discussed at the summit with the U.S.S.R., at least if some kind of disarmament could be agreed on that would free funds for development. (W. DD.)

UNITED STATES OF AMERICA.

Federal republic in North America composed of 50 separate and (theoretically) sovereign states; fifth largest country of the world in area, fourth in population, but foremost in industrial production and financial resources; bounded N. by Canada, S. by Mexico, E. by the Atlantic ocean and W. by the Pacific ocean. Area (including Alaska and Hawaii): 3,615,212 sq.mi. (incl. 62,996 sq.mi. of inland water). For territories and outlying possessions *see* Table I. Population: (1950 census, 48 states) 150,697,361; (mid-1959 est., 50 states): 177,725,900. Race (1950): white 134,942,028 (89·5%), Negro 15,042,286 (10%), other 713,047. Foreign-born white population 10,161,168 (6·7%); American Indians 343,410; Japanese 141,768; Chinese 117,629. Mother tongue (1940): English 78·6%, German 4·2%, Italian 3·2%, Polish 2·0%, Spanish 1·6%, Yiddish 1·5%, Swedish 0·7%, Norwegian 0·6%, Russian 0·5%, other or non-reported 7·1%. In 1956 there were in the United States 53 religious bodies of more than 50,000 members, and a total of about 100·2 million members. Though " Protestants " (12 Baptist bodies, 5 Methodist, 7 Lutheran, 4 Presbyterian, Protestant Episcopal Church, etc.) as a group claimed 60·1 million, the Roman Catholic Church, with an estimated total of 34·6 million, was far ahead of any single denomination. There were 2·6 million Orthodox (Greeks, Ukrainians, Russians, Serbs, Rumanians, etc.) and 480,000 Gregorian Armenians. The largest non-Christian congregation was Jewish (about 5·5 million). Monetary unit: U.S. dollar ($2·80 = £1 sterling).

President of the United States, Dwight D. Eisenhower; vice-president, Richard M. Nixon. At Dec. 31, 1959, the cabinet was as follows: secretary of state, Christian A. Herter; secretary of defence, Thomas S. Gates; secretary of the treasury, Robert B. Anderson; attorney-general, William P. Rogers; postmaster-general, Arthur E. Summerfield; secretary of the interior, Frederick A. Seaton; secretary of agriculture, Ezra T. Benson; secretary of commerce, Frederick H. Mueller; secretary of health, education and welfare, Arthur S. Flemming; and secretary of labour, James P. Mitchell.

History. *Eisenhower's Leadership.* The old but still effective technique of personal diplomacy was used by President Dwight D. Eisenhower in 1959 to try to break the east-west stalemate which had dominated the history of the United States as well as much of the rest of the world since World War II ended. The president's efforts to use his great personal prestige to ease the tensions of the " cold war " between the western world and the U.S.S.R. were a dramatic departure from previous U.S. attempts since World War II to resolve the differences between the western world and the Communist countries.

In Sept. 1959, Nikita S. Khrushchev, head of the Soviet government, flew to the United States and journeyed throughout the country. After his ten-day trip from New York to Los Angeles and from San Francisco to Des Moines, Khrushchev met Eisenhower for a weekend at the president's rustic retreat at Camp David in the Catoctin mountains of Maryland where the leaders of the two most powerful nations informally discussed their differences. Khrushchev's welcome was polite in most cities that he visited, but the people who saw him could hardly be considered enthusiastic.

TABLE I. TERRITORIES AND POSSESSIONS OF THE UNITED STATES

Territory or Possession	Area (sq.mi.)	Population (1959 est.)	Territory or Possession	Area (sq.mi.)	Population (1959 est.)
Bonin Islands	40	184	Panama Canal		
Marshall, Caroline and			Zone	553	57,000
Mariana Islands	687	70,594	Puerto Rico	3,435	2,340,000
American Samoa	76	20,154	Ryukyu Is.	848	830,400
Guam	206	38,578*	Virgin Islands	133	31,250

* Excludes military personnel.

NOTE. In addition to these possessions there are at least nine islands in the Pacific ocean, which have a total land area of approximately 20 sq.mi.: Baker, Howland, Jarvis, Johnston (pop., 1950 census, 46), Sand, Kingman Reef, Midway (pop. 416), Palmyra and Wake (pop. 349). There are also two U.S.-U.K. condominiums: Canton Island (pop. 272) and Enderbury Island.

TABLE II. CHIEF CITIES OF THE UNITED STATES
(Population, 1950 census)

City	Population	City	Population
Washington, D.C., cap.	802,178	Houston, Tex.	596,163
New York, N.Y.	7,891,957	Buffalo, N.Y.	580,132
Chicago, Ill.	3,620,962	New Orleans, La.	570,445
Philadelphia, Pa.	2,071,605	Minneapolis, Minn.	521,718
Los Angeles, Calif.	1,970,358	Cincinnati, O.	503,998
Detroit, Mich.	1,849,568	Seattle, Wash.	467,591
Baltimore, Md.	949,708	Kansas City, Mo.	456,622
Cleveland, O.	914,808	Newark, N.J.	438,776
St. Louis, Mo.	856,796	Dallas, Tex.	434,462
Boston, Mass.	801,444	Indianapolis, Ind.	427,173
San Francisco, Calif.	775,357	Denver, Colo.	415,786
Pittsburgh, Pa.	676,806	San Antonio, Tex.	408,442
Milwaukee, Wis.	637,392	Memphis, Tenn.	396,000

TABLE III. THE STATES OF THE UNITED STATES OF AMERICA

State	Population 1950 census	Increase* over 1940	Land area (sq.mi.)	Capital city
Alabama (Ala.)	3,061,743	228,782	51,078	Montgomery
Alaska	128,643	56,119	571,065	Juneau
Arizona (Ariz.)	749,587	250,326	113,575	Phoenix
Arkansas (Ark.)	1,909,511	—39,876	52,675	Little Rock
California (Calif.)	10,586,223	3,678,836	156,740	Sacramento
Colorado (Colo.)	1,325,089	201,793	103,922	Denver
Connecticut (Conn.)	2,007,280	298,038	4,899	Hartford
Delaware (Del.)	318,085	51,580	1,978	Dover
Florida (Fla.)	2,771,305	873,891	54,262	Tallahassee
Georgia (Ga.)	3,444,578	320,855	58,483	Atlanta
Hawaii	499,794	77,024	6,407	Honolulu
Idaho (Ida.)	588,637	63,764	82,769	Boise
Illinois (Ill.)	8,712,176	814,935	55,935	Springfield
Indiana (Ind.)	3,934,224	506,428	36,205	Indianapolis
Iowa (Ia.)	2,621,073	82,805	56,045	Des Moines
Kansas (Kan.)	1,905,299	104,271	82,108	Topeka
Kentucky (Ky.)	2,944,806	99,179	39,864	Frankfort
Louisiana (La.)	2,683,516	319,636	45,162	Baton Rouge
Maine (Me.)	913,774	66,548	31,040	Augusta
Maryland (Md.)	2,343,001	521,757	9,881	Annapolis
Massachusetts (Mass.)	4,690,514	373,793	7,867	Boston
Michigan (Mich.)	6,371,766	1,115,660	57,022	Lansing
Minnesota (Min.)	2,982,483	190,183	80,009	St. Paul
Mississippi (Miss.)	2,178,914	—4,882	47,248	Jackson
Missouri (Mo.)	3,954,653	169,989	69,226	Jefferson City
Montana (Mont.)	591,024	31,568	145,878	Helena
Nebraska (Neb.)	1,325,510	9,676	76,336	Lincoln
Nevada (Nev.)	160,083	49,836	109,789	Carson City
New Hampshire (N.H.)	533,242	41,718	9,017	Concord
New Jersey (N.J.)	4,835,329	675,164	7,522	Trenton
New Mexico (N.M.)	681,187	149,369	121,517	Santa Fé
New York (N.Y.)	14,830,192	1,351,050	47,944	Albany
North Carolina (N.C.)	4,061,929	490,306	49,097	Raleigh
North Dakota (N.D.)	619,636	—22,299	70,057	Bismarck
Ohio (O.)	7,946,627	1,039,015	41,000	Columbus
Oklahoma (Okla.)	2,233,351	—103,083	69,031	Oklahoma City
Oregon (Ore.)	1,521,341	431,657	96,315	Salem
Pennsylvania (Pa.)	10,498,012	597,832	45,045	Harrisburg
Rhode Island (R.I.)	791,896	78,550	1,057	Providence
South Carolina (S.C.)	2,117,027	217,223	30,305	Columbia
South Dakota (S.D.)	652,740	9,779	76,536	Pierre
Tennessee (Tenn.)	3,291,718	375,877	41,797	Nashville
Texas (Tex.)	7,711,194	1,296,370	263,513	Austin
Utah	688,862	138,552	82,346	Salt Lake City
Vermont (Vt.)	377,747	18,516	9,278	Montpelier
Virginia (Va.)	3,318,680	640,907	39,893	Richmond
Washington (Wash.)	2,378,963	642,772	66,786	Olympia
West Virginia (W. Va.)	2,005,552	103,578	24,080	Charleston
Wisconsin (Wis.)	3,434,575	296,988	54,705	Madison
Wyoming (Wyo.)	290,529	39,787	97,596	Cheyenne
District of Columbia (D.C.)	803,178	139,087	61	—

* A minus sign (—) denotes decrease.

John Foster Dulles (second from right) was sworn in as special consultant on foreign affairs in a Washington hospital on April 23. Present were President Eisenhower (right), Christian Herter (second from left), the new secretary of state, Richard Nixon and Mrs. Dulles.

Before Khrushchev arrived in the United States the president visited Bonn, London and Paris late in August and early in September to reassure the European allies that the United States would not try to negotiate unilaterally with the U.S.S.R.

In December, in the longest trip ever undertaken by a U.S. president, Eisenhower travelled 22,000 mi. to visit 11 countries in 19 days. He went as far east as India and Pakistan, visited Morocco in Africa and also stopped in Afghanistan and Persia as well as in Italy, Turkey, Greece, Spain, Portugal and France. The president said that the purpose of his trip was to demonstrate to the world the peaceful intentions of the United States. His journey seemed to have been a great personal success, although it remained to be seen what effect it would have on east-west tensions and on the policies of such countries as India and Afghanistan which were trying to remain neutral and uncommitted in the " cold war ".

Foreign Policy. In January Anastas I. Mikoyan, first deputy premier of the Soviet Union, visited the United States. His visit was awaited with interest because U.S. officials felt that he might have some new proposals to make on the question of the future of Berlin. Little more than a month before Mikoyan arrived in the United States Khrushchev had warned the west that the Soviet Union would give it six months to remove western occupation forces from the city and to make Berlin a " free city ". Khrushchev's statements were regarded throughout the west as an ultimatum and were one of the important reasons why Eisenhower decided to pursue a policy of personal diplomacy. Mikoyan did not present any new proposals to the United States, however, although his visit was considered to have been useful. For the first time since the 1930s a high Soviet official had been able to see the United States for himself. (*See* also SUMMIT CONFERENCE, APPROACHES TO.)

Foreign policy continued to dominate thoughts and discussions during the late winter and early spring. In February John Foster Dulles, the secretary of state, entered Walter Reed hospital in Washington for an operation, his second in a little more than two years. He died in May (*see* OBITUARIES). By far the strongest man in the president's cabinet, he had been allowed by Eisenhower to conduct the country's foreign policy very much as he thought it should be conducted. Dulles did not trust the U.S.S.R. and he believed that the United States should approach any discussions with the Soviet Union in a most cautious manner. Dulles also believed that the Soviet Union would eventually collapse through its own dictatorial blunders. He was succeeded as secretary of state by Christian A. Herter (*see* BIOGRAPHIES). A man well-liked on Capitol Hill, Herter did not demonstrate much of the tenacity and toughness which were the hallmarks of the diplomacy of Dulles. As the year wore on Eisenhower took over more and more of the diplomatic functions which he had delegated to Dulles.

Other developments affecting foreign policy in the late winter and early spring included visits to the United States by Harold Macmillan, the British prime minister, and by Eisenhower to Mexico.

The inability of the foreign ministers of the United States, Great Britain, France and the U.S.S.R. to reach agreement at Geneva generated pessimism in Washington, even though the May 27 ultimatum deadline that Khrushchev had set for a Berlin settlement had passed almost unnoticed. But soon after the Geneva talks recessed in June it became apparent that Eisenhower was going to disregard the many solemn warnings of Dulles against dealing directly with the Soviet Union and that the president would make a last supreme effort, before his second term of office expired in Jan. 1961, to reach a *rapprochement* with the U.S.S.R. The president went to New York city to tour the Soviet exhibition there with Frol R. Kozlov, the Soviet first deputy premier, and the announcement of Khrushchev's trip to the United States soon followed. It was greeted with approval by most U.S. citizens as well as by most people in the rest of the world. In 1959 the world seemed to be sick of the " cold war " and ready to accept any efforts to bring about a more permanent peace, however unorthodox the attempts at negotiating might seem to be in the light of previous disappointments.

The Congressional Session. While Mikoyan was visiting the United States in January, the first session of the 86th congress, with an overwhelming Democratic majority in both the Senate and the House of Representatives, got under way. There was an unusual amount of activity for the first month of a new congress. In his State of the Union message Eisenhower stressed the need for economy in government, an issue which dominated much of the session of the congress. Joseph W. Martin (Rep., Mass.), who had been the leader of the Republicans in the house for 20 years, lost his post to Charles A. Halleck (Rep., Ind.) after Republican representatives decided that they wanted a more aggressive leadership. In January the Senate debated proposals to make it more difficult if not impossible to talk legislation to death with a filibuster. The debate ended with the adoption of a compromise plan under which two-thirds of the senators present and voting on a motion, rather than two-thirds of all the members of the Senate, could halt a filibuster. The compromise was sponsored by Lyndon B. Johnson (Dem., Texas), the Senate Democratic leader. William J. Fulbright (Dem., Ark.) succeeded Theodore F. Green (Dem., R.I.) as chairman of the Senate Foreign Relations committee. Green was 91 years old and the oldest man ever to serve in the Senate.

Late in the spring, controversies in the Senate over the nominations of Lewis L. Strauss to be secretary of commerce and Clare Booth Luce to be U.S. ambassador to Brazil overshadowed such foreign policy developments as Richard M. Nixon's decision to go to Moscow in July to open a U.S. exhibition there and the plans for a " Big Four " foreign ministers' conference in May in Geneva. Mrs. Luce was confirmed by the Senate as ambassador to Brazil, but two days after her confirmation she resigned. Wayne Morse (Dem., Ore.) led the attack on her qualifications, declaring that she was too " political " a person to send abroad as an ambassador. The Senate, however, refused to confirm the nomination of Strauss, a former chairman of the Atomic Energy commission, following several weeks of hearings on his qualifications by the Senate Commerce committee. The opposition to Strauss was led by Clinton P. Anderson (Dem., N.M.) and was based largely on a belief held by many senators that Strauss had not been frank in his dealings with them over the years. It was the first time that a cabinet nomination had been turned down by the Senate since 1925.

In 1959, for the first time since 1912 when Arizona became the 48th state, the union was enlarged by the admission of the 49th and 50th states. Although congress had approved the admission of Alaska in 1958, Alaska did not formally become a state until Jan. 1959. In the spring of 1959 congress also voted statehood for Hawaii, and Hawaii was officially admitted to the union as the 50th state in August. The admission of both Hawaii and Alaska was the climax of 50 years of effort by their people to gain admission to the union.

In the autumn a special house subcommittee held a series of hearings which revealed that many of the television quiz programmes which had been so popular since 1955 had been rigged. Several contestants—including Charles Van Doren— admitted to the subcommittee that not only had they been told the questions and answers in advance of their appearances,

but they had also been coached in the way they should grimace in giving the answers.

In 1959 congress passed the first major labour legislation to be enacted since the Taft-Hartley bill became law in 1947. The 1959 legislation, known as the Landrum-Griffith act, sought to prevent corruption in labour unions and to assure democratic procedures within the unions. Demands for the legislation arose after a special Senate committee headed by John McClellan (Dem., Ark.) conducted a two-year investigation which exposed corrupt and questionable activities in the Teamsters union and several other unions.

The $77,000 million budget approved by congress was almost exactly what the president had requested. Eisenhower made economy in government one of the principal issues in 1959. Despite much criticism in congress of the president for seemingly placing fiscal soundness above the military and domestic needs of the nation, congress went along with the administration's scaled-down spending programmes.

Although the 86th congress had the largest Democratic majority in 20 years, Eisenhower was in control of the legislative situation during practically all the session. The president never hesitated to veto bills he did not like. He turned down legislation which would have taken from the secretary of agriculture authority to approve loans made by the Rural Electrification administration, and the house sustained the president's veto. Eisenhower vetoed two housing bills before congress passed one which was in line with his fiscal programme and which he then approved. Only once did congress override a presidential veto—on legislation involving the authorization of rivers and harbours projects. By his vetoes and other actions, Eisenhower showed once again how a president is uniquely able to lead the nation, whatever the size and composition of the majorities in congress. Most of the members of congress did not object to the president's policy, for it reflected the dominant middle-of-the-road feeling among the senators and representatives who made up the 86th congress.

The Steel Strike. The president was not able, however, to settle the dispute between labour and management which closed almost all the nation's steel plants from mid-July until November. The strike was suspended by the Steelworkers union after 116 days when the U.S. Supreme Court upheld a federal district court ruling that the government had the power under the Taft-Hartley act to order strikers back to work for 80 days if a strike imperilled the national health or safety. The two major issues in the strike were an increase

A bungalow at Folly Beach, a seaside resort, wrecked by a hurricane which swept through South Carolina, United States, on Sept. 29.

in pay demanded by the union and a revision of work rules sought by the steel companies. In June the U.S. bureau of labour statistics reported that the average pay in steel mills was $3·11 an hour, which was one of the highest rates of pay in U.S. industry. Work rules included such provisions as the number of men who would be assigned to a given job, authority for men to take rest periods during the day and restrictions on the kind of work that men in certain job classifications could do. Although the issues which led to the steel impasse were not seen by many observers as questions of principle, the employers' spokesmen indicated that they felt the union had usurped too many of management's prerogatives over the years and that the time had come for these to be reasserted.

Under the Taft-Hartley act the 500,000 steelworkers were free to resume their strike on Jan. 16, 1960, but at the end of December a settlement was in view.

In 1959, in spite of the steel strike, the United States had recovered from the effects of the recession which began in 1957 and continued into 1958. In congress, for example, proposals to expand public works programmes and to give greater assistance to persons who were out of work received little support because the economy came out of the recession

A policeman on duty at a junior high school at Arlington, Virginia, U.S., where in 1959 for the first time Negroes were enrolled.

remarkably quickly and with few permanent scars.

Desegregation. One of the most significant domestic events in the United States during 1959 was the final breakdown of Virginia's "massive resistance" to desegregation. In February, which marked the 150th anniversary of the birth of Abraham Lincoln, schools in two Virginia communities, Norfolk and Arlington, were desegregated. In August the four high schools in Little Rock, Arkansas, which had been closed by a desegregation dispute during the 1958-1959 school year, were reopened without incident and without interference from Governor Orval E. Faubus.

The Space Programme. Man's efforts to learn more about space continued in 1959, as did the race between the United States and the U.S.S.R. to see which nation could be the first to push scientific instruments and even men across the frontiers of outer space. The United States continued, however, to lag behind the Soviet Union in the race into space. Although the United States selected seven men to participate in the Project Mercury man-in-space programme and began to put them through rigorous training, the Soviet Union managed to send a rocket around the moon and take a picture of the side of the moon which had never been seen by man and which had never

before been photographed. The picture indicated, as one newspaper headline put it, that the other side of the moon is a rather dull and drab place. By the end of the year it was generally conceded that, however much the United States had accomplished with its space programmes, the Soviet Union still seemed to be in the lead. (Js. D.)

UNITED STATES TERRITORIES AND POSSESSIONS: *see* HAWAII; PACIFIC ISLANDS, U.S.; PUERTO RICO; VIRGIN ISLANDS, U.S.

UNIVERSITIES AND COLLEGES. A feature of 1958-59 was the number of new and projected universities. In Nov. 1958 the Atatürk university at Erzurum in Turkey was formally opened. Built to meet the needs of eastern Turkey, the university is a joint Turkish-U.S. enterprise on the land-grant pattern, with emphasis on agricultural studies. The University of Nebraska is providing initially the teachers and equipment. The university opened with 200 students in two faculties—agriculture, and letters and science. In May 1959 the Turkish Grand National Assembly approved a charter for a Middle East Technical university, aided by the United Nations, which had been in process of formation since 1958. Intended ultimately to have up to 15,000 students, it had in 1959 about 350 in three faculties—architecture, engineering and public administration. Permanent building was expected to begin in 1959 on a site of 11,000 ac. 10 mi. S.W. of Ankara. The university is a Turkish institution, but with international (mainly middle eastern) membership. The teaching language is English. Harold Stassen (United States) was in Oct. 1958 appointed by Unesco as chief adviser.

In Dec. 1958 it was announced that the Jamia Saifiyah, an institute of Arabic studies at Surat, India, was to be expanded and raised to university status. It drew students from many countries in western Asia. Because of pressure on the University of Ceylon a commission was set up in 1958 to study its future development. In 1959 Vidyodaya, the principal Buddhist school in Ceylon, was formally opened as a university.

In Feb. 1959 the working party appointed by the British secretary of state for the colonies to investigate proposals for a university of east Africa recommended that such a university be established at latest by 1966, and that the Royal Technical College of East Africa, at Nairobi, Kenya, be made a university college immediately. By June 1959 the governments of Kenya, Tanganyika and Uganda were discussing a phased programme to implement the working party's report. In Feb. 1959 Queen Elizabeth the Queen Mother formally opened the £150,000 library of the University College of East Africa (Makerere college) at Kampala, Uganda. Among the graduates she received was Josephine Namboze, the first African woman to qualify as a doctor in east Africa. It was reported in 1959 that the Liberian government had given a 50,000-ac. site for a university of west Africa, to be partly financed by U.S. business, and that the U.S. Baptist mission in Lagos intended to build a university in Western Nigeria.

In Nov. 1958 a 287-ac. site 12 mi. S.E. of Melbourne was selected for the Monash university of Victoria. Building was expected to begin in 1959 and the first students to be admitted in 1960. In May 1959 J. A. L. Matheson, professor of engineering at Manchester university, was appointed first vice-chancellor. In 1959 the New Zealand government approved requests from the University of New Zealand for means to enable the Wellington University college to establish a branch college at Palmerston North, and the Auckland University college one at Hamilton. Both branches were expected to open early in 1960, offering to begin with first-year arts subjects only. In June 1959 the Hong Kong government announced its intention to establish a second university in the colony, with Chinese as the teaching language. The

(Left) Nearing completion at the end of 1959, the University of Queensland, Australia, covering an area of 242 ac. (Right) A view of Cripps hall, the new hall of residence at Nottingham university, which was opened in October. To the right stands the clock tower.

university would be built up from three existing post-secondary colleges: Chung Chi, New Asia and United College of Hong Kong. In 1958 the Singapore government decided to grant-aid the independent Nanyang university, established in 1954 for Chinese in Malaya. In July 1959 an academic commission of inquiry published a severely critical report of standards and staffing. In June the £2 million buildings of the Kuala Lumpur division of the University of Malaya were officially opened.

The committee appointed to review future policy for the University College of the West Indies, in Jamaica, recommended in Dec. 1958 that a royal charter be sought to raise the college to university status in 1963. The committee further recommended that the offer of the Imperial College of Tropical Agriculture in Trinidad to become the college's school of agriculture be accepted, and that faculties of engineering (towards which the Trinidad government had given The West Indies $1 million) and of social science be established.

In England local interests advocated the establishment of universities at Norwich, Coventry, Hereford, Cheltenham-Gloucester and in Kent. In Scotland there was demand for a fifth university.

International Co-operation. A conference of Commonwealth ministers held at Montreal in Sept. 1958 decided to establish a new scheme of 1,000 Commonwealth scholarships and fellowships. The United Kingdom offered 500 and Canada 250. To work out details the largest Commonwealth Education conference ever held met at Oxford in July 1959. Representative of all the independent countries of the Commonwealth and 17 colonial territories, it agreed to the scholarship scheme and proposed that an additional £10 million for education be provided by the Commonwealth countries during the next five years.

In Sept. 1958 the Australian minister for external affairs announced that the number of Asian students in Australia under the Colombo plan would be increased by 20% during the current financial year. There were at the time over 6,000 Asian students in Australian universities, a higher proportion than in any European country. The Canadian British Education committee announced in June 1959 that the scheme for admitting British schoolboys and girls into Canadian universities, hitherto restricted to McGill, Toronto and British Columbia, had been joined by 13 other universities. In 1959 Leeds university announced its intention to establish the first professorship in the United Kingdom of American literature, and London university a lectureship. Both posts were to be grant-aided by the U.S. government.

The first African inter-collegiate conference on university work was held at Salisbury, Rhodesia, in Sept. 1958, attended by delegates from Basutoland, the Belgian Congo, Ghana, Kenya, Natal, Nigeria, Sierra Leone and the Federation of Rhodesia and Nyasaland. The subject discussed was teacher training. In Dec. 1958 the Rhodes trustees decided to establish Rhodes scholarships for Ceylon, Ghana, Nigeria, the Caribbean region and the Malayan region. A commission of inquiry of Africans, Americans and British, led by Sir Eric Ashby, vice-chancellor of Belfast university, in May 1959 began a survey of Nigeria's higher education needs.

Gifts. Among large gifts recorded were: $4·5 million (£1,650,000) from the J. W. McConnell foundation to McGill university, Canada, for engineering and science; £1 million (by bequest) from William Stone to Peterhouse college, Cambridge; a further Kr.8 million (£400,000) from Anders Jahre to Oslo university for the Anders Jahre Fund for the Advancement of Science; £300,000 from the Isaac Wolfson foundation to Glasgow university for a men's hall of residence; over £250,000 from the Wellcome trustees to English, Scottish and Australian universities for medical and scientific research; £150,000 from G. A. Vandervell, and £100,000 from J. Cotton, to the Royal College of Surgeons, London, for chairs of pharmacology and biochemistry respectively; $350,000 (£125,000) from the Ford foundation to the university colleges of British East Africa, Ghana, Nigeria and the Federation of Rhodesia and Nyasaland; $340,000 (£120,000) from the U.S. public health service to Montreal university for medical research; £100,000 from Rolls-Royce Ltd. to Nottingham university for a chair in thermodynamics; £100,000 from Joseph Lucas Ltd. to Birmingham university for a hall of residence for engineering students; and £100,000 from Messrs. Abe and Harry Sherman to the Hebrew University of Jerusalem.

Racial Relations. Despite widespread protest, from within the Union of South Africa and outside, the Extension of University Education bill was passed in June 1959. It prohibited the entry of non-white students into the previously multi-racial universities of Cape Town and Witwatersrand, and provided for the creation of separate colleges of higher education for Coloured, Asian, Sotho and Zulu students, which would be under direct government control. In the same month the parliament passed a bill restricting entry into the University College of Fort Hare, previously open to all, to members of the Xosa tribe, affiliating the college to the University of South Africa (in place of Rhodes university, Grahamstown) and placing it under direct government control. In Dec. 1959 Dr. Bernard Chidzero, a Southern Rhodesian African, was held to have forfeited his chance of an appointment to the academic staff of the University College of

Rhodesia and Nyasaland because he had married a white girl. In April 1959, 37 members of the academic staff of the college protested to the prime minister of Southern Rhodesia against the government's Preventive Detention bill. As a result the Salisbury city council and the Nyasaland Tobacco association withheld grants from the college.

Demonstrations and Disputes. In Oct. 1958 the Benaras Hindu university was closed indefinitely because of systematic acts of indiscipline by students. In March 1959 students of Calcutta university caused the intermediate examination in chemistry to be abandoned; they thought the paper too hard. The western German students' association in Oct. 1958 protested against the shortage of accommodation. In November and December French students made widespread demonstrations about shortages of teachers, buildings and amenities. In Jan. 1959 the faculty of commerce of the new University of Libya at Benghazi was closed, the students having complained that some of the lecturers were unqualified and inexperienced. In May students of Zagreb and Skoplje universities in Yugoslavia demonstrated, complaining in particular about their canteen food. In April 1959 200 Iraqi students in Great Britain who had ceased membership of the Iraqi Students' society in the United Kingdom on the grounds that it was Communist-led, and had formed an Iraqi Republican Students' society, were threatened by the Iraq government with loss of their scholarships unless they withdrew from the latter society. Cape Town university students demonstrated in June 1959 against the government's withdrawal of a passport from a coloured student who had been given a three-year scholarship at Oslo university. In April 1959 five Dresden university students were given prison sentences totalling 36 years for alleged sabotage and subversive activities.

Miscellanea. It was announced in March 1959 that the chairman of the new Australian University Grants committee would be Sir Leslie Martin, professor of physics at Melbourne university and the federal government's scientific adviser on defence. In 1959 Delhi university announced that it would substitute Hindi for English as the medium of instruction from 1962. J. S. Fulton, principal of Swansea university college, in Feb. 1959 was appointed principal of the University College of Sussex.

Cambridge University. At the suggestion of the home secretary the university agreed to establish an institute of criminology as a development of the existing department of criminal science. The Isaac Wolfson foundation offered £150,000 for the endowment of the institute, including the establishment of a Wolfson professorship of criminology. Another major benefaction was a grant of £120,000 from the Wellcome trust towards the cost of adding a new wing to the department of biochemistry. On Nov. 6, 1958, Princess Margaret opened the Lensfield chemical laboratories and accepted conferment of the honorary degree of doctor of law. The first lecture-room block for arts faculties on the Sidgwick avenue site was completed in July 1959.

In May 1959 the Regent House voted by 325 votes to 278 that a knowledge of a classical language should no longer be a compulsory requirement for entrance to the university. A syndicate was appointed to review the regulations for the Previous examination and suggest alternative requirements.

It was decided that the university club for members of the graduate staff should be established in the Old Schools and in the building to be vacated by Fitzwilliam House when the latter moved to its new site. A one-year course and examination in the principles of industrial management was introduced, intended mainly for graduates in science and engineering. General approval was given to a proposal for a central university science library, incorporating the philosophical library and the scientific and technological books from the university library.

Professor H. Butterfield, master of Peterhouse, was elected vice-chancellor at the end of the Lord Adrian's term of office on Oct. 1, 1959. Professor N. F. Mott succeeded Sir James Chadwick as master of Gonville and Caius college, the Rev. J. S. Boys Smith succeeded Sir James Wordie as master of St. John's college, and Professor D. L. Page succeeded Dr. E. M. W. Tillyard as master of Jesus college. Sir John Cockcroft was appointed first master of Churchill college. A personal professorship of radio astronomy was established for M. Ryle, and other chairs were filled by the election of P. V. Danckwerts as professor of chemical engineering, Dr. W. A. Lloyd as professor of education, Dr. J. M. Thoday as professor of genetics, Dr. C. F. A. Pantin as professor of zoology, and E. V. Rostow as Pitt professor of American history and institutions for the academic year 1959-60.

In 1958-59 there were 8,824 students in residence, and the government grant amounted to £2,185,500, or about 55% of the university's total income.

London University. The Courtauld Institute galleries in Woburn square were opened in Oct. 1958 by the Earl of Crawford and Balcarres. They house an important collection of French Impressionist paintings presented by Samuel Courtauld and collections presented by Lord Lee, Roger Fry and Sir Robert Witt. The University Computer unit in Gordon square began its work equipped with a Mercury Mark II electronic computer. Sir Leslie Martin presented his outline plan for development of the 35-ac. university precinct between the British Museum and Euston road. University college completed conversion of the former Seamen's hospital, Gordon street, for use by the students' union and the departments of physics and mathematics. Imperial college demolished part of the former Imperial institute buildings to provide a site for college expansion.

The university and the colleges decided to plan residential accommodation for at least 10,000 as against the 3,300 student places in 1959. The Isaac Wolfson foundation agreed to give £250,000 towards a men's international hall of residence in Cartwright gardens, primarily for Commonwealth students. It was decided that Charing Cross Hospital Medical school should be rebuilt at Fulham and the Royal Free Hospital School of Medicine at Hampstead.

Dr. C. F. Harris (St. Bartholomew's Hospital Medical college) succeeded Dr. J. F. Lockwood as vice-chancellor. Four additional members of the Senate were appointed: the director of the School of Oriental and African Studies, the director of the British Postgraduate Medical federation and additional representatives of the registered graduates in engineering and of the faculty of medicine. Sir John Cockcroft was appointed a member of the court. Newly-appointed heads of schools and institutes included: Prof. J. N. D. Anderson (Institute of Advanced Legal Studies), Prof. E. H. J. Gombrich (Warburg institute), Prof. R. B. Lucas (Royal Dental Hospital School of Dental Surgery) and Prof. R. V. Bradlaw (Institute of Dental Surgery).

Prof. R. C. FitzGerald (University college) and Prof. W. K. Matthews (School of Slavonic and East European Studies) died during the year.

The number of full-time and part-time students at grant-receiving schools and institutions of the university was 21,179 (including 5,121 in medicine), and there were a further 4,482 internal students in institutions outside the university having recognized teachers. The number of external students was 24,479 including 2,168 in university colleges overseas in special relation.

The total income for recurrent purposes of the university in 1957-58 was £14,382,581.

Oxford University. The new building for the department of metallurgy was completed and work begun on extensions

HIGHER EDUCATION
(Statistics refer to 1957 unless otherwise stated)

Country	Universities	Other institutions	Students	Teachers
EUROPE				
Austria[1]	4	10	27,296	2,759
Belgium	5	15	30,142[1]	...
Bulgaria	1	19	36,705	3,026
Czechoslovakia[1]	4	36	77,555	8,573
Denmark	2	6	12,991	1,348
Finland[1]	3	11	18,086	1,881
France	17	...	170,000	...
German Dem. Rep.	6	40	66,618	2,764
German Fed. Rep.[2]	18	50	166,071	...
Greece	3	6[3]	18,720[4]	...
Hungary[1]	4	26	32,900	...
Ireland, Rep. of	2	...	8,940	745
Italy	27	12	212,412	19,872
Malta	1[2]	...	283[2]	64
Netherlands	11	...	32,385	1,414[5]
Norway	2	6	6,216	856[6]
Poland	8	68	162,680	17,448
Portugal	4	45	19,161	863[6]
Rumania[1]	4	46	80,919	8,982
Spain	12	15	61,459	4,711
Sweden	5	11	26,106	2,717
Switzerland[1]	7	2	17,625	2,171
United Kingdom[1]	27	528[7]	188,869[7]	26,489
U.S.S.R.[1]	31	732	2,099,600[8]	...
Yugoslavia	5	98[9]	71,852	6,418
ASIA				
Burma[2]	2	4	12,712	...
Ceylon	1	2	4,961	307
China	15	212	292,000	...
India	37	...	720,000[5]	...
Indonesia[10]	6	36	25,387	2,197
Iraq	1	1	5,599	...
Israel[1]	4	...	7,824	1,250
Japan[5]	6	528	629,839	67,024[11]
Korea (South)	...	74	92,087	...
Lebanon[2]	3	7	5,092	...
Malaya, Fed. of[12]	1	2	2,256	181[13]
Pakistan[1]	6	157	84,652	...
Persia	3	5	10,400[14]	...
Philippines[6]	...	...	182,450	4,034
Syria[1]	1	—	7,696	267[10]
Thailand	5	11	28,544[13]	1,425[13]
Turkey[1]	6	—	33,393[15]	2,070[15]
AFRICA				
Algeria	1	...	4,815	244
Egypt	4	16	78,141[16]	2,937[16]
Ghana	1	5	3,126[17]	...
Kenya[18]	—	1	252	64
Morocco[19]	1	7[20]	c. 5,500	...
Nigeria	1	3	1,650	...
Rhodesia and Nyasaland, Fed. of[2]	1	—	125	40
South Africa, Union of	10	...	30,293	2,438[6]
Tunisia	1	6	2,163	...
Uganda[2]	1	...	823	149
NORTH AMERICA				
Canada	32	247	86,500	11,789[6]
Costa Rica	1	...	2,474	319
Guatemala	1	—	4,000[6]	550[6]
Honduras	1	—	900[6]	130[5]
Mexico	20	...	55,277	9,549
Nicaragua	1	—	1,100[6]	105[6]
Panama	1	—	3,027	127
Salvador, El	1	...	1,336[13]	248[13]
United States	...	1,937[2][21]	3,068,000	265,911[19][2]
SOUTH AMERICA				
Argentina[19]	7	126	141,893	4,660
Bolivia	7[1]	—	4,600[23]	245[23]
Brazil	11	377[9]	79,505	11,688
Chile	7	...	21,163[19]	...
Colombia	13	24	15,971	3,259
Ecuador	6	1	5,239[5]	720[5]
Paraguay	1	...	3,484	...
Peru	5	2	16,789[6]	1,720[6][13]
Uruguay	1	...	11,369[24]	...
Venezuela	6	...	9,184[5][25]	1,101[23]
OCEANIA				
Australia	10	...	36,903	3,769[17]
New Zealand[2]	1[26]	—	13,486	840

NOTE. National definitions of universities and other institutions of higher education differ widely.

[1] 1957-58. [2] 1958. [3] Excl. 14 teacher training colleges. [4] Excl. 2,507 student teachers. [5] 1956. [6] 1955. [7] Excl. further education institutions in Scotland and N. Ireland. [8] Incl. those taking correspondence courses. [9] Incl. faculties of the universities. [10] 1955-56. [11] Incl. teacher training staff. [12] With Singapore. [13] At universities only. [14] Tehran university only. [15] Excl. Ataturk universities opened Nov. 1957. [16] Excl. El Azhar Moslem university. [17] Incl. part-time. [18] 1958-59. [19] 1954. [20] Incl. private European but not private Moslem. [21] Incl. approx. 150 universities. [22] Incl. administrative staff. [23] 1953. [24] 1950. [25] Excl. 1 university. [26] Comprising 4 univ. colleges (granted titles of " university " in 1957) and Canterbury (Lincoln) and Massey (Palmerston North) agric. colleges.

to the departments of biochemistry, pharmacology and engineering. The restoration of the south front of the Sheldonian theatre, the most important university building to be restored from the funds of the historic buildings appeal, was completed and work begun on the remainder of the exterior.

University legislation establishing the new St. Catherine's college was approved and A. L. C. Bullock was appointed master-designate. Arne Jacobsen was to be the architect. By the end of December the amount generously contributed to the new college from the University Grants committee, industry and other sources had risen to more than £1·5 million. Legislation was approved making the societies for women students full colleges of the university and the heads of women's colleges eligible for appointment as vice-chancellor. The women's colleges will elect annually in turn a representative who will play a part in university business similar to that of the proctors, though she will not have disciplinary powers. By a narrow majority the university rejected legislation which would have made Latin an optional subject for entry into the university, but a committee was appointed to review entrance requirements.

W. L. Ferrar succeeded N. R. Murphy as principal of Hertford college; the Rev. S. L. Greenslade was to succeed the Rev. C. Jenkins as regius professor of ecclesiastical history; D. Hawkes succeeded H. H. Dubs as professor of Chinese; W. D. M. Paton succeeded J. H. Burn as professor of pharmacology; A. J. Ayer succeeded H. H. Price as Wykeham professor of logic; M. V. Laurie succeeded Sir Harry Champion as professor of forestry; N. Davis succeeded J. R. R. Tolkien as Merton professor of English language and literature; E. L. Stahl succeeded J. Boyd as Taylor professor of German language and literature; D. Donald succeeded A. D. Link as Harmsworth professor of American history; H. A. Thompson succeeded G. W. Beadle as George Eastman professor; a second professorship of experimental physics was established to which D. H. Wilkinson was appointed.

The Earl of Halifax, who had been chancellor of the university since 1933, died on Dec. 23 (see OBITUARIES).

The government grant for 1958-59 was £2,192,002, which was 65·3% of the university's total income. (If the income of the colleges were taken into account, the percentage would be about 36%.) The total number of undergraduates in residence increased from 8,234 in 1957-58 to 8,699 in 1958-59. (See also FURTHER EDUCATION.)

(H. C. D.; R. M. Ry.; J. H. Ps.; F. H. Sd.)

UPPER VOLTA, REPUBLIC OF (RÉPUBLIQUE DE HAUTE-VOLTA), a member state of the French Community. Upper Volta is bounded E. by the Republic of Niger, S. by the Republic of Dahomey, the autonomous Republic of Togo, Ghana and the Republic of Ivory Coast and W. and N. by the Republic of Soudan. Area: 121,892 sq.mi. Pop.: (1951 est.) 3,116,000; (1959 est.) 3,500,000, all Negroes. Language: Mossi and other Negro dialects. Religion: animist, Moslem, Christian minorities. Chief towns (pop., 1957 est.): Ouagadougou (cap., 47,500, incl. 1,600 Europeans); Bobo-Dioulasso (41,700). Prime minister, Maurice Yaméogo. French high commissioner, Paul Masson. Chief exports: groundnuts, livestock. Monetary unit: *franc CFA* = metropolitan Fr.2.

History. The Republic of Upper Volta was established on Dec. 11, 1958, and Maurice Yaméogo became prime minister. The constitution, approved by the territorial assembly on March 1, 1959, was ratified by referendum (793,000 votes as against 214,000). At the election for the first National Assembly, held on April 21, 64 supporters of the Rassemblement Démocratique Africain and 11 members of the Parti Fédéraliste Africain were elected. Upper Volta joined the Sahel-Bénin *entente* (see IVORY COAST). (HU. DE.)

URUGUAY. Republic in southeastern South America, bounded N. by Brazil, S. by Rio de la Plata, E. by the Atlantic ocean and W. by Argentina. Area: 72,152 sq.mi. Pop.: (1958 est.) 2,800,900, mostly of European extraction. Language: Spanish. Religion: mostly Roman Catholic. Capital: Montevideo (pop. 1954 est.) 810,969. Presidents of the governing national council in 1959: Carlos L. Fischer and (from March 1) Martín R. Etchegoyen. Main imports: raw materials (incl. sugar), machinery and parts, fuel and lubricants, motor vehicles. Main exports: wool, meat and products, textiles. Monetary unit: *peso* (25·85 pesos = £1 sterling).

History. The election results of Nov. 30, 1958, had swept the Blancos into office over the opposition party (Colorados). Of the two major groups of the Blanco party, the one headed by 85-year-old Luis Alberto de Herrera and dominated largely by rural voters, obtained a slight margin over the strongly urban group (Unión Blanca Demócrata) and succeeded in electing the entire six-member majority representation on the nine-member national council. However, this majority group soon split into two rival factions. A last-minute truce made it possible to reach agreement on a cabinet composed of a coalition of Herreristas, Ruralistas and members of the urban wing of the party. Although the agreement had been supported by his own followers, Herrera rejected the arrangement and found himself under sharp attack from the Ruralistas, but on April 8 he died.

In the spring of 1959 Uruguay suffered one of the worst disasters in its history. Torrential rains caused the rivers forming the northern and western boundaries to overflow and inundate lands aggregating approximately one-third of the country's area. In addition to heavy loss of life, the country suffered a severe economic blow through the destruction of crops, the loss of livestock and the flooding of the vital hydro-electric plant at Rincón del Bonete.

In addition to strikes, which continued to be troublesome throughout 1959, the chronic problems relating to the distribution of meat persisted. (A. E. TR.)

U.S.S.R.: *see* UNION OF SOVIET SOCIALIST REPUBLICS.

VATICAN CITY STATE. Sovereign state, situated upon the Vatican hill in the city of Rome, established by the Lateran treaty between the Holy See and Italy on Feb. 11, 1929. The pope is the sovereign. Area: 0·5 sq.mi., excluding the papal estate of Castelgandolfo and the basilicas of St. John Lateran, St. Paul-Outside-the-Walls and St. Mary Major which belong to the Vatican City state. Pop.: (1952 census) 1,025. Sovereign: Pope John XXIII.

History. During 1959 Pope John XXIII was more actively the bishop of Rome than any pope since it became the Italian capital. Not only did he summon the first synod for the diocese of Rome for six and a half centuries (*see* ROMAN CATHOLIC CHURCH); he left the territory of the Vatican to visit his diocese, usually on pastoral errands, more than twice as often during his first year as did Pius XII in nearly 20 years of the previous pontificate. His Christmas 1958 visits to the Regina Coeli prison, and to Roman hospitals and orphanages, were followed by many more pastoral visits; he went in procession during Lent to the stational churches of Rome, as no pope had done since the middle ages, and he gave benediction on the feast of Corpus Christi beneath the arch of Constantine. His visit to the North American college for its centenary on Oct. 11, 1959, was one of many to Roman colleges, churches and other ecclesiastical institutions. Another characteristic of the new pontificate, the pope's warm sympathy for non-Catholics, was shown when he revised the liturgy of Good Friday to eliminate a phrase which in the past had been misunderstood and resented by the Jews, and when he revised a prayer recited on the feast of Christ the King to omit phrases which had given offence to both Jews and Moslems.

Four encyclical letters were published during 1959: *Ad Petri cathedram*, " On truth, unity and peace ", on June 29; *Sacerdotii nostri primordia*, to mark the centenary of the death of the *curé* d'Ars, on Aug. 1; *Grata recordatio*, for the recitation of the rosary during the month of October, on Sept. 26; and *Princeps pastorum*, on the foreign missions, on Nov. 28. B. Carlo de Sezze and B. Joaquina de Vedruna de Mas were canonized on April 12; Elena Guerra and Marie Marguerite d'Youville were beatified on April 26 and May 3, respectively, the latter being the first native Canadian to be so honoured.

President Dwight D. Eisenhower, on Dec. 6, 1959, was the 11th head of state to be received by the pope during the year, the others, in the order of their visits, having been those of Persia, Jordan, Italy, Indonesia, Turkey, France, Greece,

Tunisia, Monaco and Denmark. The prime ministers of Canada, Italy and Japan were also received, as were Queen Elizabeth the Queen Mother and Princess Margaret (on April 22).

Cardinal Domenico Tardini became cardinal secretary of state at the beginning of the year, in the most important of several offices left vacant during the later years of Pius XII and now filled. The routine curial audiences *di tabella* were resumed. Cardinal Santiago Luis Copello, formerly archbishop of Buenos Aires, assumed on May 25 the duties of chancellor of the Holy Roman Church. It was announced on Oct. 22 that Cardinal Giuseppe Pizzardo had resigned, at the age of 82, from the position of secretary of the Holy office which he had held since 1951; Cardinal Alfredo Ottaviani, assessor of the Holy office from 1935 to 1953 and pro-secretary since 1953, became secretary, and Archbishop Pietro Parente, archbishop of Perugia, became assessor, a position vacant since 1953. Mgr. Giuseppe Ferretto succeeded Cardinal Alberto di Jorio as secretary of the college of cardinals. On Nov. 16 Cardinal Eugène Tisserant, secretary of the Congregation for the Eastern Church since 1936, resigned, being succeeded by Cardinal Amleto Cicognani, and Cardinal Gaetano Cicognani was succeeded as pro-prefect of the Segnatura by Cardinal Francesco Roberti. Cardinal Paolo Giobbè followed Cardinal Federico Tedeschini as datary. Three cardinals died during 1959: Crisanto Luque, of Bogota (Colombia), on May 7; Georges Grente, of Le Mans (France), on May 9; and Federico Tedeschini, archpriest of St. Peter's and apostolic datary, on Nov. 2. Eight new cardinals were created on Dec. 14: Paolo Marella, Gustavo Testa and Francesco Morano (Italy), Albert Gregory Meyer, archbishop of Chicago, and Aloisius Joseph Muench (U.S.), Arcadio Larraona (Spain), Augustin Bea (German Federal Republic) and William Theodore Heard, the first Scottish-born cardinal since the Reformation.

Substantial increases in pay, dated from July 1, with pension rights, were given to all employed by the Vatican, from curial cardinals to gardeners; the increases were considerably more favourable to the lower-paid lay workers. (*See also* ROMAN CATHOLIC CHURCH.) (M. DK.)

VEGETABLE OILS AND ANIMAL FATS. World production of vegetable oils and animal fats in 1959 was about 5% greater than in 1958, rising to the new record of 28·0 million tons. Increased supplies of edible and technical oils more than offset the decline in " palm " products, while among the animal fats tallow and lard output increased but butter production declined. Some reduction in the output of whale oil also occurred. The 1958-59 world harvests of the main field crops were all larger, but olive oil output in the Mediterranean basin fell by one-tenth and tung oil supplies also declined. The Indian groundnut harvest amounted to a record 4·8 million tons and that in China also increased, but the commercially important Nigerian and French west African crops were both lighter. The world soya bean harvest rose to 27·4 million tons, mainly as the result of a new record crop in the United States, but a heavier Chinese crop was also claimed. There was a marked increase in the important Soviet sunflower seed crop to 4·5 million tons, but floods halved the harvest in Argentina. There were heavier sesame and rapeseed crops in India and China, world output of the two crops being estimated at 1·6 and 3·6 million tons respectively. Both the United States and China harvested larger cottonseed crops, world production being reckoned at 18·5 million tons. Larger crops in Canada and the United States raised the world linseed harvest to 3·6 million tons. Output of copra again declined fairly sharply in 1959 to an estimated 2·8 million tons; palm kernel and palm oil supplies showed little significant change. Most vegetable oil and oilseeds prices rose sharply in the first half of the year and averaged higher than in 1958, quotations for lauric acid oils being particularly high; soya bean and oil prices, however, tended to move downwards. Declining output, especially in Europe, raised world butter prices; but increased production, mainly in the United States, lowered lard and tallow prices.

World exports of oils and fats displayed a marked recovery, heavy movements of soya beans, groundnuts, cottonseed, linseed and their oils, lard and tallow more than offsetting the fall in shipments of copra, palm oil and kernels, butter and whale oil. United States exports of soya beans and oil, cottonseed oil, lard and tallow were all considerably greater, and North American linseed shipments also rose. Linseed oil exports from Argentina increased, but edible oil sales were small. The recovery in Indonesian copra exports and Ceylonese copra and coconut oil shipments was insufficient to compensate for the fall in supplies from the Philippines. Indian oil exports were again small, but Chinese soya bean sales were considerably greater. Malayan coconut oil shipments were reduced, but palm oil and kernel exports again rose. There were increased shipments of Nigerian groundnuts and oil, palm kernels and palm oil, while French west African supplies of these oils and oilseeds were well maintained. Exports of palm kernels and palm oil from the Belgian Congo rose, but palm kernel oil supplies were practically unchanged. Net imports into western Europe rose sharply following a large restocking movement which took place about the middle of the year.

Oil seedcrops of the United States in 1959 totalled 58% above the 1947-49 average, but were low compared with 81% above average in 1958. The cottonseed crop was 6,142,000 tons, 28% more than in 1958; the peanut crop of 1,656 million lb. was down from 1,835·8 million lb. in 1958; the second largest soya bean crop of 528,111,000 bu. was nevertheless 8% below the 1958 record; 21,790,000 bu. of flaxseed (raw material for linseed oil) was little more than a half crop compared with the 39,543,000 bu. in 1958. (J. J. McN.; J. K. R.)

VEGETABLES: *see* Foodstuffs.
VENEREAL DISEASES: *see* Diseases.

VENEZUELA. Federal republic of 20 states, 2 territories, a federal district and island dependencies, on the north coast of South America, bounded W. by Colombia, S. by Brazil and E. by British Guiana. Area: 352,142 sq.mi. Pop.: (1950 census) 5,091,543; (1958 est.) 6,320,000; population mostly *mestizo*, Negro and mulatto. Language: Spanish. Religion: mainly Roman Catholic. Chief towns (1950 census; 1957 est. in brackets): Caracas (cap.) 495,064 (800,000); Maracaibo 235,750 (400,000); Lagunillas 34,928 (190,000); Barquisimeto 105,108 (175,000); Valencia 88,701 (125,000); Maracay 64,535 (100,000). President, Rómulo Betancourt. Main imports: machinery and transportation equipment (35%), metals and manufactures (27%), food, beverages and tobacco (9%), textiles (5%). Main exports: petroleum and products (92%), iron ore (5%). Monetary unit: *bolivar* (Bol. 9·40 = £1 sterling).

History. The provisional government remained in power in 1959, until the inauguration, on Feb. 13, of Rómulo Betancourt, who had been elected constitutional president on Dec. 7, 1958. The new regime began as a coalition. Three parties were given posts in the congress (Acción Democratica, the party of the president, receiving the presidency of the Senate, and the Christian Democratic party the presidency of the Chamber of Deputies), in the state governments (where the two parties just mentioned and the Democratic-Republican union shared the governorships and the various executive posts) and in the national cabinet. An air force general, Josué Lopez Henriquez, was entrusted with the ministry of defence.

The effort of the new regime to dissociate itself from the radical tendencies which the Acción Democratica had revealed in its previous tenure of power (1945-48) was apparent from the outset, both in the public utterances of the president and in his ceaseless endeavour to placate the military leadership,

Police and soldiers in Caracas, Venezuela, form up after dispersing unemployed demonstrators with tear gas on Jan. 31.

which still remembered his advocacy in 1947-48 of a popular militia to replace the armed forces.

The president's main concern was with the left wing of his own party, which expressed loudly its discontent that it should receive so little patronage and even less voice in policy. The Communists, more active in 1959 than in 1958, although shut out of the principal executive posts were vociferous in the congress and dominant in the press, the ministry of education and the university; and the Communist influence in labour unions was considerable.

Venezuela sent a large delegation to the petroleum conference in Cairo in April, when it endeavoured to persuade the middle eastern countries to curtail production and bring about the sale of their oil at higher prices in Europe. Extensive exchange of views took place, but no firm conclusion was reached. Throughout the spring and summer, Venezuela repeatedly protested against the United States law controlling oil imports and assigning quotas, and in the early autumn it asked Washington to be put upon the same special basis as Canada—not subject to quantitative limitation. Revenue from petroleum continued to diminish because of falling prices abroad and declining exports.

Late in the year, the congress reconvened to discuss the draft of a new constitution, and a comprehensive plan for agrarian reform. The latter was not focused upon wholesale expropriation, but rather upon inducement to owners of unproductive land to put it into cultivation. The government would use the extensive national domain, parcelling it out, with long-term credit, and providing for necessary clearing and irrigation. The programme was expected to cost from $200 million to $300 million a year, for ten years; and it was hoped to raise most of the money through the issue of long-term bonds, fully guaranteed by the government.

(C. McG.)

VETERINARY MEDICINE. The main feature of 1959 was the International Veterinary congress held in Madrid with Spain as the host nation. The congress was attended by veterinarians from all over the world and all aspects of veterinary medicine were discussed, including more especially the international control of zoonoses and epizootic disease.

Virus Diseases. Throughout the world, rabies had been recognized as occurring in two epidemiological forms, the sylvatic or campestial type in wild life and the disease as it occurs in domestic dogs, particularly in urban areas. The strains of virus concerned are antigenically identical and it was probably the success of the control of rabies in the dog by vaccination and strict police measures that resulted in the focus of interest being directed to wild life. In the United States it was stated that 20% of human rabies deaths were caused by bites from rabid wild animals. Wild vectors included foxes, skunks, raccoons, mongooses, wolves, jackals, murats and haematophagus and non-haematophagus bats. Small wild rodents were not incriminated as carriers. In some countries egg-passaged chicken embryo vaccines were being used in the mass immunization of cattle. Blue tongue, a virus disease of sheep and cattle, had shown a tendency to spread and, as well as occurring in the eastern Mediterranean, central Africa, the United States and Australia, was reported in Spain and Portugal. The disease might have been introduced by animals harbouring the infection, but the control of the arthropod vector presented difficulties and blue tongue was liable to spread to other European countries. Live attenuated virus was considered the only reliable vaccine for sheep in enzootic areas and it was suggested that research into the control of this and other virus diseases of a similar epidemiology should be co-ordinated on an international level. Scrapie, a nervous disease of sheep due apparently to an ultravisible agent, was successfully transmitted to goats; this species proved a useful animal for experimental studies.

Bacterial Diseases. Staphylococcal mastitis in dairy cattle appeared to be the most prevalent form of mastitis in dairy herds in developed countries; the organism was shown to be present in cowsheds and conventional methods of cleaning teat cups between cows were not adequate in preventing its spread.

It was announced that the eradication of bovine tuberculosis in Britain was nearly completed and the whole country would be declared free in 1960. *Salmonella pullorum,* the bacterium causing bacillary white diarrhoea in chicks and pullorum disease in adult fowls, was incriminated as a cause of infectious arthritis and synovitis in fowls kept under intensive systems of husbandry such as in broiler production. Brucellosis, especially in goats, received much attention and in north Africa particularly trials with *Brucella melitensis* vaccines were under way. *Brucella* infection appeared to be widely distributed in hares in parts of Europe and was considered a source of infection to pigs and possibly sheep.

Protozoal Diseases. A blood parasite, provisionally designated as *Eperythrozoon felis,* was demonstrated in cats in Britain, the infection being associated with anaemia. Toxoplasmosis was diagnosed in sheep in parts of England. Drugfast strains of the various coccidia species affecting poultry were demonstrated and the selective action of various drugs against different species observed.

Parasitic Diseases. The successful development and use on the farm of a live attenuated larval vaccine in the prevention of lungworm infection in cattle stimulated an interest in this method of control and vigorous studies were in progress in regard to other helminth infestations. This was the first time a vaccine had been successfully produced as a prophylactic against a parasitic infestation.

Intense study of liver fluke infestation in sheep and the ecology of the snail intermediate host, resulted in a technique for forecasting outbreaks of fluke which was dependent on such factors as population, weather and temperature.

Non-Infectious Diseases. It was shown in a number of temperate countries that the metal selenium had a sparing effect on vitamin E in cattle and sheep, and its use prevented the development of muscular dystrophy in vitamin-E-deficient animals. Workers in Britain and the United States had shown that early foetal mortality in cattle was associated with the geno-

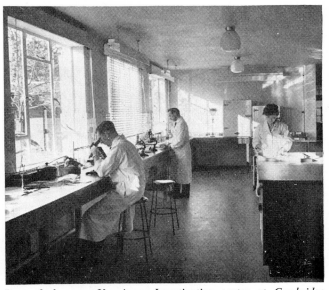

Part of the new Veterinary Investigation centre at Cambridge which was opened by Princess Frederick of Prussia on Oct. 21.

type of the sire and dam. Infertility in cattle was also associated with the fact that the oestrogens in grass might affect the speed of passage of the ovum from the ovary to the uterus, a big factor in successful implantation. (W. R. W.; K. C. S.)

BIBLIOGRAPHY (all 1959). G. C. Ainsworth, and P. K. C. Austwick, *Fungal Diseases of Animals* (Farnham Royal); H. P. Hoskins and others (eds.), *Canine Medicine,* 2nd ed. revised (Santa Barbara); *XVIth Int. vet. Congr. Report,* 2 vols. (Madrid); H. E. Biester and L. H. Schwarte (eds.), *Diseases of Poultry,* 4th ed. (Iowa); Organization for European Economic Co-operation, *Livestock Diseases and the Organization of Veterinary Services in Europe* (Paris); T. G. Hungerford, *Diseases of Livestock,* 4th ed. (Sydney); R. H. Smythe, *Clinical Veterinary Surgery,* vol. 1, *General Principles and Diagnosis* (London).

VIETNAM.

VIETNAM. A country forming the easternmost part of the Indochinese peninsula. Until World War II it was divided into two French colonies and the French protectorate of Annam. After an eight-year war, civil, local and international at the same time, on July 21, 1954, Vietnam was *de facto* divided into two independent republics. Areas and populations are:

	Area (sq.mi.)		Population	
	1943	1959	1943	1959 (est.)
Republic of Vietnam	129,086	65,726	22,612,870	12,000,000
Democratic Republic of Vietnam		63,360		13,000,000

Three-quarters of the total population live on coastal plains; *i.e.,* on 10% of the total territory, the Red River delta (north Vietnam) being among the world's most densely populated areas. In 1943 the population of Vietnam comprised 19,479,000 Vietnamese, 466,000 Chinese, 2,624,000 other national minorities (Thai, Moi, etc.), 39,100 French and 4,770 other foreigners. Religion: Buddhist and a Roman Catholic minority.

REPUBLIC OF VIETNAM. It comprises the former French colony of Cochin-China and the southern part of the Empire of Annam with its old capital Hué. It is bounded N. by the Democratic Republic of Vietnam (along the 17th parallel), W. by Laos, Cambodia and the Gulf of Siam, and S.E. and E. by the South China sea. National minorities: (1956 est.) Chinese 701,000, Cambodian and Laotian 300,300; European 10,700. Chief towns (pop. 1956 est.): Saigon (cap.), incl. the port of Cholon, 1,794,000; Dalat 250,000; Turan 101,000; Hué 90,600. President of the republic and prime minister, Ngo Dinh Diem. Main exports: rubber, rice. Main imports: textiles, machinery, petrol. Monetary unit: *piastre* (VN$98·00 = £1 sterling).

DEMOCRATIC REPUBLIC OF VIETNAM. It comprises the former French colony of Tongking and the northern part of the Empire of Annam. It is bounded N. by China, W. by Laos, S. by the Republic of Vietnam and E. by the South China sea. Chief towns (pop. 1957 est.): Hanoi (cap.) 405,000; Haiphong (chief port) 170,000. President of the republic and chairman of the Lao Dong (Communist) party, Ho Chi Minh; chairman of the executive committee of the National Assembly, Ton Duk Thang; chairman of the council of ministers, Pham Van Dong. Monetary unit: *dong.*

History. *General.* As in the previous four years, no progress was made towards Vietnamese re-unification in 1959. On the other hand, political stability increased in both republics and their economic position improved. At the end of Dec. 1958, Pham Van Dong, prime minister of north Vietnam, sent another note to Ngo Dinh Diem, president of south Vietnam, suggesting negotiations in order to " normalize " the relations between the two republics. Ngo did not reply.

Republic of Vietnam. Five years after the Geneva agreements of July 20, 1954, which ended the Indochinese war, the danger of military aggression from the north had receded, but Communist efforts at subversion in south Vietnam were intensified. These were connected not only with the general

An aged calligrapher in Saigon, south Vietnam, inscribes traditional Chinese scrolls for the lunar new year celebrations.

election to be held in the south, but apparently also with the events in Laos (*q.v.*). By April Communist underground activity was especially apparent in Cochin-China. On July 8 two members of the U.S. Military Assistance Advisory group were killed by a bomb in a U.S. compound at Bienhoa, 20 mi. north-east of Saigon.

The general election of Aug. 30 produced overwhelming support for the policies of President Ngo. The composition of the 123-member National Assembly was as follows: National Revolutionary movement (Ngo's party) 78 seats; Independents 34; Vietnam Socialist party 4; Social Democratic party 3; opposition 4. There were 6,302,000 voters, comprising 86% of the electorate. However, two opposition deputies, both elected in Saigon, were not allowed to take their seats in the assembly because they had been found guilty of " infraction of the electoral law ". They were Phan Quang Dan, who for more than 18 months had tried to obtain permission to register his proposed Democratic party, and Nguyen Tran, an Independent. At a ceremony in Saigon's former opera house, Ngo opened the republic's second National Assembly on Oct. 5. He referred to the ever-present danger of Communist subversion but declared that there was " a general regression of Communist influence in the countries of Asia and Africa".

On May 13, an agreement on war reparations between Japan and south Vietnam was signed in Saigon by the foreign ministers of the two countries, Aiichiro Fujiyama and Vu Van Mau. South Vietnam would receive $39 million in a direct grant and $16·6 million in loans and credits. The whole amount of $55·6 million would be delivered in Japanese goods and services. Carlos P. Garcia, president of the Philippine Republic, paid an official visit to Saigon in April.

On Aug. 3, Prince Norodom Sihanouk, prime minister of Cambodia, conferred with President Ngo in Saigon. Because of the Cambodian policy of neutrality, no formal diplomatic relations existed between Cambodia and south Vietnam, but the meeting of the two leaders was described as ending mutual misunderstandings and creating an atmosphere of goodwill between the two countries.

Democratic Republic of Vietnam. On Jan. 23, 1959, in a letter to the Indian chairman of the International Commission for Supervision and Control in Laos, Pham Van Dong protested against the alleged Laotian " violations " of the north Vietnamese frontier. On Feb. 4, he addressed notes to the Soviet and British governments, whose foreign ministers had been co-chairmen of the 1954 Geneva conference, drawing their attention to the danger of Laos becoming linked with Seato. At the same time north Vietnamese press and broadcasts accused the south Vietnamese government of " persecution of patriots " and of a U.S.-south Vietnamese conspiracy to keep Vietnam divided permanently.

On Feb. 10, in Peking, Ho Chi Minh, president of north Vietnam, and Hoang Van Hoan, a member of the Politburo of the Lao Dong (Communist) party, conferred with Mao Tse-tung, Liu Shao-chi and Chou En-lai. On Feb. 18 an agreement was concluded by which the Chinese People's Republic granted north Vietnam a gift of P.B.$300 million (*c.* £43·5 million) and a loan of P.B.$100 million (*c.* £14·5 million), both for economic development.

In March Ho Chi Minh visited Indonesia. On June 2 he arrived in Moscow. He left the U.S.S.R. on Aug. 1 for another visit to China, where on Aug. 21 he conferred with Chou En-lai before returning to Hanoi. During the year north Vietnam was visited in January by a German delegation led by Otto Grotewohl, prime minister of the German Democratic Republic, and in October by a Polish delegation headed by A. Zawadzki, chairman of the council of state.

The three-year development plan (1958-60) was said to be progressing satisfactorily. It was hoped that by 1960 agricultural production would be 74% greater than in 1957 and that the growth of industrial production during the same period would amount to 85%. The rice crop in 1960 was expected to be 7·6 million tons. The number of pupils in all schools would rise to 1,630,000—an increase of 65% compared with 1957. Between 1955 and 1959 the extraction of coal rose from 600,000 tons to 2 million tons, the generation of electricity from 33 million kwh. to 200 million kwh., the production of cement from 8,000 tons to 370,000 tons and the production of cotton fabrics from 8 million m. to 76 million m. (K. M. S.)

VIRGIN ISLANDS, BRITISH. British colony; a group of 36 islands (11 inhabited) forming part of the Leeward Islands, lying at the eastern extremity of the Greater Antilles in the Caribbean. The colony has in common with the other Leeward Islands governor and (with Windward Islands) Supreme Court, but a separate legislature. (*See* WEST INDIES, THE). Total area: *c.* 59 sq.mi. Total pop.: (1958 est.) 7,600. Population, mainly Negro. Language: English. Religion: Christian. Capital: Road Town (pop. 1,500 [1958 est.]) on Tortola Island. Administration: administrator; executive council; legislative council with elected majority. Administrator, G. P. Allsebrook. Main imports: food, building materials, apparel, cotton piecegoods and non-edible oils. Main exports: livestock, vegetables, fish, fruit and nuts, charcoal. Monetary unit: U.S. dollar ($2·80=£1 sterling).

History. Following the visit of a delegation from the Virgin Islands to London in July 1959 it was announced that when the office of governor of the Leeward Islands was abolished in 1960, the head of the government of the Virgin Islands would be an administrator directly responsible to the secretary of state for the colonies. It was also agreed in London that the executive council of the colony should be increased by the addition of a third member, but this recommendation was not accepted by the legislative council. During 1959 1,232 head of cattle were exported from the colony compared with 1,210 in 1958. (*See also* WEST INDIES, THE.) (X.)

VIRGIN ISLANDS, U.S.

An organized but unincorporated territory of the United States, 40 mi. E. of Puerto Rico. The three largest islands, with a total area of 133 sq.mi. and a total pop. (1950 census) of 26,665, are: St. Croix, pop. 12,103; St. Thomas 13,813; and St. John 749. Pop. (1958 est.): 31,250. Language: mainly English. Religion: Christian. Capital: Charlotte Amalie, on St. Thomas, pop. (1950) 11,469. Governor, John D. Merwin. Monetary unit: *U.S. dollar*.

History. In 1959 the three major islands had 29 state schools, consisting of 7 kindergartens, 12 rural schools, 7 city elementary schools, 1 junior high school and 2 junior-senior high schools. Total enrolment in state schools was 6,466. Total revenue for 1958-59 amounted to $9,826,532.

While much of St. Croix's income is obtained from agriculture, that of St. Thomas derives largely from the manufacture of rum and from handicrafts, tourism, trade and shipping. During the year ending June 30, 1959, tourist income was estimated at $21,738,000. (J. D. MN.)

VITAL STATISTICS.

Births. In all western European countries, except Denmark, the birthrate rose in 1959, judging from information available at the end of the year. However, even the largest increases (in Austria and the German Federal Republic) were less than 1 per thousand population. The birthrates ranged from 14·3 per thousand in Sweden to 23·7 in Portugal. The Swedish rate, though it rose fractionally, was still well below the Danish one of 16·2 which was the next lowest. The four countries with birthrates greater than 20 per thousand were Portugal, Spain, the Netherlands and the Republic of Ireland. In the United Kingdom the number of births in the first half of the year was 457,000. The birth-

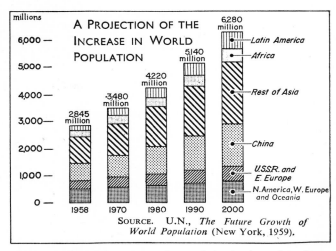

SOURCE. U.N., *The Future Growth of World Population* (New York, 1959).

The projections of the increases in population in the various demographic regions are based on the assumption that trends in fertility and mortality observed in some populations will recur in others.

rate increased for the fourth year in succession and was expected to be 10% higher in 1959 than in 1955, though still much less than the rate just after World War II. In the 1950s there had been no general trend in birthrates in western Europe. In Austria, the German Federal Republic, Spain and the United Kingdom they were rather higher in the early part of 1959 than in 1951; in Finland, France, Portugal and Sweden they were rather lower; and the rest had scarcely changed. In eastern Europe, on the other hand, birthrates were falling, even where they were already low. The only exception was in the German Democratic Republic where there were 16·7 births per thousand population (deducing the 1959 rate from births in the first nine months of the year) compared with 15·6 in 1958. The highest rate was in Poland where it was 26·3 in 1958.

Among the non-European countries of predominantly European stock, the Canadian birthrate was the highest; it had been stable around 28·0 per thousand population from 1951 to 1959. The others had also been level during that period, apart from a remarkable increase in the New Zealand rate, which was 25·2 in 1958 and 27·6 in 1959 (the first half of the year at an annual rate). In the United States there were probably nearly 4·4 million births in 1959; the rate had been between 24 and 25 births per thousand population since 1950.

In most of Asia the birthrates were greater than 30 but Japan was an outstanding exception; the preliminary estimate of the 1959 birthrate was 17·7. In India also the rate was relatively low: 23·9 in 1958. In 1958 birthrates greater than 40 were known to have occurred in several Latin American countries, the islands in the Caribbean and Malaya. The highest, 48·7, was reported in Guatemala.

Marriages. In most industrialized countries marriage rates in 1959 were still showing a slight but steady decline. In the Scandinavian countries it was sharper and the Swedish rate, which even in 1958 was one of the lowest at 6·8, fell to 6·3 in the first six months of 1959. The only western European countries where marriages in the same period indicated a higher annual rate than the average in the years 1951-56 were Greece, Italy and Spain. The Irish marriage rate, 5·3 per thousand population, was again the lowest in western Europe.

Japan still had one of the highest marriage rates in the world; the preliminary estimate of the 1959 rate was 9·2. Several countries in eastern Europe also had more than 9 marriages per thousand population. The marriage rate in the United States was stable at 8·4.

In the United Kingdom 306,000 marriages were registered

TABLE I. BIRTHRATES
(Number of live births per thousand inhabitants)

	1911-13 (average)	1926-30 (average)	1935-39 (average)	1951-56 (average)	1959*
Austria	24·9	17·6	14·8	15·3	17·6
Belgium	22·7	18·6	15·4	16·7	17·3
Czechoslovakia	29·6	23·2	17·1	21·2	16·5
Denmark	26·3	19·4	17·9	17·6	16·2
France	18·1	18·2	15·1	19·0	18·3
German Dem. Rep.	27·0	18·4	19·3	16·4	16·7
German Fed. Rep.	27·0	18·4	19·3	16·1	17·1
Greece	...	30·1	26·8	19·3	19·5
Ireland	22·6	20·1	19·4	21·3	21·2
Italy	31·7	26·8	23·2	18·1	18·1
Netherlands	28·1	23·2	20·3	21·8	21·4
Norway	25·4	18·0	15·1	18·6	18·2
Poland	38·7†	32·3	25·4‡	29·4	...
Portugal	35·3	31·2	27·2	23·7	23·7
Spain	31·2	28·5	22·0	20·5	22·0
Sweden	23·6	15·9	14·5	15·1	14·3
Switzerland	23·8	17·6	15·4	17·2	17·9
United Kingdom	24·3	17·2	15·3	15·8	17·2
Yugoslavia	...	34·2	27·8	27·7	23·4
Canada	...	24·1	20·2	28·0	28·0
Mexico	...	36·7	43·8	45·5	46·9
United States	25·1§	19·7	17·1	24·7	24·2
India‖	38·6	33·3	33·8	24·4	...
Israel	...	34·3¶	27·1¶	31·0	27·0
Japan	34·9	33·5	29·1	21·4	17·7
South Africa (Europeans)	31·9	25·9	24·7	24·8	25·5
Australia	28·0	21·0	17·3	22·8	22·8
New Zealand (excl. Maoris)	26·2	19·7	17·3	24·6	27·6

* Six or nine months, annual rate. † 1909-11. ‡ 1935-38. § 1915. ‖ Incl. Pakistan until 1939 and Burma until 1930. ¶ Jewish population of Palestine.
SOURCE. League of Nations *Statistical Yearbooks*; U.N. *Demographic Yearbooks*; U.N. *Monthly Statistical Bulletin*.

TABLE II. MARRIAGE RATES
(Number of marriages per thousand inhabitants)

	1925-29 (average)	1935-39 (average)	1940-44 (average)	1951-56 (average)	1959*
Austria . .	7·5	10·3	8·2	8·2	7·9
Belgium . .	9·2	7·4	6·0	7·8	7·2
Czechoslovakia .	9·3	8·5	8·5	8·5	7·4
Denmark . .	7·6	9·2	9·2	8·1	6·9
France . .	8·3	6·7	5·6	7·2	6·9
German Dem. Rep. ⎫ German Fed. Rep. ⎭	8·5	9·7	7·7†	⎧ 9·1 ⎨ 9·3 ⎩	9·2 9·0
Greece . .	7·4	6·4	...	7·6	7·9
Ireland . .	4·6	5·0	5·5	5·5	5·3
Italy . .	7·4	7·5	5·8	7·3	7·7
Netherlands .	7·6	7·9	7·5	8·4	7·7
Norway . .	5·9	8·0	8·4	7·9	6·5
Poland . .	8·9	8·2‡	...	10·0	...
Portugal . .	6·9	6·5	7·1	7·9	7·9
Spain . .	7·2	5·5	7·3	8·0	8·2
Sweden . .	6·5	8·9	9·6	7·4	6·3
Switzerland .	7·4	7·3	8·2	7·9	7·7
United Kingdom .	7·5	8·9	8·7	7·9	7·4
Yugoslavia . .	9·4	7·7	...	9·8	9·0
Canada . .	7·3	7·9	10·0	8·6	7·5
Mexico . .	4·7	6·8	7·4	6·9	6·7
United States .	10·1	10·7	12·1	9·7	8·4
Japan . .	8·1	8·1	9·8†	8·0	9·2
Israel . .	8·0§‖	12·2‖	12·0‖	9·6	7·9
Australia . .	7·8	8·8	10·5	8·2	7·6
New Zealand .	7·7§	9·5	8·8	8·4	7·9

* Six or nine months, annual rate. † 1940-43. ‡ 1935-38. § 1926-30. ‖ Jewish population of Palestine.
SOURCE. League of Nations *Statistical Yearbooks*; U.N. *Demographic Yearbooks*; U.N. *Monthly Statistical Bulletin*.

TABLE III. DIVORCE RATES
(Number granted per 1,000 population)

	1937-39 (average)	1947-49 (average)	1953	1956	1957
Austria . .	0·52	1·94	1·35	1·22	1·17
Belgium . .	0·40	0·76	0·47	0·48	0·54
Czechoslovakia .	0·54	0·93	0·89	1·10	1·07
Denmark . .	0·92	1·67	1·49	1·46	...
England and Wales	0·15	1·04	0·67	0·59	0·52
Finland . .	0·44	1·09	0·83	0·85	0·81*
France . .	0·57	1·17	0·70	0·68	0·66
German Dem. Rep. ⎫ German Fed. Rep. ⎭	0·77	⎧ 2·05 ⎨ 1·77 ⎩	1·61 0·97	1·25 0·81	1·25 0·81
Netherlands .	0·38	0·81	0·52	0·51	0·48
Norway . .	0·39	0·70	0·62	0·60	0·58
Portugal . .	0·11	0·13	0·12	0·11	0·09
Scotland . .	0·16	0·45	0·45	0·36	0·33
Sweden . .	0·54	1·04	1·17	1·18	1·23
Switzerland .	0·78	0·93	0·90	0·85	0·89
Yugoslavia . .	0·38	1·31	0·94	1·09	1·10
Canada . .	0·18	0·55	0·41	0·37	0·40
Mexico . .	0·23	0·31	0·32	0·41	0·30
United States* .	1·91	2·94	2·46	2·28	2·22
Japan . .	0·64	1·01	0·87	0·80	0·78
South Africa (Europeans)	0·87	1·48	1·41	1·34	1·32
Australia . .	0·44	0·97	0·90	0·68	0·65
New Zealand† .	0·66*	1·11	0·75	0·66	0·62

* Including annulments. † Prior to 1949, excl. Maoris.
SOURCE. U.N. *Demographic Yearbook 1958*.

TABLE IV. MARRIAGES AND DIVORCES IN ENGLAND AND WALES

	Marriages	Decrees Absolute		Marriages	Decrees Absolute
1937 .	359,160	4,886	1951 .	360,624	28,767
1938 .	361,768	6,250	1952 .	349,308	33,922
1939 .	439,694	8,254	1953 .	344,998	30,326
1940-44*	365,640	8,813	1954 .	341,731	28,027
1946 .	385,606	29,829	1955 .	357,918	26,816
1947 .	401,210	60,254	1956 .	352,944	26,265
1948 .	396,891	43,698	1957 .	346,903	23,785
1949 .	375,041	34,856	1958 .	339,913	22,654
1950 .	358,490	30,870	1959† .	267,633	...

* Average. † First nine months.
SOURCE. *Annual Abstracts of Statistics*; Registrar-General's Quarterly Returns, England and Wales; *Civil Judicial Statistics 1958*.

in the first nine months of 1959, 4,000 less than in the same period in 1958. The marked tendency to marry younger continued. The number of divorces in Great Britain con-

tinued to fall; in 1957 25,508 were granted, in 1958 24,413. The rate relative to the population was less than one quarter of that in the United States, and was one of the lowest in Europe.

Deaths. Western European deathrates (except the Swedish and Italian ones) in the first half of 1959 were slightly above the 1958 level. In five countries the rates were considerably higher than the average for 1951-56: Austria, Denmark, the German Federal Republic, Norway and the United Kingdom. In the latter there had been 460,000 deaths by the end of September, so the annual rate would probably be 12·0 per thousand population; it had not been as high as that since 1951. The highest deathrates in Europe in the first half of 1959 were in the German Democratic Republic (13·0), Austria (12·6) and the Republic of Ireland (12·5). The lowest ones were those in Greece (7·3) and the Netherlands (7·6). Bulgaria, Poland and Rumania also had deathrates less than 9 per thousand population in 1958 but no statistics were available for 1959. The deathrate among the population of Israel was one of the lowest in the world though it increased in 1959. In Syria it was even lower: 5·6 in 1958. The variation in deathrates reflected the different age distribution of

TABLE V. DEATHRATES
(Number of deaths per thousand inhabitants)

	1911-13 (average)	1926-30 (average)	1935-39 (average)	1951-56 (average)	1959*
Austria . .	18·8	14·4	14·0	12·2	12·6
Belgium . .	15·3	13·7	13·1	12·2	12·0
Czechoslovakia .	20·4	15·3	13·2	10·4	9·5
Denmark . .	13·0	11·1	10·6	8·9	9·5
France . .	19·0	16·8	15·3	12·6	11·5
German Dem. Rep. ⎫ German Fed. Rep. ⎭	14·8	11·8	11·8	⎧ 11·9 ⎨ 10·9 ⎩	13·0 11·0
Greece . .	...	16·6	14·5	7·2	7·3
Ireland . .	16·4	14·4	14·3	12·4	12·5
Italy . .	19·3	16·0	13·9	9·9	9·0
Netherlands .	13·1	9·9	8·7	7·6	7·6
Norway . .	13·3	11·0	10·3	8·5	9·0
Poland . .	22·4†	16·8	14·0‡	10·4	...
Portugal . .	20·7	18·4	16·0	11·6	10·7
Spain . .	22·2	17·9	17·9	9·9	9·3
Sweden . .	13·9	12·1	11·7	9·7	9·4
Switzerland .	14·8	12·1	11·6	10·2	9·5
United Kingdom .	14·2	12·3	12·2	11·7	12·0
Yugoslavia . .	...	20·0	15·9	12·0	9·6
Canada . .	...	11·1	9·7	8·5	8·0
Mexico . .	...	25·6	23·4	14·5	12·2
United States .	14·1	11·8	11·0	9·5	9·4
India§ . .	29·9	24·3	22·6	12·7	11·2
Israel . .	...	11·7‖	8·2‖	6·7	6·4
Japan . .	20·7	19·3	17·3	8·6	7·5
South Africa (Europeans)	10·3	9·7	9·8	8·5	8·5
Australia . .	10·9	9·3	9·6	9·2	8·8
New Zealand (excl. Maoris) .	9·2	8·6	9·0	9·2	9·2

* Six or nine months, annual rate. † 1909-11. ‡ 1935-38. § Incl. Pakistan up to 1939 and Burma up to 1930. ‖ Jewish population of Palestine.
SOURCE. League of Nations *Statistical Yearbooks*; U.N. *Demographic Yearbooks*; U.N. *Monthly Statistical Bulletin*.

populations—for instance, Greece, India and Japan had a relatively small number of old people—rather than differences in the current expectation of life of the inhabitants of a country.

Infant Mortality. Although the decline in infant mortality continued in 1958, it was much less steep. This was because in many countries there were already few deaths of babies aged one week to one year and mortality among those less than a week old was more difficult to prevent. In England and Wales it had scarcely been reduced since 1948 and accounted for 10,214 of the 16,685 infant deaths in 1958. There were also 16,309 stillbirths. The country with the lowest infant mortality rate—16 per thousand live births— was Sweden. In Iceland and the Netherlands it was 17. Rates in Czechoslovakia and the German Federal Republic had shown the most spectacular falls; they had both been in the

TABLE VI. INFANT MORTALITY

(Deaths under one year per thousand live births)

	1921-25 (average)	1938	1947	1957	1958
Austria	136*	80	78	44	41
Belgium	100	81	69	35	31
Czechoslovakia	156	110	89	34	30
Denmark	82	59	40	23	23
Finland	96	68	58	28	24
France	95	71	71	33	32
Germany	122	59	84	36†	39†
Greece	86	99	42‡	44	42
Hungary	187	131	107	63	58
Ireland	70	67	68	33	35
Italy	126	106	84	50	48
Netherlands	69	37	34	17	17
Norway	52	37	35	20	...
Portugal	146	137	107	88	86
Spain	143	124	76	48	42
Sweden	60	42	25	17	16
Switzerland	65	43	39	23	22
United Kingdom	78	55	44	24	23
Yugoslavia	151§	140	102‡	102	87
Argentina	116	105	78	66	...
Chile	265	213	145	118	123
Canada	98	64	46	31	30
Mexico	223*	128	95	79	80
United States	74	51	32	26	27
Israel	126‖	59‖	30	33	31
Japan	159	115	77	40	36
South Africa (Europeans)	73	52	34	29	...
Australia	58	38	29	21	21
New Zealand	43¶	50	30	24	23

* 1922-25. † German Federal Republic. ‡ 1949. § 1926-29. ‖ Jewish population of Palestine. ¶ Excl. Maoris.
SOURCE. U.N. *Demographic Yearbooks*; W.H.O. *Epidemiological and Vital Statistics Report*, vol. xii, no. 9.

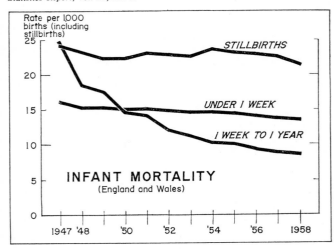

INFANT MORTALITY
(England and Wales)

80s in 1947 and were 30 and 39 respectively in 1958. Several African and South American countries had rates well over 100, as did Indonesia, where the official estimate was 150. Nearly all of these, however, had been falling year by year. (*See* also IMMIGRATION AND EMIGRATION.) (E. I. U.)

BIBLIOGRAPHY. United Nations, *The Future Growth of World Population* (New York, 1959); R. L. Meier, *Modern Science and the Human Fertility Problem* (London, 1959); Bernard Okun, *Trends in Birth Rates in the United States since 1870* (London, 1958); George W. Barclay, *Techniques of Population Analysis* (London, 1959); P. C. Bansil, *India's Food Resources and Population* (Bombay 1959).

WAGES AND HOURS.

Recovery from the world recession of 1958 was reflected in the statistics available of hours worked and wages paid in 1959. The statistics available, however, tended to relate only to the more developed countries and were best for manufacturing industries. In most countries the average number of hours worked per week in June 1959 was rather higher than a year earlier, but was rarely back to the level of June 1957. In Japan, however, the reduction in hours worked had been slight and the recovery marked so

that in June 1959 the average working week was 1·25% longer than in June 1957. In the United States, too, the average working week was longer, by about 1·75%, than two years previously. Here the recovery was certainly exaggerated by expectation of the steel strike. In Canada there had been no reduction in the number of hours worked in 1958 but there was a slight reduction in 1959.

In Canada and the United States the average working week of between 40 hours and 41 hours was still markedly shorter than elsewhere. Japan was at the other extreme with an average of 51·6 hours in June 1959. This was more than 25% longer than in North America and about 15% longer than the typical 45 hours elsewhere.

Hourly money earnings also tended to rise in 1959, but in most countries at a slightly lower rate than in the previous year. However, with a tendency for the cost of living to be stable, the real value of hourly earnings may have risen slightly more than in 1958. The most typical increase in hourly money earnings was about 3% (as in Australia, Canada, Norway, Sweden and the United Kingdom). In France, the German Federal Republic, the United States and Finland the increase was about 5%. In France, nevertheless, this represented a marked degree of stabilization in earnings.

Table II gives figures of hours worked and weekly earnings in a selection of British and U.S. industries. In British industry the changes in the average number of hours worked per week were mainly negligible, but there was an average increase of half-an-hour in the textile and clothing industries. In marked contrast there were increases averaging between three hours and five hours per week in such industries as the U.S. coal, primary metal, automobile and textile industries. In each country the changes approximately compensated changes in the opposite direction the year before. However, the depression and recovery had not influenced in either direction the average number of hours worked in food industries, gas and electricity, bus concerns or retail establishments.

The greater volatility of the U.S. economy in 1957-59 is illustrated to an even more marked extent by weekly earnings. Earnings in most U.K. industries in April 1959 were some 3% or 4% higher than a year earlier, although there was a 5% increase in the vehicles industry, one of 7% for dock workers and, very exceptionally, a reduction of 3% for coal miners. In the United States typical increases were between 3% and 6% with outstanding increases of 22% in metal industries, 16% in automobiles and 15% in textiles.

Output per man per year in U.K. manufacturing industry, which had remained stable in 1957 and 1958, started to rise in 1959 and in the second and third quarters was about 6% higher than in 1958. However, the depression had restrained wage claims after increases of typically 4% to 4·5% late in 1958 and wage rates remained almost unchanged throughout most of 1959. Indeed, the only real upheaval in the labour market was the printing strike. Towards the end of the year the marked recovery in industrial activity, the boom in ordinary shares and the return of the Conservative government augmented the claims for increased wages, which were now being supplemented by claims for shorter recognized working weeks. Though the trade unions could no longer claim increases because of the rising cost of living they had, nevertheless, become accustomed to increases roughly every 15 months and the need for some concessions was becoming urgent. Towards the end of the year agreements were reached to reduce hours of work from 44 to 42 per week without loss of pay for chemical workers and workers in the electricity supply industry, to operate from dates early in 1960. Farm workers' wages were to be increased by 4s. a week and their recognized working week reduced from 47 hours to 46 hours as from Feb. 1960. Decisions were still being awaited by the

TABLE I. AVERAGE WEEKLY HOURS AND HOURLY EARNINGS, MANUFACTURING, CERTAIN COUNTRIES

Weekly Hours		Month	1958	1959
United States	. . .	June	39·2	40·7
United Kingdom	. . .	April	45·5	45·7
Men only	. . .	April	47·6	47·6
Women only	. . .	April	41·2	41·5
Canada	. . .	June	40·7	41·0
Finland	. . .	June	41·7	43·0
France	. . .	June	45·2	45·2
German Fed. Rep.	. .	June	45·7	46·0
Japan	. . . .	June	50·6	51·6
Switzerland	. .	June	46·9	46·6
Hourly Earnings	*Month*	*Unit*	*1958*	*1959*
United States	June	Dollar	2·12	2·24
United Kingdom	April	Pence	55·9	57·9
Men only	April	Pence	65·9	68·5
Women only	April	Pence	38·3	39·8
Australia (Men only)	June	Pence	95·5	99
Canada	June	Dollar	1·67	1·73
Finland (Men only)	2nd Qtr.	Markka	218	229
France	June	Franc	185·8	195·1
German Fed. Rep.	May	D. Mark	2·28	2·39
Norway (Men only)	2nd Qtr.	Krone	5·86	6·35
Sweden	May	Krona	4·83	5·06

SOURCE. U.N. *Monthly Bulletin of Statistics.*

TABLE II. AVERAGE WEEKLY HOURS AND EARNINGS IN CERTAIN INDUSTRIES, UNITED KINGDOM AND UNITED STATES

	April 1958			April 1959		
	Hours	Earnings		Hours	Earnings	
	No.	s.	d.	No.	s.	d.
United Kingdom						
Coal mining (Men only)	...	324	3	...	312	6
Metal manufacture	46·4	261	10	46·0	270	2
Engineering	46·8	229	3	46·6	237	4
Vehicles	46·3	251	7	46·6	264	10
Chemicals	46·7	223	7	46·6	233	1
Textiles	43·6	166	10	44·3	174	0
Clothing	40·9	143	3	41·4	148	1
Food, drink and tobacco	46·5	186	8	46·3	192	6
Paper and printing	45·3	228	0	45·5	235	3
Laundries	43·1	131	5	43·0	134	7
Building and contracting	49·1	234	11	48·9	241	10
Gas, electricity and water	48·2	226	11	48·2	237	10
Bus and train services	48·8	220	10	48·9	228	9
Dock workers	...	271	11	...	291	0
United States	No.	$		No.	$	
Coal mining (bituminous)	30·0	90·60		35·2	114·75	
Primary metal industries	36·9	95·20		41·2	116·60	
Electrical machinery	39·0	83·46		40·2	88·84	
Automobiles	38·4	96·00		41·7	111·34	
Chemicals	40·7	92·39		41·6	98·18	
Textiles	36·6	54·90		40·3	63·27	
Apparel	34·5	51·75		36·6	55·63	
Food and beverages	39·7	79·80		40·2	84·42	
Printing and publishing	37·7	96·14		38·1	102·11	
Laundries	39·2	44·30		39·9	46·28	
Construction	36·2	107·88		37·0	113·59	
Gas and electricity	40·8	99·55		40·7	103·79	
Bus lines, local railways	42·7	90·10		42·9	93·95	
Retail trade	37·8	63·50		37·9	66·33	

SOURCE. U.K. Ministry of Labour *Gazette*; U.S. *Survey of Current Business.*

engineering, shipbuilding, railway and road transport workers.

One very striking break with tradition related to building workers. These had become used to annual wage increases granted in two parts, first an automatic increase in February according to a sliding scale linked with the retail price index and then a further increase negotiated later in the year. In 1959 they had their automatic increase of 1*d.* per hour (about 2%) in February but no supplement. (The supplements had been 2½*d.* per hour in 1956, 1½*d.* per hour in 1957 and 1*d.* per hour in 1958.) Further, in 1960, with stable retail prices, there would be no automatic increase for them in February, although they were claiming much as usual a negotiated 4*d.* per hour. (*See also* COST OF LIVING; PRICES; WEALTH AND INCOME, DISTRIBUTION OF.) (H. S. B.)

WALES. Principality forming part of Great Britain. Area (incl. Monmouthshire) 8,016 sq.mi. Pop.: (1951 census) 2,598,675.

Chief towns (pop. 1951): Cardiff (cap.) 243,632; Swansea 160,832; Rhondda 111,357; Newport (Mon.) 105,285. For language and religions *see* GREAT BRITAIN AND NORTHERN IRELAND, UNITED KINGDOM OF. Minister for Welsh affairs, Henry Brooke (also U.K. minister of housing and local government); minister of state for Welsh affairs, Lord Brecon. Main Welsh contributions to U.K. economy: steel, tinplate, coal, port and dock facilities.

History. *Government.* At the general election Wales and Monmouthshire returned 7 Conservatives, 27 Labour and 2 Liberal M.P.s. The majority of the south Wales constituencies returned Labour representatives, four seats only going to the Conservatives. The two mid-Wales counties of Cardigan and Montgomery returned Liberals. In the north, Anglesey, west Caernarvon and Merioneth chose Labour members, as did the industrial east, but the central areas of east Caernarvon, west Denbigh and west Flint returned Conservatives.

Employment. At the end of 1958 adverse changes in employment outweighed favourable ones, but the picture for 1959 was more encouraging. Redundancy in the tinplate industry accounted for much of the fall in the labour force. At the beginning of 1959 approximately 9,000 men had been discharged from hand tinplate and steel works. Unemployment went up sharply in western south Wales, and was highest in northwest Wales, but in south Pembroke improvement was shown at the beginning of the year as developments around Milford Haven took shape. The percentage of unemployment continued at almost twice the rate for the United Kingdom. In January it stood at 4·1%, compared with 2·4% for the United Kingdom as a whole; at the end of October it was 3·4% compared with 1·9%.

Iron and Steel. In 1959 Wales produced about 30% of the United Kingdom output of crude steel and made virtually all the tinplate. The construction of the new strip mill at Newport meant that the plant would ultimately have a capacity of 3 million ingot tons of steel per annum.

Fuel and Power. The decrease in coal consumption by industry was further felt in the Welsh coalfields and gradually extending restrictions were put upon coal output. The Coal board announced the closure in 1959 of six of the less productive pits in south Wales. On Jan. 1, 1959, industrial consumption was 77% of the consumption on Jan. 1, 1958. The gas industry made increased use of coke, oven gas and methane.

The use of electricity in south Wales in the ten years 1949 to 1959 had more than doubled. Figures showed 200,000 more consumers, 5,000 mi. of new mains and £35 million spent on extending and strengthening the distribution system. The construction of access roads and of the dams for the nuclear power station at Trawsfynydd were well under way. Good progress was made on the Festiniog pumped storage scheme. In both undertakings local labour was employed as far as possible.

Work continued satisfactorily at the new deepwater terminal for large tankers of the British Petroleum company at Pepton point, Milford Haven, and also on the Esso refinery there.

Ports. The British Transport commission's development scheme designed to increase efficiency in cargo handling in the main south Wales ports at Newport, Barry, Swansea and Port Talbot progressed well. Electrification schemes at Cardiff and Swansea docks were well advanced, and publicity was given to the facilities which the ports had to offer industrialists in England.

Agriculture. It was the government's policy to devolve to Wales as large a share of responsibility for agricultural administration as possible. The trend towards decentralization meant that decisions affecting Welsh farmers were taken in Wales. It was announced on Oct. 1 that the eradication of bovine tuberculosis from all cattle herds in the principality

Miners leaving Aberbaiden colliery, south Wales, for the last time on Jan. 31 when, with six other Welsh mines, it closed down.

had been achieved and that Wales and Monmouthshire had been declared an attested area. The Ministry of Agriculture had under consideration the recommendation of the Seaborne Davies committee that a national agricultural college for Wales be established in Aberystwyth for the provision of diploma courses in agriculture and dairying. The National Farmers' union had recognized that the government's policy of integrating forestry with agriculture should be implemented. In the past relations between the Forestry commission and farming interests in Wales had not been easy. The commission had said that it would not take the best farming land, and wanted to avoid compulsion.

Health. Outstanding success had been achieved in the treatment of tuberculosis. Deaths had fallen from 1,607 in 1948 to fewer than 350 in 1959, and the number of beds reduced from 3,020 to 2,489. Improvement was attributed to more effective chemotherapy, widespread early detection by mass radiography examination and prompt isolation and treatment. The gradual elimination of bovine infection had also played its part.

Education. At the beginning of 1959 approximately 114,000 new school places had been provided in Wales by the post-war educational building programmes. Some 250 new schools or departments had been built.

Included in the grant-in-aid to the National Museum of Wales for 1958-59 was the first provision for the staffing and running of a department of industry described as " a science museum for Wales ".

General. On June 19 a meeting was held in Cardiff to celebrate the publication by the Honourable Society of Cymmrodorion of the *Dictionary of Welsh Biography*. Lord Justice Morris, himself one of the nine Welshmen judges, addressed the assembly.

The year marked the centenary of the birth of T. E. (Tom) Ellis, the Welsh parliamentarian.   (E. H. R.)

WATER SUPPLY. The spring and summer of 1959 were exceptionally dry and very many waterworks authorities were concerned about the reliability of their sources in meeting the extraordinary high demands which they experienced. For example, on July 8 the Metropolitan Water board pumped

into supply the record quantity of 468 m.g. (million gallons), equivalent to more than 20% above the normal demand at that time of the year. This quantity may be compared with the average consumption of 334 m.g.d. (million gallons per day) for 1958. In numerous towns restrictions on the use of water for gardens and car-washing were introduced, and many authorities imposed rationing and shut off supplies during the night. During the five months from May to September the average rainfall over England and Wales was the lowest ever recorded and only a little over 50% of the long term average. In many areas the drought did not break until October.

Reports of two subcommittees of the Central Advisory Water committee set up in 1955 were published in 1959 dealing with *The Growing Demand for Water* and *Information on Water Resources*. In the first report the conclusion was reached that there was sufficient rainfall in England and Wales to ensure an adequate supply of water provided that the proper means of conservation and distribution were developed. The committee expressed the opinion that in the more distant future there need be no shortage of water in any part of England and Wales provided that development schemes were prepared well in advance of demand; that the necessary statutory powers were granted; that capital expenditure was permitted; and that the location of industries which require large quantities of water would be regulated with the water supply situation in mind. The future requisite scale of investment by water supply undertakers was estimated to be greater than £35 million per annum to keep pace with the increasing demand, bearing in mind that new sources would be more difficult and costly to develop and that water would have to be carried for longer distances. The report referred to the demand likely to be brought about by agricultural irrigation, and the committee were investigating this subject further. They were also asked to consider and report on the extent of uncontrolled abstractions of surface water and the possible need for controlling them. In the second report it was considered that

The parched bed of Burrator reservoir, which normally supplies Plymouth with 9 million gallons of water daily, in September.

there was a need for further investigation into hydrological relationships and that more co-ordination of this work was desirable. The committee recommended a more frequent investigation of rainfall stations, the more accurate recording of snowfall, the further recording of data in connection with ground water and advocated that vigorous action be taken to increase the number of river-gauging stations.

The policy of regrouping water authorities into fewer but larger units was continued and several private parliamentary bills and water orders were promoted during the year. It was estimated that at the beginning of 1959 the number of undertakings in England and Wales stood at 970 and, of these,

A Lancashire farmer empties water carried two miles in milk churns into his well, which had dried up during the rainless summer.

about 340 were concerned in various stages of the preparation of orders by agreement, or had already committed themselves to regrouping, and another 380 were engaged in discussions.

Among the larger schemes where construction had commenced or was about to be put in hand were the Tryweryn reservoir project for Liverpool, estimated to cost about £20 million; the Balderhead reservoir and other works for the Tees Valley and Cleveland Water board at a cost of some £8 million; and the Derwent reservoir for the joint use of the Sunderland Water company and the Durham County Water board. Birmingham and the South Staffordshire Water company were both considering abstraction schemes for taking large quantities of water from the River Severn and Bedford brought into commission a scheme for obtaining up to 9 m.g.d. from the Great Ouse. The establishment of the nuclear power station at Chapelcross and the resultant need to meet additional demands for water in that area caused the Dumfriesshire County council to advance by several years the construction of the Black Esk reservoir scheme.

Through its Department of Scientific and Industrial Research the government decided to give financial aid to the Water Research association and, as a result, the association was establishing new laboratories on the Thames in Buckinghamshire. There it was proposed to augment its research programme by the addition of filtration studies, investigations on the disposal and reclamation of sludge, methods of biological and chemical analysis, and methods of control of algal growth. It was also proposed to pursue some of the hydrological interests of the industry. Other bodies actively engaged in conducting research into various aspects of hydrological engineering were the British Hydromechanics Research association and the Water Pollution Research board.

A continuous watch was kept on discharges of radioactive waste both by the Atomic Energy authority and by other users of radioactive materials and, as part of the national monitoring programme of radioactive fallout from nuclear weapon tests, arrangements were made with the water undertakers concerned for samples from selected sources of drinking water to be analysed. The first results indicated that the levels of activity were well within safe limits and, in particular, that the amount of strontium-90 taken up from water was only a small fraction of the amount ingested from all sources. In Feb. 1959 a report was published by H.M.S.O. entitled *A Preliminary Survey of Radiostrontium and Radiocaesium in Drinking Water in the United Kingdom*.

Commonwealth. The discovery and development of underground water resources in the Bornu area of Northern Nigeria

ranked as one of the most important events in the history of the area. More than 50 boreholes were sunk by the Ministry of Works but it was not possible to predict whether artesian water would be found in all of them. The work was going ahead rapidly to provide water in an area where owing to the acute shortage of water the population was sparse. The Wemmershoek reservoir scheme for Cape Town was inaugurated in Dec. 1958 thus providing additional storage of some 13,000 m.g. This scheme would make available a supply of over 30 m.g.d. for urban purposes and also substantial amounts of compensation water for irrigation. It was expected that at the present rate of expansion Cape Town and the adjoining local authorities would be adequately supplied with water for about the next 30 years. The National Chemical Research laboratory at Pretoria conducted experiments with a small unit to desalt brackish water available from small farms and it was hoped to produce water at 10s. per 1,000 gal.

New water schemes were to be provided for the towns of Accra and Takoradi in Ghana following recent acute shortages. For Accra a dam was to be built on the Kuia river and for Takoradi water was to be conveyed from the Prah river to a reservoir at Inchaban. A new reservoir some 36 mi. from Salisbury, Rhodesia, was decided upon to increase the water resources of that town and to meet a consumption which had been doubling itself every four years.

Under the National Water Supply and Sanitation programme of the Ministry of Health some 275 urban and 206 rural schemes were under construction in India at an estimated cost of more than £6 million. Provision of more than £38 million was made in state plans for further schemes under the second five-year plan.

The completion of large schemes in Malta enabled the island to experience a summer entirely free of water restriction. Galleries and shafts in the limestone near the middle of the island produced 2 m.g.d., and a small concrete dam was constructed to ensure that the water would be retained and allowed to percolate to the collecting works.

Netherlands Antilles. The largest saltwater conversion plant in the world was placed in service on the Caribbean island of Aruba. This multiple-effect distillation unit uses exhaust steam from the turbo-generators of the local power plant to provide up to $2 \cdot 7$ million gal. of potable water per day to serve 55,000 inhabitants of the island, as well as some process needs of a nearby oil refinery. Production cost was given as $\$1 \cdot 75$ per 1,000 gal.

United States. The Department of the Interior made commitments for the first three of five planned installations for producing fresh water from brackish and sea water, including two types of distillation units and an electrodialysis unit. One of the distillation units would utilize a nuclear reactor for steam supply to provide a capacity of 1 m.g.d. at a cost of $\$1$ per 1,000 gal. Work was begun on the revision of the Public Health Service recommended drinking water standards. Concern was expressed for more adequate delineation of limits for non-living contaminants such as radio-nuclides, synthetic organics and toxic metals, many of which were derived from increasing re-use of water. Municipal and industrial wastes which were disposed in surface streams or found their way into ground water supplies for later re-use as public water supplies added components which natural and artificial purification mechanisms could not always correct. Because of concern over a lack of knowledge in this field, arrangements were made for a national conference on physiological effects of water quality to be held in 1960.

(J. Kd.; F. K. En.)

WEALTH AND INCOME, DISTRIBUTION OF.

United Kingdom. Between 1957 and 1958 total personal

TABLE I. DISTRIBUTION OF PERSONAL INCOME IN THE
UNITED KINGDOM, 1958*

Range of income (£ p.a.)		Number of incomes† ('000)	Amount of income before tax (£ million)	Amount of income after income tax and surtax (£ million)
50-250	. .	5,250	1,200	1,199
250-500	. .	7,110	2,662	2,546
500-800	. .	8,460	5,439	5,059
800-1,000	. .	3,120	2,761	2,531
1,000-1,500	. .	1,470	1,736	1,523
1,500-2,000	. .	335	571	443
2,000-5,000	. .	338	980	669
5,000-10,000	. .	52	350	177
10,000 and over	.	15	250	73
Total	. .	26,150	15,949	14,220

* No account is taken of £2,979 million accruing to persons which, for lack of information, could not be allocated to particular ranges of income. † A married couple is for this purpose counted as a single income recipient.
SOURCE. *National Income and Expenditure* (Cmnd. H.M.S.O., London, 1959).

TABLE II. DISTRIBUTION OF PERSONAL INCOME AFTER TAX
IN THE UNITED KINGDOM, 1949, 1954 AND 1958

Range of income after tax (£ p.a.)				Number of incomes 1949 ('000)	1954 ('000)	1958 ('000)
50-250	.	.	.	13,040	8,980	5,420
250-500	.	.	.	10,140	9,040	8,130
500-750	.	.	.	2,020	5,770	7,690
750-1,000	.	.	.	442	1,600	3,250
1,000-2,000	.	.	.	368	721	1,465
2,000-4,000	.	.	.	85	131	178
4,000 and over	.	.	.	5	8	17
Total	.	.	.	26,100	26,250	26,150

SOURCE. *National Income and Expenditure* (Cmnd. H.M.S.O., London, 1959).

income increased by 6% to £18,928 million without any accompanying rise in national output. Taxes on income took 9% of total personal income, national insurance contributions 4·5% and indirect taxes (less subsidies) 11·5%.

The general upward shift of incomes continued. Between 1957 and 1958 the number of incomes under £250 per annum fell by 700,000, but there were increases in each income bracket over £600 per annum, especially in the range £800 to £1,500 per annum. Table I shows that by 1958 more than half the number of incomes exceeded £500 per annum.

Table II shows changes in the distribution of income after tax between 1949 and 1958. The number of incomes over £750 per annum net of tax doubled between 1954 and 1958. Even then, less than 0·1% of income recipients had incomes over £4,000 per annum net of tax.

Australia. Between 1955-56 and 1956-57 the number of taxpayers increased by 3% and income by 8%, continuing previous trends. As Table III shows, in two years the number of incomes had increased in all brackets over £A1,000 per annum. There was a sharp increase in the number of incomes over £A10,000 per annum, from 4,063 to 5,670, following a temporary dip in 1955-56.

TABLE III. DISTRIBUTION OF INCOME IN AUSTRALIA,
1954-55 AND 1956-57

Range of income (£A p.a.)	1954-55 Number of taxpayers ('000)	Income ('£A million)	Income tax and social services contribution (£A million)	1956-57 Number of taxpayers ('000)	Income ('£A million)	Income tax and social services contribution (£A million)
105-500	911	294	9	927	298	11
501-1,000	1,804	1,368	78	1,638	1,253	77
1,001-2,000	823	1,037	89	1,174	1,503	125
2,001-5,000	122	351	68	166	476	87
5,001-10,000	17	115	40	23	155	56
10,001 and over	4	67	31	6	93	46
Total	3,681	3,232	315	3,934	3,778	401

SOURCE. Commonwealth of Australia: *Thirty-Seventh Report of The Commissioner of Taxation, 1957-1958.*

United States. The 1959 *Survey of Consumer Finances in the United States*, published by the board of governors of the federal reserve system, supplied information on the distribution of income in 1958 and liquid assets in early 1959. The survey was again based on small field canvasses of consumer spending units, defined as all related persons who pooled their incomes for their major items of expenditure. Survey data on the percentage distribution of spending units according to size of holdings and liquid assets—U.S. government savings bonds, deposits in savings and current accounts at banks and shares in savings and loan associations—are shown in Table IV. In early 1959, 75% of spending units owned liquid assets—a proportion which was slightly higher than in 1958 and considerably higher than in 1950.

TABLE IV. DISTRIBUTION OF SPENDING UNITS IN THE UNITED STATES
BY SIZE OF LIQUID ASSET HOLDINGS

Amounts of liquid assets held*				1946	1950	1956	1958	1959
None	.	.	.	24%	31%	28%	26%	25%
$1-$199	.	.	.	15	16	15	17	18
$200-$499	.	.	.	14	11	12	14	13
$500-$999	.	.	.	14	10	12	11	12
$1,000-$1,999	.	.	.	14	10	11	10	10
$2,000-$4,999	.	.	.	13	13	12	12	12
$5,000-$9,999	.	.	.	4	6	6	5	6
$10,000 and over	.	.	.	2	3	4	5	4

* Includes U.S. government savings bonds, current accounts, savings accounts in banks, postal savings, and shares in savings and loan associations and credit unions; excludes currency holdings.
SOURCE. Board of Governors of the Federal Reserve System.

Table V summarizes data provided by the surveys on the distribution of spending units and total money income (before

TABLE V. DISTRIBUTION IN THE UNITED STATES OF SPENDING UNITS
AND MONEY INCOME RECEIVED, BY INCOME GROUPS

Annual income (money income before taxes)	1946 (1)	(2)	1950 (1)	(2)	1957 (1)	(2)	1958 (1)	(2)
Under $1,000	17%	3%	13%	2%	8%	1%	7%	1%
$1,000-$1,999	23	12	17	7	13	4	13	4
$2,000-$2,999	25	21	19	13	11	5	12	6
$3,000-$3,999	17	20	19	18	13	9	12	8
$4,000-$4,999	8	13	12	16	12	11	12	10
$5,000-$7,499	6	11	14	23	25	28	24	27
$7,500 and over	4	20	6	21	18	42	20	43

(1) Spending units. (2) Total money income.
SOURCE. Board of Governors of the Federal Reserve System.

taxes) according to size of income. From 1957 to 1958 there was little change in the income distribution, whereas in most of the postwar period there had been an upward movement. The expansion of total money income in the postwar years resulted in a shifting of many consumers to higher income levels. The shifting pervaded the income distribution. However, when the nation's spending units were ranked into tenths by size of income, it was found that the proportionate share of total money income received by each tenth was fairly stable throughout the postwar years. For the continental United States as a whole, personal income in 1958 totalled $356,000 million, about 2% more than in 1957.

For the country as a whole, *per capita* personal income amounted to $2,057 in 1958, compared with $2,043 in the previous year. By regions, 1958 *per capita* income was almost one-fifth above the national average in the far west and mideast and was more than one-quarter below it in the southeast. The range among the states, of course, was much greater. (*See* also BUDGETS; COST OF LIVING; NATIONAL INCOME; WAGES AND HOURS.) (T. BAR.; C. F. Sz.)

WEATHER: *see* METEOROLOGY.

WESTERN EUROPEAN UNION. An organization of seven countries (Belgium, France, the German Federal Republic, Italy, Luxembourg, the Netherlands and the United Kingdom) charged with promoting military, economic and cultural co-operation between its members and, since 1954, of exercising some control over their military strength and dispositions. It consists of a permanent council situated in London and a consultative assembly which normally meets twice a year. Secretary-general, Louis Goffin (Belgium); president of the assembly, V. Badini Confalonieri (Italy).

History. The improvement in the working relations between the council and the assembly was maintained. While, for instance, the council had side-stepped the assembly's 1958 resolution calling for a committee of investigation on the question of an armaments production pool, its spokesmen now let it be known that the alternative of a liaison sub-committee would be acceptable. On one major issue, however, the assembly was distinctly unhappy: the projected transfer of W.E.U. competence in social and cultural matters to the Council of Europe. For, after the foreign ministers, meeting in Strasbourg in April, in the guise of the committee of ministers of the Council of Europe, decreed this initial measure of rationalization, the W.E.U. council had meekly acquiesced, without any consultation with the assembly. Consequently, at the assembly's fifth session, in Strasbourg (June 15-18), several voices were raised in protest.

An assembly resolution at the June session expressed the view that neither the control of armaments as provided for in the treaty nor the common production of armaments as subsequently agreed was being pursued with vigour. The council's defence was, of course, that certain decisions had still to be taken within the member countries before the W.E.U. agencies could really get down to their job. Incidentally, the council had earlier rejected as impracticable the assembly's suggestion that a distinction should be made between weapons and equipment which could be produced within Nato, those which would be better suited to production within W.E.U. and, finally, those which had to be produced on a national basis. The council's view was that the governments must continue to proceed on a case-by-case basis, working alongside the Standing Committee on Armaments.

The assembly's defence committee continued its review of European security with a second report by Frederick Mulley (Great Britain), which was devoted in June particularly to measures designed to improve and rationalize naval defence. It included an assessment of the over-all strategic position of the west, with a gentle complaint that the council did not accord the same urgency to the provision of adequate Nato ground forces as did the assembly. But, on the whole, W.E.U. parliamentarians accepted that the role of W.E.U. was, primarily, to be an adjunct to Nato.

The fifth assembly meeting was notable for a period of closed session for the hearing of a statement by General J. E. Valluy, c.-in-c., Allied forces, Central Europe. (*See* also NORTH ATLANTIC TREATY ORGANIZATION.)   (W. H. CTR.)

WEST INDIES, THE.

A federation of British West Indian territories, comprising ten colonies each consisting of one or more islands lying in, or on the borders of, the Caribbean sea. They are: Barbados; Cayman Islands; Jamaica; Leeward Islands (Antigua, Montserrat, St. Kitts-Nevis-Anguilla); Trinidad and Tobago; Turks and Caicos Islands; Windward Islands (Dominica, Grenada, St. Lucia, St. Vincent). Total land area: 8,005 sq.mi. Total pop.: (1958 est.) 3,153,450. Provincial seat of federal government: Port of Spain, Trinidad. Administration: governor-general; council of state, comprising the governor-general as president, the prime minister and ten other ministers; appointed senate; elected House of Representatives with speaker. Governor-general, Lord Hailes; federal prime minister, Sir Grantley H. Adams.

At the end of 1958 the Commission on Trade and Tariffs presented its report. It dealt with the various problems raised by the proposed customs union of the various territories of The West Indies, and it prepared a scheme for bringing this into effect by 1970. The publication of the report and a statement by the federal prime minister, Sir Grantley H. Adams, about the power of the federal government to levy taxes after the first five years of the federation's existence brought sharp protests from the government of Jamaica, which feared that its economic development would

become subject to the control of the federal government.

During the course of 1959 various points of difference appeared between the units of the federation. In September-October the postponed conference on revision of the federal constitution met and accepted the principle that representation of the units in the House of Assembly should be based as closely as possible on population, but referred the mode of implementation of the principle to a committee. (H. D. Hs.)

Barbados. British colony, the most easterly of the Caribbean Islands. Area: 166 sq.mi. Pop.: (1946 census) 192,841 (77·24% Negro, 17·55% mixed, 5·10% Europeans); (1958 est.) 236,812. Language: English. Religion: Christian (c. 70% Anglican). Capital and chief port: Bridgetown, pop. (1955 est.) 18,500 (metropolitan area, 70,900). Administration: governor; cabinet (premier and six other ministers); nominated executive council (incl. premier); executive committee; appointed legislative council; elected House of Assembly. Governors in 1959: Sir Robert Arundell and (from Sept. 29) Sir John Stow. Premier, H. G. H. Cummins. Main imports: foodstuffs, machinery and other metal manufactures, textile and textile manufactures. Main exports: sugar, molasses, rum, confectionery. Monetary unit: British West Indian dollar ($4·80 = £1 sterling).

History.   During 1959 constitutional advances were announced involving further limitation of the powers of the governor. Henceforth he would be obliged to accept the advice of his ministers in executive committee in all circumstances. The ministers were given greater responsibilities

At a reception given in their honour in Barbados: cricketers of the M.C.C. touring team in conversation with other guests.

and the nominated members were removed from the executive committee. The service commissions were made executive and would thus exercise local control over the public service. A new system of local government came into force in June, whereby the 11 vestries were replaced by three district councils. New public health and public assistance measures were made law. Interim town and country development planning legislation was also enacted to give some measure of control to development. A new terminal building at Seawell airport was put into service. Hotel development went forward at a faster pace, encouraged both by legislation and by the heavily increased demand for accommodation for visitors. This demand was greatly fostered by the reorganized Tourist board with a guaranteed budget of $200,000 per annum. Banks Barbados Breweries, Ltd., began building a brewery, estimated to cost $2·1 million.   (D. A. Ws.)

Cayman Islands. British colony, three islands in the Caribbean. Area: 100 sq.mi. Pop. (1956 est.) 9,045. Chief town: Georgetown (on Grand Cayman), pop., c. 1,700. Administration: governor; administrator; executive council; legislative assembly with elected majority. Governor (who is also governor of Jamaica and Turks Caicos Islands), Sir Kenneth Blackburne; administrator, A. H. Donald. Main imports: foodstuffs. Main exports: turtles and turtle products, rope. Currency: sterling.

History. By an order-in-council dated May 13, 1959, the Cayman Islands received their own constitution. They therefore ceased to be a dependency of Jamaica, although the governor of Jamaica remained governor of the Cayman Islands. The constitutional position of the islands as a member of The West Indies was not yet clear, and they had no separate representation in either house of the federal legislature. Elections under the new constitution were held in September and the new legislative assembly was declared open by the governor on Oct. 2.

It was reported during the year that a search for oil was being conducted in the islands. (H. D. Hs.)

Jamaica. British internally self-governing colony in the Caribbean. Area: 4,411 sq.mi. Pop.: (1943 census) 1,237,063, (77% Negro, 18% mixed, less than 2% white); (1958 est.) 1,651,500. Language: English. Religion: Christian, incl. (1943) Anglican 350,311; Baptist 318,655; Methodist 109,466; Presbyterian 92,975; Roman Catholic 70,535. Chief towns (pop., 1943 census): Kingston (cap., 1943 census of Kingston parish) 109,056, (1957 est., metropolitan area) 308,000; Spanish Town 12,007; Montego Bay 11,547. Administration: governor; privy council; council of ministers presided over by the premier; legislative council (upper legislative house); House of Representatives (elected lower legislative house). Governor, Sir Kenneth Blackburne. Premier, Norman Manley. Main imports: machinery and vehicles, flour, textile piecegoods, fuel oil, fish and fish preparations. Main exports: sugar, bananas, alumina, bauxite, rum, coffee, citrus. Currency: sterling with local notes and coinage.

History. By an order-in-council dated May 13, 1959, the constitutional changes agreed upon in 1958 came into effect. Henceforth, Jamaica would have full internal self-government —defence and external relations being reserved for the U.K. government. In future the governor could exercise his veto only on the advice of the council of ministers. The House of Representatives was increased to 45 members. Elections held in July resulted in the People's National party being returned to power with 30 out of the 45 seats, the others being won by the Jamaica Labour party.

On the whole, economic activity showed recovery from the slight recession experienced at the end of 1958. However, difficulties appeared in the agricultural sector. Export crops generally were affected by a fall in prices, and the situation in both the banana and sugar industries was considered so serious that commissions of inquiry were appointed to investigate them.

Jamaica attracted more tourists than ever during both winter and summer seasons (the estimated number for 1959 being 200,000). The increase in tourist traffic over 1958 was estimated at about 12%. Five new hotels were opened in 1959 and others were under construction.

The Industrial Development corporation announced the establishment of a number of new industries during the year.

The Jamaica Broadcasting corporation set up by the government joined Radio Jamaica on the air in June.

Migration to the United Kingdom decreased noticeably during the last half of 1958, and this trend continued through the first half of 1959. Some 62% of the migrants leaving between January and June were women and children. At the same time the flow of returning migrants increased considerably. (H. D. Hs.)

Leeward Islands. British colonies of Antigua, St. Kitts-Nevis-Anguilla, Montserrat and British Virgin Islands (see VIRGIN ISLANDS, BRITISH) forming the northern part of the Lesser Antilles and the eastern extremity of the Greater Antilles in the Caribbean. The colonies have in common governor and (with Windwards) Supreme Court, but separate legislatures.

	Area (sq.mi.)	Population (1946 census)	(1958 est.)	Capital (pop., 1957 est.)
Antigua	171*	41,757	56,777	St. Johns† 12,500
Montserrat	32	14,333	14,465	Plymouth 2,500
St. Kitts‡-Nevis-Anguilla	153§	46,243	58,579	Basseterre 13,500
	356	102,333	129,821	

* Incl. Barbuda (62 sq.mi.), Redonda (0·5 sq.mi.), dependencies. † Seat of governor. ‡ Properly St. Christopher. § Incl. Sombrero (2 sq.mi.).

Population, mainly Negro. Language: English. Religion: Christian. Administration: governor with reserve executive powers and, in each colony, administrator; executive council (incl. three ministers, in Antigua and St. Kitts-Nevis-Anguilla); legislative council with elected majority. Governor, Sir Alexander Williams. Administrator: I. G. Turbott (Antigua); A. F. Dawkins (Montserrat); and Lieut.-Col. Hon. H. A. C. Howard (St. Kitts). Main imports: food, building materials, cotton piecegoods, inedible oils, tobacco. Main exports: sugar, cotton. Monetary unit: British West Indian dollar ($4·80 = £1 sterling).

History. Constitutional reform in the Leeward Islands was discussed at a conference held in London in June 1959. As a result it was agreed that from Jan. 1, 1960, the islands would become autonomous units within the federation of The West Indies, with an administrator appointed by the U.K. government as head of government in each territory. The post of governor of the Leeward Islands was abolished at the end of the year.

Weather conditions were good in 1959. There was no longer a labour shortage in Antigua and sugar output rose to 31,828 tons. In St. Kitts and Nevis sugar output was 46,441 tons. In Antigua the sea island cotton crop amounted to 352,192 lb. of clean lint, while in St. Kitts, Nevis and Anguilla it was 529,886 lb. of clean lint and 33,940 lb. of stained cotton. In Montserrat the cotton crop amounted to 382,913 lb. of clean lint. (O. R. K.)

Trinidad and Tobago. British colony, two islands off the coast of Venezuela, north of the Orinoco delta. Area: 1,980 sq.mi. (Tobago, 116 sq.mi.). Pop.: (1946 census) 557,970 (Tobago 27,161), incl. 261,485 Africans, 195,747 East Indians and 78,775 coloured (mixed); (1958 est.) 789,000 with c. 5% in Tobago. Languages: English (lingua franca), Hindi, French, Spanish. Religion: Christian 70% (of which one-half Roman Catholic, one-third Anglican), Hindu 23%, Moslem 6%. Chief towns (pop., 1957): Port of Spain (cap.) 120,650; San Fernando (port) 38,850; Arima 12,050. Administration: governor; cabinet presided over by premier; legislative council with speaker and elected majority. Governor, Sir Edward Beetham; premier, Eric Williams. Main imports: fuels and lubricants, food, machinery and vehicles, iron and steel. Main exports: petroleum and products, sugar and rum, cocoa. Monetary unit: British West Indian dollar ($4·80 = £1 sterling).

History. In Jan. 1959 an economic mission from the Canadian Chamber of Commerce visited Trinidad. The same month a bill to remedy slum conditions in the colony was passed by the legislature.

A cabinet system of government was introduced in July and the chief minister, Eric Williams, assumed the title of premier.

During October the legislature approved the raising of two loans, one of $25 million for supplementary development works and another of $4·4 million to finance the Hilton hotel. At the end of the month a delegation left for London for official talks on constitutional reform.

At the beginning of December impounding was started at the new Navet dam. (H. E. CN.)

Turks and Caicos Islands. British colony, a group of islands in the Caribbean. Area 166 sq.mi. Pop. (1956 est.) 6,793. Chief town: Grand Turk (on Grand Turk Island), pop., c. 1,800. Administration: governor; administrator; executive council; legislative assembly with elected majority. Governor (who is also governor of Jamaica and Cayman Islands), Sir Kenneth Blackburne; administrator, G. C. Guy. Main imports: foodstuffs. Main exports: salt, sisal, crawfish. Currency: sterling.

History. By an order-in-council of May 13, 1959, the Turks and Caicos Islands received their own constitution and ceased to be a dependency of Jamaica. However, their constitutional position in relation to the federation of The West Indies (like that of the Cayman Islands) was not clear. Elections were held under the new constitution during September and on Oct. 9 the new legislature was inaugurated by the governor. (H. D. Hs.)

Windward Islands. British colonies of Dominica, Grenada, St. Lucia and St. Vincent, forming the southern part of the Lesser Antilles in the Caribbean. The colonies have in common governor and (with Leewards) Supreme Court, but separate legislatures.

	Area (sq.mi.)	Population (1946 census)	(1958 est.)	Capital (with pop., 1958 est.)	
Dominica .	305	47,624	65,436	Roseau	15,000
Grenada .	133*	72,387	91,661	St. George's†	26,863
St. Lucia .	238	70,113	92,089	Castries	25,000
St. Vincent .	150*	61,647	81,282	Kingstown	8,171
	826	251,771	330,468		

* Including the Grenadines attached in part to Grenada and in part to St. Vincent.   † Seat of governor.

Pop.: 95% Negro and mixed; some Caribs on Dominica and St. Vincent. Language: English; on Dominica and St. Lucia also French *patois*. Religion: Christian. Administration: governor with reserve executive powers and (in each colony) administrator, executive council with voting majority for elected members (incl. three ministers) and legislative council with elected majority. Governor, Sir Colville Deverell. Acting governors in 1959: H. L. Lindo (from July 25) and (from Dec. 16) L. Cools-Lartigue. Administrators: (Dominica) H. L. Lindo, (from July 25) A. D. W. Johnson and (from end-Sept.) N. A. Berridge; (Grenada) J. M. Lloyd; (St. Lucia) The Earl of Oxford and Asquith; (St. Vincent) A. F. Giles. Main imports: foodstuffs, textiles, machinery and metal manufactures, building materials. Main exports: cocoa, bananas, spices, arrowroot, coconut products, sea island cotton. Monetary unit: British West Indian dollar ($4·80 = £1 sterling).

History. Constitutional reform in the Windward Islands was discussed at a conference held in London in June 1959. As a result it was agreed that from Jan. 1, 1960, the islands would become autonomous units within the federation of The West Indies, with an administrator appointed by the U.K. government as head of government in each territory. The post of governor of the Windward Islands was abolished at the end of the year.

Budget estimates for 1959 (excluding grants-in-aid and grants and expenditure from Colonial Development and Welfare funds) were: Dominica, revenue $2,845,873, expenditure, $4,125,873; Grenada, revenue $4,860,481, expenditure, $6,266,188; St. Lucia, revenue $3,960,985, expenditure $4,959,715; and St. Vincent, revenue $3,174,510, expenditure $4,538,510. (*See* also BRITISH GUIANA; BRITISH HONDURAS.)

(L. C.-LE.)

WILD LIFE CONSERVATION.

The International Union for Conservation of Nature and Natural Resources (I.U.C.N.), having established an international committee on national parks, suggested to the secretary-general of the United Nations that he should draw up an international list of satisfactory nature reserves and national parks. In April this proposal was considered by the United Nations Economic and Social council at its meeting in Mexico City, in the form of a resolution sponsored by France, Mexico, Pakistan, Sudan, the United Kingdom, the United States and Venezuela. The resolution drew attention to the value to mankind of these reserves and parks and approved the establishment of a world list by the secretary-general. The Survival Service commission of the union, which is concerned with the preservation of animals in danger of extermination, opened an office in London. In June the International Committee for Bird Preservation organized a conference in Copenhagen on the prevention of oil pollution of the sea. The conference came to the conclusion that as a result of the working of the 1954 International Convention for the Prevention of Pollution of the Sea by Oil, pollution generally had become no worse in spite of the enormous increase in tanker tonnage. The most important omissions among the list of nations which had ratified the convention were the U.S.S.R., Poland, Italy, the United States, Panama and Liberia. News was received during the conference which made it extremely probable that the United States would soon ratify, a very important matter not only because of its own shipping, but because of U.S. influence on the "flags of convenience" countries Panama and Liberia.

Great Britain. The Nature conservancy established ten new nature reserves, including Skomer island off the coast of Pembrokeshire, Wales, where great numbers of sea birds breed regularly. There is also a large colony of the Atlantic grey seal and the unique Skomer vole. The Council for Nature, established in 1958 to co-ordinate the efforts of local natural history societies for the protection of unspoilt areas and to mobilize public interest in conservation, formed a conservation corps to develop and maintain nature reserves. Two hundred and fifty volunteers, men and women between 18 and 25 years of age, worked on 12 nature reserves, clearing scrub, and draining and planting marram grass to protect sand dunes. The Royal Society for the Protection of Birds succeeded in protecting the breeding site of ospreys at Loch Garten, Scotland, thus re-establishing the osprey as a British breeding species. The position of the kite and the black-tailed godwit also improved.

Commonwealth. Because of alarming reports that the great Indian rhinoceros had been almost exterminated in Nepal (see *Britannica Book of the Year 1959*) the Survival Service commission of I.U.C.N. sent E. P. Gee from India to investigate the situation and to make recommendations for the preservation of this rhinoceros. His report, showing that the position of the rhinoceros, though very serious, was not so disastrous as had been reported, was published by the Fauna Preservation society of London. In Tanganyika progress was made in establishing the Serengeti national park within its new boundaries and also the accompanying Serengeti Conservation unit (see *Britannica Books of the Year 1957* and *1958*). A grant of £182,000 was made by the Colonial Development and Welfare fund to the Conservation unit; the Nuffield foundation gave £20,000 to establish a pasture research unit within it. The problems facing the unit were the conservation of the forests, water and soil of the conservation area against ever increasing wood-cutting, burning, overgrazing and erosion, a special problem being the preservation of the spectacular wild life of the Ngorongoro crater. In Uganda A. H. Harthoorn of Makerere college continued his work on the growth-rate of the African buffalo. His preliminary report was precipitated because of the slaughter of

The organized poaching of African animals has been described as " commercialized carnage ". Here is a zebra caught in a snare.

wild life in Uganda in attempts to control the tsetse fly. It tended to show that the wild buffalo—and presumably other wild animals also not susceptible to nagana (cattle trypanosomiasis carried by the tsetse fly)—could, if properly conserved and utilized, become a good source of protein for human consumption. Moreover these wild ungulates were hardly ever guilty of causing soil erosion, as cattle undoubtedly were. Harthoorn also participated with J. A. Lock, head of the Department of Pharmacology at Makerere college, in experiments in marking wild animals so that individuals could be recognized later. By this means information—vital for preservation—on food, breeding and herd movements could be obtained. The animals were harmlessly immobilized by being shot with a syringe carrying a drug.

In Rhodesia the River Zambesi, dammed at Kariba gorge, started to flood more than 2,000 sq.mi. of big game country, a process which would not be completed until 1963. Thousands of wild animals, trapped on islands made by the rising floods, began to starve and drown and public outcry arose both in Northern and Southern Rhodesia. In Southern Rhodesia the government shouldered its responsibility for the rescue of the animals, but in Northern Rhodesia, where a fall in the price of copper had been followed by a drastic cut in the Game department, the burden of rescue fell at first upon private subscriptions. The Game Preservation and Hunting Association of Northern Rhodesia appealed to the Fauna Preservation society for help from Britain and a fund for " Operation Noah ", as it was called, was opened in London. By the end of 1959 more than £10,000 had been sent to Northern Rhodesia, boats had been bought, camps set up on the lake shores and many animals rescued. In November it was learned that the Northern Rhodesian government had voted £30,000 to provide more boats and an increased European and African staff for " Operation Noah " during the next two years.

United States. Conservationists interested in wild life in the United States in 1959 were especially concerned with programmes to control the use of chemical pesticides, eliminate or abate the pollution of streams, provide protected areas of land and water and deal with an emergency decline in the numbers of waterfowl as a result of drought on the breeding grounds and continuing hunting pressure.

Abnormally low snow and rainfall in the prairie states over a two-year period had failed to supply the usual duck-breeding areas; nearly 50% of the productive water areas in Minnesota and the Dakotas, for example, had dried up and similar conditions prevailed in southern parts of the Canadian prairie provinces. This misfortune for the waterfowl was intensified when the birds flew farther north to reach areas beyond the drought, and then experienced a late spring in these second-choice regions. Cold rains and snow, the Fish and Wildlife service reported, swept across those lands in May, the ice was slow in thawing and the birds were thus squeezed by an unusually late spring in the north and by drought in the south. The outcome was not known by the end of the year, but special care was being taken in the regulation of the hunting seasons. Conditions were reminiscent of those in the drought years of the 1930s when waterfowl experienced a " crisis " out of which came part of the current emphasis on care in establishing hunting regulations and persistence in developing the refuge programme.

Other migratory game birds, excepting white-winged doves, were reported up to the previous year's level, and it was believed that the doves had enjoyed a spring nesting success that compensated for earlier decreases. Among especially endangered species, the whooping crane, which continued to attract public attention, seemed to have fared better in 1959 than it had for 20 years. The Fish and Wildlife service reported nine young reared in 1959 among the 32 whooping cranes successfully wintering at the Aransas refuge in Texas. (*See* also COUNTRY LIFE; NATIONAL PARKS; ORNITHOLOGY.)

(C. L. BE.; H. Z.)

WINDWARD ISLANDS: *see* WEST INDIES, THE.

WINES. According to the provisional estimates the amount of wine produced in 1959 would be the greatest of the century. It would probably reach 230 million hl.; that is to say, it would

A bowl of wine is presented for sampling by visitors to the wine-mulling at Vintner's Hall in the City of London on Oct. 26.

exceed the amount produced in 1958, which was particularly abundant. This increase was due to the exceptional atmospheric conditions which favoured Europe and north Africa. It must be noted, however, that Italy, Spain and Portugal, which had heavy rain towards the end of summer, had poorer harvests than had been expected. Thus, the main producing regions of the continent, thanks to their dry summer, would give wines which would be more alcoholized, but whose range would be less complete. On the other hand the countries close to the Mediterranean would give wines of low strength.

France. After the disastrous harvest of 1957 (32·5 million hl.) and the 1958 one which was considered very poor (46,145,700 hl.), France had in 1959 a good harvest of about 58,276,000 hl., to which must be added about 18·6 million hl. from Algeria. This was a satisfactory yield, but the quality would vary between very good and poor.

In the Bordeaux region the spring frosts and the dryness of the summer damaged a considerable portion of the harvest. Nevertheless the harvest benefited from fine, and at times, hot weather. As regards quality the red wines of 1959 were placed between those of 1947 and of 1953. In the Sauternes region the strength of unfermented wine was satisfactory and the year was considered a very good one. On the whole less wine —both red and white—was produced than was forecast.

In Burgundy the prolonged good weather and the high temperatures were very favourable to the development of the grape. Moreover, the harvesting, begun on Sept. 15, took place in exceptionally favourable conditions. Never in the memory of vine-growers had the harvest been such a fine one, both as regards quantity and quality. The wines were well balanced, of a fine colour, rich in body and promising a good bouquet. In Beaujolais too the quality was excellent.

In Champagne the harvest was less abundant than was expected, but nevertheless reached a good average. The quality of the wine, however, would be exceptional. Because of the splendid weather enjoyed by this region, the grapes had a very fine appearance and would produce an extra-ordinary degree of alcohol (12°-13·5° and sometimes up to 14°). It could therefore be predicted that 1959 would be a better year than 1928, 1911 and even 1893.

Italy. The storms which came towards the end of summer damaged in part a harvest which promised to be a very considerable one. The final figure was 63,640,000 hl., 5·6% less than the previous year, and the quality of the wine would be rather uneven. In Tuscany and Sicily, for example, the wines would be successful, but elsewhere, notably in Apulia, they would be markedly less good.

Spain. The situation in this country was likewise more serious. Mildew and rot, the consequences of a rainy and humid period, affected the vineyards severely. The grapes were often gathered in the rain, an extremely rare occurrence. The result was a decrease of 14% on the previous harvest.

Portugal. Owing to its geographical position this country had atmospheric conditions which were more or less the same as in the two preceding years. Consequently total production in 1959 reached only 8 million hl., about 700,000 hl. less than in 1958. The harvests in the Douro region took place in good weather and the results were not so bad as had been expected. The percentage of sugar was in general greater than that of the previous year, about 13-14°.

Australia. Wine production in 1959 was 1,497,000 hl. (32,923,000 gal.) compared with 1,529,000 hl. (33,643,000 gal.) in 1958. About 750,000 hl. (16·5 million gal.) of the wine produced in 1958 was to be used for the distillation and elaboration of fortified wines. In its annual report the Australian Wine board pointed out that exports to Canada could be increased. In fact Canada was Australia's second most important customer. Australia also exported wine to the New Hebrides, Malaya, Singapore and Hong Kong.

Cyprus. The harvest was an excellent one from the point of view of both quantity and quality. Maturation was slow, but the quality of the wines would be very satisfactory, as a result of the fine weather. The clusters were sound, and there was every reason to think that the wine would be good. However, since the wineries had reduced their purchases of fresh grapes, it would be noticed that this year a more substantial part of the harvest than usual would be used for the prepara-tion of currants. Moreover, the quantity to be used in the production of crude alcohol would be appreciably increased. The conclusion to be drawn was that there would be more grapes in 1959 but perhaps less wine.

Other Countries. Among the great wine-growing countries were Argentina, the U.S.S.R., Yugoslavia, the United States, Hungary and Rumania. Other less important countries providing appreciable quantities of wine for either the domestic or the international market included Greece, Chile and the German Federal Republic. Among the producing countries in the Commonwealth of Nations the most import-ant was the Union of South Africa.   (R. Pn.)

WOOL. The world wool industry began to recover from the recession of 1958 in the closing months of that year, but recovery only really gathered momentum during 1959. The Commonwealth Economic committee estimated that the daily rate of wool usage in the ten leading consuming countries in the non-Communist world showed a distinct rise in the last quarter of 1958. The rise continued in the first quarter of 1959, when consumption was 6% higher than in the corre-sponding period of the previous year. Countries first affected by recovery were the United States, the United Kingdom, Japan, the German Federal Republic and Italy. In France, however, the rate of activity continued to decline during the early part of 1959. The sharpest rise in consumption took place in the second quarter of the year, when there was an increase of 21% compared with the same period of the previous year, and it then became clear that activity in the wool textile industry throughout the world was back to normal or moving rapidly in that direction.

Measured by day-to-day fluctuations, price levels reached their lowest point in Oct. 1958. But when measurement is by monthly averages the lowest point occurred in Jan. 1959, and it was not until March and April that a pronounced upward movement was clear.

The average price for merino wool of 64s quality in May 1957 was 140d. per lb., according to figures published by the New Zealand Wool commission (London agency). By Jan. 1959 the comparable price was 73d. The decline in medium crossbred wool prices was from 92d. for 50s quality in May 1957 to 56d. in Jan. 1959. A sharp rise in prices did not take place until March and April, and by May the average price for 64s quality was 94d. per lb., representing a rise of almost 30% since January. Crossbred wool prices were similarly affected, the rise being to 69d. for 50s in May, an advance of almost 25% on the January figure.

The sharp rise in prices during March and April undoubt-edly helped to end the recession which was still affecting the wool textile industries of some countries, and made the pace of recovery much more rapid in others. Employment had suffered during most of 1958, but the position improved during the first half of 1959 and was normal thereafter. In many instances wool consumption and production of wool textiles had by the summer made up all the ground lost during the recession, and the contrast in rates of activity within the space of only a few months was very sharp.

The sudden rise in prices and demand also enabled the New Zealand and South African Wool commissions to dis-pose of the bulk of the wool which they had bought during the recession with the aim of maintaining a floor price and injecting confidence into the market. Within a few weeks it was clear that the existence of these commission-held stocks was not of sufficient importance to affect the upward course of prices significantly, once it could be seen that the trend was in fact upward and that recovery was established.

In the latter half of the year prices improved further, and although much of the ground gained during July and August was subsequently lost after the opening of the Australian

ANNUAL WORLD PRODUCTION OF WINES*
(In thousands of hectolitres)

	1934-38	1948-52	1958	1959†
World	195,000	186,000	227,704	230,000
Italy	38,450	43,420	67,389	63,640
France	62,640	52,450	46,146	58,276
Algeria	17,880	13,500	13,827	18,601
Argentina	9,262	11,640	14,041	17,700
Spain	19,760‡	14,990	19,513	16,800
Portugal	7,890	8,020	8,694	8,000
Yugoslavia	4,420	4,140	5,759	5,200
U.S.S.R.	...	1,430	5,774	5,100
United States	2,692	4,573	5,552	...
German Fed. Rep.	2,700	2,320	4,796	4,110
Rumania	...	4,050	6,000	4,000
Hungary	3,259	3,300	5,456	4,000
Greece	3,740	3,700	3,802	3,465
Chile	3,595	3,200	3,750	...
Union of S. Africa	1,631	2,280	2,850	...
Morocco	630	640	2,008	...
Bulgaria	2,373	2,000	1,968	...
Tunisia	1,590	740	1,911	1,500
Austria	1,171	920	1,885	900
Brazil	750	860	1,698	...
Australia	928	1,444	1,529	1,497
Uruguay	705	840	663	...
Switzerland	345	677	589	...
Czechoslovakia	150	280§	410	...
Cyprus	...	130	316	...
Canada	178	220	250	...
Turkey	123	150	244	...

* Only countries with a yearly production exceeding 200,000 hl. (1 hl.=21·99 Imperial gal.) are specified. † Estimates. ‡ Average of 1931-35. § Average of 1948-51.

SEASONAL PRODUCTION OF WOOL IN THE PRINCIPAL PRODUCING
COUNTRIES (in million lb.)

Greasy Basis				1957-58	1958-59	1959-60*
Australia	.	.	.	1,434	1,577	1,670
New Zealand	.	.	.	496	540	565
Argentina	.	.	.	409	421	400
South Africa	.	.	.	299	315	323
United States	.	.	.	293	293	305
Uruguay	.	.	.	200	175	150
United Kingdom	.	.	.	114	117	119
Spain	.	.	.	81	82	82
India	.	.	.	76	76	76
Pakistan	.	.	.	42	42	42
Other	.	.	.	1,576	1,668	1,728
World total	.	.	.	5,020	5,306	5,460
Clean Basis						
Merino	.	.	.	1,096	1,183	1,229
Crossbred	.	.	.	1,188	1,256	1,291
Total apparel	.	.	.	2,284	2,439	2,520
Other	.	.	.	582	593	601
World total†	.	.	.	2,866	3,032	3,121

* Provisional.   † Clean basis.
SOURCE. Based on figures prepared by the Commonwealth Economic Committee, London.

selling season, the background of activity in the wool textile industry remained encouraging.

International trade in wool textiles improved in line with conditions in the industry, but artificial barriers in the form of quotas and tariffs led as usual to varied changes in trade between different countries. The increase in earnings of foreign exchange caused by the rise in the price of wool and other commodities led Australia and New Zealand to relax import restrictions to some extent, but in New Zealand the relaxation did not apply to imports of wool textiles. Quotas for 1960 in this field were cut in many instances, with a view to encouraging New Zealand's own wool textile production.

The tariff quota arrangements in the U.S. market for wool textiles, under which imports were permitted up to a quantity equivalent to 5% of average domestic production in the previous three years, continued in operation for the third successive year. The quota was filled much earlier than in 1958, and some of the countries exporting wool textiles to the United States protested strongly at the dislocating effect of these arrangements and their tendency to penalize higher quality, specially ordered fashion goods. Other countries, notably Japan and Italy, were able to take advantage of this situation and increase their share of the market at the expense of the United Kingdom. Protests did eventually lead the U.S. government to start the process of re-negotiating the clauses under which the tariff quota was imposed.

The far east continued to grow in importance in the wool industry, with Japan prominent as a consumer of wool and an exporter of wool textiles, and with China becoming increasingly important as a buyer of raw wool and of wool tops.

The year 1959 saw the wool industry recover buoyantly from the recession of 1958, and it seemed that demand for wool on the lower-priced basis was stronger than before. Developments in the scientific field were probably among the most important of the year, and processes for permanent creasing, shrink-proofing and moth-proofing were more widely used and publicized throughout the world. (*See* also TEXTILE INDUSTRY.)

(H. M. F. M.)

WORDS AND MEANINGS, NEW.

In 1959, as in previous years, the main additions to the vocabulary of English resulted from new factors in the fields of science, military technology and politics. One of the most outstanding events of the year in the scientific field was the orbiting of the moon by the Soviet projectile Lunik III. LUNIK, like its predecessor sputnik, gave English (and other languages) a new word. Another expression connected with the exploration of the moon was SOFT LANDING, the projected gentle landing, on the moon's surface, of a package containing scientific instruments. The phrase SURVIVAL CAPSULE was used to mean the pilot's detachable compartment in a manned rocket.

A British invention which attracted some attention was the HOVERCRAFT, a craft capable of hovering or propelling itself at a height of a few inches above flat surfaces, on generated cushions of air. Of scientific terms the word MOHOLE—meaning a projected hole through the earth's crust to the boundary between the crust and the inner mantle surrounding the earth's centre—was one of the more picturesque. Others were POLYPROPYLENE, a plastic related to polythene but able to stand higher temperatures, and RING ANGELS, a mysterious new phenomenon which starts as dots on a radar screen; rings spread out from the dots like ripples from a stone in a pond. Electronic computers were much in evidence, and the word INPUT was used to describe the information which was fed into these machines.

The never-absent subject of nuclear warfare gave a few new terms. PENTOMIC described a division composed of five battle groups armed with nuclear weapons. HEAVY WEAPON was used to distinguish major nuclear devices from lesser, " tactical " weapons and HARDENED BASE was an underground base for firing ballistic missiles. Another term was STAND-OFF BOMB, a bomb containing a guidance system which made it possible for an aircraft to release the bomb and turn away before it exploded.

UNILATERALISM, the policy of abandoning all nuclear arms whatever a potential enemy might do, and UNILATERALIST, an advocate of such a policy, were words frequently used, as were the terms NUCLEAR CLUB and NON-NUCLEAR CLUB to describe groups of countries possessing, or not possessing nuclear arms.

Economic events gave the term HEAVY FRANC, a new unit of French currency worth 100 " old " francs. OUTER SEVEN was the name given to the countries which came together to form the European Free Trade association. The growing feeling of solidarity among African peoples was high-lighted by the term PAN-AFRICANISM.

There were many other words reflecting various aspects of life in the 20th century. PHONEVISION was a pay-dial system of television, the dial used to select the programme being known as a DECODER. MUZAK was a system of relayed music, used to stimulate production in factories in the United States, and introduced into England as PLANNED MUSIC. ADMAG was used to mean a collective series of television advertisements. During the year there was much discussion about the appropriate times for showing " commercials " on television. While it was generally agreed that these should be broadcast during a NATURAL BREAK, there was some dispute as to what in fact constituted a natural break.

The characteristic dress of juvenile delinquents in several countries produced the term LEATHER JACKETS, meaning delinquents, and the need for an especial penal code for juveniles prompted the coinage CUSTODIAL TRAINING, training given during imprisonment. CALL-GIRL, an expression which had long been used in the United States, had become current in Britain in 1959 to describe a prostitute with whom assignations were made by telephone.

Marine design produced an attractive term, SEAKINDLINESS, the adaptability of a ship to rough weather, and Britain imported from the United States the term SEAQUARIUM, a huge aquarium containing large sea fishes.

Vladimir Nabokov, author of the novel *Lolita*, coined the term NYMPHET, a girl in her early teens attractive to older men.

The word ESTABLISHMENT acquired a new significance although there was some confusion over its precise meaning. In the book which he edited, *The Establishment*, Hugh Thomas defined it as: " the assumption of the attributes of a state church by certain powerful institutions and people; in general these may be supposed to be effectively beyond democratic control."

The attempt by companies or financial groups to buy sufficient voting shares in other enterprises to obtain control of them brought the phrase TAKE-OVER BID into prominence.

Traffic problems were much in the news and the word CLEARWAY, meaning a stretch of trunk road on which parking was not allowed, came into use.

United States. The vigorous and continuous expansion of English in the United States resulted in hundreds of new words and new usages in 1959. Words associated with scientific and technical progress were, as usual, numerous. The development of the science of rocketry gave COSMIC ROCKET, a rocket that escapes the gravitational influence of the earth, SILO, a concrete " nest " for launching an intercontinental ballistic missile, and COUNTY BUSTER, a nickname for a nuclear warhead. Work on space travel and artificial satellites produced such terms as CATEGORIALIZING, the identifying and reporting of space vehicles, PLANETEER, a space-traveller, SUNIK, a Soviet cosmic missile, and PADDLE WHEEL SATELLITE, a name for the U.S. satellite Explorer VI. The use of atomic energy for non-destructive purposes gave FALL-IN, the radioactive waste resulting from the peaceful use of atomic power, while the increasing use of computers and calculators was reflected in AUTOMETROLOGY, the science of automatic measurement. The curious form DUBBIDOBBER was a name for a small part of the seat-ejection mechanism of the experimental X-15 rocket plane.

TURBOCOPTER was a word coined to describe a turbine-powered helicopter, while an AMBUCOPTER was a helicopter used as an ambulance. Another term derived from the sphere of air travel was JET-WALK, a system of corridors used in boarding a jet liner.

The motor car inevitably produced a fresh crop of terms. DE-SMOGGING was an adjective describing a device to remove smog-producing agents from a car-exhaust. Two terms relating to one of the motorist's most pressing problems were SKIP-STOP PARKING and VALET PARKING. The first described a system of curb parking in an area containing three " boxes ", the central box being left free for manoeuvring, whilst the second referred to a system in which an attendant was responsible for parking the car. Another word was GO-KARTING, the sport of racing with a GO-KART, or midget car.

Some coinages from the realm of television and broadcasting were SPIKE MIKE, a microphone which could be " spiked " into a wall or some other surface, SUBCHANNEL, a division of a radio channel, TELEGOGUE, a television demagogue, THINK CONTRACT, a contract research programme calling for theoretical work rather than construction, and ANCHOR TABLE, the table where the chief telecaster of a group works.

Political and economic coinages were OPEN CURTAIN, an adjective describing open dealings with a Russian, and CLIENT STATE, a country transacting a large amount of business with another country.

The business world produced SALES KIT, the whole process of entertaining a prospective customer, and WETSELL, a business deal facilitated by alcohol. The alcoholic motif was also present in SOCIAL HANGOVER, the embarrassment felt by an over-hilarious guest on the morning after a party, and in HALF-JAIL, a punitive institution from which an alcoholic is sent to work each day, and to which he returns at the end of his work. A new kind of phobia manifested itself in NYMPHETITIS, the fear of prococious sex-manifestations, a new adjective was coined in UNBEAT, meaning normal, and a new fashion appeared in the form of LEOTIGHTS or LEGO-TARDS, combination tights and stockings. A DUTCH DOOR was not a door at all, but a pull-out folded advertisement in a magazine. A BUDGET-BUSTER was a person spending, or voting to spend, beyond the power of his, or his organization's purse.

Some curious formations and one interesting new usage appeared. BEER-B-Q meant a barbecue at which the main beverage was beer, and WAKEATHON (like other coinages of the same kind, based on " marathon ") meant the act of staying awake, or a contest in the power of staying awake. A notable example of the portmanteau word was WHYE, to describe the crossing of wheat with rye, and a verb used with a new sense was EVANGELIZE, to advocate something vigorously.

The word PAYOLA was coined to describe the practice of undercover payments in return for the mention of certain products or personalities in news stories or other features in newspapers, radio or television programmes.

(W. N.; I. W. R.)

WORLD HEALTH ORGANIZATION.

This body came into official existence as a specialized agency of the United Nations on April 1, 1948, when 26 members of the United Nations had ratified its constitution. The following 90 states were members or associate members of W.H.O. at the end of 1959:

Afghanistan	El Salvador	Lebanon	*†Rhod. & Nyasa-
Albania	Ethiopia	Liberia	land, Fed. of
Argentina	Finland	Libya	Rumania
Australia	France	Luxembourg	*Saudi Arabia
Austria	*German Fed. Rep.	Malaya,Fed.of	*†Sierra Leone
Belgium	Ghana	Mexico	S. Africa, Un. of
Bolivia	Greece	*Monaco	Spain
Brazil	Guatemala	Morocco	Sudan
Bulgaria	Guinea, Rep. of	Nepal	Sweden
Burma	Haiti	Netherlands	*Switzerland
Byelorussia	Honduras	New Zealand	Thailand
Cambodia	Hungary	Nicaragua	Tunisia
Canada	Iceland	*†Nigeria	Turkey
Ceylon	India	Norway	Ukraine
Chile	Indonesia	Pakistan	U.S.S.R.
China (Nat.)	Iraq	Panama	Un. Arab Rep.
Colombia	Ireland, Rep. of	Paraguay	Un. Kingdom
Costa Rica	Israel	Persia	United States
Cuba	Italy	Peru	Uruguay
Czechoslovakia	Japan	Philippines	Venezuela
Denmark	Jordan	Poland	*Vietnam,Rep.of
Dominican Rep.	*Korea, Rep. of	Portugal	Yemen
Ecuador	Laos		Yugoslavia

* Not a member of the United Nations. † Associate member.

W.H.O. consists of a World Health assembly, an executive board, six regional government committees and a secretariat working at W.H.O. headquarters in Geneva, at six regional offices (Alexandria, Brazzaville, Copenhagen, Manila, New Delhi and Washington) and on field assignments in member countries. Director-general, Dr. Marcelino Gomez Candau (Brazil).

History. In Jan. 1959, a ceremony held at the Swiss radio studios in Geneva marked the tenth anniversary of the W.H.O. intelligence service on outbreaks of quarantinable diseases. During the year ending June 30, 1959, smallpox was imported into 11 countries and occurred on 11 ships and 2 aircraft engaged in international travel. The largest outbreak in Europe occurred in the German Federal Republic. Of the other quarantinable diseases, plague continued the downward trend noted in recent years, with less than 300 cases notified during 1959 throughout the world. During the same period, about 160 cases of yellow fever were reported. Typhus continued to have its main focus in Ethiopia, but a considerable number of cases occurred in Egypt, Ecuador, Mexico, Korea and Yugoslavia. The 14,000 cases of cholera notified in India and East Pakistan during the first nine months of 1959 indicated an unusually low incidence of this disease. (*See* EPIDEMICS.)

The World Health assembly met in Geneva in May and adopted a regular budget of $16·9 million for 1960. It called for renewed efforts to eradicate smallpox, recommended that countries should give priority to the provision of safe and adequate water supplies, and requested the director-general to develop medical research beyond that relating directly to

Gomez Candau (centre), the director-general of W.H.O., at a press conference at the Ministry of Health, Moscow, in November.

the organization's field activities. W.H.O. thus concentrated on better co-ordination of medical research internationally and better use of research potential nationally. It was not intended that W.H.O. should create research institutes of its own.

Progress of the malaria eradication campaign was especially marked in the Americas and in Europe. This undertaking was however threatened by lack of funds. In September the Malaria Eradication Special account, a voluntary fund, had received $8·5 million, of which $8 million was contributed by the United States. A further contribution of $3 million was subsequently announced by the U.S. government.

Since the creation of an international standard for diphtheria antitoxin by the League of Nations in 1922, biological standards have been established for over 100 substances. During 1959, work continued on some 35 substances including vaccines, diagnostic reagents and long-acting penicillin, which is widely used in campaigns against yaws and syphilis.

In July, a committee of experts reviewed the W.H.O. fellowship programme, under which the 10,000th fellowship was awarded in August.

Two new member states joined the organization in 1959: Colombia and the Republic of Guinea. (Ms. Sr.)

X-RAY AND RADIOLOGY.

Much was written in 1959 about the " radiosensitivity " and " radiocurability " of various types of tumours and the important relationship of accumulated total dosage. Paul W. Scanlon, however, stressed the importance of the timing of the dosage (*Amer. J. Roentgenol.*, 81, 433-455, 1959). He called his method the interrupted or broken dosage method, in contradistinction to that advocated by Coutard, which had been in use about 30 years. Coutard's method is the daily treatment of an increment dose until the total accumulated depth dose is received by the patient.

The ultimate goal of any method of cancer radiation is cellular degeneration of the tumour cell. Radiobiologists found that the radiation effect on a given cell was greatest during the mitotic phase of its life cycle and they also showed that the direct effect of the initial radiation was to suppress the mitotic activity of the cell. The duration and magnitude of the mitotic suppression depended primarily on the amount of the initial dose and secondarily on the type of tissue radiated. They also found that further irradiation, during the period of mitotic suppression, was relatively ineffective, as there was no differential effect between the adult resting malignant cell and the surrounding normal tissue. However, if therapy was interrupted for sufficient time to allow restoration of the mitotic activity, the radiosensitivity of the tumour was increased and the effect of the further radiation was enhanced.

Scanlon analysed 46 cases of cancer of the palatine tonsil,

88 cases of cancer of the nasopharynx and 43 cases of cancer of the anus, in which the two methods of therapy were involved. Of all the factors considered in these cases, the most conspicuous was the difference in method of treatment. The broken dose or interrupted method of therapy showed a marked improvement in the five-year survival rate of the order of three or four to one over that of the conventional daily fractional therapy method. However, because of the increased biological effect of the broken dose method, there was a potential danger in so far as latent effects were concerned. The initial acute reaction from daily treatment was not as evident, but the late reactions were more severe.

Because the conclusions of experimental geneticists were questioned by many in view of the absence of any valid data concerning radiation-induced genetic damage to the human off-spring, Ira Kaplan made an analysis (*Radiology*, 72, 518-521, 1959) of the genetic changes in two successive generations of the offspring of 644 women who had received röntgen therapy for infertility and sterility. These patients had received a tissue dose of approximately 65 röntgens to the ovaries and 90 röntgens to the pituitary gland. Although these amounts were not high in the field of X-ray therapy, they were extremely high from a diagnostic X-ray point of view, where the dosage is usually measured on the basis of milliröntgens per examination. The conclusion, based on a careful study of the children and grandchildren of this irradiated group, were that there was no increased genetic damage. (*See* also Diseases.) (Be. B.)

YACHTING.

There were 59 starters—a record entry—in the 1959 Fastnet race. Fitful breezes made it a long struggle to the Lizard but there were high winds for the return from the Fastnet rock. The winner (also first in Class II) was " Anitra ", a new Swedish yawl designed by Sparkman and Stephens. The U.S. yawl " Carina " was first in Class I. First in Class III was " Danegeld ", a new sloop of unusually heavy displacement designed by David Cheverton. The Fastnet was the decisive race for the Admiral's cup, for which France and the Netherlands were challengers; broken gear forced the retirement of all three yachts in the French team, and Britain retained the cup by 135 points to 123 scored by the Netherlands.

There was a good number of additions to the offshore fleet, mostly tending towards greater beam, longer overhangs and heavier displacement. However, light displacement could

J. M. Laing's " Vashti " under sail in the Thames Estuary race on June 7; she came first in her class and second over-all.

hardly be called a thing of the past when the 12-year-old " Myth of Malham " again headed Class II in the Royal Ocean Racing club's points championship. The winners in Classes I and III were " Ramrod " and " Meon Maid II ".

The International 12-metres were racing as a class at Cowes, but without " Sceptre ", which was taking part in handicap racing on the Clyde. During Clyde week there was keen racing in the 8-metre cruiser/racers, a class which was still expanding. International 6-metres from four countries went to Poole to race for the One Ton cup against " Royal Thames ", the 1958 winner. The cup was won by " Maybe VIII " (Norway). Two new International 5·5-metres raced at Cowes, and " Vision II ", designed by C. A. Nicholson, proved an outstanding boat. For International Dragons, there was competition of a high standard at Copenhagen, where the gold cup was won by " Tip " (Canada) and the best British boat, " Salamander ", came tenth.

The dinghy classes kept on growing, and a sign of the times was a massed start of 220 dinghies during Firefly week. Fifteen countries were represented at Whitstable for the International Flying Dutchman world championship; the winner was Mario Capio (Italy) and Adrian Jardine was second. British helmsmen did not do well in the International Finn gold cup races at Copenhagen. On Long Island Sound the international challenge cup for sailing canoes was regained for Britain by Bill Kempner and Alan Emuss. Catamarans showed their paces at a " one of a kind " meeting at Westcliff-on-Sea, and it was hoped that a national class might be established.

Motor-boat enthusiasts welcomed the news that Canada had won the British (Harmsworth) international trophy for boats of unlimited power, after the United States had held it for 39 years. In Poole Harbour, the 100-mi. Duchess of York trophy race for outboard runabouts was won by R. May in a 14-ft. Derry boat powered by a Mercury engine. During the summer many runabouts came into use for joy-riding and water-skiing, but it was hard to find sheltered waters where speed would not cause danger or annoyance.

For yachtsmen, as for others, it was a long and memorable summer. Calms spoilt some of the racing during Cowes week and Clyde week, but there was no lack of breeze for either Medway week or Burnham week. It was a year that saw the launching of " Carita ", a 484-ton three-masted schooner, designed by Robert Clark and built at Amsterdam by G. de Vries Lentsch Jr. By contrast, a circumnavigation of the world was completed by John Guzzwell in " Trekka ", a ketch of 18 ft. 6 in. waterline, designed by Laurent Giles and built by Guzzwell in British Columbia. (*See* also SPORTING RECORD.) (R. J. S.)

YEMEN. Arab kingdom in southwestern coastal region of Arabian peninsula, between Saudi Arabia (N.W. and N.E.), Aden (S.E.) and the Red sea (S.W.). Area: *c.* 75,000 sq.mi. Pop.: *c.* 4,500,000. Language: Arabic. Religion: Moslem. Chief towns (pop., est.): Sana (cap.) 60,000; Taiz (seat of imam) 12,000; Hodeida (port) 30,000. Imam (king), Ahmed ibn Yahya ibn Mohammed Hamid ed-Din; prime minister, Crown Prince Seif el-Islam Mohammed el-Badr. Main exports: coffee, grain, hides. Monetary unit: *riyal* (Maria Theresa dollar).

History. In May 1959 the imam left Yemen for medical treatment in Italy. During his absence Crown Prince Mohammed el-Badr, a keen supporter of President Gamal Abd-ul-Nasser, set up a representative council of seven and carried out an army purge, announcing that Yemen " had entered the modern era ". Speculation as to whether these reforms were carried out with or without the knowledge of the imam was ended when the latter returned in August and proceeded to restore the old order, denouncing " alien tools " and having several people executed. Rebel elements fled the country.

Crown Prince Seif el-Islam Mohammed el-Badr, who acted as regent of Yemen in the absence of the imam from May to August.

On May 18 a Yemen delegation arrived in Aden to discuss problems between the two countries, but since the Aden delegation included four rulers of the federated amirates, the Yemenis refused to negotiate with it, on the grounds that Yemen did not recognize the federation.

Technicians from the U.S.S.R., the Chinese People's Republic and Czechoslovakia visited Yemen during the year. The Yemen government agreed to the building—with assistance from the United States—of a road between Mokha and Taiz. (E. S. A.)

YOUTH EMPLOYMENT. In 1959 the number of boys and girls reaching the statutory minimum school-leaving age continued to rise, a consequence of the higher birth-rate at the close of World War II. As a result the employment situation for young persons was less favourable than for many years; there was some unemployment and the placing of school leavers took longer. Difficulty was experienced in finding satisfactory openings for boys and girls suitable for training, and this focused attention on provision for apprenticeship. The report of the sub-committee under the chairmanship of Robert Carr, entitled *Training for Skill*, continued to receive consideration (*see* YOUTH EMPLOYMENT in *Britannica Book of the Year 1959*). It urged industry to take advantage of the extra number of school leavers and extend and improve apprenticeship provision. As an outcome of this and other recommendations an Industrial Training council was established in July 1958 by the British Employers' confederation, the Trades Union congress and the boards of nationalized industries. The council's aim was to keep under review the recruitment and training of workpeople, help industries in dealing with training and disseminate information about training including particulars of training practices in other countries. During 1958 new schemes of training were introduced for young workers employed in the manufacture of leather goods in the London area, in the wholesale clothing industry, the agricultural machinery industry in England and Wales, and the manufacture of woven wire in Scotland. A second scheme was introduced in the hotel and catering industry, mainly to meet the special needs of smaller establishments. There were 116 schemes in operation at the end of 1958. Local Youth Employment committees were asked to relate the recommendations of the Carr committee to local circumstances and promote action by industry at the local level. Some committees arranged public meetings to discuss action on the report. But much remained to be done before the opportunities for training matched the need for them. The Commonwealth Education conference, meeting at Oxford in July 1959, stressed the importance of industrial training and considered how countries of the Commonwealth could co-operate in promoting it.

The number of school leavers advised about careers by youth employment officers in 1958 was 555,000 as against 521,000 in the previous year. The totals of young people under 18 years of age in employment showed little change; the figures in May 1958 were 660,000 boys and 666,000 girls, representing 4·6% and 8·8% of the total numbers of male and female employees, respectively. In most industrial groups the changes in the number of boys and girls employed were small. The most marked variation was in the distributive trades, which showed an increase of 17,300. There were 6,600 fewer boys employed in transport and communications, 5,400 fewer in building and contracting and 4,500 fewer in mining and quarrying. Among girls the only substantial decrease was one of 5,200 in textiles. Eight new booklets were published in the "Choice of Careers" series (H.M.S.O., London) with the titles: *Engineering Work for Boys*; *Engineering Work for Girls*; *Nursing and Midwifery*; *Nursing for Men*; *Journalism and Press Photography*; *Agriculture and Horticulture*; *Farm and Horticultural Workers*; and *Surveying*. The Kent Education committee again organized a course for prospective youth employment officers, and the four-week course for serving youth employment officers at Birkbeck college, University of London, was duplicated because of the number of additional officers appointed to cope with the increased number of school leavers.

The report of the Oversea Migration board (Cmnd. 619, H.M.S.O., London), published in Dec. 1958, devoted a chapter to the work of voluntary societies concerned with migration. Brief summaries were given of the work of each organization, some of which are specially interested in the emigration of young people. The Catholic Child Welfare council, one of the societies described in the report, had embarked, with official approval, on a limited scheme for the settlement of boys and girls between the ages of 16 and 19 in Queensland, Australia.

Nearly half of the 14- to 17-year-old youths in the United States worked at some time during 1959. Most of these were students employed part time outside school hours or during school holidays. In the year ending June 1959, employment of youths outside school hours averaged 2·2 million. About 700,000 out-of-school youths under 18, mainly 16- and 17-year-olds, were in employment in Oct. 1958. The usually high unemployment rate for such youths was higher (at nearly one-quarter) in 1958 than in the previous year (15%), reflecting the general increase in unemployment during this period. Concern for educationally disadvantaged children of migrant agricultural workers was manifested in intensified efforts to get these children into the regular schools of the local areas where their parents were temporarily employed, and in development of special summer schools. States which received large numbers of migrants during harvest seasons, such as New York, Pennsylvania, Ohio, Oregon and Colorado, employed measures such as vigorous enforcement of school-attendance laws, reimbursement of local schools for heavy

enrolment of migrant children and summer sessions. (*See* also JUVENILE DELINQUENCY.) (W. O. L. S.; E. KE.)

YUGOSLAVIA. Federal people's republic of southeastern Europe, bounded N. by Austria, N. and N.E. by Hungary and Rumania, E. by Bulgaria, S. by Greece and W. by Albania, the Adriatic sea and Italy. Area: 99,271 sq.mi. Pop.: (1953 census) 16,936,573; (June 1958 est.) 18,397,000. Chief towns, other than republican capitals (pop. 1953 census): Subotica 115,402; Novi Sad 83,223; Maribor 77,124; Split 75,377; Rijeka 75,112; Niš 60,677; Osijek 57,320. Nationalities: (1953 census) Serb 42%; Croat 23·2%; Slovene 8·9%; Macedonian 3·7%; Montenegrin 3%; undefined (Bosnian, Istrian, etc.) 5·8%; others (national minorities) 13·4%. Religion: (1948 est.) Orthodox 49·53%; Roman Catholic 36·7%; other Christian 1·14%; Moslem 12·52%; other 0·11%; at the 1953 census 13·6% replied "no religion". President of the republic, chairman of the federal executive council (government) and supreme commander of the armed forces, Marshal Tito (Josip Broz). Deputy chairmen of the executive council: Edvard Kardelj, Aleksandar Ranković, Rodoljub Čolaković and Mijalko Todorović. Main imports: machinery and vehicles, iron, steel and manufactures, coal, petroleum and products, cotton. Main exports: timber, tobacco. Monetary unit: *dinar* (D.1,068 = £1 sterling).

History. The year 1959 opened with a fresh round of furious attacks upon Yugoslavia in the Chinese periodical, *Hung Chi* ("Red Flag"), which denounced Tito as "the tool of American imperialism". Marshal Tito used the occasion of the 40th birthday of the Yugoslav Communist party in April to reply, not without dignity. In an interview with the paper *Komunist* he said that Yugoslavia must on no account allow itself to be provoked or to become isolated. Speaking on April 19 at the celebration of the party's birthday he referred to the constant struggle between the progressive and conservative forces within the Communist world and declared that Socialism was "nobody's monopoly". He believed that reconciliation with the U.S.S.R.—he did not apparently refer

Wheat stored in a schoolroom at Srbobran, Yugoslavia. Improved cultivation and Italian seed produced a record harvest in 1959.

to China—would take a long time although it was historically inevitable. He claimed that the Soviet Union had several times followed the Yugoslav example, for instance in the matter of decentralization.

On May 25 N. S. Khrushchev, who was visiting Albania, made a point of congratulating Marshal Tito on his 67th birthday, and even the animosity of the Albanian and Bulgarian press died down for a time. After his return to Moscow, Khrushchev on June 6 expressed appreciation of Yugoslavia's support of an atom-free zone in the Balkans. A month later, on July 7, not only a Soviet but also an eastern German trade delegation arrived in Belgrade to re-open discussions of the plan for Soviet and eastern German credits to Yugoslavia which had been postponed in 1957. On Sept. 20, when he was touring Montenegro, Tito, in a speech at the mining

Federal Republics	Population (1953 census)	Capital	Population (1953 census)	President of the Republican People's assembly	Chairman of the republican executive council
Serbia*	6,979,154	Belgrade	469,988	Petar Stambolić	Miloš Minić
Croatia	3,918,817	Zagreb	350,452	Vladimir Bakarić	Jakov Blažević
Slovenia	1,466,425	Ljubljana	138,211	Miha Marinko	Boris Krajger
Bosnia-Hercegovina . . .	2,847,790	Sarajevo	135,657	Djuro Pucar	Osman Karabegović
Macedonia	1,304,514	Skopje	121,551	Lazar Koliševski	Ljubčo Arsov
Montenegro	419,873	Titograd	16,333	Blažo Jovanović	Filip Bajković

*Including the autonomous province of Vojvodina (1,712,619) and the autonomous region of Kosovo-Metohija (808,141).

centre of Nikšić, expressed his satisfaction over Khrushchev's visit to the United States as a genuine contribution to a general *détente*. Only a few days later renewed Chinese abuse of Yugoslavia was not only echoed by the Albanian prime minister, Mehmet Shehu (then in Peking), but also repeated in the Soviet press: the policy of Moscow towards Belgrade still seemed impenetrably obscure. Yugoslavia, on the other hand, while keeping all its bridges open to western Europe and the United States, made several deliberately anti-western gestures during the year. As one of these might be classed the visit of the Algerian rebel leader Ferhat Abbas to Belgrade on June 12. But this was also part of Tito's patronage of Asian and African nationalism.

Although in his speech at Nikšić Tito said with apparent satisfaction " We are revisionists ", internal Yugoslav policy showed a tendency towards further nationalization during the year. At Christmas 1958 house property was nationalized, other than small houses containing not more than two large or three small dwellings. Early in May 1959 Edvard Kardelj made a speech about agricultural policy in which he emphasized a resolution which the federal parliament had passed in April 1957 in favour of closer collaboration between the state farms and co-operatives and the independent peasants.

In practice the peasants were bound to depend on at least the co-operatives, if they were to make any technical progress. It was through advice and credits made available directly or indirectly by the state that British tractors and Italian wheat seed had come into use. Improvements of this kind together with good weather conditions made it possible already in June to forecast a record harvest for 1959 such as at last to make the country independent of wheat imports from the United States. Independence of foreign wheat was also an important gain in relation to the U.S.S.R., with whom discussions about the delivery of Soviet wheat to Yugoslavia had been suspended in May.

A trade agreement between Belgrade and Moscow on Jan. 29 provided for a total exchange of goods to the value of $108 million compared with $124 million in 1958. In the early months of the year trade with the other Communist countries became increasingly difficult and by April, owing to a sharp increase in imports, the Yugoslav trade deficit had grown alarmingly. During May, however, exports rose considerably, and by the end of July the economic news was good, not only in relation to the harvest. It was found that during the first half of the year Yugoslavia had produced 13% more coal, 14% more electricity and 24% more oil than in the first half of 1958, an important new oilfield having been opened near Sisak in Croatia; among exports the ships built in Yugoslav ports ranked high on the list. In July a credit of $9 million for the thermo-electric plant at Kosovo came from the United States; the Americans also provided a loan of $15 million at about the same time for a power station at Trebišnjica in Hercegovina. On July 15 Italy agreed to provide Yugoslavia with a credit up to the value of $50 million to be paid in investment goods, and credits were also offered by the German Federal Republic and France. By the end of September Yugoslavia's trade deficit was reduced to D.3,680 million, and its exports for the first nine months of 1959 were found to be more than 8% higher than during the first nine months of 1958. There was no doubt that the

general level of comfort had risen, particularly in the most economically advanced republic in Yugoslavia, Slovenia.

Thus, although there were only about 1·5 million of them, the Slovenes carried a good deal of weight. This partially explained the Yugoslav quarrel with Austria about the Slovene minority in southern Carinthia. On March 19, 1959, the Austrian parliament passed a law limiting the area in Carinthia in which the Slovenes were to have minority rights to something smaller than Yugoslavs believed to be justified. Ill-feeling was caused by aggressive German-speaking organizations in Carinthia which sabotaged the use of Slovene even in the Slovene-speaking districts. On Good Friday students in the Slovene capital, Ljubljana, demonstrated against Austria, and in April there were anti-Austrian demonstrations at Maribor. At this time the Yugoslav foreign minister, Koča Popović, complained in parliament in Belgrade that the new Austrian law was inconsistent with Article 7 of the Austrian state treaty; he added pointedly that similar problems had been settled in a friendly spirit with Italy, thus referring to the position of the Slovenes in Trieste. On April 21 a Yugoslav note of protest was delivered in Vienna.

Bulgarian attacks upon the supposed Yugoslav oppression of the Macedonians helped to bring Patriarch Djoris German to Macedonia in Aug. 1959. Although he resided in Belgrade he was patriarch of the Macedonian as well as the Serbian Church, and the visit was intended to emphasize the national autonomy of Macedonia.

In Jan. 1959 a new law restored to the government the right to banish suspects for a period up to two years. But on May 19 legal changes were proposed—and accepted by the Yugoslav National Assembly on June 30—which lessened legal severity. Except in the case of serious political crimes, capital punishment, life imprisonment and the loss of civil rights were abolished, the maximum sentence becoming 20 years. It was also provided that work in prison was to be paid and that those serving sentence for more than one year should be allowed a fortnight's annual holiday at home. It was interesting that, after a Swiss representative of the International Red Cross, H. G. Beckh, had visited Yugoslavia, he reported in October that Yugoslavia's prisons made the country a pioneer in the treatment of criminals; he made it clear that he had been allowed the necessary unimpeded intercourse with prisoners in a number of prisons.   (E. Wi.)

ZANZIBAR. British-protected sultanate comprising islands of Zanzibar (640 sq.mi.) and Pemba (380 sq.mi.) off the east coast of Africa; the sultan's mainland dominions are leased to, and protected by, the British government and administered with Kenya (*q.v.*). Pop. of Zanzibar proper with Pemba (1958 census) 299,111, comprising 228,815 Africans, 46,989 Arabs, 18,334 Asians, 507 Europeans and 4,466 others. Religion: mainly Moslem (Shafi Sunni). Capital: Zanzibar, pop. (1958) 57,923. Administration: sultan; British resident: privy council presided over by sultan; executive council and legislative council with official majority, both presided over by the British resident. Sultan, Seyyid Sir Khalifa bin Harub. Resident, Sir Henry Potter. Main imports: foodstuffs, textiles, machinery and transport equipment. Main exports: cloves, coconut oil. Monetary unit: East African shilling (= 1s. sterling).

History. In Aug. 1959 the sultan received congratulations from many parts of the world on the occasion of his 80th birthday. Among the presents sent to mark the event was a gold and silver cigar box from Queen Elizabeth II.

In September it was announced that the deputy governor of the Western Region of Nigeria, Sir George Mooring, would succeed Sir Henry Potter as British resident on the latter's retirement later in the year.

In June a member of the Zanzibar Nationalist party, Rutti Bulsara, was bound over for two years after being found guilty of publishing a seditious newspaper article. (K. I.)

ZOOLOGICAL GARDENS.

The remarkably good weather during 1959, at least in northern Europe, was reflected in the increased attendances at most zoological gardens and the general interest in animal collections continued to expand. Extensive building operations were in progress at many zoos, also various developments in the feeding and display of animals. Some of these problems were discussed at the annual meeting of the International Union of Directors of Zoological Gardens, held at Copenhagen at the end of August and early September; altogether 27 zoos were represented, mostly European, but also some from the United States. It was decided, if possible, to affiliate the organization to the International Union of Biological Sciences. Among other problems discussed was the feeding of animals by the general public. The meeting was very definitely against this practice and various examples were given of the harm resulting from such an injudicious and uncontrolled diet.

A new method of capturing and handling the larger wild animals was also discussed. Experiments were currently being made with an automatic projectile type of syringe which is fired into any muscular area of the animal concerned from a specially designed pneumatic rifle. When the needle of the syringe enters the muscle a dose of immobilizing drug is injected by means of a loaded plunger which comes into action when the syringe strikes the body of the animal. This method promised to be of great use in the capture of wild animals and also in the administration of drugs such as tranquillizers to captive animals requiring veterinary treatment. It had been used with success in the recapture of escaped zoo animals and was likely to revolutionize the handling of dangerous animals, but further experiments were necessary to determine the most efficient drug for different species and also the best dosage.

Among additions to zoological collections, one of the most interesting at the London zoo was a young male giant armadillo, *Priodontes giganteus*, from Guiana, already more than 4 ft. in length and 48 lb. in weight, with phenomenal digging powers. This was the first occasion this species had been exhibited in Great Britain. The London zoo also received Baikal seals, a freshwater species rarely seen in captivity outside the Soviet Union.

Flamingoes feeding at Chessington zoo, Surrey. A diet has been developed which improves the colouring of captive flamingoes.

The feeding of wild animals often presents considerable difficulty; in some cases it is almost impossible to provide the natural diet and it is necessary to find some substitute. Some species of animals, especially birds, tend to lose their colour in captivity, a very striking example being the flamingo which had been the subject of innumerable attempts to preserve its

Ranee the tigress, her markings blending with the branches and the broken sunlight in her enclosure at Whipsnade zoo, washes one of her week-old cubs while the other plays. Ranee and her mate Rajah were presented to the zoo by the Sultan of Johore in 1956.

natural bright red colour. Recently a new ration for flamingoes was described by W. G. Conway of the New York Zoological society (*Avicult. Mag.* 65, 108) which promised a method of producing a really deep flamingo red. Various sources of animal carotenoids such as astaxanthin were known to be responsible for the development of the pigment, but there was considerable difficulty in providing sufficient numbers of fresh crustacea, such as shrimps, which are the usual sources of animal carotenoids. A proprietary U.S. substance known as " 180 D. Super Caradee " containing 250,000 units of vitamin A per pound, which is a carrot oil concentrate in an alfalfa leaf carrier supplemented with D vitamins, was found to give excellent results. The diet was 10% " Caradee ", 55% " Super Laying Mash " (a poultry food) and 35% ground raw carrots, par-boiled ground horse meat and bone meal. Three species of flamingo, *Phoenicopterus ruber*, *P. antiquorum* and *P. chilensis*, were fed on this diet and after moulting all changed from the usual pale pink of captive birds to the deep flamingo red of freshly captured adults. (*See also* WILD LIFE CONSERVATION.)   (E. HIN.)

ZOOLOGY.

The increased interest in all branches of natural history including zoology was shown in 1959 by the popularity of broadcasts and films dealing with this subject, and also by the activities of local and school natural history societies. There was also an increased number of zoology graduates, as, in addition to teaching appointments in schools and universities, there were also more openings in other fields, such as pest control, administration of nature reserves and field centres, apart from entomology, museum work, fisheries investigations, etc. The increasing specialization within the subject resulted in the development of various societies concerned with particular branches and in Great Britain especially those dealing with animal behaviour, systematics, mammalogy and herpetology had all expanded, in addition to those with wider interests such as experimental biology and the various ornithological and entomological organizations. One of the results was the increasing number of symposia being held in limited fields. The only international meeting of a general character during 1959 was the 14th Limnological congress held at Salzburg and Vienna from Aug. 20 to Sept. 3.

Publication and Research. Various new periodicals started during the year including *Developmental Biology*, an international journal dealing with the broad aspects of the subject, in English, French and German, and *Journal of Insect Pathology*, edited by Edward A. Steinhaus, Berkeley, California, with an international editorial board. The latter journal established two grades of subscription, one (personal) being for private use only and costing only two-thirds of the ordinary rate. *The Proceedings of the 15th International Congress of Zoology* (London), published at the end of 1958, contained summaries of the papers presented at the congress. The reports of symposia included *Perspectives in Marine Biology*, a symposium held at the Scripps Institution of Oceanography, edited by A. A. Buzzati-Traverso (Berkeley). Recommending that non-marine biologists should read this book, the editor remarked that 90% to 95% of biologists were concerned only with terrestrial biology, whereas the seas occupy a much larger area of the world than land. *Zoogeography*, edited by Carl L. Hubbs (Washington, D.C.), contained articles contributed to a symposium arranged by the American Association for the Advancement of Science. *The Numbers of Man and Animals*, edited by J. B. Cragg and N. W. Pirie (Edinburgh), was the report of a symposium arranged by the Institute of Biology in London. *Regeneration in Vertebrates*, by C. S. Thornton (Chicago), was a report of the Developmental Biology Conference series.

Textbooks included *The Invertebrates*, vol. v, by Libbie H. Hyman (New York), completing the description of the smaller coelomate groups, Chaetognatha, Hemichordata, Pogonophora, Phoronida, Ectoprocta, Brachiopoda and Sipunculida, leaving only the Echiurida, which would be described in a later volume. *The Vertebrate Story*, by A. S. Romer (Chicago), was a new, completely rewritten, edition of *Man and the Vertebrates*, and contained accounts of the many new discoveries since 1933 when the first edition was published. *Fundamentals of Ornithology*, by J. Van Tyne and A. J. Berger (New York), was an important textbook on the subject, including references to all the families of birds. *Cours d'anatomie comparée des vertébrés*, by Jean G. Baer (Paris), was a useful summary issued in two volumes, the second comprising 68 plates with 523 figures in black and white and also in colour. *Reproduction in Domestic Animals*, edited by H. H. Cole and P. T. Cupps (New York), was the first volume of a comprehensive account of this subject by many authors. *The Ecology of Invasions by Animals and Plants*, by C. E. Elton (London), was a valuable summary of this important problem by an authority on the subject.

Monographs on special groups of animals included *The Mammals of North America*, by Raymond E. Hall and K. R. Kelson (New York), a well illustrated account with figures of 500 skulls and maps showing the distribution of each species; *Diseases of Laboratory Primates*, by T. C. Ruch (London), was the first volume of a projected handbook; *The Birds of the Palearctic Fauna*, vol. i, *Order Passeriformes*, by C. Vaurie (London), was a systematic reference work; and *Digenetic Trematodes of Vertebrates*, by S. Yamaguchi (London), was the first volume of a work, *Systema Helminthum*, to be issued in three volumes. It comprised 1,591 pages and 1,300 figures. More general topics included *The Open Sea*, part 2, *Fish and Fisheries*, with chapters on whales, turtles and animals of the sea floor, by Sir Alister Hardy (London), an excellent popular account; *Listening in the Dark*, by Donald R. Griffin (Yale), a study of acoustic orientation of bats and man; and *Animals in Motion*, by E. Muybridge (New York), a series of 380 superb plates edited by L. S. Brown. " The Anatomy of *Callimico goeldii* (Thomas) " (*Trans. Amer. phil. Soc.*, 49), by W. C. Osman Hill, was the first account of the structure of this primitive American primate.

The Zoological Record (93, London), dealing mainly with the literature of 1956, was issued in bound form at the end of the year, although the individual sections had been available much earlier. The respective lengths of the various sections give an indication of the amount of research work being conducted in different groups of the animal kingdom. This shows only slight variations from year to year and as usual Insecta headed the list with 536 pages. The list of new genera and subgenera at the end of the volume comprised 21 pages, an indication of the amount of taxonomic work in progress. (*See* also ENTOMOLOGY; GENETICS; MARINE BIOLOGY; ORNITHOLOGY; PALAEONTOLOGY; PHYSIOLOGY.)   (E. HIN.)

INDEX

INCLUDING A TEN-YEAR INDEX OF ARTICLES

Entries printed in heavy type refer to articles and do not show page notations because the articles are to be found in their alphabetical position in the body of the book. For example, the entry **ADVERTISING** indicates that this article appears in all ten issues, 1951-60. However, articles which do not appear in all ten issues show, in heavy type, the dates of issue of the *Britannica Book of the Year* in which they do appear. Thus, **OFFICE EQUIPMENT 57** indicates that an article on Office Equipment is to be found only in the *Britannica Book of the Year* 1957.

Light type entries refer to information in the text not given a special article. All page references refer to this issue only, those following the article headings referring to relevant articles elsewhere in the text of this issue only. Thus **COCOA 58, 57, 56, 55, 54, 53, 52, 51**; 212c indicates that an article on Cocoa is to be found alphabetically in the Year Books of the first eight years of the ten-year period and that, on page 212c of this issue, there is a section devoted to Cocoa.

Page references show the exact quarter of the page by means of the letters *a*, *b*, *c* and *d*, signifying respectively the upper and lower halves of the first column and the upper and lower halves of the second column.

A TEN-YEAR INDEX OF BIOGRAPHIES
To be found in Britannica Books of the Year 1951-60

The articles listed below will be found in *Britannica Books of the Year 1951-60* inclusive. The numbers given in the Index against the names indicate the years of publication of the Year Books. Only the last two figures of the year are shown in each case. Biographical articles will be found in alphabetical order throughout the Year Books up to and including *Britannica Book of the Year 1954*. Thereafter entries are consolidated alphabetically in the article BIOGRAPHIES.

A TEN-YEAR INDEX OF OBITUARIES
To be found in Britannica Books of the Year 1951-60

The Obituaries listed below will be found in *Britannica Books of the Year 1951-60* inclusive in the article entitled OBITUARIES. The number given in the Index against each name indicates the year of publication of the Year Book. The last two figures only for the year are shown. Obituaries of a length of four lines or less are not included in the Index.

LIST OF ILLUSTRATIONS